Prepare for the New York Regents Examination

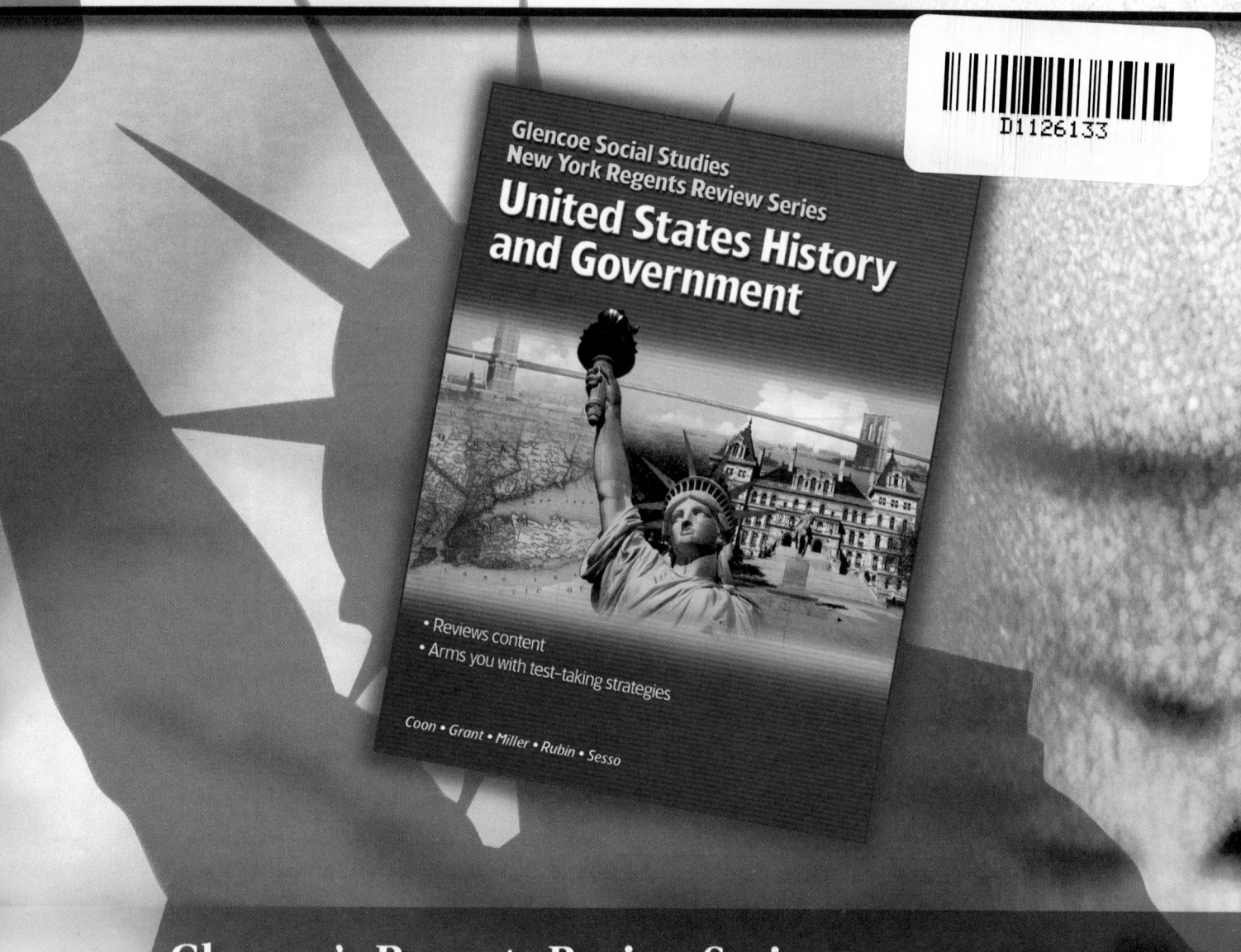

Glencoe Social Studies
New York Regents Review Series

United States History and Government

- Reviews content
- Arms you with test–taking strategies

Coon • Grant • Miller • Rubin • Sesso

Glencoe's Regents Review Series

- Provides content students need to master the New York Standards
- Acquaints students with the types and styles of questions found on the Regents Examination
- Includes the most comprehensive preparation available

The AMERICAN VISION

New York Edition

Joyce Appleby, Ph.D.   Alan Brinkley, Ph.D.   Albert S. Broussard, Ph.D.

James M. McPherson, Ph.D.   Donald A. Ritchie, Ph.D.

NATIONAL GEOGRAPHIC

Authors

Joyce Appleby, Ph.D., is Professor of History at UCLA. Dr. Appleby's published works include *Inheriting the Revolution: The First Generation of Americans; Capitalism and a New Social Order: The Jeffersonian Vision of the 1790s;* and *Ideology and Economic Thought in Seventeenth-Century England,* which won the Berkshire Prize. She served as president of both the Organization of American Historians and the American Historical Association. Dr. Appleby has been elected to the American Philosophical Society and the American Academy of Arts and Sciences, and is a Corresponding Fellow of the British Academy.

Alan Brinkley, Ph.D., is Allan Nevins Professor of American History at Columbia University. His published works include *Voices of Protest: Huey Long, Father Coughlin, and the Great Depression,* which won the 1983 National Book Award; *The End of Reform: New Deal Liberalism in Recession and War; The Unfinished Nation: A Concise History of the American People;* and *Liberalism and its Discontents.*

Albert S. Broussard, Ph.D., is Professor of History and Graduate Coordinator at Texas A&M University. Among his publications are the books *Black San Francisco: The Struggle for Racial Equality in the West, 1900–1954* and *African American Odyssey: The Stewarts, 1853–1963.*

James M. McPherson, Ph.D., is George Henry Davis Professor of American History at Princeton University. Dr. McPherson is the author of 11 books about the Civil War era. These include *Battle Cry of Freedom: The Civil War Era,* for which he won the Pulitzer Prize in 1989, and *For Cause and Comrades: Why Men Fought in the Civil War,* for which he won the 1998 Lincoln Prize.

Donald A. Ritchie, Ph.D., is Associate Historian of the United States Senate Historical Office. Dr. Ritchie received his doctorate in American history from the University of Maryland after service in the U.S. Marine Corps. He edits the Historical Series of the Senate Foreign Relations Committee and is the author of several books, including *Doing Oral History, The Oxford Guide to the United States Government,* and *Press Gallery: Congress and the Washington Correspondents,* which received the Organization of American Historians Richard W. Leopold Prize. Dr. Ritchie has served as president of the Oral History Association and as a council member of the American Historical Association.

The National Geographic Society, founded in 1888 for the increase and diffusion of geographic knowledge, is the world's largest nonprofit scientific and educational organization. The School Publishing Division supports the Society's mission by developing innovative educational programs—ranging from traditional print materials to multimedia programs including CD-ROMs, DVDs, and software.

Contributing Author

Dinah Zike, M.Ed., is an award-winning author, educator, and inventor known for designing three-dimensional hands-on manipulatives and graphic organizers known as Foldables™. She is the author of *The Big Book of Books and Activities,* which was awarded Learning Magazine's Teachers' Choice Award.

About the Cover The images on the cover are (from left to right): the March on Selma, a Polish immigrant arriving at Ellis Island, Benjamin Franklin, Ulysses S. Grant, Firefighters raising the U.S. flag on 9/11, Zora Neale Hurston, and *Oregon Trail* by Alfred Bierstadt.

The McGraw·Hill Companies

 Glencoe

Send all inquiries to: Glencoe/McGraw-Hill, 8787 Orion Place, Columbus, OH 43240-4027

ISBN: 978-0-07-879225-0
MHID: 0-07-879225-8

Printed in the United States of America.

1 2 3 4 5 6 7 8 9 10 027/055 11 10 09 08 07

A Note from the Authors

Welcome to United States History and *The American Vision*. We have written this text with several goals in mind. First, we want you to succeed in this course. We also want you to succeed on the New York Regents Examination. To help you, we have provided a correlation chart which tells you what you are expected to learn throughout the school year and where the textbook teaches the New York Core Curriculum for United States History and Government. In addition, each section begins with the objectives covered in the section, and each chapter assessment is modeled on the design of the New York Regents Examination. As you study United States history, pay attention to the curriculum and be prepared to become a successful student.

This section of your book contains the following:

How Does *The American Vision* Help Me Succeed?

When you study United States History with Glencoe's *The American Vision*, you are learning the Core Curriculum for United States History and Government. The sections in each chapter help you learn the Core Curriculum.

Section 1

The Imperialist Vision

Guide to Reading

Big Ideas
Economics and Society In the late 1800s, many Americans wanted the United States to expand its military and economic power overseas.

Content Vocabulary
• imperialism (p. 490)
• protectorate (p. 490)

Academic Vocabulary
• expansion (p. 491)
• conference (p. 495)

People and Events to Identify
• Anglo-Saxonism (p. 492)
• Matthew C. Perry (p. 493)
• Queen Liliuokalani (p. 494)
• Pan-Americanism (p. 495)

Reading Strategy
Organizing As you read about the development of the United States as a world power, use the major headings of the section to create an outline similar to the one below.

The Imperialist Vision
I. Building Support for Imperialism
   A.
   B.
   C.
II.
   A.
   B.

NEW YORK CORE CURRICULUM
U.S. History and Government

Unit 4:
II.A.1.a Role of increased American power
II.A.1.b Perry and the "opening" of Japan (1854)
II.A.2.c Acquisition of Hawaii

490 Chapter 14 Becoming a World Power

During the late 1800s, the desire to find new markets, increase trade, and build a powerful navy caused the United States to become more involved in international affairs.

Building Support for Imperialism

MAIN Idea A desire for world markets and belief in the superiority of Anglo-Saxon culture led the United States to assert itself as a world power.

HISTORY AND YOU Do you remember what role George Washington thought the United States should play in world affairs? Read to learn why Americans' opinions changed in the 1880s.

In the years immediately following the Civil War, most Americans showed little interest in expanding their nation's territory outside the United States or increasing its international influence. Instead, they focused on reconstructing the South, building up the nation's industries, and settling the West. Beginning in the 1880s, however, economic and military competition from other nations, as well as a growing feeling of cultural superiority, convinced many Americans that the United States should become a world power.

A Desire for New Markets

Several European nations were already expanding overseas, a development known as the New Imperialism. **Imperialism** is the economic and political domination of a strong nation over weaker ones. Europeans expanded their power overseas for many reasons. Factories depended on raw materials from all over the world. No country had all of the resources its economy needed. In addition, by the late 1800s, most industrialized countries had placed high tariffs against each other. These tariffs were intended to protect a nation's industries from foreign competition. The tariffs reduced trade between industrialized countries, forcing companies to look for other markets overseas.

At the same time, the growth of investment opportunities in Western Europe had slowed. Most of the factories, railroads, and mines that Europe's economy needed had been built. Increasingly Europeans began looking overseas for places to invest their capital. They started to invest in industries located in other countries, particularly in Africa and Asia.

To protect their investments, European nations began to control over those territories. Some areas became colonies; others became protectorates. In a **protectorate**, the imp

---

At the opening of each section, you will find the Core Curriculum content that is found in the section.

What do these numbers mean?

For example,

The numbers identify one of the seven historical units and the content, concepts, and themes needed to master the Core Curriculum and prepare for the Regents Exam.

NEW YORK CORE CURRICULUM
U.S. History and Government

Unit 4:
II.A.1.a Role of increased American power
II.A.1.b Perry and the "opening" of Japan (1854)
II.A.2.c Acquisition of Hawaii

Glencoe's *The American Vision* also helps you practice for the U.S. History and Government Regents Examination that you will take. Although the activity is based on chapter content, it is organized and presented in a way that is similar to the Regents Exam.

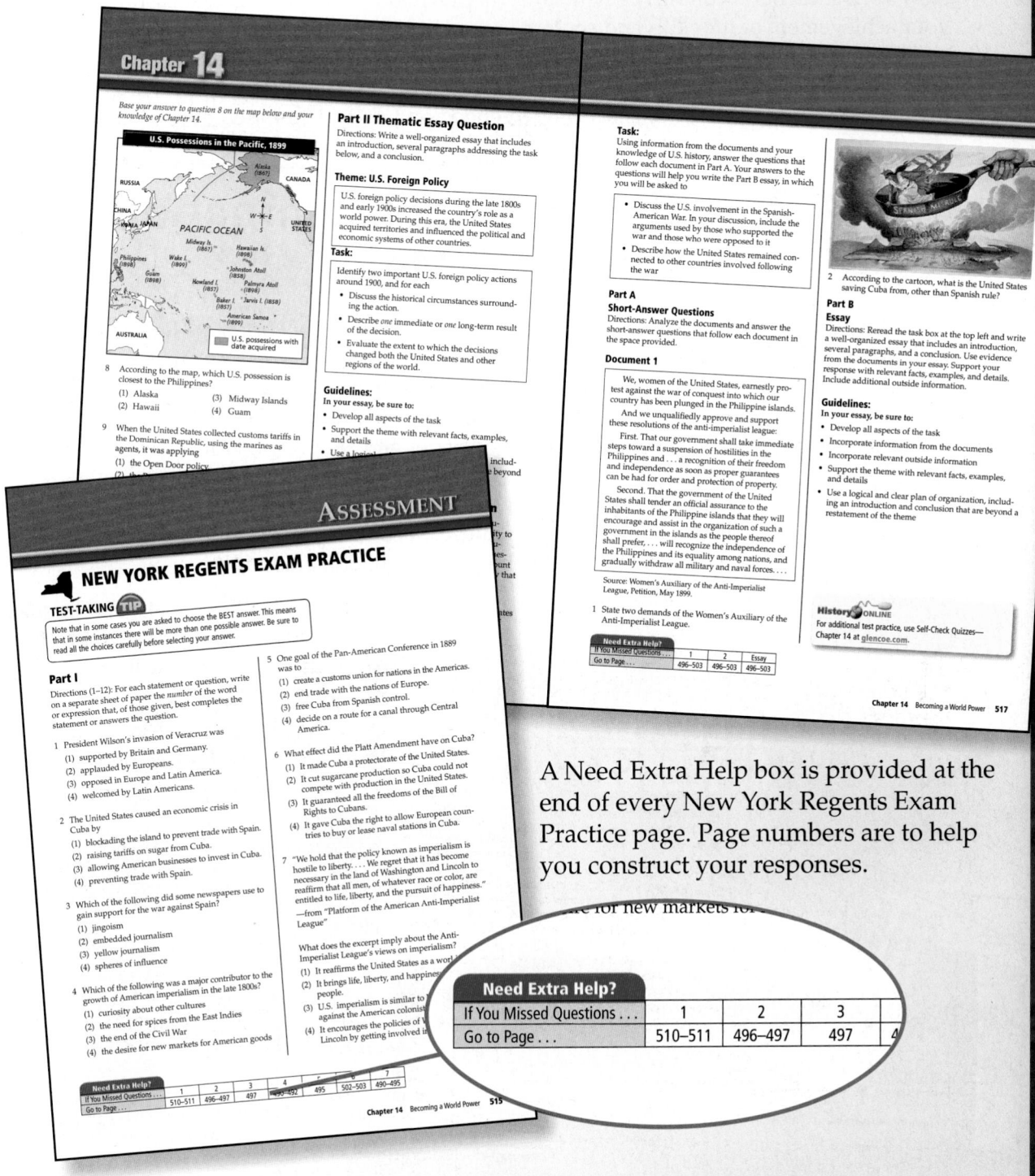

A Need Extra Help box is provided at the end of every New York Regents Exam Practice page. Page numbers are to help you construct your responses.

Need Extra Help?			
If You Missed Questions . . .	1	2	3
Go to Page . . .	510–511	496–497	497

What Is the Regents Examination?

The Regents Examination for United States History and Government is given to all New York students at commencement level (high school). It is intended to measure your achievement of the skills and content in your study of United States History and Government. Students are allowed up to three hours to complete the exam. The exam consists of three parts. Part I consists of multiple-choice questions; part II is a thematic essay; and part III consists of open-ended and document-based questions.

Why Does the Regents Examination Matter to Me?

All public schools in the state are required to administer the New York State Regents Examination for U.S. History and Government. The exam is based on New York State's Social Studies Core Curriculum. The test is used to evaluate your progress in achieving mastery of the five New York State Learning Standards in Social Studies at the commencement level: History of the United States and New York; World History; Geography; Economics; and Civics, Citizenship, and Government. These learning standards describe the facts that you need to know and the expected level of thinking and problem-solving skills you should achieve. Success on the exam helps to ensure that you have the skills you need to be successful upon graduation.

© Royalty-Free/CORBIS

▼ Flags in Ellis Island Immigration Museum Hall

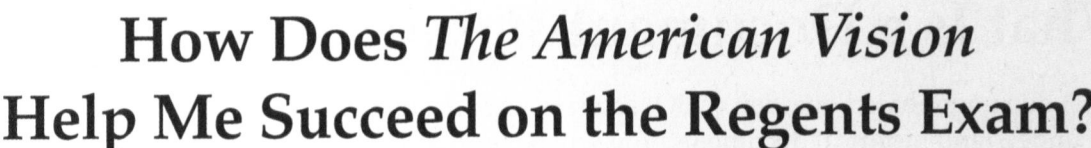

How Does *The American Vision* Help Me Succeed on the Regents Exam?

When you study United States history with Glencoe's *The American Vision* textbook, you are also preparing yourself for the New York State Regents Exam in U.S. History and Government. By mastering the content in the textbook, you are taking the most important step in preparing for the Regents Exam. In addition to the narrative, however, there are other elements of the textbook to make your test preparations easier.

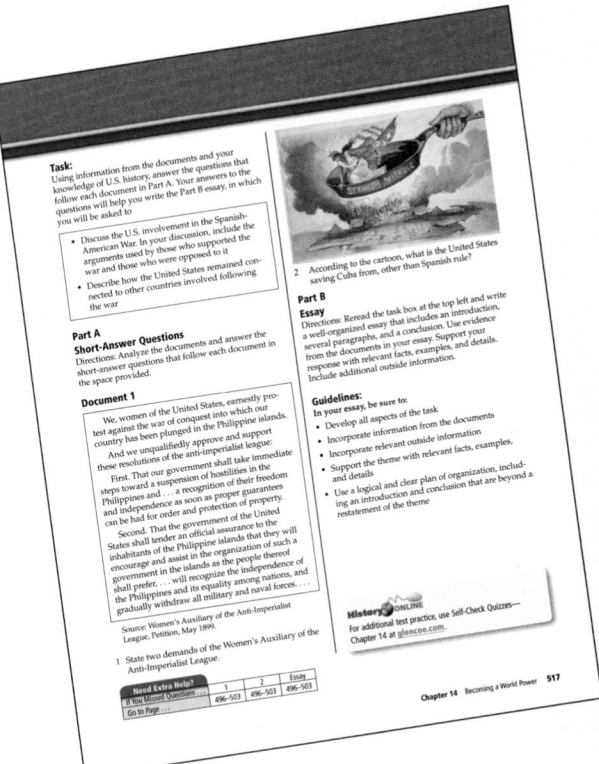

- Glencoe's *The American Vision* provides a Correlation to the New York Core Curriculum for U.S. History and Government on pages NY16–NY40. This chart will tell you what you are expected to learn throughout the school year and where the textbook teaches the Core Curriculum. By working through the Correlation Chart throughout the school year you can prepare for the Regents Exam.

- You will find many graphs, tables, and maps in *The American Vision*, each of them with questions based on the content of the visual. The Regents Exam also asks questions based on maps and other visuals, so your textbook helps you prepare for these questions.

- Each chapter assessment features multiple-choice questions in the same style as the questions in the Regents Exam. Completing these questions as you review each chapter will help you prepare for the Regents Exam.

- Each chapter assessment features at least two document-based questions and a thematic essay question. Completing these questions as you review each chapter will help you prepare for the Regents Exam. Also, tips for writing the thematic essay are included on pages NY10–NY15.

What Is a Document-Based Question?

A document-based question (DBQ) assesses your ability to analyze, interpret, and understand historical documents. You will be presented with a series of documents. These documents could appear in various forms. For example, they could be text excerpts, cartoons, or pictures. The exam will present a historical context and a task to help put the documents in perspective. The questions you answer about each document will help you write your essay in the second part of the question.

For the DBQ, you are asked to:

1. Answer specific short-answer questions about each document.

2. Write an essay drawing upon your understanding of a group of the documents.

The following example is based on a DBQ from the June 2007 Regents Exam for U.S. History and Government. The following represents only a *partial* example of the number of documents you will see on the exam.

DOCUMENT-BASED QUESTION

This question is based on the accompanying documents. It is designed to test your ability to work with historical documents. Some of the documents have been edited for the purposes of the question. As you analyze the documents, take into account the source of each document and any point of view that may be presented in the document.

Historical Context: The woman's suffrage movement of the 1800s and early 1900s and the civil rights movement of the 1950s and 1960s had many similar goals and used similar methods to achieve these goals. Yet these movements also had many different goals and used different methods to achieve them.

Task: Using information from the documents and your knowledge of United States history, answer the questions that follow each document in Part A. Your answers will help you write the Part B essay.

Part A Short-Answer Questions
Directions: Analyze the documents and answer the short-answer questions that follow each document in the space provided.

Document 1
On November 5, 1872, Susan B. Anthony, along with sixteen other women, went to the local polling booth in Rochester to vote in the general election. She was arrested and made this statement during her trial. In the trial, she was convicted and fined.

> . . . Miss Anthony.[speaking]—May it please your honor, I will never pay a dollar of your unjust penalty. All the stock in trade I possess is a debt of $10,000, incurred by publishing my paper—The Revolution—the sole object of which was to educate all women to do precisely as I have done, rebel against your man-made, unjust,

unconstitutional forms of law, which tax, fine, imprison and hang women, while denying them the right of representation in the government; and I will work on with might and main to pay every dollar of that honest debt, but not a penny shall go to this unjust claim. And I shall earnestly and persistently continue to urge all women to the practical recognition of the old Revolutionary maxim, "Resistance to tyranny is obedience to God.". . .

Source: Ida Husted Harper, *The Life and Work of Susan B. Anthony, Vol. I,*
The Hollenbeck Press, 1898

1 According to Susan B. Anthony, why did she refuse to pay a fine? [1]

_____

Document 2

. . . At these meetings [about the treatment of African Americans on buses], we discussed . . . a number of additional bus incidents that never found their way into court. . . . Several of the white drivers were determined to harass our people at every opportunity. For example, when the bus was even slightly crowded, they would make blacks pay their fare, then get off, and go to the back door to enter. Sometimes they would even take off with a squeal as a passenger trudged toward the rear after paying. . . . Clearly this kind of gratuitous [unnecessary] cruelty was contributing to an increasing tension on Montgomery buses. We tried to reason with local authorities and with bus company officials. They were polite, listened to our complaints with serious expressions on their faces, and did nothing. On December 1, 1955, Mrs. Parks took her now-famous bus ride and set events in motion that would lead to a social revolution of monumental proportions. . . .

Source: Ralph David Abernathy, *And the Walls Came Tumbling Down,* Harper & Row

2 According to Ralph David Abernathy, what was a goal of African Americans in Montgomery, Alabama? [1]

_____

Part B Essay
Directions: Write a well-organized essay that includes an introduction, several paragraphs, and a conclusion. Use evidence from *at least* **five** documents in the body of the essay. Support your response with relevant facts, examples, and details. Include additional outside information.

- Discuss the similarities *and/or* the differences between the woman's suffrage movement of the 1800s and early 1900s and the civil rights movement of the 1950s and 1960s in terms of
  —the goals of the movements *and*
  —the methods used by the movements to achieve these goals

Thematic Essay

Introduction

The thematic essay portion of the Regents Exam requires you to write a well-developed essay based upon a specific theme/concept that is found in the New York State Education Department Core Curriculum. This part of the examination is worth approximately 15 percent of your total score of 100 (it can vary somewhat from examination to examination based upon how the exam is scored). The specific theme/concept will change from examination to examination.

The thematic essay is different than the essay you will write for the document-based question (see page NY7). With the document-based question, you are given a set of documents to be used in developing the essay. The thematic essay is a more challenging task; you have nothing in front of you other than the concept and a question based upon that concept.

What should you do as a student to prepare for this portion of the examination? It is very important that you create a list of the themes/concepts that were covered in your class during the course. After you identify the themes/concepts, you should be able to develop a working definition for as many of them as possible. Your teacher should have provided you with this material during the course of the school year.

What Are Themes/Concepts?

You should be familiar with the major themes that might be tested in the Regents Exam for the United States History and Government Core Curriculum. Concepts/themes are found in the *Social Studies Resource Guide with Core Curriculum* document from the New York State Education Department. Your teacher can provide you with this *Resource Guide,* or you can download it from the Internet at www.nysed.gov.

The *Resource Guide* includes a listing of concepts and themes for United States History and Government. You should realize that many of these concepts and themes are very general and can fit into U.S. history in different eras and in a variety of places.

How do you know which concept/theme goes with certain content? At any point in the *Resource Guide* you should look at the concepts/themes column and also the content column. The thematic essay is created from a common theme that recurs across time and place in history. Your essay should be developed from the content with which you are most familiar, based upon what you have been taught and what you have read and know about.

A Sample Thematic Essay

Following is the thematic essay question that appeared on the June 2007 United States History and Government Regents Examination.

THEMATIC ESSAY QUESTION

Directions: Write a well-organized essay that includes an introduction, several paragraphs addressing the task below, and a conclusion.

Theme: Change—Industrialization

> During the 19th century, the United States experienced tremendous industrial growth. This industrial growth resulted in many changes in American life.

Task:

> Identify *two* changes in American life that resulted from industrial growth in the United States and for *each* change
> - Explain how industrialization contributed to this change
> - Discuss *one* positive *or* one negative effect of this change on American life

You may use any appropriate change in American life that resulted from industrial growth. Some suggestions you might wish to consider include increased immigration, new inventions or technologies, growth of labor unions, growth of monopolies, growth of reform movements, and increased urbanization.

You are *not* limited to these suggestions.

Guidelines:

In your essay, be sure to:
- Develop all aspects of the task
- Support the theme with relevant facts, examples, and details
- Use a logical and clear plan of organization, including an introduction and a conclusion that are beyond a restatement of the theme

Breaking Down the Question

The first thing that you should do as the test taker is to read the thematic essay question carefully so you can fully understand what the question requires you to answer.

Using the sample on the previous page, let us analyze the question.

- What is the theme in this essay? *The theme is Industrialization.*

- What is the task or question to be answered? *You must identify two changes in American life that were results of Industrialization. For each change, explain how industrial growth contributed to the change. Also discuss the positive and negative effects of the change on American life.*

- What changes in American life should you avoid writing about in your essay? *You SHOULD AVOID writing about changes in American life that were NOT results from industrialization.*

- What changes in American life may you write about in your essay? *You may choose to write about any change in American life resulting from industrial growth that you studied in class or about which you read a great deal. You are not limited to the list of suggestions.*

- You now have broken down the question into its separate components.

Outlining Your Answer to the Thematic Essay

Before you begin to write your answer to the thematic essay, it is generally wise to outline what you are going to include. Remember, you have three hours to finish the Regents examination, and you certainly have the time to plan what you are going to write. Remember that an essay in social studies is really a composition with a specific content focus.

Following is a simple, skeletal outline that you could use to answer the sample essay. Each bullet represents a potential paragraph.

- A change in American life that resulted from industrial growth in the United States during the 19th century was . . .

  - Industrialization contributed to this change by . . .

  - The major positive and negative effects of this change were . . .

- Another change in American life that resulted from industrial growth in the United States during the 19th century was . . .

  - Industrialization contributed to this change by . . .

  - The major positive and negative effects of this change were . . .

Following is a more detailed outline for writing a thematic essay.

Paragraph 1: Introductory Paragraph

Look at the statement of the theme and then try to rewrite the theme in your own words. You should establish a framework that is beyond a simple restatement of the task. You also should name the two changes in American life that you are going to write about, and you should specify whether you are discussing their positive or negative effects. You also should include a discussion of how the changes you have chosen were a result of industrialization. An example follows:

> Industrial growth rapidly changed American society during the nineteenth century. Two significant changes were the rise of cities and the increase in immigration because . . .

Paragraph 2: the Rise of Cities

Industrialization contributed to this change because

- Large factories constructed in cities provided jobs for immigrants and individuals that migrated from rural areas.

- With a larger population in the cities, industries were developed such as mass transportation and construction.

- Cities offered lights and modern plumbing and cultural attractions such as museums and libraries.

One negative effect of the rise of cities was that many factory workers and other residents had to live in crowded, small apartments called tenements. By living in the cities, individuals were more likely to face crime, violence, disease, and pollution.

Paragraph 3: the Increase in Immigration

Industrialization contributed to this change because

- The construction of large factories and increased consumer demand created a need for unskilled labor.

- Social and economic conditions convinced many people to immigrate to the United States for a better life.

One positive effect of increased immigration was the availability of cheap labor for big business and factories. Immigrants provided the necessary labor to help with the construction of skyscrapers and railroads.

Paragraph 4: Conclusion to the Essay

The final paragraph should restate the main ideas developed in your essay and then conclude with a summation of the theme or problem.

Scoring the Thematic Essay

The thematic essay is worth approximately 15 percent of your total examination grade. However, based upon a conversion chart for the specific examination, this can vary from 12 to 18 percent of your final grade. Your grade for the thematic essay is generated from a generic scoring rubric that has been developed by the New York State Education Department. On the rubric, the highest score is a five and the lowest score is a zero. Ask your teacher how to access the generic scoring rubric from the New York State Education Department Web site.

Now, let us look at the key elements of the thematic essay rubric. A 5 (the highest score) must fulfill certain criteria. The most critical criteria are italicized.

What constitutes a 5 essay?

- *Thoroughly* develops *all* aspects of the task *evenly* and *in depth*

- Is more *analytical* than *descriptive*, showing an ability to *analyze, evaluate, compare and/or contrast* issues and events and create information

- Richly supports the theme with many *relevant facts*, *examples*, and *details*

- Demonstrates *a logical and clear plan of organization;* includes an *introduction* and a *conclusion* that are *beyond* a restatement of the theme

Analysis of a 5 Essay

Let us take a look at the italicized words from the bulleted list above to understand the criteria that are needed for a superior thematic essay.

- The word "thorough" means complete. If the essay demonstrates only a "good" and not a "thorough" understanding, it is scored a 4. All aspects of the task must be addressed for a 4 or a 5.

- An analysis, evaluation, comparison, and/or contrasting of issues and events must be done in depth for a 4 or a 5. Remember, a 5 is more analytical than descriptive.

- A rich inclusion of supporting facts, examples, and details distinguishes a 5 from a 4 essay.

- A logical and clear plan of organization is utilized consistently in a 5 essay. A framework for the task that is beyond just a simple restatement is required for either a 4 or a 5. You need to be able to write your essay with an introduction and a conclusion that is developed in the overall context of the significance of the theme in your study of U.S. History and Government.

Analysis of a 2 Essay

For comparison purposes, let us look at a 2 essay in the rubric.

- *Minimally* develops all aspects of the task or develops some aspects of the task in some depth

- Is primarily descriptive; may include *faulty*, *weak*, or *isolated* application or analysis

- Includes *few relevant facts*, *examples*, and *details*; may include some *inaccuracies*

- Demonstrates a general plan of organization; may *lack focus*; may *contain digressions*; may not clearly identify which aspect of the task is being addressed; may *lack an introduction and/or a conclusion*

How to Practice for the Thematic Essay

It should be obvious to you that there are vast differences between an excellent essay and one that does not reach the level of being satisfactory. It is most important that you familiarize yourself with the generic rubric. Please note that the scoring is on a continuum from 5 to 0. A zero is a blank or illegible paper. Most of the answers to the thematic essay are somewhere in between.

You can take action to help ensure that you earn a satisfactory grade. For example, you can practice writing an outline for the thematic essay. You can then practice writing a thematic essay based on your outline. The outline that you use should be logical and sequential. Make certain that you always have an introduction and a conclusion to your essay.

New York Core Curriculum

United States History and Government Standards	Student Edition Pages
Unit One: Introduction **I. Geography**	
A. The physical/cultural setting in the Americas	A1, A2–A3, A4–A5, A14–A15, 7, 9, 10, 11, 23, 33, 35, 37, 197, 204, 207, 410–411
1. Size and location	A1, A2–A3, A4–A5, A14–A15, 9, 10, 11, 23, 33, 35, 37, 197, 204, 207

2. Major zones/areas
    a. Climate zones
    b. Vegetation zones
    c. Agricultural zones
    d. Natural resources
	7, 10, 11, 35, 37, 197, 204

3. Factors that shaped the identity of the United States
    a. Major mountain ranges
    b. Major river systems
    c. Great Plains
    d. Atlantic/Pacific oceans
    e. Coastlines
    f. Climate
    g. Abundance of natural resources
	9, 10, 11, 37, 197, 207, 410–411

4. Barriers to expansion/development
    a. Climate
    b. Mountain ranges
    c. Arid lands
    d. Great Plains
	A6–A7, 9, 23, 33, 37

B. Role/influence of geography on historical/cultural development	6–8, 10, 32, 35, 37, 39, 163, 169, 172–173, 178–179, 181, 193, 195, 254, 256, 563
1. Influences on early Native American Indians	6–8, 10
2. Influence on colonization patterns and colonial development	32, 35, 37, 39
3. Territorial expansion	163, 169, 195, 254, 256
4. Impact during wartime	163, 178–179, 181, 563
5. Effect of location on United States foreign policy	163, 172, 173, 193
C. Geographic issues today	1025
1. Waste disposal	1025
2. Water/air pollution	1025
3. Shifting populations	1025
4. Energy usage	1025
5. Urban problems/challenges	1025

United States History and Government Standards	Student Edition Pages
D. Demographics	42, 43–45, 47, 200–201, 230, 232–234, 254, 256, 606–607, 971, 1051–1052

1. Characteristics
  a. Gender
  b. Age
  c. Ethnicity
  d. Religion
  e. Economic variables
  f. Nature of household
  g. Marital status
	42, 43–45, 47, 200–201, 230, 232–234, 254, 256, 606–607, 971

2. Immigration	42, 43, 230, 606–607
3. Migration	254, 256, 971

4. Population relationships/trends since 1865
  a. Population growth
  b. Distribution
  c. Density
	971

5. Current issues
  a. Graying of America
  b. Effects of the baby boom generation
  c. Changing composition of populations
	1051–1052

Unit Two: Constitutional Foundations for the United States Democratic Republic **I. The Constitution: The Foundation of American Society**	
A. Historical foundations	4–8, 10–11, 12, 17–22, 23, 24–25, 26–29, 31–34, 36, 40, 40–42, 44–47, 51, 53, 55, 57–63, 64–68, 74–77, 78–85, 86, 87–90, 95, 98–103, 116, 119

1. 17th- and 18th-century Enlightenment thought
  a. European intellectuals (Locke, Montesquieu, Voltaire, Rousseau)
  b. Key events (Magna Carta, habeas corpus, English Bill of Rights, Glorious Revolution)
	40, 45–47

2. The peoples and peopling of the American colonies (voluntary and involuntary)
  a. Native American Indians (relations between colonists and Native American Indians, trade, alliances, forced labor, warfare)
  b. Slave trade
  c. Varieties of immigrant motivation, ethnicities, and experiences
	4–8, 10, 12, 17–22, 24–25, 28–29, 33–34, 51

United States History and Government Standards	Student Edition Pages

3. Colonial experience: political rights and mercantile relationships
   a. Colonial charters and self-government: Mayflower Compact, town meetings, House of Burgesses, local government, property rights, enforceable contracts, Albany Plan of Union
   b. Native American governmental systems
   c. Colonial slavery (evolution and variation of slavery in Chesapeake, South Carolina and Georgia, lower Mississippi Valley, middle colonies, and the North; slave resistance; influence of Africa and African-American culture upon colonial cultures; contradiction between slavery and emerging ideals of freedom and liberty)
   d. Freedom of the press: the Zenger case
   e. Salutary neglect, rights of English citizens in America
	5–8, 10–11, 23, 26–29, 31–33, 36, 38–39, 40–42, 44–46, 53, 55, 57–63, 66–67, 86, 89, 95

4. The Revolutionary War and the Declaration of Independence
   a. Causes of the Revolution
   b. Revolutionary ideology (republican principles, natural rights)
   c. Revolutionary leaders: Benjamin Franklin, George Washington, John Adams, Samuel Adams, Patrick Henry
   d. Slavery, African-Americans, and the outcome of the American Revolution (African-American role in the Revolution, growth of the "free black" population)
	53, 57–61, 64–68, 70–73, 74–77 78–85, 88–90

5. New York State Constitution based on republican principles
   a. New York State Constitution
   b. State constitutions (ratification by the people, unicameral versus bicameral legislatures, branches of government)
   c. Guaranteeing religious liberty (disestablishment of churches, the growth of religious pluralism)
   d. The abolition of slavery in the North
	87–90

6. Articles of Confederation	98–103, 116, 119
7. Northwest Ordinance	98–99
B. Constitutional Convention	87, 104–109, 110–115, 119, 120–129, R59

1. Representation and process
   a. Framers of the Constitution (James Madison)
   b. Plans of government (Virginia plan, New Jersey plan, Connecticut plan)
	104–107, 119, R59

2. Conflict and compromise: seeking effective institutions
   a. Protecting liberty against abuses or power
   b. Power separated and balanced
   c. The Constitution, slavery, and fear of tyrannical powers of government
	87, 106–109, 119

3. The document: structure of government	106–109, 120–129

4. Ratification
   a. The Federalist Papers—a New York activity with widespread influence
   b. The debate: Federalist and Anti-Federalist arguments
	110–115

United States History and Government Standards	Student Edition Pages
C. The Bill of Rights	113–115, 141–142, 154–155
D. Basic structure and function: three branches and their operation	108–109, 120–129
E. Basic constitutional principles	87, 120–129, 130–149, 155

(1) national power—limits and potentials
    (2) federalism—balance between nation and state
    (3) the judiciary—interpreter of the Constitution or shaper of public policy
    (4) civil liberties—protecting individual liberties from governmental abuses; the balance between government and the individual
    (5) criminal procedures—the balance between the rights of the accused and protection of the community and victims
    (6) equality—its historic and present meaning as a constitutional value
    (7) the rights of women under the Constitution
    (8) the rights of ethnic and racial groups under the Constitution
    (9) Presidential power in wartime and in foreign affairs
    (10) the separation of powers and the capacity to govern
    (11) avenues of representation
    (12) property rights and economic policy
    (13) constitutional change and flexibility
	87, 120–129, 130–149, 155

F. Implementing the new constitutional principles	154, 155, 156, 157, 158, 159, 162, 163, 164, 165, 166, 167, 170–171, 172–173, 176–181, 185, 188, 190–191, 192, 193
1. Creating domestic stability through sound financial policies: Hamilton's financial plans	155, 156, 157, 158
2. Development of unwritten constitutional government under Washington, Adams, and Jefferson: cabinet, political parties, judicial review, executive and Congressional interpretation, lobbying; the Marshall Court (*Marbury* v. *Madison*, 1803, *McCulloch* v. *Maryland*, 1819, and *Gibbons* v. *Ogden*, 1824)	154, 159, 170–171, 185, 190–191

3. Establishing a stable political system
    a. The Federalist and Republican parties (philosophies of Hamilton and Jefferson)
    b. Suppressing dissent (the Whiskey Rebellion, the Alien and Sedition Acts)
	158, 159, 166, 167

4. Neutrality and national security, Washington through Monroe: foreign affairs, establishing boundaries
    a. Neutrality: A key element of American foreign policy—influence of geography
    b. A new nation in a world at war
    c. Economic pressures as a tool of diplomacy
    d. The failure of Republican diplomacy: War of 1812 (significance of the War for Native American Indians, Spain, the growth of industry)
    e. Monroe Doctrine
	162, 163, 164, 165, 172–173, 176–181, 185, 188, 192, 193

United States History and Government Standards	Student Edition Pages
II. The Constitution Tested: Nationalism and Sectionalism	
A. Factors unifying the United States, 1789–1861	159, 166, 167, 170, 187, 189, 190, 191,197, 215
1. The first and second two-party systems	159, 166, 167, 215
2. The market economy and interstate commerce	187, 189, 197
3. The Marshall Court	170, 190, 191
B. Constitutional stress and crisis	164, 178, 187, 189, 192, 193, 194–196, 197, 198, 199, 200–201, 202–205, 206–209, 210–211, 212, 213, 214–215, 219, 221–222, 224, 225, 226–229, 230–232, 232–235, 236–241, 242–247, 251, 285, 287, 288, 289–291, R66–R69

1. Developing sectional differences and philosophies of government
  a. The growth of urban and industrial patterns of life in the North
    (1) the transportation revolution (Erie Canal, rise of the port of New York, New York City's rise as a trade and manufacturing center)
    (2) the introduction of the factory system
    (3) working conditions
    (4) women and work
    (5) urban problems
  b. Middle-class and working-class life in the pre-Civil War North (families, gender roles, schooling, childhood, living conditions, status of free blacks)
  c. Foreign immigration and nativist reactions (Jews; Irish mass starvation, 1845–1850; Germans; 1848 refugees; Know Nothings)
  d. Patterns of Southern development (growth of cotton cultivation, movement into the Old Southwest, women on plantations)
  e. Life under slavery (slave laws; material conditions of life; women and children; religious and cultural expression; resistance)
	187, 189, 194–196, 197, 198, 199, 200–201, 202–205, 206–209, 210–211, 219, 230–232, 251

2. Equal rights and justice: expansion of franchise; search for minority rights; expansion of slavery; abolitionist movement; the underground railroad; denial of Native American Indian rights and land ownership
  a. Political democratization: national political nominating convention, secret ballot
  b. The rise of mass politics (John Quincy Adams, Andrew Jackson, the spoils system, the bank war, Martin Van Buren)
  c. Native Americans
    (1) History of Indian relations from 1607
    (2) Native American cultural survival strategies (cultural adaptation, cultural revitalization movements, Pan-Indian movements, resistance)
    (3) The removal policy: *Worcester* v. *Georgia*, 1832
  d. The birth of the American reform tradition (religious and secular roots; public schools; care for the physically disabled and the mentally ill; the problems of poverty and crime; antislavery; women's rights movement)
	164, 178, 192, 193, 214–215, 221–222, 224, 226–229, 232–235, 236–241, 242–247, 289–291, R66–R69

United States History and Government Standards	Student Edition Pages
3. The great constitutional debates: states' rights versus federal supremacy (nullification); efforts to address slavery issue (Missouri Compromise, Compromise of 1850, fugitive slave law, *Dred Scott* v. *Sanford*, 1857); preservation of the Union	212, 213, 225, 285, 287, 288
C. Territorial expansion through diplomacy, migration, annexation, and war; Manifest Destiny	163, 164, 168, 169, 170, 254–259, 260–263, 264–269, 270–275, 298
1. The Louisiana Purchase	168, 169, 170
2. Exploring and settling the West (explorers, Lewis and Clark expedition, naturalists, trappers and traders, trailblazers, missionaries, pioneers, the Mormon Church)	169, 170, 254–259
3. The Spanish, Mexican, and Native American West	163, 164, 260–263
4. Motives for and implications of expansion and western settlement	164, 170, 254, 256
5. Politics of western expansion (Manifest Destiny, the Texas and Oregon questions, the Mexican War)	164, 264–269, 270–275
6. Impact of western expansion upon Mexicans and Native Americans	164, 265, 275, 298
D. The Constitution in jeopardy: The American Civil War	212, 291–293, 294–296, 297, 298–300, 301, 302–307, 315, 316, 318, 319, 320–326, 327, 328–330, 331–332, 333, 334–335, 336–341, 344

1. United States society divided
  a. Party disintegration and realignment and sectional polarization (Kansas-Nebraska Act, disintegration of the Whig Party and the rise of the Republican Party, *Dred Scott* decision, John Brown's raid)
  b. Abraham Lincoln, the secession crisis, and efforts at compromise (Lincoln-Douglas debates, election of 1860, secession, compromise plans, Fort Sumter)
	212, 291–293, 294–296, 297, 298–300, 301, 302–307

2. Wartime actions
  a. Military strategy, major battles (Antietam, Gettysburg), and human toll
  b. Impact of war on home front (civil liberties during the Civil War, women's roles)
  c. Government policy during the war (wartime finances, creating a national currency, transcontinental railroad, Homestead Act)
  d. Lincoln and Emancipation (the Emancipation Proclamation, the Gettysburg Address, African-American participation in the Civil War, the 13th Amendment)
	291, 315, 316, 318, 319, 320–326, 327, 328–330, 331–332, 333, 334–335, 336–341, 344

Unit Three: Industrialization of the United States **I. The Reconstructed Nation**	
A. Reconstruction plans	356–363
1. Lincoln's plan	356–357
2. Congressional Reconstruction	357–358, 362
3. Post-Civil War amendments (13th, 14th, and 15th)	360, 361, 363
4. Impeachment of Andrew Johnson	363
5. The reconstructed nation and shifting relationships between the federal government, state governments, and individual citizens	362

United States History and Government Standards	Student Edition Pages
B. The North	372–377, 412–415, 422
1. Economic and technological impacts of the Civil War	372, 412, 413, 414
2. Expanding world markets	415
3. Developing labor needs	422
C. The New South	358–359, 360, 366–371, 372–377, 478
1. Agriculture: land and labor (sharecropping and tenant farming)	377

2. Status of freedmen
   a. The economic, political, social, and educational experiences of formerly enslaved African-Americans
   b. From exclusion to segregation
	358–359, 367–370, 371, 375, 478

3. Struggle for political control in the New South	367–368
4. Supreme Court interpretations of the 13th and 14th amendments (*Civil Rights* Cases, 1883)	478
5. The emerging debate over "proper" role of African-Americans	360, 478
D. End of Reconstruction	360, 375–376, 478, 479
1. Disputed election of 1876	375
2. End of military occupation	375, 376
3. Restoration of white control in the South (1870s and 1880s) and abridgment of rights of freed African-Americans	360, 375–376
4. *Plessy* v. *Ferguson*, 1896: "separate but equal"	478, 479
E. The Impact of the Civil War and Reconstruction: Summary	356–363, 366–371, 372–377, 410–415
1. On political alignments	367–368, 373
2. On the nature of citizenship	360, 361, 363
3. On federal-state relations	362
4. On the development of the North as an industrial power	410–415
5. On American society	358–359, 367–369
II. The Rise of American Business, Industry, and Labor, 1865–1920	
A. Economic transformation and the "search for order"	410, 415, 422–427, 438
1. Business response to change: organize and rationalize	422–427

2. Organizational responses
   a. From proprietorships and partnerships to the rise of monopolies
   b. Incorporation
   c. Capital concentration; consolidation
   d. Expanding markets: national and international
   e. Merchandising changes, department stores, mail order catalogs
	410, 415, 422, 424–426, 438

United States History and Government Standards	Student Edition Pages
B. Major areas of growth in business and industry	199, 410, 414, 416–421, 424–425
1. Transportation: railroads and automobiles; urban transportation	416–419
2. Building materials: steel	424–425
3. Energy sources: coal, oil, electricity	410
4. Communications: telegraph, telephone	199, 414
C. Representative entrepreneurs: Case studies in concentrated wealth and effort (other personalities may be substituted; local examples of enterprise should also be used)	422–427, 458–467
1. John D. Rockefeller: oil; Andrew Carnegie: steel; Ford: auto	424–426, 459, 460
2. Work ethic: Cotton Mather to Horatio Alger	458–459
3. Conflict between public good and private gain, e.g., use of resources	462–463
D. New business and government practices: Popular and government responses	414–415, 419–421, 422–427, 459, 463–465
1. Laissez-faire and government support; interpretation of 14th Amendment by Supreme Court	414, 415, 459, 465
2. Railroad "pooling"; rate inequities (*Wabash, St. Louis, and Pacific Railway* v. *Illinois*, 1886); railroad regulation: state and national ICC.	419–421, 463
3. Competition and absorption; mergers and trusts; Sherman Antitrust Act, 1890 (*United States* v. *E.C. Knight*, 1895)	423–426, 464
E. Labor's response to economic change: Organize	428–435
1. Efforts at national labor unions: Knights of Labor (1869); AF of L (1881–1886); ILGWU (1900) **a.** "Bread and butter" objectives **b.** Unions and social issues (education) **c.** Attitudes toward immigrants, African-Americans, women **d.** Union leadership (Gompers, Debs)	428, 432, 434, 435
2. Struggle and conflict **a.** Major strikes: gains and losses—Homestead, Pullman (In *Re Debs*, 1895), Lawrence **b.** Management's position **c.** Weapons or tactics employed in disputes between labor and management **d.** Attitude and role of government	429, 430, 431, 432, 433, 435
F. Agrarian response to economic change: Organize and protest	463, 470–475
a. The Grange movement as agrarian protest **b.** Populism: a political response—William Jennings Bryan and the election of 1896 **(1)** Case study: The Populists as a grassroots political party **c.** National government response: Interstate Commerce Act, 1887	463, 470–475

United States History and Government Standards	Student Edition Pages
III. Adjusting Society to Industrialism: American People and Places	
A. Impact of industrialization	442–447, 450–455, 458–459, 460–467, 498, R70–R71

1. Urban growth
  a. Attractions: jobs, education, culture, public education system
  b. Problems (slums, increased crime, inadequate water and sanitation services)
  c. Skyscrapers and elevators; tenements and walk-ups
  d. Social Darwinism, increased class division, conspicuous consumption, social conscience, philanthropy
	450, 451, 452, 454, 455, 458, 459, 464–465, 498, R70–R71

2. Work and workers
  a. Factories and people—immigrant patterns of settlement
  b. Geographic, economic, social, and political considerations
  c. Working conditions: "wage slavery"
  d. Living conditions: company towns and urban slums
  e. The Great Migration: The migration of African-Americans to the North
	442, 444, 453

3. Women, families, and work
  a. Traditional roles—Victorian ideal and reality
  b. Outside and inside their homes: double drudgery
  c. Jobs for domestics, laundresses, and textile workers; technology brought jobs as telephone operators and typists
  d. Emerging family patterns: two wage earners, broken homes
  e. Problems of child labor, elderly, disabled, and African-American women
    (1) Case study: child labor
  f. Role of religion in a pluralistic society
    (1) Religious tolerance develops slowly
    (2) Puritan beliefs and values influenced our historical development
    (3) Religion and party politics to 1896
	446, 453, 454, 460, 467

4. The growing middle class (consumerism and its material benefits and effects)	452–453
5. Art and literature (Mark Twain and penny dailies)	458, 461, 466
B. Immigration, 1850–1924	442–447, 448–449, 450–455, 464–467, 498
1. New sources: eastern/southern Europe; Asia—the "new ethnicity" **a.** Case studies: Italian immigration, Chinese immigration (1850–1924, West to East migration), Russian/Jewish immigration	445, 447
2. The impulses abroad	442
3. The attractions here: labor shortages, liberty, and freedoms	442, 445, 448–449
4. Urbanization: ghettos	444, 498
5. "Americanization" process	467
6. Impacts on family, religion, education, and politics	452–455, 464–467
7. Contributions to American society **a.** Diversity of the United States population	443–445, 464–467

United States History and Government Standards	Student Edition Pages
C. Reactions to the "new" immigration	446
1. Cultural pluralism: assimilation (Americanization), acculturation ("melting pot" or cultural pluralism), or both	467
2. Nativist reactions: stereotyping and prejudice **(1)** Case study: Irish immigration	446–447, 604–606
3. Impact on African-Americans and other established minorities	604–606
4. "Yellow Peril," West Coast restrictions	445, 447
5. Literacy testing, 1917	447
6. The Red Scare	579–581
7. Quota acts of 1921 and 1924	606
D. The frontier (1850–1890)	386–393, 394–397, 398–403,

1. Land west of the Mississippi
  a. Rolling plains and the Great American Desert
  b. Native American Indian nations; concept of oneness with the environment
  c. The Homestead Act, 1862, and the settlement of the West
	394, 395, 396, 398, 407

2. The impact of industrialization
  a. Improved transportation facilitated shipping of foodstuffs and migration of population
  b. Western migration of immigrants
  c. Potential for investment: development of key urban centers
	394, 397

3. Native American Indians
  a. Pressures of advancing white settlement: differing views of land use and ownership
  b. Treaties and legal status
  c. The Indian wars: 1850–1900
  d. Legislating Indian life: reservations; Dawes Act (1887)
  e. Indian civil rights laws—legal status of Native American Indians, 1887–1970: citizenship, 1924; self-government, 1934; self-determination, 1970
	398, 399, 400–401, 402, 403

Unit Four: The Progressive Movement: Responses to the Challenges Brought About by Industrialization and Urbanization **I. Reform in America**	
A. Pressures for reform	452–455, 520–527
1. Progressives supported the use of government power for different reform purposes	522, 526, 527
2. Effects of developing technologies and their social, ethical, and moral impacts	412–414, 450–451, 454–455
3. Struggle for fair standards of business operation and working conditions (*Lochner* v. *New York*, 1905; *Muller* v. *Oregon*, 1908)	526–527
4. Increasing inequities between wealth and poverty	452, 454–455
5. Rising power and influence of the middle class	452–453

United States History and Government Standards	Student Edition Pages
B. Progress: Social and economic reform and consumer protection	450–455, 466–467, 480, 498, 520–527, 530, 533, 541, 607, 621, R72–R73

1. The "Muckrakers" and reform
  a. Magazine writers (Steffens, Tarbell)
  b. Novelists (Norris, Sinclair)
  c. Legislation (Pure Food and Drug Act, 1906; Meat Inspection Act, 1906)
	498, 521, 530, 533, R72, R73

2. Other areas of concern
  a. Social settlement movement and the problems of poverty (Jacob Riis, Jane Addams)
  b. Women's rights and efforts for peace
    (1) The suffrage movement (Elizabeth Cady Stanton, Susan B. Anthony); Seneca Falls
    (2) Beginnings of fight for birth control (Margaret Sanger)
    (3) Peace movement
  c. The black movement and reform (Booker T. Washington and W.E.B. DuBois)
    (1) Formation of NAACP (1912)
    (2) Ida Wells (anti-lynching)
    (3) Marcus Garvey
  d. Temperance/prohibition
  e. Formation of Anti-Defamation League (1913)
	455, 466, 467, 480, 498, 521, 524–525, 527, 541, 607, 621

C. Progressivism and government action	520–527, 528–535, 536–541

1. Emerging Progressive movement: political reform
  (1) Influence of America's urban middle class
  a. Municipal and state reform
    (1) Municipal reform: response to urban problems
    (2) Sudden growth and needed services
  b. Progressive state reform: e.g., Wisconsin (Robert LaFollette); New York (Theodore Roosevelt); Massachusetts (initiative, referendum, recall); economic, social, environmental reforms
	522–523

2. Theodore Roosevelt and the Square Deal
  a. The stewardship theory of the Presidency
  b. Legislation strengthening railroad regulation and consumer protection
  c. "Trust-busting" court cases (*Northern Securities Co.* v. *United States*, 1904); rule of reason: Standard Oil
	528–529, 530, 531, 533

3. Conservation
  a. Theodore Roosevelt's concern for nature, land, and resources
  b. Federal legislation and projects: effects on states' limits
  c. Roles of Gifford Pinchot and John Muir
	532, 533

United States History and Government Standards	Student Edition Pages

4. Woodrow Wilson and the New Freedom
   a. Progressivism at its zenith; the 1912 election: Taft, Roosevelt, Wilson
   b. The Underwood Tariff and the graduated income tax
   c. Clayton Antitrust Act and the Federal Trade Commission
   d. The Federal Reserve System (monetary controls)
   e. Women's suffrage amendment
	525, 535, 536, 537, 538, 539

5. World War I: effect on domestic reform	576–581
II. The Rise of American Power	
A. An emerging global involvement	490–495, 496–503, 504–511

1. From old diplomacy to new, 1865–1900
   a. Role of increased American power
     (1) Communications technology
     (2) American attitudes toward international role
     (3) Growth of naval power
   b. Perry and the "opening" of Japan (1854)
	490–495

2. Other Pacific overtures
   a. United States and China; the Chinese perspective (Boxer Rebellion)
   b. The Open-Door policy
   c. Acquisition of Hawaii
   d. Naval bases: Samoa
	494, 504–507

3. Imperialism: the Spanish-American War
   a. Causes for war
   b. United States empire—Puerto Rico; Cuban protectorate (the Platt Amendment)
     (1) Acquisition of the Philippines: "the great debate"
     (2) Disposition of territories
     (3) Constitutional issues
	496–503

4. Latin American affairs
   a. Monroe Doctrine update (Roosevelt corollary): the view from Latin America
   b. West Indies protectorates ("the big stick")
   c. Panama Canal: acquisition and construction; Canal retrocession treaty
   d. Taft and dollar diplomacy
	506–511

B. Restraint and involvement: 1914–1920	548–581

1. United States involvement
   a. Efforts at neutrality and "preparedness"
   b. Causes of United States entry into World War I
   c. United States role in the war
   d. United States reaction to the Russian Revolution
	548–581

New York Core Curriculum

United States History and Government Standards	Student Edition Pages
C. Wartime constitutional issues	558, 559, 560–561, 579–581
1. War opposition and patriotism: the draft issue	560–561
2. Espionage and Sedition acts	558, 559, 585
3. *Schenck* v. *United States*, 1919; clear and present danger doctrine	559
4. Red Scare, 1918–1919	579–581
D. The search for peace and arms control: 1914–1930	552, 564, 570–573, 585, 594–595
1. The peace movement: Women's International League for Peace and Freedom	552
2. War aims: The Fourteen Points	570–571
3. Treaty of Versailles: Wilson's role	570–573
4. League of Nations: Henry Cabot Lodge and the United States Senate rejection	572–573, 585
5. Washington Naval Disarmament Conference (1920s)	595
6. Reparations and war debts (United States as a world banker)	564, 594, 595
7. Kellogg-Briand Pact (1928)	595
8. Establishment of the World Court	594
Unit Five: At Home and Abroad: Prosperity and Depression, 1917–1940 **I. War and Prosperity: 1917–1929**	
A. Impact of war	558, 578, 560–561, 578, 581, 590, 619–621
1. War's effects on gender roles, on African-Americans, and other minority groups	558, 560–561, 578, 619–621
2. Case study: Movement of African-Americans from the South to northern cities	558, 578, 620–621
3. Return to "normalcy": 1918–1921	581, 590
B. The twenties: Business boom or false prosperity?	576–577, 590–593, 602–603, 628–629
1. Post-World War I recession	576–577
2. Avarice and scandal: Teapot Dome	590–592
3. Coolidge prosperity; not for everyone	592, 593, 602

4. Problems on the farm
    a. Expansion, mortgages, and advancing technology
    b. Farmers and minorities fail to share in economic benefit
	602, 603

5. Speculative boom: the "big bull market"	628–629
C. Mass consumption and the clash of cultural values	525, 596–603, 604–609, 610–614, 616–619, R74–R75

1. Mass consumption
    a. The automobile: new industries, products, and services
    b. Installment buying: consumer durable goods (appliances)
    c. Real estate boom and suburban development; its economic and geographic implications: decline of trolleys and trains, improvement of roads
        (1) The emergence of new regional, political, and economic units
    d. Entertainment: radio; motion pictures; advertising and cultural homogenization
	596–599, 600–601, 612–613

United States History and Government Standards	Student Edition Pages

2. Constitutional and legal issues
  a. Threats to civil liberties: Red Scare, Ku Klux Klan, and Sacco and Vanzetti
  b. Prohibition (18th Amendment) and the Volstead Act: stimulus to crime, public attitudes, repeal (21st Amendment)
  c. Science, religion, and education: the Scopes trial (1925)
  d. Restrictions on immigration: closing the "golden door"
	604–605, 606, 608–609, R74–R75

3. Shifting cultural values
  a. Revolution in morals and manners: fads, flappers, and Freud
  b. Women's changing roles
    (1) Effect of World War I
    (2) Involvement in the political process: the 19th Amendment
    (3) Health and working conditions
    (4) Women in the workforce
    (5) Emerging role: emphasis on wife rather than mother
  c. The literary scene
    (1) Sinclair Lewis, Ernest Hemingway, Edith Wharton, Willa Cather, and F. Scott Fitzgerald
    (2) The Harlem Renaissance: Duke Ellington, Langston Hughes, Bessie Smith
	525, 606–607, 611–614, 616–619

II. The Great Depression	
A. Onset of the Depression	628–633, 640–643

1. Weakness in the economy
  a. Overproduction/underconsumption (maldistribution of wealth)
  b. Overexpansion of credit (e.g., buying stock on margin)
	629, 631, 632, 633

2. The stock market crash
  a. Worldwide nature—Growing financial interdependence
  b. Interdependent banking systems
  c. International trade
  d. Political repercussions
	630, 631, 633

3. The Hoover response
  a. Rugged individualism; "trickle down" economics
  b. Reconstruction Finance Corporation
	640–643

4. Unemployment, the Bonus Army, Hoovervilles; impact on women and minorities	642–643
B. Franklin D. Roosevelt and the New Deal: Relief, recovery, and reform programs	635–637, 650–659, 662–667, 668–673

1. Relief of human suffering
  a. Bank "holiday"; Emergency Banking Act
  b. Federal Emergency Relief Act
  c. Unemployment: WPA, PWA, CCC; troubling equity issues
	652, 653, 654, 658–659, 664

New York Core Curriculum

United States History and Government Standards	Student Edition Pages

2. Recovery of the United States economy
   a. NRA: "codes of fair competition"
   b. Mortgage relief: HOLC, FHA
   c. First and second AAA, scarcity and parity
	654–655, 656, 657

3. Search for effective reform (program examples)
   a. Banking: Glass-Steagall Act (FDIC)
   b. Stock market: SEC
   c. Social Security
   d. Labor
      (1) Wagner Act (NLRB)
      (2) Labor Standards Act
	654, 665, 667, 672

4. Labor's response: Formation of CIO	666, 667

5. Controversial aspects of the New Deal
   a. Constitutional issues
      (1) Supreme Court and the NRA (*Schechter Poultry Corp.* v. *United States*, 1935)
      (2) Supreme Court and the AAA
      (3) TVA: model yardstick or creeping socialism
   b. 1936 election "mandate"
   c. Roosevelt's "Court-packing" proposal: failure and success
   d. 1940: third-term controversy (the unwritten constitution)
   e. Passage of the 22nd Amendment (1951)
	656, 664–665, 669, 670, 671

6. The human factor
   a. FDR as communicator and his efforts to restore public confidence; press conferences, "fireside chats," and effective use of the radio
   b. Eleanor Roosevelt as the President's eyes and ears
   c. The Dust Bowl and the Okies
   d. The New Deal and women (Frances Perkins)
   e. The New Deal and minorities (shift in African-American vote): discriminatory results
   f. Indian Reorganization Act (1934)
	635, 650–651, 653, 668, 669, 672

7. Culture of the Depression
   a. Literature: John Steinbeck and Langston Hughes
   b. Music: jazz, swing (big bands)
   c. Art: WPA, fine arts, Hollywood, comic books
	635–637

8. Opposition to the New Deal: Al Smith, Norman Thomas, Huey Long, Father Coughlin, Dr. Townsend	662–663
Unit Six: The United States in an Age of Global Crisis: Responsibility and Cooperation **I. Peace in Peril: 1933–1950**	
A. Isolation and neutrality	686–687
1. Causes of disillusion and pacifism	686
2. Neutrality Acts of 1935–37	686–687

NY30

United States History and Government Standards	Student Edition Pages
3. Spanish Civil War: testing war technology and ideology	686–687
4. FDR's "quarantine" speech (1937)	687
B. Failure of peace; triumph of aggression	682–685, 688–693
1. Aggressions of Japan, Germany, Italy: 1932–1940	682, 684–686, 687, 688, 690–693
2. Appeasement: The Munich Conference (1938)	689
3. German attack on Poland; start of World War II in Europe	690–693

4. Gradual United States involvement
  a. Neutrality Act of 1939 ("cash and carry")
  b. Lend-Lease Act and 50 overage destroyers deal
  c. The moral dimension: The Atlantic Charter (August 1941)
	702, 703, 704–705

C. The United States in World War II	705–707, 714–753
1. Pearl Harbor	705–707

2. The human dimensions of the war
  a. The "arsenal of democracy" (feats of productivity)
  b. Role of women: WACs; Rosie the Riveter; return of the retired
  c. Mobilization: the draft; minority issues
  d. Financing the war: war bond drives; Hollywood goes to war
  e. Rationing
  f. Experiences of men and women in military service
	714–717, 718–721, 728–730, 734–735, 742

3. Allied strategy and leadership
  a. Assistance to Soviet Union
  b. Europe first
  c. A two-front war
	714, 722–727, 736–740, 746–747, 748–750

4. The atomic bomb
  a. The Manhattan Project (role of refugees)
  b. Truman's decision to use the atomic bomb against Japan: Hiroshima and Nagasaki
  c. United States occupation of Japan; the "MacArthur constitution"
  d. Japanese war crime trials
	750–753, 770

5. The war's impact on minorities
  a. Incarceration of West Coast Japanese-Americans; Executive Order 9066; *Korematsu* v. *United States* (1944)
  b. Extent of racially integrated units in the military
  c. The Nazi Holocaust: United States and world reactions
  d. The Nuremberg war crimes trials; later trials of other Nazi criminals, e.g., Eichmann, Barbie
	694–699, 700–701, 719–721, 730, 732, 733, 752, 753, R76

United States History and Government Standards	Student Edition Pages
6. Demobilization **a.** Inflation and strikes **b.** The G.I. Bill; impact on education and housing **c.** Truman's Fair Deal **d.** Partisan problems with Congress **e.** Minorities continued to find it difficult to obtain fair practices in housing, employment, education **f.** Upset election of 1948; Truman versus Dewey **g.** Truman and civil rights	794–797
II. Peace with Problems: 1945–1960	
A. International peace efforts	752–753
1. Formation of the United Nations	752–753
2. United Nations Universal Declaration of Human Rights **a.** Eleanor Roosevelt's role **b.** Senate response	752–753
3. Displaced persons: refugee efforts	696–697, 760, 761
B. Expansion and containment: Europe	760–769
1. Summitry: Yalta and Potsdam, establishing "spheres of influence"	760, 761–765
2. The Iron Curtain: Winston Churchill	764, 765

3. Postwar uses for United States power
 a. The Truman Doctrine: Greece and Turkey
 b. The Marshall Plan
    (1) Aid for Europe
    (2) The Common Market
    (3) European Parliament
 c. Berlin airlift
 d. Formation of NATO alliance
	767, 768–769

C. Containment in Asia, Africa, and Latin America	771–773, 784–787
1. The United States and Japan **a.** Separate peace treaty (1951) **b.** Reconstruction of Japan **2.** The United States and China **a.** Rise to power of Mao Zedong and the People's Republic of China **b.** Chiang Kai-shek to Taiwan (1949) **3.** USSR tests an A-bomb (1949) **4.** The "hot war" in Asia: Korean War **a.** The Yalu River: China enters the war **b.** United Nations efforts: MacArthur, Truman, and "limited war" **c.** Stalemate and truce (1953) **5.** Point four aid: Africa, Asia, Latin America	770–772, 773, 780, 782, 784–787

United States History and Government Standards	Student Edition Pages
D. The Cold War at home	774–778, 782, 784, 796, 798
1. Truman and government loyalty checks; Case studies: The Smith Act and the House Un-American Activities Committee (Watkins v. United States, 1957); the Alger Hiss case (1950); the Rosenberg trial (1950)	774, 775, 776, 779
2. Loyalty and dissent: the case of Robert Oppenheimer	775
3. McCarthyism	777, 778

4. Politics of the Cold War
  a. Loss of China
  b. Stalemate in Korea
  c. Truman's falling popularity
	782, 784, 796, 798

Unit Seven: World in Uncertain Times: 1950–Present **I. Toward a Postindustrial World: Living in a Global Age**	
A. Changes within the United States	794–795, 802–803, 813–814, 958–961, 1002–1005, 1022
1. Energy sources (nuclear power) **2.** Materials (plastics, light metals) **3.** Technology (computers) **4.** Corporate structures (multinational corporations) **5.** Nature of employment (agriculture to industry to service) **6.** Problems (waste disposal, air/water pollution, growing energy usage, depleting resources, e.g., domestic oil supply)	794–795, 802–803, 813–814, 958–961, 982–985, 1002–1005, 1022
II. Containment and Consensus: 1945–1960	
A. Review postwar events	765, 769, 770–772, 773, 784–787, 830–832
1. Emerging power relationships: East/West; North/South; (haves/have-nots; developed/developing nations)	765, 769, 770–772, 773, 830–832, 1022–1025
B. Eisenhower foreign policies	784–787
1. The end of the Korean War	784
2. John Foster Dulles, the domino theory and massive retaliation; brinkmanship posture	782–783
3. The H-bomb; atoms for peace	780, 782–783
4. Summits and U-2s	786–787
5. Establishment of SEATO	773
6. Controversy: Aswan Dam and Suez Canal	786–787
7. Polish and Hungarian uprisings	786
8. Eisenhower Doctrine: intervention in Lebanon	787
9. Sputnik: initiating the space race	784, 787, 815

New York Core Curriculum

United States History and Government Standards	Student Edition Pages
C. Domestic politics and constitutional issues	794–799, 827, 828–829, 850–851, 852, 853–857
1. The Eisenhower peace 　**a.** Returning the United States to a peacetime economy 　**b.** Interstate Highway Act (1956) 　**c.** Suburbanization 　**d.** The Warren Court	798–799, 800–801, 827, 828–829
2. Civil rights 　**a.** Jackie Robinson breaks the color barrier 　**b.** *Brown* v. *Board of Education of Topeka*, 1954 　**c.** Beginnings of modern civil rights movement 　　**(1)** Rosa Parks and the Montgomery bus boycott 　　**(2)** Little Rock: school desegregation 　　**(3)** Segregation in public transportation ruled unconstitutional 　　**(4)** Sit-ins: nonviolent tactic 　　**(5)** Civil Rights Act of 1957	850–851, 852, 853, 854–855, 856–857, 858, 859
D. The people	794–795, 800–802, 804–807, 808–809, 810–815
1. Prosperity and conservatism 　**a.** Postwar consumption: homes, autos, and television 　**b.** New educational opportunities: G.I. Bill 　**c.** The baby boom and its effects	794–795, 800, 801, 804–805, 815, 826
2. Migration and immigration 　**a.** Suburbanization: Levittowns 　**b.** Cities: declining 　**c.** New immigration patterns: Caribbean focus	800–801, 810–813
III. Decade of Change: 1960s	
A. The Kennedy years	824–835, 858–863
1. The New Frontier: dreams and promises 　**a.** Civil rights actions 　　**(1)** James Meredith at the University of Mississippi 　　**(2)** Public career of Dr. Martin Luther King, Jr., Birmingham protest ("Letter from Birmingham Jail") 　　**(3)** Assassination of Medgar Evers 　　**(4)** March on Washington	825–826, 854–855, 861, 862, 863, 864, 872, 875

United States History and Government Standards	Student Edition Pages

2. Foreign policy and Cold War crises
   a. Bay of Pigs invasion
   b. Vienna Summit/Berlin Wall
   c. Cuban missile crisis
   d. Laos and Vietnam
   e. Latin America and the Alliance for Progress
   f. Peace Corps
   g. Launching the race to the Moon
   h. Nuclear Test Ban Treaty 1963, 1967; Hot Line established
	830–832, 832–833, 834–835, 882, 884, 889

3. Movement for rights of disabled citizens
   a. Background
     (1) Historic attitude that disabled were defective
     (2) Emergence of humanitarian view in 19th century, development of large institutions
     (3) Development of the concept of normalization; early-20th-century programs of education and training
   b. Kennedy administration, 1961–1963; beginning awareness, changing attitudes
     (1) President's Council on Mental Retardation
     (2) Special Olympics
   c. Litigation and legislation; 1960–present
     (1) Education of the Handicapped Act, 1966
     (2) Education for All Handicapped Children Act, 1971
     (3) Rehabilitation Act of 1973, Section 504
     (4) Americans with Disabilities Act, 1990
   d. Dependence to independence
     (1) Activism by disabled veterans
     (2) Deinstitutionalization
     (3) Mainstreaming
	446, 453, 826, 957

4. Assassination in Dallas	835
B. Johnson and the Great Society	838–843

1. Expanding on the Kennedy social programs
   a. War on poverty; VISTA
   b. Medicare
   c. Federal aid to education
   d. Environmental issues and concerns
	838–839, 840–843

2. The Moon landing: the challenge of space exploration	832, 833

United States History and Government Standards	Student Edition Pages

3. Continued demands for equality: civil rights movement
  a. Black protest, pride, and power
    (1) NAACP (National Association for the Advancement of Colored People): legal judicial leadership, Urban League
  b. Case studies
    (1) SNCC (Student Nonviolent Coordinating Committee): sit-in movement among college students
    (2) SCLC (Southern Christian Leadership Conference): promote nonviolent resistance, sit-ins, boycotts
    (3) CORE (Congress of Racial Equality): "Freedom Riders"
    (4) Testing of segregation laws
    (5) Others: Black Muslims; prominence of Malcolm X: advocating separation of races, separate state in the United States
    (6) Civil unrest: Watts riot, 1965, as example; Kerner Commission
    (7) Assassination of Malcolm X (February 1965)
  c. Legislative impact
    (1) Civil Rights Act of 1964 (*Heart of Atlanta Motel, Inc.* v. *United States*, 1964), modifications since 1964
    (2) 24th Amendment (eliminating poll tax)
    (3) Voting Rights Act, 1965
    (4) Court decisions since 1948 upholding or modifying preferential treatment in employment; equal access to housing; travel and accommodations; voting rights; educational equity
    (5) Fair Housing Act, 1968
	828, 841, 850–851, 854, 855, 858–859, 860–861, 862, 863, 864–865, 866–867, 868–869, 870–871, 872–874, 875

4. **Demands for equality: women**
  a. The modern women's movement
    (1) Kennedy Commission and the Civil Rights Act, 1963–1964
    (2) NOW (1966) to present
  b. Issues
    (1) Shifting roles and images
    (2) Equal Rights Amendment (failure to ratify)
    (3) *Roe* v. *Wade*, 1973
    (4) Equality in the workplace: compensation, the glass ceiling
    (5) Increased focus on domestic abuse
	826, 914–915, 916, 917–919

5. Rising consciousness of Hispanic-Americans
  a. "Brown power" movement
  b. Organizing farm labor (Cesar Chavez)
  c. Cuban and Haitian immigration
  d. Increasing presence in American politics
	920–922, 923–925

6. Demands for equality: American Indian Movement (AIM) and other protests
  a. Occupation of Alcatraz
  b. The "long march"
  c. Wounded Knee, 1973
	955–956

United States History and Government Standards	Student Edition Pages

7. Rights of the accused
  a. *Mapp* v. *Ohio*, 1961
  b. *Gideon* v. *Wainwright*, 1963
  c. *Miranda* v. *Arizona*, 1966
	827, 828–829

8. Legislative reapportionment: *Baker* v. *Carr*, 1962	827, 828
IV. The Limits of Power: Turmoil at Home and Abroad, 1965–1972	
A. Vietnam: sacrifice and turmoil	882–904, 910–913
1. The French-Indochinese War: early United States involvement; Truman, Eisenhower, and Kennedy policies (review how foreign policy is formulated)	882–883, 884, 885
2. United States and the spread of communism; domino theory; credibility of other United States commitments	883
3. Civil war in South Vietnam; concept of guerrilla warfare	883–884, 888–889

4. LBJ and the Americanization of the war
  a. Fear of "losing" Vietnam
  b. Escalation and United States assumptions; Tet offensive
	886–889, 895

5. Student protests at home
  a. Draft protesters
  b. Political radicals: protests, Students for a Democratic Society (SDS), antiwar
  c. Cultural radicals: hippies and communalists
	892–894, 898–900, 910–913

6. 1968: A year of turmoil
  a. President Johnson's decision not to seek reelection
  b. Assassinations of Dr. Martin Luther King, Jr. (April 1968) and Robert Kennedy (June 1968)
  c. The Democratic Convention; war protesters disrupt proceedings
  d. Impact of the Vietnam War on society
	896–899, 901, 902–903

V. The Trend Toward Conservatism, 1972–1985	
A. Nixon as President, 1969–1974	934–944

1. Domestic policies and events
  a. Modifications to Great Society programs (OSHA, Federal Energy Office, DEA, Clean Air Act, food stamps, revenue sharing)
  b. The Moon landing
  c. Environmental Protection Agency (1970)
  d. Self-determination for American Indians (1970)
  e. Ratification of the 26th Amendment (1971)
  f. Title IX—equal education access (1972)
	832, 833, 894, 918, 936, 956, 960

United States History and Government Standards	Student Edition Pages

2. Nixon's internationalism
   a. Henry Kissinger and realpolitik
     (1) Withdrawal from Vietnam and Cambodia; peace talks and signing of Paris Peace Accords (Pentagon papers, *New York Times* v. *United States*, 1971)
     (2) Nixon Doctrine
     (3) Opening to China
     (4) Detente: SALT and grain
	898–900, 901, 937, 938–939

3. The Presidency in crisis
   a. Resignation of Spiro Agnew
   b. Watergate affair and its constitutional implications
   c. *United States* v. *Nixon*, 1974
   d. The impeachment process and resignation
	933, 940–942, 943, 944–945

B. The Ford and Carter Presidencies	946–951
1. The appointive Presidency: Ford and Rockefeller (the constitutional aspects)	945

2. Domestic policy issues
   a. Pardon for Nixon and amnesty for draft evaders
   b. Oil crisis: shifting energy priorities
   c. Environmental concerns
     (1) Three Mile Island
     (2) Acid rain
     (3) Toxic waste
	945, 946–947, 948–949, 958–961

3. Foreign policy issues: the United States after Vietnam
   a. Fall of South Vietnam, 1975
   b. Oil crisis: Middle East in turmoil
   c. Middle East mediation: Camp David Accords
   d. The Afghanistan invasion: Olympics and grain—diplomatic weapons
   e. Iranian hostage crisis: 1979–1981
	900, 946, 950–951

C. Reagan and Bush, the "new" federalism and growth of conservatism	968–996
1. Supply-side economics	976
2. Tax policy and deficits	976–977
3. Environmental and civil rights policies	978
4. Effects on minorities	936, 952–957, 986

5. The Supreme Court and the schools
   a. *Engle* v. *Vitale*, 1962
   b. *Tinker* v. *Des Moines School District*, 1969
   c. *New Jersey* v. *TLO*, 1985
   d. *Vernonia School District* v. *Acton*, 1995
	828–829, 986

United States History and Government Standards	Student Edition Pages
D. New approaches to old problems	936, 986, 971, 1016–1019, 1020–1021, 1051–1052
1. Feast and famine: the farmer's dilemma	986
2. The problems of poverty in an affluent society—"the underclass"	936
3. The "new" immigrants; (Immigration Reform and Control Act of 1986)	1016–1019, 1020–1021
4. Changing demographic patterns (growing numbers of elderly)	971, 1051–1052
E. Renewed United States power image	979, 980–981
1. Central America and the Caribbean: debt and stability; Sandinistas, Contras, El Salvadorians	979, 980
2. Middle East: war and hostages	951, 980
F. Trade imbalance and divesting	947
1. Japan: trade imbalance **2.** United States and South Africa	947
G. United States–Soviet relations	979, 980–981, 990–991
1. Gorbachev and Soviet relations	979, 980–981, 990–991
2. "Star Wars" and arms limitation efforts	981
3. Cuts in defense spending and the fall of the Soviet Union	990–992
VI. Approaching The Next Century, 1986–1999	
A. The Bush Presidency	990–995

1. Case study: The election of 1988
   a. Effects of demographics
   b. Rise of a third party (H. Ross Perot)
   c. Increasing influence of political action committees
	990, 995

2. Domestic issues
   a. Environmental concerns
   b. Immigration issues
   c. Savings and loan scandal
   d. Social concerns (*Cruzan* v. *Director, Missouri Department of Health*, 1990 and *Planned Parenthood of Southeastern Pennsylvania, et.al.* v. *Casey*, 1992)
	986–987, 994–995, 1016–1019, 1020–1021, 1025

3. Foreign policy issues
   a. Dissolution of the Soviet Union
   b. Fall of the Berlin Wall and German reunification (1990)
   c. Crisis in Bosnia
   d. Persian Gulf crisis
	990–992, 993, 1014–1015

United States History and Government Standards	Student Edition Pages
B. The Clinton Presidency	1008–1015, 1023–1025

1. Domestic issues
  a. Social concerns
    (1) Health care
    (2) Education
    (3) Welfare reform
    (4) Stability of the Social Security system
  b. Economic concerns
    (1) Role of technologies
    (2) Impact of the baby boom generation
    (3) Balanced budget amendment (debate)
    (4) Market trends: The bull market of the 1990s
  c. Political concerns
    (1) Senate Whitewater investigations
    (2) Gun control
    (3) Campaign finance reform (debate)
  d. Impeachment and acquittal
	1002–1005, 1008–1009, 1010–1012, 1013, 1022

2. Foreign policy issues
  a. United States—Middle East relations: Israeli—PLO agreement (Rabin—Arafat)
  b. United States in the global economy
    (1) NAFTA
    (2) GATT
    (3) Economic aid to Russia
    (4) United States trade with China, Japan, and Latin America
  c. Intervention in Somalia, Haiti, Bosnia, and Yugoslavia
  d. United States—Russian relations; 1990 to the present
  e. United States—European relations: European Union (EU), NATO
	990–992, 1014–1015, 1023–1024

The AMERICAN VISION

Joyce Appleby, Ph.D.   Alan Brinkley, Ph.D.   Albert S. Broussard, Ph.D.

James M. McPherson, Ph.D.   Donald A. Ritchie, Ph.D.

NATIONAL
GEOGRAPHIC

About the Cover The images on the cover are (from left to right): the March on Selma, a Polish immigrant arriving at Ellis Island, Benjamin Franklin, Ulysses S. Grant, Firefighters raising the U.S. flag on 9/11, Zora Neale Hurston, and *Oregon Trail* by Alfred Bierstadt.

*The **McGraw·Hill** Companies*

 Glencoe

Send all inquiries to: Glencoe/McGraw-Hill, 8787 Orion Place, Columbus, OH 43240-4027

ISBN: 978-0-07-874521-8
MHID: 0-07-874521-7

Printed in the United States of America.

2 3 4 5 6 7 8 9 10 027/055 11 10 09 08 07

Joyce Appleby, Ph.D., is Professor of History at UCLA. Dr. Appleby's published works include *Inheriting the Revolution: The First Generation of Americans; Capitalism and a New Social Order: The Jeffersonian Vision of the 1790s;* and *Ideology and Economic Thought in Seventeenth-Century England,* which won the Berkshire Prize. She served as president of both the Organization of American Historians and the American Historical Association, and chaired the Council of the Institute of Early American History and Culture at Williamsburg. Dr. Appleby has been elected to the American Philosophical Society and the American Academy of Arts and Sciences, and is a Corresponding Fellow of the British Academy.

Alan Brinkley, Ph.D., is Allan Nevins Professor of American History at Columbia University. His published works include *Voices of Protest: Huey Long, Father Coughlin, and the Great Depression,* which won the 1983 National Book Award; *The End of Reform: New Deal Liberalism in Recession and War; The Unfinished Nation: A Concise History of the American People; and Liberalism and its Discontents.* He received the Levenson Memorial Teaching Prize at Harvard University.

Albert S. Broussard, Ph.D., is Professor of History and Graduate Coordinator at Texas A&M University. Before joining the Texas A&M faculty, Dr. Broussard was Assistant Professor of History and Director of the African American Studies Program at Southern Methodist University. Among his publications are the books *Black San Francisco: The Struggle for Racial Equality in the West, 1900– 1954* and *African American Odyssey: The Stewarts, 1853–1963.* Dr. Broussard has also served as president of the Oral History Association.

James M. McPherson, Ph.D., is George Henry Davis Professor of American History at Princeton University. Dr. McPherson is the author of 11 books about the Civil War era. These include *Battle Cry of Freedom: The Civil War Era,* for which he won the Pulitzer Prize in 1989, and *For Cause and Comrades: Why Men Fought in the Civil War,* for which he won the 1998 Lincoln Prize. He is a member of many professional historical associations, including the Civil War Preservation Trust.

Donald A. Ritchie, Ph.D., is Associate Historian of the United States Senate Historical Office. Dr. Ritchie received his doctorate in American history from the University of Maryland after service in the U.S. Marine Corps. He has taught American history at various levels, from high school to university. He edits the Historical Series of the Senate Foreign Relations Committee and is the author of several books, including *Doing Oral History, The Oxford Guide to the United States Government, and Press Gallery: Congress and the Washington Correspondents,* which received the Organization of American Historians Richard W. Leopold Prize. Dr. Ritchie has served as president of the Oral History Association and as a council member of the American Historical Association.

The National Geographic Society, founded in 1888 for the increase and diffusion of geographic knowledge, is the world's largest nonprofit scientific and educational organization. Since its earliest days, the Society has used sophisticated communication technologies, from color photography to holography, to convey knowledge to its worldwide membership. The School Publishing Division supports the Society's mission by developing innovative educational programs—ranging from traditional print materials to multimedia programs including CD-ROMs, dvds, and software.

Contributing Author

Dinah Zike, M.Ed., is an award-winning author, educator, and inventor known for designing three-dimensional hands-on manipulatives and graphic organizers known as Foldables™. Foldables are used nationally and internationally by teachers, parents, and educational publishing companies. Dinah has developed over 150 supplemental educational books and materials. She is the author of *The Big Book of Books and Activities,* which was awarded Learning Magazine's Teachers' Choice Award. In 2004 Dinah was honored with the CESI Science Advocacy Award. Dinah received her M.Ed. from Texas A&M, College Station, Texas.

Consultants & Reviewers

Academic Consultants

David Berger
Broeklundian Professor of History
Brooklyn College and the Graduate Center
City University of New York
Brooklyn, New York

Paul Cimbala
Professor of History
Fordham University, Rose Hill Campus
Bronx, New York

Linda Clemmons
Assistant Professor of History
Illinois State University
Normal, Illinois

Charles Eagles
Professor of History
University of Mississippi
University, Mississippi

Neil Foley
Associate Professor of History
University of Texas at Austin
Austin, Texas

Allison Gough
Assistant Professor of History
Hawaii Pacific University
Honolulu, Hawaii

K. Austin Kerr
Emeritus Professor of History
The Ohio State University
Columbus, Ohio

Jeffrey Ogbar
Associate Professor of History and Director of
    the Institute for African American Studies
University of Connecticut, Storrs
Storrs, Connecticut

Elizabeth Pleck
Professor of History
University of Illinois at Urbana-Champaign
Urbana, Illinois

William Bruce Wheeler
Emeritus Professor of History
University of Tennessee
Knoxville, Tennessee

Shawn Johansen
Professor of History
Brigham Young University Idaho
Rexburg, Idaho

Teacher Reviewers

Joanna Ackley
John F. Kennedy High School
Taylor, Michigan

Pat Ambrose
Adlai E. Stevenson High School
Lincolnshire, Illinois

Sharon K. Anderson
Cookeville High School
Cookeville, Tennessee

Fred Barnett
Cibola High School
Albuquerque, New Mexico

Shawn Barnum
Tonawanda High School
Tonawanda, New York

Vincent Beasley
Eastern Wayne High School
Goldsboro, North Carolina

Jeremiah Bergan
Baker High School
Baldwinsville, New York

Randy Bishop
Middleton High School
Middleton, Tennessee

Patrick Boyd
Ravenwood High School
Brentwood, Tennessee

Suzanne Brock
Vestavia Hills High School
Vestavia Hills, Alabama

Joyce Brown
LaFayette High School
LaFayette, Georgia

David Chapman
Bentonville High School
Bentonville, Arkansas

Teresa Cooper
Battle Creek Central High School
Battle Creek, Michigan

Timothy Davish
Lakota East High School
Liberty Township, Ohio

Peter DeWolf
First Colonial High School
Virginia Beach, Virginia

Glenn DiTomaso
Norwell High School
Norwell, Massachusetts

Kimberly Dunn
Chase High School
Forest City, North Carolina

Bre England
Warren Central High School
Indianapolis, Indiana

Robert Fenster
Hillsborough High School
Hillsborough, New Jersey

James A. Field
Morgantown High School
Morgantown, West Virginia

Shane Gardner
Freedom High School
Morganton, North Carolina

Diane Gebel
Attica High School
Attica, New York

James Gill
Binghamton High School
Binghamton, New York

Mary Ellen Goergen
Amherst High School
Amherst, New York

Teacher Reviewers

Robert Haley
Cleveland Hill High School
Cheektowaga, New York

Ken Hall
Larkin High School
Elgin, Illinois

Roberta Heath
Capital High School
Charleston, West Virginia

Cliff Hong
Liverpool High School
Liverpool, New York

George Irby
Miami Killian Senior High School
Miami, Florida

JeTaun Jamerson
Lake View High School
Chicago, Illinois

Carol Johnson
Cary High School
Cary, North Carolina

Harry F. Jones
Panther Creek High School
Cary, North Carolina

Shirley Jones
Hillcrest High School
Memphis, Tennessee

Joe Leonard
Southport High School
Indianapolis, Indiana

Tom Long
Buffalo Gap High School
Swoope, Virginia

Rebecca Mabrey
Central Cabarrus High School
Concord, North Carolina

Amy MacIntosh
Fairfield Warde High School
Fairfield, Connecticut

Shannon W. McDonald
Harding University High School
Charlotte, North Carolina

Chad McGee
Warren County High School
McMinnville, Tennessee

Marty McNeil
Akron East High School
Akron, Ohio

Kathryn Merritt
Hillcrest High School
Tuscaloosa, Alabama

Rita Morgan
Beaverton High School
Beaverton, Oregon

Jimmy Neal
Beech High School
Hendersonville, Tennessee

Teresa Pardee
East Mecklenburg High School
Charlotte, North Carolina

Patricia Radigan
Thomas Dale High School
Chester, Virginia

Steven Reeder
Cordova High School
Cordova, Tennessee

Debi Reeves
Liberty High School
Bedford, Virginia

Connie Schlieker
Atherton High School
Louisville, Kentucky

Mark Schuler
North Springs High School
Atlanta, Georgia

Russ Smith
Ashley High School
Wilmington, North Carolina

Mitzi Terry
Franklin High School
Franklin, Tennessee

Dal Tomlinson
Dixon High School
Holly Ridge, North Carolina

Penny Toneatti
Half Hollow Hills High School East
Dix Hills, New York

Lisa Valentine
Harding University High School
Charlotte, North Carolina

Stan Vickers
Westview High School
Martin, Tennessee

Danielle Walsh
Emmaus High School
Emmaus, Pennsylvania

Joshua White
Charlotte High School
Rochester, New York

Gerald Wild II
Alden High School
Alden, New York

Amy Working
Central High School
Memphis, Tennessee

Table of Contents

Table of Contents

Unit 2

Table of Contents

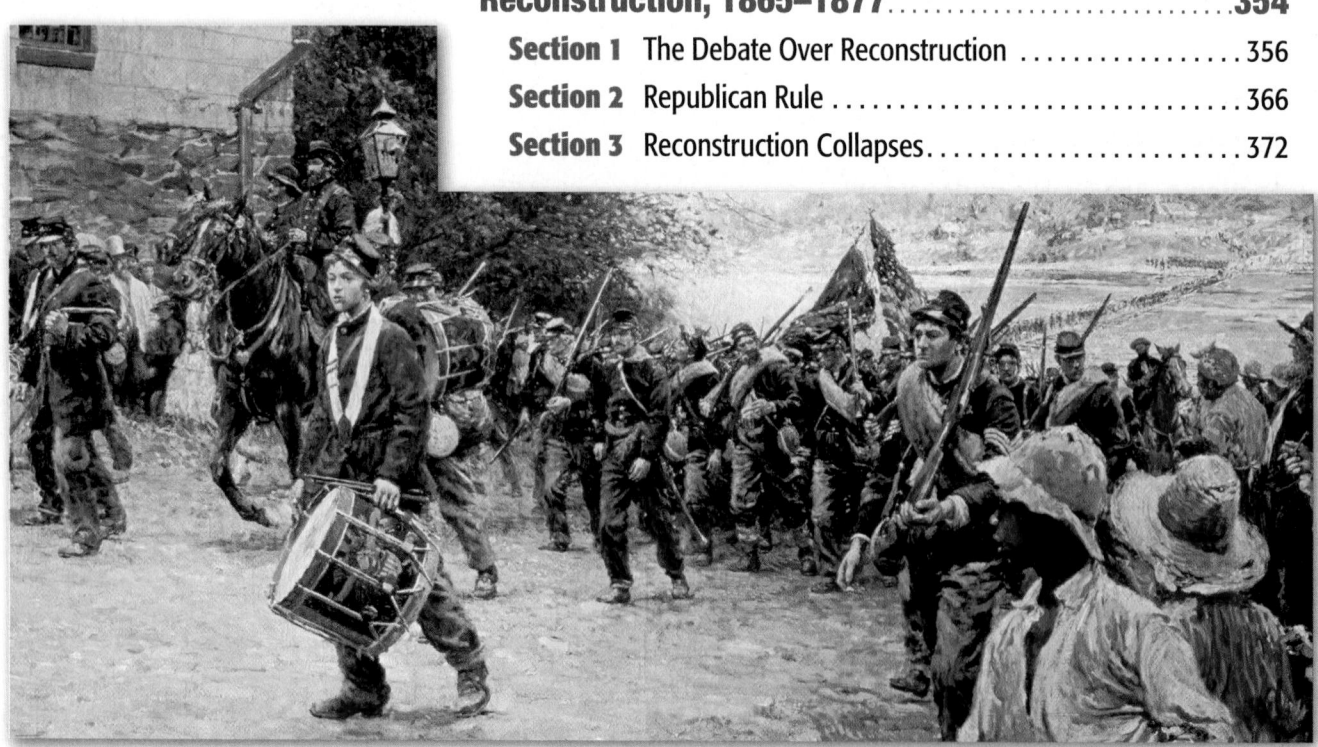

Unit 4

The Birth of Modern America 382
1865–1901

Table of Contents

NO MOLLY-CODDLING HERE

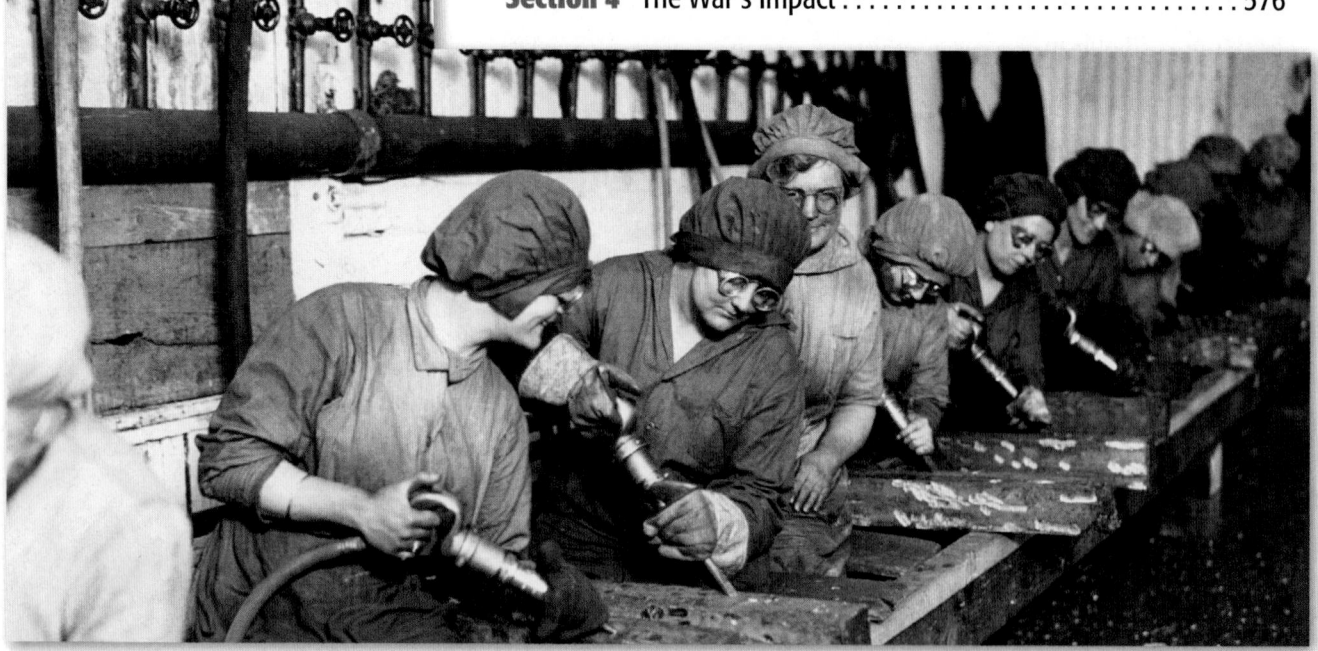

Table of Contents

Unit 6

Table of Contents

Table of Contents

Table of Contents

Appendix

Features

ANALYZING PRIMARY SOURCES

★★★★★★★★★★★★★★★★

Debates IN HISTORY

Turning Point

ANALYZING SUPREME COURT CASES

Features

A variety of quotations and excerpts throughout the text express the thoughts, feelings, and life experiences of people, past and present.

Primary Source Quotes

Primary Source Quotes

Primary Source Quotes

Maps

Maps In MOtion See *StudentWorks™ Plus*
or glencoe.com.

Maps labeled with the In Motion icon have been
specially enhanced on the StudentWorks™ Plus
DVD and on glencoe.com. These In Motion maps
allow you to interact with layers of displayed data
and to listen to audio components.

Entries in **blue** are In Motion maps.

REPUBLIC OF TEXAS

Boundary claimed by Mexico

Colorado R.

La.

Washington-on-the-Brazos

Alamo, March 6, 1836

HOUSTON 1836

San Jacinto April 21, 1836

San Antonio
Bexar, Dec. 10, 1835

SANTA ANNA 1836

Gonzales, Oct. 2, 1835

Brazoria

Goliad, March 20, 1836

URREA 1836

Refugio, March 14, 1836

Nueces R.

San Patricio Feb. 27, 1836

28°N

Boundary claimed by Texas

Rio Grande

Gulf of Mexico

26°N

MEXICO

	Mexican forces
	Mexican victory
	Texan forces
	Texan victory
	Austin's colony
	Disputed territory

0   200 kilometers

0   200 miles

Albers Equal-Area projection

96°W   94°W

24°N

Charts & Graphs

The American Vision contains a wealth of information. The trick is to know where to look to access all the information in the book. If you go through this scavenger hunt, either alone or with your teacher or parents, you will quickly learn how the textbook is organized and how to get the most out of your reading and study time. Let's get started!

1. How many units and chapters are in the book?
2. What is the difference between the glossary and the index?
3. Most sections of a chapter open with a primary source—a document or other testimony dating from the period. Where else can you find primary sources in the textbook?
4. In what special feature can you find the definition of a physical map, a political map, and a special-purpose map?
5. If you want to quickly find all the maps, charts, and graphs about World War II, where in the front do you look?
6. How can you find information about William Penn's colonization of Pennsylvania?
7. Where can you find a graphic organizer that summarizes the major events of the Civil War discussed in Chapter 9?
8. What are the key terms and names for Chapter 8, Section 3, and how are they highlighted in the text?
9. The Web site for the book is listed three times in Chapter 16. After finding all three, list how the Web site can help you.
10. Which of the book's main features will provide you with strategies for improving your studying and writing skills?

THEMES IN THE
AMERICAN VISION

As you read THE AMERICAN VISION, *you will be given help in sorting out all the information you encounter. This textbook organizes the events of your nation's past and present around 10 themes. A theme is a concept, or main idea, that happens again and again throughout history. By recognizing these themes, you will better understand events of the past and how they affect you today.*

Culture and Beliefs

Being aware of cultural differences helps us understand ourselves and others. People from around the world for generations have sung of the "land of the Pilgrims' pride, land where our fathers died," even though their ancestors arrived on these shores long after these events occurred.

Past and Present

Recognizing our historic roots helps us understand why things are the way they are today. This theme includes political, social, religious, and economic changes that have influenced the way Americans think and act.

Geography and History

Understanding geography helps us understand how humans interact with their environment. The United States succeeded in part because of its rich natural resources and its vast open spaces. In many regions, the people changed the natural landscape to fulfill their wants and needs.

Individual Action

Responsible individuals have often stepped forward to help lead the nation. Americans' strong values helped create such individuals. These values spring in part from earlier times when the home was the center of many activities, including work, education, and spending time with one's family.

Group Action

Identifying how political and social groups and institutions operate helps us work together. From the beginning, Americans formed groups and institutions to act in support of their economic, political, social, and religious beliefs.

Government and Society

Understanding the workings of government helps us become better citizens. Abraham Lincoln explained the meaning of democracy as "government of the people, by the people, for the people." Democracy, at its best, is "among" the people.

Science and Technology

Americans have always been quick to adopt innovations. The nation was settled and built by people who gave up old ways in favor of new. Americans' lives are deeply influenced by technology, the use of science, and machines. Perhaps no machine has so shaped modern life as the automobile. Understanding the role of science and technology helps us see their impact on our society and the roles they will play in the future.

Economics and Society

The free enterprise economy of the United States is consistent with the nation's history of rights and freedoms. Freedom of choice in economic decisions supports other freedoms. Understanding the concept of free enterprise is basic to studying American history.

Trade, War, and Migration

Events much bigger than any individual also shape the course of history. Being aware of global interdependence helps us make decisions and deal with the difficult issues we will encounter. Trade, war, and the movement of people between nations have altered the nation's history.

Struggles for Rights

For a democratic system to survive, its citizens must take an active role in government. The foundation of democracy is the right of every person to take part in government and to voice one's views on issues. An appreciation for the struggle to preserve these freedoms is vital to the understanding of democracy.

USING THE BIG IDEAS

You will find Big Ideas at the beginning of every section of every chapter. You are asked questions that help you put it all together to better understand how ideas and themes are connected across time—and to see why history is important to you today.

REFERENCE ATLAS

ATLAS KEY

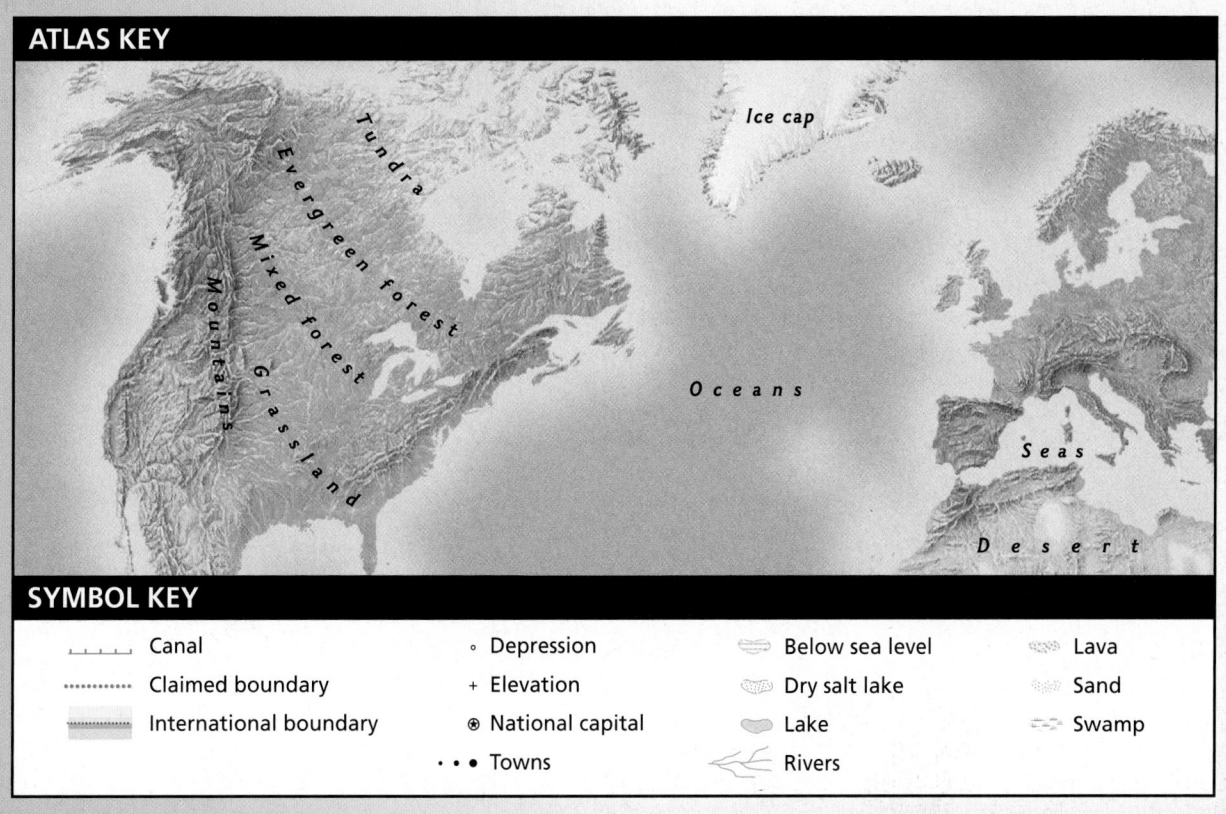

SYMBOL KEY

Canal	Depression	Below sea level	Lava
Claimed boundary	+ Elevation	Dry salt lake	Sand
International boundary	⊛ National capital	Lake	Swamp
	• • Towns	Rivers	

Column labels (top and bottom): 1 2 3 4 5 6 7 8

Row labels (left): A B C D E F G H J K

Longitude/Latitude labels (top): 130°W 125°W 120°W 50°N 115°W 110°W 105°W 100°W

C A N A

Missouri

Cape Flattery
Mt. Olympus
7,965 ft
2,428 m
Seattle

45°N

130°W

Columbia

COAST RANGE

CASCADE RANGE

COLUMBIA PLATEAU

Blue Mts.

Clearwater Mts.

Bitterroot Range

ROCKY

G R E A T

Absaroka Range

Bighorn Mts.

Salmon River Mts.

Black Hills

Missouri

Cape Mendocino

130°W
40°N

Snake

Snake River Plain

Shoshone Falls

Wind River Range

Laramie Mts.

N. Platte

Platte

Great Sandy Desert

Great Salt Lake

GREAT BASIN

Uinta Mts.

M O U N T A I N S

Sand Hills

H i g h   P l a i n s

SIERRA NEVADA

Central Valley

Lake Tahoe

Wasatch Range

San Francisco

PACIFIC

OCEAN

35°N

Mt. Whitney
14,494 ft
4,418 m

Lake Powell

Colorado

Lake Mead

14,433 ft
4,399 m
Mt. Elbert

Denver

Sangre de Cristo Mts.

Arkansas

Point Conception

Death Valley
-282 ft, -86 m

Mojave Desert

Grand Canyon

Colorado Plateau

San Juan Mts.

R A N G E S

Channel Islands

Los Angeles

Colorado

Sacramento Mts.

Llano Estacado

Red

125°W

Salton Sea

San Diego

Phoenix

Sonoran Desert

Rio Grande

Dallas

Brazos

30°N

120°W

115°W

Edwards Plateau

C O

Rio Grande

ARCTIC OCEAN

Point Barrow

68°N
180°

Chukchi Sea

North Slope

Beaufort Sea

68°N

RUSSIA

Bering Strait

ARCTIC CIRCLE

Brooks Range

CANADA

Seward Pen.

ALASKA

St. Lawrence Island

Yukon

Kuskokwim

Tanana

Alaska Range

Mt. McKinley (Denali)
20,320 ft, 6,194 m

110°W

172°W
60°N

Nunivak Island

Anchorage

60°N

25°N

Bering Sea

Bristol Bay

Gulf of Alaska

Alexander Archipelago

MEXICO

Alaska Peninsula

Kodiak I.

52°N

ALASKA

0 mi   300

0 km   300

PACIFIC OCEAN

52°N

TROPIC OF CANCER

164°W   156°W   148°W   140°W   132°W   105°W   100°W

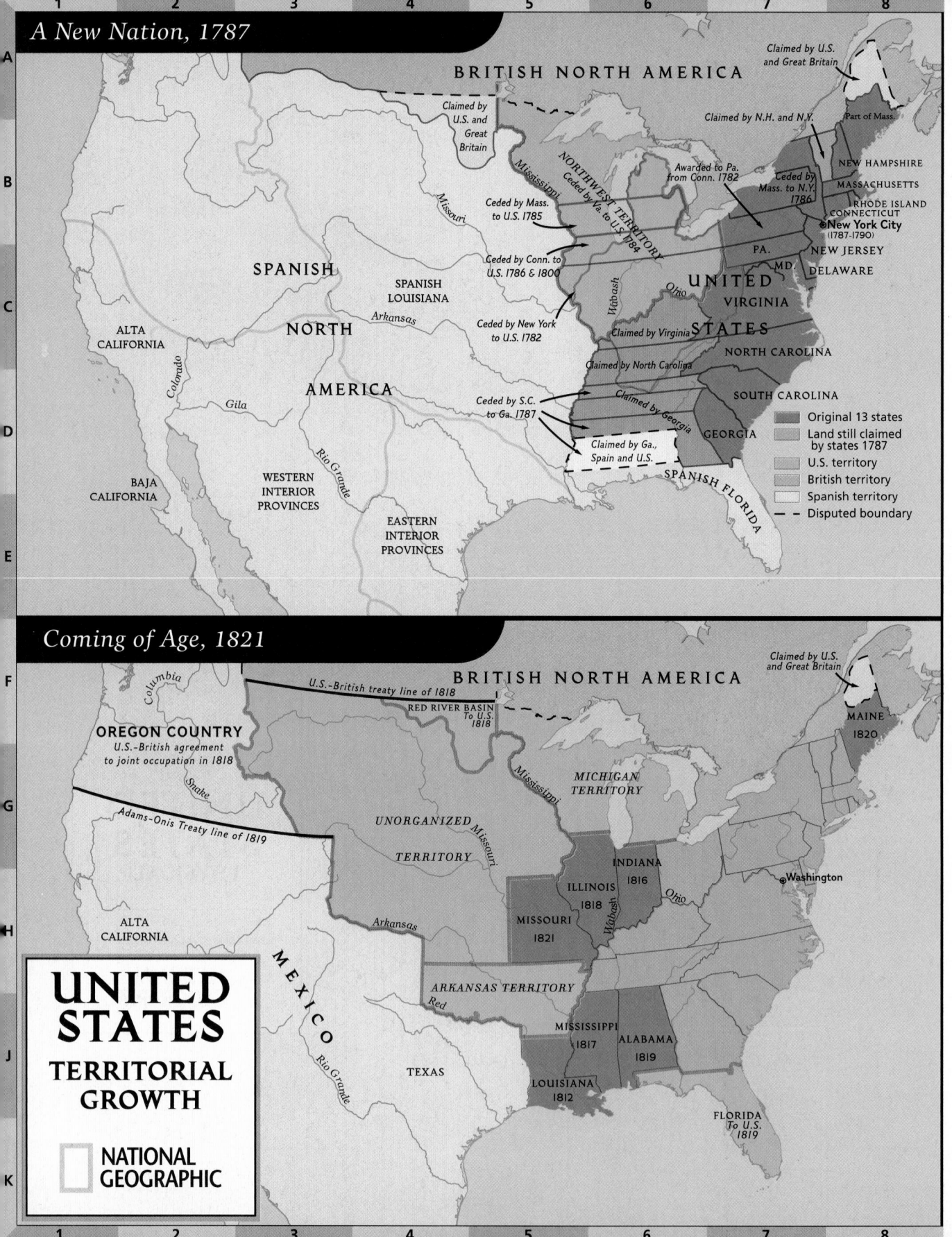

A New Nation, 1787

BRITISH NORTH AMERICA

Claimed by U.S. and Great Britain

Claimed by U.S. and Great Britain

Claimed by N.H. and N.Y.

Part of Mass.

NEW HAMPSHIRE

MASSACHUSETTS

RHODE ISLAND

CONNECTICUT

Awarded to Pa. from Conn. 1782

Ceded by Va. to U.S. 1784

Ceded by Mass. to N.Y. 1786

NORTHWEST TERRITORY

Ceded by Mass. to U.S. 1785

New York City (1787-1790)

NEW JERSEY

DELAWARE

Ceded by Conn. to U.S. 1786 & 1800

PA.

MD.

UNITED

SPANISH

Ohio

VIRGINIA

Wabash

STATES

NORTH

Ceded by New York to U.S. 1782

Missouri

Mississippi

Claimed by Virginia

NORTH CAROLINA

AMERICA

SPANISH LOUISIANA

Arkansas

Claimed by North Carolina

Colorado

SPANISH NORTH

SOUTH CAROLINA

Gila

Claimed by Georgia

Ceded by S.C. to Ga. 1787

GEORGIA

ALTA CALIFORNIA

Rio Grande

WESTERN INTERIOR PROVINCES

Claimed by Ga., Spain and U.S.

SPANISH FLORIDA

BAJA CALIFORNIA

EASTERN INTERIOR PROVINCES

Original 13 states

Land still claimed by states 1787

U.S. territory

British territory

Spanish territory

Disputed boundary

Coming of Age, 1821

Columbia

U.S.-British treaty line of 1818

BRITISH NORTH AMERICA

Claimed by U.S. and Great Britain

OREGON COUNTRY

U.S.-British agreement to joint occupation in 1818

RED RIVER BASIN To U.S. 1818

MAINE 1820

Snake

Mississippi

MICHIGAN TERRITORY

Adams-Onis Treaty line of 1819

UNORGANIZED

Missouri

TERRITORY

INDIANA 1816

Washington

ILLINOIS 1818

Ohio

ALTA CALIFORNIA

Arkansas

MISSOURI 1821

Wabash

MEXICO

ARKANSAS TERRITORY

Red

MISSISSIPPI 1817

ALABAMA 1819

Rio Grande

TEXAS

LOUISIANA 1812

FLORIDA To U.S. 1819

UNITED STATES TERRITORIAL GROWTH

NATIONAL GEOGRAPHIC

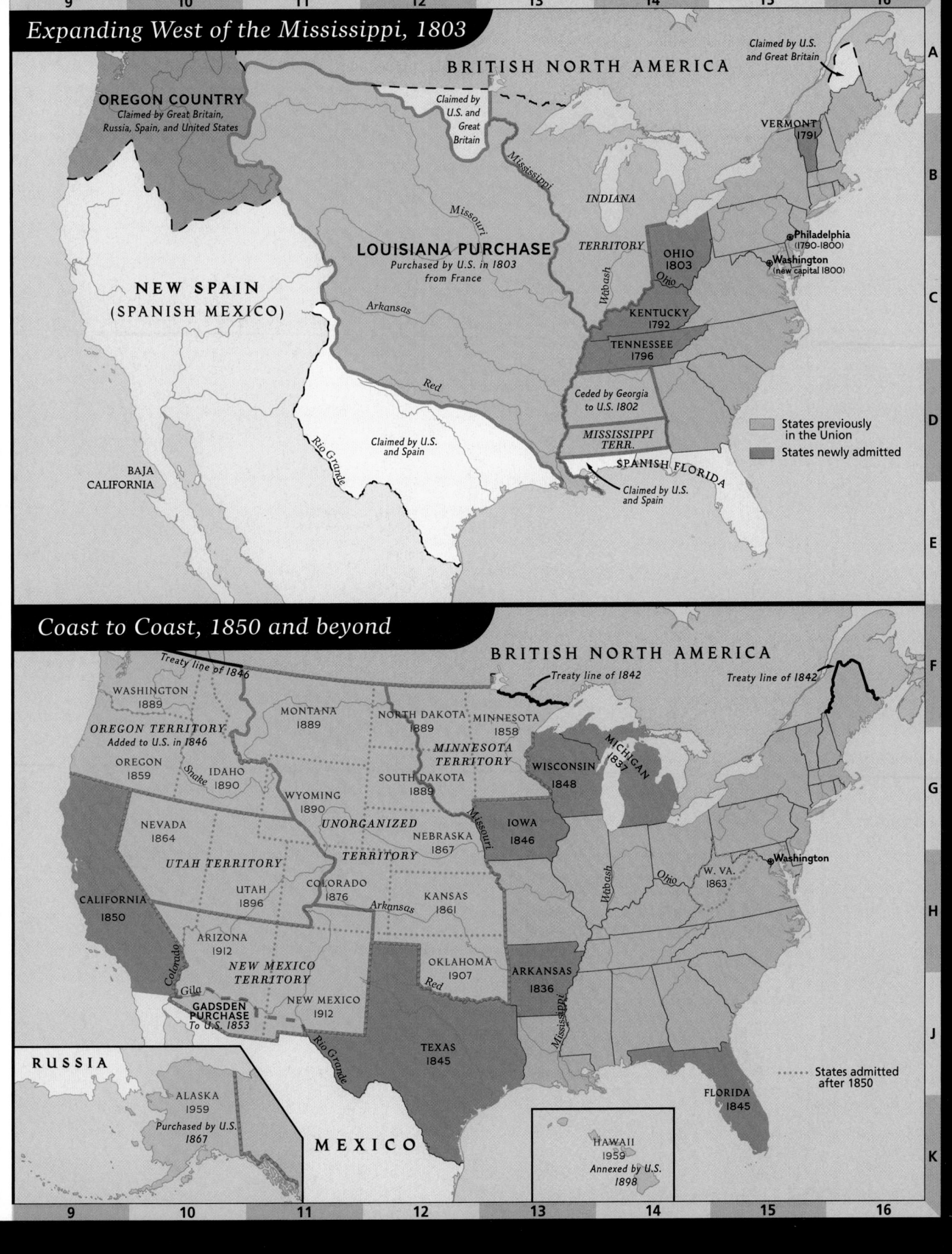

Expanding West of the Mississippi, 1803

BRITISH NORTH AMERICA

Claimed by U.S. and Great Britain

OREGON COUNTRY
Claimed by Great Britain, Russia, Spain, and United States

Claimed by U.S. and Great Britain

VERMONT (1791)

Mississippi

Missouri

INDIANA

LOUISIANA PURCHASE
Purchased by U.S. in 1803 from France

TERRITORY

OHIO 1803

Ohio

Philadelphia (1790-1800)
Washington (new capital 1800)

NEW SPAIN (SPANISH MEXICO)

Arkansas

Wabash

KENTUCKY 1792

TENNESSEE 1796

Red

Rio Grande

Ceded by Georgia to U.S. 1802

MISSISSIPPI TERR.

Claimed by U.S. and Spain

SPANISH FLORIDA

Claimed by U.S. and Spain

BAJA CALIFORNIA

States previously in the Union

States newly admitted

Coast to Coast, 1850 and beyond

BRITISH NORTH AMERICA

Treaty line of 1846

Treaty line of 1842

Treaty line of 1842

WASHINGTON 1889

MONTANA 1889

NORTH DAKOTA 1889

MINNESOTA 1858

OREGON TERRITORY
Added to U.S. in 1846

MINNESOTA TERRITORY

MICHIGAN 1837

OREGON 1859

Snake

IDAHO 1890

SOUTH DAKOTA 1889

WISCONSIN 1848

WYOMING 1890

NEVADA 1864

UNORGANIZED

NEBRASKA 1867

IOWA 1846

Missouri

Washington

UTAH TERRITORY

TERRITORY

COLORADO 1876

UTAH 1896

KANSAS 1861

Arkansas

W. VA. 1863

Wabash

Ohio

CALIFORNIA 1850

Colorado

ARIZONA 1912

Gila

NEW MEXICO TERRITORY

OKLAHOMA 1907

Red

ARKANSAS 1836

GADSDEN PURCHASE
To U.S. 1853

NEW MEXICO 1912

Rio Grande

Mississippi

RUSSIA

ALASKA 1959
Purchased by U.S. 1867

TEXAS 1845

FLORIDA 1845

MEXICO

HAWAII 1959
Annexed by U.S. 1898

States admitted after 1850

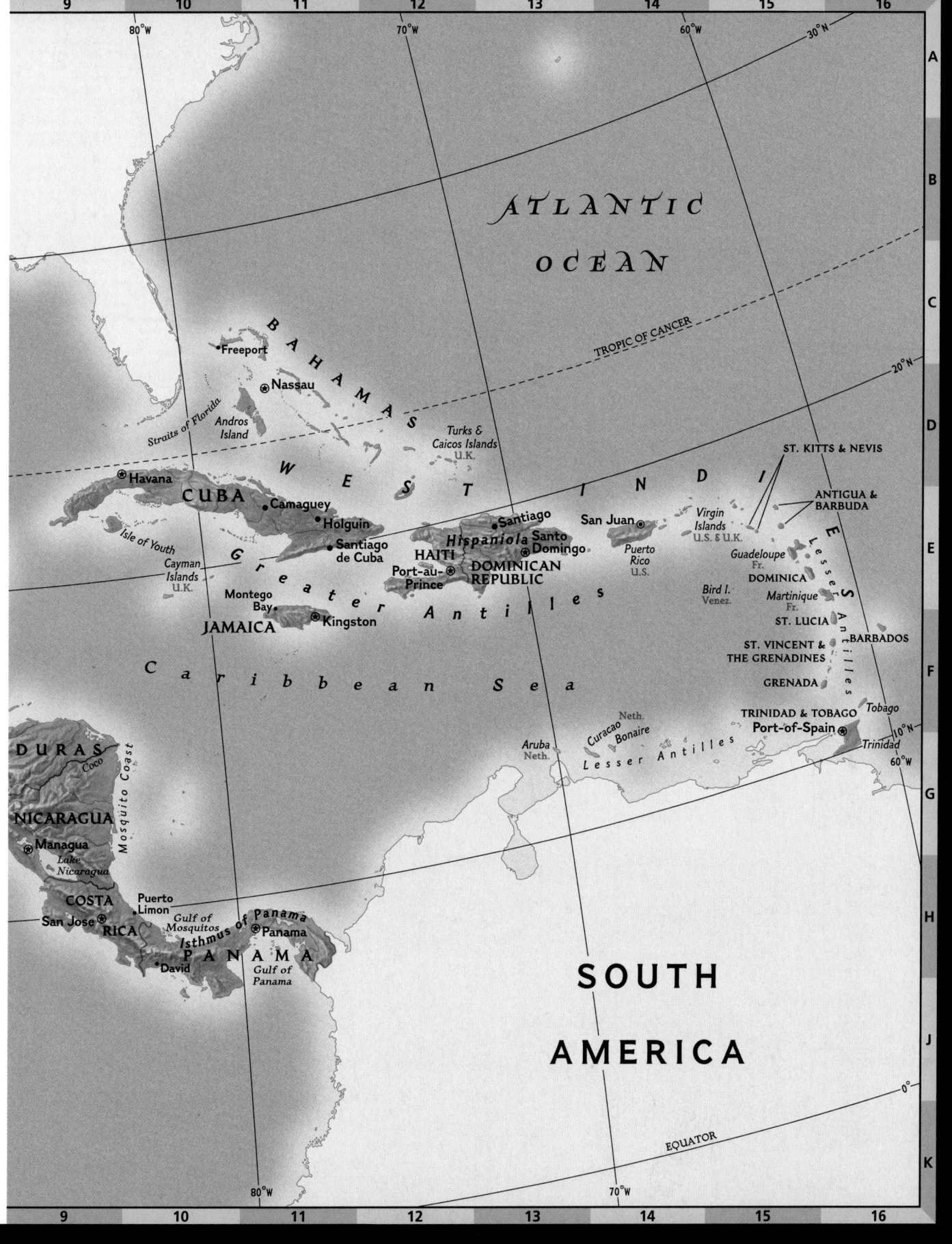

ATLANTIC

OCEAN

TROPIC OF CANCER

20°N

BAHAMAS

•Freeport

⊛ Nassau

Andros
Island

Straits of Florida

Turks &
Caicos Islands
U.K.

ST. KITTS & NEVIS

ANTIGUA &
BARBUDA

⊛ Havana

CUBA

• Camaguey

• Holguin

Santiago •

San Juan ⊛

Virgin
Islands
U.S. & U.K.

Isle of Youth

• Santiago
de Cuba

Hispaniola   Santo
Domingo

Puerto
Rico
U.S.

Guadeloupe
Fr.

Lesser Antilles

Cayman
Islands
U.K.

G

r

e

a

t

e

r

A

n

t

i

l

l

e

s

HAITI

Port-au-
Prince

⊛

DOMINICAN
REPUBLIC

Bird I.
Venez.

DOMINICA

Martinique
Fr.

W

E

S

T

I

N

D

I

E

S

Montego
Bay •

⊛ Kingston

ST. LUCIA

JAMAICA

ST. VINCENT &
THE GRENADINES

BARBADOS

C

a

r

i

b

b

e

a

n

S

e

a

GRENADA

Tobago

TRINIDAD & TOBAGO
Port-of-Spain ⊛

Trinidad

10°N

60°W

Neth.
Curacao

Bonaire

D U R A S

Coco

Mosquito Coast

Aruba
Neth.

Neth.

Lesser Antilles

NICARAGUA

⊛ Managua

Lake
Nicaragua

SOUTH

COSTA

Puerto
• Limon

Gulf of
Mosquitos

San Jose ⊛

RICA

Isthmus of

Gulf of
Panama

Panama

⊛
Panama

AMERICA

PANAMA

David

0°

EQUATOR

RUSSIA

ARCTIC OCEAN

Queen

60°N
170°W
70°N
ARCTIC CIRCLE
130°W
120°W
North Magnetic Pole
Elizabeth

Islands

Prince Patrick I.

ALASKA
U.S.

Beaufort Sea

Melville Island

Bathurst Island

Banks Island

Somerset Island

Prince of Wales I.

YUKON TERRITORY

Mt. Logan
19,551 ft
+ 5,959 m

Yukon Plateau

Mackenzie Mts.

Mackenzie

Inuvik

Great Bear Lake

Victoria Island

N U N

C A N A D A

NORTHWEST TERRITORIES

Whitehorse

Virginia Falls

Yellowknife

Great Slave Lake

150°W
50°N

Slave

Peace

Lake Athabasca

PACIFIC

Queen Charlotte Islands

Fraser Plateau

BRITISH COLUMBIA

Prince George

Fraser

Columbia Mts.

ROCKY MOUNTAINS

ALBERTA

Athabasca

GREAT PLAINS

Churchill

Churchill

Nelson

SASKATCHEWAN

MANITOBA

Edmonton

Saskatchewan

Lake Winnipegosis

Lake Winnipeg

Vancouver Island

Calgary

Saskatoon

140°W

OCEAN

Vancouver
Victoria

Regina

Winnipeg

40°N

Lake of the Woods

UNITED STATES

130°W
120°W
110°W
100°W

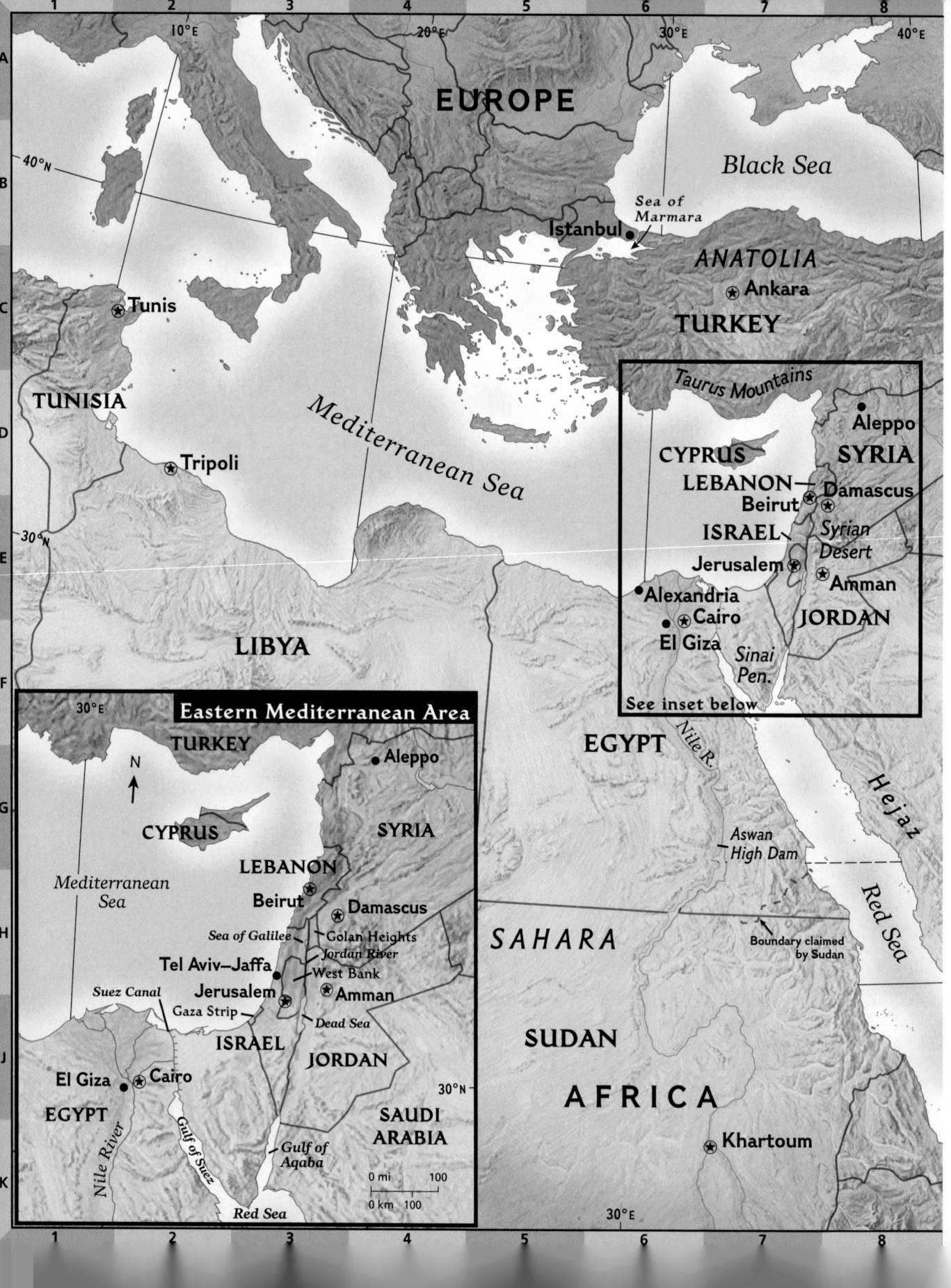

EUROPE

Black Sea

Sea of Marmara

●Istanbul

ANATOLIA

⊛ Ankara

TURKEY

Taurus Mountains

●Tunis

CYPRUS

● Aleppo

SYRIA

LEBANON—

Beirut●

⊛Damascus

ISRAEL

Syrian Desert

Jerusalem●⊛

⊛ Amman

●Alexandria

⊛ Cairo

JORDAN

El Giza●

Sinai Pen.

See inset below

TUNISIA

⊛ Tripoli

Mediterranean Sea

30°N

LIBYA

EGYPT

Nile R.

Hejaz

Eastern Mediterranean Area

30°E

N

TURKEY

● Aleppo

CYPRUS

SYRIA

Mediterranean Sea

LEBANON

Beirut ⊛

⊛ Damascus

Sea of Galilee

Golan Heights

Jordan River

Tel Aviv–Jaffa ●

West Bank

Jerusalem ●⊛

⊛ Amman

Suez Canal

Gaza Strip

Dead Sea

ISRAEL

JORDAN

El Giza ● ⊛ Cairo

Nile River

EGYPT

Gulf of Suez

Gulf of Aqaba

30°N

SAUDI ARABIA

0 mi   100

0 km   100

Red Sea

SAHARA

Aswan High Dam

Boundary claimed by Sudan

Red Sea

SUDAN

AFRICA

⊛ Khartoum

30°E

Aral
Sea

50°E   60°E   70°E   40°N

UZBEKISTAN

★ Tashkent

TAJIKISTAN

Caucasus Mountains

GEORGIA
Tbilisi ★

Yerevan ★
ARMENIA

▲ Mt. Ararat
(16,854 ft.
5,137 m)

Baku ★

Caspian Sea

AZERBAIJAN

Elburz Mountains

Tigris R.

Zagros Mountains

Euphrates R.

IRAQ

★ Baghdad

Al Basrah ●

KUWAIT

Kuwait ●

Persian Gulf
(Arabian Gulf)

TURKMENISTAN

Ashkhabad ★

Mashhad ●

Tehran ★

Plateau
of Iran

IRAN

Dushanbe ★

A S I A

Kabul ★

AFGHANISTAN

PAKISTAN

Manama ★
BAHRAIN

QATAR
★ Doha

Abu
Dhabi ★

Masqat ●

Gulf of Oman

TROPIC OF CANCER

Arabian
Sea

SAUDI
ARABIA

★ Riyadh

UNITED
ARAB
EMIRATES

OMAN

20°N

ARABIAN
PENINSULA

Makkah
(Mecca) ●

Asir

Rub al Khali
(Empty Quarter)

H

N
↑

Sanaa ●

YEMEN

J

0 mi   500

0 km   500

AZIMUTHAL EQUIDISTANT PROJECTION

MIDDLE EAST

PHYSICAL / POLITICAL

NATIONAL
GEOGRAPHIC

40°E   Aden ●   Gulf of Aden   50°E

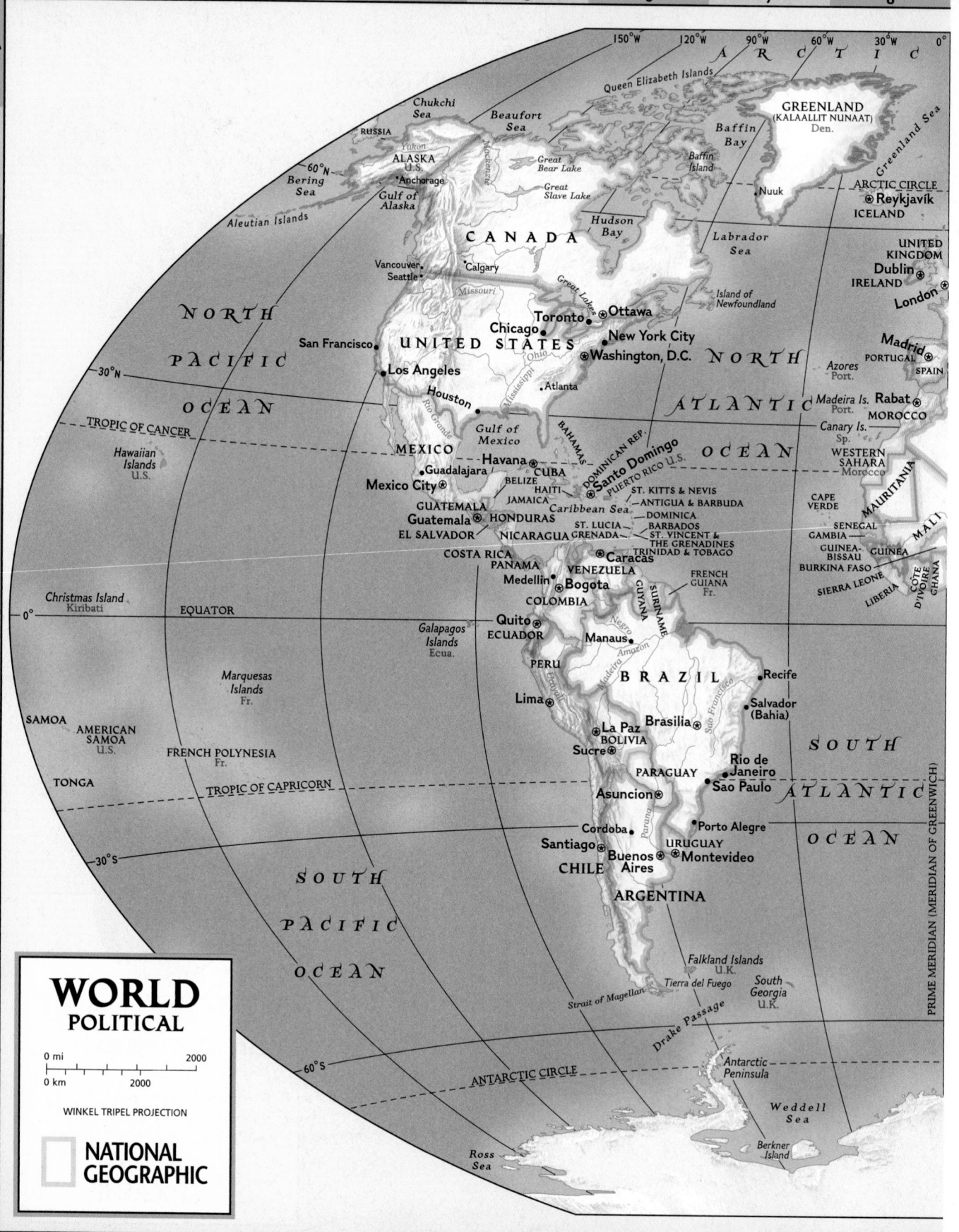

ARCTIC

150°W   120°W   90°W   60°W   30°W   0°

Chukchi
Sea

Beaufort
Sea

Queen Elizabeth Islands

GREENLAND
(KALAALLIT NUNAAT)
Den.

Greenland Sea

RUSSIA

ALASKA
U.S.

Great
Bear Lake

Baffin
Bay

Baffin
Island

Nuuk

60°N

Anchorage

Bering
Sea

Gulf of
Alaska

Great
Slave Lake

Mackenzie

ARCTIC CIRCLE

Reykjavík
ICELAND

Aleutian Islands

Hudson
Bay

Labrador
Sea

CANADA

Yukon

Vancouver
Seattle

Calgary

Missouri

Great Lakes

Island of
Newfoundland

UNITED
KINGDOM

Dublin
IRELAND

London

NORTH

San Francisco

UNITED STATES

Chicago

Toronto Ottawa

New York City
Washington, D.C.

NORTH

Madrid
PORTUGAL   SPAIN

PACIFIC

Los Angeles

Ohio

Atlanta

ATLANTIC

Azores
Port.

30°N

Houston

Rio Grande

Mississippi

Madeira Is. Rabat
Port.   MOROCCO

OCEAN

TROPIC OF CANCER

Gulf of
Mexico

Canary Is.
Sp.   Morocco

WESTERN
SAHARA

Hawaiian
Islands
U.S.

MEXICO

Havana
CUBA

BAHAMAS

DOMINICAN REP.

Santo Domingo
PUERTO RICO U.S.

OCEAN

MAURITANIA

Guadalajara

BELIZE
HAITI
JAMAICA

ST. KITTS & NEVIS
ANTIGUA & BARBUDA

CAPE
VERDE

Mexico City

GUATEMALA

Caribbean Sea

DOMINICA
BARBADOS

SENEGAL

GAMBIA

MALI

Guatemala   HONDURAS
EL SALVADOR   NICARAGUA

ST. LUCIA
GRENADA

ST. VINCENT &
THE GRENADINES
TRINIDAD & TOBAGO

GUINEA-
BISSAU   GUINEA

BURKINA FASO

COSTA RICA

Caracas

FRENCH
GUIANA
Fr.

SIERRA LEONE

LIBERIA

CÔTE D'IVOIRE

GHANA

Christmas Island
Kiribati

PANAMA

VENEZUELA

Medellin Bogota
COLOMBIA

GUYANA

SURINAME

EQUATOR

0°

Galapagos
Islands
Ecua.

Quito
ECUADOR

Manaus

Negro

Amazon

PERU

BRAZIL

Marquesas
Islands
Fr.

Lima

Madeira

Recife

Salvador
(Bahia)

SAMOA

AMERICAN
SAMOA
U.S.

FRENCH POLYNESIA
Fr.

La Paz
BOLIVIA

Sucre

Brasilia

São Francisco

SOUTH

TONGA

TROPIC OF CAPRICORN

PARAGUAY

Rio de
Janeiro
Sao Paulo

ATLANTIC

Asuncion

Parana

Porto Alegre

OCEAN

SOUTH

Cordoba

URUGUAY

Santiago
CHILE

Buenos
Aires

Montevideo

30°S

PACIFIC

ARGENTINA

OCEAN

Falkland Islands
U.K.

Tierra del Fuego

South
Georgia
U.K.

Strait of Magellan

PRIME MERIDIAN (MERIDIAN OF GREENWICH)

WORLD
POLITICAL

0 mi   2000

0 km   2000

Drake Passage

60°S

Antarctic
Peninsula

WINKEL TRIPEL PROJECTION

ANTARCTIC CIRCLE

Weddell
Sea

NATIONAL
GEOGRAPHIC

Ross
Sea

Berkner
Island

9 10 11 12 13 14 15 16

A B C D E F G H J K

OCEAN
30°E 60°E 90°E 120°E 150°E
Franz Josef Land
Severnaya Zemlya
New Siberian Islands
East Siberian Sea
Laptev Sea
Barents Sea
Kara Sea
Svalbard Nor.
Novaya Zemlya
Norwegian Sea
60°N
Bering Sea
Ob
Yenisey
Lena
Yakutsk
R U S S I A
Amur
Sakhalin
Sea of Okhotsk
Kamchatka Peninsula
Oslo
St. Petersburg
SWEDEN
FINLAND
NORWAY
EST.
LATVIA
LITH.
Yekaterinburg
Omsk
Novosibirsk
Moscow
Samara
Volga
Ural
Astana
Irtysh
Lake Baikal
Ulaanbaatar
MONGOLIA
Harbin
NORTH KOREA
Sapporo
Hokkaido
Honshu
DENMARK
NETH.
POLAND BELARUS
GERMANY
BELG. CZECH
REP. SLOVAKIA
AUST. HUNG. MOLD.
SWITZ. SLOV.
FRANCE CROAT.
KAZAKHSTAN
Aral Sea
Almaty
Tashkent
Bishkek
KYRGYZSTAN
Shenyang
Beijing
Tianjin
P'yŏngyang
Seoul
SOUTH KOREA
JAPAN
Tokyo
Osaka
Kyushu
NORTH
Paris
UKRAINE
Kyiv (Kiev)
ROMANIA AZERBAIJAN
Caspian Sea
UZBEKISTAN
TURKMENISTAN
TAJIKISTAN
Dushanbe
C H I N A
Hwang Ho (Yellow)
Chang Jiang (Yangtze)
PACIFIC
Rome
ITALY
BULGARIA
GEORGIA
ARMENIA
Black Sea
SERB.
MONT.
ALBANIA
MACED.
GREECE
TURKEY
Ankara
Ashkhabad
Tehran
AFGHANISTAN
Islamabad
PAKISTAN
Lahore
Chengdu
Wuhan
Shanghai
30°N
OCEAN
Mediterranean Sea
CYPRUS
LEBANON
ISRAEL
SYRIA
IRAQ
Baghdad
JORDAN
KUWAIT
Delhi
New Delhi
NEPAL
Brahmaputra
BHUTAN
BANGLADESH
Guangzhou
Taipei
TAIWAN
Hong Kong
Philippine Sea
The People's Republic of China claims Taiwan as its 23rd province.
Algiers
TUNISIA
Tripoli
Cairo
BAHRAIN
QATAR
U.A.E.
Riyadh
OMAN
Karachi
Masqat
Dhaka
Kolkata (Calcutta)
MYANMAR (BURMA)
LAOS
Hanoi
Hainan
South China Sea
Manila
PHILIPPINES
Luzon
NORTHERN MARIANA ISLANDS
U.S.
MARSHALL ISLANDS
ALGERIA
LIBYA
EGYPT
Nile
Red Sea
SAUDI ARABIA
Mumbai (Bombay)
INDIA
Nay Pyi Taw
Bay of Bengal
THAILAND
Bangkok
Phnom Penh
CAMBODIA
VIETNAM
Ho Chi Minh City
Mindanao
PALAU
FEDERATED STATES OF MICRONESIA
NIGER
CHAD
ERITREA
Khartoum
SUDAN
Sanaa
YEMEN
DJIBOUTI
Arabian Sea
Hyderabad
Bengaluru (Bangalore)
Chennai (Madras)
SRI LANKA
BRUNEI
KIRIBATI
Niamey
N'Djamena
CENTRAL AFRICAN REPUBLIC
Addis Ababa
ETHIOPIA
Socotra Yemen
SOMALIA
Colombo
MALDIVES
EQUATOR
Kuala Lumpur
MALAYSIA
SINGAPORE
Borneo
Celebes
NAURU
NIGERIA
Lagos
CAMEROON
BENIN
TOGO
EQ. GUINEA
GABON
SAO TOME & PRINCIPE
CABINDA Ang.
DEM. REP. OF THE CONGO
Bangui
Brazzaville
Kinshasa
Congo
UGANDA
KENYA
Nairobi
RWANDA
BURUNDI
Mogadishu
SEYCHELLES
INDONESIA
New Guinea
PAPUA NEW GUINEA
Port Moresby
SOLOMON ISLANDS
TUVALU
Luanda
ANGOLA
ZAMBIA
Lusaka
Dodoma
Dar es Salaam
TANZANIA
MALAWI
COMOROS
Jakarta
Java
Surabaya
EAST TIMOR (TIMOR-LESTE)
Darwin
Arafura Sea
Coral Sea
VANUATU
FIJI ISLANDS
Harare
ZIMBABWE
NAMIBIA
Windhoek
BOTSWANA
Gaborone
Antananarivo
MADAGASCAR
MAURITIUS
Reunion Fr.
MOZAMBIQUE
I N D I A N
New Caledonia Fr.
Zambezi
Maputo
SWAZILAND
Tshwane (Pretoria)
Bloemfontein
SOUTH AFRICA
LESOTHO
Orange
O C E A N
AUSTRALIA
Perth
Darling
Murray
Brisbane
Sydney
Canberra
Melbourne
SOUTH PACIFIC OCEAN
North Island
Cape Town
Kerguelen Islands Fr.
Tasmania
Tasman Sea
Auckland
NEW ZEALAND
Wellington
South Island
60°S
A N T A R C T I C A
Ross Sea

ABBREVIATIONS

AUST.	AUSTRIA
B.&H.	BOSNIA & HERZEGOVINA
BELG.	BELGIUM
CROAT.	CROATIA
CZECH REP.	CZECH REPUBLIC
DEM. REP. OF THE CONGO	DEMOCRATIC REPUBLIC OF THE CONGO
EQ. GUINEA	EQUATORIAL GUINEA
EST.	ESTONIA
HUNG.	HUNGARY
LITH.	LITHUANIA
MACED.	MACEDONIA
MOLD.	MOLDOVA
NETH.	NETHERLANDS
SERB.	SERBIA
MONT.	MONTENEGRO
SLOV.	SLOVENIA
SWITZ.	SWITZERLAND
U.A.E.	UNITED ARAB EMIRATES

9 10 11 12 13 14 15 16

Geography Skills Handbook

How Do I Study Geography?

Geographers have tried to understand the best way to teach and learn about geography. In order to do this, geographers created the *Five Themes of Geography*. The themes acted as a guide for teaching the basic ideas about geography to students like yourself.

People who teach and study geography, though, thought that the Five Themes were too broad. In 1994, geographers created 18 national geography standards. These standards were more detailed about what should be taught and learned. The Six Essential Elements act as a bridge connecting the Five Themes with the standards.

These pages show you how the Five Themes are related to the Six Essential Elements and the 18 standards.

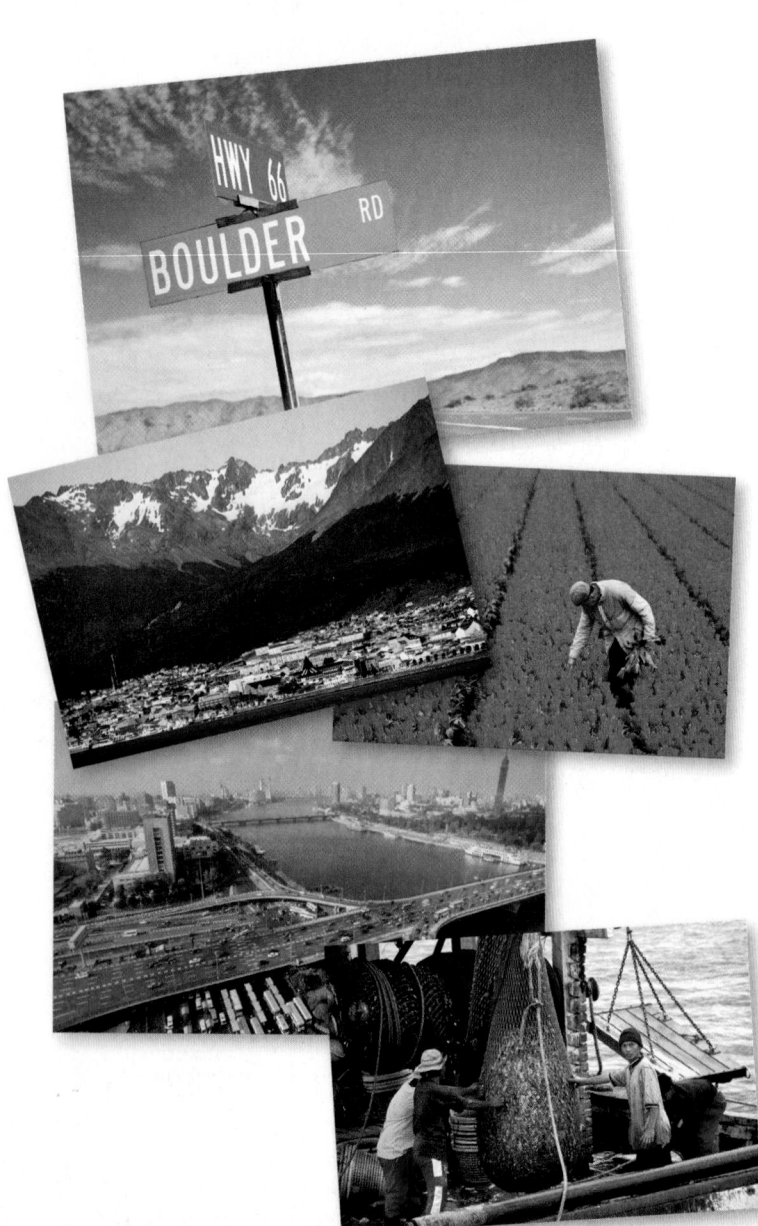

5
Themes of Geography

1 Location
Location describes where something is. Absolute location describes a place's exact position on the Earth's surface. Relative location expresses where a place is in relation to another place.

2 Place
Place describes the physical and human characteristics that make a location unique.

3 Regions
Regions are areas that share common characteristics.

4 Movement
Movement explains how and why people and things move and are connected.

5 Human-Environment Interaction
Human-Environment Interaction describes the relationship between people and their environment.

6
Essential Elements

18
Geography Standards

I. The World in Spatial Terms
Geographers look to see where a place is located. Location acts as a starting point to answer "Where Is It?" The location of a place helps you orient yourself as to where you are.

1 How to use maps and other tools

2 How to use mental maps to organize information

3 How to analyze the spatial organization of people, places, and environments

II. Places and Regions
Place describes physical characteristics such as landforms, climate, and plant or animal life. It might also describe human characteristics, including language and way of life. Places can also be organized into regions. **Regions** are places united by one or more characteristics.

4 The physical and human characteristics of places

5 How people create regions to interpret Earth's complexity

6 How culture and experience influence people's perceptions of places and regions

III. Physical Systems
Geographers study how physical systems, such as hurricanes, volcanoes, and glaciers, shape the surface of the Earth. They also look at how plants and animals depend upon one another and their surroundings for their survival.

7 The physical processes that shape Earth's surface

8 The distribution of ecosystems on Earth's surface

9 The characteristics, distribution, and migration of human populations

10 The complexity of Earth's cultural mosaics

11 The patterns and networks of economic interdependence

IV. Human Systems
People shape the world in which they live. They settle in certain places but not in others. An ongoing theme in geography is the movement of people, ideas, and goods.

12 The patterns of human settlement

13 The forces of cooperation and conflict

14 How human actions modify the physical environment

V. Environment and Society
How does the relationship between people and their natural surroundings influence the way people live? Geographers study how people use the environment and how their actions affect the environment.

15 How physical systems affect human systems

16 The meaning, use, and distribution of resources

VI. The Uses of Geography
Knowledge of geography helps us understand the relationships among people, places, and environments over time. Applying geographic skills helps you understand the past and prepare for the future.

17 How to apply geography to interpret the past

18 How to apply geography to interpret the present and plan for the future

NATIONAL GEOGRAPHIC

Contents

Geography Skills Handbook

Throughout this text, you will discover how geography has shaped the course of events in United States history. Landforms, waterways, climate, and natural resources all have helped or hindered human activities. Usually people have learned either to adapt to their environments or to transform it to meet their needs. The resources in this handbook will help you get the most out of your textbook—and provide you with skills you will use for the rest of your life.

The study of geography is more than knowing a lot of facts about places. Rather, it has more to do with asking questions about the Earth, pursuing their answers, and solving problems. Thus, one of the most important geographic tools is inside your head: the ability to think geographically.

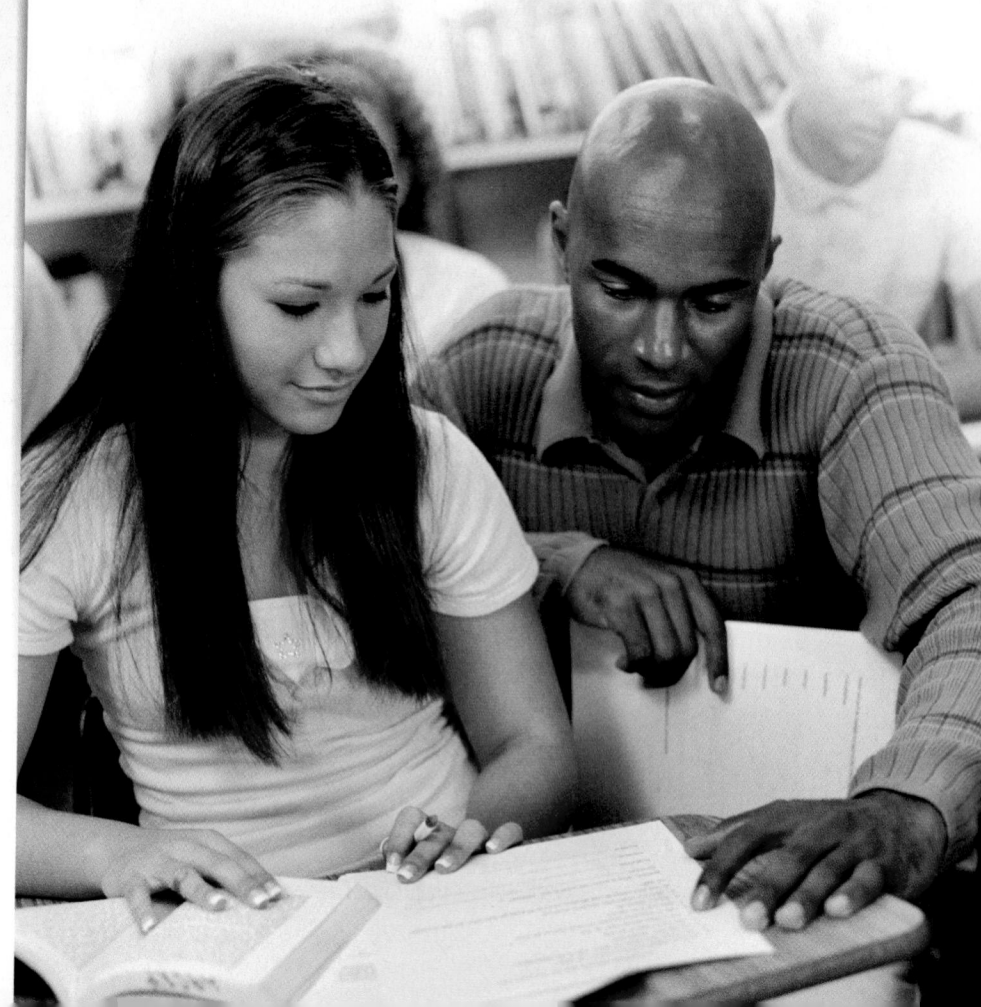

Globes and Maps

A **globe** is a scale model of the Earth. Because Earth is round, a globe presents the most accurate depiction of geographic information such as area, distance, and direction. However, globes show little close-up detail. A printed **map** is a symbolic representation of all or part of the planet. Unlike globes, maps can show small areas in great detail.

From 3-D to 2-D

Think about the surface of the Earth as the peel of an orange. To flatten the peel, you have to cut it like the globe shown here. To create maps that are not interrupted, mapmakers, or **cartographers**, use mathematical formulas to transfer information from the three-dimensional globe to the two-dimensional map. However, when the curves of a globe become straight lines on a map, distortion of size, shape, distance, or area occurs.

globe accurately shows a great circle route, as indicated on the map below. However, as shown on the flat map, the great circle distance (dotted line) between Tokyo and Los Angeles appears to be far longer than the true direction distance (solid line). In fact, the great circle distance is 345 miles (555 km) shorter.

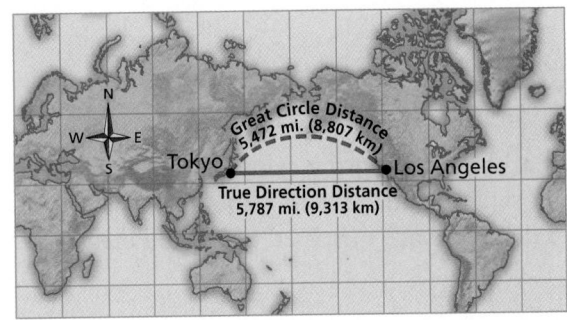

Great Circle Routes

A straight line of true direction—one that runs directly from west to east, for example—is not always the shortest distance between two points. This is due to the curvature of the Earth. To find the shortest distance, stretch a piece of string around a globe from one point to the other. The string will form part of a *great circle*, an imaginary line the follows the curve of the Earth. Ship captains and airline pilots use these **great circle routes** to reduce travel time and conserve fuel.

The idea of a great circle route is an important difference between globes and maps. A round

Practicing SKILLS

1. **Explain** the significance of: globe, map, cartographer, great circle route.

2. **Describe** the problems that arise when the curves of a globe become straight lines on a map.

3. **Use** a Venn diagram like the one below to identify the similarities and differences between globes and maps.

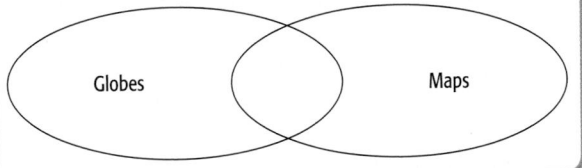

Projections

To create maps, cartographers project the round Earth onto a flat surface—making a **map projection.** Distance, shape, direction, or size may be distorted by a projection. As a result, the purpose of the map usually dictates which projection is used. There are many kinds of map projections, some with general names and some named for the cartographers who developed them. Three basic categories of map projections are shown here: **planar, cylindrical,** and **conic.**

Planar Projection

A planar projection shows the Earth centered in such a way that a straight line coming from the center to any other point represents the shortest distance. Also known as an azimuthal projection, it is most accurate at its center. As a result, it is often used for maps of the Poles.

Cylindrical Projection

A cylindrical projection is based on the projection of the globe onto a cylinder. This projection is most accurate near the Equator, but shapes and distances are distorted near the Poles.

Conic Projection

A conic projection comes from placing a cone over part of a globe. Conic projections are best suited for showing limited east-west areas that are not too far from the Equator. For these uses, a conic projection can indicate distances and directions fairly accurately.

Common Map Projections

Each type of map projection has advantages and some degree of inaccuracy. Four of the most common projections are shown here.

Winkel Tripel Projection

Most general reference world maps are the Winkel Tripel projection. It provides a good balance between the size and shape of land areas as they are shown on the map. Even the polar areas are depicted with little distortion of size and shape.

Goode's Interrupted Equal-Area Projection

An **interrupted projection** resembles a globe that has been cut apart and laid flat. Goode's Interrupted Equal-Area projection shows the true size and shape of Earth's landmasses, but distances are generally distorted.

Robinson Projection

The Robinson projection has minor distortions. The sizes and shapes near the eastern and western edges of the map are accurate, and outlines of the continents appear much as they do on the globe. However, the polar areas are flattened.

Mercator Projection

The Mercator projection increasingly distorts size and distance as it moves away from the Equator. However, Mercator projections do accurately show true directions and the shapes of landmasses, making these maps useful for sea travel.

Practicing SKILLS

1. **Explain** the significance of: map projection, planar, cylindrical, conic, interrupted projection.

2. **How** does a cartographer determine which map projection to use?

3. **How** is Goode's Interrupted Equal-Area projection different from the Mercator projection?

4. **Which** of the four common projections described above is the best one to use when showing the entire world? Why?

5. **Use** a Venn diagram like the one below to identify the similarities and differences between the Winkel Tripel and Mercator projections.

Winkel Tripel projection · Mercator projection

Determining Location

Geography is often said to begin with the question: *Where?* The basic tool for answering the question is **location.** Lines on globes and maps provide information that can help you locate places. These lines cross one another forming a pattern called a **grid system,** which helps you find exact places on the Earth's surface.

A **hemisphere** is one of the halves into which the Earth is divided. Geographers divide the Earth into hemispheres to help them classify and describe places on Earth. Most places are located in two of the four hemispheres.

Latitude

Lines of **latitude,** or parallels, circle the Earth parallel to the Equator and measure the distance north or south of the Equator in degrees. The Equator is measured at 0° latitude, while the Poles lie at latitudes 90°N (north) and 90°S (south). Parallels north of the Equator are called north latitude. Parallels south of the Equator are called south latitude.

Longitude

Lines of **longitude,** or meridians, circle the Earth from Pole to Pole. These lines measure distance east or west of the **Prime Meridian** at 0° longitude. Meridians east of the Prime Meridian are known as east latitude. Meridians west of the Prime Meridian are known as west longitude. The 180° meridian on the opposite side of the Earth is called the International Date Line.

The Global Grid

Every place has a global address, or **absolute location.** You can identify the absolute location of a place by naming the latitude and longitude lines that cross exactly at that place. For example, Tokyo, Japan, is located at 36°N latitude and 140°E longitude. For more precise readings, each degree is further divided into 60 units called minutes.

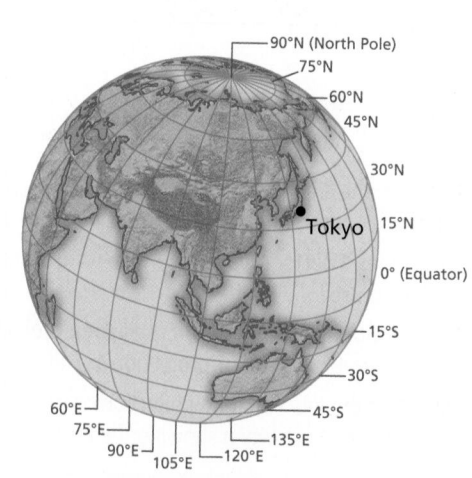

Northern and Southern Hemispheres

The diagram below shows that the Equator divides the Earth into the Northern and Southern Hemispheres. Everything north of the Equator is in the **Northern Hemisphere.** Everything south of the Equator is in the **Southern Hemisphere.**

Northern Hemisphere

Southern Hemisphere

Eastern and Western Hemispheres

The Prime Meridian and the International Date Line divide the Earth into the Eastern and Western Hemispheres. Everything east of the Prime Meridian for 180° is in the **Eastern Hemisphere.** Everything west of the Prime Meridian for 180° is in the **Western Hemisphere.**

Eastern Hemisphere

Western Hemisphere

Practicing SKILLS

1. **Explain** the significance of: location, grid system, hemisphere, Northern Hemisphere, Southern Hemisphere, Eastern Hemisphere, Western Hemisphere, latitude, longitude, Prime Meridian, absolute location.

2. **Why** do all maps label the Equator 0° latitude and the Prime Meridian 0° longitude?

3. **Which** lines of latitude and longitude divide the Earth into hemispheres?

4. **Using** the Reference Atlas maps, fill in a chart like the one below by writing the latitude and longitude of three world cities. Have a partner try to identify the cities.

5. **Use** a chart like the one below to identify the continents in each hemisphere. Some may be in more than one hemisphere.

Hemisphere	Continents
Northern	
Southern	
Eastern	
Western	

Reading a Map

In addition to latitude and longitude, maps feature other important tools to help you interpret the information they contain. Learning to use these map tools will help you read the symbolic language of maps more easily.

Title

The title tells you what kind of information the map is showing.

Key

The **key** lists and explains the symbols, colors, and lines used on the map. The key is sometimes called a legend.

Scale Bar

The **scale bar** shows the relationship between map measurements and actual distances on the Earth. By laying a ruler along the scale bar, you can calculate how many miles or kilometers are represented per inch or centimeter. The map projection used to create the map is often listed near the scale bar.

Compass Rose

The **compass rose** indicates directions. The four **cardinal directions**—north, south, east, and west—are usually indicated with arrows or the points of a star. The **intermediate directions**—northeast, northwest, southeast, and southwest—may also be shown.

Cities

Cities are represented by a dot. Sometimes the relative sizes of cities are shown using dots of different sizes.

Capitals

National capitals are often represented by a star within a circle.

Boundary Lines

On political maps of large areas, boundary lines highlight the borders between different countries or states.

Using Scale

All maps are drawn to a certain scale. **Scale** is a consistent, proportional relationship between the measurements shown on the map and the measurement of the Earth's surface.

Small-Scale Maps A small-scale map, like this political map of France, can show a large area but little detail. Note that the scale bar on this map indicates that about 1 inch is equal to 200 miles.

Large-Scale Maps A large-scale map, like this map of Paris, can show a small area with a great amount of detail. Study the scale bar. Note that the map measurements correspond to much smaller distances than on the map of France.

Absolute and Relative Location

As you learned on page GH6, absolute location is the exact point where a line of latitude crosses a line of longitude. Another way to indicate location is by **relative location**, or the location of one place in relation to another. To find relative location, find a reference point—a location you already know—on a map. Then look in the appropriate direction for the new location. For example, locate Paris (your reference point) on the map of France above. The relative location of Lyon can be described as southeast of Paris.

Practicing SKILLS

1. **Explain** the significance of: key, compass rose, cardinal directions, intermediate directions, scale bar, scale, relative location.

2. **Describe** the elements of a map that help you interpret the information displayed on the map.

3. **How** does the scale bar help you determine distances on the Earth's surface?

4. **Describe** the relative location of your school in two different ways.

5. **Use** a Venn diagram to identify the similarities and differences of small-scale maps and large-scale maps.

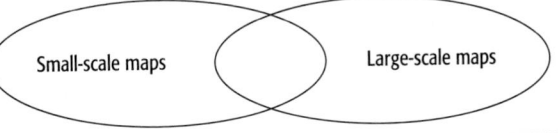

Geography Handbook   GH9

Physical Maps

A **physical map** shows the location and the **topography,** or shape of the Earth's physical features. A study of a country's physical features often helps to explain the historical development of the country. For example, mountains may be barriers to transportation, and rivers and streams can provide access into the interior of a country.

Water Features

Physical maps show rivers, streams, lakes, and other water features.

Landforms

Physical maps may show landforms such as mountains, plains, plateaus, and valleys.

Relief

Physical maps use shading and texture to show general **relief**—the differences in **elevation,** or height, of landforms.

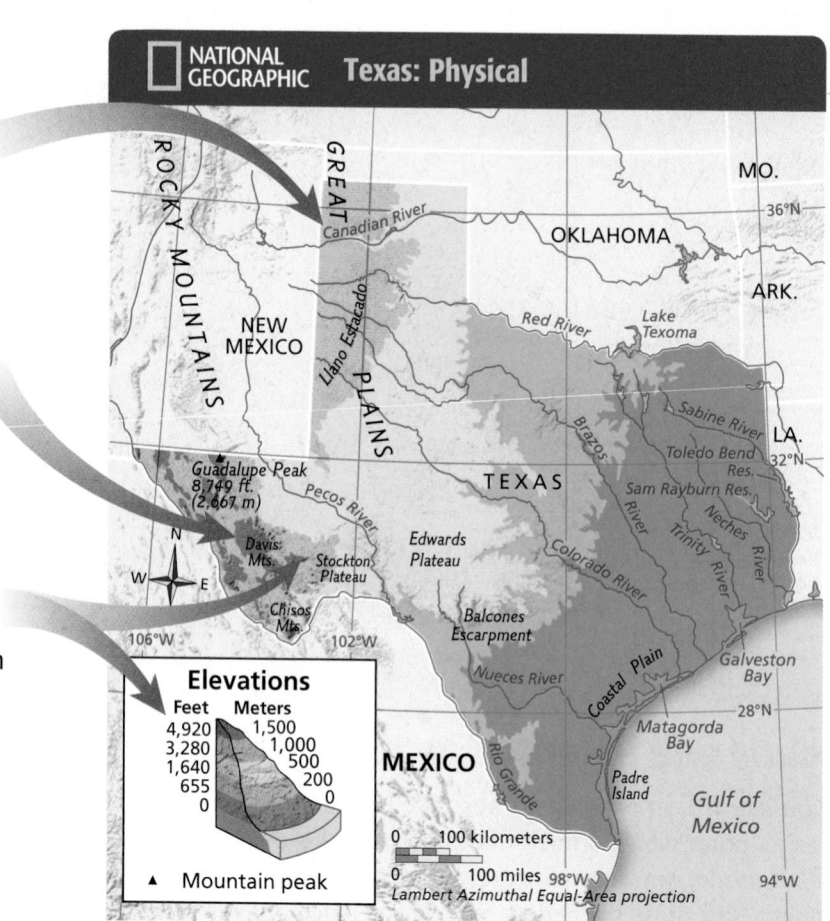

Texas: Physical

Practicing SKILLS

1. **Explain** the significance of: physical map, topography, relief, elevation.
2. **Complete** a table like the one to the right to explain what you can learn from the map about each of the physical features listed.

Physical Feature	What You Can Learn from the Map
Davis Mountains	
Red River	
Gulf Coastal Plains	

Political Maps

A **political map** shows the boundaries and locations of political units such as countries, states, counties, cities, and towns. Many features depicted on a political map are **human-made,** or determined by humans rather than by nature. Political maps can show the networks and links that exist within and between political units.

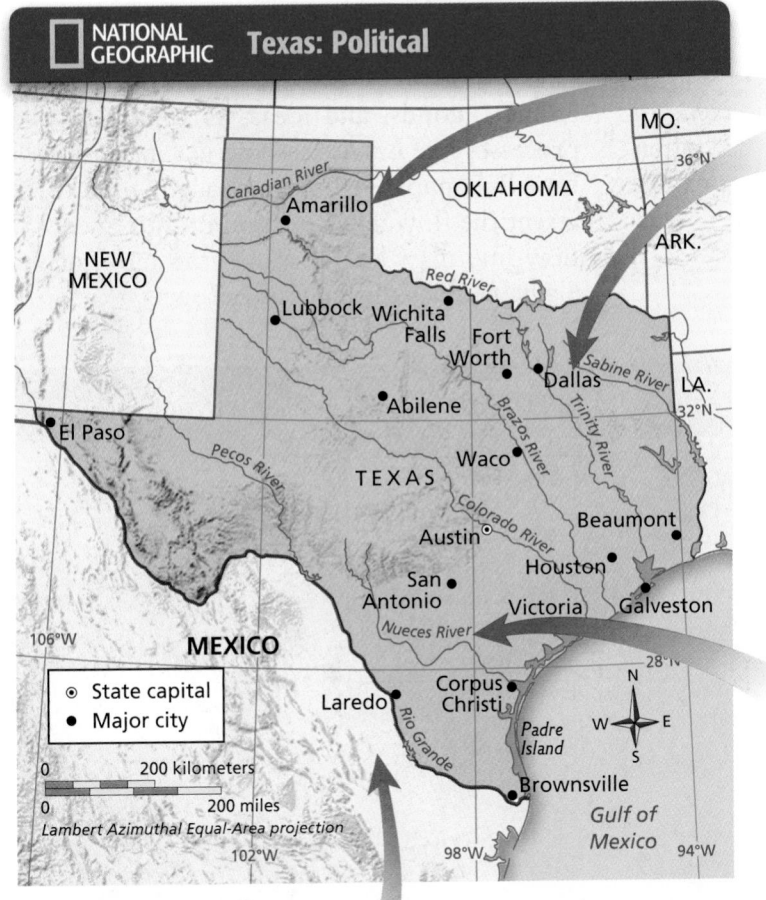

NATIONAL GEOGRAPHIC **Texas: Political**

Human-Made Features

Political maps show human-made features such as boundaries, capitals, cities, roads, highways, and railroads.

Physical Features

Political maps may show some physical features such as relief, rivers, and mountains.

Nonsubject Area

Areas surrounding the subject area of the map are usually a different color to set them apart. They are labeled to give you a context for the area you are studying.

Practicing SKILLS

1. **Explain** the significance of: political map, human-made.
2. **What** types of information would you find on a political map that would not appear on a physical map?
3. **Complete** a table like the one to the right to explain what you can learn from the map about each of the human-made features listed.

Human-Made Feature	What You Can Learn from the Map
Austin	
El Paso	
Texas state boundary	

Thematic Maps

Maps that emphasize a single idea or a particular kind of information about an area are called **thematic maps**. There are many kinds of thematic maps, each designed to serve a different need. This textbook includes thematic maps that show exploration and trade, migration of peoples, economic activities, and war and political conflicts.

Qualitative Maps

Maps that use colors, symbols, lines, or dots to show information related to a specific idea are called **qualitative maps**. Such maps are often used to depict historical information. For example, the qualitative map below shows the spread of farming in Latin America over time.

Flow-Line Maps

Maps that illustrate the movement of people, animals, goods, and ideas, as well as physical processes like hurricanes and glaciers, are called **flow-line maps**. Arrows are usually used to represent the flow and direction of movement. The flow-line map below shows the movement of Slavic peoples throughout Europe.

Geographic Information Systems

Modern technology has changed the way maps are made. Most cartographers use computers with software programs called **geographic information systems (GIS)**. A GIS is designed to accept data from different sources—maps, satellite images, printed text, and statistics. The GIS converts the data into a digital code, which arranges it in a database. Cartographers then program the GIS to process the data and produce maps. With GIS, each kind of information on a map is saved as a separate electronic layer.

1 *The first layer of information in a GIS pinpoints the area of interest. This allows the user to see, in detail, the area he or she needs to study. In this case, the area of study is a 5 mile (8 km) radius around Christ Hospital in Jersey City, New Jersey.*

2 *Additional layers of information are added based on the problem or issue being studied. In this case, hospital administrators want to find out about the population living in neighborhoods near the hospital so they can offer the community what it needs. A second layer showing African Americans who live within the 5 mile (8 km) radius has been added to the GIS.*

3 *Complex information can be presented using more than one layer. For example, the hospital's surrounding neighborhoods include other groups in addition to African Americans. A third layer showing whites who live within the 5 mile (8 km) radius has been added to the GIS. Administrators can now use this information to help them make decisions about staffing and services associated with the hospital.*

Practicing SKILLS

1. **Explain** the significance of: thematic map, qualitative maps, flow-line maps.

2. **Which** type of thematic map would best show the spread of Islam during Muhammad's time?

3. **Which** type of thematic map would best show average income per capita in the United States?

4. **How** does GIS allow cartographers to create maps and make changes to maps quickly and easily?

5. **Complete** a chart like the one below by identifying three examples of each type of thematic map found in this textbook. Note the page numbers of each.

Qualitative Maps	Flow-Line Maps

Geographic Dictionary

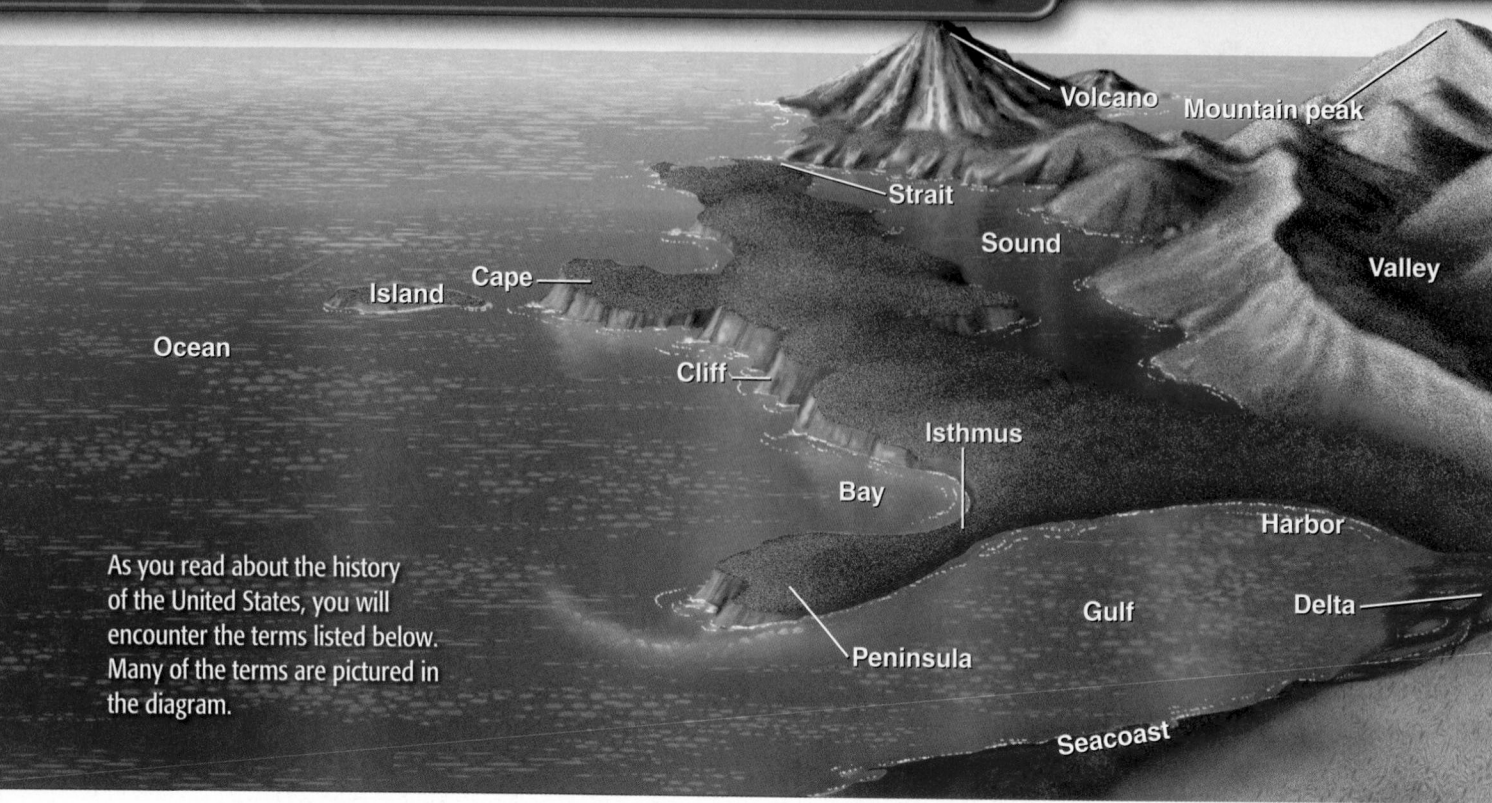

Volcano | Mountain peak | Strait | Sound | Valley | Cape | Island | Ocean | Cliff | Isthmus | Bay | Harbor | Peninsula | Gulf | Delta | Seacoast

As you read about the history of the United States, you will encounter the terms listed below. Many of the terms are pictured in the diagram.

absolute location exact location of a place on the earth described by global coordinates

basin area of land drained by a given river and its branches; area of land surrounded by lands of higher elevations

bay part of a large body of water that extends into a shoreline, generally smaller than a gulf

canyon deep and narrow valley with steep walls

cape point of land that extends into a river, lake, or ocean

channel wide strait or waterway between two landmasses that lie close to each other; deep part of a river or other waterway

cliff steep, high wall of rock, earth, or ice

continent one of the seven large landmasses on the earth

cultural feature characteristic that humans have created in a place, such as language, religion, housing, and settlement pattern

delta flat, low-lying land built up from soil carried downstream by a river and deposited at its mouth

divide stretch of high land that separates river systems

downstream direction in which a river or stream flows from its source to its mouth

elevation height of land above sea level

Equator imaginary line that runs around the earth halfway between the North and South Poles; used as the starting point to measure degrees of north and south latitude

glacier large, thick body of slowly moving ice

gulf part of a large body of water that extends into a shoreline, generally larger and more deeply indented than a bay

harbor a sheltered place along a shoreline where ships can anchor safely

highland elevated land area such as a hill, mountain, or plateau

hill elevated land with sloping sides and rounded summit; generally smaller than a mountain

island land area, smaller than a continent, completely surrounded by water

isthmus narrow stretch of land connecting two larger land areas

lake a large inland body of water

latitude distance north or south of the Equator, measured in degrees

longitude distance east or west of the Prime Meridian, measured in degrees

lowland land, usually level, at a low elevation

map drawing of the earth shown on a flat surface

meridian one of many lines on the global grid running from the North Pole to the South Pole; used to measure degrees of longitude

Mountain range

Source of river

Channel

Glacier

Highland

Lake

Hills

Plateau

Mouth of river

Canyon

Desert

River

Upstream

Downstream

Plain

Lowland

Basin

Tributary

mesa broad, flat-topped landform with steep sides; smaller than a plateau

mountain land with steep sides that rises sharply (1,000 feet or more) from surrounding land; generally larger and more rugged than a hill

mountain peak pointed top of a mountain

mountain range a series of connected mountains

mouth (of a river) place where a stream or river flows into a larger body of water

ocean one of the four major bodies of salt water that surround the continents

ocean current stream of either cold or warm water that moves in a definite direction through an ocean

parallel one of many lines on the global grid that circle the earth north or south of the Equator; used to measure degrees of latitude

peninsula body of land jutting into a lake or ocean, surrounded on three sides by water

physical feature characteristic of a place occurring naturally, such as a landform, body of water, climate pattern, or resource

plain area of level land, usually at a low elevation and often covered with grasses

plateau large area of flat or rolling land at a high elevation, about 300–3,000 feet high

Prime Meridian line of the global grid running from the North Pole to the South Pole at Greenwich, England; starting point for measuring degrees of east and west longitude

relief changes in elevation over a given area of land

river large natural stream of water that runs through the land

sea large body of water completely or partly surrounded by land

seacoast land lying next to a sea or ocean

sea level position on land level with surface of nearby ocean or sea

sound body of water between a coastline and one or more islands off the coast

source (of a river) place where a river or stream begins, often in highlands

strait narrow stretch of water joining two larger bodies of water

tributary small river or stream that flows into a larger river or stream; a branch of the river

upstream direction opposite the flow of a river; toward the source of a river or stream

valley area of low land between hills or mountains

volcano mountain created as ash or liquid rock erupts from inside the earth

Unit 1

Creating A Nation

Beginnings to 1789

Why It Matters

The settlement of North America brought together three cultures—European, African, and Native American—and created several new colonial societies. In 1776 anger at British policies caused thirteen British colonies to declare independence and create the United States of America. The American Revolution led to a new form of government. Americans created a democratic republic with a federal constitution and began expanding across the continent.

Signing the Declaration of Independence

Chapter 1

Colonizing America
Prehistory to 1754

Pilgrims worshipping at Plymouth in 1621

U.S. EVENTS

1492
• Christopher Columbus lands in America

1519
• Hernán Cortés conquers the Aztec

1607
• The English found Jamestown in Virginia

1619
• First Africans arrive in North America via Dutch traders

1450   1500   1550   1600

WORLD EVENTS

c. 1450
• Songhai Empire expands in West Africa

1498
• Vasco da Gama sails around Africa to India, locating a water route to Asia from Europe

1520
• Ferdinand Magellan sails into Pacific Ocean

1527
• Henry VIII breaks with Catholic Church

1588
• English defeat Spanish Armada

1600
• Tokugawa period of feudal rule begins in Japan

Why Do People Migrate to New Lands?

Europeans began leaving their continent in the 1500s to settle in the Americas. Their colonies reflected the values and traditions of their homelands, but they were also shaped by the geography of the new land they settled.

- *Why do you think Europeans came to America?*
- *How might the location of a colony affect its development?*

1630
- Massachusetts Bay Colony is established

1660
- British Navigation Acts regulate American colonial trade

1681
- William Penn receives charter for Pennsylvania

1734
- Libel trial of publisher John Peter Zenger helps establish free press

1642
- English Civil War begins

1688
- Glorious Revolution establishes limited monarchy in England

1707
- Act of Union creates United Kingdom

1650   1700   1750

Analyzing Colonial Experiments Create a Two-Tab Book Foldable to help analyze the colonial experiences of the French and Spanish. As you read, identify the successes and failures for each country under its tab.

French | Spanish

History ONLINE Chapter Overview
Visit glencoe.com to preview Chapter 1.

North America Before Columbus

Guide to Reading

Big Ideas
Geography and History Native American groups developed cultures based on the geography of the region in which they lived.

Content Vocabulary
- agricultural revolution *(p. 4)*
- tribute *(p. 6)*
- kiva *(p. 7)*
- pueblo *(p. 7)*

Academic Vocabulary
- decline *(p. 5)*
- technology *(p. 6)*
- eventually *(p. 8)*

People and Events to Identify
- Beringia *(p. 4)*
- Mesoamerica *(p. 4)*
- Maya *(p. 5)*
- Aztec *(p. 6)*
- Cahokia *(p. 8)*
- Iroquois Confederacy *(p. 11)*

Reading Strategy
Categorizing Complete a chart similar to the one below by filling in the names of the groups who lived in each region.

Region	Groups
Mesoamerica	
West	
Midwest	
Northeast	

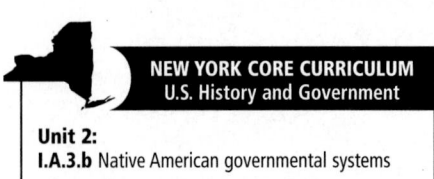

NEW YORK CORE CURRICULUM
U.S. History and Government

Unit 2:
I.A.3.b Native American governmental systems

Before 1492 the peoples of the Americas had almost no contact with the rest of the world. The societies and languages that developed varied widely. In North America, some Native Americans lived as nomadic hunters, while others lived in large, complex cities.

Mesoamerican Cultures

MAIN Idea An agricultural revolution led to the first civilizations in Mesoamerica, whose people built large, elaborate cities.

HISTORY AND YOU What is the largest city you have visited? Read to learn about the origins of Mexico City, the largest city in North America.

No one knows for certain when the first people arrived in the Americas. Current scientific evidence suggests that the first humans arrived between 15,000 and 30,000 years ago. Based on DNA tests and other evidence, some scientists think the earliest Americans came from northeast Asia. Some may have arrived during the last Ice Age, when much of the earth's water became frozen and created a land bridge between Alaska and Asia along the Bering Strait. Along this stretch of land, known as **Beringia,** nomadic hunters may have crossed to the Americas as they followed large prey, such as the wooly mammoth, antelope, and caribou. These people did not come all at once, and some may have come by boat.

Over time, the descendants of these early settlers spread southward and eastward across the Americas. Between 9,000 and 10,000 years ago, some early Americans learned to plant and raise crops. This **agricultural revolution** began in **Mesoamerica,** the region that today includes central and southern Mexico and Central America. The agricultural revolution made possible the rise of Mesoamerica's first civilizations.

Anthropologists think the first people to develop a civilization in Mesoamerica were the Olmec. Olmec culture emerged between 1500 and 1200 B.C., near where Veracruz, Mexico, is located today. The Olmec developed a sophisticated society with large villages, temple complexes, and pyramids. They also sculpted huge monuments, including 8-foot-high heads weighing up to 20 tons, from a hard rock known as basalt. Olmec culture lasted until about 300 B.C.

Olmec ideas spread throughout Mesoamerica, influencing other peoples. One of these peoples constructed the first large city in the Americas, called Teotihuacán (TAY·oh·TEE·wah·KAHN), about 30 miles northeast of where Mexico City is today. The city was built near a volcano, where there were large deposits of obsidian, or volcanic glass. Obsidian was very valuable. Its sharp, strong edges were perfect for tools and weapons.

0   200 kilometers
0   200 miles
*Lambert Azimuthal
Equal-Area projection*

Gulf of Mexico

N
W — E
S

Tula
Teotihuacán
Tenochtitlán

Uxmal
Chichén Itzá
Tulum
Yucatán
Peninsula

Palenque
Tikal

Copán

PACIFIC OCEAN

TROPIC OF CANCER

30°N
20°N
15°N

100°W   95°W   90°W   80°W

- Olmec, c. 500 B.C.
- Maya, c. A.D. 750
- Toltec, c. A.D. 1200
- Aztec, c. A.D. 1500

▲ *This temple pyramid was built at the Maya city of Tikal.*

◄ *The Aztec Temple of the Moon was built in the ancient city of Teotihuacán.*

Analyzing GEOGRAPHY

1. **Location** Where was the Maya city of Chichén Itzá located?
2. **Place** In what way do the photos show how the Mesoamericans modified the environment?

The people of Teotihuacán built up a trade network based on obsidian, which influenced the development of Mesoamerica. The city lasted from about 300 B.C. to about A.D. 650.

The Maya

Around A.D. 200, as Teotihuacán's influence spread, the Maya civilization emerged in the Yucatán Peninsula and expanded into what is now Central America and southern Mexico. The **Maya** had a talent for engineering and mathematics. They developed complex and accurate calendars linked to the positions of the stars. They also built great temple pyramids. These pyramids formed the centerpieces of Maya cities, such as Tikal and Chichén Itzá. Marvels of engineering, some pyramids were 200 feet (61 m) high. At the top of each pyramid was a temple where priests performed ceremonies dedicated to the many Maya gods.

Although trade and a common culture linked the Maya, they were not unified. Each city-state controlled its own territory. Because of the fragmented nature of their society, the different cities frequently went to war.

The Maya continued to thrive until the A.D. 900s, when they abandoned their cities in the Yucatán for unknown reasons. Some anthropologists believe Maya farmers may have exhausted the region's soil. This in turn would have led to famine, riots, and the collapse of the cities. Others believe that invaders from the north devastated the region. Maya cities in what is today Guatemala flourished for several more centuries, although by the 1500s they too were in **decline.**

History ONLINE
Student Web Activity Visit glencoe.com and complete the activity on American prehistory.

The Toltec and the Aztec

North of the Maya civilization, the Toltec people built a large city called Tula. The Toltec were master architects. They built large pyramids and huge palaces with pillared halls. They were among the first American peoples to use gold and copper in art and jewelry.

About A.D. 1200, Tula fell to invaders from the north, known as the Chichimec. One group of Chichimec, called the Mexica, built the city of Tenochtitlán (tay·NAWCH·teet·LAHN) in 1325 on the site of what is today Mexico City. The Mexica took the name **Aztec** for themselves, from the name of their original homeland, Aztlán. Aztlán is thought to have been located in the American Southwest.

The Aztec created a mighty empire by conquering neighboring cities. Using their military power, they controlled trade in the region and demanded **tribute,** or payment, from the cities they conquered. They also brought some of the people they conquered to Tenochtitlán to sacrifice in their religious ceremonies. When the Europeans arrived in the 1500s, an estimated 5 million people were living under Aztec rule.

✔ **Reading Check** **Examining** What are some of the theories that explain the decline of Maya cities?

Western Cultures

MAIN Idea Depending on their local environment, the Native Americans of western North America pursued agriculture, fishing, and hunting.

HISTORY AND YOU Do you have a particular household chore assigned to you? Read how some Native American families divided household work.

North of Mesoamerica, other peoples developed their own cultures. Many anthropologists think that agricultural **technology** spread from Mesoamerica into the American Southwest and up the Mississippi River. There, it transformed many hunter-gatherer societies into farming societies.

The Hohokam

Beginning in A.D. 300, in what is now south-central Arizona, a group called the Hohokam built a system of irrigation canals. The Hohokam used the Gila and Salt Rivers as their water supply. Their canals carried water hundreds of miles to their farms.

The Hohokam grew corn, cotton, beans, and squash. They also made decorative red-on-buff-colored pottery and turquoise pen-

PRIMARY SOURCE
The Aztec Capital, Tenochtitlán

The Aztec were master builders who filled their cities with wide plazas and spectacular temples.

The Great Temple had two shrines at the top, dedicated to the rain god and the sun god.

Aztecs played a ritual ball game on the ball court near the Great Temple.

▲ At the top, Aztecs sit in their home in front of the hearth, which was sacred to them, while an Aztec is shown cooking below.

Analyzing VISUALS

1. **Identifying** What was the main feature of the city of Tenochtitlán?

2. **Making Inferences** Why would the hearth be sacred to the Aztecs?

dants, and used cactus juice to etch shells. Hohokam culture flourished for more than 1,000 years, but in the 1300s they began to abandon their irrigation systems, likely due to floods and increased competition for farmland. By 1500, the Hohokam had left the area.

The Anasazi

Between A.D. 700 and 900, the people living in villages in what is called the Four Corners area—where Utah, Colorado, Arizona, and New Mexico now meet—developed another culture. We know these people by the name the Navajo gave them—Anasazi, or "ancient ones." Today they are often called "ancestral Puebloan" people. In the harsh desert, the Anasazi accumulated water by building networks of basins and ditches to channel rain into stone-lined depressions.

Between A.D. 850 and 1100, the Anasazi living in Chaco Canyon in what is now northwest New Mexico began constructing large, multistory buildings of adobe and cut stone, with connecting passageways and circular ceremonial rooms called **kivas.** Early Spanish explorers called these structures **pueblos,** the Spanish word for "villages." Those who built them are sometimes referred to as Pueblo people.

The Anasazi built these pueblos at junctions where streams of rainwater ran together. A pueblo in Chaco Canyon, called Pueblo Bonito, had 600 rooms and probably housed at least 1,000 people. Later, at Mesa Verde in what is today southwestern Colorado, the Anasazi built impressive cliff dwellings.

Beginning around A.D. 1130, Chaco Canyon experienced a devastating drought that lasted at least 50 years. This probably caused the Anasazi to abandon their pueblos. The Mesa Verde pueblos lasted for another 200 years, but when another drought struck in the 1270s, they too were abandoned.

The Southwest

The descendants of the Anasazi and Hohokam live in the arid Southwest. At the time of European contact, there were over 50 groups. These groups included the Zuni, Hopi, and other Pueblo peoples. Corn was essential to their survival in the arid climate because its long taproot could reach moisture deep beneath the surface. The farmers also grew squash and beans.

The Pueblo people assigned different tasks to men and women. Men farmed, performed most ceremonies, made moccasins, and wove clothing and blankets. Women made the meals, crafted pottery and baskets, and hauled water. The men and women worked together when harvesting crops and building houses.

Sometime between A.D. 1200 and 1500, two other peoples—the Apache and the Navajo— came to the region from the far northwest of North America. Some anthropologists think that their arrival might have been what drove the Chichimec people into Mexico, where they formed the Aztec Empire. Although many of the Apache remained primarily nomadic hunters, the Navajo learned farming from the Pueblo people and lived in widely dispersed settlements.

The Pacific Coast

Many different groups, including the Tlingit, Haida, Kwakiutl, Nootka, Chinook, and Salish peoples, lived in the lands bordering the Pacific Ocean from what is now southeastern Alaska to Washington State. Although they did not practice agriculture, these groups dwelt in permanent settlements. They looked to the dense coastal forests for lumber, which they used not only to build homes and to fashion ocean-going canoes, but also to create elaborate works of art, ceremonial masks, and totem poles. They were able to stay in one place because the region's coastal waters and many rivers teemed with fish.

In what is today central California, several groups hunted the abundant wildlife and flourished in the mild climate. The Pomo, for example, gathered acorns, caught fish in nets and traps, and snared small game and birds. Pomo hunters, working together, would drive deer toward a spot where the village's best archer waited, hidden and disguised in a deer-head mask. Sometimes, the hunters stampeded game into a corral, where the animals could be easily killed. When game was scarce, however, the Pomo relied on the acorn, which they had learned to convert from a hard, bitter nut into edible flour.

✔ Reading Check **Analyzing** How did societies of the Southwest cope with the dry climate?

Mississippian Culture and Its Descendants

MAIN Idea Along the Mississippi River, Native Americans built Cahokia and other large cities, while those on the Great Plains hunted buffalo herds.

HISTORY AND YOU Have you seen photos of pyramids in Egypt or Mexico? Read to learn about the large pyramids built in the Mississippi River valley.

Between A.D. 700 and 900, as agricultural technology and improved strains of maize and beans spread north from Mexico and up the Mississippi River, another new culture—the Mississippian—emerged. It began in the Mississippi River valley, where the rich soil of the floodplains was perfectly suited to the intensive cultivation of maize and beans.

The Mississippians were great builders. Eight miles from what is now St. Louis, Missouri, are the remains of one of their largest cities, which anthropologists named **Cahokia.** At its peak between about A.D. 1050 and 1250, Cahokia covered five square miles (13 sq km), contained more than 100 flat-topped pyramids and mounds, and was home to an estimated 16,000 people. Most of the people lived in pole-and-thatch houses that spread out over 2,000 acres (810 ha). The largest pyramid, named Monks Mound, was 100 feet (30.5 m) high, had four levels, and covered 16 acres (6.5 ha)—more than any pyramid in Egypt or Mexico. A log wall with watchtowers and gates surrounded the central plaza and the larger pyramids.

As it expanded across the American South, Mississippian culture led to the rise of at least three other large cities with flat-topped mounds—at present-day Spiro, Oklahoma; Moundville, Alabama; and Etowah, Georgia. Mississippian culture also spread north and west along the great rivers of the region: the Missouri, Ohio, Red, and Arkansas.

Peoples of the Southeast

The population of Cahokia mysteriously declined around A.D. 1300. The city may have been attacked by other Native Americans or its population may have become too large to support, resulting in famine and emigration. Another possibility is that the city was struck by an epidemic.

Although Cahokia came to an end, many aspects of Mississippian culture survived in the Southeast until the Europeans arrived. Almost all the people in the Southeast lived in towns. The buildings were arranged around a central plaza. Stockades usually surrounded the towns, although moats and earthen walls were also used. The houses were built out of poles and covered with grass, mud, or thatch. Women did most of the farming, while men hunted deer, bear, wildfowl, and even alligator.

The Cherokee were the largest group in the Southeast. They were located in what is today western North Carolina and eastern Tennessee. About 20,000 Cherokee lived in some 60 towns when the Europeans arrived. Other peoples in the Southeast included the Choctaw, Chickasaw, Natchez, and Creek. The Creek were a large group living in some 50 villages spread across Georgia and Alabama.

The Great Plains

When Europeans arrived, the people of the Great Plains were nomads, who had only recently abandoned farming. Until about 1500 the societies of the Great Plains had been shaped by Mississippian culture. The people of the region lived near rivers, where they could plant corn and find wood to build their homes.

Around the year 1500, the peoples of the western Plains abandoned their villages and became nomads, possibly because of war or drought. Those in the east, including the Pawnee, Kansas, and Iowa peoples, continued to farm, as well as hunt. Peoples of the western Plains, including the Sioux, became nomadic. They hunted migrating buffalo herds on foot and lived in cone-shaped tents called tepees.

Life for the Sioux and others on the Great Plains changed dramatically after they began taming horses. The Spanish brought horses to North America in the 1500s. Over the next few centuries, as horses either escaped or were stolen, the animals spread northward, **eventually** reaching the Great Plains. There, the Sioux encountered and mastered them. The Sioux soon became some of the world's greatest mounted hunters and warriors.

✓ Reading Check **Contrasting** How did the Mississippian culture affect the peoples of the Southeast?

◀ Great Plains peoples, such as the Sioux, tamed horses and lived in temporary tepee villages.

▶ The Eastern Woodlands peoples known collectively as the Iroquois lived in permanent, well-defended communities.

Legend

California	Northwest Coast	Subarctic		
Great Basin	Plateau	HOPI Tribal group		
Great Plains	Southeast			
Northeast	Southwest			

KWAKIUTL
LILLOOET
NOOTKA
THOMPSON
OKANAGAN
(BLOOD)
PLAINS CREE
MAKAH
SALISH
SANPOIL
KUTENAI
PIEGAN
PUYALLUP
COLVILLE
KALISPEL
ASSINIBOIN
CHEHALIS
NISQUALLY
SPOKANE
COEUR
CHINOOK
PALUS
D'ALENE
ATSINA
(GROS VENTRE)
COWLITZ
WALLA
HURON
TILLAMOOK
YAKIMA
WALLA
FLATHEAD
HIDATSA
MANDAN
OTTAWA
KLIKITAT
MOLALA
NEZ
CROW
HURON
KALAPUYA
PERCE
ARIKARA
MENOMINI
TIONONTATI
MOHAWK
MICMAC
COOS UMPQUA CAYUSE
OJIBWA
SANTEE
DAKOTA
SAUK
WINNEBAGO
ONEIDA
ONONDAGA
MALECITE
TAKELMA KLAMATH
BANNOCK
TETON
DAKOTA
FOX
POTAWATOMI
CAYUGA
SENECA
PASSAMAQUODDY
YUROK
KAROK
MODOC
ACHOMAWI
SHOSHONE
(SNAKE)
NORTHERN
CHEYENNE
YANKTON
DAKOTA
KICKAPOO
ERIE
SUSQUEHANNOCK
(CONESTOGA)
MAHICAN
ABENAKI
PENOBSCOT
WIYOT
SHASTA ATSUGEWI
PONCA
KASKASKIA
MIAMI
DELAWARE
(LENI LENAPE)
PENNACOOK
HUPA
YANA
PAVIOTSO
PAWNEE
OMAHA
IOWA
PEORIA
WEA
PAMUNKEY
NANTICOKE
MASSACHUSET
WAMPANOAG
MATTOLE
MAIDU
NORTHERN
PAIUTE
GOSIUTE
OTO
MISSOURI
PIANKASHAW
POWHATAN
NIPMUC
NARRAGANSET
POMO
YUKI
WASHO
ARAPAHO
KANSA
SHAWNEE
CHICKAHOMINY
MATTAPONI
PEQUOT
MOHEGAN
WAPPINGER
WINTUN
MIWOK
OSAGE
TUTELO
PAMLICO
NOTTOWAY
COSTANOAN
YOKUTS
KAWAIISU
UTE
SOUTHERN
CHEYENNE
CHEROKEE
TUSCARORA
SALINAN
MONO
SOUTHERN
PAIUTE
NAVAJO
JICARILLA
APACHE
KIOWA
QUAPAW
CATAWBA
CHUMASH
PANAMINT
HAVASUPAI
HOPI
KIOWA
APACHE
CHICKASAW
YUCHI
TUSKEGEE
ATLANTIC
OCEAN
CHEMEHUEVI
WALAPAI
ZUÑI
PUEBLO
TAWAKONI
CREEK
YAMASEE
SERRANO
YAVAPAI
MOJAVE
MESCALERO
APACHE
WICHITA
CHOCTAW
HICHITI
GUALE
PACIFIC
OCEAN
CAHUILLA
YUMA
MARICOPA
PIMA
COMANCHE
CADDO
TUNICA
ALABAMA
APALACHEE
TIMUCUA
PAPAGO
WESTERN
APACHE
KICHAI
WACO
NATCHEZ
BILOXI MOBILE
OPATA
LIPAN
APACHE
TONKAWA
ATAKAPA
CHITIMACHA
SEMINOLE
CONCHO
KARANKAWA
Gulf of Mexico
CALUSA
TARAHUMARA
CAHITA

40°N
120°W
30°N
110°W
100°W
90°W
80°W

0   400 kilometers
0   400 miles
Lambert Azimuthal Equal-Area projection

N E S W (compass)

◀ Pueblo peoples of the Southwest built multistory complexes out of adobe.

◀ The Cherokee established permanent settlements throughout the Southeast.

Analyzing GEOGRAPHY

1. **Movement** Why did some of the people of the Great Plains become nomadic?

2. **Human-Environment Interaction** How does the housing style of each group reflect its environment?

Northeastern Peoples

MAIN Idea Most Eastern Woodlands peoples spoke Algonquian or Iroquoian languages; combined hunting, fishing, and farming; and lived in small villages.

HISTORY AND YOU Can you think of an organization intended to stop conflict between nations today? Read on to learn about the origins and purpose of the Iroquois Confederacy.

When Europeans arrived, almost a million square miles of woodlands lay east of the Mississippi River and south of the Great Lakes. This landscape supported an amazing range of plant and animal life. Almost all the Eastern Woodlands peoples provided for themselves by combining hunting and fishing with farming. Deer were plentiful in the region, and deer meat regularly supplemented the corn, beans, and squash the people planted. Deer hide was also used for clothing.

The Algonquian Peoples

Most peoples in the Northeast belonged to one of two language groups: those who spoke Algonquian languages and those who spoke Iroquoian languages. The Algonquian-speaking peoples included most of the groups living in the area known today as New England. Among these peoples were the Wampanoag in Massachusetts, the Narragansett in Rhode Island, and the Pequot in Connecticut. Farther south, in what is today Virginia, lived the Algonquian-speaking peoples of the Powhatan Confederacy. Native Americans in New England and Virginia were among the first to encounter English settlers.

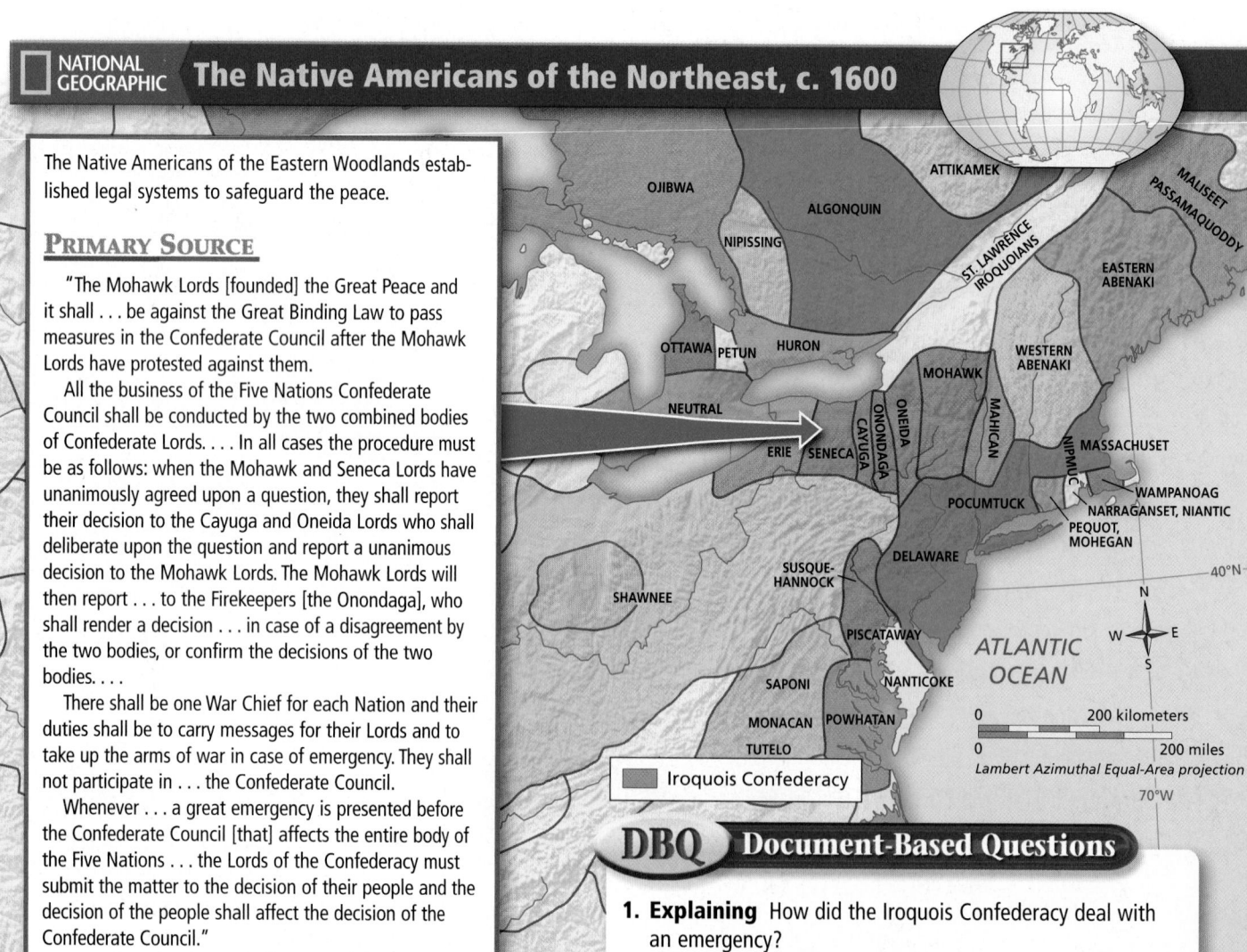

NATIONAL GEOGRAPHIC **The Native Americans of the Northeast, c. 1600**

The Native Americans of the Eastern Woodlands established legal systems to safeguard the peace.

PRIMARY SOURCE

"The Mohawk Lords [founded] the Great Peace and it shall . . . be against the Great Binding Law to pass measures in the Confederate Council after the Mohawk Lords have protested against them.

All the business of the Five Nations Confederate Council shall be conducted by the two combined bodies of Confederate Lords. . . . In all cases the procedure must be as follows: when the Mohawk and Seneca Lords have unanimously agreed upon a question, they shall report their decision to the Cayuga and Oneida Lords who shall deliberate upon the question and report a unanimous decision to the Mohawk Lords. The Mohawk Lords will then report . . . to the Firekeepers [the Onondaga], who shall render a decision . . . in case of a disagreement by the two bodies, or confirm the decisions of the two bodies. . . .

There shall be one War Chief for each Nation and their duties shall be to carry messages for their Lords and to take up the arms of war in case of emergency. They shall not participate in . . . the Confederate Council.

Whenever . . . a great emergency is presented before the Confederate Council [that] affects the entire body of the Five Nations . . . the Lords of the Confederacy must submit the matter to the decision of their people and the decision of the people shall affect the decision of the Confederate Council."

—from the *Great Binding Law of the Five Nations*

Iroquois Confederacy

ATLANTIC OCEAN

0   200 kilometers
0   200 miles
Lambert Azimuthal Equal-Area projection

40°N

70°W

DBQ **Document-Based Questions**

1. **Explaining** How did the Iroquois Confederacy deal with an emergency?

2. **Drawing Conclusions** Why do you think the Iroquois did not let the war chiefs take part in the Confederate Council?

Other Algonquian peoples included the Delaware, who lived near the Delaware River in what is today eastern Pennsylvania and New Jersey; and the Shawnee, who lived in the Ohio River valley. Words from the Algonquian language used in English today include *succotash, hominy, moccasin,* and *papoose.*

Many peoples in the Northeast, including the Algonquians and the Iroquoians, practiced slash-and-burn agriculture. By cutting down parts of forests and burning the wood, they were left with nitrogen-rich ashes. They then worked the ashes into the soil, making it more fertile for a few years. After exhausting the soil, the people of the village would move to a new location and burn down another section of forest for farming.

Native Americans of the Northeast built several types of houses. Many villages had large rectangular longhouses with barrel-shaped roofs covered in bark. Other groups built wigwams. These dwellings were either conical or dome-shaped and were formed using bent poles covered with hides or bark.

The Iroquois Confederacy

Stretching west from the Hudson River across what is today New York and southern Ontario and north to Georgian Bay lived the Iroquoian-speaking peoples. They included the Huron, Neutral, Erie, Wenro, Seneca, Cayuga, Onondaga, Oneida, and Mohawk.

All the Iroquoian peoples had similar cultures. They lived in longhouses in large towns, which they protected by building stockades. Women were responsible for the planting and harvesting of crops while men hunted. The people lived in large kinship groups, or extended families, headed by the elder women of each kinship group. Up to 10 related families lived together in each longhouse.

Iroquois women occupied positions of power and importance in their communities. Although all 50 chiefs of the Iroquois ruling council were men, the women who headed the kinship groups selected them. Council members were appointed for life, but the women could remove an appointee if they disagreed with his actions. In this way, Iroquois women enjoyed considerable political influence.

War often erupted among the Iroquoians. In the late 1500s, five of the nations in western New York—the Seneca, Cayuga, Onondaga, Oneida, and Mohawk—formed an alliance to maintain peace and oppose their common enemy—the more powerful Huron people, who lived across the Niagara River in what is now southwestern Ontario. This alliance was later called the **Iroquois Confederacy.** Europeans called these five nations the Iroquois, even though other nations spoke Iroquoian as well.

According to Iroquoian tradition, Dekanawidah, a shaman or tribal elder, and Hiawatha, a chief of the Mohawk, founded the confederacy. They were worried that war was tearing the five nations apart when the more powerful Huron people threatened them all. The five nations agreed to the Great Binding Law, an oral constitution that defined how the confederacy worked.

Reading Check **Analyzing** How did some Eastern Woodlands groups increase their crop yield?

Section 1 REVIEW

Vocabulary

1. **Explain** the significance of: Beringia, agricultural revolution, Mesoamerica, Maya, Aztec, tribute, kiva, pueblo, Cahokia, Iroquois Confederacy.

Main Ideas

2. **Describing** What route did humans take when they first came to North America?

3. **Identifying** What happened to change life for the peoples of the Great Plains?

4. **Explaining** Why did the Iroquoians form a confederacy?

Critical Thinking

5. **Big Ideas** How did geography and climate affect the cultures and traditions of Native American groups?

6. **Categorizing** Use a graphic organizer to list North American regions and the ways in which groups living in these regions obtained food.

Region	Methods of Getting Food

7. **Analyzing Visuals** Examine the map on page 10. Which groups are members of the Iroquis Confederacy?

Writing About History

8. **Expository Writing** Using library or Internet resources, find more information about the groups discussed in this section. Use the information to create a database about these civilizations. Write a one-page report with your findings.

History ONLINE
Study Central™ To review this section, go to glencoe.com and click on Study Central.

GEOGRAPHY & HISTORY

The Columbian Exchange

The arrival of Europeans in the Americas set in motion a series of complex interactions between peoples and environments. These interactions, called the Columbian Exchange, permanently altered the world's ecosystems and changed nearly every culture around the world.

Native Americans introduced Europeans to new crops. Corn, squash, pumpkins, beans, sweet potatoes, tomatoes, chili peppers, peanuts, chocolate, and potatoes all made their way to Europe, as did tobacco and chewing gum. Perhaps the most significant import for Europeans was the potato. European farmers learned that four times as many people could live off the same amount of land when potatoes were planted instead of grain.

The Europeans introduced Native Americans to wheat, oats, barley, rye, rice, onions, bananas, coffee, and citrus fruits such as lemons and oranges. They also brought over livestock such as cattle, pigs, sheep, and chickens. Perhaps the most important form of livestock was the horse—which dramatically changed life for many Native Americans on the Great Plains.

How Did Geography Shape the Exchange?

The isolation of the Americas from the rest of the world meant that Native Americans had no resistance to diseases that were common in other parts of the world, such as influenza, measles, chicken pox, mumps, typhus, and smallpox. The consequences were devastating. Epidemics killed millions of Native Americans. This catastrophe also reduced the labor supply available to Europeans, who then turned to the slave trade, eventually bringing millions of Africans to the Americas.

Horses

Horses allowed some Native Americans to become nomadic hunters.

Corn

Peppers

Cocoa

Analyzing GEOGRAPHY

1. **Movement** What new crops were introduced in Europe from the Americas? How did these crops improve the diet of Europeans?

2. **Human-Environment Interaction** How did geography play a role in the spread of diseases?

Pigs

European diseases decimated Native American populations.

Disease

Citrus Fruit

Grains

Sugarcane planters imported millions of enslaved Africans to the Americas.

Sugarcane

Cattle

Honeybees

Bananas

Coffee

Potatoes increased northern Europe's population and changed Ireland's diet.

Potatoes

Beans

Squash and Pumpkins

Peanuts improved people's health in West Africa by providing protein.

Peanuts

Disease

Tobacco use killed tens of millions in only a few hundred years.

Tobacco

Tomatoes became popular in Europe and greatly changed the cuisine of Italy.

Tomatoes

Section 2

Europe Begins to Explore

Guide to Reading

Big Ideas

Science and Technology The Renaissance brought about a scientific revolution that enabled Europeans to explore the world.

Content Vocabulary
• astrolabe *(p. 16)*
• caravel *(p. 16)*
• circumnavigate *(p. 19)*
• conquistador *(p. 20)*
• encomienda *(p. 22)*

Academic Vocabulary
• route *(p. 15)*
• acquire *(p. 16)*
• labor *(p. 17)*

People and Events to Identify
• Henry the Navigator *(p. 16)*
• Amerigo Vespucci *(p. 18)*
• Hernán Cortés *(p. 20)*
• Francisco Pizarro *(p. 20)*
• Samuel de Champlain *(p. 23)*

Reading Strategy

Organizing Complete a chart similar to the one below by filling in the outcome of each exploration listed in the chart.

Exploration	Outcome
Columbus	
Vespucci	
Balboa	
Magellan	

NEW YORK CORE CURRICULUM
U.S. History and Government

Unit 2:
I.A.2.a Native American Indians (relations between colonists and Native American Indians, trade, alliances, forced labor, warfare)
I.A.2.b Slave trade
I.A.2.c Varieties of immigrant motivation, ethnicities, and experiences

During the Renaissance, increased trade and new technology led Europeans to embark on overseas exploration. First, Europeans sailed around Africa to reach Asia. Later, Christopher Columbus sailed west and reached the Americas. Spain became the first European colonial power in the Americas.

European Explorations

MAIN Idea Beginning in the 1400s, Europe entered a new era of intellectual and technological advancement known as the Renaissance.

HISTORY AND YOU Have you tried food from a different culture? Read to learn how Europeans developed a taste for spices and produce from Asia.

For centuries, the Roman Empire dominated Europe, imposing a unified and stable social and political order. By A.D. 500, however, the Roman political and economic system collapsed, disconnecting western Europe from the rest of the world. Without a central authority, the region experienced a decline in trade, and the political system became more fragmented. Most people lived on manors or in villages ruled by local lords, who kept the peace only in the lands they controlled. This period, lasting from roughly A.D. 500 to 1500, is known as the Middle Ages.

Expanding Horizons

In 1095 Pope Urban II called for Christians to free their religion's holy places in the Middle East from Muslim control. The resulting Crusades brought western Europeans into contact with the Arab civilization of the Middle East. The Europeans began trading with the Arabs, and in particular, began buying luxury goods that Arab traders obtained from East Asia: spices, sugar, melons, tapestries, silk, and other items. As demand for East Asian goods increased, Italian city-states such as Venice, Pisa, and Genoa grew wealthy moving goods between the Middle East and western Europe. By 1200, Italian and Arab merchants controlled most of the trade in the eastern Mediterranean and charged high prices for the goods that western Europeans wanted.

By the 1300s, Europeans had a strong economic motive to begin exploring the world for a route to Asia that bypassed the Italian city-states and the Arab kingdoms. Yet western Europe did not have the technology or wealth to begin exploring. All that started to change in the 1400s. The rise of towns and the merchant class provided kings

TECHNOLOGY & HISTORY

Age of Exploration New or newly discovered technologies helped launch the European age of exploration in the 1400s.

The triangular lateen sail caught wind that blew perpendicular to the ship, providing more maneuverability and the ability to sail against the wind.

▲ The astrolabe helped sailors stay on course by using the position of the sun and stars to determine time, direction, and latitude.

◄ The compass was invented by the Chinese. Made using a lodestone, it would always point to magnetic north.

Relocating the rudder to the back of the ship made it much easier to steer.

▲ The caravel was perfect for exploration. These small ships ranged from 70 to 90 feet (23 to 27 m). They were highly maneuverable and very fast. Their smaller size enabled them to sail along shallow coastlines and explore up rivers much farther than other ships.

Analyzing VISUALS

1. **Explaining** How did lateen sails improve navigation?
2. **Making Inferences** How would knowing the time help sailors navigate?

and queens with a new source of wealth they could tax. They used their armies to open up and protect trade **routes** and to enforce uniform trade laws and a common currency within their kingdoms.

The revenue from trade meant rulers in western Europe did not have to rely as much upon the nobility for support. Increasingly, they unified their kingdoms and created strong central governments. By the mid-1400s, four strong states—Portugal, Spain, England, and France—had emerged. Starting with Portugal in the early 1400s, all four began financing exploration in the hope of expanding their trade by finding a new route to Asia.

Scientific Advances

The political and economic changes that encouraged western Europeans to explore the world would not have mattered had they not had the technology necessary to launch their expeditions. In order to find a water route to Asia, western Europeans needed navigational instruments and ships capable of long-distance travel. Fortunately, at about the same time that the new, unified kingdoms were emerging in western Europe, an intellectual revolution known as the Renaissance began as well. It quickly led to new scientific and technological advances.

Lasting from about 1350 to 1600, the Renaissance marked an artistic flowering and a rebirth of interest in ancient Greece and Rome. European scholars rediscovered the works of ancient poets, philosophers, geographers, and mathematicians. In their quest for learning, they also read the teachings of Arab scholars.

The Renaissance started with a renewed interest in the past, but it quickly led to a renewed commitment to reason, which later helped trigger a scientific revolution.

By studying Arab texts, western Europeans **acquired** the knowledge of a key navigational instrument, the **astrolabe**—a device invented by the ancient Greeks and refined by Arab navigators. An astrolabe uses the position of the sun to determine direction, latitude, and local time. Europeans also acquired the compass from Arab traders. Invented in China, the compass reliably shows the direction of magnetic north.

Navigational tools were vital to exploration, but the most important requirement was a ship capable of long-distance travel. Late in the 1400s, European shipwrights began to outfit ships with triangular-shaped lateen sails perfected by Arab traders. These sails made it possible for ships to sail against the wind. Shipwrights also began using multiple masts with several smaller sails hoisted one above the other, which made the ships travel much faster. They also moved the rudder from the side to the stern, making ships easier to steer.

In the 1400s a Portuguese ship called the caravel incorporated all of these improvements. A **caravel** was a small vessel capable of carrying about 130 tons (118 t) of cargo. A caravel needed little water to sail, so it allowed explorers to venture up shallow inlets and to beach their ships to make repairs.

Portuguese Exploration

Sailing their caravels, Portuguese explorers became the first Europeans to search for a sea route to Asia. In 1419 Prince Henry of Portugal, known as **Henry the Navigator,** set up a center for astronomical and geographical studies at Sagres on Portugal's southwestern tip. He invited mapmakers, astronomers, and shipbuilders from throughout the Mediterranean world to come there to study and plan voyages of exploration.

In 1420 Portuguese explorers began mapping Africa's west coast. In 1488 a Portuguese ship commanded by Bartholomeu Dias reached the southern tip of Africa. A decade later, four ships commanded by Vasco da Gama sailed from Portugal, rounded Africa, and reached the southwest coast of India. The long-sought water route to eastern Asia had been found.

✔ Reading Check **Examining** What developments made it possible for Europeans to begin exploring the world?

African Cultures

MAIN Idea Three great empires arose in West Africa and prospered from the gold trade.

HISTORY AND YOU What are some of the valuable things countries trade today? Read how trade influenced the rise and fall of African states.

Three great empires arose in West Africa between the 400s and 1400s. All three gained wealth and power by controlling the trade in gold and salt. Between the A.D. third and fifth centuries, Arab merchants began using camels to transport salt, gold, ivory, ostrich feathers, and furs from regions south of the Sahara to North Africa. Around the northern and southern boundaries of the Sahara, large trading settlements developed. Ideas, as well as goods, traveled the African trade routes. The Muslim nomads who controlled the caravans spread Islam into West Africa as well.

The Empires of West Africa

In the A.D. 400s the empire of Ghana emerged. Located between the salt mines of the Sahara and the gold mines to the south, Ghana prospered by taxing trade. Ghana became a Muslim kingdom in the 1100s, but frequent wars with the Muslims of the Sahara took their toll. Equally damaging was a decline in food production. Intensive cultivation had left Ghana's land exhausted and its farmers unable to feed its people. At the same time, new gold mines opened to the east. Trade routes to these mines bypassed Ghana and, by the early 1200s, the empire collapsed.

East of Ghana the empire of Mali arose. Mali also built its wealth and power by controlling the salt and gold trade. By the mid-1300s, Mali had extended eastward along the Niger River past the trading center of Timbuktu and westward to the Atlantic Ocean. Although the rulers and merchants of Mali adopted Islam, many of the people clung to their traditional belief in "spirits of the land," who they thought ensured the growth of their crops.

Mali reached its peak in the 1300s under the leadership of Mansa Musa. By that time, the opening of new gold mines had shifted the trade routes farther east and helped make Timbuktu a great center of trade and Muslim scholarship.

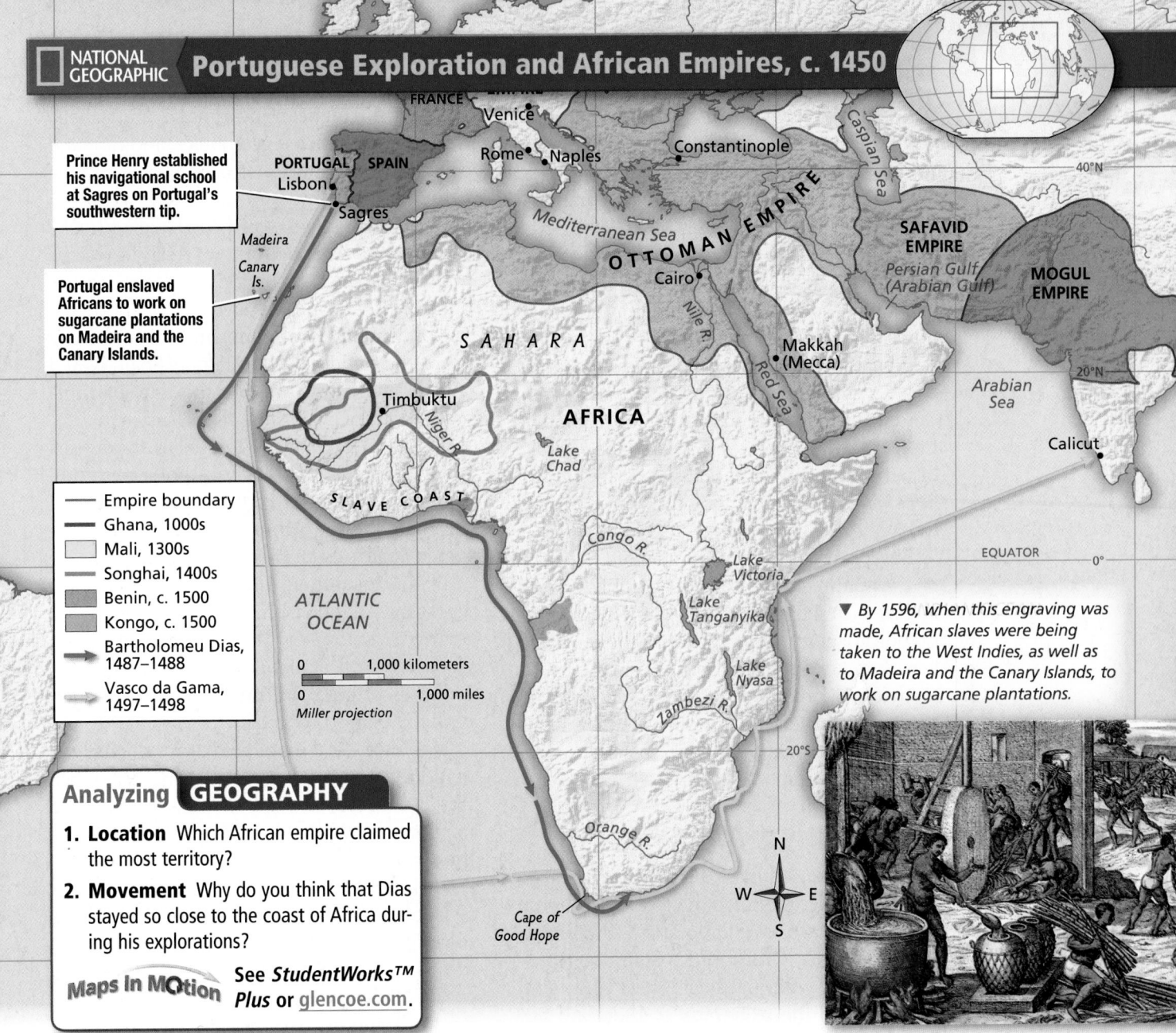

Prince Henry established his navigational school at Sagres on Portugal's southwestern tip.

Portugal enslaved Africans to work on sugarcane plantations on Madeira and the Canary Islands.

FRANCE
Venice
Rome • Naples
Constantinople
PORTUGAL SPAIN
Lisbon
Sagres
Madeira
Canary Is.
Mediterranean Sea
OTTOMAN EMPIRE
Cairo
Caspian Sea
40°N
SAFAVID EMPIRE
Persian Gulf (Arabian Gulf)
MOGUL EMPIRE
S A H A R A
Timbuktu
Niger R.
Nile R.
Makkah (Mecca)
Red Sea
20°N
Arabian Sea
Calicut
AFRICA
Lake Chad
SLAVE COAST
Congo R.
Lake Victoria
EQUATOR   0°
ATLANTIC OCEAN
Lake Tanganyika
Lake Nyasa
Zambezi R.
Orange R.
Cape of Good Hope
20°S

Empire boundary
Ghana, 1000s
Mali, 1300s
Songhai, 1400s
Benin, c. 1500
Kongo, c. 1500
Bartholomeu Dias, 1487–1488
Vasco da Gama, 1497–1498

0   1,000 kilometers
0   1,000 miles
Miller projection

▼ By 1596, when this engraving was made, African slaves were being taken to the West Indies, as well as to Madeira and the Canary Islands, to work on sugarcane plantations.

N
W   E
S

Analyzing GEOGRAPHY

1. **Location** Which African empire claimed the most territory?
2. **Movement** Why do you think that Dias stayed so close to the coast of Africa during his explorations?

Maps In M**O**tion See *StudentWorks™ Plus* or glencoe.com.

Along the Niger River, the empire of Songhai emerged. When Mali began to decline, the ruler of Songhai, Sonni Ali, seized Timbuktu in 1468. He then pushed north into the Sahara and south along the Niger River. According to legend, Sonni Ali's army never lost a battle. Songhai remained a powerful empire until 1591, when Moroccan troops shattered its army.

Slavery and Sugar

As in other parts of the world, slavery existed in African society. Most of the people enslaved in African societies had been captured in war. Most African societies would either ransom captives back to their people or absorb them into their own society. West African slavery began to change with the arrival of Arab traders, who exchanged horses, cotton, and other goods for enslaved people.

Sugar growers from Spain and Portugal also sought enslaved Africans. In the 1400s Spain and Portugal established sugarcane plantations on the Canary and Madeira Islands. The climate and soil there were favorable for growing sugarcane, a crop that requires much manual **labor.** Sugarcane must be chopped with heavy knives. Sugar growers brought in enslaved Africans to do the work.

✔ Reading Check **Analyzing** Why did Europeans begin to acquire enslaved Africans?

Exploring America

MAIN Idea Spain led in the early European exploration and colonization of the Americas.

HISTORY AND YOU Do you know how your community got its name? Read to find out how the names for Florida and the Pacific Ocean came about.

By the 1400s, most educated Europeans knew that the world was round. On European maps of the time, only the Mediterranean, Europe, the Middle East, and Africa's northern coast were shown any detail. At that time, Europeans rediscovered the works of Claudius Ptolemy, written in the A.D. 100s. His *Geography* became very influential. His basic system of lines of latitude and longitude is still used today.

European mariners also consulted the work of a twelfth-century Arab geographer named al-Idrisi. In 1154 al-Idrisi published a geographical survey of as much of the world as was then known to Europeans and Arabs. By studying the maps of Ptolemy and al-Idrisi, Western mariners finally obtained a reliable idea of the geography of the eastern African coast and the Indian Ocean.

Spain Claims America

Despite its usefulness, Ptolemy's *Geography* seriously underestimated the size of the earth. Basing his own calculations on Ptolemy's, Italian mariner Christopher Columbus predicted with wild optimism that "the end of Spain and the beginning of India are not far apart."

Columbus needed financial backing to make a voyage across the Atlantic to Asia. For six years he tried to persuade various European rulers to fund his expedition. Finally, in 1492, Spain's King Ferdinand and Queen Isabella agreed to finance his venture.

Columbus and his three ships—the *Niña,* the *Pinta,* and the *Santa Maria*—left Spain in August 1492. He sailed westward across the uncharted Atlantic until he reached the Bahamas in October. He probably landed on present-day San Salvador Island. There, Columbus encountered the Taino people. He called them "Indians" because he thought he had reached the fabled Indies. He then headed farther into the Caribbean, searching for gold. He found the islands of Cuba and Hispaniola.

In March 1493 Columbus made a triumphant return to Spain with gold, parrots, spices, and Native Americans. Ferdinand and Isabella were pleased with Columbus's findings and prepared to finance further expeditions. However, they were now involved in a competition with Portugal, which had claimed control over the Atlantic route to Asia. To resolve the rivalry, the two nations appealed to the pope. In 1493 Pope Alexander VI established a line of demarcation, an imaginary line running down the middle of the Atlantic. Spain would control everything west of the line; Portugal would control everything to the east.

In 1494, in the Treaty of Tordesillas, the demarcation line was approved by both countries. The treaty confirmed Portugal's right to control the route around Africa to India. It also confirmed Spain's claim to most of the Americas.

In the meantime, Columbus headed back across the Atlantic with 17 ships and over 1,200 Spanish colonists. Later, they accused Columbus of misleading them with false promises of gold, and many of them headed back to Spain to complain.

Hoping to find more gold and save his reputation, Columbus began exploring Hispaniola. He discovered enough loose gold to make mining worthwhile. He then decided to enslave the local Taino people and force them to mine gold and plant crops.

In 1496 Columbus returned to Spain. In the meantime, his brother Bartholomew founded a town named Santo Domingo on the south coast of Hispaniola, closer to the gold mines. Santo Domingo became the first capital of Spain's empire in America. Columbus made two more trips to America, mapping part of the coastline of South America and Central America. He died without obtaining the riches he had hoped to find.

Naming America In 1499 an Italian named **Amerigo Vespucci,** sailing under the Spanish flag, repeated Columbus's attempt to sail west to Asia. Exploring the coast of South America, Vespucci, like Columbus, assumed he had reached outermost Asia. In 1501 he made another voyage, this time for Portugal. After sailing along the coast of South America, he realized that this landmass could not be part of Asia. In 1507 a German mapmaker proposed that the new continent be named *America* for "Amerigo, the discoverer."

Turning Point

► Although no images of Christopher Columbus exist from his lifetime, this painting from about 1525 is considered to be the closest likeness.

Columbus Arrives in America

Columbus's first voyage to the Americas was a major turning point in world history. For Europeans, it opened up new areas of exploration and discovery, and provided vast wealth through trade. The event was devastating, however, for native peoples of the Americas whose cultures were changed or destroyed by war, disease, and enslavement.

ANALYZING HISTORY Describe one positive and one negative effect of Columbus's voyage to the Americas.

▲ The Landing of Columbus *was painted by American artist Albert Bierstadt in 1892, the year of the 400th anniversary of Columbus's arrival in North America. Note that the artist portrayed the indigenous people as shrouded in darkness and shadow, emerging to kneel worshipfully before the Europeans, who bring with them the "light" of civilization. Unfortunately, the arrival of Europeans did more to destroy the indigenous cultures than to enlighten them.*

Later Spanish Expeditions In 1513 the Spanish governor of Puerto Rico, Juan Ponce de León, sailed north. Legend has it that he was searching for a fountain that could magically restore youth. He never found the fabled fountain, but he did discover a land full of blooming wildflowers and fragrant plants. He claimed the area for Spain and named it *Florida,* which means "land of flowers."

Spanish explorers continued to search for a passage to China and India. In 1510 Vasco de Balboa, a planter from Hispaniola, founded a colony on the Isthmus of Panama. After hearing tales of a "south sea" that led to an empire of gold, he hacked his way across steamy, disease-ridden jungles and swamps until he reached the opposite coast. There, in 1513,

Balboa became the first European to reach the Pacific coast of America.

In 1520 Ferdinand Magellan, a Portuguese mariner working for Spain, discovered the strait later named for him at the southern tip of South America. After navigating its stormy narrows, he sailed into the ocean Balboa had seen. Its waters seemed so calm that Magellan named it *Mare Pacificum,* Latin for "peaceful sea"—the Pacific Ocean. Although Magellan was killed in the Philippine Islands, his crew continued west, arriving in Spain in 1522. They became the first known people to **circumnavigate,** or sail around, the globe.

✔ Reading Check **Describing** What were the results of Columbus's voyages across the Atlantic?

New Spain

MAIN Idea After defeating the Aztec Empire, the Spanish established the colony of New Spain.

HISTORY AND YOU Have you seen unusual animals at the zoo? Read how one Spanish explorer went looking for gold but found only "shaggy cows."

In 1519 a Spaniard named **Hernán Cortés** sailed from Cuba to explore the Yucatán Peninsula with 11 ships, 550 men, and 16 horses. Soon after arriving, thousands of warriors attacked Cortés's party. Although outnumbered, the Spanish had superior weapons. Their swords, crossbows, guns, and cannons quickly killed more than 200 warriors. As a peace offering, the Native Americans gave Cortés 20 women, including Malinche, who helped translate for Cortés. He had her baptized and called her Doña Marina.

From local rulers, Cortés learned that the Aztec had conquered many people and were at war with others, including the powerful Tlaxcalan. Cortés wanted the Tlaxcalan to join him against the Aztec. His army helped him gain their support. The local people had never seen horses before. Their foaming muzzles and glistening armor astonished them. Equally amazing were the "shooting sparks" of the Spanish cannons. Impressed, the Tlaxcalan agreed to ally with Cortés against the Aztec.

Meanwhile, the Aztec emperor Montezuma was worried. He believed in a prophecy that Quetzalcóatl—a fair-skinned, bearded deity—would someday return to conquer the Aztec. Montezuma did not know if Cortés was Quetzalcóatl, but he sent envoys promising a yearly payment to the Spanish king if Cortés halted his advance. Cortés refused to stop.

With the Spanish and Tlaxcalan heading toward him, Montezuma tried to ambush them at the city of Cholula. Warned in advance, the Spanish struck first, killing over 6,000 Cholulans. Believing Cortés was unstoppable, Montezuma allowed the Spanish troops to enter Tenochtitlán peacefully.

Defeat of the Aztec

Sitting on an island in the center of a lake, the city of Tenochtitlán impressed the Spanish. Larger than most European cities, Tenochtitlán had more than 200,000 residents and an elaborate system of canals. In the central plaza, a large double pyramid and a huge rack displayed thousands of human skulls.

Surrounded by thousands of Aztec, Cortés decided to take Montezuma hostage. Montezuma did not resist. Following orders from Cortés, he stopped all human sacrifices and had statues of the Aztec gods replaced with Christian crosses and images of the Virgin Mary. Aztec priests were furious and organized a rebellion in early 1520. The battle raged for days before the Spanish retreated to Tlaxcala. Over 450 Spaniards and more than 4,000 Aztec had died, including Montezuma.

Meanwhile, smallpox erupted in the region, devastating the defenders of Tenochtitlán. As one Aztec recounted:

PRIMARY SOURCE

"While the Spaniards were in Tlaxcala, a great plague broke out here in Tenochtitlán. . . . Sores erupted on our faces, our breasts, our bellies; we were covered with agonizing sores from head to foot. The illness was so dreadful that no one could walk or move."

—from *The Broken Spears: The Aztec Account of the Conquest of Mexico*

In 1521 Cortés returned with reinforcements and destroyed Tenochtitlán. On its ruins, the Spanish built Mexico City, which became the capital of the colony of New Spain. Cortés then sent several expeditions to conquer the rest of Central America. The men who led these expeditions became known as **conquistadors,** or "conquerors."

New Explorations In 1526 Spanish explorer **Francisco Pizarro** reached Peru. Six years later he returned with a small band of infantry. With superior weapons, Pizarro's force plundered the wealthy Inca Empire.

The Spanish had heard tales of the Seven Golden Cities of Cíbola, rumored to exist north of New Spain. In 1540, hoping to find Cíbola, Francisco Vásquez de Coronado led an expedition northward and explored the region between the Colorado River and the Great Plains. Instead of cities of gold, however, Coronado found only windswept plains and "shaggy cows," as he described the buffalo.

ATLANTIC OCEAN

St. Augustine

Gulf of Mexico

TROPIC OF CANCER

Havana

20°N

Mexico

PACIFIC OCEAN

Santo Domingo

Caribbean Sea

Panama

EQUATOR

0°

Cuzco

Spanish territories, c. A.D. 1600

Cortés, 1519–1524

Pizarro, 1526–1527

Narváez, 1528

Cabeza de Vaca, 1535–1536

de Soto, 1539–1542

Coronado, 1539–1543

Cabrilho, 1542

120°W   100°W   80°W   60°W   40°W

▲ This image depicts the battle at Tenochtitlán between the Aztec and the Spanish in 1519.

◀ Mission San Carlos Borromeo de Carmelo in California is one of many missions the Spanish built throughout their American colonies.

0   1,000 kilometers
0   1,000 miles
Miller projection

N W E S

Analyzing GEOGRAPHY

1. **Movement** By 1600, which explorer had ventured farthest north in North America?

2. **Human-Environment Interaction** In what part of South America was most of the territory held by Spain? Why do you think that was?

Meanwhile, Hernando de Soto led an expedition into the region north of Florida, exploring parts of what are today North Carolina, Tennessee, Alabama, Arkansas, and Texas. As they crisscrossed the region, the Spanish killed many local people and raided their villages for supplies. De Soto became ill and died; soon after, his men abandoned the mission and headed home.

Settling the Southwest Because no gold or other wealth was found north of New Spain, Spanish settlement of the region was slow. It was not until 1598 that settlers, led by Juan de Oñate, pushed north of the Rio Grande. When they finally reached the Rio Grande, the survivors organized a feast to give thanks to God.

This "Spanish Thanksgiving" is still celebrated each April in El Paso, Texas.

The Spanish gave the name New Mexico to the territory north of New Spain. Throughout the region, they built forts called presidios to protect settlers and serve as trading posts. Despite these efforts, few Spaniards settled in the harsh region. Instead, the Catholic Church began colonizing the Southwest.

In the 1600s and 1700s, Spanish priests built missions and spread the Christian faith among the Navajo and Pueblo peoples of the Southwest. Beginning in 1769, missionaries, led by Franciscan priest Junípero Serra, took control of California by establishing a chain of missions from San Diego to just north of San Francisco.

People IN HISTORY

Bartolomé de Las Casas
1474–1566

In the years following the Spanish conquest, many people began to protest against the abuses of the *encomienda* system. Among them was Bartolomé de Las Casas, Bishop of Chiapas. In 1502 Las Casas traveled to Hispaniola and was horrified by what he saw. The Spanish tortured, burned, and cut off the hands and noses of Native Americans to force them to obey.

Las Casas maintained that the Church and the king had a duty to protect Native Americans. In this view, he had the support of the pope who declared the Native Americans should not be enslaved. Las Casas wrote several books that were widely read in Europe, describing the treatment of the Native Americans. In response, the Spanish government stopped granting *encomiendas* and banned Native American slavery. Slowly, as *encomiendos* died without heirs, the *encomienda* system came to an end. However, Las Casas died outraged. "Surely," he wrote in his will, "God will wreak his fury and anger against Spain some day for the unjust wars waged against American Indians."

Why did the Spanish government think that ending the encomienda system was a way to stop the abuses of Native Americans?

Peninsulares, people of Spanish birth, leaders of the government and church, and landowners

Criollos, born in the colonies to Spanish parents, wealthy merchants, government officials, and landowners

Mestizos, people of Spanish and Native American parentage, artisans, farmworkers

Native Americans, Africans, people of mixed ancestry, poor, servants, often enslaved, physical labor on farms and in mines

---

The priests and missionaries in California forced the mostly nomadic Native Americans to live in villages near the missions. In New Mexico, the priests and missionaries adapted their efforts to fit into the lifestyle of the Pueblo peoples. They built churches near where the Pueblo people lived and farmed.

The Spanish priests tried to end traditional Pueblo religious practices that conflicted with Catholic beliefs. Some priests beat and whipped Native Americans who defied them. In response, a Pueblo religious leader named Popé organized an uprising in 1680. Some 17,000 warriors destroyed most of the missions in New Mexico. It took the Spanish more than a decade to regain control of the region.

Spanish American Society

Cortés rewarded his men by giving them control of some towns in the Aztec Empire. This became the **encomienda** system. Each Spaniard deserving a reward was made an *encomendero,* or commissioner, and was given control over a group of villages. Villagers paid their *encomendero* a share of the harvest and also worked part-time for him for free. The *encomendero* was supposed to protect them and convert them to Christianity. Sadly, many *encomenderos* abused their power and worked the Native Americans to death.

New Spain had a highly structured society based on birth, income, and education. At the top were *peninsulares,* those who were born in Spain. They held the top government and church positions. Next were the *criollos*—those born in the colonies to Spanish parents. Many *criollos* were wealthy, but they held slightly lesser positions. Next came the *mestizos,* people of Spanish and Native American parentage. Their social status could vary, but most were poor and relegated to the lowest class, along with people of other mixed ancestry, Native Americans, and Africans. These people provided most of the labor for New Spain's farms, mines, and ranches.

In the 1540s the Spanish discovered silver ore in northern Mexico and set up mining camps using Native American labor. Work in the dark, damp mineshafts was very difficult. Explosions and cave-ins killed many miners. Others died from exhaustion. To feed the miners, the Spanish established large cattle ranches called haciendas.

Reading Check **Describing** Why did the Spanish set up mines and cattle ranches in Mexico?

New France

MAIN Idea France claimed a vast territory in North America, but its colony had a small French population.

HISTORY AND YOU Did you know that one-third of Canadians speak French? Read to learn about French settlements in North America.

In 1524 King Francis I of France sent Giovanni da Verrazano to find the Northwest Passage—the hoped-for northern route through North America to the Pacific. Verrazano explored the Atlantic coast from North Carolina to Newfoundland, but found no sign of a passage. Ten years later, Jacques Cartier made three trips to North America, exploring and mapping the St. Lawrence River.

In 1602 King Henry IV of France authorized a group of French merchants to establish a colony. The merchants hired **Samuel de Champlain** to help them. In 1608 Champlain founded Quebec, which became the capital of the colony of New France.

The company that founded New France wanted to make money from the fur trade, so they did not need settlers to clear the land and build farms. As a result, the colony grew slowly. Most of the fur traders preferred to make their homes among the Native Americans with whom they traded. Jesuit missionaries, known as "black robes," likewise lived among the local people. In 1663 King Louis XIV made New France a royal colony and sent 4,000 new settlers. By the 1670s, New France had nearly 7,000 people, and by 1760, more than 60,000.

As their colony grew, the French continued to explore North America. In 1673 a fur trader named Louis Joliet and a Jesuit priest named Jacques Marquette began searching for a waterway the Algonquian people called the "big river." The two men finally found it—the Mississippi. In 1682 René-Robert Cavelier de La Salle followed the Mississippi all the way to the Gulf of Mexico, becoming the first European to do so. He claimed the region for France and named the territory Louisiana in honor of Louis XIV.

The geography of the lower Mississippi hindered settlement. The oppressive heat caused food to spoil quickly and mosquito-filled swamps made the climate unhealthy. The first permanent French settlement in the region was Biloxi, founded in 1699. Mobile, New Orleans, and several forts followed. The French in Louisiana realized that the crops that could be grown there, such as sugar, rice, and indigo, required abundant labor. As a result, they began importing enslaved Africans to work on their plantations.

The Spanish had always been concerned about the French in North America. Indeed, they founded St. Augustine, Florida, in 1565 to counter French settlement attempts in what became the Carolinas. St. Augustine prospered and became the first permanent town established by Europeans in what is today the United States. The arrival of the French at the mouth of the Mississippi River convinced the Spanish in 1690 to build their first mission in East Texas, San Francisco de los Tejas. Spanish settlers arrived in 1716 to secure Spain's claim and block French expansion in the area.

Reading Check **Explaining** Why do you think the French established forts and settlements in Louisiana?

Section 2 REVIEW

Vocabulary

1. **Explain** the significance of: astrolabe, caravel, Henry the Navigator, Amerigo Vespucci, circumnavigate, Hernán Cortés, conquistador, Francisco Pizarro, *encomienda*, Samuel de Champlain.

Main Ideas

2. **Examining** What led Europeans to begin exploring in the 1400s?

3. **Identifying** On what did African kingdoms base their wealth and power?

4. **Explaining** How did the Americas receive that name?

5. **Organizing** Use a graphic organizer similar to the one below to list characteristics of Spanish colonies in the Americas.

Spanish Colonies

6. **Explaining** Why was New France so sparsely populated?

Critical Thinking

7. **Big Ideas** How did scientific advancements affect geographic knowledge?

8. **Analyzing Visuals** Study the photograph of the mission on page 21. How did the Catholic Church contribute to the Spanish settlement in North America?

Writing About History

9. **Descriptive Writing** Take on the role of a sailor on Columbus's first voyage to the Americas. Write a journal entry about the Caribbean islands you explore.

History ONLINE

Study Central™ To review this section, go to glencoe.com and click on Study Central.

Founding the Thirteen Colonies

Guide to Reading

Big Ideas
Geography and History The headright system provided English settlers with a new way to acquire more land.

Content Vocabulary
• joint-stock company *(p. 25)*
• privateer *(p. 26)*
• headright *(p. 27)*
• proprietary colony *(p. 27)*
• heretic *(p. 29)*

Academic Vocabulary
• migration *(p. 24)*
• grant *(p. 26)*

People and Events to Identify
• Jamestown *(p. 26)*
• Powhatan Confederacy *(p. 26)*
• John Winthrop *(p. 29)*
• Roger Williams *(p. 30)*
• Anne Hutchinson *(p. 30)*
• Henry Hudson *(p. 31)*

Reading Strategy
Organizing Complete a graphic organizer similar to the one below by listing the problems faced by the Jamestown colonists.

Jamestown's Troubles

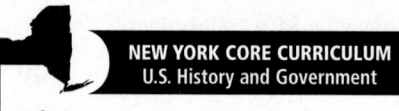

NEW YORK CORE CURRICULUM
U.S. History and Government

Unit 2:
A.2.c Varieties of immigrant motivation, ethnicities, and experiences
A.3.a Colonial charters and self-government: Mayflower Compact, town meetings, House of Burgesses, local government, property rights, enforceable contracts, Albany Plan of Union

England was late to establish colonies in the Americas. Joint-stock companies established the first English colonies with the intention of making profits. Many settlers, however, went to the Americas to escape religious persecution.

England's First Colonies

MAIN Idea While Spain was establishing an overseas empire in the 1500s, England was distracted by problems at home.

HISTORY AND YOU Religion and politics were inseparable in the 1500s and led to many conflicts. Can you think of some religious-based conflicts in the world today? Read on to learn how the Reformation divided Europe.

The first English expedition to arrive in North America was led by Italian navigator John Cabot. In 1497 Cabot sailed to present-day Nova Scotia, hoping to discover a sea route through North America to China. For the next 80 years, the English made no effort to settle in America. Cabot had found no riches that would spur **migration.** In the late 1500s, religious, economic, and political changes encouraged the founding of the first English colonies in North America.

The Protestant Reformation

At the time Cabot sailed to America, most of western Europe was Roman Catholic. This unity began to break apart in 1517, when a German monk named Martin Luther published an attack on the Church, accusing it of corruption. Luther's call for reform launched the Protestant Reformation. The Catholic Church excommunicated, or expelled, Luther, but his ideas continued to spread.

In England the rebellion against Catholicism began in 1527, when Henry VIII asked the pope to annul his marriage to Catherine of Aragon. The pope refused. Infuriated, Henry broke with the Church and declared himself the head of England's church. He then arranged his own divorce. The new church, the Anglican Church, was Protestant, but its organization and rituals retained many Catholic elements.

Some English people supported the new church, but others wanted to go further. Puritans wanted to "purify" the Anglican Church of any remaining Catholic elements. They also disapproved of the monarch having the power to appoint bishops to run the church. In their view, each congregation should elect its own leaders.

The Puritan cause suffered a serious setback in 1603, when James I became king. Although King James was Protestant, he refused to tolerate any changes in the structure of the Anglican Church. James's

The Causes of English Settlement in America

Three major factors led the English to found colonies in the Americas.

RELIGIOUS PERSECUTION

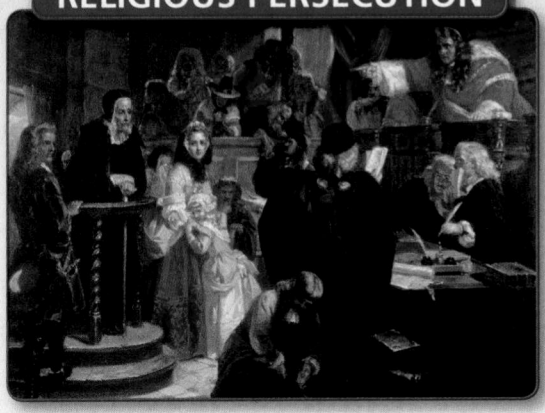

◀ *English Puritans and other non-Anglicans faced prejudice and legal harassment. Many fled to North America where they could worship as they wished.*

ECONOMIC CHANGES

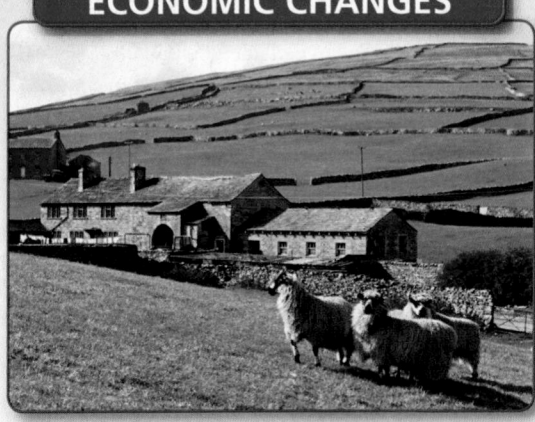

▲ *The enclosure movement displaced thousands of tenant farmers. Many English leaders thought that having colonies would help absorb England's unemployed people.*

RIVALRY WITH SPAIN

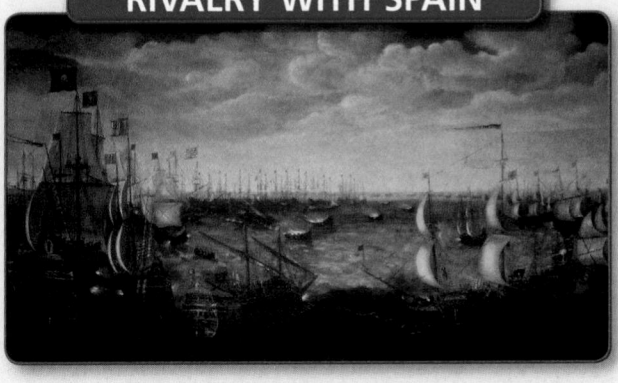

◀ *The Protestant English wanted to share the riches of the Americas that Catholic Spain was monopolizing.*

Analyzing VISUALS

1. **Determining Cause and Effect** How did England's rivalry with Spain drive the nation to establish new colonies in North America?
2. **Explaining** Why did religious groups found colonies?

refusal to reform the Anglican Church eventually caused many Puritans to leave England—some for America.

Economic Changes in England

Economic changes in England also created a motive to found colonies in America. Traditionally, English nobles who owned large estates rented their land to tenant farmers. In the 1500s, however, a large market for wool cloth developed. Landowners discovered they could make more money by evicting their tenants, enclosing the land, and raising sheep. This left thousands of tenant farmers homeless and destitute. At the same time, England's population was rising rapidly in the 1500s. Many English leaders concluded that colonies were necessary to provide land and work to the kingdom's rising number of unemployed.

The wool market had another impact on American settlement. To market their woolen goods, some merchants began organizing **joint-stock companies**. By joining together and issuing stock, merchants were able to raise large amounts of money to fund major projects. Joint-stock companies could also afford the cost of setting up colonies in other parts of the world.

England Returns to America

Hoping to share in the lucrative trade with Asia, English merchants also began searching for a water route through North America to Asia. England's new interest in the Americas contributed to its growing rivalry with Spain. England was the leading Protestant power, while Spain remained strongly Catholic.

People IN HISTORY

Captain John Smith
1580–1631

John Smith had a lifetime of adventures before he set foot in Virginia. Smith began his career as a soldier, fighting for the Dutch in their war against Spain. He later fought with the Austrians against the Turks in eastern Europe. Smith was a prolific writer, and many details about his life come from his own accounts.

After returning to England, Smith joined the expedition that settled Jamestown. He quickly began exploring the region and trading with the local Native Americans. It was on one such expedition that Smith later claimed he was taken prisoner by Chief Powhatan and that Pocahontas saved him from being killed. After Smith became president of Jamestown in 1608, he instituted rigid discipline. He required all members of the colony to work, declaring "he that does not worke shall not eate." Smith's rules led to fewer deaths. In 1609 he returned to England, where he continued to promote colonization of Virginia.

How did Smith contribute to English efforts to colonize America?

▲ *Captain John Smith helped save early Jamestown by trading with the local Native Americans.*

When the Spanish tried to suppress Protestantism in the Netherlands, the Dutch rebelled. To help the Dutch, Queen Elizabeth I allowed English **privateers** to attack Spanish ships. Privateers are privately owned ships licensed by the government to attack ships of other countries.

To attack Spanish ships in the Caribbean, Elizabeth's advisers recommended that England establish outposts in the Americas. Elizabeth agreed, but the early attempts at colonization were not promising.

In 1578 and 1583 Sir Humphrey Gilbert tried to create a colony but failed. After Gilbert was lost at sea, his half-brother, Walter Raleigh, sent two ships to scout the American coastline. Along the outer banks of what is now North Carolina, the ships found an island the Native Americans called Roanoke. Impressed, Queen Elizabeth knighted Raleigh, who had named the colony Virginia—in honor of Elizabeth, "the Virgin Queen."

Raleigh sent settlers to Roanoke Island twice, once in 1585 and again in 1587. The first group returned to England after a difficult winter. The fate of the second group is unknown. When English ships arrived in 1590, the colonists had vanished.

The Chesapeake Colonies

In 1606 King James I **granted** a charter to a new company—the Virginia Company—giving its stockholders permission to start colonies in Virginia. The company sent three small ships and 144 men to Virginia in late 1606. After a difficult trip, the ships sailed into Chesapeake Bay in the spring of 1607. The 104 men who survived the trip founded a settlement on the James River, which they named **Jamestown** in honor of their king.

Early Troubles Most of Jamestown's colonists were townspeople who knew little about living in the woods. They did not know how to fish or hunt for food, nor could they raise livestock or cultivate crops. Furthermore, the "gentlemen" among them refused to do manual labor. Lawlessness, sickness, and food shortages were the result. In late 1607, with winter approaching and the colony short of food, Captain John Smith began bartering goods for food with the **Powhatan Confederacy.** This trade helped the colony survive the next two winters.

To entice settlers, the company offered free land to anyone who worked for the colony for seven years. The offer produced results, and 400 new settlers arrived in Jamestown in 1609. The arrival of so many settlers created a crisis. There was not enough food, nor could enough be grown before winter. As winter neared, settlers began raiding the food stores of local Native Americans. In response, Powhatan cut off trade with the colonists, and his warriors began attacking settlers.

The winter of 1609–1610 became known as the "starving time." In their hunger, colonists resorted to extreme measures. George Percy, an early settler, described their desperation:

PRIMARY SOURCE

"Having fed upon horses and other beasts as long as they lasted, we were glad to make shift with vermin, as dogs, cats, rats, and mice. . . . Nothing was spared to maintain life and to do those things which seem incredible, as to dig up corpses out of graves and to eat them."

—from *The Jamestown Adventure*

By spring, only 60 settlers were still alive. The survivors abandoned Jamestown and headed downriver. On the way, they met three English ships bringing supplies, 150 more settlers, and the new governor, Lord De La Warr, who convinced the settlers to stay. His deputy, Thomas Dale, then drafted a harsh law code. Settlers were organized into work gangs and had to work at least six hours per day. The death penalty was imposed for many crimes, including rape, swearing, desertion, theft, lying, and expressing disrespect for the Bible.

Tobacco Saves the Colony

The colony still had to find a way to make a profit. The solution was a cash crop: tobacco. Smoking tobacco had become popular in Europe, although King James had condemned tobacco as a "vile weed [of] black stinking fumes [that are] baleful to the nose, harmful to the brain, and dangerous to the lungs."

The Jamestown settlers had tried growing tobacco, but the local variety was too bitter. A colonist named John Rolfe then began to experiment with seeds from Trinidad. He also developed a new method for curing tobacco, and in 1614 sent his first shipment to England. Rolfe's tobacco sold for a good price, and the settlers began planting large quantities of it.

In 1618 the Virginia Company granted the colonists the right to elect a lawmaking body.

Virginia's first general assembly met in the Jamestown church on July 30, 1619. The new government included a governor, six councilors, and 20 representatives—two from each of the colony's 10 towns. The representatives were called burgesses, and the assembly was called the House of Burgesses.

The Virginia Company also introduced the system of **headrights.** Settlers who paid their own passage to Virginia received 50 acres of land. Settlers also received 50 acres of land for each family member over 15 years of age and each servant they transported to Virginia.

In 1619 the first Africans were brought to Virginia. A Dutch slave ship stopped to trade for supplies, and the Jamestown settlers purchased 20 African men as "Christian servants," not slaves. Within a few years, however, enslaved Africans were being brought to the colony.

By 1622, more than 4,500 settlers had arrived in Virginia. This alarmed the Native Americans, and they attacked Jamestown in March 1622. They burned homes, destroyed food supplies, and killed nearly 350 settlers. The settlers eventually put an end to the uprising, but the colony was devastated. After blaming the Virginia Company, an English court revoked its charter. Virginia became a royal colony run by a governor who was appointed by the king.

Maryland Is Founded

In England, Catholics were persecuted because they did not accept the monarch as head of the Church. They were viewed as potential traitors who might help Catholic countries overthrow the English monarchy. Catholics were forbidden to practice law or teach school. They were also fined for not attending Anglican services.

The persecution of his fellow Catholics convinced George Calvert, who held the title Lord Baltimore, to found a colony where Catholics could practice their religion freely. In 1632 King Charles granted him a large area of land northeast of Virginia. Baltimore named the new colony Maryland.

Lord Baltimore owned Maryland, making it a **proprietary colony.** The proprietor, or owner, had almost unlimited authority over the colony. He could appoint a government, establish courts, coin money, impose taxes, grant lands, create towns, and raise an army. The only restriction on a proprietor was that he could do nothing that was contrary to established English law.

For the complete text of The Mayflower Compact, see page R39 in **Documents in American History.**

Lord Baltimore died shortly before settlers arrived in his colony. In 1634, 20 gentlemen, mostly Catholic, and 200 servants and artisans, mostly Protestant, arrived from England. Despite Baltimore's hope that Maryland would become a Catholic refuge, most of its settlers were Protestant, although the government officials and most owners of large estates were Catholic. As in England, religious differences led to social conflict. To reduce friction between the two groups, the colonial assembly passed the Toleration Act in 1649. This act mandated religious toleration for all Christians but made denying the divinity of Jesus a crime punishable by death.

✔ **Reading Check** **Analyzing** Why was Maryland founded?

Pilgrims and Puritans

MAIN Idea Both the Pilgrims and the Puritans founded colonies to escape religious persecution.

HISTORY AND YOU Have you ever thought that an authority figure was too strict? Read on to learn what happened to those who challenged Puritan authorities.

In England, a group of Puritans, called Separatists, concluded that the Anglican Church was too corrupt to be reformed. They formed their own congregations, and in 1608, one group fled to the Netherlands to escape persecution. These Separatists, later known as Pilgrims, later sailed to America in 1620.

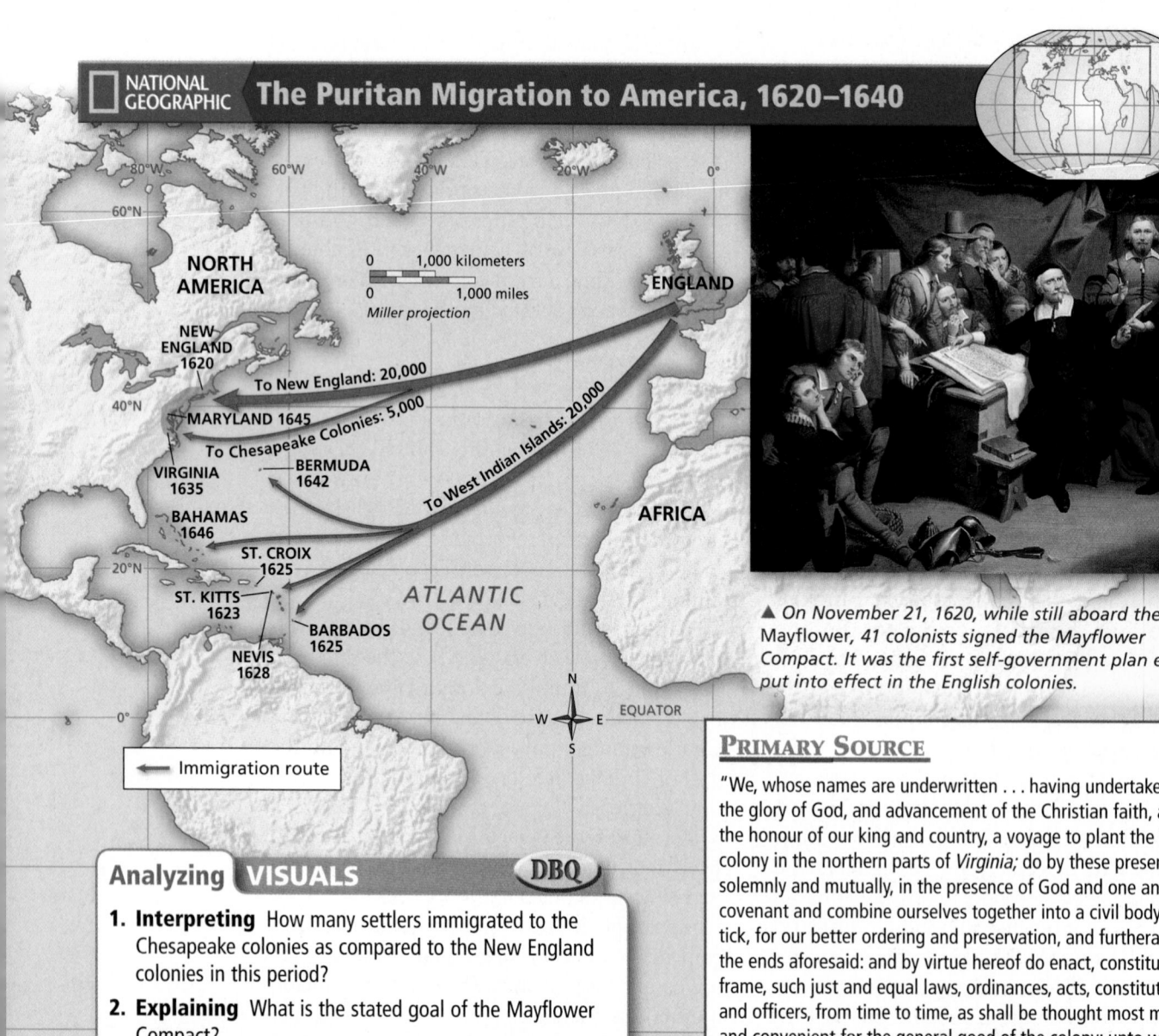

NATIONAL GEOGRAPHIC **The Puritan Migration to America, 1620–1640**

NORTH AMERICA

0   1,000 kilometers
0   1,000 miles
Miller projection

ENGLAND

NEW ENGLAND 1620

To New England: 20,000

MARYLAND 1645

To Chesapeake Colonies: 5,000

VIRGINIA 1635

BERMUDA 1642

To West Indian Islands: 20,000

BAHAMAS 1646

ST. CROIX 1625

AFRICA

ST. KITTS 1623

ATLANTIC OCEAN

BARBADOS 1625

NEVIS 1628

EQUATOR

← Immigration route

▲ On November 21, 1620, while still aboard the Mayflower, 41 colonists signed the Mayflower Compact. It was the first self-government plan ever put into effect in the English colonies.

Analyzing VISUALS **DBQ**

1. **Interpreting** How many settlers immigrated to the Chesapeake colonies as compared to the New England colonies in this period?

2. **Explaining** What is the stated goal of the Mayflower Compact?

PRIMARY SOURCE

"We, whose names are underwritten . . . having undertaken for the glory of God, and advancement of the Christian faith, and the honour of our king and country, a voyage to plant the first colony in the northern parts of *Virginia;* do by these presents, solemnly and mutually, in the presence of God and one another, covenant and combine ourselves together into a civil body politick, for our better ordering and preservation, and furtherance of the ends aforesaid: and by virtue hereof do enact, constitute, and frame, such just and equal laws, ordinances, acts, constitutions, and officers, from time to time, as shall be thought most meet and convenient for the general good of the colony; unto which we promise all due submission and obedience."

Source: *The Mayflower Compact*

Plymouth Colony

Before crossing the Atlantic, the Pilgrims returned to England, where they joined other emigrants aboard a ship called the *Mayflower.* On September 16, 1620, 102 passengers set sail for Virginia. During the trip, most of the food ran out, many passengers became ill, and one died. In November they sighted land on Cape Cod. Although they had planned to settle farther south, they were not completely lost. In 1614 the Virginia Company had hired Captain John Smith to explore the region. The Pilgrims had a copy of John Smith's "Map of New England," and they decided to settle in the area labeled "Plymouth."

According to William Bradford, one of the colony's leaders, the Pilgrims went to work building homes as soon as they arrived at Plymouth. After constructing a "common house," the settlers built modest homes of frame construction and thatched roofs. Soon, however, a plague swept through the colony, sparing only 50 settlers.

Even the surviving Pilgrims might have perished were it not for the help of Squanto, a Wampanoag man. Bradford wrote that Squanto "directed them how to set their corn, where to take fish and [how] to procure other commodities." The following autumn, the Pilgrims joined with the Wampanoag in a three-day festival to celebrate the harvest and give thanks to God for their good fortune. This celebration later became the basis for the Thanksgiving holiday.

Massachusetts Bay Colony

In 1625 Charles I took the throne, and persecution of the Puritans increased. At the same time, a depression struck England's wool industry. The depression caused high unemployment, particularly in the southeastern counties where large numbers of Puritans lived.

As he watched his fellow Puritans suffering both religious and economic hardships, **John Winthrop** grew concerned. Winthrop and several other wealthy Puritans were stockholders in the Massachusetts Bay Company. The company had already received a charter from King Charles to create a colony in New England. Winthrop decided to turn his business investment into a refuge for Puritans in America.

Other Puritans embraced the idea, and in 1630, 11 ships carrying about 900 settlers set sail. En route, in a sermon titled "A Model of Christian Charity," John Winthrop preached that the new colony should be an example to the world: "We shall be like a City upon a Hill; the eyes of all people are on us."

By the end of the year, another 1,000 settlers had arrived. As conditions in England worsened, large numbers of people began to leave in what was later called the Great Migration. By 1643, an estimated 20,000 settlers had arrived in New England.

The charter of the Massachusetts Bay Company defined the colony's government. People who owned stock in the company were called "freemen." Upon arrival all male household heads became freemen. All the freemen together were called the General Court. The General Court was to make the laws and elect the governor. John Winthrop was chosen as the first governor. He ignored the charter, however, and told the settlers that only he and his assistants could make laws for the colony. No one knew that this violated the charter, because Winthrop kept it locked in a chest.

The freemen elected Winthrop in four consecutive, annual elections. In 1634 the freemen demanded to see the charter. Winthrop had no grounds to refuse. As they read the charter, they realized that the General Court was supposed to make the laws. When the General Court assembled, they reorganized the government. The General Court became a representative assembly, with the freemen from each town electing deputies to send to the Court each year.

The Puritans believed that each congregation should control its own church. Although only church members could vote and hold office, Puritans kept the governance of church and state separate. The General Court passed laws regulating moral behavior and collected taxes for the support of their churches. Gambling, blasphemy, adultery, and drunkenness were all illegal and punished severely.

Puritans did not tolerate the expression of different religious ideas. **Heretics**—people who disagree with established religious beliefs—were considered a threat to the community. Those who voiced ideas that contradicted Puritan beliefs could be charged with heresy and banished.

People IN HISTORY

Roger Williams
1603?–1683

Shortly after his arrival in Boston in 1631, Roger Williams declared he was a Separatist and began criticizing Puritan leaders. He served as a minister in Salem, moved briefly to Plymouth Colony in 1632, and then returned to preach at Salem.

When Williams returned to Salem, he continued to criticize Puritan leaders for not making a complete break from the corrupt Anglican Church. He also insisted on greater separation of church and state. Finally, he denounced Massachusetts Bay's charter because it assumed the king had the right to give away land belonging to Native Americans. As Puritan leaders prepared to banish him, Williams fled.

In 1636 he founded Providence—later to be part of Rhode Island—on land he purchased from the Narragansetts. In his new colony, Williams created a haven for Quakers, Separatists, Jews, and others whose religious practices or views were not tolerated elsewhere. Most important, Williams championed religious freedom, which later became an important American principle.

What significant contribution to civil rights did Roger Williams make?

Anne Hutchinson
1591–1643

Anne Hutchinson, an experienced midwife and the wife of a prosperous merchant, arrived in Boston in 1634. There, she began to hold meetings with other women to discuss sermons, express her own beliefs, and evaluate the ministers.

Hutchinson stirred up controversy with her discussions of how salvation could be obtained. To most Puritans, this was heresy. In 1637 Hutchinson was tried for sedition by the Massachusetts General Court. Hutchinson did not repent. She said that God "hath let me see which was the clear [correct] ministry and which the wrong. . . . " When asked how God let her know, she replied that God spoke to her "by an immediate revelation." The Court ordered her banished.

Hutchinson, her family, and some of her followers founded a settlement in what is today Rhode Island. After the death of her husband, she moved to Long Island. In 1643 she and all but one of her children were killed in an attack by Native Americans. Some Puritans viewed her tragic death as God's judgment against a heretic.

How did Hutchinson challenge Puritan authority in the Massachusetts Bay Colony?

Puritan efforts to suppress other religious beliefs inevitably sparked conflict. Eventually, Puritan intolerance led to the founding of other colonies in New England.

Rhode Island and Dissent

In 1631 a young minister named **Roger Williams** arrived in Massachusetts. Williams was a Separatist who believed Puritans corrupted themselves by staying within the Anglican Church. Williams angered many people by condemning the Puritan churches, as well as declaring that the king had no right to give away land belonging to Native Americans.

In 1635 the Massachusetts General Court ordered him to be deported back to England, but Williams instead escaped south with a few followers. He then purchased land from the Narragansett people and founded the town of Providence in 1636. In Providence, the government had no authority over religious matters. Different religious beliefs were tolerated rather than suppressed.

In the midst of the uproar over Roger Williams, a devout Puritan named **Anne Hutchinson** began causing a stir in Boston. Hutchinson held religious discussion meetings in her home and questioned the authority of several ministers. In late 1637 the General Court charged her with heresy and banished her. Hutchinson and a few followers headed south and founded the town of Portsmouth.

Over the next few years, Massachusetts banished other dissenting Puritans. They too headed south and founded Newport in 1639 and Warwick in 1643. In 1644 these two towns joined Portsmouth and Providence to become the single colony of Rhode Island and Providence Plantations. Religious freedom became a key part of the new colony's charter.

New England Expands

In 1636 Reverend Thomas Hooker asked the General Court of Massachusetts for permission to move his congregation to the Connecticut River valley. Hooker was frustrated by the Massachusetts political system. He thought that voting should not be limited to male church members. The General Court granted Hooker's request, and he and some 100 settlers headed to the Connecticut River and founded the town of Hartford. Two years later, Hooker helped write the Fundamental Orders of Connecticut, a constitution that allowed all adult men, not just church members, to vote and serve in government. This marked the beginning of the colony of Connecticut.

Much of the territory north of Massachusetts had been granted to two men, Sir Fernando Gorges and Captain John Mason. Mason took the southern part and named it New Hampshire, while Gorges's territory in the north came to be called Maine. The government of Massachusetts claimed both New Hampshire and Maine and challenged the claims of Mason and Gorges in court. In 1677 an English court ruled against Massachusetts. Two years later, New Hampshire became a royal colony. Massachusetts, however, bought Maine from Gorges's heirs, and Maine remained part of Massachusetts until 1820.

King Philip's War

In 1637 war broke out between the English settlers and the Pequot people of New England. This conflict ended with the near extermination of the Pequot people. In the following decades, however, English settlers and Native Americans lived in relative peace.

The fur trade, in particular, facilitated peace. It enabled Native Americans to acquire tools, guns, and other European goods in exchange for furs. By the 1670s, however, the fur trade was in decline. At the same time, colonial governments began to demand that Native Americans follow English laws and customs. Native Americans reacted angrily, considering such demands arrogant and insulting.

Tensions peaked in 1675 when Plymouth Colony arrested, tried, and executed three Wampanoag men for murder. This touched off what came to be called King Philip's War, named after the Wampanoag leader Metacomet, whom the settlers called King Philip. Colonists killed Metacomet in 1676 and then mounted his head on a pike and paraded it through their settlements. By the time the war ended in 1678, few Native Americans were left in New England.

✔ **Reading Check** **Explaining** Why were Roger Williams and Anne Hutchinson banished from Massachusetts?

England's Civil War and New Colonies

MAIN Idea The English Civil War interrrupted colonization. After it ended, new colonies were founded.

HISTORY AND YOU Have you ever watched television programs about New York City? Read to learn how it became an English colony.

The English Civil War arose from a power struggle between King Charles I and Parliament. In 1642 this struggle erupted into armed conflict after the king sent troops into the Puritan-dominated Parliament to arrest Puritan leaders. In response, Parliament organized an army. After years of battles, Parliament's forces defeated the king's troops and beheaded him in 1649. Oliver Cromwell, the commander of Parliament's army, then seized power, took the title "Lord Protector," and in a few years ruled as a dictator of the new English Commonwealth.

After Cromwell died in 1658 and his son unsuccessfully tried to rule in his place, Parliament invited King Charles's son, Charles II, to take the throne. With the monarchy restored in 1660, the English government began backing a new round of colonization in America.

New York and New Jersey

Located between England's Chesapeake and New England colonies was a Dutch colony. In 1609 the Dutch East India Company hired English navigator **Henry Hudson** to search for a river that flowed through North America. Instead, he found the wide river that came to bear his name. The Dutch claimed the region, named it New Netherland, and established a settlement at New Amsterdam on Manhattan Island.

The colony grew slowly, partly because the fur trade was the focus of activity. To increase the population, the Dutch allowed anyone from any country to buy land. The strategy worked. By 1664 the population of the colony exceeded 10,000 people, with immigrants from the Netherlands, Britain, Scandinavia, Germany, and France. The first enslaved Africans arrived in the 1620s.

For an excerpt from the Fundamental Orders of Connecticut, see page R40 in **Documents in American History.**

Settled by 1660
Settled by 1700
Settled by 1760

New York
England took New York from the Dutch in 1664 and continued its focus on trade.

Pennsylvania
William Penn established Pennsylvania in 1681 as a place of religious freedom.

Virginia
The Virginia Company established its colony in 1607 as a money-making venture.

The Carolinas
The Carolina colony was chartered in 1663 as a proprietary colony; its proprietors hoped to make money growing cash crops.

Georgia
James Oglethorpe founded Georgia in 1733 as a refuge for England's poor.

Massachusetts
The Pilgrims arrived in Plymouth in 1620, and the Puritans arrived in Massachusetts Bay 10 years later; both groups fled religious persecution in England.

Rhode Island
Roger Williams founded Providence in 1636 as a place of religious toleration.

Connecticut
Thomas Hooker founded Hartford in 1636 to escape Massachusetts' Puritan political system.

Maryland
Lord Baltimore established Maryland in 1634 as a refuge for Catholics.

Maine (part of Mass.)
N.H. (1623)
Portsmouth
Boston
Plymouth
Providence
Hartford
New Haven
New Amsterdam
Philadelphia
N.J. (1664)
Baltimore
Del. (1638)
Williamsburg
Jamestown
Wilmington
Charles Towne
Savannah

L. Huron
L. Ontario
L. Erie
St. Lawrence R.
Connecticut R.
Hudson R.
Ohio R.
Tennessee R.
APPALACHIAN MOUNTAINS
40°N
80°W
30°N

ATLANTIC OCEAN

0   200 kilometers
0   200 miles
Lambert Azimuthal Equal-Area projection

Analyzing GEOGRAPHY

1. **Location** Why were the earliest settlements on the coast?
2. **Place** Which colony was founded as a haven for debtors?

England and the Netherlands were commercial rivals. In 1664 Charles II successfully took New Netherland from the Dutch. The king granted the land to his brother, James, Duke of York, who renamed the colony New York. James also received land between Delaware Bay and the Connecticut River. James later granted some of this land to two of the king's advisers and named it New Jersey. To attract settlers, New Jersey offered generous land grants, religious freedom, and the right to have a legislative assembly.

Pennsylvania and Delaware

The origins of the colony of Pennsylvania lay in a persecuted religious group and a large unpaid debt. The religious group was the Society of Friends, also known as the Quakers (because of founder George Fox's instruction to "tremble at the word of the Lord"). The debt was owed by King Charles II to the deceased father of William Penn.

William Penn was a member of the Quakers. The Quakers were considered a radical group because they saw no need for ministers and viewed the Bible as less important than each person's "inner light" from God. Quakers believed in religious toleration and pacifism, or opposition to war.

In 1681, to settle the debt owed to Penn's father, Charles II granted William Penn a large tract of land between New York and Maryland. Penn wanted his new colony of Pennsylvania to be a place where complete political and religious freedom would be practiced. He also tried to treat Native Americans fairly, and many years of peaceful relations resulted.

Penn named the capital of the colony Philadelphia, Greek for "city of brotherly love." The colony's government provided for an elected assembly and guaranteed religious freedom. The right to vote was limited, however, to Christian men who owned 50 acres of land.

Greater religious freedom and available land attracted immigrants of a variety of faiths from England, Scotland, Ireland, Scandinavia, and Germany. By 1684, Pennsylvania had more than 7,000 residents, and by 1750, Philadelphia was the largest city in the colonies. In 1682 Penn bought three counties south of Pennsylvania from the Duke of York. These "lower counties" became the colony of Delaware.

The Carolinas

Charles II also took a keen interest in the unsettled land between Virginia and Spanish Florida. Charles awarded much of this territory to eight friends in 1663. The land was named Carolina—Latin for "Charles."

Although Carolina was not divided into two distinct colonies until 1729, it developed as two separate regions. North Carolina was home to a small and scattered population of farmers. The lack of good harbors hindered its growth. Eventually, the farmers began growing tobacco as a cash crop. They also used native pine to make and export shipbuilding supplies.

The proprietors of Carolina were far more interested in the southern half of their holdings, where they hoped to cultivate sugarcane. In 1670 three ships brought settlers to South Carolina. They named their first settlement Charles Town. Sugarcane, however, did not grow well there. Instead, early colonists sold deerskins obtained from nearby Native Americans and started a slave trade in Native American prisoners of war.

The Georgia Experiment

Georgia began as a refuge for England's "worthy poor." In the 1720s James Oglethorpe, a member of Parliament, investigated English prisons. He was appalled to find that so many of the imprisoned were debtors, not strictly criminals. Oglethorpe asked the king for a colony where the poor could start over. In 1732 King George II made Oglethorpe and 19 other philanthropists the trustees for the territory between the Savannah and Altamaha rivers. Oglethorpe named the new colony Georgia, in honor of the king. Settlers arrived in 1733.

Oglethorpe and his fellow trustees banned slavery, rum, and brandy in Georgia, and they limited the size of land grants. Still, the colony attracted settlers from all over Europe. Increasingly, the settlers objected to the colony's strict rules. In the 1740s the trustees lifted the restrictions on brandy, rum, and slavery; in 1750 they granted the settlers their own elected assembly. The next year, Georgia became a royal colony.

By 1775, roughly 2.5 million people lived in England's thirteen American colonies. Despite the stumbling starts in Roanoke and Jamestown, the English had succeeded in building a large and prosperous society on the east coast of North America.

✔ **Reading Check** **Summarizing** How did William Penn acquire Pennsylvania?

Section 3 REVIEW

Vocabulary

1. **Explain** the significance of: joint-stock company, privateer, grant, Jamestown, Powhatan Confederacy, headright, proprietary colony, John Winthrop, heretic, Roger Williams, Anne Hutchinson, Henry Hudson.

Main Ideas

2. **Summarizing** How did the Protestant Reformation affect England's colonization efforts?

3. **Explaining** Why did people leave the Massachusetts Bay Colony to begin new colonies?

4. **Describing** On what principles did William Penn develop his colony?

Critical Thinking

5. **Big Ideas** How did the headright system encourage settlement in the English colonies?

6. **Organizing** Use a graphic organizer similar to the one below to list the colonies and the reasons for their founding.

Colony	Reason for Founding

7. **Analyzing Visuals** Study the painting of the signing of the Mayflower Compact on page 28. Why did the Pilgrims feel that it was necessary to create their own government?

Writing About History

8. **Persuasive Writing** Take the role of Captain John Smith. Write a speech explaining to your fellow Jamestown colonists why trading with the Powhatan Confederacy is a good survival strategy.

History ONLINE

Study Central™ To review this section, go to glencoe.com and click on Study Central.

Economics, Trade, and Rebellion

Differences in geography and patterns of settlement caused colonies to develop differently. Political changes in England affected the economy and governance of the thirteen colonies because they were part of the English imperial system.

Guide to Reading

Big Ideas
Geography and History Geography shaped the development of distinct regions within the English colonies.

Content Vocabulary
• indentured servant *(p. 34)*
• town meeting *(p. 38)*
• triangular trade *(p. 38)*
• mercantilism *(p. 40)*

Academic Vocabulary
• distinct *(p. 35)*
• reliable *(p. 40)*

People and Events to Identify
• Nathaniel Bacon *(p. 36)*
• English Bill of Rights *(p. 41)*

Reading Strategy
Organizing Complete a graphic organizer similar to the one below showing the ranking of classes in the colonial South.

Planter Elite

NEW YORK CORE CURRICULUM
U.S. History and Government

Unit 2:
I.A.1.a European intellectuals (Locke, Montesquieu, Voltaire, Rousseau)
I.A.1.b Key events (Magna Carta, habeas corpus, English Bill of Rights, Glorious Revolution)
I.A.2.a Native American Indians (relations between colonists and Native American Indians, trade, alliances, forced labor, warfare)
I.A.2.b Slave trade
I.A.3.a Colonial charters and self-government: Mayflower Compact, town meetings, House of Burgesses, local government, property rights, enforceable contracts, Albany Plan of Union
I.A.3.c Colonial slavery

Southern Society

MAIN Idea Society in the Southern Colonies was sharply divided between the wealthy elite and the backcountry farmers.

HISTORY AND YOU What kinds of produce are grown in your state? Read on to learn how the cultivation of cash crops helped the economies of the Southern colonies to grow.

In the South, wealthy planters stood on society's top rung and led very different lives from small farmers in the middle and enslaved Africans at the bottom. What linked all groups, however, was an economy based on growing crops for export. Tobacco was the South's first successful cash crop, or crop grown primarily to be sold at market. It was grown in Virginia and Maryland and, to a lesser extent, in North Carolina. In early colonial days, there was plenty of land, but not enough workers to produce the crop.

England had the opposite problem. The English enclosure movement had forced many farmers off their land. Many of them, hoping to acquire their own land in America, left England, agreeing to become **indentured servants** to cover the cost of their transportation to the colonies. Indentured servants were not enslaved, but neither were they free. The person who bought a servant's contract, or indenture, promised to provide food, clothing, and shelter to the servant until the indenture expired. In return, the servant agreed to work for the owner of the contract for a specific number of years, which varied from four to seven.

For most of the 1600s, indentured servitude benefited tobacco planters. Indentured servants could produce five times the price of their contracts in tobacco in the first year alone. Under the headright system, every indentured servant transported to America also earned the landowner another 50 acres of land. As indentured servants arrived in Virginia and Maryland, tobacco production rose steadily.

Unfortunately, almost half the indentured servants who came to Virginia and Maryland in the 1600s died before earning their freedom. Of those who survived their term of servitude, less than half ever acquired their own land.

In South Carolina, meanwhile, after trying unsuccessfully to grow sugarcane, settlers turned to rice. This failed at first, but in the 1690s a

NATIONAL GEOGRAPHIC

The Economy of the Colonial South, c. 1750

Wheat and corn
Tobacco
Rice and indigo

Maryland
• Baltimore
• Annapolis
Alexandria

Virginia

James R.
Williamsburg

Norfolk

Roanoke R.

North Carolina

Pee Dee R.

New Bern

Savannah R.

South Carolina

Wilmington

Georgia

ATLANTIC OCEAN

Charles Towne

0   100 kilometers
0   100 miles
Albers Equal-Area projection

Ocmulgee R.
Savannah

82°W   80°W   78°W

38°N

36°N

34°N

32°N

Exports to England, 1715–1775

Pounds (thousands)

70
60
50
40
30
20
10

1715   1730   1745   1760   1775

—— Tobacco   —— Rice

Source: *Historical Statistics of the United States.*

Harvesting tobacco in colonial Virginia

Analyzing GEOGRAPHY

1. **Location** Why were tobacco and rice plantations located on or near rivers?
2. **Movement** About how much tobacco was exported to England from the Southern Colonies in 1745?

new variety was introduced, and planters imported enslaved Africans to cultivate it. West Africans had grown rice for centuries and knew how to raise and harvest it. Rice rapidly became a major cash crop in South Carolina and Georgia.

Planters had also tried another crop, indigo, without much success. Indigo was used to make blue dye for cloth. It was rare and in high demand, and anyone who could grow it could make a large profit. In the early 1740s a 17-year-old named Eliza Lucas discovered that indigo needed high ground and sandy soil, not the wetlands that suited rice. Indigo quickly became another important cash crop.

Disparities in Wealth

Although many immigrants to the Southern Colonies hoped to become wealthy, very few succeeded. The plantation system tended to create a society with **distinct** social classes.

The wealthy plantation owners, sometimes referred to as the Southern gentry or the planter elite, were few in number, and they enjoyed enormous economic and political influence. They served in the governing councils and assemblies, commanded the local militias, and became county judges. With few towns or roads in the region, their plantations functioned as self-contained communities. The residents lived near each other in a group of buildings, including the planter's great house, stables, barns, and the workers' cabins. Plantations often had a school, a chapel, and workshops for blacksmiths, carpenters, weavers, coopers, and leatherworkers.

The majority of landowners in the colonial South, however, were small farmers living inland. These "backcountry" farmers worked small plots of land and lived in tiny houses. Although they grew some tobacco, they largely practiced subsistence farming, producing only enough to feed their families.

Landless tenant farmers made up another large group in the South. Although land itself was easy to acquire, many settlers and former indentured servants could not afford the costs of the deed, land survey, tools, seed, and livestock. Instead, they worked land that they rented from the planter elite. Tenant farmers led difficult lives but had higher social status than indentured servants.

Bacon's Rebellion

By the 1660s, Virginia's government was dominated by wealthy planters led by the governor, Sir William Berkeley. Berkeley assembled a majority of supporters in the House of Burgesses and arranged to restrict the vote to people who owned property. This cut the number of voters in half. Berkeley also exempted himself and his councilors from taxation. These actions angered backcountry and tenant farmers. Ultimately, however, it was the governor's policies toward Native American lands that led to a rebellion.

Acquiring land was the goal of most colonists. Many indentured servants and tenant farmers wanted to own farms eventually. Backcountry farmers wanted to increase their holdings. By the 1670s, however, most uncultivated land was in areas belonging to Native Americans in the Piedmont, the region of rolling hills between the coastal plains and the Appalachians.

Most wealthy planters lived near the coast in the region known as the Tidewater. They had no interest in the backcountry and did not want to endanger their plantations by risking war with the Native Americans. Therefore, they opposed expanding Virginia's territory into Native American lands.

In 1675 war broke out between backcountry settlers and the Susquehannock people. When Berkeley refused to support further military action, backcountry farmers were outraged. In April 1676, **Nathaniel Bacon,** a well-to-do but sympathetic planter on the governor's council, took up their cause. Bacon organized his own militia and attacked the Susquehannock. He then won a seat in the House of Burgesses. The assembly then authorized another attack on the Native Americans. It also restored the right to vote to all free white men and took away the tax exemptions Berkeley had given his supporters.

These reforms did not satisfy Bacon, however. He marched to Jamestown in July 1676 with several hundred armed men and charged Berkeley with corruption. Berkeley fled to raise his own army, and a civil war erupted. The two sides battled for control of the colony. In September 1667 Bacon's army burned Jamestown to the ground. The following month, the rebellion ended abruptly when Bacon became sick and died. Without his leadership, his army rapidly fell apart, and Berkeley returned to power.

Bacon's Rebellion convinced many wealthy planters that land should be made available to backcountry farmers. From the 1680s onward, Virginia's government generally supported expanding the colony westward, regardless of the impact on Native Americans.

The Rise of Slavery

Bacon's Rebellion also accelerated an existing trend in Virginia. By the 1670s, many planters had begun using enslaved Africans instead of indentured servants to work their plantations. In the 1680s, after the rebellion, the number of Africans brought to the colony rose rapidly.

Planters began to switch to enslaved African labor for several reasons. Enslaved workers did not have to be freed and would never have to be given their own land. In addition, when cheap land became available in the 1680s in other colonies, fewer English settlers were willing to become indentured servants.

At the same time, the English government adopted policies that encouraged slavery. English law limited trade between the English colonies and other countries. Before the 1670s, if settlers wanted to acquire enslaved Africans, they had to buy them from the Dutch or Portuguese, which was difficult to arrange. In 1672, however, King Charles II granted a charter to the Royal African Company to engage in the slave trade. This made it easier to acquire enslaved people. Planters also discovered another advantage to slavery; because enslaved Africans, unlike indentured servants, were considered property, planters could use them as collateral to borrow money and expand their plantations.

✓ Reading Check **Identifying** What government policies caused backcountry farmers in Virginia to rebel?

New England Society

MAIN Idea New England's economy was based on fishing, family farms, and lumber mills.

HISTORY AND YOU Have you attended a meeting of your local government? Read on to learn about early New England town meetings.

New England's thin and rocky soil was ill-suited to cash crops and the development of large plantations. Instead, on small farms from Connecticut to Maine, New England colonists practiced subsistence farming. The main crop was wheat, but farmers also grew other grains and vegetables, tended apple orchards, and raised dairy cattle, sheep, and pigs.

More than any other industry, fishing and whaling brought prosperity to New England. Nearby lay the Grand Banks, a shallow area in the Atlantic Ocean that teemed with cod, mackerel, halibut, and herring. In addition, New England had good harbors and plenty of timber for building fishing boats. Colonists found markets for their fish in the colonies, southern Europe, and the Caribbean. Whale blubber was used to make candles and lamp oil, and whale bones were used to fashion buttons, combs, and other items.

New England also developed a thriving lumber industry. Maine and New Hampshire had many waterfalls near the coast that could power sawmills. Demand for lumber never waned. It was used for furniture, buildings, and products such as barrels, which were used to ship almost everything in the colonial era.

Shipbuilding also became an important business. With forests and sawmills close to the coast, ships could be built quickly and cheaply—for 30 to 50 percent less than in England. By the 1770s, one out of every three English ships was built in America.

While self-sufficient plantations defined the social unit in the South, New England's social life centered on the towns. Puritans believed that Christians should form groups united by a church covenant—a voluntary agreement to worship together. The commitment to a church covenant encouraged the development of small towns surrounded by farms.

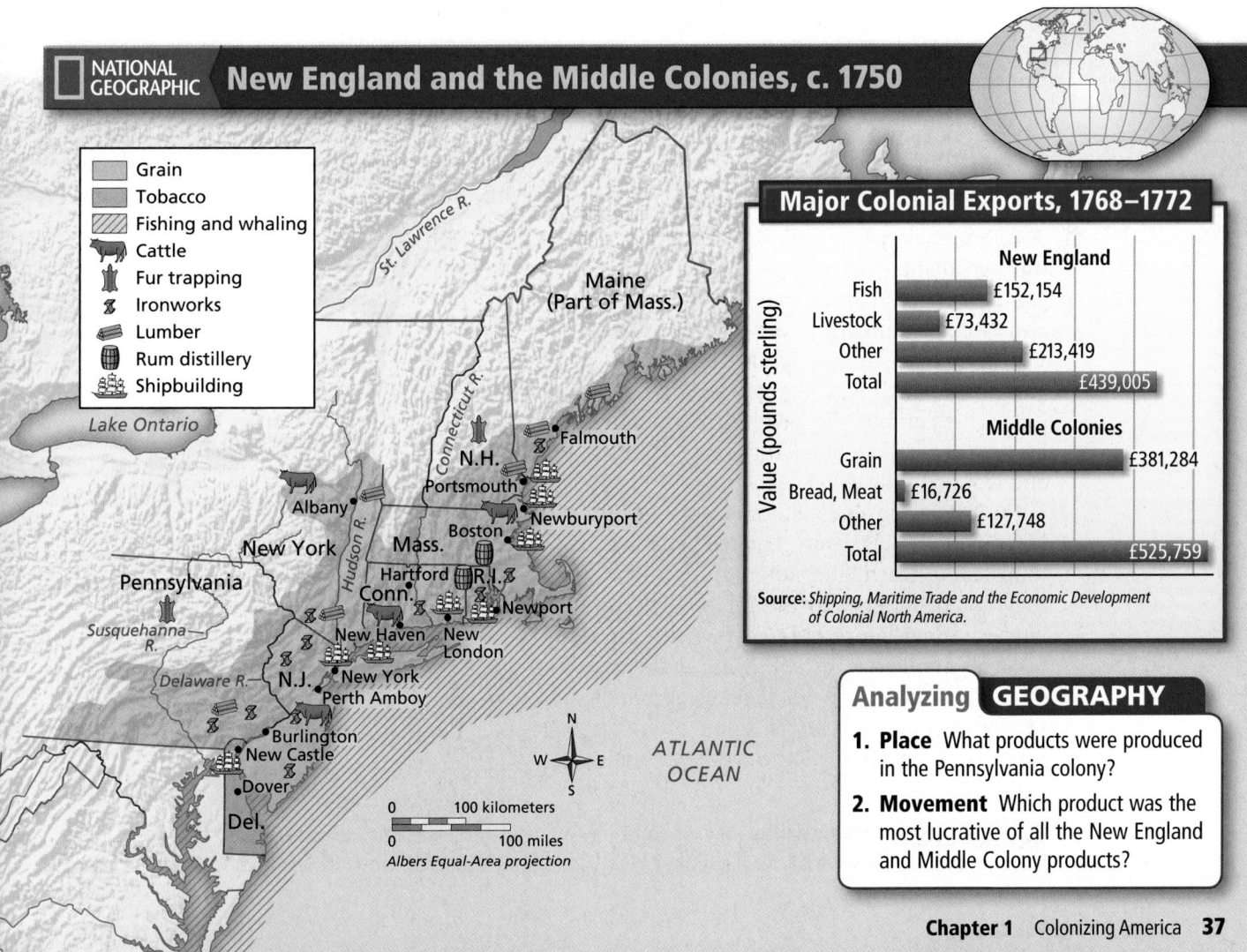

NATIONAL GEOGRAPHIC New England and the Middle Colonies, c. 1750

Legend:
- Grain
- Tobacco
- Fishing and whaling
- Cattle
- Fur trapping
- Ironworks
- Lumber
- Rum distillery
- Shipbuilding

Major Colonial Exports, 1768–1772

Value (pounds sterling)

New England

Fish	£152,154
Livestock	£73,432
Other	£213,419
Total	£439,005

Middle Colonies

Grain	£381,284
Bread, Meat	£16,726
Other	£127,748
Total	£525,759

Source: *Shipping, Maritime Trade and the Economic Development of Colonial North America.*

Analyzing GEOGRAPHY

1. **Place** What products were produced in the Pennsylvania colony?

2. **Movement** Which product was the most lucrative of all the New England and Middle Colony products?

Life in these small communities revolved around a "town common," or open public area. The marketplace, school, and "meetinghouse" (or church) bordered the common. Each family had a home lot where they could build a house and storage buildings and plant a garden.

Local Government

In the early days of colonial New England, the General Court appointed town officials and managed the town's affairs. Over time, however, townspeople began discussing local problems and issues at **town meetings.** These developed into local governments, with landowners holding the right to vote and pass laws. They elected selectmen to oversee town matters and appoint clerks, constables, and other officials. Any resident, however, could attend a town meeting and express an opinion.

Because the settlers in New England, unlike English tenants, were allowed to participate in local government, they developed a strong belief in their right to govern themselves. Town meetings thus helped set the stage for the American Revolution and the emergence of democratic government.

Puritan Society

New England Puritans valued religious devotion, hard work, and obedience to strict rules regulating daily life. Card playing and gambling were banned, and "stage-players" and "mixed dancing" were frowned upon. Watching over one's neighbors' behavior, or "holy watching," was elevated to a religious duty. The Puritans did not lead pleasureless lives, however. They drank rum, enjoyed music, and wore brightly colored clothing.

Puritans also valued education. In 1642 the Massachusetts legislature required parents and ministers to teach all children to read so that they could understand the Bible. Five years later, the legislature ordered towns with at least 50 families to establish an elementary school and those with 100 families or more to set up secondary schools. Soon afterward, other New England colonies adopted similar legislation.

Reading Check **Synthesizing** How did town meetings prepare the colonists for the future?

Trade and the Rise of Cities

MAIN Idea Cities prospered and grew through trade with England, Africa, and other colonies.

HISTORY AND YOU Does today's society have distinct social classes? Read on to learn how social classes developed in the colonies.

In the early colonial era, settlers lacked money to invest in local industry. As a result, they had to import most manufactured goods from England. Unfortunately, they produced few goods that England wanted in return.

Triangular Trade

Instead of trading directly with England, colonial merchants developed systems of **triangular trade** involving a three-way exchange of goods. New England merchants, for example, traded fish, lumber, and meat to sugar planters in the Caribbean. In return, they received raw sugar or bills of exchange—credit slips from English merchants. New England merchants would then trade the bills and sugar to English merchants for hardware, linens, and other English goods.

Trade with the Caribbean sugar plantations made many New England merchants rich. With their new wealth, they built factories to refine raw sugar and distilleries to turn molasses into rum. They also traded with the Southern Colonies, exchanging fish, rum, and grain for rice, tobacco, and indigo.

A New Urban Society

The rise of trade caused several Northern ports—including Boston, New York City, and Philadelphia—to grow into cities. In the South, trade made Charles Town, South Carolina, the region's largest urban center. In all of these cities and others, a new society with distinct social classes developed.

At the top of the social structure were wealthy merchants who controlled the city's trade. These rich merchants composed a tiny minority. Skilled artisans and their families made up nearly half of the urban population. Artisans were skilled workers such as carpenters, smiths, glassmakers, coopers, bakers, masons, and shoemakers. Alongside the

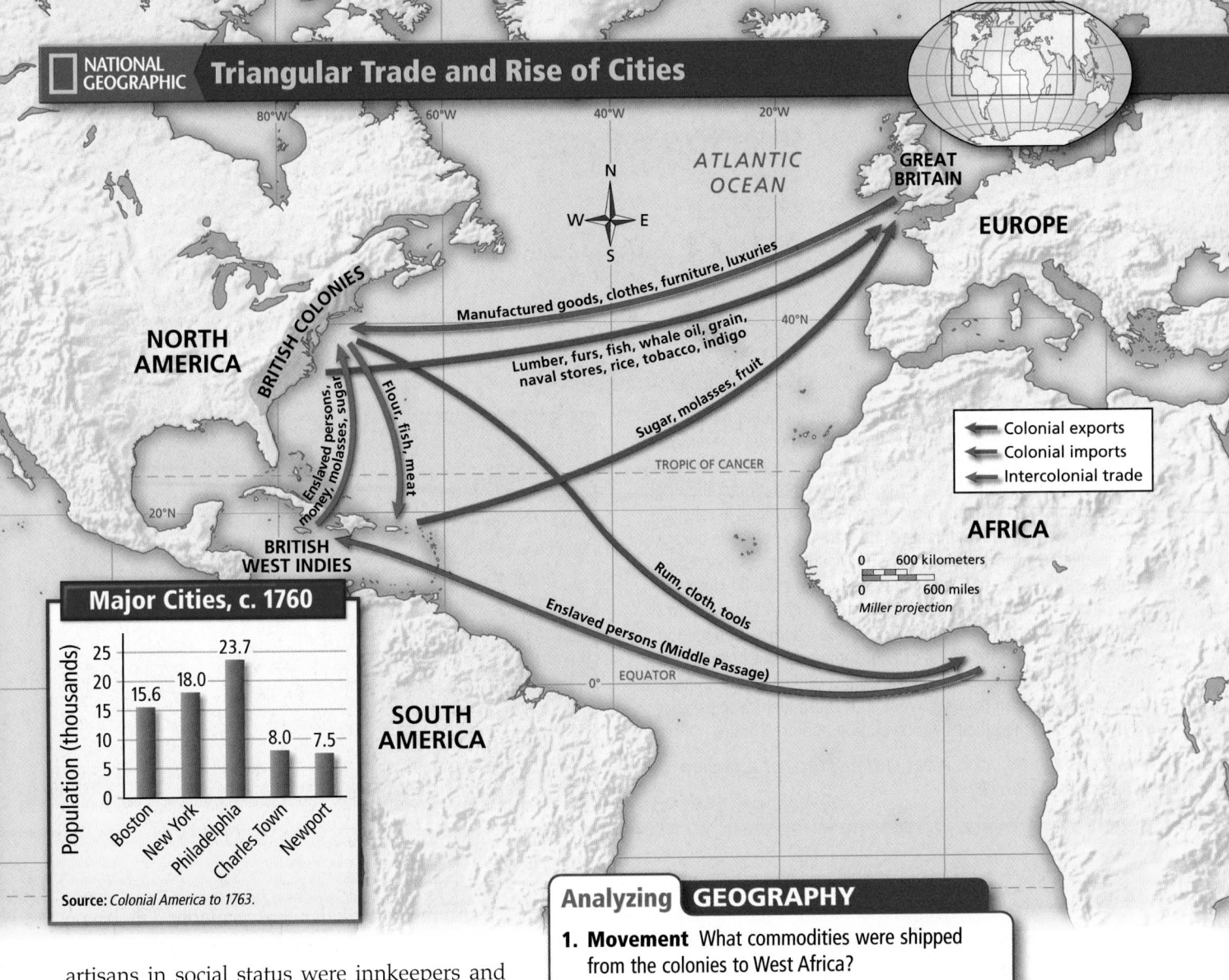

ATLANTIC OCEAN

GREAT BRITAIN

EUROPE

NORTH AMERICA

BRITISH COLONIES

Manufactured goods, clothes, furniture, luxuries

Lumber, furs, fish, whale oil, grain, naval stores, rice, tobacco, indigo

Sugar, molasses, fruit

TROPIC OF CANCER

Enslaved persons, money, molasses, sugar

Flour, fish, meat

AFRICA

BRITISH WEST INDIES

Rum, cloth, tools

Enslaved persons (Middle Passage)

EQUATOR

SOUTH AMERICA

← Colonial exports
← Colonial imports
← Intercolonial trade

0   600 kilometers
0   600 miles
Miller projection

Major Cities, c. 1760

Population (thousands)

City	Population
Boston	15.6
New York	18.0
Philadelphia	23.7
Charles Town	8.0
Newport	7.5

Source: *Colonial America to 1763.*

Analyzing GEOGRAPHY

1. **Movement** What commodities were shipped from the colonies to West Africa?
2. **Human-Environment Interaction** What types of goods did the American colonies export?

artisans in social status were innkeepers and retailers who owned their own businesses.

Beneath the artisans in urban society were people without skills or property. Many of these people loaded and serviced ships at the harbor. Others worked as servants. These people made up about 30 percent of urban society. Below them in status were indentured servants and enslaved Africans. Relatively few enslaved people lived in the North. Those who did usually lived in cities, making up between 10 and 20 percent of the population.

Life in the Middle Colonies

The Middle Colonies—Pennsylvania, New York, New Jersey, and Delaware—combined aspects of New England's economy with that of the South. As in New England, trade led to the rise of cities along the coast. As in the South, colonists benefited from fertile soil and a long growing season. Farmers produced

abundant crops of rye, oats, barley, potatoes, and especially wheat. And just as the Southern economy was based on exporting cash crops, so too did the Middle Colonies develop an economy with an important cash crop: wheat.

As merchants in the Middle Colonies began selling wheat and flour to colonies in the Caribbean, they benefited from the region's geography. Three wide rivers—the Hudson, the Delaware, and the Susquehanna—ran deep into the interior, making it easy for farmers to ship their crops to the coast.

In the early and mid-1700s, the demand for wheat soared, thanks to population growth in Europe resulting from a decline of disease. Between 1720 and 1770, wheat prices more than doubled, bringing great prosperity.

People IN HISTORY

John Locke
1632–1704

The Glorious Revolution of 1688 set a very important precedent. It suggested that there were times when revolution was justified. In 1690, John Locke, a philosopher allied with those who had overthrown King James II, wrote *Two Treatises of Government* on this topic.

Locke argued that a government's right to rule came from the people. All people, he said, were born with certain natural rights, including the right to life, liberty, and property. To protect their rights, people created government. In effect, they had made a contract—they agreed to obey the government's laws, and the government agreed to protect their rights. If a ruler violated those rights, the people were justified in rebelling.

Locke's ideas greatly influenced the American colonists because they seemed to fit colonial history. The Mayflower Compact, the Fundamental Orders of Connecticut, and other colonial charters were all agreements between the people and their government. When Locke referred to "natural rights" the colonists understood those to be the specific rights of Englishmen set out in such documents as the Magna Carta and the English Bill of Rights. By the 1770s, the American colonies would put these ideas into practice when they launched their own revolution against Britain.

According to Locke, what is the source of a government's right to rule?

▼ *John Locke wrote* Two Treatises of Government *to justify Parliament's decision to put William and Mary on the throne and require them to accept the English Bill of Rights (shown being presented below).*

📜 For an excerpt from the *Second Treatise of Government*, see page R42 in **Documents in American History.**

The wheat boom created a new group of wealthy capitalists who had money to invest in businesses. Industry did not develop on a large scale in the colonial era, but these capitalists did build many large mills near New York and Philadelphia that produced vast quantities of flour for export. Other capitalists in the Middle Colonies established glass and pottery works.

The Imperial System

Mercantilism is an economic theory about the world economy. Mercantilists believed that to become wealthy, a country must acquire gold and silver. A country could do this by selling more goods to other countries than it buys from them. This would cause more gold and silver to flow into the country than flowed out to pay for products from other countries. Mercantilists also argued that a country should be self-sufficient in raw materials. If it had to buy raw materials from another country, gold and silver would flow out to pay for them. Thus to be self-sufficient, a country needed colonies

where raw materials were available. The home country would then buy raw materials from its colonies and sell them manufactured goods in return.

Mercantilism provided some benefits to colonies. It gave them a **reliable** market for some of their raw materials and an eager supplier of manufactured goods. Mercantilism also had drawbacks, however. It prevented colonies from selling goods to other nations, even if they could get a better price. Furthermore, if a colony produced nothing the home country needed, it could not acquire gold or silver to buy manufactured goods. This was a serious problem in New England, and it partly explains why merchants there turned to the triangular trade and smuggling.

The Navigation Acts When Charles II assumed the throne in 1660, he and his advisers were determined to generate wealth for England in America and they established policies based on mercantilist ideas. Beginning in 1660, the king asked Parliament to pass a series of Navigation Acts that imposed restrictions on colonial trade. These acts required that all goods shipped to and from the colonies be carried on English ships, and listed specific products that could be sold only to England or other English colonies. Many of these goods—including sugar, tobacco, lumber, cotton, wool, and indigo—were the major products that earned money for the American colonies.

Anger at the Navigation Acts encouraged colonists to break the new laws. New England merchants began smuggling goods to Europe, the Caribbean, and Africa in large quantities. In 1686, soon after King James II succeeded his brother Charles, England took decisive action to end the smuggling. Massachusetts, Plymouth, and Rhode Island were merged into a new royal province called the Dominion of New England to be governed by an English governor-general appointed by the king. The following year, Connecticut and New Jersey were added to the Dominion, and by early 1688, New York was added as well.

King James II appointed Sir Edmund Andros to be the Dominion's first governor-general. Andros became very unpopular because he levied new taxes and rigorously enforced the Navigation Acts. Equally disturbing to Puritans were Andros's efforts to undermine their congregations. For example, he declared that only marriages performed in Anglican churches were legal.

The Glorious Revolution While Andros was angering New England colonists, James II was losing support in England. He offended many by disregarding Parliament, revoking town charters, prosecuting Anglican bishops, and practicing Catholicism.

The birth of James's son in 1688 triggered a crisis. Opponents of James had been content to wait until he died, because they expected his Protestant daughter Mary to succeed him. The son, however, was now first in line for the throne, and would be raised Catholic. To prevent a Catholic dynasty, Parliament invited Mary and her Dutch husband, William of Orange, to claim the throne. James fled in what became known as the Glorious Revolution.

Soon afterward, the colonists ousted Governor-General Andros. William and Mary permitted Rhode Island and Connecticut to resume their previous forms of government, but in 1691 they merged Massachusetts Bay, Plymouth, and Maine into the new royal colony of Massachusetts. The colony was headed by a governor appointed by the king, but the colonists were allowed to elect an assembly.

Before assuming the throne, William and Mary had to swear their acceptance of the **English Bill of Rights.** This document, written in 1689, said monarchs could not suspend Parliament's laws or create their own courts, nor could they impose taxes or raise an army without Parliament's consent. The Bill of Rights also guaranteed freedom of speech within Parliament, banned excessive bail and cruel and unusual punishments, and guaranteed every English subject the right to an impartial jury in legal cases. The ideas in this document would later help shape the American Bill of Rights.

Reading Check **Examining** In what ways did the Navigation Acts affect trade in the colonies?

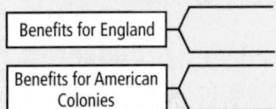

Section 4 REVIEW

Vocabulary

1. **Explain** the significance of: indentured servant, Nathaniel Bacon, town meeting, triangular trade, mercantilism, English Bill of Rights.

Main Ideas

2. **Explaining** How did the development of cash crops in the Southern colonies encourage the trade in enslaved people?

3. **Identifying** How did Puritan ideals lead to the development of town meetings?

4. **Analyzing** How did life in the Middle Colonies differ from life in the Southern Colonies?

5. **Categorizing** Complete a graphic organizer similar to the one below by filling in the benefits of mercantilism.

> Benefits for England
>
> Benefits for American Colonies

Critical Thinking

6. **Big Ideas** What role did geography play in developing different economies in the colonies?

7. **Analyzing Visuals** Study the bar graph showing the populations of major colonial cities on page 39 and the product map and graph on page 37. Why do you think Philadelphia was the largest city at this time?

Writing About History

8. **Expository Writing** Take on the role of a colonial merchant. Write a letter to a relative in England explaining how the Navigation Acts have affected your business.

History ONLINE

Study Central™ To review this section, go to <u>glencoe.com</u> and click on Study Central.

A Diverse Society

Guide to Reading

Big Ideas

Trade, War, and Migration
Immigrants from Europe and those brought by force from Africa greatly increased the population of the American colonies in the 1700s.

Content Vocabulary

• slave code *(p. 44)*
• rationalism *(p. 45)*
• pietism *(p. 47)*
• revival *(p. 47)*

Academic Vocabulary

• contract *(p. 43)*
• widespread *(p. 47)*

People and Events to Identify

• Cotton Mather *(p. 42)*
• Stono Rebellion *(p. 45)*
• John Locke *(p. 46)*
• Baron Montesquieu *(p. 47)*
• Jonathan Edwards *(p. 47)*
• George Whitefield *(p. 47)*

Reading Strategy

Categorizing Complete a graphic organizer similar to the one below by identifying why immigrants settled in the colonies.

Group	Where They Settled	Reasons for Immigrating
Germans		
Scots-Irish		
Jews		

NEW YORK CORE CURRICULUM
U.S. History and Government

Unit 2:
I.A.1.a European intellectuals (Locke, Montesquieu, Voltaire, Rousseau)
I.A.2 The peoples and peopling of the American colonies (voluntary and involuntary)
I.A.3.c Colonial slavery
I.A.3.d Freedom of the press: the Zenger case

The American colonies experienced rapid growth through natural increase and immigration. The importation of enslaved Africans continued even as colonists engaged in philosophical and religious discussions about the rights of individuals.

Colonial America Grows

MAIN Idea The American colonies experienced tremendous growth due to high birth rates, long life spans, and immigration.

HISTORY AND YOU Do you remember getting vaccinated against certain diseases? Read to find out how inoculation was introduced in the colonies.

The population of the American colonies grew rapidly in the eighteenth century. A major factor was the era's high birth rate. Most women married in their early twenties, typically to men about the same age. On average, colonial women gave birth to seven children, although giving birth to twice that number of children was not uncommon. Between 1640 and 1700, the colonial population increased from 25,000 to more than 250,000. In the 1700s the population doubled every 25 years. By the time of the American Revolution, the colonial population had reached roughly 2.5 million.

An important factor in population growth was improved housing and sanitation. Although women often died in childbirth, many adults lived into their early sixties. Contagious diseases, however, such as typhoid fever, tuberculosis, cholera, diphtheria, and scarlet fever, continued to ravage residents in colonial cities.

When an epidemic of deadly smallpox swept through Boston in 1721, Reverend **Cotton Mather,** a Puritan leader, promoted "the new Method used by the Africans and Asiaticks, to prevent and abate the Dangers of the Small-Pox." This method, inoculation, proved highly successful. Of 6,000 people who were not inoculated and caught smallpox, about 900, or 15 percent, died. In contrast, only 6 of the 241 people who received inoculation died of the disease.

Immigration

Immigration also contributed to population growth. Some 300,000 European immigrants arrived between 1700 and 1775. Most settled in the Middle Colonies, especially eastern Pennsylvania. Many others headed to the frontier, where land was free, and settled in the backcountry of Pennsylvania and the colonial South. At the same time, traders brought large numbers of enslaved Africans to America, mostly to the Southern Colonies.

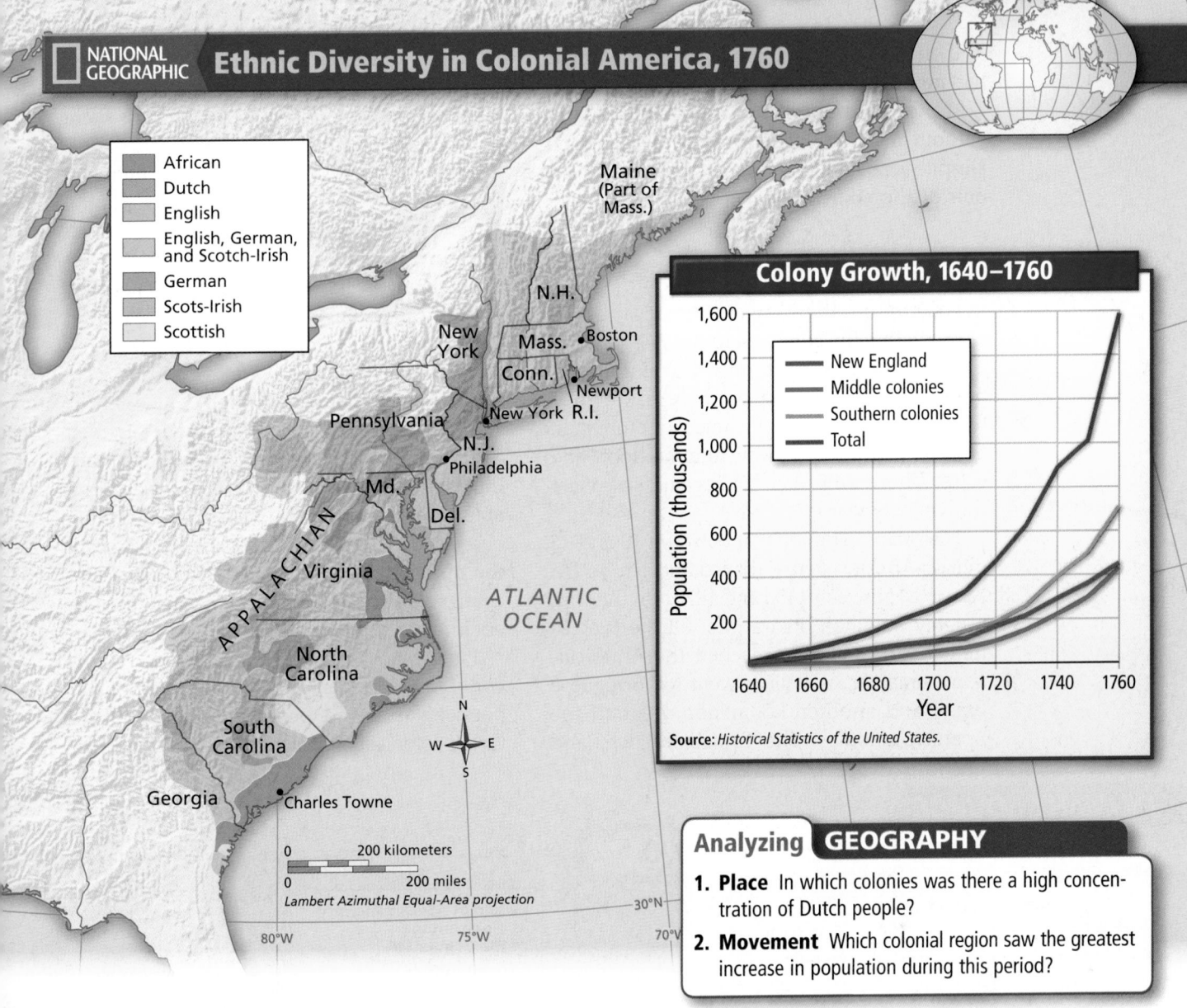

NATIONAL GEOGRAPHIC

Ethnic Diversity in Colonial America, 1760

Legend:
- African
- Dutch
- English
- English, German, and Scotch-Irish
- German
- Scots-Irish
- Scottish

Maine (Part of Mass.)

N.H.

New York

Mass. • Boston

Conn. • Newport

New York R.I.

Pennsylvania

N.J.

Philadelphia

Md.

Del.

APPALACHIAN

Virginia

ATLANTIC OCEAN

North Carolina

South Carolina

Georgia • Charles Towne

0   200 kilometers
0   200 miles
Lambert Azimuthal Equal-Area projection

30°N

80°W   75°W   70°W

N W E S

Colony Growth, 1640–1760

- New England
- Middle colonies
- Southern colonies
- Total

Population (thousands): 200, 400, 600, 800, 1,000, 1,200, 1,400, 1,600

Year: 1640, 1660, 1680, 1700, 1720, 1740, 1760

Source: *Historical Statistics of the United States.*

Analyzing GEOGRAPHY

1. **Place** In which colonies was there a high concentration of Dutch people?
2. **Movement** Which colonial region saw the greatest increase in population during this period?

In 1683 German Mennonites had come to Pennsylvania to escape religious wars at home, and by the early 1700s, a large wave of German immigration had begun. By 1775, more than 100,000 Germans lived in the colony, making up about one-third of the population. Most were farmers.

The Scots-Irish were descendants of the Scots who had helped England claim control of Northern Ireland. Beginning in 1717, rising taxes, poor harvests, and religious persecution convinced many to flee Ireland. An estimated 150,000 Scots-Irish came to the American colonies between 1717 and 1776. Most headed for the western frontier, settling in the backcountry of Pennsylvania and the South.

Jews seeking religious tolerance also began moving to America in colonial times. In 1654 a small group of Portuguese Jews arrived in New York, which was then called New Amsterdam. There they founded one of the first synagogues in North America. By 1776, approximately 1,500 Jews lived in the colonies.

Women

Women did not have equal rights in colonial America. In the early colonial era, married women could not own property or make **contracts** or wills. Husbands were the sole guardians of the children and were allowed to physically discipline both them and their wives. Single women and widows, however, had more rights. They could own property, file lawsuits, and run businesses.

By the 1700s, the status of married women had improved. In most colonies, for example, a husband could not sell or mortgage his land without his wife's signature on the contract. Despite legal limitations, many women worked outside the home.

Africans in the Colonies

For Africans, the voyage to America usually began with a forced march to the West African coast, where they were traded to Europeans, branded, and crammed onto ships. Chained together in the ships' filthy holds for more than a month, they were given minimal food and drink. Those who died or became sick were thrown overboard.

Historians estimate that between 10 and 12 million Africans were enslaved and sent to the Americas between 1450 and 1870. On the way, roughly 2 million died at sea. Of the 8 to 10 million Africans who reached the Americas, approximately 3.6 million went to Portuguese Brazil and another 1.5 million went to the Spanish colonies. The British, French, and Dutch colonies in the Caribbean imported nearly 3.7 million others to work on their plantations. Approximately 500,000 Africans were transported to British North America.

When the first Africans arrived in Virginia in 1619, English law did not recognize chattel slavery—the actual ownership of one human being by another. As a result, slavery developed slowly in the Chesapeake colonies. The first Africans brought to Virginia and Maryland were treated in a manner similar to indentured servants, and children born to Africans were not always considered enslaved.

At first, enslaved Africans could obtain their freedom by converting to Christianity. To many English settlers, enslaving Africans was acceptable, not because they were not white, but because they were not Christian. Over time, as the number of Africans increased, their status changed. By the 1660s, new laws changed slavery into a hereditary system based on race.

Finally, in 1705 Virginia created a **slave code**—a set of laws defining the relationship between enslaved people and free people. Other colonies followed suit. Enslaved persons

The Atlantic Slave Trade c. 1500–1800

In 1619 the first Africans arrived in the English colonies, beginning the brutal African slave trade. After a nearly fatal voyage across the Atlantic, known as the Middle Passage, under stifling, dirty, and crowded conditions, those starved and exhausted Africans who managed to survive were sold in markets or at auction.

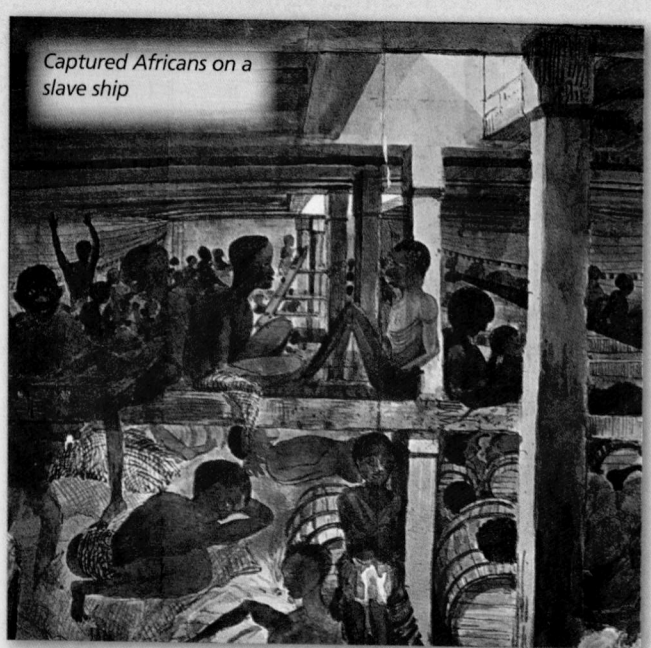

Captured Africans on a slave ship

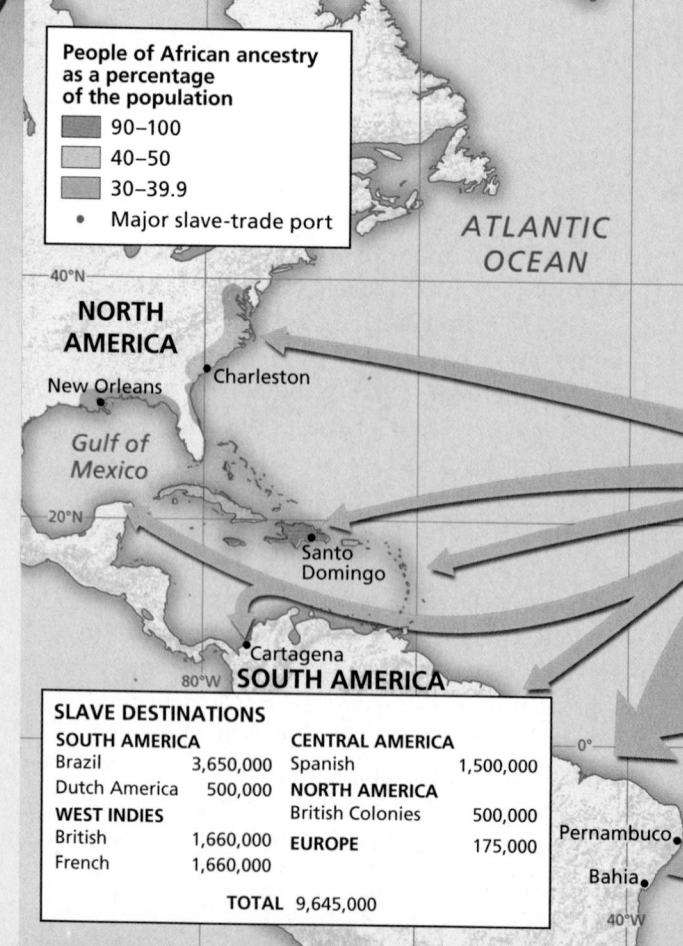

People of African ancestry as a percentage of the population
- 90–100
- 40–50
- 30–39.9
- • Major slave-trade port

ATLANTIC OCEAN

NORTH AMERICA

New Orleans • Charleston

Gulf of Mexico

Santo Domingo

• Cartagena

SOUTH AMERICA

Pernambuco

Bahia

SLAVE DESTINATIONS			
SOUTH AMERICA		**CENTRAL AMERICA**	
Brazil	3,650,000	Spanish	1,500,000
Dutch America	500,000	**NORTH AMERICA**	
WEST INDIES		British Colonies	500,000
British	1,660,000	**EUROPE**	175,000
French	1,660,000		
		TOTAL 9,645,000	

could not own property, testify against whites in court, move about freely, or assemble in large numbers. By the early 1700s, slavery had become generally accepted in colonial society. By 1775, roughly 20 percent of the colonial population was of African heritage.

No group in the American colonies endured lower status or more hardship than enslaved Africans. Most lived on Southern plantations, where they worked long days and were beaten and branded by planters. Planters also controlled enslaved Africans by threatening to sell them away from their families.

Family and religion helped the enslaved Africans maintain their dignity. Some resisted by escaping to the North; others refused to work hard or broke or lost their tools. In 1739 a group of Africans living near the Stono River in South Carolina rebelled against their white overseers and tried to escape to Spanish Florida. The militia quickly ended the **Stono Rebellion,** which took the lives of 21 whites and 44 Africans.

Reading Check **Summarizing** In what ways did enslaved people resist their enslavement?

New Ideas

MAIN Idea The ideas of the Enlightenment and the Great Awakening made the colonists question their role as subjects of the English monarchy.

HISTORY AND YOU Have you ever read a book that changed the way you thought about a subject? Read how two cultural developments influenced American colonists.

During the 1700s the English colonies came under the influence of the Enlightenment and the Great Awakening. The first championed human reason, while the second stressed a new personal relationship with God.

The Enlightenment

Enlightenment thinkers came to believe that natural laws applied to social, political, and economic relationships, and that people could figure out these natural laws if they employed reason. This emphasis on logic and reasoning was known as **rationalism.**

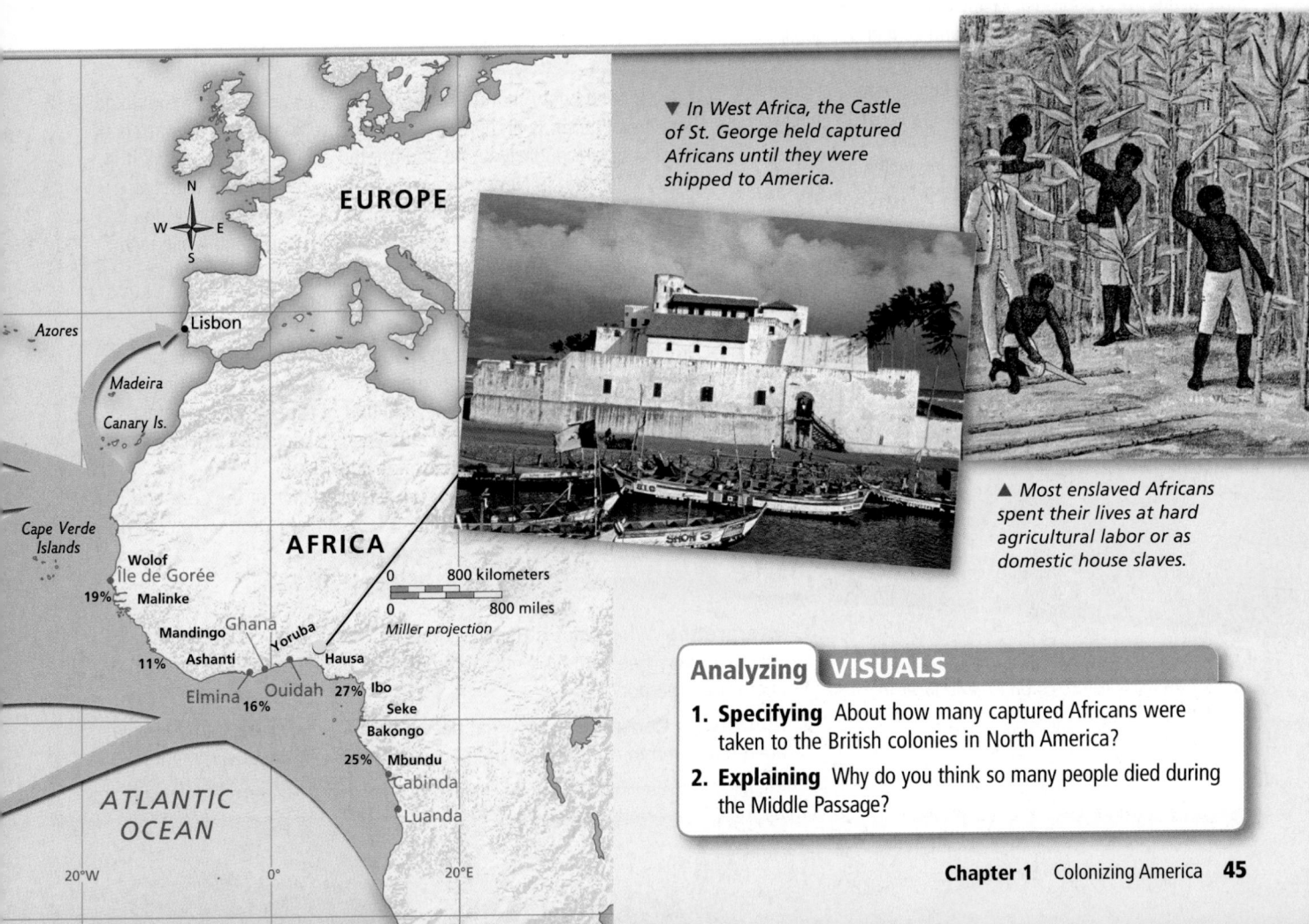

▼ In West Africa, the Castle of St. George held captured Africans until they were shipped to America.

▲ Most enslaved Africans spent their lives at hard agricultural labor or as domestic house slaves.

Analyzing VISUALS

1. **Specifying** About how many captured Africans were taken to the British colonies in North America?

2. **Explaining** Why do you think so many people died during the Middle Passage?

John Locke One of the earliest and most influential Enlightenment writers was **John Locke.** His contract theory of government and natural rights profoundly influenced the thinking of American political leaders. In his work *Two Treatises of Government,* Locke attempted to use reason to discover natural laws that applied to politics and society:

PRIMARY SOURCE

"123. If man in the state of nature be so free . . . why will he part with his freedom? . . . [T]he enjoyment of the property he has in this state is very unsafe, very unsecure. This makes him willing . . . to join in society with others . . . for the mutual *preservation* of their lives, liberties and estates. . . .

192. For no government can have a right to obedience from a people who have not freely consented to it; which they can never be supposed to do till . . .

they are put in a full state of liberty to choose their government. . . ."

—from *Two Treatises of Government*

Equally important was Locke's *Essay on Human Understanding.* In this work he argued that, contrary to what most Christians believed, people were not born sinful. Instead, their minds were blank slates that could be shaped by society and education, making people better. These ideas, that all people have rights and that society can be improved, became core beliefs in American society.

Rousseau and Montesquieu French thinker Jean Jacques Rousseau carried Locke's ideas further. In *The Social Contract,* he argued that a government should be formed by the consent of the people, who would then make

PRIMARY SOURCE
The Trial of John Peter Zenger, 1735

In 1733 John Peter Zenger began printing the *New York Weekly Journal,* a newspaper highly critical of New York Governor William Cosby. Unable to identify the anonymous writers and publisher, Cosby ordered Zenger's arrest for printing libel. The jury found Zenger not guilty. In doing so, the jury engaged in "jury nullification." Zenger was clearly guilty—but the jury, in effect, decided the law itself was wrong and refused to convict Zenger.

▲ *The Zenger case established a precedent for a free press in the colonies, and later in the United States.*

In his summation to the jury, Zenger's attorney Andrew Hamilton compared free speech and free press to freedom of religion and noted that liberty depends upon the ability to publish criticisms of the government:

PRIMARY SOURCE

". . . we well know that it is not two centuries ago that a man would have been burnt as an heretic for owning such opinions in matters of religion as are publicly wrote and printed at this day. . . . I think it is pretty clear that in New York a man may make very free with his God, but he must take special care what he says of his governor. It is agreed upon by all men that this is a reign of liberty, and while men keep within the bounds of truth I hope they may with safety both speak and write their sentiments of the conduct of men in power. I mean of that part of their conduct only which affects the liberty or property of the people under their administration; were this to be denied, then the next step may make them slaves; For what notions can be entertained of slavery beyond that of suffering the greatest injuries and oppressions without the liberty of complaining, or if they do, to be destroyed, body and estate, for so doing?"

—from *A Brief Narrative of the Case and Trial of John Peter Zenger*

DBQ Document-Based Questions

1. **Interpreting** What point is Hamilton making when he says that "a man may make very free with his God," but must be careful about what he says about the governor?

2. **Identifying Central Issues** What does Hamilton say will happen if people are not allowed to express their opinions about those in the government?

their own laws. Another influential writer was **Baron Montesquieu.** In his work, *The Spirit of Laws,* Montesquieu suggested that there were three types of political power—executive, legislative, and judicial. These powers should be separated into different branches to protect people's liberty:

PRIMARY SOURCE

"In order to have this liberty, it is necessary the government be so constituted as one man need not be afraid of another.

When the legislative and executive powers are united in the same body of magistrates, there can be no liberty. . . .

Again, there is no liberty, if the judiciary power be not separated from the legislative and executive. Were it joined with the legislative, the life and liberty of the subject would be exposed to arbitrary [control], for the judge would be then the legislator. Were it joined to the executive power, the judge might behave with violence and oppression."

—from *The Spirit of Laws*

Montesquieu's ideas were widely debated. They had a great influence on the leaders who wrote the United States Constitution.

The Great Awakening

While some Americans turned away from a religious world view, others renewed their Christian faith. Many Americans embraced a European religious movement called **pietism,** which stressed an individual's piety (devoutness) and an emotional union with God. Throughout the colonies, ministers held **revivals**—large public meetings for preaching and prayer. This **widespread** resurgence of religious fervor became known as the Great Awakening.

In 1734 a Massachusetts preacher named **Jonathan Edwards** helped launch the Great Awakening. In powerful, terrifying sermons, he invoked the "forbearance of an incensed [angry] God" and argued that a person had to repent and convert. His emotional, as opposed to rational, style of preaching was typical of the fervor of the Great Awakening. **George Whitefield,** an Anglican minister from England, also attracted and inspired many listeners.

The Great Awakening peaked around 1740. Many churches split into factions called the New Lights and the Old Lights. Those who embraced the new ideas—including Baptists, some Presbyterians and Congregationalists, and a new group called Methodists—won many converts, while traditional churches lost members.

In the South, the Baptists gained a strong following among poor farmers. Baptists also welcomed Africans at their revivals and condemned slavery. Despite violent attempts by planters to break up Baptist meetings, about 20 percent of Virginia's whites and thousands of enslaved Africans had become Baptists by 1775.

The Enlightenment and the Great Awakening had different origins, but both profoundly affected colonial society. The Enlightenment provided arguments against British rule. The Great Awakening undermined allegiance to traditional authority.

✔ **Reading Check** **Determining Cause and Effect** Why did the Great Awakening cause division in established churches?

Section 5 REVIEW

Vocabulary

1. **Explain** the significance of: Cotton Mather, slave code, Stono Rebellion, rationalism, John Locke, Baron Montesquieu, pietism, revival, Jonathan Edwards, George Whitefield.

Main Ideas

2. **Describing** What was slavery like in the early colonies?

3. **Identifying** What are two beliefs of John Locke that later became core American values?

Critical Thinking

4. **Big Ideas** What factors and motivations brought people to the American colonies in the 1700s?

5. **Organizing** Use a graphic organizer similar to the one below to explain the reasons for the population increase in the colonies in the 1700s.

Factors Contributing to Colonial Population Increase

6. **Analyzing Visuals** Examine the map on pages 44–45. In which area of the Americas did African Americans become the greatest percentage of the population?

Writing About History

7. **Persuasive Writing** Suppose that you are a German immigrant to the colonies in 1725. Write a letter to relatives in Germany explaining what your life in the colonies has been like and encouraging them to join you.

History ONLINE

Study Central™ To review this section, go to <u>glencoe.com</u> and click on Study Central.

Causes of European Exploration

- The Crusades broaden European horizons and stimulate interest in luxury goods from Asia.
- The rise of towns and the growth of the merchant class enrich monarchs and make them less dependent on the nobility.
- Monarchs want to find trade routes to Asia, by passing Italy and the Muslim states.
- The Renaissance promotes a scientific view of the world.
- New technologies such as the compass and astrolabe make sea exploration possible.

▲ The English founded their first permanent colony in North America at Jamestown in 1607.

▲ Trading ships like these vessels of the Dutch East India Company carried goods around the world.

Causes of English Colonization

- The wealth Spain acquired from conquering the Aztec and mining gold encourages others to consider creating colonies.
- The Protestant Reformation in England leads to the rise of Puritans who are persecuted by the English government, as are Catholics and others who disagree with the Anglican Church.
- Puritans, Catholics, and other religious dissenters, such as the Quakers, seek religious freedom by migrating to America.
- The growth of trade and the rising demand for English wool lead to landowners evicting peasants so as to raise sheep. Some of the peasants migrate to America to escape poverty and obtain land.

Effects of European Colonization

- Europeans explore West Africa; they begin enslaving Africans and forcing them to work on sugarcane plantations.
- European explorers land in the Americas, map the eastern coastline, and begin exploring the interior.
- Beginning with Cortés, Spanish conquistadors conquer Mexico, Peru, and the Maya people of Central America.
- An exchange of plants, animals, goods, and ideas begins between Europe and the Americas; European diseases devastate Native American populations; American diseases spread to Europe.
- Spain establishes colonies in the Caribbean; France establishes colonies along the St. Lawrence River; England establishes colonies along the east coast, from Massachusetts to Georgia.
- Cash crops, such as rice, tobacco, and sugarcane, allow Southern Colonies to flourish; they also lead to the rise of the slave trade.
- Triangular trade allows northern American colonies to prosper and leads to the rise of cities along the American East Coast.

▲ In the South, a plantation economy developed in which many planters grew rich by exporting their cash crops to Britain.

NEW YORK REGENTS EXAM PRACTICE

TEST-TAKING TIP

When possible, depending on the form of the test, underline or circle key words in the question stem so that you know what to focus on as you read the answer choices. For example, some questions ask for a specific number of items in an answer.

Part I

Directions (1–10): For each statement or question, write on a separate sheet of paper the number of the word or expression that, of those given, best completes the statement or answers the question.

1 What did the Aztecs demand from areas they conquered?

(1) praise
(2) maize
(3) silver
(4) tribute

2 The Reformation encouraged the creation of English colonies because

(1) the English monarchs wanted to banish all non-Anglicans.
(2) new religious groups sought religious freedom outside of England.
(3) Protestants wanted land for new churches.
(4) Martin Luther told his followers to leave their homes and start new lives.

3 In Roger Williams's colony of Rhode Island,

(1) only Puritans could worship publicly.
(2) the government controlled all aspects of daily life.
(3) different religious practices were tolerated.
(4) Native Americans were assimilated.

4 Because Pennsylvania was owned by William Penn, it was considered

(1) a charter colony.
(2) a joint-stock company.
(3) a proprietary colony.
(4) part of the headright system.

5 Bacon's Rebellion began because

(1) farmers wanted to take more land from Native Americans.
(2) farmers were tired of paying high taxes.
(3) farmers were not allowed to serve in the House of Burgesses.
(4) farmers wanted to acquire enslaved Africans.

6 The Iroquois Confederacy was formed to

(1) stop the constant warfare.
(2) unite against the English.
(3) better compete with the Algonquian peoples.
(4) invade the Great Lakes region.

7 At first slavery developed slowly in the colonies because

(1) English law made it illegal to enslave colonists.
(2) King Charles II granted a charter that encouraged the slave trade in the colonies.
(3) English law allowed Africans to sue for their freedom.
(4) English law did not allow slavery in the colonies.

8 The Treaty of Tordesillas established which of the following?

(1) European Christians would fight the Crusades to retake holy places from Muslims in the Middle East.
(2) Spain, Portugal, England, and France would all have equal rights to colonies in the Americas.
(3) The Aztec would surrender their lands and possessions to Hernán Cortés and the rulers of Spain.
(4) Spain would control everything west of a line of demarcation; Portugal would control everything to the east.

Need Extra Help?								
If You Missed Questions . . .	1	2	3	4	5	6	7	8
Go to Page . . .	6	24–25	30	32–33	36	11	44–45	18

[OVER]

Base your answer to question 9 on the map below and your knowledge of Chapter 1.

Settlement of the Colonies, 1587–1700

- Settled by 1660
- Settled by 1700
- Settled by 1760

N.H.
Portsmouth
Mass.
New York
Boston • Plymouth
Hartford • Providence
New Haven • R.I.
New Amsterdam
Conn.
Pennsylvania
Philadelphia • N.J.
Md. Del.
ATLANTIC
OCEAN
Virginia
Jamestown • Williamsburg
APPALACHIAN MOUNTAINS
North Carolina
N
W ← → E
S
South Carolina • Wilmington
0   200 kilometers
0   200 miles
Georgia • Charles Towne
Savannah
Lambert Azimuthal Equal-Area projection

9   Which of the following colonies had the largest settled areas by 1660?

(1) Massachusetts
(2) North Carolina
(3) New Hampshire
(4) Virginia

10 In the 1700s the English colonies were affected by a resurgence of religious zeal known as

(1) the Enlightenment.
(2) the Glorious Revolution.
(3) the Renaissance.
(4) the Great Awakening.

Part II Thematic Essay Question

Directions: Write a well-organized essay that includes an introduction, several paragraphs addressing the task below, and a conclusion.

Theme: European and Native American Interaction

The Spanish, English, and French who settled in the Americas each had a particular approach, generally, in how they related to or treated the native peoples they encountered.

Task:

Consider the interaction between Native Americans and each of the three groups of European colonists and

- Compare and contrast the interactions of each of the three groups with Native Americans
- Evaluate the lasting impact of colonization on Native American groups

Guidelines:

In your essay, be sure to:

- Develop all aspects of the task
- Support the theme with relevant facts, examples, and details
- Use a logical and clear plan of organization, including an introduction and a conclusion that are beyond a restatement of the theme

Part III Document-Based Question

This question is based on the accompanying documents. It is designed to test your ability to work with historical documents. Some of the documents have been edited for the purposes of the question. As you analyze the documents, take into account both the source of each document and any point of view that may be presented in the document.

Historical Context:

As they explored the Americas, Europeans encountered and interacted with the native peoples of the Americas.

Need Extra Help?		
If You Missed Questions . . .	9	10
Go to Page . . .	32	47

Task:

Using information from the documents and your knowledge of United States history, answer the questions that follow each document in Part A. Your answers to the questions will help you write the Part B essay, in which you will be asked to

- Discuss the overall attitude toward native people held by Europeans
- Evaluate the effectiveness of Penn's treaty with the Native Americans at establishing friendly relations and how this approach to establishing North American colonies was unusual

Part A
Short-Answer Questions

Directions: Analyze the documents and answer the short-answer questions that follow each document on a separate sheet of paper.

Document 1

"When the Spaniards were installed in the palace, they asked Motecuhzoma [Montezuma] about the city's resources and reserves. . . . They questioned him closely and then demanded gold. Motecuhzoma guided them to it. . . . When they arrived at the treasure house called Teucalco, the riches of gold and feathers were brought out to them. . . . Next they went to Motecuhzoma's storehouse, in the place called Totocalco, where his personal treasures were kept. The Spaniards grinned like little beasts and patted each other with delight. When they entered the hall of treasures, it was as if they had arrived in Paradise. They searched everywhere and coveted everything; they were slaves to their own greed. . . . They seized these treasures as if they were their own, as if this plunder were merely a stroke of good luck."

Source: *The Broken Spears: The Aztec Account of the Conquest of Mexico*

1 How does the author of this account characterize the Spanish?

Document 2

Source: Edward Hicks, *Penn's Treaty*, 1830–1840

2 What is William Penn most likely doing in this painting?

Part B
Essay

Directions: Reread the task box at the top left and write a well-organized essay that includes an introduction, several paragraphs, and a conclusion. Use evidence from the documents in your essay. Support your response with relevant facts, examples, and details. Include additional outside information.

Guidelines:
In your essay, be sure to:

- Develop all aspects of the task
- Incorporate information from the documents
- Incorporate relevant outside information
- Support the theme with relevant facts, examples, and details
- Use a logical and clear plan of organization, including an introduction and a conclusion that are beyond a restatement of the theme

For additional test practice, use Self-Check Quizzes—Chapter 1 at glencoe.com.

Need Extra Help?			
If You Missed Questions . . .	1	2	Essay
Go to Page . . .	20	32	32

The American Revolution

1754–1783

SECTION 1 The Colonies Fight for Their Rights

SECTION 2 The Revolution Begins

SECTION 3 The War for Independence

SECTION 4 The War Changes American Society

George Washington at Valley Forge

U.S. PRESIDENTS

U.S. EVENTS

WORLD EVENTS

1745   1755   1765

1754
- French and Indian War begins

1765
- Parliament passes the Stamp Act, triggering protests throughout the colonies

1770
- British troops fire on colonists in Boston Massacre

1748
- Montesquieu's *Spirit of Laws* is published

1751
- Chinese invade Tibet and control succession to the throne

1755
- Samuel Johnson's *Dictionary of the English Language* is published

1769
- Steam engine is patented by James Watt

Why Do People Rebel?

Even today, Americans grow frustrated when the government raises taxes. In the early colonial era, Americans grew accustomed to running their own affairs. So when Britain tried to reestablish control, tensions mounted over taxes and basic rights.

- *Why do you think colonists became angry at Britain?*
- *When do you think it is acceptable to rebel against a government?*

1781
- Cornwallis surrenders at Yorktown, marking the end of the Revolutionary War

1783
- Treaty of Paris is signed, officially recognizing the independence of the United States

1775
- First shots of the War are fired at Lexington and Concord

1776
- Declaration of Independence is signed

1775

1785

1776
- Adam Smith's treatise on mercantilism, *Wealth of Nations,* is published

1780
- Empress Maria Theresa of Austria-Hungary dies

FOLDABLES™

Generalizing on the American Revolution Create a Concept-Map Book Foldable that details the causes and the course of the American Revolutionary War. Select the most important causes of the war and list them inside one-half of the Concept-Map. Use the other half to list the outcomes of battles during the war.

American Revolution
Causes of the War | Course of the War

History ONLINE **Chapter Overview**
Visit glencoe.com to preview Chapter 2.

The Colonies Fight for Their Rights

Guide to Reading

Big Ideas
Struggles for Rights The colonists used economic protest to fight the power of the British Parliament.

Content Vocabulary
- customs duty (p. 57)
- inflation (p. 58)
- nonimportation agreement (p. 59)
- writ of assistance (p. 60)

Academic Vocabulary
- dominance (p. 54)
- substitute (p. 59)

People and Events to Identify
- Albany Plan of Union (p. 55)
- French and Indian War (p. 56)
- Stamp Act (p. 58)
- Sons of Liberty (p. 59)
- Townshend Acts (p. 60)
- Boston Massacre (p. 61)

Reading Strategy
Organizing Complete a graphic organizer similar to the one below by listing the causes of the French and Indian War.

NEW YORK CORE CURRICULUM
U.S. History and Government

Unit 2:
I.A.3.a Colonial charters and self-government: Mayflower Compact, town meetings, House of Burgesses, local government, property rights, enforceable contracts, Albany Plan of Union

In the mid-1700s, England and France fought a war for control of North America. Britain emerged from the conflict victorious. After the war Parliament's attempts to raise revenue from the colonies met with resistance and protests.

The French and Indian War

MAIN Idea Rivalry between France and England turned into a war for control of North America.

HISTORY AND YOU During the colonial era, France and England were frequently at war. Can you think of similar national conflicts today? Read on to learn about George Washington's role in the French and Indian War.

The French and English had been vying for **dominance** in Europe since the late 1600s, fighting three major wars between 1689 and 1748. Most of the fighting took place in Europe, but whenever France and England were at war, their colonies went to war as well. In 1754 a fourth struggle began.

The First Skirmish

In the 1740s, the British and French both became interested in the Ohio River valley. By crossing from Lake Ontario to the Ohio River and following the river south to the Mississippi River, the French could travel from New France to Louisiana very easily. Meanwhile, British fur traders had begun entering the Ohio River valley, and British land speculators—people who bought empty land hoping to sell it to settlers for a profit—had become interested in the region.

To block British claims in the region, the French built a chain of forts from Lake Ontario to the Ohio River. The British governor of Virginia tried to counter the French by building a British fort in western Pennsylvania. Before the British fort was completed, the French seized it and built Fort Duquesne at the site. Virginia's governor then asked George Washington, a young officer in the Virginia militia, to raise a force and expel the French.

As Washington's troops marched toward the Ohio River in the spring of 1754, they encountered a small French force near Great Meadows. After a brief battle, Washington retreated a short distance and built a stockade named Fort Necessity. A little over a month later, a large French force arrived and forced Washington to surrender. As the fighting between France and Britain expanded into a world war, the 22-year-old Washington became a hero in the colonies for his courageous attempt to resist the French.

NEWFOUNDLAND

Gulf of St. Lawrence

JOIN, or DIE.

▲ *After developing the Albany Plan, Benjamin Franklin drew this cartoon urging the colonies to stand together. A popular legend at the time said that a snake could put itself back together and live if it did so before sunset.*

NEW FRANCE

Sept. 18, 1759: British forces led by Wolfe capture Quebec

Sept. 8, 1760: French surrender Montreal

July 26, 1758: French surrender Louisbourg

ALGONQUIN

July 26, 1759: British troops capture Fort Carillon (Ticonderoga)

August 27, 1758: Fort Frontenac captured by the British

Fort Oswego

Lake Ontario

Fort Niagara

IROQUOIS CONFEDERACY

Lake Erie

New York

Albany

Maine (part of Mass.)

Port Royal

NOVA SCOTIA

Lake Champlain

Fall of 1755: Colonial troops are defeated at Crown Point

August 9, 1757: British surrender Fort William Henry

N.H.

Boston

Mass.

Conn. R.I.

October, 1755: British deport 6,000 Acadian farmers and disperse them among the colonies

ATLANTIC OCEAN

NEW FRANCE

July 9, 1755: Braddock defeated by French and Indian troops at Fort Duquesne

Pennsylvania

Philadelphia

Maryland

Virginia

New York

New Jersey

Delaware

Hudson R.

Ohio R.

July 4, 1754: Washington surrenders at Fort Necessity

— British advance
— French advance
✳ British victory
✳ French victory
□ Fort

0 200 kilometers
0 200 miles
Albers Equal-Area projection

Analyzing GEOGRAPHY

1. **Location** Where did most of the British victories occur?
2. **Movement** From which colonial port did the British fleet sail to conquer Quebec?

▲ *High cliffs protected Quebec, the capital of New France. As this painting depicts, British General James Wolfe found a path from the river up the steep cliffs. After defeating the French forces at Quebec, the British captured the city.*

The Albany Conference

Even before fighting started, the British government had urged its colonies to work together to prepare for the coming war. The government also suggested that the colonies negotiate an alliance with the Iroquois. The Iroquois controlled western New York—territory the French had to pass through to reach the Ohio River. In response, delegates from seven colonies met with Iroquois leaders at Albany, New York, in June 1754.

This meeting, known as the Albany Conference, achieved several things. Although the Iroquois refused an alliance with the British, they did promise to remain neutral. The colonies agreed that Britain should appoint one supreme commander of all British troops in the colonies. The conference also issued the **Albany Plan of Union,** a proposal developed by a committee led by Benjamin Franklin. The Plan of Union proposed that the colonies unite to form a federal government. Although the colonies rejected the plan, it showed that many colonial leaders had begun to think about joining together for their common defense.

The British Triumph

In 1755 the new British commander in chief, General Edward Braddock, arrived in Virginia with 1,400 British troops. After linking up with 450 local militia troops, Braddock appointed Lieutenant Colonel George Washington to serve as his aide. He then marched west intending to attack Fort Duquesne.

Seven miles from the fort, French and Native American forces ambushed the British. Braddock was killed. His troops panicked and only Washington saved them from disaster. As shots whizzed past him—leaving four holes in his hat and clothes—Washington rallied the men and organized a retreat.

The successful ambush emboldened the Delaware people, and they began attacking British settlers in western Pennsylvania. For the next two years, the **French and Indian War,** as it was called, raged along the frontier. In 1756 the fighting between Britain and France spread to Europe, where it later became known as the Seven Years' War.

Gradually, the British fleet cut off the flow of supplies and reinforcements to the colonies from France. The Iroquois, realizing the tide was turning in favor of the British, pressured the Delaware to end their attacks. With their Native American allies giving up, the French found themselves badly outnumbered. In 1759 a British fleet commanded by General James Wolfe sailed to Quebec, the capital of New France. After defeating the French troops defending the city, the British seized Quebec and took control of New France. Elsewhere in the world, the fighting continued. When the Spanish joined forces with the French in 1761, Britain seized Spain's colonies in Cuba and the Philippines.

The Treaty of Paris finally ended the war in 1763. Except for a few offshore islands, the treaty eliminated French power in North America. New France became part of the British Empire, as did all of Louisiana east of the Mississippi, except for New Orleans. To get Cuba and the Philippines back, Spain gave Florida to Britain. To compensate Spain, the French then signed a separate treaty giving the Spanish control of New Orleans and all of Louisiana west of the Mississippi.

✔ **Reading Check** **Examining** Why were the French and the British interested in the Ohio River valley?

Growing Discontent

MAIN Idea The British decision to stop colonists from settling new western lands and to impose new taxes led to widespread protests.

HISTORY AND YOU The English Bill of Rights guarantees certain individual rights. Can you recall some of these rights? Read on to learn how Parliament denied these rights to colonists.

Great Britain's victory in 1763 left the country deeply in debt. It had to pay not only the cost of the war but also the cost of governing and defending its new territories. Many British officials thought that the colonies should pay part of the costs, especially the cost of stationing British troops there. As the British government adopted new policies to solve its financial problems, resentment began to grow in the American colonies.

The Proclamation of 1763

In the spring of 1763, Pontiac, the chief of the Ottawa people, decided to go to war against the British. After uniting several Native American groups, including the Ottawa, Delaware, Shawnee, and Seneca peoples, Pontiac's forces attacked forts along the frontier and burned down several towns before British troops were able to stop them. Pontiac's War did not surprise British officials. They had been expecting trouble since 1758, when reports first indicated that settlers were moving into western Pennsylvania in defiance of the colony's treaty with the region's Native Americans.

British leaders did not want to bear the cost of another war. Many officials also owned shares in fur-trading companies operating in the region, and they knew a war would disrupt trade. They decided that the best solution was to limit western settlement until new treaties could be negotiated.

In early October, King George III issued the Proclamation of 1763. The Proclamation drew a line from north to south along the Appalachian Mountains and declared that colonists could not settle west of that line without the British government's permission. This enraged many farmers and land speculators, who wanted access to the land.

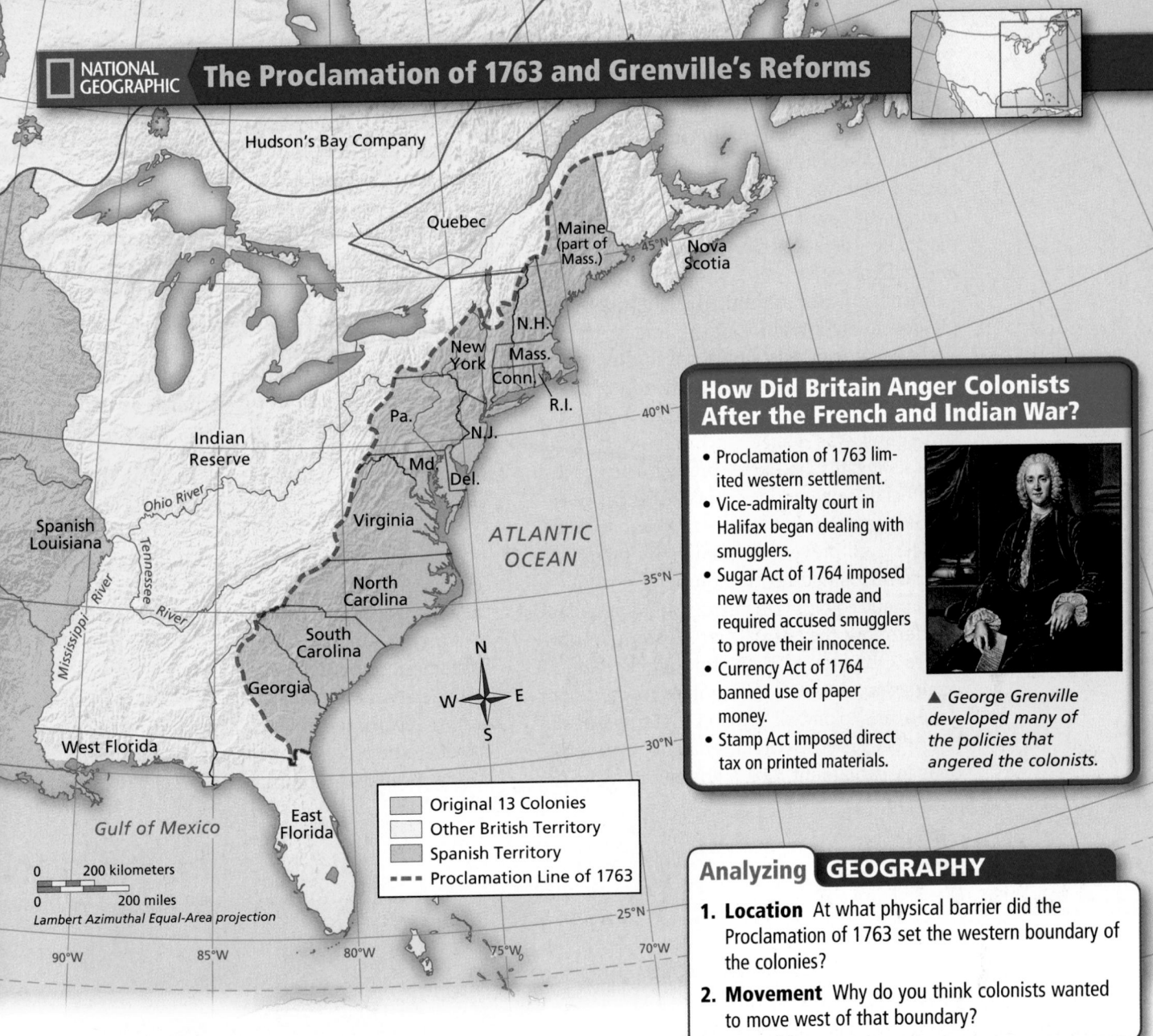

Hudson's Bay Company

Quebec

Maine (part of Mass.)

Nova Scotia

45°N

N.H.

New York

Mass.

Conn.

R.I.

Pa.

N.J.

Md.

Del.

Indian Reserve

Ohio River

Spanish Louisiana

Tennessee River

Mississippi River

Virginia

North Carolina

South Carolina

Georgia

West Florida

East Florida

Gulf of Mexico

ATLANTIC OCEAN

40°N

35°N

30°N

25°N

N
W E
S

0   200 kilometers
0   200 miles
Lambert Azimuthal Equal-Area projection

Original 13 Colonies
Other British Territory
Spanish Territory
- - - Proclamation Line of 1763

90°W   85°W   80°W   75°W   70°W

How Did Britain Anger Colonists After the French and Indian War?

- Proclamation of 1763 limited western settlement.
- Vice-admiralty court in Halifax began dealing with smugglers.
- Sugar Act of 1764 imposed new taxes on trade and required accused smugglers to prove their innocence.
- Currency Act of 1764 banned use of paper money.
- Stamp Act imposed direct tax on printed materials.

▲ George Grenville developed many of the policies that angered the colonists.

Analyzing GEOGRAPHY

1. **Location** At what physical barrier did the Proclamation of 1763 set the western boundary of the colonies?
2. **Movement** Why do you think colonists wanted to move west of that boundary?

Customs Reform

At the same time the Royal Proclamation Act was angering western farmers, eastern merchants were objecting to new tax policies. In 1763 George Grenville became prime minister and first lord of the Treasury. Grenville had to find a way to reduce Britain's debt and pay for the 10,000 British troops now stationed in North America.

Grenville knew that merchants were smuggling many goods into and out of the colonies without paying **customs duties,** taxes on imports and exports. He convinced Parliament to pass a law allowing smugglers to be tried at a new vice-admiralty court in Halifax, Nova

Scotia. Unlike colonial courts, where the juries were often sympathetic to smugglers, vice-admiralty courts were run by naval officers. These courts had no juries and did not follow British common law because Admiralty cases involved property not people. Still colonists objected, particularly to having to go to Nova Scotia to prove the legality of their property.

Among those tried by the vice-admiralty court was John Hancock. Hancock had made a fortune in the sugar trade, smuggling molasses from French colonies in the Caribbean. Defending Hancock was a young lawyer named John Adams. Adams argued that the use of vice-admiralty courts denied colonists their rights as British citizens.

The Sugar Act

In addition to stepping up enforcement of customs duties, Grenville introduced the American Revenue Act of 1764, better known as the Sugar Act. The act raised the tax rates on imports of raw sugar and molasses. It also placed new taxes on silk, wine, coffee, pimento, and indigo.

Merchants throughout the colonies complained to Parliament that the Sugar Act hurt trade. Many were also furious that the act violated several traditional English rights. Under the act, the property of merchants accused of smuggling was seized and presumed illegal until its legality had been proved. The act also let officials seize goods without due process—proper court procedures—in some circumstances, and prevented lawsuits by merchants whose goods had been improperly seized.

In many colonial cities, pamphlets circulated condemning the Sugar Act. In one pamphlet James Otis argued that although Parliament could impose taxes to regulate trade, taxing Americans to pay for British programs was different because the colonies had no representatives in Parliament. Otis's arguments gave rise to the popular expression, "No taxation without representation."

Despite the protests, the Sugar Act remained in force, and Grenville pressed ahead with other new policies. To slow **inflation,** Parliament passed the Currency Act of 1764. This act banned the use of paper money in the colonies, because it tended to lose its value quickly. The act angered colonial farmers and artisans who liked paper money precisely because it lost value quickly. They could use paper money to repay their loans, and since the money was not worth as much as when they borrowed it, the loans were easier to pay back.

The Stamp Act Crisis

Although the Sugar Act began to bring in revenue for Britain, Grenville did not believe it would cover all of the government's expenses in America. To raise more money, he asked Parliament to pass the **Stamp Act.**

Enacted in March 1765, the Stamp Act taxed almost all printed materials, including newspapers, pamphlets, posters, wills, mortgages, deeds, licenses, diplomas, and even playing

PAST & PRESENT

Protesting Government Actions

Americans have a long tradition of exercising freedom of speech and assembly to protest unpopular government actions. In 1765, for example, the British Stamp Act enraged the colonists. Many, like Patrick Henry of Virginia, spoke publicly against the act. At the same time, groups such as the Sons of Liberty organized demonstrations and other forms of protest. The tradition continues today. In Seattle, Washington, in 2002, thousands of angry protesters demonstrated for days against United States involvement in the World Trade Organization (WTO). These demonstrators believed the WTO's support for globalization damages local economies at home and abroad.

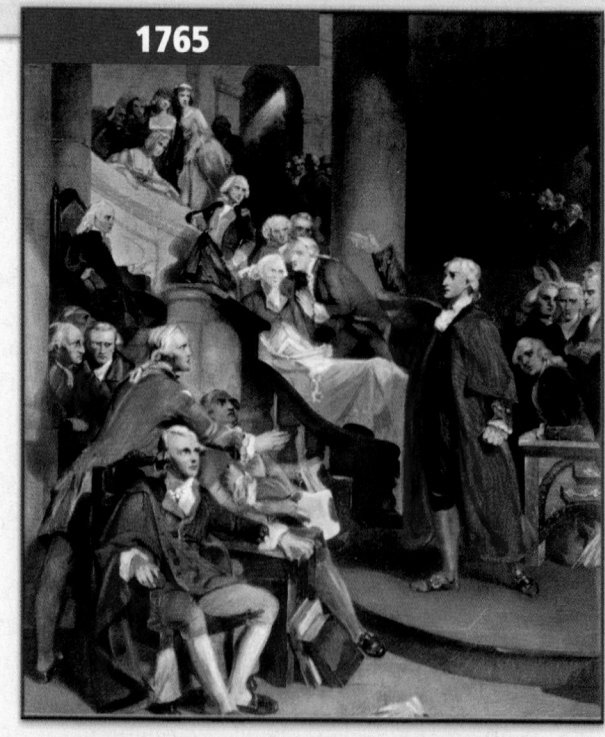

1765

▲ *Patrick Henry speaks out in protest against the Stamp Act in the Virginia House of Burgesses.*

cards. Unlike previous taxes, which had always been imposed on trade, the stamp tax was a direct tax—the first Britain had ever levied on the colonists.

As word of the Stamp Act spread through the colonies in the spring of 1765, a huge debate began. Roused by Patrick Henry's speeches, the Virginia House of Burgesses passed resolutions declaring that Virginians were entitled to the rights of British people and could be taxed only by their own representatives. Other colonial assemblies passed similar resolutions.

By the summer of 1765, a group called the **Sons of Liberty** was organizing huge demonstrations and intimidating stamp distributors. In August, a crowd in Boston hung effigies—crude stuffed figures meant to represent persons—of several British officials, including Boston's stamp agent.

In October, representatives from nine colonies met for what became known as the Stamp Act Congress. Together, they issued the Declaration of Rights and Grievances, drafted by a wealthy lawyer from Pennsylvania named John Dickinson. The resolutions declared that because taxation depended upon representation, only the colonists' political representa-

tives, and not Parliament, had the right to tax them. The congress further petitioned King George III for relief and asked Parliament to repeal the Stamp Act.

When the Stamp Act went into effect on November 1, 1765, the colonists ignored it. Instead, they began to boycott all British goods. People **substituted** sage and sassafras for imported tea. They stopped buying British cloth. In New York, 200 merchants signed a **nonimportation agreement,** pledging not to buy any British goods until Parliament repealed the Stamp Act.

The boycott had a powerful effect in Britain. Thousands of workers lost their jobs as orders from the colonies were cancelled, and British merchants could not collect money the colonies owed them. With protests mounting in both Britain and the American colonies, British lawmakers repealed the act in 1766. To assert its authority, Parliament passed the Declaratory Act. This act affirmed that Parliament had the power to make laws for the colonies.

Reading Check **Evaluating** How was the Stamp Act different from other taxes Britain had imposed on the colonies?

2002

▼ *Thousands gathered in Seattle, Washington, to protest policies of the World Trade Organization.*

MAKING CONNECTIONS

1. **Identifying Central Issues** What were the reasons for the protests in 1765 and 2002?

2. **Comparing** How were the protests in 1765 against the Stamp Act similar to the protests in 2002 against the WTO policies?

The Townshend Acts

MAIN Idea Colonists continued to deny that Parliament had the right to tax them and began organizing resistance to new taxes.

HISTORY AND YOU Have you ever disagreed with a policy at your school? Did you speak up about it? Read on to learn how the colonists reacted to the Townshend Acts.

During the Stamp Act crisis, Britain's financial problems worsened. Protests in Britain forced Parliament to lower property taxes there, yet somehow the government had to pay for its troops in America. In 1767 Charles Townshend, the new chancellor of the Exchequer, introduced new regulations and taxes. These came to be called the **Townshend Acts.**

One of the Townshend Acts was the Revenue Act of 1767. This act put new customs duties on glass, lead, paper, paint, and tea imported by the colonies. Violators of the Revenue Act had to face trial in vice-admiralty courts, which did not have juries or follow the common law.

The Townshend Acts, like the Sugar Act, also allowed officials to seize private property under certain circumstances without following due process.

To help customs officers arrest smugglers, the Revenue Act legalized the use of **writs of assistance.** The writs were general search warrants that enabled customs officers to enter any location during the day to look for evidence of smuggling.

Action and Reaction

The Townshend Acts infuriated many colonists. During the winter of 1767–1768, John Dickinson published a series of essays entitled *Letters From a Farmer in Pennsylvania.* Dickinson reasserted that only assemblies elected by the colonists had the right to tax them. In addition, he called on the colonies to become "firmly bound together" to "form one body politic" to resist the Townshend Acts.

Less than a month after Dickinson's first essay appeared, the Massachusetts assembly

People IN HISTORY

Samuel Adams
1722–1803

A passionate defender of colonial rights, Boston's Sam Adams was either a saint or a scoundrel—depending on who was describing him. Adams enjoyed his reputation as a fiery agitator. "Where there is a spark of patriotic fire," he once declared, "we will enkindle it."

Born in Boston, Adams graduated from Harvard College in 1740. He briefly studied law, worked as a clerk and merchant, and managed a brewery before being elected tax collector for Boston. As tensions with Britain increased, Adams discovered his true talents: speaking out against British tax laws and organizing resistance against them. He helped organize the Boston chapter of the Sons of Liberty. Adams forged an anti-British alliance of merchants, lawyers, and other members of the social elite with artisans, shopkeepers, and common laborers, all of whom worked together to protest British tax policies.

How did Sam Adams become a leader in the protests against British tax laws?

Sam Adams played an important role in organizing resistance to the Stamp Act and the Townshend Acts in Boston. To the right, an engraving shows protestors in Boston burning British stamps. The British cartoon above shows George Grenville carrying a tiny coffin labeled "Miss Ame-Stamp born 1765 died 1766."

began organizing resistance against Britain. Among the leaders of this resistance was Sam Adams, cousin of John Adams. In February 1768, Sam Adams, with the help of James Otis, drafted a "circular letter" for the Massachusetts assembly to pass and circulate to other colonies criticizing the Townshend Acts. British officials ordered the Massachusetts assembly to withdraw the letter. The assembly refused. Furious, the British government ordered the Massachusetts assembly dissolved. In August 1768, the merchants of Boston and New York responded by signing nonimportation agreements, promising not to import any goods from Britain. Philadelphia's merchants joined the boycott in March 1769.

In May 1769 Virginia's House of Burgesses passed the Virginia Resolves, stating that only the House could tax Virginians. When Britain dissolved the House of Burgesses, its leaders—including George Washington, Patrick Henry, and Thomas Jefferson—immediately called the members to a convention. This convention then passed a nonimportation law, blocking the sale of British goods in Virginia.

As the boycott spread, Americans again stopped drinking British tea and buying British cloth. Women's groups, known as the Daughters of Liberty, began spinning their own rough cloth, called "homespun." Wearing homespun became a sign of patriotism. Throughout the colonies, the Sons of Liberty encouraged people to support the boycotts. In 1769 colonial imports from Britain declined sharply from what they had been in 1768.

The Boston Massacre

In the fall of 1768, as violence against customs officers in Boston increased, Britain dispatched roughly 1,000 troops to the city to maintain order. Bostonians referred to the British troops stationed there as "lobster backs" because of the red coats they wore. Crowds constantly heckled and harassed the troops. On March 5, 1770, a crowd of colonists began taunting and throwing snowballs at a British soldier guarding a customs house. His call for help brought Captain Thomas Preston and a squad of soldiers.

In the midst of the tumult, the troops began firing into the crowd. According to accounts, the first colonist to die was a man of African and Native American descent known as both Michael Johnson and Crispus Attucks. When the smoke cleared, three people lay dead, two more would die later, and six others were wounded. The shootings became known as the **Boston Massacre.** Colonial newspapers portrayed the British as tyrants who were willing to kill people who stood up for their rights.

News of the Boston Massacre raced like lightning across the colonies. It might have set off a revolution, but only a few weeks later, news arrived that the British had repealed almost all of the Townshend Acts. Parliament kept one tax—a tax on tea—to uphold its right to tax the colonies. At the same time, it allowed the colonial assemblies to resume meeting. Peace and stability returned to the colonies, but only temporarily.

✓ **Reading Check** **Examining** What was stated in the Virginia Resolves passed by Virginia's House of Burgesses?

Section 1 REVIEW

Vocabulary

1. **Explain** the significance of: Albany Plan of Union, French and Indian War, customs duty, inflation, Stamp Act, Sons of Liberty, nonimportation agreement, Townshend Acts, writ of assistance, Boston Massacre.

Main Ideas

2. **Explaining** What did the Albany Plan of Union demonstrate?

3. **Describing** How did the colonists fight the Stamp Act, and what was the result?

4. **Stating** What did John Dickinson suggest that the colonies should do in his *Letters From a Farmer in Pennsylvania?*

Critical Thinking

5. **Big Ideas** What argument did the Stamp Act Congress make in protest against the British taxes?

6. **Categorizing** Use a graphic organizer similar to the one below to list the acts passed by the British Parliament and the colonists' reactions to each.

Act → Colonists' Reactions
——— → ———
——— → ———
——— → ———
——— → ———
——— → ———

7. **Analyzing Visuals** Study the political cartoon on page 55, and then summarize its main idea.

Writing About History

8. **Persuasive Writing** Suppose that you are a member of the Sons of Liberty. Write a pamphlet explaining what your group does and urging other colonists to join.

History ONLINE

Study Central™ To review this section, go to glencoe.com and click on Study Central.

Boston: Hotbed of Revolution

The growing dispute between colonists and British authorities centered on the extent of Parliament's power over the colonies, particularly the power to levy taxes. Boston was a center of protest against British policies. When, on the night of March 5, 1770, British soldiers fired into a crowd, killing or injuring 11 people, colonists were quick to declare the event a "massacre," even though exactly what occurred is debatable.

Study these primary sources and answer the questions that follow.

PRIMARY SOURCE 1

Engraving, 1774

▼ *"The Bostonians Paying the Excise-man, or Tarring and Feathering" depicts the Sons of Liberty tarring and feathering a British customs officer.*

PRIMARY SOURCE 2

Political Essay, 1767

"From what has been said, I think this uncontrovertible conclusion may be deduced, that when a ruling state obliges a dependent state to take certain commodities from her alone, it is implied in the nature of that obligation; is essentially requisite to give it the least degree of justice; and is inseparably united with it, in order to preserve any share of freedom to the dependent state; that those commodities should never be loaded with duties, FOR THE SOLE PURPOSE OF LEVYING MONEY ON THE DEPENDENT STATE.

Upon the whole, the single question is, whether the parliament can legally impose duties to be paid by the people of these colonies only, FOR THE SOLE PURPOSE OF RAISING A REVENUE, on commodities which she obliges us to take from her alone, or, in other words, whether the parliament can legally take money out of our pockets, without our consent."

—John Dickinson, "Letter From a Farmer in Pennsylvania, to the Inhabitants of the British Colonies," *Pennsylvania Gazette*, December 10, 1767

PRIMARY SOURCE 3

Political Essay, 1774

"To suppose, that by sending out a colony, the nation established an independent power; that when, by indulgence and favour, emigrants are become rich, they shall not contribute to their own defence, but at their own pleasure; and that they shall not be included, like millions of their fellow subjects, in the general system of representation; involves such an accumulation of absurdity, as nothing but the show of patriotism could palliate.

He that accepts protection, stipulates obedience. We have always protected the Americans; we may therefore subject them to government.

The less is included in the greater. That power which can take away life, may seize upon property. The parliament may enact, for America, a law of capital punishment; it may therefore establish a mode and proportion of taxation."

—Samuel Johnson, *The Patriot*

PRIMARY SOURCE 4

Letter, 1770

"[T]he Mob proceeded to a [S]entinel posted upon the Custom House, at a small Distance from the Guard, and Attacked him. . . . Captain Preston . . . hearing the [S]entinel was in Danger of being Murdered, he detached a sergeant and twelve Men to relieve him. . . . This Party as well as the [S]entinel was immediately attacked, Some [colonists] throwing Bricks, Stones, Pieces of Ice and Snow-Balls at them, whilst others advanced up to their Bayonets, and endeavored to close with them, to use their Bludgeons and Clubs; calling out to [the soldiers] to fire if they dared, and provoking them to it by the most Opprobrious Language.

Captain Preston stood between the Soldiers and the Mob . . . using every conciliating Method to perswade [sic] them to retire peaceably. . . . All he could say had no Effect, and one of the Soldiers, receiving a violent Blow, instantly fired . . . and the Mob . . . attacked with greater Violence, continually Striking at the Soldiers and pelting them, and calling out to them to fire. The Soldiers at length perceiving their Lives in Danger, and hearing the Word Fire all round them, three or four of them fired one after another, and again three more in the same hurry and Confusion. . . .

Some have swore Captain Preston gave Orders to fire; others who were near, that the Soldiers fired without Orders from the Provocation they received. None can deny the Attack made upon the Troops, but differ in the Degree of violence in the Attack."

—Thomas Gage, commander in chief of all British
North American soldiers,
explaining the events of March 5, 1770

PRIMARY SOURCE 5

Engraving, 1770

▼ *The Bloody Massacre,* by Paul Revere

PRIMARY SOURCE 6

Newspaper Account, 1770

"Thirty or forty persons, mostly lads, being . . . gathered in King-street, Capt. Preston, with a party of men with charged bayonets, came from the main guard to the Commissioners house, the soldiers pushing their bayonets, crying, Make way! They took place by the custom-house, and continuing to push to drive the people off, pricked some in several places; on which [the colonists] were clamorous, and, it is said, threw snow-balls. On this, the Captain commanded them to fire, and more snow-balls coming, he again said, Damn you, Fire, be the consequence what it will! One solider then fired . . . [and] the soldiers continued the fire, successively, till 7 or 8, or as some say 11 guns were discharged."

—"A Particular Account of the Most Barbarous
and Horrid Massacre,"
Essex [Mass.] Gazette, March 6, 1770

DBQ Document-Based Questions

1. **Identifying** Consider the image presented in Source 1 from a British point of view. What is going on in the picture? What image of American colonists is presented?

2. **Contrasting** Compare the arguments made in Source 2 and Source 3. How do they differ on the right of Parliament to tax the colonists?

3. **Contrasting** How do the accounts of the events of March 5, 1770, differ in Source 4 and Source 6? Which do you find more convincing?

4. **Analyzing** How does the engraving in Source 5 portray the Boston Massacre? Does this depiction more accurately reflect the account given in Source 4 or Source 6? Why?

Section 2

The Revolution Begins

Guide to Reading

Big Ideas
Government and Society The colonists formed the Continental Congress to act as a government during the American Revolution.

Content Vocabulary
• committee of correspondence (p. 64)
• minuteman (p. 68)

Academic Vocabulary
• enforce (p. 67)
• submit (p. 73)

People and Events to Identify
• Boston Tea Party (p. 66)
• Intolerable Acts (p. 67)
• Loyalist (p. 68)
• Patriot (p. 68)
• Battle of Bunker Hill (p. 70)
• Thomas Paine (p. 73)
• Declaration of Independence (p. 73)

Reading Strategy
Organizing Use the major headings of the section to create an outline similar to the one below, with information about the rising tensions between the colonies and Britain.

```
The Revolution Begins
I. Massachusetts Defies Britain
   A.
   B.
   C.
   D.
II.
```

NEW YORK CORE CURRICULUM
U.S. History and Government

Unit 2:
I.A.4.a Causes of the Revolution
I.A.4.b Revolutionary ideology (republican principles, natural rights)
I.A.4.c Revolutionary leaders: Benjamin Franklin, George Washington, John Adams, Samuel Adams, Patrick Henry

After years of escalating tensions, a true revolt against British rule began in the colonies in the 1770s. The colonists established a new government for themselves and organized militias to combat what they saw as British tyranny.

Massachusetts Defies Britain

MAIN Idea When Parliament punished Massachusetts for the Boston Tea Party, the colonists organized the First Continental Congress.

HISTORY AND YOU Is it ever acceptable to break the law to make a political point? Read how some colonists responded to unpopular laws.

Despite the tragedy of the Boston Massacre, the British decision to repeal the Townshend Acts had ended another crisis in colonial relations. For more than two years, the situation remained calm. Then, in the spring of 1772, a new crisis began. Britain introduced several new policies that again ignited the flames of rebellion in the American colonies. This time the fire could not be put out.

The *Gaspee* Affair

After Britain repealed the Townshend Acts, trade with the American colonies resumed, and so did smuggling. To intercept smugglers, the British sent customs ships to patrol North American waters. One such ship was the *Gaspee,* stationed off the coast of Rhode Island. Many Rhode Islanders hated the commander of the *Gaspee* because he often searched ships without a warrant and sent his crew ashore to seize food without paying for it. In June 1772, when the *Gaspee* ran aground, some 150 colonists seized and burned the ship.

The attack outraged the British. They sent a commission to investigate and gave it authority to take suspects to Britain for trial. This angered the colonists, who believed it violated their right to a trial by a jury of their peers. Rhode Island's assembly then sent a letter to the other colonies asking for help.

After the Virginia House of Burgesses received the letter in March 1773, one of its members, Thomas Jefferson, suggested that each colony create a **committee of correspondence** to communicate with the other colonies about British activities. These committees of correspondence helped unify the colonies and shape public opinion. They also helped colonial leaders coordinate their plans for resisting the British.

The Boston Tea Party, December 1773

Some 150 raiders disguised themselves as Native Americans, boarded the British ships, and threw the tea overboard.

A large crowd gathered on the pier to cheer the raiders and to make it difficult for any British troops that might arrive to get to the ships.

▲ *This lithograph, titled* The Destruction of Tea at Boston Harbor, *was created by engravers Currier & Ives in 1846. The engravers depict the scene in daylight—most likely to make the image clearer—although it happened at night.*

What Were the Coercive Acts?

Britain responded to the Boston Tea Party with four acts intended to punish Massachusetts and reassert British authority:

1. Boston Port Act
   - Closed the port of Boston until Massachusetts paid for the tea
2. Massachusetts Government Act
   - Banned town meetings
   - Required all sheriffs, council members, and judges to be appointed by the British governor
3. Administration of Justice Act
   - Allowed trials of British soldiers and officials to be transferred to Britain to protect them from American juries
4. Quartering Act
   - Required local officials to lodge British troops at the scene of a disturbance; in private homes, if necessary

Analyzing VISUALS

1. **Explaining** What was the purpose of the Boston Port Act?
2. **Drawing Conclusions** Why would the British want to ban town meetings?

The Boston Tea Party

In May 1773, Britain's new prime minister, Lord North, made a serious mistake. He decided to help the struggling British East India Company. Corrupt management and costly wars in India had put the company deeply in debt. At the same time, British taxes on tea had encouraged colonial merchants to smuggle in cheaper Dutch tea. As a result, the company had in its warehouses over 17 million pounds of tea that it needed to sell quickly.

To help the company, Parliament passed the Tea Act of 1773. The Tea Act refunded four-fifths of the taxes the company had to pay to ship tea to the colonies, leaving only the Townshend Tax. East India Company tea could now be sold at lower prices than smuggled Dutch tea. The act also allowed the East India Company to sell directly to shopkeepers, bypassing American merchants who usually distributed the tea. The Tea Act enraged the colonial merchants, who feared it was the first step by the British to squeeze them out of business.

In October 1773, the East India Company shipped 1,253 chests of tea to Boston, New York, Philadelphia, and Charles Town. The committees of correspondence decided that they must not allow the tea to be unloaded. When the first shipments arrived in New York and Philadelphia, the colonists forced the agents for the East India Company to return home with the tea. In Charles Town, customs officers seized the tea and stored it in a local warehouse where it remained unsold.

The most dramatic event occurred in Boston Harbor, shortly after the tea ships arrived. On December 17, 1773, the night before customs officials planned to bring the tea ashore, a group of approximately 150 men secretly gathered at the Boston dock. One of the men was George Hewes, a struggling Boston shoemaker who had grown to despise the British. Hewes had taken offense when British soldiers stopped and questioned him on the street and when they refused to pay him for shoes. After witnessing the Boston Massacre, his hatred grew deeper and more political.

So, after he "daubed his face and hands with coal dust, in the shop of a blacksmith," Hewes gladly joined the other volunteers as they prepared to sneak aboard several British ships anchored in Boston Harbor and destroy the tea stored on board:

PRIMARY SOURCE

"When we arrived at the wharf . . . they divided us into three parties for the purpose of boarding the three ships which contained the tea. . . . We then were ordered by our commander to open the hatches and take out all the chests of tea and throw them overboard, and we immediately proceeded to execute his orders, first cutting and splitting the chests with our tomahawks, so as thoroughly to expose them to the effects of the water. . . . In about three hours . . . we had thus broken and thrown over board every tea chest . . . in the ship."

—quoted in *The Spirit of 'Seventy-Six*

Several thousand people on the shore cheered as Hewes and the other men dumped 342 chests of tea into Boston Harbor. Although the men were disguised as Native Americans, many knew who they were. A witness later testified that Sam Adams and John Hancock were among those who boarded the ships. The raid came to be called the **Boston Tea Party.**

The Coercive Acts

The Boston Tea Party was the last straw for the British. King George III informed Lord North that "concessions have made matters worse. The time has come for compulsion." In the spring of 1774, Parliament passed four new

Countdown to Revolution, 1763–1776

1763
Proclamation of 1763 bans colonists from settling west of the Proclamation Line

1765
Stamp Act Congress issues Declaration of Rights and Grievances

1767
Townshend Acts impose new taxes on trade goods; violators to be tried in vice admiralty courts

1768
Colonial merchants begin nonimportation campaign, refuse to import British goods; Daughters of Liberty help by spinning cloth

1764 **1766** **1768** **1770**

1764
Sugar Act imposes new taxes on trade; James Otis argues that taxation without representation violates colonists' liberties

1765
The Stamp Act imposes taxes on printed materials; Sons of Liberty organize protests and boycotts

1770
British troops shoot colonists at Boston Massacre; most Townshend Acts are repealed

laws that came to be known as the Coercive Acts. These laws were intended to punish Massachusetts and end colonial challenges to British authority.

The first act was the Boston Port Act. It shut down Boston's port until the city paid for the tea that had been destroyed. The second act was the Massachusetts Government Act. It required all council members, judges, and sheriffs in Massachusetts to be appointed by the governor instead of being elected. This act also banned most town meetings.

The third act, the Administration of Justice Act, allowed the governor to transfer trials of British soldiers and officials to Britain to protect them from American juries. The final act was a new Quartering Act. It required local officials to provide lodging for British soldiers, in private homes if necessary. To **enforce** the acts, the British moved 2,000 troops to New England and appointed General Thomas Gage as the new governor of Massachusetts.

The Coercive Acts violated several traditional English rights, including the right to trial by a jury of one's peers and the right not to have troops quartered in one's home. The king was also not supposed to maintain a standing army in peacetime without Parliament's consent. Although the British Parliament had authorized the troops, colonists believed that their own local assemblies had to give their consent as well.

In July 1774, a month after the last Coercive Act had become law, the British introduced the Quebec Act. This law had nothing to do with events in the American colonies, but it, too, angered colonists. The Quebec Act stated that a governor and council appointed by the king would run Quebec. It also extended Quebec's boundaries to include much of what is today Ohio, Illinois, Michigan, Indiana, and Wisconsin. If colonists moved west, they would have to live in territory where they had no elected assembly. The Quebec Act, coming so soon after the Coercive Acts, seemed to imply that the British were trying to seize control of the colonial governments.

As other colonies learned of the harsh measures imposed on Massachusetts, they reacted with sympathy and outrage. The Coercive Acts and the Quebec Act together became known as the **Intolerable Acts.**

1773
At Boston Tea Party, colonists toss British tea into Boston Harbor

1774
Britain imposes Coercive Acts; First Continental Congress meets, passes the Suffolk Resolves, and issues Declaration of Rights and Grievances

January 1776
Tom Paine publishes *Common Sense*, arguing for independence

July 4, 1776
Congress issues Declaration of Independence

1772   1774   1776

1775
British battle colonial militia at Lexington and Concord; Second Continental Congress meets, selects George Washington to head Continental Army

Analyzing TIME LINES

1. **Stating** When and under what circumstances did the concept of "taxation without representation" first appear?

2. **Specifying** Which occurred first—the Boston Tea Party or the battles at Lexington and Concord?

The First Continental Congress

In May 1774, the Virginia House of Burgesses declared the arrival of British troops in Boston a "military invasion" and called for a day of fasting and prayer. When Virginia's governor dissolved the House of Burgesses, its members went to a nearby tavern and issued a resolution urging the colonies to suspend trade with Britain and to send delegates to a colonial congress to discuss what to do next. At least one burgess, Patrick Henry, was ready for war: "I know not what course others may take, but as for me, give me liberty or give me death!"

In New York and Rhode Island, similar calls for a congress had already been made. The committees of correspondence coordinated the different proposals, and on September 5, 1774, the First Continental Congress met in Philadelphia. The 55 delegates to the Congress represented 12 of Britain's North American colonies. Florida, Georgia, Nova Scotia, and Quebec did not attend. The delegates from the 12 colonies represented a wide range of opinion. Moderate delegates opposed the Intolerable Acts but believed a compromise was possible. Other, more radical, delegates believed the time had come to fight.

The Congress's first order of business was to endorse the Suffolk Resolves. These resolutions, prepared by Bostonians and other residents of Suffolk County, Massachusetts, urged colonists not to obey the Coercive Acts. They also called on the people of Suffolk County to arm themselves and stop buying British goods.

While discussing what other steps to take, the Congress learned that the British had suspended the Massachusetts assembly. In response, the Congress voted to issue the Declaration of Rights and Grievances. The declaration expressed loyalty to the king, but it also condemned the Coercive Acts and stated that the colonies would form a nonimportation association. Several days later, the delegates approved the Continental Association, a plan for every county and town to form committees to enforce a boycott of British goods. The delegates then agreed to hold a second Continental Congress in May 1775 if the crisis had not been resolved.

Reading Check **Examining** How did the British react to the Boston Tea Party?

The Revolution Begins

MAIN Idea Colonists organized alternative governments and formed militias to oppose British "tyranny."

HISTORY AND YOU Your political views are partly shaped by your personal background. Read on to learn why some colonists supported the British while others fought for independence.

In October 1774, members of the suspended Massachusetts assembly defied the British and organized the Massachusetts Provincial Congress. They then formed the Committee of Safety and chose John Hancock to lead it, giving him the power to call up the militia. In effect, the Provincial Congress had made Hancock a rival governor to General Gage.

A full-scale rebellion was now underway. Militias began to drill and practice shooting. The town of Concord created a special unit of men trained and ready to "stand at a minute's warning in case of alarm." These were the famous **minutemen**. All through the summer and fall of 1774, British control of the colonies weakened as colonists created provincial congresses and militias raided military depots for ammunition and gunpowder. These rebellious acts infuriated British officials.

Loyalists and Patriots

Although many colonists did not agree with Parliament's policies, they were still loyal to the king and to Britain and believed that British law should be upheld. Americans who supported the British side in the conflict became known as **Loyalists** or Tories.

Loyalists came from all parts of American society. Many were government officials or Anglican ministers. Others were prominent merchants and landowners. Many backcountry farmers on the frontier remained loyal as well, because they regarded the king as their protector against the planters and merchants who controlled the local governments.

On the other side were those who believed that the British had become tyrants. These people were known as **Patriots** or Whigs. Patriots also represented a wide cross-section of society. They were artisans, farmers, merchants, planters, lawyers, and urban workers. The Patriots were strong in New England and Virginia, while

◀ This engraving, one of a famous series by Amos Doolittle, shows the initial exchange of fire on Lexington Green between the colonists and the British soldiers.

▼ Later in the battle at Lexington, the colonial militia took cover behind stone walls, and harassed the British as they moved out of town toward Concord.

3. Colonial militia inflict 14 casualties on British at Concord's North Bridge

4. In retreat to Boston, British suffer over 250 casualties, and Americans suffer 95

PRESCOTT MINUTEMEN

Concord

Lexington

Massachusetts

Menotomy (Arlington)

Medford

2. Revere is captured; Dawes turns back; Prescott gets through

Sudbury R.

1. April 19, 1775, fighting begins on Lexington Common: 8 Americans die, 10 are wounded

Mystic R.

REVERE

0   2 kilometers
0   2 miles
Albers Equal-Area projection

Cambridge

DAWES

Charles R.

Charlestown

Boston

Boston Harbor

Roxbury

← Colonial messengers	✶ American victory
← Colonial troops	✶ British victory
← British troops	� Bridge
←-- British retreat	

Analyzing GEOGRAPHY

1. **Movement** Which side suffered the highest number of casualties at Lexington and Concord?

2. **Location** About how far was Lexington from Boston?

most of the Loyalists lived in Georgia, the Carolinas, and New York. Political differences divided communities and even split families. The American Revolution was not simply a war between the Americans and the British. It was also a civil war between Patriots and Loyalists.

Even before the Revolution, Patriot groups brutally enforced the boycott of British goods. They tarred and feathered Loyalists, and broke up Loyalist gatherings. Loyalists fought back, but there were not as many of them and they were not as well organized. Caught between the two groups were many people, possibly a majority, who did not favor either side and would support whichever side won.

Lexington and Concord

In April 1775, the British government ordered General Gage to arrest the Massachusetts Provincial Congress, even if it meant risking armed conflict. Gage did not know where the Congress was sitting, so he decided to seize the militia's supply depot at Concord instead. On April 18, about 700 British troops set out for Concord on a road that took them through the town of Lexington.

Patriot leaders heard about the plan and sent Paul Revere and William Dawes to spread the alarm. The two men made it to Lexington and warned people that the British were coming. Along with a third man, Dr. Samuel Prescott, they then headed for Concord. A British patrol stopped Revere and Dawes, but Prescott got through in time to warn Concord.

On April 19, British troops arrived in Lexington and spotted some 70 minutemen lined up on the village green. The British marched onto the field and ordered them to disperse. The minutemen had begun to back away when a shot was fired; no one is sure by whom. The British soldiers then fired at the minutemen, killing 8 and wounding 10.

The British then headed to Concord, where they found that most of the military supplies had been removed. When they tried to cross the North Bridge on the far side of town, they ran into some 400 colonial militia. A fight broke out, forcing the British to retreat.

As the British headed back to Boston, militia and farmers fired at them from behind trees, stone walls, barns, and houses. By the time the British reached Boston, they had lost 99 men, and another 174 were wounded. The colonial forces had lost 49 militia, and another 46 were wounded. News of the fighting spread across the colonies. Militia from all over New England raced to the area to help fight the British. By May 1775, the militia had surrounded Boston, trapping the British.

The Second Continental Congress

Three weeks after the battles at Lexington and Concord, the Second Continental Congress met in Philadelphia. The first issue was defense. The Congress voted to "adopt" the militia army surrounding Boston, and they named it the Continental Army. On June 15, 1775, the Congress selected George Washington to command the new army.

Before Washington could get to his new command, however, the British landed reinforcements in Boston. Determined to gain control of the area, the British decided to seize the hills north of the city. Warned in advance, the militia acted first. On June 16, 1775, they dug in on Breed's Hill near Bunker Hill and began building a fort at the top.

The following day, General Gage sent 2,200 troops to take the hill. According to legend, an American commander named William Prescott told his troops, "Don't fire until you see the whites of their eyes." When the British closed to within 50 yards, the Americans fired. They stopped two British attacks and were forced to retreat only after running out of ammunition.

The **Battle of Bunker Hill,** as it came to be called, helped to build American confidence. It showed that the colonial militia could stand up to one of the world's most feared armies. The British suffered more than 1,000 casualties in the fighting. Shortly afterward, General Gage resigned and was replaced by General William Howe. The situation became a stalemate, with the British troops encircled by colonial militia.

Reading Check **Interpreting** Why was the Battle of Bunker Hill important to the Americans?

Debates IN HISTORY

Should the American Colonies Declare Independence?

Although it may seem like the only natural course today, in 1776 independence was not the obvious choice for the 13 British colonies. While many were fed up with British actions and thought that it was time to institute true self-rule, others felt loyalty to what they considered their mother country and wanted to pursue a resolution of their grievances through political and diplomatic, not military, means. British-born Thomas Paine was one who strongly supported independence, as he discussed in his famous pamphlet, *Common Sense.* American-born John Dickinson, while angered at the behavior of the British, expressed in a speech to the Congress his arguments against splitting from Great Britain.

The Decision to Declare Independence

MAIN Idea After more than a year of war, the Continental Congress issued the Declaration of Independence.

HISTORY AND YOU Have you ever tried to mediate a disagreement between siblings or friends? Read on to learn about the Olive Branch Petition and how it failed to achieve peace.

Despite the onset of fighting, many colonists in the summer of 1775 were not prepared to break away from Great Britain. Most members of the Second Continental Congress wanted the right to govern themselves, but they did not want to break with the British Empire. By 1776, however, opinions had changed. Frustrated by Britain's refusal to compromise, many Patriot leaders began to call for independence.

Efforts at Peace

In July 1775, as the siege of Boston continued, the Continental Congress sent a document known as the Olive Branch Petition to King George III. Written by John Dickinson, the petition stated that the colonies were still loyal to the king and asked him to call off hostilities and resolve the situation peacefully.

In the meantime, the radical delegates of the Congress convinced the body to order an attack on the British troops based in Quebec. They hoped the attack would convince the French in Quebec to rebel and join in fighting the British. The American forces captured the city of Montreal, but the French did not rebel.

History ONLINE
Student Web Activity Visit glencoe.com and complete the activity on the American Revolution.

YES

Thomas Paine
Writer

PRIMARY SOURCE

"It is the good fortune of many to live distant from the scene of present sorrow; . . . But let our imaginations transport us for a few moments to Boston. . . . The inhabitants of that unfortunate city who but a few months ago were in ease and affluence, have now no other alternative than to stay and starve, or turn out to beg. . . .

Men of passive tempers look somewhat lightly over the offenses of Britain and, still hoping for the best, are apt to call out, *Come, come we shall be friends again for all this.* But examine the passions and feelings of mankind; Bring the doctrine of reconciliation to the touchstone of nature, and then tell me whether you can hereafter love, honour, and faithfully serve the power that hath carried fire and sword into your land?"

—from *Common Sense*

NO

John Dickinson
Delegate, Continental Congress

PRIMARY SOURCE

"Even those Delegates who are not restrained by Instructions [from their legislatures] have no Right to establish an independent separate Government for a Time of Peace. . . . without a full & free Consent of the People plainly exprest [sic]. . . . We are now acting on a principle of the English Constitution in resisting the assumption or Usurpation of an unjust power. We are now acting under that Constitution. Does that Circumstance [support] its Dissolution? But granting the present oppression to be a Dissolution, the Choice of . . . Restoring it, or forming a new one is vested in our Constituents, not in Us. They have not given it to Us. We may pursue measures that will force them into it. But that implies not a Right so to force them."

—from *Letters of Delegates to Congress, 1774–1789*

DBQ Document-Based Questions

1. **Finding the Main Idea** What are the main ideas in Paine's argument?
2. **Paraphrasing** Why does Dickinson believe that the Congress has no right to form a new government?
3. **Assessing** Which argument do you think is the most logical? Explain.

Turning Point

▼ Colonists in Manhattan pull down a statue of King George III upon hearing the news of the Declaration.

▲ Benjamin Franklin, John Adams, and Thomas Jefferson are shown here working to draft the Declaration of Independence.

The Colonies Declare Independence

The Declaration of Independence was an important turning point in the political history of the world. Not until this event had a colony declared itself truly independent of its ruling nation in a written document that specified the legal and moral reasons for that separation. The precedent set by the Declaration and the American Revolution was repeatedly followed over the next two hundred years by other colonies and nations. Additionally, in the United States, minority groups and women would use the language of the Declaration in their arguments for increased equality and civil rights.

ANALYZING HISTORY Why was the Declaration of Independence a turning point in political history?

▲ In this 1779 English cartoon, a horse named "America" throws its rider, King George.

The attack on Quebec convinced British officials that there was no hope of reconciliation. When the Olive Branch Petition arrived in Britain, King George III refused to look at it. Instead he proclaimed that the colonies were now "open and avowed enemies" and ordered the military to suppress the rebellion in America.

With no compromise likely, the Continental Congress increasingly began to act like an independent government. It sent people to negotiate with the Native Americans and established a postal system, a Continental Navy, and a Marine Corps. By March 1776, the Continental Navy had raided the Bahamas and had begun seizing British merchant ships.

History ONLINE
Student Web Activity Visit glencoe.com and complete the activity on the Declaration of Independence.

The Fighting Spreads

As the Revolution began, Governor Dunmore of Virginia organized two Loyalist armies to assist the British troops in Virginia, one composed of white Loyalists, the other of enslaved Africans. Dunmore proclaimed that Africans enslaved by rebels would be freed if they fought for the Loyalists. The announcement convinced many Southern planters that the colonies had to declare independence. Otherwise, they might lose their lands and labor force. They also increased their efforts to raise a large Patriot army.

In December 1775, the Patriot troops attacked and defeated Dunmore's forces near Norfolk,

Virginia. The British then pulled their soldiers out of Virginia, leaving the Patriots in control. In North Carolina, Patriot troops dispersed Loyalists at the Battle of Moore's Creek in February 1776. The British then decided to seize Charles Town, South Carolina, but the city militia thwarted their attack.

While fighting raged in the South, Washington ordered his troops to capture the hills south of Boston. After the Americans seized the hills by surprise and surrounded Boston, the British navy evacuated the British troops, leaving the Patriots in control.

Despite their defeats, it was clear that the British were not backing down. In December 1775 the king issued the Prohibitory Act, shutting down trade with the colonies and ordering a naval blockade. The British also began expanding their army by recruiting mercenaries, or soldiers for hire, from Germany.

Common Sense and Independence

As the war dragged on, more and more Patriots began to think that the time had come to declare independence, although they feared that most colonists were still loyal to the king. In January 1776, however, public opinion began to change when **Thomas Paine** published a lively and persuasive pamphlet called *Common Sense*. Until *Common Sense* appeared, nearly everyone viewed Parliament, not the king, as the enemy. In *Common Sense,* Paine attacked King George III. Parliament, he wrote, did nothing without the king's support. Paine argued that monarchies had been set up by seizing power from the people. King George III was a tyrant, and it was time to declare independence:

PRIMARY SOURCE

"Everything that is right or reasonable pleads for separation. The blood of the slain, the weeping voice of nature cries, 'TIS TIME TO PART. . . . Every spot of the old world is over-run with oppression. Freedom hath been hunted round the globe . . . and England hath given her warning to depart. Oh receive the fugitive, and prepare in time an asylum for mankind."

—from *Common Sense*

Within three months, *Common Sense* had sold 100,000 copies. George Washington noted that "*Common Sense* is working a powerful change in the minds of men." One by one the provincial congresses and legislatures told their representatives at the Continental Congress to vote for independence.

In early July a committee comprised of John Adams, Benjamin Franklin, Roger Sherman, Robert Livingston, and Thomas Jefferson **submitted** a document that Jefferson drafted, explaining why it was time for independence. On July 4, 1776, the Continental Congress issued this **Declaration of Independence.** The colonies had now become the United States of America. The American Revolution had begun.

Reading Check **Analyzing** How did Thomas Paine help persuade colonists to declare independence?

Section 2 REVIEW

Vocabulary

1. **Explain** the significance of: committee of correspondence, Boston Tea Party, Intolerable Acts, minuteman, Loyalist, Patriot, Battle of Bunker Hill, Thomas Paine, Declaration of Independence.

Main Ideas

2. **Summarizing** What were the first two actions of the First Continental Congress?

3. **Explaining** What was significant about the battles at Lexington and Concord?

4. **Making Connections** What motivated the Southern colonists to join the Revolution?

Critical Thinking

5. **Big Ideas** After King George III rejected the Olive Branch Petition, in what ways did the Continental Congress begin to act like an independent government?

6. **Organizing** Use a graphic organizer similar to the one below to indicate ways in which colonists defied Britain after the repeal of the Townshend Acts.

Colonists Acts of Defiance

7. **Analyzing Visuals** Study the painting of the colonists toppling King George's statue on page 72. What did the colonists hope to accomplish by this act?

Writing About History

8. **Descriptive Writing** Suppose that you were a participant in the Boston Tea Party. Write a diary entry describing the event.

History ONLINE

Study Central™ To review this section, go to glencoe.com and click on Study Central.

THE DECLARATION OF INDEPENDENCE

In Congress, July 4, 1776. The unanimous Declaration of the thirteen united States of America,

[Preamble]

When in the Course of human events, it becomes necessary for one people to dissolve the political bands which have connected them with another, and to assume among the Powers of the earth, the separate and equal station to which the Laws of Nature and of Nature's God entitle them, a decent respect to the opinions of mankind requires that they should declare the causes which **impel** them to the separation.

[Declaration of Natural Rights]

We hold these truths to be self-evident, that all men are created equal, that they are **endowed** by their Creator with certain unalienable Rights, that among these are Life, Liberty, and the pursuit of Happiness.

That to secure these rights, Governments are instituted among Men, deriving their just powers from the consent of the governed,

That whenever any Form of Government becomes destructive of these ends, it is the Right of the People to alter or to abolish it, and to institute new Government, laying its foundation on such principles and organizing its powers in such form, as to them shall seem most likely to effect their Safety and Happiness. Prudence, indeed, will dictate that Governments long established should not be changed for light and transient causes; and accordingly all experience hath shown, that mankind are more disposed to suffer, while evils are sufferable, than to right themselves by abolishing the forms to which they are accustomed. But when a long train of abuses and usurpations, pursuing invariably the same Object evinces a design to reduce them under absolute **Despotism,** it is their right, it is their duty, to throw off such Government, and to provide new Guards for their future security.

[List of Grievances]

Such has been the patient sufferance of these Colonies; and such is now the necessity which constrains them to alter their former Systems of Government. The history of the

---

What It Means
The Preamble The Declaration of Independence has four parts. The Preamble explains why the Continental Congress drew up the Declaration.

impel *force*

What It Means
Natural Rights The second part, the Declaration of Natural Rights, states that people have certain basic rights and that government should protect those rights. John Locke's ideas strongly influenced this part. In 1690 Locke wrote that government was based on the consent of the people and that people had the right to rebel if the government did not uphold their right to life, liberty, and property.

endowed *provided*

despotism *unlimited power*

What It Means
List of Grievances The third part of the Declaration lists the colonists' complaints against the British government. Notice that King George III is singled out for blame.

present King of Great Britain is a history of repeated injuries and **usurpations,** all having in direct object the establishment of an absolute Tyranny over these States. To prove this, let Facts be submitted to a candid world.

He has refused his Assent to Laws, the most wholesome and necessary for the public good.

He has forbidden his Governors to pass Laws of immediate and pressing importance, unless suspended in their operation till his Assent should be obtained; and when so suspended, he has utterly neglected to attend to them.

He has refused to pass other Laws for the accommodation of large districts of people, unless those people would **relinquish** the right of Representation in the Legislature, a right **inestimable** to them and formidable to tyrants only.

He has called together legislative bodies at places unusual, uncomfortable, and distant from the depository of their Public Records, for the sole purpose of fatiguing them into compliance with his measures.

He has dissolved Representative Houses repeatedly, for opposing with manly firmness his invasions on the rights of the people.

He has refused for a long time, after such dissolutions, to cause others to be elected; whereby the Legislative Powers, incapable of **Annihilation,** have returned to the People at large for their exercise; the State remaining in the mean time exposed to all the dangers of invasion from without, and **convulsions** within.

He has endeavoured to prevent the population of these States; for that purpose obstructing the Laws for **Naturalization of Foreigners;** refusing to pass others to encourage their migrations hither, and raising the conditions of new Appropriations of Lands.

He has obstructed the Administration of Justice, by refusing his Assent to Laws for establishing Judiciary Powers.

He has made Judges dependent on his Will alone, for the **tenure** of their offices, and the amount and payment of their salaries.

He has erected a multitude of New Offices, and sent hither swarms of Officers to harass our people, and eat out their substance.

He has kept among us, in times of peace, Standing Armies without the Consent of our legislature.

He has affected to render the Military independent of and superior to the Civil Power.

He has combined with others to subject us to a jurisdiction foreign to our constitution, and unacknowledged by our laws; giving his Assent to their acts of pretended legislation:

For **quartering** large bodies of troops among us:

For protecting them, by a mock Trial, from Punishment for any Murders which they should commit on the Inhabitants of these States:

usurpations *unjust uses of power*

relinquish *give up*
inestimable *priceless*

annihilation *destruction*

convulsions *violent disturbances*

Naturalization of Foreigners *process by which foreign-born persons become citizens*

tenure *term*

quartering *lodging*

render *make*

abdicated *given up*

perfidy *violation of trust*

insurrections *rebellions*

petitioned for redress *asked formally for a correction of wrongs*

unwarrantable jurisdiction *unjustified authority*

consanguinity *originating from the same ancestor*

For cutting off our Trade with all parts of the world:

For imposing taxes on us without our Consent:

For depriving us in many cases, of the benefits of Trial by Jury:

For transporting us beyond Seas to be tried for pretended offences:

For abolishing the free System of English Laws in a neighbouring Province, establishing therein an Arbitrary government, and enlarging its Boundaries so as to **render** it at once an example and fit instrument for introducing the same absolute rule into these Colonies:

For taking away our Charters, abolishing our most valuable Laws, and altering fundamentally the Forms of our Governments:

For suspending our own Legislature, and declaring themselves invested with Power to legislate for us in all cases whatsoever.

He has **abdicated** Government here, by declaring us out of his Protection and waging War against us.

He has plundered our seas, ravaged our Coasts, burnt our towns, and destroyed the lives of our people.

He is at this time transporting large armies of foreign mercenaries to compleat the works of death, desolation and tyranny, already begun with circumstances of Cruelty & **perfidy** scarcely paralleled in the most barbarous ages, and totally unworthy the Head of a civilized nation.

He has constrained our fellow Citizens taken Captive on the high Seas to bear Arms against their Country, to become the executioners of their friends and Brethren, or to fall themselves by their Hands.

He has excited domestic **insurrections** amongst us, and has endeavoured to bring on the inhabitants of our frontiers, the merciless Indian Savages, whose known rule of warfare, is an undistinguished destruction of all ages, sexes and conditions.

In every stage of these Oppressions We have **Petitioned for Redress** in the most humble terms: Our repeated Petitions have been answered only by repeated injury. A Prince, whose character is thus marked by every act which may define a Tyrant, is unfit to be the ruler of a free People.

Nor have We been wanting in attention to our British brethren. We have warned them from time to time of attempts by their legislature to extend an **unwarrantable jurisdiction** over us. We have reminded them of the circumstances of our emigration and settlement here. We have appealed to their native justice and magnanimity, and we have conjured them by the ties of our common kindred to disavow these usurpations, which, would inevitably interrupt our connections and correspondence. They too have been deaf to the voice of justice and of **consanguinity.** We must, therefore, acquiesce in the necessity, which denounces our Separation, and hold them, as we hold the rest of mankind, Enemies in War, in Peace Friends.

[Resolution of Independence by the United States]

We, therefore, the Representatives of the united States of America, in General Congress, Assembled, appealing to the Supreme Judge of the world for the **rectitude** of our intentions, do, in the Name, and by Authority of the good People of these Colonies, solemnly publish and declare, That these United Colonies are, and of Right ought to be Free and Independent States; that they are Absolved from all Allegiance to the British Crown, and that all political connection between them and the State of Great Britain, is and ought to be totally dissolved; and that as Free and Independent States, they have full Power to levy War, conclude Peace, contract Alliances, establish Commerce, and to do all other Acts and Things which Independent States may of right do.

And for the support of this Declaration, with a firm reliance on the Protection of Divine Providence, we mutually pledge to each other our Lives, our Fortunes and our sacred Honor.

What It Means
Resolution of Independence The final section declares that the colonies are "Free and Independent States" with the full power to make war, to form alliances, and to trade with other countries.

rectitude *rightness*

John Hancock
President from
Massachusetts

Georgia
Button Gwinnett
Lyman Hall
George Walton

North Carolina
William Hooper
Joseph Hewes
John Penn

South Carolina
Edward Rutledge
Thomas Heyward, Jr.
Thomas Lynch, Jr.
Arthur Middleton

Maryland
Samuel Chase
William Paca
Thomas Stone
Charles Carroll
of Carrollton

Virginia
George Wythe
Richard Henry Lee
Thomas Jefferson
Benjamin Harrison
Thomas Nelson, Jr.
Francis Lightfoot Lee
Carter Braxton

Pennsylvania
Robert Morris
Benjamin Rush
Benjamin Franklin
John Morton
George Clymer
James Smith
George Taylor
James Wilson
George Ross

Delaware
Caesar Rodney
George Read
Thomas McKean

New York
William Floyd
Philip Livingston
Francis Lewis
Lewis Morris

New Jersey
Richard Stockton
John Witherspoon
Francis Hopkinson
John Hart
Abraham Clark

New Hampshire
Josiah Bartlett
William Whipple
Matthew Thornton

Massachusetts
Samuel Adams
John Adams
Robert Treat Paine
Elbridge Gerry

Rhode Island
Stephen Hopkins
William Ellery

Connecticut
Samuel Huntington
William Williams
Oliver Wolcott
Roger Sherman

What It Means
Signers of the Declaration The signers, as representatives of the American people, declared the colonies independent from Great Britain. Most members signed the document on August 2, 1776.

Section 3

The War for Independence

The Continental Army experienced several setbacks while fighting against the British military in a war that lasted many years. Eventually, the Americans, with the help of the French and other nations, were able to foil the British war strategy to win independence.

The Opposing Sides

MAIN Idea The Continental Army and local militias had to fight more experienced and better equipped British troops.

HISTORY AND YOU Have you ever tried something new without having time to prepare? Read on to learn how the Americans fought a war without proper training or equipment.

On the same day that the Continental Congress voted for independence, the British began landing troops in New York Harbor. By mid-August, they had assembled an estimated 32,000 men under the command of General **William Howe.** British officials did not expect the rebellion to last long. Their troops were disciplined, well trained, and well **equipped.**

Compared to the British troops, the Continental Army was inexperienced and poorly equipped. Although more than 230,000 men served in the Continental Army at various times, it rarely numbered more than 20,000 at any one time. Many soldiers deserted or refused to reenlist when their term was up. Others left their posts and returned to their farms at planting or harvest time.

Paying for the war was equally difficult. Lacking the power to tax, the Continental Congress issued paper money. These "Continentals" were not backed by gold or silver and became almost worthless very quickly. Fortunately, Robert Morris, a wealthy Pennsylvania merchant and banker, personally pledged large amounts of money for the war effort. Morris also set up an efficient method of buying rations and uniforms, arranged for foreign loans, and convinced the Congress to create the Bank of North America to finance the military.

Not only did the British have to worry about fighting the Continental Army, they also had to contend with the local militias. The militias were poorly trained, but they fought differently. They did not always line up for battle. They hid behind trees and walls and ambushed British troops and supply wagons. This kind of fighting is called **guerrilla warfare,** and it is very difficult to defeat.

Another problem for the British was that they were not united at home. Many merchants and members of Parliament opposed the war. The British had to win quickly and cheaply; otherwise, opinions in Parliament would shift against the war. The United States did not have

Guide to Reading

Big Ideas
Trade, War, and Migration Hostility between France and Britain caused France to enter the Revolution on the side of the colonies.

Content Vocabulary
- guerrilla warfare *(p. 78)*
- letter of marque *(p. 82)*

Academic Vocabulary
- equip *(p. 78)*
- objective *(p. 83)*

People and Events to Identify
- William Howe *(p. 78)*
- Nathan Hale *(p. 80)*
- Valley Forge *(p. 81)*
- Marquis de Lafayette *(p. 81)*
- Saratoga *(p. 82)*
- John Paul Jones *(p. 82)*
- Charles Cornwallis *(p. 84)*
- Battle of Kings Mountain *(p. 84)*
- Treaty of Paris *(p. 85)*

Reading Strategy
Sequencing Complete a time line similar to the one below to record the major battles of the American Revolution and their outcomes.

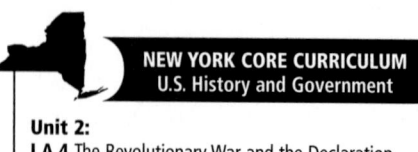

NEW YORK CORE CURRICULUM
U.S. History and Government

Unit 2:
I.A.4 The Revolutionary War and the Declaration of Independence

Why Did Britain Lose the Revolutionary War?

At the time of the Revolution, the British military was among the most powerful forces in the world. Pitted against this formidable fighting machine, the ragtag colonial forces did not seem to have a chance. Yet perseverance and the desire to secure individual freedoms eventually tipped the scales in the colonists' favor.

▶ *The British army, though extremely disciplined and well-trained, fought in the traditional way, by marching forward across an open space in tight formation. This approach made the soldiers easy targets when colonial troops fought in a guerrilla style.*

The Opposing Sides

Colonial Advantages
- Fighting on home ground
- Good decisions by generals
- Fighting for their rights and freedoms
- French alliance providing loans, naval support, and troops
- Time: the longer the war dragged on, the more likely the British were to give up

Colonial Disadvantages
- Untrained soldiers
- Food and ammunition shortages
- Weak and divided central government

British Advantages
- Well-trained, well-supplied army and navy
- Wealthy nation with substantial resources
- Strong central government

British Disadvantages
- Fighting in unfamiliar, hostile territory
- Fighting far from Britain
- Many troops were mercenaries, many indifferent to the cause
- Half-hearted support at home

Analyzing VISUALS

1. **Comparing** How did different approaches to warfare sometimes give the Americans the advantage over the better-trained and better-supplied British army?

2. **Summarizing** What other advantages did the Americans have in the war?

---

to defeat Britain—it simply had to survive until the British became tired of paying for the war.

The European balance of power also hampered the British. The French, Dutch, and Spanish were all eager to exploit Britain's problems. As a result, Britain had to station much of its military elsewhere in the world to defend its empire. The European balance of power also meant that the Patriots might be able to find allies against the British.

All these factors meant that the British had to win quickly. To do so, they had to convince Americans that their cause was hopeless and that they could safely surrender without being hanged for treason. General Howe's strategy,

therefore, had two parts. First, he sent a large number of troops to capture New York City. This would separate New England from the South and demonstrate to Americans that they could not win. The second part of Howe's strategy was diplomatic. He invited delegates from the Continental Congress to a peace conference. Howe promised that rebels who laid down their arms and swore loyalty to the king would be pardoned. When the Americans realized that Howe had no authority to negotiate a compromise, they refused to talk further.

✔ Reading Check **Identifying** What three major disadvantages did the British face in the American Revolution?

Battles in the North

MAIN Idea Early setbacks plagued the Continental Army, but the victory at Saratoga convinced France to enter the war.

HISTORY AND YOU Can you think of other wars in which the weaker side managed to defeat a stronger power? Read on to learn how the Battle of Saratoga was a turning point in the war.

Although the British had sent a huge force to seize New York City, the Congress asked Washington to try to defend it. Congressional leaders feared that if New York fell without a fight it would hurt American morale. Washington agreed and moved much of his army to Long Island to intercept the British.

The inexperience of Washington's troops became obvious when British troops attacked them in the summer of 1776. Many American soldiers fled, and some 1,500 were wounded or killed. Fortunately, the British were slow to advance, and the surviving American troops were able to escape to Manhattan. There, they joined the remainder of Washington's army defending New York City. As the British advanced, Washington abandoned the city and retreated to the northern end of Manhattan. The British then captured New York and used it as their headquarters for the rest of the war.

About this time, Washington sent volunteer Captain **Nathan Hale** to spy on the British. Although Hale was disguised as a Dutch schoolteacher, he was caught by the British and hanged. Brave until the end, Hale's last words were: "I only regret that I have but one life to lose for my country." Shortly afterward, Washington moved most of his troops from Manhattan Island to White Plains, New York.

Crossing the Delaware

At the Battle of White Plains in October 1776, the British forced Washington to retreat again. Then they surprised him. Instead of coming after the Continental Army, the British troops headed toward Philadelphia, where the Continental Congress was meeting. Caught by surprise, Washington's troops had to move quickly to get there ahead of the British.

While this march was taking place, Thomas Paine wrote another pamphlet to help boost American morale. In *The American Crisis,* he reminded Americans that "the harder the conflict, the more glorious the triumph":

PRIMARY SOURCE

"These are the times that try men's souls. The summer soldier and the sunshine patriot will in this crisis shrink from the service of their country; but he that stands it now deserves the love and thanks of man and woman."

—from *The American Crisis*

As the armies headed toward Philadelphia, winter began. The British stopped their advance and dispersed into winter camps in New Jersey. In the 1700s, armies did not usually fight in the winter because of the weather and scarce food supplies.

At this point Washington tried something daring—a winter attack. On December 25, 1776, he led some 2,400 men across the icy Delaware River and attacked a British camp at Trenton in the middle of a sleet storm. They killed or captured almost 1,000 British. Several days later, Washington's forces scattered three British regiments near Princeton. After these small victories, Washington headed into the hills of northern New Jersey for the winter.

Philadelphia Falls

In March 1777 General John Burgoyne, based in Quebec, developed a plan to isolate New England from the other American states. Burgoyne proposed a three-pronged attack on New York. He would take a large force south from Montreal. Another force would move from Montreal up the St. Lawrence River to Lake Ontario, and then head east into New York. A third force, led by General Howe, would march north from New York City. The three forces would meet near Albany and then march east into New England.

Unfortunately for the British, they did not coordinate the plan. By the time Burgoyne began marching south, General Howe had already moved 13,000 men by ship to Maryland and attacked Philadelphia from the south. Howe believed capturing Philadelphia and the Continental Congress would cripple the Revolution and convince Loyalists to rise up and take control of Pennsylvania.

Howe's action was a military success but a political failure. He defeated Washington at the Battle of Brandywine Creek and captured

NATIONAL GEOGRAPHIC   The War for Independence, 1776–1777

- ← American forces
- ← British forces
- ✳ American victory
- ✳ British victory
- ☐ Fort

Quebec

Nova Scotia

Maine (part of Mass.)

Montreal

BURGOYNE 1777

St. Lawrence R.

ST. LEGER 1777

Ft. Ticonderoga July 6, 1777

N.H.

Oct. 17, 1777: Burgoyne surrenders at Saratoga

Saratoga

Bennington Aug. 16, 1777

Oriskany Aug. 6, 1777

Albany

Bemis Heights Oct. 7, 1777

Mass.

Boston

GENERAL HOWE MARCH 17, 1776

Kingston

Conn.

R.I.

Sept. 1776: British capture New York City

N.Y.

Fort Montgomery ☐

ATLANTIC OCEAN

Pennsylvania

New York City

Brooklyn Heights Aug. 27, 1776

N.J.

Princeton

40°N

GENERAL HOWE 1776

Germantown Oct. 4, 1777

Brandywine Creek Sept. 11, 1777

Trenton

Philadelphia

Dec. 1776, Jan. 1777: Americans attack British at Trenton and Princeton

Maryland

Del.

GENERAL HOWE 1777

Sept. 1777: Howe captures Philadelphia

Virginia

0   100 kilometers
0   100 miles
Albers Equal-Area projection

Chesapeake Bay

75°W

70°W

▲ The famous Washington Crossing the Delaware was painted by Emanuel Gottlieb Leutze in 1851.

▲ This painting depicts the surrender of British General John Burgoyne to American General Horatio Gates at Saratoga on October 17, 1777. The American victory there encouraged the French to support the Americans.

Analyzing GEOGRAPHY

1. **Location** What are two colonial victories that occurred in New Jersey?
2. **Movement** What was the role of the British navy in the Revolution?

Philadelphia, but the Continental Congress escaped and no Loyalist uprising occurred.

Howe also failed to destroy the Continental Army, which set up its winter camp at **Valley Forge.** There, bitter cold and food shortages killed nearly 2,500 men.

Joining Washington at Valley Forge were two European military officers, the **Marquis de Lafayette** from France and Baron Friedrich von Steuben from Prussia. These officers helped Washington improve discipline and boost morale among the weary troops despite the camp's harsh conditions.

The Battle of Saratoga

General Burgoyne did not know Howe had gone south to attack Philadelphia. In June 1777, he and an estimated 8,000 troops marched south from Quebec into New York. Another 900 troops under the command of Colonel Barry St. Leger headed down the St. Lawrence to the eastern end of Lake Ontario. There they joined more than 1,000 Iroquois warriors and headed east toward Albany. The Iroquois had allied with the British hoping to keep American settlers off Iroquois lands.

At first, Burgoyne's march south went smoothly. His troops easily seized Fort Ticonderoga with its large store of gunpowder and supplies. In response, the Congress fired the commander defending the region and replaced him with General Horatio Gates.

After this early victory, Burgoyne's march slowed to a crawl. American troops felled trees in front of the British army and removed all the crops and cattle from the region in an effort to cut off the British food supply. Meanwhile, the British and Iroquois forces marching east from Lake Ontario were ambushed by militia and then driven back by American troops under General Benedict Arnold.

In desperation, Burgoyne retreated to **Saratoga,** where he was quickly surrounded by an American army nearly three times the size of his own. On October 17, 1777, he surrendered to General Gates. More than 5,000 British soldiers were taken prisoner. The American victory at Saratoga was astonishing and marked a turning point in the war. It not only dramatically improved American morale, it also convinced the French that the time had come to commit troops to the American cause.

Both Spain and France had been secretly sending arms and supplies to the United States well before Saratoga. The Congress appreciated the supplies but wanted the French to send troops, too. In September 1776, the Congress sent Benjamin Franklin, Arthur Lee, and Silas Deane to France to ask for troops. The French, however, were not willing to risk war until they believed the Americans could win. The victory at Saratoga convinced them, and shortly afterward they began negotiations to enter the war against Britain.

On February 6, 1778, the United States signed its first two treaties. In the first treaty, France became the first country to recognize the United States as an independent nation. The second treaty was an alliance between the United States and France. By June 1778, Britain and France were at war. In 1779 Spain entered the war as well, as an ally of France but not of the United States.

The War in the West

Not all the fighting in the Revolutionary War took place in the East. In 1778 Patriot George Rogers Clark took 175 troops down the Ohio River and captured several towns. By February 1779, the British had surrendered, giving the Americans control of the region.

While Clark fought the British in the West, Chief Joseph Brant, also known as Thayendanegea, convinced four Iroquois nations to join the British. In July 1778, British troops and Iroquois warriors attacked western Pennsylvania, burning towns and killing over 200 militia. The following summer, American troops defeated the British and Iroquois in western New York. These battles destroyed the power of the Iroquois people.

Farther south, the Cherokee people suffered a similar fate. After the Revolution began, a delegation of Shawnee, Delaware, and Mohawk convinced the Cherokee that the time had come to drive American settlers off Cherokee lands. The Cherokee attacked settlers in Virginia and North Carolina, but the American militia units were too strong. By 1780, militia units had burned down hundreds of Cherokee towns.

The War at Sea

Americans fought the British at sea, as well as on land. Instead of attacking the British fleet directly, American warships attacked British merchant ships. To further disrupt British trade, the Congress began issuing **letters of marque** (mark), or licenses, to private ship owners authorizing them to attack British merchant ships. By the war's end, millions of dollars of cargo had been seized, seriously harming Britain's trade and economy.

Perhaps the most famous naval battle of the war involved the American naval officer **John Paul Jones.** Jones commanded a ship named the *Bonhomme Richard.* While sailing near Britain in September 1779, Jones encountered a group of British merchant ships protected by the warships *Serapis* and *Countess of Scarborough.* Jones attacked the *Serapis,* but the heavier guns of the British ship nearly sank the *Bonhomme Richard.* With the American ship in distress, the British commander called on Jones to surrender. Jones replied, "I have not yet begun to fight." He lashed his ship to *Serapis* so it could not sink, and then boarded the British ship. The battle lasted more than three hours before the British surrendered.

✔ Reading Check **Summarizing** What was significant about the first U.S. treaty with France?

Battles in the South

MAIN Idea The British strategy to control the Southern states failed with their surrender at Yorktown.

HISTORY AND YOU Have you ever changed your opinion about an event because of the actions of the people or groups involved? Read on to learn how the Battle of Kings Mountain encouraged Southern farmers to organize forces.

After the British defeat at Saratoga, General Howe resigned. He was replaced by Sir Henry Clinton, who ordered the British troops in Philadelphia to abandon the city and return to New York City. Clinton wanted to gather all his forces in one place before beginning a new campaign. Washington ordered his forces at Valley Forge to intercept the British. The two sides met at the Battle of Monmouth—the largest battle of the war. Neither side won, but for the first time American troops were able to stand against the British in a regular battle.

After Clinton reached New York, he was ordered to begin a campaign in the South, where the British had the strongest Loyalist support. The Southern states were also valuable because they produced tobacco and rice. The British hoped they could keep the South, even if they lost the North.

The Struggle in the Carolinas

In December 1778, some 3,500 British troops captured Savannah, Georgia. They seized control of Georgia's backcountry and returned the British royal governor to power. The next **objective** was to capture Charles Town, South Carolina—the largest city in the South.

NATIONAL GEOGRAPHIC The War for Independence, 1778–1781

Lake Huron
Lake Michigan
Lake Ontario
Lake Erie
Ft. Detroit
HAMILTON
Ft. Miami
40°N
Cahokia July 9, 1778
Vincennes Feb. 25, 1779
CLARK
Ft. Pitt
Valley Forge
N.Y.
N.H.
Mass.
West Point
Conn.
R.I.
New York City
Pa.
N.J.
Md.
Del.
Va.
BRITISH FLEET, 1781

Washington and Rochambeau rush toward Virginia, August 1781

Kaskaskia July 4, 1778
N W E S
35°N
GREENE
Cowpens
Kings Mtn.
N.C.
CORNWALLIS
Yorktown
Wilmington
DE GRASSE
ATLANTIC OCEAN

Cornwallis is trapped; British surrender at Yorktown, 1781

French Admiral de Grasse keeps British ships away

British capture Charleston and Camden, but are defeated at Kings Mountain in 1780 and at Cowpens in 1781

S.C.
Camden
Charleston
MARION
CLINTON, 1780
Ga.
Savannah
CAMPBELL, 1778

British capture Savannah, 1778

Gulf of Mexico
85°W
80°W
75°W
30°N

0 200 kilometers
0 200 miles
Lambert Azimuthal Equal-Area projection

→ American and/or allied forces
→ British forces
✳ American victory
✳ British victory
□ Fort

▲ This painting celebrates the courage of Mary Ludwig Hays, known as "Molly Pitcher," who according to tradition carried water to the troops during the Battle of Monmouth and helped fire a cannon after the crew was killed.

Analyzing GEOGRAPHY

1. **Movement** How did the French help the American forces?

2. **Location** Where did the final battle of the war occur?

Maps In MOtion See StudentWorks™ Plus or glencoe.com.

160°W

CIRCLE

60°N

Hudson
Bay

**BRITISH
NORTH AMERICA**

140°W

40°N

**UNITED
STATES**

**SPANISH
LOUISIANA**

PACIFIC
OCEAN

**NEW
SPAIN**

ATLANTIC
OCEAN

Gulf of
Mexico

TROPIC OF CANCER

60°W

20°N

N
W E
S

0   800 kilometers
0   800 miles
Lambert Azimuthal Equal-Area
projection

120°W

100°W

80°W

British	Spanish
French	United States
Russian	Disputed

▲ The British surrender at Yorktown.
John Trumbull was not present at the
surrender but did his best to depict true
likenesses of those he knew personally,
such as George Washington, shown on
horseback in front of the flag.

Analyzing GEOGRAPHY

1. **Location** After the American Revolution, what
were the borders of the United States in the
north? In the south? In the west?

2. **Regions** Which foreign colonies shared a border
with the United States in 1783?

Charles Town Falls Clinton attacked Charles Town with nearly 14,000 British soldiers. His forces quickly surrounded the city, trapping the American forces inside. On May 12, 1780, the Americans surrendered. Nearly 5,500 Americans were taken prisoner, the greatest American defeat in the war.

After capturing Charles Town, Clinton returned to New York, leaving General **Charles Cornwallis** in command. The Continental Congress then sent General Horatio Gates, the hero of Saratoga, to defend the South Carolina backcountry. Gates attempted to destroy a British supply base at Camden, South Carolina, but failed.

The Battle of Kings Mountain After the Battle of Camden, the British began subduing the Carolina backcountry. At first, everything went well for them. Many of the settlers were Loyalists and agreed to fight for Britain. Two British cavalry officers, Banastre Tarleton and Patrick Ferguson, led many of the Loyalist forces in the region. These troops became known for their brutality.

Ferguson finally went too far when he tried to subdue the people living in the Appalachian Mountains. Enraged at his tactics, the "over-mountain" men, as they were known, put together a militia. They intercepted Ferguson at Kings Mountain on October 7, 1780, and destroyed his army. The **Battle of Kings Mountain** was a turning point in the South. Southern farmers, furious with British treatment, began organizing their own forces.

The new American commander in the region, General Nathaniel Greene, decided to wear down the British in battle while militia destroyed their supplies. He organized the militia into small units to carry out hit-and-run raids against British camps and supply wagons. Francis Marion, known as the "Swamp Fox," led the most famous of these units. The strategy worked. By late 1781, the British controlled very little of the South except for Savannah, Charles Town, and Wilmington.

The Battle of Yorktown

In late April 1781, Cornwallis marched into Virginia. As long as the Americans controlled Virginia, he believed, new troops and supplies could keep coming south. With more French troops on the way to America, the British knew they had very little time left to win the war. They had to secure Virginia.

When he reached Virginia, Cornwallis linked up with forces under the command of Benedict Arnold. Arnold had been an American general early in the war but had later sold military information to the British. When his treason was discovered, Arnold fled to British-controlled New York City. There, he was given command of British troops and ordered to Virginia.

After Arnold's forces joined those of Cornwallis, the British began to conquer Virginia. Their combined forces encountered very little resistance until June 1781, when a large American force led by General Anthony Wayne arrived in Virginia. Outnumbered and too far inland, Cornwallis retreated to the coastal town of Yorktown to protect his supplies and to maintain communications by sea.

Cornwallis's retreat created an opportunity for the Americans and their French allies. The previous year, 6,000 French troops had arrived in New England. With this support, Washington decided to march on New York City. As the troops headed to New York, the French general Rochambeau learned that a French fleet commanded by Admiral de Grasse was on its way north from the Caribbean.

When he learned of the French fleet, Washington canceled the attack on New York City. Instead, he and Rochambeau headed to Yorktown. As their troops raced south, Admiral de Grasse moved into Chesapeake Bay near Yorktown. His fleet cut off the flow of supplies to Cornwallis and prevented him from escaping by sea.

On September 28, 1781, American and French forces surrounded Yorktown and began to bombard it. On October 14, Washington's aide, Alexander Hamilton, led an attack that captured key British defenses. Three days later, Cornwallis began negotiations to surrender, and on October 19, 1781, approximately 8,000 British soldiers marched out of Yorktown and laid down their weapons.

The Treaty of Paris

When Lord North, the British prime minister, learned of the surrender at Yorktown, he knew the war was over. In March 1782, Parliament voted to begin peace negotiations. John Adams, Benjamin Franklin, and John Jay conducted most of the negotiations for the United States.

The final settlement, known as the **Treaty of Paris,** was signed on September 3, 1783. In this treaty, Britain recognized the United States of America as a new nation, with the Mississippi River as its western border. Britain also gave Florida back to Spain. France received colonies in Africa and the Caribbean that the British had seized from them in 1763. On November 24, 1783, the last British troops left New York City. The American Revolution was over. The creation of a new nation was about to begin.

✔ **Reading Check** **Describing** How was the war won at Yorktown?

Section 3 REVIEW

Vocabulary

1. **Explain** the significance of: William Howe, guerrilla warfare, Nathan Hale, Valley Forge, Marquis de Lafayette, Saratoga, letter of marque, John Paul Jones, Charles Cornwallis, Treaty of Paris.

Main Ideas

2. **Explaining** Why did the Continental Congress have trouble paying for the war?

3. **Describing** Before they officially joined the war effort, how were European countries helping the Americans fight the British?

4. **Summarizing** What was General Nathaniel Greene's strategy for fighting the British in the South?

Critical Thinking

5. **Big Ideas** Why were the French at first reluctant to make an alliance with the colonies?

6. **Categorizing** Use a graphic organizer similar to the one below to list the provisions of the Treaty of Paris.

```
┌─────────────────────┐
│   Provisions of     │
│ Treaty of Paris, 1783│
└─────────────────────┘
     │    │    │
  ┌────┐┌────┐┌────┐
  │    ││    ││    │
  └────┘└────┘└────┘
```

7. **Analyzing Visuals** Study the map on page 84. Which nation controlled most of North America at the end of the American Revolution?

Writing About History

8. **Persuasive Writing** Suppose that you are a colonial leader during the American Revolution. Write a letter to convince the ruler of a European nation to support the Americans in the war.

History ONLINE
Study Central™ To review this section, go to glencoe.com and click on Study Central.

Section 4

The War Changes American Society

Guide to Reading

Big Ideas
Culture and Beliefs As the American Revolution ended, a unique culture arose in the new United States.

Content Vocabulary
- republic *(p. 86)*
- emancipation *(p. 89)*
- manumission *(p. 90)*

Academic Vocabulary
- contradiction *(p. 86)*
- revolutionary *(p. 88)*

People and Events to Identify
- Virginia Statute for Religious Freedom *(p. 88)*
- John Trumbull *(p. 91)*
- Charles Willson Peale *(p. 91)*

Reading Strategy
Organizing Complete a graphic organizer similar to the one below by listing the features of the U.S. political system set up after the Revolution.

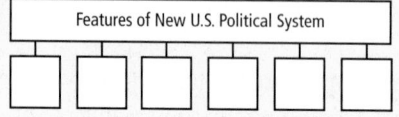

Features of New U.S. Political System

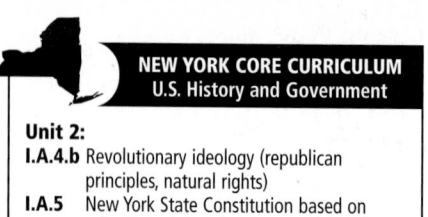

NEW YORK CORE CURRICULUM
U.S. History and Government

Unit 2:
I.A.4.b Revolutionary ideology (republican principles, natural rights)
I.A.5 New York State Constitution based on republican principles

---

The American Revolution changed society in a variety of ways. New forms of government encouraged new political ideas. Additionally, many of those who had been loyal to Britain left; this strengthened the development of a new, American cultural identity.

New Political Ideas

MAIN Idea Republican ideals changed American government by allowing some citizens voting rights and granting greater religious freedom.

HISTORY AND YOU Have you ever made up your own rules for a game? Read on to learn how the Founders experimented with new forms of government.

When American leaders declared independence and founded the United States of America, they were very much aware that they were creating something new. By breaking away from the king, they had established a **republic.** A republic is a form of government in which power resides with a body of citizens entitled to vote. The power is exercised by elected officials who are responsible to the citizens and who must govern according to laws or a constitution.

While many Europeans viewed a republic as radical and dangerous, Americans believed it could be better than other forms of government. In an ideal republic, all citizens are equal under the law, regardless of their wealth or social class. These ideas conflicted with many traditional beliefs, including ideas about slavery, about women not being allowed to vote or own property, and about certain families being "better" than others. Despite these **contradictions,** republican ideas began to change American society after the war.

New State Constitutions

Events before the Revolution led many Americans to believe that each state's constitution should be written down and that it should limit the government's power over the people. At the same time, many, including John Adams, worried that democracy could endanger a republican government and lead to tyranny. When Adams used the word *democracy,* he meant a society where the majority rules. He and other founders feared that in a pure democracy, minority groups would not have their rights protected. For example, the poor might vote to take everything away from the rich. Adams argued that government needed "checks and balances" to prevent any group in society from becoming strong enough to take away the rights of the minority.

The Revolution Changes Government

Wealth of Elected Officials

Northern States

1765–1775 / 1783–1790

Southern States

1765–1775 / 1783–1790

Over £5,000 | £2,000–£5,000 | Under £2,000

Source: "Government by the People: The American Revolution and the Democratization of the Legislatures."

Analyzing VISUALS

1. **Analyzing** In the North after the Revolution, how much did the percentage of wealthy officeholders increase?

2. **Specifying** In which region did the greater number of middle-class people enter public office after the Revolution?

▲ After the Revolution, voting rights expanded. In New Jersey, between 1790 and 1807, even women were able to vote. However, the percentage of wealthy people who actually held office increased.

Adams favored a "mixed government" with a separation of powers; he believed the executive, legislative, and judicial branches should be independent of one another. He also argued that the legislature should be bicameral; that is, it should have two houses: a senate to represent people of property and an assembly to protect the rights of the common people. Adams's ideas influenced several states as they drafted new constitutions during the Revolution. Virginia's constitution of 1776, New York's constitution of 1777, and Massachusetts's constitution of 1780 all established an elected governor, senate, and assembly. By the 1790s, most of the other states had created similar institutions.

Many states also attached a list of rights to their constitutions. This began in 1776, when George Mason drafted Virginia's Declaration of Rights, which guaranteed Virginians freedom of speech, freedom of religion, the right to bear arms, and the right to trial by jury. It barred the state from searching anyone's home without a warrant or taking their property without proper court proceedings.

Voting Rights Expand

The Revolution led to an expansion of voting rights. The experience of fighting side by side with people from every social class and region increased Americans' belief in equality. If all men were fighting for the same cause and risking death for the same ideas, then all deserved the right to vote for their leaders.

The war also weakened feelings of deference toward the upper class. The war had shown many farmers and artisans that they were equal to the rich planters and merchants they fought beside. While sitting in a tavern with farmers who were spitting and pulling off their muddy boots, one wealthy Virginian noted: "Every one who bore arms esteems himself upon an equal footing with his neighbors. . . . Each of these men considers himself, in every respect, my equal."

As a result of these ideas, in almost every state, the new constitutions made it easier for men to gain the right to vote. Many states allowed any white male who paid taxes to vote, whether or not he owned property.

Although voting rights expanded, people still had to own a certain amount of property to hold elective office, although usually much less than before the Revolution. The practice of giving veterans land grants as payment for their military service increased the number of people eligible to hold office. In the North, before the Revolution, over 80 percent of people elected were wealthy. Ten years after the war, only a little over one-third of officeholders were wealthy. In the South, higher property qualifications kept the wealthy in power, but their numbers dropped from almost 90 percent of officeholders before the war to 70 percent after the war.

Freedom of Religion

For the text of the Virginia Statute for Religious Freedom, see page R43 in **Documents in American History.**

The Revolution also led to changes in the relationship between church and state. Many of the Revolution's leaders feared "ecclesiastical tyranny"—the power of a church, backed by the government, to make people worship in a certain way. In Virginia, Baptists led a movement to abolish taxes collected to support the Anglican Church. Governor Thomas Jefferson wrote the **Virginia Statute for Religious Freedom,** and James Madison convinced the legislature to pass it in 1786. The statute declared:

PRIMARY SOURCE

"[N]o man shall be compelled to . . . support any religious worship, place, or Ministry . . . nor shall otherwise suffer on account of his religious opinions or belief; but that all men shall be free to profess . . . their opinion in matters of religion."

—from the Virginia Statute for Religious Freedom

The statute also declared that Virginia no longer had an official church and that the state could not collect taxes for churches.

The idea of denying tax support to churches spread slowly. In Massachusetts, the state constitution originally provided for the collection of funds to support churches. Quakers and Baptists were permitted to assign their taxes to their own churches instead of to the Congregational churches (the successors to the Puritan churches), but the state did not abolish religious taxes entirely until 1833.

Reading Check **Examining** Which freedoms did Virginia's constitution guarantee in its bill of rights?

The War and American Society

MAIN Idea After the war, women gained more rights, Northern states outlawed slavery, and many Loyalists fled the new nation.

HISTORY AND YOU Can you think of modern examples of how war changes the way people live? Read on to learn how the Revolution changed American society.

The American ideals of equality and liberty did not generally apply to women and African Americans. Both groups did, however, find their lives changed by the Revolution, as did the Loyalists who had supported Britain.

Women at War

Women played a vital role in the Revolutionary War, contributing on both the home front and the battlefront. With their husbands, brothers, and sons at war, some women took over running family farms. Others traveled with the army—cooking, washing, and nursing the wounded. Women also served as spies and couriers, and a few even joined the fighting. Deborah Samson of Massachusetts fought in the Continental Army disguised as a man under the name Robert Shurtleff. Margaret Corbin accompanied her husband to battle, and after his death she took his place at his cannon until the battle ended.

After the war, as Americans began to think about what their **revolutionary** ideals implied, women made some advances. They could more easily obtain a divorce and gained greater access to education. In 1779 Judith Sargent Murray wrote an essay entitled "On the Equality of the Sexes." The essay argued that women were as intelligent as men but lacked the education needed to achieve more in life. After the Revolution, many schools for girls were founded, and the number of women who were able to read increased.

African Americans

Thousands of enslaved African Americans obtained their freedom during the Revolution. Although British officials seized numerous enslaved people and shipped them to British plantations in the Caribbean, they also freed

0   200 kilometers
0   200 miles
Lambert Azimuthal Equal-Area projection

Area claimed by Britain and U.S.

Maine (part of Mass.) **1780**

Vt. **1777**

N.H.

New York **1799**

Mass. **1780**

R.I. **1784**

Pennsylvania **1780**

Conn. **1784**

N.J. **1804**

Md.

Del.

Virginia

ATLANTIC OCEAN

North Carolina

South Carolina

Georgia

N W E S

1780 Date of emancipation
Immediate emancipation
Gradual emancipation
Slaveholders could legally free slaves
Slaveholders required to obtain county court approval to free slaves
Slaveholders could not legally free slaves
No formal abolition

▲ *Dinah Morris of Vermont was granted her freedom in 1777. She was the first enslaved person to be freed in the North.*

Analyzing GEOGRAPHY

1. **Region** Which region made it difficult to emancipate enslaved people?
2. **Human-Environment Interaction** Why do you think slavery remained firmly entrenched in certain areas?

many others in exchange for military service. Many planters freed slaves who agreed to fight the British, and General Washington permitted African Americans to join the Continental Army. He also urged state militias to admit African Americans and to offer freedom to all who served. About 5,000 African Americans served in the militias and the Continental Army during the American Revolution.

After the Revolution, many Americans realized that enslaving people did not fit in with the new ideals of liberty and equality. Opposition to slavery had been growing steadily even before the Revolution, especially in the Northern and middle states. After the war began, **emancipation,** or freedom from enslavement, became a major issue. Many Northern states took steps to end slavery. Vermont banned slavery in 1777. In 1780 Pennsylvania freed all children born enslaved when they reached age 28. Rhode Island decreed in 1784 that enslaved men born

thereafter would be freed when they turned 21 and enslaved women when they turned 18. In 1799 New York freed enslaved men born in that year or later when they reached age 28 and women when they reached age 25. The eradication of slavery in the North was thus a gradual process that took several decades, but it demonstrated that slavery could be abolished.

Discrimination against African Americans did not disappear with emancipation, however. African Americans were often unable to get more than menial jobs—digging, carrying, or sweeping. Free African Americans also faced voting restrictions, segregation, and possible kidnapping and transportation to the South, where they would again be enslaved. Despite the hardships, freedom offered choices. Once free, many African Americans moved to the cities to find employment. Some found opportunities in previously barred occupations, such as artists or ministers.

People IN HISTORY

Elizabeth Freeman (Mumbet)
c. 1742–1829

Elizabeth Freeman, later called Mumbet, began life as an enslaved African American. At the age of six months she was acquired, along with her sister, by John Ashley, a wealthy western Massachusetts lawyer and businessman. The family called her Betty or Bett. For nearly 40 years, Bett worked for the Ashley family. One day, Ashley's wife tried to strike Bett's sister with a shovel. Bett intervened and took the blow instead. Furious, she stormed out of the house and refused to come back. When the Ashleys tried to force her to return, Bett consulted a local lawyer named Thomas Sedgewick. With his help, Bett sued for her freedom.

While serving the Ashleys, Bett had listened to many discussions about the new Massachusetts constitution. If the constitution said that all people were free and equal, then she thought that should apply to her. In 1781 a jury agreed, and Bett won her freedom—and took Freeman as her last name. Elizabeth Freeman was the first enslaved person in Massachusetts to gain freedom under the new constitution, and probably the first woman to be granted her freedom in the entire 13 states. Her case helped to end slavery in Massachusetts.

What is the significance of Elizabeth Freeman's court case?

Quock Walker
1753–?

Between 1781 and 1783, an enslaved Massachusetts man named Quock Walker also took the extraordinary step, in a series of cases, of suing a white man who had assaulted him. That man, Nathaniel Jennison, also claimed to own Walker, who had escaped from Jennison's farm after a severe beating.

Given the times, this was a bold step, but Walker believed,

▲ *Chief Justice William Cushing*

as Freeman did, that the law was on his side. Massachusetts's new constitution referred to the "inherent liberty" of all men. The judge, Chief Justice William Cushing, agreed and found in his favor. "Our [state] Constitution," Cushing said, "sets out with declaring that all men are born free and equal . . . and in short is totally repugnant to the idea of [people] being born slaves. This being the case, I think the idea of slavery is inconsistent with our own conduct and Constitution."

While the Walker and Freeman cases did not abolish slavery, they demonstrated that the Massachusetts courts would not support the institution. As a result of the rulings and various antislavery efforts, slavery ceased to exist in Massachusetts by 1790.

How was slavery "inconsistent" with the Massachusetts constitution?

A small group of African Americans achieved some wealth and social status. The discrimination they faced encouraged them to build their own distinct culture. Religion played an important role in that emerging culture, and African Americans created their own style of worship. In 1816 African American church leaders formed the first independent African American denomination, the African Methodist Episcopal (AME) Church.

The story was quite different in the South. The South relied heavily on enslaved labor to sustain its agricultural economy. As a result, Southern leaders showed little interest in abolishing slavery. Only Virginia took steps toward ending the institution. In 1782 the state passed a law encouraging **manumission,** or the voluntary freeing of enslaved people, especially for those who had fought in the Revolution. Through this law, about 10,000 slaves obtained their freedom, but the vast majority remained in bondage.

The Loyalists Flee

Many women and African Americans found their lives little changed as a result of the Revolution, but for many Loyalists, the end of the war changed everything. Because of their support for the British, Loyalists often found themselves shunned by former friends, and state governments sometimes seized their property.

Unwilling to live under the new government and often afraid for their lives, approximately 100,000 Loyalists fled the United States after the war. Some went to Great Britain or the British West Indies, but most moved to British North America, particularly to Nova Scotia, New Brunswick, and the region near Niagara Falls. This region was part of Quebec at the time, but in 1791 Britain made it a separate colony called Upper Canada. Today it is the province of Ontario.

Americans grappled with what to do with the property and assets of Loyalists. In North

Carolina, Patriots confiscated Loyalist lands outright. Officials in New York also seized Loyalists' lands and goods, claiming the "sovereignty of the people of this state in respect to all property." Other public officials opposed such actions. The Massachusetts Constitution of 1780, for example, extended the rights of "life, liberty, and property" to Loyalists, and gave much of the land seized from departing Loyalists to their agents or relatives who had remained.

An American Culture Emerges

In the United States, victory over the British united Americans and created powerful nationalist feelings. The Revolution helped this process in two ways. First, Americans in all the states had battled a common enemy. Soldiers from all over the country had fought side by side in each other's states. Second, stories of the Revolution and its heroes encouraged Americans to think of themselves as all belonging to the same group.

American Painters The Revolution also sparked the creativity of American painters, including **John Trumbull** and **Charles Willson Peale.** Their work and that of other artists contributed to an American identity. Trumbull served in the Continental Army as an aide to Washington. He is best known for his depiction of battles and important events in the Revolution. Peale fought at Trenton and Princeton and survived the winter at Valley Forge. He is best known for his portraits of Washington and other Patriot leaders.

Changes in Education As they started a new nation, American leaders considered an educated public to be critical to the republic's success. Jefferson called it the "keystone of our arch of government." Several state constitutions provided for government-funded universities. In 1795 the University of North Carolina became the first state university in the nation. At the same time, elementary schools instituted an American-centered style of teaching. Tossing out British textbooks, they taught republican ideas and the history of the struggle for independence.

Noah Webster, a teacher from Connecticut, was one of the educators who believed that Americans needed to develop their own educational system based on their own culture. In 1783 he wrote a textbook titled *A Grammatical Institute of the English Language,* which included *The American Spelling Book.* American teachers used this textbook for over 100 years, and it is still in print. Although he also published magazines and newspapers, as well as his best-selling textbook, Webster is probably most famous for his *American Dictionary of the English Language,* published in 1828. In that two-volume work, he purposefully set out to regularize American English, but especially to underscore its differences from British English.

As Americans began to build a national identity separate from Britain's, leaders of the United States turned their attention to the creation of a government that could promote the ideals and beliefs that the colonists had fought so hard to secure.

Reading Check **Summarizing** How did life change for women, African Americans, and Loyalists after the Revolutionary War?

Section 4 REVIEW

Vocabulary

1. **Explain** the significance of: republic, Virginia Statute for Religious Freedom, emancipation, manumission, John Trumbull, Charles Willson Peale.

Main Ideas

2. **Describing** What ideas of John Adams did Massachusetts and other states include in their constitutions?

3. **Explaining** How did the Revolution help to create powerful nationalist feelings in the United States?

Critical Thinking

4. **Big Ideas** What new aspects of culture emerged after the American Revolution?

5. **Categorizing** Use a graphic organizer similar to the one below to list the position of women, African Americans, and Loyalists in American society after the Revolution.

	Position in American Society
Women	
African Americans	
Loyalists	

6. **Analyzing Visuals** Review the graph on the wealth of elected officials on page 87. Which group lost the greatest percentage of representation among elected officials in both regions?

Writing About History

7. **Expository Writing** Suppose that you are on a committee to write a new state constitution. List the freedoms you want protected in that constitution, and explain why you feel it is important to guarantee each one.

History ONLINE

Study Central™ To review this section, go to glencoe.com and click on Study Central.

Causes of the American Revolution

- Defending the colonies in the French and Indian War costs Britain a great deal of money; Britain seeks ways to cover the costs incurred.
- Britain issues the Proclamation Act of 1763, banning colonists from moving west of the Proclamation line.
- The British crack down on smuggling by enforcing customs duties and creating a vice-admiralty court to try smugglers; merchants are angered, and colonists believe their rights are being violated.
- The Sugar Act is attacked by colonists as taxation without representation.
- The Currency Act banning paper money angers farmers and artisans.
- The 1765 Stamp Act leads to widespread colonial protests, the holding of the Stamp Act Congress, and a boycott of British goods.
- The 1767 Townshend Acts lead to further protests and another boycott.
- The Boston Massacre convinces many that the British are tyrants.
- In 1773, British efforts to help the East India Company lead to the Boston Tea Party and other protests against the tea shipments.
- Britain issues the Coercive Acts, banning Massachusetts town meetings, closing Boston's port, and quartering troops in private homes.
- Neither King George nor British officials agree to compromise with the Continental Congress, and Congress orders a boycott of British goods.
- British troops fire on militia at Lexington and Concord; the Revolution begins; and the Declaration of Independence is issued, July 4, 1776.

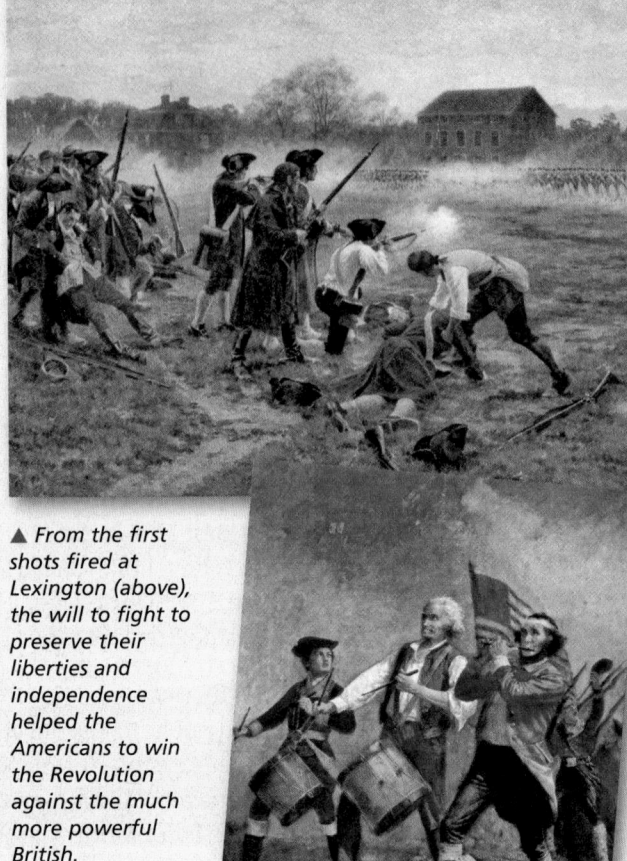

▲ From the first shots fired at Lexington (above), the will to fight to preserve their liberties and independence helped the Americans to win the Revolution against the much more powerful British.

▲ The British surrender at Saratoga. The victory at Saratoga boosted morale and helped Americans gain the support of France and Spain.

Effects of the American Revolution

- The American colonies form a new nation: the United States of America.
- A Revolutionary War between American forces led by George Washington, and British forces, rages from 1775–1780.
- The American victory at Saratoga brings France into the war as an American ally.
- The American victory at Yorktown leads to Britain agreeing to negotiate; the Treaty of Paris of 1783 formally ends the Revolutionary War.
- American states begin writing constitutions based on republican ideas.
- Voting rights expand.
- Northern American states adopt laws that gradually end slavery.
- Americans loyal to Britain flee north, leading to the creation of the new colonies of Upper and Lower Canada.
- A new American culture emerges based on the republican values.

NEW YORK REGENTS EXAM PRACTICE

TEST-TAKING TIP

As you read each question, be sure to look for main ideas. A main idea or a key word repeated in an answer choice may be a clue that it is the right answer.

Part I

Directions (1–10): For each statement or question, write on a separate sheet of paper the number of the word or expression that, of those given, best completes the statement or answers the question.

1 King George III issued the Proclamation of 1763 to
   (1) make peace with the French and Spanish.
   (2) give more lands to the colonists.
   (3) make peace with Native Americans.
   (4) punish the port of Boston.

2 In which document did John Dickinson urge colonial unity to resist the Townshend Acts?
   (1) *Letters From a Farmer in Pennsylvania*
   (2) *Common Sense*
   (3) *The American Crisis*
   (4) the Declaration of Rights

3 The First Continental Congress was formed in reaction to the
   (1) Coercive Acts.
   (2) Tea Act.
   (3) Townshend Acts.
   (4) Stamp Act.

4 The Battle of Bunker Hill demonstrated
   (1) the British ignorance of Boston's geography.
   (2) the colonists' great skill with cannons.
   (3) that the colonial militia could stand up to a professional army.
   (4) that more people were loyal to the British than Patriot leaders had thought.

5 Which of the following was one disadvantage the British faced during the Revolution?
   (1) They did not have enough money to pay their soldiers.
   (2) Their navy was weak and inexperienced.
   (3) The war did not have total support at home.
   (4) They could not get France to fight as an ally against the colonists.

6 Under the Treaty of Paris ending the Revolution, the western boundary of the United States would become the
   (1) Appalachian Mountains.
   (2) Mississippi River.
   (3) Rocky Mountains.
   (4) Pacific Ocean.

7 Virginia's Declaration of Rights was written to protect
   (1) land rights.
   (2) fishing rights.
   (3) civil rights.
   (4) mining rights.

8 The significance of the Albany Plan of Union was that it
   (1) marked the first time that the colonists had met with Native Americans.
   (2) explained clearly to the British why independence was necessary.
   (3) created a new nation out of the 13 separate colonies.
   (4) demonstrated an interest in unifying the colonies.

Need Extra Help?								
If You Missed Questions . . .	1	2	3	4	5	6	7	8
Go to Page . . .	56	60	68	70	78	85	87	55

[OVER]

Base your answer to question 9 on the map below and on your knowledge of Chapter 2.

Battles in the Revolutionary War, 1776–1777

9 How did American troops slow Burgoyne's march to seal off New England from the rest of the United States?

(1) American troops defeated the British at Philadelphia.

(2) American troops retreated from Ft. Ticonderoga, where the British gained supplies.

(3) American troops cut off the British food supply by removing cattle and crops from the region.

(4) American warships attacked British merchant ships to disrupt trade.

Need Extra Help?	
If You Missed Questions . . .	9
Go to Page . . .	80

Part II Thematic Essay Question

Directions: Write a well-organized essay that includes an introduction, several paragraphs addressing the task below, and a conclusion.

Theme: American Culture

After the American Revolution, a new culture emerged in the United States that led to changes in government, society, the arts, and education.

Task:

Compare and contrast American culture before and after the American Revolution. In your essay, be sure to

- Compare and contrast cultural changes in government, society, the arts, and education

- Discuss the reasons for the emergence of a new culture after the Revolution

- Evaluate the long-term effects of this cultural change and explain how the new culture helped shape American culture in future years

Guidelines:

In your essay, be sure to:

- Develop all aspects of the task
- Support the theme with relevant facts, examples, and details
- Use a logical and clear plan of organization, including an introduction and a conclusion that are beyond a restatement of the theme

Part III Document-Based Question

This question is based on the accompanying documents. It is designed to test your ability to work with historical documents. Some of the documents have been edited for the purposes of the question. As you analyze the documents, take into account both the source of each document and any point of view that may be presented in the document.

Historical Context:

In the American colonies, resentment over British taxation and other restrictions soon caused colonists to question and actively resist British control.

Task:

Using information from the documents and your knowledge of United States history, answer the questions that follow each document in Part A. Your answers to the questions will help you write the Part B essay, in which you will be asked to

- Discuss what caused Britain to impose new regulations and taxes on the colonies
- Evaluate how the protests over these taxes grew into a desire to be free from British rule

Part A
Short-Answer Questions

Directions: Analyze the documents and answer the short-answer questions that follow each document on a separate sheet of paper.

Document 1

"**Q.** Don't you know that the money [tax] arising from the stamps was all to be laid out in America?
A. I know it is appropriated by the act to the American service; but it will be spent in the conquered colonies where the soldiers are, not in the colonies that pay it. . . .

Q. Do you think it right that America should be protected by this country and pay no part of the expense?
A. That is not the case. The colonies raised, clothed, and paid, during the last war, near 25,000 men and spent many millions.

Q. Were you not reimbursed by Parliament?
A. We were only reimbursed what, in your opinion, we had advanced beyond our proportion, or beyond what might reasonably be expected from us; and it was a very small part of what we spent. Pennsylvania, in particular, disbursed about 500,000 pounds, and the reimbursements, in the whole, did not exceed 60,000 pounds. . . ."

Source: Benjamin Franklin, testimony before Parliament, 1766

1   Where does Franklin say the British will spend the revenue from the Stamp Act, and why does he say the tax is unfair?

Document 2

Source: "An Astronomical diary, or,
An almanack . . . " by Nathaniel Ames, 1772

2   Based on this cartoon, what was John Dickinson's belief about English rule in the colonies?

Part B
Essay

Directions: Reread the task box at the top left and write a well-organized essay that includes an introduction, several paragraphs, and a conclusion. Use evidence from the documents in your essay. Support your response with relevant facts, examples, and details. Include additional outside information.

Guidelines:

In your essay, be sure to:

- Develop all aspects of the task
- Incorporate information from the documents
- Incorporate relevant outside information
- Support the theme with relevant facts, examples, and details
- Use a logical and clear plan of organization, including an introduction and a conclusion that are beyond a restatement of the task

History ONLINE

For additional test practice, use Self-Check Quizzes—Chapter 2 at glencoe.com.

Need Extra Help?			
If You Missed Questions . . .	1	2	Essay
Go to Page . . .	95	95	95

Chapter 3

Creating a Constitution

1781–1789

SECTION 1 The Confederation

SECTION 2 A New Constitution

SECTION 3 Ratifying the Constitution

George Washington presides over the Constitutional Convention.

1781
- The Articles of Confederation are ratified by the states

1783
- Treaty of Paris ends Revolutionary War

1784
- American ships begin trading with China at the port of Canton

U.S. PRESIDENTS

U.S. EVENTS 1781   1783   1785

WORLD EVENTS

1781
- William Herschel discovers the planet Uranus using a telescope

1783
- Latin American soldier and statesman Simón Bolivár is born

How Are Governments Created?

After the American Revolution, the new nation struggled to draw up a plan for government. Americans wanted to make sure the government did not have too much power. Eventually they came up with a way to balance federal and state powers and to divide federal power into three branches.

- *Why do you think the United States scrapped its first constitution?*

- *Why did many Americans want a system of checks and balances?*

1786
- Shays's Rebellion begins in western Massachusetts

1787
- Constitutional Convention in Philadelphia drafts the Constitution of the United States

1788
- Constitution is ratified by 11 of 13 states and goes into effect

1789
- George Washington is elected president of the United States
  Washington 1789–1797

1787

1789

1786
- British appoint Cornwallis to be Governor-General of British India

1787
- Sierra Leone is founded by freed Africans

1789
- French Revolution begins

FOLDABLES

Analyzing Constitutional Powers Create a Trifold Book to analyze the Constitution by listing the various functions of government using a Venn diagram. As you read the chapter, list the powers exclusive to the state, those exclusive to the nation, and the shared powers.

The Constitution of the U. S.
State Authority | Shared Powers | National Authority

History ONLINE Chapter Overview
Visit glencoe.com to preview Chapter 3.

Section 1

The Confederation

Guide to Reading

Big Ideas
Government and Society The Articles of Confederation provided a workable but faulty national government.

Content Vocabulary
• duty (p. 101)
• recession (p. 102)

Academic Vocabulary
• explicitly (p. 98)
• occupy (p. 101)

People and Events to Identify
• Articles of Confederation (p. 98)
• Northwest Ordinance (p. 99)
• Shays's Rebellion (p. 103)

Reading Strategy
Organizing Complete a graphic organizer similar to the one below by listing the achievements of the Confederation Congress.

Achievements of the Confederation Congress

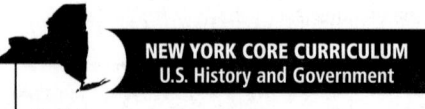

NEW YORK CORE CURRICULUM
U.S. History and Government

Unit 2:
I.A.6 Articles of Confederation
I.A.7 Northwest Ordinance

The Articles of Confederation became the first national constitution of the United States. Written during the Revolutionary War, the Articles of Confederation created a weak national government, which proved to be ineffective.

The Continental Congress Under the Articles of Confederation

MAIN Idea The Articles of Confederation gave the national government few powers.

HISTORY AND YOU Have you ever tried an experiment that failed? Read on to learn about the first national government of the United States.

Even before independence was declared, Patriot leaders at the Continental Congress realized that the colonies needed to be united under some type of central government. In November 1777 the Continental Congress adopted the Articles of Confederation and Perpetual Union—a plan for a loose union of the states under the authority of the Congress.

The Articles of Confederation

The **Articles of Confederation** established a very weak central government. The states had spent several years fighting for independence from Britain. They did not want to give up that independence to a new central government that might become tyrannical.

Under the Articles, once a year, each state would select a delegation to send to the capital city. This group, generally referred to as the Congress, was the entire government. There were no separate executive and judicial branches.

The Congress had the right to declare war, raise armies, and sign treaties. Although these powers were significant, the Congress was not given the power to impose taxes, and it was **explicitly** denied the power to regulate trade.

Western Policies

Lacking the power to tax or regulate trade, the Confederation depended on state contributions to fund the government. Congress also raised money by selling the land it controlled west of the

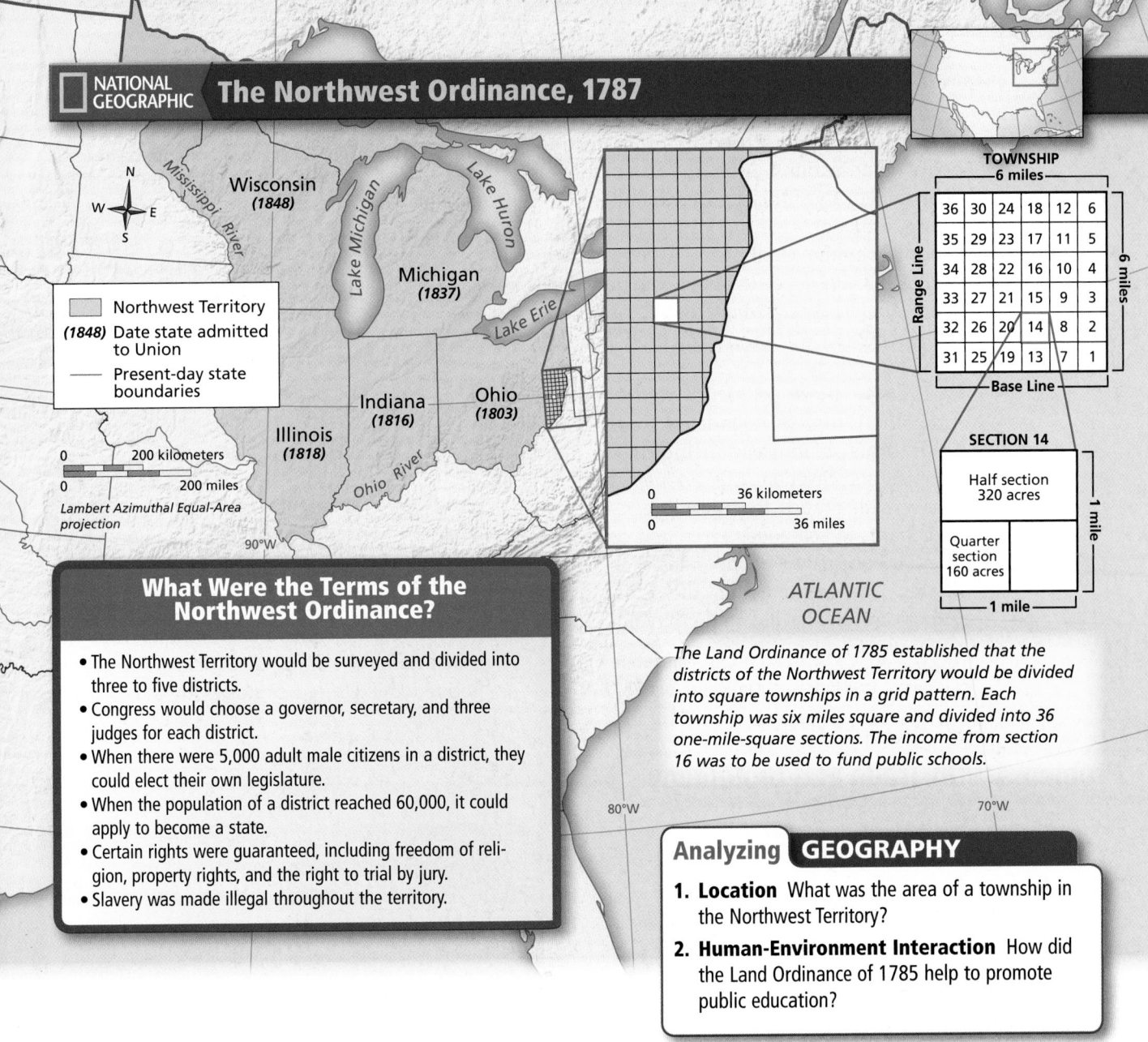

Wisconsin
(1848)

Michigan
(1837)

Lake Michigan

Lake Huron

Mississippi River

Lake Erie

Indiana
(1816)

Ohio
(1803)

Illinois
(1818)

Ohio River

Northwest Territory

(1848) Date state admitted
to Union

— Present-day state
boundaries

0   200 kilometers
0   200 miles
Lambert Azimuthal Equal-Area
projection

90°W

80°W

70°W

ATLANTIC
OCEAN

36 kilometers
0   36 miles

TOWNSHIP
6 miles

36	30	24	18	12	6
35	29	23	17	11	5
34	28	22	16	10	4
33	27	21	15	9	3
32	26	20	14	8	2
31	25	19	13	7	1

Range Line

6 miles

Base Line

SECTION 14

Half section
320 acres

Quarter
section
160 acres

1 mile

1 mile

The Land Ordinance of 1785 established that the
districts of the Northwest Territory would be divided
into square townships in a grid pattern. Each
township was six miles square and divided into 36
one-mile-square sections. The income from section
16 was to be used to fund public schools.

What Were the Terms of the Northwest Ordinance?

- The Northwest Territory would be surveyed and divided into three to five districts.
- Congress would choose a governor, secretary, and three judges for each district.
- When there were 5,000 adult male citizens in a district, they could elect their own legislature.
- When the population of a district reached 60,000, it could apply to become a state.
- Certain rights were guaranteed, including freedom of religion, property rights, and the right to trial by jury.
- Slavery was made illegal throughout the territory.

Analyzing GEOGRAPHY

1. **Location** What was the area of a township in the Northwest Territory?
2. **Human-Environment Interaction** How did the Land Ordinance of 1785 help to promote public education?

Appalachian Mountains. To get people to buy the land and settle in the region, the Congress established an orderly system for dividing and selling the land and governing the new settlements. The Land Ordinance of 1785 set up a method for surveying the western lands. It arranged the land into townships, six miles square. Each township was divided into 36 sections, one mile square.

Two years later, the Congress passed the **Northwest Ordinance,** which provided the basis for governing much of the western territory. The law created a new territory north of the Ohio River and east of the Mississippi, which could eventually be divided into three to five states. Initially the Congress would choose a governor, a secretary, and three judges for

the territory. When 5,000 adult male citizens had settled in a territory, they could elect a territorial legislature. When the population of a territory reached 60,000, the territory could apply to become a state "on an equal footing with the original states."

The Northwest Ordinance also guaranteed certain rights to people living in the territory. These included freedom of religion, property rights, and the right to trial by jury. The ordinance also stated that "there [would] be neither slavery nor involuntary servitude in the said territory." The exclusion of slavery from the Northwest Territory meant that as the United States expanded in future years, it would be divided between Southern slaveholding states and Northern free states.

Success in Trade

In addition to organizing western settlement, the Congress tried to promote trade with other nations. After the Revolutionary War ended, the British government imposed sharp restrictions on American access to British colonies in the Caribbean. American ships could still carry goods to Britain, but only goods from their respective states. A ship from Massachusetts, for example, could not carry New York goods.

To solve these problems, representatives from the Congress negotiated trade treaties with other countries, including Holland, Prussia, and Sweden. A previous commercial treaty with France also permitted American merchants to sell goods to French colonies in the Caribbean. By 1790, the trade of the United States was greater than the trade of the American colonies before the Revolution.

✔ Reading Check) **Describing** What were the provisions of the Northwest Ordinance of 1787?

The Congress Falters

MAIN Idea The first national government could not regulate trade, collect taxes, or enforce treaties, which led to calls for a stronger national government.

HISTORY AND YOU Is it better for government to be too strong or too weak? Read on to learn about problems facing the Confederation Congress.

The Congress's commercial treaties and its system of settling the West were two of its major achievements. Other problems were not so easily solved.

Problems With Trade

During the boycotts of the 1760s and the Revolutionary War, American artisans and manufacturers had prospered by making goods that people had previously bought from the British. After the war ended, British merchants flooded the United States with inexpensive

HISTORY AND GEOGRAPHY
Problems With Trade and Diplomacy

The weak confederation government was powerless to solve economic and diplomatic problems.

British Exports to American Colonies

Value (millions pounds sterling)

2.0
1.5
1.0
0.5

1750 1755 1760 1765 1770 1775 1780
Year

Source: *Historical Statistics of the United States.*

How Did the Articles of Confederation Affect Foreign Policy?

Weakness	Problem Caused
• No power to regulate commerce	• States impose trade restrictions and tariffs
• No power to compel states to obey international treaties signed by the Congress	• States restrict Britain's ability to collect American debts; Congress cannot reach a financial settlement with Britain; Britain refuses to evacuate forts on American soil
• Cannot declare war without unanimous support of all states	
• No power to tax	• Spain denies Americans permission to deposit goods at mouth of Mississippi; Congress has no leverage with Spain
• No power to print or coin money	

British Forts in the United States, 1787

BRITISH NORTH AMERICA

St. Lawrence R.

Ft. Mackinac

Pointe-au-Fer
Oswegatchie
Ft. Oswego
Fort Detroit
Ft. Niagara

Vt. Me.
Dutchman's Pt.
N.Y. N.H.
Mass.
R.I.
Penn. Conn.
N.J.
Del.
Va. Md.

Mississippi R.

ATLANTIC OCEAN

N.C.

◄ *Americans resented the continued British military presence in the United States.*

☐ United States, 1787
☐ United States territory, 1787
☐ British territory
■ British fort

Analyzing VISUALS

1. **Explaining** Why did British exports to the American colonies drop so steeply after 1775?

2. **Determining Cause and Effect** What was the effect of the national government's inability to regulate interstate trade under the Articles of Confederation?

British goods, driving many American artisans out of business.

British trade practices convinced many states to fight back by restricting British imports. Unfortunately, the states did not all impose the same **duties,** or taxes, on imported goods. The British would then take their goods to the states that had the lowest taxes or fewest restrictions. Once British goods were in the United States, they moved overland into the states that had tried to keep them out.

Because the Articles of Confederation did not allow the Congress to regulate commerce, the states began setting up customs posts on their borders to prevent the British from exploiting the different trade laws. They also levied taxes on each other's goods to raise revenue. New York, for example, taxed firewood from Connecticut and cabbage from New Jersey. New Jersey retaliated by charging New York for a harbor lighthouse on the New Jersey side of the Hudson River. Each state was beginning to act as an independent country, and this behavior threatened the unity of the new United States.

Problems With Diplomacy

The Articles of Confederation also created problems for Congress in other areas of foreign policy. The first problems surfaced immediately after the Treaty of Paris, which ended the Revolutionary War, was signed. Neither Britain nor the United States carried out the terms of the treaty, primarily because the Congress lacked the power to uphold its side of the treaty. Problems also arose with America's ally Spain soon after the war ended.

Problems With Britain Before the war, many American merchants and planters had borrowed money from British lenders. In the peace treaty, the United States had agreed that the states should allow British creditors to recover their prewar debts by suing in American courts. The Congress had no power to compel the states to do this, however, and many states placed restrictions on Britain's ability to collect its debts.

Even when the British were able to get the matter into court, they often found that American judges and juries sided with the American debtors. The United States had also agreed that the states should return the property that had been confiscated from Loyalists during the war. Again, the Congress could not compel the states to do this, further angering the British.

In retaliation, the British refused to evacuate American soil, as specified in the treaty. British forces continued to **occupy** a string of frontier posts south of the Great Lakes, inside American territory. The Congress had no way to resolve these problems. It did not have the power to impose taxes, so it could not raise the money to pay a financial settlement to Britain for the debts and Loyalist property. It also could not afford to raise an army to expel the British from American territory.

Problems With Spain American dealings with Spain also showed the weaknesses of the Articles of Confederation. After the revolutionary war, Spain's support for the United States came to an end. Instead, Spain began to regard the United States as a rival wanting to claim land in North America that Spain also claimed.

The first major dispute between Spain and the United States involved the border between Spanish territory and the state of Georgia. To pressure the United States into accepting the border where Spain wanted it to be, the Spanish withdrew permission for Americans to deposit their goods on Spanish territory at the mouth of the Mississippi River. This effectively closed the Mississippi River to frontier farmers, who used the river to ship their goods to market.

Unfortunately, the negotiators for the Congress had no leverage to pressure the Spanish to change their policy. The best American negotiators could do was to get Spain to agree to a trade treaty, in exchange for the United States withdrawing its demand for navigation rights on the Mississippi.

The proposed treaty enraged people in the Southern states. They believed the Northern states had given in on the issue simply to help Northern merchants increase their trade with Spain. Without Southern support, the treaty could not pass Congress and was withdrawn from consideration. The dispute over Georgia's border and navigation on the Mississippi remained unresolved. Again, the limited powers of the Congress under the Articles of Confederation had prevented any diplomatic solution from being worked out.

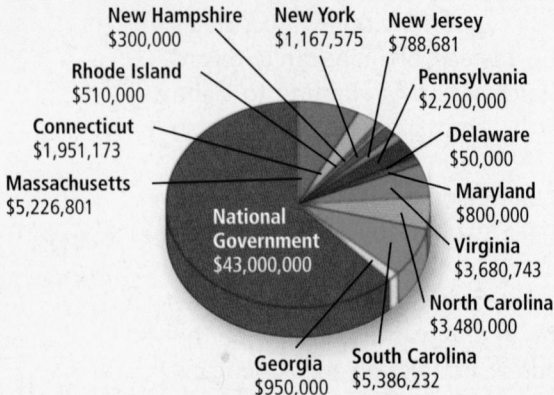

▲ Rebels occupy a courthouse in western Massachusetts.

Revolutionary Debt

New Hampshire $300,000
New York $1,167,575
New Jersey $788,681
Rhode Island $510,000
Pennsylvania $2,200,000
Connecticut $1,951,173
Delaware $50,000
Massachusetts $5,226,801
Maryland $800,000
National Government $43,000,000
Virginia $3,680,743
North Carolina $3,480,000
Georgia $950,000
South Carolina $5,386,232

Sources: *The American States During and After the Revolution;*
The Price of Liberty: The Public Debt of the American Revolution.

In the midst of Shays's Rebellion, George Washington wrote to James Madison agreeing that the rebellion showed the need to revise the Articles of Confederation:

"What stronger evidence can be given of the want of energy in our governments than these disorders? If there exists not a power to check them, what security has a man for life, liberty, or property? To you, I am sure I need not add aught on this subject, the consequences of a lax, or inefficient government, are too obvious to be dwelt on. Thirteen Sovereignties pulling against each other, and all tugging at the federal head will soon bring ruin on the whole; whereas a liberal, and energetic Constitution, well guarded and closely watched, to prevent incroachments, might restore us to that degree of respectability and consequence, to which we had a fair claim, and the brightest prospect of attaining."

—from George Washington's letter to James Madison, November 5, 1786

DBQ) Document-Based Questions

1. **Specifying** Where did Massachusetts rank among the states in terms of the amount of its Revolutionary debt?

2. **Explaining** What did Washington feel was the significance of Shays's Rebellion?

The Economic Crisis

While the Congress struggled with diplomatic issues, many other Americans were struggling financially. The end of the Revolutionary War and the decline of trade with Britain had plunged the United States into a severe economic **recession.**

Farmers were among those most affected by the recession. They were not earning as much money as they once did, and they had to keep borrowing to get their next crop in the ground. Many also had mortgages to pay. At the same time, the Revolutionary War had left both the Congress and many states in debt. To pay for the war, many states had issued bonds as a way to borrow money from wealthy merchants and planters. With the war over, the people holding those bonds wanted them to be redeemed for gold or silver.

To pay off their debts, the states could raise taxes, but farmers and other people in debt urged the state governments to issue paper money instead. They also wanted the states to make the paper money available to farmers through government loans on farm mortgages.

Since paper money would not be backed up by gold and silver, and people would not trust it, inflation—a decline in the value of money—began. Debtors would be able to pay their debts using paper money that steadily lost its value. This would let them pay off their debts more easily. Lenders, on the other hand, including many merchants and importers, strongly opposed paper money because they would not be receiving the true amount they were owed. Beginning in 1785, seven states began issuing paper money.

In Rhode Island, paper money eventually became so worthless that merchants refused to accept it. After an angry mob rioted against the merchants, Rhode Island's assembly passed a law forcing people to accept the paper money. Those who refused could be arrested and fined.

The violence in Rhode Island demonstrated two things to many American leaders. The Rhode Island assembly, influenced by the mob, had forced wealthy creditors to accept worthless money. This showed that unless a government was properly designed, the people could use the power of government to steal from the wealthy. The events also suggested that a strong central government was needed to take on the country's debts and stabilize the currency.

Shays's Rebellion

Property owners' fears seemed justified when a rebellion, known as **Shays's Rebellion,** erupted in Massachusetts in 1786. The conflict started when the government of Massachusetts decided to raise taxes instead of issuing paper money to pay off its debts. The taxes fell most heavily on farmers, particularly poor farmers in the western part of the state. As the recession grew worse, many found it impossible to pay their debts. Those who could not pay often faced the loss of their farms.

Angry at the legislature's indifference to their plight, farmers in western Massachusetts rebelled in late August 1786. They closed down several county courthouses to prevent farm foreclosures and then marched to the state supreme court. At this point, Daniel Shays, a former captain in the Continental Army who was now a bankrupt farmer, emerged as one of the rebellion's leaders.

In January 1787 Shays and about 1,200 farmers headed to a state arsenal intending to seize weapons before marching on Boston. In response, the governor sent a force under the command of General Benjamin Lincoln to defend the arsenal. Before Lincoln arrived, Shays attacked, and the militia defending the arsenal opened fire. Four farmers died in the fighting. The rest scattered. The next day Lincoln's troops arrived and ended the rebellion. The fears the rebellion had raised, however, were harder to disperse.

People with greater income and social status tended to see the rebellion, as well as inflation and an unstable currency, as signs that the republic itself was at risk. They feared that as state legislatures became more democratic and responsive to poor people, they would weaken property rights and vote to take property from the wealthy. As General Henry Knox, a close aide to George Washington, concluded: "What is to afford our security against the violence of lawless men? Our government must be braced, changed, or altered to secure our lives and property."

These concerns were an important reason that many people, including merchants, artisans, and creditors, began to argue for a stronger central government, and several members of the Congress called on the states to correct "such defects as may be discovered to exist" in the present government. The Confederation's failure to deal with conditions that might lead to rebellion, as well as the problems with trade and diplomacy, only added fuel to their argument.

Reading Check **Explaining** What caused Shays's Rebellion?

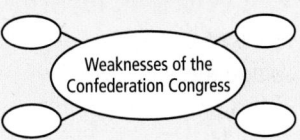

Section 1 REVIEW

Vocabulary

1. **Explain** the significance of: Articles of Confederation, Northwest Ordinance, duty, recession, Shays's Rebellion.

Main Ideas

2. **Describing** What were some accomplishments of the U.S. government under the Articles of Confederation?

3. **Explaining** Why did Shays's Rebellion lead to a call for a stronger national government?

Critical Thinking

4. **Big Ideas** What do you think was the most serious flaw of the Articles of Confederation? Explain.

5. **Organizing** Use a graphic organizer similar to the one below to list the weaknesses of the Confederation Congress.

Weaknesses of the Confederation Congress

6. **Analyzing Visuals** Study the map of the Northwest Ordinance on page 99. What significant provision of this law would contribute to dividing the nation into competing regions?

Writing About History

7. **Persuasive Writing** Take on the role of a newspaper publisher during the time of the Confederation Congress. Write an editorial expressing your opinion of Shays's Rebellion, and suggest how the government might handle such situations better in the future.

History ONLINE

Study Central™ To review this section, go to glencoe.com and click on Study Central.

A New Constitution

Guide to Reading

Big Ideas

Government and Society In the new Constitution, the Framers tried to uphold the rights of the states while providing needed national authority.

Content Vocabulary
- popular sovereignty *(p. 108)*
- federalism *(p. 108)*
- separation of powers *(p. 108)*
- checks and balances *(p. 109)*
- veto *(p. 109)*
- amendment *(p. 109)*

Academic Vocabulary
- financier *(p. 104)*

People and Events to Identify
- James Madison *(p. 104))*
- Great Compromise *(p. 106)*
- Three-Fifths Compromise *(p. 107)*

Reading Strategy

Categorizing As you read, use the major headings of the section to fill in an outline similar to the one below.

```
A New Constitution
I. The Constitutional Convention
   A.
   B.
II.
   A.
   B.
```

NEW YORK CORE CURRICULUM
U.S. History and Government

Unit 2:
I.B.1.a Framers of the Constitution (James Madison)
I.B.1.b Plans of government (Virginia plan, New Jersey plan, Connecticut plan)
I.B.2.b Power separated and balanced
I.B.2.c The Constitution, slavery, and fear of tyrannical powers of government
I.D Basic structure and function: three branches and their operation

In 1787 the delegates to the Constitutional Convention intended to revise the Articles of Confederation. Instead, they began drafting a constitution for a new national government. The delegates negotiated many difficult compromises before agreeing on the framework for the new federal system.

The Constitutional Convention

MAIN Idea The delegates to the convention tried to create a stronger national government that gave fair representation to big and small states.

HISTORY AND YOU Who do you think should be chosen to create a government? Should it be the smartest people or the richest, or should other criteria be used? Read to learn about the men who designed the Constitution.

The political and economic problems facing the United States in 1787 worried many American leaders. They believed that the new nation would not survive without a strong central government and that the Articles of Confederation had to be revised or replaced. People who supported a stronger central government became known as "nationalists." Prominent nationalists included Benjamin Franklin, George Washington, John Adams, and the **financier** Robert Morris.

One of the most influential nationalists was **James Madison,** a member of the Virginia Assembly and head of its commerce committee. As head of the commerce committee, Madison was well aware of Virginia's trade problems with the other American states and with Britain. He firmly believed that a stronger national government was needed.

In 1786 Madison convinced Virginia's assembly to call a convention of all the states to discuss trade and taxation problems. Representatives from the states were to meet in Annapolis, Maryland, but when the convention began, delegates from only five states were present, too few to reach a final decision on the problems facing the states. The delegates did discuss the weakness of the Articles of Confederation and expressed interest in modifying them.

Another important nationalist, New York delegate Alexander Hamilton, recommended that the Congress itself call for a convention. Members of the Congress were initially reluctant to call a convention, but news of Shays's Rebellion changed many minds. In February 1787, Congress called for a convention of the states "for the sole purpose of revising the Articles of Confederation."

Every state except Rhode Island sent delegates to what became known as the Constitutional Convention. In May 1787 the delegates

PRIMARY SOURCE
Creating a Constitution

George Washington

William Paterson drafted the New Jersey Plan.

Roger Sherman came up with the Connecticut, or Great, Compromise.

Alexander Hamilton

Benjamin Franklin

James Madison

Analyzing VISUALS

1. **Making Inferences** Why do you think Benjamin Franklin is pictured in the middle of this painting?

2. **Describing** How would you describe Washington's attitude in the painting, and how do you think it expresses his role at the Convention?

took their places in the Pennsylvania state-house in Philadelphia. They knew they faced a daunting task: to balance the rights of the states with the need for a stronger national government.

The Framers

The 55 delegates who attended the convention in Philadelphia included some of the shrewdest and most distinguished leaders in the United States. The majority were attorneys, and most of the others were planters and merchants. Most had experience in colonial, state, or national government. Seven had served as state governors. Thirty-nine had been members of the Congress. Eight had signed the Declaration of Independence. In the words of Thomas Jefferson, who was unable to attend the convention because he was serving as American minister to France, the convention

in Philadelphia was no less than "an assembly of demigods."

The delegates chose George Washington of Virginia, hero of the American Revolution, as presiding officer. Benjamin Franklin was a delegate from Pennsylvania. Now 81 years old, he tired easily and had other state delegates read his speeches for him. He provided assistance to many of his younger colleagues, and his experience and good humor helped smooth the debates.

Other notable delegates included New York's Alexander Hamilton and Connecticut's Roger Sherman. Virginia sent a well-prepared delegation, including the scholarly James Madison, who kept a record of the debates. Madison's records provide the best source of information about what went on in the sessions. The meetings were closed to the public to help ensure honest and open discussion free from outside political pressures.

The Virginia Plan

History ONLINE
Student Web Activity Visit glencoe.com and complete the activity on the Constitution.

The Virginia delegation arrived at the convention with a detailed plan—mostly the work of James Madison—for a new national government. A few days into the proceedings, the governor of Virginia, Edmund Randolph, introduced the plan. "A national government," he declared, "ought to be established, consisting of a supreme Legislative, Executive, and Judiciary." The Virginia Plan, as it came to be called, proposed scrapping the Articles of Confederation and creating a new national government with the power to make laws binding upon the states and to raise its own money through taxes.

The Virginia Plan proposed that the legislature be divided into two houses. The voters in each state would elect members of the first house. Members of the second house would be nominated by the state governments but actually elected by the first house. In both houses, the number of representatives for each state would reflect that state's population. The Virginia Plan would benefit large states like Virginia, New York, and Massachusetts, which had more votes than the smaller states.

The Virginia Plan drew sharp reactions. The delegates accepted the idea of dividing the government into executive, legislative, and judicial branches, but the smaller states strongly opposed having representation based on population. They feared that larger states would outvote them. William Paterson, a New Jersey delegate, offered a counterproposal that came to be called the New Jersey Plan.

The New Jersey Plan did not abandon the Articles of Confederation. Instead it modified them to make the central government stronger. Under the plan, Congress would have a single house in which each state was equally represented, but it would also have the power to raise taxes and regulate trade.

The delegates had to choose one plan for further negotiation. After debating on June 19, the convention voted to proceed with the Virginia Plan. With this vote, the convention delegates decided to go beyond their original purpose of revising the Articles of Confederation. Instead, they began work on a new constitution for the United States.

✔ **Reading Check** **Explaining** Why did small states oppose the Virginia Plan?

A Union Built on Compromise

MAIN Idea American leaders created a new constitution based on compromise.

HISTORY AND YOU Have you ever had to compromise on something you felt strongly about? Read on to learn how slavery divided the delegates at the Constitutional Convention.

As the convention worked out the details of the new constitution, the delegates found themselves divided geographically. The small states demanded changes that would protect them from the voting power of the big states. At the same time, Northern and Southern states were divided over how to treat slavery in the new constitution. The only way to resolve the differences was through compromise.

The Connecticut Compromise

After the convention voted to proceed with the Virginia Plan, tempers flared as delegates from the small states insisted that each state had to have an equal vote in Congress. Angry delegates from the larger states threatened to walk out. By July 1787, the convention had reached a turning point. As a delegate from North Carolina warned, "If we do not concede on both sides, our business must soon end."

The convention appointed a special committee to negotiate a compromise. Delegates who were strongly committed to one side or the other were left off the committee, leaving only those who were undecided or willing to change their minds. Benjamin Franklin chaired the proceedings.

The compromise the committee worked out was based on an idea proposed by Roger Sherman of Connecticut. Although sometimes called the Connecticut Compromise, it is also known as the **Great Compromise.** The committee proposed that in one house of Congress—the House of Representatives—the states would be represented according to the size of their populations. In the other house—the Senate—each state would have equal representation. Voters in each state would elect the House of Representatives, but the state legislatures would choose the senators.

People IN HISTORY

James Madison
1751–1836

Although many individuals contributed to the framing of the U.S. Constitution, the master builder was James Madison. In the year preceding the Constitutional Convention, the 36-year-old Virginia planter read volume after volume on political history. "From a spirit of industry and application," said one colleague, Madison was "the best-informed man on any point in debate."

Based on his experience in helping to draft Virginia's constitution, Madison created the Virginia Plan. Perhaps his greatest achievement was in defining the true source of political power. He argued that all power, at all levels of government, flowed ultimately from the people.

At the Convention, Madison served his nation well. The ordeal, he later said, almost killed him. In the years to come, though, the nation would call on him again. In 1801 he became President Thomas Jefferson's secretary of state. In 1808 he was elected the fourth president of the United States.

How did Madison contribute to the drafting of the U.S. Constitution?

Roger Sherman
1721–1793

Roger Sherman was born in Massachusetts but in 1743 moved to Connecticut, where he studied law and eventually became a superior court judge. Sherman was enormously respected for his knowledge, judgment, and integrity. He was a delegate to the Continental Congress and was a member of the group who drafted the Declaration of Independence. He also helped to write the Articles of Confederation.

A skilled legislator and master of political compromise, Sherman was a logical choice to serve as one of Connecticut's delegates to the Constitutional Convention. There, he ably defended the interests of the smaller states and developed the famous Connecticut Compromise that saved the convention from breaking up. Sherman was elected to the House of Representatives, where he helped to prepare the Bill of Rights. He is the only person to have signed the Declaration of Independence, the Articles of Confederation, and the Constitution—and he played an important role in drafting all three.

Why do you think that Sherman is not as well-known as some other Founders?

Compromise Over Slavery

Franklin's committee also proposed that each state could elect one member to the House of Representatives for every 40,000 people in the state. This caused a split between Northern and Southern delegates. Southern delegates wanted to count enslaved people when determining how many representatives they could elect. Northern delegates objected, pointing out that the enslaved could not vote.

Northern delegates also suggested that if slaves were counted for representation, they should be counted for purposes of taxation as well. In the end, a solution, referred to as the **Three-Fifths Compromise,** was worked out. Every five enslaved people would count as three free people for determining both representation and taxes.

The dispute over how to count enslaved people was not the only issue dividing North and South. Southerners feared that a strong national government might impose taxes on the export of farm products or ban the import of enslaved Africans. The Southern delegates insisted that the new constitution forbid interference with the slave trade and limit Congress's power to regulate trade. Northern delegates, on the other hand, knew that

Northern merchants and artisans needed a government capable of controlling foreign imports into the United States.

Eventually, another compromise was worked out. The delegates agreed that the new Congress could not tax exports. They also agreed that it could not ban the slave trade until 1808 or impose high taxes on the importation of slaves. The Great Compromise and the compromises between Northern and Southern delegates ended most of the major disputes between the state delegations. This enabled the convention to focus on the details of how the new government would operate.

By mid-September, the delegates had completed their task. Although everyone made compromises, the 39 delegates who signed the new Constitution believed it was a vast improvement over the Articles of Confederation. On September 20, they sent it to the Confederation Congress for approval. Eight days later, the Congress voted to submit the Constitution to the states for approval. The Constitution specified that nine of the thirteen states had to ratify the Constitution for it to take effect.

✔ Reading Check **Describing** What was the Three-Fifths Compromise, and why was it necessary?

A Framework for Limited Government

MAIN Idea The Framers created a federal system that provided for a separation of powers along with checks and balances to keep any one branch of government from becoming too powerful.

HISTORY AND YOU Can you think of situations when dividing responsibilities makes it harder to get things done? Read to learn why the Framers created checks and balances.

The new constitution that the states were considering was based on the idea of **popular sovereignty,** or rule by the people. Rather than a direct democracy, it created a representative system of government in which elected officials represented the voice of the people. The new constitution also established a **federal** system. It divided government power between the federal, or national, government and the state governments.

The United States Constitution provides for a **separation of powers** among the three branches of the federal government. The two houses of Congress compose the legislative branch of the government. They make the laws. The executive branch, headed by a president, implements and enforces the laws passed by Congress. The judicial branch—a system of

INFOGRAPHIC
Comparing Constitutions

The Articles of Confederation		The Federal Constitution
One—the Confederation Congress	**How Many Houses in the Legislature?**	Two—the House of Representatives and the Senate
Members of Congress appointed annually by state legislatures	**How Are Delegates Chosen?**	Representatives elected every two years by voters; senators originally chosen by state legislatures for a six-year term (today voters elect senators as well)
No separate executive; members of the Congress elect a president annually; government departments are run by committees created by the Congress	**How Is Executive Power Exercised?**	Separate executive branch; president elected every four years by Electoral College; president conducts policy, selects officers to run government departments, appoints ambassadors and judges
Judicial matters left to the states and local courts; the Congress acts as a court for disputes between states	**How Is Judicial Power Exercised?**	Separate judicial branch with a Supreme Court and lower courts created by Congress; judges appointed by the president but confirmed by the Senate
Only states can levy taxes	**What Taxes Can Be Levied?**	Federal government can levy taxes
The Congress regulated foreign trade but had no power to regulate interstate trade	**Can Trade Be Regulated?**	Federal government regulates both interstate commerce and foreign commerce

Analyzing VISUALS

1. **Contrasting** How was the election of members of the House of Representatives different from the election of members of the Confederation Congress?

2. **Evaluating** How did the Constitution solve the problems experienced under the Articles with interstate and foreign trade?

federal courts—interprets federal laws and renders judgment in cases involving those laws. No one serving in one branch can serve in any other branch at the same time.

Checks and Balances

In addition to separating the powers of the government into three branches, the delegates to the convention created a system of **checks and balances** to prevent any one of the three branches from becoming too powerful. Within this system, each branch has some ability to limit the power of the other branches.

Under the Constitution, the president—as head of the executive branch—is given far-reaching powers. The president can propose legislation, appoint judges, put down rebellions, and **veto,** or reject, acts of Congress. The president is also the commander in chief of the armed forces. According to one delegate in Philadelphia, these powers might not have been so great "had not many of the members cast their eyes towards George Washington as president."

Although the president can veto acts of Congress, the legislature can override a veto with a two-thirds vote in both houses. The Senate also has to approve or reject presidential appointments to the executive branch as well as any treaties. Furthermore, Congress can, if necessary, impeach, or formally accuse of misconduct, and then remove the president or other high officials.

Members of the judicial branch of government can hear all cases arising under federal law and the Constitution. The powers of the judiciary are balanced by the other two branches. The president can nominate members of the judiciary, but the Senate has to confirm or reject such nominations. Once appointed, however, federal judges serve for life, thus ensuring their independence from both the executive and the legislative branches.

Amending the Constitution

The delegates in Philadelphia recognized that the new constitution might need to be amended, or changed over time. To ensure this, they created a clear system for making **amendments,** or changes. To prevent the constitution from being changed constantly, they made the process difficult.

The amendment process had two steps—proposal and ratification. An amendment could be proposed by a vote of two-thirds of the members of both houses of Congress. Alternatively, two-thirds of the states could call a constitutional convention to propose new amendments. The proposed amendment then had to be ratified by three-fourths of the state legislatures or by conventions in three-fourths of the states.

The success of the Philadelphia Convention in creating a government that reflected the country's many different viewpoints was, in Washington's words, "little short of a miracle." The convention, John Adams declared, was "the single greatest effort of national deliberation that the world has ever seen."

Reading Check **Explaining** How is power divided under the system of federalism?

Section 2 REVIEW

Vocabulary

1. **Explain** the significance of: James Madison, Great Compromise, Three-Fifths Compromise, popular sovereignty, federalism, separation of powers, checks and balances, veto, amendment.

Main Ideas

2. **Contrasting** How did the New Jersey Plan differ from the Virginia Plan?

3. **Explaining** How did the Great Compromise meet the needs of both large and small states?

4. **Identifying** What provision did the Framers make in the Constitution to limit the powers of each branch of the government?

Critical Thinking

5. **Big Ideas** How did the Constitution uphold the rights of the states while strengthening the national government?

6. **Organizing** Use a graphic organizer to list the compromises that the Framers reached in creating the new Constitution.

7. **Analyzing Visuals** Study the chart on page 108. What was significant about the fact that the federal government under the new Constitution could now levy taxes?

Writing About History

8. **Descriptive Writing** Imagine you are at the Constitutional Convention. Write a journal entry describing the arguments from each side as well as your own opinion on them.

History ONLINE

Study Central™ To review this section, go to glencoe.com and click on Study Central.

109

Ratifying the Constitution

Guide to Reading

Big Ideas
Government and Society
Ratification of the Constitution moved to the states, where Federalists and Anti-Federalists argued their opposing views.

Content Vocabulary
• bill of rights *(p. 113)*

Academic Vocabulary
• framework *(p. 112)*
• specific *(p. 113)*

People and Events to Identify
• Federalist *(p. 110)*
• Anti-Federalist *(p. 111)*
• John Hancock *(p. 111)*
• Patrick Henry *(p. 111)*

Reading Strategy
Complete a graphic organizer similar to the one below by listing the supporters and goals of the Federalists and Anti-Federalists.

	Federalists	Anti-Federalists
Source of Support		
Goals		

NEW YORK CORE CURRICULUM
U.S. History and Government

Unit 2:
I.B.4.a The Federalist Papers—a New York activity with widespread influence
I.B.4.b The debate: Federalist and Anti-Federalist arguments
I.C The Bill of Rights

Once the work of the Constitutional Convention was complete, the campaign for ratification began. Each state elected delegates to a convention to vote on the new framework of government. Nine of the thirteen states had to ratify it to put it into effect.

A Great Debate

MAIN Idea Federalists supported the Constitution, but Anti-Federalists thought it endangered states' independence and gave the national government too much power.

HISTORY AND YOU Has a political advertisement ever changed your mind on an issue? Read on to learn about the tactics used by Federalists to promote their cause.

As soon as the Philadelphia Convention ended, delegates rushed home to begin the campaign for ratification. Each state would elect a convention to vote on the new constitution. Nine states had to vote for the Constitution to put it into effect. As Americans learned about the new Constitution, they began to argue over whether it should be ratified. The debate took place in state legislatures, in mass meetings, in the columns of newspapers, and in everyday conversations.

Federalists and Anti-Federalists

Supporters of the Constitution called themselves **Federalists.** The name was chosen with care. It emphasized that the Constitution would create a federal system. They believed that power should be divided between a central government and regional governments. They hoped the name would remind Americans who feared a central government that the states would retain many of their powers.

Supporters of the Federalists and the new Constitution included large landowners who wanted the property protection a strong central government could provide. Supporters also included merchants and artisans living in large coastal cities. The inability of the Confederation Congress to regulate trade had hit these citizens hard. They believed that an effective federal government that could impose taxes on foreign goods would help their businesses.

Many farmers who lived near the coast or along rivers that led to the coast also supported the Constitution, as did farmers who shipped goods across state borders. These farmers depended on trade for their livelihood and had been frustrated by the different tariffs and duties the states imposed. They wanted a strong central government that could regulate trade consistently.

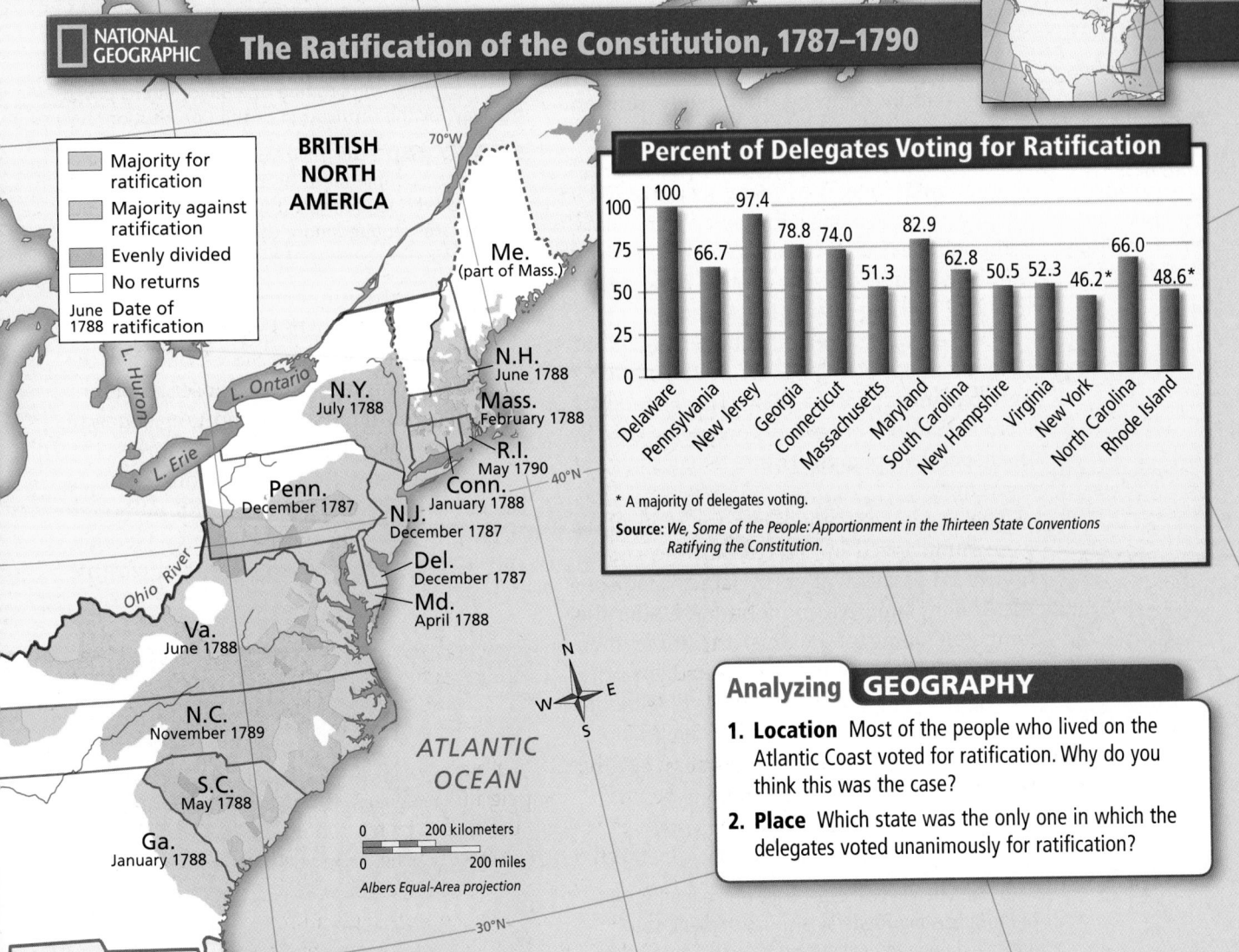

Map Legend:
- Majority for ratification
- Majority against ratification
- Evenly divided
- No returns
- June 1788 Date of ratification

BRITISH NORTH AMERICA

70°W

Me. (part of Mass.)

L. Huron
L. Ontario
L. Erie
Ohio River

N.H. June 1788
N.Y. July 1788
Mass. February 1788
R.I. May 1790
Conn. January 1788
Penn. December 1787
N.J. December 1787
Del. December 1787
Md. April 1788
Va. June 1788
N.C. November 1789
S.C. May 1788
Ga. January 1788

40°N
30°N

ATLANTIC OCEAN

0   200 kilometers
0   200 miles
Albers Equal-Area projection

Percent of Delegates Voting for Ratification

State	Percent
Delaware	100
Pennsylvania	66.7
New Jersey	97.4
Georgia	78.8
Connecticut	74.0
Massachusetts	51.3
Maryland	82.9
South Carolina	62.8
New Hampshire	50.5
Virginia	52.3
New York	46.2*
North Carolina	66.0
Rhode Island	48.6*

* A majority of delegates voting.

Source: *We, Some of the People: Apportionment in the Thirteen State Conventions Ratifying the Constitution.*

Analyzing GEOGRAPHY

1. **Location** Most of the people who lived on the Atlantic Coast voted for ratification. Why do you think this was the case?

2. **Place** Which state was the only one in which the delegates voted unanimously for ratification?

Opponents of the Constitution were called **Anti-Federalists,** a misleading name, as they were not against federalism. They accepted the need for a national government. The real issue for them was whether the national government or the state governments would be supreme. Prominent Anti-Federalists included **John Hancock, Patrick Henry,** Richard Henry Lee of Virginia, and George Clinton, governor of New York. Two members of the Constitutional Convention, Edmund Randolph and George Mason, became Anti-Federalists because they believed the new Constitution should have included a bill of rights. Sam Adams agreed. He opposed the Constitution because he believed it endangered the independence of the states.

Many Anti-Federalists were western farmers living far from the coast. These people considered themselves self-sufficient and were suspicious of the wealthy and powerful. Many of them were also deeply in debt and suspected that the new Constitution was simply a way for wealthy creditors to get rid of paper money and foreclose on their farms. A farmer named Amos Singletary expressed views shared by many western farmers:

PRIMARY SOURCE

"These lawyers and men of learning, and moneyed men, that talk so finely, and gloss over matters so smoothly, to make us poor, illiterate people swallow down the pill, expect to get into Congress themselves; they expect to be managers of this Constitution, and get all the power and all the money into their own hands, and then they will swallow up all us little folks. . . ."

—*The Massachusetts Gazette*, February 15, 1788

The Federalist

For excerpts from *Federalist 10*, *Federalist 51*, and *Federalist 59*, see pages R44–R45 in **Documents in American History**.

Although many influential leaders in the young nation opposed the newly drafted Constitution, several factors worked against the Anti-Federalists. First of all, their campaign was a negative one. The Federalists presented a definite program to meet the nation's problems. Although the Anti-Federalists complained that the Constitution failed to protect basic rights, they had nothing to offer in its place.

The Federalists were also better organized than their opponents. Most of the nation's newspapers supported them. The Federalists were able to present a very convincing case in their speeches, pamphlets, and debates in state conventions.

The Federalists' arguments for ratification were summarized in *The Federalist*—a collection of 85 essays written by James Madison, Alexander Hamilton, and John Jay. Under the joint pen name of Publius, the three men published most of the essays in New York newspapers in late 1787 and early 1788 before collecting them in *The Federalist.* Federalist No. 1, the first essay in the series, tried to set the **framework** for the debate:

PRIMARY SOURCE

"After an unequivocal experience of the inefficacy of the subsisting Foederal [sic] Government, you are called upon to deliberate on a new Constitution for the United States of America. . . . It has been frequently remarked that it seems to have been reserved to the people of this country, by their conduct and example, to decide the important question, whether societies of men are really capable or not of establishing good government from reflection and choice, or whether they are forever destined to depend for their political constitutions on accident and force."

—from *The Independent Journal*, October 27, 1787

The essays explained how the new Constitution worked and why it was needed. The essays were very influential. Even today, judges, lawyers, legislators, and historians rely upon *The Federalist* to help them interpret the Constitution and understand what the original Framers intended.

✓ Reading Check **Summarizing** Which groups of people in the United States tended to support the new Constitution?

Battle for Ratification

MAIN Idea The promise of a Bill of Rights paved the way for the ratification of the Constitution.

HISTORY AND YOU Have you ever had to convince a friend to do something? Read on to learn why some states quickly decided to ratify the Constitution, but others states required more convincing.

As the ratifying conventions began to gather, the Federalists knew that they had clear majorities in some states but that the vote was going to be much closer in others, including the large and important states of Massachusetts, Virginia, and New York.

The first state conventions took place in December 1787 and January 1788. Although Delaware, Pennsylvania, New Jersey, Georgia, and Connecticut all quickly ratified the

Debates IN HISTORY

Should the Federal Constitution Be Ratified?

The debate over ratification of the Constitution was often heated. Many important figures of the time, such as Patrick Henry, were concerned about the loss of state power and the fact that the Constitution did not mention protections of civil liberties. Others, such as James Madison, were convinced that only a strong federal government would protect people's liberties and ensure the success of the new United States of America.

Constitution, the most important battles still lay ahead.

The Debate in Massachusetts

In Massachusetts, opponents of the Constitution held a clear majority when the convention met in January 1788. Among the opponents were Massachusetts Governor John Hancock and Samuel Adams, both of whom had signed the Declaration of Independence. Adams refused to support the new Constitution unless Federalists could give him a guarantee "that the said Constitution be never construed to authorize Congress to infringe the just liberty of the press, or the rights of conscience; or to prevent the people of the United States ... from keeping their own arms; ... or to subject the people to unreasonable searches and seizures of their persons, papers or possessions."

Federalists moved quickly to meet Adams's objections to the Constitution. **Specifically,** Federalists promised to attach a **bill of rights** to the Constitution once it was ratified. Federalists also agreed to support an amendment that would reserve for the states all powers not specifically granted to the federal government.

These concessions, combined with most artisans siding with the Federalists, persuaded Adams to vote for ratification. John Hancock and his supporters were won over by hints from local Federalists that they would support him for president of the United States. In the final vote, 187 members of the convention voted in favor of the Constitution, while 168 voted against it.

YES

James Madison
Delegate to the Constitutional Convention

PRIMARY SOURCE

"In a single republic ... usurpations are guarded against by a division of the government into distinct and separate departments. In the compound republic of America, the power surrendered by the people, is first divided between two distinct governments, and then the portion allotted to each, subdivided among the rights of the people. The different governments will controul [sic] each other; at the same time that each will be controuled [sic] by itself....

In the extended republic of the United States, and among the great variety of interests, parties and sects which it embraces, a coalition of a majority of the whole society could seldom take place on any other principles than those of justice and the general good."
—from *Federalist No. 51*

NO

Patrick Henry
Member of the Virginia Ratifying Convention

PRIMARY SOURCE

"This proposal of altering our federal government is of a most alarming nature: make the best of this new government—say it is composed by anything but inspiration—you ought to be extremely cautious, watchful, jealous of your liberty; for instead of securing your rights, you may lose them forever.... My political curiosity ... leads me to ask, who authorized [the Framers] to speak the language of *We, the People*, instead of *We, the States*? States are the characteristics, and the soul of a confederation. If the states be not the agents of this compact, it must be one great consolidated national government, of the people of all the states."
—from *The Debates in the Several State Conventions on the Adoption of the Federal Constitution*

DBQ Document-Based Questions

1. **Summarizing** According to Madison, how is power to be divided under the Constitution?

2. **Explaining** According to Henry, why should people be cautious about the new national government?

3. **Identifying Points of View** How do Madison and Henry disagree over the role of the states in the federal republic?

The Debate in Virginia

By the end of June 1788, Maryland, South Carolina, and New Hampshire had ratified the Constitution. The Federalists had reached the minimum number of states required to put the new Constitution into effect, but Virginia and New York still had not ratified. Without the support of these two large states, many feared the new government would not succeed.

Patrick Henry, Richard Henry Lee, George Mason, and other Anti-Federalists argued strongly against ratification. George Mason raised an argument similar to the one Sam Adams had made in Massachusetts:

PRIMARY SOURCE

"... the State Legislatures have no Security for the Powers now presumed to remain to them; or the People for their Rights. There is no Declaration of any kind, for preserving the Liberty of the Press, or the [trial] by Jury in civil [causes]; nor against the Danger of standing [armies] in time of Peace."

—George Mason, from "Objections to This Constitution of Government," 1787

George Washington and James Madison presented the arguments for ratification to the Virginia convention. In the end, Madison's promise to add a bill of rights won the day for the Federalists. Upon hearing the proposal for a bill of rights, Virginia Governor Edmund Randolph agreed to support the new Constitition. Randolph had attended the Constitutional Convention but had refused to sign the final document, worried that it lacked sufficient protections of the people's rights. His decision to change sides convinced others to change their votes as well. The Virginia convention voted narrowly for the new Constitution, 89 in favor and 79 against.

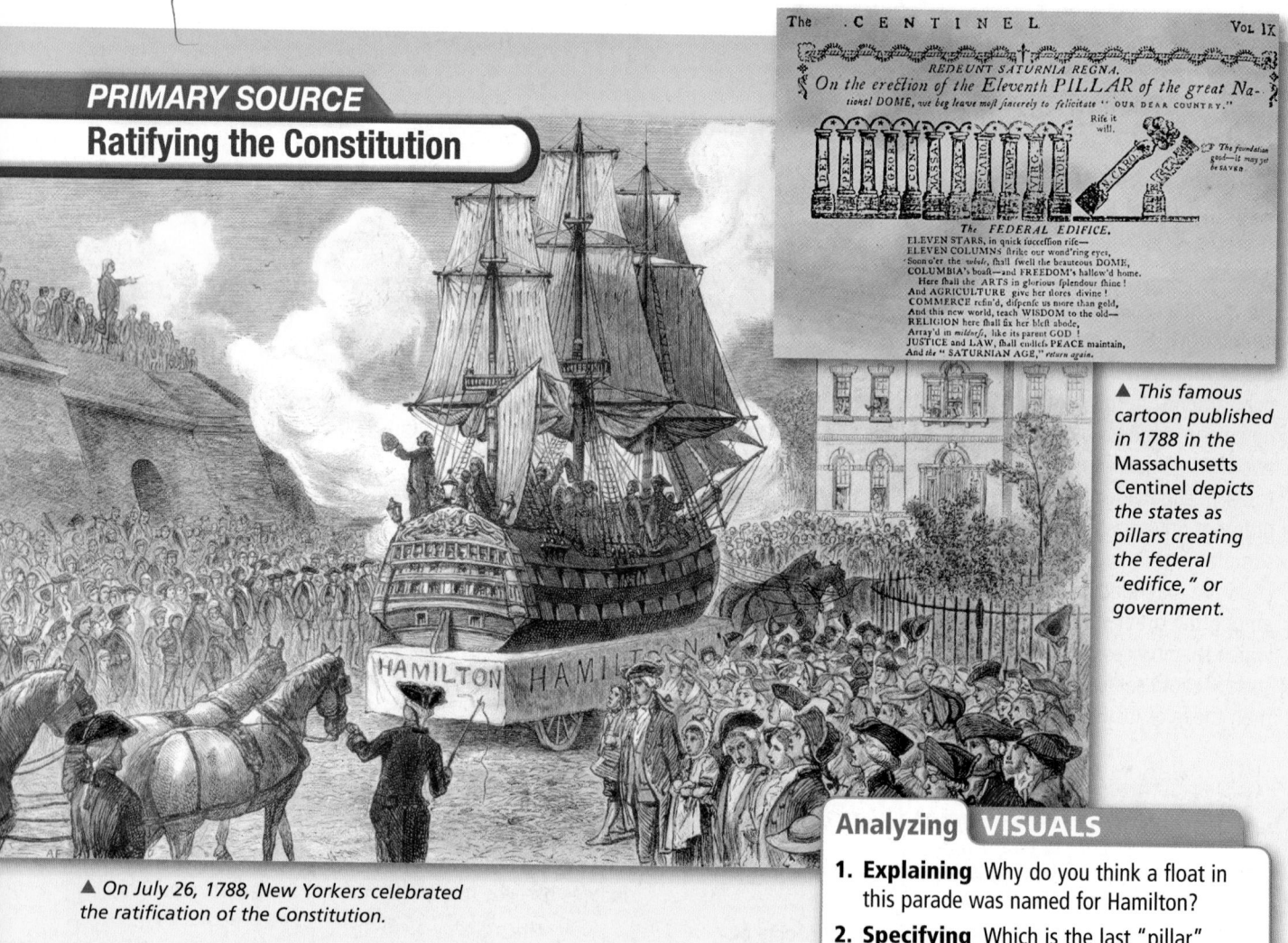

PRIMARY SOURCE
Ratifying the Constitution

▲ On July 26, 1788, New Yorkers celebrated the ratification of the Constitution.

▲ This famous cartoon published in 1788 in the Massachusetts Centinel depicts the states as pillars creating the federal "edifice," or government.

Analyzing VISUALS

1. **Explaining** Why do you think a float in this parade was named for Hamilton?

2. **Specifying** Which is the last "pillar" shown being added to the federal "edifice"?

New York Votes to Ratify

In New York, two-thirds of the members elected to the state convention, including New York Governor George Clinton, were Anti-Federalists. During the debate over ratification, the Federalists, led by Alexander Hamilton and John Jay, repeatedly tried to assure the Anti-Federalists that the new federal government would pose no threat to liberty. Hamilton stressed that the new constitution had been specifically designed to limit the growth of tyranny:

PRIMARY SOURCE

"On whatever side we view this subject, we discover various and powerful checks to the encroachments of Congress. The true and permanent interests of the members are opposed to corruption. Their number is vastly too large for easy combination. The rivalship between the houses will forever prove an insuperable obstacle. The people have an obvious and powerful protection in their state governments. Should any thing dangerous be attempted, these bodies of perpetual observation will be capable of forming and conducting plans of regular opposition."

—from "Speech Urging Ratification of the Constitution by New York State, 1788"

The Federalists managed to delay the final vote until news arrived that New Hampshire and Virginia had both ratified the Constitution and that the new federal government was now in effect. If New York refused to ratify, it would be in a very awkward position. It would have to operate independently of all of the surrounding states. Soon after, delegates from New York City warned that the city would secede from the state of New York and join the United States independently if the new Constitution was not ratified. These arguments convinced enough Anti-Federalists to change sides. The vote was very close, 30 to 27, but the Federalists won.

By July 1788, all the states except Rhode Island and North Carolina had ratified the Constitution. Because ratification by nine states was all that the Constitution required, the new government could be launched without them. In mid-September 1788, the Confederation Congress established a timetable for the election of the new government. It chose March 4, 1789, as the date for the first meeting of the new Congress.

The two states that had held out finally ratified the Constitution after the new government was in place. North Carolina waited until a bill of rights had actually been proposed, then voted to ratify the Constitution in November 1789. Rhode Island, still nervous about losing its independence, did not ratify the Constitution until May 1790, and even then the vote was very close—34 to 32.

The United States now had a new government, but no one knew if the new Constitution would work any better than the Articles had. With both anticipation and nervousness, the American people waited for their new government to begin. Many expressed great confidence, because George Washington was the first president under the new Constitution.

Reading Check **Examining** Why was it important for Virginia and New York to ratify the Constitution, even after the required nine states had done so?

Section 3 REVIEW

Vocabulary

1. **Explain** the significance of: Federalist, Anti-Federalist, John Hancock, Patrick Henry, bill of rights.

Main Ideas

2. **Explaining** What did supporters of the Constitution hope to achieve with the selection of the name *Federalists*?

3. **Identifying** What two promises did Federalists make to win the support of those who initially opposed the Constitution?

Critical Thinking

4. **Big Ideas** Do you think it was important for all the states to ratify the Constitution? Why or why not?

5. **Organizing** Use a graphic organizer similar to the one below to list the factors that worked against the Anti-Federalists.

Factors Working Against Anti-Federalists

6. **Analyzing Visuals** Study the cartoon on page 114. The Latin phrase at the top means "a return to the Age of Saturn," or a golden age. Why do you think that phrase was included in this cartoon?

Writing About History

7. **Persuasive Writing** Take on the role of a Federalist or an Anti-Federalist at a state ratifying convention. Write a speech in which you try to convince your audience to either accept or reject the new Constitution.

History ONLINE

Study Central™ To review this section, go to glencoe.com and click on Study Central.

115

The Articles of Confederation

Weaknesses

- No power to regulate commerce
- No power to compel states to obey international treaties signed by the Congress
- No power to tax
- No power to print or coin money

Effects

- States impose trade restrictions and tariffs on each other's goods
- States restrict Britain's ability to collect debts from Americans; Congress cannot reach a financial settlement with Britain; Britain refuses to evacuate forts on American soil
- Spain denies Americans permission to deposit goods at mouth of Mississippi; Congress has no leverage to force Spain to negotiate
- States issue money, inflation makes the currency worthless; debt problems lead to rebellion in Massachusetts and riots in Rhode Island

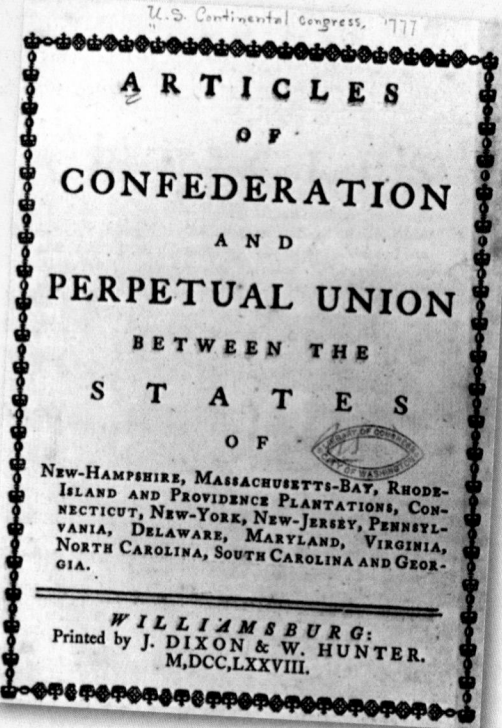

▲ The Articles of Confederation

◄ George Washington headed the Constitutional Convention that drafted a new plan of government.

▼ Many Americans celebrated the ratification of the new Constitution and hoped for greater stability and less chaos.

The Federal Constitution

Decisions at the Constitutional Convention

- New Jersey Plan to amend the Articles of Confederation is rejected
- Virginia Plan to create a federal Constitution is approved
- Connecticut Compromise (Great Compromise) gets both small and large states to support the constitution: Congress will have House of Representatives elected by the people and a Senate, whose members are chosen by the states, and each state has equal representation
- Three-Fifths Compromise gets Southern and Northern states to support the constitution: enslaved people will count as three-fifths of a free person for determining representation in Congress and taxes owed

Checks and Balances of the Federal Constitution

- Federal government has three branches: executive (headed by a president), legislative (Congress), and judicial
- President can veto laws but Congress can override a veto
- President commands the military; Congress votes all funds and taxes
- President selects his cabinet and nominates judges, but the Senate must approve the nominations
- Congress can impeach the president and judges and remove them from office
- To get the Constitution ratified, supporters also promised to add a bill of rights (Amendments 1–10) to further limit federal power

NEW YORK REGENTS EXAM PRACTICE

TEST-TAKING TIP

Pace yourself when taking a test so that you will have time to go back and check your answers or try to answer any questions you may have skipped.

Part I

Directions (1–11): For each statement or question, write on a separate sheet of paper the number of the word or expression that, of those given, best completes the statement or answers the question.

1 The Northwest Ordinance outlined the process for

(1) ratification of the Constitution.

(2) achieving statehood.

(3) negotiating international treaties.

(4) extending slavery north of the Ohio River.

2 Shays's Rebellion was viewed by many powerful people as

(1) evidence that the Articles were working.

(2) a righteous fight of the oppressed.

(3) a sign that the national government was too weak.

(4) a major blow to democracy.

3 At the Constitutional Convention of 1787, the Great Compromise resolved the issue of

(1) representation.

(2) taxation.

(3) slavery.

(4) control of trade.

4 The Framers ensured that the Constitution could evolve over time by

(1) establishing a process for replacing it.

(2) establishing a bill of rights.

(3) establishing that the states could veto federal laws.

(4) establishing a process for amending it.

5 Most Anti-Federalists fought against ratification of the Constitution because it

(1) had been written by Federalists.

(2) gave too much power to the states.

(3) did not protect civil liberties or states' rights.

(4) gave more power to the Northern states than the Southern states.

6 North Carolina ratified the Constitution only after

(1) All the other states ratified it.

(2) Rhode Island had ratified it.

(3) New York had ratified it.

(4) A bill of rights had been proposed.

7 The Framers provided for a separation of powers in the federal government by

(1) establishing executive, legislative, and judicial branches.

(2) giving the president the power to command the army.

(3) making the Supreme Court the most important court in the nation.

(4) establishing a process for changing the Constitution.

8 Which of the following is an *opinion* about the Constitution?

(1) By 1790, all states had ratified the Constitution.

(2) A major concern in writing the Constitution was how many representatives each state would have.

(3) Under the Constitution, the federal government could raise money to operate.

(4) Because of the Constitution, the United States has the best government in the world.

Need Extra Help?								
If You Missed Questions . . .	1	2	3	4	5	6	7	8
Go to Page . . .	98–99	103	106–107	108–109	110–111	113–115	108–109	110–115

[OVER]

Base your answer to question 9 on the map below and on your knowledge of Chapter 3.

Western Land Claims of the Original States, 1787

BRITISH NORTH AMERICA

Vermont, 1791 (Claimed by N.Y., Mass., and N.H.)

Maine (Part of Mass.)

N.H.

N.Y. Mass.

Conn. R.I.

Mass., 1785
Conn., 1786

Pa. N.J.

Ceded by Conn., 1800

Md. Del.

Va.

ATLANTIC OCEAN

LOUISIANA (Ceded to France by Spain, 1800)

North Carolina, 1790

N.C.

S.C.

South Carolina, 1787

Georgia, 1802

Ga.

Ceded by Spain, 1795
Ceded by Georgia, 1802

SPANISH FLORIDA

Gulf of Mexico

Land ceded

Boundary of land ceded by New York, 1782

Boundary of land ceded by Virginia, 1784

State of Franklin

Thirteen original states after land cessions

9 Which state had the largest land claims in the West?

(1) Massachusetts   (3) Georgia

(2) North Carolina   (4) Virginia

10 Large landowners and merchants supported the Constitution because it

(1) allowed for states to trade with foreign powers with fewer regulations.

(2) enabled the original states to settle lands in the West.

(3) gave the national government power to protect property and regulate trade.

(4) eased trade laws and lowered taxes on land.

11 Which of the following proposed a legislature that was divided into two houses?

(1) the Virginia Plan

(2) the New Jersey Plan

(3) the Three-Fifths Compromise

(4) the Missouri Plan

Need Extra Help?

If You Missed Questions . . .	9	10	11
Go to Page . . .	118	110	106

Part II Thematic Essay Question

Directions: Write a well-organized essay that includes an introduction, several paragraphs addressing the task below, and a conclusion.

Theme: The United States Constitution

The U.S. Constitution provides a framework for government by establishing a federal government. It provided for a separation of powers.

Task

• Describe how the system of checks and balances functions

• Discuss how this system has been applied in United States history

• Evaluate how this system can adapt to the needs of American political life

Guidelines:

In your essay, be sure to:

• Develop all aspects of the task

• Support the theme with relevant facts, examples, and details

• Use a logical and clear plan of organization, including an introduction and a conclusion that are beyond a restatement of the theme

Part III Document-Based Question

This question is based on the accompanying documents. It is designed to test your ability to work with historical documents. Some of the documents have been edited for the purposes of the question. As you analyze the documents, take into account both the source of each document and any point of view that may be presented in the document.

Historical Context:

The weak national government established by the Articles of Confederation led to the drafting and eventual ratification of the U.S. Constitution.

Task:

Using information from the documents and your knowledge of United States history, answer the questions that follow each document in Part A. Your answers to the questions will help you write the Part B essay, in which you will be asked to

- Discuss the reasons that the Articles of Confederation established a weak central government and compare it to the federal system established by the Constitution
- Evaluate the events that led to ratification of the Constitution

Part A

Short-Answer Questions

Directions: Analyze the documents and answer the short-answer questions that follow each document on a separate sheet of paper.

Document 1

Source: American Antiquarian Society

1 To what does the cartoonist compare the states that have ratified the Constitution?

Document 2

[The Articles of Confederation] were framed during the rage of war, when a principle of common safety supplied the place of a coercive power in government. . . .

When resolutions were passed in Congress, there was no power to compel obedience. . . . Had one state been invaded by its neighbour, the union was not constitutionally bound to assist in repelling the invasion. . . .

Source: Reverend Jedediah Morse, *The American Geography*, 1789

2 What defects in the Articles of Confederation does Morse see?

3 Why does Morse think that the Articles were effective during the American Revolution but not afterward?

Part B

Essay

Directions: Read the task box at the top left and write a well-organized essay that includes an introduction, several paragraphs, and a conclusion. Use evidence from the documents in your essay. Support your response with relevant facts, examples, and details. Include additional outside information.

Guidelines:

In your essay, be sure to:

- Develop all aspects of the task
- Incorporate information from the documents
- Incorporate relevant outside information
- Support the theme with relevant facts, examples, and details
- Use a logical and clear plan of organization, including an introduction and a conclusion that are beyond a restatement of the theme

History ONLINE

For additional test practice, use Self-Check Quizzes— Chapter 3 at glencoe.com.

Need Extra Help?				
If You Missed Questions . . .	1	2	3	Essay
Go to Page . . .	119	119	119	98–116

THE CONSTITUTION HANDBOOK

S erving as the framework of national government and the source of American citizens' basic rights, the Constitution is the most important document of the United States. To preserve self-government, all citizens need to understand their rights and responsibilities.

Major Principles

MAIN Idea The Constitution's basic principles assure people's rights and provide for a balance among the different branches of government.

HISTORY AND YOU If you had to create the rules for a new organization, would you give all members an equal voice? Read on to learn how the Constitution reflects representative government.

The principles outlined in the Constitution were the Framers' solution to the complex problems of a representative government. The Constitution rests on seven major principles of government: (1) **popular sovereignty,** (2) republicanism, (3) limited government, (4) **federalism,** (5) separation of powers, (6) checks and balances, and (7) individual rights.

Popular Sovereignty and Republicanism

The opening words of the Constitution, "We the people," reinforce the idea of popular sovereignty, or "authority of the people." In the Constitution, the people consent to be governed and specify the powers and rules by which they shall be governed.

The Articles of Confederation's government had few powers, and it was unable to cope with the many challenges facing the nation. The new federal government had greater powers, but it also had specific limitations. A system of interlocking responsibilities kept any one branch of government from becoming too powerful.

Voters are sovereign, that is, they have ultimate authority in a republican system. They elect representatives and give them the responsibility to make laws and run the government. For most Americans today, the terms republic and representative democracy mean the same thing: a system of limited government where the people are the final source of authority.

Guide to Reading

Big Ideas
Government and Society A written contract between the people and their government can preserve natural rights and allow for change over time.

Content Vocabulary
- popular sovereignty *(p. 120)*
- federalism *(p. 120)*
- enumerated powers *(p. 121)*
- reserved powers *(p. 121)*
- concurrent powers *(p. 122)*
- impeach *(p. 123)*
- bill *(p. 124)*
- cabinet *(p. 125)*
- judicial review *(p. 127)*
- due process *(p. 127)*

Academic Vocabulary
- grant *(p. 121)*
- responsive *(p. 129)*

Reading Strategy
Taking Notes As you read about the Constitution, use the major headings of the handbook to fill in an outline.

I. Major Principles
   A.
   B.
   C.
   D.
   E.
   F.
II.

NEW YORK CORE CURRICULUM
U.S. History and Government

Unit 2:
I.B.2.a Protecting liberty against abuses of power
I.B.2.b Power separated and balanced
I.B.3 The document: structure of government
I.E Basic constitutional principles
I.F Implementing the new constitutional principles

Limited Government

Although the Framers agreed that the nation needed a stronger central authority, they feared misuse of power. They wanted to prevent the government from using its power to give one group special advantages or to deprive another group of its rights. By creating a limited government, they restricted the government's authority to specific powers **granted** by the people.

The delegates to the Constitutional Convention were very specific about the powers granted to the new government. Their decision to provide a written outline of the government's structure also served to show what they intended. Articles I, II and III of the Constitution describe the powers of the federal government and the limits on those powers. Other limits are set forth in the Bill of Rights, which guarantees certain rights to the people.

Federalism

In establishing a strong central government, the Framers did not deprive states of all authority. The states gave up some powers to the national government but retained others. This principle of shared power is called federalism. The federal system allows the people of each state to deal with their needs in their own way, but at the same time, it lets the states act together to deal with matters that affect all Americans.

The Constitution defines three types of government powers. Certain powers belong only to the federal government. These **enumerated powers** include the power to coin money, regulate interstate and foreign trade, maintain the armed forces, and create federal courts (Article I, Section 8).

The second kind of powers are those retained by the states, known as **reserved powers,** including the power to establish schools, set marriage and divorce laws, and regulate trade within the state. Although reserved powers are not specifically listed in the Constitution, the Tenth Amendment says that all powers not granted to the federal government "are reserved to the States."

The third set of powers defined by the Constitution is **concurrent powers**—powers the state and federal governments share. They include the right to raise taxes, borrow money, provide for public welfare, and administer criminal justice. Conflicts between state law and federal law must be settled in a federal court. The Constitution declares that it is "the supreme Law of the Land."

Separation of Powers

To prevent any single group or institution in government from gaining too much authority, the Framers divided the federal government into three branches: legislative, executive, and judicial. Each branch has its own functions and powers. The legislative branch, Congress, makes the laws. The executive branch, headed by the president, carries out the laws. The judicial branch, consisting of the Supreme Court and other federal courts, interprets and applies the laws.

In addition to giving separate responsibility to separate branches, the membership of each branch is chosen in different ways. The president nominates federal judges and the Senate confirms the appointments. People vote for members of Congress. Voters cast ballots for president, but the method of election is indirect. On Election Day the votes in each state are counted. Whatever candidate receives a majority receives that state's electoral votes, which total the number of senators and representatives the state has in Congress. Electors from all states meet to formally elect a president. A candidate must receive at least 270 of 538 electoral votes to win.

Checks and Balances

The Framers who wrote the Constitution deliberately created a system of checks and balances in which each branch of government can check, or limit, the power of the other branches. This system helps balance the power of the three branches and prevents any one branch from becoming too powerful. For example, imagine that Congress passes a law. The president can reject the law by vetoing it. However, Congress can override, or reverse, the president's veto if two-thirds of the members of both the Senate and the House of Representatives vote again to approve the law.

Individual Rights

Ten amendments to the Constitution were approved in 1791 to protect certain basic rights, including freedom of speech, religion, and the right to a trial by jury. These ten amendments are referred to as the Bill of Rights. Over the years, 17 more amendments were added to the Constitution. Some give additional rights to Americans and some modify how the government works. Included among them are amendments that abolish slavery, guarantee voting rights, authorize an income tax, and set a two-term limit on the presidency.

✔ Reading Check **Explaining** What are the three branches of government?

INFOGRAPHIC
The Federal Government

The Constitution divides power in three ways:

1. Between the federal and state governments
2. Between three branches of government
3. By providing checks and balances

The Federal System

Enumerated Powers
Powers *enumerated* to national government; for example, declaring war

Concurrent Powers
Powers *concurrent* to national and state governments; for example, the power to tax

Reserved Powers
Powers *reserved* for state governments; for example, setting up educational system

The Legislative Branch

MAIN Idea The Legislative branch makes the nation's laws and appropriates funds.

HISTORY AND YOU Have you ever written to your representative to support or oppose a bill? Read to find out how Congress makes laws.

The legislative branch includes the two houses of Congress: the Senate and the House of Representatives. Congress's two primary roles are to make the nation's laws and to decide how federal funds are spent.

The government cannot spend any money unless Congress appropriates, or sets aside, funds. All tax and spending bills must originate in the House of Representatives and be approved in both the House and the Senate before moving to the president for signature.

Congress also monitors the executive branch and investigates possible abuses of power. The House of Representatives can **impeach,** or bring formal charges against, any federal official it suspects of wrongdoing or misconduct. If an official is impeached, the Senate acts as a court and tries the accused official. Officials who are found guilty may be removed from office.

The Senate has certain additional powers. Two-thirds of the Senate must ratify treaties made by the president. The Senate must also confirm presidential appointments of federal officials such as department heads, ambassadors, and federal judges.

Checks and Balances

Legislative Branch
- **Congress Makes the Law**

Judicial Branch
- **Supreme Court Interprets the Law**

Checks on the Legislative Branch:
- Can declare acts of Congress unconstitutional

Checks on the Executive Branch:
- Can declare executive actions unconstitutional

Executive Branch
- **President Carries Out the Law**

Checks on the Judicial Branch:
- Creates lower federal courts
- Can impeach and remove judges
- Can propose amendments to overrule judicial decisions
- Approves appointments of federal judges

Checks on the Executive Branch:
- Can override presidential veto
- Confirms executive appointments
- Ratifies treaties
- Can declare war
- Appropriates money
- Can impeach and remove president

Checks on the Legislative Branch:
- Can propose laws
- Can veto laws
- Can call special sessions of Congress
- Makes appointments to federal posts
- Negotiates foreign treaties

Checks on the Judicial Branch:
- Appoints federal judges
- Can grant pardons to federal offenders

Analyzing VISUALS

1. **Explaining** How can the president help control the judiciary?
2. **Summarizing** What checks does the legislative branch have on the president?

All members of Congress have the responsibility to represent their constituents, the people of their home states and districts. As a constituent, you can expect your senators and representative to promote national and state interests. Thousands of **bills**—proposed laws—are introduced in Congress every year. Because individual members of Congress cannot possibly study all these bills carefully, both houses use committees of selected members to evaluate proposed legislation.

Standing committees are permanent committees in both the House and the Senate that specialize in a particular topic, such as agriculture, commerce, or veterans' affairs. These committees are usually divided into subcommittees that focus on a particular aspect of an issue. The House and the Senate also form temporary select committees to deal with issues requiring special attention. These committees meet only until they complete their task.

Occasionally the House and the Senate form joint committees with members from both houses. These committees meet to consider specific issues. One type of joint committee, a conference committee, has a special function. If the House and the Senate pass different versions of the same bill, a conference committee meets to work out a compromise bill acceptable to both houses.

Once a committee in either house of Congress approves a bill, it is sent to the full Senate or House for debate. After debate the bill may be passed, rejected, or returned to the committee for further changes. When both houses pass a bill, it goes to the president. If the president approves the bill and signs it, the bill becomes law. If the president vetoes the bill, it does not become law unless Congress takes it up again and votes to override the veto.

✔ Reading Check **Analyzing** What is the most important power of the legislative branch?

INFOGRAPHIC
How a Bill Becomes Law

The legislative process is complex. It begins with a representative in Congress introducing a bill and eventually works its way to the president who either signs the bill into law or vetoes it.

How a Bill Becomes Law

1. A legislator introduces a bill in the House or Senate, where it is referred to a committee for review.

2. After review, the committee decides whether to shelve it or to send it back to the House or Senate with or without revisions.

3. The House or Senate then debates the bill, making revisions if desired. If the bill is passed, it is sent to the other house.

4. If the House and Senate pass different versions of the bill, the houses must meet in a conference committee to decide on a compromise version.

5. The compromise bill is then sent to both houses.

6. If both houses pass the bill, it is sent to the president to sign.

7. If the president signs the bill, it becomes law.

8. The president may veto the bill, but if two-thirds of the House and Senate vote to approve it, it becomes law without the president's approval.

The Executive Branch

MAIN Idea As the nation's leader, the president carries out laws with the help of executive offices, departments, and agencies.

HISTORY AND YOU What would you do if you were the student council president? Read on to learn about the roles of the U.S. president.

The executive branch of government includes the president, the vice president, and various executive offices, departments, and agencies. The executive branch executes, or carries out, the laws that Congress passes.

The President's Roles

The president plays a number of different roles in government. These roles include serving as the nation's chief executive, chief diplomat, commander in chief of the military, chief of state, and legislative leader.

▲ President Bush signs the Voting Rights Act of 2006.

Analyzing VISUALS

1. **Describing** What is the role of a conference committee?

2. **Analyzing** How can a bill become law without the approval of the president?

Chief Executive As chief executive, the president is responsible for carrying out the nation's laws. As chief diplomat, the president directs foreign policy, appoints ambassadors, and negotiates treaties with other nations.

Commander in Chief As commander in chief of the armed forces, the president can give orders to the military and direct its operations. The president cannot declare war; only Congress holds this power. The president can send troops to other parts of the world for up to 60 days but must notify Congress when doing so. The troops may remain longer only if Congress gives its approval or declares war.

Chief of State As chief of state, the president is symbolically the representative of all Americans. The president fulfills this role when receiving foreign ambassadors or heads of state, visiting foreign nations, or honoring Americans.

Legislative Leader The president serves as a legislative leader by proposing laws to Congress and working to see that they are passed. In the annual State of the Union address, the president presents his goals for legislation in the upcoming year.

The Executive at Work

Many executive offices, departments, and independent agencies help the president carry out and enforce the nation's laws. The Executive Office of the President (EOP) is made up of individuals and agencies that directly assist the president. Presidents rely on the EOP for advice and for gathering information needed for decision making.

The executive branch has 15 executive departments, each responsible for a different area of government. For example, the Department of State carries out foreign policy, and the Department of the Treasury manages the nation's finances. The department heads have the title of secretary, and are members of the president's **cabinet.** The cabinet helps the president set policies and make decisions.

Reading Check **Explaining** What are the major roles of the president?

The Judicial Branch

MAIN Idea The judicial branch consists of different federal courts that review and evaluate laws and interpret the Constitution.

HISTORY AND YOU The Constitution did not specifically give the judicial branch the power to review laws. Do you think it is a reasonable task? Read to learn about the role of federal judges and the Supreme Court.

Article III of the Constitution calls for the creation of a Supreme Court and "such inferior [lower] courts as Congress may from time to time ordain and establish." Today the judicial branch consists of three main categories of courts, including:

District and Appellate Courts

United States district courts are the lowest level of the federal court system. These courts consider criminal and civil cases that come under federal authority, such as kidnapping, federal tax evasion, claims against the federal government, and cases involving constitutional rights, such as free speech. There are 91 district courts, with at least one in every state.

The appellate courts, or appeals courts, consider district court decisions in which the losing side has asked for a review of the verdict. If an appeals court disagrees with the lower court's decision, it can overturn the verdict or order a retrial. There are 14 appeals courts, one for each of 12 federal districts, one military appeals court, and an appellate court for the federal circuit.

The Supreme Court

The Supreme Court is the final authority in the federal court system. It consists of a chief justice and eight associate justices. Most of the Supreme Court's cases come from appeals of lower court decisions. Only cases involving foreign ambassadors or disputes between states can begin in the Supreme Court.

INFOGRAPHIC
The Federal Court System

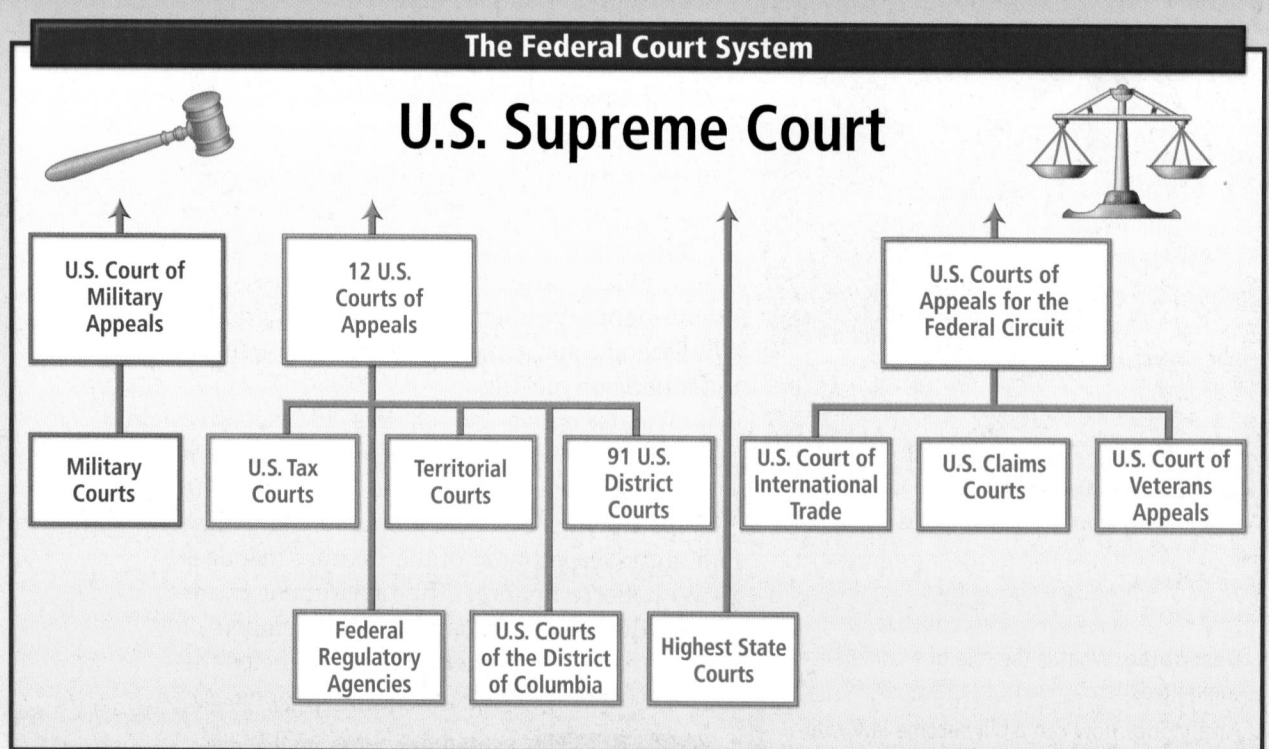

The Federal Court System

U.S. Supreme Court

- U.S. Court of Military Appeals
- 12 U.S. Courts of Appeals
- U.S. Courts of Appeals for the Federal Circuit

- Military Courts
- U.S. Tax Courts
- Territorial Courts
- 91 U.S. District Courts
- U.S. Court of International Trade
- U.S. Claims Courts
- U.S. Court of Veterans Appeals

- Federal Regulatory Agencies
- U.S. Courts of the District of Columbia
- Highest State Courts

Supreme Court Independence The president appoints the Court's justices for life, and the Senate confirms the appointments. The public has no input. The Framers hoped that by appointing judges, they would be free to evaluate the law with no concern for pleasing voters.

Judicial Review The role of the judicial branch is not described in detail in the Constitution, but the role of the courts has grown as powers implied in the Constitution have been put into practice. In 1803 Chief Justice John Marshall expanded the power of the Supreme Court by striking down an act of Congress in the case of *Marbury* v. *Madison*. Although not mentioned in the Constitution, judicial review has become a major power of the judicial branch. **Judicial review** gives the Supreme Court the ultimate authority to interpret the meaning of the Constitution.

✔ Reading Check **Analyzing** How does the Supreme Court protect the Constitution?

▲ The U.S. Supreme Court, front row, left to right, Justices Anthony Kennedy and John Paul Stevens, Chief Justice John Roberts, Justices Antonin Scalia and David Souter; back row, left to right, Justices Stephen Breyer, Clarence Thomas, Ruth Bader Ginsburg, Samuel Alito

Analyzing VISUALS

1. **Interpreting** How many routes to the U.S. Supreme Court are depicted in the chart?

2. **Analyzing** How would a case originating in Puerto Rico be appealed to the U.S. Supreme Court?

Rights and Responsibilities

MAIN Idea The Constitution and the Bill of Rights provide Americans with protection and freedoms.

HISTORY AND YOU How do you think the Constitution protects your rights as a student? Read on to find out about the major rights of Americans.

All American citizens have certain basic rights, but they also have specific responsibilities. Living in a system of self-government means ultimately that every citizen is partly responsible for how their society is governed and for the actions the government takes on their behalf.

The Rights of Americans

The rights of Americans fall into three broad categories: the right to be protected from unfair actions of the government, to receive equal treatment under the law, and to retain certain basic freedoms.

Protection from Unfair Actions Parts of the Constitution and the Bill of Rights protect all Americans from unfair treatment by the government or the law. Among these rights are the right to a lawyer when accused of a crime and the right to trial by jury when charged with a crime. In addition, the Fourth Amendment protects us from unreasonable searches and seizures. This provision requires police to have a court order before searching a person's home for criminal evidence. To obtain this, the police must have a very strong reason to suspect the person of committing a crime.

Equal Treatment All Americans, regardless of race, religion, or political beliefs, have the right to be treated the same under the law. The Fifth Amendment states that no person shall "be deprived of life, liberty, or property, without due process of law." **Due process** means that the government must follow procedures established by law and guaranteed by the Constitution, treating all people equally. The Fourteenth Amendment requires every state to grant its citizens "equal protection of the laws."

Basic Freedoms The basic freedoms are described in the First Amendment—freedom of speech, freedom of religion, freedom of the press, freedom of assembly, and the right to petition. In a democracy, power rests in the hands of the people. Therefore, citizens in a democratic society must be able to exchange ideas freely. The First Amendment allows citizens to criticize the government, in speech or in the press, without fear of punishment.

In addition, the Ninth Amendment states that the rights of Americans are not limited to those in the Constitution. This has allowed Americans to assert other basic rights over the years that have been upheld in court, or assured by amending the Constitution.

Limits on Rights The rights of Americans are not absolute. They are limited based on the principle of respecting everyone's rights equally. For example, many cities and towns require groups to obtain a permit to march on city streets. Such laws do limit free speech, but they also protect the community by ensuring that the march will not endanger other people.

In this and other cases, the government balances an individual's rights, the rights of others, and the community's health and safety. Most Americans are willing to accept some limitations on their rights to gain these protections as long as the restrictions are reasonable and apply equally to all. A law banning all marches would violate the First Amendment rights of free speech and assembly and be unacceptable. Similarly, a law preventing only certain groups from marching would be unfair because it would not apply equally to everyone.

Citizens' Responsibilities

Citizens in a democratic society have both duties and responsibilities. Duties are actions required by law. Responsibilities are voluntary actions. Fulfilling both your duties and your responsibilities helps ensure good government and protects your rights.

Duties One basic duty of all Americans is to obey the law. Laws serve three important functions. They help maintain order; they protect

INFOGRAPHIC
Amending the Constitution

Article V of the Constitution enables Congress and the states to amend, or change, the Constitution.

The Amendment Process

Proposal

Amendment proposed by a vote of two-thirds of both houses of Congress

or

Amendment proposed by a national convention requested by two-thirds of states

Ratification

After approval by three-fourths of state legislatures

or

After approval by three-fourths of state ratifying conventions

New amendment to the Constitution

Analyzing VISUALS

1. **Summarizing** What role do the states play in the amendment process?

2. **Explaining** How many approvals by state legislatures are required for an amendment to the Constitution?

the health, safety, and property of all citizens; and they make it possible for people to live together peacefully. If you believe a law is wrong, you can work through your representatives to change it.

Americans also have a duty to pay taxes. The government uses tax money to defend the nation, to build roads and bridges, and to assist people in need. Americans benefit from services provided by the government. Another duty of citizens is to defend the nation. All males aged 18 and older must register with the government in case the nation needs to call on them for military service. Military service is not automatic, but a war could make it necessary.

The Constitution guarantees all Americans the right to a trial by a jury of their equals. For this reason, you may be called to jury duty when you reach the age of 18. Having a large group of jurors on hand is necessary to guarantee the right to a fair and speedy trial. You also have a duty to serve as a trial witness if called to do so.

Most states require you to attend school until a certain age. School is where you gain the knowledge and skills needed to be a good citizen. In school you learn to think more clearly, to express your opinions more accurately, and to analyze the ideas of others. These skills will help you make informed choices when you vote.

Responsibilities The responsibilities of citizens are not as clear-cut as their duties, but they are as important because they help maintain the quality of government and society. One important responsibility is to be well informed. You need to know what is happening in your community, your state, your country, and the world. Knowing what your government is doing and expressing your thoughts about its actions helps to keep it **responsive** to the wishes of the people. You also need to be informed about your rights and to assert them when necessary. Knowing your rights helps preserve them. Other responsibilities include accepting responsibility for your actions, and supporting your family.

To enjoy your rights to the fullest, you must be prepared to respect the rights of others. Respecting the rights of others also means respecting the rights of people with whom you disagree. Respecting and accepting others regardless of race, religion, beliefs, or other differences is essential in a democracy.

Vote, Vote, Vote! Perhaps the most important responsibility of American citizens is to vote when they reach the age of 18. Voting allows you to participate in government and to guide its direction. When you vote for people to represent you in government, you will be exercising your right of self-government. If you disapprove of the job your representatives are doing, it will be your responsibility to help elect other people in the next election. You can also let your representatives know what you think about issues through letters, telephone calls, and petitions and by taking part in public meetings or political rallies.

Reading Check **Describing** What are the major rights and responsibilities of an American citizen?

Vocabulary

1. **Explain** the significance of: popular sovereignty, federalism, enumerated powers, reserved powers, concurrent powers, impeach, bill, cabinet, judicial review, due process.

Main Ideas

2. **Explaining** What are the provisions of the First Amendment?

3. **Summarizing** How are popular sovereignty and voting connected?

Critical Thinking

4. **Big Ideas** What is the difference between a duty and a responsibility?

5. **Organizing** Use a graphic organizer similar to the one below to list reasons why the framers of the Constitution provided for separation of powers.

Separation of Powers

6. **Analyzing Visuals** Study the photograph on page 127. How has the composition of the Supreme Court changed over time?

Writing About History

7. **Expository Writing** Working with a partner, choose one of the constitutional rights listed below. Write a report that traces the right's historical development, from the time the Constitution was ratified to the present.

suffrage
freedom of speech
freedom of religion
equal protection of law

History ONLINE

Study Central™ To review this section, go to glencoe.com and click on Study Central.

THE
CONSTITUTION
OF THE UNITED STATES

The Constitution of the United States is a truly remarkable document. It was one of the first written constitutions in modern history. The entire text of the Constitution and its amendments follow. For easier study, those passages that have been set aside or changed by the adoption of amendments are printed in blue. Also included are explanatory notes that will help clarify the meaning of important ideas presented in the Constitution.

A burst of fireworks over the Lincoln Memorial in Washington, D.C.

Preamble

We the People of the United States, in Order to form a more perfect Union, establish Justice, insure domestic Tranquility, provide for the common defence, promote the general Welfare, and secure the Blessings of Liberty to ourselves and our Posterity, do ordain and establish this **Constitution** for the United States of America.

Article I
Section 1

All legislative Powers herein granted shall be vested in a Congress of the United States, which shall consist of a Senate and House of Representatives.

Section 2

[1.] The House of Representatives shall be composed of Members chosen every second Year by the People of the several States, and the Electors in each State shall have the Qualifications requisite for Electors of the most numerous Branch of the State Legislature.

[2.] No person shall be a Representative who shall not have attained to the Age of twenty five Years, and been seven Years a Citizen of the United States, and who shall not, when elected, be an Inhabitant of that State in which he shall be chosen.

[3.] Representatives and direct Taxes shall be apportioned among the several States which may be included within this Union, according to their respective Numbers, which shall be determined by adding to the whole Number of free Persons, including those bound to Service for a Term of Years, and excluding Indians not taxed, three fifths of all other Persons. The actual **Enumeration** shall be made within three Years after the first Meeting of the Congress of the United States, and within every subsequent Term of ten Years, in such Manner as they shall by Law direct. The Number of Representatives shall not exceed one for every thirty Thousand, but each State shall have at Least one Representative; and until such enumeration shall be made, the State of New Hampshire shall be entitled to chuse three; Massachusetts eight, Rhode-Island and Providence Plantations one, Connecticut five, New-York six, New Jersey four, Pennsylvania eight, Delaware one, Maryland six, Virginia ten, North Carolina five, South Carolina five, and Georgia three.

[4.] When vacancies happen in the Representation from any State, the Executive Authority thereof shall issue Writs of Election to fill such Vacancies.

[5.] The House of Representatives shall chuse their Speaker and other Officers; and shall have the sole Power of **Impeachment.**

The Preamble introduces the Constitution and sets forth the general purposes for which the government was established. The Preamble also declares that the power of the government comes from the people.

The printed text of the document shows the spelling and punctuation of the parchment original.

Article I. The Legislative Branch

The Constitution contains seven divisions called articles. Each article covers a general topic. For example, Articles I, II, and III create the three branches of the national government—the legislative, executive, and judicial branches. Most of the articles are divided into sections.

> ### Section 1. Congress
> **Lawmaking** The power to make laws is given to a Congress made up of two chambers to represent different interests: the Senate to represent the states and the House to be more responsive to the people's will.

> ### Section 2.
> ### House of Representatives
> **Division of Representatives Among the States** The number of representatives from each state is based on the size of the state's population. Each state is entitled to at least one representative. The Constitution states that each state may specify who can vote, but the Fifteenth, Nineteenth, Twenty-fourth, and Twenty-sixth Amendments have established guidelines that all states must follow regarding the right to vote. What are the qualifications for members of the House of Representatives?

Vocabulary

preamble: *introduction*
constitution: *principles and laws of a nation*
enumeration: *census or population count*
impeachment: *bringing charges against an official*

Section 3. The Senate
Voting Procedure Originally, senators were chosen by the legislators of their own states. The Seventeenth Amendment changed this, so that senators are now elected by their state's people. There are 100 senators, 2 from each state.

What Might Have Been
Electing Senators South Carolina delegate Charles Pinckney suggested during the Convention that the members of the Senate come from four equally proportioned districts within the United States and that the legislature elect the executive every seven years.

Section 3. The Senate
Trial of Impeachments One of Congress's powers is the power to impeach—to accuse government officials of wrongdoing, put them on trial, and, if necessary, remove them from office. The House decides if the offense is impeachable. The Senate acts as a jury, and when the president is impeached, the Chief Justice of the United States serves as the judge. A two-thirds vote of the members present is needed to convict impeached officials. What punishment can the Senate give if an impeached official is convicted?

Vocabulary
president pro tempore: *presiding officer of Senate who serves when the vice president is absent*

quorum: *minimum number of members that must be present to conduct sessions*

adjourn: *to suspend a session*

Section 3
[1.] The Senate of the United States shall be composed of two Senators from each State, chosen by the Legislature thereof, for six Years; and each Senator shall have one Vote.
[2.] Immediately after they shall be assembled in Consequence of the first Election, they shall be divided as equally as may be into three Classes. The Seats of the Senators of the first Class shall be vacated at the Expiration of the second Year, of the second Class at the Expiration of the fourth Year, and of the third Class at the Expiration of the sixth Year, so that one third may be chosen every second Year; and if Vacancies happen by Resignation, or otherwise, during the Recess of the Legislature of any State, the Executive thereof may make temporary Appointments until the next Meeting of the Legislature, which shall then fill such Vacancies.
[3.] No Person shall be a Senator who shall not have attained to the Age of thirty Years, and been nine Years a Citizen of the United States, and who shall not, when elected, be an Inhabitant of that State for which he shall be chosen.
[4.] The Vice President of the United States shall be President of the Senate, but shall have no Vote, unless they be equally divided.
[5.] The Senate shall chuse their other Officers, and also a **President pro tempore,** in the Absence of the Vice-President, or when he shall exercise the Office of the President of the United States.
[6.] The Senate shall have the sole Power to try all Impeachments. When sitting for that Purpose, they shall be on Oath or Affirmation. When the President of the United States is tried, the Chief Justice shall preside: And no Person shall be convicted without the Concurrence of two thirds of the Members present.
[7.] Judgment in Cases of Impeachment shall not extend further than to removal from Office, and disqualification to hold and enjoy any Office of honor, Trust or Profit under the United States: but the Party convicted shall nevertheless be liable and subject to Indictment, Trial, Judgment and Punishment, according to Law.

Section 4
[1.] The Times, Places and Manner of holding Elections for Senators and Representatives, shall be prescribed in each State by the Legislature thereof; but the Congress may at any time by Law make or alter such Regulations, except as to the Places of chusing Senators.
[2.] The Congress shall assemble at least once in every Year, and such Meeting shall be on the first Monday in December, unless they shall by Law appoint a different Day.

Section 5
[1.] Each House shall be the Judge of the Elections, Returns and Qualifications of its own Members, and a Majority of each shall constitute a **Quorum** to do Business; but a smaller Number may **adjourn** from day to day, and may be

authorized to compel the Attendance of absent Members, in such Manner, and under such Penalties as each House may provide.

[2.] Each House may determine the Rules of its Proceedings, punish its Members for disorderly Behaviour, and, with the **Concurrence** of two thirds, expel a Member.

[3.] Each House shall keep a Journal of its Proceedings, and from time to time publish the same, excepting such Parts as may in their Judgment require Secrecy; and the Yeas and Nays of the Members of either House on any question shall, at the Desire of one fifth of those Present, be entered on the Journal.

[4.] Neither House, during the Session of Congress, shall, without the Consent of the other, adjourn for more than three days, nor to any other Place than that in which the two Houses shall be sitting.

Section 6

[1.] The Senators and Representatives shall receive a Compensation for their Services, to be ascertained by Law, and paid out of the Treasury of the United States. They shall in all Cases, except Treason, Felony and Breach of the Peace, be privileged from Arrest during their Attendance at the Session of their respective Houses, and in going to and returning from the same; and for any Speech or Debate in either House, they shall not be questioned in any other Place.

[2.] No Senator or Representative shall, during the Time for which he was elected, be appointed to any civil Office under the Authority of the United States, which shall have been created, or the **Emoluments** whereof shall have been encreased during such time; and no Person holding any Office under the United States, shall be a Member of either House during his Continuance in Office.

Section 7

[1.] All Bills for raising **Revenue** shall originate in the House of Representatives; but the Senate may propose or concur with Amendments as on other **Bills.**

[2.] Every Bill which shall have passed the House of Representatives and the Senate, shall, before it become a Law, be presented to the President of the United States; If he approve he shall sign it, but if not he shall return it, with his Objections to that House in which it shall have originated, who shall enter the Objections at large on their Journal, and proceed to reconsider it. If after such Reconsideration two thirds of that House shall agree to pass the Bill, it shall be sent, together with the Objections, to the other House, by which it shall likewise be reconsidered, and if approved by two thirds of that House, it shall become a Law. But in all such Cases the Votes of both Houses shall be determined by yeas and Nays, and the Names of the Persons voting for and against the Bill shall be entered on the Journal of each House respectively. If any Bill shall not be returned by the President within ten Days (Sundays excepted) after it shall have been presented to him, the Same shall be a Law, in like Manner as if he had signed it, unless the Congress by their Adjournment prevent its Return, in which Case it shall not be a Law.

Section 6. Privileges and Restrictions
Pay and Privileges To strengthen the federal government, the Founders set congressional salaries to be paid by the United States Treasury rather than by members' respective states. Originally, members were paid $6 per day. In 2002, all members of Congress received a base salary of $150,000.

Section 7. Passing Laws
Revenue Bill All tax laws must originate in the House of Representatives. This ensures that the branch of Congress that is elected by the people every two years has the major role in determining taxes.

Section 7. Passing Laws
How Bills Become Laws A bill may become a law only by passing both houses of Congress and by being signed by the president. The president can check Congress by rejecting–vetoing–its legislation. How can Congress override the president's veto?

[3.] Every Order, **Resolution,** or Vote to which the Concurrence of the Senate and House of Representatives may be necessary (except on a question of Adjournment) shall be presented to the President of the United States; and before the Same shall take Effect, shall be approved by him, or being disapproved by him, shall be repassed by two thirds of the Senate and House of Representatives, according to the Rules and Limitations prescribed in the Case of a Bill.

Section 8

[1.] The Congress shall have the Power to lay and collect Taxes, Duties, Imposts and Excises, to pay the Debts and provide for the common Defence and general Welfare of the United States; but all Duties, Imposts and Excises shall be uniform throughout the United States;

[2.] To borrow Money on the credit of the United States;

[3.] To regulate Commerce with foreign Nations, and among the several States, and with the Indian Tribes;

[4.] To establish an uniform Rule of **Naturalization,** and uniform Laws on the subject of Bankruptcies throughout the United States;

[5.] To coin Money, regulate the Value thereof, and of foreign Coin, and fix the Standard of Weights and Measures;

[6.] To provide for the Punishment of counterfeiting the Securities and current Coin of the United States;

[7.] To establish Post Offices and post Roads;

[8.] To promote the Progress of Science and useful Arts, by securing for limited Times to Authors and Inventors the exclusive Right to their respective Writings and Discoveries;

[9.] To constitute Tribunals inferior to the supreme Court;

[10.] To define and punish Piracies and Felonies committed on the high Seas, and Offences against the Law of Nations;

[11.] To declare War, grant Letters of Marque and Reprisal, and make Rules concerning Captures on Land and Water;

[12.] To raise and support Armies, but no Appropriation of Money to that Use shall be for a longer Term than two Years;

[13.] To provide and maintain a Navy;

[14.] To make Rules for the Government and Regulation of the land and naval Forces;

[15.] To provide for calling forth the Militia to execute the Laws of the Union, suppress Insurrections and repel Invasions;

[16.] To provide for organizing, arming, and disciplining, the Militia, and for governing such Part of them as may be employed in the Service of the United States, reserving to the States respectively, the Appointment of the Officers, and the Authority of training the Militia according to the discipline prescribed by Congress;

[17.] To exercise exclusive Legislation in all Cases whatsoever, over such District (not exceeding ten Miles square) as may, by Cession of particular States, and the Acceptance of Congress, become the Seat of Government of the United States, and to exercise like Authority over all Places purchased by the Consent of the Legislature of the State in which the Same shall be, for the Erection of Forts, Magazines, Arsenals, dock-Yards, and other needful Buildings; And

Section 8.
Powers Granted to Congress
Expressed Powers Expressed powers are those powers directly stated in the Constitution. Most of the expressed powers of Congress are itemized in Article I, Section 8. These powers are also called enumerated powers because they are numbered 1 to 18. Which clause gives Congress the power to declare war?

Vocabulary
resolution: *legislature's formal expression of opinion*
naturalization: *procedure by which a citizen of a foreign nation becomes a citizen of the United States*

[18.] To make all Laws which shall be necessary and proper for carrying into Execution the foregoing Powers, and all other Powers vested by this Constitution in the Government of the United States, or in any Department or Officer thereof.

Section 9

[1.] The Migration or Importation of such Persons as any of the States now existing shall think proper to admit, shall not be prohibited by the Congress prior to the Year one thousand eight hundred and eight, but a Tax or duty may be imposed on such Importation, not exceeding ten dollars for each Person.

[2.] The Privilege of the Writ of Habeas Corpus shall not be suspended, unless when in Cases of Rebellion or Invasion the public Safety may require it.

[3.] No Bill of Attainder or ex post facto Law shall be passed.

[4.] No Capitation, or other direct, Tax shall be laid, unless in Proportion to the Census or Enumeration herein before directed to be taken.

[5.] No Tax or Duty shall be laid on Articles exported from any State.

[6.] No Preference shall be given by any Regulation of Commerce or Revenue to the Ports of one State over those of another: nor shall Vessels bound to, or from, one State, be obliged to enter, clear, or pay Duties in another.

[7.] No Money shall be drawn from the Treasury, but in Consequence of Appropriations made by Law; and a regular Statement and Account of the Receipts and Expenditures of all public Money shall be published from time to time.

[8.] No Title of Nobility shall be granted by the United States:And no Person holding any Office of Profit or Trust under them, shall, without the Consent of the Congress, accept of any present, Emolument, Office, or Title, of any kind whatever, from any King, Prince, or foreign State.

Section 10

[1.] No State shall enter into any Treaty, Alliance, or Confederation; grant Letters of Marque and Reprisal; coin Money; emit Bills of Credit; make any Thing but gold and silver Coin a Tender in Payment of Debts; pass any Bill of Attainder, ex post facto Law, or Law impairing the Obligation of Contracts, or grant any Title of Nobility.

[2.] No State shall, without the Consent of the Congress, lay any Imposts or Duties on Imports or Exports, except what may be absolutely necessary for executing it's inspection Laws: and the net Produce of all Duties and Imposts, laid by any State on Imports and Exports, shall be for the Use of the Treasury of the United States; and all such Laws shall be subject to the Revision and Controul of the Congress.

[3.] No State shall, without the Consent of Congress, lay any Duty of Tonnage, keep Troops, or Ships of War in time of Peace, enter into any Agreement or Compact with another State, or with a foreign Power, or engage in War, unless actually invaded, or in such imminent Danger as will not admit of delay.

Section 8.
Powers Granted to Congress

Elastic Clause The final enumerated power is often called the "elastic clause." This clause gives Congress the right to make all laws "necessary and proper" to carry out the powers expressed in the other clauses of Article I. It is called the elastic clause because it lets Congress "stretch" its powers to meet situations the Founders could not have anticipated.

What does the phrase "necessary and proper" in the elastic clause mean? It was a subject of dispute from the beginning. The issue was whether a strict or a broad interpretation of the Constitution should be applied. The dispute was first addressed in 1819, in the case of *McCulloch* v. *Maryland,* when the Supreme Court ruled in favor of a broad interpretation. The Court stated that the elastic clause allowed Congress to use its powers in any way that was not specifically prohibited by the Constitution.

Section 9. Powers Denied to the Federal Government

Original Rights A writ of habeas corpus issued by a judge requires a law official to bring a prisoner to court and show cause for holding the prisoner. A bill of attainder is a bill that punishes a person without a jury trial. An "ex post facto" law is one that makes an act a crime after the act has been committed. What does the Constitution say about bills of attainder?

Section 10.
Powers Denied to the States

Limitations on Powers Section 10 lists limits on the states. These restrictions were designed, in part, to prevent an overlapping in functions and authority with the federal government.

Article II. The Executive Branch

Article II creates an executive branch to carry out laws passed by Congress. Article II lists the powers and duties of the president, describes qualifications for office and procedures for electing the president, and provides for a vice president.

What Might Have Been

Term of Office Alexander Hamilton also provided his own governmental outline at the Constitutional Convention. Some of its most distinctive elements were that both the executive and the members of the Senate were "elected to serve during good behaviour," meaning there was no specified limit on their time in office.

Section 1.
President and Vice President

Former Method of Election In the election of 1800, the top two candidates received the same number of electoral votes, making it necessary for the House of Representatives to decide the election. To eliminate this problem, the Twelfth Amendment, added in 1804, changed the method of electing the president stated in Article II, Section 3. The Twelfth Amendment requires that the electors cast separate ballots for president and vice president.

Section 1.
President and Vice President

Qualifications The president must be a citizen of the United States by birth, at least 35 years of age, and a resident of the United States for 14 years.

What Might Have Been

Qualifications At the Constitutional Convention, the New Jersey Amendments, sponsored by the smaller states, raised the possibility of making the executive a committee of people rather than a single individual. Also, executives were not allowed to run for a second term of office under this plan.

Article II
Section 1

[1.] The executive Power shall be vested in a President of the United States of America. He shall hold his Office during the Term of four Years, and, together with the Vice-President, chosen for the same Term, be elected, as follows

[2.] Each State shall appoint, in such Manner as the Legislature thereof may direct, a Number of Electors, equal to the whole Number of Senators and Representatives to which the State may be entitled in the Congress: but no Senator or Representative, or Person holding an Office of Trust or Profit under the United States, shall be appointed an Elector.

[3.] The Electors shall meet in their respective States, and vote by Ballot for two Persons, of whom one at least shall not be an Inhabitant of the same State with themselves. And they shall make a List of all the Persons voted for, and of the Number of Votes for each; which List they shall sign and certify, and transmit sealed to the Seat of the Government of the United States, directed to the President of the Senate. The President of the Senate shall, in the Presence of the Senate and House of Representatives, open all the Certificates, and the Votes shall then be counted. The Person having the greatest Number of Votes shall be the President, if such Number be a Majority of the whole Number of Electors appointed; and if there be more than one who have such Majority, and have an equal Number of Votes, then the House of Representatives shall immediately chuse by Ballot one of them for President; and if no person have a Majority, then from the five highest on the List the said House shall in like Manner chuse the president. But in chusing the President, the Votes shall be taken by States, the Representation from each State having one Vote; A quorum for this Purpose shall consist of a Member or Members from two thirds of the States, and a Majority of all the States shall be necessary to a Choice. In every Case, after the Choice of the President, the Person having the greatest Number of Votes of the Electors shall be the Vice-President. But if there should remain two or more who have equal Votes, the Senate shall chuse from them by Ballot the Vice President.

[4.] The Congress may determine the Time of chusing the Electors, and the Day on which they shall give their Votes; which Day shall be the same throughout the United States.

[5.] No Person except a natural born Citizen, or a Citizen of the United States, at the time of the Adoption of this Constitution, shall be eligible to the Office of President; neither shall any Person be eligible to that Office who shall not have attained to the Age of thirty five Years, and been fourteen Years a Resident within the United States.

[6.] In Case of the Removal of the President from Office, or of his Death, Resignation, or Inability to discharge the Powers and Duties of the said Office, the Same shall devolve on the Vice-President, and the Congress may by Law provide for the Case of Removal, Death, Resignation or Inability, both of the President and Vice-President, declaring what Officer shall then act as President, and such Officer shall act accordingly, until the Disability be removed, or a President shall be elected.

[7.] The President shall, at stated Times, receive for his Services, a Compensation, which shall neither be encreased nor diminished during the Period for which he shall have been elected, and he shall not receive within that Period any other Emolument from the United States, or any of them.

[8.] Before he enter on the Execution of his Office, he shall take the following Oath or Affirmation—"I do solemnly swear (or affirm) that I will faithfully execute the Office of President of the United States, and will to the best of my Ability, preserve, protect and defend the Constitution of the United States."

Section 2

[1.] The President shall be Commander in Chief of the Army and Navy of the United States, and of the Militia of the several States, when called into the actual Service of the United States; he may require the Opinion, in writing, of the principal Officer in each of the executive Departments, upon any Subject relating to the Duties of their respective Offices, and he shall have Power to grant Reprieves and Pardons for Offences against the United States, except in Cases of Impeachment.

[2.] He shall have Power, by and with the Advice and Consent of the Senate, to make Treaties, provided two thirds of the Senators present concur; and he shall nominate, and by and with the Advice and Consent of the Senate, shall appoint Ambassadors, other public Ministers and Consuls, Judges of the supreme Court, and all other Officers of the United States, whose Appointments are not herein otherwise provided for, and which shall be established by Law: but the Congress may by Law vest the Appointment of such inferior Officers, as they think proper, in the President alone, in the Courts of Law, or in the Heads of Departments.

[3.] The President shall have Power to fill up all Vacancies that may happen during the Recess of the Senate, by granting Commissions which shall expire at the End of their next Session.

Section 3

He shall from time to time give to the Congress Information of the State of the Union, and recommend to their Consideration such Measures as he shall judge necessary and expedient; he may, on extraordinary Occasions, convene both Houses, or either of them, and in Case of Disagreement between them, with Respect to the Time of Adjournment, he may adjourn them to such Time as he shall think proper; he shall receive Ambassadors and other public Ministers; he shall take Care that the Laws be faithfully executed, and shall Commission all the Officers of the United States.

Section 1.
President and Vice President
Vacancies If the president dies, resigns, is removed from office by impeachment, or is unable to carry out the duties of the office, the vice president becomes president.

Section 1.
President and Vice President
Salary Originally, the president's salary was $25,000 per year. The president's current salary is $400,000 plus a $50,000 expense account per year. The president also receives living accommodations in the White House and Camp David.

Section 2.
Powers of the President
Cabinet Mention of "the principal officer in each of the executive departments" is the only suggestion of the president's cabinet to be found in the Constitution. The cabinet is an advisory body, and its power depends on the president. Section 2, Clause 1 also makes the president the head of the armed forces. This established the principle of civilian control of the military.

Section 2.
Powers of the President
Treaties The president is responsible for the conduct of relations with foreign countries. What role does the Senate have in approving treaties?

Section 3.
Duties of the President
Executive Orders An important presidential power is the ability to issue executive orders. An executive order is a rule or command the president issues that has the force of law. Only Congress can make laws under the Constitution, but executive orders are considered part of the president's duty to "take care that the laws be faithfully executed." This power is often used during emergencies. Over time the scope of executive orders has expanded. Decisions by federal agencies and departments are also considered to be executive orders.

Section 4. Impeachment
Reasons for Removal From Office This section states the reasons for which the president and vice president may be impeached and removed from office. Only Andrew Johnson and Bill Clinton have been impeached by the House. Richard Nixon resigned before the House could vote on possible impeachment.

Article III. The Judicial Branch

The term *judicial* refers to courts. The Constitution set up only the Supreme Court but provided for the establishment of other federal courts. The judiciary of the United States has two different systems of courts. One system consists of the federal courts, whose powers derive from the Constitution and federal laws. The other includes the courts of each of the 50 states, whose powers derive from state constitutions and laws.

Section 2. Jurisdiction
General Jurisdiction Federal courts deal mostly with "statute law," or laws passed by Congress, treaties, and cases involving the Constitution itself.

Section 2. Jurisdiction
The Supreme Court A court with "original jurisdiction" has the authority to be the first court to hear a case. The Supreme Court generally has "appellate jurisdiction" in that it mostly hears cases appealed from lower courts.

Section 2. Jurisdiction
Jury Trial Except in cases of impeachment, anyone accused of a crime has the right to a trial by jury. The trial must be held in the state where the crime was committed. Jury trial guarantees were strengthened in the Sixth, Seventh, Eighth, and Ninth Amendments.

Vocabulary

original jurisdiction: *authority to be the first court to hear a case*

appellate jurisdiction: *authority to hear cases that have been appealed from lower courts*

Section 4

The President, Vice-President and all civil Officers of the United States, shall be removed from Office on Impeachment for, and Conviction of, Treason, Bribery, or other high Crimes and Misdemeanors.

Article III
Section 1

The judicial Power of the United States, shall be vested in one supreme Court, and in such inferior Courts as the Congress may from time to time ordain and establish. The Judges, both of the supreme and inferior Courts, shall hold their Offices during good Behaviour, and shall, at stated Times, receive for their Services, a Compensation, which shall not be diminished during their Continuance in Office.

Section 2

[1.] The judicial Power shall extend to all Cases, in Law and Equity, arising under this Constitution, the Laws of the United States, and Treaties made, or which shall be made, under their Authority;—to all Cases affecting Ambassadors, other public Ministers and Consuls;—to all Cases of admiralty and maritime Jurisdiction;—to Controversies to which the United States shall be a Party;—to Controversies between two or more States;—between a State and Citizens of another State;—between Citizens of different States,—between Citizens of the same State claiming Lands under Grants of different States, and between a State, or the Citizens thereof, and foreign States, Citizens or Subjects.

[2.] In all Cases affecting Ambassadors, other public Ministers and Consuls, and those in which a State shall be Party, the supreme Court shall have **original Jurisdiction.** In all the other Cases before mentioned, the supreme Court shall have **appellate Jurisdiction,** both as to Law and Fact, with such Exceptions, and under such Regulations as the Congress shall make.

[3.] The Trial of all Crimes, except in Cases of Impeachment, shall be by Jury; and such Trial shall be held in the State where the said Crimes shall have been committed; but when not committed within any State, the Trial shall be at such Place or Places as the Congress may by Law have directed.

Section 3

[1.] Treason against the United States, shall consist only in levying War against them, or in adhering to their Enemies, giving them Aid and Comfort. No Person shall be convicted of Treason unless on the Testimony of two Witnesses to the same overt Act, or on Confession in open Court.

[2.] The Congress shall have Power to declare the Punishment of Treason, but no Attainder of Treason shall work Corruption of Blood, or Forfeiture except during the Life of the Person attainted.

Article IV

Section 1

Full Faith and Credit shall be given in each State to the public Acts, Records, and judicial Proceedings of every other State. And the Congress may by general Laws prescribe the Manner in which such Acts, Records and Proceedings shall be proved, and the Effect thereof.

Section 2

[1.] The Citizens of each State shall be entitled to all Privileges and Immunities of Citizens in the several States. [2.] A Person charged in any State with **Treason,** Felony, or other Crime, who shall flee from Justice, and be found in another State, shall on Demand of the executive Authority of the State from which he fled, be delivered up, to be removed to the State having Jurisdiction of the Crime. [3.] No Person held to Service of Labour in one State, under the Laws thereof, escaping into another, shall, in Consequence of any Law or Regulation therein, be discharged from such Service or Labour, but shall be delivered up on Claim of the Party to whom such Service or Labour may be due.

Section 3

[1.] New States may be admitted by the Congress into this Union; but no new State shall be formed or erected within the Jurisdiction of any other State; nor any State be formed by the Junction of two or more States, or Parts of States, without the Consent of the Legislatures of the States concerned as well as of the Congress. [2.] The Congress shall have Power to dispose of and make all needful Rules and Regulations respecting the Territory or other Property belonging to the United States; and nothing in this Constitution shall be so construed as to Prejudice any Claims of the United States, or of any particular State.

Section 4

The United States shall guarantee to every State in this Union a Republican Form of Government, and shall protect each of them against Invasion; and on Application of the Legislature, or of the Executive (when the Legislature cannot be convened) against domestic Violence.

Article V

The Congress, whenever two thirds of both Houses shall deem it necessary, shall propose **Amendments** to this Constitution, or, on the Application of the Legislatures of two thirds of the several States, shall call a Convention for proposing Amendments, which, in either Case, shall be valid to all Intents and Purposes, as Part of this Constitution, when ratified by the Legislatures of three fourths of the several States, or by Conventions in three fourths thereof, as the one or the other Mode of **Ratification** may be proposed by the Congress; Provided

Article IV. Relations Among the States

Article IV explains the relationship of the states to one another and to the national government. This article requires each state to give citizens of other states the same rights as its own citizens, addresses the admission of new states, and guarantees that the national government will protect the states.

Section 1. Official Acts
Recognition by States This provision ensures that each state recognizes the laws, court decisions, and records of all other states. For example, a marriage license issued by one state must be accepted by all states.

Vocabulary

treason: *violation of the allegiance owed by a person to his or her own country, for example, by aiding an enemy*

amendment: *a change to the Constitution*

ratification: *process by which an amendment is approved*

Section 3.
New States and Territories
New States Congress has the power to admit new states. It also determines the basic guidelines for applying for statehood. Two states, Maine and West Virginia, were created within the boundaries of another state. In the case of West Virginia, President Lincoln recognized the West Virginia government as the legal government of Virginia during the Civil War. This allowed West Virginia to secede from Virginia without obtaining approval from the Virginia legislature.

Article V. The Amendment Process

Article V explains how the Constitution can be amended, or changed. All of the 27 amendments were proposed by a two-thirds vote of both houses of Congress. Only the Twenty-first Amendment was ratified by constitutional conventions of the states. All other amendments have been ratified by state legislatures. What is an amendment?

Article VI. Constitutional Supremacy

Article VI contains the "supremacy clause." This clause establishes that the Constitution, laws passed by Congress, and treaties of the United States "shall be the supreme Law of the Land." The "supremacy clause" recognizes the Constitution and federal laws as supreme when in conflict with those of the states.

Article VII. Ratification

Article VII addresses ratification and states that, unlike the Articles of Confederation, which required approval of all thirteen states for adoption, the Constitution would take effect after it was ratified by nine states.

that no Amendment which may be made prior to the Year One thousand eight hundred and eight shall in any Manner affect the first and fourth Clauses in the Ninth Section of the first Article; and that no State, without its Consent, shall be deprived of its equal Suffrage in the Senate.

Article VI

[1.] All Debts contracted and Engagements entered into, before the Adoption of this Constitution, shall be as valid against the United States under this Constitution, as under the Confederation.

[2.] This Constitution, and the Laws of the United States which shall be made in Pursuance thereof; and all Treaties made, or which shall be made, under the Authority of the United States, shall be the supreme Law of the Land; and the Judges in every State shall be bound thereby, any Thing in the Constitution or Laws of any State to the Contrary notwithstanding.

[3.] The Senators and Representatives before mentioned, and the Members of the several State Legislatures, and all executive and judicial Officers, both of the United States and of the several States, shall be bound by Oath or Affirmation, to support this Constitution; but no religious Test shall ever be required as a Qualification to any Office or public Trust under the United States.

Article VII

The Ratification of the Conventions of nine States, shall be sufficient for the Establishment of this Constitution between the States so ratifying the same.

Done in Convention by the Unanimous Consent of the States present the Seventeenth Day of September in the Year of our Lord one thousand seven hundred and Eighty seven and of the Independence of the United States of America the Twelfth. In witness whereof We have hereunto subscribed our Names,

Signers

George Washington,
President and Deputy from Virginia

New Hampshire
John Langdon
Nicholas Gilman

Massachusetts
Nathaniel Gorham
Rufus King

Connecticut
William Samuel Johnson
Roger Sherman

New York
Alexander Hamilton

New Jersey
William Livingston
David Brearley
William Paterson
Jonathan Dayton

Pennsylvania
Benjamin Franklin
Thomas Mifflin
Robert Morris
George Clymer
Thomas FitzSimons
Jared Ingersoll
James Wilson
Gouverneur Morris

Delaware
George Read
Gunning Bedford, Jr.
John Dickinson
Richard Bassett
Jacob Broom

Maryland
James McHenry
Daniel of St. Thomas
    Jenifer
Daniel Carroll

Virginia
John Blair
James Madison, Jr.

North Carolina
William Blount
Richard Dobbs Spaight
Hugh Williamson

South Carolina
John Rutledge
Charles Cotesworth
    Pinckney
Charles Pinckney
Pierce Butler

Georgia
William Few
Abraham Baldwin

Attest:
William Jackson,
    Secretary

Amendment I

Congress shall make no law respecting an establishment of religion, or prohibiting the free exercise thereof; or abridging the freedom of speech, or of the press; or the right of the people peaceably to assemble, and to petition the Government for a redress of grievances.

Amendment II

A well regulated Militia, being necessary to the security of a free State, the right of the people to keep and bear Arms, shall not be infringed.

Amendment III

No Soldier shall, in time of peace be **quartered** in any house, without the consent of the Owner, nor in time of war, but in a manner to be prescribed by law.

Amendment IV

The right of the people to be secure in their persons, houses, papers, and effects, against unreasonable searches and seizures, shall not be violated, and no **Warrants** shall issue, but upon **probable cause,** supported by Oath or affirmation, and particularly describing the place to be searched, and the persons or things to be seized.

Amendment V

No person shall be held to answer for a capital, or otherwise infamous crime, unless on a presentment or indictment of a Grand Jury, except in cases arising in the land or naval forces, or in the Militia, when in actual service in time of War or public danger; nor shall any person be subject for the same offence to be twice put in jeopardy of life or limb; nor shall be compelled in any criminal case to be a witness against himself, nor be deprived of life, liberty, or property, without due process of law; nor shall private property be taken for public use without just compensation.

Amendment VI

In all criminal prosecutions, the accused shall enjoy the right to a speedy and public trial, by an impartial jury of the State and district wherein the crime shall have been committed, which district shall have been previously ascertained by law, and to be informed of the nature and cause of the accusation; to be confronted with the witnesses against him; to have compulsory process for obtaining Witnesses in his favor, and to have the assistance of counsel for his defence.

Amendment VII

In Suits at common law, where the value in controversy shall exceed twenty dollars, the right of trial by jury shall be preserved, and no fact tried by a jury, shall be otherwise reexamined in any Court of the United States, than according to the rules of **common law.**

The Amendments

This part of the Constitution consists of changes and additions. The Constitution has been amended 27 times throughout the nation's history.

The Bill of Rights

The first 10 amendments are known as the Bill of Rights (1791). These amendments limit the powers of the federal government. The First Amendment protects the civil liberties of individuals in the United States. The amendment freedoms are not absolute, however. They are limited by the rights of other individuals. What freedoms does the First Amendment protect?

Vocabulary

quarter: *to provide living accommodations*
warrant: *document that gives police particular rights or powers*
probable cause: *police must have a reasonable basis to believe a person is linked to a crime*

Amendment 5
Rights of the Accused This amendment contains important protections for people accused of crimes. One of the protections is that government may not deprive any person of life, liberty, or property without due process of law. This means that the government must follow proper constitutional procedures in trials and in other actions it takes against individuals. According to Amendment V, what is the function of a grand jury?

Amendment 6
Right to Speedy and Fair Trial A basic protection is the right to a speedy, public trial. The jury must hear witnesses and evidence on both sides before deciding the guilt or innocence of a person charged with a crime. This amendment also provides that legal counsel must be provided to a defendant. In 1963, in *Gideon* v. *Wainwright*, the Supreme Court ruled that if a defendant cannot afford a lawyer, the government must provide one to defend him or her. Why is the right to a "speedy" trial important?

Vocabulary

common law: *law established by previous court decisions*

Vocabulary

bail: *money that an accused person provides to the court as a guarantee that he or she will be present for a trial*

Amendment 9
Powers Reserved to the People This amendment prevents government from claiming that the only rights people have are those listed in the Bill of Rights.

Amendment 10
Powers Reserved to the States This amendment protects the states and the people from the federal government. It establishes that powers not given to the national government and not denied to the states by the Constitution belong to the states or to the people. These are checks on the "necessary and proper" power of the federal government, which is provided for in Article I, Section 8, Clause 18.

Amendment 11
Suits Against States The Eleventh Amendment (1795) provides that a lawsuit brought by a citizen of the United States or a foreign nation against a state must be tried in a state court, not in a federal court. The Supreme Court had ruled in *Chisholm* v. *Georgia* (1793) that a federal court could try a lawsuit brought by citizens of South Carolina against a citizen of Georgia.

Vocabulary

majority: *more than half*

Amendment 12
Election of President and Vice President The Twelfth Amendment (1804) corrects a problem that had arisen in the method of electing the president and vice president, which is described in Article II, Section 1, Clause 3. This amendment provides for the Electoral College to use separate ballots in voting for president and vice president. If no candidate receives a majority of the electoral votes, who elects the president?

Amendment VIII

Excessive **bail** shall not be required, nor excessive fines imposed, nor cruel and unusual punishments inflicted.

Amendment IX

The enumeration in the Constitution, of certain rights, shall not be construed to deny or disparage others retained by the people.

Amendment X

The powers not delegated to the United States by the Constitution, nor prohibited by it to the States, are reserved to the States respectively, or to the people.

Amendment XI

The Judicial power of the United States shall not be construed to extend to any suit in law or equity, commenced or prosecuted against one of the United States by Citizens of another State, or by Citizens or Subjects of any Foreign State.

Amendment XII

The electors shall meet in their respective states and vote by ballot for President and Vice-President, one of whom, at least, shall not be an inhabitant of the same state with themselves; they shall name in their ballots the person voted for as President, and in distinct ballots the person voted for as Vice-President, and they shall make distinct lists of all persons voted for as President, and of all persons voted for as Vice-President, and of the number of votes for each, which lists they shall sign and certify, and transmit sealed to the seat of the government of the United States, directed to the President of the Senate;—The President of the Senate shall, in the presence of the Senate and House of Representatives, open all the certificates and the votes shall then be counted;—The person having the greatest number of votes for President, shall be the President, if such number be a **majority** of the whole number of Electors appointed; and if no person have such majority, then from the persons having the highest numbers not exceeding three on the list of those voted for as President, the House of Representatives shall choose immediately, by ballot, the President. But in choosing the President, the votes shall be taken by states, the representation from each state having one vote; a quorum for this purpose shall consist of a member or members from two-thirds of the states, and a majority of all the states shall be necessary to a choice. And if the House of Representatives shall not choose a President whenever the right of choice shall devolve upon them, before the fourth day of March next following, then the Vice-President shall act as President, as in the case of the death or other constitutional disability of the President. The person having the greatest number of votes as Vice-President, shall be the Vice-President, if such number be a majority of the whole number of Electors appointed, and if no person have a majority, then from the two highest numbers on the list, the Senate shall choose the Vice-President; a quorum for the purpose shall consist of two-thirds of the whole number of Senators, and a majority of the whole number shall be necessary to a choice. But no person constitutionally ineligible to the office of President shall be eligible to that of Vice-President of the United States.

Amendment XIII
Section 1
Neither slavery nor involuntary servitude, except as a punishment for crime whereof the party shall have been duly convicted, shall exist within the United States, or any place subject to their jurisdiction.

Section 2
Congress shall have power to enforce this article by appropriate legislation.

Amendment XIV
Section 1
All persons born or naturalized in the United States, and subject to the jurisdiction thereof, are citizens of the United States and of the State wherein they reside. No State shall make or enforce any law which shall **abridge** the privileges or immunities of citizens of the United States; nor shall any State deprive any person of life, liberty, or property, without due process of law; nor deny to any person within its jurisdiction the equal protection of the laws.

Section 2
Representatives shall be apportioned among the several States according to their respective numbers, counting the whole number of persons in each State, excluding Indians not taxed. But when the right to vote at any election for the choice of electors for President and Vice-President of the United States, Representatives in Congress, the Executive and Judicial officers of a State, or the members of the Legislature thereof, is denied to any of the male inhabitants of such State, being twenty-one years of age, and citizens of the United States, or in any way abridged, except for participation in rebellion, or other crime, the basis of representation therein shall be reduced in the proportion which the number of such male citizens shall bear to the whole number of male citizens twenty-one years of age in such State.

Section 3
No person shall be a Senator or Representative in Congress, or elector of President and Vice-President, or hold any office, civil or military, under the United States, or under any State, who, having previously taken an oath, as a member of Congress, or as an officer of the United States, or as a member of any State legislature, or as an executive or judicial officer of any State, to support the Constitution

Amendment 13
Abolition of Slavery Amendments Thirteen (1865), Fourteen, and Fifteen often are called the Civil War amendments because they grew out of that conflict. The Thirteenth Amendment outlaws slavery.

Amendment 14
Rights of Citizens The Fourteenth Amendment (1868) originally was intended to protect the legal rights of the freed slaves. Its interpretation has been extended to protect the rights of citizenship in general by prohibiting a state from depriving any person of life, liberty, or property without "due process of law." In addition, it states that all citizens have the right to equal protection of the laws in all states.

Amendment 14. Section 2
Representation in Congress This section reduced the number of members a state had in the House of Representatives if it denied its citizens the right to vote. Later civil rights laws and the Twenty-fourth Amendment guaranteed the vote to African Americans.

Vocabulary
abridge: *to reduce*

Amendment 14. Section 3
Penalty for Engaging in Insurrection The leaders of the Confederacy were barred from state or federal offices unless Congress agreed to remove this ban. By the end of Reconstruction, all but a few Confederate leaders were allowed to return to public service.

of the United States, shall have engaged in insurrection or rebellion against the same, or given aid or comfort to the enemies thereof. But Congress may by a vote of two-thirds of each House, remove such disability.

Section 4

The validity of the public debt of the United States, authorized by law, including debts incurred for payment of pensions and bounties for service, in suppressing insurrection or rebellion, shall not be questioned. But neither the United States nor any State shall assume or pay any debt or obligation incurred in aid of **insurrection** or rebellion against the United States, or any claim for the loss or emancipation of any slave; but all such debts, obligations and claims shall be held illegal and void.

Section 5

The Congress shall have power to enforce, by appropriate legislation, the provisions of this article.

Amendment XV

Section 1

The right of citizens of the United States to vote shall not be denied or abridged by the United States or by any State on account of race, color, or previous condition of servitude.

Section 2

The Congress shall have power to enforce this article by appropriate legislation.

Amendment XVI

The Congress shall have power to lay and collect taxes on incomes, from whatever source derived, without **apportionment** among the several States and without regard to any census or enumeration.

Amendment XVII

Section 1

The Senate of the United States shall be composed of two Senators from each State, elected by the people thereof, for six years; and each Senator shall have one vote. The electors in each State shall have the qualifications requisite for electors of the most numerous branch of the State legislatures.

Section 2

When **vacancies** happen in the representation of any State in the Senate, the executive authority of such State shall issue writs of election to fill such vacancies: *Provided,* That the legislature of any State may empower the executive thereof to make temporary appointments until the people fill the vacancies by election as the legislature may direct.

Amendment 14. Section 4
Public Debt The public debt acquired by the federal government during the Civil War was valid and could not be questioned by the South. However, the debts of the Confederacy were declared to be illegal. Could former slaveholders collect payment for the loss of their slaves?

Amendment 15
Voting Rights The Fifteenth Amendment (1870) prohibits the government from denying a person's right to vote on the basis of race. Despite the law, many states denied African Americans the right to vote by such means as poll taxes, literacy tests, and white primaries.

Amendment 16
Income Tax The origins of the Sixteenth Amendment (1913) date back to 1895, when the Supreme Court declared a federal income tax unconstitutional. To overturn this decision, this amendment authorizes an income tax that is levied on a direct basis.

Amendment 17
Direct Election of Senators The Seventeenth Amendment (1913) states that the people, instead of state legislatures, elect United States senators. How many years are in a Senate term?

Vocabulary

insurrection: *rebellion against the government*
apportionment: *distribution of seats in House based on population*
vacancy: *an office or position that is unfilled or unoccupied*

Section 3

This amendment shall not be so construed as to affect the election or term of any Senator chosen before it becomes valid as part of the Constitution.

Amendment XVIII
Section 1

After one year from ratification of this article, the manufacture, sale, or transportation of intoxicating liquors within, the importation thereof into, or the exportation thereof from the United States and all territory subject to the jurisdiction thereof for beverage purposes is hereby prohibited.

Section 2

The Congress and the several States shall have concurrent power to enforce this article by appropriate legislation.

Section 3

This article shall be inoperative unless it shall have been ratified as an amendment to the Constitution by the legislatures of the several States, as provided in the Constitution, within seven years from the date of the submission hereof to the States by the Congress.

Amendment XIX
Section 1

The right of citizens of the United States to vote shall not be denied or abridged by the United States or by any state on account of sex.

Section 2

Congress shall have power by appropriate legislation to enforce the provisions of this article.

Amendment XX
Section 1

The terms of the President and Vice President shall end at noon on the 20th day of January, and the terms of the Senators and Representatives at noon on the 3rd day of January, of the years in which such terms would have ended if this article had not been ratified; and the terms of their successors shall then begin.

Section 2

The Congress shall assemble at least once in every year, and such meeting shall begin at noon on the 3rd day of January, unless they shall by law appoint a different day.

Amendment 18
Prohibition The Eighteenth Amendment (1919) prohibited the production, sale, or transportation of alcoholic beverages in the United States. Prohibition proved to be difficult to enforce. This amendment was later repealed by the Twenty-first Amendment.

Amendment 19
Woman Suffrage The Nineteenth Amendment (1920) guaranteed women the right to vote. By then women had already won the right to vote in many state elections, but the amendment made their right to vote in all state and national elections constitutional.

Amendment 20
"Lame Duck" The Twentieth Amendment (1933) sets new dates for Congress to begin its term and for the inauguration of the president and vice president. Under the original Constitution, elected officials who retired or who had been defeated remained in office for several months. For the outgoing president, this period ran from November until March. Such outgoing officials, referred to as "lame ducks," could accomplish little. What date was fixed as Inauguration Day?

Amendment 20. Section 3
Succession of President and Vice President This section provides that if the president-elect dies before taking office, the vice president-elect becomes president.

Vocabulary

president-elect: *individual who is elected president but has not yet begun serving his or her term*

Amendment 21
Repeal of Prohibition The Twenty-first Amendment (1933) repeals the Eighteenth Amendment. It is the only amendment ever passed to overturn an earlier amendment. It is also the only amendment ratified by special state conventions instead of state legislatures.

Section 3

If, at the time fixed for the beginning of the term of the President, the President elect shall have died, the Vice President elect shall become President. If a President shall not have been chosen before the time fixed for the beginning of his term, or if the **President elect** shall have failed to qualify, then the Vice President elect shall act as President until a President shall have qualified; and the Congress may by law provide for the case wherein neither a President elect nor a Vice President elect shall have qualified, declaring who shall then act as President, or the manner in which one who is to act shall be selected, and such person shall act accordingly until a President or Vice President shall have qualified.

Section 4

The Congress may by law provide for the case of the death of any of the persons from whom the House of Representatives may choose a President whenever the right of choice shall have devolved upon them, and for the case of the death of any of the persons from whom the Senate may choose a Vice President whenever the right of choice shall have devolved upon them.

Section 5

Sections 1 and 2 shall take effect on the 15th day of October following the ratification of this article.

Section 6

This article shall be inoperative unless it shall have been ratified as an amendment to the Constitution by the legislatures of three-fourths of the several States within seven years from the date of its submission.

Amendment XXI
Section 1

The eighteenth article of amendment to the Constitution of the United States is hereby repealed.

Section 2

The transportation or importation into any State, Territory, or possession of the United States for delivery or use therein of intoxicating liquors, in violation of the laws thereof, is hereby prohibited.

Section 3

This article shall be inoperative unless it shall have been ratified as an amendment to the Constitution by conventions in the several States, as provided in the Constitution, within seven years from the date of the submission hereof to the States by the Congress.

Amendment XXII

Section 1

No person shall be elected to the office of the President more than twice, and no person who had held the office of President, or acted as President, for more than two years of a term to which some other person was elected President shall be elected to the office of the President more than once. But this Article shall not apply to any person holding the office of President when this Article was proposed by the Congress, and shall not prevent any person who may be holding the office of President, or acting as President, during the term within which this Article becomes operative from holding the office of President or acting as President during the remainder of such term.

Section 2

This article shall be inoperative unless it shall have been ratified as an amendment to the Constitution by the legislatures of three-fourths of the several States within seven years from the date of its submission to the States by the Congress.

Amendment XXIII

Section 1

The District constituting the seat of Government of the United States shall appoint in such manner as the Congress may direct:

A number of electors of President and Vice President equal to the whole number of Senators and Representatives in Congress to which the District would be entitled if it were a State, but in no event more than the least populous State; they shall be in addition to those appointed by the States, but they shall be considered, for the purposes of the election of President and Vice President, to be electors appointed by a State; and they shall meet in the District and perform such duties as provided by the twelfth article of amendment.

Section 2

The Congress shall have power to enforce this article by appropriate legislation.

Amendment XXIV

Section 1

The right of citizens of the United States to vote in any primary or other election for President or Vice President, for electors for President or Vice President, or for Senator or Representative in Congress, shall not be denied or abridged by the United States or any State by reason of failure to pay any poll tax or other tax.

Amendment 22
Presidential Term Limit The Twenty-second Amendment (1951) limits presidents to a maximum of two elected terms. The amendment wrote into the Constitution a custom started by George Washington. It was passed largely as a reaction to Franklin D. Roosevelt's election to four terms between 1933 and 1945. It also provides that anyone who succeeds to the presidency and serves for more than two years of the term may not be elected more than one more time.

Amendment 23
D.C. Electors The Twenty-third Amendment (1961) allows citizens living in Washington, D.C., to vote for president and vice president, a right previously denied residents of the nation's capital. The District of Columbia now has three presidential electors, the number to which it would be entitled if it were a state.

Amendment 24
Abolition of the Poll Tax The Twenty-fourth Amendment (1964) prohibits poll taxes in federal elections. Prior to the passage of this amendment, some states had used such taxes to keep low-income African Americans from voting. In 1966 the Supreme Court banned poll taxes in state elections as well.

Section 2

The Congress shall have power to enforce this article by appropriate legislation.

Amendment XXV

Section 1

In case of the removal of the President from office or his death or resignation, the Vice President shall become President.

Section 2

Whenever there is a vacancy in the office of the Vice President, the President shall nominate a Vice President who shall take the office upon confirmation by a majority vote of both Houses of Congress.

Section 3

Whenever the President transmits to the President pro tempore of the Senate and the Speaker of the House of Representatives his written declaration that he is unable to discharge the powers and duties of his office, and until he transmits to them a written declaration to the contrary, such powers and duties shall be discharged by the Vice President as Acting President.

Section 4

Whenever the Vice President and a majority of either the principal officers of the executive departments or of such other body as Congress may by law provide, transmit to the President pro tempore of the Senate and the Speaker of the House of Representatives their written declaration that the President is unable to discharge the powers and duties of his office, the Vice President shall immediately assume the power and duties of the office of Acting President.

Thereafter, when the President transmits to the President pro tempore of the Senate and the Speaker of the House of Representatives his written declaration that no inability exists, he shall resume the powers and duties of his office unless the Vice President and a majority of either the principal officers of the executive department or of such other body as Congress may by law provide, transmit within four days to the President pro tempore of the Senate and the Speaker of the House of Representatives their written declaration that the President is unable to discharge the powers and duties of his office. Thereupon Congress shall decide the issue, assembling within forty-eight hours for that purpose if not in session. If the Congress, within twenty-one days after receipt of the latter written declaration, or, if Congress is not in session, within twenty-one days after Congress is required to assemble, determines by two-thirds vote of both Houses that the President is unable to discharge the powers and duties of his office, the Vice President shall continue to discharge the same as Acting President; otherwise, the President shall resume the power and duties of his office.

Amendment 25
Presidential Disability and Succession The Twenty-fifth Amendment (1967) established a process for the vice president to take over leadership of the nation when a president is disabled. It also set procedures for filling a vacancy in the office of vice president.

This amendment was used in 1973, when Vice President Spiro Agnew resigned from office after being charged with accepting bribes. President Richard Nixon then appointed Gerald R. Ford as vice president in accordance with the provisions of the Twenty-fifth Amendment. A year later, President Nixon resigned during the Watergate scandal, and Ford became president. President Ford then had to fill the vice presidency, which he had left vacant upon assuming the presidency. He named Nelson A. Rockefeller as vice president. Thus individuals who had not been elected held both the presidency and the vice presidency. Whom does the president inform if he or she cannot carry out the duties of the office?

Amendment XXVI

Section 1
The right of citizens of the United States, who are eighteen years of age or older, to vote shall not be denied or abridged by the United States or by any State on account of age.

Section 2
The Congress shall have power to enforce this article by appropriate legislation.

Amendment XXVII

No law, varying the compensation for the services of Senators and Representatives, shall take effect, until an election of representatives shall have intervened.

Amendment 26
Voting Age of 18 The Twenty-sixth Amendment (1971) lowered the voting age in both federal and state elections to 18.

Amendment 27
Congressional Salary Restraints The Twenty-seventh Amendment (1992) makes congressional pay raises effective during the term following their passage. James Madison offered the amendment in 1789, but it was never adopted. In 1982 Gregory Watson, then a student at the University of Texas, discovered the forgotten amendment while doing research for a school paper. Watson made the amendment's passage his crusade.

The Young Republic

1789–1850

Why It Matters

Internal improvements and industrial development began to transform the United States in the early 1800s, but these changes also highlighted the growing differences between the North and South and set the stage for civil war. At the same time, Americans fought a war with Mexico and continued to expand west, building a nation that stretched from the Atlantic to the Pacific.

The bustle and excitement of an Election Day in Philadelphia in the early 1800s

151

Chapter 4

Federalists and Republicans

1789–1816

SECTION 1 Washington and Congress

SECTION 2 Partisan Politics

SECTION 3 Jefferson in Office

SECTION 4 The War of 1812

This detail from Jean Leon Gerome Ferris's painting Washington's Inauguration at Independence Hall, 1793 *shows Washington being greeted by John Adams and Thomas Jefferson.*

1789
- Washington becomes president

Washington 1789–1797

1794
- Jay's Treaty is signed

J. Adams 1797–1801

Jefferson 1801–1809

1803
- Louisiana Purchase doubles size of the nation

1804
- Lewis and Clark begin to explore the Louisiana Purchase

U.S. PRESIDENTS

U.S. EVENTS

1790   1795   1800

WORLD EVENTS

1789
- French Revolution begins

1793
- Louis XVI is guillotined during French Revolution

1798
- Quasi-War between France and the U.S. begins

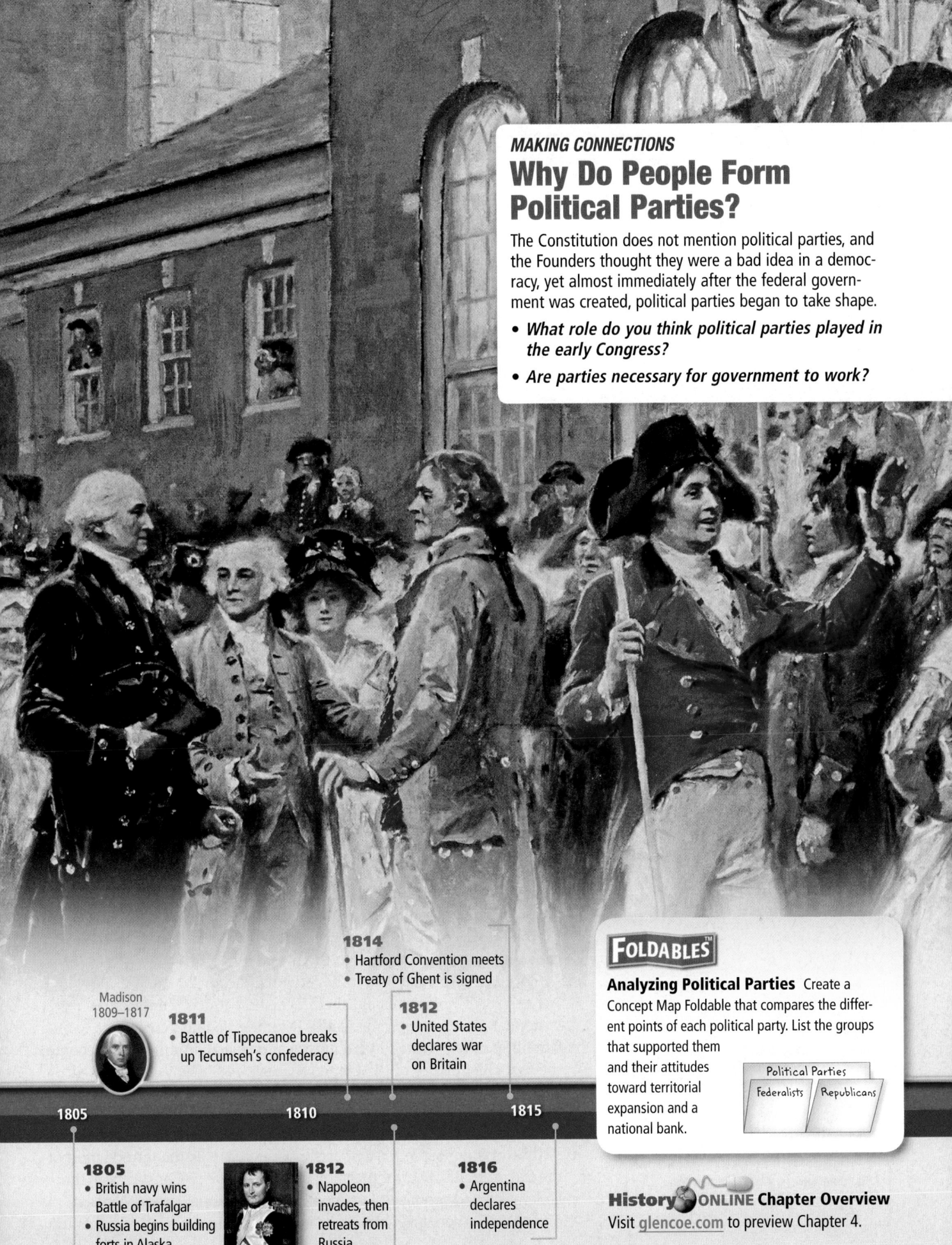

1814
- Hartford Convention meets
- Treaty of Ghent is signed

Madison
1809–1817

1811
- Battle of Tippecanoe breaks up Tecumseh's confederacy

1812
- United States declares war on Britain

1805

1810

1815

1805
- British navy wins Battle of Trafalgar
- Russia begins building forts in Alaska

1812
- Napoleon invades, then retreats from Russia

1816
- Argentina declares independence

FOLDABLES™

Analyzing Political Parties Create a Concept Map Foldable that compares the different points of each political party. List the groups that supported them and their attitudes toward territorial expansion and a national bank.

Political Parties
Federalists | Republicans

History ONLINE **Chapter Overview**
Visit glencoe.com to preview Chapter 4.

Washington and Congress

Guide to Reading

Big Ideas
Individual Action George Washington helped define the new American presidency.

Content Vocabulary
- cabinet *(p. 154)*
- bond *(p. 156)*
- speculator *(p. 157)*
- enumerated powers *(p. 157)*
- implied powers *(p. 157)*
- agrarianism *(p. 159)*

Academic Vocabulary
- revenue *(p. 155)*
- creditor *(p. 156)*

People and Events to Identify
- Tariff of 1789 *(p. 156)*
- Bank of the United States *(p. 158)*
- Whiskey Rebellion *(p. 158)*

Reading Strategy
Organizing Complete a graphic organizer similar to the one below by indicating the tasks completed by the first Congress under the Constitution.

Tasks of Congress

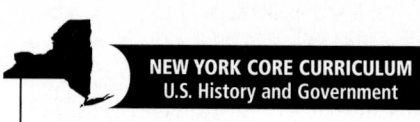

NEW YORK CORE CURRICULUM
U.S. History and Government

Unit 2:
I.C The Bill of Rights
I.F.1 Creating domestic stability through sound financial policies: Hamilton's financial plans
I.F.3 Establishing a stable political system
I.F.3.b Suppressing the dissent (the Whiskey Rebellion, the Alien and Sedition Acts.)

President Washington and the First Congress had to decide how to make the new government function effectively. The conflicting philosophies of Thomas Jefferson and Alexander Hamilton became the basis for two new political parties.

Creating a New Government

MAIN Idea With the adoption of the Constitution, American leaders had to establish a new national government to deal effectively with the challenges facing the nation.

HISTORY AND YOU Have you ever had to accomplish something based on a complicated plan? Read on to find out how American leaders carried out the specifications of the new Constitution.

The Philadelphia Convention had given the nation a new Constitution. George Washington's task, and the task facing the newly elected Congress, was to take the words of the Constitution and turn them into an effective government for the United States. To get the government up and running, the president needed a bureaucracy to handle different responsibilities. In 1789 Congress created the Department of State, the Department of the Treasury, the Department of War, and the Office of the Attorney General.

To manage these departments, Washington wanted individuals who were "disposed to measure matters on a Continental Scale," instead of thinking only of their own states. He chose Thomas Jefferson as secretary of state, Alexander Hamilton as secretary of the treasury, and General Henry Knox as secretary of war. For attorney general, Washington selected Edmund Randolph, the former governor of Virginia. Washington regularly met with these men to ask for their advice. The department heads came to be known as the **cabinet,** a group of advisers to the president.

Congress also established the federal judiciary. In the Judiciary Act of 1789, Congress established 13 district courts, three courts of appeal, and the Supreme Court. With the Senate's consent, Washington chose the federal judges and selected John Jay to become the first chief justice of the United States.

The Bill of Rights

One of the most important acts of Congress was the introduction of the Bill of Rights. During the campaign to ratify the Constitution, the Federalists had promised to add such amendments. James Madison, one of the leaders in Congress, made the passage of a bill of rights top

Origins of the Bill of Rights

Basic Rights	Magna Carta (1215)	English Bill of Rights (1689)	Virginia Declaration of Rights (1776)	Virginia Statute for Religious Freedom (1786)	American Bill of Rights (1791)
No state religion				●	●
Freedom of worship		● limited	●	●	●
Freedom of speech		●	●		●
Right to petition		● limited			●
Right to bear arms					●
No quartering troops in private homes without permission					●
No searches and seizures without a specific search warrant	●		●		●
Government cannot take away life, liberty, or property unless it follows proper court procedures (due process)	●	●	●		●
Right to a speedy public trial by jury and to a lawyer	●	●	●	●	●
No excessive bail, fines, or cruel and unusual punishment	●	●	●		●

Steps to the Bill of Rights

In creating the Bill of Rights, the first ten amendments to the Constitution, James Madison drew on the great founding documents of English legal history and tradition: the Magna Carta, the English Bill of Rights, the Virginia Declaration of Rights, and the Virginia Statute for Religious Freedom. Beginning in 1215, these and other documents had established protections of individual rights and freedoms designed to safeguard citizens from oppression and tyrannical government.

Analyzing VISUALS

1. **Specifying** Which right was established in the Magna Carta and appears in all subsequent documents?
2. **Explaining** Which two rights are the only ones unique to the American Bill of Rights, and why do you think that is?

priority. He hoped it would demonstrate the good faith of federal leaders and build support for the new government.

In drafting the Bill of Rights, Madison relied heavily on the Virginia Declaration of Rights that George Mason prepared in 1776 and the Virginia Statute for Religious Freedom that Thomas Jefferson wrote in 1786. In late September 1789, Congress agreed on 12 constitutional amendments. They were then sent to the states for ratification, but only 10 were approved. These 10 went into effect and are generally referred to as the Bill of Rights. The first eight protect the rights of individuals against actions of the federal government. The last two set limits on the powers of the new national government. The Ninth Amendment states that the people have other rights not listed. The Tenth Amendment states that any powers not specifically given to the federal government are reserved for the states.

Financing the Government

Having organized the new federal government, the next most pressing need was a source of **revenue.** Without money, the government could not operate. Madison and Hamilton responded to this need with different plans for financing the government.

The Tariff of 1789 James Madison suggested that the federal government raise most of its money by taxing imports. After much discussion, Congress passed the **Tariff of 1789.** This law required importers to pay a percentage of the value of their cargo when they landed it in the United States. Shippers also had to pay tonnage—a tax based on how much their ships carried.

The tariffs and tonnage rates angered many Southern planters. High tonnage rates meant they would be charged higher rates to ship their rice and tobacco to Europe. The new tariff also meant that the imported goods the South needed would cost more. Many Southerners began to suspect that the federal government was opposed to their region's interests.

Hamilton's Financial Program Hamilton supported the Tariff of 1789, but he believed the government also needed the ability to borrow money. To fund the Revolutionary War, the Congress under the Articles of Confederation had issued **bonds**—paper notes promising to repay money after a certain length of time with interest. By 1789, the United States owed roughly $40 million to American citizens and another $11.7 million to lenders in France,

Spain, and the Netherlands. Few believed the bonds would be repaid in full, and they had fallen in value to as little as 10 cents on the dollar. In 1790 Hamilton asked Congress to redeem the bonds at full value.

Hamilton believed that if the United States accepted these debts at full value, then wealthy **creditors,** bankers, and merchants who owned the bonds would have enough confidence in its financial stability to lend it money in the future. Hamilton had described the importance of debt several years earlier:

PRIMARY SOURCE

"A national debt if it is not excessive will be to us a national blessing; it will be a powerfull cement of our union. It will also create a necessity for keeping up taxation . . . which without being oppressive, will be a spur to industry. . ."

—from Alexander Hamilton, letter to Robert Morris, April 30, 1781

Opposition to Hamilton's Plan Led by Madison, critics argued that Hamilton's plan was unfair to the original purchasers of the bonds. These people—who included farmers, war veterans, and widows—fearing they would

PRIMARY SOURCE
Funding a New Government

For the new federal government to succeed, it needed money. Secretary Alexander Hamilton wanted the government to do four things to secure its ability to raise money: 1. tax imports, 2. take on the debts of the Continental Congress, 3. establish a national bank, and 4. impose an excise tax on whiskey. All were controversial.

1. THE TARIFF OF 1789

◀ The Tariff of 1789 levied a tax on the value of goods imported and on the weight of the shipment (tonnage).

2. THE NATION'S FINANCES, 1792

Debts

• Foreign debt:	$11.7 million
• State debt the federal government agreed to pay:	$21.5 million
• Domestic debts (bonds):	$42.4 million
• Total:	$75.6 million

Annual interest on the debts (must be paid every year):	$4.6 million

Income

• Customs revenue (tariffs and tonnage):	$4.4 million
• Excise taxes (whiskey tax):	$1.2 million
• Funds remaining (after paying interest):	$1.0 million

▲ Hamilton believed that establishing a national bank that would take on prior debts would give lenders a stake in the new government's success.

never be paid, had sold their bonds to **speculators.** Madison was outraged that speculators who had paid as little as $10 for a $100 bond would now receive full value.

Madison and other Southerners were also upset because Northerners owned most of the bonds, while much of the tax money that would be used to pay off the bonds would come from the South. Madison also worried that creditors would eventually dominate American society and endanger liberty.

The debate over Hamilton's proposals raged for months. Finally, in July 1790, Hamilton, Madison, and Jefferson struck a deal. Madison and Jefferson would use their influence to convince Southerners in Congress to vote for Hamilton's plan. In return, the United States capital would move from New York City to an area along the Potomac River to be called the District of Columbia. Southerners believed that having the capital in the South would help offset the strength of the Northern states.

The Bank of the United States

With his system of public credit finally in place, Hamilton asked Congress to create a national bank. He argued that the government needed the bank to manage its debts and interest payments. The bank would also issue bank notes—paper money. The notes would provide a national currency that would promote trade, encourage investment, and stimulate economic growth.

Southerners opposed the plan. They pointed out that Northern merchants would own most of the bank's stock. Madison argued that Congress could not establish a bank because it was not among the federal government's **enumerated powers,** or powers specifically mentioned in the Constitution.

Despite Madison's objections, Congress passed the bank bill. Washington realized that his decision to sign the bill or to veto it would set an important precedent. Attorney General Randolph and Secretary of State Jefferson argued that the Constitution did not give the federal government the power to create a bank. Hamilton disagreed, noting that Article I, Section 8, of the Constitution gave the federal government the power "to make all laws which shall be necessary and proper" to execute its responsibilities. The "necessary and proper" clause created **implied powers**—powers not listed in the Constitution but necessary for the government to do its job.

---

3. THE NATIONAL BANK

Hamilton explains why a national bank is constitutional:

"[I]f the measure have an obvious relation to that end, and is not forbidden by any particular provision of the Constitution—it may safely be deemed to come within the compass of the national authority. There is also this further criterion, which may materially assist the decision. Does the proposed measure abridge a preexisting right of any State or of any individual? If it does not, there is a strong presumption in favour of its constitutionality. . . ."

—from Alexander Hamilton, *Opinion on the Constitutionality of Establishing a National Bank,* February 23, 1791

Jefferson argues that a national bank is unconstitutional:

"I consider the foundation of the Constitution as laid on this ground that 'all powers not delegated to the U.S. by the Constitution, nor prohibited by it to the States, are reserved to the States or to the people.' . . . To take a single step beyond the boundaries thus specially drawn around the powers of Congress, is to take possession of a boundless feild [sic] of power, no longer susceptible of any definition."

—from Thomas Jefferson, *Opinion on the Constitutionality of Establishing a National Bank,* February 15, 1791

4. EXCISE TAXES

▲ *The excise tax on whiskey was especially despised and led to a rebellion in 1794 quelled by federal troops sent by George Washington.*

DBQ Document-Based Questions

1. **Synthesizing** Why did Hamilton want to establish credit for the new nation?
2. **Explaining** Why did Jefferson argue against a national bank?

A national bank, Hamilton argued, was necessary to collect taxes, regulate trade, and provide for defense. Jefferson agreed that implied powers existed, but believed "necessary and proper" meant absolutely necessary, not simply convenient. After studying the issue, Washington agreed to sign the bill. In 1791 the **Bank of the United States** was created with a 20-year charter.

History ONLINE
Student Web Activity Visit glencoe.com and complete the activity on the rise of political parties.

The Whiskey Rebellion

Hamilton also believed the government had to establish its right to impose direct taxes. In 1791 Congress imposed a tax on the manufacture of whiskey. The new tax enraged western farmers who distilled their grain into whiskey before shipping it to market. The **Whiskey Rebellion** erupted in western Pennsylvania in 1794. Farmers terrorized tax collectors, stopped court proceedings, and robbed the mail. In August 1794, Washington sent about 15,000 troops to crush the rebellion. The rebels dispersed without a fight. This willingness to use armed troops against civilians, however, worried many people.

✔ Reading Check **Explaining** Why did Madison object to Hamilton's plan for a national bank?

The Rise of Political Parties

MAIN Idea Federalists backed a stronger government and manufacturers; Republicans supported a weaker government and farmers.

HISTORY AND YOU The Federalists were more popular in some parts of the nation, the Democratic-Republicans in others. Is one political party more popular than others in your state?

During Washington's first term in office, the debate over Hamilton's financial program divided Congress into factions based on their views of the federal government's role. These factions became the nation's first political parties. Hamilton's supporters called themselves Federalists. His opponents, led by Madison and Jefferson, took the name Democratic-Republicans, although most people at the time referred to them as Republicans.

Decades later, the Democratic-Republicans became known as the Democrats, the name they are known by today. The party known today as the Republican Party is a different party that was founded in 1854. The Federalist Party does not exist today.

People IN HISTORY

Alexander Hamilton
1755/57–1804

Alexander Hamilton was born in the British West Indies and immigrated to America in 1772. An attorney by profession, Hamilton represented New York at the Constitutional Convention of 1787 and, as author of many of the *Federalist* papers, was instrumental in getting the Constitution ratified.

As secretary of the treasury in the new government, Hamilton advocated his vision for a powerful national government, a national bank, and the assumption of Revolutionary-era debts. His ideas became the foundation of the Federalist Party.

Hamilton resigned as treasury secretary in 1795, but remained influential. In 1804 he was killed in a duel with Aaron Burr, a political enemy. An ambitious, brilliant, pragmatic, and innovative statesman, Alexander Hamilton's legacy is the strong national government we have today.

How did Alexander Hamilton contribute to the formation of the U.S. government?

Thomas Jefferson
1743–1826

Thomas Jefferson was a man of contradictions. He wrote elegantly about American ideals of rights and liberties, yet he was a slaveholder. Jefferson was the chief drafter of the Declaration of Independence and the author of the Virginia Statute for Religious Freedom.

During the Revolution, Jefferson served as United States minister to France. He remained in that post until 1789, when he returned to the United States to become secretary of state in Washington's administration.

With James Madison, Jefferson formed the Democratic-Republican Party in opposition to the Federalists, whom he felt were betraying the ideals of the American Revolution by attempting to set up a government as authoritarian as the British monarchy. Jefferson believed that the power of the national government should be minimized. In 1800 he was elected to be the third president of the United States.

What was Jefferson's vision for the nation?

Hamilton and the Federalists

Hamilton favored a strong national government. He believed that democracy was dangerous to liberty and stated that "the people are turbulent and changing; they seldom judge or determine right." This distrust led him to favor putting government into the hands of the "rich, well born, and able."

Hamilton also believed that manufacturing and trade were the basis of national wealth and power. He favored policies that would support these areas of the economy. Supporters of the Federalist Party often included artisans, merchants, manufacturers, and bankers. The party also attracted urban workers and Eastern farmers who benefited from trade.

Jefferson and the Republicans

Although James Madison led the opposition to Hamilton's program in Congress, Thomas Jefferson emerged as the leader of the Democratic-Republicans. Jefferson believed that the strength of the United States was its independent farmers. His ideas are sometimes referred to as **agrarianism.** Jefferson argued that owning land enabled people to be independent. As long as most people owned their own land, they would fight to preserve the Republic.

Jefferson feared that too much emphasis on commerce would lead to a society sharply divided between the rich, who owned everything, and the poor, who worked for wages. He also believed that the wealthy would corrupt the government and threaten the rights and liberties of ordinary people.

PRIMARY SOURCE

"Dependence begets subservience and venality, suffocates the germ of virtue. . . . While we have land to labour . . . let us never wish to see our citizens occupied at a work-bench, or twirling a distaff. . . .[L]et our work-shops remain in Europe. It is better to carry provisions and materials to workmen there, than bring them to the provisions and materials, and with them their manners and principles. . . . The mobs of great cities add just so much to the support of pure government, as sores do to the strength of the human body."

—from *Notes on the State of Virginia*

In general, Democratic-Republicans supported agriculture over commerce and trade. They also expressed concern that Hamilton's policies tended to favor the North. Over time, they became the party that stood for the rights of states against the federal government.

The development of America's first two political parties divided the country regionally. The rural South and West tended to support the Republicans, while the more urban Northeast tended to support the Federalists. Although these parties emerged during the dispute over Hamilton's programs, events in Europe would deepen the divisions between them and create new crises for the young nation.

Reading Check **Classifying** What were the nation's first two political parties, and what issues did they favor?

Section 1 REVIEW

Vocabulary

1. **Explain** the significance of: cabinet, Tariff of 1789, bond, speculator, enumerated powers, implied powers, Bank of the United States, Whiskey Rebellion, agrarianism.

Main Ideas

2. **Listing** What actions of the new federal government started and ended the Whiskey Rebellion?

3. **Identifying** Who was the main leader of each of the new American political parties?

Critical Thinking

4. **Big Ideas** What precedents did George Washington set as president of the United States?

5. **Categorizing** Use a graphic organizer similar to the one below to list the first political parties in the United States, their supporters, and the issues they promoted.

Political Party	Supporters	Issues Supported

6. **Analyzing Visuals** Study the chart on the Bill of Rights on page 155. What new protection originated in the Virginia Statute for Religious Freedom?

Writing About History

7. **Persuasive Writing** Suppose you are James Madison. Write a speech to persuade others not to support Alexander Hamilton's financial program.

History ONLINE

Study Central™ To review this section, go to glencoe.com and click on Study Central.

HULTON GETTY

Profile

GEORGE WASHINGTON *At the age of 16, George Washington carefully transcribed in his own hand the* Rules of Civility and Decent Behaviour in Company and Conversation. *Among the rules our first president lived by:*

- Every action done in company ought to be with some sign of respect to those that are present.

- When in company, put not your hands to any part of the body, not usually [un]covered.

- Put not off your clothes in the presence of others, nor go out your chamber half dressed.

- Sleep not when others speak.

- Spit not in the fire, nor stoop low before it. Neither put your hands into the flames to warm them, nor set your feet upon the fire, especially if there is meat before it.

- Shake not the head, feet or legs. Roll not the eyes. Lift not one eyebrow higher than the other. Wry not the mouth, and bedew no man's face with your spittle, by approaching too near him when you speak.

- Show not yourself glad at the misfortune of another though he were your enemy.

- Be not hasty to believe flying reports to the disparagement of any.

- Think before you speak.

- Cleanse not your teeth with the Table Cloth.

VERBATIM

WAR'S END

❝I hope you will not consider yourself as commander-in-chief of your own house, but be convinced, that there is such a thing as equal command.❞

> **LUCY FLUCKER KNOX,**
> *to her husband Henry Knox, upon his return as a hero from the Revolutionary War*

❝The American war is over, but this is far from being the case with the American Revolution. Nothing but the first act of the drama is closed.❞

> **BENJAMIN RUSH,**
> *signer of the Declaration of Independence and member of the Constitutional Convention*

❝You could not have found a person to whom your schemes were more disagreeable.❞

> **GEORGE WASHINGTON,**
> *to Colonel Lewis Nicola, in response to his letter urging Washington to seize power and proclaim himself king*

❝It appears to me, then, little short of a miracle that the delegates from so many states . . . should unite in forming a system of national government.❞

> **GEORGE WASHINGTON,**
> *in a letter to the Marquis de Lafayette at the close of the Constitutional Convention*

❝It astonishes me to find this system approaching to near perfection as it does; and I think it will astonish our enemies.❞

LEONARD DESELVA/CORBIS

> **BENJAMIN FRANKLIN,**
> *remarking on the structure of the new United States government*

Annual Salaries

Annual federal employee salaries, 1789

President (he refused it) $25,000	
Vice President $5,000	
Secretary of State $3,500	
Chief Justice $4,000	
Senator ....$6 per day	
Representative ....$6 per day	
Army Captain $420	
Army Private $48	

CORBIS

1780s WORD PLAY

Dressing the "Little Pudding Heads"

Can you match these common items of Early American clothing with their descriptions?

1. clout

a. a band of strong fabric wrapped around a baby to suppress the navel

2. stays

b. a diaper

3. surcingle

c. the wool cover worn over a diaper

4. pilch

d. a head covering for a child learning to walk to protect its brain from falls

5. pudding cap

e. a garment worn by children to foster good posture, made from linen and wood or baleen splints

answers: 1. b; 2. e; 3. a; 4. c; 5. d

Milestones

SETTLED, 1781. LOS ANGELES, by a group of 46 men and women, most of whom are of Native American and African descent.

CALLED, 1785. LEMUEL HAYNES, as minister to a church in Torrington, Connecticut. Haynes, who fought at Lexington during the Revolutionary War, is the first African American to minister to a white congregation. A parishioner insulted Haynes by refusing to remove his hat in church, but minutes into the sermon, the parishioner was so moved that the hat came off. He is now a prayerful and loyal member of the congregation.

PUBLISHED, 1788. *THE ELEMENTARY SPELLING BOOK,* by Noah Webster, a 25-year-old teacher from Goshen, N.Y. The book standardizes American spelling and usage that differs from the British.

NUMBERS

5 Number of years younger average American bride compared to her European counterpart

6 Average number of children per family to survive to adulthood

7 Average number of children born per family

8 Number of Daniel Boone's surviving children

68 Number of Daniel Boone's grandchildren

$5 Average monthly wage for male agricultural laborer, 1784

$3 Average monthly wage for female agricultural laborer, 1784

PIX/FPG

CRITICAL THINKING

1. *Contrasting* Benjamin Rush made a distinction between the American war and the American Revolution. What do you think he meant by his statement?

2. *Making Inferences* Based on the rules George Washington lived by, how would you describe his character?

Partisan Politics

Guide to Reading

Big Ideas
Government and Society
Disagreements between the political parties early in the nation's history threatened citizens' rights.

Content Vocabulary
- most-favored nation (p. 163)
- alien (p. 166)
- sedition (p. 166)
- interposition (p. 167)
- nullification (p. 167)

Academic Vocabulary
- radical (p. 162)
- neutral (p. 162)

People and Events to Identify
- Jay's Treaty (p. 163)
- Pinckney's Treaty (p. 164)
- Quasi-War (p. 165)
- Alien and Sedition Acts (p. 166)

Reading Strategy
Categorizing Complete a graphic organizer by listing the provisions of treaties made by the United States.

Treaty	Provisions
Jay's Treaty	
Pinckney's Treaty	
Convention of 1800	

NEW YORK CORE CURRICULUM
U.S. History and Government

Unit 2:
I.F.3.b Suppressing dissent (the Whiskey Rebellion, the Alien and Sedition Acts)
I.F.4 Neutrality and national security, Washington through Monroe: foreign affairs, establishing boundaries
II.C Territorial expansion through diplomacy, migration, annexation, and war; Manifest Destiny
II.C.4 Motives for and implications of expansion and western settlement

Although Washington wanted to remain neutral in the ongoing war between France and Britain, staying out of the conflict was not easy. In 1800 the United States underwent its first transfer of political power—from the Federalist Party to the Democratic-Republican Party.

Trade and Western Expansion

MAIN Idea During Washington's presidency, the United States faced several challenges in foreign policy and territorial expansion; the French Revolution and conflict between Britain and France divided Americans.

HISTORY AND YOU Have you ever been involved in a dispute between two friends? Read on to find out how events in France forced Americans to take sides in political struggles at home.

Shortly after George Washington was inaugurated in 1789, the French Revolution began in Europe. At first, most Americans sympathized with the revolutionaries, who seemed to be fighting for the same rights Americans had won a few years earlier. By the spring of 1793, however, a new group of French **radicals** had seized control. They stripped aristocrats of their property and executed thousands of people, including the king and queen. These events divided Americans. Many Federalists, horrified by the violence and chaos, opposed the revolutionaries, but many Republicans supported them, despite the bloodshed, because they seemed to be fighting for liberty.

When France declared war on Britain, President Washington found himself in a difficult position. Both Britain and France traded with the United States. Furthermore, the Treaty of 1778 with France required the United States to help defend France's colonies in the Caribbean. Fulfilling this agreement might mean war with Great Britain. In April 1793, Washington declared the United States to be "friendly and impartial" toward both warring powers.

Jay's Treaty

Despite Washington's declaration, the British began intercepting all **neutral** ships carrying goods to French ports, including hundreds of American ships. At the same time, reports appeared that the British, operating out of forts they still occupied on American territory, were inciting Native Americans to attack western settlers. Together, these events pushed Congress to the brink of war in 1794.

Determined to avoid war, Washington sent John Jay to Britain to seek a solution. The British were busy fighting France. They did not want to fight the Americans, but they knew that the United States

Diplomacy and Westward Expansion, 1790–1796

NATIONAL GEOGRAPHIC

Legend:
— Line of Pinckney's Treaty
— Line of Treaty of Greenville
▨ Maximum Spanish claim, 1784
▨ New states, 1791–1796
✳ Major battle
■ British-held fort
■ Spanish-held fort

CANADA

Vermont (1791) Maine

N.H.

New York Mass.

R.I.

Pennsylvania Conn. 40°N

N.J.

Md. Del. 70°W

Fallen Timbers Aug. 20, 1794
Harmer's Defeat Oct. 22, 1790
St. Clair's Defeat Nov. 4, 1791
Northwest Territory Ohio R.

Virginia

ATLANTIC OCEAN

Kentucky (1792)

Tennessee (1796) North Carolina

Mississippi R. Tennessee R.

South Carolina

Georgia

SPANISH FLORIDA

0   200 kilometers
0   200 miles
Lambert Azimuthal Equal-Area projection

Jay's Treaty, 1794: The British agree to give up their forts on U.S. territory, but the U.S. has to agree that the British navy can intercept U.S. ships going to France.

Pinckney's Treaty, 1795: Spain gives up all land claims north of the treaty line and allows U.S. merchants to use the Mississippi and leave goods at New Orleans.

▲ Anti-Federalists burn a figure representing John Jay after Jay's Treaty with England was signed in 1794.

Analyzing GEOGRAPHY

1. **Location** Which three states joined the Union between 1790 and 1800?
2. **Human-Environment Interaction** How do you think that Pinckney's Treaty probably helped the economies of Tennessee and Kentucky?

depended on trade with Britain. They agreed to sign a treaty but drove a hard bargain.

Jay was forced to agree that Britain had the right to seize cargoes bound for French ports. He also failed to get compensation for merchants whose goods had been seized. The British did agree, however, to submit the issue to international arbitration—a hearing by neutral third countries. The British also agreed to give up their forts on American territory and granted the United States **most-favored nation** status. American merchants would no longer be discriminated against when trading with Britain. They were also allowed limited trade with Britain's colonies in the Caribbean.

When **Jay's Treaty** was sent to the Senate for ratification, the senators were shocked by its terms and tried to keep them secret. Although they eventually ratified the treaty, news of its terms leaked to the public. The Republicans immediately attacked the treaty,

accusing the Federalists of being pro-British. Across much of the country, public protests were held condemning the treaty. After prolonged deliberation, Washington agreed to implement the treaty. The decision prevented war with Great Britain and protected the fragile American economy.

Pinckney's Treaty

Jay's Treaty also helped the United States win concessions from Spain, which still controlled Florida and territory west of the Mississippi River. In 1795 Spain joined France in its war against Britain. The signing of the treaty had raised fears in Spain that the British and Americans might now join forces to seize Spain's North American holdings. Spain quickly offered to negotiate all outstanding issues with the United States. Washington sent Thomas Pinckney to Spain to negotiate.

In 1795 the Spanish signed the Treaty of San Lorenzo—better known as **Pinckney's Treaty.** The treaty granted the United States the right to navigate the Mississippi and to deposit goods at the port of New Orleans. The treaty won broad acceptance, especially among western farmers who wanted to use the Mississippi to get crops to market.

Westward Expansion

In the 1780s, drawn by abundant land, fertile soil, wide rivers, and a wide variety of fish and game, Americans flocked to the area between the Appalachian Mountains and the Mississippi River. In less than a decade, Kentucky grew from a few hundred settlers to over 70,000, and in 1792, it became a state. Four years later, Tennessee became a state as well. In the meantime, other settlers moved into the Northwest Territory, where they clashed with the region's Native Americans.

In the Northwest Territory, a chief of the Miami named Little Turtle united the Miami, Shawnee, Delaware, and other groups into a confederacy to defend their lands against white settlers. In late 1790, Little Turtle's forces defeated American troops led by General Josiah Harmar. A year later, they ambushed an American force led by General Arthur St. Clair, killing nearly half his men.

After these disasters, Washington sent General Anthony Wayne to stop the Native American attacks. In August 1794, a large force made up of Shawnee, Ottawa, Chippewa, and Potawatomi warriors, led by the Shawnee chief Blue Jacket, attacked Wayne's troops at the Battle of Fallen Timbers. Wayne's forces won the battle, inflicting heavy losses.

Wayne's victory dealt a decisive blow to Native American resistance in the Northwest Territory. In August 1795, 12 Native American nations signed the Treaty of Greenville. They agreed to give up part of southern Ohio and Indiana in exchange for a yearly payment of $10,000 from the federal government. They also gave up land near where Chicago, Detroit, and Vincennes, Indiana, are located today. After the treaty was signed, the flow of settlers into the region rapidly increased. By 1803, Ohio had enough settlers to become a state.

✔ **Reading Check** **Examining** Why did Little Turtle form a confederacy?

The War Between the Parties

MAIN Idea Conflict between Federalists and Republicans began to threaten social stability.

HISTORY AND YOU Do you think that the federal government should be able to suspend civil rights? Read on to learn how the Federalists suppressed criticism of their leadership.

With Washington stepping down, the United States held its first openly contested election. The Federalists rallied around John Adams for president, while the Republicans nominated Thomas Jefferson. Anger over Jay's Treaty made the election close, but when the electoral votes were tallied, John Adams edged out Jefferson 71 to 68 and became the second president of the United States.

The Quasi-War With France

President Adams faced troubled times at home and abroad. Enraged by Jay's Treaty, the French began stopping American ships en route to Britain and seizing their goods. France's actions led many Federalists to call for war. Although critical of the French, Adams, like Washington, was reluctant to go to war. Instead, he sent Charles Pinckney, Elbridge Gerry, and John Marshall to Paris to negotiate with the French government.

After weeks of waiting, three agents representing Charles Maurice de Talleyrand, the French minister of foreign affairs, approached the Americans. They asked for a bribe of $250,000 just to initiate talks, and also sought an American loan of $12 million. In a letter, John Marshall recounted an exchange with "Mr. X," one of the agents:

PRIMARY SOURCE

"Mr. X. again returned to the subject of money; said he, Gentlemen, you do not speak to the point—it is money: it is expected that you will offer money. We said we had spoken to that point very explicitly: we had given an answer. No, said he, you have not; what is your answer? We replied, it is no; no; not a sixpence."

—from *Official Correspondence . . . Between C. C. Pinckney, John Marshall, and Elbridge Gerry*

Washington's Farewell Address, 1796

Before leaving office, George Washington wrote a letter to the American people. Widely reprinted, Washington's Farewell Address warned Americans against sectionalism, political parties, and the dangers of becoming too attached to any foreign nation:

"... The name of American, which belongs to you in your national capacity, must always exalt the just pride of patriotism. ... With slight shades of difference, you have the same religion, manners, habits, and political principles. You have in a common cause fought and triumphed together; the independence and liberty you possess are the work of joint counsels, and joint efforts of common dangers, sufferings, and successes.

... In contemplating the causes which may disturb our Union, it occurs as matter of serious concern that any ground should have been furnished for characterizing parties by geographical discriminations, Northern and Southern, Atlantic and Western. ... You cannot shield yourselves too much against the jealousies and heartburnings which spring from these misrepresentations.

... Let me now take a more comprehensive view, and warn you in the most solemn manner against the baneful effects of the spirit of party generally. ... The disorders and miseries, which result, gradually incline the minds of men to seek security and repose in the absolute power of an individual.

... Of all the dispositions and habits which lead to political prosperity, religion and morality are indispensable supports. In vain would that man claim the tribute of patriotism, who should labor to subvert these great pillars of human happiness, these firmest props of the duties of men and citizens. ...

... The great rule of conduct for us in regard to foreign nations is in extending our commercial relations, to have with them as little political connection as possible. ... It is our true policy to steer clear of permanent alliances with any portion of the foreign world. ... we may safely trust to temporary alliances for extraordinary emergencies."

—From "A Letter to the American People," Sept. 17, 1796

▲ *George Washington at Versailles, France, 1796*

DBQ Document-Based Questions

1. **Identifying** About what three main issues does Washington warn Americans?

2. **Discussing** How do you think Washington would feel about the activities of the national government today?

When President John Adams informed Congress of the incident, he referred to the French agents as X, Y, and Z. Newspapers began referring to the incident as the XYZ Affair. Federalist newspapers later turned Pinckney's response into a stirring campaign slogan, "Millions for defense, but not one cent for tribute."

Irate Americans, who had been angry with Britain a few years earlier, now called for war against France. Resolutions and mass meetings further aroused the public. In June 1798 Congress suspended trade with France and directed the navy to capture French ships.

The two nations were soon fighting an undeclared war at sea that came to be known as the **Quasi-War.** In the fall of 1798, France proposed new negotiations. In September 1800 the two countries signed the Convention of 1800. The United State gave up all claims against France for damages to American shipping. In return, France released the United States from the Treaty of 1778. The signing of the Convention of 1800 brought the Quasi-War to an end.

The Alien and Sedition Acts

The Quasi-War also affected domestic politics in the United States. Many Federalists resented the harsh criticisms printed in Republican newspapers. They remembered the angry Republican crowds that had protested Jay's Treaty. Now, the Quasi-War had reversed the situation, and Federalists decided to strike back at the Republicans.

Turning Points

The Election of 1800

The election of 1800 was a major turning point in American political history. This is because it was the first transfer of power between parties under the federal Constitution, and, despite the enormous political and personal hatred between the party members, it was accomplished peacefully. It demonstrated the commitment on all sides to the Constitution and to a democratic republic despite partisan passions.

ANALYZING HISTORY What made the election of 1800 so significant in American political history?

▲ This cartoon reveals the emotions in American politics and the divisive nature of the relationship between the parties in the early years of the nation. The scene depicts a fight in the House of Representatives in 1798, begun when Federalist Roger Griswold of Connecticut assaulted Republican Matthew Lyon of Vermont.

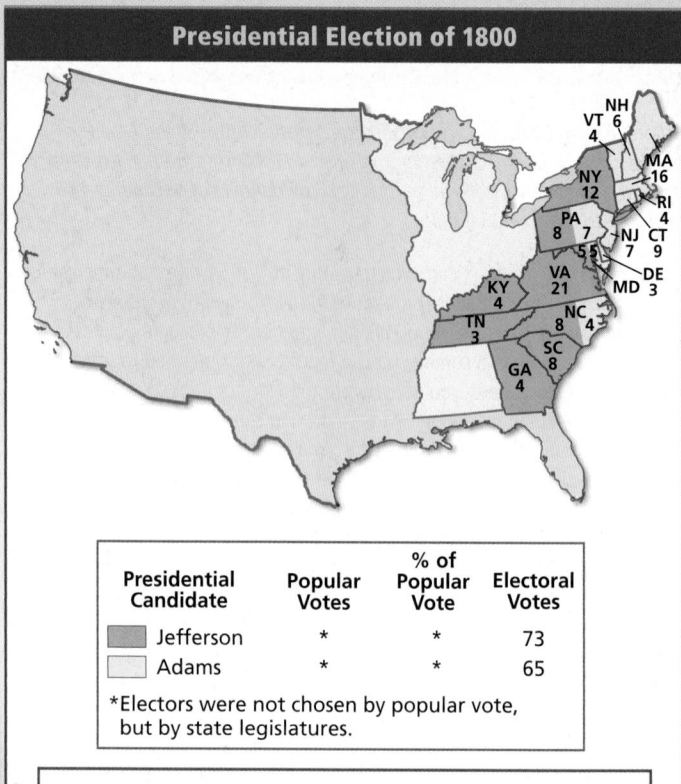

Presidential Election of 1800

Presidential Candidate	Popular Votes	% of Popular Vote	Electoral Votes
Jefferson	*	*	73
Adams	*	*	65

*Electors were not chosen by popular vote, but by state legislatures.

According to the original terms of the Constitution, each elector in the Electoral College voted for two people in a presidential election. The person receiving the most votes became president, and the person receiving the second-highest number of votes became vice president. Under this system a tie was possible, as happened in the case of the tie between Thomas Jefferson and Aaron Burr in 1800. The House of Representatives then elected Jefferson after 35 rounds of voting in which there was no clear winner. To prevent such confusion in the future, the Twelfth Amendment was added to the Constitution in 1804. The amendment stipulates that electoral votes for president and vice president are counted and listed separately.

For the text of the Kentucky Resolution, see page R47 in Documents in American History.

At the height of public anger at France in 1798, the Federalists pushed four laws through Congress. These laws became known as the **Alien and Sedition Acts.**

The first three laws were aimed at **aliens**—people living in the country who were not citizens. The Federalists knew that many recent immigrants had come from France and Ireland. These immigrants were often anti-British and tended to vote for the Republicans when they became citizens.

The first law changed the period for people waiting to become citizens from 5 to 14 years. The next two laws gave the president the power to deport without trial any alien deemed dangerous to the nation.

The fourth law tried to prevent **sedition,** or incitement to rebellion. This law made it illegal to say or print anything "false, scandalous, and malicious" about the federal government or any government officer. In short, the act deprived citizens of their right to criticize public officials. The government indicted 21 people and convicted 11 under this act, most of them Republican newspaper editors and politicians.

In 1798 and 1799, the Republican-controlled legislatures of Kentucky and Virginia passed resolutions, secretly written by Jefferson and Madison, criticizing the Alien and Sedition Acts. Both resolutions argued that since the states had created the Constitution, they could declare federal laws unconstitutional.

The Virginia Resolutions introduced the theory of **interposition.** They argued that if the federal government did something unconstitutional, the state could interpose between the federal government and the people and stop the illegal action. The Kentucky Resolutions advanced the theory of **nullification.** According to this theory, if the federal government passed an unconstitutional law, the states had the right to nullify the law, or declare it invalid. Although these resolutions had little effect in 1800, states used these ideas in later decades to defend their regional interests.

The Election of 1800

John Adams hoped to win reelection in 1800 but he faced an uphill battle. The Alien and Sedition Acts had angered many people, as had new taxes on houses, land, and enslaved Africans. The Republican nominees, Thomas Jefferson for president and Aaron Burr for vice president, campaigned against the taxes and the national bank. They accused the Federalists of favoring monarchy and discouraging political participation.

The election was closely contested and had an unexpected outcome, one that revealed a flaw in the system for selecting the president. The Constitution does not let citizens vote directly for the chief executive. Instead, each state chooses electors—the same number as it has senators and representatives. This group, known as the Electoral College, then votes for the president.

According to the original terms of the Constitution, each elector in the Electoral College voted for two people. The normal practice was for an elector to cast one vote for his party's presidential candidate and another for the vice presidential candidate. To avoid a tie between Jefferson and Burr, the Republicans had intended for one elector to refrain from voting for Burr, but when the votes were counted, Jefferson and Burr each had 73. Since no candidate had a majority, the Federalist-controlled House of Representatives had to choose a president.

Many Federalists despised Jefferson and wanted to choose Burr, but Alexander Hamilton preferred Jefferson. He urged his followers to support Jefferson, leading to a tie in the House of Representatives. Finally, in February 1801, Federalist James Bayard cast a blank ballot so that Jefferson received more votes than Burr and became president. Historians are not sure why this happened. They have inferred that Bayard did it because Jefferson had let him know that if elected, he would keep Hamilton's financial system and not fire all Federalists in the government.

The election of 1800 was an important turning point in American history. At the time, the Federalists controlled the army, the presidency, and the Congress. They could have refused to step down and overthrown the Constitution. Instead, they respected the people's right to choose the president. The election of 1800 demonstrated that power in the United States could be peacefully transferred despite strong disagreements between the parties.

✔ Reading Check **Analyzing** What was the purpose of the Alien and Sedition Acts?

Vocabulary

1. **Explain** the significance of: most-favored nation, Jay's Treaty, Pinckney's Treaty, Quasi-War, Alien and Sedition Acts, alien, sedition, interposition, nullification.

Main Ideas

2. **Identifying** What were the positive outcomes of Jay's Treaty?

3. **Determining Cause and Effect** What were the causes of the Quasi-War?

Critical Thinking

4. **Big Ideas** How did the Alien and Sedition Acts interfere with the lives of Americans?

5. **Organizing** Use a graphic organizer similar to the one below to list the foreign policy challenges that Washington and Adams faced during their presidencies.

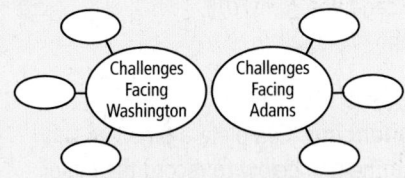

6. **Analyzing Visuals** Study the map of the presidential election of 1800 on page 166. Which three states split their electoral votes between Adams and Jefferson?

Writing About History

7. **Persuasive Writing** Assume the role of an American citizen in 1798. Write a letter to the editor explaining why you do or do not support the Alien and Sedition Acts.

History ONLINE

Study Central™ To review this section, go to glencoe.com and click on Study Central.

Section 3

Jefferson in Office

Guide to Reading

Big Ideas
Government and Society Jefferson worked to limit the scope of the government, obtain the Louisiana Territory, and keep the nation out of European wars.

Content Vocabulary
• judicial review (p. 170)
• embargo (p. 173)

Academic Vocabulary
• license (p. 173)

People and Events to Identify
• Louisiana Purchase (p. 169)
• Meriwether Lewis (p. 169)
• William Clark (p. 169)
• Sacagawea (p. 170)
• John Marshall (p. 170)

Reading Strategy
Sequencing Complete a time line similar to the one below to record the major events of Thomas Jefferson's presidency.

NEW YORK CORE CURRICULUM
U.S. History and Government

Unit 2:
I.F.2 Development of unwritten constitutional government under Washington, Adams, and Jefferson: cabinet, political parties, judicial review, executive and Congressional interpretation, lobbying; the Marshall Court (*Marbury* v. *Madison*, 1803, *McCulloch* v. *Maryland*, 1819, and *Gibbons* v. *Ogden*, 1824)
I.F.4 Neutrality and national security, Washington through Monroe: foreign affairs, establishing boundaries
II.C.1 The Louisiana Purchase
II.C.2 Exploring and settling the West (explorers, Lewis and Clark expedition, naturalists, trappers and traders, trailblazers, missionaries, pioneers, the Mormon Church)

President Thomas Jefferson worked to limit the scope of the federal government, purchased the Louisiana Territory, and tried to keep the United States out of European conflicts. The Supreme Court, under John Marshall, established the power of judicial review.

Jefferson's Administration

MAIN Idea During Jefferson's presidency the nation more than doubled in size, while the federal judiciary established its authority.

HISTORY AND YOU Today, we await a Supreme Court decision to determine whether a law is constitutional. However, the Court did not start out with this power. Read on to find out how the Supreme Court established this authority.

Thomas Jefferson privately referred to his election as the "Revolution of 1800." He believed that Washington and Adams had acted too much like royalty, and he tried to create a less formal style for the presidency. He rode horseback rather than traveling in carriages. In place of formal receptions, he entertained at more intimate dinners around a circular table so that, as he said, "When brought together in society, all are perfectly equal."

Although Jefferson set a new style for the presidency, he did not overturn all of the Federalists' policies. Instead he sought to integrate Republican ideas into the policies that the Federalists had already put in place. A strong believer in small government, Jefferson hoped to limit federal power. He began paying off the federal debt, cut government spending, and did away with the hated whiskey tax. Instead of a standing army, he planned to rely on local militia.

Jefferson's economic ideas had worried many Federalists, who expected the new president to close the national bank. Jefferson's choice of Albert Gallatin as secretary of the treasury reassured them. Gallatin was a skilled financier who supported Hamilton's system.

The Louisiana Purchase

One of Jefferson's strongest beliefs was that a republic could survive only if most of the people owned land. This belief led him to support the idea of expanding the country farther west.

In 1800 French leader Napoleon Bonaparte convinced Spain to give Louisiana back to France in exchange for helping Spain take control of part of Italy. Napoleon's deal worried Jefferson because it gave France control of the lower Mississippi. Jefferson believed that having France back in North America would force the United States

0   200 kilometers
0   200 miles
Lambert Azimuthal Equal-Area projection

BRITISH TERRITORY

Ft. Clatsop, winter quarters 1805–1806

OREGON TERRITORY

Ft. Mandan, winter quarters 1804–1805

Columbia R.

Lewis
Clark

Snake R.

50°N

40°N   120°W

LOUISIANA PURCHASE

Missouri R.

Pikes Peak

Colorado R.

Santa Fe

Arkansas R.

Indiana Territory   Ohio   Pa.

Ohio R.

St. Louis   Va.

Kentucky

Tenn.   N.C.

Red R.

SPANISH TERRITORY

Brazos R.

30°N

Rio Grande

Chihuahua

100°W

Mississippi
Territory   Ga.

Natchitoches

S.C.

ATLANTIC OCEAN

New Orleans   Spanish Florida

Gulf of Mexico

90°W   80°W

N
W   E
S

← Lewis and Clark's expedition
← Zebulon Pike's expedition
United States, 1803

▲ Meriwether Lewis and William Clark, with their Native American guide, Sacagawea.

Analyzing GEOGRAPHY

1. **Location** Where did Lewis and Clark begin their expedition?

2. **Movement** What two rivers in Spanish territory did Pike cross during his explorations?

into an alliance with the British, whom Jefferson despised. Jefferson ordered Robert Livingston, his ambassador to France, to try to block the deal or gain concessions for the United States. Livingston arrived in Paris in the spring of 1801, but he accomplished little until 1803.

By 1803, Napoleon had begun making plans to conquer Europe. If France resumed its war against Britain, the last thing the French wanted was an alliance between the United States and Great Britain. Furthermore, France's government was short on funds. In 1803, therefore, Napoleon offered to sell all of the Louisiana Territory, as well as New Orleans, to the United States. Livingston immediately accepted.

On April 30, 1803, the United States bought Louisiana from France for $11.25 million. It also agreed to take on French debts owed to

American citizens. These debts were worth about $3.75 million, making the total cost about $15 million. The Senate overwhelmingly approved the **Louisiana Purchase.** The deal more than doubled the size of the United States and gave the nation control of the entire Mississippi River.

Lewis and Clark Even before Louisiana became a part of the United States, Jefferson asked Congress to fund a secret expedition into the Louisiana Territory to trace the Missouri River and find a route to the Pacific Ocean. After Congress approved the expedition, Jefferson chose **Meriwether Lewis,** his private secretary, and **William Clark,** the brother of Revolutionary War hero George Rogers Clark, to lead the expedition.

In May 1804 the "Corps of Discovery," as the expedition was called, headed west up the Missouri River. Along the way they met **Sacagawea,** a Shoshone woman who joined the expedition as a guide and interpreter. The expedition found a path through the Rocky Mountains and eventually traced the Columbia River to the Pacific Ocean. The expedition also gave the United States a claim to the Oregon territory along the coast.

The Pike Expedition Lewis and Clark's expedition was not the only one exploring the Louisiana Purchase. In 1805 Zebulon Pike mapped much of the upper Mississippi, and in 1806 he headed west to find the headwaters of the Arkansas River. Pike traveled to Colorado, where he charted the mountain now known as Pikes Peak. He also mapped part of the Rio Grande and traveled across northern Mexico and what is now southern Texas. Pike provided Americans with detailed description of the Great Plains and the Rocky Mountains.

The Essex Junto The Louisiana Purchase alarmed New England Federalists. It meant that, eventually, their region would lose its influence in national affairs while the South and West gained political strength through new states. In Massachusetts, a small group of Federalists known as the Essex Junto drafted a plan to take New England out of the Union.

Hoping to expand their movement, they persuaded Vice President Aaron Burr to run for governor of New York in 1804. During the campaign, Alexander Hamilton called Burr "a dangerous man, and one who ought not be trusted with the reins of government." Offended, Burr challenged Hamilton to a duel. When the two met on July 11, 1804, though, Hamilton refused to fire. Burr shot and killed his foe. In 1807, Burr was accused of plotting to create his own country in the western U.S. He was charged with treason but acquitted.

An Independent Judiciary

At the end of their term, the Federalist majority in Congress enacted the Judiciary Act of 1801. This act created 16 new federal judges. President Adams then appointed Federalists to these positions. These judges were nicknamed "midnight judges" because Adams supposedly stayed up signing appointments until midnight on his last day in office.

Republicans in Congress were not pleased that the Federalists controlled the courts. One of the first acts of Congress after Jefferson took office was to repeal the Judiciary Act of 1801, thereby doing away with the "midnight judges" by abolishing their offices.

Impeaching Judges The Republicans then tried to remove other Federalists from the judiciary by impeachment. Republican leaders believed that the impeachment power was one of the checks and balances in the Constitution. Congress could impeach and remove judges for arbitrary or unfair decisions, not just for criminal behavior.

In 1804, the House impeached Supreme Court Justice Samuel Chase. During one trial, Chase had ordered Democratic-Republicans removed from the jury. He had also denounced Jefferson to another jury. The Senate, however, did not convict Chase. Many senators did not think he was guilty of "treason, bribery, or other high crimes and misdemeanors" that the Constitution required for his removal. The impeachment of Justice Chase established that judges could be removed only for criminal behavior, not simply because Congress disagreed with their decisions.

John Marshall and *Marbury* **v.** *Madison* The most important judicial appointment President Adams made before leaving office was the choice of **John Marshall** as Chief Justice of the United States. Marshall served as Chief Justice for 34 years. He was more responsible than any other justice for making the Supreme Court into a powerful, independent branch of the federal government.

Marshall increased the power of the Supreme Court in 1803 with the decision in *Marbury* v. *Madison.* In this case, the Supreme Court ruled part of the Judiciary Act of 1789 to be unconstitutional. The decision marked the first time the Supreme Court asserted the power of **judicial review**—the power to decide whether laws passed by Congress were constitutional and to strike down those that were not. Although the Supreme Court would not strike down another federal law until the case of *Dred Scott* v. *Sanford* 54 years later, the power to do so had been established.

✔ **Reading Check** **Explaining** Why did Congress repeal the Judiciary Act of 1801?

ANALYZING SUPREME COURT CASES

Should the Supreme Court Have the Power of Judicial Review?

★ *Marbury* v. *Madison*, 1803

Background to the Case

William Marbury had been appointed a justice of the peace shortly before President Adams left office. Adams had signed Marbury's appointment, but the documents had not been delivered when Adams left office. The new secretary of state, James Madison, was supposed to deliver the documents, but President Jefferson told him to hold them, hoping Marbury would quit and allow Jefferson to appoint someone else. Marbury then asked the Supreme Court to issue a court order telling Madison to deliver the documents.

How the Court Ruled

Marbury based his request for a court order on the Judiciary Act of 1789, which said that requests for federal court orders go directly to the Supreme Court. In *Marbury* v. *Madison,* the Supreme Court decided that part of the Judiciary Act was unconstitutional and thus invalid. The Constitution specifies which cases can go directly to the Supreme Court, and court orders are not mentioned. The decision established the Court's power to declare laws unconstitutional and invalid.

▲ *Chief Justice John Marshall (1755–1835) established many precedents that helped to make the judiciary branch powerful enough to check and balance the other two branches of the federal government.*

PRIMARY SOURCE

The Court's Opinion

"It is emphatically the province and duty of the judicial department to say what the law is. Those who apply the rule to particular cases must of necessity expound and interpret that rule. If two laws conflict with each other, the courts must decide on the operation of each.

So, if a law be in opposition to the Constitution; if both the law and the Constitution apply to a particular case, so that the court must either decide that case conformably to the law, disregarding the Constitution, or conformably to the Constitution, disregarding the law, the court must determine which of these conflicting rules governs the case. This is of the very essence of judicial duty."

—Chief Justice John Marshall in *Marbury* v. *Madison*

PRIMARY SOURCE

Federalist No. 78 and the Court's Decision

Some scholars argue that the Court was wrong to claim the power of judicial review, but no one who helped write the Constitution objected. In Federalist No. 78, Alexander Hamilton implies that judicial review is to be expected:

"The interpretation of the laws is the proper and peculiar province of the courts. A constitution is in fact, and must be, regarded by the judges as a fundamental law. It therefore belongs to them to ascertain its meaning as well as the meaning of any particular act proceeding from the legislative body. If there should happen to be an irreconcilable variance between the two, that which has the superior obligation and validity ought of course to be preferred; or in other words, the constitution ought to be preferred to the statute. . ."

—from *Federalist No. 78*

DBQ Document-Based Questions

1. **Identifying** What does Chief Justice John Marshall say is the main duty of the judiciary?
2. **Describing** How does Alexander Hamilton uphold the principle of judicial review?
3. **Contrasting** On what point do Marshall and Hamilton disagree?

Rising International Tensions

MAIN Idea To avoid getting drawn into the war between France and England, Jefferson banned trade with other countries.

HISTORY AND YOU Jefferson used a trade embargo as a tool of diplomacy. Are there countries today with which the U.S. does not trade?

In addition to acquiring Louisiana from the French, Jefferson had to contend with pirate raids against American ships traveling in the Mediterranean. Then, during his second term, he also had to focus his efforts on keeping the United States out of the war between Britain and France.

The Barbary Pirates

For years, the Barbary States on the North African coast—Morocco, Algiers, Tunis, and Tripoli—had menaced Mediterranean ship-ping. European nations had routinely paid "tribute" to these countries so that their ships would be undisturbed, believing that it was less expensive than fighting. In 1795 the United States paid nearly $1 million to the ruler of Algiers for the release of a ship and its crew.

Jefferson refused to continue such payments. In 1801 Tripoli declared war on the United States and, in turn, Jefferson sent a naval squadron into the Mediterranean. For four years the United States fought its first foreign military conflict. In 1805 an American threat to force a coup in Tripoli ended hostilities. It took a second conflict with the Barbary States in 1815, however, to finally end American tribute payments.

Economic Warfare

In mid-1803, Napoleon's armies surged out of France and headed east. France and Britain were at war again. At first, the war actually benefited American merchants. As the British seized French ships, American merchants began trad-

King George threatens to break Jefferson's arms and legs if he misbehaves. His club is labeled "Heart of Oak," a reference to the British navy.

Unable to escape, Jefferson complains that Britain and France are free to assault him on "the Highway of all Nations,"—the seas.

Napoleon praises Jefferson for making noise, but demands the money for Louisiana.

▲ *This 1809 cartoon expresses anger at Jefferson's embargo policy, which hurt American trade but did not stop the British and French from seizing American ships.*

Analyzing VISUALS

1. **Identifying** In the cartoon, what are King George and Napoleon doing?
2. **Explaining** What is the figurative meaning of this cartoon?

ing with French colonies. The British left the American ships alone because the United States had proclaimed neutrality.

In 1806 Britain issued regulations known as the Orders in Council. These declared that all ships going to Europe needed British **licenses** and would be searched for contraband. In response, Napoleon declared that merchants who obeyed the British system would have their goods confiscated when they reached Europe. American merchants were caught in the middle. No matter whom they obeyed, they were going to lose their goods.

Impressment The British navy was short of recruits because of low pay and terrible shipboard conditions. British sailors often deserted to American vessels. Britain tried to solve this problem by impressment, a legalized form of kidnapping that forced people into military service. Britain claimed the right to stop American ships and search for deserters. On many occasions they impressed American citizens into service as well.

In June 1807 these tensions reached the boiling point when the British warship *Leopard* stopped the American warship *Chesapeake* to search for British deserters. When the captain of the *Chesapeake* refused to comply, the *Leopard* opened fire, killing three Americans. After the Americans surrendered, the British went aboard and seized four sailors.

The Embargo of 1807 The attack on the *Chesapeake* enraged the public, and American newspapers clamored for war. Like Washington and Adams before him, however, President Jefferson did not want to entangle the United States in the affairs of Europe. Instead of going to war, he asked Congress to pass the Embargo Act of 1807, halting all trade between the United States and Europe.

The **embargo,** a government ban on trade with other countries, wound up hurting the United States more than France or Britain. In the Northeast, the shipping business came to a standstill. Farmers in the South and West saw the demand for their crops plummet. In Congress, Maryland's Philip Barton Key railed against the embargo:

PRIMARY SOURCE

"In a commercial point of view, it has annihilated our trade. In an agricultural point of view. it has paralised [sic] industry. . . . Our most fertile lands are reduced to sterility, so far as it respects our surplus product. . . . [I]t will drive (if continued) our seamen into foreign employ, and our fishermen to foreign sand banks. In a financial point of view, it has dried up our revenue."

—from *The National Intelligencer and Washington Advertiser,* May 27, 1808

Realizing the embargo was not working, Congress repealed it in March 1809, shortly before Jefferson left office. After his second term, President Jefferson gladly retired to his estate, Monticello, in Virginia. While the embargo made Jefferson unpopular, his administration had reversed the Federalist course by limiting the power of the federal government. It had also acquired a vast new territory in the West.

✓ Reading Check **Examining** Why did Jefferson have Congress pass the Embargo Act?

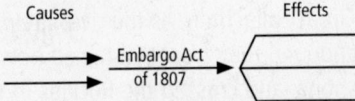

Section 3 REVIEW

Vocabulary

1. **Explain** the significance of: Louisiana Purchase, Meriwether Lewis, William Clark, Sacagawea, John Marshall, judicial review, embargo.

Main Ideas

2. **Explaining** Why did Napoleon sell Louisiana to the United States?

3. **Determining Cause and Effect** What led to the war with the Barbary States?

Critical Thinking

4. **Big Ideas** How did the Supreme Court decision in *Marbury* v. *Madison* strengthen the federal judiciary?

5. **Organizing** Use a graphic organizer similar to the one below to list the causes and effects of the Embargo Act of 1807.

Causes   Effects

Embargo Act of 1807

6. **Analyzing Visuals** Study the map of the Louisiana Purchase on page 169. In what territories did Lewis and Clark make their winter camps during their expedition?

Writing About History

7. **Descriptive Writing** Suppose that you are a member of the Lewis and Clark or Zebulon Pike expedition. Write a journal entry describing what you have done or seen on your trip.

History ONLINE

Study Central™ To review this section, go to glencoe.com and click on Study Central.

GEOGRAPHY & HISTORY

The Lewis and Clark Expedition

When Thomas Jefferson asked Congress to fund an expedition to explore the Louisiana Territory, his goal was to find a water route—the fabled "Northwest Passage"—to the Pacific Ocean. The Corps of Discovery set out in May 1804. It was led by Captain Meriwether Lewis and Captain William Clark and included some 40 people—36 soldiers, 2 civilian employees, and 2 dependents.

After sailing up the Missouri River into the Great Plains, the expedition spent the winter with the Mandan people. In the spring of 1805, they headed into the Rocky Mountains. The group spent a month carrying their boats and supplies 18 miles around Great Falls. Then, as the river grew shallow, they abandoned their boats, obtained horses from the Shoshone, and crossed the Rockies in the fall of 1805. Once across the mountains, they built dugout canoes and headed down the Columbia River to the Pacific Coast where they waited for the winter to pass. They then headed back across the Rockies, down the Missouri and home.

What Was Learned About the West's Geography?

The Lewis and Clark expedition recorded 178 new species of plant life and 122 previously unknown species of animal life. Numerous specimens and sketches were brought back, and to this day, the expedition's journals remain a vital source of information about the region in the early 1800s. The expedition found a route from the Missouri through the Rockies to the Pacific, and demonstrated that no Northwest Passage existed because the Rocky Mountains divided the continent.

Analyzing GEOGRAPHY

1. **Movement** How did the geography of the route followed by the Corps of Discovery make movement difficult for the explorers?

2. **Human-Environment Interaction** How did the explorers adapt to the physical barriers they faced?

The Mandan of the upper Missouri were farmers as well as hunters. While men hunted deer, buffalo, and small game, the women grew corn, squash, and beans. Each family had its own plot of land.

7. Reaching the Pacific
Finding no ocean-going ships to take them home, the Corps spends the winter at Fort Clatsop before the long trip back.

6. Canoe Camp, Sept.–Oct. 1805
A Nez Percé chief shows Clark how to use fire to hollow out canoes. The Columbia River and its tributaries now carry the Corps to the Pacific.

4. Great Falls, June 1805
The Corps' boats are stopped by a series of great waterfalls. Two wagons made on the spot are loaded with canoes and baggage and pulled over 18 miles.

2. Council Bluffs, August 1804
Now entering the Great Plains, the Corps continues to pole, pull, row, and sail their boats upriver.

OREGON COUNTRY

Columbia R.

Snake R.

Missouri R.

LOUISIANA PURCHASE

Mississippi R.

5. Over the Rockies
With horses carrying their baggage, the Corps struggles through snowstorms over steep trails. On Sept. 17, they reach their highest point, 7,032 feet above sea level.

3. Fort Mandan, Winter 1804–1805
The Corps spends a very cold winter with the Mandan people, surviving on their beans, corn, and squash. Sacagawea joins them as a Shoshone translator. Six canoes replace the large keelboat.

1. Camp Dubois, May 14, 1804
A 55-foot keelboat and two smaller pirogues carry some 40 members of the expedition, a Newfoundland dog, and supplies.

The officers, sergeants, and corporals wore red, white and blue uniforms. Privates wore white.

Different groups of Plains Indians used sign language to talk to each other. Members of the expedition knew this sign language, but it was a slow way to communicate. At the Mandan village, Lewis hired Toussaint Charbonneau, and his wife Sacagawea, a Shoshone woman who knew the language of people further upriver.

The expedition spent the winter of 1805 with the Mandan people. The Mandan lived in earthen lodges near the Missouri River, in what is today North Dakota. They were friendly to visitors as their villages were important regional trading centers.

York, an enslaved man who served Captain Clark, was the only African American on the expedition. York is shown tending Lewis's dog Seaman—a Newfoundland who served as a watchdog and helped the expedition hunt.

The expedition used three boats to travel up the Missouri River—a large keelboat and two pirogues, one red and one white. The expedition abandoned the keelboat at the Mandan village and used six canoes to travel further upriver.

The War of 1812

Guide to Reading

Big Ideas
Individual Action Military leaders, including William Henry Harrison, Tecumseh, Oliver Perry, and Andrew Jackson, contributed to the outcome of the War of 1812.

Content Vocabulary
• nationalism *(p. 181)*

Academic Vocabulary
• overseas *(p. 177)*
• enable *(p. 178)*

People and Events to Identify
• Non-Intercourse Act *(p. 176)*
• War Hawks *(p. 177)*
• Tecumseh *(p. 178)*
• William Henry Harrison *(p. 178)*
• Oliver Perry *(p. 179)*
• Hartford Convention *(p. 181)*
• Treaty of Ghent *(p. 181)*

Reading Strategy
Organizing Complete a graphic organizer similar to the one below by listing the causes of the War of 1812.

Causes

War of 1812

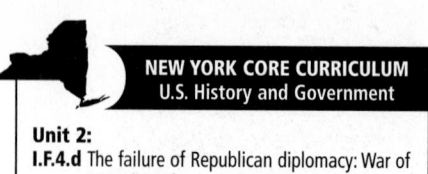

NEW YORK CORE CURRICULUM
U.S. History and Government

Unit 2:
I.F.4.d The failure of Republican diplomacy: War of 1812 (significance of the War for Native American Indians, Spain, the growth of industry)

The War of 1812 was the second major clash between the United States and Britain in North America. Although neither side won a clear victory, the war gave Americans a strong sense of national pride.

The Decision for War

MAIN Idea Trade restrictions and the belief that the British encouraged Native American attacks on Americans led to war.

HISTORY AND YOU Do you remember reading about Pontiac's rebellion? Read how conflicts in western territories influenced the decision to go to war.

After Thomas Jefferson announced that he would not run again for president in 1808, the Republican Party nominated James Madison. The Federalists nominated Charles Pinckney. Despite some lingering anger about the Embargo Act of 1807, Madison won the election easily. He assumed office in the midst of an international crisis. Tensions between the United States and Britain were rising, and it would fall to Madison to decide whether or not to lead the United States into its first full-scale war since the Revolution.

Economic Pressures

Like Jefferson, Madison wanted to avoid war. To force the British to stop seizing American ships, he asked Congress to pass the **Non-Intercourse Act.** This act forbade trade with France and Britain while authorizing the president to reopen trade with whichever country removed its trade restrictions first. The idea was to play France and Britain against each other, but the plan failed.

In May 1810, Congress took a different approach with a plan drafted by Nathaniel Macon of North Carolina. The plan, called Macon's Bill Number Two, reopened trade with both Britain and France, but stated that if either nation dropped its restrictions on trade, the United States would stop importing goods from the other nation. Soon afterward, Napoleon announced that France would no longer restrict American trade, although his statement still allowed for the seizure of American ships. Madison accepted Napoleon's statement, despite its conditions, hoping to pressure the British into dropping their trade restrictions, as well. When the British refused, Congress passed a non-importation act against Britain in early 1811.

Madison's strategy eventually worked. By early 1812, the refusal of the United States to buy British goods had begun to hurt the British economy. British merchants began to pressure their government to repeal its restrictions on trade. Finally, in June 1812, Britain ended all

The Causes of the War of 1812

The War of 1812 had four main causes: the British policy of intercepting U.S. ships trading with France; British impressments of American sailors; problems with Native Americans on the frontier; and a group of Congressmen from the South and West who strongly pushed for war.

NATIVE AMERICAN ATTACKS

▲ Americans blamed the British for tensions with Native Americans that led to confrontations such as the Battle of Tippecanoe in 1811 (above).

▶ British impressment of American sailors angered many Americans.

THE WAR HAWKS

"Has not Congress solemnly pledged itself to the world not to surrender our rights? And has not the nation . . . resolved to maintain at all hazards our maritime independence?

. . . No man in the nation wants peace more than I: but I prefer the troubled ocean of war, demanded by the honor and independence of the country, with all its calamities and desolation, to the tranquil and putrescent pool of igno-minious peace. . . . Britain stands pre-eminent in her outrage on us, by her violation of the sacred personal rights of American freemen, in the arbitrary and lawless imprisonment of our seamen, the attack on the *Chesapeake*—the murder, sir."

—Henry Clay, speech before the Senate, February 22, 1810

▲ Henry Clay

▲ John C. Calhoun

IMPRESSMENT

DBQ Document-Based Questions

1. **Paraphrasing** What does Clay say that war with Great Britain is "demanded by"?

2. **Summarizing** According to Clay, why does "Britain stand pre-eminent in her outrage on" the United States?

restrictions on American trade, but it was too late. Two days later, the British learned that the United States had declared war.

The War Hawks

Although it seemed that Britain's actions had hurt Eastern merchants, most members of Congress who wanted war came from the South and West. Nicknamed the **War Hawks** by their opponents, they were led by Henry Clay of Kentucky, John C. Calhoun of South Carolina, and Felix Grundy of Tennessee. The War Hawks believed economic pressure had failed and the nation's reputation was in danger if it did not go to war to stop the British from seizing American sailors.

Americans in the South and West wanted war for two more reasons. British trade restrictions had hurt Southern planters and Western farmers, who earned much of their income by shipping tobacco, rice, wheat, and cotton **overseas.** Eastern merchants could still make a profit despite British restrictions because they passed the cost of losing their ships and goods onto the farmers.

Westerners also blamed the British for clashes with Native Americans along the frontier. In the early 1800s, settlers had begun moving past the line established by the Treaty of Greenville. As clashes with Native Americans increased, many settlers accused the British in Canada of arming the Native Americans and encouraging them to attack American settlements.

Tecumseh and Tippecanoe

Although western settlers blamed the British for their problems with the Native Americans, it was the increasing demands of speculators and settlers that sparked Native American resistance. **Tecumseh,** a Shawnee leader, believed that Native Americans needed to unite to protect their lands.

While Tecumseh worked for political union, his brother Tenskwatawa (known as "the Prophet") called for a spiritual rebirth of Native American cultures. His followers lived in Prophetstown on the Tippecanoe River in Indiana, where they tried to practice traditional Native American ways of living.

Aware that Tecumseh's movement was gaining strength, **William Henry Harrison,** governor of the Indiana Territory, prepared to stamp it out. In November 1811, after learning that Tecumseh had gone south to recruit more followers, Harrison gathered troops and marched toward Prophetstown. Tenskwatawa sent fighters to intercept Harrison near the Tippecanoe River. The Battle of Tippecanoe left nearly 200 of Harrison's troops dead or wounded, but it shattered Native American confidence in the Prophet. Many, including Tecumseh, fled to Canada.

Tecumseh's flight to Canada seemed to prove that the British were supporting the Native Americans, as did the British-made rifles his forces left behind on the battlefield. Many western farmers argued that war with Britain would **enable** the United States to seize Canada and end Native American attacks. In June 1812, President Madison gave in to the pressure and asked Congress to declare war. The vote in Congress split along regional lines. The South and West generally voted for war; the Northeast did not.

✔ **Reading Check** **Examining** Why did Americans in the South and West favor war with Great Britain?

The Invasion of Canada

MAIN Idea Americans attacked British Canada at several points along the border and fought for control of the Great Lakes.

HISTORY AND YOU Can you think of any war that has deeply divided Americans? Read how Americans disagreed about the War of 1812.

Although the Republican-led Congress had called for war, the nation was not ready to fight. The army had fewer than 7,000 troops and little equipment. The navy had only 16 ships. Also, Americans were deeply divided over the war. Many people in New York and New England called it "Mr. Madison's War," implying that it was a private fight that did not deserve the nation's support.

Paying for the war also posed a problem. The year before the war, Republicans had shut down the Bank of the United States by refusing to renew its charter. This made it difficult for the government to borrow money because most private bankers were located in the Northeast. They opposed the war and would not lend money to the government. Despite the nation's military and financial weaknesses, President Madison ordered the military to invade Canada.

Three Strikes Against Canada

American military leaders planned to attack Canada from three directions—from Detroit, from Niagara Falls, and up the Hudson River valley toward Montreal. All three attacks failed. The British navy on Lake Erie rapidly shuttled troops to Detroit and forced the American commander, General William Hull, to surrender.

The British then shifted their troops to the Niagara peninsula, where they took up positions on Queenston Heights along the Niagara River. From there, they easily drove off some 600 American troops who had landed on the Canadian side of the Niagara River. The American force would have been larger, except that the New York militia, many of whom opposed the war, refused to cross the river. They argued that the terms of their military service did not require them to leave the country.

80°W

BRITISH NORTH AMERICA
(CANADA)

L. Superior

Indiana
Territory

- American offensive
- British offensive
- ★ American victory
- ★ British victory

L. Huron

Montreal
Châteaugay
Oct. 25, 1813
Prevost
Aug.–Sept.
1814

Chrysler's Farm
Nov. 11, 1813   Plattsburgh
Lake Champlain
Sept. 11, 1814

York (Toronto)
burned
Apr. 27, 1813
Wilkinson,
1813
Dearborn, 1813

L. Ontario

Vt.

N.H.

L.
Michigan

Michigan Terr.

Thames River
Oct. 5, 1813
Brock
July 1812
Ft. Niagara
Queenstown Heights
Oct. 13, 1812

New York

Mass.

Detroit
surrendered
Aug. 16, 1812
L. Erie
Presque Isle (Erie)

Conn.

Ft. Dearborn

Perry
Sept. 1813

Illinois
Terr.
Tippecanoe
Nov. 7, 1811
Put-in-Bay
Sept. 10, 1813
Harrison
Oct. 1813

blockade

Indiana
Territory
Hull
Aug. 1812
Ohio

Pennsylvania

New
Jersey

naval

40°N

Ohio R.

Fort McHenry
Sept. 13–14, 1814   Baltimore
Washington, D.C.
burned Aug. 24,
1814
Del.

ATLANTIC
OCEAN

British

Virginia

Maryland

Ross
Aug. 1814

Analyzing GEOGRAPHY

1. **Regions** Where did most of the battles of the war occur?
2. **Place** On what date did the British burn Washington, D.C.?

0   100 kilometers
0   100 miles
Lambert Azimuthal Equal-Area projection

Maps In Motion See *StudentWorks™ Plus* or glencoe.com.

The third American attack fared no better than the first two. General Henry Dearborn, marching up the Hudson River toward Montreal, called off the attack after the militia refused to cross the border.

Perry's Victory on Lake Erie

The following year, the United States had more success after Commodore **Oliver Perry** secretly arranged for the construction of a fleet on the coast of Lake Erie in Ohio. On September 10, 1813, Perry's fleet attacked the British fleet on Lake Erie near Put-in-Bay. When his own ship was no longer able to fight, Perry rowed to another vessel. After a grueling four-hour battle, the British surrendered.

Perry's victory gave the Americans control of Lake Erie. It also enabled General Harrison to recover Detroit and march into Canada, where he defeated a combined force of British troops and Native Americans at the Battle of the Thames River.

Harrison's troops from the west were supposed to meet up with American troops from Niagara Falls in the east. British troops and Canadian militia, however, stopped the American attack from the east at the Battle of Stony Creek. When Harrison learned of the defeat, he retreated to Detroit. By the end of 1813, the United States still had not conquered any territory in Canada.

✔ Reading Check **Explaining** Why was conquering Canada an important American goal in the War of 1812?

The War Ends

MAIN Idea After more than two years of fighting, the war ended with a treaty that left boundaries the same and did not address the causes of the war.

HISTORY AND YOU When was the last time you heard the national anthem, "The Star-Spangled Banner"? Read about the attack on Fort McHenry that inspired the lyrics by Francis Scott Key.

In 1814 Napoleon's empire collapsed. With the war against France over, the British were able to send much of their navy and many more troops to deal with the United States. The British strategy for the war had three parts. First, the British navy would raid American cities along the coast. Second, they would march south into New York from Montreal, cutting New England off from the rest of the country. Third, they would seize New Orleans and close the Mississippi River to western farmers. The British believed this strategy would force the United States to make peace.

British Forces Attack Washington and Baltimore

With attention focused on Canada, in August 1814, a British fleet sailed into Chesapeake Bay and landed troops within marching distance of Washington, D.C. The British easily dispersed the poorly trained militia defending the capital and entered the city unopposed. Madison and other government officials hastily fled. The British set fire to the White House and the Capitol. They then prepared to attack Baltimore.

Unlike Washington, D.C., Baltimore was ready for the British. The city militia inflicted heavy casualties on the British troops that went ashore. After bombarding Fort McHenry throughout the night of September 13, the

PRIMARY SOURCE
The War of 1812 Ends

▼ Although it took place after the peace treaty had been signed in Ghent, the Battle of New Orleans made future president Andrew Jackson a national hero, easing his entrance into politics.

The Battle of New Orleans, 1815

Red R.
Mississippi R.
Mississippi Territory
Mobile Bay
Lake Pontchartrain
Jackson, 1814
SPANISH FLORIDA
Louisiana
New Orleans
Jan. 8, 1815
30°N
British naval blockade
Pakenham, 1814
Gulf of Mexico

0 — 100 kilometers
0 — 100 miles
Lambert Azimuthal Equal-Area projection
90°W

United States
American offensive
British offensive
American victory

The Effects of the War of 1812

• Increased the prestige of the United States
• Generated a new spirit of patriotism among Americans
• Fostered national unity
• Greatly weakened the Federalist Party

Analyzing VISUALS

1. **Explaining** How did the War of 1812 affect national politics?
2. **Determining Cause and Effect** In 1818 Britain and the United States reached an agreement on the border between Canada and the United States. How might the outcome of the war have helped them reach agreement?

British abandoned their attack on the city. Francis Scott Key, a young lawyer held aboard a British ship during the shelling, was elated to see the American flag still flying above the fort at dawn. On the back of a letter, he scribbled a poem about the battle that would later become the national anthem of the United States. The final lines of the poem evoke the powerful symbolism of the flag: "O say does that Star-Spangled Banner yet wave / O'er the land of the free and the home of the brave?"

The same month the British attacked Washington and Baltimore, they sent a force of 15,000 well-trained British soldiers south from Montreal into New York. The key to the British advance was control of Lake Champlain. On September 11, 1814, the American fleet on the lake defeated the British fleet; realizing that the Americans could use their control of the lake to surround them, the British abandoned the attack and retreated to Montreal.

Events in New England and New Orleans

The British offensive increased New England's opposition to the war. In December 1814, Federalists from the region met in Hartford, Connecticut, to discuss what they could do independently of the United States. Although members of the Essex Junto urged New England to secede, moderate delegates refused to support such extreme action. Instead, the **Hartford Convention** called for several constitutional amendments to increase the region's political power.

Less than a month after the Hartford Convention began, an American victory in the South put a stop to Federalist complaints. In January 1815, a British fleet with some 7,500 men landed near New Orleans. The American commander, General Andrew Jackson, quickly improvised a defense using cotton bales. The thick bales absorbed the British bullets, while the British advancing in the open provided easy targets for the American troops. The fighting ended in a decisive American victory.

The Battle of New Orleans made Andrew Jackson a national hero. It also helped to destroy the Federalist Party. As **nationalism,** or feelings of strong patriotism, surged, the Federalists at the Hartford Convention appeared divisive and unpatriotic. They never recovered nationally, and within a few years the party ceased to exist.

Peace negotiations began in the Belgian city of Ghent even before the major battles of 1814. On December 24, 1814, the negotiators signed the **Treaty of Ghent,** ending the War of 1812. The treaty restored prewar boundaries but did not mention neutral rights or impressment, and no territory changed hands. Still, the War of 1812 increased the nation's prestige overseas and generated a new spirit of patriotism and national unity.

Four years later in the Convention of 1818, the United States and Great Britain set the U.S.-Canadian border from what is now Minnesota to the Rocky Mountains at 49° north latitude. The countries also agreed to claim jointly for the next ten years a region farther west known as the Oregon Country.

✔ **Reading Check** **Examining** What were the effects of the Battle of New Orleans?

Section 4 REVIEW

Vocabulary

1. **Explain** the significance of: Non-Intercourse Act, War Hawks, Tecumseh, William Henry Harrison, Oliver Perry, Hartford Convention, Treaty of Ghent.

Main Ideas

2. **Explaining** What was the significance of the Battle of Tippecanoe?

3. **Determining Cause and Effect** What was the outcome of Oliver Perry's attack on the British on Lake Erie?

4. **Identifying** What happened in 1814 that enabled the British to focus on the war with the United States?

Critical Thinking

5. **Big Ideas** How did the Battle of Tippecanoe affect the Native Americans of the Northwest Territory?

6. **Organizing** Use a graphic organizer similar to the one below to list how Americans in different regions felt about war with Great Britain.

Section of U.S.	Position on War	Reason for War Position
West		
South		
North		

7. **Analyzing Visuals** Study the map about the War of 1812 on page 179. Which battle of the war was fought furthest north, and which side had the victory?

Writing About History

8. **Descriptive Writing** Suppose you are an American citizen at the beginning of the War of 1812. Write a letter to a friend describing how the idea of the war makes you feel.

History ONLINE
Study Central™ To review this section, go to glencoe.com and click on Study Central.

Organizing the Government and Expanding the Nation

- Washington creates the first cabinet: a secretary of war, a secretary of the treasury, a secretary of state, and an attorney general.
- Congress passes the Judiciary Act, establishing federal courts, including the Supreme Court.
- The Bill of Rights is added to the Constitution.
- To finance the new government, Alexander Hamilton proposes a national tariff, excise taxes, a Bank of the United States, and redeeming Revolutionary War bonds at full value.
- In *Marbury* v. *Madison,* the Supreme Court asserts the power of judicial review.
- The Louisiana Purchase nearly doubles the size of the United States. Lewis and Clark, and Zebulon Pike explore the territory.
- Jay's Treaty improves trade relations with the British Empire.
- Pickney's Treaty secures use of the lower Mississippi River from Spain.
- The debate over Hamilton's plans leads to the emergence of the first two political parties—the Federalists, supported by artisans and merchants in the Northeast, and the Democratic-Republicans, supported by farmers in the South and the West.
- Jay's Treaty with Britain angers Republicans.
- France's attacks on American ships leads to the Quasi-War, and Federalists try to limit political criticism with the Alien and Sedition Acts.

▲ *Washington's first cabinet, from left to right: Secretary of War Henry Knox, Secretary of State Thomas Jefferson, Attorney General Edmund Randolph, and Secretary of the Treasury Alexander Hamilton.*

▲ *In one of the most spectacular American victories of the War of 1812, the USS* Constitution *defeated the British HMS* Guerriere.

Causes of the War of 1812

- The French Revolution leads to a war between Britain and France; the British and French start seizing merchant ships—including American ships—headed to each other's ports. The war increases party divisions; the Federalists support Britain and the Republicans support France.
- When the Republicans gain control of Congress and the presidency, tensions with Britain grow worse.
- British impressment of American sailors angers Americans.
- British support of Native Americans, including Tecumseh, angers settlers in the West.
- British trade restrictions and seizure of merchant cargo heading to France angers Southern planters and frontier farmers.
- An American embargo fails to convince the British to change their policies.
- A group of congressmen, known as War Hawks, call for war, both to avenge Britain's violations of American sovereignty and to protect the interests of the South and the West.

NEW YORK REGENTS EXAM PRACTICE

TEST-TAKING TIP

Often it is helpful to identify the key term in a question and then locate its synonym in an answer choice to identify the correct answer.

Part I

Directions (1–11): For each statement or question, write on a separate sheet of paper the number of the word or expression that, of those given, best completes the statement or answers the question.

1 One of the most important acts of the first U.S. Congress under the Constitution was to
(1) elect George Washington as the first president.
(2) establish a federal banking system.
(3) pass the Tariff of 1789.
(4) add a Bill of Rights to the Constitution.

2 The Democratic-Republican Party was started mainly to oppose the ideas of
(1) Thomas Jefferson.
(2) John Adams.
(3) Alexander Hamilton.
(4) George Washington.

3 In 1795 Pinckney's Treaty granted the United States the right to which of the following?
(1) take over British forts in the Northwest Territory
(2) navigate the Mississippi River
(3) impress British sailors
(4) remain neutral between Britain and France

4 The Convention of 1800 ended which conflict?
(1) Little Turtle's War
(2) the War of 1812
(3) the Franco-British War
(4) the Quasi-War

5 In 1804, Lewis and Clark set off to explore
(1) the Louisiana Territory.
(2) the Colorado Territory.
(3) Spanish Florida.
(4) the Mississippi River.

6 The Supreme Court decision in *Marbury* v. *Madison* established the principle of
(1) judicial review.
(2) democratic republicanism.
(3) nullification.
(4) constitutionality.

7 In the Battle of Tippecanoe, U.S. General William Henry Harrison defeated the forces of
(1) Little Turtle.
(2) Great Britain.
(3) Tecumseh and Tenskwatawa.
(4) Napoleon.

8 At the Hartford Convention in 1814, some delegates urged New England to
(1) boycott British goods.
(2) fight against the national bank.
(3) establish a whiskey tax.
(4) secede from the United States.

Need Extra Help?								
If You Missed Questions . . .	1	2	3	4	5	6	7	8
Go to Page . . .	154–155	158–159	164	164–165	169	171	178	181

[OVER]

Base your answer to questions 9 and 10 on the map below and on your knowledge of Chapter 4.

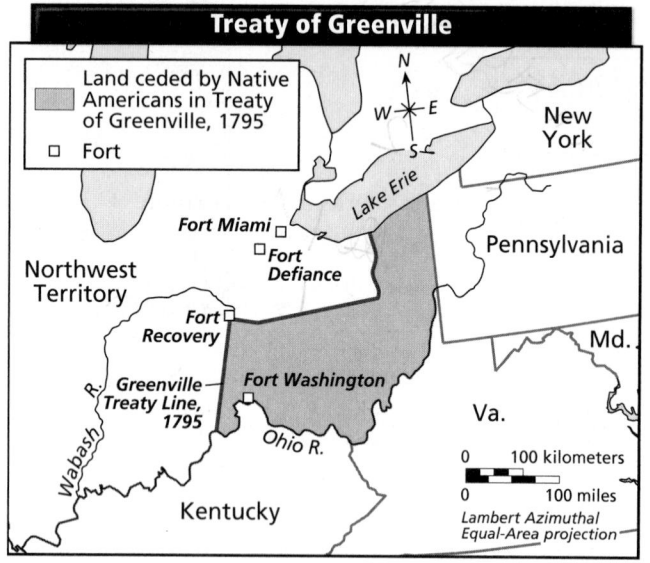

Treaty of Greenville

Land ceded by Native Americans in Treaty of Greenville, 1795

☐ Fort

New York

Lake Erie

Fort Miami

Fort Defiance

Pennsylvania

Northwest Territory

Fort Recovery

Md.

Greenville Treaty Line, 1795

Fort Washington

Va.

Ohio R.

Wabash

Kentucky

0   100 kilometers

0   100 miles

Lambert Azimuthal Equal-Area projection

9 In the Treaty of Greenville, Native Americans gave up most of which present-day state?

(1) Ohio

(2) Pennsylvania

(3) Kentucky

(4) Virginia

10 The new territory acquired by this treaty gave the United States access to which of the following?

(1) Lake Michigan

(2) the Atlantic Ocean

(3) Lake Erie

(4) the Mississippi River

11 After the War of 1812, the United States experienced an upsurge of which of the following?

(1) internationalism

(2) nationalism

(3) agrarianism

(4) republicanism

Need Extra Help?			
If You Missed Questions . . .	9	10	11
Go to Page . . .	184	184	181

Part II Thematic Essay Question

Directions: Write a well-organized essay that includes an introduction, several paragraphs addressing the task below, and a conclusion.

Theme: The Early Presidents

George Washington, John Adams, and Thomas Jefferson were the first three presidents of the United States. Each of these presidents under the new Constitution experienced both successes and failures.

Task:

Identify the successes and failures of the presidencies of Washington, Adams, and Jefferson and

• Describe the historical circumstances surrounding each high and low point.

• Discuss each president's response.

• Evaluate the short- and long-term effects of each presidents' actions during these points.

Guidelines:

In your essay, be sure to:

• Develop all aspects of the task

• Support the theme with relevant facts, examples, and details

• Use a logical and clear plan of organization, including an introduction and a conclusion that are beyond a restatement of the theme

Part III Document-Based Question

This question is based on the accompanying documents. This question is designed to test your ability to work with historical documents. Some of the documents have been edited for the purposes of the question. As you analyze the documents, take into account the source of each document and any point of view that may be presented in the document.

Historical Context:

The new nation of the United States of America faced a number of foreign policy issues that led to conflict with other nations.

Task:

Using information from the documents and your knowledge of United States history, answer the questions that follow each document in Part A. Your answers to the questions will help you write the Part B essay in which you will be asked to

- Discuss at least two foreign policy issues that led to conflict during the terms of the first three U.S. presidents
- Evaluate the conflicts including background, public opinion, outcome, and long-term effects

Part A
Short-Answer Questions

Directions: Analyze the documents and answer the short-answer questions that follow each document on a separate sheet of paper.

Document 1

> In attending to the *reasons* for the present states of warfare as exhibited to our view by public documents, we lament that they do not furnish to our minds satisfactory evidence of its prosperity. . . .
>
> We ask leave in conclusion to state that about three fourths of our townsmen depend on the sea for means of subsistence for themselves and families. By the recent declaration of war more than one half of that proportion is liable to fall into the hands of the enemy with a large proportion of their property, and many of their wives and children may thereby be reduced to extreme poverty. We would be permitted to further remark that out of this large proportion of [seamen] belonging to this town, we have but *four* detained by foreign nations. . . .

Source: *The Repertory and General Advertiser,* July 31, 1812

1 What reasons do the residents give for opposing the war?

2 According to the petition, were the residents of Brewster worried more about losing townsmen and property to impressment by foreign nations or to fighting the British? What reasoning do the residents use?

Document 2

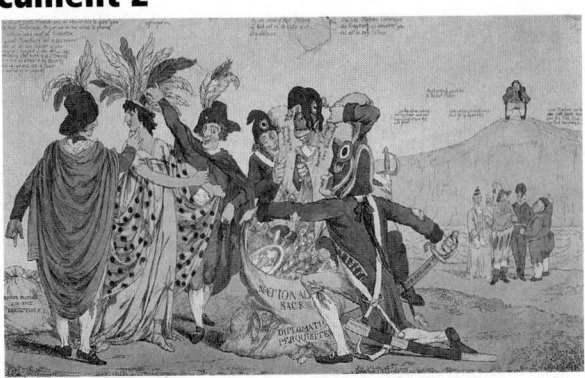

3 This cartoon, in which French leaders harass a woman symbolizing the United States, was created in response to what scandal?

Part B
Essay

Directions: Reread the task box at the top left and write a well-organized essay that includes an introduction, several paragraphs, and a conclusion. Use evidence from the documents in your essay. Support your response with relevant facts, examples, and details. Include additional outside information.

Guidelines:

In your essay, be sure to:

- Develop all aspects of the task
- Incorporate information from the documents
- Incorporate relevant outside information
- Support the theme with relevant facts, examples, and details
- Use a logical and clear plan of organization, including an introduction and a conclusion that are beyond a restatement of the theme

History ONLINE

For additional test practice, use Self-Check Quizzes—Chapter 4 at glencoe.com.

Need Extra Help?				
If You Missed Questions . . .	1	2	3	Essay
Go to Page . . .	176–181	176–181	164–165	154–181

Growth and Division

1816–1832

SECTION 1 American Nationalism

SECTION 2 Early Industry

SECTION 3 The Land of Cotton

SECTION 4 Growing Sectionalism

Boats use the locks on the Erie Canal in Lockport, New York, in the 1830s.

U.S. PRESIDENTS

Madison
1809–1817

Monroe
1817–1825

U.S. EVENTS

1816
• Congress establishes Second Bank of the United States

1819
• Spain cedes Florida to the United States

1820
• Henry Clay guides the Missouri Compromise through Congress

1823
• Monroe Doctrine declared

WORLD EVENTS

1815

1820

1815
• Napoleon is defeated at Battle of Waterloo

1817
• Exploration of Australia's interior begins

1821
• Mexico declares independence from Spain

1822
• Greece declares independence from the Ottoman Empire

Can Economics Shape Politics?

After the War of 1812, a new spirit of nationalism took hold in American society. New roads and canals helped connect the country. Industry developed in the North, while agriculture based on slave labor grew strong in the South. By the 1830s, the two regions were increasingly at odds with each other.

- *Why do you think roads and canals helped build nationalism?*

- *How did the economic differences between North and South cause tensions?*

1825
- Erie Canal opens

J. Q. Adams
1825–1829

1828
- Jackson defeats Adams's reelection bid

Jackson
1829–1837

1831
- Nat Turner slave rebellion

1825

1830

1829
- Slavery abolished in Mexico

1830
- French seize control of Algiers

FOLDABLES™

Describing Innovations Create a Three-Tab Book Foldable that describes the advances and innovations in transportation for the following: roads, railroads, and travel by water. Describe the location and routes and list the relevant dates, legislation, and building projects for each category.

Transportation

Roads *Rails* *Water*

History ONLINE Chapter Overview
Visit glencoe.com to preview Chapter 5.

American Nationalism

Actions

NEW YORK CORE CURRICULUM
U.S. History and Government

Unit 2:
I.F.2 Development of unwritten constitutional government under Washington, Adams, and Jefferson: cabinet, political parties, judicial review, executive and Congressional interpretation, lobbying; the Marshall Court (*Marbury v. Madison*, 1803, *McCulloch v. Maryland*, 1819, and *Gibbons v. Ogden*, 1824)
I.F.4.e Monroe Doctrine
II.A.3 The Marshall Court

The United States entered an "Era of Good Feelings" after the War of 1812. The federal government began building the national road, defended its authority to regulate interstate commerce, and declared the Western Hemisphere off-limits for future colonization.

Economic Nationalism

MAIN Idea The surge of nationalism and the survival of only one political party created an atmosphere in which some economic proposals of the Federalists were enacted.

HISTORY AND YOU Do you think the government should place tariffs on imports or practice free trade? Read how tariffs became a bitterly debated issue in the early republic.

After the War of 1812, a strong sense of national pride swept the United States. The *Columbian Centinel,* a Boston newspaper, called this time the **"Era of Good Feelings."** The name came to describe the period of James Monroe's presidency.

During the last two years of James Madison's second term, American leaders launched an ambitious program to bind the nation together. The program included creating a new national bank, protecting American manufacturers from foreign competition, and building new canals and roads to improve transportation and link the country together.

Partisan infighting had largely ended in national politics because only one major political party—the Republicans—remained. The Federalist Party rapidly lost political influence after the War of 1812, in part because of public disapproval of the Hartford Convention. At the same time, the war taught Republican leaders that a stronger federal government was necessary. This new perspective allowed many who might have been Federalists to join the Republicans instead. James Monroe won the presidency in 1816 with 83 percent of the electoral vote. By the election of 1820, the Federalist Party was gone. All the presidential candidates were Republicans.

The Second Bank

Republicans traditionally had opposed the idea of a national bank. They had blocked the charter renewal of the First Bank of the United States in 1811 and offered nothing in its place. The results were disastrous. State-chartered banks and other private banks greatly expanded their lending with bank notes that were used as money. Without a national bank to regulate currency, prices rose rapidly

90°W 87°W 84°W 81°W 78°W

Michigan Territory

Lake Michigan

42°N

CANADA

Lake Erie

▶ Conestoga wagons carried pioneers west

━━━ National Road
─── 1820 boundary

Wabash River

Ohio

Pennsylvania

Illinois

Indiana

Richmond
Indianapolis
Terre Haute
Effingham
Vandalia

Columbus
Springfield

Wheeling
Zanesville

Uniontown

Cumberland

Maryland

Del.

St. Louis

Ohio River

Virginia

District of Columbia

Potomac River

Kentucky

0   100 kilometers
0   100 miles
Albers Equal-Area projection

In 1806 Congress funded the building of a major east-west highway to connect the eastern United States to St. Louis and the Missouri River, the gateway to the territory of the new Louisiana Purchase. In 1811 laborers started cutting the roadbed westward from Cumberland, Maryland. The 32-foot-wide bed had a surface of sand and gravel. By the 1820s the National Road was a heavily traveled superhighway for its time. It was completed to Vandalia, Illinois, when funding ceased. The National Road turned out to be the only great federally funded transportation project of its time. President Madison vetoed a bill to fund further roads and canals. He did not think the Constitution gave the federal government the authority to make "internal improvements."

Analyzing GEOGRAPHY

1. **Location** Where did the National Road begin and end?
2. **Movement** How long was the stretch of National Road that was federally funded?

during the War of 1812. When the government borrowed money to pay for the war, it had to pay high interest rates on the loans.

Because of these problems, many Republicans changed their minds after the war. In 1816 Representative **John C. Calhoun** of South Carolina introduced a bill proposing the Second Bank of the United States. With the support of Henry Clay of Kentucky and Daniel Webster of Massachusetts, the bill passed in 1816. This legislation gave the bank the power to issue notes that would serve as a national currency and to control state banks.

Tariffs and Transportation

Protection of manufacturers was another part of the Republican program. Because an embargo had prevented Americans from buying British goods during the War of 1812, American manufacturers had increased their output to meet the demand. Once the war was over, however, British goods flowed into the United States at such low prices that they

threatened to put American manufacturers out of business.

Congress responded with the Tariff of 1816. Unlike earlier **revenue tariffs,** which provided income for the federal government, this tariff was a **protective tariff,** designed to protect American manufacturers by taxing imports to drive up their prices. New England shippers and Southern farmers opposed the tariff and the higher prices it caused, but they could not block its passage.

The Republicans also wanted to improve the nation's transportation system. In 1816 Calhoun sponsored a federal internal improvement plan, but President Madison vetoed it, arguing that spending money to improve transportation was not expressly granted in the Constitution. Nevertheless, road and canal construction soon began, with private businesses and state and local governments funding much of the work.

✓ Reading Check **Summarizing** What are three examples of economic nationalism after the War of 1812?

Judicial Nationalism

MAIN Idea Under Chief Justice John Marshall, the Supreme Court issued decisions that helped strengthen the national government.

HISTORY AND YOU Do you recall the earlier debate over the meaning of the "necessary and proper" clause in the Constitution? Read on to find out how the Supreme Court interpreted its meaning.

The judicial philosophy of Chief Justice John Marshall boosted the forces helping to unify the nation after the war. Between 1816 and 1824, the Supreme Court issued rulings that established the dominance of the nation over the states.

For further information on the cases of *Martin* v. *Hunter's Lessee* and *Gibbons* v. *Ogden*, see page R59 in **Supreme Court Case Summaries**.

Martin v. Hunter's Lessee

In 1816 the Court decided in *Martin* v. *Hunter's Lessee* that it had the authority to hear all appeals of state court decisions in cases involving federal statutes and treaties. In this case, Denny Martin, a British subject, tried to sell land in Virginia inherited from his uncle, Lord Fairfax, a British Loyalist during the war. However, Virginia law stated that no "enemy" could inherit land. The Supreme Court upheld Martin's case, ruling that Virginia's law conflicted with Jay's Treaty, which stated that land belonging to Loyalists before the war was still theirs. This historic decision helped establish the Supreme Court as the nation's court of final appeal.

McCulloch v. Maryland

This 1819 case concerned Maryland's attempt to tax the Second Bank of the United States. Before addressing Maryland's right to tax the national bank, the Supreme Court ruled on the federal government's right to create a national bank in the first place. In the Court's opinion, written by Marshall, the bank was constitutional, even though the Constitution did not specifically give Congress the power to create one.

As had been the case during the struggle to establish the first national bank, the conflict over the second centered on the "necessary and proper" clause. Marshall observed that the Constitution gave the federal government the power to collect taxes, to borrow money, to regulate commerce, and to raise armies and navies. He noted that the national bank helped the federal government exercise these powers. He concluded that the Constitution's "necessary and proper" clause allowed the federal government to create a bank.

Opponents argued that the "necessary and proper" clause meant the government could only do things absolutely necessary, but Marshall rejected that idea. Instead, he held that "necessary and proper" meant the government could use any method that was convenient for carrying out its powers as long as the method was not expressly forbidden.

Marshall then argued that the federal government was "supreme in its own sphere of action." This meant that a state government could not interfere with an agency of the federal government exercising its specific constitutional powers within a state's borders. Taxing the national bank was a form of interference and, therefore, unconstitutional.

Gibbons v. Ogden

This 1824 case involved a company that had been granted a monopoly by the state of New York to control all steamboat traffic in New York waters. When the company tried to expand its monopoly to New Jersey, the matter went to court. The Supreme Court declared the monopoly unconstitutional. Marshall noted that the Constitution gave the federal government control over interstate commerce, which the Court **interpreted** to include all trade along the coast or on waterways dividing the states.

In writing the Supreme Court's decision, Marshall defined interstate commerce in a way that went beyond the exchange of goods between states. The Court ensured that federal law would take precedence over state law in interstate transportation.

All these cases strengthened the power of the federal government at the expense of the states. Although defenders of states' rights bitterly attacked Marshall's opinions, his views helped make the "necessary and proper" clause and the interstate commerce clause major vehicles for expanding federal power.

✔ **Reading Check** **Identifying** How did the Supreme Court establish and expand federal power over the states?

ANALYZING SUPREME COURT CASES

What Does "Necessary and Proper" Mean?

★ *McCulloch* v. *Maryland*, 1819

Background to the Case

In 1816, President James Madison and Congress worked to establish the Second Bank of the United States. Two years later, the state of Maryland passed legislation imposing a tax on the Second Bank. The cashier at the Second Bank's branch in Baltimore, Maryland, James McCulloch, refused to pay the tax, and the matter went to the Supreme Court.

How the Court Ruled

In a unanimous decision the Court found that, under the "necessary and proper" clause, the federal government did have the unenumerated power to establish a national bank and that, while the states had the power to tax, they could not interfere with instruments of the federal government, and the tax was construed to be interference. This established the supremacy of the federal government over the governments of the states.

▲ *The Second Bank of the United States was located in Philadelphia. The Supreme Court held with the* McCulloch v. Maryland *ruling that the federal government had the right to establish a national bank and that the states could not tax it or otherwise interfere in any federal enterprise.*

PRIMARY SOURCE

The Court's Opinion

Can the Federal Government Create a Bank?

" . . . Although, among the enumerated powers of government, we do not find the word 'bank' or 'incorporation,' we find the great powers, to lay and collect taxes; to borrow money; to regulate commerce; to declare and conduct a war; and to raise and support armies and navies. . . . But it may with great reason be contended, that a government, entrusted with such ample powers . . . must also be entrusted with ample means for their execution.

. . . To its enumeration of powers is added, that of making 'all laws which shall be necessary and proper, for carrying into execution the foregoing powers, and all other powers vested by this constitution, in the government of the United States, or in any department thereof.'. . . [I]t is the unanimous and decided opinion of this Court, that the act to incorporate the Bank of the United States is . . . constitutional."

Can a State Tax a Federal Agency or Activity?

" . . . the power to tax involves the power to destroy. . . . If the states may tax one instrument, employed by the government . . . they may tax all the means employed by the government, to an excess which would defeat all the ends of government. . . . The result is a conviction that the states have no power, by taxation or otherwise, to retard, impede, burden, or in any manner control, the operations of the constitutional laws enacted by congress to carry into execution the powers vested in the general government. This is, we think, the unavoidable consequence of that supremacy which the constitution has declared."

—Chief Justice John Marshall writing for the Court in *McCulloch* v. *Maryland*

DBQ Document-Based Questions

1. **Specifying** What two questions did the decision in *McCulloch* v. *Maryland* address?
2. **Describing** How did Marshall interpret the "necessary and proper" clause in this case?
3. **Summarizing** How did Marshall's decision establish the authority of the federal government over the states?

Nationalist Diplomacy

MAIN Idea The surge of national pride and confidence after the War of 1812 led the United States to push to expand its borders.

HISTORY AND YOU Can you think of a time when success at one endeavor gave you confidence to stretch yourself in other ways? Read on to find out how the young United States began to assert itself in foreign affairs.

Read the Monroe Doctrine on page R48 in **Documents in American History.**

The wave of nationalism within Congress and among voters influenced the nation's foreign affairs, too. Led by President Monroe, the United States expanded its borders and asserted itself internationally.

Jackson Invades Florida

In the early 1800s, Spanish-held Florida was a source of anger and frustration for Southerners. Many runaway slaves fled there, knowing that Americans had no authority to capture them in Spanish territory. Similarly, many Creek groups had retreated to Florida as American settlers seized their lands. These peoples united with escaped slaves and other Native Americans and took a new name for themselves—*Seminole,* meaning "runaway." The **Seminoles** in Spanish Florida and Americans in Georgia staged raids against each other. Spain was unable to control the border, and many Americans clamored for the United States government to step in. As tensions heightened in the region, the Seminole leader Kinache warned an American general to stay out of Florida:

PRIMARY SOURCE

"You charge me with killing your people, stealing your cattle and burning your houses; it is I that have cause to complain of the Americans. . . . I shall use force to stop any armed Americans from passing my towns or my lands."

—quoted in *The Seminoles of Florida*

PRIMARY SOURCE
Nationalism and Diplomacy, 1818–1823

British Treaty Line, 1818

Oregon Country

Adams-Onís Treaty Line, 1819

CANADA

Unorganized Territory

Michigan Territory

N.H.
Vt.
Me. (part of Mass.)
Mass.
N.Y.
R.I.
Conn.
Pa.
N.J.
Del.
Md.

Ill. Ind. Ohio

Missouri Territory

Ky.

Va.

Arkansas Territory

Tenn.

N.C.

S.C.

ATLANTIC OCEAN

Miss. Ala. Ga.

NEW SPAIN

La.

Fla.

Gulf of Mexico

40°N
30°N
110°W
90°W
80°W

Claimed area
Unorganized territory
Territory
Established state

0   600 kilometers
0   600 miles
Albers Equal-Area projection

PRIMARY SOURCE

"[T]he occasion has been judged proper for asserting . . . that the American continents . . . are henceforth not to be considered as subjects for future colonization by any European powers . . .

. . . In the wars of the European powers in matters relating to themselves we have never taken any part. . . . With the movements in this hemisphere we are of necessity more immediately connected. . . . We owe it, therefore, to candor and to the amicable relations existing between the United States and those powers to declare, that we should consider any attempt on their part to extend their system to any portion of this hemisphere as dangerous to our peace and safety. With the existing colonies or dependencies of any European power we have not interfered and shall not interfere. But, with the Governments who have declared their independence, and maintained it . . . we could not view any interposition for the purpose of oppressing them, or controlling, in any other manner, their destiny, by any European power, in any other light than as the manifestation of an unfriendly disposition toward the United States."

—from President Monroe's message to Congress, December 2, 1823

DBQ Document-Based Questions

1. **Identifying Central Issues** What does the Monroe Doctrine prohibit?

2. **Analyzing** According to the Monroe Doctrine, what is the United States position on existing colonies?

The warning fell on deaf ears. In 1818 former member of Congress, John C. Calhoun, now secretary of war, ordered U.S. troops under the command of General Andrew Jackson into Florida to stop the Seminole raids. After destroying several Seminole villages, Jackson disobeyed orders and seized the Spanish settlements of St. Marks and Pensacola. He then removed the Spanish governor of Florida from power.

Furious, Spanish officials demanded that Jackson be punished. Secretary of State John Quincy Adams, however, defended Jackson and argued that the cause of the dispute was Spain's failure to keep order in Florida. Adams used this incident to put pressure on Spain during the ongoing negotiations to settle the border. Occupied with problems throughout its Latin American empire, Spain gave in and ceded all of Florida to the United States in the **Adams-Onís Treaty** of 1819. The treaty also **finalized** the western border of the Louisiana Purchase, which now lay along the Sabine, Red, and Arkansas Rivers to the Rocky Mountains and then followed the 42nd parallel west to the Pacific Ocean.

The Monroe Doctrine

In 1809 rebellions began to erupt in Spain's colonies. By 1824, all of Spain's colonies on the American mainland had declared independence. Spain's once vast empire had been reduced to three islands: Cuba, Puerto Rico, and Santo Domingo.

Meanwhile, a group of European countries—Great Britain, Austria, Prussia, and Russia (later joined by France)—formed the Quadruple Alliance in an effort to suppress movements against monarchies in Europe. Over Britain's objection, in 1822 the alliance raised the possibility of helping Spain regain control of its overseas colonies. Great Britain and the United States made a great deal of money trading with Latin America and did not want the Spanish to reassert control. In August 1823, British officials suggested that the two nations issue a joint statement supporting the independence of the new Latin American countries.

At the same time, Russia's growing presence on North America's Pacific Coast also worried the American government. Russia already claimed Alaska, and in 1821 it announced that its empire extended south into the Oregon Country between Russian Alaska and the western United States.

Secretary Adams urged Monroe to avoid working with the British when dealing with Spain and Russia. He did not want the United States to be regarded as Britain's junior partner. Monroe agreed, and in 1823, without consulting the British, he declared that the American continents were "henceforth not to be considered as subjects for future colonization by any European power."

The president's proclamation, later called the **Monroe Doctrine,** marked the beginning of a long-term American policy of trying to prevent European powers from interfering in Latin American political affairs. The Monroe Doctrine upheld Washington's policy of avoiding entanglements in European power struggles.

✓ Reading Check **Examining** In what ways did U.S. foreign policy become more assertive in the early 1800s?

Section 1 REVIEW

Vocabulary

1. **Explain** the significance of: Era of Good Feelings, John C. Calhoun, revenue tariff, protective tariff, Seminoles, Adams-Onís Treaty, Monroe Doctrine.

Main Ideas

2. **Contrasting** How was the Tariff of 1816 different from previous tariffs?

3. **Summarizing** What did the Marshall Court interpret the "necessary and proper" clause to mean?

4. **Determining Cause and Effect** What caused the United States to send Andrew Jackson into Spanish Florida?

Critical Thinking

5. **Big Ideas** How did the Monroe Doctrine reinforce President Washington's ideas about foreign policy?

6. **Categorizing** Use a graphic organizer to list examples of nationalism in the United States after the War of 1812.

Examples of Nationalism		
Economic	Judicial	Diplomatic

7. **Analyzing Visuals** Study the map on page 192. What areas of the present-day United States were in dispute or held by another nation at this time?

Writing About History

8. **Persuasive Writing** Suppose you are a newspaper publisher in Georgia in 1818. Write an editorial in which you defend Andrew Jackson's actions in seizing Spanish settlements in Florida.

History ONLINE

Study Central™ To review this section, go to glencoe.com and click on Study Central.

Early Industry

Guide to Reading

Big Ideas
Science and Technology New manufacturing techniques reshaped the way Americans worked.

Content Vocabulary
• free enterprise system *(p. 197)*
• interchangeable parts *(p. 198)*
• labor union *(p. 199)*
• strike *(p. 199)*

Academic Vocabulary
• transportation *(p. 194)*
• extraction *(p. 196)*

People and Events to Identify
• Erie Canal *(p. 194)*
• National Road *(p. 194)*
• Robert Fulton *(p. 196)*
• Industrial Revolution *(p. 197)*
• Francis C. Lowell *(p. 198)*
• Eli Whitney *(p. 198)*
• Samuel F. B. Morse *(p. 199)*

Reading Strategy
Categorizing Complete a graphic organizer by listing the major milestones in transportation and industrialization that occurred in the United States in the early 1800s.

Transportation	Industrialization

NEW YORK CORE CURRICULUM
U.S. History and Government

Unit 2:
II.B.1.a The growth of urban and industrial patterns of life in the North
II.B.1.b Middle-class and working-class life in the pre-Civil War North (families, gender roles, schooling, childhood, living conditions, status of free blacks)

A technological revolution in transportation and industry swept through the North. This revolution led to dramatic social and economic changes. Early industrialization also led to the growth of towns and cities in the North.

A Revolution in Transportation

MAIN Idea New modes of transportation unified the nation and strengthened its economy.

HISTORY AND YOU How do you think life would be without highways, trains, and other ways to move people and goods quickly? Read on to learn how new forms of transportation developed in the United States.

In the summer of 1817, explosions suddenly began disturbing the peace and quiet of rural upstate New York. What had started was not a war but a great engineering challenge: a canal 40 feet (12.2 m) wide and 4 feet (1.2 m) deep, connecting the Hudson River at Albany to Lake Erie at Buffalo. The longest canal in the nation at that time was almost 28 miles (45 km) long. The new **Erie Canal** would span a colossal 363 miles (584.1 km).

Building the canal was difficult and dangerous. Canal beds collapsed, burying diggers. Blasting accidents killed other workers. In 1819 alone more than 1,000 men were stricken with diseases contracted in the swamps through which they dug. Despite the dangers they faced, the canal workers pressed on and completed the immense project in 1825. The Erie Canal was a striking example of a revolution in **transportation** that swept through the Northern states in the early 1800s. This revolution led to dramatic social and economic changes.

Roads and Turnpikes

As early as 1806, the nation took the first steps toward a transportation revolution when Congress funded the building of a major east–west highway, the **National Road.** In 1811 laborers started cutting the roadbed westward from the Potomac River at Cumberland, Maryland. By 1818, the roadway had reached Wheeling, Virginia (now West Virginia), on the Ohio River. The route was almost parallel to the military road George Washington helped open in 1754. Conestoga wagons drawn by teams of oxen or mules carried migrating pioneers west on this road, while livestock and wagonloads of farm produce traveled the opposite way, toward the markets of the East.

Rather than marking the start of a federal campaign to improve transportation, the National Road turned out to be the only great

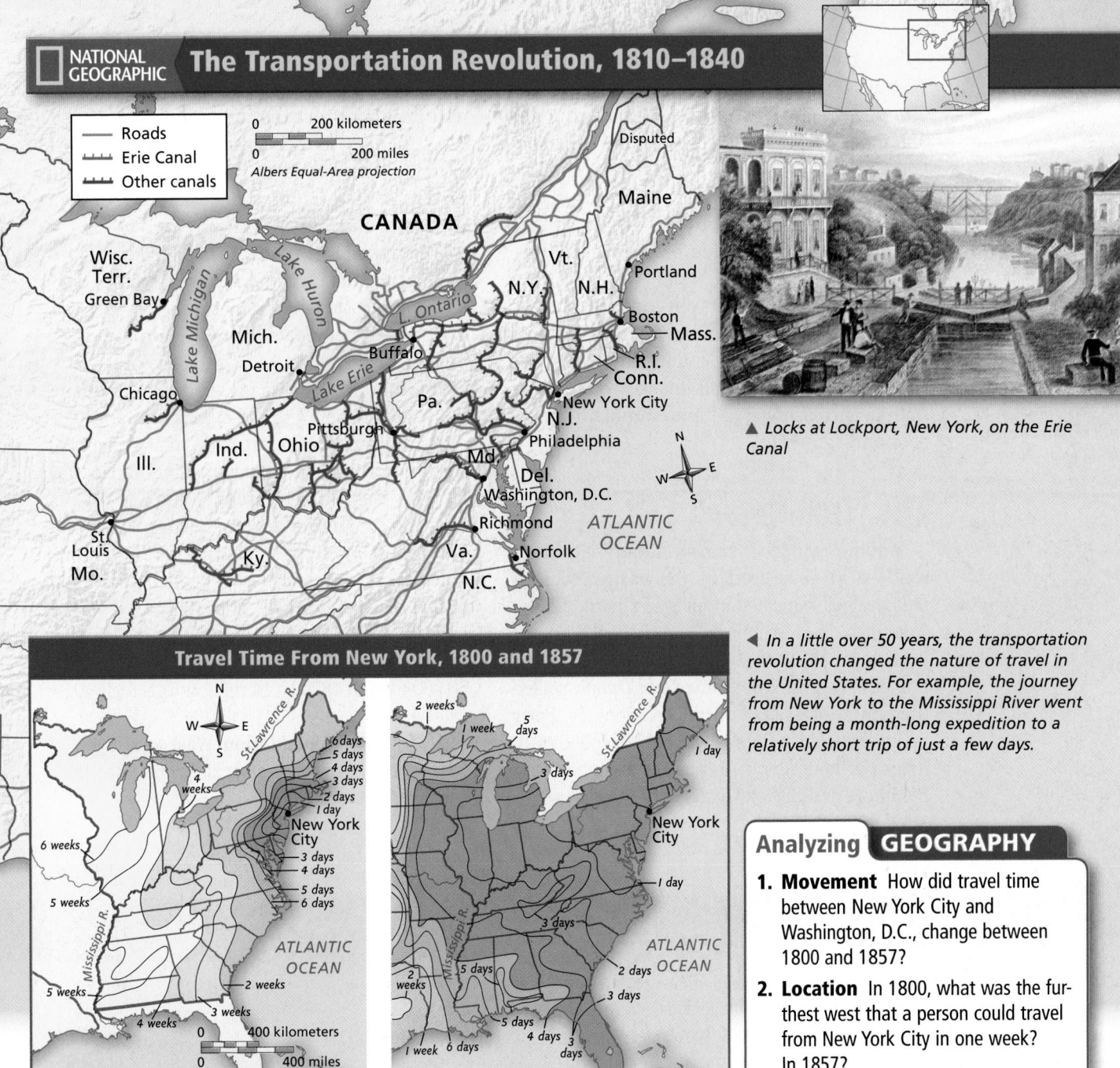

The Transportation Revolution, 1810–1840

Roads
Erie Canal
Other canals

0   200 kilometers
0   200 miles
Albers Equal-Area projection

CANADA

Disputed

Maine

Wisc. Terr.
Green Bay

Lake Michigan
Lake Huron
L. Ontario
Lake Erie

Vt.
Portland
N.Y.   N.H.
Boston
Mass.

Mich.
Buffalo
Detroit

R.I.
Conn.
New York City
N.J.
Philadelphia

Chicago

Pa.

Pittsburgh

Ill.   Ind.   Ohio
Md.
Del.
Washington, D.C.

Richmond
St. Louis
Mo.   Ky.   Va.   Norfolk
N.C.

ATLANTIC OCEAN

▲ Locks at Lockport, New York, on the Erie Canal

Travel Time From New York, 1800 and 1857

N   W   E   S

St. Lawrence R.

6 days
5 days
4 days
3 days
2 days
1 day
New York City
3 days
4 days
5 days
6 days

4 weeks

6 weeks

5 weeks

5 weeks

Mississippi R.

ATLANTIC OCEAN

2 weeks

3 weeks

4 weeks

Gulf of Mexico

0   400 kilometers
0   400 miles
Albers Equal-Area projection

2 weeks
1 week
5 days

St. Lawrence R.

3 days
1 day

New York City

1 day

Mississippi R.

3 days

2 days

5 days

ATLANTIC OCEAN

3 days

2 weeks

5 days
4 days   3 days
1 week   6 days

Gulf of Mexico

◄ In a little over 50 years, the transportation revolution changed the nature of travel in the United States. For example, the journey from New York to the Mississippi River went from being a month-long expedition to a relatively short trip of just a few days.

Analyzing GEOGRAPHY

1. **Movement** How did travel time between New York City and Washington, D.C., change between 1800 and 1857?

2. **Location** In 1800, what was the furthest west that a person could travel from New York City in one week? In 1857?

federally funded transportation project of its time. Madison and his successors believed in a strict interpretation of the Constitution and doubted that the federal government had the power to fund roads and other "internal improvements."

Instead, states, localities, and private businesses took the initiative. Private companies laid down hundreds of miles of toll roads. By 1821 some 4,000 miles (6,400 km) of toll roads had been built, mainly to connect Eastern cities, where heavy traffic made the roads extremely profitable. Even so, major roads going west had also been built, connecting Pittsburgh, Pennsylvania, and Buffalo, New York, to Eastern markets.

Steamboats and Canals

Rivers offered a far faster, more efficient, and cheaper way to move goods than did roads, which were often little more than wide paths. A barge could hold many wagonloads of grain or coal. Loaded boats and barges, however, could usually travel only downstream, as moving against the current with heavy cargoes proved difficult.

The steamboat changed all that. In 1807 **Robert Fulton** and Robert R. Livingston stunned the nation when the *Clermont* chugged 150 miles up the Hudson River from New York City to Albany in just 32 hours. The steamboat made river travel more reliable and upstream travel easier. By 1850 over 700 steamboats, also called riverboats, traveled along the nation's waterways.

The growth of river travel—and the success of the Erie Canal—spurred a wave of canal building throughout the country. By 1840 more than 3,300 miles of canals snaked through the nation, increasing trade and stimulating new economic growth.

History ONLINE
Student Web Activity Visit glencoe.com and complete the activity on the Erie Canal.

The "Iron Horse"

Another mode of transportation—the railroad—also developed in the early 1800s. A wealthy, self-educated industrialist named Peter Cooper built an American engine based on the ones developed in Great Britain. In 1830 Cooper's tiny but powerful locomotive, *Tom Thumb*, pulled the nation's first load of train passengers. Forty people traveled at the then incredible speed of 10 miles per hour along 13 miles of track between Baltimore and Ellicott City, Maryland.

The new machines did not win universal favor. Some said they were not only dangerous and uncomfortable, but dirty and ugly as well. "It is the Devil's own invention," declared one critic, "compounded of fire, smoke, soot, and dirt, spreading its infernal poison throughout the fair countryside."

The advantages of train travel, however, soon became apparent to almost everyone. Trains traveled much faster than stagecoaches or wagons, and, unlike steamboats, they could go nearly anywhere track was laid. More than any other form of transportation, railroads sped the settlement of the American West and expanded trade.

As railroads expanded, they created national markets for many goods by making transportation cheaper. They increased the demand for iron and coal even more directly. Between 1830 and 1861, the United States laid more than 30,000 miles of railroad track—so it needed more than 60,000 miles of iron rail. Since mills used coal to make iron, the need for rails added to the increasing demand for coal. Coal **extraction** shot up from 50,000 tons in 1820 to 14 million tons in 1860.

Reading Check **Evaluating** What were two advantages of trains over other kinds of transportation in the 1800s?

TECHNOLOGY & HISTORY

New technologies developed in the North revolutionized transportation and communications, and helped begin the transformation of the United States from an agricultural to an industrial nation.

▲ **The Steamboat**
Paddle-wheeled steamboats, such as Robert Fulton's *Clermont*, made river travel easier and more reliable.

▲ **The Railroad Locomotive**
The *Tom Thumb* was the first American locomotive. Railroads transformed the nation, allowing people and goods to move quickly from city to city and helping to encourage settlement in the West.

A New System of Production

MAIN Idea A revolution in manufacturing—the Industrial Revolution—dramatically changed the American economy and way of life.

HISTORY AND YOU How would your life be different without instant electronic communication? Read how one man developed the first method of communicating instantly over long distances.

Along with dramatic changes in transportation, a revolution occurred in business and industry. The **Industrial Revolution,** which began in Great Britain in the mid-1700s, consisted of several basic developments. Manufacturing shifted from hand tools to large, complex machines. Skilled artisans gave way to workers, organized by specific tasks, and often unskilled. Factories, some housing hundreds of machines and workers, replaced home-based workshops. Manufacturers sold their wares nationwide or abroad instead of just locally.

Industry developed quickly in the United States in the early 1800s for several reasons. Perhaps the most important factor was the American **free enterprise system** based on private property rights. Individuals could acquire capital and decide how to use it without strict government controls.

The free enterprise system also encouraged industrialization because companies in competition with each other were always willing to experiment with new technologies to make goods cheaper and to transport them more quickly. The era's low taxes also meant that entrepreneurs had more money to invest.

Beginning in the 1830s, many states encouraged industrialization by passing general incorporation laws. These laws allowed companies to become corporations and to raise money by issuing stock without having to obtain a charter from the state legislature. These laws also limited investor liability. If a person bought stock in a company and it went bankrupt, the person risked losing his or her investment but was not responsible for the company's debts. By limiting liability, the new state laws encouraged people to invest money, spurring economic growth.

Industrialization began in the Northeast, where many streams and rivers could provide mills with waterpower. The region was also home to many entrepreneurs who were willing to invest in British industrial techniques.

◀ **The Water Frame**
The water frame allowed cotton fibers to be easily spun into cotton thread.

▲ **The Telegraph**
The first modern breakthrough in communications was the telegraph and Morse code. Suddenly, news and other information could be sent via telegraph keys over long distances nearly instantly.

Sewing Machines ▶
By the mid 1840s, mass-produced cloth could be sewn into mass-produced clothing with sewing machines invented by Elias Howe.

Analyzing VISUALS

1. **Making Connections** How were the inventions of the water frame and the sewing machine connected?

2. **Discussing** Which invention do you think was the most significant? Why?

Working at the Lowell Mills

In 1846 a visitor to the Lowell mills described the employees' work schedule:

"The operatives work *thirteen hours* a day in the summer time, and *from daylight to dark* in the winter. At half past four in the morning the factory bell rings, and at five the girls must be in the mills. . . . At seven the girls are allowed thirty minutes for breakfast, and at noon thirty minutes more for dinner. . . . But within this time they must hurry to their boarding-houses and return to the factory. . . . At seven o'clock in the evening the factory bell sounds the close of the day's work.

. . . So fatigued . . . are numbers of the girls, that they go to bed soon after their evening meal and endeavor . . . to resuscitate their weakened frames for the toils of the coming day."

—from *The Harbinger*, November 14, 1846

DBQ Document-Based Questions

1. **Drawing Conclusions** Why are working days shorter in the mills during the winter?

2. **Making Inferences** What does the writer mean by "resuscitate their weakened frames"?

Importing British technology was not easy. Britain had passed strict laws making it illegal to share industrial technology with foreigners. A young English textile worker named Samuel Slater was willing to take the risk. In 1789 he moved to Rhode Island, where he received funding from Moses Brown, a wealthy merchant who had been trying to duplicate British technology. Slater built a British water frame from memory. The frame stretched and spun raw cotton fiber into cotton thread.

The American textile industry took a huge step forward when entrepreneur **Francis C. Lowell** began opening a series of mills in northeastern Massachusetts in 1814. Using machinery he had built after touring British textile mills, Lowell introduced mass production of cotton cloth to the United States. In Waltham, Massachusetts, the site of the first mill, his Boston Manufacturing Company built residences for workers. The company employed thousands of workers—mostly women and children, who would work for lower wages than men. By 1840 dozens of textile mills had been built in the Northeast. Industrialists also began applying factory techniques to the production of lumber, shoes, leather, wagons, and other products.

Technological Advances

A wave of inventions and technological innovations further spurred the nation's industrial growth. An ingenious young New Englander named **Eli Whitney**—perhaps most famous for inventing the cotton gin—also popularized the concept of **interchangeable parts,** transforming gun-making from a one-by-one process into a factory process. Using this process, machines turned out large quantities of identical pieces that workers assembled into finished weapons.

Communications improved as well. American inventor **Samuel F. B. Morse** began work on the telegraph in 1832 and developed the Morse code for sending messages. By 1844 the first long-distance telegraph line connected Washington, D.C., and Baltimore. Morse publicly demonstrated the device, tapping out in code the words "What hath God wrought?" From Baltimore came a reply: "What is the news from Washington?"

Journalists saw the telegraph as a tool for speedy transmission of the news. In 1848 a group of newspapers pooled their resources to collect and share news over the telegraph wires. This organization was the Associated Press. Spurred by the demands of journalists and other businesses that needed quick reliable communications with distant markets, more than 50,000 miles of telegraph wire connected most parts of the country by 1860.

The Rise of Large Cities

The industrialization of the United States drew thousands of people from farms and villages to towns in search of factory jobs with higher wages. Many city populations doubled or tripled. In 1820 only one American city boasted more than 100,000 residents. By 1860, eight cities had reached that size.

The growing cities provided opportunities for many different occupations. One group was printers and publishers, who shared the goal of keeping the public informed. America had always claimed a high literacy rate, and by 1840, over 75 percent of the total population and over 90 percent of the white population could read. The publishing industry grew to meet demand for reading materials.

Many of the early writers, editors, and teachers were educated women. Sarah Buell Hale and Lydia Howard Huntley Sigourney were leading editors and literary figures of their day. Unlike women who worked in factories, women in publishing generally came from the nation's growing middle class.

Workers Begin to Organize

The industrial boom created a new kind of laborer, the factory worker, whose ranks swelled to 1.3 million by 1860. Although the owners of early factory mills expressed a paternalistic concern for their workers, the relationship between management and labor became more strained whenever prices slumped and wages dropped.

Eleven-year-old Lucy Larcom went to work at the Lowell mills after her father's death left her family in financial hardship. At first she felt excited by the change from farm life, but she soon came to dread the drudgery of her work:

PRIMARY SOURCE

"I know that sometimes the confinement of the mill became very wearisome to me. In the sweet June weather I would lean far out of the window, and try not to hear the unceasing clash of the sound inside. Looking away to the hills, my whole stifled being would cry out, 'Oh, that I had wings!'"

—from *A New England Girlhood*

Hoping to help improve working conditions, some workers began to join together in **labor unions.** During the late 1820s and early 1830s, about 300,000 men and women belonged to some form of union. Most of the organizations were local and focused on a single trade, such as printing or shoemaking. Although these unions worked separately, they began pushing for similar changes, such as higher wages or a shorter, 10-hour workday.

During this time, unions had little success. Most employers refused to recognize or bargain with them. Unions also had little power or money to support **strikes,** or work stoppages, to achieve their goals. The courts often ruled against these early unions, seeing them as unlawful conspiracies that limited free enterprise. "Competition is the life of trade," a New York court declared in an 1835 case involving a union's demand that its workers be paid at least one dollar to make a pair of shoes. "If the defendants cannot make coarse boots for less than one dollar per pair, let them refuse to do so: but let them not directly or indirectly undertake to say that others shall not do the same work for less price."

Unions did make some gains, however. In 1840 President Martin Van Buren showed his gratitude for labor's political support by reducing the workday for federal employees to 10 hours. Two years later, in *Commonwealth* v. *Hunt,* the Massachusetts Supreme Court ruled that union strikes were legal.

Reading Check **Explaining** What was life like for a factory worker in the early 1820s?

Life in the North

MAIN Idea The rise of industrialization and the growth of cities led to change and reform in American society.

HISTORY AND YOU What is life like in your community? Read on to find out how people lived in the North in the early 1800s.

Most of the cities in the North were still relatively small before the Civil War, compared to the expansion that would come later. They had, however, begun to suffer some of the negative results of growth: crime, overcrowding, and public health problems. Immigration from Europe also added to the growing population and its problems.

Life in Northern Cities

The population growth in urban centers provided many challenges to city leaders. To combat rising crime and frequent labor riots, many cities established police departments. Fire, which had long been a concern in crowded conditions when many structures were still made of wood, was also a major urban danger. Volunteer or loosely organized fire departments that had existed since colonial times in cities such as Boston, New York, and Philadelphia, were professionalized during this period.

Crime and fire were not the only dangers in early nineteenth-century cities—they were also extremely unsanitary. Transportation was horse-based, making animal waste an enormous problem, along with human waste, in the era before sewer systems. Additionally, people and industries dumped waste and garbage into public water supplies, such as local rivers. Diseases such as cholera, typhoid, and yellow fever raged through urban areas. Water supplies were made safe only after medical advances in the latter nineteenth century.

Families in the growing cities retained the same structure as they had in the country or in the lands they emigrated from. In general, a family consisted of two parents, often with many children. Infant mortality remained commonplace. Men worked and were expected to

PRIMARY SOURCE
Life in the North, 1820–1860

The County Election by George Caleb Bingham shows how festive and inclusive elections had become by the 1850s. He created the work to celebrate the democratic principles of the Whig Party.

Upper class men voting

Farmers come to the courthouse to vote

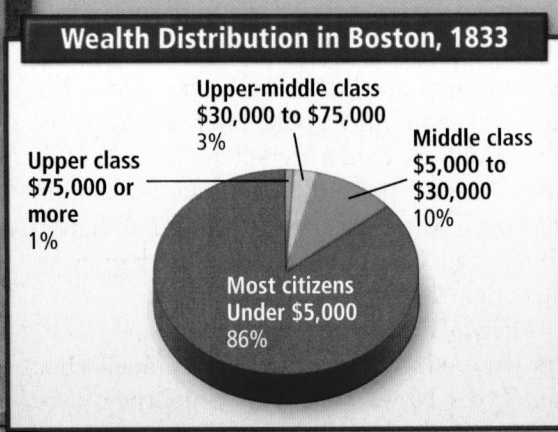

Wealth Distribution in Boston, 1833

Upper-middle class $30,000 to $75,000 — 3%

Upper class $75,000 or more — 1%

Middle class $5,000 to $30,000 — 10%

Most citizens Under $5,000 — 86%

▲ In 1833, most people in the Northeast were farmers who made a moderate or low income.

Analyzing VISUALS

1. **Expressing** What is the overall tone of this painting?

2. **Specifying** What income group was the second-largest in 1833 in the North?

rule their families. If they did not share in running a family business, women, especially in the middle class, were expected to remain at home to create an orderly, nurturing environment. In towns, women found that bakeries, butcher shops, clothiers, and candle shops offered goods that women once had to labor long hours to produce at home. Institutions of higher education were not available to women until the 1830s, and even then few had the prior education or resources to attend college.

Until the 1850s, public schools did not exist in many cities, or attendance was not mandatory. Before that time, middle-class boys generally finished high school and the wealthy might attend college. Their sisters went to "academies" for young ladies, if they were not tutored at home. Working-class boys might attend school briefly before joining the workforce; working-class girls had to be taught at home if they were to learn to read at all.

Northern cities became havens for runaway slaves as well as free African Americans, but most African Americans remained poor. Many African American women worked as domestic servants, as maids and laundresses. Many African American men found work in New England's shipping industry, as sailors or dock workers. In cities with larger African American populations, such as New York and Philadelphia, a small African American middle class emerged, including carpenters, shoemakers, schoolteachers, and ministers.

Life on the Farm

Even though industry and cities expanded in the Northeast during the first half of the nineteenth century, agriculture remained the country's leading economic activity. On most farms, the entire family shared the work. Fields had to be planted, tended, and plowed. Cows, pigs, and chickens had to be cared for. In the winter months, men and boys made repairs and cut wood for the fire while women spun thread into yarn and wove cloth for clothing. Until late in the century, farming employed more people and produced more wealth than any other kind of work.

A reporter traveling through Ohio in 1851 described a scene that resembled much of the North at that time:

"As far as the eye can stretch in the distance nothing but corn and wheat fields are to be seen; and on some points in the Scioto Valley as high as a thousand acres of corn may be seen in adjoining fields, belonging to some eight or ten different proprietors."

—from *The Cultivator*, September 1851

Northern farmers produced enough to sell their surplus in the growing Eastern cities and towns. The farmers' labors not only helped feed the population but also nourished the region's economy. As parts of the North began concentrating on manufacturing, the South continued to tie its fortunes to agriculture—and to the institution of slavery.

✓ Reading Check **Comparing** Why was farming more important in the South than in the North?

Section 2 REVIEW

Vocabulary

1. **Explain** the significance of: Erie Canal, National Road, Robert Fulton, Industrial Revolution, free enterprise system, Francis C. Lowell, Eli Whitney, interchangeable parts, Samuel F. B. Morse, labor union, strike.

Main Ideas

2. **Describing** How did the building of canals and railways boost the U.S. economy?

3. **Summarizing** What factors contributed to the development of industry in the North?

4. **Identifying** What was the leading economic activity in the United States in the early 1800s?

Critical Thinking

5. **Big Ideas** How did interchangeable parts revolutionize the manufacturing process?

6. **Organizing** Use a graphic organizer to list the effects of some of the technological advances of the early 1800s.

Technological Advances	Effects
Steamboat →	
Railroad →	

7. **Analyzing Visuals** Study the maps on page 195. What inventions helped to decrease the amount of time required to travel from New York City?

Writing About History

8. **Descriptive Writing** Suppose that you are a teenager working in a textile factory in the early 1800s. Write a letter to your family describing what your life is like there.

History ONLINE

Study Central™ To review this section, go to glencoe.com and click on Study Central.

The Land of Cotton

Guide to Reading

Big Ideas
Science and Technology The invention of the cotton gin made cotton a key part of the South's economy and ensured that slavery continued to shape the South's society and culture.

Content Vocabulary
- cotton gin *(p. 202)*
- yeoman farmer *(p. 205)*
- task system *(p. 206)*

Academic Vocabulary
- annual *(p. 202)*
- ambiguous *(p. 208)*

People and Events to Identify
- Frederick Douglass *(p. 207)*
- Gabriel Prosser *(p. 209)*
- Nat Turner *(p. 209)*

Reading Strategy
Organizing Complete a graphic organizer similar to the one below by listing the main categories of Southern society.

Southern Society

Highest _____

_____

_____

Lowest _____

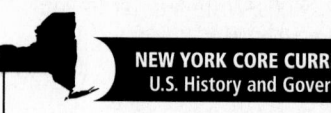

NEW YORK CORE CURRICULUM
U.S. History and Government

Unit 2:
II.B.1.d Patterns of Southern development (growth of cotton cultivation, movement into the Old Southwest, women on plantations)
II.B.1.e Life under slavery (slave laws; material conditions of life; women and children; religious and cultural expression; resistance)

The economy of the South was based on the production of cash crops, including tobacco, rice, and cotton, for export. Southern society had a distinct class system made up of the planter elite, yeoman farmers, and enslaved people.

The Southern Economy

MAIN Idea The cotton gin made cotton the most important cash crop in the South and deepened the region's dependency on enslaved labor.

HISTORY AND YOU Do you know how the clothing you wear is made? What is the cloth made from? Read on to learn how the invention of the cotton gin transformed the economy and society of the South.

The South thrived on the production of several major cash crops. In the upper Southern states—Maryland, Virginia, Kentucky, and Tennessee—farmers grew tobacco. Rice paddies dominated the coastal regions of South Carolina and Georgia. In Louisiana and parts of eastern Texas, fields of sugarcane stretched for miles. No crop, however, played a greater role in the South's fortunes than cotton. It was grown in a wide belt stretching from inland South Carolina, west through Georgia, Alabama, and Mississippi, and into eastern Texas.

During a visit to the South in 1793, Eli Whitney, the inventive young New Englander, noticed that removing cotton seeds by hand from the fluffy bolls was so tedious that it took a worker an entire day to separate a pound of cotton lint. An acquaintance knew of Whitney's mechanical ingenuity and suggested that he try building a machine to pick out the seeds. In only ten days, Whitney built a simple **cotton gin**—*gin* being short for *engine*—that quickly and efficiently combed the seeds out of cotton balls. The machine pulled the cotton through a rotating cylinder with openings that were too small for the seeds to pass through.

The invention of the cotton gin happened at the same time that textile mills were expanding in Europe. Mills in England and France clamored for all the cotton they could get. In 1792, the year before Whitney invented his cotton gin, the South produced about 6,000 bales of cotton. By 1801, **annual** production reached 100,000 bales.

Cotton Becomes King

Cotton soon dominated the region. By the late 1840s, Southerners were producing more than 2 million bales of cotton annually, and in 1860 production reached almost 4 million bales.

TECHNOLOGY & HISTORY

The Cotton Gin

In 1793 Eli Whitney built a device that removed the seeds of the "green-seed" cotton. Whitney's "gin" combed the seeds out of the cotton. The cotton gin was easy to mass produce, and quickly increased the profitability of cotton, which, in turn, increased the size and number of plantations and the need for enslaved laborers.

Slots in the grate allow the cotton to pass but not the seeds. Brushes pull the cotton off the cylinder and out of the gin.

Cotton bolls are dumped into the hopper.

A crank turns the cylinder with wire teeth. The teeth pull the cotton past a grate.

◀ Eli Whitney

Cotton Production in the South

Illinois, Indiana, Ohio, Md., Del., Virginia, Missouri, Kentucky, North Carolina, Tennessee, South Carolina, Arkansas, Mississippi, Alabama, Georgia, Texas, Louisiana, Florida

ATLANTIC OCEAN

Gulf of Mexico

Cotton production
- 1790
- 1820
- 1840
- 1860

N S E W

0 200 kilometers
0 200 miles
Albers Equal-Area projection

Cotton Production, 1790–1860

Bales (millions) vs Year (1790 1800 1810 1820 1830 1840 1850 1860)

Source: *Historical Statistics of the United States.*

Analyzing VISUALS

1. **Explaining** How did the cotton gin affect slavery in the South?
2. **Identifying** Where did cotton production spread most widely between 1820 and 1840?

In that year, Southern cotton sold for a total of $191 million in European markets—nearly two-thirds of the total export trade of the United States. Southerners began saying, "Cotton is King."

"The whole interior of the Southern states was languishing," observed one Southern judge, but Whitney's invention changed everything. "Individuals who were depressed with poverty, and sunk with idleness, have suddenly risen to wealth and respectability. Our debts have been paid off, our capitals increased; and our lands are treble [triple] in value."

While the cotton gin made some Southern planters rich, it also strengthened the institution of slavery. The spread of cotton plantations across the Deep South made the demand for slave labor skyrocket. Congress had outlawed the foreign slave trade in 1808, but a high birthrate among enslaved women—encouraged by slaveholders eager to sell new laborers at high prices—meant that the enslaved population kept growing. Between 1820 and 1850, the number of people who were enslaved in the South rose from about 1.5 million to nearly 4 million.

Industry Lags

Although the South became prosperous from agriculture, it did not industrialize as quickly as the North. For the most part, the South remained a region of rural villages and plantations, with only three large cities: Baltimore, Charleston, and New Orleans.

The South did have some industry. Coal, iron, salt, and copper mines, as well as ironworks and textile mills, could be found there. The region still relied heavily on imported goods, however, which worried some people. As one Southerner noted, "For what have we not looked to our Northern friends? From them we get not only our clothes, carriages, saddles, hats, shoes, flour, potatoes, but even our onions and horn buttons." At this time, in 1860, manufacturing in the South accounted for only 16 percent of the nation's manufacturing total. Most Southerners were content to rely on agriculture.

✔ Reading Check **Synthesizing** What effect did the cotton gin have on slavery in the South?

Society in the South

MAIN Idea In contrast to the North, the South had a rigid social class system dominated by a planter elite.

HISTORY AND YOU What mental images do you have of the Old South? What are they based on? Read on to learn more about how Southern society was organized.

The economy of the South resulted in a society with rigid and clearly defined class structure. At the top of Southern society was the planter elite, who owned the larger plantations. The 1850 census showed that in a Southern white population of just over 6 million, a total of 347,725 families were slaveholders. Of this number, around 37,000 were planters, defined as those who held 20 or more enslaved people. Fewer than 8,000 planters held 50 or more people in slavery; only 11 held 500 or more.

A very small percentage of Southern slaveholders lived a life of gentility in grand

PRIMARY SOURCE
Life in the Old South

Many enslaved African Americans worked on cotton plantations during the early 1800s. Cotton was the main cash crop for the South and required large amounts of manual labor to harvest. Cotton plantations located near rivers, similar to the one below, would transport bales of cotton to the docks to be sent to markets in the North or in Europe.

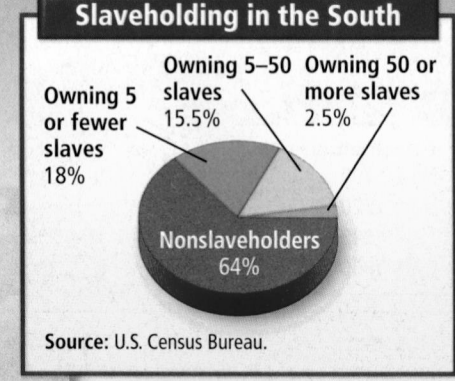

Slaveholding in the South

Owning 5 or fewer slaves 18%

Owning 5–50 slaves 15.5%

Owning 50 or more slaves 2.5%

Nonslaveholders 64%

Source: U.S. Census Bureau.

Most workers lived in small shacks—located right on the plantation.

The plantation owner's home was usually much larger and more luxurious than the workers' homes.

This wagon loaded with bales of cotton would probably be driven down to docks on the river, seen in the distance.

mansions. Many planter mansions were little more than cottages with newly built facades.

Although wealthy planters made up a tiny group—representing less than half of one percent of white Southern families and slightly over two percent of slaveholding families—they dominated the region's economy and its political system.

Ordinary farmers—often called **yeoman farmers**—and their families made up the vast majority of the white population. They may have held four or fewer enslaved persons, though most held none at all, and they worked on the land themselves. In his novel *Huckleberry Finn* author Mark Twain gives his impressions of a typical small Southern farm:

PRIMARY SOURCE

"A rail fence around a two-acre yard . . . big double log house for the white folks—hewed logs, with the chinks stopped up with mud or mortar . . . outside of the fence a garden; . . . then the cotton fields begin; and after the fields, the woods."

—from *Huckleberry Finn*

Near the bottom of the social ladder stood the white, rural poor. This group, made up mostly of families living on land too barren for successful farming, scratched a meager existence from hunting and fishing, vegetable gardening, and raising a few half-wild hogs and chickens. They made up less than 10 percent of the white population.

At the bottom of society were African Americans, 93 percent of them enslaved. In 1850 nearly 3.6 million African Americans lived in the South—about 37 percent of the total Southern population.

Rounding out Southern society was a small urban class of lawyers, doctors, merchants, and other professionals. Agriculture's influence was so great that even many of these city dwellers invested in or owned farms. As one observer noted, "No matter how one might begin, as lawyer, physician, clergyman, mechanic, or merchant, he ended, if prosperous, as proprietor of a rice or cotton plantation."

☑ Reading Check **Identifying** What classes made up the South's social structure?

THE PLANTER CLASS

◄ The planter elite lived extremely comfortable lives of wealth, leisure, and privilege.

THE YEOMAN CLASS

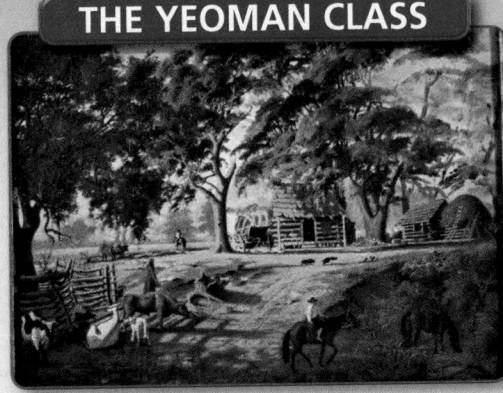

▲ Yeoman farmers did not have the wealth or power of the planter elite but lived comfortably. They may have owned enslaved persons though most held none.

THE ENSLAVED

◄ Most enslaved people lived hard lives as either field hands or house servants.

Analyzing VISUALS

1. **Specifying** What percentage of white Southerners owned more than six slaves?
2. **Explaining** If most southern whites did not own slaves, why do you think that Southerners still held on so tightly to the institution?

Slavery

MAIN Idea Enslaved African Americans had no legal rights; resistance and rebellion were two ways of coping with enslavement.

HISTORY AND YOU Do you remember reading about the Stono Rebellion? Read on to learn about slave revolts and attempted revolts in the 1800s.

The rice and cotton plantations depended on enslaved labor for their existence. The overwhelming majority of enslaved African Americans toiled in the South's fields. Some, however, worked in the region's few industrial plants or as skilled workers, such as blacksmiths, carpenters, and coopers. Others became house servants.

Enslaved people had few legal rights. State slave codes forbade enslaved men and women from owning property or leaving a slaveholder's premises without permission. They could not bring a lawsuit or sign a contract. They could not possess firearms or testify in court against a white person. Laws banned them from learning to read and write. Society viewed enslaved persons as property.

Plantation Life

Enslaved African Americans working in the fields were organized using two basic labor systems. On farms and small plantations that held few enslaved people, the **task system** was used. Under this system, workers were given a specific set of jobs to accomplish every day. After completing their tasks, they were allowed to spend the remainder of the day as they chose. Some enslaved people earned money through their skills as artisans. Others cultivated personal gardens for extra food.

In the 1800s, as cotton production became more common and slavery more widespread, slaveholders who owned large plantations adopted the gang system of labor. Under this system, enslaved people were organized into work gangs that labored from sunup to sundown—plowing, planting, cultivating, or picking, depending on the season.

INFOGRAPHIC
Slavery in America, 1800–1860

Percentage of the Enslaved Population, 1860

Percentage of total population enslaved
- More than 50%
- 30%–50%
- 10%–30%
- Less than 10%
- None, or no statistics available

◄ *Enslaved African Americans on a Southern plantation*

A driver acted as the director of a work gang. Often these individuals were enslaved people themselves, chosen for their loyalty or willingness to cooperate. They ensured that the workers labored continuously. No matter which labor system was used, slavery was a degrading experience. **Frederick Douglass,** who rose from slavery to become a prominent leader of the antislavery movement, recalled how life as an enslaved person affected him:

PRIMARY SOURCE

"My natural elasticity was crushed; my intellect languished; the disposition to read departed; the cheerful spark that lingered about my eye died; the dark night of slavery closed in upon me, and behold a man transformed to a brute."

—from *Narrative of the Life of Frederick Douglass*

Enslaved Women and Children

African American women did not have an easier time than men as enslaved people. They worked long, hard days in the fields or in the plantation house, where they served as maids, nannies, or cooks. These jobs may have seemed less arduous than fieldwork, but the responsibilities were greater and the demands were constant, as was the scrutiny of the master or mistress of the house. On larger plantations, older enslaved women cared for the babies of other enslaved women in nurseries while they worked. Where family relationships were allowed, they also cooked and cared for their own families.

Young enslaved children might be allowed to play, often with the plantation owner's own children, but as soon as they were able, they were given chores. They were not allowed to attend school, although there were rare occasions when some children learned to read.

Free African Americans

Although most African Americans of the time lived in slavery, some did not. By 1850, some 225,000 free African Americans resided in the South. Most lived in the cities, especially in Maryland and Virginia.

NATIONAL GEOGRAPHIC   An Economy Built on Enslaved Labor, c. 1850

Distribution of Slave Labor

- Rice, Sugar, Hemp 10%
- Tobacco 10%
- Cotton 55%
- Mining, Lumbering, Industry, Construction 10%
- Domestic Servants 15%

Legend:
- Cotton
- Rice
- Sugarcane
- Tobacco
- Coal
- Iron
- Lumber

0   200 kilometers
0   200 miles
Albers Equal-Area projection

Analyzing GEOGRAPHY

1. **Regions** Review the map on page 206. Which states had the highest percentage of enslaved people in the total population?

2. **Human-Environment Interaction** Study the map and graph on page 207. How does the information on the map relate to the percentage of slave labor used in farming?

Maps In MOtion   See *StudentWorks™ Plus* or glencoe.com.

People IN HISTORY

Nat Turner
1800–1831

The man who led the nation's best-known slave revolt believed from an early age—through his mother's encouragement—that he was divinely inspired. "I was intended for some great purpose," he once declared.

Although many considered Nat Turner a religious fanatic—he claimed to take his directions from mysterious voices and the movements of heavenly bodies—others knew he had a sharp mind. "He certainly never had the advantages of education," said the man appointed to be his lawyer, "but he can read and write . . . and for natural intelligence and quickness of apprehension is surpassed by few men I have ever seen."

As he awaited execution, Turner reportedly showed little remorse for his deeds, certain that he had acted in the name of God to free his people. "I am here loaded with chains and willing to suffer the fate that awaits me," he said.

Turner's revolt sent a wave of terror through the South and heightened fears of future uprisings. As a result, many states adopted even harsher restrictions on both enslaved and free African Americans.

What was the result of Turner's revolt?

▲ Nat Turner, an enslaved minister, led a group of African Americans in an armed uprising in August 1831.

A few enslaved persons were descended from Africans brought to the United States as indentured servants in the 1700s, before the slave system became universal. Some had earned their freedom fighting in the American Revolution, and still others were the half-white children of slaveholders, who had granted them freedom. There were also some formerly enslaved persons whose slaveholders had freed them or who had managed to buy freedom for themselves and their families.

Free African Americans had an **ambiguous** position in Southern society. The experiences of freed African Americans differed from state to state. In some states they had to obtain special licenses to preach or to own firearms. In cities like Charleston and New Orleans, some were successful enough to become slaveholders themselves. One such African American was Cecee McCarty, who amassed a fortune in New Orleans by retailing imported dry goods. She eventually had a sales force of 32 enslaved African Americans who she sent across the state to sell her wares.

Another 196,000 free African Americans lived in the North, where slavery had been outlawed, but they were not accepted into white society. African American educator and minister Samuel Ward of New York lamented that racial prejudice was "ever at my elbow":

PRIMARY SOURCE

"As a servant, it denied me a seat at the table with my white fellow servants . . . along the streets it ever pursued, ever ridiculed, ever abused me. If I sought redress, the very complexion I wore was pointed out as the best reason for my seeking it in vain; if I desired to turn to account a little learning, in the way of earning a living by it, the idea of employing a black clerk was preposterous—too absurd to be seriously entertained."

—from *Autobiography of a Fugitive Negro*

Still, free African Americans could organize their own churches and voluntary associations, and publish newspapers, as well as earn money from the jobs they held.

One African American who not only kept his wages but also multiplied them many times over was James Forten of Philadelphia. He went to sea in his teens as a powder monkey—the person on board a warship who handled explosives. Later, he worked as a sailmaker. By the age of 32, he owned a thriving sail factory employing 40 African American and white workers. He devoted much of his wealth to the cause of abolishing slavery.

Coping With Enslavement

African Americans dealt with the horrors of slavery in a variety of ways. From language to music to religion, they developed a culture that provided them with a sense of mutual support.

African American Culture Songs were important to many enslaved people. Field-workers often used songs to pass the long workdays. Some songs were more provocative than most plantation owners knew, using subtle language and secret meanings to lament the singers' bondage and to express a continuing hope for freedom.

Songs also played a key role in one of the most important aspects of African American culture: religion. By the early 1800s, large numbers of African Americans were Christians. The religious services enslaved people held often centered on praying about their particular concern—their dreams of freedom or a better life in the next world.

Resistance and Rebellion Many enslaved men and women found ways to oppose the dreadful lives forced on them. Some quietly staged work slowdowns. Others broke tools or set fire to houses and barns. Still others risked beatings or mutilations to run away. Some African Americans turned on their slaveholders and killed them. On occasion, enslaved people also plotted uprisings.

The first major slave uprising in the United States occurred in 1800. It was organized by an enslaved man named **Gabriel Prosser.** Prosser learned to read and grew deeply religious. Inspired by the Biblical story of the Israelite struggle for freedom from their enslavement in Egypt, Prosser began to organize those among the enslaved who were willing to revolt. They made their own weapons and ammunition and planned to capture Richmond, kill all whites living there, except for French people, Methodists, and Quakers—groups whom Prosser felt were against slavery—and establish a separate African American nation.

On the night of August 30, 1800, about 1,000 armed enslaved people approached Richmond but in the end were forced to turn back due to a heavy storm. The plot, however, was exposed, and Governor James Monroe then sent out the state militia, who eventually captured Prosser. He, along with 34 other leaders of the revolt, was shortly hanged.

In 1822 Denmark Vesey, a free African American who operated a woodworking shop in Charleston, South Carolina, was accused of planning an armed revolt to free the region's slaves. Whether or not Vesey actually planned an uprising is not known. The Charleston authorities claimed to have learned of the plot from an informer, and in 1822 Vesey was tried, convicted, and hanged.

A group of African Americans in Virginia did carry out an armed uprising on August 22, 1831. Leading the attack was **Nat Turner,** an enslaved minister who believed God had chosen him to bring his people out of bondage. Turner and his followers killed more than 50 white men, women, and children before state and local troops put down the uprising.

✔ **Reading Check** **Describing** What was life like for African Americans in the 1800s?

Section 3 REVIEW

Vocabulary

1. **Explain** the significance of: cotton gin, yeoman farmer, task system, Frederick Douglass, Gabriel Prosser, Nat Turner.

Main Ideas

2. **Analyzing** What happened at the same time as the invention of the cotton gin to increase the importance of cotton in the South?

3. **Identifying** Which class in the South during the early 1800s made up the largest percentage of the white population?

4. **Discussing** How was working within the task system different than working within the gang system?

Critical Thinking

5. **Big Ideas** How did the cotton gin and cotton farming change the South?

6. **Organizing** Complete a graphic organizer by listing the provisions of some slave codes.

Slave Codes

7. **Analyzing Visuals** Study the graph about slave labor on page 207. After those who worked to produce cotton, what was the next-largest group of enslaved workers?

Writing About History

8. **Expository Writing** Suppose you are a European visitor to the South in 1830. Write a newspaper article explaining your impressions of life in this region.

History ONLINE

Study Central™ To review this section, go to glencoe.com and click on Study Central.

ANALYZING PRIMARY SOURCES

Living Under Slavery

Enslaved persons were not free. That fundamental fact meant they could be sold and separated from their families. They could not legally marry or leave their slaveholder's property without permission. Slaveholders held such power that they controlled access to basic life necessities and could physically punish, even kill, the people they held in slavery without breaking the law.

Study these primary sources and answer the questions that follow.

PRIMARY SOURCE 1

Autobiography, 1845

"The men and women slaves received, as their monthly allowance of food, eight pounds of pork, or its equivalent in fish, and one bushel of corn meal. Their yearly clothing consisted of two coarse linen shirts, one pair of linen trousers, like the shirts, one jacket, one pair of trousers for winter, made of coarse negro cloth, one pair of stockings, and one pair of shoes; the whole of which could not have cost more than seven dollars. The allowance of the slave children was given to their mothers, or the old women having the care of them. The children unable to work in the field had neither shoes, stockings, jackets, nor trousers, given to them; their clothing consisted of two coarse linen shirts per year. When these failed them, they went naked until the next allowance-day. Children from seven to ten years old, of both sexes, almost naked, might be seen at all seasons of the year.

There were no beds given the slaves, unless one coarse blanket be considered such, and none but the men and women had these. This, however, is not considered a very great privation. They find less difficulty from the want of beds, than from the want of time to sleep; for when their day's work in the field is done, the most of them having their washing, mending, and cooking to do, and having few or none of the ordinary facilities for doing either of these, very many of their sleeping hours are consumed in preparing for the field the coming day; and when this is done, old and young, male and female, married and single, drop down side by side, on one common bed,—the cold, damp floor,—each covering himself or herself with their miserable blankets; and here they sleep till they are summoned to the field by the driver's horn."

—from *Narrative of the Life of Frederick Douglass, an American Slave*

PRIMARY SOURCE 2

Advertisement, 1829

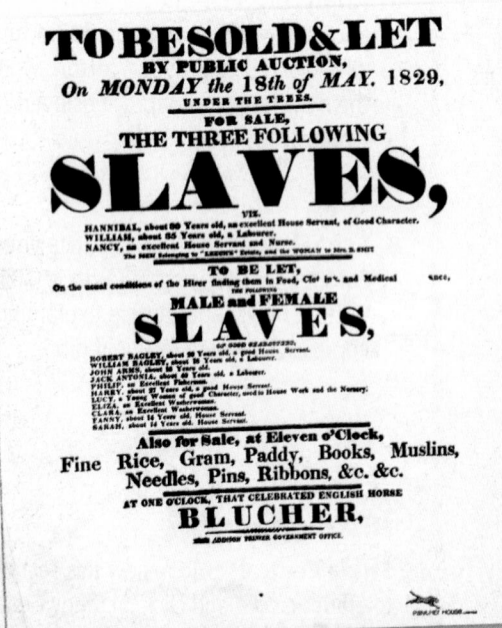

PRIMARY SOURCE 3

Photograph, 1863

▼ *Gordon escaped from his slaveholder in Mississippi during the Civil War. In this photograph, he shows the scars from a brutal whipping.*

PRIMARY SOURCE 4

Autobiography, 1861

"I once saw two beautiful children playing together. One was a fair white child; the other was her slave, and also her sister. When I saw them embracing each other, and heard their joyous laughter, I turned sadly away from the lovely sight. I foresaw the inevitable blight that would fall on the little slave's heart. I knew how soon her laughter would be changed to sighs. The fair child grew up to be a still fairer woman. From childhood to womanhood her pathway was blooming with flowers, and overarched by a sunny sky. Scarcely one day of her life had been clouded when the sun rose on her happy bridal morning.

How had those years dealt with her slave sister, the little playmate of her childhood? She, also, was very beautiful; but the flowers and sunshine of love were not for her. She drank the cup of sin, and shame, and misery, whereof her persecuted race are compelled to drink."

—from *Incidents in the Life of a Slave Girl*

PRIMARY SOURCE 5

Painting, c. 1852

Slave Auction of African Family

PRIMARY SOURCE 6

Photograph, 1858

▶ *Louisa, an enslaved teenager from St. Louis, Missouri, is shown photographed with her slaveholders' son.*

DBQ Document-Based Questions

1. **Analyzing** What does Source 1 reveal about the daily lives of enslaved persons?

2. **Interpreting** Examine Sources 2 and 3. What do these images demonstrate about the status and treatment of enslaved persons?

3. **Comparing and Contrasting** Read Source 4. How were the lives of the two girls similar when they were young but different when they became young women?

4. **Analyzing Visuals** Look at Source 5 and examine the people in the painting. Write a paragraph describing what you see going on in this scene.

5. **Speculating** Study Source 6. How do you think Louisa felt about taking care of this young boy? How might slavery complicate personal relationships?

Growing Sectionalism

Guide to Reading

Big Ideas
Government and Society The rise of a new political party represented a disagreement between those who wanted to expand federal power and those who wanted to limit it.

Content Vocabulary
• favorite son (p. 214)
• corrupt bargain (p. 215)
• mudslinging (p. 215)

Academic Vocabulary
• controversy (p. 213)
• ignorance (p. 215)

People and Events to Identify
• Missouri Compromise (p. 213)
• Henry Clay (p. 213)
• William Crawford (p. 214)
• American System (p. 214)

Reading Strategy
Organizing Complete a graphic organizer similar to the one below by listing the divisive issues of the 1820s.

NEW YORK CORE CURRICULUM
U.S. History and Government

Unit 2:
II.B.1 Developing sectional differences and philosophies of government
II.B.2.b The rise of mass politics (John Quincy Adams, Andrew Jackson, the spoils system, the bank war, Martin Van Buren)
II.B.3 The great constitutional debates: states' rights versus federal supremacy (nullification); efforts to address slavery issue (Missouri Compromise, Compromise of 1850, fugitive slave law, *Dred Scott* v. *Sanford*, 1857); preservation of the Union

S ectional disputes over slavery and its westward spread eroded the spirit of nationalism that swept the nation after the War of 1812. The one-party political system—dominated by the Democratic-Republicans—began to unravel in the 1820s.

The Missouri Compromise

MAIN Idea The Missouri Compromise tried to resolve, at least temporarily, the growing disagreement between Northern and Southern states over the issue of slavery.

HISTORY AND YOU Have you ever used compromise to solve a dispute with a friend? Read on to find out how Congress established a compromise that maintained a political balance of power.

The Monroe administration's Era of Good Feelings could not ward off the nation's growing sectional disputes and the passionately differing opinions over slavery. Tensions rose to the boiling point in 1819, when Missouri's application for statehood stirred up the country's most divisive issue: whether slavery should expand westward.

In 1819 the Union consisted of 11 free and 11 slave states. While the House of Representatives already had a majority of Northerners, admitting any new state, either slave or free, would upset the balance in the Senate and touch off a bitter struggle over political power.

Missouri's territorial government requested admission into the Union as a slave state in 1819. Acting for slavery's opponents, Congressman James Tallmadge, Jr., of New York proposed a resolution that prohibited slaveholders from bringing new slaves into Missouri. The resolution also called for all enslaved children currently living in Missouri to be freed at age 25. The House accepted the proposal, but the Senate rejected it. Most Senators and members of the House of Representatives from the South voted against the ban, while most from the North voted in favor of it.

Finally, a solution emerged when Maine, which for decades had been part of Massachusetts, requested admission to the Union as a separate state. The Senate decided to combine Maine's request with Missouri's, and it voted to admit Maine as a free state and Missouri as a slave state. This solution preserved the balance in the Senate. Senator Jesse Thomas of Illinois then proposed an amendment that would prohibit slavery in the Louisiana Purchase territory north of Missouri's southern border. This would allow slavery to expand into Arkansas territory south of Missouri, but it would keep it out of the rest of the Louisiana Purchase.

The Missouri Compromise

NATIONAL GEOGRAPHIC

Legend:
- Slave state/territory
- Free state/territory
- Territory opened to slavery by the Missouri Compromise
- Closed to slavery by the Missouri Compromise

0 400 kilometers
0 400 miles
Albers Equal-Area projection

Maine Admitted as free state in 1820

CANADA

Michigan Territory

Unorganized Territory

N.H.
Vt.
N.Y.
Conn.
Mass.
R.I.
40°N
Pa.
N.J.
Del.
Md.

Ill. Ind. Ohio

Mo. Admitted as slave state in 1821

Missouri Compromise Line 36°30'N

Arkansas Territory

Ky.

Va.

N.C.

S.C.

ATLANTIC OCEAN

30°N

Tenn.

Miss. Ala. Ga.

NEW SPAIN

La.

Fla.

Gulf of Mexico

90°W

80°W

Voting for the Compromise

Maine

Missouri

House of Representatives, 1820
- Vote yes to Missouri as slave state and Maine as free state and for compromise line
- Vote yes to Missouri and Maine, but no for compromise line
- Votes no on Missouri and Maine, but yes on compromise line
- Votes no on Missouri and Maine, and no to compromise line

Analyzing GEOGRAPHY

1. **Regions** Most representatives from which region of the country voted for both provisions of the Missouri Compromise?
2. **Place** Which state came into the Union as a slave state, and which came in as a free state?

Since many people at the time thought the Great Plains area north of Missouri was not suitable for farming, it appeared that this **Missouri Compromise** benefited the South. By a very close vote, carefully managed by **Henry Clay** of Kentucky, the House of Representatives voted to accept the Compromise. The Compromise held out the hope that pairing the admission of free and slave states together would quiet the dispute over the expansion of slavery.

Once the issue was settled, however, a new problem developed. Pro-slavery members of the Missouri constitutional convention added a clause to the proposed state constitution prohibiting free African Americans from entering the state. This new **controversy** threatened final approval of Missouri's admission to the Union. Clay again engineered a solution by getting the Missouri legislature to state that they would not honor the spirit of the clause's wording.

Despite Clay's efforts, many leaders feared that the Missouri Compromise was only a temporary solution. "I take it for granted," John Quincy Adams wrote, "that the present question is a mere preamble—a title page to a great tragic volume." The Compromise merely postponed a debate over the future of slavery.

Reading Check **Examining** Why was the Missouri Compromise proposed?

The Elections of 1824 and 1828

MAIN Idea The presidential elections of 1824 and 1828 highlighted the growing sectionalism in the nation.

HISTORY AND YOU Do you recall the divisions that led to the creation of the Federalist Party and the Democratic-Republican Party? Read on to learn how the Democratic-Republican Party split over issues in the 1820s.

Politics reflected the sectional tensions of the day. Although the Republicans had supporters throughout the nation, the presidential campaigns of 1824 and 1828 showed how deeply the party was torn along regional lines.

A Battle of Favorite Sons

Four candidates ran for president in 1824. All belonged to the Republican Party and all were **"favorite sons,"** men who enjoyed the support of leaders from their own state and region. Two candidates, Henry Clay of Kentucky and Andrew Jackson of Tennessee, represented the West. John Quincy Adams, the

Massachusetts son of John Adams, who was serving as President Monroe's secretary of state, was New England's favorite son. **William Crawford** of Georgia represented the South.

Crawford ran on the original principles of Jefferson's party—states' rights and strict interpretation of the Constitution. Clay favored the national bank, the protective tariff, and nationwide internal improvements—collectively known as the **American System.** Adams also favored internal improvements but was less enthusiastic about tariffs. Jackson avoided taking a stand on specific issues. His campaign focused on his leadership qualities and heroism at the Battle of New Orleans.

On Election Day, Jackson won the most popular votes, but no candidate won a majority in the Electoral College. Following constitutional procedure, the election went to the House of Representatives, which would select the president from the three candidates who had received the most electoral votes. Clay, who had placed fourth, was eliminated.

As the Speaker of the House, Henry Clay had tremendous influence, and few doubted whom he would support. Clay and Jackson had been rivals for political leadership in the West. Clay once described Jackson as "igno-

The Election of 1824

A Westerner cheers for Jackson reflecting sectional views.

Two men discuss how Crawford will never catch up to Adams.

An Irishman declares his dislike for Adams.

Henry Clay drops out of the race.

Adams

Crawford

Jackson

Analyzing VISUALS

1. **Explaining** Why is Clay scratching his head over the race?

2. **Summarizing** Why is Jackson shown running in third place?

rant, passionate, hypocritical, [and] corrupt." Jackson referred to Clay as the "meanest scoundrel that ever disgraced the image of his god."

On a snowy February 9, 1825, the representatives met to make their choice. As expected, Clay threw his support behind Adams, and he won the House election easily. Adams received 13 votes, while Jackson won 7, and Crawford won 4. Many Jackson supporters accused Clay of arranging votes for Adams in return for a cabinet post. When Adams took office, he did indeed name Clay as his secretary of state, and Jackson's supporters accused Adams and Clay of striking a **"corrupt bargain."** Adams and Clay denied any wrongdoing, but the incident split the party. Jackson's supporters began referring to themselves as Democrats, while Henry Clay and his supporters formed a new party called the National Republicans.

John Quincy Adams Takes Office

In his first message to Congress, John Quincy Adams announced an ambitious program of nationalist legislation that exceeded even Clay's American System. In addition to standard internal improvements, Adams urged that federal revenue also be used to build a national university and astronomical observatories, and to fund scientific research. His proposals, however, struck many legislators as a return to Federalist ideas. His opponents in Congress argued that it was a waste of taxpayers' money.

In the end, Congress granted the president funds for improving rivers and harbors and for extending the National Road westward, but this was far less than he had wanted. The repeated rebuffs he suffered in Congress set the stage for Adams's defeat in 1828.

The Election of 1828

The election of 1828 pitted John Quincy Adams against Andrew Jackson. Jackson fought to achieve a victory that his supporters believed had been unjustly denied him four years earlier. Both candidates engaged in **mudslinging,** criticizing each other's personalities and morals. Adams called his opponent "incompetent both by his **ignorance** and by the fury of his passions." Jackson portrayed himself as the candidate of the common man and attacked Adams as an out-of-touch aristocrat. Jackson also revived the alleged "corrupt bargain" between Adams and Clay to show that the president was untrustworthy.

When the results came in, Jackson had 56 percent of the popular vote and 178 of the 261 electoral votes, a clear victory. Many of the voters who supported Jackson were from the West and the South, rural and small-town men who saw Jackson as the candidate most likely to represent their interests. The man whose fiery personality had earned him the nickname "Old Hickory," after a tough, hard wood found on the frontier, finally had reached the White House.

Reading Check **Identifying** What did John Quincy Adams hope to accomplish during his presidency?

Section 4 REVIEW

Vocabulary

1. **Explain** the significance of: Missouri Compromise, Henry Clay, favorite son, William Crawford, American System, corrupt bargain, mudslinging.

Main Ideas

2. **Explaining** How did the Missouri Compromise maintain the balance of power in the Senate?

3. **Describing** What events helped John Quincy Adams win the presidency in 1824?

Critical Thinking

4. **Big Ideas** Why was the Democratic Party formed after the election of 1824?

5. **Organizing** Use a graphic organizer similar to the one below to list the terms of the Missouri Compromise.

Missouri Compromise

6. **Analyzing Visuals** Study the maps on page 213. Why was the Missouri Compromise only a temporary measure?

Writing About History

7. **Expository Writing** Suppose that you are a voter in the election of 1828. Write a letter to a family member explaining which presidential candidate you support and why.

History ONLINE

Study Central™ To review this section, go to glencoe.com and click on Study Central.

Effects of Nationalism

Economic Nationalism

- Second Bank of the United States is created.
- Tariff of 1816 is passed to protect the nation's industries.
- The federal government funds the National Road, and states fund other roads and canals, helping to tie the nation together.

Judicial Nationalism

- In *Martin* v. *Hunter's Lessee,* Supreme Court asserts right to hear appeals from state courts in cases involving federal law.
- In *McCulloch* v. *Maryland,* Supreme Court establishes that the "necessary and proper" clause has broad meaning and that the federal government is supreme in its own sphere.
- In *Gibbons* v. *Ogden,* the Supreme Court gives the federal government broad power to regulate interstate commerce.

Nationalism in Foreign Policy

- Andrew Jackson invades Florida; Spain cedes the territory to the United States in 1819.
- The United States issues the Monroe Doctrine, telling Europeans they may no longer colonize the Americas.

▲ *The Erie Canal was one of several developments in transportation that changed the economy and society of the United States in the first half of the nineteenth century.*

▲ *The invention of the cotton gin and an increase in demand in the market led to the spread of cotton plantations and a further entrenchment of slavery as an institution in the South.*

Causes of Sectionalism

Life in the North

- Construction of canals, roads, and railroads is widespread.
- Development of steam engine leads to the first railroads and extensive use of steamboats.
- Industrialization begins, and factories begin to be built to manufacture textiles and other goods.
- Large cities develop as does an urban working class.
- Northern farmers live on individual family farms.

Life in the South

- Eli Whitney's cotton gin makes cotton production with slave labor feasible; cotton becomes main product of the South.
- Southern society is generally divided into elite planters, yeoman farmers, and enslaved African Americans.
- Enslaved Americans generally live on plantations helping to plant and harvest cotton, rice, and sugarcane, although some are employed in other industries.
- A distinct African American culture develops among the enslaved who develop many strategies to cope with and resist slavery.

NEW YORK REGENTS EXAM PRACTICE

TEST-TAKING

As you read a question, underline key phrases so that you can easily refer to them as you review the answer choices.

Part I

Directions (1–10): For each statement or question, write on a separate sheet of paper the number of the word or expression that, of those given, best completes the statement or answers the question.

1. Which of the following cases established the Supreme Court as the final court of appeal?

    (1) *Commonwealth* v. *Hunt*

    (2) *Martin* v. *Hunter's Lessee*

    (3) *McCulloch* v. *Maryland*

    (4) *Gibbons* v. *Ogden*

2. "The American continents, by the free and independent condition which they have assured and maintain, are henceforth not to be considered as subjects for future colonization by any European powers. . . .

    We should consider any attempt on their part to extend their system to any portion of this hemisphere as dangerous to our peace and safety."

    —from the Monroe Doctrine

    Based on the excerpt above, what was the Doctrine designed to do?

    (1) preserve U.S. trade routes with Europe

    (2) prohibit European nations from colonizing any lands in the Western Hemisphere

    (3) prevent Central American countries from declaring war against the United States

    (4) protect the United States from invasion by Central American nations

3. The Erie Canal connected Lake Erie to

    (1) the Missouri River.

    (2) the Hudson River.

    (3) the St. Lawrence River.

    (4) the Mississippi River.

4. In 1814 Francis Lowell introduced

    (1) interchangeable parts in the production of weapons.

    (2) mass-produced textiles into the United States.

    (3) the idea of a Second Bank of the United States in Congress.

    (4) a bill to complete the National Road.

5. In the social class system of the South, which of the following groups was at the top?

    (1) yeoman farmers

    (2) planters

    (3) urban professionals

    (4) merchants

6. In the early 1800s, slavery expanded in the South after

    (1) the invention of the cotton gin.

    (2) industry flourished in the North.

    (3) Spain ceded Florida.

    (4) Gabriel Prosser's rebellion was discovered.

7. The Missouri Compromise maintained a balance of power between the North and South in the Senate by

    (1) allowing slavery in all new states that joined the Union.

    (2) splitting Massachusetts into two free states.

    (3) allowing slavery in no portion of the Louisiana Territory.

    (4) adding a slave state and a free state to the Union simultaneously.

Need Extra Help?							
If You Missed Questions . . .	1	2	3	4	5	6	7
Go to Page . . .	190	193	194	198	204	203	212

[OVER]

Base your answer to question 8 on the map below and your knowledge of Chapter 5.

The United States in 1824

0   400 kilometers
0   400 miles
Albers Equal-Area projection

British Treaty Line, 1818
BRITISH NORTH AMERICA
Disputed area

Oregon Country (Occupied jointly by Britain and the U.S.)

Adams-Onís Treaty Line, 1819

Unorganized territory

MEXICO

Arkansas Territory

N.H.
Vt.
Me.
Michigan Territory
N.Y.
Mass.
R.I.
Conn.
Pa.
N.J.
Ind. Ohio
Del.
Ill.
Va.
Md.
Mo.
Ky.
Tenn.
N.C.
S.C.
Miss. Ala. Ga.
La.
Fla. Terr.

ATLANTIC OCEAN

Gulf of Mexico

☐ British territory
▨ Mexico
— Louisiana Purchase
☐ United States

8   Which future state was jointly occupied by Britain and the U.S. in 1824?

A   Texas

B   Oregon

C   Michigan

D   Arkansas

9   After the election of 1824, the Democratic-Republican Party split into which two new parties?

(1)   National Republicans and Democrats

(2)   Democratic-Republicans and Federalists

(3)   Democrats and Republicans

(4)   Federalists and Republicans

10   During his administration, President John Quincy Adams called for Congress to provide the funds for

(1)   the Second Bank of the United States.

(2)   the fulfillment of the Adams-Onís Treaty.

(3)   a national university.

(4)   the building of the Erie Canal.

Need Extra Help?			
If You Missed Questions . . .	8	9	10
Go to Page . . .	R15	214	193

Part II Thematic Essay Question

Directions: Write a well-organized essay that includes an introduction, several paragraphs addressing the task below, and a conclusion.

Theme: The Southern Economy

While in the North an industrial economy was developing and an infrastructure, such as the National Road, was being built, industry lagged behind agriculture as the main way to make a living in the South. Partly, this was due to the rise of cotton as the dominant crop in that region.

Task:

Explore the state of the Southern economy, and make sure to

• Discuss the economy before the cotton boom

• Explain why cotton became "king" in the South

• Describe the effects, in the South and in the nation, of that development

Guidelines:

In your essay, be sure to:

• Develop all aspects of the task

• Support the theme with relevant facts, examples, and details

• Use a logical and clear plan of organization, including an introduction and a conclusion that are beyond a restatement of the theme

Part III Document-Based Question

This question is based on the accompanying documents. It is designed to test your ability to work with historical documents. Some of the documents have been edited for the purposes of the question. As you analyze the documents, take into account both the source of each document and any point of view that may be presented in the document.

Historical Context:

Enslaved African Americans led difficult lives with no legal rights, while the position of free African Americans was complex and challenging.

Task:

Using information from the documents and your knowledge of United States history, answer the questions that follow each document in Part A. Your answers to the questions will help you write the Part B essay, in which you will be asked to

- Discuss the development of slavery in the South
- Describe the lives of enslaved Africans in the South, and compare their lives with those of free African Americans
- Evaluate social effects of slavery on the South and on the nation as a whole

Part A
Short-Answer Questions

Directions: Analyze the documents and answer the short-answer questions that follow each document on a separate sheet of paper.

Document 1

"She was the daughter of a planter . . . who, at his death, left her mother and his three children free, with money to go to St. Augustine. . . . It was during the Revolutionary War; and they were captured. . . . She was a little girl when she was captured and sold to the keeper of a large hotel. . . . But as she grew older she evinced so much intelligence, and was so faithful, that her master and mistress could not help seeing it was for their interest to take care of such a valuable piece of property. She became an indispensable personage in the household, officiating in all capacities, from cook and wet nurse to seamstress. She was much praised for her cooking. . . . In consequence of numerous requests . . . she asked permission of her mistress to bake crackers at night, after all the household work was done; and she obtained leave to do it, provided she would clothe herself and her children from the profits."

Source: Harriet Ann Jacobs, *Incidents in the Life of a Slave Girl*, 1861

1 In what ways was Jacobs' grandmother treated like property and not a person?

Document 2

Source: William A. Stephens, *The Parting*, Library of Congress, 1863

2 What does the cartoonist imply about slavery?

Part B
Essay

Directions: Reread the task box at the left and write a well-organized essay that includes an introduction, several paragraphs, and a conclusion. Use evidence from the documents in your essay. Support your response with relevant facts, examples, and details. Include additional outside information.

Guidelines:

In your essay, be sure to:

- Develop all aspects of the task
- Incorporate information from the documents
- Incorporate relevant outside information
- Use a logical and clear plan of organization, including an introduction and a conclusion that are beyond a restatement of the theme

For additional test practice, use Self-Check Quizzes—Chapter 5 at glencoe.com.

Need Extra Help?			
If You Missed Questions . . .	1	2	Essay
Go to Page . . .	219	R18	202–209

The Spirit of Reform

1828–1845

Town members listen to a local politician in the early 1800s.

1830
• Mormon religion officially organizes

1832
• Democrats hold their first presidential nominating convention

1828
• North-South rift develops over tariff

Jackson
1829–1837

1833
• American Anti-slavery Society is founded by William Lloyd Garrison

Van Buren
1837–1841

U.S. PRESIDENTS

U.S. EVENTS

WORLD EVENTS

1825

1830

1835

1826
• First railway tunnel built in England

1829
• Mexico abolishes slavery

1835
• Fairy tales of Hans Christian Andersen are published

1837
• Queen Victoria ascends to English throne

Can Average Citizens Change Society?

In the 1830s and 1840s, reformers tried to change American society. Some worked to end slavery, others to give women the vote or to give all Americans access to public education. Some sought to reform prisons, while others tried to reduce alcohol abuse. The issues of the era still shape the concerns of reformers today as they try to improve education, reduce social problems and end discrimination toward minorities and women.

- *How did reforms of this era increase the tensions between North and South?*
- *What do you think is the best way to get a society to accept reform?*

1838
- Cherokee embark on the Trail of Tears

W. Harrison 1841

Tyler 1841–1845

1848
- Women's rights convention is held at Seneca Falls, New York

1840

1845

1839
- Slave revolt occurs aboard the *Amistad*

1842
- China is opened by force to foreign trade

1845
- The Great Irish Famine begins

FOLDABLES™

Identifying Reform Movements
Create a Four-Tab Book Foldable in order to identify the major reform movements in American society in the early nineteenth century. For each reform movement, list when it began, its causes, its leadership, and its accomplishments.

Education Reform
Temperance Movement
Prison Reform
Abolitionism

History ONLINE Chapter Overview
Visit glencoe.com to preview Chapter 6.

Jacksonian America

Guide to Reading

Big Ideas
Government and Society The American political system became more democratic during the Jacksonian era.

Content Vocabulary
- suffrage *(p. 223)*
- spoils system *(p. 224)*
- caucus system *(p. 224)*
- secede *(p. 225)*

Academic Vocabulary
- evident *(p. 223)*
- exposure *(p. 227)*

People and Events to Identify
- Tariff of Abominations *(p. 225)*
- Daniel Webster *(p. 225)*
- Force Bill *(p. 226)*
- Indian Removal Act *(p. 226)*
- Trail of Tears *(p. 227)*
- Panic of 1837 *(p. 229)*

Reading Strategy
Organizing Complete a graphic organizer, similar to the one below, listing the positions of Jackson and Calhoun during the nullification crisis.

Nullification → Jackson's Position / Calhoun's Position

NEW YORK CORE CURRICULUM
U.S. History and Government

Unit 2:

II.B.2.a	Political democratization: national political nominating convention, secret ballot
II.B.2.b	The rise of mass politics (John Quincy Adams, Andrew Jackson, the spoils system, the bank war, Martin Van Buren)
II.B.2.c.(3.)	The removal policy: *Worcester* v. *Georgia,* 1832
II.C.6	Impact of western expansion upon Mexicans and Native Americans

A ndrew Jackson was elected with wide popular support. As president, he stood up for federal authority, tried to move Native Americans to the West, and fatally undermined the Bank of the United States. A new party, the Whigs, emerged to oppose him.

A New Era in Politics

MAIN Idea States expanded voting rights in the late 1820s, making the nation more democratic, which in turn helped Andrew Jackson win election. As president, Jackson opposed South Carolina's nullification vote, supported the Indian Removal Act, and closed the Bank of the United States.

HISTORY AND YOU Have you ever felt that someone "played favorites"? Read how Andrew Jackson used the "spoils system" to reward his political supporters.

Margaret Bayard Smith was one of the thousands of Americans who attended the presidential inauguration of Andrew Jackson in 1829. She later wrote to a friend about how much the atmosphere in Washington, D.C., impressed her. "Thousands and thousands of people, without distinction of rank, collected in an immense mass around the Capitol, silent, orderly and tranquil," she explained.

On that day, President Jackson broke a long tradition by inviting the public to his reception. When Smith later attended the White House gala, however, she quickly formed a different opinion about the crowd she had so admired just hours before.

PRIMARY SOURCE

"The *Majesty of the People* had disappeared, and a rabble, a mob, of boys, . . . women, children—[were] scrambling, fighting romping. . . . The President, after having been *literally* nearly pressed to death and almost suffocated and torn to pieces by the people in their eagerness to shake hands with Old Hickory, had retreated through the back way. . . . Cut glass and china to the amount of several thousand dollars had been broken in the struggle to get refreshments. . . . Ladies and gentlemen, only had been expected at this Levee [reception], not the people en masse. But it was the People's day, and the People's President, and the People would rule."

—from *The First Forty Years of Washington Society*

The citizens who had turned the normally dignified inauguration reception into a boisterous affair represented a new class of American voters and a new era in American politics. Beginning in the early 1800s and continuing through the presidency of Andrew Jackson, the nation's political system became more democratic, and ordinary citizens became a greater political force.

The Election of 1828

More than three times the number of voters turned out for the election of 1828 than had participated in the presidential election four years earlier. This surge had two sources. First, Andrew Jackson's supporters encouraged high voter turnout by using tactics to appeal to average citizens—parades, speeches, barbecues, and even a popular campaign song. Second, and more important, more men were eligible to vote in 1828. Most states had lowered or eliminated property requirements for voters, allowing many more white men to vote. These new voters heavily favored Andrew Jackson.

ANALYZING HISTORY Do you think that the election of 1828 indicated a change in the way government worked? Write a brief essay to explain your opinion.

The Election of 1828

Jackson   Adams

ME 9
1 (Jackson)
8 (Adams)
NY 36
20 (Jackson)
16 (Adams)
NH 8
VT 7
MA 15
RI 4
CT 8
NJ 8
DE 3
MD 11
5 (Jackson)
6 (Adams)
PA 28
MI TERR.
UNORGANIZED TERRITORY
IL 3
IN 5
OH 16
VA 24
MO 3
KY 14
NC 15
AR TERR.
TN 11
SC 11
MS 3
AL 5
GA 9
LA 5
FL TERR.

Presidential Candidate	Popular Vote	% of Popular Vote	Electoral Vote
Jackson	647,286	56.03%	178
Adams	508,064	43.97%	83

▲ Excited that a western war hero of humble origins had made it to the White House, crowds flocked to see Andrew Jackson as he traveled to his inauguration as president in 1829.

Voter Participation

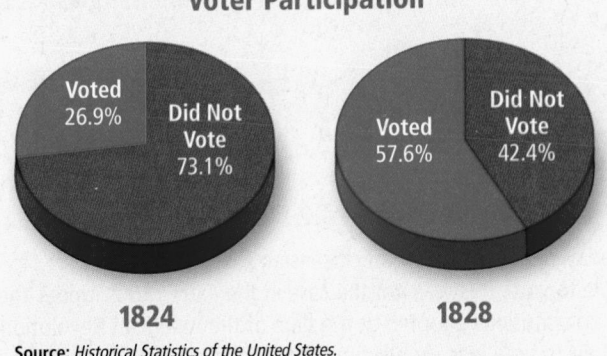

Voted 26.9%   Did Not Vote 73.1%

Voted 57.6%   Did Not Vote 42.4%

1824   1828

Source: *Historical Statistics of the United States.*

States Expand Voting Rights

In the early 1800s, hundreds of thousands of Americans, mostly white men, gained the right to vote. This happened because many states lowered or eliminated property ownership as a voting qualification. In addition, as cities and towns grew, the percentage of working people who did not own property increased. These people paid taxes and had an interest in political affairs—and they too wanted a greater voice in electing those who represented them.

The expansion of **suffrage**—the right to vote—was **evident** in the turnout for the presidential election of 1828. In 1824 about 355,000 Americans had voted for president. Four years later, more than 1.1 million citizens cast a ballot in the presidential election. Eventually every state made its voting qualifications more democratic, and by 1840, over 2 million Americans voted in the presidential election.

In 1828 Andrew Jackson benefited from the large number of new voters, many of whom lived on the frontier. Many of the citizens who voted for the first time in 1828 saw in Jackson a man whose origins were little different from their own, and whose achievements they greatly admired.

The Spoils System

Andrew Jackson had great confidence in the capability and intelligence of average Americans. He believed that the majority should rule in a democracy and that ordinary citizens should play a role in government.

These beliefs led Jackson to support the **spoils system**—the practice of giving people government jobs on the basis of party loyalty. Rewarding supporters with jobs had long been part of American politics, but Jackson was the first president to fire a large number of federal employees so as to appoint his own followers. A shocked John Quincy Adams warned that the policy would make government "a perpetual . . . scramble for office."

Jackson considered the spoils system to be democratic because it put an end to a permanent, nonelected office-holding class. Because government jobs were "so plain and simple," in his opinion, they could easily be rotated at will and given to supporters.

From Caucus to Convention

Jackson's supporters also changed the way presidential candidates were chosen. At that time, political parties used the caucus system to select presidential candidates. Members of the party who served in Congress, known as the party caucus, would meet to choose the nominee for president. Jackson's supporters believed that the **caucus system** restricted nominations to the elite and well-connected.

The Jacksonians replaced the caucus with a national nominating convention. At nominating conventions, delegates from the states gathered to decide on the party's presidential nominee. Supporters believed that conventions allowed the people, not the elite, to decide on party nominees. In 1832 the Democrats held a convention and renominated Andrew Jackson for president.

✔ **Reading Check** **Examining** In what ways did the United States become more democratic in the early 1800s?

PAST & PRESENT

Choosing a President

Today, nearly all American citizens age 18 and older are eligible to vote. This was not the case in the early 1800s. Under the state constitutions adopted at the time of the American Revolution, the right to vote was usually limited to white males who owned property. Over the next few decades, however, states began lowering or eliminating property requirements for voters. Women could not vote, nor could the overwhelming majority of African American men, even those living in the North who met other requirements for voting. Still, changes in the Jacksonian era meant many more Americans could participate in presidential elections.

The rise of national nominating conventions also changed the process of choosing a president. Rather than congressional party leaders deciding on the party's candidate, delegates from the states could participate in the decision at a nominating convention.

Today, parties still hold national conventions in presidential election years, but voting to choose the party's nominee for president has become largely symbolic. The party's nominee has generally been decided in advance, through state primaries and state caucuses.

1844

▲ Men crowd around the ballot boxes at a New York City polling station, waiting for their chance to vote in the presidential election of 1844.

The Nullification Crisis

MAIN Idea Resentment about high tariffs led Southern states to claim that states could declare a federal law null or void.

HISTORY AND YOU Have you ever felt so strongly about an issue that you wrote a letter of complaint? Read how Southern states were outraged about tariff rates.

Jackson had not been in office long before he had to focus on a national crisis. It centered on South Carolina, but it also highlighted the growing rift between the nation's Northern and Southern regions.

The Debate Over Nullification

In the early 1800s, South Carolina's economy began to decline. Many of the state's residents blamed this situation on the nation's tariffs. Because it had few industries, South Carolina purchased many of its manufactured goods, such as cooking utensils and tools, from England, but tariffs made them extremely expensive. When Congress levied yet another new tariff in 1828—which critics called the **Tariff of Abominations**—many South Carolinians threatened to **secede,** or withdraw, from the Union.

The growing turmoil troubled one politician in particular: John C. Calhoun, the nation's vice president and a resident of South Carolina. Calhoun felt torn between upholding the country's policies and helping his fellow South Carolinians. Rather than support secession, Calhoun put forth the idea of nullification to defuse the situation. He explained this idea in an anonymously published work, *The South Carolina Exposition and Protest,* which argued that states had the right to declare a federal law null, or not valid. Calhoun theorized that the states had this right because they had created the federal Union.

The issue continued to simmer beneath the surface until January 1830, when Robert Hayne of South Carolina and **Daniel Webster** of Massachusetts confronted each other on the floor of the Senate. The debate consisted of several speeches delivered for over a week. Webster, perhaps the greatest orator of his day, was a ferocious defender of the Union. Hayne was an eloquent champion of the right of states to chart their own course.

2004

▲ Today, electronic voting is becoming common. Nearly all U.S. citizens older than 18 years of age may vote.

▲ George W. Bush accepts the presidential nomination at the Republican National Convention in 2004.

MAKING CONNECTIONS

1. **Contrasting** How is the electorate different today than it was in the early 1800s?

2. **Synthesizing** How have national party conventions changed since the early 1800s?

Hayne asserted that the Union was no more than a voluntary association of states and advocated the motto, "Liberty first and Union afterward." Webster countered that liberty depended on the strength of the Union:

PRIMARY SOURCE

"I have not allowed myself, sir, to look beyond the Union, to see what might lie hidden in the dark recess behind. I have not coolly weighed the chances of preserving liberty when the bonds that unite us together shall be broken asunder. I have not accustomed myself to hang over the precipice of disunion, to see whether, with my short sight, I can fathom the depth of the abyss below. . . . Liberty and Union, now and for ever, one and inseparable!"

—from *The Writings and Speeches of Daniel Webster*

Jackson Defends the Union

Several months after the Webster-Hayne debate, President Jackson let everyone know his position on the issue. During a political dinner, Jackson stood to make a toast. Looking directly at John Calhoun, he said, "Our federal Union—it must be preserved." Calhoun's hand shook, but he rose to counter with, "The Union—next to our liberty, most dear."

The war of words erupted into a full confrontation in 1832, when Congress passed yet another tariff law. At President Jackson's request, the new law cut tariffs significantly, but South Carolinians were not satisfied. The state legislature asked South Carolina voters to elect a special state convention. In November 1832 the convention adopted an ordinance of nullification declaring the tariffs of 1828 and 1832 to be unconstitutional.

Jackson considered the nullification ordinance an act of treason, and he sent a warship to Charleston. In 1833 Congress passed the **Force Bill,** authorizing the president to use the military to enforce acts of Congress. As tensions rose, Senator Henry Clay pushed through Congress a bill that would lower the nation's tariffs gradually until 1842. In response, South Carolina repealed its nullification of the tariff law. Both sides claimed victory, and the issue was laid to rest—at least temporarily.

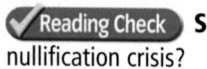 **Reading Check** **Summarizing** What caused the nullification crisis?

Policies Toward Native Americans

MAIN Idea During Andrew Jackson's administration Native American groups were forced to relocate onto western reservations.

HISTORY AND YOU Do you know a family that was forced to move from their home by the government? Read on to learn how Native Americans reacted to the Indian Removal Act.

Andrew Jackson's commitment to extending democracy did not benefit everyone. His attitude toward Native Americans reflected the views of many westerners at that time. Jackson had fought the Creek and Seminole people in Georgia and Florida, and in his inaugural address he declared his intention to move all Native Americans to the Great Plains.

This idea had been gaining support in the United States since the Louisiana Purchase. John C. Calhoun had formally proposed it in 1823, when he was secretary of war. Many Americans believed that the Great Plains was a wasteland that would never be settled. They thought that if they moved Native Americans to that region, the nation's conflict with them would be over. In 1830 Jackson pushed through Congress the **Indian Removal Act,** which provided money for relocating Native Americans.

Most Native Americans eventually gave in and resettled on the Great Plains, but not the Cherokee of Georgia. Over the years, this Native American group had adopted many aspects of white culture. The Cherokee had adopted a written language, drawn up a written constitution modeled on the United States Constitution, and sent many of their children to schools established by white missionaries.

The Cherokee hired lawyers to sue the state of Georgia in order to challenge the state's attempt to extend its authority over Cherokee lands. Their case, *Worcester* v. *Georgia*, eventually reached the Supreme Court. In 1832 Chief Justice John Marshall ordered state officials to honor Cherokee property rights. Jackson refused to support the decision. "Marshall has made his opinion," the president reportedly said, "now let him enforce it."

Most Cherokee resisted the government's offers of western land. Jackson's successor, Martin Van Buren, sent in the army to end the conflict in 1838. The army forced the remaining people from their homes and marched them to what is now Oklahoma. About 2,000 Cherokee died in camps while waiting for the relocation to begin. Roughly 2,000 more died of starvation, disease, and **exposure** on the journey, which became known as the **Trail of Tears.**

By 1838, most Native Americans living east of the Mississippi had been moved to reservations. Most American citizens supported the removal policies. Only a few denounced the harsh treatment of Native Americans. Nonsupporters included some National Republicans and a few religious denominations, especially the Quakers and Methodists.

✔ **Reading Check** **Interpreting** What was the Trail of Tears?

Jackson Battles the National Bank

MAIN Idea Jackson deliberately destroyed the national bank; his opponents formed a new political party.

HISTORY AND YOU Do you know of any political parties other than the Democratic and Republican parties? Read how the Whigs fared in the 1836 presidential election.

One of the biggest controversies of Jackson's presidency was his campaign against the Second Bank of the United States. Like most Westerners, and many working people in the East, Jackson regarded the Bank as a monopoly that benefited the wealthy elite.

NATIONAL GEOGRAPHIC **Effects of the Indian Removal Act, 1831–1842**

In 1832 Sauk and Fox warriors led by Chief Black Hawk fought to reclaim territory east of the Mississippi River, but were defeated.

▲ Cherokee travel the Trail of Tears.

The Cherokee took their refusal to move to the Supreme Court—and won. Federal troops forced them to leave in 1838.

Chief Osceola led the Seminole in rebellion.

Multigroup removal route
Trail of Tears
■ Fort
— 1840 border

0   400 kilometers
0   400 miles
Albers Equal-Area projection

Analyzing GEOGRAPHY

1. **Interpreting** Name two Native American groups in the northern half of the United States that were forced to relocate.

2. **Locating** Where did the Trail of Tears end?

Maps In MOtion *See StudentWorks™ Plus* **or** glencoe.com.

▲ Democrats Andrew Jackson, Thomas Hart Benton, and Martin Van Buren are depicted as quack doctors trying to cure Uncle Sam of his economic ills. Uncle Sam complains that their remedies are making him worse.

▲ Jackson holds up an order removing federal deposits from the National Bank. The Bank begins to collapse. The tiny figures scurrying away are newspaper publishers, bankers, and other Bank supporters.

Analyzing VISUALS

1. **Interpreting Points of View** Which cartoon is pro-Jackson? Why do you think so?

2. **Analyzing** What does the artist of the cartoon on the left think of Jackson and the Democrats' plans for the bank?

Despite its reputation, the Bank played an important role in keeping the money supply of the United States stable. At the time, most paper money consisted of bank notes issued by private state banks. State banks promised that the notes could always be turned in for "hard" money—gold or silver coins. The state banks, however, would often issue more paper money than they could redeem in gold or silver. This allowed them to make more loans at lower interest rates, but it created the danger of inflation—that money might lose its value.

To prevent the state banks from lending too much money, the Bank of the United States regularly collected bank notes and asked state banks to redeem them for gold and silver. This action forced state banks to be careful about how much money they loaned, and it also limited inflation.

Many western settlers, who needed easy credit to run their farms, were unhappy with the Bank's policies. President Jackson also believed the Bank to be unconstitutional, despite the Supreme Court's ruling in *McCulloch v. Maryland.*

To make the Bank an issue in the 1832 election, Jackson's opponents in Congress introduced a bill extending the Bank's charter for another 20 years. Congress passed the bill, but Jackson vetoed it. It quickly became clear that most Americans supported Jackson as he easily went on to win a second term.

Jackson took his reelection as a directive from the people to destroy the Bank at once, even though its charter did not run out until 1836. He removed the government's deposits from the Bank and placed them in state banks. The removal of the deposits greatly weakened the bank, leading to a slow death. Jackson had won a major political victory by attacking the Bank. Later, however, critics would charge that destroying the Bank contributed significantly to the financial woes that plagued the country in the years ahead.

Andrew Jackson's forceful style earned him plenty of detractors, and by the mid-1830s a new party had emerged to oppose him. The group named itself the Whigs after the party in England that had worked to limit the king's power. The Whigs advocated a stronger federal government and support for industrial and commercial development. Jackson's Democrats, on the other hand, continued to favor a limited federal government.

Martin Van Buren

The Whigs were united in opposing Jackson, but they were unable to settle on a leader. During the 1836 presidential election, Jackson's popularity and the nation's continuing prosperity helped Democrat Martin Van Buren defeat the Whigs, who ran three candidates for president.

The new president had little time to savor his victory. Shortly after Van Buren took office, a crippling economic crisis hit the nation. During this **Panic of 1837,** as the crisis was called, many banks and businesses failed. Thousands of farmers lost their land, and unemployment soared among eastern factory workers. Van Buren, a firm believer in his party's philosophy of a limited federal government, did little to ease the crisis.

"Tippecanoe and Tyler Too"

With the nation experiencing hard times, the Whigs looked forward to ousting the Democrats in the presidential election of 1840. They nominated General William Henry Harrison, who was regarded as a hero for his role in the Battle of Tippecanoe and in the War of 1812. John Tyler, a Southerner and former Democrat who had left his party in protest over the nullification issue, joined the ticket as the vice presidential candidate. Adopting the campaign slogan "Tippecanoe and Tyler too," the Whigs blamed Van Buren for the economic depression and presented Harrison, a man born to wealth and privilege, as a simple frontiersman.

The strategy worked. Harrison won a decisive victory—234 electoral votes to 60, although the popular vote was much closer. On March 4, 1841, Harrison delivered his inauguration speech. The weather that day was bitterly cold, but Harrison insisted on delivering his nearly two-hour address without a hat or coat. He came down with pneumonia and died 32 days later, thereby serving the shortest term of any American president. Vice President John Tyler then became president.

Tyler's rise to the presidency shocked Whig leaders. Tyler actually opposed many Whig policies, and party leaders had placed him on the ticket mainly to attract Southern voters. The Whigs in Congress tried to push through their agenda anyway, including a Third Bank of the United States and a higher tariff, but Tyler sided with the Democrats on these key issues.

Foreign relations occupied the country's attention during much of Tyler's administration, especially relations with Great Britain. Disputes over the Maine-Canadian border, and other issues, resulted in the 1842 Webster-Ashburton Treaty, which established the border between the United States and Canada from Maine to Minnesota.

✓ **Reading Check** **Identifying** What new political party won the presidential election of 1840?

Section 1 REVIEW

Vocabulary

1. **Explain** the significance of: suffrage, spoils system, caucus system, Tariff of Abominations, secede, Daniel Webster, Force Bill, Indian Removal Act, Trail of Tears, Panic of 1837.

Main Ideas

2. **Explaining** Why did President Jackson support the spoils system?

3. **Describing** How was the nullification crisis resolved?

4. **Summarizing** How did the system of checks and balances in the federal government fail during the struggle over the Indian Removal Act?

5. **Organizing** Use a graphic organizer, similar to the one below, to list the policies of the Whigs and Jacksonian Democrats.

Party	Policies
Whigs	
Democrats	

Critical Thinking

6. **Big Ideas** In what ways did the United States become more democratic during Jackson's administration?

7. **Analyzing Visuals** Study the circle graphs on page 223. How much had voter participation increased in 1828 over 1824?

Writing About History

8. **Persuasive Writing** Suppose that you are a Native American living in the United States during Andrew Jackson's presidency. Write an essay giving your opinion of the Indian Removal Act.

History ONLINE

Study Central™ To review this section, go to glencoe.com and click on Study Central.

Section 2

A Changing Culture

Guide to Reading

Big Ideas
Group Action The Second Great Awakening increased membership in many religious groups in the United States.

Content Vocabulary
- nativism *(p. 232)*
- utopia *(p. 234)*
- romanticism *(p. 234)*
- transcendentalism *(p. 234)*

Academic Vocabulary
- predominantly *(p. 232)*
- philosopher *(p. 234)*

People and Events to Identify
- Know-Nothings *(p. 232)*
- Second Great Awakening *(p. 232)*
- Charles Grandison Finney *(p. 233)*
- Joseph Smith *(p. 233)*

Reading Strategy
Categorizing Complete a graphic organizer, similar to the one below, by listing the beliefs of religious groups during the Second Great Awakening.

Religious Groups	Beliefs

NEW YORK CORE CURRICULUM
U.S. History and Government

Unit 2:
II.B.c Foreign immigration and nativist reactions (Jews; Irish mass starvation, 1845–1850; Germans; 1848 refugees; Know-Nothings)

Between 1815 and 1860, over 5 million immigrants arrived in the United States. Most of these newcomers found opportunity and a fresh start, but some also found discrimination and prejudice. At the same time, a new religious movement began to change American society.

The New Wave of Immigrants

MAIN Idea In the early 1800s, millions of Irish and Germans immigrated to the United States. The many Catholics among them encountered religious prejudice.

HISTORY AND YOU Recall what you may have read about conflicts between Protestants and Catholics in Europe. During the 1800s, many Protestant Americans disliked the large numbers of Catholics coming into the country. Read on to learn about nativism in the early 1800s in the United States.

In June 1850 Daniel Guiney decided to leave his impoverished town in Ireland and move to the United States. Ireland was suffering a devastating famine. Tens of thousands of citizens were dying of starvation, while many more were fleeing the country. By August, Guiney had moved to Buffalo, New York. After settling in, Guiney wrote home about the wondrous land where he now resided:

PRIMARY SOURCE

"We mean to let you know our situation at present. . . . We arrived here about five o'clock in the afternoon of yesterday, fourteen of us together, where we were received with the greatest kindness of respectability. . . . When we came to the house we could not state to you how we were treated. We had potatoes, meat, butter, bread, and tea for dinner. . . . If you were to see Denis Reen when Daniel Danihy dressed him with clothes suitable for this country, you would think him to be a boss or steward, so that we have scarcely words to state to you how happy we felt at present."

—from *Out of Ireland*

Daniel Guiney was just one of the millions of immigrants who came to the United States in search of a better life in the mid-1800s. Between 1815 and 1860, the United States experienced a massive influx of immigrants, mostly from Europe. Many had fled violence and political turmoil at home, while others sought to escape starvation and poverty. Although immigrants provided a large source of labor for America's industries, many citizens feared the influence of so many foreigners.

PRIMARY SOURCE
The Irish Famine and Immigration to America

Irish Population Decline, 1841–1851

ATLANTIC OCEAN

Irish Sea

◇ Dublin

- 30% & over
- 25% to 29%
- 15% to 24%
- 0% to 14%
- Population rise

▲ Starving peasants try to break into a workhouse during the Great Irish Famine of 1846-47.

Irish Immigration to the U.S., 1830–1860

Immigrants (thousands) — Year

Source: *Historical Statistics of the United States: Colonial Times to 1970.*

Analyzing VISUALS

1. **Interpreting** In what year did Irish immigration to the United States peak? Why might it have declined afterward?

2. **Explaining** What was the main pull factor that brought Irish immigrants to the United States?

▲ Irish immigrants arrive in New York in 1847. Economic opportunities brought the Irish to America. Irish men worked in factories, helped build railroads, and took part in other construction projects. Irish women took jobs in factories and as domestic servants in the homes of the growing middle and upper classes.

Germans and Irish Arrive

The largest wave of immigrants, almost two million, came from Ireland. The Irish were fleeing a famine that began in 1845, when a fungus destroyed much of the nation's potato crop—a mainstay of the Irish diet. Most Irish immigrants arrived with no money and few skills. They generally settled in the industrialized cities of the Northeast, where many worked as unskilled laborers and servants.

Germans were the second-largest group of immigrants to arrive. At the time, Germany was divided into many states and, in 1848, revolutionaries across Germany tried and failed to impose reforms. The ensuing violence and repression convinced many Germans to emigrate. By 1860, over 1.5 million had arrived in the United States. Most had enough money to buy land and settle in Ohio and Pennsylvania, where they became farmers or went into business.

Nativism

While immigrants often found a new sense of freedom in the United States, some encountered discrimination. The presence of people from different cultures, with different languages and different religions, produced feelings of **nativism,** or hostility toward foreigners.

In the 1800s, many Americans were anti-Catholic. Many Protestant ministers preached anti-Catholic sermons and, occasionally, anti-Catholic riots erupted. The arrival of millions of **predominantly** Catholic Irish and German immigrants led to the rise of several nativist groups, such as the Supreme Order of the Star-Spangled Banner, founded in 1849. These groups pledged never to vote for a Catholic and pushed for laws banning immigrants and Catholics from holding public office. In July 1854 delegates from these groups formed the American Party. Membership in the party was secret, and those questioned about it were obliged to answer, "I know nothing." The **Know-Nothings,** as the party was nicknamed, built a large following in the 1850s.

✔ Reading Check **Analyzing** Why did nativism become so strong in the mid-1800s?

A Religious Revival

MAIN Idea During the Second Great Awakening, many revivals were held, and new religious denominations formed.

HISTORY AND YOU Have you ever been inspired by a gifted speaker? Read on to learn how ministers used emotional sermons to reach their audiences.

While immigrants added to the diversity of society, Americans were transforming society in their own ways. One important change occurred in religious life, where Protestantism experienced a dramatic revival, and new forms of worship emerged.

The Second Great Awakening

By the end of the 1700s, many church leaders had grown concerned that Americans' commitment to the Christian faith was weakening. In the early 1800s, ministers began an effort to revive people's commitment to religion. The resulting movement came to be called the **Second Great Awakening.** It began in Kentucky among frontier farmers and spread to the rest of the country. Leaders of various Protestant denominations—most

PRIMARY SOURCE
The Second Great Awakening

▲ *Charles Grandison Finney (above) was a founder of modern revivalism. Finney's emotional sermons helped launch the Second Great Awakening, which was spread across the nation at outdoor camp meetings (left).*

often Methodists, Baptists, and Presbyterians—held camp meetings that attracted thousands of followers for several days of song, prayer, and emotional outpourings of faith.

The basic message of the Second Great Awakening was that individuals must re-admit God and Christ into their daily lives. The new revivalism rejected the traditional Calvinist idea that only a chosen few were predestined for salvation. Instead, ministers preached that all people could attain grace through faith.

One of the most prominent advocates of this new message was a Presbyterian minister named **Charles Grandison Finney.** Finney preached that each person contained within himself or herself the capacity for spiritual rebirth and salvation. Finney helped found modern revivalism. His camp meetings were carefully planned and rehearsed to create as much emotion as possible. He compared his methods to those used by politicians and sales-people, and he used emotion to focus people's attention on his message.

Finney began preaching in upstate New York, where he launched a series of revivals in towns along the Erie Canal. He then took his message to the cities of the Northeast. Finney warned against using politics to change soci-ety. He believed that if Christian ideas reformed people from within, society would become better, but if people remained selfish and immoral, political reforms would not make any difference.

New Religious Groups

A number of new religious groups also emerged during the Second Great Awakening. Many Americans were looking for spiritual answers to the problems in their lives but chose to look to new religious ideas rather than return to traditional Protestant beliefs.

Unitarians and Universalists Two groups that grew rapidly in the 1830s were the Unitarians and Universalists. Unitarians reject the idea that Jesus was the son of God, arguing instead that he was a great teacher. Their name comes from the belief that God is a unity, rather than a trinity of Father, Son, and Holy Spirit. Universalists believe in the universal salvation of souls. They reject the idea of hell and believe that God intends to save everyone.

The Mormons Another group that began during this period was the Church of Jesus Christ of Latter-day Saints, whose followers are commonly known as Mormons. **Joseph Smith,** a New Englander living in western New York, began preaching Mormon ideas in 1830 after claiming to have been called to restore the Christian church to its original form. Smith published *The Book of Mormon* in that year, saying it was a translation of words inscribed on golden plates he had received from an angel. The text told of the coming of God and the need to build a king-dom on Earth. Smith made hundreds of con-verts across New England and the Midwest.

After enduring harassment in Ohio, Missouri, and elsewhere, Mormons moved to Commerce, Illinois, in 1839. They bought the town and renamed it Nauvoo. The group prospered in the Midwest, and Nauvoo grew to about 15,000 by 1844. Persecution contin-ued, however, and that same year local resi-dents murdered Smith. Brigham Young then became the leader of the Church. The Mormons left Illinois and headed west to Utah Territory, where they established permanent roots.

▲ Finney's success enabled him to build the Broadway Tabernacle in New York City. The church opened in 1836 and held 2,400 people.

Analyzing VISUALS

1. **Interpreting** Study the picture on page 232. How is the audience reacting?

2. **Theorizing** Why do you think revivalism was effective in spreading Christian ideas?

Utopian Communities

For an excerpt of Emerson's writing, see pages R66–67 in **American Literature Library.**

Some Americans in the 1830s concluded that society had corrupted human nature. They decided that the solution was to separate from society and form a **utopia,** or ideal society. Cooperative living and the absence of private property characterized these communities. Perhaps the best known were Brook Farm, a cooperative community in Massachusetts, and the Oneida Community, a religious society in upstate New York.

The Shakers were a religious group that established utopian communities. The group got its name from a ritual "shaking" dance its members performed. The society believed in social and spiritual equality for all of its members. The first Shaker communities had been founded in the 1780s. They peaked with some 6,000 members before their numbers began to decline. Since they did not believe in marrying or having children, the group could only expand by making converts.

Reading Check **Summarizing** What was the basic message of the Second Great Awakening?

Cultural Renaissance

MAIN Idea Nationalism and sectionalism gave rise to a creative period for American writers and artists.

HISTORY AND YOU Do you read a newspaper regularly? Read on to learn how the "penny press" made newspapers affordable for average people.

The optimism of the Second Great Awakening also influenced **philosophers** and writers. Many leading thinkers of the day adopted the tenets of **romanticism,** a movement that began in Europe in the late 1700s. Romanticism advocated feeling over reason, inner spirituality over external rules, the individual above society, and nature over environments created by humans.

One notable expression of American romanticism came from New England writers and philosophers, who were known as the transcendentalists. **Transcendentalism** urged people to transcend, or overcome, the limits of their minds and let their souls reach out to embrace the beauty of the universe.

People IN HISTORY

Henry David Thoreau
1817–1862

One of America's most admired thinkers, Henry David Thoreau lived in Concord, Massachusetts, and became a protégé of transcendentalist Ralph Waldo Emerson. Thoreau is particularly famous for his experiment in living the transcendentalist life. In one of his most popular works, *Walden*, he recounts his feelings and experiences during a two-year period in which he lived in a shack by Walden Pond outside Concord.

He said of his stay there, "I went to the woods because I wished to live deliberately, to front only the essential facts of life, and see if I could not learn what it had to teach, and not, when I came to die, discover that I had not lived."

In 1849 Thoreau published "Civil Disobedience." In this influential essay, he discussed issues of personal conscience versus the demands of the government. Thoreau was inspired to write the essay after he spent a night in jail for refusing to pay a tax. He felt the tax supported an immoral government that condoned slavery and was fighting what he believed was an imperialist war with Mexico. The ideas in "Civil Disobedience" would influence future civil rights leaders, such as Mahatma Gandhi and Martin Luther King, Jr.

How did Thoreau's purpose for living on Walden Pond reflect transcendentalist ideas?

Margaret Fuller
1810–1850

As a young woman, Margaret Fuller was another member of the prominent group of New England writers and philosophers who developed transcendentalism. In 1840, with the help of Ralph Waldo Emerson, she founded the magazine *The Dial,* in which she published writings of the transcendentalist movement.

Fuller also organized groups of Boston women to promote their educational and intellectual development. These meetings convinced her to write the book *Women in the Nineteenth Century,* in which she argued that women deserve equal political rights.

Fuller's success in editing *The Dial* caught the eye of Horace Greeley, the famous editor of the *New York Tribune,* and in 1844 he hired Fuller to be the *Tribune's* literary critic. In 1846 Greeley sent Fuller to Europe to cover reform efforts there. While in Italy, Fuller married Giovanni Angelo Ossoli, a revolutionary fighting to unite Italy. Fuller sent home reports about the Italian revolution of 1848, becoming the first American woman foreign-war correspondent. Tragically, in 1850, on a trip to the United States, Fuller, Ossoli, and their young son were drowned when their ship sank as it approached New York.

How was Fuller unusual among the women of her time?

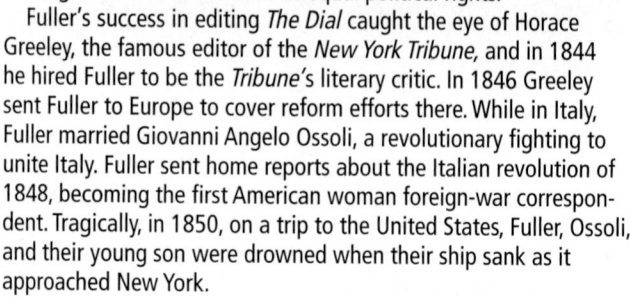

American Writers Emerge

The most influential transcendentalist was Ralph Waldo Emerson. In his 1836 essay "Nature," Emerson wrote that those who wanted fulfillment should try to commune with nature. Emerson influenced other writers, including Margaret Fuller and Henry David Thoreau. Thoreau believed that individuals must fight the pressure to conform. "If a man does not keep pace with his companions, perhaps it is because he hears a different drummer," he wrote. "Let him step to the music which he hears, however measured or far away."

Emerson and Thoreau were only two of many writers who set out to create uniquely American works. Washington Irving, famous for writing "The Legend of Sleepy Hollow" (1819), became the first internationally prominent American writer. James Fenimore Cooper romanticized Native Americans and frontier explorers in his Leatherstocking Tales, the most famous being *The Last of the Mohicans* (1826). Nathaniel Hawthorne, a New England customs official and resident of Brook Farm, wrote more than 100 short stories and novels. His novel *The Scarlet Letter* (1850), with its Puritan setting, explored the persecution and psychological suffering that may result from sin. Herman Melville, another New Englander, wrote the great *Moby Dick* (1851). Edgar Allan Poe, a poet and short story writer, achieved fame as a writer of terror and mystery. Perhaps the era's most important poet was Walt Whitman, who published *Leaves of Grass* in 1855. Whitman loved nature, the common people, and American democracy, and his famous work reflects these passions. Another major poet of the era, Emily Dickinson, wrote unconventional, mystical, and deeply personal works.

The Penny Press

Another important development of the early 1800s was the rise of the mass distribution newspaper. Before the 1800s, most newspapers catered to well-educated readers. They were typically published once a week and cost around six cents—too much for the average worker.

As more Americans learned to read and gained the right to vote, publishers began producing inexpensive newspapers, known as penny papers, which provided the kind of content most people wanted. Reports of fires, crimes, marriages, gossip, politics, and other local news made the papers an instant success with a mass audience.

General interest magazines that catered to a more specialized readership also emerged around this time. In 1830 Louis A. Godey founded *Godey's Lady's Book,* the first American magazine for women. The poet James Russell Lowell launched *Atlantic Monthly,* another magazine for the well educated, in 1857, while *Harper's Weekly* covered everything from book reviews to news reports.

Reading Check **Evaluating** What were the main themes of American writers in the early 1800s?

Vocabulary

1. **Explain** the significance of: nativism, Know-Nothings, Second Great Awakening, Charles Grandison Finney, Joseph Smith, utopia, romanticism, transcendentalism.

Main Ideas

2. **Explaining** What pushed Irish and German people to immigrate to the United States in the mid-1800s?

3. **Specifying** What new religious group formed in the 1830s?

4. **Identifying** What was the penny press?

Critical Thinking

5. **Big Ideas** Which religious denominations increased their influence in the Second Great Awakening?

6. **Organizing** Use a graphic organizer, similar to the one below, to list American cultural movements in the mid-1800s.

Movements in American Culture in the Mid-1800s

7. **Analyzing Visuals** Study the map on page 231. What level of population decrease did most of Ireland experience?

Writing About History

8. **Expository Writing** Suppose you are an Irish or German immigrant to the United States in the mid-1800s. Write an article to be published in your home country that contrasts your new life in the United States with how your life was in your home country.

History ONLINE

Study Central™ To review this section, go to glencoe.com and click on Study Central.

Section 3

Reforming Society

Guide to Reading

Big Ideas
Past and Present Reform movements sought to change American society in ways that upheld American values and ideals.

Content Vocabulary
• benevolent society (p. 237)
• temperance (p. 238)
• penitentiary (p. 238)

Academic Vocabulary
• institution (p. 236)
• imposition (p. 238)

People and Events to Identify
• Dorothea Dix (p. 236)
• Lyman Beecher (p. 236)
• Horace Mann (p. 238)
• Elizabeth Cady Stanton (p. 241)
• Seneca Falls Convention (p. 241)

Reading Strategy
Organizing Use the major headings in Section 3 to create an outline, similar to the one below, about American reform efforts in the first half of the nineteenth century.

Reforming Society
I. The Reform Spirit
   A.
   B.
   C.
   D.
II.

NEW YORK CORE CURRICULUM
U.S. History and Government

Unit 2:
II.B.2.d The birth of the American reform tradition (religious and secular roots; public schools; care for the physically disabled and the mentally ill; the problems of poverty and crime; antislavery; women's rights movement)

The Second Great Awakening created an environment for social change. Spurred on by this revival of religion, as well as a heightened belief in the power of individuals to improve society and themselves, Americans engaged in reform movements.

The Reform Spirit

MAIN Idea Inspired by the Second Great Awakening, reformers tried to tackle many problems in society.

HISTORY AND YOU Identify a local, national, or world issue that you believe citizens and lawmakers need to address. Why is this issue important to you? Read on to learn about reformers during the mid-1800s.

In 1841 a clergyman asked schoolteacher **Dorothea Dix** to lead a Sunday school class at a local prison. What Dix saw there appalled her. Mentally ill persons lay neglected in dirty, unheated rooms. Putting aside her teaching career, she began a crusade to improve conditions for the mentally ill and to provide them with the facilities and treatment they needed.

In 1843 Dix composed a letter to the Massachusetts legislature, calling for a new approach to mental illness. She gave the history of a local woman as evidence that more humane treatment might help many of the mentally ill: "Some may say these things cannot be remedied . . . I know they can. . . . A young woman, a pauper . . . was for years a raging maniac. A cage, chains, and the whip were the agents for controlling her, united with harsh tones and profane language." Dix explained that a local couple took the woman in and treated her with care and respect. "They are careful of her diet. They keep her very clean. She calls them 'father' and 'mother.' Go there now, and you will find her 'clothed,' and though not perfectly in her 'right mind,' so far restored as to be a safe and comfortable inmate."

Largely through the efforts of Dorothea Dix, more than a dozen states enacted sweeping prison reforms that created special **institutions,** often referred to as asylums, for the mentally ill. As influential as she was, Dix was just one of many citizens who worked to reform various aspects of American society in the mid 1800s.

The reform movements of the mid-1800s stemmed in large part from the revival of religious fervor. Revivalists preached the power of individuals to improve themselves and the world. **Lyman Beecher,** a prominent minister, insisted that it was the nation's citizenry, more than its government, that should take charge of building a better society. True reform, he said, could take place only through "the voluntary energies of the nation itself."

The Beechers: A Family of Reformers

Henry Ward Beecher supported abolition-ist causes before the Civil War. After-ward, he became one of the best known ministers of the late 1800s.

Edward and Charles Beecher became ministers and were active in the abolitionist movement. Edward founded the first antislavery society in Illinois.

Harriet Beecher Stowe was the author of *Uncle Tom's Cabin*—a novel that greatly helped the abolitionist cause.

Isabella Beecher was a leader of the woman suffrage move-ment. She founded the Con-necticut Woman Suffrage Association and lobbied the Connecticut legislature to give women the same property rights as their husbands.

Catharine Beecher was a leader in the education reform movement who worked to increase women's access to higher education.

Lyman Beecher, father of the family, was one of the nation's best known preachers. He helped trigger the Second Great Awakening and urged citizens to work to reform their society.

Analyzing VISUALS

1. **Describing** How did the Beecher family reflect the historical developments and social concerns of the 1800s?
2. **Specifying** What causes did the Beecher daughters support?

Under the guidance of Beecher and other religious leaders, associations known as **benevolent societies** sprang up in cities and towns across the country. At first, they focused on spreading the word of God and attempting to convert nonbelievers. Soon, however, they sought to combat a number of social problems.

One striking feature of the reform effort was the overwhelming presence of women. Young women in particular had joined the revivalist movement in much larger numbers than men. One reason was that many unmarried women with uncertain futures discovered in religion a foundation on which to build their lives.

As more women turned to the church, many also joined religious-based reform groups. These reform groups targeted aspects of American society they considered in dire need of change. Among these issues were excessive consumption of alcohol, prisons, and education.

The Temperance Movement

Many reformers argued that no behavior caused more crime, disorder, and poverty than the abuse of alcohol. Men who drank too much, they argued, spent their money on liquor rather than necessities for their families, and they sometimes abused their wives and children. While not everyone agreed, no one doubted that alcoholism was widespread in the early 1800s. In small towns throughout the West, citizens drank to ease the isolation and loneliness of rural life, while in the pubs and saloons in Eastern cities, drinking was the main leisure activity for many workers.

Although advocates of **temperance,** or moderation in the consumption of alcohol, had been active since the late 1700s, the new reformers energized the campaign. Across the country, temperance groups began preaching the evils of alcohol and persuading heavy drinkers to give up liquor. In 1833 several of the groups united to form the American Temperance Union.

Temperance societies also pushed for laws prohibiting the sale of liquor. In 1851 Maine passed the first state prohibition law, an example followed by a dozen other states by 1855. Other states passed "local option" laws, which allowed towns and villages to prohibit liquor sales within their boundaries.

Prison Reform

The spirit of reform also prompted some people to try to improve the prison system. Inmates of all kinds, from violent offenders to debtors and the mentally ill, were often indiscriminately crowded together in jails and prisons, which were literally holes in the ground in some cases. One jail in Connecticut, for example, was an abandoned mineshaft. Beginning around 1816, many states began building new facilities to provide a better environment for inmates.

Underlying the prison reform movement was a belief in rehabilitating prisoners rather than merely locking them up. Officials imposed rigid discipline to rid criminals of the "laxness" they believed had led them astray. Solitary confinement and the **imposition** of silence on work crews were meant to give prisoners the chance to meditate and think about their wrongdoing. The name of these new prisons, **penitentiaries,** expressed the idea that they were places where prisoners would work to achieve penitence, or remorse.

Educational Reform

In the early 1800s, many reformers sought to establish a system of public education—government-funded schools open to all citizens. The increase in the number of voters in the 1820s and 1830s and the arrival of millions of new immigrants convinced many people of the need for public education. Most American leaders and social reformers believed that a

Reforming Society, 1830–1860

Reformers of the mid-1800s saw it as their Christian duty to improve society. They wanted to alleviate suffering in society.

▲ Reformers in the 1800s pushed for more education for women. The Emerson School for Girls in Boston (above) was an early example of a girls' school.

democratic republic could only survive if the electorate was well educated.

Massachusetts legislator **Horace Mann** was a leader of the movement for public education. As president of the Massachusetts Senate, Mann pressed for more public education and helped create a state board of education in 1837. He then left the state senate to serve as secretary of the new board. During his 12 years in that post, he doubled teachers' salaries, opened 50 new high schools, and established training schools for teachers. Massachusetts quickly became a model for other states. As he wrote in one report, Mann was convinced the nation needed public education to survive:

PRIMARY SOURCE

"The establishment of a republican government, without well-appointed and efficient means for the universal education of the people, is the most rash and foolhardy experiment ever tried by man. . . . It may be an easy thing to make a republic, but it is a very laborious thing to make republicans; and woe to the republic that rests upon no better foundations than ignorance, selfishness and passion!"

—from "Report of the Massachusetts Board of Education," 1848

▲ Sing Sing prison, built in 1828 in New York, was an example of the new approach favored by reformers. This woodcut shows prisoners arriving at the dining room, marching in hand-on-shoulder lockstep. They were required to eat in silence.

▲ Temperance groups used images such as the one above, entitled "The Drunkard's Progress," to warn people about drinking. The image shows the progress from taking one drink to a ruined life of poverty and crime. Below, a wife and child weep at the loss of their husband and father.

Analyzing VISUALS

1. **Synthesizing** In the image of Sing Sing prison, how would you describe the environment? What was the goal of creating such a prison environment?

2. **Analyzing** From "The Drunkard's Progress," what indicates that women were often temperance supporters?

In 1852 Massachusetts passed the first mandatory school attendance law; New York passed a similar measure the next year. Reformers focused on creating elementary schools to teach all children the basics of reading, writing, and arithmetic, and to instill a work ethic. These schools were open to all and supported by local and state taxes and tuition.

By the 1850s, tax-supported elementary schools had gained widespread support in the northeastern states and had begun to spread to the rest of the country. Rural areas responded more slowly because children were needed to help with planting and harvesting for large portions of the year.

In the South, reformer Calvin Wiley played a similar role in North Carolina to that of Horace Mann in Massachusetts. In 1839 North Carolina began providing aid to local communities that established taxpayer-funded schools. Wiley traveled throughout the state, building support for public education. By 1860, about two-thirds of North Carolina's white children attended school for part of the year. The South as a whole responded less quickly, and only about one-third of white children were enrolled by 1860. African American children were excluded almost entirely.

Women's Education

When officials talked about educating voters, they had men in mind, as women were still not allowed to vote in the early 1800s. Nonetheless, women reformers, such as Catharine Beecher, seized the opportunity to push for more educational opportunities for girls and women.

Emma Willard, who founded a girls' school in Vermont in 1814, was another educational pioneer. Her school covered the usual subjects for young women, such as cooking and etiquette, but it also taught academic subjects, such as history, math, and literature, which were rarely taught to women. In 1837 another educator, Mary Lyon, opened Mount Holyoke Female Seminary in Massachusetts, the first institution of higher education for women only.

In 1849 new opportunities for higher education enabled Elizabeth Blackwell to become the first woman to earn a medical degree. In 1857 she founded the New York Infirmary for Women and Children—a hospital staffed entirely by women.

✓ Reading Check **Identifying** What three areas of social reform did reformers target?

The Early Women's Movement

MAIN Idea Women were generally expected to be homemakers and models for their children, but some began demanding greater rights.

HISTORY AND YOU How did you think the lives of women changed from the colonial period to the mid-1800s? Read on to learn about the early women's movement.

For the text of the Seneca Falls Declaration, see page R48 in **Documents in American History.**

In the early 1800s, the Industrial Revolution began to change the economic roles of men and women. In the 1700s, most economic activity took place in or near the home because most Americans lived and worked in a rural farm setting. Although husbands and wives had distinct chores, maintaining the farm was the focus of their efforts. By the mid-1800s, these circumstances had started to change, especially in the northeastern states. The development of factories and other work centers separated the home from the workplace. Men now often left home to go to work, while women tended the house and children. In time, this development led to the emergence of the first women's movement.

"True Womanhood"

As the nature of work changed, many Americans began to divide life into two spheres of activity—the home and the workplace. Many believed the home to be the proper sphere for women, partly because the outside world was seen as corrupt and dangerous, and partly because of popular ideas about the family.

The Christian revivalism of the 1820s and 1830s greatly influenced the American family. For many parents, raising children was treated as a solemn responsibility because it prepared young people for a disciplined Christian life.

PRIMARY SOURCE
The Seneca Falls Declaration

PRIMARY SOURCE

Declaration of Sentiments

". . . We hold these truths to be self-evident: that all men and women are created equal; that they are endowed by their Creator with certain inalienable rights. . . .

The history of mankind is a history of repeated injuries and usurpations on the part of man toward woman, having in direct object the establishment of an absolute tyranny over her. . . .

Resolutions

Resolved, That all laws which prevent woman from occupying such a station in society as her conscience shall dictate, or which place her in a position inferior to that of man, are contrary to the great precept of nature, and therefore of no force or authority.

Resolved, That woman is man's equal—was intended to be so by the Creator, and the highest good of the race demands that she should be recognized as such.

. . . *Resolved,* That it is the duty of women of this country to secure to themselves their sacred right to the elective franchise.

. . . *Resolved,* therefore, That, being invested by the Creator with the same capabilities, and the same consciousness of responsibility for their exercise, it is demonstrably the right and duty of woman, equally with man, to promote every righteous cause by every righteous means . . . both in private and in public, by writing and by speaking, by any instrumentalities proper to be used, and in any assemblies proper to be held. . . ."

—from The Seneca Falls Declaration

▲ Susan B. Anthony (left) and Elizabeth Cady Stanton (right) were two of the most prominent women's suffrage advocates. Stanton attended the Seneca Falls Convention that issued the Declaration of Sentiments.

DBQ Document-Based Questions

1. **Identifying** According to the third resolution, what is the duty of American women?

2. **Paraphrasing** What does the Declaration ask all women to do?

Women often were viewed as more moral and charitable than men, and they were expected to be models of piety and virtue to their children and husbands.

The idea that women should be homemakers and should take responsibility for developing their children's characters evolved into a set of ideas known as "true womanhood." Magazine articles and novels aimed at women reinforced the value of their role at home. In 1841 Catharine Beecher, a daughter of minister and reformer Lyman Beecher, wrote a book called *A Treatise on Domestic Economy.* The popular volume argued that women could find fulfillment at home and gave instruction on childcare, cooking, and health matters.

Women Seek Greater Rights

Many women did not believe the ideas of true womanhood were limiting. Instead, the new ideas implied that wives were now partners with their husbands and in some ways were morally superior to them. Women were held up as the conscience of the home and society.

The idea that women had an important role to play in building a virtuous home was soon extended to making society more virtuous. As women became involved in the great moral crusades of the era, some began to argue that they needed greater political rights to promote their ideas.

An advocate of this idea was Margaret Fuller. Fuller argued that every woman had her own relationship with God and needed "as a soul to live freely and unimpeded." She declared, "We would have every arbitrary barrier thrown down and every path laid open to women as freely as to men." Fuller believed that if men and women, whom she called the "two sides" of human nature, were treated equally, it would end injustice in society.

In 1848 Lucretia Mott and **Elizabeth Cady Stanton,** two women active in the antislavery movement, organized the **Seneca Falls Convention.** This gathering of women reformers marked the beginning of an organized women's movement. The convention issued a "Declaration of Sentiments and Resolutions" that began with words expanding the Declaration of Independence: "We hold these truths to be self-evident: that all men and women are created equal. . . ." Stanton shocked many of the women present by proposing that they focus on gaining the right to vote. Nevertheless, the Seneca Falls Convention is considered by many to be the unofficial beginning of the struggle for women's voting rights.

Throughout the 1850s, women continued to organize conventions to gain greater rights for themselves. The conventions did meet with some success. By 1860, for example, reformers had convinced 15 states to pass laws permitting married women to retain their property if their husbands died. Above all, these conventions drew attention to their cause and paved the way for a stronger women's movement to emerge after the Civil War.

Reading Check **Examining** What events of the mid-1800s sparked the first women's movement?

Section 3 REVIEW

Vocabulary

1. **Explain** the significance of: Dorothea Dix, Lyman Beecher, benevolent society, temperance, penitentiary, Horace Mann, Elizabeth Cady Stanton, Seneca Falls Convention.

Main Ideas

2. **Explaining** What principle was the basis for the drive for public education?

3. **Specifying** On what document did the Seneca Falls Convention base the "Declaration of Sentiments"?

Critical Thinking

4. **Big Ideas** How did the Second Great Awakening affect the reform movements of the mid-1800s?

5. **Organizing** Use a graphic organizer, similar to the one below, to list the major areas of reform in the mid-1800s.

Areas of Reform

6. **Analyzing Visuals** Study the photograph of the classroom on page 238. How is your classroom similar to or different from this one?

Writing About History

7. **Persuasive Writing** Think of one social reform that you believe is needed today. Write a letter to a legislator explaining why you believe the reform is needed and how it might be achieved. Give examples of specific problems in your community or state to support your argument.

History ONLINE

Study Central™ To review this section, go to glencoe.com and click on Study Central.

The Abolitionist Movement

Guide to Reading

Big Ideas
Individual Action Abolitionists challenged the morality and legality of slavery in the United States.

Content Vocabulary
- gradualism *(p. 242)*
- abolition *(p. 243)*
- emancipation *(p. 244)*

Academic Vocabulary
- compensate *(p. 242)*
- demonstration *(p. 245)*

People and Events to Identify
- American Colonization Society *(p. 243)*
- William Lloyd Garrison *(p. 244)*
- American Anti-Slavery Society *(p. 244)*
- Frederick Douglass *(p. 245)*
- Sojourner Truth *(p. 246)*

Reading Strategy
Sequencing Complete a time line similar to the one below to record early events of the abolitionist movement.

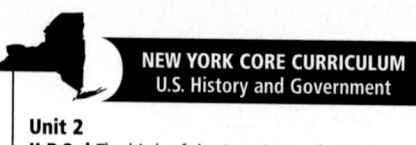

NEW YORK CORE CURRICULUM
U.S. History and Government

Unit 2
II.B.2.d The birth of the American reform tradition (religious and secular roots; public schools; care for the physically disabled and the mentally ill; the problems of poverty and crime; antislavery; women's rights movement)

In the early and mid-1800s, some Americans, mainly in the North, embarked on a crusade to abolish slavery in the United States. As the country became more polarized about the issue, the work of abolitionists created controversy and sometimes led to violence.

The New Abolitionists

MAIN Idea In the early years of the United States, some religious groups proposed ending slavery gradually, but by the 1830s, a new generation of abolitionists demanded an immediate end to slavery.

HISTORY AND YOU Have you ever tried to do something slowly to make it less difficult? Is it better to do something difficult quickly to get it over with? What is the best approach when the choice affects human lives? Read to learn about the different proposals for ending slavery.

In the 1830s a growing number of Americans had begun to demand an immediate end to slavery in the South. Of all the reform movements that began in the early 1800s, the movement to end slavery was the most divisive. By pitting North against South, it polarized the nation and helped bring about the Civil War.

Early Opposition to Slavery

From the earliest days of the Republic, many Americans had opposed slavery. Many of the country's founders knew that a nation based on the principles of liberty and equality would have difficulty remaining true to its ideals if it continued to enslave human beings. Quakers and Baptists in both the North and South had long argued that slavery was a sin. After the Revolution, Baptists in Virginia called for "every legal measure to [wipe out] this horrid evil from the land."

Gradualism Early antislavery societies generally supported an approach known as **gradualism,** or the belief that slavery had to be ended gradually. First they would stop slave traders from bringing new slaves into the country. Then they would phase out slavery in the North and the Upper South before finally ending slavery in the Lower South. Slaveholders would also be **compensated** for their loss. Supporters of gradualism believed it would give the South's economy time to adjust to the loss of enslaved labor.

Colonization The first antislavery societies also believed that ending slavery would not end racism in the United States. Many thought that the best solution was to send African Americans back to their ancestral homelands in Africa. In December 1816, antislavery reformers founded

Turning Point ▶

The Abolitionist Movement Begins

Since colonial times, many Americans had believed slavery was immoral. The Second Great Awakening and the general spirit of reform in the 1830s, however, created an environment in which abolitionism began to gain widespread support. William Lloyd Garrison sparked the movement by publishing the *Liberator*, through which he spread his ideas, and by founding the American Anti-Slavery Society. Garrison's energy, moral certitude, and strong rhetoric attracted fellow activists, as well as new converts, and gave the movement momentum on a national scale.

ANALYZING HISTORY How did William Lloyd Garrison start the abolitionist movement of the 1830s?

▲ William Lloyd Garrison, editor of the Liberator, supported the immediate abolition of slavery.

◀ The Philadelphia Anti-Slavery Society was one example of the abolitionist groups that formed in the North in the 1830s. Lucretia Mott, also a supporter of women's suffrage, is in the front row, second from right.

---

the **American Colonization Society** (ACS) to move African Americans to Africa. The society had the support of many prominent Americans, including James Madison, James Monroe, Henry Clay, Daniel Webster, and John Marshall.

By 1821 the ACS had acquired land in West Africa. The following year, free African Americans began boarding ships chartered by the society to take them to Africa. There they established a colony that eventually became the country of Liberia. It declared its independence as a republic in 1847 and adopted a constitution based on the U.S. Constitution. The capital, Monrovia, was named for President Monroe.

Colonization was never a realistic solution to racism. The cost of transportation to Africa was high, and the ACS had to depend on donations. Moving roughly 1.5 million African Americans from the United States to Africa was nearly impossible. Furthermore, most

African Americans regarded the United States as their home and did not want to move to another continent. Only an estimated 12,000 African Americans moved to Africa between 1821 and 1860.

Abolitionism

Gradualism and colonization remained the main goals of antislavery groups until the 1830s, when a new idea, **abolition,** began to gain ground. Abolitionists argued that enslaved African Americans should be freed immediately, without gradual measures or compensation to former slaveholders.

Abolitionism began to gain support in the 1830s for several reasons. As with other reform movements of the era, it drew its strength from the Second Great Awakening, with its focus on sin and repentance. In the eyes of abolitionists, slavery was an enormous evil for which the country needed to repent.

**History ONLINE
Student Web Activity** Visit glencoe.com and complete the activity on abolitionism.

The Abolitionist Movement

In the 1830s a vigorous movement to end slavery developed, mainly in the North. The abolitionist movement began a fight to end slavery.

▲ Minister Theodore Weld, his wife Angelina Grimké, and her sister Sarah were radical activists in the abolitionist movement. The Grimké sisters had grown up in the South and witnessed slavery firsthand. In the course of their activism, Angelina Grimké became the first woman to address the Massachusetts legislature. The three wrote regularly for abolitionist newspapers, such as the Liberator, and worked together on the influential book Slavery As It Is: Testimony of a Thousand Witnesses (1839).

◄ In 1850 a convention was held in Cazenovia, New York, to oppose the Fugitive Slave Law. Many abolitionist leaders attended. Frederick Douglass is seated left of the table; Theodore Weld is in front.

The first well-known advocate of abolition was a free African American from North Carolina named David Walker, who published *Appeal to the Colored Citizens of the World.* In this pamphlet, Walker advocated violence and rebellion as the only way to end slavery. Although Walker's ideas were influential, the rapid development of a large national abolitionist movement in the 1830s was largely due to the efforts of **William Lloyd Garrison.**

William Lloyd Garrison In 1829 Garrison became an assistant to Benjamin Lundy, the Quaker publisher of the Baltimore antislavery newspaper *Genius of Universal Emancipation.* Garrison admired Lundy but grew impatient with his gradualist approach. In 1831 Garrison moved to Boston where he founded the antislavery newspaper, the *Liberator.*

In the pages of the *Liberator,* Garrison published caustic attacks on slavery and called for an immediate end to it. He condemned colonization and attacked the Constitution because it did not ban slavery. To those who objected to his fiery language, he responded that the time for moderation was over:

PRIMARY SOURCE

"I am aware that many object to the severity of my language; but is there not cause for severity? I *will be* as harsh as truth and as uncompromising as justice. On this subject, I do not wish to think, or speak, or write, with moderation. No! No! Tell a man whose house is on fire, to give a moderate alarm; tell him to moderately rescue his wife from the hands of the ravisher; tell the mother to gradually [remove] her babe from the fire into which it has fallen—but urge me not to use moderation in a cause like the present. I am in earnest—I will not equivocate—I will not excuse—I will not retreat a single inch—AND I WILL BE HEARD."

—from the *Liberator,* January 1, 1831

In Garrison's opinion, the situation was clear: Slavery was immoral and slaveholders were evil. The only option was immediate and complete **emancipation,** or the freeing of all enslaved people. In 1833 Garrison founded the **American Anti-Slavery Society.** Membership grew quickly. By the mid-1830s, there were hundreds of society chapters, and by 1838, there were more than 1,350 chapters and over 250,000 members.

NARRATIVE
OF THE
LIFE
OF
FREDERICK DOUGLASS,
AS
AMERICAN SLAVE.

WRITTEN BY HIMSELF.

BOSTON:
PUBLISHED AT THE ANTI-SLAVERY OFFICE,
No. 25 Cornhill.
1845.

▲ Frederick Douglass was a powerful advocate for the abolitionist movement. His autobiography (above) helped build support for the abolition of slavery.

In 1852 abolitionist and former slave Frederick Douglass gave a speech at the Fourth of July celebration in Rochester, New York:

PRIMARY SOURCE

"What, to the American slave, is your 4th of July? I answer; a day that reveals to him, more than all other days in the year, the gross injustice and cruelty to which he is the constant victim. To him, your celebration is a sham; your boasted liberty, an unholy license; your national greatness, swelling vanity; your sounds of rejoicing are empty and heartless; . . . a thin veil to cover up crimes which would disgrace a nation of savages. There is not a nation on the earth guilty of practices more shocking and bloody than are the people of the United States, at this very hour."

—from *The Frederick Douglass Papers*

DBQ **Document-Based Questions**

1. **Making Inferences** Why do you think Douglass was invited to speak on the Fourth of July?

2. **Summarizing** How does Douglass characterize the Fourth of July celebrations from the viewpoint of an enslaved person?

Other Abolitionist Leaders Garrison was not the only leader of the abolitionist movement. Theodore Weld, a disciple of the evangelist Charles Grandison Finney, was one of the most effective leaders, recruiting and training many abolitionists for the American Anti-Slavery Society. Arthur and Lewis Tappan, two devout and wealthy brothers from New York City, helped to finance the movement. The orator Wendell Phillips, the poet John Greenleaf Whittier, and many others became active in the cause as well.

Many women also gave their efforts to the abolitionist movement. Prudence Crandall worked as a teacher and an abolitionist in Connecticut, and Lucretia Mott—the women's rights advocate—often spoke out in favor of abolitionism as well. Some Southern women also joined the crusade. Among the earliest were Sarah and Angelina Grimké, South Carolina sisters who moved north to work openly against slavery.

African American Abolitionists Not surprisingly, free African Americans played a prominent role in the abolitionist movement.

African Americans in the North, who numbered over 190,000 by 1850, endured much prejudice, but they cherished their freedom nonetheless. Even before Garrison launched his movement, African Americans had established at least 50 abolitionist societies in the North. When Garrison launched his newspaper, African Americans rushed to his support, not only buying the paper but also helping to sell it. Many began writing and speaking out against slavery and taking part in protests and **demonstrations**.

Frederick Douglass was one of the most prominent African Americans in the abolitionist movement. In 1838 Douglass had escaped from slavery in Maryland by posing as a free African American sailor. "I appear before the immense assembly this evening as a thief and a robber," he told one Massachusetts group in 1842. "I stole this head, these limbs, this body from my master, and ran off with them." Douglass published his own antislavery newspaper, the *North Star*, and wrote an autobiography, *Narrative of the Life of Frederick Douglass*, which quickly sold 4,500 copies after its publication in 1845.

Another important African American abolitionist was **Sojourner Truth.** She gained freedom in 1827 when New York freed all remaining enslaved people in the state. In the 1840s her antislavery speeches—eloquent, joyous, and deeply religious—drew huge crowds. Though lacking a formal education, Truth enthralled listeners with her folksy wit, engaging stories, contagious singing, and strong message:

PRIMARY SOURCE

"I have had five children and never could take one of them up and say, 'My child' or 'My children,' unless it was when no one could see me. . . . I was forty years a slave but I did not know how dear to me was my posterity."

—from the *Anti-Slavery Bugle*, 1856

✓**Reading Check** **Summarizing** How did William Lloyd Garrison work to end slavery?

The Response to Abolitionism

MAIN Idea Many people in both the North and the South opposed abolitionism for economic, political, and cultural reasons.

HISTORY AND YOU Would you be willing to go to jail to defend a principle? Read on to learn the risks taken by abolitionists to defend their position.

Abolitionism was a powerful force, and it provoked a powerful public response. In the North, citizens looked upon the abolitionist movement with views ranging from support to indifference to opposition. In the South, many residents feared that their entire way of life was under attack. They rushed to defend the institution of slavery, which they saw as the key to the region's economy.

POLITICAL CARTOONS   PRIMARY SOURCE
Should Slavery Be Abolished?

▲ This cartoon shows pro-slavery forces raiding a post office in Charleston, South Carolina, and destroying abolitionist materials, including copies of the Liberator. The reward sign refers to Arthur Tappan, president of the American Anti-Slavery Society.

▲ This cartoon, titled "Southern Ideas of Liberty," denounces southern attempts to suppress abolitionism. A judge with donkey ears and whip sits on bales of cotton with his feet on the Constitution and condemns an abolitionist to be lynched.

Analyzing VISUALS

1. **Identifying Points of View** In what region of the country do you think these cartoons were created? Why?
2. **Interpreting** How do these cartoons reflect the seriousness of sectional tensions?

Reaction in the North

While many Northerners disapproved of slavery, some opposed abolitionism even more. They viewed the movement as a threat to the existing social system. Some whites, including many prominent businesspeople, warned it would lead to war between the North and the South. Others feared it might create an influx of freed African Americans to the North, overwhelming the labor and housing markets. Many in the North also had no desire to see the South's economy crumble. If that happened, they might lose the money Southern planters owed to Northern banks, as well as the cotton that fed Northern textile mills.

Given such attitudes, it was not surprising that mobs in Northern cities also attacked abolitionists. A mob in Boston stoned and almost hanged Garrison, and Weld was frequently attacked following his public speeches. Arthur Tappan's home was sacked by a New York mob in 1834, and in 1837 abolitionist publisher Reverend Elijah P. Lovejoy was killed trying to protect his printing press. Yet Northerners also resented Southern slave-catchers, who kidnapped African American runaways in the North and hauled them back south. In response, several states in the North passed personal liberty laws restricting slave recapture.

Reaction in the South

To most Southerners, slavery was a "peculiar institution" vital to Southern life. While the North was building factories, the South remained agricultural, tied to cotton and the enslaved people who harvested it. Southerners responded to criticisms of slavery by defending the institution. South Carolina's governor called it a "national benefit," while Thomas Dew, a leading Southern academic, claimed that most slaves had no desire for freedom because of their close relationship with their slaveholders. "[T]hroughout the whole slaveholding country," he declared, "the slaves of good [slaveholders] are his warmest, most constant, and most devoted friends."

Eight months after Garrison first printed the *Liberator* in 1831, Nat Turner, an enslaved preacher, led a revolt that killed over 50 Virginians. Many Southerners thought papers like the *Liberator* sparked the rebellion. Garrison's paper did not even circulate in the South, but furious Southerners demanded the suppression of abolitionist material as a condition for remaining in the Union. Southern postal workers refused to deliver abolitionist newspapers. In 1836, under Southern pressure, the House of Representatives passed a gag rule providing that all abolitionist petitions be shelved without debate.

For all the uproar it caused, the abolitionist movement remained small. Few people accepted the idea that slavery should be immediately eliminated. The crusade that William Lloyd Garrison started, however, and that thousands of men and women struggled to keep alive, became a powerful reminder that the institution of slavery fundamentally divided the nation.

Reading Check **Evaluating** How did Northerners and Southerners view abolitionism differently?

Section 4 REVIEW

Vocabulary

1. **Explain** the significance of: gradualism, American Colonization Society, abolition, William Lloyd Garrison, emancipation, American Anti-Slavery Society, Frederick Douglass, Sojourner Truth.

Main Ideas

2. **Identifying** What were two early proposals for ending slavery in the early 1800s?

3. **Describing** How did Congress react to the growing conflict over slavery?

Critical Thinking

4. **Big Ideas** Which individuals helped to build support for abolition, and what did they do to gain that support?

5. **Organizing** Use a graphic organizer, similar to the one below, to list the reasons why many Northerners opposed extreme abolitionism.

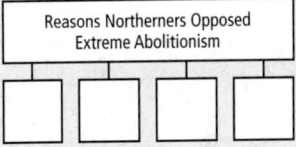

```
Reasons Northerners Opposed
Extreme Abolitionism
```

6. **Analyzing Visuals** Examine the cartoon on the left on page 246. What is the meaning of the judge having his feet on the Constitution?

Writing About History

7. **Descriptive Writing** Suppose you are writing for the *Liberator* in the 1830s. Write a letter to a friend describing what you hope to accomplish as a member of the staff of an abolitionist newspaper. Be sure to explain why you sought the job.

History ONLINE

Study Central™ To review this section, go to glencoe.com and click on Study Central.

Causes of Social Change and Reform in the 1830s and 1840s

Political Change

- States expand voting rights for white males by lowering or eliminating property qualifications.
- Andrew Jackson wins the presidency in the 1828 election.

Social Change

- Large numbers of Irish and German immigrants enter the United States.
- A religious revival—the Second Great Awakening—sweeps the country.
- New religious ideas and philosophies, such as romanticism, transcendentalism, and utopianism, gain support.
- Newspapers become cheap and are widely read, helping create a common popular culture.

▲ Painter George Caleb Bingham depicts the bustle and energy of a county election in the early 1800s. The painting shows that elections in America involved all social classes.

▲ An anti-Catholic mob battles militia during a riot in Philadelphia in 1844. Nativism became strong in the 1840s as people objected to the arrival of Irish Catholic immigrants.

▶ An abolitionist poster from 1835

Effects of Social Change and Reform in the 1830s and 1840s

Political Effects

- Andrew Jackson wins the presidency and supports the spoils system.
- Political parties begin using the convention to nominate candidates instead of the caucus system.
- Government becomes more responsive to public opinion.
- Jackson blocks South Carolina's attempts at nullification, pulls funds from the unpopular Bank of the United States, and supports the Indian Removal Act.
- Women begin demanding more political rights. Susan B. Anthony, Elizabeth Cady Stanton, and others organize the woman suffrage movement and issue the Declaration of Sentiments and Resolutions.

Social Effects

- Nativism gains support, leading to the creation of the anti-immigrant American Party—the "Know-Nothings."
- New American literature is written, including works by Emerson, Thoreau, Irving, Hawthorne, Melville, Poe, Whitman, and Dickinson.
- Religious enthusiasm helps trigger a series of new reform movements, including efforts to reform prisons, mental institutions, and schools, and to reduce the consumption of alcohol.
- Efforts to end slavery gradually and through colonization give way to a rising abolition movement led by William Lloyd Garrison, Frederick Douglass, and others.

NEW YORK REGENTS EXAM PRACTICE

TEST-TAKING TIP

Unless you are sure you know the answer, always try to narrow down answer choices to at least two before making a final selection.

Part I

Directions (1–11): For each statement or question, write on a separate sheet of paper the number of the word or expression that, of those given, best completes the statement or answers the question.

1 In 1828 passage of which legislation caused South Carolinians to threaten to secede from the Union?

(1) the Second Bank of the United States charter

(2) the Tariff of Abominations

(3) the Force Bill

(4) the Indian Removal Act

2 Which Whig presidential candidate won in 1840?

(1) William Henry Harrison

(2) John Tyler

(3) Andrew Jackson

(4) John C. Calhoun

3 The Know-Nothings developed in reaction to

(1) Jackson's push for expanded democracy.

(2) the Second Great Awakening.

(3) the transcendentalists.

(4) a huge influx of immigrants.

4 How did the teachings of the Second Great Awakening differ from earlier Protestant teachings?

(1) Its ministers preached that all people could attain salvation.

(2) Its ministers preached that God was a trinity.

(3) Its ministers preached that women could belong to the church.

(4) Its ministers preached the idea of nativism.

5 In the 1840s Dorothea Dix became the foremost reformer in the area of

(1) woman suffrage.

(2) temperance.

(3) mental illness.

(4) education.

6 At the Seneca Falls Convention in 1848, attendees were shocked when Elizabeth Cady Stanton

(1) wore pants to all the meetings.

(2) proposed that women seek the right to vote.

(3) insisted that African Americans be admitted.

(4) announced that she would run for Congress.

7 The goal of the American Colonization Society was to move

(1) all enslaved people to the West.

(2) free African Americans to West Africa.

(3) free Africans to Canada.

(4) formerly enslaved and free African Americans to the North.

8 Which of the following people were former slaves who fought hard for abolition in the mid-1800s?

(1) David Walker and Frederick Douglass

(2) Angelina Grimké and Sarah Grimké

(3) Sojourner Truth and Benjamin Lundy

(4) Frederick Douglass and Sojourner Truth

Need Extra Help?								
If You Missed Questions . . .	1	2	3	4	5	6	7	8
Go to Page . . .	225–226	229	232	232–234	236	240–241	243	245–246

[OVER]

Base your answer to question 9 on the chart below and your knowledge of Chapter 6.

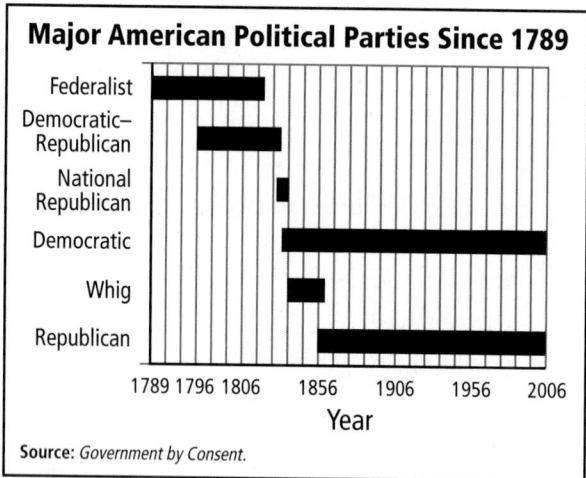

Major American Political Parties Since 1789

Federalist
Democratic–Republican
National Republican
Democratic
Whig
Republican

1789 1796 1806   1856   1906   1956   2006
Year

Source: *Government by Consent.*

9   What party shown had the shortest life span?

(1) Federalist

(2) Democratic-Republican

(3) Whig

(4) National Republican

10 Which party emerged to oppose Andrew Jackson and his policies?

(1) Democratic

(2) Federalist

(3) Whig

(4) Republican

11 One reason many Americans were in favor of the Indian Removal Act was that they

(1) thought the East had become too crowded.

(2) wanted remaining Native American lands in the Southeast.

(3) felt guilty about earlier treatment of Native Americans.

(4) wanted to expand democracy to include Native Americans.

Need Extra Help?

If You Missed Questions . . .	9	10	11
Go to Page . . .	250	228–229	226

Part II Thematic Essay Question

Directions: Write a well-organized essay that includes an introduction, several paragraphs addressing the task below, and a conclusion.

Theme: Romanticism, Transcendentalism, and Reform

In the 1800s, several important themes developed among America's writers and philosophers, including transcendentalism and romanticism, which influenced society.

Discuss how romanticism and transcendentalism affected the reforms of the time. Be sure to

• Define and explain romanticism and transcendentalism.

• Describe at least two reform movements that were influenced by these themes.

• Describe at least two effects of these themes on the movements you choose.

Guidelines:

In your essay, be sure to:

• Develop all aspects of the task

• Support the theme with relevant facts, examples, and details

• Use a logical and clear plan of organization, including an introduction and a conclusion that are beyond a restatement of the theme

Part III Document-Based Question

This question is based on the accompanying documents. It is designed to test your ability to work with historical documents. Some of the documents have been edited for the purposes of the question. As you analyze the documents, take into account the source of each document and any point of view that may be presented in the document.

Historical Context:

During the early and mid-1800s, a number of Americans participated in reform movements. These movements varied in their focus, but all shared the goal of improving society. However, not all people agreed with the reformers and their goals.

Task:
Using information from the documents and your knowledge of United States history, answer the questions that follow each document in Part A. Your answers to the questions will help you write the Part B essay in which you will be asked to

- Discuss the social conditions during the early and mid-1800s that spurred people to push for social change
- Discuss the viewpoints of those who were for and those who were against reform movements
- Evaluate the effects of these reform movements on Americans

Part A
Short-Answer Questions
Directions: Analyze the documents and answer the short-answer questions that follow each document on a separate sheet of paper.

Document 1

Source: Bernard F. Reilly, *American Political Prints, 1776–1876*

1 What does Jackson appear to be trampling underfoot?

Document 2

Common schools indeed! Money is very scarce, and the times are unusually hard. . . . Gentlemen, it appears to me that schools are sufficiently plenty, and that the people have no desire they should be increased. Those now in operation are not filled, and it is very doubtful if they are productive or of much real benefit. Would it not redound as much to the advantage of young persons, and to the honour of the State, if they should pass their days in the cotton patch, or at the plow, or in the cornfield, instead of being [confined] in a school house, where they are earning nothing?

Source: *Raleigh Register*, November 9, 1829

2 What reasons does the author give for opposing free public education?

Part B
Essay
Directions: Reread the text at the top left and write a well-organized essay that includes an introduction, several paragraphs, and a conclusion. Use evidence from the documents in your essay. Support your response with relevant facts, examples, and details. Include additional outside information.

Guidelines:
In your essay, be sure to:
- Develop all aspects of the task
- Incorporate information from the documents
- Incorporate relevant outside information
- Use a logical and clear plan of organization, including an introduction and a conclusion that are beyond a restatement of the theme

History ONLINE
For additional test practice, use Self-Check Quizzes—Chapter 6 at glencoe.com.

Need Extra Help?			
If You Missed Questions . . .	1	2	Essay
Go to Page . . .	R18	251	230–241

Manifest Destiny

1820–1848

SECTION 1 The Western Pioneers

SECTION 2 The Hispanic Southwest

SECTION 3 Independence for Texas

SECTION 4 The War With Mexico

Settlers head west in covered wagons, carrying all their belongings with them.

1836
- Texas wins independence from Mexico

Van Buren
1837–1841

1841
- President Harrison becomes first president to die in office

W. Harrison
1841

Tyler
1841–1845

U.S. PRESIDENTS

U.S. EVENTS

1836

1839

WORLD EVENTS

1842

1839
- First pedal-propelled bicycle is designed by Kirkpatrick MacMillan of Scotland

1842
- China cedes Hong Kong to Britain

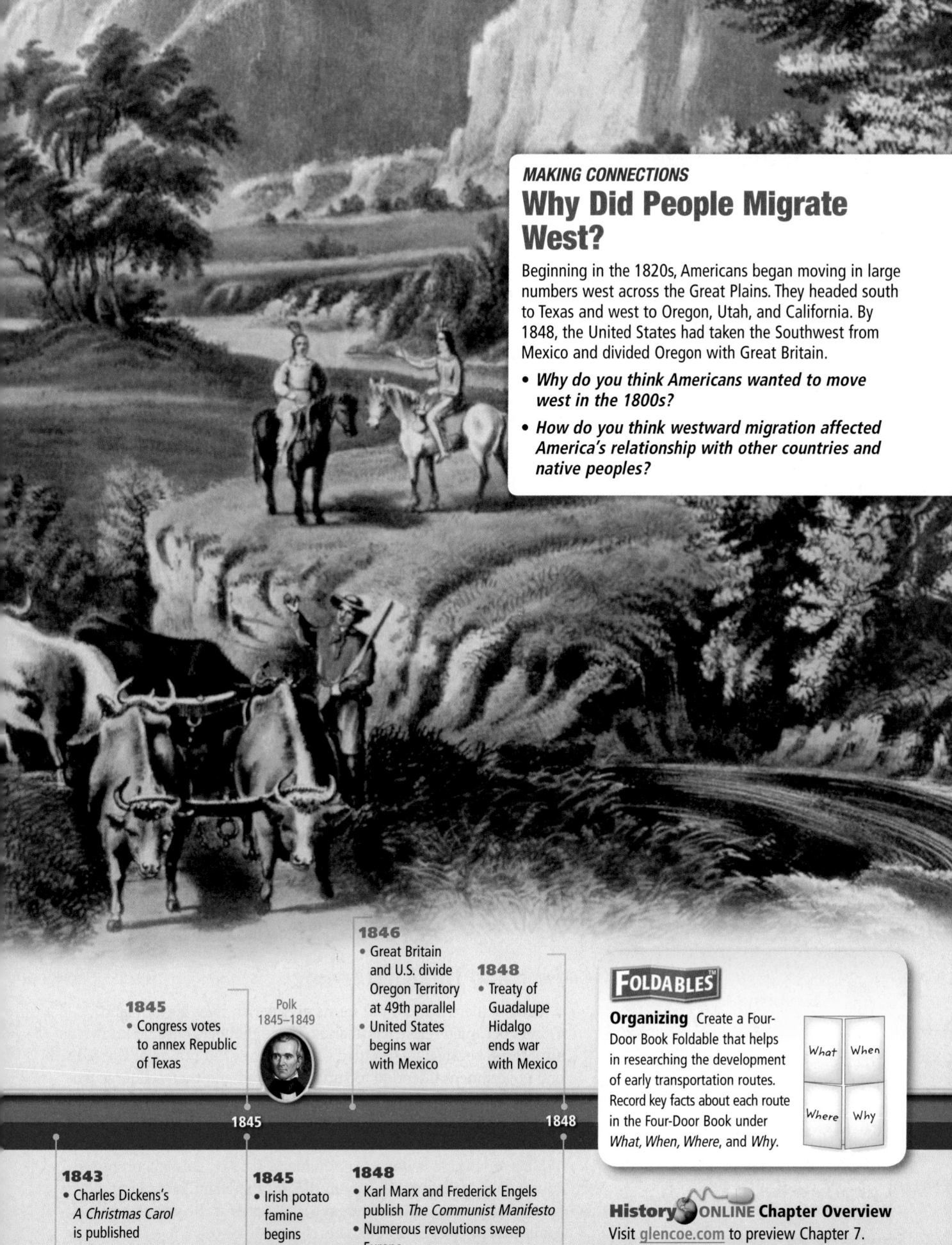

MAKING CONNECTIONS

Why Did People Migrate West?

Beginning in the 1820s, Americans began moving in large numbers west across the Great Plains. They headed south to Texas and west to Oregon, Utah, and California. By 1848, the United States had taken the Southwest from Mexico and divided Oregon with Great Britain.

- *Why do you think Americans wanted to move west in the 1800s?*

- *How do you think westward migration affected America's relationship with other countries and native peoples?*

1845
- Congress votes to annex Republic of Texas

Polk
1845–1849

1846
- Great Britain and U.S. divide Oregon Territory at 49th parallel
- United States begins war with Mexico

1848
- Treaty of Guadalupe Hidalgo ends war with Mexico

1845

1848

1843
- Charles Dickens's *A Christmas Carol* is published

1845
- Irish potato famine begins

1848
- Karl Marx and Frederick Engels publish *The Communist Manifesto*
- Numerous revolutions sweep Europe

FOLDABLES™

Organizing Create a Four-Door Book Foldable that helps in researching the development of early transportation routes. Record key facts about each route in the Four-Door Book under *What, When, Where,* and *Why.*

What | When
Where | Why

History ONLINE Chapter Overview
Visit glencoe.com to preview Chapter 7.

Chapter 7 Manifest Destiny **253**

The Western Pioneers

Guide to Reading

Big Ideas

Science and Technology Several inventions in the early 1800s helped make it possible to settle the West.

Content Vocabulary
• squatter (p. 254)
• overlander (p. 256)

Academic Vocabulary
• guarantee (p. 254)
• convert (p. 255)

People and Events to Identify
• Manifest Destiny (p. 254)
• Jethro Wood (p. 255)
• John Deere (p. 255)
• Cyrus McCormick (p. 255)
• Kit Carson (p. 256)

Reading Strategy

Organizing Use a graphic organizer, like the one below, to list the trails to the West used by settlers in the 1840s.

Trails to the West

NEW YORK CORE CURRICULUM
U.S. History and Government

Unit 2:
II.C.2 Exploring and settling the West (explorers, Lewis and Clark expedition, naturalists, trappers and traders, trailblazers, missionaries, pioneers, the Mormon Church)
II.C.4 Motives for and implications of expansion and western settlement
II.C.5 Politics of western expansion (Manifest Destiny, the Texas and Oregon questions, the Mexican War)
II.C.6 Impact of western expansion upon Mexicans and Native Americans

In the 1840s, Americans made the grueling trek west to the frontier states of the Midwest and the rich lands of the Oregon Country. The invention of new farming equipment made it easier to clear and cultivate new land, thus encouraging settlement of the Midwest.

Settling New Lands

MAIN Idea Americans moved westward and established new farms in the Midwest; later settlers traveled in wagon trains to the Pacific Coast.

HISTORY AND YOU Have you ever packed for a long trip? What things did you take with you? Read on to learn how settlers faced difficult times on the trail west.

In 1800 only around 387,000 white settlers lived west of the Appalachian Mountains. By 1820, that number had grown to more than 2.4 million, and the numbers continued to rise rapidly. By the time the Civil War began, more Americans lived west of the Appalachians than lived in states along the Atlantic Coast.

Some Americans headed west for religious reasons. Others were lured by the chance to own their own farms. While most settled east of the Mississippi River, more than 250,000 Americans continued farther west, across the Great Plains and Rocky Mountains to California and the Pacific Northwest.

In 1845 a magazine editor named John Louis O'Sullivan declared that it was the "manifest destiny" of Americans "to overspread the continent allotted by Providence." Many Americans believed in this concept of **Manifest Destiny**—the idea that God had given the entire continent to Americans and wanted them to settle western land.

Farming the New Lands

Early settlers marked out farms on the rich river bottom land. Others occupied fertile woodlands. These pioneers became known as **squatters,** because they settled on lands they did not own. The federal government intended to survey the land and then sell large parcels to real estate companies, but squatters wanted to buy the land they occupied directly from the government.

Bowing to public pressure, Congress passed the Preemption Act of 1830, a renewable law made permanent in 1841. This law protected squatters by **guaranteeing** them the right to claim land before it was surveyed and the right to buy up to 160 acres at the government's minimum price of $1.25 per acre.

The Idea of Manifest Destiny

▲ Entitled "American Progress," this famous painting of the idea of Manifest Destiny depicts America as a woman, leading the country into the West. She carries a book, which represents American enlightenment and is laying a telegraph wire.

PRIMARY SOURCE

Although John L. O'Sullivan did not use the phrase "manifest destiny" until 1845, as early as 1839 he was declaring that it was America's destiny to spread its ideas to the world:

". . . our national birth was the beginning of a new history. . . . [W]e are the nation of progress, of individual freedom, of universal enfranchisement. . . . We must onward to the fulfilment [sic] of our mission— to the entire development of the principle of our organization—freedom of conscience, freedom of person, freedom of trade and business pursuits, universality of freedom and equality. This is our high destiny. . . . For this blessed mission to the nations of the world . . . has America been chosen; and her high example shall smite unto death the tyranny of kings, hierarchs, and oligarchs. . . ."

—from "The Great Nation of Futurity," *The United States Democratic Review*

DBQ Document-Based Questions

1. **Analyzing** What symbolizes progress in the painting? Why is the left portion of the painting darker than the right?
2. **Paraphrasing** For what does O'Sullivan say that the United States has been chosen?

Plows and Reapers

A few decades earlier, farmers had only wooden plows to break the grass cover and roots of Midwestern sod. **Jethro Wood** patented an iron-bladed plow in 1819, and in 1837 **John Deere** engineered a plow with sharp-edged steel blades that cut cleanly through the sod. This reduced, by half, the labor needed to prepare an acre for farming.

Midwestern agriculture also received a boost from the mechanical reaper, which **Cyrus McCormick** patented in 1834. For centuries farmers had cut grain by hand, using a sickle or a scythe—exhausting and time-consuming work. Switching from a sickle to a McCormick reaper pulled by horses or mules, farmers could harvest far more grain with far less effort.

Settling the Pacific Coast

Latecomers to the Midwest set their sights on the Pacific Coast, partly because emigrants assumed that the treeless Great Plains had poor land for farming. The United States and Great Britain—as well as Native Americans—laid claim to Oregon Country, a region that included present-day Oregon, Washington, and British Columbia. In 1818 Britain and the United States had agreed to occupy the land jointly. In the 1830s, American missionaries began arriving in Oregon to **convert** Native Americans. These missionaries spread the word about Oregon and persuaded others to come to the lush Willamette Valley.

✔ **Reading Check** **Describing** How did Congress help squatters attain land in the West?

History ONLINE
Student Web Activity Visit glencoe.com and complete the activity on the Oregon Trail.

Westward Migration

MAIN Idea Emigrant groups followed specific trails through territory belonging to Native Americans.

HISTORY AND YOU Do you remember which religious groups came to America to escape religious persecution? Read on to learn why the Mormons left the United States to practice their religion freely.

Much of the terrain from the edge of the frontier to the Pacific was difficult. A small number of trailblazers—mountain men like **Kit Carson** and Jim Bridger—made their living by trapping beaver and selling the furs to traders. At the same time, they gained a thorough knowledge of the territory and the local Native Americans.

By the 1840s, the mountain men had carved out several East-to-West trails that helped settlers travel. The most popular route was the Oregon Trail. Others included the California Trail and the Santa Fe Trail.

Emigrants made the journey in groups of covered wagons called wagon trains. Before starting out, the trains assembled at staging areas outside a frontier town. There, families exchanged information about routes, bought supplies, trained oxen, and practiced steering the cumbersome wagons, which new drivers were apt to tip over.

The first wagon trains hired mountain men to guide them. Once the trails became well worn, most of the travelers—known as **overlanders**—found their own way with the help of guidebooks. Sometimes the guidebooks were wrong, leading to tragedy. In 1846 a group of 87 overlanders known as the Donner Party, after the two brothers who led them, were trapped by winter snows high up in the Sierra Nevada. After 41 died of starvation, those still alive resorted to cannibalism in order to survive.

NATIONAL GEOGRAPHIC Overland Trails West, 1840–1860

BRITISH NORTH AMERICA

Portland · Washington Terr. · Ft. Walla Walla · Columbia R. · Missouri R. · Unorg. Terr. · Minn. · Wis.

Oregon · Snake R. · Ft. Boise · OREGON TRAIL · Nebraska Territory · Mississippi R. · Iowa

CALIFORNIA TRAIL · Donner Pass · South Pass · Ft. Laramie · MORMON TRAIL · Platte R. · Council Bluffs

Sacramento · Great Salt L. · Ft. Bridger · Salt Lake City · Ft. Kearny · Nauvoo · Ill.

San Francisco · Utah Terr. · PONY EXPRESS · Denver · Kansas Terr. · St. Joseph · Independence · St. Louis · Mo. · Ky. · Va.

California · OLD SPANISH TRAIL · Colorado R. · Bent's Fort · SANTA FE TRAIL · Arkansas R. · Ark. · Tenn. · N.C.

Los Angeles · New Mexico Territory · Santa Fe · CIMARRON CUTOFF · Unorganized Terr. · Red R. · Fort Smith · Miss. · Ala. · Ga. · S.C. · ATLANTIC OCEAN

PACIFIC OCEAN · Tucson · El Paso · BUTTERFIELD OVERLAND MAIL · Texas · La.

MEXICO · Rio Grande · Gulf of Mexico

Legend:
- - - - Continental Divide
✕ Pass
■ Fort
—— 1860 border

0 400 kilometers
0 400 miles
Lambert Azimuthal Equal-Area projection

Analyzing GEOGRAPHY

1. **Location** Name three Missouri cities that served as starting points for western emigrants.
2. **Regions** Why did emigrants bypass the Great Plains and travel all the way to the Far West?

Maps In Motion See *StudentWorks™ Plus* or glencoe.com.

The typical trip west took five to six months, with the wagon trains progressing about 15 miles (24 km) per day. Generally, men drove the wagons, hunted game, and fed and cared for the animals at night, while women looked after the children, cooked the meals, cleaned the camp, and laundered the clothes. As Elizabeth Geer recounts, the journey was exhausting and difficult:

PRIMARY SOURCE

"I carry my babe and lead, or rather carry, another through snow, mud, and water, almost to my knees. It is the worst road. . . . [T]here was not one dry thread on one of us—not even my babe. . . . I have not told you half we suffered. I am not adequate to the task."

—quoted in *Women's Diaries of the Westward Journey*

Native Americans

Early travelers feared attacks by Native American warriors, but such encounters were rare. By one estimate, only 362 emigrants died due to Native American attacks between 1840 and 1860, while emigrants killed 426 Native Americans in the same period. In fact, Native Americans often gave emigrants gifts of food, as well as helpful information about routes, edible plants, and sources of water. They often traded fresh horses for items such as cotton clothing and ammunition.

As the overland traffic increased, Native Americans on the Great Plains became concerned and angry over the threat this influx of people posed to their way of life. The Sioux, Cheyenne, Arapaho, and other groups relied on buffalo for food, shelter, clothing, tools, and countless other necessities of everyday life. Now they feared that the age-old wanderings of the buffalo herds would be disrupted.

Hoping to ensure peace, the federal government negotiated the Treaty of Fort Laramie in 1851. In that document, the United States promised eight Native American groups that specific territories in the region of the Great Plains would belong to them as long as they allowed settlers to pass through peacefully. The government also agreed to make payments to the groups.

The Mormon Migration

Unlike those bound for the West in search of land, the Mormons followed a deeply rooted American tradition—the quest for religious freedom. The Mormons, however, had to seek that freedom by leaving the Eastern states, instead of coming to them.

In 1844, after a mob murdered their leader, Joseph Smith, the church's new leader, Brigham Young, took his people west to escape further persecution. Several thousand Mormons forged their way along a path that became known as the Mormon Trail. It served as a valuable route into the western United States. In 1847 the Mormons stopped at the Great Salt Lake in what is now Utah. Undeterred by the wildness of the area, they staked a claim on the land they called "Deseret."

✔ Reading Check **Describing** What difficulties did settlers face in the American West?

Section 1 REVIEW

Vocabulary

1. **Explain** the significance of: Manifest Destiny, squatters, Jethro Wood, John Deere, Cyrus McCormick, Kit Carson, overlander.

Main Ideas

2. **Specifying** Who encouraged settlers to emigrate to the Oregon Territory?

3. **Describing** What was the purpose of the 1851 Treaty of Fort Laramie, and what were its main points?

Critical Thinking

4. **Big Ideas** What two inventions made it easier to farm on the frontier?

5. **Organizing** Use a graphic organizer, similar to the one below, to list the reasons that Americans emigrated to the West.

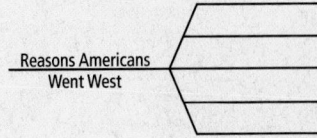

Reasons Americans Went West

6. **Analyzing Visuals** Study the map of overland trails to the West on page 256. Where did the Old Spanish Trail begin, and where did it end?

Writing About History

7. **Descriptive Writing** Suppose that you emigrated from the East to a frontier farm in the West. Write a journal entry describing a day in your journey.

History ONLINE

Study Central™ To review this section, go to glencoe.com and click on Study Central.

EDWARD S. CURTIS/CORBIS

Eulogy

CHIEF JOSEPH (*above*), *a leader of the Nez Perce of the Wallowa Valley in eastern Oregon, remembers his father, Old Joseph. The Nez Perce were forced to leave the Wallowa Valley less than a decade after Old Joseph's death.*

MY FATHER SENT FOR ME. I SAW HE WAS DYING. I TOOK HIS HAND IN MINE. He said, "My son, my body is returning to my mother earth, and my spirit is going very soon to see the Great Spirit Chief. When I am gone, think of your country. You are the chief of these people. They look to you to guide them. Always remember that your father never sold his country. You must stop your ears whenever you are asked to sign a treaty selling your home. A few years more, and white men will be all around you. They have their eyes on this land. My son, never forget my dying words. This country holds your father's body. Never sell the bones of your father and your mother."

I pressed my father's hand and told him I would protect his grave with my life. My father smiled and passed to the spirit land.

I buried him in that beautiful valley of winding rivers. I love that land more than all the rest of the world. A man who would not love his father's grave is worse than a wild animal.

Baseball for Beginners

Thinking of taking up the new game of baseball? Watch out! The rules keep changing!

1845
- Canvas bases will be set 90 feet apart in a diamond shape.
- Only nine men will play on each side.
- Pitches are to be thrown underhanded.
- A ball caught on the first bounce is an out.

1846
- At first base, a fielder can tag the bag before the runner reaches it and so make an out.

1847
- Players may no longer throw the ball at a runner to put him out.

These changes may be coming:
- A poor pitch is a ball; nine balls gives the runner first base, a walk.
- A ball caught on the first bounce is no longer an out.

O. PIERRE HAVENS/CORBIS

An early New York baseball team

WESTERN WORD PLAY
Word Watch

Can you talk Western? Match the word to its meaning.

1. maverick

2. Hangtown fry

3. grubstake

4. bonanza

5. palo alto

6. pard or rawwheel

a. gold rush favorite, made of eggs, bacon, and oysters

b. inexperienced '49er, Eastern type not used to wearing boots

c. a lucky discovery of gold; a source of sudden wealth

d. a style of hat worn by gold rush miners

e. a lone dissenter who takes an independent stand, from the name of a Texas cattleman who left his herd unbranded

f. food provided by an investor to a gold prospector in exchange for a share of whatever gold he finds

answers: 1.e; 2.a; 3.f; 4.c; 5.d; 6.b

Milestones

SETTLED, 1847. THE VALLEY OF THE GREAT SALT LAKE, by Brigham Young, leader of the Mormons, and a party of 143, to escape hostility toward their group in Illinois. Young plans to return to Council Bluffs, Iowa, and lead the rest of the members of his faith to a permanent home in Utah.

MOVED, 1845. HENRY DAVID THOREAU, writer, to Walden Pond, Concord, Massachusetts. Thoreau intends to build his own house on the shore of the pond and earn his living by the labor of his hands only. "Many of the so-called comforts of life," writes Thoreau, "are not only not indispensable, but positive hindrances to the elevation of mankind."

AILING, 1847. EDGAR ALLAN POE, in Baltimore, following the death of his wife, Virginia. Other than a poem on death, Poe has written little this year, devoting his dwindling energies to plagiarism suits against other authors.

LIBRARY OF CONGRESS/CORBIS

Frederick Douglass

EMIGRATED, 1845. FREDERICK DOUGLASS, former slave, author, and abolitionist leader, to England to escape the danger of re-enslavement in reaction to his autobiography, *Narrative of the Life of Frederick Douglass.* On his 1845 trip across the Atlantic, Douglass was not permitted cabin accommodations. After a lecture during the crossing, some passengers threatened to throw him overboard.

NUMBERS

18,000 Miles from New York to California by sea route around Cape Horn

90,000 People arriving in California in 1849, half by sea, half by overland route

BETTMANN/CORBIS

Panning for gold

$20 Average earned per day by California gold miners in 1849

$435 Value of miners' average daily earnings in 2006 dollars

50 Number of years after the signing of the Declaration of Independence that Thomas Jefferson and John Adams die—within hours of each other.

17,069,453 U.S. population in 1840

55,000 Number of emigrants moving west along the Oregon Trail in 1850

CRITICAL THINKING

1. Categorizing As a leader, Old Joseph combined spiritual beliefs with practical politics. Give examples of each.

2. Identifying Points of View Thoreau believed that the basics in life rather than the extra comforts made people better human beings. Do you agree or disagree with his view? Why?

The Hispanic Southwest

Guide to Reading

Big Ideas
Trade, War, and Migration
Americans began to settle in the Mexican borderlands, leading to conflict with the Mexican government.

Content Vocabulary
- secularize *(p. 261)*
- mestizo *(p. 262)*
- vaqueros *(p. 262)*

Academic Vocabulary
- civil *(p. 261)*
- ultimately *(p. 263)*

People and Events to Identify
- John Sutter *(p. 263)*
- William Becknell *(p. 263)*
- Santa Fe Trail *(p. 263)*
- *Tejano* *(p. 263)*

Reading Strategy
Categorizing Use a graphic organizer, similar to the one below, to list features of each Mexican territory after Mexico gained independence.

Territory	Features
California	
New Mexico	
Texas	

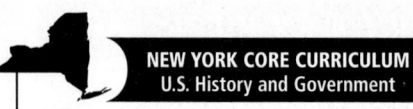

NEW YORK CORE CURRICULUM
U.S. History and Government

Unit 2:
II.C.3 The Spanish, Mexican, and Native American West
II.C.6 Impact of western expansion upon Mexicans and Native Americans

Mexico won its independence from Spain in 1821. For the next quarter century, the Mexican government neglected its far northern territories. American influence grew as more Americans settled in the region.

Mexican Independence and the Borderlands

MAIN Idea Far from Mexico City, the Mexican borderlands were sparsely populated; the region's economy centered on cattle and sheep ranching.

HISTORY AND YOU Have you ever visited or seen pictures of an old Spanish mission in the Southwest? Read on to learn about the purpose of the missions, the way they functioned, and why they were abandoned after Mexican independence.

In 1821, after more than a decade of fighting, Mexico won its independence from Spain. During the decades that followed, Mexico experienced great turmoil and political chaos. The far northern territories of California, New Mexico, and Texas remained part of Mexico, although their great distance from the capital, Mexico City, allowed for considerable political independence. As the young Mexican republic struggled to establish a stable national government, it neglected its northern borderlands.

Located more than 1,000 miles from Mexico City, this region was sparsely populated by Native Americans and Hispanic settlers. Thus, the Mexican frontier was threatened on several fronts. Settlements in Texas and New Mexico faced attacks by Apaches, Comanches, and other Native American groups. In addition, the under-populated northern territories were threatened by the westward expansion of the United States and the southward expansion of Russian settlements along the Pacific Coast. (Russia had begun colonizing Alaska in the 1780s.)

The Spanish had expanded the territory of New Spain by establishing missions on the northern frontier. The purpose of the state-financed missions was to spread the Christian faith and Spanish culture to Native Americans. Missions controlled vast tracts of land on which grazed cattle, sheep, and horses. Native Americans tended to the livestock and did other work at the missions under conditions of near slavery.

By the early 1800s, the mission system was in decline. By the time Mexico became independent, it had nearly collapsed, having received little financial support during the struggle for independence. In 1821

INFOGRAPHIC
Spanish Missions

▼ Spanish missions were self-sufficient, fortified, religious communities used to convert Native Americans.

Blacksmith

Living Quarters

tholic Church

Oven

Stables

Granary

Tannery and Workshops

Analyzing VISUALS DBQ

1. **Analyzing** What factors do you think determined the selection of a mission site?
2. **Identifying** What was the most dominant feature of a mission complex?

California had only 36 Franciscan friars to run 21 missions.

Many Mexicans believed that maintaining state-supported religious institutions was not appropriate for a republic. In 1834 the Mexican government **secularized**—or transferred from religious control to **civil** control—the missions and then transferred the land to private ownership. Although the goal of reformers was to divide mission lands among Native Americans, most land ended up in the hands of cattle ranchers who then relied on Native Americans for labor. The frontier presidios, or forts, established by the Spanish similarly became weak due to labor shortages and reduced funding. This left frontier settlers vulnerable to attack.

In the borderlands, political chaos followed Mexican independence. In 1837 a visitor described conditions in frontier California:

PRIMARY SOURCE

"The old monastic order is destroyed and nothing seems to have replaced it except anarchy. The official power is weak and flutters irresolutely in the hands of its holders. Doubtless a new political order will arise out of this chaos but while waiting for it the country is badly administered, society is without ties, without guarantees, and the people are wretched."

—quoted in *The Mexican Frontier 1821–1846*

California

In the 1810s and 1820s, most of the approximately 3,200 Hispanic Californians took no direct role in Mexico's struggle for independence. Secularization of the missions had a tremendous impact on life in California, because it freed up land for cattle ranching, which became the mainstay of the economy.

Rancheros, or ranchers, owned sprawling tracts of land. These predominantly white "Spanish Dons" and their families constituted less than 10 percent of California's population but dominated California society.

Beneath these elites was a class of **mestizos** (persons of mixed European and Native American ancestry). Some of this middle class worked as **vaqueros** (cowboys), but many were skilled craftspeople.

At the bottom of society were Native Americans. They had suffered high mortality rates under Spanish rule. After Mexican independence, their situation improved little. Although freed from the missions, they were often exploited by the new class of rancheros. Many escaped to live among the independent Native Americans on the edges of the California frontier.

In the California territory, men played a powerful role in the family, and only men could vote or hold elective office. Yet women, especially upper-class women, had rights and privileges as well. Unlike American women of the era, Hispanic women retained control over their own property after marriage and could seek legal redress in the courts.

New Mexico

As in California, Mexican independence brought little immediate change to New Mexico (which included present-day Arizona). New Mexico remained largely rural. Sheep ranching thrived in the region's dry climate. Large ranches were established south of Santa Fe. North of Santa Fe, Hispanic settlers focused more on farming.

In the 1820s, when the Navajo and Apache launched a series of attacks on New Mexico, the Mexican government was unable to provide protection. This fed a growing dissatisfaction with the national government. Finally, in 1837, Pueblo people and Hispanic settlers north of Santa Fe launched a rebellion and killed the unpopular territorial governor and 16 other government officials.

✔ **Reading Check** **Identifying** What were the major social classes in California?

Life on the California Frontier

DBQ Document-Based Questions

1. **Drawing Conclusions** Why do you think horses were driven into the sea in 1807?

2. **Analyzing Visuals** How can you tell that the horse was important on the California frontier?

▲ The painting Los Californios depicts three California ranchers of Hispanic descent, known as los Californios, *lassoing a steer.*

PRIMARY SOURCE

"In the old days every one seemed to live out-doors. There was much gaiety and social life, even though people were widely scattered. We traveled as much as possible on horseback. . . . Young men would ride from one ranch to another for parties, and whoever found his horse tired would let him go and catch another. In 1806 there were so many horses in the valleys about San José that seven or eight thousand were killed. Nearly as many were driven into the sea at Santa Barbara in 1807, and the same thing was done at Monterey in 1810. Horses were given to the runaway sailors, and to trappers and hunters who came over the mountains, for common horses were plenty, but fast and beautiful horses were never more prized in any country than in California, and each young man had his favorites."

—from Guadalupe Vallejo, "Ranch and Mission Days in Alta California," *Century Magazine* (December 1890)

Americans Arrive in the Borderlands

MAIN Idea Trade between the borderlands and the United States increased after Mexican independence; Americans began to settle in the Southwest.

HISTORY AND YOU What can you recall about how trade restrictions imposed by Britain angered American colonists? Read to learn how trade with foreign nations grew after Mexico became independent from Spain.

After Mexican independence, American influence in the borderlands increased. Americans had begun moving into California before Mexican independence, and immigration increased after 1821. Trade with California rose significantly once Mexico was no longer part of Spain's empire. Traders from the United States, Russia, and other countries arrived in California ports to exchange manufactured goods for sea otter skins and hides and tallow derived from cattle.

In 1839, hoping to attract more settlers, Juan Bautista Alvarado, governor of California, granted 50,000 acres in the Sacramento Valley to **John Sutter,** a Swiss immigrant from Germany. There, Sutter built a trading post and cattle ranch. "Sutter's Fort" was often the first stopping point for Americans reaching California. As more Americans arrived, the differences between California and southern Mexico increased. This fueled political tensions between frontier leaders and the Mexican national government. The American population, however, was still small. Only about 700 Americans lived in California in 1845.

During the Spanish colonial period, New Mexicans received most manufactured goods from traders who came north from the state of Chihuahua. This began to change in 1821, the year of Mexican independence, when an American trader named **William Becknell** arrived in Santa Fe. He opened the **Santa Fe Trail,** which became a major trade route connecting Santa Fe with Independence, Missouri. Caravan wagons brought American manufactured goods to New Mexico and exchanged them for silver, mules, and furs. As trade increased, a small American population settled in Santa Fe.

East of New Mexico, Texas had long served as a buffer territory between the United States and the rest of Mexico. Texas was a sparsely populated region where settlers faced recurring raids by the Comanche and Apache. Most of the 2,500 Spanish-speaking *Tejanos* were concentrated in the towns of San Antonio and Goliad (then called La Bahía). Just before Mexican independence, Spain began allowing foreigners to settle in Texas. Mexico continued this policy, and Americans soon began to flood into that territory.

The decision to invite Americans to settle led, **ultimately,** to a revolt against Mexican rule and independence for Texas. California and New Mexico remained Mexican territory for 25 years after Mexican independence. Texas—where Americans soon vastly outnumbered *Tejanos*—broke away after fifteen years.

✔ **Reading Check** **Summarizing** In what ways did Americans have an influence in the Mexican borderlands?

Section 2 REVIEW

Vocabulary

1. **Explain** the significance of: secularize, mestizo, vaquero, John Sutter, William Becknell, Santa Fe Trail, *Tejano.*

Main Ideas

2. **Describing** What happened to the mission system in California after Mexican independence?

3. **Determining Cause and Effect** What caused Americans to settle in Santa Fe?

Critical Thinking

4. **Big Ideas** Why do you think the conflict in Texas between American settlers and the Mexican government was more serious than the conflict in California?

5. **Organizing** Use a time line, similar to the one below, to list some events that occurred in Mexican territories after Mexico achieved independence.

1821	1837
1834	1839

6. **Analyzing Visuals** Study the image of the mission on page 261. Why do you think the missions had troops stationed within them? Why would they have been built with the living quarters all facing inward?

Writing About History

7. **Expository Writing** Review the section and then write a short essay to summarize the state of the Mexican borderlands in the period after Mexico achieved independence.

Study Central™ To review this section, go to glencoe.com and click on Study Central.

Independence for Texas

Guide to Reading

Big Ideas
Culture and Beliefs Americans in Texas hoped to transplant American institutions to their new homeland.

Content Vocabulary
- *empresario* (p. 264)
- annexation (p. 269)

Academic Vocabulary
- convention (p. 266)
- reinforcement (p. 268)

People and Events to Identify
- National Colonization Act (p. 264)
- Washington-on-the-Brazos (p. 265)
- Antonio López de Santa Anna (p. 266)
- Sam Houston (p. 267)
- Alamo (p. 267)
- William B. Travis (p. 267)

Reading Strategy
Categorizing Complete a graphic organizer, similar to the one below, by filling in the major battles of the Texas war for independence and the outcome of each battle.

Major Battle	Outcome

NEW YORK CORE CURRICULUM
U.S. History and Government

Unit 2:
II.C.5 Politics of western expansion (Manifest Destiny, the Texas and Oregon questions, the Mexican War)

Americans who settled in Texas did not assimilate as the Mexican government had hoped. The struggle over control of that border territory resulted in rebellion and, after some dramatic military encounters, independence for Texas.

Opening Texas to Americans

MAIN Idea Mexico invited Americans to settle in Texas but insisted that they adopt local customs, obey Mexican law, and convert to Catholicism.

HISTORY AND YOU Why do you think Mexico required Americans to become Mexican citizens? Read on to learn how *empresarios* brought American settlers to Texas.

In July 1821 Stephen F. Austin set off from Louisiana for the Texas territory in the northeastern corner of Mexico. The Spanish government had promised to give his father, Moses, a huge tract of Texas land if the elder Austin settled 300 American families there. Moses died before he could fulfill his end of the deal. On his deathbed, he asked Stephen to take his place in Texas.

When Austin settled in Texas, it was not a wild and empty land. Spanish-speaking *Tejanos* had established such settlements as San Antonio de Bexar and Hidalgo in the southern portion of the region. The land north of these settlements was the territory of the Apache, Comanche, and other Native American groups. In 1824 Texas was joined with Coahuila to become part of the Mexican state of Coahuila y Texas.

Unable to persuade its own citizens to settle on this frontier, Mexico decided to continue Spanish policy and allow foreigners to settle there. Between 1823 and 1825, Mexico passed three colonization laws, which offered cheap land to nearly anyone willing to come. The last law granted new immigrants a ten-year exemption from paying taxes but required that they become Mexican citizens, abide by Mexican law, and convert to Roman Catholicism.

Empresarios and Settlers

Although some American emigrants headed to Texas on their own, most came at the encouragement of ***empresarios,*** a Spanish word meaning "agents" or "contractors." Under the **National Colonization Act,** Mexico gave 26 *empresarios* large grants of Texas land. In exchange, the *empresarios* promised to fill it with a certain number of settlers. The *empresarios* assigned a plot to each family and governed the colonies they established.

PRIMARY SOURCE

"The Americans from the north have taken possession of practically all the eastern part of Texas, in most cases without the permission of the authorities. . . .

[In San Felipe de Austin, the] population is nearly 200 persons, of which only ten are Mexicans, for the balance are all Americans from the North with an occasional European. . . . Beyond . . . are scattered the families brought by Stephen Austin, which today number more than two thousand persons. . . . [T]he spark that will start the conflagration that will deprive us of Texas, will start from this colony."

—from José María Sánchez, "A Trip to Texas in 1828"

Map Legend:
- Texas
- Other Mexican states
- International boundary
- Mexico state boundary
- Empresario boundary
- Burnet (1826) Empresario name and date land granted

Analyzing GEOGRAPHY

1. **Human-Environment Interaction** How many parcels of land did Stephen Austin hold in Texas?
2. **Place** What three other Mexican states bordered Texas?

Stephen Austin was the most successful *empresario*. He founded the town **Washington-on-the-Brazos** and, by the mid-1830s, had persuaded 1,500 American families to immigrate.

Americanizing Texas

Americans in Texas initially accepted Mexican citizenship. The government assumed they would adopt Mexican customs and come to see Mexico as their own country, but few did. Mexican customs and the Roman Catholic Church were alien to most American settlers.

Many Mexicans, in turn, distrusted the settlers because of their American lifestyle and rejection of Mexican ways. Mexicans' unease increased in 1826, when Benjamin Edwards, the brother of *empresario* Haden Edwards, led a rebellion against Mexican authority. Angry over disputes about whether Mexico or the *empresario* ruled the region, Edwards declared that the settlements of Americans in Texas now constituted the independent nation of Fredonia.

When threatened by Mexican troops and a party of *Tejanos* led by Stephen Austin, the rebels dispersed.

Although most settlers ignored Edwards's call for revolution, the Mexican government feared it signaled an American plot to acquire Texas. In 1830 Mexico closed its borders to further immigration by Americans and banned the import of enslaved labor. It also taxed goods imported from foreign countries, hoping to discourage trade with the United States.

These new laws infuriated the settlers. Without immigration their settlements could not grow. The import tax meant higher prices for goods they were accustomed to purchasing from the United States. Perhaps worst of all, the Mexican government was making rules for them. They saw no reason to obey a government they hardly considered their own.

Reading Check **Examining** What did Mexico's colonization laws offer settlers in northern Texas, and what did the laws require of these settlers?

Texas Goes to War

MAIN Idea When Mexico tried to enforce its laws, American settlers rebelled and established an independent state.

HISTORY AND YOU Have you heard the motto "Remember the Alamo"? Read on to learn how Texas became an independent nation.

With tensions simmering, settlers met at two **conventions** in the Texas town of San Felipe in 1832 and 1833. At the first convention, settlers chose Stephen Austin to be the convention's president. The convention asked Mexico to reopen Texas to American immigrants and to loosen the taxes on imports. The second convention recommended separating Texas from Coahuila and creating a new Mexican state. The convention also created a constitution for the new state and designated Austin to travel to Mexico City to negotiate with the Mexican government.

In the fall of 1833 negotiations stalled. An irritated Austin sent a letter to *Tejano* leaders in San Antonio, suggesting that Texas start peacefully organizing its own state government. Then he visited Mexican President **Antonio López de Santa Anna** in Mexico City and persuaded him to agree to several demands, including lifting the hated ban on immigration.

As Austin was returning home, he was arrested on January 3, 1834, by Mexican officials, who had intercepted his letter to the *Tejanos.* He was taken back to Mexico City and imprisoned for treason, without trial. Shortly afterward, in April 1834, President Santa Anna denounced Mexico's constitution of 1824 and declared himself dictator.

Austin was released from prison in July 1835. Even he saw that further negotiation with Santa Anna was pointless and, in September, he urged Texans to organize an army, which they quickly did.

The Early Battles

The Mexican army had serious problems. Continuing political instability in Mexico City had denied the army sound leadership, training, and support. Against this handicapped

History of Texas, 1819–1836

1819
Spain and the United States sign the Adams-Onís Treaty recognizing Spanish sovereignty over Texas

1824
The new Mexican government establishes the state of Coahuila y Texas, combining Texas with Coahuila to the south

1827
New constitution of the State of Coahuila y Texas declares that from this point forward no one born in the state can be born into slavery and bans the importation of enslaved persons after six months

1819   1821   1823   1825   1827   1829

1821
Stephen F. Austin arrives in San Antonio

1826–1827
American settlers Haden and Benjamin Edwards lead a revolt against Mexican rule; the brothers briefly declare an independent state called "Fredonia"; the rebellion falls apart without any violence

1828
Mexican General Manuel de Mier y Terán reports *Tejanos* are still importing slaves and ignoring Mexican law; warns Texas is likely to revolt

force, the Texan army enjoyed its first taste of victory at the military post of Gonzales, about 75 miles east of San Antonio. There, Mexican soldiers ordered the Texans to surrender their arms. In response, the rebels pointed a cannon at the Mexican force and held up a cloth sign painted with the taunt, "Come and Take It." Having no orders to attack, the Mexicans retreated to San Antonio, and the Texans followed them. The rebels, numbering only about 350, drove the much larger Mexican force out of San Antonio in December 1835.

On March 2, 1836, Texas declared its independence from Mexico. Shortly thereafter, the Texans drafted a new constitution that drew heavily from the U.S. Constitution and specifically protected slavery.

The Alamo

Few of the Texas rebels had any military training, and at first, no one could agree on who should lead them. Finally, a former governor of Tennessee and proven military leader named **Sam Houston** took command. In the meantime, Santa Anna organized a force of about 6,000 troops to put down the rebellion.

When Santa Anna's forces arrived at San Antonio in February 1836, they found over 180 Texas rebels holed up in an abandoned Catholic mission called the **Alamo.** Under the command of Lieutenant Colonel **William B. Travis,** the small force sought to delay Santa Anna and give Houston's army more time to prepare. From within the mission, Travis dispatched a courier with a plea to fellow Texans and U.S. citizens for help:

PRIMARY SOURCE

"I am besieged with a thousand or more of the Mexicans under Santa Anna. . . . I shall never surrender or retreat. Then, I call on you in the name of Liberty, of patriotism, and of everything dear to the American character, to come to our aid with all dispatch. . . . If this call is neglected, I am determined to sustain myself as long as possible, and die like a soldier who never forgets what is due to his own honor and that of his country. VICTORY OR DEATH!"

—quoted in *Lone Star*

1834
Stephen F. Austin is arrested for writing a letter that calls for establishing a separate Mexican state of Texas

1835
At Gonzales and San Antonio, Texas rebels force Mexican military to retreat

April 1836
Santa Anna surrenders to Texans after defeat at the Battle of San Jacinto

1831 › 1833 › 1835 › 1837 ›

1830
Mexico passes law barring Americans from immigration to Texas, increasing military forces in Texas, and forbidding the importation of slaves

February 1836
Alamo falls to Santa Anna

Analyzing TIME LINES

1. **Specifying** What event occurred in 1827, and what was the result?
2. **Identifying** In what year did Texas achieve independence?

The Texas War for Independence, 1835–1836

Unorganized Terr.

UNITED STATES

Ark.

Red R.

Brazos R.

REPUBLIC OF TEXAS

La.

Colorado R.

Boundary claimed by Mexico

Washington-on-the-Brazos

Alamo, March 6, 1836

HOUSTON 1836

San Jacinto April 21, 1836

San Antonio
Bexar, Dec. 10, 1835

Gonzales, Oct. 2, 1835

Brazoria

SANTA ANNA 1836

Goliad, March 20, 1836

Refugio, March 14, 1836

Boundary claimed by Texas

Nueces R.

URREA 1836

San Patricio Feb. 27, 1836

28°N

Rio Grande

Gulf of Mexico

26°N

MEXICO

N
W   E
S

0   200 kilometers
0   200 miles
Albers Equal-Area projection

Mexican forces
Mexican victory
Texan forces
Texan victory
Austin's colony
Disputed territory

24°N

96°W   94°W

▲ The Battle of San Jacinto (above) was a decisive victory for American forces. The victory secured Texas's independence and ended the war.

▲ Texan rebels fought valiantly to defend the Alamo (above), but were overwhelmed by Mexican forces. Their heroism bought time for the main Texas army to prepare for war.

Analyzing GEOGRAPHY

1. **Locating** The boundary claimed by Texas lies along what river?

2. **Identifying** What were the first and last battles of the war?

Maps In Motion See *StudentWorks™ Plus* or glencoe.com.

The call for **reinforcements** went almost unanswered. Only 32 settlers from Gonzales, deciding on their own to join the fight, made it into the Alamo. Running low on ammunition and gunpowder, the Texans held off Santa Anna's besieging army for 13 days. It was during the standoff that the new Texas government met at Washington-on-the-Brazos and formally declared independence.

On March 6, 1836, Santa Anna's army stormed the Alamo. The Texans fought off the attackers for six hours, killing or wounding about 600 before being overrun. Although the defenders of the Alamo had been defeated, they had bought Houston's army nearly two extra weeks to organize.

Goliad

Two weeks later the Mexican army overwhelmed Texan troops led by James W. Fannin at Goliad, a town southeast of San Antonio near the Gulf Coast. Fannin and his men surrendered, hoping that the Mexicans would disarm them and expel them from Texas. Though the Mexican field general at Goliad wrote to

Santa Anna requesting clemency, Santa Anna demanded execution. At dawn on March 27, 1836, a firing squad executed more than 300 men. The losses at the Alamo and Goliad devastated Texans but also united them in support of their new country.

The Battle of San Jacinto

With the Texan army in disarray, Sam Houston desperately needed more time to recruit fresh volunteers and to train the soldiers who remained. Rather than fight, he chose to retreat, heading east toward Louisiana.

Houston was biding his time. Up against a larger, more disciplined army, he decided to wait for Santa Anna to make a mistake. The mistake occurred on April 21, when both armies were encamped along the San Jacinto River near what is now the city of Houston. Santa Anna no longer saw Houston's army as a threat, so he allowed his men to sleep in the afternoon, confident that Houston would wait until the next day to launch an attack.

Eager for a fight, Houston's soldiers convinced the officers to launch an afternoon assault. Shielded from sight by a hill, Houston's troops crept up on Santa Anna's sleeping soldiers and charged. The surprise attack threw the Mexican soldiers into a panic.

The Battle of San Jacinto lasted less than 20 minutes, but the killing continued for hours. Yelling "Remember the Alamo" and "Remember Goliad," Houston's men attacked the Mexican troops with guns, knives, and clubs. In addition to the hundreds killed, over 700 members of Santa Anna's force were taken captive. The Texans suffered only 9 killed and 34 wounded.

Among the captured troops was Santa Anna himself. Houston forced Santa Anna to order his army out of Texas and sign a treaty recognizing independence for the Republic of Texas. The Mexican Congress refused to accept the treaty, but it was unwilling to launch another military campaign. Texas had won the war.

The Republic of Texas

In September 1836 the newly independent republic called its citizens to the polls. They elected Sam Houston as their first president and voted 3,277 to 91 in favor of **annexation,** or becoming part of the United States.

Given that Americans had enthusiastically supported the war, most Texans assumed the United States would want to annex the republic. Many northern members of Congress, however, opposed admitting Texas as a slave state.

President Andrew Jackson did not want to increase North-South tensions or risk a costly war with Mexico, which continued to claim ownership of Texas. Jackson made no move toward annexation, although on his last day in office he did sign a resolution officially recognizing Texas as an independent nation.

Reading Check **Summarizing** What difficulties did the Texans face in their war against Mexico?

Section 3 REVIEW

Vocabulary

1. **Explain** the significance of: *empresario*, National Colonization Act, Washington-on-the-Brazos, Antonio López de Santa Anna, Sam Houston, Alamo, William B. Travis, annexation.

Main Ideas

2. **Identifying** What was Fredonia?

3. **Stating** What was the military contribution of the soldiers defending the Alamo during the Texas war for independence?

Critical Thinking

4. **Big Ideas** What aspects of their culture did American settlers in Texas refuse to change?

5. **Organizing** Use a graphic organizer, similar to the one below, to list the reasons that Texans did not wish to become Mexican citizens.

Reasons Texans Opposed Mexican Citizenship

6. **Analyzing Visuals** Examine the time line on pages 266–267. How many years after Stephen Austin arrived in Texas did the Texans win the Battle of San Jacinto?

Writing About History

7. **Persuasive Writing** Suppose you live in Texas in the late 1830s. Write a letter to the U.S. Congress to persuade them to vote for or against the annexation of Texas.

History ONLINE

Study Central™ To review this section, go to glencoe.com and click on Study Central.

The War With Mexico

Guide to Reading

Big Ideas
Trade, War, and Migration War with Mexico brought new territories under the control of the United States.

Content Vocabulary
- envoy *(p. 272)*
- cede *(p. 275)*

Academic Vocabulary
- resolution *(p. 272)*
- secure *(p. 275)*

People and Events to Identify
- James K. Polk *(p. 271)*
- "Fifty-four Forty or Fight" *(p. 272)*
- Zachary Taylor *(p. 272)*
- John C. Frémont *(p. 275)*
- Bear Flag Republic *(p. 275)*
- Winfield Scott *(p. 275)*
- Treaty of Guadalupe Hidalgo *(p. 275)*

Reading Strategy
Taking Notes As you read about the war with Mexico, use the major headings of the section to complete the outline started below.

> The War With Mexico
> I. The Lingering Question of Texas
>   A.
>   a.

NEW YORK CORE CURRICULUM
U.S. History and Government

Unit 2:
II.C.5 Politics of western expansion (Manifest Destiny, the Texas and Oregon questions, the Mexican War)

By 1844, control of Oregon and the annexation of Texas had become major political issues. After the annexation of Texas, the border between the United States and Mexico was in dispute. The United States declared war on Mexico and took Mexico's northern territories.

The Lingering Question of Texas

MAIN Idea In 1844 James K. Polk was elected president and promised to annex Texas and Oregon and to buy California from Mexico.

HISTORY AND YOU Can you remember a slogan from a recent election campaign? Find out what "Fifty-four Forty or Fight" referred to and why it is still remembered.

Territorial disputes between the United States and Mexico began as far back as 1803, when the United States claimed Texas as part of the Louisiana Purchase. The United States renounced that claim in the Adams-Onís Treaty of 1819, but the idea of Manifest Destiny and of acquiring Mexican territory had strong popular support.

Tensions increased during the administration of John Tyler, who hoped to bring Texas into the Union. Because Texas already had a large population of Southerners who had taken slaves into Texas, Texans were certain to support the cause of slavery. Antislavery leaders in Congress, therefore, opposed annexation. Moreover, Mexico had never recognized the independence of Texas. Although militarily unable to regain control over Texas, Mexico still regarded the Republic of Texas as Mexican territory.

Texas and Oregon Enter the Union

In early 1844, after spearheading a publicity campaign in favor of annexation, President Tyler brought the matter before the Senate. He blundered, however, by including in the supporting documents a letter written by Secretary of State John C. Calhoun that contained a fierce defense of slavery. Outraged Northerners pointed to the letter as evidence that annexation was nothing but a pro-slavery plot, and by a count of 35 to 16, the Senate voted against annexation. The maneuver that Tyler believed would win him a second term instead destroyed his chances of retaining the presidency.

The Election of 1844 As the presidential race began later that year, the front-runners for the nomination were Whig Senator Henry Clay and former Democratic president Martin Van Buren. Although

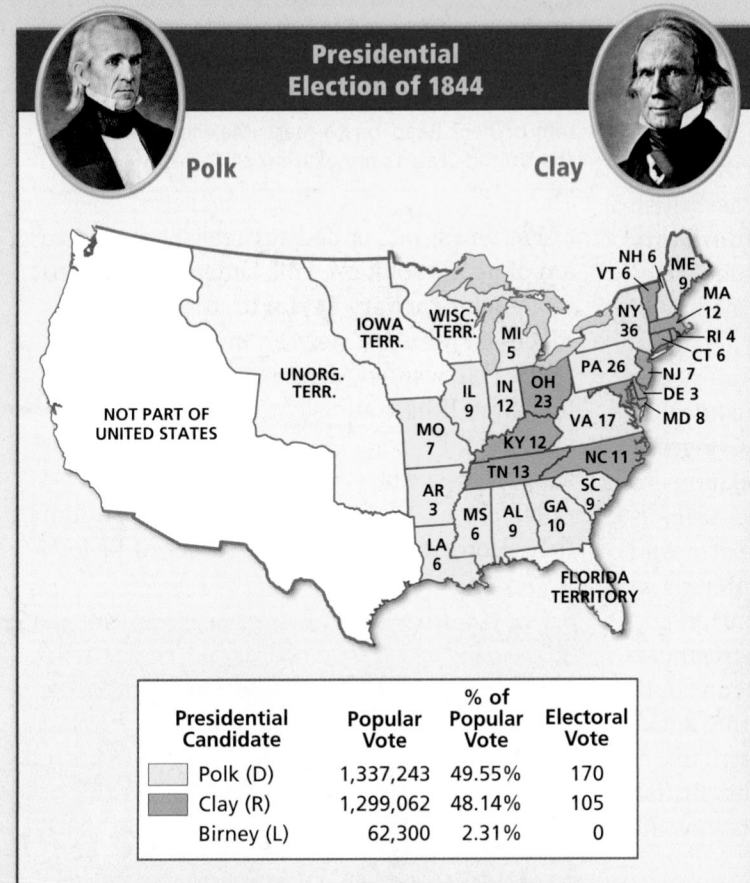

Presidential Election of 1844

Polk   **Clay**

NOT PART OF UNITED STATES

UNORG. TERR.

IOWA TERR.

WISC. TERR.

MI 5

NH 6
VT 6
ME 9
MA 12
NY 36
RI 4
CT 6
PA 26
NJ 7
DE 3
VA 17
MD 8

IL 9
IN 12
OH 23

MO 7
KY 12
NC 11

AR 3
TN 13
SC 9

MS 6
AL 9
GA 10

LA 6

FLORIDA TERRITORY

Presidential Candidate	Popular Vote	% of Popular Vote	Electoral Vote
Polk (D)	1,337,243	49.55%	170
Clay (R)	1,299,062	48.14%	105
Birney (L)	62,300	2.31%	0

▲ A ship symbolizing Texas carries James K. Polk to victory as it enters the Union. Henry Clay, and other Whigs who oppose Texas's annexation, are pulled into Salt River. In the 1800s, if someone "fell into Salt River," it meant the person had ruined his political career.

▲ James K. Polk's bridge across Salt River collapses under the weight of his pack, labeled Texas Annexation. Meanwhile, Henry Clay safely crosses "The People's Bridge" to the presidential chair.

Analyzing VISUALS   DBQ

1. **Comparing and Contrasting** How are the two cartoons alike and how are they different?

2. **Identifying** Which states did Clay win in the election of 1844?

---

politicians on both sides of the annexation issue pressed the candidates to state their positions, both responded cautiously to avoid losing supporters.

Van Buren's indecision cost him the Democratic nomination. His party instead chose **James K. Polk,** a former member of Congress and governor of Tennessee. Polk promised to annex not only Texas but also the contested Oregon Territory in the Northwest. In addition, he vowed to buy California from Mexico. This ambitious platform appealed to both Northerners and Southerners because it expanded the country while promising to maintain the delicate balance between free and slave states.

The Democrats' unity on annexation caused Clay to backpedal. Reversing a statement made in the spring of 1844 against immediate annexation, Clay now supported annexation of Texas as long as it was done without causing war with Mexico. This so angered antislavery Whigs in his party that they threw their support to the Liberty Party—a small third party that supported abolition. With the Whig vote split, Polk won the election.

The Oregon Question Polk took a strong stance on what came to be known as the Oregon Question. Despite British claims to the region, which had been established in the Convention of 1818, Polk and the Democrats held that the United States had a "clear and unquestionable" right to *all* of the Oregon Country, including the region north of the 49th parallel that is today known as British Columbia. Their rallying cry, **"Fifty-four Forty or Fight,"** declared that the United States should control all of Oregon below the line of 54° 40' north latitude.

Despite such slogans, few Americans wanted to fight the British to gain control of Oregon. After lengthy debates in Congress, Polk agreed to use diplomatic negotiations to settle the Oregon Question. In June 1846, as the United States fought with Mexico, and Great Britain was dealing with problems in Ireland, the two nations negotiated the Oregon Treaty to settle the dispute. In this agreement, the United States received all of Oregon south of 49° north latitude and west of the Rocky Mountains, except for the southern tip of Vancouver Island. In exchange, the British were guaranteed navigation rights on the Columbia River.

The Annexation of Texas Even before Polk took office, outgoing President Tyler pushed an annexation **resolution** through Congress in February 1845, and Texas joined the Union that year. As predicted, Mexico was outraged and broke diplomatic relations with the United States government. Matters worsened when the two countries disputed the location of Texas's southwestern border. Mexico said it was at the Nueces River. Texans, and then the United States, claimed the Rio Grande, about 150 miles (240 km) farther west and south, as the boundary. The Texas–United States claim covered far more territory than the Mexican claim.

Polk's intentions in California added to the growing strife with Mexico. In November 1845 he sent John Slidell as a special **envoy,** or representative, to Mexico City to try to purchase the territory. Mexico's new president, José Joaquín Herrera, refused even to meet with Slidell.

Reading Check **Examining** What did James Polk promise to do if elected president?

The War With Mexico

MAIN Idea Hostilities over the southwestern boundary of Texas led to war with Mexico.

HISTORY AND YOU Have you ever thought that someone took something that did not belong to him or her? Read on to learn Mexico's reaction to the United States's annexation of Texas.

Herrera's snub ended any realistic chance of a diplomatic solution. Polk ordered troops led by General **Zachary Taylor** to cross the Nueces River—in Mexico's view, an invasion of its territory. Polk wanted Mexican soldiers to fire the first shot. If he could say that Mexico was the aggressor, he could more easily win popular support for a war.

Finally, on May 9, 1846, news reached him that a force of Mexicans had attacked Taylor's

Debates IN HISTORY

Should the United States Go to War With Mexico?

Although many Americans supported war with Mexico for personal or political gain or because they subscribed to the principle of Manifest Destiny, many were against it. Debates raged between citizens, in newspapers, and in Congress over President Polk's motives and the tactics he had used to force a declaration of war against America's southern neighbor. While Polk insisted that Mexico had been the aggressor, many thought that the United States had purposefully incited the war to gain more land or, as Frederick Douglass believed, to extend slavery into new territory.

men. In an address to Congress, Polk declared that the United States was at war "by the act of Mexico herself." Hoping to incite the public's indignation, he added that "American blood has been shed on the American soil!"

Many Whigs opposed the war as yet another plot to extend slavery. Most Washington politicians, though, recognized that, no matter how questionable Polk's actions were, the United States was committed to war. On May 13 the Senate voted 40 to 2 and the House voted 174 to 14 in favor of war. Critics quickly dubbed the conflict "Mr. Polk's War."

Calling All Volunteers

Polk and his advisers developed a three-pronged military strategy. Taylor's troops would continue to move south, crossing the Rio Grande near the Gulf of Mexico. A separate force to the northwest would capture Santa Fe, an important trading center and now the capital of New Mexico, and then march west to take control of California with the help of the American navy. Finally, U.S. forces would advance on Mexico City and force Mexico to surrender.

To implement the ambitious plan, the United States needed to expand its army. Congress authorized the president to call for 50,000 volunteers, and men from all over the country rushed to enlist. Almost 73,000 answered the call.

Undisciplined and unruly, the volunteers proved to be less than ideal soldiers. As one officer observed, "They will do well enough to defend their own firesides, but they can not endure the fatigue incident to an invading army."

YES

James K. Polk
U.S. President

PRIMARY SOURCE

"Upon the pretext that Texas, a nation as independent as [Mexico], thought proper to unite its destinies with our own, [Mexico] has affected to believe that we have severed her rightful territory, and in official proclamations and manifestoes has repeatedly threatened to make war upon us for the purpose of reconquering Texas. In the meantime we have tried every effort at reconciliation. . . . But now, after reiterated menaces, Mexico has . . . invaded our territory and shed American blood upon the American soil. . . .

As war exists, and, notwithstanding all our efforts to avoid it, exists by the act of Mexico herself, we are called upon by every consideration of duty and patriotism to vindicate with decision the honor, the rights, and the interests of our country."

—from *The Congressional Globe*, May 11, 1846

NO

Frederick Douglass
American Abolitionist

PRIMARY SOURCE

"The war . . . was [begun] with no higher or holier motive than that of upholding and propagating slavery. In 1829 Mexico . . . had declared the entire abolition of slavery in her territories. The consequence was a decrease in the value of slaves in the border states of America, . . . What was the desperate purpose of the United States? . . . [T]hey stirred up a revolt against Mexico in Texas, which, . . . ultimately severed from the mother country. Their next step was kindly to recognise the independence of Texas, and in 1844 it was annexed to the Union. An army of men was sent to protect the Texians [sic]; . . . and the Mexicans firing at the invaders, the United States at once recognised a war, . . ."

—from *The Frederick Douglass Papers*

DBQ Document-Based Questions

1. **Paraphrasing** According to President Polk, what was the United States's attitude toward war with Mexico before Mexican forces attacked?

2. **Specifying** What reasons does Polk give for declaring war on Mexico?

3. **Summarizing** According to Frederick Douglass, what steps did the United States take to incite the war?

4. **Identifying Central Issues** What does Douglass say is the true reason for the war with Mexico?

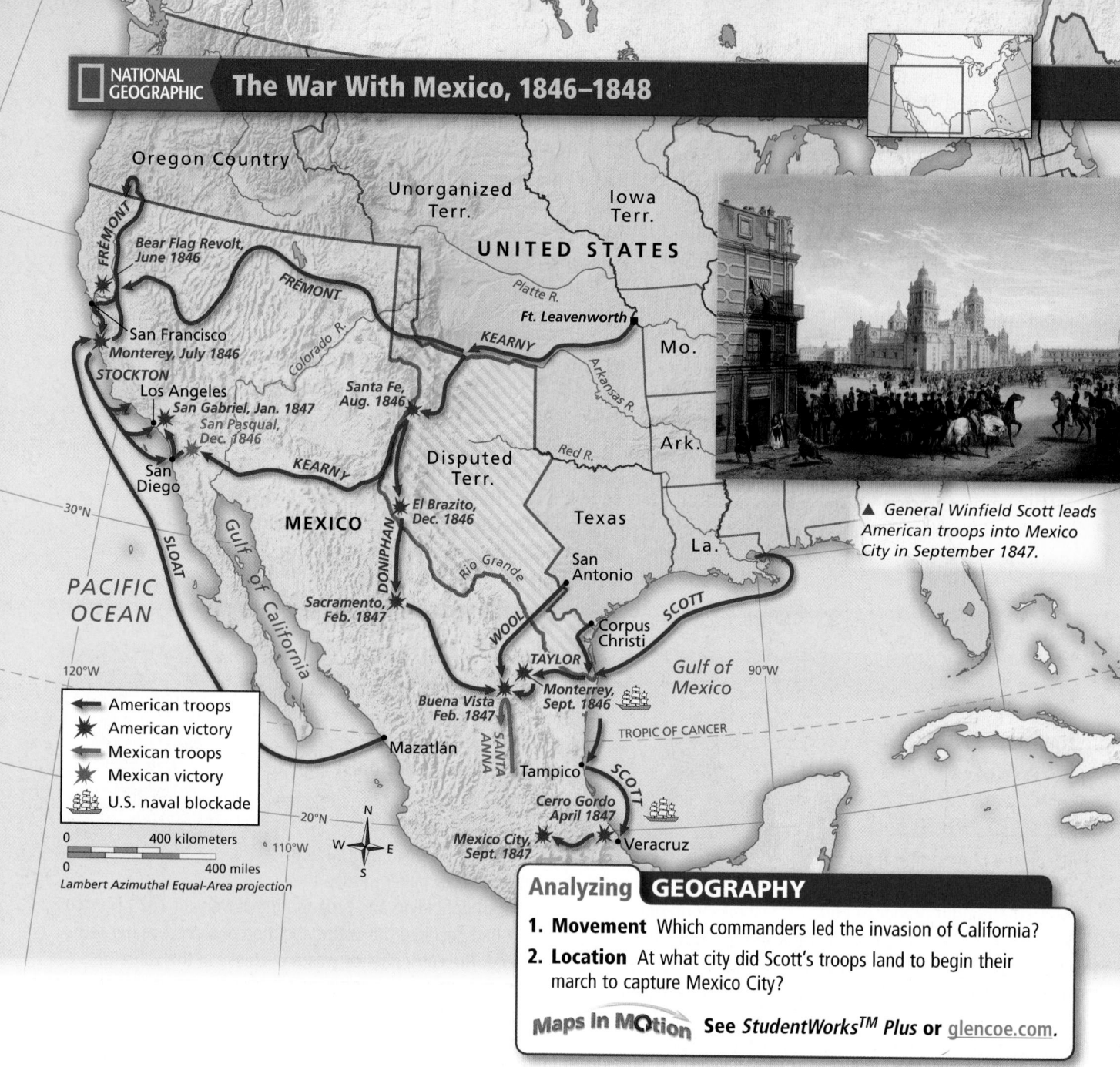

The War With Mexico, 1846–1848

Oregon Country

UNITED STATES

Unorganized Terr.

Iowa Terr.

Platte R.

Ft. Leavenworth

Mo.

Ark.

Arkansas R.

Red R.

FRÉMONT

Bear Flag Revolt, June 1846

San Francisco

Monterey, July 1846

STOCKTON

Los Angeles

San Gabriel, Jan. 1847

San Pasqual, Dec. 1846

San Diego

KEARNY

Santa Fe, Aug. 1846

Colorado R.

MEXICO

DONIPHAN

El Brazito, Dec. 1846

Disputed Terr.

Texas

San Antonio

La.

SLOAT

PACIFIC OCEAN

Gulf of California

Rio Grande

Sacramento, Feb. 1847

WOOL

TAYLOR

Corpus Christi

SCOTT

Gulf of Mexico

Buena Vista Feb. 1847

Monterrey, Sept. 1846

30°N

120°W

90°W

SANTA ANNA

Mazatlán

Tampico

TROPIC OF CANCER

SCOTT

20°N

110°W

Cerro Gordo April 1847

Mexico City, Sept. 1847

Veracruz

Legend:
- → American troops
- ✸ American victory
- → Mexican troops
- ✸ Mexican victory
- ⛵ U.S. naval blockade

0 — 400 kilometers

0 — 400 miles

Lambert Azimuthal Equal-Area projection

N W E S

▲ General Winfield Scott leads American troops into Mexico City in September 1847.

Analyzing GEOGRAPHY

1. **Movement** Which commanders led the invasion of California?
2. **Location** At what city did Scott's troops land to begin their march to capture Mexico City?

Maps In MOtion See *StudentWorks™ Plus* or glencoe.com.

Other officers saw similar problems. One bemoaned in a half-comical way that the green recruits constantly demanded his attention:

PRIMARY SOURCE

"[O]ne wanted me to read a letter he had just received; another wanted me to write one for him; another wanted me to send his money home; another wanted me to keep it for him. . . . [O]ne complained that his uniform was too large, another that his was too small."

—From *Memoirs of a Maryland Volunteer*

The Fighting Begins

In early May, several days before Polk signed the declaration of war, Taylor's troops defeated Mexican forces, first at Palo Alto and then at Resaca de la Palma. Taylor then moved south, defeating Mexican forces at Matamoros. By late September, he had marched about 200 miles (322 km) west from the coast of the Gulf of Mexico and captured Monterrey.

In the meantime, Colonel Stephen W. Kearny led troops from Fort Leavenworth, west of Missouri, toward Santa Fe. The march through the dry countryside was brutal, but when Kearny's men reached the city in August, the Mexican force there had already fled. With Santa Fe **secured,** Kearny led a small U.S. force into California.

Before Kearny arrived, and even before war with Mexico was officially declared, settlers in northern California led by American General **John C. Frémont** had begun an uprising. The official Mexican presence in the territory had never been strong, and the settlers had little trouble overcoming it. On June 14, 1846, they declared California independent of Mexico and renamed the region the **Bear Flag Republic.** A few weeks later, the Bear Flag Republic came to an end when American naval forces arrived and took possession of California for the United States.

To Mexico City

Despite having lost vast territories, Mexico's leaders refused to surrender. Polk decided to force things to a conclusion by sending soldiers on ships to the Mexican port of Veracruz. From there they would march west and capture the Mexican capital, Mexico City.

Polk, seeing Taylor as a potential rival in the 1848 election, eased him out of the war by placing General **Winfield Scott,** a member of the Whig Party, in command of this campaign. In March 1847 Scott's force landed at Veracruz, which his forces took after a three-week siege. Having taken control of this strategic port, the American troops then headed for Mexico City, fighting vicious and bloody battles with Mexican forces along the way. On September 14, after storming Chapultepec Castle, which guarded the city, they finally captured the capital after a hard fight at the city gates. With the Americans in control of the capital, a group of city leaders finally surrendered to General Scott unconditionally. American forces went on to establish a formal occupation of Mexico.

The Peace Treaty

On February 2, 1848, Mexican leaders signed the **Treaty of Guadalupe Hidalgo.** In the agreement, Mexico **ceded,** or gave up, more than 500,000 square miles (1,295,000 sq. km) of territory to the United States. Mexico also accepted the Rio Grande as the southern border of Texas. In exchange, the United States paid Mexico $15 million and agreed to take over $3.25 million in debts Mexico owed to American citizens.

With Oregon and the former Mexican territories now under the American flag, the dream of Manifest Destiny was finally realized: the United States now stretched from ocean to ocean. Valuable ports on the West Coast opened up new markets to the Pacific nations of Asia. The question of whether the new lands should allow slavery, however, would soon lead the country into a bloody civil war. The experience that such men as Robert E. Lee and Ulysses S. Grant gained during the war with Mexico would soon be used to lead Americans in battle against each other.

Reading Check **Summarizing** What was President Polk's military strategy in the war with Mexico?

Section 4 REVIEW

Vocabulary

1. **Explain** the significance of: James K. Polk, "Fifty-four Forty or Fight," envoy, Zachary Taylor, John C. Frémont, Bear Flag Republic, Winfield Scott, Treaty of Guadalupe Hidalgo, cede.

Main Ideas

2. **Specifying** What were the provisions of the Oregon Treaty?

3. **Explaining** What brought an end to the Bear Flag Republic?

Critical Thinking

4. **Big Ideas** The idea of Manifest Destiny was realized as a result of the war with Mexico. What new problem did the additional territories cause for the United States?

5. **Organizing** Use a graphic organizer, similar to the one below, to list the provisions of the Treaty of Guadalupe Hidalgo.

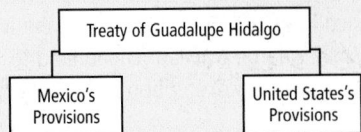

Treaty of Guadalupe Hidalgo	
Mexico's Provisions	United States's Provisions

6. **Analyzing Visuals** Study the painting of Scott's entry into Mexico City on page 274. How does the artist depict the event? How might the real event have differed from the painting?

Writing About History

7. **Expository Writing** Suppose you are James K. Polk, the Democratic candidate for president in 1844. Write a speech in which you explain your platform.

History ONLINE

Study Central™ To review this section, go to glencoe.com and click on Study Central.

Causes of Western Expansion

- The idea of Manifest Destiny influences many political leaders who believe the nation is destined to expand across the continent.

- The Preemption Act of 1830 gives settlers the right to claim land.

- New technology, including plows and reapers, enables settlers to farm the Midwest.

- Lush soil and moderate climate lures settlers to Oregon Territory and northern California.

- Christian beliefs lead missionaries to head west to try to convert Native Americans.

- Trailblazers map paths across the plains and mountains, making it easier for settlers to head west safely in long wagon trains.

- Treaty of Fort Laramie limits attacks by Native Americans on settlers and wagon trains heading west.

- Religious persecution leads Mormons to migrate west to Utah, where they can practice their religion freely.

- Mission system had already brought Spanish to the Southwest in the 1600s and 1700s.

- Hispanics move to California to establish large ranches.

- Mexico lures settlers to Texas with the National Colonization Act, giving large tracts of cheap land to *empresarios* and granting settlers exemption from taxes for 10 years.

▲ Astoria (above) was the first permanent settlement in the Oregon Territory.

▶ Vaqueros rest outside Santa Inez mission in California. Ranching and missionary work brought many Spanish settlers to the region.

Effects of Western Expansion

- Texas becomes American in culture, and Texans grow frustrated with Mexican laws, specifically the tariffs on trade with the United States, the ban on slavery, and the requirement that settlers become Catholic.

- Led by Stephen Austin and Sam Houston, Texans rebel against Mexico, declare independence, and defeat the Mexican forces led by Santa Anna.

- Americans in Texas and Oregon want to join the United States.

- The debate over Texas triggers a sectional crisis—Northerners believe the South wants Texas in order to expand slavery.

- James K. Polk campaigns, promising to get both Texas and Oregon, and wins the presidency.

- Britain and the United States agree to divide the Oregon territory.

- Congress approves the annexation of Texas.

- After fighting begins between American and Mexican forces on the Texas border, the United States declares war and invades Mexico.

- In the peace treaty, Mexico cedes much of its northern territory to the United States, including California and the American Southwest.

▲ American troops land at Monterey in Mexico in 1846. The War with Mexico ended with the United States in control of much of the Southwest.

NEW YORK REGENTS EXAM PRACTICE

TEST-TAKING

Be sure to examine carefully statements that contain the words *always*, *not*, and *never*. These are strong words that give clues to the incorrect answer.

Part I

Directions (1–11): For each statement or question, write on a separate sheet of paper the number of the word or expression that, of those given, best completes the statement or answers the question.

1 The term "Manifest Destiny" describes the idea that
  (1) European nations have no right to establish new colonies in the Western Hemisphere.
  (2) Protestantism should be the official religion of the United States.
  (3) God wants the United States to control all of North America.
  (4) Native Americans should be allowed to retain all their original lands.

2 Which group left the United States to establish a settlement called Deseret in the West?
  (1) Mormons
  (2) *empresarios*
  (3) Seminoles
  (4) mountain men

3 In the early 1800s, California society was dominated by which group?
  (1) mestizos   (3) rancheros
  (2) vaqueros   (4) *empresarios*

4 In 1821 William Becknell arrived in New Mexico and opened up trade in that border territory by
  (1) establishing the Santa Fe Trail.
  (2) starting the first American department store.
  (3) building a railroad line from Missouri.
  (4) leading a revolt against Mexico.

5 What did the saying "Fifty-four Forty or Fight" refer to?
  (1) the large number of Americans seeking farmland in California
  (2) the war with Mexico over boundary disputes at the Rio Grande
  (3) the area of land Polk supporters wanted in Oregon
  (4) the annexation of Texas and the battle at the Alamo

6 Who was Brigham Young?
  (1) a mountain man
  (2) a squatter
  (3) an overlander
  (4) a leader of the Mormons

7 The result of the Battle of San Jacinto was that
  (1) California became an independent republic.
  (2) the Cherokee were forced to leave the Southeast.
  (3) Texas became an independent republic.
  (4) the Mormons were forced to leave Ohio.

8 As part of his platform in the 1844 presidential election, James Polk promised to
  (1) extend American power around the world.
  (2) create a large, standing army.
  (3) remove all Native Americans from the Midwest.
  (4) annex Texas and Oregon.

Need Extra Help?								
If You Missed Questions . . .	1	2	3	4	5	6	7	8
Go to Page . . .	254	257	262	263	272	257	269	271

[OVER]

Base your answer to question 9 on the map below and on your knowledge of Chapter 7.

Treaty of Guadalupe Hidalgo, 1848

OREGON COUNTRY

Unorganized territory

Great Salt Lake

Colorado R.

PACIFIC OCEAN

0   200 kilometers
0   200 miles
Albers Equal-Area projection

Texas

Rio Grande

MEXICO

Area gained by the United States as a result of the Treaty of Guadalupe Hildago, 1848

9 Which of the following states now include territory acquired as a result of the war with Mexico?

(1) Oregon and Washington
(2) Montana and Idaho
(3) California and Nevada
(4) Texas and Oklahoma

10 The war with Mexico was officially ended by which of the following events?

(1) the signing of the Oregon Treaty
(2) the signing of the Treaty of Guadalupe Hidalgo
(3) the annexation of Texas
(4) the establishment of the Bear Flag Republic

11 The invention of the McCormick reaper encouraged

(1) settlement of the Great Plains.
(2) trade with New Mexico.
(3) mountain men to create trails to California.
(4) the expansion of slavery into new territories.

Need Extra Help?			
If You Missed Questions . . .	9	10	11
Go to Page . . .	278	275	255

Part II Thematic Essay Question

Directions: Write a well-organized essay that includes an introduction, several paragraphs addressing the task below, and a conclusion.

Theme: The War With Mexico

Even at the time, many Americans questioned the motives and goals of the war with Mexico, while others felt it was necessary to fulfill America's Manifest Destiny and the needs of a nation.

Task:

Discuss whether you think the war with Mexico was justified or not. Be sure to

- Discuss Manifest Destiny and how it was used as justification for expansion
- Evaluate arguments both for and against the Mexican War
- Describe at least one positive and one negative result of the war

Guidelines:
In your essay, be sure to:

- Develop all aspects of the task
- Support the theme with relevant facts, examples, and details
- Use a logical and clear plan of organization, including an introduction and a conclusion that are beyond a restatement of the theme

Part III Document-Based Question

This question is based on the accompanying documents. It is designed to test your ability to work with historical documents. Some of the documents have been edited for the purposes of the question. As you analyze the documents, take into account the source of each document and any point of view that may be presented in the document.

Historical Context:

The 1800s were a time of rapid expansion in the United States. Americans moved westward and established farms in the Midwest; later settlers traveled in wagon trains to the Pacific Coast and to Mexican territories.

Task:

Using information from the documents and your knowledge of United States history, answer the questions that follow each document in Part A. Your answers to the questions will help you write the Part B essay in which you will be asked to

- Discuss how the settlement of the West led to American annexation of new territories
- Describe how annexation and the acquisition of territory often led to fundamental disagreements in American government
- Evaluate the political consequences and effects of the annexation of new territory

Part A
Short-Answer Questions

Directions: Analyze the documents and answer the short-answer questions that follow each document on a separate sheet of paper.

Document 1

"It can no longer be doubted that this is a war of conquest. . . . In a letter to Commodore Sloat, . . . the Secretary [of War] says, 'You will take such measures as will render that vast region [California] a desirable place of residence for emigrants from our soil.' In a letter to Colonel Kearny . . . he says: 'Should you conquer and take possession of New Mexico and Upper California, you will establish civil governments therein. You may assure the people of these provinces that it is the wish of the United States to provide for them a free government with the least possible delay. . . .'"

Source: Charles Sumner, "Report on the War with Mexico," April 1847

1 What evidence does Sumner provide to show that war with Mexico was the U.S. government's intention?

Document 2

2 How does this image convey the attitudes of Texans during early battles with the Mexican army?

Part B
Essay

Directions: Reread the task box at the top left and write a well-organized essay that includes an introduction, several paragraphs, and a conclusion. Use evidence from the documents in your essay. Support your response with relevant facts, examples, and details. Include additional outside information.

Guidelines:
In your essay, be sure to:

- Develop all aspects of the task
- Incorporate information from the documents
- Incorporate relevant outside information
- Support the task with relevant facts, examples, and details
- Use a logical and clear plan of organization, including an introduction and a conclusion that are beyond a restatement of the task

 History ONLINE

For additional test practice, use Self-Check Quizzes—Chapter 7 at glencoe.com.

Need Extra Help?			
If You Missed Questions . . .	1	2	Essay
Go to Page . . .	279	279	279

Unit 3

The Crisis of Union

1848–1877

Why It Matters

The growing sectional crisis in the 1800s led to the Civil War, the most wrenching war in American history. The Civil War fundamentally altered American society. It ended slavery, destroyed the economy of the Old South, and changed the relationship between the federal government and the state governments. It also resulted in several changes to the United States Constitution.

Confederate soldiers of the 6th Virginia Infantry charge troops of the Union 9th Corps at the Battle of the Crater in Petersburg, Virginia, 1864.

Sectional Conflict Intensifies

1848–1860

SECTION 1 Slavery and Western Expansion

SECTION 2 The Crisis Deepens

SECTION 3 The Union Dissolves

African Americans escape from slavery and head north to freedom

U.S. PRESIDENTS

Polk
1845–1849

Taylor
1849–1850

1850
- Compromise of 1850 is adopted in an attempt to ease sectional tensions

Fillmore
1850–1853

Pierce
1853–1857

1854
- Republican Party is founded

1856
- Violence erupts between proslavery and antislavery forces in Kansas

KANSAS & FREEDOM !
Gen. Samuel C. Pomeroy,

FIRST CONGREGATIONAL CHURCH

On Tuesday Evening,

U.S. EVENTS

1848   1850   1852   1854   1856

WORLD EVENTS

1847
- Working hours in Britain are limited

1848
- Serfdom is abolished in Austrian Empire

1852
- Livingstone explores Africa's Zambezi River

1853
- Crimean War begins, pitting Russia against Great Britain and Turkey

MAKING CONNECTIONS
What Keeps Nations United?

From the days of the Constitutional Convention until the late 1840s, people in the North and South had made compromises to keep the nation united. That began to change in the 1850s as the nation expanded westward rapidly and the controversy over slavery in the new territories intensified.

- *Why do you think Northerners and Southerners became less willing to compromise in the 1850s?*
- *Was the Civil War inevitable?*

1860
- South Carolina secedes from the Union

Buchanan
1857–1861

1859
- John Brown raids the federal arsenal at Harpers Ferry, Virginia

CHARLESTON
MERCURY
EXTRA.

UNION
DISSOLVED!

Lincoln
1861–1865

1861
- Fort Sumter is bombarded by Confederate forces; the Civil War begins

1858

1860

1858
- First transatlantic telegraph cable laid between Europe and North America

1859
- Darwin's *Origin of Species is* published

FOLDABLES™

Analyzing Events Create a Trifold Book Foldable about one of the following events: the Fugitive Slave Act, the *Dred Scott* decision, the Lincoln-Douglas debates, the Missouri Compromise, the Kansas-Nebraska Act, or John Brown's raid. Describe the event, how it influenced events leading to the Civil War, and what might have happened if the event had turned out differently.

History ONLINE Chapter Overview
Visit glencoe.com to preview Chapter 8.

Section 1

Slavery and Western Expansion

Guide to Reading

Big Ideas
Struggles for Rights As sectional tensions rose, some Americans openly defied laws they thought were unjust.

Content Vocabulary
- popular sovereignty (p. 285)
- secession (p. 287)
- transcontinental railroad (p. 291)

Academic Vocabulary
- survival (p. 286)
- perception (p. 291)

People and Events to Identify
- Wilmot Proviso (p. 284)
- Free-Soil Party (p. 285)
- "Forty-Niners" (p. 286)
- Compromise of 1850 (p. 288)
- Fugitive Slave Act (p. 288)
- Underground Railroad (p. 289)
- Harriet Tubman (p. 289)
- *Uncle Tom's Cabin* (p. 291)
- Gadsden Purchase (p. 291)
- Kansas-Nebraska Act (p. 292)

Reading Strategy
Categorizing Complete a graphic organizer similar to the one below by pairing the presidential candidates of 1848 with their positions on slavery in the West.

Candidate	Position

NEW YORK CORE CURRICULUM
U.S. History and Government

Unit 2:
II.D.1.a Party disintegration and realignment and sectional polarization (Kansas-Nebraska Act, disintegration of the Whig Party and the rise of the Republican Party, *Dred Scott* decision, John Brown's raid)

The spread of slavery into new territory became the overriding political issue of the 1850s. Admitting new slave states or new free states would upset the balance of power between Northern states and Southern states in the national government.

The Search for Compromise

MAIN Idea Continuing disagreements over the westward expansion of slavery increased sectional tensions between the North and South.

HISTORY AND YOU What do you recall about the compromise Henry Clay previously negotiated between Northerners and Southerners? Read on to learn about the Great Compromise of 1850 and how it allowed California to be admitted to the Union.

As many people in both the North and South had anticipated, the Mexican War greatly increased sectional tensions. The war had opened vast new lands to American settlers raising, once again, the divisive issue of whether slavery should be allowed to spread westward into the new lands. As part of the debate over the new western territories, Southerners also demanded new laws to help them retrieve slaves who escaped to free states.

The Wilmot Proviso

In August 1846 Representative David Wilmot, a Democrat from Pennsylvania, proposed an addition to a war appropriations bill. His amendment, known as the **Wilmot Proviso,** proposed that in any territory that the United States gained from Mexico "neither slavery nor involuntary servitude shall ever exist."

Wilmot's proposal outraged Southerners. They believed that any antislavery decision about the territories would threaten slavery everywhere. Despite fierce Southern opposition, a coalition of Northern Democrats and Whigs passed the Wilmot Proviso in the House of Representatives. The Senate, however, refused to vote on it. During the debate, Senator John C. Calhoun of South Carolina prepared a series of resolutions to counter the Wilmot Proviso. The Calhoun Resolutions never came to a vote, but they demonstrated the growing anger of many Southerners.

In the resolutions, Calhoun argued that the states owned the territories of the United States in common, and that Congress had no right to ban slavery in them. Calhoun warned somberly that "political revolution, anarchy, [and] civil war" would surely erupt if the North failed to heed Southern concerns.

That's you Dad! more **"FREE SOIL."** *We'll rat 'em out yet. Long life to Davy Wilmot.*

Martin van Buren

Lewis Cass

Analyzing VISUALS   DBQ

1. **Finding the Main Idea** What is the main idea of this cartoon?

2. **Identifying Central Issues** Is the cartoon supporting free soil or popular sovereignty? How do you know?

In the nineteenth century, farmers would sometimes burn down their barns to kill all the rats. Democrats who supported free soil—many of whom, like Martin Van Buren, came from New York—were nicknamed Barn Burners. They opposed the nomination of Lewis Cass for president and supported the Wilmot Proviso.

Popular Sovereignty

With the country increasingly divided along sectional lines over the issue of slavery's expansion in the territories, many moderates began searching for a solution that would spare Congress from having to deal with the issue. Senator Lewis Cass of Michigan proposed one solution. Cass suggested that the citizens of each new territory should be allowed to decide for themselves whether or not they wanted to permit slavery. This idea came to be called **popular sovereignty.**

Popular sovereignty appealed to many members of Congress because it removed the slavery issue from national politics. It also appeared democratic since settlers themselves would make the decision. Abolitionists argued that it denied African Americans their right to freedom, but many Northerners supported the idea because they believed Northerners would settle most of the new territory and then ban slavery there.

The Free-Soil Party Emerges With the 1848 election approaching, the Whigs chose Zachary Taylor, hero of the war with Mexico, to run for president. The Whig Party in the North was split. Many Northern Whigs, known as Conscience Whigs, opposed slavery. They also opposed Taylor, a large slaveholder, because they believed he wanted to expand slavery westward. Other Northern Whigs supported Taylor and voted with the Southern Whigs to nominate him. These Northern Whigs were known as Cotton Whigs because many of them were linked to Northern textile manufacturers who needed Southern cotton.

The decision to nominate Taylor convinced many Conscience Whigs to quit the party. They then joined antislavery Democrats from New York, who were frustrated that their party had nominated Lewis Cass instead of Martin Van Buren. These two groups then joined members of the abolitionist Liberty Party to form the **Free-Soil Party,** which opposed slavery in the "free soil" of western territories.

Although some Free-Soilers condemned slavery as immoral, most simply wanted to preserve the western territories for white farmers. They believed that allowing slavery to expand would make it difficult for free men to find work. The Free-Soil Party's slogan summed up their views: "Free soil, free speech, free labor, and free men."

Candidates from three parties campaigned for the presidency in 1848. Democrat Lewis Cass supported popular sovereignty, although this support was not mentioned in the South. His promise to veto the Wilmot Proviso, should Congress pass it, however, was often reported. Former president Martin Van Buren led the Free-Soil Party, which took a strong position against slavery in the territories and backed the Wilmot Proviso. General Zachary Taylor, the Whig candidate, avoided the whole issue. On Election Day, support for the Free-Soilers split the Democratic vote in New York. This enabled Taylor to win the state, and with it, enough electoral votes to win the election.

The Forty-Niners Head to California

Within a year of Taylor's inauguration, the issue of slavery again took center stage. In 1848 gold was discovered in California, and thousands of people headed west, hoping to become rich. By the end of 1849, more than 80,000 **"Forty-Niners"** had arrived to look for gold—more than enough people for California to apply for statehood. Congress had to decide whether California would enter the Union as a free state or a slave state.

Before leaving office, President Polk had urged Congress to create territorial governments for California and New Mexico, but Congress had not been able to agree on whether to allow slavery in these territories. Although President Taylor was himself a slaveholder, he did not think slavery's **survival** depended on its expansion westward. He believed that the way to avoid a fight in Congress was to have Californians make their own decision about slavery. With Taylor's encouragement, California applied for admission as a free state in late 1849. Thus, the Gold Rush had forced the nation once again to confront the divisive issue of slavery.

The Great Debate Begins

If California became a free state, the slaveholding states would be in the minority in the Senate. Southerners dreaded this, fearing it

---

PRIMARY SOURCE
The Compromise of 1850

Leaders in the California Territory submitted their request to become a state in 1849. Debate in Congress over California's entry into the Union as a free state ended in the Compromise of 1850. California joined the Union in September 1850 as part of the Compromise.

PRIMARY SOURCE

". . . [I]t is this circumstance, Sir, the prohibition of slavery . . . which has contributed to raise . . . the dispute as to the propriety of the admission of California into the Union under this constitution."

—Daniel Webster, speech in the Senate, March 7, 1850

► Daniel Webster, Henry Clay, and John Calhoun were the main participants in the 1850 debate over the slavery issue and California's entry into the Union.

◄ As word of the discovery of gold in California spread through the nation, Americans rushed to the mountains in search of gold.

might result in limits on slavery and states' rights. A few Southern leaders began to talk openly of **secession**—of taking their states out of the Union.

Clay's Proposal In early 1850 one of the most senior and influential leaders in the Senate, Henry Clay of Kentucky, tried to find a compromise that would enable California to join the Union. Clay—nicknamed "The Great Compromiser" because of his role in promoting the Missouri Compromise in 1820 and solving the nullification crisis in 1833—proposed eight resolutions to solve the crisis.

Clay grouped the resolutions in pairs, offering concessions to both sides. The first pair allowed California to come in as a free state but organized the rest of the Mexican cession without any restrictions on slavery. The second pair settled the border between New Mexico and Texas in favor of New Mexico but compensated Texas by having the federal government take on its debts. This would win Southern votes because many Southerners held Texas bonds.

Clay's third pair of resolutions outlawed the slave trade in the District of Columbia but did not outlaw slavery itself. The final two resolutions were concessions to the South. Congress would be prohibited from interfering with the slave trade and would pass a new fugitive slave act to help Southerners recover enslaved African Americans who had fled to the North. These concessions were intended to reassure the South that after California joined the Union, the North would not use its control of the Senate to abolish slavery.

Clay's proposals triggered a massive debate. Any compromise would need the approval of Senator John C. Calhoun, the great defender of the South's rights. Calhoun was too ill to address the Senate. He wrote a speech and then sat, hollow-eyed and shrouded in flannel blankets, as another senator read it aloud.

Calhoun's Response Calhoun's address was brutally frank. It asserted flatly that Northern agitation against slavery threatened to destroy the South. He did not think Clay's compromise would save the Union. The South needed an acceptance of its rights, the return of fugitive slaves, and a guarantee of a balance of power between the sections. If the Southern states could not live in safety within the Union, Calhoun darkly predicted, secession was the only honorable solution.

<u>PRIMARY SOURCE</u>

"[T]he equilibrium between [the North and the South] . . . has been destroyed. . . . [o]ne section has the exclusive power of controlling the government, which leaves the other without any adequate means of protecting itself against its encroachment and oppression."

—John C. Calhoun, speech in the Senate, March 4, 1850

The Compromise of 1850

- California admitted to the Union as a free state
- Popular sovereignty to determine slavery issue in Utah and New Mexico territories
- Texas border dispute with New Mexico resolved
- Texas receives $10 million
- Slave trade, but not slavery itself, abolished in the District of Columbia
- New, stringent Fugitive Slave Law adopted

<u>PRIMARY SOURCE</u>

"California, with suitable boundaries, ought, upon her application, to be admitted as one of the States of this Union, without the imposition by Congress of any restriction in respect to the exclusion or introduction of slavery within those boundaries."

—Henry Clay's resolution, January 29, 1850

DBQ **Document-Based Questions**

1. **Summarizing** How does Clay think slavery should be treated in California?

2. **Finding Main Ideas** What is Calhoun's concern about adding California to the Union?

3. **Generalizing** Do you think the North or the South achieved more of its goals in the Compromise of 1850? Why?

Three days later, Senator Daniel Webster of Massachusetts rose to respond to Calhoun's talk of secession. Calling on the Senate to put national unity above sectional loyalties, Webster voiced his support for Clay's plan, claiming that it was the only hope for preserving the Union. Although he sought conciliation, Senator Webster did not back away from speaking bluntly—and with chilling foresight:

PRIMARY SOURCE

"I wish to speak to-day, not as a Massachusetts man, nor as a Northern man, but as an American. . . . I speak to-day for the preservation of the Union. 'Hear me for my cause'. . . . There can be no such thing as a peaceable secession. Peaceable secession is an utter impossibility. . . . I see as plainly as I see the sun in heaven what that disruption itself must produce; I see that it must produce war, and such a war as I will not describe."

—from the *Congressional Globe*

The Compromise of 1850

At first, Congress did not pass Clay's bill, in part because President Taylor opposed it. Then, unexpectedly, Taylor died in office that summer. Vice President Millard Fillmore succeeded him and quickly threw his support behind the compromise.

By the end of summer, Calhoun was dead, Webster had accepted the position of secretary of state, and Clay was exhausted, leaving leadership of the Senate to younger men. Thirty-seven-year-old Stephen A. Douglas of Illinois took charge of the effort to resolve the crisis. Douglas divided the large compromise initiative into several smaller bills. This allowed his colleagues from different sections to abstain or vote against whatever parts they disliked while supporting the rest. By fall, Congress had passed all the parts of the original proposal as Clay had envisioned it, and President Fillmore had signed them into law.

Fillmore called the compromise a "final settlement" between the North and South. For a short time, the **Compromise of 1850** did ease the tensions over slavery. In the next few years, however, more conflicts arose, and the hope of a permanent solution through compromise would begin to fade.

Reading Check **Summarizing** How did the Gold Rush affect the issue of slavery?

The Fugitive Slave Act

MAIN Idea Many Northerners opposed the Fugitive Slave Act and vowed to disobey it.

HISTORY AND YOU Under what circumstances, if any, do you believe citizens should disobey a law? Read to learn how some Northerners responded to the Fugitive Slave Act of 1850.

Although Henry Clay had conceived the **Fugitive Slave Act** as a benefit to slaveholders, it actually hurt the Southern cause by creating active hostility toward slavery among many Northerners who had been indifferent.

Northern Resistance Grows

Under the Fugitive Slave Act of 1850, a person claiming that an African American had escaped from slavery had only to point out that person as a runaway to take him or her into custody. The accused then would be brought before a federal commissioner. With no right to testify on their own behalf, African Americans had no way to prove their cases. An affidavit asserting that the captive had escaped from a slaveholder or testimony by white witnesses was all a court needed to order the person sent south. Furthermore, federal commissioners had an incentive to rule in favor of the slaveholder; such judgments earned the commissioner a $10 fee, but judgments in favor of the accused paid only $5.

The law also required federal marshals to assist slave catchers, and it authorized marshals to deputize citizens on the spot to help capture fugitives. A citizen who refused to cooperate could be jailed.

Newspaper accounts of the unjust seizure of African Americans fueled Northern indignation. One Northern newspaper proclaimed that "almost no colored man is safe in our streets." As outraged as Northerners were over such seizures, they were even angrier over the requirement that ordinary citizens help capture runaways. This provision drove many into active defiance. Frederick Douglass emphasized this part of the law over and over again in his speeches. A powerful orator, Douglass would paint an emotional picture of an African American fleeing kidnappers. Then he would ask his audience whether they would give the runaway over to the "pursuing bloodhounds." "No!" the crowd would roar.

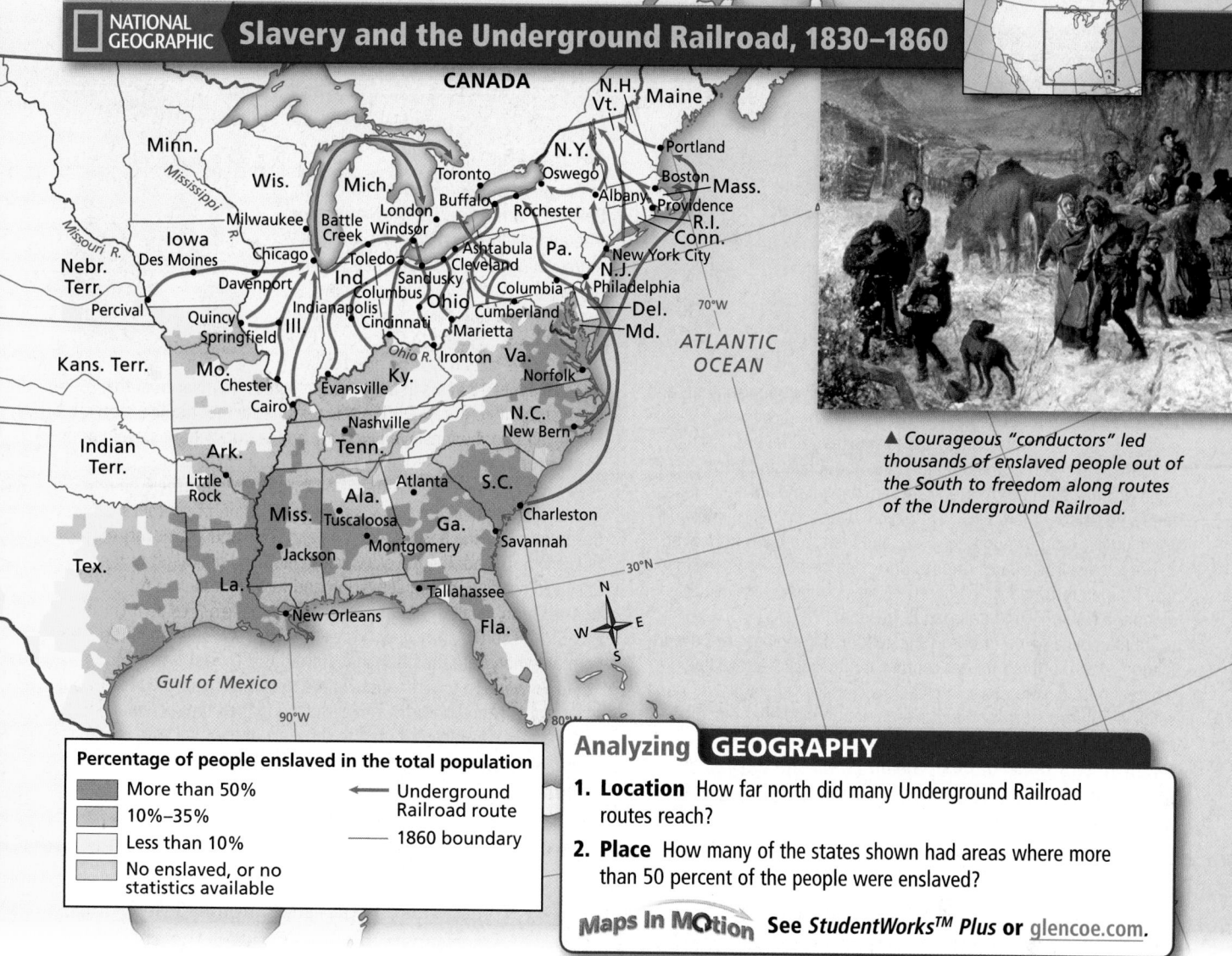

CANADA

N.H.
Vt. Maine

Minn.

Wis. Mich.

Toronto
Portland

N.Y.
Oswego
Boston Mass.
Albany Providence
R.I.
Conn.

Buffalo
Rochester

Milwaukee
Battle
Creek
London
Windsor

Iowa
Des Moines
Chicago
Toledo
Sandusky
Cleveland
Ashtabula
Pa.
New York City
N.J.

Nebr.
Terr.

Davenport
Ind
Columbus
Ohio
Columbia
Philadelphia

Percival
Indianapolis
Cincinnati
Marietta
Del.
70°W

Quincy
Springfield
Ill
Cumberland
Md.

ATLANTIC
OCEAN

Mo.
Ohio R.
Ironton
Va.

Kans. Terr.
Chester
Evansville
Ky.
Norfolk

Cairo
Nashville
N.C.
New Bern

Indian
Terr.
Ark.
Tenn.

Little
Rock
Atlanta
S.C.

Ala.
Miss.
Tuscaloosa
Ga.
Charleston

Tex.
Jackson
Montgomery
Savannah
30°N

La.
Tallahassee

New Orleans
Fla.

Gulf of Mexico

90°W
80°W

Mississippi R.
Missouri R.

N
W E
S

Percentage of people enslaved in the total population

- More than 50%
- 10%–35%
- Less than 10%
- No enslaved, or no statistics available

← Underground Railroad route
— 1860 boundary

▲ Courageous "conductors" led thousands of enslaved people out of the South to freedom along routes of the Underground Railroad.

Analyzing GEOGRAPHY

1. **Location** How far north did many Underground Railroad routes reach?
2. **Place** How many of the states shown had areas where more than 50 percent of the people were enslaved?

Maps In Motion See *StudentWorks™ Plus* or glencoe.com.

The Underground Railroad

Antislavery activists often used the words of writer Henry David Thoreau to justify defying the Fugitive Slave Act. In his 1849 essay, "Civil Disobedience," Thoreau advocated disobeying laws on moral grounds. "Unjust laws exist," he wrote. "Shall we be content to obey them, or shall we endeavor to amend them, and obey them until we have succeeded, or shall we transgress them at once?" For many, the answer was to disobey them without delay.

Although the Fugitive Slave Act included heavy fines and prison terms for helping a runaway, whites and free African Americans continued their work with the **Underground Railroad.** This informal but well-organized system was legendary during the 1840s and 1850s and helped thousands of enslaved persons escape. Members, called "conductors," transported runaways north in secret, gave

them shelter and food along the way, and saw them to freedom in the Northern states or in Canada, with some money for a fresh start.

Dedicated people, many of them African Americans, made dangerous trips into the South to guide enslaved persons along the Underground Railroad to freedom. The most famous of these conductors was **Harriet Tubman,** herself a runaway. She risked many trips to the South, even after slaveholders offered a large reward for her capture.

In Des Moines, Iowa, Isaac Brandt used secret signals to communicate with conductors on the Underground Railroad—a hand lifted palm outwards, for example, or a certain kind of tug at the ear. "I do not know how these signs or signals originated," he later remembered, "but they had become well understood. Without them the operation of the system of running slaves into free territory would not have been possible."

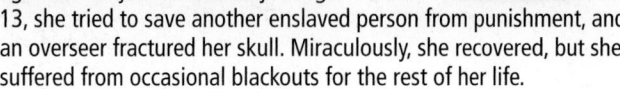

People IN HISTORY

Harriet Tubman
1820–1913

Known as "Moses" for her courage in leading enslaved people to freedom as Moses had led the Hebrews out of slavery in Egypt, Harriet Tubman was a heroine of the antislavery movement. Tubman was born into slavery in Maryland and struggled early against the system's brutality. At age 13, she tried to save another enslaved person from punishment, and an overseer fractured her skull. Miraculously, she recovered, but she suffered from occasional blackouts for the rest of her life.

Tubman escaped to freedom in 1849. About crossing into Pennsylvania, she later wrote, "I looked at my hands to see if I was the same person. There was such a glory over everything. The sun came up like gold through the trees, and I felt like I was in Heaven."

Her joy inspired others. After Congress passed the Fugitive Slave Act, Tubman returned to the South 19 times to guide enslaved people along the Underground Railroad to freedom.

Tubman became notorious in the eyes of slaveholders, but despite a large reward offered for her capture, no one ever betrayed her whereabouts. Furthermore, in all her rescues, she never lost a "passenger." Tubman's bravery and determination made her one of the most important figures in the antislavery movement.

What do you think Tubman meant when she wrote, "I looked at my hands to see if I was the same person?"

Harriet Beecher Stowe
1811–1896

Daughter of reformer-minister Lyman Beecher, Harriet Beecher Stowe was born into a family of high achievers. Unlike many young women of the time, Stowe received a good education, including teacher training in Hartford, Connecticut. In 1832 Stowe moved to Cincinnati, Ohio. There, Stowe began writing and teaching. She spent 18 years in Ohio—right across the river from the slave state of Kentucky. During this period, she met fugitive slaves, employed a former enslaved woman, and learned about slavery from Southern friends.

In 1850 Stowe moved with her husband to Maine. There, in reaction to the Fugitive Slave Law, she began writing *Uncle Tom's Cabin*, based on what she had learned while in Ohio and antislavery materials she had read. The novel, which humanized the plight of the enslaved, was an instant sensation and further hardened the positions of both abolitionists and slaveholders. When President Lincoln met Stowe, so the story goes, he exclaimed, "So you're the little woman who wrote the book that started this Great War!"

Stowe went on to write many more novels, stories, and articles but is today best known for the novel that so fanned the sectional flames over slavery that it contributed to the start of the Civil War.

What was the effect of Uncle Tom's Cabin on the slavery debate?

Levi Coffin was born to a Quaker family in North Carolina. As a boy, he witnessed a group of African Americans in chains being led to an auction. The incident deeply affected him, and years later, he allowed escaped African Americans to stay at his home in Indiana, where three Underground Railroad routes from the South converged.

To read an excerpt from **Uncle Tom's Cabin**, see page R68 in **American Literature Library**.

PRIMARY SOURCE

"We knew not what night or what hour of the night we would be roused from slumber by a gentle rap at the door. . . . Outside in the cold or rain, there would be a two-horse wagon loaded with fugitives, perhaps the greater part of them women and children. I would invite them, in a low tone, to come in, and they would follow me into the darkened house without a word, for we knew not who might be watching and listening."

—quoted in *The Underground Railroad*

An estimated 2,000 African Americans stopped at Coffin's Indiana house on their way to freedom. Coffin later moved to Cincinnati, Ohio, where he assisted another 1,300 African Americans who had crossed the river from Kentucky to freedom. A thorn in the side of slaveholders, the Underground Railroad deepened Southern mistrust of Northern intentions.

Uncle Tom's Cabin

One evening in 1851, the well-educated, deeply religious Stowe family sat in their parlor in Brunswick, Maine, listening to a letter being read aloud. The letter was from Harriet Beecher Stowe's sister, Isabella, in Boston.

The new Fugitive Slave Act, part of the Compromise of 1850, had gone into effect, Isabella reported, and slave catchers prowled the streets. They pounced on African Americans without warning, breaking into their houses, destroying their shops, and carrying them off. Isabella described daily attacks. She also told of outraged Bostonians, white and African American alike, who rallied to resist the kidnappers.

Harriet Beecher Stowe listened with growing despair. She had lived for many years in Cincinnati, across the Ohio River from the slave state of Kentucky. There, she had met many runaways from slavery and heard their tragic tales. She had also visited Kentucky and witnessed slavery firsthand.

As the reading of her sister's letter continued, Stowe, who was an accomplished author, received a challenge. "Now Hattie," Isabella wrote, "if I could use a pen as you can, I would write something that would make this whole nation feel what an accursed thing slavery is." Stowe suddenly rose from her chair and announced, "I will write something. I will if I live." That year, she began writing sketches for a book called *Uncle Tom's Cabin.*

After running as a serial in an antislavery newspaper, *Uncle Tom's Cabin* came out in book form in 1852 and sold 300,000 copies in its first year—an astounding number for the time. Today, the writing may seem overly sentimental, but to Stowe's original readers, mostly Northerners, it was powerful. Her depiction of the enslaved hero Tom and the villainous overseer Simon Legree changed Northern **perceptions** of African Americans and slavery.

Stowe presented African Americans as real people imprisoned in dreadful circumstances. Because she saw herself as a painter of slavery's horrors rather than an abstract debater, Stowe was able to evoke pity and outrage even in readers who were unmoved by rational arguments.

Theatrical dramatizations of *Uncle Tom's Cabin* increased the story's appeal. The plays reached a wider audience than the novel and specifically attracted the working class, which tended to ignore abolitionism.

Southerners tried unsuccessfully to have the novel banned and attacked its portrayal of slavery, accusing Stowe of writing "distortions" and "falsehoods." One Southern editor said he wanted a review of *Uncle Tom's Cabin* to be "as hot as hellfire, blasting and searing the reputation of the vile wretch in petticoats."

Despite Southern outrage, the book eventually sold millions of copies. It had such a dramatic impact on public opinion that many historians consider it one of the causes of the Civil War.

✔ **Reading Check** **Examining** What was an unintended consequence of the Fugitive Slave Act?

The Kansas-Nebraska Act

[MAIN Idea] In the 1850s the debate over the spread of slavery became increasingly heated and sometimes turned violent.

HISTORY AND YOU Have you ever watched Congress on television? Do you think politicians behave differently when they know the public is watching? Read on to find out how debate gave way to a physical assault on the Senate floor in 1856.

The opening of Oregon and the admission of California to the Union had convinced Americans that a **transcontinental railroad** should be built to connect the West Coast to the rest of the country. In the 1850s getting to the West Coast required many grueling weeks of travel overland or a long sea voyage around the tip of South America. A transcontinental railroad would reduce the journey to four relatively easy days, while promoting further settlement and growth in the territories along the route.

Debating the Route of the Transcontinental Railroad

The transcontinental railroad had broad appeal, but the choice of its eastern starting point became a new element in the sectional conflict. Two routes were initially proposed—a northern route and a southern route.

Many Southerners preferred a southern route from New Orleans, but the geography of the Southwest required the railroad to pass through northern Mexico. Secretary of War Jefferson Davis, a supporter of the South's interests, convinced President Franklin Pierce to send James Gadsden, a South Carolina politician and railroad promoter, to buy the land from Mexico. In 1853 Mexico accepted $10 million for the **Gadsden Purchase**—a 30,000-square-mile strip of land that today is part of southern Arizona and New Mexico.

Meanwhile, Senator Stephen A. Douglas of Illinois, the head of the Senate committee on territories, had his own ideas for a transcontinental railroad. Douglas wanted the eastern terminus to be in Chicago, but he knew that northern route required Congress to organize the unsettled lands west of Missouri and Iowa.

NATIONAL GEOGRAPHIC "Bleeding Kansas," 1855–1856

Proslavery capital Lecompton

Topeka

Antislavery capital Lawrence

Kansas River

Kansas City

Missouri River

May 21, 1856: "Border ruffians" from proslavery Missouri destroy printing press and burn buildings

Wakarusa River

Kansas Territory

Missouri

* Major attack by free-state forces

* Major attack by proslavery forces

May 24, 1856: John Brown massacres proslavery settlers at Pottawatomie Creek

Osawatomie

Pottawatomie Creek

Marais des Cygnes River

May 19, 1858: Proslavery men execute free-state men in a ravine

N W E S

0   10 kilometers
0   10 miles
Albers Equal-Area projection

SOUTHERN CHIVALRY — ARGUMENT versus CLUB'S.

▲ Representative Preston Brooks beat Senator Charles Sumner for criticizing Brooks's cousin, Senator Andrew Butler. While many Northerners were outraged over the incident, Southerners voiced their approval by sending Brooks canes.

Analyzing VISUALS

1. **Interpreting** According to the map, how many governments were in the Kansas Territory in 1856?

2. **Analyzing** In the cartoon shown above depicting the beating of Charles Sumner, which side do you think the cartoonist favored? Explain.

In 1853 Douglas prepared a bill to organize the region into a new territory to be called Nebraska. Although the House of Representatives passed the bill quickly, Southern senators who controlled key committees refused to go along, and they prevented the bill from coming to a vote. These senators made it clear to Douglas that if he wanted Nebraska organized, he needed to work to repeal the Missouri Compromise and allow slavery in the new territory.

Repealing the Missouri Compromise

Douglas knew that any attempt to repeal the Missouri Compromise would divide the country. Nevertheless, he wanted to open the northern Great Plains to settlement. At first he tried to dodge the issue and gain Southern support for his bill by saying that any states organized in the new Nebraska territory would be allowed to exercise popular sovereignty, deciding for themselves whether to allow slavery.

History ONLINE
Student Web Activity Visit glencoe.com and complete the activity on Bleeding Kansas.

Southern leaders in the Senate were not fooled. If the Missouri Compromise remained in place while the region was settled, slaveholders would not move there. As a result, the states formed in the region would naturally become free states. Determined to get the territory organized, Douglas's next version of the bill proposed to undo the Missouri Compromise and allow slavery in the region. He also proposed dividing the region into two territories. Nebraska would be to the north, adjacent to the free state of Iowa, and Kansas would be to the south, west of the slave state of Missouri. This looked like Nebraska was intended to be free territory, while Kansas was intended for slavery.

Douglas's bill outraged Northern Democrats and Whigs. Free-Soilers and antislavery Democrats called the act an "atrocious plot." They claimed abandoning the Missouri Compromise broke a solemn promise to limit the spread of slavery. Despite this opposition, the leaders of the Democrats in Congress won enough support to pass the **Kansas-Nebraska Act** in May 1854.

"Bleeding Kansas"

Kansas became the first battleground between those favoring the extension of slavery and those opposing it. Since eastern Kansas offered the same climate and rich soil as the slave state of Missouri, settlers moving there from Missouri were likely to bring enslaved persons with them and claim Kansas for the South. Northerners responded by hurrying into the territory themselves, intent on creating an antislavery majority. Northern settlers could count on the support of the New England Emigrant Aid Society, an abolitionist group founded to recruit and outfit antislavery settlers bound for Kansas. Carrying supplies and rifles, hordes of Northerners headed for the new territory.

Pro-slavery Senator David Atchison of Missouri responded by calling on men from his state to storm into Kansas. In the spring of 1855, thousands of Missourians—called "border ruffians" in the press—voted illegally in Kansas, helping to elect a proslavery legislature. Antislavery settlers countered by holding a convention in Topeka and drafting their own constitution that banned slavery. By March 1856, Kansas had two governments.

On May 21, 1856, border ruffians, worked up by the arrival of more Northerners, attacked the town of Lawrence, a stronghold of antislavery settlers. The attackers wrecked newspaper presses, plundered shops and homes, and burned a hotel and the home of the elected free-state governor.

"Bleeding Kansas," as newspapers dubbed the territory, became the scene of a territorial civil war between pro-slavery and antislavery settlers. By the end of 1856, 200 people had died in the fighting and $2 million worth of property had been destroyed.

The Caning of Charles Sumner

While bullets flew and blood ran in Kansas, the Senate hotly debated the future of the western territories. In mid-May 1856, Senator Charles Sumner of Massachusetts, a fiery abolitionist, delivered a speech accusing pro-slavery senators of forcing Kansas into the ranks of slave states. He singled out Senator Andrew P. Butler of South Carolina, saying Butler had "chosen a mistress . . . the harlot, Slavery."

Several days later, Butler's second cousin, Representative Preston Brooks, approached Sumner at his desk in the Senate chamber. Brooks shouted that Sumner's speech had been "a libel on South Carolina, and Mr. Butler, who is a relative of mine." Before Sumner could respond, Brooks raised a gold-handled cane and beat him savagely, leaving the senator severely injured.

Many Southerners considered Brooks a hero. Some sent him canes inscribed "Hit Him Again." Shocked by the attack and outraged by the flood of Southern support for Brooks, Northerners strengthened their determination to resist the "barbarism of slavery." One New York clergyman wrote in his journal that "no way is left for the North, but to strike back, or be slaves."

Reading Check **Describing** Why did Stephen Douglas propose repealing the Missouri Compromise?

Section 1 REVIEW

Vocabulary

1. **Explain** the significance of: Wilmot Proviso, popular sovereignty, Free-Soil Party, "Forty-Niners," secession, Compromise of 1850, Fugitive Slave Act, Underground Railroad, Harriet Tubman, *Uncle Tom's Cabin*, transcontinental railroad, Gadsden Purchase, Kansas-Nebraska Act.

Main Ideas

2. **Describing** How did Stephen Douglas achieve passage of the Compromise of 1850?

3. **Explaining** How could *Uncle Tom's Cabin* be considered a cause of the Civil War?

4. **Summarizing** How did the Kansas Territory become an arena of civil war?

Critical Thinking

5. **Big Ideas** How did antislavery activists justify disobeying the Fugitive Slave Act?

6. **Organizing** Use a graphic organizer similar to the one below to list the main elements of the Compromise of 1850.

Compromise of 1850

7. **Analyzing Visuals** Study the photo on page 286. What does the photo reveal about the people who traveled to California to find gold?

Writing About History

8. **Expository Writing** Suppose you are a reporter for a Southern or a Northern newspaper in the 1850s. Write an article on public reaction to *Uncle Tom's Cabin*.

History ONLINE

Study Central™ To review this section, go to glencoe.com and click on Study Central.

Section 2

The Crisis Deepens

Guide to Reading

Big Ideas

Group Action Due to differing opinions within established parties, Americans forged new political alliances in the 1850s.

Content Vocabulary
- referendum (p. 298)
- insurrection (p. 301)

Academic Vocabulary
- correspondence (p. 294)
- formulate (p. 300)

People and Events to Identify
- Republican Party (p. 294)
- Dred Scott (p. 296)
- Lecompton constitution (p. 298)
- Freeport Doctrine (p. 300)
- John Brown (p. 301)

Reading Strategy

Categorizing As you read about the North-South split, complete a graphic organizer like the one below to categorize events as executive, legislative, judicial, or nongovernmental.

Executive	
Legislative	
Judicial	
Nongovernmental	

NEW YORK CORE CURRICULUM
U.S. History and Government

Unit 2:
II.D.1.a Party disintegration and realignment and sectional polarization (Kansas-Nebraska Act, disintegration of the Whig Party and the rise of the Republican Party, *Dred Scott* decision, John Brown's raid)
II.D.1.b Abraham Lincoln, the secession crisis, and efforts at compromise (Lincoln-Douglas debates, election of 1860, secession, compromise plans, Fort Sumter)

The controversy over slavery accelerated the breakdown of the major political parties and the formation of new ones, including the party of future president Abraham Lincoln. Friction intensified until the North and South became unable to compromise any further.

The Birth of the Republican Party

MAIN Idea Continuing disagreements over the expansion of slavery—most notably the Kansas-Nebraska Act—led to the formation of the Republican Party.

HISTORY AND YOU Do you know of any foreign governments that are controlled by a coalition of political parties? Read on to learn how the Republican Party was formed by a coalition of political parties.

When the Kansas-Nebraska Act repealed the Missouri Compromise, it had a dramatic effect on the political system. Proslavery Southern Whigs and antislavery Northern Whigs had long battled for control of their party, but the Kansas-Nebraska Act finally split the party. Every Northern Whig in Congress had voted against the bill, while most Southern Whigs had voted for it. "We Whigs of the North," wrote one member from Connecticut, "are unalterably determined never to have even the slightest political **correspondence** or connexion" with the Southern Whigs.

Anger over the Kansas-Nebraska Act convinced former Whigs, members of the Free-Soil Party, and a few antislavery Democrats to work together during the congressional elections of 1854. Their coalitions took many different names, including the Anti-Nebraska Party, the Fusion Party, the People's Party, and the Independent Party. The most popular name was the **Republican Party.**

Republicans Organize

At a convention in Michigan in July 1854, the Republican Party was officially organized. In choosing the same name as Thomas Jefferson's original party, the Republicans declared their intention to revive the spirit of the American Revolution. Just as Jefferson had chosen the name because he wanted to prevent the United States from becoming a monarchy, the new Republicans chose their name because they feared that the Southern planters were becoming an aristocracy that controlled the federal government.

Republicans did not agree on whether slavery should be abolished in the Southern states, but they did agree that it had to be kept out of the territories. A large majority of Northern voters seemed to agree,

The Politics and Election of 1856

In 1856 three candidates ran for president: James Buchanan for the Democrats, John Frémont for the Republicans, and Millard Fillmore for the American Party. None of them had wide support because of their position for or against abolition. The fractured electorate chose Buchanan.

▼ Fremont pulls ahead in the presidential race. Buchanan has crashed into the Democratic platform and blames the slavery plank in the platform for scaring his mount and causing the crash. Fillmore rides a goose and holds a Know-Nothing lantern. He warns that if he loses, the Union will be dissolved. Spectators note that the goose has a curved spine—with no back bone.

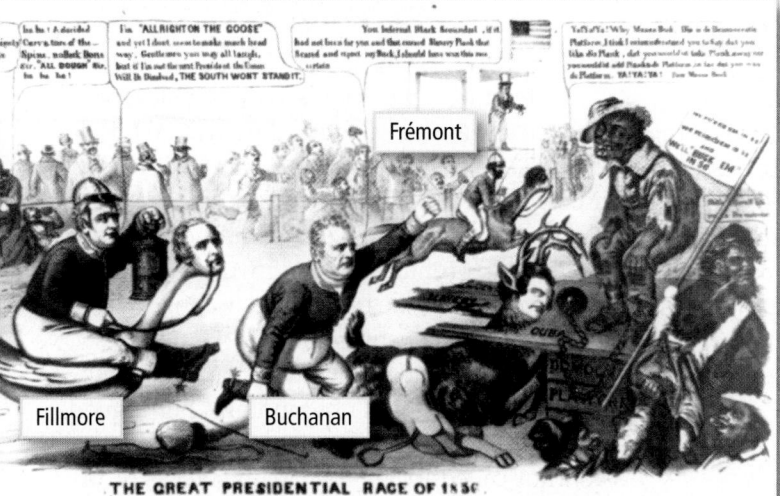

THE GREAT PRESIDENTIAL RACE OF 1856.

▲ The cartoon above shows Buchanan as a "buck"— a play on his name—winning the presidential race. Fillmore is shown as an underfed horse that has collapsed. Frémont is shown trying to win by riding two horses—a wooly nag labeled "abolitionism" and a horse with Horace Greeley's face. Greeley was editor of the New York Tribune—a very popular paper that supported antislavery causes.

Analyzing VISUALS

1. **Making Inferences** Why do you think that both cartoons are so critical of Fillmore?
2. **Identifying Points of View** Which cartoon do you think might have appeared in the North and which in the South? Why?

enabling the Republicans and the other anti-slavery parties to make great strides in the elections of 1854.

The Know-Nothings

At the same time, Northern anger against the Democrats enabled the American Party—also known as the Know-Nothings—to make gains, particularly in the Northeast. The American Party was an anti-Catholic and nativist party. It opposed immigration, especially Catholic immigration. Prejudice, and fear that immigrants would take away jobs, enabled the American Party to win many seats in Congress and state legislatures in 1854.

Soon after the election, the Know-Nothings suffered the same fate as the Whigs. Many Know-Nothings had been elected from the Upper South, particularly Maryland, Tennessee, and Kentucky. They quickly split with Know-Nothings from the North over their support for the Kansas-Nebraska Act. Furthermore, the violence in Kansas and the beating of Charles Sumner made slavery a far more important issue to most Americans than immigration. Eventually, the Republican Party absorbed most Northern Know-Nothings.

The Election of 1856

To gain the widest possible support in the 1856 campaign, Republicans nominated John C. Frémont, a famous Western explorer nicknamed "The Pathfinder." Frémont had spoken in favor of Kansas becoming a free state. He had little political experience but also no embarrassing record to defend.

The Democrats nominated James Buchanan. Buchanan had served in Congress for 20 years and had been the American ambassador to Russia and then to Great Britain. He had been in Great Britain during the debate over the Kansas-Nebraska Act and had not taken a stand on the issue, but his record in Congress showed that he believed the best way to save the Union was to make concessions to the South.

The American Party tried to reunite its Northern and Southern members at its convention, but most of the Northern delegates walked out when the party refused to call for the repeal of the Kansas-Nebraska Act. The rest of the convention then chose former president Millard Fillmore to represent the American Party, hoping to attract the vote of former Whigs.

The campaign was really two separate contests: Buchanan against Frémont in the North, and Buchanan against Fillmore in the South. Buchanan had solid support in the South and only needed his home state of Pennsylvania and one other state to win the presidency. Democrats campaigned on the idea that only Buchanan could save the Union and that the election of Frémont would cause the South to secede. When the votes were counted, Buchanan had won.

The *Dred Scott* Decision

In his March 1857 inaugural address, James Buchanan suggested that the nation let the Supreme Court decide the question of slavery in the territories. Most people who listened to the address did not know that Buchanan had contacted members of the Supreme Court and therefore knew that a decision was imminent.

Many Southern members of Congress had quietly pressured the Supreme Court justices to issue a ruling on slavery in the territories. They expected the Southern majority on the court to rule in favor of the South. They were not disappointed. Two days after the inauguration, the Court released its opinion in the case of *Dred Scott* v. *Sandford*.

Dred Scott was an enslaved man whose Missouri slaveholder had taken him to live in free territory before returning to Missouri. Assisted by abolitionists, Scott sued to end his slavery, arguing that the time he had spent in free territory meant he was free.

Scott's case went all the way to the Supreme Court. On March 6, 1857, Chief Justice Roger B. Taney delivered the majority opinion in the case. Taney ruled against Scott because, he claimed, African Americans were not citizens and therefore could not sue in the courts. Taney then addressed the Missouri Compromise's ban on slavery in territory north of Missouri's southern border:

PRIMARY SOURCE

"[I]t is the opinion of the court that the act of Congress which prohibited a citizen from holding and owning [enslaved persons] in the territory of the United States north of the line therein mentioned is not warranted by the Constitution and is therefore void."

—from *Dred Scott* v. *Sandford*

Instead of removing the issue of slavery in the territories from politics, the *Dred Scott* decision itself became a political issue that further intensified the sectional conflict. The Supreme Court had said that the federal government could not prohibit slavery in the territories. Free soil, one of the basic ideas uniting Republicans, was unconstitutional.

Democrats cheered the decision, but Republicans claimed it was not binding. They argued that it was an *obiter dictum*, an incidental opinion not called for by the circumstances of the case. Southerners, on the other hand, called on Northerners to obey the decision if they wanted the South to remain in the Union.

Many African Americans, among them Philadelphia activist Robert Purvis, publicly declared contempt for any government that could produce such an edict:

PRIMARY SOURCE

"Mr. Chairman, look at the facts—here, in a country with a sublimity of impudence that knows no parallel, setting itself up before the world as a free country, a land of liberty!, 'the land of the free, and the home of the brave,' the 'freest country in all the world' . . . and yet here are millions of men and women . . . bought and sold, whipped, manacled, killed all the day long."

—quoted in *Witness for Freedom*

✔ Reading Check **Explaining** How did the *Dred Scott* decision contribute to the growing split between North and South?

ANALYZING SUPREME COURT CASES
Can the Government Ban Slavery in Territories?

★ *Dred Scott* v. *Sandford*, 1857

Background to the Case

Between 1833 and 1843, enslaved African American Dred Scott and his wife Harriet had lived in the free state of Illinois and in the part of the Louisiana Territory that was considered free under the Missouri Compromise. When he was returned to Missouri, Scott sued his slaveholder, John Sandford, based on the idea that he was free because he had lived in free areas, and won. That decision was reversed by the Missouri Supreme Court, and Scott's case went to the U.S. Supreme Court.

How the Court Ruled

The 7-2 decision enraged many Northerners, and delighted many in the South. In his lengthy opinion for the Court, Chief Justice Roger B. Taney found that enslaved descendants of enslaved Africans were property, could not be citizens of the United States, or of a state, and that therefore Scott had no rights under the Constitution and no right to sue Sandford. Further, Taney decreed that Congress did not have the authority to prohibit slavery in the territories. This made the Missouri Compromise unconstitutional.

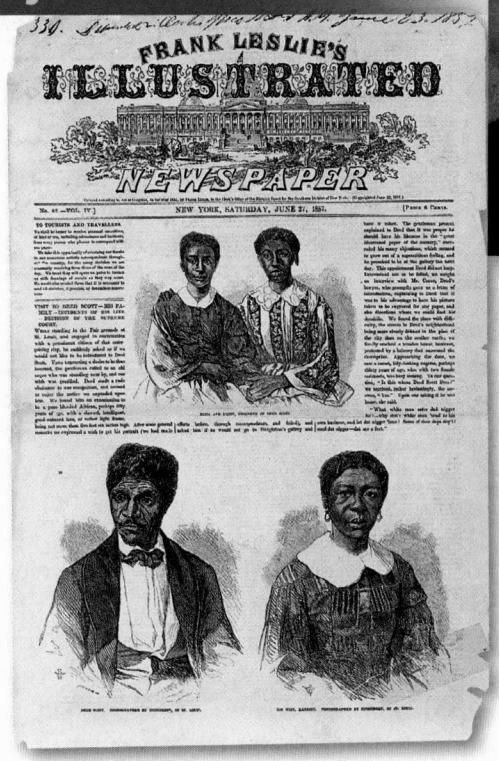

▲ Chief Justice Roger B. Taney (above, right) delivered the Supreme Court's ruling in the *Dred Scott* case. The decision made Scott and his family a topic for the nation's press.

PRIMARY SOURCE

The Court's Opinion

"[T]he right of property in a slave is distinctly and expressly affirmed in the Constitution. . . . And no word can be found in the Constitution which gives Congress a greater power over slave property, or which entitles property of that kind to less protection than property of any other description. . . . Upon these considerations, it is the opinion of the court that the act of Congress which prohibited a citizen from holding and owning property of this kind in the territory of the United States north of the line therein mentioned, is not warranted by the Constitution, and is therefore void; and that neither Dred Scott himself, nor any of his family, were made free by being carried into this territory."

—Chief Justice Roger B. Taney, writing for the Court in *Dred Scott* v. *Sandford*

PRIMARY SOURCE

Dissenting Views

"The prohibition of slavery north of thirty-six degrees thirty minutes, and of the State of Missouri . . . was passed by a vote of 134, in the House of Representatives, to 42. Before [President] Monroe signed the act, it was submitted by him to his Cabinet, and they held the restriction of slavery in a Territory to be within the constitutional powers of Congress. It would be singular, if in 1804 Congress had power to prohibit the introduction of slaves in Orleans Territory [the future state of Louisiana] from any other part of the Union, under the penalty of freedom to the slave, if the same power, embodied in the Missouri compromise, could not be exercised in 1820."

—Justice John McLean, dissenting in *Dred Scott* v. *Sandford*

DBQ Document-Based Questions

1. **Finding the Main Idea** What is the main idea of Chief Justice Roger B. Taney's opinion in *Dred Scott* v. *Sandford*?

2. **Summarizing** What argument does Justice John McLean offer in favor of Congress's right to prohibit slavery in the territories?

3. **Expressing** Which argument do you feel is stronger? Explain.

The Emergence of Abraham Lincoln

MAIN Idea Stephen Douglas took positions on Kansas and the *Dred Scott* case that reduced his popularity while Abraham Lincoln gained a reputation within the Republican Party.

HISTORY AND YOU What do you know about Abraham Lincoln? Read on to find out how he rose to national prominence in the 1850s through a series of famous debates.

After losing in 1856, Republicans realized they needed a candidate who could win every Northern state. They also knew that Senator Stephen Douglas of Illinois was a rising star in the Democratic Party and a Northerner whom the South might trust with the presidency in order to stop a Republican victory. To win, Republicans needed a candidate who could defeat Douglas in his home state of Illinois. They also needed Douglas to take unpopular positions on the issues under consideration.

By late 1858, both conditions had been fulfilled. Douglas had taken positions on Kansas and the *Dred Scott* case that made him less popular in both the North and the South. At the same time, Republicans had found a candidate from Illinois who might be able to challenge Douglass—a relatively unknown politician named Abraham Lincoln.

Kansas's Constitution

Douglas began to lose popularity in the South because of events in Kansas. Hoping to end the troubles there, President Buchanan urged the territory to apply for statehood. The proslavery legislature scheduled an election for delegates to a constitutional convention, but antislavery Kansans boycotted it, claiming it was rigged. The resulting constitution, drafted in the town of Lecompton in 1857, legalized slavery in the territory.

Each side then held its own **referendum,** or popular vote, on the constitution. Antislavery forces voted down the constitution; proslavery forces approved it. Buchanan accepted the proslavery vote and asked Congress to admit Kansas as a slave state. The Senate quickly voted to accept the **Lecompton constitution,** but the House of Representatives blocked it. Many members of Congress became so angry

during the debates that fistfights broke out. Southern leaders were stunned when even Stephen Douglas refused to support them. Many had thought that Douglas was one of the few Northern leaders who understood the South's concerns and would be willing to compromise.

Finally, to get the votes they needed, Southern leaders in Congress agreed to allow Kansas to hold another referendum on the constitution. Southern leaders expected to win this referendum. If settlers in Kansas rejected the Lecompton constitution, they would delay statehood for Kansas for at least two more years. Despite these conditions, the settlers in Kansas voted overwhelmingly in 1858 to reject the Lecompton constitution. They did not want slavery in their state. As a result, Kansas did not become a state until 1861.

Debates IN HISTORY

Can Slavery be Prohibited in the Western Territories?

In the 1850s, much of the political debate over slavery centered on the spread of slavery into the western territories. The *Dred Scott* decision held that the federal government could not ban slavery in the territories. Opponents of slavery then debated whether residents of a territory could ban slavery. This became a central issue in the Lincoln-Douglas debates of 1858.

Lincoln and Douglas

In 1858 Illinois Republicans chose Abraham Lincoln to run for the Senate against the Democratic incumbent, Stephen A. Douglas. Lincoln launched his campaign in June with a memorable speech, in which he declared:

PRIMARY SOURCE

"A house divided against itself cannot stand. I believe this Government cannot endure, permanently half *slave* and half *free.* I do not expect the Union to be dissolved—I do not expect the house to *fall*—but I *do* expect it will cease to be divided. It will become *all* one thing or *all* the other."

—from *Abraham Lincoln, Slavery, and the Civil War*

The nationally prominent Douglas, a short, stocky man nicknamed "The Little Giant," regularly drew large crowds on the campaign trail. Seeking to overcome Douglas's fame, Lincoln proposed a series of debates between the candidates, which would expose him to larger audiences than he could attract on his own. Douglas confidently accepted.

Although not an abolitionist, Lincoln believed slavery to be morally wrong and opposed its spread into western territories. Douglas, by contrast, supported popular sovereignty. During a debate in Freeport, Lincoln asked Douglas if the people of a territory could legally exclude slavery before achieving statehood. If Douglas said yes, he would appear to be opposing the *Dred Scott* ruling, which would cost him Southern support. If he said no, it would make it seem as if he had abandoned popular sovereignty, the principle on which he had built his following in the North.

YES

Stephen Douglas
United States Senator

PRIMARY SOURCE

"It matters not what way the Supreme Court may hereafter decide as to the abstract question whether slavery may or may not go into a territory under the constitution, the people have the lawful means to introduce it or exclude it as they please, for the reason that slavery cannot exist a day or an hour anywhere, unless it is supported by local police regulations. Those police regulations can only be established by the local legislature, and if the people are opposed to slavery they will elect representatives to that body who will by unfriendly legislation effectually prevent the introduction of it into their midst. If, on the contrary, they are for it, their legislation will favor its extension."

—speech delivered August 27, 1858

NO

Abraham Lincoln
Former Congressman

PRIMARY SOURCE

"What is Popular Sovereignty? Is it the right of the people to have Slavery or not have it, as they see fit, in the territories? I will state . . . my understanding is that Popular Sovereignty, as now applied to the question of Slavery, does allow the people of a Territory to have Slavery if they want to, but does not allow them not to have it if they do not want it. I do not mean that if this vast concourse of people were in a Territory of the United States, any one of them would be obliged to have a slave if he did not want one; but I do say that, as I understand the Dred Scott decision, if any one man wants slaves, all the rest have no way of keeping that one man from holding them."

—speech delivered August 21, 1858

DBQ Document-Based Questions

1. **Finding the Main Idea** According to Abraham Lincoln, why could territorial residents *not* ban slavery through popular sovereignty?

2. **Comparing** Why does Stephen Douglas think popular sovereignty can effectively limit slavery?

3. **Speculating** After reading both points of view, which author do you think had a more realistic assessment of the effectiveness of popular sovereignty to stop the spread of slavery?

John Brown Becomes a Martyr

Issued in the North in 1863, in the middle of the Civil War, this print depicts John Brown being led to his execution. The symbols in the print show how John Brown had become a martyr to many Northerners.

The flag says *Sic Semper Tyrannis*—Latin for "as always with tyrants" and refers to the idea that tyrants must be killed.

Brown is shown standing upright, unhurt, and uncowed as he is led to his death.

A figure wearing a tri-cornered hat of the American Revolution with the number *76* emblazoned on it looks on with concern.

Brown's jailers look malevolent, with angry snarls and hands on weapons.

A statue of Justice is shown with her arms and scales broken.

According to tradition, Brown kissed an enslaved child as he was led to the scaffold. This enslaved child and its mother are portrayed in a way that would remind viewers of paintings of Jesus and his mother Mary.

Analyzing VISUALS

1. **Identifying Central Issues** How is John Brown portrayed in this image?
2. **Drawing Conclusions** Why do you think that the statue of Justice is depicted as broken?

Douglas tried to avoid the dilemma, **formulating** an answer that became known as the **Freeport Doctrine.** He replied that he accepted the *Dred Scott* ruling, but he argued that people could still keep slavery out by refusing to pass the laws needed to regulate and enforce it. "Slavery cannot exist . . . anywhere," argued Douglas, "unless it is supported by local police regulations." Douglas's response pleased Illinois voters but angered Southerners.

Lincoln also attacked Douglas's claim that he "cared not" whether Kansans voted for or against slavery. Denouncing "the modern Democratic idea that slavery is as good as freedom," Lincoln called on voters to elect Republicans, "whose hearts are in the work, who do care for the result":

PRIMARY SOURCE

"Has any thing ever threatened the existence of this Union save and except this very institution of Slavery? What is it that we hold most dear amongst us? Our own liberty and prosperity. What has ever threatened our liberty and prosperity save and except this institution of Slavery? If this is true, how do you propose to improve the condition of things by enlarging Slavery—by spreading it out and making it bigger? You may have a wen [sore] or cancer upon your person and not be able to cut it out lest you bleed to death; but surely it is no way to cure it, to engraft it and spread it over your whole body. That is no proper way of treating what you regard a wrong."

—from *Abraham Lincoln, Slavery, and the Civil War*

Douglas won the election, but Lincoln did not come away empty-handed. He had used the debates to make clear the principles of the Republican Party. He had also established a national reputation for himself as a man of clear, insightful thinking who could argue with force and eloquence. Within a year, however, national attention shifted to another figure, a man who opposed slavery not with well-crafted phrases, but with a gun.

✓ Reading Check **Examining** What were the positions of Stephen Douglas and Abraham Lincoln on slavery?

John Brown's Raid

MAIN Idea Abolitionist John Brown planned to free and arm enslaved African Americans to stage a rebellion against slaveholders.

HISTORY AND YOU Do you recall a previous time in American history when citizens revolted against what they believed was an unfair government? Read on to learn about John Brown's raid at Harpers Ferry.

John Brown was a fervent abolitionist who believed, as one minister who knew him in Kansas said, "that God had raised him up on purpose to break the jaws of the wicked." In 1859 he developed a plan to seize the federal arsenal at Harpers Ferry, Virginia (today in West Virginia), free and arm the enslaved people in the area, and begin an **insurrection,** or rebellion, against slaveholders.

On the night of October 16, 1859, Brown and 18 followers seized the arsenal. To the terrified night watchman, he announced, "I have possession now of the United States armory, and if the citizens interfere with me I must only burn the town and have blood."

Soon, however, Brown was facing a contingent of U.S. Marines, rushed to Harpers Ferry from Washington, D.C., under the command of Colonel Robert E. Lee. Just 36 hours after it had begun, Brown's attempt to start a slave insurrection ended with his capture. A Virginia court tried and convicted him and sentenced him to death. In his last words to the court, Brown, repenting nothing, declared:

PRIMARY SOURCE

"I believe that to have interfered as I have done, as I have always freely admitted I have done in behalf of [God's] despised poor, I did no wrong, but right. Now if it is deemed necessary that I should forfeit my life for the furtherance of the ends of justice and mingle my blood . . . with the blood of millions in this slave country whose rights are disregarded by wicked, cruel and unjust enactments, I say, let it be done!"

—from *The Life and Letters of Captain John Brown*

On December 2, the day of his execution, Brown handed one of his jailers a prophetic note: "I, John Brown, am now quite certain that the crimes of this guilty land will never be purged away but with Blood. I had as I now think vainly flattered myself that without very much bloodshed it might be done."

Many Northerners viewed Brown as a martyr in a noble cause. The execution, Henry David Thoreau predicted, would strengthen abolitionist feeling in the North. "He is not old Brown any longer," Thoreau declared, "he is an angel of light."

For most Southerners, however, Brown's raid offered all the proof they needed that Northerners were actively plotting the murder of slaveholders. "Defend yourselves!" cried Georgia Senator Robert Toombs. "The enemy is at your door!"

Reading Check **Evaluating** In what ways might a Northerner and a Southerner view John Brown's action differently?

Section 2 REVIEW

Vocabulary

1. **Explain** the significance of: Republican Party, Dred Scott, referendum, Lecompton constitution, Freeport Doctrine, John Brown, insurrection.

Main Ideas

2. **Listing** What were the two rulings in *Dred Scott* v. *Sandford* that increased sectional divisiveness?

3. **Explaining** What was the ultimate fate of the Lecompton constitution?

4. **Synthesizing** How did Americans react to John Brown's raid?

Critical Thinking

5. **Big Ideas** What were the main goals of the Republican and American parties?

6. **Organizing** Use a graphic organizer similar to the one below to list causes of the growing tensions between the North and South.

Causes

Growing Tensions

7. **Analyzing Visuals** Study the image of John Brown's martyrdom on page 300. What do you think is the signficance of the figure in the tri-cornered hat?

Writing About History

8. **Expository Writing** Suppose that you have just read the Supreme Court's ruling in the *Dred Scott* case. Write a letter to the editor explaining your reaction to the decision.

History ONLINE
Study Central™ To review this section, go to glencoe.com and click on Study Central.

Section 3

The Union Dissolves

Guide to Reading

Big Ideas
Struggles for Rights After Lincoln's election to the presidency, many Southerners placed state loyalty above loyalty to the Union.

Content Vocabulary
• martial law (p. 307)

Academic Vocabulary
• commitment (p. 306)
• impose (p. 307)

People and Events to Identify
• John C. Breckinridge (p. 303)
• John Bell (p. 303)
• Fort Sumter (p. 304)
• Crittenden's Compromise (p. 305)
• Confederacy (p. 305)
• Jefferson Davis (p. 305)

Reading Strategy
Taking Notes Use the major headings of this section to outline the events that led to the U.S. Civil War.

```
The Union Dissolves
I. The Election of 1860
    A.
    B.
    C.
    D.
II.
```

NEW YORK CORE CURRICULUM
U.S. History and Government

Unit 2:
II.D.1.b Abraham Lincoln, the secession crisis, and efforts at compromise (Lincoln-Douglas debates, election of 1860, secession, compromise plans, Fort Sumter)

In the end, all attempts at compromise between the North and South over slavery failed to end the sectional differences. Finally, the outcome of the 1860 election triggered a showdown and the first shots of the long, bloody Civil War.

The Election of 1860

MAIN Idea The election of Abraham Lincoln led the Southern states to secede from the Union.

HISTORY AND YOU Is it always important to give someone a chance to keep a promise? Lincoln had promised not to free slaves in the Southern states. Read on to learn how South Carolina decided to secede anyway.

John Brown's raid on Harpers Ferry was a turning point for the South. The possibility of a slave uprising had long haunted many Southerners, but they were frightened and angered by the idea that Northerners would deliberately try to arm enslaved people and encourage them to rebel.

Although the Republican leaders quickly denounced Brown's raid, many Southerners blamed Republicans. To them, the key point was that both the Republicans and John Brown opposed slavery. As one Atlanta newspaper noted: "We regard every man who does not boldly declare that he believes African slavery to be a social, moral, and political blessing as an enemy to the institutions of the South."

In the Senate, Robert Toombs of Georgia warned that the South would "never permit this Federal government to pass into the traitorous hands of the Black Republican party." In April 1860, with the South in an uproar, Democrats headed to Charleston, South Carolina, to choose their nominee for president.

The Democrats Split

In 1860 the debate over slavery in the western territories finally tore the Democratic Party apart. Their first presidential nominating convention ended in dispute. Northern delegates wanted to support popular sovereignty, while Southern delegates wanted the party to uphold the *Dred Scott* decision and endorse a federal slave code for the territories. Stephen Douglas was not able to get the votes needed to be nominated for president, but neither was anyone else.

In June 1860 the Democrats met again, this time in Baltimore, to select their candidate. Douglas's supporters in the South had organized rival delegations to ensure Douglas's endorsement. The original Southern delegations objected to these rival delegates and again

The Election of 1860

After the slavery issue split the Democratic Party, the election of 1860 evolved into a four-way race. In the cartoon, the artist implies that Lincoln won because he had the best bat, which is labeled "equal rights and free territories," while the other candidates were for compromise or the extension of slavery.

Stephen Douglas holds a bat labeled "Non-intervention" and blames Lincoln's rail for his loss.

John Breckinridge's bat is labeled "slavery extension" and his belt says Disunion Club.

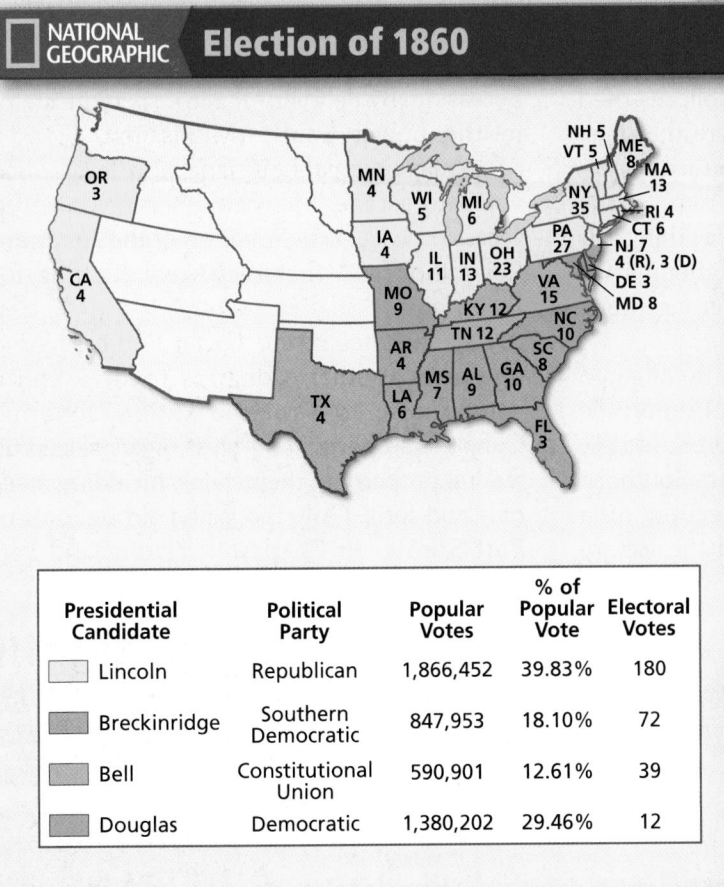

NATIONAL GEOGRAPHIC Election of 1860

John Bell's bat is labeled "Fusion" and his belt says Union Club.

Abraham Lincoln, the winner, stands on home base holding a rail labeled "Equal Rights and Free Territory."

Presidential Candidate	Political Party	Popular Votes	% of Popular Vote	Electoral Votes
Lincoln	Republican	1,866,452	39.83%	180
Breckinridge	Southern Democratic	847,953	18.10%	72
Bell	Constitutional Union	590,901	12.61%	39
Douglas	Democratic	1,380,202	29.46%	12

Analyzing VISUALS DBQ

1. **Interpreting** How does the map show that Lincoln was a sectional candidate?

2. **Identifying Points of View** Do you think that the artist was sympathetic to abolition or not? Explain.

walked out. The remaining Democrats then chose Douglas to run for president.

The Southern Democrats who had walked out organized their own convention and nominated the current vice president, **John C. Breckinridge** of Kentucky, for president. Breckinridge supported the *Dred Scott* decision and agreed to endorse the idea of a federal slave code for the western territories.

The split in the Democratic Party greatly improved Republican prospects, which was what some of the more radical Southern delegates had intended all along. They hoped that a Republican victory would be the final straw that would convince the Southern states to secede.

Other people, including many former Whigs, were greatly alarmed at the danger to the Union. They created another new party, the Constitutional Union Party, and chose former Tennessee senator **John Bell** as their candidate. The Constitutional Unionists campaigned on a position of upholding both the Constitution and the Union.

Lincoln Is Elected

With no chance of winning electoral votes in the South, the Republican candidate had to sweep the North. The most prominent Republican at the time was Senator William Seward from New York. Delegates at the Republican convention in Chicago did not think Seward had a wide enough appeal. Instead they nominated Abraham Lincoln, whose debates with Douglas had made him very popular in the North.

During the campaign, the Republicans tried to persuade voters they were more than just an antislavery party. They denounced John Brown's raid and reaffirmed the right of the Southern states to preserve slavery within their borders. They also supported higher tariffs, a new homestead law for western settlers, and a transcontinental railroad.

The Republican proposals greatly angered many Southerners. However, with Democratic votes split between Douglas and Breckinridge, Lincoln won the election without Southern support. For the South, the election of a Republican president represented the victory of the abolitionists. The survival of Southern society and culture seemed to be at stake. For many, there was now no choice but to secede.

Secession Begins

The dissolution of the Union began with South Carolina, where anti-Northern, secessionist sentiment had long been intense. Shortly after Lincoln's election, the state legislature called for a convention. The convention unanimously voted for the Ordinance of Secession. By February 1, 1861, six more states in the Lower South—Mississippi, Florida, Alabama, Georgia, Louisiana, and Texas—had voted to secede. Many Southerners believed secession was in the tradition of the American Revolution and that they were fighting for their rights.

As the states of the Lower South seceded one after another, Congress tried to find a compromise to save the Union. Ignoring Congress's efforts, the secessionists seized all federal property in their states, including arsenals and forts. Only the island strongholds of **Fort Sumter** in Charleston Harbor and Fort

Steps to Civil War, 1846–1860

▲ David Wilmot

1846
Wilmot Proviso proposing to ban slavery in Mexican cession enrages Southerners

1848
Free-Soil Party is founded by Northern antislavery Whigs, Democrats, and members of the Liberty Party

1850
Compromise of 1850 allows California to enter Union as a free state, giving free states a Senate majority, but the new Fugitive Slave law enrages Northerners

CAUTION!!
COLORED PEOPLE
OF BOSTON, ONE & ALL,
You are hereby respectfully CAUTIONED and advised, to avoid conversing with the
Watchmen and Police Officers of Boston,
For since the recent ORDER OF THE MAYOR & ALDERMEN, they are empowered to act as
KIDNAPPERS AND **Slave Catchers,**
And they have already been actually employed in KIDNAPPING, CATCHING, AND KEEPING SLAVES. Therefore, if you value your LIBERTY, and the Welfare of the Fugitives among you, Shun them in every possible manner, as so many HOUNDS on the track of the most unfortunate of your race.
Keep a Sharp Look Out for KIDNAPPERS, and have TOP EYE open.
APRIL 24, 1851.

1846 **1848** **1850** **1852**

1847
Vice President George Dallas proposes popular sovereignty; Democrat Lewis Cass popularizes the idea, angering Northern antislavery Democrats

1849
California Gold Rush brings flood of settlers; California applies for statehood

1852
Uncle Tom's Cabin is published

Pickens in Pensacola Harbor, as well as a few other islands off the coast of Florida, remained out of Southern hands.

Although horrified at the seizure of federal property by the secessionists, many members of Congress were still willing to compromise to avoid civil war. To that end, Kentucky senator John J. Crittenden proposed several amendments to the Constitution. One would guarantee slavery where it already existed. Another would also reinstate the Missouri Compromise line, extending it to the California border. Slavery would be prohibited north of the line and protected south of it. Lincoln, however, asked congressional Republicans to stand firm, and **Crittenden's Compromise** did not pass.

Virginia—a slave state but still in the Union—then proposed a peace conference. Delegates from 21 states attended the conference in Washington, D.C. The majority came from Northern and border states. None came from the secessionist states. The delegates met for three weeks, but came up with little more than a modified version of Crittenden's Compromise. When presented to Congress, the plan went down in defeat.

Founding the Confederacy

On the same day the peace conference met, delegates from the seceding states met in Montgomery, Alabama. There, in early February, they declared themselves to be a new nation—the Confederate States of America—or the **Confederacy,** as it became known. The convention then drafted a constitution based largely on the U.S. Constitution but with some important changes. It declared that each state was independent and guaranteed the existence of slavery in Confederate territory. It did ban the import of slaves from other countries. It also banned protective tariffs and limited the presidency to a single six-year term.

The delegates to the convention chose **Jefferson Davis,** a former senator from Mississippi, as president of the Confederate States of America. In his inaugural address, Davis declared, "The time for compromise has now passed. The South is determined to . . . make all who oppose her smell Southern powder and feel Southern steel."

✔ **Reading Check** **Identifying** What main event triggered the secession of Southern states?

1854
Kansas-Nebraska Act crafted by Stephen Douglas repeals Missouri Compromise; Republican Party is founded

1856
Charles Sumner is caned in the Senate

1858
Abraham Lincoln wins national attention during Lincoln-Douglas debates

1859
John Brown raids Harpers Ferry

1860
Lincoln is elected; secession begins

1854   **1856**   **1858**   **1860**

1856
Border ruffians attack antislavery settlers in Lawrence, Kansas; John Brown leads attack on pro-slavery settlers in Pottawatomie Creek, Kansas

1857
Dred Scott decision allowing slavery in all federal territories enrages Northerners

▲ *Antislavery settlers in Kansas*

Analyzing TIME LINES

1. **Specifying** How many years elapsed between the Compromise of 1850 and the beginning of the Civil War?

2. **Identifying** Which came first—the *Dred Scott* decision or the Wilmot Proviso?

The Civil War Begins

MAIN Idea The plan to resupply Fort Sumter triggered the beginning of the Civil War.

HISTORY AND YOU Do you think it is ever appropriate for the government to declare martial law? Why or why not? Read to learn how Lincoln used martial law to keep Maryland from seceding.

In his inaugural address on March 4, 1861, Lincoln spoke directly to the seceding states. He repeated his **commitment** not to interfere with slavery where it existed but insisted that "the Union of these States is perpetual." Lincoln did not threaten the seceded states, but he said he intended to "hold, occupy, and possess" federal property in those states. Lincoln also encouraged reconciliation:

PRIMARY SOURCE

"In your hands, my dissatisfied countrymen, and not in mine is the momentous issue of civil war. The government will not assail you. You can have no conflict, without yourselves being the aggres-sors. . . . We are not enemies, but friends. We must not be enemies. Though passion may have strained, it must not break our bonds of affection."

—from Lincoln's first Inaugural Address

Fort Sumter Falls

In April Lincoln announced that he would resupply Fort Sumter. Confederate President Jefferson Davis now faced a dilemma. Leaving federal troops in the South's most vital harbor was unacceptable if the Confederacy was to be an independent nation. Firing on the supply ship, however, would undoubtedly lead to war with the United States.

Davis decided to capture Fort Sumter before the supply ship arrived. If he was successful, peace might be preserved. Confederate leaders sent a note to Major Robert Anderson, the fort's commander, demanding Fort Sumter's surrender by the morning of April 12, 1861.

Anderson stood fast. The fateful hour came and went, and cannon fire suddenly shook the

Turning Point

The Fall of Fort Sumter

When the Confederacy took Fort Sumter, it fired the first shots of the American Civil War. The Civil War was the most serious test of the strength of the Union up to that point, or since. The North, led by President Lincoln, was determined to preserve the United States as a whole, while the South, led by Jefferson Davis and Robert E. Lee, was determined to start a new nation of its own to preserve the institution of slavery.

ANALYZING HISTORY Why was the shelling of Fort Sumter a turning point in American history?

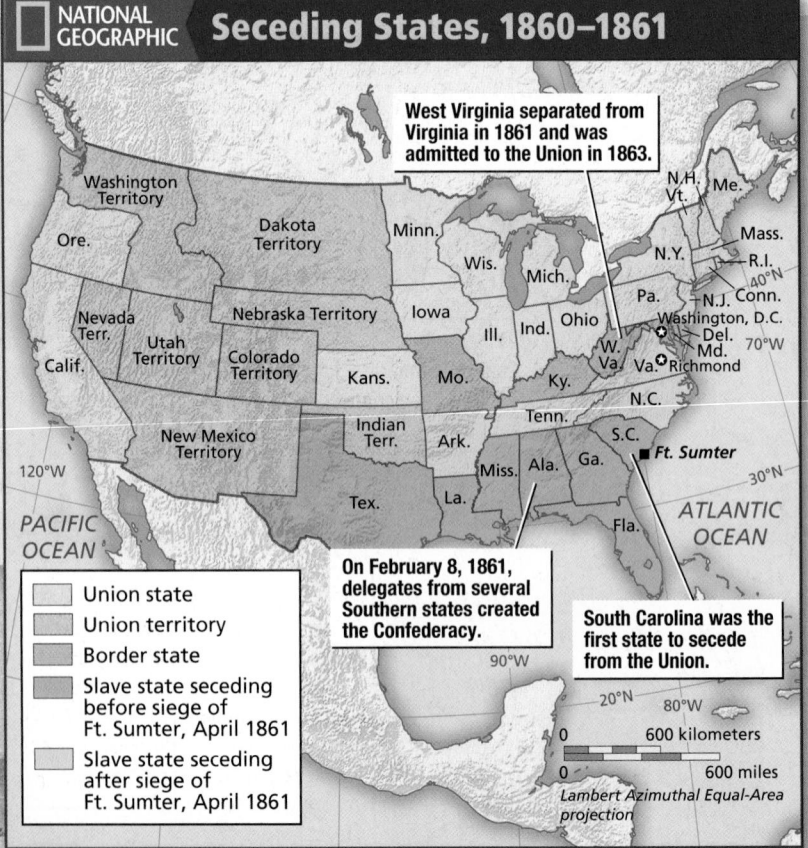

NATIONAL GEOGRAPHIC Seceding States, 1860–1861

West Virginia separated from Virginia in 1861 and was admitted to the Union in 1863.

On February 8, 1861, delegates from several Southern states created the Confederacy.

South Carolina was the first state to secede from the Union.

Union state
Union territory
Border state
Slave state seceding before siege of Ft. Sumter, April 1861
Slave state seceding after siege of Ft. Sumter, April 1861

600 kilometers
600 miles
Lambert Azimuthal Equal-Area projection

◄ The attack on Fort Sumter sparked the Civil War.

air. Confederate forces bombarded Fort Sumter for 33 hours, wrecking the fort but killing no one, until Anderson and his exhausted men finally surrendered. The Civil War had begun.

The Upper South Secedes

After the fall of Fort Sumter, President Lincoln called for 75,000 volunteers to serve in the military for 90 days. The call for troops created a crisis in the Upper South. Many people there did not want to secede, but faced with the prospect of civil war, they believed they had no choice but to leave the Union. Virginia acted first, passing an Ordinance of Secession on April 17, 1861. The Confederate Congress responded by moving the capital of the Confederacy to Richmond, Virginia. By early June of 1861, Arkansas, North Carolina, and Tennessee had also seceded.

Hanging On to the Border States

With the upper South gone, Lincoln was determined to keep the slaveholding border states from seceding. Delaware seemed safe, but Lincoln worried about Kentucky, Missouri, and Maryland. Virginia's secession had placed a Confederate state across the Potomac River from the nation's capital. If Maryland seceded, Washington would be surrounded by Confederate territory.

To prevent Maryland's secession, Lincoln **imposed martial law** in Baltimore, where mobs had already attacked federal troops. Under martial law, the military takes control of an area, replaces civilian authorities, and suspends many civil rights. Secessionists could be arrested and held without trial. Union Army officers imprisoned dozens of suspected secessionist leaders.

Lincoln knew that Kentucky was divided over whether to secede and that its control of the Ohio River's south bank was strategically important. When Kentucky declared itself neutral, Lincoln promised to leave the state alone so long as the Confederacy did the same.

Kentucky stayed neutral until September 1861, when Confederate forces occupied part of the state, prompting Union troops to move in as well. The Confederate invasion angered many in the Kentucky legislature, which now voted to fight the Confederacy. This led other Kentuckians who supported the Confederacy to create a rival government and secede.

The third border state Lincoln worried about was Missouri. Although many people in the state sympathized strongly with the Confederacy, its convention voted almost unanimously against secession. A struggle then broke out between the convention and pro-secession forces led by Governor Claiborne F. Jackson. In the end, Missouri stayed with the Union with the support of federal forces. From the very beginning of the Civil War, Lincoln had been willing to take political, even constitutional, risks to preserve the Union. The issue of its preservation now shifted to the battlefield.

Reading Check **Describing** Why were the border states of Maryland and Kentucky important to the Union?

Section 3 REVIEW

Vocabulary

1. **Explain** the significance of: John C. Breckinridge, John Bell, Fort Sumter, Crittenden's Compromise, Confederacy, Jefferson Davis, martial law.

Main Ideas

2. **Explaining** How did problems in the Democratic Party help Abraham Lincoln win the 1860 election?

3. **Identifying** Where and under what circumstances did the American Civil War begin?

Critical Thinking

4. **Big Ideas** How did Lincoln prevent Kentucky, Missouri, and Maryland from seceding? Was Lincoln justified in his actions? Why or why not?

5. **Categorizing** Use a graphic organizer similar to the one below to list the various parties' candidates and political positions in the 1860 election.

Party	Candidate	Position
Northern Democrat		
Southern Democrat		
Constitutional Unionist		
Republican		

6. **Analyzing Visuals** Examine the map on the election of 1860 on page 303. Explain why Douglas won only one state.

Writing About History

7. **Persuasive Writing** Suppose you are an adviser to President Lincoln and have just heard about the firing on Fort Sumter. Write a brief report for the president, advising him on what steps to take next.

History ONLINE

Study Central™ To review this section, go to glencoe.com and click on Study Central.

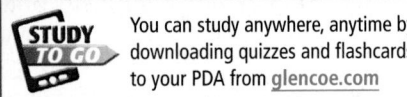

Causes of Sectional Tensions

- Disagreement continues over the legality, morality, and politics of slavery.
- Congressman David Wilmot proposes the Wilmot Proviso to ban slavery in territory acquired from Mexico.
- The concept of popular sovereignty—that local settlers can decide whether their state will be a free state or slave state—is popularized.
- The California Gold Rush leads to Californians applying for statehood as a free state, creating the possibility of more free states than slave states in the Senate.
- The Compromise of 1850 leads to the Fugitive Slave Law.
- Harriet Beecher Stowe publishes *Uncle Tom's Cabin* in 1852.
- The Kansas-Nebraska Act repeals the Missouri Compromise.
- The *Dred Scott* case results in the Supreme Court declaring the Missouri Compromise unconstitutional.
- John Brown launches a raid on Harpers Ferry, hoping to incite a slave rebellion.
- Lincoln wins the presidency in 1860.

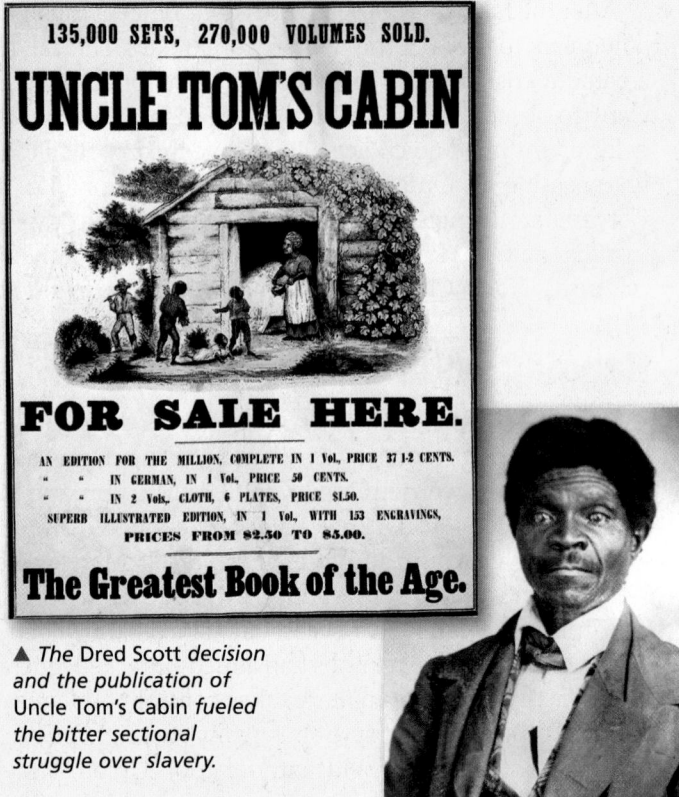

▲ The Dred Scott *decision and the publication of* Uncle Tom's Cabin *fueled the bitter sectional struggle over slavery.*

◀ *When Northern settlers organized to stop slavery from spreading into Kansas (left), their efforts were met with a violent response by Southerners. Ultimately, the struggle over slavery led to Civil War, when the Confederacy fired on Fort Sumter (above)*

Effects of Sectional Tensions

- The Free-Soil Party, seeking to stop the spread of slavery into western territories, is formed.
- The Republican Party is formed by antislavery Whigs, Democrats, Free-Soilers, and members of the abolitionist Liberty Party.
- Some Northerners actively resist the Fugitive Slave Law and help escaped slaves; the Underground Railroad moves runaway slaves from the South to freedom in Canada.
- Violence erupts between proslavery and antislavery settlers in Kansas.
- John Brown and *Uncle Tom's Cabin* polarized the North and South.
- Missouri Compromise is found unconstitutional by the Supreme Court in *Dred Scott* v. *Sandford*.
- John Brown's raid convinces many Southerners that secession is necessary to keep the South safe.
- Lincoln's election is the final straw. Several Southern states secede from the Union and form the Confederacy.
- Confederates attack Fort Sumter in South Carolina and take it.
- Lincoln calls for troops to put down the rebellion; the Civil War begins.

NEW YORK REGENTS EXAM PRACTICE

TIP

When a question contains a negative, try to reword the sentence or phrase to make it positive.

Part I

Directions (1–10): For each statement or question, write on a separate sheet of paper the number of the word or expression that, of those given, best completes the statement or answers the question.

1 The Wilmot Proviso declared that there would be no

(1) more slavery in the United States.

(2) slavery in the lands won from Mexico.

(3) further territorial acquisitions.

(4) new states added to the Union.

2 Which was an effect of the Fugitive Slave Law?

(1) Southerners had no more problems with escaped enslaved people.

(2) Enslaved people could now leave slavery whenever they wished.

(3) California came into the Union as a free state.

(4) Northerners who had been neutral about slavery were now outraged.

3 In the *Dred Scott* decision, the Supreme Court determined that it was unconstitutional to

(1) allow slavery in the territories.

(2) prohibit slavery in the territories.

(3) free slaves in the United States.

(4) bring enslaved people from one state to another.

4 Which of the following best describes the party called the Know-Nothings?

(1) proslavery and antigovernment

(2) antislavery and pro-immigration

(3) pro-Catholic and pro-immigration

(4) anti-immigration and anti-Catholic

5 The South saw the election of Abraham Lincoln in 1860 as a

(1) political victory for pro-slavery supporters.

(2) chance to take over Congress.

(3) victory for the abolitionists.

(4) good opportunity to end years of sectionalism.

6 The Civil War began when

(1) Lincoln refused to send troops into Kentucky.

(2) Fort Sumter fell to the Confederacy.

(3) Virginia seceded from the Union.

(4) army officers imprisoned many suspected secessionists.

7 "A house divided against itself cannot stand. . . . I do not expect the Union to be dissolved; I do not expect the house to fall; but I do expect it will cease to be divided. It will become all one thing, or all the other. . . ."

—Abraham Lincoln, 1858

The "divided house" referred to in this speech was caused primarily by

(1) expansionism.

(2) war with Mexico.

(3) slavery.

(4) the suffrage movement.

Need Extra Help?							
If You Missed Questions . . .	1	2	3	4	5	6	7
Go to Page . . .	284	288	296	295	304	306	302

[OVER]

Base your answers to questions 8 and 9 on the map below and on your knowledge of Chapter 8.

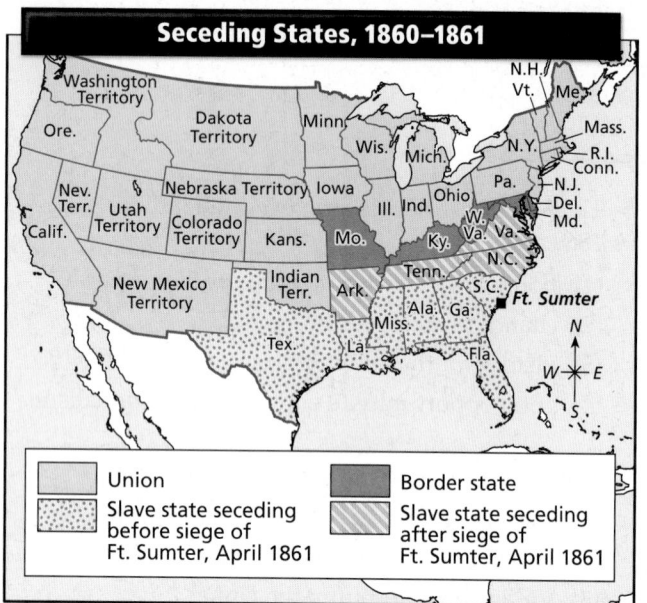

Seceding States, 1860–1861

Legend:
- Union
- Slave state seceding before siege of Ft. Sumter, April 1861
- Border state
- Slave state seceding after siege of Ft. Sumter, April 1861

8   Which slave state remained in the Union after the Fort Sumter attack?

(1) Arkansas

(2) Virginia

(3) Missouri

(4) Texas

9   Which states did not secede until after the Fort Sumter attack?

(1) North Carolina, South Carolina, and Virginia

(2) Arkansas, Tennessee, and Kentucky

(3) Alabama, Georgia, and South Carolina

(4) Tennessee, North Carolina, and Virginia

10 Anger over the Kansas-Nebraska Act brought about the formation of which party?

(1) the American Party

(2) the Republican Party

(3) the Cotton Whig Party

(4) the Free-Soil Party

Need Extra Help?			
If You Missed Questions . . .	8	9	10
Go to Page . . .	307	307	294

Part II Thematic Essay Question

Directions: Write a well-organized essay that includes an introduction, several paragraphs addressing the task below, and a conclusion.

Theme: The Raid on Harpers Ferry

The abolitionist movement at times took a violent turn. In October 1859 abolitionist John Brown and 18 men seized the arsenal at Harpers Ferry. Brown's goal was to begin a rebellion against slaveholders.

Task:

Discuss the raid, and be sure to

- Explain the goals of the abolitionist movement and the factors that caused Brown to attempt the raid

- Describe the events of the raid and the outcome

- Evaluate the lasting effect of the raid on the abolitionist movement and its contribution to the split between the North and the South

Guidelines:

In your essay, be sure to:

- Develop all aspects of the task

- Support the theme with relevant facts, examples, and details

- Use a logical and clear plan of organization, including an introduction and a conclusion that are beyond a restatement of the theme

Part III Document-Based Question

This question is based on the accompanying documents. It is designed to test your ability to work with historical documents. Some of the documents have been edited for the purposes of the question. As you analyze the documents, take into account the source of each document and any point of view that may be presented in the document.

Historical Context:

Throughout the early 1800s, tensions between the North and the South increased. During the 1850s, the sectional differences that had always existed became a rift.

Task:

Using information from the documents and your knowledge of United States history, answer the questions that follow each document in Part A. Your answers to the questions will help you write the Part B essay in which you will be asked to

- Discuss the differences between the North and the South that contributed to sectionalism

- Evaluate the role of slavery and the abolitionist movement in the growing divide between the North and South

Part A
Short-Answer Questions

Directions: Analyze the documents and answer the short-answer questions that follow each document on a separate sheet of paper.

Document 1

> "In the ante-revolutionary period, the differences between the populations of the Northern and Southern colonies had already been strongly developed. The early colonists did not bear with them from the mother-country to the shores of the New World any greater degree of congeniality than existed among them at home. They had come not only from different stocks of population, but from different feuds in religion and politics. There could be no congeniality between . . . New England, and the South. . . ."

Source: Edward A. Pollard, *The Lost Cause*

1 According to Pollard, when did differences between the North and South begin and what did he believe caused the differences between the people of the North and the South?

Document 2

Source: Bernard F. Reilly, *American Political Prints,* 1776–1876, Boston, 1991

2 What do you think this cartoon is satirizing?

Part B
Essay

Directions: Write a well-organized essay that includes an introduction, several paragraphs, and a conclusion. Use evidence from the documents in your essay. Support your response with relevant facts, examples, and details. Include additional outside information.

Guidelines:

In your essay, be sure to:

- Develop all aspects of the task
- Incorporate information from the documents
- Incorporate relevant outside information
- Support the theme with relevant facts, examples, and details
- Use a logical and clear plan of organization, including an introduction and a conclusion that are beyond a restatement of the theme

History ONLINE

For additional test practice, use Self-Check Quizzes—Chapter 8 at glencoe.com

Need Extra Help?			
If You Missed Questions . . .	1	2	Essay
Go to Page . . .	311	302	302

The Civil War

1861–1865

The Third Minnesota Infantry Regiment marches into Little Rock, Arkansas, September 11, 1863.

U.S. PRESIDENTS

U.S. EVENTS

WORLD EVENTS

1860   1861   1862

1859
- John Brown leads raid on federal arsenal at Harpers Ferry, Virginia

1861
- Fort Sumter attacked
- First Battle of Bull Run

Lincoln
1861–1865

1862
- Battle of Antietam halts Lee's invasion
- Lincoln presents Emancipation Proclamation

1859
- Work on the Suez Canal begins in Egypt

1861
- Russian serfs emancipated by Czar Alexander II

1862
- British firm builds Confederate warship *Alabama* which begins sinking Union shipping

How Is Modern Warfare Different?

The Civil War was in many respects the first modern war. Both sides fielded large armies equipped with mass-produced weapons. Railroads and the telegraph ensured rapid communications and troop movements. Hundreds of thousands of soldiers were killed.

- *Why was the North able to defeat the South?*
- *How did specific battles affect President Lincoln's political decisions?*

1863
- Battle of Gettysburg
- Vicksburg is captured

1864
- Atlanta falls; Sherman begins march to the sea
- Grant battles Lee in Virginia

1865
- Lee surrenders to Grant
- Abraham Lincoln assassinated

A. Johnson 1865–1869

1863   1864   1865

1863
- French troops occupy Mexico City

1864
- Karl Marx founds First International Workingmen's Association to promote socialism

FOLDABLES

Outlining Compromise Efforts Create a Half Book Foldable that lists the failure of compromise efforts before the Civil War. Complete the chart by showing the series of compromises attempted. Describe each compromise effort in the left-hand column. In the right-hand column, describe the outcome of each compromise.

Compromise Efforts | Outcomes

History **ONLINE Chapter Overview**
Visit glencoe.com to preview Chapter 9.

The Opposing Sides

Guide to Reading

Big Ideas

Government and Society The Confederacy's weak central government had difficulty coordinating the war effort.

Content Vocabulary
- greenback (p. 315)
- conscription (p. 316)
- habeas corpus (p. 316)
- attrition (p. 319)

Academic Vocabulary
- sufficient (p. 316)
- implement (p. 319)

People and Events to Identify
- Robert E. Lee (p. 314)
- Copperheads (p. 316)
- James Mason (p. 317)
- John Slidell (p. 317)
- *Trent* Affair (p. 317)
- Anaconda Plan (p. 319)

Reading Strategy

Taking Notes Use the major headings in this section to create an outline similar to the one below, to record the advantages and disadvantages of the North and the South at the start of the Civil War.

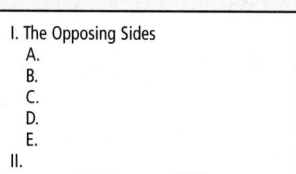

```
I. The Opposing Sides
   A.
   B.
   C.
   D.
   E.
II.
```

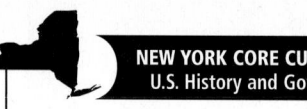

NEW YORK CORE CURRICULUM
U.S. History and Government

Unit 2:
II.D.2.a Military strategy, major battles (Antietam, Gettysburg), and human toll
II.D.2.c Government policy during the war (wartime finances, creating a national currency, transcontinental railroad, Homestead Act)

At the start of the Civil War, the North and South each had distinct advantages and disadvantages. Both sides expected the conflict to end quickly. Instead, the Civil War became a long, bloody, and bitter struggle in which neither side won an easy triumph.

Choosing Sides

MAIN Idea The Union had economic advantages at the start of the Civil War, but was politically divided; if the Confederacy could gain European support and wear down the North, it had a chance at victory.

HISTORY AND YOU Do you believe the government should limit civil liberties during wartime? Read on to learn how President Lincoln decided to suspend writs of habeas corpus during the Civil War.

On the same day that he learned his home state of Virginia had voted to secede from the Union, **Robert E. Lee**—one of the most respected senior officers in the United States Army—received an offer from General Winfield Scott to command the Union's troops. Although Lee had spoken against secession and considered slavery "a moral and political evil," he wrote, "I cannot raise my hand against my birthplace, my home, my children." Instead, he resigned from the army and offered his services to the Confederacy.

Lee was only one of hundreds of military officers who had to choose whether to support the Union or the Confederacy. Eventually 313 officers, or about one-third of the total, resigned to join the Confederacy. The South had a strong military tradition. In 1860 the United States had eight military colleges, and seven of them were in the South. These colleges provided the South with a large number of trained officers to lead its armies.

Just as the South had a strong military tradition, the North had a strong naval tradition. More than three-quarters of the United States Navy's officers came from the North. Perhaps even more important, most of the navy's warships and all but one of the country's shipyards remained under Union control.

The Opposing Economies

Although the South had many experienced officers to lead its troops in battle, the North had several economic advantages. In 1860 the population of the North was about 22 million, while the South had about 9 million people, more than one-third of whom were enslaved. The North's larger population gave it a great advantage in raising an army and in supporting the war effort. The North's

▲ Confederate soldiers of the 3rd Georgia Infantry (above) fought under Lee's command during the Peninsula campaign. The Confederacy had fewer soldiers but many of the nation's best officers.

▲ Men of the 110th Pennsylvania Infantry Regiment at Falmouth, Virginia, April 1863. Union troops were generally better equipped than Confederate forces.

Analyzing VISUALS

1. **Interpreting** Based on the graph, what were the North's greatest advantages over the South?

2. **Assessing** Which of the North's advantages do you think were most important in winning the war? Why?

Resources of the Union and of the Confederacy

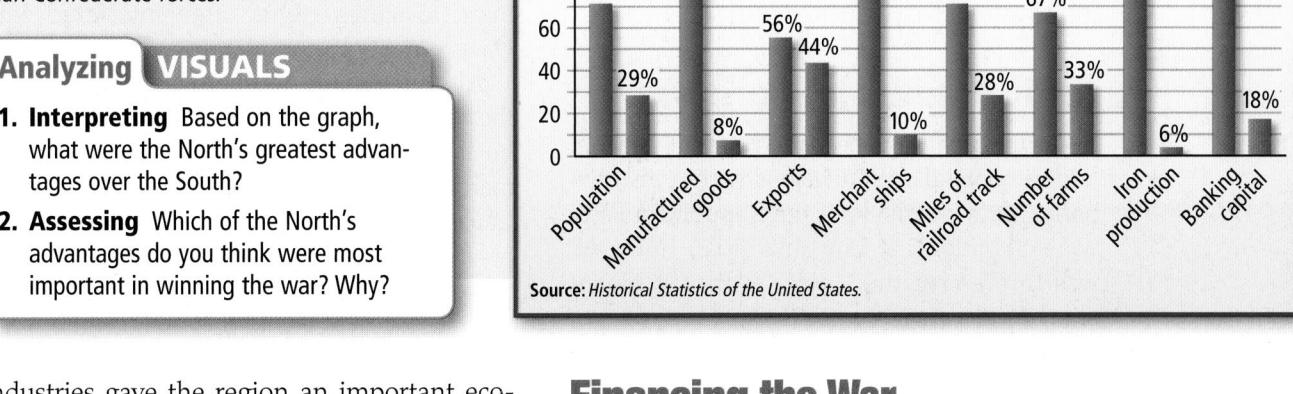

Union   Confederacy

	Union	Confederacy
Population	71%	29%
Manufactured goods	92%	8%
Exports	56%	44%
Merchant ships	90%	10%
Miles of railroad track	72%	28%
Number of farms	67%	33%
Iron production	94%	6%
Banking capital	82%	18%

Source: *Historical Statistics of the United States.*

industries gave the region an important economic advantage over the South as well. In 1860 almost 90 percent of the nation's factories were in the North. They produced more than 90 percent of the country's clothing, boots, and shoes, and 94 percent of its pig iron (unrefined iron), vital for manufacturing weapons and equipment.

Both sides were able to produce the food they needed. Although much of the South's fertile land was used for the production of cash crops, such as cotton and tobacco, Southern farmers also grew rice and great quantities of corn. The problem facing the South was not its ability to produce food, but its ability to distribute it once the war began. It had only half as many miles of railroad track as the North and had only one line—from Memphis to Chattanooga—connecting the western states of the Confederacy to the east. This made it much easier for Northern forces to disrupt the movement of food and troops.

Financing the War

Both the North and the South had to act quickly to raise money for the war. The North enjoyed several financial advantages. In addition to controlling the national treasury, the Union could expect continued revenue from tariffs. Many Northern banks also held large reserves of cash, which they lent the government by purchasing bonds.

Concern about the North's ability to win the war caused many people to withdraw gold and silver from the banks. Without gold and silver, the banks could not buy government bonds, and without the gold and silver from the sale of bonds, the government could not pay its suppliers and troops. To solve this problem, Congress passed the Legal Tender Act in February 1862. This act created a national currency and allowed the government to issue paper money. These paper bills came to be known as **greenbacks** because of their color.

In contrast to the Union, the Confederacy's financial situation was poor, and it became worse over time. Most Southern planters were in debt and unable to buy bonds. At the same time, Southern banks were small and had few cash reserves. As a result, they could not buy many bonds.

The best hope for the South to raise money was by taxing trade. Shortly after the war began, however, the Union Navy blockaded Southern ports, which reduced trade and revenue. The Confederacy then imposed new taxes on property and farm products, but many Southerners refused to pay.

Lacking **sufficient** money from taxes or bonds, the Confederacy was forced to print paper money to pay its bills. This caused rapid inflation in the South. Confederate paper money became almost worthless. By the end of the war, the South had experienced 9,000 percent inflation, compared to only 80 percent in the North.

Party Politics in the North

As the Civil War began, President Lincoln had to contend with divisions within his own party. Many members of the Republican Party were abolitionists. Lincoln's goal, however, was to preserve the Union, even if it meant allowing slavery to continue.

The president also had to contend with the Democrats. One faction, known as the War Democrats, supported a war to restore the Union but opposed ending slavery. Another faction, known as the Peace Democrats, opposed the war and called for reuniting the states through negotiation. Many Republicans viewed them as traitors and referred to them as **Copperheads,** after the poisonous snake.

One major disagreement between Republicans and Democrats concerned the use of **conscription,** or forcing people into military service. In 1862 Congress passed a militia law requiring states to use conscription if they could not recruit enough volunteers. Many Democrats opposed the law, and riots erupted in several strongly Democratic districts in Indiana, Ohio, Pennsylvania, and Wisconsin.

To enforce the militia law, Lincoln suspended writs of **habeas corpus.** Habeas corpus refers to a person's right not to be imprisoned unless charged with a crime and given a trial. A writ of habeas corpus is a court order that requires the government either to charge an imprisoned person with a crime or let the person go free. When writs of habeas corpus are suspended, a person can be imprisoned indefinitely without trial. In this case, President Lincoln suspended the writ for anyone who openly supported the rebels or encouraged others to resist the militia draft. Lincoln justified imposing limits on speech in wartime: "Must I shoot a simple-minded soldier boy who deserts," the president asked, "while I must not touch a hair of a wily agitator who induces him to desert?"

Weak Southern Government

Although the South had no organized opposition party, President Jefferson Davis still faced many problems. The Confederate constitution emphasized states' rights and limited the central government's power. This commitment to states' rights often interfered with Davis's ability to conduct the war.

Although many Southern leaders supported the war, some opposed Jefferson Davis when he supported conscription and established martial law early in 1862. Leaders from North Carolina and Georgia, including Davis's vice president, Alexander Stephens, were among those who dissented. They objected to the Confederacy forcing people to join the army and opposed Davis's decision to suspend writs of habeas corpus.

The Diplomatic Challenge

The outbreak of the Civil War put the major governments of Europe in a difficult position. The United States did not want the Europeans interfering in the war and expected them to respect the North's blockade of Southern ports. Confederate leaders, on the other hand, wanted the Europeans, particularly the British, to recognize the Confederate States of America as an independent country, and to provide military assistance to the South. Southern leaders knew that British and French textile factories depended on Southern cotton. To pressure these nations, Southern planters stopped selling their cotton to them until they recognized the Confederacy.

The British and French met informally with Confederate representatives in May 1861. The French promised to recognize the Confederacy

The Politics of the Civil War

▲ The cartoon above is entitled "The Copperhead Plan for Subjugating the South." It shows Peace Democrats meeting with a Southerner (possibly Jefferson Davis). The Peace Democrats are saying: "Please come back" and "We will do anything you want." The Southerner is saying, "Oh Dear, I can't stand this much longer."

▲ The cartoon above shows "Union" fighting "Secession." Union's feet are entangled by a copperhead snake, and his arms are bound by the Constitution. Secession tramples the flag, and holds a club labeled Pirate Alabama—referring to a Southern warship the British let the South build in Britain. Behind the fighters are two men—one representing France and the other Britain. The British figure is handing clubs to Secession to help him beat Union.

Analyzing VISUALS   DBQ

1. **Making Inferences** Do you think the cartoon on the left was created by a Northerner or a Southerner? Why?

2. **Identifying Points of View** What opinion of the Peace Democrats does the cartoon on the right express?

if the British did so, as well. British leaders, however, were not ready to risk war with the United States. Until the Confederacy won decisive victories on the battlefield and proved it would survive and eventually win the war, the British would not risk recognizing it.

In late 1861, the Confederacy decided to send **James Mason** of Virginia to Britain, and **John Slidell** of Louisiana, to France. The two men were to negotiate on behalf of the Confederacy. Mason and Slidell traveled to Havana, Cuba, and boarded the *Trent*, a British ship. When the *Trent* left Havana, it was intercepted by the Union warship *San Jacinto*.

The British were furious the United States had stopped one of their ships. They sent an ultimatum to the United States, demanding the release of the two Confederates. Britain then sent troops to Canada and strengthened its Atlantic fleet. After a few tense weeks, Lincoln freed Mason and Slidell, commenting, "One war at a time."

After being freed, the diplomats continued on their journey to seek Confederate allies. Although the arrest of Mason and Slidell in the so-called *Trent Affair* had excited interest worldwide, their diplomatic mission failed to gain the support the South wanted.

✓ Reading Check) **Explaining** How would British and French recognition of the Confederacy have helped the South to overcome the North's advantages in the war?

The First Modern War

MAIN Idea Unlike previous wars, the Civil War was fought with huge, mostly volunteer armies equipped with new technologies.

HISTORY AND YOU Do you know what types of weapons and other gear soldiers carry today? Read on to learn about the weapons and supplies available to soldiers in the Civil War.

The economic and political situation in the North and South was very important to the outcome of the war because, in many respects, the Civil War was the first "modern" war. Unlike most of the wars fought in Europe during the previous two centuries, the Civil War was not fought by small disciplined armies with limited goals. It involved huge armies, made up mostly of civilian volunteers, that required vast quantities of supplies and equipment.

Military Technology

Many of the top officers who led the Union and Confederate troops had studied Napoleon's campaigns and had fought in the war with Mexico in the 1840s. They believed that the best way to win a battle was to organize troops into tight columns and march toward the enemy, firing in massed volleys. When the troops got close enough, they would charge the enemy and attack with bayonets. These tactics had been necessary in the early 1800s because soldiers used smooth bore muskets firing round metal balls. They were very inaccurate except at close range.

By the 1850s, French and American inventors had developed a new, inexpensive conoidal— or cone-shaped—bullet for rifles. Rifles firing conoidal bullets were accurate at much greater ranges. This meant that troops would be fired on several more times while charging enemy lines.

TECHNOLOGY & HISTORY

Civil War Technology Military conflict often leads to the use of new technologies. The Civil War was no exception. New weapons, ships and means of communication greatly changed the nature of warfare.

▲ Conoidal Bullets

These new bullets made gunfire more accurate at greater ranges and increased the number of casualties.

▲ Telegraph

Invented before the war, the telegraph let generals learn the results of battles almost immediately, and change their strategy and give new orders quickly.

▲ Balloons

The Civil War marked the first time aerial reconnaissance was used in war. Both sides used balloons to observe enemy troops.

◄ Ironclads

To operate on enemy rivers and coast lines guarded by shore-based cannon, both sides built armor-plated steamships. Ironclads marked the beginning of the shift from wooden ships to steel ships.

Analyzing VISUALS

1. **Explaining** How did balloons change warfare?

2. **Describing** How did the telegraph help both sides fight the war?

The Civil War also marked the first time that troops defending their positions protected themselves with trenches and barricades instead of standing upright in a line. By combining rifles firing conoidal bullets with the protection of trenches, defenders were able to inflict very high casualties on attacking forces. High casualties meant that armies had to keep replacing their soldiers. **Attrition**—the wearing down of one side by the other through exhaustion of soldiers and resources—played a critical role as the war dragged on. The North, with its large population, could replace its troops much more easily than the South.

The South's Strategy

Early in the war, Jefferson Davis imagined a struggle similar to the Revolutionary War. His generals would pick their battles carefully, attacking and retreating when necessary and avoiding large battles that might risk heavy losses. Davis believed that if the South waged a defensive war of attrition in this manner, it would force the Union to spend its resources until it became tired of the war and agreed to negotiate.

The idea of a defensive war of attrition, however, outraged many Southerners. Believing themselves superior fighters, they scorned the idea of defensive warfare. "The idea of waiting for blows, instead of inflicting them, is altogether unsuited to the genius of our people," declared the *Richmond Examiner* in 1861.

The Southern disdain for remaining on the defensive meant that when battles occurred, Southern troops often went on the offensive, charging enemy lines and suffering very high casualties. In 1862 and 1863, Confederate armies fought nine large battles. In six of them, they went on the offensive, and they suffered 20,000 more casualties than the Union forces.

The Union's Anaconda Plan

Early in the war, the general in chief of the United States, Winfield Scott, proposed a strategy for defeating the South. Scott suggested that the Union blockade Confederate ports and send gunboats down the Mississippi to divide the Confederacy. The South, thus separated, would gradually run out of resources and surrender. The plan would take time, Scott admitted, but it would defeat the South with the least amount of bloodshed.

Many Northerners rejected the plan as too slow and indirect for certain victory. Northern newspapers referred to the strategy as the **Anaconda Plan,** after the snake that slowly strangles its prey to death. Opponents argued that a rapid and massive invasion of the South would bring victory more quickly. Although Lincoln agreed to **implement** Scott's suggestions, and imposed a blockade of Southern ports, he hoped that a quick victory over the Southern forces massing in Virginia might discredit the secessionists and bring an end to the crisis. Ultimately, he and other Union leaders realized that only a long war that focused on destroying the South's armies had any chance of success.

✔ Reading Check **Describing** What war strategy did Jefferson Davis develop for the South?

Vocabulary

1. **Explain** the significance of: Robert E. Lee, greenback, Copperheads, conscription, habeas corpus, James Mason, John Slidell, *Trent* Affair, attrition, Anaconda Plan.

Main Ideas

2. **Explaining** Why did some members of Lincoln's own Republican Party disagree with him over the war?

3. **Describing** How did Southern pride and tradition interfere with the South's ability to win the war?

Critical Thinking

4. **Big Ideas** How did the belief in states' rights hamper the Confederate government during the war?

5. **Organizing** Using a graphic organizer similar to the one below, list the military innovations of the Civil War era.

Military Innovations

6. **Analyzing Visuals** Examine the conoidal bullets shown on page 318. How did conoidal bullets affect the war effort? What other innovations made the Civil War the first "modern" war?

Writing About History

7. **Descriptive Writing** Suppose that you are living in one of the border states at the beginning of the Civil War. Write a letter to a relative explaining why you are planning to join either the Union or the Confederate army.

History ONLINE

Study Central™ To review this section, go to glencoe.com and click on Study Central.

The Early Stages

Guide to Reading

Big Ideas

Geography and History The Union hoped to seize the Mississippi River valley and cut the Confederacy in two.

Content Vocabulary
- bounty *(p. 321)*
- blockade runner *(p. 322)*

Academic Vocabulary
- assemble *(p. 324)*
- crucial *(p. 326)*

People and Events to Identify
- "Stonewall" Jackson *(p. 320)*
- David G. Farragut *(p. 322)*
- Ulysses S. Grant *(p. 323)*
- George B. McClellan *(p. 324)*
- Emancipation Proclamation *(p. 327)*

Reading Strategy

Categorizing Complete a graphic organizer similar to the one below by filling in the results of each early Civil War battle listed.

Battle	Results
First Battle of Bull Run	
Battle of Shiloh	
Battle of Murfreesboro	
Seven Days' Battle	
Second Battle of Bull Run	

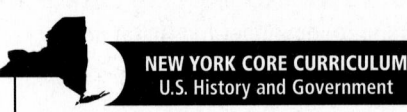

NEW YORK CORE CURRICULUM
U.S. History and Government

Unit 2:
II.D.2.a Military strategy, major battles (Antietam, Gettysburg), and human toll
II.D.2.d Lincoln and Emancipation (the Emancipation Proclamation, the Gettysburg Address, African-American participation in the Civil War, the 13th Amendment)

Both the North and the South developed strategies to win the Civil War. Both sides, however, experienced military setbacks and high casualties early in the war. President Lincoln issued the Emancipation Proclamation and put ending slavery at the heart of the Union war effort.

Mobilizing the Troops

MAIN Idea To fight the war successfully, it became clear to leaders on both sides that they would need conscription to ensure the necessary numbers of troops.

HISTORY AND YOU Do you know anyone who was drafted into military service? Read on to find out how the Union had to draft men into service during the Civil War.

In the first months of the Civil War, President Lincoln was under great pressure to strike quickly against the South. Confederate troops, led by General P.G.T. Beauregard, were gathering 25 miles (40 km) south of Washington, D.C., along the Bull Run River near Manassas Junction, an important railroad center in northern Virginia. Lincoln approved an assault on these forces, hoping that a Union victory would lead to a quick end to the conflict.

Expecting a short exciting fight, hundreds of spectators from Washington, D.C., picnicked a few miles away to watch the battle. They were soon horrified and dismayed by the chaos and death that they witnessed. At first, the attack went well for the Union. Its forces slowly pushed the Confederates back from their positions behind the Bull Run. During the fighting, Confederate reinforcements from Virginia, led by Thomas J. Jackson, moved into the line. As Confederate troops retreated past Jackson, their commander yelled: "There is Jackson standing like a stone wall! Rally behind the Virginians!" Afterward, Jackson became known as **"Stonewall" Jackson,** and went on to become one of the most effective commanders in the Confederate army.

As Confederate reinforcements arrived, Union commander General Irwin McDowell decided to fall back. The retreat quickly turned into a panic, although the exhausted Confederate troops did not pursue the Union forces very far. The Union defeat at the First Battle of Bull Run made it clear that the North would need a large, well-trained army to defeat the South. Lincoln had originally called for 75,000 men to serve for three months. The day after Bull Run, he signed another bill for the enlistment of 500,000 men for three years.

At first, excitement about the war inspired many men to enlist on both sides, swamping recruitment offices and training camps. As the

The Naval War

An important element in the Union's success in the Civil War was its ability to blockade most of the Confederacy's ports. Because of the blockade, trade goods became very scarce in the South, which hurt morale.

▲ Admiral David Farragut's daring and successful capture of New Orleans gave the North control of the most important port in the South and control of the lower part of the Mississippi River.

▲ The Civil War witnessed the first use of metal warships, known as ironclads, because they were covered in sloped iron plates. The most famous battle of ironclads took place in March 1862, when the South tried to break the Union blockade of Virginia using an ironclad built from the captured Union ship Merrimack. Renamed the Virginia, the ironclad sank two Union ships. The next day, the Union's newly built ironclad, the Monitor, challenged the Virginia. The ships battled for hours, but neither was able to sink the other. The Monitor's presence, however, kept the Virginia from breaking the blockade.

Analyzing VISUALS DBQ

1. **Describing** How did the *Virginia* and the *Monitor* represent a new type of war technology?

2. **Explaining** What was the significance of Farragut's capture of New Orleans?

war dragged on and casualties rose, however, fewer young men volunteered, forcing both governments to resort to conscription. The South introduced conscription in April 1862 for all white men between the ages of 18 and 35. The draft, however, exempted certain people, including key government workers, teachers, and after 1862, planters who held at least 20 enslaved African Americans.

The North at first tried to encourage voluntary enlistment by offering a **bounty**—a sum of money given as a bonus—to individuals who promised to serve three years in the military. Congress also passed the Militia Act in July 1862, giving Lincoln the authority to call state militias, which included drafted troops, into federal service. Finally, after these measures failed to meet military needs, Congress introduced a national draft in 1863 to raise the necessary troops.

✓ **Reading Check** **Summarizing** What was the significance of the First Battle of Bull Run?

The Naval War

MAIN Idea Although the Union had experienced setbacks on land, its naval forces successfully blockaded Southern ports and took control of the mouth of the Mississippi River.

HISTORY AND YOU Is there a military leader from a recent war that you consider to be a "hero"? Read on to find out how a Southerner became a naval hero in the North during the Civil War.

While the Union and Confederacy mobilized their armies, the Union navy began operations against the South. In April 1861, President Lincoln proclaimed a blockade of all Confederate ports. By the spring of 1862, the Union navy had sealed off every major Southern harbor along the Atlantic coast, except for Charleston, South Carolina, and Wilmington, North Carolina. Lincoln intended to hurt the South's economy as much as possible by cutting its trade with the world.

The Blockade

Although the Union blockade became increasingly effective as the war dragged on, Union vessels were thinly spread and found it difficult to stop all of the **blockade runners**—small, fast vessels the South used to smuggle goods past the blockade, usually under cover of night. By using blockade runners, the South could ship at least some of its cotton to Europe in exchange for shoes, rifles, and other supplies. The amount of material that made it through the blockade, however, was much less than the amount that had been shipped before the war.

At the same time, Confederate ships operating out of foreign ports attacked Northern merchant ships at sea. Two of the most famous Confederate raiders were the warships *Alabama* and *Florida,* both of which the Confederacy had built in Great Britain. The *Alabama* captured 64 ships before a Union warship sank it off the coast of France in 1864. The *Florida* destroyed 38 merchant ships before being captured at a harbor in Brazil.

The damage done by these two ships strained relations between the United States and Great Britain. Union officials did not think Great Britain should have allowed the ships to be built, and they demanded Britain pay damages for the losses the Union suffered.

Farragut Seizes New Orleans

While the Union navy fought to seal off the Confederacy's Atlantic ports, it also began preparations to seize New Orleans and gain control of the lower Mississippi River. In February 1862, **David G. Farragut** took command of a Union force of 42 warships and 15,000 soldiers led by General Benjamin Butler.

At the time, Farragut was 60 years old. He had gone to sea at age 9 and was a veteran of the War of 1812 and the war with Mexico. His father had moved to the United States from Spain in 1776 and had fought in the Revolutionary War and served as governor of the Mississippi Territory. Although he was born in Tennessee, Farragut was a staunch supporter of the Union.

Farragut's actions at the battle for New Orleans made him a hero in the North. In early April, his fleet began bombarding Confederate forts defending the lower Mississippi River. When the attack failed to destroy the forts, Farragut made a daring decision. At 2:00 A.M. on April 24, 1862, his ships headed upriver past the forts in single file, exposing themselves to attack. The forts opened fire with more than 80 guns, while Confederate gunboats tried to ram the fleet and tugboats placed flaming rafts in front of the Union ships. Remarkably, all but four of Farragut's ships survived the battle and continued upriver.

On April 25, 1862, Farragut arrived at New Orleans. Six days later, General Butler's troops took control of the city. The South's largest city, and a center of the cotton trade, was now in Union hands.

✔ Reading Check **Explaining** How did the Confederates try to break the Union blockade?

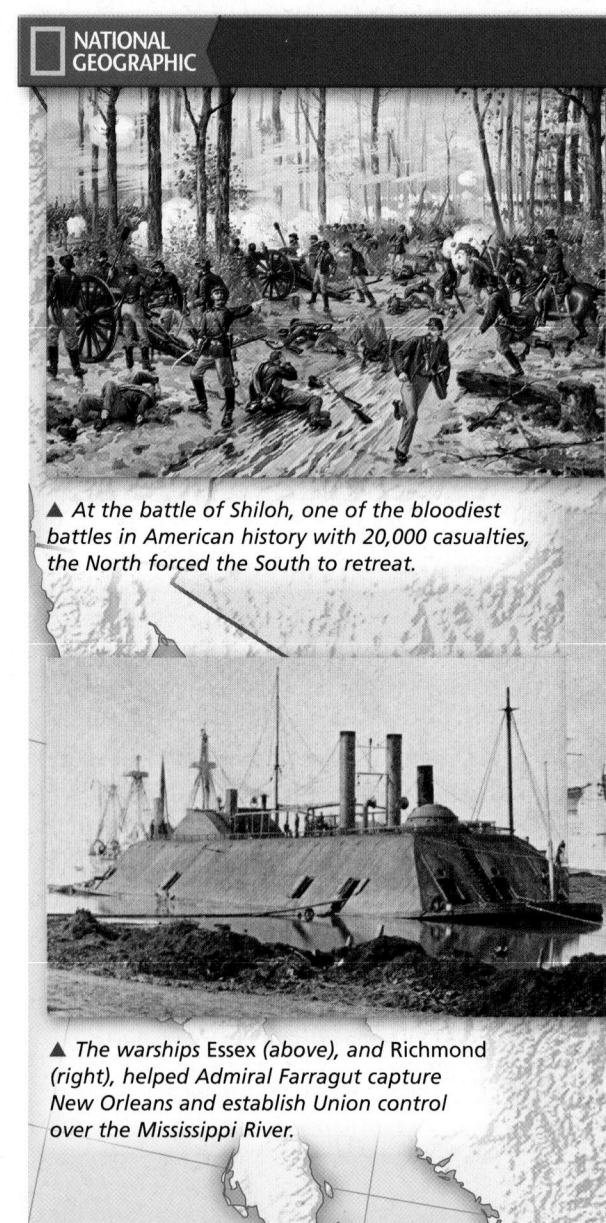

NATIONAL GEOGRAPHIC

▲ At the battle of Shiloh, one of the bloodiest battles in American history with 20,000 casualties, the North forced the South to retreat.

▲ The warships Essex (above), and Richmond (right), helped Admiral Farragut capture New Orleans and establish Union control over the Mississippi River.

The War in the West

MAIN Idea After the Union victory at Shiloh, the Union took control of eastern Tennessee.

HISTORY AND YOU Do you know someone with great perseverance? Read on to learn how General Grant demonstrated his worth to President Lincoln with his actions at the Battle of Shiloh.

In February 1862, as Farragut prepared for his attack on New Orleans, Union general **Ulysses S. Grant** began a campaign to seize control of the Cumberland and Tennessee Rivers. Control of these rivers would cut Tennessee in two and provide the Union with a river route deep into the Confederacy.

Backed by armored gunboats, Grant seized Fort Henry, the Confederacy's main fort on the Tennessee River. He then marched his troops east and surrounded Fort Donelson on the Cumberland River, forcing its garrison to surrender. With the fall of Fort Donelson and Fort Henry, all of Kentucky and most of western Tennessee came under Union control.

Shiloh

Next, Grant led his troops up the Tennessee River to attack Corinth, Mississippi. Seizing Corinth would cut the Confederacy's only rail line connecting Mississippi and western Tennessee. Determined to stop the Union advance, Confederate forces launched a surprise attack on Grant's troops early on April 6, 1862. The battle took place about 20 miles (32 km) north of Corinth near a small church named Shiloh.

The War in the West, 1862–1863

Legend:
- Union states
- Confederate states
- Union forces
- Confederate forces
- Union victory
- Confederate victory

Kansas

Missouri

Illinois

Indiana

Louisville
Kentucky

Perryville
Oct. 8, 1862

Paducah

Ft. Donelson
Feb. 16, 1862

Ft. Henry
Feb. 6, 1862

Nashville
Murfreesboro
Dec. 31, 1862–Jan. 2, 1863

Tenn.

Pea Ridge
March 6–8, 1862

Shiloh
April 6–7,
1862

Chattanooga
Nov. 23–25, 1863

Indian Territory

Memphis

Corinth

Chickamauga
Sept. 19–20, 1863

Arkansas

Corinth
Oct. 4,
1862

Atlanta

Birmingham

Mississippi

Alabama

Georgia

Red R.

Sabine R.

Texas

Vicksburg
May–July 1863

Jackson
May 14, 1863

Jackson

Natchez

Louisana

Port Hudson
May–July 1863

Mobile

Florida

Sabine Pass
Sept. 24–25, 1862

Baton Rouge

New Orleans
April 1862

30°N

New Orleans

Gulf of Mexico

Galveston
Oct. 4, 1862

Analyzing GEOGRAPHY

1. **Location** Which of the battles listed on the map is farthest west?
2. **Location** Most of the battles in this phase of the war took place in which state?

0   200 kilometers

0   200 miles

Albers Equal-Area projection

95°W   90°W   85°W

Hearing the attack, Grant raced from his headquarters to the battle. Although the Union troops were forced back, Grant rushed around the battlefield and managed to **assemble** a defensive line that held off repeated Southern attacks. The next morning, knowing reinforcements were coming, Grant went on the offensive, surprising the Confederates and forcing General Beauregard, their commander, to order a retreat.

The Battle of Shiloh stunned people in both the North and the South. Twenty thousand troops were killed or wounded, more than in any other battle up to that point. When newspapers demanded Grant be fired because of the high casualties, Lincoln refused, saying, "I can't spare this man; he fights."

Murfreesboro

Grant's victory at Shiloh cheered Lincoln, but the fighting was not over. Confederate troops evacuated Corinth and quickly moved east by railroad to Chattanooga, Tennessee, where they were placed under the command of General Braxton Bragg.

Bragg took his troops into Kentucky, hoping the Union armies would follow. He also hoped that his invasion of Kentucky would lead to an uprising of pro-Confederate supporters in the state. Bragg's invasion failed. Union troops led by General Don Carlos Buell stopped Bragg's forces at the Battle of Perryville.

After Bragg retreated, Lincoln ordered Buell to seize Chattanooga and cut the railroad lines that passed through the city. Lincoln knew that eastern Tennessee was home to many Union sympathizers, and he wanted it under Union control. He also knew that cutting the rail lines would deprive the Confederacy of "hogs and hominy"—vital supplies of meat and corn that the South needed.

Frustrated at Buell's slow advance, Lincoln fired him and put General William Rosecrans in command. As Rosecrans's forces headed south, Bragg's forces attacked them west of the Stones River near Murfreesboro. Although the Union lines fell back, they did not break, and the battle ended inconclusively. Four days later, with Union reinforcements arriving from Nashville, Bragg decided to retreat.

✓ **Reading Check** **Evaluating** What was the significance of the Battle of Shiloh?

The War in the East

MAIN Idea After the Union defeated Lee at Antietam, Britain decided to stay out of the conflict and Lincoln issued a proclamation to end slavery.

HISTORY AND YOU Can you think of a point in your life when things suddenly improved? Read how victory at Antietam improved Northern morale and made the war more challenging for the South.

While Union and Confederate troops were struggling for control of Tennessee and the Mississippi River, another major campaign was being waged in the east to capture Richmond, Virginia. After General McDowell's failure at the First Battle of Bull Run, President Lincoln ordered General **George B. McClellan** to lead the Union army in the east.

The Peninsula Campaign

After taking several months to prepare his forces, McClellan began transporting the troops by ship to the mouth of the James River, southeast of Yorktown, Virginia. From there, he intended to march up the peninsula formed by the James and York Rivers toward Richmond, only 70 miles (113 km) away.

Although popular with the troops, McClellan proved overly cautious and unwilling to attack unless he had overwhelming strength. He took 30 days to capture Yorktown, giving the Confederates time to move their troops into position near Richmond.

As McClellan advanced toward Richmond, he made another mistake. He allowed his forces to become divided by the Chickahominy River. Seizing this opportunity, the Confederate commander, General Joseph E. Johnston, attacked McClellan's army, inflicting heavy casualties. After Johnston was wounded in the battle, General Robert E. Lee was placed in command.

In late June of 1862, Lee began a series of attacks on McClellan's army that became known collectively as the Seven Days' Battle. Although Lee was unable to decisively defeat the Union army, he inflicted heavy casualties and forced McClellan to retreat to the James River. Together, the two sides suffered more than 30,000 casualties. Despite McClellan's protests, Lincoln ordered him to withdraw

Chambersburg

Wrightsville

Pennsylvania

Gettysburg
July 1–3, 1863

Westminster

Antietam
September 17, 1862

Maryland

West
Virginia

Frederick

Potomac

Washington, D.C.

Manassas
Junction

Second Bull Run
August 29–30, 1862

Chancellorsville
May 1–4, 1863

Fredericksburg
December 13, 1862

Virginia

Shenandoah

Chesapeake Bay

Rappahannock R.

Seven Days
June 25–July 1, 1862

Richmond

Chickahominy R.

York R.

James R.

Yorktown

Hampton Roads
March 8–9, 1862

Ft. Monroe

▲ Union troops lay a pontoon bridge across the Rappahannock River in preparation for the assault on Fredericksburg. The battle was a major victory for the South.

0   30 kilometers
0   30 miles
Albers Equal-Area projection

- ∿∿∿ Fortification
- ← Union advance
- ◄┅┅ Union retreat
- ← Confederate advance
- ◄┅┅ Confederate retreat
- ✸ Union victory
- ✸ Confederate victory
- ✻ Other battle

▲ The soldiers of the Union Army sit above their encampment at Cumberland Landing during the Peninsula Campaign.

Analyzing GEOGRAPHY

1. **Interpreting** Which battles shown above took place outside Virginia's borders?
2. **Applying** How far apart are the two capital cities of Richmond and Washington, D.C.?

from the peninsula and bring his troops back to Washington.

As McClellan's troops withdrew, Lee decided to attack the Union forces that were defending Washington. The maneuvers by the two sides led to another battle at Bull Run, near Manassas Junction—the site of the first major battle of the war. Again, the South forced the North to retreat, leaving the Confederate forces only 20 miles (32 km) from Washington. Soon after, word arrived at the White House that Lee's forces had crossed into Maryland and begun an invasion of the North.

The Battle of Antietam

Lee decided to invade Maryland for several reasons. Both he and Jefferson Davis believed that an invasion might convince the North to accept the South's independence. They also thought that a victory on Northern soil might help the South win recognition from the British and help the Peace Democrats gain control of Congress in the upcoming elections. By heading north, Lee could also feed his troops from Northern farms and draw Union troops out of Virginia during harvest season.

▲ President Lincoln meets General George McClellan (left center, facing Lincoln) after the battle of Antietam.

◄ With their backs to Antietam Creek, Union troops under the command of General McClellan attack Confederate positions, September 17, 1862.

The Battle of Antietam and the Emancipation Proclamation

The Battle of Antietam marked an important turning point in the war. The Union's victory kept Britain from recognizing the Confederacy as a separate nation. If Britain had taken this action, the balance in the struggle might have tipped in favor of the Confederacy. Also, the victory at Antietam and the terribly high casualties brought President Lincoln to the decision that the time had come to end slavery in the South by issuing the Emancipation Proclamation. The Proclamation was the first step toward finally outlawing slavery throughout the United States.

ANALYZING HISTORY How did emancipation change the war? Write a brief essay explaining your opinion.

▲ Lincoln reads the Emancipation Proclamation to members of his cabinet. Left of Lincoln are Secretary of War Edwin M. Stanton and Secretary of the Treasury Salmon P. Chase. In front of the table sits Secretary of State William Seward.

For the text of the Emancipation Proclamation, see page R49 in **Documents in American History.**

When he learned that McClellan had been sent after him, Lee ordered his troops to congregate near Sharpsburg, Maryland. Meanwhile, McClellan's troops took positions along Antietam (an·TEE·tuhm) Creek, east of Lee. On September 17, 1862, McClellan ordered his troops to attack.

The Battle of Antietam, the bloodiest one-day battle in the war and in American history, ended with over 6,000 men killed and 16,000 wounded. Although McClellan did not break Lee's lines, he inflicted so many casualties that Lee decided to retreat to Virginia.

The Battle of Antietam was a **crucial** victory for the Union. The British government had been ready to intervene in the war as a mediator if Lee's invasion had succeeded. It had also begun making plans to recognize the Confederacy in the event the North rejected mediation. Lee's defeat at Antietam changed everything. The British decided once again to wait and see how the war progressed, and with this decision the South lost its best chance at gaining international recognition and support. The South's defeat at Antietam had an even greater political impact in the United States. It convinced Lincoln that the time had come to end slavery in the South.

The Emancipation Proclamation

Although most Democrats opposed any move to end slavery, Republicans were divided on the issue. Many Republicans were strong abolitionists, but others, like Lincoln, did not want to risk losing the loyalty of the slaveholding border states that had chosen to remain in the Union. During the first year of the war, Lincoln had described the conflict as a war to preserve the Union, never as a battle against slavery. In August 1861, for example, General John C. Frémont had declared that all enslaved African Americans who worked for rebels in his region were now free. Worried that Frémont's policy would cost the Union support in border states, such as Kentucky, Lincoln overturned the order and insisted that Union officers could only seize enslaved African Americans who worked directly for Confederate troops.

A year later, however, with Northern casualties rising to staggering levels, many Northerners, including the president, began to conclude that slavery had to end—in part to punish the South and in part to make the soldiers' sacrifices worthwhile. George Julian, a Republican from Indiana, summed up the argument for freeing the slaves in an important speech delivered early in 1862:

PRIMARY SOURCE

"When I say that this rebellion has its source and life in slavery, I only repeat a simple truism. . . . The mere suppression of the rebellion will be an empty mockery of our sufferings and sacrifices, if slavery shall be spared to canker the heart of the nation anew, and repeat its diabolical misdeeds."

—quoted in *Battle Cry of Freedom*

As Lee's forces marched toward Antietam, Lincoln said that if the Union could drive those forces from Northern soil, he would issue a proclamation ending slavery. On September 22, 1862, just five days after the battle, Lincoln publicly announced that he would issue the **Emancipation Proclamation**—a decree freeing all enslaved persons in states still in rebellion after January 1, 1863. The Proclamation freed enslaved African Americans only in states at war with the Union. It did not address slavery in the border states. Short of a constitutional amendment, however, Lincoln could not end slavery in the border states, nor did he want to risk losing their loyalty.

The proclamation, by its very existence, transformed the conflict from a war to preserve the Union to a war of liberation. "We shout for joy that we live to record this righteous decree," exulted Frederick Douglass. Abolitionists rejoiced at the announcement, and looked forward to new energy among Union forces. "We were no longer merely the soldiers of a political controversy," recalled Union officer Regis de Trobiand. "We were now the missionaries of a great work of redemption, the armed liberators of millions."

✔ **Reading Check** **Examining** Why did Lincoln issue the Emancipation Proclamation and what events affected the timing of the proclamation?

Vocabulary

1. **Explain** the significance of: "Stonewall" Jackson, bounty, blockade runner, David G. Farragut, Ulysses S. Grant, George B. McClellan, Emancipation Proclamation.

Main Ideas

2. **Explaining** Why did both sides begin to use conscription early in the war?

3. **Paraphrasing** Why did Lincoln refuse to fire Grant after the Battle of Shiloh?

4. **Identifying Central Issues** What was the significance of the Battle of Antietam?

Critical Thinking

5. **Big Ideas** Why was seizing control of the Mississippi River an important strategy of the Union Navy?

6. **Organizing** Use a graphic organizer similar to the one below to explain President Lincoln's reasons for issuing the Emancipation Proclamation and the effects it had on the war.

7. **Analyzing Visuals** Examine the painting of the battle between the *Monitor* and the *Virginia* on page 321. What made these vessels superior to regular warships?

Writing About History

8. **Persuasive Writing** Suppose that you are asked to advise President Lincoln about issuing the Emancipation Proclamation. Write a short paper in which you advise him on whether or not to issue it and explain the reasons for your position.

History ONLINE

Study Central™ To review this section, go to glencoe.com and click on Study Central.

Life During the War

Guide to Reading

Big Ideas
Trade, War, and Migration The Civil War brought great suffering and widespread changes to civilians, as well as soldiers, on both sides of the conflict.

Content Vocabulary
• hardtack *(p. 331)*
• prisoner of war *(p. 333)*

Academic Vocabulary
• denial *(p. 331)*
• supplement *(p. 331)*

People and Events to Identify
• 54th Massachusetts *(p. 330)*
• Elizabeth Blackwell *(p. 332)*
• United States Sanitary Commission *(p. 332)*
• Clara Barton *(p. 333)*

Reading Strategy
Organizing Complete a graphic organizer similar to the one below to list the reasons that the North experienced a wartime economic boom.

Reason for North's Economic Boom

NEW YORK CORE CURRICULUM
U.S. History and Government

Unit 2:
II.D.2.b Impact of war on home front (civil liberties during the Civil War, women's roles)
II.D.2.d Lincoln and Emancipation (the Emancipation Proclamation, the Gettysburg Address, African-American participation in the Civil War, the 13th Amendment)

While the economic hardships of the Civil War began to wear down the morale of Southerners, the North experienced an economic boom. Life for soldiers in the field was difficult; medical treatment was primitive, and conditions in prison camps were horrific.

The Wartime Economies

MAIN Idea While the South suffered inflation and food shortages, the North prospered during the war.

HISTORY AND YOU Do you know anyone who experienced rationing during World War II? Read on to learn how the South struggled to produce enough food.

Pressed by the costs of the war, both the North and the South struggled to keep their economies working. The South, with few financial resources and little industry, suffered more from wartime inflation and critical shortages. In contrast, the North, supported by banks and industries, responded quickly to the demands of the war.

Southern Shortages, Falling Morale

By the end of 1862, the South's economy had begun to suffer from the war. The collapse of the South's transportation system, the blockade of Southern ports, and the presence of Union troops in several important agricultural regions led to severe food shortages during the winter of 1862–1863.

Southerners began to question the sacrifices they were being called upon to make—or to demand of others. Hearing of the hardships faced by their families, many Confederate soldiers deserted and returned home to help.

In the spring of 1863, Southern food shortages led to riots. In several communities, mobs of women armed with knives and guns marched into shops to seize food. In the Confederate capital, Richmond, several hundred women broke into shops, yelling, "Bread! Bread!" and then began to loot the stores for food, clothing, shoes, and other goods. The riot finally ended when Jefferson Davis sent troops to confront the mob and order the rioters to disperse.

The Union's War Boom

In contrast, the North experienced an economic boom because of the war. Its growing industries supplied the troops with uniforms, munitions, and other necessities.

Life on the Home Front

The Civil War affected people other than soldiers. It changed the economy for people on the home front, required women to take on new jobs, and led to civil unrest as well.

▲ Opposition to the draft led to riots in New York in July 1863. Local military police fired on the rioters to stop the violence.

▲ The Union Army's requirements led to an economic boom in the North. These factory workers were hired by the Union to make wagon wheels.

▲ Women helped produce goods needed for the war effort. While most worked on their farms, others went to work in factories to produce goods for the war effort. Above, women work in a munitions factory in Massachusetts.

Analyzing VISUALS

1. **Explaining** How did the war help the economy of the North?
2. **Describing** What kinds of social changes did the war cause?

The expanded use of mechanized reapers and mowers made farming possible with fewer workers, many of whom were women. One missionary in Iowa in late 1862 commented that he "met more women driving teams on the road and saw more at work in the fields than men."

Women also filled labor shortages in various industries. New sewing machines greatly increased the productivity of seamstresses. As more women entered the textile industry, the North produced an abundance of uniforms for its soldiers.

The North, however, also experienced episodes of mob violence. In 1863 riots broke out across the North over the Union's new conscription legislation. In March of that year,

Congress had passed the Union Conscription Act, making all healthy males aged 20 to 45 eligible for military service. However, if a man could find a replacement or pay a $300 fee, he did not have to serve. This meant that wealthy men were able to buy their way out of fighting in the war. In New York City, the most infamous of the draft riots occurred over four days in July. Rioters, mainly recent immigrants from Ireland and Germany, killed about 100 people and destroyed over $1 million worth of property. Militia regiments had to be called away from the war to restore order.

Reading Check **Explaining** What were the effects of food shortages on the South?

History ONLINE
Student Web Activity Visit glencoe.com and complete the activity on Civil War letters.

African Americans in the Military

MAIN Idea Many African Americans eagerly enlisted in the Union war effort.

HISTORY AND YOU Do you know anyone who joined the military after September 11, 2001? Read how the Emancipation Proclamation inspired African Americans to join the Union forces.

The Emancipation Proclamation officially permitted African Americans to enlist in the Union forces. Almost immediately, thousands of African Americans, including Frederick Douglass's two sons, Charles and Lewis, rushed to join the military. Douglass approved; he believed serving in the military would help African Americans overcome discrimination:

PRIMARY SOURCE

"Once let the black man get upon his person the brass letters U.S.; let him get an eagle on his button, and a musket on his shoulder and bullets in his pocket, and there is no power on earth which can deny that he has earned the right to citizenship."

—quoted in *Battle Cry of Freedom*

About 180,000 African Americans served in the Union army during the Civil War, roughly 9 percent of the army's total soldiers. Another 10,000 to 15,000 served in the Union navy.

Among the first African American regiments organized in the North was the **54th Massachusetts.** The regiment fought valiantly at Fort Wagner near Charleston Harbor in July 1863, losing nearly half of its soldiers in the battle. "Men all around me would fall and roll down the slope into the ditch," remembered Lewis Douglass. "Swept down like chaff, still our men went on and on." The *New York Tribune* applauded the regiment's achievement:

PRIMARY SOURCE

"... if this Massachusetts Fifty-Fourth had faltered when its trial came, two hundred thousand [African Americans] for whom it was a pioneer would never have been put into the field.... But it did not falter. It made Fort Wagner such a name to [African Americans] as Bunker Hill has been for ninety years to white Yankees."

—from *Like Men of War*

✔ **Reading Check** **Analyzing** Why might African Americans have wanted to fight in the Civil War?

PRIMARY SOURCE
African Americans Fight for the Union

The bravery of African American units, such as the 54th Massachusetts Regiment, demonstrated that they could fight as well as white soldiers, and, in the long term, it may have helped to overcome discrimination.

African American servicemen, such as the sailors of the USS Vermont (above) and the members of Fourth Colored Regiment (left), fought bravely for the Union. African Americans made up about 9 percent of the Union army and nearly 12 percent of the Union navy.

Military Life

MAIN Idea Soldiers suffered physical hardship and women provided medical assistance.

HISTORY AND YOU You probably know that it is important to clean and sanitize a wound. Read to learn how doctors performed surgery during the Civil War.

Early in the war, General Irwin McDowell's troops stopped to pick berries and foolishly wasted water from their canteens to wash them. "They were not used to denying themselves much; they were not used to journeys on foot," McDowell later reflected. Self-**denial** and long marches would prove to be only the first of the harsh realities of the war.

The Soldiers in the Field

Union and Confederate soldiers suffered many hardships during the long days and weeks between battles. Some Southern soldiers had to sleep without blankets and tramp the roads shoeless. Union soldier Elisha Rhodes wrote home that "all that we have to eat is the cattle killed by the way. No bread or salt in the Regiment and I am most starved."

For the Union soldier, meals often consisted of **hardtack** (a hard biscuit made of wheat flour), potatoes, and beans, flavored at times with dried salt pork (pork fat cured in salty brine). Confederate bread was usually made of cornmeal instead of wheat. Whenever possible, soldiers **supplemented** their diet with fruit or vegetables seized or purchased from farms they passed.

Battlefield Medicine

When Americans went to war in 1861, most were not prepared for the horrors of battle. "The sights and smells that assailed us were simply indescribable," wrote one Southern soldier. "Corpses were swollen to twice their size, some actually burst asunder. . . . The odors were so deadly that in a short time we all sickened [and] . . . most of us [were] vomiting profusely."

The Civil War produced huge numbers of casualties, and doctors struggled to tend to the wounded. In the mid-1800s doctors had little understanding of infection and germs. They used the same unsterilized instruments on all patients and, as a result, infection spread quickly in the field hospitals.

The Battle of Fort Wagner

On July 18 the Union tried to capture Fort Wagner with the 54th Massachusetts, one of the first African American regiments. Although they did not capture the fort, their valor and willingness to die for the Union underscored the worth of African American soldiers to the Union.

Analyzing VISUALS

1. **Identifying** Who mainly made up the 54th Massachusetts?

2. **Explaining** How did African American troops contribute to the success of the Union in the Civil War?

Nurses and Field Hospitals

▲ Nurses and doctors of the U.S. Sanitary Commission stand outside their hospital in Fredericksburg, Virginia, 1864. The Commission was started by Dr. Elizabeth Blackwell.

▲ Soldiers wounded at the Battle of the Wilderness in 1864 rest at a Fredericksburg hospital.

▲ Thousands of women, such as Union nurse Anne Bell, volunteered to care for wounded soldiers during the war.

Analyzing VISUALS DBQ

1. **Explaining** What were the conditions in Civil War field hospitals?
2. **Describing** What medical role did women play during the war?

Disease was one of the greatest threats facing Civil War soldiers. In many cases, regiments lost half their men to illness. Crowded together in army camps, drinking from unsanitary water supplies, many soldiers became sick. Smallpox, dysentery, typhoid, and pneumonia killed thousands of soldiers.

Battlefield physicians also used extreme measures in treating casualties. Faced with appalling wounds, doctors often amputated arms and legs to prevent gangrene and other infections from spreading. General Carl Schurz described the scene in a field hospital:

PRIMARY SOURCE

"As a wounded man was lifted on the table, often shrieking with pain . . . the surgeon quickly examined the wound and resolved upon cutting off the wounded limb. Some ether was administered. . . . The surgeon snatched the knife from between his teeth, where it had been while his hands were busy, wiped it rapidly once or twice across his blood-stained apron, and the cutting began. The operation accomplished, the surgeon would look around with a deep sigh, and then—'Next!'"

—quoted in *The Civil War*

Women Serve As Nurses

Women helped the war effort at home by managing family farms and businesses. On the battlefield, women made dramatic contributions to the Civil War by serving as nurses. Before the war, most army nurses had been men. Inspired by the famous British nurse Florence Nightingale, American women took on many of the nursing tasks in Civil War army hospitals.

In 1861 **Elizabeth Blackwell,** the first female physician in the United States, started the nation's first training program for nurses. Her work led to the creation of the **United States Sanitary Commission,** an organization that provided medical assistance and supplies to army camps and hospitals. Tens of thousands of women volunteered to work for the Commission, and raised money to send bandages, medicine, clothing, and food to army camps.

Not all women helping at the front lines were members of the Sanitary Commission. On her own, **Clara Barton** left her job in a patent office to nurse soldiers on the battlefield. With her face sometimes bluish with gunpowder, Barton fed the sick, bandaged the wounded, and even dug out bullets with her own small knife.

Although Southern women were encouraged to stay at home and support the troops by making bandages and other supplies, many founded small hospitals or braved the horrors of the battlefield. Kate Cumming of Mobile, Alabama, served as a nurse following the Battle of Shiloh. In her diary she vividly described a makeshift hospital:

PRIMARY SOURCE

"Nothing that I had ever heard or read had given me the faintest idea of the horrors witnessed here. . . . The men are lying all over the house. . . . The foul air from this mass of human beings at first made me giddy and sick, but I soon got over it. . . . "

—quoted in *Battle Cry of Freedom*

The Civil War was a turning point for the nursing profession. The courage and energy of the women also helped to break down the belief that women were weaker than men.

Military Prisons

The horrors of the battlefield and danger of disease were not the only hardships endured by soldiers during the Civil War. **Prisoners of war**—soldiers captured by the enemy in battle—also suffered terribly during the conflict.

Early in the war, the United States and the Confederacy held formal prisoner exchanges. After Lincoln issued the Emancipation Proclamation, however, the Confederacy announced that it would not exchange freed African Americans for Southern white prisoners. Instead, it would either re-enslave or execute all African American troops captured in battle.

In response to the South's treatment of African American troops, Lincoln stopped all prisoner exchanges. As a result, both the North and the South found themselves with large and growing numbers of prisoners of war. Taking care of them proved difficult, especially in the South. While conditions were bad in Northern prisons, the South could not even feed their prisoners adequately because of food shortages.

The most infamous prison in the South, Andersonville in Georgia, had no shade or shelter. Exposure, overcrowding, lack of food, and disease killed more than 100 men per day during the sweltering summer of 1864. In all, 13,000 of the 45,000 prisoners sent to Andersonville died there. After the war, Henry Wirz, Andersonville's commandant, became the only person executed for war crimes during the Civil War.

✔ **Reading Check** **Summarizing** What medical problems did Union and Confederate soldiers face?

Vocabulary

1. **Explain** the significance of: 54th Massachusetts, hardtack, Elizabeth Blackwell, United States Sanitary Commission, Clara Barton, prisoner of war.

Main Ideas

2. **Determining Cause and Effect** What was the cause of rioting in the North during the Civil War?

3. **Explaining** Why was the performance of the 54th Massachusetts significant for African Americans?

4. **Organizing** Complete a graphic organizer similar to the one below by listing the contributions of women during the Civil War.

Women's Contributions to the Civil War

Critical Thinking

5. **Big Ideas** How did the Emancipation Proclamation affect African Americans in the military?

6. **Analyzing Visuals** Examine the photographs of battlefield hospitals on page 332. Why do you think infections spread so easily in these hospitals, resulting in numerous deaths from disease, rather than from battle wounds?

Writing About History

7. **Descriptive Writing** Suppose that you are a nurse on one of the battlefields during the Civil War. Write a journal entry describing the conditions of the soldiers and your reaction to the situation.

History ONLINE

Study Central™ To review this section, go to glencoe.com and click on Study Central.

333

ANALYZING PRIMARY SOURCES

The Emancipation Proclamation

The secession of the Southern states was prompted by fears that the institution of slavery was under attack. The Civil War, however, began as a battle over the question of the right of the Southern states to secede. When Abraham Lincoln decided to issue the Emancipation Proclamation, he put ending slavery at the heart of the Union effort. In doing so, he changed the meaning of the war. The proclamation was the first bold step in the abolition of slavery throughout the nation.

Study these primary sources and answer the questions that follow.

PRIMARY SOURCE 1

Political Speech, 1861

"[The Confederate States of America's] constitution has put at rest, *forever*, all the agitating questions relating to our peculiar institution—African slavery as it exists among us—the proper *status* of the negro in our form of civilization. . . . The prevailing ideas entertained by . . . most of the leading statesmen at the time of the formation of the old constitution, were that the enslavement of the African was in violation of the laws of nature; that it was wrong in *principle*, socially, morally, and politically. . . .

Our new government is founded upon exactly the opposite idea; its foundations are laid, its corner-stone rests, upon the great truth that the negro is not equal to the white man; that slavery—subordination to the superior race—is his natural and normal condition."

—Alexander H. Stephens, vice president of the Confederate States of America, March 21, 1861

PRIMARY SOURCE 3

Political Speech, 1862

"Mr. Speaker . . . the people of the loyal States . . . know that slavery lies at the bottom of all our troubles. They know that but for this curse this horrid revolt against liberty and law would not have occurred. They know that all the unutterable agonies of our many battle-fields, all the terrible sorrows which rend so many thousands of loving hearts, all the ravages and desolation of this stupendous conflict, are to be charged to slavery. They know that its barbarism has molded the leaders of this rebellion into the most atrocious scoundrels of the nineteenth century. . . . What I said on this floor in January last, I repeat now, that the mere suppression of this rebellion will be an empty mockery of our sufferings and sacrifices, if slavery shall be spared to canker the heart of the nation anew, and repeat its diabolical deeds."

—Representative George W. Julian of Indiana in the U.S. House of Representatives, May 23, 1862

PRIMARY SOURCE 2

Political Cartoon, 1864

▼ "Lincoln Writing the Emancipation Proclamation," by Adalbert J. Volck

PRIMARY SOURCE 4

Letters, 1862

"To Abraham Lincoln, president of the United States:

". . . On the face of this wide earth, Mr. President, there is not one disinterested, determined, intelligent champion of the Union cause who does not feel that all attempts to put down the Rebellion, and at the same time uphold its inciting cause, are preposterous and futile—that the Rebellion, if crushed out tomorrow, would be renewed within a year if Slavery were left in full vigor— that Army officers who remain to this day devoted to Slavery can at best be but halfway loyal to the Union—and that every hour of deference to Slavery is an hour of added and deepened peril to the Union."

—Horace Greeley, editor of the *New York Tribune*,
August, 19, 1862

"Dear Sir—

". . . If there be those who would not save the Union unless they could at the same time save slavery, I do not agree with them—If there be those who would not save the Union unless they could at the same time destroy slavery, I do not agree with them.

"My paramount object in this struggle is to save the Union, and is not either to save or destroy slavery—If I could save the Union without freeing any slave, I would do it; and if I could save it by freeing all the slaves, I would do it; and if I could do it by freeing some and leaving others alone, I would also do that."

—Abraham Lincoln's response,
August 22, 1862

PRIMARY SOURCE 5

Political Cartoon, 1864

▼ "President Lincoln Writing the Proclamation of Freedom," by Daniel G. Blythe

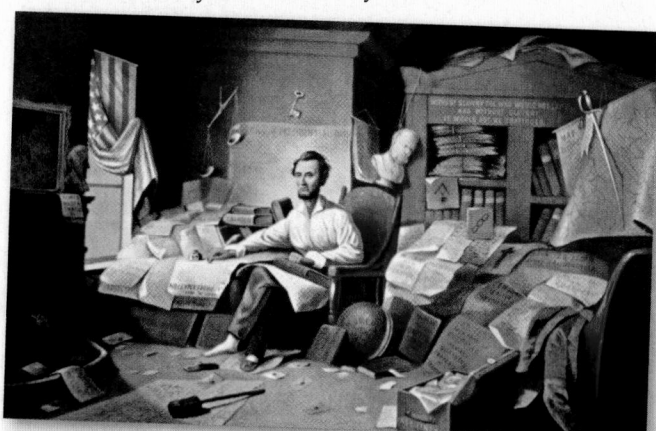

PRIMARY SOURCE 6

Letter, 1863

"My dear Sir—

". . . After the commencement of hostilities I struggled nearly a year and a half to get along without touching the 'institution' [of slavery]; and when finally I conditionally determined to touch it, I gave a hundred days fair notice of my purpose, to all the States and people, within which time they could have turned it wholly aside, by simply again becoming good citizens of the United States. They chose to disregard it, and I made the peremptory proclamation on what appeared to me to be a military necessity. And being made, it must stand. As to the States not included in it, of course they can have their rights in the Union as of old. Even the people of the states included, if they choose, need not to be hurt by it. Let them adopt systems of apprenticeship . . . conforming substantially to the most approved plans of gradual emancipation; and, with the aid they can have from the general government, they may be nearly as well off, in this respect, as if the present trouble had not occurred, and much better off than they can possibly be if the contest continues persistently."

—Abraham Lincoln, letter to Major General John A. McClernand,
January 8, 1863

DBQ Document-Based Questions

1. **Summarizing** According to Alexander H. Stephens's speech in Source 1, how does the government of the Confederacy differ from that of the Union?

2. **Contrasting** Study the images in Sources 2 and 5. What views of the Emancipation Proclamation do they present? How is Abraham Lincoln portrayed?

3. **Assessing** In Source 3, why does Representative George W. Julian believe the war must put an end to slavery?

4. **Contrasting** Read the letters in Source 4 and Source 6. How do the positions of Horace Greeley and Abraham Lincoln toward ending slavery differ? How does Lincoln's position change over time?

Section 4

The Turning Point

Guide to Reading

Big Ideas
Geography and History The Union victory at Vicksburg cut the Confederacy in two.

Content Vocabulary
- forage *(p. 337)*
- siege *(p. 337)*

Academic Vocabulary
- encounter *(p. 339)*
- promote *(p. 341)*

People and Events to Identify
- Ambrose Burnside *(p. 338)*
- Joseph Hooker *(p. 338)*
- George Meade *(p. 339)*
- Gettysburg *(p. 339)*
- Pickett's Charge *(p. 339)*
- William Tecumseh Sherman *(p. 341)*

Reading Strategy
Categorizing Complete a graphic organizer to record the results of the listed battles that shaped the Union victory.

Battle	Results
Vicksburg	
Chancellorsville	
Gettysburg	
Chickamauga Creek	
Missionary Ridge	

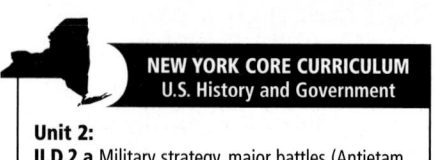

NEW YORK CORE CURRICULUM
U.S. History and Government

Unit 2:
II.D.2.a Military strategy, major battles (Antietam, Gettysburg), and human toll

For a while, the North floundered under a series of generals who were overly cautious or intimidated by the reputation of General Robert E. Lee. The tide of the war began to turn after the North won pivotal victories at Vicksburg and Gettysburg.

Vicksburg Falls

MAIN Idea General Grant captured Vicksburg, thus gaining control of the Mississippi River and dividing the South.

HISTORY AND YOU How long do you think you could go hungry to defend a cause? Read how Confederate soldiers surrendered after their food supply was cut off.

In April 1862, Admiral David G. Farragut captured New Orleans and secured control of the Mississippi River delta for the Union. Later that year, General Ulysses S. Grant seized control of the river as far south as Memphis after his victory at Shiloh. Despite these successes, there remained one major Confederate stronghold on the river—Vicksburg, Mississippi.

"Vicksburg is the key," Lincoln said. "The war can never be brought to a close until the key is in our pocket." If Grant could take Vicksburg, the Confederacy would be cut in two. If not, as Lincoln commented, the earlier victories in the west would make little difference: "We can take all the northern ports of the Confederacy, and they can still defy us from Vicksburg. It means hog and hominy without limit, fresh troops from the States of the far South, and a cotton country where they can raise the staple without interference."

Grierson's Raid

The city of Vicksburg was located on the east bank of the Mississippi River. At first, Grant tried to approach the city from the north, but the land was too swampy, and the rivers in the area were covered with vegetation and blocked by trees. To get at Vicksburg, Grant decided to move his troops across the Mississippi to the west bank and then march south. Once he was past the city, he intended to cross back to the east bank and attack the city from the south.

To distract the Confederates while he carried out this difficult maneuver, Grant ordered Colonel Benjamin Grierson to take 1,700 cavalry troops on a raid through Mississippi. Grierson's forces traveled 600 miles (965 km) in two weeks, tearing up railroads, burning depots, and fighting skirmishes. His raid enabled Grant to move his troops south of the city.

PRIMARY SOURCE
The Siege of Vicksburg

▲ Union ironclads commanded by Rear Admiral David Porter sealed off Vicksburg's access to the Mississippi and bombarded the city's defenses.

Grant Closes in on Vicksburg, March–July 1863

0   10 kilometers
0   10 miles
Albers Equal-Area projection

Yazoo R.
Siege of Vicksburg May 18–July 4
Big Black River Bridge May 17
Champion Hill May 16
Jackson May 14
Vicksburg
Louisiana
Mississippi
Jackson
Big Black R.
Mississippi R.
Raymond May 12
Pearl R.
Port Gibson May 1

Union advance
Confederate position
Union victory

During the siege of Vicksburg, Union troops dug 13 "approach trenches" along their lines, allowing them to get close to the Confederate fortifications. In the meantime, the gunboats bombarded the city. The city was unable to receive food and other supplies. The city surrendered on July 4, 1863.

Analyzing VISUALS   DBQ

1. **Describing** How did the Union work to break down the defenses at Vicksburg?
2. **Making Inferences** At Vicksburg, the siege was successful, but under what circumstances might a siege be risky for the attackers?

The Siege of Vicksburg

After returning to the east bank of the Mississippi River, Grant embarked on a daring march east, ordering his troops to live off the country. **Foraging**—or searching and raiding for food—as they marched, Grant's troops headed east into Mississippi. They captured the town of Jackson before turning back west toward Vicksburg. Grant's troops marched an astonishing 180 miles (290 km) in 17 days, fought 5 battles, and inflicted 7,200 casualties on the Confederates. The march ended by driving the Confederate forces back into their defenses at Vicksburg.

In May 1863 Grant launched two assaults on Vicksburg, but the city's defenders repulsed both attacks and inflicted high casualties. Grant decided that the only way to take the city was to put it under **siege**—to cut off its food and supplies and bombard it until its defenders gave up. The siege of Vicksburg lasted for six weeks, with Confederate troops and the city's residents facing near-starvation. On July 4, 1863, the Confederate commander at Vicksburg surrendered. The Union victory had cut the Confederacy in two.

✔ Reading Check **Explaining** Why did President Lincoln want the Union army to capture Vicksburg?

The Road to Gettysburg

MAIN Idea Gettysburg was the bloodiest battle of the war and the last time the Confederates invaded the North.

HISTORY AND YOU Have you read the Gettysburg Address? Read on to learn about the battle that inspired one of the greatest speeches in American history.

Shortly after General McClellan's victory at Antietam, Lincoln became frustrated with him. At Antietam, McClellan might have destroyed Lee's army, but he let it slip away. He then moved so slowly after the battle that Lee was able to recover and block McClellan's advance on Richmond. On November 7, 1862, Lincoln fired McClellan and gave command of the army to General **Ambrose Burnside.**

Lincoln wanted a general who was not intimidated by Lee's reputation. He urged Burnside to push south into Virginia and destroy Lee's army. Lincoln did not know that the turning point in the east would come not in Virginia but to the north, in Pennsylvania.

Fredericksburg and Chancellorsville

On December 13, 1862, Burnside ordered a series of assaults against Lee's Confederate troops entrenched in the hills south of Fredericksburg, Virginia. The Union troops suffered over 12,000 casualties, more than twice the loss suffered by the Confederates. Faced with complaints about Burnside from other officers, Lincoln replaced him with General **Joseph Hooker.**

General Hooker devised a plan to get at Lee's troops on the hills near Fredericksburg. First, he left a large part of his army at Fredericksburg to keep Lee's troops from moving. He then took the rest of the army west to

PRIMARY SOURCE
The Gettysburg Address

The bloody victory at Gettysburg was a major turning point in the Civil War. It kept Britain out of the war, inflicted serious losses on the Confederacy and helped restore Union morale. In November 1863 Lincoln went to Gettysburg to dedicate part of the battlefield as a cemetery. His speech, the Gettysburg Address, became one of the best-known orations in American history.

▼ On July 3, 1863, the Confederate forces launched an attack known later as Pickett's Charge. Charging up Cemetery Ridge into withering cannon fire, the Confederates suffered nearly 7000 casualties in less than two hours. Soon after the attack failed, General Lee ordered Southern forces to withdraw.

circle around behind Lee's troops and attack them from the rear. Realizing what was going on, Lee also divided his forces. He left a small force at Fredericksburg and headed west with most of his troops to stop Hooker.

On May 2, 1863, Lee's troops attacked Hooker's in dense woods known as the Wilderness near Chancellorsville, Virginia. Although outnumbered two to one, Lee's forces repeatedly defeated the Union troops. On May 5, Hooker decided to retreat.

The Battle of Gettysburg

Having weakened the Union forces at Chancellorsville, Lee decided to invade the North again. In June 1863, he marched into Pennsylvania. After Hooker failed to stop Lee, Lincoln removed him from command and appointed General **George Meade** as his replacement. Meade immediately headed north to intercept Lee.

At the end of June, as Lee's army foraged in the Pennsylvania countryside, some of his troops headed into the town of **Gettysburg,** to scout for the enemy. When they arrived near the town, however, they **encountered** Union cavalry. On July 1, 1863, the Confederates pushed the Union troops out of the town into the hills to the south. At the same time, the main forces of both armies hurried to the scene of the fighting.

On July 2, Lee attacked, but the Union troops held their ground. The following day, he ordered nearly 15,000 men under the command of General George E. Pickett and General A.P. Hill to undertake a massive assault. The attack came to be known as **Pickett's Charge.** A mile-wide line of Confederate troops marched across open farmland toward Union positions on Cemetery Ridge. Union cannons and guns opened fire, inflicting 7,000 casualties in less than half an hour of fighting.

▲ More than 50,000 Americans were killed or wounded during the battle of Gettysburg.

DBQ Document-Based Questions

1. **Specifying** To what event is Lincoln referring that occurred "fourscore and seven years ago"?
2. **Identifying Central Issues** What does Lincoln say is the main purpose of the Civil War and the rea-son for the sacrifices at Gettysburg?

The Aftermath

Fewer than 5,000 Confederate troops made it up the ridge, and Union troops quickly overwhelmed those who did. Lee then quickly rallied his troops and began a retreat to Virginia on a rainy July 4. Confederate forces soon became trapped between a swollen Potomac River and pursuing Union troops, but General Meade, with his army depleted by the battle, decided not to attack the defenses put up by the retreating Confederate forces.

At Gettysburg, Confederate forces lost approximately 28,000 killed or wounded. This amounted to over one-third of Lee's entire force. The Union army suffered about 23,000 casualties, but could better afford the losses.

Gettysburg proved to be the turning point of the war. The Union's victory strengthened the Republicans politically and ensured that Britain would not recognize the Confederacy. For the rest of the war, Lee's forces fought on the defensive, slowly giving ground.

✔ **Reading Check** **Summarizing** What was the result of Pickett's Charge?

Battle for Tennessee

MAIN Idea After Grant won control of Tennessee, Lincoln appointed him general in chief.

HISTORY AND YOU Have you ever planned a strategy to win a game? Read on to learn how Grant's planned assault on Chattanooga was even more successful than expected.

After the Union's major victories at Vicksburg and Gettysburg, fierce fighting erupted in Tennessee near Chattanooga. Chattanooga was a vital railroad junction. Both sides knew that if the Union forces captured Chattanooga, they would control a major railroad running south to Atlanta.

Chickamauga

During the summer of 1863, Union General William Rosecrans outmaneuvered Confederate General Braxton Bragg. In early September, Rosecrans forced the Confederates to evacuate Chattanooga without a fight. Bragg did not retreat far, however. When Rosecrans advanced

---

People IN HISTORY

Ulysses S. Grant
1822–1885

Before his victories in Kentucky and Tennessee, Ulysses S. Grant had been an average West Point cadet, a failed businessman, and had served in the Mexican War. More than any other Union commander, however, Grant changed the strategy—and the outcome—of the Civil War. Grant's restless urge for offensive fighting and his insistence on "unconditional surrender" at Fort Donelson convinced Lincoln to place the general in command of all Union troops in 1864. Lincoln's confidence was not misplaced. Despite mounting casualties and accusations that he was a "butcher," Grant pushed relentlessly until Lee finally surrendered at Appomattox.

The Union's enthusiasm for its victorious general made Grant a two-term president after the war, although scandals in his administration marred his reputation. The Civil War had been the high point of Grant's life, the challenge that brought out his abilities as a leader.

How did Grant change the outcome of the Civil War?

Robert E. Lee
1807–1870

The son of a distinguished—though not wealthy—Virginia family, Robert E. Lee was raised in the socially exclusive world of the aristocratic South. From the beginning, he seemed marked by fate for brilliant success. At West Point he excelled in both his studies and his social life, impressing teachers and fellow cadets with his talent and good nature. As an army officer in the war with Mexico, he performed with brilliance and courage.

Offered command of Union troops at the beginning of the Civil War, Lee refused, unable to oppose his fellow Virginians. A hero to Southerners during the war, Lee felt a responsibility to set an example of Southern honor in defeat. His swearing of renewed allegiance to the United States after the war inspired thousands of former Confederate soldiers to do the same. As president of Washington College in Virginia (later renamed Washington and Lee), Lee encouraged his students to put the war behind them and to behave as responsible citizens.

How did Lee work to heal the wounds of the Civil War?

---

into Georgia, Bragg launched an assault against him at Chickamauga Creek on September 19, 1863. Bragg soon smashed through part of the Union defenses, and Rosecrans ordered his troops to fall back to Chattanooga, where he found himself almost completely surrounded by Bragg's forces.

The Battle of Chattanooga

In an effort to save the Union troops in Chattanooga, Lincoln decided to send some of Meade's forces to help Rosecrans. Dozens of trains were assembled, and 11 days later 20,000 men with their artillery, horses, and equipment arrived near Chattanooga after traveling more than 1,200 miles (1,930 km).

Lincoln also decided to reorganize the military leadership in the west, and he placed Grant in overall command. Grant then hurried to Chattanooga to take charge of the coming battle. In late November, he ordered his troops to attack Confederate positions on Lookout Mountain. Charging uphill through swirling fog, the Union forces quickly drove the Confederate troops off the mountain.

Confederate soldiers retreating from Lookout Mountain hurried to join other Confederate forces at Missionary Ridge east of Chattanooga. The Confederates were outnumbered, but they awaited a Union attack, secure on a high rugged position, just as the Union troops had been at Cemetery Ridge near Gettysburg.

Grant did not intend to storm Missionary Ridge. He believed an all-out assault would be suicidal. Instead, he ordered General **William Tecumseh Sherman** to attack Confederate positions on the north end of the ridge. When Sherman failed to break through, Grant ordered 23,000 men under General George Thomas to launch a limited attack against the Confederates in front of Missionary Ridge as a diversion.

To Grant's astonishment, Thomas's troops overran the Confederate trenches and charged up the steep slope of Missionary Ridge itself. "They shouted 'Chickamauga,'" one Confederate remembered, "as though the word itself were a weapon." The rapid charge scattered the surprised Confederates, who retreated in panic, leaving Missionary Ridge—and Chattanooga—to the Union army.

Grant Becomes General in Chief

By the spring of 1864, Grant had accomplished two crucial objectives for the Union. His capture of Vicksburg had given the Union control of the Mississippi River, while his victory at Chattanooga had secured eastern Tennessee and cleared the way for an invasion of Georgia. Lincoln rewarded Grant by appointing him general in chief of the Union forces and **promoting** him to lieutenant general, a rank no one had held since George Washington. When the president met Grant in March 1864 he told him, "I wish to express my satisfaction with what you have done. . . . The particulars of your plan I neither know nor seek to know." The president had finally found a general he trusted to win the war.

✔ **Reading Check** **Examining** Why was capturing Chattanooga important to the Union?

Section 4 REVIEW

Vocabulary

1. **Explain** the significance of: forage, siege, Ambrose Burnside, Joseph Hooker, George Meade, Gettysburg, Pickett's Charge, William Tecumseh Sherman.

Main Ideas

2. **Explaining** What was the purpose of Grierson's Raid?

3. **Identifying Central Issues** How was Gettysburg a turning point in the war?

4. **Summarizing** Why did Lincoln make Grant general in chief of the army?

Critical Thinking

5. **Big Ideas** Why was capturing Vicksburg important to the Union?

6. **Organizing** Using a graphic organizer, list the results of the Battle of Gettysburg. Consider both the Union and the Confederacy.

7. **Analyzing Visuals** Study the map of Grant's approach to Vicksburg on page 337. Why do you think he fought several battles outside Vicksburg before he laid siege to the city itself?

Writing About History

8. **Descriptive Writing** Take on the role of a Confederate soldier at the Battle of Gettysburg. Write a letter to your family describing the battle and your feelings about its result.

History ONLINE

Study Central™ To review this section, go to glencoe.com and click on Study Central.

GEOGRAPHY & HISTORY

The Battle of Gettysburg

The Confederate invasion of the North in 1863 was a bold stroke. By moving north, General Robert E. Lee gained access to the rich farms and other resources of Pennsylvania. When his troops arrived in Gettysburg on July 1, they forced Union troops to flee to the hills south of the town. Had Confederate forces attacked the Union troops in the hills immediately, they might have won. The decision not to attack enabled Union troops to reinforce their position and build a formidable defensive line.

How Did Geography Shape the Battle?

The Union line stretched from Culp's Hill and Cemetery Hill in the north, south along Cemetery Ridge to another hill called Little Round Top. The Union forces controlled the high ground and were deployed in such a way that troops could easily be moved from one part of the line to another depending on where the enemy attacked.

On July 2, Lee tried to seize Little Round Top. Controlling the hill would have let his artillery fire down the length of the Union line. After savage fighting, his attack was repulsed, but Lee believed the Union had shifted so many troops south to hold Little Round Top that it had left its line on Cemetery Ridge vulnerable to attack.

On July 3, Lee ordered some 12,500 troops to attack Cemetery Ridge in what became known as Pickett's Charge. Union artillery ripped holes in the Confederate line as it advanced. When the Confederates neared the crest of the ridge, Union troops, protected by trenches and barricades they had built, unleashed volley after volley. Firing at point-blank rage, stabbing with bayonets, and battering with rifle butts, the Union soldiers drove the Confederates back. Lee knew he had been beaten. The next day he began his retreat to Virginia.

Town of Gettysburg

Culp's Hill

Seminary Ridge

**Army of Northern Virginia
Robert E. Lee**

Analyzing GEOGRAPHY

1. **Place** Why was the Union army in such a strong position in the Battle of Gettysburg?

2. **Movement** What made Pickett's charge so difficult? Why did Lee think it would succeed?

On July 3, Lee ordered some 12,500 men to attack Cemetery Ridge. The Confederates marched three-quarters of a mile across open fields and then uphill toward Union lines. Although the attack is known as Pickett's Charge, General Pickett's troops made up only about one-third of the Confederate force that attacked.

Pennsylvania

Carlisle

Wrightsville

Chambersburg

Gettysburg

MEADE

Frederick   Baltimore

Maryland

West Virginia

Winchester

Front Royal

Potomac R.

Shenandoah R.

HOOKER

Washington D.C.

LEE

Virginia

Fredericksburg

Chancellorsville

Rappahannock R.

Chesapeake Bay

Richmond

← Union advance
← Confederate advance

0   40 kilometers
0   40 miles
Albers Equal-Area projection

N W E S

Cemetery Ridge

Army of the Potomac
General George G. Meade

Little Round Top

The Devil's Den

Peach Orchard

On July 2, Lee ordered Longstreet to attack the Union lines near the hill named Little Round Top. Savage fighting erupted in the Peach Orchard, on the slopes of Little Round Top, and near a jumble of boulders called the Devil's Den. The Union forces held Little Round Top and drove back the Confederates.

The War Ends

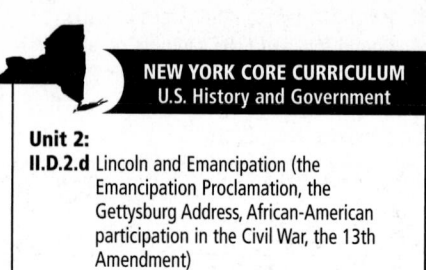
After four bloody years of fighting, Union forces began to wear down the Confederate army. As the war neared its conclusion, however, the assassination of President Lincoln left the nation with many questions about how to reunite the Union.

Grant Versus Lee

MAIN Idea During the final year of the war, Grant's forces battled Lee's forces for control of Virginia.

HISTORY AND YOU Have you read about trench warfare during World War I? Read to learn how the Confederate Army used trenches to defend Petersburg, Virginia.

In the spring of 1864, the most successful general of the Union Army faced the most renowned Confederate commander. Grant put his most trusted **subordinate,** William Tecumseh Sherman, in charge of operations in the west. He then headed to Washington, D.C., to take command of the Union troops facing Lee.

From the Wilderness to Cold Harbor

"Whatever happens, there will be no turning back," Grant promised Lincoln. He was determined to march southward, attacking Lee's forces relentlessly, until the South surrendered.

The first battle of Grant's campaign erupted in the Wilderness, a densely forested area near Fredericksburg, Virginia. The battle lasted for two days, continuing even after the woods caught fire, blinding and choking the combatants. Despite suffering heavy casualties, Grant attacked again near Spotsylvania Courthouse. First in terrible heat and then in pouring rain, the two armies battled for 11 days, often in bloody hand-to-hand combat that left many traumatized.

Unlike past campaigns, in which several weeks of reinforcing and resupplying followed battles, warfare now continued without pause. Savage combat, advances and retreats, and the digging of defensive trenches filled most days and nights. One Union officer noted that the men "had grown thin and haggard. The experience . . . seemed to have added twenty years to their age."

Unable to break Lee's lines at Spotsylvania, Grant headed toward Cold Harbor, a strategic crossroads northeast of Richmond. Convinced that his relentless attacks had weakened and demoralized Lee's troops, Grant decided to launch an all-out assault at Cold Harbor. The attack cost his army 7,000 casualties, compared to 1,500 for the South.

Grant v. Lee, 1864–1865

Fortification
Union advance
Confederate advance
Confederate retreat
Union victory
Confederate victory
Inconclusive battle

Potomac R.

Maryland

Washington, D.C.

Delaware

N
W   E
S

▲ Union soldiers sit in trenches during the siege of Petersburg, Virginia. The siege lasted from June 1864 to April 1865.

Shenandoah R.

Rappahannock Station
Culpeper
Brandy Station
The Wilderness May 5–7, 1864
Chancellorsville
Fredericksburg
Rapidan R.
Spotsylvania Courthouse May 8–19, 1864

Staunton
Gordonsville
North Anna R.
Charlottesville
South Anna R.
North Anna May 23–26, 1864

Potomac R.
Rappahannock R.

James R.
Pamunkey R.
Mattaponi R.

Richmond
Amelia Courthouse, April 5, 1865
Sayler's Creek April 6, 1865
Lynchburg
Farmville
Appomattox R.
Cold Harbor
Cold Harbor, June 3, 1864
York R.
Chickahominy R.

Chesapeake Bay

ATLANTIC OCEAN

Petersburg
Petersburg siege June 1864–April 1865
James R.

Appomattox Courthouse, April 9, 1865: Lee surrenders to Grant

Five Forks April 1, 1865

Roanoke R.

0   40 kilometers
0   40 miles
Albers Equal-Area projection

Analyzing GEOGRAPHY

1. **Movement** How long did the final contest between Grant and Lee take, from the battle of the Wilderness to the surrender at Appomattox Courthouse?

2. **Location** Based on the positions of the armies on the map, why do you think Lee chose to surrender at Appomattox?

The Siege of Petersburg

Stopped by Lee at Cold Harbor, Grant tried another plan similar to the one he had used near Vicksburg. He ordered General **Philip Sheridan** to stage a cavalry raid north and west of Richmond. While Sheridan's troops distracted Lee, Grant headed southeast, crossed the James River, and then turned west toward Petersburg. Capturing Petersburg would cut the only railroad line into Richmond.

When the first Union troops reached the outskirts of Petersburg, they paused. The city was defended by miles of barricades 20 feet (7 m) thick. In front of the Confederate trenches were ditches up to 15 feet (4.6 m) deep to slow down attackers. Carefully positioned cannons supported Confederate lines.

The strength of the defenses the Confederates had erected at Petersburg intimidated the Union troops, who were already exhausted. Realizing a full-scale frontal assault would be suicidal, Grant ordered his troops to put the city under siege.

✓ **Reading Check** **Summarizing** Why did General Grant decide to capture Petersburg?

The Union Advances

MAIN Idea After the fall of Atlanta, General Sherman led his troops across the state of Georgia, causing mass destruction along the way.

HISTORY AND YOU Do you think that armies should treat civilians differently from soldiers during a war? Read on to learn how General Sherman treated Southerners during his March to the Sea.

While Grant fought Lee, General Sherman marched his army from Chattanooga toward Atlanta and the Union navy prepared to seal the last major port on the Gulf of Mexico east of the Mississippi—Mobile, Alabama.

Farragut Attacks Mobile

On August 5, 1864, Admiral Farragut took 18 ships past the three Confederate forts defending Mobile Bay. As the fleet headed into the bay, a mine—which in the 1860s was called a torpedo—blew up a Union ship. The explosion brought the fleet to a halt, right in front of a fort's guns. "Damn the torpedoes! Full speed ahead!" cried Farragut, whose ship led the way through the minefield.

After getting past the Confederate forts, Farragut's ships destroyed a Confederate fleet defending Mobile Bay. Although Farragut did not capture Mobile, he did seal off the bay. Blockade runners moving goods in and out of the Deep South east of the Mississippi could no longer use any port on the Gulf of Mexico.

Sherman's March to the Sea

In late August 1864, Sherman sent his troops south around Atlanta to cut the roads and railways leading into the city. His troops destroyed the rail lines by heating the rails and twisting them into snarls of steel nicknamed **"Sherman neckties."** To avoid being trapped in the city, Confederate General John B. Hood ordered his troops to evacuate Atlanta on September 1, 1864.

After occupying Atlanta, Sherman proposed to march across Georgia. "I could cut a swath to the sea," he explained, "and divide the Confederacy in two." The march would be "a demonstration to the world . . . that we have a power that Davis cannot resist. I can make the march, and make Georgia howl!"

Sherman ordered all civilians to leave Atlanta. He explained to the city's mayor that he was "not only fighting hostile armies, but a hostile people." To end the war, he believed, he had no choice but to "make old and young, rich and poor, feel the hard hand of war." Sherman then ordered his troops to destroy everything of military value, including mills, warehouses, factories, railroads, and machine shops. Sherman's troops set fires to destroy these **structures,** but the fires quickly spread, burning down more than one-third of the city.

On November 15, 1864, Sherman began his **March to the Sea.** His troops cut a path of destruction through Georgia that was, in places, 60 miles (97 km) wide. They ransacked houses, burned crops, and killed cattle. By December 21, 1864, they had reached the coast and seized the city of Savannah.

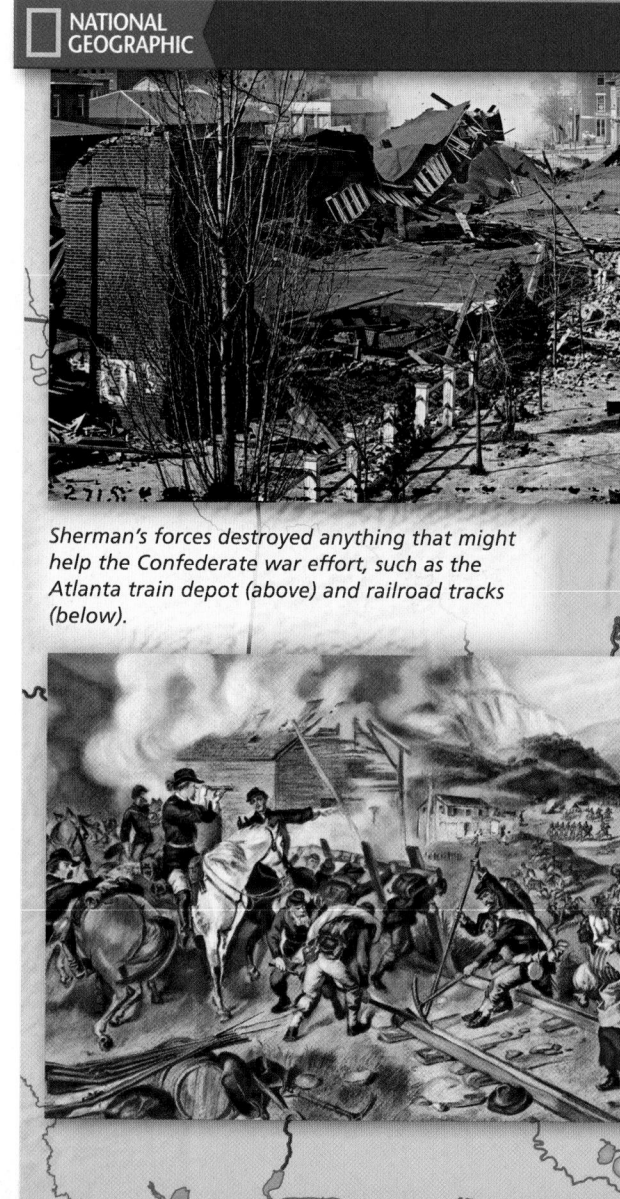

NATIONAL GEOGRAPHIC

Sherman's forces destroyed anything that might help the Confederate war effort, such as the Atlanta train depot (above) and railroad tracks (below).

After reaching the sea, Sherman ordered his troops to turn north and head into South Carolina—the state that many people believed had started the Civil War. "The whole army," Sherman wrote, "is burning with an insatiable desire to wreak vengeance upon South Carolina." As one Union soldier declared, "Here is where treason began and . . . here is where it shall end."

As the troops marched north, they burned and **pillaged,** or looted, nearly everything in front of them. At least 12 towns were set on fire, including Columbia, the state capital. The march demoralized Southerners. As one South Carolinian wrote, "All is gloom, despondency and inactivity. Our army is demoralized and the people panic stricken . . . to fight longer seems madness."

✔ Reading Check **Examining** Why did General Sherman march his army through Georgia?

The South Surrenders

MAIN Idea After Lee surrendered, Lincoln was assassinated before the country had agreed on the future of former slaves and the defeated South.

HISTORY AND YOU When do you think disloyalty amounts to treason? Read on to learn why Grant promised not to prosecute Confederate soldiers for taking up arms against the government.

When Sherman and Grant began their campaigns in the spring of 1864, Lincoln knew that his own reelection depended on their success. By summer, sensing the public's anger over the costly war, Lincoln confided to an army officer, "I am going to be beaten." He did not know, however, that the war was nearly over. Only a few months later, the Confederacy was on the verge of collapse.

Sherman's March to the Sea

Union states
Confederate states
Union forces
Area of Sherman's March
Confederate forces
Union victory
Confederate victory

Kentucky

Virginia

Richmond

North Carolina

Raleigh

April 13, 1865: Union troops occupy Raleigh; Johnston surrenders April 18, 1865

Nashville
Nashville
Dec. 15–16, 1864
Franklin
Nov. 30, 1864
Tennessee

Fayetteville
March 11, 1865

Bentonville
March 19, 1865

ATLANTIC OCEAN

34°N

Kennesaw Mtn.
June 27, 1864

South Carolina

Wilmington

Atlanta
Battles of Atlanta
July 20, 22, 28, 1864

Columbia

Feb. 17, 1865: Union troops occupy Columbia

0   100 kilometers
0   100 miles
Albers Equal-Area projection

Alabama

Georgia

SHERMAN

Charleston

76°W

Sept. 2, 1864: Union troops occupy Atlanta

Macon

Montgomery

Savannah

32°N

Dec. 21, 1864: Union troops occupy Savannah

80°W

Analyzing GEOGRAPHY

1. **Movement** Compare this map to the map on page 345. Why did Lee's forces retreat west instead of south?

2. **Location** Through which state did Sherman's "march to the sea" pass? Where did it end, and on what date?

The Cost of the Civil War

▲ Robert E. Lee surrenders to General Grant at Appomattox Courthouse on April 9, 1865.

▲ The war devastated the South. Hundreds of thousands of people were dead, and several major cities, including Richmond (above), lay in ruins.

Casualties of the Civil War

Troops (thousands)

North South

| | Total Deaths | Battle-related deaths | Non-battle deaths |

Source: *For the Common Defense.*

American War Deaths*

War with Mexico 13,000
Revolutionary War 25,000
Korean War 36,500
Vietnam War 58,000
World War I 107,000

War on Terror 3,500
Other major wars 5,000

Civil War 620,000
World War II 407,000

*approximate figures
Sources: United States Civil War Center; *For the Common Defense*

Analyzing VISUALS

1. **Identifying** The Civil War cost more American lives than any other conflict. What were the next two most deadly wars?

2. **Specifying** Which region suffered the highest number of battle-related deaths?

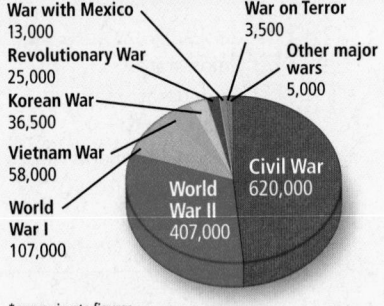

History ONLINE
Student Skill Activity To learn how to create and modify spreadsheets, visit glencoe.com and complete the Skill activity.

The Election of 1864

To oppose Lincoln in the 1864 election, the Democrats nominated General George B. McClellan, whose popularity had remained high despite his dismissal earlier in the war. Knowing the country was growing weary of the war, McClellan promised to stop the hostilities and open negotiations with the South to restore the Union peaceably.

The capture of Atlanta came just in time to revitalize Northern support for the war and for Lincoln himself. The president won reelection with 55 percent of the popular vote. Lincoln interpreted his reelection as a **mandate,** or a command from the voters, to end slavery permanently by amending the Constitution. To get the amendment through Congress, Republicans asked Democrats who were against slavery to help them. On January 31, 1865, the **Thirteenth Amendment** to the Constitution, banning slavery in the United States, narrowly passed the House of Representatives and was sent to the states for ratification.

Surrender

Meanwhile, in the trenches near Petersburg, Lee knew that time was running out. On April 1, 1865, Union troops led by Sheridan cut the last railroad line into Petersburg at the Battle of Five Forks. The following night, Lee's troops withdrew from their positions near the city and raced west.

Lee's desperate attempt to escape Grant's forces failed when Sheridan's cavalry got ahead of Lee's troops and blocked the road at **Appomattox Courthouse.** When his troops failed to break through, Lee sadly observed, "There is nothing left for me to do but go and see General Grant, and I would rather die a thousand deaths." With his ragged and battered troops surrounded and outnumbered, Lee surrendered to Grant at Appomattox Courthouse on April 9, 1865.

Grant's generous terms of surrender guaranteed that the United States would not prosecute Confederate soldiers for treason. When Grant agreed to let Confederates take their horses home "to put in a crop to carry themselves and their families through the next winter," Lee thanked him, adding that the kindness would "do much toward conciliating our people." As Lee left, he shook hands with Ely Parker, a Senecan who served as Grant's secretary. "I am glad to see a real American here," Lee told the Native American. Parker replied, "We are all Americans."

Lincoln's Assassination

With the war over, Lincoln described his plan to restore the Southern states to the Union. In the speech, he mentioned including African Americans in Southern state governments. One listener, the actor John Wilkes Booth, sneered to a friend, "That is the last speech he will ever make." The president's advisers repeatedly warned him not to appear unescorted in public. Nevertheless, on the evening of April 14, 1865, Lincoln went to Ford's Theatre with his wife to see a play. During the third act, Booth slipped quietly behind him and shot the president in the back of the head.

Lincoln's death shocked the nation. Once viewed as a rustic, unsophisticated man not suited for the presidency, Lincoln had become the Union's greatest champion. The usually stern General Grant wept openly as Lincoln's body lay in state at the White House. Tens of thousands of men, women, and children lined railroad tracks across the nation as Lincoln's body was transported back to Springfield, Illinois, for burial.

Aftermath of the Civil War

The North's victory in the Civil War strengthened the power of the federal government over the states. It also transformed American society by finally ending the enslavement of millions of African Americans. At the same time, it left the South socially and economically devastated.

Following the war, many questions remained unresolved. When would the Southern states be permitted back into the Union? Under what conditions would that occur? What would be the status of newly freed African Americans? Americans from the North and the South tried to answer these questions in the years following the Civil War—an era known as Reconstruction.

Reading Check **Explaining** Why did President Lincoln doubt he could win the 1864 election?

Section 5 REVIEW

Vocabulary

1. **Explain** the significance of: Philip Sheridan, "Sherman neckties," March to the Sea, pillage, mandate, Thirteenth Amendment, Appomattox Courthouse.

Main Ideas

2. **Describing** What was the fighting like at Spotsylvania?

3. **Analyzing** What was the effect of Farragut's blockade of Mobile Bay?

4. **Listing** What were three short-term consequences of the Civil War?

Critical Thinking

5. **Big Ideas** How did Northern military strategy change after Ulysses S. Grant took command of the Union Army?

6. **Organizing** Complete a graphic organizer that lists the purposes of the Union march on Atlanta and the effects of the city's capture on both sides.

| Purpose | | Union March on Atlanta | | Effects |

7. **Analyzing Visuals** Examine the graphs of war deaths on page 348. Create a spreadsheet of battles, and for each, list the outcome and number of lives lost to analyze the overall outcome of the Civil War.

Writing About History

8. **Descriptive Writing** Take on the role of a reporter living in Georgia during Sherman's March. Write a brief article describing the Union's actions and their effects on the people of Georgia.

History ONLINE

Study Central™ To review this section, go to glencoe.com and click on Study Central.

▲ *Jefferson Davis meets with his cabinet and General Lee.*

▲ *After the Battle of Antietam (above), Lincoln issued the Emancipation Proclamation.*

▲ *Grant's forces wore down Lee's troops in a series of battles in northern Virginia. At Cold Harbor (above), the Union suffered heavy losses.*

North v. South

1861

- Lincoln orders a blockade of Southern ports.
- The Confederacy organizes its government.
- The South wins the First Battle of Bull Run.
- Both sides begin building up their forces.

1862

- Farragut captures New Orleans.
- After the Battles of Shiloh and Murfreesboro, the Union gains control of western Tennessee.
- Led by McClellan, Union troops land in Virginia to begin the Peninsular Campaign; after a series of battles with Lee's forces, McClellan's forces withdraw.
- Lee invades the North, but is defeated at the Battle of Antietam.

1863: The Turning Point

- Lincoln issues the Emancipation Proclamation.
- Grant captures Vicksburg after a long siege and cuts the Confederacy in two.
- After winning the battles of Fredericksburg and Chancellorsville, Lee invades the north but is defeated at the Battle of Gettysburg.
- After losing the Battle of Chickamauga, Union forces drive back Southern forces at the Battle of Chattanooga.
- Grant is given command of all Union forces.

1864

- Grant battles Lee's forces in northern Virginia; Lee retreats into Petersburg, which Grant puts under siege.
- Sherman captures Atlanta, then begins his March to the Sea across Georgia.

1865

- Lee attempts to escape from Petersburg but is surrounded by Grant's forces and surrenders at Appomattox Courthouse; other Confederate forces surrender as well.
- Lincoln is assassinated.

▼ *The capture of New Orleans (below) gave the Union control of the mouth of the Mississippi River.*

▼ *The failure of Pickett's Charge convinced Lee to withdraw from Gettysburg. It was the turning point of the war.*

▼ *Mourners surround Lincoln's hearse in Philadelphia in April 1865.*

NEW YORK REGENTS EXAM PRACTICE

TEST-TAKING TIP

Be sure to read each question carefully to identify any key words that may help you either to choose the correct answer choice or eliminate incorrect answer choices.

Part I

Directions (1–10): For each statement or question, write on a separate sheet of paper the number of the word or expression that, of those given, best completes the statement or answers the question.

1 Which of the following was part of the Union's Anaconda Plan for defeating the Confederacy?

(1) a blockade of Southern ports

(2) a quick ground offensive

(3) the assassination of Jefferson Davis

(4) a defensive war of attrition

2 The damage done by the *Alabama* and the *Florida* created tension between the Union and Great Britain because

(1) it helped the Confederacy to nearly win the war.

(2) Great Britain had joined the war on the side of the Confederacy.

(3) the ships initially had been promised to the Union.

(4) Great Britain had allowed the ships to be built in Britain by the Confederacy.

3 One result of the Battle of Antietam was that

(1) Lincoln decided to issue the Emancipation Proclamation.

(2) the Confederacy was split in two.

(3) Great Britain decided to support the Confederacy.

(4) David Farragut became a hero in the North.

4 In the Civil War, women made huge contributions for the first time as

(1) nurses.

(2) soldiers.

(3) reporters.

(4) teachers.

5 One outcome of the Battle of Gettysburg was that the British

(1) were determined to support the Confederacy.

(2) would never now support the Confederacy.

(3) wanted to support the Union.

(4) decided to sell ships to the Union.

6 After the successful capture of Chattanooga, Lincoln

(1) recalled General Sherman to Washington, D.C.

(2) issued the Emancipation Proclamation.

(3) began negotiations for peace with the Confederacy.

(4) made General Grant general in chief of the army.

7 The institution of slavery was formally abolished in the United States by the

(1) Compromise of 1850.

(2) Emancipation Proclamation of 1863.

(3) creation of the Freedmen's Bureau in 1865.

(4) Ratification of the Thirteenth Amendment in 1865.

Need Extra Help?							
If You Missed Questions . . .	1	2	3	4	5	6	7
Go to Page . . .	319	322	326	332	340	341	348

[OVER]

Base your answer to question 8 on the map below and on your knowledge of Chapter 9.

Peninsula Campaign, April–May 1862

Hanover Courthouse
May 27, 1862

Seven Pines
May 31–
June 1, 1862

Eltham's Landing
May 7, 1862

Richmond

MAGRUDER

Drewry's Bluff
May 15, 1862

Yorktown Siege
April 5–
May 4, 1862

Williamsburg
May 5, 1862

Virginia

Fort
Monroe

Rappahannock R.

York R.

James R.

MCCLELLAN

Chesapeake Bay

Legend:
★ Union victory
✦ Confederate victory
✸ Other battle
⌐⌐⌐ Fortification
+—+ Railroad
← Union advance
← Confederate advance
◄---- Confederate retreat

0   20 kilometers
0   20 miles
Albers Equal-Area projection

8 How did General McClellan move his troops to Virginia?

(1) railroad.

(2) wagon.

(3) land.

(4) water.

9 By 1864, when Grant faced Lee at Spotsylvania, the nature of the war had changed in which of the following ways?

(1) It had been fought mostly in the South and was now fought mostly in the North.

(2) Where there had been long breaks between battles, there was now continuous fighting.

(3) The Confederacy, not the Union, now began to win most of the battles.

(4) Both sides now introduced new technologies, such as ironclads and conoidal bullets.

10 The Civil War ended when

(1) Sherman reached Savannah.

(2) the Thirteenth Amendment was ratified.

(3) Lee surrendered to Grant at Appomattox.

(4) Lincoln was assassinated.

Need Extra Help?			
If You Missed Questions . . .	8	9	10
Go to Page . . .	352	344	348

Part II Thematic Essay Question

Directions: Write a well-organized essay that includes an introduction, several paragraphs addressing the task below, and a conclusion.

Theme: Civil Liberties in Wartime

President Lincoln suspended the writ of habeas corpus during the Civil War to prevent interference with the draft.

Task:

Consider the suspension of civil liberties during wartime.

- Explain the extent of the suspension of civil liberties during the Civil War, including the reasoning behind it and the public's reaction

- Discuss your beliefs on the suspension of civil liberties during wartime

- Evaluate the impact of the suspension of civil liberties on the outcome of the war and on the U.S. citizens

Guidelines:

In your essay, be sure to:

- Develop all aspects of the task

- Support the theme with relevant facts, examples, and details

- Use a logical and clear plan of organization, including an introduction and a conclusion that are beyond a restatement of the theme

Part III Document-Based Question

This question is based on the accompanying documents. It is designed to test your ability to work with historical documents. Some of the documents have been edited for the purposes of the question. As you analyze the documents, take into account the source of each document and any point of view that may be presented in the document.

Historical Context:

As the nation perched on the brink of the Civil War, people across the nation were divided by their beliefs and feelings. However, many opposed the idea of fighting against fellow citizens.

Task:

Using information from the documents and your knowledge of United States history, answer the questions that follow each document in Part A. Your answers to the questions will help you write the Part B essay, in which you will be asked to

- Discuss the beliefs and attitudes of those who were against a war
- Evaluate how political and sectional differences influenced opinions for and against the war
- Explain why many people were against the idea of war but were still willing to fight, and the reasons why they might do so

Part A
Short-Answer Questions

Directions: Analyze the documents and answer on a separate sheet of paper the short-answer questions that follow each document.

Document 1

My Dear Sister:

. . . With all my devotion to the Union and the feeling of loyalty and duty of an American citizen, I have not been able to make up my mind to raise my hand against my relatives, my children, my home. I have, therefore, resigned my commission in the Army, and, save in defense of my native state . . . I hope I may never be called on to draw my sword. I know you will blame me; but you must think as kindly of me as you can. . . .

Source: Robert E. Lee, *Personal Reminiscences, Anecdotes, and Letters of General Robert E. Lee*

1 Why did Robert E. Lee think it was necessary to resign from the U.S. Army?

2 What do you think Lee's feelings were about the war?

Document 2

Source: *Harper's Weekly*, February 28, 1863

3 Based on this cartoon, about Peace Democrats or "Copperheads," what is the artist trying to show?

Part B
Essay

Directions: Reread the task box at the top left and write a well-organized essay that includes an introduction, several paragraphs, and a conclusion. Use evidence from the documents in your essay. Support your response with relevant facts, examples, and details. Include additional outside information.

Guidelines:
In your essay, be sure to:

- Develop all aspects of the task
- Incorporate information from the documents
- Incorporate relevant outside information
- Support the theme with relevant facts, examples, and details
- Use a logical and clear plan of organization, including an introduction and a conclusion that are beyond a restatement of the theme

History ONLINE

For additional test practice, use Self-Check Quizzes—Chapter 9 at glencoe.com.

Need Extra Help?				
If You Missed Questions . . .	1	2	3	Essay
Go to Page . . .	353	353	353	353

Reconstruction
1865–1877

SECTION 1 The Debate Over Reconstruction

SECTION 2 Republican Rule

SECTION 3 Reconstruction Collapses

Richmond, Virginia, lies in ruins after the city falls to Union troops in April 1865.

1865
- Freedmen's Bureau is founded
- Lincoln is assassinated

A. Johnson
1865–1869

1866
- Congress passes the Fourteenth Amendment

1867
- Radical Republicans take control of Congress

Grant
1869–1877

1870
- Fifteenth Amendment ratified

1871
- Congress passes the Ku Klux Klan Act

U.S. PRESIDENTS

U.S. EVENTS

1865   1867   1869   1871

WORLD EVENTS

1866
- Transatlantic cable is completed

1868
- Meiji Restoration begins Japanese modernization

1869
- First ships pass through Suez Canal

1871
- Germany is unified; German Empire is proclaimed

How Do Nations Recover From War?

After war devastates a country, it needs to feed and house refugees, repair damage, create jobs, and get the economy growing again. The United States faced all of these problems after the Civil War, but it also had to find a way to reconcile Northerners and Southerners and protect the rights of the formerly enslaved.

- *What did the United States do to reconstruct the South?*

- *Considering both the short term and the long term, was Reconstruction a success or a failure?*

1875
- "Whiskey Ring" scandal breaks

Hayes
1877–1881

1877
- Compromise of 1877 ends Reconstruction efforts

1873   1875   1877

1874
- First Impressionist art exhibit opens in Paris

FOLDABLES™

Contrasting Before and After Collect information about life in the South before and after the Civil War. List the most important facts in a Two-Tab Foldable. Include information about all levels of Southern society—rich and poor, white and African American, native-born and immigrant—and how conditions changed for each group.

Before | After

Life in the South

History ONLINE Chapter Overview
Visit glencoe.com to preview Chapter 10.

The Debate Over Reconstruction

NEW YORK CORE CURRICULUM
U.S. History and Government

Unit 3:
I.A.1 Lincoln's Plan
I.A.2 Congressional Reconstruction
I.A.3 Post-Civil War amendments (13th, 14th, and 15th)
I.A.4 Impeachment of Andrew Johnson
I.A.5 The reconstructed nation and shifting relationships between the federal government, state governments, and individual citizens

I n the months after the Civil War ended, the nation began to rebuild and reunite. Almost immediately, fierce struggles began over how long it should take to restore the Southern states to the Union and how punitive Reconstruction should be.

The Reconstruction Battle Begins

MAIN Idea Presidents Lincoln and Johnson, as well as Radical Republicans in Congress, put forward different plans for reconstructing the Union.

HISTORY AND YOU Think of another war that you have studied. What were the peace terms, and who benefited? Read on to learn about different plans for peace following the American Civil War.

By 1865, large areas of the former Confederacy lay in ruins, and the South's economy was in a state of collapse. The value of land had fallen significantly. Confederate money was worthless. Roughly two-thirds of the transportation system no longer functioned, with dozens of bridges destroyed and miles of railroad twisted and rendered useless. Most dramatically of all, the emancipation of African Americans had thrown the agricultural system into chaos. Until the South developed a new system to replace enslaved labor, it could not maintain its agricultural output.

While some Southerners felt bitter over the Union's military victory, for many the more important struggle was rebuilding their land and their lives. Meanwhile, the president and Congress grappled with the difficult task of Reconstruction, or rebuilding after the war. They had to decide under what terms and conditions the former Confederate states could rejoin the Union.

Lincoln's Plan

President Lincoln wanted a moderate policy that would reconcile Southerners with the Union, instead of punishing them for treason. In December 1863 he offered a general **amnesty,** or pardon, to all Southerners who took an oath of loyalty to the United States and accepted the Union's proclamations concerning slavery. When 10 percent of a state's voters in the 1860 presidential election had taken this oath, they could organize a new state government. The only people not offered a pardon were officials of the former Confederate government, officers of the Confederate army, and former federal judges, members of Congress, and military officers who had left their posts to help the Confederacy.

Three Plans for Reconstruction

After the Civil War, three plans were proposed to restore the South to the Union. The political struggle that resulted revealed that sectional tensions had not ended with the Civil War.

1. Lincoln's Plan for Reconstruction

- Amnesty to all but a few Southerners who took an oath of loyalty to the United States and accepted its proclamations concerning slavery
- When 10 percent of a state's voters in the 1860 presidential election had taken the oath, they could organize a new state government
- Members of the former Confederate government, officers of the Confederate army, and former federal judges, members of Congress, and military officers who had left their posts to help the Confederacy would not receive amnesty

2. Congressional Reconstruction

- Passed the Fourteenth and Fifteenth Amendments
- Military Reconstruction Act divided the South into five military districts
- New state constitutions required to guarantee voting rights
- Military rule protected voting rights for African Americans
- Empowered African Americans in government and supported their education

▲ *Thaddeus Stevens*

▶ *Charles Sumner*

3. Johnson's Plan for Reconstruction

- Amnesty for those taking an oath of loyalty to the United States; excluded high-ranking Confederates and those with property over $20,000, but they could apply for pardons individually
- Required states to ratify the Thirteenth Amendment abolishing slavery

Analyzing VISUALS

1. **Identifying** Which plan made the most provisions for formerly enslaved African Americans?
2. **Specifying** Which plan was most forgiving of former Confederate political and military leaders?

The Radical Republicans

Resistance to Lincoln's plan surfaced at once among the more radical Republicans in Congress. Led by Representative Thaddeus Stevens of Pennsylvania and Senator Charles Sumner of Massachusetts, the radicals did not want to reconcile with the South. They wanted, in Stevens's words, to "revolutionize Southern institutions, habits, and manners."

The **Radical Republicans** had three main goals. First, they wanted to prevent the leaders of the Confederacy from returning to power after the war. Second, they wanted the Republican Party to become a powerful institution in the South. Third, they wanted the federal government to help African Americans achieve political equality by guaranteeing their right to vote in the South.

Republicans knew that, once the South was restored to the Union, it would gain about 15 seats in the House of Representatives. Before the Civil War, the number of Southern seats in the House was based on the Three-Fifths Compromise in the Constitution. According to this compromise, only three-fifths of the enslaved population counted toward representation. The abolition of slavery entitled the South to more seats in the House. This would endanger Republican control of Congress, unless Republicans could find a way to protect African Americans' voting rights.

Although Radical Republicans knew that giving African American men in the South the right to vote would help their party win elections, most were not acting cynically. Many had been abolitionists before the Civil War and had pushed Lincoln into making emancipation a goal of the war. They believed in a right to political equality for all men, regardless of race. Senator Henry Wilson of Massachusetts summarized their position:

PRIMARY SOURCE

"[Congress] must see to it that the man made free by the Constitution . . . is a freeman indeed; that he can go where he pleases, work when and for whom he pleases . . . go into schools and educate himself and his children; that the rights and guarantees of the good old common law are his, and that he walks the earth, proud and erect in the conscious dignity of a free man."

—from the *Congressional Globe*, December 21, 1865

History ONLINE
Student Web Activity Visit glencoe.com and complete the activity on Southern Reconstruction.

The Wade-Davis Bill

Caught between Lincoln and the Radical Republicans were a large number of moderate Republicans. The moderates thought Lincoln was too lenient but that the radicals were going too far in supporting African Americans.

By the summer of 1864, the moderates and radicals had agreed on an alternative plan to Lincoln's and introduced it in Congress as the **Wade-Davis Bill.** This bill required the majority of the adult white males in a former Confederate state to take an oath of allegiance to the Union. The state could then hold a constitutional convention to create a new state government. Each state's convention would then have to abolish slavery, reject all debts the state had acquired as part of the Confederacy, and deprive all former Confederate government officials and military officers of the right to vote or hold office.

Although Congress passed the Wade-Davis Bill, Lincoln blocked it with a **pocket veto**—that is, he let the session of Congress expire without signing the legislation. He thought that imposing a harsh peace would be counterproductive. The president wanted "no persecution, no bloody work."

✔ **Reading Check** **Summarizing** Why did President Lincoln favor a lenient policy toward the South?

Freedmen's Bureau

MAIN Idea The Freedmen's Bureau helped newly freed African Americans obtain food, find work, and get an education.

HISTORY AND YOU Do you remember the slave codes that denied African Americans basic rights, including an education? Read on to learn how the Freedmen's Bureau tried to help former slaves start their new lives.

After considering different approaches to restoring the Southern states to the Union, Lincoln decided that harsh terms would only alienate many whites in the South. The devastation of the war and the collapse of the economy had left hundreds of thousands of people unemployed, homeless, and hungry. At the same time, the victorious Union armies had to contend with the thousands of African Americans who had fled to Union lines as the war progressed. As Sherman marched through Georgia and South Carolina, thousands of freed African Americans—now known as freedmen—began following his troops, seeking food and shelter.

To help the freedmen feed themselves, Sherman reserved all abandoned plantation land within 30 miles of the coast from Charleston, South Carolina, to Jacksonville, Florida, for the use of freed African Americans. Over the next few months, Union troops settled more than 40,000 African Americans on roughly half a million acres of land in South Carolina and Georgia.

The refugee crisis prompted Congress to establish the Bureau of Refugees, Freedmen, and Abandoned Lands—better known as the **Freedmen's Bureau.** The bureau was part of the War Department, and General Oliver O. Howard was appointed its commissioner. With the army's support, the bureau played a key role in Reconstruction. It was given the task of feeding and clothing war refugees in the South using surplus army supplies. Beginning in September 1865, the bureau provided nearly 30,000 rations a day for the next year and helped prevent mass starvation in the South.

The Bureau also helped formerly enslaved people find work on plantations. It negotiated labor contracts with planters, specifying the amount of pay workers would receive and the number of hours they had to work. It also established special courts to deal with grievances between workers and planters.

Although many Northerners backed the Bureau, some argued that freedmen should be given "forty acres and a mule" to support themselves. These people urged the federal government to seize Confederate land and distribute it to emancipated slaves. To others, however, taking land from plantation owners was wrong because it violated individual property rights. Ultimately, Congress rejected land confiscation.

The Freedmen's Bureau made an important contribution in the field of education. The Bureau worked closely with Northern charities to educate formerly enslaved African Americans. It provided buildings for schools, paid teachers, and helped to establish colleges for training African American teachers.

✓ Reading Check **Explaining** What were the purposes of the Freedmen's Bureau?

Johnson Takes Office

MAIN Idea President Johnson wanted to readmit Southern states on generous terms; meanwhile, Southern states passed laws restricting the rights of African Americans.

HISTORY AND YOU Have you ever had a dispute with a longtime friend? After it was over, did the situation improve? Read to learn how Southern states passed laws to limit African Americans' rights.

Lincoln's assassination drastically changed the politics of Reconstruction. Lincoln's vice president, Andrew Johnson, now became president. Johnson had been a Southern Democrat before the Civil War. A resident of Tennessee, he had served as a mayor and state legislator before being elected to the United States Senate. When Tennessee seceded, Johnson remained loyal and stayed in the Senate, making him a hero in the North.

PRIMARY SOURCE
The Freedmen's Bureau in Action

The Freedmen's Bureau was established by the Union to help formerly enslaved people make new lives for themselves. Headed by Union General Oliver Otis Howard, the Bureau provided food, clothing, and medical care. It also helped African Americans to build and manage many schools, such as those pictured here, throughout the South.

▲ Schools funded by the Freedmen's Bureau, such as the one above, led to a dramatic increase in literacy among African Americans. By 1870, more than 1,000 new schools had been established.

▲ Formerly enslaved African Americans await the distribution of food at office of the Freedmen's Bureau in South Carolina in 1865.

Analyzing VISUALS

1. **Specifying** Aside from basic relief efforts, what other services did the Freedmen's Bureau provide?

2. **Explaining** Why do you think education was a priority for formerly enslaved people?

As Union troops advanced into Tennessee in 1862, Lincoln appointed Johnson military governor of the state. The president then approved Johnson's nomination as vice president in 1864, hoping to convince some Democrats to vote Republican. Johnson was hot-tempered and stubborn at times, but, like Lincoln, he believed that a moderate policy was needed to bring the South back into the Union and to win Southern loyalty.

Johnson's Plan

In the summer of 1865, with Congress in recess, Johnson initiated what he called his restoration program, which closely resembled Lincoln's plan. In late May 1865, he issued an amnesty proclamation to supplement the one Lincoln had issued earlier. Johnson offered to pardon all former citizens of the Confederacy who took an oath of loyalty to the Union and to return their property. He excluded from the pardon former Confederate officers and officials, as well as former Confederates who owned property worth more than $20,000. These were the people—the rich planter elite—who Johnson believed had caused the Civil War. Those who were excluded could apply individually for a pardon.

On the same day that he issued the pardon, Johnson issued another proclamation for North Carolina. This became a model of how he wanted to restore the South to the Union. Under it, each former Confederate state had to call a constitutional convention to revoke its ordinance of secession, ratify the Thirteenth Amendment, and reject all Civil War debts.

The former Confederate states, for the most part, met Johnson's conditions. While they organized their new governments and elected members to Congress, Johnson began granting pardons to thousands of Southerners.

By the time Congress gathered for its next session in December 1865, Johnson's plan was well under way. Many members of Congress were astonished and angered when they realized that Southern voters had elected to Congress many former Confederate officers and political leaders, including Alexander Stephens, the former vice president of the Confederacy. Many Republicans found this unacceptable and voted to reject the new Southern members of Congress.

Black Codes

The election of former Confederate leaders to Congress was not the only development that angered congressional Republicans. The new Southern state legislatures also passed a series of laws known as **black codes,** which severely limited African Americans' rights.

The black codes varied from state to state, but they all seemed intended to keep African Americans in a condition similar to slavery. African Americans were generally required to enter into annual labor contracts. Their children had to accept apprenticeships in some states and could be whipped or beaten while serving in these apprenticeships. Several state codes set specific work hours for African Americans and required them to get licenses to work in nonagricultural jobs.

The black codes enraged many Northerners. Gideon Welles, the secretary of the navy, warned, "The entire South seem to be stupid and vindictive, know not their friends, and are pursuing just the course which their opponents, the Radicals, desire."

✓ Reading Check **Summarizing** Whom did President Johnson blame for the Civil War?

The Fourteenth Amendment

The passage of the Fourteenth Amendment was a turning point in American political and legal history. Since its ratification, the amendment has been used to expand federal power over the states and to extend civil rights through its equal protection clause. It also provided the foundation for the doctrine of incorporation—the concept that the rights and protections in the Bill of Rights apply to the states. This doctrine was first upheld by the Supreme Court in *Gitlow* v. *New York* in 1925. In the 1950s and 1960s, the Warren Court used the clause extensively to extend civil rights in cases such as *Brown* v. *Board of Education, Gideon* v. *Wainwright,* and *Reynolds* v. *Sims,* among others.

ANALYZING HISTORY **What is significant about the ratification of the Fourteenth Amendment? Write a brief essay to explain your answer.**

Radical Republicans Take Control

MAIN Idea Radical Republicans, angered by President Johnson's actions, designed their own policies to reconstruct the South.

HISTORY AND YOU If you disagree with a political decision, what can you do to change it? Read how Republicans responded to Johnson's plan.

The election of former Confederate leaders to Congress and the introduction of the black codes convinced many moderate Republicans to join the Radicals. In late 1865, House and Senate Republicans created a Joint Committee on Reconstruction. Their goal was to develop their own program for rebuilding the Union.

The Fourteenth Amendment

In an effort to override the black codes, Congress passed the **Civil Rights Act of 1866.** The act granted citizenship to all persons born in the United States except Native Americans. It allowed African Americans to own property and stated that they were to be treated equally in court. It also gave the federal government the power to sue people who violated those rights.

Worried that the Supreme Court might overturn the Civil Rights Act, the Republicans then introduced the **Fourteenth Amendment** to the Constitution. This amendment granted citizenship to all persons born or naturalized in the United States and declared that no state could deprive any person of life, liberty, or property "without due process of law." It also declared that no state could deny any person "equal protection of the laws."

Increasing violence in the South convinced moderates to support the amendment. The most dramatic incident occurred in Memphis, Tennessee, in May 1866, when white mobs killed 46 African Americans and burned hundreds of their homes, churches, and schools. Congress passed the amendment in June and sent it to the states for ratification.

President Johnson attacked the amendment and made it the major issue of the 1866 congressional elections. He hoped voters would reject the Radical Republicans and elect a new majority in Congress that would support his plan for Reconstruction instead.

The Fourteenth Amendment

"No State shall make or enforce any law which shall abridge the privileges or immunities of citizens of the United States; nor shall any State deprive any person of life, liberty, or property, without due process of law; nor deny to any person within its jurisdiction the equal protection of the laws."

▲ In 1964, in Reynolds v. Sims, *the Court used the Fourteenth Amendment's equal protection clause to ensure that state voting districts were of equal size.*

◀ Clarence Gideon

▶ Ernesto Miranda

▲ In two major cases, Gideon v. Wainwright *in 1963 and* Miranda v. Arizona *in 1966, the Court clarified that the Fifth and Sixth Amendments of the Bill of Rights had to be upheld by the states.*

▶ In 1925, in Gitlow v. New York, *the Supreme Court began using the Fourteenth Amendment to apply the Bill of Rights to the states. In this case, it held that state laws had to protect free speech.*

▲ Benjamin Gitlow

◀ In 1954 the Supreme Court based its decision ending school segregation, Brown v. Board of Education, *on the Fourteenth Amendment's equal protection clause.*

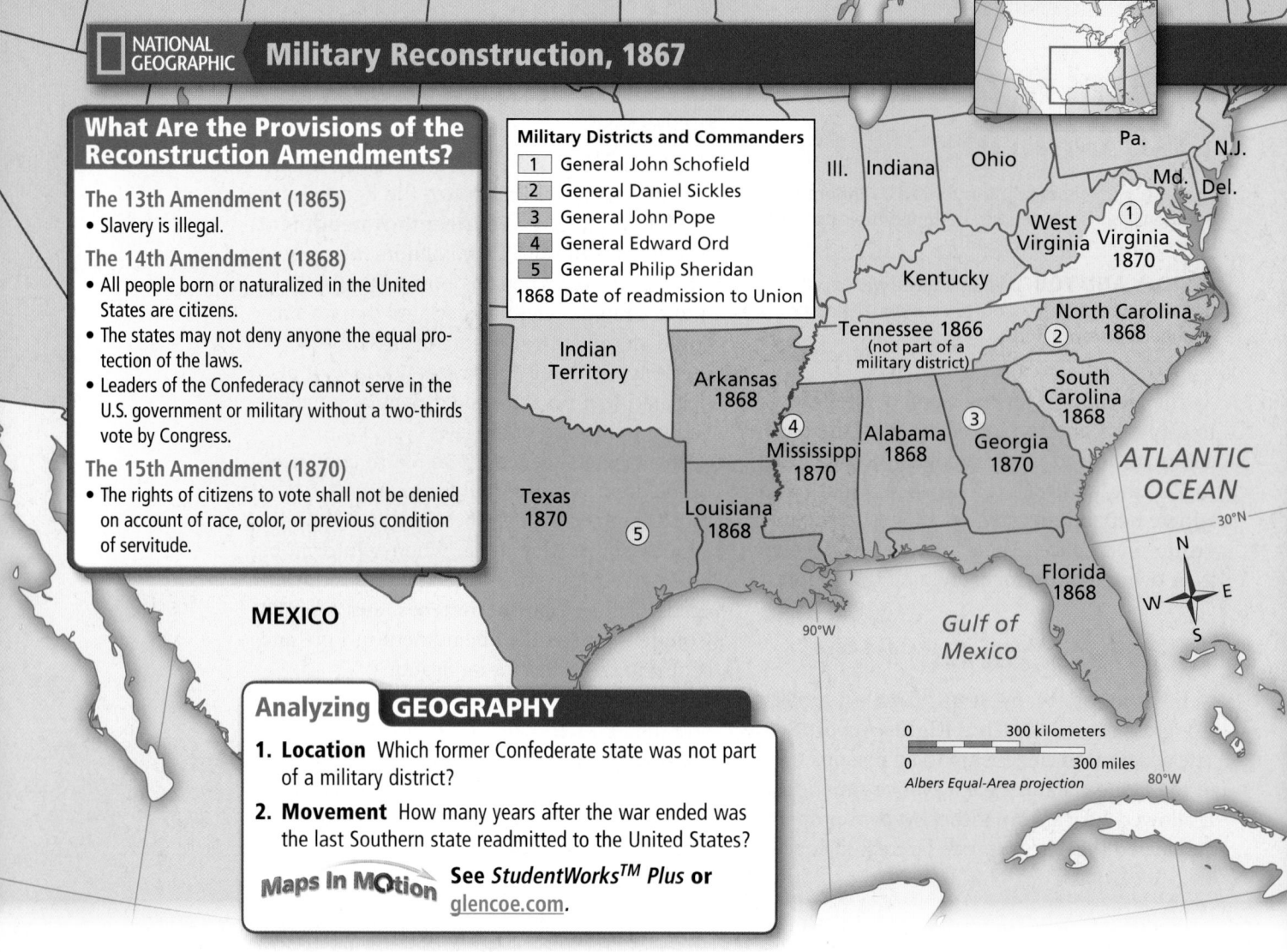

NATIONAL GEOGRAPHIC   Military Reconstruction, 1867

What Are the Provisions of the Reconstruction Amendments?

The 13th Amendment (1865)
• Slavery is illegal.

The 14th Amendment (1868)
• All people born or naturalized in the United States are citizens.
• The states may not deny anyone the equal protection of the laws.
• Leaders of the Confederacy cannot serve in the U.S. government or military without a two-thirds vote by Congress.

The 15th Amendment (1870)
• The rights of citizens to vote shall not be denied on account of race, color, or previous condition of servitude.

Military Districts and Commanders
1	General John Schofield
2	General Daniel Sickles
3	General John Pope
4	General Edward Ord
5	General Philip Sheridan

1868 Date of readmission to Union

Indian Territory

Texas 1870

MEXICO

Arkansas 1868

Louisiana 1868

Mississippi 1870

Alabama 1868

Tennessee 1866 (not part of a military district)

Georgia 1870

Kentucky

West Virginia   Virginia 1870

North Carolina 1868

South Carolina 1868

Florida 1868

Ill.   Indiana   Ohio   Pa.   N.J.   Md.   Del.

ATLANTIC OCEAN

Gulf of Mexico

0   300 kilometers
0   300 miles
Albers Equal-Area projection

30°N
80°W
90°W

Analyzing GEOGRAPHY

1. **Location** Which former Confederate state was not part of a military district?

2. **Movement** How many years after the war ended was the last Southern state readmitted to the United States?

Maps In Motion See *StudentWorks™ Plus* or glencoe.com.

As the election campaign got under way, more violence erupted in the South. In July 1866, a white mob attacked delegates to a convention in New Orleans that supported African American voting rights. As Johnson attacked Radical Republicans, Republicans responded by accusing Democrats of being traitors and starting the Civil War. When the votes were counted, the Republicans had won a roughly three-to-one majority in Congress. The Fourteenth Amendment was ratified by the states in 1868.

Military Reconstruction

In March 1867 congressional Republicans passed the Military Reconstruction Act, which essentially wiped out Johnson's programs. The act divided the former Confederacy, except for Tennessee—which had ratified the Fourteenth Amendment in 1866—into five military districts. A Union general was placed in charge of each district.

In the meantime, each former Confederate state had to hold another constitutional convention. The new state constitutions had to give the right to vote to all adult male citizens, regardless of their race. After a state had ratified its new constitution, it had to ratify the Fourteenth Amendment before it would be allowed to elect members to Congress.

With military officers supervising voter registration, the Southern states began holding elections and organizing constitutional conventions. By the end of 1868, six former Confederate states—North Carolina, South Carolina, Florida, Alabama, Louisiana, and Arkansas—had met all the **requirements** and were readmitted to the Union.

Johnson Is Impeached The Republicans knew that they had the votes to override any veto of their policies, but they also knew that President Johnson could interfere with their plans by refusing to enforce the laws they passed. Although they distrusted Johnson, Republicans in Congress knew that Secretary of War Edwin M. Stanton agreed with their program and would enforce it. They also trusted General Ulysses S. Grant, the head of the army, to support their policies.

To prevent Johnson from bypassing Grant or firing Stanton, Congress passed the Command of the Army Act and the Tenure of Office Act. The Command of the Army Act required all orders from the president to go through the headquarters of the general of the army—Grant's headquarters. The Tenure of Office Act required the Senate to approve the removal of any government official whose appointment had required the Senate's consent.

Determined to challenge the Tenure of Office Act, Johnson fired Stanton on February 21, 1868. Stanton barricaded himself inside his office and refused to leave. Three days later, the House of Representatives voted to **impeach** Johnson, meaning that they charged him with "high crimes and misdemeanors" in office. The main charge against Johnson was that he had broken the law by refusing to uphold the Tenure of Office Act.

As provided in the Constitution, the Senate put the president on trial. If two-thirds of the senators found the president guilty, he would be removed from office. On May 16, 1868, the Senate voted 35 to 19 that Johnson was guilty—one vote short of conviction. Seven Republicans joined the Democrats in refusing to convict Johnson. These senators believed that it would set a dangerous **precedent** to impeach a president simply because he did not agree with congressional policies.

Although Johnson remained in office, he finished his term quietly and did not run for reelection in 1868. That year the Republicans nominated General Grant to run for president. During the campaign, ongoing violence in the South convinced many Northern voters that the Southern states could not be trusted to reorganize their governments without military supervision. At the same time, the presence of Union troops in the South enabled African Americans to vote in large numbers. As a result, Grant won six Southern states and most of the Northern states. The Republicans retained large majorities in both houses of Congress.

The Fifteenth Amendment With their majority secure and a trusted president in office, Republicans moved to expand their Reconstruction program. Realizing the importance of African American voters, Congress passed the **Fifteenth Amendment** to the Constitution. This amendment declared that the right to vote "shall not be denied . . . on account of race, color, or previous condition of servitude." By March 1870, enough states had ratified the amendment to make it part of the Constitution.

Radical Reconstruction had a dramatic impact on the South, particularly in the short term. It changed Southern politics by bringing hundreds of thousands of African Americans into the political process for the first time. It also began to change Southern society. This angered many white Southerners, who began to fight back against the federal government's policies.

✔ **Reading Check** **Identifying** What two laws did the Radical Republicans pass to reduce presidential power?

Section 1 REVIEW

Vocabulary

1. **Explain** the significance of: amnesty, Radical Republicans, Wade-Davis Bill, pocket veto, Freedmen's Bureau, black codes, Civil Rights Act of 1866, Fourteenth Amendment, impeach, Fifteenth Amendment.

Main Ideas

2. **Identifying** What were the three main goals of the Radical Republicans?

3. **Specifying** In what area did the Freedmen's Bureau have the most impact?

4. **Explaining** Under what circumstances did Andrew Johnson become president?

5. **Listing** What were the main provisions of the Military Reconstruction Act?

Critical Thinking

6. **Big Ideas** What services did the Freedmen's Bureau provide?

7. **Listing** Use a graphic organizer to list the effects of the Civil War on the South.

```
I. Johnson Takes Office
    A.
    B.
    C.
II.
    A.
    B.
    C.
```

8. **Analyzing Visuals** Review the images on page 361. How has the Fourteenth Amendment changed over time?

Writing About History

9. **Descriptive Writing** Take on the role of a Southerner after the Civil War. Write a journal entry describing the postwar South and what you hope the future will hold for the region.

History ONLINE

Study Central™ To review this section, go to glencoe.com and click on Study Central.

TIME NOTEBOOK

PHOTOWORLD/FPG

Eyewitness

WILLIAM H. CROOKE *served as a bodyguard for President Andrew Johnson and witnessed the decisive vote by Edmund Ross during the impeachment trial in the Senate on Saturday, May 16, 1868. Here, Crooke recalls the scene:*

The tension grew. There was a weary number of names before that of Ross was reached. When the clerk called it, and Ross [senator from Kansas] stood forth, the crowd held its breath.

'Not guilty,' called the senator from Kansas. It was like the babbling [sic] over of a caldron. The Radical Senators, who had been laboring with Ross only a short time before, turned to him in rage; all over the house people began to stir. The rest of the roll-call was listened to with lessened interest. . . . When it was over, and the result—35 to 19—was announced, there was a wild outburst, chiefly groans of anger and disappointment, for the friends of the president were in the minority.

It was all over in a moment, and Mr. Johnson was ordering some whiskey from the cellar. [President Johnson was not convicted.]

VERBATIM

❝If the South is ever to be made a safe Republic, let her lands be cultivated by the toil of the owners, or the free labor of intelligent citizens.❞

THADDEUS STEVENS,
arguing for land redistribution in the South during Reconstruction

❝In the South, the [Civil] war is what A.D. is elsewhere; they date from it.❞

MARK TWAIN,
from Life on the Mississippi

❝For we colored people did not know how to be free and the white people did not know how to have a free colored person about them.❞

HOUSTON HARTSFIELD HOLLOWAY,
freedman, on the problem of Reconstruction

❝As in the war, freedom was the keynote of victory, so now is universal suffrage the keynote of Reconstruction.❞

ELIZABETH CADY STANTON,
arguing for universal suffrage, 1867

❝We thought we was goin' to be richer than the white folks, 'cause we was stronger and knowed how to work, and the whites didn't and they didn't have us to work for them anymore. But it didn't turn out that way. We soon found out that freedom could make folks proud but it didn't make 'em rich.❞

FELIX HAYWOOD,
former slave

PRESIDENTIAL SUPERLATIVES

While he was neither "first in war, first in peace" nor "first in the hearts of his countrymen," President Andrew Johnson left his mark on history:

- First to have never attended school
- First to be impeached
- First to be elected to the Senate both before and after being president
- First to host a queen at the White House

- First tailor/president who made his own clothes
- Last not to attend successor's inauguration
- Most vetoes overridden
- Father of the Homestead Act

BETTMANN/CORBIS

Andrew Johnson

(Re)inventing America

Patents awarded to African American inventors during the Reconstruction period:

ALEXANDER ASHBOURNE biscuit cutter

LANDROW BELL locomotive smokestack

LEWIS HOWARD LATIMER water closets (toilets) for railway cars, electric lamp with cotton filament, dough kneader

THOMAS ELKINS refrigerator with cooling coils

THOMAS J. MARTIN fire extinguisher

ELIJAH MCCOY automatic oil cup and 57 other devices and machine parts, including an ironing board and lawn sprinkler

BETTMANN/CORBIS

Refrigerators keep foods cool.

NUMBERS

$7,200,000
Purchase price paid by U.S. to Russia for Alaska in 1867

2¢ Price paid per acre for Alaska

$30 Boarding and tuition, per quarter in 1870, at Saint Frances Academy, boarding school for African American girls in Baltimore, Maryland. Students come from states as distant as Florida and Missouri for an education "productive of the happiest effects among individuals and in society."

$5 Extra charge for instruction in embroidery

$25 Extra charge for instruction in making wax fruit

$3 Tuition, per quarter, for local "day scholars"

5,407 Number of pupils in Mississippi Freedmen's schools in 1866

50 Number of schools established for freed African Americans in Mississippi in 1866

20% Percentage of state income of Mississippi spent on artificial arms and legs for war veterans in 1866

Milestones

REEXAMINED, 1870. THE ROMANTIC STORY OF POCAHONTAS, based on the written account of Captain John Smith. *The London Spectator,* reporting on the work of Mr. E. Neils, debunks Smith's tale of the young Pocahontas flinging herself between him and her father's club. The young girl was captured and held prisoner on board a British ship and then forcibly married to Mr. John Rolfe. Comments *Appleton's Journal* in 1870: "All that is heroic, picturesque, or romantic in history seems to be rapidly disappearing under the microscopic scrutiny of modern critics."

FOUNDED, 1877. NICODEMUS, KANSAS, by six African American and two white Kansans. On the high, arid plains of Graham County, the founders hope to establish a community of homesteading former slaves.

TOPPED, 1875. THE ONE MILLION MARK FOR POPULATION, by New York City. New York is the ninth city in the history of the world to achieve a population level of more than one million. The first was Rome in 133 B.C.

MPI/HULTON GETTY PICTURE LIBRARY/LIAISON

Pocahontas

EXTINGUISHED, 1871. THE PESHTIGO FOREST FIRE in Wisconsin. The conflagration caused 2,682 deaths. The Peshtigo tragedy has been overshadowed by the Great Chicago Fire of the same year, which killed 300.

PUBLISHED, 1865. *DRUM TAPS,* by Walt Whitman. Based on his experiences as a hospital volunteer, Whitman's new poems chronicle the horrors of the Civil War.

CRITICAL THINKING

1. *Theorizing* Do you think the quote from *Appleton's Journal* can be applied to events in America today? Explain your thinking.

2. *Comparing* What do the quotes by Felix Haywood and Houston Hartsfield Holloway reveal about the views of African Americans during Reconstruction?

Republican Rule

Big Ideas
Group Action Despite opposition, African Americans took active roles in politics during Reconstruction.

Content Vocabulary
• carpetbagger *(p. 366)*
• scalawag *(p. 366)*
• graft *(p. 368)*

Academic Vocabulary
• commissioner *(p. 368)*
• comprehensive *(p. 369)*

People and Events to Identify
• Ku Klux Klan Act *(p. 371)*

Reading Strategy
Organizing Complete a graphic organizer similar to the one below to identify how African Americans helped to govern the South during Reconstruction.

African Americans' Political Roles

NEW YORK CORE CURRICULUM
U.S. History and Government

Unit 3:
I.C.2.a The economic, political, social, and educational experiences of formerly enslaved African-Americans
I.C.3 Struggle for political control in the New South

Under the Republican-controlled Congress, the South began to rebuild. During this time, African Americans gained some new opportunities, particularly in politics, while some white Southerners organized to resist the changes that were occurring.

Republican Rule in the South

MAIN Idea During Reconstruction, African Americans organized politically and took part in governing the South.

HISTORY AND YOU What are the factors that help you decide to support a political party? Read on to learn why the Republican Party won the support of African Americans during Reconstruction.

By late 1870, all the former Confederate states had rejoined the Union under the congressional Reconstruction plan. Throughout the South, the Republican Party took power and introduced major reforms. Most white Southerners scorned the Republicans, however, partly because the party included Northerners and African Americans. Southerners also believed that the Union Army had forced the new Republican governments on them.

Carpetbaggers and Scalawags

As Reconstruction began, many Northerners moved to the South. Quite a few were eventually elected or appointed to positions in the South's new state governments. Southerners, particularly Democratic Party supporters, referred to these newcomers as **carpetbaggers** because some arrived with suitcases made of carpet fabric. Many local residents viewed the Northerners as intruders seeking to exploit the South.

Some carpetbaggers did seek to take advantage of the war-torn region, and corruption plagued parts of the South. Others, however, hoped to find more opportunities than existed for them in the North or the West. Some simply wanted to help. Many Northern schoolteachers, for example, moved south to help educate whites and African Americans.

While many Southerners despised carpetbaggers, they also disliked white Southerners who worked with the Republicans and supported Reconstruction. They called these people **scalawags**—an old Scotch-Irish term for weak, underfed, worthless animals.

The scalawags were a diverse group. Some were former Whigs who had grudgingly joined the Democratic Party before the war. Many were owners of small farms who did not want the wealthy

African Americans Enter Politics

Reconstruction provided African Americans with new opportunities to participate in politics. Many took part in the state constitutional conventions and were elected to state legislatures—achieving a majority in South Carolina's state assembly—and to local offices.

▲ This drawing from 1867 depicts the primary groups that became political leaders of the South's African American community—artisans (shown with tools), the middle class, and Union soldiers.

▲ This sketch from 1868 shows African Americans campaigning. African Americans were excited to participate in politics. The sketch shows women and children as well, suggesting that the entire community regarded political issues as important, even though only adult males could vote.

Analyzing VISUALS

1. **Identifying Central Issues** Why do you think African Americans were so enthusiastic about participating in politics?
2. **Explaining** What about the illustration above indicates the political position of women?

▲ The sketch above from the 1870s shows South Carolina's legislature—the only state legislature with an African American majority during Reconstruction.

planters to regain power. Still others were business people who favored Republican plans for developing the South's economy.

African Americans in Politics

The Fifteenth Amendment allowed many freedmen to take part in governing the South. With the right to vote, African American men could organize politically. "You never saw a people more excited on the subject of politics than are the [African Americans] of the South," wrote one plantation manager.

At first, the leadership of the African American community came from among those individuals who had been educated before the war. These included artisans, shopkeepers, and ministers. Many had lived in the North and fought in the Union Army. Aided by the Republican Party, these leaders delivered speeches to former plantation workers, drawing them into politics. Within a few remarkable years, many African Americans went from enslaved laborers to legislators and administrators working in nearly all levels of government.

Hundreds of formerly enslaved men served as delegates to state constitutional conventions. They also won election to numerous local offices, from mayor to police chief to school **commissioner.** Dozens of African Americans served in Southern state legislatures, while 14 were elected to the U.S. House of Representatives, and two, Hiram Revels and Blanche K. Bruce, were elected to the Senate.

Republican Reforms

With formerly enslaved men making such political gains, many Southerners claimed that "Black Republicanism" ruled the South. Such claims, however, were greatly exaggerated. No African American was ever elected governor. In South Carolina, African Americans did gain control of the legislature, but were able to hold power for only one term.

The Republican Party took power in the South because it also had the support of a large number of white Southerners. Poor white farmers, who resented the planters and the Democratic Party that dominated the South before the Civil War, often joined with African American voters to elect Republicans.

The newly elected Republican governments instituted a number of reforms. They repealed the black codes and made many more state offices elective. They established state hospitals and institutions for orphans, the mentally ill, and the hearing and visually impaired. They rebuilt roads, railways, and bridges, and funded the construction of new railroads and industries in the South. They also established a system of public schools.

The Republican reforms did not come without cost. Many state governments were forced to borrow money and to impose high property taxes to pay for the repairs and new programs. Many property owners, unable to pay these new taxes, lost their land.

Although many Republicans wanted to help the South, others were corrupt. One Republican governor accepted more than $40,000 in bribes. **Graft,** or gaining money illegally through politics, was common in the South, just as it was in the North at the time, but it gave Democrats another issue that would help them regain power in the 1870s.

✓ Reading Check **Summarizing** Which groups helped elect Republicans in the South during Reconstruction?

PAST & PRESENT

The African American Church

Since colonial times, churches have been important to African Americans as both religious and social institutions. After Reconstruction ended, churches became the only institution that remained under their control once they lost voting rights and segregation was imposed. African American ministers were community leaders in places where political leaders did not exist. Later, during the civil rights struggles of the 1950s and 1960s, the churches and their ministers took the lead in organizing the community for political action. For example, Martin Luther King, Jr., was one of a long line of pastors who worked to help protect and advance their communities. His Dexter Avenue Baptist Church in Montgomery, Alabama, became the headquarters for the famous bus boycott in that city in 1955.

An African American congregation (above) listens as their minister preaches in a Washington, D.C. church in 1876. Henry Turner (left) was a bishop of the African Methodist Episcopalian (AME) Church. He and others helped make black churches places of social and religious leadership.

African American Communities

MAIN Idea Reconstruction governments expanded public education to all children, and African Americans built their own churches.

HISTORY AND YOU Do you remember how Horace Mann started a movement for public education? Read on to learn how new schools were built in the South during Reconstruction.

In addition to entering politics, African Americans worked to improve their lives in other ways during Reconstruction. Many sought to establish their own thriving communities and to gain an education.

African American Churches

Religion had long played a central role in the lives of many African Americans, and with the shackles of slavery now gone, formerly enslaved people across the South began building their own churches. Churches frequently became the center of African American communities, as they housed schools and hosted social events and political gatherings. In rural areas, church picnics, festivals, and other activities provided residents with many of their recreational and social opportunities. In many communities, churches acted as unofficial courts by promoting social values, settling disputes among residents, and disciplining individuals for improper behavior.

A Desire to Learn

Once freed, many African Americans immediately sought an education. In the first years of Reconstruction, the Freedmen's Bureau, with the help of Northern charities, established schools for African Americans across the South. By 1870, some 4,000 schools and 9,000 teachers—roughly half of them African American—taught 200,000 formerly enslaved people of all ages. In the 1870s Reconstruction governments built a **comprehensive** public school system in the South, and by 1876, about 40 percent of all African American children (roughly 600,000 students) attended school.

2000s

▼ Churches played a key role in the struggle for civil rights and have produced many prominent African American leaders. They still play an important role in the African American community today.

MAKING CONNECTIONS

1. **Describing** What role did churches take in the lives of African Americans after Reconstruction?

2. **Explaining** How have African American churches expanded their role in modern times?

The White League and Ku Klux Klan

▲ This cartoon from 1874 reads "Everything points to a Democratic victory this fall" and shows members of the White League—a group similar to the Ku Klux Klan—denying African Americans the right to vote.

▲ Ku Klux Klansmen (top) disguised their identities. The cartoon says that White Leagues and the KKK made life worse for African Americans than it had been under slavery.

Analyzing VISUALS

1. **Summarizing** What methods did the White League and the Ku Klux Klan use to deny African Americans their civil rights?

2. **Expressing** Do you think the cartoon on the right is correct in its assumption? Why or why not?

Several African American academies were established in the South. These academies grew into an important network of African American colleges and universities, including Fisk University in Tennessee and Atlanta University and Morehouse College in Georgia. The institution that would become Howard University was founded in 1867 in Washington, D.C., by a group of Congregationalists who wanted to establish a seminary for African American ministers. Soon the idea expanded to the creation of an entire university, named for one of the founders and head of the Freedmen's Bureau, General Oliver Howard. Howard University quickly expanded to include the first law school, established in 1869, for African Americans.

The Hampton Institute was started in 1868 in Virginia to teach African Americans a trade or agricultural techniques. In 1881, after Reconstruction, Spelman College—the first college for African American women—and the Tuskegee Institute, now Tuskegee University, were founded. The first teacher at Tuskegee was Booker T. Washington, who later became an important African American leader.

African Americans also established thousands of other organizations to support each other. These organizations ranged from burial societies and debating clubs to drama societies and trade associations.

Reading Check **Examining** How did education for African Americans change during Reconstruction?

The Ku Klux Klan Forms

MAIN Idea Some Southerners hated the "Black Republican" governments and started groups such as the Ku Klux Klan that terrorized African Americans.

HISTORY AND YOU Have you heard of recent activities of the Ku Klux Klan? Read on to learn when and why the organization was founded.

At the same time as these changes were taking place, African Americans faced intense resentment from many Southern whites. Many Southerners also despised the "Black Republican" governments, which they believed vindictive Northerners had forced upon them.

Unable to strike openly at the Republicans running their states, some Southerners organized secret societies. The largest of these groups was the Ku Klux Klan. Started in 1866 by former Confederate soldiers in Pulaski, Tennessee, the Klan grew rapidly throughout the South. Its goal was to drive out the carpetbaggers and intimidate African American voters so as to regain control of the South for the Democratic Party.

Hooded, white-robed Klan members rode in bands at night, terrorizing supporters of the Republican governments. They broke up Republican meetings, drove Freedmen's Bureau officials out of their communities, burned African American homes, schools, and churches, and attempted to keep African Americans and white Republicans from voting.

Some Republicans and African Americans formed their own militia groups and fought back. As the violence perpetrated by both sides increased, one African American organization sent a report to the federal government asking for help:

PRIMARY SOURCE

"We believe you are not familiar with the description of the Ku Klux Klan's riding nightly over the country, going from county to county, and in the county towns spreading terror wherever they go by robbing, whipping, ravishing, and killing our people without provocation, compelling colored people to break the ice and bathe in the chilly waters of the Kentucky River. . . . We pray you will take some steps to remedy these evils."

—from a petition to Congress, March 25, 1871, National Archives

The Ku Klux Klan's activities outraged President Ulysses S. Grant and congressional Republicans. In 1870 and 1871, Congress passed three Enforcement Acts to combat the acts of violence in the South. The first act made it a federal crime to interfere with a citizen's right to vote. The second put federal elections under the supervision of federal marshals. The third act, also known as the **Ku Klux Klan Act,** outlawed the activities of the Klan. Local authorities and federal agents, acting under the Enforcement Acts, arrested more than 3,000 Klan members throughout the South. Southern juries, however, convicted only about 600, and fewer still served any time in prison.

Reading Check **Describing** Why did Congress pass the Enforcement Acts?

Section 2 REVIEW

Vocabulary

1. **Explain** the significance of: carpetbagger, scalawag, graft, Ku Klux Klan Act.

Main Ideas

2. **Identifying** In what state did African Americans gain control of the legislature for a time, and why did this occur?

3. **Specifying** Where and when was the first law school for African Americans established?

4. **Explaining** What were the three main provisions of the Enforcement Acts?

Critical Thinking

5. **Big Idea** How did the establishment of schools, churches, and social organizations benefit African Americans during Reconstruction?

6. **Categorizing** Use a graphic organizer to identify both the negative and positive aspects of carpetbagger rule.

Carpetbagger Rule	
Positives	Negatives

7. **Analyzing Visuals** Study the images on page 367. What do they suggest about the African American community in the South after the Civil War?

Writing About History

8. **Descriptive Writing** Suppose you are a Northerner who has recently moved to the Reconstruction South. Write a letter to a friend describing your life in the South at this time.

History ONLINE

Study Central™ To review this section, go to glencoe.com and click on Study Central.

Reconstruction Collapses

Guide to Reading

Big Ideas
Economics and Society After Reconstruction the South tried to build a new economy but problems lingered.

Content Vocabulary
- "sin tax" (p. 372)
- tenant farmer (p. 377)
- sharecropper (p. 377)
- crop lien (p. 377)
- debt peonage (p. 377)

Academic Vocabulary
- outcome (p. 375)
- circumstance (p. 377)

People and Events to Identify
- Horace Greeley (p. 373)
- "Whiskey Ring" (p. 373)
- Panic of 1873 (p. 374)
- Compromise of 1877 (p. 375)
- "New South" (p. 377)

Reading Strategy
Taking Notes Use the major headings of Section 3 to create an outline listing the major events of the Grant administration and the end of Reconstruction.

```
I. The Grant Administration
    A.
    B.
II.
    A.
```

NEW YORK CORE CURRICULUM
U.S. History and Government

Unit 3:
I.C.1 Agriculture: land and labor (sharecropping and tenant farming)
I.C.3 Struggle for political control in the New South
I.C.5 The emerging debate over "proper" role of African-Americans
I.D.1 Disputed election of 1876
I.D.3 Restoration of white control in the South (1870s and 1880s) and abridgment of rights of freed African-Americans

As Reconstruction came to an end in the late 1870s, the gains made by African Americans after the Civil War were steadily eroded by Southern whites as they reclaimed control of state legislatures. In the meantime, Southerners were developing strategies for a rebirth of the region's economy.

The Grant Administration

MAIN Idea Political scandals and an economic depression tarnished Grant's presidency.

HISTORY AND YOU Can you think of any recent political scandals? Read on to learn how bribery and corruption hurt the Grant administration.

As commander of the Union forces, Ulysses S. Grant had led the North to victory in the Civil War. His reputation had then carried him into the White House in the election of 1868. Unfortunately, Grant had little experience in politics. He believed that the president's role was to carry out the laws and leave the development of policy to Congress. This approach pleased the Radical Republicans in Congress, but it left the president weak and ineffective when dealing with other issues. Eventually, Grant's lack of political experience helped to divide the Republican Party and to undermine public support for Reconstruction.

The Republicans Split

During Grant's first term in office, the Republican-controlled Congress continued to enforce Reconstruction. At the same time, it expanded the programs it had introduced during the Civil War to promote commerce and industry. It kept tariffs high, tightened banking regulations, promised to repay its debts with gold—not paper money—and increased federal spending on railroads, port facilities, and the national postal system.

The Republican Congress also kept in place the taxes on alcohol and tobacco that had been introduced as emergency measures during the war. These taxes, nicknamed **"sin taxes,"** helped the government pay off the bonds that had been issued to pay for the Civil War.

Democrats attacked these Republican economic policies, arguing that they benefited the wealthy, such as government bondholders, at the expense of the poor, who paid most of the sin taxes. They argued that wealthy Americans were gaining too much influence in Grant's administration.

The Scandals of the Grant Administration

▲ In this cartoon, Grant, the Civil War hero of Vicksburg and Appomattox Courthouse, is "dogged" by the men in his administration who have been involved in various scandals.

▼ This cartoonist shows the Grant administration looking for those guilty of fraud in a whiskey barrel—symbol of the "Whiskey Ring."

I BEG TO REPEAT THAT THESE FRAUDS ON THE GOVERNMENT SHALL BE PROBED TO THE VERY BOTTOM.

Analyzing VISUALS

1. **Interpreting** What is Uncle Sam's mood in the cartoon above, and why do you think he has this attitude?

2. **Making Inferences** In the cartoon on the right, how far does the cartoonist suggest that the corruption in government has spread?

Some Republicans, known as Liberal Republicans, agreed with the Democrats. They were concerned that men who were in office to make money and sell influence were beginning to dominate the Republican Party. The Liberal Republicans tried to prevent Grant's renomination in 1872. When that failed, they left the Republican Party and nominated their own candidate, **Horace Greeley,** the influential newspaper publisher.

To attract Southern support, the Liberal Republicans promised to pardon nearly all former Confederates and to remove Union troops from the South. As a result, the Democratic Party, believing that only a united effort would defeat Grant, also nominated Greeley. Despite the split in his own party and Greeley's passionate campaigning, Grant won the election easily.

During Grant's second term, a series of scandals hurt the reputation of his administration. Grant's secretary of war, William Belknap, had accepted bribes from merchants operating at army posts in the West. He was impeached but resigned before the Senate could try him. Then, in 1875, the **"Whiskey Ring"** scandal broke. A group of government officials and distillers in St. Louis, Missouri, cheated the government out of millions of dollars by filing false tax reports. Reportedly, Orville E. Babcock, Grant's private secretary, was involved, although this was never proved.

The Panic of 1873

In addition to the political scandals of Grant's second term, the nation endured a severe economic crisis. The turmoil started in 1873, when a series of bad railroad investments forced the powerful banking firm of Jay Cooke and Company to declare bankruptcy. A wave of fear known as the **Panic of 1873** quickly spread through the financial community. Dozens of smaller banks closed, and the stock market plummeted. Thousands of businesses shut down, and unemployment soared.

The scandals in the Grant administration and the deepening economic depression hurt the Republicans politically. In the 1874 midterm elections, the Democrats won control of the House of Representatives and made gains in the Senate.

✓ **Reading Check** **Explaining** Why did the Liberal Republicans oppose President Grant?

Reconstruction Ends

MAIN Idea After Republican Rutherford B. Hayes became president in a disputed election, he removed the last federal troops from the South.

HISTORY AND YOU What is the process by which presidents are elected? Read on to learn how contested returns in three states created a political crisis in 1876.

The rising power of the Democrats made enforcing Reconstruction more difficult. At the same time, many Northerners were more concerned with their own economic problems than with the political situation in the South.

"Redeeming" the South

In the 1870s, Southern Democrats had worked to regain control of their state and local governments from Republicans. Southern

POLITICAL CARTOONS PRIMARY SOURCE
The Compromise of 1877

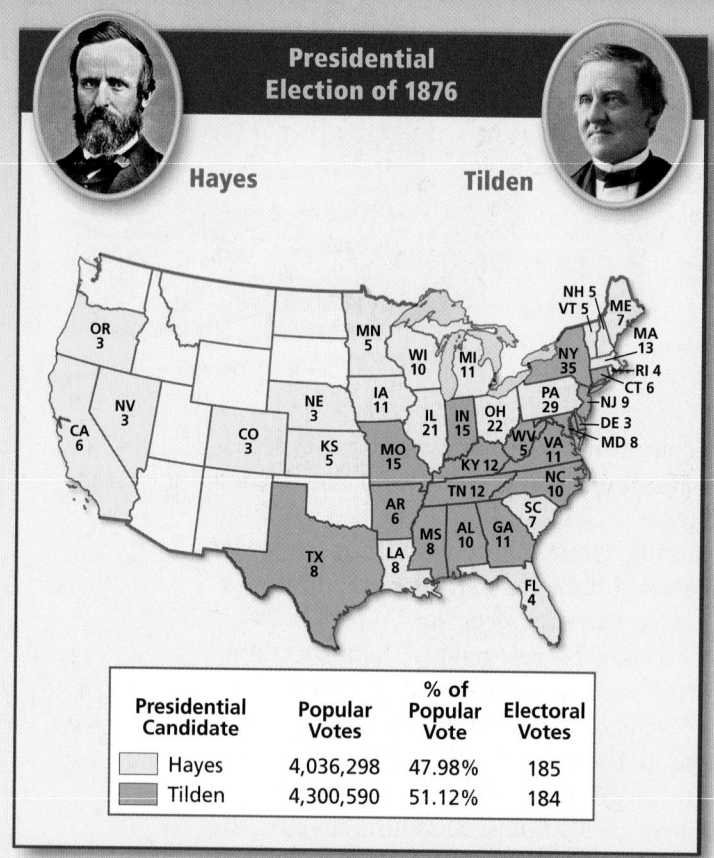

Presidential Election of 1876

Hayes   Tilden

Presidential Candidate	Popular Votes	% of Popular Vote	Electoral Votes
Hayes	4,036,298	47.98%	185
Tilden	4,300,590	51.12%	184

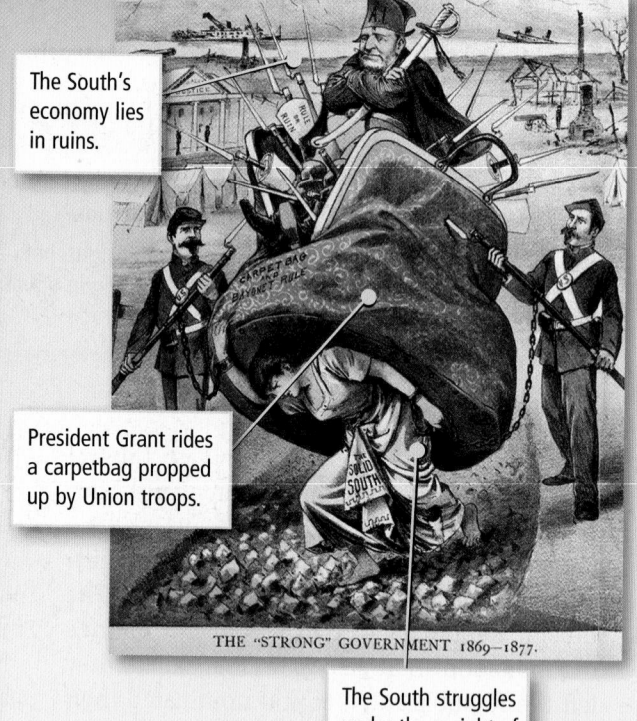

The South's economy lies in ruins.

President Grant rides a carpetbag propped up by Union troops.

THE "STRONG" GOVERNMENT 1869–1877.

The South struggles under the weight of the carpetbag.

▲ In the 1876 presidential election, 20 electoral votes were in dispute. They were eventually awarded to Hayes, and many believed he made a deal with Southern Democrats in Congress to win the presidency. Whether or not this was true, Hayes's election signified the end of Reconstruction.

terrorist groups, such as the Ku Klux Klan and Knights of the White Camellia, intimidated African American and white Republican voters, while some Democrats resorted to various forms of election fraud, such as stuffing ballot boxes, bribing vote counters, and stealing ballot boxes in Republican precincts. Southern Democrats also called on all whites to help "redeem"—or save—the South from "Black Republican" rule.

By appealing to white racism and defining elections as a struggle between whites and African Americans, Democrats were able to win back the support of white owners of small farms who had supported Republicans. By 1876, the Democrats had taken control of all Southern state legislatures except those of Louisiana, South Carolina, and Florida. In those states, the large number of African American voters, protected by Union troops, was able to keep the Republicans in power.

The South's economy booms.

President Hayes uses a plow labeled "Let Em Alone Policy" to bury rifles and carpetbags.

THE "WEAK" GOVERNMENT 1877–1881.

Analyzing VISUALS

1. **Identifying Points of View** Which government did the cartoonist approve of more? How can you tell?

2. **Identifying Central Issues** What criticism of Hayes is the cartoonist responding to with this cartoon?

The Compromise of 1877

With Grant's reputation damaged by scandals, the Republicans decided not to nominate him for a third term in 1876. Instead, they nominated Rutherford B. Hayes, a former governor of Ohio. Many Americans regarded Hayes as a moral man untainted by scandal. Hayes wanted to end Radical Reconstruction.

The Democrats responded by nominating Samuel Tilden, a wealthy corporate lawyer and former governor of New York who had tried to end the corruption in New York City's government. On Election Day, Tilden clearly won 184 electoral votes, 1 short of a majority. Hayes clearly won 165 electoral votes, leaving 20 votes in dispute. Nineteen of the votes were in the three Southern states Republicans still controlled: Louisiana, South Carolina, and Florida. There had been so much election fraud on both sides that no one could tell which candidate had won.

To resolve the situation, Congress appointed a 15-person commission made up equally of members of the House, the Senate, and the Supreme Court. The commission had 8 Republicans and 7 Democrats, and eventually voted along party lines, 8 to 7, to give the votes to Hayes. The commission's recommendations, however, were not binding if either house of Congress rejected them.

After much debate, several Southern Democrats joined with Republicans in the Democrat-controlled House of Representatives and voted to accept the commission's findings. This gave the election to Hayes. Noting that Hayes could not have won without the support of Southern Democrats, many people concluded that a deal had been made. This is why the **outcome** of the election is known as the **Compromise of 1877.**

Historians are not sure if a deal was actually made or, if so, what its exact terms were. The Compromise of 1877 reportedly included a promise by the Republicans to pull federal troops out of the South if Hayes were elected, and that is, in fact, what happened within a month of Hayes taking office. It is also true, however, that the nation was tired of the politics of Reconstruction and that even Republican leaders were ready to put an end to it. Indeed, President Grant pulled troops out of Florida even before Hayes took office, so it is possible that no deal was actually made.

The New South

The New South was a blend of the old and the new. Industry began to develop, but agriculture remained vital to the economy. By the 1890s, the South was exporting more cotton, rice, and tobacco than before the Civil War. Although slavery had ended, many African Americans were poor sharecroppers who harvested crops for landowners.

Sharecropping in the South, 1880

Percentage of sharecropped farms by county

- 34.2% to 81.0%
- 25.8% to 34.1%
- 19.6% to 25.7%
- 12.7% to 19.5%
- 0% to 12.6%

▲ The industry of the "New South" was still driven by agricultural products, such as tobacco. The workers shown above are processing tobacco in a Richmond tobacco factory in 1899.

Analyzing VISUALS

1. **Specifying** In which three states was sharecropping most common?
2. **Explaining** Why do you think the South's economy remained so dependent on agriculture after Reconstruction?

▲ Sharecroppers harvest cotton in Georgia in 1898.

During his inaugural speech on March 5, 1877, President Hayes expressed his desire to move the country beyond the quarrelsome years of Reconstruction:

PRIMARY SOURCE

"Let me assure my countrymen of the Southern States that it is my earnest desire to regard and promote their truest interests—the interests of the white and colored people both equally—and to put forth my best efforts in behalf of a civil policy which will forever wipe out . . . the distinction between North and South, . . . that we may have not merely a united North or a united South, but a united country."

—quoted in *The Life of Rutherford Birchard Hayes*

Whether the speech expressed Hayes's real thoughts is unknown, but in April 1877 he pulled federal troops out of the South. Without soldiers to support them, the last Republican governments in South Carolina and Louisiana collapsed. The Democrats had "redeemed" the South. Reconstruction was now over.

✔ Reading Check **Explaining** What major issue was settled by the Compromise of 1877?

A "New South" Arises

MAIN Idea The postwar South developed more industry, but most people still worked in agriculture.

HISTORY AND YOU What do you recall about the disadvantages of the South during the Civil War? Read on to learn how the region tried to industrialize in the postwar period.

Many Southern leaders realized that the South could never return to the pre–Civil War agricultural economy once dominated by the planter elite. Instead, they called for the creation of a **"New South"**—a phrase coined by Henry W. Grady, editor of the *Atlanta Constitution*. They believed the region had to develop a strong industrial economy.

Powerful white Southerners and Northern financiers brought great economic changes to parts of the South. Northern capital helped to build railroads, and by 1890 almost 40,000 miles of track crisscrossed the South. Southern industry also grew. A thriving iron and steel industry developed around Birmingham, Alabama. In North Carolina, tobacco processing became big business, and cotton mills appeared in numerous small towns.

In other ways, the South changed little. Despite its industrial growth, the region remained agrarian. As late as 1900, only 6 percent of the Southern labor force worked in manufacturing. For many African Americans, the end of Reconstruction meant a return to the "Old South," where they had little political power and were forced to labor under difficult and unfair conditions.

The collapse of Reconstruction ended African Americans' hopes of being granted their own land in the South. Instead, many returned to plantations owned by whites, where they either worked for wages or became **tenant farmers,** paying rent for the land they farmed. Most tenant farmers eventually became **sharecroppers.** Sharecroppers did not pay their rent in cash. Instead, they paid a share of their crops—often as much as one-half to two-thirds.

Many sharecroppers also needed more seed and other supplies than their landlords could provide. As a result, country stores and local suppliers provided them with the supplies they needed on credit and at interest rates often as high as 40 percent. To make sure that sharecroppers paid their debts, laws allowed merchants to put liens on their crops. These **crop liens** meant that the merchants could take crops to cover the debts.

The crop-lien system and high interest rates led many sharecroppers into a financial condition called **debt peonage.** Debt peonage trapped sharecroppers on the land because they could not make enough money to pay off their debts and leave, nor could they declare bankruptcy. Failure to pay off debts could lead to imprisonment or forced labor. The Civil War had ended slavery, but the failure of Reconstruction trapped many African Americans in economic **circumstances** that severely limited their newly gained freedom.

Reading Check **Summarizing** What factors brought about an economic rebuilding of the South?

Section 3 REVIEW

Vocabulary

1. **Explain** the significance of: "sin tax," Horace Greeley, "Whiskey Ring," Panic of 1873, Compromise of 1877, "New South," tenant farmer, sharecropper, crop lien, debt peonage.

Main Ideas

2. **Analyzing** What caused the Panic of 1873?

3. **Explaining** How did Reconstruction end?

4. **Describing** How did conditions for African Americans in the post-Reconstruction South resemble conditions before the Civil War?

Critical Thinking

5. **Big Ideas** What factors contributed to the improving economy of the South after Reconstruction?

6. **Organizing** Use a graphic organizer to identify the problems faced by Grant's administration.

Problems Faced by Grant's Administration

7. **Analyzing Visuals** Study the map of the election of 1876 on page 374. Which candidate won the popular vote?

Writing About History

8. **Expository Writing** Write a short essay explaining what you consider to be the three most important events of the Reconstruction period. Explain why you chose those events.

History ONLINE

Study Central™ To review this section, go to glencoe.com and click on Study Central.

Plans for Reconstruction

Lincoln's Plan

- Amnesty for all Southerners who take an oath of loyalty and accept the end of slavery, excluding former Confederate officials

- Once 10 percent had taken the oath, new state governments could be formed

Congressional Plan—The Wade-Davis Bill

- A majority of southerners must take an oath of loyalty in order for new state governments to form

- Each state must hold a convention to abolish slavery, reject Confederate debts, and deprive former Confederate officials and officers of the right to vote or hold office

Johnson's Plan

- Amnesty for all Southerners who take an oath of loyalty, excluding former Confederate officers and owners of large amounts of property

- Confederate states must hold a convention to revoke secession and ratify the 13th Amendment

▲ During Reconstruction, many African American men held elected offices, some as state senators and representatives.

▲ After the Civil War, the South's agricultural economy revived, and many African Americans found themselves doing much the same work they had when enslaved. Many became sharecroppers, trapped on the land because of the high debts they were forced to accumulate.

The Events of Reconstruction

The White Southern Response

- The South elects many former Confederate officials to Congress

- Southern states introduce black codes to restrict African American freedom and force them into labor contracts

- White mobs riot and attack African Americans

- Militant groups, such as the Ku Klux Klan, organize to oppose reconstruction and prevent African Americans from voting

- Southern Democrats slowly regain power by using racism to bring poor white voters back to the Democratic party

Congress

- Congress passes the Civil Rights Act of 1866 and the Fourteenth Amendment

- Congress imposes Military Reconstruction, requiring former Confederate states to give the right to vote to all adult males

- Congress passes the Fifteenth Amendment

African Americans

- Freedman's Bureau and Reconstruction governments build schools enabling formerly enslaved African Americans to get an education

- During Reconstruction, African Americans enter politics in large numbers, holding many political offices in the South

- As Reconstruction ends and the South's agrarian economy revives, many African Americans become sharecroppers

NEW YORK REGENTS EXAM PRACTICE

TEST-TAKING TIP

Be sure to evaluate each possible answer before you make your final choice. Do not just choose the first one that you think is correct.

Part I

Directions (1–11): For each statement or question, write on a separate sheet of paper the number of the word or expression that, of those given, best completes the statement or answers the question.

1 The Freedmen's Bureau made the most lasting and important impact in
  (1) education.
  (2) land redistribution.
  (3) voter registration.
  (4) labor negotiations.

2 The first African American leaders who emerged during Reconstruction came from which group?
  (1) scalawags who wanted to strengthen the Republican Party
  (2) those who had been educated before the Civil War
  (3) those who had just been freed from enslavement
  (4) former Confederate political leaders

3 The third Enforcement Act was passed by Congress in 1871 to
  (1) divide the Confederacy into five military districts.
  (2) provide all adult males with the right to vote.
  (3) outlaw the activities of the Ku Klux Klan.
  (4) establish the Freedmen's Bureau.

4 One way in which Reconstruction failed was that, in the end, it
  (1) did not reunite the Confederate states with the Union.
  (2) led to much corruption in the Grant administration.
  (3) gave the Democrats complete control of every level of government.
  (4) allowed African Americans to lose many of their new rights.

5 What effect did the system of sharecropping have on the South after the Civil War?
  (1) It kept formerly enslaved persons economically dependent.
  (2) It brought investment capital to the South.
  (3) It encouraged Northerners to migrate South.
  (4) It provided for a fairer distribution of farm profits.

6 Which of the following groups was among the scalawags during Reconstruction?
  (1) formerly enslaved African Americans
  (2) Southern whites who owned small farms
  (3) Northern Radical Republicans
  (4) members of the Ku Klux Klan

7 Following the Civil War, many Southern states enacted black codes to
  (1) provide free farmland for African Americans.
  (2) guarantee equal civil rights for African Americans.
  (3) restrict the rights of formerly enslaved persons.
  (4) support the creation of the Freedmen's Bureau.

Need Extra Help?							
If You Missed Questions . . .	1	2	3	4	5	6	7
Go to Page . . .	359	367	371	377	377	366	360

[OVER]

Base your answer to questions 8 and 9 on the map below and your knowledge of Chapter 9.

Military Districts

Military District Commander
1	Gen. Schofield	4	Gen. Ord
2	Gen Sickles	5	Gen. Sheridan
3	Gen. Pope	1868	Date of readmission to Union

*Tennessee was not part of a military district.

8 Which General commanded a district comprised only of states that had been readmitted to the Union in 1868?

(1) General Sickles

(2) General Pope

(3) General Ord

(4) General Sheridan

9 What were the last states to be readmitted to the Union?

(1) Arkansas, Louisiana, Alabama

(2) Texas, Mississippi, Georgia

(3) North Carolina, South Carolina, Virginia

(4) Virginia, Texas, Arkansas

10 In the Compromise of 1877, what did Rutherford B. Hayes supposedly promise to do as president?

(1) free all enslaved African Americans in the Southern states

(2) ensure the passage of the Enforcement Acts

(3) pardon members of President Grant's administration

(4) remove all federal troops from the Southern states

Need Extra Help?			
If You Missed Questions . . .	8	9	10
Go to Page . . .	380	380	375

Part II Thematic Essay Question

Directions: Write a well-organized essay that includes an introduction, several paragraphs addressing the task below, and a conclusion.

Theme: Approaches to Reconstruction

When the Civil War ended, individuals or groups in the federal government had different ideas about the form that Reconstruction should take.

Task:

Consider the approaches to Reconstruction taken by President Lincoln, President Johnson, and Congress and

• Discuss their different motivations and actions

• Describe the successes and failures of each Reconstruction plan

• Evaluate the long-term impact of Reconstruction legislation and programs

Guidelines:

In your essay, be sure to:

• Develop all aspects of the task

• Support the theme with relevant facts, examples, and details

• Use a logical and clear plan of organization, including an introduction and a conclusion that are beyond a restatement of the theme

Part III Document-Based Question

This question is based on the accompanying documents. It is designed to test your ability to work with historical documents. Some of the documents have been edited for the purposes of the question. As you analyze the documents, take into account the source of each document and any point of view that may be presented in the document.

Historical Context:

At the end of the Civil War, the nation's effort to rebuild and reunite began. A struggle ensued over which plan to follow to reconstruct the South and how best to protect the rights of the newly freed African Americans.

Task:

Using information from the documents and your knowledge of United States history, answer the questions that follow each document in Part A. Your answers to the questions will help you write the Part B essay in which you will be asked to

- Discuss the status of African Americans immediately following the Civil War
- Evaluate the actions taken to protect the rights of newly freed African Americans

Part A
Short-Answer Questions

Directions: Analyze the documents and answer the short-answer questions that follow each document on a separate sheet of paper.

Document 1

"Four million of persons [former slaves] have just been freed from a condition of dependence, . . . Make them independent of their old masters, so that they may not be compelled to work for them upon unfair terms, which can only be done by giving them a small tract of land to cultivate for themselves, . . . Nothing is so likely to make a man a good citizen as to make him a freeholder. Nothing will so multiply the productions of the South as to divide it into small farms. Nothing will make men so industrious and moral as to let them feel that they are above want and are the owners of the soil which they till. It will also be of service to the white inhabitants. They will have constantly among them industrious laborers, anxious to work for fair wages. How is it possible for them to cultivate their lands if these people were expelled? If Moses should lead or drive them into exile, or carry out the absurd idea of colonizing them, the South would become a barren waste."

Source: *Congressional Globe*, speech to House of Representatives, March 19, 1867

1   What was Thaddeus Stevens arguing that the federal government should do?

Document 2

Source: Joseph Keppler, *Puck*, Feb. 4, 1880

2   What is the cartoonist saying about Grant and his administration?

Part B
Essay

Directions: Reread the task box at the top left and write a well-organized essay that includes an introduction, several paragraphs, and a conclusion. Use evidence from the documents in your essay. Support your response with relevant facts, examples, and details. Include additional outside information.

For additional test practice, use Self-Check Quizzes—Chapter 10 at glencoe.com.

Need Extra Help?			
If You Missed Questions . . .	1	2	Essay
Go to Page . . .	381	381	381

The Birth of Modern America

1865–1901

Why It Matters

Following the turmoil of the Civil War and Reconstruction, the United States began its transformation from a rural nation to an industrial, urban nation linked together by railroads. New inventions and scientific discoveries fundamentally altered how Americans lived and worked. New factories employed thousands of workers; cities grew dramatically in size, and tens of millions of new immigrants flooded into the country.

Wabash Avenue and the elevated railroad in downtown Chicago, 1900

Settling the West
1865–1890

SECTION 1 Miners and Ranchers

SECTION 2 Farming the Plains

SECTION 3 Native Americans

Cattle ranching in the American West has changed little in 140 years. Here an Apache cowboy herds cattle into a corral during spring roundup on an Arizona ranch.

U.S. PRESIDENTS

U.S. EVENTS

WORLD EVENTS

1862
- Homestead Act makes cheap land available to settlers

1864
- Sand Creek Massacre takes place

Johnson 1865–1869

1867
- Chisholm Trail cattle drive begins

Grant 1869–1877

1876
- Battle of the Little Bighorn

Hayes 1877–1881

Garfield 1881

1860

1870

1880

1867
- British colonies unite to form Canada

1871
- Prussia unites German states to create Germany

1876
- Porfirio Diaz becomes dictator of Mexico

1879
- Zulu launch war against British settlers

Why Did Settlers Move West?

After the Civil War, many American settlers continued migrating to the western frontier. The lives of western miners, farmers, and ranchers were filled with hardships.

- *Why do you think settlers continued migrating west when life on the Great Plains was so difficult?*
- *When the frontier closed what effect do you think this had on American society?*

1887
- Dawes Act eliminates communal ownership of Native American reservations

Arthur
1881–1885

Cleveland
1885–1889

Harrison
1889–1893

Cleveland
1893–1897

McKinley
1897–1901

1890

1900

1886
- Gold is discovered in South Africa

1891
- Russia begins Trans-Siberian railway and many settlers head east to Siberia

FOLDABLES

Summarizing Displacement Make a Sentence Strips Foldable to represent how the arrival of settlers changed the American West. Choose an event and create a flip book. On the front of each strip write the event and its location. Write a brief explanation of how the event changed the West.

History ONLINE Chapter Overview
Visit glencoe.com to preview Chapter 11.

Miners and Ranchers

Guide to Reading

Big Ideas
Geography and History Miners and ranchers settled large areas of the West.

Content Vocabulary
- vigilance committee *(p. 387)*
- hydraulic mining *(p. 389)*
- open range *(p. 390)*
- long drive *(p. 391)*
- hacienda *(p. 392)*
- barrios *(p. 393)*

Academic Vocabulary
- extract *(p. 388)*
- adapt *(p. 390)*
- prior *(p. 390)*

People and Events to Identify
- Henry Comstock *(p. 386)*
- boomtown *(p. 386)*

Reading Strategy
Organizing As you read about the development of the mining industry, complete a graphic organizer listing the locations of mining booms and the discoveries made there.

Mining Booms & Discoveries

NEW YORK CORE CURRICULUM
U.S. History and Government

Unit 2:	
II.C.3	The Spanish, Mexican, and Native American West
II.C.6	Impact of western expansion upon Mexicans and Native Americans
Unit 3:	
III.D.1.a	Rolling plains and the Great American Desert

Mining and ranching attracted settlers to western territories that soon had populations large enough to qualify for statehood. People mined for gold, silver, and lead, or shipped longhorn cattle to the East.

Growth of the Mining Industry

MAIN Idea The discovery of gold, silver, and other minerals attracted thousands of settlers who established new states on the frontier.

HISTORY AND YOU Do you remember reading about the 1849 California gold rush? Read on to learn how mineral discoveries shaped the settlement of the West.

Mining played an important role in the settling of the American West. Beginning with the California gold rush, and continuing throughout the late 1800s, wave after wave of prospectors came to the region hoping to strike it rich mining gold, silver, and other minerals. Demand for minerals rose dramatically after the Civil War as the United States changed from a farming nation to an industrial nation. Mining in the West also encouraged the building of railroads to connect the mines to factories back east.

Boomtowns

In 1859 a prospector named **Henry Comstock** staked a claim in Six-Mile Canyon, near Virginia City, Nevada. Frustrated by his failure to find any gold, Comstock sold his claim a few months later. He had not realized that the sticky, blue-gray clay that made mining in the area difficult was in fact nearly pure silver ore.

News of the Comstock Lode, as the strike came to be called, brought a flood of eager prospectors to Virginia City. So many people arrived that, in 1864, Nevada was admitted as the 36th state. The Comstock Lode generated more than $230 million and helped the Union finance the Civil War.

The story of the Comstock Lode was replayed many times in the American West. News of a mineral strike would start a stampede of prospectors. Almost overnight, tiny frontier towns were transformed into small cities. Virginia City, for example, grew from a town of a few hundred people to nearly 30,000 in just a few months. It had an opera house, shops with furniture and fashions from Europe, several newspapers, and a six-story hotel.

These quickly growing towns were called **boomtowns.** Using the word "boom" this way began in the late 1800s. It refers to a time of rapid economic growth.

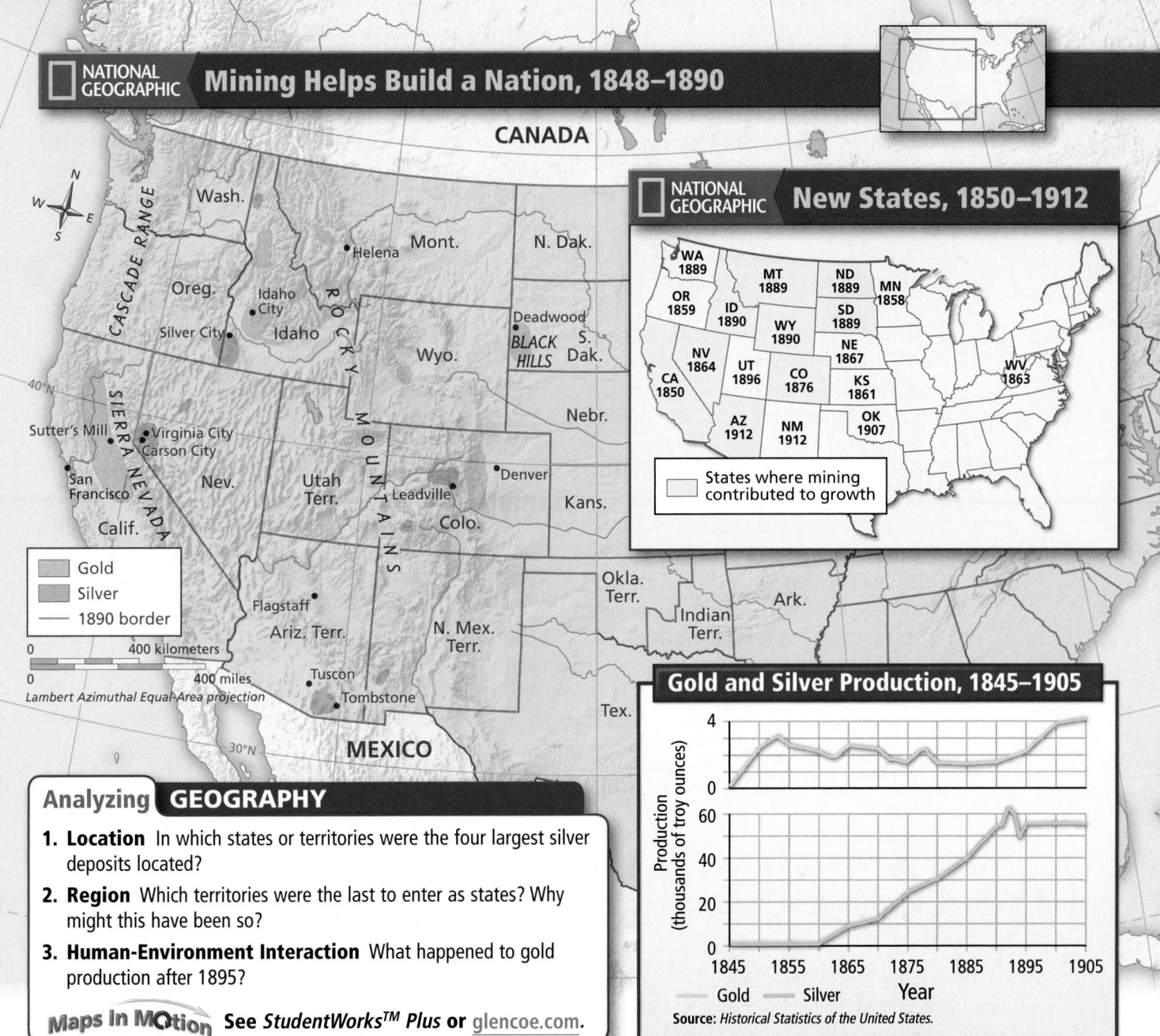

NATIONAL GEOGRAPHIC Mining Helps Build a Nation, 1848–1890

CANADA

Wash.

Oreg.

Idaho City

Silver City

Helena

Mont.

N. Dak.

Idaho

Wyo.

Deadwood
BLACK
HILLS

S.
Dak.

Nebr.

Sutter's Mill
Virginia City
Carson City

San
Francisco

Calif.

Nev.

Utah
Terr.

Leadville

Denver

Colo.

Kans.

Gold
Silver
1890 border

0   400 kilometers
0   400 miles
Lambert Azimuthal Equal-Area projection

Flagstaff
Ariz. Terr.

N. Mex.
Terr.

Tuscon
Tombstone

MEXICO

Okla.
Terr.

Indian
Terr.

Ark.

Tex.

NATIONAL GEOGRAPHIC New States, 1850–1912

WA 1889	MT 1889	ND 1889	MN 1858
OR 1859	ID 1890	SD 1889	
	WY 1890	NE 1867	
NV 1864	UT 1896	CO 1876	KS 1861	WV 1863
CA 1850	AZ 1912	NM 1912	OK 1907	

☐ States where mining contributed to growth

Gold and Silver Production, 1845–1905

Production (thousands of troy ounces)

4

0

60

40

20

0

1845 1855 1865 1875 1885 1895 1905

—— Gold   —— Silver   Year

Source: *Historical Statistics of the United States.*

Analyzing GEOGRAPHY

1. **Location** In which states or territories were the four largest silver deposits located?

2. **Region** Which territories were the last to enter as states? Why might this have been so?

3. **Human-Environment Interaction** What happened to gold production after 1895?

Maps In Motion See *StudentWorks*™ *Plus* or glencoe.com.

Boomtowns were rowdy places. Prospectors fought over claims, and thieves haunted the streets and trails. Often, "law and order" was enforced by **vigilance committees**—self-appointed volunteers who would track down and punish wrongdoers. In some cases, they punished the innocent or let the guilty go free, but most people respected the law and tried to deal firmly but fairly with the accused.

Men were usually first to arrive at a mining site, but women soon followed. Many found work in laundries or as cooks. Others worked at "hurdy-gurdy" houses (named after the mechanical violin), where they waited on tables and danced with men for the price of a drink. Some women became property owners and community leaders.

Boomtowns could not last forever because, eventually, the mines that supported the economy would be used up. A few boomtowns were able to survive when the mines closed, but many did not. Instead, they went "bust"—a term borrowed from card games that refers to players losing all of their money. In Virginia City, for example, the mines were exhausted by the late 1870s, and the economy collapsed. Most residents moved on; by 1930, Virginia City had only 500 residents. Other towns were completely abandoned, becoming "ghost-towns."

Mining Leads to Statehood

Mining also spurred the development of Colorado, Arizona, the Dakotas, and Montana. After gold was discovered in 1858 in Colorado near Pikes Peak, miners rushed to the area, declaring "Pikes Peak or Bust." Many panned for gold without success and headed home, complaining of a "Pikes Peak hoax."

In truth, the Colorado mountains contained plenty of gold and silver, although much of it was hidden beneath the surface and hard to **extract.** Deep deposits of lead mixed with silver were found at Leadville in the 1870s. News of the strike attracted as many as 1,000 newcomers a week, making Leadville one of the West's most famous boomtowns.

Operations at Leadville and other mining towns in Colorado yielded more than $1 billion worth of silver and gold (many billions in today's money). This bonanza spurred the building of railroads through the Rocky Mountains and transformed Denver, the supply point for the mining areas, into the second largest city in the West, after San Francisco.

Three railroads, the Denver and Rio Grande Western, the South Park and Pacific, and the Colorado Midland all made stops at towns in the mining region.

The discovery of gold in the Black Hills of the Dakota Territory and copper in Montana drew miners to the region in the 1870s. When the railroads were completed, many farmers and ranchers settled the area. In 1889 Congress admitted three new states: North Dakota, South Dakota, and Montana.

In the Southwest, the Arizona Territory followed a similar pattern. Miners had already begun moving to Arizona in the 1860s and 1870s to work one of the nation's largest copper deposits. When silver was found at the town of Tombstone in 1877, however, it set off a boom that attracted a huge wave of prospectors to the territory.

The boom lasted less than 10 years, but in that time, Tombstone became famous for its lawlessness. Marshall Wyatt Earp and his brothers gained their reputations during the famous gunfight at the O. K. Corral there in 1881. Although Arizona did not grow as quickly as Colorado, Nevada, or Montana, by 1912 it had enough people to apply for statehood, as did the neighboring territory of New Mexico.

PAST & PRESENT

New Mining Technology

In the late 1800s, mining companies developed a new technology—hydraulic mining—to remove large quantities of earth and process it for minerals. Miners generated a high-pressure spray by directing water from nearby rivers into narrower and narrower channels, through a large canvas hose and out a giant iron nozzle called a monitor. Using a powerful high-pressure blast of water, "a handful of men," as one journalist wrote, "took out the very heart of a mountain."

Although hydraulic mining is no longer used in the United States, the invention of earth-moving machines such as bulldozers and excavators has made it possible to continue to dig for minerals by removing large quantities of earth. This kind of mining is called open-pit mining or strip mining. It has many of the same problems faced by hydraulic miners. Specifically, something has to be done with the leftovers. The processed ore is usually pumped to a pond, where the water evaporates. These ponds can often be toxic because of the chemicals and minerals that are left after the ore is removed.

1866

▲ The high-pressure water washed the loose earth into large sluices, or ditches that carried the water and earth into riffle boxes. The boxes agitated the water, causing the silver or gold to settle out. The leftover debris, called tailings or "slickens," was then washed into a nearby stream.

Mining Technology

Extracting minerals from the rugged mountains of the American West required ingenuity and patience. Early prospectors extracted shallow deposits of ore in a process called placer mining, using simple tools like picks, shovels, and pans.

Other prospectors used sluice mining. Sluices were used to search riverbeds more quickly than the panning method. A sluice diverted the current of a river into trenches. The water was directed to a box with metal "riffle" bars that caused heavier minerals to settle to the bottom of the box. A screen at the end of the box prevented the minerals from escaping with the water and sediment.

When deposits near the surface ran out, miners began **hydraulic mining** to remove large quantities of earth and process it for minerals. Miners sprayed water at very high pressure against the hill or mountain they were mining. The water pressure washed away the dirt, gravel, and rock, and exposed the minerals beneath the surface.

Hydraulic mining began in California, near Nevada City. It effectively removed large quantities of minerals and generated a lot of tax money for local and state governments. Unfortunately, it also had a devastating effect on the local environment. Millions of tons of silt, sand, and gravel were washed into local rivers. The sediment raised the riverbed, and the rivers began overflowing their banks, causing major floods that wrecked fences, destroyed orchards, and deposited rocks and gravel on what had been good farm soil.

In the 1880s farmers fought back by suing the mining companies. In 1884 federal judge Lorenzo Sawyer ruled in favor of the farmers. He declared hydraulic mining a "public and private nuisance" and issued an injunction stopping the practice.

Congress eventually passed a law in 1893 allowing hydraulic mining if the mining company created a place to store the sediment. By then most mining companies had moved to quartz mining—the kind of mining familiar to people today—in which deep mine shafts are dug, and miners go underground to extract the minerals.

Reading Check **Explaining** What role did mining play in the development of the American West?

August 1995

▼ Mining is still very important to the western economy. The Kennecott Copper Mine in Bingham Canyon, Utah, is the largest human-made excavation in the world. The mine is 2½ miles wide and ¾ mile deep. It supplies approximately 15% of all copper used in the United States.

▲ An example of the problems of open-pit mining can be seen at the Berkeley Pit copper mine in Montana (above). When the mine closed, groundwater flooded the pit. The water passed through mineral deposits and became very acidic and contaminated with chemicals. Cleanup is scheduled for 2018 once a treatment plant has been built.

MAKING CONNECTIONS

1. **Comparing** How was mining in the 1880s similar to mining today?

2. **Problem-Solving** How might mining companies avoid damaging the environment and still extract the minerals they need?

Ranching and Cattle Drives

MAIN Idea Ranchers built vast cattle ranches on the Great Plains and shipped their cattle on railroads to eastern markets.

HISTORY AND YOU What images come to mind when you think of cowboys? Read on to learn about the realities of life as a cowboy in the West.

While many Americans headed to the Rocky Mountains to mine gold and silver, others began herding cattle on the Great Plains. Americans had long believed it was impossible to raise cattle in the region. Water was scarce, and cattle from the East could not survive on the tough prairie grasses. In Texas, however, lived a breed of cattle that had **adapted** to the Great Plains—the Texas longhorn.

The longhorn was descended from Spanish cattle introduced two centuries earlier. These cattle had been allowed to run wild and, slowly, a new breed—the longhorn—had emerged.

Lean and rangy, the longhorn could easily survive the harsh climate of the Plains. By 1865, some 5 million roamed the Texas grasslands.

Cattle ranching also prospered on the Plains because of the **open range,** a vast area of grassland that the federal government owned. The open range covered much of the Great Plains and provided land where ranchers could graze their herds free of charge and unrestricted by private property.

The Long Drive Begins

Prior to the Civil War, ranchers had little incentive to round up the longhorns. Beef prices were low, and moving cattle to eastern markets was not practical. The Civil War and the coming of the railroads changed this situation. During the Civil War, eastern cattle were slaughtered in huge numbers to feed the armies of the Union and the Confederacy. After the war, beef prices soared and ranchers looked for a way to round up the longhorns and sell them to eastern businesses.

NATIONAL GEOGRAPHIC Cattle Ranching and the Long Drive, c. 1870

Cattle trails
Railroads
1890 border

0 200 kilometers
0 200 miles
Lambert Azimuthal
Equal-Area projection

PRIMARY SOURCE

Charles Goodnight and Oliver Loving carved out the Goodnight-Loving Trail from Texas to Colorado, New Mexico, and Wyoming. Goodnight spoke of the dangers of a night stampede:

"The cattle were nervous and easily frightened, and the slightest noise might startle them into running. The heat developed by a large drove of cattle during a stampede was surprising .... Animal heat seems to attract electricity, especially when the cattle are wet, and after a storm I have seen the faces of men riding with a herd scorched as if some furnace blast had blazed against them."

—from *The West*

By the 1860s, railroads had reached the Great Plains. Lines ended at Abilene and Dodge City in Kansas and at Sedalia in Missouri. Ranchers and livestock dealers realized that if they could move the cattle as far as the railroad, the longhorns could be sold for a huge profit and shipped east to market.

In 1866 ranchers began rounding up the longhorns and drove about 260,000 of them to Sedalia, Missouri. Most of the cattle did not survive this first **long drive,** but those that survived sold for 10 times the price they would have brought in Texas. Other trails soon opened. The route to Abilene, Kansas, became the major route north. Between 1867 and 1871, cowboys drove nearly 1.5 million head of cattle up the Chisholm Trail from southern Texas to Abilene. As the railroads expanded in the West, other trails reached from Texas to more towns in Kansas, Nebraska, Montana, and Wyoming.

A long drive was a spectacular sight. In the spring, ranchers met with their cowboys to round up cattle from the open range. Stock from many different owners made up these herds. Cowboys from major ranches went north with the herds. The only way to tell them apart was by the brands burned onto their hides by branding irons. Stray calves without brands were called mavericks. These were divided and branded. The herds could number anywhere from 2,000 to 5,000 cattle.

Ranching Becomes Big Business

Cowboys drove millions of cattle north from Texas to Kansas and points beyond. Some of the longhorns went straight to slaughterhouses, but others were sold to ranchers who were building up herds in Wyoming, Montana, and other territories. Sheep herders moved their flocks onto the range and farmers settled there, blocking the trails. "Range wars" broke out among groups competing for land. Eventually, after much loss of life, hundreds of square miles were fenced cheaply and easily with a new invention—barbed wire.

At first, ranchers did not want to abandon open grazing and complained when farmers put up barriers that prevented the ranchers' livestock from roaming. Soon, however, ranchers used barbed wire to shut out those competing with them for land and to keep their animals closer to sources of food and water. For cowboys, however, barbed wire ended the adventure of the long cattle drive.

The fencing of the range was not the only reason the long drives ended. Investors from the East and from Britain had poured money into the booming cattle business, causing an oversupply of animals on the market. Prices plummeted in the mid-1880s and many ranchers went bankrupt. Then, in the winter of 1886–1887, blizzards buried the Plains in deep snow, and temperatures dropped as low as 40 degrees below zero. Massive numbers of cattle froze or starved to death.

The cattle industry survived this terrible blow, but it was changed forever. The day of the open range had ended. From that point on, herds were raised on fenced-in ranches. New European breeds replaced longhorns, and the cowboy became a ranch hand.

Reading Check Analyzing How did heavy investment in the cattle industry affect the industry as a whole?

▼ Women help rope and brand cattle at the J. W. Lough ranch in Kansas, 1891.

Analyzing VISUALS **DBQ**

1. **Explaining** What were two by-products of a cattle stampede?
2. **Analyzing** Why did the cattle trails north stop where they did?

Settling the Hispanic Southwest

MAIN Idea The arrival of new settlers changed life for Hispanics in the Southwest.

HISTORY AND YOU Do you remember reading about New Spain? Read on to learn how the Hispanic community changed when the Southwest became part of the United States.

For centuries, much of what is today the American Southwest belonged to Spain's empire. After Mexico won its independence, the region became the northern territories of the Republic of Mexico. When the United States defeated Mexico in 1848 and took control of the region, it acquired the Spanish-speaking population living there. According to the Treaty of Guadalupe Hidalgo ending the war, the region's residents retained their property rights and became American citizens.

In California, the Spanish mission system had collapsed by the early 1800s. In its place, a society dominated by a landholding elite had emerged. These landowners owned vast **haciendas**—huge ranches that covered thousands of acres. The heavy influx of "Forty-Niners" during the California gold rush, however, changed this society dramatically. California's population grew from 14,000 to 100,000 in two years. Suddenly, Hispanic Californians were vastly outnumbered.

Some Hispanic Californians welcomed the newcomers and the economic growth that resulted. Others distrusted the English-speaking prospectors, who tried to exclude them from the mines. When California achieved statehood in 1850, Hispanics served in many state and local offices. Increasingly, however, the original Hispanic population found their status diminished and, frequently, they were relegated to lower-paying and less desirable jobs.

As they had done with Native Americans, settlers from the East clashed with Mexican Americans over land. Across the region, many Hispanics lost their land to the new settlers.

PRIMARY SOURCE
Hispanics in the Southwest

In the mid-19th century, most Hispanics in the Southwest lived on large haciendas where they worked in the fields harvesting crops or helped tend cattle.

A fancily dressed vaquero, known as a *charro*, poses for a photo in 1890.

PRIMARY SOURCE

"As a horseman, [the vaquero] has no superiors, and it is mounted that he operates with such sure effect against the wild animals. The sport of 'lassoing' wild bulls and other cattle is highly exciting, and one of which all Spanish Americans are passionately fond. To catch the animal by his horns or neck requires much skill, yet to seize him with certainty by the leg, when at the top of his speed, requires greater practice and dexterity."

—from *Gleason's Pictorial Drawing-Room Companion*, 1852

▲ Hispanic farmworkers harvest grapes in southern California in 1905.

Analyzing VISUALS

1. **Making Generalizations** Based on the appearance of the vaquero in the photo at left, what generalizations can you make about the man?

2. **Analyzing** What do you notice about the types of people who were farmworkers? Why might this be so?

Mexican American claims to the land often dated back to Spanish land grants. These grants were hundreds of years old and defined the boundaries of property in vague terms. When ownership of a property was claimed by more than one person, American courts frequently held that the old land grants were insufficient proof of ownership. This allowed others to stake claim to the property. In some instances, outright fraud was used to take land illegally from Mexican Americans.

The cattle boom of the 1870s and 1880s had a tremendous impact on Hispanics in the Southwest, where many had long worked as vaqueros (the Spanish word for "cowboys"). Vaqueros developed the tools and techniques for managing cattle. They taught American cowboys their trade and enriched the English language with words of Spanish origin, including "lariat," "lasso," and "stampede."

With the increasing demand for beef in the eastern United States, English-speaking ranchers wanted to expand their herds and claimed large tracts of land of Mexican origin. In some cases, the Hispanic population fought back. In New Mexico, residents of the town of Las Vegas were outraged when English-speaking ranchers tried to fence in land that had long been used by the community to graze livestock. In 1889 a group of Hispanic New Mexicans calling themselves *Las Gorras Blancos* (white caps) raided ranches owned by English-speakers, tore down their fences, and burned their barns and houses. The raids finally ended in 1890 when the governor threatened to call in federal troops.

Despite the influx of English-speaking settlers, the Hispanic population of New Mexico remained more influential in public affairs than did their counterparts in California and Texas. Hispanics remained the majority, both in population and in the state legislature. In addition, a Hispanic frequently served as New Mexico's territorial delegate to Congress.

As more railroads were built in the 1880s and 1890s, the population of the Southwest continued to swell. The region not only attracted Americans and European immigrants, but also immigrants from Mexico. Mexican immigrants worked mainly in agriculture and on the railroads. In the growing cities of the Southwest—such as El Paso, Albuquerque, and Los Angeles—Hispanics settled in neighborhoods called **barrios.** Barrios had Spanish-speaking businesses and Spanish-language newspapers and they helped keep Hispanic cultural and religious traditions alive. As native Californian Mariano Guadalupe Vallejo explained in 1890:

PRIMARY SOURCE

"No class of American citizens is more loyal than the Spanish Californians, but we shall always be especially proud ... to honor the founders of our ancient families, and the saints and heroes of our history since the days when Father Junipero planted the cross at Monterey."

—quoted in *Foreigners in Their Native Land*

Reading Check **Describing** How did vaqueros contribute to the cattle industry in the West?

Section 1 REVIEW

Vocabulary

1. **Explain** the significance of: Henry Comstock, boomtown, vigilance committee, hydraulic mining, open range, long drive, hacienda, barrios.

Main Ideas

2. **Explaining** How did hydraulic mining affect the environment?

3. **Stating** What caused the decline of the cattle business in the late 1800s?

4. **Describing** How did the gold rush change society in California?

Critical Thinking

5. **Big Ideas** How did mining contribute to the development of the West?

6. **Organizing** Use a graphic organizer similar to the one below to list the ways barbed wire was used and the result of using barbed wire on the Great Plains.

7. **Analyzing Visuals** Sketch a map of the western cattle trails. Then compare your map to the one on page 390, and list the differences between the two maps.

Writing About History

8. **Descriptive Writing** Write a summary for a story line for a Hollywood movie. Your script should realistically portray the life of either a miner or rancher in the West in the mid- to late 1800s.

History ONLINE
Study Central™ To review this section, go to glencoe.com and click on Study Central.

Section 2

Farming the Plains

Guide to Reading

Big Ideas
Group Action After 1865 settlers staked out homesteads and began farming the Great Plains.

Content Vocabulary
- homestead *(p. 395)*
- dry farming *(p. 396)*
- sodbuster *(p. 396)*
- bonanza farm *(p. 397)*

Academic Vocabulary
- prospective *(p. 394)*
- innovation *(p. 396)*

People and Events to Identify
- Great Plains *(p. 394)*
- Stephen Long *(p. 394)*
- Homestead Act *(p. 395)*
- Wheat Belt *(p. 397)*

Reading Strategy
Organizing As you read about the settlement of the Great Plains, complete a graphic organizer similar to the one below by listing the ways the government encouraged settlement.

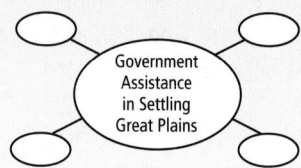

Government Assistance in Settling Great Plains

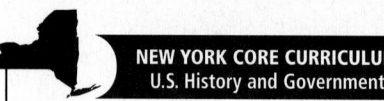

NEW YORK CORE CURRICULUM
U.S. History and Government

Unit 3:
III.D.1.a Rolling plains and the Great American Desert
III.D.1.c The Homestead Act, 1862, and the settlement of the West
III.D.2.a Improved transportation facilitated shipping of foodstuffs and migration of population

The Homestead Act encouraged settlers to move to the Great Plains. Although life was difficult, settlers discovered that wheat could be grown on the Great Plains using new technologies. By 1890 there was no longer a true frontier in the United States.

The Beginnings of Settlement

MAIN Idea Settlers staked out homesteads and began farming the region.

HISTORY AND YOU Would you move to a region with extreme weather such as drought and blizzards? Read on to learn how settlers coped with the harsh environment of the Great Plains.

The population of the **Great Plains** grew steadily in the decades after the Civil War. Land once thought to be worthless for farming was transformed into America's wheat belt. Homesteaders faced many challenges. Without trees to use as timber, many early settlers built their homes from chunks of sod, densely packed soil held together by grass roots. To obtain water, they had to drill wells more than 100 feet deep and operate the pump by hand. Nothing was wasted. Homesteader Charley O'Kieffe recalled eating weeds from the garden, as well as the vegetables, joking that he was obeying the rule, "If you can't beat 'em, eat 'em."

O'Kieffe and his neighbors were early settlers on the Great Plains. This region extends westward to the Rocky Mountains from around the 100th meridian—a line of longitude running north and south from the central Dakotas through western Texas. It is dry grassland where trees grow naturally only along rivers and streams. For centuries this open country had been home to vast herds of buffalo that grazed on the prairie grasses. Nomadic Native American groups had hunted the buffalo for food and used buffalo hides for clothing and shelter.

Major **Stephen Long,** who explored the region with an army expedition in 1819, called it the "Great American Desert" and concluded that it was "almost wholly unfit for cultivation." He predicted that the scarcity of wood and water would prove to be "an insuperable obstacle in . . . settling the country."

During the late 1800s, several developments undermined the assumption that the region was uninhabitable. One important factor was the construction of the railroads. Railroad companies sold land along the rail lines at low prices and provided credit to **prospective** settlers. Pamphlets and posters spread the news to city dwellers across Europe and America that cheap farm land was theirs to claim if they were willing to move.

Corn
Cotton
Wheat
Cattle

0   200 kilometers
0   200 miles
Lambert Azimuthal
Equal-Area projection

TROPIC OF CANCER

PACIFIC OCEAN

▲ A family stands outside their sod house on the Great Plains in 1880. There were very few trees on the Great Plains, and wood was expensive because it had to be shipped to the region. So settlers cut chunks of earth from the ground to build their homes.

What Was the Homestead Act?

The Homestead Act of 1862 created a procedure for people who wanted to settle on federal land in the West.

Requirements of the Act
• Settlers had to be 21 years of age.
• Settlers had to be head of a household.
• Settlers had to pay a $10 filing fee and $2 commission to the land agent to be given 160 acres of land.
• To gain title to the land, settlers had to live on it for five years, and make improvements such as building a house and clearing land for farming.
• Alternatively, settlers could buy the land for $1.25 per acre after six months.

Analyzing GEOGRAPHY

1. **Human-Environment Interaction** What were the similarities and differences in land use between Iowa and California?

2. **Region** In what region of the country were both cattle raised and cotton grown?

A Nebraskan coined the slogan "Rain follows the plow" to sell the idea that cultivating the Plains would increase rainfall. The weather seemed to cooperate. For more than a decade beginning in the 1870s, rainfall on the Plains was well above average. The lush green of the plains contradicted assertions that the region was a desert.

In 1862 the government encouraged settlement on the Great Plains by passing the **Homestead Act.** For a $10 registration fee, an individual could file for a **homestead**—a tract of public land available for settlement. A homesteader could claim up to 160 acres of land and could receive title to that land after living there for five years. Later government legislation increased the size of the tracts available. With

their property rights assured, more settlers moved to the Plains.

Settlers often found life very difficult on the Plains. In addition to building sod houses and drilling deep wells for water, they faced summer temperatures greater than 100°F. Prairie fires were a frequent danger. Sometimes swarms of grasshoppers swept over farms and destroyed the crops. In winter there were terrible blizzards and extreme cold. Despite these challenges and hardships, most homesteaders persisted and gradually learned how to live in the difficult environment.

✔ Reading Check **Analyzing** What is the relationship between private property rights and the settlement of the Great Plains?

The Wheat Belt

MAIN Idea As a result of new farming methods and machinery, settlers on the Great Plains were able to produce large amounts of wheat.

HISTORY AND YOU Do you remember learning about the way the cotton gin changed Southern life? Read on to learn how agricultural practices changed life on the Plains.

Many new farming methods and inventions in the nineteenth century revolutionized agriculture. One approach, called **dry farming,** was to plant seeds deep in the ground, where there was enough moisture for them to grow. By the 1860s farmers on the Plains were using plows, seed drills, reapers, and threshing machines. These new steel machines made dry farming possible. Unfortunately, soil on the plains could blow away during a dry season. Many **sodbusters,** as those who plowed the Plains were called, eventually lost their homesteads through the combined effects of drought, wind erosion, and overuse of the land.

Large landholders could invest in mechanical reapers and steam tractors that made it easier to harvest a large crop. Threshing machines knocked kernels loose from the stalks. Mechanical binders tied the stalks into bundles for collection. These **innovations** were well suited for harvesting wheat, a crop that could endure the dry conditions of the Great Plains.

During the 1880s many farmers from the Midwest moved to the Great Plains to take advantage of the inexpensive land and the new

TECHNOLOGY & HISTORY

Farm Machinery Farmers are indebted to the inventions of John Deere and Cyrus McCormick. Deere's steel plow broke through the hard ground. McCormick's mechanical reaper did the work of five men. Later inventions included a mechanical harrow to help prepare the ground for seeds and a grain drill to plant seeds.

The tail keeps the rotor oriented into the wind.

▼ Technology made farming the vast open plains of America feasible. Here, horse-drawn binders are being used to gather hay in the late 1800s.

▼ Windmills were vital to settling the Great Plains where farmers faced one major problem: a lack of water. There were few rivers, and it rarely rained. To get water, settlers drilled deep wells and used windmills to pump the water to the surface. The strong winds on the flat, treeless plains were an ideal power source.

In the 1870s, the rotor was made of wooden blades. In high winds, the sections could tilt open to let wind through and protect the rotor from damage.

The pump is run by a crank in the gear box that is connected to a shaft in the tower.

Analyzing VISUALS
1. **Identifying** What was used to power the windmill?
2. **Analyzing Visuals** In addition to field hands, what else did farmers using mechanical harvesting machines need?

farming technology. The **Wheat Belt** began at the eastern edge of the Great Plains and encompassed much of the Dakotas and parts of Nebraska and Kansas. The new machines allowed a single family to bring in a substantial harvest on a wheat farm covering several hundred acres. Some wheat farms covered up to 50,000 acres. These were called **bonanza farms** because they yielded big profits. Like mine owners, bonanza farmers formed companies, invested in property and equipment, and hired laborers as needed.

Farmers Fall on Hard Times

The bountiful harvests in the Wheat Belt helped the United States become the world's leading exporter of wheat by the 1880s. Then things began to go wrong. A severe drought struck the Plains in the late 1880s, destroying crops and turning the soil to dust. In addition, competition from farmers in other countries began to increase. By the 1890s a glut of wheat on the world market caused prices to drop. Some farmers tried to make it through these difficult times by mortgaging their land—that is, they borrowed money based on the value of their land. If they failed to meet their mortgage payments, they forfeited the land to the bank. Some who lost their land continued to work it as tenant farmers, renting the land from its new owners. By 1900 tenants cultivated about one-third of the farms on the Plains.

Closing the Frontier

On April 22, 1889, the government opened one of the last large territories for settlement. Within hours, more than 10,000 people raced to stake claims in an event known as the Oklahoma Land Rush. The next year, the Census Bureau reported that there was no longer a true frontier left in America. In reality, there was still a lot of unoccupied land, and new settlement continued into the 1900s, but the "closing of the frontier" marked the end of an era. It worried many people, including historian Frederick Jackson Turner. Turner believed that the frontier had provided a "safety-valve of social discontent." It was a place where Americans could always make a fresh start.

Most settlers did indeed make a fresh start, adapting to the difficult environment of the Plains. Water from their deep wells enabled them to plant trees and gardens. Railroads brought lumber and brick to replace sod as a building material, as well as coal for fuel. They also brought manufactured goods from the East, such as clothes and household goods. Small-scale farmers rarely became wealthy, but they could be self-sufficient. Typical homesteaders raised cattle, chickens, and a few crops. The real story of the West was not one of limitless opportunity, nor one in which heroes rode off into the sunset. It was about ordinary people who settled down and built homes and communities through great effort.

✓ Reading Check **Identifying** What technological innovations helped farmers cultivate the Plains?

Section 2 REVIEW

Vocabulary

1. **Explain** the significance of: Great Plains, Stephen Long, Homestead Act, homestead, dry farming, sodbuster, Wheat Belt, bonanza farm.

Main Ideas

2. **Identifying** How did the Homestead Act encourage settlement of the Plains?

3. **Explaining** What factors contributed to the making of the Wheat Belt in the Great Plains and then to troubled times for wheat farmers in the 1890s?

Critical Thinking

4. **Big Ideas** What challenges did Plains farmers face?

5. **Organizing** Make a graphic organizer similar to the one below that lists the effects of technology on farming in the Great Plains.

Invention	Advantage for Farmers

6. **Analyzing Visuals** Examine the photograph on page 396 of farmers using machinery. Based on the terrain and the type of work they needed to do, what other types of technology would have helped farmers on the Plains?

Writing About History

7. **Persuasive Writing** Write an advertisement to persuade people from the East and Europe to establish homesteads on the Great Plains.

History ONLINE

Study Central™ To review this section, go to glencoe.com and click on Study Central.

Native Americans

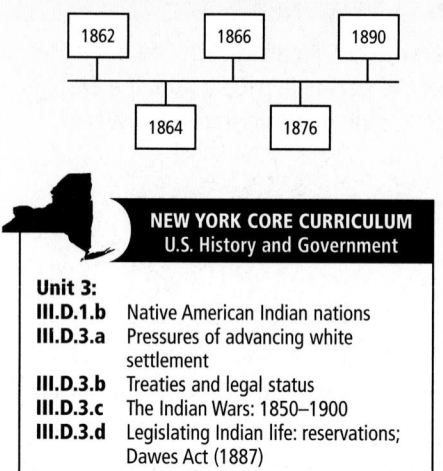

As settlers entered Native American lands on the Great Plains, clashes grew more common. Conflicts continued as the government tried to force Native Americans onto reservations and encouraged them to assimilate into the culture of the United States.

Struggles of the Plains Indians

MAIN Idea The settlement of the West dramatically altered the way of life of the Plains Indians.

HISTORY AND YOU Can you recall a situation in which someone broke a promise to you? Do you remember your reaction? Read on to learn how Native Americans responded when the federal government broke treaties.

For centuries the Great Plains were home to many groups of Native Americans. Some lived in communities as farmers and hunters, but many were **nomads** who roamed vast distances, following their main source of food—the buffalo.

The groups of Plains Indians were similar in many ways. Plains Indian nations were divided into bands consisting of up to 500 people. A governing council headed each band, but most members participated in making decisions. Most lived in extended family groups and believed in the spiritual power of the natural world.

The ranchers, miners, and farmers who moved onto the Plains deprived Native Americans of their hunting grounds, broke treaties guaranteeing certain lands to the Plains Indians, and often forced them to **relocate** to new territory. Native Americans resisted by attacking wagon trains, stagecoaches, and ranches. Occasionally, an entire group would go to war against nearby settlers and troops.

The Dakota Sioux Uprising

The first major clash began in 1862, when the Dakota people (also known as the Sioux) launched a major uprising in Minnesota. The Sioux had agreed to live on a reservation in exchange for **annuities,** or annual payments from the government. The annuities, however, frequently got caught up in bureaucracy and corruption and never reached them. By 1862 many lived in desperate poverty and faced possible starvation. When Chief Little Crow asked local traders to provide food on credit, one replied, "If they are hungry, let them eat grass or their own dung." Two weeks later, when the Dakota took up arms, that trader was found dead with his mouth stuffed with grass.

Little Crow reluctantly agreed to lead this uprising. He wanted to wage war against soldiers, not civilians, but he was unable to keep

Native American Battles and Reservations, 1860–1890

NATIONAL GEOGRAPHIC

CANADA

Wash.

Oreg.

Idaho

Mont.

N. Dak.

Minn.

Bear Paw Mountain 1877

Little Bighorn 1876

Fetterman Massacre 1866

Ft. Kearney

S. Dak.

Dakota Sioux Uprising 1862

Wyo.

BLACK HILLS

Wounded Knee 1890

Iowa

Fort Laramie Treaties:
1851: Native Americans agree to the construction of roads and forts on their lands
1868: The Sioux agree to move to a reservation in the Black Hills

Ft. Laramie

Nebr.

Nev.

Utah Terr.

Colo.

Ft. Lyon

Sand Creek 1864

Kans.

Mo.

Calif.

NO MAN'S LAND

Medicine Lodge

Treaty of Medicine Lodge, 1867:
Southern Plains Indians agree to move to Indian Territory

Ft. Defiance

Ariz. Terr.

N. Mex. Terr.

CHEYENNE AND ARAPAHO

CHEROKEE OUTLET

OSAGE

CHEROKEE

CREEK

Ark.

BOSQUE REDONDO (1863–1868)

Ft. Sumner

UNASSIGNED LANDS

SEMINOLE

CHOCTAW

Miss.

CHICKASAW

COMANCHE, KIOWA, AND APACHE

Texas

La.

Skeleton Canyon, 1886:
Apache leader Geronimo surrenders

Native American Population

Population (500,000 to 100,000)

1850 1860 1870 1880 1890 1900

Year

Sources: *Nations Within a Nation;* U.S. Census Bureau.

Legend:
- Reservation in 1890
- Route of Chief Joseph and the Nez Perce, 1877
- Battle
- Fort
- Treaty Site
- 1890 border

0   400 kilometers
0   400 miles
Lambert Azimuthal Equal-Area projection
120°W   110°W

MEXICO

Analyzing VISUALS

1. **Analyzing** What happened to the Native American population between 1850 and 1900?

2. **Locating** From what state to what state did the Nez Perce travel in 1877? Through what other states did they pass?

Maps In MOtion See *StudentWorks™ Plus* or glencoe.com.

---

angry Dakota from slaughtering hundreds of settlers in the area.

After the rebellion was suppressed, a military tribunal sentenced 307 Dakota to death. After reviewing the evidence, President Lincoln reduced the number to 38. Others fled the reservation when federal troops arrived and became exiles in a region that bore their name—the Dakota Territory.

Red Cloud's War

The Dakota Territory was home to another Sioux tribe, the Lakota. The Lakota were a nomadic tribe who fought hard to keep control

of their hunting grounds, which extended from the Black Hills westward to the Bighorn Mountains. They had battled rival groups for this country and did not intend to let settlers have it. Leading them were chiefs Red Cloud, Crazy Horse, and Sitting Bull.

The army suffered a major defeat during "Red Cloud's War" of 1866–1868. The army was constructing forts along the Bozeman Trail, the path used to reach the Montana gold mines. In December 1866, Crazy Horse, a religious leader and war chief, tricked the fort's commander into sending Captain William Fetterman and about 80 soldiers out to pursue what they thought was a small raiding party.

Hundreds of warriors were waiting in ambush and wiped out the entire unit (an event that became known as Fetterman's Massacre). The Sioux continued to resist any military presence in the region, and in 1868 the army abandoned its posts along the trail.

Sand Creek

In the 1860s tensions began to rise between the miners coming into Colorado in search of silver and gold and the Cheyenne and Arapaho who already lived there. As the number of settlers increased, bands of Native Americans began raiding wagon trains and stealing cattle and horses from ranches. By the summer of 1864, trade had come to a standstill, dozens of homes had been burned, and an estimated 200 settlers had been killed. The territorial governor, John Evans, ordered the Native Americans to surrender at Fort Lyon, where he said they would be given food and protection. Those who failed to report would be subject to attack.

Although several hundred Native Americans surrendered at the fort, many others did not. In November 1864, Chief Black Kettle brought several hundred Cheyenne to the fort, not to surrender but to negotiate a peace deal. The fort's commander did not have the authority to negotiate, and he told Black Kettle to make camp at Sand Creek while he waited for orders. Shortly afterward, Colonel John Chivington of the Colorado Volunteers was ordered to attack the Cheyenne at Sand Creek.

When Chivington stopped at Fort Lyon, he was told that the Native Americans at Sand Creek were waiting to negotiate. Chivington replied that, since the Cheyenne had been attacking settlers, including women and children, there could be no peace. The events that followed became known as the **Sand Creek Massacre.**

What actually happened at Sand Creek is unclear. Some witnesses stated afterward that Black Kettle had been flying both an American flag and a white flag of truce, which Chivington ignored. Others reported that the American troops fired on the unsuspecting Native Americans and then brutally murdered hundreds of women and children. Still others described a savage battle in which both sides fought ferociously for two days. Fourteen sol-

diers died, but the number of Native Americans reported killed varied from 69 to 600. One general later called Chivington's attack "the foulest and most unjustifiable crime in the annals of America." The truth of what really happened is still debated.

A Doomed Plan for Peace

In light of escalating conflict with Native Americans on the Great Plains, Congress took action. In 1867 Congress formed an **Indian Peace Commission,** which proposed creating two large reservations on the Plains, one for the Sioux and another for Native Americans of the southern Plains. Agents from the federal government's Bureau of Indian Affairs would run the reservations. The army would deal with any groups that refused to report or remain there.

Reservations were not a new idea. Both Puritan and Jesuit missionaries had used them in colonial days to separate Native American nations from one another. The reservations were also intended to encourage Native Americans to adopt white culture. After the American Revolution, the Iroquois (who called themselves the Haudenosaunee) were placed on reservations in western New York. These reservations, however, existed to separate Native Americans and citizens of the United States. Nearly a century later, reservations were based exclusively on keeping the Native Americans separate from American citizens.

The reservation system was again tested after the California gold rush. California, Oregon, and Washington all tried reservations as a way to minimize conflicts between Native Americans and settlers.

The Indian Peace Commission's plan was doomed to failure. Pressuring Native American leaders into signing treaties, as negotiators did at Medicine Lodge Creek in 1867, did not **ensure** that chiefs or their followers would abide by them, nor could they prevent settlers from violating their terms. Those who did move to reservations faced much the same conditions that drove the Dakota Sioux to violence—poverty, despair, and the corrupt practices of American traders.

✔ Reading Check **Explaining** What proposal did the Indian Peace Commission present to the Plains Indians?

The Last Native American Wars

MAIN Idea Settlers and Native Americans fought for land and cultural traditions.

HISTORY AND YOU Can you identify parts of the world where development is destroying local cultures? Read how the destruction of the buffalo changed some Native American cultures.

By the 1870s many Native Americans on the southern Plains had left the reservations in disgust. They preferred hunting buffalo on the open plains, so they joined others who had also shunned the reservations. Buffalo, however, were rapidly disappearing as settlers killed off thousands of the animals.

Following the Civil War, professional buffalo hunters invaded the area, seeking buffalo hides for markets in the East. Other hunters killed merely for sport, leaving carcasses to rot. Then railroad companies hired sharpshooters to kill large numbers of buffalo that were obstructing rail traffic and used them to feed the workers.

The army, determined to force Native Americans onto reservations, encouraged buffalo killing. By 1889 very few of the animals remained.

Battle of the Little Bighorn

In 1876 prospectors overran the Lakota Sioux reservation in the Dakota Territory to mine gold in the Black Hills. The Lakota saw no reason they should abide by a treaty that American settlers were violating, so many left the reservation that spring to hunt near the Bighorn Mountains in southeastern Montana.

The government responded by sending an expedition commanded by General Alfred H. Terry. Lieutenant Colonel **George A. Custer** and the Seventh Cavalry were with the expedition. Custer underestimated the fighting capabilities of the Lakota and Cheyenne. On June 25, 1876, ignoring orders, and acting on his own initiative, he launched a three-pronged attack in broad daylight on one of the largest groups of Native American warriors ever assembled on the Great Plains.

POLITICAL CARTOONS PRIMARY SOURCE
Government Native American Policies

▲ This cartoon from 1878 shows Secretary of the Interior Carl Schurz investigating the Indian "bureau."

THE REASON OF THE INDIAN OUTBREAK.
General Miles declares that the Indians are starved into rebellion.

▲ This cartoon is labeled "The Reason of the Indian Outbreak" and quotes General Miles who said the "Indians are starved into rebellion."

Analyzing VISUALS — DBQ

1. **Examining** Who does the cartoon on the right blame for the problems of Native Americans?

2. **Analyzing** According to the cartoon on the left, why was the Indian Bureau unable to help Native Americans?

People IN HISTORY

George Custer
1839–1876

George Custer, who graduated at the bottom of his West Point class, became an unlikely hero during the Civil War. During the many cavalry charges he led, 11 horses were shot out from under him. At the age of 23, he became the youngest Union Army general. When Custer later commanded the Seventh Cavalry in the West, the Cheyenne called him "Yellow Hair," because he wore his curly blond hair to his shoulders. Custer wore buckskins for battle, though he wore velveteen uniforms in the camp. He spent many hours studying military tactics and reading military history. He risked his own career to testify against the corruption of the Indian Bureau. In anger at his testimony, President Grant removed him from command. However, the public outcry in favor of Custer led to his return to command, a decision that cost the lives of Custer and all his troops.

How did Custer's actions in the Civil War indicate what he might do in other combat situations?

Sitting Bull
c. 1831–1890

The great Lakota chief Sitting Bull faced his first battle at age 14, in a raid against the Crow tribe. As a young man he joined two groups, a warrior society known as Strong Heart and a group that worked for tribal welfare, Silent Eaters. Sitting Bull became chief when he was 37 years old. A holy man as well as a warrior, Sitting Bull led Native Americans in sun dances and prayers to the Great Spirit. After his victory at the Little Bighorn, Sitting Bull led his people to Canada to avoid the reservation system. In 1881, with his people facing starvation, Sitting Bull led them to Montana. He asked his son to hand the commanding officer of Fort Buford his rifle, hoping to show that "he has become a friend of the Americans." Sitting Bull also asked it to be remembered that "I was the last man of my tribe to surrender my rifle." Four years later, he briefly joined Buffalo Bill's Wild West show. He was killed by a Lakota, as he had seen in a vision five years before: A Lakota policeman shot him in a scuffle trying to keep the great chief from joining a Ghost Dance, which had been outlawed.

How did Sitting Bull wish to be remembered?

The Native American forces first repulsed a cavalry charge from the south. Then they turned on Custer and his 210 soldiers and killed all but one of them. One Lakota warrior recalled the scene afterward: "The soldiers were piled one on top of another, dead, with here and there, an Indian among the soldiers. Horses lay on top of men, and men on top of horses."

Newspaper accounts portraying Custer as a victim of a massacre produced a public outcry in the East, and the army stepped up its campaign against Native Americans on the Plains. Sitting Bull fled with his followers to Canada, but the other Lakota were forced to return to the reservation and give up the Black Hills.

Flight of the Nez Perce

Farther west, the Nez Perce people, led by **Chief Joseph,** refused to be moved to a smaller reservation in Idaho in 1877. When the army came to relocate them, they fled their homes and embarked on a journey of more than 1,300 miles. Finally, in October 1877, Chief Joseph surrendered, and he and his followers were exiled to Oklahoma. His speech summarized the hopelessness of their cause:

PRIMARY SOURCE

"Our chiefs are killed. . . . The little children are freezing to death. My people . . . have no blankets, no food. . . . Hear me, my chiefs; I am tired; my heart is sick and sad. From where the sun now stands I will fight no more forever."

—quoted in *Bury My Heart at Wounded Knee*

Tragedy at Wounded Knee

Native American resistance came to a final and tragic end on the Lakota Sioux reservation in 1890. Defying the orders of the government, the Lakota continued to perform the Ghost Dance, a ritual that celebrated a hoped-for day of reckoning when settlers would disappear, the buffalo would return, and Native Americans would reunite with their dead ancestors.

Federal authorities had banned the ceremony fearing it would lead to violence. They blamed the latest defiance on Chief Sitting Bull, who had returned from Canada, and sent police to arrest the chief. Sitting Bull's supporters tried to stop the arrest. In the exchange of gunfire that followed, the chief himself was killed.

A group of Ghost Dancers then fled the reservation, and the army went after them. On December 29, 1890, as troops tried to disarm them at Wounded Knee Creek, gunfire broke out. A deadly battle ensued, taking the lives of 25 U.S. soldiers and **approximately** 200 Lakota men, women, and children.

The Dawes Act

Some Americans had long opposed the treatment of Native Americans. In her 1881 book *A Century of Dishonor*, Helen Hunt Jackson detailed the years of broken promises and injustices. Her descriptions of events such as the massacre at Sand Creek sparked new debate on the issue. Some Americans believed the solution was to encourage Native Americans to **assimilate,** or be absorbed, into American society as landowners and citizens. This meant dividing reservations into individual **allotments,** where families could become self-supporting.

This policy became law in 1887 when Congress passed the **Dawes Act.** This act allotted to each head of household 160 acres of reservation land for farming; single adults received 80 acres, and 40 acres were allotted for children. The land that remained after all members had received allotments would be sold to American settlers, with the proceeds going into a trust for Native Americans.

This plan failed to achieve its goals. Some Native Americans succeeded as farmers or ranchers, but many had little training or enthusiasm for either pursuit. Like homesteaders, they often found their allotments too small to be profitable, so they sold them. Some Native American groups had grown attached to their reservations and hated to see them transformed into homesteads for settlers as well as Native Americans.

In the end, the assimilation policy proved a dismal failure. No legislation could provide a satisfactory solution to the Native American issue, because there was no entirely satisfactory solution to be had. The Native Americans were doomed because they were dependent on buffalo for food, clothing, fuel, and shelter. When the herds were wiped out, Native Americans on the Plains had no way to sustain their way of life, and few adopted American settlers' lifestyles in place of their traditional cultures.

The Dawes Act granted citizenship to Native Americans who stayed on their allotments for 25 years. Few qualified, and it was not until 1924 that Congress passed the Citizenship Act, granting all Native Americans citizenship. Some states—Arizona, Maine, and New Mexico—did not grant Native Americans the right to vote until after World War II.

Under Franklin Roosevelt's New Deal, the policies of assimilation and allotments finally ended in 1934. The Indian Reorganization Act reversed the Dawes Act's policy of assimilation. It restored some reservation lands, gave Native American tribes control over those lands, and permitted them to elect tribal governments.

✔ **Reading Check** **Cause and Effect** What effect did Helen Hunt Jackson's book *A Century of Dishonor* have?

Section 3 REVIEW

Vocabulary

1. **Explain** the significance of: nomad, annuity, Sand Creek Massacre, Indian Peace Commission, George A. Custer, Chief Joseph, assimilate, allotment, Dawes Act.

Main Ideas

2. **Comparing** In what ways were the different groups of the Plains Indians similar?

3. **Discussing** Why do you think the government's policy of assimilation of Native Americans was a failure?

Critical Thinking

4. **Big Ideas** How did Native Americans respond to the loss of land from white settlement of the Great Plains?

5. **Organizing** Use a graphic organizer similar to the one below to list the reasons the government's plans to move the Plains Indians onto reservations failed.

6. **Analyzing Visuals** Examine the map of battle sites and reservations on page 399. Then, from the point of view of a historian, explain the actions taken against Native Americans within the historical context of the time.

Writing About History

7. **Descriptive Writing** Assume the role of a Plains Indian. Write a journal entry describing how you feel about the Dawes Act and how it has affected your life.

History ONLINE

Study Central™ To review this section, go to glencoe.com and click on Study Central.

Causes of Settlers Moving West to the Great Plains

Mining

- Deposits of gold, silver, and copper are discovered.
- New technologies, such as hydraulic mining, make it possible to remove vast quantities of ore.

Ranching

- Wild longhorn cattle, found to survive well on the Plains, are available in large numbers to be rounded up.
- Railroads provide an easy way to ship cattle to eastern markets.

Farming

- Congress passes the Homestead Act in 1862.
- New farming technologies, including new plows, reapers, and drills, make it possible to farm on the Plains.
- Railroads advertise for settlers and bring necessities such as lumber and coal to the Plains.

► *Tens of thousands of settlers headed west, lured by the possibility of striking it rich mining gold or silver. This photo shows miners standing beside a stack of silver ingots in Leadville, Colorado, c. 1880.*

► *A Plains family stands atop their reaper on their Nebraska farm in the 1890s. Technology such as the reaper made farming the Great Plains practical.*

▲ *Although the Dawes Act was intended to assimilate Native Americans, traditional ways of life persisted. Above, a Cheyenne woman uses a stone mortar and pestle to grind wild cherries outside her home in the 1890s.*

Effects of Settling the Great Plains

- Miners arrive in such large numbers that Colorado, the Dakotas, Nevada, and Montana are able to become states.
- Hydraulic mining damages the environment in some areas and interferes with farming.
- The Great Plains becomes the nation's Wheat Belt, growing tens of thousands of acres of wheat.
- The arrival of miners, ranchers, and farmers leads to conflict with Native Americans.
- The federal government fights several wars with the Native Americans, establishes reservations, and passes the Dawes Act to assimilate Native Americans.

NEW YORK REGENTS EXAM PRACTICE

 TEST-TAKING TIP

Look at each question to find clues to support your answer. Try not to get confused by the wording of the question. Then look for an answer that best fits the question.

Part I

Directions (1–10): For each statement or question, write on a separate sheet of paper the number of the word or expression that, of those given, best completes the statement or answers the question.

1 In 1889 the discovery of gold and copper led to the rapid development of the northern Great Plains and formation of which of the following states?

(1) Montana, North Dakota, South Dakota

(2) Montana, Wyoming, Idaho

(3) North Dakota, South Dakota, Iowa

(4) North Dakota, South Dakota, Nebraska

2 Which of the following factors provided an incentive for people to farm the Great Plains?

(1) long cattle drives

(2) large amounts of rainfall

(3) the Homestead Act

(4) dry, windy weather

3 The open range was closed to grazing with the use of

(1) the long drive.

(2) barbed wire.

(3) the railroads.

(4) placer mining.

4 The Native American wars that occurred between 1860 and 1890 were mainly the result of

(1) disputes over the spread of slavery.

(2) conflict with Mexico over Texas and California.

(3) the search for gold in California.

(4) the movement of settlers onto the Great Plains.

5 Why did *Las Gorras Blancos* carry out night raids in New Mexico?

(1) The English-speaking ranchers claimed land used by the community to graze livestock.

(2) Vaqueros were outlawed by the English-speaking ranchers.

(3) The English-speaking majority in the legislature closed the barrios.

(4) The Hispanic minority did not want New Mexico to join the United States.

6 Placer mining is a process by which

(1) deep mine shafts are dug and miners go underground to extract the minerals.

(2) miners use simple tools like picks, shovels, and pans to extract shallow deposits of minerals.

(3) men use a high-pressure blast of water to loosen large quantities of earth and extract minerals.

(4) earth-moving machines remove large quantities of earth to extract the minerals.

7 The aim of the Dawes Act of 1887 was to

(1) restore previously taken land to Native Americans.

(2) maintain traditional Native American cultures.

(3) end all governmental contact with Native Americans.

(4) assimilate Native Americans into American culture.

8 The Indian Peace Commission proposed

(1) a treaty to end the Battle of the Little Bighorn.

(2) federal regulations for hunting buffalo.

(3) creating two large reservations for the Plains Indians.

(4) removing Sitting Bull from power.

Need Extra Help?								
If You Missed Questions . . .	1	2	3	4	5	6	7	8
Go to Page . . .	388	394–395	390–391	401–403	392–393	388–389	402–403	400

[OVER]

Base your answer to question 9 on the chart below and your knowledge of Chapter 11.

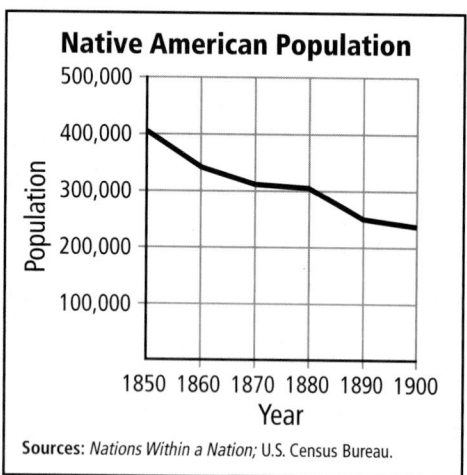

Native American Population

Sources: *Nations Within a Nation;* U.S. Census Bureau.

9   What does the chart indicate about the Native American population between 1850 and 1900?

(1) The Native American population was over 400,000 in 1860.

(2) The Native American population increased over 50 years.

(3) The Native American population declined between 1840 and 1850.

(4) The Native American population was less than 300,000 in 1890.

10 Cattle ranching prospered because of the vast area of grassland owned by the government that was called

(1) the open range.

(2) the long drive.

(3) barbed wire.

(4) the Chisholm Trail.

11 In the early 1800s, society in California was dominated by landowners who lived on

(1) barrios.

(2) haciendas.

(3) bonanza farms.

(4) homesteads.

Need Extra Help?			
If You Missed Questions . . .	9	10	11
Go to Page . . .	398–403	390–391	392

Part II Thematic Essay Question

Directions: Write a well-organized essay that includes an introduction, several paragraphs addressing the task below, and a conclusion.

Theme: Settling the West

Mining and ranching led to the rapid development of the American West. Boomtowns and cattle drives dramatically altered the Western landscape.

Discuss the two industries that altered the frontier

• Describe the boom and bust cycle of a mining town

• Discuss how long drives were affected by settlement

• Evaluate the changes in the environment caused by both industries

Guidelines:

In your essay, be sure to:

• Develop all aspects of the task

• Support the theme with relevant facts, examples, and details

• Use a logical and clear plan of organization, including an introduction and a conclusion that are beyond a restatement of the theme

Part III Document-Based Question

This question is based on the accompanying documents. This question is designed to test your ability to work with historical documents. Some of the documents have been edited for the purposes of the question. As you analyze the documents, take into account the source of each document and any point of view that may be presented in the document.

Historical Context:

During the mid- to late 1800s, the expansion of the West resulted in clashes between white settlers and Native Americans and government policies that led to the unfair treatment of Native Americans.

Task:
Using information from the documents and your knowledge of United States history, answer the questions that follow each document in Part A. Your answers to the questions will help you write the Part B essay in which you will be asked to

- Discuss the actions of the U.S. government toward Native Americans. In your discussion, use arguments by those who supported the government actions and those who opposed them
- Evaluate the effect of these government policies on Native Americans

Part A
Short-Answer Questions
Directions: Analyze the documents and answer the short-answer questions that follow each document on a separate sheet of paper.

Document 1

"I have heard that you intend to settle us on a reservation near the mountains. I don't want to settle. I love to roam over the prairies. There I feel free and happy, but when we settle down we grow pale and die. I have laid aside my lance, bow, and shield, and yet I feel safe in your presence. I have told you the truth. I have no little lies hid about me, but I don't know how it is with the commissioners. Are they as clear as I am? A long time ago this land belonged to our fathers; but when I go up to the river I see camps of soldiers on its banks. These soldiers cut down my timber; they kill my buffalo; and when I see that, my heart feels like bursting; I feel sorry. . . . Has the white man become a child that he should recklessly kill and not eat? When the red men slay game, they do so that they may live and not starve."

Source: *Bury My Heart at Wounded Knee*

1 How does the writer view the white settlers' approach to the land and the resources on it?

Document 2

"Judéwin knew a few words of English; and she had overheard the paleface woman talk about cutting our long, heavy hair. Our mothers had taught us that only unskilled warriors who were captured had their hair shingled by the enemy. Among our people, short hair was worn by mourners, and shingled hair by cowards! . . .

"I cried aloud, shaking my head all the while until I felt the cold blades of the scissors . . . and heard them gnaw off one of my thick braids. Then I lost my spirit. Since the day I was taken from my mother I had suffered extreme indignities. . . . I had been tossed about in the air like a wooden puppet. And now my long hair was shingled like a coward's! In my anguish I moaned for my mother, but no one came to comfort me. Not a soul reasoned quietly with me, as my own mother used to do; for now I was only one of many little animals driven by a herder."

Source: Zitkala-Sä, "School Days of an Indian Girl"

2 Based on this excerpt, what indignities did the little girl experience?

Part B
Essay
Directions: Reread the task box at the top left and write a well-organized essay that includes an introduction, several paragraphs, and a conclusion. Use evidence from the documents in your essay. Support your response with relevant facts, examples, and details. Include additional outside information.

Guidelines:
In your essay, be sure to:
- Develop all aspects of the task
- Incorporate information from the documents
- Incorporate relevant outside information
- Use a logical and clear plan of organization, including an introduction and a conclusion

History ONLINE
For additional test practice, use Self-Check Quizzes—Chapter 11 at glencoe.com.

Need Extra Help?			
If You Missed Questions . . .	1	2	Essay
Go to Page . . .	407	407	398–403

Industrialization

1865–1901

A steel-mill worker gathers a ball of molten iron at the U.S. Steel plant in Gary, Indiana. At the time of this photo, steelworkers were planning to strike for higher wages.

U.S. PRESIDENTS

U.S. EVENTS

WORLD EVENTS

1869
• Transcontinental railroad is completed

1876
• Alexander Graham Bell invents telephone

1879
• Thomas Edison perfects lightbulb

1882
• Standard Oil forms trust

Hayes 1877–1881

Garfield 1881

Arthur 1881–1885

Cleveland 1885–1889

1865

1875

1885

1865
• Dmitri Mendeleyev creates periodic table of elements

1876
• Nicholas Otto builds first practical gasoline engine

1880
• John Milne develops seismograph

1885
• Canada's transcontinental railway is completed

Did Industry Improve Society?

Many factors promoted industrialization, including cheap labor, new inventions and technology, and plentiful raw materials. Railroads rapidly expanded, while government policies encouraged economic growth.

- *What changes in lifestyle do you think occurred because of industrialization?*

- *How do you think industrialization changed American politics?*

1886
- Haymarket riot occurs

1892
- Homestead strike occurs

B. Harrison
1889–1893

Cleveland
1893–1897

1894
- Pullman strike begins

McKinley
1897–1901

1901
- J.P. Morgan forms U.S. Steel

1895

1892
- Rudolf Diesel patents diesel engine

1895
- Louis and Auguste Lumière introduce motion pictures

FOLDABLES™

Analyzing Organizations Make a Three-Tab Book Foldable to help you analyze how the Civil War transformed the nature of industry. As you read the chapter, write details under the corresponding tab.

Before the Civil war | Both | After the Civil war

INDUSTRIALIZATION

History ONLINE Chapter Overview
Visit glencoe.com to preview Chapter 12.

The Rise of Industry

Guide to Reading

Big Ideas
Government and Society The United States government adopted a policy of laissez-faire economics, allowing business to expand.

Content Vocabulary
• gross national product (p. 410)
• laissez-faire (p. 414)
• entrepreneur (p. 415)

Academic Vocabulary
• resource (p. 410)
• practice (p. 415)

People and Events to Identify
• Edwin Drake (p. 410)
• Alexander Graham Bell (p. 412)
• Thomas Alva Edison (p. 412)
• Morrill Tariff (p. 415)

Reading Strategy
Organizing As you read about the changes brought about by industrialization, complete a graphic organizer similar to the one below, listing the causes of industrialization.

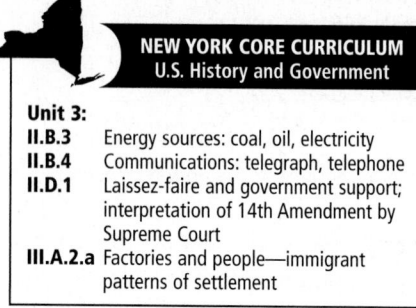

NEW YORK CORE CURRICULUM
U.S. History and Government

Unit 3:
II.B.3 Energy sources: coal, oil, electricity
II.B.4 Communications: telegraph, telephone
II.D.1 Laissez-faire and government support; interpretation of 14th Amendment by Supreme Court
III.A.2.a Factories and people—immigrant patterns of settlement

American business and industry grew rapidly after the end of the Civil War. Industrialization changed the way people lived and worked.

The United States Industrializes

MAIN Idea Natural resources and a large labor force allowed the United States to industrialize rapidly.

HISTORY AND YOU What natural resources are located in your area? Read to learn how the availability of raw materials encouraged industrialization.

Although the Industrial Revolution reached the United States in the early 1800s, most Americans still lived on farms. Out of a population of over 30 million, only 1.3 million Americans worked in industry when the Civil War began in 1861. After the war, industry rapidly expanded, and millions of Americans left their farms to work in mines and factories. Factories began to replace smaller workshops as complex machinery began to substitute for simpler hand tools.

By the late 1800s, the United States was the world's leading industrial nation. By 1914 the nation's **gross national product** (GNP)—the total value of all goods and services that a country produces—was eight times greater than it had been in 1865 when the Civil War came to an end.

Natural Resources

An abundance of raw materials was one reason for the nation's industrial success. The United States had vast natural **resources,** including timber, coal, iron, and copper. This meant that American companies could obtain them cheaply and did not have to import them from other countries. Many of these resources were located in the American West. The settlement of this region helped accelerate industrialization, as did the transcontinental railroad. Railroads took settlers and miners to the region and carried resources back to factories in the East.

At the same time, people began using a new resource, petroleum. Even before the automotive age, petroleum was in high demand because it could be turned into kerosene. The American oil industry was built on the demand for kerosene, a fuel used in lanterns and stoves. The industry began in western Pennsylvania, where residents had long noticed oil bubbling to the surface of area springs and streams. In 1859 **Edwin Drake** drilled the first oil well near Titusville, Pennsylvania. By 1900 oil fields from Pennsylvania to Texas had been drilled. As oil production rose, it led to economic expansion.

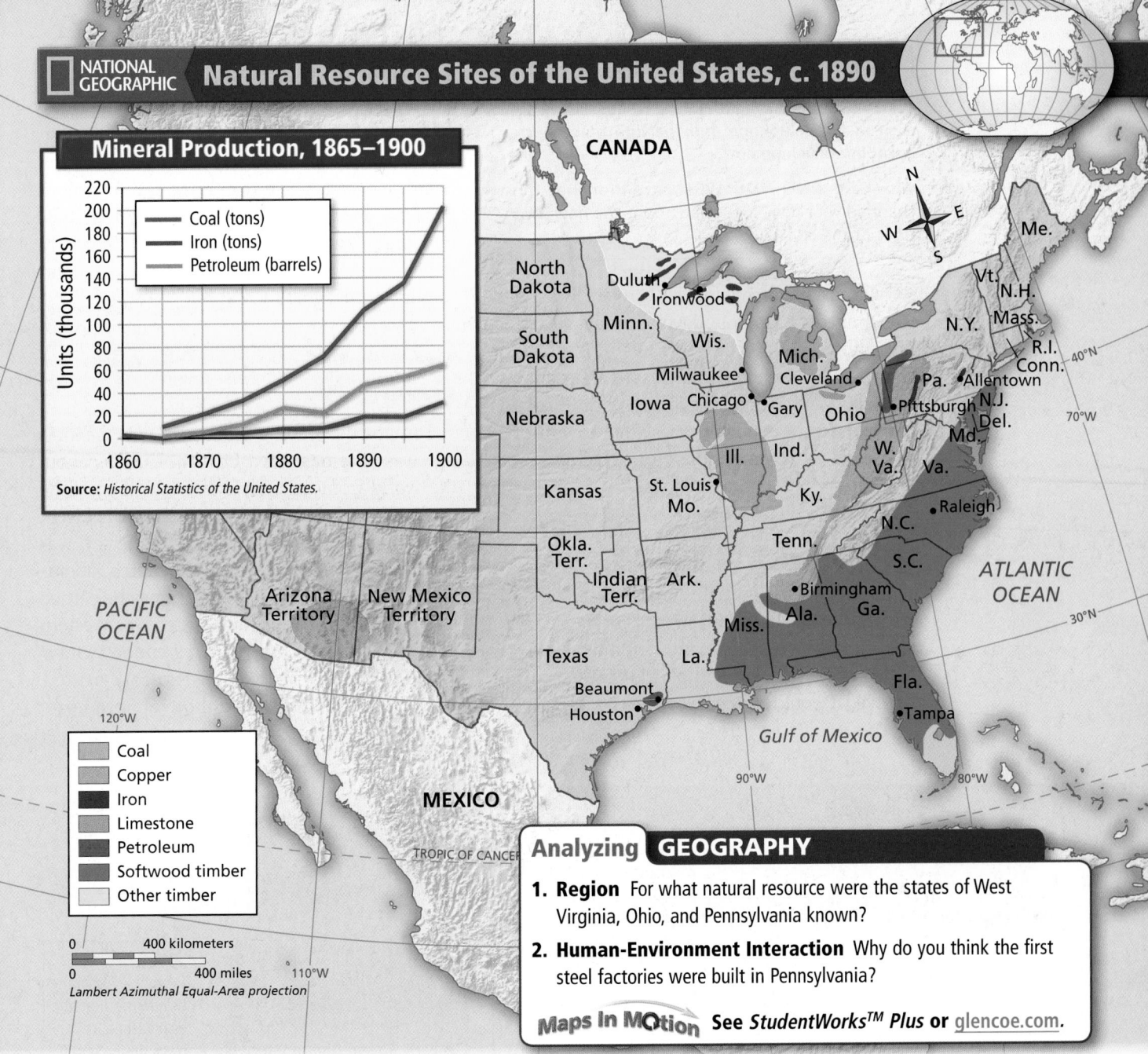

Mineral Production, 1865–1900

Units (thousands)

- Coal (tons)
- Iron (tons)
- Petroleum (barrels)

220
200
180
160
140
120
100
80
60
40
20
0

1860 1870 1880 1890 1900

Source: *Historical Statistics of the United States.*

CANADA

North Dakota
South Dakota
Minn.
Wis.
Duluth
Ironwood
Mich.
Milwaukee
Cleveland
Pa. Allentown
Iowa
Chicago
Gary
Ohio
Pittsburgh
N.J.
Nebraska
Ind.
Del.
Ill.
W. Va.
Md.
Kansas
St. Louis
Mo.
Ky.
Va.
Okla. Terr.
Tenn.
N.C.
Raleigh
Indian Terr.
Ark.
S.C.
Birmingham
Ala.
Ga.
Miss.
Texas
La.
Fla.
Beaumont
Houston
Tampa

Me.
Vt.
N.H.
N.Y.
Mass.
R.I.
Conn.

PACIFIC OCEAN
Arizona Territory
New Mexico Territory
MEXICO
TROPIC OF CANCER
Gulf of Mexico
ATLANTIC OCEAN

40°N
70°W
30°N
80°W
90°W
120°W
110°W

Coal
Copper
Iron
Limestone
Petroleum
Softwood timber
Other timber

0   400 kilometers
0   400 miles
Lambert Azimuthal Equal-Area projection

Analyzing GEOGRAPHY

1. **Region** For what natural resource were the states of West Virginia, Ohio, and Pennsylvania known?

2. **Human-Environment Interaction** Why do you think the first steel factories were built in Pennsylvania?

Maps In Motion See *StudentWorks*™ **Plus** or glencoe.com.

A Large Workforce

The human resources available to American industry were as important as natural resources in enabling the nation to industrialize rapidly. Between 1860 and 1910 the population of the United States nearly tripled. This population growth provided industry with an abundant workforce and also created greater demand for the consumer goods manufactured by factories.

Population growth stemmed from two causes—large families and a flood of immigrants. Because of better living conditions, more children survived and grew to adulthood. American industry began to grow at a time when social and economic conditions in eastern Europe and China convinced many people to immigrate to the United States in search of a better life. Many were also seeking to escape oppressive governments and religious persecution. Between 1870 and 1910, more than 17 million immigrants arrived in the United States. These multitudes entered the growing industrial workforce, helped factories increase production, and became consumers of industrial products.

Reading Check **Explaining** How did oil production affect the American economy?

New Inventions

MAIN Idea During the late 1800s, inventions such as the telephone and the lightbulb spurred economic development.

HISTORY AND YOU What invention has most changed your daily life? Read about the new inventions of the late 1800s.

Natural resources and labor were essential to America's economic development, but new inventions and technology were important as well. New technology increased the nation's productivity and improved transportation and communications networks. New inventions also resulted in new industries, which in turn produced more wealth and jobs.

Bell and the Telephone

In 1874 a Scottish immigrant named **Alexander Graham Bell** suggested the idea of a telephone to his assistant, Thomas Watson. Watson recalled, "He had an idea by which he believed it would be possible to talk by telegraph."

Bell began experimenting with ways to transmit sound via an electrical current of varying intensity. In 1876 he succeeded. Picking up the crude telephone, he placed a call to the next room, saying, "Come here, Watson, I want you." Watson heard and came. The telephone revolutionized business and personal communication. In 1877 Bell organized the Bell Telephone Company, which eventually became the American Telephone and Telegraph Company (AT&T).

Edison, Westinghouse, and Electricity

Perhaps the leading pioneer in new technology was **Thomas Alva Edison.** Curious about the world from an early age, he learned all he could about the mechanical workings of objects. His laboratory at Menlo Park, New Jersey, was the forerunner of the modern research laboratory. Edison set up his lab with money he earned by improving the telegraph system for Western Union. He referred to it as an "invention factory." During the first five years Menlo Park existed, Edison patented an invention almost every

American Inventions, 1865–1895

1872
Elijah McCoy invents automatic lubricator for steam engines, allowing trains to run faster with less maintenance

1877
Thomas Edison develops phonograph

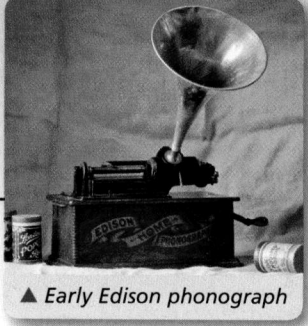
▲ Early Edison phonograph

1886
Josephine Cochrane develops automatic dishwasher; its basic design is still used today

1870 **1875** **1880** **1885**

1873
Christopher Sholes develops typewriter and sells it to Remington and Sons

▲ Alexander Graham Bell

1876
Alexander Graham Bell invents telephone

▲ Bell's first telephone

1882
Lewis Latimer invents the carbon filament for light-bulbs, allowing them to last much longer

▲ Edison's first commercial lightbulb

month. By the time he died, Edison held more than one thousand patents.

Edison first achieved international fame in 1877 with the invention of the phonograph. Two years later he perfected the electric generator and the lightbulb. Although Edison had expected to produce an inexpensive lightbulb in six weeks, the task took more than a year. His laboratory then went on to invent or improve several other major devices, including the battery, the dictaphone, and the motion picture.

An Edison company began to transform American society in 1882 when it started supplying electric power to New York City. In 1889 several Edison companies merged to form the Edison General Electric Company (today known as GE).

Engineer and industrialist George Westinghouse invented an air-brake system for railroads. Unlike earlier manual systems that required brakes to be applied to each car, Westinghouse's invention provided a continuous braking system, so that all the cars' brakes were applied at the same time. Because the trains could brake rapidly and smoothly, they could safely travel at higher speeds.

Westinghouse also developed an alternating current (AC) system to distribute electricity using transformers and generators. Working with inventor Nikola Tesla, Westinghouse further improved his system. His Westinghouse Electric Company lit Chicago's Columbia Exhibition in 1893. It was also the first to use the hydroelectric power of Niagara Falls to generate electricity for streetcars and lights in Buffalo, New York, 22 miles away.

Technology's Impact

In ways big and small, technology changed the way people lived. Shortly after the Civil War, Thaddeus Lowe invented the ice machine, the basis of the refrigerator. In the early 1870s Gustavus Swift, founder of Swift Meatpacking, hired an engineer to develop a refrigerated railroad car. Swift shipped the first refrigerated load of fresh meat in 1877. The widespread use of refrigeration kept food fresh longer and reduced the risk of food poisoning.

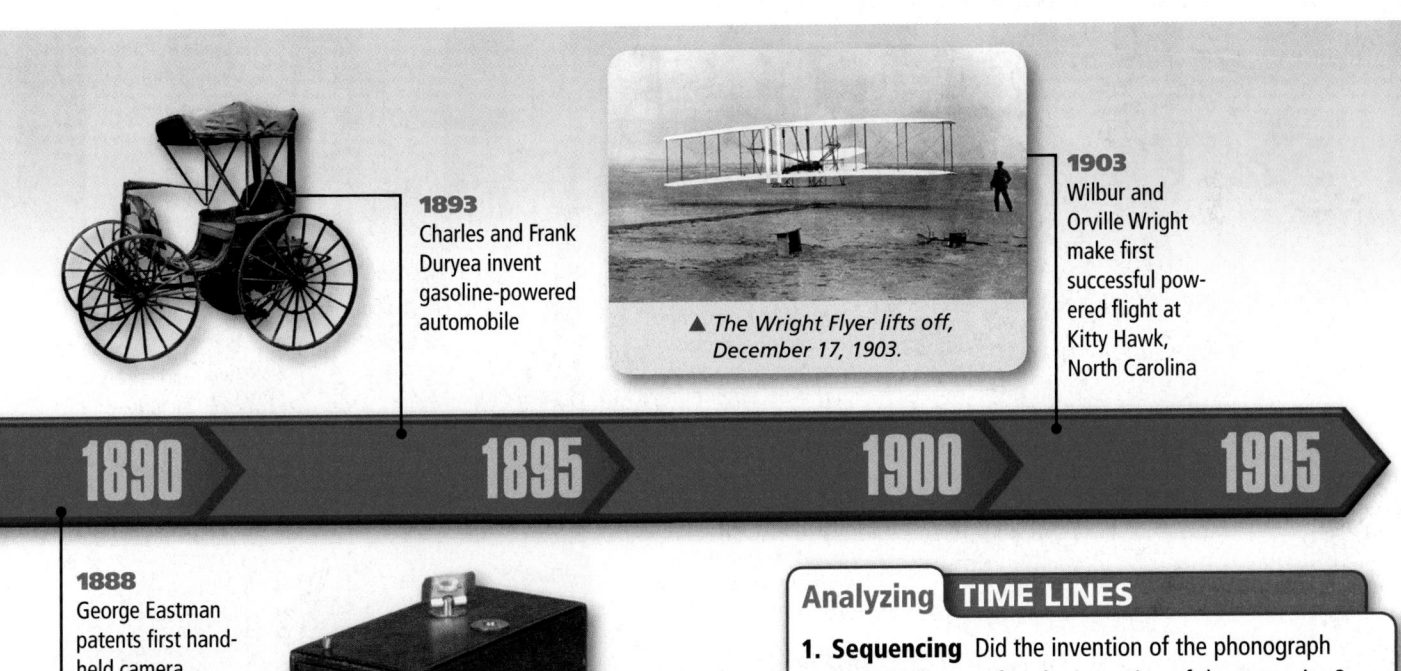

1893 Charles and Frank Duryea invent gasoline-powered automobile

▲ *The Wright Flyer lifts off, December 17, 1903.*

1903 Wilbur and Orville Wright make first successful powered flight at Kitty Hawk, North Carolina

1890 1895 1900 1905

1888 George Eastman patents first handheld camera, the Kodak

Analyzing TIME LINES

1. **Sequencing** Did the invention of the phonograph occur before or after the invention of the typewriter?

2. **Calculating** How much time elapsed between the invention of a gasoline-powered automobile and the first flight of the Wright brothers?

3. **Identifying** For what invention is Josephine Cochrane known?

The textile industry had long depended on machines to turn fibers into cloth. By the mid-1800s, the introduction of the Northrop automatic loom allowed cloth to be made at a much faster rate. Bobbins, which had to be changed by hand, could now be changed automatically.

Changes also took place in the clothing industry. Standard sizes were used in making ready-made clothes. Power-driven sewing machines and cloth cutters rapidly moved the clothing business from small tailor shops to large factories. Similar changes took place in shoemaking. By 1900 cobblers had nearly disappeared.

Technology's impact also included improved communications. Cyrus Field laid a telegraph cable across the Atlantic Ocean in 1866. This cable provided instant contact between the United States and Europe.

✓ **Reading Check** **Explaining** How did the use of electric power affect economic development?

Free Enterprise

MAIN Idea Laissez-faire economics promoted industrialization, but tariffs protected American companies from competition.

HISTORY AND YOU Do you remember how Americans objected to British taxes on trade before the American Revolution? Read how tariffs affected American industries in the late 1800s.

Another important reason the United States was able to industrialize rapidly was its free enterprise system. In the late 1800s, many Americans embraced the idea of **laissez-faire** (leh•say•FARE), a French phrase meaning "let people do as they choose." Supporters of laissez-faire believe the government should not interfere in the economy other than to protect private property rights and maintain peace. They argue that if the government regulates the economy, it increases costs and eventually hurts society more than it helps.

POLITICAL CARTOONS PRIMARY SOURCE
Should Government Regulate the Economy?

◀ Entitled "The Consumer Consumed," this cartoon shows a shopper being told that if he buys domestic goods, he has to pay extra money to trusts (monopolies), and if he buys foreign goods, he has to pay extra money (duties) to the government.

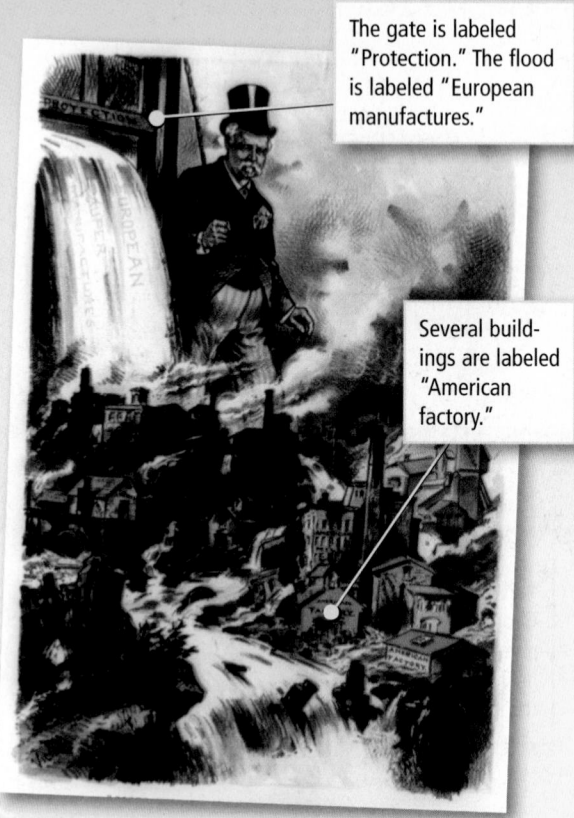

The gate is labeled "Protection." The flood is labeled "European manufactures."

Several buildings are labeled "American factory."

▲ The original caption for this cartoon read "Goods will be so much cheaper—Democratic argument. But what will happen to all the American factories?"

Analyzing VISUALS DBQ

1. **Interpreting** What is happening to American factories after the protection gate is opened?

2. **Analyzing** What argument does the cartoon on the left give in favor of free trade?

Laissez-faire relies on supply and demand, rather than the government, to regulate wages and prices. Supporters believe a free market with competing companies leads to greater efficiency and creates more wealth for everyone. Laissez-faire advocates also support low taxes and limited government debt to ensure that private individuals, not the government, will make most of the decisions about how the nation's wealth is spent.

In the late 1800s, the profit motive attracted many capable and ambitious people into business. **Entrepreneurs**—people who risk their capital to organize and run businesses—were attracted by the prospect of making money in manufacturing and transportation. Many entrepreneurs from New England, who had accumulated money by investing in trade, fishing, and textile mills, now invested in factories and railroads. An equally important source of private capital was Europe, especially Great Britain. Foreign investors saw great opportunities for profit in the United States.

In many ways, the United States **practiced** laissez-faire economics in the late 1800s. State and federal governments kept taxes and spending low. They did not impose costly regulations on industry or try to control wages and prices. In other ways, however, the government went beyond laissez-faire and introduced policies intended to promote business.

Since the early 1800s, leaders in the Northeast and the South had different ideas about the proper role of the government in the economy. Northern leaders wanted high tariffs to protect manufacturers from foreign competition and also supported federal subsidies for companies building roads, canals, and railroads. Southern leaders opposed subsidies and favored low tariffs to promote trade and to keep the cost of imported goods low.

The Civil War ended the debate. After the Southern states seceded, the Republican-controlled Congress passed the **Morrill Tariff,** which greatly increased tariff rates. By 1865 tariffs had nearly tripled. Congress also gave vast tracts of Western land and nearly $65 million in loans to Western railroads, and sold public lands with mineral resources for much less than their market value.

In the late 1800s, the United States was one of the largest free trade areas in the world. The Constitution bans states from imposing tariffs, and there were few regulations on commerce or immigration. Supporters of laissez-faire say these factors played a major role in the country's tremendous economic growth.

High tariffs, however, contradicted laissez-faire ideas. When the nation raised tariffs on foreign goods, other countries raised their tariffs on American goods. This hurt American companies trying to sell goods abroad, particularly farmers who sold their products overseas. Despite these problems, many business leaders and members of Congress believed tariffs were necessary. Few believed that new American industries could compete with established European factories without tariffs to protect them. Later, in the early 1900s, after American companies had become large and efficient, business leaders began to push for free trade. They believed they could now compete internationally and win sales in foreign markets.

✔️ Reading Check **Analyzing** Do you think government policies at this time helped or hindered industrialization? Why?

Section 1 REVIEW

Vocabulary

1. **Explain** the significance of: gross national product, Edwin Drake, Alexander Graham Bell, Thomas Alva Edison, laissez-faire, entrepreneur, Morrill Tariff.

Main Ideas

2. **Explaining** How did an abundance of natural resources contribute to economic growth in the United States in the late 1800s?

3. **Organizing** Use a graphic organizer similar to the one below to indicate how the inventions listed affected the nature of American work and business.

Invention	Effects
telephone	
lightbulb	
automatic loom	

4. **Describing** How did the principles of the free enterprise system, laissez-faire, and profit motive encourage the rise of industry?

Critical Thinking

5. **Big Ideas** What role did the federal government play in increasing industrialization after the Civil War?

6. **Analyzing Visuals** Examine the time line on pages 412–413. Choose one invention and explain how it changed society.

Writing About History

7. **Descriptive Writing** Imagine you are a young person living in this country in the late 1800s. Choose one of the inventions discussed in the section and write a journal entry describing its impact on your life.

History ONLINE

Study Central™ To review this section, go to glencoe.com and click on Study Central.

Section 2

The Railroads

Guide to Reading

Big Ideas
Science and Technology The growth of railroads encouraged development of the Plains and Western regions.

Content Vocabulary
• time zone *(p. 419)*
• land grant *(p. 420)*

Academic Vocabulary
• integrate *(p. 419)*
• investor *(p. 420)*

People and Events to Identify
• Pacific Railway Act *(p. 416)*
• Grenville Dodge *(p. 416)*
• Leland Stanford *(p. 417)*
• Cornelius Vanderbilt *(p. 419)*
• Jay Gould *(p. 420)*
• Crédit Mobilier *(p. 421)*
• James J. Hill *(p. 421)*

Reading Strategy
Organizing As you read about the development of a nationwide rail network, complete a graphic organizer similar to the one below, listing the effects of this rail network on the nation.

Effects

Nationwide Rail Network

NEW YORK CORE CURRICULUM
U.S. History and Government

Unit 3:
II.B.1 Transportation: railroads and automobiles; urban transportation
II.C Representative entrepreneurs: Case studies in concentrated wealth and effort (other personalities may be substituted; local examples of enterprise should also be used)

Major railroads, including the transcontinental railroad, were constructed rapidly after the Civil War ended. Railroads required major capital investment and government land grants. The huge profits to be made, however, led to some corruption as well.

Linking the Nation

MAIN Idea After the Civil War, the rapid construction of railroads accelerated the nation's industrialization and linked the country together.

HISTORY AND YOU How has technology helped unify the United States in recent years? Read to learn how railroads helped connect the nation.

In 1865 the United States had about 35,000 miles of railroad track, almost all of it east of the Mississippi River. After the Civil War, railroad construction expanded dramatically, linking the distant regions of the nation in a transportation network. By 1900 the United States, now a booming industrial power, had more than 200,000 miles of track.

The Transcontinental Railroad

The railroad boom began in 1862, when President Abraham Lincoln signed the **Pacific Railway Act.** This act provided for the construction of a transcontinental railroad by two corporations. To encourage rapid construction, the government offered each company land along its right-of-way. A competition between the two companies developed, as each raced to obtain as much land and money as possible.

The Union Pacific Under the direction of engineer **Grenville Dodge,** a former Union general, the Union Pacific began pushing westward from Omaha, Nebraska, in 1865. The laborers faced blizzards in the mountains, scorching heat in the desert, and, sometimes, angry Native Americans. Labor, money, and engineering problems plagued the supervisors of the project. As Dodge observed:

PRIMARY SOURCE

"Everything—rails, ties, bridging, fastenings, all railway supplies, fuel for locomotives and trains, and supplies for men and animals on the entire work—had to be transported from the Missouri River."

—quoted in *The Growth of the American Republic*

The railroad workers of the Union Pacific included Civil War veterans, newly recruited Irish immigrants, frustrated miners and farmers, cooks, adventurers, and ex-convicts. At the height of the project, the Union

The Transcontinental Railroad Connects the Nation

NATIONAL GEOGRAPHIC

The two railroads join at Promontory Summit, Utah, 1869.

Wash. Terr.
Oreg.
Idaho Terr.
Mont. Terr.
Wyo. Terr.
Nebr.
Omaha
CENTRAL PACIFIC
UNION PACIFIC
Sacramento
Nev.
Calif.
Utah Terr.
Colo. Terr.
Kans.
Ariz. Terr.
N. Mex. Terr.
Indian Terr.
Tex

▲ Led by Grenville Dodge (top right), workers built the Union Pacific Railroad from Omaha, across the Great Plains, to Utah. Many Irish immigrants worked on the railroad.

▲ The Union Pacific and Central Pacific met in Utah, where a ceremonial gold spike was driven, joining the two lines.

▲ Led by Theodore Judah (above, left), workers built the Central Pacific Railroad eastward from Sacramento, through the Rocky Mountains to Utah. Many Chinese immigrants worked on the railroad.

Analyzing VISUALS

1. **Analyzing** Based on the map and photos, why do you think Union Pacific workers were able to lay so many more miles of track than Central Pacific workers?

2. **Describing** Based on the photos, why do you think life as a railroad worker was so difficult?

Pacific employed about 10,000 workers. Camp life was rough, dirty, and dangerous, with lots of gambling, hard drinking, and fighting.

The Central Pacific The Central Pacific Railroad began as the dream of engineer Theodore Judah. He sold stock in his fledgling Central Pacific Railroad Company to four Sacramento merchants: grocer **Leland Stanford,** shop owner Charley Crocker, and hardware store owners Mark Hopkins and Collis P. Huntington. These "Big Four" eventually made huge fortunes, and Stanford became governor of California, served as a United States senator, and founded Stanford University.

Because of a shortage of labor in California, the Central Pacific Railroad hired about 10,000 workers from China and paid them about $1.00 a day. All the equipment—rails, cars, locomotives, and machinery—was shipped from the eastern United States, either around Cape Horn at the tip of South America or over the isthmus of Panama in Central America.

TECHNOLOGY & HISTORY

Railroads and the Economy Building the railroad system led to the creation of new technologies and jobs. Economists refer to this as the "multiplier effect." Whenever a new technology becomes widely used, it creates many new jobs in other industries that are needed to support it.

Building railroad engines and cars created many jobs in other industries. For example, textile workers made fabric for seats in passenger cars, glassworkers made the lenses for the lamps, and metalworkers cast the bronze bells.

Railroads greatly increased the demand for coal, both to power locomotives and to melt iron in steel refineries. This created a huge coal-mining industry in Pennsylvania and West Virginia. In 1860, some 36,000 people were coal miners; by 1889, there were more than 290,000.

Railroads created many new jobs. Engineers, firemen, and brakemen were needed to run the trains; mechanics, machinists, oilers, dispatchers, track workers, loaders, and many others were needed to keep the railway running. By 1900, more than 1 million people worked for the railroads.

In 1860 the nation had 30,000 miles of railroad track. By 1890, another 130,000 miles had been laid. Track-laying crews employed thousands of workers. In addition, the lumber industry needed tens of thousands of workers to make railroad ties. Thousands of others worked in iron mines and in the steel industry, helping make rails, engine boilers, and other steel components.

History ONLINE
Student Web Activity Visit glencoe.com and complete the activity on industrialization.

The Last Spike Workers completed the Transcontinental Railroad in only four years, despite the physical challenges. Each mile of track required 400 rails; each rail took 10 spikes. The Central Pacific, starting from the west, laid a total of 688 miles of track. The Union Pacific laid 1,086 miles.

On May 10, 1869, hundreds of spectators gathered at Promontory Summit, Utah, to watch dignitaries hammer five gold and silver spikes into the final rails that would join the Union Pacific and Central Pacific. General Grenville Dodge was at the ceremony:

PRIMARY SOURCE

"The trains pulled up facing each other, each crowded with workmen. . . . The officers and invited guests formed on each side of the track. . . . Prayer was offered; a number of spikes were driven in the two adjoining rails . . . and thus the two roads were welded into one great trunk line from the Atlantic to the Pacific."

—from *Mine Eyes Have Seen*

After Leland Stanford hammered in the last spike, telegraph operators sent the news across the nation. Cannons blasted in New York City, Chicago held a parade, and citizens in Philadelphia rang the Liberty Bell.

Railroads Spur Growth

The transcontinental railroad was the first of many lines that began crisscrossing the nation after the Civil War. By linking the nation, railroads increased the markets for many products, spurring American industrial growth. Railroads also stimulated the economy by spending huge amounts of money on steel, coal, timber, and other materials.

Hundreds of small, unconnected railroads had been built before the Civil War. Gradually, however, large rail lines took them over. By 1890, for example, the Pennsylvania Railroad had consolidated 73 smaller companies. Eventually, seven giant systems with terminals in major cities and scores of branches

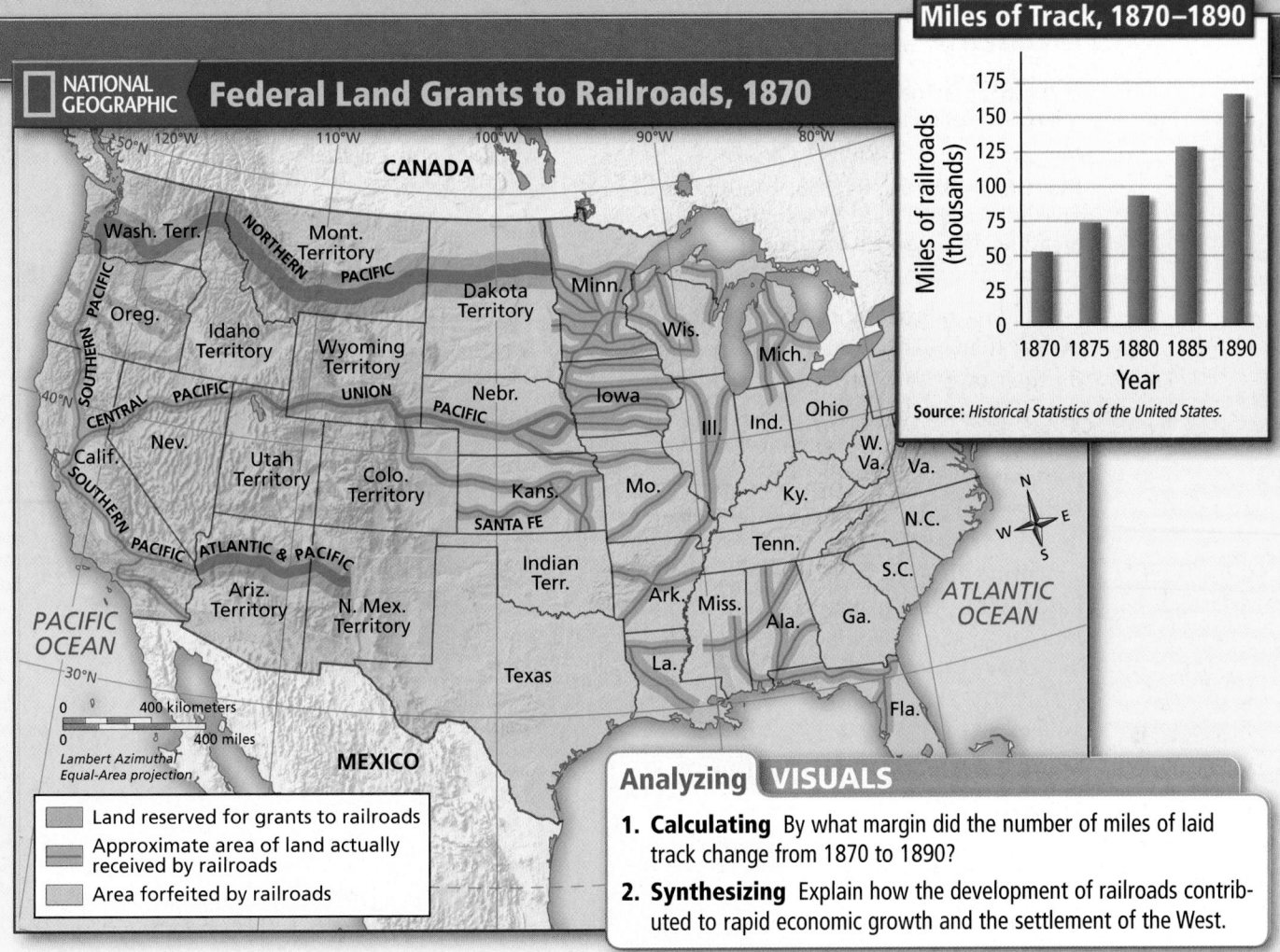

Federal Land Grants to Railroads, 1870

NATIONAL GEOGRAPHIC

CANADA

Wash. Terr.
Oreg.
Idaho Territory
Mont. Territory
Dakota Territory
Wyoming Territory
UNION PACIFIC
Nev.
Calif.
Utah Territory
Colo. Territory
Nebr.
Kans.
SANTA FE
ATLANTIC & PACIFIC
Ariz. Territory
N. Mex. Territory
Indian Terr.
Texas
PACIFIC OCEAN
MEXICO

NORTHERN PACIFIC
SOUTHERN PACIFIC
CENTRAL PACIFIC
SOUTHERN PACIFIC

Minn.
Wis.
Mich.
Iowa
Ill.
Ind.
Ohio
Mo.
Ky.
W. Va.
Va.
N.C.
Tenn.
S.C.
Ark.
Miss.
Ala.
Ga.
La.
Fla.
ATLANTIC OCEAN

0 ——— 400 kilometers
0 ——— 400 miles
Lambert Azimuthal Equal-Area projection

Land reserved for grants to railroads
Approximate area of land actually received by railroads
Area forfeited by railroads

Miles of Track, 1870–1890

Miles of railroads (thousands)

175
150
125
100
75
50
25
0

1870 1875 1880 1885 1890
Year

Source: *Historical Statistics of the United States.*

Analyzing VISUALS

1. **Calculating** By what margin did the number of miles of laid track change from 1870 to 1890?

2. **Synthesizing** Explain how the development of railroads contributed to rapid economic growth and the settlement of the West.

reaching into the countryside controlled most rail traffic.

One of the most successful railroad consolidators was **Cornelius Vanderbilt.** By 1869, Vanderbilt had purchased and merged three short New York railroads to form the New York Central, running from New York City to Buffalo. Within four years he had extended his control over lines all the way to Chicago, which enabled him to offer the first direct rail service between New York City and Chicago. In 1871 Vanderbilt began building New York's Grand Central Terminal.

Before the 1880s each community set its clocks by the sun's position at noon. Having many local time zones interfered with train scheduling, however, and at times even threatened passenger safety. When two trains traveled on the same track, collisions could result from scheduling errors caused by variations in time. To make rail service safer and more reliable, the American Railway Association divided the country into four **time zones** in

1883. The federal government ratified this change in 1918.

Meanwhile, new locomotive technology and the invention of air brakes enabled railroads to put longer and heavier trains on their lines. When combined with large, **integrated** railroad systems, operations became so efficient that the average rate per mile for a ton of freight dropped from two cents in 1860 to three-quarters of a cent in 1900.

The nationwide rail network also helped unite Americans in different regions. The *Omaha Daily Republican* observed in 1883 that railroads had "made the people of the country homogeneous, breaking through the peculiarities and provincialisms which marked separate and unmingling sections." This was a bit of an overstatement, but it recognized that railroads were changing American society.

Reading Check **Explaining** Why was the country divided into four time zones?

Robber Barons

MAIN Idea The government helped finance railroad construction by providing land grants, but this system also led to corruption.

HISTORY AND YOU Have you heard of any recent financial scandals? Read to learn how government grants led to large-scale corruption.

Building railroad lines often required more money than most private **investors** could raise on their own. To encourage railroad construction across the Great Plains, the federal government gave **land grants** to many railroad companies. The railroads then sold the land to settlers, real estate companies, and other businesses to raise money to build the railroad.

During the 1850s and 1860s, the federal land grant system gave railroad companies more than 120 million acres of public land, an area larger than New England, New York, and Pennsylvania combined. Several railroads, including the Union Pacific and Central Pacific, received enough land to cover most of the cost of building their lines.

The great wealth many railroad entrepreneurs acquired in the late 1800s led to accusations that they had built their fortunes by swindling investors and taxpayers, bribing officials, and cheating on their contracts and debts. Infamous for manipulating stock, **Jay Gould** was the most notoriously corrupt railroad owner.

Bribery occurred frequently, partly because government helped fund the railroads. Some investors quickly discovered that they could make more money by acquiring government land grants than by operating a railroad. To get more grants, some investors began bribing members of Congress.

The Robber Barons

▲ Jay Gould bowls on Wall Street with balls labeled "Trickery," and "False Reports." The pins are labeled "Banker," "Inexperienced Investor," "Small Operator," and "Stock Broker."

▲ Railroad owners Jay Gould (lower left), Cornelius Vanderbilt (upper left), Russell Sage (upper right), and Cyrus W. Field (lower right) carve up the United States. The figure in back is lowering an envelope to European royalty labeled "Sealed proposals for the purchase of Europe."

Analyzing VISUALS

1. **Analyzing Visuals** What "pins" has Jay Gould managed to knock down, and what does this suggest?

2. **Interpreting** What do the faces and actions of the five men in the cartoon suggest?

The Crédit Mobilier Scandal

Corruption in the railroad industry became public in 1872, when the **Crédit Mobilier** scandal erupted. Crédit Mobilier was a construction company set up by several stockholders of the Union Pacific Railroad, including Oakes Ames, a member of Congress. Acting for both the Union Pacific and Crédit Mobilier, the investors signed contracts with themselves. Crédit Mobilier greatly overcharged Union Pacific and added miles to the railroad construction. Because the same investors controlled both companies, the railroad agreed to pay the inflated bills without questions.

By the time the Union Pacific railroad was completed, these investors had made millions of dollars, but the railroad itself had used up its federal grants and was almost bankrupt. To convince Congress to give the railroad more grants, Ames sold other members of Congress shares in the Union Pacific at a price well below their market value.

During the election campaign of 1872, an angry associate of Ames sent a letter to the *New York Sun* listing the members of Congress who had accepted shares. The scandal led to an investigation that implicated several members of Congress, including Speaker of the House James G. Blaine and Representative James Garfield, who later became president. It also revealed that Vice President Schuyler Colfax had accepted stock from the railroad. Neither criminal nor civil charges were filed against anyone involved with Crédit Mobilier, however, nor did the scandal affect the outcome of the elections.

The Great Northern Railroad

The Crédit Mobilier scandal created the impression that all railroad entrepreneurs were "robber barons"—people who loot an industry and give nothing back. Some, like Jay Gould, deserved this reputation, but others did not.

James J. Hill was clearly no robber baron. Hill built and operated the Great Northern Railroad from Wisconsin and Minnesota in the East to Washington in the West, without any federal land grants or subsidies. He had carefully planned the railroad's route to pass close to established towns in the region.

To increase business, he offered low fares to settlers who homesteaded along his route. Later, he sold homesteads to the Norwegian and Swedish immigrants coming to the region. He then identified American products that were in demand in China, including cotton, textiles, and flour, and arranged to haul those goods to Washington for shipment to Asia. This enabled the railroad to earn money by hauling goods both east and west, instead of simply sending lumber and farm products east and coming back empty, as many other railroads did at that time. The Great Northern became the most successful transcontinental railroad and the only one that was not eventually forced into bankruptcy.

Reading Check **Describing** How was the Great Northern different from other railroads of its time?

Section 2 REVIEW

Vocabulary

1. **Explain** the significance of: Pacific Railway Act, Grenville Dodge, Leland Stanford, Cornelius Vanderbilt, time zone, land grant, Jay Gould, Crédit Mobilier, James J. Hill.

Main Ideas

2. **Describing** How did Grenville Dodge contribute to the economic growth of the United States in the late 1800s?

3. **Listing** Use a graphic organizer similar to the one below to list the different ways by which railroads were financed.

Ways Railroads Were Financed

Critical Thinking

4. **Big Ideas** How did railroad expansion lead to industrial growth?

5. **Theorizing** Why might politicians be tempted to accept gifts of railroad stock? Why did Crédit Mobilier become a scandal?

6. **Analyzing Visuals** Examine the map and graph on page 419. Then make up a quiz of at least five questions based on the information presented.

Writing About History

7. **Persuasive Writing** Take on the role of an employee of a major railroad corporation. Your job is to write an advertisement to recruit workers for your corporation. After writing the advertisement, present it to your class.

Study Central™ To review this section, go to glencoe.com and click on Study Central.

Section 3

Big Business

Guide to Reading

Big Ideas
Economics and Society Business people such as Andrew Carnegie developed new ways to expand business.

Content Vocabulary
- corporation *(p. 422)*
- stock *(p. 422)*
- economies of scale *(p. 422)*
- pool *(p. 424)*
- vertical integration *(p. 425)*
- horizontal integration *(p. 425)*
- monopoly *(p. 425)*
- trust *(p. 426)*
- holding company *(p. 426)*

Academic Vocabulary
- distribution *(p. 422)*
- consumer *(p. 424)*

People and Events to Identify
- Andrew Carnegie *(p. 424)*
- John D. Rockefeller *(p. 425)*

Reading Strategy
Organizing As you read about the rise of corporations in the United States, complete a graphic organizer showing the steps large business owners took to weaken or eliminate competition.

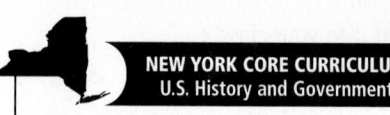

NEW YORK CORE CURRICULUM
U.S. History and Government

Unit 3:
II.A.1 Business response to change: organize and rationalize
II.A.2 Organizational responses
II.C.1 John D. Rockefeller: oil; Andrew Carnegie: steel; Ford: auto
II.D.1 Laissez-faire and government support; interpretation of 14th Amendment by Supreme Court

Following the Civil War, large corporations developed that could consolidate various business functions and produce goods more efficiently. Retail stores began using advertising and mail-order catalogs to attract new consumers.

The Rise of Big Business

MAIN Idea Corporations could produce goods more efficiently, which allowed the rise of big business.

HISTORY AND YOU Do you own stock in a corporation or know someone who does? Read to learn why corporations issue stock.

Before the Civil War, most manufacturing enterprises were owned by just a few people working in partnership. Everything had changed by 1900. Big businesses dominated the economy, operating vast complexes of factories, warehouses, and **distribution** facilities.

Big business would not have been possible without the **corporation.** A corporation is an organization owned by many people but treated by law as though it were a person. It can own property, pay taxes, make contracts, and sue and be sued. The people who own the corporation are called stockholders because they own shares of ownership called **stock.** Issuing stock allows a corporation to raise large amounts of money for big projects while spreading out the financial risk.

Before the 1830s there were few corporations, because entrepreneurs had to convince a state legislature to issue them a charter. In the 1830s, however, states began passing general incorporation laws, allowing companies to become corporations and issue stock without charters from the legislature.

With the money they raised from the sale of stock, corporations could invest in new technologies, hire large workforces, and purchase many machines, greatly increasing their efficiency. This enabled them to achieve **economies of scale:** the cost of manufacturing is decreased by producing goods quickly in large quantities.

All businesses have two kinds of costs, fixed costs and operating costs. Fixed costs are costs a company has to pay, whether or not it is operating. For example, a company has to pay its loans, mortgages, and taxes, regardless of whether it is operating. Operating costs are costs that occur when running a company, such as paying wages and shipping costs and buying raw materials and supplies.

The small manufacturers that were common before the Civil War usually had low fixed costs but high operating costs. If sales dropped, it was cheaper to shut down temporarily. Big manufacturers,

Types of Business Organizations

	Sole proprietorship	Partnership	Corporation
Who owns the business?	One person owns the business and often manages it	Two or more people own and manage the business	All investors who own its stock; managers are hired
How is money raised?	Owner uses savings and borrows money from a bank	Partners each invest some of their own money and borrow money from a bank	Shares of stock are sold to finance business; bank loans are also used
Advantages	Easy to start Low fixed costs, as facilities are usually small and inexpensive to maintain	Partners share responsibility for running the business Low fixed costs	Limited liability for investors Low operating costs; can stay open if economy slows
Disadvantages	Difficult to raise money; limited opportunities for growth; owner has unlimited liability; high operating costs may force business to shut down if the economy is weak	Partners may disagree on direction the company should take; owners have unlimited liability High operating costs	Often have high fixed costs because of size of facilities and equipment needed

▶ The rise of corporations whose stock could be sold publicly also led to the rise of stock exchanges, where stockbrokers bought and sold stock for investors. The photo shows the trading floor of the New York Stock Exchange (NYSE) in 1908. By the late 1800s, the NYSE was the nation's most important stock exchange.

U.S. Businesses, 1870–1900

Source: *Historical Statistics of the United States.*

Analyzing VISUALS

1. **Making Inferences** After comparing proprietorships and corporations, why do you think both still exist today?
2. **Making Generalizations** Based on the chart, what generalization can you make about the growth of U.S. businesses during those three decades? What explanation can you offer?

however, had the high fixed costs of building and maintaining a factory. Compared to their fixed costs, the operating costs of big businesses were low. Operating costs, such as wages, were such a small part of a corporation's costs that it made sense to continue operating, even in a recession.

In these circumstances, big corporations had several advantages. They could produce more goods cheaply and efficiently. They could continue to operate in poor economic times by cutting prices to increase sales rather than shutting down. Many were also able to negotiate rebates from the railroads, further lowering their operating costs.

Small businesses with high operating costs found it difficult to compete with large corporations, and many were forced out of business. At the time, many people criticized corporations for cutting prices and negotiating rebates. They believed the corporations were behaving unethically by driving small companies out of business. In many cases, it was the changing nature of business organization and the new importance of fixed costs that caused competition to become so severe and led to so many small companies going out of business.

Reading Check **Describing** What factors led to the rise of big business in the United States?

Consolidating Industry

MAIN Idea Business leaders devised new and larger forms of business organizations and new ways to promote their products.

HISTORY AND YOU How does advertising reach you today? How has technology created new ways to market and sell goods? Read to learn how an increase in new products led to new selling methods.

Many business leaders did not like the intense competition that had been forced on them. Although falling prices benefited **consumers,** they cut into profits. To stop prices from falling, many companies organized **pools,** or agreements, to keep prices at a certain level.

American courts and legislatures were suspicious of pools because they interfered with competition and property rights. As a result, companies that formed pools had no legal protection and could not enforce their agreements in court. Pools generally did not last long anyway. They broke apart whenever one member cut prices to steal the market share from another. By the 1870s, competition had reduced many industries to a few large and highly efficient corporations.

Andrew Carnegie and Steel

The remarkable life of **Andrew Carnegie** illustrates many of the factors that led to the rise of big business in the United States. Born in Scotland, Carnegie was the son of a poor hand weaver who moved to the United States in 1848. At age 12, Carnegie went to work as a bobbin boy in a textile factory earning $1.20 per week. After two years, he became a messenger in a telegraph office, then worked as secretary to Thomas Scott, a superintendent and, later, president of the Pennsylvania Railroad. Carnegie's energy impressed Scott, and when Scott was promoted, Carnegie became the new superintendent.

As a railroad supervisor, Carnegie knew that he could make a lot of money by investing in companies that served the railroad industry. He bought shares in iron mills and factories that made sleeping cars and locomotives. He also invested in a company that built railroad bridges. By his early 30s, he was earning $50,000 per year and decided to quit his job to concentrate on his own business investments.

As part of his business activities, Carnegie frequently traveled to Europe. On one trip, he

INFOGRAPHIC
The Rise of the Steel Industry

Several factors led to the rise of big business in the late 1800s: the use of new technology, the advantages of economies of scale, and the process of vertical and horizontal integration.

Coke, iron ore, and limestone are hoisted to the top of the blast furnace and sprinkled into the furnace. Blasts of super-hot air melt the ore as it falls.

Blast furnace

Impurities rise to the top of the molten iron and are skimmed off. The iron drains out the bottom of the furnace and is carried to the Bessemer converter.

Carnegie's use of a Bessemer converter enabled his steel mills to make large quantities of inexpensive steel. Molten iron is poured into the converter and then air is blown in, separating the impurities, and leaving high grade steel to pour out.

Bessemer converter

Coke (from coal)   Iron ore   Limestone

met Sir Henry Bessemer, who had invented a new process for making high-quality steel efficiently and cheaply. After meeting Bessemer, Carnegie opened a steel company in Pittsburgh in 1875 and began using the Bessemer process. Carnegie often boasted about how cheaply he could produce steel:

PRIMARY SOURCE

"Two pounds of iron stone mined upon Lake Superior and transported nine hundred miles to Pittsburgh; one pound and one-half of coal mined and manufactured into coke, and transported to Pittsburgh; one-half pound of lime, mined and transported to Pittsburgh; a small amount of manganese ore mined in Virginia and brought to Pittsburgh—and these four pounds of materials manufactured into one pound of steel, for which the consumer pays one cent."

—quoted in *The Growth of the American Republic*

To make his company more efficient, Carnegie began the **vertical integration** of the steel industry. A vertically integrated company owns all of the different businesses on which it depends for its operation. Instead of paying companies for coal, lime, and iron, Carnegie's steel company bought coal mines, limestone quarries, and iron ore fields. Vertical integration saved money and enabled many companies to become even bigger.

Rockefeller and Standard Oil

Successful business leaders also pushed for **horizontal integration,** or combining firms in the same business into one large corporation. Horizontal integration took place as companies competed. When a company began to lose market share, it would often sell out to competitors to create a larger organization.

Perhaps the most famous industrialist who achieved almost complete horizontal integration of his industry is **John D. Rockefeller.** When oil was discovered in Pennsylvania, many entrepreneurs started drilling for oil, hoping to strike it rich. Rockefeller decided to build oil refineries instead. By 1870, his company, Standard Oil, was the nation's largest oil refiner. He then began buying out his competitors. By 1880, the company controlled about 90 percent of the oil-refining industry in the United States. When a single company achieves control of an entire market, it becomes a **monopoly.**

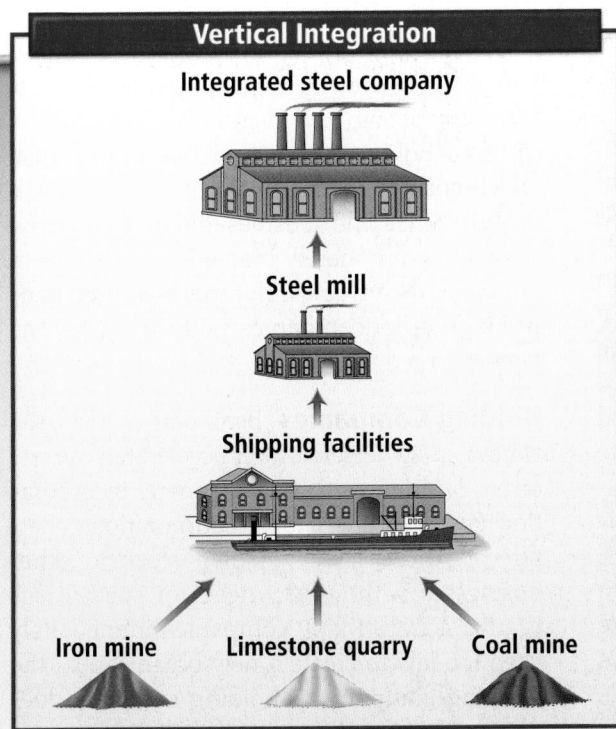

▲ In a vertically integrated industry, a company owns all parts of the industrial process. In this case, a steel company owns the iron and coal mines, the limestone quarries, and the ships and trains that move the materials, as well as the steel mills.

▲ When one company grows by buying up its competitors, it is using horizontal integration to expand.

Analyzing VISUALS

1. **Analyzing Visuals** What enabled entrepreneurs such as Andrew Carnegie to build large steel factories?

2. **Explaining** Why did business owners want to vertically integrate their companies?

People IN HISTORY

John D. Rockefeller
1839–1937

John Davison Rockefeller was one of the foremost industrialists of the late 1800s. Born in upstate New York, Rockefeller moved with his family to Cleveland, Ohio, as a teenager. As a young man, he established a grain and livestock business that made huge profits during the Civil War.

Meanwhile, Cleveland had emerged as a center for refining the oil extracted from the oil fields of western Pennsylvania. In 1863 Rockefeller used his wartime profits to start an oil-refining company. He then began buying up other oil refineries. In 1870 Rockefeller and some associates founded the Standard Oil Company. Rockefeller invested in the newest and most efficient refining technology. He also became known for using ruthless tactics to get preferential shipping rates from railroad companies and acquire competing oil refineries.

By the early 1880s, Rockefeller had created the Standard Oil Trust. With a near-monopoly on American oil refining, Standard Oil made Rockefeller one of the richest men in the world. Rockefeller later donated much of his wealth to philanthropic causes, most notably funding colleges and universities.

What made Standard Oil so successful?

J. P. Morgan
1837–1913

John Pierpont Morgan, the most powerful and influential financier of his era, built a financial empire that became known as the "House of Morgan." The son of a successful Boston banker, Morgan began his career working in the New York City branch of his father's bank.

Morgan soon developed a reputation for shrewd business sense. He specialized in financing railroads, an industry plagued by cutthroat competition and instability. Before Morgan would agree to rescue a troubled railroad company, he insisted the company reorganize to become more efficient, combine smaller railway lines to create a larger coordinated railroad system, and agree to have a representative from Morgan's firm oversee future decisions.

During the depression of the 1890s, Morgan used his immense fortune to finance a bond to rescue the federal government's depleted gold reserve. In 1901 Morgan made history when he organized the first billion-dollar corporation, U.S. Steel, by merging the Carnegie Steel Company and several other steel companies.

How did Morgan try to help the railroad industry?

New Business Organizations

Many Americans feared monopolies because they believed that a monopoly could charge whatever it wanted for its products. Others, however, believed that monopolies had to keep prices low because raising prices would encourage competitors to reappear and offer the products for a lower price. In some industries, one company had a near-monopoly in the United States but was competing on a global scale. Standard Oil, for example, came very close to having a monopoly in the United States, but international competition forced the company to keep its prices low in the late 1800s and early 1900s.

In the late 1800s, in an effort to stop horizontal integration and the rise of monopolies, many states made it illegal for one company to own stock in another company. It did not take long, however, for companies to discover ways around the laws.

Trusts In 1882 Standard Oil formed the first **trust,** a new way of merging businesses that did not violate such laws. A trust is a legal arrangement that allows one person to manage another person's property. The person who manages that property is called a trustee.

Instead of buying a company outright, Standard Oil had stockholders give their stocks to a group of Standard Oil trustees. In exchange, the stockholders received shares in the trust, which entitled them to a portion of the trust's profits. Since the trustees did not own the stock but were merely managing it, they were not violating any laws. The trustees could control a group of companies as if they were one large, merged company.

Holding Companies Beginning in 1889, the state of New Jersey further accelerated the rise of big business with a new general incorporation law. This law allowed corporations chartered in New Jersey to own stock in other businesses without any need for special legislative action. Many companies immediately used the law to create a new organization, the **holding company.** A holding company does not produce anything itself. Instead, it owns the stock of companies that do produce goods. The holding company manages the companies it owns, effectively merging them into one large enterprise.

Investment Banking Another increase in the size of corporations began in the mid-1890s, when investment bankers began to help put new holding companies together. Perhaps the most famous and successful investment banker of the era was J. P. Morgan. John Pierpont Morgan began his career in 1857 as an agent for his father's banking company in New York, America's financial capital. Investment bankers like Morgan specialized in helping companies issue stock. Companies would sell large blocks of stock to investment bankers at a discount. The bankers would then find people willing to buy the stock and sell it for a profit.

In the mid-1890s, investment bankers became interested in selling stock in holding companies that merged many of America's already large corporations. In 1901, J. P. Morgan bought out Andrew Carnegie. Morgan then merged Carnegie Steel with other large steel companies into an enormous holding company called the United States Steel Company. U.S. Steel, worth $1.4 billion, was the first billion-dollar company in American history. By 1904, the United States had 318 holding companies. Together, these giant corporations controlled over 5,300 factories and were worth more than $7 billion.

Selling the Product

The creation of giant manufacturing companies in the United States forced retailers—companies that sell products directly to consumers—to expand in size as well. The vast array of products that American industries produced led retailers to look for new ways to attract consumers. N. W. Ayer and Son, the first advertising company, began creating large illustrated ads instead of relying on the old small print line ads previously used in newspapers. By 1900, retailers were spending over $90 million a year on advertising in newspapers and magazines.

Advertising attracted readers to the newest retail business, the department store. In 1877 advertisements billed John Wanamaker's new Philadelphia department store, the Grand Depot, as the "largest space in the world devoted to retail selling on a single floor." When it opened, only a handful of department stores existed in the United States; soon hundreds sprang up. Department stores provided a huge selection of products in one large, elegant building. The store atmosphere made shopping seem glamorous and exciting.

Chain stores, a group of retail outlets owned by the same company, first appeared in the mid-1800s. In contrast to department stores, which offered many services, chain stores focused on offering low prices. Woolworth's, which opened in 1879, became one of the most successful retail chains in American history.

To reach the millions of people who lived in rural areas far from chain stores or department stores, retailers began issuing mail-order catalogs. Two of the largest mail-order retailers were Montgomery Ward and Sears, Roebuck and Co. Their huge catalogs, widely distributed through the mail, used attractive illustrations and appealing descriptions to advertise thousands of items for sale.

Reading Check **Explaining** What techniques did corporations use to consolidate their industries?

Vocabulary

1. **Explain** the significance of: corporation, stock, economies of scale, pool, Andrew Carnegie, vertical integration, horizontal integration, John D. Rockefeller, monopoly, trust, holding company.

Main Ideas

2. **Stating** Why did the number of corporations increase in the late 1800s?

3. **Comparing** Use a graphic organizer to list ways business leaders in the 1800s tried to eliminate competition.

Attempts to Eliminate Competition

Critical Thinking

4. **Big Ideas** What techniques were used by Carnegie and others to consolidate their industries? How did state governments respond?

5. **Forming an Opinion** Do you think an individual today can rise from "rags to riches" like Andrew Carnegie did? Why or why not?

6. **Analyzing Visuals** Look again at the chart on page 423. During which decade did the number of U.S. businesses increase the most? By how many?

Writing About History

7. **Expository Writing** Write a newspaper editorial in which you explain why entrepreneurs were a positive or a negative force on the U.S. economy in the late 1800s.

History ONLINE

Study Central™ To review this section, go to glencoe.com and click on Study Central.

Section 4

Unions

Guide to Reading

Big Ideas
Struggles for Rights Unions grew and labor unrest intensified as workers fought for more rights.

Content Vocabulary
- deflation *(p. 428)*
- trade union *(p. 429)*
- industrial union *(p. 429)*
- blacklist *(p. 429)*
- lockout *(p. 430)*
- arbitration *(p. 432)*
- injunction *(p. 433)*
- closed shop *(p. 434)*

Academic Vocabulary
- restraint *(p. 430)*
- constitute *(p. 435)*

People and Events to Identify
- Marxism *(p. 430)*
- Knights of Labor *(p. 432)*
- American Federation of Labor *(p. 434)*
- Samuel Gompers *(p. 434)*

Reading Strategy
Sequencing As you read about the increase of American labor unions in the late 1800s, complete a time line similar to the one below by filling in the incidents of labor unrest discussed and the results of each incident.

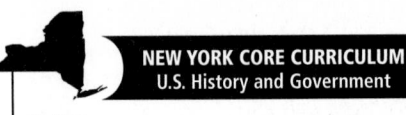

NEW YORK CORE CURRICULUM
U.S. History and Government

Unit 3:
II.E.1 Efforts at national labor unions: Knights of Labor (1869); AF of L (1881–1886); ILGWU (1900)
II.E.2 Struggle and conflict

Workers tried to form unions in the late 1800s, hoping to improve wages, hours, and working conditions. Business leaders were willing to deal with some trade unions but generally opposed industrial unions. Many strikes in this era led to violence, which hurt the image of unions and slowed their growth.

Working in the United States

MAIN Idea Low wages, long hours, and difficult working conditions caused resentment among workers and led to efforts to organize unions.

HISTORY AND YOU Have you ever felt that you were underpaid for an after-school job? Read about the conditions that made workers want to organize.

Life for workers in industrial America was difficult. Many workers had to perform dull, repetitive tasks in working conditions that were often unhealthy and dangerous. Workers breathed in lint, dust, and toxic fumes. Heavy machines lacking safety devices caused many injuries. Despite the difficult working conditions, industrialism led to a dramatic rise in the standard of living. The average worker's wages rose by 50 percent between 1860 and 1890. Nonetheless, the uneven division of income between the wealthy and the working class caused resentment among workers. In 1900 the average industrial worker made 22¢ per hour and worked 59 hours per week.

Deflation, or a rise in the value of money, added to tensions between workers and employers. Between 1865 and 1897, deflation caused prices to fall, which increased the buying power of workers' wages. Although companies cut wages regularly in the late 1800s, prices fell even faster, so that wages were actually still going up in buying power. Workers, however, resented getting less money. Eventually, many concluded that they needed a union to bargain for them in order to get higher wages and better working conditions.

Early Unions

There were two basic types of industrial workers in the United States in the 1800s—craft workers and common laborers. Craft workers had special skills and training. They included machinists, iron molders, stonecutters, shoemakers, printers, and many others. Craft workers received higher wages and had more control over how they organized their time. Common laborers had few skills and received lower wages.

Struggling to Organize

MAIN Idea Workers began to form unions to fight for better wages and working conditions but had few successes.

HISTORY AND YOU Do you sometimes feel that you spend too many hours a day in school? Read to learn how workers sought an eight-hour workday.

Although workers attempted on many occasions to create large industrial unions, they rarely succeeded. In many cases the confrontations with owners and the government led to violence and bloodshed. In 1868 William Sylvis, president of the Iron Molders' Union, wrote to Karl Marx in support of his work and to express his own beliefs:

PRIMARY SOURCE

"... monied power is fast eating up the substance of the people. We have made war upon it, and we mean to win it. If we can we will win through the ballot box; if not, we will resort to sterner means. A little bloodletting is sometimes necessary in desperate causes."

—quoted in *Industrialism and the American Worker*

The Great Railroad Strike

The panic of 1873 was a severe recession that struck the American economy and forced many companies to cut wages. The economy had still not recovered when, in July 1877, the Baltimore and Ohio Railroad announced it was cutting wages, for the third time. In Martinsburg, West Virginia, workers walked off the job and blocked the tracks.

As word spread, railroad workers across the country walked off the job. The strike eventually involved 80,000 railroad workers and affected two-thirds of the nation's railways. Angry strikers smashed equipment, tore up tracks, and blocked rail service in New York, Baltimore, Pittsburgh, St. Louis, and Chicago. The governors of several states called out their militias. In many places, gun battles erupted between the militia and the strikers.

Declaring a state of "insurrection," President Hayes sent federal troops to Martinsburg, Baltimore, Pittsburgh, and elsewhere. It took 12 bloody days for police, state militias, and

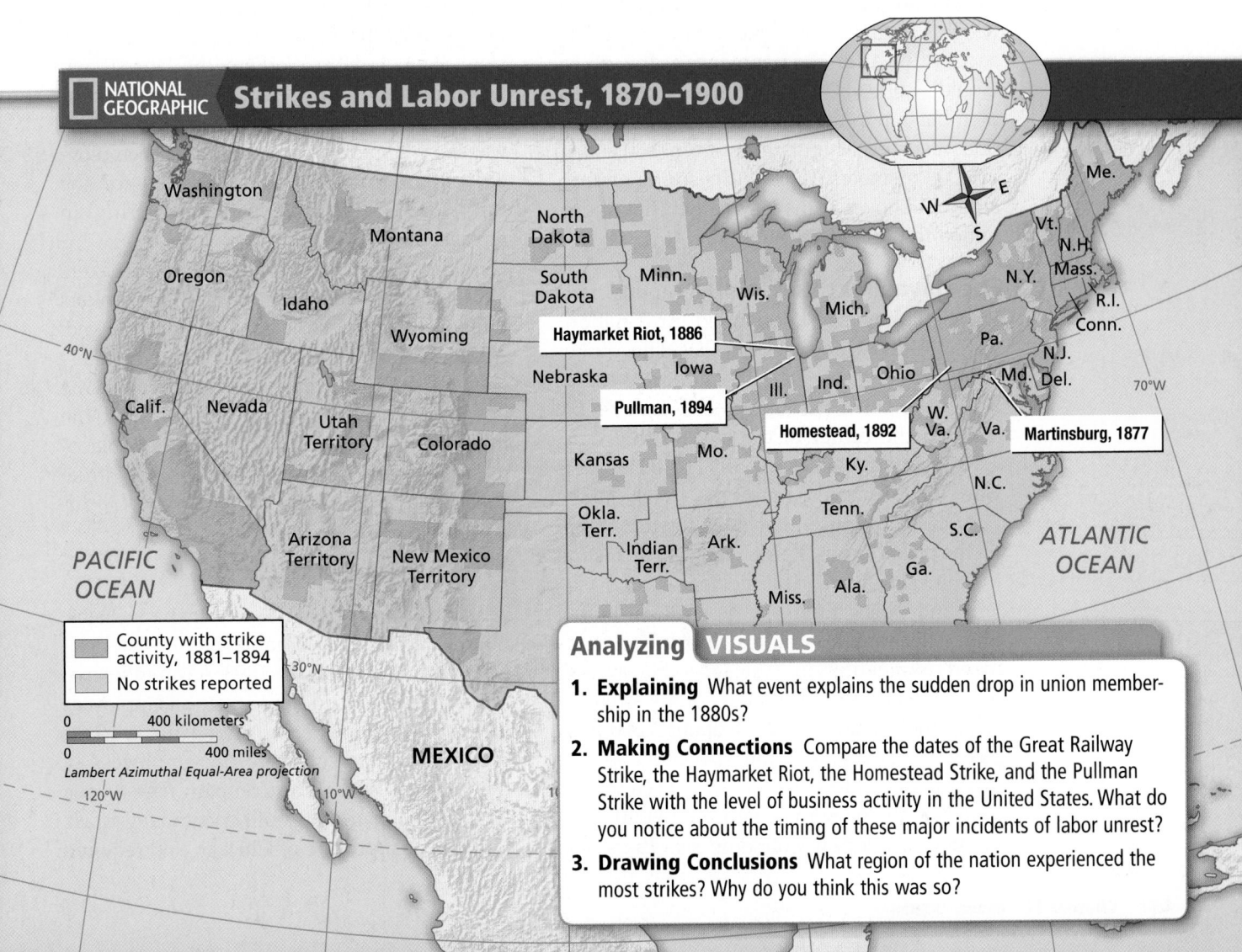

NATIONAL GEOGRAPHIC **Strikes and Labor Unrest, 1870–1900**

County with strike activity, 1881–1894

No strikes reported

0   400 kilometers
0   400 miles
Lambert Azimuthal Equal-Area projection

Analyzing VISUALS

1. **Explaining** What event explains the sudden drop in union membership in the 1880s?

2. **Making Connections** Compare the dates of the Great Railway Strike, the Haymarket Riot, the Homestead Strike, and the Pullman Strike with the level of business activity in the United States. What do you notice about the timing of these major incidents of labor unrest?

3. **Drawing Conclusions** What region of the nation experienced the most strikes? Why do you think this was so?

federal troops to restore order. By the time the strike collapsed, more than 100 people lay dead, and over $10 million in railroad property had been destroyed. The violence of this strike alarmed many Americans and pointed to the need for more peaceful means to settle labor disputes.

The Knights of Labor

The **Knights of Labor,** founded in 1869, took a different approach to labor issues. Its leader, Terrence Powderly, opposed strikes, preferring to use boycotts to pressure employers. The Knights of Labor also supported **arbitration,** a process in which a third party helps workers and employers reach an agreement. The Knights called for an eight-hour workday and supported equal pay for women, the abolition of child labor, and the creation of worker-owned factories. Unlike many organizations of the era, the Knights welcomed women and African Americans as members.

Early Successes In the early 1880s, the Knights began to use strikes and were initially successful. After they convinced one of Jay Gould's railroads to reverse wage cuts in 1885, membership in the union soared. In less than one year, the Knights grew from 100,000 to 700,000 members. Then, in the spring of 1886, an event known as the Haymarket Riot undermined the Knights' reputation.

The Haymarket Riot In 1886 supporters of the eight-hour workday called for a nationwide strike on May 1st. On that date, strikes took place in many cities. In Chicago, the local Knights of Labor led a march of 80,000 people through the center of the city on that date. Over the next few days, nearly 70,000 workers went on strike across the city.

On May 3, police intervened to stop a fight on the picket line at the McCormick Harvesting Machine Company. The incident turned violent and police fired on the strikers, killing four. Afterward, a local anarchist group organized a meeting in Chicago's Haymarket Square to protest the shooting of the strikers.

On the evening of May 4, about 3,000 people gathered to hear the speeches. As the meeting began to break up, the police moved in to keep order. Someone threw a bomb, killing one officer and wounding six others. The police opened fire, and workers shot back. About 100 people, including nearly 70 police officers, were injured.

The police arrested eight people for the bombing. Seven were German immigrants and advocates of anarchism. The incident horrified people across the country. Although the evidence was weak, all eight men were convicted, and four were executed.

Critics long opposed to the union movement pointed to the Haymarket riot to claim that unions were dominated by dangerous radicals. One of the men arrested was a member of the Knights of Labor. This association hurt the Knights' reputation and, coupled with lost strikes, led to a steady decline in membership and influence.

The Homestead Strike

In the summer of 1892, another labor dispute led to bloodshed. A steel mill owned by Andrew Carnegie in Homestead, Pennsylvania, was managed by an anti-union business partner, Henry Clay Frick. The mill's employees belonged to the Amalgamated Association of Iron, Steel, and Tin Workers, the largest craft union in the country. When the union's contract was about to expire, Frick proposed to cut wages by 20 percent. He then locked employees out of the plant and arranged for the Pinkerton Detective Agency to bring in replacement workers.

When the Pinkertons and strikebreakers approached the plant on barges, the strikers refused to let them land. Gunfire followed. After 14 hours, several Pinkertons and strikers were dead, and dozens more were injured. The governor of Pennsylvania then ordered the militia to take control and protect the replacement workers. After four months, the strike collapsed.

The Pullman Strike

Under the leadership of Eugene V. Debs, railroad employees organized the American Railway Union (ARU) in 1893. As an industrial union, the ARU tried to organize all employees of the railroad industry. Among the workers the union organized were the employees of the Pullman Palace Car Company. The owner, George Pullman, had built a company town, Pullman, just outside of Chicago and required

Comparing Major Strikes

	Homestead Steel Strike, 1892	Pullman Railroad Strike, 1895	Lawrence Textile Strike, 1912
Conditions	Seeking to break the union, the Carnegie Steel Company rejects wage increase and proposes a 20% wage cut	Deep wage cuts without cuts in rent and food prices at company housing and company stores	Very low wages; high mortality among workers (many workers are young girls); extreme poverty among workers; strike begins after new wage cuts
Union	Amalgamated Association of Iron, Steel, and Tin Workers	American Railway Union	International Workers of the World (IWW); strikers mostly female, immigrant textile workers
Tactics	**Workers:** Surround factory with pickets and armed workers to keep it shut down and keep strikebreakers out **Employer:** Locks workers out of the plant; hires Pinkertons to break strike	**Workers:** Refuse to handle any railcars built by Pullman; railroads are tied up nationwide **Employer:** Locks workers out of factory	**Workers:** Picketing; union provides food and money to strikers; gains support by touring child workers around country **Employer:** Uses firehoses on picketing workers
Role of Government	State government sends in militia to end violence between strikers and Pinkertons	Federal government gets court injunction to end strike because it interferes with shipment of U.S. mail; federal troops end strike	Local police and state and local militia make mass arrests, attack picketers; after attack on women and children, strike is publicized; Congress and President Taft investigate
Outcome	Company hires strikebreakers; strike collapses after anarchist tries to kill plant manager	ARU leaders are jailed, strike ends unsuccessfully; ARU membership declines	Employers give in, grant workers' demands

Analyzing VISUALS

1. **Contrasting** How does the Lawrence Textile Strike differ from the others?
2. **Analyzing Visuals** In which instance do federal troops break the strike, and on what grounds?

his workers to live there and to buy goods from company stores. In 1893 the Pullman Company laid off workers and slashed wages. The wage cuts made it difficult for workers to pay their rent and the high prices at the company stores. After the company refused to discuss workers' grievances, a strike began. To show support for the Pullman strikers, other ARU members across the United States refused to handle Pullman cars.

This boycott tied up the railroads and threatened to paralyze the economy. Determined to break the strike, railroad managers arranged for U.S. mail cars to be attached to the Pullman cars. If the strikers refused to handle the Pullman cars, they would be interfering with the U.S. mail, a violation of federal law. President Grover Cleveland then sent in troops, claiming it was his responsibility to keep the mail running. Then a federal court issued an **injunction,** or formal court order, directing the union to halt the boycott. Debs went to jail for violating the injunction, but both the strike at Pullman and the ARU strike collapsed. In the case *In re Debs* (1895), the Supreme Court upheld the right to issue such an injunction. This gave business a powerful tool for dealing with labor unrest.

✔ Reading Check **Summarizing** Why was it difficult for unions to succeed in the 1800s?

New Unions Emerge

MAIN Idea The AFL fought for skilled workers; new unions tried to organize unskilled workers.

HISTORY AND YOU Do you know anyone who belongs to a union? Read on to learn about the different types of unions and how they tried to help their members.

Although workers often shared the same complaints about wage rates and working hours, unions took very different approaches to how they tried to improve workers' lives. Trade unions remained the most common type of labor organization. Of course, most workers were unskilled and unrepresented by trade unions. Thus, new types of unions emerged that tried to reach out to those workers and had different ideas about how to help them.

The Rise of the AFL

The **American Federation of Labor** (AFL) was the dominant union of the late 1800s. In 1886 leaders of several national trade unions came together to create the AFL. From its beginning, the AFL focused on promoting the interests of skilled workers.

Samuel Gompers was the first president of the AFL, a position he held until 1924 (with the exception of one year). While other unions became involved in politics, Gompers tried to steer away from controversy and stay focused on "pure and simple" unionism. That is, he thought it best that the AFL stay focused on "bread and butter" issues—wages, working hours, and working conditions. He was willing to use the strike but preferred to negotiate.

The AFL had three main goals. First, it tried to convince companies to recognize unions and to agree to collective bargaining. Second, it pushed for **closed shops,** meaning that companies could only hire union members. Third, it promoted an eight-hour workday.

The AFL grew slowly, but by 1900 it was the biggest union in the country, with over 500,000 members. Still, at that time, the AFL represented less than 15 percent of all nonfarm workers. Most AFL members were white men, because the unions discriminated against African Americans, and only a few would admit women.

The IWW

In 1905 a group of labor radicals, many of them socialists, created the Industrial

People IN HISTORY

Samuel Gompers
1850–1924

Samuel Gompers was the longest-serving president of the American Federation of Labor. Born in London to a Dutch Jewish family, Gompers quit school at 10 to earn money for his family, working as a cigarmaker. He and his family moved to the United States in 1863.

In 1877 Gompers became president of the Cigarmakers' Union. In 1886 he persuaded other craft unions to form the American Federation of Labor and became its first president. Within four years, the AFL had a quarter of a million members. That number grew to one million during the next two years.

A practical man who distrusted socialism, Gompers avoided political ideas and concentrated on improving working conditions. He believed that a just society was built on a fair labor policy. "Show me the country in which there are no strikes and I will show you that country in which there is no liberty," he said.

Do you agree that a union can try to improve working conditions without becoming involved in politics? Explain your answer.

Eugene V. Debs
1855–1926

Eugene Victor Debs was a prominent labor leader and member of the American Socialist Party. Born in Terre Haute, Indiana, Debs went to work at age 15 as a railroad fireman. He helped found the Brotherhood of Locomotive Firemen.

In 1893 Debs helped organize the American Railway Union (ARU). At the time, railway engineers, firemen, conductors, and switchmen all had separate unions. The ARU tried to organize all railroad employees into one union. Debs was arrested for interfering with the U.S. mail during the ARU's unsuccessful Pullman strike. While in prison, Debs read works by Karl Marx and became very critical of capitalism.

Debs ran for president five times between 1900 and 1920 as the nominee of the American Socialist Party. He waged his last campaign from prison while serving time for speaking against America's involvement in World War I.

What did Debs think about combining politics with union activities? How does this differ from Gompers's approach?

Workers of the World (IWW). Nicknamed "the Wobblies," the IWW wanted to organize all workers according to industry, without making distinctions between skilled and unskilled workers. The IWW endorsed using strikes and believed "The working class and the employing class have nothing in common."

The IWW believed all workers should be organized into "One Big Union." In particular, the IWW tried to organize the unskilled workers who were ignored by most unions.

In 1912 the IWW led a successful strike of textile workers in Lawrence, Massachusetts. After textile companies cut wages, 25,000 workers went on strike. During the strike, the children of strikers were sent out of town—in case things became violent. The companies reversed the wage cuts after ten weeks. The Lawrence strike was the IWW's greatest victory. Most IWW strikes failed.

The IWW never gained a large membership, but its radical philosophy and controversial strikes led many to condemn the organization as subversive.

Working Women

After the Civil War, the number of women wage earners began to increase. By 1900 women made up more than 18 percent of the labor force. The type of jobs women did outside the home reflected society's ideas about what **constituted** "women's work." About one-third of women wage earners worked as domestic servants. Another third worked as teachers, nurses, and sales clerks. The remaining third were industrial workers. Many worked in the garment industry and food-processing plants.

Regardless of the job, women were paid less than men even when they performed the same jobs. It was assumed that a woman had a man helping to support her, and that a man needed higher wages to support a family. Most unions excluded women.

One of the most famous labor leaders of the era was Mary Harris Jones, also known as "Mother Jones." An Irish immigrant, Jones began as a labor organizer for the Knights of Labor, then helped to organize mine workers. Her persuasiveness as a public speaker made her a very successful organizer, leading John D. Rockefeller to label her "the most dangerous woman in America."

In 1900 Jewish and Italian immigrants who worked in the clothing business in New York City founded the International Ladies' Garment Workers Union. The membership, composed mostly of female workers, expanded rapidly in a few years. In 1909 a strike of 20,000 garment workers won union recognition in the industry and better wages and benefits for employees.

In 1903 Mary Kenney O'Sullivan and Leonora O'Reilly decided to establish a separate union for women. With the help of Jane Addams and Lillian Wald, they established the Women's Trade Union League (WTUL), the first national association dedicated to promoting women's labor issues. The WTUL pushed for an eight-hour workday, the creation of a minimum wage, an end to evening work for women, and the abolition of child labor.

Reading Check **Comparing** How were female industrial workers treated differently from male workers in the late 1800s?

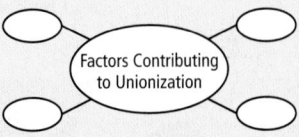

Section 4 REVIEW

Vocabulary

1. **Explain** the significance of: deflation, trade union, industrial unions, blacklist, lockout, Marxism, Knights of Labor, arbitration, injunction, American Federation of Labor, Samuel Gompers, closed shop.

Main Ideas

2. **Identifying** Use a graphic organizer similar to the one below to list the factors that led to an increase in unions in the late 1800s.

Factors Contributing to Unionization

3. **Describing** What groups of workers were represented by the Knights of Labor?

4. **Discussing** How did employers and unions treat women differently from men? What reasons were given for the differences?

Critical Thinking

5. **Big Ideas** Why did industrial unions frequently fail in the late 1800s?

6. **Determining Cause and Effect** Why do you think the rise of unions might have led to increased opposition to immigrants in the United States?

7. **Analyzing Visuals** Look at the map on page 431. In what state did two major disturbances occur? How do you explain this?

Writing About History

8. **Persuasive Writing** Imagine that you are an American worker living in one of the nation's large cities. Write a letter to a friend explaining why you support or oppose the work of labor unions.

History ONLINE
Study Central™ To review this section, go to glencoe.com and click on Study Central.

Causes of Industrialization

- Abundant natural resources
- Cheap immigrant labor force
- High tariffs reduce the import of foreign goods
- National transportation and communication networks

▶ *The Central Pacific Railroad Company changed the way companies did business and helped link the nation together.*

Causes of the Growth of Big Business

- Little or no government intervention
- Development of pools, trusts, holding companies, and monopolies
- Small businesses could not compete with economies of scale of larger businesses
- Practices of some big businesses sometimes limited competition

▲ *Blast furnaces of a U.S. Steel plant line the Monongahela River east of Pittsburgh in Braddock, Pennsylvania, in 1905. New technology and new forms of business organization made possible the rise of large-scale industrial factories in the late 1800s.*

Effects on the Workplace

- Rural migration and immigration created large, concentrated workforce
- Low wages, long hours, and dangerous working conditions were common in large-scale industries
- First large unions formed but had little bargaining power against larger companies

▶ *Workers fill molds with molten steel at a foundry in 1905. Working conditions of the era led to many industrial accidents and contributed to the rise of unions.*

NEW YORK REGENTS EXAM PRACTICE

TEST-TAKING

> Be sure to pay close attention to specific words in a question. Words can change the meaning of the sentence and of the correct answer.

Part I

Directions (1–11): For each statement or question, write on a separate sheet of paper the number of the word or expression that, of those given, best completes the statement or answers the question.

1 What factors contributed to industrialization?

  (1) lack of natural resources

  (2) free enterprise system

  (3) limited workforce

  (4) deteriorating railroad system

2 What economic policy results in little government interaction with business practices?

  (1) capitalism

  (2) protectionism

  (3) supply-side

  (4) laissez-faire

3 The Pacific Railway Act provided for the construction of a railway

  (1) by offering right-of-way land grants to railroad companies.

  (2) along the Pacific coast from California north to Canada.

  (3) by the Union Pacific Railroad company.

  (4) by the Central Pacific Railroad company.

4 Corporations are organizations that

  (1) receive federal funding.

  (2) sell stock to the public.

  (3) have a monopoly on a product or service.

  (4) earn profits for their workers.

5 In the late 1800s, which of the following helped business leaders eliminate competition?

  (1) strikes

  (2) labor unions

  (3) closed shops

  (4) monopolies

6 Which of the following events hurt the membership of the Knights of Labor?

  (1) the Pullman Strike

  (2) the panic of 1873

  (3) the Haymarket Riot

  (4) the Great Railroad Strike of 1877

7 Which of the following was a goal of the AFL under Samuel Gompers?

  (1) having the union represent women in the garment and textile industries

  (2) promoting the ten-hour workday

  (3) having companies recognize unions and bargain collectively

  (4) pushing for closed shops and lower wages for workers

8 How did the federal government aid railroad construction in the 1850s and 1860s?

  (1) advertised overseas to attract immigrants to help build tracks

  (2) used tax dollars to fund many railroad projects

  (3) passed laws to legalize railroad monopolies

  (4) granted public lands to railroads to sell to raise funds

Need Extra Help?								
If You Missed Questions ...	1	2	3	4	5	6	7	8
Go to Page ...	414–415	414–415	416	422	425–427	432	434–435	420

[OVER]

Base your answer to question 9 on the chart below and on your knowledge of Chapter 12.

Steel Production, 1865–1895

Source: *Historical Statistics of the United States.*

9   Between what years did steel production increase the most?

   (1) 1865–1870
   (2) 1885–1890
   (3) 1890–1895
   (4) 1895–1900

10 Closed shops and eight-hour workdays were goals of which of the following groups?

   (1) farmers
   (2) politicians
   (3) industrialists
   (4) organized labor

11 Which of the following statements about labor unions in the late 1800s is accurate?

   (1) Strikes by labor unions usually gained public support.
   (2) Labor union activities were frequently opposed by the government.
   (3) Demands by labor union were usually met.
   (4) Arbitration was commonly used to end labor unrest.

Need Extra Help?			
If You Missed Questions . . .	9	10	11
Go to Page . . .	422–427	428–435	428–430

Part II Thematic Essay Question

Directions: Write a well-organized essay that includes an introduction, several paragraphs addressing the task below, and a conclusion.

Theme: Labor Unions

In the late 1800s and early 1900s, workers in the United States began to unite and form labor unions. During this era, labor unions made great strides in helping workers fight for improved wages, better hours, and safer working conditions.

Identify at least two labor unions formed during the late 1800s and early 1900s, and for each

• Discuss each organization's views, goals, and activities.

• Evaluate the extent to which each union and its members changed the role of labor in the United States.

Guidelines:
In your essay, be sure to:

• Develop all aspects of the task

• Support the theme with relevant facts, examples, and details

• Use a logical and clear plan of organization, including an introduction and a conclusion that are beyond a restatement of the theme

Part III Document-Based Question

This question is based on the accompanying documents. This question is designed to test your ability to work with historical documents. Some of the documents have been edited for the purposes of the question. As you analyze the documents, take into account the source of each document and any point of view that may be presented in the document.

Historical Context:
During the late 1800s and the early 1900s, large corporations such as U.S. Steel and Standard Oil Company monopolized certain industries. Many Americans were critical of the business practices large corporations employed to eliminate competition and increase profits.

ASSESSMENT

Task:

Using information from the documents and your knowledge of United States history, answer the questions that follow each document in Part A. Your answers to the questions will help you write the Part B essay in which you will be asked to

- Discuss the rise of big business and criticisms of its actions
- Evaluate the long-term effects of the business practices of big business, including government responses

Part A
Short-Answer Questions

Directions: Analyze the documents and answer the short-answer questions that follow each document on a separate sheet of paper.

Document 1

> Very often people who admit the facts, who are willing to see that Mr. Rockefeller has employed force and fraud to secure his ends, justify him by declaring, 'It's business.' That is, 'It's business' has come to be a legitimate excuse for hard dealing, sly tricks, special privileges. It is a common enough thing to hear men arguing that the ordinary laws of morality do not apply in business.
>
> As for the ethical side, there is no cure but in an increasing scorn of unfair play.... When the businessman who fights to secure special privileges, to crowd his competitor off the track by other than fair competitive methods, receives the same summary disdainful ostracism by his fellows that the doctor or lawyer who is 'unprofessional,' the athlete who abuses the rules, receives, we shall have gone a long way toward making commerce a fit pursuit for our young men.

Source: Ida Tarbell, *History of the Standard Oil Company*

1 In what way did Tarbell believe the attitudes of the American people contributed to Rockefeller's business practices?

Source: Bernhard Gillam, *Puck*, February 7, 1883

2 What does the cartoon say about Gould and Vanderbilt?

Part B
Essay

Directions: Reread the task box at the top left and write a well-organized essay that includes an introduction, several paragraphs, and a conclusion. Use evidence from the documents in your essay. Support your response with relevant facts, examples, and details. Include additional outside information.

Guidelines:

In your essay, be sure to:

- Develop all aspects of the task
- Incorporate information from the documents
- Incorporate relevant outside information
- Support the task with relevant facts, examples, and details
- Use a logical and clear plan of organization, including an introduction and a conclusion that are beyond a restatement of the task

History ONLINE

For additional test practice, use Self-Check Quizzes—Chapter 12 at glencoe.com.

Need Extra Help?			
If You Missed Questions . . .	1	2	Essay
Go to Page . . .	425–427	425–427	422–427

Urban America

1865–1896

Immigrants look toward New York City while waiting on a dock at Ellis Island in the early 1900s.

U.S. PRESIDENTS

U.S. EVENTS

WORLD EVENTS

1883
- Brooklyn Bridge completed
- Civil Service Act adopted

1870
- Fifteenth Amendment ratified
- Farmers' Alliance founded

Hayes
1877–1881

1881
- President Garfield assassinated

Garfield
1881

Arthur
1881–1885

Cleveland
1885–1889

1870   1875   1880   1885

1872
- Ballot Act makes voting secret in Britain

1876
- Porfiro Diaz becomes dictator of Mexico

1881
- Anti-Jewish pogroms erupt in Russia

1884
- First subway in London opens

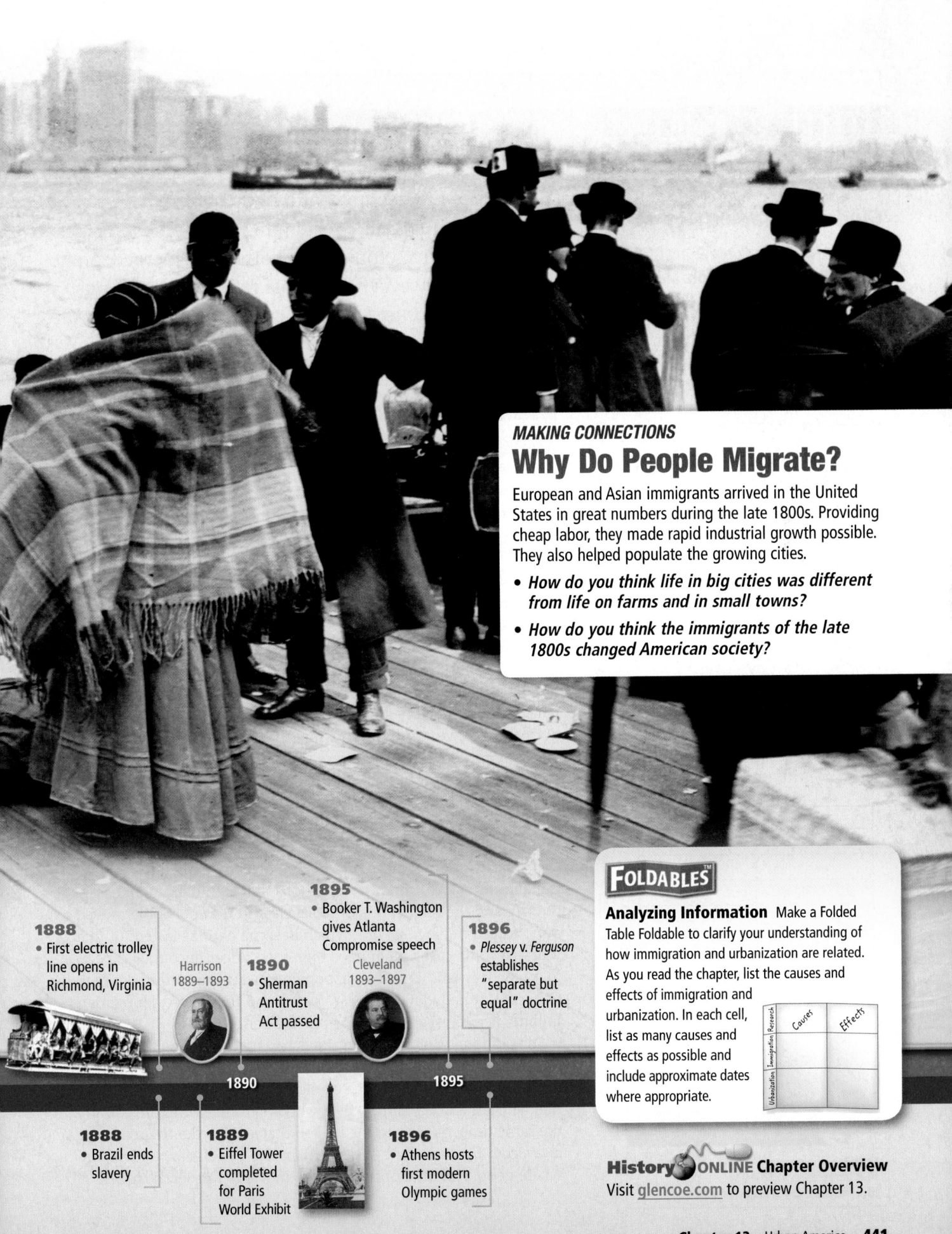

MAKING CONNECTIONS
Why Do People Migrate?

European and Asian immigrants arrived in the United States in great numbers during the late 1800s. Providing cheap labor, they made rapid industrial growth possible. They also helped populate the growing cities.

- *How do you think life in big cities was different from life on farms and in small towns?*

- *How do you think the immigrants of the late 1800s changed American society?*

1888
- First electric trolley line opens in Richmond, Virginia

Harrison 1889–1893

1890
- Sherman Antitrust Act passed

1895
- Booker T. Washington gives Atlanta Compromise speech

Cleveland 1893–1897

1896
- *Plessey* v. *Ferguson* establishes "separate but equal" doctrine

1890

1895

1888
- Brazil ends slavery

1889
- Eiffel Tower completed for Paris World Exhibit

1896
- Athens hosts first modern Olympic games

FOLDABLES™

Analyzing Information Make a Folded Table Foldable to clarify your understanding of how immigration and urbanization are related. As you read the chapter, list the causes and effects of immigration and urbanization. In each cell, list as many causes and effects as possible and include approximate dates where appropriate.

Immigration Research	Causes	Effects
Urbanization		

History ONLINE Chapter Overview
Visit glencoe.com to preview Chapter 13.

Immigration

Guide to Reading

Big Ideas
Trade, War, and Migration Many people from Europe came to the United States to escape war, famine, or persecution or to find better jobs.

Content Vocabulary
- steerage *(p. 443)*
- nativism *(p. 446)*

Academic Vocabulary
- immigrant *(p. 442)*
- ethnic *(p. 444)*

People and Events to Identify
- Ellis Island *(p. 443)*
- Jacob Riis *(p. 444)*
- Angel Island *(p. 445)*
- Chinese Exclusion Act *(p. 447)*

Reading Strategy
Categorizing Complete a graphic organizer similar to the one below by filling in the reasons people left their homelands to immigrate to the United States.

Reasons for Immigrating	
Push Factors	Pull Factors

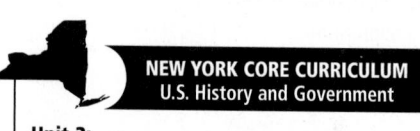

NEW YORK CORE CURRICULUM
U.S. History and Government

Unit 3:
III.B Immigration, 1850–1924
III.C Reactions to the "new" immigration

In the late nineteenth century, a major wave of immigration began. Most immigrants settled in cities, where distinctive ethnic neighborhoods emerged. Some Americans, however, feared that the new immigrants would not adapt to American culture or might be harmful to American society.

Europeans Flood Into America

MAIN Idea Immigrants from Europe came to the United States for many reasons and entered the country through Ellis Island.

HISTORY AND YOU Have you ever been to an ethnic neighborhood where residents have re-created aspects of their homeland? Read on to learn how immigrants adjusted to life in the United States.

Between 1865—the year the Civil War ended—and 1914—the year World War I began—nearly 25 million Europeans immigrated to the United States. By the late 1890s, more than half of all **immigrants** in the United States were from eastern and southern Europe, including Italy, Greece, Austria-Hungary, Russia, and Serbia. This period of immigration is known as "new" immigration. The "old" immigration, which occurred before 1890, had been primarily of people from northern and western Europe. More than 70 percent of these new immigrants were men; they were working either to be able to afford to purchase land in Europe or to bring family members to America.

Europeans immigrated to the United States for many reasons. Many came because American industries had plenty of jobs available. Europe's industrial cities, however, also offered plenty of jobs, so economic factors do not entirely explain why people migrated. Many came in the hope of finding better jobs that would let them escape poverty and the restrictions of social class in Europe. Some moved to avoid forced military service, which in some nations lasted for many years. In some cases, as in Italy, high food prices encouraged people to leave. In Poland and Russia, population pressure led to emigration. Others, especially Jews living in Russia and the Austro-Hungarian Empire, fled to escape religious persecution.

In addition, most European states had made moving to the United States easy. Immigrants were allowed to take their savings with them, and most countries had repealed old laws forcing peasants to stay in their villages and banning skilled workers from leaving the country. At the same time, moving to the United States offered a chance to break away from Europe's class system and move to a democratic nation where people had the opportunity to move up the social ladder.

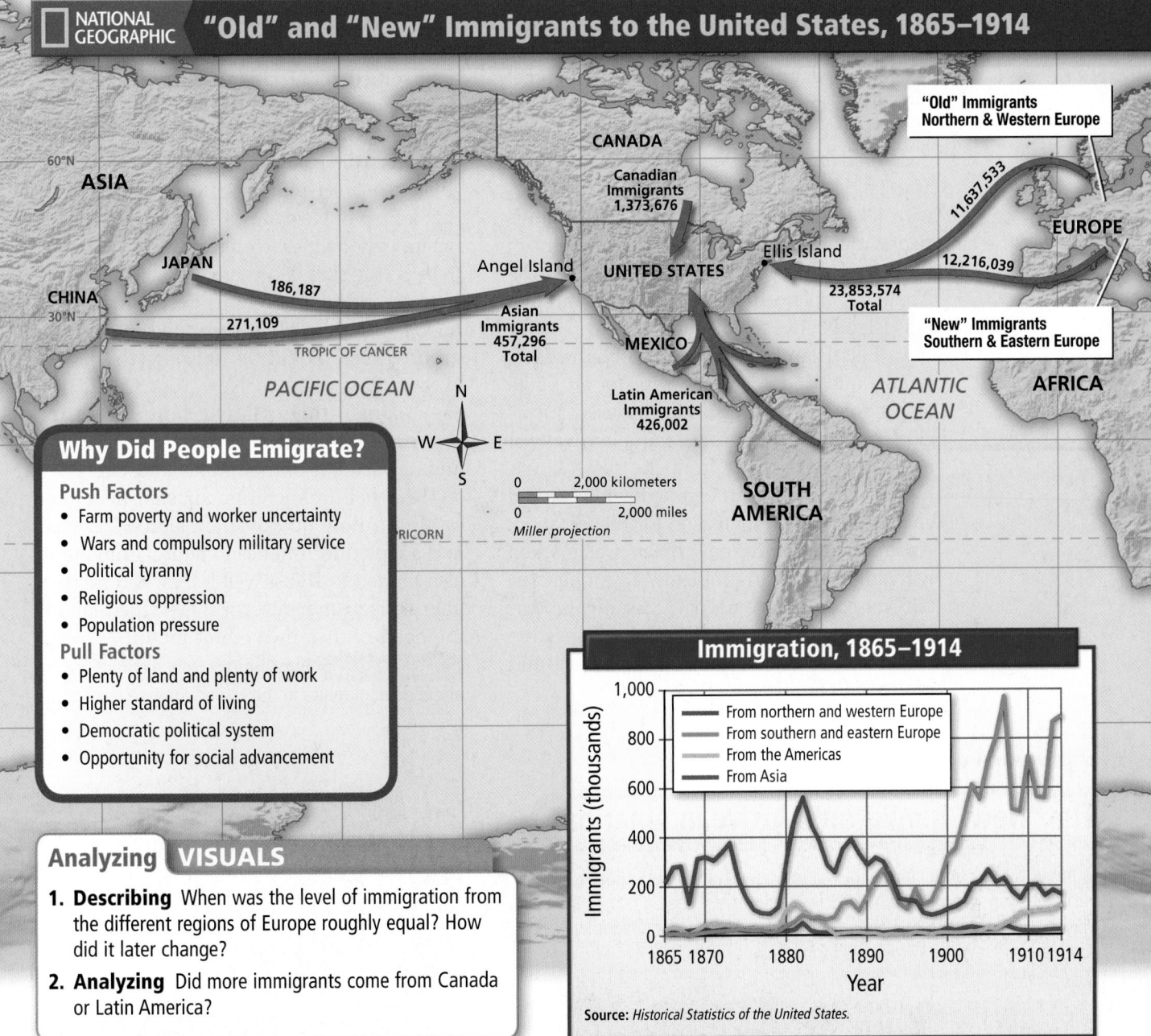

"Old" and "New" Immigrants to the United States, 1865–1914

"Old" Immigrants
Northern & Western Europe

"New" Immigrants
Southern & Eastern Europe

CANADA

Canadian Immigrants 1,373,676

ASIA

JAPAN

CHINA

186,187

271,109

Angel Island

Ellis Island

UNITED STATES

Asian Immigrants 457,296 Total

MEXICO

Latin American Immigrants 426,002

11,637,533

12,216,039

23,853,574 Total

EUROPE

AFRICA

ATLANTIC OCEAN

TROPIC OF CANCER

PACIFIC OCEAN

SOUTH AMERICA

PRICORN

N W E S

0   2,000 kilometers
0   2,000 miles
Miller projection

60°N

30°N

Why Did People Emigrate?

Push Factors
- Farm poverty and worker uncertainty
- Wars and compulsory military service
- Political tyranny
- Religious oppression
- Population pressure

Pull Factors
- Plenty of land and plenty of work
- Higher standard of living
- Democratic political system
- Opportunity for social advancement

Analyzing VISUALS

1. **Describing** When was the level of immigration from the different regions of Europe roughly equal? How did it later change?

2. **Analyzing** Did more immigrants come from Canada or Latin America?

Immigration, 1865–1914

Immigrants (thousands)

1,000
800
600
400
200
0

From northern and western Europe
From southern and eastern Europe
From the Americas
From Asia

1865 1870   1880   1890   1900   1910 1914

Year

Source: *Historical Statistics of the United States.*

The Atlantic Voyage

The voyage to the United States was often very difficult. Most immigrants booked passage in **steerage,** the cheapest accommodations on a steamship. Edward Steiner, an Iowa clergyman who posed as an immigrant in order to write a book on immigration, described the miserable quarters:

PRIMARY SOURCE

"Narrow, steep and slippery stairways lead to it. Crowds everywhere, ill smelling bunks, uninviting washrooms—this is steerage. The odors of scat-tered orange peelings, tobacco, garlic and disinfectants meeting but not blending. No lounge or chairs for comfort, and a continual babble of tongues—this is steerage. The food, which is miserable, is dealt out of huge kettles into the dinner pails provided by the steamship company."

—quoted in *World of Our Fathers*

At the end of a 14-day journey, the passengers usually disembarked at **Ellis Island,** a tiny island in New York Harbor. There, a huge three-story building served as the processing center for many of the immigrants arriving from Europe after 1892.

Ellis Island

Most immigrants passed through Ellis Island in about a day. They would not soon forget their hectic introduction to the United States. A medical examiner who worked there later described how "hour after hour, ship load after ship load ... the stream of human beings with its kaleidoscopic variations was ... hurried through Ellis Island by the equivalent of 'step lively' in every language of the earth." About 12 million immigrants passed through Ellis Island between 1892 and 1954.

In Ellis Island's enormous hall, crowds of immigrants filed past the doctor for an initial inspection. "Whenever a case aroused suspicion," an inspector wrote, "the alien was set aside in a cage apart from the rest ... and his coat lapel or shirt marked with colored chalk" to indicate the reason for the isolation. About one out of five newcomers was marked with an "H" for heart problems, "K" for hernias, "Sc" for scalp problems, or "X" for mental disability. Newcomers who failed the inspection might be separated from their families and returned to Europe.

Ethnic Cities

Many of those who passed these inspections settled in the nation's cities. By the 1890s, immigrants made up a large percentage of the population of major cities, including New York, Chicago, Milwaukee, and Detroit. **Jacob Riis,** a Danish-born journalist, observed in 1890 that a map of New York City, "colored to designate nationalities, would show more stripes than on the skin of a zebra."

In the cities, immigrants lived in neighborhoods that were often separated into **ethnic** groups, such as "Little Italy" or the Jewish "Lower East Side" in New York City. There they spoke their native languages and re-created the churches, synagogues, clubs, and newspapers of their homelands.

How well immigrants adjusted depended partly on how quickly they learned English and adapted to American culture. Immigrants also tended to adjust well if they had marketable skills or money, or if they settled among members of their own ethnic group.

✔ Reading Check **Explaining** How did immigration affect demographics in the United States?

PRIMARY SOURCE
The "New" Immigrants Arrive in America

In the late 1800s, the number of immigrants coming from northwest Europe began to decline, while "new immigrants," fleeing war, poverty, and persecution, began to arrive in large numbers from southern and eastern Europe, and from Asia.

▲ Jewish people migrated to the United States from all across Europe seeking an opportunity to better their lives. Many Jews from Eastern Europe (such as those above) were also fleeing religious persecution.

▲ Many Italian immigrants took jobs as construction workers, bricklayers, and dockworkers in urban areas, but this group is building a railroad, c. 1900.

◀ Many Chinese came to America to escape poverty and civil war. Many helped build railroads. Others set up small businesses. These children were photographed in San Francisco's Chinatown, c. 1900.

Asian Immigration

MAIN Idea Asian immigrants arrived on the West Coast, where they settled mainly in cities.

HISTORY AND YOU Do you know someone who has moved to the United States from Asia? What motivated that person to come here? Read on to learn about the experiences of earlier generations of Asian immigrants.

In the mid-1800s, China's population reached about 430 million, and the country was suffering from severe unemployment, poverty, and famine. Then, in 1850, the Taiping Rebellion erupted in China. This insurrection caused such suffering that thousands of Chinese left for the United States. In the early 1860s, as construction began on the Central Pacific Railroad, the demand for railroad workers led to further Chinese immigration.

Chinese immigrants settled mainly in western cities, where they often worked as laborers or servants or in skilled trades. Others became merchants. Because native-born Americans kept them out of many businesses, some Chinese immigrants opened their own.

Japanese also began immigrating to the United States. Although some came earlier, the number of Japanese immigrants soared upward between 1900 and 1910. As Japan industrialized, economic problems caused many Japanese to leave their homeland for new economic opportunities.

Until 1910 Asian immigrants arriving in San Francisco first stopped at a two-story shed at the wharf. As many as 500 people at a time were often squeezed into this structure, which Chinese immigrants from Canton called *muk uk*, or "wooden house." In January 1910 California opened a barracks on **Angel Island** for Asian immigrants. Most were young men in their teens or twenties, who nervously awaited the results of their immigration hearings. The wait could last for months. On the walls of the barracks, several immigrants wrote anonymous poems in pencil or ink.

✓ **Reading Check** **Making Generalizations** Why did Chinese immigrants come to the United States?

NATIONAL GEOGRAPHIC — Immigration Settlement Patterns

Legend:
- China
- Germany
- Ireland
- Italy
- Japan
- Mexico
- Poland
- Russia
- Scandinavia

Settlement figures in thousands

New York: 480, 425, 182, 165, 66, 42, 7
Massachusetts: 249, 32, 28, 26
Wisconsin: 242, 61, 30, 23
Illinois: 332, 129, 114, 64, 28, 23
Ohio: 204, 55
Pennsylvania: 212, 205, 72, 66, 50
California: 72, 44, 40, 10, 8
Texas: 72, 48

Why Did Immigrants Come to America?

Italians
- cholera epidemic in 1880s
- land shortage for peasants; landlords charge high rent
- food shortages
- poverty, unemployment

East Europeans
- Russians, Poles: land shortages for peasants, unemployment, high taxes; long military draft
- Jews: discrimination, poverty, and recurring pogroms

Chinese
- famine
- land shortage for peasants
- civil war (Taiping rebellion)

Typical Occupations in America

Italians
- unskilled labor—dock work, construction, railroads
- some skilled labor, such as bricklayers, stonemasons, and other trades

East Europeans
- Poles: farmers, coal miners, steel and textile millworkers; meatpacking
- Jews: laborers, garment workers, merchants

Chinese
- railroad and construction workers; some skilled labor
- merchants, small businesses

Analyzing VISUALS

1. **Analyzing Visuals** To which city did most Russian immigrants come to live?
2. **Contrasting** How would you contrast the immigration settlement patterns of Texas and Ohio?

Nativism Resurges

MAIN Idea Economic concerns and religious and ethnic prejudices led some Americans to push for laws restricting immigration.

HISTORY AND YOU In what ways does immigration affect the area in which you live? Read on to learn why nativists tried to stop immigration.

Eventually the wave of immigration led to increased feelings of nativism on the part of many Americans. **Nativism** is an extreme dislike of immigrants by native-born people. It had surfaced during the heavy wave of Irish immigration in the 1840s and 1850s. In the late 1800s, anti-immigrant feelings focused mainly on Asians, Jews, and eastern Europeans.

Nativists opposed immigration for many reasons. Some feared that the influx of Catholics from countries such as Ireland, Italy, and Poland would swamp the mostly Protestant United States. Many labor unions also opposed immigration, arguing that immigrants undermined American workers because they would work for low wages and accept jobs as strikebreakers.

Prejudice Against Catholics

Increased feelings of nativism led to the founding of anti-immigrant organizations. The American Protective Association, founded by Henry Bowers in 1887, was an anti-Catholic organization. Its members vowed not to hire or vote for Catholics.

The Irish were among the immigrants who suffered most from the anti-Catholic feeling. Arriving to escape famine and other hardships, many were illiterate and found only the lowest-paying work as miners, dockhands, ditch-diggers, and factory workers. Irish women worked as cooks, servants, and mill-workers. The dominant Protestant, British culture in America, which considered Irish poverty to be the result of laziness, superstition, and ignorance, had no use for the Catholic Irish.

Although several presidents vetoed legislation that would have limited immigration, prejudice

POLITICAL CARTOONS PRIMARY SOURCE
Prejudice Against Catholic Immigrants

Anti-Catholic prejudice was strong in the United States for most of the 1800s. Many Americans tried to prevent Catholic immigration to the United States, fearing Catholic beliefs were incompatible with American values.

THE AMERICAN RIVER GANGES.

▲ Catholic priests crawl ashore as children are tossed to them by New York politicians in this 1871 cartoon criticizing New York's decision to fund Catholic schools.

PRIMARY SOURCE

"We unite to protect our country and its free institutions against the secret, intolerant, and aggressive efforts . . . by a certain religious political organization to control the government of the United States. . . .

. . . We have men born in several countries remote from this that are as loyal as any native, but they are not Romanists [Catholics]. American loyalty consists in devotion to our Constitution, laws, institutions, flag, and, above all, our public schools, for without intelligence this representative republic will go to pieces. . . . We are opposed to priests and prelates as such 'taking part in elections' and voting their laity as a unit in the interests of a foreign corporation . . ."

—from the platform of the American Protective Association, 1894

DBQ Document-Based Questions

1. **Explaining** What does the American Protective Association believe is incompatible with American citizenship? To what power does the statement refer?

2. **Detecting Bias** How does the cartoon express hostility toward Catholicism? Why might the cartoonist have depicted the public school on the hill in ruins?

against immigrants stimulated the passage of a new federal law. Enacted in 1882, the law banned convicts, paupers, and the mentally disabled from immigrating to the United States. The law also placed a 50¢ per head tax on each newcomer.

Restrictions on Asian Immigration

In the West, anti-Chinese sentiment sometimes led to racial violence. Denis Kearney, himself an Irish immigrant, organized the Workingman's Party of California in the 1870s to fight Chinese immigration. The party won seats in California's legislature and pushed to cut off Chinese immigration.

In 1882 Congress passed the **Chinese Exclusion Act.** The law barred Chinese immigration for 10 years and prevented the Chinese already in the country from becoming citizens. The Chinese in the United States organized letter-writing campaigns, petitioned the president, and even filed suit in federal court, but their efforts failed. Congress renewed the law in 1892 and made it permanent in 1902. It was not repealed until 1943.

On October 11, 1906, in response to rising Japanese immigration, the San Francisco Board of Education ordered "all Chinese, Japanese and Korean children" to attend the racially segregated "Oriental School" in the city's Chinatown neighborhood. (Students of Chinese heritage had been forced to attend racially segregated schools since 1859.) The directive caused an international incident. Japan took great offense at the insulting treatment of its people.

In response, Theodore Roosevelt invited school board leaders to the White House. He proposed a deal. He would limit Japanese immigration, if the school board would rescind its segregation order. Roosevelt then carried out his end of the deal. He began talks with Japan, and negotiated an agreement whereby Japan agreed to curtail the emigration of Japanese to the continental United States. The San Francisco school board then revoked its segregation order. This deal became known as the "Gentleman's Agreement" because it was not a formal treaty and depended on the leaders of both countries to uphold the agreement.

The Literacy Debate

In 1905 Theodore Roosevelt commissioned a study on how immigrants were admitted to the nation. The commission recommended an English literacy test. Two years later, another commission suggested literacy tests—in any language—for immigration. These recommendations reflected the bias of people against the "new immigrants," who were thought to be less intelligent than the "old immigrants." Although Presidents Taft and Wilson both vetoed legislation to require literacy from immigrants, the legislation eventually passed in 1917 over Wilson's second veto. The purpose of the law was to reduce immigration from southeastern European nations.

Reading Check **Explaining** Why did the federal government pass the Chinese Exclusion Act?

Vocabulary

1. **Explain** the significance of: steerage, Ellis Island, Jacob Riis, Angel Island, nativism, Chinese Exclusion Act.

Main Ideas

2. **Listing** Why did European immigrants come to the United States?

3. **Describing** What caused the increase in Chinese immigration in the 1860s?

4. **Organizing** Complete a graphic organizer by listing the reasons nativists opposed immigration to the United States.

Reasons Nativists Opposed Immigration

Critical Thinking

5. **Big Ideas** Where did most immigrants settle in the late 1800s? How did this benefit ethnic groups?

6. **Interpreting** Why did some Americans blame immigrants for the nation's problems?

7. **Analyzing Visuals** Select one of the people featured in any photo in this section. Write a journal entry about his or her experience, based on what you see in the photo.

Writing About History

8. **Descriptive Writing** Imagine that you are an immigrant who arrived in the United States in the 1800s. Write a letter to a relative in your home country describing your feelings during processing at either Ellis Island or Angel Island.

History ONLINE

Study Central™ To review this section, go to glencoe.com and click on Study Central.

ANALYZING PRIMARY SOURCES

Immigration

The United States is a nation of immigrants. In the late nineteenth century, more immigrants arrived on American shores than ever before. Some came from places such as the British Isles and Germany, from which many earlier immigrants had arrived. Others came from southern and eastern Europe, Asia, and other parts of the Americas. As the United States welcomed this mixture of ethnicities, religions, and languages, immigration became a subject of heated political debate.

Study these primary sources and answer the questions that follow.

PRIMARY SOURCE 2

Photograph, 1905

▼ *Immigrants are checked for trachoma and other contagious eye diseases at Ellis Island. The inspector is using a buttonhook, normally used to fasten ladies' gloves, to lift this woman's eyelid. The instrument was "cleaned" between inspections by wiping it on the towel hanging nearby.*

PRIMARY SOURCE 1

Political Cartoon, 1880

▼ *"Welcome to All," by J. Keppler,* Puck *(1880)*

PRIMARY SOURCE 3

Memoir Reflecting on Arrival at Ellis Island

"A group of Slovenian immigrants, of which this writer was one, arrived in New York from . . . Austria. . . . It was a beautiful morning in May 1906. After leaving the French ship LA TOURAINE, we were transported to Ellis Island for landing and inspection. There we were 'sorted out' as to the country we came from and placed in a 'stall' with the letter 'A' above us. ('A' was for Austria.)

There were at least a hundred Slovenian immigrants. We separated ourselves, as was the custom at home—men on the right and women and children on the left. All of us were waiting to leave for all parts of the United States.

The day was warm and we were very thirsty. An English-speaking immigrant asked the near-by guard where we could get a drink of water. The guard withdrew and returned shortly with a pail of water, which he set before the group of women. Some men stepped forward quickly to have a drink, but the guard pushed them back saying: 'Ladies first!' When the women learned what the guard had said, they were dumbfounded, for in Slovenia . . . women always were second to men. . . . Happy at the sudden turn of events, one elderly lady stepped forward, holding a dipper of water, and proposed this toast:

'Živijo Amerika, kjer so ženske prve!'
(Long live America, where women are first!)"

—Marie Priesland, recalling her arrival in the United States

PRIMARY SOURCE 4

Magazine Article, 1903

"When I went to work for that American family I could not speak a word of English, and I did not know anything about housework. The family consisted of husband, wife and two children. They were very good to me and paid me $3.50 a week, of which I could save $3.

"I did not understand what the lady said to me, but she showed me how to cook, wash, iron, sweep, dust, make beds, wash dishes, clean windows, paint and brass, polish the knives and forks, etc., by doing the things herself and then overseeing my efforts to imitate her. . . . In six months I had learned how to do the work of our house quite well, and . . . I had also learned English. . . . I worked for two years as a servant . . . . and I was now ready to start in business."

—Chinese immigrant Lee Chew, reflecting on his first years in America

PRIMARY SOURCE 5

Questions Asked Immigrants, c. 1907

U.S. IMMIGRATION SERVICE		
1	Calling or Occupation?	farmer
2	Able to Read?	yes
3	Able to Write?	yes
4	Nationality?	Germany
5	Whether having a ticket to final destination?	yes
6	By whom was passage paid?	father
7	Whether in possession of $50, and if less, how much?	$20
8	Whether going to join a relative or friend?	friend
9	Ever in prison or almshouse or institution for care or treatment of the insane or supported by charity?	no
10	Whether a Polygamist?	no
11	Whether an Anarchist?	no
12	Whether coming by reason of any offer, solicitation, promise, or agreement, express or implied, to labor in the United States? Condition of Health, Mental and Physical.	no no health problem
13	Deformed or Crippled. Nature, length of time and cause.	no

PRIMARY SOURCE 6

Political Cartoon, 1896

"*The Immigrant: The Stranger at Our Gate*," *The Ram's Horn (April 25, 1896)*
Emigrant: "Can I come in?"
Uncle Sam: "I 'spose you can; there's no law to keep you out."

THE STRANGER AT OUR GATE.
EMIGRANT.—Can I come in?   UNCLE SAM.—I 'spose you can; there's no law to keep you out.

DBQ Document-Based Questions

1. **Analyzing Visuals** Compare the political cartoons in Sources 1 and 6. How do the two depictions differ on the reasons why immigrants left their homeland and why they came to the United States?

2. **Making Inferences** Why did immigrants have to undergo health inspections? What do you suppose happened when an immigrant was found to have a contagious illness?

3. **Interpreting** Why do you think the author of Source 3 remembered Ellis Island so clearly decades later?

4. **Evaluating** According to Lee Chew in Source 4, what were some factors that helped him adapt as an immigrant and become a small business owner?

5. **Making Inferences** Study the questions listed in Source 5. Why do you think immigrants were required to answer these questions?

Section 2

Urbanization

Guide to Reading

Big Ideas
Government and Society The growth of and problems in major cities led to political machines that controlled local politics.

Content Vocabulary
- skyscraper *(p. 450)*
- tenement *(p. 453)*
- political machine *(p. 455)*
- party boss *(p. 455)*
- graft *(p. 455)*

Academic Vocabulary
- incentive *(p. 450)*
- trigger *(p. 455)*

People and Events to Identify
- Louis Sullivan *(p. 451)*
- George Plunkitt *(p. 455)*
- William "Boss" Tweed *(p. 455)*

Reading Strategy
Organizing As you read about urbanization in the United States in the late 1800s, complete a graphic organizer similar to the one below by filling in the problems the nation's cities faced.

Urban Problems

NEW YORK CORE CURRICULUM
U.S. History and Government

Unit 3:
III.A.1.a Attractions: jobs, education, culture, public education system
III.A.1.b Problems (slums, increased crime, inadequate water and sanitation services)
III.A.1.c Skyscrapers and elevators: tenements and walk-ups
III.A.2.d Living conditions: company towns and urban slums

Native-born Americans and immigrants were drawn to cities by the jobs available in America's growing industries. The new, modern cities had skyscrapers, public transportation systems, and neighborhoods divided by social class. In many cities, political machines controlled city government.

Americans Migrate to the Cities

MAIN Idea Rural Americans and immigrants moved to the cities where skyscrapers and mass transit were developed to deal with congestion.

HISTORY AND YOU Have you ever ridden the bus, subway, or railway system? How do you think your ride to school or the store would be different without mass transportation? Read on to learn why cities developed mass transportation systems.

After the Civil War, the urban population of the United States grew from around 10 million in 1870 to more than 30 million in 1900. New York City, which had more than 800,000 inhabitants in 1860, grew to almost 3.5 million by 1900. During the same period, Chicago swelled from 109,000 residents to more than 1.6 million. The United States had only 131 cities with populations of 2,500 or more residents in 1840; by 1900, there were more than 1,700 such urban areas.

Most of the immigrants who poured into the United States in the late 1800s lacked both the money to buy farms and the education to obtain higher-paying jobs. Thus, they settled in the nation's growing cities, where they toiled long hours for little pay in the rapidly expanding factories of the United States. Despite the harshness of their new lives, most immigrants found that the move had improved their standard of living.

Rural Americans also began moving to the cities at this time. Farmers moved to cities because urban areas offered more and better-paying jobs than did rural areas. Cities had much to offer, too—bright lights, running water, and modern plumbing, plus attractions such as museums, libraries, and theaters.

The physical appearance of cities also changed dramatically. As city populations grew, demand raised the price of land, creating the **incentive** to build upward rather than outward. Soon, tall, steel frame buildings called **skyscrapers** began to appear. Chicago's ten-story Home Insurance Building, built in 1885, was the first skyscraper, but other buildings quickly dwarfed it. New York City, with its business district on the narrow island of Manhattan, boasted more skyscrapers than any other city in the world. With limited space, New Yorkers had to build up, not out.

TECHNOLOGY & HISTORY

The Technology of Urbanization

Before the mid-1800s, few buildings exceeded four or five stories. To make wooden and stone buildings taller required enormously thick walls in the lower levels. This changed when steel companies began mass-producing cheap steel girders and steel cable.

Completed in 1913, the Woolworth Building is 792 feet high. It was the tallest building in the world until 1930.

A steel frame carries the weight, allowing the building to be much taller than stone or wood structures.

▲ Steel Cable

Steel also changed the way bridges were built. Engineers could now suspend bridges from steel towers using thick steel cables. Using this technique, engineer John Roebling designed New York's Brooklyn Bridge— the world's largest suspension bridge at the time. It was completed in 1883.

With steel beams instead of walls supporting the building, windows could be larger.

► Elevators

Elisha Otis invented the safety elevator in 1852. By the late 1880s, the first electric elevators had been installed, making tall buildings practical.

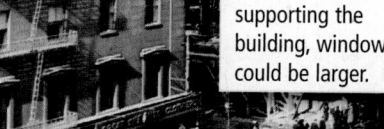

Analyzing VISUALS

1. **Theorizing** What other technologies were necessary in order to build modern skyscrapers?
2. **Predicting** What long-term effects do you think the new building technologies had on cities?

No one contributed more to the design of skyscrapers than Chicago's **Louis Sullivan.** "What people are within, the buildings express without," explained Sullivan, whose lofty structures featured simple lines and spacious windows using new, durable plate glass.

To move people around cities quickly, various kinds of mass transit developed. At first, almost all cities relied on the horsecar, a railroad car pulled by horses. In 1890 horsecars moved about 70 percent of urban traffic in the United States.

More than 20 cities, beginning with San Francisco in 1873, installed cable cars, which were pulled along tracks by underground cables. Then, in 1887, engineer Frank J. Sprague developed the electric trolley car. The country's first electric trolley line opened the following year in Richmond, Virginia.

In the largest cities, congestion became so bad that engineers began looking for ways to move mass transit off the streets. Chicago responded by building an elevated railroad, while Boston, followed by New York, built the first subway systems.

✔ Reading Check **Summarizing** What new technologies helped people in the late 1800s get to and from work?

Separation by Class

MAIN Idea In the cities, society was separated by classes, with the upper, middle, and working classes living in different neighborhoods.

HISTORY AND YOU Do you know the history of certain neighborhoods in your city or town? Can you see where the classes were divided? Read on to learn how each class lived in the cities.

In the growing cities, the wealthy people and the working class lived in different parts of town. So, too, did members of the middle class. The boundaries between neighborhoods were quite definite and can still be seen in many American cities today.

High Society

During the last half of the 1800s, the wealthiest families established fashionable districts in the heart of a city. Americans with enough money could choose to construct homes in the style of a feudal castle, an English manor house, a French château, a Tuscan villa, or a Persian pavilion. In Chicago, merchant and real estate developer Potter Palmer chose a castle. In New York, Cornelius Vanderbilt's grandson commissioned a $3 million French château with a two-story dining room, a gymnasium, and a marble bathroom.

As their homes grew larger, wealthy women managed an increasing number of servants, such as cooks, maids, butlers, coachmen, nannies, and chauffeurs, and spent a great deal of money on social activities. In an age in which many New Yorkers lived on $500 a year, socialite hostess Cornelia Sherman Martin spent $360,000 on a dance.

Middle-Class Gentility

American industrialization also helped expand the middle class. The nation's rising middle class included doctors, lawyers, engineers, managers, social workers, architects, and teachers. Many people in the middle class moved away from the central city so as to escape the crime and pollution and be able to afford larger homes. Some took advantage of the new commuter rail lines to move to "streetcar suburbs."

PRIMARY SOURCE
Urban Society

Urban industrial society in the late 1800s was divided into social classes. The upper class and middle class lived well, but conditions for the working class and poor were often abysmal.

THE UPPER CLASS

▲ The upper class could afford elaborate mansions and many servants. Men typically owned or managed large businesses. Women almost never worked. Clothing was elaborate and expensive. Events, such as afternoon tea in their garden (above), required formal dress and shows they had substantial leisure time.

THE MIDDLE CLASS

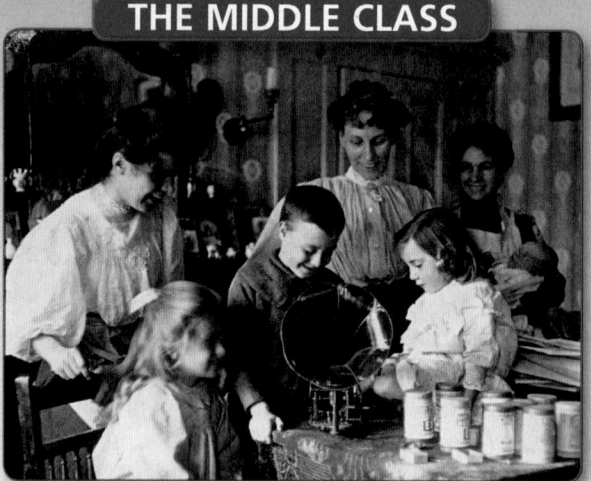

▲ Middle class families could generally afford their own homes and better quality clothing. Women rarely worked—and if they did it was usually because they wanted a career, not out of necessity. Many families had at least one servant (shown above in back holding the baby) and enough money left over to buy luxuries, such as the new gramophone shown above.

In the late nineteenth century, most middle class families had at least one live-in servant. This gave the woman of the house more time to pursue activities outside the home. "Women's clubs" became popular. At first, these clubs focused on social and educational activities. Over time, however, "club women" became very active in charitable and reform activities. In Chicago, for example, the Women's Club helped establish juvenile courts and exposed the terrible conditions at the Cook County Insane Asylum.

The Working Class

Few families in the urban working class could hope to own a home. Most spent their lives in crowded **tenements,** or apartment buildings. The first tenement in the United States was built in 1839. In New York, three out of four residents squeezed into tenements, dark and crowded multi-family apartments. To supplement the average industrial worker's annual income of $445, many families rented precious space to a boarder. Zalmen Yoffeh, a journalist, lived in a New York tenement as a child. He recalled:

History ONLINE
Student Web Activity Visit glencoe.com and complete the activity on tenement life.

The Family Economy

Within the working class, some people were better off than others. White native-born men earned higher wages than African American men, immigrants, and women.

One economist estimated that 64 percent of working class families relied on more than one wage earner in 1900. In some cases, the whole family worked, including the children. The dangerous working conditions faced by child workers, and the fact that they were not in school, alarmed many reformers.

THE WORKING CLASS

▲ Most working class families lived in apartments, often only a single room in size. They had no servants, and often husbands and wives both had to work.

WORKING WOMEN

▶ Many young women, such as this one making a straw hat in a factory, worked long hours for little pay.

URBAN POVERTY

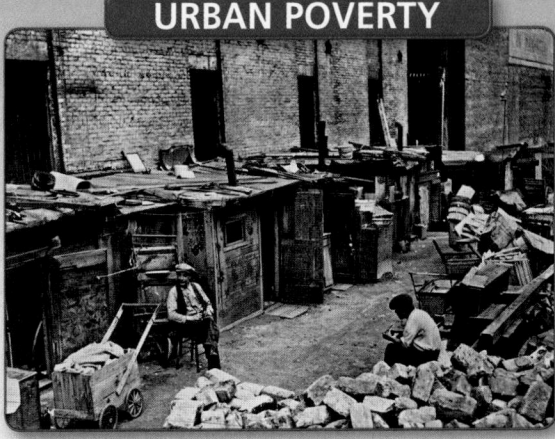

▲ Unable to afford homes, the urban poor slept on the street or built shacks in back alleys like these in New York City in the early 1900s.

Analyzing VISUALS

1. **Comparing and Contrasting** What do the upper class and middle class have in common compared to the working class and poor?

2. **Drawing Conclusions** How effective was industrial society at meeting people's needs?

A growing number of women took jobs outside the home. Native-born white women typically had more years of education than other women. Thus, many used their literacy to work as teachers or do clerical work.

The largest source of employment for women, however, remained domestic service. Immigrant women often worked as domestic servants in the North; African American women usually worked as domestic servants in the South. Such work involved long hours, low wages, and social isolation.

When people were physically unable to work, they had to rely on family members or charity. When a worker was maimed or killed on the job, there was usually no compensation. Most older Americans lived with family members. Nearly 70 percent of those 65 or older lived with their grown children. A growing number, however, lived independently or in homes for the aged.

Reading Check **Explaining** Who was in the "middle class" in the late 1800s? Where did they live?

Urban Problems

MAIN Idea Major problems plagued the cities; political machines provided help for some residents but were frequently corrupt.

HISTORY AND YOU What kinds of programs are used in your area to deal with urban problems? Read about political machines and how they ran city government.

City living posed the risks of crime, violence, fire, disease, and pollution. The rapid growth of cities only made these problems worse and complicated the ability of urban governments to respond to these problems.

Crime and Pollution

Crime was a growing problem in American cities. Minor criminals, such as pickpockets, swindlers, and thieves, thrived in crowded urban living conditions. Major crimes multiplied as well. From 1880 to 1900, the murder rate jumped sharply from 25 per million people to more than 100 per million people.

POLITICAL CARTOONS   PRIMARY SOURCE
Were Political Machines Bad for Cities?

Critics of political machines said that they took bribes and gave contracts to friends, robbing cities of resources. Defenders argued that they provided services and kept the city running.

EMPTY.   "WHAT ARE YOU GOING TO DO ABOUT IT?"   FULL.

EMPTY TO THE WORKMEN.   THE FOUR MASTERS THAT EMPTIED IT.

▲ *Workers in New York find the city treasury empty, while behind the scenes, Boss Tweed and other city politicians enjoy a sumptuous feast.*

DBQ   **Document-Based Questions**

1. **Analyzing Primary Sources** How does Plunkitt say he learns of people in need in his district?

2. **Determining Cause and Effect** What is the result of Plunkitt's care for the needy in his district?

Alcohol contributed to violent crime, both inside and outside the home. Danish immigrant Jacob Riis, who documented slum life in his 1890 book *How the Other Half Lives,* accused saloons of "breeding poverty," corrupting politics, bringing suffering to the wives and children of drunkards, and fostering "the corruption of the child" by selling beer to minors.

Disease and pollution posed even bigger threats. Improper sewage disposal contaminated city drinking water and **triggered** epidemics of typhoid fever and cholera. Though flush toilets and sewer systems existed in the 1870s, pollution remained a severe problem as horse manure was left in the streets, smoke belched from chimneys, and soot and ash accumulated from coal and wood fires.

Machine Politics

The **political machine,** an informal political group designed to gain and keep power, came about partly because cities had grown much faster than their governments. New city dwellers needed jobs, housing, food, heat, and police protection. In exchange for votes, political machines and the **party bosses** who ran them eagerly provided these necessities.

Graft and Fraud The party bosses who ran the political machines also controlled the city's finances. Many machine politicians grew rich as the result of fraud or **graft**—getting money through dishonest or questionable means. **George Plunkitt,** one of New York City's most powerful party bosses, defended what he called "honest graft." For example, a politician might find out in advance where a new park was to be built and buy the land near the site. The politician would then sell the land to the city for a profit. As Plunkitt stated, "I see my opportunity, and I take it."

Outright fraud occurred when party bosses accepted bribes from contractors who were supposed to compete fairly to win contracts to build streets, sewers, and buildings. Corrupt bosses also sold permits to their friends to operate public utilities, such as railroads, waterworks, and power systems.

Tammany Hall Tammany Hall, the New York City Democratic political machine, was the most infamous such organization. **William "Boss" Tweed** was its leader during the 1860s and 1870s. Tweed's corruptness led to a prison sentence in 1874.

City machines often controlled all the city services, including the police department. In St. Louis, the "boss" never feared arrest when he called out to his supporters at the police-supervised voting booth, "Are there any more repeaters out here that want to vote again?"

Opponents of political machines, such as political cartoonist Thomas Nast, blasted bosses for their corruption. Defenders, though, argued that machines provided necessary services and helped to assimilate the masses of new city dwellers.

Reading Check **Evaluating** Why did political machines help city dwellers in the late 1800s?

Section 2 REVIEW

Vocabulary

1. **Explain** the significance of: skyscraper, Louis Sullivan, tenement, political machine, party boss, graft, George Plunkitt, William "Boss" Tweed.

Main Ideas

2. **Identifying** What technologies made the building of skyscrapers possible?

3. **Comparing** How did the living conditions of the upper, middle, and the working classes in the late 1800s compare?

4. **Organizing** Complete the graphic organizer below by listing the effects of many Americans moving from rural to urban areas in the late 1800s.

```
                              Effects
 ┌──────────┐            _____
 │ Migration │  ───────▶  _____
 └──────────┘            _____
```

Critical Thinking

5. **Big Ideas** How did political machines respond to the needs of the people?

6. **Synthesizing** Why were pollution and sewage a problem in American cities in the late 1800s?

7. **Analyzing Visuals** Look at the photos on pages 452–453. How did industrialization affect the class structure in the United States?

Writing About History

8. **Persuasive Writing** Take on the role of an urban planner in a major city in the late 1800s. Write a letter to members of the city government listing specific reasons for the importance of setting aside city land for parks and recreational areas.

History ONLINE

Study Central™ To review this section, go to glencoe.com and click on Study Central.

GEOGRAPHY & HISTORY

Italian Immigration to America

Italians from southern Italy were among the largest group of the "new immigrants"—the peoples who flooded American shores between 1880 and 1920. In Italy, most were poor peasants who worked for absentee landlords and lived in extreme poverty. They were often illiterate and had never traveled even as far as the next village. Leaving for America was daunting. "Make yourself courage"—those were the last words one boy heard his father say as they said goodbye in Naples.

How Did Geography Shape Urban Life?

In New York City, these peasant-immigrants congregated in Little Italy in lower Manhattan. They would find an apartment on the street where people from their village in Italy lived. In 1910, as many as 40,000 people were packed in a 17-block area of Little Italy. As they mingled with other Italians, they began thinking of themselves as Italians, not Neapolitans (from Naples) or Sicilians (from Sicily).

New York's Little Italy bustled with peddlers, bakers, and laborers, but also with immigrants moving in or out of the area. Italian families were hardworking and thrifty. As soon as possible, they moved to cleaner, sunnier places, such as Brooklyn or Long Island. By 1914, one reformer said there were at least 1500 lawyers, 500 physicians, and a growing number of merchants, bankers, and businessmen in New York City who were of Italian heritage. It was a very American success story.

Women worked long hours. They went out once or even twice a day to shop from pushcarts for their meals. They often cooked and did the washing for their family and for male boarders, too.

Analyzing GEOGRAPHY

1. **Place** What drew Italian immigrants to specific areas of New York City?
2. **Movement** What years represented the peak period for the new immigrants to the United States?

Mulberry Street was the heart of Little Italy. Neapolitans (people from Naples) tended to settle on Mulberry Street, while Sicilians crowded the tenements on Elizabeth Street two blocks away.

Around 1900, roughly 4,300 tenement apartments were occupied with large families who lived in just a few rooms.

Street vendors often sold foods that were popular in Italy. They were very busy during holidays. In Little Italy, one of the biggest holidays was the feast of Saint Gennaro, patron saint of Naples—still celebrated in Little Italy in New York today.

Bread was often sold on the streets because tenement ovens could not produce the traditional Italian crust. Young children ran many errands, like buying food and gathering wood for fuel.

Section 3

The Gilded Age

Guide to Reading

Big Ideas
Past and Present Ideas about wealth during the last part of the 1800s continue to affect society today.

Content Vocabulary
- individualism *(p. 458)*
- Social Darwinism *(p. 459)*
- philanthropy *(p. 460)*
- settlement house *(p. 467)*
- Americanization *(p. 467)*

Academic Vocabulary
- evolution *(p. 459)*
- publish *(p. 461)*

People and Events to Identify
- Gilded Age *(p. 458)*
- Gospel of Wealth *(p. 460)*
- Mark Twain *(p. 461)*
- Social Gospel *(p. 466)*
- Jane Addams *(p. 467)*

Reading Strategy
Categorizing Complete a graphic organizer similar to the one below by filling in the main idea of each of the theories and movements listed.

Theory or Movement	Main Idea
Social Darwinism	
Laissez-Faire	
Gospel of Wealth	
Realism	

NEW YORK CORE CURRICULUM
U.S. History and Government

Unit 3:
II.D.3 Sherman Antitrust Act, 1890
III.A.1.d Social Darwinism, increased class division, conspicuous consumption, social conscience, philanthropy
III.A.5 Art and literature (Mark Twain)
III.B.5 "Americanization" process
Unit 4:
I.B.2.a Social settlement movement and the problems of poverty (Jacob Riis, Jane Addams)

The industrialization of the United States led to new art and literature and new ideas about government's role in society. Social Darwinists believed society developed through "survival of the fittest." Other Americans thought steps needed to be taken to help the less fortunate.

Social Darwinism

MAIN Idea Individualism and Social Darwinism shaped Americans' attitudes toward industrial society.

HISTORY AND YOU Do you think each individual person should be left on his or her own to succeed, or should people help those who fall behind? Read to learn about people who applied the notion of "survival of the fittest" to human society.

In 1873 Mark Twain and Charles Warner wrote a novel entitled *The Gilded Age: A Tale of Today*. Historians later adopted the term and applied it to the era in American history that began about 1870 and ended around 1900. The era was in many ways a time of marvels. Amazing new inventions led to rapid industrial growth. Cities expanded to sizes never seen before. Masses of workers thronged the streets. Skyscrapers reached to the sky, electric lights banished the darkness, and wealthy entrepreneurs built spectacular mansions.

By calling this era the **Gilded Age,** Twain and Warner were sounding an alarm. Something is gilded if it is covered with gold on the outside but made of cheaper material inside. A gilded age might appear to sparkle, but critics pointed to corruption, poverty, crime, and great disparities in wealth between the rich and the poor.

Whether the era was golden or merely gilded, it was certainly a time of great cultural activity. Industrialism and urbanization altered the way Americans looked at themselves and their society, and these changes gave rise to new values, new art, and new entertainment.

The Idea of Individualism

One of the strongest beliefs of the era—and one that remains strong today—was the idea of **individualism.** Many Americans firmly believed that no matter how humble their origins, they could rise in society and go as far as their talents and commitment would take them. No one expressed the idea of individualism better than Horatio Alger, who wrote more than 100 "rags-to-riches" novels. In his books, a poor person goes to the big city and, through a combination of hard work and luck,

PRIMARY SOURCE

The Gospel of Wealth

"In bestowing charity, the main consideration should be to help those who will help themselves; to provide part of the means by which those who desire to improve may do so; to give those who desire to rise the aids by which they may rise; to assist, but rarely or never to do all. Neither the individual nor the race is improved by almsgiving. Those worthy of assistance, except in rare cases, seldom require assistance. The really valuable men of the race never do, except in cases of accident or sudden change.... He is the only true reformer who is as careful and as anxious not to aid the unworthy as he is to aid the worthy, and, perhaps, even more so, for in almsgiving more injury is probably done by rewarding vice than by relieving virtue.... "

—Andrew Carnegie, quoted in *The North American Review*, June 1889

PRIMARY SOURCE

"Robert was very different. He inherited from his father an unusual amount of courage and self-reliance, and if one avenue was closed to him, he at once set out to find another. It is of this class that successful men are made, and we have hopes that Robert will develop into a prosperous and successful man."

—from Horatio Alger, *Brave and Bold*

DBQ **Document-Based Questions**

1. **Analyzing Primary Sources** What does Carnegie believe is the way to dignify the lives of rich people?

2. **Describing** On what does Alger base Robert's chances of success? Do you agree with his criteria? Why or why not?

becomes successful. His popular books convinced many young people that no matter how many obstacles they faced, success was possible.

Social Darwinism

Another powerful idea of the era was **Social Darwinism.** This philosophy, loosely derived from Darwin's theories, strongly reinforced the idea of individualism.

Herbert Spencer British philosopher Herbert Spencer applied Charles Darwin's theory of **evolution** and natural selection to human society. In his 1859 book *On the Origin of Species by Means of Natural Selection*, Darwin argued that plant and animal life had evolved over the years by a process he called natural selection. In this process, those species that cannot adapt to the environment in which they live gradually die out, while those that do adapt thrive and live on.

Spencer took this theory intended to explain developments over millions of years and argued that human society also evolved through competition and natural selection. He argued that society progressed and became better because only the fittest people survived. Spencer and others, such as American scholar William Graham Sumner, who shared his views, became known as Social Darwinists, and their ideas became known as Social Darwinism. "Survival of the fittest" became the catchphrase of their philosophy.

Social Darwinism also paralleled the economic doctrine of laissez-faire that opposed any government programs that interfered with business. Not surprisingly, industrial leaders heartily embraced the theory. John D. Rockefeller maintained that survival of the fittest, as demonstrated by the growth of huge businesses like his own Standard Oil, was "merely the working out of the law of nature and the law of God."

Darwinism and the Church For many devout Christians, however, Darwin's conclusions were upsetting and offensive. They rejected the theory of evolution because they believed it contradicted the Bible's account of creation. Some ministers, however, concluded that evolution may have been God's way of creating the world. One of the most famous ministers of the era, Henry Ward Beecher, called himself a "Christian evolutionist."

Carnegie's Gospel of Wealth Andrew Carnegie advocated a gentler version of Social Darwinism that he called the **Gospel of Wealth.** This philosophy held that wealthy Americans should engage in **philanthropy** and use their great fortunes to create the conditions that would help people help themselves. Building schools and hospitals, for example, was better than giving handouts to the poor. Carnegie himself helped fund the creation of public libraries in cities across the nation because libraries provided the information people needed to get ahead in life.

✔ Reading Check **Summarizing** What was the main idea of Social Darwinism?

A Changing Culture

MAIN Idea Artists and writers began portraying life in America more realistically, and cities offered new forms of entertainment.

HISTORY AND YOU Have you read Mark Twain's *The Adventures of Huckleberry Finn*? Read to learn about how Twain portrayed American life in a realistic way.

The late 1800s was a period of great cultural change for writers and artists, and for many urban Americans who sought new forms of entertainment.

Realism

A new movement in art and literature called realism began in the 1800s. Just as Darwin tried to explain the natural world scientifically, artists and writers tried to portray the world realistically. European realists included Edgar Degas and Edouard Manet. Perhaps the best known American realist painter was Thomas Eakins. In realistic detail, he painted young men rowing and athletes playing baseball, and he showed surgeons and scientists in action.

PRIMARY SOURCE
Realism in Art and Literature

Realist writers and artists did not want to portray people and the world idealistically. Instead they sought to present things as accurately as possible.

PRIMARY SOURCE

"'Say, who is you? Whar is you? Dog my cats ef I didn' hear sumf'n. Well, I know what I's gwyne to do: I's gwyne to set down here and listen tell I hears it agin.'"

So he set down on the ground betwixt me and Tom. He leaned his back up against a tree, and stretched his legs out till one of them most touched one of mine. My nose begun to itch. It itched till the tears come into my eyes. But I dasn't scratch. Then it begun to itch on the inside. Next I got to itching underneath. I didn't know how I was going to set still. This miserableness went on as much as six or seven minutes; but it seemed a sight longer than that."

—from *The Adventures of Huckleberry Finn* by Mark Twain

▲ Realist painters did not generally choose heroic or historical topics for their art. Instead they preferred to depict ordinary people doing ordinary things. Thomas Eakins, perhaps the best-known American realist, depicted various aspects of American life, including a carriage ride by the wealthy (above) or a professional baseball game (right).

Writers also attempted to capture the world as they saw it. In several novels, William Dean Howells presented realistic descriptions of American life. For example, his novel *The Rise of Silas Lapham* (1885) described the attempts of a self-made man to enter Boston society. Also an influential literary critic, Howells was the first to declare **Mark Twain** an incomparable American genius.

Twain, whose real name was Samuel Clemens, **published** his masterpiece, *The Adventures of Huckleberry Finn*, in 1884. In this novel, the title character and his friend Jim, an escaped slave, float down the Mississippi River on a raft. Twain wrote in local dialect with a lively sense of humor. He had written a true American novel, in which the setting, subject, characters, and style were clearly American.

Popular Culture

Popular culture changed considerably in the late 1800s. Industrialization improved the standard of living for many people, enabling them to spend money on entertainment and recreation. Increasingly, urban Americans divided their lives into separate units—that of

For examples of literature from the Gilded Age, read excerpts from the writings of Mark Twain and Carl Sandburg on pages R70–71 in **American Literature Library.**

work and that of home. People began "going out" to public entertainment.

The Saloon In cities, saloons often outnumbered groceries and meat markets. As a place for social gathering, saloons played a major role in the lives of male workers. Saloons offered drinks, free toilets, water for horses, and free newspapers for customers. They even offered the first "free lunch": salty food that made patrons thirsty and eager to drink more. Saloons also served as political centers and saloonkeepers were often key figures in political machines.

Amusement Parks and Sports Working-class families and single adults could find entertainment at new amusement parks such as New York's Coney Island. Amusements such as water slides and railroad rides cost only a nickel or dime.

Watching professional sports also became popular during the late 1800s. Formed in 1869, the first professional baseball team was the Cincinnati Red Stockings. Other cities soon fielded their own teams. In 1903 the first official World Series was played between the Boston Red Sox and the Pittsburgh Pirates. Football also gained in popularity and by the late 1800s had spread to public colleges.

As work became less strenuous, many people looked for activities involving physical exercise. Tennis, golf, and croquet became popular. In 1891 James Naismith, athletic director for a college in Massachusetts, invented a new indoor game called basketball.

Vaudeville and Ragtime Adapted from French theater, vaudeville took on an American flavor in the early 1880s with its hodgepodge of animal acts, acrobats, and dancers. The fast-paced shows went on continuously all day and night.

Like vaudeville, ragtime music echoed the hectic pace of city life. Its syncopated rhythms grew out of the music of riverside honky-tonks, saloon pianists, and banjo players, using the patterns of African American music. Scott Joplin, one of the most important African American ragtime composers, became known as the "King of Ragtime." He wrote his most famous piece, "The Maple Leaf Rag," in 1899.

✔ Reading Check **Describing** What was the importance of the saloon in city life?

Analyzing VISUALS DBQ

1. **Analyzing** How does Twain's writing reflect a realist approach to writing?
2. **Making Inferences** Why might Realist art have become popular in the late 1800s?

Politics in Washington

MAIN Idea The two major parties were closely competitive in the late 1800s; tariff rates and big business regulation were hotly debated political issues.

HISTORY AND YOU Have you ever considered getting a job working for the government once you graduate? Read to learn why you will have to take an examination if you want a government job.

After President James A. Garfield was elected in 1880, many of his supporters tried to claim the "spoils of office"—the government jobs that are handed out following an election victory. President Garfield did not believe in the spoils system. One of these job seekers made daily trips to the White House in the spring of 1881 asking for a job. He was repeatedly rejected. Reasoning that he would have a better chance for a job if Vice President Chester A. Arthur were president, this man shot President Garfield on July 2, 1881. Weeks later, Garfield died from his wounds.

Civil Service Reform

For many, Garfield's assassination highlighted the need to reform the political system. Traditionally, under the spoils system, elected politicians extended patronage—the power to reward supporters by giving them government jobs. Many Americans believed the system made government inefficient and corrupt. In the late 1870s, reformers had begun pushing him for an end to patronage.

When Rutherford B. Hayes became president in 1877, he tried to end patronage by firing officials who had been given their jobs because of their support of the party and replacing them with reformers. His actions divided the Republican Party between "Stalwarts" (who supported patronage) and the "Halfbreeds" (who opposed it), and no reforms were passed. In 1880 the Republicans nominated James Garfield, a "Halfbreed," for president and Chester A. Arthur, a "Stalwart," for vice president. Despite the internal feud over patronage, the Republicans managed to win the election, only to have Garfield assassinated a few months later.

Garfield's assassination turned public opinion against the spoils system. In 1883 Congress responded by passing the Pendleton Act. This law required that some jobs be filled by competitive written examinations, rather than through patronage. This marked the beginning of professional civil service—a system where most government workers are given jobs based on their qualifications rather than on their political affiliation. Although only about 10 percent of federal jobs were made civil service positions in 1883, the percentage steadily increased over time.

The Election of 1884

In 1884 the Democratic Party nominated Grover Cleveland, the governor of New York, for president. Cleveland was a reformer with a reputation for honesty. The Republican Party nominated James G. Blaine, a former Speaker of the House rumored to have accepted bribes. Some Republican reformers were so unhappy with Blaine that they supported Cleveland. They became known as "Mugwumps," from an Algonquian word meaning "great chief." If Blaine was their party's candidate, declared the Mugwumps, they would vote for Cleveland, "an honest Democrat."

Blaine hoped to make up for the loss of the Mugwumps by courting Catholic voters. Shortly before the election, however, Blaine met with a Protestant minister who denounced the Democrats for having ties to Catholicism. When Blaine was slow to condemn the remark, he lost many Catholic votes. Cleveland narrowly won the election.

As the first elected Democratic president since 1856, Grover Cleveland faced a horde of supporters who expected him to reward them with jobs. Mugwumps, on the other hand, expected him to increase the number of jobs protected by the civil service system. Cleveland chose a middle course and angered both sides. Economic issues, however, soon replaced the debate about patronage reform.

The Interstate Commerce Commission

Many Americans were concerned by the power of large corporations. Small businesses and farmers had become particularly angry at the railroads. While large corporations such as Standard Oil were able to negotiate rebates and lower rates because of the volume of goods they shipped, others were forced to pay much higher rates. Although the high fixed costs and low operating costs of railroads caused much

Political Debates of the Gilded Age

▲ Senator Pendleton is congratulated for his civil service bill; behind him a trash bin overflows with papers saying reform is impossible.

JOHN BULL AND HIS FRIEND CLEVELAND.

"THAT SUITS ME MR.CLEVELAND, KEEP MY MILLS AND FACTORIES GOING IF THE REST OF MANKIND STARVE—I AM GLAD TO SEE YOU SPORT MY COLORS THE RED BANDANNA"

"I AM PROUD OF YOUR APPROVAL MR. BULL AND AM DOING MY BEST TO SERVE YOU AS YOU SAY—I WEAR THE REAL BRITISH RED THERE ISN'T ANYTHING GREEN ABOUT ME"

▲ John Bull, symbol of Britain, thanks Grover Cleveland for free trade because it keeps British workers employed even if everyone else starves.

Analyzing VISUALS

1. **Analyzing** Does the cartoon on the right say free trade is a good idea? How do you know?
2. **Explaining** Did the artist who drew the cartoon on the left favor civil service reform? How does he indicate his opinion?

of this problem, many Americans believed railroads were gouging customers.

Neither party moved quickly at the federal level to address these problems. Both believed that government should not interfere with corporations' property rights, which courts had held to be the same as those of individuals. Many states, however, passed laws regulating railroad rates; in 1886 the Supreme Court ruled in the case of *Wabash, St. Louis, and Pacific Railway* v. *Illinois* that states could not regulate railroad rates for traffic between states because only the federal government could regulate interstate commerce.

Public pressure forced Congress to respond to the Wabash ruling. In 1887 Cleveland signed the Interstate Commerce Act. This act, which created the Interstate Commerce Commission (ICC), was the first federal law to regulate interstate commerce. The legislation limited railroad rates to what was "reasonable and just," forbade rebates to high-volume users, and made it illegal to charge higher rates for shorter hauls. The commission was not very effective in regulating the industry, however, because it had to rely on the courts to enforce its rulings.

Debating Tariffs Another major economic issue concerned tariffs. Many Democrats thought that Congress should cut tariffs because these taxes had the effect of raising the price of manufactured goods. Although it may have made sense to protect weak domestic manufacturing after the Civil War, many questioned the need to maintain high tariffs in the 1880s, when large American companies were fully capable of competing internationally. High tariffs also forced other nations to respond in kind, making it difficult for farmers to export their surpluses.

In December 1887 President Cleveland proposed lowering tariffs. The House, with a Democratic majority, passed moderate tariff reductions, but the Republican-controlled Senate rejected the bill. With Congress deadlocked, tariff reduction became a major issue in the election of 1888.

Republicans Regain Power

The Republicans and their presidential candidate, Benjamin Harrison, received large campaign contributions in 1888 from industrialists who benefited from high tariffs. Cleveland and the Democrats campaigned against high tariff rates. In one of the closest races in American history, Harrison lost the popular vote but won the electoral vote.

The McKinley Tariff The election of 1888 gave the Republicans control of both houses of Congress as well as the White House. Using this power, the party passed legislation to address points of national concern. In 1890 Representative William McKinley of Ohio pushed through a tariff bill that cut tobacco taxes and tariff rates on raw sugar but greatly increased rates on other goods, such as textiles, to discourage people from buying those imports.

The McKinley Tariff was intended to protect American industry from foreign competition and encourage consumers to buy American goods. Instead, it helped to trigger a steep rise in the price of all goods that angered many Americans and may have contributed to President Harrison's defeat in the 1892 election.

The Sherman Antitrust Act Congress also responded to popular pressure to do something about the power of the large business combinations known as trusts. In 1890 Congress passed the Sherman Antitrust Act, which prohibited any "combination . . . or conspiracy, in restraint of trade or commerce among the several States." The law, however, was vaguely worded, poorly enforced, and weakened by judicial interpretation. Most significantly, the Supreme Court ruled the law did not apply to manufacturing, holding that manufacturing was not interstate commerce. Thus the law had little impact. In the 1890s businesses formed trusts and combinations at a great rate. Like the ICC, the Sherman Antitrust Act was more important for establishing a precedent than for its immediate impact.

✔ **Reading Check** **Summarizing** What actions did Congress take to regulate big business?

The Rebirth of Reform

MAIN Idea Reformers developed new methods and philosophies for helping the urban poor.

HISTORY AND YOU Have you ever been to a YMCA? What activities can you do there? Read on to find out the origin of the YMCA and other community centers.

The tremendous changes that industrialism and urbanization brought triggered a debate over how best to address society's problems. While many Americans embraced the ideas of individualism and Social Darwinism, others disagreed, arguing that society's problems could be fixed only if Americans and their government began to take a more active role in regulating the economy and helping those in need.

Debates IN HISTORY

Is Social Darwinism the Best Approach for Ensuring Progress and Economic Growth?

The social problems that came with industrialization led to a debate over government's role in the economy. Some believed that government should intervene to help the poor and solve problems while others argued that leaving things alone was the best solution.

Challenging Social Darwinism

In 1879 journalist Henry George published *Progress and Poverty*, a discussion of the American economy that quickly became a national bestseller. In his book George observed, "The present century has been marked by a prodigious increase in wealth-producing power." This should, he asserted, have made poverty "a thing of the past." Instead, he claimed, the "gulf between the employed and the employer is growing wider; social contrasts are becoming sharper." In other words, laissez-faire economics was making society worse—the opposite of what Social Darwinists believed.

Most economists now argue that George's analysis was flawed. Industrialism did make some Americans very wealthy, but it also improved the standard of living for most others as well. At the time, however, in the midst of poverty, crime, and harsh working conditions, many Americans did not believe things were improving. George's economic theories encouraged other reformers to challenge the assumptions of the era.

Lester Frank Ward In 1883 Lester Frank Ward published *Dynamic Sociology*, in which he argued that humans were different from animals because they had the ability to make plans to produce the future outcomes they desired.

Ward's ideas came to be known as Reform Darwinism. People, he insisted, had succeeded in the world because of their ability to cooperate; competition was wasteful and time-consuming. Government, he argued, could regulate the economy, cure poverty, and promote education more efficiently than competition in the marketplace could.

YES

William Graham Sumner

Professor

PRIMARY SOURCE

"The moment that government provided work for one, it would have to provide work for all, and there would be no end whatever possible. Society does not owe any man a living. In all the cases that I have ever known of young men who claimed that society owed them a living, it has turned out that society paid them—in the State prison ... The fact that a man is here is no demand upon other people that they shall keep him alive and sustain him. He has got to fight the battle with nature as every other man has; and if he fights it with the same energy and enterprise and skill and industry as any other man, I cannot imagine his failing—that is, misfortune apart."

—testimony before the U.S. House of Representatives, 1879

NO

Lester Frank Ward

Sociologist

PRIMARY SOURCE

"The actions of men are a reflex of their mental characteristics. Where these differ so widely the acts of their possessors will correspondingly differ. Instead of all doing the same thing they will do a thousand different things. The natural and necessary effect of this is to give breadth to human activity. Every subject will be looked at from all conceivable points of view, and no aspect will be overlooked or neglected. It is due to this multiplicity of viewpoints, growing out of natural inequalities in the minds of men, that civilization and culture have moved forward along so many lines and swept the whole field of possible achievement."

—from "Social Classes in the Light of Modern Sociological Theory," 1908

DBQ Document-Based Questions

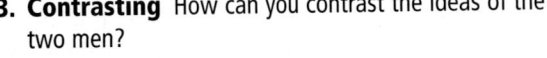

1. **Summarizing** What argument does Professor Sumner make against government assisting people?

2. **Paraphrasing** How does Professor Ward believe that different abilities aid society?

3. **Contrasting** How can you contrast the ideas of the two men?

4. **Evaluating** Which opinion do you agree with? Write a brief essay explaining your ideas.

People IN HISTORY

Jane Addams
1860–1935

After visiting a settlement house in London, England, Jane Addams decided to open Hull House in 1889 to assist poor immigrants in Chicago.

That assistance took on many forms: day care, kindergartens, libraries, an art gallery, an employment agency, and a meeting place for trade unions. The women who worked at Hull House, many of them college-educated in social work, pushed for protective legislation for children and women, which was enacted first in Illinois and then nationally.

Addams wrote books about her experiences at Hull House, giving an example to many others throughout the nation who also founded settlement houses. She favored woman suffrage and supported the founding of the American Civil Liberties Union and the National Association for the Advancement of Colored People. She was active in the peace movement, serving as first president of the organization that became the Women's International League for Peace and Freedom. For her efforts, she was awarded the Nobel Peace Prize in 1931.

What kind of assistance did Hull House provide immigrants?

▲ *Children stand in front of Hull House in 1905.*

Looking Backward Writer Edward Bellamy promoted another alternative to Social Darwinism and laissez-faire economics. In 1888 he published *Looking Backward,* a novel about a man who falls asleep in 1887 and awakens in the year 2000 to find that the nation has become a perfect society with no crime, poverty, or politics. In this fictional society, the government owns all industry and shares the wealth equally with all Americans. Bellamy's ideas were essentially a form of socialism. His book became a bestseller and helped to shape the thinking of some American reformers.

Naturalism in Literature Criticism of industrial society also appeared in literature in a new style of writing known as naturalism. Social Darwinists argued that people could make choices to improve their situation. Naturalists challenged this idea by suggesting that some people failed in life simply because they were caught up in circumstances they could not control. Sometimes people's lives were destroyed through no fault of their own.

Among the most prominent naturalist writers were Stephen Crane, Jack London, and Theodore Dreiser. Stephen Crane's novel

Maggie, A Girl of the Streets (1893), told the story of a girl's descent into prostitution and death. Jack London's tales of the Alaskan wilderness demonstrated the power of nature over civilization. Theodore Dreiser's novels, such as *Sister Carrie* (1900), painted a world where people sinned without punishment and where the pursuit of wealth and power often destroyed their character.

Helping the Urban Poor

The plight of the urban poor prompted some reformers to find new ways to help. Their efforts gave rise to the Social Gospel movement, the Salvation Army, the YMCA, and settlement houses.

The Social Gospel The **Social Gospel** movement worked to better conditions in cities according to the biblical ideals of charity and justice. Washington Gladden, a minister, was an early advocate who popularized the movement in writings such as *Applied Christianity* (1887). Walter Rauschenbusch, a Baptist minister from New York, became the leading voice in the Social Gospel movement.

The Church, he argued, must "demand protection for the moral safety of the people." The Social Gospel movement inspired many churches to take on new community functions. Some churches built gyms and provided social programs and child care. Others focused exclusively on helping the poor.

The Salvation Army and the YMCA The Salvation Army and the YMCA also combined faith and an interest in reform. The Salvation Army offered practical aid and religious counseling to the urban poor. The Young Men's Christian Association (YMCA) tried to help industrial workers and the urban poor by organizing Bible studies, citizenship training, and group activities. YMCAs, or "Ys," offered libraries, gymnasiums, auditoriums, and low-cost hotel rooms available on a temporary basis to those in need.

The head of the Chicago YMCA, Dwight L. Moody, was a gifted preacher who founded his own church, today known as Moody Memorial Church. By 1867, Moody had begun to organize revival meetings in other American cities, which drew thousands of people. Moody rejected both the Social Gospel and Social Darwinism. He believed the way to help the poor was not by providing them with services but by redeeming their souls and reforming their character.

The Settlement House Movement The **settlement house** movement began as an offshoot of the Social Gospel movement. In the late 1800s idealistic reformers—including many college-educated women—established settlement houses in poor, often heavily immigrant neighborhoods. A settlement house was a community center where reformers resided and offered everything from medical care and English classes to kindergartens and recreational programs. **Jane Addams** opened the famous Hull House in Chicago in 1889. Her work inspired others, including Lillian Wald, who founded the Henry Street Settlement in New York City.

Public Education As the United States became increasingly industrialized and urbanized, it needed more workers who were trained and educated. The number of public schools increased dramatically after the Civil War. The number of children attending school rose from 6,500,000 in 1870 to 17,300,000 in 1900. Public schools were often crucial to the success of immigrant children. At public schools, immigrant children were taught English and learned about American history and culture, a process known as **Americanization.**

Schools also tried to instill discipline and a strong work ethic. Grammar schools divided students into grades and drilled them in punctuality, neatness, and efficiency—necessary habits for the workplace. At the same time, vocational education in high schools taught skills required in specific trades.

Not everyone had access to school. Cities were far ahead of rural areas. Many African Americans also did not have equal "educational opportunities. Some African Americans started their own schools, following the example of Booker T. Washington, who founded the Tuskegee Institute in 1881.

✔ **Reading Check** **Explaining** What was the purpose of a settlement house?

Section 3 REVIEW

Vocabulary

1. **Explain** the significance of Gilded Age, individualism, Social Darwinism, Gospel of Wealth, philanthropy, Mark Twain, Social Gospel, settlement house, Jane Addams, Americanization.

Main Ideas

2. **Defining** What were the defining characteristics of the Gilded Age?

3. **Describing** How did changes in art and literature reflect the issues and characteristics of the late 1800s?

4. **Explaining** Why was the Sherman Antitrust Act ineffective?

5. **Categorizing** Complete a chart like the one below by listing the names and goals of reform movements that arose in the late 1800s to help the urban poor.

Reform Movement	Goals

Critical Thinking

6. **Big Ideas** Do you think the idea of the Gospel of Wealth is still alive today? Why or why not?

7. **Analyzing Visuals** Look at the cartoon on the right on page 463. What do the figures in the background suggest?

Writing About History

8. **Descriptive Writing** Imagine that you are a newspaper editor in the late 1800s. Write an editorial in which you support or oppose the philosophy of Social Darwinism.

History ONLINE

Study Central™ To review this section, go to glencoe.com and click on Study Central.

Eyewitness

BROWN BROTHERS

In his exposé of urban poverty, How the Other Half Lives (1890), **JACOB RIIS** *documented the living conditions in New York City tenements:*

"The statement once made a sensation that between seventy and eighty children had been found in one tenement. It no longer excites even passing attention, when the sanitary police report counting 101 adults and 91 children in a Crosby Street house, one of twins, built together. The children in the others, if I am not mistaken, numbered 89, a total of 180 for two tenements! Or when midnight inspection in Mulberry Street unearths a hundred and fifty "lodgers" sleeping on filthy floors in two buildings. In spite of brown-stone fittings, plate-glass and mosaic vestibule floors, the water does not rise in summer to the second story, while the beer flows unchecked to the all-night picnics on the roof. The saloon with the side-door and the landlord divide the prosperity of the place between them, and the tenant, in sullen submission, foots the bill."

VERBATIM

❝Tell 'em quick, and tell 'em often.❞

WILLIAM WRIGLEY,
*soap salesman and promoter of chewing gum,
on his marketing philosophy*

❝A pushing, energetic, ingenious person, always awake and trying to get ahead of his neighbors.❞

HENRY ADAMS,
historian, describing the average New Yorker or Chicagoan

❝We cannot all live in cities, yet nearly all seem determined to do so.❞
HORACE GREELEY,
newspaper editor

INDICATORS:
Livin' in the City

Moving off the farm for a factory job? Sharpen your pencil. You'll need to budget carefully to buy all you will need.

Here are the numbers for a Georgia family of four in 1890. The husband is a textile worker, and the wife works at home. There is one child, age 4, and a boarder. They share a two-room, wood-heated, oil-lighted apartment.

INCOME: (annual)

husband's income	$312.00
boarder's rent	10.00
TOTAL INCOME.	**$322.00**

EXPENSES: (annual)

medical.	$65.00
furniture	46.90
clothing	46.00
rent.	21.00
flour/meal	25.00
hog products	17.00
other meat.	13.00
vegetables	13.00
lard.	6.50
potatoes.	6.40
butter.	5.00
sugar	4.00
charitable donations.	6.10
vacation	3.25
alcohol	3.25
tobacco	3.00
molasses.	2.00
other food	27.80
miscellaneous	68.20
TOTAL EXPENSES.	**$382.40**

Milestones

ON THE RUN, 1881. THE JESSE JAMES GANG, after robbing a Chicago, Rock Island, and Pacific train near Winston, Missouri, and killing the conductor and a passenger.

OVERTURNED, 1878. BY THE SUPREME COURT, a Louisiana court decision that awarded damages to an African American woman who had been refused admission to a steamship stateroom reserved for whites.

PLAGUED BY GRASSHOPPERS, 1874. THE AMERICAN GREAT PLAINS. Insect swarms a mile wide blot out the midday sun. Two inches deep on the ground, they leave "nothing but the mortgage," as one farmer put it.

CELEBRATED IN EUROPE, 1887. ANNIE OAKLEY, star of Buffalo Bill's Wild West Show. Oakley shot a cigarette from the lips of Crown Prince Wilhelm of Germany. Years later, when the U.S. goes to war against Kaiser Wilhelm, Oakley will quip: "I wish I'd missed that day!"

Jesse James

REMOVED, 1884. IDA B. WELLS, journalist and former slave, from a ladies coach on a train. Wells refused to move to the smoking car where African Americans were to be seated.

ARRESTED, 1872. SUSAN B. ANTHONY, for casting a ballot in Rochester, New York. Anthony argued that the Fourteenth and Fifteenth Amendments applied to women.

Susan B. Anthony

NUMBERS

1 in 12 Americans living in cities of 100,000 or more in 1865

A crowded New York City street

1 in 5 Americans living in cities in 1896

522 Inhabitants in a one-acre area in the Bowery, New York City

$2 Daily wage for a farm laborer, New York, 1869

$4 Daily wage for a plumber, New York City, 1869

50¢ Price of a pair of boy's knee pants, a parasol, button boots, or a necktie (1870s)

$8 Price of a "Fine All-Wool Suit," 1875

25¢ Admission to "Barnum's American Museum" (featuring the smallest pair of human beings ever seen!), 1896

CRITICAL THINKING

1. Analyzing Visuals Look at the Jacob Riis photo of an urban family and the photo of a New York City street. What do the pictures tell you about urban life in the 1890s?

2. Comparing What character traits do you think Ida B. Wells and Susan B. Anthony may have shared?

Populism

Guide to Reading

Big Ideas
Economics and Society The Populist movement and its presidential candidate William Jennings Bryan strongly supported silver as the basis for currency.

Content Vocabulary
• populism (p. 470)
• greenbacks (p. 470)
• inflation (p. 470)
• deflation (p. 470)
• cooperatives (p. 471)
• graduated income tax (p. 473)

Academic Vocabulary
• bond (p. 470)
• currency (p. 471)
• strategy (p. 472)

People and Events to Identify
• Farmers' Alliance (p. 472)
• People's Party (p. 473)
• William Jennings Bryan (p. 474)
• William McKinley (p. 475)

Reading Strategy
Taking Notes As you read about the emergence of populism in the 1890s, use the major headings of the section to create an outline similar to the one below.

```
Populism
I. Unrest in Rural America
   A.
   B.
   C.
II.
   A.
   B.
```

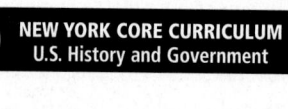

NEW YORK CORE CURRICULUM
U.S. History and Government

Unit 3:
II.F.1.a The Grange movement as agrarian protest
II.F.1.b Populism: a political response—William Jennings Bryan and the election of 1896
II.F.1.b.(1) Case study: The Populists as a grass-roots political party

After the Civil War, falling crop prices and deflation made it hard for farmers to make a living. Farmers tried to overcome these problems by forming organizations such as the Grange and the Farmers' Alliance. In the 1890s, many farmers joined the Populist Party.

Unrest in Rural America

MAIN Idea Deflation, low crop prices, and tariffs hurt farmers economically.

HISTORY AND YOU What can you buy for a dollar today? Read on to learn how the value of a dollar has changed over time.

Populism was a movement to increase farmers' political power and to work for legislation in their interest. Farmers joined the Populist movement because they were in the midst of an economic crisis. New technology enabled farmers to produce more crops, but the greater supply had caused prices to fall. High tariffs also made it hard for farmers to sell their goods overseas. Farmers also felt they were victimized by large and faraway entities: the banks from which they obtained loans and the railroads that set their shipping rates.

The Money Supply

Some farmers thought adjusting the money supply would solve their economic problems. During the Civil War, the federal government had expanded the money supply by issuing millions of dollars in **greenbacks**—paper currency that could not be exchanged for gold or silver coins. This increase in the money supply without an increase in goods for sale caused **inflation,** or a decline in the value of money. As the paper money lost value, the prices of goods soared.

After the Civil War ended, the United States had three types of currency in circulation—greenbacks, gold and silver coins, and national bank notes backed by government **bonds.** To get inflation under control, the federal government stopped printing greenbacks and began paying off its bonds. In 1873 Congress also decided to stop making silver into coins. These decisions meant that the money supply was not large enough for the country's growing economy. In 1865, for example, there was about $30 in circulation for each person. By 1895, there was only about $23. As the economy expanded, **deflation**—or an increase in the value of money and a decrease in prices—began. As money increased in value, prices fell.

Deflation hit farmers especially hard. Most farmers had to borrow money for seed and other supplies to plant their crops. Because

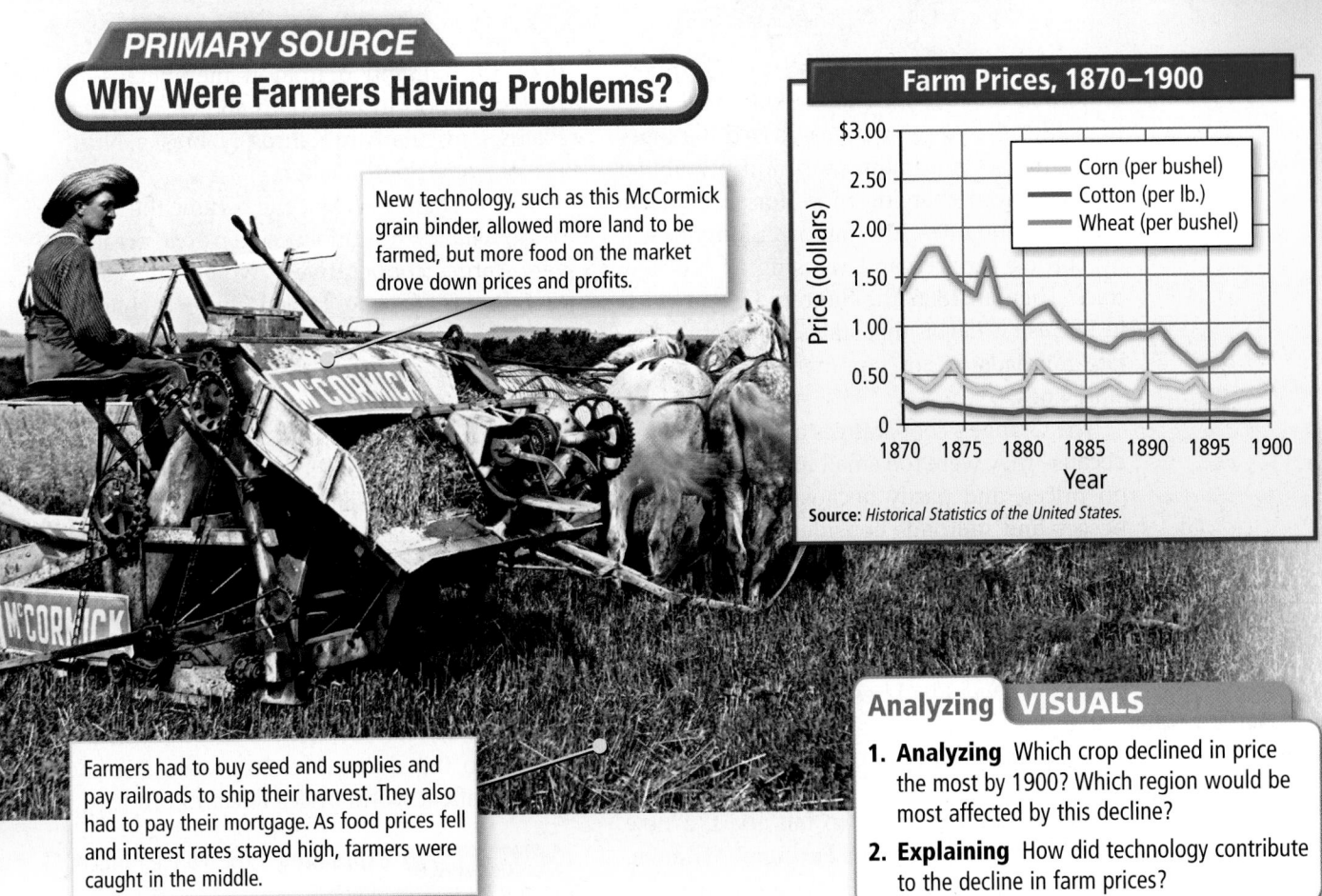

New technology, such as this McCormick grain binder, allowed more land to be farmed, but more food on the market drove down prices and profits.

Farm Prices, 1870–1900

Corn (per bushel)
Cotton (per lb.)
Wheat (per bushel)

Price (dollars)

Year

Source: *Historical Statistics of the United States.*

Farmers had to buy seed and supplies and pay railroads to ship their harvest. They also had to pay their mortgage. As food prices fell and interest rates stayed high, farmers were caught in the middle.

Analyzing VISUALS

1. **Analyzing** Which crop declined in price the most by 1900? Which region would be most affected by this decline?

2. **Explaining** How did technology contribute to the decline in farm prices?

money was in short supply, interest rates began to rise, which increased the amount farmers owed. Rising interest rates also made mortgages more expensive, but falling prices meant the farmers sold their crops for less, and they still had to make the same mortgage payments to the banks.

Realizing that their problems were partly caused by a shortage of **currency,** many farmers concluded that Eastern bankers had pressured Congress into reducing the money supply. Some farmers called for the printing of more greenbacks. Others, particularly those in the West where new silver mines had been found, wanted the government to mint silver coins. They referred to the decision to stop minting silver as "The Crime of '73."

The Grange Takes Action

In 1866 the Department of Agriculture sent Oliver H. Kelley to tour the rural South and report on the condition of the region's farmers. Realizing how isolated farmers were from each other, Kelley founded the first national farm

organization, the Patrons of Husbandry, better known as the Grange, in 1867.

At first Grangers met largely for social and educational purposes. Then, in 1873, the nation plunged into a severe recession, and farm income fell sharply. Farmers looking for help joined the Grange in large numbers. By 1874, the Grange had between 800,000 and 1.5 million members.

Grangers responded to the crisis by pressuring state legislatures to regulate railroad and warehouse rates. They also tried to create **cooperatives**—marketing organizations that try to increase prices and lower costs for their members.

One of the reasons farmers could not charge higher prices for their crops was that there were so many farmers in competition. If a farmer raised prices, a buyer could always go elsewhere and pay less. Cooperatives pooled farmers' crops and held them off the market in order to force up prices. Because a cooperative controlled a large quantity of farm products, it could also negotiate better shipping rates with the railroads.

None of the **strategies** the Grangers employed improved farmers' economic conditions. Several Western states passed "Granger laws" that set maximum rates and prohibited railroads from charging more for short hauls than for long ones. The railroads fought back by cutting services and refusing to lay new track. Then, in 1886, the Supreme Court ruled in *Wabash* v. *Illinois* that states could not regulate railroads or any commerce that crossed state lines.

The Grange's cooperatives also failed, partly because they were too small to have any effect on prices, and partly because Eastern businesses and railroads considered them to be similar to unions—illegitimate conspiracies that restricted trade—so they refused to do business with them. By the late 1870s, farmers began to leave the Grange for organizations they hoped would address their problems.

The Farmers' Alliance

As the Grange began to fall apart, a new organization, known as the **Farmers' Alliance,** began to form. By 1890, the Alliance had between 1.5 and 3 million members, with strong support in the South and on the Great Plains, particularly in Kansas, Nebraska, North Dakota, and South Dakota.

When Charles W. Macune became the leader of the Alliance, he announced a plan to organize very large cooperatives, which he called exchanges. Macune hoped these exchanges would be big enough to force farm prices up and to make loans to farmers at low interest rates. The exchanges had some success. The Texas Exchange successfully marketed cotton at prices slightly higher than those paid to individual farmers, while the Illinois Exchange negotiated slightly better railroad rates for wheat farmers.

Ultimately, the large cooperatives failed. Many overextended themselves by lending too much money at low interest rates that was never repaid. In many cases, wholesalers, railroads, and bankers discriminated against them, making it difficult for them to stay in business. They also failed because they were still too small to affect world prices for farm products.

Reading Check **Explaining** How did the Farmers' Alliance try to help farmers?

POLITICAL CARTOONS PRIMARY SOURCE
Who Is to Blame for Farmers' Problems?

▲ A farmer wearing a Granger hat tries to warn people about the railroad.

THE POLITICAL POOR RELATION.—AN UNWELCOME GUEST

▲ A thin farmer is an unwelcome guest at the Congressional kitchen, where businessmen are enjoying their meals.

Analyzing VISUALS

1. **Analyzing** What is the cartoon on the left implying about the railroad's relationship to farmers?

2. **Explaining** Who does the cartoon on the right blame for the problems facing farmers?

The Rise of Populism

MAIN Idea Farmers started the People's Party to fight for their interests and attracted many supporters when a depression hit in the 1890s.

HISTORY AND YOU Do you remember reading about the creation of the Republican Party in the 1850s? Read how another new party, the Populists, shook up politics in the 1890s.

By 1890 the Alliance's lack of success had started a debate in the organization. Some Alliance leaders, particularly in the western states, wanted to form a new party and push for political reforms. Members of the Kansas Alliance formed the **People's Party,** also known as the Populists, and nominated candidates to run for Congress and the state legislature. Alliances in Nebraska, South Dakota, and Minnesota quickly followed Kansas's example.

Most Southern leaders of the Alliance opposed the idea of a third party. They did not want to undermine the Democrats' control of the South. Instead, they suggested that the Alliance produce a list of demands and promise to vote for candidates who supported those demands. They hoped this would force Democrats to adopt the Alliance program.

The Subtreasury Plan

To get Southern Democrats to support the Alliance, Charles Macune introduced the subtreasury plan, which called for the government to set up warehouses called subtreasuries. Farmers would store their crops in the warehouses, and the government would provide low-interest loans to the farmers.

Macune believed the plan would enable farmers to hold their crops off the market in large enough quantities to force prices up. The Alliance also called for the free coinage of silver, an end to protective tariffs and national banks, tighter regulation of the railroads, and direct election of senators by voters.

Macune's strategy seemed to work at first. In 1890 the South elected four governors, all Democrats, who had pledged to support the Alliance program. Several Southern legislatures now had pro-Alliance majorities, and more than 40 Democrats who supported the Alliance program were elected to Congress.

A Populist Runs for President

Meanwhile, the new People's Party did equally well in the West. Populists took control of the Kansas and Nebraska legislatures. Populists also held the balance of power in Minnesota and South Dakota. Eight Populist representatives and two Populist senators were elected to the United States Congress.

At first, Southern members of the Alliance were excited over their success in electing so many pro-Alliance Democrats to Congress and to Southern state legislatures, but over the next two years, their excitement turned into frustration. Despite their promises, few Democrats followed through in their support of the Alliance program.

In May 1891 Western populists met with some labor and reform groups in Cincinnati. There, they endorsed the creation of a new national People's Party to run candidates for president. The following year, many Southern farmers had reached the point where they were willing to break with the Democratic Party and join the People's Party.

In July 1892 the People's Party held its first national convention in Omaha, Nebraska. James B. Weaver was nominated to run for president. The Omaha convention endorsed a platform that denounced the government's refusal to coin silver as a "vast conspiracy against mankind" and called for a return to unlimited coinage of silver at a ratio that gave 16 ounces of silver the same value as one ounce of gold. It also called for federal ownership of railroads and a **graduated income tax,** one that taxed higher earnings more heavily.

Populists also adopted proposals designed to appeal to organized labor. The Omaha platform also called for an eight-hour workday and immigration restrictions, but workers found it hard to identify with a party focused on rural problems and the coinage of silver. The Populists had close ties to the Knights of Labor, but that organization was in decline, and the fast-growing American Federation of Labor had steered clear of an alliance with them. As a result, most urban workers continued to vote for the Democrats, whose candidate, Grover Cleveland, won the election.

✓ Reading Check **Summarizing** What was the main outcome of the Populist campaign in the elections of 1892?

The Election of 1896

MAIN Idea Although William Jennings Bryan had the support of the Populists and the Democrats, Republican William McKinley defeated him.

HISTORY AND YOU What was the best speech you have ever heard? How did the speaker draw you in? Read on to learn how a powerful speech won the presidential nomination for William Jennings Bryan.

As the election of 1896 approached, leaders of the People's Party decided to make the free coinage of silver the focus of their campaign. They also decided to hold their convention after the Republican and Democratic conventions. They believed the Republicans would endorse a gold standard, and they did. They also expected the Democrats to nominate Grover Cleveland, even though Cleveland also strongly favored a gold standard. The People's Party hoped that when they endorsed silver, pro-silver Democrats would abandon their party and vote for the Populists.

Unfortunately for the Populists, their strategy failed. The Democrats did not waiver on the silver issue. Instead, they nominated **William Jennings Bryan,** a strong supporter of silver. When the Populists gathered in St. Louis for their own convention, they faced a difficult choice: endorse Bryan and risk undermining their identity as a separate party, or nominate their own candidate and risk splitting the silver vote. They eventually decided to support Bryan as well.

Bryan's Campaign

William Jennings Bryan, a former member of Congress from Nebraska, was only 36 years old when the Democrats and the Populists nominated him for president. Bryan had served in Congress as a representative from Nebraska. He was a powerful speaker and he won the Democratic nomination by delivering an electrifying address in defense of silver—one of the most famous in American political history.

Turning Point

The Election of 1896

Before the Civil War, farmers of the West and the South determined the outcome of elections. As industrialization caused Eastern cities to grow, the balance of political power shifted. From the 1870s to the 1890s, elections became very close, and power swung back and forth between the parties. The election of 1896 marked a turning point. Political power shifted from voters in the rural parts of the country to those in urban areas in the Northeast and industrial Midwest. Never again would farm votes determine the winner of a presidential election. The South and West did not regain their political importance until their urban areas grew to match those in the Northeast and Midwest.

MAKING CONNECTIONS Does the pattern of 1896's election resemble recent elections? Write an essay comparing a recent election to the 1896 election.

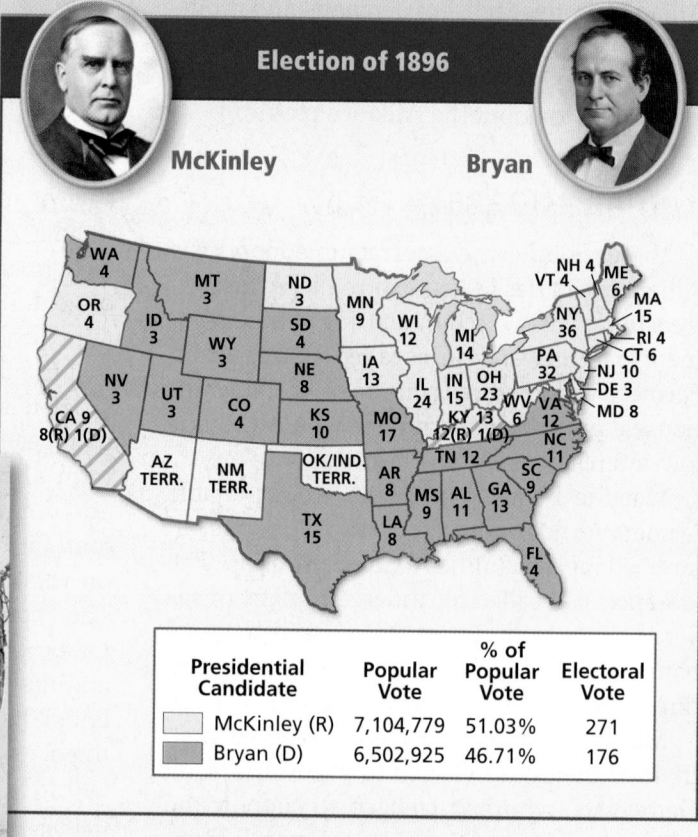

Election of 1896

McKinley   Bryan

Presidential Candidate	Popular Vote	% of Popular Vote	Electoral Vote
☐ McKinley (R)	7,104,779	51.03%	271
☐ Bryan (D)	6,502,925	46.71%	176

◀ For many, the campaign to elect William Jennings Bryan was viewed as both a crusade and a revolution, as the symbols and slogans on this 1896 poster show.

With a few well-chosen words, Bryan transformed the campaign for silver into a crusade:

PRIMARY SOURCE

"Having behind us the producing masses of this nation and the world, supported by the commercial interests, the laboring interests and the toilers everywhere, we will answer their demand for a gold standard by saying to them: You shall not press down upon the brow of labor this crown of thorns; you shall not crucify mankind upon a cross of gold."

—quoted in *America in the Gilded Age*

Bryan waged an energetic campaign, traveling thousands of miles and delivering 600 speeches in 14 weeks. Some found his relentless campaigning undignified, and Catholic immigrants and other city dwellers cared little for the silver issue. They did not like Bryan's speaking style either. It reminded them of rural Protestant preachers, who were sometimes anti-Catholic. Republicans knew that Democrats and Populists would be hard to beat in the South and the West. To regain the White House, they had to sweep the Northeast and the Midwest. They decided on **William McKinley,** the governor of Ohio, as their candidate.

The Front Porch Campaign

Unlike Bryan, McKinley launched a "Front Porch Campaign," greeting delegates who came to his home in Canton, Ohio. The Republicans campaigned against the Democrats by promising workers that McKinley would provide a "full dinner pail." This meant more to urban workers than the issue of silver money because the economy was in a severe recession following the Panic of 1893. At the same time, most business leaders supported the Republicans, convinced that unlimited silver coinage would ruin the country. Many employers warned workers that if Bryan won, businesses would fail and unemployment would rise further.

McKinley's reputation as a moderate on labor issues and as tolerant toward ethnic groups helped improve the Republican Party's image with urban workers and immigrants. When the votes were counted, McKinley had won with a decisive victory. He captured 51 percent of the popular vote and had a winning margin of 95 electoral votes—hefty numbers in an era of tight elections. As expected, Bryan won the South and most of the West, but few of the states he carried had large populations or delivered many electoral votes. By embracing populism and its rural base, Bryan and the Democrats lost the northeastern industrial areas, where votes were concentrated.

The Populist Party declined after 1896. Their efforts to ease the economic hardships of farmers and to regulate big business had not worked. Some of the reforms they favored, including the graduated income tax and some governmental regulation of the economy—however, came about in the subsequent decades.

Reading Check **Evaluating** What were the results of the 1896 presidential election?

Section 4 REVIEW

Vocabulary

1. **Explain** the significance of: populism, greenbacks, inflation, deflation, cooperatives, Farmers' Alliance, People's Party, graduated income tax, William Jennings Bryan, William McKinley.

Main Ideas

2. **Organizing** Use a graphic organizer that lists the factors that contributed to and the results of farmers' unrest in the 1890s.

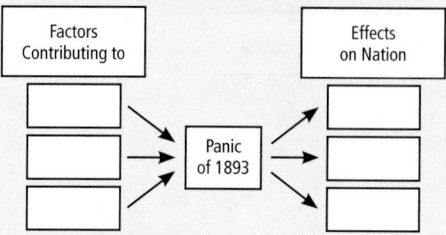

3. **Describing** What economic factors caused farmers to support populism?

4. **Listing** What issues did the Democrats endorse in the 1896 presidential election?

Critical Thinking

5. **Big Ideas** Why did the Populists support William Jennings Bryan?

6. **Synthesizing** How did the Farmers' Alliance contribute to the rise of a new political party?

7. **Analyzing Visuals** Look at the campaign poster on page 474. Choose one of the symbols or slogans and explain its meaning to Bryan's campaign.

Writing About History

8. **Persuasive Writing** Imagine you support the Populist Party and that you have been asked to write copy for a campaign poster. Include a slogan that provides reasons for people to support the Populists.

History ONLINE

Study Central™ To review this section, go to glencoe.com and click on Study Central.

The Rise of Segregation

Guide to Reading

Big Ideas
Individual Action Several prominent African Americans led the fight against racial discrimination.

Content Vocabulary
- poll tax *(p. 478)*
- segregation *(p. 478)*
- Jim Crow laws *(p. 478)*
- lynching *(p. 480)*

Academic Vocabulary
- discrimination *(p. 478)*

People and Events to Identify
- Ida B. Wells *(p. 480)*
- Booker T. Washington *(p. 481)*
- W. E. B. Du Bois *(p. 481)*

Reading Strategy
Organizing As you read, complete a web diagram listing ways that states disenfranchised African Americans and legalized discrimination.

Factors Contributing to Discrimination

NEW YORK CORE CURRICULUM
U.S. History and Government

Unit 3:	
I.C.4	Supreme Court interpretations of the 13th and 14th amendments
I.D.3	Restoration of white control in the South (1870s and 1880s) and abridgment of rights of freed African-Americans
I.D.4	*Plessy v. Ferguson,* 1896
Unit 4:	
I.B.2.c	The black movement and reform
I.B.2.c.(2)	Ida Wells (anti-lynching)

After Reconstruction ended, Southern states began passing laws that eroded the rights of African Americans by introducing segregation and denying voting rights. African American leaders struggled to protect civil rights and improve quality of life but could not always agree on the most effective strategy.

Resistance and Repression

MAIN Idea Many African Americans fled the South, but some stayed and joined the Populist Party.

HISTORY AND YOU Do you remember reading about the rise of sharecropping after the Civil War? Read how African American farmers tried to work together in the late 1800s.

After Reconstruction, many African Americans in the rural South lived in conditions of grinding poverty. Most were sharecroppers, landless farmers who gave their landlords a large portion of their crops as rent, rather than paying cash. Sharecropping usually left farmers in chronic debt. Many eventually left farming and sought jobs in Southern towns or headed west to claim homesteads.

The Exodusters Head to Kansas

In the mid-1870s, Benjamin "Pap" Singleton, a former slave, became convinced that African Americans would never be given a chance to get ahead in the South. He began urging African Americans to move west, specifically to Kansas, and form their own independent communities where they could help each other get ahead. His ideas soon set in motion a mass migration. In the spring of 1879, African American communities in Louisiana, Mississippi, and Texas were swept with a religious enthusiasm for moving to Kansas—seeing it as a new promised land. In less than two months, approximately 6,000 African Americans left their homes in the rural South and headed to Kansas. The newspapers called it "an Exodus," like the Hebrews' escape from Egyptian bondage. The migrants themselves came to be known as "Exodusters."

One of the migrants to Kansas later explained why they went: "The whole South—every State in the South—had got into the hands of the very men that held us as slaves." The first Exodusters, many possessing little more than hope and the clothes on their backs, arrived in Kansas in the spring of 1879. A journalist named Henry King described the scene:

NATIONAL GEOGRAPHIC | **The Exodus to Kansas**

Legend:
- State abandoned by Exodusters
- State where Exodusters settled
- ← Route of migration

States shown on map: Kansas, Missouri, Illinois, Ind., W. Va., Virginia, Kentucky, N.C., Oklahoma, Tennessee, S.C., Ark., Miss., Ala., Georgia, Texas, La., Florida

▲ In 1879, soon after Reconstruction ended, an estimated 6,000–15,000 African Americans left the rural South and headed to Kansas where they hoped to build a better life for themselves.

Analyzing VISUALS

1. **Analyzing** According to the map, which states were departure points for the Exodusters?
2. **Making Connections** What earlier events in American history would have made the Exodusters think Kansas was a good place to settle?

PRIMARY SOURCE

"One morning in April, 1879, a Missouri steamboat arrived at Wyandotte, Kansas, and discharged a load of negro men, women and children, with ... barrels, boxes, and bundles of household effects.... [T]heir garments were incredibly patched and tattered ... and there was not probably a dollar in money in the pockets of the entire party.... They looked like persons coming out of a dream. And, indeed, such they were .... for this was the advance guard of the Exodus."

—quoted in *Eyewitness: The Negro in History*

Forming a Separate Alliance

While some African Americans fled the South, others joined with poor white farmers who had created the Farmers' Alliance. Alliance leaders urged African Americans to form a similar organization. In 1886 African American farmers established the Colored Farmers' National Alliance. By 1890, the organization had about 1.2 million members.

When the Populist Party formed in 1891, many African American farmers joined the new organization. This posed a major challenge to the Democratic Party in the South. If poor whites left the party and joined with African Americans in voting for the Populists, the coalition might be unbeatable.

To win back the poor white vote, Democratic leaders began appealing to racism, warning whites that support for Populism would return the South to "Black Republican" rule, similar to Reconstruction. In addition, election officials began using various methods to make it harder and harder for African Americans to vote. As one Democratic leader in the South told a reporter, "Some of our people, some editors especially, deny that [African Americans] are hindered from voting; but what is the good of lying? They are interfered with, and we are obliged to do it, and we may as well tell the truth."

Reading Check **Examining** Who were the Exodusters, and why did they migrate to Kansas?

Imposing Segregation

MAIN Idea Southern states passed laws that imposed segregation and denied African American men their voting rights.

HISTORY AND YOU Can you think of a rule that is unfairly or unevenly enforced? Read about the tactics used to disfranchise African Americans.

After Reconstruction ended in 1877, the rights of African Americans were gradually undermined. Attempts to unify whites and African Americans politically and economically failed. Instead, a movement to diminish the civil rights of African Americans gained momentum as the century ended.

Taking Away the Vote

The Fifteenth Amendment prohibits states from denying citizens the right to vote on the basis of "race, color, or previous condition of servitude," but it does not bar states from denying the right to vote on other grounds. In the late 1800s, Southern states began imposing restrictions that, while not mentioning race, were designed to make it difficult or impossible for African Americans to vote.

In 1890 Mississippi began requiring all citizens registering to vote to pay a **poll tax** of $2, a sum beyond the means of most poor African Americans. Mississippi also instituted a literacy test, requiring voters to read and understand the state constitution. Few African Americans born after the Civil War had been able to attend school and those who had grown up under slavery were largely illiterate. Even those who knew how to read often failed the test because officials deliberately picked passages that few people could understand.

Other Southern states adopted similar restrictions. In Louisiana the number of African Americans registered to vote fell from about 130,000 in 1890 to around 5,300 in 1900. In Alabama the number fell from about 181,000 to about 3,700.

Election officials were far less strict in applying the poll tax and literacy requirements to whites, but the number of white voters also fell significantly. To let more whites vote, Louisiana introduced the "grandfather clause," which allowed any man to vote if he had an ancestor who could vote in 1867. This provision, which was adopted in several Southern states, exempted most whites from voting restrictions such as literacy tests.

Legalizing Segregation

African Americans in the North were often barred from public places, but **segregation,** or the separation of the races, was different in the South. Southern states passed laws that enforced **discrimination**. These laws became known as **Jim Crow laws.** The term probably refers to the song "Jump Jim Crow," which was popular in minstrel shows of the day.

Civil Rights Cases In 1883 the Supreme Court set the stage for legalized segregation when it overturned the Civil Rights Act of 1875. That law had prohibited keeping people out of public places on the basis of race and barred racial **discrimination** in selecting jurors. The 1883 Supreme Court decision, however, said that the Fourteenth Amendment provided only that "no state" could deny citizens equal protection under the law. Private organizations—such as hotels, theaters, and railroads—were free to practice segregation.

Encouraged by the Supreme Court's ruling and by the decline of congressional support for civil rights, Southern states passed a series of laws that established racial segregation in virtually all public places. Southern whites and African Americans could no longer ride together in the same railroad cars, eat in the same dining halls, or even drink from the same fountains.

Plessy v. _Ferguson_ In 1892 an African American named Homer Plessy challenged a Louisiana law that forced him to ride in a separate railroad car from whites. He was arrested for riding in a "whites-only" car. In 1896 the Supreme Court, in _Plessy_ v. _Ferguson_, upheld the Louisiana law and set out a new doctrine of "separate but equal" facilities for African Americans. The ruling established the legal basis for discrimination in the South for more than 50 years. While public facilities for African Americans in the South were always separate, they were far from equal. In many cases, they were inferior.

✓ Reading Check **Summarizing** How did the Supreme Court help to legalize segregation?

ANALYZING SUPREME COURT CASES

Do states have the right to segregate citizens by race?

★ *Plessy* v. *Ferguson*, 1896

Background to the Case

When Homer Adolph Plessy, a light-skinned man who was one-eighth African American, took a seat in the whites-only section of an East Louisiana Railway train and refused to move, he was arrested. Convicted of breaking a Louisiana law enacted in 1890, Plessy appealed his case to the Louisiana Supreme Court, then to federal Supreme Court. The incident was planned in advance to test the statute, using Plessy, who appeared to be white, to show the folly of the law. Although the words "separate but equal" do not appear in the court responses, the term came to describe a condition that persisted until 1954.

How the Court Ruled

The Court upheld the right of states to make laws that sustained segregation. The majority of justices wanted to distinguish between political rights guaranteed by the Fourteenth and Fifteenth Amendments and social rights.

▲ *A conductor orders Homer Plessy to leave the white section of the railroad car.*

PRIMARY SOURCE

The Court's Opinion

"The object of the [Fourteenth] amendment was undoubtedly to enforce the absolute equality of the two races before the law, but . . . it could not have been intended to abolish distinctions based upon color, or to enforce social, as distinguished from political equality, or a commingling of the two races upon terms unsatisfactory to either. Laws permitting, and even requiring, their separation in places where they are liable to be brought into contact do not necessarily imply the inferiority of either race to the other . . . We cannot say that a law which authorizes or even requires the separation of the two races in public conveyances is unreasonable."

—Justice Henry Billings Brown writing for the Court in *Plessy* v. *Ferguson*

PRIMARY SOURCE

Other Views

"Our constitution is color-blind, and neither knows nor tolerates classes among citizens. In respect of civil rights, all citizens are equal before the law. . . . We boast of the freedom enjoyed by our people above all other peoples. But it is difficult to reconcile that boast with a state of law which, practically, puts the brand of servitude and degradation upon a large class of our fellow citizens—our equals before the law. The thin disguise of 'equal' accommodations for passengers in railroad coaches will not mislead any one, nor atone for the wrong this day done."

—Justice John Marshall Harlan writing the lone dissent in *Plessy* v. *Ferguson*

DBQ Document-Based Questions

1. **Analyzing Primary Sources** What distinction does Justice Brown make about the rights of citizens?
2. **Identifying Points of View** How does Justice Harlan regard the Court's decision?
3. **Evaluating** What rights do you think all states should extend to their citizens? Why do you think so?

The African American Response

MAIN Idea Some African American leaders focused on practical vocational education, while others pushed for full civil rights and educational opportunities.

HISTORY AND YOU How would your life be different without an education? Read on to learn why some early civil rights leaders focused on access to education.

The African American community responded to violence and discrimination in several ways. Ida B. Wells used the press to end violence, while Mary Church Terrell worked in education. Booker T. Washington proposed that African Americans focus on achieving economic goals, rather than political goals. W. E. B. Du Bois argued African Americans should demand equal rights immediately.

Ida B. Wells

In the late 1800s, mob violence increased in the United States, particularly in the South. Between 1890 and 1899, there was an average of 187 **lynchings**—hangings without proper court proceedings—each year.

In 1892 **Ida B. Wells,** a fiery young African American woman from Tennessee, launched a fearless crusade against lynching. After a mob drove Wells out of town, she settled in Chicago and continued her campaign. In 1895 she published a book denouncing mob violence and demanding "a fair trial by law for those accused of crime, and punishment by law after honest conviction." Although Congress rejected an anti-lynching bill, the number of lynchings decreased significantly in the 1900s, due in great part to the efforts of activists such as Wells.

Mary Church Terrell

One lynching victim had been a close friend of Mary Church Terrell, a college-educated woman who'd been born during the Civil War. This death, and President Harrison's refusal to publicly condemn lynching, started Terrell on her lifelong battle against lynching, racism, and sexism.

Terrell also worked with woman suffrage workers such as Jane Addams and Susan B. Anthony. In addition to helping found the

---

People IN HISTORY

Booker T. Washington
1856–1915

Born into slavery on a plantation in Virginia, Booker T. Washington spent his childhood working in the coal mines of West Virginia. At age 16, he heard about the Hampton Institute in Virginia, where African Americans could learn farming or a trade. With little money in his pockets, Washington left home and walked nearly 500 miles to the school, where he was able to work as a janitor to pay for his education.

When the Alabama legislature decided in 1881 to begin a school to train black leaders, Washington was recommended for the job. He borrowed money to buy an abandoned plantation; the students built classrooms, a chapel, and dormitories. The Tuskegee Institute became well-known, attracting prominent scholars such as George Washington Carver to the faculty.

Washington used his influence with white businessmen to raise money for the school. He encouraged the development of black-owned businesses, and he organized the National Negro Business League in 1900. He was a nationally known spokesperson for the African American community and advised presidents William Howard Taft and Theodore Roosevelt on political appointments.
What were Booker T. Washington's most important achievements?

W. E. B. Du Bois
1868–1963

W. E. B. Du Bois was born in Massachusetts a few years after the end of the Civil War. After graduating from Fisk University, Du Bois earned a Ph.D. from Harvard. As a professor at Atlanta University, Du Bois focused his research on race relations in the United States.

The Souls of Black Folk, Du Bois's 1903 collection of essays, had a major impact on its readers. In them, Du Bois directly criticized Booker T. Washington for being too cautious and conservative on civil rights issues. Du Bois believed African Americans needed to insist upon equal treatment and voting rights. He also helped to found the Niagara Movement, the forerunner of the NAACP. In 1910 he began publishing *The Crisis*, the official magazine of the NAACP.

In his later years, Du Bois turned to socialism and became active in the peace movement. This led to political censure and the State Department's refusal to allow Du Bois to travel outside the country. When he was permitted to leave, he went to Ghana, where he became a citizen the year he died.
How did W. E. B. Du Bois's approach to civil rights differ from Washington's approach?

National Association of Colored Women and the National Association for the Advancement of Colored People, Terrell formed the Women Wage-Earners Association, which assisted African American nurses, waitresses, and domestic workers.

Terrell led a boycott against department stores in Washington, D.C., that refused to serve African Americans. In an address to the National American Women's Suffrage Association Terrell said, "With courage, born of success achieved in the past, with a keen sense of the responsibility which we shall continue to assume, we look forward to a future large with promise and hope. Seeking no favors because of our color, nor patronage because of our needs, we knock at the bar of justice, asking an equal chance."

Calls for Compromise

The most famous African American of the late nineteenth century was the influential educator **Booker T. Washington.** He proposed that African Americans concentrate on achieving economic goals rather than political ones. In 1895 Washington summed up his views in a speech before a mostly white audience in Atlanta. Known as the Atlanta Compromise, the speech urged African Americans to postpone the fight for civil rights and instead concentrate on preparing themselves educationally and vocationally for full equality:

PRIMARY SOURCE

"The wisest among my race understand that the agitation of questions of social equality is the extremest folly, and that the enjoyment of all the privileges that will come to us must be the result of severe and constant struggle rather than of artificial forcing.... It is important and right that all privileges of the law be ours, but it is vastly more important that we be prepared for the exercise of these privileges. The opportunity to earn a dollar in a factory just now is worth infinitely more than the opportunity to spend a dollar in an opera-house."

—adapted from *Up From Slavery*

Du Bois Rejects Compromise

The Atlanta Compromise speech provoked a strong challenge from **W. E. B. Du Bois,** the leader of a new generation of African American activists. In his 1903 book *The Souls of Black Folk,* Du Bois explained why he saw no advantage in giving up civil rights, even temporarily. He was particularly concerned with protecting and exercising voting rights. "Negroes must insist continually, in season and out of season," he wrote, "that voting is necessary to proper manhood, that color discrimination is barbarism." In the years that followed, many African Americans worked to win the vote and end discrimination. The struggle, however, would prove to be a long one.

✓ **Reading Check** **Describing** How did Ida B. Wells try to stop the practice of lynching?

Section 5 REVIEW

Vocabulary

1. **Explain** the significance of: poll tax, segregation, Jim Crow laws, lynching, Ida B. Wells, Booker T. Washington, W. E. B. Du Bois.

Main Ideas

2. **Describing** Under what kind of conditions did many African Americans in the South live in after Reconstruction?

3. **Identifying** How did Southern states restrict African American voting in the 1890s?

4. **Organizing** Use a graphic organizer similar to the one below to list the responses of some prominent African Americans to racial discrimination.

African American	Response to Discrimination
Ida B. Wells	
Booker T. Washington	
W.E.B. Du Bois	

Critical Thinking

5. **Big Ideas** How did Booker T. Washington's answer to racial discrimination differ from that of W. E. B. Du Bois?

6. **Analyzing Visuals** Look at the cartoon on page 479. How does the cartoonist play into white fears?

Writing About History

7. **Expository Writing** Imagine that you are living in the 1890s. Write a letter to the editor of the local newspaper explaining your view of the Supreme Court ruling in *Plessy* v. *Ferguson.*

History ONLINE

Study Central™ To review this section, go to glencoe.com and click on Study Central.

Effects of Industrialization:

1. Immigration and Urbanization

- Rise of large factories greatly increases the demand for labor in the United States, encouraging immigrants to move to America in large numbers.

- The increase in industrial jobs encourages large numbers of Americans and immigrants to settle in cities.

- As cities grow large, pollution, crime, disease, and fire become serious problems.

- New industrial technology allows cities to grow even larger with the development of the skyscraper, the elevator, and the trolley car.

- Large urban areas change the nature of politics creating corrupt urban political "machines" such as Tammany Hall in New York.

▲ *A crowded immigrant community in New York in the early 1900s*

Effects of Industrialization:

2. Farm Problems

- Industrialization and new technology increases farm production and creates the ability to ship farm products across the country.

- Farmers produce huge surpluses, driving down food prices, while a money shortage leads to high interest rates; farmers grow deeper in debt while income falls.

- High railroad rates in the West combine with high rents for tenant farmers in the South to create a crisis for farmers.

- Farmers form the Grange, the Alliance, and the Populist Party to help address their concerns.

▲ *Sharecroppers in the South were often trapped in poverty and debt.*

Effects of Industrialization:

3. Changes in Culture

- Industrial society initially leads to a strong belief in individualism; Social Darwinism emerges as the idea that government should not interfere in society.

- Ongoing social problems caused by industrialization lead to Reform Darwinism and the emergence of reformers who want to use government to help solve society's problems and regulate the economy.

- New forms of realist and naturalist art and literature depict industrial life in serious and realistic ways.

▲ *Settlement houses, such as Hull House (above), helped poor immigrants educate their children and adapt to life in the United States.*

NEW YORK REGENTS EXAM PRACTICE

TEST-TAKING

Read the questions carefully. From the wording of each question, you can see that some have two or three concepts in common. Find the one choice that best answers each question.

Part I

Directions (1–9): For each statement or question, write on a separate sheet of paper the number of the word or expression that, of those given, best completes the statement or answers the question.

1 In the late nineteenth century, many labor unions opposed immigration, arguing that immigrants

  (1) would work for higher wages.

  (2) eased financial drains on social services.

  (3) assimilated into American culture.

  (4) would accept jobs as strikebreakers.

2 What was the major reason for Chinese immigration to the United States in the early nineteenth century?

  (1) Many Chinese were escaping severe unemployment and famine.

  (2) Many Chinese were escaping religious persecution.

  (3) Many Chinese left to avoid required military service.

  (4) Many Chinese left to escape the class system and move up the social ladder.

3 Working class individuals residing in cities usually lived

  (1) in the streetcar suburbs.

  (2) in tenements.

  (3) in fashionable downtown districts.

  (4) away from the central city.

4 The nineteenth-century philosophy of Social Darwinism maintained that

  (1) the government should have control over the means of production and the marketplace.

  (2) all social class distinctions in American society should be eliminated.

  (3) economic success comes to those who are the hardest working and most competent.

  (4) wealth and income should be more equally distributed.

5 The Interstate Commerce Act (1887) was designed to regulate interstate commerce by requiring

  (1) railroads to increase rebates to high-volume users.

  (2) railroads to charge higher rates for short hauls.

  (3) states to regulate interstate railroad traffic.

  (4) the federal government to regulate railroad rates.

6 The Populist Party supported government ownership of railroads and telegraph lines because government ownership would

  (1) increase railroad and telegraph lines across rural areas.

  (2) make these services more reliable.

  (3) keep prices more stable.

  (4) provide enough revenue to allow the government to eliminate the graduated income tax.

7 Which of the following concepts is associated with the Gospel of Wealth?

  (1) survival of the fittest

  (2) laissez-faire

  (3) unregulated competition

  (4) philanthropy

Need Extra Help?							
If You Missed Questions . . .	1	2	3	4	5	6	7
Go to Page . . .	446	445	453	458–459	462–463	473	458–461

[OVER]

Base your answer to question 8 on the chart below and your knowledge of Chapter 13.

Farm Prices, 1870–1900

Source: *Historical Statistics of the United States.*

8   What happened to crop prices between 1870 and 1880?

   (1) The price of cotton increased as the price of wheat and corn decreased.

   (2) The price of wheat, corn, and cotton increased.

   (3) The price of cotton, wheat, and corn stayed the same following an initial increase.

   (4) The price of wheat significantly decreased as the price of cotton decreased steadily.

9   In 1890 the Populists formed the People's Party and supported

   (1) the subtreasury plan where farmers could store crops in warehouses to force prices up.

   (2) limited governmental regulations for the railroad companies.

   (3) the election of senators by state legislatures.

   (4) the free coinage of gold.

Need Extra Help?		
If You Missed Questions . . .	8	9
Go to Page . . .	471	473

Part II Thematic Essay Question

Directions: Write a well-organized essay that includes an introduction, several paragraphs addressing the task below, and a conclusion.

Theme: Immigration

From 1870 to 1900 the urban population of the United States grew from 10 million to 30 million. Many immigrants stayed in the cities, while rural Americans moved to cities.

Task:

- Discuss the reasons immigrants remained in the cities and rural Americans moved to urban areas
- Discuss the problems resulting from urbanization
- Evaluate the effectiveness of reform movements that addressed society's problems.

Guidelines:

In your essay, be sure to:

- Develop all aspects of the task
- Support the theme with relevant facts, examples, and details
- Use a logical and clear plan of organization, including an introduction and a conclusion that are beyond a restatement of the theme

Part III Document-Based Question

This question is based on the accompanying documents. It is designed to test your ability to work with historical documents. Some of the documents have been edited for the purposes of the question. As you analyze the documents, take into account both the source of each document and any point of view that may be presented in the document.

Historical Context:

In the late nineteenth century, a major wave of immigrants began coming to the United States, most from southern and eastern Europe. Distinctive ethnic neighborhoods emerged in cities, where most of the new immigrants settled.

Task:

Using information from the documents and your knowledge of United States history, answer the questions that follow each document in Part A. Your answers to the questions will help you write the Part B essay, in which you will be asked to

- Discuss the cultural and economic contributions of immigrants
- Discuss the ideas of assimilation and acculturation
- Evaluate the effects of nativist reactions to new immigration

Part A

Short-Answer Questions

Directions: Analyze the documents and answer the short-answer questions that follow each document on a separate sheet of paper.

Document 1

> In the very act of coming and traveling to reach his destination, he [the immigrant] adds ... to the immediate prosperity and success of certain lines of business. Not only do the ocean steamers ... get very large returns in carrying passengers of this description, but in forwarding them to the places chosen by the immigrants as their future homes the railroad companies also derive great benefit and their passenger traffic is greatly swelled....
>
> ... These immigrants not only produce largely, ... but, having wants which they cannot supply themselves, create a demand for outside supplies.... Thus it is that the Eastern manufacturer finds the call upon him for his wares and goods growing more urgent all the time, thus the consumption of coal keeps on expanding notwithstanding the check to new railroad enterprises, and thus there is a more active and larger interchange of all commodities.

Commercial and Financial Chronicle, editorial, 1882

1 According to the editorial, what effect did immigration have on the nation's economy?

Need Extra Help?			
If You Missed Questions . . .	1	2	Essay
Go to Page . . .	R19	R18	442–447

Document 2

—Frank Beard, from *Judge,* 1885

2 According to the cartoon, why were people concerned about immigrants coming to the United States?

Part B

Essay

Directions: Reread the task box at the top left and write a well-organized essay that includes an introduction, several paragraphs, and a conclusion. Use evidence from the documents in your essay. Support your response with relevant facts, examples, and details. Include additional outside information.

Guidelines:

In your essay, be sure to:

- Develop all aspects of the task
- Incorporate information from the documents
- Incorporate relevant outside information
- Support the theme with relevant facts, examples, and details
- Use a logical and clear plan of organization, including an introduction and a conclusion that are beyond a restatement of the theme

History ONLINE

For additional test practice, use Self-Check Quizzes—Chapter 13 at glencoe.com.

Imperialism and Progressivism

1890–1920

Why It Matters

Between 1890 and 1920 two very important developments took place in American history. First, the United States began its rise to the global superpower it is today. Second, reformers began changing the government to solve problems caused by industrialism. Government became more involved in society than ever before.

U.S. warships battle the Spanish off the coast of Cuba, 1898.

Becoming a World Power

1872–1917

SECTION 1 The Imperialist Vision

SECTION 2 The Spanish-American War

SECTION 3 New American Diplomacy

A tugboat tows the battleship USS Ohio through the recently completed Panama Canal, July 1915.

1878
• U.S. signs treaty with Samoa to use Pago Pago harbor

1893
• Americans overthrow Queen Liliuokalani of Hawaii

U.S. PRESIDENTS

Hayes
1877–1881

Garfield
1881

Arthur
1881–1885

Cleveland
1885–1889

B. Harrison
1889–1893

Cleveland
1893–1897

U.S. EVENTS

1872

1882

1892

WORLD EVENTS

1874
• Britain annexes Fiji Islands

1882
• Germany, Austria, and Italy form Triple Alliance

1889
• First Pan-American conference is held

1894
• Sino-Japanese War breaks out

How Are Empires Built?

International economic and military competition convinced the United States it must become a world power. In the late 1800s, the United States increased its trade and military presence in East Asia and Latin America, and by the early 1900s, it had created an American empire.

- *Why do you think the United States focused on East Asia and Latin America?*

- *What factors make a nation a world power?*

1898
- U.S. declares war on Spain

McKinley
1897–1901

T. Roosevelt
1901–1909

1904
- Panama Canal construction begins
- Roosevelt Corollary is issued

Taft
1909–1913

1902

1912

1899
- John Hay sends Open Door notes

1900
- Boxer Rebellion begins in China

1904
- Russo-Japanese War begins

FOLDABLES™

Taking Notes Create a Concept-Map Book Foldable to help you take basic notes about the relationship between economic and military power. As you read the chapter, write details under each tab and be careful to note the years in which events and developments occurred.

U.S. Expansion
↓   ↘
Economic Power   Military Power

History ONLINE **Chapter Overview**
Visit glencoe.com to preview Chapter 14.

Section 1

The Imperialist Vision

Guide to Reading

Big Ideas
Economics and Society In the late 1800s, many Americans wanted the United States to expand its military and economic power overseas.

Content Vocabulary
- imperialism *(p. 490)*
- protectorate *(p. 490)*

Academic Vocabulary
- expansion *(p. 491)*
- conference *(p. 495)*

People and Events to Identify
- Anglo-Saxonism *(p. 492)*
- Matthew C. Perry *(p. 493)*
- Queen Liliuokalani *(p. 494)*
- Pan-Americanism *(p. 495)*

Reading Strategy
Organizing As you read about the development of the United States as a world power, use the major headings of the section to create an outline similar to the one below.

```
The Imperialist Vision
I. Building Support for Imperialism
    A.
    B.
    C.
II.
    A.
    B.
```

NEW YORK CORE CURRICULUM
U.S. History and Government

Unit 4:
II.A.1.a Role of increased American power
II.A.1.b Perry and the "opening" of Japan (1854)
II.A.2.c Acquisition of Hawaii

During the late 1800s, the desire to find new markets, increase trade, and build a powerful navy caused the United States to become more involved in international affairs.

Building Support for Imperialism

MAIN Idea A desire for world markets and belief in the superiority of Anglo-Saxon culture led the United States to assert itself as a world power.

HISTORY AND YOU Do you remember what role George Washington thought the United States should play in world affairs? Read to learn why Americans' opinions changed in the 1880s.

In the years immediately following the Civil War, most Americans showed little interest in expanding their nation's territory outside the United States or increasing its international influence. Instead, they focused on reconstructing the South, building up the nation's industries, and settling the West. Beginning in the 1880s, however, economic and military competition from other nations, as well as a growing feeling of cultural superiority, convinced many Americans that the United States should become a world power.

A Desire for New Markets

Several European nations were already expanding overseas, a development known as the New Imperialism. **Imperialism** is the economic and political domination of a strong nation over weaker ones. Europeans expanded their power overseas for many reasons. Factories depended on raw materials from all over the world. No country had all of the resources its economy needed. In addition, by the late 1800s, most industrialized countries had placed high tariffs against each other. These tariffs were intended to protect a nation's industries from foreign competition. The tariffs reduced trade between industrialized countries, forcing companies to look for other markets overseas.

At the same time, the growth of investment opportunities in Western Europe had slowed. Most of the factories, railroads, and mines that Europe's economy needed had been built. Increasingly, Europeans began looking overseas for places to invest their capital. They started to invest in industries located in other countries, particularly in Africa and Asia.

To protect their investments, European nations began exerting control over those territories. Some areas became colonies. Many others became protectorates. In a **protectorate,** the imperial power

Causes of American Imperialism

American imperialism had three main causes:

1. The belief in the superiority of American culture
2. The belief that the nation needed a large navy for security, with bases overseas
3. The belief that the economy needed overseas markets

1. ANGLO-SAXONISM

"The work which the English race began when it colonized North America is destined to go on until every land . . . that is not already the seat of an old civilization shall become English in its language, in its religion, in political habits and traditions, and to a predominant extent in the blood of its people."
—John Fiske, quoted in *The Expansionists of 1898*

2. MILITARY BASES

". . . [T]he ships of war of the United States, in war, will be like land birds, unable to fly far from their own shores. To provide resting-places for them, where they can coal and repair, would be one of the first duties of a government proposing to itself the development of the power of the nation at sea."
—Alfred Thayer Mahan, *The Influence of Sea Power Upon History*

3. OVERSEAS MARKETS

"[W]e are raising more than we can consume, . . . making more than we can use. Therefore we must find new markets for our produce…"
—Albert Beveridge, quoted in *The Meaning of the Times and Other Speeches*

Exports and Imports, 1865–1900

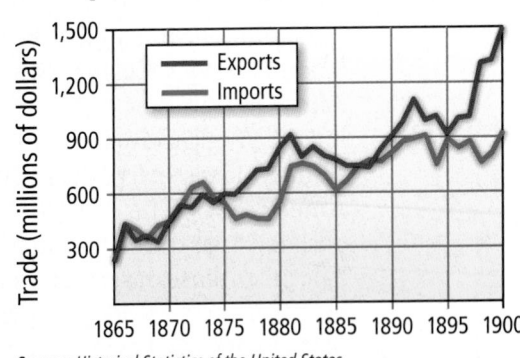

Source: *Historical Statistics of the United States.*

DBQ · Document-Based Questions

1. **Interpreting** Based on the quote above, how do you think Albert Beveridge would use the data shown in the graph to support his argument?
2. **Comparing** What is the difference between Fiske's support for expanding American power overseas and Mahan's support for establishing military bases overseas?

allowed the local rulers to stay in control and protected them against rebellions and invasion. In exchange, the local rulers usually had to accept advice from the Europeans on how to govern their countries.

The United States noticed the **expansion** of European power overseas. As the United States industrialized, many Americans took an interest in the new imperialism. Until the late 1800s, the United States had expanded by settling more territory in North America. Now, with settlers finally filling up the western frontier, many Americans concluded that the nation needed new overseas markets to keep its economy strong.

A Feeling of Superiority

In addition to economic concerns, certain other key ideas convinced many Americans to encourage their nation's expansion overseas. Many supporters of Social Darwinism argued that nations competed with each other politically, economically, and militarily, and that only the strongest would survive. To them, this idea justified increasing American influence abroad.

Many Americans, such as the well-known writer and historian John Fiske, took this idea even further. Fiske argued that English-speaking nations had superior character, ideas, and systems of government.

Fiske's ideas, known as **Anglo-Saxonism,** were popular in Britain and the United States. Many Americans linked it with the idea of Manifest Destiny. They believed the nation's destiny had been to expand westward to the Pacific Ocean. Now they believed the United States was destined to expand overseas and spread its civilization to other people.

Another influential advocate of Anglo-Saxonism was Josiah Strong, a popular American minister in the late 1800s. Strong linked Anglo-Saxonism to Christian missionary ideas. His ideas influenced many Americans. "The Anglo-Saxon," Strong declared, "[is] divinely commissioned to be, in a peculiar sense, his brother's keeper." By linking missionary work with Anglo-Saxonism, Strong convinced many Americans to support an expansion of American power overseas.

Building a Modern Navy

As imperialism and Anglo-Saxonism gained support, the United States became increasingly assertive in foreign affairs. Three international crises illustrated this new approach. In 1888 the country risked war to prevent Germany from taking control of Samoa in the South Pacific. Three years later, when a mob in Chile attacked American sailors in the port of Valparaíso, the United States threatened to go to war unless Chile paid reparations. Then, in 1895, the United States backed Venezuela against Great Britain in a border dispute with British Guiana. After Britain rejected an American ultimatum, many newspapers and members of Congress called for war. All three crises were eventually resolved peacefully.

As Americans became increasingly willing to risk war to defend American interests overseas, support for building a large modern navy began to grow. Supporters argued that if the United States did not build up its navy and acquire bases overseas, European nations would shut it out of foreign markets.

Captain Alfred T. Mahan, an officer in the U.S. Navy who taught at the Naval War College, best expressed this argument. In 1890 Mahan published his lectures in a book called *The*

Influence of Sea Power upon History, 1660–1783. In this book Mahan pointed out that many prosperous peoples in the past, such as the British and Dutch, had built large fleets of merchant ships to trade with the world. He then suggested that a nation also needed a large navy to protect its merchant ships and to defend its right to trade with other countries.

Mahan's book became a best-seller, helping to build public support for a big navy. Two powerful senators, Henry Cabot Lodge and Albert J. Beveridge, pushed for constructing a new navy. In the executive branch, Benjamin Tracy, secretary of the navy under President Harrison, and John D. Long, secretary of the navy under President McKinley, strongly supported Mahan's ideas.

By the 1890s, several different ideas had come together in the United States. Business leaders wanted new markets overseas. Anglo-Saxonism had convinced many Americans of their destiny to dominate the world. Growing European imperialism threatened America's security. Combined with Mahan's theories, these ideas convinced Congress to authorize the construction of a large, modern navy.

✔ **Reading Check** **Summarizing** How did Americans' opinions about overseas expansion change in the late 1800s?

PRIMARY SOURCE
Perry Arrives in Japan

In 1853 Japan was a closed society. Its rulers had deliberately ended contact with the outside world, permitting only a small amount of trade with the Dutch and the Chinese. They were largely unaware of the changes the industrial revolution had brought to Europe and the United States. Perry's black steamships, belching smoke, and moving without any visible sails, were something the Japanese had never seen before.

The Japanese had cannons and guns, but Perry's ships carried 65 large cannons—a staggering number that represented immense power—and a direct threat to Japan's many coastal castles and towns. Perry's arrival carried different meanings for people living in the two countries, as shown in the two images to the right—one from Japan and the other from the United States.

American Expansion in the Pacific

MAIN Idea The desire for new markets led to trade with Japan and the annexation of Hawaii.

HISTORY AND YOU What products do you use that are made in Japan? Read how the United States and Japan first became trading partners.

From the earliest days of the Republic, Americans had expanded their nation by moving westward. When Americans began looking overseas for new markets in the 1800s, therefore, they naturally tended to look toward the Pacific. Even before imperialist ideas became popular, American businesses had begun sending ships to trade in East Asia.

Perry Opens Japan

Many American business leaders believed that the United States would benefit from trade with Japan, as well as with China. Japan's rulers, however, who believed that excessive contact with the West would destroy their culture, allowed only the Chinese and Dutch to trade with their nation. In 1852, after receiving several petitions from Congress, President Millard Fillmore decided to force Japan to trade with the United States. He ordered Commodore **Matthew C. Perry** to take a naval expedition to Japan to negotiate a trade treaty.

On July 8, 1853, four American warships under Perry's command entered Edo Bay (today known as Tokyo Bay). The display of American technology and firepower impressed the Japanese, who had never before seen steamships. Realizing that they could not resist modern Western technology and weapons, the Japanese agreed to sign the Treaty of Kanagawa. In addition to granting the United States permission to trade at two ports in Japan, the treaty called for peace between the two countries; promised help for any American ships and sailors shipwrecked off the Japanese coast; and gave American ships permission to buy supplies such as wood, water, food, and coal in the Japanese ports.

The American decision forcing Japan to open trade played an important role in Japanese history. Japanese leaders concluded that it was time to remake their society. They adopted Western technology and launched their own industrial revolution. By the 1890s, the Japanese had a powerful navy and had begun building their own empire in Asia.

▶ American painter James Evans entitled his work "Commodore Perry Carrying the Gospel of God to the Heathen, 1853."

U.S. JAPAN FLEET, Com PERRY. carrying the 'GOSPEL of GOD'. to the HEATHEN, 1853.

▼ This Japanese color print depicts one artist's perspective of Perry's "black ships" that arrived in Japan in 1853.

Analyzing VISUALS

1. **Comparing** What elements did both the American and Japanese artists depict the same way? Which were different?

2. **Making Inferences** What impression of the Americans does the Japanese image convey? What is the American painting communicating about Perry's mission?

People IN HISTORY

Queen Liliuokalani
1838–1917

Queen Liliuokalani was the last ruling monarch of the Hawaiian Islands. A group of white sugar planters had forced her predecessor to accept a new constitution that minimized the power of the monarchy, gave voting rights to Americans and Europeans, and denied voting rights to most Hawaiians and all Asians.

As queen, Liliuokalani was determined to regain royal power and reduce the power of foreigners. On January 14, 1893, she issued a new constitution, which restored the power of the monarchy and the rights of the Hawaiian people. In response, a group of planters led by Sanford B. Dole launched a revolt. Under protest, Liliuokalani surrendered her throne on January 17. After supporters led a revolt in an attempt to restore her to power in 1895, Liliuokalani was placed under house arrest for several months. After her release, she lived out her days in Washington Palace in Honolulu.

Why did sugar planters lead a revolt against Queen Liliuokalani?

▲ *Sanford B. Dole gives Hawaii, represented as the bride, to Uncle Sam.*

For an example of American views on annexing Hawaii read "President Harrison on Hawaiian Annexation" on page R51 in **Documents in American History.**

Annexing Hawaii

As trade with Asia grew during the 1800s, Americans began seeking ports where they could refuel and resupply while crossing the Pacific Ocean. Pago Pago, in the Samoan Islands, had one of the finest harbors in the South Pacific. In 1878 the United States negotiated permission to open a base there.

More important was Hawaii. Whaling ships and merchant vessels crossing the Pacific often stopped there to rest and to take on supplies. In 1819 missionaries from New England arrived in Hawaii. American settlers found that sugarcane grew well in Hawaii's climate and soil. By the mid-1800s, businessmen had established many plantations on the islands.

A severe recession struck Hawaii in 1872. Three years later, worried that the economic crisis might force the Hawaiians to turn to the British or French for help, the United States signed a treaty exempting Hawaiian sugar from tariffs. When the treaty came up for renewal several years later, the Senate insisted that Hawaii grant the United States exclusive rights to a naval base at Pearl Harbor.

The treaty led to a boom in the Hawaiian sugar industry and wealth for the planters. In 1887 prominent planters pressured the Hawaiian king into accepting a constitution

that limited the king's authority. As tensions mounted between the planters and Hawaiians, Congress passed a new tariff in 1890 that gave subsidies to sugar producers in the United States. The subsidies made Hawaiian sugar more expensive than American sugar. Unable to sell much sugar, planters concluded that the only way to increase sales was to have Hawaii become part of the United States.

In 1891 **Queen Liliuokalani** ascended the Hawaiian throne. Liliuokalani disliked the influence that American settlers had gained in Hawaii. In January 1893 she tried to impose a new constitution reasserting her authority as ruler of Hawaii. In response, a group of planters tried to overthrow the monarchy. Supported by the marines from the *USS Boston*, they forced the queen to step down. Then they set up a provisional government and asked the United States to annex Hawaii.

President Cleveland strongly opposed imperialism. He withdrew the annexation treaty from the Senate and tried to return Liliuokalani to power. Hawaii's new leaders refused to restore the queen and decided to wait until Cleveland left office. Five years later, the United States annexed Hawaii.

✔ **Reading Check** **Explaining** How did the search for new markets push the United States to become a world power?

Diplomacy in Latin America

MAIN Idea The United States worked to increase trade with Latin America.

HISTORY AND YOU What products have you used that come from Latin America? Read to learn how the United States tried to expand its trade relations with Latin America.

The Pacific was not the only region where the United States sought to increase its influence in the 1800s. It also focused on Latin America. Although the United States bought raw materials from this region, Latin Americans bought most of their manufactured goods from Europe. American business leaders and government officials wanted to increase the sale of American products to the region. They also wanted the Europeans to understand that the United States was the dominant power in the region.

James G. Blaine, who served as secretary of state in three administrations in the 1880s, led early efforts to expand American influence in Latin America. "What we want," Blaine explained, "are the markets of these neighbors of ours that lie to the south of us. . . . With these markets secured new life would be given to our manufacturers, the product of the western farmer would be in demand, the reasons for and inducements to strikers, with all their attendant evils, would cease." Blaine proposed that the United States invite the Latin American nations to a **conference** in Washington, D.C. The conference would discuss ways in which the American nations could work together to support peace and to increase trade. The idea that the United States and Latin America should work together came to be called **Pan-Americanism.**

On October 2, 1889, Washington, D.C., hosted the first modern Pan-American conference, which all Latin American nations except the Dominican Republic attended. Blaine had two goals for the conference. First, he wanted to create a customs union between Latin America and the United States. He also wanted to create a system for American nations to work out their disputes peacefully.

A customs union would require all of the American nations to reduce their tariffs against each other and to treat each other equally in trade. Blaine hoped that a customs union would turn the Latin Americans away from European products and toward American products. He also hoped that a common system for settling disputes would keep the Europeans from meddling in American affairs.

Although the warm reception they received in the United States impressed the Latin American delegates to the conference, they rejected both of Blaine's ideas. They did agree, however, to create the Commercial Bureau of the American Republics, an organization that worked to promote cooperation among the nations of the Western Hemisphere. In 1920 the name was changed to the International Bureau of the American Republics. This organization was later known as the Pan-American Union and is today called the Organization of American States (OAS).

✓ Reading Check **Summarizing** How did Secretary of State Blaine attempt to increase American influence in Latin America?

Section 1 REVIEW

Vocabulary

1. **Explain** the significance of: imperialism, protectorate, Anglo-Saxonism, Matthew C. Perry, Queen Liliuokalani, Pan-Americanism.

Main Ideas

2. **Listing** Use a graphic organizer to list the factors that led the United States to adopt an imperialist policy in the 1890s.

> Factors Leading to U.S. Imperialist Policy

3. **Describing** Why and how did the Americans force the Japanese to trade with the United States?

4. **Explaining** Why did Secretary of State James G. Blaine convene the Pan-American conference in 1889?

Critical Thinking

5. **Big Ideas** Do you think the United States should have supported the planters in their attempt to overthrow Queen Liliuokalani of Hawaii? Why or why not?

6. **Evaluating** How did trade with the United States change Japanese society?

7. **Analyzing Visuals** Study the two images of Perry's ship on page 493. How do the artists' perspectives vary? Do you think the artists show any bias in their representations? Why or why not?

Writing About History

8. **Persuasive Writing** Imagine that you are living in the United States in the 1890s. Write a letter to the president persuading him to support or oppose an imperialist policy for the United States.

History ONLINE

Study Central™ To review this section, go to glencoe.com and click on Study Central.

The Spanish-American War

Guide to Reading

Big Ideas

Trade, War, and Migration The United States defeated Spain in a war, acquired new overseas territories, and became an imperial power.

Content Vocabulary
- yellow journalism *(p. 497)*
- autonomy *(p. 498)*
- jingoism *(p. 499)*

Academic Vocabulary
- intervene *(p. 498)*
- volunteer *(p. 500)*

People and Events to Identify
- José Martí *(p. 496)*
- William Randolph Hearst *(p. 497)*
- Joseph Pulitzer *(p. 497)*
- Emilio Aguinaldo *(p. 500)*
- Platt Amendment *(p. 502)*
- Foraker Act *(p. 503)*

Reading Strategy
Organizing As you read about the Spanish-American War, complete a graphic organizer like the one below by listing the circumstances that contributed to war with Spain.

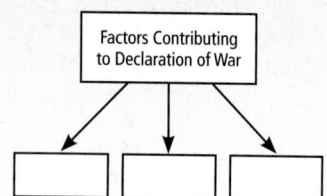

Factors Contributing
to Declaration of War

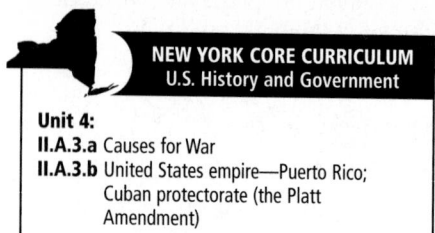

NEW YORK CORE CURRICULUM
U.S. History and Government

Unit 4:
II.A.3.a Causes for War
II.A.3.b United States empire—Puerto Rico; Cuban protectorate (the Platt Amendment)

During the Spanish-American War, the United States defeated Spanish troops in Cuba and the Philippines. Afterward, the United States annexed the Philippines and became an imperial power.

The Coming of War

MAIN Idea In support of the Cuban rebellion and in retaliation for the loss of the USS *Maine*, the United States declared war on Spain.

HISTORY AND YOU Do you remember what led the American colonists to declare their independence from Britain? Read about another colony that fought for independence from a colonial ruler.

By 1898 Cuba and Puerto Rico were Spain's last remaining colonies in the Western Hemisphere. Cubans had periodically revolted against Spanish rule, and many Americans regarded the Spanish as tyrants. Ultimately, the United States issued a declaration of war. Although the fighting lasted only a few months, the "splendid little war," as Secretary of State John Hay described it, dramatically altered the position of the United States on the world stage.

The Cuban Rebellion Begins

Cuba was one of Spain's oldest colonies in the Americas. Its sugar-cane plantations generated considerable wealth for Spain and produced nearly one-third of the world's sugar in the mid-1800s. Until Spain abolished slavery in 1886, about one-third of the Cuban population was enslaved and forced to work for wealthy landowners on the plantations.

In 1868 Cuban rebels declared independence and launched a guerrilla war against Spanish authorities. Lacking internal support, the rebellion collapsed a decade later. Many Cuban rebels then fled to the United States. One of the exiled leaders was **José Martí,** a writer and poet. While living in New York City in the 1880s, Martí brought together Cuban exile groups living in the United States. The groups raised funds, purchased weapons, and trained troops in preparation for an invasion of Cuba.

By the early 1890s, the United States and Cuba had become closely linked economically. Cuba exported much of its sugar to the United States, and Americans had invested approximately $50 million in Cuba's sugar plantations, mines, and railroads. These economic ties created a crisis in 1894, when the United States imposed a new tariff on sugar that devastated Cuba's economy. With Cuba in financial

Causes of the Spanish-American War

The Spanish-American War had four main causes:

1. The Cuban Rebellion against Spain
2. American desire to protect its investments in Cuba
3. Yellow journalism that intensified public anger at Spain
4. The explosion of the USS *Maine*

CUBANS REBEL AGAINST SPAIN

◀ *Spanish oppression of the Cuban people triggered a rebellion that earned the sympathy of many Americans, some of whom began providing arms and money to the rebels.*

U.S. Investment in Cuba, 1897

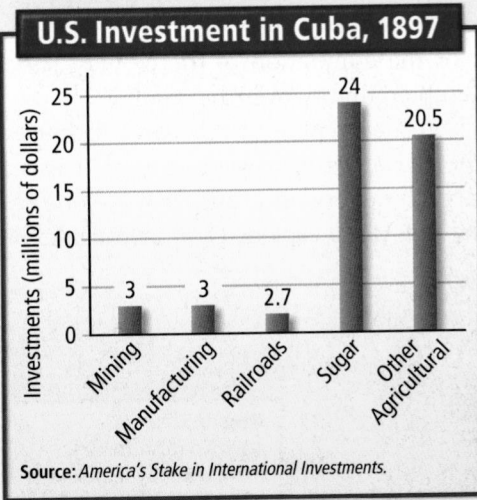

Source: *America's Stake in International Investments.*

◀ *With $30 to $50 million invested in Cuba and nearly $100 million in annual trade, American business leaders wanted Spain out of Cuba and an end to the rebellion.*

YELLOW JOURNALISM

NEW YORK JOURNAL
AND ADVERTISER.

DESTRUCTION OF THE WAR SHIP MAINE WAS THE WORK OF AN ENEMY

$50,000!
$50,000 REWARD!
For the Detection of the
Perpetrator of
the Maine Outrage!

Assistant Secretary Roosevelt
Convinced the Explosion of
the War Ship Was Not
an Accident.

The Journal Offers $50,000 Reward for the
Conviction of the Criminals Who Sent
258 American Sailors to Their Death.
Naval Officers Unanimous That
the Ship Was Destroyed

$50,000!
$50,000 REWARD!
For the Detection of the
Perpetrator of
the Maine Outrage!

▲ *Dramatic and emotional stories in newspapers owned by Hearst and Pulitzer described Spanish atrocities in Cuba and enraged the American people, some of whom began to call for war.*

THE *MAINE* EXPLODES, 1898

▲ *President McKinley sent the battleship* Maine *to Cuba to help Americans evacuate. When the ship exploded, an enraged nation blamed Spain, and "Remember the Maine!" became the battle cry for war.*

Analyzing VISUALS

1. **Interpreting** What do you think contributed to American sympathy with the Cubans?
2. **Identifying Central Issues** What role did economics play in the lead-up to war with Spain?

distress, Martí's followers launched a new rebellion in February 1895. Although Martí died during the fighting, the rebels seized control of eastern Cuba, declared independence, and formally established the Republic of Cuba in September 1895.

America Supports Cuba

When the uprising in Cuba began, President Grover Cleveland declared the United States neutral. Outside the White House, however, many people openly supported the rebels. Some citizens compared the Cubans' struggle to the American Revolution. A few sympathetic Americans even began smuggling guns from Florida to the Cuban rebels.

What caused most Americans to support the rebels were the stories of Spanish atrocities reported in two of the nation's major newspapers, the *New York Journal* and the *New York World*. The *Journal*, owned by **William Randolph Hearst,** and *The World*, owned by **Joseph Pulitzer,** competed with each other to increase their circulation. The *Journal* reported outrageous stories of the Spanish feeding Cuban prisoners to sharks and dogs. Not to be outdone, *The World* described Cuba as a place with "blood on the roadsides, blood in the fields, blood on the doorsteps, blood, blood, blood!" This kind of sensationalist reporting, in which writers often exaggerated and even made up stories to attract readers, became known as **yellow journalism.**

Although the press invented sensational stories, Cubans indeed suffered horribly. The Spanish sent nearly 200,000 troops to the island to put down the rebellion and appointed General Valeriano Weyler as governor. Weyler's harsh policies quickly earned him the nickname "El Carnicero" ("The Butcher").

The Cuban rebels staged hit-and-run raids, burned plantations and sugar mills, tore up railroad tracks, and attacked supply depots. Knowing that many American businesses had investments in Cuba, the rebels hoped that the destruction of American property would lead to American intervention in the war.

To prevent Cuban villagers from helping the rebels, Weyler herded hundreds of thousands of rural men, women, and children into "reconcentration camps," where tens of thousands died of starvation and disease. News reports of these camps enraged Americans.

Calls for War

In 1897 Republican William McKinley became president of the United States. The new president did not want to **intervene** in the war, believing it would cost too many lives and hurt the economy. In September 1897, he asked the Spanish if the United States could help negotiate an end to the conflict. He made it clear that if the war did not end soon, the United States might have to intervene.

Spain removed Weyler from power and offered the Cubans **autonomy**—the right to their own government—but only if Cuba remained part of the Spanish empire. The Cuban rebels refused to negotiate.

Spain's concessions enraged many Spanish loyalists in Cuba. In January 1898, the loyalists rioted in Havana. Worried that Americans in Cuba might be attacked, McKinley sent the battleship USS *Maine* to Havana in case the Americans had to be evacuated.

On February 9, 1898, the *New York Journal* printed a letter intercepted by a Cuban agent. Written by Enrique Dupuy de Lôme, the Spanish ambassador to the United States, the letter described McKinley as "weak and a bidder for the admiration of the crowd." The nation erupted in fury over the insult.

Then, on the evening of February 15, 1898, while the *Maine* sat in Havana Harbor, it was ripped apart by an explosion and sank. No one is sure why the *Maine* exploded. An investigation

PRIMARY SOURCE
The Spanish-American War

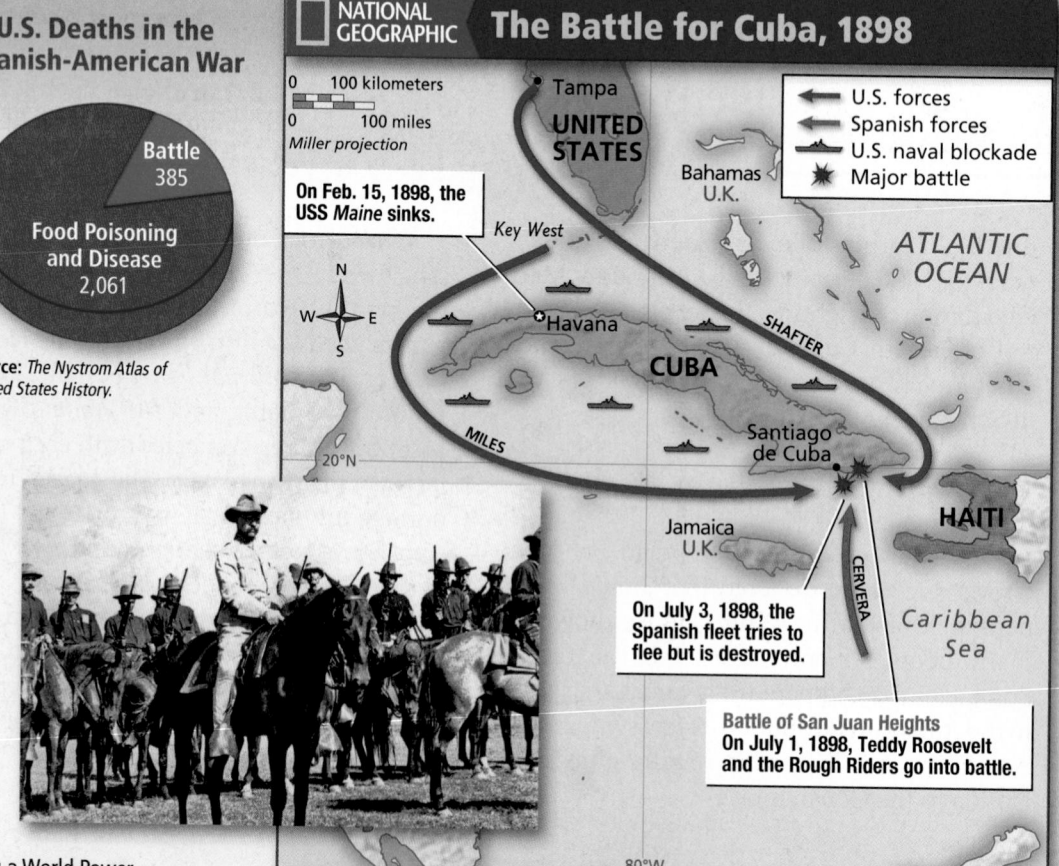

When the United States declared war on Spain, the U.S. Army had approximately 25,000 soldiers. Spain had roughly 200,000 in Cuba alone. To expand its forces, the government called into service soldiers from the state militias and also enlisted 20,000 volunteers in the army. Among those volunteers was the First Volunteer Cavalry, nicknamed the Rough Riders, under the command of Colonels Leonard Wood and Theodore Roosevelt.

U.S. Deaths in the Spanish-American War

Battle 385

Food Poisoning and Disease 2,061

Source: *The Nystrom Atlas of United States History.*

NATIONAL GEOGRAPHIC — The Battle for Cuba, 1898

0   100 kilometers
0   100 miles
Miller projection

On Feb. 15, 1898, the USS *Maine* sinks.

UNITED STATES
Tampa
Key West
Havana
CUBA
Santiago de Cuba
Bahamas U.K.
ATLANTIC OCEAN
HAITI
Jamaica U.K.
Caribbean Sea
SHAFTER
MILES
CERVERA
20°N
80°W

U.S. forces
Spanish forces
U.S. naval blockade
Major battle

On July 3, 1898, the Spanish fleet tries to flee but is destroyed.

Battle of San Juan Heights
On July 1, 1898, Teddy Roosevelt and the Rough Riders go into battle.

in the 1970s suggested that the spontaneous combustion of a coal bunker aboard the ship caused the explosion, but a study in the 1990s concluded that a mine could have done the damage. In 1898, however, many Americans believed it was an act of sabotage by Spanish agents. "Remember the *Maine!*" became the rallying cry for those demanding a declaration of war against Spain.

In response, Congress authorized McKinley to spend $50 million for war preparations. McKinley faced tremendous pressure to go to war. Within the Republican Party, **jingoism**—aggressive nationalism—was very strong. Many Democrats also demanded war, and Republicans feared that if McKinley did not go to war, the Democrats would win the elections in 1900. Finally, on April 11, 1898, McKinley asked Congress to authorize the use of force.

On April 19, Congress proclaimed Cuba independent, demanded that Spain withdraw from the island, and authorized the president to use armed force if necessary. In response, on April 24, Spain declared war on the United States. For the first time in 50 years, the United States was at war with another nation.

Reading Check **Examining** What conditions led to the Cuban rebellion in 1895?

A War on Two Fronts

MAIN Idea The United States fought and defeated Spain in both the Caribbean and the Pacific.

HISTORY AND YOU Have you ever had to plan a trip or an event? Read to learn about the problems American troops encountered in the war of 1898.

The United States Navy was ready for war with Spain. The navy's North Atlantic Squadron blockaded Cuba, and Commodore George Dewey, commander of the American naval squadron based in Hong Kong, was ordered to attack the Spanish fleet based in the Philippines. The Philippines was a Spanish colony, and American naval planners wanted to prevent the Spanish fleet based there from sailing east to attack the United States.

The Battle of Manila Bay

A short time after midnight, on May 1, 1898, Dewey's squadron entered Manila Bay in the Philippines. As dawn broke, four American ships in the squadron opened fire and rapidly destroyed all eight of the severely outgunned Spanish warships.

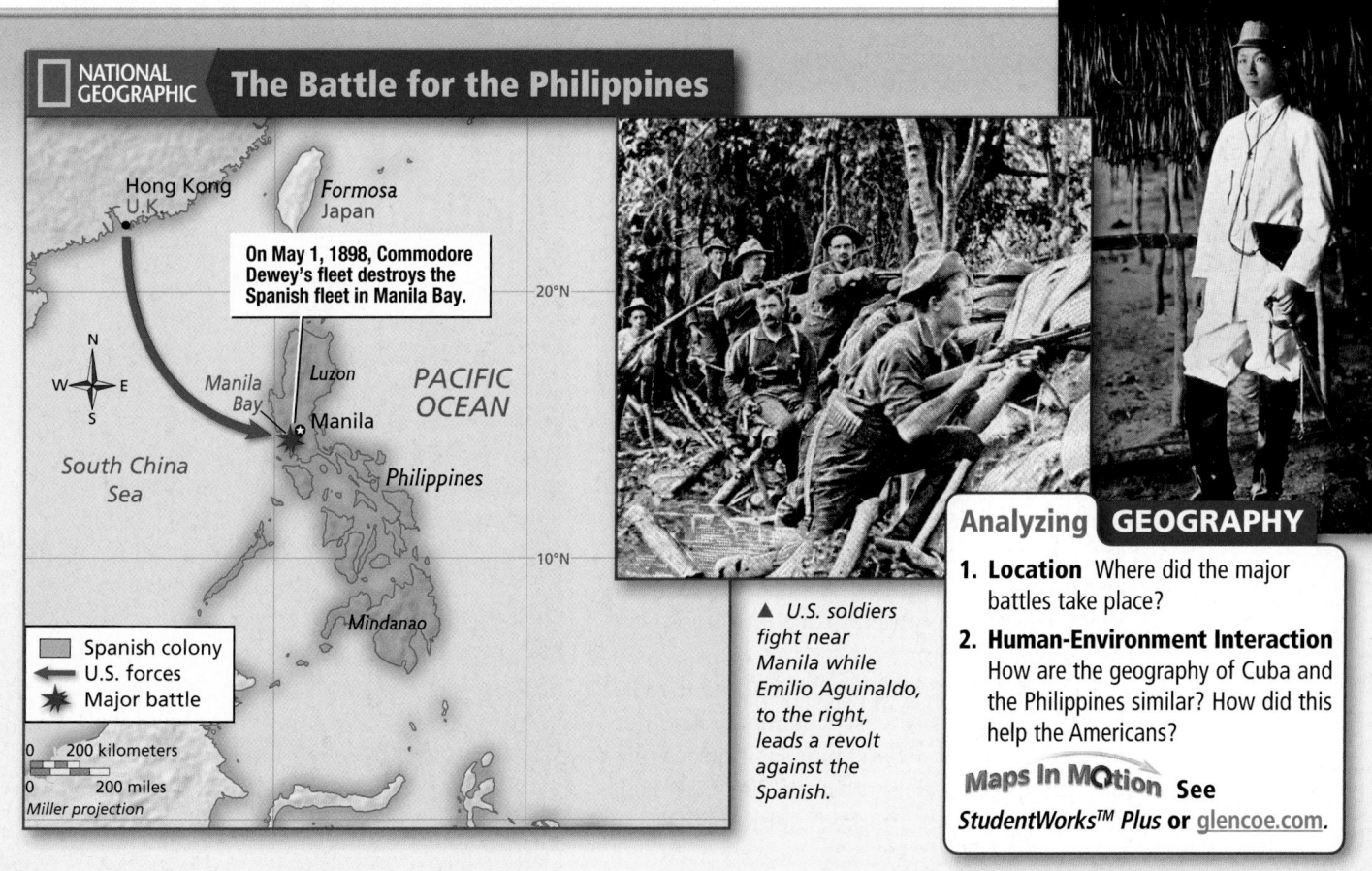

NATIONAL GEOGRAPHIC **The Battle for the Philippines**

Hong Kong U.K.
Formosa Japan
On May 1, 1898, Commodore Dewey's fleet destroys the Spanish fleet in Manila Bay.
20°N
N W E S
Manila Bay
Luzon
Manila
PACIFIC OCEAN
South China Sea
Philippines
10°N
Mindanao

Spanish colony
U.S. forces
Major battle

0 200 kilometers
0 200 miles
Miller projection

▲ U.S. soldiers fight near Manila while Emilio Aguinaldo, to the right, leads a revolt against the Spanish.

Analyzing GEOGRAPHY

1. **Location** Where did the major battles take place?
2. **Human-Environment Interaction** How are the geography of Cuba and the Philippines similar? How did this help the Americans?

Maps In Motion See *StudentWorks™ Plus* or glencoe.com.

Dewey's quick victory took McKinley and his advisers by surprise. The army was not yet ready to send troops to help Dewey. Hastily, the army assembled 20,000 troops to sail from San Francisco to the Philippines. On the way, the Americans also seized the island of Guam, another Spanish possession in the Pacific.

While waiting for the American troops to arrive, Dewey contacted **Emilio Aguinaldo,** a Filipino revolutionary leader who had staged an unsuccessful uprising against the Spanish in 1896. Aguinaldo quickly launched a new rebellion against the Spanish. While the rebels took control of most of the islands, American troops seized the Philippine capital of Manila.

American Forces in Cuba

The Spanish in Cuba were not prepared for war. Tropical diseases and months of fighting rebels had weakened their soldiers. Their warships were old and their crews poorly trained. Both sides knew that the war would ultimately be decided at sea. If the United States could defeat the Spanish fleet, Spain would not be able to supply its troops in Cuba. Eventually, they would have to surrender.

The United States Army was not prepared for war either. Although there were many **volunteers,** the army lacked the resources to train and equip them. In many training camps, conditions were so unsanitary that epidemics broke out, and hundreds died—far more than would be killed in battle with the Spanish.

Finally, on June 14, 1898, a force of about 17,000 troops landed east of the city of Santiago, Cuba. The Spanish fleet, well-protected by powerful shore-based guns, occupied Santiago Harbor. American military planners wanted to capture those guns to drive the Spanish fleet out of the harbor and into battle with the American fleet waiting nearby.

Among the American troops advancing toward Santiago was a volunteer cavalry unit from the American west. They were a flamboyant mix of cowboys, miners, and law officers known as the "Rough Riders." Colonel Leonard Wood commanded them. Theodore Roosevelt was second in command.

On July 1, American troops attacked the village of El Caney northeast of Santiago. Another force attacked the San Juan Heights. While one group of soldiers attacked San Juan Hill, the Rough Riders attacked Kettle Hill. After seizing Kettle Hill, Roosevelt and his men assisted in the capture of San Juan Hill.

The all-black 9th and 10th Cavalry Regiments accompanied the Rough Riders up Kettle Hill. Roughly one-fourth of the American troops fighting in Cuba were African Americans, four of whom received the Medal of Honor for their bravery during the war.

The Spanish commander in Santiago panicked after the American victories at El Caney and the San Juan Heights and ordered the Spanish fleet in the harbor to flee. As they exited the harbor on July 3, American warships attacked them, sinking or beaching every Spanish vessel. Two weeks later, the Spanish troops in Santiago surrendered. Soon afterwards, American troops occupied the nearby Spanish colony of Puerto Rico as well.

✔ Reading Check **Comparing** How prepared was the U.S. Army as compared to the U.S. Navy to fight a war against Spain?

Debates
IN HISTORY

Should the United States Annex the Philippines?

In the Treaty of Paris of 1898, Spain ceded control of the Philippine Islands to the United States. Americans were divided over whether the United States should give the Filipinos their independence or become an imperial power by annexing the Philippines. Supporters of annexation argued the United States would benefit economically and the Filipinos would benefit from exposure to American values and principles. Opponents, however, considered it hypocritical for the United States, with its own colonial past, to become an imperial nation.

An American Empire

MAIN Idea In defeating Spain, the United States acquired an overseas empire.

HISTORY AND YOU Do you think Puerto Rico should become the 51st state? Read how Puerto Rico became an American territory.

As American and Spanish leaders met to discuss the terms for a peace treaty, Americans debated what to do about their newly acquired lands. Cuba would receive its independence as promised, and Spain had agreed to the U.S. annexation of Guam and Puerto Rico. The big question was what to do with the Philippines. The United States faced a difficult choice—remain true to its republican ideals or become an imperial power that ruled a foreign country without the consent of its people. The issue sparked an intense political debate.

The Debate Over Annexation

Many people who supported annexing the Philippines emphasized the economic and military benefits of taking the islands. They would provide the United States with another Pacific naval base, a stopover on the way to China, and a large market for American goods.

Other supporters believed America had a duty to help "less civilized" peoples. "Surely this Spanish war has not been a grab for empire," commented a New England minister, "but a heroic effort [to] free the oppressed and to teach the millions of ignorant, debased human beings thus freed how to live."

Not all Americans supported annexation. Anti-imperialists included William Jennings Bryan, industrialist Andrew Carnegie, social worker Jane Addams, writer Samuel Clemens (Mark Twain), and Samuel Gompers, leader of the American Federation of Labor.

YES

Albert J. Beveridge
United States Senator

PRIMARY SOURCE

"The Opposition tells us that we ought not to govern a people without their consent. I answer, The rule of liberty that all just government derives its authority from the consent of the governed, applies only to those who are capable of self-government. We govern the Indians without their consent, we govern our territories without their consent, we govern our children without their consent. . . . Would not the people of the Philippines prefer the just, humane, civilizing government of this Republic to the savage, bloody rule of pillage and extortion from which we have rescued them?"

—from *The Meaning of the Times*

NO

William Jennings Bryan
Presidential Candidate

PRIMARY SOURCE

"It is not necessary to own people in order to trade with them. We carry on trade today with every part of the world, and our commerce has expanded more rapidly than the commerce of any European empire. . . . A harbor and coaling station in the Philippines would answer every trade and military necessity and such a concession could have been secured at any time without difficulty.

. . . Imperialism finds no warrant in the Bible. The command 'Go ye into all the world and preach the gospel to every creature' has no Gatling gun attachment. . . ."

—from *Speeches of William Jennings Bryan*

DBQ Document-Based Questions

1. **Making Inferences** According to Albert Beveridge, why is annexation of the Philippines an honorable decision?

2. **Recognizing Bias** What does Beveridge think of the people of the Philippines?

3. **Analyzing** What are William Jennings Bryan's two main criticisms of imperialism?

4. **Drawing Conclusions** After studying both sides of the issue, who do you think was right? Explain.

The Debate Over Empire

▲ President McKinley raises the American flag over the Philippines while William Jennings Bryan tries to chop it down.

WELL, I HARDLY KNOW WHICH TO TAKE FIRST!

▲ President McKinley (the waiter) prepares to take Uncle Sam's order. The menu posted on the wall shows three regions of choice: the Cuba steak, the Porto [Puerto] Rico pig; and the Philippines and Sandwich Islands (Hawaii) in the Pacific.

Analyzing VISUALS

1. **Identifying Central Issues** Based on the cartoon on the left, what do you think McKinley is trying to accomplish? What about Bryan?

2. **Making Inferences** What does the cartoon on the right suggest that Uncle Sam is going to do? On what basis do you infer that?

History ONLINE
Student Web Activity Visit glencoe.com and complete the activity on American imperialism.

Andrew Carnegie argued that the cost of an empire far outweighed the economic benefits it provided. Gompers worried that competition from cheap Filipino labor would drive down American wages. Addams, Clemens, and others believed imperialism violated American principles. Despite the objections of the anti-imperialists, President McKinley ultimately decided to annex the islands. He later explained his reasoning as follows:

PRIMARY SOURCE

"And one night late it came to me this way. . . (1) that we could not give them back to Spain— that would be cowardly and dishonorable; (2) that we could not turn them over to France or Germany. . . that would be bad for business and discreditable; (3) that we could not leave them to themselves—they were unfit for self-government. . . and (4) that there was nothing left for us to do but to take them all, and to educate the Filipinos, and uplift and civilize and Christianize them."

—A Diplomatic History of the American People

On December 10, 1898, the United States and Spain signed the Treaty of Paris. Under the treaty, Cuba became an independent nation, and the United States acquired Puerto Rico and Guam and agreed to pay Spain $20 million for the Philippines. After an intense debate, the Senate ratified the treaty in February 1899. The United States had become an imperial power.

The Platt Amendment

Although the United States had promised to grant Cuba its independence, President McKinley took steps to ensure that Cuba would remain tied to the United States. He allowed the Cubans to prepare a new constitution for their country but attached conditions. The **Platt Amendment,** submitted by Senator Orville Platt, specified the following: (1) Cuba could not make any treaty with another nation that would weaken its independence; (2) Cuba had to allow the United States to buy or lease naval stations in Cuba; (3) Cuba's debts had to be kept low to prevent foreign countries from landing troops to enforce payment; and (4) the United States would have the right to intervene to protect Cuban independence and keep order.

Reluctantly, the Cubans added the amendment to their constitution. The Platt Amendment, which effectively made Cuba an American protectorate, remained in effect until its repeal in 1934.

Governing Puerto Rico

Another pressing question was how to govern Puerto Rico. In 1900 Congress passed the **Foraker Act,** establishing a civil government for the island. The law provided for an elected legislature, but also called for a governor and executive council, to be appointed by the president, who held final authority. Supreme Court rulings subsequently held that Puerto Ricans were not American citizens and so did not possess the constitutional rights of citizens.

Congress gradually allowed Puerto Ricans greater self-government. In 1917 it granted Puerto Ricans American citizenship. Thirty years later, islanders were allowed to elect their own governor. At this time a debate began over whether Puerto Rico should become a state, become independent, or continue as a self-governing commonwealth of the United States. This debate over Puerto Rico's status continues today.

Rebellion in the Philippines

The United States quickly learned that controlling its new empire would not be easy. Emilio Aguinaldo called the American decision to annex his homeland a "violent and aggressive seizure" and ordered his troops to attack American soldiers. The Philippine-American war, or Philippine Insurrection as it was referred to at the time, lasted for more than three years. Approximately 126,000 American soldiers were sent to the Philippines to fight the insurgency. More than 4,300 American soldiers died, either from combat or disease, as did an estimated 50,000–200,000 Filipinos.

To fight the Filipino guerrillas, the United States military adopted many of the same policies that America had condemned Spain for using in Cuba. Reconcentration camps were established to separate Filipino guerrillas from civilians. Consequently, thousands of people died from disease and starvation, just as they had in Cuba.

While American troops fought the guerrillas, the first U.S. civilian governor of the islands, William Howard Taft, tried to win over the Filipinos by improving education, transportation, and health care. Railroads and bridges were built. Public schools were set up, and new health-care policies virtually eliminated diseases such as cholera and smallpox. These reforms slowly reduced Filipino hostility.

In March 1901, American troops captured Aguinaldo. A month later, Aguinaldo called on the guerrillas to surrender. On July 4, 1902, the United States declared the war over. Eventually the United States allowed the Filipinos a greater role in governing their own country. By the mid-1930s, they were permitted to elect their own congress and president. Finally, in 1946, the United States granted independence to the Philippines.

Reading Check **Explaining** What were the arguments for and against establishing an American empire?

Section 2 REVIEW

Vocabulary

1. **Explain** the significance of: José Martí, William Randolph Hearst, Joseph Pulitzer, yellow journalism, autonomy, jingoism, Emilio Aguinaldo, Platt Amendment, Foraker Act.

Main Ideas

2. **Explaining** Why did many Americans blame Spain for the explosion of the USS *Maine*?

3. **Identifying** How did the U.S. fight the Spanish-American War on two fronts?

4. **Categorizing** Complete the table by summarizing the effects of the United States annexing lands obtained after the Spanish-American War.

Lands Annexed	Effects

Critical Thinking

5. **Big Ideas** How has the government of Puerto Rico changed since the Foraker Act was passed in 1900?

6. **Evaluating** Why did Filipinos feel betrayed by the U.S. government after the Spanish-American War?

7. **Analyzing Visuals** Study the circle graph on page 498. What caused the most casualties during the war? Explain.

Writing About History

8. **Descriptive Writing** Imagine that you are a Filipino living during the time of the U.S. annexation of the Philippine Islands. Write a journal entry in which you describe your feelings about American control of the islands.

History ONLINE

Study Central™ To review this section, go to glencoe.com and click on Study Central.

Section 3

New American Diplomacy

Guide to Reading

Big Ideas
Trade, War, and Migration Under President Theodore Roosevelt, the United States increased its power on the world stage.

Content Vocabulary
- sphere of influence *(p. 504)*
- Open Door policy *(p. 505)*
- dollar diplomacy *(p. 509)*
- guerrilla *(p. 511)*

Academic Vocabulary
- access *(p. 505)*
- tension *(p. 508)*

People and Events to Identify
- Boxer Rebellion *(p. 506)*
- Hay-Pauncefote Treaty *(p. 508)*
- Roosevelt Corollary *(p. 508)*
- Victoriana Huerta *(p. 511)*
- Pancho Villa *(p. 511)*

Reading Strategy
Organizing As you read about American diplomacy complete a graphic organizer by listing the reasons the U.S. wanted a canal through Central America.

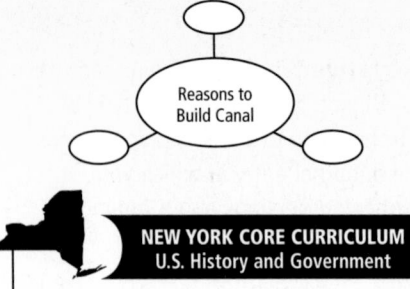

NEW YORK CORE CURRICULUM
U.S. History and Government

Unit 4:
II.A.4.a Monroe Doctrine update (Roosevelt corollary): the view from Latin America
II.A.4.b West Indies protectorates ("the big stick")
II.A.4.c Panama Canal: acquisition and construction: Canal retrocession treaty
II.A.4.d Taft and dollar diplomacy

Succeeding President McKinley, President Theodore Roosevelt mediated disputes in Asia and Latin America and acquired the Panama Canal Zone. Presidents Taft and Wilson worked to increase American trade and influence in Latin America.

American Diplomacy in Asia

MAIN Idea The United States pursued an Open Door policy to allow all nations access to China's markets.

HISTORY AND YOU Do you remember reading about a trade agreement with Japan in the 1850s? Read to learn about America's efforts to keep trade open with China in the 1900s.

In 1899 the United States was a major power in Asia, with naval bases all across the Pacific. Operating from those bases, the United States Navy—by then the third-largest navy in the world—could exert American power anywhere in East Asia. The nation's primary interest in Asia, however, was not conquest but commerce. Between 1895 and 1900, American exports to China increased fourfold. Although China bought only about two percent of American exports, the vast Chinese markets excited American business leaders, especially those in the textile, oil, and steel industries.

The Open Door Policy

In 1894 war erupted between China and Japan over Korea, which at that time was part of the Chinese empire. Western observers were astonished when Japan easily defeated China's massive military. In the peace treaty, China granted Korea independence and gave Japan territory in Manchuria. The war showed that Japan had mastered Western technology and industry. It also demonstrated that China was far weaker than anyone had thought.

The Russians were concerned about Japan's rising power. They did not want Japan to acquire the territory in Manchuria, because it bordered Russia. Backed by France and Germany, Russia forced Japan to return the Manchurian territory it had acquired. Then, in 1898, Russia demanded China lease the territory to Russia instead.

Leasing a territory meant that it would still belong to China, even though a foreign government would maintain overall control. Soon Germany, France, and Britain demanded "leaseholds" in China as well. Each "leasehold" became the center of a country's **sphere of influence,** an area where a foreign nation controlled economic development such as railroad construction and mining.

In June 1900, Boxer rebels attack foreign compounds in Peking and Tientsin.

What Was the Open Door Policy?

1. Within its sphere of influence, each power agreed not to interfere with any existing business interests or port treaties of other powers.

2. Existing Chinese tariffs would remain unchanged in all spheres of influence and would be collected by the Chinese government.

3. Within each sphere of influence, harbor fees and railroad charges would be the same for all countries, giving no special rates to the countries whose businesses owned and operated the harbors and railroads.

▲ *Secretary of State John Hay*

Empire / Sphere of Influence
- British
- French
- Japanese
- Russian
- German

0   1000 kilometers
0   1000 miles
Miller projection

Analyzing VISUALS

1. **Interpreting** What do you think Britain was attempting with the locations of their spheres of influence?

2. **Analyzing** Based on the map, which country do you believe had the most influence?

▲ *International soldiers pose in Tianjin after rescuing their besieged delegations during the Boxer Rebellion. The American is second from left.*

Politicians and businessmen in the United States worried about these events. President McKinley and Secretary of State John Hay both supported what they called an **Open Door policy,** in which all countries would be allowed to trade with China. In 1899 Hay sent notes to countries with leaseholds in China asking them not to discriminate against other nations wanting to do business in their sphere of influence. Each of the nations responded by saying they accepted the Open Door policy but would not act on it unless all of the others agreed. Once Hay had received assurances from all of the nations with leaseholds, he declared that the United States expected the other powers to uphold the policy.

The Boxer Rebellion

While foreign countries debated **access** to China's market, secret Chinese societies organized to fight foreign control. Westerners referred to one such group, the Society of Harmonious Fists, as the Boxers. In 1900 the group decided to destroy both the "foreign devils" and their Chinese Christian converts, whom they believed were corrupting Chinese society.

In what became known as the **Boxer Rebellion,** the Boxers, supported by some Chinese troops, besieged foreign embassies in Beijing and Tianjin, killing more than 200 foreigners and taking others prisoner. After the German ambassador to China was killed, eight nations—Germany, Austria-Hungary, Britain, France, Italy, Japan, Russia, and the United States—decided to intervene. A large international force of nearly 50,000 troops, including 3,400 Americans, landed in China to rescue the foreigners and smash the rebellion.

During the crisis, Secretary of State John Hay worked with British diplomats to persuade the other powers not to partition China. In a second set of Open Door notes, Hay convinced the participating powers to accept compensation from China for damages caused by the rebellion. After some discussion, the powers agreed not to break up China into European-controlled colonies. The United States retained access to China's lucrative trade in tea, spices, and silk and maintained an increasingly larger market for its own goods.

✔ **Reading Check** **Explaining** What was the purpose of the Open Door policy?

Roosevelt's Diplomacy

MAIN Idea Presidents Roosevelt and Taft continued to support a policy of expanding United States influence in foreign countries.

HISTORY AND YOU Do you know of a country that is trying to expand its influence today? Read to find out about expansion of United States influence in the early 1900s.

The election of 1900 once again pitted President McKinley against William Jennings Bryan. Bryan, an anti-imperialist, attacked the Republicans for their support of imperialism in Asia. McKinley, who chose war hero Theodore Roosevelt as his running mate, focused on the country's increased prosperity and ran on the slogan "Four Years More of the Full Dinner Pail." He won the election by a wide margin.

On September 6, 1901, while visiting Buffalo, New York, President McKinley was attacked by Leon Czolgosz, an anarchist who opposed all forms of government. Czolgosz fired two shots and hit the president. A few days later, McKinley died from his wounds. Theodore Roosevelt took over the presidency.

PAST & PRESENT

The Great White Fleet

In 1907 President Theodore Roosevelt sent 16 new battleships on a voyage around the world to showcase the nation's ability to project power to any place in the world. Painted white, the ships became known as the "Great White Fleet." The tour made a stop in Japan to demonstrate that the United States would uphold its interests in Asia. The visit did not help ease the growing tensions between the United States and Japan.

The use of naval power to send a diplomatic message continues today. Just as the battleship symbolized naval power in 1900, so too today does the aircraft carrier symbolize the power and global reach of the United States Navy. In March 1996, for example, a strike force led by the aircraft carrier *Kitty Hawk* was sent to the Taiwan Straits. This show of force came after China tested missiles in the area. The carrier sent the message to China that the United States would protect Taiwan from aggression.

1907

Great White Fleet

▲ *The Great White Fleet gets underway in December 1907.*

◄ *The Great White Fleet circumnavigated the globe.*

Theodore Roosevelt, just 42 years old at the time, was the youngest person ever to become president. Republican leaders had asked him to run for vice president because his charisma and status as a war hero would win votes, but they had hoped the relatively powerless position of vice president would keep him from causing political problems. Now they cringed at the thought of him in the White House. Ohio Republican senator Mark Hanna exclaimed, "Now look, that . . . cowboy is president of the United States!"

Roosevelt favored increasing American power on the world stage. He warned Americans not to become "an assemblage of well-to-do hucksters who care nothing for what happens beyond." Roosevelt also accepted some of Anglo-Saxonism's ideas. He believed that the United States had a duty to shape the "less civilized" corners of the earth.

Balancing Power in East Asia

As president, Theodore Roosevelt supported the Open Door policy in China and worked to prevent any single nation from monopolizing trade there. This concern prompted Roosevelt to help negotiate an end to the war between Japan and Russia that had broken out in 1905. At a peace conference in Portsmouth, New Hampshire, Roosevelt convinced the Russians to recognize Japan's territorial gains and persuaded the Japanese to stop fighting and to seek no further territory. For his efforts in ending the war, Roosevelt won the Nobel Peace Prize in 1906.

In the years after the peace treaty, relations between the United States and Japan grew steadily worse. As the two nations vied for greater influence in Asia, they held each other in check through a series of agreements. They pledged to respect each other's territorial possessions, to uphold the Open Door policy, and to support China's independence.

The Panama Canal

Theodore Roosevelt believed in a strong global military presence. He insisted that displaying American power to the world would make nations think twice about fighting, and thus promote peace. He often expressed this belief with a West African saying, "Speak softly and carry a big stick."

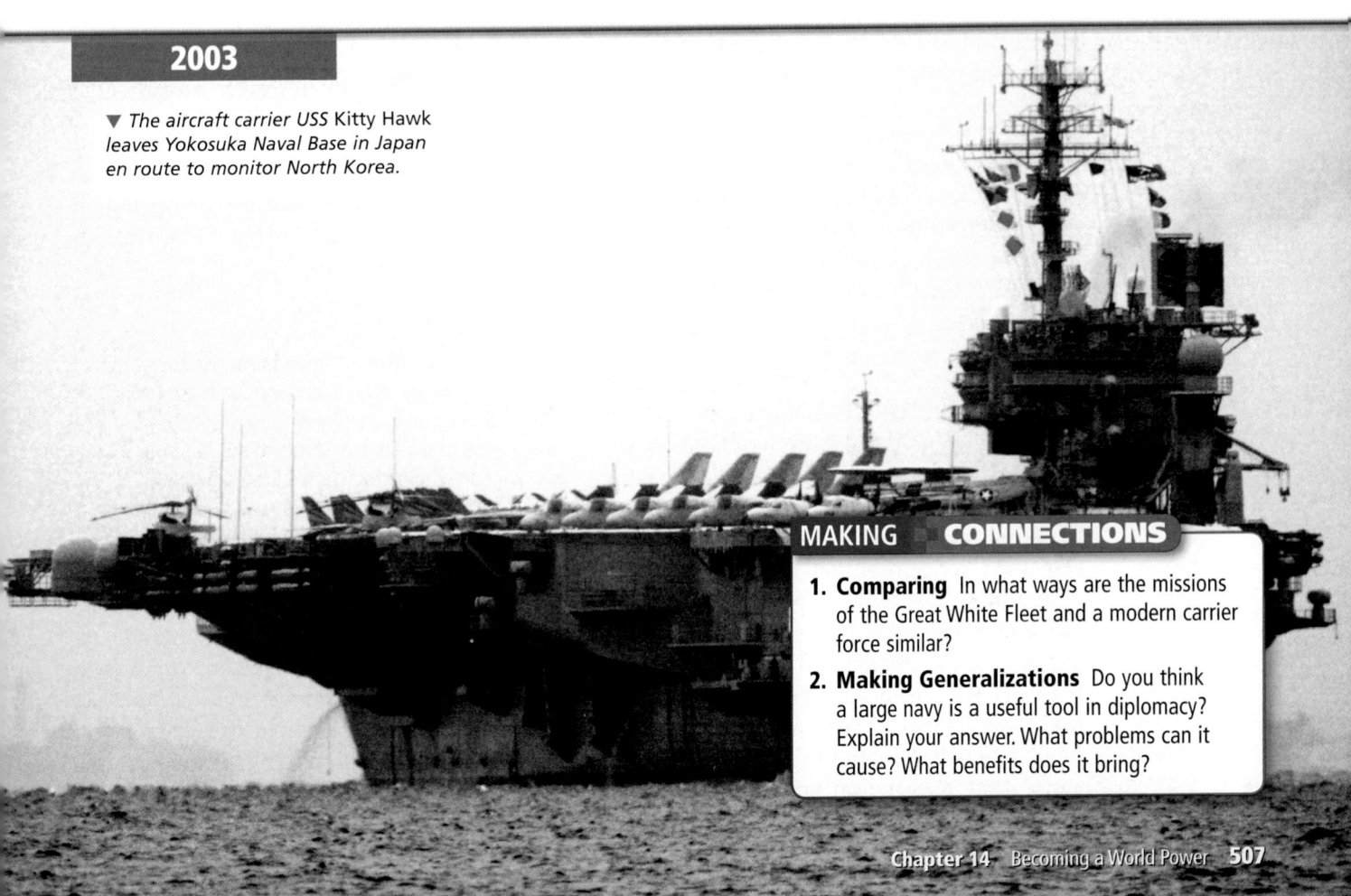

2003

▼ The aircraft carrier USS Kitty Hawk leaves Yokosuka Naval Base in Japan en route to monitor North Korea.

MAKING CONNECTIONS

1. **Comparing** In what ways are the missions of the Great White Fleet and a modern carrier force similar?

2. **Making Generalizations** Do you think a large navy is a useful tool in diplomacy? Explain your answer. What problems can it cause? What benefits does it bring?

Roosevelt's "big stick" policy was perhaps most evident in the Caribbean. There the world witnessed one of the most dramatic acts of his presidency—the acquisition and construction of the Panama Canal. Roosevelt and others believed that having a canal through Central America was vital to American power in the world. A canal would save time and money for both commercial and military shipping.

Acquiring the Canal Zone As early as 1850, the United States and Great Britain had agreed not to build a canal without the other's participation. In 1901 the United States and Great Britain signed the **Hay-Pauncefote Treaty,** which gave the United States the exclusive right to build any proposed canal through Central America.

A French company had begun digging a canal through Panama in 1881. By 1889, however, it abandoned its efforts because of bankruptcy and terrible losses from disease among the workers. The company was reorganized in 1894, but it hoped only to sell its rights to dig the canal.

The United States had long considered two possible canal sites, one through Nicaragua and one through Panama. The French company eased this choice by offering to sell its rights and property in Panama to the United States.

In 1903 Panama was Colombia's most northern province. Secretary of State Hay offered Colombia $10 million and a yearly rent of $250,000 for the right to construct the canal and to control a narrow strip of land on either side of it. Considering the price too low and afraid of losing control of Panama, the Colombian government refused the offer.

Panama Revolts Some Panamanians feared losing the commercial benefits of the canal. Panama had opposed Colombian rule since the mid-1800s, and the canal issue added to the **tension.** In addition, the French company remained concerned that the United States would build the canal in Nicaragua instead. The French company's agent, Philippe Bunau-Varilla, and Panamanian officials decided that the only way to ensure the canal would be built was to make their own deal with the United States. Bunau-Varilla arranged for a small army to stage an uprising in Panama.

Meanwhile, to prevent Colombian interference, President Roosevelt ordered U.S. warships to the area.

On November 3, 1903, with ten U.S. warships looming offshore, Bunau-Varilla's forces revolted. Within a few days, the United States recognized Panama's independence, and the two nations soon signed a treaty allowing the canal to be built.

Protesters in the United States and throughout Latin America condemned Roosevelt's actions as unjustifiable aggression. The president countered that he had advanced "the needs of collective civilization" by building a canal that shortened the distance between the Atlantic and the Pacific by about 8,000 nautical miles (14,816 km).

The Roosevelt Corollary

By the early 1900s, American officials had become very concerned about the size of the debts Latin American nations owed to European banks. In 1902, after Venezuela defaulted on its debts, Great Britain, Germany, and Italy blockaded Venezuelan ports. The crisis was resolved peacefully after the United States intervened and put pressure on both sides to reach an agreement.

To address the problem, Roosevelt gave an address to Congress in which he declared what came to be known as the **Roosevelt Corollary** to the Monroe Doctrine. The corollary stated that the United States would intervene in Latin American affairs when necessary to maintain economic and political stability in the Western Hemisphere:

PRIMARY SOURCE

"Chronic wrongdoing . . . may, in America, as elsewhere, ultimately require intervention by some civilized nation, and in the Western Hemisphere the adherence of the United States to the Monroe Doctrine may force the United States, however reluctantly, in flagrant cases of such wrongdoing or impotence, to the exercise of an international police power."

—quoted in *The Growth of the United States*

The goal of the Roosevelt Corollary was to prevent European powers from using the debt problems of Latin America to justify intervening in the region. The United States first applied the Roosevelt Corollary in the

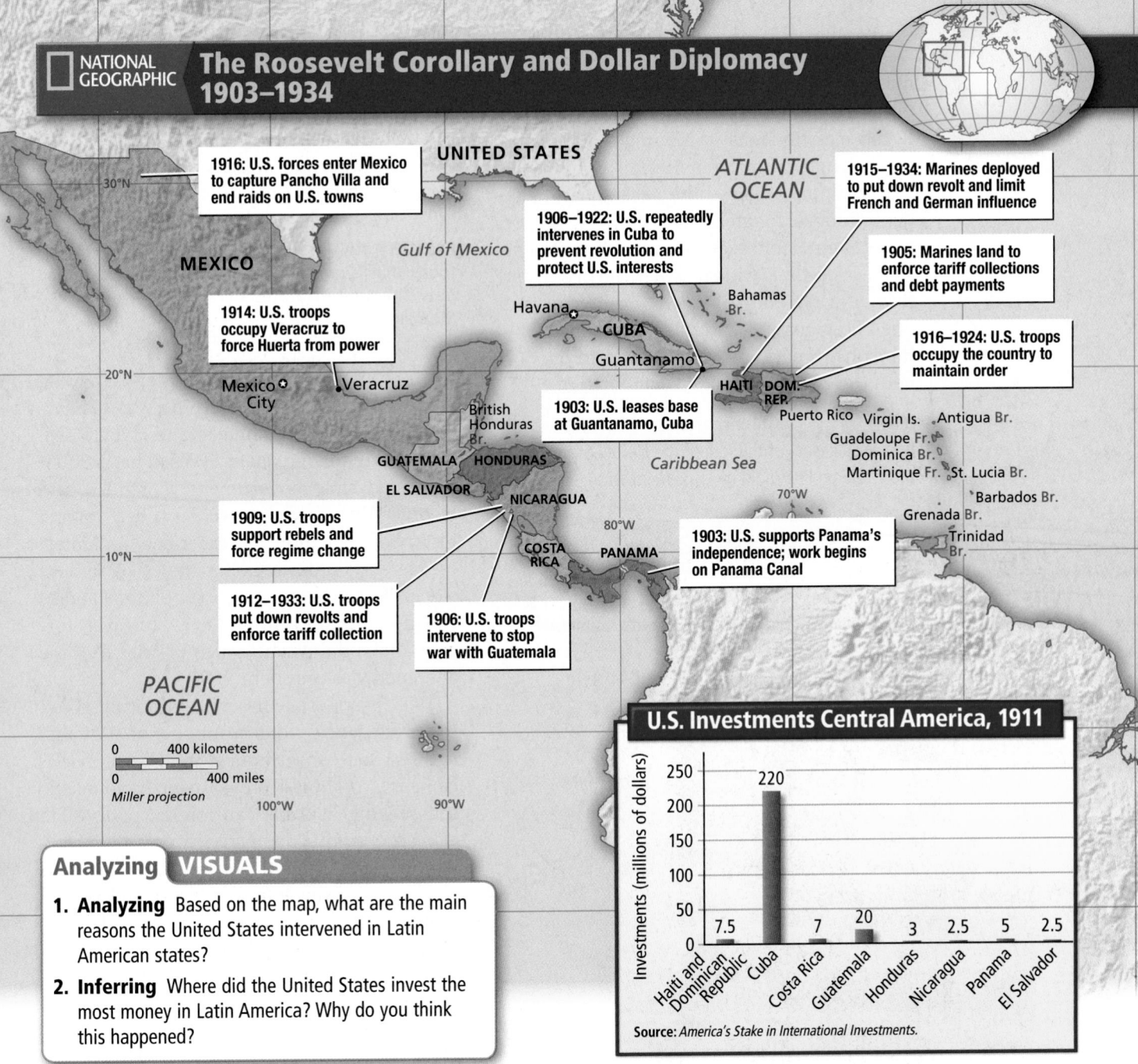

The Roosevelt Corollary and Dollar Diplomacy 1903–1934

UNITED STATES

ATLANTIC OCEAN

1916: U.S. forces enter Mexico to capture Pancho Villa and end raids on U.S. towns

1906–1922: U.S. repeatedly intervenes in Cuba to prevent revolution and protect U.S. interests

1915–1934: Marines deployed to put down revolt and limit French and German influence

Gulf of Mexico

MEXICO

1905: Marines land to enforce tariff collections and debt payments

1914: U.S. troops occupy Veracruz to force Huerta from power

Bahamas Br.

Havana **CUBA**

1916–1924: U.S. troops occupy the country to maintain order

Guantanamo

HAITI **DOM. REP.**

Mexico City • Veracruz

British Honduras Br.

1903: U.S. leases base at Guantanamo, Cuba

Puerto Rico Virgin Is. Antigua Br.
Guadeloupe Fr.
Dominica Br.
Martinique Fr. St. Lucia Br.

GUATEMALA **HONDURAS**

Caribbean Sea

EL SALVADOR

NICARAGUA

Barbados Br.

Grenada Br.

70°W

Trinidad Br.

1909: U.S. troops support rebels and force regime change

80°W

COSTA RICA **PANAMA**

1903: U.S. supports Panama's independence; work begins on Panama Canal

1912–1933: U.S. troops put down revolts and enforce tariff collection

1906: U.S. troops intervene to stop war with Guatemala

PACIFIC OCEAN

0 400 kilometers
0 400 miles
Miller projection
100°W   90°W

U.S. Investments Central America, 1911

Investments (millions of dollars)

Haiti and Dominican Republic	7.5
Cuba	220
Costa Rica	7
Guatemala	20
Honduras	3
Nicaragua	2.5
Panama	5
El Salvador	2.5

Source: *America's Stake in International Investments.*

Analyzing VISUALS

1. **Analyzing** Based on the map, what are the main reasons the United States intervened in Latin American states?

2. **Inferring** Where did the United States invest the most money in Latin America? Why do you think this happened?

Dominican Republic, which had fallen behind on its debt payments to European nations. In 1905 the United States assumed the responsibility of collecting customs tariffs in the Dominican Republic, using the United States Marine Corps as its agent.

Dollar Diplomacy

Latin American nations resented the growing American influence in the region, but Roosevelt's successor, William Howard Taft, continued his policies. Taft placed much less emphasis on military force and more on helping Latin American industry. He believed that

if American business leaders supported Latin American development, everyone would benefit. American businesses would increase their trade and profits, and countries in Latin America would rise out of poverty and social disorder. Taft's policy came to be called **dollar diplomacy.**

Administration officials also worked hard to replace European loans with loans from American banks. The goal of this policy was to give the Europeans fewer reasons to intervene in Latin American affairs. During Taft's administration, American bankers took over debts that Honduras owed to Britain and took control of Haiti's national bank.

Although Taft described his brand of diplomacy as "substituting dollars for bullets," in Nicaragua he used both. American bankers began making loans to Nicaragua to support its shaky government in 1911. The following year, civil unrest forced the Nicaraguan president to appeal for greater assistance. American marines entered the country, replaced the collector of customs with an American agent, and formed a committee of two Americans and one Nicaraguan to control the customs commissions. American troops stayed to support both the government and customs until 1925.

✔ Reading Check **Summarizing** What was Roosevelt's view of the role of the United States in the world and how did he implement it?

POLITICAL CARTOON PRIMARY SOURCE
Wilson and Mexico

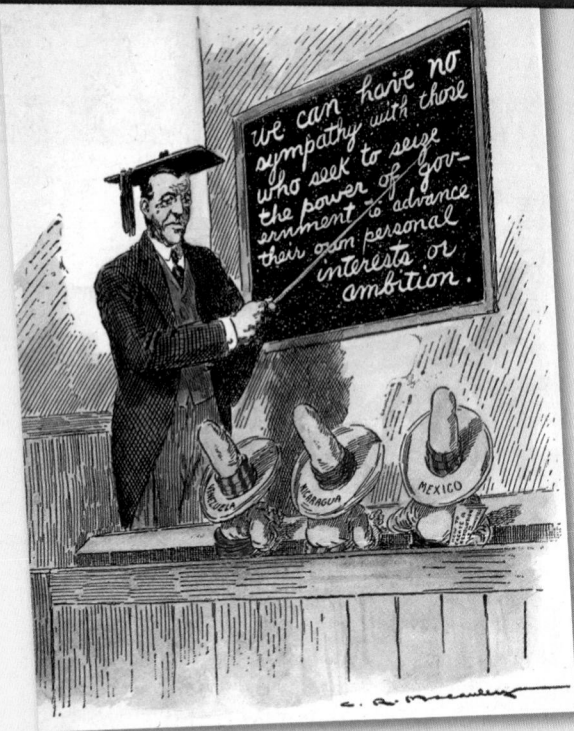

we can have no sympathy with those who seek to seize the power of government to advance their own personal interests or ambition.

▲ *President Wilson (who had a Ph.D.) is shown teaching Venezuela, Nicaragua, and Mexico that revolution for personal gain is wrong, while Mexico is shown hiding a note labeled "How to create a revolution."*

Analyzing VISUALS

1. **Analyzing** In what ways is the cartoon making fun of President Wilson?

2. **Inferring** What is the cartoon implying about Mexico?

Woodrow Wilson's Diplomacy in Mexico

MAIN Idea Wilson believed in "moral diplomacy" and tried to encourage democracy in Latin America.

HISTORY AND YOU Can you think of a country today that is going through a long civil war? Read how the United States became involved in the Mexican Revolution.

"It would be the irony of fate," remarked Woodrow Wilson just before he was inaugurated in 1913, "if my administration had to deal chiefly with foreign affairs." Wilson had written books on state government, Congress, and George Washington, as well as a five-volume history of the nation. His experience and interest were in domestic policy. He was a university professor before entering politics. He also was a committed progressive. However, foreign affairs did absorb much of Wilson's time and energy as president.

Wilson opposed imperialism and resolved to "strike a new note in international affairs" and see that "sheer honesty and even unselfishness . . . should prevail over nationalistic self-seeking in American foreign policy." He also believed that democracy was essential to a nation's stability and prosperity. To ensure a world free of revolution and war, the United States should promote democracy. During Wilson's presidency, however, other forces frustrated his hope to lead the world by moral example. In fact, Wilson's first international crisis was awaiting him when he took office.

The Mexican Revolution

For more than 30 years, Porfirio Díaz ruled Mexico as a dictator. During his reign, Mexico became much more industrialized, but foreign investors owned and financed the new railroads and factories that were built. Most Mexican citizens remained poor and landless. In 1911 widespread discontent erupted into revolution.

Francisco Madero, a reformer who appeared to support democracy, constitutional government, and land reform, led the revolution. Madero, however, proved to be an unskilled administrator. Worried about Madero's plans for land reform, conservative forces plotted against him. In February 1913, General **Victoriano Huerta** seized power; Madero was murdered, presumably on Huerta's orders.

Huerta's brutality repulsed Wilson, who refused to recognize the new government. Instead, Wilson announced a new policy. Groups that seized power in Latin America would have to set up "a just government based upon law, not upon arbitrary or irregular force," in order to win American recognition. Wilson was convinced that, without the support of the United States, Huerta soon would be overthrown. Meanwhile, Wilson ordered the navy to intercept arms shipments to Huerta's government. He also permitted Americans to arm Huerta's opponents.

Wilson Sends Troops Into Mexico

In April 1914, American sailors visiting the city of Tampico were arrested after entering a restricted area. Although they were quickly released, their American commander demanded an apology. The Mexicans refused. Wilson saw the refusal as an opportunity to overthrow Huerta. He asked Congress to authorize the use of force, and shortly after Congress passed the resolution, he learned that a German ship was unloading weapons at the Mexican port of Veracruz. Wilson immediately ordered American warships to shell the Veracruz harbor and then sent marines to seize the city.

Although the president expected the Mexican people to welcome his action, anti-American riots broke out. Wilson then accepted international mediation to settle the dispute. Venustiano Carranza, whose forces had acquired arms from the United States, became Mexico's president.

Mexican forces opposed to Carranza were not appeased, and they conducted raids into the United States, hoping to force Wilson to intervene. In March 1916, **Pancho Villa** (VEE•yah) and a group of **guerrillas**—an armed band that uses surprise attacks and sabotage rather than open warfare—burned the town of Columbus, New Mexico, and killed 16 Americans. Wilson responded by sending 6,000 troops under General John J. Pershing across the border to find and capture Villa. The expedition dragged on with no success. Wilson's growing concern over the war raging in Europe finally caused him to recall Pershing's troops in 1917.

Wilson's Mexican policy damaged U.S. foreign relations. The British ridiculed the president's attempt to "shoot the Mexicans into self-government." Latin Americans regarded his "moral imperialism" as no improvement over Theodore Roosevelt's "big stick" diplomacy. In fact, Wilson followed Roosevelt's example in the Caribbean. In 1914 he negotiated exclusive rights for naval bases and a canal with Nicaragua. In 1915 he sent marines into Haiti to put down a rebellion. The marines remained there until 1934. In 1916 he sent troops into the Dominican Republic to preserve order and to set up a government he hoped would be more stable and democratic than the current regime.

✔ Reading Check **Examining** Why did President Wilson intervene in Mexico?

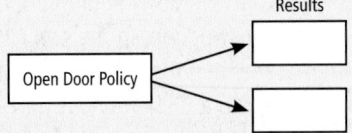

Section 3 REVIEW

Vocabulary

1. **Explain** the significance of: sphere of influence, Open Door policy, Boxer Rebellion, Hay-Pauncefote Treaty, Roosevelt Corollary, dollar diplomacy, Victoriano Huerta, Pancho Villa, guerrilla.

Main Ideas

2. **Summarizing** Use a graphic organizer to list the results of the Open Door policy.

```
                          Results
                        ┌────────┐
              ┌────────→│        │
┌──────────────┐        └────────┘
│Open Door Policy│
└──────────────┘        ┌────────┐
              └────────→│        │
                        └────────┘
```

3. **Identifying** Why did President Theodore Roosevelt want to increase U.S. influence overseas?

4. **Specifying** How did Latin Americans view Wilson's "moral imperialism"?

Critical Thinking

5. **Big Ideas** Why did the United States decide to build a canal through Panama? How did Roosevelt assist Panama in becoming independent?

6. **Analyzing** How did the Roosevelt Corollary and dollar diplomacy affect U.S. relations with other countries?

7. **Analyzing Visuals** Study the map on page 509. To which countries did the U.S. send troops most often?

Writing About History

8. **Expository Writing** Imagine that you are a Mexican citizen during Wilson's presidency. Write a radio news broadcast expressing your feelings about American actions in Mexico.

History ONLINE

Study Central™ To review this section, go to glencoe.com and click on Study Central.

GEOGRAPHY & HISTORY

The Panama Canal

The idea of a canal connecting the Atlantic and Pacific oceans had been around for a long time before a French company began digging a canal across Panama in 1882. Disease and mud slides killed more than 20,000 workers before financial setbacks halted construction. In the early 1900s, the United States negotiated rights to build the canal with Colombia (Panama was part of Colombia at that time), but Colombia's Senate refused to ratify the treaty. With the support of the United States, Panama declared independence from Colombia and signed a treaty giving the United States a perpetual lease on the canal site in exchange for $10 million and annual payments. Construction resumed in 1904, and the canal was opened in 1914.

How Does Geography Affect the Canal?

Before the canal opened, ships sailing from New York to San Francisco traveled 12,600 miles (20,277 km) around the treacherous tip of South America. Afterwards, the trip was only 4,900 miles (7,886 km) and could be completed in less than half the time. Panama's geography made building the canal a challenge because the center of the country was much higher than sea level. Engineers built a series of lakes and concrete locks to raise and lower ships as they traveled the 51-mile canal. In each chamber of the locks, some 26 million gallons of water are pumped in or drained out in only 7 minutes to raise or lower a ship. At the artificial Gatun Lake, a dam generates electricity that powers the locks while gravity adjusts the water level.

Ships transit the canal more than 14,000 times each year, generating over $1 billion in tolls.

Analyzing GEOGRAPHY

1. **Human-Environment Interaction** How were the geographical features of Panama used or overcome in order to build the canal?

2. **Location** Why do you think the Panama site was ultimately selected for the canal?

Pacific Ocean

Panama City •

Atlantic Ocean

Pacific Ocean

Miraflores Locks

Pedro Miguel Lock

Lake Gatún

Gatún Locks

Atlantic Ocean

Cross Section of the Panama Canal

Gatún Dam created Lake Gatún—one of the largest artificial lakes in the world. A hydroelectric station at the dam generates power to run the pumps and gates of the locks.

Gatún Locks has 3 chambers for each direction. Together they raise ships at sea level up 86 feet to the level of Lake Gatún.

Lake Gatún

• Colón

▲ The Miraflores locks (above) are one of three sets of locks on the Panama Canal, and the first set for ships entering from the Pacific. After a ship enters a lock chamber, water is pumped in raising the ship up 27 feet to the next level. The ship then moves to the next chamber and is raised another 27 feet.

Causes of American Imperialism

- The United States wanted new markets for its products, particularly its manufactured goods.
- Many Americans believed it was the destiny of the United States to spread its power and civilization to other parts of the world.
- American leaders believed that having a powerful navy and controlling trade were key to being a world power.

▶ *USS* Texas *docks in port in 1896*

▲ *American soldiers in Cuba cheer the news that the city of Santiago, Cuba, has surrendered during the Spanish-American War, 1898.*

Effects of the Spanish-American War

- Cuba officially became an independent nation, although the United States claimed control over its foreign relations and exerted influence over internal politics.
- The United States acquired Puerto Rico, Guam, and the Philippines.
- Americans debated the morality and wisdom of becoming an imperial nation.
- The United States fought a three-year war to secure control over the Philippines.

The United States Acts As a World Power

- The United States used diplomatic means to establish the Open Door policy in China.
- President Theodore Roosevelt negotiated a peace agreement between Russia and Japan.
- The United States completed construction of the Panama Canal.
- The United States intervened, with the intent to provide stability, in the affairs of several Caribbean nations.
- The United States twice intervened in the lengthy Mexican Revolution.

▲ *After supporting a revolution in Panama, the United States begins construction of the Panama Canal.*

NEW YORK REGENTS EXAM PRACTICE

TEST-TAKING

Note that in some cases you are asked to choose the BEST answer. This means that in some instances there will be more than one possible answer. Be sure to read all the choices carefully before selecting your answer.

Part I

Directions (1–12): For each statement or question, write on a separate sheet of paper the *number* of the word or expression that, of those given, best completes the statement or answers the question.

1 President Wilson's invasion of Veracruz was
   (1) supported by Britain and Germany.
   (2) applauded by Europeans.
   (3) criticized in Europe and Latin America.
   (4) welcomed by Latin Americans.

2 The United States caused an economic crisis in Cuba by
   (1) blockading the island to prevent trade with Spain.
   (2) raising tariffs on sugar from Cuba.
   (3) allowing American businesses to invest in Cuba.
   (4) preventing trade with Spain.

3 Which of the following did some newspapers use to gain support for the war against Spain?
   (1) anti-Americanism
   (2) objective reporting
   (3) yellow journalism
   (4) spheres of influence

4 Which of the following was a major contributor to the growth of American imperialism in the late 1800s?
   (1) curiosity about other cultures
   (2) the need for spices from the East Indies
   (3) the end of the Civil War
   (4) the desire for new markets for American goods

5 One goal of the Pan-American Conference in 1889 was to
   (1) create a customs union for nations in the Americas.
   (2) end trade with the nations of Europe.
   (3) free Cuba from Spanish control.
   (4) decide on a route for a canal through Central America.

6 What effect did the Platt Amendment have on Cuba?
   (1) It effectively made Cuba a protectorate of the United States.
   (2) It cut sugarcane production so Cuba could not compete with production in the United States.
   (3) It guaranteed all the freedoms of the Bill of Rights to Cubans.
   (4) It gave Cuba the right to allow European countries to buy or lease naval stations in Cuba.

7 "We hold that the policy known as imperialism is hostile to liberty. . . . We regret that it has become necessary in the land of Washington and Lincoln to reaffirm that all men, of whatever race or color, are entitled to life, liberty, and the pursuit of happiness."
   —from "Platform of the American Anti-Imperialist League"

   What does the excerpt imply about the Anti-Imperialist League's views on imperialism?
   (1) It reaffirms the United States as a world power.
   (2) It brings life, liberty, and happiness to more people.
   (3) U.S. imperialism is similar to British actions against the American colonists.
   (4) It encourages the policies of Washington and Lincoln by getting involved in foreign affairs.

Need Extra Help?							
If You Missed Questions . . .	1	2	3	4	5	6	7
Go to Page . . .	510–511	496–497	497	490–492	495	502–503	490–495

[OVER]

Base your answer to question 8 on the map below and your knowledge of Chapter 14.

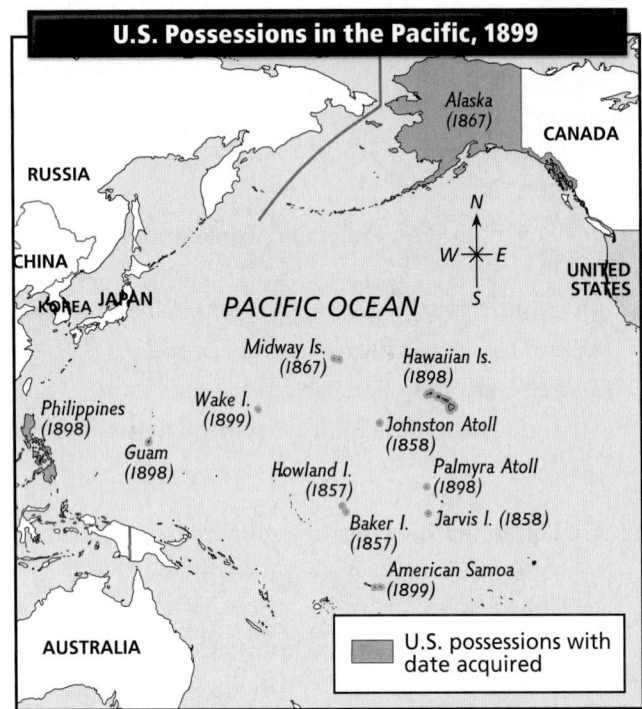

U.S. Possessions in the Pacific, 1899

8 According to the map, which U.S. possession is closest to the Philippines?

(1) Alaska (3) Midway Islands

(2) Hawaii (4) Guam

9 When the United States collected customs tariffs in the Dominican Republic, using the marines as agents, it was applying

(1) the Open Door policy.

(2) the Roosevelt Corollary.

(3) dollar diplomacy.

(4) the Platt Amendment.

10 In 1898 President McKinley sent the battleship *Maine* to Havana to

(1) protect American citizens and interests, if necessary.

(2) put down riots by Spanish loyalists.

(3) put down the Cuban rebellion.

(4) negotiate peace with Spain.

Need Extra Help?

If You Missed Questions . . .	8	9	10
Go to Page . . .	499–502	508–509	498

Part II Thematic Essay Question

Directions: Write a well-organized essay that includes an introduction, several paragraphs addressing the task below, and a conclusion.

Theme: U.S. Foreign Policy

U.S. foreign policy decisions during the late 1800s and early 1900s increased the country's role as a world power. During this era, the United States acquired territories and influenced the political and economic systems of other countries.

Task:

Identify two important U.S. foreign policy actions around 1900, and for each

• Discuss the historical circumstances surrounding the action.

• Describe *one* immediate or *one* long-term result of the decision.

• Evaluate the extent to which the decisions changed both the United States and other regions of the world.

Guidelines:

In your essay, be sure to:

• Develop all aspects of the task

• Support the theme with relevant facts, examples, and details

• Use a logical and clear plan of organization, including an introduction and a conclusion that are beyond a restatement of the theme

Part III Document-Based Question

This question is based on the accompanying documents. This question is designed to test your ability to work with historical documents. Some of the documents have been edited for the purposes of the question. As you analyze the documents, take into account the source of each document and any point of view that may be presented in the document.

Historical Context:

During the late 1800s and early 1900s, the United States was involved in the political and economic affairs of other countries around the world.

Task:

Using information from the documents and your knowledge of U.S. history, answer the questions that follow each document in Part A. Your answers to the questions will help you write the Part B essay, in which you will be asked to

- Discuss the U.S. involvement in the Spanish-American War. In your discussion, include the arguments used by those who supported the war and those who were opposed to it
- Describe how the United States remained connected to other countries involved following the war

Part A
Short-Answer Questions

Directions: Analyze the documents and answer the short-answer questions that follow each document in the space provided.

Document 1

We, women of the United States, earnestly protest against the war of conquest into which our country has been plunged in the Philippine islands.

And we unqualifiedly approve and support these resolutions of the anti-imperialist league:

First. That our government shall take immediate steps toward a suspension of hostilities in the Philippines and . . . a recognition of their freedom and independence as soon as proper guarantees can be had for order and protection of property.

Second. That the government of the United States shall tender an official assurance to the inhabitants of the Philippine islands that they will encourage and assist in the organization of such a government in the islands as the people thereof shall prefer, . . . will recognize the independence of the Philippines and its equality among nations, and gradually withdraw all military and naval forces. . . .

Source: Women's Auxiliary of the Anti-Imperialist League, Petition, May 1899.

1 State two demands of the Women's Auxiliary of the Anti-Imperialist League.

2 According to the cartoon, what is the United States saving Cuba from, other than Spanish rule?

Part B
Essay

Directions: Reread the task box at the top left and write a well-organized essay that includes an introduction, several paragraphs, and a conclusion. Use evidence from the documents in your essay. Support your response with relevant facts, examples, and details. Include additional outside information.

Guidelines:

In your essay, be sure to:

- Develop all aspects of the task
- Incorporate information from the documents
- Incorporate relevant outside information
- Support the theme with relevant facts, examples, and details
- Use a logical and clear plan of organization, including an introduction and conclusion that are beyond a restatement of the theme

For additional test practice, use Self-Check Quizzes—Chapter 14 at glencoe.com.

Need Extra Help?			
If You Missed Questions . . .	1	2	Essay
Go to Page . . .	496–503	496–503	496–503

The Progressive Movement

1890–1920

SECTION 1 The Roots of Progressivism

SECTION 2 Roosevelt and Taft

SECTION 3 The Wilson Years

Women wearing academic dress march in a New York City parade for woman suffrage in 1910.

1889
- Hull House opens in Chicago

1890
- Jacob Riis's *How the Other Half Lives* is published

1902
- Maryland passes first U.S. workers' compensation laws

1906
- Pure Food and Drug Act passed

B. Harrison 1889–1893

Cleveland 1893–1897

McKinley 1897–1901

T. Roosevelt 1901–1909

U.S. PRESIDENTS

U.S. EVENTS   1890   1900

WORLD EVENTS

1884
- Toynbee Hall, first settlement house, is established in London

1903
- Russian Bolshevik Party is established by Lenin

1906
- British pass workers' compensation law

Can Politics Fix Social Problems?

Industrialization changed American society. Cities were crowded, working conditions were often bad, and the old political system was breaking down. These conditions gave rise to the Progressive movement. Progressives campaigned for both political and social reforms.

- *What reforms do you think progressives wanted to achieve?*
- *Which of these reforms can you see in today's society?*

Taft
1909–1913

Wilson
1913–1921

1910
- Mann-Elkins Act passed

1913
- Seventeenth Amendment requires direct election of senators

1920
- Nineteenth Amendment gives women voting rights

1910

1920

1908
- Germany limits working hours for children and women

1911
- British create national health insurance program

1914
- World War I begins in Europe

1917
- Russian Revolution begins

FOLDABLES

Analyzing Reform Programs Create a Pocket Book Foldable that divides the Progressive agenda into political reforms and social reforms. Take notes on a wide range of reforms, placing each one in the proper column of the Foldable.

Progressive Political Reform

Progressive Social Reforms

History ONLINE Chapter Overview
Visit glencoe.com to preview Chapter 15.

Section 1

The Roots of Progressivism

Guide to Reading

Big Ideas
Group Action The progressives sought to improve life in the United States with social, economic, and political reforms.

Content Vocabulary
- muckraker *(p. 521)*
- direct primary *(p. 522)*
- initiative *(p. 523)*
- referendum *(p. 523)*
- recall *(p. 523)*
- suffrage *(p. 524)*
- prohibition *(p. 527)*

Academic Vocabulary
- legislation *(p. 523)*
- advocate *(p. 527)*

People and Events to Identify
- Jacob Riis *(p. 521)*
- Robert M. La Follette *(p. 522)*
- Carrie Chapman Catt *(p. 525)*

Reading Strategy
Organizing As you read about the beginnings of progressivism, complete a graphic organizer similar to the one below by filling in the beliefs of progressives.

Progressive Beliefs

NEW YORK CORE CURRICULUM
U.S. History and Government

Unit 4:
I.A.3 Struggle for fair standards of business operation and working conditions
I.B.1 The "Muckrakers" and reform
I.B.2.b Women's rights and efforts for peace
I.B.2.d Temperance/prohibition
I.C.1 Progressivism and government action
I.C.4.e Women's suffrage amendment

The Progressive Era was a time when many Americans tried to improve their society. They tried to make government honest, efficient, and more democratic. The movement for women's suffrage gained more support, as did efforts to limit child labor and reduce alcohol abuse.

The Rise of Progressivism

MAIN Idea Progressives tried to solve the social problems that arose as the United States became an urban, industrialized nation.

HISTORY AND YOU What areas of public life do you believe need to be reformed? Read on to learn about a movement that tried to fix many of society's problems.

Progressivism was a collection of different ideas and activities. It was not a tightly organized political movement with a specific set of reforms. Rather, it was a series of responses to problems in American society that had emerged from the growth of industry. Progressives had many different ideas about how to fix the problems they saw in American society.

Who Were the Progressives?

Progressivism was partly a reaction against laissez-faire economics and its emphasis on an unregulated market. Progressives generally believed that industrialization and urbanization had created many social problems. After seeing the poverty of the working class and the filth and crime of urban society, reformers began doubting the free market's ability to address those problems.

Progressives belonged to both major political parties. Most were urban, educated, middle-class Americans. Among their leaders were journalists, social workers, educators, politicians, and members of the clergy. Most agreed that government should take a more active role in solving society's problems. At the same time, they doubted that the government in its present form could fix those problems. They concluded that government had to be fixed before it could be used to fix other problems.

One reason progressives thought they could improve society was their strong faith in science and technology. The application of scientific knowledge had produced the lightbulb, the telephone, and the automobile. It had built skyscrapers and railroads. Science and technology had benefited people; thus, progressives believed using scientific principles could also produce solutions for society.

PRIMARY SOURCE

The Photojournalism of Jacob Riis

Photography offered a new tool in combating injustice. One of the most famous early photojournalists was Jacob Riis, whose book, *How the Other Half Lives*, helped stir progressives to action:

<u>PRIMARY SOURCE</u>

"Look into any of these houses, everywhere the same piles of rags, of malodorous bones and musty paper. . . . Here is a 'flat' or 'parlor' and two pitch-dark coops called bedrooms. Truly, the bed is all there is room for. The family teakettle is on the stove, doing duty for the time being as a wash-boiler. By night it will have returned to its proper use again, a practical illustration of how poverty in 'the Bend' makes both ends meet. One, two, three beds are there, if the old boxes and heaps of foul straw can be called by that name; a broken stove with crazy pipe from which the smoke leaks at every joint, a table of rough boards propped up on boxes, piles of rubbish in the corner. The closeness and smell are appalling. How many people sleep here? The woman with the red bandanna shakes her head sullenly, but the bare-legged girl with the bright face counts on her fingers—five, six!"

—from *How the Other Half Lives*

DBQ Document-Based Questions

1. **Analyzing Visuals** What effect do Riis's photos convey?
2. **Making Inferences** Based on the quotation above, how could you summarize Riis's views on changing life in the slums?

▲ New York slum dwellers in this Jacob Riis photograph, taken about 1890, lived in wooden shacks in a city alley.

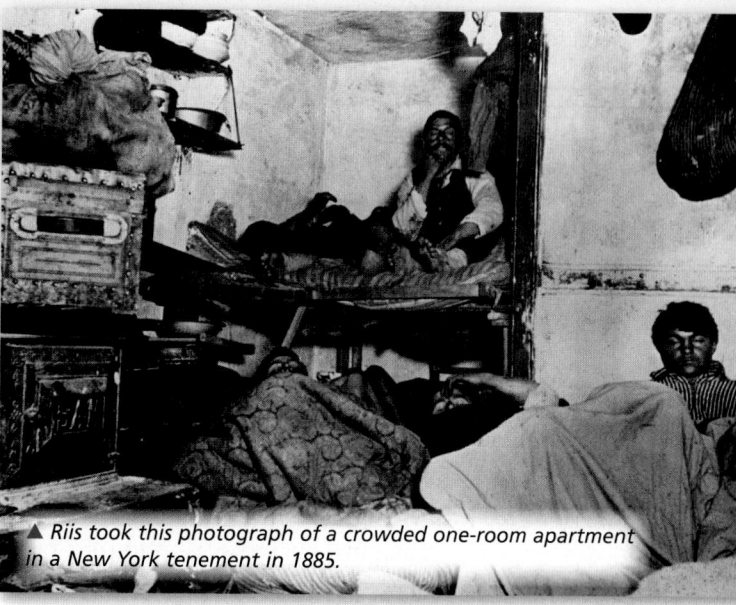

▲ Riis took this photograph of a crowded one-room apartment in a New York tenement in 1885.

The Muckrakers

Among the first people to articulate progressive ideas was a group of crusading journalists who investigated social conditions and political corruption. President Theodore Roosevelt nicknamed these writers "**muckrakers.**" The term referred to a character in John Bunyan's book *Pilgrim's Progress*, who single-mindedly scraped up the filth on the ground, ignoring everything else. These journalists, according to Roosevelt, were obsessed with scandal and corruption. Widely circulated, cheap newspapers and magazines helped to spread the muckrakers' ideas.

Muckrakers uncovered corruption in many areas. Some concentrated on exposing the unfair practices of large corporations. In *Everybody's Magazine*, Charles Edward Russell attacked the beef industry. In *McClure's*, Ida Tarbell published a series of articles critical of the Standard Oil Company. Other muckrakers targeted government and social problems. Lincoln Steffens reported on vote stealing and other corrupt practices of urban political machines. These articles were later collected into a book, *The Shame of the Cities*.

Still other muckrakers concentrated on social problems. In his influential book, *How the Other Half Lives* (1890), **Jacob Riis** published photographs and descriptions of the poverty, disease, and crime that afflicted many immigrant neighborhoods in New York City. By raising public awareness of these problems, the muckrakers stimulated calls for reform.

Read literature from the era on pages R72–R73 in the **American Literature Library.**

✔ Reading Check **Describing** How did the muckrakers help spark the Progressive movement?

Reforming Government

MAIN Idea Progressives tried to make government more efficient and more responsive to citizens.

HISTORY AND YOU How do you use your time and resources wisely? Read on to learn how progressives tried to make the government more efficient.

Progressivism included a wide range of reform activities. Different issues led to different approaches, and progressives even took opposing positions on how to address some problems. They condemned corruption in government but did not always agree on the best way to fix the problem.

Making Government Efficient

One group of progressives focused on making government more efficient by using ideas from business. Theories of business efficiency first became popular in the 1890s. Books such as Frederick W. Taylor's *The Principles of Scientific Management* (1911) described how a company could increase efficiency by managing time, breaking tasks down into small parts, and using standardized tools. In his book, Taylor argued that this "scientific method" of managing businesses optimized productivity and provided more job opportunities for unskilled workers. Many progressives argued that managing a modern city required the use of business management techniques.

Progressives saw corruption and inefficiency in municipal government where, in most cities, the mayor or city council chose the heads of city departments. Traditionally, they gave these jobs to political supporters and friends, who often knew little about managing city services.

Progressives supported two proposals to reform city government. The first, a commission plan, divided city government into several departments, each one under an expert commissioner's control. The second approach was a council-manager system. The city council would hire a city manager to run the city instead of the mayor. In both systems, experts play a major role in managing the city. Galveston, Texas, adopted the commission system in 1901. Other cities soon followed.

Democratic Reforms

Another group of progressives focused on making the political system more democratic and more responsive to citizens. Many believed that the key to improving government was to make elected officials more responsive and accountable to the voters.

La Follette's Laboratory of Democracy
Led by Republican governor **Robert M. La Follette,** Wisconsin became a model of progressive reform. La Follette attacked the way political parties ran their conventions. Party bosses controlled the selection of convention delegates, which meant they also controlled the nomination of candidates. La Follette pressured the state legislature to pass a law requiring parties to hold a **direct primary,** in which all party members could vote for a candidate to run in the general election. This and other successes earned Wisconsin a reputation as the "laboratory of democracy." La Follette later recalled:

PRIMARY SOURCE
New Types of Government

The most deadly hurricane in United States history slammed into Galveston, Texas, on September 8, 1900, killing about 6,000 people. Because the political machine running the city was incapable of responding to the disaster, local business leaders convinced the state to allow them to take control. The following April, Galveston introduced the commission system of local government, which replaced the mayor and city council with five commissioners. Sometimes referred to as the Galveston Plan, its constitutionality was confirmed and took effect.

Four of those commissioners were local business leaders. Reformers in other cities were impressed by the city's rapid recovery. Clearly, the city benefited from dividing the government into departments under the supervision of an expert commissioner. Soon, other cities adopted either the commission or council-manager systems of government.

▶ *A house sits on its side after a hurricane ripped through Galveston, Texas, in September 1900.*

"It was clear to me that the only way to beat boss and ring rule was to keep the people thoroughly informed. Machine control is based upon misrepresentation and ignorance. Democracy is based upon knowledge. It is of first importance that the people shall know about their government and the work of their public servants."

—from La Follette's *Autobiography*

Wisconsin's use of the direct primary soon spread to other states, but to force legislators to listen to the voters, progressives also pushed for three additional reforms: the initiative, the referendum, and the recall. The **initiative** permitted a group of citizens to introduce **legislation** and required the legislature to vote on it. The **referendum** allowed citizens to vote on proposed laws directly without going to the legislature. The **recall** provided voters an option to demand a special election to remove an elected official from office before his or her term had expired.

Direct Election of Senators

Progressives also targeted the Senate. As originally written, the federal constitution directed each state legislature to elect two senators. Political machines and business interests often influenced these elections. Some senators, once elected, repaid their supporters with federal contracts and jobs.

To counter Senate corruption, progressives called for direct election of senators by the state's voters. In 1912, Congress passed a direct-election amendment. Although the direct election of senators was intended to end corruption, it also removed one of the state legislatures' checks on federal power. In 1913 the amendment was ratified and became the Seventeenth Amendment to the Constitution.

Reading Check **Evaluating** What was the impact of the Seventeenth Amendment? What problem was it intended to solve?

Analyzing VISUALS

1. **Differentiating** In what forms of government do voters elect the City Council?
2. **Analyzing** In a mayor-council form of government, who is responsible to carry out policy?

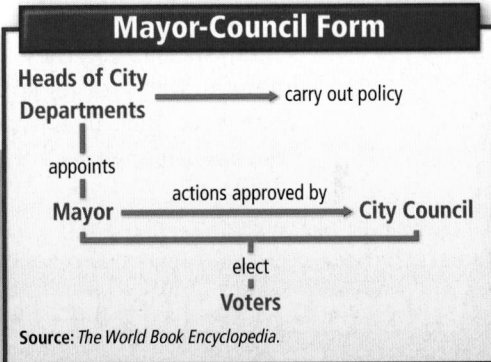

Mayor-Council Form

Heads of City Departments → carry out policy

appoints

Mayor — actions approved by → City Council

elect

Voters

Source: *The World Book Encyclopedia.*

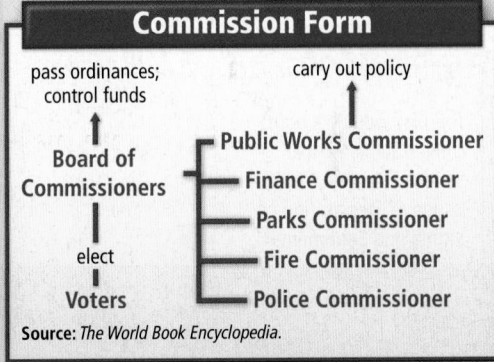

Commission Form

pass ordinances; control funds   carry out policy

Board of Commissioners — Public Works Commissioner

Finance Commissioner

Parks Commissioner

Fire Commissioner

elect

Voters — Police Commissioner

Source: *The World Book Encyclopedia.*

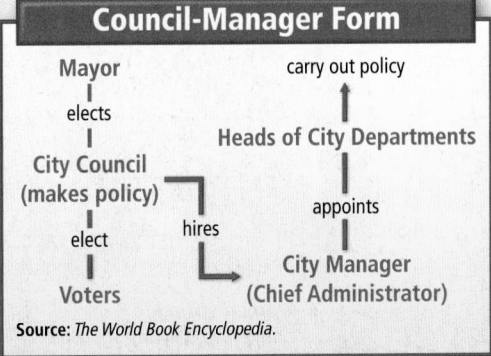

Council-Manager Form

Mayor

elects   carry out policy

City Council (makes policy)   Heads of City Departments

elect   hires   appoints

Voters   City Manager (Chief Administrator)

Source: *The World Book Encyclopedia.*

Suffrage

MAIN Idea Many progressives joined the movement to win voting rights for women.

HISTORY AND YOU Do you remember reading about the Seneca Falls Convention in 1848? Read about the momentum of the women's rights movement in the 1910s.

For an example of the early woman suffrage movement read "The Seneca Falls Declaration" on page R48 in **Documents in American History.**

At the first women's rights convention in Seneca Falls, New York, in 1848, Elizabeth Cady Stanton convinced the delegates that their first priority should be the right to vote. Decades later, universal woman **suffrage**—the right to vote—still had not been granted. It became a major goal for women progressives.

Early Problems

The woman suffrage movement got off to a slow start. Some people threatened women suffragists and said they were unfeminine and immoral. Many of its supporters were abolitionists, as well. In the years before the Civil War, abolishing slavery took priority.

After the Civil War, Congress introduced the Fourteenth and Fifteenth Amendments to grant citizenship to African Americans and voting rights to African American men. Leaders of the woman suffrage movement wanted these amendments to give women the right to vote, as well. They were disappointed when Republicans refused.

The debate over the Fourteenth and Fifteenth Amendments split the suffrage movement into two groups: the New York City–based National Woman Suffrage Association, which Elizabeth Cady Stanton and Susan B. Anthony founded in 1869, and the Boston-based American Woman Suffrage Association, which Lucy Stone and Julia Ward Howe led.

The first group wanted to focus on passing a constitutional amendment. The second group believed that the best strategy was convincing state governments to give women voting rights before trying to amend the Constitution. This split weakened the movement, and by 1900 only Wyoming, Idaho, Utah, and Colorado had granted women full voting rights.

THE Woman Suffrage Movement

1848
The first women's rights convention is held in Seneca Falls, New York, and issues a "Declaration of Rights and Sentiments"

1872
Susan B. Anthony votes illegally in the presidential election in Rochester, New York, claiming the Fourteenth Amendment gives her that right; she is arrested and found guilty

▲ Susan B. Anthony

1850   1870   1890

▲ Women voting in Cheyenne, Wyoming, 1869

1869
Territory of Wyoming becomes the first state or territory to grant women the right to vote

▲ Elizabeth Cady Stanton

1890
Elizabeth Cady Stanton becomes president of the National American Woman Suffrage Association

Building Support

In 1890 the two groups united to form the National American Woman Suffrage Association (NAWSA) but still had trouble convincing women to become politically active. As the Progressive movement gained momentum, however, many middle-class women concluded that they needed the vote to promote the reforms they favored. Many working-class women also wanted the vote to pass labor laws protecting women.

As the movement grew, women began lobbying lawmakers, organizing marches, and delivering speeches on street corners. On March 3, 1913, the day before President Wilson's inauguration, suffragists marched on Washington, D.C.

Alice Paul, a Quaker social worker who headed NAWSA's congressional committee, had organized the march. Paul wanted to use protests to confront Wilson on suffrage. Other members of NAWSA who wanted to negotiate with Wilson were alarmed. Paul left NAWSA and formed the National Woman's Party. Her supporters picketed the White House, blocked sidewalks, chained themselves to lampposts, and went on hunger strikes if arrested.

In 1915 **Carrie Chapman Catt** became NAWSA's leader and tried to mobilize the suffrage movement in one final nationwide push. She also threw NAWSA's support behind Wilson's reelection campaign.

As more states granted women the right to vote, Congress began to favor a constitutional amendment. In 1918 the House of Representatives passed a women's suffrage amendment. The Senate voted on the amendment, but it failed by two votes.

During the midterm elections of 1918, Catt used NAWSA's resources to defeat two antisuffrage senators. In June 1919 the Senate passed the amendment by slightly more than the two-thirds vote needed. On August 26, 1920, after three-fourths of the states had ratified it, the Nineteenth Amendment, guaranteeing women the right to vote, went into effect.

Reading Check **Evaluating** How successful were women in lobbying for the Nineteenth Amendment?

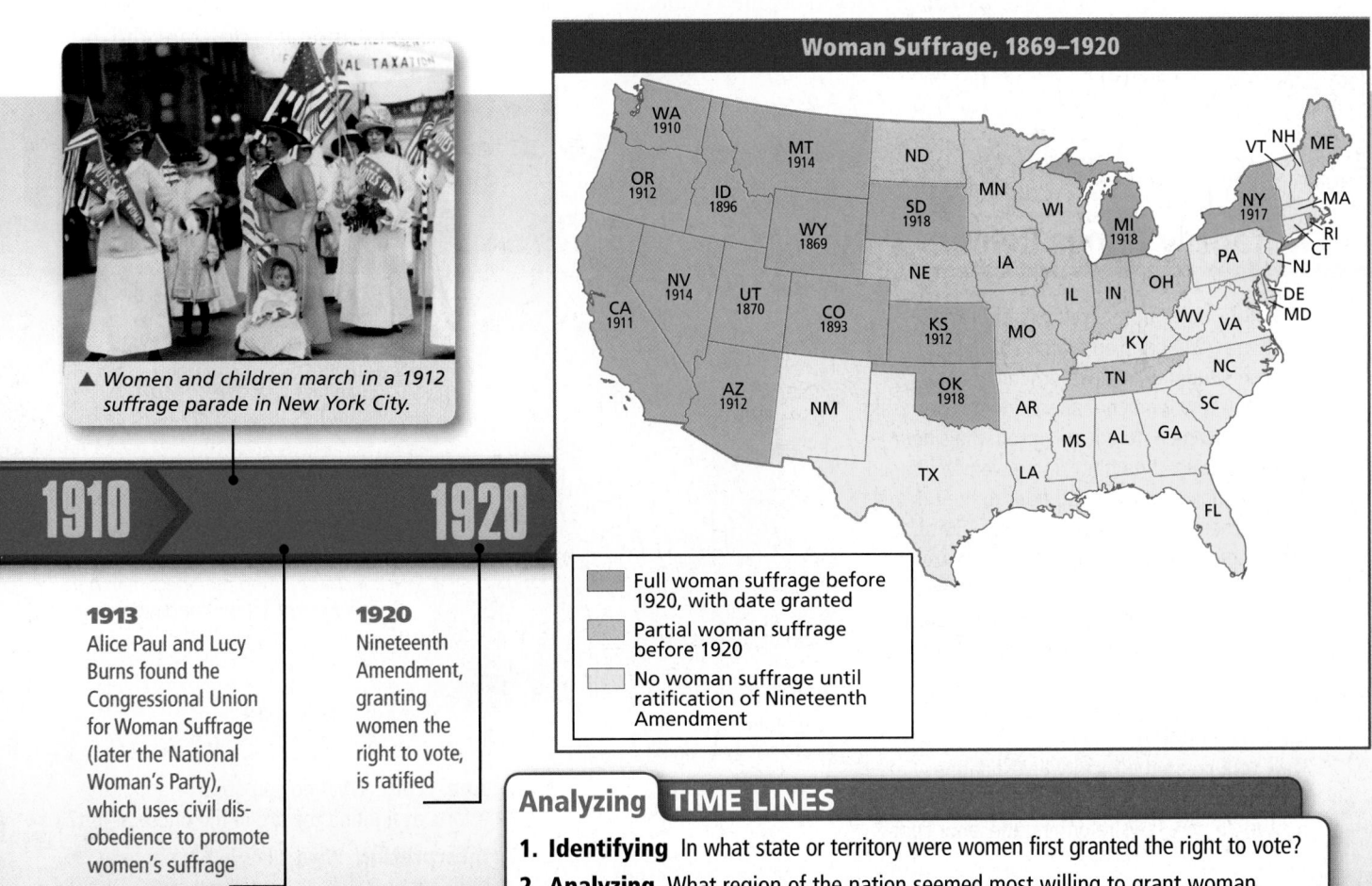

▲ Women and children march in a 1912 suffrage parade in New York City.

1910 ▶ **1920**

1913
Alice Paul and Lucy Burns found the Congressional Union for Woman Suffrage (later the National Woman's Party), which uses civil disobedience to promote women's suffrage

1920
Nineteenth Amendment, granting women the right to vote, is ratified

Woman Suffrage, 1869–1920

WA 1910
OR 1912
ID 1896
MT 1914
ND
MN
WI
VT
NH
ME
NV 1914
UT 1870
WY 1869
SD 1918
NE
IA
MI 1918
NY 1917
MA
RI
CT
CA 1911
CO 1893
KS 1912
MO
IL
IN
OH
PA
NJ
DE
MD
AZ 1912
NM
OK 1918
AR
KY
WV
VA
TN
NC
TX
LA
MS
AL
GA
SC
FL

- ▢ Full woman suffrage before 1920, with date granted
- ▢ Partial woman suffrage before 1920
- ▢ No woman suffrage until ratification of Nineteenth Amendment

Analyzing TIME LINES

1. **Identifying** In what state or territory were women first granted the right to vote?

2. **Analyzing** What region of the nation seemed most willing to grant woman suffrage without a national amendment?

Reforming Society

MAIN Idea Many progressives focused on social welfare problems such as child labor, unsafe working conditions, and alcohol abuse.

HISTORY AND YOU Have you heard of companies using "sweatshop" labor in foreign countries? Read on to learn how progressives tried to ban child labor and make factories safer for workers.

History ONLINE
Student Skill Activity To learn how to create and modify a database, visit glencoe.com and complete the skill activity.

While many progressives focused on reforming the political system, others focused on social problems. These social-welfare progressives created charities to help the poor and disadvantaged. They also pushed for new laws they hoped would fix social problems.

Child Labor

Probably the most emotional progressive issue was the campaign against child labor. Children had always worked on family farms, but mines and factories presented more dangerous and unhealthy working conditions. Muckraker John Spargo's 1906 book, *The Bitter Cry of the Children,* presented detailed evidence of child labor conditions. It told of coal mines that hired thousands of 9- or 10-year-old

"breaker boys" to pick slag out of coal, paying them 60 cents for a 10-hour day. It described the way that the work bent their backs permanently and often crippled their hands.

Reports like these convinced states to pass laws that set a minimum age for employment and established other limits on child labor, such as maximum hours children could work.

Health and Safety Codes

Many adult workers also labored in difficult conditions. When workers were injured or killed on the job, they and their families received little or no compensation. Progressives joined union leaders to pressure states for workers' compensation laws. These laws established insurance funds that employers financed. Workers injured in accidents received payments from the funds.

In two cases, *Lochner* v. *New York* (1905) and *Muller* v. *Oregon* (1908), the Supreme Court addressed government's authority to regulate business to protect workers. In the Lochner case, the Court ruled that a New York law forbidding bakers to work more than 10 hours a day was unconstitutional. The state did not have the right to interfere with the liberty of

PRIMARY SOURCE
A Tragedy Brings Reform

Fire broke out on the top floors of the Triangle Shirtwaist Company on March 25, 1911. Young women struggled against locked doors to escape. A few women managed to get out using the fire escape before it collapsed. The single elevator stopped running. Some women jumped from windows on the ninth floor to their death, while others died in the fire. Nearly 150 of the 500 employees lost their lives in the blaze.

The Triangle factory was a nonunion shop. Health and safety issues were a major concern for unions. The disaster illustrated that fire precautions and inspections were inadequate. Exit doors were kept locked, supposedly to prevent theft. As a result of the fire and loss of life, New York created a Factory Investigating Commission. Between 1911 and 1914, the state passed 36 new laws reforming the labor code.

▲ Firemen fight Triangle Shirtwaist fire, March 25, 1911.

▲ Trade union members march in support of the women who died.

Analyzing VISUALS

1. **Analyzing** What do you observe about the efforts at fighting the fire in the photo at left?

2. **Interpreting** What clues in the photo at right suggest that at least some of the women who died were immigrants?

employers and employees. In the case of women working in laundries in Oregon, however, the Court upheld the state's right to limit hours. The different judgments were based on gender differences. The Court stated that healthy mothers were the state's concern and, therefore, the limits on women's working hours did not violate their Fourteenth Amendment rights.

Some progressives also favored zoning laws as a method of protecting the public. These laws divided a town or city into zones for commercial, residential, or other development, thereby regulating how land and buildings could be used. Building codes set minimum standards for light, air, room size, and sanitation, and required buildings to have fire escapes. Health codes required restaurants and other facilities to maintain clean environments for their patrons.

The Prohibition Movement

Many progressives believed alcohol explained many of society's problems. Settlement house workers knew that hard-earned wages were often spent on alcohol and that drunkenness often led to physical abuse and sickness. Some employers believed drinking hurt workers' efficiency. The temperance movement—which **advocated** that people stop, or at least moderate, their alcohol consumption—emerged from these concerns.

For the most part, women led the temperance movement. In 1874 a group of women formed the Woman's Christian Temperance Union (WCTU). By 1911 the WCTU had nearly 250,000 members. In 1893 evangelical Protestant ministers formed another group, the Anti-Saloon League. When the temperance movement began, it concentrated on reducing alcohol consumption. Later it pressed for **prohibition**—laws banning the manufacture, sale, and consumption of alcohol.

Progressives Versus Big Business

Many progressives agreed that big business needed regulation. Some believed the government should break up big companies to restore competition. This led to the Sherman Antitrust Act in 1890. Others argued that big business was the most efficient way to organize the economy. They pushed for government to regulate big companies and prevent them from abusing their power. The Interstate Commerce Commission (ICC), created in 1887, was an early example of this kind of thinking.

Some progressives went even further and advocated socialism—the idea that the government should own and operate industry for the community. They wanted the government to buy up large companies, especially industries that affected everyone, such as utilities. At its peak, socialism had some national support. Eugene V. Debs, the former American Railway Union leader, won nearly a million votes as the American Socialist Party candidate for president in 1912. Most progressives and most Americans, however, believed the American system of free enterprise was superior.

Reading Check **Comparing** In what ways were progressive efforts to end child labor and impose safety codes similar?

Section 1 REVIEW

Vocabulary

1. **Explain** the significance of: muckraker, Jacob Riis, Robert M. La Follette, direct primary, initiative, referendum, recall, suffrage, Carrie Chapman Catt, prohibition.

Main Ideas

2. **Organizing** Use a graphic organizer similar to the one below to list the kinds of problems that muckrakers exposed.

```
       ┌──────────────────┐
       │ Problems Exposed │
       │  by Muckrakers   │
       └──────────────────┘
   ↙    ↓    ↓    ↓    ↓    ↘
  □    □    □    □    □    □
```

3. **Summarizing** How did initiative, referendum, and recall change democracy in the United States?

4. **Stating** What key provision did the Nineteenth Amendment make?

5. **Describing** Explain the various zoning laws and codes favored by progressives.

Critical Thinking

6. **Big Ideas** Identify the different social issues associated with progressives. How do these ideals influence society today?

7. **Analyzing Visuals** Study the charts on page 523. Which system gives voters the most control over department heads? How?

Writing About History

8. **Expository Writing** Create a database of progressive ideas of the period. Then write a one-page report using a word processor to summarize the progressive ideals.

History ONLINE

Study Central™ To review this section, go to glencoe.com and click on Study Central.

Roosevelt and Taft

Guide to Reading

Big Ideas
Individual Action Presidents Theodore Roosevelt and William Taft worked to improve labor conditions, control big business, and support conservation.

Content Vocabulary
- Social Darwinism *(p. 528)*
- arbitration *(p. 529)*
- insubordination *(p. 535)*

Academic Vocabulary
- regulate *(p. 530)*
- environmental *(p. 532)*

People and Events to Identify
- Square Deal *(p. 528)*
- United Mine Workers *(p. 529)*
- Hepburn Act *(p. 530)*
- Upton Sinclair *(p. 530)*
- Meat Inspection Act *(p. 530)*
- Pure Food and Drug Act *(p. 530)*
- Gifford Pinchot *(p. 532)*
- Richard A. Ballinger *(p. 534)*
- Children's Bureau *(p. 535)*

Reading Strategy
Notes As you read about the Roosevelt and Taft administrations, use the headings of the section to create an outline similar to the one below.

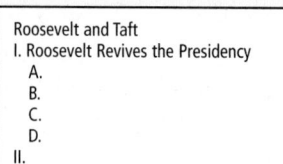

```
Roosevelt and Taft
I. Roosevelt Revives the Presidency
    A.
    B.
    C.
    D.
II.
```

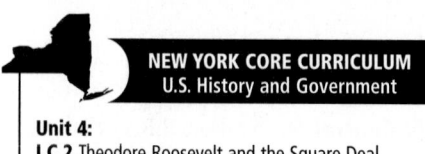

NEW YORK CORE CURRICULUM
U.S. History and Government

Unit 4:
I.C.2 Theodore Roosevelt and the Square Deal
I.C.3 Conservation

A s president, Theodore Roosevelt extended the federal government's ability to curb the power of big business and to conserve natural resources. His successor, William Howard Taft, was less popular with progressives.

Roosevelt Revives the Presidency

MAIN Idea Theodore Roosevelt, who believed in progressive ideals for the nation, took on big business.

HISTORY AND YOU How much do you think a president's personal beliefs should shape national policy? Read on to learn how Theodore Roosevelt used his ideas to change trusts and big business.

Theodore Roosevelt became president at age 42—the youngest person ever to take office. Roosevelt was intensely competitive, strong-willed, and extremely energetic. In international affairs, Roosevelt was a Social Darwinist. He believed the United States was in competition with the other nations of the world and that only the fittest would survive. Domestically, however, Roosevelt was a committed progressive, who believed that government should actively balance the needs of competing groups in American society.

"I shall see to it," Roosevelt declared in 1904, "that every man has a square deal, no less and no more." His reform programs soon became known as the **Square Deal.** To Roosevelt, it was not inconsistent to believe in **Social Darwinism** and progressivism at the same time.

Roosevelt Takes on the Trusts

Roosevelt believed that trusts and other large business organizations were very efficient and part of the reason for America's prosperity. Yet Roosevelt remained concerned that the monopoly power of some trusts hurt the public interest. His goal was to ensure that trusts did not abuse their power. When the *New York Sun* declared that Roosevelt was "bringing wealth to its knees," the president disagreed. "We draw the line against misconduct," he declared, "not against wealth."

Roosevelt decided to make an example out of major trusts that he believed were abusing their power. His first target was J. P. Morgan's railroad holding company, Northern Securities. Established in 1901, the company proposed, through an exchange of stock, to merge existing railroad systems to create a monopoly on railroad traffic in the Northwest. As a monopoly, Northern Securities would have no competition. Farmers and business owners feared it would raise rates and hurt their profits. In 1902 the president ordered the attorney

Jay Gould was a well-known railroad speculator who had been involved in many scandals. At one point, he controlled the four largest western railroads, including the Union Pacific.

John D. Rockefeller, founder of Standard Oil, which controlled most oil production in the United States

James J. Hill, founder of the Great Northern Railway Company and a partner with J. P. Morgan in Northern Securities

J. P. Morgan controlled a huge banking and financial empire. He also created the U.S. Steel Corporation and helped finance several railroads.

Theodore Roosevelt, shown standing in the middle of Wall Street carrying a sword labeled "Public Service"

Analyzing VISUALS **DBQ**

1. **Inferring** Why do you think the scene is set on Wall Street?
2. **Analyzing** What do the giants represent?

general to file suit under the Sherman Antitrust Act, charging the company was a "combination in restraint of trade."

Roosevelt's action baffled J. P. Morgan. Expecting to resolve the suit without legal action, he inquired what could be done to "fix it up." Unmoved, Roosevelt proceeded with the case. In 1904, in *Northern Securities* v. *United States*, the Supreme Court ruled that Northern Securities had indeed violated the Sherman Antitrust Act. Roosevelt proclaimed, "The most powerful men in the country were held to accountability before the law." Newspapers hailed Roosevelt as a "trustbuster," and his popularity with the American public soared.

The Coal Strike of 1902

As president, Roosevelt regarded himself as the nation's head manager. He believed it was his job to keep society operating efficiently by mediating conflicts between different groups and their interests. In the fall of 1902, he put these beliefs into practice.

The previous spring, the **United Mine Workers** (UMW) had launched a strike by the anthracite (hard coal) miners of eastern Pennsylvania. Nearly 150,000 workers walked out, demanding increased pay, reduced work hours, and union recognition. Coal prices began to rise. Roosevelt viewed it as another example of groups pursuing their private interests at the nation's expense. If the strike dragged on too long, the country would face a coal shortage that could shut down factories and leave many homes unheated.

Roosevelt urged the union and the owners to accept **arbitration**—a settlement negotiated by an outside party. The union agreed; the mine owners did not. The mine owners' stubbornness infuriated Roosevelt, as well as the public. Roosevelt threatened to order the army to run the mines. Fearful of this, the mine owners finally accepted arbitration. By intervening in the dispute, Roosevelt took the first step toward establishing the federal government as an honest broker between powerful groups in society.

Regulating Big Business

Despite his lawsuit against Northern Securities and his role in the coal strike, Roosevelt believed most trusts benefited the economy and that breaking them up would do more harm than good. Instead, he proposed creating a new federal agency to investigate corporations and publicize the results. He believed the most effective way to keep big business from abusing its power was to keep the public informed.

In 1903 Roosevelt convinced Congress to create the Department of Commerce and Labor. The following year, this department began investigating U.S. Steel, a gigantic holding company that had been created in 1901. Worried about a possible antitrust lawsuit, the company's leaders met privately with Roosevelt and offered a deal. They would open their account books and records for examination. In exchange, if any problems were found, the company would be advised privately and allowed to correct them without having to go to court.

Roosevelt accepted this "gentlemen's agreement," as he called it, and soon made similar deals with other companies. These arrangements gave Roosevelt the ability to **regulate** big business without having to sacrifice economic efficiency by breaking up the trusts.

In keeping with his belief in regulation, Roosevelt pushed the **Hepburn Act** through Congress in 1906. This act was intended to strengthen the Interstate Commerce Commission (ICC) by giving it the power to set railroad rates. At first, railroad companies were suspicious of the ICC and tied up its decisions by challenging them in court. Eventually, the railroads realized that they could work with the ICC to set rates and regulations that limited competition and prevented new competitors from entering the industry. Over time, the ICC became a supporter of the railroads' interests, and by 1920 it had begun setting rates at levels intended to ensure the industry's profits.

Consumer Protection

By 1905 consumer protection had become a national issue. That year, a journalist named Samuel Hopkins Adams published a series of articles in *Collier's* magazine describing the patent medicine business.

Many companies patented and marketed potions they claimed would cure a variety of ills. Many of these medicines were little more than alcohol, colored water, and sugar. Others contained caffeine, opium, cocaine, and other dangerous compounds. Consumers had no way to know what they were taking, nor did they receive any assurance that the medicines worked as claimed. Adams's articles pointed out that these supposed cures could cause health problems. The articles in *Collier's* outraged many Americans.

Many Americans were equally concerned about the food they ate. Dr. W. H. Wiley, chief chemist at the United States Department of Agriculture, had issued reports documenting the dangerous preservatives being used in what he called "embalmed meat." Then, in 1906, **Upton Sinclair** published his novel *The Jungle*. Based on Sinclair's close observations of the slaughterhouses of Chicago, the powerful book featured appalling descriptions of conditions in the meatpacking industry:

PRIMARY SOURCE

"[T]here would come all the way back from Europe old sausage that had been rejected, and that was [moldy] and white—it would be dosed with borax and glycerine, and dumped into the hoppers, and made over again for home consumption. . . . There would be meat stored in great piles in rooms; and the water from leaky roofs would drip over it, and thousands of rats would race about [upon] it."

—from *The Jungle*

Sinclair's book was a best-seller. It made consumers ill—and angry. Many became vegetarians after reading the book. Roosevelt and Congress responded with the **Meat Inspection Act,** passed in 1906. It required federal inspection of meat sold through interstate commerce and required the Agriculture Department to set standards of cleanliness in meatpacking plants. The **Pure Food and Drug Act,** passed on the same day in 1906, prohibited the manufacture, sale, or shipment of impure or falsely labeled food and drugs.

✔ Reading Check **Identifying** What term was used to describe Roosevelt's policies and how accurate was it?

★ *Northern Securities v. United States,* 1904

Background to the Case

In 1901 three powerful businessmen, J. P. Morgan, James J. Hill, and Edward H. Harriman, created Northern Securities—a holding company that owned the majority of the stock in several major railroads. The government sued the company for violating the Sherman Antitrust Act, and a court ordered the company broken up.

How the Court Ruled

The Constitution gives the federal government the power to regulate interstate commerce—but did "commerce" mean all business activity, or just the movement of goods across state lines? The owners of Northern Securities argued that their company was a holding company set up to buy stock. It had been created legally under New Jersey law, and federal laws should not apply because the company itself did not engage in interstate commerce. In a 5-4 decision, the Court concluded that the commerce clause allows the federal government to regulate the ownership of companies.

NO MOLLY-CODDLING HERE

▲ President Roosevelt once said "Speak softly and carry a big stick." This cartoon shows Roosevelt swinging his stick and knocking down the trusts—and everything else, as well.

<u>PRIMARY SOURCE</u>

The Court's Opinion

"No state can, by merely creating a corporation . . . project its authority into other states, and across the continent, so as to prevent Congress from exerting the power it possesses under the Constitution over interstate and international commerce. . . .

. . . Every corporation created by a state is necessarily subject to the supreme law of the land. . . . In short, the court may make any order necessary to bring about the dissolution or suppression of an illegal combination that restrains interstate commerce. All this can be done without infringing in any degree upon the just authority of the states."

—Justice John Marshall Harlan, writing for the Court

<u>PRIMARY SOURCE</u>

Dissenting Views

"Commerce depends upon population, but Congress could not, on that ground, undertake to regulate marriage and divorce. If the act before us is to be carried out according to what seems to me the logic of the argument . . . I can see no part of the conduct of life with which . . . Congress might not interfere.

. . . This act is construed by the Government to affect the purchasers of shares in two railroad companies because of the effect it may have . . . upon the competition of these roads. If such a remote result of the exercise of an ordinary incident of property and personal freedom is enough to make that exercise unlawful, there is hardly any transaction concerning commerce between the States that may not be made a crime by the finding of a jury or a court."

—Justice Oliver Wendell Holmes, dissenting

DBQ Document-Based Questions

1. **Interpreting** How does Justice Harlan view the rights of states and the authority of Congress?
2. **Defining** How does Justice Harlan refer to the Sherman Antitrust Act?
3. **Analyzing** What does Justice Holmes fear in narrowly applying a law?

Conservation

MAIN Idea New legislation gave the federal government the power to conserve natural resources.

HISTORY AND YOU Have you ever visited a national park or forest? Read on to find out how Roosevelt made some national parks and forests possible.

Roosevelt put his stamp on the presidency most clearly in the area of **environmental** conservation. Realizing that the nation's bountiful natural resources were being used up at an alarming rate, Roosevelt urged Americans to conserve those resources.

An enthusiastic outdoorsman, Roosevelt valued the country's minerals, animals, and rugged terrain. He cautioned against unregulated exploitation of public lands and believed in conservation to manage the nation's resources. Roosevelt argued that the government must distinguish "between the man who skins the land and the man who develops the country. I am going to work with, and only with, the man who develops the country."

Western Land Development

Roosevelt quickly applied his philosophy in the dry Western states, where farmers and city dwellers competed for scarce water. In 1902 Roosevelt supported passage of the Newlands Reclamation Act, authorizing the use of federal funds from public land sales to pay for irrigation and land development projects. The federal government thus began transforming the West's landscape and economy on a large scale.

Gifford Pinchot

Roosevelt also backed efforts to save the nation's forests through careful management of the timber resources of the West. He appointed his close friend **Gifford Pinchot** to head the United States Forest Service established in 1905. "The natural resources," Pinchot said, "must be developed and preserved for the benefit of the many and not merely for the profit of a few."

As progressives, Roosevelt and Pinchot both believed that trained experts in forestry and resource management should apply the same scientific standards to the landscape that others were applying to managing cities and industry. They rejected the laissez-faire argument that the best way to preserve public land was to sell it to lumber companies, who would then carefully conserve it because it was the source of their profits. With the president's support, Pinchot's department drew up regulations controlling lumbering on federal lands. Roosevelt also added over 100 million acres to the protected national forests and established five new national parks and 51 federal wildlife reservations.

Roosevelt's Legacy

President Theodore Roosevelt changed the role of the federal government and the nature of the presidency. He used his power in the

Debates
IN HISTORY

Should Resources Be Preserved?

The origins of the environmentalist movement can be traced back to the Progressive Era. Then, as now, people disagreed over the best approach to the environment. Their disagreements were represented in the differing views of John Muir, founder of the Sierra Club, who worked with Roosevelt to create Yosemite National Park, and Gifford Pinchot, head of the U.S. Forest Service under Theodore Roosevelt. Muir was a preservationist, hoping that wild places could be left as they were. Pinchot was a conservationist who believed in managing the use of land for the benefit of the nation's citizens.

White House to present his views, calling it his "bully pulpit." Increasingly, Americans began looking to the federal government to solve the nation's economic and social problems.

Under Roosevelt, the power of the executive branch of government had dramatically increased. The Hepburn Act gave the Interstate Commerce Commission the power to set rates, the Meat Inspection Act stated that the Agriculture Department could inspect food, the Department of Commerce and Labor could monitor business, the Bureau of Corporations could investigate corporations and issue reports, and the attorney general could rapidly bring antitrust lawsuits under the Expedition Act.

Reading Check **Examining** How did Roosevelt's policies help the conservation of natural resources?

Taft's Reforms

MAIN Idea William Howard Taft broke with progressives on tariff and conservation issues.

HISTORY AND YOU Have you ever been judged in comparison with the accomplishments of a sibling or friend? Read on to learn how Taft had to deal with comparisons with Roosevelt.

Roosevelt believed William Howard Taft to be the ideal person to continue his policies. Taft had worked closely with Roosevelt. He had served as a judge, as governor of the Philippines, and as Roosevelt's secretary of war. Taft easily received his party's nomination. His victory in the general election in November 1908 was a foregone conclusion. The Democratic candidate, William Jennings Bryan, lost for a third time.

YES

John Muir
Sierra Club Founder

PRIMARY SOURCE

"The making of gardens and parks goes on with civilization all over the world, and they increase both in size and number as their value is recognized.

Everybody needs beauty as well as bread, places to play in and pray in, where Nature may heal and cheer and give strength to body and soul alike. . . . Nevertheless, like anything else worth while . . . they have always been subject to attack by despoiling gainseekers . . . eagerly trying to make everything immediately and selfishly commercial, with schemes disguised in smug-smiling philanthropy, industriously, shampiously crying, 'Conservation, conservation, panutilization,' that man and beast may be fed and the dear Nation made great."

—from *The Yosemite*

NO

Gifford Pinchot
Chief of U.S. Forest Service

PRIMARY SOURCE

"The first principle of conservation is development, the use of the natural resources now existing on this continent for the benefit of the people who live here now. There may be just as much waste in neglecting the development and use of certain natural resources as there is in their destruction. . . .

Conservation stands emphatically for the development and use of water-power now, without delay. It stands for the immediate construction of navigable waterways . . . as assistants to the railroads. . . .

In addition . . . natural resources must be developed and preserved for the benefit of the many, and not merely for the profit of the few."

—from *The Fight for Conservation*

DBQ Document-Based Questions

1. **Contrasting** How do the two men differ in their views about nature?

2. **Making Connections** Which view do you think is more common today? Why do you think so?

3. **Speculating** Which viewpoint do you think was more likely to be held by ranchers and farmers in California in the early twentieth century?

Campaigning Against Child Labor

In 1900, 18 percent of children were employed. Mary Harris Jones, "Mother" Jones, as she was called, campaigned against child labor. After working with children in an Alabama cotton mill, she wrote, "Little girls and boys . . . reaching thin little hands into the machinery to repair snapped threads. They replaced spindles all day long; all night through . . . six-year-olds with faces of sixty did an eight-hour shift for ten cents a day . . ."

Using posters like the one shown at right to build public support, the campaign against child labor made steady progress. Between 1880 and 1910, 36 states passed laws on the minimum age for manufacturing workers.

Analyzing VISUALS

1. **Analyzing** What in the photo indicates that the children could easily be injured?
2. **Hypothesizing** What effect do you think the images on the inset poster may have had on people in the early 1900s?

▲ *At a Georgia cotton mill in 1909, two boys keep a spinning machine running by repairing broken thread and replacing bobbins as they are filled.*

The Payne-Aldrich Tariff

Like many progressives, Taft believed high tariffs limited competition, hurt consumers, and protected trusts. Roosevelt had warned him to stay away from tariff reform because it would divide the Republican Party. Taft, however, called Congress into special session to lower tariff rates.

As Roosevelt predicted, the tariff debate divided progressives, who favored tariff reduction, and conservative Republicans who wanted to maintain high tariffs. In the prolonged negotiations on the bill, Taft's support for tariff reductions wavered, and then collapsed. In the end, Taft signed into law the Payne-Aldrich Tariff, which cut tariffs hardly at all and actually raised them on some goods.

Progressives felt outraged by Taft's decision: "I knew the fire had gone out of [the progressive movement]," recalled the head of the U.S. Forest Service, Gifford Pinchot, after Roosevelt left office. "Washington was a dead town. Its leader was gone, and in his place [was] a man whose fundamental desire was to keep out of trouble."

Ballinger Versus Pinchot

With Taft's standing among Republican progressives deteriorating, a sensational controversy broke out late in 1909 that helped permanently destroy Taft's popularity with reformers. Many progressives were unhappy when Taft replaced Roosevelt's secretary of the interior, James R. Garfield, an aggressive conservationist, with **Richard A. Ballinger,** a more conservative corporate lawyer. Suspicion of Ballinger grew when he tried to make nearly a million acres of public forests and mineral reserves available for private development.

In the midst of this mounting concern, Gifford Pinchot charged the new secretary with having once plotted to turn over valuable public lands in Alaska to a private business group for personal profit. Taft's attorney general investigated the charges and decided they were groundless. Not satisfied, Pinchot leaked the story to the press and asked Congress to investigate. Taft fired Pinchot for **insubordination,** or disobedience to authority. The congressional investigation cleared Ballinger.

By the second half of his term of office, many Americans believed that Taft had "sold the Square Deal down the river." Popular indignation was so great that the congressional elections of 1910 resulted in a sweeping Democratic victory, with Democrats taking the majority in the House, and Democrats and progressive Republicans grabbing control of the Senate from conservative Republicans.

Taft's Achievements

Despite his political problems, Taft also had several successes. Although Roosevelt was nicknamed the "trustbuster," Taft was a strong opponent of monopoly and actually brought twice as many antitrust cases in four years as his predecessor had in seven. In other areas, too, Taft pursued progressive policies. Taft established the **Children's Bureau** in 1912, an agency that investigated and publicized the problems of child labor. The agency exists today, and deals with issues such as child abuse prevention, adoption, and foster care.

The Ballinger-Pinchot controversy aside, Taft was also a dedicated conservationist. His contributions in this area actually equaled or surpassed those of Roosevelt. He set up the Bureau of Mines in 1910 to monitor the activities of mining companies, expand the national forests, and protect waterpower sites from private development. Most of the new and emerging technologies in the minerals field were partly made possible by the existence of the Bureau of Mines.

After Taft took office in 1909, Roosevelt left for a big-game hunt in Africa, followed by a tour of Europe. He did not return to the United States until June 1910. Although disturbed by stories of Taft's "betrayal" of progressivism, Roosevelt at first refused to criticize the president.

In October 1911 Taft announced an antitrust lawsuit against U.S. Steel, claiming that the company's decision to buy the Tennessee Coal and Iron Company in 1907 had violated the Sherman Antitrust Act. The lawsuit was the final straw for Roosevelt. As president, he had approved U.S. Steel's plan to buy the company.

Roosevelt believed Taft's focus on breaking up trusts was destroying the carefully crafted system of cooperation and regulation that Roosevelt had established with big business. In November 1911 Roosevelt publicly criticized Taft's decision. Roosevelt argued that the best way to deal with the trusts was to allow them to exist while continuing to regulate them.

After Roosevelt broke with Taft, it was only a matter of time before progressives convinced him to reenter politics. In late February 1912, Roosevelt announced that he would enter the presidential campaign of 1912 and attempt to replace Taft as the Republican nominee for president.

Reading Check **Evaluating** How did Taft's accomplishments regarding conservation and trust-busting compare to Roosevelt's?

Section 2 REVIEW

Vocabulary

1. **Explain** the significance of: Square Deal, Social Darwinism, United Mine Workers, arbitration, Hepburn Act, Upton Sinclair, Meat Inspection Act, Pure Food and Drug Act, Gifford Pinchot, Richard A. Ballinger, insubordination, Children's Bureau.

Main Ideas

2. **Explaining** What was the intent of the Hepburn Act?

3. **Describing** How did Roosevelt's policies change the Western landscape?

4. **Discussing** How did Taft help conservation efforts and child labor problems?

Critical Thinking

5. **Big Ideas** How did Upton Sinclair contribute to involving the federal government in protecting consumers?

6. **Organizing** Use a graphic organizer to list Taft's progressive reforms.

Taft's Progressive Reforms

7. **Analyzing Visuals** Study the photo on page 534. Could this photo be used to rally the cause against child labor? Explain the dangerous elements of the job.

Writing About History

8. **Expository Writing** Suppose that you are living in the early 1900s and have just read Sinclair's *The Jungle*. Write a letter to a friend summarizing the plot and how it characterizes the Progressive Era.

History ONLINE
Study Central™ To review this section, go to glencoe.com and click on Study Central.

535

The Wilson Years

Guide to Reading

Big Ideas
Individual Action Woodrow Wilson increased the control of the government over business.

Content Vocabulary
• income tax (p. 538)
• unfair trade practices (p. 539)

Academic Vocabulary
• academic (p. 536)
• unconstitutional (p. 540)

People and Events to Identify
• Progressive Party (p. 536)
• New Nationalism (p. 537)
• New Freedom (p. 537)
• Federal Reserve Act (p. 539)
• Federal Trade Commission (p. 539)
• Clayton Antitrust Act (p. 539)
• National Association for the Advancement of Colored People (p. 541)

Reading Strategy
Organizing As you read about progressivism during the Wilson administration, complete a chart similar to the one below by listing Wilson's progressive economic and social reforms.

Economic Reforms	Social Reforms

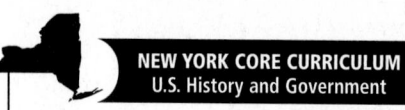

NEW YORK CORE CURRICULUM
U.S. History and Government

Unit 4:
I.C.4 Woodrow Wilson and the New Freedom
I.B.2.c The black movement and reform (Booker T. Washington and W.E.B. Du Bois)

Woodrow Wilson, a progressive Democrat, won the election of 1912. While in office, he supported lower tariffs, more regulation of business, and creation of a federal reserve banking system.

The Election of 1912

MAIN Idea Woodrow Wilson was elected after Republican voters split between Taft and Roosevelt.

HISTORY AND YOU Do you remember a catchy slogan from a political campaign? Read about the competing slogans and platforms in the 1912 election.

The 1912 presidential campaign featured a current president, a former president, and an **academic** who had entered politics only two years earlier. The election's outcome determined the path of the Progressive movement.

Picking the Candidates

Believing that President Taft had failed to live up to progressive ideals, Theodore Roosevelt informed seven state governors that he was willing to accept the Republican nomination. "My hat is in the ring!" he declared. "The fight is on."

The struggle for control of the Republican Party reached its climax at the national convention in Chicago in June 1912. Conservatives rallied behind Taft. Most of the progressives supported Roosevelt. When it became clear that Taft's delegates controlled the nomination, Roosevelt decided to leave the party and campaign as an independent.

Declaring himself "fit as a bull moose," Roosevelt became the presidential candidate for the newly formed **Progressive Party,** which quickly became known as the Bull Moose Party. Because Taft had alienated so many groups, the election of 1912 became a contest between two progressives: Roosevelt and the Democratic candidate, Woodrow Wilson.

After a university teaching career that ended in his becoming the president of Princeton University, Woodrow Wilson entered politics as a firm progressive. As governor of New Jersey, he pushed through one progressive reform after another. He signed laws that introduced the direct primary, established utility regulatory boards, and allowed cities to adopt the commissioner form of government. In less than two years, New Jersey became a model of progressive reform.

New Nationalism Versus New Freedom

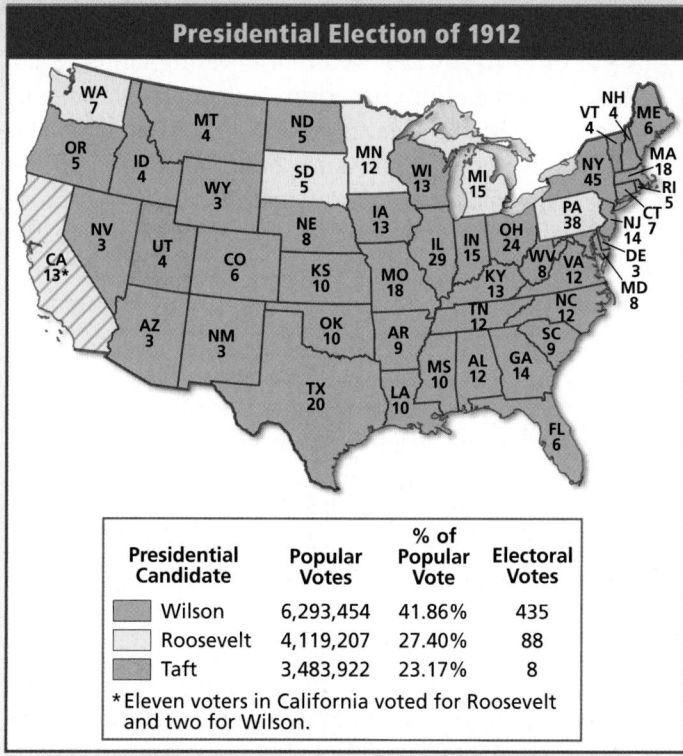

Presidential Election of 1912

Presidential Candidate	Popular Votes	% of Popular Vote	Electoral Votes
Wilson	6,293,454	41.86%	435
Roosevelt	4,119,207	27.40%	88
Taft	3,483,922	23.17%	8

*Eleven voters in California voted for Roosevelt and two for Wilson.

DBQ Document-Based Questions

1. **Analyzing Visuals** From which state did Roosevelt gain the most Electoral College votes?

2. **Analyzing Primary Sources** How do Wilson and Roosevelt differ on trusts?

3. **Making Generalizations** What can you generalize about the two men based solely on their appearance in giving a speech?

Maps In Motion See *StudentWorks™ Plus* or glencoe.com.

WILSON'S NEW FREEDOM

"I am perfectly willing that [a business] should beat any competitor by fair means . . . But there must be no squeezing out the beginner . . . no secret arrangements against him. All the fair competition you choose, but no unfair competition of any kind. . . . A trust is an arrangement to get rid of competition. . . . A trust does not bring efficiency . . . it *buys efficiency out of business*. I am for big business, and I am against the trusts . . . any man who can put others out of business by making the thing cheaper to the consumer . . . I take off my hat to . . . "

—from *The New Freedom*

ROOSEVELT'S NEW NATIONALISM

"Combinations in industry [trusts] are the result of an imperative economic law which cannot be repealed by political legislation. . . . The way out lies, not in attempting to prevent such combinations, but in completely controlling them in the interest of the public welfare. . . . The absence of an effective state, and, especially national, restraint upon unfair money getting has tended to create a small class of enormously wealthy and economically powerful men. . . . The prime need is to change the conditions which enable these men to accumulate power."

—from *The New Nationalism*

Wilson Versus Roosevelt

The election of 1912 was a contest between two progressives with different approaches to reform. Roosevelt accepted the large trusts as a fact of life and set out proposals to increase regulation. Roosevelt also outlined a complete program of reforms. He favored legislation to protect women and children in the labor force and supported workers' compensation for those injured on the job. Roosevelt called his program the **New Nationalism.**

Wilson countered with what he called the **New Freedom.** He criticized Roosevelt's New Nationalism for supporting "regulated monopoly." Monopolies, he believed, should be destroyed, not regulated. Wilson argued that Roosevelt's approach gave the federal government too much power in the economy and did nothing to restore competition. Freedom, in Wilson's opinion, was more important than efficiency. "The history of liberty," Wilson declared, "is the history of the limitation of governmental power. . . . If America is not to have free enterprise, then she can have freedom of no sort whatever."

As expected, Roosevelt and Taft split the Republican voters, enabling Wilson to win the Electoral College with 435 votes and the election, even though he received less than 42 percent of the popular vote.

Reading Check **Summarizing** Who were the major candidates in the election of 1912?

Wilson's Reforms

MAIN Idea President Wilson reformed tariffs and banks and oversaw the creation of the Federal Trade Commission.

HISTORY AND YOU Are you aware of recent economic concerns and presidential responses to them? Read to learn of Wilson's economic actions after his election.

The new chief executive lost no time in embarking on his program of reform. "The president is at liberty, both in law and conscience, to be as big a man as he can," Wilson had once written. "His capacity will set the limit." During his eight years as president, Wilson demonstrated his executive power as he crafted reforms affecting tariffs, the banking system, trusts, and workers' rights.

Reforming Tariffs

Five weeks after taking office, Wilson appeared before Congress, the first president to do so since John Adams. He had come to present his bill to reduce tariffs. Wilson personally lobbied members of Congress to support the tariff reduction bill. Not even Roosevelt had taken such an active role in promoting legislation.

Wilson believed that lowering tariffs would benefit both American consumers and manufacturers. If tariff rates were lowered, he reasoned, the pressure of foreign competition would lead American manufacturers to improve their products and lower their prices. In the long term, businesses would benefit from the "constant necessity to be efficient, economical, and enterprising."

In 1913 Congress passed the Underwood Tariff, and Wilson signed it into law. This law reduced the average tariff on imported goods to about 30 percent of the value of the goods, or about half the tariff rate of the 1890s.

An important section of the Underwood Tariff Act provided for levying an **income tax,** or a direct tax on the earnings of individuals. The Constitution originally prohibited direct taxes on individuals. Ratification of the Sixteenth Amendment in 1913, however, gave the federal government the power to tax the income of individuals directly.

INFOGRAPHIC

Progressives Reform the Economic System

During Wilson's presidency, Congress passed several major reforms affecting the nation's economy. The Federal Reserve and the Federal Trade Commission were created, federal income tax was introduced, and unions were legalized.

The Federal Reserve

Why Was the Federal Reserve Created?
- to create national supervision of the banking industry
- to decentralize banking institutions and access to credit
- to prevent recurring "panics," such as the Panic of 1907
- to allow the demands of business to control the expanding and contracting of currency

What Does the Federal Reserve Do?
- controls the money supply and credit policies
- raises interest rates to member banks in times of plenty so that people won't borrow or spend too much money
- lowers interest rates to member banks during recessions so that people can more easily obtain needed credit
- supervises and supports Federal Reserve banks in twelve regions
- buys and sells government bonds and other securities

NATIONAL GEOGRAPHIC Federal Reserve System

6 Federal Reserve District
★ Federal Reserve Bank
• Federal Reserve Branch Bank

Reforming the Banks

The United States had not had a central bank since the 1830s. During the economic depressions that hit the country periodically after that time, hundreds of small banks collapsed, wiping out the life savings of many of their customers.

To restore public confidence in the banking system, President Wilson supported the establishment of a federal reserve system. Banks would have to keep a portion of their deposits in a regional reserve bank, which would provide a financial cushion against unanticipated losses. The **Federal Reserve Act** of 1913 created 12 regional banks to be supervised by a Board of Governors, appointed by the president. This allowed national supervision of the banking system. The Board could set the interest rates the reserve banks charged other banks, thereby indirectly controlling the interest rates of the entire nation and the amount of money in circulation. The Federal Reserve Act became one of the most significant pieces of legislation in American history.

Other Reforms

Why Was the Federal Trade Commission Created?
- to advise business people on the legality of their actions
- to protect consumers from false advertising
- to investigate unfair trade practices

What Was the Clayton Antitrust Act?
- outlawed unfair trade practices
- made it illegal for a company to hold stock in another, if by doing so, it reduced competition
- made owners and directors of businesses guilty of violating antitrust laws criminally liable
- allowed private parties who had been injured by trusts to collect any damages in legal suits
- banned use of injunctions against strikes
- farm and labor organizations could no longer be considered illegal combinations in restraint of trade

Analyzing VISUALS

1. **Analyzing** What do the Federal Trade Commission and the Clayton Antitrust Act have in common?
2. **Identifying** What do you notice about the Western states and the locations of the Federal Reserve Banks? Why do you think this pattern exists?

Antitrust Action

During his campaign, Wilson had promised to restore competition to the economy by breaking up monopolies. Roosevelt had argued this was unrealistic, because big businesses were more efficient and unlikely to be replaced by smaller, more competitive firms. Once in office, Wilson's opinion shifted and he came to agree with Roosevelt. Progressives in Congress, however, continued to demand action against big business.

In the summer of 1914, at Wilson's request, Congress created the **Federal Trade Commission** (FTC) to monitor American business. The FTC had the power to investigate companies and issue "cease and desist" orders against companies engaging in **unfair trade practices,** or those that hurt competition. The FTC could be taken to court if a business disagreed with its rulings.

Wilson did not want the FTC to break up big business. Instead, it was to work toward limiting business activities that unfairly limited competition. He deliberately appointed conservative business leaders to serve as the FTC's first commissioners.

Unsatisfied by Wilson's approach, progressives in Congress responded by passing the **Clayton Antitrust Act** in 1914. The act outlawed certain practices that restricted competition. For example, it forbade agreements that required retailers who bought from one company to stop selling a competitor's products. It also banned price discrimination. Businesses could not charge different customers different prices. Manufacturers could no longer give discounts to some retailers who bought a large volume of goods, but not to others. Farm and labor organizations could no longer be considered illegal combinations in restraint of trade. The passing of the Clayton Antitrust Act corrected deficiencies in the Sherman Antitrust Act of 1890, which was the first federal antitrust law.

Before the Clayton act passed, labor unions lobbied Congress to exempt unions from antitrust legislation. The Clayton Antitrust Act specifically declared that its provisions did not apply to labor organizations or agricultural organizations. When the bill became law, Samuel Gompers, the head of the American Federation of Labor, called the act the workers' "Magna Carta" because it gave unions the right to exist.

Regulating Business

Despite his accomplishments, Wilson was not guaranteed reelection. In the congressional elections of 1914, Democrats suffered major losses. The Republican Party was also not likely to be divided as it had been in the election of 1912.

In 1916 Wilson signed the first federal law regulating child labor. The Keating-Owen Child Labor Act prohibited the employment of children under the age of 14 in factories producing goods for interstate commerce. In 1918 the Supreme Court declared the law **unconstitutional** on the grounds that child labor was not interstate commerce and therefore only states could regulate it. Wilson's effort, however, helped his reputation with progressive voters. Wilson also supported the Adamson Act, which established the eight-hour workday for railroad workers, and the Federal Farm Loan Act, which helped provide farmers with loans at low interest rates.

✔ **Reading Check** **Evaluating** What was the impact of the passage of the Sixteenth Amendment?

Progressivism's Legacy and Limits

MAIN Idea Progressivism changed many people's ideas about the government's role in social issues.

HISTORY AND YOU Do you believe that groups of people have been left out of "the American dream"? Read on to find out about progressivism's failures and successes.

During his presidency, Wilson had built upon Roosevelt's foundation. He expanded the role of the federal government and the power of the president.

A New Kind of Government

Progressivism made important changes in the political life of the United States. Before this era, most Americans did not expect the government to pass laws protecting workers or regulating big business. In fact, many courts had previously ruled the passage of such laws unconstitutional.

Founding of the NAACP

W.E.B. Du Bois was one of six founders of the NAACP. In *The Crisis*, the journal of the NAACP, Du Bois wrote:

PRIMARY SOURCE

"The object of this publication is to set forth those facts and arguments which show the danger of race prejudice. . . . It takes its name from the fact that the editors believe that this is a critical time in the history. . . . Catholicity and tolerance, reason and forbearance can today make the world-old dream of human brotherhood approach realization: while bigotry and prejudice, emphasized race consciousness and force can repeat the awful history of the contact of nations and groups in the past. We strive for this higher and broader vision of Peace and Good Will."

—from *The Crisis*, November 1910

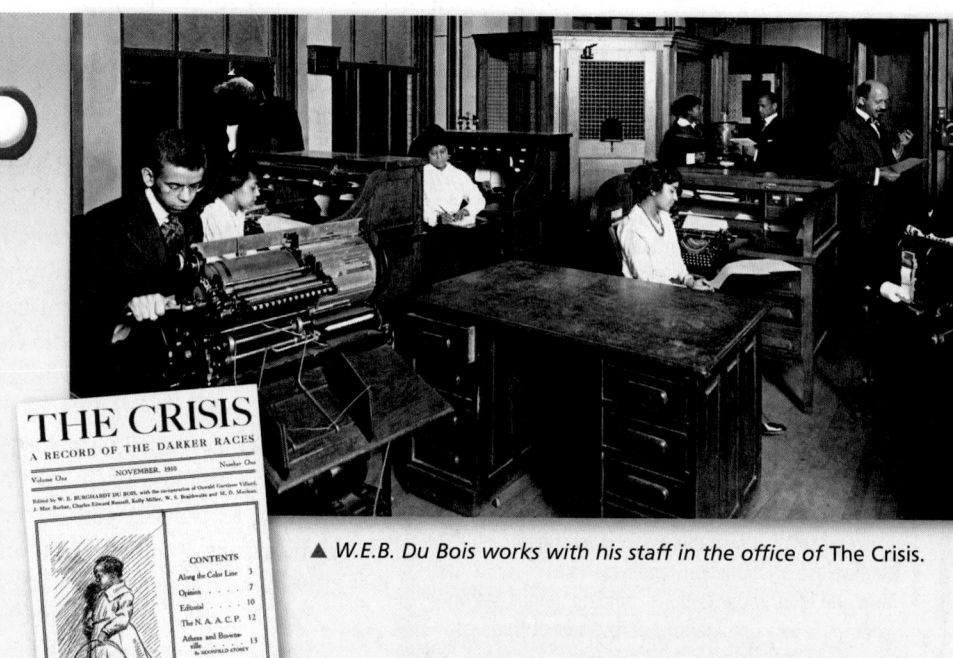

▲ *W.E.B. Du Bois works with his staff in the office of* The Crisis.

▲ *The first issue of* The Crisis, November 1910

DBQ **Document-Based Questions**

1. **Analyzing** According to Du Bois, why was the magazine given its name?

2. **Analyzing Primary Sources** What "vision" does Du Bois recommend to his readers?

By the end of the Progressive Era, however, both legal and public opinion had shifted. Increasingly, Americans expected the government, particularly the federal government, to play a more active role in regulating the economy and solving social problems.

The Limits of Progressivism

The most conspicuous limit to progressivism was its failure to address racial and religious discrimination. African Americans themselves, however, were absorbing the reform spirit, which fueled their longstanding desire for advancement.

In 1905 W.E.B. Du Bois and 28 other African American leaders met at Niagara Falls to demand full rights for African Americans. They met on the Canadian side of the falls because no hotel on the American side would accept them. There, they launched what became known as the Niagara Movement. This meeting was one of many steps leading to the founding of the **National Association for the Advancement of Colored People** (NAACP) in 1909. Du Bois and other NAACP founders believed that voting rights were essential to end lynching and racial discrimination. "The power of the ballot we need in sheer self-defense," Du Bois said, "else what shall save us from a second slavery? Freedom too, the long-sought we still seek,—the freedom of life and limb, the freedom to work and think, the freedom to love and aspire. Work, culture, liberty,—all these we need, not singly, but together."

In 1908 race riots in Springfield, Illinois, shocked many people, including Mary White Ovington, a settlement house worker. She had been studying African Americans in New York, determined to do something to improve their situation. Other progressives, including Jane Addams of Hull House, and muckrakers Ida Wells-Barnett and Lincoln Steffens, joined Ovington in calling for change. Capitalizing on Springfield as Lincoln's hometown and his centennial birthday on February 12, 1909, they organized a national conference to take stock of the progress in emancipation. At a second conference the following year, the NAACP was born. Through Du Bois, the members learned of the Niagara Movement, and the two groups eventually merged.

African Americans were not the only minority group facing discrimination. Jewish people also lived in fear of mob violence. In 1913 Leo Frank, a Jew being tried in Atlanta for a murder he did not commit, was sentenced to death. Although his sentence was changed to life imprisonment, a mob lynched him two years later.

In this context, lawyer Sigmund Livingston started the Anti-Defamation League (ADL) to combat stereotypes and discrimination. The ADL worked to remove negative portrayals of Jews in movies, in print, and on stage. For example, the League protested an army manual published during World War I that targeted Jews as likely to pretend to be sick to escape work or battle. When the ADL complained, President Wilson had the manual recalled.

Reading Check **Evaluating** How did progressivism change American beliefs about the federal government?

Section 3 REVIEW

Vocabulary

1. **Explain** the significance of: Progressive Party, New Nationalism, New Freedom, income tax, Federal Reserve Act, Federal Trade Commission, unfair trade practices, Clayton Antitrust Act, National Association for the Advancement of Colored People.

Main Ideas

2. **Discussing** Explain how Wilson won the presidency without winning the popular vote.

3. **Identifying** Why did Wilson propose the Federal Reserve system?

4. **Organizing** Use a graphic organizer similar to the one below to list the effects progressivism had on American society.

Critical Thinking

5. **Big Ideas** What new federal agencies increased the government's power to regulate the economy?

6. **Forming an Opinion** Which of Wilson's reforms do you consider to be most important? Why?

7. **Analyzing Visuals** Study the chart on page 538. What was the purpose of the Federal Reserve?

Writing About History

8. **Expository Writing** Suppose that you are a newspaper editor during Wilson's administration. Write an article about the failure of Progressives to address African American reform issues.

History ONLINE

Study Central™ To review this section, go to glencoe.com and click on Study Central.

Causes of the Progressive Movement

- People thought progress in science and knowledge could improve society.

- People thought immigration, urbanization, and industrialization had created social problems.

- People thought laissez-faire economics and an unregulated market led to social problems and that government could fix them.

- Political corruption prevented the government from helping its citizens.

▶ In 1910 a young boy works in a glass factory, an example of the type of child labor progressive reformers wanted to end.

Effects on Business and Society

- Interstate Commerce Commission is strengthened.
- Consumer protection laws are passed.
- Federal Trade Commission is created.
- Federal Reserve System is created to regulate the money supply.
- Clayton Antitrust Act grants labor unions more rights.
- Zoning laws and building codes improve urban housing.
- Child labor laws are passed, regulating time and conditions for minors to work.
- Workers' compensation laws are passed.
- Temperance movement begins seeking limitations on the production and consumption of alcohol.

▲ Trade unions begin their march honoring victims of the Triangle Shirtwaist Factory fire.

Effects on Politics

- Cities begin adopting commission and city-manager forms of government.
- States begin to adopt the direct primary system, allowing voters to choose candidates for office.
- States begin to allow initiatives, referendums, and recall votes.
- Seventeenth Amendment is ratified, requiring direct election of senators.
- Nineteenth Amendment is ratified, guaranteeing women the right to vote.

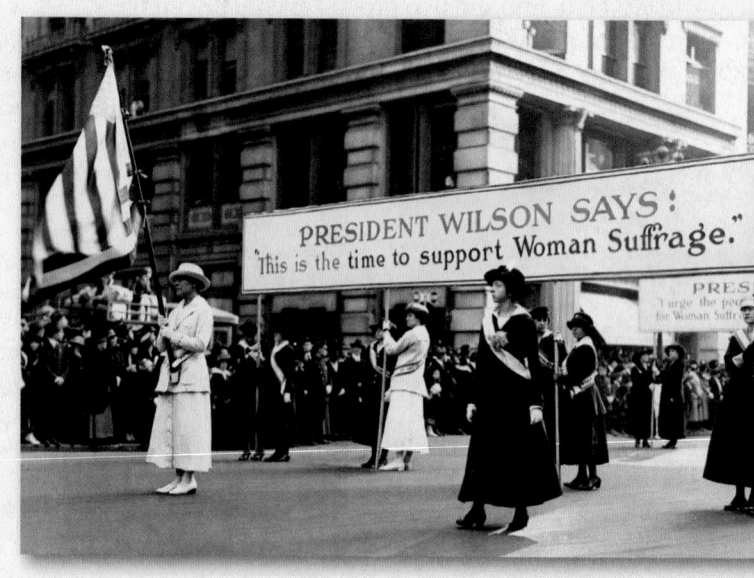
▶ Women march in 1916 in support of Woodrow Wilson's efforts to grant women the right to vote.

NEW YORK REGENTS EXAM PRACTICE

TEST-TAKING

> You can eliminate some answers by using your own knowledge and common sense. Read through each option and decide if it fits with what you know; if it does not, discard it.

Part I

Directions (1–11): For each statement or question, write on a separate sheet of paper the number of the word or expression that, of those given, best completes the statement or answers the question.

1 The term "muckraker" was used to describe
  (1) street sweepers.
  (2) investigative journalists.
  (3) farmers.
  (4) garden designers.

2 What placed proposed legislation on the ballot for voter approval?
  (1) direct primary
  (2) referendum
  (3) initiative
  (4) veto

3 How did Governor La Follette help expand democracy?
  (1) by favoring women's suffrage
  (2) by requiring political parties to hold a direct primary
  (3) by allowing recall elections
  (4) by providing absentee ballots for voters

4 What did Du Bois and other NAACP founders believe was essential to end racial violence?
  (1) establishment of African American colleges
  (2) higher-paying jobs for low-income citizens
  (3) voting rights for African Americans
  (4) private schools for African American children

5 The Progressive movement strengthened the cause of women's suffrage by
  (1) drawing attention to child labor.
  (2) encouraging trustbusting.
  (3) making government more efficient.
  (4) showing women they needed the vote to get the reforms they wanted.

6 Upton Sinclair's novel *The Jungle* was instrumental in exposing which industry?
  (1) steel
  (2) meatpacking
  (3) oil
  (4) alcohol

7 Theodore Roosevelt became known as a trustbuster for his actions against
  (1) the Northern Securities company.
  (2) the United Mine Workers.
  (3) the automobile industry.
  (4) national parks.

8 What did the Nineteenth Amendment, ratified in 1920, accomplish?
  (1) It required colleges to accept women.
  (2) It guaranteed child care for workers' children.
  (3) It granted women the right to vote.
  (4) It guaranteed equal pay for equal work.

Need Extra Help?								
If You Missed Questions . . .	1	2	3	4	5	6	7	8
Go to Page . . .	521	523	522–523	541	522–525	530	528–529	524–525

[OVER]

Base your answer to question 9 on the map below and on your knowledge of Chapter 15.

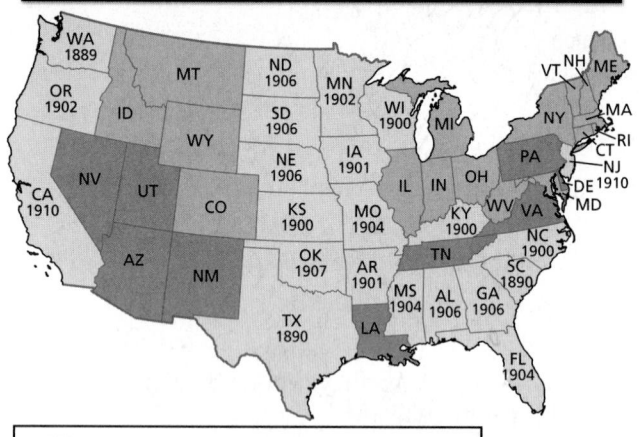

Progressives and State Governments, 1889–1912

Reformers control state legislatures
Reformers influence state government
Reformers not effective
1900   Date reformers came to power

9   What generalization can you make about progressives in state governments?

   (1)   Progressives were most active in the Far West, the Great Plains, and the South.

   (2)   They had no influence in New England.

   (3)   Reformers controlled few state legislatures by 1910.

   (4)   Reformers had little success in the Deep South.

10   How did President Wilson attempt to reform the banking industry?

   (1)   He created the Federal Reserve System.

   (2)   He vetoed the Underwood Tariff Act.

   (3)   He opposed the Sixteenth Amendment.

   (4)   He refused to break up monopolies.

11   What was the temperance movement linked to?

   (1)   the prohibition of alcohol

   (2)   the production of alcohol

   (3)   the reduction of alcohol

   (4)   the requisition of alcohol

Need Extra Help?			
If You Missed Questions . . .	9	10	11
Go to Page . . .	522–523	539	527

Part II Thematic Essay Question

Directions: Write a well-organized essay that includes an introduction, several paragraphs addressing the task below, and a conclusion.

Theme: The Progressive Movement

> In the early twentieth century, the Progressive movement responded to challenges brought about by urbanization and industrialization.

> Identify two important actions of the progressives during this era and for each
> - Discuss the background and circumstances surrounding the action.
> - Describe one immediate or one long-term result.
> - Evaluate the extent to which the decisions changed the economic, social, and political landscape of the nation.

Guidelines:

In your essay, be sure to:

- Develop all aspects of the task
- Support the theme with relevant facts, examples, and details
- Use a logical and clear plan of organization, including an introduction and a conclusion that are beyond a restatement of the theme

Part III Document-Based Question

This question is based on the accompanying documents. This question is designed to test your ability to work with historical documents. Some of the documents have been edited for the purposes of the question. As you analyze the documents, take into account the source of each document and any point of view that may be presented in the document.

Historical Context:

During the early twentieth century, progressives were involved in trying to make improvements to society, the economy, and government. During this time, Presidents Roosevelt, Wilson, and Taft were considered progressive presidents.

Task:
Using information from the documents and your knowledge of United States history, answer the questions that follow each document in Part A. Your answers to the questions will help you write the Part B essay in which you will be asked to

- Discuss the woman suffrage movement and the progressive presidents and how they contributed to the successes or failures of the progressive movement
- Evaluate the long-term effects of progressive reforms

Part A
Short-Answer Questions
Directions: Analyze the documents and answer the short-answer questions that follow each document on a separate sheet of paper.

Document 1

> "The suffragettes had a big headquarters in downtown Washington. My mother would take me up there on Saturdays when she volunteered to help out with mailings. The backbone of the suffrage movement was composed of well-to-do, middle-class women, both Republicans and Democrats. There weren't many working-class women in the movement. . . .
>
> The suffragettes organized pickets and marches and rallies. I was only ten years old the first time I went to a march with my mother. She told me, 'Oh, you're too young, you can't go.' But I said, 'I am going, because you're going to win the right to vote and I'm going to vote when I'm grown-up.' So she let me march. . . . The more marches that were held, the more you could feel the movement just building and building. In my heart, I knew that this movement was going to go somewhere. . . ."

Source: Lucy Haessler, quoted in
The Century for Young People

1 Who does Haessler say were the backbone of the movement? Why do you think working-class women were not involved?

Source: S.D. Ehrhart, *Puck*, February 24, 1909

2 How is William Howard Taft portrayed in this cartoon?

Part B
Essay
Directions: Reread the task box at the top left and write a well-organized essay that includes an introduction, several paragraphs, and a conclusion. Use evidence from the documents in your essay. Support your response with relevant facts, examples, and details. Include additional outside information.

Guidelines:
In your essay, be sure to:
- Develop all aspects of the task
- Incorporate information from the documents
- Incorporate relevant outside information
- Support the task with relevant facts, examples, and details
- Use a logical and clear plan of organization, including an introduction and conclusion that are beyond a restatement of the task

For additional test practice, use Self-Check Quizzes—Chapter 15 at glencoe.com.

Need Extra Help?			
If You Missed Questions . . .	1	2	Essay
Go to Page . . .	524–525	533–535	524–541

Chapter 16

World War I and Its Aftermath

1914–1920

SECTION 1 The United States Enters World War I

SECTION 2 The Home Front

SECTION 3 A Bloody Conflict

SECTION 4 The War's Impact

American soldiers fire on German positions during the Battle of the Argonne Forest, 1918

Wilson
1913–1921

U.S. PRESIDENTS

U.S. EVENTS

WORLD EVENTS

1915
• German submarine sinks the *Lusitania*

1917
• U.S. enters the war
• Selective Service Act passed

1914

1916

1914
• Franz Ferdinand assassinated; war begins in Europe

1916
• Battle of Verdun begins in February
• Battle of the Somme begins in July

1917
• Bolshevik Revolution begins in October

Why Do Nations Go to War?

World War I was the first time in American history that the United States sent troops to fight in Europe. This decision ended the long-standing policy of remaining neutral in Europe's wars.

- *Why do you think the United States changed its policy and sent troops to Europe?*
- *Do you think it was a difficult decision?*

FOLDABLES

Organizing Information As you read the chapter, write information under each tab, listing which country is in the alliance, why it joined the alliance, or what reasons it had for disagreeing with the countries in the opposing alliance.

Central Powers | Allied Powers

World War I

1918
- Congress passes Sedition Act
- Armistice ends fighting on November 11

1919
- Race riots and strikes take place in Northern cities

1920
- Red scare and Palmer Raids

1918

1920

1918
- Treaty of Brest-Litovsk ends Russian-German war

1919
- Versailles Peace Conference begins

History ONLINE **Chapter Overview**
Visit glencoe.com to preview Chapter 16.

Section 1

The United States Enters World War I

Guide to Reading

Big Ideas
Trade, War, and Migration Although the United States tried to stay neutral, events pushed the nation into war.

Content Vocabulary
- militarism *(p. 549)*
- nationalism *(p. 550)*
- propaganda *(p. 552)*
- contraband *(p. 554)*

Academic Vocabulary
- emphasis *(p. 550)*
- erode *(p. 554)*

People and Events to Identify
- Balkans *(p. 550)*
- Franz Ferdinand *(p. 550)*
- Sussex pledge *(p. 555)*
- Zimmermann telegram *(p. 555)*

Reading Strategy
Organizing Complete the graphic organizer shown below by identifying the factors that contributed to the conflict.

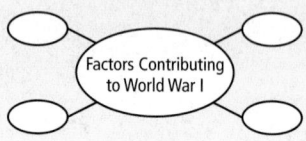

Factors Contributing to World War I

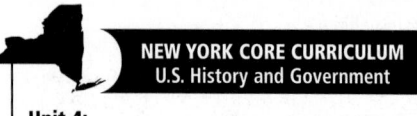

NEW YORK CORE CURRICULUM
U.S. History and Government

Unit 4:
II.B.1.a Efforts at neutrality and "preparedness"
II.B.1.b Causes of United States entry into World War I

Militarism, alliances, imperialism, and nationalism led to World War I in Europe. Attacks on U.S. ships and American support for the Allies eventually caused the United States to enter the war.

World War I Begins

MAIN Idea Old alliances and nationalist sentiments among European nations set the stage for World War I.

HISTORY AND YOU Does your school have a long-standing rivalry with another school? Read how European nations formed political alliances that brought most of the continent into war.

Despite more than 40 years of general peace, tensions among European nations were building in 1914. Throughout the late 1800s and early 1900s, a number of factors created problems among the powers of Europe and set the stage for a monumental war.

Militarism and Alliances

The roots of World War I date back to the 1860s. In 1864, while Americans fought the Civil War, the German kingdom of Prussia launched the first of a series of wars to unite the various German states into one nation. By 1871 Prussia had united Germany and proclaimed the birth of the German Empire. The new German nation rapidly industrialized and quickly became one of the most powerful nations in the world.

The creation of Germany transformed European politics. In 1870, as part of their plan to unify Germany, the Prussians had attacked and defeated France. They then forced the French to give up territory along the German border. From that point forward, France and Germany were enemies. To protect itself, Germany signed alliances with Italy and with Austria-Hungary, a huge empire that controlled much of southeastern Europe. This became known as the Triple Alliance.

The new alliance alarmed Russian leaders, who feared that Germany intended to expand eastward into Russia. Russia and Austria-Hungary were also competing for influence in southeastern Europe. Many of the people of southeastern Europe were Slavs— the same ethnic group as the Russians—and the Russians wanted to support them against Austria-Hungary. As a result, Russia and France had a common interest in opposing Germany and Austria-Hungary. In 1894 they signed the Franco-Russian Alliance, promising to come to each other's aid in a war with the Triple Alliance.

In 1839, Britain gave Belgium a guarantee that it would protect Belgium's neutrality.

Triple Entente
Triple Alliance
Other European states

Germany took Alsace-Lorraine from France in 1870. The French were determined to recover the territory.

Russia and Serbia were both Slavic countries. Russia did not have an alliance with Serbia but was determined to help Serbia against Austria-Hungary.

Balkan Nationalism
Southeastern Europe is known as the Balkans. In the 1800s, two empires controlled this region—Austria-Hungary and the Turkish Ottoman Empire. As the ideas of nationalism spread across Europe, the people in the region fought a series of wars to gain their independence. By 1914, most of the Balkans were free, except for the Slavs living in Bosnia.

The Growth of Armies, 1870–1914

1870   1914

0   400 kilometers
0   400 miles
Lambert Azimuthal Equal-Area projection

Analyzing VISUALS

1. **Interpreting** Study the map and chart above. Why might Britain think it had to have the strongest navy in Europe?

2. **Analyzing** Germany feared France might go to war with them. Based on the map and chart, why would German leaders have reached this conclusion?

Maps In Motion See *StudentWorks™ Plus* or glencoe.com.

The system of alliances in Europe encouraged **militarism**—the aggressive build-up of armed forces to intimidate and threaten other nations. German militarism eventually forced Britain to become involved in the alliance system. Britain's policy was to support weaker countries against stronger ones so as to make sure no country conquered all of Europe. By the late 1800s, it was clear that Germany had become the strongest nation in Europe.

In 1898 Germany began building a large modern navy as well. A strong German navy threatened the British, who depended on their naval strength to protect their island from invasion. By the early 1900s, an arms race had begun between Great Britain and Germany, as both nations raced to build warships.

The naval race greatly increased tensions between Germany and Britain and convinced the British to establish closer relations with France and Russia. The British still refused to sign a formal alliance, so their new relationship with the French and Russians became known as an entente cordiale—a friendly understanding. Britain, France, and Russia became known as the Triple Entente.

Causes of World War I

Use the acronym MAIN to remember the four main causes of World War I: Militarism, Alliances, Imperialism, Nationalism.

MILITARISM

▲ Warships of the German Imperial fleet are shown anchored near Kiel, Germany in 1911. The naval race between Britain and Germany caused tension in Europe prior to World War I.

ALLIANCES

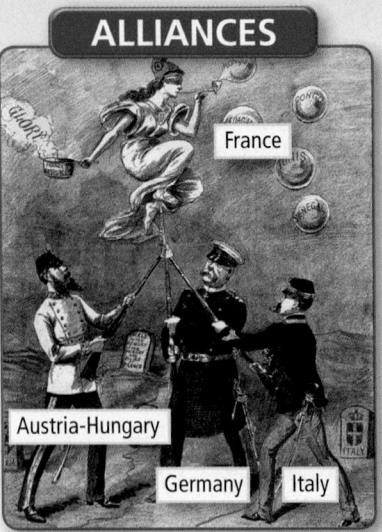

France
Austria-Hungary
Germany
Italy

▲ An 1883 British cartoon illustrates the Triple Alliance.

IMPERIALISM

▲ Franz Joseph, Emperor of Austria-Hungary, and Wilhelm II, Emperor of Germany, salute during a parade in Berlin in 1889.

Imperialism and Nationalism

By the late 1800s, **nationalism,** or a feeling of intense pride in one's homeland, had become a powerful idea in Europe. Nationalists place primary **emphasis** on promoting their homeland's culture and interests above those of other countries. Nationalism was one of the reasons for the tensions among the European powers. Each nation viewed the others as competitors, and many people were willing to go to war to expand their nation at the expense of others.

One of the basic ideas of nationalism is the right to self-determination—the idea that people who share a national identity should have their own country and government. In the 1800s nationalism led to a crisis in southeastern Europe in the region known as the **Balkans.** Historically, the Ottoman Empire and the Austro-Hungarian Empire had ruled the Balkans. Both of these empires were made up of many different nations.

Imperialism—the idea that a country can increase its power and wealth by controlling other peoples—had convinced the major European powers to build empires in the 1700s and 1800s. Nationalism ran counter to imperialism. As the idea of nationalism spread in the late 1800s and early 1900s, the different

national groups within Europe's empires began to press for independence.

Among the groups pushing for independence were the Serbs, Bosnians, Croats, and Slovenes. These people all spoke similar languages and had come to see themselves as one people. They called themselves South Slavs, or Yugoslavs. The first of these people to obtain independence were the Serbs, who formed a nation called Serbia between the Ottoman and Austro-Hungarian Empires. Serbs believed their nation's mission was to unite the South Slavs.

Russia supported the Serbs, while Austria-Hungary did what it could to limit Serbia's growth. In 1908 Austria-Hungary annexed Bosnia, which had belonged to the Ottoman Empire. The Serbs were furious. They wanted Bosnia to be part of their nation. The annexation demonstrated to the Serbs that Austria-Hungary had no intention of letting the Slavic people in its empire become independent.

A Terrorist Attack Brings War

In late June 1914 the heir to the Austro-Hungarian throne, the Archduke **Franz Ferdinand,** visited the Bosnian capital of Sarajevo. As he and his wife rode through the city, a Bosnian revolutionary named Gavrilo

NATIONALISM

▲ Serbian nationalist Gavrilo Princip is dragged into police headquarters in Sarajevo shortly after killing Archduke Franz Ferdinand, heir to the Austro-Hungarian throne.

Analyzing VISUALS

1. **Interpreting** What point is the cartoonist trying to make about the Triple Alliance?

2. **Explaining** How did Austrian imperialism and Balkan nationalism contribute to the outbreak of World War I?

Princip rushed their open car and shot the couple to death. The assassin was a member of a Serbian nationalist group nicknamed the "Black Hand." The assassination took place with the knowledge of Serbian officials who hoped to start a war that would bring down the Austro-Hungarian Empire.

The Alliances Are Triggered The Austro-Hungarian government blamed Serbia for the attack and decided the time had come to crush Serbia in order to prevent Slavic nationalism from undermining its empire. Knowing an attack on Serbia might trigger a war with Russia, the Austrians asked their German allies for support. Germany promised to support Austria-Hungary if war erupted.

Austria-Hungary then issued an ultimatum to the Serbian government. The Serbs counted on Russia to back them up, and the Russians, in turn, counted on France. French leaders were worried that they might someday be caught alone in a war with Germany, so they promised to support Russia if war began.

On July 28 Austria-Hungary declared war on Serbia. Russia immediately mobilized its army, including troops stationed on the German border. On August 1 Germany declared war on Russia. Two days later, it declared war on France. World War I had begun.

Germany's Plan Fails Germany had long been prepared for war against France and Russia. It immediately launched a massive invasion of France, hoping to knock the French out of the war. It would then be able to send its troops east to deal with the Russians.

The German plan had one major problem. It required the German forces to advance through neutral Belgium in order to encircle the French troops. The British had guaranteed Belgium's neutrality. When German troops crossed the Belgian frontier, Britain declared war on Germany.

Those fighting for the Triple Entente were called the Allies. France, Russia, and Great Britain formed the backbone of the Allies along with Italy, which joined them in 1915 after the other Allies promised to cede Austro-Hungarian territory to Italy after the war. What remained of the Triple Alliance—Germany and Austria-Hungary—joined with the Ottoman Empire and Bulgaria to form the Central Powers.

The German plan seemed to work at first. German troops swept through Belgium and headed into France, driving back the French and British forces. Then, to the great surprise of the Germans, Russian troops invaded Germany. The Germans had not expected Russia to mobilize so quickly. They were forced to pull some of their troops away from the attack on France and send them east to stop the Russians. This weakened the German forces just enough to give the Allies a chance to stop them. The Germans drove to within 30 miles (48 km) of Paris, but stubborn resistance by British and French troops at the Battle of the Marne finally stopped the German advance. Because the swift German attack had failed to defeat the French, both sides became locked in a bloody stalemate along hundreds of miles of trenches that would barely change position for the next three years.

The Central Powers had greater success on the Eastern Front. German and Austro-Hungarian forces stopped the Russian attack and then went on the offensive. They swept across hundreds of miles of territory and took hundreds of thousands of prisoners. Russia suffered 2 million killed, wounded, or captured in 1915 alone, but it kept fighting.

✔ Reading Check **Explaining** What incident triggered the beginning of World War I?

America Declares War

MAIN Idea British propaganda and business interests led most Americans to a pro-British stance on the war.

HISTORY AND YOU Do you recall a time when you tried to remain neutral in a fight between friends? Read how the United States tried to stay out of World War I.

When the fighting began, President Wilson was determined to keep the country out of a European war. He immediately declared the United States to be neutral in the conflict. "We must be impartial in thought as well as in action," Wilson stated. For many Americans that proved difficult to do.

Americans Take Sides

Despite the president's plea, many Americans supported one side or the other. Many of the country's 8 million German Americans, for example, supported their homeland. Many of the nation's 4.5 million Irish Americans, whose homeland endured centuries of British rule, also sympathized with the Central Powers.

In general, however, American public opinion favored the Allied cause. Many Americans valued the heritage, language, and political ideals they shared with Britain. Others treasured America's links with France, a great friend to America during the Revolutionary War.

For more than two years, the United States officially remained neutral. During this time a great debate began over whether the United States should prepare for war. Supporters of the "preparedness" movement believed that preparing for war was the best way to stay out of the conflict. They also argued that if the United States was pulled into the war, it was better to be prepared.

Other Americans disagreed. In 1915 Carrie Chapman Catt and Jane Addams—leaders of the woman suffrage movement—founded the Women's Peace Party (later known as the International League for Peace and Freedom). This organization, along with others such as the League to Limit Armament, worked to keep America out of the war by urging the president not to build up the military.

Government Officials Back Britain One select group of Americans was decidedly pro-British: President Wilson's cabinet. Only Secretary of State William Jennings Bryan favored neutrality. The other cabinet members, as well as Bryan's chief adviser, Robert Lansing, and Walter Hines Page, the American ambassador to London, argued forcefully on behalf of Britain. Many American military leaders also backed the British. They believed that an Allied victory was the only way to preserve the international balance of power.

British officials worked diligently to win American support. One method they used was **propaganda,** or information designed to influence opinion. Both sides used propaganda, but German propaganda was mostly anti-Russian and did not appeal to most Americans. British propaganda, on the other hand, was extremely skillful.

Debates IN HISTORY

Should America Stay Neutral in World War I?

Americans were deeply divided about whether the United States should remain neutral in World War I. Despite President Wilson's pronouncement that Americans should remain neutral in thought as well as action, many Americans, including those working for the government, had very definite opinions as to whether or not the United States should enter the war.

To control the flow of news to the United States, the British cut the transatlantic telegraph cable from Europe to the United States. This meant that most war news would be based on British reports. The American ambassador to Britain, Walter Hines Page, himself strongly pro-British, gave the reports legitimacy by endorsing many of them. When stories arrived describing German atrocities, enough Americans believed them to help sway American support in favor of the Allies.

Business Supports Britain American business interests also leaned toward the Allies. Companies in the United States, particularly on the East Coast, had strong ties with businesses in the Allied countries. As business leader Thomas W. Lamont stated, "Our firm had never for one moment been neutral: we did not know how to be. From the very start we did everything that we could to contribute to the cause of the Allies."

Many American banks began to invest heavily in an Allied victory. American loans to the cash-hungry Allies skyrocketed. By 1917 such loans would total over $2 billion. Other American banks, particularly in the Midwest, where pro-German feelings were strongest, also lent some $27 million to Germany.

More money might have been lent to Germany, but most foreign loans required the approval of William McAdoo, the secretary of the Treasury. McAdoo was strongly pro-British and did what he could to limit loans to Germany. As a result, the country's prosperity was intertwined with the military fortunes of Britain, France, and Russia. If the Allies won, the money would be paid back; if not, the money might be lost forever.

YES

John Works
Civil War Veteran and U.S. Senator

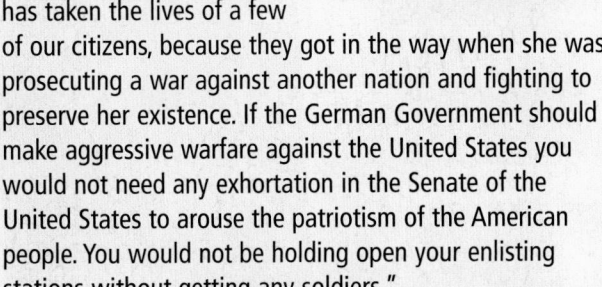

PRIMARY SOURCE

"Germany is not moving against this country. She has not been guilty of any aggression against us. She has taken the lives of a few of our citizens, because they got in the way when she was prosecuting a war against another nation and fighting to preserve her existence. If the German Government should make aggressive warfare against the United States you would not need any exhortation in the Senate of the United States to arouse the patriotism of the American people. You would not be holding open your enlisting stations without getting any soldiers."

—from *The Congressional Record*, March 4, 1917

NO

Robert Lansing
Secretary of State

PRIMARY SOURCE

"I have come to the conclusion that the German Government is utterly hostile to all nations with democratic institutions because those who compose it see in democracy a menace to absolutism and the defeat of the German ambition for world domination....

... Germany must not be permitted to win this war and to break even, though to prevent it this country is forced to take an active part. This ultimate necessity must be constantly in our minds in all our controversies with the belligerents. American public opinion must be prepared for the time, which may come, when we will have to cast aside our neutrality and become one of the champions of democracy."

—from *War Memoirs of Robert Lansing*

 DBQ Document-Based Questions

1. **Summarizing** When does Senator Works believe war is justified?

2. **Explaining** Why does Secretary of State Lansing believe Germany is a threat to the United States?

3. **Comparing** Based on these sources, what is the focus of the neutrality debate? What is not being discussed?

4. **Evaluating** Which position do you agree with? Write an essay explaining why the other side is wrong.

Moving Toward War

Although most Americans supported the Allies and hoped for their victory, they did not want to join the conflict. However, a series of events gradually **eroded** American neutrality and drew the nation into the war.

German Submarines Go Into Action

Shortly after the war began, the British declared a blockade of German ports and began intercepting neutral merchant ships sailing to Europe. They forced the ships to land at British ports where they were inspected for **contraband,** or goods prohibited from shipment to Germany and its allies.

Although Britain's decision to intercept neutral ships, including American ships, led to protests from the U.S. government, the German response angered Americans even more. Britain and France depended on food, equipment, and other supplies from both the United States and their overseas empires. To stop those shipments, Germany deployed submarines known as U-boats—from the German word *Untersee-boot* ("underwater boat"). In February 1915, the Germans announced that they would sink without warning any ship they found in the waters around Britain.

Germany's announcement triggered outrage in the United States and elsewhere. Germany had signed an international treaty that banned attacks on civilian ships without warning. The Germans claimed that their U-boats would be placed at great risk if they had to surface and give a warning before firing.

The Germans Sink the *Lusitania*

The issue reached a crisis on May 7, 1915, when the British passenger ship *Lusitania* entered the war zone. A German submarine sunk the ship, killing nearly 1,200 passengers—including 128 Americans. The attack outraged Americans who saw the sinking as a terrorist attack on civilians, including women and children, not as a legitimate act of war.

Wilson tried to defuse the crisis. He refused to threaten Germany with war saying that the United States was "too proud to fight." Instead, he sent several official protests to Germany insisting that it stop endangering the lives of noncombatants in the war zone.

Late in March 1916, Wilson's policy was tested when a U-boat torpedoed the French passenger ship *Sussex*, injuring several Americans on board. Although Wilson's closest advisers favored breaking off diplomatic relations with Germany, the president chose

Turning Points

The Sinking of the *Lusitania*

When World War I began, many Americans supported one side or the other, but most agreed the United States should stay out of the war. Eight months later, when the German submarine U-20 sank the *Lusitania*, killing 1,195 people, including 128 Americans, attitudes began to shift.

The attack seemed to prove that Germany was acting in an uncivilized way and it gave credibility to British propaganda. Even though the United States would not enter the war for nearly two more years, the attack on the *Lusitania* marked a turning point in the war because it changed American attitudes and set the stage for the American entry into the war.

ANALYZING HISTORY Do you think the use of submarines in World War I was justified? Write a brief essay explaining your opinion.

▲ A mass funeral for Lusitania victims was held in Queenston, Ireland, on May 23, 1915. **How do you think people reacted when they saw photos like this in the newspaper?**

▲ After the sinking, the Boston Committee of Public Safety issued this poster showing a drowning woman and baby and urging Americans to prepare for war by building up the military.

to issue one last warning. He demanded that the German government abandon its methods of submarine warfare or risk war with the United States.

Germany did not want to strengthen the Allies by drawing the United States into the war. It promised with certain conditions to sink no more merchant ships without warning. The **Sussex Pledge,** as it was called, met the foreign-policy goals of both Germany and President Wilson by keeping the United States out of the war a little longer.

Wilson's efforts to keep American soldiers at home played an important part in his reelection bid in 1916. Campaigning as the "peace" candidate, his campaign slogan, "He kept us out of the war," helped Wilson win a narrow victory over the Republican nominee, Charles Evans Hughes.

The United States Declares War

Following Wilson's reelection, events quickly brought the country to the brink of war. In January 1917, a German official named Arthur Zimmermann sent a telegram to the German ambassador in Mexico asking him to make an offer to the Mexican government: If Mexico agreed to become an ally of Germany in a war with the United States, Germany promised Mexico would regain its "lost territory in Texas, New Mexico, and Arizona" after the war. British intelligence intercepted the **Zimmermann telegram.** Shortly afterward, it was leaked to American newspapers. Furious, many Americans now concluded war with Germany was necessary.

Then, on February 1, 1917, Germany resumed unrestricted submarine warfare. German military leaders believed that they could starve Britain into submission in four to six months if their U-boats began sinking all ships on sight. Although they knew this decision might draw the United States into the war, they did not believe the Americans could raise an army and transport it to Europe in time. Between February 3 and March 21, German U-boats sank six American ships. Finally roused to action, President Wilson appeared before a special session of Congress on April 2, 1917. Declaring that "the world must be made safe for democracy," Wilson asked Congress to declare war on Germany.

PRIMARY SOURCE

"It is a fearful thing to lead this great peaceful people into war. . . . But the right is more precious than peace, and we shall fight for the things which we have always carried nearest to our hearts—for democracy, for the right of those who submit to authority to have a voice in their own governments, for the rights and liberties of small nations. . . ."

—quoted in the Congressional Record, 1917

After a debate, the Senate passed the resolution on April 4 by a vote of 82 to 6. The House concurred 373 to 50 on April 6, and Wilson signed the resolution. America was at war.

Reading Check **Summarizing** How did Germany's use of unrestricted submarine warfare bring America into World War I?

Section 1 REVIEW

Vocabulary

1. **Explain** the significance of: militarism, nationalism, Balkans, Franz Ferdinand, propaganda, contraband, Sussex Pledge, Zimmermann telegram.

Main Ideas

2. **Identifying** Name the two alliances in Europe at the start of World War I, and list the members of each alliance.

3. **Explaining** Why did many Americans support the British in the war even though the United States was officially neutral?

Critical Thinking

4. **Big Ideas** How did trade and economics contribute to America's entry into World War I?

5. **Organizing** Use a graphic organizer similar to the one below to identify the events that led the United States to enter World War I.

6. **Analyzing Visuals** Examine the images on page 554. How did images like these contribute to America's eventual entry into the war?

Writing About History

7. **Expository Writing** Imagine you are an American survivor of the sinking of the *Lusitania*. Write a letter to President Wilson about what you think he should do.

History ONLINE

Study Central™ To review this section, go to glencoe.com and click on Study Central.

Section 2

The Home Front

Guide to Reading

Big Ideas

Government and Society To successfully fight the war, the United States government had to mobilize the entire nation.

Content Vocabulary
• victory garden (p. 556)
• espionage (p. 558)

Academic Vocabulary
• migrate (p. 558)
• draft (p. 560)

People and Events to Identify
• War Industries Board (p. 556)
• National War Labor Board (p. 557)
• Committee on Public Information (p. 558)
• selective service (p. 560)

Reading Strategy

Taking Notes Use the major headings of this section to create an outline similar to the one below.

> The Home Front
> I. Organizing the Economy
>   A.
>   B.
>   C.
> II.
>   A.
>   B.

NEW YORK CURRICULUM
U.S. History and Government

Unit 4:
II.C.1 War opposition and patriotism: the draft issue
II.C.2 Espionage and Sedition Acts
II.C.3 *Schenck* v. *United States*, 1919; clear and present danger doctrine

Unit 5:
I.A.1 War's effects on gender roles, on African-Americans, and other minority groups
I.A.2 Case study: Movement of African-Americans from the South to northern cities

To fight World War I, the American government used progressive ideas and new government agencies to mobilize the population and organize the economy.

Organizing the Economy

MAIN Idea The government used progressive ideas to manage the economy and pay for the war.

HISTORY AND YOU How do you help conserve food or fuel resources? Read how Americans made sacrifices to aid the war effort.

When the United States entered the war in April 1917, progressives controlled the federal government. Rather than abandon their ideas during wartime, they applied progressive ideas to fighting the war. Their ideas about planning and scientific management shaped how the American government organized the war effort.

Wartime Agencies

To efficiently manage the relationship between the federal government and private companies, Congress created new agencies to coordinate mobilization and ensure the efficient use of national resources. These agencies emphasized cooperation between big business and government, not direct government control. Business executives, managers, and government officials staffed the new agencies.

Managing the Economy Perhaps the most important of the new agencies was the **War Industries Board** (WIB), established in July 1917 to coordinate the production of war materials. At first, the WIB's authority was limited, but problems with production convinced Wilson to expand its powers and appoint Bernard Baruch, a Wall Street stockbroker, to run it. The WIB told manufacturers what they could produce, allocated raw materials, ordered the construction of new factories, and, in a few instances, set prices.

Perhaps the most successful agency was the Food Administration, run by Herbert Hoover. This agency was responsible for increasing food production while reducing civilian consumption. Using the slogan "Food Will Win the War—Don't Waste It," it encouraged families to conserve food and grow their own vegetables in **victory gardens.** By having Wheatless Mondays, Meatless Tuesdays, and Porkless Thursdays, families would leave more food for the troops.

While Hoover managed food production, the Fuel Administration, run by Harry Garfield, tried to manage the nation's use of coal and oil.

"SHALL WE BE MORE TENDER WITH OUR DOLLARS THAN WITH THE LIVES OF OUR SONS ?"
W.G.McAdoo
WE DEFEND YOU
BUY A UNITED STATES GOVERNMENT BOND
OF THE
2ND LIBERTY LOAN
OF 1917

REMEMBER!
THE FLAG OF LIBERTY SUPPORT IT !
BUY
U.S.Government Bonds
3RD. LIBERTY LOAN

▶ The actor Douglas Fairbanks urges Americans to buy Liberty Bonds at a rally held in New York City in 1918.

Paying for World War I

Billions of dollars

First Liberty Loan — 2.0
Second Liberty Loan — 3.8
Third Liberty Loan — 4.2
Fourth Liberty Loan — 7.0
Victory Loan — 4.4
Other Loans — 3.0
Taxation — 7.2

Analyzing VISUALS

To pay for World War I, the U.S. government increased taxes and issued bonds. Progressives liked bonds because they were voluntary and Americans could buy them based on their financial situation. Officials worried, however, that the war had so divided Americans that few would buy them. To get people to buy bonds, the government printed posters, organized parades, and asked movie stars to promote them.

1. **Analyzing** What was the total revenue raised by loans? What percentage of the cost of the war was paid by taxes?

2. **Interpreting** What point is the poster for the 2nd Liberty Loan making? What group of people does the poster for the 3rd Liberty Loan address?

To conserve energy, Garfield introduced daylight savings time and shortened workweeks for factories that did not make war materials. He also encouraged Americans to observe Heatless Mondays.

Paying for the War By the end of the war, the United States had spent about $32 billion. To fund the war effort, Congress raised income tax rates, placed new taxes on corporate profits, and imposed an extra tax on the profits of arms factories.

Taxes, however, did not cover the entire cost of the war. The government also borrowed over $20 billion through the sale of Liberty Bonds and Victory Bonds. Americans who bought bonds were lending money to the government that would be repaid with interest in a specified number of years.

Mobilizing the Workforce

The success of the war effort also required the cooperation of workers. To prevent strikes from disrupting the war effort, the government established the **National War Labor Board** (NWLB) in March 1918. Chaired by William Howard Taft and Frank Walsh, a prominent labor attorney, the NWLB attempted to mediate labor disputes that might otherwise lead to strikes.

The NWLB often pressured industry to improve wages, adopt an eight-hour workday, and allow unions the right to organize and bargain collectively. In exchange, labor leaders agreed not to disrupt war production with strikes or other disturbances. As a result, membership in unions increased by just over one million between 1917 and 1919.

History ONLINE
Student Web Activity Visit glencoe.com and complete the activity on wartime propaganda.

For an example of government efforts to promote patriotism, read "The American's Creed" on page R51 in **Documents in American History.**

Women Support Industry With large numbers of men in the military, employers were willing to hire women for jobs that had traditionally been limited to men. Some one million women joined the workforce for the first time during the war, and another 8 million switched to higher paying industrial jobs. Women worked in factories, shipyards, and railroad yards and served as police officers, mail carriers, and train engineers.

The wartime changes in female employment were not permanent. When the war ended, most women returned to their previous jobs or stopped working. Although the changes were temporary, they demonstrated that women were capable of holding jobs that many had believed only men could do.

The Great Migration Begins

Women were not the only group in American society to benefit economically. Desperate for workers, Henry Ford sent company agents to the South to recruit African Americans. Other companies quickly followed Ford's example. Their promises of high wages and plentiful work convinced between 300,000 and 500,000 African Americans to leave the South and move to northern cities.

This massive population movement became known as the "Great Migration." It greatly altered the racial makeup of such cities as Chicago, New York, Cleveland, and Detroit. It would also, eventually, change American politics. In the South, African Americans were generally denied the right to vote, but in the northern cities they were able to vote and affect the policies of northern politicians.

Mexican Americans Head North

The war also encouraged other groups to **migrate.** Continuing political turmoil in Mexico and the wartime labor shortage in the United States convinced many Mexicans to head north. Between 1917 and 1920, over 100,000 Mexicans migrated into the Southwest, providing labor for farmers and ranchers.

Meanwhile, Mexican Americans found new opportunities in factory jobs in Chicago, St. Louis, Omaha, and other cities. Many faced hostility and discrimination when they arrived in American cities. Like other immigrant groups before them, they tended to settle in their own separate neighborhoods, called barrios, where they could support each other.

Shaping Public Opinion

Progressives did not think that organizing the economy was enough to ensure the success of the war effort. They also believed the government needed to shape public opinion.

Selling the War Eleven days after asking Congress to declare war, President Wilson created the **Committee on Public Information** (CPI) to "sell" the war to the American people. Headed by George Creel, a journalist, the CPI recruited advertising executives, artists, authors, songwriters, entertainers, public speakers, and motion picture companies to help sway public opinion in favor of the war.

The CPI distributed pamphlets and arranged for thousands of short patriotic talks, called "four-minute speeches," to be delivered at movie theaters and other public places. Some 75,000 speakers, known as Four-Minute Men, urged audiences to support the war in various ways, from buying war bonds to reporting draft dodgers to the authorities.

Civil Liberties Curtailed Besides using propaganda, the government also passed legislation to limit opposition to the war and fight **espionage,** or spying to acquire government information. The Espionage Act of 1917 made it illegal to aid the enemy, give false reports, or interfere with the war effort. The Sedition Act of 1918 made it illegal to speak against the war publicly. In practice, it allowed officials to prosecute anyone who criticized the government. These two laws led to over 1,000 convictions.

Wartime fears also led to attacks on German Americans, labor activists, socialists, and pacifists. Ads urged Americans to monitor their fellow citizens. Americans even formed private groups, such as the American Protective League and the Boy Spies of America, to spy on neighbors and coworkers.

Despite protests, the Espionage and Sedition Acts were upheld in court. Although the First Amendment specifically states that "Congress shall make no law . . . abridging the freedom of speech, or of the press," the Supreme Court departed from a strict literal interpretation of the Constitution. The Court ruled that the government could restrict speech when the words constitute a "clear and present danger."

Reading Check Explaining Why did Congress pass the Espionage Act in 1917?

ANALYZING SUPREME COURT CASES

Can Government Limit Free Speech?

* *Schenck* v. *United States*, 1919
* *Abrams* v. *United States*, 1919

Background to the Cases

In the fall of 1917, Charles Schenck mailed pamphlets to draftees telling them the draft was wrong and urging them to write protest letters. In August 1918, Jacob Abrams wrote pamphlets denouncing the war and criticizing the decision to send troops to Russia to fight communist forces. Both men were convicted of violating the Espionage Act. Both appealed their convictions all the way to the Supreme Court.

How the Court Ruled

The Schenck and Abrams cases raised the question: Are there some circumstances in which the First Amendment's protection of free speech no longer applies? In both cases, the Supreme Court upheld the Espionage Act, concluding that under certain circumstances, the government can indeed limit free speech. In the Schenck case, the Supreme Court decision was unanimous, but in the Abrams case, the Court split 7-2 in their decision.

▲ Eugene Debs, leader of the American Socialist Party, delivers a speech protesting the war in Canton, Ohio, in 1918. Debs was arrested for making the speech and convicted under the Espionage Act. He appealed to the Supreme Court, but the Court upheld his conviction, citing the *Schenck* case as the precedent.

PRIMARY SOURCE

The Court's Opinion

"The most stringent protection of free speech would not protect a man in falsely shouting fire in a theatre and causing a panic. . . . The question in every case is whether the words used are used in such circumstances and are of such a nature as to create a clear and present danger that they will bring about the substantive evils that Congress has a right to prevent. It is a question of proximity and degree. When a nation is at war, many things that might be said in time of peace are such a hindrance to its effort that their utterance will not be endured so long as men fight, and that no Court could regard them as protected by any constitutional right."

—Justice Oliver Wendell Holmes writing for the Court in *Schenck* v. *U.S.*

PRIMARY SOURCE

Dissenting Views

"It is only the present danger of immediate evil or an intent to bring it about that warrants Congress in setting a limit to the expression of opinion where private rights are not concerned. . . . Now nobody can suppose that the surreptitious publishing of a silly leaflet by an unknown man, without more, would present any immediate danger that its opinions would hinder the success of the government arms. . . .

. . . the ultimate good desired is better reached by free trade in ideas—that the best test of truth is the power of the thought to get itself accepted in the competition of the market . . ."

—Justice Oliver Wendell Holmes dissenting in *Abrams* v. *U.S.*

DBQ   Document-Based Questions

1. **Explaining** When does Holmes think the government can restrict speech?

2. **Analyzing** What does Holmes mean by referring to the "free trade in ideas?"
   Do you think the government should ever be allowed to restrict free speech? Why or why not?

3. **Making Inferences** Why do you think Holmes regarded *Schenck* as a much more immediate danger than *Abrams*? What was the difference between their actions?

Building the Military

MAIN Idea The United States instituted a draft for military service, and African Americans and women took on new roles.

HISTORY AND YOU Describe a time you were required to do something that you might not have done otherwise. Read on to learn about the selective service system.

Progressives did not abandon their ideas when it came to building up the military. Instead, they applied their ideas and developed a new system for recruiting a large army.

Volunteers and Conscripts

When the United States entered the war in 1917, the army and National Guard together had slightly more than 300,000 troops. Many men volunteered after war was declared, but many more were still needed.

Selective Service Many progressives believed that conscription—forced military service—was a violation of democratic and republican principles. Believing a **draft** was necessary, however, Congress, with Wilson's support, created a new conscription system called **selective service.**

Instead of having the military run the draft from Washington, D.C., the Selective Service Act of 1917 required all men between 21 and 30 to register for the draft. A lottery randomly determined the order in which they were called before a local draft board in charge of selecting or exempting people from military service.

The thousands of local boards were the heart of the system. The members of the draft boards were civilians from local communities. Progressives believed local people, understanding community needs, would know which men to draft and would do a far better job than a centralized government bureaucracy. Eventually about 2.8 million Americans were drafted.

Volunteers for War Not all American soldiers were drafted. Approximately 2 million men volunteered for military service. Some had heard stories of German atrocities and wanted to fight back. Others believed democracy was at stake. Many believed they had a duty to respond to their nation's call. They had

▲ A 1918 poster commemorates the 369th Regiment—the first Americans to see combat in World War I.

"Liberty And Freedom Shall Not Perish" A. Lincoln

COLORED MEN The First Americans Who Planted Our Flag on the Firing Line

▼ African American soldiers march near Verdun, France, November 1918.

Analyzing VISUALS

1. **Theorizing** Why do you think the French were willing to use African Americans in combat?
2. **Analyzing** Why do you think the poster includes a quote from Abraham Lincoln?

grown up listening to stories of the Civil War and the Spanish-American War. They saw World War I as a great adventure and wanted to fight for their country.

Although the horrors of war soon became apparent to the American troops, their morale remained high, helping to ensure victory. More than 50,000 Americans died in combat and over 200,000 were wounded. Another 60,000 soldiers died from disease, mostly from the influenza epidemic of 1918 and 1919.

The flu epidemic was not limited to the battlefield. It spread around the world and made more than a quarter of all Americans sick. The disease killed an estimated 25–50 million people worldwide, including more than 500,000 Americans.

African Americans in the War Of the nearly 400,000 African Americans who were drafted, about 42,000 served overseas as combat troops. African American soldiers encountered discrimination and prejudice in the army, where they served in racially segregated units, almost always under the supervision of white officers.

Despite these challenges, many African American soldiers fought with distinction. For example, the African American 92nd and 93rd Infantry Divisions fought in bitter battles along the Western Front. Many of them won praise from both the French commander, Marshal Henri Pétain, and the United States commander, General John Pershing.

Women Join the Military

World War I was the first war in which women officially served in the armed forces, although only in noncombat positions. As the military prepared for war in 1917, it faced a severe shortage of clerical workers because so many men were assigned to active duty. Early in 1917, the navy authorized the enlistment of women to meet its clerical needs.

Women serving in the navy wore a standard uniform and were assigned the rank of yeoman. By the end of the war, over 11,000 women had served in the navy. Although most performed clerical duties, others served as radio operators, electricians, pharmacists, chemists, and photographers.

Unlike the navy, the army refused to enlist women. Instead, it began hiring women as temporary employees to fill clerical jobs. The only women to actually serve in the army were in the Army Nursing Corps.

Women nurses had served in both the army and navy since the early 1900s, but as auxiliaries. They were not assigned ranks, and were not technically enlisted in the army or navy. Army nurses were the only women in the military sent overseas during the war. More than 20,000 nurses served in the Army Nursing Corps during the war, including more than 10,000 overseas.

✔ **Reading Check** **Describing** How did Congress ensure that the United States would have enough troops to serve in World War I?

Section 2 REVIEW

Vocabulary

1. **Explain** the significance of: War Industries Board, victory gardens, National War Labor Board, Committee on Public Information, espionage, selective service.

Main Ideas

2. **Examining** How did government efforts to ensure public support for the war conflict with ideas about civil rights?

3. **Describing** What were the contributions of African Americans during the war?

Critical Thinking

4. **Big Ideas** How did progressives use their ideas to mobilize both the economy and the American people during the war?

5. **Organizing** Use a graphic organizer similar to the one below to identify the effects of the war on the American workforce.

U.S. Groups	Effects
Women	
African Americans	
Hispanics	

6. **Analyzing Visuals** Examine the graph on page 557. How much did World War I cost? Do you think the government should rely on taxes or loans to fund a war? Explain.

Writing About History

7. **Persuasive Writing** Imagine that you are working for the Committee on Public Information. Write text for an advertisement or lyrics to a song in which you attempt to sway public opinion in favor of the war.

History ONLINE

Study Central™ To review this section, go to glencoe.com and click on Study Central.

ANALYZING PRIMARY SOURCES

Propaganda in World War I

All of the warring nations in World War I used propaganda to boost support for their side. Many Americans believed the propaganda coming from Europe, particularly from the British government and press. When the United States entered the war, the American government also began using propaganda in an attempt to unite Americans behind the war effort.

Read the passages and study the posters. Then answer the questions that follow.

Movie Poster, 1918

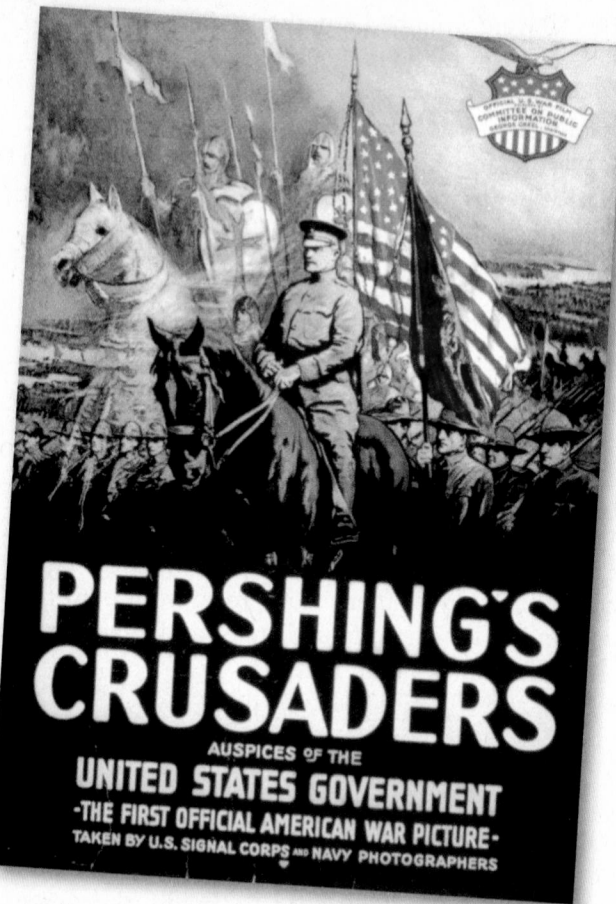

PERSHING'S CRUSADERS

AUSPICES OF THE
UNITED STATES GOVERNMENT
-THE FIRST OFFICIAL AMERICAN WAR PICTURE-
TAKEN BY U.S. SIGNAL CORPS AND NAVY PHOTOGRAPHERS

PRIMARY SOURCE 2

Government War Bond Advertisement, 1918

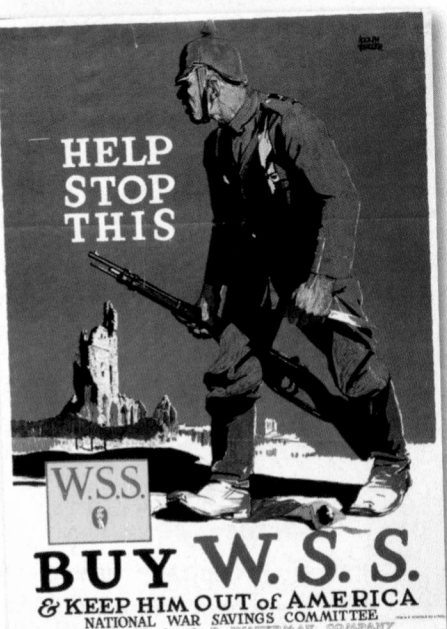

HELP STOP THIS

W.S.S.

BUY W.S.S.
& KEEP HIM OUT of AMERICA
NATIONAL WAR SAVINGS COMMITTEE

PRIMARY SOURCE 3

American Soldier's Diary, 1918

"Germans, and a German—so different. Fishing through the poor torn pockets of shabby German body, drooped over wreck of machine gun, to find well-thumbed photograph of woman and little boy and little girl—so like one's own . . . impossible to hate what had been that body.

Nothing so revolting as bitter, pitiless cruelty of those who know nothing of reality of it all. Those . . . Germano-baiters at home, so much more cruel than those who have the right— and are not."

—Diary of Lieutenant Howard V. O'Brien, October 6, 1918

PRIMARY SOURCE 4

Newspaper Column, *New York Times*, May 1915

▼ *Great Britain established the Bryce Committee to investigate German atrocities in Belgium. Its findings, released just five days after the sinking of the* Lusitania, *increased anti-German sentiment in the United States. Investigations after the war, however, found that many of the stories were false or gross exaggerations.*

GERMAN ATROCITIES ARE PROVED, FINDS BRYCE COMMITTEE

Not Only Individual Crimes, but
Premeditated Slaughter
in Belgium.

YOUNG AND OLD MUTILATED

Women Attacked, Children Brutally Slain, Arson and
Pillage Systematic.

COUNTENANCED BY OFFICERS

Wanton Firing on Red Cross and
White Flag; Prisoners and
Wounded Shot.

CIVILIANS USED AS SHIELDS

Proof That Belgians Did Not Fire
on Germans at Louvain—Germans Received Kindness.

PRIMARY SOURCE 5

U.S. Government Pamphlet, 1918

"Fear, perhaps, is rather an important element to be bred in the civilian population. It is difficult to unite a people by talking only on the highest ethical plane. To fight for an ideal, perhaps, must be coupled with thoughts of self-preservation. So a truthful appeal to the fear of men, the recognition of the terrible things that would happen if the German Government were permitted to retain its prestige, may be necessary in order that all people unite in the support of the needed sacrifices."

—Pamphlet for speakers from the Committee on Public Information, quoted in the *New York Times,* February 4, 1918

PRIMARY SOURCE 6

American Red Cross Poster, c. 1916

CIVILIZATION VS. BARBARISM

FOR HUMANITY'S SAKE
SAVE A LIFE -
RED CROSS WEEK
JUNE 18TH TO 25TH.

DBQ Document-Based Questions

1. **Explaining** Examine Primary Source 1. What is the underlying message behind the poster for "Pershing's Crusaders"?

2. **Identifying** What images of the Germans do Primary Sources 2 and 6 promote?

3. **Analyzing** Study Primary Source 4. How do you think stories of German atrocities affected American neutrality?

4. **Making Connections** Read Primary Sources 3 and 5. Why do you think the government used propaganda? Do you think propaganda is a good idea in wartime?

5. **Evaluating** According to Primary Sources 2, 5, and 6, what is at stake in the war? What should citizens do to help the war effort?

A Bloody Conflict

Guide to Reading

Big Ideas
Individual Action American troops played a major role in helping end the war.

Content Vocabulary
• convoy *(p. 567)*
• armistice *(p. 569)*
• national self-determination *(p. 570)*
• reparations *(p. 572)*

Academic Vocabulary
• network *(p. 564)*
• adequately *(p. 567)*
• resolve *(p. 570)*

People and Events to Identify
• no-man's-land *(p. 564)*
• John J. Pershing *(p. 568)*
• Treaty of Versailles *(p. 570)*
• Fourteen Points *(p. 570)*
• League of Nations *(p. 571)*

Reading Strategy
Organizing Complete a graphic organizer similar to the one below by listing the kinds of warfare and technology used in the fighting.

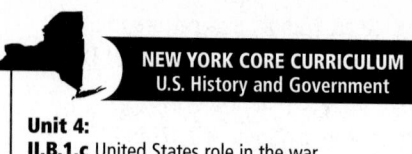

NEW YORK CORE CURRICULUM
U.S. History and Government

Unit 4:
II.B.1.c United States role in the war
II.D.2 War aims: The Fourteen Points
II.D.3 Treaty of Versailles: Wilson's role
II.D.4 League of Nations: Henry Cabot Lodge and the United States Senate rejection

Technology caused both sides to lose millions of men during World War I. The arrival of American troops helped the Allies win, but the peace treaty set the stage for another war to come.

Combat in World War I

MAIN Idea New technologies made World War I the first modern war.

HISTORY AND YOU What new technologies have been developed or proposed in your lifetime? Read on to learn about the weapons that World War I personnel faced.

By the spring of 1917, World War I had devastated Europe. Old-fashioned strategies and new technologies resulted in terrible destruction. Many Americans believed, however, that their troops would make a difference and quickly bring the war to an end.

Trench Warfare

Early offensives in 1914 demonstrated that warfare had changed. Powerful artillery guns were placed several miles behind the front lines. From there, they hurled huge explosive shells onto the battlefield. More people were killed by artillery fire than by any other weapon in World War I. Artillery fire produced horrific scenes of death and destruction, as one American noted in his diary:

PRIMARY SOURCE

"Many dead Germans along the road. One heap on a manure pile. . . . Devastation everywhere. Our barrage has rooted up the entire territory like a ploughed field. Dead horses galore, many of them have a hind quarter cut off—the Huns [Germans] need food. Dead men here and there."

—quoted in *The American Spirit*

To protect themselves from artillery, troops began digging trenches. On the Western Front—where German troops confronted French, British, and Belgian forces—the troops dug a **network** of trenches that stretched from the English Channel to the Swiss border. To prevent the enemy from overrunning the trenches, troops relied upon a new weapon, the machine gun, to hold off the attackers. The space between opposing trenches was called **no-man's-land.** It was a rough barren landscape filled with craters from artillery fire. To prevent troops from crossing no-man's-land, both sides built barbed wire entanglements and obstacles in front of their trenches.

NATIONAL GEOGRAPHIC — The War in the Trenches, 1914–1916

Major Battles

1 **Tannenberg,** Aug. 1914. Germans stop Russian invasion.

2 **Marne,** Sept. 1914. French stop German advance on Paris; trench warfare begins.

3 **1st Ypres,** Oct.–Nov. 1914. British stop German advance on French ports.

4 **Gallipoli,** Feb.–Dec. 1915. Turks block British and French effort to secure a supply route to Russia.

5 **2nd Ypres,** April–May 1915. Germans use poison gas for the first time, but British lines hold.

6 **Isonzo,** June–Dec. 1915. Austrians block Italian efforts to take Trieste.

7 **Somme,** July–Nov. 1916. British and French push back German lines. British use tanks for the first time.

8 **Verdun,** Feb.–Dec. 1916. Massive German attack, but French lines hold.

Legend:
- Allied Powers
- Central Powers
- Neutral Powers
- Line of trench warfare, 1915–1917
- Allied victory
- Central Powers victory

0 — 400 kilometers
0 — 400 miles
Lambert Azimuthal Equal-Area projection

Trench Warfare

Machine gun nests
Reserve trench
Support trench
Front-line trench
Artillery guns several miles behind the lines
Barbed wire
No-man's-land

Analyzing GEOGRAPHY

1. **Location** Along what nations' boundaries did the Western Front lie?
2. **Human-Environment Interaction** In addition to weapons, what other dangers did troops in the trenches face?

To break through enemy lines, the attacker would begin with a massive artillery barrage. Soldiers would then scramble out of their trenches, race across no-man's-land while enemy machine guns fired at them, and try to capture the enemy's trenches.

Before charging enemy trenches, troops fixed bayonets—long knives—to their rifles. For those troops that made it across no-man's-land, fighting in the trenches was brutal. Troops threw grenades—small bombs—at each other, and used bayonets, rifle butts, knives, axes, pistols and even rocks and fists to kill the enemy.

The results of this kind of warfare were horrific. In major battles, both sides often lost hundreds of thousands of men, yet neither side was able to break through the other's lines.

New Technology

New technologies were needed to break through enemy lines. In April 1915, the Germans first used poison gas in the Second Battle of Ypres. The fumes caused vomiting, blindness, and suffocation. Soon afterward the Allies also began using gas. To counter gas attacks, both sides developed gas masks.

In late 1915, the British introduced the armored tank into battle. These tanks were slow and mechanically unreliable, but they could crush barbed wire and cross trenches. Unfortunately, there were not enough of them. The tanks could support the troops, but they did not revolutionize warfare in World War I. By the time World War II broke out, however, tanks had replaced cavalry in most modern armies and made trench warfare obsolete.

World War I also marked the first use of aircraft in war. In addition, it was the first and last time that zeppelins were used in combat. Zeppelins are giant rigid balloons, also known as blimps or dirigibles. Early in the war, the Germans sent squadrons of zeppelins to drop bombs on British warships in the North Sea.

At first, airplanes were used as scouts. They flew over enemy territory, as well as the English Channel and the North Sea, spying on enemy troops and ships. Before long, however, the Allies equipped them with machine guns to attack the German zeppelin fleet. The machine guns were timed to fire through the aircraft's propeller as it spun so that the bullets did not hit the propeller. A few airplanes even carried rockets to destroy the zeppelins. Others carried small bombs to drop on enemy lines.

As technology advanced, aircraft were used to shoot down other aircraft. Battles between aircraft became known as dogfights. Early military aircraft were difficult to fly and easy to destroy. The wings and body frame were covered in cloth and easily caught fire. Pilots did not carry parachutes. The average life expectancy of a combat pilot in World War I was about two weeks.

✔ **Reading Check** **Describing** What new technologies were introduced in World War I?

The Americans Arrive

MAIN Idea The arrival of Americans changed the course of the war and helped the Allies win.

HISTORY AND YOU Have you ever had to boost someone's morale? Read on to learn about Americans who helped the Allies win World War I.

Waves of American troops marched into this bloody stalemate—nearly 2 million before the war's end. Although the "doughboys," as American soldiers were nicknamed, were inexperienced, they were fresh and eager to fight. Their presence boosted the morale of Allied forces. It also demoralized the German soldiers, who now faced large numbers of fresh troops. As the Americans began to arrive, many in Germany concluded that the war was lost.

Winning the War at Sea

No American troopships were sunk on their way to Europe thanks to the efforts of American Admiral William S. Sims. The British preferred to fight German submarines by sending warships to find them, while merchant ships would race across the Atlantic individually. This approach enabled German submarines to inflict heavy losses on British shipping. Sims

TECHNOLOGY & HISTORY

New Weapons World War I is often called the first modern war because troops used new technology that is still widely used in warfare today. Much of this new technology developed in response to trench warfare.

◀ **Artillery Forces Troops into Trenches**
Australian soldiers load an artillery shell during the Battle of Passchendaele in 1917. Powerful long-range artillery fire from guns like this forced troops to build trenches for protection.

▲ **Machine Guns Defend Trenches**
Machine guns made it very difficult to capture enemy trenches. They could fire thousands of bullets per minute. A small team with a machine gun could down hundreds of troops crossing open terrain. This photo shows a German machine gun crew.

proposed that merchant ships and troop transports be gathered into groups, called **convoys.** Small highly maneuverable warships called destroyers would protect and escort the convoys across the Atlantic.

Convoys also saved lives. If a ship was sunk, other ships in the convoy could rescue survivors. The system worked. Convoys greatly reduced shipping losses and ensured that a large number of American troops arrived safely in Europe in time to help stop Germany's last great offensive on the Western Front.

Russia Leaves the War

In March 1917, riots broke out in Russia over the government's handling of the war and the scarcity of food and fuel. Czar Nicholas II, the leader of the Russian Empire, abdicated his throne. This marked the beginning of the Russian Revolution.

Political leadership in Russia passed to a provisional, or temporary, government. The leaders of the provisional government wanted Russia to stay in the war. However, the government was unable to deal **adequately** with the major problems afflicting the nation, such as food shortages. The Bolshevik Party, led by Vladimir Lenin, overthrew the provisional government and established a Communist government in November 1917.

Germany's military fortunes improved with the Bolshevik takeover of Russia. Lenin's first act after seizing power was to pull Russia out of the war and concentrate on establishing a Communist state. Lenin agreed to the Treaty of Brest-Litovsk with Germany on March 3, 1918. Under this treaty, Russia lost substantial territory. It gave up the Ukraine, its Polish and Baltic territories, and Finland.

With the Eastern Front settled, Germany could now concentrate its forces in the west. German leaders knew this was their last chance to win. If the troops transferred from Russia could not break Allied lines, it was only a matter of time before Germany would have to surrender.

Americans Enter Combat

At the time World War I began, many Americans knew that the French had helped the United States during the American Revolution. American school children still learned the story of the Marquis de Lafayette, who had brought French officers to America to help train American soldiers and who had served on George Washington's staff during the Revolutionary War. Many Americans regarded the French people as friends and believed the nation owed the French a debt for their help in the revolution.

◀ **Poison Gas vs. Trenches**
To break through trench lines, both sides began using poison gas. To protect against gas attacks, troops were forced to carry gas masks similar to those shown here worn by American soldiers in France in 1917.

▲ **Airplanes Bomb Trenches**
Airplanes offered both sides a way to counter trench warfare. Several types of aircraft, including the British Sopwith Camel shown above, could carry 4–5 small bombs to drop on enemy artillery and trenches. They also attacked troops using their machine guns.

Tanks vs. Trenches ▶
To help capture trenches, the Allies built tanks that were immune to machine gun fire and able to smash through barbed wire. Tanks had tracks instead of wheels, enabling them to cross the mud and craters of no-man's-land.

Analyzing VISUALS

1. **Analyzing** Modern militaries do not use trench warfare. Which weapons pictured eventually ended the use of trenches?

2. **Synthesizing** Explain how the different technologies of World War I worked together to kill so many people.

When General **John J. Pershing,** commander of the American Expeditionary Force (AEF), arrived in Paris on July 4, 1917, he and his officers headed to Picpus Cemetery where Lafayette was buried. One of Pershing's officers, Colonel Charles E. Stanton, raised his hand in salute and proclaimed, "Lafayette, we are here!" France had helped the United States gain its freedom. Now American soldiers would help the French to preserve theirs.

When American troops began arriving in France, the British and French commanders wanted to integrate them into their armies under British and French command. Pershing refused, and President Wilson supported him. Pershing insisted that American soldiers fight in American units under American command.

Despite French and British pleas that they needed American soldiers to replace their own losses, Pershing held firm with one exception. The 93rd Infantry Division—an African American unit—was transferred to the French. Its soldiers became the first Americans to enter combat.

Germany's Last Offensive

On March 21, 1918, the Germans launched a massive attack along the Western Front, beginning with gas attacks and a huge artillery bombardment. German forces, strengthened by reinforcements from the Russian front, pushed deep into Allied lines. By early June, they were less than 40 miles (64 km) from Paris.

American troops played an important role in containing the German offensive. In late May, as the German offensive continued, the Americans launched their first major attack, quickly capturing the village of Cantigny. On June 1, American and French troops blocked the German drive on Paris at the town of Château-Thierry. On July 15, the Germans launched one last massive attack in an attempt to take Paris, but American and French troops held their ground.

The Battle of the Argonne Forest

With the German drive stalled, French Marshal Ferdinand Foch, supreme commander of the Allied forces, ordered massive counterattacks. In mid-September, American troops drove back German forces at the battle of Saint-Mihiel. Next, an American offensive was launched in the region between the Meuse River and the Argonne Forest. General Pershing

assembled over 600,000 American troops, 40,000 tons of supplies, and roughly 4,000 artillery pieces for the most massive attack in American history.

The attack began on September 26, 1918. German positions slowly fell to the advancing American troops. The Germans inflicted heavy casualties, but by early November the Americans had shattered German defenses and opened a hole on the eastern flank of the German lines. Soon after, all across the Western Front, the Germans began to retreat.

American Heroes

Although the brutal trench warfare of World War I led to many acts of astonishing bravery, the actions of two Americans, Corporal Alvin York and Captain Eddie Rickenbacker, captured the nation's imagination.

Alvin York Born in 1887, Alvin York grew up poor in the mountains of Tennessee, where he learned to shoot by hunting wild game. Opposed to war, he initially tried to avoid the draft as a conscientious objector—a person who refuses to obey the law because of his moral or religious beliefs. As a Christian, York

Alvin York and the Battle of the Argonne Forest

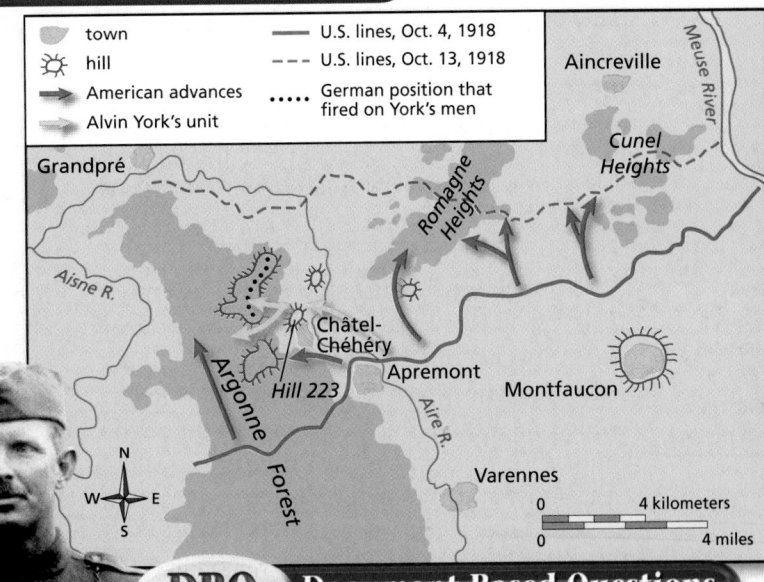

October 8th 1918, Argonne Forest, France.

"So on the morning of the 8th, just before day-light, we started for the hill of Chattel Chehery. So before we got there it got light, and the Germans sent over a heavy barrage and also gas, and we put on our gas masks and just pressed right on through those shells and got to the top of hill 223.... [A]t the zero hour ... we done went over the top.... The Germans ... jes stopped us in our tracks. Their machine guns were up there on the heights overlooking us and well hidden, and we couldn't tell for certain where the terrible heavy fire was coming from.... So we decided to try and get them by a surprise attack in the rear.... So there was 17 of us boys went around on the left flank to see if we couldn't put those guns out of action."

—from *Sergeant York*

Map legend:
- town
- hill
- American advances
- Alvin York's unit
- U.S. lines, Oct. 4, 1918
- U.S. lines, Oct. 13, 1918
- German position that fired on York's men

Map labels: Aincreville, Meuse River, Cunel Heights, Grandpré, Romagne Heights, Aisne R., Châtel-Chéhéry, Apremont, Montfaucon, Hill 223, Argonne Forest, Aire R., Varennes

0 4 kilometers / 0 4 miles

DBQ Document-Based Questions

1. **Extrapolating** Why was the American victory in the Argonne Forest important?

2. **Explaining** What made capturing enemy positions in the Argonne Forest so difficult?

Maps In Motion See *StudentWorks™ Plus* or glencoe.com.

believed he was not allowed to kill anyone. Eventually, he decided that he could fight in a war if the cause was just.

On October 8, 1918, during the Battle of the Argonne Forest, German machine guns on a fortified hill fired on York's platoon and killed nine men. York took command and charged the machine guns. By the end of the battle, York had killed between 9 and 25 Germans, captured the machine guns, and taken 132 prisoners. For his actions, he received the Medal of Honor and the French Croix de Guerre. After returning home, he used his fame to raise money for the Alvin York Institute—a school for poor Tennessee children.

Eddie Rickenbacker Born in Columbus, Ohio, Eddie Rickenbacker was a famous race car driver before the war. Rickenbacker's car-racing reflexes served him well as a combat pilot. He was named commander of the 94th Aero Squadron, the first all-American squadron to enter combat. In all, he fought in 134 air battles and shot down 26 aircraft, becoming the top American combat pilot. In one battle, he single-handedly fought seven German aircraft—a feat for which he was later awarded the Congressional Medal of Honor.

The War Ends

While fighting raged along the Western Front, a revolution engulfed Austria-Hungary. In October 1918, Poland, Hungary, and Czechoslovakia declared independence. By early November, the governments of the Austro-Hungarian Empire and the Ottoman Empire had surrendered to the allies.

On November 3, sailors in Kiel, the main base of the German fleet, mutinied. Within days, groups of workers and soldiers seized power in other German towns. As the revolution spread, the German emperor decided to step down. On November 9, Germany became a republic. Two days later the government signed an **armistice**—a truce, or an agreement to stop fighting. At the 11th hour on the 11th day of the 11th month, 1918, the fighting stopped.

✔ **Reading Check** **Interpreting** Why would Pershing want to keep U.S. soldiers in their own units?

A Flawed Peace

MAIN Idea The United States Senate refused to ratify the Treaty of Versailles and rejected the League of Nations.

HISTORY AND YOU How might your feelings toward a peace plan differ if you lived in a defeated country compared to a victorious country? Read on to learn why the U.S. Senate did not ratify the Treaty of Versailles.

📜 Read Wilson's "Fourteen Points" on page R52 in **Documents in American History.**

Although the fighting stopped in November 1918, World War I was not over. A peace treaty had to be negotiated and signed. In January 1919, delegates from 27 countries traveled to France to attend the peace conference. The conference took place at the Palace of Versailles, near Paris, and the treaty with Germany that resulted came to be called the **Treaty of Versailles.** The conference also negotiated the Treaty of Saint-Germain, ending the war with Austria-Hungary.

Negotiations on the Treaty of Versailles lasted five months. The most important participants were the so-called "Big Four" of the Allies: President Wilson of the United States, British Prime Minister David Lloyd George, French Premier Georges Clemenceau, and Italian Prime Minister Vittorio Orlando.

Representatives from Russia were not invited to the conference. Wilson and the other Allied leaders refused to recognize Lenin's government as legitimate. At the time of the peace conference, a civil war was raging in Russia between communist and non-communist forces. In mid-1918, the United States, Great Britain, and Japan had sent troops to Russia to help the anti-communist forces. Nearly 15,000 American troops remained in Russia—which had been renamed the Soviet Union by the Bolsheviks—until the spring of 1920. By that time, it had become clear that the Bolsheviks had won the civil war.

The Fourteen Points

When President Wilson arrived in Paris in January 1919, he brought with him a peace plan known as the **Fourteen Points.** Wilson had presented the plan to Congress in January 1918 to explain the goals of the United States in the war. The president believed that if the Fourteen Points were implemented, they would establish the conditions for a lasting peace in Europe.

What Did President Wilson Want?

The Fourteen Points

1. End secret treaties and secret diplomacy among nations.
2. Guarantee freedom of navigation on the seas for all nations.
3. Create free trade among nations.
4. Reduce armed forces as much as possible consistent with domestic safety.
5. Settle all colonial claims fairly taking into account the views of both the colonial peoples and the imperial nations.
6. Evacuate German troops from Russia and restore all conquered territory.
7. Restore Belgium's independence.
8. Restore all French territory occupied by Germany, including Alsace-Lorraine.
9. Adjust Italy's borders based on where Italians live.
10. Divide Austria-Hungary into new nations for each ethnic group.
11. Base borders of the Balkan states on nationality.
12. Break up the Ottoman Empire and make Turkey a separate country.
13. Create an independent Poland.
14. Create a League of Nations.

The Fourteen Points were based on "the principle of justice to all peoples and nationalities." In the first five points, Wilson proposed to eliminate the causes of the war through free trade, freedom of the seas, disarmament, an impartial adjustment of colonial claims, and open diplomacy instead of secret agreements.

The next eight points addressed the right of **national self-determination.** This is the idea that the borders of countries should be based on ethnicity and national identity. A group of people who feel that they are a nation should be allowed to have their own country. Wilson and other supporters of national self-determination believed that when borders are not based on national identity, border disputes will occur and nations are more likely to go to war to **resolve** them.

The principle of national self-determination also meant that no nation should be allowed to keep territory taken from another nation. Wilson's Fourteen Points required the Central Powers to evacuate all of the countries invaded during the war. Wilson also wanted the territory

What Did the Allies Agree to Do?

Treaty of Versailles (peace with Germany)

- German troops will return all captured territory to Belgium, Russia, and France.
- Germany will be divided in two; some German territory will be given to Denmark, France, Poland, Czechoslovakia, and Belgium.
- Germany will be held responsible for all wartime losses and must pay reparations.
- Germany's army and navy will be limited in size. Germany cannot have an air force, and cannot have military forces west of the Rhine.

Treaty of Saint-Germain (peace with Austria)

- The Austro-Hungarian Empire is dissolved and replaced by the nation of Austria.
- Four new nations are recognized: Czechoslovakia, Hungary, Poland, and Yugoslavia.
- Austria may not unite with Germany; its army is limited to 30,000 men.

The Covenant of the League of Nations (included in both peace treaties above)

- Members agree to reduce armaments.
- Members agree to protect each other against aggression.
- Colonies of the Central Powers will now be supervised by League members.
- Parts of the Ottoman Empire will be made independent under League supervision.

NATIONAL GEOGRAPHIC — **Changes in Europe, 1919**

Former Austria-Hungary boundary
Former German boundary
Former Russian boundary

0 500 kilometers
0 500 miles
Lambert Azimuthal Equal-Area projection

Analyzing VISUALS

1. **Comparing** How many of the Fourteen Points were accepted at the Paris Peace Conference?
2. **Analyzing** What nations received territory from the Austro-Hungarian Empire?

Maps In Motion See *StudentWorks™ Plus* or glencoe.com.

of Alsace-Lorraine that Germany had taken in 1871 restored to France.

The fourteenth point was most important to Wilson. It called for the creation of a "general association of nations" that would later be called the **League of Nations.** The League's member nations would help preserve peace by pledging to respect and protect each other's territory and political independence. Wilson was so determined to get agreement on the League of Nations that he was willing to give up other goals in the Fourteen Points in exchange for support for the League.

The Treaty of Versailles

Wilson received an enthusiastic reception from crowds in Paris and other national capitals that he visited. Many people believed that the American intervention had brought an end to four grim years of war. Wilson's popularity in Europe put him in a strong negotiating position. He was delighted when the peace conference decided to use the Fourteen Points as the basis for negotiations.

Not everyone was impressed by President Wilson's ideas. Premier Clemenceau of France, in particular, wanted to punish the Germans for the suffering they had inflicted on the French people. He was also determined to end the German threat once and for all. Other Allied governments tended to agree.

Despite Wilson's hopes, the peace terms were harsh. The Treaty of Versailles, reluctantly signed by Germany on June 28, 1919, included many terms designed to punish and weaken Germany. Germany's armed forces were greatly reduced in size and Germany was not allowed to put troops west of the Rhine River—the region near the French border. The treaty also specifically blamed Germany for the war, stating that it had been caused by "the aggression of Germany."

When the German government signed the treaty, it, in effect, acknowledged that Germany was guilty of causing the war. This allowed the Allies to demand that Germany pay **reparations**—monetary compensation for all of the war damage it had caused. A commission set up after the treaty was signed decided that Germany owed the Allies approximately $33 billion. This sum was far more than Germany could pay all at once and was intended to keep Germany's economy weak for a long time.

Wilson had somewhat better success in promoting national self-determination. Four empires were dismantled as a result of World War I and the peace negotiations: the Austro-Hungarian Empire, the Russian Empire, the German Empire, and the Ottoman Empire. The various peace treaties signed after the war created nine new nations in Europe: Austria, Czechoslovakia, Estonia, Finland, Hungary, Latvia, Lithuania, Poland and Yugoslavia. In general, the majority of people in these new countries were from one ethnic group.

National self-determination was not, however, applied to Germany. Both Poland and Czechoslovakia were given territory where the majority of the people were German. Germany was even split in two in order to give Poland access to the Baltic Sea. By leaving a large number of Germans living outside Germany, the Treaty of Versailles helped set the stage for a new series of crises in the 1930s.

The Treaty of Versailles did not address several of Wilson's Fourteen Points. It did not mention freedom of the seas or free trade. It also ignored Wilson's goal of a fair settlement of colonial claims. No colonial people in Asia or Africa were granted independence. Germany's colonies in Africa and the Middle East were placed under the supervision of Britain and France. Japan was given responsibility for Germany's colonies in East Asia.

The treaty also stated that new countries were to be created from the Ottoman Empire. In 1920 the Ottoman Empire was divided into the nations of Turkey, Syria (including Lebanon), Iraq, Palestine, and Transjordan. Syria was put under French supervision and Iraq, Palestine, and Transjordan were put under British supervision.

Although disappointed with many parts of the Treaty of Versailles, Wilson achieved his

POLITICAL CARTOONS PRIMARY SOURCE
Debating the Treaty of Versailles

◄ Senator Henry Cabot Lodge escorts the peace treaty out of the Senate.

◄ In the original caption of this cartoon, President Wilson is saying: "Build your house up there where it can't be washed away."

Analyzing VISUALS DBQ

1. **Identifying** What point is the cartoon on the right trying to make?

2. **Interpreting** Why does the cartoon on the left suggest that international agreement on a peace treaty is important?

primary goal. The treaty called for the creation of a League of Nations. League members promised to reduce armaments, to submit all disputes that endangered the peace to arbitration, and to come to the aid of any member who was threatened with aggression by another state.

The U.S. Senate Rejects the Treaty

President Wilson was confident the American people would support the Treaty of Versailles, but he had badly underestimated the opposition in Congress. All treaties signed by the United States must be ratified by two-thirds of the Senate, and in November 1918, the Democratic Party had lost control of the Senate. Even though he needed Republican support to ratify the treaty, Wilson refused to take any Republican leaders with him to the peace conference. This ensured that Wilson's views prevailed, but it also meant that Republican concerns were not addressed.

Opposition in the Senate focused on the League of Nations. One group of senators, nicknamed the "Irreconcilables," refused to support the treaty under any circumstances. They assailed the League as the kind of "entangling alliance" that the Founders had warned against. A larger group of senators, known as the "Reservationists," was led by the powerful chairman of the Foreign Relations committee, Henry Cabot Lodge. The Reservationists were willing to support the treaty if certain amendments were made to the League of Nations.

The Reservationists pointed out that the Constitution requires Congress to declare war. Yet the League of Nations could require member states to aid any member who was attacked. The Reservationists argued that this might force the United States into a war without Congressional approval. They agreed to ratify the treaty if it was amended to say that any military action by the United States required the approval of Congress. Wilson refused, fearing the change would undermine the League's effectiveness.

To overcome Senate opposition, Wilson decided to take his case directly to the American people. If public support for the treaty was strong enough, the senators would back down. Starting in September 1919, Wilson traveled 8,000 miles and made over 30 major speeches in three weeks. On September 25, the president collapsed from the physical strain and soon afterward suffered a stroke. Bedridden, Wilson ignored the advice of his wife and Democratic leaders and refused to compromise on the treaty.

The Senate finally voted in November 1919. It voted again in March 1920. Both times it refused to ratify the treaty. After Wilson left office in 1921, the United States negotiated separate peace treaties with each of the Central Powers. The League of Nations, the foundation of President Wilson's plan for lasting world peace, took shape without the United States.

Reading Check **Examining** What was national self-determination and why did Wilson think it would help prevent war?

Section 3 REVIEW

Vocabulary

1. **Explain** the significance of: no-man's-land, convoy, John J. Pershing, armistice, Treaty of Versailles, Fourteen Points, national self-determination, League of Nations, reparations.

Main Ideas

2. **Explaining** How did technology change the way World War I was fought?

3. **Analyzing** What impact did John J. Pershing and the Battle of the Argonne Forest have on World War I?

4. **Organizing** Use a graphic organizer to list the results of World War I.

Critical Thinking

5. **Big Ideas** Why did President Wilson propose his Fourteen Points?

6. **Analyzing** What countries were involved in the Paris peace conference in 1919? Which country was not invited to participate? Why?

7. **Analyzing Maps and Charts** Examine the map and chart on page 571. Prepare a quiz with questions based on information from both. Give the quiz to some of your classmates.

Writing About History

8. **Descriptive Writing** Imagine that you are an American soldier fighting in Europe during World War I. Write a letter home describing your situation and how you feel about fighting there.

History ONLINE

Study Central™ To review this section, go to glencoe.com and click on Study Central.

American soldiers set sail for Europe.

World War Firsts

Human ingenuity goes to work in the service of war:

AERIAL COMBAT, 1914. War takes to the air. Two Allied aircraft chase two German planes across Britain.

GAS ATTACKS, 1915. The German High Command admits to using chlorine gas bombs and shells on the field of combat. Deadly mustard gas is used in 1917.

GAS MASKS. Issued to Allied soldiers in 1915.

DONKEY'S EARS. A new trench periscope enables soldiers to observe the battleground from the relative safety of a trench without risking sniper fire.

BIG BERTHA. Enormous howitzer gun bombards Paris. "Big Bertha," named after the wife of its manufacturer, is thought to be located nearly 63 miles behind German lines. Moving at night on railroad tracks, the gun is difficult for the Allies to locate.

Color My World

Some bright spots in a dark decade:

- Color newspaper supplements (1914)
- 3-D films (1915)
- Nail polish (1916)
- Three-color traffic lights (1918)
- Color photography introduced by Eastman Kodak (1914)

One of the first color photographs

VERBATIM

"My message was one of death for young men. How odd to applaud that."
WOODROW WILSON,
on returning to the White House after asking Congress for a declaration of war, 1917

"Food is Ammunition—Don't Waste It"
POSTER FROM U.S. FOOD ADMINISTRATION,
administered by Herbert Hoover

"I have had a hard time getting over this war. My old world died."
RAY STANNARD BAKER,
journalist

"Let us, while this war lasts, forget our special grievances and close our ranks shoulder to shoulder with our own white fellow citizens and the allied nations that are fighting for democracy."
W.E.B. DU BOIS,
African American scholar and leader, 1918

"America has at one bound become a world power in a sense she never was before."
BRITISH PRIME MINISTER DAVID LLOYD GEORGE,
on the U.S. entry into World War I, 1917

"In the camps I saw barrels mounted on sticks on which zealous captains were endeavoring to teach their men how to ride a horse."
THEODORE ROOSEVELT,
on touring U.S. military training facilities, 1917

"The war was over, and it seemed as if everything in the world were possible, and everything was new, and that peace was going to be all we dreamed about."
FLORENCE HARRIMAN,
Red Cross volunteer, in Paris on Armistice Day, 1918

How to Make a Doughboy

Take one American infantryman.

1. Arm with 107 pieces of fighting equipment, including:

   - ☒ rifle
   - ☒ rifle cartridges
   - ☒ cartridge belt
   - ☒ steel helmet
   - ☒ clubs
   - ☒ knives
   - ☒ gas mask
   - ☒ wire cutters
   - ☒ trench tool
   - ☒ bayonet and scabbard
   - ☒ grenades

2. Add 50 articles of clothing, including 3 wool blankets and a bedsack.

3. Equip with eating utensils and 11 cooking implements.

4. Train well.

TOTAL COST: $156.30

(not including training and transportation to Europe)

Milestones

SHOT DOWN AND KILLED, APRIL 22, 1918. "THE RED BARON," Manfred von Richthofen, Germany's ace pilot. Von Richthofen destroyed more than 80 Allied aircraft. The English fighter pilot Edward Mannock said, "I hope he roasted all the way down."

Jeannette Rankin

ELECTED, NOVEMBER 7, 1916. JEANNETTE RANKIN of Montana, to the U.S. Congress. The first woman congressional representative explained her victory by saying that women "got the vote in Montana because the spirit of pioneer days was still alive."

Vladimir Lenin

REPATRIATED, APRIL 10, 1917. VLADIMIR ILYICH LENIN, to Russia, after an 11-year absence. The leader of the leftist Bolshevik party hopes to reorganize his revolutionary group.

NUMBERS 1915

$1,040 Average annual income for workers in finance, insurance, and real estate

$687 Average income for industrial workers (higher for union workers, lower for nonunion workers)

$510 Average income for retail trade workers

$355 Average income for farm laborers

$342 Average income for domestic servants

$328 Average income for public school teachers

$11.95 Cost of a bicycle

$1.15 Cost of a baseball

$1 Average cost of a hotel room

39¢ Cost of one dozen eggs

5¢ Cost of a glass of cola

7¢ Cost of a large roll of toilet paper

CRITICAL THINKING

1. Analyzing What pioneer qualities was Jeannette Rankin referring to when she said women "got the vote in Montana because the spirit of pioneer days was still alive"?

2. Drawing Conclusions How do you think the inventions in "Color My World" kept up spirits on the home front during World War I? Why was this important?

Section 4

The War's Impact

Guide to Reading

Big Ideas
Economics and Society The change from wartime to peacetime caused many economic and social problems.

Content Vocabulary
• cost of living *(p. 576)*
• general strike *(p. 577)*
• deport *(p. 580)*

Academic Vocabulary
• widespread *(p. 577)*
• authorities *(p. 580)*

People and Events to Identify
• Calvin Coolidge *(p. 577)*
• Red Scare *(p. 579)*
• A. Mitchell Palmer *(p. 579)*
• J. Edgar Hoover *(p. 580)*

Reading Strategy
Organizing Complete a graphic organizer similar to the one below to list the effects of the end of World War I on the American economy.

NEW YORK CORE CURRICULUM
U.S. History and Government

Unit 4:
II.B.1.d United States reaction to the Russian Revolution
II.C.4 Red Scare, 1918–1919

Unit 5:
I.A.1 War's effects on gender roles, on African-Americans, and other minority groups
I.A.3 Return to "normalcy": 1918–1921
I.B.1 Post World War I recession

America's victory overseas led to turmoil at home. The end of the wartime economy led to a depression and fears of communism, as strikes, riots, and bombings took place.

An Economy in Turmoil

MAIN Idea The country suffered economic uncertainty, strikes, and riots in the year after the war.

HISTORY AND YOU Do you know anyone who has participated in a strike? Read why millions of workers went on strike in 1919.

With the war over, Americans welcomed the soldiers back as heroes. Parades were thrown in their honor, and a new organization, the American Legion, was created to support the veterans. But their arrival home was also bittersweet. Two million men now needed to find jobs in an economy that was shutting down its production of war materials and sliding into recession.

When the war ended, government agencies removed their controls from the economy. People raced to buy goods that had been rationed, while businesses rapidly raised prices they had been forced to keep low during the war. The result was rapid inflation. In 1919 prices rose more than 15 percent. Inflation greatly increased the **cost of living**— the cost of food, clothing, shelter, and other essentials that people need to survive. Orders for war materials evaporated, so factories laid off workers. Soldiers returned home looking for civilian employment but found jobs scarce. In short, 1919 was a year of economic turmoil.

Inflation Leads to Strikes

Many companies had been forced to raise wages during the war, but inflation now threatened to wipe out the gains workers had made. While workers wanted higher wages to keep up with inflation, companies resisted because inflation was also driving up their operating costs.

During the war, the number of workers in unions had increased dramatically. By the time the war ended, workers were better organized and much more capable of implementing strikes. Many business leaders, on the other hand, were determined to break the power of the unions and roll back the gains labor had made. These circumstances led to an enormous wave of strikes in 1919. By the end of the year, more than 3,600 strikes involving more than 4 million workers had taken place.

▲ National Guard troops get rioting under control in Boston during the Police Strike of 1919

Workers on Strike, 1916–1921

Graph: Thousands of Workers (y-axis: 1,000 to 4,500) vs. Year (x-axis: 1916–1921). The line starts around 1,500 in 1916, dips to about 1,250 in 1917–1918, peaks at about 4,200 in 1919, then declines to about 1,500 in 1920 and 1,200 in 1921.

Analyzing VISUALS

1. **Evaluating** Why do you think strikes in 1919 worried the government more than strikes in previous years?

2. **Making Inferences** Why do you think the Boston Police Strike received so much attention? Why were officials willing to use military force in Boston so quickly?

The Seattle General Strike The first major strike took place in Seattle, where some 35,000 shipyard workers walked off the job demanding higher wages and shorter hours. Other unions in Seattle soon joined the shipyard workers and organized a general strike.

A **general strike** is a strike that involves all workers in a community, not just workers in a particular industry. The Seattle general strike involved more than 60,000 people and paralyzed the city for five days. Although the strikers returned to work without making any gains, their actions worried many Americans because the general strike was a common tactic used in Europe by communists and other radical groups.

The Boston Police Strike Perhaps the most famous strike of 1919 took place in Boston, where roughly 75 percent of the police force walked off the job. Riots and looting soon erupted in the city, forcing the governor, **Calvin Coolidge,** to call in the National Guard. When the strikers tried to return to work, the police commissioner then fired the strikers and hired a new police force instead.

Despite protests, Coolidge agreed that the men should be fired, declaring: "There is no right to strike against the public safety by anybody, anywhere, anytime." Coolidge's response earned him **widespread** public support and convinced the Republicans to make him their vice presidential candidate in the 1920 election.

The Steel Strike Shortly after the police strike ended, one of the largest strikes in American history began when an estimated 350,000 steelworkers went on strike for higher pay, shorter hours, and recognition of their union. Elbert H. Gary, the head of U.S. Steel, refused even to talk to union leaders. Instead, he set out to break the union by using anti-immigrant feelings to divide the workers.

Many steelworkers were immigrants. The company blamed the strike on foreign radicals and called for loyal Americans to return to work. Meanwhile, to keep the mills running, the company hired African Americans and Mexicans as replacement workers. Clashes between company guards and strikers were frequent. In Gary, Indiana, a riot left 18 strikers dead. The strike collapsed in early 1920 and its failure set back the union cause in the steel industry. Steel workers remained unorganized until 1941.

Racial Unrest

The economic turmoil after the war also contributed to widespread racial unrest. Many African Americans had moved north during the war to take factory jobs. As people began to be laid off and returning soldiers found it hard to find work and affordable housing, many gave in to feelings of racism and blamed African Americans for taking their jobs. Frustration and racism combined to produce violence.

In the summer of 1919, 25 race riots broke out across the nation. African American leader James Weldon Johnson called the summer of 1919, "the red summer" because of the amount of blood that was spilled. The riots began in July, when a mob of angry white people burned shops and homes in an African American neighborhood in Longview, Texas. A week later, in Washington, D.C., gangs of African Americans and whites fought each other for four days before troops got the riots under control.

The worst violence occurred in Chicago. On a hot July day, African Americans went to a whites-only beach. Both sides began throwing stones at each other. Whites also threw stones at an African American teenager swimming near the beach to prevent him from coming ashore, and he drowned. A full-scale riot then erupted in the city.

Angry African Americans attacked white neighborhoods while whites attacked African American neighborhoods. The Chicago riot lasted for almost two weeks and the government was forced to send in National Guard troops to impose order. By the time the rioting ended, 38 people had been killed—15 white and 23 black—and over 500 had been injured.

The race riots of 1919 disillusioned some African Americans who felt their wartime contributions had been for nothing. For others, however, the wartime struggle for democracy encouraged them to fight for their rights at home.

The race riots of 1919 were different in one respect. For the first time, African Americans organized and fought back against the white mobs. Many African Americans also dedicated themselves to fighting for their rights politically. The NAACP surged in membership after the war, and in 1919, it launched a new campaign for a federal law against lynching.

✔ Reading Check Analyzing Why did the end of the war lead to race riots?

PAST & PRESENT

Terrorists Attack America

When terrorists attacked the United States on September 11, 2001, many Americans believed the United States was experiencing something new—multiple attacks by a terrorist organization.

It is almost forgotten by the American people that in June 1919, eight bombs exploded in eight American cities within minutes of each other, and another 30 bombs sent through the mail were intercepted before they exploded. In September 1920 an even larger bomb exploded in New York. As it did after 9/11, the United States government created a new federal agency to protect the American people. In 1919 the government created the General Intelligence Division, headed by Herbert Hoover, who later headed the FBI. In 2002 the government created the Department of Homeland Security.

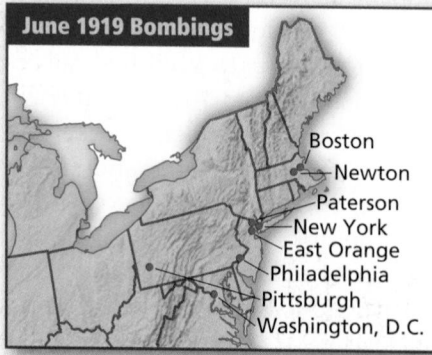

June 1919 Bombings

Boston
Newton
Paterson
New York
East Orange
Philadelphia
Pittsburgh
Washington, D.C.

September, 1920

▲ *In September 1920, a bomb made of 100 lbs. of dynamite and 500 lbs. of steel fragments exploded in New York City, killing 38 people and injuring 300 others.*

The Red Scare

MAIN Idea Fear of a Communist revolution caused a nationwide panic.

HISTORY AND YOU Many Americans believed the country was in danger in 1919. Read on to see similarities with today's concerns about security.

The wave of strikes in 1919 helped to fuel fears that Communists were conspiring to start a revolution in the United States. Americans had been stunned when Communists seized power in Russia and negotiated a separate peace agreement with Germany. Many Americans viewed this as a betrayal, and hostility toward Communists increased. Communism became associated with disloyalty and treachery.

Americans had long been suspicious of communist ideas. Since the late 1800s, many Americans had accused immigrants of importing radical socialist and communist ideas and blamed them for labor unrest and violence. Events in Russia seemed to justify fears of a Communist revolution. The Soviet establishment of the Communist International in 1919—an organization for coordinating Communist parties in other countries—appeared to be further proof of a growing threat.

The strikes of 1919 fueled fears that Communists, or "reds," as they were called, might seize power. This led to a nationwide panic known as the **Red Scare.** Many people were particularly concerned about workers using strikes to start a revolution. Seattle's mayor, Ole Hanson, for example, claimed that the Seattle general strike was part of an attempt to "take possession of our American government and try to duplicate the anarchy of Russia."

In April, the postal service intercepted more than 30 parcels containing homemade bombs addressed to prominent Americans. In May, union members, socialists, and communists organized a parade in Cleveland to protest the jailing of American Socialist Party leader Eugene Debs. The parade turned into a series of riots. By the time police and army units got the violence under control, two people were dead and another 40 were injured.

In June, eight bombs in eight cities exploded within minutes of one another, suggesting a nationwide conspiracy. One of them damaged the home of United States Attorney General **A. Mitchell Palmer.** Most people believed the bombings were the work of radicals trying to destroy the American way of life.

September, 2001

▼ *Firefighters search for victims in the rubble of the World Trade Center in September 2001.*

MAKING CONNECTIONS

1. **Comparing** How was the government's response to the 1919 and 1920 attacks similar to its response to the attacks of September 11, 2001? How was it different?

2. **Synthesizing** How do you think the government should have responded to the bombings of 1919 and 1920? In what ways were the government's policies inappropriate?

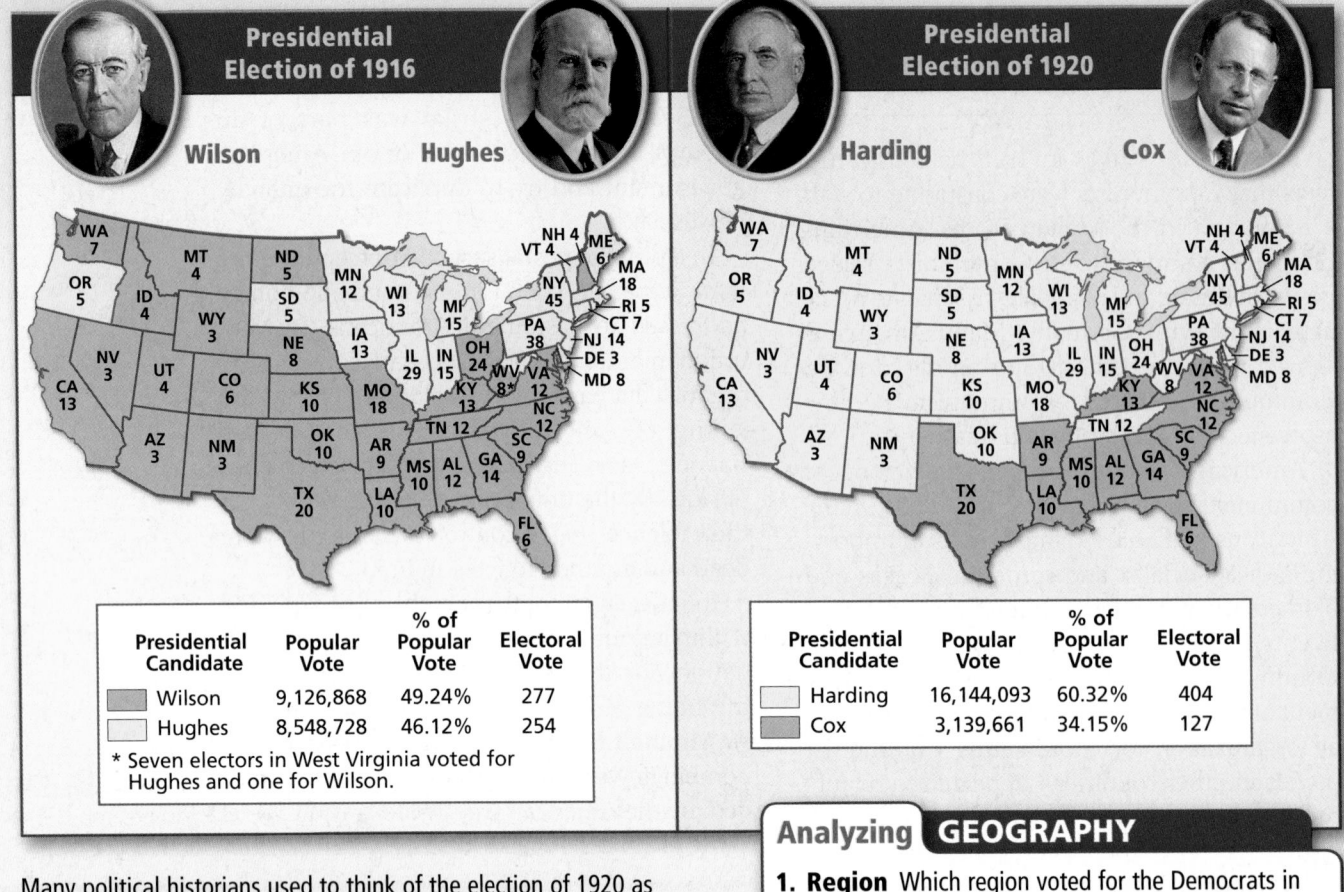

Presidential Election of 1916

Wilson   Hughes

Presidential Candidate	Popular Vote	% of Popular Vote	Electoral Vote
Wilson	9,126,868	49.24%	277
Hughes	8,548,728	46.12%	254

* Seven electors in West Virginia voted for Hughes and one for Wilson.

Presidential Election of 1920

Harding   Cox

Presidential Candidate	Popular Vote	% of Popular Vote	Electoral Vote
Harding	16,144,093	60.32%	404
Cox	3,139,661	34.15%	127

Many political historians used to think of the election of 1920 as the end of the Progressive Era. It is true that the 1920 election represented a dramatic shift from the progressive Woodrow Wilson to the much more traditionally conservative Warren Harding. But did the election really show a great change in voting habits throughout the country?

Analyzing GEOGRAPHY

1. **Region** Which region voted for the Democrats in both elections? Which region voted Republican in both elections?

2. **Region** What region of the country changed its vote between 1916 and 1920? Why do you think this happened? Does this change suggest people's views of progressivism had changed?

The Palmer Raids

Declaring that a "blaze of revolution" was "burning up the foundations of society," Palmer took action. He established a special division within the Justice Department, the General Intelligence Division. This division, headed by **J. Edgar Hoover,** eventually became the Federal Bureau of Investigation (FBI).

Although evidence pointed to no single group as the bombers, Palmer's agents targeted the foreign-born. On November 7, 1919, Palmer ordered a series of raids on offices of the Union of Russian Workers in 12 cities. Less than seven weeks later, a transport ship left New York for Russia carrying 249 immigrants who had been deported, or expelled from the country.

In January 1920, Palmer ordered another series of raids, this time on the headquarters of various radical organizations. Nearly 6,000 people were arrested. That same month, the New York state legislature expelled five members of the Socialist Party who had been elected to the legislature. Over the next few months, 32 states passed sedition laws making it illegal to join groups advocating revolution. Palmer's raids continued until the spring of 1920. **Authorities** detained thousands of suspects and nearly 600 people were **deported.**

Palmer's agents often ignored the civil liberties of the suspects. Officers entered homes and offices without search warrants. People were mistreated. Some were jailed for indefinite periods of time and were not allowed to talk to their attorneys. Many of the immigrants who were deported were never granted a court hearing to challenge the evidence against them or to contest the deportation order.

For a while, Palmer was regarded as a national hero. His raids, however, failed to turn up any hard evidence of revolutionary conspiracy. When his prediction that violence would rock the nation on May Day 1920—a celebration of workers in Europe—proved wrong, Palmer lost much of his credibility and support.

The Red Scare greatly influenced people's attitudes during the 1920s. Americans often linked radicalism with immigrants, and that attitude led to a call for Congress to limit immigration.

The Election of 1920

Economic problems, labor unrest, and racial tensions, as well as the fresh memories of World War I, all combined to create a general sense of disillusionment in the United States. By 1920 Americans wanted an end to the upheaval.

During the 1920 campaign, Ohio governor James M. Cox and his running mate, Assistant Secretary of the Navy Franklin D. Roosevelt, ran on a platform of progressive ideals. President Wilson tried to convince the Democrats to make the campaign a referendum on the Treaty of Versailles and the League of Nations, but the party chose not to take a strong stand on the issue for fear of alienating voters.

The Republican candidate, Warren G. Harding, called for a return to "normalcy." His vice-presidential running mate, Calvin Coolidge, was chosen because people admired the way he had handled the Boston police strike. Harding argued that what the United States needed was a return to simpler days before the Progressive Era reforms:

PRIMARY SOURCE

"[Our] present need is not heroics, but healing; not nostrums, but normalcy; not revolution, but [bold] restoration; not agitation, but adjustment; not surgery, but serenity; not the dramatic, but the dispassionate; . . . not submergence in internationality, but sustainment in triumphant nationality."

—quoted in *Portrait of a Nation*

Harding's sentiments struck a chord with voters, and he won the election by a landslide margin of over 7 million votes. Many Americans were weary of more crusades to reform society and the world. They hoped to put the country's racial and labor unrest and economic troubles behind them and build a more prosperous and stable society.

✓ Reading Check **Examining** After World War I, why were Americans suspicious of some union leaders?

Section 4 REVIEW

Vocabulary

1. **Explain** the significance of: cost of living, general strike, Calvin Coolidge, Red Scare, A. Mitchell Palmer, J. Edgar Hoover, deport.

Main Ideas

2. **Identifying** Use a chart like the one below to list the various causes of labor unrest in 1919.

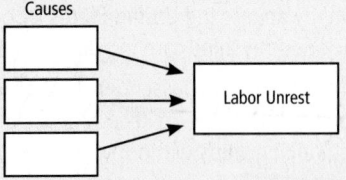

3. **Describing** What events made many Americans believe a revolution was imminent in 1919?

Critical Thinking

4. **Big Ideas** Why did the end of World War I bring such turmoil to the United States?

5. **Analyzing** Provide evidence to explain whether or not the Palmer raids deprived some people of their civil rights.

6. **Analyzing Visuals** Examine the photograph on page 577. What do you notice about the rioters? What does this tell you about the riots?

Writing About History

7. **Persuasive Writing** Imagine that you are a European immigrant working in a factory in the United States in 1919. Write a letter to a relative in Europe describing the feelings of Americans toward you and other immigrants.

History ONLINE

Study Central™ To review this section, go to glencoe.com and click on Study Central.

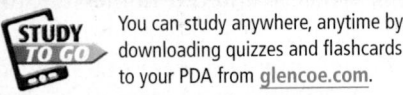

STUDY TO GO

You can study anywhere, anytime by downloading quizzes and flashcards to your PDA from glencoe.com.

Causes of America's Entry Into World War I

- Americans hear stories of German atrocities and many become anti-German.

- Many of President Wilson's advisors support the Allies.

- American banks lend the Allies large amounts of money and American companies sell the Allies food, weapons, and military supplies.

- Germany angers the United States by ordering submarines to attack neutral ships carrying goods to the Allies.

- Germany sinks the passenger ships *Lusitania* and *Sussex*, enraging Americans. To keep America out of the war, Germany stops sinking ships without warning in 1916.

- Germany tries to make an alliance with Mexico, further angering Americans.

- In a last attempt to win the war, Germany orders submarines to attack ships without warning in 1917; six American ships are sunk.

- The United States declares war, April 1917.

▶ German U-boats helped cause the United States to enter the war.

▲ World War I enabled women to take jobs traditionally reserved for men.

Social and Cultural Effects of World War I

- Northern factories recruit African Americans from the rural South; African Americans migrate to northern cities in large numbers, improving their standard of living and changing politics in northern cities.

- In search of workers, companies also hire large numbers of women for jobs traditionally reserved for men.

- Labor shortages cause many Mexicans to migrate north to take work in the United States. Many Hispanic Americans leave farmwork for factory work.

- Laws limiting civil rights in wartime are upheld by the Supreme Court in the cases of *Schenck* v. *U.S.* and *Abrams* v. *U.S.*

- During the war, anti-German feelings are widespread.

- The end of the war leads to economic and social tensions; many workers go on strike; race riots erupt in many cities.

- After the war, many Americans become anti-immigrant, anti-communist, and anti-union.

NEW YORK REGENTS EXAM PRACTICE

TEST-TAKING TIP

Eliminate answers that do not make sense. For instance, if an answer refers to World War II, you know it cannot be correct.

Part I

Directions (1–10): For each statement or question, write on a separate sheet of paper the number of the word or expression that, of those given, best completes the statement or answers the question.

1 Which of the following was a primary cause of World War I?

   (1) a complex set of alliances among European nations

   (2) the exile of Mexican General Victoriano Huerta

   (3) the dissatisfaction of Russian peasants

   (4) the breakup of the Austro-Hungarian Empire

2 The event that triggered the American entry into World War I was

   (1) the sinking of the *Lusitania*.

   (2) the resumption of unrestricted submarine warfare.

   (3) the invasion of neutral Belgium.

   (4) the interception of the Zimmermann telegram.

3 Which federal mobilization agency introduced daylight savings time and shortened the workweek?

   (1) War Industries Board

   (2) Committee on Public Information

   (3) National War Labor Board

   (4) Fuel Administration

4 Both the Espionage Act and the Sedition Act of 1918 were designed to

   (1) provide plans for rebuilding Germany.

   (2) help the British and French economies.

   (3) limit opposition to the war in the United States.

   (4) protect the rights of German Americans.

5 Which of the following technologies was first used during World War I?

   (1) tanks

   (2) cannons

   (3) aircraft carriers

   (4) hot-air balloons

6 Why did the Senate reject the Versailles Treaty?

   (1) to keep the United States free from foreign entanglements

   (2) to express opposition to the harsh sanctions imposed on Germany

   (3) to avoid the dues for membership in the League of Nations

   (4) to reduce United States military forces in Europe

7 The Red Scare was a fear that

   (1) nuclear power would result in widespread destruction in the United States.

   (2) Communists would seize power in the United States.

   (3) fire would spread quickly through overcrowded American cities.

   (4) the Soviet Union would develop an atomic bomb.

8 The organization that eventually became the Federal Bureau of Investigation was originally formed to

   (1) uncover German spies during World War I.

   (2) spread propaganda within the United States in support of World War I.

   (3) infiltrate unions to prevent strikes.

   (4) raid the headquarters of radical organizations in order to look for evidence of a Communist conspiracy.

Need Extra Help?

If You Missed Questions . . .	1	2	3	4	5	6	7	8
Go to Page . . .	548–550	554–555	556–557	558	565–567	571–573	579	580

[OVER]

Base your answer to question 9 on the map below and your knowledge of Chapter 16.

Europe after WWI

9 Which countries lost territory as a result of World War I?

(1) Germany, Russia, France

(2) Germany, France, England

(3) Germany, Italy, Austria-Hungary

(4) Germany, Austria-Hungary, Russia

10 How did Congress ensure that the United States had enough troops to serve in World War I?

(1) Congress allowed women to serve in combat.

(2) The Selective Service Act of 1917 required all men ages 21 to 30 to register for the draft.

(3) Congress allowed African Americans to serve in the armed forces.

(4) Congress offered a free education and cheap land prices to anyone willing to serve.

Part II Thematic Essay Question

Directions: Write a well-organized essay that includes an introduction, several paragraphs addressing the task below, and a conclusion.

Theme: World War I

> Prior to World War I, European countries were at odds over territory and the right of self-determination. Eventually, these differences led to World War I. The United States tried to remain neutral but ultimately joined the war.

> • Discuss the causes of World War I. In your discussion, include specific details that explain why each nation became involved in the war.
>
> • Evaluate the effectiveness of U.S. troops and the Allies in the fight against the Axis powers.

Guidelines:

In your essay, be sure to:

• Develop all aspects of the task.

• Support the theme with relevant facts, examples, and details.

• Use a logical and clear plan of organization, including an introduction and a conclusion that are beyond a restatement of the theme.

Part III Document-Based Question

This question is based on the accompanying documents. This question is designed to test your ability to work with historical documents. Some of the documents have been edited for the purposes of the question. As you analyze the documents, take into account the source of each document and any point of view that may be presented in the document.

Historical Context:

Following World War I, the Treaty of Versailles did not fully implement Wilson's Fourteen Points. However, it did call for the creation of the League of Nations. Wilson attempted to rally support in the Senate for ratification of the treaty, but opposition to the League of Nations had grown strong.

Need Extra Help?		
If You Missed Questions . . .	9	10
Go to Page . . .	570–571	560–561

Task:

Using information from the documents and your knowledge of United States history, answer the questions that follow each document in Part A. Your answers to the questions will help you write the Part B essay in which you will be asked to

- Discuss the goals of the Fourteen Points and the reasons why the Treaty of Versailles did not implement these points more fully.
- Explain the factors for the Senate's failure to ratify the Treaty of Versailles.

Part A
Short-Answer Questions

Directions: Analyze the documents and answer the short-answer questions that follow each document on a separate sheet of paper.

Document 1

"I personally went over this reservation to Article 10 ... with groups of Senators and with individual members. Finally, I asked Senator McCumber. ... we took up the reservation. ... After much discussion, he and I agreed upon the reservation ... presented to the Senate and finally adopted. The reservation was as follows:

'The United States assumed no obligation to preserve the territorial integrity or political independence of any country or to interfere in controversies between nations—whether members of the league or not—under the provisions of Article 10 or to employ the military or naval forces of the United States under any article of the treaty for any purpose, unless in any particular case the Congress, which, under the Constitution, has the sole power to declare war or authorize the employment of the military or naval forces of the United States, shall by act or joint resolution so provide.'"

Source: Henry Cabot Lodge, *The Senate and the League of Nations*, Charles Scribner's Sons

1 Based on this document, under what circumstances may the United States send troops to protect political independence abroad?

Need Extra Help?			
If You Missed Questions . . .	1	2	Essay
Go to Page . . .	570–573	570–573	570–573

Document 2

Letter from Robert Lansing to Frank L. Polk, 19 November 1919:

"The treaty when laid before the Senate was tremendously handicapped by two things: first, the Covenant ... was open to valid criticism because it apparently was in defiance of certain constitutional provisions; and second, the insensate animosity of a considerable group of Republican Senators to the President personally. This latter feeling enhanced the objections to the League because he ... was looked upon as author. ... If his enemies could practically destroy the League or render it worthless, they were particularly desirous of doing so because they felt that it would humble his pride of authorship and prove to the world that he was by no means so great and powerful as had been supposed."

Source: Arthur S. Link, ed. *The Papers of Woodrow Wilson*, Princeton University Press

2 What did Lansing believe were two major reasons for the failure of ratification?

Part B
Essay

Directions: Reread the task at the top left and write a well-organized essay that includes an introduction, several paragraphs, and a conclusion. Use evidence from the documents in your essay. Support your response with relevant facts, examples, and details. Include additional outside information.

Guidelines:

In your essay, be sure to:

- Develop all aspects of the task
- Incorporate information from the documents
- Incorporate relevant outside information
- Use a logical and clear plan of organization, including an introduction and conclusion that are beyond a restatement of the theme

History ONLINE

For additional test practice, use Self-Check Quizzes—Chapter 16 at glencoe.com.

Unit 6

Boom and Bust
1920–1941

Why It Matters

In the 1920s, new technology, including automobiles, airplanes, radios, and electric appliances helped create a booming economy with rising stock prices and increased consumer spending. In 1929, economic problems triggered the Great Depression. This led to increased federal regulation of the economy and several new programs, such as Social Security as the federal government took on the task of protecting people from economic hardship

The Great White Way, Times Square, New York, 1925

Chapter 17

The Jazz Age
1921–1929

Joe "King" Oliver's jazz band plays in San Francisco in 1921, with singer Lil Hardin.

1921
• Washington Conference convenes

Harding 1921–1923

1922
• Claude McKay's *Harlem Shadows* is published

1923
• Teapot Dome scandal erupts

Coolidge 1923–1929

1924
• Congress passes National Origins Act

1925
• Scopes trial begins

U.S. PRESIDENTS

U.S. EVENTS
1921   1923   1925

WORLD EVENTS

1921
• Ireland becomes independent country

1922
• Mussolini and Fascists take power in Italy

1923
• France invades Ruhr
• Hitler writes *Mein Kampf*

1924
• Vladimir Lenin dies

Why Does Culture Change?

In the 1920s, technology spurred economic growth and cultural change. Although not everyone approved, young people adopted new styles of dress, listened to jazz music, and had more independence than earlier generations.

- *What technologies changed life in the 1920s?*
- *How do you think the invention of radio and movies changed popular culture?*

1927
- Lindbergh completes first solo transatlantic flight

Hoover
1929–1933

1928
- Kellogg-Briand Pact signed

1927   1929

1926
- British General Strike paralyzes British economy

1927
- Stalin gains control of Soviet Union

1928
- Chiang Kai-shek becomes leader of China

FOLDABLES™

Categorizing the Harlem Renaissance
Create a Trifold Book Foldable to present a brief biography, with artistic works, of major figures in the Harlem Renaissance under the category of writers, poets, and musicians. You may want to expand on your entries by using the Internet.

Writers	Poets	Musicians

History ONLINE Chapter Overview
Visit glencoe.com to preview Chapter 17.

The Politics of the 1920s

Guide to Reading

Big Ideas
Economics and Society Government policies helped create prosperity in the 1920s.

Content Vocabulary
- supply-side economics *(p. 593)*
- cooperative individualism *(p. 593)*
- isolationism *(p. 594)*

Academic Vocabulary
- investigation *(p. 591)*
- revelation *(p. 592)*

People and Events to Identify
- Teapot Dome *(p. 591)*
- Charles G. Dawes *(p. 595)*
- Charles Evans Hughes *(p. 595)*
- Kellogg-Briand Pact *(p. 595)*

Reading Strategy
Taking Notes As you read about Presidents Harding and Coolidge, create an outline similar to the one below.

> The Politics of the 1920s
> I. The Harding Administration
>   A.
>   B.
> II.
> III.
>   A.
>   B.

NEW YORK CORE CURRICULUM
U.S. History and Government

Unit 4:
II.D.5 Washington Naval Disarmament Conference (1920s)
II.D.6 Reparations and war debts
II.D.7 Kellogg-Briand Pact (1928)
II.D.8 Establishment of the World Court
Unit 5:
I.A.3 Return to "normalcy": 1918–1921
I.B.2 Avarice and scandal: Teapot Dome
I.B.3 Coolidge prosperity; not for everyone

Warren G. Harding's administration suffered from corruption and scandals. His successor, Calvin Coolidge, worked hard to restore the American public's faith in their government and to promote a healthy economy.

The Harding Administration

MAIN Idea President Harding staffed his administration with political friends from Ohio; his presidency was marred by many scandals.

HISTORY AND YOU If you were choosing teammates, would you pick a friend or a better player? Read on to learn about the problems Harding created by making poor choices for government appointments.

Warren G. Harding was born in 1865 in Corsica, Ohio. In 1898 voters elected Harding to the Ohio General Assembly, where he fit in comfortably with the powerful Ohio Republican political machine. Voters elected him as Ohio's lieutenant governor in 1903 and United States senator in 1914. After serving one term in the Senate, Harding ran for and won the presidency in 1920.

Harding's political philosophy fit in well with the times. In his campaign, he had promised "a return to normalcy," by which he meant "normal" life after the war. His charm and genial manner endeared him to the nation, and people applauded when the open, easygoing atmosphere of the Harding administration replaced the quiet gloom of President Wilson's last years.

Teapot Dome and Other Scandals

Harding made several distinguished appointments to the cabinet, including former Supreme Court Justice Charles Evans Hughes as secretary of state, former Food Administrator Herbert Hoover as secretary of commerce, and business tycoon Andrew Mellon as secretary of the treasury. All three men would play an important role in supporting and shaping the economic prosperity of the 1920s.

Many of Harding's other appointments, however, were disastrous. He gave cabinet posts and other high-level jobs to friends and political allies from Ohio. Harding named Harry M. Daugherty, his campaign manager and boss of the Ohio Republican Party, attorney general. He made his boyhood friend Daniel Crissinger chairman of the Federal Reserve Board and selected Colonel Charles R. Forbes—another Ohio acquaintance—to head the Veterans Bureau.

Harding felt more comfortable among his old poker-playing friends, known as the Ohio Gang, than he did around such sober and

An Administration Plagued by Scandal

▲ "Bargain Day in Washington" shows the U.S. Capitol, the Washington Monument, the army, the White House, and the navy as having been "sold" to the highest bidder.

▲ This cartoon shows politicians on the slippery "White House Highway" trying to outrun the scandal of Teapot Dome.

Analyzing VISUALS — DBQ

1. **Drawing Conclusions** What does the cartoon on the left suggest about politicians?
2. **Analyzing** What does the cartoon on the right imply about corruption in the federal government?

serious people as Herbert Hoover. According to Alice Roosevelt Longworth, the White House study resembled a speakeasy.

PRIMARY SOURCE

"The air [would be] heavy with tobacco smoke, trays with bottles containing every imaginable brand of whiskey . . . cards and poker chips at hand—a general atmosphere of waistcoat unbuttoned, feet on desk, and spittoons alongside."

—quoted in *The Perils of Prosperity, 1914–1932*

The Ohio Gang did more than drink, smoke, and play poker with the president. Some members used their positions to sell government jobs, pardons, and protection from prosecution. Forbes sold scarce medical supplies from veterans' hospitals and kept the money for himself, costing the taxpayers about $250 million. When Harding learned what was going on, he complained privately that he had been betrayed. He said that he had no troubles with his enemies, but his friends were a different story: "They're the ones that keep me walking the floor nights!"

In June 1923 Harding left to tour the West. En route from Alaska to California, he became ill with what was probably a heart attack. He died in San Francisco on August 2, shortly before the news of the Forbes scandal broke. Early the next morning, the vice president, Calvin Coolidge, took the oath of office and became president.

The Forbes scandal was only the latest in a series of scandals and accusations that had marked the Harding administration. The most famous scandal, known as **Teapot Dome,** began in early 1922 when Harding's secretary of the interior, Albert B. Fall, secretly allowed private interests to lease lands containing U.S. Navy oil reserves at Teapot Dome, Wyoming, and Elk Hills, California. In return, Fall received bribes from these private interests totaling more than $300,000.

After the *Wall Street Journal* broke the story, the Senate launched an **investigation** that took most of the 1920s to complete. Trials followed; the Supreme Court invalidated the leases in 1927, and in 1929 Secretary Fall became the first cabinet officer in American history to go to prison.

Another Harding administration scandal involved Attorney General Harry Daugherty. During World War I, the federal government had seized a German-owned company in the United States as enemy property. To acquire the company and its valuable chemical patents, a German agent bribed a "go-between" politician, and a portion of the bribe ended up in a bank account that Daugherty controlled.

Under investigation by his own Justice Department, Daugherty refused to turn over requested files and bank records. He also refused to testify under oath, claiming immunity, or freedom from prosecution, on the grounds that he had had confidential dealings with the president. Daugherty's actions disgusted the new president, Calvin Coolidge, who demanded his resignation.

"Silent Cal" Takes Over

Calvin Coolidge was very different from Harding. Harding had enjoyed the easy conversation and company of old friends. Coolidge, joked a critic, could be "silent in five languages." Although he quickly distanced himself from the Harding administration, Coolidge asked the most capable cabinet members—Hughes, Mellon, and Hoover—to remain in the cabinet. Coolidge's philosophy of government was simple. He believed that prosperity rested on business leadership and that part of his job as president was to make sure that government interfered with business and industry as little as possible.

In the year following Harding's death and the **revelations** of the scandals, Coolidge avoided crises and adopted policies to help keep the nation prosperous. He easily won the Republican nomination for president in 1924.

The Republicans campaigned using the slogan "Keep Cool with Coolidge." They promised the American people that the policies that had brought prosperity would continue. Coolidge won the election easily, winning more than half the popular vote and 382 electoral votes.

✔ Reading Check **Analyzing** What do the scandals of the Harding administration have in common with each other?

PRIMARY SOURCE
Coolidge and Prosperity

Critics have accused Calvin Coolidge of catering to big business and cite his comment that the "business of the American people is business." This quote comes from his 1925 speech to the American Society of Newspaper Editors. Examine the graphs and the speech to assess if his policies benefited business at the expense of the public.

PRIMARY SOURCE

"After all, the chief business of the American people is business. They are profoundly concerned with producing, buying, selling, investing and prospering in the world. . . . In all experience, the accumulation of wealth means the multiplication of schools, the increase of knowledge, the dissemination of intelligence, the encouragement of science, the broadening of outlook, the expansion of liberties, the widening of culture. . . . We make no concealment of the fact that we want wealth, but there are many other things that we want very much more. We want peace and honor, and that charity which is so strong an element of all civilization.

The chief ideal of the American people is idealism. I cannot repeat too often that America is a nation of idealists."

—*New York Times,* January 18, 1925

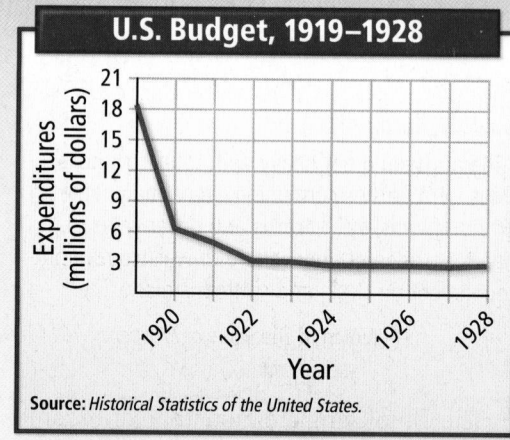

U.S. Budget, 1919–1928

Expenditures (millions of dollars)

Year

Source: *Historical Statistics of the United States.*

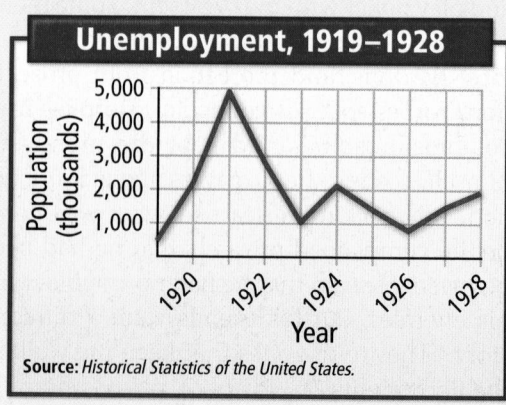

Unemployment, 1919–1928

Population (thousands)

Year

Source: *Historical Statistics of the United States.*

Policies of Prosperity

MAIN Idea During the 1920s, the government cut taxes and spending to encourage economic growth.

HISTORY AND YOU Do you have a sales tax in your state? Do you think taxes are too high? How do you know? Read to learn about changes to American taxes in the 1920s.

Although Harding gave many corrupt friends government jobs, he also selected several highly qualified individuals for his cabinet. Among them were Andrew Mellon and Herbert Hoover. Both of these men were responsible for policies that contributed to the economic growth and prosperity of the 1920s.

At the beginning of the 1920s, the nation had a large national debt, and many people were worried that it would not recover from the postwar recession. Harding chose Andrew Mellon, a successful banker and industrialist, to be secretary of the treasury. Mellon became the chief architect of economic policy and served as secretary of the treasury for three Republican presidents.

When Mellon took office, he had three major goals: to balance the budget, to reduce the government's debt, and to cut taxes. He was convinced these policies would promote economic growth and prosperity. He also firmly believed that the government should apply business principles to its operations.

In 1921 Mellon convinced Congress to create both the Bureau of the Budget to prepare a unified federal budget, and the General Accounting Office to track spending. He then began cutting spending. The federal budget fell from $6.4 billion to less than $3 billion in seven years. He also cut tax rates.

Mellon argued that high tax rates actually reduced the amount of tax money the government collected. If taxes were lower, businesses and consumers would spend and invest their extra money, causing the economy to grow. As the economy grew, Americans would earn more money, and the government would actually collect more taxes at a lower rate than it would if it kept tax rates high. This idea is known today as **supply-side economics,** or "trickle-down" economics.

At Mellon's urging, Congress dramatically reduced tax rates. When Mellon took office, most taxpayers paid 4 percent federal income tax, while wealthy Americans in the highest bracket paid 73 percent. By 1928, Congress had reduced the rate most Americans paid to 0.5 percent and cut the rate for the wealthiest Americans to 25 percent.

Secretary of Commerce Herbert Hoover also sought to promote economic growth. He tried to balance government regulation with his own philosophy of **cooperative individualism.** This idea involved encouraging businesses to form trade associations that would voluntarily share information with the federal government. Hoover believed this system would reduce costs and promote economic efficiency.

To assist businesses, Hoover directed the Bureau of Foreign and Domestic Commerce to find new markets for companies. He also established the Bureau of Aviation to regulate and promote the growth of the airline industry and the Federal Radio Commission to help the young radio industry by regulating radio frequencies and the power of transmitters.

✓ **Reading Check** **Summarizing** What strategies did Mellon use to promote economic growth?

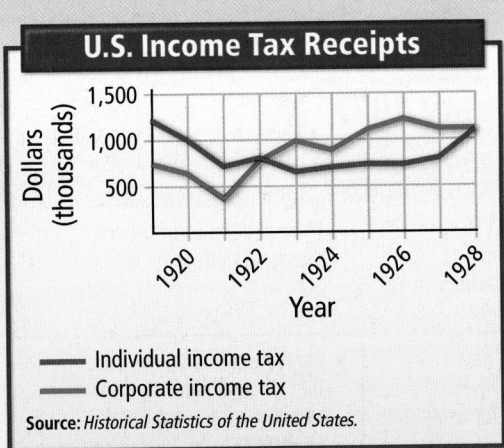

U.S. Income Tax Receipts

Dollars (thousands) — 1,500 / 1,000 / 500

Year — 1920, 1922, 1924, 1926, 1928

— Individual income tax
— Corporate income tax

Source: *Historical Statistics of the United States.*

Analyzing VISUALS **DBQ**

1. **Analyzing Primary Sources** What does Coolidge believe is the point of accumulating wealth? Do you believe that the United States has achieved Coolidge's goals? Explain.

2. **Evaluating** Based on the graphs, what did Coolidge's economic policies achieve in the 1920s?

Trade and Arms Control

MAIN Idea During the 1920s, the United States tried to promote peace and stability through economic policies and arms control agreements.

HISTORY AND YOU Do you remember reading about the Treaty of Versailles and how the United States never ratified it? Read to learn how America initiated other treaties in the 1920s.

Before World War I the United States was a debtor nation. By the end of the war, the situation was reversed. Wartime allies owed the United States more than $10 billion in war debts. By the 1920s, the United States was the dominant economic power in the world. Under the leadership of Secretary of State Charles Evan Hughes, the nation tried to use its economic power to promote peace and stability.

The Myth of Isolationism

The majority of Americans—tired of being entangled in the baffling, hostile, and danger-ous politics of Europe—favored **isolationism.** This is the idea that the United States will be safer and more prosperous if it stays out of world affairs.

To many people at the time, it appeared that the United States had become isolationist. The United States had not ratified the Treaty of Versailles and had not joined the League of Nations. The Permanent Court of International Justice, better known as the World Court, opened in 1921, but the United States refused to join it as well.

Despite appearances, the United States was too powerful and too interconnected with other countries economically to be truly isolationist. Instead of relying on armed force and the collective security of the League of Nations, the United States tried to promote peace by using economic policies and arms control agreements.

The Dawes Plan

America's former allies had difficulty making the payments on their immense war debts. High American tariffs hampered their economic

The Washington Conference, November 1921–February 1922

Treaty	Signers	Terms	Weaknesses
Four-Power Treaty	United States, Great Britain, France, Japan	• All agreed to respect the others' territory in the Pacific • Full and open negotiations in the event of disagreements	• Mutual defense of other co-signers not specified
Five-Power Treaty	United States, Great Britain, France, Japan, Italy	• All agreed to freeze naval production at 1921 levels and halt production of large warships for 10 years • U.S. and Great Britain agreed not to build new naval bases in the western Pacific	• No restrictions on the construction of smaller battle craft such as submarines and naval destroyers • Did not place restrictions on the ground forces
Nine-Power Treaty	United States, Great Britain, France, Japan, Italy, Belgium, China, the Netherlands, Portugal	• All agreed to preserve equal commercial rights to China—a reassertion of the Open Door policy	• No enforcement of the terms of the Open Door policy specified

Analyzing VISUALS

1. **Interpreting Charts** Which countries signed the Five-Power Treaty?

2. **Analyzing** Why do you think the terms of the treaties focused on the Pacific region?

recovery by making it difficult to sell their products in the United States. This meant they could not acquire the money to pay off their war debts. These countries also were receiving reparations—huge cash payments Germany was required to make as punishment for starting the war. These payments, however, were crippling the German economy.

It was vital for the United States that European economies be healthy so that the Europeans could buy American exports and repay their debts. Thus, in 1924, American diplomat **Charles G. Dawes** negotiated an agreement with France, Britain, and Germany by which American banks would make loans to Germany that would enable it to make reparations payments. In exchange, Britain and France would accept less in reparations and pay back more on their war debts.

The Washington Conference

Despite their debts, the major powers were involved in a costly postwar naval arms race. To end the weapons race, the United States invited representatives from eight major countries—Great Britain, France, Italy, China, Japan, Belgium, the Netherlands, and Portugal—to Washington, D.C., to discuss disarmament. The Washington Conference opened on November 12, 1921.

In his address to the delegates, Secretary of State **Charles Evans Hughes** proposed a 10-year moratorium, or halt, on the construction of new warships. He also proposed a list of warships in each country's navy to be destroyed, beginning with some American battleships. The discussions that followed produced the Five-Power Naval Limitation Treaty in which Britain, France, Italy, Japan, and the United States essentially formalized Hughes's proposal.

As a long-term effort to prevent war, the conference had some serious shortcomings. It did nothing to limit land forces. It also angered the Japanese because it required Japan to maintain a smaller navy than either the United States or Great Britain. It did, however, give Americans cause to look forward to a period of peace, recovery, and prosperity.

Abolishing War

The apparent success of the Washington Conference boosted hopes that written agreements could end war altogether. Perhaps the highest expression of that idea occurred when U.S. Secretary of State Frank Kellogg and French Foreign Minister Aristide Briand proposed a treaty to outlaw war. On August 27, 1928, the United States and 14 other nations signed the **Kellogg-Briand Pact.** Although it had no binding force, the pact was hailed as a victory for peace. It stated that all signing nations agreed to abandon war and to settle all disputes by peaceful means. The Kellogg-Briand Pact and the Dawes Plan were perhaps the most notable foreign policy achievements of the Coolidge administration.

Reading Check **Identifying** What problem was the Dawes Plan intended to solve?

Section 1 REVIEW

Vocabulary

1. **Explain** the significance of: Teapot Dome, supply-side economics, cooperative individualism, isolationism, Charles G. Dawes, Charles Evans Hughes, Kellogg-Briand Pact.

Main Ideas

2. **Summarizing** What scandals marred Harding's presidency?

3. **Explaining** What strategies did Andrew Mellon and Herbert Hoover use to stimulate economic growth?

4. **Describing** In what two ways did the United States try to promote peace during the 1920s?

Critical Thinking

5. **Big Ideas** What efforts did the United States make to promote worldwide economic recovery?

6. **Categorizing** Use a graphic organizer like the one below to list the major terms of the treaties resulting from the Washington Conference.

Major Terms of Treaties	

7. **Analyzing Visuals** Examine the charts on page 592. What explanation can you offer for the drop in the United States's budget from 1919 to 1928?

Writing About History

8. **Persuasive Writing** Imagine that you are an American business owner or farmer in the 1920s. Write a letter to your representatives in Congress explaining why you think cutting taxes is a good or bad idea.

History ONLINE
Study Central™ To review this section, go to glencoe.com and click on Study Central.

A Growing Economy

Guide to Reading

Big Ideas
Economics and Society The United States experienced stunning economic growth during the 1920s.

Content Vocabulary
• mass production (p. 596)
• assembly line (p. 596)
• Model T (p. 596)
• welfare capitalism (p. 602)
• open shop (p. 602)

Academic Vocabulary
• disposable (p. 598)
• credit (p. 600)

People and Events to Identify
• Charles Lindbergh (p. 600)

Reading Strategy
Organizing As you read about the booming era of the 1920s, complete a graphic organizer to analyze the causes of economic growth and prosperity in the 1920s.

NEW YORK CORE CURRICULUM
U.S. History and Government

Unit 5:
I.B.3 Coolidge prosperity; not for everyone
I.B.4 Problems on the farm
I.C.1.a The automobile: new industries, products, and services
I.C.1.b Installment buying: consumer durable goods (appliances)
I.C.1.c Real Estate boom and suburban development; its economic and geographic implications: decline of trolleys and trains, improvement of roads
I.C.1.d Entertainment: radio; motion pictures; advertising and cultural homogenization

In the 1920s widespread ownership of automobiles, radios, and other innovations changed how Americans lived. The Coolidge administration encouraged business growth and tried to promote stability in international affairs.

The Rise of New Industries

MAIN Idea Mass production and the assembly line allowed new industries, such as automobile and airplane manufacturing, to grow.

HISTORY AND YOU How would businesses, governments, and your family be affected if air travel did not exist? Read to learn how the transportation industry changed during the 1920s and 1930s.

By the 1920s, the automobile had become an accepted part of American life. In a 1925 survey conducted in Muncie, Indiana, 21 out of 26 families who owned cars did not have bathtubs with running water. When asked why her family decided a car was more important than indoor plumbing, a farm wife explained, "You can't ride to town in a bathtub."

The automobile was just one part of a rising standard of living that Americans experienced in the 1920s. Real per capita earnings soared 22 percent between 1923 and 1929. Meanwhile, as Americans' wages increased, their work hours decreased. In 1923 U.S. Steel cut its daily work shift from 12 hours to 8 hours. In 1926 Henry Ford cut the workweek for his employees from six days to five, and International Harvester, a maker of farm machinery, instituted an annual two-week paid vacation for employees. These changes took place because **mass production,** or large-scale manufacturing done with machinery, increased supply and reduced costs. Workers could be paid more and the consumer goods they bought cost less.

The Assembly Line and the Model T

First adopted by carmaker Henry Ford, the moving **assembly line** divided operations into simple tasks and cut unnecessary motion to a minimum. In 1913 Ford installed the first moving assembly line at his plant in Highland Park, Michigan. By the following year, workers were building an automobile every 93 minutes. Before, the task had taken 12 hours. By 1925 a Ford car was rolling off the line every 10 seconds. Ford was the first person to build factories based on the concept of the assembly line.

Ford's assembly-line product was the **Model T**—affectionately called the "Tin Lizzie" or "Flivver." In 1908, the Model T's first year,

The Car Changes America

Many industries that were needed to build cars prospered. Car manufacturers needed steel for the car body, glass for the windows, and rubber for the tires. The automobile also led to changes in society. People moved to the suburbs, but were less isolated from the benefits of the city. At the same time, there was a decline in mass transportation such as railroads and trolleys.

▲ Cars greatly increased the demand for oil, leading to a boom in the oil business, as shown by the forest of oil wells in Signal Hills, California in 1930. To keep cars refueled, roadside gas stations sprang up across the country.

▲ Cars allowed people greater mobility and freedom. These young women drove to the country to have a picnic.

▶ The auto industry spurred a boom in other industries, as well. These workers at Goodyear Tire and Rubber in Akron, Ohio, are removing car tires from curing pits.

▲ The car let people live further out in the suburbs and commute to jobs in the city.

Analyzing VISUALS · DBQ

1. **Determining Cause and Effect** How did the automobile help other industries grow? Which industries were most affected?

2. **Drawing Conclusions** Based on the images above, how did the car change people's lives?

---

it sold for $850. In 1914 mass production reduced the price to $490. Three years later, improved assembly-line methods and a high volume of sales brought the price down to $360. By 1924 Model Ts were selling for $295, and Ford sold millions of them. His business philosophy was: lower the cost per car and thereby increase the volume of sales.

The low prices made possible by Ford's mass-production methods not only created an immense market for his cars but also spawned imitators. By the mid-1920s, other car manufacturers, notably General Motors and Chrysler, competed successfully with Ford. The auto industry also spurred growth in other industries, such as rubber, plate glass, nickel, and lead. The auto industry alone consumed 15 percent of the nation's steel and led to a huge expansion of the petroleum industry.

High Wages for Workers Ford also increased his workers' wages in 1914 to $5 a day (doubling their pay) and reduced the workday to eight-hour shifts. Ford took these dramatic steps to build up workers' loyalty and to undercut union organizers.

There were strings attached, however. Ford created a "Sociological Department," which set requirements workers had to meet. For example, renting space in one's home to nonfamily members was strictly forbidden. Investigators visited employees' homes to verify their eligibility and workers who broke the rules could be disqualified from extra pay, suspended, or even fired.

The Social Impact of the Automobile

Cars revolutionized American life. They eased the isolation of rural life and enabled more people to live farther from work. An entirely new kind of worker, the auto commuter, appeared. Since commuters could drive from their homes in suburbia to their workplaces, other forms of urban transportation, such as the trolley, became less popular.

Consumer Goods

In response to rising **disposable** income, many other new goods came on the market. Americans bought such innovations as electric razors, facial tissues, frozen foods, and home hair color.

Companies created many new products for the home. As indoor plumbing became more common, Americans' concern for hygiene led to the development of numerous household cleaning products. By appealing to people's health concerns, advertisers convinced homemakers to buy cleansers in hopes of protecting their families from disease.

New appliances advertised as labor-savers changed the home. Electric irons, vacuum cleaners, washing machines, and refrigerators changed the way people cleaned their homes and prepared meals.

Another lucrative category of consumer products focused on Americans' concern with fashion and youthful appearance. Mouthwash, deodorants, cosmetics, and perfumes became popular products in the 1920s.

Birth of the Airline Industry

In the early 1900s, many people were trying to build the first powered airplane that could

TECHNOLOGY & HISTORY

Labor- and Time-saving Machines The technology of the 1920s changed the way many people lived. Applying electric motors to items such as washers, dryers, food mixers, and refrigerators revolutionized household tasks. Improved technology helped raise many Americans' standard of living.

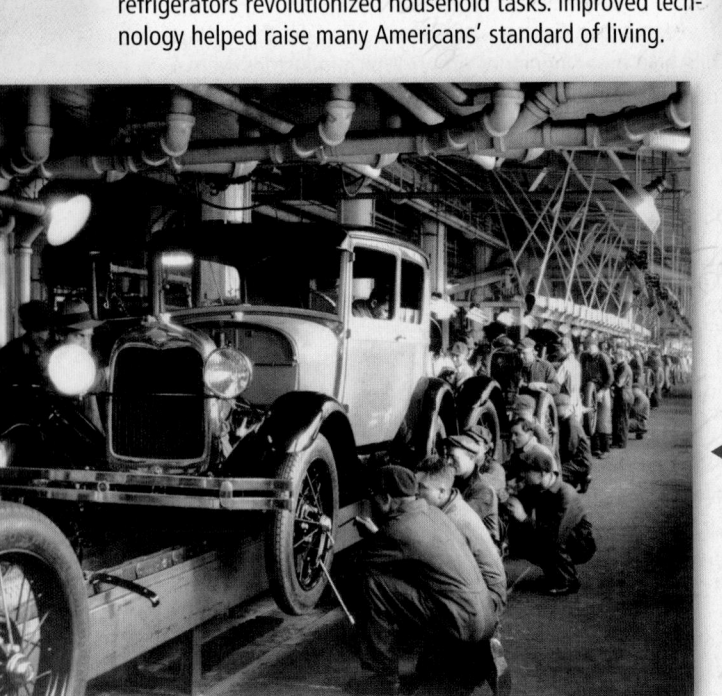

◀ **Assembly Lines Reduce Prices**

The moving assembly line and standardized parts made auto assembly fast, efficient and cheap. As a result, most Americans could afford to buy a car.

Electric Appliances Save Time and Labor

New electrical appliances changed life for the growing middle class that could afford them. Refrigerators, such as the 1926 Kelvinator (above left) made it practical to buy and store larger quantities of food. The electric washer with hand wringer (above center) and the vacuum cleaner saved cleaning time. The Air-Way Sanitizor vacuum cleaner (above right) was the first to have a disposable bag.

carry a human being. Samuel Langley, secretary of the Smithsonian Institution, was perhaps best known for his attempts at the time. Langley had built small model airplanes powered by steam engines, and the War Department had awarded him $50,000 to build an airplane that could carry a person. On December 8, 1903, Langley demonstrated his plane to government officials in Washington, D.C. Unfortunately, his plane broke apart on takeoff and crashed into the Potomac River.

The War Department, in its final report on the Langley project, concluded that "[W]e are still far from the ultimate goal, and it would seem as if years of constant work and study by experts, together with the expenditure of thousands of dollars, would still be necessary before we can hope to produce an apparatus of practical utility on these lines."

Nine days later, Wilbur and Orville Wright, two inventors from Dayton, Ohio, tested the airplane they had built using only $1,000 of their personal savings. The Wright brothers had carefully studied the problems of earlier airplanes and had designed one with better wings, a more efficient propeller, and a strong but very light engine. On December 17, 1903, at Kitty Hawk, North Carolina, Orville made the first crewed, powered flight in history.

After the Wright brothers' successful flight, the aviation industry began developing rapidly. Leading the way was American inventor Glenn Curtiss. Curtiss owned a motorcycle company in Hammondsport, New York. Fascinated by airplanes, he agreed in 1907 to become director of experiments at the Aerial Experiment Association, an organization that Alexander Graham Bell founded. Within a year, Curtiss had invented ailerons—surfaces attached to wings that can be tilted to steer the plane. Ailerons made it possible to build rigid wings and much larger aircraft. They are still used today.

Curtiss's company began building aircraft and sold the first airplanes in the United States. The company grew from a single factory to a huge industrial enterprise during World War I, as orders for his biplanes and engines flooded in from Allied governments. Although Curtiss retired in 1920, his inventions made possible the airline industry that emerged in the 1920s.

Airlines Speed Travel

The aviation industry developed quickly after the Wright brothers' first successful flight in 1903 (above). Below, passengers are shown boarding a Northwest Orient Airlines Ford Tri-motor. Although seating was cramped (right), passenger airlines carried increasing numbers of people in the 1920s.

Radio Links the Nation Together ▶

Commercial radio grew rapidly in the 1920s. It helped create a national community as people across the country could listen to the same music, sports, news, and entertainment programs. The technicians shown at right are preparing for the first NBC radio show, which was broadcast in 1926.

Analyzing VISUALS **DBQ**

1. **Making Connections** Which of the inventions pictured is most important to your life? Which do you think is most important to the nation as a whole?

2. **Making Generalizations** How have advances in transportation and communication changed life in the United States in the past 100 years?

After Curtiss and other entrepreneurs started building practical aircraft, the federal government began to support the airline industry. President Wilson's postmaster general introduced the world's first regular airmail service in 1918 by hiring pilots to fly mail between Washington, D.C., and New York. In 1919 the Post Office expanded airmail service across the continent.

The aviation industry received an economic boost in 1925 when Congress passed the Kelly Act, authorizing postal officials to contract with private airplane operators to carry mail. The following year Congress passed the Air Commerce Act, which provided federal aid for building airports. Former airmail pilot **Charles Lindbergh** made an amazing transatlantic solo flight in 1927, showing the possibilities of commercial aviation. By the end of 1928, 48 airlines were serving 355 American cities.

The Radio Industry

In 1913 Edwin Armstrong, an American engineer, invented a special circuit that made it practical to transmit sound via long-range radio. The radio industry began a few years later. In November 1920 the Westinghouse Company broadcast the news of Harding's landslide election victory from station KDKA in Pittsburgh—one of the first public broadcasts in history. That success persuaded Westinghouse to open other stations.

In 1926 the National Broadcasting Company (NBC) set up a network of stations to broadcast daily programs. By 1927, almost 700 stations dotted the country. Sales of radio equipment grew from $12.2 million in 1921 to $842.5 million in 1929, by which time 10 million radios were in use across the country.

In 1928 the Columbia Broadcasting System (CBS) assembled a coast-to-coast network of stations to rival NBC. The two networks sold advertising time and hired musicians, actors, and comedians from vaudeville, movies, and the nightclub circuit to appear on their shows. Americans experienced the first presidential election campaign to use radio broadcasts in 1928, when the radio networks sold more than $1 million in advertising time to the Republican and Democratic Parties.

✓Reading Check **Analyzing** How did the automobile change the way people lived?

The Consumer Society

MAIN Idea Consumer credit and advertising helped to create a nation of consumers.

HISTORY AND YOU Have you ever purchased something on credit or bought an item because of advertising? Read to discover the beginnings of the widespread consumer culture in America.

Higher wages and shorter workdays resulted in a decade-long buying spree that kept the economy booming. Shifting from traditional attitudes of thrift and prudence, Americans in the 1920s enthusiastically accepted their new role as consumers.

Easy Consumer Credit

One notable aspect of the economic boom was the growth of individual borrowing. **Credit** had been available before the 1920s, but most Americans had considered debt shameful. Now, however, attitudes toward debt started changing as people began believing in their ability to pay their debts over time. Many

PRIMARY SOURCE
Advertising to Consumers

The early advertising age used techniques that continue to persuade consumers today. Easy credit terms and installment plans, envy of peers and neighbors, and the link of a product with a famous, attractive person all convinced people that they needed the flood of newly available consumer goods.

listened to the sales pitch "Buy now and pay in easy installments," and racked up debts. Americans bought 75 percent of their radios and 60 percent of their automobiles on the installment plan. Some started buying on credit at a faster rate than their incomes increased.

Mass Advertising

When inventor Otto Rohwedder developed a commercial bread slicer in 1928, he faced a problem common to new inventions: the invention—sliced bread—was something no one knew was needed. To attract consumers, manufacturers turned to advertising, another booming industry in the 1920s.

Advertisers linked products with qualities associated with the modern era, such as progress, convenience, leisure, success, and style. In a 1924 magazine advertisement for deodorant, the headline read, "Flappers they may be—but they know the art of feminine appeal!" An advertisement for a spaghetti product told homemakers that heating is the same as cook-

ing: "Just one thing to do and it's ready to serve." Advertisers also preyed on consumers' fears and anxieties, such as jarred nerves due to the hectic pace of modern life or insecurities about one's status or weight.

The Managerial Revolution

By the early 1920s, many industries had begun to create modern organizational structures. Companies were split into divisions with different functions, such as sales, marketing, and accounting. To run these divisions, businesses needed to hire managers. Managers freed executives and owners from the day-to-day running of the companies.

The managerial revolution in companies created a new career—the professional manager. The large numbers of new managers helped expand the size of the middle class, which in turn added to the nation's prosperity. Similarly, so many companies relied on new technology that engineers were also in very high demand. They, too, joined the ranks of the growing middle class.

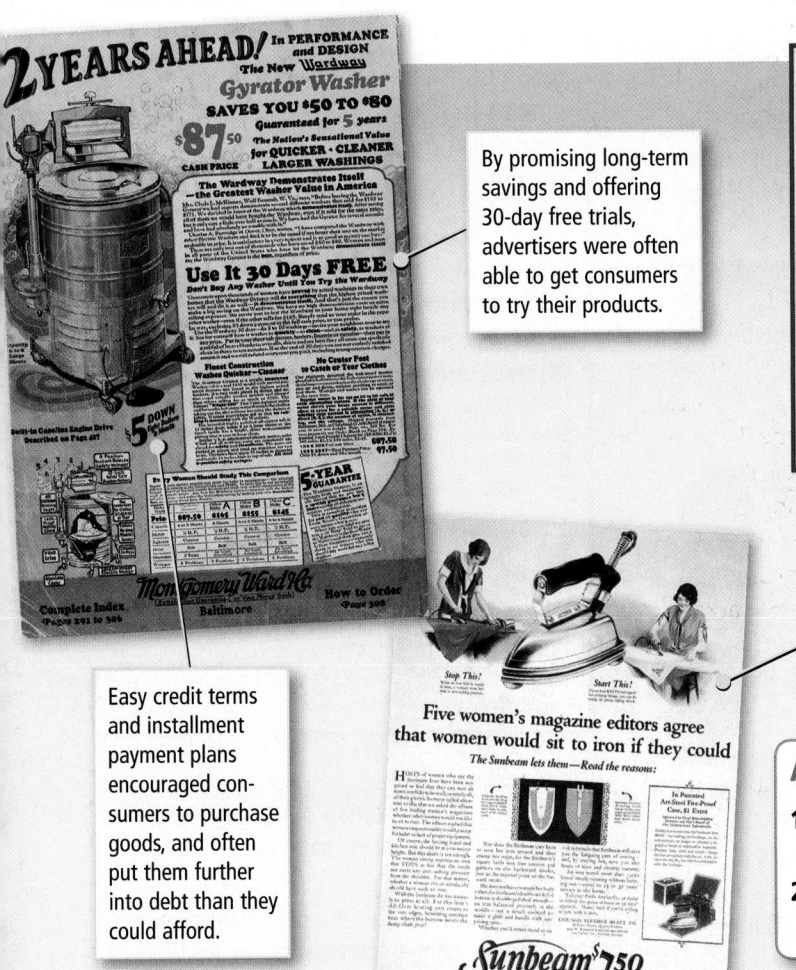

By promising long-term savings and offering 30-day free trials, advertisers were often able to get consumers to try their products.

Easy credit terms and installment payment plans encouraged consumers to purchase goods, and often put them further into debt than they could afford.

This 1928 advertisement appeals to "expert opinion" to sell the product. It also shows that 1920s advertisers believed ironing to be a woman's job.

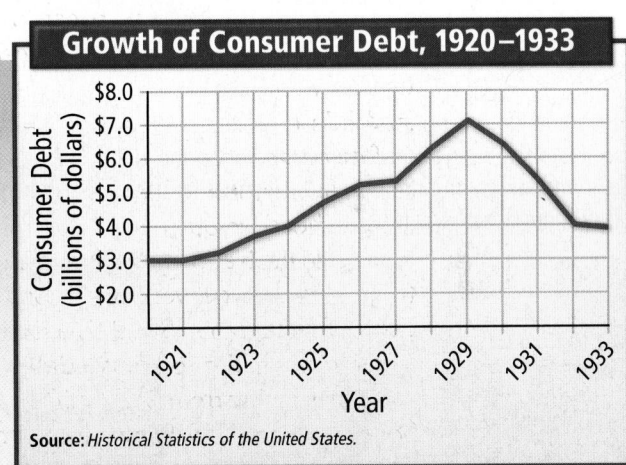

Growth of Consumer Debt, 1920–1933

Source: *Historical Statistics of the United States.*

Analyzing VISUALS

1. **Making Connections** What techniques do advertisers use today to sell automobiles?

2. **Analyzing Visuals** What happened to consumer debt between 1921 and 1929? Why might this have happened?

Welfare Capitalism

Middle-class Americans were not the only members of the new consumer society. Industrial workers also had more disposable income, partly due to rising wages and partly because many corporations introduced what came to be called **welfare capitalism.** Companies allowed workers to buy stock, participate in profit sharing, and receive medical care and pensions.

The Decline of Unions Benefits programs also made unions seem unnecessary to many workers. During the 1920s, unions lost both influence and membership. Employers promoted the **open shop**—a workplace where employees were not required to join a union. With benefits covering some of their basic needs, workers were able to spend more of their income to improve their quality of life. Many purchased consumer goods they previously could not afford.

Uneven Prosperity Not all Americans shared in this economic boom. Thousands of African Americans had factory jobs during World War I. When servicemen returned from the war, they replaced both African Americans and women.

Native Americans were also excluded from prosperity. Although granted citizenship in 1924, they were often isolated on reservations, where there was little productive work.

The majority of immigrants to the United States continued to come from Europe. Even these people often found it difficult to find work; most of them were farmers and factory workers whose wages were pitifully low.

Many people in the Deep South were also left out of the economic boom. The traditional agricultural economic base eroded after the war ended. Farmers in general failed to benefit from the growing economy.

✓ Reading Check **Analyzing** How did advertisers try to convince Americans to buy their products?

PRIMARY SOURCE
Prosperity for Whom?

Although many people benefited from the economic boom of the 1920s, several groups did not share in the general prosperity, nor did all regions of the country. Members of minority groups, newly arrived immigrants, and farmers often struggled economically. During the 1920s, for example, laborers in manufacturing not only outnumbered farmers but also acquired three times more actual wealth.

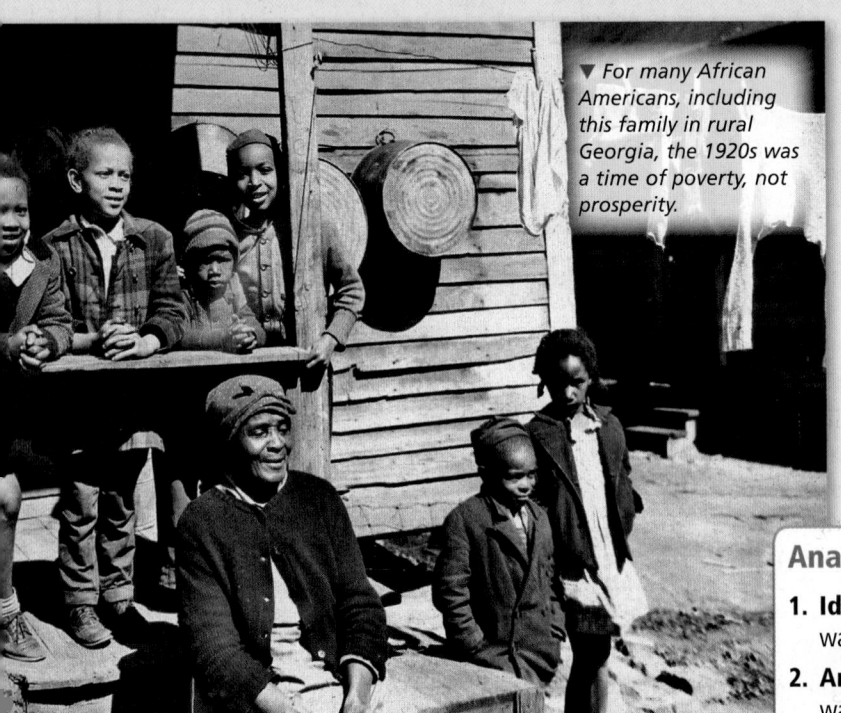

▼ For many African Americans, including this family in rural Georgia, the 1920s was a time of poverty, not prosperity.

Average Hourly Earnings, 1929

Northeast: 0.47, Midwest: 0.45, South: 0.31, West: 0.47

Source: *Manpower in Economic Growth.*

Annual Earnings, 1920–1930

— Nonfarm Employees
— Agricultural Employees

Source: *Manpower in Economic Growth.*

Analyzing VISUALS

1. **Identifying** In what region of the nation were hourly wages lowest in 1929?

2. **Analyzing** What pattern characterizes the gap between wages of farm and nonfarm employees during the 1920s?

The Farm Crisis

MAIN Idea Increases in farm productivity and decreases in foreign markets led to lower prices for farmers.

HISTORY AND YOU Do you remember reading about the platform of the Populist Party in the 1890s? Read to learn about farmers' troubles in the 1920s.

American farmers did not share in the prosperity of the 1920s. On average, they earned less than one-third of the income of workers in the rest of the economy. Technological advances in fertilizers, seed varieties, and farm machinery allowed them to produce more, but higher yields without a corresponding increase in demand meant that they received lower prices. Between 1920 and 1921, corn prices dropped almost 19 percent, and wheat went from $1.83 a bushel to $1.03. The cost of the improved farming technology, meanwhile, continued to increase.

Changing Market Conditions

Many factors contributed to this "quiet depression" in American agriculture. During the war, the government had urged farmers to produce more to meet the great need for food supplies in Europe. Many farmers borrowed heavily to buy new land and new machinery to raise more crops. Sales were strong, prices were high, and farmers prospered. After the war, however, European farm output rose, and the debt-ridden countries of Europe had little money to spend on American farm products. Congress had unintentionally made matters worse when it passed the Fordney-McCumber Act in 1922. This act raised tariffs dramatically in an effort to protect American industry from foreign competition. By dampening the American market for foreign goods, however, it provoked a reaction in foreign markets against American agricultural products. Farmers in the United States could no longer sell as much of their crops overseas, and prices tumbled.

Helping Farmers

Some members of Congress tried to help the farmers sell their surplus. Every year from 1924 to 1928, Senator Charles McNary of Oregon and Representative Gilbert Haugen of Iowa proposed the McNary-Haugen Bill, a plan in which the government would boost farm prices by buying up surpluses and selling them, at a loss, overseas.

Congress passed the bill twice, but President Coolidge vetoed it both times. He argued that with money flowing to farmers under this law, they would be encouraged to produce even greater surpluses. American farmers remained mired in a recession throughout the 1920s.

Reading Check **Synthesizing** What factors led to the growing economic crisis in farming?

Section 2 REVIEW

Vocabulary

1. **Explain** the significance of: mass production, assembly line, Model T, Charles Lindbergh, welfare capitalism, open shop.

Main Ideas

2. **Evaluating** How did the automobile affect American society?

3. **Summarizing** What factors led to the new consumer society in the United States during the 1920s?

4. **Analyzing** What conditions contributed to the tough times farmers faced in the early 1920s?

Critical Thinking

5. **Big Ideas** How did the availability of credit change society?

6. **Organizing** Use a graphic organizer like the one below to list some of the new industries that grew in importance during the 1920s.

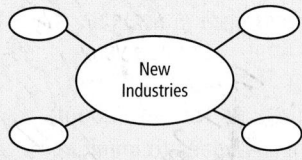

New Industries

7. **Analyzing Visuals** Study the Technology & History on pages 598–599. How do appliances, cars, and airplanes differ today? How do you think new products change society today?

Writing About History

8. Write an article for a contemporary newspaper analyzing the impact of Charles Lindbergh's transatlantic flight on the development of aviation in the United States and the world.

A Clash of Values

Guide to Reading

Big Ideas
Past and Present The struggles of the 1920s regarding immigration and proper behavior continue to affect current events.

Content Vocabulary
- nativism *(p. 604)*
- anarchist *(p. 604)*
- evolution *(p. 608)*
- creationism *(p. 608)*
- speakeasy *(p. 609)*

Academic Vocabulary
- source *(p. 606)*
- deny *(p. 608)*

People and Events to Identify
- Emergency Quota Act *(p. 606)*
- National Origins Act *(p. 606)*
- Fundamentalism *(p. 608)*

Reading Strategy
Organizing As you read about Americans' reactions to immigrants during the 1920s, complete a graphic organizer similar to the one below by filling in the causes and effects of anti-immigrant prejudices.

NEW YORK CORE CURRICULUM
U.S. History and Government

Unit 5:
I.C.2.a Threats to civil liberties: Red Scare, Ku Klux Klan, and Sacco and Vanzetti
I.C.2.b Prohibition (18th Amendment) and the Volstead Act
I.C.2.c Science, religion, and education: the Scopes Trial (1925)
I.C.2.d Restrictions on immigration: closing the "golden door"
I.C.3.a Revolution in morals and manners: fads, flappers, and Freud
I.C.3.b Women's changing roles

The 1920s are often called the "Roaring Twenties" because to many the decade seemed to be one long party. Urban Americans celebrated the new "modern" culture, but not everyone agreed that the new trends were a good thing. Rural Americans believed traditional society and morality were under attack.

Nativism Resurges

MAIN Idea Nativism and racism increased in the 1920s and led to changes in immigration laws.

HISTORY AND YOU In your school, is there a limit to the number of students in each class? Read to learn why the United States imposed new rules in the 1920s limiting the number of immigrants admitted each year.

The 1920s was a time of economic growth, but it was also a time of cultural turmoil. When the 1920s began, an economic recession, an influx of immigrants, and cultural tensions combined to create an atmosphere of disillusionment and intolerance. The fear and prejudice many felt toward Germans and communists during and after World War I expanded to include all immigrants. This triggered a general rise in racism and **nativism**—a belief that one's native land needs to be protected against immigrants.

During World War I, immigration to the United States had dropped sharply. By 1921, however, it had returned to prewar levels, with the majority of immigrants coming from southern and eastern Europe. Many Americans reacted to the bombings, strikes, and recession of the postwar years by blaming immigrants. Many believed immigrants were taking jobs that would otherwise have gone to soldiers returning home from the war.

The Sacco-Vanzetti Case

The controversial Sacco-Vanzetti case reflected the prejudices and fears of the era. On April 15, 1920, two men robbed and murdered two employees of a shoe factory in Massachusetts. Police subsequently arrested two Italian immigrants, Nicola Sacco and Bartolomeo Vanzetti, for the crime.

The case created a furor when newspapers revealed that the two men were **anarchists,** or people who oppose all forms of government. They also reported that Sacco owned a gun similar to the murder weapon and that the bullets used in the murders matched those in Sacco's gun. The evidence was questionable, but the fact that the accused men were anarchists and foreigners led many people to assume they were guilty, including the jury. On July 14, 1921,

Hostility Toward Immigrants

In the 1920s, many Americans believed that immigrants from southern and eastern Europe would not assimilate into American culture. These concerns led to the rise of a new Ku Klux Klan and efforts in Congress to pass legislation that would keep "undesirable" immigrants out.

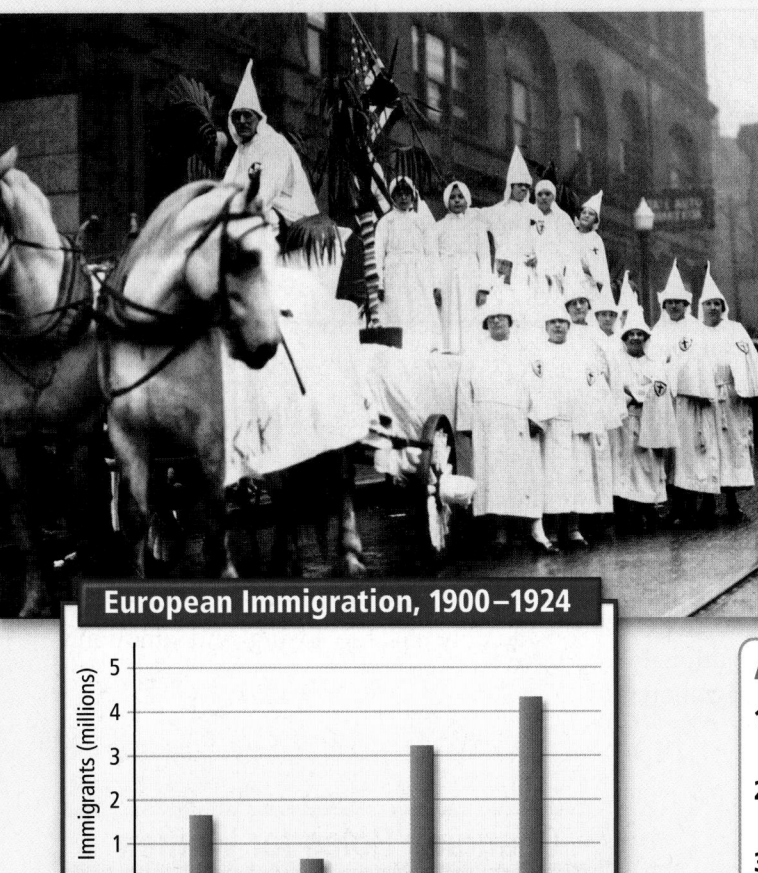

Men, women, and children participate in a Klan march in Cincinnati, Ohio, in 1925 (left). Membership in the KKK soared in the early 1920s because of its opposition to immigrants. Not everyone agreed with the Klan, however; the cartoon above mocks a proposal to impose a literacy test on immigrants.

European Immigration, 1900–1924

Immigrants (millions)

Region	
United Kingdom	~1.6
Germany	~0.6
Eastern Europe	~3.2
Southern Europe	~4.3

Source: *Historical Statistics of the United States.*

Analyzing VISUALS   DBQ

1. **Making Inferences** What does the presence and membership of children in the Klan suggest to others?
2. **Analyzing Visuals** What is the "wall" made of in the cartoon?
3. **Making Connections** From which two regions did the majority of immigrants come? Why were so many people from these regions willing to leave their homelands and come to the United States?

Sacco and Vanzetti were found guilty and sentenced to death. After six years of appeals, Sacco and Vanzetti were executed on August 23, 1927.

Return of the Ku Klux Klan

At the forefront of the movement to restrict immigration was the Ku Klux Klan, or KKK. The old KKK had flourished in the South after the Civil War and used threats and violence to intimidate newly freed African Americans. The new Klan had other targets as well: Catholics, Jews, immigrants, and other groups said to be "un-American." In the 1920s, the Klan claimed it was fighting for "Americanism."

William J. Simmons founded the new Ku Klux Klan in Georgia, in 1915. A former preacher, Simmons pledged to preserve America's white, Protestant civilization. The Klan attracted few members until 1920, when Simmons began using professional promoters to sell Klan memberships. By 1924 membership had reached nearly 4 million as it spread beyond the South into Northern cities.

The Klan began to decline in the late 1920s, however, largely as a result of scandals and power struggles between its leaders. Membership shrank, and politicians backed by the Klan were voted out of office. In addition, new restrictions on immigration deprived the Klan of one of its major issues.

Read "Sacco and Vanzetti Must Die" by John Dos Passos on pages R74–R75 of the **American Literature Library.**

Controlling Immigration

American immigration policies changed in response to the postwar recession and nativist pleas to "Keep America American." Even some business leaders, who had favored immigration as a **source** of cheap labor, now saw the new immigrants as radicals.

In 1921 President Harding signed the **Emergency Quota Act.** The act restricted annual admission to the United States to only 3 percent of the total number of people in any ethnic group already living in the nation. Ethnic identity and national origin thus determined admission to the United States.

In 1924 the **National Origins Act** made immigration restriction a permanent policy. The law set quotas at 2 percent of each national group represented in the U.S. Census of 1890. Thus, immigration quotas were based on the ethnic composition of the country more than 30 years earlier—before the heavy wave of immigration from southern and eastern Europe. The new quotas deliberately favored immigrants from northwestern Europe. Although subsequent legislation made some changes in immigration laws, the National Origins Act set the framework for immigration for the next four decades.

Hispanic Immigration

While workers and unions rejoiced at the reduction in competition with European immigrants for jobs, employers desperately needed laborers for agriculture, mining, and railroad work. Mexican immigrants were able to fill this need because the National Origins Act of 1924 exempted natives of the Western Hemisphere from the quota system.

Large numbers of Mexican immigrants had already begun moving to the United States after the passage of the Newlands Reclamation Act of 1902. The act funded irrigation projects in the Southwest and led to the creation of large factory farms that needed thousands of farmworkers. As the demand for cheap farm labor steadily increased, Mexican immigrants crossed the border in record numbers. By the end of the 1920s, nearly 700,000 had migrated to the United States.

✔ **Reading Check** **Explaining** How was the Ku Klux Klan of the 1920s different from the earlier Klan?

A Clash of Cultures

MAIN Idea Supporters of the new morality in the 1920s clashed with those who supported more traditional values.

HISTORY AND YOU How do you think older generations view your generation? Read about the changes in morality during the 1920s.

Many groups that wanted to restrict immigration also wanted to preserve what they considered to be traditional values. They feared that a "new morality" was taking over the nation. Challenging traditional ways of behaving, the new morality glorified youth and personal freedom and changed American society—particularly the status of women.

Women in the 1920s

Having won the right to vote in 1920, many women sought to break free of the traditional roles and behaviors that were expected of them. Attitudes toward marriage—popularized by magazines and other media—changed considerably. As the loving and emotional aspects of marriage grew in importance, the

PRIMARY SOURCE
Changing Roles for Women

As women achieved greater independence, access to higher education, and professional opportunities in the 1920s, they adopted new clothing styles that expressed their identities.

▶ *Many young women adopted the flapper style in the 1920s. They stopped wearing corsets, bobbed their hair, and wore short skirts, high heels, and rounded hats with almost no brim. The style expressed the sense of freedom many women felt in the 1920s.*

ideas of romance, pleasure, and friendship became linked to successful marriages.

The popularizing of Sigmund Freud's psychological theories also changed people's ideas about relationships. Freudian psychology emphasized human sexuality and his theories (often oversimplified) became acceptable subjects of public conversation.

The automobile played a role in encouraging the new morality. Cars allowed young people to escape the careful watch of their parents. Instead of socializing at home with the family, many youths could now use cars to "go out" with their friends.

Women in the workforce began to define the new morality. Many working-class women took jobs because they or their families needed the wages but for some young, single women, work was a way to break away from parental authority and establish financial independence. Earning money also allowed women to participate in the consumer culture.

Fashion, too, changed during the 1920s, particularly for women, who "bobbed," or shortened, their hair, wore flesh-colored silk stockings, and copied the glamorous look of movie stars. The flapper personified these changes, even though she was not typical of most women. The flapper smoked cigarettes, drank prohibited liquor, and wore makeup and sleeveless dresses with short skirts.

Women who attended college in the 1920s often found support for their emerging sense of independence. Women's colleges, in particular, encouraged their students to pursue careers and to challenge traditional ideas about women's role in society.

Many professional women made major contributions in science, medicine, law, and literature in the 1920s. In medicine, Florence Sabin's research led to a dramatic drop in death rates from tuberculosis while Edith Wharton, Willa Cather, and Edna Ferber each won a Pulitzer Prize in fiction for their novels.

Public health nurse Margaret Sanger believed that families could improve their standard of living by limiting the number of children they had. She founded the American Birth Control League in 1921 to promote knowledge about birth control. This organization became Planned Parenthood in the 1940s. During the 1920s and 1930s, the use of birth control increased dramatically, particularly among middle-class couples.

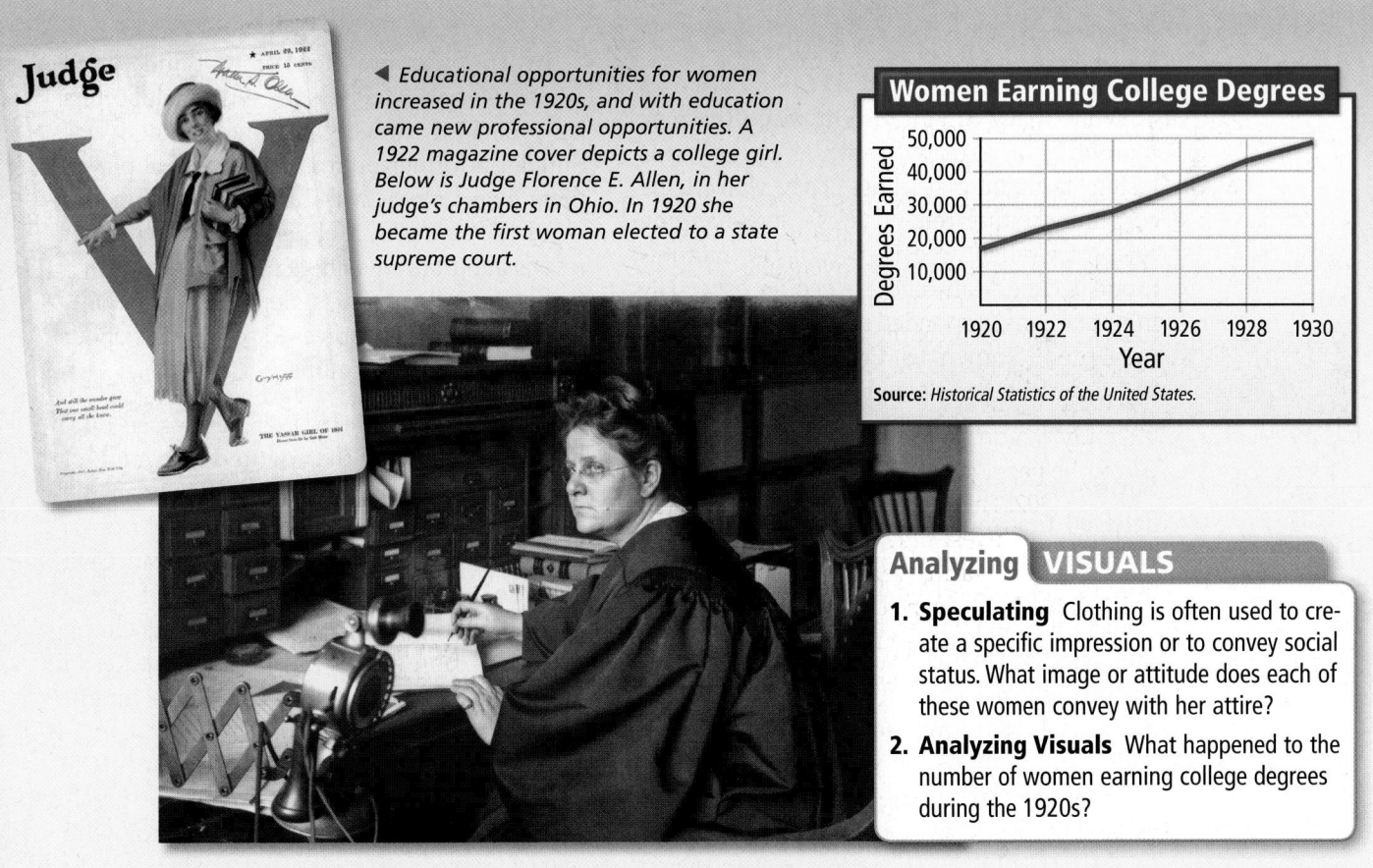

◀ Educational opportunities for women increased in the 1920s, and with education came new professional opportunities. A 1922 magazine cover depicts a college girl. Below is Judge Florence E. Allen, in her judge's chambers in Ohio. In 1920 she became the first woman elected to a state supreme court.

Women Earning College Degrees

Source: *Historical Statistics of the United States.*

Analyzing VISUALS

1. **Speculating** Clothing is often used to create a specific impression or to convey social status. What image or attitude does each of these women convey with her attire?

2. **Analyzing Visuals** What happened to the number of women earning college degrees during the 1920s?

The War Against Alcohol

Prohibition supporters argued that it reduced violence, illness, and poverty. Critics argued that it increased violence because gangs fought to control the sale of illegal alcohol, and that it led to illness because many people drank unsafe "moonshine."

The Shadow of Danger

If you believe that the traffic in Alcohol does more harm than good—*help stop it!*

Strengthen America Campaign
Strengthen America Campaign · 100 East Twenty Second Street, New York City, N.Y.

▲ Supporters of Prohibition portrayed the sale of alcohol as a danger to mothers and children.

◄ Prohibition led to the creation of a special federal bureau charged with stopping the sale of illegal alcohol. In this photo, a federal agent cracks open barrels of illegal rum in San Francisco in 1927.

Murder Rate, 1920–1940

*per 100,000 residents

Source: *Historical Statistics of the United States.*

Analyzing VISUALS — DBQ

1. **Theorizing** How might opponents of Prohibition use the murder rate in the 1920s and 1930s to support their argument? Can you think of other reasons the murder rate might have fallen in the 1930s?

2. **Analyzing Visuals** How does the poster use emotional appeal to strengthen its argument?

Fundamentalism

While many Americans embraced the new morality, others feared that the country was losing its traditional values. They viewed the consumer culture, relaxed ethics, and changing roles of women as evidence of the nation's moral decline. Many of these people, especially in rural towns, responded by joining a religious movement known as **Fundamentalism,** a name derived from a series of Christian religious pamphlets titled "The Fundamentals."

Fundamentalist Beliefs Fundamentalists believed that the Bible was literally true and without error. They rejected the idea that human beings derived their moral behavior from society and nature, not God. In particular, they rejected Charles Darwin's theory of **evolution,** which said that human beings had developed from lower forms of life over the course of millions of years. Instead, they believed in **creationism**—the belief that God created the world as described in the Bible.

Two popular preachers, Billy Sunday and Aimee Semple McPherson, stirred supporters by preaching in very nontraditional ways. Sunday, a former professional baseball player, drew huge crowds with his showmanship and rapid-fire sermons. McPherson conducted her revivals and faith healings in Los Angeles in a flamboyant theatrical style, using stage sets and costumes that expressed the themes of her highly emotional sermons.

The Scopes Trial In 1925 Tennessee outlawed any teaching that **denied** "the story of the Divine Creation of man as taught in the Bible," or taught that "man descended from a lower order of animals." The American Civil Liberties Union (ACLU) advertised for a teacher willing to be arrested for teaching evolution. John T. Scopes, a biology teacher in Dayton, Tennessee, volunteered. He taught evolution and was arrested.

The trial took place in the summer of 1925. William Jennings Bryan, a three-time presidential candidate, was the prosecutor who represented the creationists. Clarence Darrow, one of the country's most celebrated trial lawyers, defended Scopes. After eight days of trial, Scopes was found guilty and fined $100, although the conviction was later overturned on a technicality. The trial had been broadcast over the radio, and Darrow's blistering cross-examination of Bryan hurt the Fundamentalist cause. Increasingly, Fundamentalists felt isolated and their commitment to political activism declined.

Prohibition

The movement to ban alcohol grew stronger in the early 1900s. People supported the prohibition of alcohol sales for many reasons. Some opposed alcohol consumption for religious reasons; others thought prohibition would reduce unemployment, domestic violence, and poverty. Prohibition supporters achieved their goal when the Eighteenth Amendment went into effect in January 1920.

Congress passed the Volstead Act, making the U.S. Treasury Department responsible for enforcing Prohibition. Treasury agents had enforced federal tax laws for many years, but police powers—a government's power to control people and property in the interest of public safety, health, welfare, and morals—had generally been reserved for state governments. The Eighteenth Amendment granted federal and state governments the power to enforce Prohibition, marking a dramatic increase in federal police powers.

The Treasury Department struggled to enforce Prohibition. During the 1920s, treasury agents made more than 540,000 arrests, but Americans persisted in blatantly ignoring the law. People flocked to secret bars called **speakeasies,** where they could purchase alcohol. In New York City alone, an estimated 32,000 speakeasies sold liquor illegally. Liquor also was readily available in rural areas, where bootlegging—the illegal production and distribution of liquor—was common.

Organized crime thrived on the illegal trade in alcohol. Huge profits could be made smuggling liquor from Canada and the Caribbean. Crime became big business, and some gangsters had enough money to corrupt local politicians. Al Capone, one of the most successful and violent gangsters of the era, had many police officers, judges, and other officials on his payroll. Capone dominated organized crime in Chicago. Finally, Eliot Ness, the leader of a special Treasury Department task force, brought Capone to justice. More than 70 federal agents were killed while enforcing Prohibition in the 1920s.

The battle to repeal Prohibition began almost as soon as the Eighteenth Amendment was ratified. The Twenty-first Amendment, ratified in 1933, repealed the Eighteenth Amendment and ended Prohibition. Prohibition had reduced alcohol consumption, but it had not improved society in the ways its supporters had hoped.

✔ **Reading Check** **Identifying** What political, social, and economic contributions did women make to American society in the 1920s?

Section 3 REVIEW

Vocabulary

1. **Explain** the significance of: nativism, anarchist, Emergency Quota Act, National Origins Act, Fundamentalism, evolution, creationism, speakeasy.

Main Ideas

2. **Identifying** What two factors influenced the limits on immigration?

3. **Summarizing** What issues caused clashes between traditional and new moralities?

Critical Thinking

4. **Big Ideas** Why did many Americans oppose immigration after World War I? What connections can you make with immigration policies today?

5. **Categorizing** Use a graphic organizer similar to the one below to list the provisions of the immigration acts passed in the 1920s.

Act	Provisions

6. **Analyzing Visuals** Look at the chart on page 605 showing European immigration. How would these figures have affected someone who was a nativist? Why?

Writing About History

7. **Persuasive Writing** Imagine it is the 1920s. Write a letter to your senator persuading him or her either to continue supporting Prohibition or to work for its repeal.

History ONLINE

Study Central™ To review this section, go to <u>glencoe.com</u> and click on Study Central.

Section 4

Cultural Innovations

Guide to Reading

Big Ideas
Culture and Beliefs Through sharing in the arts and sports of the time, Americans embraced new ways of thinking.

Content Vocabulary
• bohemian *(p. 610)*
• mass media *(p. 613)*

Academic Vocabulary
• diverse *(p. 610)*
• unify *(p. 613)*

People and Events to Identify
• Carl Sandburg *(p. 611)*
• Willa Cather *(p. 611)*
• Ernest Hemingway *(p. 612)*
• F. Scott Fitzgerald *(p. 612)*
• Edith Wharton *(p. 612)*

Reading Strategy
Organizing As you read about the 1920s, complete a graphic organizer like the one below by filling in the main characteristics of art, literature, and popular culture that reflect the era.

Cultural Movement	Main Characteristics
Art	
Literature	
Popular Culture	

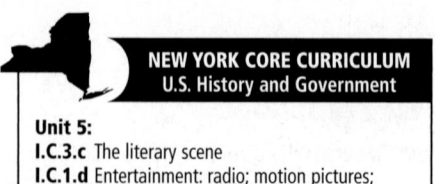

NEW YORK CORE CURRICULUM
U.S. History and Government

Unit 5:
I.C.3.c The literary scene
I.C.1.d Entertainment: radio; motion pictures; advertising and cultural homogenization

The 1920s was an era of great artistic innovation. Artists and writers experimented with new techniques. Popular culture also changed. Broadcast radio introduced Americans around the country to the latest trends in music and entertainment, and motion pictures became a major leisure-time activity.

Art and Literature

MAIN Idea New York City's Greenwich Village and Chicago's South Side became known as centers for new artistic work.

HISTORY AND YOU Is there a neighborhood with many art galleries in your community? Read about the flowering of the arts during the 1920s in the United States.

During the 1920s, American artists and writers challenged traditional ideas. These artists explored what it meant to be "modern," and they searched for meaning in the emerging challenges of the modern world. Many artists, writers, and intellectuals of the era flocked to Manhattan's Greenwich Village and Chicago's South Side. The artistic and unconventional, or **bohemian,** lifestyle of these neighborhoods allowed young artists, musicians, and writers greater freedom to express themselves.

Modern American Art

European art movements greatly influenced the modernists of American art. Perhaps most striking was the **diverse** range of artistic styles, each attempting to express the individual, modern experience. American painter John Marin drew on nature as well as the urban dynamics of New York for inspiration, explaining, "the whole city is alive; buildings, people, all are alive; and the more they move me the more I feel them to be alive." Painter Charles Scheeler applied the influences of photography and the geometric forms of Cubism to urban and rural American landscapes. Edward Hopper revived the visual accuracy of realism in his haunting scenes. His paintings conveyed a modern sense of disenchantment and isolation. Georgia O'Keeffe's landscapes and flowers were admired in many museums throughout her long life.

Poets and Writers

Poets and writers of the 1920s varied greatly in their styles and subject matter. Chicago poet, historian, folklorist, and novelist **Carl**

Ashcan Realists and the Lost Generation

Many artists and writers focused on the isolation and alienation of modern society. A group of artists who painted urban life became known as the Ashcan Realists. The writers who described modern life as spiritually empty and materialistic became known as the "Lost Generation."

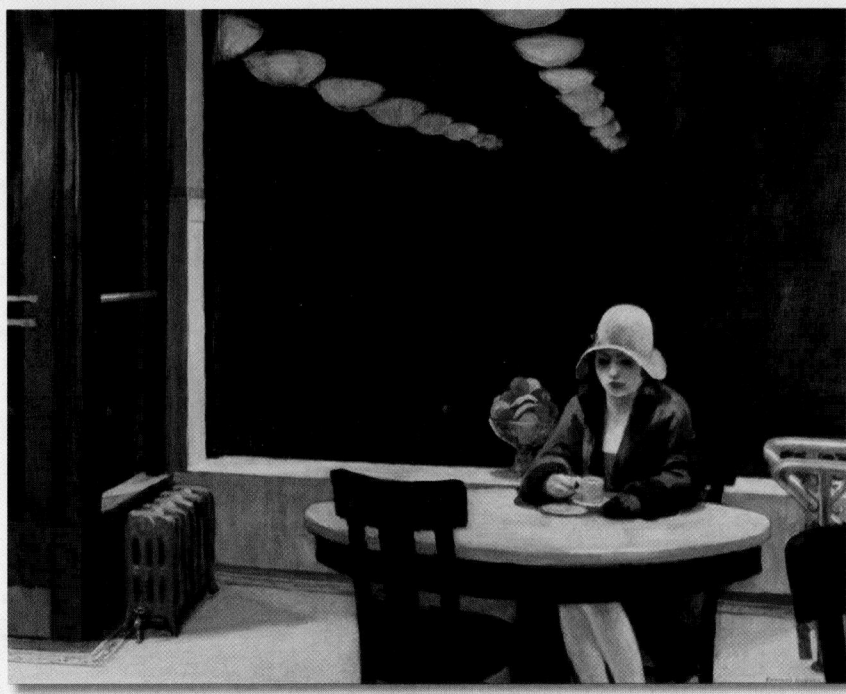

Excerpt from
"The Hollow Men" (1925)
by T.S. Eliot

We are the hollow men
We are the stuffed men
Leaning together
Headpiece filled with straw. Alas!
Our dried voices, when
We whisper together
Are quiet and meaningless
As wind in dry grass
Or rats' feet over broken glass
In our dry cellar
Shape without form, shade without colour,
Paralysed force, gesture without motion;
Those who have crossed
With direct eyes, to death's other Kingdom
Remember us—if at all—not as lost
Violent souls, but only
As the hollow men
The stuffed men.

◀ *Edward Hopper studied with one of the founders of the Ashcan Realist movement. His painting,* Automat, *(left) expresses the loneliness and isolation many young people felt during the 1920s. An automat was a place where a person could buy food or drinks from vending machines.*

Excerpt from *The Great Gatsby* (1925)
by F. Scott Fitzgerald

"They were careless people, Tom and Daisy—they smashed up things and creatures and then retreated back into their money or their vast carelessness or whatever it was that kept them together, and let other people clean up the mess they had made. . . .

I shook hands with him; it seemed silly not to, for I felt suddenly as though I were talking to a child. Then he went into the jewelry store to buy a pearl necklace—or perhaps only a pair of cuff buttons—rid of my provincial squeamishness forever."

DBQ Document-Based Questions

1. **Analyzing Primary Sources** How does Fitzgerald characterize Tom and Daisy? What does their attitude say about the culture of the 1920s?

2. **Explaining** Eliot uses the adjectives *hollow* and *stuffed* to describe contemporary people. How can both be true?

3. **Analyzing Primary Sources** How is Hopper's painting similar to Eliot's poem and Fitzgerald's novel?

Sandburg used common speech to glorify the Midwest, as did Pulitzer Prize–winner **Willa Cather,** who wrote about life on the Great Plains. In Greenwich Village, another Pulitzer Prize winner, Edna St. Vincent Millay, expressed women's equality and praised a life intensely lived.

Several poets had an important impact on the literary culture. Gertrude Stein, an avant-garde poet of the era, was a mentor to many writers, including Ernest Hemingway. Some poets, including Ezra Pound, Amy Lowell, and William Carlos Williams, used clear, concise images to express moments in time. Others concentrated on portraying what they perceived to be the negative effects of modernism. In "The Hollow Men," for example, T.S. Eliot described a world filled with empty dreams that would end "not with a bang but a whimper."

Among playwrights, one of the most innovative was Eugene O'Neill. His plays, filled with bold artistry and modern themes, portrayed realistic characters and situations, offering a vision of life that sometimes touched on the tragic.

Many American writers wrote about their disillusionment with World War I. Some, known as the "Lost Generation," moved to Paris or other cities in Europe. There, they often wrote about "heroic antiheroes"—flawed individuals who still had heroic qualities. **Ernest Hemingway** was one such writer. In direct simple prose, he described the experience of war in such novels as *For Whom the Bell Tolls* and *A Farewell to Arms.*

Sinclair Lewis wrote about the absurdities of small-town life in *Main Street* and *Babbitt.* **F. Scott Fitzgerald's** colorful characters chased futile dreams in *The Great Gatsby,* a novel critical of modern society's superficiality. Similarly, **Edith Wharton** used irony and humor to criticize upper-class ignorance and pretensions. Her 1920 novel, *The Age of Innocence,* won the Pulitzer Prize.

✔ Reading Check **Examining** Why did many creative people flock to Greenwich Village during the 1920s?

Popular Culture

MAIN Idea Broadcast radio and "talking" pictures were new forms of popular entertainment.

HISTORY AND YOU What forms of entertainment make up today's popular culture? Read how Americans spent their leisure time in the 1920s.

The economic prosperity of the 1920s provided many Americans with more leisure time and more spending money, which they devoted to making their lives more enjoyable. Millions of Americans eagerly watched sports and enjoyed music, theater, and other forms of popular entertainment. They also fell in love with motion pictures and radio programs.

Movies and Radio Shows

For many Americans in the 1920s, nothing quite matched the allure of motion pictures. Before technology made sound possible in

PRIMARY SOURCE
Entertainment Brings Americans Together

Part of what made the 1920s feel "new" and "modern" was the rise of mass culture. Popular entertainment—whether movies or sports—brought Americans together in a shared experience.

Movies were very popular in the 1920s. Note the live musicians playing music to accompany the silent film. On screen is actress Clara Bow. At left are actors Douglas Fairbanks, Sr., Mary Pickford, Charlie Chaplin, and director D. W. Griffith. They founded the United Artists movie studio in 1919.

Professional sports drew huge crowds in the 1920s. Top players such as Babe Ruth (left) and Ty Cobb (above) became celebrities and were among the first to be paid to endorse products in advertisements.

Analyzing **VISUALS**

1. **Making Connections** How does the experience of seeing a movie today compare or contrast with what you observe in the photograph of early filmgoers?

2. **Analyzing** What do you observe about the crowds at the baseball games?

films, theaters hired piano players to provide music during the feature, while subtitles explained the plot. Audiences thronged to see such stars as Mary Pickford, Charlie Chaplin, Tom Mix, Douglas Fairbanks, Sr., Rudolph Valentino, and Clara Bow. In 1927 the golden age of Hollywood began when the first "talking" picture—*The Jazz Singer*—was produced.

Entertainment programs broadcast over the radio also had a large following during the Jazz Age. Most stations in the 1920s played the popular songs of the day, such as "Yes! We Have No Bananas" and "Ain't We Got Fun." Broadcasts such as *The Eveready Hour* offered everything from classical music to comedy. In one of the most popular shows, *Amos 'n' Andy*, the trials and tribulations of two African American characters (portrayed by white actors) captured the nation's attention every evening.

The **mass media**—radio, movies, newspapers, and magazines aimed at a broad audience—did more than just entertain. Their easy availability to millions helped break down patterns of provincialism, or narrow focus on local interests. They fostered a sense of shared experience that helped **unify** the nation and spread new ideas and attitudes.

Sports

Thanks to motion pictures and radio, sports such as baseball and boxing reached new heights of popularity in the 1920s. Baseball star Babe Ruth became a national hero, famous for hitting hundreds of home runs. As one broadcaster later remarked, "He wasn't a baseball player. He was a worldwide celebrity, an international star, the likes of which baseball has never seen since."

Sports fans also idolized boxer Jack Dempsey. Dempsey held the title of world heavyweight champion from 1919 until 1926, when he lost it to Gene Tunney. When Dempsey attempted to win back the title in 1927, fans' enthusiasm for the rematch reached such a frenzy that one store sold $90,000 worth of radios—an incredible sum at that time—in the two weeks before the event.

Americans eagerly followed other sports and sports figures, too. Newspaper coverage helped generate enthusiasm for college football. One of the most famous players of the 1920s was Red Grange of the University of Illinois. Grange was known as the "Galloping Ghost" because of his speed and ability to evade members of opposing teams.

The triumphs of Bobby Jones, the best golfer of the decade, and tennis players Bill Tilden and Helen Wills, who dominated world tennis, also thrilled sports fans. In 1926 Jones became the first golfer to win the U.S. Open and the British Open in the same year. When swimmer Gertrude Ederle shattered records by swimming the English Channel in a little over 14 hours in 1927, Americans were enchanted.

Reading Check **Summarizing** How did the economy of the 1920s affect popular culture?

Section 4 REVIEW

Vocabulary

1. **Explain** the significance of: bohemian, Carl Sandburg, Willa Cather, Ernest Hemingway, F. Scott Fitzgerald, Edith Wharton, mass media.

Main Ideas

2. **Describing** What were the main themes of artists and writers during the 1920s?

3. **Discussing** How did Americans enjoy their leisure time in the 1920s? What made these activities possible?

Critical Thinking

4. **Big Ideas** How did writers, artists, and popular culture of the 1920s affect traditional ideas in the United States?

5. **Organizing** Use a graphic organizer similar to the one below to list the effects of mass media on American culture.

Effects

Mass Media of 1920s

6. **Analyzing Visuals** Look at the painting on page 611. How does Edward Hopper create a sense of alienation in this painting?

Writing About History

7. **Descriptive Writing** Imagine that you have moved to New York's Greenwich Village in the 1920s. Write a letter to a friend describing the atmosphere in your neighborhood.

History ONLINE

Study Central™ To review this section, go to glencoe.com and click on Study Central.

BETTMANN/CORBIS

Appreciation

LOUIS DANIEL ARMSTRONG *Writer Stanley Crouch remembers Louis Armstrong, a Jazz Age great.*

Pops. Sweet Papa Dip. Satchmo. He had perfect pitch and perfect rhythm. His improvised melodies and singing could be as lofty as a moon flight or as low-down as the blood drops of a street thug dying in the gutter. The extent of his influence across jazz and across American music continues to this day.

Not only do we hear Armstrong in trumpet players who represent the present renaissance in jazz, we can also detect his influence in certain rhythms that sweep from country-and-western music to rap.

Louis Daniel Armstrong was born in New Orleans on August 4, 1901. It was at a home for troubled kids that young Louis first put his lips to the mouthpiece of a cornet and, later, a trumpet.

In 1922 Armstrong went to Chicago, where he joined King Oliver and his Creole Jazz Band. The band brought out the people and all the musicians, black and white, who wanted to know how it was truly done.

When he first played in New York City in 1924, his improvisations set the city on its head. The stiff rhythms of the time were slashed away by his combination of the percussive and the soaring. He soon returned to Chicago, perfected what he was doing, and made one record after another.

Louis Armstrong was so much, in fact, that every school of jazz since has had to address how he interpreted the basics of the idiom—swing, blues, ballads, and Afro-Hispanic rhythms. His freedom, his wit, and his discipline give his music a perpetual position in the wave of the future that is the station of all great art.

VERBATIM

"The great creators of the government . . . thought of America as a light to the world, as created to lead the world in the assertion of the right of peoples and the rights of free nations. "

WOODROW WILSON,
in defense of the League of Nations, 1920

"We seek no part in directing the destinies of the Old World. "

WARREN G. HARDING,
Inaugural Address, 1921

"Here was a new generation, . . . dedicated more than the last to the fear of poverty and the worship of success; grown up to find . . . all wars fought, all faiths in man shaken. "

CULVER PICTURES

F. Scott Fitzgerald

F. SCOTT FITZGERALD,
author, This Side of Paradise

"There has been a change for the worse during the past year in feminine dress, dancing, manners and general moral standards. [One should] realize the serious ethical consequences of immodesty in girls' dress. "

from the **PITTSBURGH OBSERVER,** *1922*

"[In New York] I saw 7,000,000 two-legged animals penned in an evil smelling cage, . . . streets as unkempt as a Russian steppe, . . . rubbish, waste paper, cigar butts. . . . One glance and you know no master hand directs. "

article in Soviet newspaper **PRAVDA**
describing New York City in 1925

WHAT'S NEW

Invented This Decade

How did we live without . . .

- push-button elevators
- neon signs
- oven thermostats
- electric razors
- tissues
- spiral-bound notebooks
- motels
- dry ice
- zippers
- pop-up toasters
- flavored yogurt
- car radios
- adhesive tape
- food disposals
- water skiing
- automatic potato peeler
- self-winding wristwatch

Milestones

EMBARRASSED, 1920. TEXAS SENATOR MORRIS SHEPPARD, a leading proponent of the Eighteenth Amendment, when a large whiskey still is found on his farm.

ERASED, 1922. THE WORD "OBEY," from the Episcopal marriage ceremony, by a vote of American Episcopal bishops.

DIED, 1923. HOMER MOREHOUSE, 27, in the 87th hour of a record-setting 90-hour, 10-minute dance marathon.

EXONERATED, 1921. EIGHT CHICAGO WHITE SOX PLAYERS charged with taking bribes to throw the 1919 World Series. The players were found "not guilty" when grand jury testimony disappeared. Newly appointed commissioner of baseball Kenesaw Mountain Landis banned the "Black Sox" from baseball.

MAKING A COMEBACK, 1926. SANTA CLAUS, after falling into low favor in the last decade. Aiming at children, advertisers are marketing St. Nick heavily.

NUMBERS

60,000
Families with radios in 1922

9,000,000
Motor vehicles registered in U.S. in 1920

33.5 Number of hours Charles Lindbergh spent in his nonstop flight from New York to Paris on May 20, 1927

1,800 Tons of ticker tape and shredded paper dropped on Charles Lindbergh in his parade in New York City

$16,000 Cost of cleaning up after the parade

7,000 Job offers received by Lindbergh

3.5 million
Number of letters received by Lindbergh

Charles Lindbergh

CRITICAL THINKING

1. *Recognizing Bias* How does the communist newspaper *Pravda* describe New York City? Why do you think the writer described the city in such negative terms?

2. *Making Connections* Why do you think Charles Lindbergh's flight caused such excitement among Americans in 1927?

Section 5
African American Culture

The Harlem Renaissance was a creative era for African American artists and writers. The growing African American population in the North meant an increasing number of African Americans had meaningful political power to continue the struggle for civil rights.

Guide to Reading

Big Ideas
Group Action The artistic and political contributions of African Americans changed American society.

Content Vocabulary
• jazz *(p. 617)*
• blues *(p. 618)*

Academic Vocabulary
• symbolize *(p. 618)*
• impact *(p. 620)*
• ongoing *(p. 621)*

People and Events to Identify
• Great Migration *(p. 616)*
• Harlem Renaissance *(p. 616)*
• Claude McKay *(p. 616)*
• Langston Hughes *(p. 616)*
• Zora Neale Hurston *(p. 616)*
• Cotton Club *(p. 618)*
• Marcus Garvey *(p. 621)*

Reading Strategy
Organizing As you read about the African American experience in the 1920s, complete a graphic organizer similar to the one below by filling in the causes and effects of the Harlem Renaissance.

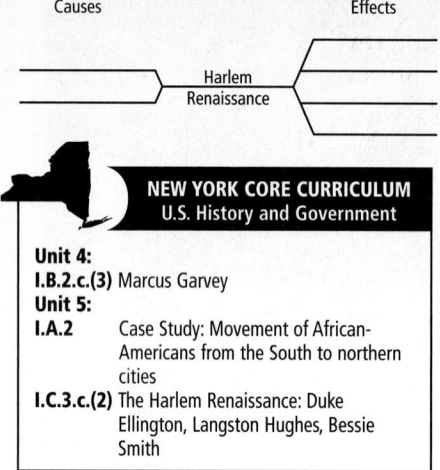

NEW YORK CORE CURRICULUM
U.S. History and Government

Unit 4:
I.B.2.c.(3) Marcus Garvey
Unit 5:
I.A.2 Case Study: Movement of African-Americans from the South to northern cities
I.C.3.c.(2) The Harlem Renaissance: Duke Ellington, Langston Hughes, Bessie Smith

The Harlem Renaissance

MAIN Idea The Harlem Renaissance sparked new trends in literature, music, and art.

HISTORY AND YOU Can you think of any examples of integrating different cultures in today's music and visual arts? Read to learn about the contributions of African Americans to the arts during the 1920s.

During World War I and the 1920s, hundreds of thousands of African Americans joined in the **Great Migration** from the rural South to industrial cities in the North. By moving north, African Americans sought to escape Southern segregation, find economic opportunities, and build better lives. Although job discrimination and economic inequality remained the norm in Northern cities, the North still offered much greater economic opportunities for African Americans compared to the South. After World War I, African American populations swelled in large Northern cities. The cities were full of nightclubs and music, particularly in the New York City neighborhood of Harlem—the heart and soul of the African American renaissance. It was there that African American artistic development, racial pride, and political organization thrived. The result was a flowering of African American arts that became known as the **Harlem Renaissance.**

The Writers

Claude McKay was the first important writer of the Harlem Renaissance. McKay translated the shock of American racism into *Harlem Shadows,* a collection of poetry published in 1922. In such poems as "The Lynching" and "If We Must Die," McKay's eloquent verse expressed a proud defiance and bitter contempt of racism—two striking characteristics of Harlem Renaissance writing. **Langston Hughes** was a prolific, original, and versatile writer. He became a leading voice of the African American experience in America.

Another important Harlem Renaissance author was **Zora Neale Hurston.** Hurston published her first novels, *Jonah's Gourd Vine* and *Their Eyes Were Watching God,* in the 1930s. Hurston's personal and spirited portrayals of rural African American culture were also the

Voices From the Harlem Renaissance

▲ Zora Neale Hurston

Excerpt from
Dust Tracks on a Road
by Zora Neale Hurston

"I can look back and see sharp shadows, high lights, and smudgy inbetweens. I have been in Sorrow's kitchen and licked out all the pots. Then I have stood on the peaky mountain wrapped in rainbows, with a harp and a sword in my hands.

"What I had to swallow in the kitchen has not made me less glad to have lived, nor made me want to low-rate the human race . . . It is the graceless acknowledgment of defeat . . . I am in the struggle with the sword in my hands, and I don't intend to run until you run me [away]."

I, Too, Sing America
by Langston Hughes

I, too, sing America.

I am the darker brother.
They send me to eat in the kitchen
When company comes,
But I laugh,
And eat well,
And grow strong.

Tomorrow,
I'll be at the table
When company comes.
Nobody'll dare
Say to me,
"Eat in the kitchen,"
Then.

Besides,
They'll see how
beautiful I am
And be ashamed—

I, too, am America.

▲ Langston Hughes stressed racial pride in his poetry. He reminded African Americans that they had their own history and achievements which were in every way as worthy of celebration as those of white people.

If We Must Die
By Claude McKay

If we must die—let it not be like hogs
Hunted and penned in an inglorious spot,
While round us bark the mad and hungry
dogs,Making their mock at our accursed
lot. If we must die—oh, let us nobly die,
So that our precious blood may not be shed
In vain; then even the monsters we defy
Shall be constrained to honor us though dead!
Oh, Kinsmen! We must meet the common foe;
Though far outnumbered, let us show us brave,
And for their thousand blows deal one deathblow!
What though before us lies the open grave?
Like men we'll face the murderous, cowardly pack,
Pressed to the wall, dying, but fighting back!

◄ Originally from Jamaica, Claude McKay wrote both poems and novels. "If We Must Die" was written shortly after World War I when race riots were erupting across the nation.

DBQ Document-Based Questions

1. **Speculating** What might have been some of the "pots" in Sorrow's kitchen for a woman in the Harlem Renaissance?

2. **Comparing and Contrasting** What does McKay's poem have in common with Hurston's excerpt and the poem by Hughes?

first major stories featuring African American women as central characters. Other notable writers of the Harlem Renaissance include Countee Cullen, Alain Locke, Dorothy West, and Nella Larsen.

Jazz, Blues, and the Theater

When New Orleans native Louis Armstrong moved to Chicago in 1922, he introduced an improvisational early form of **jazz,** a style of music influenced by Dixieland blues and ragtime, with its syncopated rhythms and improvisational elements. Three years later, Armstrong awed fellow musicians with a series of recordings made with his group, the Hot Five. In these recordings, especially in the song "Cornet Chop Suey," Armstrong broke away from the New Orleans tradition of ensemble or group playing by performing highly imaginative solos. He became the first great cornet and trumpet soloist in jazz music. The artistic freedom of Chicago's South Side gave Armstrong the courage to create his own type of jazz.

History ONLINE
Student Web Activity Visit glencoe.com and complete the activity on the Jazz Age.

Ragtime also influenced the composer, pianist, and bandleader Edward "Duke" Ellington, who listened as a teenager to ragtime piano players in Washington, D.C. In 1923 Ellington, also known simply as "Duke," formed a small band, moved to New York, and began playing in speakeasies and clubs. He soon created his own sound, a blend of improvisation and orchestration using different combinations of instruments. In fact, Ellington often did not like to use the word "jazz," since he believed it put a restriction on the general concept of his music. The Ellington style appeared in such hits as "Mood Indigo" and "Sophisticated Lady." Ellington, who had to be forced to practice piano as a child, eventually composed nearly 6,000 musical pieces, about a third of them jazz numbers. He also wrote religious music, the scores for five movies, and a ballet.

Like many other African American entertainers, Ellington got his start at the **Cotton Club,** the most famous nightclub in Harlem (but one that served only white customers). Years later, reflecting on the music of this era, Ellington said, "Everything, and I repeat, every-thing had to swing. And that was just it, those cats really had it; they had that soul. And you know you can't just play some of this music without soul. Soul is very important."

Bessie Smith seemed to **symbolize** soul. Her emotional singing style and commanding voice earned her the title "the Empress of the Blues." Smith sang of unfulfilled love, poverty, and oppression—the classic themes of the **blues,** a soulful style of music that evolved from African American spirituals. Born in Tennessee, Smith started performing in tent shows, saloons, and small theaters in the South. Discovered by Ma Rainey, one of the early great blues singers, Smith later performed with many of the greatest jazz bands of the era, including those of Louis Armstrong, Fletcher Henderson, and Benny Goodman. Her first recorded song, "Down Hearted Blues," became a major hit in 1923.

While jazz and blues filled the air during the Harlem Renaissance, the theater arts were also flourishing. *Shuffle Along*, the first musical written, produced, and performed by African Americans, made its Broadway debut in 1921. The show's success helped launch a number of

Scenes From the Harlem Renaissance

The Harlem Renaissance made both jazz and blues music popular and enabled African American entertainers to reach a wide audience.

▲ Louis Armstrong and his band, the Hot Five

▲ Many famous acts got their start at Harlem's Cotton Club. Patrons flocked there to hear the latest jazz music—African American music played by African American musicians—but the audience was limited to whites.

 Duke Ellington and his band at a Chicago nightclub

careers, including those of Florence Mills and Paul Robeson.

Robeson first gained recognition as an athlete at Rutgers University, where he was valedictorian of his class. After graduating from law school, he focused on an acting career. A celebrated singer and actor, Robeson received wide acclaim in the title role of a 1924 New York production of *Emperor Jones,* a play by Eugene O'Neill. Four years later, Robeson gained fame for his work in the musical, *Show Boat.* He also often appeared at the Apollo Theater, another famous club in Harlem.

Perhaps the most daring performer of the era, Josephine Baker transformed a childhood knack for flamboyance into a career as a well-known singer and dancer. Baker performed on Broadway but later moved to Paris and launched an international career.

The Harlem Renaissance succeeded in bringing international fame to African American arts. It also sparked a political transformation in the United States.

✓ **Reading Check** **Analyzing** How did African Americans help shape the national identity through the use of music?

African Americans and 1920s Politics

MAIN Idea While the NAACP pursued racial equality through the courts, black nationalists supported independence and separation from whites.

HISTORY AND YOU How does a sense of positive self-esteem help you perform better? Read how African Americans developed a new sense of pride.

In 1919, 1,300 African American veterans of World War I marched through Manhattan to Harlem. The march symbolized the new aspirations of African Americans in the 1920s. W. E. B. Du Bois captured the new sense of dignity and defiance of African Americans:

PRIMARY SOURCE

"We return. We return from fighting. We return fighting. Make way for democracy! We saved it in France, and by the Great Jehovah, we will save it in the United States of America, or know the reason why."

—quoted in *When Harlem Was in Vogue*

Excerpt from Bessie Smith's first hit song, 1923

Down Hearted Blues

Gee, but it's hard to love someone when that someone don't love you!

I'm so disgusted, heart-broken, too; I've got those down-hearted blues;

Once I was crazy 'bout a man; he mistreated me all the time,

The next man I get has got to promise me to be mine, all mine!

Trouble, trouble, I've had it all my days,

Trouble, trouble, I've had it all my days;

It seems like trouble going to follow me to my grave.

◀ *Bessie Smith was one of the earliest and most famous women blues singers.*

▲ *Singer and actor Paul Robeson created a sensation in a 1925 production of Eugene O'Neill's play* Emperor Jones.

▶ *Dancer Josephine Baker*

Analyzing **VISUALS**

1. **Hypothesizing** Why do you think many African American performers of the 1920s dressed so formally?

2. **Speculating** How might the Harlem Renaissance have helped overcome racism in American society?

During World War I, thousands of African Americans began the Great Migration from the rural South to the industrial cities of the North. Many African American neighborhoods, including Harlem in New York City, developed at this time.

African American Population

Legend: ■ 1910 ■ 1920

City	1910	1920
Chicago	44.1	109.4
New York	91.7	152.4
Detroit	5.7	40.8
Cleveland	8.4	34.4
St. Louis	43.9	69.8
Philadelphia	84.4	134.2

(Y-axis: Population, 0 to 160,000)

Source: U.S. Department of Commerce.

Analyzing GEOGRAPHY

1. **Movement** To what three Midwestern cities did many of the African Americans from the South migrate?

2. **Location** In which cities was the African American population highest in 1920?

Maps In Motion See *StudentWorks™ Plus* or glencoe.com.

(Map of the eastern United States showing African American migration, with state labels and cities: Detroit, Chicago, St. Louis, New York, Philadelphia, Baltimore, Washington D.C.)

Legend: ▨ African American migration

The Black Vote in the North

World War I set the stage for African Americans to reenter federal politics in the United States, although perhaps not in the way many expected. The Great Migration of African Americans to the North to take jobs in the war factories had a significant **impact** on the political power of African Americans in the United States as well. As their numbers grew in city neighborhoods, African Americans became a powerful voting bloc that could sometimes sway the outcome of elections.

At election time, most African American voters in the North cast their votes for Republicans, the party of Abraham Lincoln. In 1928 African American voters in Chicago achieved a significant political breakthrough.

Voting as a bloc, they helped elect Oscar DePriest, the first African American representative in Congress from a Northern state. During his three terms in Congress, DePriest introduced laws to oppose racial discrimination and make lynching a federal crime.

The NAACP Battles Injustice

The National Association for the Advancement of Colored People (NAACP) battled valiantly—but often unsuccessfully—against segregation and discrimination against African Americans. Its efforts focused primarily on lobbying public officials and working through the court system.

The NAACP also lobbied and protested against the horrors of lynching. The NAACP's persistent efforts led to the passage of antilynching legislation in the House of Representatives in 1922. The Senate defeated the bill, but the NAACP continued the fight. Its **ongoing** efforts to end lynching kept the issue in the news and probably helped to reduce the number of lynchings that took place.

One of the NAACP's greatest political triumphs occurred in 1930 with the defeat of Judge John J. Parker's nomination to the U.S. Supreme Court. The NAACP joined with labor unions to launch a highly organized national campaign against the North Carolina judge, who allegedly was racist and antilabor. By a narrow margin, the Senate refused to confirm Parker's nomination. His defeat demonstrated that African American voters and lobby groups had finally achieved enough influence to affect national politics and change decisions in Congress.

Black Nationalism and Marcus Garvey

While the NAACP fought for integration and improvement in the economic and political position of African Americans, other groups began to emphasize black nationalism and black pride. Eventually, some began calling for black separation from white society.

A dynamic black leader from Jamaica, **Marcus Garvey,** captured the imagination of millions of African Americans with his "Negro Nationalism," which glorified the black culture and traditions. Inspired by Booker T. Washington's call for self-reliance, Garvey founded the Universal Negro Improvement Association (UNIA), an organization aimed at promoting black pride and unity. The central message of Garvey's Harlem-based movement was that African Americans could gain economic and political power by educating themselves. Garvey also advocated separation and independence from whites. In 1920, at the height of his power, Garvey told his followers they would never find justice or freedom in America, and he proposed leading them to Africa.

The emerging African American middle class and intellectuals distanced themselves from Garvey and his push for racial separation. FBI officials saw UNIA as a dangerous catalyst for black uprisings in urban areas. Garvey also alienated key figures in the Harlem Renaissance by characterizing them as "weak-kneed and cringing . . . [flatterers of] the white man." Convicted of mail fraud in 1923, Garvey served time in prison. In 1927 President Coolidge commuted Garvey's sentence and used Garvey's immigrant status to have him deported to Jamaica.

Despite Garvey's failure to keep his movement alive, he instilled millions of African Americans with a sense of pride in their heritage and inspired hope for the future. That sense of pride and hope survived long after Garvey and his "back to Africa" movement was gone. This pride and hope reemerged strongly during the 1950s and played a vital role in the civil rights movement of the 1960s.

✔ Reading Check **Summarizing** How did World War I change attitudes among African Americans toward themselves and their country?

Section 5 REVIEW

Vocabulary

1. **Explain** the significance of: Great Migration, Harlem Renaissance, Claude McKay, Langston Hughes, Zora Neale Hurston, jazz, Cotton Club, blues, Marcus Garvey.

Main Ideas

2. **Analyzing** What musical style did Duke Ellington create? How was it different from other styles of music?

3. **Synthesizing** How did the Great Migration affect the political power of African Americans in the North?

Critical Thinking

4. **Big Ideas** What actions did the NAACP take to expand political rights for African Americans?

5. **Organizing** Use a graphic organizer similar to the one below to describe the impact of the Harlem Renaissance on U.S. society.

6. **Analyzing Visuals** Look at the photographs of Harlem Renaissance writers on page 617. Select one person and write a description of him or her, based only on what you see in the photo.

Writing About History

7. **Descriptive Writing** Imagine that you witnessed the African American men of the 369th Infantry, who had come back from the war, march through Manhattan and home to Harlem. Write a paragraph describing your feelings upon seeing these men.

History ONLINE
Study Central™ To review this section, go to glencoe.com and click on Study Central.

Causes of Prosperity

Government's Role

- Limits interference with business
- Cuts taxes, debt, and government spending
- Imposes higher tariffs to protect young industries

Business Innovation and Technology

- Mass production creates a wide range of consumer goods sold at low prices.
- Technology such as autos, airplanes, and radio leads to new industries and economic growth.
- Business pays high wages.

New Consumer Society

- People have more disposable income and leisure time
- Credit is more readily available
- Mass advertising begins

▲ The moving assembly line, pioneered by Henry Ford, made building automobiles efficient and greatly reduced prices.

▲ Joe "King" Oliver's band, with Louis Armstrong on slide trumpet, performs in Chicago in 1923, introducing the sound of jazz to America.

A Changing Society

Cultural Changes

- A new youth culture with a "new morality" develops.
- Young people and women gain more independence.
- The working class enjoys more leisure time.
- New mass media in radio, movies, and sports develops.

Changes for African Americans

- Harlem Renaissance begins.
- Literature reveals racial pride and contempt of racism.
- Jazz and blues are popularized.
- Great Migration during the war creates strong African American voting blocs in Northern cities.
- First African American from the North is elected to Congress.
- NAACP battles segregation and discrimination.

Opposition to Change

- Nativists and a new Ku Klux Klan target immigrants, Catholics, Jews, and African Americans.
- Government imposes new quotas on immigration.
- Fundamentalists push for traditional values.
- Prohibition is implemented.

◄ A federal agent enforces Prohibition by dumping barrels of illegal alcohol as neighborhood children watch.

NEW YORK REGENTS EXAM PRACTICE

TEST-TAKING **TIP**

Make sure that you can define the chapter's vocabulary terms. You will see these words in questions on standardized tests. By understanding their meanings you can omit incorrect answers through the process of elimination.

Part I

Directions (1–9): For each statement or question, write on a separate sheet of paper the number of the word or expression that, of those given, best completes the statement or answers the question.

1 Teapot Dome is an example of a scandal during the administration of

(1) Calvin Coolidge.

(2) Warren G. Harding.

(3) Woodrow Wilson.

(4) William Howard Taft.

2 What agreement involved American banks giving loans to Germany to pay war reparations to France and Britain?

(1) the Washington Conference

(2) the Kellogg-Briand Pact

(3) the Dawes Plan

(4) the Four-Power Treaty

3 Which of the following changed Americans' ideas about spending more money on items that were once considered luxury goods?

(1) mass production

(2) consumer credit

(3) advertising

(4) welfare capitalism

4 The passage of the Eighteenth Amendment was seen as a victory for

(1) opponents of alcohol consumption.

(2) supporters of women's suffrage.

(3) nativists.

(4) Sacco and Vanzetti.

5 The artistic developments of African Americans in the 1920s were known as the

(1) Great Migration.

(2) Saint Louis blues.

(3) New Orleans sound.

(4) Harlem Renaissance.

6 What effect did greater education and job opportunities for women create?

(1) Many women began earning as much money as men did.

(2) Women contributed to both scientific and artistic knowledge.

(3) More women preferred to remain at home.

(4) Most women working outside the home gained leadership positions.

7 What was an idea of black nationalism?

(1) integration and political improvement in society

(2) separation and independence from whites

(3) emigration from the United States to Jamaica

(4) support for the arts as a way to improve African American society

Need Extra Help?							
If You Missed Questions . . .	1	2	3	4	5	6	7
Go to Page . . .	590–592	594–595	600–601	609	616	606–607	621

[OVER]

Base your answer to question 8 on the map below and your knowledge of Chapter 17.

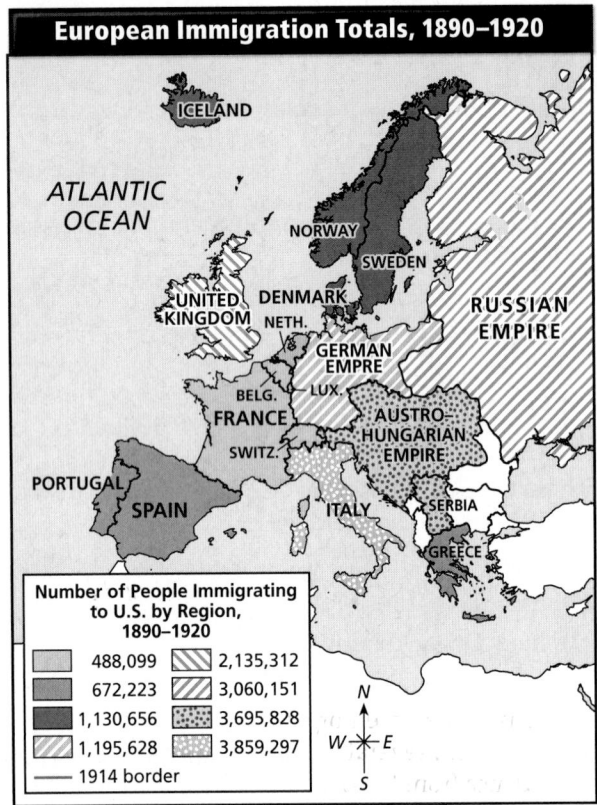

European Immigration Totals, 1890–1920

Number of People Immigrating to U.S. by Region, 1890–1920

488,099	2,135,312
672,223	3,060,151
1,130,656	3,695,828
1,195,628	3,859,297
1914 border	

8 Which area sent the greatest number of immigrants to the United States between 1890 and 1920?

(1) Italy
(2) Russian Empire
(3) German Empire
(4) Spain

9 What written agreement declared war illegal in 1928?

(1) the Washington Conference
(2) the Dawes Plan
(3) the Kellogg-Briand Pact
(4) the League of Nations Charter

Part II Thematic Essay Question

Directions: Write a well-organized essay that includes an introduction, several paragraphs addressing the task below, and a conclusion.

Theme: World Conflict

The Harding and Coolidge administrations promoted economic prosperity and world peace. Consider how both administrations attempted this difficult task.

Identify at least two methods used by the administrations to promote economic and political stability
- Discuss each method and the desired goals
- Evaluate the success of each method in achieving peace and prosperity

Guidelines:
In your essay, be sure to:
- Develop all aspects of the task
- Support the theme with relevant facts, examples, and details
- Use a logical and clear plan of organization, including an introduction and a conclusion that are beyond a restatement of the theme

Part III Document-Based Question

This question is based on the accompanying documents. This question is designed to test your ability to work with historical documents. Some of the documents have been edited for the purposes of the question. As you analyze the documents, take into account the source of each document and any point of view that may be presented in the document.

Historical Context:
The years following World War I were characterized by prosperity, economic and technological growth, and great artistic innovation.

Need Extra Help?		
If You Missed Questions . . .	8	9
Go to Page . . .	605–606	595

Task:

Using information from the documents and your knowledge of United States history, answer the questions that follow each document in Part A. Your answers to the questions will help you write the Part B essay in which you will be asked to

- Discuss the rise of new technology, such as the airplane
- Evaluate the effects of economic prosperity on the nation and its leaders

Part A
Short-Answer Questions

Directions: Analyze the documents and answer the short-answer questions that follow each document on a separate sheet of paper.

Document 1

"What endless hours I worked over this chart in California, measuring, drawing, rechecking each 100-mile segment of its great-circle route, each theoretical hour of my flight. . . . A few lines and figures on a strip of paper, a few ounces of weight, this [map] strip is my key to Europe. With it, I can fly the ocean. With it, that black dot at the other end marked 'Paris' will turn into a famous French city with an aerodrome where I can land. But without this chart, all my years of training, all that went into preparing for this flight, no matter how perfectly the engine runs or how long the fuel lasts, all would be as directionless as those columns of smoke in the New England valleys behind me."

Source: Charles Lindbergh, *The Spirit of St. Louis*

1 What does Lindbergh believe is the most valuable tool he has?

2 Based on this excerpt what conclusions can you draw about Lindbergh as a person?

Document 2

Source: Clifford Berryman, *The Evening Star,* c. 1928

3 What does the cartoon imply about Coolidge?

Part B
Essay

Directions: Write a well-organized essay that includes an introduction, several paragraphs, and a conclusion. Use evidence from the documents in your essay. Support your response with relevant facts, examples, and details. Include additional outside information.

Guidelines:
In your essay, be sure to:

- Develop all aspects of the task
- Incorporate information from the documents
- Incorporate relevant outside information
- Support the task with relevant facts, examples, and details
- Use a logical and clear plan of organization, including an introduction and a conclusion that are beyond a restatement of the task

ONLINE
For additional test practice, use Self-Check Quizzes—Chapter 17 at glencoe.com.

Need Extra Help?				
If You Missed Questions . . .	1	2	3	Essay
Go to Page . . .	600	600	596–603	592–601

The Great Depression Begins

1929–1932

SECTION 1 The Causes of the Great Depression

SECTION 2 Life During the Depression

SECTION 3 Hoover Responds to the Depression

Women and children wait in a bread line at New York City's New Hope Mission in the early 1930s.

Hoover
1929–1933

U.S. PRESIDENTS

U.S. EVENTS

1929
• Stock market crashes on Black Tuesday

1930
• Congress passes Hawley-Smoot Tariff

1929

1930

1931

WORLD EVENTS

1928
• Soviets introduce First Five-Year Plan to industrialize the country

1929
• Mexico passes 8-hour day, right to strike, and unemployment insurance

1930
• France creates a health and old age insurance plan

1931
• Collapse of large Austrian bank triggers bank failures across Europe

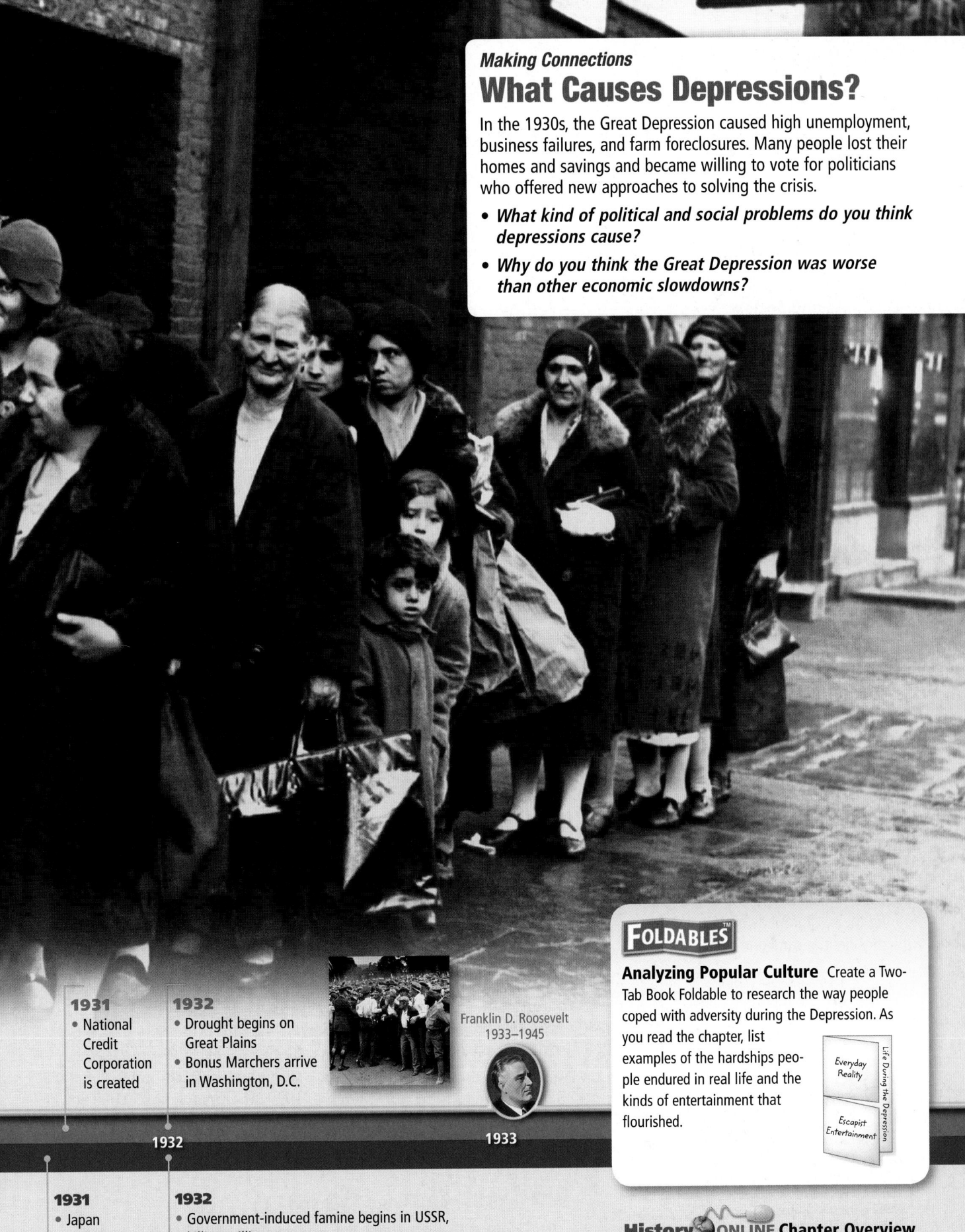

What Causes Depressions?

In the 1930s, the Great Depression caused high unemployment, business failures, and farm foreclosures. Many people lost their homes and savings and became willing to vote for politicians who offered new approaches to solving the crisis.

- *What kind of political and social problems do you think depressions cause?*
- *Why do you think the Great Depression was worse than other economic slowdowns?*

FOLDABLES™

Analyzing Popular Culture Create a Two-Tab Book Foldable to research the way people coped with adversity during the Depression. As you read the chapter, list examples of the hardships people endured in real life and the kinds of entertainment that flourished.

Everyday Reality

Escapist Entertainment

Life During the Depression

1931
- National Credit Corporation is created

1932
- Drought begins on Great Plains
- Bonus Marchers arrive in Washington, D.C.

Franklin D. Roosevelt 1933–1945

1932

1933

1931
- Japan invades Manchuria

1932
- Government-induced famine begins in USSR, killing millions
- Unemployment in Germany reaches 6 million

History ONLINE Chapter Overview
Visit glencoe.com to preview Chapter 18.

The Causes of the Great Depression

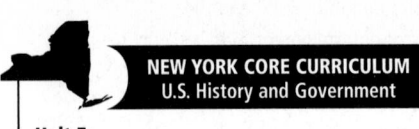
Although the 1920s were prosperous, speculation in the stock market, risky lending policies, overproduction, and uneven income distribution eventually undermined the economy and led to the Great Depression.

The Long Bull Market

MAIN Idea A strong economy helped Herbert Hoover win the 1928 election, but increasing speculation in the stock market set the stage for a crash.

HISTORY AND YOU Have you ever taken a risk while playing a game or sport? How did you decide if the risk was worth it? Read on to learn about the risks people were willing to take in the stock market in the 1920s.

The economic **collapse** that began in 1929 seemed unimaginable only a year earlier. In the 1928 election, both presidential candidates tried to paint a rosy picture of the future. Republican Herbert Hoover declared, "We are nearer to the final triumph over poverty than ever before in the history of any land."

The Election of 1928

When Calvin Coolidge declined to run for reelection in 1928, the Republicans nominated his secretary of commerce, Herbert Hoover. Hoover was well-known to Americans because he had run the Food Administration during World War I. The Democrats chose **Alfred E. Smith,** four-time governor of New York. Smith was the first Roman Catholic to win a major party's nomination for president.

Smith's beliefs became a campaign issue. Some Protestants claimed that the Catholic Church financed the Democratic Party and would rule the United States if Smith became president. These slurs embarrassed Hoover, a Quaker, and he tried to quash them, but the charges damaged Smith's candidacy.

Smith's biggest challenge, however, was the prosperity of the 1920s, for which the Republicans took full credit. Hoover defeated Smith by more than 6 million votes and won the Electoral College in a landslide, 444 to 87. On March 4, 1929, an audience of 50,000 stood in the rain to hear Hoover's inaugural speech. "I have no fears for the future of our country," Hoover said. "It is bright with hope."

The Stock Market Soars

The optimism that swept Hoover into the White House also drove stock prices to new highs. Sometimes the **stock market** experiences

Hoover and "Rugged Individualism"

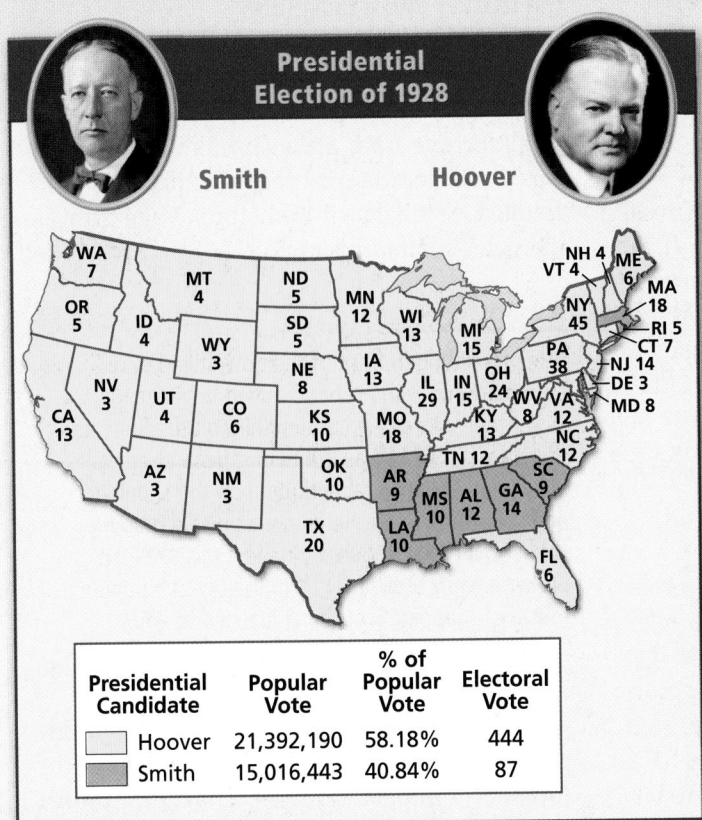

Presidential Election of 1928

Smith   Hoover

Presidential Candidate	Popular Vote	% of Popular Vote	Electoral Vote
Hoover	21,392,190	58.18%	444
Smith	15,016,443	40.84%	87

PRIMARY SOURCE

"We were challenged with a peacetime choice between the American system of rugged individualism and a European philosophy of diametrically opposed doctrines—doctrines of paternalism and state socialism. . . . [T]hese ideas would have meant the destruction of self-government through centralization of government. It would have meant the undermining of . . . individual initiative and enterprise . . .

". . . You cannot extend the mastery of the government over the daily working life of a people without at the same time making it the master of the people's souls and thoughts. . . . Free speech does not live many hours after free industry and free commerce die. . . . Every step of bureaucratizing of the business of our country poisons the very roots of liberalism—that is, political equality, free speech, free assembly, free press, and equality of opportunity. It is the road not to more liberty, but to less liberty."

—Herbert Hoover, speech delivered October 22, 1928

DBQ Document-Based Questions

1. **Contrasting** Against what other system does Hoover contrast "rugged individualism"?

2. **Analyzing Primary Sources** What does Hoover believe is at stake if free industry and free commerce die? Do you agree or disagree? Explain your position.

---

a long period of rising stock prices, or a **bull market.** In the late 1920s a prolonged bull market convinced many people to **invest** in stocks. By 1929 approximately 10 percent of American households owned stocks.

As the market continued to soar, many investors began buying stocks on **margin,** making only a small cash down payment (as low as 10 percent of the price). With $1,000, an investor could buy $10,000 worth of stock. The other $9,000 would come as a loan from a stockbroker, who earned both a commission on the sale and interest on the loan. The broker held the stock as collateral.

If the price of the stock kept rising, the investor could make a profit. For example, the investor who borrowed to buy $10,000 worth of stock had only to wait for it to rise to $11,000 in value. The investor could then sell the stock, repay the loan, and make $1,000 in profit. The problem came if the stock price began to fall.

To protect the loan, a broker could issue a **margin call,** demanding the investor repay the loan at once. As a result, many investors were very sensitive to any fall in stock prices. If prices fell, they had to sell quickly, or they might not be able to repay their loans.

Before the late 1920s, the prices investors paid for stocks had generally reflected the stocks' true value. If a company made a profit or had good future sales prospects, its stock price rose; prices fell when earnings dropped. In the late 1920s, however, many investors bid prices up without considering a company's earnings and profits. Buyers, hoping for a quick windfall, engaged in **speculation.** They bet the market would continue to climb, thus enabling them to sell the stock and make money quickly.

Reading Check **Summarizing** What was the stock market like in the 1920s?

The Great Crash

MAIN Idea Rising stock prices led to risky investment practices; when the stock market crashed, banks were in trouble.

HISTORY AND YOU Have you ever paid more for something than it was worth? Read on to learn why the stock market collapsed in 1929.

The bull market lasted only as long as investors continued putting new money into it. By the latter half of 1929, the market was running out of new customers. In September, professional investors sensed danger and began to sell off their holdings. Prices slipped. Other investors sold shares to pay the interest on their brokerage loans. Prices fell further.

The Stock Market Crash

On Monday, October 21, 1929, the comedian Groucho Marx was awakened by a telephone call from his broker. "You'd better get down here with some cash to cover your margin," the broker said. The stock market had plunged. The dazed comedian had to pay back the money he had borrowed to buy stocks, which were now selling for far less than he had paid for them. Other brokers made similar margin calls. Nervous customers put their stocks up for sale at a frenzied pace, driving the market into a tailspin.

On October 24, a day that came to be called Black Thursday, the market plummeted further. Marx was wiped out. He had earned a small fortune from plays and films, but now it was gone, and he was deeply in debt. His son recalled his final visit to the brokerage firm, as Groucho spotted his broker:

PRIMARY SOURCE

"He was sitting in front of the now-stilled ticker-tape machine, with his head buried in his hands. Ticker tape was strewn around him on the floor, and the place . . . looked as if it hadn't been swept out in a week. Groucho tapped [him] on the shoulder and said, 'Aren't you the fellow who said nothing could go wrong?' 'I guess I made a mistake,' the broker wearily replied. 'No, I'm the one who made a mistake,' snapped Groucho. 'I listened to you.'"

—quoted in *1929: The Year of the Great Crash*

The following week, on October 29, a day that was later dubbed **Black Tuesday,** prices took the steepest dive yet. That day, almost 16 million shares of stock were sold; the stock

---

Turning Point

A Crash Becomes a Depression

When the stock market crashed in October 1929, it exposed many weaknesses in the American economy. By 1932 over 25 percent of American workers were unemployed. Charities could not help all who were in need. Many cities had gone bankrupt and newly created state relief agencies had insufficient funds to help.

The Great Depression prompted major political changes. When Franklin D. Roosevelt ran for president in 1932, he had offered few details about how he would save the economy. Once in office, however, he launched a massive program to rescue the banking system, stabilize industry, and aid the unemployed. By the late 1930s, the federal government had taken on huge new responsibilities for the health of the economy and welfare of American families.

ANALYZING HISTORY Do you think the Great Depression required government intervention to resolve? Write a brief essay explaining your opinion.

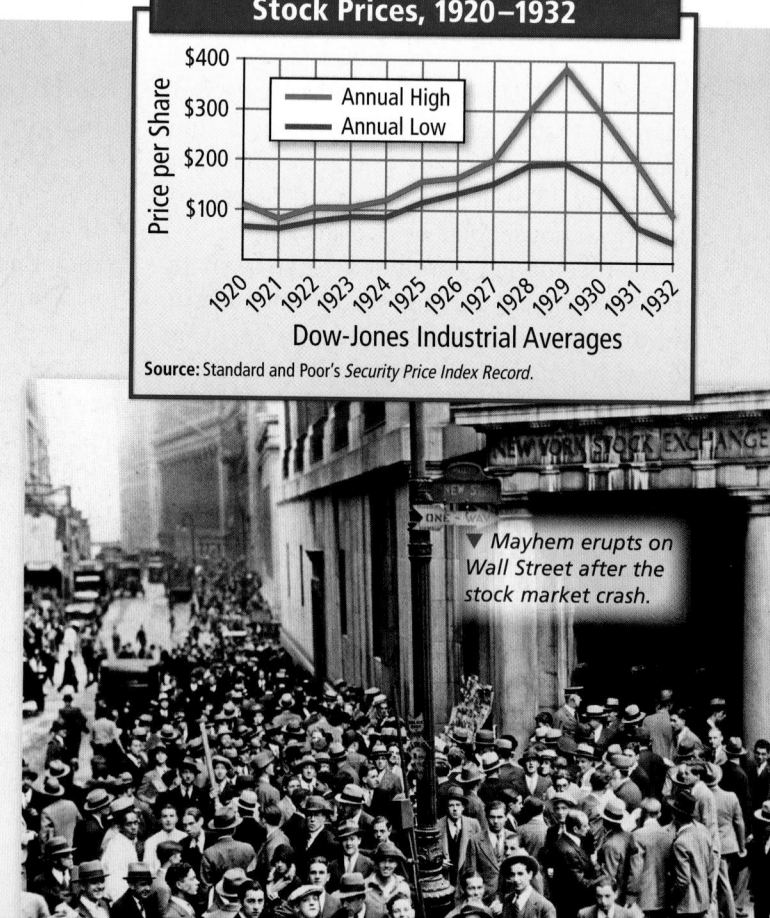

Stock Prices, 1920–1932

Price per Share / Dow-Jones Industrial Averages

— Annual High
— Annual Low

Source: Standard and Poor's *Security Price Index Record.*

▼ *Mayhem erupts on Wall Street after the stock market crash.*

market lost between $10 billion and $15 billion in value. By mid-November, stock prices had dropped by more than one-third. Some $30 billion was lost, a **sum** roughly equal to the total wages Americans earned in 1929. Although the stock market crash was not the major cause of the Great Depression, it undermined the economy's ability to overcome other weaknesses.

Banks Begin to Close

The market crash severely weakened the nation's banks in two ways. First, by 1929 banks had loaned nearly $6 billion to stock speculators. Second, many banks had invested depositors' money in the stock market, hoping for higher returns than they could get by using the money for loans.

When stock values collapsed, banks lost money on their investments, and speculators defaulted on their loans. Having suffered serious losses, many banks cut back drastically on the loans they made. With less credit available, consumers and businesses were not able to borrow as much money. This helped to send the economy into a recession.

Some banks could not absorb the losses they suffered and were forced to close. The government did not insure bank deposits, so if a bank collapsed, customers, including those who did not invest in the stock market, lost their savings. Bank failures in 1929 and 1930 created a crisis of confidence in the banking system.

News of bank failures worried Americans. Some depositors made runs on banks, causing the banks to collapse. A **bank run** takes place when many depositors decide to withdraw their money at one time, usually because of fear that the bank is going to collapse.

Most banks make a profit by lending money received from depositors and collecting interest on the loans. The bank keeps only a fraction of depositors' money in reserve to cover daily business and withdrawals. Usually, that reserve is enough to meet the bank's needs. If too many people withdraw their money, however, the bank will collapse. More than 10 percent of the nation's banks—nearly 3,500—had closed by 1932.

Reading Check **Determining Cause and Effect** What chain of events led to the economic crash of 1929?

Bank Failures, 1928–1933

Number of Failures

4,000
3,000
2,000
1,000
0

1928 1929 1930 1931 1932 1933

Source: *Historical Statistics of the United States.*

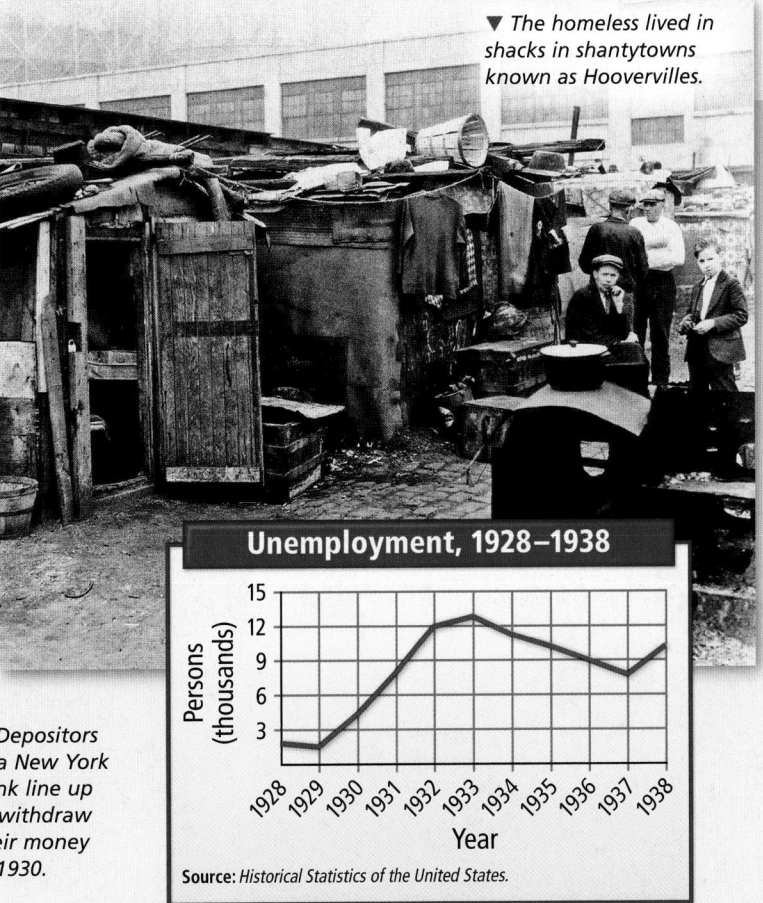

▼ The homeless lived in shacks in shantytowns known as Hoovervilles.

◀ Depositors at a New York bank line up to withdraw their money in 1930.

Unemployment, 1928–1938

Persons (thousands)

15
12
9
6
3

1928 1929 1930 1931 1932 1933 1934 1935 1936 1937 1938

Year

Source: *Historical Statistics of the United States.*

The Roots of the Great Depression

MAIN Idea An uneven distribution of income, tariff policies, and the Federal Reserve Board's mistakes contributed to the Great Depression.

HISTORY AND YOU How evenly is wealth distributed in your community? Read about the uneven distribution of income in the late 1920s.

The stock market crash played a major role in putting the economy into a recession. Yet the crash would not have led to a long-lasting depression if other forces had not been at work. The roots of the Great Depression were deeply entangled in the economy of the 1920s.

The Uneven Distribution of Income

Overproduction was one factor contributing to the onset of the Great Depression. More efficient machinery increased the production capacity of both factories and farms. Most Americans, however, did not earn enough to buy up the flood of goods they helped produce. While manufacturing output per person-hour rose 32 percent, the average worker's wage increased only 8 percent. In 1929 the top 5 percent of all American households earned 30 percent of the nation's income. In contrast, about two-thirds of families earned less than $2,500 a year, leaving them with little disposable income.

INFOGRAPHIC
Causes of the Great Depression

What Caused the Economy to Collapse?

- **Low Interest Rates** Federal Reserve kept interest rates low; companies borrowed money and expanded more than necessary.
- **Overproduction** Companies made more goods than could be sold.
- **Uneven Distribution of Wealth** Not everyone who wanted consumer goods could afford them.
- **High Tariffs** Tariffs restricted foreign demand for American goods.
- **Falling Demand** With too many goods unsold, production was cut back and employees were laid off.
- **Stock Market Speculation** Low interest rates encouraged borrowing money to speculate, endangering bank solvency.

Cyclical Effect

Automobile sales declined. This loss of demand meant less demand for:

Textiles — Oil — Steel — Rubber

Industry slowed, which caused: Unemployment — Lower wages — Which helped contribute further to:

Income and Spending

Dollars (billions) / Year 1929–1934

— Personal Spending
— Personal Income

Source: *Historical Statistics of the United States.*

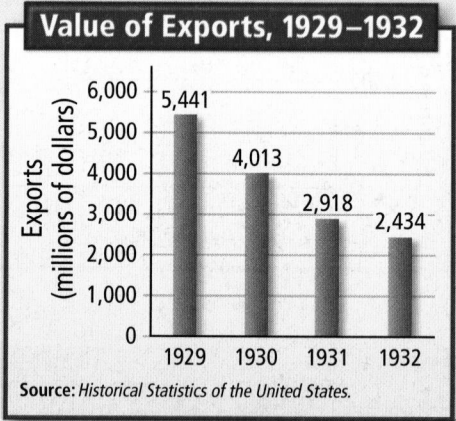

Value of Exports, 1929–1932

Exports (millions of dollars): 5,441 (1929), 4,013 (1930), 2,918 (1931), 2,434 (1932)

Source: *Historical Statistics of the United States.*

Analyzing VISUALS — DBQ

1. **Analyzing** What effect did the decline in automobile sales have on the steel industry?
2. **Calculating** Between what two years was the decrease in the value of exports the greatest?

During the 1920s many Americans had purchased high-cost items, such as refrigerators and cars, on the **installment** plan. Purchasers could make small down payments and pay the remainder of the item's price in monthly installments. Paying off such debts eventually forced some buyers to stop making new purchases. Because of the decrease in sales, manufacturers in turn cut production and laid off employees.

The slowdown in retail sales reverberated throughout the economy. When radio sales slumped, for example, makers cut back on orders for copper wire, wood cabinets, and glass radio tubes. Montana copper miners, Minnesota lumberjacks, and Ohio glassworkers, in turn, lost their jobs. Jobless workers cut back on purchases, further cutting sales. This kind of chain reaction put more and more Americans out of work. Many families had little or no savings. They had nothing to support themselves when they lost their jobs. In 1930 alone, about 26,000 businesses collapsed.

The Loss of Export Sales

Many jobs might have been saved if American manufacturers had sold more goods abroad. As the bull market of the 1920s sped up, U.S. banks made loans to speculators rather than loans to foreign companies. Foreign countries were also facing a recession after World War I. Many nations did not have the money to buy American-manufactured goods or crops.

In 1929 Hoover wanted to encourage overseas trade by lowering tariffs. Conservative Republicans, however, wanted to protect American industry from foreign competition by raising tariffs. The resulting legislation, the **Hawley-Smoot Tariff,** raised the average tariff rate to the highest level in American history. In the end, it failed to help American businesses, because foreign countries responded by raising their own tariffs. This meant fewer American products were sold overseas. By 1932 exports had fallen to about one-fifth of what they had been in 1929, which hurt both American companies and farmers.

Mistakes by the Federal Reserve

Just as consumers were able to buy more goods on credit, access to easy money propelled the stock market. Instead of raising interest rates to curb excessive speculation, the Federal Reserve Board kept its rates very low throughout the 1920s.

The Board's failure to raise interest rates significantly helped cause the Depression in two ways. First, by keeping rates low, it encouraged member banks to make risky loans. Second, its low interest rates led business leaders to think the economy was still expanding. As a result, they borrowed more money to expand production, a serious mistake because it led to overproduction when sales were falling. When the Depression finally hit, companies had to lay off workers to cut costs. Then the Federal Reserve made another mistake. It raised interest rates, tightening credit. The economy continued to spiral downward.

✔ Reading Check **Listing** What were three factors that contributed to the Great Depression?

Section 1 REVIEW

Vocabulary

1. **Explain** the significance of: Alfred E. Smith, stock market, bull market, margin, margin call, speculation, Black Tuesday, bank run, installment, Hawley-Smoot Tariff.

Main Ideas

2. **Identifying** What factors contributed to Herbert Hoover's election in 1928?

3. **Examining** How did the stock market collapse affect banks?

4. **Explaining** What effect did tariff policies have on the Great Depression?

Critical Thinking

5. **Big Ideas** How did the practice of buying on margin and speculation cause the stock market to rise?

6. **Organizing** Use a graphic organizer similar to the one below to list the causes of the Great Depression.

Causes

Great Depression

7. **Analyzing Visuals** Look at the graph on page 630. What generalization can you make about the variation in highs and lows of the stock market from 1920 to 1932?

Writing About History

8. **Expository Writing** Write an article for a financial magazine explaining the stock market's rapid decline in 1929 and the reasons for the crash on Black Tuesday.

History ONLINE

Study Central™ To review this section, go to glencoe.com and click on Study Central.

Life During the Depression

Guide to Reading

Big Ideas
Past and Present As the Great Depression and the drought worsened, thousands of people tried to find work and shelter in other places.

Content Vocabulary
- bailiff *(p. 634)*
- hobo *(p. 634)*
- soap opera *(p. 637)*

Academic Vocabulary
- suspend *(p. 634)*
- colleague *(p. 636)*
- technique *(p. 637)*

People and Events to Identify
- Dust Bowl *(p. 635)*
- Walt Disney *(p. 636)*
- John Steinbeck *(p. 637)*
- William Faulkner *(p. 637)*
- Grant Wood *(p. 637)*

Reading Strategy
Taking Notes As you read about life in the United States during the Great Depression, use the major headings of the section to create an outline similar to the one below.

Life During the Depression
I. The Depression Worsens
    A.
    B.
II.

NEW YORK CORE CURRICULUM
U.S. History and Government

Unit 5:
II.A.3 The Hoover response
II.A.4 Unemployment, the Bonus Army, Hoovervilles; impact on women and minorities
II.B.6.c The Dust Bowl and the Okies
II.B.7.a Literature: John Steinbeck
II.B.7.c Art: fine arts, Hollywood, comic books

The Great Depression caused large numbers of people to lose their jobs and property. To help people escape their misery, popular entertainment offered humorous and optimistic movies and radio programs. Novelists and photographers created more realistic portrayals of American life.

The Depression Worsens

MAIN Idea Hunger and homelessness became severe problems by the early 1930s; then, a terrible drought devastated the Great Plains.

HISTORY AND YOU Have you ever been caught outside in a thunderstorm? Read about the deadly dust storms of the 1930s.

The Depression grew steadily worse during Hoover's administration. In 1930, 1,352 banks **suspended** operations across the nation, more than twice the number of bank failures in 1929. More than 9,000 banks had failed by 1933. In 1932 alone, some 30,000 companies went out of business. By 1933 more than 12 million workers, or roughly one-fourth of the workforce, were unemployed.

Struggling to Get By

People without jobs often went hungry. Whenever possible they stood in bread lines—sometimes blocks long—for free food or lined up outside soup kitchens, which private organizations set up to give the poor meals. New York City's YMCA fed up to 12,000 people daily.

Families or individuals who could not pay their rent or mortgage lost their homes. Some of them, paralyzed by fear and humiliation over their sudden misfortune, simply would not or could not move. Their landlord would then ask the court for an eviction notice. Court officers known as **bailiffs** then ejected the nonpaying tenants, piling their belongings in the street.

Throughout the country, newly homeless people put up shacks on unused or public lands, forming communities called shantytowns. Blaming the president for their plight, people referred to such places as Hoovervilles.

In search of work or a better life, many homeless and unemployed Americans began to wander around the country—walking, hitchhiking, or, most often, "riding the rails." These wanderers, called **hobos,** would sneak past railroad police to slip into open boxcars on freight trains. Hundreds of thousands of people, mostly boys and young men, wandered from place to place in this fashion.

Fleeing the Dustbowl

The fierce dust storms of the 1930s destroyed farms and caused many to flee the Great Plains. Below, girls pump water during a dust storm in Springfield, Colorado.

About 40 percent of migrant farmers who fled the Dust Bowl went to California's San Joaquin Valley to pick cotton and grapes. In his novel *The Grapes of Wrath*, John Steinbeck describes what these migrants found when they arrived to harvest crops:

PRIMARY SOURCE

"Maybe he [the owner of the fields] needs two hunderd men, so he talks to five hunderd, an' they tell other folks, an' when you get to the place, they's a thousan' men. This here fella says, 'I'm payin' twenty cents an hour.' An' maybe half the men walk off. But they's still five hunderd that's so . . . hungry they'll work for nothin' but biscuits. Well, this here fella's got a contract to pick them peaches or—chop that cotton. You see now? The more fellas he can get, an' the hungrier, less he's gonna pay. An' he'll get a fella with kids if he can."

—from *The Grapes of Wrath*

DBQ Document-Based Questions

1. **Analyzing Primary Sources** What advantage does the owner of the fields have when it comes to paying people to work?

2. **Drawing Conclusions** Why might the owners of the fields prefer to get "a fella with kids"?

The Dust Bowl

Farmers soon faced a new disaster. Since homesteading had begun on the Great Plains, farmers' plows had uprooted the wild grasses that held the soil's moisture. When crop prices dropped in the 1920s, farmers left many of their fields uncultivated. Then, a terrible drought struck the Great Plains. With neither grass nor wheat to hold the scant rainfall, the soil dried to dust. From the Dakotas to Texas, America's wheat fields became a vast **"Dust Bowl."**

Winds whipped the arid earth, blowing it aloft and blackening the sky for hundreds of miles. When the dust settled, it buried crops and livestock. Humans and animals caught outdoors sometimes died of suffocation when the dust filled their lungs. The number of yearly dust storms grew, from 22 in 1934 to 72 in 1937. Will and Carolyn Henderson farmed in western Oklahoma. Carolyn wrote a series of articles for the *Atlantic Monthly* about their life during the drought.

PRIMARY SOURCE

"At the little country store, after one of the worst of these storms, the candies in the show case all looked alike and equally brown. Dust to eat and dust to breathe and dust to drink. Dust in the beds and in the flour bin, on dishes and walls and windows, in hair and eyes and ears and teeth and throats. . . ."

—from *Dust to Eat: Drought and Depression in the 1930s*

Some Great Plains farmers managed to hold on to their land, but many had no chance. If their withered fields were mortgaged, they had to turn them over to the banks. Then, nearly penniless, many families headed west, hoping for a better life in California. Because many migrants were from Oklahoma, they became known as "Okies." In California, they lived in roadside camps and remained homeless and impoverished.

✓ Reading Check **Explaining** What chain of events turned the once-fertile Great Plains into the Dust Bowl?

History ONLINE Student Web Activity Visit glencoe.com and complete the activity on hobo life during the Depression.

Art and Entertainment

MAIN Idea Movies and radio shows were very popular during the 1930s, a period that also produced new art and literature.

HISTORY AND YOU Has a movie ever helped you get through a difficult time? Read to learn ways that people coped with the Great Depression.

The hard times of the 1930s led many Americans to prefer entertainment that let them escape their worries. For this reason, movies and radio plays grew increasingly popular. Also, in the 1930s, comic books grew rapidly in popularity. The first comic books cheered people by reprinting newspaper comics, but in the late 1930s, the "superhero" genre was born with the printing of the first tales of *Superman* in 1938 and *Batman* in 1939.

Hollywood

During the 1930s more than 60 million Americans went to the movies each week. Child stars such as Shirley Temple and Jackie Coogan delighted viewers. Groucho Marx wisecracked while his brothers amused audiences in such films as *Animal Crackers,* and comedies became very popular because they provided a release from daily worries.

King Kong, first released in 1933, showcased new special effects. Moviegoers also loved cartoons. **Walt Disney,** who brought Mickey Mouse to life in 1928, produced the first feature-length animated film, *Snow White and the Seven Dwarfs,* in 1937.

Even serious films were optimistic. In *Mr. Smith Goes to Washington,* Jimmy Stewart played a naïve scout leader who becomes a senator. He exposes the corruption of some of his **colleagues** and calls upon senators to view American government as a high achievement.

In 1939 MGM produced *The Wizard of Oz,* a colorful musical that lifted viewers' spirits. That same year, Vivien Leigh and Clark Gable thrilled audiences in *Gone with the Wind,* a Civil War epic that won nine Academy Awards. Hattie McDaniel, who won the award for Best Supporting Actress, was the first African American to win an Academy Award.

On the Air

While movies captured the imagination, radio offered information and entertainment as near as the living room. Tens of millions of people listened to the radio daily, and radio comedians such as Jack Benny, George Burns, and Gracie Allen were popular, as were the radio adventures of superheroes such as the Green Hornet and the Lone Ranger.

People IN HISTORY

Margaret Bourke-White
1904–1971

While a student at Columbia University, Margaret Bourke-White took a course on photography. She went on to become one of the leading photographers of her time. In 1927 she began photographing architectural and industrial subjects. Her originality led to jobs at major magazines such as *Fortune* and *Life.* During World War II she became the first woman photographer attached to the U.S. armed forces. She covered the Italian campaign and the siege of Moscow. She was among those who photographed concentration camp survivors. Bourke-White traveled to India after the war to document Gandhi's efforts to gain that nation's independence from Great Britain. During the Korean War, she traveled with South Korean troops.

What made Margaret Bourke-White's career and photography unusual for the time?

▲ *African American flood victims wait for food and clothing from the Red Cross in 1937 in one of Margaret Bourke-White's most famous photos. The people contrast sharply with the billboard.*

Daytime radio dramas carried over their story lines from day to day. Programs such as *The Guiding Light* presented middle-class families confronting illness, conflict, and other problems. The shows' sponsors were often makers of laundry soaps, so the shows were nicknamed **soap operas.** Radio created a new type of community. Even strangers found common ground in discussing the lives of radio characters.

Literature and Art

Literature and art also flourished during the 1930s. Writers and artists tried to portray life around them, using the homeless and unemployed as their subjects in stories and pictures.

Novelist **John Steinbeck** added flesh and blood to journalists' reports of poverty and misfortune. His writing evoked both sympathy for his characters and indignation at social injustice. In *The Grapes of Wrath* (1939), which was awarded the Pulitzer Prize and was made into a movie, Steinbeck tells the story of the Joad family fleeing the Dust Bowl to find a new life in California after losing their farm. The novel was based on Steinbeck's visits to migrant camps and his interviews with migrant families. In one article he described typical housing for the migrants, for which they paid the growers as much as $2.00 daily:

PRIMARY SOURCE

"[They have] one-room shacks usually about 10 by 12 feet, have no rug, no water, no bed. In one corner there is a little iron wood stove. Water must be carried from the faucet at the end of the street."

—from *Dust to Eat: Drought and Depression*

Other novelists developed new writing techniques. In *The Sound and the Fury,* **William Faulkner,** who later won the Nobel Prize for Literature, shows what his characters are thinking and feeling before they speak. Using this stream of consciousness **technique,** he exposes hidden attitudes of Southern whites and African Americans in a fictional Mississippi county.

Although written words remained powerful, images were growing more influential. Photographers roamed the nation with the new 35-millimeter cameras, seeking new subjects. In 1936, *Time* magazine publisher Henry Luce introduced *Life,* a weekly photojournalism magazine that enjoyed instant success. The striking pictures of photojournalists Dorothea Lange and Margaret Bourke-White showed how the Great Depression had affected average Americans.

Painters in the 1930s included Thomas Hart Benton and **Grant Wood,** whose styles were referred to as the regionalist school. Their work emphasized traditional American values, especially those of the rural Midwest and South. Wood's painting that is best-known today is *American Gothic.* The portrait pays tribute to no-nonsense Midwesterners while gently making fun of their severity.

Reading Check **Examining** What subjects did artists, photographers, and writers emphasize during the 1930s?

Section 2 REVIEW

Vocabulary

1. **Explain** the significance of: bailiff, hobo, Dust Bowl, Walt Disney, soap opera, John Steinbeck, William Faulkner, Grant Wood.

Main Ideas

2. **Analyzing** What environmental event of the 1930s worsened the Great Depression?

3. **Explaining** How did people try to escape the realities of life during the Great Depression?

Critical Thinking

4. **Big Ideas** How did some Great Plains farmers respond to the loss of their fields to the banks?

5. **Organizing** Use a graphic organizer such as the one below to identify the effects of the Great Depression.

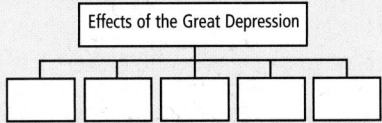

Effects of the Great Depression

6. **Analyzing Visuals** Look at the photo on page 635. What details indicate that this is a severe dust storm?

Writing About History

7. **Descriptive Writing** Imagine you are writing the catalogue for an art show of photographs by Dorothea Lange or Margaret Bourke-White. Write a paragraph describing one of the images in this section or discussing their photographic skill.

History ONLINE

Study Central™ To review this section, go to glencoe.com and click on Study Central.

GEOGRAPHY & HISTORY

The Dust Bowl

In the late nineteenth century, settlers on the Great Plains turned the semiarid region into the bread-basket of America, growing vast fields of wheat and other crops. Intensive farming destroyed the region's native grasses and loosened the soil. At first, this was not a problem, as the Great Plains experienced higher than normal rainfall in the late 1800s. Over time, how-ever, farmers exhausted the soil. When rainfall began to decline and temperatures rose in the 1920s, the soil began to dry out. In 1932, a full-scale drought hit. The fierce heat dried the exhausted soil into fine dustlike particles. The high winds of the open plains easily lifted the dirt into the air creating "dust storms." In 1932 alone, 14 dust storms struck the Great Plains. These storms carried the soil of the Great Plains hundreds of miles. In May 1934, a huge storm dumped piles of dirt in Chicago. Further east, silt from the storm collected on the windows of the White House.

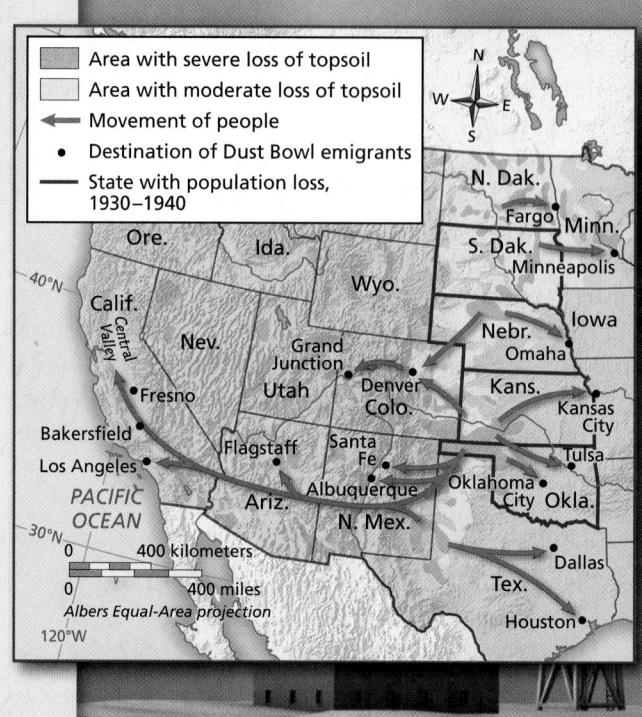

How Did the Dust Bowl Affect Americans?

The "Dust Bowl" is sometimes called a human-made natural disaster. The drought and rising temperatures of the 1930s were a natural disaster. But the dust storms were human-made, the result of decades of overcultivation. These "black blizzards" scoured and buried homes, ruined vehicle engines, and diminished visibility. The blowing dirt could injure eyes and damage lungs; it even suffocated people. As the drought destroyed their livelihood, and the dust storms destroyed their belongings, many farmers abandoned the land, packed up their families, and fled the region in search of work elsewhere.

Analyzing GEOGRAPHY

1. **Movement** Which states lost population in the 1930s? In which direction did most people fleeing the Dust Bowl move?

2. **Human-Environment Interaction** Study the image at right. What problems and dangers does the dust storm create?

The drought on the Great Plains in the 1930s was the worst ever recorded in U.S. history. Summer temperatures soared above 110 degrees in many locations, setting records that still stand. The lack of water and fierce heat dried the soil to a fine dust. An estimated 200 million acres of land lost some or all of its topsoil.

Dust storms towered thousands of feet in the air and moved rapidly across the open plains. When a storm hit, it became dark outside, and visibility often dropped to only a few feet.

▲ Many farmers in the dust bowl, such as Elmer Thomas and his family of Muskogee, Oklahoma (above), decided to leave the region. Many became migrant workers, traveling from across the west in search of short-term employment.

The fine grit of dust storms could clog car engines and other mechanical devices beyond repair.

People raced for cover when a storm hit. The grit stung the skin and eyes. Breathing the dust could cause dust pneumonia. Many people, especially children and senior citizens, became sick, and many died.

Hoover Responds to the Depression

President Hoover tried to fix the economy by providing loans to banks and corporations and by starting public works projects. Later, he reluctantly supported direct aid to impoverished families. By the early 1930s, more Americans were demanding the government's help.

Guide to Reading

Big Ideas
Government and Society President Hoover's ideas about government shaped his response to the Great Depression, making the government slow to respond.

Content Vocabulary
- public works *(p. 640)*
- relief *(p. 642)*
- foreclose *(p. 643)*

Academic Vocabulary
- series *(p. 640)*
- community *(p. 641)*

People and Events to Identify
- Reconstruction Finance Corporation *(p. 641)*
- Bonus Army *(p. 643)*

Reading Strategy
Categorizing As you read about Herbert Hoover's response to the Depression, create a graphic organizer listing his major initiatives and their results.

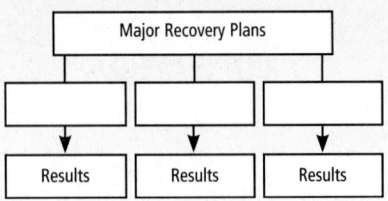

Major Recovery Plans

Results Results Results

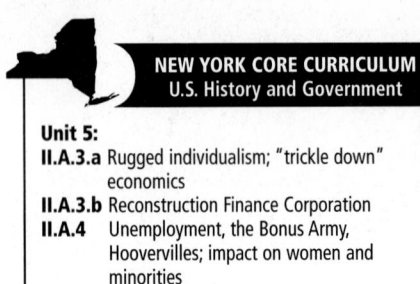

NEW YORK CORE CURRICULUM
U.S. History and Government

Unit 5:
II.A.3.a Rugged individualism; "trickle down" economics
II.A.3.b Reconstruction Finance Corporation
II.A.4 Unemployment, the Bonus Army, Hoovervilles; impact on women and minorities

Promoting Recovery

MAIN Idea Hoover encouraged businesses to stop laying off workers and created public works projects.

HISTORY AND YOU What efforts would you have taken to help the economy if you had been president? Read about the public works efforts of the early 1930s.

On Friday, October 25, 1929, the day after Black Thursday, President Herbert Hoover declared that "the fundamental business of the country . . . is on a sound and prosperous basis." On March 7, 1930, he told the press that "the worst effects of the crash upon employment will have passed during the next sixty days." Critics derided his optimism as conditions worsened. Hoover, however, hoped to downplay the public's fears. He wanted to avoid more bank runs and layoffs by urging consumers and business leaders to make rational decisions. In the end, Hoover's efforts failed to inspire the public's confidence, and the economy continued its downward slide.

President Hoover believed that the American system of "rugged individualism" would keep the economy moving. He felt that the government should not step in to help individuals out. After World War I, many European countries had implemented a form of socialism, which Hoover felt contributed to their lack of economic recovery. In 1922 Hoover had written a book, *American Individualism,* which presented arguments for why the American system of individualism was the best social, political, spiritual, and economic system in the world. Thus, it was difficult for Hoover to propose policies that had the government taking more control.

Despite his public statements that the economy was not in trouble, Hoover was worried. To devise strategies for improving the economy, he organized a **series** of conferences, bringing together the heads of banks, railroads, and other big businesses, as well as labor leaders and government officials.

Industry leaders pledged to keep factories open and to stop slashing wages. By 1931, however, they had broken those pledges. Hoover then increased the funding for **public works,** or government-financed building projects. The resulting construction jobs were intended to replace some of those lost in the private sector.

▲ While the Democratic Party donkey marches outside singing old songs, Hoover tries to deal with economic problems caused by high tariffs, depression and drought.

▲ Herbert Hoover reassures a farmer his scarecrow labeled farm relief will help.

Analyzing VISUALS DBQ

1. **Analyzing** What does the cartoon on the right suggest about Hoover's plan to help farmers?

2. **Analyzing** How are Hoover and the Democrats portrayed in the cartoon on the left?

Public works projects did create some jobs but for only a small fraction of the millions who were unemployed. The government could create enough new jobs only by massively increasing government spending, which Hoover refused to do.

Someone had to pay for public works projects. If the government raised taxes to pay for them, consumers would have less money to spend, further hurting already struggling businesses. If the government kept taxes low and ran a budget deficit instead—spending more money than it collected in taxes—it would have to borrow the money. Borrowing would mean less money available for businesses to expand and for consumer loans. Hoover feared that deficit spending would actually delay an economic recovery.

As the 1930 congressional elections approached, most Americans felt threatened by rising unemployment. Citizens blamed the party in power for the ailing economy. The Republicans lost 49 seats and their majority in the House of Representatives; they held on to the Senate by a single vote.

Trying to Rescue the Banks

To get the economy growing again, Hoover focused on expanding the money supply. The government, he believed, had to help banks make loans to corporations, which could then expand production and rehire workers.

The president asked the Federal Reserve Board to put more currency into circulation, but the Board refused. In an attempt to ease the money shortage, Hoover set up the National Credit Corporation (NCC) in October 1931. The NCC created a pool of money that allowed troubled banks to continue lending money in their **communities.** This program, however, failed to meet the nation's needs.

In 1932 Hoover requested Congress to set up the **Reconstruction Finance Corporation** (RFC) to make loans to businesses. By early 1932 the RFC had lent about $238 million to approximately 160 banks, 60 railroads, and 18 building-and-loan organizations. The RFC was overly cautious, however. It failed to increase its lending sufficiently to meet the need, and the economy continued its decline.

Direct Help for Citizens

From the start, Hoover strongly opposed the federal government's participation in **relief**—money given directly to impoverished families. He believed that only state and local governments should dole out relief. Any other needs should be met by private charity, not by the federal government. By the spring of 1932, however, state and local governments were running out of money, and private charities lacked the resources to handle the crisis.

That year, political support for a federal relief measure increased, and Congress passed the Emergency Relief and Construction Act in July. Reluctantly, Hoover signed the bill. The new act called for $1.5 billion for public works and $300 million in emergency loans to the states for direct relief. For the first time in United States history, the federal government was supplying direct relief funds, although governors of the states had to apply for the loans. By this time, however, the new program could not reverse the accelerating collapse.

Reading Check **Summarizing** Why did Hoover oppose a federal relief program?

In an Angry Mood

MAIN Idea Farmers, veterans, and others who were suffering grew frustrated and demanded the government do something to help.

HISTORY AND YOU Have you ever felt strongly enough about an issue to take part in a protest? Read what happened when veterans of World War I demonstrated in Washington, D.C., in 1932.

In the months after the Wall Street crash, most Americans were resigned to bad economic news. By 1931, however, many people were becoming increasingly discontent.

Hunger Marches and Protests by Farmers

In January 1931 about 500 residents of Oklahoma City looted a grocery store. Crowds began showing up at rallies and "hunger marches" organized by the American Communist Party. On December 5, 1932, in Washington, D.C., a group of about 1,200 hunger marchers chanted, "Feed the hungry, tax the rich." Police herded them into a cul-de-sac

An Angry Nation

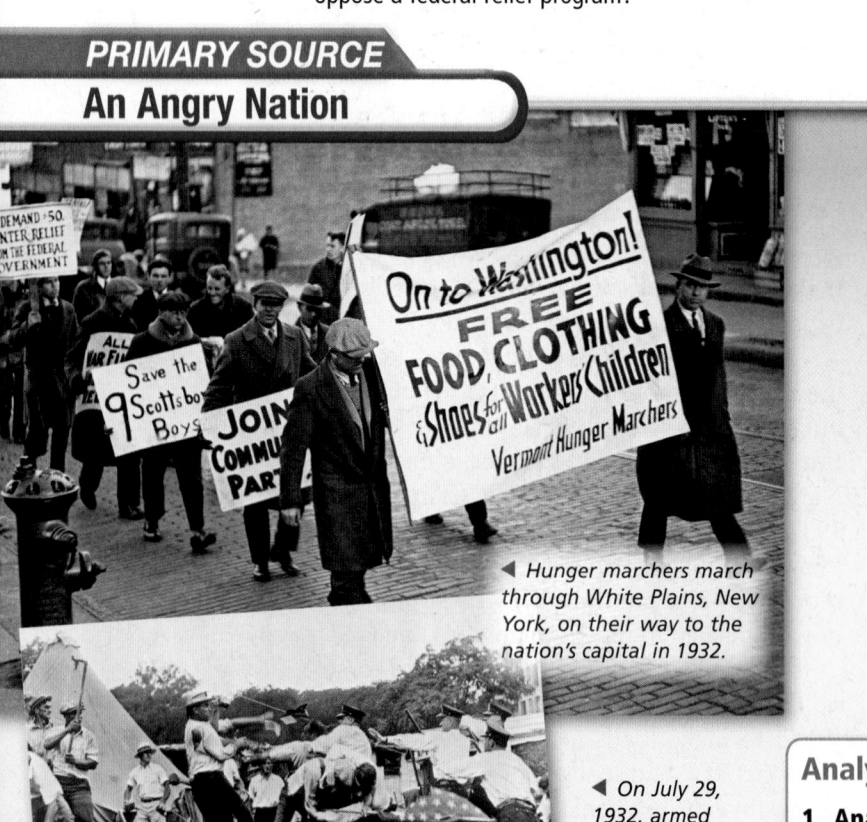

◀ Hunger marchers march through White Plains, New York, on their way to the nation's capital in 1932.

◀ On July 29, 1932, armed guards use tear gas and clubs to move Bonus Army marchers.

▲ Angry at low prices, dairy farmers dump milk in an attempt to drive up prices and draw attention to their problems.

Analyzing VISUALS DBQ

1. **Analyzing Visuals** What do you observe about the Bonus Army's attempt to defend itself?

2. **Speculating** How do you think poor and hungry people would have responded to the photo at top right?

and denied them food and water, until some members of Congress insisted on the marchers' right to petition their government. They were then permitted to march to Capitol Hill.

The hungry poor were not the only people who began to protest conditions during the Depression. During World War I's agricultural boom, many farmers had heavily mortgaged their land to pay for seed, feed, and equipment. After the war, prices sank so low that farmers began losing money. Creditors **foreclosed** on nearly one million farms between 1930 and 1934, taking ownership of the land and evicting the families. Some farmers began destroying their crops, desperately trying to raise prices by reducing the supply. In Nebraska, farmers burned corn to heat their homes. Georgia dairy farmers blocked highways and stopped milk trucks, dumping the milk into ditches.

The Bonus Marchers

After World War I, Congress had enacted a $1,000 bonus for each veteran, to be distributed in 1945. In 1931 Texas congressman Wright Patman introduced a bill that would authorize early payment of these bonuses. In May 1932 several hundred Oregon veterans began marching to Washington to lobby for passage of the legislation. As they moved east, other veterans joined them until they numbered about 1,000. Wearing ragged military uniforms, they trudged along the highways or rode the rails, singing old war songs. The press termed the marchers the **"Bonus Army."**

Once in Washington, the marchers camped in Hoovervilles. More veterans joined them until the Bonus Army swelled to 15,000. President Hoover acknowledged the veterans' right to petition but refused to meet with them. When the Senate voted down the bonus bill, veterans outside the Capitol began to grumble. Many returned home, but some marchers stayed on. Some squatted in vacant buildings downtown.

In late July, Hoover ordered the buildings cleared. The police tried, but when an officer panicked and fired into a crowd, killing two veterans, the city government called in the army. General Douglas MacArthur ignored Hoover's orders to clear the buildings but to leave the camps alone. McArthur sent in cavalry, infantry, and tanks to clear the camps.

Soon unarmed veterans were running away, pursued by 700 soldiers. The soldiers tear-gassed stragglers and burned the shacks. National press coverage of troops assaulting veterans further harmed Hoover's reputation and hounded the president throughout the 1932 campaign.

Although Hoover failed to resolve the economic crisis, he did more than any prior president to expand the federal government's economic role. The Reconstruction Finance Corporation was the first federal agency created to stimulate the economy during peacetime. The route of the Bonus Army marchers and the lingering Depression, however, tarnished Hoover's public image.

Reading Check **Evaluating** How did Americans react as the Depression continued?

Section 3 REVIEW

Vocabulary

1. **Explain** the significance of: public works, Reconstruction Finance Corporation, relief, foreclose, Bonus Army.

Main Ideas

2. **Identifying** What two major strategies did President Hoover use to promote economic recovery?

3. **Explaining** What did World War I veterans do to try to get their service bonuses early?

Critical Thinking

4. **Big Ideas** How did President Hoover's philosophy of government guide his response to the Depression?

5. **Organizing** Use a graphic organizer similar to the one below to list American reactions to the Great Depression.

American Reactions

6. **Analyzing Visuals** Look at the photo of the Hunger Marchers on page 642. How would you compare their approach and style to protestors today?

Writing About History

7. **Persuasive Writing** Imagine that you are a World War I veteran in 1931. Write a persuasive letter to your congressperson explaining why you need your bonus now, not in 1945.

History ONLINE

Study Central™ To review this section, go to glencoe.com and click on Study Central.

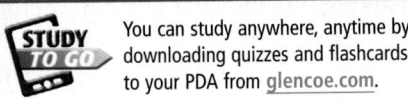

You can study anywhere, anytime by downloading quizzes and flashcards to your PDA from glencoe.com.

Causes of the Depression

Long-Range Causes

- Uneven distribution of wealth ensures that many consumers do not have enough income to purchase the goods being produced.
- Interest rates are kept too low by the Federal Reserve, which encourages businesses to borrow money and to expand production beyond market demand.
- Overproduction by business eventually floods the market with goods that cannot be sold. Businesses begin laying off workers and shutting down production.

Immediate Causes

- People and businesses borrow money to invest in the stock market; speculation drives stock prices too high and when they collapse, many people lose all of their money, and many banks collapse when loans are not repaid.
- As companies lay off workers, demand for goods falls as workers lack the income to purchase goods being produced. This in turn causes even more layoffs and a cyclical effect sets in, driving up unemployment.
- In order to protect American companies from competition, Congress raises tariffs. When other countries respond in kind, foreign demand for American goods falls, further hurting American companies.

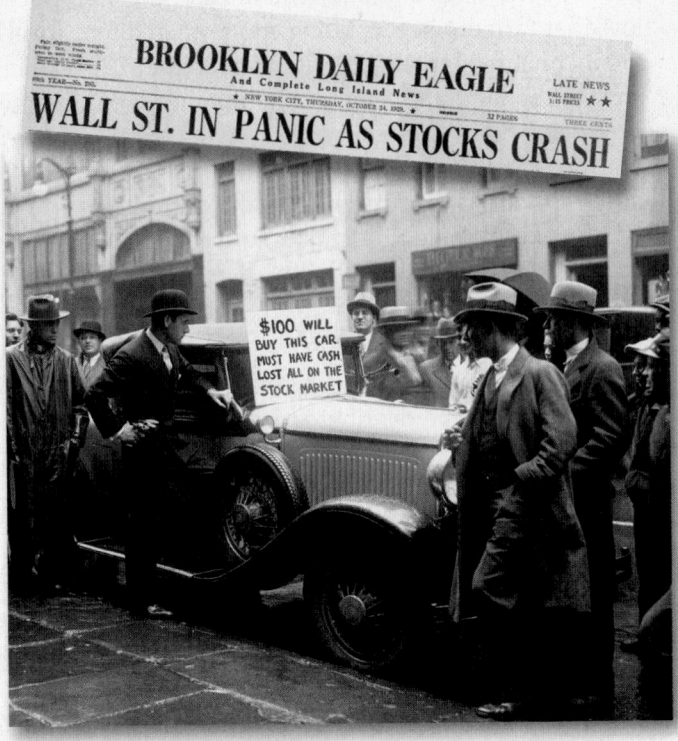

▲ A New York paper trumpets the stock crash. To raise cash to pay their stock debts, people began selling anything of value, including this car.

▲ Shantytowns appeared in many cities during the Depression as homelessness and unemployment rose.

Effects of the Depression

- Unemployment rises to record levels.
- Many people, unable to pay their debts, lose their homes and farms; the homeless create shantytowns, nicknamed Hoovervilles, on the edges of cities.
- Hunger marches, protests by farmers, and marches by veterans seeking their bonuses indicate growing anger among the population at economic conditions.
- The Republican Party rapidly loses political support, enabling the Democrats to take control of Congress.
- The federal government, for the first time, begins providing direct relief to citizens in need.
- Forms of entertainment, including movies, radio shows, and comic books, focus on distracting people from their daily lives.

NEW YORK REGENTS EXAM PRACTICE

TEST-TAKING

If you are not sure of the answer, try to narrow the options. First, eliminate any choices that you know are clearly wrong. Then, if necessary, make a guess among the remaining choices.

Part I

Directions (1–9): For each statement or question, write on a separate sheet of paper the number of the word or expression that, of those given, best completes the statement or answers the question.

1 One of the major problems with the stock market in the late 1920s was the number of people who bought stocks
  (1) on margin, with borrowed money.
  (2) in companies that they supported.
  (3) only after carefully studying a company's history.
  (4) without knowing their stockbroker's reputation.

2 Which of the following was a root cause of the Great Depression?
  (1) prohibiting the sale of alcohol
  (2) giving women the right to vote
  (3) uneven distribution of income
  (4) the end of federal control of banks

3 Herbert Hoover won the 1928 election in a landslide, in part because of
  (1) fears of another world war.
  (2) prosperity under Calvin Coolidge.
  (3) having been vice president.
  (4) his support for unions.

4 Hoover was slow to respond to the economic crisis because he opposed
  (1) all public works projects.
  (2) deficit spending.
  (3) investing in stocks.
  (4) private charities.

5 How did American citizens respond to the Great Depression in the 1930 midterm election?
  (1) by reelecting Hoover
  (2) by voting for socialist candidates
  (3) by staying away from the polls
  (4) by voting for Democrats

6 What was Hoover's response to the Bonus Army marchers who came to Washington, D.C.?
  (1) He ordered them to be paid their bonuses.
  (2) He had the army remove them.
  (3) He visited them and listened to them.
  (4) He set up soup kitchens to feed them.

7 During the Great Depression, the expression *Hooverville* showed that President Hoover
  (1) was seen as a role model.
  (2) used the military to aid the unemployed.
  (3) was blamed for the suffering of the poor.
  (4) supported relief and public housing for the needy.

Need Extra Help?							
If You Missed Questions . . .	1	2	3	4	5	6	7
Go to Page . . .	628–629	632–633	628	641	641	643	634

[OVER]

Base your answer to question 8 on the map below and on your knowledge of Chapter 18.

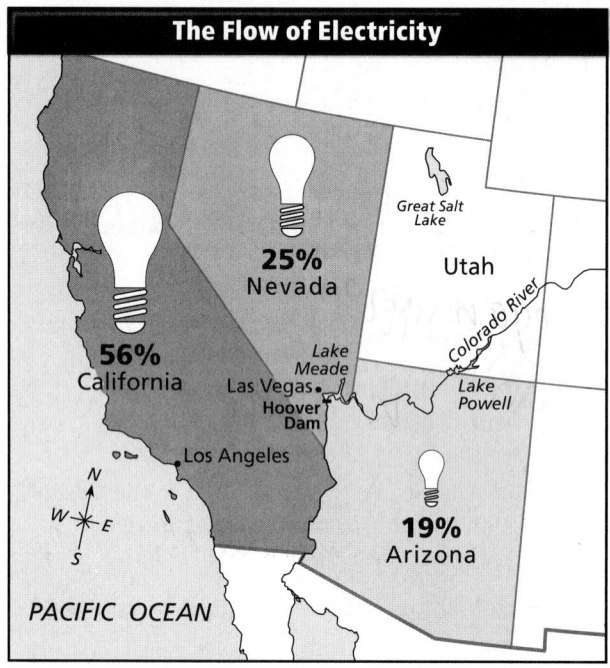

The Flow of Electricity

8 The federal government began building Hoover Dam in 1931. What body of water was it designed to control?

(1) the Pacific Ocean

(2) Lake Powell

(3) the Great Salt Lake

(4) the Colorado River

9 Despite the poverty of the 1930s, more than 60 million people went to the movies weekly. Why were movies so popular?

(1) Special effects used in the movies were amazing.

(2) The first talking picture was released.

(3) Movies offered an escape from viewers' hard lives.

(4) Theaters were air conditioned and offered free popcorn.

Need Extra Help?		
If You Missed Questions . . .	8	9
Go to Page . . .	R15	636–637

Part II Thematic Essay Question

Directions: Write a well-organized essay that includes an introduction, several paragraphs addressing the task below, and a conclusion.

Theme: The Great Depression

The 1920s were prosperous, but the American economy was vulnerable. By the 1930s, hunger and homelessness were severe problems throughout the nation.

Task:

Identify at least two causes of the Great Depression in the United States and for each

- Describe one immediate and one long-term effect of the cause
- Evaluate the extent to which the cause contributed to the collapse of the economy and the Great Depression

Guidelines:

In your essay, be sure to:

- Develop all aspects of the task
- Support the theme with relevant facts, examples, and details
- Use a logical and clear plan of organization, including an introduction and a conclusion that are beyond a restatement of the theme

Part III Document-Based Question

This question is based on the accompanying documents. It is designed to test your ability to work with historical documents. Some of the documents have been edited for the purposes of the question. As you analyze the documents, take into account both the source of each document and any point of view that may be presented in the document.

Historical Context:

During the late 1920s and 1930s, the United States experienced the Great Depression, which caused widespread economic hardship and changed the lives of Americans.

Task:

Using information from the documents and your knowledge of United States history, answer the questions that follow each document in Part A. Your answers to the questions will help you write the Part B essay in which you will be asked to

- Describe the effects of the Great Depression on the lives of Americans throughout the nation
- Evaluate the effectiveness of the Hoover administration at alleviating the problems of the Depression

Part A

Short-Answer Questions

Directions: Analyze the documents and answer the short-answer questions that follow each document on a separate sheet of paper.

Document 1

> The newspapers were full of it, and I read everything I could get my hands on, gathering in the full meaning of such terms as Black Thursday, deflation and depression. I couldn't imagine such financial disaster touching my small world; it surely concerned only the rich. But by the first week of November I too knew differently; along with millions of others across the nation, I was without a job. All that next week I searched for any kind of work that would prevent my leaving school. Again it was, 'We're firing, not hiring.' 'Sorry, sonny, nothing doing here.' Finally, on the seventh of November I went to school and cleaned out my locker, knowing it was impossible to stay on. A piercing chill was in the air as I walked back to the rooming house. The hawk had come. I could already feel his wings shadowing me.

Source: Gordon Parks, *A Choice of Weapons*

1 Why did Parks at first think he was safe from the effects of the stock market crash? What changed his mind?

Document 2

Source: John T. McCutcheon, *Chicago Tribune*, 1931

2 How does the cartoon inspire sympathy for the character?

Part B

Essay

Directions: Reread the task box at the top left and write a well-organized essay that includes an introduction, several paragraphs, and a conclusion.

Guidelines:

In your essay, be sure to:

- Develop all aspects of the task
- Incorporate information from the documents
- Incorporate relevant outside information
- Support the theme with relevant facts, examples, and details
- Use a logical and clear plan of organization, including an introduction and a conclusion that are beyond a restatement of the theme

For additional test practice, use Self-Check Quizzes—Chapter 18 at glencoe.com.

Need Extra Help?			
If You Missed Questions . . .	1	2	Essay
Go to Page . . .	630–632	630–632	634–637

Chapter 18   The Great Depression Begins   **647**

Chapter 19

Roosevelt and the New Deal

1933–1941

SECTION 1 The First New Deal

SECTION 2 The Second New Deal

SECTION 3 The New Deal Coalition

WE DO OUR PART

During the 1932 presidential campaign, New York governor Franklin D. Roosevelt greets a coal miner in West Virginia.

Hoover
1929–1933

Franklin D.
Roosevelt
1933–1945

1933
- Unemployment peaks at 24.9%
- FDR's "100 Days" results in 9 new federal programs

1934
- Securities and Exchange Commission is created

1935
- Social Security Act and Wagner Act are passed
- Supreme Court strikes down NIRA

U.S. PRESIDENTS

U.S. EVENTS   1931   1933   1935

WORLD EVENTS

1933
- Hitler becomes German chancellor
- World Economic Conference fails to reduce tariffs

1935
- Hitler denounces Treaty of Versailles
- Canada creates minimum wage and unemployment insurance

MAKING CONNECTIONS

Can Government Fix the Economy?

During the 1930s, New Deal programs increased government regulation of banking, industry, and farming; gave greater rights to workers; and provided government aid to the unemployed and senior citizens.

- *What kind of problems do you think government can solve?*
- *What difficulties can result when the government tries to regulate the economy?*

Analyzing Long-Term Effects Make a Folded Chart Foldable showing major New Deal programs and their long-term effects. In one column, describe the program's original purpose. In the second column, identify how those programs still influence government and society today.

New Deal Measures	Purpose in the 1930s	Effects Today
Social Security		
National Labor Relations Board		
Federal Deposit Insurance Corporation		

1936
- "Court-packing" plan creates controversy

1937
- Sit-down strikes force General Motors to recognize UAW

1938
- Fair Labor Standards Act sets minimum wage and 40-hour workweek

1937

1939

1936
- Wave of sit-down strikes in France leads to 40-hour workweek
- Spanish Civil War begins

1938
- Germany annexes Austria
- Mexico takes control of U.S. oil companies in Mexico

1939
- World War II begins

History ONLINE Chapter Overview
Visit glencoe.com to preview Chapter 19.

The First New Deal

Guide to Reading

Big Ideas
Individual Action Franklin Delano Roosevelt's character and experiences prepared him for the presidency.

Content Vocabulary
- polio *(p. 650)*
- gold standard *(p. 652)*
- bank holiday *(p. 652)*
- fireside chats *(p. 653)*

Academic Vocabulary
- apparent *(p. 651)*
- ideology *(p. 652)*
- fundamental *(p. 658)*

People and Events to Identify
- New Deal *(p. 651)*
- Hundred Days *(p. 652)*
- Civilian Conservation Corps *(p. 658)*

Reading Strategy
Sequencing As you read about Roosevelt's first three months in office, complete a time line to record the major problems he addressed during this time.

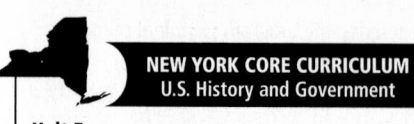

NEW YORK CORE CURRICULUM
U.S. History and Government

Unit 5:
II.B.1 Relief of human suffering
II.B.2 Recovery of the United States economy
II.B.3.b Stock market: SEC
II.B.6.a FDR as communicator and his efforts to restore public confidence; press conferences, "fireside chats," and effective use of the radio
II.B.6.b Eleanor Roosevelt as the President's eyes and ears

Franklin Delano Roosevelt was elected president in 1932, following his promise of a "new deal" for Americans. In his first 100 days in office, he let loose a flood of legislation designed to rescue banks, industry, and agriculture and provide jobs for the unemployed.

Roosevelt's Rise to Power

MAIN Idea Franklin D. Roosevelt was governor of New York when he was elected president in 1932, promising a New Deal for the American people.

HISTORY AND YOU Do you believe your past experiences can make you stronger? Read how FDR's experiences helped prepare him to be president.

A distant cousin of Theodore Roosevelt, Franklin Delano Roosevelt grew up in Hyde Park, New York. In his youth he learned to hunt, ride horses, and sail; he also developed a lifelong commitment to conservation and a love of rural America. Roosevelt was educated at Harvard and Columbia Law School. While at Harvard, he became friends with Theodore Roosevelt's niece Eleanor, whom he later married.

Intensely competitive, Roosevelt liked to be in control. He also liked being around people. His charming personality, deep rich voice, and wide smile expressed confidence and optimism. In short, his personality seemed made for a life in politics.

Roosevelt began his political career in 1910, when he was elected to the New York State Senate. Three years later, having earned a reputation as a progressive reformer, he became assistant secretary of the navy in the Wilson administration. In 1920 his reputation (and famous surname) helped him win the vice presidential nomination on the unsuccessful Democratic ticket.

After losing the election, Roosevelt temporarily withdrew from politics. The next year he caught the dreaded paralyzing disease **polio.** Although there was no cure, Roosevelt refused to give in. He began a vigorous exercise program to restore muscle control. Eventually, by wearing heavy steel braces on his legs, he was able to walk short distances by leaning on a cane and someone's arm and swinging his legs forward from his hips.

While recovering from polio, Roosevelt depended on his wife and his aide Louis Howe to keep his name prominent in the New York Democratic Party. Eleanor Roosevelt became an effective public speaker, and her efforts kept her husband's political career alive.

By the mid-1920s, Roosevelt was again active in the Democratic Party. In 1928 he ran for governor of New York. He campaigned hard

Roosevelt's First Inaugural Address

March 4, 1933

"This is preeminently the time to speak the truth, the whole truth, frankly and boldly. Nor need we shrink from honestly facing conditions in our country today. This great Nation will endure as it has endured, will revive and will prosper. So, first of all, let me assert my firm belief that the only thing we have to fear is fear itself—nameless, unreasoning, unjustified terror which paralyzes needed efforts to convert retreat into advance.

. . . Restoration calls, however, not for changes in ethics alone. This Nation asks for action, and action now.

. . . Our greatest primary task is to put people to work. This is no unsolvable problem if we face it wisely and courageously. It can be accomplished in part by direct recruiting by the Government itself, treating the task as we would treat the emergency of a war.

. . . Action in this image and to this end is feasible under the form of government which we have inherited from our ancestors. Our Constitution is so simple and practical that it is possible always to meet extraordinary needs by changes in emphasis and arrangement without loss of essential form.

We do not distrust the future of essential democracy. The people of the United States have not failed. In their need they have registered a mandate that they want direct, vigorous action."

—from *The Public Papers and Addresses of Franklin D. Roosevelt*

▲ *Franklin Roosevelt delivers his First Inaugural Address.*

DBQ Document-Based Questions

1. **Analyzing Primary Sources** Why does Roosevelt think that "nameless, unreasoning, unjustified terror" is such a big problem?

2. **Identifying Central Issues** What unspoken fear does Roosevelt address in the final two paragraphs?

---

to demonstrate that his illness had not slowed him down, and he narrowly won the election. Two years later he was reelected in a landslide. As governor, Roosevelt oversaw the creation of the first state relief agency to aid the unemployed.

Roosevelt's popularity in New York paved the way for his presidential nomination in 1932. Americans saw in him an energy and optimism that gave them hope despite the tough economic times. After Roosevelt became president, his serenity and confidence amazed people. When one aide commented on his attitude, Roosevelt replied, "If you had spent two years in bed trying to wiggle your big toe, after that anything else would seem easy."

In mid-June 1932, with the country deep in the Depression, Republicans gathered in Chicago and nominated Herbert Hoover to run for a second term as president. Later that month, the Democrats also held their national convention in Chicago. When Roosevelt won the nomination, he broke with tradition by flying to Chicago to accept it in person. His speech set the tone for his campaign:

"Let it be from now on the task of our Party to break foolish traditions. . . . It is inevitable that the main issue of this campaign should revolve about . . . a depression so deep that it is without precedent. . . . Republican leaders not only have failed in material things, they have failed in national vision, because in disaster they have held out no hope. . . . I pledge you, I pledge myself, to a new deal for the American people."

—from *The Public Papers and Addresses of Franklin D. Roosevelt*

From that point forward, Roosevelt's policies for ending the Depression became known as the **New Deal.** Roosevelt's confidence that he could make things better contrasted sharply with Herbert Hoover's **apparent** failure to do anything effective. On Election Day, Roosevelt won in a landslide, receiving the electoral vote of all but six states.

Reading Check **Interpreting** What events in Roosevelt's life shaped his ideas and character?

The Hundred Days

MAIN Idea Upon taking office, FDR launched the New Deal by sending 15 major pieces of legislation to Congress.

HISTORY AND YOU Do you remember reading about the "New Nationalism" and "New Freedom"? Read how those ideas influenced New Deal legislation.

Although Roosevelt won the presidency in November 1932, the country's unemployed and homeless had to endure another winter as they waited for his inauguration on March 4, 1933. All through the winter, unemployment continued to rise and bank runs increased, further threatening the banking system.

Some of the bank runs occurred because people feared that Roosevelt would abandon the **gold standard** and reduce the value of the dollar in order to fight the Depression. Under the gold standard, one ounce of gold equaled a set number of dollars. To reduce the value of the dollar, the United States would have to stop exchanging dollars for gold. Many Americans, and many foreign investors with deposits in American banks, decided to take their money out of the banks and convert it to gold before it lost its value.

Across the nation, people stood in long lines with paper bags and suitcases, waiting to withdraw their money from banks. By March 1933, more than 4,000 banks had collapsed, wiping out nine million savings accounts. In 38 states, governors declared **bank holidays**—closing the remaining banks before bank runs could put them out of business.

By the day of Roosevelt's inauguration, most of the nation's banks were closed. One in four workers was unemployed. The economy seemed paralyzed. Roosevelt knew he had to restore the nation's confidence. "First of all," the president declared in his Inaugural Address, "let me assert my firm belief that the only thing we have to fear is fear itself. . . . This nation asks for action, and action now!"

The New Deal Begins

Roosevelt and his advisers, sometimes called the "brain trust," came into office bursting with ideas about how to end the Depression. Roosevelt had no clear agenda, nor did he have a strong political **ideology.** The previous spring, during his campaign for the presidential nomination, Roosevelt had revealed the approach he would take as president. "The country needs," Roosevelt explained, "bold, persistent experimentation . . . . Above all, try something."

The new president began to send bill after bill to Congress. Between March 9 and June 16, 1933—which came to be called the **Hundred Days**—Congress passed 15 major acts to resolve the economic crisis, setting a pace for new legislation that has never been equaled. Together, these programs made up what would later be called the First New Deal.

A Divided Administration

To generate new ideas and programs, Roosevelt deliberately chose advisers who disagreed with each other. He wanted to hear many different points of view, and by setting his advisers against one another, Roosevelt ensured that he alone made the final decision on what policies to pursue.

Despite their disagreements, Roosevelt's advisers generally favored some form of government intervention in the economy—although they disagreed over what the government's role should be.

One influential group during the early years of Roosevelt's administration supported the "New Nationalism" of Theodore Roosevelt. These advisers believed that if government agencies worked with businesses to regulate wages, prices, and production, they could lift the economy out of the Depression.

A second group of Roosevelt's advisers went even further. They distrusted big business and blamed business leaders for causing the Depression. These advisers wanted government planners to run key parts of the economy.

A third group in Roosevelt's administration supported the "New Freedom" of Woodrow Wilson. These advisers wanted Roosevelt to support "trust busting" by breaking up big companies and allowing competition to set wages, prices, and production levels. They also thought the government should impose regulations to keep economic competition fair.

✔ **Reading Check** **Summarizing** What ideas did Roosevelt's advisers support?

People IN HISTORY

Eleanor Roosevelt
1884–1962

Orphaned at age 10, Eleanor Roosevelt was raised by relatives and later attended boarding school in England. When she returned home as a young woman, she devoted time to a settlement house on Manhattan's Lower East Side. During this time, she became engaged to Franklin D. Roosevelt, a distant cousin. They were married in 1905. At their wedding, Eleanor's uncle, President Theodore Roosevelt, gave her away.

During FDR's presidency, Eleanor Roosevelt transformed the role of First Lady. Rather than restricting herself to traditional hostess functions, she became an important figure in his administration. She traveled extensively, toured factories and coal mines, and met with factory workers and farmers. She then told her husband what people were thinking. In doing so, she became FDR's "eyes and ears" when his disability made travel difficult.

Eleanor was also a strong supporter of civil rights and prodded her husband to stop discrimination in New Deal programs. When the Daughters of the American Revolution barred African American singer Marian Anderson from performing in its auditorium, Eleanor intervened and arranged for Anderson to perform at the Lincoln Memorial instead.

After FDR's death, Eleanor remained politically active. She continued to write her syndicated newspaper column, "My Day," which she began in 1936, and became a delegate to the United Nations where she helped draft the Universal Declaration of Human Rights.

How might Franklin Roosevelt's political career have been different if Eleanor had not been his wife?

▲ *In this 1935 photo, Eleanor Roosevelt speaks to Geraldine Walker, a five-year-old from Detroit, Michigan, as slums in that city were about to be cleared.*

Banks and Debt Relief

MAIN Idea President Roosevelt took steps to strengthen banks and the stock market and to help farmers and homeowners keep their property.

HISTORY AND YOU Have you ever watched a presidential address? Read about Roosevelt's "fireside chats" and how they encouraged optimism that the economy would get better.

As the debate over policies and programs swirled around him, President Roosevelt took office with one thing clear in his mind. Very few of the proposed solutions would work as long as the nation's banks remained closed. The first thing he had to do was restore confidence in the banking system.

On his very first night in office, Roosevelt told Secretary of the Treasury William H. Woodin that he wanted an emergency banking bill ready for Congress in less than five days. The following afternoon, Roosevelt declared a national bank holiday, temporarily closing all banks, and called Congress into a special session scheduled to begin on March 9, 1933.

When Congress convened, the House of Representatives unanimously passed the Emergency Banking Relief Act after only 38 minutes of debate. The Senate approved the bill that evening, and Roosevelt signed it into law shortly afterward. The new law required federal examiners to survey the nation's banks and issue Treasury Department licenses to those that were financially sound.

On March 12 President Roosevelt addressed the nation by radio. Sixty million people listened to this first of many "**fireside chats,**" direct talks in which Roosevelt let the American people know what he was trying to accomplish. He told people that their money would be secure if they put it back into the banks: "I assure you that it is safer to keep your money in a reopened bank than under the mattress." When banks opened the day after the speech, deposits far outweighed withdrawals. The banking crisis was over.

The FDIC and SEC

Although President Roosevelt had restored confidence in the banking system, many of his advisers urged him to go further. They pushed for new regulations for both banks and the stock market. Roosevelt agreed with their ideas and supported the Securities Act of 1933 and the Glass-Steagall Banking Act.

The Securities Act required companies that sold stocks and bonds to provide complete and truthful information to investors. The following year, Congress created a government agency, the Securities and Exchange Commission (SEC), to regulate the stock market and prevent fraud.

The Glass-Steagall Act separated commercial banking from investment banking. Commercial banks handle everyday transactions. They take deposits, pay interest, cash checks, and lend money for mortgages. Under the Glass-Steagall Act, these banks were no longer allowed to risk depositors' money by using it to speculate on the stock market.

To further protect depositors, the Glass-Steagall Act also created the Federal Deposit Insurance Corporation (FDIC) to provide government insurance for bank deposits up to a certain amount. By protecting depositors in this way, the FDIC greatly increased public confidence in the banking system.

Mortgage and Debt Relief

While some of Roosevelt's advisers believed low prices had caused the Depression, others believed that debt was the main obstacle to economic recovery. With incomes falling, people had to use most of their money to pay their debts and had little left over to buy goods or services. Many Americans, terrified of losing their homes and farms, cut back on their spending to make sure they could pay their mortgages. Roosevelt responded to the crisis by introducing several policies intended to assist Americans with their debts.

The Home Owners' Loan Corporation To help homeowners make their mortgage payments, Roosevelt asked Congress to establish the Home Owners' Loan Corporation (HOLC). The HOLC bought the mortgages of many

THE First Hundred Days

March 9
Roosevelt signs the Emergency Banking Relief Act and 3 days later delivers his first fireside chat

▲ Farmers in Texas receive their AAA checks.

May 12
The Agricultural Adjustment Act is signed, and farmers soon begin receiving payments to destroy their crops in an effort to push up prices

April 1933 ▶ May 1933 ▶

March 31
The Civilian Conservation Corps is created and soon afterward begins hiring 3 million young men to work in the nation's forests

May 12
The Federal Emergency Relief Administration begins making grants to states to help the unemployed

homeowners who were behind in their payments. It then restructured them with longer terms of repayment and lower interest rates. Roughly 10 percent of homeowners received HOLC loans.

The HOLC did not help everyone. It made loans only to homeowners who were not farm owners and who were still employed. When people lost their jobs and could no longer make their mortgage payments, the HOLC foreclosed on their property, just as a bank would have done. Between 1933 and 1936, the three years during which it functioned as a loan source, the HOLC made loans to cover one million mortgages—one out of every ten in the United States.

The Farm Credit Administration Three days after Congress authorized the creation of the HOLC, it authorized the Farm Credit Administration (FCA) to help farmers refinance their mortgages. Over the next seven months, the FCA lent four times as much money to farmers as the entire banking system had the year before. It was also able to push interest rates substantially lower. These loans saved millions of farms from foreclosure.

Although FCA loans helped many farmers in the short term, their long-term value can be questioned. FCA loans helped less efficient farmers keep their land, but giving loans to poor farmers meant that the money was not available to lend to more efficient businesses in the economy. Although FCA loans may have slowed the overall economic recovery, they did help many desperate and impoverished people hold onto their land.

✔ **Reading Check** **Explaining** How did the government restore confidence in the banking system?

▲ *Workers of the Grand Coulee Dam in Washington.*

May 18
Congress creates the Tennessee Valley Authority

June 13
The Home Owners' Loan Corporation is authorized to make low interest mortgage loans to homeowners

June 16
The Public Works Administration is created. Under the leadership of Harold Ickes, it begins spending over $3 billion on public works such as new highways, dams, and public buildings. The agency begins spending.

June 1933

June 16
The National Recovery Administration is authorized to begin setting codes and regulations for industry

Analyzing TIME LINES

1. **Analyzing** What groups of people were targeted for help in the first hundred days of Roosevelt's first term?

2. **Drawing Conclusions** What was Roosevelt's first act after becoming president? Why do you think he chose this as a first step?

Farms and Industry

MAIN Idea New Deal legislation tried to raise crop prices and stabilize industry.

HISTORY AND YOU Can you think of a product that gets more expensive when less of it is available? Read to learn how some New Deal programs tried to raise prices.

Many of Roosevelt's advisers believed that both farmers and businesses were suffering because prices were too low and production too high. Several advisers believed competition was inefficient and bad for the economy. They favored creating federal agencies to manage the economy.

The AAA

To further help the nation's farmers, Secretary of Agriculture Henry Wallace drafted the Agricultural Adjustment Act. President Roosevelt asked Congress to pass the act. This legislation was based on a simple idea—that prices for farm goods were low because farmers grew too much food. Under Roosevelt's program, the government would pay some farmers *not* to raise certain livestock, and *not* to grow certain crops. Some farmers were also asked *not* to produce dairy products. As the program went into effect, farmers slaughtered 6 million piglets and 200,000 sows and plowed under 10 million acres of cotton—all in an effort to raise prices. The program was administered by the Agricultural Adjustment Administration (AAA).

Over the next two years, farmers withdrew millions more acres from cultivation and received more than $1 billion in support payments. The program accomplished its goal: the farm surplus fell greatly by 1936. Food prices then rose, as did total farm income, which quickly increased by more than 50 percent.

In a nation caught in a Depression, however, raising food prices drew harsh criticism. Furthermore, not all farmers benefited. Large commercial farmers who concentrated on one crop profited more than smaller farmers who raised several products. Worse, thousands of poor tenant farmers, many of them African Americans, became homeless and jobless when landlords took their fields out of production.

PAST & PRESENT

The TVA

The Tennessee Valley Authority (TVA) was a New Deal project that produced visible benefits. The TVA built dams to control floods, conserve forest lands, and bring electricity to rural areas.

Today, TVA power facilities include 17,000 miles of transmission lines, 29 hydroelectric dams, 11 fossil-fuel plants, 4 combustion-turbine plants, 3 nuclear power plants, and a pumped-storage facility. These combine to bring power to nearly 8 million people in a seven-state region.

Since 1998, the TVA has been working to reduce air pollution. Projects are designed to cut harmful emissions released into the air. The TVA is committed to developing programs that protect the environment.

The TVA, 1940

Area served by TVA

Major dam

Power plant

0   100 kilometers
0   100 miles
Albers Equal-Area projection

The NRA

The government turned its attention to manufacturing in June 1933, when Roosevelt and Congress enacted the National Industrial Recovery Act (NIRA). The NIRA suspended antitrust laws and allowed business, labor, and government to cooperate in setting up voluntary rules for each industry.

These rules were known as codes of fair competition. Some codes set prices, established minimum wages, and limited factories to two shifts per day so that production could be spread to as many firms as possible. Other codes shortened workers' hours, with the goal of creating additional jobs. Another provision in the law guaranteed workers the right to form unions. The codes also helped businesses develop codes of fair competition within industries.

Under the leadership of Hugh Johnson, the National Recovery Administration (NRA) ran the entire program. Business owners who signed code agreements received signs displaying the National Recovery Administration's symbol—a blue eagle—and the slogan, "We Do Our Part." The NRA had limited power to enforce the codes, but urged consumers to buy goods only from companies that displayed the blue eagle.

The NRA did revive a few American industries, but its gains proved short-lived. Small companies complained, justifiably, that large corporations wrote the codes to favor themselves. American employers disliked codes that gave workers the right to form unions and bargain collectively over wages and hours. They also argued that paying high minimum wages forced them to charge higher prices to cover their costs.

The codes were also difficult to administer, and business leaders often ignored them. Furthermore, businesses could choose not to sign code agreements and thus not be bound by their rules. It became obvious that the NRA was failing when industrial production actually fell after the organization was established. By the time the Supreme Court declared the NRA unconstitutional in 1935, it had already lost much of its political support.

Reading Check **Examining** What were the goals of the Agricultural Adjustment Act and the National Industrial Recovery Act?

2006

This photo shows the completed Cherokee Hydroelectric Dam.

Tennessee's Cherokee Dam is today part of the TVA. Workers (upper right) built it in the late 1930s.

MAKING CONNECTIONS

1. **Listing** Look at the map on page 656. What states other than Tennessee benefited from the TVA projects?

2. **Examining** Where were most of the projects located?

Maps In Motion See *StudentWorks*™ *Plus* or glencoe.com.

Relief Programs

MAIN Idea Programs such as the CCC, the PWA, and the WPA provided jobs for some unemployed workers.

HISTORY AND YOU Do you know who built your school, post office, or playground? Read about the projects completed by the New Deal workers.

History ONLINE
Student Skill Activity To learn how to use a word processor, visit glencoe.com and complete the Skill activity.

While many of President Roosevelt's advisers emphasized tinkering with prices and providing debt relief to solve the Depression, others maintained that its **fundamental** cause was low consumption. They thought getting money into the hands of needy individuals would be the fastest remedy. Because neither Roosevelt nor his advisers wanted simply to give money to the unemployed, they supported work programs for the unemployed.

The CCC

The most highly praised New Deal work relief program was the **Civilian Conservation Corps** (CCC). The CCC offered unemployed young men 18 to 25 years old the opportunity to work under the direction of the forestry service planting trees, fighting forest fires, and building reservoirs. To prevent a repeat of the Dust Bowl, the workers planted a line of more than 200 million trees, known as a Shelter Belt, from north Texas to North Dakota.

The young men lived in camps near their work areas and earned $30 a month, $25 of which was sent directly to their families. The average CCC worker returned home after six to twelve months, better nourished and with greater self-respect. CCC programs also taught more than 40,000 of its recruits to read and write. By the time the CCC closed down in 1942, it had put 3 million young men to work outdoors—including 80,000 Native Americans, who helped to reclaim land they had once owned. After a second Bonus Army March on Washington in 1933, Roosevelt added some 250,000 veterans to the CCC as well.

FERA and the PWA

A few weeks after authorizing the CCC, Congress established the Federal Emergency Relief Administration (FERA). Roosevelt chose

POLITICAL CARTOONS PRIMARY SOURCE
Did the New Deal Help Americans?

▲ This cartoon, entitled "How Much More Do We Need?" shows Uncle Sam grasping New Deal lifesavers to stay afloat.

► This 1935 cartoon shows FDR as a doctor with a variety of medicines to help ailing Uncle Sam.

Analyzing VISUALS **DBQ**

1. **Interpeting** In the cartoon at the left, what is happening to the dock, and why?

2. **Analyzing** With whom is President Roosevelt conferring in the cartoon at right?

Harry Hopkins, a former social worker, to run the agency. FERA did not initially create projects for the unemployed. Instead, it channeled money to state and local agencies to fund their relief projects.

Half an hour after meeting with Roosevelt to discuss his new job, Hopkins set up a desk in the hallway outside of his office. In the next two hours, he spent $5 million on relief projects. When critics charged that some of the projects did not make sense in the long run, Hopkins replied, "People don't eat in the long run—they eat every day."

In June 1933 Congress authorized another relief agency, the Public Works Administration (PWA). One-third of the nation's unemployed were in the construction industry. To put them back to work, the PWA began building highways, dams, sewer systems, schools, and other government facilities. In most cases, the PWA did not hire workers directly but instead awarded contracts to construction companies. By insisting that contractors not discriminate against African Americans, the agency broke down some of the long-standing racial barriers in the construction trades.

The CWA

By the fall of 1933 neither FERA nor the PWA had reduced unemployment significantly. Hopkins realized that unless the federal government acted quickly, a huge number of unemployed citizens would be in severe distress once winter began. After Hopkins explained the situation, President Roosevelt authorized him to set up the Civil Works Administration (CWA).

Unlike the PWA, the CWA hired workers directly. That winter the CWA employed 4 million people, including 300,000 women. Under Hopkins's direction, the agency built or improved 1,000 airports, 500,000 miles of roads, 40,000 school buildings, and 3,500 playgrounds and parks. The cost of the CWA was huge—the program spent nearly $1 billion in just five months.

Although the CWA helped many people get through the winter, President Roosevelt was alarmed by how quickly the agency was spending money. He did not want Americans to get used to the federal government providing them with jobs. Warning that the CWA would "become a habit with the country," Roosevelt insisted that it be shut down the following spring.

Success of the First New Deal

During his first year in office, Roosevelt convinced Congress to pass an astonishing array of legislation. The programs enacted during the first New Deal did not restore prosperity, but they reflected Roosevelt's zeal for action and his willingness to experiment. Banks were reopened, many more people retained their homes and farms, and more people were employed. Perhaps the most important result of the first New Deal was a noticeable change in the spirit of the American people. Roosevelt's actions had inspired hope and restored Americans' faith in their nation.

Reading Check **Identifying** What types of projects did public works programs undertake?

Section 1 REVIEW

Vocabulary

1. **Explain** the significance of: polio, New Deal, gold standard, bank holiday, Hundred Days, fireside chats, Civilian Conservation Corps.

Main Ideas

2. **Describing** What actions did Roosevelt take during the Hundred Days?

3. **Explaining** How did government regulate banks and the stock market in the first Roosevelt administration?

4. **Interpreting** How did the AAA affect farm prices?

5. **Organizing** Use a graphic organizer to list the major organizations of the First New Deal.

Critical Thinking

6. **Big Ideas** In what ways did FDR's early experiences shape his political ideology?

7. **Analyzing Charts** Look at the time line on pages 654–655. How did the various agencies listed change the role of government?

Writing About History

8. **Expository Writing** Interview a member of your community who lived during the Great Depression. How did the New Deal programs affect your community? Create a one-page report using a word processor to summarize your findings.

History ONLINE

Study Central™ To review this section, go to glencoe.com and click on Study Central.

ANALYZING PRIMARY SOURCES

The First New Deal

When FDR took office in 1933, the economy had been getting worse for more than three years. During the first one hundred days of his presidency, he oversaw 15 major pieces of legislation that attempted to revive the nation's economy and provide relief to the unemployed. Never before had the federal government intervened so directly in the economy. Key to stopping the economic downslide was FDR's ability to inspire confidence that the nation's economic problems could be solved.

Study these primary sources and answer the questions that follow.

PRIMARY SOURCE 1

Inaugural Address, 1933

"I am certain that my fellow Americans expect that on my induction into the Presidency I will address them with a candor and a decision which the present situation of our nation impels. This is pre-eminently the time to speak the truth, the whole truth, frankly and boldly. . . .

"So, first of all, let me assert my firm belief that the only thing we have to fear is fear itself—nameless, unreasoning, unjustified terror which paralyzes needed efforts to convert retreat into advance. In every dark hour of our national life a leadership of frankness and vigor has met with that understanding and support of the people themselves which is essential to victory. I am convinced that you will again give that support to leadership in these critical days. . . .

"This Nation asks for action, and action now.

"Our greatest primary task is to put people to work. This is no unsolvable problem if we face it wisely and courageously. It can be accomplished in part by direct recruiting by the Government itself, treating the task as we would treat the emergency of a war, but at the same time, through this employment, accomplishing greatly needed projects to stimulate and reorganize the use of our natural resources."

—President Franklin D. Roosevelt,
first inaugural address, delivered March 4, 1933

Excerpted from *The Public Papers and Addresses of Franklin D. Roosevelt*

PRIMARY SOURCE 2

Oral History Interview

"During the whole '33 one-hundred days' Congress, people didn't know what was going on, the public. Couldn't understand these things that were being passed so fast. They knew something was happening, something good for them. They began investing and working and hoping again. . . .

"A Depression is much like a run on a bank. It's a crisis of confidence. People panic and grab their money."

—Raymond Moley, original member of FDR's "brains trust"

Excerpted from *Hard Times: An Oral History of the Great Depression* (1970)

PRIMARY SOURCE 3

Magazine Cover, 1933

▶ *"The Faces of Victory and Defeat," portrayal of Herbert Hoover and Roosevelt on inauguration day, March 4, 1933*

Mar. 4, 1933   THE NEW YORKER   Price 15 cents

PRIMARY SOURCE 4

New Deal poster for the CCC, c. 1935 ▼

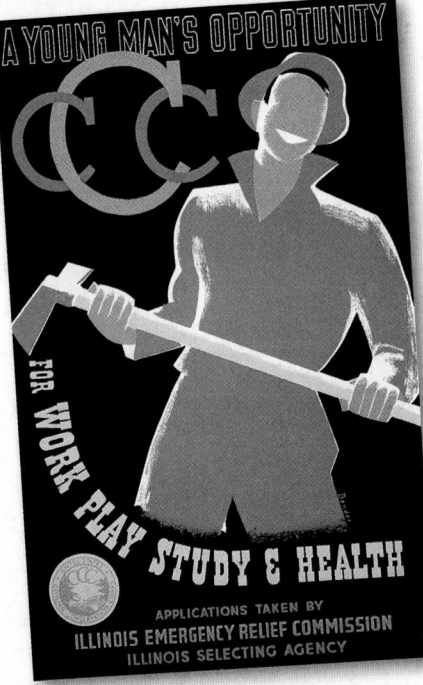

PRIMARY SOURCE 5

Oral History Interview

"What Roosevelt and the New Deal did was to turn about and face the realities. . . . A hundred years from now, when historians look back on it, they will say a big corner was turned. People agreed that old things didn't work. What ran through the whole New Deal was finding a way to make things work.

"Before that, Hoover would loan money to farmers to keep their mules alive, but wouldn't loan money to keep their children alive. This was perfectly right within the framework of classical thinking. If an individual couldn't get enough to eat, it was because he wasn't on the ball. It was his responsibility. The New Deal said: Anybody who is unemployed isn't necessarily unemployed because he's shiftless."

—Economist Gardiner C. Means,
economic adviser in the Roosevelt administration

Excerpted from *Hard Times: An Oral History of the Great Depression* (1970)

PRIMARY SOURCE 7

Magazine Cover, 1934

▶ *Uncle Sam being tattooed with the initials of New Deal agencies (October 1934).*

PRIMARY SOURCE 6

Contemporary Book, 1934

"Even if the government conduct of business could give us the maximum of efficiency instead of least efficiency, it would be purchased at the cost of freedom. It would increase rather than decrease abuse and corruption, stifle initiative and invention, undermine the development of leadership, cripple the mental and spiritual energies of our people and the forces which make progress."

—Former president Herbert Hoover in his book,
The Challenge to Liberty (1934)

Excerpted from *The Era of Franklin D. Roosevelt, 1933–1945*

DBQ Document-Based Questions

1. **Evaluating** What themes did Roosevelt emphasize in his inaugural address? How would you have responded to this speech if you had been an unemployed worker?

2. **Explaining** Study Sources 2 and 3. How did FDR inspire confidence and optimism? What effect did this have on the economy?

3. **Describing** In Source 4, the poster highlights four opportunities offered by the CCC. Describe some specific ways the CCC provided such opportunities.

4. **Paraphrasing** In Source 5, how does the author define Roosevelt's attitude toward unemployment and Hoover's approach to unemployment?

5. **Evaluating** In Source 6, why does Herbert Hoover object to the New Deal? What programs do you think he found most objectionable?

6. **Speculating** Study the picture in Source 7. How does the artist feel about the New Deal? What symbols are used to convey that message?

The Second New Deal

Guide to Reading

Big Ideas

Economics and Society In 1935 Roosevelt introduced new programs to help unions, senior citizens, and the unemployed.

Content Vocabulary
- deficit spending (p. 662)
- binding arbitration (p. 666)
- sit-down strike (p. 666)

Academic Vocabulary
- benefit (p. 663)
- finance (p. 664)
- thereby (p. 665)

People and Events to Identify
- American Liberty League (p. 663)
- Works Progress Administration (p. 664)
- National Labor Relations Board (p. 665)
- Congress of Industrial Organizations (p. 667)
- Social Security Act (p. 667)

Reading Strategy

Organizing As you read about President Roosevelt's Second New Deal, complete a graphic organizer similar to the one below by filling in his main legislative successes during this period.

Legislation	Provisions

NEW YORK CORE CURRICULUM
U.S. History and Government

Unit 5:
II.B.1.c Unemployment: WPA, PWA, CCC; troubling equity issues
II.B.3.c Social Security
II.B.3.d.(1) Wagner Act (NLRB)
II.B.4 Labor's response: Formation of CIO
II.B.5.a.(1) Supreme Court and NRA (*Schechter Poultry Corp. v. United States*, 1935)

In response to criticisms of the New Deal, President Roosevelt introduced several major pieces of legislation in 1935. These laws created the Works Progress Administration, the National Labor Relations Board, and the Social Security Administration.

Launching the Second New Deal

MAIN Idea By 1935, the New Deal faced political and legal challenges, as well as growing concern that it was not ending the Depression.

HISTORY AND YOU Do you know anyone who can easily convince others to follow his or her ideas? Read about several people who used this power against Roosevelt and his New Deal policies.

Harry Hopkins, head of the Federal Emergency Relief Administration, worked long hours in his Washington office, a bare, dingy room with exposed water pipes. Hopkins also took to the road to explain the New Deal. Once in Iowa, where he was discussing spending programs, someone called out, "Who's going to pay for it?" Hopkins peeled off his jacket, loosened his tie, and rolled up his sleeves, before roaring his response: "You are!"

President Roosevelt appreciated Harry Hopkins's feistiness. He needed effective speakers who were willing to contend with his adversaries. Although Roosevelt had been tremendously popular during his first two years in office, opposition to his policies had begun to grow.

The economy had shown only a slight improvement, even though the New Deal had been in effect for two years. Although the programs had created more than 2 million new jobs, more than 10 million workers remained unemployed, and the nation's total income was about half of what it had been in 1929.

Criticism From Left and Right

Hostility toward Roosevelt came from both the political right and the left. People on the right generally believed the New Deal regulated business too tightly. The right wing also included many Southern Democrats who believed the New Deal had expanded the federal government's power at the expense of states' rights.

The right wing, which had opposed the New Deal from the beginning, increased that opposition by late 1934. To pay for his programs, Roosevelt had started **deficit spending,** abandoning a balanced budget and borrowing money. Many business leaders became greatly alarmed at the government's growing deficit.

Opposition to the New Deal

By 1935 some Americans had grown impatient with the New Deal economic recovery. They believed that the reforms did not go far enough and called for wider-ranging change.

THE TOWNSEND PLAN
$200, PER MONTH FOR THOSE OVER 60 YRS OF AGE - THE SPENDING OF THIS MONEY WILL PUT THE CONTROL OF CREDIT IN THE HANDS OF THE PEOPLE - PREVENTING ECONOMIC CHAOS

◀ *Dr. Francis Townsend explains his ideas to offer pensions to business leaders at a 1936 luncheon in Philadelphia.*

▶ *Huey Long, who served Louisiana in the U.S. Senate, looked for ways to redistribute wealth.*

▲ *Father Coughlin speaks to a crowd of 6,000 members of the National Union for Social Justice at the Hippodrome in Detroit shortly after the stock market collapse in 1929. By the mid-1930s, Coughlin favored massive taxes.*

Analyzing VISUALS

1. **Comparing and Contrasting** What strikes you as the same and different about these three men?

2. **Assessing** Which man do you think would have the largest audience, and why?

In August 1934 business leaders and anti–New Deal politicians from both parties joined together to create the **American Liberty League.** Its purpose was to organize opposition to the New Deal and "teach the necessity of respect for the rights of person and property."

While criticisms from the right threatened to split the Democratic Party and reduce business support for Roosevelt, another serious challenge to the New Deal came from the political left. People on the left believed Roosevelt had not gone far enough. They wanted even more dramatic government economic intervention to shift wealth from the rich to middle-income and poor Americans.

Huey Long Perhaps the most serious threat came from Huey Long of Louisiana. As governor of Louisiana, Long had championed the poor and downtrodden. He had improved schools, colleges, and hospitals, and built roads and bridges. These **benefits** made Long popular, enabling him to build a powerful—but

corrupt—political machine. In 1930 Long was elected to the U.S. Senate.

Long's attacks on the rich were popular in the midst of the Great Depression. He captivated audiences with folksy humor and fiery oratory. By 1934, he had established a national organization, the Share Our Wealth Society, to promote his plan for massive redistribution of wealth. Long announced he would run for president in 1936.

Father Coughlin Roosevelt also faced a challenge from Father Charles Coughlin, a Catholic priest in Detroit. About 30 to 45 million listeners heard his weekly radio show.

Originally an ardent New Deal supporter, Coughlin had become impatient with its moderate reforms. He called instead for inflating the currency and nationalizing the banking system. In 1935 Coughlin organized the National Union for Social Justice, which some Democrats feared would become a new political party.

History ONLINE
Student Web Activity Visit glencoe.com and complete the activity on the New Deal.

The Townsend Plan A third challenge came from Francis Townsend, a California physician. Townsend proposed that the federal government pay citizens over age 60 a pension of $200 a month. Recipients would have to retire and spend their entire pension check each month. He believed the plan would increase spending and remove people from the workforce, freeing up jobs for the unemployed.

Townsend's proposal attracted millions of supporters, especially among older Americans, who mobilized as a political force for the first time. Townsend's program was particularly popular in the West. When combined with Long's support in the Midwest and South, and Coughlin's support among urban Catholics in the Northeast, Roosevelt faced the possibility of a coalition that would draw enough votes to prevent his reelection.

The WPA

Roosevelt was also disturbed by the failure of the New Deal to generate a rapid economic recovery. In 1935 he launched a series of programs now known as the Second New Deal.

Among these new programs was the **Works Progress Administration** (WPA). Headed by Harry Hopkins, the WPA was the largest public works program of the New Deal. Between 1935 and 1941, the WPA spent $11 billion. Its 8.5 million workers constructed about 650,000 miles of highways, roads, and streets, 125,000 public buildings, and more than 8,000 parks. It built or improved more than 124,000 bridges and 853 airports.

The WPA's most controversial program was Federal Number One, a program for artists, musicians, theater people, and writers. The artists created thousands of murals and sculptures for public buildings. Musicians established 30 symphony orchestras, as well as hundreds of smaller musical groups. The Federal Theater Project **financed** playwrights, actors, and directors. It also funded writers who recorded the stories of former slaves and others whose voices were not often heard.

The Supreme Court's Role

In May 1935, in *Schechter Poultry Company* v. *United States*, the Supreme Court unanimously struck down the authority of the National Recovery Administration. The Schechter broth-

ers had been convicted of violating the NRA's poultry code.

The Court ruled that the Constitution did not allow Congress to delegate its legislative powers to the executive branch. Thus, it declared the NRA's codes unconstitutional. Although relieved to be rid of that "awful headache," the NRA, Roosevelt still worried about the ruling. It suggested that the Court could strike down the rest of the New Deal.

Roosevelt knew he needed a new series of programs to keep voters' support. He called congressional leaders to a White House conference. Pounding his desk, he thundered that Congress could not go home until it passed his new bills. That summer, Congress worked busily to pass Roosevelt's programs.

Reading Check **Identifying Points of View** What criticisms prompted the Second New Deal?

Debates IN HISTORY

Was the New Deal Socialistic?

Franklin Roosevelt took extraordinary measures to stimulate the economy with his New Deal programs. Many Americans were divided on the issue of increased government intervention in the economy. Some claimed the New Deal was socialistic and a violation of American values. Others thought the New Deal did not do enough to help Americans.

Reforms for Workers and Senior Citizens

MAIN Idea Roosevelt asked Congress to pass the Wagner Act and Social Security to build support among workers and older Americans.

HISTORY AND YOU Do you have an older relative who has retired from his or her job? Read about benefits created by the Social Security Act.

When the Supreme Court struck down the NRA, it also invalidated the section of the NIRA that gave workers the right to organize. President Roosevelt and the Democrats in Congress knew that the working-class vote was very important in winning reelection in 1936. They also believed that unions could help end the Depression. They thought that high union wages would give workers more money to spend, **thereby** boosting the economy. Opponents disagreed, arguing that high wages forced companies to charge higher prices and hire fewer people. Despite these concerns, Congress pushed ahead with new labor legislation.

The Wagner Act

In July 1935 Congress passed the National Labor Relations Act (also called the Wagner Act after its author, Senator Robert Wagner of New York). The act guaranteed workers the right to organize unions and to bargain collectively. It also set up the **National Labor Relations Board** (NLRB), which organized factory elections by secret ballot to determine whether workers wanted a union.

YES

Alfred E. Smith
Former Democratic Candidate

PRIMARY SOURCE

"Now what would I have my party do? I would have them re-declare the principles that they put forth in that 1932 platform [reduce the size of government, balance the federal budget] . . .

Just get the platform of the Democratic party and get the platform of the Socialist party and . . . make your mind up to pick up the platform that more nearly squares with the record, and you will have your hand on the Socialist platform. . . .

[I]t is all right with me, if they want to disguise themselves as Karl Marx or Lenin or any of the rest of that bunch, but I won't stand for their allowing them to march under the banner of Jackson or Cleveland."

—speech delivered January 25, 1936

NO

Norman Thomas
Socialist Party Candidate

PRIMARY SOURCE

"All of these leaders or would-be leaders out of our wilderness, however they may abuse one another, however loosely they may fling around the charge of socialism or communism—still accept the basic institutions and loyalties of the present system. A true Socialist is resolved to replace that system. . . .

The New Deal did not say, as socialism would have said, 'Here are so many millions of American people who need to be well fed and well clothed. How much food and cotton do we require?' We should require more, not less. What Mr. Roosevelt said was 'How much food and cotton can be produced for which the exploited masses must pay a higher price?'"

—speech delivered February 2, 1936

DBQ Document-Based Questions

1. **Distinguishing Fact From Opinion** Compare Smith's attack on the New Deal with what you have read about it elsewhere. Does he make any valid points?

2. **Contrasting** According to Thomas, how are the principles of the New Deal and those of the Socialist Party different?

3. **Evaluating** Which speaker do you find more persuasive? Why?

4. **Hypothesizing** Do you think either speaker would be able to persuade someone who did not agree with him to reconsider his or her attitudes?

The Wagner Act also set up a process called **binding arbitration** whereby dissatisfied union members could take their complaints to a neutral party who would listen to both sides and decide on the issues. The NLRB could investigate employers' actions and stop unfair practices, such as spying on workers.

The CIO Is Formed The Wagner Act led to a burst of labor activity. John L. Lewis led the United Mine Workers union. He worked with several other unions to organize industrial workers. They formed the Committee for Industrial Organization (CIO) in 1935.

The CIO set out to organize unions that included all workers, skilled and unskilled, in a particular industry. It focused first on the automobile and steel industries—two of the largest industries in which workers were not yet unionized.

Sit-Down Strikes Union organizers used new tactics, such as the **sit-down strike,** in which employees stopped work inside the factory and refused to leave. (This technique prevented management from sending in replacement workers.) First used effectively to organize rubber workers, the sit-down strike became a common CIO tactic for several years.

The United Auto Workers (UAW), a CIO union, initiated a series of sit-down strikes against General Motors. On December 31, 1936, the workers at General Motor's plant in Flint, Michigan, began a sit-down strike. The UAW strikers held the factory for weeks, while spouses, friends, and other supporters passed them food and other provisions through windows. A journalist who was allowed to enter the plant reported on conditions in the factory:

PRIMARY SOURCE

"Beds were made up on the floor of each car, the seats being removed if necessary. . . . I could not see—and I looked for it carefully—the slightest damage done anywhere to the General Motors Corporation. The nearly completed car bodies, for example, were as clean as they would be in the salesroom, their glass and metal shining."

—quoted in *The Great Depression*

Violence broke out in Flint when police launched a tear gas assault on one of the plants. The police wounded 13 strikers, but the strike held. On February 11, 1937, the company gave in and recognized the UAW as its employees' sole bargaining agent. The UAW became one of the most powerful unions in the United States.

PRIMARY SOURCE
The CIO Uses Sit-Down Strikes

▲ *Sit-down strikers at the GM Fisher Body plant in Flint, Michigan, take over the plant on December 30, 1936. Their action led to a national strike that lasted until February 11, 1937.*

Union Membership, 1933–1940

Members (thousands)

Source: *Historical Statistics of the United States.*

Analyzing VISUALS

1. **Analyzing** How can you tell from the men's appearance and activities that they intend to stay?

2. **Summarizing** When did union membership increase the most? How can you account for this jump?

U.S. Steel, the nation's largest steel producer and a long-standing opponent of unionizing, decided it did not want to repeat the General Motors experience. In March 1937 the company recognized the CIO's steelworkers union. Smaller steel producers did not follow suit and suffered bitter strikes. By 1941, however, the steelworkers union had won contracts throughout the industry.

In the late 1930s, workers in other industries worked hard to gain union recognition from their employers. Union membership tripled from roughly 3 million in 1933 to about 9 million in 1939. In 1938 the CIO changed its name to the **Congress of Industrial Organizations** and became a federation of industrial unions.

Social Security

After passing the Wagner Act, Congress began work on one of America's most important pieces of legislation. This was the **Social Security Act.** Its major goal was to provide some security for older Americans and unemployed workers.

Roosevelt and his advisers spent months preparing the bill, which they viewed primarily as an insurance measure. Workers earned the right to receive benefits because they paid premiums, just as they did in buying a life insurance policy. The premiums were a tax paid to the federal government. The legislation also provided modest welfare payments to other needy people, including those with disabilities and poor mothers with dependent children.

The core of Social Security was the monthly retirement benefit, which people could collect when they stopped working at age 65. Another important benefit, unemployment insurance, supplied a temporary income to unemployed workers looking for new jobs. Some critics did not like the fact that the money came from payroll taxes imposed on workers and employers, but to Roosevelt these taxes were crucial: "We put those payroll contributions there so as to give the contributors a legal, moral, and political right to collect their pensions and their unemployment benefits."

Since the people receiving benefits had already paid for them, he explained, "no . . . politician can ever scrap my social security program." What Roosevelt did not anticipate was that, in the future, Congress would borrow money from the Social Security fund to pay for other programs while failing to raise payroll deductions enough to pay for the benefits.

Although Social Security helped many people, initially it left out many of the neediest—farm and domestic workers. Some 65 percent of all African American workers in the 1930s fell into these two categories. Nevertheless, Social Security established the principle that the federal government should be responsible for those who, through no fault of their own, were unable to work.

Reading Check **Explaining** How did the Social Security Act protect workers?

Vocabulary

1. **Explain** the significance of: deficit spending, American Liberty League, Works Progress Administration, National Labor Relations Board, binding arbitration, sit-down strike, Congress of Industrial Organizations, Social Security Act.

Main Ideas

2. **Summarizing** How did the ideas of Father Coughlin, Senator Long, and Dr. Townsend differ?

3. **Analyzing** Why was the Social Security Act an important piece of legislation?

Critical Thinking

4. **Big Ideas** How did the New Deal contribute to the growth of industrial unions?

5. **Organizing** Use a graphic organizer similar to the one below to list the political challenges Roosevelt faced in his first term.

6. **Analyzing Visuals** Look again at the photo of Dr. Townsend on page 663. How does he intend to prevent economic chaos?

Writing About History

7. **Persuasive Writing** Choose one of the figures who criticized the New Deal. Write an editorial to the local newspaper expressing why people should be in favor of or opposed to that person's ideas.

History ONLINE

Study Central™ To review this section, go to glencoe.com and click on Study Central.

The New Deal Coalition

Guide to Reading

Big Ideas

Group Action Backed by a new coalition of voters FDR easily won reelection, but conservative opposition prevented the passage of additional reforms.

Content Vocabulary

- court-packing *(p. 670)*
- broker state *(p. 673)*
- safety net *(p. 673)*

Academic Vocabulary

- recovery *(p. 670)*
- mediate *(p. 673)*

People and Events to Identify

- Frances Perkins *(p. 669)*
- Henry Morgenthau *(p. 670)*
- John Maynard Keynes *(p. 670)*

Reading Strategy

Taking Notes As you read, create an outline similar to the one below.

> The New Deal Coalition
> I. Roosevelt's Second Term
>   A.
>   B.
>   C.
> II.
>   A.
>   B.

NEW YORK CORE CURRICULUM
U.S. History and Government

Unit 5:

II.B.5.a.(1)	Supreme Court and the NRA (*Schechter Poultry Corp.* v. *United States*, 1935)
II.B.6.b	Eleanor Roosevelt as the President's eyes and ears
II.B.5.c	Roosevelt's "Court-packing" proposal: failure and success
II.B.6.d	The New Deal and women (Frances Perkins)
II.B.6.e	The New Deal and minorities (shift in African-American vote): discriminatory results
II.B.6.f	Indian Reorganization Act (1934)

President Roosevelt won a landslide reelection victory in 1936. Early in his second term, however, his court-packing plan and a new recession hurt him politically. The Fair Labor Standards Act, the last significant piece of New Deal legislation, provided new protections for workers.

Roosevelt's Second Term

MAIN Idea Roosevelt was easily reelected, but the New Deal lost momentum during his second term due to his court-packing plan and a new recession.

HISTORY AND YOU Does your family rent or own your home? Read how the New Deal started programs that tried to make home ownership more affordable.

Since the Civil War, African Americans had been reliable Republican voters. The Republican Party was the party of both Abraham Lincoln and emancipation. In the 1930s, however, this allegiance unraveled. The Great Depression had hit African Americans hard, and the Republican Party had done little to help. To many African Americans, it seemed their votes were taken for granted. That was certainly the sentiment of Robert L. Vann, editor of the *Pittsburgh Courier,* Pennsylvania's leading African American newspaper. Vann decided it was time for a change and started a campaign to persuade African Americans to join the Democratic Party. "My friends, go turn Lincoln's picture to the wall," he told audiences. "That debt has been paid in full."

The dramatic shift in party allegiance by African Americans was part of a historic political realignment the New Deal triggered. As the election of 1936 approached, millions of voters owed their jobs, mortgages, and bank accounts to the New Deal, and they knew it.

The white South, which had been the core of the Democratic Party, now became just one part of a new coalition that included farmers, industrial workers, African Americans, new immigrants, ethnic minorities, women, progressives, and intellectuals. First Lady Eleanor Roosevelt helped bring about the change in the African American and women's vote. She had demonstrated strong sympathies toward African Americans in her many tours of the country. She recounted her experiences to her husband and persuaded him to address at least some of their problems in his New Deal programs.

African Americans made some modest gains during the New Deal. The president appointed several African Americans to positions in his administration, where they informally became known as the Black Cabinet. FDR also tried to see that public works projects included African Americans.

Building the New Deal Coalition

By creating programs that addressed the needs of different groups in American society, the New Deal created a new voting coalition: African Americans, women, and laborers.

▲ **New Deal Raises African American Hopes**
Mary McLeod Bethune, shown with Eleanor Roosevelt, was appointed in 1936 as director of the Office of Minority Affairs within the National Youth Association. Bethune became the first black woman to head a federal agency. Roosevelt also relied on an informal advisory group, the "Black Cabinet," also known as the "Black Brain Trust." FDR failed in some areas of civil rights, such as not opposing poll taxes for fear of causing Southern Democrats to block New Deal programs.

▲ **Appealing to Women and Workers**
The appointment of Secretary of Labor Frances Perkins, shown surveying work on the Golden Gate Bridge in 1935, was one example of Roosevelt's effort to bring women voters into the New Deal coalition. Perkins headed the team that designed the Social Security program and the Fair Labor Standards Act. Social Security, along with the New Deal's labor programs, helped bring many workers into the New Deal coalition.

Analyzing VISUALS

1. **Analyzing** Look at the photo of Frances Perkins and the workers. What clues do you get that she took her job seriously?

2. **Evaluating** What mood does the photograph of Mary McLeod Bethune and Eleanor Roosevelt convey?

▲ **A New Deal for Native Americans**
Commissioner of Indian Affairs John Collier, shown here consulting with Native American leaders in South Dakota, helped create the Indian Reorganization Act of 1934. The act reversed the Dawes Act's policy of assimilation. It restored some reservation lands, gave Native Americans control over those lands, and permitted them to elect their own governments.

A similar policy guided FDR's approach to women. He appointed the first woman to a cabinet post, Secretary of Labor **Frances Perkins,** and appointed many other women to lower-level posts. He also appointed two female diplomats and a female federal judge. Despite these gains, New Deal programs paid women lower wages than men.

The Election of 1936

To challenge President Roosevelt's reelection bid, the Republicans nominated Alfred Landon, the governor of Kansas. Although Landon favored some New Deal policies, he declared it was time "to unshackle initiative and free the spirit of American enterprise." Landon was unable to convince the majority of American voters it was time for a change. Roosevelt and the New Deal that he represented remained very popular, and on Election Day, Roosevelt swept to victory in one of the largest landslides in American history. He won more than 60 percent of the popular vote and carried every state except Maine and Vermont.

The Court-Packing Plan

Although many people supported the New Deal, the Supreme Court saw things differently. In January 1936, in *United States* v. *Butler*, the Court had declared the Agricultural Adjustment Act unconstitutional. With cases pending on Social Security and the Wagner Act, it was possible that the Court would strike down most of the major New Deal programs.

Roosevelt was furious that a handful of jurists, "nine old men" as he called them, were blocking the wishes of a majority of the people. After winning reelection, he decided to try to change the political balance on the Court. In March 1937 he sent Congress a bill to increase the number of justices. It proposed that if any justice had served for 10 years and did not retire within six months after reaching the age of 70, the president could appoint an additional justice to the Court. Since four justices were in their 70s and two more were in their late 60s, the bill, if passed, would allow Roosevelt to quickly appoint as many as six new justices.

The **court-packing** plan, as the press called it, was Roosevelt's first serious political mistake. Although Congress had the power to change the Court's size, the scheme created the impression that the president was trying to undermine the Court's independence.

The issue split the Democratic Party. Many Southern Democrats feared Roosevelt's plan would put justices on the Court who would overturn segregation. At the same time, African American leaders worried that once Roosevelt set the precedent of changing the Court's makeup, a future president might pack the Court with justices opposed to civil rights. Many Americans believed the plan would give the president too much power.

Despite the uproar, Roosevelt's actions appeared to force the Supreme Court to back down. In April 1937, the Court upheld the constitutionality of the Wagner Act by a vote of 5-4 in the case *National Labor Relations Board* v. *Jones and Laughlin Steel Corporation*. In May the Court narrowly upheld the Social Security Act in *Steward Machine Company* v. *Davis*. Shortly afterward, a conservative justice resigned, enabling Roosevelt to appoint a New Deal supporter to the Court.

In mid-July the Senate quietly killed the court-packing bill without bringing it to a vote.

Roosevelt achieved his goal of changing the Court's view of the New Deal. The fight over the court-packing plan, however, hurt his reputation and encouraged conservative Democrats to work with Republicans to block any further New Deal proposals.

The Recession of 1937

In late 1937 Roosevelt's reputation again suffered when unemployment suddenly surged. Early in the year, the economy had seemed on the verge of full **recovery.** Industrial output was almost back to pre-Depression levels, and many people believed the worst was over. Roosevelt decided it was time to balance the budget. Concerned about the dangers of too much debt, Roosevelt ordered the WPA and the PWA to be cut significantly. Unfortunately, Roosevelt cut spending just as the first Social Security payroll taxes removed $2 billion from the economy, which plummeted. By the end of 1937, about 2 million people had been thrown out of work.

The recession of 1937 led to a debate inside Roosevelt's administration. Treasury Secretary **Henry Morgenthau** favored balancing the budget and cutting spending. This would encourage business leaders to invest in the economy. Harry Hopkins, head of the WPA, and Harold Ickes, head of the PWA, both disagreed. They pushed for more government spending using a new theory called Keynesianism to support their arguments.

Keynesianism was based on the theories of an influential British economist named **John Maynard Keynes.** In 1936 Keynes published a book arguing that government should spend heavily in a recession, even if it required deficit spending, to jump-start the economy.

According to Keynesian economics, Roosevelt had done the wrong thing when he cut back programs in 1937. At first, Roosevelt was reluctant to begin deficit spending again. Many critics believed the recession proved the public was becoming too dependent on government spending. Finally, in the spring of 1938, with no recovery in sight, Roosevelt asked Congress for $3.75 billion for the PWA, the WPA, and other programs.

✔ Reading Check **Summarizing** What events weakened Roosevelt's reputation in 1937?

ANALYZING SUPREME COURT CASES

Can Government Regulate Business?

★ *Schechter Poultry v. United States* (1935)
★ *NLRB v. Jones & Laughlin Steel Corp.* (1937)

Background to the Cases

These two cases look at the federal government's right to regulate interstate commerce. In the *Schechter* case, the Court overturned the NIRA and the industrial codes that regulated business. In the *Jones & Laughlin* case, Chief Justice Hughes switched sides from the *Schechter* case and upheld the Wagner Act's labor regulations. The case marks the Supreme Court's shift toward upholding New Deal legislation.

How the Court Ruled

Both cases addressed the question of federal power to regulate interstate commerce. In the *Schechter* case, the Court ruled that the federal government could regulate only business activity that was *directly* related to interstate commerce. In the *NLRB* case, the Court extended congressional power to regulate commerce and upheld the constitutionality of the Wagner Act.

▲ *In this 1937 cartoon, the donkey, a symbol of the Democratic Party, kicks up a storm and the dove of peace flies off, dropping the olive branch, in response to FDR's court-packing plan.*

The Court's Opinion

"The persons employed in slaughtering and selling in local trade are not employed in interstate commerce. Their hours and wages have no direct relation to interstate commerce. The question of how many hours these employees should work and what they should be paid differs in no essential respect from similar questions in other local businesses which handle commodities brought into a state and there dealt in as a part of its internal commerce. . . .

On both the grounds we have discussed, the attempted delegation of legislative power and the attempted regulation of intrastate transactions which affect interstate commerce only indirectly, we hold the code provisions here in question to be invalid."

—Chief Justice Charles E. Hughes
writing for the Court in *Schechter v. U.S.*

Dissenting Views

"The fundamental principle is that the power to regulate commerce is the power to enact 'all appropriate legislation' for its 'protection or advancement' . . . Although activities may be intrastate in character when separately considered, if they have such a close and substantial relation to interstate commerce that their control is essential or appropriate to protect that commerce from burdens and obstructions, Congress cannot be denied the power to exercise that control.

When industries organize themselves on a national scale . . . . how can it be maintained that their industrial labor relations constitute a forbidden field into which Congress may not enter when it is necessary to protect interstate commerce from the paralyzing consequences of industrial war?"

—Chief Justice Charles E. Hughes
writing for the Court in *NLRB v. Jones & Laughlin Steel Corporation*

DBQ Document-Based Questions

1. **Explaining** In *Schechter,* why does the Court assert that poultry workers are not engaged in interstate commerce?

2. **Analyzing** In the *NLRB* decision, how has the Court's reasoning changed?

3. **Drawing Conclusions** How would you explain the shift in the Court's attitude toward federal labor regulations?

The New Deal Ends

MAIN Idea The New Deal expanded federal power over the economy and established a social safety net.

HISTORY AND YOU Do you think the government should help those in need? Read how people felt about the government as the New Deal came to an end.

In his second Inaugural Address, Roosevelt had pointed out that despite the nation's progress in climbing out of the Depression, many Americans were still poor:

PRIMARY SOURCE

"I see one-third of a nation ill-housed, ill-clad, ill-nourished. . . . The test of our progress is not whether we add more to the abundance of those who have much; it is whether we provide enough for those who have too little."

—from *The Public Papers and Addresses of Franklin D. Roosevelt*

The Last New Deal Reforms

One of the president's goals for his second term was to provide better housing for the nation's poor. Eleanor Roosevelt, who had toured poverty-stricken Appalachia and the rural South, strongly urged the president to do something. Roosevelt responded with the National Housing Act, establishing the United States Housing Authority. This organization received $500 million to subsidize loans for builders willing to provide low-cost housing.

Roosevelt also sought to help the nation's tenant farmers. Before being shut down, the AAA had paid farmers to take land out of production. In doing so, it had inadvertently hurt tenant farmers. Landowners had expelled tenants from the land to take it out of production. As a result, some 150,000 white and 195,000 African American tenants left farming during the 1930s. To stop this trend, Congress created the Farm Security Administration to give loans to tenants so they could purchase farms.

INFOGRAPHIC
What New Deal Programs Still Exist Today?

▲ All workers are required to have a Social Security card, printed on bank paper to decrease forgeries.

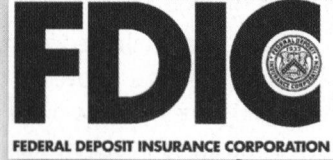

▶ The Federal Deposit Insurance Corporation sign is posted at most banks.

Program	Purpose Today
Social Security	The Social Security Administration provides old age pensions, unemployment insurance, and disability insurance.
National Labor Relations Board	The NLRB oversees union elections, investigates complaints of unfair labor practices, and mediates labor disputes.
Securities and Exchange Commission	The SEC regulates and polices the stock market.
Federal Deposit Insurance Corporation	The FDIC insures deposits up to $100,000.
Tennessee Valley Authority	The TVA provides electrical power to more than 8 million consumers.
Federal Housing Authority	Renamed the Department of Housing and Urban Development (HUD) in 1965, it insures mortgage loans, assists low-income renters, and fights housing discrimination.

◀ The Federal Housing Administration Web site uses this logo.

Analyzing VISUALS

1. **Identifying** Which organization regulates and oversees the stock market policies?
2. **Listing** What is the new name for the Federal Housing Authority?

To further help workers, Roosevelt pushed through Congress the Fair Labor Standards Act, which abolished child labor, limited the workweek to 44 hours for most workers, and set the first federal minimum wage at 25 cents an hour. The Fair Labor Standards Act was the last major piece of New Deal legislation. The recession of 1937 enabled the Republicans to win seats in Congress in the midterm elections of 1938. Together with conservative Southern Democrats, they began blocking further New Deal legislation. By 1939, the New Deal era had come to an end.

The New Deal's Legacy

The New Deal had only limited success in ending the Depression. Unemployment remained high, and economic recovery was not complete until after World War II. Even so, the New Deal gave many Americans a stronger sense of security and stability.

As a whole, the New Deal tended to balance competing economic interests. Business leaders, farmers, workers, homeowners, and others now looked to government to protect their interests. The federal government's ability to take on this new role was enhanced by two important Supreme Court decisions. In 1937, in *NLRB* v. *Jones and Laughlin Steel,* the Court ruled that the federal government had the authority to regulate production within a state. Later, in 1942, in *Wickard* v. *Filburn,* the Court used a similar argument to allow the federal government to regulate consumption in the states. These decisions increased federal power over the economy and allowed it to **mediate** between competing groups.

In taking on this mediating role, the New Deal established what some have called the **broker state,** in which the government works out conflicts among different interests. This broker role has continued under the administrations of both parties ever since. The New Deal also brought about a new public attitude toward government. Roosevelt's programs had succeeded in creating a **safety net** for Americans—safeguards and relief programs that protected them against economic disaster. By the end of the 1930s, many Americans felt that the government had a duty to maintain this safety net, even though doing so required a larger, more expensive federal government.

Critics continue to argue that the New Deal made the government too powerful. Thus, another legacy of the New Deal is a continuing debate over how much the government should intervene in the economy or support the disadvantaged. Throughout the hard times of the Depression, most Americans maintained a surprising degree of confidence in the American system. Journalist Dorothy Thompson expressed this feeling in 1940:

PRIMARY SOURCE

"We have behind us eight terrible years of a crisis. . . . Here we are, and our basic institutions are still intact, our people relatively prosperous and most important of all, our society relatively affectionate. . . . No country is so well off."

—from the *Washington Post,* October 9, 1940

Reading Check **Summarizing** What was the legacy of Roosevelt's New Deal?

Vocabulary

1. **Explain** the significance of: Frances Perkins, court-packing, Henry Morgenthau, John Maynard Keynes, broker state, safety net.

Main Ideas

2. What caused a recession early in Roosevelt's second term?

3. How did the New Deal expand federal power over the economy?

Critical Thinking

4. **Big Ideas** What groups made up the New Deal coalition?

5. **Organizing** Use a chart like the one below to list the achievements and defeats of Roosevelt's second term.

Achievements	Defeats

6. **Analyzing Visuals** Choose one of the photos on page 669 and write a brief account of the day's activities from the viewpoint of one of the people in the photograph.

Writing About History

7. **Persuasive Writing** Imagine that you are a staff member in Roosevelt's cabinet. Write a short paper criticizing or defending FDR's court-packing plan.

History ONLINE

Study Central™ To review this section, go to glencoe.com and click on Study Central.

The New Deal in Action

Banking and Finances

- Emergency Banking Relief Act regulated banks.
- Federal Deposit Insurance Corporation insured bank deposits.
- Farm Credit Administration refinanced farm mortgages.
- Home Owners' Loan Corporation financed homeowners' mortgages.

Agriculture and Industry

- Agricultural Adjustment Administration paid farmers to limit surplus production.
- National Industrial Recovery Act limited industrial production and set prices.
- National Labor Relations Act gave workers the right to organize unions and bargain collectively.
- Tennessee Valley Authority financed rural electrification and helped develop the economy of a seven-state region.

▲ A steel worker labors on the Grand Coulee Dam on the Columbia River in eastern Washington.

Work and Relief

- Civilian Conservation Corps created forestry jobs for young men.
- Federal Emergency Relief Administration funded city and state relief programs.
- Public Works Administration created work programs to build public projects, such as roads, bridges, and schools.

◄ A Civilian Conservation Corps member plants trees.

Social "Safety Net"

- Social Security Act provided
  - income for senior citizens, handicapped, and unemployed
  - monthly retirement benefit for people over 65

▶ In 1935 President Roosevelt signs the Social Security Bill while Secretary of Labor Perkins and legislators observe.

NEW YORK REGENTS EXAM PRACTICE

TEST-TAKING

Questions sometimes ask for the exception, rather than the one right answer. Be sure to read through the question carefully, as well as each response, to see which one does not fit.

Part I

Directions (1–11): For each statement or question, write on a separate sheet of paper the number of the word or expression that, of those given, best completes the statement or answers the question.

1 One of the ways in which Franklin Roosevelt gained political experience before being president was being elected
   (1) senator from Maine.
   (2) mayor of Boston.
   (3) governor of New York.
   (4) representative from Connecticut.

2 Which of the following was created to protect bank deposits?
   (1) Agricultural Adjustment Act
   (2) Home Owners' Loan Corporation
   (3) Securities and Exchange Commission
   (4) Federal Deposit Insurance Corporation

3 Why did the Agricultural Adjustment Act pay farmers not to grow certain crops?
   (1) to raise farm prices
   (2) to lower farm prices
   (3) to stabilize prices
   (4) to let farmers relax

4 The New Deal was being criticized in 1935 because it
   (1) had created too many new programs.
   (2) was focusing only on the South.
   (3) had spent too much money.
   (4) had not ended the Great Depression.

5 Benefits for older Americans were guaranteed by the
   (1) Congress of Industrial Organizations.
   (2) Works Progress Administration.
   (3) Social Security Act.
   (4) Wagner Act.

6 During Roosevelt's second term, he split his own party by suggesting the need to
   (1) appoint additional Supreme Court judges.
   (2) include African Americans in New Deal programs.
   (3) appoint women to his cabinet.
   (4) follow Keynesian economics.

7 Part of the New Deal's legacy was an expansion of
   (1) state power over the courts.
   (2) federal power over the economy.
   (3) federal power over the Constitution.
   (4) state power over social safety nets.

8 What prevented banks from being closed completely because of bank runs?
   (1) New Deal
   (2) bank holiday
   (3) gold standard
   (4) fireside chat

Need Extra Help?								
If You Missed Questions . . .	1	2	3	4	5	6	7	8
Go to Page . . .	650–651	654	656	662–664	667	670	673	652

[OVER]

Base your answer to question 9 on the map below and on your knowledge of Chapter 19.

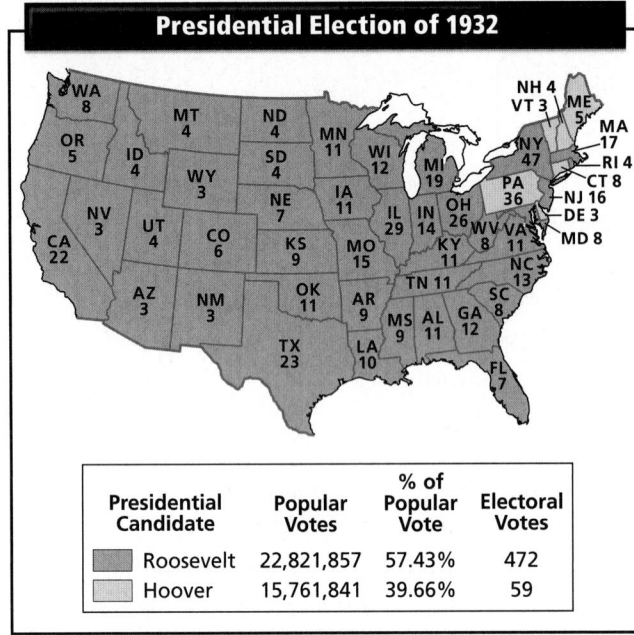

Presidential Election of 1932

Presidential Candidate	Popular Votes	% of Popular Vote	Electoral Votes
Roosevelt	22,821,857	57.43%	472
Hoover	15,761,841	39.66%	59

9 Which state gave Hoover the largest number of votes in the Electoral College?
(1) Pennsylvania
(2) New York
(3) Connecticut
(4) Texas

10 The New Deal changed Americans' attitudes toward government and
(1) the desire for easy wealth.
(2) the challenge of unionization.
(3) the duty to regulate industry.
(4) the need to provide a safety net.

11 Paying for programs with borrowed money is called
(1) deficit spending.
(2) the gold standard.
(3) states' rights.
(4) binding arbitration.

Need Extra Help?			
If You Missed Questions . . .	9	10	11
Go to Page . . .	R15	673	662

Part II Thematic Essay Question

Directions: Write a well-organized essay that includes an introduction, several paragraphs addressing the task below, and a conclusion.

Theme: The New Deal

The programs of the New Deal and the Second New Deal helped ease hardships caused by the Great Depression and increased the role of the federal government.

Task:

Review the various New Deal programs, select one that you think could be used or adapted to a current situation, and

• Explain what groups would benefit
• Describe how the program would help the current situation

Guidelines:

In your essay, be sure to:

• Develop all aspects of the task
• Support the theme with relevant facts, examples, and details
• Use a logical and clear plan of organization, including an introduction and a conclusion that are beyond a restatement of the theme

Part III Document-Based Question

This question is based on the accompanying documents. It is designed to test your ability to work with historical documents. Some of the documents have been edited for the purposes of the question. As you analyze the documents, take into account both the source of each document and any point of view that may be presented in the document.

Historical Context:

The New Deal programs of Franklin D. Roosevelt's administration provided relief from the Great Depression.

Task:

Using information from the documents and your knowledge of United States history, answer the questions that follow each document in Part A. Your answers to the questions will help you write the Part B essay, in which you will be asked to

- Discuss the motivations and inspirations behind New Deal programs
- Evaluate the reasons why many government officials supported the programs and the reasons for opposition to the programs

Part A

Short-Answer Questions

Directions: Analyze the documents and answer the short-answer questions that follow each document on a separate sheet of paper.

Document 1

"This trip to the mining areas was my first contact with the work being done by the Quakers. I liked the theory of trying to put people to work to help themselves. The men were started on projects and taught to use their abilities to develop new skills. The women were encouraged to revive any household arts they might once have known but which they had neglected in the drab life of the mining village.

This was only the first of many trips into the mining districts but it was the one that started the homestead idea [placing people in communities with homes, farms, and jobs] . . . . It was all experimental work, but it was designed to get people off relief, to put them to work building their own homes and to give them enough land to start growing food."

Source: *The Autobiography of Eleanor Roosevelt*, Da Capo Press

1 Why did Eleanor Roosevelt like the Quaker project?

Document 2

Source: The Granger Collection, New York

2 What message does this cartoon communicate about Roosevelt?

Part B

Essay

Directions: Reread the task box at the top left and write a well-organized essay that includes an introduction, several paragraphs, and a conclusion. Use evidence from the documents in your essay. Support your response with relevant facts, examples, and details. Include additional outside information.

Guidelines:

In your essay, be sure to:

- Develop all aspects of the task
- Incorporate information from the documents
- Incorporate relevant outside information
- Use a logical and clear plan of organization, including an introduction and a conclusion that are beyond a restatement of the theme

ONLINE

For additional test practice, use Self-Check Quizzes—Chapter 19 at glencoe.com.

Need Extra Help?			
If You Missed Questions . . .	1	2	Essay
Go to Page . . .	R18	R19	652–659

Unit 7

Global Struggles
1931–1960

Why It Matters

The rise of dictatorships in the 1930s led to World War II, the most destructive war in world history. The United States played a major role in the war, fighting in Europe, Africa, and Asia. Afterwards, the United States emerged as a global superpower, abandoned isolationism, and began building alliances around the world. Confrontation with the Soviet Union led to the Cold War, as the United States sought to contain the spread of communism.

678

Despite the fog, American soldiers march in Belgium during the winter of 1944–1945.

A World in Flames

1931–1941

Italian dictator Benito Mussolini, at left, walks in Munich, Germany, with German dictator Adolf Hitler, center, in 1938.

U.S. PRESIDENTS

Roosevelt
1933–1945

1934
- Nye Committee holds hearings on causes of World War I

1935
- First Neutrality Act bars sale of weapons to warring nations

1937
- Neutrality Act limits trade with all warring nations

U.S. EVENTS

1931   1933   1935   1937

WORLD EVENTS

1931
- Japan invades Manchuria

1933
- Hitler becomes chancellor of Germany

1935
- Hitler denounces Treaty of Versailles
- Italy invades Ethiopia

1936
- Spanish Civil War begins
- Hitler reoccupies the Rhineland

1937
- Japan invades China

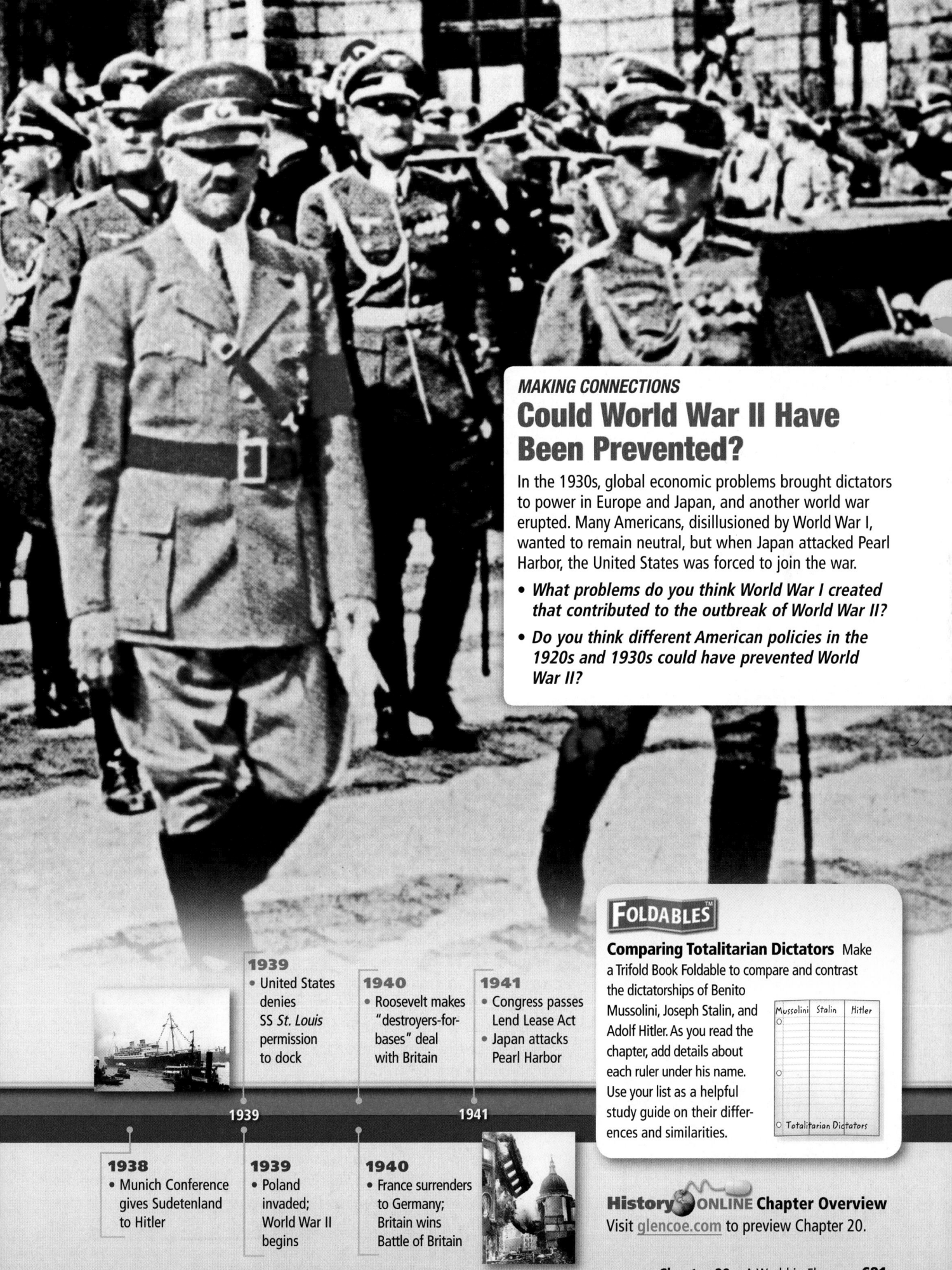

MAKING CONNECTIONS
Could World War II Have Been Prevented?

In the 1930s, global economic problems brought dictators to power in Europe and Japan, and another world war erupted. Many Americans, disillusioned by World War I, wanted to remain neutral, but when Japan attacked Pearl Harbor, the United States was forced to join the war.

• *What problems do you think World War I created that contributed to the outbreak of World War II?*

• *Do you think different American policies in the 1920s and 1930s could have prevented World War II?*

FOLDABLES™

Comparing Totalitarian Dictators Make a Trifold Book Foldable to compare and contrast the dictatorships of Benito Mussolini, Joseph Stalin, and Adolf Hitler. As you read the chapter, add details about each ruler under his name. Use your list as a helpful study guide on their differences and similarities.

1938
• Munich Conference gives Sudetenland to Hitler

1939
• United States denies SS *St. Louis* permission to dock

1939
• Poland invaded; World War II begins

1940
• Roosevelt makes "destroyers-for-bases" deal with Britain

1940
• France surrenders to Germany; Britain wins Battle of Britain

1941
• Congress passes Lend Lease Act
• Japan attacks Pearl Harbor

1939

1941

History ONLINE Chapter Overview
Visit glencoe.com to preview Chapter 20.

Chapter 20 A World in Flames **681**

America and the World

Guide to Reading

Big Ideas
Government and Society In the years following World War I, aggressive and expansionistic governments took power in both Europe and Asia.

Content Vocabulary
- fascism *(p. 682)*
- collective *(p. 683)*
- internationalism *(p. 687)*

Academic Vocabulary
- exploit *(p. 682)*
- dominate *(p. 685)*

People and Events to Identify
- Benito Mussolini *(p. 682)*
- Vladimir Lenin *(p. 683)*
- Joseph Stalin *(p. 683)*
- Adolf Hitler *(p. 684)*
- Manchuria *(p. 685)*
- Neutrality Act of 1935 *(p. 686)*
- Axis Powers *(p. 687)*

Reading Strategy
Taking Notes As you read about the events in Europe and Asia after World War I, use the major headings of the section to create an outline similar to the one below.

> America and the World
> I. The Rise of Dictators
>   A.
>   B.
>   C.
>   D.
> II.

NEW YORK CORE CURRICULUM
U.S. History and Government

Unit 6:
I.A Isolation and neutrality
I.A.2 Neutrality Acts of 1935–1937
I.A.3 Spanish Civil War: testing war technology and ideology
I.A.4 FDR's "quarantine" speech (1937)
I.B.1 Aggressions of Japan, Germany, Italy: 1932–1940

In the years following World War I, aggressive and expansionist governments took power in Europe and Asia. Meanwhile, most Americans did not want to get involved in another foreign war.

The Rise of Dictators

MAIN Idea Dictators took control of the governments of Italy, the Soviet Union, Germany, and Japan.

HISTORY AND YOU Can you think of a country today that is ruled by a dictator? Read about the repressive governments that arose during the 1920s and 1930s.

When World War I ended, President Wilson had hoped that the United States could "aid in the establishment of just democracy throughout the world." Instead, the treaty that ended the war, along with the economic depression that followed, contributed to the rise of antidemocratic governments in both Europe and Asia.

Mussolini and Fascism in Italy

One of Europe's first dictatorships arose in Italy. In 1919 **Benito Mussolini** founded Italy's Fascist Party. **Fascism** was an aggressive nationalistic movement that considered the nation more important than the individual. Fascists believed that order in society would come only through a dictator who led a strong government. They also thought nations became great by building an empire.

Fascism was also strongly anticommunist. After the Russian Revolution, many Europeans feared that communists, allied with labor unions, were trying to bring down their governments. Mussolini **exploited** these fears by portraying fascism as a bulwark against communism. Fascism began to stand for the protection of private property and the middle class. Mussolini also promised the working class full employment and social security. He pledged to return Italy to the glories of the Roman Empire.

Backed by the Fascist militia known as the Blackshirts, Mussolini threatened to march on Rome in 1922, claiming he was coming to defend Italy against a communist revolution. Liberal members of the Italian parliament insisted that the king declare martial law. When he refused, the cabinet resigned. Conservative advisers then persuaded the king to appoint Mussolini as the premier.

Once in office, Mussolini worked quickly to set up a dictatorship. Weary of strikes and riots, many Italians welcomed Mussolini's leadership. With the support of industrialists, landowners, and the Roman

0 1,000 kilometers
0 1,000 miles
Lambert Equal-Area projection

ARCTIC OCEAN

ATLANTIC OCEAN

PACIFIC OCEAN

In 1926 Joseph Stalin becomes dictator of the Soviet Union and begins to collectivize agriculture and industrialize the economy. His policies kill millions of rural peasants.

In 1936 General Francisco Franco launches a military revolt that overthrows Spain's democratic government; Franco then establishes a dictatorship.

In 1933, high unemployment and fears of communism enable Adolf Hitler and the Nazi Party to take power. Hitler imposed a dictatorship, enacted anti-Jewish policies, and began rebuilding the military.

Sea of Okhotsk

GERMANY

SPAIN

EUROPE

ITALY

SOVIET UNION

JAPANESE EMPIRE

Black Sea

Caspian Sea

ASIA

In 1931, the militarist Empire of Japan invades Manchuria; six years later, Japan attacks China. In 1941 General Hideki Tōjō becomes prime minister and led the nation into war with the United States.

In 1922 fears of communism and economic chaos enable Benito Mussolini to lead the Fascists to power in Italy.

Red Sea

Arabian Sea

AFRICA

Analyzing GEOGRAPHY

1. **Region** In which region of the world did a dictator first come to power, and when?

2. **Human-Environment Interactions** What effect did Stalin's policies have on the Soviet Union?

Catholic Church, Mussolini—who took the title of Il Duce, or "The Leader"—embarked on an ambitious program of bringing order to Italy.

Stalin Takes Over the USSR

After the Russian Revolution, the Communist Party, led by **Vladimir Lenin,** established communist governments throughout the Russian Empire. In 1922 they renamed these territories the Union of Soviet Socialist Republics (USSR). The Communists instituted one-party rule, suppressed individual liberties, and punished opponents.

After Lenin died in 1924, a power struggle began between Leon Trotsky and **Joseph Stalin.** Born with the surname of Dzuhgashvili, Stalin replaced his last name with the Russian word *stal,* meaning "steel." Between 1902 and 1913, he had been imprisoned or exiled seven times, but he always escaped.

By 1926, Stalin had become the new Soviet dictator. He began a massive effort to industrialize his country, using Five-Year Plans. During the first two of these Five-Year Plans, from 1928 to 1937, steel production increased from 4 million to 18 million tons (3.628 to 16.326 million t). At the same time, however, industrial wages declined by 43 percent from 1928 to 1940. Family farms were combined and turned into **collectives,** or government-owned farms. Peasants who resisted by killing livestock or hoarding crops faced show trials or death from starvation. As many as 10 million peasants died in famines during 1932 and 1933.

Stalin tolerated no opposition, targeting not only political enemies but also artists and intellectuals. During the late 1930s, the USSR was a nation of internal terrorism, with public trials that featured forced confessions. A new constitution, passed in 1936, promised many freedoms but was never enforced.

Stalin also used concentration camps; by 1935 some 2 million people were in camps, most of which were located in the Arctic. Prisoners were used as slave labor. Between 8 and 10 million people died as a result of Stalin's rule, which lasted until his death in 1953.

Hitler and Nazi Germany

Adolf Hitler was a fervent anticommunist and an admirer of Mussolini. A native Austrian, Hitler had fought for Germany in World War I. Germany's surrender and the subsequent Treaty of Versailles caused him and many other Germans to hate both the victorious Allies and the German government that had accepted the peace terms.

Postwar Germany's political and economic chaos led to the rise of new political parties. One of these was the National Socialist German Workers' Party, or the Nazi Party. The party was nationalistic and anticommunist, calling for Germany to expand its territory and not abide by the terms of the Treaty of Versailles. It also was anti-Semitic. Using the words *Socialist* and *Workers* in its name, the party

hoped to attract unhappy workers. Adolf Hitler was one of the party's first recruits.

In November 1923, the Nazis tried to seize power by marching on city hall in Munich, Germany. Hitler intended to seize power locally and then march on Berlin, the German capital, but the plan failed. The Nazi Party was banned for a time, and Hitler was arrested.

While in prison, Hitler wrote *Mein Kampf* ("My Struggle"), in which he called for the unification of all Germans under one government. He claimed that Germans, particularly blond, blue-eyed Germans, belonged to a "master race" called Aryans. He argued that Germans needed more space and called for Germany to expand east into Poland and Russia. According to Hitler, the Slavic peoples of eastern Europe belonged to an inferior race, which Germans should enslave. Hitler's racism was strongest, however, toward Jews. He believed that Jews were responsible for many of the world's problems, especially for Germany's defeat in World War I.

After his release, Hitler changed his tactics. Instead of trying to seize power violently, he focused on getting Nazis elected to the

▼ *Japanese officers targeted resource-rich Manchuria as the first goal in their drive to build an empire.*

Japan Invades Manchuria, 1931

Japanese invasion of Manchuria

Italy Invades Ethiopia, 1935

Italian-held territory
Ethiopia (Abyssinia)
Italian invasion route

▲ *Mussolini, the dictator of Italy, wanted to build a new Roman Empire in Africa. In 1935 the Italian army invaded Ethiopia, then known as Abyssinia. The emperor, Haile Selassie, went into exile.*

Reichstag, the lower house of the German parliament. When the Great Depression struck Germany, many desperate Germans began to vote for radical parties, including the Nazis and Communists. By 1932, the Nazis were the largest party in the Reichstag. The following year, the German president appointed Hitler as chancellor, or prime minister.

After taking office, Hitler called for new elections. He then ordered the police to crack down on the Socialist and Communist Parties. Storm troopers, as the Nazi paramilitary units were called, began intimidating voters. After the election, the Reichstag, dominated by the Nazis and other right-wing parties, voted to give Hitler dictatorial powers. In 1934 Hitler became president, which gave him control of the army. He then gave himself the new title of Der Führer, or "The Leader."

Militarists Control Japan

In Japan, as in Germany, difficult economic times helped undermine the political system. Japanese industries had to import nearly all of the resources they needed to produce goods. During the 1920s Japan did not earn enough money from its exports to pay for its imports, which limited economic growth. When the Depression struck, other countries raised their tariffs. This made the situation even worse.

Many Japanese military officers blamed the country's problems on corrupt politicians. Most officers believed that Japan was destined to **dominate** East Asia and saw democracy as "un-Japanese" and bad for the country.

Japanese military leaders and their civilian supporters argued that seizing territory was the only way Japan could get the resources it needed. In September 1931, the Japanese army invaded **Manchuria,** a resource-rich region of northern China. When the Japanese prime minister tried to stop the war by negotiating with China, officers assassinated him. From that point forward, the military controlled the country. Japan's civilian government supported the nationalist policy of expanding the empire and appointed a military officer to serve as prime minister.

✓ Reading Check **Examining** How did postwar conditions contribute to the rise of dictatorships in Europe?

The Spanish Civil War, 1936–1939

In 1936 a civil war broke out in Spain when Fascist General Francisco Franco attempted a military coup. With aid from Hitler and Mussolini, Spain became a testing ground for new military ideas such as air strikes. On April 26, 1937, planes released 100,000 pounds of bombs, destroying 70% of Guernica, shown at left after the bombing. A mere 15 days after the bombing, the artist Pablo Picasso began painting Guernica *(above).*

Analyzing VISUALS

1. **Comparing** In what way were the three wars shown on the map all a prelude to World War II?

2. **Analyzing** How does Picasso show the terror of the Guernica bombing?

American Neutrality

MAIN Idea Most Americans did not want to get involved in another European war, despite Franklin Roosevelt's emphasis on internationalism.

HISTORY AND YOU Do you think the United States should become involved in the wars of other nations even when it is not under attack? Read to learn about American attitudes during the 1930s.

The rise of dictatorships and militarism discouraged many Americans. The sacrifices they had made during World War I seemed pointless. Once again, Americans began supporting isolationism and trying to avoid involvement in international conflicts.

The Nye Committee

Isolationist ideas became stronger in the early 1930s for two reasons. When the Depression began, many European nations found it difficult to repay money they had borrowed during World War I. In 1934 all of the debtor nations except Finland announced they would no longer repay their war debts.

Meanwhile, dozens of books and articles appeared arguing that arms manufacturers had tricked the United States into entering World War I. In 1934 Senator Gerald P. Nye of North Dakota held hearings to investigate these allegations. The Nye Committee documented the huge profits that arms factories had made during the war. The report created the impression that these businesses influenced the decision to go to war. Coupled with the European refusal to repay their loans, the Nye Committee's findings turned even more Americans toward isolationism.

Legislating Neutrality

Italian and German aggression increased under Mussolini and Hitler. Worried that the actions of these nations might lead to war, Congress passed the **Neutrality Act of 1935.** This legislation—reflecting the belief that arms sales had helped bring the United States into World War I—made it illegal for Americans to sell arms to any country at war.

In 1936 a rebellion erupted in Spain after voters elected a coalition of Republicans, Socialists, and Communists. General Francisco Franco led the rebellion, backed by Spanish Fascists, army officers, landowners, and Catholic Church leaders. The revolt became a civil war and attracted

INFOGRAPHIC
The Neutrality Acts, 1935–1937

Causes
- Nye Senate Committee report suggesting that the American arms industry had pushed the nation into World War I for its own profit
- growing belief that America should have stayed out of World War I

The Neutrality Act of 1935
- mandatory embargo on selling or exporting arms, ammunition, or implements of war to nations at war
- discretionary travel restrictions
- set to expire after 6 months

Causes
- Italy's invasion of Ethiopia; FDR encourages a moral embargo against Italy, which he could not enforce

The Neutrality Act of 1936
- arms embargo with countries at war
- discretionary travel restrictions
- ban on loans to nations fighting, but short-term credits exempted
- republics in the Americas exempted

Causes
- Spanish Civil War
- sale of aviation parts to rebels in Spain, which FDR thought unpatriotic
- agreements creating the Axis alliance

The Neutrality Act of 1937
- arms embargo against nations at war
- travel ban on warring nations' ships
- trade with countries at war on a cash-and-carry basis allowed if goods were not contraband or sent on foreign ships

▲ Republican Senator Gerald Nye headed the Senate Munitions Committee, whose findings convinced many that arms makers were "merchants of death" and that the United States should remain neutral.

Analyzing VISUALS
1. **Analyzing** What impact did the Nye Committee's findings have on public opinion?
2. **Evaluating** Why did so many Americans support neutrality?

worldwide attention. Congress passed a second neutrality act, banning the sale of arms to either side in a civil war.

Shortly after the Spanish Civil War began, Hitler and Mussolini pledged to cooperate on several international issues. Mussolini termed this new relationship the Rome-Berlin Axis. The following month, Japan aligned itself with Germany and Italy when it signed the Anti-Comintern Pact with Germany. The pact required the two countries to exchange information about communist groups. Together, Germany, Italy, and Japan became known as the **Axis Powers,** although they did not formally become military allies until September 1940.

With tensions in Europe worsening, Congress passed the Neutrality Act of 1937. This act not only continued the ban on selling arms to warring nations, but also required them to buy all nonmilitary supplies from the United States on a "cash-and-carry" basis. Countries at war had to send their own ships to the United States to pick up the goods, and they had to pay cash. Loans were not allowed. Isolationists knew that attacks on American ships carrying supplies to Europe had helped bring the country into World War I. They wanted to prevent such attacks from involving the nation in another European war.

Roosevelt's Internationalism

When he took office in 1933, President Roosevelt knew that ending the Great Depression was his first priority. He was not, however, an isolationist. He supported **internationalism,** the idea that trade between nations creates prosperity and helps prevent war. Internationalists also believed that the United States should try to preserve peace in the world. Roosevelt warned that the neutrality acts "might drag us into war instead of keeping us out," but he did not veto the bills.

In July 1937, Japanese forces in Manchuria launched a full-scale attack on China. Roosevelt decided to help the Chinese. Because neither China nor Japan had actually declared war, Roosevelt claimed the Neutrality Act of 1937 did not apply, and he authorized the sale of weapons to China. He warned that the nation should not stand by and let an "epidemic of lawlessness" infect the world:

PRIMARY SOURCE

"When an epidemic of physical disease starts to spread, the community ... joins in a quarantine of the patients in order to protect the health of the community against the spread of the disease. . . . War is a contagion, whether it be declared or undeclared. . . . There is no escape through mere isolation or neutrality. . . . "

—quoted in *Freedom From Fear*

Despite his words, Americans were still not willing to risk another war. "It is a terrible thing," the president said, "to look over your shoulder when you are trying to lead—and find no one there."

Reading Check **Evaluating** Why did many Americans support isolationism?

Section 1 REVIEW

Vocabulary

1. **Explain** the significance of: Benito Mussolini, fascism, Vladimir Lenin, Joseph Stalin, collectives, Adolf Hitler, Manchuria, Neutrality Act of 1935, Axis Powers, internationalism.

Main Ideas

2. **Identifying** Which nations did dictators govern during the years after World War I?

3. **Analyzing** What events caused Roosevelt to become more of an internationalist?

Critical Thinking

4. **Big Ideas** Why did antidemocratic governments rise to power in postwar Europe and Asia?

5. **Organizing** Use a graphic organizer similar to the one below to compare the governments opposed to democracy in Europe and Asia.

Country	Dictator	Ideology

6. **Analyzing Visuals** Look at the photograph on page 685 of Guernica after it was destroyed. How might both isolationists and internationalists have used the image to win support for their cause?

Writing About History

7. **Persuasive Writing** Write a newspaper editorial supporting either isolationism or internationalism after World War I. Include reasons that support your ideas and that help convince others to embrace your position.

History ONLINE

Study Central™ To review this section, go to glencoe.com and click on Study Central.

World War II Begins

Guide to Reading

Big Ideas
Trade, War, and Migration World War II officially began with the Nazi invasion of Poland and the French and British declarations of war on Germany in September 1939.

Content Vocabulary
• appeasement *(p. 689)*
• blitzkrieg *(p. 690)*

Academic Vocabulary
• violation *(p. 688)*
• regime *(p. 688)*
• concentrate *(p. 690)*
• transport *(p. 693)*

People and Events to Identify
• *Anschluss* *(p. 688)*
• Munich Conference *(p. 689)*
• Maginot Line *(p. 690)*
• Winston Churchill *(p. 693)*
• Battle of Britain *(p. 693)*

Reading Strategy
Sequencing As you read about the events leading up to World War II, record them by completing a time line similar to the one below.

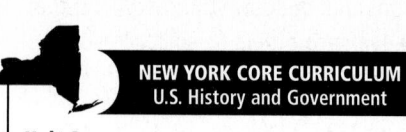

NEW YORK CORE CURRICULUM
U.S. History and Government

Unit 6:
I.B.1 Aggressions of Japan, Germany, Italy: 1932–1940
I.B.2 Appeasement: The Munich Conference (1938)
I.B.3 German attack on Poland; start of World War II in Europe

The shadow of World War I loomed large in the minds of European leaders in the late 1930s. Although Nazi Germany appeared increasingly aggressive, Britain and France wanted to avoid another bloody conflict. Efforts to negotiate peaceful agreements with Nazi Germany ultimately failed.

Path to War

MAIN Idea European nations tried to prevent war by giving in to Adolf Hitler's demands.

HISTORY AND YOU Do you remember reading how Europe was divided after World War I? Read to learn how German demands for more territory started World War II.

In 1935 Hitler began to defy the Treaty of Versailles that had ended World War I. He announced that Germany would build a new air force and begin a military draft that would greatly expand its army—actions in direct **violation** of the treaty. Rather than enforce the treaty by going to war, European leaders tried to negotiate with Hitler. At the time, the Nazi **regime** was weaker than it later would become. If European leaders had responded more aggressively, could war have been avoided? Historians still debate this question today.

Europe's leaders had several reasons for believing—or wanting to believe—that a deal could be reached with Hitler and that war could be avoided. First, they wanted to avoid a repeat of the bloodshed of World War I. Second, some thought most of Hitler's demands were reasonable, including his demand that all German-speaking regions be united. Third, many people assumed that the Nazis would be more interested in peace once they gained more territory.

The Austrian *Anschluss*

In late 1937 Hitler again called for the unification of all German-speaking people, including those in Austria and Czechoslovakia. He believed that Germany could expand its territory only by "resort[ing] to force with its attendant risks."

In February 1938 Hitler threatened to invade German-speaking Austria unless Austrian Nazis were given important government posts. Austria's chancellor gave in to this demand, but then tried to put the matter of unification with Germany to a democratic vote. Fearing the outcome, Hitler sent troops into Austria in March and announced the *Anschluss,* or unification, of Austria and Germany.

0   200 kilometers

0   200 miles

Lambert Azimuthal
Equal-Area projection

Hitler demands the
return of Danzig to
Germany, October 1938.

In August 1939, the Nazi-
Soviet Pact is signed. One
week later, on Sept. 1,
Germany invades Poland.

In March 1936, Germany sends
troops into the Rhineland,
defying the Treaty of Versailles.

Austrian *Anschluss*, 1938—
Germany annexes Austria.

▲ At Munich in 1938, Britain's Neville Chamberlain (left), Mussolini (second from left), and Hitler (right) reached a deal that prevented war but required Czechoslovakia to give up the Sudetenland (brown area on the Czech border above) to Germany. Six months later, Germany occupied all of Czechoslovakia.

Analyzing GEOGRAPHY

1. **Region** Why do you think Hitler's first military action was in the Rhineland?

2. **Region** Why might Hitler have welcomed a nonaggression pact with the Soviets?

Maps in Motion See *StudentWorks™ Plus* or glencoe.com.

The Munich Crisis

Hitler next announced German claims to the Sudetenland, an area of Czechoslovakia with a large German-speaking population. The Czechs strongly resisted Germany's demands for the Sudetenland. France threatened to fight if Germany attacked Czechoslovakia, and the Soviet Union also promised aid. Prime Minister Neville Chamberlain pledged Britain's support to France, its ally.

Representatives of Britain, France, Italy, and Germany agreed to meet in Munich to decide Czechoslovakia's fate. At the **Munich**

Conference, on September 29, 1938, Britain and France agreed to Hitler's demands, a policy that came to be known as **appeasement.** In other words, they made concessions in exchange for peace. Supporters of appeasement believed that Hitler had a few limited demands. They felt that if they gave him what he wanted, they could avoid war. Czechoslovakia was told to give up the Sudetenland or fight Germany on its own. When Chamberlain returned home, he promised "a peace with honor . . . peace in our time," but he also began to speed up British rearmament—in case appeasement failed.

Appeasement did fail to preserve the fragile peace. In March 1939 Germany sent troops into Czechoslovakia and divided the country. Slovakia became independent in name, but it was actually under German control. The Czech lands became a German protectorate.

Hitler Demands Danzig

A month after the Munich Conference, Hitler demanded that the city of Danzig be returned to German control. Although Danzig was more than 90 percent German, it had been part of Poland since World War I. Hitler also requested a highway and railroad across the Polish Corridor, an area that separated western Germany from the German state of East Prussia.

Hitler's new demands convinced Britain and France that war was inevitable. On March 31, 1939, Britain announced that if Poland went to war to defend its territory, Britain and France would come to its aid. This declaration encouraged Poland to refuse Hitler's demands. In May 1939, Hitler ordered the German army to prepare to invade Poland. He also ordered his foreign minister to begin negotiations with the USSR. If Germany was going to fight Britain and France, Hitler did not want to have to fight the Soviets, too.

The Nazi-Soviet Pact

When German officials proposed a nonaggression treaty to the Soviets, Stalin agreed. He believed the best way to protect the USSR was to turn the capitalist nations against each other. If the treaty worked, Germany would go to war against Britain and France, and the USSR would be safe.

The nonaggression pact, signed by Germany and the USSR on August 23, 1939, shocked the world. Communism and Nazism were supposed to be totally opposed to each other. Leaders in Britain and France understood, however, that Hitler had made the deal to free himself for war against their countries and Poland. They did not know that the treaty also contained a secret deal to divide Poland between Germany and the Soviet Union.

✔ **Reading Check** **Identifying** What regions did Hitler take or demand in the lead-up to the war?

The War Begins

MAIN Idea After Poland and France fell to the Nazis, the British evacuated thousands of trapped troops from Dunkirk.

HISTORY AND YOU Can you think of a contemporary situation in which people acted heroically to save others in danger? Read to learn about the heroism of civilians and soldiers in World War II.

On September 1, 1939, Germany invaded Poland. Two days later, Britain and France declared war on Germany. World War II had begun.

Poland bravely resisted Germany's onslaught, but its army was outdated. The Polish army rode horses and carried lances against German tanks. In addition, the Germans used a new type of warfare called **blitzkrieg,** or "lightning war." Blitzkrieg used large numbers of massed tanks to break through and rapidly encircle enemy positions. To support the tanks, waves of aircraft bombed enemy positions and dropped paratroopers to cut their supply lines. The Polish army could not repel the attack. Warsaw, the Polish capital, fell to the Germans on September 27. By October 5, 1939, the Germans had defeated the Polish military.

The Fall of France

In contrast to the war in Poland, western Europe remained eerily quiet. The Germans referred to this situation as the *sitzkrieg*, or "sitting war." The British called it the "Bore War," while American newspapers nicknamed it the "Phony War." The British had sent troops to France, and both countries remained on the defensive, waiting for the Germans to attack.

After World War I, the French had built a line of concrete bunkers and fortifications called the **Maginot Line** along the German border. Rather than risk their troops by attacking, the French preferred to wait behind the Maginot Line for the Germans to approach. This decision proved to be disastrous for two reasons. First, it allowed Germany to **concentrate** on Poland first before turning west to face the British and French. Second, Hitler decided to go around the Maginot Line, which protected France's border with Germany but not France's border with Belgium.

To get around the Maginot Line, the Germans would have to invade the Netherlands, Belgium, and Luxembourg first—which is exactly what they did. On May 10, Hitler launched a new blitzkrieg. While German troops parachuted into the Netherlands, an army of tanks rolled into Belgium and Luxembourg.

The British and French had expected the German attack. As soon as it began, British and French forces raced north into Belgium. This was a mistake. Instead of sending their tanks through the open countryside of central Belgium, the Germans sent their main force through the Ardennes Mountains of Luxembourg and eastern Belgium. The French did not think that large numbers of tanks could move through the mountains, and had left only a few troops to defend that part of the border. The Germans easily smashed through the French lines, and then turned west across northern France to the English Channel. The British and French armies were still in Belgium and could not move back into France quickly enough. They were now trapped in Belgium.

The Miracle at Dunkirk

After trapping the Allied forces in Belgium, the Germans began to drive them toward the English Channel. The only hope for Britain and France was to evacuate their surviving troops by sea, but the Germans had captured all but one port, Dunkirk, in northern France near the Belgian border.

TECHNOLOGY & HISTORY

Blitzkrieg In 1939 Germany unleashed blitzkrieg—lightning war—on Europe. Blitzkrieg combined several technologies—aircraft, tanks, parachutes, and radios—to produce a highly mobile, fast-moving army that could coordinate multiple attacks, break through lines, and rapidly encircle enemy positions.

◀ A superior air force led to Germany's defeat of western Europe by summer 1940. The aircraft could drop paratroopers behind enemy lines as well as bomb targets.

▲ German tanks rolled into Poland in 1939, ahead of the infantry, which followed to end any resistance. The bombers supported the swift-moving tanks from the air. The armored tanks, known as Panzers, often moved so rapidly that they had to wait for the infantry to catch up.

Analyzing VISUALS

1. **Drawing Conclusions** What do you observe about the advance of the Panzer tanks in the photo on the left?

2. **Evaluating** What dangers do you think the paratroopers in the center photo may have faced?

As German forces closed in on Dunkirk, Hitler suddenly ordered them to stop. No one is sure why he gave this order. Historians know that Hitler was nervous about risking his tank forces, and he wanted to wait until more infantry arrived. Hermann Goering, the head of the German air force, also assured Hitler that aircraft alone could destroy the trapped soldiers. There is also some evidence that Hitler thought that the British would be more willing to accept peace if the Germans did not humiliate them by destroying their forces at Dunkirk.

Whatever Hitler's reasons, his order provided a three-day delay. This gave the British time to strengthen their lines and begin the evacuation. Some 850 ships of all sizes—from navy warships to small sailboats operated by civilian volunteers—headed to Dunkirk from England, many of them making the 48-mile trip multiple times. French, Dutch, and Belgian ships joined British ones in "Operation Dynamo." The British had hoped to rescue about 45,000 troops. Instead, when the evacu-ation ended on June 4, an estimated 338,000 British and French troops had been saved. This became known as the "Miracle at Dunkirk."

The evacuation had its price, however. Almost all of the British army's equipment remained at Dunkirk—90,000 rifles, 7,000 tons of ammunition, and 120,000 vehicles. If Hitler invaded Britain, it would be almost impossible to stop him from conquering the country.

Three weeks later, on June 22, 1940, Hitler accepted the French surrender in the same railway car in which the Germans had surrendered at the end of World War I. Germany now occupied much of northern France and its Atlantic coastline. To govern the rest of France, Germany installed a puppet government at the town of Vichy and made Marshal Philippe Pétain the new government's figurehead leader. Pétain predicted that Britain "will have her neck wrung like a chicken."

Reading Check **Explaining** By what means did Hitler overtake both Poland and France?

PRIMARY SOURCE
The Battle of Britain, 1940

During the Battle of Britain, bombs fell around London's St. Paul's Cathedral, a famous architectural treasure as well as a place of worship. Some of the subways no longer ran but were converted to air-raid shelters where people could sleep.

PRIMARY SOURCE

"Even though large tracts of Europe and many old and famous States have fallen or may fall into the grip of the Gestapo and all the odious apparatus of Nazi rule, we shall not flag or fail, we shall go on to the end, we shall fight in France, we shall fight on the seas and oceans, we shall fight with growing confidence and growing strength in the air, we shall defend our island, whatever the cost may be, we shall fight on the beaches, we shall fight on the landing grounds, we shall fight in the fields and in the streets, we shall fight in the hills; we shall never surrender...."

—Winston Churchill, Speech to Parliament, June 4, 1940

▲ Winston Churchill

DBQ Document-Based Questions

1. **Identifying Points of View** What effect does Churchill suggest the fall of other European states will have on Britain?

2. **Analyzing Primary Sources** What does Churchill expect to grow as the Allied forces fight the Nazis?

3. **Hypothesizing** What effect do you think Churchill's words had on those who heard or read the speech?

Britain Remains Defiant

MAIN Idea Despite the bombing of London and other major cities, Britain's Winston Churchill stood firm against the threat of Nazi invasion.

HISTORY AND YOU Think of a time when the odds were against you. How did you react? Read about British resolve when faced with Nazi air raids.

Neither Pétain nor Hitler anticipated the bravery of the British people or the spirit of their leader, **Winston Churchill,** who had replaced Neville Chamberlain as prime minister. Hitler expected Britain to negotiate peace after France surrendered, but on June 4, 1940, Churchill delivered a defiant speech in Parliament, vowing that Britain would never surrender. The speech was intended to rally the British people and to alert the isolationist United States to Britain's plight.

Realizing Britain would not surrender, Hitler ordered his commanders to prepare to invade. Getting across the English Channel, however, posed a major challenge. Germany had few **transport** ships, and the British air force would sink them if they tried to land troops in England. To invade, therefore, Germany first had to defeat the British Royal Air Force.

In June 1940, the German air force, called the *Luftwaffe,* began to attack British shipping in the English Channel. Then, in mid-August, the *Luftwaffe* launched an all-out air battle to destroy the Royal Air Force. This air battle, which lasted into the fall of 1940, became known as the **Battle of Britain.**

On August 23, German bombers accidentally bombed London, the British capital. This attack on civilians enraged the British, who responded by bombing Berlin the following night. For the first time in the war, bombs fell on the German capital. Infuriated, Hitler ordered the *Luftwaffe* to stop its attacks on British military targets and to concentrate on bombing London.

Hitler's goal was to terrorize the British people into surrendering. The British endured, however, taking refuge in cellars and subway stations whenever German bombers appeared.

Although the Royal Air Force was greatly outnumbered, the British had one major advantage. They had developed a new technology called radar. Using radar stations placed along their coast, the British were able to detect incoming German aircraft and direct British fighters to intercept them.

Day after day, the British fighters inflicted more losses on the Germans than they suffered. During the long battle, Germany lost 1,733 aircraft while the British lost 915 fighter planes, along with 449 pilots. The skill of more than 2,000 British and 500 foreign pilots—including many Poles, Canadians, Frenchmen, and a few Americans—successfully thwarted Hitler's plan to invade Britain. These pilots flew as often as five times a day. Praising them, Churchill told Parliament, "Never in the field of human conflict was so much owed by so many to so few." On October 12, 1940, Hitler canceled the invasion of Britain.

Reading Check **Evaluating** How was Britain able to resist Hitler and the Nazis?

Section 2 REVIEW

Vocabulary

1. **Explain** the significance of: *Anschluss*, Munich Conference, appeasement, blitzkrieg, Maginot Line, Winston Churchill, Battle of Britain.

Main Ideas

2. **Explaining** Why did Europe's leaders first try to deal with Hitler through appeasement?

3. **Analyzing** Why was the decision to leave French forces behind the Maginot Line disastrous for Europe?

4. **Summarizing** In what ways did Winston Churchill prove to be an effective leader for Britain as the war began?

Critical Thinking

5. **Big Ideas** What was the new type of warfare used by Germany against Poland? Explain the technique.

6. **Organizing** Use a graphic organizer similar to the one below to list early events of the war in Poland and western Europe.

Events

7. **Analyzing Visuals** Look again at the photograph on page 689. What do you observe about the participants at the Munich Conference?

Writing About History

8. **Expository Writing** Choose one dramatic incident from the beginnings of World War II and write a news story explaining what happened.

History ONLINE

Study Central™ To review this section, go to glencoe.com and click on Study Central.

Section 3

The Holocaust

Guide to Reading

Big Ideas
Group Action The Nazis believed Jews to be subhuman. They steadily increased their persecution of Jews and eventually set up death camps and tried to kill all the Jews in Europe.

Content Vocabulary
• concentration camp *(p. 698)*
• extermination camp *(p. 698)*

Academic Vocabulary
• prohibit *(p. 694)*
• assume *(p. 696)*
• virtually *(p. 699)*

People and Events to Identify
• *Shoah* *(p. 694)*
• Nuremberg Laws *(p. 694)*
• Gestapo *(p. 696)*
• Wannsee Conference *(p. 698)*

Reading Strategy
Organizing As you read about the Holocaust, complete a graphic organizer similar to the one below by listing examples of Nazi persecution of European Jews.

Examples of Persecution

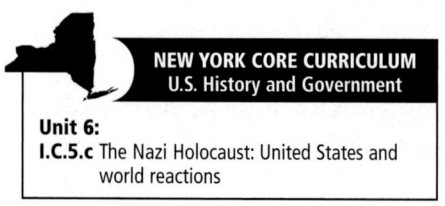

NEW YORK CORE CURRICULUM
U.S. History and Government

Unit 6:
I.C.5.c The Nazi Holocaust: United States and world reactions

Nazis first acted upon their racist ideology when they imposed restrictions on Jews and stripped them of basic rights. Eventually, Nazi Germany created concentration camps and systematically attempted to kill all European Jews and others whom they regarded as inferior.

Nazi Persecution of the Jews

MAIN Idea Nazi laws stripped Jews of citizenship and all fundamental rights; immigration restrictions in other countries made leaving Germany difficult.

HISTORY AND YOU Do you know anyone who came to the United States as a refugee? Read how Jewish refugees were turned away in the late 1930s.

During the Holocaust, the Nazis killed nearly 6 million European Jews. The Nazis also killed millions of people from other groups they considered inferior. The Hebrew term for the Holocaust is *Shoah,* meaning "catastrophe," but it is often used specifically to refer to the Nazi campaign to exterminate the Jews during World War II.

The Nuremberg Laws

Although the Nazis persecuted anyone who dared oppose them, as well as the disabled, Gypsies, homosexuals, and Slavic peoples, they reserved their strongest hatred for the Jews. This loathing went far beyond the European anti-Semitism that was common at the time. Over the centuries, people who were prejudiced against Jews had discriminated against them in many ways. For example, Jews had sometimes been segregated in ghettos or **prohibited** from owning land.

After the Nazis took power, they quickly moved to deprive German Jews of many established rights. In September 1935, the **Nuremberg Laws** took citizenship away from Jewish Germans and banned marriage between Jews and other Germans. Two months later, another decree defined a Jew as a person with at least one Jewish grandparent and barred Jews from holding public office or voting. Another law compelled Jews with German-sounding names to adopt "Jewish" names. Soon the passports of Jews were marked with a red *J* to identify them as Jewish.

By the summer of 1936, at least half of Germany's Jews were jobless, having lost the right to work as civil servants, journalists, farmers, teachers, and actors. In 1938 the Nazis also banned Jews from practicing law and medicine and from operating businesses. With no source of income, life became very difficult.

The Persecution Begins, 1935–1938

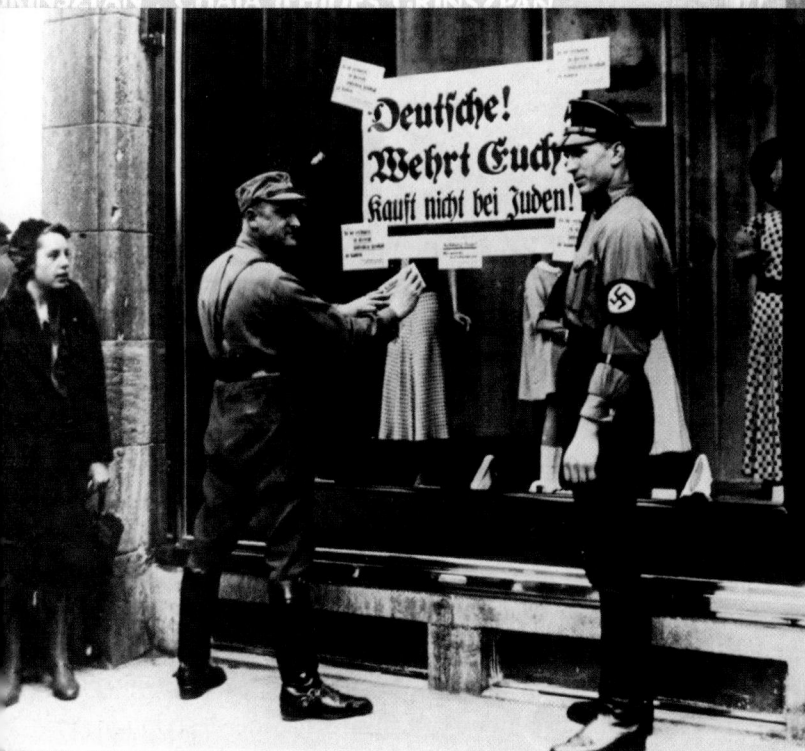
▼ Nazi storm troopers place warning signs encouraging a boycott on Jewish-owned businesses in 1933.

▲ On Kristallnacht, *November 7, 1938, roaming bands of Nazi storm troopers destroyed Jewish property and terrorized Jewish families across the Third Reich.*

Analyzing VISUALS

1. **Hypothesizing** What effect do you think the signs might have had on the woman in the photograph on the left?

2. **Making Connections** How do you think publication of the photograph of the synagogue would have affected world opinion toward the Nazis?

Despite worsening conditions, many Jews chose to remain in Germany during the early years of Nazi rule. Well integrated into German society before this time, they were reluctant to leave and give up the lives they had built there. Many also thought that conditions would surely improve after a time. In fact, conditions soon became worse.

Kristallnacht

On November 7, 1938, a young Jewish refugee named Herschel Grynszpan shot and killed a German diplomat in Paris. Grynszpan's father and 10,000 other Jews had been deported from Germany to Poland, and the distraught young man was seeking revenge for this act and for the persecution of the Jews in general.

In retaliation, an infuriated Hitler ordered his minister of propaganda, Joseph Goebbels, to stage attacks against the Jews that would seem like a spontaneous popular reaction to news of the murder. On the night of November 9, this plan played out in a spree of destruction. In Vienna, a Jewish child named Frederic Morton watched in terror that night as Nazi storm troopers broke into his family's apartment:

PRIMARY SOURCE

"They yanked out every drawer in every one of our chests and cupboards, and tossed each in the air. They let the cutlery jangle across the floor, the clothes scatter, and stepped over the mess to fling the next drawer.... 'We might be back,' the leader said. On the way out he threw our mother-of-pearl ashtray over his shoulder, like confetti. We did not speak or move or breathe until we heard their boots against the pavement."

—quoted in *Facing History and Ourselves*

The anti-Jewish violence that erupted throughout Germany and Austria that night came to be called *Kristallnacht,* or "night of broken glass," because broken glass littered the streets afterward. By the following morning, more than 90 Jews were dead, hundreds were badly injured, and thousands more were terrorized. The Nazis had forbidden police to interfere while bands of thugs destroyed 7,500 Jewish businesses and wrecked more than 180 synagogues.

The lawlessness of *Kristallnacht* persisted. Following that night of violence, the **Gestapo,** the government's secret police, arrested at least 20,000 wealthy Jews, releasing them only if they agreed to emigrate and surrender all their possessions. The state also confiscated insurance payments owed to Jewish owners of ruined businesses.

Jewish Refugees Try to Flee

Kristallnacht and its aftermath marked a significant escalation of Nazi persecution against the Jews. Many Jews, including Frederick Morton's family, decided that it was time to leave and fled to the United States. Between 1933, when Hitler took power, and the start of

World War II in 1939, some 350,000 Jews escaped Nazi-controlled Germany. These emigrants included prominent scientists, such as Albert Einstein, and business owners like Otto Frank, who resettled his family in Amsterdam in 1933. Otto's daughter Anne kept a diary of her family's life in hiding after the Nazis overran the Netherlands. The "secret annex," as she called their hiding place, has become a museum.

Limits on Jewish Immigration By 1938, one American consulate in Germany had a backlog of more than 100,000 visa applications from Jews trying to leave for the United States. Following the Nazi *Anschluss,* some 3,000 Austrian Jews applied for American visas each day. Many never received visas to the United States or to the other countries where they applied. As a result, millions of Jews remained trapped in Nazi-dominated Europe.

Several factors limited Jewish immigration to the United States. Nazi orders prohibited Jews from taking more than about four dollars out of Germany. American immigration law, however, forbade granting a visa to anyone "likely to become a public charge." Customs officials tended to **assume** that this description

PRIMARY SOURCE
The Holocaust

▼ After World War II broke out, the Nazis methodically deprived Jews of their rights, confining many to overcrowded ghettos. After weeks of fierce resistance, Jews in the Warsaw ghetto in Poland (below) were rounded up for deportation to concentration camps in May 1943.

▲ By 1943, the Nazis had started to implement their plans to exterminate the Jews. The system of ghettos was abandoned in favor of herding men, women, and children onto cattle cars for transport to death camps.

applied to Jews, because Germany had forced them to leave behind any wealth. High unemployment rates in the 1930s also made immigration unpopular. Few Americans wanted to raise immigration quotas, even to accommodate European refugees. Others did not want to admit Jews because they held anti-Semitic attitudes. The existing immigration policy allowed only 150,000 immigrants annually, with a fixed quota from each country. The law permitted no exceptions for refugees or victims of persecution.

International Response At an international conference on refugees in 1938, several European countries, the United States, and Latin America stated their regret that they could not take in more of Germany's Jews without raising their immigration quotas. Meanwhile, Nazi propaganda chief Joseph Goebbels announced that "if there is any country that believes it has not enough Jews, I shall gladly turn over to it all our Jews." Hitler also declared himself "ready to put all these criminals at the disposal of these countries . . . even on luxury ships."

As war loomed in 1939, many ships departed from Germany crammed with Jews desperate to escape. Some of their visas, however, had been forged or sold illegally, and Mexico, Paraguay, Argentina, and Costa Rica all denied access to Jews with such documents. So, too, did the United States.

The *St. Louis* Affair On May 27, 1939, the SS *St. Louis* entered the harbor in Havana, Cuba, with 930 Jewish refugees on board. Most of these passengers hoped to go to the United States eventually, but they had certificates improperly issued by Cuba's director of immigration giving them permission to land in Cuba. When the ships arrived in Havana, the Cuban government revoked the certificates and refused to let the refugees come ashore. For several days, the ship's captain steered his ship in circles off the coast of Florida, awaiting official permission to dock at an American port. Denied permission, the ship turned back toward Europe. The passengers finally disembarked in France, Holland, Belgium, and Great Britain. Within two years, the first three of these countries fell under Nazi domination. Many of the refugees brought to these countries perished in the Nazis' "final solution."

✔ **Reading Check** **Analyzing** Why did many Jews stay in Germany despite being persecuted?

In 1944 Elie Wiesel was taken to a concentration camp. In the excerpt below, he describes his wait during a move from one camp to another in 1944:

PRIMARY SOURCE

"The snow fell thickly. We were forbidden to sit down or even to move. The snow began to form a thick layer over our blankets. They brought us bread—the usual ration. We threw ourselves upon it. Someone had the idea of appeasing his thirst by eating the snow. Soon the others were imitating him. As we were not allowed to bend down, everyone took out his spoon and ate the accumulated snow off his neighbor's back. A mouthful of bread and a spoonful of snow. The SS [guards] who were watching laughed at the spectacle."

—Elie Wiesel, *Night*

▲ When the war ended, Allied troops managed to liberate the few surviving inmates of the death camps—many of whom were too shocked to believe they were being freed.

DBQ **Document-Based Questions**

1. **Explaining** How did the prisoners in Weisel's account try to quench their thirst?

2. **Describing** How did the guards react?

The Final Solution

MAIN Idea Nazi atrocities included sending millions of Jews, Gypsies, Slavs, the disabled, and others to concentration camps and extermination camps.

HISTORY AND YOU Can you think of a conflict today where violence is motivated by ethnic or religious hatred? Read to learn how prejudice led to mass murder in Nazi Germany.

On January 20, 1942, Nazi leaders met at the **Wannsee Conference** to determine the "final solution of the Jewish question." Previous "solutions" had included rounding up Jews, Gypsies, Slavs, and others from conquered areas, shooting them, and piling them into mass graves. Another method forced Jews and other "undesirables" into trucks and then piped in exhaust fumes to kill them. These methods, however, had proven too slow and inefficient for the Nazis.

At Wannsee, the Nazis made plans to round up Jews from the vast areas of Nazi-controlled Europe and take them to detention centers known as **concentration camps.** There, healthy individuals would work as slave laborers until they dropped dead of exhaustion, disease, or malnutrition. Most others, including the elderly, the infirm, and young children, would be sent to **extermination camps,** attached to many of the concentration camps, to be executed in massive gas chambers.

NATIONAL GEOGRAPHIC The Holocaust, 1939–1945

Key:
- ■ Concentration camp
- ■ Extermination camp
- ■ Location of *Einsatzgruppen*
- — International boundary, January 1938

0   400 kilometers
0   400 miles
Lambert Azimuthal Equal-Area projection

Map labels: NORWAY, FINLAND, SWEDEN, ESTONIA, LATVIA, Moscow, DENMARK, North Sea, Baltic Sea, LITHUANIA, EAST PRUSSIA (Ger.), UNITED KINGDOM, Bergen-Belsen, Ravensbrück, NETH., Treblinka, UNION OF SOVIET SOCIALIST REPUBLICS, GERMANY, POLAND, BELG., Buchenwald, Chelmno, Sobibor, Majdanek, Paris, LUX., CZECHOSLOVAKIA, Auschwitz-Birkenau, Dachau, FRANCE, SWITZ., AUSTRIA, HUNGARY, ROMANIA, ITALY, Adriatic Sea, YUGOSLAVIA, Black Sea, BULGARIA, Rome, ALBANIA, GREECE, Mediterranean

Jewish Losses, 1939–1945	
Baltic States	228,000
Belgium	40,000
Bulgaria	14,000
Byelorusian SSR	245,000
Czechoslovakia	155,000
Denmark	500
France	90,000
Germany and Austria	210,000
Greece	54,000
Hungary	450,000
Italy	8,000
Netherlands	195,000
Poland	3,000,000
Romania	300,000
Russian SSR	107,000
Ukrainian SSR	900,000
Yugoslavia	26,000

◀ A survivor of the Buchenwald camp drinks water outside the camp barracks, April 1945

Analyzing GEOGRAPHY

1. **Place** Where were most of the extermination camps located?
2. **Region** Which three nations had the highest number of Jewish losses?

Maps In Motion See *StudentWorks™ Plus* or <u>glencoe.com</u>.

Concentration Camps

The Nazis had established their first concentration camps in 1933 to jail political opponents. After the war began, the Nazis built concentration camps throughout Europe.

Buchenwald, one of the largest concentration camps, was built near the town of Weimar in Germany in 1937. During its operation, more than 200,000 prisoners worked 12-hour shifts as slave laborers in nearby factories. Although Buchenwald had no gas chambers, hundreds of prisoners died there every month from exhaustion and horrible living conditions.

Leon Bass, a young American soldier, saw Buchenwald at the end of the war. A room built to hold 50 people had housed more than 150, with bunk beds built almost to the ceiling. Bass recalled:

PRIMARY SOURCE

"I looked at a bottom bunk and there I saw one man. He was too weak to get up; he could just barely turn his head. He was skin and bones. He looked like a skeleton; and his eyes were deep set. He didn't utter a sound; he just looked at me with those eyes, and they still haunt me today."

—quoted in *Facing History and Ourselves*

Extermination Camps

After the Wannsee Conference, the Nazis built extermination facilities in a number of the concentration camps, mostly in Poland, to kill Jews more efficiently. At these camps, including the infamous Treblinka and Auschwitz, Jews were the Nazis' main victims. Auschwitz alone housed about 100,000 people in 300 prison barracks. Its gas chambers, built to kill 2,000 people at a time, sometimes gassed 12,000 people in a day. Of the estimated 1,600,000 people who died at Auschwitz, about 1,300,000 were Jews. The other 300,000 were Poles, Soviet prisoners of war, and Gypsies.

Upon arrival at Auschwitz, healthy prisoners were selected for slave labor. Elderly or disabled people, the sick, and mothers and children went immediately to the gas chambers, after which their bodies were burned in giant crematoriums.

In only a few years, Jewish culture, which had existed in Europe for over 1,000 years, had been **virtually** obliterated by the Nazis in the lands they conquered. Despite exhaustive debate, there is still great controversy about why and how an event so horrifying as the Holocaust could have occurred. No consensus has been reached, but most historians point to a number of factors: the German people's sense of injury after World War I; severe economic problems; Hitler's control over the German nation; the lack of a strong tradition of representative government in Germany; German fear of Hitler's secret police; and a long history of anti-Jewish prejudice and discrimination in Europe.

Reading Check **Summarizing** How did Hitler try to exterminate Europe's Jewish population?

Section 3 REVIEW

Vocabulary

1. **Explain** the significance of: *Shoah*, Nuremberg Laws, Gestapo, Wannsee Conference, concentration camp, extermination camp.

Main Ideas

2. **Listing** What early steps did Germany take in persecution of Jewish people?

3. **Analyzing** What was the purpose of the Wannsee Conference?

Critical Thinking

4. **Big Ideas** Do you think the German people or other nations could have prevented the Holocaust? Why or why not?

5. **Organizing** Use a graphic organizer similar to the one below to list the methods the Nazis used to try to destroy the Jewish population.

Extermination Methods

6. **Analyzing Visuals** Study the photos on pages 695–696. How do the images show the destruction of Jewish life?

Writing About History

7. **Persuasive Writing** Imagine that you are living in the United States during the 1930s. You believe that more Jewish immigrants should be allowed to come into the country. Write a letter to your representative or senator in Congress to express your point of view.

History ONLINE
Study Central™ To review this section, go to glencoe.com and click on Study Central.

ANALYZING PRIMARY SOURCES

The Holocaust

As the Allies liberated areas from German control in the spring of 1945, they discovered horrifying scenes in Nazi concentration camps. The Nazi regime had systematically murdered six million Jews and killed another six million Poles, Slavs, Gypsies, homosexuals, communists, and mentally disabled persons. Photographs of the newly liberated camps shocked the American public, although the Roosevelt administration and the State Department had evidence of the death camps as early as 1942.

Study these primary sources and answer the questions that follow.

Eyewitness Account

"[There] were two barracks: the men stood on one side, the women on the other. They were addressed in a very polite and friendly way: 'You have been on a journey. You are dirty. You will take a bath. Get undressed quickly.' Towels and soap were handed out, and then suddenly the brutes woke up and showed their true faces: this horde of people, these men and women were driven outside with hard blows and forced both summer and winters to go the few hundred metres to the 'Shower Room.' Above the entry door was the word 'Shower'. One could even see shower heads on the ceiling which were cemented in but never had water flowing through them.

These poor innocents were crammed together, pressed against each other. Then panic broke out, for at last they realized the fate in store for them. But blows with rifle butts and revolver shots soon restored order and finally they all entered the death chamber. The doors were shut and, ten minutes later, the temperature was high enough to facilitate the condensation of the hydrogen cyanide for the condemned were gassed with hydrogen cyanide. This was the so-called 'Zyklon B' . . . which was used by the German barbarians. . . . One could hear fearful screams, but a few moments later there was complete silence."

—André Lettich, Jewish prisoner assigned to remove bodies from the gas chambers at Birkenau from *Nazism 1919–1945, Volume 3: Foreign Policy, War and Racial Extermination—A Documentary Reader*

PRIMARY SOURCE 2

Photograph, 1945

▼ *Newly liberated survivors at Dachau concentration camp, May 4, 1945*

PRIMARY SOURCE 3

Nazi Decree, 1941

I (1) Jews over six years of age are prohibited from appearing in public without wearing a Jewish star.
   (2) The Jewish star is a yellow piece of cloth with a black border, in the form of a six-pointed star the size of the palm of the hand. The inscription reads "JEW" in black letters. It shall be worn visibly, sewn on the left chest side of the garment.
II Jews are forbidden:
   (a) to leave their area of residence without written permission of the local police, carried on their person.
   (b) to wear medals, decorations or other insignia.

—Nazi decree issued September 1, 1941 from *Nazism 1919–1945, Volume 3: Foreign Policy, War and Racial Extermination—A Documentary Reader*

PRIMARY SOURCE 4

American Soldier's Diary, 1945

"One thousand Weimar citizens toured the Buchenwald camp in groups of 100. They saw blackened skeletons and skulls in the ovens of the crematorium. In the yard outside, they saw a heap of white human ashes and bones. . . .

The living actually looked worse than the dead. Those who lived wore striped uniforms, with the stripes running up and down. Those who were dead were stripped of their clothing and lay naked, many stacked like cordwood waiting to be burned in the crematory. At one time, 5,000 had been stacked on the vacant lot next to the crematory.

Often . . . the SS wished to make an example of someone in killing him. They hung him on the lot adjacent to the crematory, and all the three sections of the camp witnessed the sight—some 30,000 prisoners. They used what I call hay hooks, catching him under the chin and the other in the back of his neck. He hung in this manner until he died."

—diary of Captain Luther D. Fletcher, from *World War II: From the Battle Front to the Home Front*

PRIMARY SOURCE 5

Photograph, April 17, 1945

PRIMARY SOURCE 6

Painting

Unable to Work, *by Auschwitz survivor David Olère*

◄ *American soldiers force German civilians to view bodies after the liberation of the Buchenwald concentration camp.*

DBQ Document-Based Questions

1. **Speculating** How do you suppose soldiers could participate in such barbaric acts?

2. **Analyzing Visuals** What does the appearance of these survivors tell you about conditions in the camps?

3. **Drawing Conclusions** What purpose did the restrictions listed in Source 3 serve?

4. **Drawing Conclusions** Study Sources 5 and 6. How do you think American troops reacted to the horrifying scenes they found in the concentration camps? Why do you think American troops made Germans tour the liberated concentration camps?

5. **Analyzing Visuals** Study the painting in Source 6. What symbols does the artist use to illustrate the fate of those too weak to work?

America Enters the War

Guide to Reading

Big Ideas
Government and Society After World War II began, the United States attempted to continue its prewar policy of neutrality.

Content Vocabulary
- hemispheric defense zone *(p. 704)*
- strategic materials *(p. 706)*

Academic Vocabulary
- revise *(p. 702)*
- purchase *(p. 702)*
- underestimate *(p. 707)*

People and Events to Identify
- America First Committee *(p. 703)*
- Lend-Lease Act *(p. 704)*
- Atlantic Charter *(p. 705)*

Reading Strategy
Organizing As you read about America's efforts to stay neutral, complete a graphic organizer similar to the one below by naming events that shifted American opinion toward helping the Allies.

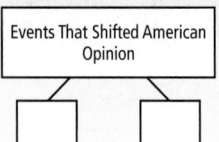

```
    Events That Shifted American
              Opinion

         ┌──────────┐
    ┌────┤          ├────┐
    │    └──────────┘    │
 ┌─────┐            ┌─────┐
 │     │            │     │
 └─────┘            └─────┘
```

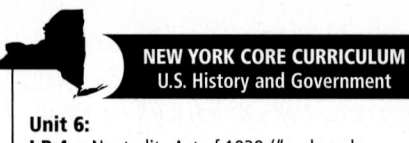

NEW YORK CORE CURRICULUM
U.S. History and Government

Unit 6:
I.B.4.a Neutrality Act of 1939 ("cash and carry")
I.B.4.b Lend-Lease Act and 50 overage destroyers deal
I.B.4.c The moral dimension: The Atlantic Charter (August 1941)
I.C.1 Pearl Harbor

As World War II began, the United States remained officially neutral but aided Great Britain considerably in its fight against Germany. In the Pacific, Japan's territorial expansion led to growing tensions with the United States, which peaked when Japan attacked Pearl Harbor.

FDR Supports England

MAIN Idea President Roosevelt favored changes in American neutrality laws, although Americans remained divided about the war and American involvement.

HISTORY AND YOU Have you ever been drawn into an argument when you just wanted to be left alone? Read about the increasing difficulties that the United States faced in trying to stay out of World War II.

President Roosevelt officially proclaimed the United States neutral two days after Britain and France declared war on Germany. Despite this proclamation, however, he was determined to help the two countries as much as possible in their struggle against Hitler.

Destroyers-for-Bases Deal

Soon after the war began, Roosevelt called Congress into a special session to **revise** the neutrality laws. He asked Congress to eliminate the ban on arms sales to nations at war. Public opinion strongly supported the president. Congress passed the new law, but isolationists demanded a price for the revision. Under the Neutrality Act of 1939, warring nations could buy weapons from the United States only on a "cash-and-carry" basis. This law was similar to the 1937 Neutrality Act governing the sale of nonmilitary items to countries that were at war.

In the spring of 1940, the United States faced its first test in remaining neutral. In May, Prime Minister Winston Churchill asked Roosevelt to transfer old American destroyers to Britain, which had lost nearly half its destroyers. To protect its cargo ships from German submarines and to block any German attempt to invade Britain, the nation needed more destroyers.

Determined to give Churchill the destroyers, Roosevelt used a loophole in the neutrality act that required cash for **purchases.** In exchange for the right to build American bases on British-controlled Newfoundland, Bermuda, and islands in the Caribbean, Roosevelt sent 50 old American destroyers to Britain. Because the deal did not involve an actual sale, the neutrality act did not apply.

The Only Way We Can Save Her

"STAY OUT! STAY OUT FOR MY SAKE, AS WELL AS YOUR OWN!"

WAR MAD EUROPE

DEMOCRACY

AMERICA, THE LAST REFUGE OF DEMOCRACY

▲ This 1939 cartoon shows Uncle Sam standing guard over Democracy, whose only refuge is America.

ISOLATION POLICY

▲ Nazi bullets whiz past Uncle Sam and his isolationist policies.

Analyzing VISUALS   DBQ

1. **Analyzing Visuals** According to the cartoon at left, what message is Democracy sending to Uncle Sam?
2. **Analyzing Visuals** What do you observe about Uncle Sam's perch in the cartoon above?

The Isolationist Debate

Widespread acceptance of the destroyers-for-bases deal reflected a change in public opinion. By July 1940, most Americans favored offering limited aid to the Allies. That spirit was hardly unanimous, however. In fact, people who wanted greater American involvement in the war and those who felt that the United States should remain neutral began debating the issue in the spring of 1940.

At one extreme was the Fight for Freedom Committee, a group that urged the repeal of all neutrality laws and stronger action against Germany. At the other extreme was the **America First Committee.** It was a staunchly isolationist group opposed to any American intervention or aid to the Allies. The committee's members included aviator Charles Lindbergh and Senator Gerald Nye.

Closer to the center, the Committee to Defend America by Aiding the Allies, which journalist William Allen White headed, pressed for increased American aid to the Allies but opposed armed intervention.

The heated neutrality debate took place during the 1940 presidential election campaign. For months, Americans had wondered whether President Roosevelt would follow the tradition George Washington had set and retire after a second term. With the United States in a precarious position, however, many believed a change of leaders might not be in the country's best interest. Roosevelt decided to run for an unprecedented third term.

During the campaign, FDR steered a careful course between neutrality and intervention. The Republican nominee, Wendell Willkie, did the same, promising he too would assist the Allies but stay out of the war. The voters reelected Roosevelt by a wide margin, preferring to keep a president they knew during this crisis period.

✔ Reading Check) **Identifying** Identify different groups and their positions on U.S. neutrality in the late 1930s.

Edging Toward War

MAIN Idea In 1940 and 1941, the United States took more steps to provide aid to Great Britain.

HISTORY AND YOU What kinds of aid does America provide other countries today? Why? Read why FDR thought it was important to "lend" Britain some help.

Read "The Four Freedoms" on page R53 in **Documents in American History**.

With the election over, Roosevelt expanded the nation's role in the war. Britain was fighting for democracy, he said, and the United States had to help. Speaking to Congress, he listed the "Four Freedoms" for which both the United States and Britain stood: freedom of speech, freedom of worship, freedom from want, and freedom from fear.

The Lend-Lease Act

By December 1940, Great Britain had run out of funds to wage its war against Germany. Roosevelt came up with a way to remove the cash requirement of the most recent neutrality act. He proposed the **Lend-Lease Act,** which allowed the United States to lend or lease arms to any country considered "vital to the defense of the United States." The act allowed Roosevelt to send weapons to Britain if the British government promised to return or pay rent for them after the war.

Roosevelt warned that, if Britain fell, an "unholy alliance" of Germany, Japan, and Italy would keep trying to conquer the world. The president argued that the United States should become the "great arsenal of democracy" to keep the British fighting and make it unnecessary for Americans to go to war.

The America First Committee disagreed, but Congress passed the Lend-Lease Act by a wide margin. By the time the program ended, the United States had "lent" more than $40 billion in weapons, vehicles, and other supplies to the Allied war effort.

While shipments of supplies to Britain began at once, lend-lease aid eventually went to the Soviet Union, as well. In June 1941, violating the Nazi-Soviet pact, Hitler invaded the Soviet Union. Although Churchill detested communism and considered Stalin a harsh dictator, he vowed that any person or state "who fights against Nazism will have our aid." Roosevelt, too, supported this policy.

A Hemispheric Defense Zone

Congressional approval of the Lend-Lease Act did not solve the problem of getting American arms and supplies to Britain. German submarines patrolling the Atlantic Ocean were sinking hundreds of thousands of tons of shipments each month; the British Navy did not have enough ships to stop them.

Because the United States was still technically neutral, Roosevelt could not order the U.S. Navy to protect British cargo ships. Instead, he developed the idea of a **hemispheric defense zone.** Roosevelt declared that the entire western half of the Atlantic was part of the Western Hemisphere and, therefore, neutral. He then ordered the U.S. Navy to patrol the western Atlantic and reveal the location of German submarines to the British.

The Atlantic Charter

In August 1941, Roosevelt and Churchill met on board American and British warships anchored near Newfoundland. During these meetings, the two men agreed on the text of

---

PRIMARY SOURCE

Aiding Britain, 1939–1941

The Four Freedoms

"In the future days, which we seek to make secure, we look forward to a world founded upon four essential human freedoms.

The first is freedom of speech and expression—everywhere in the world.

The second is freedom of every person to worship God in his own way—everywhere in the world.

The third is freedom from want—which . . . will secure to every nation a healthy peacetime life for its inhabitants—everywhere in the world.

The fourth is freedom from fear—which, translated into world terms, means a world-wide reduction of armaments to such a point and in such a thorough fashion that no nation will be in a position to commit an act of physical aggression against any neighbor—anywhere in the world."

—Address to Congress, January 6, 1941

the **Atlantic Charter.** This agreement committed both nations to a postwar world of democracy, nonaggression, free trade, economic advancement, and freedom of the seas. By late September, an additional 15 anti-Axis nations had signed the charter. Churchill later said that FDR pledged to "force an 'incident' . . . which would justify him in opening hostilities" with Germany.

An incident quickly presented itself. In early September, a German submarine, or U-boat, fired on an American destroyer that had been radioing the U-boat's position to the British. Roosevelt promptly responded by ordering American ships to follow a "shoot-on-sight" policy toward German submarines.

The Germans escalated hostilities the following month, targeting two American destroyers. One of them, the *Reuben James,* sank after being torpedoed, killing 115 sailors. As the end of 1941 drew near, Germany and the United States continued a tense standoff.

✔ Reading Check **Evaluating** How did the Lend-Lease Act help the Allied war effort?

Japan Attacks

MAIN Idea The Japanese attack on Pearl Harbor led the United States to declare war on Japan.

HISTORY AND YOU Do you remember how the United States acquired territory in the Pacific? Read about the threats to American interests as Japan expanded its empire.

Despite the growing tensions in the Atlantic, the Japanese attack on Pearl Harbor finally brought the United States into World War II. Ironically, Roosevelt's efforts to help Britain fight Germany resulted in Japan's decision to attack the United States.

America Embargoes Japan

Roosevelt knew that Britain needed much of its navy in Asia to protect its territories there from Japanese attack. As German submarines sank British ships in the Atlantic, however, the British began moving warships from Southeast Asia, leaving India and other colonial possessions vulnerable.

How Did FDR Help Britain While the U.S. Remained Neutral?

- Neutrality Act of 1939 allowed warring nations to buy weapons from the United States if they paid cash and transported arms on their own ships
- Destroyers-for-bases provided old American destroyers in exchange for the right to build U.S. defense bases in British-controlled Bermuda, Caribbean Islands, and Newfoundland
- Lend-Lease Act permitted U.S. to lend or lease arms to any country "vital to the defense of the United States"
- Hemispheric defense zone established the entire western half of the Atlantic as part of the Western Hemisphere and, therefore, neutral

What Did the Atlantic Charter Declare?

1. The U.S. and Britain do not seek to expand their territories.
2. Neither seeks territorial changes against the wishes of the people involved.
3. Both respect people's right to select their own government.
4. All nations should have access to trade and raw materials.
5. Improved labor standards and economic advances are vital.
6. Both nations hope people will be free from want and fear.
7. Everyone should be able to freely travel the high seas.
8. All nations must abandon the use of force; disarmament is necessary after the war.

NATIONAL GEOGRAPHIC **Sending Aid to Britain, 1939–1941**

EUROPE

September 4, 1941: Attack on the *Greer* prompts FDR's "shoot-on-sight" policy.

NORTH AMERICA

AFRICA

ATLANTIC OCEAN

0   800 kilometers
0   800 miles
Miller projection

SOUTH AMERICA

····· Hemispheric Defense Zone
→ Lend-Lease convoy route
⟵ Area with German submarines

DBQ **Document-Based Questions**

1. **Drawing Conclusions** Why do you think it was important to begin the Atlantic Charter with the first three points?
2. **Analyzing Primary Sources** How does the Atlantic Charter echo FDR's Four Freedoms speech?

Turning Point

Japan Attacks Pearl Harbor

Pearl Harbor was an important turning point because it not only brought the United States into the war but also decisively marked an end to U.S. isolationism. After the war ended, the nation did not withdraw from its role in international affairs, as it had done following World War I. Involvement in the war signaled the beginning of a global role for the United States that has continued to the present day. With the decision to support the United Nations and efforts to rebuild Europe, the nation became actively involved in international events.

HYPOTHESIZING Do you believe the United States would have entered the war regardless of the attack on Pearl Harbor? Support your ideas with reasons.

▲ Rescue boats approach the burning USS West Virginia and USS Tennessee, which were hit by enemy fire on December 7, 1941. In the photo to the right, President Roosevelt addresses Congress the following day.

◀ Although ideas to create a memorial of Pearl Harbor were put forth as early as 1946, not until 1958 did President Eisenhower sign the bill that authorized this memorial, a bridge built over the sunken USS Arizona. The completed memorial was dedicated in 1962.

History ONLINE
Student Web Activity Visit glencoe.com and complete the activity on Pearl Harbor.

History ONLINE
Student Skill Activity To learn how to create multimedia presentations, visit glencoe.com and complete the skill activity.

To hinder Japanese aggression, Roosevelt began applying economic pressure. Japan depended on the United States for many key materials, including scrap iron, steel, and especially oil. At that time, the United States supplied roughly 80 percent of Japan's oil. In July 1940 Congress gave the president the power to restrict the sale of **strategic materials** (materials important for fighting a war). Roosevelt immediately blocked the sale of airplane fuel and scrap iron to Japan. Furious, the Japanese signed an alliance with Germany and Italy, becoming a member of the Axis.

In 1941 Roosevelt began sending lend-lease aid to China. Japan, which had invaded China in 1937, controlled much of the Chinese coast by 1941. Roosevelt hoped that lend-lease aid would enable the Chinese to tie down the Japanese and prevent them from attacking elsewhere. The strategy failed. By July 1941,

Japan had sent military forces into southern Indochina, posing a direct threat to the British Empire.

Roosevelt responded. He froze all Japanese assets in the United States, reduced the amount of oil being shipped to Japan, and sent General Douglas MacArthur to the Philippines to build up American defenses there.

Roosevelt made it clear that the oil embargo would end only if Japan withdrew from Indochina and made peace with China. With its war against China in jeopardy because of a lack of oil and other resources, the Japanese military planned to attack the resource-rich British and Dutch colonies in Southeast Asia. They also decided to seize the Philippines and to attack the American fleet at Pearl Harbor. While the Japanese prepared for war, negotiations with the Americans continued, but neither side would back down. In late November

1941, six Japanese aircraft carriers, two battleships, and several other warships set out for Hawaii.

Japan Attacks Pearl Harbor

The Japanese government appeared to be continuing negotiations with the United States in good faith. American intelligence, however, had decoded Japanese communications that made it clear that Japan was preparing to go to war against the United States.

On November 27, American commanders at the Pearl Harbor naval base received a war warning from Washington, but it did not mention Hawaii as a possible target. Because of the great distance from Japan to Hawaii, officials doubted that Japan would attempt such a long-range attack.

The U.S. military's inability to correctly interpret the information they were receiving left Pearl Harbor an open target. The result was devastating. Japan's surprise attack on December 7, 1941, sank or damaged eight battleships, three cruisers, four destroyers, and six other vessels. The attack also destroyed 188 airplanes and killed 2,403 Americans. Another 1,178 were injured.

That night, a gray-faced Roosevelt met with his cabinet, telling them the country faced the most serious crisis since the Civil War. The next day, he asked Congress to declare war:

PRIMARY SOURCE

"Yesterday, December 7, 1941—a date which will live in infamy—the United States of America was suddenly and deliberately attacked by naval and air forces of the Empire of Japan. . . . No matter how long it may take us . . . the American people in their righteous might will win through to absolute victory."

—from *The Public Papers and Addresses of Franklin D. Roosevelt*

The Senate voted 82 to 0 and the House 388 to 1 to declare war on Japan.

Germany Declares War

Although Japan and Germany were allies, Hitler was not bound to declare war against the United States. The terms of the alliance specified that Germany had to come to Japan's aid only if Japan was attacked, not if it attacked another country. Hitler had grown frustrated with the American navy's attacks on German submarines, however, and he believed the time had come to declare war.

Hitler greatly **underestimated** the strength of the United States. He expected the Japanese to easily defeat the Americans in the Pacific. By helping Japan, he hoped for Japanese support against the Soviet Union after they had defeated the Americans. On December 11, Germany and Italy both declared war on the United States.

Reading Check **Examining** Why did military officials not expect an attack on Pearl Harbor?

Section 4 REVIEW

Vocabulary

1. **Explain** the significance of: America First Committee, Lend-Lease Act, hemispheric defense zone, Atlantic Charter, strategic materials.

Main Ideas

2. **Analyzing** What early efforts did Roosevelt make to help the British?

3. **Explaining** What was the hemispheric defense zone? Why was it developed?

4. **Summarizing** Why was the United States unprepared for Japan's attack on Pearl Harbor?

Critical Thinking

5. **Big Ideas** After Roosevelt's efforts to help Britain, some people accused him of being a dictator. Do you agree or disagree with this label? Explain your answer.

6. **Organizing** Use a graphic organizer similar to the one below to show how Roosevelt helped Britain while remaining officially neutral.

7. **Analyzing Visuals** Study the images on page 706. Then create a multimedia presentation that traces the Japanese attack on Pearl Harbor.

Writing About History

8. **Expository Writing** Write a letter to the editor of your newspaper explaining why you think the United States should either remain neutral or become involved in World War II.

History ONLINE

Study Central™ To review this section, go to <u>glencoe.com</u> and click on Study Central.

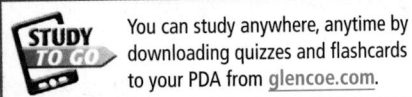

Causes of the Rise of Dictators

Italy

- Mussolini's Fascist Party believed in the supreme power of the state.
- In 1922 Mussolini threatened to march on Rome; the king appointed Mussolini as the premier.

Germany

- Hitler's Nazi Party believed in an all-powerful state, territorial expansion, and ethnic purity.
- Hitler believed that Germans needed more living space and called for Germany to expand east into Poland and Russia.
- Germany invaded Poland in 1939, France in 1940, and the USSR in 1941.

Japan

- Military leaders pushed for territorial expansion.
- Japan attacked Manchuria in 1931.
- Japan invaded China in 1937.
- Japan attacked Pearl Harbor in 1941.

▲ German tanks move down a highway near Soissons, France in May 1940.

▲ These survivors of Buchenwald, liberated in 1945, show the horrifying conditions under which they lived.

Effects

Holocaust

- During the Holocaust, the Nazis killed an estimated 6 million Jews.
- Jews were targeted and sent to concentration or extermination camps throughout Europe.

World War II

- Leaders of France and Britain tried to appease Hitler by allowing territorial growth.
- Britain and France declared war on Germany following the invasion of Poland.
- The United States sent aid to the Allied forces through the lend-lease program and cash-and-carry provision.
- France was defeated by the Nazis, who occupied the country in 1940.
- The United States declared war on Japan in 1941, after the bombing of Pearl Harbor.

ASSESSMENT

NEW YORK REGENTS EXAM PRACTICE

TEST-TAKING TIP

Look at each question to find clues to support your answer. Try not to get confused by the wording of the question. Then look for an answer that best fits the question.

Part I

Directions (1–11): For each statement or question, write on a separate sheet of paper the number of the word or expression that, of those given, best completes the statement or answers the question.

1 • cash-and-carry (1937)
   • destroyers-for-bases deal (1940)
   • Lend-Lease Act (1941)

Which change in United States foreign policy is demonstrated by the passage of these acts prior to World War II?
(1) a shift from neutrality toward more direct involvement
(2) an effort to become more neutral
(3) a movement from isolationism to containment of communism
(4) a desire to provide aid to both Allied and Axis Powers

2 In the 1930s the United States responded to the rise of fascism in Europe by
(1) invading Germany and Italy.
(2) forming military alliances.
(3) passing a series of neutrality laws.
(4) joining the League of Nations.

3 What began when Germany annexed Austria?
(1) *Kristallnacht*
(2) *Anschluss*
(3) Munich Conference
(4) Nazi-Soviet Nonaggression Pact

4 When France fell to the Nazis, the French and British evacuated thousands of troops from
(1) Dunkirk.
(2) Danzig.
(3) Buchenwald.
(4) Poland.

5 Which factor encouraged an American policy of neutrality during the 1930s?
(1) disillusionment with World War I and its results
(2) decline in the military readiness of other nations
(3) repeal of Prohibition
(4) economic prosperity of the period

6 Concentration camps and extermination camps were part of what Nazis called
(1) justice for all.
(2) the "final solution."
(3) population control.
(4) the last straw.

7 The neutrality laws passed in the 1930s assumed that the surest way to avoid war was for the U.S. to
(1) maintain a superior army and navy.
(2) restrict loans to and limit trade with warring nations.
(3) discourage aggressors by threatening military reprisals.
(4) enter alliances with other democratic nations.

8 What did Hitler call Germany's quick air strikes?
(1) blitzkrieg
(2) *Kristallnacht*
(3) *Anschluss*
(4) gestapo

Need Extra Help?								
If You Missed Questions . . .	1	2	3	4	5	6	7	8
Go to Page . . .	702–707	686	688	690–692	686–687	698–699	686–687	690

[OVER]

Base your answer to question 9 on the chart below and your knowledge of Chapter 20.

Nazi Concentration and Extermination Camps

9   In which two countries were most of the concentration and extermination camps located?

(1) Germany and France

(2) Germany and Poland

(3) Germany and the Soviet Union

(4) Germany and Austria

10   Which of the following was one step that America took to aid Great Britain?

(1) created a hemispheric defense zone

(2) founded the America First Committee

(3) called for the Wannsee Conference

(4) attended the Munich Conference

11   What event caused the United States to enter the war in 1941?

(1) the blitzkrieg over Poland

(2) the bombing of Pearl Harbor

(3) the embargo on Japan

(4) the sinking of the *Lusitania*

Need Extra Help?			
If You Missed Questions . . .	9	10	11
Go to Page . . .	698–699	704–705	705–707

Part II Thematic Essay Question

Directions: Write a well-organized essay that includes an introduction, several paragraphs addressing the task below, and a conclusion.

Theme: The Holocaust

During the Holocaust, the Nazis killed an estimated 6 million European Jews. The Nazis also sent millions of Jews, Gypsies, Slavs, the disabled, and others to concentration camps and extermination camps.

Task:

• Explain actions the Allies could have taken to aid the Jews, Gypsies, Slavs, and others

• Describe the possible effects of Allied intervention in the Holocaust

• Explain how the short- and long-term outcome of the Nazis' Final Solution may have been affected by intervention

Guidelines:

In your essay, be sure to:

• Develop all aspects of the task

• Support the theme with relevant facts, examples, and details

• Use a logical and clear plan of organization, including an introduction and a conclusion that are beyond a restatement of the theme

Part III Document-Based Question

This question is based on the accompanying documents. It is designed to test your ability to work with historical documents. Some of the documents have been edited for the purposes of the question. As you analyze the documents, take into account both the source of each document and any point of view that may be presented in the document.

Historical Context:

As the Axis Powers waged war in Europe, the United States attempted to stay out of the conflict. The bombing of Pearl Harbor by Japan finally compelled the United States to declare war.

Task:

Using information from the documents and your knowledge of United States history, answer the questions that follow each document in Part A. Your answers to the questions will help you write the Part B essay, in which you will be asked to

- Discuss the motivations of the United States to remain neutral
- Discuss the impact of the bombing of Pearl Harbor on the nation
- Evaluate how the United States slowly became involved in the war, and finally joined in combat to support the Allied forces

Part A
Short-Answer Questions

Directions: Analyze the documents and answer the short-answer questions that follow each document on a separate sheet of paper.

Document 1

As soon as I finished brushing my teeth and pulled on my trousers, I automatically clicked on the little radio that stood on the shelf above my bed. I remember that I was buttoning my shirt and looking out the window . . . when the hum of the warming set gave way to a frenzied voice. "This is no test," the voice cried out. "Pearl Harbor is being bombed by the Japanese!"

[The family ran outside to look toward the naval base at Pearl Harbor.]

And then we saw the planes. They came zooming up out of that sea of gray smoke, flying north toward where we stood and climbing into the bluest part of the sky, and they came in twos and threes, in neat formations, and if it hadn't been for that red ball on their wings, the rising sun of the Japanese Empire, you could easily believe that they were Americans, flying over in precise military salute.

—quoted in *Eyewitness to America*

1 What makes Inouye certain that the planes are Japanese, not American?

Document 2

Source: Chicago Historical Society

2 According to the cartoon, how did Americans feel about assisting the Allies?

Part B
Essay

Directions: Reread the task box at the top left and write a well-organized essay that includes an introduction, several paragraphs, and a conclusion. Use evidence from the documents in your essay. Support your response with relevant facts, examples, and details. Include additional outside information.

Guidelines:

In your essay, be sure to:

- Develop all aspects of the task
- Use a logical and clear plan of organization, including an introduction and a conclusion that are beyond a restatement of the theme

History ONLINE

For additional test practice, use Self-Check Quizzes—Chapter 20 at glencoe.com.

Need Extra Help?			
If You Missed Questions . . .	1	2	Essay
Go to Page . . .	R19	R18	R3

Chapter 21

America and World War II

1941–1945

SECTION 1 Mobilizing for War

SECTION 2 The Early Battles

SECTION 3 Life on the Home Front

SECTION 4 Pushing Back the Axis

SECTION 5 The War Ends

Allied troops land in Normandy on D-Day, 1944.

U.S. PRESIDENTS

1941
- United States enters World War II
- Roosevelt bans discrimination in defense industries

Franklin D. Roosevelt 1933–1945

1942
- Women's Army Auxiliary Corps established
- Japanese American relocation ordered

1943
- Detroit race riots
- Zoot-suit riots in Los Angeles

U.S. EVENTS

WORLD EVENTS

1941 — 1942 — 1943

1941
- Japan attacks Pearl Harbor

1942
- Japan captures the Philippines
- Americans win Battle of Midway

1943
- Germans defeated at Stalingrad
- Allied forces land in Italy

MAKING CONNECTIONS

What Kinds of Sacrifices Does War Require?

During World War II, millions of Americans enlisted in the armed forces, risking their lives in the struggle. On the home front, Americans also helped the war effort by giving up goods needed by the military and buying war bonds.

- *Why do you think so many Americans volunteered to fight in World War II?*
- *Should civilians have to make sacrifices in wartime?*

FOLDABLES

Summarizing American Life During World War II Make a Pocket Book Foldable to summarize various aspects of daily life that World War II affected.

Label the two pockets as Economic and Social. Include general effects as well as specific programs under each pocket.

Economic   Social

1944
- Supreme Court rules in *Korematsu v. United States* that Japanese American relocation is constitutional

Harry Truman
1945–1953

1945
- Franklin Roosevelt dies in office; Harry S. Truman becomes president

1944

1945

1944
- Eisenhower leads D-Day invasion
- MacArthur's forces land in the Philippines

1945
- U.S. Marines capture Iwo Jima
- United States drops atomic bomb on Japan

History ONLINE **Chapter Overview**
Visit glencoe.com to preview Chapter 21.

Mobilizing for War

Guide to Reading

Big Ideas
Economics and Society Americans quickly converted to a wartime economy to support the war effort.

Content Vocabulary
- cost-plus *(p. 716)*
- disenfranchised *(p. 719)*

Academic Vocabulary
- vehicle *(p. 717)*
- draft *(p. 718)*

People and Events to Identify
- War Production Board *(p. 717)*
- Office of War Mobilization *(p. 717)*
- "Double V" campaign *(p. 720)*
- Tuskegee Airmen *(p. 720)*
- Oveta Culp Hobby *(p. 721)*
- Women's Army Corps *(p. 721)*

Reading Strategy
Organizing Complete a graphic organizer similar to the one below by filling in the agencies that the U.S. government created to mobilize the nation for war.

Government Agencies Created to Mobilize the Economy

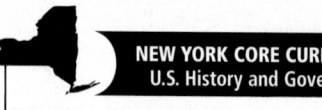

NEW YORK CORE CURRICULUM
U.S. History and Government

Unit 6:
I.C.2.a The "arsenal of democracy" (feats of productivity)
I.C.2.b Role of women: WACs; Rosie the Riveter; return of the retired
I.C.2.c Mobilization: the draft; minority issues
I.C.2.f Experiences of men and women in military service

After World War I, America returned to isolationism. When the nation entered World War II in 1941, its armed forces ranked nineteenth in might, behind the tiny European nation of Belgium. Three years later, the United States was producing 40 percent of the world's arms.

Converting the Economy

MAIN Idea The United States quickly mobilized the economy to fight the war.

HISTORY AND YOU Have you ever changed the way you performed a task in order to do it faster or more efficiently? What steps did you take to speed things up? Read on to learn how the United States changed the way factories produced goods during World War II.

Shortly after 1:30 P.M. on December 7, 1941, Secretary of the Navy Frank Knox phoned President Roosevelt at the White House. "Mr. President," Knox said, "it looks like the Japanese have attacked Pearl Harbor." A few minutes later, Admiral Harold Stark, chief of naval operations, phoned and confirmed the attack.

Although President Roosevelt remained calm when he heard the news, he later expressed his concerns to his wife Eleanor: "I never wanted to have to fight this war on two fronts. We haven't got the Navy to fight in both the Atlantic and Pacific. . . . We will have to build up the Navy and the Air Force and that will mean we will have to take a good many defeats before we can have a victory."

Although the difficulties of fighting a global war troubled the president, British prime minister Winston Churchill was not worried. Churchill knew that victory in modern war depended on a nation's industrial power. He compared the American economy to a gigantic boiler: "Once the fire is lighted under it there is no limit to the power it can generate."

Churchill was right. The industrial output of the United States during the war astounded the rest of the world. American workers were twice as productive as German workers and five times more productive than Japanese workers. In 1943 the Soviet leader Joseph Stalin toasted "American production, without which this war would have been lost." American war production turned the tide in favor of the Allies. In less than four years, the United States and its allies achieved what no other group of nations had ever done—they fought and won a two-front war against two powerful military empires, forcing each to surrender.

The Arsenal of Democracy

Analyzing VISUALS

1. **Determining Cause and Effect** When did tank production begin to drop? Why might this be so?

2. **Making Connections** How do you think the workers felt as they watched the tanks rolling out of the factory?

U.S. Output of Military Products

Products (y-axis): 80,000 / 60,000 / 40,000 / 20,000

Year (x-axis): 1941, 1942, 1943, 1944, 1945

— Combat aircraft — Ships — Tanks

Source: *The Big 'L': American Logistics in World War II.*

The United States rapidly increased its war production after the attack on Pearl Harbor. The expansion was possible in part because the government had already begun mobilizing the economy before the country entered the war. When the German blitzkrieg swept into France in May 1940, President Roosevelt declared a national emergency and announced a plan to build 50,000 warplanes a year. Two months later he asked Congress for $4 billion to build a "Two-Ocean" Navy.

Shocked by the success of the German attack, many Americans were willing to build up the country's defenses. By October 1940, Congress had increased the defense budget to more than $17 billion. The Army-Navy Munitions Board—the military agency in charge of buying equipment—began signing contracts with American companies for new aircraft, ships, and equipment.

Roosevelt believed that government and business had to work together to prepare for war. He created the National Defense Advisory Committee to help mobilize the economy and asked several business leaders to serve on the committee. The president and his advisers believed that giving industry an incentive to move quickly was the best way to rapidly mobilize the economy. As Henry Stimson, the new secretary of war, wrote in his diary: "If you are going to try and go to war, or to prepare for war, in a capitalist country, you have got to let business make money out of the process or business won't work."

Normally when the government needed military equipment, it would ask companies to bid for the contract, but that system was too slow in wartime. Instead of asking for bids, the government signed **cost-plus** contracts. The government agreed to pay a company whatever it cost to make a product plus a guaranteed percentage of the costs as profit.

Under the cost-plus system, the more a company produced and the faster it did the work, the more money it would make. The system was not cheap, but it did get war materials produced quickly and in quantity.

Cost-plus convinced many companies to convert to war production. Other firms, however, could not afford to reequip their factories to make military goods. To convince more companies to convert, Congress gave new authority to the Reconstruction Finance Corporation (RFC). That government agency, set up during the Depression, could make loans to companies wanting to convert their factories to war production.

✓ **Reading Check** **Analyzing** What government policies helped American industry to produce large quantities of war materials?

American Industry Gets the Job Done

MAIN Idea Factories built tanks, airplanes, trucks, and jeeps for military use, as well as safer ships.

HISTORY AND YOU Has a coach or an instructor ever challenged you to improve your speed or efficiency at a task? Read on to learn how American industry helped the war effort.

By the fall of 1941, much had already been done to prepare the economy for war, but it was still only partially mobilized. Although many companies were producing military equipment, most still preferred to make consumer goods. The Great Depression was ending, demand was up, and sales were rising. The Japanese attack on Pearl Harbor, however, changed everything. A flood of orders by the government for war materials began, and by the summer of 1942, almost all major industries and some 200,000 companies had converted to war production. Together they made the nation's wartime "miracle" possible.

PRIMARY SOURCE
Building the Liberty Ships

▲ *In this 1942 photograph, workers construct a Liberty ship in San Francisco.*

PRIMARY SOURCE

"I took classes on how to weld. I had leather gloves, leather pants, a big hood, goggles and a leather jacket. . . .
They put me forty feet down in the bottom of the ship to be a tacker. I filled the long seams of the cracks in the ship corners full of hot lead and then brushed them good and you could see how pretty it was. The welders would come along and weld it so it would take the strong waves and deep water and heavy weight."

—Katie Grant, World War II riveter at Kaiser Richmond Shipyard, California

DBQ **Document-Based Questions**

1. **Interpreting** Why would Katie Grant have had to wear leather clothing?
2. **Summarizing** What was her job?

Tanks Replace Cars

The automobile industry was uniquely suited to the mass production of military equipment. Automobile factories began producing trucks, jeeps, and tanks. Mass production was critical in modern warfare, because the country that could move troops and supplies most quickly usually won the battle. As General George C. Marshall, chief of staff for the United States Army, observed:

PRIMARY SOURCE

"The greatest advantage . . . the United States enjoyed on the ground in the fighting was . . . the jeep and the two-and-a-half ton truck. These are the instruments that moved and supplied United States troops in battle, while the German army . . . depended heavily on animal transport. . . . The United States, profiting from the mass production achievements of its automotive industry . . . had mobility that completely outclassed the enemy."

—quoted in *Miracle of World War II*

Automobile factories did not just produce **vehicles.** They also built artillery, rifles, mines, helmets, pontoon bridges, and dozens of other pieces of military equipment. Henry Ford created an assembly line for the enormous B-24 bomber known as the "Liberator" at Willow Run Airport near Detroit. By the end of the war, the factory had built more than 8,600 aircraft. Overall, the auto industry produced nearly one-third of all military equipment manufactured during the war.

Building the Liberty Ships

Ford's remarkable achievement in aircraft production was more than matched by Henry Kaiser's shipyards. Henry Kaiser started in the construction industry, but when World War II began, Kaiser shifted from the construction industry to shipbuilding.

German submarines were sinking American cargo ships at a terrifying rate. The United States had to find a way to build cargo ships as quickly as possible. Kaiser believed that speed was more important than quality and that cost was less important than results. He spent whatever it took to get the job done quickly. To save time, he applied techniques from the construction industry to shipbuilding. Instead of building an entire ship in one place from the keel up, parts were prefabricated and brought to the shipyard for assembly.

Kaiser's shipyards built many different kinds of ships, but they were best known for Liberty ships. The Liberty ship was the basic cargo ship used during the war. Liberty ships were welded instead of riveted. Although welded ships tended to crack, Vice Admiral Emory Land, head of the U.S. Maritime Commission, preferred the Liberty ships:

PRIMARY SOURCE

"Every time a riveted ship goes into dock you have a lot of repairs to do. You do not have them in welded ships. . . . On combat damage, comparing the welded Liberty ships and others, everything is in favor of the Liberty. . . . riveted ships are apt to go to the bottom if they are bombed or mined or torpedoed. . . . Never mind about the fractures or the cracks—[the Liberty ships] get into port."

—quoted in *Miracle of World War II*

When the war began, it took 244 days to build the first Liberty ship. After Kaiser shipyards applied their mass-production techniques, average production time dropped to 41 days. Kaiser's shipyards built 30 percent of all American ships constructed during the war, including nearly 3,000 Liberty ships.

The War Production Board

As American companies converted to war production, many business leaders became frustrated with the mobilization process. Government agencies argued constantly about supplies and contracts and whose orders had the highest priority.

After Pearl Harbor, President Roosevelt tried to improve the system by creating the **War Production Board** (WPB). He gave the WPB the authority to set priorities and production goals and to control the distribution of raw materials and supplies. Almost immediately, the WPB clashed with the military. Military agencies continued to sign contracts without consulting with the WPB. Finally, in 1943, Roosevelt established the **Office of War Mobilization** (OWM) to settle arguments among the different agencies.

Reading Check **Explaining** What military need led to the production of Liberty ships?

Building an Army

MAIN Idea Minorities and women played an important role in the United States armed forces during World War II.

HISTORY AND YOU Do you think the United States should have a military draft? Read to learn about the first peacetime draft in American history.

Converting factories to war production was only part of the mobilization process. To fight and win the war, the United States also needed to build up its armed forces.

Creating an Army

Within days of Germany's attack on Poland in 1939, President Roosevelt expanded the army to 227,000 soldiers. Before the spring of 1940, college students, unions, isolationists, and most members of Congress had opposed a peacetime **draft.** Opinions changed after France surrendered to Germany in June 1940. Two members of Congress introduced the Selective Service and Training Act, a plan for the first peacetime draft in American history. In September, Congress approved the draft by a wide margin.

You're in the Army Now

More than 60,000 men enlisted in the month after the attack on Pearl Harbor. At first, the flood of recruits overwhelmed the army's training facilities. Many recruits had to live in tents rather than barracks. The army also experienced equipment shortages. Troops carried sticks representing guns, threw stones simulating grenades, and practiced maneuvers with trucks labeled "TANK."

New recruits were initially sent to a reception center, where they were given physical exams and injections against smallpox and typhoid. The draftees were then issued uniforms, boots, and whatever equipment was available. The clothing bore the label "G.I.," meaning "Government Issue," which is why American soldiers were called GIs.

After taking aptitude tests, recruits went to basic training for eight weeks. They learned

PRIMARY SOURCE
Creating an American Army

▲ Soldiers from a Mexican-American platoon train at Fort Benning in 1943.

U.S. Armed Forces, 1939–1946

Military personnel (millions) vs. Year

Legend: Army, Navy, Marines

Source: *Historical Statistics of the United States.*

PRIMARY SOURCE

For many Americans, entering the army changed their perspective, as historian Carl Degler recalls:

"Entrance into the Army in August, 1942, widened my horizons literally as well as experientially: for the first time I travelled beyond a 200 mile radius from Newark. I marvelled at the flatness of the prairie in Illinois . . . . Stops at posts in Miami Beach, Florida, and Richmond, Virginia, were my introduction to the American South."

—from *The History Teacher,* vol. 23, 1990

how to handle weapons, load backpacks, read maps, pitch tents, and dig trenches. Trainees drilled and exercised constantly and learned how to work as a team.

Basic training helped to break down barriers between soldiers. Recruits came from all over the country, and training together created a "special sense of kinship," as one soldier noted. "The reason you storm the beaches is not patriotism or bravery. It's that sense of not wanting to fail your buddies."

A Segregated Army

Although basic training promoted unity, most recruits did not encounter Americans from every part of society. At the start of the war, the U.S. military was segregated. White recruits did not train alongside African Americans. African Americans had separate barracks, latrines, mess halls, and recreational facilities. Once trained, African Americans were organized into their own military units, but white officers generally commanded them. Most military leaders also wanted to keep African American soldiers out of combat and assigned them to construction and supply units.

Some African Americans did not want to support the war. As one student at a black college noted: "The Army Jim Crows us. . . . Employers and labor unions shut us out. Lynchings continue. We are **disenfranchised** . . . and spat upon. What more could Hitler do to us than that?" Despite the bitterness, most African Americans agreed with African American writer Saunders Redding that they should support their country:

PRIMARY SOURCE

"There are many things about this war that I do not like . . . yet I believe in the war. . . . [W]e know that whatever the mad logic of [Hitler's] New Order there is no hope for us under it. The ethnic theories of the Hitler 'master folk' admit of no chance of freedom. . . . This is a war to keep [people] free. The struggle to broaden and lengthen the road of freedom—our own private and important war to enlarge freedom here in America—will come later. . . . I believe in this war because I believe in America. I believe in what America professes to stand for."

—from "A Negro Looks at This War"

A Segregated Army

Although the U.S. armed forces were segregated, discrimination did not prevent minority groups from performing with courage. Two of the best-known examples are the Tuskegee Airmen (right), comprised of African American volunteers, and the 442nd Regimental Combat Team (below), made up of Japanese American volunteers. The 450 Tuskegee Airmen fought in North Africa, Sicily, and Italy. The 442nd Regimental Combat Team became the most decorated unit in U.S. history.

Analyzing VISUALS

1. **Identifying** In what year did the army experience the most rapid growth? Why do you think that is the case?

2. **Evaluating** What do the expressions on the faces of the Tuskegee Airmen convey?

History ONLINE
Student Skill Activity To learn how to conduct an interview, visit glencoe.com and complete the Skill activity.

Pushing for "Double V" Many African American leaders combined patriotism with protest. In 1941 the National Urban League asked its members to encourage African Americans to join the war effort. It also asked them to make plans for building a better society in the United States after the war. The *Pittsburgh Courier*, a leading African American newspaper, launched the **"Double V" campaign.** The campaign urged African Americans to support the war to achieve a double victory—over both Hitler's racism abroad and the racism at home.

African Americans in Combat Under pressure from African American leaders, President Roosevelt ordered the army, air force, navy, and marines to recruit African Americans, and he told the army to put African Americans into combat. He also promoted Colonel Benjamin O. Davis, Sr., the highest-ranking African American officer, to the rank of brigadier general.

In early 1941 the air force created its first African American unit, the 99th Pursuit Squadron. The pilots trained in Tuskegee, Alabama, and became known as the **Tuskegee Airmen.** In April 1943, after General Davis urged the military to put African Americans into combat as soon as possible, the squadron was sent to the Mediterranean. Lieutenant Colonel Benjamin O. Davis, Jr., General Davis's son, commanded the squadron and helped win the battle of Anzio in Italy.

In late 1943 Colonel Davis took command of three new squadrons that had trained at Tuskegee. Known as the 332nd Fighter Group, these squadrons were ordered to protect American bombers as they flew to their targets. The 332nd Fighter Group flew 200 such missions and did not lose a single member to enemy aircraft.

African Americans also performed well in the army. The all–African American 761st Tank Battalion was commended for its service during the Battle of the Bulge. Although the

PRIMARY SOURCE
Women in World War II

About 400,000 American women played a major role in the military side of the war effort, if not in direct combat. Sixteen American women were awarded the Purple Heart for being injured as a result of enemy action. More than 400 American military women lost their lives.

◀ *In this 1943 photo, Nancy Nesbit checks with the control tower from her plane at Avenger Field in Sweetwater, Texas, where the Women's Auxiliary Ferrying Squadron of the U.S. Army trained.*

▲ *A doctor and an army nurse tend to a patient at a U.S. Army hospital in Leyte in the Philippines.*

Analyzing VISUALS

1. **Inferring** Why might the military have been reluctant to allow women in combat?

2. **Evaluating** What does the photo above suggest about conditions in military hospitals?

military did not end all segregation during the war, it did integrate military bases in 1943 and steadily expanded the role of African Americans within the armed forces. These successes paved the way for President Truman's decision to fully integrate the military in 1948.

Other Minorities in the Military Japanese Americans were not allowed to serve in the military at first. As the war progressed, however, second-generation Japanese Americans served in the 100th Infantry Battalion and the 442nd Regimental Combat Team. Almost half had been in internment camps in the American Southwest. Together these units became the most decorated in the history of the United States military. Many Mexican Americans had joined the National Guard during the 1930s and served on the front lines. Most minorities were allowed only in noncombat positions, such as kitchen workers. Native Americans, who were regarded as fierce warriors, were an exception to that policy. One-third of all healthy Native American men aged 18–50 served during the war.

Women Join the Armed Forces

Women joined the armed forces, as they had done during World War I. The army enlisted women for the first time, although they were barred from combat. Many jobs in the army were administrative and clerical. Assigning women to these jobs made more men available for combat.

Congress first allowed women in the military in May 1942, when it established the Women's Army Auxiliary Corps (WAAC) and appointed **Oveta Culp Hobby,** an official with the War Department, to serve as its first director. Although pleased about the establishment of the WAAC, many women were unhappy that it was an auxiliary corps and not part of the regular army. A little over a year later, the army replaced the WAAC with the **Women's Army Corps** (WAC). Director Hobby was assigned the rank of colonel. "You have a debt and a date," Hobby explained to those training to be the nation's first women officers. "A debt to democracy, a date with destiny."

As early as 1939, pilot Jackie Cochran had written to Eleanor Roosevelt suggesting that women pilots could aid the war effort. The following year, Nancy Love wrote to army officials to suggest that women be allowed to deliver planes. (The air force was not yet a separate branch of the military.) Training programs began in 1942; the Women Airforce Service Pilots (WASPs) began the next year. Although the WASPs were no longer needed after 1944, about 300 women pilots made more than 12,000 deliveries of 77 different kinds of planes.

The Coast Guard, the navy, and the marines quickly followed the army and set up their own women's units. In addition to serving in these new organizations, another 68,000 women served as nurses in the army and navy.

Reading Check **Summarizing** How did the status of women and African Americans in the armed forces change during the war?

Vocabulary

1. **Explain** the significance of: cost-plus, War Production Board, Office of War Mobilization, disenfranchised, "Double V" campaign, Tuskegee Airmen, Oveta Culp Hobby, Women's Army Corps.

Main Ideas

2. **Describing** How did Congress support factories that converted to war production?

3. **Analyzing** What role did the OWM play in the war production effort?

4. **Explaining** How were minorities discriminated against in the military?

Critical Thinking

5. **Big Ideas** How did American industry rally behind the war effort?

6. **Organizing** Use a graphic organizer like the one below to list the challenges facing the United States as it mobilized for war.

Challenges to Mobilization

7. **Analyzing Visuals** Look again at the photograph on page 716. What do you observe about the construction process?

Writing About History

8. **Expository Writing** Interview a World War II veteran or research your community during the war. How did industry rally behind the war effort? Write a one-page report to summarize your findings.

History ONLINE

Study Central™ To review this section, go to glencoe.com and click on Study Central.

Section 2

The Early Battles

Guide to Reading

Big Ideas
Individual Action Several key people made decisions that changed the course of the war.

Content Vocabulary
• periphery *(p. 725)*
• convoy system *(p. 727)*

Academic Vocabulary
• code *(p. 724)*
• target *(p. 726)*

People and Events to Identify
• Chester Nimitz *(p. 722)*
• Douglas MacArthur *(p. 722)*
• Bataan Death March *(p. 723)*
• Corregidor *(p. 723)*
• James Doolittle *(p. 723)*

Reading Strategy
Organizing Complete a time line similar to the one below to record the major battles discussed and the victor in each.

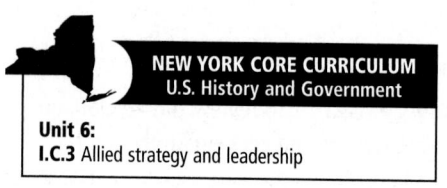

NEW YORK CORE CURRICULUM
U.S. History and Government

Unit 6:
I.C.3 Allied strategy and leadership

The early battles of the war on both fronts required changes in strategy from all sides. In the Pacific, the Battle of Midway was a major turning point against the Japanese, while the Battle of the Atlantic and the Battle of Stalingrad made it clear that Germany would not win the war.

Holding the Line Against Japan

MAIN Idea The Japanese continued to win victories in the Pacific until the Battle of Midway.

HISTORY AND YOU Have you ever continued toward a goal even though the odds were against you? Read on to learn about the early battles in the Pacific.

Admiral **Chester Nimitz,** the commander of the United States Navy in the Pacific, began planning operations against the Japanese Navy. Although the Japanese had badly damaged the American fleet at Pearl Harbor, the American aircraft carriers, which were on a mission at sea, were safe. The United States had several carriers in the Pacific, and Nimitz was determined to use them. In the days just after Pearl Harbor, however, he could do little to stop Japan's advance into Southeast Asia.

The Fall of the Philippines

A few hours after bombing Pearl Harbor, the Japanese attacked American airfields in the Philippines. Two days later, they landed troops. The American and Filipino forces defending the Philippines were badly outnumbered. Their commander, General **Douglas MacArthur,** retreated to the Bataan Peninsula. Using the peninsula's rugged terrain, the troops held out for more than three months.

By March, in desperation, the troops ate cavalry horses and mules. The lack of food and supplies, along with diseases such as malaria, scurvy, and dysentery, took their toll. The women of the Army Nurse Corps worked on Bataan in primitive conditions. Patients slept in the open air. One nurse, Rose Meier, reported, "If we needed more room, we got our axes and chopped some bamboo trees down."

Realizing MacArthur's capture would demoralize the American people, President Roosevelt ordered the general to evacuate to Australia. MacArthur promised, "I came through, and I shall return."

On April 9, 1942, the weary defenders of the Bataan Peninsula finally surrendered. Nearly 78,000 prisoners of war were forced

The Bataan Death March, April 1942

Private Leon Beck was taken prisoner when Bataan surrendered and took part in the Bataan Death March for 13 days before escaping:

PRIMARY SOURCE

"They'd halt us in front of these big artesian wells . . . so we could see the water and they wouldn't let us have any. Anyone who would make a break for water would be shot or bayoneted. Then they were left there. Finally, it got so bad further along the road that you never got away from the stench of death. There were bodies laying all along the road in various degrees of decomposition—swollen, burst open, maggots crawling by the thousands. . . ."

—from *Death March: The Survivors of Bataan*

DBQ Document-Based Questions

1. **Making Inferences** Why did the Japanese captors stop at the wells?

2. **Hypothesizing** Why might the captors treat the captives as they did on this march?

to march—sick, exhausted, and starving—65 miles (105 km) to a Japanese prison camp. Almost ten thousand troops died on this march, which was later called the **Bataan Death March.** Sixty-six women nurses were also captured and sent to the University of Santo Tomas in Manila. They remained there—with 11 navy nurses and some 3,000 Allied civilians—until early in 1945.

Although the troops in the Bataan Peninsula surrendered, a small force held out on the island of **Corregidor** in Manila Bay. Finally, in May 1942, Corregidor surrendered. The Philippines had fallen to the Japanese.

The Doolittle Raid on Tokyo

Even before the Philippines fell, President Roosevelt was searching for a way to raise the morale of the American people. He wanted to bomb Tokyo, but American planes could reach Tokyo only if an aircraft carrier brought them close enough. Unfortunately, Japanese ships in the North Pacific prevented carriers from getting near Japan.

In early 1942, a military planner suggested replacing the carrier's usual short-range bombers with long-range B-25 bombers that could attack from farther away. The only problem was that, although B-25s could take off from a carrier, the bombers could not land on its short deck. After attacking Japan, they would have to land in China.

President Roosevelt put Lieutenant Colonel **James Doolittle** in command of the mission to bomb Tokyo. At the end of March, a crane loaded sixteen B-25s onto the aircraft carrier *Hornet.* The next day, the *Hornet* headed west across the Pacific. On April 18, American bombs fell on Japan for the first time.

Japan Changes Strategy

While Americans rejoiced in the air force's success, Japanese leaders were aghast at the raid. Those bombs could have killed the emperor, who was revered as a god. The Doolittle raid convinced Japanese leaders to change their strategy.

Before the raid, the Japanese navy had disagreed about the next step. The officers in charge of the navy's planning wanted to cut American supply lines to Australia by capturing the south coast of New Guinea. The commander of the fleet, Admiral Yamamoto, wanted to attack Midway Island—the last American base in the North Pacific west of Hawaii. Yamamoto believed that attacking Midway would lure the American fleet into battle and enable his fleet to destroy it.

After Doolittle's raid, the Japanese war planners dropped their opposition to Yamamoto's idea. The American fleet had to be destroyed to protect Tokyo from bombing. The attack on New Guinea would still go ahead, but only three aircraft carriers were assigned to the mission. All of the other carriers were ordered to assault Midway.

The Battle of the Coral Sea

The Japanese believed that they could safely proceed with two attacks at once because they thought their operations were secret. What the Japanese did not know was that an American team of code breakers based in Hawaii had already broken the Japanese navy's secret **code** for conducting operations.

In March 1942, decoded Japanese messages alerted the United States to the Japanese attack on New Guinea. In response, Admiral Nimitz sent two carriers, the *Yorktown* and the *Lexington,* to intercept the Japanese in the Coral Sea. There, in early May, carriers from both sides launched all-out airstrikes against each other. Although the Japanese sank the *Lexington* and badly damaged the *Yorktown,* the American attacks prevented the Japanese from landing on New Guinea's south coast and kept the supply lines to Australia open.

The Battle of Midway

Back at Pearl Harbor, the code-breaking team now learned of the plan to attack Midway. With so many ships at sea, Admiral Yamamoto transmitted the plans for the Midway attack by radio, using the same code the Americans had already cracked.

Admiral Nimitz had been waiting for the opportunity to ambush the Japanese fleet. He

NATIONAL GEOGRAPHIC **The Battle of Midway, 1942**

- Course of *Enterprise* and *Hornet*

8 **June 4, 5:01 P.M.** *Yorktown* fliers join *Enterprise* attack on the *Hiryu,* setting it ablaze.

Course of *Yorktown*

9 **June 6, 1:31 P.M.** Japanese submarine *I-168* torpedoes the *Yorktown,* which sinks the next morning.

Hiryu sinks ✖

Course of Japanese fleet

Akagi sinks *Soryu* sinks
Kaga sinks

7 **June 4, noon.** Planes from the *Hiryu* attack U.S. carriers. *Yorktown* hit. The ship is abandoned but remains afloat.

Yorktown sinks

6 **June 4, 10:22–10:28 A.M.** U.S. Dive-bombers score direct hits on *Kaga, Akagi,* and *Soryu.*

1 **June 4, 4:30 A.M.** Japanese carriers launch 108 warplanes to strike U.S. base at Midway.

2 **June 4, 6:16 A.M.** U.S. fighters clash with attackers.

5 **June 4, 9:17 A.M.** Japanese planes return. Fleet turns to engage U.S. carriers.

4 **June 4, 7:08 A.M.** U.S. fliers from Midway begin attacking Japanese fleet.

U.S. Dauntless dive-bomber

Line of U.S. submarines stationed 170 miles from Midway.

3 **June 4, 6:30 A.M.** Japanese begin bombing Midway.

Midway Islands (U.S.)

Kure Atoll (U.S.)

PACIFIC OCEAN

N W E S

- U.S. actions
- Japanese actions

immediately ordered carriers to take up positions near Midway. Unaware that they were heading into an ambush, the Japanese launched their aircraft against Midway on June 4, 1942. The Americans were ready. The Japanese ran into a blizzard of antiaircraft fire, and 38 planes were shot down.

As the Japanese prepared a second wave to attack Midway, aircraft from the American carriers *Hornet, Yorktown,* and *Enterprise* launched a counterattack. The American planes caught the Japanese carriers with fuel, bombs, and aircraft exposed on their flight decks. Within minutes, three Japanese carriers were reduced to burning wrecks. A fourth was sunk a few hours later, and Admiral Yamamoto ordered his remaining ships to retreat.

The Battle of Midway was a turning point in the war. The Japanese navy lost four large carriers—the heart of its fleet. Just six months after Pearl Harbor, the United States had stopped the Japanese advance. The victory was not without cost, however. The battle killed 362 Americans and 3,057 Japanese.

✔ **Reading Check** **Explaining** Why was the United States able to ambush the Japanese at Midway?

▼ *Japanese aircraft bomb the USS Yorktown near Midway, June 1942.*

Analyzing VISUALS

1. **Interpreting** When did Japan launch the attack on Midway?
2. **Drawing Conclusions** Why were aircraft carriers so vital to the war in the Pacific?

Maps In MOtion See *StudentWorks™ Plus* or glencoe.com.

Stopping the Germans

MAIN Idea The Allies defeated Germany in Africa and in the Battle of the Atlantic. The Soviet victory at Stalingrad was a turning point of the war.

HISTORY AND YOU Have you ever tried something simple before attempting a more challenging problem? Read on to learn about the Allied strategy for attacking the Germans.

In 1942 Allied forces began to win victories in Europe as well. Almost from the moment the United States entered the war, Joseph Stalin, the leader of the Soviet Union, urged President Roosevelt to open a second front in Europe. Stalin appreciated the lend-lease supplies that the United States had sent, but the Soviets were doing most of the fighting. If British and American troops opened a second front by attacking Germany from the west, it would take pressure off the Soviet Union.

Roosevelt wanted to get American troops into battle in Europe, but Prime Minister Churchill urged caution. He did not believe the United States and Great Britain were ready to launch a full-scale invasion of Europe. Instead, Churchill wanted to attack the **periphery,** or edges, of the German empire. Roosevelt agreed, and in July 1942, he ordered the invasion of Morocco and Algeria—two French territories indirectly under German control.

The Struggle for North Africa

Roosevelt decided to invade Morocco and Algeria for two reasons. First, the invasion would give the army some experience without requiring a lot of troops. More important, once American troops were in North Africa, they would be able to help the British troops fight the Germans in Egypt.

Great Britain needed Egypt because the Suez Canal was located there. Most of Britain's empire, including India, Hong Kong, Singapore, Malaya, and Australia, sent supplies to Britain through the canal. General Erwin Rommel—a brilliant leader whose success earned him the nickname "Desert Fox" —commanded the German forces in the area, known as the "Afrika Korps."

History ONLINE
Student Web Activity Visit glencoe.com and complete the activity on America and World War II.

El Alamein and Stalingrad, November 1942

Just as the Battle of Midway was a turning point in the war in the Pacific, so too were the battles of El Alamein in North Africa and Stalingrad in Europe. The British victory over German General Rommel at El Alamein secured the Suez Canal and kept the Germans away from the oil resources of the Middle East. Germany's defeat at the Battle of Stalingrad was a major turning point by ending Hitler's plans to dominate Europe.

◀ A British tank successfully navigates a wide ditch outside a town in North Africa.

▲ A Soviet gun crew fights against Nazi forces in Stalingrad. Only one day after the Nazis publicly boasted that the city would fall to them, the Red Army turned the tide of battle.

Analyzing VISUALS

1. **Assessing** How do you think the environment made combat at El Alamein and Stalingrad challenging?

2. **Evaluating** Why were the battles shown so important to the Allies?

Although the British forced Rommel to retreat in November 1942, after a 12-day battle against the coastal city of El Alamein near the Suez Canal, German forces remained a serious threat. Later that month, Americans under General Dwight D. Eisenhower's command invaded North Africa. He planned to trap Rommel between two Allied forces. The American forces in Morocco, led by General George Patton, quickly captured the city of Casablanca, while those in Algeria seized the cities of Oran and Algiers. The Americans then headed east into Tunisia, while British forces headed west into Libya.

When the American troops advanced into the mountains of western Tunisia, they had to fight the German army for the first time. They did not do well. At the Battle of Kasserine Pass, the Americans were outmaneuvered and outfought. They suffered roughly 7,000 casualties and lost nearly 200 tanks. Eisenhower fired the general who led the attack and put Patton in command. Together, the American and British forces finally pushed the Germans back. On May 13, 1943, the last German troops in North Africa surrendered.

The Battle of the Atlantic

As American and British troops fought the German army in North Africa, the war against German submarines in the Atlantic Ocean intensified. After Germany declared war on the United States, German submarines entered American coastal waters. American cargo ships were easy **targets,** especially at night when the glow from the cities in the night sky silhouetted the vessels. To protect the ships, cities on the East Coast dimmed their lights every evening. People also put up special "blackout curtains" and, if they had to drive at night, did so with their headlights off.

By August 1942, German submarines had sunk about 360 American ships along the East Coast. So many oil tankers were sunk that gasoline and fuel oil had to be rationed. To keep oil flowing, the government built the first long-distance oil pipeline, stretching some 1,250 miles (2,010 km) from Texas to Pennsylvania.

The loss of so many ships convinced the U.S. Navy to set up a **convoy system.** Under this system, cargo ships traveled in groups escorted by navy warships. The convoy system improved the situation dramatically. It made it much more difficult for a submarine to torpedo a cargo ship and escape without being attacked.

The spring of 1942 marked the high point of the German submarine campaign. In May and June alone, over 1.2 million tons of shipping were sunk. Yet in those same two months, American and British shipyards built more than 1.1 million tons of new shipping. From July 1942 onward, American shipyards produced more ships than German submarines managed to sink. At the same time, American airplanes and warships began to use new technology, including radar, sonar, and depth charges, to locate and attack submarines. As the new technology began to take its toll on German submarines, the Battle of the Atlantic turned in favor of the Allies.

The Battle of Stalingrad

In the spring of 1942, before the Battle of the Atlantic turned against Germany, Adolf Hitler was very confident that he would win the war. The German army was ready to launch a new offensive to knock the Soviets out of the war.

Hitler was convinced that only by destroying the Soviet economy could he defeat the Soviet Union. In May 1942, he ordered his army to capture strategic oil fields, factories, and farmlands in southern Russia and Ukraine. The city of Stalingrad, which controlled the Volga River and was a major railroad junction, was the key to the attack. If the German army captured Stalingrad, they would cut off the Soviets from the resources they needed to stay in the war.

When German troops entered Stalingrad in mid-September, Stalin ordered his troops to hold the city at all costs. Retreat was forbidden. The Germans were forced to fight from house to house, losing thousands of soldiers in the process. They were not equipped to fight in the bitter cold, but Soviet troops had quilted undersuits, felt boots, fur hats, and white camouflaged oversuits.

On November 23, Soviet reinforcements arrived and surrounded Stalingrad, trapping almost 250,000 German troops. When the battle ended in February 1943, some 91,000 Germans had surrendered, although only 5,000 of them survived the Soviet prison camps and returned home after the war. Each side lost nearly half a million soldiers. The Battle of Stalingrad was a major turning point in the war. Just as the Battle of Midway put the Japanese on the defensive for the rest of the war, the Battle of Stalingrad put the Germans on the defensive as well.

Reading Check **Describing** How did the United States begin winning the Battle of the Atlantic?

Section 2 REVIEW

Vocabulary

1. **Explain** the significance of: Chester Nimitz, Douglas MacArthur, Bataan Death March, Corregidor, James Doolittle, periphery, convoy system.

Main Ideas

2. **Explaining** Briefly explain the causes and effects of the effort to defeat the Japanese in 1942.

3. **Analyzing** Why did Churchill want to defeat the Germans in Africa before staging a European invasion?

Critical Thinking

4. **Big Ideas** Explain the significance of one person whose actions made a difference in the war.

5. **Organizing** Use a graphic organizer like the one below to list the reasons that the Battle of Midway is considered a turning point of the war.

6. **Analyzing Visuals** Look again at the map on page 724. How long did the Battle of Midway last?

Writing About History

7. **Expository Writing** Much of the course of wars is determined by the need for supply lines to remain open. Write a brief essay explaining how this need shaped early battles in which the United States was involved.

History ONLINE

Study Central™ To review this section, go to glencoe.com and click on Study Central.

Section 3

Life on the Home Front

Guide to Reading

Big Ideas
Trade, War, and Migration During World War II, Americans faced demands and new challenges at home.

Content Vocabulary
- Sunbelt *(p. 730)*
- zoot suit *(p. 732)*
- victory suit *(p. 732)*
- rationing *(p. 734)*
- victory garden *(p. 735)*

Academic Vocabulary
- coordinate *(p. 731)*
- justify *(p. 732)*

People and Events to Identify
- A. Philip Randolph *(p. 730)*
- Bracero Program *(p. 730)*
- Great Migration *(p. 731)*
- Office of Price Administration *(p. 734)*

Reading Strategy
Organizing Complete a graphic organizer listing opportunities for women and African Americans before and after the war. Evaluate what progress was still needed after the war.

Opportunities

	Before War	After War	Still Needed
Women			
African Americans			

NEW YORK CORE CURRICULUM
U.S. History and Government

Unit 6:
I.C.2.b Role of women: WACs; Rosie the Riveter
I.C.2.c Mobilization: the draft, minority issues
I.C.2.d Rationing
I.C.2.f Experiences of men and women in military service
I.C.5.a Incarceration of West Coast Japanese-Americans; Executive Order 9066; *Korematsu* v. *United States* (1944)
I.C.5.b Extent of racially integrated units in the military

Although women and African Americans gained new work opportunities, Latinos and Japanese Americans faced violence in American cities. To assist with the war effort, the government controlled wages and prices, rationed goods, encouraged recycling, and sold bonds.

Women and Minorities Gain Ground

MAIN Idea With many men on active military duty, women and minorities found factory and other jobs open to them.

HISTORY AND YOU Do you remember reading about the unequal treatment of African American soldiers in World War I? Read on to learn how desegregation of the military began in World War II.

As American troops fought their first battles against the Germans and Japanese, the war began dramatically changing American society at home. In contrast to the devastation that large parts of Europe and Asia experienced, American society gained some benefits from World War II. The war finally ended the Great Depression. Mobilizing the economy created almost 19 million new jobs and nearly doubled the average family's income. For Robert Montgomery, a worker at an Ohio machine tool plant, "one of the most important things that came out of World War II was the arrival of the working class at a new status level in this society. . . . The war integrated into the mainstream a whole chunk of society that had been living on the edge."

The improvement in the economy did not come without cost. American families had to move to where the defense factories were located. Housing conditions were terrible. The pressures and prejudices of the era led to strikes, race riots, and rising juvenile delinquency. Goods were rationed and taxes were higher than ever before. Workers were earning more money, but they were also working an average of 90 hours per week. Despite the hardships, James Covert, whose mother owned a grocery store during the war, was probably right when he said that the war "changed our lifestyle and more important, our outlook. . . . There was a feeling toward the end of the war that we were moving into a new age of prosperity."

When the war began, American defense factories wanted to hire white men. With so many men in the military, however, there simply were not enough white men to fill all of the jobs. Under pressure to produce, employers began to recruit women and minorities.

Women Working in the Defense Plants

We Can Do It!

At left, a riveter works on a bomber in Fort Worth, Texas. Posters such as those above and to the right encouraged women to participate in the war effort.

"THE GIRL HE LEFT BEHIND" IS STILL BEHIND HIM
She's a WOW
WOMAN ORDNANCE WORKER

Women Working

Labor force (millions)

20
18
16
14

1940 1942 1944 1946

Source: *Historical Statistics of the United States.*

Analyzing VISUALS

1. **Listing** During what years did women's employment outside the home hit its highest levels?

2. **Analyzing** How are the women portrayed in the posters?

Women in the Defense Plants

During the Great Depression, many people believed married women should not work outside the home, especially if they took jobs that could go to men trying to support their families. Most working women were young, single, and employed in traditional female jobs such as domestic work or teaching. The wartime labor shortage, however, forced factories to recruit married women for industrial jobs traditionally reserved for men.

Although the government hired nearly 4 million women, primarily for clerical jobs, the women working in the factories captured the public's imagination. The great symbol of the campaign to hire women was "Rosie the Riveter," a character from a popular song by the Four Vagabonds. The lyrics told of Rosie, who worked in a factory while her boyfriend

served in the marines. Images of Rosie appeared on posters, in newspapers, and in magazines. Eventually 2.5 million women worked in shipyards, aircraft factories, and other manufacturing plants. Working in a factory changed the perspectives of many middle-class women like Inez Sauer:

PRIMARY SOURCE

"I learned that just because you're a woman and have never worked is no reason you can't learn. The job really broadened me. . . . I had always been in a shell; I'd always been protected. But at Boeing I found a freedom and an independence I had never known. After the war I could never go back to playing bridge again, being a club woman. . . . when I knew there were things you could use your mind for. The war changed my life completely."

—quoted in *The Homefront*

By the end of the war, the number of working women had increased from 12.9 million to 18.8 million. Although most women were laid off or left their jobs voluntarily after the war, their success permanently changed American attitudes about women in the workplace.

African Americans Demand War Work

Although factories were hiring women, they resisted hiring African Americans. Frustrated by the situation, **A. Philip Randolph,** the head of the Brotherhood of Sleeping Car Porters—a major union for African American railroad workers—decided to take action. He informed President Roosevelt that he was organizing "from ten to fifty thousand [African Americans] to march on Washington in the interest of securing jobs . . . in national defense and . . . integration into the military and naval forces."

In response, Roosevelt issued Executive Order 8802, on June 25, 1941. The order declared, "there shall be no discrimination in the employment of workers in defense industries or government because of race, creed, color, or national origin." To enforce the order, the president created the Fair Employment Practices Commission—the first civil rights agency the federal government had established since the Reconstruction Era.

Mexican Farmworkers

American citizens were not the only ones who gained in the wartime economy. In 1942 the federal government arranged for Mexican farmworkers to help with the harvest in the Southwest. The laborers were part of the **Bracero Program.** *Bracero* is a Spanish word meaning "worker." More than 200,000 Mexicans came to help harvest fruit and vegetables. Many also helped to build and maintain railroads. The Bracero Program continued until 1964. Migrant farmworkers thus became an important part of the Southwest's agricultural system.

✔ **Reading Check** **Describing** How did mobilizing the economy help end the Depression?

A Nation on the Move

MAIN Idea Millions of Americans relocated during the war to take factory jobs or to settle in less prejudiced areas.

HISTORY AND YOU Has someone in your family moved because of a job transfer? Read on to find out about relocations that resulted from the war.

The wartime economy created millions of new jobs, but the Americans who wanted these jobs did not always live near the factories. To get to the jobs, 15 million Americans moved during the war. The Midwest assembly plants and Northeast and Northwest shipyards attracted many workers. Most Americans, however, headed west and south in search of jobs.

The growth of southern California and the expansion of cities in the Deep South created a new industrial region—the **Sunbelt.** For the first time since the Industrial Revolution began

PRIMARY SOURCE
A Nation on the Move

During the war, millions of Americans flocked to the cities to work in factories. Many immigrants stayed on after the war to become citizens. As a result, the populations of Northern cities became more ethnically diverse, and these cities remained more populous after the war.

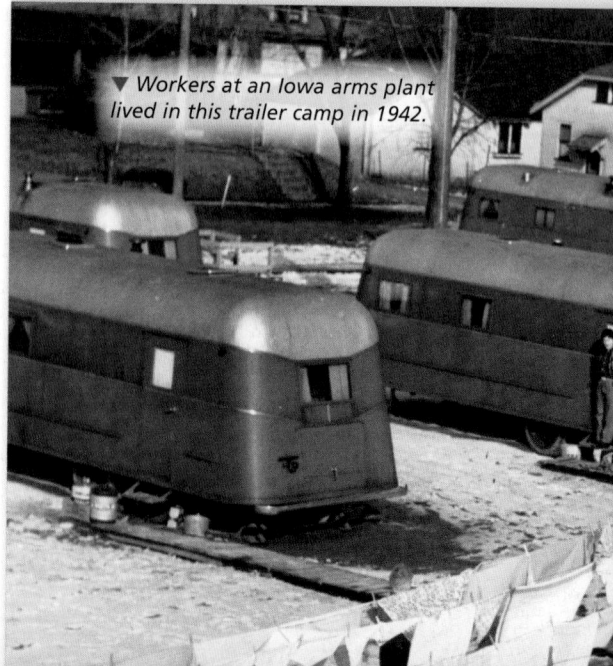

▼ *Workers at an Iowa arms plant lived in this trailer camp in 1942.*

in the United States, the South and West led the way in manufacturing and urbanization.

The Housing Crisis

In many ways, the most difficult task facing cities with war industries was where to put the thousands of workers arriving in their communities. Tent cities and parks filled with tiny trailers sprang up. Landlords began renting "hot beds." The worker paid 25 cents for eight hours in the bed, then went to work while the bed was rented to another worker.

Anticipating the housing crisis, Congress had passed the Lanham Act in 1940. The act provided $150 million for housing. In 1942 President Roosevelt created the National Housing Agency (NHA) to **coordinate** all government housing programs. By 1943, those programs had been allocated over $1.2 billion. Although prefabricated public housing had tiny rooms, thin walls, poor heating, and almost no privacy, it was better than no housing at all. Nearly 2 million people lived in government-built housing during the war.

Racism Leads to Violence

African Americans left the South in large numbers during World War I, but this "**Great Migration,**" as historians refer to it, slowed during the Great Depression. When jobs in war factories opened up for African Americans during World War II, the Great Migration resumed. In the crowded cities of the North and West, however, African Americans were often met with suspicion and intolerance. Sometimes these attitudes led to violence.

The worst racial violence of the war erupted in Detroit on Sunday, June 20, 1943. The weather that day was sweltering. To cool off, nearly 100,000 people crowded into Belle Isle, a park on the Detroit River. Gangs of white and African American teenage girls began fighting. These fights triggered others, and a full-scale riot erupted across the city. By the time the violence ended, 25 African Americans and 9 whites had been killed. Despite the appalling violence in Detroit, African American leaders remained committed to their "Double V" campaign.

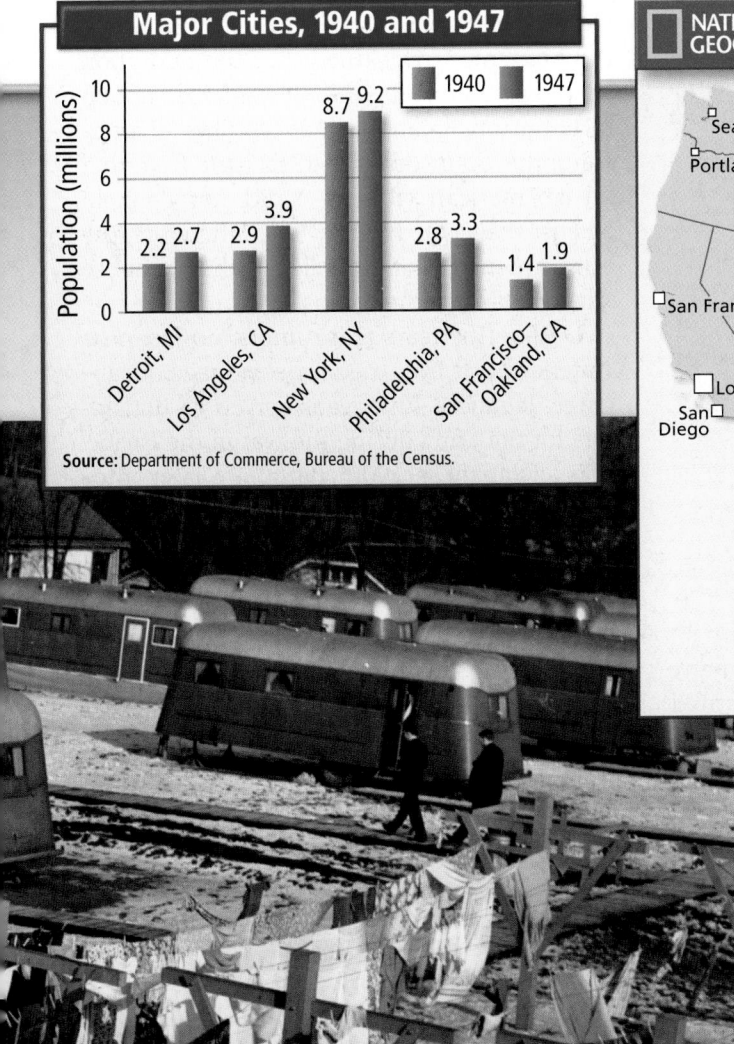

Major Cities, 1940 and 1947

Population (millions), 1940 and 1947:

City	1940	1947
Detroit, MI	2.2	2.7
Los Angeles, CA	2.9	3.9
New York, NY	8.7	9.2
Philadelphia, PA	2.8	3.3
San Francisco–Oakland, CA	1.4	1.9

Source: Department of Commerce, Bureau of the Census.

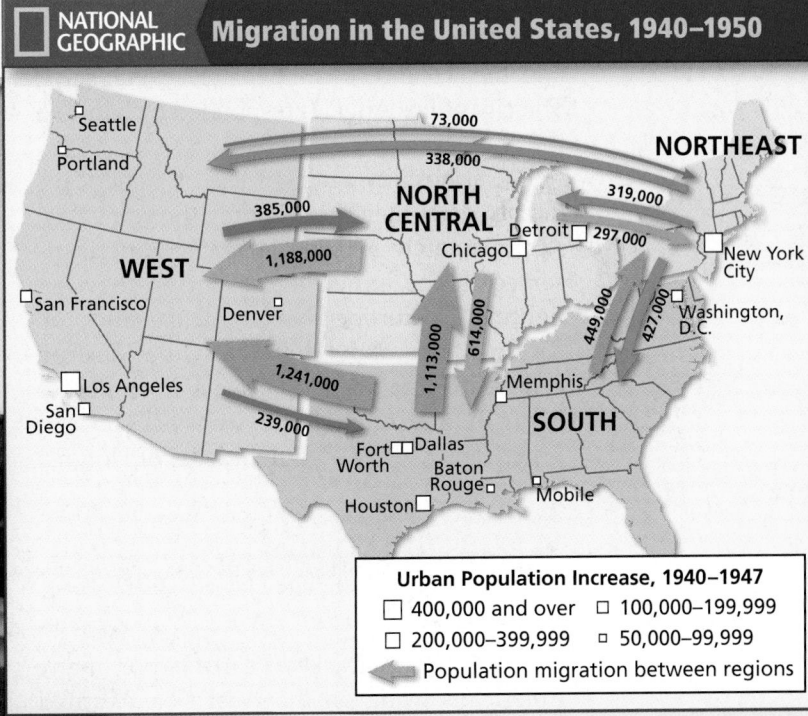

NATIONAL GEOGRAPHIC **Migration in the United States, 1940–1950**

Seattle
Portland
73,000
338,000
NORTHEAST
319,000
385,000
NORTH CENTRAL
1,188,000
Detroit 297,000
Chicago
New York City
WEST
San Francisco
Denver
Washington, D.C.
449,000
427,000
1,113,000
614,000
Los Angeles
1,241,000
Memphis
San Diego
239,000
SOUTH
Fort Worth
Dallas
Baton Rouge
Mobile
Houston

Urban Population Increase, 1940–1947
- ☐ 400,000 and over
- ☐ 100,000–199,999
- ☐ 200,000–399,999
- ☐ 50,000–99,999
- ⬅ Population migration between regions

Analyzing GEOGRAPHY

1. **Movement** What region of the nation had the most total population gain?
2. **Movement** What region of the nation had the largest population loss?

The Zoot Suit Riots

Wartime prejudice boiled over elsewhere as well. In southern California, racial tensions became entangled with juvenile delinquency. Across the nation, the number of crimes committed by young people rose dramatically. In Los Angeles, racism against Mexican Americans and the fear of juvenile crime became linked because of the "zoot suit."

A **zoot suit** had very baggy, pleated pants and an overstuffed, knee-length jacket with wide lapels. Accessories included a wide-brimmed hat and a long key chain. Zoot-suit wearers usually wore their hair long, gathered into a ducktail. The zoot suit angered many Americans. In order to save fabric for the war, most men wore a "**victory suit**"—a suit with no vest, no cuffs, a short jacket, and narrow lapels. To many, the zoot suit was unpatriotic.

In California, Mexican American teenagers adopted the zoot suit. In June 1943, after hearing rumors that zoot-suiters had attacked several sailors, some 2,500 soldiers and sailors stormed into Mexican American neighborhoods in Los Angeles. They attacked Mexican American teenagers, cut their hair, and tore off their zoot suits. The police did not intervene, and the violence continued for several days. The city of Los Angeles responded by banning the zoot suit.

Racial hostility against Mexican Americans did not deter them from joining the war effort. Approximately 500,000 Hispanic Americans served in the armed forces during the war, fighting in Europe, North Africa, and the Pacific. Most—about 400,000—were Mexican American. Another 65,000 were from Puerto Rico. By the end of the war, 17 Mexican Americans had received the Medal of Honor.

Japanese American Relocation

When Japan attacked Pearl Harbor, many Americans living on the West Coast turned their anger against Japanese immigrants and Japanese Americans. Mobs attacked their businesses and homes. Banks would not cash their checks, and grocers refused to sell them food.

Newspapers printed rumors about Japanese spies in the Japanese American community.

Members of Congress, mayors, and many business and labor leaders demanded that all people of Japanese ancestry be removed from the West Coast. They did not believe that Japanese Americans would remain loyal to the United States in the war with Japan.

On February 19, 1942, President Roosevelt signed an order allowing the War Department to declare any part of the United States a military zone and to remove people from that zone. He must have felt **justified** only four days later, when a Japanese submarine surfaced north of Santa Barbara, California, and shelled an oil refinery, or in September of that year, when Japanese bombers twice dropped bombs on an Oregon forest. American fears of a Japanese attack on the West Coast must have seemed reasonable. Secretary of War Henry Stimson declared most of the West Coast a military zone and ordered all people of Japanese ancestry to evacuate to 10 internment camps further inland.

Not all Japanese Americans accepted the relocation without protest. Fred Korematsu argued that his rights had been violated and took his case to the Supreme Court. In December 1944, in *Korematsu* v. *United States,* the Supreme Court ruled that the relocation was constitutional because it was based not on race, but on "military urgency." Shortly afterward, the Court did rule in *Ex parte Endo* that loyal American citizens could not be held against their will. In early 1945, therefore, the government began to release the Japanese Americans from the camps.

Despite the fears and rumors, no Japanese American was ever tried for espionage or sabotage. Japanese Americans served as translators for the army during the war in the Pacific. The all-Japanese 100th Battalion, later integrated into the 442nd Regimental Combat Team, was the most highly decorated unit in World War II.

After the war, the Japanese American Citizens League (JACL) tried to help Japanese Americans who had lost property during the relocation. In 1988 President Ronald Reagan apologized to Japanese Americans on behalf of the U.S. government and signed legislation granting $20,000 to each surviving Japanese American who had been interned.

✔ Reading Check **Comparing** Why did millions of people relocate during the war?

ANALYZING SUPREME COURT CASES

Can the Government Limit Civil Liberties in Wartime?

Korematsu v. United States, 1944

Background to the Case

During World War II, President Roosevelt's Executive Order 9066 and other legislation gave the military the power to exclude people of Japanese descent from areas that were deemed important to U.S. national defense and security. In 1942, Toyosaburo Korematsu refused to leave San Leandro, California, which had been designated as a "military area," based on Executive Order 9066. Korematsu was found guilty in federal district court of violating Civilian Exclusion Order No. 34. Korematsu petitioned the Supreme Court to review the federal court's decision.

How the Court Ruled

In their decision, the majority of the Supreme Court, with three dissenting, found that, although exclusion orders based on race are constitutionally suspect, the government is justified in time of "emergency and peril" to suspend citizens' civil rights. A request for a rehearing of the case in 1945 was denied.

▲ *Japanese American women and their children talk together at the Heart Mountain Relocation Camp.*

The Court's Opinion

"It should be noted, to begin with, that all legal restrictions which curtail the civil rights of a single racial group are immediately suspect. That is not to say that all such restrictions are unconstitutional. It is to say that courts must subject them to the most rigid scrutiny. Pressing public necessity may sometimes justify the existence of such restrictions; racial antagonism never can. . . . Korematsu was not excluded from the Military Area because of hostility to him or his race. He was excluded because . . . the properly constituted military authorities feared an invasion of our West Coast [by Japan] and felt constrained to take proper security measures, because they decided that the military urgency of the situation demanded that all citizens of Japanese ancestry be segregated from the West Coast temporarily, and finally, because Congress . . . determined that they should have the power to do just this."

—Justice Hugo Black
writing for the court in
Korematsu v. United States

Dissenting View

"I dissent, because I think the indisputable facts exhibit a clear violation of Constitutional rights. This is not . . . a case of temporary exclusion of a citizen from an area for his own safety or that of the community, nor a case of offering him an opportunity to go temporarily out of an area where his presence might cause danger to himself or to his fellows. On the contrary, it is the case of convicting a citizen as a punishment for not submitting to imprisonment in a concentration camp, based on his ancestry, and solely because of his ancestry, without evidence or inquiry concerning his loyalty and good disposition towards the United States. If this be a correct statement of the facts disclosed by this record, and facts of which we take judicial notice, I need hardly labor the conclusion that Constitutional rights have been violated."

—Justice Owen J. Roberts, dissenting in
Korematsu v. United States

DBQ Document-Based Questions

1. **Explaining** Why did the Supreme Court find in favor of the government in this case, even though the justices were suspicious of exclusion based on race?

2. **Contrasting** Why did Justice Roberts disagree with the majority opinion?

3. **Analyzing** Under what circumstances, if any, do you think the government should be able to suspend civil liberties of all or specific groups of American citizens?

Daily Life in Wartime

MAIN Idea The federal government took steps to stabilize wages and prices, as well as to prevent strikes. Americans supported the war through rationing, growing food, recycling, and buying bonds.

HISTORY AND YOU Have you ever given up something you enjoyed for a short period of time to gain something greater? Read on to learn how Americans sacrificed during the war.

Housing shortages and racial tensions were serious difficulties during the war, but mobilization strained society in other ways as well. Prices rose, materials were in short supply, and the question of how to pay for the war loomed ominously over the war effort.

Wage and Price Controls

Both wages and prices began to rise quickly during the war because of the high demand for workers and raw materials. The president worried about inflation. To stabilize both wages and prices, Roosevelt created the **Office of Price Administration** (OPA) and the Office of Economic Stabilization (OES). The OES regulated wages and the price of farm products. The OPA regulated all other prices. Despite some problems with labor unions, the OPA and OES kept inflation under control. At the end of the war, prices had risen only about half as much as they had during World War I.

While the OPA and OES worked to control inflation, the War Labor Board (WLB) tried to prevent strikes. In support, most American unions issued a "no strike pledge." Instead of striking, unions asked the WLB to mediate wage disputes. By the end of the war, the WLB had helped to settle more than 17,000 disputes involving more than 12 million workers.

Blue Points, Red Points

The demand for raw materials and supplies created shortages. The OPA began **rationing,** or limiting the purchase of, many products to make sure enough were available for military use. Meat and sugar were rationed. Gasoline was rationed, driving distances were restricted, and the speed limit was set at 35 miles per hour to save gas and rubber.

Hollywood Goes to War

In 1942 President Roosevelt created the Office of War Information (OWI). The OWI's role was to improve the public's understanding of the war and to act as a liaison office with the various media. The OWI established detailed guidelines for filmmakers, including a set of questions to be considered before making a movie, such as, "Will this picture help win the war?"

▲ Movies ranged from a comic Daffy Duck cartoon to a serious portrayal of a bombing raid on Germany.

◄ Chaplin, noted as a comic and a director, made this movie in 1940, before the United States entered the war.

Analyzing VISUALS

1. **Interpreting** How would heroic movies like *The Memphis Belle* help win the war?

2. **Analyzing** Why do you think so many movies about Hitler were comedies?

A person from each household picked up a book of ration coupons every month. Blue coupons, called blue points, controlled processed foods. Red coupons, or red points, controlled meats, fats, and oils. Other coupons controlled items such as coffee, shoes, and sugar. Thirteen rationing programs were in effect at the height of the program. When people bought food, they also had to give enough coupon points to cover their purchases. Most rationing ended before the war was over. Sugar and rubber rationing continued after the war; sugar was rationed until 1947.

Victory Gardens and Scrap Drives

Americans also planted gardens to produce more food for the war effort. Any area of land might become a garden—backyards, school yards, city parks, and empty lots. The government encouraged **victory gardens** by praising them in film reels, pamphlets, and official statements.

Certain raw materials were so vital to the war effort that the government organized scrap drives. Volunteers collected spare rubber, tin, aluminum, and steel. They donated pots, tires, tin cans, car bumpers, broken radiators, and rusting bicycles. Oils and fats were so important to the production of explosives that the WPB set up fat-collecting stations. Americans would exchange bacon grease and meat drippings for extra ration coupons. The scrap drives boosted morale and did contribute to the success of American industry during the war.

Paying for the War

The federal government spent more than $300 billion during World War II—more money than it had spent from Washington's administration to the end of Franklin Roosevelt's second term. To raise money, the government raised taxes. Because most Americans opposed large tax increases, Congress refused to raise taxes as high as Roosevelt requested. As a result, the extra taxes collected covered only 45 percent of the war's cost.

The government issued war bonds to make up the difference between what was needed and what taxes supplied. Buying bonds is a way to lend money to the government. In exchange for the money, the government promises to repay the bonds' purchase price plus interest at some future date. The most common bonds during World War II were E bonds, which sold for $18.75 and could be redeemed for $25.00 after 10 years. Individuals bought nearly $50 billion worth of war bonds. Banks, insurance companies, and other financial institutions bought the rest— more than $100 billion worth of bonds.

Despite the hardships, the overwhelming majority of Americans believed the war had to be fought. Although the war brought many changes to the United States, most Americans remained united behind one goal—winning the war.

Reading Check **Evaluating** How did rationing affect daily life in the United States? How did it affect the economy?

Section 3 REVIEW

Vocabulary

1. **Explain** the significance of: A. Philip Randolph, Bracero Program, Sunbelt, Great Migration, zoot suit, victory suit, Office of Price Administration, rationing, victory garden.

Main Ideas

2. **Assessing** Why were jobs suddenly available to women and minorities?

3. **Evaluating** For what reasons did Americans relocate during the war?

4. **Explaining** How did the federal government control the economy during the war?

Critical Thinking

5. **Big Ideas** What challenges did Americans at home face during the war?

6. **Organizing** Use a graphic organizer like the one below to list the results of increased racial tensions during the war.

Racial Tensions

Result   Result   Result

7. **Analyzing Visuals** Look again at the photograph on pages 730–731. How does the photographer capture the feeling of people settling into a new area?

Writing About History

8. **Persuasive Writing** Write a newspaper editorial urging fellow citizens to conserve resources so that those resources can be used in the war effort.

History ONLINE

Study Central™ To review this section, go to <u>glencoe.com</u> and click on Study Central.

Section 4

Pushing Back the Axis

Guide to Reading

Big Ideas

Geography and History The Allies slowly pushed back the German and Japanese forces during 1943 and 1944.

Content Vocabulary
- amphtrac (p. 742)
- kamikaze (p. 743)

Academic Vocabulary
- briefly (p. 740)
- intense (p. 740)

People and Events to Identify
- Casablanca Conference (p. 736)
- D-Day (p. 740)
- Omar Bradley (p. 740)
- Guadalcanal (p. 743)

Reading Strategy

Organizing Complete a graphic organizer similar to the one below by filling in the names and battles fought. Indicate whether Allied or Axis forces won the battle.

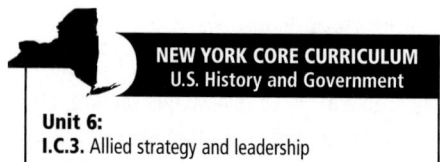

NEW YORK CORE CURRICULUM
U.S. History and Government

Unit 6:
I.C.3. Allied strategy and leadership

After British and American troops won victories over the Axis in North Africa and Italy, Allied leaders made plans for an invasion of Europe. Led by Admiral Nimitz and General MacArthur, American forces steadily advanced across the Pacific.

Striking Germany and Italy

MAIN Idea The Allies stepped up bombing of Germany and invaded Sicily and Italy.

HISTORY AND YOU Have you ever talked over your ideas with a good friend whose opinion you value? Read on to learn about FDR's meetings with Churchill and Stalin.

The Allied invasion of North Africa in November 1942 had shown that a large-scale invasion from the sea was possible. The success of the landings convinced Roosevelt to meet again with Churchill to plan the next stage of the war. In January 1943, FDR headed to Casablanca, Morocco, to meet the prime minister.

At the **Casablanca Conference,** Roosevelt and Churchill agreed to step up the bombing of Germany. The goal of this new campaign was "the progressive destruction of the German military, industrial, and economic system, and the undermining of the morale of the German people." The Allies also agreed to attack the Axis on the island of Sicily. Churchill called Italy the "soft underbelly" of Europe. He was convinced that the Italians would quit the war if the Allies invaded their homeland.

Strategic Bombing

The Allies had been bombing Germany even before the Casablanca Conference. Britain's Royal Air Force had dropped an average of 2,300 tons (2,093 t) of explosives on Germany every month for more than three years. The United States Eighth Army Air Force had dropped an additional 1,500 tons (1,365 t) of bombs during the last six months of 1942. These numbers were small, however, compared to the massive new campaign. Between January 1943 and May 1945, the Royal Air Force and the United States Eighth Army Air Force dropped approximately 53,000 tons (48,230 t) of explosives on Germany every month.

The bombing campaign did not destroy Germany's economy or undermine German morale, but it did cause a severe oil shortage and wrecked the railroad system. It also destroyed so many aircraft factories that Germany's air force could not replace its losses. By the time

Important Battles of World War II

1 **El Alamein,** Nov. 1942. British forces defeat German forces commanded by Rommel, preventing German control of North Africa.

2 **Stalingrad,** Nov. 1942. A large German force is defeated at the city of Stalingrad, ending German hopes of defeating the Soviet Union.

3 **Kasserine Pass,** Feb.–May 1943. American troops fight German forces for the first time and are badly beaten.

4 **Leningrad,** Sept. 1941–Jan. 1944. The Russians hold off the Germans besieging the city of Leningrad for 900 days.

5 **Sicily,** July–Aug. 1943. Allies land in Sicily; begin the liberation of Italy.

6 **Anzio,** Jan.–May 1944. U.S. forces land near Rome behind German lines.

7 **D-Day,** June 1944. Allies land at Normandy; begin liberation of France.

8 **Operation Market Garden,** Sept. 1944. Allied troops parachute into the Netherlands to seize bridges across the Rhine, but attack fails.

9 **Battle of the Bulge,** Dec. 1944–Jan. 1945. Last large German counter-attack against American and British troops is halted.

Analyzing GEOGRAPHY

1. **Place** Into what country did the Allies land for Operation Market Garden?

2. **Region** What Allied victories are shown in North Africa?

Maps In Motion See *StudentWorks™ Plus* or glencoe.com.

the Allies landed in France, they had control of the air, ensuring that their troops would not be bombed.

Striking the Soft Underbelly

As the bombing campaign against Germany intensified, plans to invade Sicily also moved ahead. General Dwight D. Eisenhower commanded the invasion, with General Patton and the British General Bernard Montgomery head-

ing the ground forces. The invasion began before dawn on July 10, 1943. Despite bad weather, the Allied troops made it ashore with few casualties. A new amphibious truck delivered supplies and artillery to the soldiers on the beach.

Eight days after the troops came ashore, American tanks smashed through enemy lines and captured the western half of the island. Patton's troops then headed east, while the British attacked from the south. By August 18, the Germans had evacuated the island.

The attack on Sicily created a crisis within the Italian government. The king of Italy, Victor Emmanuel, and a group of Italian generals decided that it was time to depose Mussolini. On July 25, 1943, the king invited the dictator to his palace. "My dear Duce," the king began, "it's no longer any good. Italy has gone to bits. The soldiers don't want to fight anymore. At this moment, you are the most hated man in Italy." The king then arrested Mussolini, and the new Italian government began negotiating a surrender to the Allies.

Following Italy's surrender, however, German troops seized control of northern Italy, including Rome, and returned Mussolini to power. The Germans then took up positions near the heavily fortified town of Cassino. The terrain near Cassino was steep, barren, and rocky. Rather than attack such difficult terrain, the Allies landed at Anzio, behind German lines. Instead of retreating, however, as the Allies had hoped, the Germans surrounded the Allied troops near Anzio.

It took the Allies five months to break through the German lines at Cassino and Anzio. Finally, in late May 1944, the Germans retreated. Less than two weeks later, the Allies captured Rome. Fighting in Italy continued, however, for another year. The Italian campaign was one of the bloodiest in the war, with more than 300,000 Allied casualties.

The Tehran Conference

Roosevelt wanted to meet with Stalin before the Allies invaded France. In late 1943, Stalin agreed, proposing that Roosevelt and Churchill meet him in Tehran, Iran.

The leaders reached several agreements. Stalin promised to launch a full-scale offensive against the Germans when the Allies invaded France in 1944. Roosevelt and Stalin then agreed to divide Germany after the war so that it would never again threaten world peace. Stalin promised that once Germany was defeated, the Soviet Union would help the United States against Japan. He also accepted Roosevelt's proposal of an international peace-keeping organization after the war.

✔ Reading Check **Explaining** What effect did the Allied victory in Sicily have on Italy?

Driving Back the Germans, 1943–1944

November 28, 1943
Stalin, Roosevelt, and Churchill meet at the Tehran Conference

January 1943
The British and American air forces begin massive strategic bombing of German industry and infrastructure

Jan. 1943 ▸ March 1943 ▸ July 1943 ▸ Dec. 1943 ▸

July 10, 1943
Patton and Montgomery land forces on Sicily, beginning the invasion of Italy

July 25, 1943
The king of Italy puts Mussolini under arrest and the new Italian government negotiates surrender with the Allies

December 4–6, 1943
Roosevelt and Churchill meet in Cairo to plan D-Day. Roosevelt selects Eisenhower to command the invasion

Landing in France

MAIN Idea The Allies landed a massive force on France's beaches on June 6, 1944, known as D-Day.

HISTORY AND YOU What has been the biggest surprise you ever successfully planned? Read on to find out how the Allies made a surprise landing in France.

After the conference in Tehran, Roosevelt headed to Cairo, Egypt, where he and Churchill continued planning the invasion of France. One major decision still had to be made. The president had to choose the commander for Operation Overlord—the code name for the invasion. Roosevelt selected General Eisenhower.

Planning Operation Overlord

Knowing that the Allies would eventually invade France, Hitler had fortified the coast along the English Channel. The Allies did have the advantage of surprise, because the Germans did not know when or where the Allies would land. The Germans believed the Allies would land in Pas-de-Calais—the area of France closest to Britain. The Allies placed dummy equipment along the coast across from Calais as decoys. The real target was to be further south, at five beaches covering a 60-mile spread along the Normandy coast.

By the spring of 1944, more than 1.5 million American soldiers, 12,000 airplanes, and 5 million tons (4.6 million t) of equipment had been sent to England. Only one thing was left to do—pick the date for the invasion and give the command to go. The invasion had to begin at night to hide the ships crossing the English Channel. The ships had to arrive at low tide so that they could see the beach obstacles. The low tide had to come at dawn so that gunners bombarding the coast could see their targets. Paratroopers, who would be dropped behind enemy lines before the main landing on the beaches, needed a moonlit night to see where to land. Perhaps most important of all, the weather had to be good. A storm would ground the airplanes, and high waves would swamp landing craft.

March 4, 1944
The Allies make their first major daylight bombing raid on Berlin

June 6, 1944
Over 130,000 American, British, and Canadian troops land in Normandy on D-Day, beginning the liberation of France

Jan. 1944 ▷ June 1944 ▷

January 1944
American forces attack Monte Cassino and land at Anzio in an attempt to break through German lines and capture Rome

Analyzing TIME LINES

1. **Identifying** On what date did Allied forces land at Normandy to begin liberating France, and what is the date known as?

2. **Determining Cause and Effect** What effect did the successful Allied invasion of Sicily have on politics in Italy?

Given all these requirements, there were only a few days each month when the invasion could begin. The first opportunity was from June 5 to 7, 1944. Eisenhower's planning staff referred to the day any operation began by the letter *D*. The date for the invasion, therefore, came to be known as **D-Day.** Heavy cloud cover, strong winds, and high waves made landing on June 5 impossible. The weather was forecast to improve **briefly** a day later. The Channel would still be rough, but the landing ships and aircraft could operate. After looking at forecasts one last time, shortly after midnight on June 6, 1944, Eisenhower gave the final order: "OK, we'll go."

The Longest Day

Nearly 7,000 ships carrying more than 100,000 soldiers headed for Normandy's coast. At the same time, 23,000 paratroopers were dropped inland, east and west of the beaches. Allied fighter-bombers raced up and down the coast, hitting bridges, bunkers, and radar sites. At dawn, Allied warships began a tremendous barrage. Thousands of shells rained down on the beaches, code-named "Utah," "Omaha," "Gold," "Sword," and "Juno."

The American landing at Utah Beach went well. The German defenses were weak, and in less than three hours the troops had captured the beach and moved inland, suffering fewer than 200 casualties. On the eastern flank, the British and Canadian landings also went well. By the end of the day, British and Canadian forces were several miles inland. Omaha Beach, however, was a different story. Under **intense** German fire, the American assault almost disintegrated. Lieutenant John Bentz Carroll was in the first wave that went ashore:

PRIMARY SOURCE

"Two hundred yards out, we took a direct hit. . . . Somehow or other, the ramp door opened up . . . and the men in front were being struck by machine-gun fire. Everyone started to jump off into the water. . . . The tide was moving us so rapidly. . . . We would grab out on some of those underwater obstructions and mines built on telephone poles and girders, and hang on. We'd take cover, then make a dash through the surf to the next one, fifty feet beyond."

—from *D-Day: Piercing the Atlantic Wall*

General **Omar Bradley,** commander of the American forces landing at Omaha and Utah, began making plans to evacuate. Slowly, however, the American troops began to knock out the German defenses. More landing craft arrived, ramming their way through the obstacles to get to the beach. Nearly 2,500 Americans were either killed or wounded on Omaha, but by early afternoon, Bradley received this message: "Troops formerly pinned down on beaches . . . [are] advancing up heights behind beaches." By the end of the day, nearly 35,000 American troops had landed at Omaha, and another 23,000 had landed at Utah. More than 75,000 British and Canadian troops were on shore as well. The invasion—the largest amphibious operation in history—had succeeded.

Reading Check **Summarizing** What conditions had to be met before Eisenhower could order D-Day to begin?

PRIMARY SOURCE

The United States began island-hopping across the Pacific with the Battle of Tarawa in November 1943. Reporter Robert Sherrod witnessed the savage hand-to-hand fighting:

"A Marine jumped over the seawall and began throwing blocks of fused TNT into a coconut-log pillbox. . . . Two more Marines scaled the seawall, one of them carrying a twin-cylindered tank strapped to their shoulders, the other holding the nozzle of the flame thrower. As another charge of TNT boomed inside the pillbox, causing smoke and dust to billow out, a khaki-clad figure ran out the side entrance. The flame thrower, waiting for him, caught him in its withering stream of intense fire. As soon as it touched him, the [Japanese soldier] flared up like a piece of celluloid. He was dead instantly . . . charred almost to nothingness."

—from *Tarawa: The Story of a Battle*

Driving Japan Back

MAIN Idea American troops slowly regained islands in the Pacific that the Japanese had captured.

HISTORY AND YOU Have you ever had to do a project over? Read to learn about American forces that took back Pacific islands from the Japanese.

While the buildup for invading France was taking place in Britain, American military leaders were also developing a strategy to defeat Japan. The American plan called for a two-pronged attack. The Pacific Fleet, commanded by Admiral Nimitz, would advance through the central Pacific by "hopping" from one island to the next, closer and closer to Japan. Meanwhile, General MacArthur's troops would advance through the Solomon Islands, capture the north coast of New Guinea, and then launch an invasion to retake the Philippines.

Island-Hopping in the Pacific

By the fall of 1943, the navy was ready to launch its island-hopping campaign, but the geography of the central Pacific posed a problem. Many of the islands were coral reef atolls. The water over the coral reef was not always deep enough to allow landing craft to get to the shore. If the landing craft ran aground on the reef, the troops would have to wade to the beach. As some 5,000 United States Marines learned at Tarawa Atoll, wading ashore could cause very high casualties. Tarawa, part of the Gilbert Islands, was the navy's first objective. The Japanese base there had to be captured in order to put air bases in the nearby Marshall Islands.

NATIONAL GEOGRAPHIC Island-Hopping in the Pacific, 1942–1945

◄ Marines are shown firing from behind sand bags during the battle of Tarawa. One Marine has just thrown a hand grenade.

SOVIET UNION
Sakhalin
Attu May 11–27, 1943
Aleutian Is.
Kiska
MONGOLIA
MANCHURIA
Kuril Is.
40°N
160°W
140°W
Beijing
Sea of Japan
Hiroshima Aug. 6, 1945
Tokyo
Japan surrenders on battleship *Missouri* Sept. 2, 1945
PACIFIC OCEAN
CHINA
Chongqing
Nanjing
Yellow R.
Shanghai
Nagasaki Aug. 9, 1945
Midway June 4–7, 1942
Yangtze R.
Okinawa
Okinawa Apr. 1– June 22, 1945
Iwo Jima Feb. 19–March 26, 1945
INDIA
Hawaiian Islands
Lashio
Hong Kong U.K.
Philippine Sea
Wake Island U.K.
Pearl Harbor
20°N
BURMA
Luzon
Manila March 4, 1945
PHILIPPINES
Saipan June 15–July 9, 1944
Marshall Islands Feb. 1944
0   1,000 kilometers
SIAM (THAILAND)
Bangkok
South China Sea
Leyte Gulf Oct. 23–26, 1944
Guam
Guam U.S.
Guam July 21– Aug. 10, 1944
Nimitz, Nov. 1943
0   1,000 miles
FRENCH INDOCHINA
Mindanao
MacArthur
Palau Is.
Miller projection
Singapore U.K.
Halsey
Tarawa Nov. 20–23, 1943
EQUATOR
0°
Borneo
Halsey
Nauru U.K.
Gilbert Is.
Batavia
Java
NEW GUINEA
Solomon Is.
Guadalcanal Aug. 7, 1942– Feb. 9, 1943
Ellice Is.
INDIAN OCEAN
Darwin
Coral Sea May 4–8, 1942
New Hebrides
100°E
120°E
Coral Sea

Japanese Empire and conquests
Farthest extent of Japan's conquests, July 1942
Allied forces
Major battle
Atomic bombing

AUSTRALIA

140°E
160°E

Analyzing GEOGRAPHY

1. **Place** When Nimitz left Pearl Harbor, what was his destination?

2. **Place** Who controlled Guam in 1942?

People IN HISTORY

The Navajo Code Talkers

When American marines stormed an enemy beach, they used radios to communicate. Using radios, however, meant that the Japanese could intercept and translate the messages. In the midst of the battle, however, there was no time to use a code-machine. Acting upon the suggestion of Philip Johnston, an engineer who had lived on a Navajo reservation as a child, the marines recruited Navajos to serve as "code talkers."

The Navajo language had no written alphabet and was known only to the Navajo and a few missionaries and anthropologists. The Navajo recruits developed code words, using their own language, that stood for military terms. For example, the Navajo word *jay-sho*, or "buzzard," was code for *bomber; lotso,* or "whale," meant *battleship;* and *na-ma-si,* or "potatoes," stood for *grenades.*

Code talkers proved invaluable in combat. They could relay a message in minutes that would have taken a code-machine operator hours to encipher and transmit. At the battle of Iwo Jima, code talkers transmitted more than 800 messages during the first 48 hours as the marines struggled to get ashore under intense bombardment. More than 400 Navajo served in the marine corps as code talkers. Sworn to secrecy, their mission was not revealed until 1971. In 2001 Congress awarded the code talkers the Congressional Gold Medal for their unique contribution during the war.

What advantage did the code talkers provide over traditional forms of communication?

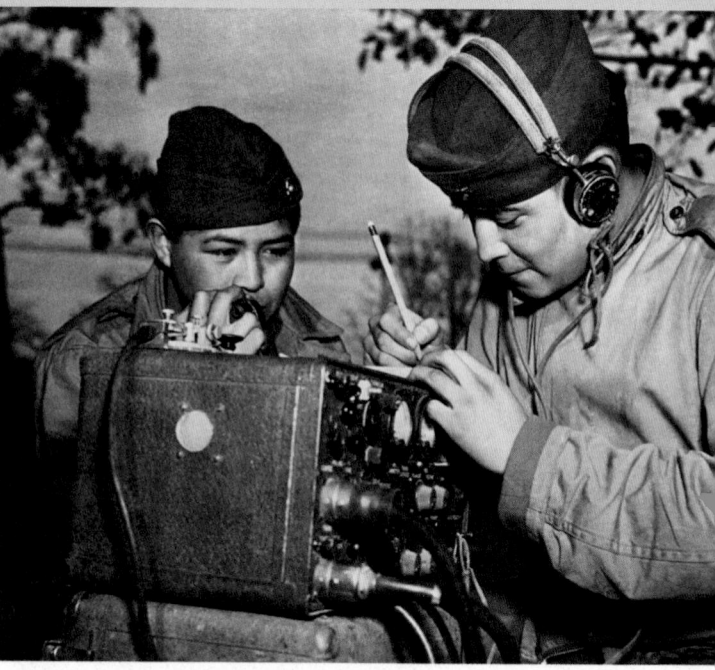

▲ *These Navajo code talkers assigned to a Pacific-based marine regiment relay orders using a field radio.*

When the landing craft hit the reef, at least 20 ships ran aground. The marines had to plunge into shoulder-high water and wade several hundred yards to the beach. Raked by Japanese fire, only one marine in three made it ashore. Once the marines reached the beach, the battle was still far from over.

Although many troops died wading ashore, one vehicle had been able to cross the reef and deliver its troops onto the beaches. The vehicle was a boat with tank tracks, nicknamed the "Alligator." This amphibious tractor, or **amphtrac,** had been invented in the late 1930s to rescue people in Florida swamps. It had never been used in combat, and the navy decided to buy only 200 of them in 1941. If more had been available at Tarawa, American casualties probably would have been much lower.

More than 1,000 marines died on Tarawa. Photos of bodies lying crumpled next to burning landing craft shocked Americans back home. Many people began to wonder how many lives would be lost in defeating Japan.

The next assault—Kwajalein Atoll in the Marshall Islands—went much more smoothly. This time all of the troops went ashore in amphtracs. Although the Japanese resisted fiercely, the marines captured Kwajalein and nearby Eniwetok with far fewer casualties.

After the Marshall Islands, the navy targeted the Mariana Islands. American military planners wanted to use the Marianas as a base for a new heavy bomber, the B-29 Superfortress. The B-29 could fly farther than any other plane in the world. From airfields in the Marianas, B-29s could bomb Japan. Admiral Nimitz decided to invade three of the Mariana Islands: Saipan, Tinian, and Guam. Despite strong Japanese resistance, American troops captured all three by August 1944. A few months later, B-29s began bombing Japan.

MacArthur Returns

As the forces under Admiral Nimitz hopped across the central Pacific, General Douglas MacArthur's troops began their own campaign in the southwest Pacific. The campaign began by invading **Guadalcanal** in the Solomon Islands, east of New Guinea, in August 1942. It continued until early 1944, when MacArthur's troops finally captured enough islands to surround the main Japanese base in the region. In response, the Japanese withdrew their ships and aircraft from the base, although they left 100,000 troops behind to hold the island.

Worried that the navy's advance across the central Pacific was leaving him behind, MacArthur ordered his forces to leap nearly 600 miles (966 km) to capture the Japanese base at Hollandia on the north coast of New Guinea. Shortly after securing New Guinea, MacArthur's troops seized the island of Morotai—the last stop before the Philippines.

To take back the Philippines, the United States assembled an enormous invasion force. In October 1944, more than 700 ships carrying more than 160,000 troops sailed for Leyte Gulf in the Philippines. On October 20, the troops began to land on Leyte, an island on the eastern side of the Philippines. A few hours after the invasion began, MacArthur headed to the beach. Upon reaching the shore, he strode to a radio and spoke into the microphone: "People of the Philippines, I have returned. By the grace of Almighty God, our forces stand again on Philippine soil."

To stop the American invasion, the Japanese sent four aircraft carriers toward the Philippines from the north and secretly dispatched another fleet to the west. Believing the Japanese carriers were leading the main attack, most of the American carriers protecting the invasion left Leyte Gulf and headed north to stop them. Seizing their chance, the Japanese warships to the west raced through the Philippine Islands into Leyte Gulf and ambushed the remaining American ships.

The Battle of Leyte Gulf was the largest naval battle in history. It was also the first time that the Japanese used **kamikaze** attacks. *Kamikaze* means "divine wind" in Japanese. It refers to the great storm that destroyed the Mongol fleet during its invasion of Japan in the thirteenth century. Kamikaze pilots would deliberately crash their planes into American ships, killing themselves but also inflicting severe damage. Luckily for the Americans, just as their situation was becoming desperate, the Japanese commander, believing more American ships were on the way, ordered a retreat.

Although the Japanese fleet had retreated, the campaign to recapture the Philippines from the Japanese was long and grueling. More than 80,000 Japanese were killed; fewer than 1,000 surrendered. MacArthur's troops did not capture Manila until March 1945. The battle left the city in ruins and more than 100,000 Filipino civilians dead. The remaining Japanese retreated into the rugged terrain north of Manila; they were still fighting in August 1945 when word came that Japan had surrendered.

✓ Reading Check **Describing** What strategy did the United States Navy use to advance across the Pacific?

Section 4 REVIEW

Vocabulary

1. **Explain** the significance of: Casablanca Conference, D-Day, Omar Bradley, amphtrac, Guadalcanal, kamikaze.

Main Ideas

2. **Determining Cause and Effect** What event prompted Italy to surrender?

3. **Describing** Why was D-Day's success so vital to an Allied victory?

4. **Summarizing** What was the military goal in the Pacific?

Critical Thinking

5. **Big Ideas** How did the geography of the Pacific affect American strategy?

6. **Organizing** Use a graphic organizer like the one below to explain the importance of each leader listed in the text.

Leader	Significance
Dwight Eisenhower	
George Patton	
George Marshall	
Omar Bradley	
Douglas MacArthur	

7. **Analyzing Visuals** Look at the photo on page 739 of the D-Day landing. What do you observe about the manner of the landing?

Writing About History

8. **Persuasive Writing** Imagine that you are living in Florida and see the potential for the amphtrac in the war. Write a letter to a member of Congress detailing reasons why it would be a good purchase for the marines.

History ONLINE

Study Central™ To review this section, go to glencoe.com and click on Study Central.

NATIONAL GEOGRAPHIC

GEOGRAPHY & HISTORY

The Battle for Omaha Beach

The selection of a site for the largest amphibious landing in history was one of the biggest decisions of World War II. Allied planners considered coastlines from Denmark to Portugal in search of a sheltered location with firm flat beaches within range of friendly fighter planes in England. There also had to be enough roads and paths to move jeeps and trucks off the beaches and to accommodate the hundreds of thousands of American, Canadian, and British troops set to stream ashore following the invasion. An airfield and a seaport that the Allies could use were also needed. Most important was a reasonable expectation of achieving the element of surprise.

How Did Geography Shape the Battle?

Surrounded at both ends by cliffs that rose wall-like from the sea, Omaha Beach was only four miles long. The entire beach was overlooked by a 150-foot high bluff and there were only five ravines leading from the beach to the top of the bluff.

The Germans made full use of the geographic advantage the 150-foot bluff gave them. They dug trenches and built concrete bunkers for machine guns at the top of the cliffs and positioned them to guard the ravines leading to the beach.

American
British
Canadian

BRITAIN

Portsmouth
Southampton
Portland
Dartmouth
UTAH
OMAHA
GOLD
JUNO
SWORD
Dover
Shoreham
Calais
Straits of Dover
Dieppe
Le Havre
English Channel
Cherbourg
St.-Lo   Caen
NORMANDY
Seine River
FRANCE

0   100 kilometers
0   100 miles
Lambert Azimuthal Equal-Area projection

Once ashore they had to cross 300 yards of open beach to the base of the bluff.

The men had to jump into the water and wade ashore against a strong tide in water that was nearly over their heads.

Analyzing GEOGRAPHY

1. **Location** Why did the Allies choose Normandy as the invasion site?

2. **Human-Environment Interaction** How did geography make the invasion of Omaha Beach difficult?

American troops were carried to Omaha Beach in landing craft. Many of the landing craft came under such intense fire that they opened their front ramp doors early.

745

The War Ends

Guide to Reading

Big Ideas
Individual Action After fierce military campaigns, President Harry S. Truman decided to use atomic weapons against Japan.

Content Vocabulary
• hedgerow (p. 746)
• napalm (p. 749)
• charter (p. 753)

Academic Vocabulary
• despite (p. 748)
• nuclear (p. 751)

People and Events to Identify
• Battle of the Bulge (p. 746)
• V-E Day (p. 747)
• Harry S. Truman (p. 748)
• Iwo Jima (p. 748)
• Manhattan Project (p. 751)
• V-J Day (p. 752)
• United Nations (p. 752)
• Nuremberg Trials (p. 753)

Reading Strategy
Create an outline of the section, using the major headings as the main points. Follow the structure shown below.

> The War Ends
> I. The Third Reich Collapses
>   A.
>   B.
> II.
>   A.
>   B.

NEW YORK CORE CURRICULUM
U.S. History and Government

Unit 6:
I.C.4.a The Manhattan Project (role of refugees)
I.C.4.b Truman's decision to use the atomic bomb against Japan: Hiroshima and Nagasaki
I.C.4.d Japanese war crime trials
I.C.5.d The Nuremberg war crimes trials; later trials of other Nazi criminals, e.g., Eichmann, Barbie

Fierce fighting in both Europe and the Pacific during 1945 led to the defeat of the Axis powers. The Allies began war crimes trials and set up a peacekeeping organization to prevent another global war.

The Third Reich Collapses

MAIN Idea The war in Europe ended in spring 1945 after major battles, as the Allies moved west toward Germany.

HISTORY AND YOU Have you ever been in a competition in which you persevered, despite fatigue, to win? Read to learn how the Allies fought in Europe to defeat Germany.

Although D-Day had been a success, it was only the beginning. Surrounding many fields in Normandy were **hedgerows**—dirt walls, several feet thick, covered in shrubbery. The hedgerows had been built to fence in cattle and crops, but they also enabled the Germans to fiercely defend their positions. The battle of the hedgerows ended on July 25, 1944, when 2,500 American bombers blew a hole in the German lines, enabling American tanks to race through the gap.

As the Allies broke out of Normandy, the French Resistance—French civilians who had secretly organized to resist the German occupation of their country—staged a rebellion in Paris. When the Allied forces liberated Paris on August 25, they found the streets filled with French citizens celebrating their victory.

The Battle of the Bulge

As the Allies advanced toward the German border, Hitler decided to stage one last desperate offensive. His goal was to cut off Allied supplies coming through the port of Antwerp, Belgium. The attack began just before dawn on December 16, 1944. Six inches (15 cm) of snow covered the ground, and the weather was bitterly cold. Moving rapidly, the Germans caught the American defenders by surprise. As the German troops raced west, their lines bulged outward, and the attack became known as the **Battle of the Bulge.**

Shortly after the Germans surrounded the Americans, Eisenhower ordered General Patton to rescue them. Three days later, faster than anyone expected in the midst of a snowstorm, Patton's troops slammed into the German lines. As the weather cleared, Allied aircraft began hitting German fuel depots.

On Christmas Eve, out of fuel and weakened by heavy losses, the German troops driving toward Antwerp were forced to halt. Two days later, Patton's troops broke through to the German line. Although

The War Ends in Europe, 1945

The Axis Before the War, 1939	The Axis at its Peak, 1942	The Axis at German Surrender, 1945

How Many People Died in World War II?		
Country	Military Deaths	Civilian Deaths
USSR	11,000,000	6,700,000
Germany	3,250,000	2,350,000
Japan	1,740,000	393,000
China	1,400,000	8,000,000
Poland	110,000	5,300,000
United States	405,000	2,000
Great Britain	306,000	61,000
Italy	227,000	60,000
France	122,000	470,000

Axis-controlled territory
Allied advances, 1944–45
0   400 kilometers
0   400 miles
Lambert Azimuthal Equal-Area projection

Analyzing VISUALS

1. **Comparing** Which nation had the greatest number of civilian casualties?
2. **Analyzing** Why did the United States have so few civilian deaths?

fighting continued for three weeks, the United States had won the Battle of the Bulge. On January 8, the Germans began to withdraw. They had suffered more than 100,000 casualties and lost many tanks and aircraft. They had very few resources left to prevent the Allies from entering Germany.

The War Ends in Europe

While American and British forces fought to liberate France, the Soviets began a massive attack on German troops in Russia. By the time the Battle of the Bulge ended, the Soviets had driven Hitler's forces out of Russia and back across Poland. By February 1945, Soviet troops were only 35 miles (56 km) from Berlin.

As the Soviets crossed Germany's eastern border, American forces attacked Germany's western border. By the end of February 1945, American troops had fought their way to the Rhine River, Germany's last major line of defense in the west. On March 7, American tanks crossed the Rhine.

As German defenses crumbled, American troops raced east to within 70 miles (113 km) of Berlin. On April 16, Soviet troops finally smashed through the German defenses and reached the outskirts of Berlin five days later.

Deep in his Berlin bunker, Adolf Hitler knew the end was near. On April 30, 1945, he committed suicide. Before killing himself, Hitler chose Grand Admiral Karl Doenitz as his successor. Doenitz tried to surrender to the Americans and British while continuing to fight the Soviets, but Eisenhower insisted on unconditional surrender. On May 7, 1945, Germany accepted the terms. The next day—May 8, 1945—was proclaimed **V-E Day,** for "Victory in Europe."

Reading Check Explaining Why was the Battle of the Bulge such a disastrous defeat for Germany?

Japan Is Defeated

MAIN Idea The United States decided to end the war with Japan by using napalm and atomic bombs.

HISTORY AND YOU When was the last time you had to make a difficult decision, with no really good choice? Read to learn about the decision President Truman made in 1945.

Unfortunately, President Roosevelt did not live to see the defeat of Germany. On April 12, 1945, while vacationing in Warm Springs, Georgia, he died of a stroke. His vice president, **Harry S. Truman,** became president during this difficult time.

The next day, Truman told reporters: "Boys, if you ever pray, pray for me now. . . . When they told me yesterday what had happened, I felt like the moon, the stars, and all the planets had fallen on me." **Despite** his feelings, Truman began at once to make decisions about the war. Although Germany surrendered a few weeks later, the war with Japan continued, and Truman was forced to make some of the most difficult decisions of the war during his first six months in office.

The Battle of Iwo Jima

On November 24, 1944, bombs fell on Tokyo. Above the city flew 80 B-29 Superfortress bombers that had traveled more than 1,500 miles (2,414 km) from new American bases in the Mariana Islands.

At first the B-29s did little damage because they kept missing their targets. By the time the B-29s reached Japan, they did not have enough fuel left to fix their navigational errors or to adjust for high winds. The pilots needed an island closer to Japan so the B-29s could refuel. American military planners decided to invade **Iwo Jima.**

Iwo Jima was perfectly located, roughly halfway between the Marianas and Japan, but its geography was formidable. At its southern tip was a dormant volcano. The terrain was rugged, with rocky cliffs, jagged ravines, and

Winning the War Against Japan, 1944–1945

March 9, 1945
Firebombing destroys most of Tokyo

April 1, 1945
American troops land on Okinawa

Feb. 1945 ▷ **April 1945** ▷ **June 1945** ▷

October 23–24, 1944
Victory in the Battle of Leyte Gulf enables MacArthur to return to the Philippines

February 19, 1945
U.S. Marines land on Iwo Jima; over 6,800 marines are killed before the island is captured

dozens of caves. Volcanic ash covered the ground. Even worse, the Japanese had built a vast network of concrete bunkers connected by miles of tunnels.

On February 19, 1945, some 60,000 Marines landed on Iwo Jima. As the troops leapt from the amphtracs, they sank up to their ankles in the soft ash. Meanwhile, Japanese artillery began to pound the invaders.

The marines crawled inland, using flame-throwers and explosives to attack the Japanese bunkers. More than 6,800 marines were killed capturing the island. Admiral Nimitz later wrote that, on Iwo Jima, "uncommon valor was a common virtue."

Firebombing Japan

While American engineers prepared airfields on Iwo Jima, General Curtis LeMay, commander of the B-29s based in the Marianas, decided to change strategy. To help the B-29s hit their targets, he ordered them to drop bombs filled with **napalm**—a kind of jellied gasoline. The bombs were designed not only to explode but also to start fires. Even if the B-29s missed their targets, the fires they started would spread to the intended targets.

The use of firebombs was very controversial because the fires would also kill civilians; however, LeMay could think of no other way to destroy Japan's war production quickly. Loaded with firebombs, B-29s attacked Tokyo on March 9, 1945. As strong winds fanned the flames, the firestorm grew so intense that it sucked the oxygen out of the air, asphyxiating thousands. As one survivor later recalled:

PRIMARY SOURCE

"The fires were incredible . . . with flames leaping hundreds of feet into the air. . . . With every passing moment the air became more foul. . . the noise was a continuing crashing roar. . . . Fire-winds filled with burning particles rushed up and down the streets. I watched people . . . running for their lives. . . . The flames raced after them like living things, striking them down. . . . Wherever I turned my eyes, I saw people . . . seeking air to breathe."

—quoted in *New History of World War II*

August 9, 1945
A second atomic bomb is dropped on Japan, destroying the city of Nagasaki

September 2, 1945
The Japanese delegation boards the battleship USS *Missouri* in Tokyo Bay for the official surrender ceremony

August 1945

August 6, 1945
An atomic bomb destroys the Japanese city of Hiroshima

Analyzing TIME LINES

1. **Listing** When was Tokyo destroyed?
2. **Sequencing** How many days lapsed between the dropping of the first and second atomic bombs?

The Tokyo firebombing killed more than 80,000 people and destroyed more than 250,000 buildings. By the end of June 1945, Japan's six most important industrial cities had been firebombed, destroying almost half of their total urban area. By the end of the war, the B-29s had firebombed 67 Japanese cities.

The Invasion of Okinawa

Despite the massive damage the firebombing caused, there were few signs in the spring of 1945 that Japan was ready to quit. Many American officials believed the Japanese would not surrender until Japan had been invaded. To prepare for the invasion, the United States needed a base near Japan to stockpile supplies and build up troops. Iwo Jima was small and still too far away. Military planners chose Okinawa—only 350 miles (563 km) from Japan.

American troops landed on Okinawa on April 1, 1945. Instead of defending the beaches, the Japanese troops took up positions in the island's rugged mountains. To dig the Japanese out of their caves and bunkers, the Americans had to fight their way up steep slopes against constant machine gun and artillery fire. More than 12,000 American soldiers, sailors, and marines died during the fighting, but by June 22, 1945, Okinawa had finally been captured.

The Terms for Surrender

Shortly after the United States captured Okinawa, the Japanese emperor urged his government to find a way to end the war. The biggest problem was the American demand for unconditional surrender. Many Japanese leaders were willing to surrender, but on one condition: the emperor had to stay in power.

American officials knew that the fate of the emperor was the most important issue for the Japanese. Most Americans, however, blamed the emperor for the war and wanted him removed from power. President Truman was reluctant to go against public opinion. Furthermore, he knew the United States was almost ready to test a new weapon that might force Japan to surrender without any conditions. The new weapon was the atomic bomb.

The Manhattan Project

In 1939 Leo Szilard, one of the world's top physicists, learned that German scientists had split the uranium atom. Szilard had been the first scientist to suggest that splitting the atom might release enormous energy. Worried that the Nazis were working on an atomic bomb, Szilard convinced the world's best-known physicist, Albert Einstein, to sign a letter Szilard had drafted and send it to President Roosevelt. In the letter, Einstein warned that by using uranium, "extremely powerful bombs of a new type may . . . be constructed."

Roosevelt responded by setting up a scientific committee to study the issue. The committee remained skeptical until 1941, when they met with British scientists who were already working on an atomic bomb. The British research so impressed the Americans that they

Debates
IN HISTORY

Should America Drop the Atomic Bomb on Japan?

More than 60 years later, people continue to debate what some historians have called the most important event of the twentieth century—President Truman's order to drop atomic bombs on Japan. Did his momentous decision shorten the war and save American lives, as Truman contended, or was it a barbaric and unnecessary show of superior military technology designed to keep the Soviet Union out of Japan?

convinced Roosevelt to begin a program to build an atomic bomb.

The secret American program to build an atomic bomb was code-named the **Manhattan Project** and was headed by General Leslie R. Groves. The first breakthrough came in 1942, when Szilard and Enrico Fermi, another physicist, built the world's first **nuclear** reactor at the University of Chicago. Groves then organized a team of engineers and scientists to build an atomic bomb at a secret laboratory in Los Alamos, New Mexico. J. Robert Oppenheimer led the team. On July 16, 1945, they detonated the world's first atomic bomb in New Mexico.

Hiroshima and Nagasaki

Even before the bomb was tested, American officials began debating how to use it. Admiral William Leahy, chairman of the Joint Chiefs of Staff, opposed using the bomb because it killed civilians indiscriminately. He believed an economic blockade and conventional bombing would convince Japan to surrender. Secretary of War Henry Stimson wanted to warn the Japanese about the bomb while at the same time telling them that they could keep the emperor if they surrendered. Secretary of State James Byrnes, however, wanted to drop the bomb without any warning to shock Japan into surrendering.

President Truman later wrote that he "regarded the bomb as a military weapon and never had any doubts that it should be used." His advisers had warned him to expect massive casualties if the United States invaded Japan. Truman believed it was his duty as president to use every weapon available to save American lives.

YES

Harry S. Truman
President of the United States

PRIMARY SOURCE

"The world will note that the first atomic bomb was dropped on Hiroshima, a military base. . . . If Japan does not surrender, bombs will have to be dropped on her war industries and, unfortunately, thousands of civilian lives will be lost. . . .

Having found the bomb we have used it. We have used it against those who attacked us without warning at Pearl Harbor, against those who have starved and beaten and executed American prisoners of war, against those who have abandoned all pretense of obeying international laws of warfare. We have used it in order to shorten the agony of war, in order to save the lives of thousands and thousands of young Americans."

—from *Public Papers of the Presidents*

NO

William Leahy
Chairman of the Joint Chiefs of Staff

PRIMARY SOURCE

"It is my opinion that the use of this barbarous weapon at Hiroshima and Nagasaki was of no material assistance in our war against Japan. The Japanese were already defeated and ready to surrender because of the effective sea blockade and the successful bombing with conventional weapons. . . .

The lethal possibilities of atomic warfare in the future are frightening. My own feeling was that in being the first to use it, we had adopted an ethical standard common to the barbarians of the Dark Ages. I was not taught to make war in that fashion, and wars cannot be won by destroying women and children."

—from *I Was There*

DBQ Document-Based Questions

1. **Explaining** What reasons does Truman offer to justify the use of the atomic bomb?
2. **Summarizing** Why does Leahy say he was against using the bomb?
3. **Evaluating** Whom do you think makes the more persuasive argument? Explain your answer.

The Allies threatened Japan with "prompt and utter destruction" if the nation did not surrender, but the Japanese did not reply. Truman then ordered the military to drop the bomb. On August 6, 1945, a B-29 bomber named *Enola Gay* dropped an atomic bomb, code-named "Little Boy," on Hiroshima, an important industrial city.

The bomb destroyed about 63 percent of the city. Between 80,000 and 120,000 people died instantly, and thousands more died later from burns and radiation sickness. Three days later, on August 9, the Soviet Union declared war on Japan. Later that day, the United States dropped another atomic bomb, code-named "Fat Man," on the city of Nagasaki, killing between 35,000 and 74,000 people.

Faced with such massive destruction and the shock of the Soviets joining the war, the Japanese emperor ordered his government to surrender. On August 15, 1945—**V-J Day**—Japan surrendered. The long war was over.

✔ Reading Check **Analyzing** What arguments did Truman consider when deciding whether to use the atomic bomb?

Building a New World

MAIN Idea The victorious Allies tried to create an organization to prevent future wars.

HISTORY AND YOU What are some of your most noble goals? Read to learn about the goals of the Allied forces after the war.

Well before the war ended, President Roosevelt had begun thinking about what the world would be like after the war. The president had wanted to ensure that war would never again engulf the world.

Creating the United Nations

President Roosevelt believed that a new international political organization could prevent another world war. In 1944, at the Dumbarton Oaks estate in Washington, D.C., delegates from 39 countries met to discuss the new organization, which was to be called the **United Nations** (UN). The delegates at the conference agreed that the UN would have a General Assembly, in which every member

Plans for a Better World

▲ *The Nuremberg trials*

DBQ **Document-Based Questions**

1. **Identifying** Which right relates to free elections?

2. **Speculating** Why do you think that the right to an education might be so far down on the list?

3. **Evaluating** Which five of the human rights included in the Declaration do you feel are the most important today? Why?

The Universal Declaration of Human Rights
Issued by the United Nations, December 10, 1948

1. All human beings are born free and equal in dignity and rights.
3. Everyone has the right to life, liberty, and security of person.
4. No one shall be held in slavery or servitude . . .
5. No one shall be subjected to torture or to cruel, inhuman or degrading treatment or punishment.
7. All are equal before the law and are entitled without any discrimination to equal protection of the law.
11. Everyone charged with a penal offense has the right to be presumed innocent until proved guilty . . .
13. Everyone has the right to freedom of movement . . .
16. Men and women . . . are entitled to equal rights as to marriage, during marriage and at its dissolution . . .
17. Everyone has the right to own property . . .
18. Everyone has the right to freedom of thought, conscience and religion . . .
19. Everyone has the right to freedom of opinion and expression . . .
20. Everyone has the right to freedom of peaceful assembly and association.
21. The will of the people . . . shall be expressed in periodic and genuine elections which shall be by universal and equal suffrage . . .
23. Everyone has the right to work . . .
25. Everyone has the right to a standard of living adequate for the health and well-being of himself and of his family, including food, clothing, housing and medical care and necessary social services, and the right to security in the event of unemployment, sickness, disability, widowhood, old age or other lack of livelihood . . .
26. Everyone has the right to education . . .

nation in the world would have one vote. The UN would also have a Security Council with 11 members. Five countries would be permanent members of the Security Council: Britain, France, China, the Soviet Union, and the United States—the five big powers that had led the fight against the Axis. These five permanent members would each have veto power.

On April 25, 1945, representatives from 50 countries came to San Francisco to officially organize the United Nations and design its **charter,** or constitution. The General Assembly was given the power to vote on resolutions, to choose the non-permanent members of the Security Council, and to vote on the UN's budget. The Security Council was responsible for international peace and security. It could investigate any international problem and propose settlements. It could also take action to preserve the peace, including asking its members to use military force to uphold a UN resolution.

Soon after its founding, the UN created a Commission on Human Rights and chose Eleanor Roosevelt to serve as its first chair. The Commission drafted the Universal Declaration of Human Rights, and the UN issued it in 1948. The document strongly reflects the ideas and principles that Eleanor Roosevelt espoused during her life. It lists 30 rights that are said to be universally applicable to all human beings in all societies.

Putting the Enemy on Trial

Although the Allies had declared their intention to punish German and Japanese leaders for war crimes, they did not work out the details until the summer of 1945. In August, the United States, Britain, France, and the Soviet Union created the International Military Tribunal (IMT). The Tribunal held trials in Nuremberg, Germany, where Hitler had staged Nazi Party rallies.

Twenty-two leaders of Nazi Germany were prosecuted at the **Nuremberg Trials.** Three were acquitted and seven were given prison sentences. The remaining 12 were sentenced to death. Trials of lower-ranking officials and military officers continued until April 1949. Those trials led to the execution of 24 more German leaders. Another 107 were given prison sentences.

Similar trials were held in Tokyo. The IMT for the Far East charged 25 Japanese leaders with war crimes. Significantly, the Allies did not indict the Japanese emperor. They feared that any attempt to put him on trial would lead to an uprising by the Japanese people. Eighteen Japanese defendants were sentenced to prison. The rest were sentenced to death by hanging.

The war crimes trials punished many of the people responsible for World War II and the Holocaust, but they were also part of the American plan for building a better world. As Robert Jackson, chief counsel for the United States at Nuremberg, observed in his opening statement to the court: "The wrongs we seek to condemn and punish have been so calculated, so malignant and so devastating, that civilization cannot tolerate their being ignored because it cannot survive their being repeated."

Reading Check **Describing** How is the United Nations organized?

Section 5 REVIEW

Vocabulary

1. **Explain** the significance of: hedgerow, Battle of the Bulge, V-E Day, Harry S. Truman, Iwo Jima, napalm, Manhattan Project, V-J Day, United Nations, charter, Nuremberg Trials.

Main Ideas

2. **Explaining** What was the significance of the Battle of the Bulge?

3. **Identifying** What was the advantage of using napalm bombs?

4. **Synthesizing** How was the United Nations designed to prevent global wars?

Critical Thinking

5. **Big Ideas** If you had been a member of President Truman's cabinet, what advice would you have given him about dropping the atomic bomb?

6. **Organizing** Using a graphic organizer like the one below, indicate the steps to victory in Europe and over Japan. Add boxes as needed.

```
        Allied Victory
        /          \
Victory in Europe   Victory over Japan
   [        ]          [        ]
```

7. **Analyzing Visuals** Look at the photo of the Japanese delegation on page 749. What do you observe about the scene?

Writing About History

8. **Descriptive Writing** Imagine that you are in a large American city when news of victory over Japan comes. Describe the celebrations and the mood of the people.

History ONLINE

Study Central™ To review this section, go to glencoe.com and click on Study Central.

The Pacific

1941
- Japan attacks Pearl Harbor, Dec. 7

1942
- The United States defeats Japan in the Battles of the Coral Sea and Midway

1943
- The United States begins its island-hopping campaign

1944
- The United States retakes the Philippines

1945
- The United States drops the atomic bomb; Japan surrenders on August 15

Europe and North Africa

1941
- Germany invades the Soviet Union

1942
- The Allies turn the tide in the Battle of the Atlantic

1943
- The Allies invade Italy; German forces in North Africa and Stalingrad surrender to Allies

1944
- The Allies invade Normandy on June 6

1945
- Germany surrenders unconditionally on May 7

The Home Front

1941
- President Roosevelt forbids race discrimination in defense industries

1942
- Congress establishes WAAC; War Department relocates Japanese Americans to internment camps

1943
- Race riots occur in Detroit and Los Angeles; Roosevelt establishes OWM

1944
- Supreme Court hears case of *Korematsu* v. *United States*

1945
- Nearly 40 nations sign the United Nations charter

▼ *A convoy of Allied M-3 tanks moves forward.*

▼ *Fire erupts on the* USS Bunker Hill *after a kamikaze attack, May 1945.*

NEW YORK REGENTS EXAM PRACTICE

TEST-TAKING

> Look at each question to find clues to support your answer. Try not to get confused by the wording of the question. Then look for an answer that best fits the question.

Part I

Directions (1–11): For each statement or question, write on a separate sheet of paper the number of the word or expression that, of those given, best completes the statement or answers the question.

1 The invasion of Normandy was important because it

(1) brought the Soviet Union into the war.

(2) forced the Germans to fight a two-front war.

(3) marked the first successful invasion by sea.

(4) protected the Pacific fleet.

2 What type of victory did African Americans push for in the war effort?

(1) Tuskegee

(2) Triple C

(3) Double V

(4) Carver

3 The Japanese were determined to destroy the American fleet in the Pacific after

(1) they were successful at Pearl Harbor.

(2) the Americans surrendered at Bataan.

(3) the crew of the *Enola Gay* dropped an atomic bomb on Hiroshima.

(4) James Doolittle dropped bombs on Tokyo.

4 To prevent huge shipping losses in the Atlantic, Americans used

(1) antisubmarine devices.

(2) a convoy system.

(3) an air force escort.

(4) minesweepers.

5 Whom did the Bracero Program bring to the United States to help with the harvest?

(1) Japanese

(2) German prisoners of war

(3) Mexican workers

(4) Jews fleeing Germany

6 What did the U.S. government do to encourage the collection of materials that could be used in the war?

(1) victory gardens

(2) scrap drives

(3) rationing

(4) war bonds

7 Where did the Allies begin their invasion of Italy?

(1) Sicily

(2) Casablanca

(3) Tehran

(4) Normandy

8 What complicated the planning for D-Day?

(1) German army

(2) amphtracs

(3) weather

(4) air forces

Need Extra Help?								
If You Missed Questions . . .	1	2	3	4	5	6	7	8
Go to Page . . .	738	720	723–724	727	730	735	737–738	739–740

[OVER]

Base your answer to question 9 on the chart below and your knowledge of Chapter 21.

Relocation Camps, 1942–1946

9 Most of the relocation camps were located in which region of the United States?

(1) the West

(2) the Southeast

(3) the Deep South

(4) the Midwest

10 What was the code name for the plan to build the atomic bomb?

(1) Manhattan Project

(2) Doolittle Raid

(3) Operation Overlord

(4) V-J Day

11 The guilt or innocence of Nazi leaders was determined by the

(1) Tokyo trials.

(2) UN Security Council cases.

(3) Dumbarton Oaks conference.

(4) Nuremberg trials.

Need Extra Help?			
If You Missed Questions . . .	9	10	11
Go to Page . . .	R15	750–751	753

Part II Thematic Essay Question

Directions: Write a well-organized essay that includes an introduction, several paragraphs addressing the task below, and a conclusion.

Theme: The United Nations

After World War I, President Wilson wanted the United States to join the League of Nations, but the Senate refused to join. As World War II ended, the United States wanted to create another international organization, the United Nations.

Task:

Discuss why the United States joined the UN and

- Describe what changed between the end of World War I and the end of World War II

- Discuss the likelihood of the UN succeeding when the League of Nations had failed

- Evaluate the long-term effects of the UN on the world

Guidelines:

In your essay, be sure to:

- Develop all aspects of the task

- Support the theme with relevant facts, examples, and details

- Use a logical and clear plan of organization, including an introduction and a conclusion that are beyond a restatement of the theme

Part III Document-Based Question

This question is based on the accompanying documents. It is designed to test your ability to work with historical documents. Some of the documents have been edited for the purposes of the question. As you analyze the documents, take into account the source of each document and any point of view that may be presented in the document.

Historical Context:

During World War II, African Americans played an important part in the war effort. Many historians believe that the civil rights movement of the 1950s and 1960s had its roots in the "Double V" campaign and the march on Washington.

Task:

Using information from the documents and your knowledge of United States history, answer the questions that follow each document in Part A. Your answers to the questions will help you write the Part B essay, in which you will be asked to

- Discuss the contributions of African Americans to the war effort
- Evaluate how the response of African American soldiers and workers helped lay a foundation for the civil rights movement

Part A
Short-Answer Questions

Directions: Analyze the documents and answer the short-answer questions that follow each document on a separate sheet of paper.

Document 1

"Up to that point the doors to industrial and economic opportunity were largely closed. Under the pressure of war, the pressures of government policy, the pressures of world opinion, the pressures of blacks themselves and their allies, all this began to change. . . .The war forced the federal government to take a stronger position with reference to discrimination, and things began to change as a result. There was a tremendous attitudinal change that grew out of the war. There had been a new experience for blacks, and many weren't willing to go back to the way it was before."

Source: John W. Jeffries, *Wartime America,*
Ivan R. Dee, 1996

1 How did the war change the status of African Americans in American society?

2 Why do you think the war forced the government to take a stronger position on discrimination in the workplace?

Document 2

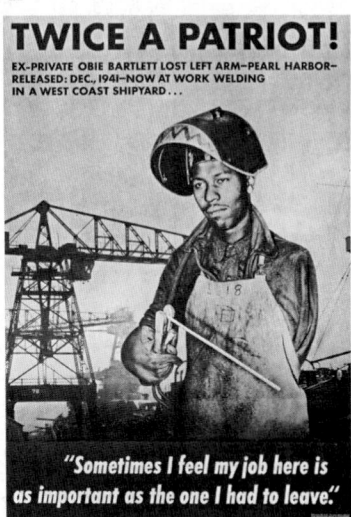

Source: U.S. Government Printing Office, 1943

3 Based on this image, what is the poster saying to African Americans?

Part B
Essay

Directions: Reread the task box at the top left and write a well-organized essay that includes an introduction, several paragraphs, and a conclusion. Use evidence from the documents in your essay. Support your response with relevant facts, examples, and details. Include additional outside information.

Guidelines:
In your essay, be sure to:

- Develop all aspects of the task
- Incorporate information from the documents
- Incorporate relevant outside information
- Support the theme with relevant facts, examples, and details
- Use a logical and clear plan of organization, including an introduction and a conclusion that are beyond a restatement of the theme

For additional test practice, use Self-Check Quizzes—Chapter 21 at glencoe.com.

Need Extra Help?				
If You Missed Questions . . .	1	2	3	Essay
Go to Page . . .	R19	R19	R9	719–721

Chapter 22

The Cold War Begins
1945–1960

SECTION 1 The Origins of the Cold War

SECTION 2 The Early Cold War Years

SECTION 3 The Cold War and American Society

SECTION 4 Eisenhower's Cold War Policies

The world's first nuclear artillery shell is test fired on May 25, 1953. Such tests were common during the early cold war.

1948
- Berlin airlift begins

1950
- McCarthy charges that Communists staff the U.S. State Department
- Korean War begins

1953
- Armistice agreement is reached in Korea

1945
- Franklin Roosevelt dies

Truman
1945–1953

1947
- Truman Doctrine is declared

Eisenhower
1953–1961

U.S. PRESIDENTS

U.S. EVENTS

1945

WORLD EVENTS

1950

March 1945
- Yalta Conference is held to plan postwar world

July 1945
- Potsdam Conference partitions Germany

1948
- State of Israel is created

1949
- Communists take power in China

758 Chapter 22 The Cold War Begins

MAKING CONNECTIONS
How Did the Atomic Bomb Change the World?

The destructiveness of the atomic bomb raised the stakes in military conflicts. Growing tensions between the United States and the Soviet Union after World War II led to a constant threat of nuclear war.

- *How did the atomic bomb change relations between nations?*
- *Do you think the invention of the atomic bomb made the world safer?*

1960
- U-2 incident occurs

1955   1960

1956
- Hungarians rebel against the Communist government

1957
- Soviet Union launches Sputnik

FOLDABLES™

Analyzing Causes Make a Two-Tab Book Foldable that lists the long-term and short-term causes of the Cold War. List the information as you read and review the chapter.

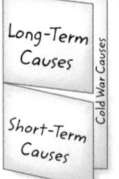

Long-Term Causes

Short-Term Causes

Cold War Causes

History ONLINE Chapter Overview
Visit glencoe.com to preview Chapter 22.

Section 1

The Origins of the Cold War

Guide to Reading

Big Ideas

Government and Society Although World War II was nearly over, personal and political differences among Allied leaders and the peoples they represented led to new global challenges.

Content Vocabulary
- satellite nations *(p. 765)*
- Iron Curtain *(p. 765)*

Academic Vocabulary
- liberate *(p. 760)*
- equipment *(p. 762)*

People and Events to Identify
- Yalta *(p. 760)*
- Cold War *(p. 762)*
- Potsdam *(p. 764)*

Reading Strategy

Categorizing Complete a graphic organizer similar to the one below by filling in the names of the conferences held among the "Big Three" Allies and the outcomes of each.

Conferences	Outcomes

NEW YORK CORE CURRICULUM
U.S. History and Government

Unit 6:
II.B.1 Summitry: Yalta and Potsdam, establishing "spheres of influence"
II.B.2 The Iron Curtain: Winston Churchill

After the war ended, tensions continued to rise over the amount of freedom the Soviets were going to allow the nations they controlled. Leaders of Britain, the United States, and the Soviet Union held conferences but could not resolve this issue.

The Yalta Conference

MAIN Idea Roosevelt, Churchill, and Stalin met at Yalta to discuss Poland, Germany, and the rights of liberated Europe.

HISTORY AND YOU Do you remember Wilson's idealistic Fourteen Points and how they were changed during negotiations after World War I? Read on to learn how negotiations during and after World War II led to results different from what Roosevelt and Truman wanted.

In February 1945, with the war in Europe almost over, Roosevelt, Churchill, and Stalin met at **Yalta**—a Soviet resort on the Black Sea—to plan the postwar world. Although the conference seemed to go well, several agreements reached at Yalta later played an important role in causing the Cold War.

Poland

The first issue discussed at Yalta was what to do about Poland. Shortly after the Germans invaded Poland, the Polish government fled to Britain. In 1944, however, Soviet troops drove back the Germans and entered Poland. As they **liberated** Poland from German control, the Soviets encouraged Polish Communists to set up a new government. This meant there were now two governments claiming the right to govern Poland: one Communist and one non-Communist.

President Roosevelt and Prime Minister Churchill both argued that the Poles should be free to choose their own government. "This is what we went to war against Germany for," Churchill explained, "that Poland should be free and sovereign."

Stalin quickly responded to Churchill's comments. According to Stalin, because Poland was on the Soviet Union's western border, the need for its government to be friendly was a matter of "life and death" from the Soviet point of view. Every time invaders had entered Russia from the west, they had come through Poland. Eventually, the three leaders compromised. Roosevelt and Churchill agreed to recognize the Polish government set up by the Soviets. Stalin agreed that the government would include members of the prewar Polish government and that free elections would be held as soon as possible.

The Yalta Conference, 1945

▲ *Churchill, Roosevelt, and Stalin at Yalta*

The Declaration of Liberated Europe

At Yalta, the Allies issued the Declaration of Liberated Europe. The Soviet Union's failure to uphold the Declaration contributed to the coming of the Cold War. The Declaration contained the following commitments:

- The peoples of Europe will be allowed to create democratic institutions of their own choice, but must destroy all remaining aspects of Nazism and fascism in their societies.
- The United States, Great Britain, and the Soviet Union will help the peoples of Europe to do the following:
  1. Establish peace in their country
  2. Provide aid to people in distress
  3. Form temporary governments that represent all democratic elements of the society and hold free elections to choose a government that responds to the will of the people
- The United States, Great Britain, and the Soviet Union will continue to support the principles expressed in the Atlantic Charter.

NATIONAL GEOGRAPHIC The Division of Germany, 1945

0 100 kilometers
0 100 miles
Albers Equal-Area projection

North Sea

Baltic Sea

POLAND

U.K.

NETH.

Elbe R.

Berlin

BELG.

Allied Occupation Zones, 1945–1949
- American
- British
- French
- Soviet
- Present-day Germany

CZECH.

FRANCE

Rhine R.

Danube R.

SWITZ.

AUSTRIA

0 6 kilometers
0 6 miles

West Berlin

East Berlin

Analyzing VISUALS

1. **Specifying** In the Declaration of Liberated Europe, what three things did the Big Three promise to help the peoples of Europe do?

2. **Locating** In what zone in the divided Germany was Berlin located?

The Declaration of Liberated Europe

After reaching a compromise on Poland, Roosevelt, Churchill, and Stalin agreed to issue the Declaration of Liberated Europe. The declaration asserted "the right of all people to choose the form of government under which they will live."

The Allies promised that the people of Europe would be allowed "to create democratic institutions of their own choice." They also promised to create temporary governments that represented "all democratic elements" and pledged "the earliest possible establishment through free elections of governments responsive to the will of the people."

Dividing Germany

After discussing Poland and agreeing to a set of principles for liberating Europe, the conference focused on Germany. Roosevelt, Churchill, and Stalin agreed to divide Germany into four zones. Great Britain, the United States, the Soviet Union, and France would each control one zone. The same four countries would also divide the German capital city of Berlin into four zones, even though it was in the Soviet zone.

Although pleased with the decision to divide Germany, Stalin also demanded that Germany pay heavy reparations for the war damage it had caused. Roosevelt agreed, but he insisted reparations be based on Germany's ability to pay. He also suggested, and Stalin agreed, that Germany pay reparations with trade goods and products instead of cash. The Allies would also be allowed to remove industrial machinery, railroad cars, and other **equipment** from Germany as reparations. This decision did not resolve the issue. Over the next few years, arguments about German reparations greatly increased tensions between the United States and the Soviet Union.

Tensions Begin to Rise

The Yalta decisions shaped the expectations of the United States. Two weeks after Yalta, the Soviets pressured the king of Romania into appointing a Communist government. The United States accused the Soviets of violating the Declaration of Liberated Europe.

Soon afterward, the Soviets refused to allow more than three non-Communist Poles to serve in the 18-member Polish government. There was also no indication that they intended to hold free elections in Poland as promised. On April 1, President Roosevelt informed the Soviets that their actions in Poland were not acceptable.

Yalta marked a turning point in Soviet-American relations. President Roosevelt had hoped that an Allied victory and the creation of the United Nations would lead to a more peaceful world. Instead, as the war came to an end, the United States and the Soviet Union became increasingly hostile toward each other. This led to an era of confrontation and competition between the two nations that lasted from about 1946 to 1990. This era became known as the **Cold War.**

Soviet Security Concerns

The tensions between the United States and the Soviet Union led to the Cold War because the two sides had different goals. As the war ended, Soviet leaders became concerned about security. They wanted to keep Germany weak and make sure that the countries between Germany and the Soviet Union were under Soviet control.

Although security concerns influenced their thinking, Soviet leaders were also communists. They believed that communism was a superior economic system that would eventually replace capitalism, and that the Soviet Union should encourage communism in other nations. Soviet leaders also accepted Lenin's theory that capitalist countries would eventually try to destroy communism. This made them suspicious of capitalist nations.

American Economic Issues

While Soviet leaders focused on securing their borders, American leaders focused on economic problems. Many American officials believed that the Depression had caused World War II. Without it, Hitler would never have come to power, and Japan would not have wanted to expand its empire.

Debates
IN HISTORY

Did the Soviet Union Cause the Cold War?

Many people have debated who was responsible for the Cold War. Most Americans, including diplomat George Kennan who had served in Russia, believed that it was Soviet ideology and insecurity that brought on the Cold War. On the other side, communist leaders, such as Stalin's adviser Andrei Zhdanov, believed that capitalism and imperialism caused the Cold War.

American advisers also thought that the Depression became so severe because nations reduced trade. They believed that when nations stop trading, they are forced into war to get resources. By 1945, Roosevelt and his advisers were convinced that economic growth was the key to peace. They wanted to promote economic growth by increasing world trade.

Similar reasoning convinced American leaders to promote democracy and free enterprise. They believed that democratic governments with protections for people's rights made countries more stable and peaceful. They also thought that the free enterprise system, with private property rights and limited government intervention in the economy, was the best route to prosperity.

✔ **Reading Check** **Identifying** What did the Allies decide at Yalta?

Truman Takes Control

MAIN Idea Although President Truman took a firm stand against Soviet aggression, Europe remained divided after the war.

HISTORY AND YOU Have you ever had to say no to someone or insist they do something? Read to learn about President Truman's actions at Potsdam.

Eleven days after confronting the Soviets on Poland, President Roosevelt died and Harry S. Truman became president. Truman was strongly anti-Communist. He also believed that World War II had begun because Britain had tried to appease Hitler. He did not intend to make the same mistake with Stalin. "We must stand up to the Russians," he told Secretary of State Edward Stettinius the day after taking office.

YES

George F. Kennan
American Diplomat

PRIMARY SOURCE

"[The] USSR still [believes] in antagonistic 'capitalist encirclement' with which in the long run there can be no permanent peaceful coexistence. . . . At bottom of [the] Kremlin's neurotic view of world affairs is traditional and instinctive Russian sense of insecurity. . . . And they have learned to seek security only in patient but deadly struggle for total destruction of rival power, never in compacts and compromises with it.

. . . In summary, we have here a political force committed fanatically to the belief that . . . it is desirable and necessary that the internal harmony of our society be disrupted, our traditional way of life be destroyed, the international authority of our state be broken, if Soviet power is to be secure."

—Moscow Embassy Telegram #511, 1946

NO

Andrei Zhdanov
Advisor to Stalin

PRIMARY SOURCE

"The more the war recedes into the past, the more distinct becomes . . . the division of the political forces operating on the international arena into two major camps. . . . The principal driving force of the imperialist camp is the U.S.A. . . . The cardinal purpose of the imperialist camp is to strengthen imperialism, to hatch a new imperialist war, to combat socialism and democracy, and to support reactionary and antidemocratic profascist regimes. . . .

. . . As embodiment of a new and superior social system, the Soviet Union reflects in its foreign policy the aspirations of progressive mankind, which desires lasting peace and has nothing to gain from a new war hatched by capitalism."

—from *For a Lasting Peace for a People's Democracy*, no. 1, November 1947

DBQ **Document-Based Questions**

1. **Paraphrasing** What belief of the Soviets does Kennan say will prevent "permanent peaceful coexistence" with the United States?

2. **Identifying Central Issues** What does Zhadanov say are the goals of the "imperialist camp" led by the United States?

Communist countries
Non-communist countries
— Iron Curtain

0   400 kilometers
0   400 miles
Lambert Azimuthal
Equal-Area projection

N
W E
S

ARCTIC CIRCLE

Reykjavik
ICELAND

70°N

60°N

NORWAY
SWEDEN
FINLAND

Oslo
Stockholm
Helsinki

North Sea

Baltic Sea

Moscow

UNITED KINGDOM
Dublin
IRELAND
London

DENMARK
Copenhagen
NETH.
The Hague

SOVIET UNION

Berlin   POLAND
Bonn   EAST GERMANY   Warsaw

Brussels
BELG.
Paris   LUX.
FRANCE

WEST GERMANY
Prague
CZECHOSLOVAKIA
Vienna
AUSTRIA
Bern
SWITZ.

Budapest
HUNGARY
ROMANIA
Bucharest

Belgrade
YUGOSLAVIA

50°N

Madrid
SPAIN

Corsica

ITALY
Rome

Sardinia

40°N

BULGARIA
Sofia

Tiranë
ALBANIA

PRIMARY SOURCE

"A shadow has fallen upon the scenes so lately light by the Allied victory.... From Stettin in the Baltic to Trieste in the Adriatic, an iron curtain has descended across the continent. Behind that line lie all the capitals of the ancient states of Central and Eastern Europe. Warsaw, Berlin, Prague, Vienna, Budapest, Belgrade, Bucharest and Sofia, all these famous cities and the populations around them lie in what I must call the Soviet sphere, and all are subject in one form or another, not only to Soviet influence, but to a very high and, in some cases, increasing measure of control from Moscow....

The Communist parties, which were very small in all these Eastern States of Europe, have been raised to pre-eminence and power far beyond their numbers and are seeking everywhere to obtain totalitarian control....

In front of the iron curtain which lies across Europe are other causes for anxiety ... in a great number of countries, far from the Russian frontiers and throughout the world, Communist fifth columns are established and work in ... absolute obedience to the directions they receive from the Communist center.... I do not believe that Soviet Russia desires war. What they desire is the fruits of war and the indefinite expansion of their power and doctrines."

—Winston Churchill, address to Westminster College, Fulton, Missouri, March 5, 1946

DBQ   Document-Based Questions

1. **Finding the Main Idea** What was the "iron curtain," and why do you think Churchill described it in that way?

2. **Identifying Central Issues** What "other causes for anxiety" did Churchill say the Soviets were creating?

Ten days later, Truman did exactly that during a meeting with Soviet Foreign Minister Molotov. Truman immediately brought up the issue of Poland and demanded that Stalin hold free elections as he had promised at Yalta. Molotov took the unexpectedly strong message back to Stalin. The meeting marked an important shift in Soviet-American relations and set the stage for further confrontations.

The Potsdam Conference

In July 1945 with the war against Japan still raging, Truman finally met Stalin at **Potsdam,** near Berlin. Both men had come to Potsdam primarily to work out a deal on Germany.

Truman was now convinced that industry was critical to Germany's survival. Unless that nation's economy was allowed to revive, the rest of Europe would never recover, and the German people might turn to communism out of desperation.

Stalin and his advisers were equally convinced that they needed reparations from Germany. The war had devastated the Soviet economy. Soviet troops had begun stripping their zone in Germany of its machinery and industrial equipment for use back home, but Stalin wanted Germany to pay much more.

At the conference, Truman took a firm stand against heavy reparations. He insisted that Germany's industry had to be allowed to recover. Truman suggested that the Soviets take reparations from their zone, while the Allies allowed industry to revive in the other zones. Stalin opposed this idea since the Soviet zone was mostly agricultural. It could not provide all the reparations the Soviets wanted.

To get the Soviets to accept the agreement, Truman offered Stalin a small amount of German industrial equipment from the other zones, but required the Soviets to pay for part of it with food shipments from their zone. He also offered to accept the new German-Polish border the Soviets had established.

Stalin did not like Truman's proposal. At Potsdam, Truman learned that the atomic bomb had been successfully tested, and he hinted to Stalin that the United States had developed a new, powerful weapon. Stalin suspected that Truman was trying to bully him into a deal and that the Americans were trying to limit reparations to keep the Soviets weak.

Despite his suspicions, Stalin had to accept the terms. American and British troops controlled Germany's industrial heartland, and there was no way for the Soviets to get any reparations except by cooperating. Nevertheless, the Potsdam conference marked yet another increase in tensions between the Soviets and the Americans.

The Iron Curtain Descends

Although Truman had won the argument over reparations, he had less success on other issues at Potsdam. The Soviets refused to make any stronger commitments to uphold the Declaration of Liberated Europe. The presence of the Soviet army in Eastern Europe ensured that pro-Soviet Communist governments would eventually be established in Poland, Romania, Bulgaria, Hungary, and Czechoslovakia. "This war is not as in the past," Stalin commented. "Whoever occupies a territory also imposes his own social system. . . . It cannot be otherwise."

The Communist countries of Eastern Europe came to be called **satellite nations** because they were controlled by the Soviets, as satellites are tied by gravity to the planets they orbit. These nations had to remain Communist and friendly to the Soviet Union. They also had to follow policies that the Soviets approved.

After watching the Communist takeover in Eastern Europe, Winston Churchill coined a phrase to describe what had happened. In a 1946 speech delivered in Fulton, Missouri, he referred to an "iron curtain" falling across Eastern Europe. The press picked up the term and, for the next 43 years, when someone referred to the Iron Curtain, they meant the Communist nations of Eastern Europe and the Soviet Union. With the **Iron Curtain** separating the Communist nations of Eastern Europe from the West, the World War II era had come to an end. The Cold War was about to begin.

✔ Reading Check Explaining How did the Potsdam Conference hurt Soviet-American relations?

Section 1 REVIEW

Vocabulary

1. **Explain** the significance of: Yalta, Cold War, Potsdam, satellite nations, Iron Curtain.

Main Ideas

2. **Identifying** At Yalta, what agreement did the "Big Three" come to about Germany's future after World War II?

3. **Summarizing** What concerns made the Soviets suspicious of the Western Allies?

4. **Explaining** How did the Potsdam Conference help bring about the Cold War?

Critical Thinking

5. **Big Ideas** How did different economic systems cause tensions between the United States and the Soviet Union?

6. **Organizing** Use a graphic organizer similar to the one below to list events that led to the Cold War.

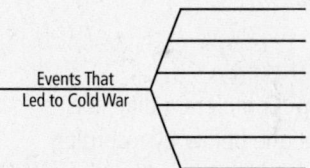

Events That Led to Cold War

7. **Analyzing Visuals** Study the map on page 764. Why did the Soviet Union want to have control over the countries on its western border?

Writing About History

8. **Expository Writing** Suppose that you are an adviser to Truman. Write a report explaining your interpretation of Churchill's "iron curtain" speech.

History ONLINE

Study Central™ To review this section, go to glencoe.com and click on Study Central.

The Early Cold War Years

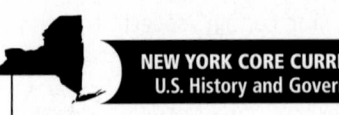

NEW YORK CORE CURRICULUM
U.S. History and Government

Unit 6:
II.B.3.a The Truman Doctrine: Greece and Turkey
II.B.3.b The Marshall Plan
II.B.3.c Berlin airlift
II.B.3.d Formation of NATO Alliance
II.C.1 The United States and Japan
II.C.2 The United States and China
II.C.4 The "hot war" in Asia: Korean War
II.D.4 Politics of the Cold War

President Truman worked to contain communism by supporting Greece, Iran, and West Germany. When Communist North Korea invaded South Korea, Truman and the UN sent troops to aid South Korea.

Containing Communism

MAIN Idea The Truman Doctrine offered aid to any nation resisting communism; the Marshall Plan aided European countries in rebuilding.

HISTORY AND YOU Is there a conflict in the world today where you think the United States should intervene? Read on to learn how President Truman adopted policies designed to stop the spread of communism.

Despite growing tensions with the Soviet Union, many American officials continued to believe cooperation with the Soviets was possible. In late 1945 the foreign ministers of the former wartime Allies met first in London, then in Moscow, to discuss the future of Europe and Asia. Although both British and American officials pushed for free elections in Eastern Europe, the Soviets refused to budge. "Our relations with the Russians," the British foreign minister gloomily concluded, "are drifting into the same condition as that in which we had found ourselves with Hitler."

The Long Telegram

Increasingly exasperated by the Soviets' refusal to cooperate, officials at the State Department asked the American Embassy in Moscow to explain Soviet behavior. On February 22, 1946, diplomat **George Kennan** responded with what became known as the **Long Telegram,** a 5,540-word message explaining his views of the Soviets.

According to Kennan, the Soviets' view of the world came from a traditional "Russian sense of **insecurity**" and fear of the West, intensified by the communist ideas of Lenin and Stalin. Because communists believed that they were in a long-term historical struggle against capitalism, Kennan argued, it was impossible to reach any permanent settlement with them.

Kennan therefore proposed what became the basic American policy throughout the Cold War: "a long-term, patient but firm and vigilant **containment** of Russian expansive tendencies." Kennan explained that, in his opinion, the Soviet system had several major economic and political weaknesses. If the United States could keep the Soviets from expanding their power, it would be only a matter of time before the Soviet system would fall apart. Communism could be beaten without going to war. The Long Telegram circulated widely in

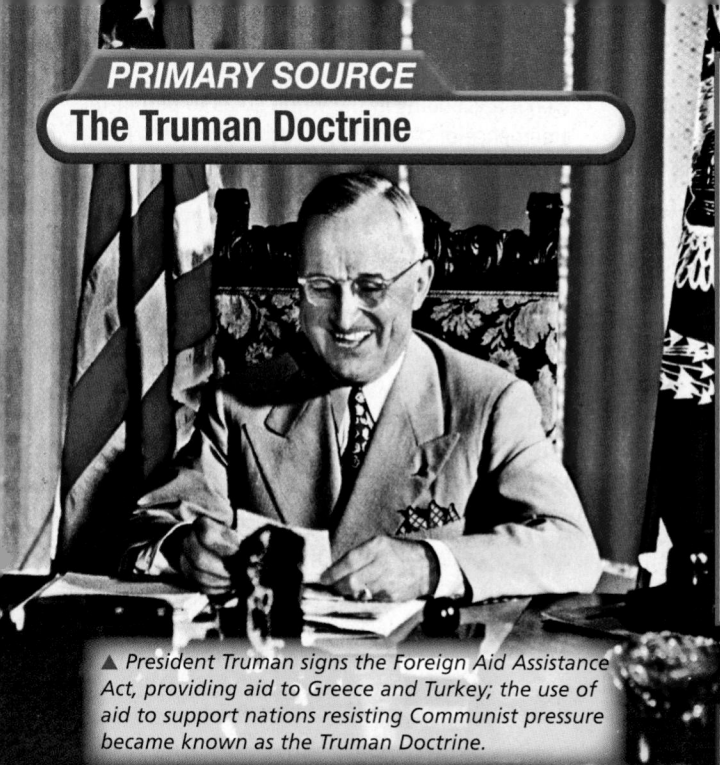

The Truman Doctrine

▲ President Truman signs the Foreign Aid Assistance Act, providing aid to Greece and Turkey; the use of aid to support nations resisting Communist pressure became known as the Truman Doctrine.

PRIMARY SOURCE

"The peoples of a number of countries of the world have recently had totalitarian regimes forced upon them against their will. The Government of the United States has made frequent protests against coercion and intimidation, in violation of the Yalta agreement in Poland, Romania, and Bulgaria. At the present moment in world history nearly every nation must choose between alternative ways of life. The choice is too often not a free one. . . . I believe that it must be the policy of the United States to support free peoples who are resisting attempted subjugation by armed minorities or by outside pressures. I believe that we must assist free peoples to work out their own destinies in their own way."

—Truman's address to Congress, March 12, 1947

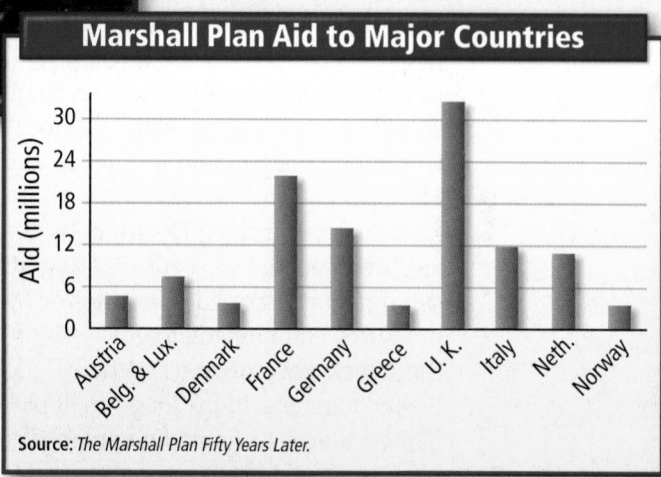

Marshall Plan Aid to Major Countries

Source: *The Marshall Plan Fifty Years Later.*

DBQ Document-Based Questions

1. **Finding the Main Idea** What was the stated goal of the Truman Doctrine?

2. **Drawing Conclusions** Which nation received the most aid through the Marshall Plan? Why do you think this might be?

Truman's administration. The administration based its policy of containment—keeping communism within its present territory through the use of diplomatic, economic, and military actions—on this document.

Crisis in Iran

While Truman's administration discussed Kennan's ideas, a series of crises erupted during the spring and summer of 1946. These crises seemed to prove that Kennan was right about the Soviets. The first crisis began in Iran in March 1946.

During World War II, the United States had put troops in southern Iran while Soviet troops occupied northern Iran to secure a supply line from the Persian Gulf. After the war, instead of withdrawing as promised, the Soviet troops remained in northern Iran. Stalin then began demanding access to Iran's oil supplies. To increase the pressure, Soviet troops helped

local Communists in northern Iran establish a separate government.

To American officials, these actions signaled a Soviet push into the Middle East. The secretary of state sent Stalin a strong message demanding that Soviet forces withdraw. At the same time, the battleship USS *Missouri* sailed into the eastern Mediterranean. The pressure seemed to work. Soviet forces withdrew, having been promised a joint Soviet-Iranian oil company, although the Iranian parliament later rejected the plan.

The Truman Doctrine

Frustrated in Iran, Stalin turned northwest to Turkey. There, the straits of the Dardanelles were a vital route from Soviet Black Sea ports to the Mediterranean. For centuries, Russia had wanted to control this strategic route. In August 1946, Stalin demanded joint control of the Dardanelles with Turkey.

For more of the text of Truman's Address to Congress, see page R54 in **Documents in American History.**

Presidential adviser Dean Acheson saw this move as another move in a Soviet plan to control the Middle East, and he advised Truman to make a show of force. The president declared, "We might as well find out whether the Russians are bent on world conquest." He then ordered the new aircraft carrier *Franklin D. Roosevelt* to join the *Missouri* in protecting Turkey and the eastern Mediterranean.

While the United States supported Turkey, Britain tried to help Greece. In August 1946 Greek Communists launched a guerrilla war against the Greek government. For about six months, British troops helped the Greeks fight the guerrillas. The effort strained Britain's economy, which was still weak from World War II. In February 1947 Britain informed the United States that it could no longer afford to help Greece.

On March 12, 1947, Truman went before Congress to ask for $400 million to fight Communist aggression in Greece and Turkey. His speech outlined a policy that became known as the Truman Doctrine. Its goal was to aid "free peoples who are resisting attempted subjugation by armed minorities or by outside pressures." Its immediate goal was to stabilize the Greek government and help Turkey resist Soviet demands. In the long run, it pledged the United States to fight the spread of communism worldwide.

The Marshall Plan

Meanwhile, postwar Western Europe faced grave problems. Economies and cities were ruined, people were nearing starvation, and political chaos was at hand. The terrible winter of 1946 made things worse.

In June 1947 Secretary of State George C. Marshall proposed the European Recovery Program, or **Marshall Plan,** which would give European nations American aid to rebuild their economies. Truman saw the Marshall Plan and the Truman Doctrine as "two halves of the same walnut," both essential for containment. Marshall offered help to all nations planning a recovery program:

PRIMARY SOURCE

"Our policy is directed not against any country or doctrine but against hunger, poverty, desperation and chaos. Its purpose should be the revival of a working economy in the world so as to permit the emergence of political and social conditions in which free institutions can exist."

—quoted in *Marshall: Hero for Our Times*

Although the Marshall Plan was offered to the Soviet Union and its satellite nations in Eastern Europe, those nations rejected the offer. Instead, the Soviets developed their own economic program. This action further separated Europe into competing regions. The Marshall Plan pumped billions of dollars worth of supplies, machinery, and food into Western Europe. Western Europe's recovery weakened the appeal of communism and opened new markets for trade.

The Berlin Airlift

President Truman and his advisers believed that Western Europe's prosperity depended on Germany's recovery. The Soviets, however, still wanted Germany to pay reparations to the Soviet Union. Eventually, the dispute over Germany brought the United States and the Soviet Union to the brink of war.

By early 1948, U.S. officials had concluded that the Soviets were deliberately trying to undermine Germany's economy. In response, the United States, Great Britain, and France announced that they were merging their zones in Germany and allowing the Germans to have their own government. They also agreed to merge their zones in Berlin and to make West Berlin part of the new German republic.

The new nation was officially called the Federal Republic of Germany, but it became known as West Germany. The Soviet zone eventually became the German Democratic Republic, also known as East Germany. West Germany was not allowed to have a military, but in most respects, it was independent.

The decision to create West Germany convinced the Soviets that they would never get the reparations they wanted. In late June 1948, Soviet troops cut all road and rail traffic to West Berlin hoping to force the United States to either reconsider its decision or abandon West Berlin. This blockade provoked a crisis. President Truman sent bombers with atomic weapons to bases in Britain and the American commander in Germany warned: "If we mean to hold Europe against communism, then we must not budge." The challenge was to keep West Berlin alive without provoking war with the Soviets. Instead of ordering troops to fight their way to Berlin, and thereby triggering war with the Soviet Union, Truman ordered the air force to fly supplies into Berlin instead.

The Berlin airlift began in June 1948 and continued through the spring of 1949, bringing in more than 2 million tons of supplies to the city. Stalin finally lifted the blockade on May 12, 1949. The airlift symbolized American determination to contain communism and not give in to Soviet demands.

NATO

The Berlin blockade convinced many Americans that the Soviets were bent on conquest. The public began to support a military alliance with Western Europe. By April 1949, an agreement had been reached to create the North Atlantic Treaty Organization (NATO)—a mutual defense alliance.

NATO initially included 12 countries: the United States, Canada, Britain, France, Italy, Belgium, Denmark, Portugal, the Netherlands, Norway, Luxembourg, and Iceland. NATO members agreed to come to the aid of any member who was attacked. For the first time in its history, the United States had committed itself to maintaining peace in Europe. Six years later, NATO allowed West Germany to rearm and join its organization. This decision alarmed Soviet leaders. They responded by organizing a military alliance in Eastern Europe known as the Warsaw Pact.

✔ **Reading Check** **Evaluating** What triggered the beginning of the Berlin airlift?

History ONLINE
Student Web Activity Visit glencoe.com and complete the activity on the Berlin Airlift.

PRIMARY SOURCE
The Berlin Airlift, 1948–1949

After the Soviet Union blockaded West Berlin, the United States delivered 4,000 tons of food, medicine, coal and other supplies that were needed every day to keep the city functioning. A cargo plane had to land with supplies every three and a half minutes. To keep the airlift running, crews stayed onboard and food was brought to them while the planes were unloaded and refueled. Meanwhile, 20,000 volunteers in Berlin built a third airport, enabling the flow of supplies to increase to 13,000 tons a day.

NATIONAL GEOGRAPHIC **NATO Is Born, 1949**

Founding members
Joined 1952
Joined 1955
Warsaw Pact

70°N
ARCTIC CIRCLE
30°W
ICELAND
60°N
20°W
NORWAY
North Sea
ATLANTIC OCEAN
DENMARK
UNITED KINGDOM
NETH.
E. GER.
POLAND
SOVIET UNION
50°N
W. GER.
BELG.
LUX.
CZECH.
FRANCE
HUNGARY
ROMANIA
ITALY
BULGARIA
PORTUGAL
40°N
ALB.
30°E
GREECE
TURKEY
0°
10°E
Mediterranean Sea
20°E
0   600 kilometers
0   600 miles
Lambert Azimuthal Equal-Area projection

Analyzing VISUALS

1. **Interpreting** Which nations are the founding members of NATO?
2. **Identifying** Which NATO nations shared a border with one or more Warsaw Pact nations?

The Korean War

MAIN Idea Attempts to keep South Korea free from communism led the United States to military intervention.

HISTORY AND YOU What happens to someone who disobeys a coach, employer, or teacher? Read on to learn what happened to General MacArthur when he criticized the president.

The Cold War eventually spread beyond Europe. Conflicts also emerged in Asia, where events in China and Korea brought about a new attitude toward Japan and sent American troops back into battle in Asia less than five years after World War II had ended.

The Chinese Revolution

In China, Communist forces led by Mao Zedong had been struggling against the Nationalist government led by Chiang Kai-shek since the late 1920s. During World War II, the two sides suspended their war to resist Japanese occupation. With the end of World War II, however, civil war broke out again. Although Mao made great gains, neither side could win nor agree to a compromise.

To prevent a Communist revolution in Asia, the United States sent the Nationalist government $2 billion in aid beginning in the mid-1940s, but the Nationalists squandered this advantage through poor military planning and corruption. By 1949, the Communists had captured the Chinese capital of Beijing, while support for the Nationalists declined.

In August 1949 the U.S. State Department discontinued aid to the Chinese Nationalists. The defeated Nationalists then fled to the small island of Taiwan (Formosa). The victorious Communists established the People's Republic of China in October 1949.

China's fall to communism shocked Americans. To make matters worse, in September 1949 the Soviet Union announced that it had successfully tested its first atomic weapon. Then, early in 1950, the People's Republic of China and the Soviet Union signed a treaty of friendship and alliance. Many Western leaders feared that China and the Soviet Union would support Communist revolutions in other nations.

The United States kept formal diplomatic relations with only the Nationalist Chinese in

NATIONAL GEOGRAPHIC

▲ **June–September 1950**

North Korean troops invade South Korea, driving South Korean and UN forces south into a small perimeter around Pusan.

	North Korean-controlled territory
	South Korean-controlled territory
←	North Korean advance
←	UN counteroffensive
—	Front line
←	Chinese counteroffensive
—	Armistice line

Taiwan. It used its veto power in the UN Security Council to keep representatives of the new Communist People's Republic of China out of the UN, allowing the Nationalists to retain their seat.

New Policies in Japan

The Chinese revolution brought about a significant change in American policy toward Japan. At the end of World War II, General Douglas MacArthur had taken charge of occupied Japan. His mission was to introduce democracy and keep Japan from threatening war again. Once the United States lost China as its chief ally in Asia, it adopted policies to encourage the rapid recovery of Japan's industrial economy. Just as

▲ September–November 1950

Led by General MacArthur, UN troops land behind North Korean lines at the port of Inchon. North Korean forces fall back rapidly, and the UN forces head north into North Korea.

▲ November 1950–January 1951

As UN forces near the Chinese border, Chinese troops cross into North Korea driving the UN back. MacArthur wants to attack Chinese territory. He publicly argues with Truman and is fired.

▲ January 1951–July 1953

Led by U.S. General Matthew Ridgway, the UN forces push the Chinese and North Korean forces out of South Korea. The war bogs down into a stalemate along the 38th parallel.

◀ Soldiers of the U.S. 2nd Infantry Division man a machine gun near the Chongchun River in Korea, December 15, 1950.

Analyzing GEOGRAPHY

1. **Human-Environment Interaction** What occurred at the port of Inchon in 1950?
2. **Location** What geographical feature forms the border between China and North Korea?

the United States viewed West Germany as the key to defending all of Europe against communism, it saw Japan as the key to defending Asia.

The Korean War Begins

At the end of World War II, American and Soviet forces entered Korea to disarm the Japanese troops stationed there. The Allies divided Korea at the 38th parallel of latitude. Soviet troops controlled the north, while American troops controlled the south.

As the Cold War began, talks to reunify Korea broke down. A Communist Korean government was organized in the north, while an American-backed government controlled the south. Both governments claimed authority over Korea, and border clashes were common. The Soviet Union provided military aid to the North Koreans, who quickly built up an army. On June 25, 1950, North Korean troops invaded the south, rapidly driving back the poorly equipped South Korean forces.

Truman saw the Communist invasion of South Korea as a test of the containment policy and ordered United States naval and air power into action. He then called on the United Nations to act. Truman succeeded because the Soviet delegate was boycotting the UN Security Council over its China policy and was not present to veto the American proposal. With the pledge of UN troops, Truman ordered General MacArthur to send American troops from Japan to Korea.

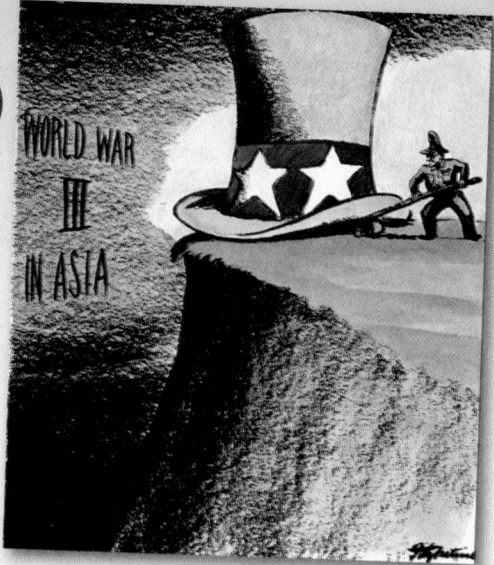

▲ Entitled "Not a General's Job," this cartoon suggests that MacArthur had overstepped his authority in Korea.

▲ President Truman, Secretary of State Dean Acheson, and "The Pentagon" are held over the flame of public opinion for firing General MacArthur. "John Q." refers to "John Q. Public," or the American people.

Analyzing VISUALS

1. **Identifying Points of View** Which of the cartoons supports President Truman's decision to fire General MacArthur? Explain.

2. **Making Inferences** What does the cartoon on the right imply MacArthur was trying to do in Asia?

The American and South Korean troops were driven back into a small pocket of territory near the port of Pusan. Inside the "Pusan perimeter," as it came to be called, the troops stubbornly resisted the North Korean onslaught, buying time for MacArthur to organize reinforcements.

On September 15, 1950, MacArthur ordered a daring invasion behind enemy lines at the port of Inchon. The Inchon landing took the North Koreans by surprise. Within weeks they were in full retreat back across the 38th parallel. Truman then gave the order to pursue the North Koreans beyond the 38th parallel. MacArthur pushed the North Koreans north to the Yalu River, the border with China.

China Enters the War The Communist People's Republic of China saw the advancing UN troops as a threat and warned the forces to halt their advance. When those warnings were ignored, Chinese forces crossed the Yalu River in November. Hundreds of thousands of Chinese troops flooded across the border, driving the UN forces back across the 38th parallel.

As his troops fell back, an angry MacArthur demanded approval to expand the war against China. He asked for a blockade of Chinese ports, the use of Chiang Kai-shek's Nationalist forces, and the bombing of Chinese cities with atomic weapons.

Truman Fires MacArthur President Truman refused MacArthur's demands because he did not want to expand the war into China or to use the atomic bomb. MacArthur persisted. He publicly criticized the president, arguing that it was a mistake to keep the war limited. "There is no substitute for victory," MacArthur insisted, by which he meant that if the United States was going to go to war, it should use all of its power to win. Keeping a war limited was, in his view, a form of appeasement, and appeasement he argued, "begets new and bloodier war."

Determined to maintain control of policy and to show that the president commanded the military, an exasperated Truman fired MacArthur for insubordination in April 1951. Later, in private conversation, Truman explained:

"I was sorry to have to reach a parting of the way with the big man in Asia, but he asked for it and I had to give it to him."

MacArthur, who remained popular despite being fired, returned home to parades and a hero's welcome. Many Americans criticized the president. Congress and other military leaders, however, supported Truman's decision and his Korean strategy. American policy in Asia remained committed to **limited war**—a war fought to achieve a limited objective, such as containing communism. Truman later explained why he favored limited war in Korea:

PRIMARY SOURCE

"The Kremlin [Soviet Union] is trying, and has been trying for a long time, to drive a wedge between us and the other nations. It wants to see us isolated. It wants to see us distrusted. It wants to see us feared and hated by our allies. Our allies agree with us in the course we are following. They do not believe we should take the initiative to widen the conflict in the Far East. If the United States were to widen the conflict, we might well have to go it alone."

—from "Address to the Civil Defense Conference," May 7, 1951

As Truman also noted, America's allies in Europe were much closer to the Soviet Union. If war broke out, Europe would suffer the most damage and might well be attacked with atomic bombs. This concern—that all-out war in Korea might lead to nuclear war—was the main reason why Truman favored limited war. This concern shaped American foreign policy throughout the Cold War.

Changes in Policy

By mid-1951, the UN forces had pushed the Chinese and North Korean forces back across the 38th parallel. The war then settled down into a series of relatively small battles over hills and other local objectives. In November 1951, peace negotiations began, but an armistice would not be signed until July 1953. More than 33,600 American soldiers died in action in the Korean War, and more than 2,800 died from accidents or disease.

The Korean War marked an important turning point in the Cold War. Until 1950, the United States had preferred to use political pressure and economic aid to contain communism. After the Korean War began, the United States embarked on a major military buildup.

The Korean War also helped expand the Cold War to Asia. Before 1950, the United States had focused on Europe as the most important area in which to contain communism. After the Korean War began, the United States became more militarily involved in Asia. In 1954 the United States signed defense agreements with Japan, South Korea, Taiwan, the Philippines, and Australia, forming the Southeast Asia Treaty Organization (**SEATO**). American aid also began flowing to French forces fighting Communists in Vietnam.

Reading Check **Analyzing** How did President Truman view the Communist invasion of South Korea?

Section 2 REVIEW

Vocabulary
1. **Explain** the significance of: George Kennan, Long Telegram, containment, Marshall Plan, NATO, limited war, SEATO.

Main Ideas
2. **Explaining** How did the Truman Doctrine and the Marshall Plan address the spread of communism?

3. **Describing** What originally led to the formation of two Koreas?

Critical Thinking
4. **Big Ideas** How did the Long Telegram influence U.S. foreign policy?

5. **Categorizing** Use a graphic organizer similar to the one below to list early conflicts between the Soviet Union and the United States.

6. **Analyzing Visuals** Study the maps of the Korean War on pages 770–771. When did the United Nations control the most territory in Korea? When did both sides finally agree on an armistice line?

Writing About History
7. **Persuasive Writing** Write a letter to the editor of a newspaper explaining why you agree or disagree with President Truman's firing of General MacArthur.

History ONLINE

Study Central™ To review this section, go to glencoe.com and click on Study Central.

Section 3

The Cold War and American Society

Guide to Reading

Big Ideas

Struggles for Rights In the early part of the Cold War, the fear of communism led to a hunt for spies and to intolerance and suspicion of people with radical ideas in the United States.

Content Vocabulary

- subversion *(p. 774)*
- loyalty review program *(p. 774)*
- perjury *(p. 776)*
- censure *(p. 778)*
- fallout *(p. 781)*

Academic Vocabulary

- manipulate *(p. 775)*
- convince *(p. 776)*

People and Events to Identify

- Red Scare *(p. 774)*
- Alger Hiss *(p. 776)*
- McCarran Act *(p. 778)*
- McCarthyism *(p. 778)*

Reading Strategy

Summarizing As you read, summarize the section content by using the major headings to create an outline similar to the one below.

> The Cold War and American Society
> I. A New Red Scare
>   A. The Loyalty Review Program
>   B.
>   C.

NEW YORK CORE CURRICULUM
U.S. History and Government

Unit 6:
II.C.3 USSR tests an A-bomb (1949)
II.D.1 Truman and government loyalty checks
Case studies: The Smith Act and the House Un-American Activities Committee (*Watkins* v. *United States*, 1957); the Alger Hiss case (1950); the Rosenberg trial (1950)
II.D.2 Loyalty and dissent: the case of Robert Oppenheimer
II.D.3 McCarthyism

Fearing subversive activity, the government tried to root out Communists in government, Hollywood, and labor unions, while Americans learned to live with the threat of nuclear attack.

A New Red Scare

MAIN Idea Public accusations and trials followed in the wake of fears of communism and spies.

HISTORY AND YOU Do you remember reading about the fears of communism during the early twentieth century? Read on to learn of a second major scare in the 1950s.

During the 1950s, thousands of ordinary people—from teachers to autoworkers to high government officials—shared a disturbing experience. Rumors and accusations of Communists in the United States and of Communist infiltration of the government tapped into fears that Communists were trying to take over the world.

The **Red Scare** began in September 1945, when a clerk named Igor Gouzenko walked out of the Soviet Embassy in Ottawa, Canada, and defected. Gouzenko carried documents revealing a massive effort by the Soviet Union to infiltrate organizations and government agencies in Canada and the United States, with the specific goal of obtaining information about the atomic bomb.

The Gouzenko case stunned Americans. It implied that spies had infiltrated the American government. Soon, however, the search for spies escalated into a general fear of Communist **subversion.** Subversion is the effort to weaken a society secretly and overthrow its government.

The Loyalty Review Program

In early 1947, just nine days after his powerful speech announcing the Truman Doctrine, the president established a **loyalty review program** to screen all federal employees. Rather than calm public suspicion, Truman's action seemed to confirm fears that Communists had infiltrated the government and helped to increase the fear of communism sweeping the nation.

Between 1947 and 1951, more than 6 million federal employees were screened for their loyalty—a term difficult to define. A person might become a suspect for reading certain books, belonging to various groups, traveling overseas, or even seeing certain foreign films. About 14,000 employees were subject to scrutiny by the Federal Bureau of Investigation (FBI). Some 2,000 employees quit their jobs

PRIMARY SOURCE
The Hunt for Spies, 1947–1954

▲ **Loyalty and Dissent, Oppenheimer, 1953**

Although he had led the effort to develop the atomic bomb, Dr. Robert Oppenheimer's left-wing views and opposition to the hydrogen bomb led to the suspension of his security clearance and controversial public hearings.

▲ ***Hiss v. Chambers*, 1948**

In 1948, Whittaker Chambers, a *TIME* magazine editor and former Communist Party member, testified that U.S. diplomat Alger Hiss was a Communist. Hiss denied being a spy or a member of the Communist Party. Evidence provided by Chambers led to Hiss being convicted of perjury.

▶ **The Rosenbergs Are Convicted, 1950**

In 1950 the hunt for spies who had given U.S. nuclear secrets to the Soviets led to the arrest of Julius and Ethel Rosenberg. Accused of running a Soviet spy network, the Rosenbergs became the first civilians executed for espionage in 1953. Their case was controversial and led to public protests.

Analyzing VISUALS

1. **Summarizing** What were the Rosenbergs accused of and what was the result?

2. **Explaining** Why was Robert Oppenheimer's security clearance suspended?

---

during the check, many under pressure. Another 212 were fired for "questionable loyalty," although no actual evidence against them was uncovered.

House Un-American Activities Committee (HUAC)

Although the FBI helped screen federal employees, FBI Director J. Edgar Hoover was not satisfied. In 1947 Hoover went before the House Un-American Activities Committee (HUAC). Formed in 1938 to investigate both Communist and Fascist activities in the United States, HUAC was a minor committee until Hoover expanded its importance.

Hoover urged HUAC to hold public hearings on Communist subversion. The committee, Hoover said, could reveal "the diabolic machinations of sinister figures engaged in un-American activities." Hoover's aim was to expose not just Communists but also "Communist sympathizers" and "fellow travelers." Under Hoover's leadership, the FBI sent agents to infiltrate groups suspected of subversion and wiretapped thousands of telephones.

Hollywood on Trial One of HUAC's first hearings in 1947 focused on the film industry as a powerful cultural force that Communists might **manipulate** to spread their ideas and influence. HUAC's interviews routinely began, "Are you now, or have you ever been, a member of the Communist Party?" Future American president Ronald Reagan was head of the Screen Actors Guild at the time and, when called before HUAC, he testified that there were Communists in Hollywood.

During the hearings, ten screenwriters, known as the "Hollywood Ten," used their Fifth Amendment right to protect themselves from self-incrimination and refused to testify. The incident led producers to blacklist, or agree not to hire, anyone who was believed to be a Communist or who refused to cooperate with the committee. In 1950 a pamphlet called *Red Channels* was published, listing 151 blacklisted actors, directors, broadcasters, and screenwriters. The blacklist created an atmosphere of distrust and fear.

Alger Hiss In 1948 Whittaker Chambers, a *TIME* magazine editor and former Communist Party member, testified to HUAC that several government officials were also former Communists or spies.

The most prominent official named by Chambers was **Alger Hiss,** a diplomat who had served in Roosevelt's administration, attended the Yalta conference, and taken part in organizing the United Nations. After Hiss sued him for libel, Chambers testified before a grand jury that, in 1937 and 1938, Hiss had given him secret documents from the State Department. Hiss denied being either a spy or a member of the Communist Party, and he also denied ever having known Chambers.

The committee was ready to drop the investigation until Representative Richard Nixon of California **convinced** his colleagues to continue the hearings to determine whether Hiss or Chambers had lied. Chambers produced copies of secret documents, along with microfilm that he had hidden in a hollow pumpkin on his farm. These "pumpkin papers," Chambers claimed, proved Hiss was lying. A jury agreed and convicted Hiss of **perjury,** or lying under oath.

The Rosenbergs Another sensational spy case centered on accusations that American Communists had sold the secrets of the atomic bomb to the Soviets. Many people did not believe that the Soviet Union could have produced an atomic bomb in 1949 without help. This belief intensified the hunt for spies.

In 1950 the hunt led to a British scientist who admitted sending information to the Soviet Union. After hearing his testimony, the FBI arrested Julius and Ethel Rosenberg, a New York couple who were members of the Communist Party. The government charged them with heading a Soviet spy ring.

The Rosenbergs denied the charges but were condemned to death for espionage. Many people believed that they were not leaders or spies but victims caught up in the wave of anti-Communist frenzy. Appeals, public expressions of support, and pleas for clemency failed, however, and the couple was executed in June 1953.

Project Venona The American public hotly debated the guilt or innocence of individuals, like the Rosenbergs, who were accused of being spies. There was, however, solid evidence of Soviet espionage, although very few Americans knew it at the time. In 1946 American and British cryptographers, working for a project code-named "Venona," cracked the Soviet spy code of the time, enabling them to read approximately 3,000 messages between Moscow and the United States collected during the Cold War.

The messages collected using Project Venona confirmed extensive Soviet spying and an ongoing effort to steal nuclear secrets. The government did not reveal Project Venona's existence until 1995. The Venona documents provided strong evidence that the Rosenbergs were indeed guilty.

The Red Scare Spreads

Following the federal government's example, many state and local governments, universities, businesses, unions, churches, and private organizations began their own efforts to find Communists. The University of California required its 11,000 faculty members to take loyalty oaths and fired 157 who refused to do so. Many Catholic groups became strongly anti-Communist and urged their members to identify Communists within the Church.

The Taft-Hartley Act of 1947 required union leaders to take oaths that they were not Communists, but many union leaders did not object. Instead, they launched their own efforts to purge Communists from their organizations. The president of the CIO called Communist sympathizers "skulking cowards" and "apostles of hate." The CIO eventually expelled 11 unions that refused to remove Communist leaders from their organization.

Reading Check **Explaining** What was the purpose of the loyalty review boards and HUAC?

McCarthyism

MAIN Idea Senator Joseph R. McCarthy used the fear of communism to increase his own power and destroy the reputations of many people.

HISTORY AND YOU Have you ever known anyone who spread untrue stories about others? Read on to find out about the false accusations that Senator McCarthy spread in the early 1950s.

In 1949 the Red Scare intensified even further. In that year, the Soviet Union successfully tested an atomic bomb, and China fell to communism. To many Americans, these events seemed to prove that the United States was losing the Cold War. Deeply concerned, they wanted to know why their government was failing. As a result, many continued to believe that Communists had infiltrated the government and remained undetected.

In February 1950, soon after Alger Hiss's perjury conviction, a little-known Wisconsin senator gave a political speech to a Republican women's group in West Virginia. Halfway through his speech, Senator Joseph R. McCarthy made a surprising statement:

PRIMARY SOURCE

"While I cannot take the time to name all the men in the State Department who have been named as members of the Communist Party and members of a spy ring, I have here in my hand a list of 205 that were known to the Secretary of State as being members of the Communist Party and who nevertheless are still working and shaping the policy of the State Department."

—quoted in *The Fifties*

The Associated Press picked up the statement and sent it to newspapers nationwide. While at an airport, reporters asked McCarthy to see his list of Communists. McCarthy replied that he would be happy to show it to them, but unfortunately, it was in his bag on the plane. In fact, the list never appeared. McCarthy, however, continued to make charges and draw attention.

McCarthy's use of sensationalist charges was not new. When he ran for the Senate in 1946, he accused his opponent, Robert M. La Follette, Jr., of being "communistically inclined." McCarthy did not provide any evidence to support his accusation, but it helped him win the election.

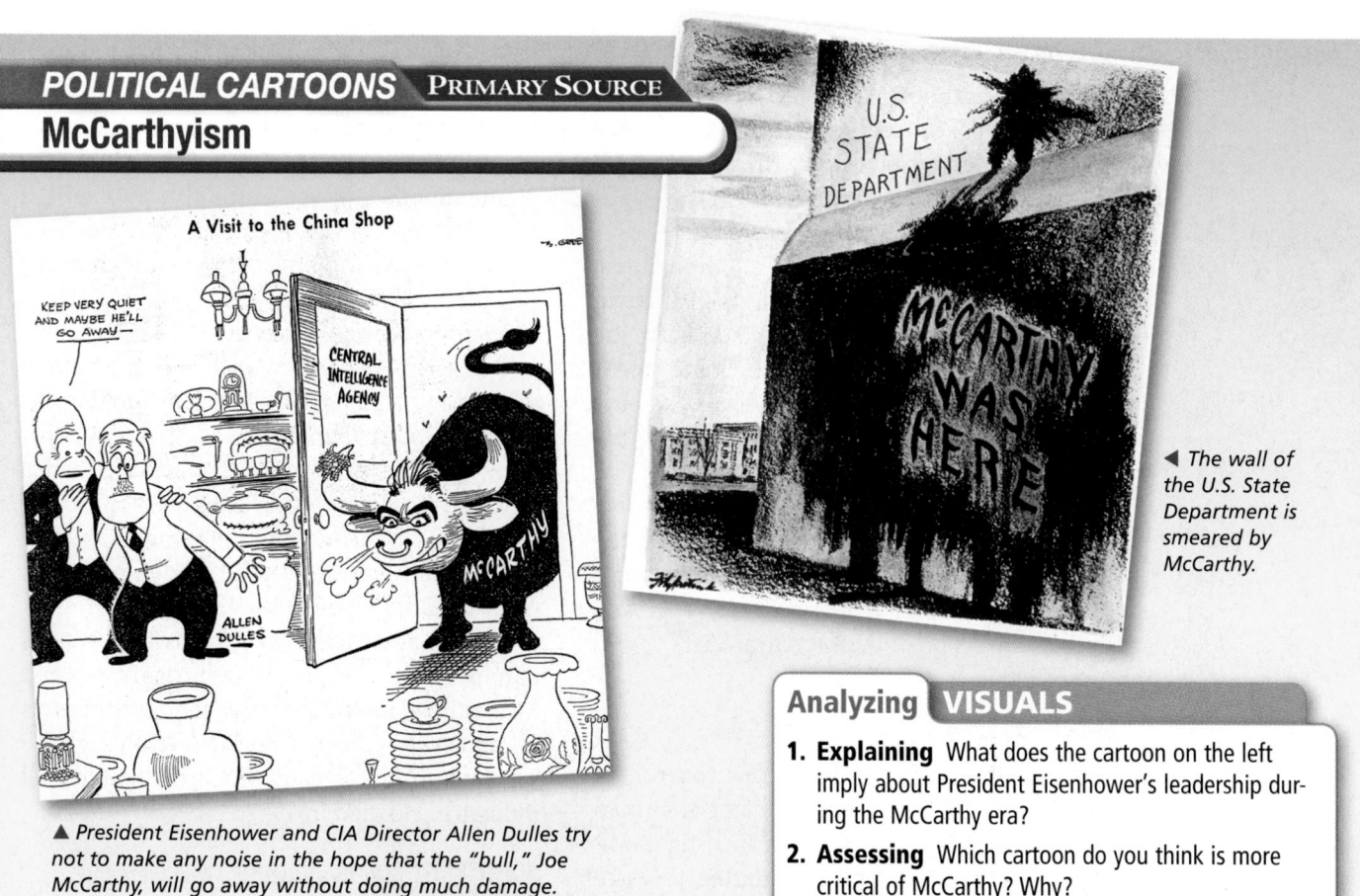

POLITICAL CARTOONS PRIMARY SOURCE
McCarthyism

A Visit to the China Shop

KEEP VERY QUIET AND MAYBE HE'LL GO AWAY—

CENTRAL INTELLIGENCE AGENCY

McCARTHY

ALLEN DULLES

▲ President Eisenhower and CIA Director Allen Dulles try not to make any noise in the hope that the "bull," Joe McCarthy, will go away without doing much damage.

U.S. STATE DEPARTMENT

McCARTHY WAS HERE

◀ The wall of the U.S. State Department is smeared by McCarthy.

Analyzing VISUALS

1. **Explaining** What does the cartoon on the left imply about President Eisenhower's leadership during the McCarthy era?

2. **Assessing** Which cartoon do you think is more critical of McCarthy? Why?

After becoming a senator, McCarthy continued to proclaim that Communists were a danger both at home and abroad. To some audiences, he distributed a booklet called "The Party of Betrayal," which accused Democratic Party leaders of corruption and of protecting Communists. Secretary of State Dean Acheson was a frequent target. According to McCarthy, Acheson was incompetent and a tool of Stalin. He also wildly accused George C. Marshall, the former army chief of staff and secretary of state, of disloyalty as a member of "a conspiracy so immense as to dwarf any previous such ventures in the history of man."

McCarthy was not alone in making such charges. In the prevailing mood of anxiety about communism, many Americans were ready to believe them.

The McCarran Act

In 1950, with the Korean War underway and McCarthy and others arousing fears of Communist spies, Congress passed the Internal Security Act, usually called the **McCarran Act.** Declaring that "world Communism has as its sole purpose the establishment of a totalitarian dictatorship in America," Senator Pat McCarran of Nevada offered a way to fight "treachery, infiltration, sabotage, and terrorism." The act made it illegal to "combine, conspire, or agree with any other person to perform any act which would substantially contribute to . . . the establishment of a totalitarian government."

The McCarran Act required all Communist Party and "Communist-front" organizations to publish their records and register with the United States attorney general. Communists could not have passports to travel abroad and, in cases of a national emergency, Communists and Communist sympathizers could be arrested and detained. Unwilling to punish people for their opinions, Truman vetoed the bill, but Congress easily overrode his veto in 1950. Later Supreme Court cases, however, limited the scope of the McCarran Act.

McCarthy's Tactics

After the Republicans won control of Congress in 1952, McCarthy became chairman of the Senate subcommittee on investigations. Using the power of his committee to force government officials to testify about alleged Communist influences, McCarthy turned the investigation into a witch hunt—a search for disloyalty based on flimsy evidence and irrational fears. His tactic of damaging reputations with vague and unfounded charges became known as **McCarthyism.**

McCarthy's sensational accusations drew the attention of the press, which put him in the headlines and quoted him widely. When he questioned witnesses, McCarthy would badger them and then refuse to accept their answers. His tactics left a cloud of suspicion that McCarthy and others interpreted as guilt. Furthermore, people were afraid to challenge him for fear of becoming targets themselves.

McCarthy's Downfall

In 1954 McCarthy began to look for Soviet spies in the United States Army. During weeks of televised Army-McCarthy hearings, millions of Americans watched McCarthy question and bully officers, harassing them about trivial details and accusing them of misconduct. His popular support began to fade.

Finally, to strike back at the army's lawyer, Joseph Welch, McCarthy brought up the past of a young lawyer in Welch's firm who had been a member of a Communist-front organization while in law school. Welch, who was fully aware of the young man's past, now exploded at McCarthy for possibly ruining the young man's career: "Until this moment, I think I never really gauged your cruelty or your recklessness. . . . You have done enough. Have you no sense of decency, sir, at long last? Have you left no sense of decency?"

Spectators cheered. Welch had said aloud what many Americans had been thinking. As Senator Stuart Symington of Missouri commented, "The American people have had a look at you for six weeks. You are not fooling anyone." McCarthy had lost the power to arouse fear. Newspaper headlines repeated: "Have you no sense of decency?"

Later that year, the Senate passed a vote of **censure,** or formal disapproval, against McCarthy—one of the most serious criticisms it can level against a member. Although he remained in the Senate, McCarthy had lost all influence. He died in 1957.

✔ Reading Check Evaluating What were the effects of McCarthyism?

ANALYZING SUPREME COURT CASES

Are There Limits on Congressional Power?

★ *Watkins* v. *United States*, 1957

Background to the Case

In 1954 labor organizer John Watkins testified before the House Un-American Activities Committee. He agreed to discuss his own connections with the Communist Party and to identify people he knew who were still members, but he refused to give information about those who were no longer members. Watkins received a misdemeanor conviction for refusing to answer questions "pertinent to the question under inquiry." In 1957 he appealed his case to the Supreme Court.

How the Court Ruled

The Watkins case raised the question: Is it constitutional for a congressional committee to ask any question or investigate any topic, whether or not it is directly related to Congress's law-making function? In a 6-to-1 decision—two members did not participate—the Supreme Court held that the activities of HUAC during its investigations were, indeed, beyond the scope of the stated aims of the committee, as well as the authority of congressional powers.

▲ Senator Joseph McCarthy (above) symbolized the fears of the early 1950s, when communist spies were suspected to have infiltrated all aspects of American society. Together, McCarthy's committee in the Senate and the House Un-American Activities Committee used their power to subpoena people to investigate their loyalty. As a result many reputations were smeared and careers ruined.

PRIMARY SOURCE

The Court's Opinion

"The power of the Congress to conduct investigations is inherent in the legislative process. That power is broad. . . . But, broad as is this power of inquiry, it is not unlimited. There is no general authority to expose the private affairs of individuals without justification in terms of the functions of the Congress. . . . Nor is the Congress a law enforcement or trial agency. These are functions of the executive and judicial departments of government. No inquiry is an end in itself; it must be related to, and in furtherance of, a legitimate task of the Congress. Investigations conducted solely for the personal aggrandizement of the investigators or to "punish" those investigated are indefensible."

—Chief Justice Earl Warren, writing for the majority in
Watkins v. *United States*

PRIMARY SOURCE

Dissenting View

"It may be that at times the House Committee on Un-American Activities has, as the Court says, "conceived of its task in the grand view of its name." And, perhaps, as the Court indicates, the rules of conduct placed upon the Committee by the House admit of individual abuse and unfairness. But that is none of our affair. So long as the object of a legislative inquiry is legitimate and the questions propounded are pertinent thereto, it is not for the courts to interfere with the committee system of inquiry. To hold otherwise would be an infringement on the power given the Congress to inform itself. . . ."

—Justice Tom Campbell Clark, author of the dissenting opinion in
Watkins v. *United States*

DBQ Document-Based Questions

1. **Explaining** On what does Warren say a congressional inquiry must always be based?
2. **Discussing** Why does Clark disagree with the majority opinion?
3. **Making Inferences** What opinion do you think Warren had of HUAC?

Life During the Early Cold War

MAIN Idea Obsessed with fear of a nuclear attack, many Americans took steps to protect themselves.

HISTORY AND YOU Have you ever felt the need to protect yourself from something dangerous or scary? Read to learn more about how Americans tried to deal with their fears during the early 1950s.

The Red Scare and the spread of nuclear weapons had a profound impact on American life in the 1950s. Fear of communism and of nuclear war affected the thinking and choices of many ordinary Americans, as well as their leaders in government. Some Americans responded by preparing to survive a nuclear attack, while others became active in politics in an effort to shape government policy. Writers responded by describing the dangers of atomic war and the threat of communism—sometimes to convince people to take action and sometimes to protest policies they feared might lead to war.

Facing the Bomb

Already upset by the first Soviet atomic test in 1949, Americans were shocked when the Soviets again successfully tested the much more powerful hydrogen bomb, or H-bomb, in 1953. The United States had tested its own H-bomb less than a year earlier.

Americans prepared for a surprise Soviet attack. Schools set aside special areas as bomb shelters. In bomb drills, students learned to

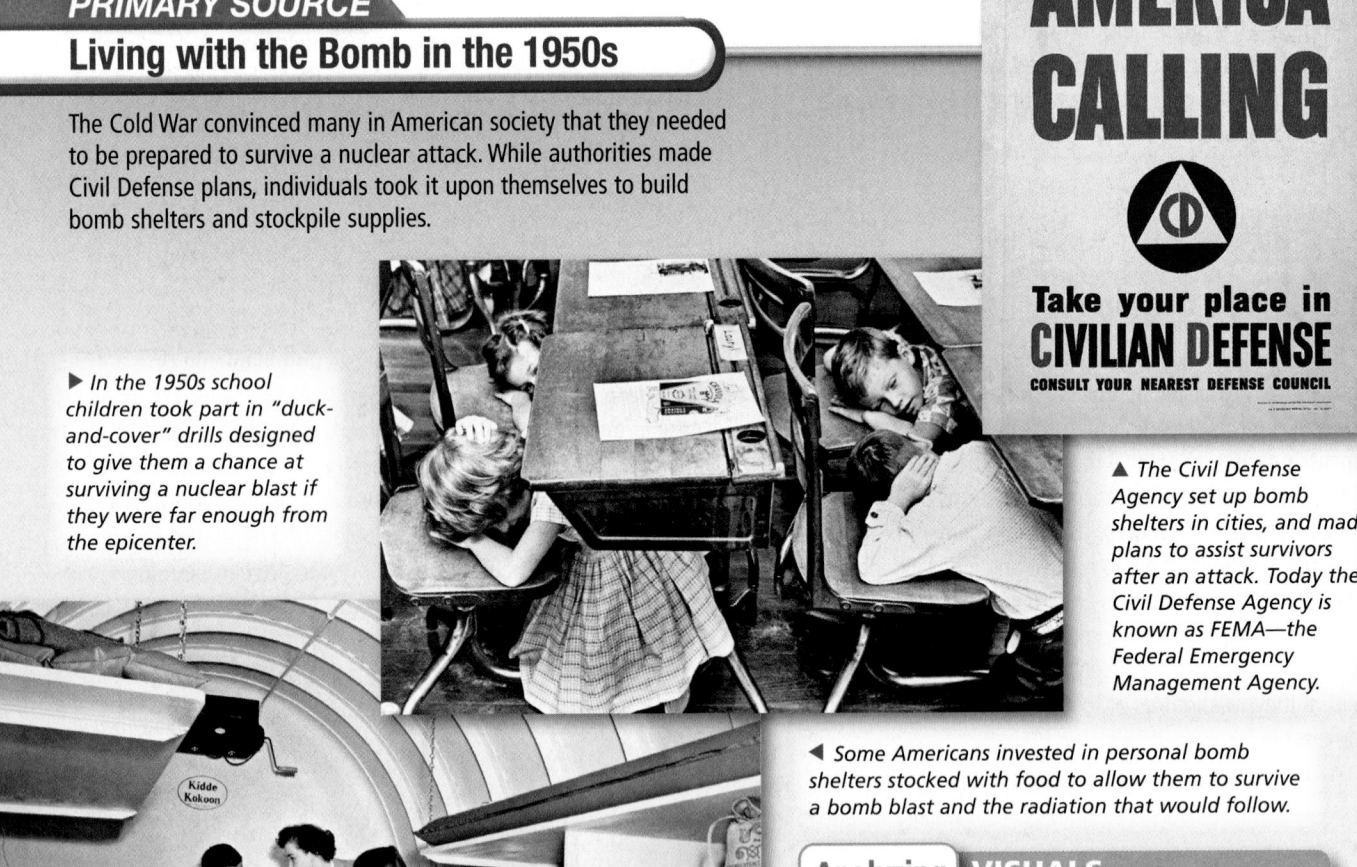

Living with the Bomb in the 1950s

The Cold War convinced many in American society that they needed to be prepared to survive a nuclear attack. While authorities made Civil Defense plans, individuals took it upon themselves to build bomb shelters and stockpile supplies.

▶ In the 1950s school children took part in "duck-and-cover" drills designed to give them a chance at surviving a nuclear blast if they were far enough from the epicenter.

AMERICA CALLING

Take your place in **CIVILIAN DEFENSE**
CONSULT YOUR NEAREST DEFENSE COUNCIL

▲ The Civil Defense Agency set up bomb shelters in cities, and made plans to assist survivors after an attack. Today the Civil Defense Agency is known as FEMA—the Federal Emergency Management Agency.

◀ Some Americans invested in personal bomb shelters stocked with food to allow them to survive a bomb blast and the radiation that would follow.

CANNED FOOD

Kidde Kokoon

Analyzing VISUALS

1. **Explaining** What was the purpose of the "duck-and-cover" drills and bomb shelters?

2. **Making Inferences** Even if some preparations would not work, why might the government have wanted people to prepare for war?

CANNED WATER

duck under their desks, turn away from the windows, and cover their heads with their hands. These "duck-and-cover" actions were supposed to protect them from a nuclear bomb blast.

Although "duck-and-cover" might have made people feel safe, it would not have protected them from deadly nuclear radiation. According to experts, for every person killed outright by a nuclear blast, four more would die later from **fallout,** the radiation left over after a blast. To protect themselves, some families built backyard fallout shelters and stocked them with canned food.

Popular Culture in the Cold War

Worries about nuclear war and Communist infiltration filled the public's imagination. Cold War themes soon appeared in films, plays, television, the titles of dance tunes, and popular fiction.

In 1953 Arthur Miller's thinly veiled criticism of the Communist witchhunts, *The Crucible,* appeared on Broadway. The play remains popular today as a cautionary tale about how hysteria can lead to false accusations. Matt Cvetic was an FBI undercover informant who secretly infiltrated the Communist Party in Pittsburgh, Pennsylvania. His story captivated magazine readers in the *Saturday Evening Post* in 1950 and came to movie screens the next year as *I Was a Communist for the FBI.* Another suspense film, *Walk East on Beacon* (1951), features the FBI's activities in an espionage case.

In 1953 television took up the theme with a series about an undercover FBI counterspy who was also a Communist Party official. Each week, *I Led Three Lives* kept television viewers on edge. Popular tunes such as "Atomic Boogie" and "Atom Bomb Baby" played on the radio.

In 1954 author Philip Wylie published *Tomorrow!* This novel describes the horrific effects of nuclear war on an unprepared American city. As an adviser on civil defense, Wylie had failed to convince the federal government to play a strong role in building bomb shelters. Frustrated, he wrote his novel to educate the public about the horrors of atomic war.

One of the most famous and enduring works of this period is John Hersey's nonfiction book *Hiroshima.* Originally published as the entire contents of the August 1946 edition of *The New Yorker* magazine, the book provides the firsthand accounts of six survivors of the U.S. dropping of the atomic bomb on Hiroshima, Japan. Not only did it make some Americans question the use of the bomb, *Hiroshima* also underscored the real and personal horrors of a nuclear attack.

At the same time that these fears were haunting Americans, the country was enjoying postwar prosperity and optimism. That spirit, combined with McCarthyism, fears of Communist infiltration, and the threat of atomic attack, made the early 1950s a time of contrasts. As the 1952 election approached, Americans were looking for someone or something that would make them feel secure.

✔ Reading Check Describing How did the Cold War affect life in the 1950s?

Section 3 REVIEW

Vocabulary

1. **Explain** the significance of: Red Scare, subversion, loyalty review program, Alger Hiss, perjury, McCarran Act, McCarthyism, censure, fallout.

Main Ideas

2. **Explaining** What was the result of President Truman's loyalty review program?

3. **Analyzing** Hearings to investigate Communist subversion in what organization led to McCarthy's downfall?

4. **Identifying** What event made Americans fearful of a nuclear attack by the Soviets?

Critical Thinking

5. **Big Ideas** How did the Red Scare and McCarthyism change American society and government?

6. **Organizing** Use a graphic organizer similar to the one below to list the causes and effects of the Red Scare of the 1950s.

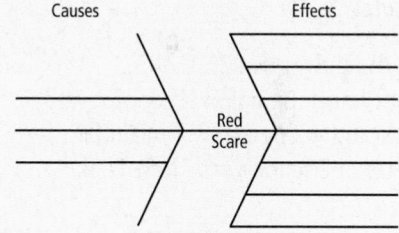

Causes   Effects

Red Scare

7. **Analyzing Visuals** Study the cartoons on page 777. Which cartoon do you think makes the stronger point? Explain.

Writing About History

8. **Persuasive Writing** Suppose that you are a newspaper editor during the Army-McCarthy hearings. Write an editorial giving reasons why people should support or condemn Senator McCarthy.

History ONLINE

Study Central™ To review this section, go to glencoe.com and click on Study Central.

Section 4

Eisenhower's Cold War Policies

Guide to Reading

Big Ideas
Science and Technology Nuclear technology enabled Eisenhower to change U.S. military policy, while new missile technology marked the beginning of the space age.

Content Vocabulary
- massive retaliation *(p. 783)*
- brinkmanship *(p. 783)*
- covert *(p. 785)*
- developing nation *(p. 785)*
- military-industrial complex *(p. 787)*

Academic Vocabulary
- imply *(p. 786)*
- response *(p. 787)*

People and Events to Identify
- Central Intelligence Agency *(p. 785)*
- *Sputnik* *(p. 787)*

Reading Strategy
Organizing Complete a concept web similar to the one below by filling in aspects of Eisenhower's "New Look."

Eisenhower's "New Look"

NEW YORK CORE CURRICULUM
U.S. History and Government

Unit 6:
II.C.4.c Stalemate and Truce (1953)
II.C.5 Point four aid: Africa, Asia, Latin America
Unit 7:
II.B Eisenhower foreign policies
II.B.2 John Foster Dulles, massive retaliation; brinkmanship
II.B.4 Summits and U-2s
II.B.7 Polish and Hungarian uprisings
II.B.8 Eisenhower Doctrine: intervention in Lebanon
II.B.9 Sputnik: initiating the space race

President Eisenhower believed developing new technology to deliver nuclear weapons would help prevent war. He also directed the CIA to use covert operations in the struggle to contain communism.

Massive Retaliation

MAIN Idea Eisenhower fought the Cold War by increasing the U.S. nuclear arsenal and using the threat of nuclear war to end conflicts in Korea, Taiwan, and the Suez.

HISTORY AND YOU Do you know anyone who uses threats to get his or her way? Read further to learn about Eisenhower's use of nuclear threats to achieve foreign policy goals.

By the end of 1952, many Americans were ready for a change in leadership. The Cold War had much to do with that attitude. Many people believed that Truman's foreign policy was not working. The Soviet Union had tested an atomic bomb and consolidated its hold on Eastern Europe. China had fallen to communism, and American troops were fighting in Korea.

Tired of the criticism and uncertain he could win, Truman decided not to run again. The Democrats nominated Adlai Stevenson, governor of Illinois. The Republicans chose Dwight D. Eisenhower, the general who had organized the D-Day invasion. Stevenson had no chance against a national hero who had helped win World War II. Americans wanted someone they could trust to lead the nation in the Cold War. Eisenhower won in a landslide.

"More Bang for the Buck"

The Cold War shaped Eisenhower's thinking from the moment he took office. He was convinced that the key to victory in the Cold War was not simply military might but also a strong economy. The United States had to show the world that free enterprise could produce a better society than communism. At the same time, economic prosperity would prevent Communists from gaining support in the United States and protect society from subversion.

As a professional soldier, Eisenhower knew the costs associated with large-scale conventional war. Preparing for that kind of warfare, he believed, was too expensive. "We cannot defend the nation in a way which will exhaust our economy," the president declared. Instead of maintaining a large and expensive army, the nation "must be prepared to use atomic weapons in all forms." Nuclear weapons, he said, gave "more bang for the buck."

TECHNOLOGY & HISTORY

Cold War Technology President Eisenhower's emphasis on nuclear weapons required new technology to deliver them. Eisenhower wanted to make sure that the United States could wage nuclear war even if the Soviets destroyed American bases in Europe or Asia. This required technology that would allow the U.S. to strike the USSR without needing bases in Europe.

▶ **ICBMs**

Because bombers could be shot down, Eisenhower also approved the development of intercontinental ballistic missiles (ICBMs) that could reach anywhere in the world in less than 30 minutes. The Atlas missile (right) was the first American ICBM. It was also used to launch the first seven U.S. astronauts. It is still used today to launch satellites.

▲ **Long-Range Bombers**

In 1955 the U.S. Air Force unveiled the huge B-52 bomber (above), which could fly across continents to drop nuclear bombs. The B-52 is still in use today.

Sixteen missiles were carried in silos located here.

◀ **Missile Submarines**

Eisenhower also began a program to build submarines capable of launching nuclear missiles from underwater. The Polaris submarine (left) launched in 1960 and carried 16 nuclear missiles.

Analyzing VISUALS

1. **Determining Cause and Effect** How did Eisenhower's nuclear strategy lead to the development of new technologies?

2. **Defining** What is an ICBM and what is its purpose?

The Korean War had convinced Eisenhower that the United States could not contain communism by fighting a series of small wars. Such wars were unpopular and too expensive. Instead, wars had to be prevented from happening in the first place. The best way to do that seemed to be to threaten to use nuclear weapons. This policy came to be called **massive retaliation.**

The new policy enabled Eisenhower to cut military spending from $50 billion to $34 billion. He did this by reducing the size of the army, which was expensive to maintain. At the same time, he increased the U.S. nuclear arsenal from about 1,000 bombs in 1953 to about 18,000 bombs in 1961.

Brinkmanship

President Eisenhower's willingness to threaten nuclear war to maintain peace worried some people. However, Secretary of State John Foster Dulles, the dominant figure in the nation's foreign policy in the 1950s, strongly defended this approach:

PRIMARY SOURCE

"You have to take chances for peace, just as you must take chances in war. Some say that we were brought to the verge of war. Of course we were brought to the verge of war. The ability to get to the verge without getting into the war is the necessary art.... If you try to run away from it, if you are scared to go to the brink, you are lost. We've had to look it square in the face.... We walked to the brink and we looked it in the face. We took strong action."

—quoted in *Rise to Globalism*

Critics called this **brinkmanship**—the willingness to go to the brink of war to force the other side to back down—and argued that it was too dangerous. During several crises, however, President Eisenhower felt compelled to threaten nuclear war.

The Korean War Ends

During his campaign for the presidency, Eisenhower had said, "I shall go to Korea," promising to end the costly and increasingly unpopular war. On December 4, 1952, he kept his promise. Bundled against the freezing Korean winter, the president-elect talked with frontline commanders and their troops.

Eisenhower became convinced that the ongoing battle was costing too many lives and bringing too few victories. He was determined to bring the war to an end. The president then quietly let the Chinese know that the United States might continue the Korean War "under circumstances of our own choosing"—a hint at a nuclear attack.

The threat to go to the brink of nuclear war seemed to work. In July 1953 negotiators signed an armistice. The battle line between the two sides in Korea, which was very near the prewar boundary, became the border between North Korea and South Korea. A "demilitarized zone" (DMZ) separated them. American troops are still based in Korea, helping to defend South Korea's border. There has never been a peace treaty to end the war.

The Taiwan Crisis

Shortly after the Korean War ended, a new crisis erupted in Asia. Although Communists had taken power in mainland China, the Nationalists still controlled Taiwan and several

Turning Point

Sputnik Launches a Space Race

As the United States began to develop ICBMs, Americans were stunned to discover that the Soviet Union already had them. On October 4, 1957, the Soviets demonstrated this technology by launching *Sputnik*, the first artificial satellite to orbit Earth.

Worried that the United States was falling behind, Congress created the National Aeronautics and Space Administration (NASA) to coordinate missile research and space exploration. It also passed the National Defense Education Act (NDEA), which provided funds for education in science, math, and foreign languages.

Sputnik marked the beginning of a new era—the use of satellites in space. Both nations in the Cold War began launching satellites to assist in communications and to spy on the other nation. Today, satellites are a vital part of modern communications and travel. They transmit television and cell phone signals, and the satellites of the Global Positioning System (GPS) help ships and airplanes to navigate. Hikers and drivers can also buy GPS receivers to help determine where they are.

ANALYZING HISTORY Do you think missile and satellite technology helped prevent conflict during the Cold War or made the Cold War worse? Create a multimedia presentation on the Space Race and how it has changed American society.

▲ Sputnik (above) was the world's first artificial satellite. It made news around the world and launched the space race.

▲ Scientists prepare the first U.S. satellite, Explorer I, for launch in 1958.

▲ Sputnik II, launched only a month after Sputnik, carried the first living creature into orbit—an "astro" dog named Laika.

small islands along China's coast. In the fall of 1954, China threatened to seize two of the islands. Eisenhower saw Taiwan as part of the "anti-Communist barrier" in Asia that needed to be protected at all costs.

When China began shelling the islands and announced that Taiwan would be liberated, Eisenhower asked Congress to authorize the use of force to defend Taiwan. He then warned the Chinese that any attack on Taiwan would be resisted by U.S. naval forces stationed nearby and hinted that they would use nuclear weapons to stop an invasion. Soon afterward, China backed down.

The Suez Crisis

The following year, a serious crisis erupted in the Middle East. Eisenhower's goal in that region was to prevent Arab nations from aligning with the Soviet Union. To build support among Arabs, Secretary of State Dulles offered to help Egypt finance the construction of a dam on the Nile River.

The deal ran into trouble in Congress, however, because Egypt had bought weapons from Communist Czechoslovakia. Dulles was forced to withdraw the offer. A week later, Egyptian troops seized control of the Suez Canal from the Anglo-French company that had controlled it. The Egyptians intended to use the canal's profits to pay for the dam.

The British and French responded quickly to the Suez Crisis. In October 1956, British and French troops invaded Egypt. Eisenhower was furious with Britain and France. The situation became even more dangerous when the Soviet Union threatened rocket attacks on Britain and France and offered to send troops to help Egypt. Eisenhower immediately put U.S. nuclear forces on alert, noting, "If those fellows start something, we may have to hit them—and if necessary, with everything in the bucket."

Under strong pressure from the United States, the British and French called off their invasion. The Soviet Union had won a major diplomatic victory, however, by supporting Egypt. Soon afterward, other Arab nations began accepting Soviet aid as well.

✔ Reading Check **Identifying** What was brinkmanship?

Covert Operations

MAIN Idea Eisenhower directed the Central Intelligence Agency to use covert operations to limit the spread of communism and Soviet influence.

HISTORY AND YOU Do you enjoy reading spy novels? Read on to learn of the development and work of a spy agency in the United States.

President Eisenhower relied on brinkmanship on several occasions, but he knew it could not work in all situations. It could prevent war, but it could not, for example, prevent Communists from staging revolutions within countries. To prevent Communist uprisings in other countries, Eisenhower decided to use **covert,** or hidden, operations conducted by the **Central Intelligence Agency (CIA).**

Many of the CIA's operations took place in **developing nations**—nations with primarily agricultural economies. Many of these countries blamed European imperialism and American capitalism for their problems. Their leaders looked to the Soviet Union as a model of how to industrialize their countries. They often threatened to nationalize, or put under government control, foreign businesses operating in their countries.

One way to stop developing nations from moving into the Communist camp was to provide them with financial aid, as Eisenhower had tried to do in Egypt. In some cases, however, where the threat of communism seemed stronger, the CIA ran covert operations to overthrow anti-American leaders and replace them with pro-American leaders.

Iran and Guatemala

Two examples of covert operations that achieved U.S. objectives took place in Iran and Guatemala. By 1953, Iranian Prime Minister Mohammed Mossadegh had already nationalized the Anglo-Iranian Oil Company. He seemed ready to make an oil deal with the Soviet Union. The pro-American Shah of Iran tried to force Mossadegh out of office, but failed and fled into exile. The CIA quickly sent agents to organize street riots and arrange a coup that ousted Mossadegh and returned the shah to power.

The following year, the CIA intervened in Guatemala. In 1951, with Communist support, Jacobo Arbenz Guzmán was elected president of Guatemala. His land-reform program took over large estates and plantations, including those of the American–owned United Fruit Company. In May 1954, Communist Czechoslovakia delivered arms to Guatemala. The CIA responded by arming the Guatemalan opposition and training them at secret camps in Nicaragua and Honduras. Shortly after these CIA-trained forces invaded Guatemala, Arbenz Guzmán left office.

Trouble in Eastern Europe

Covert operations did not always work as Eisenhower hoped. Stalin died in 1953, and a power struggle began in the Soviet Union. By 1956, Nikita Khrushchev had emerged as the leader of the Soviet Union. That year, Khrushchev delivered a secret speech to Soviet officials. He attacked Stalin's policies and insisted that there were many ways to build a communist society. Although the speech was secret, the CIA obtained a copy of it. With Eisenhower's permission, the CIA arranged for it to be broadcast to Eastern Europe.

Many Eastern Europeans had long been frustrated with Communist rule. Hearing Khrushchev's speech further discredited communism. In June 1956 riots erupted in Eastern Europe. By late October, a full-scale uprising had begun in Hungary. Although Khrushchev was willing to tolerate greater freedom in Eastern Europe, he had never meant to **imply** that the Soviets would tolerate an end to communism in the region. Soon after the uprising began, Soviet tanks rolled into Budapest, the capital of Hungary, and crushed the rebellion.

The Eisenhower Doctrine

The United States was not the only nation using covert means to support its foreign policy. President Gamal Abdel Nasser of Egypt had emerged from the Suez crisis as a hero to the Arab people, and by 1957 he had begun working

The U-2 Incident

In 1960, the Soviet Union shot down an American U-2 spy plane in Soviet air space. The incident led to a dramatic confrontation at the U.S-Soviet summit in Paris in 1960.

◀ Calling President Eisenhower "a thief caught red-handed," Soviet Premier Khrushchev warns the Paris summit that further spy flights will lead to war.

▲ The U-2 (above left) was America's most sophisticated spy plane, able to fly higher than any other plane at the time. The pilot, Francis Gary Powers (above right), was captured but later released.

Analyzing VISUALS

1. **Paraphrasing** What did Nikita Khrushchev say would be the result of further U.S. aerial spying?
2. **Making Inferences** Why was the U-2 used as a spy plane?

with Jordan and Syria to spread pan-Arabism—the idea that all Arab people should be united into one nation. Eisenhower and Dulles worried about Nasser's links to the Soviets and feared that he was laying the groundwork to take control of the Middle East. In late 1957 Eisenhower asked Congress to authorize the use of military force whenever the president thought it necessary to assist Middle East nations resisting Communist aggression. The policy came to be called the Eisenhower Doctrine. It essentially extended the Truman Doctrine and the policy of containment to the Middle East.

In February 1958 Eisenhower's concerns appeared to be confirmed when left-wing rebels, believed to be backed by Nasser and the Soviet Union, seized power in Iraq. Fearing that his government was next, the president of Lebanon asked the United States for help. Eisenhower immediately ordered 5,000 marines to Lebanon to protect its capital, Beirut. At the same time, British forces went into Jordan at the request of King Hussein to protect his government. Once the situation stabilized, the U.S. forces withdrew.

A Spy Plane Is Shot Down

After the Hungarian uprising, Khrushchev reasserted Soviet power and the superiority of communism. Although he had supported "peaceful coexistence" with capitalism, he began accusing the "capitalist countries" of starting a "feverish arms race." In 1957 after the launch of *Sputnik,* Khrushchev boasted, "We will bury capitalism. . . . Your grandchildren will live under communism."

Late the following year, Khrushchev demanded the withdrawal of Allied troops from West Berlin. Secretary of State Dulles rejected Khrushchev's demands. If the Soviets threatened Berlin, Dulles announced, NATO would respond, "if need be by military force." Brinkmanship worked again, and Khrushchev backed down.

At Eisenhower's invitation, Khrushchev visited the United States in late 1959. After the success of that visit, the two leaders agreed to hold a summit in Paris. A summit is a formal face-to-face meeting of leaders from different countries to discuss important issues.

Shortly before the summit was to begin in 1960, the Soviet Union shot down an American U-2 spy plane. At first, Eisenhower claimed that the aircraft was a weather plane that had strayed off course. Then Khrushchev dramatically produced the pilot. Eisenhower refused to apologize, saying the flights had protected American security. In **response,** Khrushchev broke up the summit.

In this climate of heightened tension, President Eisenhower prepared to leave office. In January 1961 he delivered a farewell address to the nation. In the address, he pointed out that a new relationship had developed between the military establishment and the defense industry. He warned Americans to be on guard against the influence of this **military-industrial complex** in a democracy. Although he had avoided war and kept communism contained, Eisenhower was also frustrated: "I confess I lay down my official responsibility in this field with a definite sense of disappointment. . . . I wish I could say that a lasting peace is in sight."

✓ Reading Check **Explaining** In what nations did the United States intervene with covert operations?

Vocabulary

1. **Explain** the significance of: massive retaliation, brinkmanship, covert, Central Intelligence Agency, developing nation, *Sputnik*, military-industrial complex.

Main Ideas

2. **Summarizing** Why did Eisenhower want to depend on nuclear weapons instead of traditional military approaches to war?

3. **Defining** What was the goal of the Eisenhower Doctrine?

Critical Thinking

4. **Big Ideas** How did technology shape Eisenhower's military policy?

5. **Organizing** Use a graphic organizer similar to the one below to list Eisenhower's strategies for containing communism.

6. **Analyzing Visuals** Study the photograph of Khrushchev on page 786. How does this photograph illustrate the U.S. and Soviet relationship at this point in the Cold War?

Writing About History

7. **Persuasive Writing** Suppose that you are a member of Eisenhower's Cabinet. Defend or attack brinkmanship as a foreign policy tactic. Be sure to provide specific reasons for your opinions.

History ONLINE
Study Central™ To review this section, go to glencoe.com and click on Study Central.

Causes of the Cold War

Long-Range Causes

- Both the United States and the Soviet Union believe their economic and political systems are superior.
- Defeat of Germany creates a power vacuum in Europe and leaves U.S. and Soviet forces occupying parts of Europe.
- The U.S. wants to rebuild Europe's economy and support democratic governments to ensure peace and security.
- The USSR wants Germany weak and believes nations on the Soviet border should have Communist governments.

Immediate Causes

- At Yalta, Soviets promise to allow free elections in Eastern Europe but instead gradually impose Communist regimes.
- At Potsdam, Soviets want German reparations, but the U.S. supports rebuilding Germany's economy.
- Soviet troops help Communists in northern Iran, but U.S. pressure forces a withdrawal.
- George Kennan sends the Long Telegram to U.S. officials, explaining that the Soviets need to be contained.
- Soviets send aid to Communist rebels in Greece and demand Turkey share control of the Dardanelles with the USSR; Truman issues the Truman Doctrine and sends aid to Greece and Turkey.

▲ From left to right: British Prime Minister Clement Atlee, U.S. President Harry Truman, and Soviet leader Joseph Stalin at the Potsdam Conference in 1945. The conference contributed to the onset of the Cold War because of disagreements over how to handle postwar Europe.

Effects of the Cold War

Effects in Europe

- U.S. launches the Marshall Plan to rebuild Europe.
- Germany is divided into two separate nations.
- The USSR blockades Berlin; U.S. organizes the Berlin Airlift.
- The U.S. creates NATO; the USSR creates the Warsaw Pact.

Global Effects

- When China falls to communism, the U.S. responds by helping Japan build up its economy and military.
- When Communist North Korea invades South Korea, the U.S. organizes an international force to stop the invasion.

Effects on the United States

- Soviet spies are arrested.
- A new Red Scare leads to laws restricting the Communist Party in the U.S. and to investigations by the House Un-American Activities Committee and Senator Joseph McCarthy.
- Americans practice civil defense; some build bomb shelters.
- President Eisenhower orders the development of new rockets, bombers, and submarines that can carry nuclear weapons.
- Eisenhower uses the CIA to covertly contain communism.

▲ The Soviet Union displays its nuclear capabilities in the form of these short-range missiles during celebrations commemorating the 40th anniversary of the Bolshevik Revolution in 1957. The nuclear arms race was a part of the Cold War for nearly 40 years.

NEW YORK REGENTS EXAM PRACTICE

TEST-TAKING

When you first start a test, review it completely so that you can budget your time most efficiently. For example, if there are essay questions at the end, you will want to be sure you leave enough time to write complete answers.

Part I

Directions (1–11): For each statement or question, write on a separate sheet of paper the number of the word or expression that, of those given, best completes the statement or answers the question.

1 Which of the following was agreed to at the Yalta Conference?

(1) the division of Germany

(2) the terms of Germany's surrender

(3) the establishment of satellite nations

(4) the establishment of NATO

2 At Potsdam, the main conflict was over which of the following?

(1) the United Nations

(2) the invasion of Japan

(3) German reparations

(4) nuclear weapons

3 George Kennan first suggested which foreign policy?

(1) brinkmanship

(2) containment

(3) massive retaliation

(4) the Marshall Plan

4 Which event set off the Korean War?

(1) The Japanese invaded South Korea.

(2) The Soviet Union invaded North Korea.

(3) Chinese-controlled North Korea invaded South Korea.

(4) Soviet-controlled North Korea invaded South Korea.

5 After World War II, the purpose of HUAC was to

(1) hold public hearings on Communist subversion.

(2) locate chapters of the Communist Party.

(3) administer the loyalty review program.

(4) create the McCarran Act.

6 The McCarran Act required

(1) every government employee to take a loyalty oath.

(2) all Communist Party chapters to disband.

(3) all Communist organizations to register with the government.

(4) the censure of members of Congress who would not support HUAC.

7 Eisenhower's administration developed an approach to foreign policy based on the threat of nuclear attack known as

(1) containment.

(2) massive retaliation.

(3) subversion.

(4) duck-and-cover.

8 After World War II, the Soviet Union wanted to establish a buffer zone on its European border that consisted of which of the following?

(1) developing nations

(2) capitalist nations

(3) satellite nations

(4) demilitarization

Need Extra Help?								
If You Missed Questions . . .	1	2	3	4	5	6	7	8
Go to Page . . .	760–761	764–765	766	771	775	778	782–783	765

[OVER]

Base your answer to question 9 on the map below and your knowledge of Chapter 22.

Berlin After World War II, 1945

0 — 6 kilometers
0 — 6 miles
Transverse Mercator projection

Havel River
Tegel
East Berlin
Brandenburg Gate
Checkpoint Charlie
Gatow
West Berlin
Tempelhof
Spree River

- American sector
- British sector
- French sector
- Soviet sector
- East Germany
- Airport

9   Why was Stalin initially able to control access to West Berlin?

   (1)   West Berlin was in the Soviet Union.

   (2)   West Berlin was ruled by Communists.

   (3)   West Berlin was in the Soviet sector of Germany.

   (4)   West Berlin was occupied by the Red Army.

10   The Eisenhower Doctrine extended the Truman Doctrine to which region?

   (1)   Asia

   (2)   Eastern Europe

   (3)   South America

   (4)   the Middle East

11   What was the underlying goal of the Marshall Plan?

   (1)   to contain Soviet expansion in the Middle East

   (2)   to rebuild European economies to prevent the spread of communism

   (3)   to monitor the growth of the military-industrial complex in the United States

   (4)   to Americanize Western European nations

Need Extra Help?			
If You Missed Questions . . .	9	10	11
Go to Page . . .	768–769	768–769	768

Part II Thematic Essay Question

Directions: Write a well-organized essay that includes an introduction, several paragraphs addressing the task below, and a conclusion.

Theme: The Cold War

After the end of World War II, a "Cold War" between the United States and the Soviet Union began, largely because of different ideas about economics. This era of confrontation and competition between the two nations lasted from about 1946 to 1990.

Task:

Identify at least two important conflicts of the Cold War and for each

- Discuss the background of the conflict, including actions of the United States and Soviet Union

- Describe one immediate and one long-term effect of each conflict

Guidelines:

In your essay, be sure to:

- Develop all aspects of the task

- Support the theme with relevant facts, examples, and details

- Use a logical and clear plan of organization, including an introduction and a conclusion that are beyond a restatement of the theme

Part III Document-Based Question

This question is based on the accompanying documents. It is designed to test your ability to work with historical documents. Some of the documents have been edited for the purposes of the question. As you analyze the documents, take into account the source of each document and any point of view that may be presented in the document.

Historical Context:

The effects of the Cold War were far-reaching and had significant social and political consequences. The fear of communism and its spread permeated the lives of Americans resulting in a new Red Scare. In addition, Americans were locked into a scientific and technological competition with the USSR.

Task:

Using information from the documents and your knowledge of United States history, answer the questions that follow each document in Part A. Your answers to the questions will help you write the Part B essay in which you will be asked to

- Discuss the social effects of the Cold War on citizens of the United States, including the Red Scare
- Evaluate the far-reaching effects of the fear of communism and the desire to surpass the Soviet Union in the space race and weapons production

Part A

Short-Answer Questions

Directions: Analyze the documents and answer the short-answer questions that follow each document on a separate sheet of paper.

Document 1

As a United States Senator, I am not proud of the way in which the Senate has been made a publicity platform for irresponsible sensationalism. I am not proud of the reckless abandon in which unproved charges have been hurled from this side of the aisle. I am not proud of the obviously staged, undignified countercharges that have been attempted in retaliation from the other side of the aisle . . . I am not proud of the way we smear outsiders from the Floor of the Senate and hide behind a cloak of congressional immunity. . . .

As an American, I am shocked at the way Republicans and Democrats alike are playing directly into the Communist design of 'confuse, divide, and conquer.'. . . I want to see our nation recapture the strength and unity it once had when we fought the enemy instead of ourselves.

Source: Margaret Chase Smith, *Declaration of Conscience*, Doubleday & Company, Inc., 1972

1 In the speech, Smith expresses anger with whom? Why?

Document 2

"So Russia Launched a Satellite, but Has It Made Cars With Fins Yet?"

Source: Milwaukee Public Library

2 What is the cartoonist comparing?

Part B

Essay

Directions: Reread the task box at the top left and write a well-organized essay that includes an introduction, several paragraphs, and a conclusion.

Guidelines:

In your essay, be sure to:

- Develop all aspects of the task
- Incorporate information from the documents
- Incorporate relevant outside information

History ONLINE

For additional test practice, use Self-Check Quizzes—Chapter 22 at glencoe.com.

Need Extra Help?			
If You Missed Questions . . .	1	2	Essay
Go to Page . . .	778	R18	774–781

Postwar America

1945–1960

SECTION 1 Truman and Eisenhower

SECTION 2 The Affluent Society

SECTION 3 The Other Side of American Life

Teens enjoy milkshakes while studying in a 1950's-style diner.

U.S. PRESIDENTS
U.S. EVENTS
WORLD EVENTS

1944
- GI Bill is enacted

Truman
1945–1953

1946
- Strikes erupt across country

1947
- Congress passes Taft-Hartley Act over Truman's veto

1951
- The *I Love Lucy* television show airs its first show

1944

1948

1952

1946
- Churchill gives "Iron Curtain" speech

1948
- South Africa introduces apartheid

1952
- Scientists led by Edward Teller develop hydrogen bomb

What Does It Mean to Be Prosperous?

After World War II, the United States experienced years of steady economic growth. Although not everyone benefited, the economic boom meant most Americans enjoyed more prosperity than earlier generations.

- *How did Americans spend this new wealth?*
- *How does prosperity change the way people live?*

FOLDABLES™

Categorizing Information Make a Folded-Table Foldable on popular culture in the 1950s and present. List the following for both time periods: data on the types of mass media and size of the audiences for them, characteristics of youth culture, and groups represented in the mass media.

Popular Culture	1950s	Present
Mass Media Types		
Youth Culture		
Groups Represented in Media		

Eisenhower
1953–1961

1955
- Salk polio vaccine becomes widely available

1956
- Congress passes Federal Highway Act

1957
- Estimated 40 million television sets in use in the United States

1956

1960

1954
- Gamal Abdel Nasser takes power in Egypt

1956
- Suez Canal crisis

1957
- USSR launches *Sputnik I* and *Sputnik II* satellites

History ONLINE **Chapter Overview**
Visit glencoe.com to preview Chapter 23.

Truman and Eisenhower

In the postwar era, Congress limited the power of unions and rejected most of President Truman's plan for a "Fair Deal." When Eisenhower became president, he cut back some government programs and launched the interstate highway system.

Return to a Peacetime Economy

MAIN Idea Despite inflation and strikes, the nation was able to shift to a peacetime economy without a recession.

HISTORY AND YOU Do you know you can get help paying for college if you serve in the military? Read to learn about the origins of the "GI Bill" and how it helped World War II veterans get a college education.

After the war many Americans feared the return to a peacetime economy. They worried that, after military production halted and millions of former soldiers glutted the labor market, unemployment and recession might sweep the country. Despite such worries, the economy continued to grow after the war as increased consumer spending helped ward off a recession. After 17 years of an economic depression and wartime shortages, Americans rushed out to buy the consumer goods they had long desired.

The Servicemen's Readjustment Act, popularly called the **GI Bill,** boosted the economy further. The act provided generous funds to veterans to help them establish businesses, buy homes, and attend college. The postwar economy did have problems, particularly in the first couple of years following the end of the war. A greater demand for goods led to higher prices, and this inflation soon triggered labor unrest. As the cost of living rose, workers in the automobile, steel, electrical, and mining industries went on strike for better pay.

Afraid that the nation's energy supply would be drastically reduced because of the striking miners, Truman ordered government seizure of the mines, while pressuring mine owners to grant the union most of its demands. The president also halted a strike that shut down the nation's railroads by threatening to draft the striking workers into the army.

Labor unrest and high prices prompted many Americans to call for a change. The Republicans seized on these sentiments during the 1946 congressional elections, winning control of both houses of Congress for the first time since 1930.

The new conservative Congress quickly set out to curb the power of organized labor. **Legislators** proposed a measure known as the Taft-Hartley Act, which outlawed the **closed shop,** or the practice of forcing business owners to hire only union members. Under this law,

The GI Bill of Rights

One reason the American economy rebounded so quickly after World War II ended was the Servicemen's Readjustment Act of 1944, popularly called the GI Bill of Rights. The act subsidized college tuition and provided zero down-payment, low-interest loans to veterans to help them buy homes and establish businesses.

Veterans flocked to colleges in large numbers after the war. Among them was William Oskay, Jr., (above) who attended Pennsylvania State University in 1946. By 1947, nearly half of all people attending college were veterans. At the University of Iowa (left), 60 percent of students were veterans in 1947. By 1956, when the GI program ended, 7.8 million veterans had used it to attend college. Another 2.4 million veterans used the program to obtain home loans.

Analyzing VISUALS

1. **Calculating** Based on the graph, what was the increase in college enrollments between 1944 and 1950?

2. **Specifying** About how many new homes were constructed in 1950?

College Enrollment

Enrollment (thousands): 0, 100, 200, 300, 400, 500
Years: 1942, 1944, 1946, 1948, 1950

Source: *Historical Statistics of the United States.*

New Home Construction

Homes (thousands): 0, 500, 1,000, 1,500, 2,000
Years: 1945, 1946, 1947, 1948, 1949, 1950

Source: *Historical Statistics of the United States.*

states could pass **right-to-work laws,** which outlawed **union shops** (shops in which new workers were required to join the union). The measure also prohibited featherbedding, the practice of limiting work output in order to create more jobs. Furthermore, the bill forbade unions from using their money to support political campaigns.

When the bill reached Truman, however, he vetoed it, arguing that it was a mistake:

PRIMARY SOURCE

"... [It would] reverse the basic direction of our national labor policy, inject the government into private economic affairs on an unprecedented scale, and conflict with important principles of our democratic society. Its provisions would cause more strikes, not fewer."

—quoted in *The Growth of the American Republic*

The president's concerns did little to sway Congress, which passed the Taft-Hartley Act in 1947 over Truman's veto. Its supporters claimed that the law held irresponsible unions in check, just as the Wagner Act of 1935 had restrained anti-union activities and employers. Labor leaders called the act a "slave labor" law and insisted that it erased many of the gains that unions had made since 1933.

✔ **Reading Check** **Explaining** Why did Truman veto the Taft-Hartley Act?

Truman's Program

MAIN Idea Truman pushed for a "Fair Deal" for Americans, despite the legislative conflicts he had with Congress.

HISTORY AND YOU Do you remember how close the last presidential election was? Read on to learn about Truman's surprise victory in 1948.

The Democratic Party's loss of control in Congress in the 1946 elections did not dampen President Truman's spirits or his plans. Shortly after taking office, Truman had proposed domestic measures seeking to continue the work of Franklin Roosevelt's New Deal. During his tenure in office, Truman worked to push this agenda through Congress.

Truman's Legislative Agenda

Truman's proposals included expansion of Social Security benefits; raising the minimum wage; a program to ensure full employment through aggressive use of federal spending and investment; public housing and slum clearance; and long-range environmental and public works planning. He also proposed a system of national health insurance.

Truman also boldly asked Congress in February 1948 to pass a broad civil rights bill that would protect African Americans' right to vote, abolish poll taxes, and make lynching a federal crime. He issued an executive order barring discrimination in federal employment and ending segregation in the armed forces. Most of Truman's legislative efforts, however, met with little success, as a coalition of Republicans and conservative Southern Democrats defeated many of his proposals.

The Election of 1948

As the presidential election of 1948 approached, most observers gave Truman little chance of winning. Some Americans still believed that he lacked the stature for the job, and they viewed his administration as weak and inept.

Divisions within the Democratic Party also seemed to spell disaster for Truman. At the Democratic Convention that summer, two factions **abandoned** the party altogether. Reacting angrily to Truman's support of civil rights, a group of Southern Democrats formed the States' Rights, or Dixiecrat, Party and nominated South Carolina Governor Strom Thurmond for president. At the same time, the party's more liberal members were frustrated by Truman's ineffective domestic policies and critical of his anti-Soviet foreign policy. They formed a new Progressive Party, with Henry A. Wallace as their presidential candidate.

The president's Republican opponent was New York Governor Thomas Dewey, a dignified and popular candidate who seemed unbeatable. After polling 50 political writers, *Newsweek* magazine declared three weeks before the election, "The landslide for Dewey will sweep the country."

Perhaps the only person who gave Truman any chance to win the election was Truman himself. "I know every one of those 50 fellows," he declared about the writers polled in *Newsweek.* "There isn't one of them has enough sense to pound sand in a rat hole." Ignoring the polls, he poured his energy into the campaign, traveling more than 20,000 miles by train and making more than 350 speeches. Along the way, Truman attacked the majority Republican Congress as "do-nothing, good-for-nothing" for refusing to enact his legislative agenda.

Truman's attacks on the "**Do-Nothing Congress**" did not mention that both he and Congress had passed the Truman Doctrine's aid program to Greece and Turkey, as well as the Marshall Plan. Congress had also enacted the National Security Act of 1947, which created the Department of Defense, the National Security Council, and the CIA; established the Joint Chiefs of Staff as a permanent organization; and made the Air Force an independent branch of the military. The 80th Congress did not "do nothing" as Truman charged, but its accomplishments were in areas that did not affect most Americans directly. As a result, Truman's charges began to stick.

With a great deal of support from laborers, African Americans, and farmers, Truman won a narrow but stunning victory over Dewey. Perhaps just as remarkable as the president's victory was the resurgence of the Democratic Party. When the dust had cleared after election day, Democrats had regained control of both houses of Congress.

The Fair Deal

Truman's 1949 State of the Union address repeated the domestic agenda he had put forth previously. "Every segment of our population and every individual," he declared, "has a right to expect from . . . government a fair deal." Whether intentional or not, the president had coined a name—the **Fair Deal**—to set his program apart from the New Deal. In February, he began to send his proposals to Congress.

The 81st Congress did not completely embrace Truman's Fair Deal. Legislators did raise the legal minimum wage to 75¢ an hour. They increased Social Security benefits by 75 percent and extended them to 10 million additional people. Congress also passed the National Housing Act of 1949, which provided for the construction of low-income housing, accompanied by long-term rent subsidies.

Congress refused, however, to pass national health insurance or to provide subsidies for farmers or federal aid for schools. In addition, legislators, led by the same coalition of conservative Republicans and Dixiecrats, opposed Truman's efforts to enact civil rights legislation. His plans for federal aid to education were also not enacted.

Reading Check **Summarizing** What did Truman and the Congress accomplish in foreign relations?

PRIMARY SOURCE
The Election of 1948

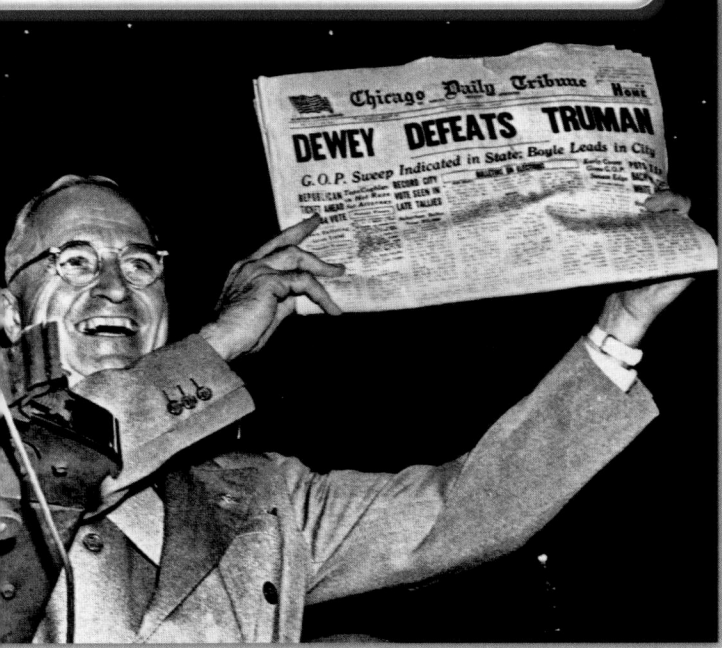

▲ *Harry Truman gleefully displays the erroneous* Chicago Daily Tribune *headline announcing his defeat by Thomas Dewey.*

What Was the Fair Deal?

In 1949 Truman outlined in his State of the Union address an ambitious legislative program that became known as the Fair Deal. Some of its main features were:

- the expansion of Social Security benefits
- an increase in the minimum wage
- a program to ensure full employment
- a program of public housing and slum clearance
- a long-range plan for environmental and public works
- a system of national health insurance
- a broad program of civil rights legislation

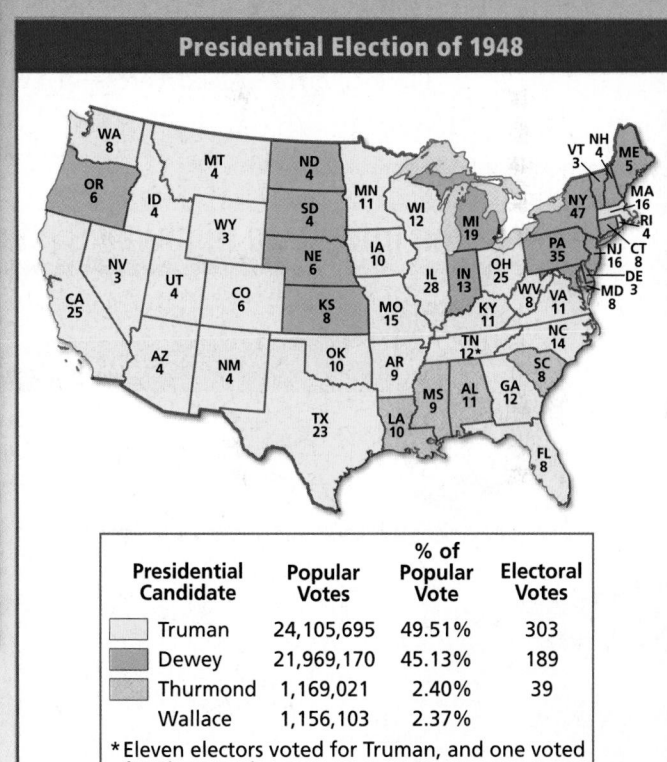

Presidential Election of 1948

Presidential Candidate	Popular Votes	% of Popular Vote	Electoral Votes
Truman	24,105,695	49.51%	303
Dewey	21,969,170	45.13%	189
Thurmond	1,169,021	2.40%	39
Wallace	1,156,103	2.37%	

*Eleven electors voted for Truman, and one voted for Thurmond.

Analyzing VISUALS

1. **Interpreting** In what regions of the nation did Thomas Dewey receive the most votes?

2. **Calculating** What was the difference in percentage of the popular vote received by Truman and Dewey?

The Eisenhower Years

MAIN Idea President Eisenhower cut federal spending, supported business, funded the interstate highway system, and extended some New Deal programs.

HISTORY AND YOU Do you think it is important for a president to have served in the military? Read to learn how Americans chose a war hero as president in the 1950s.

In 1950 the United States went to war in Korea. The war consumed the nation's attention and resources and effectively ended Truman's Fair Deal. By 1952, with the war at a bloody stalemate and his approval rating dropping quickly, Truman declined to run again for the presidency.

With no Democratic incumbent to face, Republicans pinned their hopes for regaining the White House in 1952 on a popular World War II hero: Dwight Eisenhower, former commander of the Allied Forces in Europe. The Democrats nominated Illinois Governor Adlai Stevenson.

The Republicans adopted the slogan: "It's time for a change!" The warm and friendly Eisenhower, known as "Ike," promised to end the war in Korea. "I like Ike" became the Republican rallying cry. Eisenhower won the election in a landslide, carrying the Electoral College, 442 votes to 89. The Republicans also gained an eight-seat majority in the House, while the Senate became evenly divided between Democrats and Republicans.

Eisenhower Takes Office

President Eisenhower had two favorite phrases. "Middle of the road" described his political beliefs and "**dynamic conservatism**" meant balancing economic conservatism with activism in areas that would benefit the country. Eisenhower wasted little time in showing his conservative side. The new president's cabinet appointments included several business

---

GEOGRAPHY AND HISTORY
Effects of the Interstate Highway System

WEST INTERSTATE 80

Interstate Highway System

Commercial Trucking *Interstate highways made distribution of goods by transport truck fast and efficient. By the 1990s, trucks moved more than 6 billion tons of goods—mostly by interstate.*

Rise of Suburbs *Interstate highways contributed to the growth of suburbs and urban sprawl. Interstates let people commute long distances from home to work.*

Analyzing GEOGRAPHY

1. **Location** Where were most of the interstate highways built? Why do you think that is?
2. **Movement** In what ways did the interstate highway system change daily life?

Road Culture *Interstate travel encouraged the development of cheap hotel chains, roadside convenience stores, and fast food restaurants located near interstate exits.*

leaders. Under their guidance, Eisenhower ended government price and rent controls, which many conservatives viewed as unnecessary federal regulation of the economy. Eisenhower's administration believed business growth was vital to the nation. His secretary of defense, formerly the president of General Motors, declared to the Senate that "what is good for our country is good for General Motors, and vice versa."

Eisenhower's conservatism showed itself in other ways as well. In an attempt to cut federal spending, the president vetoed a school construction bill and agreed to slash government aid to public housing. Along with these cuts, he supported some modest tax cuts.

Eisenhower also targeted the federal government's continuing aid to businesses, or what he termed "creeping socialism." Shortly after taking office, the president abolished the Reconstruction Finance Corporation (RFC), which since 1932 had lent money to banks, railroads, and other large institutions in financial trouble. Another Depression-era agency, the Tennessee Valley Authority (TVA), also came under Eisenhower's scrutiny. During his presidency, appropriations for the TVA fell from $185 million to $12 million.

In some areas, President Eisenhower took an activist role. For example, he pushed for two large government projects. During the 1950s, as the number of Americans who owned cars increased, so too did the need for greater and more efficient travel routes. In 1956 Congress responded to this growing need by passing the **Federal Highway Act,** the largest public works program in American history. The act appropriated $25 billion for a 10-year effort to construct more than 40,000 miles (64,400 km) of interstate highways. Congress also authorized construction of the Great Lakes–St. Lawrence Seaway to connect the Great Lakes with the Atlantic Ocean through a series of locks on the St. Lawrence River. Three previous presidents had been unable to reach agreements with Canada to build this waterway to aid international shipping. Through Eisenhower's efforts, the two nations finally agreed on a plan to complete the project.

Extending Social Security

Although President Eisenhower cut federal spending and tried to limit the federal government's role in the economy, he agreed to extend the Social Security system to an additional 10 million people. He also extended unemployment compensation to an additional 4 million citizens and agreed to raise the minimum wage and continue to provide some government aid to farmers.

By the time Eisenhower ran for a second term in 1956, the nation had successfully shifted back to a peacetime economy. The battles between liberals and conservatives over whether to continue New Deal policies would continue. In the meantime, however, most Americans focused their energy on enjoying what had become a decade of tremendous prosperity.

Reading Check **Evaluating** What conservative and activist measures did Eisenhower take during his administration?

Vocabulary

1. **Explain** the significance of: GI Bill, closed shop, right-to-work laws, union shop, "Do-Nothing Congress," Fair Deal, dynamic conservatism, Federal Highway Act.

Main Ideas

2. **Identifying** What difficulties could have hindered the return to a peacetime economy?

3. **Analyzing** Why did Congress oppose some of Truman's Fair Deal policies?

4. **Describing** How did Eisenhower describe his approach to politics?

Critical Thinking

5. **Big Ideas** How did President Eisenhower aid international shipping during his administration?

6. **Organizing** Use a graphic organizer like the one below to compare the agendas of the Truman and Eisenhower administrations.

7. **Analyzing Visuals** Study the map on page 797. In which part of the country did Strom Thurmond receive the most votes? Why do you think this is?

Writing About History

8. **Persuasive Writing** Assume the role of a member of Congress during Truman's administration. Write a speech convincing Congress to pass or defeat Truman's Fair Deal measures.

History ONLINE

Study Central™ To review this section, go to glencoe.com and click on Study Central.

Section 2

The Affluent Society

Guide to Reading

Big Ideas
Culture and Beliefs Postwar abundance and new technologies changed American society.

Content Vocabulary
- baby boom *(p. 801)*
- white-collar job *(p. 802)*
- blue-collar worker *(p. 802)*
- multinational corporation *(p. 802)*
- franchise *(p. 802)*
- rock 'n' roll *(p. 805)*
- generation gap *(p. 807)*

Academic Vocabulary
- phenomenon *(p. 800)*
- conform *(p. 802)*

People and Events to Identify
- Levittown *(p. 800)*
- Jonas Salk *(p. 803)*
- Elvis Presley *(p. 805)*
- Jack Kerouac *(p. 807)*

Reading Strategy
Sequencing Use a time line to record major events of science, technology, and popular culture during the 1950s.

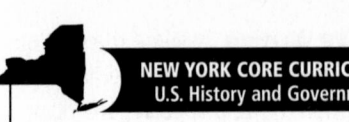

NEW YORK CORE CURRICULUM
U.S. History and Government

Unit 7:
I.A.3 Technology (computers)
I.A.4 Corporate structures (multinational corporations)
I.A.5 Nature of employment (agriculture to industry to service)
II.D.1.a Postwar consumption: homes, autos, and television
II.D.1.c The baby boom and its effects
II.D.2.a Suburbanization: Levittowns

For many Americans, the 1950s was a time of affluence, with many new technological breakthroughs. In addition, new forms of entertainment created a generational divide between young people and adults.

American Abundance

MAIN Idea America entered a period of postwar abundance, with expanding suburbs, growing families, and more white-collar jobs.

HISTORY AND YOU Have you ever noticed that every restaurant in a pizza chain looks alike? Read on to learn about the rise of franchises.

The 1950s was a decade of incredible prosperity. Between 1940 and 1955, the average income of American families roughly tripled. Americans in all income brackets—poor, middle-class, and wealthy—experienced this rapid rise in income. In 1958 economist John Kenneth Galbraith published *The Affluent Society,* in which he claimed that the nation's postwar prosperity was a new **phenomenon.** In the past, Galbraith said, all societies had an "economy of scarcity," meaning that a lack of resources and overpopulation had limited economic productivity. Now, the United States had created what Galbraith called an "economy of abundance." New business techniques and improved technology enabled the nation to produce an abundance of goods and services, thereby dramatically raising the standard of living for Americans.

The economic boom of the 1950s provided most Americans with more disposable income than ever before and, as in the 1920s, they began to spend it on new consumer goods, including refrigerators, washing machines, televisions, and air conditioners. Advertising helped fuel the nation's spending spree. Advertising became the fastest-growing industry in the United States, as manufacturers employed new marketing techniques to sell their products. These techniques were carefully planned to whet the consumer's appetite. A second car became a symbol of status, a freezer became a promise of plenty, and mouthwash was portrayed as the key to immediate success.

The Growth of Suburbia

Advertisers targeted consumers who had money to spend. Many of these consumers lived in new mass-produced suburbs that grew up around cities in the 1950s. **Levittown,** New York, was one of the earliest of the mass-produced suburbs. The driving force behind this planned residential community was Bill Levitt, who mass-produced hundreds of simple and similar-looking homes in a potato field 10 miles east of New York City. Between 1947 and 1951, thousands of

A New America: Suburbs and Highways

The Baby Boom, 1940–1970

per 1,000 population for women 15–44 years old.
Source: *Historical Statistics of the United States.*

Thanks to the GI Bill, many people could afford the cheap mass-produced houses of suburban developments, such as Levittown, New York (above). Suburban living led to crowded highways (right) as commuters headed to work.

Analyzing VISUALS

1. **Interpreting** In what year was there the greatest increase in the number of live births? Why might this be?
2. **Drawing Conclusions** Why might the number of live births have started to decline by the late 1950s?

families rushed to buy the inexpensive homes. These new suburbs multiplied throughout the United States. Suburbs became increasingly popular during the 1950s, accounting for about 85 percent of new home construction. The number of suburban dwellers doubled, while the population of cities rose only 10 percent.

Reasons for the rapid growth of suburbia varied. Some people wanted to escape the crime and congestion of city neighborhoods. Others believed the suburbs would provide a better life for themselves and their children. For millions of Americans, the suburbs came to symbolize the American dream.

Affordability was a key reason that home buyers moved to the suburbs. With the GI Bill providing low-interest loans to veterans, buying a new house was more affordable than at any previous time in American history. The government's decision to give income tax deductions for home-mortgage interest payments and property taxes made owning a home even more

attractive. Between 1940 and 1960, the number of Americans who owned their own homes rose from about 41 percent to about 61 percent.

The Baby Boom

The American birthrate exploded after World War II. From 1945 to 1961, a period known as the **baby boom,** more than 65 million children were born in the United States. At the height of the baby boom, a child was born every seven seconds.

Several factors contributed to the baby boom. First, young couples who had delayed marriage during World War II and the Korean War could now marry, buy homes, and begin their families. In addition, the government encouraged the growth of families by offering generous GI benefits for home purchases. Finally, on television and in magazines, popular culture celebrated pregnancy, parenthood, and large families.

The Changing Workplace

Dramatic changes in the workplace accompanied the country's economic growth. The ongoing mechanization of farms and factories accelerated in the 1950s. As a result, more Americans began working in offices. These jobs came to be referred to as **white-collar jobs,** because employees typically wore a white shirt and tie to work, instead of the blue denim of factory workers and laborers. In 1956, for the first time, white-collar workers outnumbered **blue-collar workers.**

Many white-collar employees worked for large corporations. As these businesses competed with each other, some expanded overseas. These **multinational corporations** located themselves closer to important raw materials and benefited from a cheaper labor pool, which made them more competitive.

The 1950s also witnessed the rise of **franchises,** in which a person owns and runs one or several stores of a chain operation. Because many business leaders believed that consumers valued dependability and familiarity, the owners of chain operations often demanded that their franchises present a uniform look and style.

Like franchise owners, many corporate leaders expected their employees to **conform** to company standards. In general, they did not want free-thinking individuals or people who might speak out or criticize the company. Some observers criticized this trend. In his 1950 book *The Lonely Crowd,* sociologist David Riesman argued that this conformity was changing people. Formerly, he claimed, people were "inner-directed," judging themselves on the basis of their own values and the esteem of their families. Now, however, people were becoming "other-directed"—concerned with winning the approval of the corporation or community.

In his 1956 book, *The Organization Man,* William H. Whyte, Jr., attacked the similarity many business organizations cultivated to keep any individual from dominating. "In group doctrine," Whyte wrote, "the strong personality is viewed with overwhelming suspicion," and the person with ideas is considered "a threat."

✔ **Reading Check** **Interpreting** Describe two causes and effects of the economic boom of the 1950s.

Scientific Advances

MAIN Idea Computers began a business revolution, and doctors discovered new ways to fight disease.

HISTORY AND YOU Do you own a computer? Read on to learn about the earliest computers.

As the United States experienced many social changes during the postwar era, the nation also witnessed several important scientific advances. In electronics and medicine, American scientists broke new ground during the 1950s.

Advances in Electronics

The electronics industry made rapid advances after World War II. In 1947 three American physicists—John Bardeen, Walter H. Brattain, and William Shockley—developed the transistor, a tiny device that generated electric signals and made it possible to miniaturize radios and calculators. Radios, once a large piece of furniture, became portable and could be easily carried to the beach or other places.

The age of computers also dawned in the postwar era. In 1946 scientists working under a U.S. Army contract developed one of the nation's earliest computers—known as ENIAC (Electronic Numerical Integrator and Computer)—to make military calculations. Several years later, a newer model called UNIVAC (Universal Automatic Computer) would process business data and launch the computer revolution. The computer, along with changes and improvements in communication and transportation systems, allowed many Americans to work more quickly and efficiently.

Medical Miracles

The medical breakthroughs of the 1950s included the development of new, powerful antibiotics and vaccines to fight infection and the introduction of new techniques to fight cancer and heart disease.

Prior to the 1950s, cancer had been thought to be untreatable. The development of radiation treatments and chemotherapy in the 1950s helped many cancer patients survive. Similarly, treatments for heart disease had eluded

People IN HISTORY

Dr. Jonas Salk
1914–1995

The man who developed the vaccine for one of the nation's most feared diseases almost did not go into medicine. Jonas Salk enrolled in college as a pre-law student but soon changed his mind. "My mother didn't think I would make a very good lawyer," Salk said, "probably because I could never win an argument with her." Salk switched his major to pre-med and went on to become a research scientist.

Every so often, Salk would make rounds in the overcrowded polio wards of a hospital near his lab, where nurses described their feelings of helpless rage. One nurse said, "I can remember how the staff used to kid Dr. Salk—kidding in earnest—telling him to hurry up and do something."

Salk became famous for the polio vaccine he developed in 1952. The shy doctor, however, did not desire fame. About becoming a celebrity, Salk observed that it was "a transitory thing and you wait till it blows over. Eventually people will start thinking, 'That poor guy,' and leave me alone. Then I'll be able to get back to my laboratory."

What character traits do you think made Dr. Salk a successful research scientist?

▲ In the 1940s and 1950s, Americans became very concerned about the epidemic of polio cases that struck so many children. Here, a device known as an iron lung helps polio patients to breathe.

scientists for decades, and when someone suffered a heart attack, nothing could be done. In 1950, however, doctors developed cardiopulmonary resuscitation (CPR), a technique that has saved many lives. Doctors also began replacing worn-out heart valves with mechanical valves and implanted the first pacemakers in 1952.

A third disease that had frightened Americans for decades was tuberculosis, a lung disease also known as the white plague. The disease was both highly infectious and contagious, so patients lived in isolation in sanatoriums. In 1956 for the first time, tuberculosis fell from the list of the top ten fatal diseases. New antibiotics and a blood test for the disease finally put an end to fear of tuberculosis.

Polio, too, finally yielded to science. Polio epidemics had been occurring in the United States since 1916. The viral disease had struck Franklin Roosevelt as a young man and forced him to use a wheelchair and wear steel braces on his legs. In the 1940s and 1950s, widespread polio epidemics terrorized the nation. Every summer, polio broke out somewhere in the country. Many died; those who did not were often confined to iron lungs—large metal tanks

with pumps that helped patients breathe. Even if they eventually recovered, they were often paralyzed for life.

Each summer, parents searched for ways to safeguard their families from the dreaded disease. Some sent their children to the country to avoid excessive contact with others. Public swimming pools and beaches were closed. Parks and playgrounds across the country stood deserted. Nevertheless, the disease continued to strike. In 1952 a record 58,000 new cases were reported.

Finally, research scientist **Jonas Salk** developed an injectable vaccine to prevent polio. Salk first tested the vaccine on himself, his wife, and his three sons, and then on 2 million schoolchildren. In 1955 the vaccine became available to the general public. American scientist Albert Sabin then developed an oral vaccine for polio. Safer and more convenient than Salk's injection vaccine, the Sabin vaccine became the most common method for preventing the disease. The threat of polio nearly disappeared.

✔ Reading Check **Examining** What medical and technological advances met specific needs in the late 1940s and 1950s?

The New Mass Media

MAIN Idea The rise of television led to changes in the movie and radio industries.

HISTORY AND YOU How many hours of television do you watch weekly? Read to find out about the early days of television broadcasting.

Although regular television broadcasts had begun in the early 1940s, there were few stations, and sets were expensive. There were estimated to be no more than 8,000 sets in use in the entire United States in 1946. By the late 1950s, however, small black-and-white-screened televisions sat in living rooms across the country. Nearly 40 million televisions had been sold by 1957, and more than 80 percent of families had at least one television.

The Rise of Television

Early television programs fell into several main categories, including comedy, action and adventure, and variety entertainment. In 1953 Lucille Ball and her real-life husband, Desi Arnaz, starred in one of the most popular shows ever to air on American television, a situation comedy (sitcom) called *I Love Lucy*. The episode in which Lucy gave birth (which paralleled Lucille Ball's actual pregnancy) had an audience of 44 million viewers. Fewer people tuned in to watch the presidential inauguration the following day.

Comedy proved popular in other formats. Many early comedy shows, such as those starring Bob Hope and Jack Benny, were adapted from radio programs. Variety shows, such as Ed Sullivan's *Toast of the Town*, provided a mix of comedy, music, dance, acrobatics, and juggling. Quiz shows also drew large audiences after the 1955 debut of *The $64,000 Question*. In this show and its many imitators, two contestants tried to answer questions from separate, soundproof booths.

Television viewers also enjoyed action shows. Westerns such as *Hopalong Cassidy, The Lone Ranger,* and *Gunsmoke* grew quickly in popularity. Viewers also enjoyed police shows

Television in the 1950s

▲ *I Love Lucy, a comedy about housewife Lucy, husband Ricky, and friends Fred and Ethel was the most popular show of the 1950s.*

▲ *Howdy Doody was the first network kids' show ever broadcast in color.*

▲ The Adventures of Ozzie and Harriet *was a comedy featuring the life of Ozzie and Harriet Nelson and their sons in a middle-class American suburb. Their portrayal of family life was idealized—father worked, mother stayed at home raising the children, and there was always plenty of food and consumer goods available.*

Analyzing VISUALS

1. **Explaining** How did *The Adventures of Ozzie and Harriet* reflect an idealized American family?

2. **Making Generalizations** To what type of audience were most of these television programs designed to appeal?

such as *Dragnet,* a hugely successful show featuring Detective Joe Friday and his partner hunting down a new criminal each week. By the late 1950s, television news had also become an important vehicle for information, and televised athletic events had made professional and college sports a popular choice for entertainment.

Hollywood Responds

As the popularity of television grew, movies lost viewers. Weekly movie attendance dropped from 82 million in 1946 to 36 million by 1950. By 1960, when some 50 million Americans owned televisions, one-fifth of the nation's movie theaters had closed.

Throughout the 1950s, Hollywood struggled to recapture its audience. When contests, door prizes, and advertising failed to lure people back, Hollywood tried 3-D films that required the audience to wear special glasses. Viewers soon tired of the glasses and the often ridiculous plots of 3-D movies.

Cinemascope—a process that showed movies on large, panoramic screens—finally gave Hollywood something television could not match. Wide-screen, full-color spectacles like *The Robe, The Ten Commandments,* and *Around the World in 80 Days* cost a great deal of money to produce. These blockbusters, however, made up for their cost by attracting huge audiences and netting large profits.

Radio Draws Them In

Television also forced the radio industry to change in order to keep its audience. Television made radio comedies, dramas, and soap operas obsolete. Radio stations responded by broadcasting recorded music, news, weather, sports, and talk shows.

Radio also had one audience that television could not reach—people traveling in their cars. In some ways, the automobile saved the radio industry. People commuting to and from work, running errands, or traveling on long road trips relied on radio for information and entertainment. As a result, radio stations survived and even flourished. The number of radio stations more than doubled between 1948 and 1957.

✔ Reading Check **Identifying** How did the television industry affect the U.S. economy?

New Music and Poetry

MAIN Idea Young people developed their own popular culture based largely on rock 'n' roll music and literature of the beat movement.

HISTORY AND YOU How do the adults you know feel about your favorite music? Read on to learn of the conflicts over musical taste that began during the 1950s.

Many teens in every generation seek to separate themselves from their parents. One way of creating that separation is by embracing different music. In that respect, the 1950s were no different from earlier decades, but the results were different for two reasons.

For the first time, teens had large amounts of disposable income that could be spent on entertainment designed specifically for them. In addition, the new mass media meant that teens across the country could hear the same music broadcast or watch the same television shows. The result was the rise of an independent youth culture separate from adult culture. The new youth culture became an independent market for the entertainment and advertising industries.

Rock 'n' Roll

In 1951 at a record store in downtown Cleveland, Ohio, radio disc jockey Alan Freed noticed white teenagers buying African American rhythm-and-blues records and dancing to the music in the store. Freed convinced his station manager to play the music on the air. Just as the disc jockey had suspected, the listeners went crazy for it. Soon, white artists began making music that stemmed from these African American rhythms and sounds, and a new form of music, **rock 'n' roll,** was born.

With a loud and heavy beat that made it ideal for dancing, along with lyrics about romance, cars, and other themes that appealed to young people, rock 'n' roll became wildly popular with the nation's teens. Before long, teenagers around the country were rushing out to buy recordings from such artists as Buddy Holly, Chuck Berry, and Bill Haley and the Comets. In 1956 teenagers found their first rock 'n' roll hero in **Elvis Presley,** who became known as the "King of Rock 'n' Roll."

Elvis Presley was born in rural Mississippi and grew up poor in Memphis, Tennessee. While in high school, Presley learned to play guitar and sing by imitating the rhythm-and-blues music he heard on the radio. By 1956, the handsome young Elvis had a record deal with RCA Victor, a movie contract, and had made public appearances on several television shows. At first, the popular television variety show host Ed Sullivan refused to invite Presley to appear, insisting that rock 'n' roll music was not fit for a family-oriented show. When a competing show featuring Presley upset Sullivan's high ratings, however, he relented. He ended up paying Presley $50,000 per performance for three appearances, more than triple the amount he had paid any other performer.

Presley owed his wild popularity as much to his moves as to his music. During his performances he would gyrate his hips and dance in ways that shocked many in the audience. Not surprisingly, parents—many of whom listened to Frank Sinatra and other more mellow, mainstream artists—condemned rock 'n' roll as loud, mindless, and dangerous. The city council of San Antonio, Texas, actually banned rock 'n' roll from the jukeboxes at public swimming pools.

The rock 'n' roll hits that teens bought in record numbers united them in a world their parents did not share. Thus, in the 1950s,

PRIMARY SOURCE
Rock 'n' Roll Sweeps the Nation

African American singers such as Chuck Berry (left), Little Richard (below left), and Fats Domino (below right) became huge stars in the popular music industry of the 1950s.

Bill Haley and His Comets (above) was one of the first popular rock 'n' roll bands. Elvis Presley (left) became rock 'n' roll's first superstar, but many disapproved of his dance moves.

▲ Little Richard

▲ Fats Domino

Analyzing VISUALS

1. **Explaining** Why did adults disapprove of rock 'n' roll?
2. **Describing** How did this disapproval contribute to the generation gap?

rock 'n' roll helped to create what became known as the **generation gap,** or the cultural separation between children and their parents.

The Beat Movement

If rock 'n' roll helped to create a generation gap, a group of mostly white writers and artists who called themselves beats, or beatniks, highlighted a values gap in 1950s America. The term "beat" may have come from the feeling among group members of being "beaten down" by American culture, or from jazz musicians who would say, "I'm beat right down to my socks."

Beat poets, writers, and artists harshly criticized what they considered the sterility and conformity of American life, the meaninglessness of American politics, and the emptiness of popular culture. In 1956, 29-year-old beat poet Allen Ginsberg published a long poem titled "Howl," which blasted modern American life. Another beat member, **Jack Kerouac,** published *On the Road* in 1957. Although Kerouac's book about his freewheeling adventures with a car thief and con artist shocked some readers, the book went on to become a classic in modern American literature. Although the beat movement remained relatively small, it laid the foundations for the more widespread youth cultural rebellion of the 1960s.

African American Entertainers

African American entertainers struggled to find acceptance in a country that often treated them as second-class citizens. With a few notable exceptions, television tended to shut out African Americans. In 1956 NBC gave a popular African American singer named Nat King Cole his own 15-minute musical variety show. In 1958, after 64 episodes, NBC canceled the show after failing to secure a national sponsor for a show hosted by an African American.

African American rock 'n' roll singers faced fewer obstacles. The talented African Americans who recorded hit songs in the 1950s included Chuck Berry, Little Richard, Fats Domino, and Ray Charles. The late 1950s and early 1960s also saw the rise of several female African American groups, including the Crystals, the Shirelles, and the Ronettes. With their catchy, popular sound, these groups were the musical predecessors of the famous late 1960s groups Martha and the Vandellas and the Supremes.

Over time, the music of the early rock 'n' roll artists had a profound influence on popular music throughout the world. Little Richard and Chuck Berry, for example, provided inspiration for the Beatles, whose music swept Britain and the world in the 1960s. Elvis Presley's music transformed generations of rock 'n' roll bands that followed him and other pioneers of rock.

Despite the innovations in music and the economic boom of the 1950s, not all Americans were part of the affluent society. For many of the country's minorities and rural poor, the American dream remained well out of reach.

✔ Reading Check **Summarizing** How did rock 'n' roll help create the generation gap?

Section 2 REVIEW

Vocabulary

1. **Explain** the significance of: Levittown, baby boom, white-collar job, blue-collar worker, multinational corporation, franchise, Jonas Salk, rock 'n' roll, Elvis Presley, generation gap, Jack Kerouac.

Main Ideas

2. **Organizing** Use a graphic organizer like the one below to list the causes and effects of the economic boom of the 1950s.

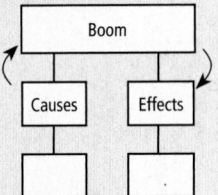

3. **Listing** What major technological breakthroughs occurred in the 1950s?

4. **Explaining** How did television affect other forms of mass media?

5. **Identifying** How did young people of the 1950s express their own culture?

Critical Thinking

6. **Big Ideas** What were the roots of rock 'n' roll, and how did it reach a mass audience?

7. **Analyzing Visuals** Study the photographs on page 804. These programs have been criticized for presenting a one-sided view of American life. Do you agree? Why or why not?

Writing About History

8. **Expository Writing** Assume the role of a media critic in the 1950s, and use the information in this section to write a critique of one television show, movie, music concert, or piece of literature.

History ONLINE

Study Central™ To review this section, go to glencoe.com and click on Study Central.

TIME NOTEBOOK

BETTMANN/CORBIS

Profile

JAMES DEAN *had a brief but spectacular career as a film star. His role in* Rebel Without a Cause *made him an icon for American youth in the mid-50s. In 1955 Dean was killed in a car crash. He was 24.*

"I guess I have as good an insight into this rising generation as any other young man my age. Therefore, when I do play a youth, I try to imitate life. *Rebel Without a Cause* deals with the problems of modern youth. . . . If you want the kids to come and see the picture, you've got to try to reach them on their own grounds. If a picture is psychologically motivated, if there is truth in the relationships in it, then I think that picture will do good."

—*from an interview for* Rebel Without a Cause

VERBATIM

❝It will make a wonderful place for the children to play in, and it will be a good storehouse, too. ❞

MRS. RUTH CALHOUN,
mother of three, on her backyard fallout shelter, 1951

❝Riddle: What's college? That's where girls who are above cooking and sewing go to meet a man they can spend their lives cooking and sewing for. ❞

ad for Gimbel's department store campus clothes, 1952

❝Radioactive poisoning of the atmosphere and hence annihilation of any life on Earth has been brought within the range of technical possibilities. ❞

ALBERT EINSTEIN,
physicist, 1950

❝If the television craze continues with the present level of programs, we are destined to have a nation of morons. ❞

DANIEL MARSH,
President of Boston University, 1950

❝Every time the Russians throw an American in jail, the House Un-American Activities Committee throws an American in jail to get even. ❞

MORT SAHL,
comedian, 1950s

WINNERS & LOSERS

UNDERWOOD & UNDERWOOD/CORBIS

Poodle Cut

POODLE CUTS
Short, curly hairstyle gains wide popularity and acceptance

TV GUIDE
New weekly magazine achieves circulation of 6.5 million by 1959

PALMER PAINT COMPANY OF DETROIT
Sells 12 million paint-by-number kits ranging from simple landscapes and portraits to Leonardo da Vinci's The Last Supper

THE DUCKTAIL
Banned in several Massachusetts schools in 1957

COLLIER'S
The respected magazine loses circulation, publishes its final edition on January 4, 1957

LEONARDO DA VINCI'S THE LAST SUPPER
Now everyone can paint their own copy to hang in their homes

The Ducktail

SUPER STOCK

1950S WORD PLAY
Translation, Please!
Match the word to its meaning.

Teen-Age Lingo
1. cool
2. hang loose
3. hairy
4. yo-yo

a. a dull person, an outsider
b. worthy of approval
c. formidable
d. don't worry

answers: 1.b; 2.d; 3.c; 4.a

American Scene, 1950–1960
(MILLIONS)

24.3 — 35.5 — 1950 1960 — **Children 5–14**

1.8 — 4.0 — 1950 1960 — **Girl Scouts & Brownies**

2.0 — 3.8 — 1950 1960 — **Bicycle Production**

BETTMANN/CORBIS

Bomb Shelter

Be Prepared
"Know the Bomb's True Dangers. Know the Steps You Can Take to Escape Them!—You Can Survive."
Government pamphlet, 1950

DIGGING YOUR OWN BOMB SHELTER? Better go shopping. Below is a list of items included with the $3,000 Mark I Kidde Kokoon, designed to accommodate a family of five for a three-to five-day underground stay.

- air blower
- radiation detector
- protective apparel suit
- face respirator
- radiation charts (4)
- hand shovel (for digging out after the blast)
- gasoline driven generator
- gasoline (10 gallons)
- chemical toilet
- toilet chemicals (2 gallons)
- bunks (5)
- mattresses and blankets (5)
- air pump (blowing up mattresses)
- incandescent bulbs (2) 40 watts
- fuses (2) 5 amperes
- clock—non-electric
- first aid kit
- waterless hand cleaner
- sterno stove
- canned water (10 gallons)
- canned food (meat, powdered milk, cereal, sugar, etc.)
- paper products

NUMBERS 1957
3¢ Cost of first-class postage stamp
19¢ Cost of loaf of bread
25¢ Cost of issue of Sports Illustrated
35¢ Cost of movie ticket
50¢ Cost of gallon of milk (delivered)
$2.05 Average hourly wage
$2,845 Cost of new car

POPPERFOTO/ARCHIVE PHOTO

$5,234 Median income for a family of four
$19,500 Median price of a home

CRITICAL THINKING
1. Predicting If the number of American children continued to grow, how would that affect bicycle production and Scout membership? How could that growth affect the American economy?

2. Hypothesizing How have attitudes towards women changed since the 1952 department store ad for campus clothes? What do you think are some reasons for the change in attitude?

The Other Side of American Life

Guide to Reading

Big Ideas
Economics and Society The postwar prosperity did not extend to all Americans. For some groups, poverty and discrimination continued during the apparent abundance of the 1950s.

Content Vocabulary
• poverty line *(p. 810)*
• urban renewal *(p. 811)*
• termination policy *(p. 813)*
• juvenile delinquency *(p. 815)*

Academic Vocabulary
• income *(p. 810)*
• entity *(p. 813)*

People and Events to Identify
• Lorraine Hansberry *(p. 812)*
• Bracero Program *(p. 812)*
• Appalachia *(p. 814)*

Reading Strategy
Taking Notes As you read about social problems in the United States in the 1950s, use the major headings of this section to create an outline similar to the one below.

> The Other Side of American Life
> I. Poverty Amidst Prosperity
>   A.
>   B.
>   C.
>   D.
>   E.
> II.

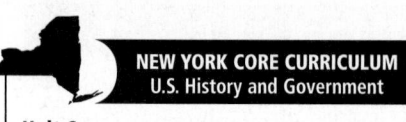

NEW YORK CORE CURRICULUM
U.S. History and Government

Unit 6:
I.C.6.e Minorities continued to find it difficult to obtain fair practices in housing, employment, education

Unit 7:
II.D.2.b Cities: declining

During the 1950s, about 20 percent of the American population—particularly people of color and those living in the inner cities and Appalachia—did not share in the general prosperity. Experts also worried about the rise in juvenile delinquency.

Poverty Amidst Prosperity

MAIN Idea Despite the growing affluence of much of the nation, many groups still lived in poverty.

HISTORY AND YOU Are the pockets of poverty in America today the same as they were in the 1950s? Read on to learn about the people and regions most affected by poverty in the 1950s.

The 1950s saw a tremendous expansion of the middle class. At least one in five Americans, or about 30 million people, however, lived below the **poverty line.** This imaginary marker is a figure the government sets to reflect the minimum **income** required to support a family. Such poverty remained invisible to most Americans, who assumed that the country's general prosperity had provided everyone with a comfortable existence.

The writer Michael Harrington, however, made no such assumptions. During the 1950s, Harrington set out to chronicle poverty in the United States. In his book *The Other America,* published in 1962, he alerted those in the mainstream to what he saw in the run-down and hidden communities of the country:

PRIMARY SOURCE

"To be sure, the other America is not impoverished in the same sense as those poor nations where millions cling to hunger as a defense against starvation. . . . That does not change the fact that tens of millions of Americans are, at this very moment, maimed in body and spirit, existing at levels beneath those necessary for human decency. If these people are not starving, they are hungry, and sometimes fat with hunger, for that is what cheap foods do. They are without adequate housing and education and medical care."

—from *The Other America*

The poor included single mothers and the elderly; minorities such as Puerto Ricans and Mexican immigrants; rural Americans—both African American and white—and inner city residents, who remained stuck in crowded slums as wealthier citizens fled to the suburbs. Many Native Americans endured grinding poverty whether they stayed on reservations or migrated to cities.

The Other America

Amid the prosperity of the 1950s, many lived in terrible poverty. While suburbs boomed, the poor, many of whom were minorities, were relegated to inner-city slums. Native Americans suffered extreme poverty and the breakdown of their culture on reservations, while Mexican migrant workers in the Southwest barely made enough to feed, clothe, and shelter themselves and their children.

▲ A poor Navajo family stands outside their home on an Arkansas reservation in 1948.

▲ Children play in the littered streets of a Chicago slum in 1954.

Analyzing VISUALS

1. **Examining** Based on the photos, what aspect of life does it seem the hardest for the poor in America to obtain?

2. **Hypothesizing** What do you think might account for minorities having a lower average income than whites in the United States in the 1940s and 1950s?

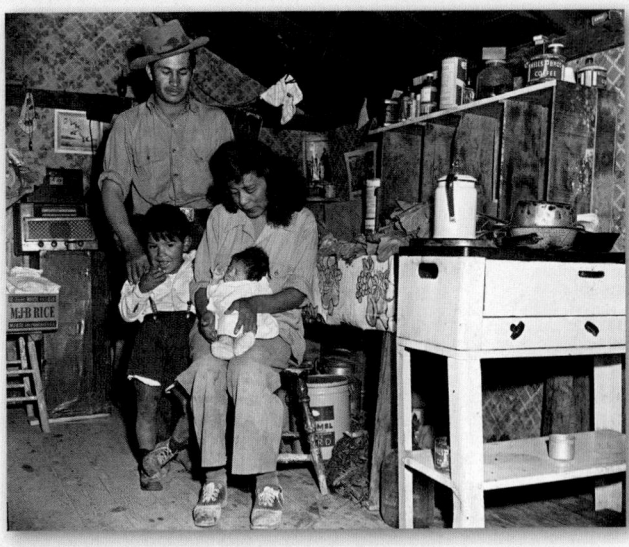

▲ The Cervantes family lived in a one-room shack at a ranch camp near Fresno, California, in 1950.

The Decline of the Inner City

The poverty of the 1950s was most apparent in the nation's urban centers. As middle-class families moved to the suburbs, they left behind the poor and less-educated. Many city centers deteriorated because the taxes that the middle class paid moved out with them. Cities no longer had the tax dollars to provide adequate public transportation, housing, and other services.

When government tried to help inner-city residents, it often made matters worse. During the 1950s, for example, **urban renewal** pro-grams tried to eliminate poverty by tearing down slums and erecting new high-rise buildings for poor residents. These crowded, high-rise projects, however, often created an atmosphere of violence. The government also unwittingly encouraged the residents of public housing to remain poor by evicting them as soon as they began earning a higher income.

In the end, urban renewal programs actually destroyed more housing space than they created. Too often, the wrecking balls destroyed poor people's homes to make way for road-ways, parks, universities, tree-lined boulevards, or shopping centers.

African Americans

Many of the citizens left behind in the cities were African American. By 1960, more than 3 million African Americans had migrated from the South to Northern cities in search of greater economic opportunity and to escape violence and racial intimidation. For many of these migrants, however, the economic boom of the war years did not continue in the 1950s.

Long-standing patterns of racial discrimination in schools, housing, hiring, and salaries in the North kept many inner-city African Americans poor. The last hired and the first fired for good jobs, they often remained stuck in the worst-paying occupations. In 1958 African Americans' salaries, on average, were only 51 percent of what whites earned. Poverty and racial discrimination also deprived many African Americans of other benefits, such as decent medical care.

In 1959 the play *A Raisin in the Sun* opened on Broadway. Written by African American author **Lorraine Hansberry**, the play told the story of a working-class African American family struggling against poverty and racism. The title referred to a Langston Hughes poem that wonders what happens to an unrealized dream: "Does it dry up like a raisin in the sun?" The play won the New York Drama Critics Circle Award for the best play of the year. Responding to a correspondent who had seen the play, Lorraine Hansberry wrote: "The ghettos are killing us; not only our dreams . . . but our very bodies. It is not an abstraction to us that the average [African American] has a life expectancy of five to ten years less than the average white."

Hispanics

African Americans were not the only minority group that struggled with poverty. Much of the nation's Hispanic population faced the same problems. During the 1950s and early 1960s, the **Bracero Program** brought nearly 5 million Mexicans to the United States to work on farms and ranches in the Southwest. Braceros were temporary contract workers. Many later returned home, but some 350,000 settled permanently in the United States.

These laborers, who worked on large farms throughout the country, lived with extreme poverty and hardship. They toiled long hours, for little pay, in conditions that were often

PAST & PRESENT

The Inner-City's Ongoing Problems

By the end of the 1950s, many major U.S. cities were in decline. "White flight" and lowered tax revenues, as well as racial discrimination and a lack of sympathy for the less fortunate, combined to create islands of decay and poverty in urban centers.

Although numerous programs were launched in the 1960s to try to improve living conditions and eliminate poverty, the problem has proven more difficult than first anticipated. Fifty years separate the two photos of inner-city slums to the right, yet, tragically, the quality of life has barely changed.

Major Cities With High Poverty Rates, 1960

Philadelphia
Detroit
Chicago
Cleveland
New York
Baltimore
St. Louis
Pittsburgh
Los Angeles
San Diego
Dallas
Houston
San Antonio
New Orleans

1940

▲ *Even in the 1940s, urban decay was characteristic of many American cities, including Washington, D.C., where people lived in dire poverty within sight of the Capitol.*

unbearable. In *The Other America*, Michael Harrington noted:

PRIMARY SOURCE

"[Migrant laborers] work ten-eleven-twelve hour days in temperatures over one hundred degrees. Sometimes there is no drinking water. . . . Women and children work on ladders and with hazardous machinery. . . . Babies are brought to the field and are placed in 'cradles' of wood boxes."

—from *The Other America*

Away from the fields, many Mexican families lived in small, crudely built shacks, while some did not even have a roof over their heads. "They sleep where they can, some in the open," Harrington noted about one group of migrant workers. "They eat when they can (and sometimes what they can)." The nation paid little attention to the plight of Mexican farm laborers until the 1960s, when the workers began to organize for greater rights.

Native Americans

Native Americans also faced challenges throughout the postwar era. By the middle of the 1900s, Native Americans—who made up less than one percent of the population—were the poorest ethnic group in the nation. Average annual family income for Native American families, for example, was $1,000 less than that of African American families.

After World War II, during which many Native American soldiers had served with distinction, the United States government launched a program to bring Native Americans into mainstream society—whether they wanted to assimilate or not.

Under the plan, which became known as the **termination policy,** the federal government withdrew all official recognition of the Native American groups as legal **entities** and made them subject to the same laws as white citizens. Native American groups were then placed under the responsibility of state governments. At the same time, the government encouraged Native Americans to blend in with the larger society by helping them move off reservations to cities.

Although the idea of integrating Native Americans into mainstream society began with good intentions, some of its supporters had more selfish goals. Speculators and developers sometimes gained rich farmland at the expense of destitute Native American groups.

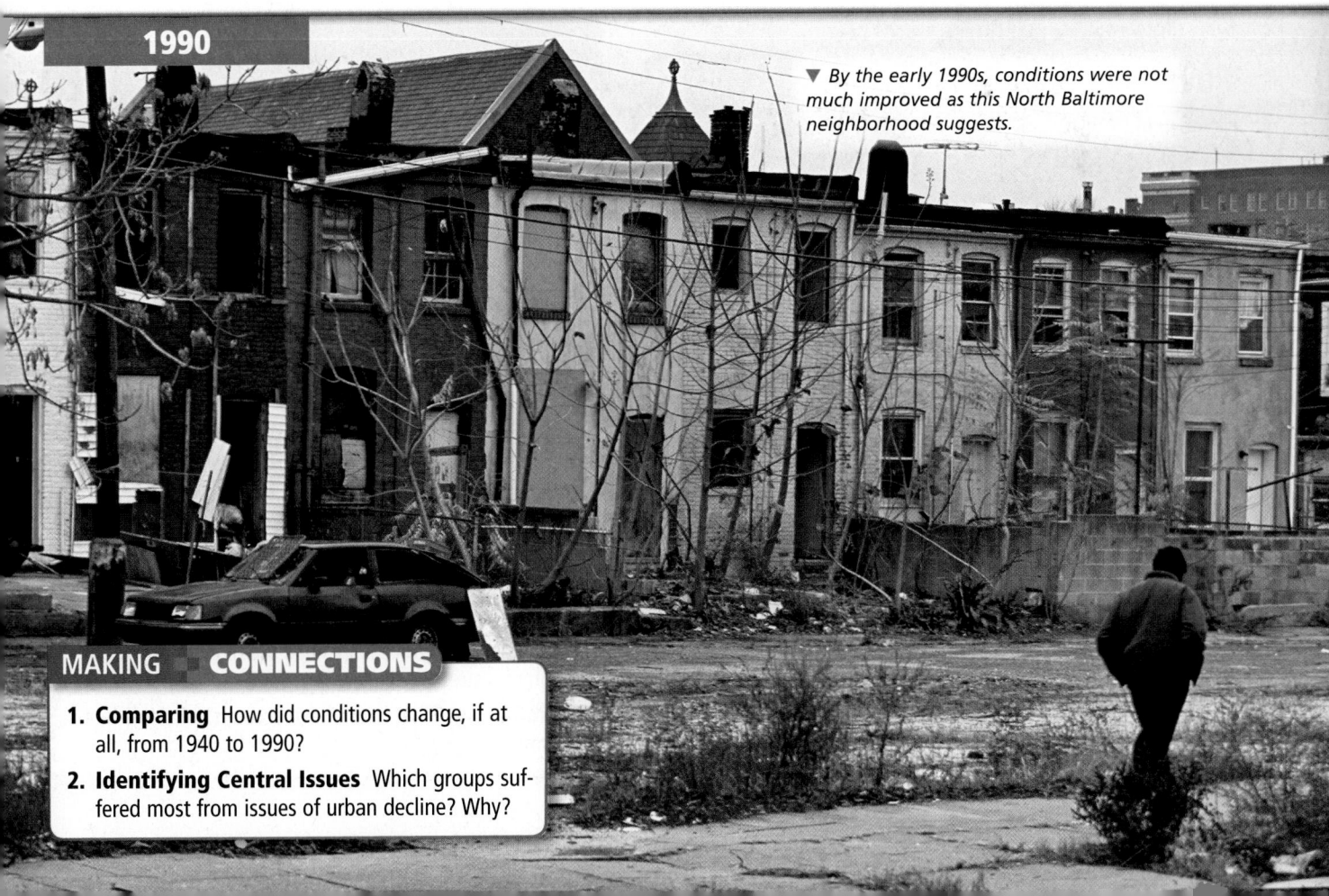

1990

▼ By the early 1990s, conditions were not much improved as this North Baltimore neighborhood suggests.

MAKING CONNECTIONS

1. **Comparing** How did conditions change, if at all, from 1940 to 1990?
2. **Identifying Central Issues** Which groups suffered most from issues of urban decline? Why?

For most Native Americans, termination was a disastrous policy that only deepened their poverty. In the mid-1950s, for example, the Welfare Council of Minneapolis described Native American living conditions in that city as miserable: "One Indian family of five or six, living in two rooms, will take in relatives and friends who come from the reservations seeking jobs until perhaps fifteen people will be crowded into the space."

During the 1950s, Native Americans in Minneapolis could expect to live only 37 years, compared to 46 years for all Minnesota Native Americans and 68 years for other Minneapolis residents. Similar patterns existed elsewhere. Benjamin Reifel, a Sioux, described the despair that the termination policy produced:

PRIMARY SOURCE

"The Indians believed that when the dark clouds of war passed from the skies overhead, their rising tide of expectations, though temporarily stalled, would again reappear. Instead they were threatened by termination. . . . Soaring expectations began to plunge."

—quoted in *The Earth Shall Weep*

Appalachia

Residents of rural **Appalachia** also failed to share in the prosperity of the 1950s. The scenic beauty of the mountainous region, which stretches from New York to Georgia, often hid desperate poverty. Coal mining had long been the backbone of the Appalachian economy. With mechanization of mining in the 1950s, unemployment soared. With no work to be had, some 1.5 million people abandoned Appalachia to seek a better life in the cities. "Whole counties," wrote one reporter, "are precariously held together by a flour-and-dried-milk paste of surplus foods. . . . The men who are no longer needed in the mines and the farmers who cannot compete . . . have themselves become surplus commodities in the mountains."

Appalachia had fewer doctors per thousand people than the rest of the country. Studies revealed high rates of nutritional deficiency and infant mortality. In addition, schooling in the region was considered even worse than in inner-city slums.

Reading Check **Identifying** Which groups were left out of the economic boom of the 1950s?

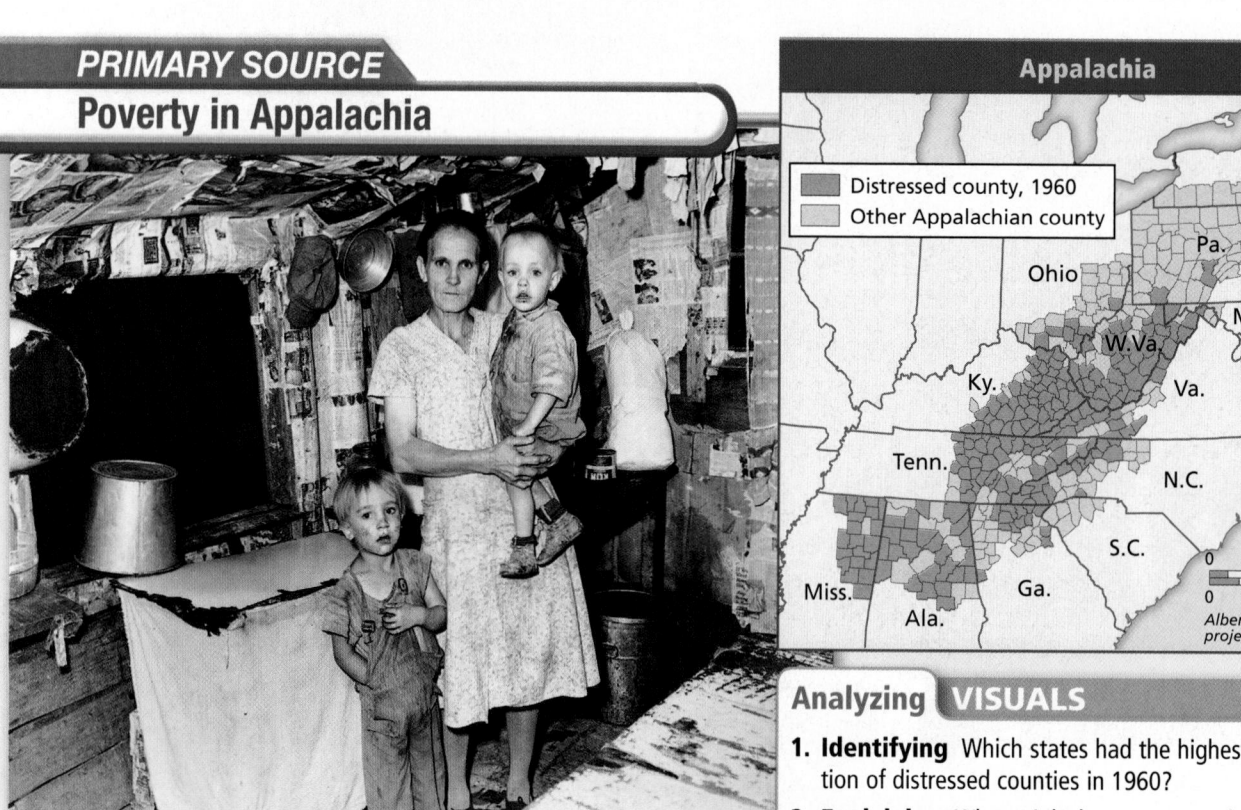

PRIMARY SOURCE
Poverty in Appalachia

▲ *Eight family members lived in this three-room house lined with newspaper in Appalachia in the 1950s.*

Appalachia

- Distressed county, 1960
- Other Appalachian county

N.Y.
Pa.
Ohio
Md.
W.Va.
Ky.
Va.
Tenn.
N.C.
S.C.
Miss.
Ga.
Ala.

0 200 kilometers
0 200 miles
Albers Equal-Area projection

Analyzing VISUALS   DBQ

1. **Identifying** Which states had the highest concentration of distressed counties in 1960?

2. **Explaining** What might have accounted for this high number?

Juvenile Delinquency

MAIN Idea Juvenile crime rates rose during the 1950s; a crisis in education occurred when the baby boomers began school.

HISTORY AND YOU Has your school placed a greater emphasis on science and math classes recently? Read to learn about a push in science and math education during the 1950s.

During the 1950s, many middle-class, white Americans found it easy to ignore the poverty and racism that afflicted many of the nation's minorities, since they themselves were removed from it. Some social problems, however, became impossible to ignore.

One problem at this time was a rise in, or at least a rise in the reporting of, **juvenile delinquency**—antisocial or criminal behavior of young people. Between 1948 and 1953, the United States saw a 45 percent rise in juvenile crime rates. A popular 1954 book titled *1,000,000 Delinquents* correctly predicted that in the following year, about 1 million young people would be involved in some kind of criminal activity.

Americans disagreed on what had triggered the rise in delinquency. Experts blamed television, movies, comic books, racism, busy parents, a rising divorce rate, lack of religion, and anxiety over the military draft. Some cultural critics claimed that young people were rebelling against the conformity of their parents. Others blamed a lack of discipline. Doting parents, complained Bishop Fulton J. Sheen, had raised bored children who sought new thrills, such as "alcohol, marijuana, even murder." Still others pointed at social causes, blaming teen violence on poverty. The problem, however, cut across class and racial lines—the majority of car thieves, for example, had grown up in middle-class homes.

Most teens, of course, steered clear of gangs, drugs, and crime. Nonetheless, the public tended to stereotype young people as juvenile delinquents, especially those teens who favored unconventional clothing and long hair, or used street slang.

Concerned about their children, many parents focused on the nation's schools as a possible solution. When baby boomers began entering the school system in the 1950s, enrollments increased by 13 million. School districts struggled to pay for new buildings and hire more teachers.

Americans' education worries only intensified in 1957 after the Soviet Union launched the world's first space satellites, *Sputnik I* and *Sputnik II*. Many Americans felt that the nation had fallen behind its Cold War enemy and blamed what they felt was a lack of technical education in the nation's schools. *Life* magazine proclaimed a "Crisis in Education" and offered a grim warning: "What has long been an ignored national problem, *Sputnik* has made a recognized crisis." In the wake of the *Sputnik* launches, efforts began to improve math and science education. Profound fears about the country's young people, it seemed, dominated the end of a decade that had brought prosperity and progress for many Americans.

✓ Reading Check **Evaluating** What were some suggested explanations of the increase in juvenile crime?

Section 3 REVIEW

Vocabulary

1. **Explain** the significance of: poverty line, urban renewal, Lorraine Hansberry, Bracero Program, termination policy, Appalachia, juvenile delinquency.

Main Ideas

2. **Evaluating** How did the federal government's termination policy affect Native Americans?

3. **Analyzing** What effects did the baby boomers have on schools?

Critical Thinking

4. **Big Ideas** Why did urban renewal fail to improve the lives of the poor in the inner cities?

5. **Organizing** Use a graphic organizer similar to the one below to list groups of Americans left out of the country's postwar economic boom.

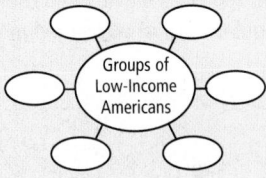

Groups of Low-Income Americans

6. **Analyzing Visuals** Study the photographs on page 811. Why were minority groups hit so hard by poverty, compared to whites, in the 1950s?

Writing About History

7. **Expository Writing** Choose a current social problem that you observe among adolescents. Describe the problem and its causes, and then recommend a solution.

History ONLINE

Study Central™ To review this section, go to glencoe.com and click on Study Central.

The Prosperity of the 1950s

Economy and Society

- The GI Bill provided funds and loans to millions of war veterans.
- Consumer spending increased rapidly.
- More Americans owned homes than ever before.

Population Patterns

- The U.S. population experienced a "baby boom."
- Millions of Americans moved out of cities to the suburbs.

Science, Technology, and Medicine

- Improvements in communication, transportation, and electronics allowed Americans to work more efficiently.
- Medical breakthroughs included the polio vaccine, antibiotics, and treatments for tuberculosis, cancer, and heart disease.

Popular Culture

- New forms of music, radio, cinema, and literature emerged.
- Television replaced movies and radio as the nation's new and most popular form of mass media.

▲ The huge, stylized automobiles of the 1950s, such as this Cadillac convertible, symbolized the good life to many Americans of the time.

The Problems of the 1950s

Economy and Society

- Workers went on strike for higher wages.
- Congress would not pass Truman's civil rights legislation.
- Eisenhower cut back on New Deal programs.

Population Patterns

- Financially able people moved from crowded cities to new suburbs.
- Poverty increased in the inner city and the poor faced ongoing social problems.
- Crime increased among young people.

Science, Technology, and Medicine

- Poor people in inner cities and rural areas had limited access to modern health care.

Popular Culture

- Not everyone could afford to buy the new consumer goods available, such as televisions.
- African Americans and other minorities were, for the most part, not depicted on television.
- Many television programs promoted stereotypical gender roles.

▲ While many prospered in the 1950s, many were excluded from achieving the American Dream.

ASSESSMENT

NEW YORK REGENTS EXAM PRACTICE

TEST-TAKING

Before answering, read the entire question and all answer choices. Then choose the answer that makes the most sense.

Part I

Directions (1–11): For each statement or question, write on a separate sheet of paper the number of the word or expression that, of those given, best completes the statement or answers the question.

1 Which of the following were two characteristics of the U.S. economy after World War II?

(1) high unemployment and scarce goods

(2) abundant goods and low unemployment

(3) low unemployment and scarce goods

(4) abundant goods and high unemployment

2 Which of the following was achieved under Truman's Fair Deal?

(1) a large increase in Social Security benefits

(2) a broad program of civil rights reforms

(3) a decrease in the funding for the TVA

(4) a federal highway bill

3 One major cause of the growth of the suburbs was the

(1) rise in blue-collar jobs.

(2) Korean War.

(3) affordability of homes.

(4) television.

4 Jonas Salk developed the first vaccine for which illness?

(1) tuberculosis

(2) cancer

(3) heart disease

(4) polio

5 The imaginary government marker setting the minimum income required to support a family is called the

(1) urban renewal.

(2) poverty line.

(3) income tax.

(4) delinquency.

6 The purpose of the Bracero Program was to

(1) bring workers into the United States from Mexico.

(2) send workers from the United States to Mexico.

(3) find housing for new immigrants.

(4) deport illegal immigrants.

7 The GI Bill boosted the postwar economy by

(1) instituting a military draft.

(2) providing veterans with generous loans.

(3) requiring all veterans to go to college.

(4) providing veterans with white-collar jobs.

Need Extra Help?							
If You Missed Questions . . .	1	2	3	4	5	6	7
Go to Page . . .	794–795	797	800–801	802–803	810	812–813	794–795

[OVER]

Base your answer to question 8 on the graph below and on your knowledge of Chapter 23.

Suburban Dwellers, 1910–1980

Source: *The First Measured Century.*

8 What trend in the percentage of suburban dwellers does this graph show?

(1) Fewer people were moving from the cities to the suburbs each year.

(2) More people lived in the suburbs in 1910 than 1950.

(3) More people lived in the cities in 1960 than 1950.

(4) More people lived in the suburbs in 1980 than 1970.

9 The invention of the transistor changed communications in which way?

(1) It made computers small and portable.

(2) It made Cinemascope possible.

(3) It made radios small and portable.

(4) It made color television possible.

10. In what year were there approximately twice the number of suburban residents as there had been in 1910?

(1) 1930

(2) 1940

(3) 1950

(4) 1960

Need Extra Help?			
If You Missed Questions . . .	8	9	10
Go to Page . . .	R16	802	815

Part II Thematic Essay Question

Directions: Write a well-organized essay that includes an introduction, several paragraphs addressing the task below, and a conclusion.

Theme: Presidents Truman and Eisenhower

Harry Truman and Dwight Eisenhower were members of two different political parties. However, the two men did not always act along party lines and, in some cases, took similar approaches to governing.

Task:

Compare and contrast the domestic agendas of these two presidents of the postwar era. Be sure to

- Discuss at least two similarities and two differences in the presidents' agendas

- Describe the immediate effects of each president's agenda on the nation

- Evaluate the long-term effects of each agenda

Guidelines:

In your essay, be sure to:

- Develop all aspects of the task

- Support the theme with relevant facts, examples, and details

- Use a logical and clear plan of organization, including an introduction and a conclusion that are beyond a restatement of the theme

Part III Document-Based Question

This question is based on the accompanying documents. It is designed to test your ability to work with historical documents. Some of the documents have been edited for the purposes of the question. As you analyze the documents, take into account both the source of each document and any point of view that may be presented in the document.

Historical Context:

The 1950s in America was a period of postwar abundance, with more middle-class jobs, consumerism, and homes in the suburbs. The economy experienced strong economic growth with dramatic changes in the workplace.

Task:
Using information from the documents and your knowledge of United States history, answer the questions that follow each document in Part A. Your answers to the questions will help you write the Part B essay, in which you will be asked to

- Discuss the changes that took place in postwar America, including changes in the workplace and the growth of entertainment, including television
- Evaluate how these changes helped shape American society, work, and education today

Part A
Short-Answer Questions

Directions: Analyze the documents and answer the short-answer questions that follow each document on a separate sheet of paper.

Document 1

"One of the real threats to America's future place in the world is a citizenry which duly elects to be entertained and not informed. From the time the typical citizen arises and looks at his morning newspaper until he turns off his radio or television set before going to bed, he has unwittingly cast his vote a hundred times for entertainment or for education. Without his knowing it, he has helped to determine the very character of our three most important media of communication—the press, radio, and television."

Source: George Gallup, quoted in *Legacy of Freedom, Vol. 2: United States History from Reconstruction to the Present*

1 According to Gallup, what is a threat to the future of the United States in the world?

2 How do American citizens determine what is read, seen, and heard in the mass media?

Document 2

"He never wastes a minute, J.P.—that's his lunch."

Source: B. Wiseman, *Hey, Can't You Forget Business?*, 1953

3 What is the main idea of this cartoon?

Part B
Essay

Directions: Reread the task box at the top left and write a well-organized essay that includes an introduction, several paragraphs, and a conclusion. Use evidence from the documents in your essay. Support your response with relevant facts, examples, and details. Include additional outside information.

Guidelines:
In your essay, be sure to:
- Develop all aspects of the task
- Incorporate information from the documents
- Incorporate relevant outside information
- Support the theme with relevant facts, examples, and details
- Use a logical and clear plan of organization, including an introduction and a conclusion that are beyond a restatement of the theme

For additional test practice, use Self-Check Quizzes—Chapter 23 at glencoe.com.

Need Extra Help?

If You Missed Questions . . .	1	2	3	Essay
Go to Page . . .	819	819	802	R13

A Time of Upheaval

1954–1980

Why It Matters

Americans in the 1960s sought to remake their society. African Americans protested for civil rights and social equality and were soon joined by women's groups, Hispanics, Native Americans, and the disabled, all of whom demanded more equal treatment. At the same time, the federal government launched several new programs, including Medicare, designed to end poverty; and the Supreme Court took a more active role in society, issuing important rulings on civil rights.

Demonstrators block the entrance to the House of Representatives as part of the "May Day" protest against the Vietnam War, 1971

The New Frontier and the Great Society

1961–1968

SECTION 1 The New Frontier

SECTION 2 JFK and the Cold War

SECTION 3 The Great Society

Future President John F. Kennedy waves to a crowd while campaigning, January 1960.

U.S. PRESIDENTS

Kennedy
1961–1963

1961
- Bay of Pigs invasion
- Peace Corps is created

Oct. 1962
- Cuban missile crisis

Nov. 1963
- Kennedy is assassinated; Johnson becomes president

Johnson
1963–1969

U.S. EVENTS

1961

1963

WORLD EVENTS

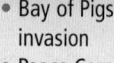

1961
- Construction of Berlin Wall begins

1964
- South Africa's Nelson Mandela sentenced to life in prison

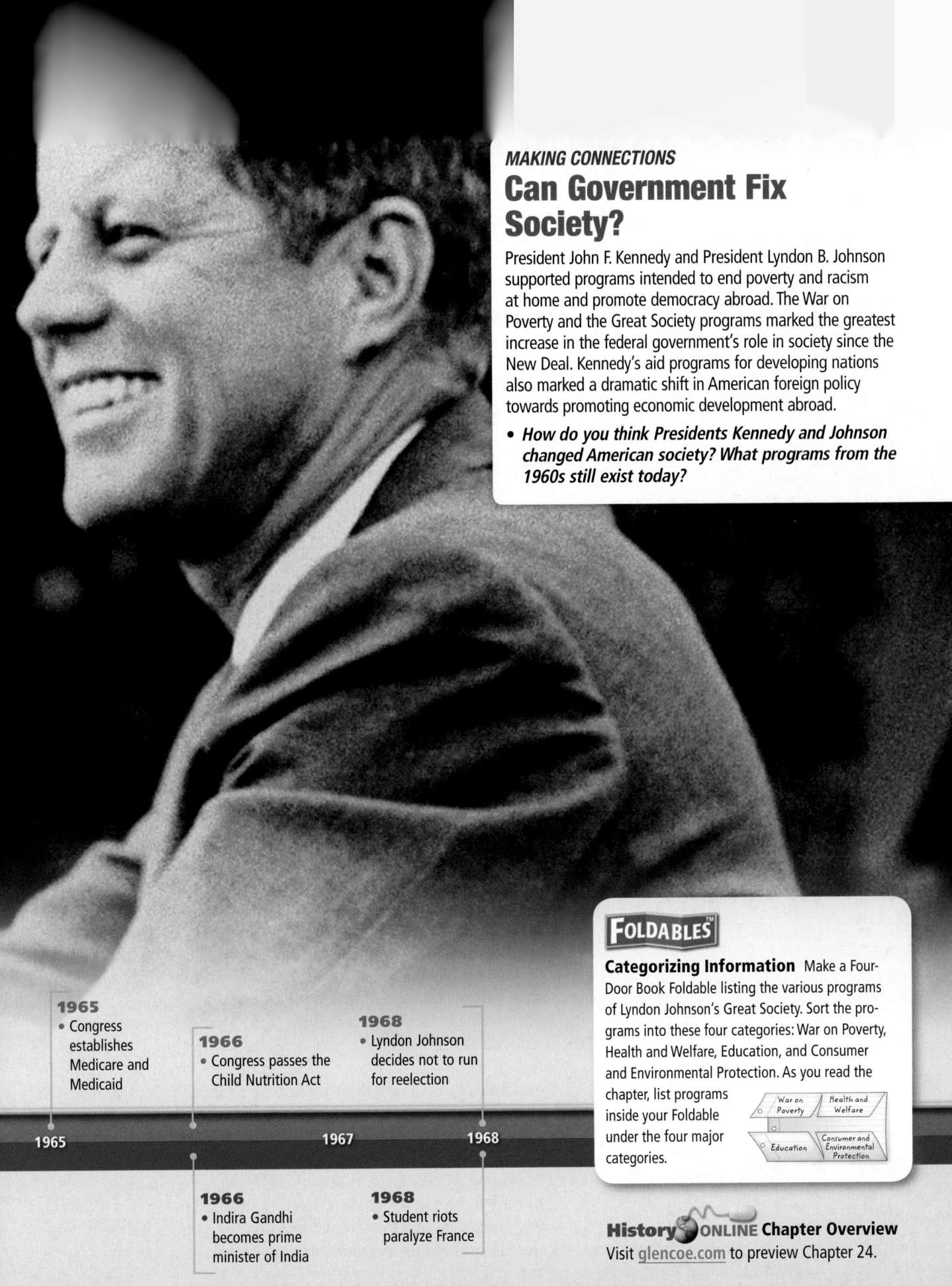

Can Government Fix Society?

President John F. Kennedy and President Lyndon B. Johnson supported programs intended to end poverty and racism at home and promote democracy abroad. The War on Poverty and the Great Society programs marked the greatest increase in the federal government's role in society since the New Deal. Kennedy's aid programs for developing nations also marked a dramatic shift in American foreign policy towards promoting economic development abroad.

- *How do you think Presidents Kennedy and Johnson changed American society? What programs from the 1960s still exist today?*

FOLDABLES™

Categorizing Information Make a Four-Door Book Foldable listing the various programs of Lyndon Johnson's Great Society. Sort the programs into these four categories: War on Poverty, Health and Welfare, Education, and Consumer and Environmental Protection. As you read the chapter, list programs inside your Foldable under the four major categories.

War on Poverty / Health and Welfare / Education / Consumer and Environmental Protection

1965
- Congress establishes Medicare and Medicaid

1966
- Congress passes the Child Nutrition Act

1968
- Lyndon Johnson decides not to run for reelection

1965   1967   1968

1966
- Indira Gandhi becomes prime minister of India

1968
- Student riots paralyze France

History ONLINE Chapter Overview
Visit glencoe.com to preview Chapter 24.

Section 1

The New Frontier

Guide to Reading

Big Ideas
Government and Society Under the programs and policies of the Kennedy administration, women, persons with disabilities, and others gained a greater share of civil rights.

Content Vocabulary
- missile gap *(p. 824)*
- reapportionment *(p. 828)*
- due process *(p. 829)*

Academic Vocabulary
- commentator *(p. 824)*
- arbitrary *(p. 829)*

People and Events to Identify
- New Frontier *(p. 825)*
- Earl Warren *(p. 828)*

Reading Strategy
Categorizing As you read about the presidency of John F. Kennedy, complete a graphic organizer similar to the one below by listing the domestic successes and setbacks of his administration.

Successes	Setbacks

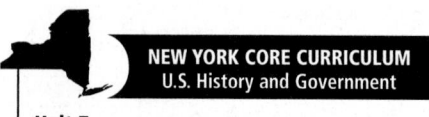

NEW YORK CORE CURRICULUM
U.S. History and Government

Unit 7:
II.C.1.d The Warren Court
III.A.1 The New Frontier: dreams and promises
III.A.3 Movement for rights of disabled citizens

In the presidential election campaign of 1960, John F. Kennedy promised to move the nation into "the New Frontier." After narrowly winning the election, Kennedy succeeded in getting only part of his agenda enacted.

The Election of 1960

MAIN Idea In 1960 a youthful John F. Kennedy narrowly defeated Richard M. Nixon in the presidential election.

HISTORY AND YOU Have you ever watched a televised political debate? Did you pay attention to the candidates' looks and mannerisms? Read on to learn how television changed people's perception of candidates.

On September 26, 1960, at 9:30 P.M. Eastern Standard Time, an estimated 75 million people sat indoors, focused on their television sets, watching the first televised presidential debate. The debate marked a new era of television politics.

During the 1960 presidential race, both parties made substantial use of television. The Democrats spent more than $6 million on television and radio spots, while the Republicans spent more than $7.5 million. Not everyone was happy with this new style of campaigning. Television news **commentator** Eric Sevareid complained that the candidates had become "packaged products" and declared, "the Processed Politician has finally arrived."

The candidates in the first televised debate differed in many ways. The Democratic nominee, John F. Kennedy, was a Catholic from a wealthy and influential Massachusetts family. Richard M. Nixon, the Republican nominee and Eisenhower's vice-president, was a Quaker from California; he had grown up in a family that struggled financially. Kennedy seemed outgoing and relaxed, while Nixon struck many as formal and even stiff in manner.

The campaign centered on the economy and the Cold War. Although the candidates presented different styles, they differed little on these two issues. Both promised to boost the economy, and both portrayed themselves as "Cold Warriors," determined to stop the forces of communism. Kennedy expressed concern about a suspected "**missile gap,**" claiming the United States lagged behind the Soviets in weaponry. Nixon warned that the Democrats' fiscal policies would boost inflation, and that only he had the necessary foreign policy experience to guide the nation.

Kennedy's Catholic faith became an issue, as Al Smith's Catholicism had in 1928. The United States had never had a Catholic president, and many Protestants had concerns about Kennedy. Kennedy decided to confront this issue openly in a speech.

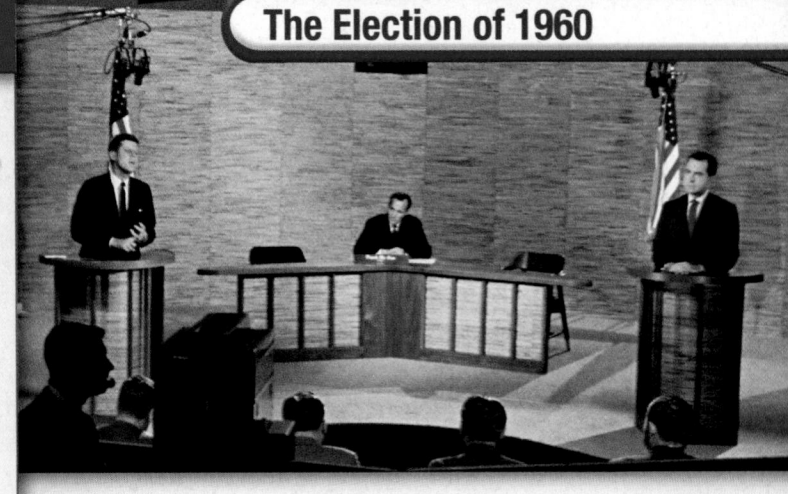

The Election of 1960

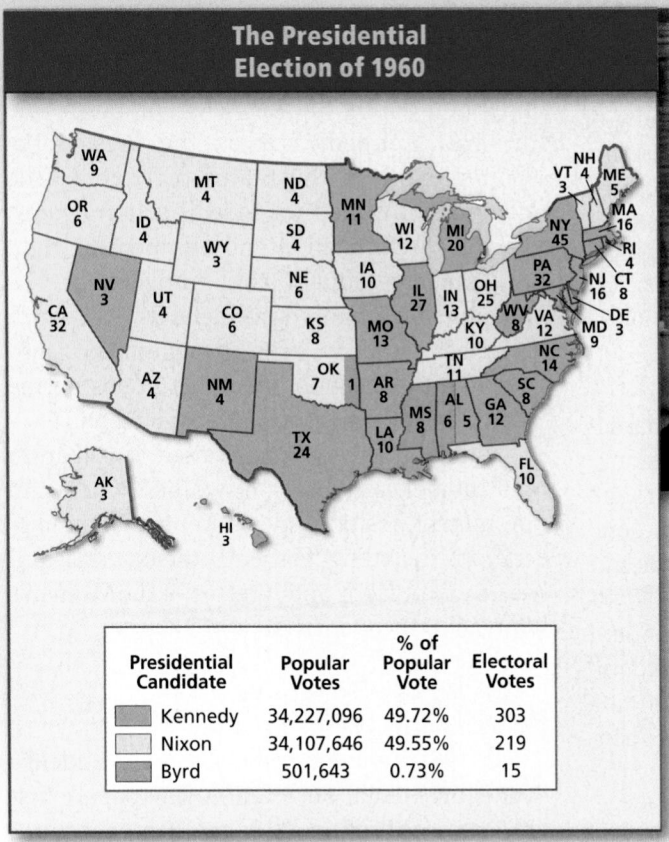

The Presidential Election of 1960

Presidential Candidate	Popular Votes	% of Popular Vote	Electoral Votes
Kennedy	34,227,096	49.72%	303
Nixon	34,107,646	49.55%	219
Byrd	501,643	0.73%	15

▲ The Kennedy-Nixon debates marked the first televised presidential campaign. Senator Kennedy matched Vice President Nixon's well-known debating skills, grasped facts about the way government worked, and showed he cared about Americans.

Analyzing VISUALS

1. **Assessing** What region of the nation went most solidly Republican?
2. **Identifying** Which states gave one or more electoral votes to Harry Byrd?

"I believe in an America where the separation of the church and state is absolute," he said, "where no Catholic prelate would tell the president, should he be a Catholic, how to act."

The four televised debates influenced the election's outcome, one of the closest in American history. Kennedy won the popular vote by 119,000 out of 68 million votes cast, and the Electoral College by 303 votes to 219.

Despite his narrow victory, John F. Kennedy captured the imagination of the American public as few presidents had before him. During the campaign, many had been taken with Kennedy's youth and optimism, and his Inaugural Address reinforced this impression.

In the speech, the new president declared that "the torch has been passed to a new generation" and called on citizens to take a more active role in making the nation better. "My fellow Americans," he exclaimed, "ask not what your country can do for you—ask what you can do for your country."

Reading Check **Identifying** What were the two main issues of the 1960 presidential election?

Kennedy Takes Office

MAIN Idea Despite an uneasy relationship with Congress, President Kennedy managed to get parts of his domestic agenda passed.

HISTORY AND YOU Do you think there are enough women in top government positions today? Read on to learn how Kennedy's programs were designed to help women.

Upon entering office, President Kennedy set out to implement a legislative agenda that became known as the **New Frontier.** He hoped to increase aid to education, provide health insurance to the elderly, and create a Department of Urban Affairs. He would soon find that transforming lofty ideals into real legislation was no easy task on Capitol Hill.

Although the Democrats had majorities in both houses of Congress, Kennedy was unable to push through many of his programs. Kennedy had trailed Nixon in many Democratic districts and had not helped many Democrats get elected. Those who did win, therefore, did not feel they owed him anything.

Southern Democrats—who were a large part of the Democratic majority in Congress—viewed the New Frontier as too expensive and, together with Republicans, were able to defeat many of Kennedy's proposals. Senator Everett Dirksen, Republican minority leader from Illinois, claimed that Kennedy's efforts to increase the power of the federal government would push the nation down an ominous path.

Successes and Setbacks

Kennedy did achieve some victories, particularly in his efforts to improve the economy. Although the economy had soared through much of the 1950s, it had slowed by the end of the decade. In an effort to increase economic growth and create more jobs, Kennedy advocated deficit spending. The new president convinced Congress to invest more funds in defense and space exploration. Such spending did indeed create more jobs and stimulate economic growth.

In addition, Kennedy asked businesses to hold down prices and labor leaders to hold down pay increases. The labor unions in the steel industry agreed to reduce their demands for higher wages, but several steel companies raised prices sharply. In response, Kennedy threatened to have the Department of Defense buy cheaper foreign steel, and instructed the Justice Department to investigate whether the steel industry was fixing prices. The steel companies backed down and cut their prices, but the victory had strained the president's relations with the business community.

Kennedy also pushed for a cut in tax rates. When opponents argued that a tax cut would help only the wealthy, Kennedy asserted that lower taxes meant businesses would have more money to expand, which would create new jobs and benefit everybody. "A rising tide lifts all boats," Kennedy explained to illustrate how tax cuts would help all Americans.

Congress refused to pass the tax cut because of fears that it would cause inflation. Congress also blocked his plans for health insurance for senior citizens and federal aid to education. However, they did agree to Kennedy's request to raise the minimum wage and his proposal for an Area Redevelopment Act and a Housing Act. These acts helped to create jobs and build low-income housing in poor areas.

Expanding Women's Rights

The issue of women's rights also received attention during the Kennedy administration. In 1961 Kennedy created the Presidential Commission on the Status of Women. The commission called for federal action against gender discrimination and affirmed the right of women to equally paid employment. The commission proposed the Equal Pay Act, which Kennedy signed in 1963. The commission also inspired the creation of similar groups on the state level to study the status of women.

Although he never appointed a woman to his cabinet, a number of women worked in prominent positions in the Kennedy administration, including Esther Peterson, assistant secretary of labor and director of the Women's Bureau of the Department of Labor.

A New View of the Disabled

In 1961 Kennedy convened the President's Panel on Mental Retardation. The panel's first report, containing 112 recommendations, called for funding of research into developmental disabilities and educational and vocational programs for people with developmental disabilities; a greater reliance on residential—as opposed to institutional—treatment centers; and grants to provide prenatal services to women in low-income groups to promote healthy pregnancies.

Responding to the report, Congress enacted the Mental Retardation Facilities and Community Mental Health Centers Construction Act of 1963. This legislation provided grants for construction of research centers; funds to train educational personnel to work with people with developmental disabilities; and grants to states for construction of mental health centers.

In 1962 Eunice Kennedy Shriver, the president's sister, began a day camp at her home for children with developmental disabilities. Camp Shriver, as it was first known, offered people with disabilities a chance to be physically competitive. That effort later grew into the Special Olympics program. The first Special Olympics Games were held in Chicago in 1968.

✔ Reading Check **Evaluating** Why did Kennedy have difficulty getting his agenda enacted?

ANALYZING SUPREME COURT CASES

Does Each Vote Really Count?

★ *Baker v. Carr, 1962*
★ *Reynolds v. Sims, 1964*

Background of the Cases

Although many more Americans were living in urban areas, most states had not redrawn their political districts to reflect this shift. This gave rural voters more political influence than urban voters. In *Baker* v. *Carr*, the Supreme Court ruled on whether federal courts had jurisdiction in lawsuits seeking to force states to redraw their electoral districts. In *Reynolds* v. *Sims*, the court decided whether uneven electoral districts violated the equal protection clause of the 14th Amendment.

How the Court Ruled

In *Baker* v. *Carr*, the Supreme Court ruled that federal courts can hear lawsuits seeking to force state authorities to redraw electoral districts. In *Reynolds* v. *Sims*, the Court ruled that the inequality of representation in the Alabama legislature did violate the equal protection clause. These rulings forced states to reapportion their political districts according to the principle of "one person, one vote."

▲ The 1962 Supreme Court. Seated left to right, Associate Justices Tom Clark and Hugo Black, Chief Justice Earl Warren, Associate Justices William O. Douglas and John Harlan; standing, left to right, Associate Justices Byron White, William Brennan, Potter Stewart, and Arthur Goldberg. Justices Byron White and Arthur Goldberg were appointed by Kennedy.

PRIMARY SOURCE

The Court's Opinion

"Legislators represent people, not trees or acres. Legislators are elected by voters, not farms or cities or economic interests. As long as ours is a representative form of government ... the right to elect legislators in a free and unimpaired fashion is a bedrock of our political system. ...

And, if a State should provide that the votes of citizens in one part of the State should be given two times, or five times, or 10 times the weight of votes of citizens in another part of the State, it could hardly be contended that the right to vote of those residing in the disfavored areas had not been effectively diluted.

—Justice William Brennan, Jr., writing for the court in *Reynolds* v. *Sims*

PRIMARY SOURCE

Dissenting Views

"As of 1961, the Constitutions of all but 11 States ... recognized bases of apportionment other than geographic spread of population. ... The consequence of today's decision is that ... state courts, are given blanket authority and the constitutional duty to supervise apportionment. ... It is difficult to imagine a more intolerable and inappropriate interference by the judiciary with the independent legislatures of the States. ... [The Court] says only that 'legislators represent people, not trees or acres,'. ... But it is surely equally obvious ... that legislators can represent their electors only by speaking for their interests—economic, social, political—many of which do reflect the place where the electors live. ... These decisions also cut deeply into the fabric of our federalism."

—Justice John Marshall Harlan dissenting in *Reynolds* v. *Sims*

DBQ Document-Based Questions

1. **Summarizing** What is the main idea of the majority decision in *Reynolds* v. *Sims*?
2. **Explaining** Why does Justice Harlan disagree with the majority in *Reynolds* v. *Sims*?
3. **Making Inferences** How do you think reapportionment according to "one person, one vote" changed state politics?

Warren Court Reforms

MAIN Idea Under Chief Justice Earl Warren, the Supreme Court issued a number of decisions that altered the voting system, expanded due process, and reinterpreted aspects of the First Amendment.

HISTORY AND YOU Do you ever watch cop shows in which police officers read suspects their "Miranda rights"? Read on to learn about the origin of this process.

For further information on the Supreme Court cases referenced on this page, see pages R58–R61 in **Supreme Court Case Summaries.**

In 1953 President Eisenhower nominated **Earl Warren,** governor of California, to be Chief Justice of the United States. Under Warren's leadership, the Supreme Court issued several rulings that dramatically reshaped American politics and society.

"One Man, One Vote"

Some of the Warren Court's more notable decisions concerned **reapportionment,** or the way in which states draw up political districts based on changes in population. By 1960, many more Americans resided in cities and suburbs than in rural areas. Yet many states had failed to change their electoral districts to reflect that population shift.

In Tennessee, for example, a rural county with only 2,340 voters had one representative in the state assembly, while an urban county with 133 times more voters had only seven. Thus, rural voters had far more political influence than urban voters. Some Tennessee voters took the matter to court and their case wound up in the Supreme Court. In *Baker* v. *Carr* (1962), the Court ruled that the federal courts had jurisdiction to hear lawsuits seeking to force states to redraw electoral districts.

The Supreme Court subsequently ruled, in *Reynolds* v. *Sims* (1964), that the current apportionment system in most states was unconstitutional. The Warren Court required states to reapportion electoral districts along the principle of "one man, one vote," so that all citizens' votes would have equal weight. The decision was a momentous one, for it shifted political

What Were the Major Decisions of the Warren Court?

Civil Rights

Brown v. Board of Education (1954)	Declared segregation in public schools unconstitutional
Baker v. Carr (1962)	Established that federal courts can hear lawsuits seeking to force state authorities to redraw electoral districts
Reynolds v. Sims (1964)	Mandated that state legislative districts be approximately equal in population
Heart of Atlanta Motel v. United States (1964)	Upheld the Civil Rights Act of 1964 provision requiring desegregation of public accommodations
Loving v. Virginia (1967)	Forbade state bans on interracial marriage

Due Process

Mapp v. Ohio (1961)	Ruled that unlawfully seized evidence cannot be used in a trial
Gideon v. Wainwright (1963)	Established suspects' right to a court-appointed attorney if suspects were unable to afford one
Escobedo v. Illinois (1964)	Affirmed right of the accused to an attorney during police questioning
Miranda v. Arizona (1966)	Required police to inform suspects of their rights during the arrest process

Freedom of Speech and Religion

Engel v. Vitale (1962)	Banned state-mandated prayer in public schools
Abington School District v. Schempp (1963)	Banned state-mandated Bible reading in public schools
New York Times v. Sullivan (1964)	Restricted circumstances in which celebrities could sue the media

Analyzing VISUALS

1. **Interpreting** How did *Brown* v. *Board of Education* and *Reynolds* v. *Sims* affect the nation?

2. **Summarizing** What three major policy areas did the Warren Court's decisions affect?

power from rural and often conservative areas to urban areas, where more liberal voters resided. The Court's decision also boosted the political power of African Americans and Hispanics, who often lived in cities.

Extending Due Process

In a series of rulings, the Supreme Court began to use the Fourteenth Amendment to apply the Bill of Rights to the states. Originally, the Bill of Rights applied only to the federal government. Many states had their own bills of rights, but some federal rights did not exist at the state level. The Fourteenth Amendment states that "no state shall . . . deprive any person of life, liberty, or property without due process of law." **Due process** means that the law may not treat individuals unfairly, **arbitrarily,** or unreasonably, and that courts must follow proper procedures when trying cases. Due process is meant to ensure that all people are treated the same by the legal system. The Court ruled in several cases that due process meant applying the federal bill of rights to the states.

In 1961 the Supreme Court ruled in *Mapp* v. *Ohio* that state courts could not consider evidence obtained in violation of the federal Constitution. In *Gideon* v. *Wainwright* (1963), the Court ruled that a defendant in a state court had the right to a lawyer, regardless of his or her ability to pay. The following year, in *Escobedo* v. *Illinois,* the justices ruled that suspects must be allowed access to a lawyer and must be informed of their right to remain silent before being questioned by the police. *Miranda* v. *Arizona* (1966) went even further, requiring that authorities immediately inform suspects that they have the right to remain silent; that anything they say can and will be used against them in court; that they have a right to a lawyer; and that, if they cannot afford a lawyer, the court will appoint one for them. Today these warnings are known as the Miranda rights.

Prayer and Privacy

The Supreme Court also handed down decisions that reaffirmed the separation of church and state. The Court applied the First Amendment to the states in *Engel* v. *Vitale* (1962). In this ruling, the Court decided that states could not compose official prayers and require those prayers to be recited in public schools. The following year, in *Abington School District* v. *Schempp*, it ruled against state-mandated Bible readings in public schools. Weighing in on another issue, the Court ruled in *Griswold* v. *Connecticut* (1965) that prohibiting the sale and use of birth-control devices violated citizens' constitutional right to privacy.

As with most rulings of the Warren Court, these decisions delighted some and deeply disturbed others. What most people did agree upon, however, was the Court's pivotal role in shaping national policy. The Warren Court, wrote *New York Times* columnist Anthony Lewis, "has brought about more social change than most Congresses and most Presidents."

✔ **Reading Check** **Examining** What was the significance of the "One Man, One Vote" ruling?

Section 1 REVIEW

Vocabulary
1. **Explain** the significance of: missile gap, New Frontier, Earl Warren, reapportionment, due process.

Main Ideas
2. **Interpreting** In what ways was the 1960 presidential election a turning point in political campaign history?

3. **Summarizing** What progress was made for women's rights during Kennedy's administration?

4. **Describing** Name three decisions of the Warren Court and explain how each protected civil rights.

Critical Thinking
5. **Big Ideas** What were some successes and failures of Kennedy's New Frontier? How did the new programs change the lives of Americans?

6. **Organizing** Use a graphic organizer similar to the one below to list the economic policies of the Kennedy administration.

Economic Policies	

7. **Analyzing Visuals** Look at the election map on page 825. Which states split their electoral votes?

Writing About History
8. **Expository Writing** In his Inaugural Address, President Kennedy asked his fellow Americans to "ask what you can do for your country." Respond to this statement in an essay.

History ONLINE

Study Central™ To review this section, go to glencoe.com and click on Study Central.

JFK and the Cold War

Guide to Reading

Big Ideas
Economics and Society The Kennedy administration used foreign aid to improve relations with Latin American countries and lessen the appeal of left-wing movements.

Content Vocabulary
• flexible response *(p. 830)*
• space race *(p. 832)*

Academic Vocabulary
• conventional *(p. 830)*
• institute *(p. 833)*
• remove *(p. 835)*

People and Events to Identify
• Peace Corps *(p. 832)*
• Berlin Wall *(p. 834)*
• Warren Commission *(p. 835)*

Reading Strategy
Sequencing As you read about the crises of the Cold War, complete a time line similar to the one below to record the major events of the Cold War in the 1950s and early 1960s.

NEW YORK CORE CURRICULUM
U.S. History and Government

Unit 7:
III.A.2.a Bay of Pigs invasion
III.A.2.b Vienna Summit/Berlin Wall
III.A.2.c Cuban missile crisis
III.A.2.e Latin America and the Alliance for Progress
III.A.2.f Peace Corps
III.A.2.g Launching the race to the Moon
III.A.4 Assassination in Dallas
V.A.1.b The Moon landing

During the Kennedy Administration, ongoing tensions with the Soviet Union led to crises over Cuba and West Berlin. To contain communism and stay ahead of the Soviet Union in technology, President Kennedy created aid programs for developing nations and expanded the space program.

Containing Communism

MAIN Idea President Kennedy developed new programs to combat the spread of communism.

HISTORY AND YOU Would you consider joining the Peace Corps and serving in a foreign country? Read on to learn about Kennedy's diplomatic efforts in Latin America.

When John F. Kennedy entered the White House, he had to devote much of his time to foreign policy. The Cold War with the Soviet Union dominated all other concerns at the time, and Kennedy attempted to stop the spread of communism with a range of programs. These included a **conventional** weaponry program to give the nation's military more flexibility, a program to provide economic aid to Latin America, and the creation of the Peace Corps to help developing nations worldwide.

A More Flexible Response

Kennedy took office at a time of growing global instability. Nationalism was exploding throughout the developing world, and the Soviet Union actively supported "wars of national liberation."

Kennedy felt that Eisenhower had relied too heavily on nuclear weapons, which could be used only in extreme situations. To allow for a "**flexible response**" if nations needed help resisting Communist movements, the president pushed for a buildup of troops and conventional weapons. Kennedy also expanded the Special Forces, an elite army unit created in the 1950s to wage guerrilla warfare in limited conflicts, and allowed the soldiers to wear their distinctive "Green Beret" headgear.

Aid to Other Countries

Kennedy wanted to renew diplomatic focus on Latin America. Conditions in many Latin American societies were not good: Governments were often in the hands of the wealthy few and many

▲ *John F. Kennedy delivers his inaugural speech, January 20, 1961. He spoke of the obligation of his generation to defend liberty. To his right is incoming Vice President Lyndon Johnson.*

PRIMARY SOURCE

"Let the word go forth from this time and place, to friend and foe alike, that the torch has been passed to a new generation of Americans—born in this century, tempered by war, disciplined by a hard and bitter peace, proud of our ancient heritage—and unwilling to witness or permit the slow undoing of those human rights to which this Nation has always been committed. . . . Let every nation know, whether it wishes us well or ill, that we shall pay any price, bear any burden, meet any hardship, support any friend, oppose any foe, in order to assure the survival and the success of liberty. . . .

To those old allies whose cultural and spiritual origins we share, we pledge the loyalty of faithful friends. . . . To those peoples in the huts and villages across the globe struggling to break the bonds of mass misery, we pledge our best efforts to help them help themselves . . . To our sister republics south of our border, we offer a special pledge—to convert our good words into good deeds—in a new alliance for progress—to assist free men and free governments in casting off the chains of poverty. . . .

Now the trumpet summons us again—not as a call to bear arms, though arms we need; not as a call to battle, though embattled we are—but a call to bear the burden of a long twilight struggle, year in and year out, "rejoicing in hope, patient in tribulation"—a struggle against the common enemies of man: tyranny, poverty, disease, and war itself. . . .

And so, my fellow Americans: ask not what your country can do for you—ask what you can do for your country. My fellow citizens of the world: ask not what America will do for you, but what together we can do for the freedom of man."

—Inaugural Address delivered January 20, 1961

DBQ   Document-Based Questions

1. **Expressing** What commitment does Kennedy make with respect to human rights?

2. **Classifying** To what three specific groups does Kennedy promise aid, and what aid is promised?

3. **Finding the Main Idea** What does Kennedy indicate are the common enemies of humankind?

---

of their citizens lived in extreme poverty. In some countries, these conditions spurred the growth of left-wing movements aimed at overthrowing their governments.

When the United States became involved in Latin America, it usually did so to help existing governments stay in power and to prevent Communist movements from flourishing. Poor Latin Americans resented this intrusion, just as they resented American corporations, whose presence was seen as a kind of imperialism.

The Alliance for Progress To improve relations between the United States and Latin America, Kennedy proposed an Alliance for Progress, a series of cooperative aid projects with Latin American governments. The alliance was designed to create a "free and prosperous Latin America" that would be more stable and less likely to support Communist-inspired revolutions.

Over a 10-year period, the United States pledged $20 billion to help Latin American countries establish better schools, housing, health care, and fairer land distribution. The results were mixed. In some countries—notably Chile, Colombia, Venezuela, and the Central American republics—the alliance did promote real reform. In others, local rulers used the money to keep themselves in power.

The Peace Corps Another program aimed at helping less-developed nations fight poverty was the **Peace Corps,** an organization that sent Americans to provide humanitarian services in less-developed nations.

After rigorous training, volunteers spent two years in countries that requested assistance. They laid out sewage systems in Bolivia and trained medical technicians in Chad. Others taught English or helped to build roads. Today, the Peace Corps is still active and remains one of Kennedy's most enduring legacies.

The Cold War in Space

In 1961 Yuri Gagarin (YHOO•ree gah•GAHR•ihn), a Soviet astronaut, became the first person to orbit Earth. Again, as in 1957 when they launched *Sputnik,* the first satellite, the Soviets had beaten the United States in the **space race.** President Kennedy worried about the impact of the flight on the Cold War. Soviet successes in space might convince the world that communism was better than capitalism.

Less than six weeks after the Soviet flight, the president went before Congress and declared: "I believe this nation should commit itself to achieving the goal, before this decade is out, of landing a man on the moon."

Kennedy's speech set in motion a massive effort to develop the necessary technology. In 1962 John Glenn became the first American to orbit Earth. Three years later, the United States sent three men into orbit in a capsule called *Apollo. Apollo* was launched using the Saturn V, the most powerful rocket ever built. The Saturn V was able to give both *Apollo* and the lunar module—which astronauts would use to land on the moon—enough velocity to reach the moon.

On July 16, 1969, a Saturn V lifted off in Florida, carrying three American astronauts: Neil Armstrong, Edwin "Buzz" Aldrin, and Michael Collins. On July 20 Armstrong and Aldrin boarded the lunar module, named *Eagle,* and headed down to the moon. Minutes later, Armstrong radioed NASA's flight center in Texas: "Houston . . . the *Eagle* has landed."

Armstrong became the first human being to walk on the moon. As he set foot on the lunar surface, he announced: "That's one small step for a man, one giant leap for mankind." The United States had won the space race and decisively demonstrated its technological superiority over the Soviet Union.

✔ **Reading Check** **Examining** What global challenges did Kennedy face during his presidency?

TECHNOLOGY & HISTORY

Space Technology Cold War tensions between the United States and the Soviet Union fueled the space race. Both countries vied for superiority in aeronautical technology and dominance in space exploration.

▲ American astronaut John Glenn is loaded into his space capsule, named *Friendship 7,* on February 20, 1962, shortly before being launched into orbit.

▲ John Glenn in orbit around Earth

◄ NASA recruited seven astronauts for its first manned space program. Each astronaut would ride in a *Mercury* capsule atop an ICBM reconfigured to lift them into space. The first American astronaut to ride into space in the capsule was Alan Shepard. The first American to orbit Earth was John Glenn.

Crises of the Cold War

MAIN Idea President Kennedy faced foreign policy crises in Cuba and Berlin.

HISTORY AND YOU Do you think the embargo against Cuba should be lifted? Read on to learn about the crises President Kennedy faced over Cuba.

President Kennedy's efforts to combat Communist influence in other countries led to some of the most intense crises of the Cold War. At times these crises left Americans and people in many other nations wondering whether the world would survive.

The Bay of Pigs

The first crisis occurred in Cuba, only 90 miles (145 km) from American shores. There, Fidel Castro had overthrown the corrupt Cuban dictator Fulgencio Batista in 1959. Almost immediately, Castro established ties with the Soviet Union, **instituted** drastic land reforms, and seized foreign-owned businesses, many of which were American. Cuba's alliance with the Soviets worried many Americans. The Communists were now too close for comfort, and Soviet premier Nikita Khrushchev was

also expressing his intent to strengthen Cuba militarily.

Fearing that the Soviets would use Cuba as a base from which to spread revolution throughout the Western Hemisphere, President Eisenhower had authorized the CIA to secretly train and arm a group of Cuban exiles, known as *La Brigada,* to invade the island. The invasion was intended to set off a popular uprising against Castro.

When Kennedy became president, his advisers approved the plan. In office less than three months and trusting his experts, Kennedy agreed to the operation with some changes. On April 17, 1961, some 1,400 armed Cuban exiles landed at the Bay of Pigs on the south coast of Cuba. The invasion was a disaster. *La Brigada*'s boats ran aground on coral reefs; Kennedy canceled their air support to keep the United States' involvement a secret; and the expected popular uprising never happened. Within two days, Castro's forces killed or captured almost all the members of *La Brigada.*

The Bay of Pigs was a dark moment for the Kennedy administration. The action exposed an American plot to overthrow a neighbor's government, and the outcome made the United States look weak and disorganized.

◄ Apollo capsule carried three astronauts.

Lunar Module

▲ To reach the Moon, NASA developed the giant Saturn V rocket, which lifted a three-person capsule, called *Apollo,* and a landing craft, called the Lunar Module, into space. Once *Apollo* and the Lunar Module entered orbit around the Moon, the Lunar Module carried two astronauts from the Apollo capsule down to the Moon's surface.

▲ Neil Armstrong was the first person to walk on the Moon.

▲ Buzz Aldrin descended to the Moon's surface, July 20, 1969, becoming the second man to walk on the Moon.

Analyzing VISUALS

1. **Calculating** What analysis can you make about the size of the space capsules and modules used in space?

2. **Describing** How does the Moon's surface appear in these photos?

3. **Identifying** What was the purpose of the Lunar Module?

The Cuban Missile Crisis, October 1962

Soviet missile sites
American quarantine zone

UNITED STATES

Gulf of Mexico

Miami

ATLANTIC OCEAN

85°W

25°N

October 27, 1962: a U2 spy plane is shot down over Cuba

BAHAMAS

TROPIC OF CANCER

Havana

CUBA

Guantanamo

Site of the Bay of Pigs Invasion: launched Apr. 15, 1961

20°N

▲ Fidel Castro in 1963

▼ USS Vesole intercepts a Soviet ship during the U.S. blockade on Cuba.

0   200 kilometers
0   200 miles
Lambert Conformal Equal-Area projection

Caribbean Sea

JAMAICA   HAITI

80°W   75°W

▲ The presence of missiles in Cuba was confirmed by aerial photographs.

Analyzing GEOGRAPHY

1. **Location** Near what major Cuban city are the missiles placed?
2. **Regions** What is the distance from those missiles to Miami?
3. **Place** Where in Cuba did the Bay of Pigs invasion begin?

Maps In Motion See *StudentWorks*™ *Plus* or glencoe.com.

The Berlin Wall Goes Up

Kennedy faced another foreign policy challenge beginning in June 1961, when he met with Soviet Premier Nikita Khrushchev in Vienna, Austria. Khrushchev wanted to stop the flood of Germans pouring out of Communist East Germany into West Berlin. He demanded that the Western powers recognize East Germany and that the United States, Great Britain, and France withdraw from Berlin, a city lying completely within East Germany. Kennedy refused and reaffirmed the West's commitment to West Berlin.

Khrushchev retaliated by building a wall through Berlin, blocking movement between the Soviet sector and the rest of the city. Guards posted along the wall shot at many of those attempting to escape from the East. For nearly 30 years afterward, the **Berlin Wall** stood as a visible symbol of Cold War divisions.

The Cuban Missile Crisis

By far the most terrifying crisis of the Kennedy era occurred the next year. During the summer of 1962, American intelligence agencies learned that Soviet technicians and equipment had arrived in Cuba and that military construction was in progress. On October 22, President Kennedy announced on television that American spy planes had taken aerial photographs showing that the Soviet Union had placed long-range missiles in Cuba. Enemy missiles stationed so close to the United States posed a dangerous threat.

Kennedy ordered a naval blockade to stop the delivery of more missiles, demanded the existing missile sites be dismantled, and warned that if attacked, the United States would respond fully against the Soviet Union. Still, work on the missile sites continued. Nuclear holocaust seemed imminent.

Then, after a flurry of secret negotiations, the Soviet Union offered a deal. It would **remove** the missiles if the United States promised not to invade Cuba and to remove its missiles from Turkey near the Soviet border. The reality was that neither Kennedy nor Khrushchev wanted nuclear war. "Only lunatics . . . who themselves want to perish and before they die destroy the world, could do this," wrote the Soviet leader. On October 28, the leaders reached an agreement. Kennedy publicly agreed not to invade Cuba and privately agreed to remove the Turkish missiles; the Soviets agreed to remove their missiles from Cuba. The world could breathe again.

The Cuban missile crisis forced the United States and the Soviet Union to consider the consequences of nuclear war. In August 1963, the two countries concluded years of negotiation by agreeing to a treaty that banned testing nuclear weapons in the atmosphere.

In the long run, however, the missile crisis had ominous consequences. The humiliating retreat the United States forced on the Soviet leadership undermined the position of Nikita Khrushchev and contributed to his fall from power a year later. The crisis also exposed the Soviets' military inferiority and prompted a dramatic Soviet arms buildup over the next two decades. This buildup contributed to a comparable military increase in the United States in the early 1980s.

Death of a President

Soon after the Senate ratified the test ban treaty, John F. Kennedy's presidency ended shockingly and tragically. On November 22, 1963, Kennedy and his wife traveled to Texas. As the presidential motorcade rode slowly through the crowded streets of Dallas, gunfire rang out. Someone had shot the president twice—once in the throat and once in the head. Horrified government officials sped Kennedy to a nearby hospital, where he was pronounced dead moments later.

Lee Harvey Oswald, the man accused of killing Kennedy, appeared to be a confused and embittered Marxist who had spent time in the Soviet Union. He himself was shot to death while in police custody two days after the assassination. The bizarre situation led some to speculate that the second gunman, local nightclub owner Jack Ruby, killed Oswald to protect others involved in the crime. In 1964 a national commission headed by Chief Justice Warren concluded that Oswald was the lone assassin. The report of the **Warren Commission** left some questions unanswered, and theories about a conspiracy to kill the president have persisted, though none has gained wide acceptance.

In the wake of the assassination, the United States and much of the world went into mourning. Thousands traveled to Washington, D.C., and waited in a line several miles long outside the Capitol to walk silently past the president's flag-draped casket.

Kennedy was president for little more than 1,000 days. Yet he made a profound impression on most Americans. Kennedy's successor, Vice President Lyndon Baines Johnson, set out to promote many of the programs that Kennedy left unfinished.

Reading Check **Summarizing** How was the Cuban missile crisis resolved?

Section 2 REVIEW

Vocabulary
1. **Explain** the significance of: flexible response, Peace Corps, space race, Berlin Wall, Warren Commission.

Main Ideas
2. **Explaining** What were the goals of the Alliance for Progress?

3. **Discussing** How did Kennedy and Khrushchev reach an agreement to end the Cuban missile crisis? What were the details of this agreement?

Critical Thinking
4. **Big Ideas** What was the role of foreign aid in relations between the United States and Latin America?

5. **Organizing** Use a graphic organizer similar to the one below to list the programs that Kennedy used to reduce the threat of nuclear war and to try to stem communism.

6. **Analyzing Visuals** Look at the photograph of John Glenn on page 832. What is the name of his craft, and why do you think the name might have been chosen?

Writing About History
7. **Descriptive Writing** Assume the role of an American citizen during the Cuban missile crisis. Write a journal entry describing the mood of the country during that time.

History ONLINE

Study Central™ To review this section, go to glencoe.com and click on Study Central.

TIME NOTEBOOK

Eyewitness

On May 22, 1964, **PRESIDENT LYNDON JOHNSON** *delivered a speech in Ann Arbor, Michigan, outlining his domestic agenda that would become known as "The Great Society." Speechwriter and policy adviser Richard Goodwin watched the speech on videotape the next morning back in Washington. He recalls his reaction:*

Then, with the cheers, at first muted as if the audience were surprised at their own response, then mounting toward unrestrained, accepting delight, Johnson concluded: "There are those timid souls who say . . . we are condemned to a soulless wealth. I do not agree. We have the power to shape civilization. . . . But we need your will, your labor, your hearts. . . . So let us from this moment begin our work, so that in the future men will look back and say: It was then, after a long and weary way, that man turned the exploits of his genius to the full enrichment of his life."

Watching the film in the White House basement, almost involuntarily I added my applause to the tumultuous acclaim coming from the sound track. . . . I clapped for the President, and for our country.

WHAT IS A PIP, ANYWAY?

Match these rock 'n' roll headliners with their supporting acts.

1. Paul Revere and
2. Martha and
3. Gary Puckett and
4. Gladys Knight and
5. Smokey Robinson and
6. Diana Ross and

a. the Union Gap
b. the Supremes
c. the Miracles
d. the Vandellas
e. the Raiders
f. the Pips

answers: 1. e; 2. d; 3. a; 4. f; 5. c; 6. b

VERBATIM

❝Is there any place we can catch them? What can we do? Are we working 24 hours a day? Can we go around the moon before them?❞

PRESIDENT JOHN F. KENNEDY,
to Lyndon B. Johnson, after hearing that Soviet cosmonaut Yuri Gagarin had orbited the Earth, 1961

❝It was quite a day. I don't know what you can say about a day when you see four beautiful sunsets. . . . This is a little unusual, I think.❞

COLONEL JOHN GLENN,
in orbit, 1962

❝There are tens of millions of Americans who are beyond the welfare state. Taken as a whole there is a culture of poverty . . . bad health, poor housing, low levels of aspiration and high levels of mental distress. Twenty percent of a nation, some 32,000,000.❞

MICHAEL HARRINGTON,
The Culture of Poverty, 1962

❝I have a dream.❞

MARTIN LUTHER KING JR.,
1963

❝I don't see an American dream; . . . I see an American nightmare . . . . Three hundred and ten years we worked in this country without a dime in return.❞

MALCOLM X,
1964

❝The Great Society rests on abundance and liberty for all. It demands an end to poverty and racial injustice.❞

LYNDON B. JOHNSON,
1964

❝In 1962, the starving residents of an isolated Indian village received 1 plow and 1,700 pounds of seeds. They ate the seeds.❞

PEACE CORPS AD,
1965

Space Race

Want to capture some of the glamour and excitement of space exploration? Create a new nickname for your city. You won't be the first.

CITY	NICKNAME
Danbury, CT	Space Age City
Muscle Shoals, AL	Space Age City
Houston, TX	Space City, USA
Galveston, TX	Space Port, USA
Cape Kennedy, FL	Spaceport, USA
Blacksburg, VA	Space Age Community
Huntsville, AL	~~Rocket City, USA~~
	~~Space City, USA~~
	~~Space Capital of the Nation~~
	Space Capital of the World

RALPH MORSE/TIMEPIX

John Glenn, first American to orbit Earth

Milestones

PERFORMED IN ENGLISH, 1962. THE CATHOLIC MASS, following Pope John XXIII's Second Vatican Council. "Vatican II" allows the Latin mass to be translated into local languages around the world.

ENROLLED, 1962. JAMES MEREDITH, at the University of Mississippi, following a Supreme Court ruling that ordered his admission to the previously segregated school. Rioting and a showdown with state officials who wished to bar his enrollment preceded Meredith's entrance to classes.

BROKEN, 1965. 25-DAY FAST BY CÉSAR CHÁVEZ, labor organizer. His protest convinced others to join his nonviolent strike against the grape growers; shoppers boycotted table grapes in sympathy.

STRIPPED, 1967. MUHAMMAD ALI, of his heavyweight champion title, after refusing induction into the army following a rejection of his application for conscientious objector status. The boxer was arrested, given a five-year sentence, and fined $10,000.

PICKETED, 1968. THE MISS AMERICA PAGEANT in Atlantic City, by protesters who believe the contest's emphasis on women's physical beauty is degrading and minimizes the importance of women's intellect.

AP

CRITICAL THINKING

1. Determining Cause and Effect Who did the Voting Rights Act of 1965 help more—whites or African Americans? Explain your answer.

2. Speculating Why do you think President Kennedy was eager to best the Soviets in space?

The Great Society

Guide to Reading

Big Ideas
Individual Action President Lyndon B. Johnson relied on his experience and persuasiveness to get civil rights and antipoverty bills enacted.

Content Vocabulary
• consensus (p. 839)

Academic Vocabulary
• confine (p. 841)
• subsidy (p. 842)

People and Events to Identify
• War on Poverty (p. 839)
• VISTA (p. 840)
• Barry Goldwater (p. 840)
• Great Society (p. 841)
• Medicare (p. 841)
• Medicaid (p. 841)
• Head Start (p. 842)
• Robert Weaver (p. 842)

Reading Strategy
Organizing As you read about Lyndon Johnson's presidency, complete a graphic organizer similar to the one below to list the social and economic programs started during his administration.

Johnson's Programs

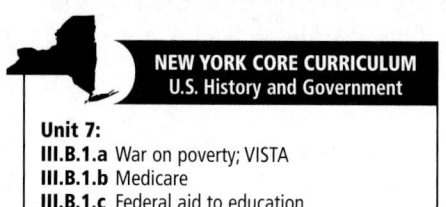

NEW YORK CORE CURRICULUM
U.S. History and Government

Unit 7:
III.B.1.a War on poverty; VISTA
III.B.1.b Medicare
III.B.1.c Federal aid to education

Lyndon B. Johnson had decades of experience in Congress and was skilled in getting legislation enacted. When he became president, he moved quickly to push for passage of a civil rights bill and antipoverty legislation.

Johnson Takes the Reins

MAIN Idea President Johnson's experience in Congress helped him push through a civil rights bill and new laws to fight poverty.

HISTORY AND YOU How do you think someone's early life affects his or her career choices? Read on to learn how Lyndon Johnson's early life prepared him for the presidency.

At 2:38 P.M. on November 22, 1963, just hours after President Kennedy had been pronounced dead, Lyndon B. Johnson stood in the cabin of *Air Force One*, the president's plane, with Kennedy's widow on one side of him and his wife, Claudia, known as "Lady Bird," on the other. Johnson raised his right hand, placed his left hand on a Bible, and took the oath of office.

Within days of the assassination, Johnson appeared before Congress and urged the nation to move forward and build on Kennedy's legacy: "The ideas and ideals which [Kennedy] so nobly represented must and will be translated into effective action," he declared. "John Kennedy's death commands what his life conveyed—that America must move forward."

The United States that President Lyndon B. Johnson inherited from John F. Kennedy appeared to be a booming, bustling place. Away from the nation's affluent suburbs, however, was another country, one inhabited by the poor, the ill-fed, the ill-housed, and the ill-educated. Writer Michael Harrington examined the nation's impoverished areas in his 1962 book, *The Other America*. Harrington claimed that, while the truly poor numbered almost 50 million, they remained largely hidden in city slums, in Appalachia, in the Deep South, and on Native American reservations. Soon after taking office, Lyndon Johnson decided to launch an antipoverty crusade.

Johnson's Leadership Style

Lyndon Baines Johnson was born and raised in the "hill country" of central Texas, near the banks of the Pedernales River. He remained a Texan in his heart, and his style posed a striking contrast with Kennedy's. He was a man of impressive stature who spoke directly, convincingly, and even roughly at times.

When President Johnson launched the War on Poverty in 1964, he wanted programs that would help all impoverished Americans, rural and urban.

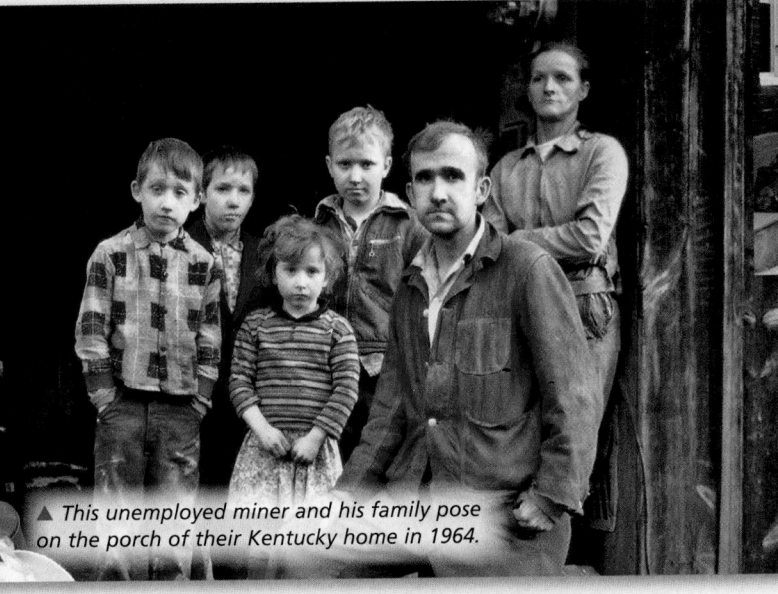

▲ This unemployed miner and his family pose on the porch of their Kentucky home in 1964.

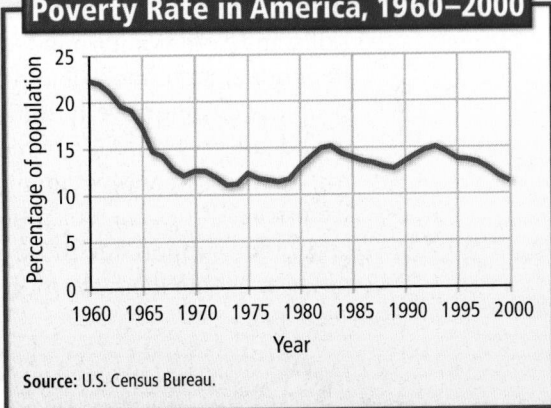

▲ Low-income residents sweep the front stoops of their row houses in Baltimore, Maryland, in the early 1960s.

Poverty Rate in America, 1960–2000

(Line graph: Percentage of population, y-axis 0 to 25; Year, x-axis 1960 to 2000)

Source: U.S. Census Bureau.

Analyzing VISUALS — DBQ

1. **Evaluating** Do you find anything hopeful in the photographs shown?
2. **Interpreting** Based on the data in the chart, how successful was Johnson's War on Poverty?

Johnson had honed his style in long years of public service. By the time he became president at age 55, he already had 26 years of congressional experience behind him. He had been a congressional staffer, a member of the House of Representatives, a senator, Senate majority leader, and vice president.

During his career Johnson earned a reputation as a man who got things done. He did favors, twisted arms, bargained, flattered, and threatened. With every technique he could think of, Johnson sought to find **consensus,** or general agreement. His ability to build coalitions had made him one of the most effective and powerful leaders in the Senate's history.

A War on Poverty

Why was this powerful man so concerned about poor people? Although Johnson liked to exaggerate the poor conditions of his child-hood for dramatic effect, he had in fact known hard times. He had also seen extreme poverty firsthand in a brief career as a teacher in a low-income area. Johnson believed deeply in social action. He felt that a wealthy, powerful government could and should try to improve the lives of its citizens. Kennedy himself had said of Johnson, "He really cares about this nation." Finally, there was Johnson's ambition. He wanted history to portray him as a great president. Attacking poverty was a good place to begin.

Kennedy had plans for an antipoverty program and a civil rights bill before his death. President Johnson knew that any program linked to the slain president would be very popular. In his State of the Union address in 1964, Johnson told his audience: "Unfortunately, many Americans live on the outskirts of hope, some because of their poverty and some because of their color and all too many because of both." He concluded by declaring an "unconditional **War on Poverty** in America."

By the summer of 1964, Johnson had convinced Congress to pass the Economic Opportunity Act. This legislation attacked inadequate public services, illiteracy, and unemployment as three major causes of poverty. The act established 10 new programs within a new government agency, the Office of Economic Opportunity (OEO). Many of the new programs were directed at young Americans living in inner cities.

The Neighborhood Youth Corps provided work-study programs to help underprivileged young men and women earn a high school diploma or college degree. The Job Corps helped unemployed people ages 16–21 acquire job skills. One of the more dramatic programs introduced was **VISTA** (Volunteers in Service to America), which was essentially a domestic Peace Corps. VISTA put young people with skills and community-minded ideals to work in poor neighborhoods and rural areas to help people overcome poverty. Additional programs included Upward Bound, which offered tutoring to high school students, and a Work Experience Program, which provided day care and other support for those in poor households to enable them to work.

The Election of 1964

In April 1964 *Fortune* magazine observed, "Lyndon Johnson has achieved a breadth of public approval few observers would have believed possible when he took office." Johnson had little time to enjoy such praise, for he was soon to run for the office he had first gained through a tragic event.

The Republican candidate in the 1964 election was Senator **Barry Goldwater** of Arizona. Known for his strong conservatism, he set the tone for his campaign when he accepted his party's nomination, declaring, "Extremism in the defense of liberty is no vice! And let me remind you also that moderation in the pursuit of justice is no virtue!"

Few Americans were ready to embrace Goldwater's message, which seemed too aggressive for a nation nervous about nuclear war. On Election Day, Johnson won in a landslide, gaining more than 61 percent of the popular vote and winning all but six states in the Electoral College.

✓ Reading Check **Examining** What inspired the War on Poverty? Why was Johnson able to convince Congress to pass it?

PAST & PRESENT

VISTA Continues the War on Poverty

Volunteers in Service to America (VISTA) began in 1965 as part of President Johnson's War on Poverty. Its focus was to help people help themselves, offering money and programs to low-income communities. Many young people during the idealistic 1960s who weren't able to serve abroad in the Peace Corps program chose instead to work with VISTA. Since the program began, more than 140,000 people have served.

In 1993 VISTA became part of the government agency AmeriCorps. Today, more than 1,200 projects across the nation attempt to make gains in bridging the technology gap, increase housing opportunities, improve health care services, and strengthen community organizations. Volunteers, who must be at least 18, usually work for a year in VISTA-sponsored projects through local, state, or federal agencies or nonprofit, public, or private organizations. In 2006 VISTA had nearly 6,000 volunteers.

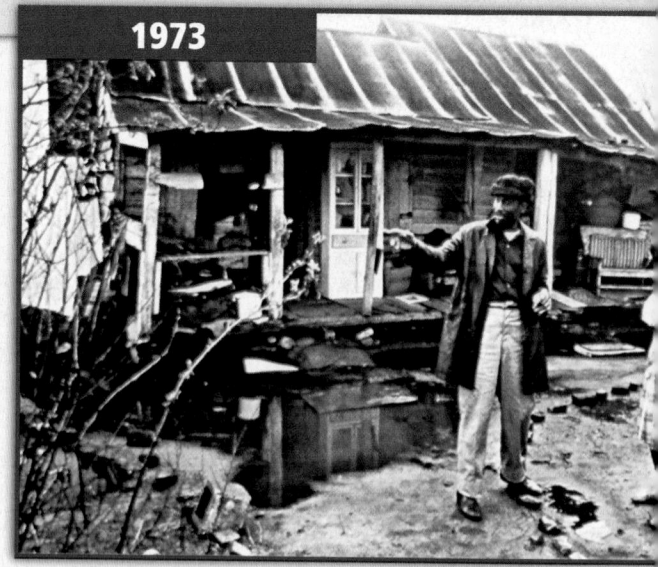

1973

▲ In 1973, Leroy Sneed was a VISTA member in his hometown of Mitchellville, South Carolina, where he was involved in home-repair and community organizing. Here he talks with a homeowner about rebuilding or repairing her home.

The Great Society

MAIN Idea Great Society programs provided assistance to disadvantaged Americans.

HISTORY AND YOU What reforms do you think might help reduce poverty today? Read on to learn about the antipoverty programs initiated by President Johnson.

After his election, Johnson began working with Congress to create the "**Great Society**" he had promised during his campaign. In this same period, major goals of the civil rights movement were achieved through the Civil Rights Act of 1964, which barred discrimination of many kinds, and the Voting Rights Act of 1965, which protected voters from discriminatory practices.

Johnson's goals were consistent with the times for several reasons. The civil rights movement had brought the grievances of African Americans to the forefront, reminding many that equality of opportunity had yet to be realized. Economics also supported Johnson's goal. The economy was strong, and many believed it would remain so indefinitely. There was no reason to believe, therefore, that poverty could not be significantly reduced.

Johnson elaborated on the Great Society's goals during a speech at the University of Michigan in May of 1964. It was clear that the president did not intend only to expand relief to the poor or to **confine** government efforts to material things. The president wanted, he said, to build a better society "where leisure is a welcome chance to build and reflect, . . . where the city of man serves not only the needs of the body and the demands of commerce but the desire for beauty and the hunger for community."

This ambitious vision encompassed more than 60 programs that were initiated between 1965 and 1968. Among the most significant programs were **Medicare** and **Medicaid.** Health care reform had been a major issue since the days of Harry Truman. By the 1960s, public support for better health care benefits had solidified. Medicare had especially strong support since it was directed at all senior citizens. In 1965 approximately half of all Americans over the age of 65 had no health insurance.

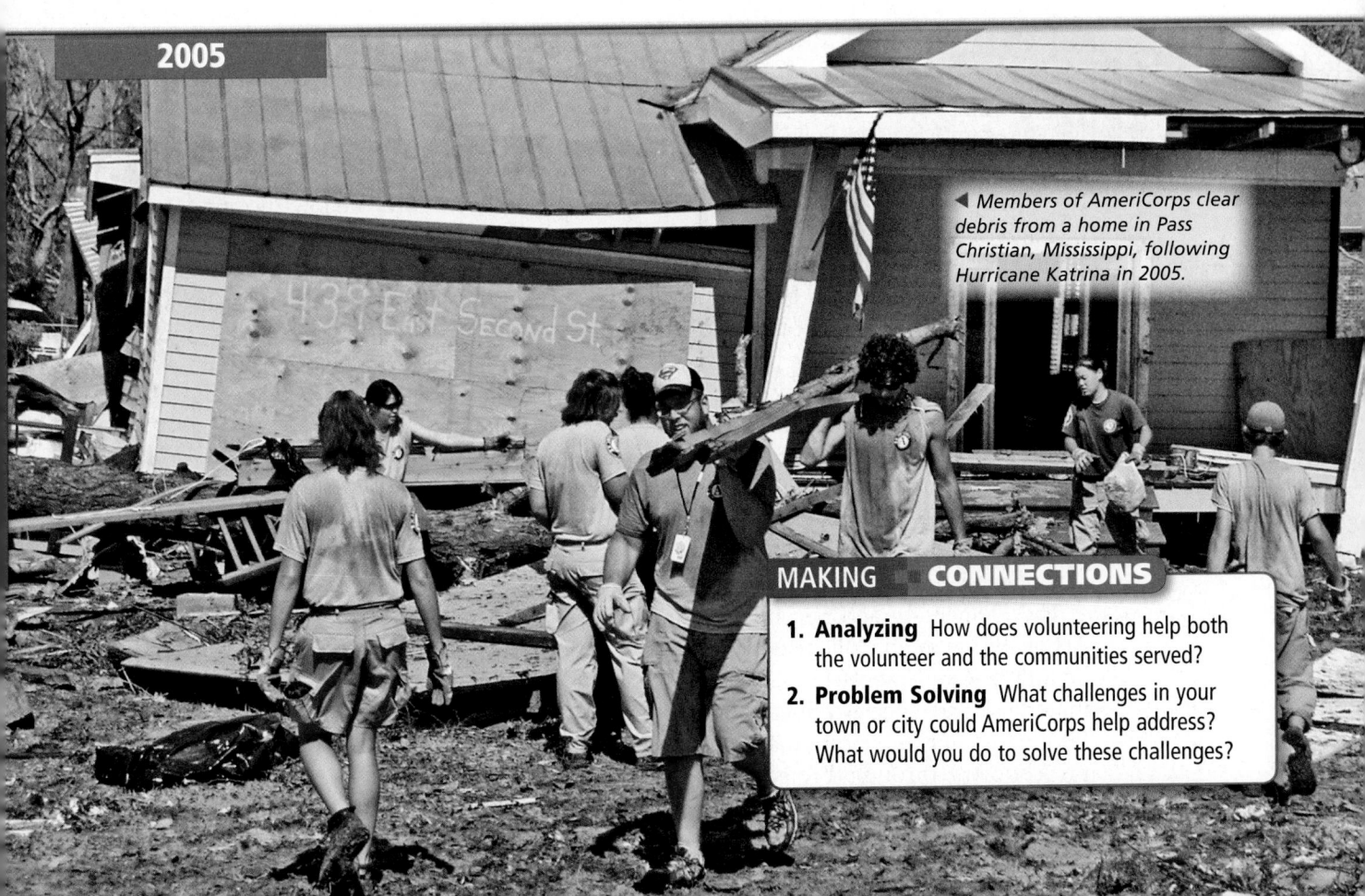

2005

◄ Members of AmeriCorps clear debris from a home in Pass Christian, Mississippi, following Hurricane Katrina in 2005.

MAKING CONNECTIONS

1. **Analyzing** How does volunteering help both the volunteer and the communities served?

2. **Problem Solving** What challenges in your town or city could AmeriCorps help address? What would you do to solve these challenges?

What Was the Great Society?

Health and Welfare

Medicare (1965) established a comprehensive health insurance program for all senior citizens; financed through the Social Security system.

Medicaid (1965) provided health and medical assistance to low-income families; funded through federal and state governments.

Child Nutrition Act (1966) established a school breakfast program and expanded the school lunch and milk programs to improve nutrition.

Education

Elementary and Secondary Education Act (1965) targeted aid to students and funded related activities such as adult education and education counseling.

Higher Education Act (1965) supported college tuition scholarships, student loans, and work-study programs for low- and middle-income students.

Project Head Start (1965) funded a preschool program for disadvantaged children.

The War on Poverty

Office of Economic Opportunity (1964) oversaw many programs to improve life in inner cities, including Job Corps, an education and job training program for at-risk youth.

Housing and Urban Development Act (1965) established new housing subsidy programs and made federal loans and public housing grants easier to obtain.

Demonstration Cities and Metropolitan Development Act (1966) revitalized urban areas through a variety of social and economic programs.

Consumer and Environmental Protection

Water Quality Act and Clean Air Acts (1965) supported development of standards and goals for water and air quality.

Highway Safety Act (1966) improved federal, state, and local coordination and created training standards for emergency medical technicians.

Fair Packaging and Labeling Act (1966) required all consumer products to have true and informative labels.

Analyzing VISUALS

1. **Interpreting** What was the purpose of the Water Quality and Clean Air Acts of 1965?

2. **Evaluating** Which of the Great Society programs do you think had the most effect on American life? Why do you think so?

Johnson convinced Congress to set up Medicare as a health insurance program funded through the Social Security system. Medicare's twin program, Medicaid, financed health care for welfare recipients who were living below the poverty line. Like the New Deal's Social Security program, both programs created what have been called "entitlements," that is, they entitle certain categories of Americans to benefits. Today, the cost of these programs has become a permanent part of the federal budget.

Great Society programs also strongly supported education. For Johnson, who had taught school as a young man, education was a personal passion. Vice President Hubert Humphrey once said that Johnson "was a nut on education.... [He] believed in it, just like some people believe in miracle cures."

The Elementary and Secondary Education Act of 1965 granted millions of dollars to public and private schools for textbooks, library materials, and special education programs. Efforts to improve education also extended to preschoolers through Project **Head Start.**

Administered by the Office of Economic Opportunity, Head Start was directed at disadvantaged children who had "never looked at a picture book or scribbled with a crayon." Another program, Upward Bound, was designed to prepare low-income teenagers for college.

Improvements in health and education were only the beginning of the Great Society programs. Conditions in the cities—poor schools, crime, slum housing, poverty, and pollution—blighted the lives of those who dwelled there. Johnson urged Congress to act on several pieces of legislation addressing urban issues. One created a new cabinet agency, the Department of Housing and Urban Development, in 1965. Its first secretary, **Robert Weaver,** was the first African American to serve in the cabinet. A broad-based program informally called "Model Cities" authorized federal **subsidies** to many cities. The funds, matched by local and state contributions, supported programs to improve transportation, health care, housing, and policing. Since many urban areas lacked sufficient or affordable housing, legislation also authorized about $8 billion to build houses for low- and middle-income people.

One notable Great Society measure changed the composition of the American population: the Immigration Act of 1965. This act eliminated the national origins system established in the 1920s, which had given preference to northern European immigrants. The new measure opened wider the door of the United States to newcomers from all parts of Europe, as well as from Asia and Africa.

The Great Society's Legacy

The Great Society programs touched nearly every aspect of American life and improved thousands, perhaps millions, of lives. In the years since President Johnson left office, however, debate has continued over whether the Great Society was truly a success.

In many ways, the impact of the Great Society was limited. In his rush to accomplish as much as possible, Johnson did not calculate exactly how his programs might work. As a result, some of them did not work as well as hoped. Furthermore, the programs grew so quickly they were often unmanageable and difficult to evaluate.

Cities, states, and groups eligible for aid began to expect immediate and life-changing benefits. These expectations left many feeling frustrated and angry. Other Americans opposed the massive growth of federal programs and criticized the Great Society for intruding too much into their lives.

A lack of funds also hindered the effectiveness of Great Society programs. When Johnson attempted to fund both his grand domestic agenda and the increasingly costly war in Vietnam, the Great Society eventually suffered. Some Great Society initiatives have survived to the present, however. These include Medicare and Medicaid, two cabinet agencies—the Department of Transportation and the Department of Housing and Urban Development (HUD)—and Project Head Start. Overall, the programs provided some important benefits to poorer communities and gave political and administrative experience to minority groups.

An important legacy of the Great Society was the questions it produced. How can the federal government help disadvantaged citizens? How much government help can a society provide without weakening the private sector? How much help can people receive without losing motivation to fight against hardships on their own?

Lyndon Johnson took office determined to change the United States in a way few other presidents had attempted. If he fell short, it was perhaps that the goals he set were so high. In evaluating the administration's efforts, the *New York Times* wrote, "The walls of the ghettos are not going to topple overnight, nor is it possible to wipe out the heritage of generations of social, economic, and educational deprivation by the stroke of a Presidential pen."

Reading Check **Summarizing** What were the Great Society programs, and what was their impact?

Vocabulary

1. **Explain** the significance of: consensus, War on Poverty, VISTA, Barry Goldwater, Great Society, Medicare, Medicaid, Head Start, Robert Weaver.

Main Ideas

2. **Analyzing** How did Johnson's War on Poverty strive to ensure greater fairness in American society?

3. **Describing** Which Great Society programs supported education? How did these programs help?

Critical Thinking

4. **Big Ideas** How did President Johnson carry on the ideals of President Kennedy?

5. **Organizing** Use a graphic organizer similar to the one below to list five of the Great Society initiatives that have survived to the present.

Great Society Initiatives

6. **Analyzing Visuals** Look at the graph on page 839. When was poverty at its lowest in the U.S.?

Writing About History

7. **Descriptive Writing** Assume the role of a biographer. Write a chapter in a biography of Lyndon Johnson in which you compare and contrast his leadership style to that of John Kennedy.

History ONLINE

Study Central™ To review this section, go to glencoe.com and click on Study Central.

Domestic Programs of the 1960s

- A growing awareness of poverty, as well as concern for women's rights and the rights of various minority groups, leads to a series of new programs known as the War on Poverty and the Great Society.
- The President's Commission on the Status of Women is established and the Equal Pay Act of 1963 is passed.
- New programs aid the developmentally disabled.
- Office of Economic Opportunity is established to fight poverty, illiteracy, unemployment, and disease.
- Civil Rights Act of 1964 prohibits race discrimination and social segregation, and the Voting Rights Act protects universal suffrage.
- Medicare and Medicaid Acts are passed to provide federal medical aid to senior citizens and poor.
- Elementary and Secondary Education Act is passed to increase aid for public schools.

▲ VISTA volunteers work to curb delinquency by counseling and helping troubled children and their families.

Foreign Policy of the 1960s

- Kennedy pledges to end Eisenhower's reliance on nuclear weapons and to use new methods to prevent the spread of communism.
- Kennedy introduces the "flexible response" policy—building up both nuclear missiles and conventional forces.
- The United States pledges aid to struggling Latin American nations.
- Peace Corps sends volunteers to help in poor countries.
- The United States aids Cuban exiles trying to overthrow Castro, but their landing at the Bay of Pigs fails.
- Soviet missiles in Cuba lead to the Cuban missile crisis; the United States blockades Cuba and the Soviets remove the missiles.
- The U.S. and Soviet Union sign the Nuclear Test Ban Treaty.

▲ The U.S. Navy ship, the Vesole, intercepts the missile-carrying Soviet ship Potzunov as it leaves Cuba during the Cuban Missile Crisis.

Supreme Court Cases of the 1960s

- Led by Chief Justice Earl Warren, the Supreme Court makes a series of decisions that dramatically change American society and the federal government's relationship to citizens.
- In *Reynolds* v. *Sims* the Court requires states to adhere to the principle of one person, one vote.
- In four cases, *Mapp* v. *Ohio*, *Gideon* v. *Wainwright*, *Escobedo* v. *Illinois*, and *Miranda* v. *Arizona*, the Court extends due process, giving more protection to those accused of crimes.
- In *Abington School District* v. *Schemp*, the Court rules that states cannot require prayer and Bible readings in public schools.

▲ Clarence Earl Gideon was denied counsel during a trial in Florida in 1961. His case eventually went to the Supreme Court.

NEW YORK REGENTS EXAM PRACTICE

TEST-TAKING TIP

To answer vocabulary questions, first try to define the word on your own, without looking at the answer choices. Then read the question and look for the answer that best matches your definition.

Part I

Directions (1–11): For each statement or question, write on a separate sheet of paper the number of the word or expression that, of those given, best completes the statement or answers the question.

1 The Warren Court ruled on many cases that dealt with reapportionment, which is

(1) the requirement of separate but equal facilities for schools.

(2) the process courts must follow when trying cases to treat individuals fairly.

(3) the way in which political districts are drawn based on population changes.

(4) the requirement of separation of church and state in schools.

2 Congress defeated which of the following proposals of Kennedy's New Frontier?

(1) raising the minimum wage

(2) investing funds in defense and space exploration

(3) health care for senior citizens

(4) providing funds to build low-incoming housing

3 Kennedy attempted to reduce the threat of nuclear war and stop the spread of communism by

(1) withdrawing aid from Latin American countries.

(2) disbanding the Special Forces and withdrawing troops from limited military conflicts.

(3) creating the Peace Corps, which provided humanitarian services to less-developed countries.

(4) encouraging growth in the automotive industry to assure that capitalism was superior.

4 How did Soviet Premier Nikita Khrushchev respond when Western powers refused to withdraw from West Berlin?

(1) He sent long-range missiles to Cuba.

(2) He built a wall through Berlin, blocking movement between the Soviet and Western nations.

(3) He enlisted *La Brigada* to invade Cuba and remove Castro from power.

(4) He had food and supplies airlifted to Berlin to end a blockade by American forces.

5 Which Johnson program provided high school and college work-study opportunities?

(1) the Neighborhood Youth Corps

(2) VISTA

(3) the Peace Corps

(4) AmeriCorps

6 The Warren Court decision requiring that a defendant in a state court had the right to a lawyer, regardless of his or her ability to pay was

(1) *Engel* v. *Vitale.*

(2) *Griswold* v. *Connecticut.*

(3) *Plessy* v. *Ferguson.*

(4) *Gideon* v. *Wainwright.*

7 How did the Immigration Reform Act of 1965 change the composition of the American population?

(1) It set strict limits on the number of immigrants admitted to the United States.

(2) It did not allow any immigrants to enter the United States from Eastern Europe.

(3) It continued the national origins system.

(4) It opened the United States to individuals from all over the world, including Asia and Africa.

Need Extra Help?							
If You Missed Questions . . .	1	2	3	4	5	6	7
Go to Page . . .	828	826	832	834	840	829	843

[OVER]

Base your answer to question 8 on the map below and on your knowledge of Chapter 24.

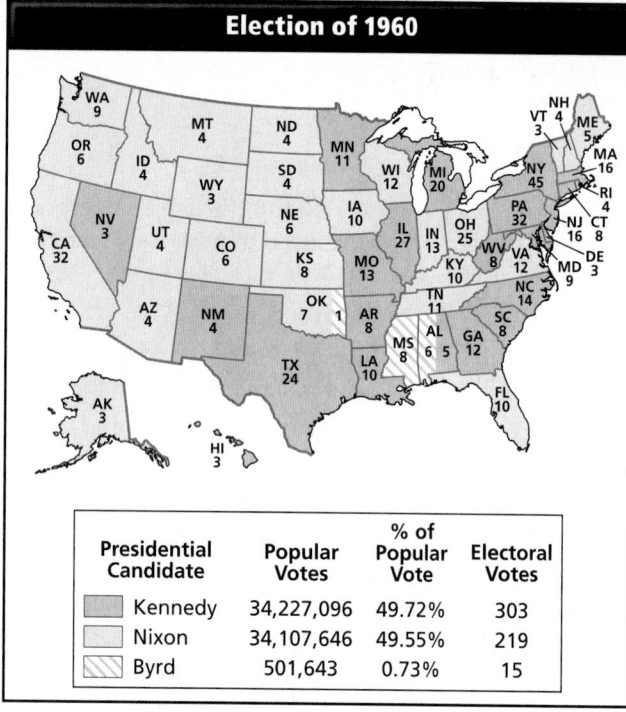

Election of 1960

Presidential Candidate	Popular Votes	% of Popular Vote	Electoral Votes
Kennedy	34,227,096	49.72%	303
Nixon	34,107,646	49.55%	219
Byrd	501,643	0.73%	15

8 What would have happened if Kennedy had lost New York to Nixon?

(1) Kennedy would have won the election since he won the popular vote.

(2) Byrd would have gained ground on both candidates, forcing a run-off.

(3) Nixon would have lost the election by six electoral votes.

(4) Nixon would have won the election by six electoral votes.

9 Which idea was part of Johnson's Great Society?

(1) eliminating government-funded health care for senior citizens

(2) increasing federal aid for education

(3) opposing civil rights legislation

(4) increasing foreign aid to Cuba

Need Extra Help?		
If You Missed Questions . . .	8	9
Go to Page . . .	R15	842

Part II Thematic Essay Question

Directions: Write a well-organized essay that includes an introduction, several paragraphs addressing the task below, and a conclusion.

Theme: The Great Society

President Johnson's Great Society programs were aimed at improving the lives of Americans and, in fact, touched nearly every aspect of American life. However, in the years since President Johnson left office, debate has continued over whether the Great Society was truly a success.

Task:

- Discuss why Johnson proposed the Great Society and how the initiatives were intended to bring about social change

- Evaluate the extent to which the Great Society was successful in bringing about that change

Guidelines:

In your essay, be sure to:

- Develop all aspects of the task

- Support the theme with relevant facts, examples, and details

- Use a logical and clear plan of organization, including an introduction and a conclusion that are beyond a restatement of the theme

Part III Document-Based Question

This question is based on the accompanying documents. It is designed to test your ability to work with historical documents. Some of the documents have been edited for the purposes of the question. As you analyze the documents, take into account the source of each document and any point of view that may be presented in the document.

Historical Context:

During his presidency, Lyndon B. Johnson declared a War on Poverty. This "war" was intended to help the nation's poor, who numbered almost 50 million in the early 1960s.

Task:

Using information from the documents and your knowledge of United States history, answer the questions that follow each document in Part A. Your answers to the questions will help you write the Part B essay, in which you will be asked to

- Discuss the state of the nation's poor in the early 1960s, including the locations of impoverished areas and the gap between the rich and the poor

- Evaluate programs that were part of the War on Poverty and discuss their effectiveness in addressing the needs of the poor

Part A
Short-Answer Questions

Directions: Analyze the documents and answer the short-answer questions that follow each document on a separate sheet of paper.

Document 1

"I come home to an empty room. I don't even have a dog. . . . No, this is not the kind of life I would choose. If a man had a little piece of land or something, a farm, or well . . . anyway, you've got to have something. You sit down in a place like this, you grit your teeth, you follow me? So many of them are doing that, they sit down, they don't know what to do, they go out. I see 'em in the middle of the night, they take a walk. Don't know what to do. Have no home environment, don't have a dog, don't have nothing . . . just a big zero."

Source: Studs Terkel, *Division Street: America,* New Press

1 What does the writer mean when he says, "You sit down in a place like this, you grit your teeth . . ."?

2 What does the person think might help him to have some purpose in his life?

Document 2

Source: Library of Congress, 1965

3 According to the cartoon, what is Johnson trying to do?

Part B
Essay

Directions: Reread the task box at the top left and write a well-organized essay that includes an introduction, several paragraphs, and a conclusion. Use evidence from the documents in your essay. Support your response with relevant facts, examples, and details. Include additional outside information.

Guidelines:
In your essay, be sure to:

- Develop all aspects of the task

- Incorporate information from the documents

- Incorporate relevant outside information

- Support the theme with relevant facts, examples, and details

- Use a logical and clear plan of organization, including an introduction and a conclusion that are beyond a restatement of the theme

For additional test practice, use Self-Check Quizzes—Chapter 24 at glencoe.com.

Need Extra Help?				
If You Missed Questions . . .	1	2	3	Essay
Go to Page . . .	R19	R19	R18	R13

The Civil Rights Movement

1954–1968

SECTION 1 The Movement Begins

SECTION 2 Challenging Segregation

SECTION 3 New Civil Rights Issues

Martin Luther King, Jr., and his wife Coretta lead the civil rights march in Selma, Alabama, 1965.

U.S. PRESIDENTS

Eisenhower 1953–1961

Kennedy 1961–1963

1954
- *Brown v. Board of Education* ruling is issued

1955
- Montgomery bus boycott begins in Alabama

1957
- Eisenhower sends troops to Little Rock to ensure integration of a high school

1960
- Greensboro sit-in begins

1963
- The March on Washington, D.C., is held to support the Civil Rights bill

U.S. EVENTS

1953

1957

1961

WORLD EVENTS

1955
- West Germany is admitted to NATO

1957
- Russia launches *Sputnik* into orbit

1960
- France successfully tests nuclear weapons

1962
- Cuban missile crisis erupts

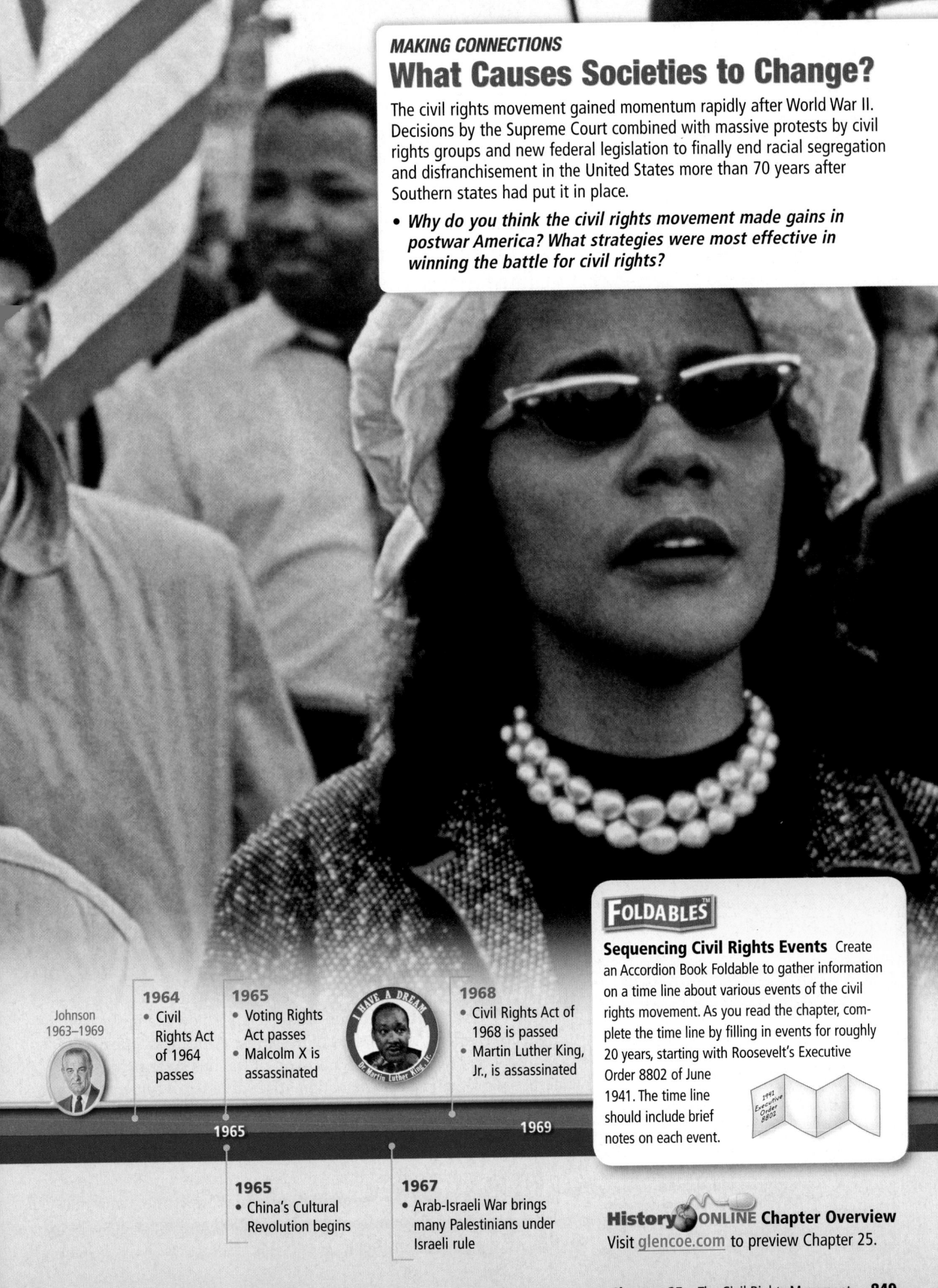

What Causes Societies to Change?

The civil rights movement gained momentum rapidly after World War II. Decisions by the Supreme Court combined with massive protests by civil rights groups and new federal legislation to finally end racial segregation and disfranchisement in the United States more than 70 years after Southern states had put it in place.

- *Why do you think the civil rights movement made gains in postwar America? What strategies were most effective in winning the battle for civil rights?*

Johnson
1963–1969

1964
- Civil Rights Act of 1964 passes

1965
- Voting Rights Act passes
- Malcolm X is assassinated

I HAVE A DREAM
Dr Martin Luther King, Jr.

1968
- Civil Rights Act of 1968 is passed
- Martin Luther King, Jr., is assassinated

1965

1969

1965
- China's Cultural Revolution begins

1967
- Arab-Israeli War brings many Palestinians under Israeli rule

FOLDABLES

Sequencing Civil Rights Events Create an Accordion Book Foldable to gather information on a time line about various events of the civil rights movement. As you read the chapter, complete the time line by filling in events for roughly 20 years, starting with Roosevelt's Executive Order 8802 of June 1941. The time line should include brief notes on each event.

1941 Executive Order 8802

History ONLINE Chapter Overview
Visit glencoe.com to preview Chapter 25.

Chapter 25 The Civil Rights Movement **849**

The Movement Begins

Guide to Reading

Big Ideas
Struggles for Rights In the 1950s, African Americans began a movement to win greater legal and social equality.

Content Vocabulary
• "separate but equal" *(p. 850)*
• de facto segregation *(p. 851)*
• sit-in *(p. 852)*

Academic Vocabulary
• facility *(p. 850)*

People and Events to Identify
• Rosa Parks *(p. 850)*
• National Association for the Advancement of Colored People (NAACP) *(p. 850)*
• Thurgood Marshall *(p. 852)*
• Linda Brown *(p. 852)*
• Martin Luther King, Jr. *(p. 854)*
• Southern Christian Leadership Conference (SCLC) *(p. 855)*

Reading Strategy
Organizing Complete a graphic organizer similar to the one below by listing the causes of the civil rights movement.

Civil Rights Movement

NEW YORK CORE CURRICULUM
U.S. History and Government

Unit 7:

II.C.2.b	*Brown* v. *Board of Education of Topeka,* 1954
II.C.2.c	Beginnings of modern civil rights movement
III.B.3.a.(1)	NAACP (National Association for the Advancement of Colored People): legal judicial leadership, Urban League
III.B.3.b.(2)	SCLC (Southern Christian Leadership Conference): promote nonviolent resistance, sit-ins, boycotts
III.B.3.b.(3)	CORE (Congress of Racial Equality)
III.B.3.b.(4)	Testing of segregation laws

After World War II, African Americans and other civil rights supporters challenged segregation in the United States. Their efforts were vigorously opposed by Southern segregationists, but the federal government began to take a firmer stand for civil rights.

The Origins of the Movement

MAIN Idea African Americans won court victories, increased their voting power, and began using "sit-ins" to desegregate public places.

HISTORY AND YOU Are you registered to vote, or do you plan to register when you are 18? Read on to learn how African Americans increased their voting power and worked to desegregate public places.

On December 1, 1955, **Rosa Parks** left her job as a seamstress in Montgomery, Alabama, and boarded a bus to go home. In 1955 buses in Montgomery reserved seats in the front for whites and seats in the rear for African Americans. Seats in the middle were open to African Americans, but only if there were few whites on the bus.

Rosa Parks took a seat just behind the white section. Soon, all of the seats on the bus were filled. When the bus driver noticed a white man standing, he told Parks and three other African Americans in her row to get up and let the white man sit down. The other three African Americans rose, but Rosa Parks did not. The driver then called the Montgomery police, who took Parks into custody.

News of the arrest soon reached E. D. Nixon, a former president of the local chapter of the **National Association for the Advancement of Colored People (NAACP).** Nixon, who wanted to challenge bus segregation in court, told Parks, "With your permission we can break down segregation on the bus with your case." Parks replied, "If you think it will mean something to Montgomery and do some good, I'll be happy to go along with it."

When Rosa Parks agreed to challenge segregation in court, she did not know that her decision would spark a new era in the civil rights movement. Within days of her arrest, African Americans in Montgomery had organized a boycott of the bus system. Mass protests soon began across the nation. After decades of segregation and inequality, many African Americans had decided the time had come to demand equal rights.

The struggle would not be easy. The Supreme Court had declared segregation to be constitutional in *Plessy* v. *Ferguson* in 1896. The ruling had established the **"separate but equal"** doctrine. Laws that segregated African Americans were permitted as long as equal **facilities** were provided for them.

Thurgood Marshall
1908–1993

Over his lifetime, Thurgood Marshall made many contributions to the civil rights movement. Perhaps his most famous accomplishment was representing the NAACP in the *Brown* v. *Board of Education* case.

Marshall's speaking style was simple and direct. During the Brown case, Justice Frankfurter asked Marshall for a definition of *equal*. Marshall replied: "*Equal* means getting the same thing, at the same time and in the same place."

Born into a middle-class Baltimore family in 1908, Marshall earned a law degree from Howard University Law School. The school's dean, Charles Hamilton Houston, enlisted Marshall to work for the NAACP. Together, the two laid out the legal strategy for challenging discrimination in many areas of American life. In 1935 Marshall won his first case regarding segregation in state institutions. The decision forced the University of Maryland to integrate. Marshall went on to win 29 of the 32 cases he argued before the Supreme Court, and became known as "Mr. Civil Rights." In 1967 Marshall became the first African American to serve on the Supreme Court, where he continued to be a voice for civil rights. In his view, the Constitution was not perfect, because it had accepted slavery. "The true miracle of the Constitution," he once wrote, "was not the birth of the Constitution, but its life."

How did Thurgood Marshall contribute to the civil rights movement?

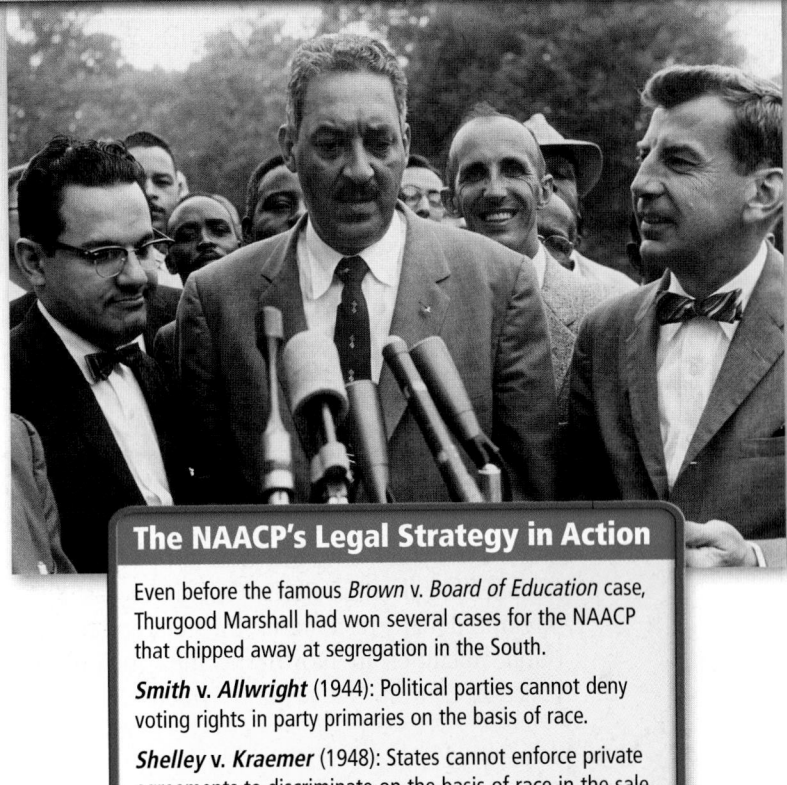

The NAACP's Legal Strategy in Action

Even before the famous *Brown* v. *Board of Education* case, Thurgood Marshall had won several cases for the NAACP that chipped away at segregation in the South.

Smith v. *Allwright* (1944): Political parties cannot deny voting rights in party primaries on the basis of race.

Shelley v. *Kraemer* (1948): States cannot enforce private agreements to discriminate on the basis of race in the sale of property.

Sweatt v. *Painter* (1950): Law schools segregated by race are inherently unequal.

After the *Plessy* decision, laws segregating African Americans and whites spread quickly. These laws, nicknamed "Jim Crow" laws, segregated buses, trains, schools, restaurants, pools, parks, and other public facilities. Usually the "Jim Crow" facilities provided for African Americans were of poorer quality than those provided for whites. Areas without laws requiring segregation often had **de facto segregation**—segregation by custom and tradition.

Court Challenges Begin

The civil rights movement had been building for a long time. Since 1909, the NAACP had supported court cases intended to overturn segregation. Over the years, the NAACP achieved some victories. In 1935, for example, the Supreme Court ruled in *Norris* v. *Alabama* that Alabama's exclusion of African Americans from juries violated their right to equal protection under the law. In 1946 the Court ruled in *Morgan* v. *Virginia* that segregation on interstate buses

was unconstitutional. In 1950 it ruled in *Sweatt* v. *Painter* that state law schools had to admit qualified African American applicants, even if parallel black law schools existed.

New Political Power

In addition to a string of court victories, African Americans enjoyed increased political power. Before World War I, most African Americans lived in the South, where they were largely excluded from voting. During the Great Migration, many moved to Northern cities, where they were allowed to vote. Increasingly, Northern politicians sought their votes and listened to their concerns.

During the 1930s, many African Americans benefited from FDR's New Deal programs and began supporting the Democratic Party. This gave the party new strength in the North. This wing of the party was now able to counter Southern Democrats, who often supported segregation.

The Push for Desegregation

During World War II, African American leaders began to use their political power to demand more rights. Their efforts helped end discrimination in wartime factories and increased opportunities for African Americans in the military.

In Chicago in 1942, James Farmer and George Houser founded the Congress of Racial Equality (CORE). CORE began using **sit-ins,** a form of protest first used by union workers in the 1930s. In 1943 CORE attempted to desegregate restaurants that refused to serve African Americans. Using the sit-in strategy, members of CORE went to segregated restaurants. If they were denied service, they sat down and refused to leave. The sit-ins were intended to shame restaurant managers into integrating their restaurants. Using these protests, CORE successfully integrated many restaurants, theaters, and other public facilities in Northern cities including Chicago, Detroit, Denver, and Syracuse.

Brown v. Board of Education

To better understand the court ruling in *Brown* v. *Board of Education*, read an excerpt from the Court's ruling on page R55 in **Documents in American History.**

After World War II, the NAACP continued to challenge segregation in the courts. From 1939 to 1961, the NAACP's chief counsel and director of its Legal Defense and Education Fund was the brilliant African American attorney **Thurgood Marshall.** After the war, Marshall focused his efforts on ending segregation in public schools.

In 1954 the Supreme Court decided to combine several cases and issue a general ruling on segregation in schools. One of the cases involved a young African American girl named **Linda Brown,** who was denied admission to her neighborhood school in Topeka, Kansas, because of her race. She was told to attend an all-black school across town. With the help of the NAACP, her parents then sued the Topeka school board.

On May 17, 1954, the Supreme Court ruled unanimously in *Brown* v. *Board of Education of Topeka, Kansas,* that segregation in public schools was unconstitutional and violated the equal protection clause of the Fourteenth Amendment. Chief Justice Earl Warren summed up the Court's decision, declaring: "In the field of public education, the doctrine of separate

but equal has no place. Separate educational facilities are inherently unequal."

Southern Resistance

The Brown decision marked a dramatic reversal of the precedent established in the *Plessy* v. *Ferguson* case in 1896. *Brown* v. *Board of Education* applied only to public schools, but the ruling threatened the entire system of segregation. Although it convinced many African Americans that the time had come to challenge segregation, it also angered many white Southerners, who became even more determined to defend segregation, regardless of what the Supreme Court ruled.

Although some school districts in border states integrated their schools, anger and opposition was a far more common reaction. In Washington, D.C., Senator Harry F. Byrd of Virginia called on Southerners to adopt "massive resistance" against the ruling. Across the South, hundreds of thousands of white Americans joined citizens' councils to pressure their local governments and school boards into defying the Supreme Court. Many states adopted pupil assignment laws. These laws established elaborate requirements other than race that schools could use to prevent African Americans from attending white schools.

The Supreme Court inadvertently encouraged white resistance when it followed up its decision in *Brown* v. *Board of Education* a year later. The Court ordered school districts to proceed "with all deliberate speed" to end school segregation. The wording was vague enough that many districts were able to keep their schools segregated for many more years.

Massive resistance also appeared in the halls of Congress. In 1956 a group of 101 Southern members of Congress signed the "Southern Manifesto," which denounced the Supreme Court's ruling as "a clear abuse of judicial power" and pledged to use "all lawful means" to reverse the decision. Although the "Southern Manifesto" had no legal standing, the statement encouraged white Southerners to defy the Supreme Court. Not until 1969 did the Supreme Court order all school systems to desegregate "at once" and operate integrated schools "now and hereafter."

Reading Check **Examining** Why was the ruling in *Brown* v. *Board of Education* so important?

ANALYZING SUPREME COURT CASES

Is Segregation Unconstitutional?

★ *Brown* v. *Board of Education*, 1954

Background to the Cases

One of the most important Supreme Court cases in American history began in 1952, when the Supreme Court agreed to hear the NAACP's case *Brown* v. *Board of Education of Topeka, Kansas,* along with three other cases. They all dealt with the question of whether the principle "separate but equal" established in *Plessy* v. *Ferguson* was constitutional with regard to public schools.

How the Court Ruled

In a unanimous decision in 1954, the Court ruled in favor of Linda Brown and the other plaintiffs. In doing so, it overruled *Plessy* v. *Ferguson* and rejected the idea that equivalent but separate schools for African American and white students were constitutional. The Court held that racial segregation in public schools violates the Fourteenth Amendment's equal protection clause because "Separate educational facilities are inherently unequal." The Court's rejection of "separate but equal" was a major victory for the civil rights movement and led to the overturning of laws requiring segregation in other public places.

▲ *The children involved in the* Brown v. Board of Education *case are shown in this 1953 photograph. They are, from front to back, Vicki Henderson, Donald Henderson, Linda Brown (of the case title), James Emanuel, Nancy Todd, and Katherine Carper. Together, their cases led to the Supreme Court decreeing that public schools could not be segregated on the basis of race.*

The Court's Opinion

"In these days, it is doubtful that any child may reasonably be expected to succeed in life if he is denied the opportunity of an education. Such an opportunity, where the state has undertaken to provide it, is a right which must be made available to all on equal terms. We come then to the question presented: Does segregation of children in public schools solely on the basis of race, even though the physical facilities and other 'tangible' factors may be equal, deprive the children of the minority group of equal educational opportunities? We believe that it does."

—Chief Justice Earl Warren writing for the Court in
Brown v. *Board of Education of Topeka, Kansas*

Dissenting Views

"We regard the decisions of the Supreme Court in the school cases as a clear abuse of judicial power. . . . In the case of *Plessy* v. *Ferguson* in 1896 the Supreme Court expressly declared that under the 14th Amendment no person was denied any of his rights if the States provided separate but equal facilities. . . . This interpretation, restated time and again, became a part of the life of the people of many of the States and confirmed their habits, traditions, and way of life. It is founded on elemental humanity and commonsense, for parents should not be deprived by Government of the right to direct the lives and education of their own children."

—from the "Southern Manifesto"

DBQ Document-Based Questions

1. **Explaining** Why did the Supreme Court find in favor of Linda Brown?
2. **Drawing Conclusions** What is the main argument against the *Brown* decision in the excerpt from the "Southern Manifesto"?
3. **Making Inferences** Do you think that the authors of the "Southern Manifesto" were including African Americans in the last sentence of the excerpt? Why or why not?

The Civil Rights Movement Begins

MAIN Idea The *Brown* v. *Board of Education* ruling ignited protest and encouraged African Americans to challenge other forms of segregation.

HISTORY AND YOU Do you think that one person has the power to change things for the better? Read on to learn how the courage and hard work of individuals helped reform society.

In the midst of the uproar over the *Brown* v. *Board of Education* case, Rosa Parks made her decision to challenge segregation of public transportation. Outraged by Parks's arrest, Jo Ann Robinson, head of a local organization called the Women's Political Council, called on African Americans to boycott Montgomery's buses on the day Rosa Parks appeared in court.

The boycott marked the start of a new era of the civil rights movement among African Americans. Instead of limiting the fight for their rights to court cases, African Americans in large numbers began organizing protests, defying laws that required segregation, and demanding they be treated as equal to whites.

The Montgomery Bus Boycott

The Montgomery bus boycott was a dramatic success. On the afternoon of Rosa Parks's court appearance, several African American leaders formed the Montgomery Improvement Association to run the boycott and to negotiate with city leaders for an end to segregation. They elected a 26-year-old pastor named **Martin Luther King, Jr.,** to lead them.

On the evening of December 5, 1955, a meeting was held at Dexter Avenue Baptist Church, where Dr. King was the pastor. In the deep, resonant tones and powerful phrases that characterized his speaking style, King encouraged the people to continue their protest. "There comes a time, my friends," he said, "when people get tired of being thrown into the abyss of humiliation, where they experience the bleakness of nagging despair." He cautioned, however, that the protest had to be peaceful:

PRIMARY SOURCE

"Now let us say that we are not advocating violence. . . . The only weapon we have in our hands this evening is the weapon of protest. If we were incarcerated behind the iron curtains of a communistic nation—we couldn't do this. If we were trapped in the dungeon of a totalitarian regime—we couldn't do this. But the great glory of American democracy is the right to protest for right!"

—quoted in *Parting the Waters: America in the King Years*

King had earned a Ph.D. in theology from Boston University. He believed that the only moral way to end segregation and racism was through nonviolent passive resistance. He told his followers, "We must use the weapon of love. We must realize that so many people are taught to hate us that they are not totally responsible for their hate." African Americans, he urged, must say to racists: "We will soon wear you down by our capacity to suffer, and in winning our freedom we will so appeal to your heart and conscience that we will win you in the process."

Turning Point

The Montgomery Bus Boycott

The act of one woman on a bus and the subsequent bus boycott in Montgomery, Alabama, brought civil rights out of the legal arena and turned it into a struggle in which ordinary Americans realized that they could make a difference. Rosa Parks's refusal to give up her seat on the bus to a white man showed that even small acts of defiance could empower people to create change.

The Montgomery bus boycott, which was begun to show support for Parks, became a huge success. It started a chain reaction—the beginning of a mass movement that would dramatically change American society over the next 20 years, and bring to prominence many influential African American leaders, including Martin Luther King, Jr.

ANALYZING HISTORY Drawing Conclusions How did the bus boycott create a mass movement for change?

King drew upon the philosophy and techniques of Indian leader Mohandas Gandhi, who had used nonviolent resistance effectively to challenge British rule in India. Believing in people's ability to transform themselves, King was certain that public opinion would eventually force the government to end segregation.

Stirred by King's powerful words, African Americans in Montgomery continued their boycott for over a year. Instead of riding the bus, they organized car pools or walked to work. Meanwhile, Rosa Parks's legal challenge to bus segregation worked its way through the courts. In November 1956, the Supreme Court affirmed the decision of a special three-judge panel declaring Alabama's laws requiring segregation on buses unconstitutional.

African American Churches

Martin Luther King, Jr., was not the only prominent minister in the bus boycott. Many of the other leaders were African American ministers. The boycott could not have suc-ceeded without the support of the African American churches in the city. As the civil rights movement gained momentum, African American churches continued to play a critical role. They served as forums for many of the protests and planning meetings, and mobilized many of the volunteers for specific civil rights campaigns.

After the Montgomery bus boycott demonstrated that nonviolent protest could be successful, African American ministers led by King established the **Southern Christian Leadership Conference (SCLC)** in 1957. The SCLC set out to eliminate segregation from American society and to encourage African Americans to register to vote. Dr. King served as the SCLC's first president. Under his leadership, the organization challenged segregation at voting booths and in public transportation, housing, and accommodations.

✓ Reading Check **Summarizing** What role did African American churches play in the civil rights movement?

History ONLINE
Student Web Activity Visit glencoe.com and complete the activity on Rosa Parks.

▲ African Americans walk to work during the third month of the Montgomery bus boycott (above). The Dexter Avenue Baptist Church in Montgomery, Alabama (right), was the Reverend Dr. Martin Luther King, Jr.'s, first church as a minister and headquarters for the organizers of the bus boycott.

▲ Rosa Parks rides a newly integrated bus after the successful boycott.

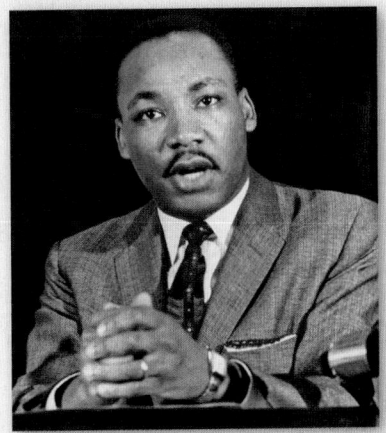

Eisenhower Responds

MAIN Idea President Eisenhower sent the U.S. Army to enforce integration in Arkansas.

HISTORY AND YOU Do you believe that the president should uphold Supreme Court rulings? Read to learn how Eisenhower responded to events in Little Rock, Arkansas.

President Eisenhower sympathized with the civil rights movement and personally disagreed with segregation. Following the precedent set by President Truman, he ordered navy shipyards and veterans' hospitals to desegregate. At the same time, however, Eisenhower disagreed with those who wanted to end segregation through protests and court rulings. He believed segregation and racism would end gradually, as values changed. With the nation in the midst of the Cold War, he worried that challenging white Southerners might divide the nation at a time when the country needed to pull together. Publicly, he refused to endorse the *Brown* v. *Board of Education* decision. Privately, he remarked, "I don't believe you can change the hearts of men with laws or decisions."

Although he believed that the *Brown* v. *Board of Education* decision was wrong, Eisenhower knew he had to uphold the authority of the federal government. As a result, he became the first president since Reconstruction to send troops into the South to protect the rights of African Americans.

Crisis in Little Rock

In September 1957, the school board in Little Rock, Arkansas, won a court order requiring that nine African American students be admitted to Central High, a school with 2,000 white students. The governor of Arkansas, Orval Faubus, was known as a moderate on racial issues, but he was determined to win reelection and began to campaign as a defender of white supremacy. He ordered troops from the Arkansas National Guard to prevent the nine students from entering the school. The next day, as the National Guard troops sur-

PRIMARY SOURCE
Little Rock School Crisis, Arkansas, 1957

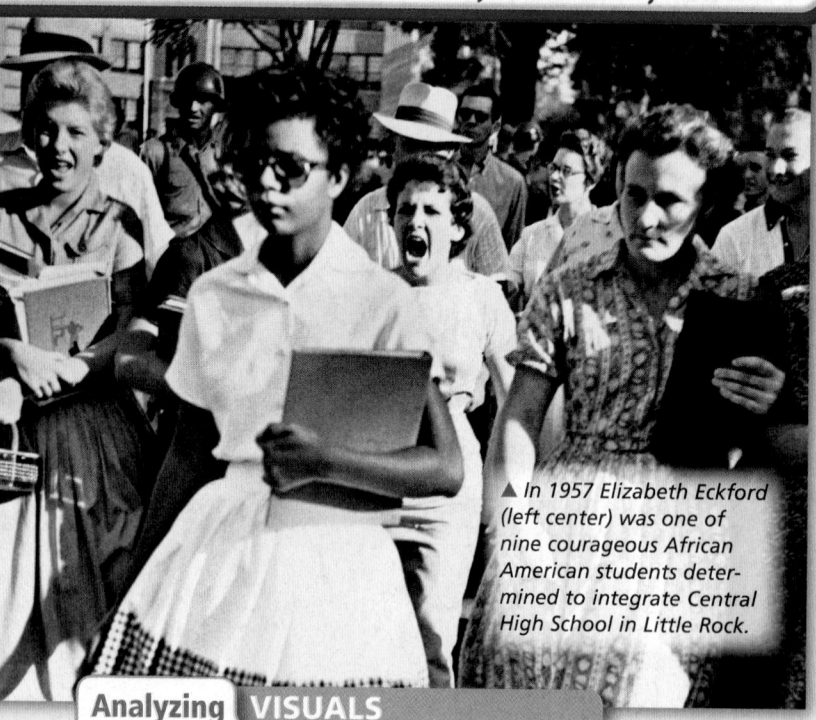

▲ In 1957 Elizabeth Eckford (left center) was one of nine courageous African American students determined to integrate Central High School in Little Rock.

▲ Arkansas governor Orval Faubus sought to block the school's integration. He is shown holding up a paper making his argument that the federal government was abusing its power in forcibly integrating Central High in Little Rock.

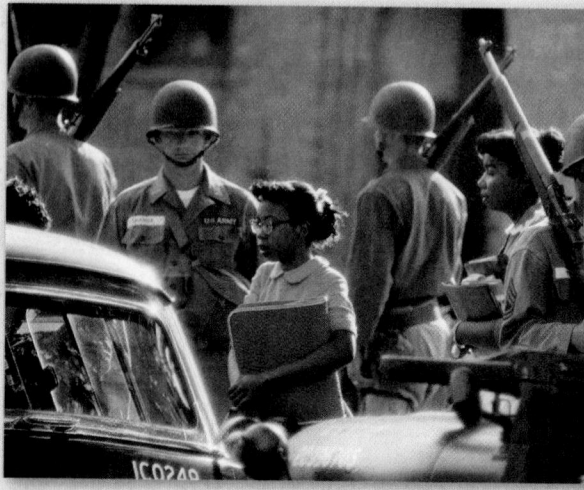

▶ Federal troops protect African American students at Central High.

Analyzing VISUALS

1. **Explaining** Why do you think the white people are shouting at Elizabeth Eckford?

2. **Identifying Central Issues** Why did President Eisenhower send troops to Little Rock?

rounded the school, an angry white mob joined the troops to protest and to intimidate the students trying to register.

Faubus had used the armed forces of a state to oppose the federal government—the first such challenge to the Constitution since the Civil War. Eisenhower knew that he could not allow Faubus to defy the federal government. After a conference between Eisenhower and Faubus proved fruitless, the district court ordered the governor to remove the troops. Instead of ending the crisis, however, Faubus simply left the school to the mob. After the African American students entered the building, angry whites beat at least two African American reporters and broke many of the school's windows.

The violence finally convinced President Eisenhower that he had to act. Federal authority had to be upheld. He immediately ordered the Army to send troops to Little Rock. In addition, he federalized the Arkansas National Guard. By nightfall, 1,000 soldiers of the elite 101st Airborne Division had arrived. By 5:00 A.M., the troops had encircled the school, bayonets ready. A few hours later, the nine African American students arrived in an army station wagon and walked into the high school. Federal authority had been upheld, but the troops had to stay in Little Rock for the rest of the school year.

Officials in Little Rock, however, continued to resist integration. Before the start of the following school year, Governor Faubus ordered the three public high schools in Little Rock closed. Steps to integrate the schools in Little Rock resumed only in 1959.

New Civil Rights Legislation

In the same year that the Little Rock crisis began, Congress passed the first civil rights law since Reconstruction. The Civil Rights Act of 1957 was intended to protect the right of African Americans to vote. Eisenhower believed firmly in the right to vote, and he viewed it as his responsibility to protect voting rights. He also knew that if he sent a civil rights bill to Congress, conservative Southern Democrats would try to block the legislation. In 1956 he did send the bill to Congress, hoping not only to split the Democratic Party but also to convince more African Americans to vote Republican.

Several Southern senators did try to stop the Civil Rights Act of 1957, but the Senate majority leader, Democrat Lyndon Johnson, put together a compromise that enabled the act to pass. Although its final form was much weaker than originally intended, the act still brought the power of the federal government into the civil rights debate. It created a civil rights division within the Department of Justice and gave it the authority to seek court injunctions against anyone interfering with the right to vote. It also created the United States Commission on Civil Rights to investigate allegations of denial of voting rights. After the bill passed, the SCLC announced a campaign to register 2 million new African American voters.

Reading Check **Explaining** Why did Eisenhower intervene in the Little Rock controversy?

Section 1 REVIEW

Vocabulary

1. **Explain** the significance of: Rosa Parks, NAACP, "separate but equal," de facto segregation, sit-in, Thurgood Marshall, Linda Brown, Martin Luther King, Jr., Southern Christian Leadership Conference.

Main Ideas

2. **Explaining** What was CORE and what were some of its tactics?

3. **Identifying** What event set off the civil rights movement of the 1950s?

4. **Summarizing** Why did Eisenhower send the 101st Airborne Division to Little Rock, Arkansas?

Critical Thinking

5. **Big Ideas** Why did the role of the federal government in civil rights enforcement change?

6. **Organizing** Use a graphic organizer similar to the one below to list the efforts made to end segregation.

Efforts to End Segregation

7. **Analyzing Visuals** Study the photograph of Elizabeth Eckford on page 856. Describe Eckford's demeanor compared to those around her. What might this indicate about her character?

Writing About History

8. **Expository Writing** Assume the role of an African American soldier returning from World War II. Write a letter to the editor of a newspaper describing your expectations of civil rights.

History ONLINE

Study Central™ To review this section, go to glencoe.com and click on Study Central.

Challenging Segregation

Guide to Reading

Big Ideas
Group Action African American citizens created organizations that directed protests to demand full civil rights.

Content Vocabulary
• filibuster (p. 864)
• cloture (p. 864)

Academic Vocabulary
• register (p. 859)

People and Events to Identify
• Student Nonviolent Coordinating Committee (SNCC) (p. 859)
• Freedom Riders (p. 860)
• James Meredith (p. 862)
• Civil Rights Act of 1964 (p. 865)
• Voting Rights Act of 1965 (p. 867)

Reading Strategy
Organizing Complete a graphic organizer about the challenges to segregation in the South.

Cause	Effect
Sit-In Movement	
Freedom Riders	

NEW YORK CORE CURRICULUM
U.S. History and Government

Unit 7:
III.B.3.a.(1) NAACP (National Association for the Advancement of Colored People): legal judicial leadership, Urban League
III.B.3.b.(1) SNCC (Student Nonviolent Coordinating Committee): sit-in movement among college students
III.B.3.b.(3) CORE (Congress of Racial Equality): "Freedom Riders"
III.B.3.b.(4) Testing of segregation laws
III.B.3.c.(1) Civil Rights Act of 1964 (*Heart of Atlanta Motel, Inc. v. United States*, 1964), modifications since 1964
III.B.3.c.(3) Voting Rights Act, 1965

In the early 1960s, the struggle for civil rights intensified. African American citizens and white supporters created organizations that directed protests, targeted specific inequalities, and attracted the attention of the mass media and the government.

The Sit-in Movement

MAIN Idea African American students staged sit-ins and formed the Student Nonviolent Coordinating Committee (SNCC) to organize efforts for desegregation and voter registration throughout the South.

HISTORY AND YOU Would you risk your personal safety to participate in a sit-in? Read on to learn of the response of young people to the sit-in movement of the early 1960s.

In the fall of 1959, four young African Americans—Joseph McNeil, Ezell Blair, Jr., David Richmond, and Franklin McCain—enrolled at North Carolina Agricultural and Technical College, an African American college in Greensboro. The four freshmen spent evenings talking about the civil rights movement. In January 1960, McNeil suggested a sit-in at the whites-only lunch counter in the nearby Woolworth's department store.

"All of us were afraid," Richmond later recalled, "but we went and did it." On February 1, 1960, the four friends entered the Woolworth's. They purchased school supplies and then sat at the lunch counter and ordered coffee. When they were refused service, Blair asked, "I beg your pardon, but you just served us at [the checkout] counter. Why can't we be served at the counter here?" The students stayed at the counter until it closed, and then announced that they would sit at the counter every day until they were given the same service as white customers.

As they left the store, the four were excited. McNeil recalled, "I just felt I had powers within me, a superhuman strength that would come forward." McCain was also energized, saying, "I probably felt better that day than I've ever felt in my life."

News of the daring sit-in at the Woolworth's store spread quickly across Greensboro. The following day, 29 African American students arrived at Woolworth's determined to sit at the counter until served. By the end of the week, over 300 students were taking part.

Starting with just four students, a new mass movement for civil rights had begun. Within two months, sit-ins had spread to 54 cities in nine states. They were staged at segregated stores, restaurants, hotels, and movie theaters. By 1961, sit-ins had been held in more than 100 cities.

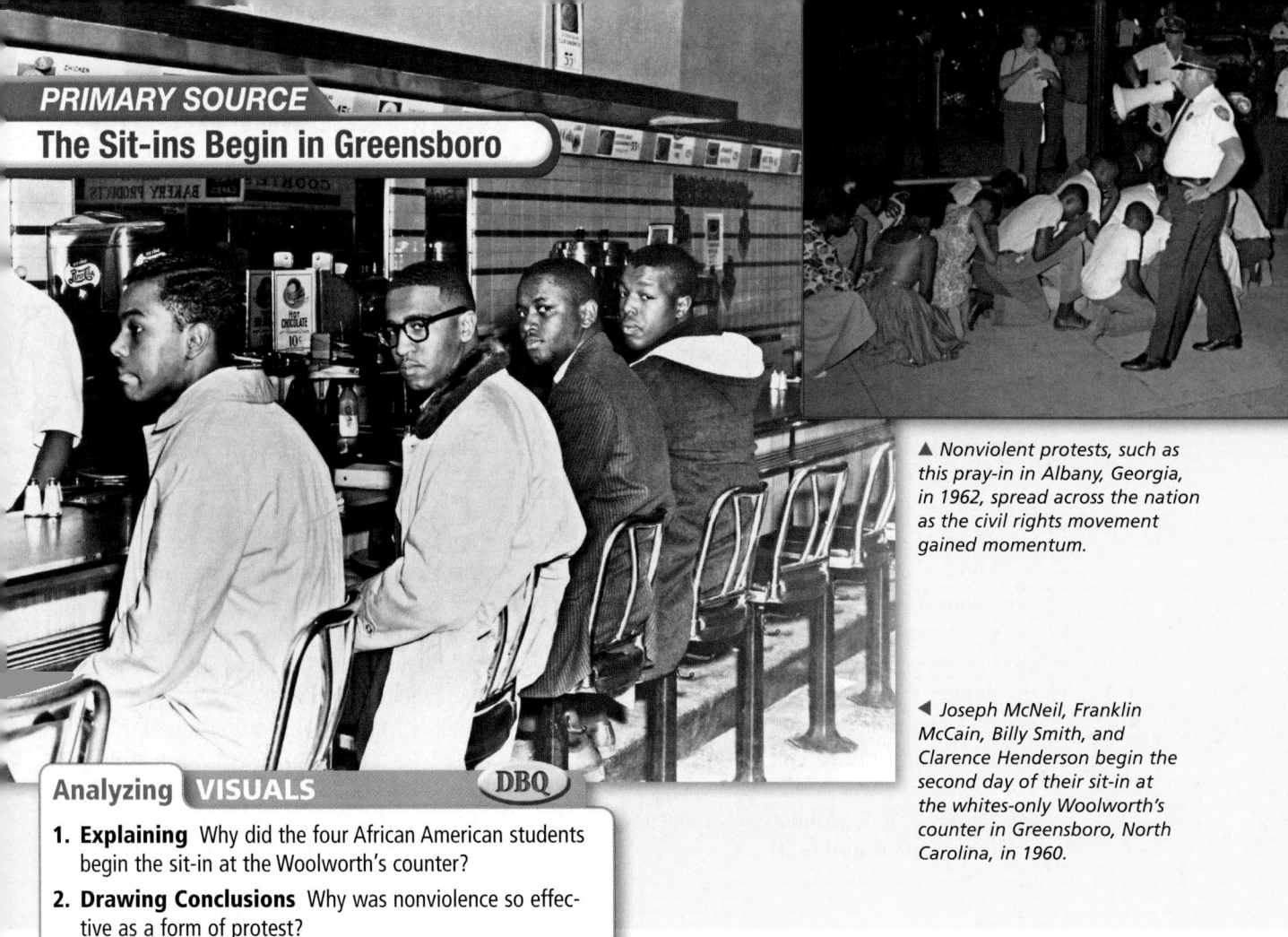

PRIMARY SOURCE
The Sit-ins Begin in Greensboro

▲ Nonviolent protests, such as this pray-in in Albany, Georgia, in 1962, spread across the nation as the civil rights movement gained momentum.

◄ Joseph McNeil, Franklin McCain, Billy Smith, and Clarence Henderson begin the second day of their sit-in at the whites-only Woolworth's counter in Greensboro, North Carolina, in 1960.

Analyzing VISUALS DBQ

1. **Explaining** Why did the four African American students begin the sit-in at the Woolworth's counter?

2. **Drawing Conclusions** Why was nonviolence so effective as a form of protest?

The sit-in movement brought large numbers of idealistic and energized college students into the civil rights struggle. Many African American students had become discouraged by the slow pace of desegregation. Students like Jesse Jackson, a student leader at North Carolina Agricultural and Technical College, wanted to see things change more quickly. The sit-in offered them a way to take matters into their own hands.

At first, the leaders of the NAACP and the SCLC were nervous about the sit-in campaign. They feared that students did not have the discipline to remain nonviolent if they were provoked enough. For the most part, the students proved them wrong. Those conducting sit-ins were heckled by bystanders, punched, kicked, beaten with clubs, and burned with cigarettes, hot coffee, and acid—but most did not fight back. Their heroic behavior grabbed the nation's attention.

As the sit-ins spread, student leaders in different states realized they needed to coordinate their efforts. The person who brought them together was Ella Baker, a former NAACP official and the executive director of the SCLC. In April 1960 Baker invited student leaders to attend a convention at Shaw University in Raleigh, North Carolina. There she urged students to create their own organization instead of joining the NAACP or the SCLC. Students, she said, had "the right to direct their own affairs and even make their own mistakes."

The students agreed with Baker and established the **Student Nonviolent Coordinating Committee (SNCC).** Among SNCC's early leaders were Marion Barry, who later served as mayor of Washington, D.C., and John Lewis, who later became a member of Congress. African American college students from all across the South made up the majority of SNCC's members, although many whites also joined. Between 1960 and 1965, SNCC played a key role in desegregating public facilities in dozens of Southern communities. SNCC also began sending volunteers into rural areas of the Deep South to **register** African Americans to vote.

The idea for what came to be called the Voter Education Project began with Robert Moses, an SNCC volunteer from New York. Moses pointed out that the civil rights movement tended to focus on urban areas. He urged the SNCC to start helping rural African Americans, who often faced violence if they tried to register to vote. Despite the danger, many SNCC volunteers headed to the Deep South. Moses himself went to Mississippi. Several had their lives threatened; others were beaten, and in 1964, local officials brutally murdered three SNCC workers.

One SNCC organizer, a sharecropper named Fannie Lou Hamer, had been evicted from her farm after registering to vote. She was arrested in Mississippi for urging other African Americans to register. Police severely beat her while she was in jail. She then helped organize the Mississippi Freedom Democratic Party and challenged the legality of Mississippi's segregated Democratic Party at the 1964 Democratic National Convention.

✔ Reading Check **Explaining** What were the effects of the sit-in movement?

The Freedom Riders

MAIN Idea Teams of African Americans and whites rode buses into the South to protest the continued illegal segregation on interstate bus lines.

HISTORY AND YOU Is it acceptable to risk provoking violence in order to advance a cause you support? Read to learn about the violence that erupted against the Freedom Riders and against Martin Luther King, Jr.'s march in Birmingham.

Despite rulings outlawing segregation in interstate bus service, bus travel remained segregated in much of the South. In 1961 CORE leader James Farmer asked teams of African American and white volunteers, many of whom were college students, to travel into the South to draw attention to its refusal to integrate bus terminals. The teams became known as the **Freedom Riders.**

In early May 1961, the first Freedom Riders boarded several southbound interstate buses. When the buses arrived in Anniston, Birmingham, and Montgomery, Alabama, angry white mobs attacked them. The mobs

The Civil Rights Movement, 1954–1965

May 1954
In *Brown* v. *Board of Education,* Supreme Court declares segregated schools unconstitutional

December 1956
Supreme Court declares separate-but-equal doctrine is no longer constitutional

January 1957
Martin Luther King, Jr., and other Southern ministers create SCLC

May 1961
James Farmer organizes the first Freedom Riders to desegregate interstate bus travel

1955   1957   1959   1961

December 1955
Rosa Parks is arrested and Montgomery Bus Boycott begins

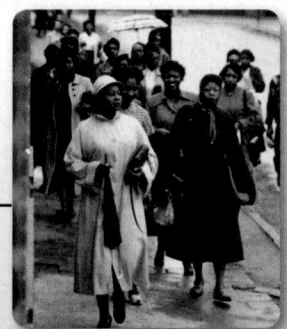

September 1957
Arkansas governor Faubus blocks desegregation of Little Rock High School, forcing Eisenhower to send troops to the school

February 1960
Students in Greensboro, North Carolina, stage a sit-in at a local lunch counter; as sit-ins spread, student leaders form SNCC in April

slit the bus tires and threw rocks at the windows. In Anniston, someone threw a firebomb into one bus, but fortunately no one was killed.

In Birmingham the riders emerged from a bus to face a gang of young men armed with baseball bats, chains, and lead pipes. The gang beat the riders viciously. One witness later reported, "You couldn't see their faces through the blood." The head of the police in Birmingham, Public Safety Commissioner Theophilus Eugene "Bull" Connor, explained that there had been no police at the bus station because it was Mother's Day, and he had given many of his officers the day off. FBI evidence later showed that Connor had contacted the local Ku Klux Klan and told them to beat the Freedom Riders until "it looked like a bulldog got a hold of them."

The violence in Alabama made national news, shocking many Americans. The attack on the Freedom Riders came less than four months after President John F. Kennedy took office. The new president felt compelled to get the violence under control.

Kennedy and Civil Rights

While campaigning for the presidency in 1960, John F. Kennedy promised to actively support the civil rights movement if elected. His brother, Robert F. Kennedy, had used his influence to get Dr. King released from jail after a demonstration in Georgia. African Americans responded by voting overwhelmingly for Kennedy. Their votes helped him narrowly win several key states, including Illinois, which Kennedy carried by only 9,000 votes.

Once in office, however, Kennedy at first seemed as cautious as Eisenhower on civil rights, which disappointed many African Americans. Kennedy knew he needed the support of many Southern senators to get other programs through Congress and that any attempt to push through new civil rights legislation would anger them. Congressional Republicans repeatedly reminded the public of Kennedy's failure to follow through on his campaign promise to push for civil rights for African Americans.

May 1963
Martin Luther King, Jr., leads protests in Birmingham, Alabama; police assault the protestors and King is jailed

March 1965
King leads a march in Selma, Alabama, to build support for a new voting rights law; police brutally attack marchers

August 3, 1965
Congress passes the Voting Rights Act of 1965

1963   1965

September 1962
James Meredith tries to register at University of Mississippi; riots force Kennedy to send troops

August 1963
King delivers his "I Have a Dream" speech during the March on Washington in support of new civil rights act

July 1964
Johnson signs Civil Rights Act of 1964 into law

Analyzing TIME LINES

1. **Identifying** According to the time line, what was the first major event in the civil rights movement?

2. **Analyzing** How many years were there between the *Brown* decision and the passage of the Civil Rights Act of 1964?

3. **Stating** When were the Freedom Riders organized?

Kennedy did, however, name approximately 40 African Americans to high-level positions in the government. He also appointed Thurgood Marshall to a federal judgeship on the Second Circuit Appeals Court in New York—one level below the Supreme Court and the highest judicial position an African American had attained to that point. Kennedy created the Committee on Equal Employment Opportunity (CEEO) to stop the federal bureaucracy from discriminating against African Americans in hiring and promotions.

The Justice Department Takes Action

Although President Kennedy was unwilling to challenge Southern Democrats in Congress, he allowed the Justice Department, run by his brother Robert, to actively support the civil rights movement. Robert Kennedy tried to help African Americans register to vote by having the civil rights division of the Justice Department file lawsuits across the South.

When violence erupted against the Freedom Riders, the Kennedys came to their aid as well, although not at first. At the time the Freedom Riders took action, President Kennedy was preparing for a meeting with Nikita Khrushchev, the leader of the Soviet Union. Kennedy did not want violence in the South to disrupt the meeting by giving the impression that his country was weak and divided.

After the Freedom Riders were attacked in Montgomery, the Kennedys publicly urged them to stop the rides and give everybody a "cooling off" period. James Farmer replied that African Americans "have been cooling off now for 350 years. If we cool off anymore, we'll be in a deep freeze." Instead, he announced that the Freedom Riders planned to head into Mississippi on their next trip.

To stop the violence, President Kennedy made a deal with Senator James Eastland of Mississippi, a strong supporter of segregation. If Eastland would use his influence in Mississippi to prevent violence, Kennedy would not object if the Mississippi police arrested the Freedom Riders. Eastland kept the deal. No violence occurred when the buses arrived in Jackson, Mississippi, but the riders were arrested.

The cost of bailing the Freedom Riders out of jail used up most of CORE's funds, which meant that the rides would have to end unless more money could be found. When Thurgood Marshall learned of the situation, he offered James Farmer the use of the NAACP Legal Defense Fund's huge bail bond account to keep the rides going.

When President Kennedy returned from meeting with Khrushchev and found that the Freedom Riders were still active, he changed his approach. He ordered the Interstate Commerce Commission (ICC) to tighten its regulations against segregated bus terminals. In the meantime, Robert Kennedy ordered the Justice Department to take legal action against Southern cities that maintained segregated bus terminals. The actions of the ICC and the Justice Department finally produced results. By late 1962, segregation in interstate bus travel had come to an end.

James Meredith As the Freedom Riders were trying to desegregate interstate bus lines, efforts continued to integrate Southern schools. On the day John F. Kennedy was inaugurated, an African American air force veteran named **James Meredith** applied for a transfer to the University of Mississippi. Up to that point, the university had avoided complying with the Supreme Court ruling ending segregated education.

In September 1962, Meredith tried to register at the university's admissions office, only to find Ross Barnett, the governor of Mississippi, blocking his path. Meredith had a court order directing the university to register him, but Governor Barnett stated emphatically, "Never! We will never surrender to the evil and illegal forces of tyranny."

Frustrated, President Kennedy dispatched 500 federal marshals to escort Meredith to the campus. Shortly after Meredith and the marshals arrived, an angry white mob attacked the campus, and a full-scale riot erupted. The mob hurled rocks, bottles, bricks, and acid at the marshals. Some people fired shotguns at them. The marshals responded with tear gas, but they were under orders not to fire.

The fighting continued all night. By morning, 160 marshals had been wounded. Reluctantly, Kennedy ordered the army to send several thousand troops to the campus. For the rest of the year, Meredith attended classes at the University of Mississippi under federal guard. He graduated in August.

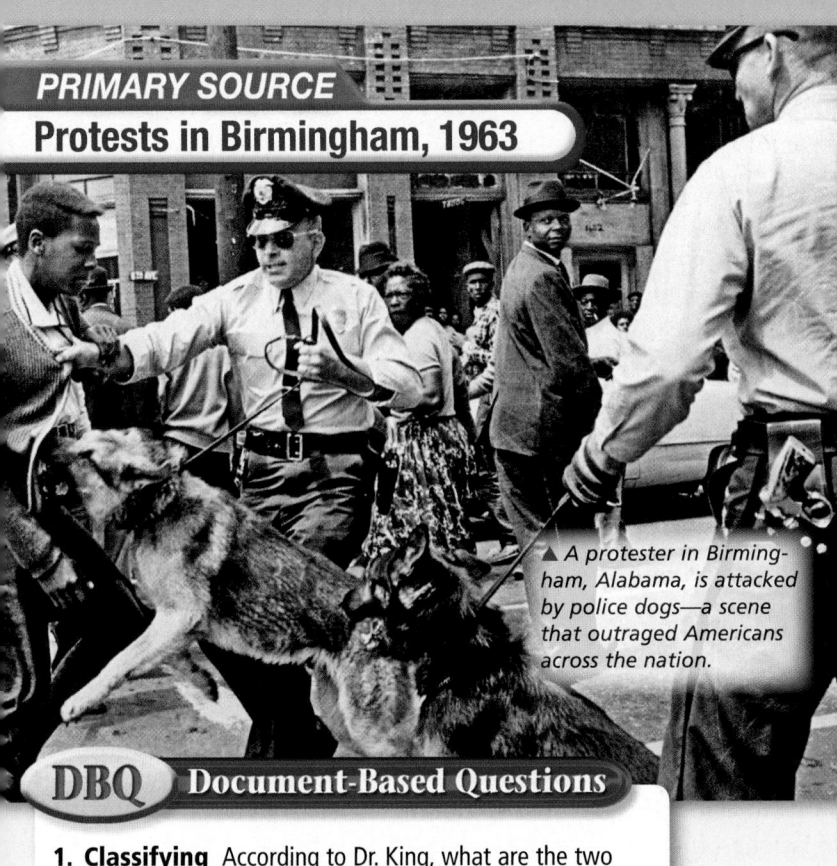

Protests in Birmingham, 1963

▲ *A protester in Birmingham, Alabama, is attacked by police dogs—a scene that outraged Americans across the nation.*

PRIMARY SOURCE

"Since we so diligently urge people to obey the Supreme Court's decision of 1954 outlawing segregation in the public schools, at first glance it may seem rather paradoxical for us consciously to break laws. One may well ask: "How can you advocate breaking some laws and obeying others?" The answer lies in the fact that there are two types of laws: just and unjust. . . . [and] one has a moral responsibility to disobey unjust laws. I would agree with St. Augustine that 'an unjust law is no law at all.'

. . . . Any law that uplifts human personality is just. Any law that degrades human personality is unjust. All segregation statutes are unjust because segregation distorts the soul and damages the personality. It gives the segregator a false sense of superiority and the segregated a false sense of inferiority. . . . An unjust law is a code that a numerical or power majority group compels a minority group to obey but does not make binding on itself. This is difference made legal. By the same token, a just law is a code that a majority compels a minority to follow and that it is willing to follow itself. This is sameness made legal."

—from Martin Luther King, Jr., "Letter from Birmingham Jail, 1963"

DBQ Document-Based Questions

1. **Classifying** According to Dr. King, what are the two types of laws? What is the difference between them?
2. **Determining Cause and Effect** What does King say are the effects of segregation on the segregator? On the segregated?

Violence in Birmingham

The events in Mississippi frustrated Martin Luther King, Jr., and other civil rights leaders. Although they were pleased that Kennedy had intervened, they were disappointed that the president had not seized the moment to push for a new civil rights law.

Reflecting on the problem, Dr. King came to a difficult decision. It seemed to him that only when violence got out of hand would the federal government intervene. "We've got to have a crisis to bargain with," one of his advisers observed. King agreed. In the spring of 1963, he decided to launch demonstrations in Birmingham, Alabama, knowing they would provoke a violent response. He believed it was the only way to get President Kennedy to actively support civil rights.

The situation in Birmingham was volatile. Public Safety Commissioner Bull Connor, who had arranged for the attack on the Freedom Riders, was now running for mayor. Eight days after the protests began, King was arrested. While in jail, King began writing on scraps of paper that had been smuggled into his cell. The "Letter from Birmingham Jail" that he produced is one of the most eloquent defenses of nonviolent protest ever written.

In his letter, King explained that although the protesters were breaking the law, they were following a higher moral law based on divine justice. Injustice, he insisted, had to be exposed "to the light of human conscience and the air of national opinion before it can be cured."

After King was released, the protests, which had been dwindling, began to grow again. Bull Connor responded with force. He ordered the Birmingham police to use clubs, police dogs, and high-pressure fire hoses on the demonstrators. Millions of Americans watched the graphic violence on the nightly news on television. Outraged by the brutality and worried that the government was losing control, Kennedy ordered his aides to prepare a new civil rights bill.

✔ Reading Check **Evaluating** How did President Kennedy help the civil rights movement?

The Civil Rights Act of 1964

MAIN Idea President Johnson used his political expertise to get the Civil Rights Act of 1964 passed.

HISTORY AND YOU Do you remember the constitutional amendments that granted African Americans civil rights after the Civil War? Read on to learn about new legal steps taken during the 1960s.

Determined to introduce a civil rights bill, Kennedy now waited for a dramatic moment to address the nation on the issue. Alabama's governor, George Wallace, gave the president his chance. At his inauguration as governor, Wallace had stated, "I draw a line in the dust . . . and I say, Segregation now! Segregation tomorrow! Segregation forever!" On June 11, 1963, Wallace stood in front of the University of Alabama's admissions office to block two African Americans from enrolling. He stayed until federal marshals ordered him to move.

The next day a white segregationist murdered Medgar Evers, a civil rights activist in Mississippi. President Kennedy seized the moment to announce his civil rights bill. That evening, he spoke to Americans about a "moral issue . . . as old as the scriptures and as clear as the American Constitution":

PRIMARY SOURCE

"The heart of the question is whether . . . we are going to treat our fellow Americans as we want to be treated. If an American, because his skin is dark, cannot eat lunch in a restaurant open to the public, if he cannot send his children to the best public school available, if he cannot vote for the public officials who represent him . . . then who among us would be content to have the color of his skin changed and stand in his place?

One hundred years of delay have passed since President Lincoln freed the slaves, yet their heirs, their grandsons, are not fully free. . . . And this Nation, for all its hopes and all its boasts, will not be fully free until all its citizens are free. . . . Now the time has come for this Nation to fulfill its promise."

—from Kennedy's White House address, June 11, 1963

The March on Washington

Dr. King realized that Kennedy would have a very difficult time pushing his civil rights bill through Congress. Therefore, he searched for a way to lobby Congress and to build more public support. When A. Philip Randolph suggested a march on Washington, King agreed.

On August 28, 1963, more than 200,000 demonstrators of all races flocked to the nation's capital. The audience heard speeches and sang hymns and songs as they gathered peacefully near the Lincoln Memorial. Dr. King then delivered a powerful speech outlining his dream of freedom and equality for all Americans.

King's speech and the peacefulness and dignity of the March on Washington built momentum for the civil rights bill. Opponents in Congress, however, continued to do what they could to slow the bill down, dragging out their committee investigations and using procedural rules to delay votes.

The Bill Becomes Law

Although the civil rights bill was likely to pass the House of Representatives, where a majority of Republicans and Northern Democrats supported the measure, it faced a much more difficult time in the Senate. There, a small group of determined Southern senators would try to block the bill indefinitely.

In the U.S. Senate, senators are allowed to speak for as long as they like when a bill is being debated. The Senate cannot vote on a bill until all senators have finished speaking. A **filibuster** occurs when a small group of senators take turns speaking and refuse to stop the debate and allow a bill to come to a vote. Today a filibuster can be stopped if at least 60 senators vote for **cloture,** a motion that cuts off debate and forces a vote. In the 1960s, however, 67 senators had to vote for cloture to stop a filibuster. This meant that a minority of senators opposed to civil rights could easily prevent the majority from enacting a new civil rights law.

Worried that the bill would never pass, many African Americans became even more disheartened. Then, President Kennedy was assassinated in Dallas, Texas, on November 22, 1963, and his vice president, Lyndon Johnson, became president. Johnson was from Texas and

Martin Luther King, Jr.'s Address, Washington, 1963

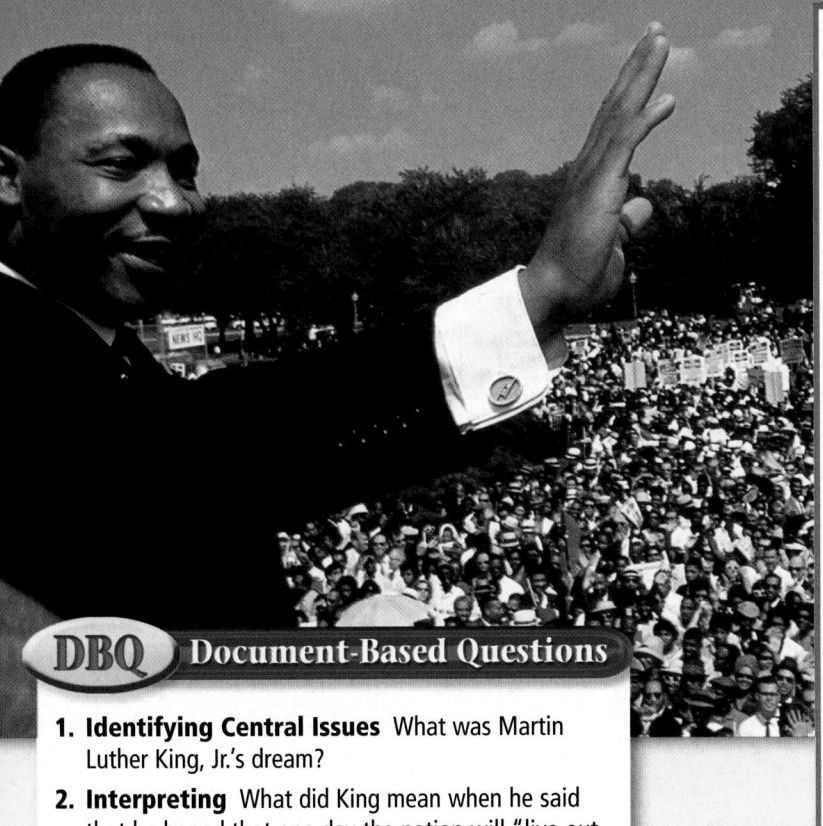

"And so even though we face the difficulties of today and tomorrow, I still have a dream. It is a dream deeply rooted in the American dream.

I have a dream that one day this nation will rise up and live out the true meaning of its creed: 'We hold these truths to be self-evident, that all men are created equal.'

I have a dream that one day on the red hills of Georgia, the sons of former slaves and the sons of former slave owners will be able to sit down together at the table of brotherhood. . . .

I have a dream that my four little children will one day live in a nation where they will not be judged by the color of their skin but by the content of their character.

I have a dream today!

. . . And when this happens, when we allow freedom to ring, when we let it ring from every village and every hamlet, from every state and every city, we will be able to speed up that day when all of God's children, black men and white men, Jews and Gentiles, Protestants and Catholics, will be able to join hands and sing in the words of the old Negro spiritual:

Free at last! Free at last!

Thank God Almighty, we are free at last!"

—Martin Luther King, Jr.,
"Address in Washington," 1963

DBQ Document-Based Questions

1. **Identifying Central Issues** What was Martin Luther King, Jr.'s dream?

2. **Interpreting** What did King mean when he said that he hoped that one day the nation will "live out the true meaning of its creed"?

had been the leader of the Senate Democrats before becoming vice president. Although he had helped pass the Civil Rights Acts of 1957 and 1960, he had done so by weakening their provisions and by compromising with other Southern senators.

To the surprise of the civil rights movement, Johnson committed himself wholeheartedly to getting Kennedy's program, including the civil rights bill, through Congress. Johnson had served in Congress for many years and was adept at getting legislation enacted. He knew how to build public support, how to put pressure on Congress, and how to use the rules and procedures to get what he wanted.

In February 1964, President Johnson's leadership began to produce results. The civil rights bill passed the House of Representatives by a majority of 290 to 130. The debate then moved to the Senate. In June, after 87 days of filibuster, the Senate finally voted to end debate by a margin of 71 to 29—four votes over the two-thirds needed for cloture. The Senate then eas-

ily passed the bill. On July 2, 1964, President Johnson signed the **Civil Rights Act of 1964** into law.

The Civil Rights Act of 1964 was the most comprehensive civil rights law Congress had ever enacted. It gave the federal government broad power to prevent racial discrimination in a number of areas. The law made segregation illegal in most places of public accommodation, and it gave citizens of all races and nationalities equal access to public facilities. The law gave the U.S. attorney general more power to bring lawsuits to force school desegregation and required private employers to end discrimination in the workplace. It also established the Equal Employment Opportunity Commission (EEOC) as a permanent agency in the federal government. This commission monitors the ban on job discrimination by race, religion, gender, and national origin.

To read more of Martin Luther King, Jr.'s "I Have a Dream" speech see page R56 in **Documents in American History.**

Reading Check **Examining** How did Dr. King lobby Congress to pass a new civil rights act?

The Struggle for Voting Rights

MAIN Idea President Johnson called for a new voting rights law after hostile crowds severely beat civil rights demonstrators.

HISTORY AND YOU Do you remember the tactics Southern states adopted to keep African Americans from voting? Read on to learn about the Voting Rights Act of 1965.

Even after the Civil Rights Act of 1964 was passed, voting rights were far from secure. The act had focused on segregation and job discrimination, and it did little to address voting issues. The Twenty-fourth Amendment, ratified in 1964, helped somewhat by eliminating poll taxes, or fees paid in order to vote, in federal (but not state) elections. African Americans still faced hurdles, however, when they tried to vote. As the SCLC and SNCC stepped up their voter registration efforts in the South, their members were often attacked and beaten, and several were murdered.

Across the South, bombs exploded in African American businesses and churches. Between June and October 1964, arson and bombs destroyed 24 African American churches in Mississippi alone. Convinced that a new law was needed to protect African American voting rights, Dr. King decided to stage another dramatic protest.

The Selma March

In January 1965, the SCLC and Dr. King selected Selma, Alabama, as the focal point for their campaign for voting rights. Although African Americans made up a majority of Selma's population, they comprised only 3 percent of registered voters. To prevent African Americans from registering to vote, Sheriff Jim Clark had deputized and armed dozens of white citizens. His posse terrorized African Americans and frequently attacked demonstrators with clubs and electric cattle prods.

In December 1964, Dr. King received the Nobel Peace Prize in Oslo, Norway, for his work in the civil rights movement. A few weeks

Marching for Freedom, Selma, 1965

The Civil Rights Act of 1964
- Gave the federal government power to prevent racial discrimination and established the Equal Employment Opportunity Commission (EEOC).
- Made segregation illegal in most places of public accommodation.
- Gave the U.S. attorney general more power to bring lawsuits to force school desegregation.
- Required employers to end workplace discrimination.

The Voting Rights Act of 1965
- Authorized the U.S. attorney general to send federal examiners to register qualified voters.
- Suspended discriminatory devices, such as literacy tests, in counties where less than half of all adults had been allowed to vote.

Martin Luther King, Jr.

Coretta Scott King, Dr. King's wife

Analyzing VISUALS

1. **Making Connections** How did the Civil Rights Act of 1964 work to end segregation?

2. **Drawing Conclusions** Why do you think counties where less than half of all adults were allowed to vote were a focus of the Voting Rights Acts of 1965?

later, King announced, "We are not asking, we are demanding the ballot." King's demonstrations in Selma led to the arrest of approximately 2,000 African Americans, including schoolchildren, by Sheriff Clark. Clark's men attacked and beat many of the demonstrators, and Selma quickly became a major story in the national news.

To keep pressure on the president and Congress to act, Dr. King joined with SNCC activists and organized a "march for freedom" from Selma to the state capitol in Montgomery, a distance of about 50 miles (80 km). On Sunday, March 7, 1965, the march began. The SCLC's Hosea Williams and SNCC's John Lewis led 500 protesters toward U.S. Highway 80, the route that marchers had planned to follow to Montgomery.

As the protesters approached the Edmund Pettus Bridge, which led out of Selma, Sheriff Clark ordered them to disperse. While the marchers kneeled in prayer, more than 200 state troopers and deputized citizens rushed the demonstrators. Many were beaten in full view of television cameras. This brutal attack, known later as "Bloody Sunday," left 70 African Americans hospitalized and many more injured.

The nation was stunned as it viewed the shocking footage of law enforcement officers beating peaceful demonstrators. Watching the events from the White House, President Johnson became furious. Eight days later, he appeared before a nationally televised joint session of the legislature to propose a new voting rights law.

The Voting Rights Act of 1965

On August 3, 1965, the House of Representatives passed the voting rights bill by a wide margin. The following day, the Senate also passed the bill. The **Voting Rights Act of 1965** authorized the U.S. attorney general to send federal examiners to register qualified voters, bypassing local officials who often refused to register African Americans. The law also suspended discriminatory devices, such as literacy tests, in counties where less than half of all adults had been registered to vote.

The results were dramatic. By the end of the year, almost 250,000 African Americans had registered as new voters. The number of African American elected officials in the South also increased. In 1965, only about 100 African Americans held elected office; by 1990 more than 5,000 did.

The passage of the Voting Rights Act of 1965 marked a turning point in the civil rights movement. The movement had now achieved its two major legislative goals. Segregation had been outlawed and new federal laws were in place to prevent discrimination and protect voting rights. After 1965, the movement began to shift its focus to the problem of achieving full social and economic equality for African Americans. As part of that effort, the movement turned its attention to the problems of African Americans trapped in poverty and living in ghettos in many of the nation's major cities.

✔ Reading Check **Summarizing** How did the Twenty-fourth Amendment affect African American voting rights?

Section 2 REVIEW

Vocabulary

1. **Explain** the significance of: SNCC, Freedom Riders, James Meredith, filibuster, cloture, Civil Rights Act of 1964, Voting Rights Act of 1965.

Main Ideas

2. **Describing** What was the purpose of the SNCC?

3. **Summarizing** How did the Freedom Riders help the civil rights movement?

4. **Explaining** Why did Dr. King lead the March on Washington in 1963?

5. **Analyzing** What was "Bloody Sunday"? How did President Johnson respond?

Critical Thinking

6. **Big Ideas** How did television help the civil rights movement?

7. **Sequencing** Use a time line similar to the one below to sequence the events in the civil rights movement.

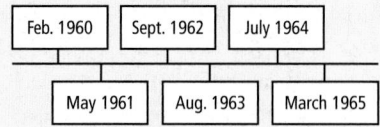

| Feb. 1960 | Sept. 1962 | July 1964 |

| May 1961 | Aug. 1963 | March 1965 |

8. **Analyzing Visuals** Study the photographs in this section. What elements of the photographs show the sacrifices African Americans made in the civil rights movement?

Writing About History

9. **Descriptive Writing** Assume the role of a journalist working for a college newspaper in 1960. Write an article for the newspaper describing the sit-in movement, including its participants, goals, and achievements.

History ONLINE

Study Central™ To review this section, go to glencoe.com and click on Study Central.

The Civil Rights Movement

Although major figures of the civil rights movement such as Martin Luther King, Jr., are widely remembered today, the movement drew its strength from the dedication of grass-roots supporters. In rural and urban areas across the South, ordinary individuals advanced the movement through their participation in marches, boy-cotts, and voter registration drives. Those who dared to make a stand against discrimi-nation risked being fired from their job, evicted from their home, and becoming the tar-get of physical violence.

Study these primary sources and answer the questions that follow.

PRIMARY SOURCE 1

Public Testimony, 1964

In 1964, the "Mississippi Freedom Democratic Party" challenged the right of Mississippi's established (all white) Democratic Party representatives to seats at the party's national convention on the grounds that African Americans had been systematically denied the right to vote.

"[M]y husband came, and said the plantation owner was raising cain because I had tried to register [to vote] and before he quit talking the plantation owner came, and said, 'Fannie Lou, do you know—did Pap tell you what I said?' And I said, 'Yes sir.' He said, 'I mean that . . . If you don't go down and withdraw . . . well—you might have to go because we are not ready for that.' . . .

And I addressed him and told him and said, 'I didn't try to register for you. I tried to register for myself.'

I had to leave the same night.

On the 10th of September, 1962, 16 bullets was fired into the home of Mr. and Mrs. Robert Tucker for me. That same night two girls were shot in Ruleville, Mississippi. Also Mr. Joe McDonald's house was shot in.

And in June, the 9th, 1963, I had attended a voter registration workshop, was returning back to Mississippi. . . . I stepped off the bus . . . and somebody screamed . . . 'Get that one there,' and when I went to get in the car, when the man told me I was under arrest, he kicked me.

I was carried to the county jail. . . . [The patrolmen] left my cell and it wasn't too long before they came back. He said 'You are from Ruleville all right,' and he used a curse word, he said, 'We are going to beat you until you wish you was dead.'. . .

All of this on account we want to register, to become first-class citizens, and if the freedom Democratic Party is not seated now, I question America, is this America, the land of the free and the home of the brave where we have to sleep with our telephones off the hooks because our lives be threatened daily because we want to live as decent human beings in America?"

—Fannie Lou Hamer testifying before the Credentials Committee of the Democratic National Convention, August 22, 1964

PRIMARY SOURCE 2

Photograph, c. 1964

"Freedom Schools" taught literacy and African American history and encouraged voter registration.

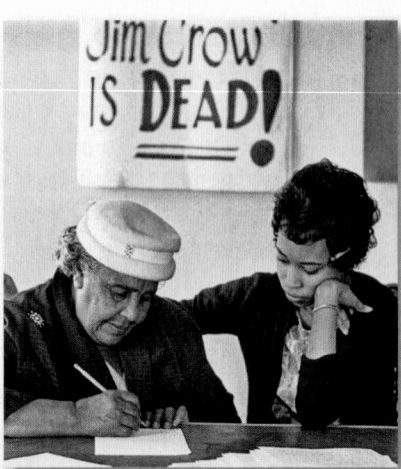

PRIMARY SOURCE 3

Strategy Memo, April 1960

"The choice of the non-violent method, 'the sit-in,' symbolizes both judgment and promise. It is a judgment upon middle-class conventional half-way efforts to deal with radical social evil. It is specifically a judgment upon contemporary civil rights attempts. As one high school student from Chattanooga exclaimed, 'We started because we were tired of waiting for you to act. . . .'"

—James M. Lawson, Jr., "From a Lunch-Counter Stool," April 1960, Student Nonviolent Coordinating Committee Papers

PRIMARY SOURCE 4

Autobiography, 1968

"[At Tougaloo College] I had become very friendly with my social science professor, John Salter, who was in charge of NAACP activities on campus. All during the year, while the NAACP conducted a boycott of the downtown stores in Jackson, I had been one of Salter's most faithful canvassers and church speakers. During the last week of school, he told me that sit-in demonstrations were about to start in Jackson and that he wanted me to be the spokesman for a team that would sit-in at Woolworth's lunch counter. The two other demonstrators would be classmates of mine, Memphis and Pearlena. . . .

Seconds before 11:15 we were occupying three seats at the previously segregated Woolworth's lunch counter. In the beginning the waitresses seemed to ignore us, as if they really didn't know what was going on. Our waitress walked past us a couple of times before she noticed we had started to write our own orders down and realized we wanted service. She asked us what we wanted. We began to read to her from our order slips. She told us that we would be served at the back counter, which was for Negroes.

'We would like to be served here,' I said.

The waitress started to repeat what she had said, then stopped in the middle of the sentence. She turned the lights out behind the counter, and she and the other waitresses almost ran to the back of the store, deserting all their white customers. I guess they thought that violence would start immediately after the whites at the counter realized what was going on.

At noon, students from a nearby white high school started pouring in to Woolworth's. When they first saw us they were sort of surprised. . . . Then the white students started chanting all kinds of anti-Negro slogans. We were called a little bit of everything. . . .

Memphis suggested that we pray. We bowed our heads, and all hell broke loose. A man rushed forward, threw Memphis from his seat, and slapped my face. Then another man who worked in the store threw me against

PRIMARY SOURCE 5

Photograph, 1963

▼ *Lunch counter sit-in May 28, 1963, in Jackson, Mississippi. Seated (from left to right) are John Salter, Joan Trumpauer, and Anne Moody.*

an adjoining counter. . . . The mob started smearing us with ketchup, mustard, sugar, pies, and everything on the counter. . . .

About ninety policemen were standing outside the store; they had been watching the whole thing through the windows, but had not come in to stop the mob or do anything. . . .

After the sit-in, all I could think of was how sick Mississippi whites were. They believed so much in the segregated Southern way of life, they would kill to preserve it. . . . Now I knew it was impossible for me to hate sickness. The whites had a disease, an incurable disease in its final stage. What were our chances against such a disease?"

—Anne Moody, *Coming of Age in Mississippi*

DBQ Document-Based Questions

1. **Identifying** In Source 1, what sorts of repercussions did Fannie Lou Hamer endure for daring to register to vote? How do you think such tactics affected the civil rights movement?

2. **Interpreting** Study the photograph in Source 2. Who seems to be teaching whom? Why do you think the civil rights movement attracted so many young people?

3. **Evaluating** Read the passage in Source 3 and study the photograph in Source 5. Why do you think nonviolent demonstrations were effective for the civil rights movement?

4. **Making Inferences** Read Source 4. Why do you think Anne Moody wanted to try to force integration of the lunch counter? Why would she risk physical harm to do so?

New Civil Rights Issues

Guide to Reading

Big Ideas
Struggles for Rights In the late 1960s, the civil rights movement tried to address the persistent economic inequality of African Americans.

Content Vocabulary
- racism *(p. 870)*
- black power *(p. 872)*

Academic Vocabulary
- enforcement *(p. 874)*

People and Events to Identify
- Kerner Commission *(p. 871)*
- Chicago Movement *(p. 872)*
- Richard J. Daley *(p. 872)*
- Stokely Carmichael *(p. 872)*
- Malcolm X *(p. 873)*
- Black Panthers *(p. 874)*

Reading Strategy
Organizing Complete a graphic organizer like the one below by listing five major violent events in the civil rights movement and their results.

Event	Result

NEW YORK CORE CURRICULUM
U.S. History and Government

Unit 7:
III.B.3.b.(5) Others: Black Muslims; prominence of Malcolm X: advocating separation of races, separate state in the United States.
III.B.3.b.(6) Civil unrest: Watts riot, 1965, as example; Kerner Commission
III.B.3.b.(7) Assassination of Malcolm X (February 1965)
IV.A.6.b Assassinations of Dr. Martin Luther King, Jr. (April 1968) and Robert Kennedy (June 1968)

By the mid-1960s, much progress had been made in the arena of civil rights. However, leaders of the movement began to understand that merely winning political rights for African Americans would not completely solve their economic problems. The struggle would continue to try to end economic inequality.

Urban Problems

MAIN Idea African Americans became impatient with the slow pace of change; this frustration sometimes boiled over into riots.

HISTORY AND YOU Have you ever seen news coverage of a riot in the United States or overseas? What triggered the outburst? Read on to learn about the factors that fed into the riots of the 1960s.

Despite the passage of civil rights laws in the 1950s and 1960s, **racism**—prejudice or discrimination toward someone because of his or her race—was still common in American society. Changing the law could not change people's attitudes, nor did it help most African Americans trapped in poverty in the nation's big cities.

In 1965 nearly 70 percent of African Americans lived in large cities. Many had moved from the South to the big cities of the North during the Great Migration of the 1920s and 1940s. There, they often found the same prejudice and discrimination that had plagued them in the South.

Even if African Americans had been allowed to move into white neighborhoods, poverty trapped many of them in inner cities. Many African Americans found themselves channeled into low-paying jobs with little chance of advancement. Those who did better typically found employment as blue-collar workers in factories, but most did not advance beyond that. In 1965 only 15 percent of African Americans held professional, managerial, or clerical jobs, compared to 44 percent of whites. The average income of an African American family was only 55 percent of that of the average white family, and almost half of African Americans lived in poverty. Their unemployment rate was typically twice that of whites.

Poor neighborhoods in the nation's major cities were overcrowded and dirty, leading to higher rates of illness and infant mortality. At the same time, the crime rate increased in the 1960s, particularly in low-income neighborhoods. Juvenile delinquency rates rose, as did the rate of young people dropping out of school. Complicating matters even more was a rise in the number of single-parent households. All poor neighborhoods suffered from these problems, but because

The Problem of Urban Poverty

"...SH! AFTER A WHILE THEY'LL GO AWAY!"

Baldy

► Congress is compared to the Roman emperor Nero, who was said to have played music as Rome burned.

◄ Barry Goldwater tries to persuade President Johnson to stop creating programs to end urban poverty.

Analyzing VISUALS DBQ

1. **Making Inferences** In the cartoon on the left, what does the man suggest about urban problems?
2. **Drawing Conclusions** Based on the cartoon above, what should Congress have done to stop the rioting?

more African Americans lived in poverty, their communities were disproportionately affected.

Many African Americans living in urban poverty knew the civil rights movement had made enormous gains, but when they looked at their own circumstances, nothing seemed to be changing. The movement had raised their hopes, but their everyday problems continued. As a result, their anger and frustration began to rise—until it finally erupted.

The Watts Riot

Just five days after President Johnson signed the Voting Rights Act, a riot erupted in Watts, an African American neighborhood in Los Angeles. Allegations of police brutality had served as the catalyst for this uprising, which lasted for six days and required over 14,000 members of the National Guard and 1,500 law officers to restore order. Rioters burned and looted entire neighborhoods and destroyed about $45 million in property. They killed 34 people and injured about 900 others.

More rioting was yet to come. Riots broke out in dozens of American cities between 1965 and 1968. The worst riot took place in Detroit in 1967. Burning, looting, and skirmishes with police and National Guard members resulted in 43 deaths and over 1,000 wounded.

Eventually the U.S. Army sent in tanks and soldiers armed with machine guns to get control of the situation. Nearly 4,000 fires destroyed 1,300 buildings, and the damage in property loss was estimated at $250 million.

The Kerner Commission

In 1967 President Johnson appointed the National Advisory Commission on Civil Disorders, headed by Governor Otto Kerner of Illinois, to study the causes of the urban riots and to make recommendations to prevent them from happening again. The **Kerner Commission,** as it became known, conducted a detailed study of the problem. The commission blamed racism for most of the problems in the inner city. "Our nation is moving toward two societies, one black, one white—separate and unequal," it concluded.

The commission recommended the creation of 2 million inner-city jobs, the construction of 6 million new units of public housing, and a renewed federal commitment to fight de facto segregation. President Johnson's War on Poverty, which addressed some of the concerns about inner-city jobs and housing, was already underway. Saddled with spending for the Vietnam War, however, Johnson never endorsed the recommendations of the commission.

The Shift to Economic Rights

By the mid-1960s, a number of African American leaders were becoming increasingly critical of Martin Luther King, Jr.'s nonviolent strategy. They felt it had failed to improve the economic position of African Americans. Dr. King came to agree with this criticism, and in 1965 he decided to address economic issues.

Dr. King decided to focus on the problems that African Americans faced in Chicago. King had never conducted a civil rights campaign in the North, but by tackling a large Northern city, he believed he could call greater attention to poverty and other racial problems that lay beneath the urban race riots.

To call attention to the deplorable housing conditions that many African American families faced, Dr. King and his wife Coretta moved into a slum apartment in an African American neighborhood in Chicago. Dr. King and the SCLC hoped to work with local leaders to improve the economic status of African Americans in poor neighborhoods.

The **Chicago Movement,** however, made little headway. When Dr. King led a march through the all-white suburb of Marquette Park to demonstrate the need for open housing, he was met by angry white mobs similar to those in Birmingham and Selma. Mayor **Richard J. Daley** ordered the Chicago police to protect the marchers, and he was determined to prevent violence. He met with Dr. King and proposed a new program to clean up the slums. Associations of realtors and bankers also agreed to promote open housing. In theory, mortgages and rental property would be available to everyone, regardless of race. In practice, little changed.

✓ Reading Check **Describing** How did Dr. King and SCLC leaders hope to address economic concerns?

Black Power

MAIN Idea Impatient with the slower gains of Martin Luther King, Jr.'s movement, many young African Americans called for "black power."

HISTORY AND YOU How did Dr. King work to avoid violence? Read on to find out how some African Americans broke with Dr. King's approach.

Dr. King's failure in Chicago seemed to show that nonviolent protests could do little to solve economic problems. After 1965, many African Americans, especially urban young people, began to turn away from King. Some leaders called for more aggressive forms of protest. Their strategies ranged from armed self-defense to promoting the idea that the government should set aside a number of states where African Americans could live separate from whites. As African Americans became more assertive, some organizations, including CORE and SNCC, voted to expel all whites from leadership positions in their organizations. They believed that African Americans alone should lead their struggle.

Many young African Americans called for **black power,** a term that had many meanings. A few interpreted black power to mean that physical self-defense and even violence were acceptable—a clear rejection of Dr. King's philosophy. To most, including **Stokely Carmichael,** the leader of SNCC in 1966, the term meant that African Americans should control the social, political, and economic direction of their struggle:

PRIMARY SOURCE

"This is the significance of black power as a slogan. For once, black people are going to use the words they want to use—not just the words whites want to hear. . . . The need for psychological equality is the reason why SNCC today believes that blacks must organize in the black community. Only black people can . . . create in the community an aroused and continuing black consciousness. . . ."

—from the *New York Review of Books,* September 1966

Black power stressed pride in the African American cultural group. It emphasized racial distinctiveness rather than assimilation—the process by which minority groups adapt to the dominant culture in a society. African Americans showed pride in their racial heritage by adopting new Afro hairstyles and African-style clothing. Many also took African names. In universities, students demanded that African and African American studies courses be made part of the standard school curriculum. Dr. King and some other leaders criticized black power as a philosophy of hopelessness and despair. The idea was very popular, however, in poor neighborhoods where many African Americans resided.

Malcolm X

By the early 1960s, a young man named **Malcolm X** had become a symbol of the black power movement. Born Malcolm Little in Omaha, Nebraska, he experienced a difficult childhood and adolescence. He drifted into a life of crime and, in 1946, was convicted of burglary and sent to prison for six years.

Prison transformed Malcolm. He began to educate himself and played an active role in the prison debate society. Eventually, he joined the Nation of Islam, commonly known as the Black Muslims, who were led by Elijah Muhammad. Despite their name, the Black

Muslims do not hold the same beliefs as mainstream Muslims. The Nation of Islam preached black nationalism. Like Marcus Garvey in the 1920s, Black Muslims believed that African Americans should separate themselves from whites and form their own self-governing communities.

Shortly after joining the Nation of Islam, Malcolm Little changed his name to Malcolm X. The "X" symbolized the family name of his African ancestors who had been enslaved. He declared that his true name had been stolen from him by slavery, and he would no longer use the name white society had given him.

The Black Muslims viewed themselves as their own nation and attempted to make themselves as self-sufficient as possible. They ran their own businesses and schools, and published their own newspaper, *Muhammad Speaks.* They encouraged their members to respect each other and to strengthen their families. Black Muslims did not advocate violence, but they did advocate self-defense. Malcolm X's criticisms of white society and the mainstream civil rights movement gained national attention for the Nation of Islam.

PRIMARY SOURCE
Black Power in the 1960s

In the late 1960s, a new group of African American leaders, such as Malcolm X, had lost patience with the slow progress of civil rights and felt that African Americans needed to act more militantly and demand equality, not wait for it to be given.

▲ *Medalists Tommie Smith and John Carlos give the black power salute at the 1968 Olympics. Above right, Stokely Carmichael speaks at a protest rally in Mississippi in 1966.*

PRIMARY SOURCE

"Since the black masses here in America are now in open revolt against the American system of segregation, will these same black masses turn toward integration or will they turn toward complete separation? Will these awakened black masses demand integration into the white society that enslaved them or will they demand complete separation from that cruel white society that has enslaved them? Will the exploited and oppressed black masses seek integration with their white exploiters and white oppressors or will these awakened black masses truly revolt and separate themselves completely from this wicked race that has enslaved us?"

—Malcolm X, from his speech "The Black Revolution," 1964

DBQ Document-Based Questions

1. **Identifying** What are two options Malcolm X thinks African Americans have regarding their relationship with whites?

2. **Drawing Conclusions** Do you think Malcolm X supported integration? Why or why not?

The Civil Rights Movement's Legacy

There have been many changes in the status of African Americans in the United States since the 1960s. Changes have taken place in politics, economics, and education.

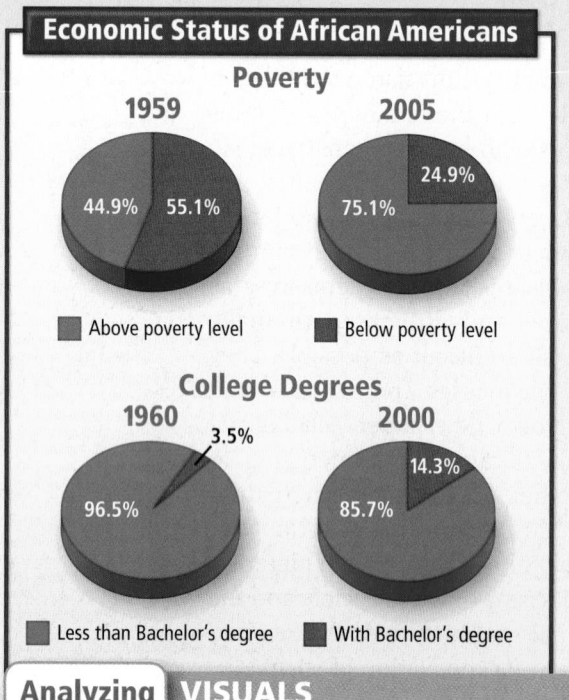

Economic Status of African Americans

Poverty

1959
- 44.9%
- 55.1%

2005
- 24.9%
- 75.1%

■ Above poverty level　■ Below poverty level

College Degrees

1960
- 3.5%
- 96.5%

2000
- 14.3%
- 85.7%

■ Less than Bachelor's degree　■ With Bachelor's degree

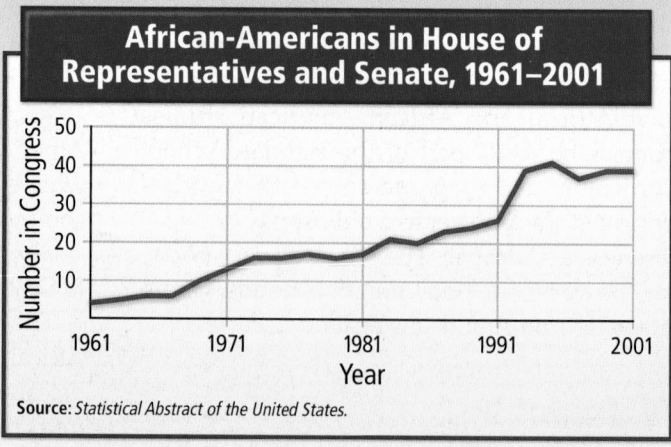

African-Americans in House of Representatives and Senate, 1961–2001

Number in Congress (y-axis: 10, 20, 30, 40, 50)
Year (x-axis: 1961, 1971, 1981, 1991, 2001)

Source: *Statistical Abstract of the United States.*

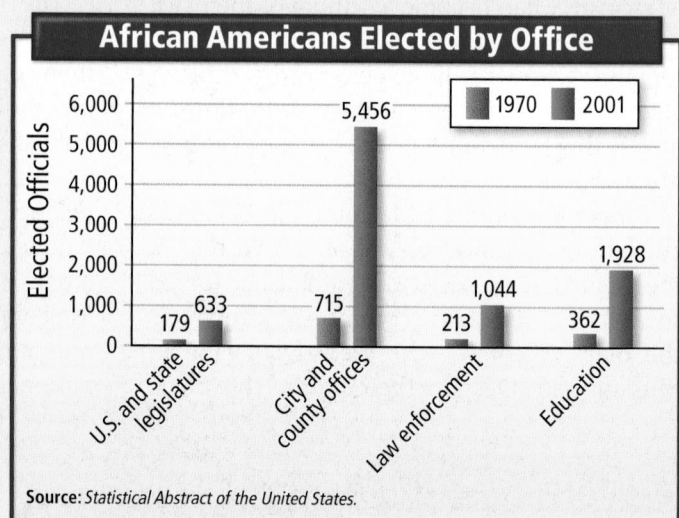

African Americans Elected by Office

Elected Officials (y-axis: 0, 1,000, 2,000, 3,000, 4,000, 5,000, 6,000)

Legend: ■ 1970　■ 2001

- U.S. and state legislatures: 179, 633
- City and county offices: 715, 5,456
- Law enforcement: 213, 1,044
- Education: 362, 1,928

Source: *Statistical Abstract of the United States.*

Analyzing VISUALS

1. **Interpreting** In which elected offices did African Americans see the greatest increase in representation?

2. **Drawing Conclusions** Does the data presented suggest that the civil rights movement was a success? Why or why not?

By 1964, Malcolm X had broken with the Black Muslims. Discouraged by scandals involving the Nation of Islam's leader, he went to the Muslim holy city of Makkah (also called Mecca) in Saudi Arabia. After seeing Muslims from many races worshipping together, he concluded that an integrated society was possible after all.

After Malcolm X broke with the Nation of Islam, he continued to criticize the organization. Because of this, organization members shot and killed him in February 1965. Although Malcolm X left the Nation of Islam before his death, his speeches and ideas from those years with the Black Muslims have influenced African Americans to take pride in their own culture and to believe in their ability to make their way in the world.

Malcolm X's ideas influenced a new generation of militant African American leaders who also preached black power, black nationalism,

and economic self-sufficiency. In 1966 in Oakland, California, Huey Newton, Bobby Seale, and Eldridge Cleaver organized the **Black Panthers.**

The Black Panthers believed that a revolution was necessary in the United States, and they urged African Americans to arm themselves and prepare to force whites to grant them equal rights. Black Panther leaders called for an end to racial oppression and control of major institutions in the African American community, such as schools, law **enforcement,** housing, and hospitals. Eldridge Cleaver, who served as the minister of culture, articulated many of the organization's aims in his 1967 best-selling book, *Soul on Ice.*

✓ Reading Check **Describing** What disagreements split Dr. Martin Luther King, Jr., and the black power movement?

King Is Assassinated

MAIN Idea After Dr. King was assassinated in Memphis, Tennessee, Congress passed the Civil Rights Act of 1968.

HISTORY AND YOU Do you know someone who remembers Dr. King's assassination? Read about the events surrounding King's death.

By the late 1960s, the civil rights movement had fragmented into dozens of competing organizations with differing philosophies for reaching equality. At the same time, the emergence of black power and the call by some African Americans for violent action angered many white civil rights supporters. This made further legislation to help African Americans economically less likely.

In this atmosphere, Dr. King went to Memphis, Tennessee, to support a strike of African American sanitation workers in March 1968. At the time, the SCLC had been planning a national "Poor People's Campaign" to promote economic advancement for all impoverished Americans. The purpose of this campaign, the most ambitious one that Dr. King would ever lead, was to lobby the federal government to commit billions of dollars to end poverty and unemployment in the United States. People of all races and nationalities were to converge on the nation's capital, as they had in 1963 during the March on Washington, where they would camp out until both Congress and President Johnson agreed to pass the requested legislation to fund the proposal.

On April 4, 1968, as he stood on his hotel balcony in Memphis, Dr. King was assassinated by a sniper. Ironically, the previous night he had told a gathering at a local church, "I've been to the mountaintop. . . . I've looked over and I've seen the Promised Land. I may not get there with you, but I want you to know tonight that we as a people will get to the Promised Land."

Dr. King's death touched off both national mourning and riots in more than 100 cities, including Washington, D.C. The Reverend Ralph Abernathy, who had served as a trusted assistant to Dr. King for many years, led the Poor People's Campaign in King's absence. The demonstration, however, did not achieve any of the major objectives that either King or the SCLC had hoped it would.

In the wake of Dr. King's death, Congress did pass the Civil Rights Act of 1968. The act contained a fair-housing provision outlawing discrimination in housing sales and rentals and gave the Justice Department authority to bring suits against such discrimination.

Dr. King's death marked the end of an era in American history. Although the civil rights movement continued, it lacked the unity of purpose and vision that Dr. King had given it. Under his leadership, and with the help of tens of thousands of dedicated African Americans, many of whom were students, the civil rights movement transformed American society. Although many problems remain to be solved, the achievements of the civil rights movement in the 1950s and 1960s dramatically improved the lives of African Americans, creating opportunities that had not existed before.

✔ Reading Check **Summarizing** What were the goals of the Poor People's Campaign?

Section 3 REVIEW

Vocabulary

1. **Explain** the significance of: racism, Kerner Commission, Chicago Movement, Richard J. Daley, black power, Stokely Carmichael, Malcolm X, Black Panthers.

Main Ideas

2. **Describing** What were the findings and the recommendations of the Kerner Commission?

3. **Assessing** How did Malcolm X's ideas about the relationship between African Americans and white Americans change by the time of his murder?

4. **Explaining** What was the general effect of Dr. King's assassination?

Critical Thinking

5. **Big Ideas** How was the Civil Rights Act of 1968 designed to improve the economic status of African Americans?

6. **Categorizing** Use a graphic organizer similar to the one below to list the main views of each leader.

Leader	Views
Dr. Martin Luther King, Jr.	
Malcolm X	
Eldridge Cleaver	

7. **Analyzing Visuals** Study the cartoons on page 871. Together, what do they imply about government response and responsibility for the problems of the inner cities?

Writing About History

8. **Expository Writing** Assume the role of a reporter in the late 1960s. Suppose that you have interviewed a follower of Dr. King and a member of the Black Panthers. Write a transcript of each interview.

History ONLINE

Study Central™ To review this section, go to glencoe.com and click on Study Central.

Origins of the Civil Rights Movement

Long-Range Causes

- Widespread racial segregation in the American South
- Lack of voting rights for African Americans in the American South

Immediate Causes

- The arrival of large numbers of African Americans in the North after the Great Migration gives them increased political influence and greater voting power.
- African American contributions during World War II lead many African Americans to believe it is time to take action to demand change.
- NAACP strategy of using lawsuits to weaken segregation scores a major victory in 1954 with the *Brown* v. *Board of Education* ruling.
- African American churches serve as organizational bases, and pastors rally African Americans and organize protests.

► *Linda Brown was the main plaintiff in* Brown v. Board of Education.

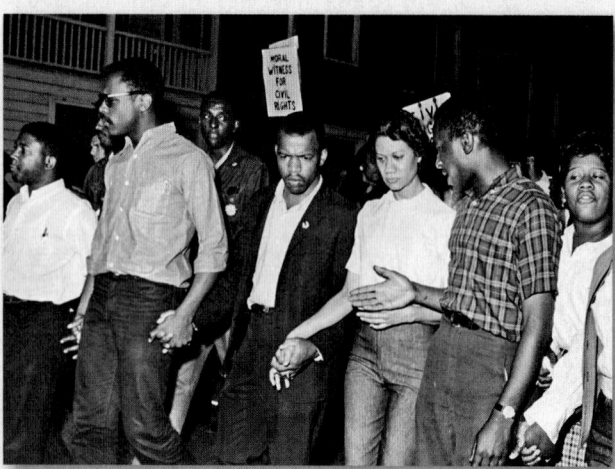

▲ *Civil rights activists march to protest a pro-segregationist speech by Alabama governor George Wallace in 1964.*

Major Events of the Civil Rights Movement

- African American community in Montgomery, Alabama, led by Dr. Martin Luther King, Jr., organizes the Montgomery bus boycott.
- African American students are blocked from entering Little Rock High School. President Eisenhower sends in federal troops and asks Congress to pass the Civil Rights Act of 1957.
- Sit-ins begin in Greensboro, and soon young people are staging sit-ins across the South to integrate public facilities.
- Freedom Riders end segregation on interstate bus travel.
- Martin Luther King, Jr., leads a march in Birmingham, then a March on Washington to support the Civil Rights Act of 1964.
- Martin Luther King, Jr., leads a march in Selma to pressure Congress to pass the Voting Rights Act of 1965.

Major Results of the Civil Rights Movement

- Civil Rights Act of 1957
- Civil Rights Act of 1964
- Voting Rights Act of 1965
- Civil Rights Act of 1968
- End of legal segregation in schools and public facilities
- Restoration of voting rights for African Americans
- Ban on discrimination based on race in the workplace
- Increased federal power to protect civil rights

▲ *A civil rights march in Montgomery, Alabama, in 1965*

NEW YORK REGENTS EXAM PRACTICE

TEST-TAKING

Look for clues in the question that help you to eliminate certain answer choices right away. For example, if a question asks for a difference between two political leaders, you know that you can eliminate answer choices that show what they have in common.

Part I

Directions (1–10): For each statement or question, write on a separate sheet of paper the number of the word or expression that, of those given, best completes the statement or answers the question.

1 Which event led to the bus boycott in Alabama?

  (1) a riot in Montgomery

  (2) the CORE sit-in

  (3) the arrest of Rosa Parks

  (4) a church bombing

2 In 1957, the Southern Christian Leadership Conference (SCLC) set out to

  (1) march on Washington and pass a civil rights bill.

  (2) encourage demonstrations and boycotts.

  (3) increase church attendance and promote brotherhood.

  (4) end segregation and encourage voter registration.

3 Why was the sit-in movement considered a major turning point in the civil rights movement?

  (1) It discouraged high school and college students from becoming involved in the civil rights movement.

  (2) It encouraged large numbers of college students to join the civil rights movement.

  (3) At first, it encouraged the NAACP and SCLC to recruit more college students, but the associated violence changed their minds.

  (4) It encouraged large numbers of Southern whites to support the civil rights movement.

4 "Bloody Sunday" occurred in reaction to

  (1) the Selma march.

  (2) the passage of the Civil Rights Act of 1964.

  (3) the March on Washington.

  (4) the assassination of Dr. Martin Luther King, Jr.

5 In response to the race riots in the mid-1960s, the federal government established which of the following?

  (1) SNCC

  (2) the EEOC

  (3) the Chicago Movement

  (4) the Kerner Commission

6 What did the Nation of Islam advocate?

  (1) African Americans should use nonviolent resistance to fight for civil rights.

  (2) African Americans should separate from whites and form their own government.

  (3) African Americans should use violence to overthrow the government and establish their own nation.

  (4) African Americans should sue the federal government to establish equality among the nation's citizens.

7 How did the Civil Rights Act of 1964 help African Americans?

  (1) The act authorized the U.S. attorney general to send federal employees to register voters.

  (2) The act suspended literacy tests in counties where less than half of all adults had been allowed to vote.

  (3) The act outlawed discrimination in housing.

  (4) The act gave the federal government more power to force school desegregation.

Need Extra Help?							
If You Missed Questions . . .	1	2	3	4	5	6	7
Go to Page . . .	854	855	858–859	866–867	871–872	873	864–865

[OVER]

Base your answers to questions 8 and 9 on the map below and on your knowledge of Chapter 25.

Route of the Freedom Riders, 1961

8 The route of the Freedom Riders focused on which region of the United States?

(1) the Midwest

(2) the South

(3) New England

(4) the West

9 The final destination of the Freedom Riders was

(1) Montgomery, Alabama.

(2) Washington, D.C.

(3) Selma, Alabama.

(4) Jackson, Mississippi.

---

10 *Brown* v. *Board of Education* was a significant case because it made it illegal to

(1) prevent African Americans from voting.

(2) segregate restaurants.

(3) segregate public schools.

(4) discriminate in the selling of a house.

Need Extra Help?

If You Missed Questions . . .	8	9	10
Go to Page . . .	R15	R15	852

Part II Thematic Essay Question

Directions: Write a well-organized essay that includes an introduction, several paragraphs addressing the task below, and a conclusion.

Theme: Civil Rights

As the 1960s passed, the civil rights movement began to fragment as major differences among African American leaders began to appear.

Task:

Select one of the African American leaders who advocated a more militant approach to the problems of racism and

• Compare the ideas of that leader with the ideas of Martin Luther King, Jr.

• Evaluate which leader was more effective and describe the long-term effects of each leader's actions.

Guidelines:

In your essay, be sure to:

• Develop all aspects of the task

• Support the theme with relevant facts, examples, and details

• Use a logical and clear plan of organization, including an introduction and a conclusion that are beyond a restatement of the theme

Part III Document-Based Question

This question is based on the accompanying documents. It is designed to test your ability to work with historical documents. Some of the documents have been edited for the purposes of the question. As you analyze the documents, take into account both the source of each document and any point of view that may be presented in the document.

Historical Context:

African Americans and others challenged segregation in the United States following World War II. Their efforts were opposed by segregationists, despite the increased involvement of the federal government. By the mid-1960s, progress had been made, including civil rights legislation, but the fight was far from over.

Task:

Using information from the documents and your knowledge of United States history, answer the questions that follow each document in Part A. Your answers to the questions will help you write the Part B essay, in which you will be asked to

- Discuss the actions of civil rights leaders and the government to further civil rights
- Evaluate the long-term effects of civil rights legislation and the actions of civil rights organizations

Part A
Short-Answer Questions

Directions: Analyze the documents and answer the short-answer questions that follow each document on a separate sheet of paper.

Document 1

"I am about to sign into law the Civil Rights Act of 1964. I want to take this occasion to talk to you about what that law means to every American. . . . We believe that all men are created equal. Yet many are denied equal treatment. We believe that all men have certain unalienable rights. Yet many Americans do not enjoy those rights. We believe that all men are entitled to the blessings of liberty. Yet millions are being deprived of those blessings—not because of their own failures, but because of the color of their skin. The reasons are deeply imbedded in history and tradition and the nature of man. We can understand—without rancor or hatred—how this all happened. But it cannot continue. Our Constitution, the foundation of our Republic, forbids it. The principles of our freedom forbid it. Morality forbids it. And the law I will sign tonight forbids it."

Source: from President Lyndon B. Johnson's radio and television remarks upon signing the Civil Rights Act of 1964

1 According to Johnson, what are the origins of racism?

Document 2

Source: Jon Kennedy, *Arkansas Democrat-Gazette*

2 What is the main idea of this cartoon?

Part B
Essay

Directions: Reread the task box at the top left and write a well-organized essay that includes an introduction, several paragraphs, and a conclusion. Use evidence from the documents in your essay. Support your response with relevant facts, examples, and details. Include additional outside information.

Guidelines:
In your essay, be sure to:

- Develop all aspects of the task
- Incorporate information from the documents
- Incorporate relevant outside information
- Support the theme with relevant facts, examples, and details
- Use a logical and clear plan of organization, including an introduction and a conclusion that are beyond a restatement of the theme

For additional test practice, use Self-Check Quizzes—Chapter 25 at glencoe.com.

Need Extra Help?			
If You Missed Questions . . .	1	2	Essay
Go to Page . . .	R19	R18	850–876

Chapter 26

The Vietnam War

1954–1975

SECTION 1 Going to War in Vietnam

SECTION 2 Vietnam Divides the Nation

SECTION 3 The War Winds Down

American soldiers march up a hill in Vietnam in 1968, as fires behind them send smoke into the air.

U.S. PRESIDENTS

Eisenhower 1953–1961

Kennedy 1961–1963

Johnson 1963–1969

U.S. EVENTS

WORLD EVENTS

1955
- U.S. military aid and advisers are sent to South Vietnam

1955

1964
- Congress passes Gulf of Tonkin Resolution

1965
- U.S. combat troops arrive in Vietnam

1960

1965

1954
- France leaves Indochina; Geneva Accords divide Vietnam in two

1958
- U.S. troops land in Lebanon

1960
- U-2 spy plane is shot down

1968
- Tet Offensive begins
- Anti-war protest in Chicago

Nixon 1969–1974

1970
- National Guard troops kill student protesters at Kent State

1973
- Last U.S. troops leave Vietnam

1970

1975

1970
- Nixon orders invasion of Cambodia

1975
- Saigon falls to North Vietnamese invasion

FOLDABLES™

Defining Vietnam Terminology

Make a Vocabulary Book Foldable to aid your review of the Vietnam War. Select terms for a 10-tab Vocabulary Book. Example terms include: *Ho Chi Minh, Containment,* and *Gulf of Tonkin Resolution.* Define the terms under the appropriate tab.

Ho Chi Minh
Containment
Gulf of Tonkin resolution

History ONLINE Chapter Overview
Visit glencoe.com to preview Chapter 26.

Going to War in Vietnam

Guide to Reading

Big Ideas

Trade, War, and Migration American involvement in the war in Vietnam was the result of its Cold War strategy.

Content Vocabulary

- domino theory *(p. 883)*
- guerrilla *(p. 883)*
- napalm *(p. 889)*
- Agent Orange *(p. 889)*

Academic Vocabulary

- strategic *(p. 885)*
- traditional *(p. 885)*

People and Events to Identify

- Ho Chi Minh *(p. 882)*
- Dien Bien Phu *(p. 884)*
- Geneva Accords *(p. 884)*
- Ngo Dinh Diem *(p. 884)*
- Vietcong *(p. 885)*
- Gulf of Tonkin Resolution *(p. 886)*
- Ho Chi Minh trail *(p. 889)*

Reading Strategy

Organizing Complete a graphic organizer similar to the one below by providing reasons why the United States aided France in Vietnam.

Reasons for U.S. Support of France

NEW YORK CORE CURRICULUM
U.S. History and Government

Unit 7:
IV.A.1 The French-Indochinese War: early United States involvement; Truman, Eisenhower, and Kennedy policies (review how foreign policy is formulated)
IV.A.2 United States and the spread of communism; domino theory; credibility of other United States commitments
IV.A.3 Civil war in South Vietnam; concept of guerilla warfare

In the late 1940s and early 1950s, most Americans knew little about Indochina, France's colony in Southeast Asia. During the Cold War, however, American officials became concerned the region might fall to communism. Eventually, American troops were sent to fight in Vietnam.

American Involvement in Vietnam

MAIN Idea The Cold War policy of containment led the United States to become increasingly involved in events in Vietnam.

HISTORY AND YOU Have you met anyone who was born in Vietnam? Do you know why he or she left? Read to learn about Vietnam's complicated and tragic history.

In 1940, the Japanese invaded Vietnam. The occupation was only the latest example of foreigners ruling the Vietnamese people. The Chinese Empire had controlled the region for hundreds of years. Then, beginning in the late 1800s and lasting until World War II, France ruled Vietnam as well as neighboring Laos and Cambodia—a region known collectively as French Indochina.

The Growth of Vietnamese Nationalism

The Vietnamese did not want to be ruled by foreigners, and by the early 1900s, nationalism had become a powerful force in the country. The Vietnamese formed several political parties to push for independence or for reform of the French colonial government. One of the leaders of the nationalist movement for almost 30 years was Nguyen Tat Thanh—better known by his assumed name, **Ho Chi Minh.** At the age of 21, Ho Chi Minh traveled to Europe where he lived in London and then Paris. In 1919 he presented a petition for Vietnamese independence at the Versailles Peace Conference, but the peace treaty ignored the issue. Ho Chi Minh later visited the Soviet Union where he became an advocate of communism. In 1930 he returned to Southeast Asia, helped found the Indochinese Communist Party, and worked to overthrow French rule.

Ho Chi Minh's activities made him a wanted man. He fled Indochina and spent several years in exile in the Soviet Union and China. In 1941 he returned to Vietnam. By then, Japan had seized control of the country. Ho Chi Minh organized a nationalist group called the Vietminh. The group united both Communists and non-Communists in the struggle to expel the Japanese forces. Soon afterward, the United States began sending aid to the Vietminh.

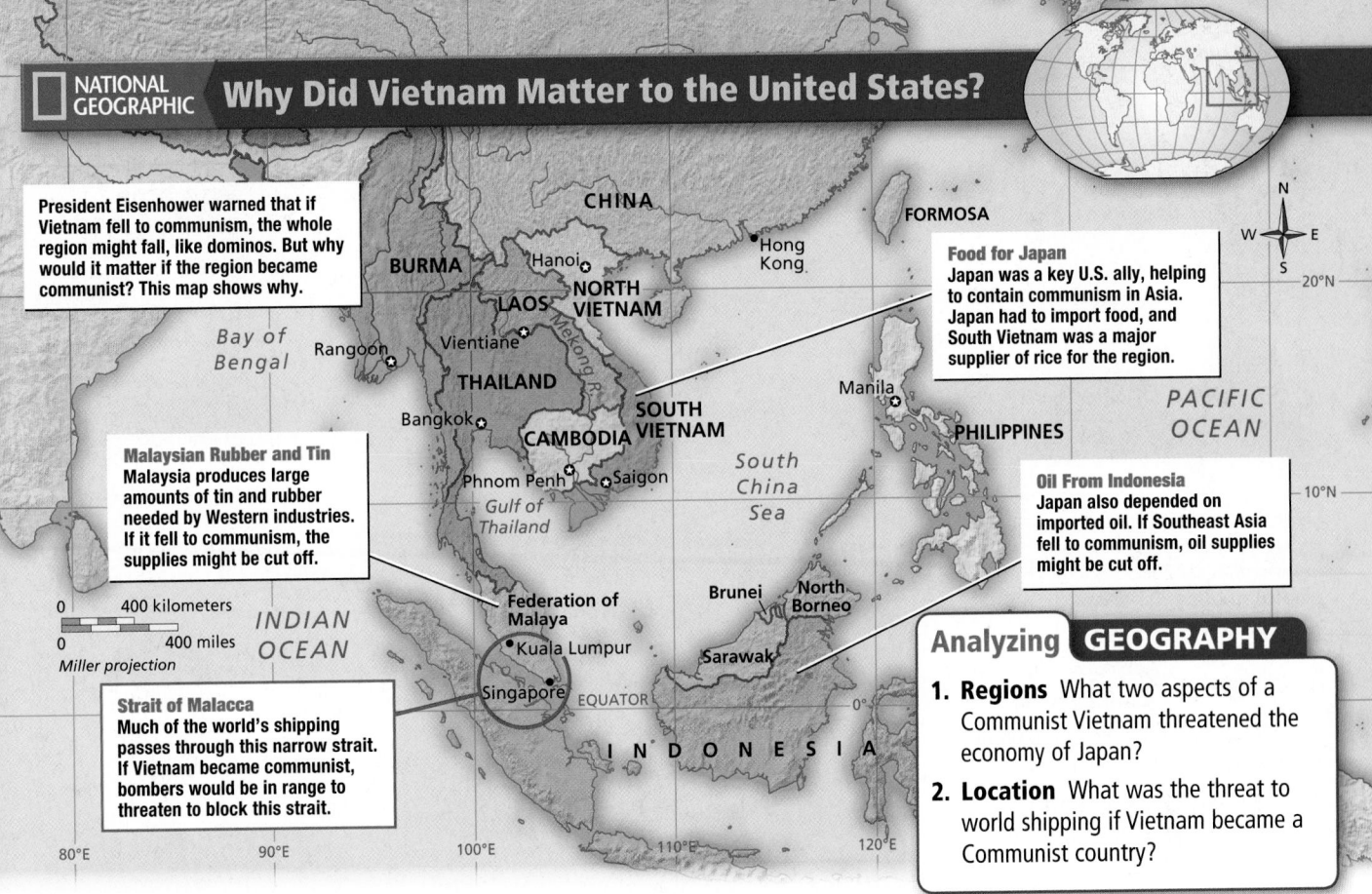

President Eisenhower warned that if Vietnam fell to communism, the whole region might fall, like dominos. But why would it matter if the region became communist? This map shows why.

Food for Japan
Japan was a key U.S. ally, helping to contain communism in Asia. Japan had to import food, and South Vietnam was a major supplier of rice for the region.

Malaysian Rubber and Tin
Malaysia produces large amounts of tin and rubber needed by Western industries. If it fell to communism, the supplies might be cut off.

Oil From Indonesia
Japan also depended on imported oil. If Southeast Asia fell to communism, oil supplies might be cut off.

Strait of Malacca
Much of the world's shipping passes through this narrow strait. If Vietnam became communist, bombers would be in range to threaten to block this strait.

0 400 kilometers
0 400 miles
Miller projection

Analyzing GEOGRAPHY

1. **Regions** What two aspects of a Communist Vietnam threatened the economy of Japan?
2. **Location** What was the threat to world shipping if Vietnam became a Communist country?

America Aids the French

When Japan surrendered to the Allies in 1945, it gave up control of Indochina. Ho Chi Minh quickly declared Vietnam to be an independent nation. France, however, had no intention of allowing Vietnam to become independent. Seeking to regain their colonial empire in Southeast Asia, French troops returned to Vietnam in 1946 and drove the Vietminh forces into hiding in the countryside.

The Vietminh fought back against the French-dominated regime and slowly gained control of large areas of the countryside. As the fighting escalated, France appealed to the United States for help. The request put American officials in a difficult position. The United States opposed colonialism. It had pressured the Dutch to give up their empire in Indonesia and supported the British decision to give India independence in 1947. In Vietnam, however, the independence movement had become entangled with the Communist movement. American officials did not want France to control Vietnam, but they also did not want Vietnam to be communist.

Two events convinced President Truman to help France—the fall of China to communism and the outbreak of the Korean War. The latter, in particular, seemed to indicate that the Soviet Union had begun a major push to impose communism on East Asia. Shortly after the Korean War began, Truman authorized military aid to French forces in Vietnam. President Eisenhower continued Truman's policy and defended his decision with what became known as the **domino theory**—the idea that if Vietnam fell to communism, the rest of Southeast Asia would follow:

PRIMARY SOURCE

"You have a row of dominoes set up, you knock over the first one, and what will happen to the last one is the certainty that it will go over very quickly. ... Asia, after all, has already lost some 450 million of its peoples to Communist dictatorship, and we simply can't afford greater losses."

—President Eisenhower, quoted in *America in Vietnam*

Defeat at Dien Bien Phu

Despite aid from the United States, the French continued to struggle against the Vietminh, who consistently frustrated the French with hit-and-run and ambush tactics. These are the tactics of **guerrillas,** irregular troops who blend into the civilian population and are difficult for regular armies to fight.

CHINA

Dien Bien Phu

Hanoi

BURMA

20°N

LAOS

Vientiane

NORTH VIETNAM

Rangoon

▲ Ho Chi Minh, Communist leader of North Vietnam, was determined to reunite Vietnam and began arming Vietcong guerrillas to seize power in South Vietnam.

THAILAND

Bangkok

CAMBODIA

SOUTH VIETNAM

Mekong River

N
W   E
S

▲ Mao Zedong, leader of Communist China, supported North Vietnam.

South China Sea

Gulf of Thailand

Phnom Penh

Saigon

Analyzing GEOGRAPHY

1. **Regions** Why do you think Mao supported North Vietnam?

2. **Human-Environment Interaction** What difficulties would North Vietnam face in sending aid to the Vietcong?

0   400 kilometers
0   400 miles

Miller projection

100°E   110°E

▲ Ngo Dinh Diem, South Vietnam's president, accepted American aid to fight the Vietcong.

The mounting casualties and the inability of the French to defeat the Vietminh made the war very unpopular in France. Finally, in 1954 the struggle reached a turning point when the French commander ordered his forces to occupy the mountain town of **Dien Bien Phu.** Seizing the town would interfere with the Vietminh's supply lines and force them into open battle. Soon afterward, a huge Vietminh force surrounded Dien Bien Phu and began bombarding the town. On May 7, 1954, the French force at Dien Bien Phu fell to the Vietminh. The defeat convinced the French to make peace and withdraw from Indochina.

Geneva Accords

Negotiations to end the conflict were held in Geneva, Switzerland. The **Geneva Accords** divided Vietnam along the 17th parallel, with Ho Chi Minh and the Vietminh in control of North Vietnam and a pro-Western regime in control of the South. In 1956 elections were to be held to reunite the country under a single government. The Geneva Accords also recog-

nized Cambodia's independence. Laos had gained independence in the previous year.

Shortly after the Geneva Accords partitioned Vietnam, the French troops left. The United States became the principal protector of the new government in the South, led by a nationalist leader named **Ngo Dinh Diem** (NOH DIHN deh•EHM). Like Ho Chi Minh, Diem had been educated abroad, but, unlike the North Vietnamese leader, Diem was pro-Western and fiercely anti-Communist. A Catholic, he welcomed the roughly one million North Vietnamese Catholics who migrated south to escape Ho Chi Minh's rule.

The elections mandated by the Geneva Accords never took place. In a special referendum, Diem became president of the new Republic of Vietnam in the South. He then refused to permit the 1956 elections, fearing Ho Chi Minh would win. Eisenhower approved Diem's actions and increased American aid to South Vietnam.

Reading Check **Summarizing** Why did Ho Chi Minh lead a resistance movement against France?

America Becomes Involved in Vietnam

MAIN Idea Political pressures in the United States led the nation to become deeply involved in the civil war in Vietnam.

HISTORY AND YOU Do you have a relative or family friend who fought in the Vietnam War? Read on to find out why the United States got involved in this complicated conflict.

After Ngo Dinh Diem refused to hold national elections and began to crack down on Communist groups in South Vietnam, Ho Chi Minh and the Communists began an armed struggle to reunify the nation. They organized a new guerrilla army of South Vietnamese Communists, which became known as the **Vietcong.** As fighting began between the Vietcong and South Vietnam's forces, President Eisenhower sent hundreds of military advisers to train South Vietnam's army.

Despite American assistance, the Vietcong continued to grow more powerful because many Vietnamese opposed Diem's government. The Vietcong's use of terror was also effective. By 1961, the Vietcong had assassinated thousands of government officials and established control over much of the countryside. In response Diem looked increasingly to the United States for help.

Kennedy Takes Over

On taking office in 1961, President Kennedy continued the nation's policy of support for South Vietnam. Like Presidents Truman and Eisenhower before him, Kennedy saw the Southeast Asian country as vitally important in the battle against communism.

In political terms, Kennedy needed to appear tough on communism, since Republicans often accused Democrats of having lost China to communism during the Truman administration. From 1961 to late 1963, the number of American military personnel in South Vietnam jumped from about 2,000 to around 15,000.

American officials believed that the Vietcong continued to grow because Diem's government was unpopular and corrupt. They urged him to create a more democratic government and to introduce reforms to help Vietnam's peasants. Diem introduced some limited reforms, but they had little effect.

One program Diem introduced, at the urging of American advisers, made the situation worse. The South Vietnamese created special fortified villages known as **strategic** hamlets. These villages were protected by machine guns, bunkers, trenches, and barbed wire. Vietnamese officials then moved villagers to the strategic hamlets. The program proved to be extremely unpopular. Many peasants resented being uprooted from their villages, where they had worked to build farms and where many of their ancestors lay buried.

The Overthrow of Diem

Diem made himself even more unpopular by discriminating against Buddhism, one of the country's most widely practiced religions. In the spring of 1963, Diem, a Catholic, banned the **traditional** religious flags for Buddha's birthday. When Buddhists took to the streets in protest, Diem's police killed 9 people and injured 14 others. In the demonstrations that followed, a Buddhist monk poured gasoline over his robes and set himself on fire, the first of several Buddhists to do so. Images of their self-destruction horrified Americans as they watched the footage on television news reports. These extreme acts of protest were a disturbing sign of the opposition to the Diem regime.

In August 1963 American ambassador Henry Cabot Lodge arrived in Vietnam. He quickly learned that Diem's unpopularity had so alarmed several Vietnamese generals that they were plotting to overthrow him. When Lodge expressed American sympathy for their cause, the generals launched a military coup. They seized power on November 1, 1963, and executed Diem shortly afterward.

Diem's overthrow only made matters worse. Despite his unpopularity with some Vietnamese, Diem had been a respected nationalist and a capable administrator. After his death, South Vietnam's government grew increasingly weak and unstable. The United States became even more deeply involved in order to prop it up. Coincidentally, three weeks after Diem's death, President Kennedy was assassinated. The presidency, as well as the growing problem of Vietnam, now belonged to Kennedy's vice president, Lyndon Johnson.

Johnson and Vietnam

Initially, President Johnson exercised caution and restraint regarding the conflict in Vietnam. "We seek no wider war," he repeatedly promised. At the same time, Johnson was determined to prevent South Vietnam from becoming communist. "The battle against communism," he declared shortly before becoming president, "must be joined ... with strength and determination."

Politics also played a role in Johnson's Vietnam policy. Like Kennedy, Johnson remembered that many Republicans blamed the Truman administration for the fall of China to communism in 1949. Should the Democrats also "lose" Vietnam, Johnson feared, it might cause a "mean and destructive debate that would shatter my Presidency, kill my administration, and damage our democracy."

For the text of the Gulf of Tonkin Resolution see R57 in Documents in American History.

The Gulf of Tonkin Resolution On August 2, 1964, President Johnson announced that North Vietnamese torpedo boats had fired on two American destroyers in the Gulf of Tonkin. Two days later, the president reported that another similar attack had taken place. Johnson was campaigning for the presidency and was very sensitive to accusations of being soft on communism. He insisted that North Vietnam's attacks were unprovoked and immediately ordered American aircraft to attack North Vietnamese ships and naval facilities. Johnson did not reveal that the American warships had been helping the South Vietnamese conduct electronic spying and commando raids against North Vietnam.

Johnson then asked Congress for the authority to defend American forces and American allies in Southeast Asia. Congress agreed to Johnson's request with little debate. Most members of Congress agreed with Republican representative Ross Adair of Indiana, who defiantly declared, "The American flag has been fired upon. We will not and cannot tolerate such things."

On August 7, 1964, the Senate and House passed the **Gulf of Tonkin Resolution,** authorizing the president to "take all necessary measures to repel any armed attack against the forces of the United States and to prevent further aggression." With only two dissenting votes, Congress had, in effect, handed its war powers over to the president.

The United States Sends in Troops

Shortly after Congress passed the Gulf of Tonkin Resolution, the Vietcong began to attack bases where American advisers were stationed in South Vietnam. The attacks began in the fall of 1964 and continued to escalate. After a Vietcong attack on a base at Pleiku in February 1965 left eight Americans dead and more than 100 wounded, President Johnson decided to respond. Less than 14 hours after the attack, American aircraft bombed North Vietnam.

After the air strikes, one poll showed that Johnson's approval rating on his handling of Vietnam jumped from 41 percent to 60 percent. Further, nearly 80 percent of Americans agreed that without American assistance, Southeast Asia would fall to the Communists. An equivalent number believed that the United States should send combat troops to Vietnam

Debates IN HISTORY

Should America Fight in Vietnam?

As the war in Vietnam dragged on, Americans became increasingly divided about the nation's role in the conflict. In January 1966, George W. Ball, undersecretary of state to President Johnson, delivered an address to indicate "how we got [into Vietnam] and why we must stay." George Kennan, a former ambassador to the Soviet Union, testified before the Senate Foreign Relations Committee in that same year, arguing that American involvement in Vietnam was "something we would not choose deliberately if the choice were ours to make all over again today."

to prevent that from happening. The president's actions also met with strong approval from his closest advisers, including Secretary of Defense Robert McNamara and National Security Adviser McGeorge Bundy.

Some officials disagreed, chief among them Undersecretary of State George Ball, who initially supported involvement in Vietnam but later turned against it. He warned that if the United States got too involved, it would be difficult to get out. "Once on the tiger's back," he warned, "we cannot be sure of picking the place to dismount."

Most of the advisers who surrounded Johnson, however, firmly believed the nation had a duty to halt communism in Vietnam, both to maintain stability in Southeast Asia and to ensure the United States's continuing power and prestige in the world. In a memo to the president, Bundy argued:

PRIMARY SOURCE

"The stakes in Vietnam are extremely high. The American investment is very large, and American responsibility is a fact of life which is palpable in the atmosphere of Asia, and even elsewhere. The international prestige of the U.S. and a substantial part of our influence are directly at risk in Vietnam."

—quoted in *The Best and the Brightest*

In March 1965, President Johnson expanded American involvement by beginning a sustained bombing campaign against North Vietnam code-named Operation Rolling Thunder. That same month, the president also ordered the first combat troops into Vietnam. American soldiers would now fight alongside South Vietnamese troops against the Vietcong.

✔ **Reading Check** **Describing** How did politics play a role in President Johnson's Vietnam policy?

YES

George W. Ball
Undersecretary of State

PRIMARY SOURCE

"[T]he conflict in Viet-Nam is a product of the great shifts and changes triggered by the Second World War. . . . [T]he Soviet Union under Stalin exploited the confusion to push out the perimeter of its power and influence in an effort to extend the outer limits of Communist domination by force or the threat of force. . . .

The bloody encounters in [Vietnam] . . . are thus in a real sense battles and skirmishes in a continuing war to prevent one Communist power after another from violating internationally recognized boundary lines fixing the outer limits of Communist dominion. . . .

In the long run our hopes for the people of South Vietnam reflect our hopes for people everywhere. What we seek is a world living in peace and freedom."

—Speech delivered January 30, 1966

NO

George F. Kennan
Former Diplomat

PRIMARY SOURCE

"Vietnam is not a region of major military-industrial importance. . . . Even a situation in which South Vietnam was controlled exclusively by the Vietcong, . . . would not present in my opinion, dangers great enough to justify our direct military intervention.

And to attempt to crush North Vietnamese strength to a point where Hanoi could no longer give any support to Vietcong political activity in the South would. . . have the effect of bringing in Chinese forces at some point. . . .

Our motives are widely misinterpreted; and the spectacle of Americans inflicting grievous injury on the lives of a poor and helpless people. . . produces reactions among millions of people throughout the world profoundly detrimental to the image we would like them to hold of this country."

—Testimony before the Senate Foreign Relations Committee, February 10, 1966

DBQ **Document-Based Questions**

1. **Summarizing** Why does Ball believe that the United States is justified in fighting in Vietnam?

2. **Explaining** What are the three main points of Kennan's argument?

3. **Contrasting** What is the fundamental difference between the views of Ball and Kennan?

4. **Evaluating** With which position do you agree? Write a paragraph to explain your choice.

A Bloody Stalemate

MAIN Idea The failure of United States forces to defeat the Vietcong and the deaths of thousands of American soldiers led many Americans to question the nation's involvement in Vietnam.

HISTORY AND YOU Have you ever heard people compare a contemporary military conflict to the Vietnam War? Read on to find out why some people fear becoming involved in a similar conflict today.

By the end of 1965, more than 180,000 American combat troops were fighting in Vietnam. In 1966 that number doubled. Since the American military was extremely strong, it marched into Vietnam with great confidence. "America seemed omnipotent then," wrote Philip Caputo, one of the first marines to arrive. "We saw ourselves as the champions of a 'cause that was destined to triumph.'"

Lacking the firepower of the Americans, the Vietcong used ambushes, booby traps, and other guerrilla tactics. Ronald J. Glasser, an American army doctor, described the devastating effects of one booby trap:

PRIMARY SOURCE

"Three quarters of the way through the tangle, a trooper brushed against a two-inch vine, and a grenade slung at chest high went off, shattering the right side of his head and body.... Nearby troopers took hold of the unconscious soldier and, half carrying, half dragging him, pulled him the rest of the way through the tangle."

—quoted in *Vietnam, A History*

The Vietcong also frustrated American troops by blending in with the general population and then quickly vanishing. "It was a sheer physical impossibility to keep the enemy from slipping away whenever he wished," explained one American general. Journalist Linda Martin noted, "It's a war where nothing is ever quite certain and nowhere is ever quite safe."

NATIONAL GEOGRAPHIC

The Vietnam War, 1965–1973

CHINA

Dien Bien Phu

Hanoi

Gulf of Tonkin

0   200 kilometers
0   200 miles
Miller projection
20°N

LAOS

NORTH VIETNAM

Vientiane

Mekong R.

Con Thien 1967

Khe Sanh 1968

Hue 1968

South China Sea

February 8–March, 1971: Invasion of Laos

THAILAND

HO CHI MINH TRAIL

Vinh Huy 1967

Dak To 1967

Cu Nghi 1966

Ia Drang 1965

May 1–June 29, 1970: Invasion of Cambodia

CAMBODIA

100°E

SOUTH VIETNAM

Phnom Penh

Saigon

10°N

⬅ Major U.S. and South Vietnamese troop movement

⬅ Major North Vietnamese supply line

✳ Major battle

110°E

▲ Although helicopters helped American troops cope with Vietnam's jungles and mountains, napalm bombs (right) were also used to counter the thick foliage.

Analyzing GEOGRAPHY

1. **Places** What countries were invaded during the Vietnam War?

2. **Movement** Why was it difficult to seal South Vietnam's border?

"Search and Destroy"

To counter the Vietcong's tactics, American troops went on "search and destroy" missions. They tried to find enemy troops, bomb their positions, destroy their supply lines, and force them out into the open for combat.

The Vietcong evaded American forces by hiding out in the thick jungle or escaping through tunnels dug in the earth. To take away the Vietcong's ability to hide, American forces literally destroyed the landscape. American planes dropped **napalm**, a jellied gasoline that explodes on contact. They also used **Agent Orange**, a chemical that strips leaves from trees and shrubs, turning farmland and forest into wasteland. For those South Vietnamese still living in the countryside, danger lay on all sides.

United States military leaders underestimated the Vietcong's strength. They also misjudged the enemy's stamina and the support they had among the South Vietnamese. American generals believed that continuously bombing and killing large numbers of Vietcong would destroy the enemy's morale and force them to give up. The guerrillas, however, had no intention of surrendering, and they were willing to accept huge losses to achieve their goals.

The Ho Chi Minh Trail

In the Vietcong's war effort, North Vietnamese support was a major factor. Although the Vietcong forces were made up of many South Vietnamese, North Vietnam provided arms, advisers, and leadership. As Vietcong casualties mounted, North Vietnam began sending North Vietnamese Army units to fight.

North Vietnam sent arms and supplies south by way of a network of jungle paths known as the **Ho Chi Minh trail.** The trail wound through the countries of Cambodia and Laos, bypassing the border between North and South Vietnam. Because the trail passed through countries not directly involved in the war, President Johnson refused to allow a full-scale attack on the trail to shut it down.

North Vietnam itself received military weapons and other support from the Soviet Union and China. One of the main reasons President Johnson refused to order a full-scale invasion of North Vietnam was his fear that such an attack would bring China into the war, as had happened in Korea. By placing limits on the war, however, Johnson made it very difficult to win. Instead of conquering enemy territory, American troops were forced to fight a war of attrition—a strategy of defeating the enemy forces by wearing them down. This strategy led troops to conduct grisly body counts after battles to determine how many enemy soldiers had been killed. The U.S. military began measuring "progress" in the war by the number of enemy dead.

Bombing from American planes killed as many as 220,000 Vietnamese between 1965 and 1967. By the end of 1966, more than 6,700 American soldiers had been killed. The notion of a quick and decisive victory grew increasingly remote. As a result, many citizens back home began to question the nation's involvement in the war.

Reading Check **Describing** What tactics did the United States adopt to fight the Vietcong?

Section 1 REVIEW

Vocabulary

1. **Explain** the significance of: Ho Chi Minh, domino theory, guerrilla, Dien Bien Phu, Geneva Accords, Ngo Dinh Diem, Vietcong, Gulf of Tonkin Resolution, napalm, Agent Orange, Ho Chi Minh trail.

Main Ideas

2. **Explaining** What convinced the French to pull out of Vietnam?

3. **Determining Cause and Effect** What was the result of the overthrow of Diem in Vietnam?

4. **Analyzing** Why did fighting in Vietnam turn into a stalemate by the mid-1960s?

Critical Thinking

5. **Big Ideas** How did American Cold War politics lead to the United States fighting a war in Vietnam?

6. **Sequencing** Use a graphic organizer similar to the one below to sequence events that led to U.S. involvement in Vietnam.

| August 1963 | November 1, 1963 | August 2, 1964 |
| August 7, 1964 | February 1965 | March 1965 |

7. **Analyzing Visuals** Study the map on page 883. Why is China's location significant in relation to the Cold War struggles in Southeast Asia?

Writing About History

8. **Persuasive Writing** Suppose you are a member of Congress in August 1964. Write a statement supporting or opposing the Gulf of Tonkin Resolution.

History ONLINE

Study Central™ To review this section, go to glencoe.com and click on Study Central.

GEOGRAPHY & HISTORY

The Ho Chi Minh Trail

North and South Vietnam were long narrow countries. As a result, the border between them was very narrow and easy to defend. In order to send supplies and troops to the south, the North Vietnamese had to find a way around the border. They achieved this by crossing (illegally) into Laos and Cambodia, two neutral nations to the west, then heading south bypassing South Vietnam's northern border. The mountains and rain forests of the region provided cover for people using the trails and roads that ran south. The Americans referred to the elaborate network of roads, trails, forest paths, bridges, tunnels, and shelters as the Ho Chi Minh Trail.

How Did Geography Influence the Ho Chi Minh Trail?

The Ho Chi Minh Trail followed the topography—or natural physical features—of the region. When viewed from aircraft, the trail often disappeared and blended into the surrounding countryside, making it very difficult to attack. Furthermore, it provided access to multiple points along South Vietnam's long western border, which was much harder for American and South Vietnamese troops to defend. By 1967, an estimated 20,000 Vietnamese soldiers traveled the route each month. The American military tried to disrupt the flow of people and goods, but this proved very difficult to do. By the end of the war, the Ho Chi Minh Trail stretched some 12,000 miles (19,312 km) through the canopied rain forests.

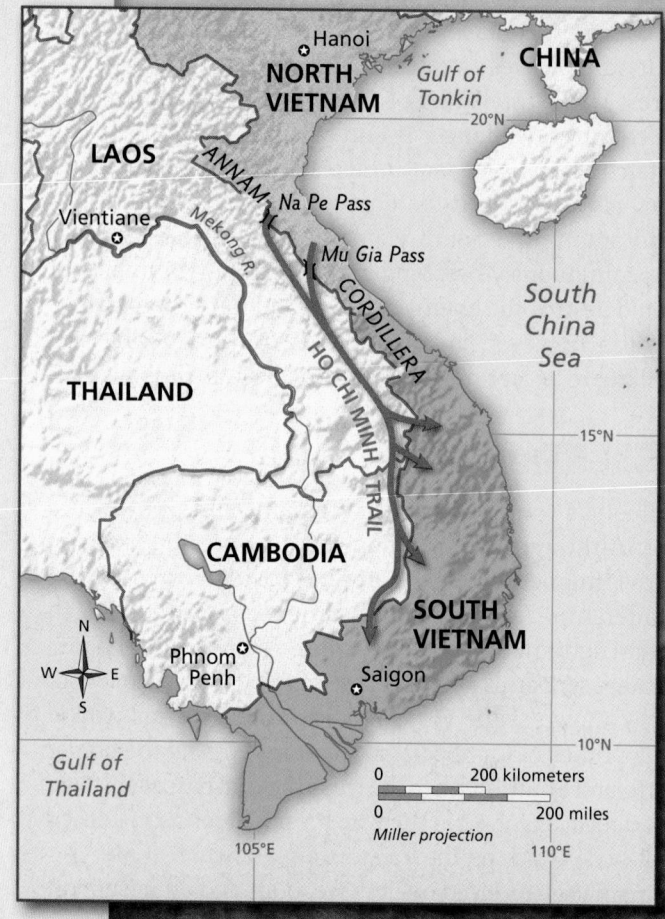

Analyzing GEOGRAPHY

1. **Movement** What diplomatic and international problems were caused by the route of the Ho Chi Minh Trail?

2. **Human-Environment Interaction** What kinds of challenges did the geography of Southeast Asia pose for fighting a war?

▲ In an effort to close the trail and ambush enemy troops using it, American troops set up "firebases" on hilltops overlooking part of the trail. Helicopters helped American troops overcome the region's difficult terrain. They could quickly move men and supplies over the rain forest.

▲ The Vietnamese moved goods along the trail in many ways. Most porters carried goods on their back; others strapped goods to bicycles. Trucks carried supplies and people on wider parts of the trail.

American aircraft tried to destroy troops and vehicles on the trail by dropping bombs, including napalm—a jellied gasoline that would catch fire and burn a wide area.

To deprive the enemy of cover, American aircraft sprayed areas near the trail with defoliants that killed all plant life, leaving a barren area. The most famous chemical used was Agent Orange.

Section 2

Vietnam Divides the Nation

Guide to Reading

Big Ideas
Group Action Many Americans protested to end their country's involvement in the Vietnam War.

Content Vocabulary
• credibility gap *(p. 892)*
• teach-in *(p. 893)*
• dove *(p. 895)*
• hawk *(p. 895)*

Academic Vocabulary
• media *(p. 892)*
• disproportionate *(p. 893)*

People and Events to Identify
• William Westmoreland *(p. 892)*
• Tet Offensive *(p. 895)*

Reading Strategy
Organizing Complete a graphic organizer similar to the one below to list the reasons for opposition to the Vietnam War.

Reasons for Opposition to Vietnam War

NEW YORK CORE CURRICULUM
U.S. History and Government

Unit 7:
IV.A.4.b Escalation and United States assumptions; Tet offensive
IV.A.5.a Draft protesters
IV.A.5.b Political radicals: protests, Students for a Democratic Society (SDS), antiwar
IV.A.6.a President Johnson's decision not to seek reelection
IV.A.6.b Assassinations of Dr. Martin Luther King, Jr. (April 1968) and Robert Kennedy (June 1968)
IV.A.6.c The Democratic Convention; war protesters disrupt proceedings
V.A.1.e Ratification of the 26th Amendment (1971)

As casualties mounted in Vietnam, many Americans began to protest against the war. Discouraged by domestic conflict over the war, rising violence, and the apparent lack of progress in Vietnam, President Johnson announced he would not seek another term as president.

An Antiwar Movement Emerges

MAIN Idea The Vietnam War produced sharp divisions between Americans who supported the war and those who did not, and the resulting political turmoil led President Johnson to decide not to run again for president.

HISTORY AND YOU Do you know people who did not support the war in Iraq and those who did? Read on to find out how differences over the Vietnam War began to divide the country.

When American troops first entered the Vietnam War in the spring of 1965, many Americans supported the military effort. A Gallup poll published soon afterward showed that 66 percent of Americans approved of the policy in Vietnam. As the war dragged on, however, public support began to drop. Suspicion of the government's truthfulness about the war was a significant reason. Throughout the early years of the war, the American commander in South Vietnam, General **William Westmoreland,** reported that the enemy was on the brink of defeat. In 1967 he confidently declared that the "enemy's hopes are bankrupt" and added, "we have reached an important point where the end begins to come into view."

Contradicting such reports were less optimistic **media** accounts, especially on television. Vietnam was the first "television war," with footage of combat appearing nightly on the evening news. Day after day, millions of people saw images of wounded and dead Americans and began to doubt government reports. In the view of many, a **credibility gap** had developed, meaning it was hard to believe what the Johnson administration said about the war.

Congress, which had given the president a nearly free hand in Vietnam, soon grew uncertain about the war. Beginning in February 1966 the Senate Foreign Relations Committee held "educational" hearings on Vietnam, calling in Secretary of State Dean Rusk and other policy makers to explain the administration's military strategy. The committee also listened to critics, such as American diplomat George Kennan. Although Kennan had helped to create the policy of containment, he argued that Vietnam was not strategically important to the United States.

'CHOPPING BLOCK'

▲ An axe labeled "Vietnam Issue" splits the nation in two.

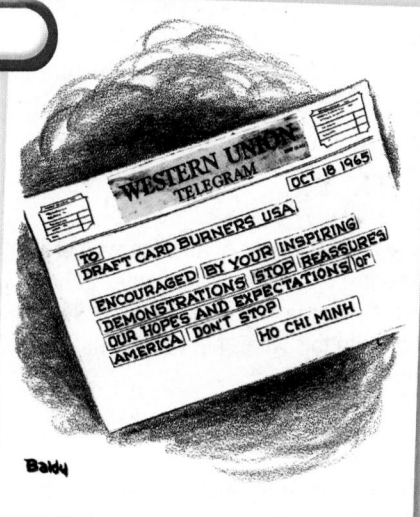

◄ Ho Chi Minh sends a telegram praising antiwar protesters.

Analyzing VISUALS

1. **Finding the Main Idea** What is the main message of the cartoon on the left?

2. **Making Inferences** The cartoon on the right was drawn before the one on the left. Do you think that differences between the two indicate a change in attitude toward antiwar protests? Explain.

Teach-ins Begin

In March 1965, a group of faculty members and students at the University of Michigan abandoned their classes and joined together in a **teach-in.** They discussed the issues surrounding the war and reaffirmed their reasons for opposing it. The gathering inspired teach-ins at many campuses. In May 1965, 122 colleges held a "National Teach-In" by radio for more than 100,000 antiwar demonstrators.

People who opposed the war did so for different reasons. Some saw the conflict as a civil war in which the United States had no business interfering. Others viewed South Vietnam as a corrupt dictatorship and believed that defending it was immoral and unjust.

Anger at the Draft

Young protesters especially focused on what they saw as an unfair draft system. Until 1969, a college student was often able to defer military service until after graduation. By contrast, young people from working-class families were more likely to be drafted and sent to Vietnam because they were unable to afford college. Draftees in the military were most likely to be assigned to combat units where they faced grave dangers. In 1969 draftees made up 62 percent of battle deaths.

The majority of soldiers who served in Vietnam, however, were volunteer enlistees. Holding out the military as an avenue to vocational training and upward social mobility, military recruiters encouraged youth in poor and working-class communities to enlist. Thus, a **disproportionate** number of working-class youths, many of them minorities, were among the volunteers who served in Vietnam.

The Vietnam War coincided with the high tide of the civil rights movement. From early in the war, the treatment of African American soldiers came under scrutiny. Between 1961 and 1966, African Americans constituted about 10 percent of military personnel while African Americans comprised about 13 percent of the total population of the United States. Because African Americans were more likely to be assigned to combat units, however, they accounted for almost 20 percent of combat-related deaths.

The high number of African Americans and poor Americans dying in Vietnam angered African American leaders, including Dr. Martin Luther King, Jr. In April 1967 King publicly condemned the conflict:

PRIMARY SOURCE

"I speak for the poor of America who are paying the double price of smashed hopes at home and death and corruption in Vietnam. . . . The great initiative in this war is ours. The initiative to stop it must be ours."

—quoted in *A Testament of Hope*

In response to such criticisms, military officials strived to lower the number of African American casualties. By the end of the conflict, African Americans accounted for about 12 percent of America's dead, roughly equivalent to their presence in the national population.

As the war escalated, American officials increased the draft call, putting many college students at risk. An estimated 500,000 draftees refused to go. Many burned their draft cards or simply did not show up for induction. Some fled the country, moving to Canada, Sweden, or other nations. Others stayed and went to prison rather than fight in a war they opposed.

Between 1965 and 1968, officials prosecuted more than 3,300 Americans for refusing to serve. The draft became less of an issue in 1969 when the government introduced a lottery system, in which only those with low lottery numbers were subject to the draft.

Protests against the war were not confined to college campuses. Demonstrators held public rallies and marches in towns across the country. In April 1965 Students for a Democratic Society (SDS), a left-wing student organization, organized a march on Washington, D.C., that drew more than 20,000 participants. Two years later, in October 1967, a rally at Washington's Lincoln Memorial drew tens of thousands of protesters, as well.

Anger over the draft also fueled discussions about the voting age. Many draftees argued that if they were old enough to fight, they were old enough to vote. In 1971 the Twenty-sixth Amendment to the Constitution was ratified, giving all citizens age 18 and older the right to vote in all state and federal elections.

PRIMARY SOURCE
A Divided Nation

▲ An antiwar protest in New York City in 1969

▲ The war split the nation. Above, construction workers march in New York City in support of the war effort.

◄ Antiwar demonstrators burn their draft cards in front of the Pentagon in 1972.

Hawks and Doves

In the face of growing opposition to the war, President Johnson remained determined to continue fighting. He assailed his critics in Congress as "selfish men who want to advance their own interests." He dismissed the college protesters as too naive to appreciate the importance of resisting communism.

The president was not alone in his views. In a poll taken in early 1968, 53 percent of the respondents favored stronger military action in Vietnam, compared to 24 percent who wanted an end to the war. Of those Americans who supported the policy in Vietnam, many openly criticized the protesters for a lack of patriotism.

By 1968 the nation seemed to be divided into two camps. Those who wanted the United States to withdraw from Vietnam were known as **doves.** Those who insisted that the country stay and fight came to be known as **hawks.** As the two groups debated, the war appeared to take a dramatic turn for the worse, and the nation endured a year of shock and crisis.

✔ **Reading Check** **Explaining** What led to the ratification of the Twenty-sixth Amendment?

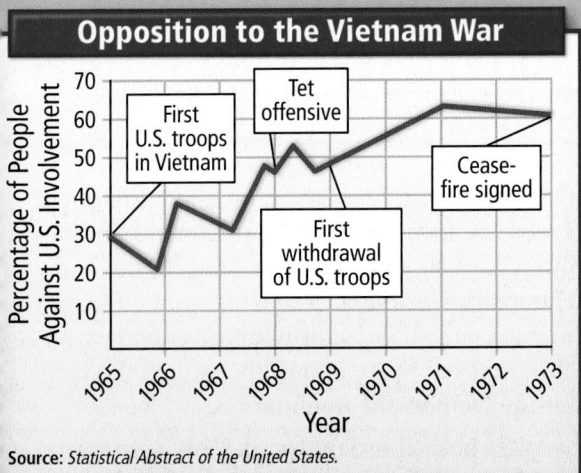

Opposition to the Vietnam War

Percentage of People Against U.S. Involvement

First U.S. troops in Vietnam

Tet offensive

First withdrawal of U.S. troops

Cease-fire signed

Year: 1965 1966 1967 1968 1969 1970 1971 1972 1973

Source: *Statistical Abstract of the United States.*

Analyzing VISUALS

1. **Interpreting** During which two years was opposition to the war lowest? What event occurred around that time?

2. **Synthesizing** In what year did opposition to the war peak? How was this sentiment logically related to the withdrawal of American troops?

1968: The Pivotal Year

MAIN Idea The Tet Offensive increased doubt that the United States could win in Vietnam.

HISTORY AND YOU Have you ever participated in a public-opinion poll? Read how Johnson's plummeting approval rating made him decide not to run for re-election in 1968.

The most turbulent year of the chaotic 1960s was 1968. The year saw a shocking political announcement, two traumatic assassinations, and a political convention held amid strident anti-war demonstrations. First, however, the nation endured a surprise attack in Vietnam.

The Tet Offensive

On January 30, 1968, during Tet, the Vietnamese New Year, the Vietcong and North Vietnamese launched a massive surprise attack. In this **Tet Offensive,** guerrilla fighters attacked most American airbases in South Vietnam and most of the South's major cities. Vietcong even blasted their way into the American embassy in Saigon.

Militarily, Tet was a disaster for the Vietcong. After about a month of fighting, the American and South Vietnamese soldiers repelled the enemy troops, inflicting heavy losses on them. President Johnson triumphantly noted that the enemy's effort had ended in "complete failure." Later, historians confirmed that Tet nearly destroyed the Vietcong.

The North Vietnamese, however, had scored a major political victory. The American people were shocked that an enemy supposedly on the verge of defeat could launch such a large-scale attack. When General Westmoreland requested 209,000 troops in addition to the 500,000 already in Vietnam, he seemed to be admitting the United States could not win.

To make matters worse, the media, which had tried to remain balanced in their war coverage, now openly criticized the effort. "The American people should be getting ready to accept, if they haven't already, the prospect that the whole Vietnam effort may be doomed," declared the *Wall Street Journal*. Television newscaster Walter Cronkite announced that it seemed "more certain than ever that the bloody experience in Vietnam is to end in a stalemate."

1968: A Year of Turmoil

The election year 1968 was tumultuous. The country was divided over Vietnam. President Johnson chose not to run again. Protesters fought with police at the Democratic National Convention. Race riots erupted in several American cities and both Martin Luther King, Jr., and Robert Kennedy were killed.

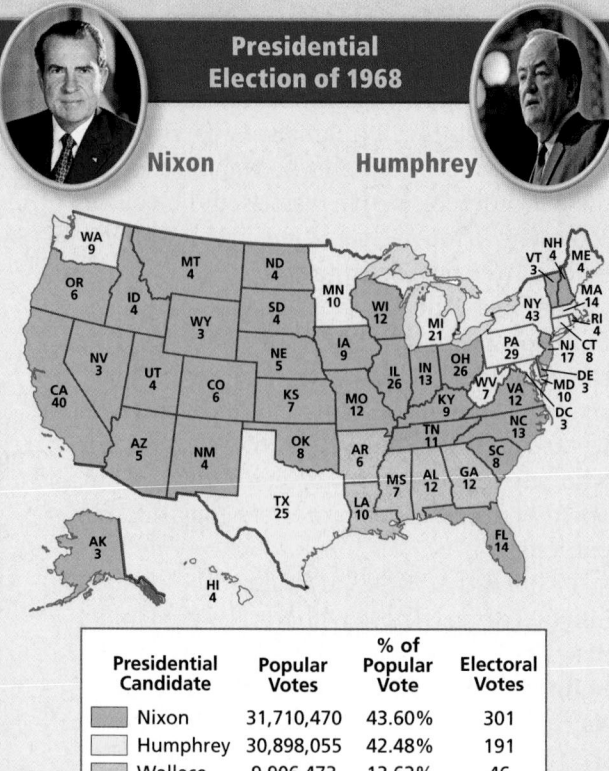

Presidential Election of 1968

Nixon   Humphrey

Presidential Candidate	Popular Votes	% of Popular Vote	Electoral Votes
Nixon	31,710,470	43.60%	301
Humphrey	30,898,055	42.48%	191
Wallace	9,906,473	13.62%	46

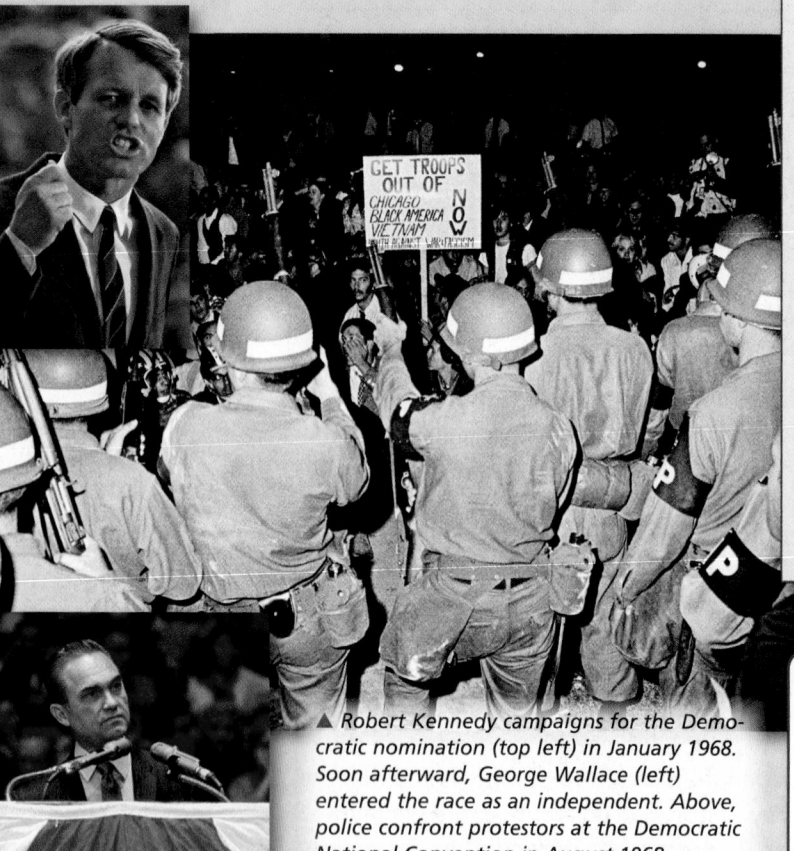

▲ Robert Kennedy campaigns for the Democratic nomination (top left) in January 1968. Soon afterward, George Wallace (left) entered the race as an independent. Above, police confront protestors at the Democratic National Convention in August 1968.

Analyzing VISUALS

1. **Regions** In what area of the country did George Wallace receive the most votes?

2. **Regions** Do you think Richard Nixon would have won if Wallace had not been in the race?

Public opinion no longer favored the president. In the weeks following the Tet Offensive, the president's approval rating plummeted to a dismal 35 percent, while support for his handling of the war fell even lower, to 26 percent. The administration's credibility gap now seemed too wide to repair.

Johnson Leaves the Race

With the war growing increasingly unpopular and Johnson's credibility all but gone, some Democrats began looking for an alternative candidate to nominate for president in 1968. In November 1967, even before the Tet disaster, a little-known liberal senator from Minnesota, Eugene McCarthy, became the first dove to declare he would challenge Johnson for the Democratic presidential nomination. In March 1968 McCarthy stunned the nation by winning more than 40 percent of the votes in the New Hampshire primary. Realizing that Johnson was vulnerable, Senator Robert Kennedy, who also opposed the war, quickly entered the race for the Democratic nomination.

With both the country and his own party deeply divided, Johnson addressed the public on television on March 31, 1968. He stunned viewers by announcing, "I have concluded that I should not permit the presidency to become involved in the partisan divisions that are developing in this political year. Accordingly, I shall not seek, and I will not accept, the nomination of my party for another term as your President."

A Season of Violence

Following Johnson's announcement, the nation endured even more shocking events. In April, James Earl Ray was arrested for killing Dr. Martin Luther King, Jr. Just two months later, another assassination rocked the country—that of Robert Kennedy. Kennedy, who appeared to be on his way to winning the Democratic nomination, was gunned down on June 5. The assassin was Sirhan Sirhan, an Arab nationalist angry over the candidate's pro-Israeli remarks a few nights before.

The violence that seemed to plague the country in 1968 culminated with a chaotic and well-publicized clash between antiwar protesters and police at the Democratic National Convention in Chicago. Thousands of protesters surrounded the convention center, demanding that the Democrats adopt an antiwar platform.

Despite the protests, the delegates chose Hubert Humphrey, President Johnson's vice president, as their presidential nominee. Meanwhile, in a park not far from the convention hall, the protesters and police began fighting. As officers tried to disperse demonstrators with tear gas and billy clubs, demonstrators taunted the authorities with the chant, "The whole world is watching!" A subsequent federal investigation of the incident described the event as a "police riot."

Nixon Wins the Presidency

The violence and chaos now associated with the Democratic Party benefited the 1968 Republican presidential candidate, Richard Nixon. Although defeated by John Kennedy in the 1960 election, Nixon had remained active in national politics. A third candidate, Governor George Wallace of Alabama, decided to run in 1968 as an independent. Wallace, an outspoken segregationist, sought to attract Americans who felt threatened by the civil rights movement and urban social unrest.

Public opinion polls gave Nixon a wide lead over Humphrey and Wallace. Nixon's campaign promise to unify the nation and restore law and order appealed to Americans who feared their country was spinning out of control. Nixon also declared that he had a plan for ending the war in Vietnam.

At first Humphrey's support of President Johnson's Vietnam policies hurt his campaign. After Humphrey broke with the president and called for a complete end to the bombing of North Vietnam, he began to move up in the polls. A week before the election, President Johnson helped Humphrey by announcing that the bombing had halted and that a cease-fire would follow.

Johnson's announcement had come too late, however. In the end, Nixon's promises to end the war and restore order at home were enough to sway the American people. On Election Day, Nixon defeated Humphrey by more than 100 electoral votes, although he won the popular vote by a slim margin of 43 percent to 42 percent. Wallace partially accounted for the razor-thin margin by winning 46 electoral votes and more than 13 percent of the popular vote.

Reading Check **Explaining** Why did President Johnson say he would not run for reelection in 1968?

Section 2 REVIEW

Vocabulary

1. **Explain** the significance of: William Westmoreland, credibility gap, teach-in, dove, hawk, Tet Offensive.

Main Ideas

2. **Explaining** Why did some people view the draft as unfair?

3. **Summarizing** What are three important events that made 1968 such a violent year in the United States?

Critical Thinking

4. **Big Ideas** Why did support of the war dwindle by the late 1960s?

5. **Organizing** Use a graphic organizer similar to the one below to list the effects of the Tet Offensive.

Effects of Tet Offensive

6. **Analyzing Visuals** Study the cartoon on the right on page 893. What is the message of the telegram beyond its literal meaning?

Writing About History

7. **Expository Writing** Suppose that you are living in 1968. Write a letter to the editor of a local newspaper in which you explain your reasons for either supporting or opposing the Vietnam War.

History ONLINE

Study Central™ To review this section, go to glencoe.com and click on Study Central.

Section 3

The War Winds Down

Guide to Reading

Big Ideas

Trade, War, and Migration
The Vietnam War changed the way Americans viewed the government and the military, and led them to question how the armed forces were deployed.

Content Vocabulary
- linkage *(p. 898)*
- Vietnamization *(p. 898)*

Academic Vocabulary
- generation *(p. 899)*
- unresolved *(p. 903)*

People and Events to Identify
- Henry Kissinger *(p. 898)*
- Pentagon Papers *(p. 900)*
- War Powers Act *(p. 903)*

Reading Strategy

Organizing Complete a graphic organizer similar to the one below by listing the steps that President Nixon took to end American involvement in Vietnam.

Steps Nixon Took

NEW YORK CORE CURRICULUM
U.S. History and Government

Unit 7:	
IV.A.5	Student protests at home
IV.A.6.d	Impact of the Vietnam War on society
V.A.2.1.(1)	Withdrawal from Vietnam and Cambodia; peace talks and signing of Paris Peace Accords (Pentagon papers, *New York Times* v. *United States*, 1971)
V.B.3.a	Fall of South Vietnam, 1975

Shortly after taking office, President Nixon moved to end the nation's involvement in the Vietnam War. The final years of the conflict, however, yielded more bloodshed and turmoil, as well as a growing cynicism in the minds of Americans about the honesty and effectiveness of the United States government.

Nixon Moves to End the War

MAIN Idea While unrest and suspicion of the government grew, the United States finally withdrew its troops from Vietnam.

HISTORY AND YOU Have you ever protested against something you felt was wrong? Read on to find out how college students reacted to what they viewed as a widening of the Vietnam War.

As a first step to fulfilling his campaign promise to end the war, Nixon appointed Harvard professor **Henry Kissinger** as special assistant for national security affairs and gave him wide authority to use diplomacy to end the conflict. Kissinger embarked upon a policy he called **linkage,** which meant improving relations with the Soviet Union and China—suppliers of aid to North Vietnam—so that he could persuade them to cut back on their aid.

Kissinger also rekindled peace talks with the North Vietnamese. In August 1969 Kissinger entered into secret negotiations with North Vietnam's negotiator, Le Duc Tho. In their talks, which dragged on for four years, Kissinger and Le Duc Tho argued over a possible cease-fire, the return of American prisoners of war, and the ultimate fate of South Vietnam.

Meanwhile, Nixon reduced the number of American troops in Vietnam. Known as **Vietnamization,** this process involved the gradual withdrawal of U.S. troops while the South Vietnamese assumed more of the fighting. On June 8, 1969, Nixon announced the withdrawal of 25,000 soldiers, but he was determined to keep a strong American presence in Vietnam to ensure bargaining power during peace negotiations. In support of that goal, the president increased air strikes against North Vietnam and—without informing Congress or the public—began secretly bombing Vietcong sanctuaries in neighboring Cambodia.

Turmoil at Home Continues

Even though the United States had begun scaling back its involvement in Vietnam, the American home front remained divided and volatile, as Nixon's war policies stirred up new waves of protest.

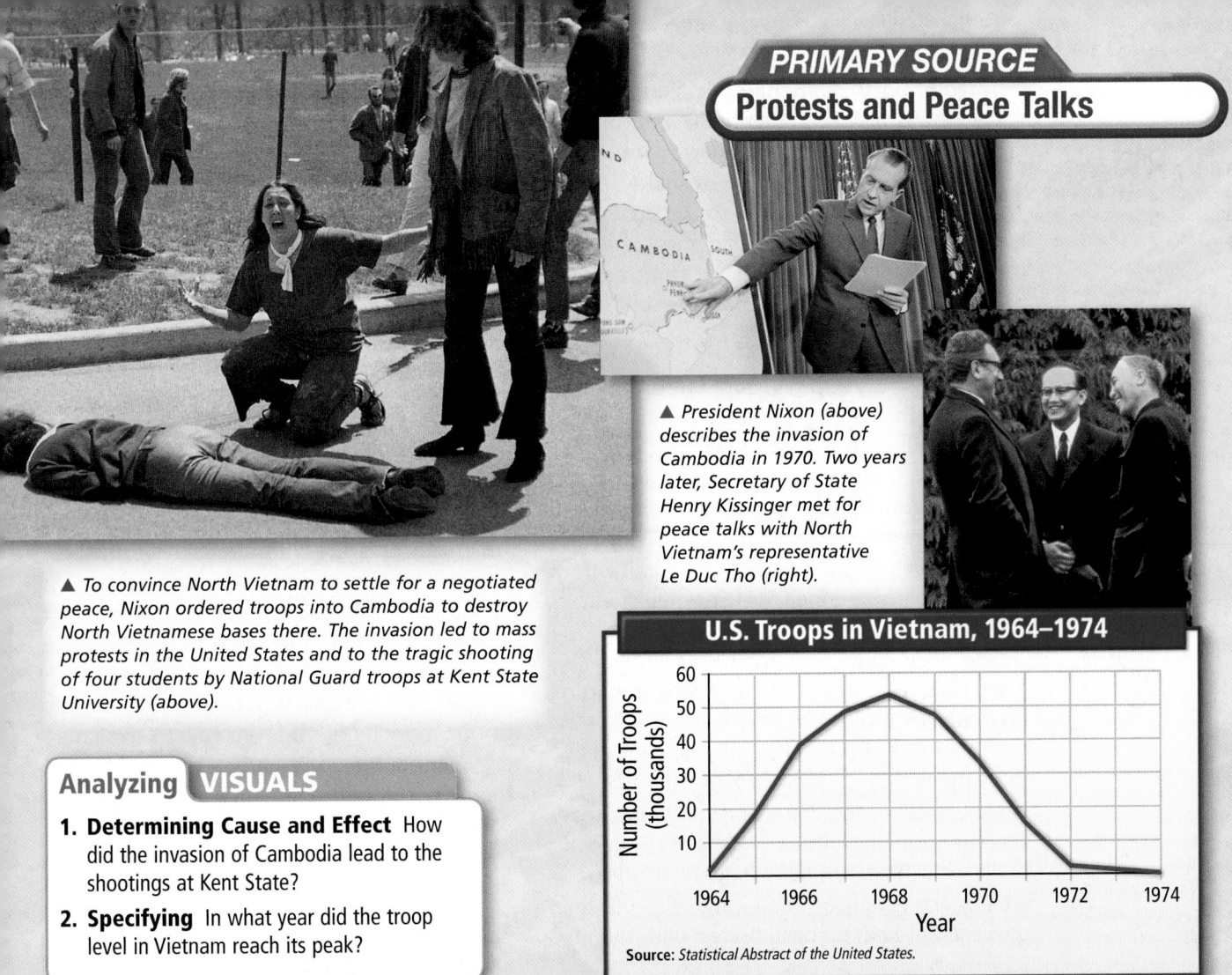

▲ President Nixon (above) describes the invasion of Cambodia in 1970. Two years later, Secretary of State Henry Kissinger met for peace talks with North Vietnam's representative Le Duc Tho (right).

▲ To convince North Vietnam to settle for a negotiated peace, Nixon ordered troops into Cambodia to destroy North Vietnamese bases there. The invasion led to mass protests in the United States and to the tragic shooting of four students by National Guard troops at Kent State University (above).

U.S. Troops in Vietnam, 1964–1974

Source: Statistical Abstract of the United States.

Analyzing VISUALS

1. **Determining Cause and Effect** How did the invasion of Cambodia lead to the shootings at Kent State?

2. **Specifying** In what year did the troop level in Vietnam reach its peak?

Massacre at My Lai In late 1969 Americans learned that, in the spring of 1968, an American platoon under the command of Lieutenant William Calley had massacred unarmed South Vietnamese civilians in the hamlet of My Lai. Most of the victims were old men, women, and children. Calley eventually went to prison for his role in the killings.

Most American soldiers acted responsibly and honorably during the war. The actions of a small group, however, convinced many people that the war was brutal and senseless. Jan Barry, a founder of the Vietnam Veterans Against the War, viewed My Lai as a symbol of the dilemma his **generation** faced in the conflict:

PRIMARY SOURCE

"To kill on military orders and be a criminal, or to refuse to kill and be a criminal is the moral agony of America's Vietnam war generation. It is what has forced upward of sixty thousand young Americans, draft resisters and deserters to Canada, and created one hundred thousand military deserters a year. . . ."

—quoted in *Who Spoke Up?*

The Invasion of Cambodia Sparks Protest Americans heard more startling news when Nixon announced in April 1970 that American troops had invaded Cambodia. The troops were ordered to destroy Vietcong military bases there.

Many viewed the Cambodian invasion as a widening of the war, and it set off many protests. At Kent State University on May 4, 1970, Ohio National Guard soldiers, armed with tear gas and rifles, fired on demonstrators without an order to do so. The soldiers killed four students. Ten days later, police killed two African American students during a demonstration at Jackson State College in Mississippi.

In addition to sparking violence on campuses, the invasion of Cambodia cost Nixon significant congressional support. Numerous legislators expressed outrage over the president's failure to notify them of the action. In December 1970 an angry Congress repealed the Gulf of Tonkin Resolution, which had given the president nearly complete power in directing the war in Vietnam.

The Pentagon Papers Support for the war weakened further in 1971 when Daniel Ellsberg, a disillusioned former Defense Department worker, leaked what became known as the **Pentagon Papers** to the *New York Times.* The documents revealed that many government officials during the Johnson administration privately questioned the war while publicly defending it.

The documents contained details of decisions that were made by the presidents and their advisers to expand the war without the consent of Congress. They also showed how the various administrations had tried to convince Congress, the press, and the public that the situation in Vietnam was better than it really was. The Pentagon Papers confirmed what many Americans had long believed: the government had not been honest with them.

The United States Pulls Out

By 1971, polls showed that nearly two-thirds of Americans wanted to end the Vietnam War as quickly as possible. In April 1972 President Nixon dropped his longtime insistence that North Vietnamese troops had to withdraw from South Vietnam before any peace treaty could be signed. In October, less than a month before the presidential election, Kissinger emerged from his secret talks with Le Duc Tho to announce that "peace is at hand."

A month later, Americans went to the polls to decide on a president. Senator George McGovern, the Democratic candidate, was an outspoken critic of the war. He did not appeal to many middle-class Americans, however, who were tired of antiwar protesters. Nixon was reelected in a landslide, winning 60.7 percent of the popular vote.

Just weeks after the presidential election, the peace negotiations broke down. South Vietnam's president, Nguyen Van Thieu, refused to agree to any plan that left North Vietnamese troops in the South. Henry Kissinger tried to win additional concessions from the Communists, but talks broke off on December 16, 1972.

The next day, to force North Vietnam to resume negotiations, the Nixon administration began the most destructive air raids of the entire war. In what became known as the "Christmas bombings," American B-52s dropped thousands of tons of bombs on North Vietnamese targets for 11 straight days, pausing only on Christmas Day.

In the wake of the bombing campaign, the United States and North Vietnam returned to the bargaining table. Thieu finally gave in to American pressure and allowed North Vietnamese troops to remain in the South. On January 27, 1973, the warring sides signed an agreement "ending the war and restoring the peace in Vietnam."

The United States promised to withdraw its troops, and both sides agreed to exchange prisoners of war. The parties did not resolve the issue of South Vietnam's future, however. After almost eight years of war—the longest war in American history—the nation ended its direct involvement in Vietnam.

South Vietnam Falls

Two years after the United States pulled its troops out of Vietnam, the peace agreement collapsed. In March 1975 the North Vietnamese army launched a full-scale invasion of the South. Thieu desperately appealed to Washington, D.C., for help.

President Nixon had assured Thieu during the peace negotiations that the United States "[would] respond with full force should the settlement be violated by North Vietnam." Nixon, however, had resigned under pressure following Watergate, a scandal that broke as the war was winding down. The new president, Gerald Ford, asked for funds to aid the South Vietnamese, but Congress refused.

Without American assistance, the South Vietnamese Army was unable to stop the invasion. On April 30, the North Vietnamese captured Saigon, South Vietnam's capital, and united Vietnam under Communist rule. They then renamed the city Ho Chi Minh City.

Reading Check **Evaluating** What did the Pentagon Papers confirm for many Americans?

Can the Government Put Limits on the Press?

★ *New York Times* v. *United States*, 1971

Background to the Case

In 1971 Daniel Ellsberg leaked classified documents, known as the Pentagon Papers, to the *New York Times* and the *Washington Post*. When the newspapers attempted to publish these documents, the Nixon administration argued that publication would threaten national security. The case centered on the First Amendment guarantee of a free press.

How the Court Ruled

In a 6-to-3 per curiam opinion—*per curiam* meaning that the decision was issued by the whole Court and not specific justices—the Court found that the Nixon administration had failed to prove that publication of the Pentagon Papers would imperil the nation in any way. The *New York Times* and the *Washington Post* could publish the Pentagon Papers.

▲ Daniel Ellsberg (above, left) leaked the classified documents known as the Pentagon Papers.

PRIMARY SOURCE

Concurring View

"The Government's power to censor the press [via the First Amendment] was abolished so that the press would remain forever free to censure the Government.... And paramount among the responsibilities of a free press is the duty to prevent any part of the government from deceiving the people and sending them off to distant lands to die of foreign fevers and foreign shot and shell. In my view, far from deserving condemnation for their courageous reporting, the *New York Times*, the *Washington Post*, and other newspapers should be commended for serving the purpose that the Founding Fathers saw so clearly. In revealing the workings of government that led to the Vietnam War, the newspapers did precisely that which the Founders hoped and trusted they would do."

—Justice Hugo Black in *New York Times* v. *United States*

PRIMARY SOURCE

Dissenting View

The First Amendment, after all, is only one part of an entire Constitution. Article II of the great document vests in the Executive Branch primary power over the conduct of foreign affairs and places in that branch the responsibility for the Nation's safety.... What is needed here is a weighing, upon properly developed standards, of the broad right of the press to print and of the very narrow right of the Government to prevent. Such standards are not yet developed. The parties here are in disagreement as to what those standards should be. But even the newspapers concede that there are situations where restraint is in order and is constitutional."

—Justice Harry Blackmun, dissenting in *New York Times* v. *United States*

DBQ Document-Based Questions

1. **Explaining** Why did Justice Black agree with the Court's decision? What did he imply about the government's actions?

2. **Contrasting** Why did Justice Blackmun disagree with the Court's decision?

3. **Assessing** Do you think the government can ever justify media censorship, even based on national security concerns? Explain.

The Legacy of Vietnam

MAIN Idea The Vietnam War made a negative impact on the way in which Americans viewed international conflicts, as well as their own government.

HISTORY AND YOU Do you think that leaders at the highest levels of the federal government are trustworthy? Read on to find out how the Vietnam War and other events led Americans to lose some trust in their leaders.

History ONLINE
Student Web Activity Visit glencoe.com and complete the activity on the Vietnam Veterans Memorial.

"The lessons of the past in Vietnam," President Ford declared in 1975, "have already been learned—learned by Presidents, learned by Congress, learned by the American people—and we should have our focus on the future." Vietnam had a deep and lasting impact on American society.

The War's Human Toll

The United States paid a heavy price for its involvement in Vietnam. The war had cost the nation over $170 billion in direct costs and much more in indirect economic expenses. It had also resulted in the deaths of approximately 58,000 young Americans and the injury of more than 300,000. In Vietnam, around one million North and South Vietnamese soldiers died in the conflict, as did countless civilians.

PRIMARY SOURCE
The Legacy of Vietnam

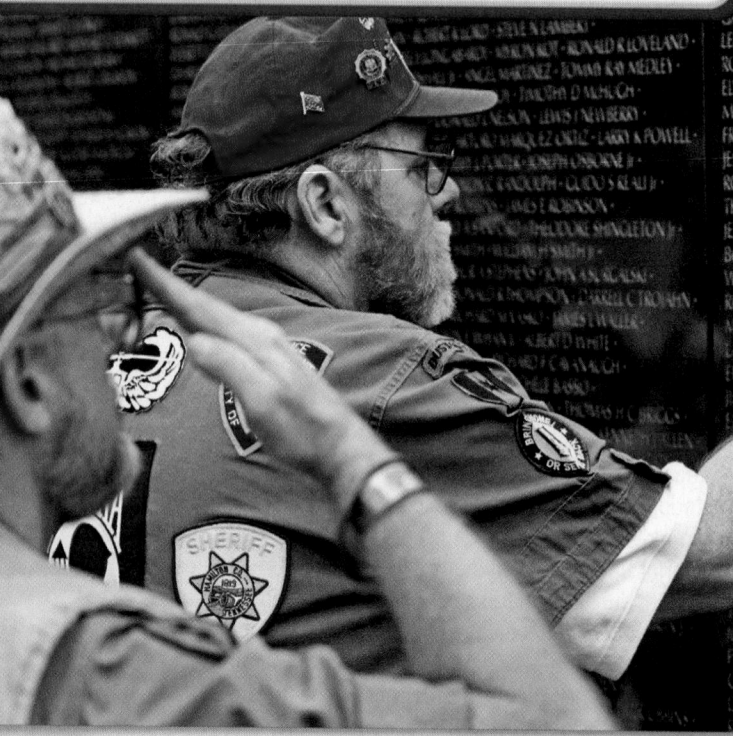

The War Powers Act

- Requires the president in all cases to consult with Congress before making any troop commitments

- Requires the president to inform Congress of any commitment of troops abroad within 48 hours

- Requires the president to withdraw troops in 60 to 90 days, unless Congress explicitly approves the troop commitment

▲ The Vietnam Veterans Memorial is inscribed with the names of the 58,249 people killed or missing in Vietnam.

▲ Along with returning troops, many freed prisoners of war, or POWs, such as Lt. Colonel Robert Stirm, were joyfully greeted by their families. Sadly, some did not come home and were labeled as MIAs, or "missing in action," and remain so to this day.

Analyzing VISUALS

1. **Explaining** How did the War Powers Act seek to curb the power of the president?

2. **Assessing** Do you think that the legacy of Vietnam has been a lasting one? Why or why not?

Even after they returned home from fighting as in other wars, soldiers found it hard to escape the war's psychological impact. Army Specialist Doug Johnson recalled the problems he faced:

PRIMARY SOURCE

"It took a while for me to recognize that I did suffer some psychological problems in trying to deal with my experience in Vietnam. The first recollection I have of the effect took place shortly after I arrived back in the States. One evening . . . I went to see a movie on post. I don't recall the name of the movie or what it was about, but I remember there was a sad part, and that I started crying uncontrollably. It hadn't dawned on me before this episode that I had. . . succeeded in burying my emotions."

—quoted in *Touched by the Dragon*

One reason why it may have been harder for some Vietnam veterans to readjust to civilian life was that many considered the war a defeat. Many Americans wanted to forget the war. Thus, the sacrifices of many veterans often went unrecognized. There were relatively few welcome-home parades and celebrations after the war.

The war also remained **unresolved** for the American families whose relatives and friends were classified as prisoners of war (POWs) or missing in action (MIA). Despite many official investigations, these families were not convinced that the government had told the truth about POW/MIA policies.

The nation finally began to come to terms with the war almost a decade later. In 1982 the nation dedicated the Vietnam Veterans Memorial in Washington, D.C., a large black granite wall inscribed with the names of those killed and missing in action in the war. "It's a first step to remind America of what we did," veteran Larry Cox of Virginia said at the dedication of the monument.

The War's Impact on the Nation

The war also left its mark on the nation as a whole. In 1973 Congress passed the **War Powers Act** as a way to reestablish some limits on executive power. The act required the president to inform Congress of any commitment of troops abroad within 48 hours, and to withdraw them in 60 to 90 days, unless Congress explicitly approved the troop commitment. No president has recognized this limitation, and the courts have tended to avoid the issue as a strictly political question. Nonetheless, every president since the law's passage has asked Congress to authorize the use of military force before committing ground troops to combat. In general, the war shook the nation's confidence and led some to embrace isolationism, while others began to question the policy of containing communism and instead urged more negotiation with the Soviet Union.

On the domestic front, the Vietnam War increased Americans' cynicism about their government. Many felt the nation's leaders had misled them. Together with Watergate, Vietnam made Americans more wary of their leaders.

Reading Check **Describing** How did the Vietnam War affect Americans' attitudes toward international conflicts?

Section 3 REVIEW

Vocabulary

1. **Explain** the significance of: Henry Kissinger, linkage, Vietnamization, Pentagon Papers, War Powers Act.

Main Ideas

2. **Explaining** Why was the United States unable to help South Vietnam following the full-scale invasion by North Vietnam in 1975?

3. **Describing** How was the aftermath of the Vietnam War different for its veterans than postwar periods had been for veterans of earlier U.S. wars?

Critical Thinking

4. **Big Ideas** Why did Congress pass the War Powers Act? How did it reflect distrust of the executive branch of government?

5. **Organizing** Use a graphic organizer similar to the one below to list the effects of the Vietnam War on the nation.

Effects of Vietnam War

6. **Analyzing Visuals** Study the left photo on page 902. Why do you think it is important for society to have war memorials?

Writing About History

7. **Descriptive Writing** Suppose you are a college student in 1970. Write a journal entry expressing your feelings about the events at Kent State University and Jackson State College.

History ONLINE

Study Central™ To review this section, go to glencoe.com and click on Study Central.

Causes of the Vietnam War

- During World War II, the United States helps the people of Indochina fight the Japanese, who had invaded the region.
- After World War II, France refuses to give independence to the people of Indochina and sends troops to reestablish control.
- Led by Ho Chi Minh, the Vietminh fight the French. Ho Chi Minh wants Vietnam to be independent but also wants to build a Communist society in Vietnam.
- Concerned about the spread of communism, President Eisenhower sends aid to help the French retain control in Vietnam.
- After losing the battle of Dien Bien Phu, France pulls out of Vietnam. The Geneva Accords create North and South Vietnam.
- Ho Chi Minh becomes the leader of North Vietnam and makes it a Communist nation allied with the USSR and China. North Vietnam begins arming guerrillas to fight the South Vietnamese government.
- American leaders become worried that a "domino effect" might cause all of Southeast Asia to fall to communism if South Vietnam falls.
- President Kennedy sharply increases military aid to South Vietnam.
- President Johnson escalates U.S. involvement and gains war powers after the Gulf of Tonkin incident.

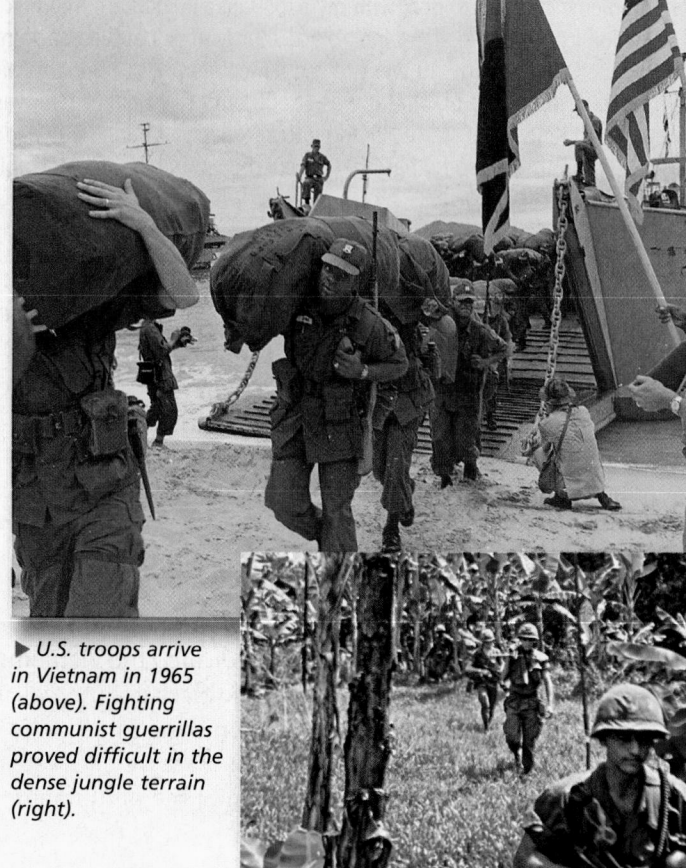

▶ U.S. troops arrive in Vietnam in 1965 (above). Fighting communist guerrillas proved difficult in the dense jungle terrain (right).

▲ The Vietnam Veterans Memorial in Washington, D.C., is a stark reminder of the costs of the Vietnam War.

Effects of the Vietnam War

- Americans applaud President Johnson's response to a Vietcong attack with aggressive air strikes.
- The United States commits over 380,000 ground troops to fighting in Vietnam by the end of 1966.
- American people question the government's honesty about the war, creating the so-called "credibility gap."
- The war casualties and the unfair draft system cause civil unrest.
- The wartime economy hurts domestic spending for programs such as the Great Society.
- President Nixon is elected largely on promises to end the war and unite a divided country.
- Congress passes the War Powers Act to limit the power of the president during wartime.

NEW YORK REGENTS EXAM PRACTICE

TEST-TAKING TIP

Do not spend too much time trying to figure out the right answer. Move on, and then come back to that question when you have answered all the questions you do know. If you still do not know the answer, select the one that you think is the most logical.

Part I

Directions (1–11): For each statement or question, write on a separate sheet of paper the number of the word or expression that, of those given, best completes the statement or answers the question.

1 Who was the leader of the North Vietnamese?

(1) Mao Zedong

(2) Ho Chi Minh

(3) Dien Bien Phu

(4) Ngo Dinh Diem

2 President Johnson did not order a full-scale attack on North Vietnam because

(1) he did not think that the U.S. could win.

(2) the military lacked the manpower to launch an assault.

(3) he did not want to bring China into the war.

(4) he did not want to lose the 1968 election.

3 Many Americans objected to the draft because it

(1) forced young men to flee to Canada.

(2) unfairly targeted the poor and minorities.

(3) did not include women.

(4) did not raise the necessary number of troops.

4 Which of the following events was significant in turning American public opinion against the war in Vietnam?

(1) the National Teach-in

(2) the 1968 Democratic National Convention

(3) the assassination of President Kennedy

(4) the Tet Offensive

5 The gradual removal of U.S. troops from Vietnam was known as

(1) Agent Orange.

(2) containment.

(3) linkage.

(4) Vietnamization.

6 Which of the following was part of the legacy of the Vietnam War?

(1) Americans' increased cynicism about their government

(2) Americans' belief that the policy of containment worked

(3) Americans' confidence that the United States would win the Cold War

(4) Americans' paranoia about the intentions of the North Vietnamese government

7 Why is the Gulf of Tonkin Resolution important?

(1) It authorized the use of force in Vietnam.

(2) It ordered U.S. forces to withdraw from Vietnam.

(3) It divided Vietnam into two countries.

(4) It required the president to consult Congress before committing troops.

8 The purpose of the War Powers Act was to ensure that the president would

(1) have greater authority over the military.

(2) consult Congress before committing troops in extended conflicts.

(3) have the authority to sign treaties without Senate approval.

(4) have a freer hand in fighting the spread of communism.

Need Extra Help?								
If You Missed Questions . . .	1	2	3	4	5	6	7	8
Go to Page . . .	882	886	895	895–896	898	902–903	886	903

[OVER]

Base your answer to question 9 on the map below and on your knowledge of Chapter 26.

The Vietnam War

9 The Ho Chi Minh Trail ran through which two nations?

(1) Laos and Japan

(2) Laos and Thailand

(3) Laos and China

(4) Laos and Cambodia

10 The Twenty-sixth Amendment says that

(1) women may serve in the armed forces.

(2) the president, not Congress, should decide where and when troops will fight.

(3) a person who is old enough to fight is old enough to vote.

(4) a draft is a poor system for selecting soldiers.

11 Which of the following temporarily established North and South Vietnam and recognized Cambodia's independence?

(1) the Treaty of Paris

(2) Gulf of Tonkin Resolution

(3) the Truman Doctrine

(4) the Geneva Accords

Need Extra Help?			
If You Missed Questions . . .	9	10	11
Go to Page . . .	R15	894–895	884

Part II Thematic Essay Question

Directions: Write a well-organized essay that includes an introduction, several paragraphs addressing the task below, and a conclusion.

Theme: Television and the Vietnam War

The conflict in Vietnam has been called the first "television war." For the first time, Americans could watch scenes of death and destruction unfold in front of them from their living rooms.

Task:

• Describe how the television coverage of the Vietnam War contributed to its unpopularity

• Evaluate the long-term effects of television on the public's views on war, including the effect of television on the current conflict in Iraq

Guidelines:

In your essay, be sure to:

• Develop all aspects of the task

• Support the theme with relevant facts, examples, and details

• Use a logical and clear plan of organization, including an introduction and a conclusion that are beyond a restatement of the theme

Part III Document-Based Question

This question is based on the accompanying documents. It is designed to test your ability to work with historical documents. Some of the documents have been edited for the purposes of the question. As you analyze the documents, take into account both the source of each document and any point of view that may be presented in the document.

Historical Context:

During the 1960s political pressures in the United States led to a deep involvement in the civil war between Communist and non-Communist forces in Vietnam. However, as casualties mounted in Vietnam, many Americans began to protest publicly against the war and to demand that the United States pull out of the conflict.

ASSESSMENT

Task:
Using information from the documents and your knowledge of United States history, answer the questions that follow each document in Part A. Your answers to the questions will help you write the Part B essay, in which you will be asked to

- Discuss the political circumstances that led to U.S. involvement in the Vietnam conflict
- Discuss public reaction to the war, both in support of U.S. involvement and against it
- Evaluate the long-term social and political effects of the Vietnam war on the nation

Part A
Short-Answer Questions
Directions: Analyze the documents and answer the short-answer questions that follow each document on a separate sheet of paper.

Document 1

"I read a lot of pacifist literature to determine whether or not I was a conscientious objector. I finally concluded that I wasn't....

The one clear decision I made in 1968 about me and the war was that if I was going to get out of it, I was going to get out in a legal way. I was not going to defraud the system in order to beat the system. I wasn't going to leave the country, because the odds of coming back looked real slim....

With all my terror of going into the Army ... there was something seductive about it, too. I was seduced by World War II and John Wayne movies.... I had been, as we all were, victimized by a romantic, truly uninformed view of war."

Source: Mark Baker, *Nam*, Berkley, 1983

1 What options did the young man have regarding going to war?

2 Do you think World War II movies gave him a realistic view of what fighting in Vietnam would be like?

Document 2

Source: *Washington Daily News*

3 What opinion is the cartoonist expressing as Johnson and his aides find their way through the dark tunnel?

Part B
Essay
Directions: Reread the task box at the top left and write a well-organized essay that includes an introduction, several paragraphs, and a conclusion. Use evidence from the documents in your essay. Support your response with relevant facts, examples, and details. Include additional outside information.

Guidelines:
In your essay, be sure to:
- Develop all aspects of the task
- Incorporate information from the documents
- Incorporate relevant outside information
- Support the theme with relevant facts, examples, and details
- Use a logical and clear plan of organization, including an introduction and a conclusion that are beyond a restatement of the theme

For additional test practice, use Self-Check Quizzes—Chapter 26 at glencoe.com.

Need Extra Help?				
If You Missed Questions . . .	1	2	3	Essay
Go to Page . . .	R19	R19	R18	R8

The Politics of Protest

1960–1980

SECTION 1 Students and the Counterculture

SECTION 2 The Feminist Movement

SECTION 3 Latino Americans Organize

▲ César Chávez leads a march in Delano, California, in 1966.

1962
• *Silent Spring* is published

Eisenhower 1953–1961

Kennedy 1961–1963

1963
• *The Feminine Mystique* is published

Johnson 1963–1969

1966
• National Organization for Women and United Farm Workers organized

Nixon 1969–1974

U.S. PRESIDENTS

U.S. EVENTS

1960

1965

1970

WORLD EVENTS

1962
• Cuban missile crisis

1964
• China becomes world's fifth nuclear power

1968
• Soviet Union halts democratic uprising in Czechoslovakia

Can Protests Bring Change?

The civil rights movement that began in the 1950s inspired other groups in American society to stage protests in the 1960s and 1970s. Students, women, and Latinos all formed organizations and began demanding changes in how American society treated them. Instead of trying to lobby legislatures or educate voters, all of these groups used mass protests and demonstrations to draw attention to their cause.

- *Why do you think these groups decided to use public protests to achieve change?*
- *How has society changed for students, women, and Latinos?*

1973
- *Roe* v. *Wade* decision on abortion
- Native Americans clash with FBI at Wounded Knee

Ford
1974–1977

Carter
1977–1981

1979
- Nuclear accident at Three Mile Island

1975

1980

1975
- Last European colonies in Africa gain independence from Portugal

1979
- Ayatollah Khomeini leads revolution against the Shah of Iran

FOLDABLES™

Organizing Information Make a Four-Door Book Foldable about the Berkeley Free Speech Movement, Students for a Democratic Society (SDS), or the National Organization for Women. As you read, complete the Four-Door Book by answering the questions *who, what, when,* and *why*.

Who | What

When | Why

History ONLINE Chapter Overview
Visit glencoe.com to preview Chapter 27.

Students and the Counterculture

Guide to Reading

Big Ideas
Struggles for Rights During the 1960s, many of the country's young people raised their voices in protest against numerous aspects of American society.

Content Vocabulary
- counterculture *(p. 912)*
- hippies *(p. 912)*
- communes *(p. 913)*

Academic Vocabulary
- rationality *(p. 912)*
- conformity *(p. 913)*

People and Events to Identify
- Port Huron Statement *(p. 911)*
- Tom Hayden *(p. 911)*
- Free Speech Movement *(p. 911)*
- Haight-Ashbury district *(p. 913)*
- Woodstock *(p. 913)*
- Bob Dylan *(p. 913)*

Reading Strategy
Organizing Use the major headings of this section to create an outline similar to the one below.

Students and the Counterculture
I. The Rise of the Youth Movement
   A.
   B.
II.
   A.
   B.

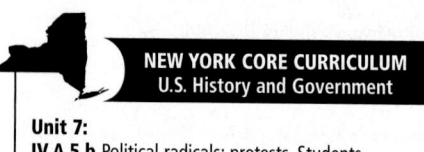

NEW YORK CORE CURRICULUM
U.S. History and Government

Unit 7:
IV.A.5.b Political radicals: protests, Students for a Democratic Society (SDS), antiwar
IV.A.5.c Cultural radicals: hippies and communalists

The 1960s was one of the most tumultuous decades in American history. The decade also gave birth to a youth movement that challenged the American political and social system and conventional middle-class values.

The Rise of the Youth Movement

MAIN Idea The youth protest movement of the 1960s included Students for a Democratic Society and the Free Speech Movement.

HISTORY AND YOU Do you know of any groups that work to improve society? Read how the youth of the 1960s protested social injustice.

The roots of the 1960s youth movement stretched back to the 1950s. In the decade after World War II, the country had enjoyed a time of peace and prosperity. Prosperity did not extend to all, however, and some, especially the artists and writers of the beat movement, had openly criticized American society. They believed American society valued conformity over independence and financial gain over spiritual and social advancement.

At the same time, the turmoil of the civil rights movement had raised serious questions about racism in American society, and the nuclear arms race between the United States and the Soviet Union made many of the nation's youth uneasy about the future. For many young people, the events of the 1950s had called into question the wisdom of their parents and their political leaders.

The youth movement originated with the baby boomers, the huge generation born after World War II. By 1970, 58.4 percent of the American population was 34 years old or younger. (By comparison, those 34 or younger in 2000 represented an estimated 48.9 percent.) The early 1960s also saw a rapid increase in enrollment at colleges. The economic boom of the 1950s meant more families could afford to send their children to college. Between 1960 and 1966, enrollment in four-year colleges rose from 3.1 million to almost 5 million. College life gave young people a sense of freedom and independence. It also allowed them to meet and bond with others who shared their feelings about society and fears about the future. It was on college campuses across the nation that youth protest movements began and reached their peak.

Students for a Democratic Society

Some young people were concerned most about the injustices they saw in the country's political and social system. In their view, a small wealthy elite controlled politics, and wealth itself was unfairly

The Student Movement

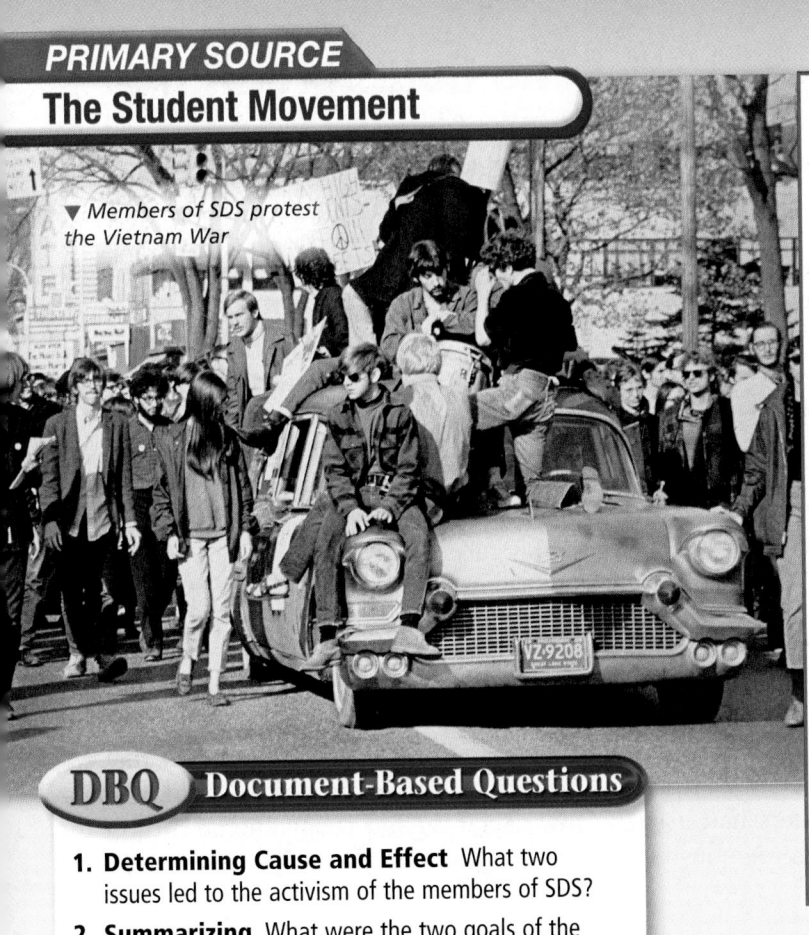

▼ Members of SDS protest the Vietnam War

In 1962 Students for a Democratic Society issued the Port Huron Statement explaining SDS and the reasons for their actions:

"We are people of this generation, bred in at least modest comfort, housed now in universities, looking uncomfortably to the world we inherit. . . .

When we were kids the United States was the wealthiest and strongest country in the world . . . Freedom and equality for each individual, government of, by, and for the people—these American values we found good. . . .

As we grew, however, our comfort was penetrated by events too troubling to dismiss. First, the permeating and victimizing fact of human degradation, symbolized by the Southern struggle against racial bigotry, compelled most of us from silence to activism. Second, the enclosing fact of the Cold War, symbolized by the presence of the Bomb, brought awareness that we ourselves, and our friends, and millions of abstract 'others' . . . might die at any time.

. . . Our work is guided by the sense that we may be the last generation in the experiment with living. . . . The search for truly democratic alternatives to the present, and a commitment to social experimentation with them, is a worthy and fulfilling human enterprise, one which moves us and, we hope, others today.

—from the *Port Huron Statement*, 1962

DBQ Document-Based Questions

1. **Determining Cause and Effect** What two issues led to the activism of the members of SDS?

2. **Summarizing** What were the two goals of the group?

---

divided. These young people formed what came to be known as the New Left. (The "new" left differed from the "old" left of the 1930s, which had advocated socialism and communism.)

A prominent organization within the New Left was Students for a Democratic Society (SDS), founded in 1959. It defined its views in a 1962 declaration known as the **Port Huron Statement.** Written largely by **Tom Hayden,** editor of the University of Michigan's student newspaper, the declaration called for an end to apathy and urged citizens to stop accepting a country run by big corporations and big government.

SDS chapters focused on protesting the Vietnam War, but they also addressed other issues, including poverty, campus regulations, nuclear power, and racism. In 1968, for example, SDS leaders assisted in an eight-day occupation of several buildings at Columbia University to protest the administration's plan to build a new gym in an area that had served as a neighborhood park near Harlem.

The Free Speech Movement

Another movement that captured the nation's attention in the 1960s was the **Free Speech Movement,** led by Mario Savio and others at the University of California at Berkeley. The movement began when the university decided, in the fall of 1964, to restrict students' rights to distribute literature and to recruit volunteers for political causes on campus. The protesters, however, quickly targeted more general campus matters as well.

Like many college students, those at Berkeley were dissatisfied with practices at their university. Officials divided huge classes into sections taught by graduate students, while many professors claimed they were too busy with research to meet with students. Faceless administrators made rules that were not always easy to obey and imposed punishments for violations. Feeling isolated in this impersonal environment, many Berkeley students rallied to support the Free Speech Movement.

The struggle between Berkeley's students and administrators peaked on December 2, 1964, with a sit-in and powerful speech by Savio. Early the next morning, 600 police officers entered the campus and arrested more than 700 protesters.

The arrests set off an even larger protest movement. Within days, a campus-wide strike had stopped classes and many members of the faculty also voiced their support for the Free Speech Movement. In the face of this growing opposition, the administration gave in to the students' demands.

Soon afterward, the Supreme Court upheld students' rights to freedom of speech and assembly on campuses. In a unanimous vote, the Court upheld the section of the Civil Rights Act assuring these rights in places offering public accommodations, which, by definition, included college campuses. The Berkeley revolt was one of the first major student protests in the 1960s, and it became a model for others. The tactics the Berkeley protesters had used were soon being used in college demonstrations across the country.

✔ **Reading Check** **Synthesizing** What were three reasons for the growth of the youth movement of the 1960s?

The Counterculture

MAIN Idea Counterculture youths tried to create an alternative to mainstream culture.

HISTORY AND YOU Do you know anyone today who rejects mainstream society? Read on to learn about the ideas of the 1960s counterculture.

While many young Americans in the 1960s sought to reform the system, others rejected it entirely and tried to create a new lifestyle based on flamboyant dress, rock music, drug use, and communal living. They created what became known as the **counterculture** and were commonly called "**hippies.**"

Hippie Culture

Originally, hippies rejected **rationality,** order, and traditional middle-class values. They wanted to build a utopia—a society that was freer, closer to nature, and full of love, empathy, tolerance, and cooperation. Much of this was a reaction to the 1950s stereotype of the white-collar "man in the gray flannel suit" who led a constricted and colorless life.

As the counterculture grew, many newcomers did not understand these ideas. For them, what mattered were the outward signs that

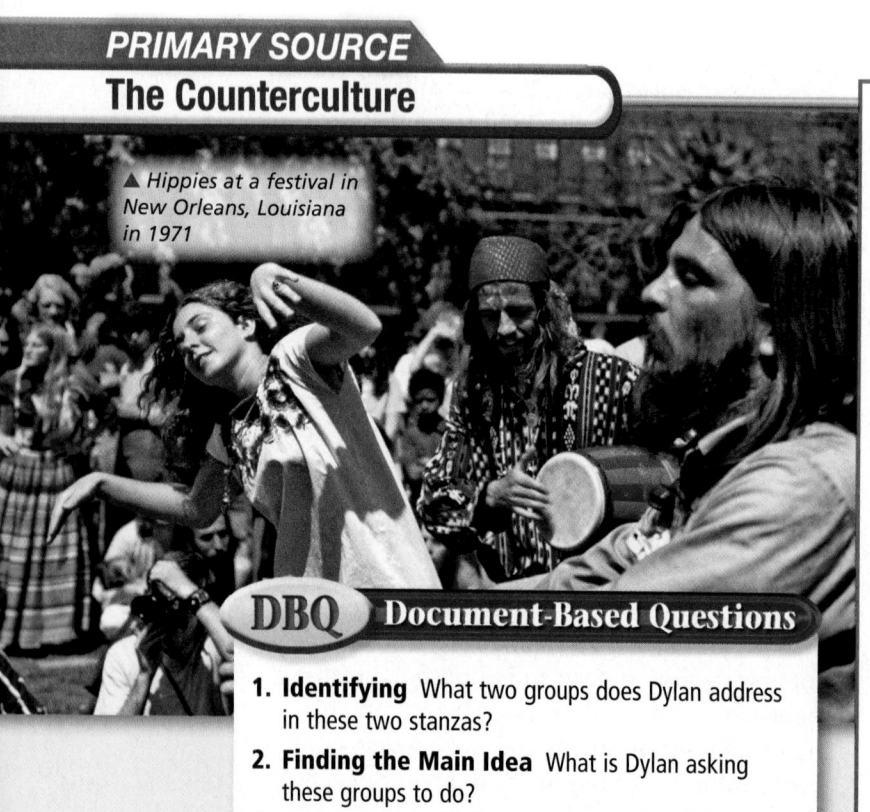

PRIMARY SOURCE
The Counterculture

▲ Hippies at a festival in New Orleans, Louisiana in 1971

DBQ **Document-Based Questions**

1. **Identifying** What two groups does Dylan address in these two stanzas?

2. **Finding the Main Idea** What is Dylan asking these groups to do?

Come senators, congressmen
Please heed the call
Don't stand in the doorway
Don't block up the hall
For he that gets hurt
Will be he who has stalled
There's a battle outside
And it is ragin'.
It'll soon shake your windows
And rattle your walls
For the times they are a-changin'.

Come mothers and fathers
Throughout the land
And don't criticize
What you can't understand
Your sons and your daughters
Are beyond your command
Your old road is
Rapidly agin'.
Please get out of the new one
If you can't lend your hand
For the times they are a-changin'.

—from *"The Times They Are A-Changin'"*

▲ Bob Dylan performs at the Newport Folk Festival in 1965.

defined the movement—long hair, Native American headbands, cowboy boots, long dresses, shabby jeans, and the use of drugs.

Many hippies wanted to drop out of society by leaving home and living together in **communes**—group living arrangements in which members shared everything and worked together. Some hippies established rural communes, while others lived together in parks or crowded apartments in large cities. One of the most famous hippie destinations was San Francisco's **Haight-Ashbury district.** By the mid-1960s, thousands of hippies had flocked there.

The Impact of the Counterculture

After a few years, the counterculture movement began to decline. Some urban hippie communities became dangerous places where muggings and other criminal activity took place. The glamour of drug use waned as more and more young people became addicted or died from overdoses. In addition, many people in the movement had gotten older and moved on. Although the counterculture declined without achieving its utopian ideals, it did change some aspects of American culture.

Fashion Protesters and members of the counterculture often expressed themselves with their clothing. By wearing cheap surplus clothes recycled from earlier decades and repaired with patches, they showed that they were rejecting both consumerism and the social class structure. Ethnic clothing was popular for similar reasons. Beads and fringes imitated Native American costumes, while tie-dyed shirts borrowed techniques from India and Africa.

Perhaps the most potent symbol of the era was hair. Long hair, beards, and mustaches on young men symbolized defiance of both 1950s **conformity**—when buzz cuts were popular—and the military, which required all recruits to have short hair. School officials at the time debated the acceptable length of a student's hair. Over time, however, longer hair on men and more individual clothing for both genders became generally accepted. What was once the clothing of defiance became mainstream.

Music Counterculture musicians made use of folk music and the rhythms of rock 'n' roll and wrote heartfelt lyrics that expressed the hopes and fears of their generation. At festivals such as **Woodstock,** held in upstate New York in August 1969, and in Altamont, California, later that year, hundreds of thousands of people gathered to listen to the new music.

Major folk singers included **Bob Dylan,** who became an important voice of the movement, as did singers Joan Baez and Pete Seeger. Rock musicians popular with the counterculture included Jimi Hendrix, Janis Joplin, and The Who. These musicians used electrically amplified instruments that drastically changed the sound of rock, and their innovations continue to influence musicians today.

Reading Check **Evaluating** What lasting impact did the counterculture have on the nation?

Section 1 REVIEW

Vocabulary

1. **Explain** the significance of: Port Huron Statement, Tom Hayden, Free Speech Movement, counterculture, hippies, communes, Haight-Ashbury district, Woodstock, Bob Dylan.

Main Ideas

2. **Describing** With what issues did SDS concern itself?

3. **Summarizing** What were the core ideals of the members of the counterculture?

Critical Thinking

4. **Big Ideas** How did the U.S. Supreme Court validate the actions of the members of the Free Speech Movement?

5. **Organizing** Use a graphic organizer similar to the one below to list the causes of the youth movement.

Causes

Youth Movement

6. **Analyzing Visuals** Study the image on page 911. Why do you think that older adults were frightened or threatened by the student movement?

Writing About History

7. **Descriptive Writing** Suppose that you are a journalist in the 1960s. Write an article in which you visit a commune and describe the hippie culture of the day.

History ONLINE

Study Central™ To review this section, go to glencoe.com and click on Study Central.

The Feminist Movement

Guide to Reading

Big Ideas
Struggles for Rights Women organized to claim their rights and responsibilities as citizens.

Content Vocabulary
• feminism *(p. 914)*

Academic Vocabulary
• gender *(p. 915)*
• compatible *(p. 919)*

People and Events to Identify
• Equal Pay Act *(p. 915)*
• Betty Friedan *(p. 915)*
• National Organization for Women (NOW) *(p. 916)*
• Gloria Steinem *(p. 916)*
• Equal Rights Amendment (ERA) *(p. 917)*
• Phyllis Schlafly *(p. 918)*
• Title IX *(p. 918)*

Reading Strategy
Categorizing Use a graphic organizer similar to the one below to list the main arguments for and against the Equal Rights Amendment (ERA).

For ERA	Against ERA

NEW YORK CORE CURRICULUM
U.S. History and Government

Unit 7:
III.B.4.a(1) Kennedy Commission and the Civil Rights Act, 1963–1964
III.B.4.a(2) NOW (1966) to present
III.B.4.b(1) Shifting roles and images
III.B.4.b(2) Equal Rights Amendment (failure to ratify)
III.B.4.b(3) *Roe* v. *Wade,* 1973
III.B.4.b(4) Equality in the workplace: compensation; the glass ceiling

By the 1960s, many women had become increasingly dissatisfied with society's perception of women and their place in society. Some women began to join organizations aimed at improving their role in society. The Equal Rights Amendment stirred a national debate.

A Renewed Women's Movement

MAIN Idea Women in the 1960s and 1970s began creating organizations to change society through education and legislative action.

HISTORY AND YOU Have you ever read a book that spurred you to action or got you excited? Read on to learn about a book that helped define and reawaken the women's movement.

African Americans and college students were not the only groups seeking to change American society in the 1960s. By the middle of the decade, a new women's movement had emerged as many women became discontent with their status and treatment in American society. This movement became known as the feminist movement, or the women's liberation movement.

Feminism—the belief that men and women should be equal politically, economically, and socially—had been a weak and often embattled force since the adoption of the Nineteenth Amendment guaranteeing women's voting rights in 1920. Soon after the amendment was ratified, the women's movement split into two camps. For the next 40 years, it had very little political influence.

The onset of World War II provided women with greater opportunity, at least temporarily. With many men enlisted in the army, women became an integral part of the nation's workforce. After the war, however, many women returned to their traditional role of homemaker. Even though 8 million American women had gone to work during the war, the new postwar emphasis on having babies and establishing families discouraged women from seeking employment. Many Americans assumed that a good mother should stay home to raise her children.

Despite the popular emphasis on homemaking, however, the number of women who held jobs outside the home actually increased during the 1950s. Most women who went to work did so in order to help their families maintain their comfortable lifestyles. By 1960, nearly one-third of all married women were part of the paid workforce. Yet many people continued to believe that women, even college-educated women, could better serve society by remaining in the home to influence the next generation of men.

What Caused the Women's Movement?

The women's movement was revitalized in the 1960s, partly because of the efforts of the President's Commission on the Status of Women, and partly because writers, such as Betty Friedan, convinced women the time had come to take action.

▲ President Kennedy meets with Eleanor Roosevelt, Representative Edith Green (center) and Esther Peterson, director of the Women's Bureau at the Department of Labor (right) in early 1962 to discuss the findings of the President's Commission on the Status of Women.

DBQ Document-Based Questions

1. **Making Inferences** What was the "feminine mystique"?
2. **Drawing Conclusions** What do you think "the problem" was?
3. **Hypothesizing** Why might President Kennedy have wanted Eleanor Roosevelt to head the commission studying the status of women?

PRIMARY SOURCE

In 1963 Betty Friedan tried to describe the feelings that would lead to the rebirth of the women's movement:

▲ Betty Friedan, 1972

"The problem lay buried, unspoken, for many years in the minds of American women. . . . Each suburban housewife struggled with it alone. As she made the beds, shopped for groceries, matched slipcover material, ate peanut butter sandwiches with her children, chauffeured Cub Scouts and Brownies . . . she was afraid to ask even of herself the silent question—'Is this all?'

. . . In the fifteen years after World War II, this mystique of feminine fulfillment became the cherished and self-perpetuating core of contemporary American culture. Millions of women lived their lives in the image of those pretty pictures of the American suburban housewife . . . Words like 'emancipation' and 'career' sounded strange and embarrassing. . . .

But on an April morning in 1959, I heard a mother of four, having coffee with four other mothers in a suburban development . . . say in a tone of quiet desperation, 'the problem.' And the others knew, without words, that she was not talking about a problem with her husband, or her children, or her home. Suddenly they realized they all shared the same problem, the problem that has no name.

. . . Sometimes a woman would say 'I feel empty somehow . . . incomplete.' Or she would say, 'I feel as if I don't exist.'"

—from *The Feminine Mystique*

Origins of the Movement

By the early 1960s, many women were increasingly resentful of a world where newspaper ads separated jobs by **gender,** banks denied them credit, and, worst of all, they often were paid less for the same work. Women found themselves shut out of higher-paying professions such as law, medicine, and finance. By the mid-1960s, about 47 percent of American women were in the workforce, but three-fourths of them worked in lower paying clerical, sales, or factory jobs, or as cleaning women and hospital attendants.

Workplace Rights One stimulus that invigorated the women's movement was the President's Commission on the Status of Women, established by President Kennedy and headed by Eleanor Roosevelt. The commission's report highlighted the problems faced by women in the workplace and helped create a network of feminist activists who lobbied Congress for women's legislation. In 1963, with the support of organized labor, they won passage of the **Equal Pay Act,** which in most cases outlawed paying men more than women for the same job.

The Feminine Mystique Although many working women were angry about inequality in the workplace, many other women who had stayed home were also discontent. **Betty Friedan** tried to describe the reasons for their discontent in her book *The Feminine Mystique,* published in 1963.

Friedan had traveled around the country interviewing women who had graduated with her from Smith College in 1942. She found that while most of these women reported having everything they could want in life, they still felt unfulfilled.

Friedan's book became a best-seller. Many women began reaching out to one another, pouring out their anger and sadness in what came to be known as consciousness-raising sessions. While they talked informally about their unhappiness, they were also building the base for a nationwide mass movement.

The Civil Rights Act and Women Congress gave the women's movement another boost by including them in the 1964 Civil Rights Act. Title VII of the act outlawed job discrimination not only on the basis of race, color, religion, and national origin, but also on the basis of gender. The law provided a strong legal basis for the changes the women's movement would later demand.

Given the era's attitudes about what kind of work was proper for women, simply having the law on the books was not enough. Even the agency charged with administering the civil rights act—the Equal Employment Opportunity Commission (EEOC)—accepted the idea that jobs could be gender-specific. In 1965 the commission ruled that gender-segregated help-wanted ads were legal.

The Time Is NOW

By June 1966, Betty Friedan returned to an idea that she and other women had been considering—the need for an organization to promote feminist goals. On the back of a napkin she scribbled that it was time "to take the actions needed to bring women into the mainstream of American society, now . . . in fully equal partnership with men." Friedan and others then set out to form the **National Organization for Women** (NOW).

In October 1966, a group of about 300 women and men held the founding conference of NOW. "The time has come," its founders declared, "to confront with concrete action the conditions which now prevent women from enjoying the equality of opportunity and freedom of choice which is their right as individual Americans and as human beings."

The new organization responded to frustrated housewives by demanding greater educational opportunities for women. The group also focused much of its energy on aiding women in the workplace. NOW leaders denounced the exclusion of women from certain professions and from most levels of politics. They lashed out against the practice of paying women less than men for equal work, a practice the Equal Pay Act had not eliminated.

When NOW set out to pass an Equal Rights Amendment to the Constitution, its membership rose to over 200,000. By July 1972, the movement had its own magazine, *Ms.*, which kept readers informed about women's issues. The editor of the magazine was **Gloria Steinem,** an author who became one of the movement's leading figures.

✔ Reading Check **Identifying** What two forces helped bring the women's movement to life again?

Debates
IN HISTORY

Should the Equal Rights Amendment Be Ratified?

In the 1970s ratification of the Equal Rights Amendment (ERA) was a hotly debated issue. Organizations such as NOW and other supporters of the amendment fought hard for its ratification. One of these was U.S. Representative Shirley Chisholm, who spoke out in support of the ERA in a speech to Congress in 1970. In 1971 conservative activist Phyllis Schlafly formed the group Stop-ERA to fight the legislation.

Successes and Failures

MAIN Idea The women's movement made gains for women in education and employment but has not achieved complete equality for women.

HISTORY AND YOU Have you ever seen men and women treated differently because of their gender? Read to learn how the women's movement tried to get equal treatment for women in the 1960s and 1970s.

During the late 1960s and early 1970s, the women's movement fought to amend the Constitution and enforce Title VII of the Civil Rights Act, lobbied to repeal laws against abortion, and worked for legislation against gender discrimination in employment, housing, and education. The movement had many successes, but also encountered strong opposition to some of the reforms it wanted.

The Equal Rights Amendment

The women's movement seemed to be off to a strong start when Congress passed the **Equal Rights Amendment** (ERA) in March 1972. The amendment specified that "Equality of rights under the law shall not be denied or abridged by the United States or by any State on account of sex." To become part of the Constitution, the amendment had to be ratified by 38 states. Many states did so—35 by 1979—but by then, significant opposition to the amendment had begun to build up.

Opponents of the ERA argued that it would take away some traditional rights, such as the right to alimony in divorce cases or the right to have single-gender colleges. They also feared it would allow women to be drafted into the military and eliminate laws that provided special protection for women in the workforce.

YES

Shirley Chisholm
Member of the U.S. House of Representatives

PRIMARY SOURCE

"Discrimination against women . . . is so widespread that it seems to many persons normal, natural and right. . . .

It is time we act to assure full equality of opportunity . . . to women.

The argument that this amendment will not solve the problem of sex discrimination is not relevant. . . . Of course laws will not eliminate prejudice from the hearts of human beings. But that is no reason to allow prejudice to continue to be enshrined in our laws. . . . The Constitution they wrote was designed to protect the rights of white, male citizens. As there were no black Founding Fathers, there were no founding mothers—a great pity, on both counts. It is not too late to complete the work they left undone."

—speech before Congress, August 10, 1970

NO

Phyllis Schlafly
Author and Conservative Activist

PRIMARY SOURCE

"This Amendment will absolutely and positively make women subject to the draft. Why any woman would support such a ridiculous and un-American proposal as this is beyond comprehension. . . . Foxholes are bad enough for men, but they certainly are *not* the place for women—and we should reject any proposal which would put them there in the name of 'equal rights.'. . .

Another bad effect of the Equal Rights Amendment is that it will abolish a woman's right to child support and alimony . . .

Under present American laws, the man is *always* required to support his wife and each child he caused to be brought into the world. Why should women abandon these good laws . . . ?"

—from the *Phyllis Schlafly Report*, February 1972

DBQ Document-Based Questions

1. **Summarizing** Why does Chisholm believe that the ERA is necessary?
2. **Explaining** What does Schlafly say was the main flaw in the arguments of the ERA supporters?
3. **Evaluating** With which position do you agree? Write a paragraph to explain your choice.

One outspoken opponent was **Phyllis Schlafly,** who organized the Stop-ERA campaign. By the end of 1979, four states had voted to rescind their approval. Many people had become worried that the amendment would give federal courts too much power to interfere with state laws. Unable to achieve ratification by three-fourths of the states by the deadline set by Congress, the Equal Rights Amendment finally failed in 1982.

Equality in Education

One major achievement of the movement came in the area of education. Kathy Striebel's experience illustrated the discrimination female students often faced in the early 1970s. In 1971 Striebel, a high school junior in St. Paul, Minnesota, wanted to compete for her school's swim team, but the school did not allow girls to join. Kathy's mother, Charlotte, was a member of the local NOW chapter. Through it, she learned that St. Paul had recently banned gender discrimination in education. She filed a grievance with the city's human rights department, and officials required the school to allow Kathy to swim.

For further information on the case of *Roe* v. *Wade*, see page R60 in **Supreme Court Case Summaries.**

Shortly after joining the team, Kathy beat out one of the boys and earned a spot at a meet. As she stood on the block waiting to swim, the opposing coach declared that she was ineligible because the meet was outside St. Paul and thus beyond the jurisdiction of its laws. "They pulled that little girl right off the block," Charlotte Striebel recalled angrily.

Recognizing the problem, leaders of the women's movement lobbied Congress to ban gender discrimination in education. In 1972 Congress responded by passing a law known collectively as the Educational Amendments. One section, **Title IX,** prohibited federally funded schools from discriminating against women in nearly all aspects of its operations, from admissions to athletics.

Roe v. Wade

One of the most important goals for many women activists was the repeal of laws against abortion. Until 1973, the right to regulate abortion was reserved to the states. This was in keeping with the original plan of the Constitution, which reserved all police power—the power to control people and property in the

---

PRIMARY SOURCE
The Changing Status of Women

Women's roles were changing in society. Although the ERA failed, more women entered the workforce and gender discrimination in schools was banned with the passage of Title IX.

Analyzing VISUALS

1. **Analyzing** By how much did the percentage of working women increase between 1950 and 2000?

2. **Interpreting** What gains, if any, did women make in median income compared to men?

Women in the Workforce

Source: *Historical Statistics of the United States: Earliest Times to the Present, Volume 2.*

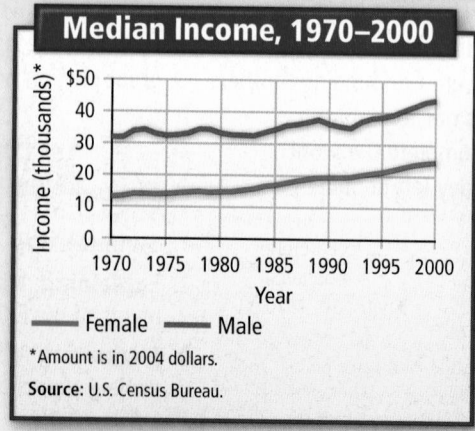

Median Income, 1970–2000

*Amount is in 2004 dollars.

Source: U.S. Census Bureau.

interest of safety, health, welfare, and morals—to the state. Early in the country's history, some abortions were permitted in the early stages of pregnancy, but by the mid-1800s, states had passed laws prohibiting abortion, except to save the life of the mother.

In the late 1960s, some states began adopting more liberal abortion laws. For example, several states allowed abortion if carrying a baby to term might endanger the woman's mental health or if she was a victim of rape or incest. The big change came with the 1973 Supreme Court decision in *Roe* v. *Wade*. The Supreme Court ruled that state governments could not regulate abortion during the first three months of pregnancy, a time that was said to be within a woman's constitutional right to privacy. During the second three months of pregnancy, states could regulate abortions on the basis of the health of the mother. States could ban abortion in the final three months except in cases of a medical emergency. Those in favor of abortion rights cheered *Roe* v. *Wade* as a victory, but the issue was far from settled politically. The decision gave rise to the right-to-life movement, whose members consider abortion morally wrong and advocate its total ban.

After the *Roe* v. *Wade* ruling, the two sides began an impassioned battle that continues today. In the 1992 case *Planned Parenthood* v. *Casey,* the Supreme Court modified *Roe* v. *Wade.* The court decided that states could place some restrictions on all abortions, such as requiring doctors to explain the risks and require their patients to give "informed consent." The court also upheld laws that required underage girls to inform their parents before obtaining an abortion. At the same time, the court struck down laws requiring women to notify their husbands before having an abortion. The court also abandoned the rule that states could ban abortion only in the final three months. Technology had now made it possible for the fetus to be viable outside the womb much earlier in a pregnancy. States could now restrict abortion based on the viability of the fetus.

The Impact of the Feminist Movement

Despite the failure of the ERA, the women's movement has brought profound changes to society. Since the 1970s, many more women have pursued college degrees and careers outside of the home, and two-career families are much more common than they were in the 1950s and 1960s. Many employers now offer options to help make work more **compatible** with family life, including flexible hours, on-site child care, and job sharing.

Even though the women's movement helped change social attitudes toward women, a significant income gap between men and women still exists. A major reason for the gap is that many working women still hold lower-paying jobs such as bank tellers, administrative assistants, cashiers, schoolteachers, and nurses. It is in professional jobs that women have made the most dramatic gains since the 1970s. By 2000, women made up over 40 percent of the nation's graduates receiving medical or law degrees.

✔ **Reading Check** **Summarizing** What successes and failures did the women's movement experience during the late 1960s and early 1970s?

Section 2 REVIEW

Vocabulary

1. **Explain** the significance of: feminism, Equal Pay Act, Betty Friedan, National Organization for Women (NOW), Gloria Steinem, Equal Rights Amendment (ERA), Phyllis Schlafly, Title IX.

Main Ideas

2. **Explaining** Why did more women work outside the home in the 1950s?

3. **Explaining** Why were some people against passage of the ERA?

Critical Thinking

4. **Big Ideas** What gains have been made in women's rights since the 1960s?

5. **Organizing** Use a graphic organizer similar to the one below to list the major achievements of the women's movement.

6. **Analyzing Visuals** Study the bar graph on page 918. What was the first year in which approximately half of all women were in the workforce?

Writing About History

7. **Persuasive Writing** Assume the role of a supporter or an opponent of the ERA. Write a letter to the editor of your local newspaper to persuade people to support your position.

History ONLINE

Study Central™ To review this section, go to glencoe.com and click on Study Central.

Section 3

Latino Americans Organize

Guide to Reading

Big Ideas
Struggles for Rights Latinos organized to fight discrimination and to gain access to better education and jobs.

Content Vocabulary
- repatriation *(p. 922)*
- bilingualism *(p. 925)*

Academic Vocabulary
- likewise *(p. 920)*
- adequate *(p. 924)*

People and Events to Identify
- League of United Latin American Citizens *(p. 923)*
- American GI Forum *(p. 924)*
- César Chávez *(p. 925)*
- Dolores Huerta *(p. 925)*
- United Farm Workers *(p. 925)*
- *La Raza Unida* *(p. 925)*
- Bilingual Education Act *(p. 925)*

Reading Strategy
Organizing Complete a time line similar to the one below to record major events in the struggle of Latinos for equal civil and political rights.

1947 — 1954 — 1966

1967 — 1968 — 1969

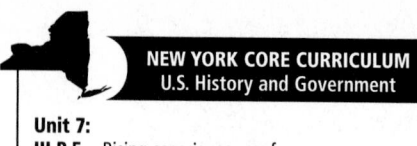

NEW YORK CORE CURRICULUM
U.S. History and Government

Unit 7:
III.B.5 Rising consciousness of Hispanic-Americans
III.B.5.b Organizing farm labor (Cesar Chavez)
III.B.5.c Cuban and Haitian immigration
III.B.5.d Increasing presence in American politics

Most Mexican Americans and Mexican immigrants lived in the Southwest, where many faced discrimination in jobs and housing. By the mid-twentieth century, more immigrants arrived from various parts of Latin America. Latinos formed civil rights organizations to challenge discrimination.

Latinos Migrate North

MAIN Idea Mexicans, the largest Spanish-speaking immigrant group, faced discrimination and segregation in the West and Southwest.

HISTORY AND YOU Have you ever heard of immigrants getting their "green cards," which permit them to work in the United States? Read on to learn how the Bracero Program allowed some Mexicans to work on a temporary basis.

Americans of Mexican heritage have lived in what is now the United States since before the founding of the republic. Their numbers steadily increased in the 1800s, in part because the United States acquired territory where Mexicans already lived, and in part because Mexicans began migrating north to live in the United States. In the twentieth century, Mexican immigration rose dramatically.

In 1910 the Mexican Revolution began and the resulting turmoil prompted a wave of emigration from Mexico that lasted more than a decade. During the 1920s, half a million Mexicans immigrated to the United States through official channels, and an unknown number entered the country through other means. Precise population estimates are impossible to determine because many Mexicans frequently moved back and forth across the border.

Not surprisingly, persons of Mexican heritage remained concentrated in the areas that were once the northern provinces of Mexico. In 1930, 90 percent of ethnic Mexicans in the United States lived in Texas, California, Arizona, New Mexico, and Colorado. In Texas, the favorite destinations for Mexican immigrants, cities such as San Antonio and El Paso, had large populations of Mexican Americans and Mexican immigrants. As a result of heavy Mexican immigration, the ethnic Mexican population in Texas grew from 71,062 in 1900 to 683,681 in 1930. Southern California, **likewise,** had a large Spanish-speaking population.

Of course, not all Mexican Americans remained in the West and Southwest. In the 1910s and 1920s, along with Americans of other ethnic backgrounds, many Mexican Americans headed for the cities of the Midwest and Northeast, where they found jobs in factories.

Latinos Arrive in America, 1910–1950

In the twentieth century, Latinos, mainly Mexicans, began to enter the United States in large numbers settling mostly in the West and Southwest. Others, who came from Puerto Rico or Cuba, often settled in the barrios of the large cities in the East.

▲ Family of Mexican migrant workers, who came to the United States as part of the Bracero program during World War II

▲ These refugees, guarded by U.S. troops at Fort Bliss, Texas, were some of the more than 500,000 who came to the United States to escape the turmoil of the Mexican Revolution.

Analyzing VISUALS

1. **Interpreting** The U.S. Latino population is made up of which main groups?
2. **Drawing Conclusions** Why have Latino Americans experienced a growing political influence in recent years?

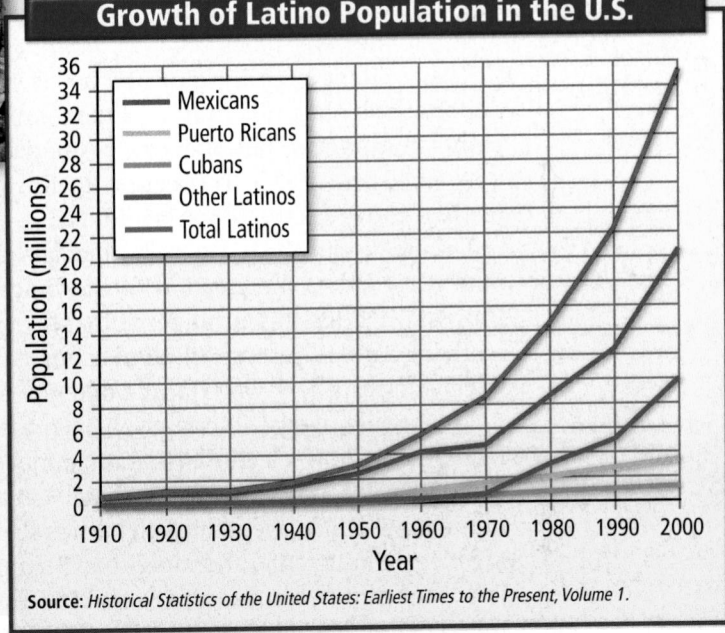

Growth of Latino Population in the U.S.

Legend:
- Mexicans
- Puerto Ricans
- Cubans
- Other Latinos
- Total Latinos

Y-axis: Population (millions), 0 to 36
X-axis: Year, 1910 to 2000

Source: *Historical Statistics of the United States: Earliest Times to the Present, Volume 1.*

Mexicans Face Discrimination

Across the Southwest, most Mexican Americans lived in barrios. Barrios were the product of a combination of the region's history and discrimination against Latinos. Los Angeles, for example, was founded as a Spanish town in 1781. When English-speaking settlers arrived a century later, they built around the older Spanish-speaking district.

Residential segregation, however, also had roots in ethnic discrimination. With heavy Mexican immigration in the early twentieth century, the ethnic Mexican population of Los Angeles grew from 5,000 in 1900 to around 190,000 in 1930. By that time, the Spanish-speaking population was segregated in the eastern part of the city, where most lived in small, dilapidated housing and suffered high rates of infant mortality and disease.

In California and across the Southwest, discrimination in employment meant that most ethnic Mexicans could find work only in low-paying jobs. Many lived in rural areas where they worked as agricultural laborers. Ernesto Galarza was eight years old when his family immigrated to California and settled in Sacramento in 1913. In his autobiography, he recalled the importance of the barrio to new immigrants:

"For the Mexicans the *barrio* was a colony of refugees. We came to know families from Chihuahua, Sonora, Jalisco, and Durango. . . . As poor refugees, their first concern was to find a place to sleep, then to eat and find work. In the *barrio* they were most likely to find all three, for not knowing English, they needed something that was even more urgent than a room, a meal, or a job, and that was information in a language they could understand."

—from *Barrio Boy*

During the Great Depression of the 1930s, approximately one-third of the Mexican population in the United States returned to Mexico. Some left voluntarily, believing it would be easier to get by in Mexico. Many Mexican Americans, however, faced increased hostility and discrimination as unemployment rates soared in the early 1930s.

Then, federal officials launched a series of deportations that not only included immigrants from Mexico but often their American-born children as well. This return to Mexico became known as the **repatriation.**

During World War II, labor shortages in the Southwest led to the creation of the Bracero Program. Under this arrangement, Mexican workers entered into short-term labor contracts, mostly as low-wage farm workers.

Meanwhile, illegal immigration increased. In 1954 Eisenhower's administration launched a program intended to deport illegal Latino immigrants. Police swept through barrios seeking illegal immigrants, and more than 3.7 million Mexicans were deported over the next three years. The raids were criticized in the United States and in Mexico for intimidating people for simply looking "Mexican." In addition, the program often failed to distinguish between individuals legally in the country (some of whom were U.S. citizens) and those who had entered illegally.

Other Latinos Arrive

Although Mexicans remained the largest group of Spanish-speaking newcomers in the 1950s, large numbers of Puerto Ricans arrived as well. American citizens since 1917, Puerto Ricans may move freely within American territory. After World War II, economic troubles in Puerto Rico prompted over a million Puerto Ricans to move to the mainland United States. American factory owners and employment agencies had also begun to recruit in Puerto Rico for workers, and the advent of relatively cheap air travel made immigration easier. The majority of Puerto Ricans settled in New York City. There, they suffered racial discrimination and alarmingly high levels of poverty.

The United States also became home to more than 350,000 Cuban immigrants in the decade after the Cuban Revolution of 1959. Many Cubans fleeing the Communist regime were professionals or business owners who settled in and around Miami, Florida. Most were welcomed in the United States because they were middle class or affluent and viewed as refugees fleeing Communist oppression. In 1960 about 3 million Latinos lived in the United States. By the late 1960s, more than 9 million Latinos lived in the United States.

✔ **Reading Check** **Summarizing** What were some of the criticisms of Eisenhower's deportation program?

PRIMARY SOURCE
Latinos in the United States

By the late 1960s, approximately 9 million Latinos lived in the United States. Although many were citizens, they still faced segregation, discrimination, and other forms of racial prejudice. However, with their increasing population and through political protest and legal action they began to work to improve conditions.

▲ *Latino dancers in a traditional dance at a fiesta in Taos, New Mexico*

Latinos Organize

MAIN Idea Latino civil rights organizations, such as LULAC and the American GI Forum, fought against discrimination.

HISTORY AND YOU Recall what you learned about the decision in the Supreme Court case *Brown v. Board of Education.* Read on to find out how LULAC filed similar lawsuits challenging discrimination against Mexican Americans.

The Latino community in the West and Southwest included American citizens and immigrant noncitizens. Regardless of their citizenship status, however, people of Mexican heritage were often treated as outsiders by the English-speaking majority. Latinos formed several organizations to work for equal rights and fair treatment.

In 1929 a number of Mexican American organizations came together to create the **League of United Latin American Citizens** (LULAC). The purpose of this organization was to fight discrimination against persons of Latin American ancestry. The organization limited its membership to people of Latin American heritage who were American citizens. LULAC encouraged assimilation into American society and adopted English as its official language.

LULAC achieved many advances for Latinos. One of its early crusades ended segregation of public places in Texas where Mexican Americans (along with African Americans) had been barred from "whites only" sections. The organization also ended the practice of segregating Spanish-speaking children in "Mexican schools."

In *Mendez* v. *Westminster* (1947), a group of Mexican parents won a lawsuit that challenged school segregation in California. Two years later, LULAC filed a similarly successful suit in Texas. During the 1950s, the organization was a frequent and vocal critic of the excesses and abuses of deportation authorities. In 1954 the Supreme Court's ruling in *Hernandez* v. *Texas* extended more rights to Latino citizens. The case ended the exclusion of Mexican Americans from juries in Texas.

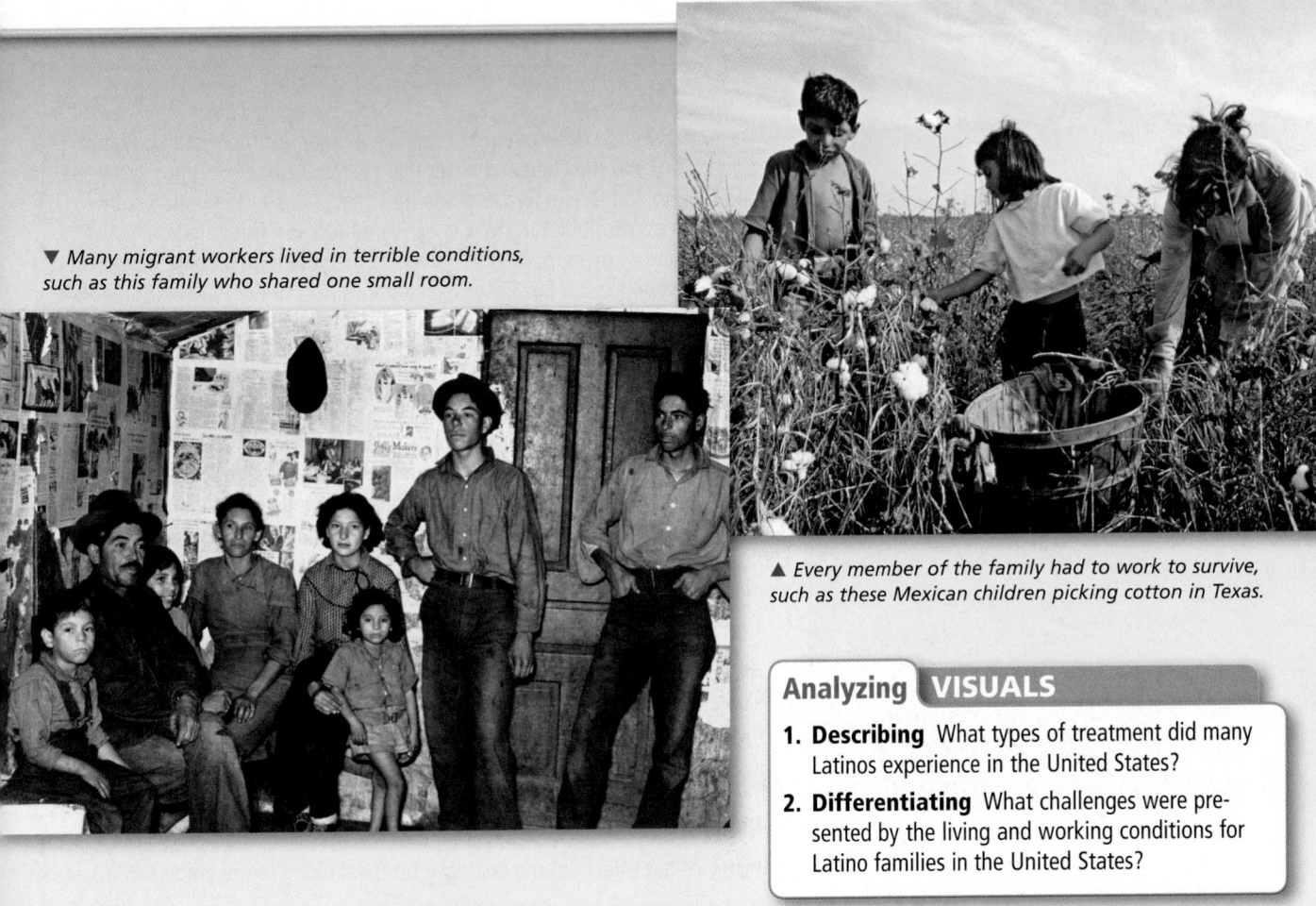

▼ *Many migrant workers lived in terrible conditions, such as this family who shared one small room.*

▲ *Every member of the family had to work to survive, such as these Mexican children picking cotton in Texas.*

Analyzing VISUALS

1. **Describing** What types of treatment did many Latinos experience in the United States?

2. **Differentiating** What challenges were presented by the living and working conditions for Latino families in the United States?

History ONLINE

Student Web Activity Visit glencoe.com and complete the activity on protest movements.

Another Latino organization, the **American GI Forum,** was founded to protect the rights of Mexican American veterans. After World War II, Latino veterans were excluded from veterans' organizations and denied medical services by the Veterans Administration.

The GI Forum's first effort to combat racial injustice involved a Mexican American soldier who was killed during World War II. A funeral home refused to hold his funeral because he was Mexican American. The GI Forum drew national attention to the incident and, with the help of Senator Lyndon Johnson, the soldier's remains were buried in Arlington National Cemetery. Initially concerned only with issues directly affecting Latino veterans, the organization later broadened its scope to challenge segregation and other forms of discrimination against all Latinos.

Reading Check **Analyzing** How did American society discriminate against Latinos?

Protests and Progress

MAIN Idea Many Latinos worked as poorly paid agricultural laborers; the United Farm Workers tried to improve their working conditions.

HISTORY AND YOU Do you think the United States should have a national language? Read how school districts set up bilingual education classes to teach immigrant students in their own language while they were still learning English.

As the 1960s began, Latino Americans continued to face prejudice and limited access to **adequate** education, employment, and housing. Encouraged by the achievements of the African American civil rights movement, Latinos launched a series of campaigns to improve their economic situation and end discrimination.

One major campaign was the effort to improve conditions for farmworkers. Most Mexican American farm laborers earned little pay, received few benefits, and had no job

PRIMARY SOURCE
César Chávez Promotes Nonviolence

▲ *Activist César Chávez was instrumental in improving conditions for Latino migrant workers.*

PRIMARY SOURCE

"Farmworkers had been trying to organize a union for more than one hundred years. In 1965 they began a bitter five-year strike against grape growers around Delano, California. Two and one-half years later, in the hungry winter of 1968 with no resolution in sight, they were tired and frustrated.

Among some of them, particularly some of the young men, there began the murmurs of violence. . . . But Cesar rejected that part of our culture 'that tells young men that you're not a man if you don't fight back.' The boycott had followed in the tradition of Cesar's hero, Mahatma Gandhi, whose practice of nonviolence he embraced. And now, like Gandhi, Cesar announced he would undertake a fast . . . .

After twenty-five days, Cesar was carried to a nearby park where the fast ended during a mass with thousands of farmworkers. He had lost thirty-five pounds, but there was no more talk of violence among the farmworkers. . . .

Cesar was too weak to speak, so his statement was read by others in both English and Spanish. 'It is my deepest belief that only by giving our lives do we find life,' they read. 'The truest act of courage . . . is to sacrifice ourselves for others in a totally nonviolent struggle for justice.'"

—Marc Grossman, UFW spokesman, quoted in *Stone Soup for the World*

DBQ Document-Based Questions

1. **Identifying** Whose ideas inspired César Chávez to begin his fast?
2. **Explaining** What effect did the fast have on the striking farmworkers?

security. In the early 1960s, **César Chávez** and **Dolores Huerta** organized two groups that fought for farmworkers. In 1965 the groups went on strike in California to demand union recognition, increased wages, and better benefits.

When employers resisted, Chávez enlisted college students, churches, and civil rights groups to organize a national boycott of table grapes, one of California's main agricultural products. An estimated 17 million citizens stopped buying grapes, and industry profits tumbled. In 1966, under the sponsorship of the American Federation of Labor and Congress of Industrial Organization (AFL-CIO), Chávez and Huerta merged their two organizations into one—the **United Farm Workers** (UFW). The new union kept the boycott going until 1970, when the grape growers finally agreed to raise wages and improve working conditions.

During the 1960s and 1970s, a growing number of Latino youths became involved in civil rights. In 1967 college students in San Antonio, Texas, led by José Angel Gutiérrez, founded the Mexican American Youth Organization (MAYO). MAYO organized walk-outs and demonstrations to protest discrimination. In 1968 about 1,000 Mexican American students and teachers in East Los Angeles walked out of their classrooms to protest racism. In Crystal City, Texas, protests organized by MAYO in 1969 led to the creation of bilingual education at the local high school.

MAYO's success and the spread of protests across the West and Southwest convinced Gutiérrez to found a new political party, ***La Raza Unida,*** or "the United People," in 1969. *La Raza* promoted Latino causes and supported Latino candidates in Texas, California, Colorado, Arizona, and New Mexico. The group mobilized Mexican American voters with calls for job-training programs and greater access to financial institutions. By the early 1970s, it had elected Latinos to local offices in several cities with large Latino populations.

La Raza was part of a larger civil rights movement among Mexican Americans (many of whom began calling themselves Chicanos). This "Brown Power" movement fought against discrimination and celebrated ethnic pride. On September 16, 1969 (Mexican Independence Day), students at the University of California at Berkeley staged a sit-in demanding a Chicano Studies program. Over the next decade, more than 50 universities created programs dedicated to the study of Latinos in the United States.

One issue many Latino leaders promoted in the late 1960s was **bilingualism**—the practice of teaching immigrant students in their own language while they also learned English. Congress supported their arguments, passing the **Bilingual Education Act** in 1968. This act directed school districts to set up classes for immigrants in their own language while they were learning English.

Later, bilingualism became politically controversial. Many Americans worried that bilingualism made it difficult for Latino immigrants to assimilate. Beginning in the 1980s, an English-only movement began, and by the 2000s, legislatures in 25 states had passed laws or amendments making English the official language of their state.

✔ Reading Check **Explaining** How did Latino Americans increase their economic opportunities in the 1960s?

Section 3 REVIEW

Vocabulary

1. **Explain** the significance of: repatriation, League of United Latin American Citizens, American GI Forum, César Chávez, Dolores Huerta, United Farm Workers, *La Raza Unida,* bilingualism, Bilingual Education Act.

Main Ideas

2. **Identifying** What are the national origins of the three main groups of Latinos in the United States?

3. **Describing** Under what circumstances did the American GI Forum first take action?

4. **Explaining** Why did some Americans worry about the Bilingual Education Act?

Critical Thinking

5. **Big Ideas** How did the judicial system support Latino civil rights in the last century? Cite two relevant court cases and their decisions.

6. **Categorizing** Use a graphic organizer similar to the one below to identify Latino groups and their achievements.

Civil Rights Group	Achievement

7. **Analyzing Visuals** Study the graph on page 921. What was the total U.S. Latino population in 2000? Which group had the largest population?

Writing About History

8. **Expository Writing** Write a magazine article about the conditions that gave rise to the Latino civil rights movement in the postwar period.

History ONLINE

Study Central™ To review this section, go to glencoe.com and click on Study Central.

Causes of the New Protest Movements

- The earlier "beat" movement questioned American values.

- The successes of African Americans' fight for civil rights demonstrated to other groups that change was possible if people demanded change.

- Many in the baby boom generation became frustrated with society as they entered college and began to advocate for social reform.

- The Vietnam War and the draft led many students to join protests.

- Women began to question their position in postwar society. Betty Friedan's book *The Feminine Mystique* influenced many young women.

- The Kennedy administration began to pay attention to women's issues, passing the Equal Pay Act and creating the President's Commission on the Status of Women.

- The Latino American population increased through immigration; Latino newcomers, as well as citizens, faced discrimination.

◀ SDS leader Mario Savio speaks at a 1966 sit-in.

▶ Latinos began to fight for improved labor conditions through the work of the United Farm Workers who held rallies such as this one in 1979.

▲ Women's rights leaders, such as Bella Abzug (left, in hat) and Betty Friedan (right, in red coat) fought for greater equality for women.

Effects of the New Protest Movements

- New student groups, including Students for a Democratic Society (SDS), were formed. Court cases affirmed student rights to free speech on campus.

- New women's groups, such as the National Organization of Women (NOW), emerged. They fought for equal economic rights in the workplace and in society, and they demanded equal opportunities in education.

- A campaign began for the Equal Rights Amendment, but the amendment was not ratified.

- The *Roe* v. *Wade* decision affirmed a constitutional right to abortion, with some limits.

- New Latino organizations emerged, such as the United Farm Workers (UFW) and *La Raza Unida*, fighting for increased economic opportunity and greater representation in political institutions.

- Latinos made substantial gains politically and economically, and many were elected to positions in Congress and state governments.

NEW YORK REGENTS EXAM PRACTICE

TEST-TAKING

Read each question carefully to understand exactly what it is asking. Then review all the answer choices before finally choosing the **best** answer to the question.

Part I

Directions (1–11): For each statement or question, write on a separate sheet of paper the number of the word or expression that, of those given, best completes the statement or answers the question.

1 SDS was begun by Tom Hayden at which university?

(1) Harvard University

(2) University of California at Berkeley

(3) Kent State University

(4) University of Michigan

2 Which of the following was an outgrowth of hippie culture?

(1) SDS

(2) rock 'n' roll music

(3) communes

(4) buzz cuts

3 The work of the President's Commission on the Status of Women led to

(1) the Equal Employment Opportunity Commission.

(2) the Equal Rights Amendment.

(3) the Equal Pay Act.

(4) the National Organization for Women.

4 Title IX of the Educational Amendments prohibited federally funded schools

(1) from paying male teachers more than female teachers.

(2) from discriminating against minorities.

(3) from providing same-gender education.

(4) from discriminating on the basis of gender.

5 Cuban immigrants arriving after the Cuban Revolution in 1959 were welcomed by Americans because

(1) there was a shortage of cheap labor.

(2) they were considered refugees from communism.

(3) most of them were fluent in English.

(4) there was a need for more doctors and other professionals.

6 Using a tactic the NAACP used to advance the rights of African Americans, LULAC fought discrimination against Latinos mainly

(1) through lobbying efforts.

(2) through demonstrations and other protests.

(3) through the court system.

(4) through periodicals and other mass media.

7 The Supreme Court upheld the Free Speech protesters' rights to free speech and assembly under which law?

(1) the Civil Rights Act of 1964

(2) the Equal Rights Amendment

(3) the Educational Amendments

(4) the Twenty-sixth Amendment

8 Why did the onset of World War II provide women with greater opportunities in the workplace?

(1) Many men enlisted in the army and women became an integral part of the nation's workforce.

(2) Soldiers were needed and women gained equality through combat positions in the military.

(3) Women were able to stay home and raise families because of the GI Bill.

(4) Women gained the right to vote while men were at war.

Need Extra Help?								
If You Missed Questions . . .	1	2	3	4	5	6	7	8
Go to Page . . .	910–911	913	915	918	922–923	923	911–912	914

[OVER]

Base your answer to questions 9 and 10 on the map below and your knowledge of Chapter 27.

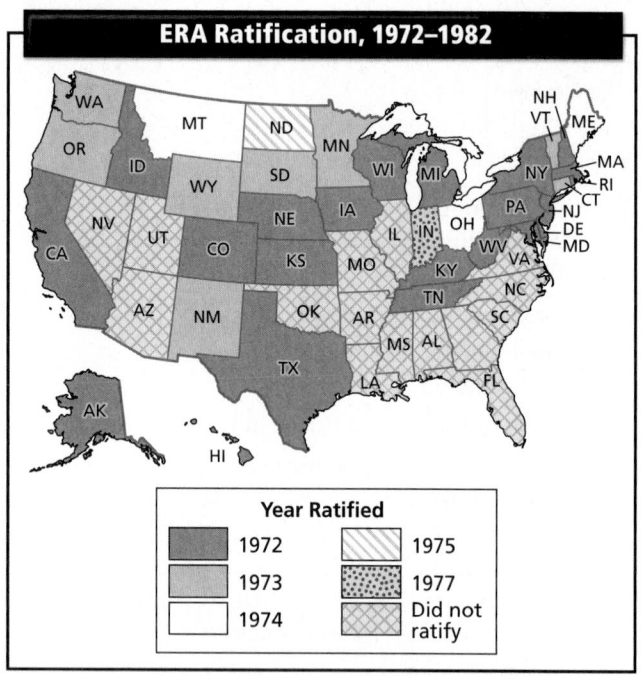

ERA Ratification, 1972–1982

Year Ratified

▨	1972	▨	1975
▨	1973	▨	1977
☐	1974	▨	Did not ratify

9   In what region of the country did most states fail to ratify the ERA?

(1) the South   (3) the West

(2) New England   (4) the Midwest

10 How many states had ratified the Equal Rights Amendment by 1977?

(1) 20   (3) 30

(2) 25   (4) 35

11 The United Farm Workers' boycott against California grape growers was effective because

(1) the grape growers gave in so quickly to the union's demands.

(2) no one thought that the grape growers could organize so well.

(3) grapes were a major agricultural product of California.

(4) the union had the support of the U.S. government.

Need Extra Help?			
If You Missed Questions . . .	9	10	11
Go to Page . . .	R15	R15	925

Part II Thematic Essay Question

Directions: Write a well-organized essay that includes an introduction, several paragraphs addressing the task below, and a conclusion.

Theme: Protest and Change

The decades of the 1960s and 1970s were a tumultuous period of great protest and change in the United States.

Task:

Identify two equality movements in the United States discussed in this chapter, and for each

• Discuss the members of the movement and the historical background of the movement

• Describe each movement's goals and the actions taken to achieve these goals

• Evaluate the long-term successes or failures of each movement

Guidelines:

In your essay, be sure to:

• Develop all aspects of the task

• Support the theme with relevant facts, examples, and details

• Use a logical and clear plan of organization, including an introduction and a conclusion that are beyond a restatement of the theme

Part III Document-Based Question

This question is based on the accompanying documents. It is designed to test your ability to work with historical documents. Some of the documents have been edited for the purposes of the question. As you analyze the documents, take into account both the source of each document and any point of view that may be presented in the document.

Historical Context:

During the 1960s and 1970s, many groups rose up in the United States to speak out about injustice and to attempt to change society and increase equality in the nation.

Task:

Using information from the documents and your knowledge of United States history, answer the questions that follow each document in Part A. Your answers to the questions will help you write the Part B essay, in which you will be asked to

- Discuss the roots of the youth movement and the counterculture and why individuals joined these movements
- Evaluate how each movement changed American society politically and socially

Part A
Short-Answer Questions

Directions: Analyze the documents and answer the short-answer questions that follow each document on a separate sheet of paper.

Document 1

> "[I]f this is a firm, and if the Board of Regents are the board of directors, and if President Kerr in fact is the manager, then I'll tell you something: the faculty are a bunch of employees, and we're the raw material! But we're a bunch of raw material[s] that don't mean to have any process upon us, don't mean to be made into any product, don't mean to end up being bought by some clients of the University, be they the government, be they industry, be they organized labor, be they anyone! We're human beings! There is a time when the operation of the machine becomes so odious, makes you so sick at heart, that you can't take part; you can't even passively take part, and you've got to put your bodies upon the gears and upon the wheels, upon the levers, upon all the apparatus, and you've got to make it stop. And you've got to indicate to the people who run it, to the people who own it, that unless you're free, the machine will be prevented from working at all!"

Source: Mario Savio, speech to Free Speech Movement protesters, University of California at Berkeley, December 2, 1964

1 What is Savio asking his fellow students to do, both literally and figuratively in this speech?

Document 2

Source: Jack Knox, *Nashville Banner*

2 According to the cartoonist, why were hippies hypocrites?

Part B
Essay

Directions: Reread the task box at the top left and write a well-organized essay that includes an introduction, several paragraphs, and a conclusion. Use evidence from the documents in your essay. Support your response with relevant facts, examples, and details. Include additional outside information.

Guidelines:
In your essay, be sure to:

- Develop all aspects of the task
- Incorporate information from the documents
- Incorporate relevant outside information
- Support the theme with relevant facts, examples, and details
- Use a logical and clear plan of organization, including an introduction and a conclusion that are beyond a restatement of the theme

 History ONLINE

For additional test practice, use Self-Check Quizzes—Chapter 27 at glencoe.com.

Need Extra Help?			
If You Missed Questions . . .	1	2	Essay
Go to Page . . .	R19	R18	R8

A Changing Society

1968–present

Why It Matters

In the last 40 years, the United States won the Cold War and the Soviet Union collapsed, bringing about dramatic changes in global politics. Americans faced many new challenges, including regional wars, environmental problems, and the rise of international terrorism. At the same time, the rise of modern American conservatism changed America's politics and led to new perspectives on the role of government in modern society.

By the early twenty-first century, American society was becoming increasingly diverse even as technology enabled people to become more interconnected.

Politics and Economics

1968–1980

Secretary of State Henry Kissinger sits with President Richard Nixon in the Oval Office to discuss foreign affairs on September 21, 1973.

U.S. PRESIDENTS

Nixon
1969–1974

Ford
1974–1977

U.S. EVENTS

WORLD EVENTS

1970
- First Earth Day observed
- Environmental Protection Agency created

1970

1972
- Nixon visits China and the Soviet Union
- Watergate burglars are arrested

1972

1973
- Senate Watergate investigations begin
- AIM and government clash at Wounded Knee, South Dakota

1974
- Nixon resigns

1974

1971
- People's Republic of China admitted to UN

1973
- Britain, Ireland, and Denmark join Common Market

1974
- India becomes world's sixth nuclear power

What Stops Government Abuse of Power?

The Watergate scandal forced Richard Nixon to become the first president to resign from office. The legacy of Watergate, together with the Vietnam War and the economic downturn of the late 1970s, caused many people to distrust the government and worry about the nation's future.

- *How do you think Watergate affected people's attitudes toward government?*
- *Do you think Nixon should have been punished for his role in the scandal?*

1975
- President Ford signs Helsinki Accords

Carter
1977–1981

1979
- Iranian revolutionaries seize U.S. embassy in Tehran

1976

1978

1977
- Human rights manifesto is signed by 241 Czech activists and intellectuals

1979
- Sandinista guerrillas overthrow Nicaraguan dictator Somoza
- Margaret Thatcher becomes prime minister of Great Britain

FOLDABLES

Analyzing Cause and Effect After you have read about the Watergate scandal, create a Shutter Fold Foldable to analyze critical information. Write a summary of Watergate events in the large middle section inside the Shutter Foldable. On the left-hand tab, list the causes of the Watergate scandal. On the right-hand tab, list the effects of Watergate on the political system.

History ONLINE Chapter Overview
Visit glencoe.com to preview Chapter 28.

Chapter 28 Politics and Economics **933**

Section 1

The Nixon Administration

Guide to Reading

Big Ideas

Individual Action One of President Nixon's most dramatic accomplishments was changing the United States's relationship with the People's Republic of China and the Soviet Union.

Content Vocabulary
- revenue sharing (p. 936)
- impound (p. 936)
- détente (p. 938)
- summit (p. 939)

Academic Vocabulary
- welfare (p. 936)
- liberal (p. 936)

People and Events to Identify
- Southern strategy (p. 935)
- New Federalism (p. 936)
- Henry Kissinger (p. 937)
- Vietnamization (p. 937)
- SALT I (p. 939)

Reading Strategy

Organizing Complete a graphic organizer similar to the one below by listing Nixon's domestic and foreign policies.

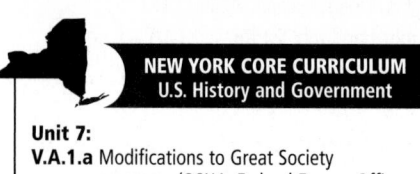

NEW YORK CORE CURRICULUM
U.S. History and Government

Unit 7:
V.A.1.a Modifications to Great Society programs (OSHA, Federal Energy Office, DEA, Clean Air Act, food stamps, revenue sharing)
V.A.2.a Henry Kissinger and realpolitik

After he won the 1968 presidential election, Richard Nixon sought to restore law and order at home. His greatest accomplishments, however, were in foreign policy, where he worked to ease Cold War tensions with China and the Soviet Union.

Appealing to Middle America

MAIN Idea Nixon won the 1968 election by appealing to a "silent majority" of Americans.

HISTORY AND YOU Do you view your community as politically and socially liberal or conservative? Read on to find out about the strategies Nixon used to convince conservative Southerners to vote for him.

While they did not shout as loudly as the protesters, many Americans supported the government and longed for an end to the violence and turmoil that seemed to be plaguing the nation. The presidential candidate in 1968 who appealed to many of these frustrated citizens was Richard Nixon, a Republican. Nixon aimed many of his campaign messages at these Americans, whom he referred to as "Middle America" and the "silent majority." He promised them "peace with honor" in Vietnam, law and order, a more streamlined government, and a return to more traditional values at home.

Nixon's principal opponent in the 1968 presidential election was Democrat Hubert Humphrey, who had served as vice president under Lyndon Johnson. Nixon also had to wage his campaign against a strong third-party candidate, George Wallace, an experienced Southern politician and avowed supporter of segregation. In a 1964 bid for the Democratic presidential nomination, the former Alabama governor had attracted considerable support.

On Election Day, Wallace captured an impressive 13.5 percent of the popular vote, the best showing of a third-party candidate since 1924. Nixon managed a victory, however, receiving 43.4 percent of the popular vote to Humphrey's 42.7, and 301 electoral votes to Humphrey's 191.

The Southern Strategy

One of the keys to Nixon's victory was his surprisingly strong showing in the South. Even though the South had long been a Democratic stronghold, Nixon had refused to concede the region. To gain Southern support, Nixon had met with powerful South Carolina senator Strom Thurmond and won his backing by promising several things: to appoint only conservatives to the federal

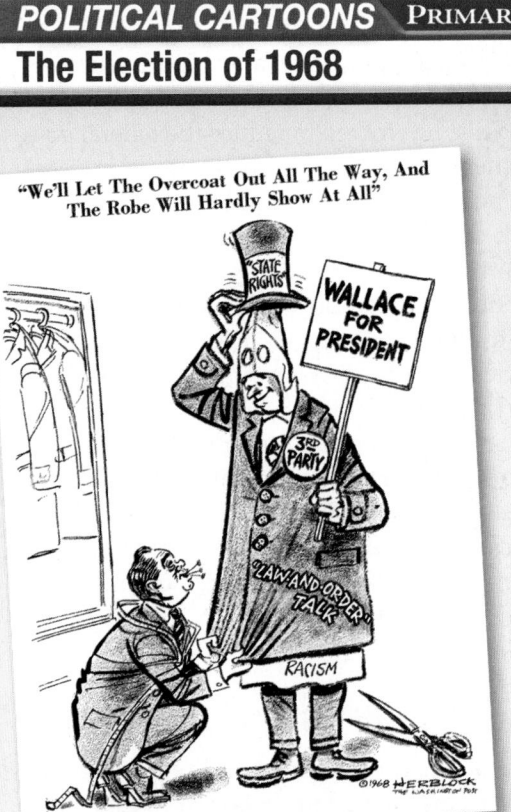

"We'll Let The Overcoat Out All The Way, And The Robe Will Hardly Show At All"

▲ Third-party presidential candidate George Wallace tailors an overcoat to cover the robe worn by one of his supporters.

"...He Doesn't Have Much of a Punch But He's Awful Fast on His Feet!"

▲ Republican Richard Nixon is fast on his feet as he spars with Democrat Hubert Humphrey. The man with the glasses represents John Q. Public, who is speaking to an elephant representing the Republican Party.

Analyzing VISUALS — DBQ

1. **Identifying** In the cartoon on the left, what is the cartoonist accusing Wallace of doing?

2. **Identifying Points of View** In the cartoon on the right, do you think the cartoonist approves of Nixon? Why or why not?

courts, to name a Southerner to the Supreme Court, to oppose court-ordered busing, and to choose a vice presidential candidate acceptable to the South. (Nixon ultimately chose Spiro Agnew, governor of the border state of Maryland.)

Nixon's efforts paid off on Election Day. Large numbers of white Southerners deserted the Democratic Party, granting Humphrey only one victory in that region—in Lyndon Johnson's home state of Texas. While Wallace claimed most of the states in the Deep South, Nixon captured Virginia, Tennessee, Kentucky, and North Carolina. Senator Strom Thurmond's support delivered his state of South Carolina for the Republicans as well.

Following his victory, Nixon set out to attract even more Southerners to the Republican Party, an effort that became known as the **Southern strategy.** Toward this end, he kept his agreement with Senator Thurmond and

took steps to slow desegregation. During his tenure, Nixon worked to overturn several civil rights policies. He reversed a Johnson administration policy, for example, that had cut off federal funds for racially segregated schools.

A Law-and-Order President

During the campaign, Nixon had also promised to uphold law and order. His administration specifically targeted the nation's antiwar protesters. Attorney General John Mitchell declared that he stood ready to prosecute "hard-line militants" who crossed state lines to stir up riots. Mitchell's deputy, Richard Kleindienst, went even further with the boast, "We're going to enforce the law against draft evaders, against radical students, against deserters, against civil disorders, against organized crime, and against street crime."

President Nixon also went on the attack against the recent Supreme Court rulings that expanded the rights of accused criminals. Nixon openly criticized the Court and its chief justice, Earl Warren. The president promised to fill vacancies on the Supreme Court with judges who would support the rights of law enforcement over the rights of suspected criminals.

When Chief Justice Warren retired shortly after Nixon took office, the president replaced him with Warren Burger, a respected conservative judge. He also placed three other conservative justices on the Court, including one from the South. The Burger Court did not reverse Warren Court rulings on the rights of criminal suspects. It did, however, refuse to expand those rights further. For example, in *Stone* v. *Powell* (1976), it agreed to limits on the rights of defendants to appeal state convictions to the federal judiciary. The Court also continued to uphold capital punishment as constitutional.

The New Federalism

Nixon had campaigned promising to reduce the size of the federal government by dismantling several federal programs and giving more control to state and local governments. Nixon called this the **New Federalism.** He argued that such an approach would make government more effective.

"I reject the patronizing idea that government in Washington, D.C., is inevitably more wise and more efficient than government at the state or local level," Nixon declared. "The idea that a bureaucratic elite in Washington knows what's best for people . . . is really a contention that people cannot govern themselves." Under the New Federalism program, Congress passed a series of **revenue-sharing** bills that granted federal funds to state and local agencies to use.

Although revenue sharing was intended to give state and local agencies more power, over time it gave the federal government new power. As states came to depend on federal funds, the federal government could impose conditions on the states. Unless they met those conditions, their funds would be cut off.

As part of the New Federalism, Nixon sought to close down many of the programs of Johnson's Great Society. He vetoed funding for the Department of Housing and Urban Development, eliminated the Office of Economic Opportunity, and tried unsuccessfully to shut down the Job Corps.

While he worked to reduce the federal government's role, Nixon also sought to increase the power of the executive branch. The president did not have many strong relationships with members of Congress. The fact that the Republicans did not control either house also contributed to struggles with the legislative branch. Nixon often responded by trying to work around Congress. For instance, when Congress appropriated money for programs he opposed, Nixon **impounded,** or refused to release, the funds. By 1973, he had impounded an estimated $15 billion. The Supreme Court eventually declared the practice of impoundment unconstitutional.

The Family Assistance Plan

One federal program Nixon sought to reform was the nation's **welfare** system—Aid to Families with Dependent Children (AFDC). The program had many critics, Republican and Democratic alike. They argued that AFDC was structured so that it was actually better for poor people to apply for benefits than to take a low-paying job. A mother who had such a job, for example, would then have to pay for child care, sometimes leaving her with less income than she had on welfare.

In 1969 Nixon proposed replacing the AFDC with the Family Assistance Plan. The plan called for providing needy families a guaranteed yearly grant of $1,600, which could be supplemented by outside earnings. Many **liberals** applauded the plan as a significant step toward expanding federal responsibility for the poor. Nixon, however, presented the program in a conservative light, arguing it would encourage welfare recipients to become more responsible.

Although the program won approval in the House in 1970, it soon came under harsh attack. Welfare recipients complained that the federal grant was too low, while conservatives, who disapproved of guaranteed income, also criticized the plan. Such opposition led to the program's defeat in the Senate.

Reading Check **Evaluating** How did Nixon's New Federalism differ from Johnson's Great Society?

Nixon's Foreign Policy

MAIN Idea With the support of national security adviser Henry Kissinger, Nixon forged better relationships with China and the Soviet Union.

HISTORY AND YOU How should a president balance his efforts between domestic and foreign affairs? Read on to learn about Nixon's strategies for dealing with communist countries.

Despite Nixon's domestic initiatives, a State Department official later recalled that the president had a "monumental disinterest in domestic policies." Nixon once expressed his hope that a "competent cabinet" of advisers could run the country. This would allow him to focus his energies on foreign affairs.

Nixon and Kissinger

In a move that would greatly influence his foreign policy, Nixon chose as his national security adviser **Henry Kissinger,** a former Harvard professor. Kissinger had served under Presidents Kennedy and Johnson as a foreign policy consultant. Although Secretary of State William Rogers outranked him, Kissinger soon took the lead in helping shape Nixon's foreign policy.

The Nixon Doctrine Nixon and Kissinger shared views on many issues. Both believed abandoning the war in Vietnam would damage the United States's position in the world. Thus, they worked toward a gradual withdrawal while simultaneously training the South Vietnamese to defend themselves.

This policy of **Vietnamization,** as it was called, was then extended globally in what came to be called the Nixon Doctrine. In July 1969, only six months after taking office, Nixon announced that the United States would now expect its allies to take care of their own defense. The United States would uphold all of the alliances it had signed, and would continue to provide military aid and training to allies, but it would no longer "conceive all the plans, design all the programs, execute all the decisions and undertake all the defense of the free nations of the world." America's allies would have to take responsibility for maintaining peace and stability in their own areas of the world.

People IN HISTORY

Henry Kissinger
1923–

Born in Germany, Henry Kissinger immigrated to the United States with his family in 1938 to escape Nazi persecution of Jews. During World War II, he served in U.S. military intelligence. After the war, Kissinger attended Harvard University and then joined the faculty there. He held various positions related to government, defense, and international affairs.

After acting as a consultant on national security under Presidents Kennedy and Johnson, Kissinger became President Nixon's national security adviser. In this capacity, he helped to establish the policy of détente with the Soviet Union and China. In 1973 he became secretary of state. Kissinger negotiated the cease-fire with North Vietnam, and along with Le Duc Tho, his co-negotiator, was awarded the Nobel Peace Prize in 1973.

In 1977 Kissinger was awarded the Presidential Medal of Freedom for his services to the nation. Today, he remains an unofficial adviser on international issues to leaders around the world.

How did Henry Kissinger influence foreign policy in the 1970s?

▲ In 1971, Time *magazine celebrated Kissinger as the driving force behind Nixon's trip to China.*

Détente With the Soviet Union and China

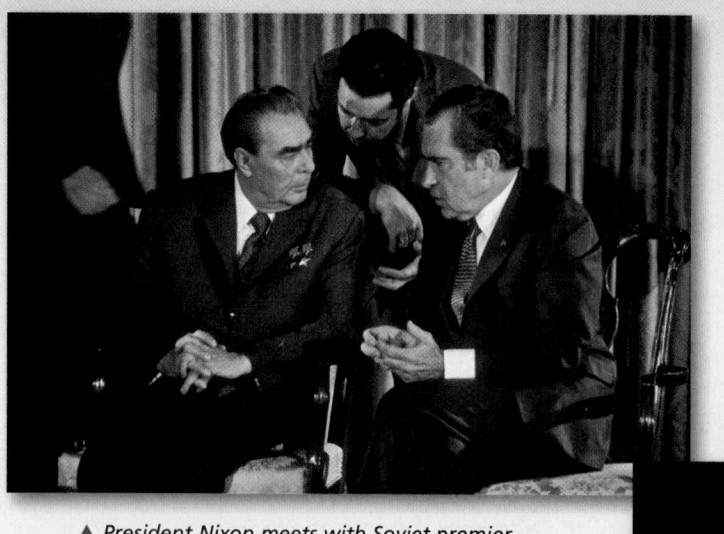

▲ President Nixon meets with Soviet premier Brezhnev to discuss limiting the number of nuclear weapons.

The Nuclear Arms Race

Number of nuclear weapons

— United States
— USSR/Russia

45,000
40,000
35,000
30,000
25,000
20,000
15,000
10,000
5,000
0

1945   1955   1965   1975   1985   1995   2005

Year

Source: *Bulletin of the Atomic Scientists.*

◄ Mao Zedong, leader of China, greets Nixon in Beijing on February 21, 1972.

Analyzing VISUALS

1. **Specifying** In what year did the number of nuclear weapons in the U.S. peak?

2. **Explaining** Why was establishing détente a significant accomplishment?

The New Policy of Détente The Soviet Union was not pleased when Nixon, a man with a history of outspoken anticommunist actions, became president. The Washington correspondent for the Soviet newspaper *Izvestia*, Yuri Barsukov, predicted that Soviet leaders "would have to deal with a very stubborn president."

Things did not turn out that way, however. Nixon was still a staunch anticommunist, but he and Kissinger rejected the notion of a bipolar world in which the superpowers of the United States and the Soviet Union confronted one another. They believed the United States needed to adjust to the growing role of China, Japan, and Western Europe. This emerging "multipolar" world demanded a different approach to American foreign policy.

Both Nixon and Kissinger wanted to continue to contain communism, but they believed that engagement and negotiation with Communists offered a better way for the United States to achieve its international goals. As a surprised nation watched, Nixon and Kissinger put their philosophy into practice. They developed a new approach called **détente,** or relaxation of tensions, between the United States and its two major Communist rivals, the Soviet Union and China. In explaining détente to the American people, Nixon said that the United States had to build a better relationship with its main rivals in the interest of world peace:

PRIMARY SOURCE

"We must understand that détente is not a love fest. It is an understanding between nations that have opposite purposes, but which share common interests, including the avoidance of a nuclear war. Such an understanding can work—that is, restrain aggression and deter war—only as long as the potential aggressor is made to recognize that neither aggression nor war will be profitable."

—quoted in *The Limits of Power*

Nixon Visits China

Détente began with an effort to improve American-Chinese relations. Since 1949, when Communists took power in China, the United States had refused to recognize the Communists as the legitimate rulers. Instead, the American government recognized the exiled regime on the island of Taiwan as the Chinese government. Having long supported this policy, Nixon now set out to reverse it. He began by lifting trade and travel restrictions and withdrawing the Seventh Fleet from defending Taiwan.

After a series of highly secret negotiations between Kissinger and Chinese leaders, Nixon announced that he would visit China in February 1972. During the historic trip, the leaders of both nations agreed to establish "more normal" relations between their countries. In a statement that epitomized the notion of détente, Nixon told his Chinese hosts during a banquet toast, "Let us start a long march together, not in lockstep, but on different roads leading to the same goal, the goal of building a world structure of peace and justice."

In taking this trip, Nixon hoped not only to strengthen ties with the Chinese, but also to encourage the Soviets to more actively pursue diplomacy. Since the 1960s, a rift had developed between the Communist governments of the Soviet Union and China. Troops of the two nations occasionally clashed along their borders. Nixon believed détente with China would encourage Soviet premier Leonid Brezhnev to be more accommodating with the United States.

United States-Soviet Tensions Ease

Nixon's strategy toward the Soviets worked. Shortly after the public learned of American negotiations with China, the Soviets proposed an American-Soviet **summit,** or high-level diplomatic meeting, to be held in May 1972. On May 22, President Nixon flew to Moscow for a weeklong summit, becoming the first American president since World War II to visit the Soviet Union.

During the historic Moscow summit, the two superpowers signed the first Strategic Arms Limitation Treaty, or **SALT I,** a plan to limit nuclear arms the two nations had been working on for years. Nixon and Brezhnev also agreed to increase trade and the exchange of scientific information. Détente profoundly eased tensions between the Soviet Union and the United States.

By the end of Nixon's presidency, one Soviet official admitted that "the United States and the Soviet Union had their best relationship of the whole Cold War period." President Nixon indeed had made his mark on the world stage. As he basked in the glow of his 1972 foreign policy triumphs, however, trouble was brewing on the home front. A scandal was about to engulf his presidency and plunge the nation into one of its greatest constitutional crises.

Reading Check **Summarizing** What were the results of the 1972 American-Soviet summit?

Section 1 REVIEW

Vocabulary

1. **Explain** the significance of: Southern strategy, New Federalism, revenue sharing, impound, Henry Kissinger, Vietnamization, détente, summit, SALT I.

Main Ideas

2. **Describing** How did President Nixon attempt to increase the power of the presidency?

3. **Explaining** How did Nixon use his visit to China to improve relations with the Soviet Union?

Critical Thinking

4. **Big Ideas** What were the results of Nixon's policy of détente?

5. **Organizing** Use a graphic organizer similar to the one below to describe how President Nixon established détente in the listed countries.

| China | |
| Soviet Union | |

6. **Analyzing Visuals** Look at the *Time* cover on page 937. What does the image portray about Nixon's foreign policy?

Writing About History

7. **Expository Writing** Take on the role of a member of President Nixon's staff. Write a press release explaining either Nixon's domestic or foreign policies.

History ONLINE
Study Central™ To review this section, go to glencoe.com and click on Study Central.

The Watergate Scandal

Guide to Reading

Big Ideas

Government and Society The Watergate scandal intensified lingering distrust of government that had arisen during the Vietnam War.

Content Vocabulary
- executive privilege *(p. 944)*
- special prosecutor *(p. 944)*

Academic Vocabulary
- incident *(p. 940)*
- challenger *(p. 941)*

People and Events to Identify
- Sam J. Ervin *(p. 942)*
- John Dean *(p. 942)*
- Federal Campaign Act Amendments *(p. 945)*

Reading Strategy

Taking Notes Use the headings in this section to create an outline similar to the one below by recording information about the Watergate scandal.

The Watergate Scandal
I. The Roots of Watergate
  A.
  B.
II.
  A.
  B.

NEW YORK CORE CURRICULUM
U.S. History and Government

Unit 7:
V.A.3.a Resignation of Spiro Agnew
V.A.3.b Watergate affair and its constitutional implications
V.A.3.c *United States v. Nixon*, 1974
V.A.3.d The impeachment process and resignation

Despite a successful first term, Richard Nixon and his supporters worried about reelection. The tactics they resorted to led the president to become embroiled in a scandal known as Watergate, one of the United States's great constitutional crises.

The Roots of Watergate

MAIN Idea Tactics used by Nixon's supporters to try to ensure his reelection in 1972 led to the Watergate scandal.

HISTORY AND YOU What do you know about Richard Nixon and the Watergate scandal? Read on to learn how the president became involved in this major governmental crisis.

The Watergate scandal is perhaps the most famous scandal in modern American history. It certainly had momentous consequences, as it led to the only time in the nation's history when the president of the United States was forced to resign from office. As reporter Bob Woodward recounts in his book, *All the President's Men*, the scandal began on the morning of June 17, 1972.

Woodward was a young reporter for the *Washington Post* at that time. His editor had ruined his Saturday by asking him to cover a seemingly insignificant but bizarre **incident.** In the early hours of that morning, five men had broken into the Democratic National Committee (DNC) headquarters in the city's Watergate apartment-office complex. Woodward was ordered to attend the arraignment and see if there was a story worth reporting.

As Woodward sat near the back of the courtroom listening to the bail proceedings for the five defendants, the judge asked each man his occupation. One of the men, James McCord, answered that he was retired from government service.

"Where in government?" asked the judge. "CIA," McCord whispered. Woodward sprang to attention. Why was a former agent of the CIA involved in what seemed to be nothing more than a burglary? Over the next two years, Woodward and another reporter, Carl Bernstein, would investigate this question. In so doing, they uncovered a scandal that helped trigger a constitutional crisis and eventually forced President Nixon to resign.

Mounting a Reelection Fight

The Watergate scandal began when the Nixon administration tried to cover up its involvement in the break-in at the Democratic National Committee headquarters, along with other illegal

The Watergate Scandal Erupts

In June 1972, five men were arrested attempting to place wiretaps on phones and stealing information from the Democratic National Headquarters at the Watergate Hotel. The subsequent investigation revealed a cover-up that reached to the White House.

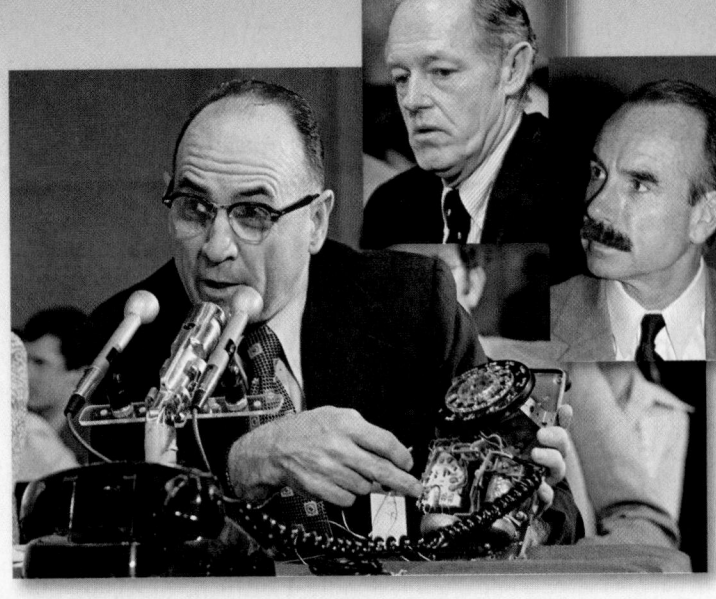

▲ James McCord shows Congress the bugging device he installed. E. Howard Hunt (center) and G. Gordon Liddy (right) also testified.

▲ The Watergate Complex gave its name to the resulting scandal. Security guard Frank Willis (right) reported to police evidence of the break-in.

▶ Counsel to the president John Dean testified that Nixon had been directly involved in the cover-up of the Watergate break-in.

Analyzing VISUALS

1. **Speculating** If you had discovered the break-in, what might make you suspicious about the burglars?

2. **Explaining** Why was John Dean's testimony damaging to the president?

actions. Although the affair began with the Watergate burglary, many scholars believe the roots of the scandal lay in Nixon's character and the atmosphere that he and his advisers created in the White House.

Richard Nixon had fought hard to become president. He had battled back from numerous political defeats, including a loss to John F. Kennedy in the 1960 presidential election. Along the way, Nixon had grown defensive, secretive, and often resentful of his critics.

Furthermore, Nixon had become president when American society was in turmoil. There were race riots, and protests over the Vietnam War continued to consume the country. In Nixon's view, protesters and other "radicals" were trying to bring down his administration. Nixon was so consumed with his opponents that he compiled an "enemies list" filled with

people—from politicians to members of the media—whom he considered a threat to his presidency.

When Nixon began his reelection campaign, his advisers were optimistic. Nixon had just finished triumphant trips to China and the Soviet Union. Former governor George Wallace, who had mounted a strong campaign in 1968, had dropped out of the race after an assassin's bullet paralyzed him, and the Democratic **challenger,** South Dakota Senator George McGovern, was viewed by many as too liberal.

Nixon's reelection was by no means certain, however. The unpopular Vietnam War still raged, and his staffers remembered how close the 1968 election had been. Determined to win at all costs, they began spying on opposition rallies and spreading rumors and false reports about their Democratic opponents.

As part of their efforts to help the president, Nixon's advisers ordered five men to break into the Democratic Party's headquarters at the Watergate complex and steal any sensitive campaign information. They were also to place wiretaps on the office telephones. While the burglars were at work, a security guard making his rounds spotted a piece of tape holding a door lock. The guard ripped off the tape, but when he passed the door later, he noticed that it had been replaced. He quickly called police, who arrived shortly and arrested the men.

The Cover-Up Begins

History ONLINE
Student Web Activity Visit glencoe.com and complete the activity on the 1970s.

After the Watergate break-in, the media discovered that one burglar, James McCord, was not only an ex-CIA officer but also a member of the Committee for the Re-election of the President (CRP). Reports soon surfaced that the burglars had been paid from a secret CRP fund controlled by the White House.

At this point, the cover-up began. White House officials destroyed incriminating documents and gave false testimony to investigators. Meanwhile, President Nixon stepped in. The president may not have ordered the break-in, but he did order a cover-up. With Nixon's consent, administration officials asked the CIA to stop the FBI from investigating the source of the money paid to the burglars. The CIA told the FBI that the investigation threatened national security. To combat efforts to block the FBI investigation, the FBI's deputy director, W. Mark Felt, secretly leaked information about Watergate to the Washington Post.

Meanwhile, Nixon's press secretary dismissed the incident as a "third-rate burglary attempt," and the president told the American public, "The White House has had no involvement whatever in this particular incident." The strategy worked. Most Americans believed President Nixon, and despite efforts by the media, in particular the *Washington Post*, to keep the story alive, few people paid much attention during the 1972 presidential campaign. On Election Day, Nixon won reelection by one of the largest margins in history with nearly 61 percent of the popular vote, compared to 37.5 percent for George McGovern.

✔ Reading Check **Examining** Why did members of the CRP break into the Democratic National Committee headquarters?

The Cover-Up Unravels

MAIN Idea The president's refusal to cooperate with Congress only focused attention on his possible involvement.

HISTORY AND YOU How far do you think that presidents should be able to go in the name of national security? Read on to learn how Nixon tried to invoke national security concerns to thwart an investigation of his involvement in Watergate.

In early 1973, the Watergate burglars went on trial. Under relentless prodding from federal judge John J. Sirica, McCord agreed to cooperate with the grand jury investigation. He also agreed to testify before the newly created Senate Select Committee on Presidential Campaign Activities. The chairman of the committee was Senator **Sam J. Ervin,** a Democrat from North Carolina.

McCord's testimony opened a floodgate of confessions, and a parade of White House and campaign officials exposed one illegality after another. Foremost among the officials was counsel to the president **John Dean,** a member of the inner circle of the White House who leveled allegations against Nixon himself.

A Summer of Shocking Testimony

In June 1973 John Dean testified before Senator Ervin's committee that former Attorney General John Mitchell had ordered the Watergate break-in and that Nixon had played an active role in attempting to cover up any White House involvement. As a shocked nation absorbed Dean's testimony, the Nixon administration strongly denied the charges.

Because Dean had no evidence to confirm his account, for the next month, the Senate committee attempted to determine who was telling the truth. Then, on July 16, the answer appeared unexpectedly. On that day, White House aide Alexander Butterfield testified that Nixon had ordered a taping system installed in the White House to record all conversations. The president had done so, Butterfield said, to help him write his memoirs after he left office. For members of the committee, however, the tapes would tell them exactly what the president knew and when he knew it, but only if the president could be forced to release them.

ANALYZING SUPREME COURT CASES

Is Executive Privilege Unlimited?

★ *United States* v. *Nixon*, 1974

Background to the Case

In 1974 Special Prosecutor Leon Jaworski issued a subpoena to gain access to tape recordings President Nixon had made of conversations in the Oval Office. Jaworski believed that the tapes would prove the active involvement of the president in the Watergate cover-up. Nixon filed a motion to prevent the subpoena, claiming executive privilege. The case went to district court, but that court withheld judgment pending the decision of the Supreme Court.

How the Court Ruled

In a unanimous 8-to-0 decision (Justice Rehnquist did not take part), the Supreme Court found that executive privilege did not protect Nixon's tape recordings, stating that while the president has a right to protect military secrets and other sensitive material and has a right to some confidentiality, the needs of a criminal trial must take precedence.

▲ The Senate committee overseeing the Watergate investigation, chaired by Senator Sam Ervin (fourth from left at the table), wanted access to Nixon's tape recordings.

PRIMARY SOURCE

The Court's Opinion

"In this case we must weigh the importance of the general privilege of confidentiality of Presidential communications in performance of the President's responsibilities against the inroads of such a privilege on the fair administration of criminal justice. The interest in preserving confidentiality is weighty indeed and entitled to great respect. However, we cannot conclude that advisers will be moved to temper the candor of their remarks by the infrequent occasions of disclosure because of the possibility that such conversations will be called for in the context of a criminal prosecution. On the other hand, the allowance of the privilege to withhold evidence that is demonstrably relevant in a criminal trial would cut deeply into the guarantee of due process of law and gravely impair the basic function of the courts. A President's acknowledged need for confidentiality in the communications of his office is general in nature, whereas the constitutional need for production of relevant evidence in a criminal proceeding is specific and central to the fair adjudication of a particular criminal case in the administration of justice. . . . The President's broad interest in confidentiality of communications will not be vitiated by disclosure of a limited number of conversations preliminarily shown to have some bearing on the pending criminal cases. We conclude that when the ground for asserting privilege as to subpoenaed materials sought for use in a criminal trial is based only on the generalized interest in confidentiality, it cannot prevail over the fundamental demands of due process of law in the fair administration of criminal justice. . . ."

—Chief Justice Warren Burger writing for the Court in
United States v. *Nixon*

DBQ Document-Based Questions

1. **Finding the Main Idea** What is the main point of the decision in *United States* v. *Nixon*?
2. **Summarizing** What does Burger say that executive privilege in this case would violate?
3. **Expressing** Do you agree with the Supreme Court's decision in this case? Explain.

The Watergate Scandal

◀ President Nixon clings to his desk as the Watergate scandal crashes like a tidal wave through the Oval Office.

"...DOWN, BOY!..."

Baldy

▲ The Watergate investigation takes the form of a search dog who has tracked the evidence directly to the president.

Analyzing VISUALS   DBQ

1. **Specifying** What does the cartoon on the left use to symbolize the Watergate scandal?
2. **Explaining** What is the meaning of Nixon's appearance and the magnifying glass in the cartoon on the right?

The Case of the Tapes

At first, Nixon refused to hand over the tapes, pleading **executive privilege**—the principle that White House conversations should remain confidential to protect national security. **Special prosecutor** Archibald Cox, the government lawyer appointed by the president to handle the Watergate cases, took Nixon to court in October 1973 to force him to give up the recordings. Nixon ordered Attorney General Elliot Richardson to fire Cox, but Richardson refused and resigned. Nixon then ordered Richardson's deputy to fire Cox, but the deputy resigned as well. Nixon's solicitor general, Robert Bork, finally fired Cox, but the incident, nicknamed the "Saturday Night Massacre" in the press, badly damaged Nixon's reputation with the public.

The fall of 1973 proved to be a disastrous time for Nixon for other reasons, as well. His vice president, Spiro Agnew, was forced to resign in disgrace after investigators learned that he had taken bribes from state contractors while governor of Maryland and that he had continued to accept bribes while serving in Washington. Gerald Ford, the Republican leader of the House of Representatives, became the new vice president.

Nixon Resigns

In an effort to quiet the growing outrage over his actions, President Nixon appointed a new special prosecutor, Texas lawyer Leon Jaworski, who proved no less determined than Cox to obtain the president's tapes. In July the Supreme Court ruled that the president had to turn over the tapes, and Nixon complied.

Several days later, the House Judiciary Committee voted to impeach Nixon, or officially charge him with misconduct. The committee charged Nixon with obstructing justice in the Watergate cover-up; misusing federal agencies to violate the rights of citizens; and defying the authority of Congress by refusing to deliver tapes and other materials as requested. Before the House of Representatives could vote on whether Nixon should be impeached, investigators found indisputable evidence against the president. One of the tapes revealed that on June 23, 1972, just six days after the Watergate burglary, Nixon had ordered the CIA to stop the FBI's investigation. With this news, even the president's strongest supporters conceded that impeachment by the House and conviction in the Senate were inevitable. On August 9, 1974, Nixon resigned his office in disgrace. Gerald Ford took the oath of office and became the nation's 38th president.

The Impact of Watergate

Upon taking office, President Ford urged Americans to put the Watergate scandal behind them. "Our long national nightmare is over," he declared. On September 8, 1974, Ford announced that he would grant a "full, free, and absolute pardon" to Richard Nixon for any crimes he "committed or may have committed or taken part in" while president. "[This] is an American tragedy in which we all have played a part," he told the nation. "It could go on and on and on, or someone must write the end to it."

The Watergate crisis led to new laws intended to limit the power of the executive branch. The **Federal Campaign Act Amendments** limited campaign contributions and established an independent agency to administer stricter election laws. The Ethics in Government Act required financial disclosure by high government officials in all three branches of government. The FBI Domestic Security Investigation Guidelines Act restricted the Bureau's political intelligence-gathering activities. Congress also established a means for appointing an independent counsel to investigate and prosecute wrongdoing by high government officials.

Despite these efforts, Watergate left many Americans with a deep distrust of their public officials. On the other hand, some Americans saw the Watergate affair as proof that in the United States, no person is above the law. As Bob Woodward observed:

PRIMARY SOURCE

"Watergate was probably a good thing for the country; it was a good, sobering lesson. Accountability to the law applies to everyone. The problem with kings and prime ministers and presidents is that they think that they are above it . . . that they have some special rights, and privileges, and status. And a process that says: No. We have our laws and believe them, and they apply to everyone, is a very good thing."

—quoted in *Nixon: An Oral History of His Presidency*

After the ordeal of Watergate, most Americans attempted to put the affair behind them. In the years ahead, however, the nation encountered a host of new troubles, from a stubborn economic recession to a heart-wrenching hostage crisis overseas.

Reading Check **Evaluating** Why did Congress pass new laws after the Watergate scandal?

Section 2 REVIEW

Vocabulary

1. **Explain** the significance of: Sam J. Ervin, John Dean, executive privilege, special prosecutor, Federal Campaign Act Amendments.

Main Ideas

2. **Explaining** How did the Watergate cover-up involve the CIA and the FBI?

3. **Determining Cause and Effect** Why did President Nixon finally resign?

Critical Thinking

4. **Big Ideas** How did the Watergate scandal alter the balance of power between the executive and legislative branches of the federal government?

5. **Organizing** Use a graphic organizer similar to the one below to record the effects of the Watergate scandal.

Effects of Watergate Scandal

6. **Analyzing Visuals** Study the photographs on page 941. How did the Watergate hearings demonstrate the effectiveness of the system of checks and balances?

Writing About History

7. **Descriptive Writing** Take on the role of a television news analyst. Write a script in which you explain the Watergate scandal and analyze the factors that led to it.

History ONLINE

Study Central™ To review this section, go to glencoe.com and click on Study Central.

Ford and Carter

Guide to Reading

Big Ideas
Economics and Society A weakening economy and growing energy crisis marred the terms of Presidents Ford and Carter.

Content Vocabulary
• inflation (p. 946)
• embargo (p. 946)
• stagflation (p. 947)

Academic Vocabulary
• theory (p. 947)
• deregulation (p. 949)

People and Events to Identify
• OPEC (p. 946)
• Helsinki Accords (p. 948)
• Department of Energy (p. 949)
• Camp David Accords (p. 951)

Reading Strategy
Organizing Complete a graphic organizer similar to the one below by listing the causes of economic problems in the 1970s.

NEW YORK CORE CURRICULUM
U.S. History and Government

Unit 7:
V.B.2.b Oil crisis: shifting energy priorities
V.B.3.b Oil crisis: Middle East in turmoil
V.B.3.c Middle East mediation: Camp David Accords
V.B.3.d The Afghanistan invasion: Olympics and grain—diplomatic weapons
V.B.3.e Iranian hostage crisis: 1979–1981

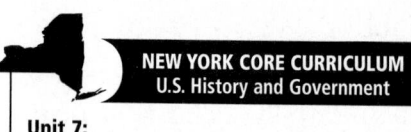

By the time Richard Nixon resigned, the boom period Americans had experienced in the previous decades was coming to an end. Through the 1970s, Presidents Gerald R. Ford and Jimmy Carter attempted, with varying levels of success, to lead the United States through both domestic and foreign crises.

The Economic Crisis of the 1970s

MAIN Idea In the 1970s Americans had to face a slowing economy and an end to plentiful, cheap energy.

HISTORY AND YOU Have you ever heard anyone describe their experiences during the energy crisis of the 1970s? Read on to learn how politics and Americans' dependency on oil imports led to a serious crisis.

During the 1950s and 1960s, many Americans enjoyed remarkable prosperity and had come to assume it was the norm. This prosperity rested in large part on easy access to raw materials around the world and a strong manufacturing base at home. In the 1970s, however, the boom years gave way to a decade of hard times.

A Mighty Economic Machine Slows

The nation's economic troubles began in the mid-1960s when President Johnson increased federal deficit spending, to fund both the Vietnam War and the Great Society programs, without raising taxes. This spending spurred **inflation** by pumping large amounts of money into the economy.

The next blow to the economy came in the early 1970s when the price of oil began to rise. By 1970, the United States had become dependent on oil imports from the Middle East and Africa. This was not a problem as long as prices remained low, but in 1973, the **Organization of Petroleum Exporting Countries (OPEC)**—a cartel dominated by Arab countries—decided to use oil as a political weapon. In 1973 a war erupted between Israel and its Arab neighbors. OPEC announced that its members would place an **embargo** on, or prohibit the shipment of, petroleum to countries that supported Israel. OPEC also raised the price of crude oil by 70 percent, and then by another 130 percent a few months later.

Although the embargo ended within a few months, oil prices continued to rise. The price of a barrel of crude oil had risen from $3 in 1973 to $30 in 1980. As oil and gasoline prices rose, Americans had less money for other goods, which contributed to a recession.

The Energy Crisis

OPEC's embargo caused long lines at gas stations and caused inflation to accelerate rapidly. The U.S. government responded by imposing price controls.

▲ The oil embargo and price increases imposed by OPEC, whose members are shown above, severely decreased supply and increased prices in the United States.

Price of Gasoline, 1970–1990

*Price of Leaded Regular Gasoline in Constant 2000 dollars.

Source: Energy Information Administration.

Analyzing VISUALS

1. **Drawing Conclusions** What problems did American consumers face because of the oil embargo?
2. **Specifying** In what year, between 1970 and 1990, did gasoline reach its highest price?

A Stagnant Economy

Another economic problem was the decline of manufacturing. By 1970, many American manufacturing plants were old and less efficient than the plants Japan and Germany had built after World War II. In 1971, for the first time since 1889, the United States imported more than it exported. Unable to compete, many factories closed, and millions of workers lost their jobs. Thus, in the early 1970s, President Nixon faced a new economic problem nicknamed **"stagflation"**—a combination of inflation and a stagnant economy with high unemployment.

Economists who emphasized the demand side of economic **theory,** including supporters of Keynesianism, did not think that inflation and recession could occur at the same time. They believed that demand drives prices and that inflation could only occur in a booming economy when demand for goods was high. As a result, they did not know what fiscal policy the government should pursue. Increased spending might help end the recession, but it would increase inflation. Raising taxes might slow inflation, but it would also keep the economy in recession.

Nixon decided to focus on controlling inflation. The government moved first to cut spending and raise taxes. The president hoped that higher taxes would prompt Americans to spend less, which would ease the demand on goods and drive down prices. Congress and much of the public, however, protested the idea of a tax hike. Nixon then tried to reduce consumer spending by getting the Federal Reserve Board to raise interest rates. When this failed, the president tried to stop inflation by imposing a 90-day freeze on wages and prices and then issuing federal regulations limiting future wage and price increases. This too met with little success.

✔ **Reading Check** **Explaining** How did President Nixon attempt to stop stagflation?

Ford and Carter Battle the Economic Crisis

MAIN Idea When Gerald Ford failed to solve the nation's problems, Americans turned to political outsider Jimmy Carter to lead the nation.

HISTORY AND YOU Do you think a president should be a Washington insider? Read how being an outsider affected Carter's ability to lead.

When Nixon resigned in 1974, inflation was still high, despite many efforts to reduce prices. Meanwhile, the unemployment rate was over 5 percent. It would now be up to the new president, Gerald Ford, to confront stagflation.

Ford Tries to "Whip" Inflation

By 1975, the American economy was in the worst recession since the Great Depression, with unemployment at nearly 9 percent. Ford responded by launching a plan called WIN— "Whip Inflation Now." He urged Americans to reduce their use of oil and gas, and take steps to conserve energy. The plan had little impact on the economic situation. The president then began cutting government spending and urged the Federal Reserve to raise interest rates to curb inflation. He also sought to balance the budget and keep taxes low. He vetoed more than 50 bills that the Democratic Congress passed during the first two years of his administration. These efforts failed to revive the economy.

Ford's Foreign Policy

In foreign policy, Ford continued Nixon's general strategy. Ford kept Kissinger on as secretary of state and continued to pursue détente with the Soviets and the Chinese. In August 1975, he met with leaders of NATO and the Warsaw Pact to sign the **Helsinki Accords.** Under the accords, the parties recognized the borders of Eastern Europe established at the end of World War II. The Soviets in return promised to uphold certain basic human rights, including the right to move across national borders. The subsequent Soviet failure to uphold these basic rights turned many Americans against détente.

Ford also met with problems in Southeast Asia. In May 1975, soon after Communists seized power in Cambodia, Cambodian forces captured the *Mayaguez,* an American cargo ship traveling near its shores. Calling the seizure an "act of piracy," Ford sent U.S. Marines to retrieve it. Cambodia secretly released the crew shortly before the marines arrived. Unaware the crew was safe, the marines attacked and recaptured the ship, but 41 servicemen died in the battle.

The Election of 1976

The presidential race pitted Gerald Ford against James Earl Carter, Jr., or Jimmy Carter, as he liked to be called. A former governor of Georgia, Carter had no political experience in Washington. Carter took advantage of his outsider status, promising to restore honesty to the federal government. He also promised new programs for energy development, tax reform, welfare reform, and national health care.

Ford characterized Carter as a liberal whose social programs would produce higher rates of inflation and require tax increases. For many voters, however, Carter's image as a moral and upstanding individual, untainted by Washington politics, made him an attractive candidate. In the end, Carter narrowly defeated Ford with 50.1 percent of the popular vote to Ford's 47.9 percent, while capturing 297 electoral votes to Ford's 240.

Carter's Economic Policies

Most of Carter's domestic policies were intended to fix the economy. At first he tried to end the recession and reduce unemployment by increasing government spending and cutting taxes. When inflation surged in 1978, he changed his mind. He delayed the tax cuts and vetoed the spending programs he had himself proposed. He tried to ease inflation by reducing the money supply and raising interest rates. In the end, none of his efforts succeeded.

Carter believed that the nation's most serious problem was its dependence on foreign oil. In one of his first national addresses, he asked Americans to support a "war" against rising energy consumption. "Our decision about energy will test the character of the American people and the ability of the president and Congress to govern this nation," Carter stated.

The Election of 1976

When President Ford failed to solve the nation's economic problems, voters decided to give Washington outsider Jimmy Carter a chance.

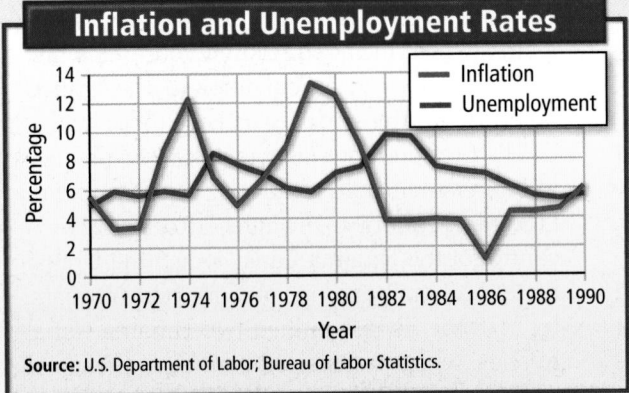

Inflation and Unemployment Rates

Source: U.S. Department of Labor; Bureau of Labor Statistics.

Analyzing VISUALS

1. **Analyzing** In what areas of the country did Carter receive the most votes? Why do you think this was so?

2. **Interpreting** What was the trend for both unemployment and inflation after 1976?

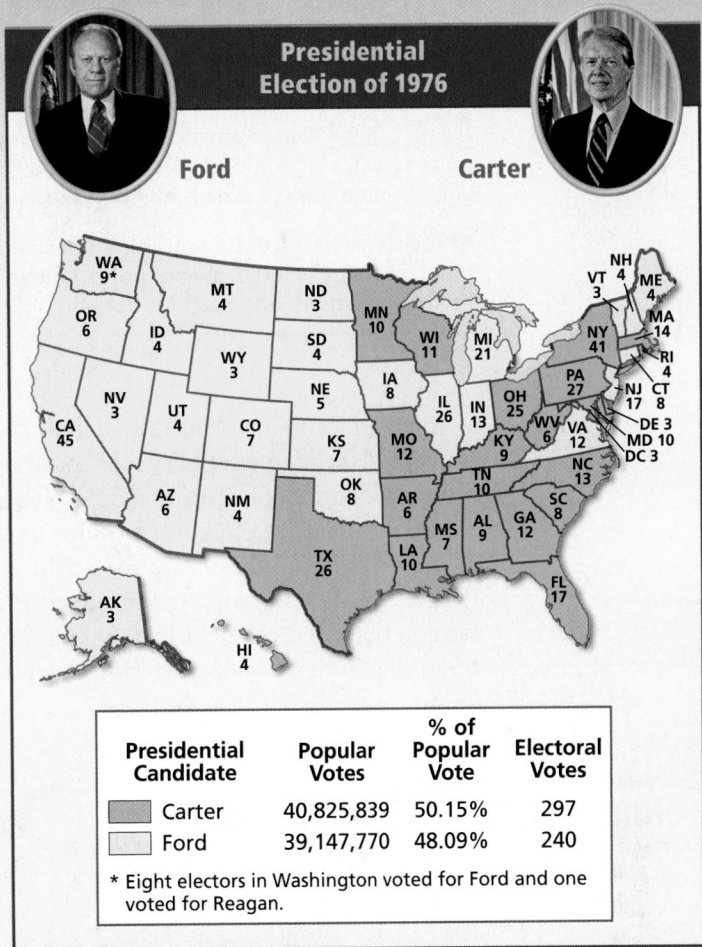

Presidential Election of 1976

Ford

Carter

Presidential Candidate	Popular Votes	% of Popular Vote	Electoral Votes
Carter	40,825,839	50.15%	297
Ford	39,147,770	48.09%	240

* Eight electors in Washington voted for Ford and one voted for Reagan.

Carter proposed a national energy program to conserve oil and to promote the use of coal and renewable energy sources such as solar power. He also convinced Congress to create a **Department of Energy,** and asked Americans to reduce their energy consumption.

Meanwhile, many business leaders and economists urged the president and Congress to deregulate the oil industry. They believed that regulations, first imposed as part of President Nixon's price control plan, made it very difficult for oil companies to make a profit. They claimed they lacked the spare capital needed to invest in new domestic oil wells. This in turn kept the nation dependent on foreign oil.

Carter agreed to support **deregulation** but insisted on a "windfall profits tax" to prevent oil companies from overcharging consumers. Critics argued that the tax conflicted with the basic idea of deregulation, which was to free up capital for use in finding new sources of oil.

In the summer of 1979, instability in the Middle East produced a second major fuel shortage and deepened the nation's economic problems. Under increasing pressure to act, Carter made several proposals in a televised address. In the speech, Carter warned about a "crisis of confidence" that had struck "at the very heart and soul of our national will." The address became known as the "malaise" speech, although Carter had not specifically used that word. Many Americans felt that Carter was blaming the people for his failures.

President Carter's difficulties in solving the nation's economic problems lay partly in his inexperience and inability to work with Congress. Carter, proud of his outsider status, made little effort to reach out to Washington's legislative leaders. As a result, Congress blocked many of his energy proposals. The president also failed to set clear goals for the nation. Instead, he followed a cautious middle course that left people confused. By 1979, public opinion polls showed that Carter's popularity had dropped lower than President Nixon's during Watergate.

Reading Check **Summarizing** To what did President Carter devote much of his domestic agenda?

Carter's Foreign Policy

MAIN Idea Carter attempted to reestablish the United States as a moral force for good on the international stage but had few successes.

HISTORY AND YOU Do you think a leader's personal morality should shape policy? Read how Carter applied his moral code to foreign policy.

In contrast to his uncertain leadership at home, Carter's foreign policy was more clearly defined. A man of strong religious beliefs, Carter argued that the United States must try to be "right and honest and truthful and decent" in dealing with other nations. Yet it was on the international front that Carter suffered one of his most devastating defeats.

Morality in Foreign Policy

President Carter set the tone for his foreign policy in his inaugural speech, when he said, "Our commitment to human rights must be absolute. . . . The powerful must not persecute the weak, and human dignity must be enhanced." Along with his foreign policy team—which included Andrew Young, the first African American ambassador to the United Nations—Carter strove to achieve these goals.

The president put his principles into practice in Latin America. To remove a major symbol of U.S. interventionism, he agreed to give Panama control of the Panama Canal, which the United States had built and operated for over 60 years. In 1978 the Senate ratified two Panama Canal treaties, which transferred control of the canal to Panama on December 31, 1999.

PRIMARY SOURCE
Jimmy Carter and the Middle East

During his administration, Jimmy Carter faced a number of challenges in the Middle East. His foreign policy there met with mixed success.

▲ **The Soviet Invasion of Afghanistan**
The Soviet invasion of Afghanistan shattered détente. Carter responded by imposing a grain embargo, but it did not force the Soviets to pull back.

▼ **The Iranian Hostage Crisis**
The Ayatollah Khomeini (right) led a revolution in Iran in 1979. Fifty-two Americans were taken hostage. Carter's inability to negotiate their release hurt his reelection campaign.

▲ **The Camp David Accords**
In 1978, Carter helped negotiate a peace treaty between Egypt and Israel. Above, Egyptian President Anwar Sadat, Carter, and Israeli Prime Minister Menachem Begin sign the accords.

Analyzing VISUALS

1. **Specifying** What was Carter's major success in foreign policy?

2. **Theorizing** Why was the Middle East a major focus of Carter's foreign policy?

Most dramatically, Carter singled out the Soviet Union as a violator of human rights. He strongly condemned, for example, the Soviet practice of imprisoning those who protested against the government. Relations between the two superpowers suffered a further setback when Soviet troops invaded the Central Asian nation of Afghanistan in December 1979. Carter responded by imposing an embargo on the sale of grain to the Soviet Union and boycotting the 1980 Summer Olympic Games in Moscow. Under the Carter administration, détente eroded further.

Triumph and Failure in the Middle East

It was in the volatile Middle East that President Carter met both his greatest foreign policy triumph and his greatest failure. In 1978 Carter helped broker a historic peace treaty, known as the **Camp David Accords,** between Israel and Egypt—two nations that had been bitter enemies for decades. The treaty was formally signed in 1979. Most other Arab nations in the region opposed the treaty, but it marked a first step to achieving peace in the Middle East.

Just months after the Camp David Accords, Carter had to deal with a crisis in Iran. The United States had long supported Iran's monarch, the Shah, because Iran was a major oil supplier and a buffer against Soviet expansion in the Middle East. The Shah, however, had grown increasingly unpopular in Iran. He was a repressive ruler and had introduced Westernizing reforms to Iranian society. The Islamic clergy fiercely opposed the Shah's reforms. Opposition to the Shah grew, and in January 1979 protesters forced him to flee. An Islamic republic was then declared.

The new regime, led by religious leader Ayatollah Khomeini, distrusted the United States because of its support of the Shah. In November 1979, revolutionaries stormed the American embassy in Tehran and took 52 Americans hostage. The militants threatened to kill the hostages or try them as spies.

The Carter administration tried unsuccessfully to negotiate for the hostages' release. In April 1980, as pressure mounted, Carter approved a daring rescue attempt. To the nation's dismay, the rescue mission failed when several helicopters malfunctioned and one crashed in the desert. Eight servicemen died in the accident. Hamilton Jordan, President Carter's chief of staff, described the atmosphere in the White House the day after the crash. The president "looked exhausted and careworn. . . . The mood at the senior staff meeting was somber and awkward. I sensed that we were all uncomfortable, like when a loved one dies and friends don't know quite what to say."

The crisis continued into the fall of 1980. Every night, news programs reminded viewers how many days the hostages had been held. The president's inability to free them cost him support in the 1980 election. Negotiations continued right up to Carter's last day in office. On January 20, 1981, the day Carter left office, Iran released the Americans, ending their 444 days in captivity.

✔ Reading Check **Summarizing** What was President Carter's main foreign policy theme?

Section 3 REVIEW

Vocabulary

1. **Explain** the significance of: inflation, OPEC, embargo, stagflation, Helsinki Accords, Department of Energy, Camp David Accords.

Main Ideas

2. **Describing** How did the OPEC embargo affect the U.S. economy?

3. **Specifying** What were two ingredients in Carter's failure to achieve success in his domestic policy?

4. **Identifying** What crisis in the Middle East occurred during the Carter administration?

Critical Thinking

5. **Big Ideas** How did Carter attempt to deal with the nation's energy crisis?

6. **Organizing** Complete a graphic organizer by listing the ways in which President Carter applied his human rights ideas to his foreign policy.

Carter's Human Rights Foreign Policy

7. **Analyzing Visuals** Study the photograph of the hostages on page 950. What effect do you think images such as this one had on Americans who were living or traveling in other countries?

Writing About History

8. **Expository Writing** Write an essay identifying what you believe to be Carter's most important foreign policy achievement. Explain your choice.

History ONLINE
Study Central™ To review this section, go to glencoe.com and click on Study Central.

New Approaches to Civil Rights

Guide to Reading

Big Ideas

Struggles for Rights African Americans, Native Americans, and people with disabilities organized to fight discrimination and gain access to better education and jobs.

Content Vocabulary

- busing *(p. 953)*
- affirmative action *(p. 953)*

Academic Vocabulary

- criteria *(p. 954)*
- appropriate *(p. 957)*

People and Events to Identify

- Allan Bakke *(p. 954)*
- Jesse Jackson *(p. 955)*
- Congressional Black Caucus *(p. 955)*
- Shirley Chisholm *(p. 955)*
- American Indian Movement (AIM) *(p. 955)*
- Section 504 *(p. 957)*

Reading Strategy

Sequencing Complete a time line similar to the one below by recording groups in the civil rights movement and their actions.

```
       1971    1974
1969                      1977
           1973
```

NEW YORK CORE CURRICULUM
U.S. History and Government

Unit 7:

III.A.3	Movement for rights of disabled citizens
III.A.3.c	Litigation and legislation; 1960–present
III.B.6.a	Occupation of Alcatraz
III.B.6.c	Wounded Knee, 1973
V.A.1	Domestic policies and events
V.A.1.d	Self-determination for American Indians (1970)
V.B.2	Domestic policy issues

Throughout the 1960s and 1970s, reforms took place in many areas of society. In this period, minority groups, such as African Americans, Native Americans, and persons with disabilities, began to develop new ways to expand opportunities and assert their civil rights.

African Americans Seek Greater Opportunity

MAIN Idea During the 1960s and 1970s, African Americans built on the civil rights achievements of the 1950s to advance their social, political, and legal status.

HISTORY AND YOU Does your school district have a program of busing? Read on to learn how such programs originated as a way to integrate public schools.

By the end of the 1960s, many African American leaders felt a growing sense of frustration. Although most legal forms of racial discrimination had been dismantled, many African Americans saw little improvement in their daily lives. Increasingly, the problems facing most African Americans lay in their lack of access to good jobs and adequate schooling. As a result, leaders of the civil rights movement began to focus their energies on these problems.

Equal Access to Education

In the 1970s, African Americans began to push harder for improvements in public education and access to good schools. Although the Supreme Court had ordered an end to segregated public schools in the 1954 case *Brown* v. *Board of Education,* many schools remained segregated because children attended schools near where they lived. As a result many schools, especially in the North, remained segregated, not by law, but because whites and African Americans lived in different neighborhoods.

In many cases where de facto segregation existed, the white schools were superior, as Ruth Baston of the NAACP noted in 1965 after visiting Boston schools:

PRIMARY SOURCE

"When we would go to white schools, we'd see these lovely classrooms with a small number of children in each class. The teachers were permanent. We'd see wonderful materials. When we'd go to our schools, we'd see overcrowded classrooms, children sitting out in the corridors. And so then we decided that

Busing to End Segregation

To end segregation in public schools, state courts ordered the busing of children to schools outside of their neighborhoods. Reaction from parents to forced busing was often violent.

▲ Supporters of busing took part in the National March on Boston in 1975. The NAACP sponsored the march to mark the anniversary of the Brown v. Board of Education *decision, which outlawed segregation in schools.*

▲ *Anger over busing was particularly virulent in some neighborhoods in Boston, Massachusetts, where police often had to escort school buses along their routes.*

Analyzing VISUALS

1. **Explaining** Why were parents in Boston neighborhoods angry over busing?

2. **Making Inferences** Why are protesters holding signs that read "21 years is too long to wait" in the photograph on the right?

where there were a large number of white students, that's where the care went. That's where the books went. That's where the money went."

—quoted in *Freedom Bound*

To solve this problem, state courts began ordering local governments to bus children to schools outside their neighborhoods to achieve greater racial balance. The practice led to protests and even riots in several white communities, including Boston. The Supreme Court, however, upheld the constitutionality of **busing** in the 1971 case *Swann* v. *Charlotte-Mecklenburg Board of Education.*

In response, many whites took their children out of public schools or moved to a district where busing had not been imposed. About 20,000 white students left Boston's public system for parochial and private schools. By late 1976, African Americans, Latinos, and other minorities made up the majority of Boston's public school students. This "white flight" also occurred in other cities. When Detroit tried to bus students from one school district to another in 1974, the Court held in *Miliken* v. *Bradley* that busing across district lines was unconstitutional unless districts had been deliberately drawn to create segregation.

Affirmative Action

In addition to supporting busing, civil rights leaders in the 1970s began advocating **affirmative action** as a new way to solve economic and educational discrimination. Enforced through executive orders and federal policies, affirmative action called for companies, schools, and institutions doing business with the federal government to recruit African Americans with the hope that this would lead to improved social and economic status. Officials later expanded affirmative action to include other minority groups and women.

For further information on the case of *Swann* v. *Charlotte-Mecklenburg Board of Education,* see page R61 in the *Supreme Court Case Summaries.*

People IN HISTORY

Jesse Jackson
1941–

An ordained Baptist minister, Jesse Jackson first became involved in social causes as an aid to Martin Luther King, Jr. Jackson went on to form Operation PUSH, an organization based in Chicago, which was founded to promote economic opportunities for African Americans. In 1984 he founded the broader National Rainbow Coalition, which advocates for the rights of African Americans, women, and others.

In the 1980s Jackson turned to politics. He ran for the Democratic presidential nomination in 1984 and 1988, placing third and then second to become the most successful African American presidential candidate to that point.

Jackson established the Wall Street Project in 1997 to increase opportunities for minorities in big business. Also in that year, President Clinton selected Jackson as a special envoy to Africa to promote democracy and human rights. In 2000 Jackson received the Presidential Medal of Freedom—the nation's highest civilian honor.

How has Jesse Jackson worked to improve the status of African Americans and promote civil rights for all Americans?

Shirley Chisholm
1924–2005

Shirley Chisholm once remarked, "Of my two 'handicaps,' being female put more obstacles in my path than being black." Her success in challenging both racism and sexism propelled the Brooklyn, New York, native into the national spotlight.

In 1968 Chisholm became the first African American woman to be elected to the United States Congress. There, Chisholm became an ardent defender of several causes, and helped to found the Congressional Black Caucus. She also worked on education and family issues and voted to increase day care programs.

In 1972 Chisholm ran for the Democratic nomination for president. Although she did not win the nomination, she did receive 28 delegates.

After the convention, Chisholm continued her crusade in Congress to help minorities and women for several more terms. She declined to run for re-election in 1982, citing the difficulties of campaigning for liberal issues in an increasingly conservative atmosphere.

On what issues did Shirley Chisholm focus?

Supporters of the policy argued that because so few companies had hired from these groups in the past, they had not necessarily developed the required job skills. If businesses opened their doors wider to minorities, more of them could begin to acquire skills and build better lives.

In one example of affirmative action's impact, Atlanta witnessed a significant increase in minority job opportunities after Maynard Jackson became its first African American mayor in 1973. When Jackson took office, less than one percent of all city contracts went to African Americans, even though they made up about half of Atlanta's population. Jackson used the expansion of the city's airport to redress this imbalance. Through his efforts, small companies and minority firms took on 25 percent of all airport construction work, earning them some $125 million in contracts.

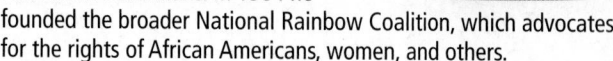

For further information on the case of *University of California Regents v. Bakke*, see page R60 in the *Supreme Court Case Summaries*.

The *Bakke* Case

Affirmative action programs did not go unchallenged, however. Critics viewed them as a form of reverse racial discrimination. They claimed that qualified white male workers and students were kept from jobs, promotions, and places in schools because a certain number of such positions had been set aside for minorities or women.

Affirmative action was addressed by the Supreme Court in 1978. The case began in 1974, after officials at the medical school of the University of California at Davis turned down the admission of a white applicant named **Allan Bakke** for a second time. When Bakke learned that slots had been set aside for minorities, he sued the school. Bakke argued that by admitting minority applicants—some of whom had scored lower than Bakke on their exams—the school had discriminated against him based on his race.

In 1978, in *University of California Regents v. Bakke*, the Supreme Court, in a 5 to 4 ruling, declared that the university had violated Bakke's civil rights. It also ruled, however, that schools had an interest in maintaining a diverse student body. Thus, universities could consider race as one part of their admissions **criteria** as long as they did not use "fixed quotas," such as the slots the UC-Davis Medical School had reserved for minority students.

New Political Leaders

New political leaders emerged in the African American community in the 1970s. **Jesse Jackson,** a former aid to Martin Luther King, Jr., was among this new generation of activists. In 1971 Jackson founded Operation PUSH (People United to Save Humanity), an organization dedicated to registering voters, developing African American businesses, and broadening educational opportunities. In 1984 and 1988, Jackson sought the Democratic presidential nomination. Although both attempts were unsuccessful, he won over millions of voters.

African Americans also became more influential in national politics for the first time since Reconstruction. In 1971 African American members of Congress organized the **Congressional Black Caucus** to more clearly represent their concerns. Another prominent leader of the era was **Shirley Chisholm** of New York. Chisholm was a founding member of the Congressional Black Caucus and the first African American woman to serve in Congress. In 1977 another former assistant to Martin Luther King, Jr., U.S. Representative Andrew Young, was selected by President Carter to become the first African American to serve as U.S. ambassador to the United Nations. He went on to become the mayor of Atlanta. By the early 1980s, African American mayors had been elected in Atlanta, Detroit, Chicago, Los Angeles, New Orleans, Philadelphia, and Washington, D.C.

Another leader who emerged in the 1980s was Louis Farrakhan, a prominent minister of the Nation of Islam. He organized the Million Man March, which attracted an enormous crowd in Washington, D.C., on October 16, 1995. Farrakhan had conceived of the march as a way to promote self-reliance and responsibility among African American men. In addition to Farrakhan, the event featured other prominent speakers, including Jesse Jackson and the poet Maya Angelou.

In 1990, voters in Virginia elected L. Douglas Wilder, who became the first African American to serve as governor of a state. In that same year, David Dinkins took office as the first African American mayor of New York City.

Reading Check **Examining** What were the goals of affirmative action policies?

Native Americans Raise Their Voices

MAIN Idea The most impoverished minority group in America, Native Americans, began organizing for civil rights.

HISTORY AND YOU What do you recall about the Black Power Movement in the 1960s? Read on to learn how some Native Americans formed the American Indian Movement.

In 1970 Native Americans were one of the nation's smallest minority groups, constituting less than one percent of the U.S. population, yet they faced enormous problems. The unemployment rate for Native Americans was ten times the national rate. Their average annual family income was $1,000 less than that of African Americans. Unemployment was very high on reservations, where nearly half of all Native Americans lived. Those living in cities often had little education or training. The bleakest statistic of all showed that the life expectancy for Native Americans was almost seven years below the national average.

A Protest Movement Emerges

In 1961 more than 400 members of 67 Native American groups gathered in Chicago to discuss ways to address their problems. They issued a manifesto, known as the Declaration of Indian Purpose, asking for federal programs to create greater economic opportunities on reservations.

Unlike some groups who wanted to be accepted by mainstream society, many Native Americans wanted more independence from it. They took a step toward this goal in 1968 when Congress passed the Indian Civil Rights Act. The legislation guaranteed reservation residents the protections of the Bill of Rights, but it also recognized local reservation law.

Native Americans who viewed the government's efforts as too modest formed more militant groups, which typically employed a more combative style. One such group, the **American Indian Movement (AIM),** staged a symbolic protest in 1969 by occupying the abandoned federal prison on Alcatraz Island in San Francisco Bay for 19 months, claiming ownership "by right of discovery."

The most famous protest by AIM took place at Wounded Knee, South Dakota, where U.S. troops had killed hundreds of Sioux in 1890. In February 1973, AIM members seized the town of Wounded Knee for 70 days. They demanded that the government honor its past treaty obligations to Native Americans and insisted that radical changes be made in the administration of reservations. A brief clash between AIM members and the FBI resulted in two Native Americans dead and several wounded on both sides. Shortly thereafter, the siege came to an end.

Native American Gains

By the mid-1970s, the Native American movement had begun to achieve some of its goals. In 1975 Congress passed the Indian Self-Determination and Educational Assistance Act, which increased funds for Native American education and expanded local control over federal programs. More Native Americans also moved into policy-making positions at the Bureau of Indian Affairs, and the agency pushed for more Native American self-determination.

Native Americans also won several court cases involving land and water rights. The people of the Pueblo of Taos, New Mexico, regained property rights to Blue Lake, a place sacred to their religion. In 1980 a federal court settled a claim of the Passamaquoddy and the Penobscot peoples. The government paid them $81.5 million to relinquish their claim to land in Maine. Other court decisions gave Native American governments the authority to tax businesses on their reservations.

Since Native Americans first began to organize, many reservations have improved their economic conditions by actively developing businesses, such as electric plants, resorts, cattle ranches, and oil and gas wells. More recently, gambling casinos have become a successful enterprise. Because of rulings on sovereignty, Native Americans in some areas are allowed to operate gaming establishments under their own laws even though state laws prevent others from doing so.

☑ **Reading Check** **Analyzing** What conditions led Native Americans to organize in the 1960s?

The Disability Rights Movement

In the 1970s, people with disabilities struggled for greater rights in education, employment, and housing. They met with success in the passage of legislation such as the Rehabilitation Act of 1973.

▲ Section 504 of the Rehabilitation Act and, later, the Americans with Disabilities Act specified that disabled people must have equal access to public facilities, such as transportation and parking.

▲ On April 5, 1977, the American Coalition of Citizens with Disabilities organized sit-ins demanding equal rights.

Analyzing VISUALS

1. **Listing** What rights did people with disabilities struggle for in the 1970s?
2. **Specifying** What two accommodations for people with disabilities are shown in the photograph on the right?

The Disability Rights Movement

MAIN Idea During the 1970s, people with disabilities fought for greater rights and access to education and jobs.

HISTORY AND YOU Do you or someone you know have a disability? Read on to learn about how people with disabilities achieved new legislation to help protect their civil rights.

The struggle for disability rights had its early expression in the independent living movement begun at the University of California at Berkeley in the early 1970s. The movement advocated for the right of people of all levels of abilities to choose to live freely in society. This was part of a new attitude that encouraged deinstitutionalization of people with disabilities.

People with disabilities also looked to the federal government to protect their civil rights. Access to public facilities and prohibitions on discrimination in employment led their demands. One victory was passage, in 1968, of the Architectural Barriers Act, which mandated that new buildings constructed with federal funds be accessible to disabled persons. The Rehabilitation Act of 1973 was even more significant. According to **Section 504,** "no otherwise qualified individual with a disability . . . shall . . . be excluded from participation in, be denied the benefits of, or be subjected to discrimination under any program or service or activity receiving Federal financial assistance . . ."

Unfortunately passage of the Rehabilitation Act meant little until procedures for enforcing its provisions were established. As of 1977, the Department of Health, Education, and Welfare (HEW) had issued no such regulations. Frustrated, the American Coalition of Citizens with Disabilities, headed by Frank Bowe, organized protests. On April 5, 1977, some 2,000 persons with disabilities in 10 cities began sit-ins at regional HEW offices. Although most protests lasted only a day or two, protesters in San Francisco maintained their sit-in for over three weeks—leaving only when HEW's director signed the regulations banning discrimination.

Changes also occurred in special education. In 1966 Congress created the Bureau for the Education of the Handicapped, which provided grants to develop programs for educating children with disabilities. In 1975 the Education for All Handicapped Children Act required that all students with disabilities receive a free, **appropriate** education. One trend was to mainstream, or bring into the regular classroom, students with disabilities.

In 1990 Congress enacted the Americans with Disabilities Act. This far-reaching legislation banned discrimination against persons with disabilities in employment, transportation, public education, and telecommunications.

Today, new technologies are important assets to people with disabilities. Innovations such as closed-captioned television broadcasts, devices for telephones, and screen readers allow people with disabilities to access information in new ways.

✓ Reading Check **Explaining** Why did the American Coalition of Citizens with Disabilities stage sit-ins in 1977?

Section 4 REVIEW

Vocabulary

1. **Explain** the significance of: busing, affirmative action, Allan Bakke, Jesse Jackson, Congressional Black Caucus, Shirley Chisholm, American Indian Movement (AIM), Section 504.

Main Ideas

2. **Specifying** How did some critics characterize affirmative action?

3. **Identifying Central Issues** What was significant about AIM's claim to Alcatraz Island?

4. **Explaining** What was the significance of the independent living movement?

Critical Thinking

5. **Big Ideas** How did the Supreme Court support civil rights during the 1970s?

6. **Organizing** Use a graphic organizer to identify civil rights leaders and their causes.

Civil Rights Leaders	Causes

7. **Analyzing Visuals** Study the images on page 953 of busing in the 1970s. Why do you think reactions to busing were so strong and at times even violent?

Writing About History

8. **Expository Writing** Write a magazine article about conditions that provoked the Native American protest movement of the 1960s and 1970s. Be sure to discuss the movement's goals and activities.

History ONLINE

Study Central™ To review this section, go to glencoe.com and click on Study Central.

Environmentalism

Guide to Reading

Big Ideas
Group Action Increased awareness of environmental issues inspired a grassroots campaign to protect nature.

Content Vocabulary
- smog *(p. 959)*
- fossil fuel *(p. 961)*

Academic Vocabulary
- intensify *(p. 961)*
- alternative *(p. 961)*

People and Events to Identify
- Rachel Carson *(p. 958)*
- Environmental Protection Agency *(p. 960)*
- Love Canal *(p. 960)*
- Three Mile Island *(p. 961)*

Reading Strategy
Organizing Complete a graphic organizer similar to the one below by including actions taken to combat the nation's environmental problems in the 1960s and 1970s.

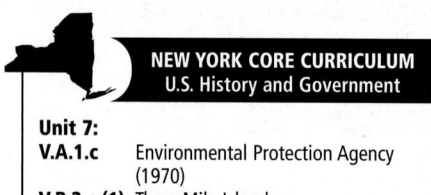

NEW YORK CORE CURRICULUM
U.S. History and Government

Unit 7:
V.A.1.c Environmental Protection Agency (1970)
V.B.2.c.(1) Three Mile Island
V.B.2.c.(3) Toxic waste

Americans became increasingly aware of the damage being done to the environment. Soon environmental issues became national concerns, and individuals, local groups, and the government acted to address the damage and protect natural resources.

The Origins of Environmentalism

MAIN Idea Concerns about the effects of a deadly pesticide, the visible signs of pollution in American cities, and an influential book inspired a movement to protect the environment.

HISTORY AND YOU Do you take action personally or with others to preserve and protect the environment? Read on to learn how one woman inspired the environmental movement.

In 1966 Carol Yannacone of Patchogue, a small community on Long Island, New York, learned that officials were using the powerful pesticide DDT as part of a mosquito control operation at a local lake. Alarmed that the pesticide might poison the lake and local streams, Yannacone and her husband Victor, an attorney, contacted several local scientists who confirmed their suspicions.

The Yannacones then successfully sued to halt the use of the pesticide. In so doing, they had discovered a new strategy for addressing environmental concerns. Shortly after the Yannacones' court victory, the scientists involved in the case established the Environmental Defense Fund and used its contributions for a series of legal actions across the country to halt DDT spraying. Their efforts led to a nationwide ban on the use of the pesticide in 1972.

The effort to ban DDT was only one part of a new environmental movement that took shape in the 1960s and 1970s. The person who helped trigger this new movement was not a political leader or prominent academic, but a soft-spoken marine biologist named **Rachel Carson.** Carson's 1962 book *Silent Spring* assailed the increasing use of pesticides, particularly DDT. She contended that while pesticides curbed insect populations, they also killed birds, fish, and other creatures that might ingest them. Carson warned Americans of a "silent spring," in which there would be no birds left to usher spring in with their songs. *Silent Spring* became a bestseller and one of the most controversial and influential books of the 1960s. The chemical industry was outraged and began an intense campaign to discredit Carson and her arguments.

Many Americans believed Carson's warnings, however, largely because of what they were seeing around them and reading in news reports. Rivers across the nation were no longer safe for

Origins of the Environmentalist Movement

▲ Industrial pollution in cities like Newark, New Jersey (above) led to thick clouds of smog that caused breathing problems for some people. Tired of the dirty air, many Americans began to demand an end to pollution.

▲ Volunteers work to clean up an oil spill off the coast of California in 1969. News of the spill helped mobilize the new environmentalist movement.

◄ In 1969, the Cuyahoga River in Ohio caught fire. The incident gained national attention and contributed to the passage of the Clean Water Act in 1972.

Analyzing VISUALS

1. **Summarizing** What events raised awareness of the need to protect the environment?
2. **Discussing** Why do you think the fire on the Cuyahoga River convinced many people of the need for action?

fishing or swimming. **Smog,** or fog made heavier and darker by smoke and chemical fumes, hung perpetually over many major cities. In the Northwest, timber companies were cutting down acres of forest. In 1969 a major oil spill off Santa Barbara, California, ruined miles of beach and killed scores of birds and aquatic animals. A dike project in Florida's Everglades indirectly killed millions of birds and animals. Pollution and garbage caused nearly all the fish to disappear from Lake Erie. By 1970, many citizens were convinced it was time to do something about protecting the environment.

A Grassroots Effort Begins

Many observers point to April 1970 as the unofficial beginning of the environmentalist movement. That month, the nation held its first Earth Day celebration, a day devoted to addressing environmental concerns. The national response was overwhelming. On 2,000 college campuses, in 10,000 secondary schools, and in hundreds of communities, millions of Americans participated in activities to show their environmental awareness.

After Earth Day, many citizens formed local environmental groups. Long-standing non-profit organizations such as the Audubon Society, the Sierra Club, and the Wilderness Society grew rapidly in membership and political influence. These organizations worked to protect the environment and promote the conservation of natural resources. In 1970 activists started the Natural Resources Defense Council to coordinate a nationwide network of scientists, lawyers, and activists working on environmental issues.

Many communities and businesses responded to these organizations. Many city planners sought to reduce urban sprawl and expand green space. Architects and builders tried to make their structures more energy efficient, and the forestry industry began reforestation programs.

✔ Reading Check **Identifying** What natural resources did environmental groups want to protect?

The Environmental Movement Blossoms

MAIN Idea Pressure from citizens and activist groups led Congress to pass major environmental legislation.

HISTORY AND YOU Can you think of a recent environmental disaster that has been in the news? Read on to learn about two of the worst environmental disasters in American history.

As the environmental movement gained support, the federal government took action. In 1970 President Nixon signed the National Environmental Policy Act, which created the **Environmental Protection Agency (EPA).** The EPA set and enforced pollution standards, promoted research, and directed anti-pollution activities with state and local governments.

The Clean Air Act also became law in 1970 after Congress overrode President Nixon's veto. This act established emissions standards for factories and automobiles. It also ordered all industries to comply with such standards within five years.

In following years, Congress passed two more pieces of significant environmental legislation. The Clean Water Act (1972) restricted the discharge of pollutants into the nation's lakes and rivers, and the Endangered Species Act (1973) established measures for saving threatened animal and plant species. These laws succeeded in reducing smog, and the pollution of many lakes, streams, and rivers declined dramatically.

Love Canal

Despite the flurry of federal environmental legislation, Americans continued to mobilize on the community level throughout the 1970s. One of the most powerful displays of community activism occurred in a housing development near Niagara Falls, New York, known as **Love Canal.**

POLITICAL CARTOONS PRIMARY SOURCE
A New Focus on the Environment

By the 1970s, the environmental movement was a strong force for change in the nation and around the world. In response, Congress passed a series of laws designed to protect the air, water, and wildlife.

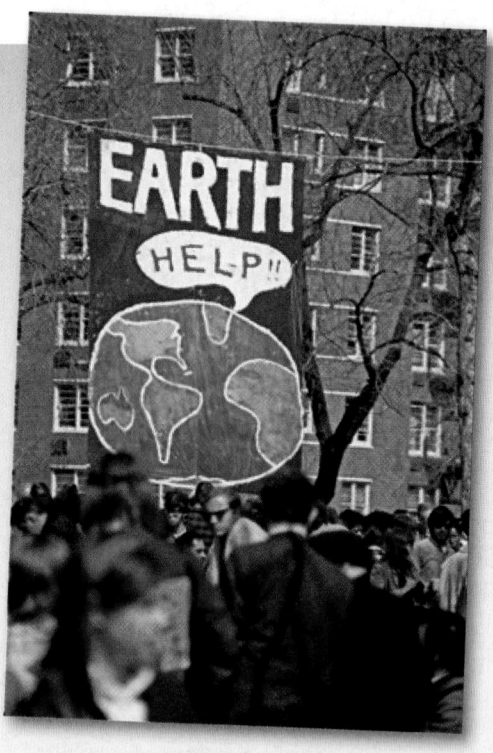

▶ Events, such as the annual Earth Day celebrations, helped environmentalists increase public awareness of environmental problems.

◀ President Ford and others are criticized for supporting industrial interests rather than protecting the environment.

Analyzing VISUALS DBQ

1. **Identifying** Who does the large figure represent in the cartoon on the left?

2. **Summarizing** What is the main idea being expressed in the Earth Day poster?

During the 1970s, residents of Love Canal began to notice increasingly high incidences of health problems in their community, including nerve damage, blood diseases, cancer, miscarriages, and birth defects. The residents soon learned that their community sat atop a decades-old toxic waste dump. Over time, its hazardous contents had spread through the ground.

Led by a local woman, Lois Gibbs, the residents joined together and demanded that the government take steps to address these health threats. Hindered at first by local and state officials, the residents refused to back down, and by 1978 they had made their struggle known to the entire nation. That year, in the face of mounting public pressure and evidence of the dangers posed by the dump, the state permanently relocated more than 200 families.

In 1980, after hearing protests from the families who still lived near the landfill, President Carter declared Love Canal a federal disaster area and moved over 600 remaining families to new locations. In 1983 Love Canal residents sued the company that had created the dump site and settled the case for $20 million. The site was cleaned up by sealing the waste within an underground bunker and burning homes located above the dumping ground.

Concerns About Nuclear Energy

During the 1970s, a number of citizens also became concerned about the use of nuclear reactors to generate electricity. As nuclear power plants began to dot the nation's landscape, the debate over their use **intensified.** Supporters of nuclear energy hailed it as a cleaner and less expensive **alternative** to **fossil fuels,** such as coal, oil, and natural gas, which are in limited supply. Opponents warned of the risks nuclear energy posed, particularly the devastating consequences of an accidental radiation release into the air.

The debate gained national attention in a shocking fashion in 1979. In the early hours of March 28, one of the reactors at the **Three Mile Island** nuclear facility outside Harrisburg, Pennsylvania, overheated after its cooling system failed. Two days later, as plant officials scrambled to fix the problem, low levels of radiation escaped from the reactor.

Officials evacuated many nearby residents, while others fled on their own. Citizens and community groups expressed outrage at protest rallies. Officials closed down the reactor and sealed the leak. The Nuclear Regulatory Commission, the federal agency that regulates the nuclear power industry, eventually declared the plant safe. President Carter even visited the site in order to allay the public's concerns.

Although no one was hurt, the accident at Three Mile Island had a powerful impact politically. Many people now doubted the safety of nuclear energy. Such doubts have continued. Since Three Mile Island, some 60 nuclear power plants have been shut down or abandoned, and no new facilities have been built since 1973.

Reading Check **Summarizing** What is the environmental movement's main goal?

Vocabulary

1. **Explain** the significance of: Rachel Carson, smog, Environmental Protection Agency, Love Canal, fossil fuel, Three Mile Island.

Main Ideas

2. **Summarizing** What were some of the dangers of DDT?

3. **Explaining** Why was Love Canal a dangerous place to live?

Critical Thinking

4. **Big Ideas** What were some groups that lobbied for legislation to protect the environment in the 1960s and 1970s?

5. **Categorizing** Use a graphic organizer similar to the one below to list the environmental laws passed in the 1970s, and explain their purposes.

Environmental Legislation	Purpose

6. **Analyzing Visuals** Study the cartoon on the left-hand side of page 960. What is the meaning of the piece of paper that reads "O.K. Gerald Ford" in the main figure's pocket?

Writing About History

7. **Descriptive Writing** Take on the role of an investigative reporter, and describe the environmental disaster at either Love Canal or Three Mile Island. Explain how community activism brought the issue to the nation's attention.

History ONLINE

Study Central™ To review this section, go to glencoe.com and click on Study Central.

A Era of Challenges

Major Domestic Issues of the 1970s

- A nation is divided and angry over the Vietnam War.
- An energy crisis is triggered by OPEC's raising of oil prices.
- A stagnant economy exists with both inflation and high unemployment.
- Ongoing racial problems occur in major cities.
- Growing awareness of environmental problems including air and water pollution, toxic waste (at Love Canal and other sites), the overuse of pesticides, plus a crisis with the nuclear power plant at Three Mile Island.

Major Foreign Policy Issues of the 1970s

- Cold War tensions continue with the Soviet Union and China.
- The Soviet Union invades Afghanistan.
- War between Israel and its Arab neighbors breaks out in 1973, and ongoing violence occurs in the Middle East.
- A revolution in Iran leads to the taking of American hostages.

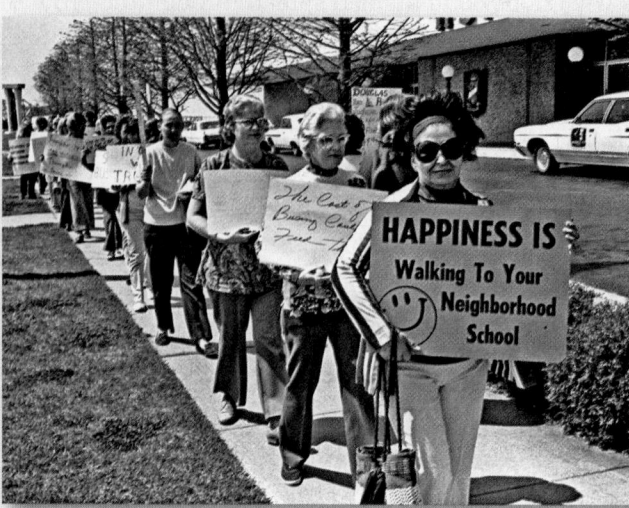

▲ In the 1970s, state courts order the forced desegregation of public schools through busing, despite protests such as the one above in Memphis, Tennessee.

▲ Americans wait in long lines to purchase gasoline during the energy crisis of the 1970s.

◀ The first Earth Day in 1970 is often seen as the start of an organized environmentalist movement, which continues to have a major influence on politics and society today.

New Policies and Activism

Responding to Domestic Issues

- Nixon attempts to win over Southern conservatives, but his administration's determination to win leads to the Watergate cover-up and Nixon's subsequent resignation.
- Ford's WIN campaign fails to overcome inflation.
- Carter urges Americans to conserve energy, creates the Department of Energy, and asks Congress to pass legislation deregulating the oil industry.
- Civil rights leaders propose affirmative action policies to reduce discrimination; the Supreme Court upholds some types of affirmative action in the *Bakke* case.
- Busing begins in northern cities to integrate schools.
- Environmentalist movement begins; Nixon creates the EPA.

Responding to Foreign Policy Issues

- Nixon and Kissinger introduce the policy of détente and begin talks with both the USSR and China.
- Carter mediates negotiations between Israel and Egypt leading to the first Arab-Israeli peace treaty.
- The United States imposes a grain embargo on the USSR for invading Afghanistan and boycotts the Moscow Olympics.
- The hostage crisis with Iran drags on for more than a year; an American rescue attempt fails, and the hostages are not released until Carter leaves office.

NEW YORK REGENTS EXAM PRACTICE

TEST-TAKING

Always manage your time during a test so you can go back and review all your answers.

Part I

Directions (1–10): For each statement or question, write on a separate sheet of paper the number of the word or expression that, of those given, best completes the statement or answers the question.

1 In the 1968 presidential election, Nixon appealed to what group of Americans by promising to appoint only conservatives to the federal courts?

(1) Native Americans

(2) Southerners

(3) Middle Americans

(4) Northeastern intellectuals

2 Nixon developed a new program to try to make government more efficient known as

(1) New Federalism.

(2) the Silent Majority.

(3) States' Rights.

(4) the Great Society.

3 Members of the Committee for the Re-election of the President broke into Democratic Party headquarters at the Watergate to

(1) leave incriminating evidence of Democratic wrongdoing.

(2) install a tape-recording device so that Nixon could write his memoirs.

(3) find information to use in the case *United States* v. *Nixon*.

(4) steal sensitive information and install wiretaps.

4 In the wake of the Watergate scandal, Congress passed a series of laws to accomplish which of the following goals?

(1) to stop tape recordings in the White House

(2) to limit the power of the presidency

(3) to pardon Richard Nixon for his part in the cover-up

(4) to remove police power from the FBI

5 In the early 1970s, OPEC began to use oil as a political weapon against countries that

(1) would not join their organization.

(2) supported the existence of Israel.

(3) refused to pay the new per-barrel oil price.

(4) supported Arab countries' disapproval of Israel.

6 To protest the Soviet Union's invasion of Afghanistan, President Carter took which of the following actions?

(1) He sent U.S. Army troops to fight on the side of the Afghans.

(2) He put NATO forces in Europe on high alert.

(3) He approved a buildup of U.S. nuclear weapons.

(4) He placed an embargo on grain shipments to the Soviet Union.

7 The 1971 case *Swann* v. *Charlotte-Mecklenburg Board of Education* upheld the constitutionality of which policy?

(1) busing

(2) affirmative action

(3) segregation

(4) revenue sharing

Need Extra Help?							
If You Missed Questions . . .	1	2	3	4	5	6	7
Go to Page . . .	934	936	940	945	946	951	953

[OVER]

Base your answer to question 8 on the map below and your knowledge of Chapter 28.

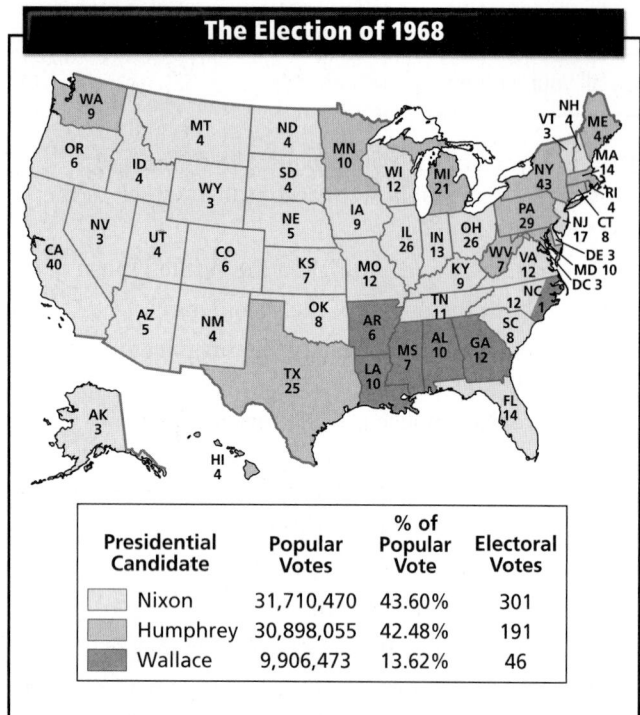

The Election of 1968

Presidential Candidate	Popular Votes	% of Popular Vote	Electoral Votes
Nixon	31,710,470	43.60%	301
Humphrey	30,898,055	42.48%	191
Wallace	9,906,473	13.62%	46

8 In which region did Nixon receive the most support?

(1) North and South.

(2) North and Midwest.

(3) Midwest and West.

(4) South and West.

9 The unofficial beginning of the environmentalist movement occurred

(1) when the Yannacones complained about the use of DDT.

(2) on the first Earth Day in 1970.

(3) when Congress passed the Clean Air Act.

(4) after Love Canal was found to be poisoned.

Part II Thematic Essay Question

Directions: Write a well-organized essay that includes an introduction, several paragraphs addressing the task below, and a conclusion.

Theme: Watergate

Secretary of State and former general Alexander Haig stated that the Watergate scandal led to a "fundamental discrediting of respect for the presidency . . . [and] a new skepticism about politics in general, . . ."

Task:

Consider Secretary of State Haig's statement and the Watergate scandal and

- Discuss whether you agree or disagree with his statement

- Evaluate the effects of Watergate in light of his statement

Guidelines:

In your essay, be sure to:

- Develop all aspects of the task

- Support the theme with relevant facts, examples, and details

- Use a logical and clear plan of organization, including an introduction and a conclusion that are beyond a restatement of the theme

Part III Document-Based Question

This question is based on the accompanying documents. It is designed to test your ability to work with historical documents. Some of the documents have been edited for the purposes of the question. As you analyze the documents, take into account the source of each document and any point of view that may be presented in the document.

Historical Context:

During the 1970s, the United States experienced a number of foreign policy issues that affected domestic policy.

Need Extra Help?		
If You Missed Questions . . .	8	9
Go to Page . . .	934	958

Task:
Using information from the documents and your knowledge of United States history, answer the questions that follow each document in Part A. Your answers to the questions will help you write the Part B essay in which you will be asked to

- Discuss the foreign policy issues that led to the energy crisis and the buildup of nuclear arms
- Evaluate the long-term effects of these issues on U.S. Foreign policy

Part A
Short-Answer Questions
Directions: Analyze the documents and answer the short-answer questions that follow each document on a separate sheet of paper.

Document 1

> Evidence of the full dimensions of the energy crisis in this country is becoming more clear every day.
>
> - As a first step to cut gasoline use, President Nixon was reportedly ready to order closing of service stations nationwide from 9 P.M. Saturday to midnight Sunday. . . .
> - Immediate rationing of gasoline and fuel oil is being urged on the President by top oil-industry executives. . . .
>
> One major piece of legislation . . . directs the President to take measures necessary to reduce the nation's energy demands by 25 percent within four weeks.
>   Speed limits would be cut nationally; lighting and heating of public and commercial buildings would be curtailed; home-owners would be given tax deductions to winterize their homes. . . .
>   Other pending measures would impose year-round daylight saving time and would open naval oil reserves for intense exploration."

Source: *U.S. News & World Report*, December 3, 1973

1 What proposals did the U.S. government make to deal with the energy crisis?

Document 2

Ranan Lurie, 1970.

2 According to this cartoon, who ultimately suffered over the arms buildup between the United States and the Soviet Union?

Part B
Essay
Directions: Reread the task box at the top left and write a well-organized essay that includes an introduction, several paragraphs, and a conclusion.

Guidelines:
In your essay, be sure to:
- Develop all aspects of the task
- Incorporate information from the documents
- Incorporate relevant outside information
- Support the theme with relevant facts, examples, and details
- Use a logical and clear plan of organization, including an introduction and a conclusion that are beyond a restatement of the theme

History ONLINE
For additional test practice, use Self-Check Quizzes—Chapter 28 at glencoe.com.

Need Extra Help?			
If You Missed Questions . . .	1	2	Essay
Go to Page . . .	948	939	948

Chapter 29

Resurgence of Conservatism

1980–1992

SECTION 1 The New Conservatism

SECTION 2 The Reagan Years

SECTION 3 Life in the 1980s

SECTION 4 The End of the Cold War

President Ronald Reagan, his wife Nancy, Vice-President George H.W. Bush, and his wife Barbara at Reagan's Second Inauguration.

U.S. PRESIDENTS

Carter 1977–1981

Reagan 1981–1989

U.S. EVENTS

1979 — 1982 — 1985

1979
- Jerry Falwell's "Moral Majority" movement begins

1981
- Launch of *Columbia*, first space shuttle
- American hostages released in Iran

1983
- Reagan announces the Star Wars program
- U.S. Marine barracks bombed in Lebanon

WORLD EVENTS

1979
- Iranian revolution brings down Shah
- Soviets invade Afghanistan

1980
- War begins between Iran and Iraq

1985
- Mikhail Gorbachev becomes leader of Soviet Union

Are There Cycles in American Politics?

After several decades where progressive and liberal ideas dominated American politics, conservatism began making a comeback in the 1970s, and in 1980 voters elected the conservative Ronald Reagan president. Reagan's commitment to less government regulation, a stronger military, and uncompromising anticommunism seemed to meet voters' concerns.

- *Why do you think conservative ideas appealed to more Americans in the 1980s?*
- *How do you think conservative ideas have changed society?*

FOLDABLES

Analyzing Information Create a Folded Chart Foldable to organize information about the government under Ronald Reagan. List domestic and foreign policy for three eras: before the Reagan era, the Reagan administration, and the post-Reagan years.

The Reagan Revolution	Before Reagan	Reagan Era	After Reagan
Domestic Policy			
Foreign Policy			

1986
- Iran-Contra scandal enters the news

1987
- INF Treaty between U.S. and USSR

1988
- More than 35,000 cases of AIDS diagnosed for the year

G. Bush 1989–1993

1991
- Persian Gulf War occurs between Iraq and UN coalition

1988

1991

1989
- Tiananmen Square protest in China
- Communist governments in Eastern Europe collapse

1990
- Germany reunites as one nation

1991
- Soviet Union dissolves

History ONLINE **Chapter Overview**
Visit glencoe.com to preview Chapter 29.

The New Conservatism

Guide to Reading

Big Ideas
Economics and Society High taxes as well as economic and moral concerns led the country toward a new conservatism.

Content Vocabulary
- liberal *(p. 968)*
- conservative *(p. 968)*
- "televangelist" *(p. 973)*

Academic Vocabulary
- indicate *(p. 973)*
- stability *(p. 973)*

People and Events to Identify
- William F. Buckley *(p. 971)*
- Sunbelt *(p. 971)*
- Billy Graham *(p. 973)*
- Jerry Falwell *(p. 973)*
- "Moral Majority" *(p. 973)*

Reading Strategy
Taking Notes Use the major headings of this section to outline information about the rise of the new conservatism in the United States.

```
The New Conservatism
I. Liberalism and Conservatism
    A.
    B.
II.
    A.
```

NEW YORK CORE CURRICULUM
U.S. History and Government

Unit 7:
V.C. Reagan and Bush, the "new" federalism and growth of conservatism

By the 1980s, new levels of discontent with government and society had left many Americans concerned about the direction of the nation. Some began to call for a return to more conservative approaches and values.

Liberalism and Conservatism

MAIN Idea Conservatives and liberals disagreed on the role of government.

HISTORY AND YOU Do you consider yourself liberal or conservative? Why? Read on to learn more about conservative and liberal ideas of government.

Midge Decter, a New Yorker and a writer for the conservative publication *Commentary*, was appalled at the violence that hit her city on a hot July night in 1977. On the night of July 13, the power failed in New York City. The blackout left millions of people in darkness, and looting and arson rocked the city. City officials and the media blamed the lawlessness on the anger and despair of youth in neglected areas. Decter disagreed:

PRIMARY SOURCE

"[T]hose young men went on their spree of looting because they had been given permission to do so . . . by all the papers and magazines, movies and documentaries—all the outlets for the purveying of enlightened liberal attitude and progressive liberal policy—which had for years and years been proclaiming that race and poverty were sufficient excuses for lawlessness. . . . "

—quoted in *Commentary*, September 1977

Midge Decter's article blaming liberalism for the New York riots illustrates one side of a debate in American politics that continues to the present day. On one side are people who call themselves **liberals;** on the other side are those who identify themselves as **conservatives.** Liberal ideas had dominated American politics in the 1960s, but conservative ideas regained significant support in the 1970s, and in 1980 Ronald Reagan, a strong conservative, was elected president.

Liberalism

In American politics today, people who call themselves liberals believe several basic ideas. In general, liberals believe that the government should regulate the economy to protect people from the

Liberalism vs. Conservatism

▲ Conservatives believe the liberal concern with achieving social equality and alleviating poverty is often taken to excess. They also disapprove of the idea of using the power of government to redistribute wealth from one group to another, preferring that the free market determine the distribution of wealth.

▲ Liberals believe that the conservative concern with keeping taxes low comes at the expense of other social needs and that conservatives who want low taxes are uncaring when it comes to helping the less fortunate.

Analyzing VISUALS

1. **Interpreting** In the cartoon on the left, what is the artist implying about Democratic policies?

2. **Identifying** In the cartoon on the right, what criticisms of tax breaks does the artist illustrate?

power of large corporations and wealthy elites. Liberals also believe that the government, particularly the federal government, should play an active role in helping disadvantaged Americans, partly through social programs and partly by putting more of society's tax burden on wealthier people.

Although liberals favor government intervention in the economy, they are suspicious of any attempt by the government to regulate social behavior. They are strong supporters of free speech and privacy, and are opposed to the government supporting or endorsing religious beliefs. They believe that a diverse society made up of different races, cultures, and ethnic groups will be more creative and energetic.

Liberals often support higher taxes on the wealthy, partly because they believe that those with greater assets should shoulder more of the costs of government and partly because it allows the government to redistribute wealth through government programs and thereby make society more equal.

Conservatism

Unlike liberals, conservatives distrust the power of government. They believe governmental power should be divided into different branches and split between the state and federal levels to limit its ability to intrude into people's lives.

Conservatives believe that when government regulates the economy, it makes the economy less efficient, resulting in less wealth and more poverty. They believe that free enterprise is the best economic system, and argue that if people and businesses are free to make their own economic choices, there will be more wealth and a higher standard of living for everyone.

For this reason, conservatives generally oppose high taxes and government programs that transfer wealth from the rich to those who are less wealthy. They believe that taxes and government programs discourage investment, take away people's incentive to work hard, and reduce the amount of freedom in society.

The more the government regulates the economy, conservatives argue, the more it will have to regulate every aspect of people's behavior. Ultimately, conservatives fear, the government will so restrict people's economic freedom that Americans will no longer be able to improve their standard of living and get ahead in life.

Many conservatives believe that religious faith is vitally important in sustaining society. They believe most social problems result from issues of morality and character—issues, they argue, that are best addressed through commitment to a religious faith and through the private efforts of churches, individuals, and communities to help those in need. Despite this general belief, conservatives do support the use of the governmental police powers to regulate social behavior in some instances.

✓ **Reading Check** **Contrasting** How do liberal and conservative opinions about government differ?

Conservatism Revives

MAIN Idea Geographical regions tend to support either liberal or conservative ideas.

HISTORY AND YOU Politically, how would you define yourself or the region in which you live? Read on to learn about the growing political power of voters in the Southwest.

During the New Deal era of the 1930s, conservative ideas lost much of their influence in national politics. Following World War II, however, conservatism began to revive.

The Role of the Cold War

Support for conservative ideas began to revive for two major reasons, both related to the Cold War. First, the struggle against communism revived the debate about the role of the government in the economy. Some Americans believed that liberal economic ideas

NATIONAL GEOGRAPHIC **The Rise of the Sunbelt, 1950–1980**

Analyzing GEOGRAPHY

1. **Location** Which Sunbelt states had more than 8 million residents in 1980?

2. **Movement** What factors might explain why some Sunbelt states experienced strong growth while others did not?

were slowly leading the United States toward communism and set out to stop this trend. They also thought the United States had failed to stop the spread of Soviet power because liberals did not fully understand the need for a strong anticommunist foreign policy.

At the same time, many Americans viewed the Cold War in religious terms. Communism rejects religion and emphasizes the material side of life. To Americans with a deep religious faith, the struggle against communism was a struggle between good and evil. Liberalism, which emphasizes economic welfare, gradually lost the support of many religious Americans, who increasingly turned to conservatism.

Conservatives Organize

In 1955 a young conservative named **William F. Buckley** founded a new magazine called *National Review*. Buckley's magazine helped to revive conservative ideas in the United States. Buckley debated in front of college students and appeared on radio and television shows, spreading conservative ideas to an even wider audience.

Within the Republican Party, conservatives, particularly young conservatives, began to demand a greater role in party decision-making. In 1960 some 90 young conservative leaders met at Buckley's family estate and founded Young Americans for Freedom (YAF), an independent conservative group, to push for their ideas and to support conservative candidates.

By 1964 the new conservative movement had achieved enough influence within the Republican Party to enable the conservative Barry Goldwater to win the nomination for president. To the dismay of the conservatives, however, President Johnson easily defeated Goldwater and won the election in a landslide.

The Rise of the Sunbelt

One of the problems facing conservatives in the 1950s and early 1960s was that their votes were split between the Republicans and the Democrats. Two regions of the country, the South and the West, were more conservative than other areas. Southern conservatives, however, usually voted for the Democrats, while conservatives in the West voted Republican. This meant that the party that won the heavily populated Northeast would win the election. Since the Northeast strongly supported liberal ideas, both parties were pulled toward liberal policies.

This pattern began to change during World War II, when large numbers of Americans moved south and west to take jobs in the war factories. The movement to the South and West—together known as the **Sunbelt**—continued after the war. As the Sunbelt's economy expanded, Americans living in those regions began to view the federal government differently from people living in the Northeast.

Sunbelt Conservatism

Industry in the Northeast was in decline, leading to the region's nickname—the Rust Belt. This region had higher unemployment than any other, and its cities were congested and polluted. These problems prompted Americans in the Northeast to look to the government for programs and regulations that would help them solve their problems.

In contrast, many Americans in the Sunbelt opposed high taxes and federal regulations that might interfere with their region's growth. Many white Southerners were also angry with the Democrats for supporting civil rights, which they interpreted as an effort by the federal government to impose its policies on the South.

When Barry Goldwater argued in 1964 that the federal government was becoming too strong, many Southerners agreed. For the first time since Reconstruction, they began voting Republican in large numbers. Although Goldwater lost, he showed Republicans that the best way to attract Southern votes was to support conservative policies.

Americans living in the West also responded to conservative criticism of the federal government. Westerners were proud of their frontier heritage and spirit of "rugged individualism." They resented federal environmental regulations that limited ranching, controlled water use, and restricted the development of the region's natural resources. Western anger over such policies inspired the "Sagebrush Rebellion" of the early 1970s—a widespread protest led by conservatives against federal laws that they felt were hindering the region's development.

The Conservative Coalition

The new conservative coalition that emerged in the 1970s was made up of people from the South and West, particularly middle class suburban voters, evangelical Christians, and people concerned about high taxes and resisting the Soviet Union in the Cold War.

▲ Voters in the suburbs (top) and rural west (above) increasingly voted conservative in the 1980s.

▲ Evangelical Christians including supporters of Jerry Falwell (photo left corner) were a major force behind the conservative resurgence.

Analyzing VISUALS

1. **Inferring** What do you notice about the ethnicity of most people in the conservative coalition? Why do you think other groups were not as well represented?

2. **Speculating** What groups in the coalition would be most likely to leave it in the future? Why?

By 1980, the population of the Sunbelt had surpassed that of the Northeast. This gave the conservative regions of the country more electoral votes. With Southerners also shifting to the Republican Party, conservatives began to build a coalition that could elect a president.

Suburban Conservatism

As riots erupted and crime soared during the 1960s and 1970s, many Americans moved to suburbs to escape the chaos of the cities. Even there, however, they found the quiet middle-class lifestyle they desired to be in danger. The rapid inflation of the 1970s had caused the buying power of middle-class families to shrink while taxes remained high.

Many Americans resented the taxes they had to pay for New Deal and Great Society programs when they themselves were losing ground economically. In 1978 Howard Jarvis, a conservative activist, launched the first successful tax revolt in California with Proposition 13, a referendum on the state ballot that greatly reduced property taxes.

Soon afterward anti-tax movements appeared in other states, and tax cuts quickly became a national issue. For many Americans, the conservative idea that the government had become too big meant simply that taxes were too high. As conservatives began to call for tax cuts, the middle class flocked to their cause.

The Religious Right

While many Americans turned to conservatism for economic reasons, others were drawn to it because they feared that American society had lost touch with its traditional values. For many Americans of conservative religious faith, the events of the 1960s and 1970s were shocking. The Supreme Court decision in *Roe* v. *Wade*, which established that the right to have an abortion was protected by the Constitution, greatly concerned them. They were also critical of other Supreme Court decisions that limited prayer in public schools and expanded protections for people accused of crimes.

The feminist movement and the push for the Equal Rights Amendment (ERA) also upset some religious Americans because it seemed to represent an assault on the traditional family. Many religious conservatives were shocked by the behavior of some university students in the 1960s, whose contempt for authority seemed to **indicate** a general breakdown in American values and morality. These concerns helped expand the conservative cause into a mass movement.

Although religious conservatives included people of many faiths, the largest group was evangelical Protestants. Evangelicals believe that they are saved from their sins through conversion (which they refer to as being "born again") and a personal commitment to follow Jesus Christ, whose death and resurrection reconciles them to God.

After World War II, a religious revival began in the United States among Protestant evangelicals. Protestant ministers, such as **Billy Graham** and Oral Roberts, built national followings. By the late 1970s, about 70 million Americans described themselves as "born again." Protestant evangelicals owned their own newspapers, magazines, radio stations, and television networks.

Television in particular allowed evangelical ministers to reach a large nationwide audience. These **"televangelists,"** as they were soon called, included Marion "Pat" Robertson, who founded the Christian Broadcasting Network, and **Jerry Falwell,** who used his television show *The Old-Time Gospel Hour* to found a movement that he called the **"Moral Majority."** Using television and mail campaigns, the Moral Majority built up a network of ministers to register new voters who backed conservative candidates and issues. Falwell later claimed to have registered 2 million new voters by 1980.

A New Coalition

By the end of the 1970s, a new conservative coalition of voters had begun to come together. Although the members of this coalition were concerned with many different issues, they were held together by a common belief that American society had somehow lost its way.

The Watergate scandal, high taxes, and special interest politics had undermined many Americans' faith in their government. Rising unemployment, rapid inflation, and the energy crisis had shaken their confidence in the economy. Riots, crime, and drug abuse suggested that society itself was falling apart. The retreat from Vietnam, the hostage crisis in Iran, and the Soviet invasion of Afghanistan seemed to make the nation look weak and helpless internationally. Many Americans were tired of change and upheaval. They wanted **stability** and a return to what they remembered as a better time. For some, the new conservatism and its most prominent spokesperson, Ronald Reagan, offered hope to a nation in distress.

✔ Reading Check **Summarizing** Why did many Americans begin to support the conservative movement?

Section 1 REVIEW

Vocabulary

1. **Explain** the significance of: liberal, conservative, William F. Buckley, Sunbelt, Billy Graham, "televangelist," Jerry Falwell, "Moral Majority."

Main Ideas

2. **Explaining** Why do liberals sometimes support higher taxes on the wealthy?

3. **Determining Cause and Effect** What was the cause of the Sagebrush Rebellion in the 1970s?

Critical Thinking

4. **Big Ideas** What kind of economy do conservatives want?

5. **Organizing** Use a graphic organizer similar to the one below to list conservative beliefs.

Conservative Beliefs

6. **Analyzing Visuals** Study the map of the Sunbelt on page 970. What impact would the migration patterns shown have on representation in the U.S. House of Representatives?

Writing About History

7. **Persuasive Writing** Many conservatives believe that "government that governs least, governs best." Write a paragraph supporting or opposing this statement.

History ONLINE

Study Central™ To review this section, go to glencoe.com and click on Study Central.

The Reagan Years

Guide to Reading

Big Ideas

Trade, War, and Migration During the Cold War, President Reagan reinforced the idea that the United States had to take strong action to resist the spread of Communist influence abroad.

Content Vocabulary
- supply-side economics *(p. 976)*
- budget deficit *(p. 977)*
- "mutual assured destruction" *(p. 981)*

Academic Vocabulary
- confirmation *(p. 978)*
- visible *(p. 979)*

People and Events to Identify
- Reaganomics *(p. 976)*
- Iran-Contra scandal *(p. 980)*
- Mikhail Gorbachev *(p. 981)*

Reading Strategy

Organizing Complete a graphic organizer similar to the one below by filling in the major points of the supply-side theory of economics.

NEW YORK CORE CURRICULUM
U.S. History and Government

Unit 7:
V.C.1 Supply-side economics
V.C.2 Tax policy and deficits
V.E Renewed United States power image
V.G United States—Soviet relations

In 1980 Americans elected Ronald Reagan president. Reagan cut taxes, deregulated several industries, and appointed conservative justices. He began a massive military buildup that greatly increased the deficit and sent aid to insurgent groups fighting communism.

The Road to the White House

MAIN Idea President Reagan's experiences in Hollywood and as governor of California led to his successful campaign for the presidency.

HISTORY AND YOU How could a previous career as a movie star help someone get elected to public office? Read on to learn more about the way that President Reagan's background helped to make him an attractive presidential candidate.

In 1926, at age fifteen, Ronald Reagan earned $15 a week working as a lifeguard on the Rock River in Illinois. Being a lifeguard, Reagan later wrote, taught him quite a bit about human nature:

PRIMARY SOURCE

"Lifeguarding provides one of the best vantage points in the world to learn about people. During my career at the park, I saved seventy-seven people. I guarantee you they needed saving—no lifeguard gets wet without good reason. . . . Not many thanked me, much less gave me a reward, and being a little money-hungry, I'd done a little daydreaming about this. They felt insulted. . . . I got to recognize that people hate to be saved. . . ."

—from *Where's the Rest of Me?*

The belief that people do not want to be saved by someone else was one of the ideas that Ronald Reagan took with him to the White House. It reflected his philosophy of self-reliance and independence.

Becoming a Conservative

Reagan grew up in Dixon, Illinois, the son of an Irish American shoe salesman. After graduating from Eureka College in 1932, Reagan worked as a sports broadcaster at an Iowa radio station. In 1937 he took a Hollywood screen test and won a contract from a movie studio. During the next 25 years he made more than 50 movies. As a broadcaster and an actor, Reagan learned how to speak publicly and how to project a strong, attractive image—skills that proved invaluable when he entered politics.

In 1947 Reagan became president of the Screen Actors Guild—the actors' union. Soon afterward, he testified about communism in

The Election of 1980

Baldy

▲ When Ronald Reagan ran for the Republican presidential nomination, he was still best known to most Americans as an actor. Critics said that while he was scripted and polished, he lacked any real substance.

▼ By 1980, Carter was so unpopular that other Democrats did not want his help in their own campaigns. Reagan soundly defeated Carter in the Election of 1980.

Baldy

' I PLEDGE TO COME OUT CAMPAIGNING VIGOROUSLY FOR ALL DEMOCRATS ! ... '

Analyzing VISUALS

1. **Making Inferences** In the cartoon above, what does the artist infer about Reagan's campaign?

2. **Interpreting** What is the artist in the cartoon to the right saying about Carter's place in the Democratic Party?

Hollywood before the House Un-American Activities Committee. Reagan had been a staunch Democrat and a supporter of the New Deal, but dealing with Communists in the union shifted him toward conservative ideas.

In 1954 Reagan became the host of the television show "General Electric Theater" and agreed to be a motivational speaker for General Electric. As he traveled the country speaking to people, he became increasingly conservative. Over and over again, he said later, he heard average Americans describe how high taxes and government regulations made it impossible for them to get ahead.

By 1964 Reagan had become such a popular national speaker that Barry Goldwater asked him to make a televised speech on behalf of Goldwater's campaign. The speech impressed several wealthy entrepreneurs in California. They convinced Reagan to run for governor of California in 1966 and helped finance his campaign. Reagan won the election and was reelected in 1970. Ten years later he won the Republican presidential nomination.

The Election of 1980

Reagan's campaign appealed to Americans who were frustrated with the economy and worried that the United States had become weak internationally. Reagan promised to cut taxes and increase defense spending. He won the support of social conservatives by calling for a constitutional amendment banning abortion. During one debate with President Carter, Reagan asked voters, "Are you better off than you were four years ago?" On Election Day, the voters answered "No." Reagan won nearly 51 percent of the popular vote and 489 electoral votes, easily defeating Carter in the Electoral College. For the first time since 1954, Republicans also gained control of the Senate.

✔ Reading Check Describing What event jump-started Ronald Reagan's political career as a conservative leader?

Domestic Policies

MAIN Idea Believing that government was part of the problem, President Reagan cut social service programs, sponsored tax cuts, and deregulated industry.

HISTORY AND YOU Do you think that cutting social programs is a good way to help the economy? Read on to learn more about Reagan's economic policies.

Ronald Reagan believed that the key to restoring the economy and overcoming problems in society was to get Americans to believe in themselves again. He expressed this idea in his Inaugural Address:

PRIMARY SOURCE

"We have every right to dream heroic dreams. . . . You can see heroes every day going in and out of factory gates. Others, a handful in number, produce enough food to feed all of us. . . . You meet heroes across a counter. . . . There are entrepreneurs with faith in themselves and faith in an idea who create new jobs, new wealth and opportunity. . . . Their patriotism is quiet but deep. Their values sustain our national life."

—from Reagan's First Inaugural Address

Reagan also told Americans that they should not expect government to help: "In this present crisis, government is not the solution to our problem. Government is the problem."

Reaganomics

History ONLINE
Student Web Activity Visit glencoe.com and complete the activity on the 1980s.

Reagan's first priority was the economy, which was suffering from stagflation—a combination of high unemployment and high inflation. According to most economists, the way to fight unemployment was to increase government spending. Increasing spending, however, made inflation worse. Conservative economists offered two competing ideas for fixing the economy. One group, known as monetarists, argued that inflation was caused by too much money in circulation. They believed the best solution was to raise interest rates. Another group supported **supply-side economics.** They argued that the economy was weak because taxes were too high.

Supply-side economists believed that high taxes took too much money away from investors. If taxes were cut, businesses and investors could use their extra capital to make new investments. Businesses would expand and create new jobs, and the result would be a larger supply of goods for consumers, who would now have more money to spend because of the tax cuts.

Reagan combined monetarism and supply-side economics. He encouraged the Federal Reserve to keep interest rates high, and asked Congress to pass a massive tax cut. Critics called his approach **Reaganomics** or "trickle-down economics." They believed Reagan's policy would help corporations and wealthy Americans, but little wealth would "trickle down" to middle-class or poor Americans.

Reagan made deals with conservative Democrats in the House and moderate Republicans in the Senate. Eventually Congress passed a 25 percent tax cut.

Debates IN HISTORY

Are Tax Cuts Good for the Economy?

Ronald Reagan believed that government regulation of the economy was harmful and that taxes should be as low as possible to promote private spending and investment. During the 1984 presidential campaign, Reagan ran against Jimmy Carter's vice president, Walter Mondale. In these excerpts from the first debate between the two candidates, Reagan and Mondale discuss their fundamentally different approaches to government. Mondale advocated for tax increases and that is often cited as a main reason why he lost the election.

Cutting Programs Cutting tax rates meant that the government would receive less money, at least until the economy started to grow. This would increase the **budget deficit**—the amount by which expenditures exceed income. To keep the deficit under control, Reagan proposed cuts to social programs. Welfare benefits, including the food-stamp program and the school-lunch program, were cut back. Medicare payments, unemployment compensation, student loans, and housing subsidies were also reduced.

After a struggle, Congress passed most of these cuts. The fight convinced Reagan that he would never get Congress to cut spending enough to balance the budget. He decided that cutting taxes and building up the military were more important than balancing the budget. He accepted a rapidly rising deficit as the price of getting his other programs passed.

Deregulation Reagan believed that excessive government regulation was another cause of the economy's problems. His first act as president was to sign an executive order to end price controls on oil and gasoline. Critics said that ending controls would drive prices up, but in fact they fell. Falling energy prices freed up money for businesses and consumers to spend elsewhere, helping the economy to recover.

Other deregulation soon followed. The Federal Communications Commission stopped trying to regulate the cable television industry. The National Highway Traffic and Safety Administration reduced requirements for air bags and higher fuel efficiency for cars. Carter had already begun deregulating the airline industry, and Reagan encouraged the process, which led to price wars, cheaper fares, and the founding of new airlines.

YES

Ronald Reagan
President

PRIMARY SOURCE

"…[T]he plan that we have had and that we are following is a plan that is based on growth in the economy. . . . Our tax cut, we think, was very instrumental in bringing about this economic recovery.

. . . So, we believe that as we continue to reduce the level of government spending…and, at the same time, as the growth in the economy increases the revenues the government gets, without raising taxes, those two lines will meet. . . . The deficit is the result of excessive government spending. . . . I don't believe that Mr. Mondale has a plan for balancing the budget; he has a plan for raising taxes. . . . And for the 5 years previous to our taking office, taxes doubled in the United States, and the budgets increased $318 billion. So, there is no ratio between taxing and balancing a budget."

—from the first presidential debate, Oct. 7, 1984

NO

Walter Mondale
Presidential candidate

PRIMARY SOURCE

"…[E]ven with historically high levels of economic growth, we will suffer a $263 billion deficit. . . . Real interest rates—the real cost of interest—will remain very, very high, and many economists are predicting that we're moving into a period of very slow growth. . . . I proposed over a hundred billion dollars in cuts in federal spending over 4 years, but I am not going to cut it out of Social Security and Medicare and student assistance and things . . . that people need. . . . The rate of defense spending increase can be slowed. . . . And there are other ways of squeezing this budget without constantly picking on our senior citizens and the most vulnerable in American life."

—from the first presidential debate, Oct. 7, 1984

DBQ Document-Based Questions

1. **Specifying** What does Reagan say his administration has done to improve economic growth?

2. **Explaining** How does Reagan propose to balance the federal budget?

3. **Summarizing** How does Mondale respond to Reagan's plan? What effects does he foresee from that course?

4. **Evaluating** Which approach do you feel will be the most effective? Why? Explain your answer.

Sandra Day O'Connor
1930–

When a Supreme Court vacancy opened up in 1981, President Reagan chose Sandra Day O'Connor, an Arizona appeals court judge. Unlike many Supreme Court justices, O'Connor had broad political experience. Appointed to a state senatorial vacancy in 1969, she successfully ran for the seat and became the state senate's first woman majority leader in 1972. O'Connor won election as a superior court judge in 1974 and was later appointed to the court of appeals.

O'Connor's nomination was opposed by the Moral Majority because she had supported the Equal Rights Amendment (ERA), and had refused to back an anti-abortion amendment, or criticize the decision in *Roe* v. *Wade*. Others, however, praised her legal judgment and conservative approach to the law. As a moderate conservative, she quickly became an important swing vote on the Court, between more liberal and more conservative justices.

Why do you think that O'Connor supported the Equal Rights Amendment?

▲ *(Above photo) From left, front row are Thurgood Marshall; William Brennan, Jr.; William Rehnquist; Byron White; and Harry Blackmun. Back row from left are Antonin Scalia; John Paul Stevens; Sandra Day O'Connor; and Anthony M. Kennedy. (Right photo) Robert Bork failed to be confirmed.*

Reagan's secretary of the interior, James Watt, increased the public land that companies could use for oil drilling, mining, and logging. Watt's actions angered environmentalists, as did the EPA's decision to ease regulations on pollution-control equipment and to reduce safety checks on chemicals and pesticides.

In 1983 the economy began to recover. By 1984, the United States had begun the biggest economic expansion in its history up to that time. The median income of families climbed steadily, rising 15 percent by 1989. Five million new businesses and 20 million new jobs were created. By 1988, unemployment had fallen to 5.5 percent, the lowest in 14 years.

Reagan Wins Reelection By 1984, the economic recovery had made Reagan very popular. Democrats nominated Jimmy Carter's vice president, Walter Mondale. He chose as his running mate Representative Geraldine Ferraro, the first woman nominated to run for vice president for a major party. Instead of arguing issues with his opponent, Reagan emphasized the good economy. In an overwhelming landslide, he won about 59 percent of the popular vote and all the electoral votes except those from Mondale's home state of Minnesota and the District of Columbia.

Shifting the Judicial Balance

Reagan did not apply his conservative ideas only to the economy. He also tried to bring a strict constructionist outlook to the federal judiciary. Reagan wanted judges who followed the original intent of the Constitution. He also changed the Supreme Court by nominating Sandra Day O'Connor, the first woman on the Supreme Court.

In 1986 Chief Justice Warren Burger retired. Reagan chose the most conservative associate justice, William Rehnquist, to succeed him. He then named Antonin Scalia, a conservative, to fill Rehnquist's vacancy. In 1987 his attempt to put Robert Bork on the Court led to a bitter fight in the Senate. Democrats saw Bork as too conservative and blocked his **confirmation.** Reagan then nominated Anthony Kennedy, a moderate, to become the new associate justice.

✔ Reading Check **Explaining** What is supply-side economics?

Reagan Oversees a Military Buildup

MAIN Idea President Reagan began a massive military buildup to weaken the Soviet economy and deter Soviet aggression.

HISTORY AND YOU Do you remember President Eisenhower's warning about the military as he left office? Read to learn how President Reagan sought to use military power to defeat the Soviets.

Reagan did not limit his reforms to the domestic scene. He adopted a new foreign policy that rejected both containment and détente. Reagan called the Soviet Union "the focus of evil in the modern world" and "an evil empire." In his view, the United States should not negotiate with or try to contain evil. It should try to defeat it.

"Peace Through Strength"

In Reagan's opinion, the only option open to the United States in dealing with the Soviet Union was "peace through strength"— a phrase he used during his campaign. The military buildup Reagan launched was the largest peacetime buildup in American history. It cost about $1.5 trillion over five years.

Reagan believed that, if the Soviets tried to match the American buildup, it might put so much pressure on their economy that they would be forced to reform their system or it would collapse. In 1982 Reagan told students at Eureka College that Soviet defense spending would eventually cause the Communist system to fall apart:

PRIMARY SOURCE

"The Soviet empire is faltering because rigid centralized control has destroyed incentives for innovation, efficiency, and individual achievement. . . . But in the midst of social and economic problems, the Soviet dictatorship has forged the largest armed force in the world. It has done so by preempting the human needs of its people and in the end, this course will undermine the foundations of the Soviet system."

—from *A Time for Choosing*

The United States also tried to stop nations from supporting terrorism. After Libya backed a terrorist bombing in Berlin, the United States launched an air attack on Libya on April 14, 1986. The raids killed 37 and injured about 200.

Reagan's military buildup created new jobs in defense industries. Supply-side economists had predicted that, despite the spending, lower taxes combined with cuts in government programs would generate enough growth to increase tax revenues and balance the budget. Tax revenues did rise, but other programs were too popular for Reagan to cut significantly. As a result, the annual budget deficit went from $80 billion to over $200 billion.

The Reagan Doctrine

Building up the military was only part of Reagan's military strategy. He also believed that the United States should support guerrilla groups who were fighting to overthrow Communist or pro-Soviet governments. This policy became known as the Reagan Doctrine.

Aid to the Afghan Rebels Perhaps the most **visible** example of the Reagan Doctrine was in Afghanistan. In late December 1979 the Soviet Union invaded Afghanistan to support a Soviet-backed government. The Soviets soon found themselves fighting Afghan guerrillas known as the mujahadeen.

President Carter sent about $30 million in military aid to the Afghan guerrillas, but Reagan sent $570 million more. The Soviets were soon trapped in a situation similar to the American experience in Vietnam. They could not defeat the Afghan guerrillas. As casualties mounted, the war strained the Soviet economy and in 1988 the Soviets decided to withdraw.

Nicaragua and Grenada Reagan was also concerned about Soviet influence in Nicaragua. Rebels known as the Sandinistas had overthrown a pro-American dictator in Nicaragua in 1979. The Sandinistas set up a socialist government and accepted Cuban and Soviet aid. They then began aiding rebels in nearby El Salvador.

In response, the Reagan administration began secretly arming an anti-Sandinista guerrilla force known as the contras, from the Spanish word for "counterrevolutionary." When Congress learned of this policy, it banned further aid to the contras.

Reagan's Foreign Policy

President Reagan launched a massive weapons buildup, believing it would weaken the Soviet Union. He also provided aid to Afghan rebels fighting Soviet forces and engaged in a series of meetings with the Soviet leader that produced a nuclear arms treaty (at right).

▲ In 1987, Reagan stood at the Brandenburg Gate in West Berlin and demanded that Gorbachev tear down the Berlin Wall.

Analyzing VISUALS

1. **Contrasting** What contradictions do the photos seem to suggest about Reagan's policies? How can you reconcile them?

2. **Evaluating** Why might a president want to make a public speech demanding another nation change its behavior? Why might it be effective?

Aiding the contras was not Reagan's only action in Latin America. In 1983 radical Marxists overthrew the left-wing government on the tiny Caribbean island of Grenada. In October, Reagan sent in American troops. The Cuban and Grenadian soldiers were quickly defeated and a new anti-Communist government was put in place.

The Iran-Contra Scandal Although Congress had prohibited aid to the Nicaraguan contras, individuals in Reagan's administration continued to illegally support the rebels. They secretly sold weapons to Iran, considered an enemy and sponsor of terrorism, in exchange for the release of American hostages being held in the Middle East. Profits from these sales were then sent to the contras.

News of the illegal operations broke in November 1986. One of the chief figures in the **Iran-Contra scandal** was Marine Colonel Oliver North, an aide to the National Security

Council (NSC). He and other senior NSC and CIA officials testified before Congress and admitted to covering up their actions.

President Reagan had approved the sale of arms to Iran, but the congressional investigation concluded that he had had no direct knowledge about the diversion of the money to the contras. To the end, Reagan insisted he had done nothing wrong, but the scandal tainted his second term in office.

Arms Control

As part of the military buildup, Reagan decided to place nuclear missiles in Western Europe to counter Soviet missiles in Eastern Europe. This decision triggered a new peace movement. Tens of thousands of protesters pushed for a "nuclear freeze"—a halt to the deployment of new nuclear missiles.

Reagan offered to cancel the deployment of the new missiles if the Soviets removed their missiles from Eastern Europe. He also proposed Strategic Arms Reduction Talks (START) to cut the number of missiles on both sides in half. The Soviets refused and walked out of the arms control talks.

"Star Wars" Despite his decision to deploy missiles in Europe, Reagan generally disagreed with the military strategy known as nuclear deterrence, sometimes called **"mutual assured destruction."** This strategy assumed that, as long as the United States and Soviet Union could destroy each other with nuclear weapons, they would be afraid to use them.

Reagan believed that mutual assured destruction was immoral because it depended on the threat to kill massive numbers of people. He also knew that if nuclear war did begin, there would be no way to defend the United States. In March 1983 Reagan proposed the Strategic Defense Initiative (SDI). This plan, nicknamed "Star Wars," called for the development of weapons that could intercept and destroy incoming missiles.

A New Soviet Leader In 1985 **Mikhail Gorbachev** became the leader of the Soviet Union and agreed to resume arms-control talks. Gorbachev believed that the Soviet Union had to reform its economic system or it would soon collapse. It could not afford a new arms race with the United States.

Reagan and Gorbachev met in a series of summits. The first of these was frustrating for both, as they disagreed on many issues. Gorbachev promised to cut back Soviet nuclear forces if Reagan would agree to give up SDI, but Reagan refused.

Reagan then challenged Gorbachev to make reforms. In West Berlin, Reagan stood at the Brandenburg Gate of the Berlin Wall, the symbol of divided Europe, and declared: "General Secretary Gorbachev, if you seek peace, if you seek prosperity for the Soviet Union and Eastern Europe . . . tear down this wall!"

Relations Improve By 1987, Reagan was convinced that Gorbachev did want to reform the Soviet Union and end the arms race. While some politicians distrusted the Soviets, most people welcomed the Cold War thaw and the reduction in the danger of nuclear war. In December 1987 the two leaders signed the Intermediate Range Nuclear Forces (INF) Treaty. It was the first treaty to call for the destruction of nuclear weapons.

No one realized it at the time, but the treaty marked the beginning of the end of the Cold War. With an arms control deal in place, Gorbachev felt confident that Soviet military spending could be reduced. He pushed ahead with economic and political reforms that eventually led to the collapse of communism in Eastern Europe and in the Soviet Union.

With the economy booming, the American military strong, and relations with the Soviet Union rapidly improving, Ronald Reagan's second term came to an end. As he prepared to leave office, Reagan assessed his presidency: "They called it the Reagan revolution. Well, I'll accept that, but for me it always seemed more like the great rediscovery, a rediscovery of our values and our common sense."

✔ **Reading Check** **Identifying** What was the Reagan Doctrine?

Section 2 REVIEW

Vocabulary

1. **Explain** the significance of: supply-side economics, Reaganomics, budget deficit, Iran-Contra scandal, "mutual assured destruction," Mikhail Gorbachev.

Main Ideas

2. **Specifying** What political office did Ronald Reagan hold before he was elected president?

3. **Explaining** How did Reagan aim to change the Supreme Court?

4. **Summarizing** What was the goal of the U.S. military buildup under President Reagan?

Critical Thinking

5. **Big Ideas** What was President Reagan's approach to foreign policy?

6. **Organizing** Use a graphic organizer similar to the one below to list the ways in which the Reagan Doctrine was implemented.

7. **Analyzing Visuals** Study the political cartoons on page 975. How do the cartoons portray Reagan and Carter?

Writing About History

8. **Expository Writing** Take on the role of a newspaper editor during the Reagan administration. Write an editorial in which you present your opinion of Reagan's plans for a military buildup.

History ONLINE
Study Central™ To review this section, go to glencoe.com and click on Study Central.

Section 3

Life in the 1980s

Guide to Reading

Big Ideas
Science and Technology
Achievements in technology during the 1980s symbolized the optimism many associated with the Reagan era.

Content Vocabulary
- yuppie *(p. 982)*
- discount retailing *(p. 983)*

Academic Vocabulary
- via *(p. 984)*
- orientation *(p. 987)*

People and Events to Identify
- Mothers Against Drunk Driving (MADD) *(p. 986)*
- AIDS *(p. 987)*
- Stonewall Riot *(p. 987)*
- American Association of Retired Persons (AARP) *(p. 987)*

Reading Strategy
Organizing Complete a graphic organizer similar to the one below by listing the kinds of social issues that Americans faced in the 1980s.

NEW YORK CORE CURRICULUM
U.S. History and Government

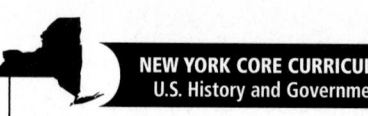

Unit 7:
V.D.1 Feast and famine: the farmer's dilemma
V.D.2 The problems of poverty in an affluent society—"the underclass"
V.D.4 Changing demographic patterns (growing number of elderly)

The 1980s was a period of increased wealth for many, as areas of the economy improved and new technologies came to market. However, cuts in social programs left many Americans in need, leading to a new sense of activism.

A Booming Economy

MAIN Idea Innovation in the retailing and broadcast industries changed American society and generated new businesses and jobs.

HISTORY AND YOU What technological devices are part of your everyday life? Read on to find out about the inventions of the 1980s.

By late 1983, the American economy had revived after the stagflation of the 1970s. Stock prices soared as many companies reported record profits. Stockbrokers, speculators, and real estate developers made multimillion-dollar deals, buying and selling hundreds of companies. Perhaps the most famous real estate developer of the era was Donald Trump, who opened Trump Tower in New York City in 1982. Many of the new moneymakers were young, ambitious, and hardworking. Journalists called them **yuppies,** from "young urban professionals."

The rapid economic growth and emphasis on accumulating wealth in the 1980s was partly caused by the baby boom. By the 1980s, many baby boomers had finished college, entered the job market, and begun building their careers. Young people entering the workforce often placed an emphasis on acquiring goods and getting ahead in their jobs. Because baby boomers were so numerous, their concerns tended to shape the culture.

The strong economic growth of the 1980s mostly benefited middle- and upper-class Americans. As a result, the emphasis on acquiring wealth had another effect on society. From 1967 to 1986, the amount of money earned by the top 5 percent of Americans fluctuated between 15.6 and 17.5 percent of the nation's total income. In the late 1980s, their share of the nation's income began to rise. By the mid-1990s, the top 5 percent of Americans earned well over 21 percent of the nation's income.

A Retail Revolution

In addition to the booming real-estate and stock markets, the economy of the 1980s witnessed a revolution in retail sales. Several entrepreneurs pioneered a new approach to retailing—or selling goods to

The Booming Economy of the 1980s

The American economy grew rapidly in the 1980s for several reasons—lower taxes spurred investment and spending while new methods of retailing lowered prices and new technology led to new businesses and the creation of many new jobs.

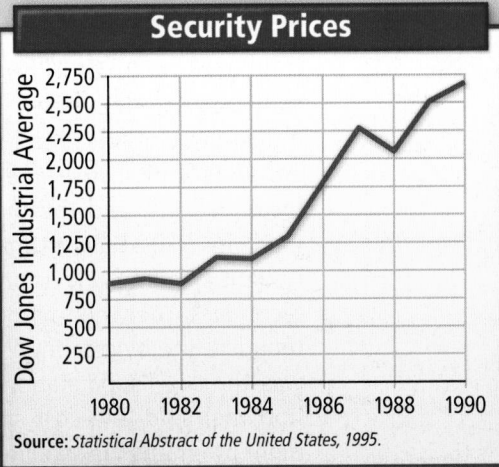

Security Prices

Source: *Statistical Abstract of the United States, 1995.*

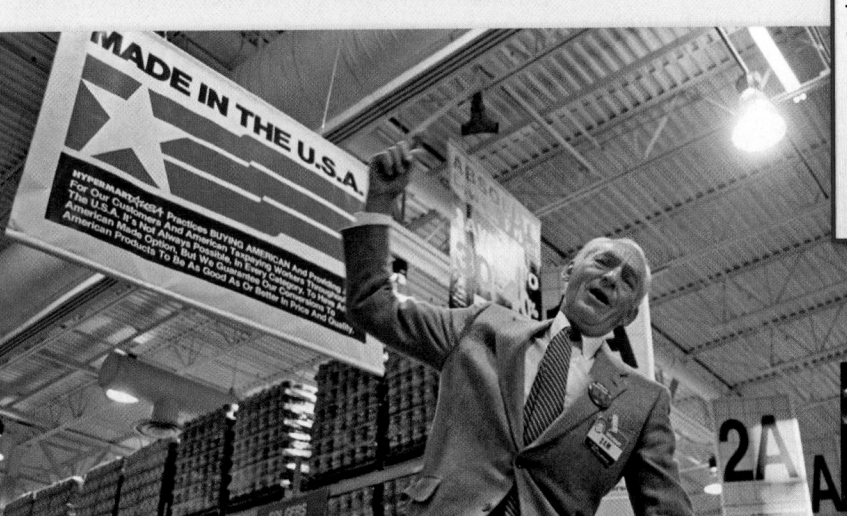

Analyzing VISUALS

1. **Identifying** In what year of the late 1980s did the Dow Jones sharply decline?

2. **Explaining** Examine the photos and then write a brief essay explaining how they demonstrate economic trends of the 1980s.

Discount retail stores (above) and cable television (right) took off in the 1980s, helping to further fuel economic growth.

consumers—that greatly reduced prices for Americans.

This new type of retailing, known as **discount retailing,** had actually begun to emerge in the 1960s—but it did not have a major impact on the economy until the 1980s. Discount retailers sell large quantities of goods at very low prices, trying to sell the goods quickly to turn over their entire inventory in a short period of time. By selling a lot of products at very low prices, they could make more money than traditional retailers who sold fewer products at higher prices. During the 1960s many new discount retail chains were founded, including K Mart, Woolco, Target, and Wal-Mart. Annual sales by discount stores grew from about $2 billion in the mid-1960s to almost $70 billion by 1985.

The most successful discount retailer was Sam Walton, the founder of Wal-Mart. Walton developed a system of distribution centers to rapidly re-supply his stores. He was one of the first retailers to use a computer database to track inventory and sales. By 1985, he was the richest person in the United States.

Others soon copied Walton's approach. By the late 1970s, discount retailers had begun to build huge "superstores" that enabled them to sell large quantities of goods very quickly at low prices. One such entrepreneur was Arthur Blank, who opened Home Depot—a chain of giant home-improvement stores—in 1978. In 1983 Richard Schulze, a former air force officer, used his technical training to found Best Buy, a huge discount retailer of consumer electronics. Dozens of other entrepreneurs started discount stores in other industries. Their innovations created millions of new jobs in the 1980s and helped fuel the era's rapid economic growth.

A Revolution in Media

In the 1980s other entrepreneurs began transforming the news and entertainment industries. Until the late 1970s television viewers were limited to three national networks, local stations, and the public television network. In 1970 a businessman named Ted Turner bought a failing television station in Atlanta, Georgia. Turner then pioneered a new type of broadcasting by creating WTBS in 1975. WTBS was the first "superstation"—a television station that sold low-cost sports and entertainment programs **via** satellite to cable companies throughout the nation.

The Rise of Cable Television Turner's innovation changed broadcasting and helped spread cable television across the country. Dozens of networks soon appeared. Many of the new networks specialized in one type of broadcasting, such as sports (ESPN), movies (HBO), or news. In 1980 Turner himself founded the Cable News Network (CNN)—the first 24-hour, all-news network.

Other new networks focused on specific audiences, such as churchgoers, shoppers, or minorities. In 1980 entrepreneur Robert Johnson created Black Entertainment Television (BET). Johnson—who had been born into a poor, rural family in Mississippi and gone on to earn a master's degree from Princeton University—was convinced that television had tremendous power to promote African American businesses and culture. BET was the first, and is still the largest, African American-owned network on cable television.

In 1981 music and technology merged when Music Television (MTV) went on the air. MTV broadcast performances of songs and images, or music videos. MTV was an instant hit, though the videos it showed were often criticized for violence and sexual content. Many performers began to produce videos along with each of their new albums. Music videos boosted the careers of artists such as Madonna and Michael Jackson.

Rap music was the new sound of the 1980s. This musical style originated in local clubs in New York City's South Bronx. Emphasizing heavy bass and very rhythmic sounds, rap artists did not usually sing but rather spoke over the music and rhythmic beats. Rap's lyrics frequently focused on the African American expe-

PAST & PRESENT

New Space Technology

After the series of moon landings of the 1970s, NASA concentrated on the space shuttle. Although it looks like a huge airplane, the shuttle is rocketed into space, then glides back to Earth for another flight. Unlike earlier spacecraft, the shuttle is reusable. Astronauts John Young and Roger Crippen made the first space shuttle flight in April 1981.

Between April 1981 and December 2006, shuttle astronauts completed 114 missions. They have placed many satellites in orbit, including the Hubble Space Telescope, and conducted numerous experiments. Tragedy has struck twice during shuttle missions. In 1986, the space shuttle *Challenger* exploded shortly after liftoff. In 2003, the shuttle *Columbia* came apart while reentering the atmosphere. Seven astronauts died in each of these accidents.

As the shuttle nears the end of its service life, both NASA and several independent companies have begun work on vehicles capable of reaching orbit. Shuttle launches are very expensive and many entrepreneurs are seeking to develop low-cost alternatives to the shuttle that will enable business to move into space and develop new industries there.

April 1981

▲ On April 12, 1981, the shuttle Columbia *lifted off on the first space shuttle flight.*

rience in the inner city. While rap was initially popular among East Coast African Americans, it grew in popularity, becoming a multimillion-dollar industry that appealed to music lovers across the country.

Technology and Media In the 1980s technology also transformed how people accessed their entertainment. Until the 1980s, most people listened to music on large stereo systems in their homes or relied on radio-station programming when they were driving. In the 1980s, the Sony Walkman made music portable. The Sony Walkman played cassette tapes, but it marked the beginning of a new way for people to access music. In the 1990s, portable compact disc (CD) players replaced the Walkman, and in the early 2000s digital audio players, such as the iPod and MP3 players, advanced the technology even further.

Video technology also began to change. Until the 1980s most people had to watch television shows when they aired. By the end of the 1980s, many people had videocassette recorders (VCRs), enabling them to tape television shows or watch taped films whenever they wished. By the 2000s, VCRs were being replaced by digital video disk (DVD) recorders. The growing use of VCRs changed the movie industry, as people increasingly chose to rent taped movies to watch at home rather than go to the theater.

Even as technology changed the music and television industries, it also brought about a new form of entertainment that competed with music and movies—the video game. Early video games grew out of military computer technology. The first video arcade game was a game called *Pong*, released in 1972. Home video games developed quickly. In the early 1980s sales reached about $3 billion with the sale of games such as *Pac-Man* and *Space Invaders.* Video arcades became the new spot for young people to meet. By the mid-1980s, home video games were able to compete with arcade games in graphics and speed. Video games have continued to grow in popularity to the present day and three major companies—Sony, Nintendo, and Microsoft—have emerged as the major developers of video games and game devices.

✔ Reading Check **Describing** What forms of entertainment gained popularity in the 1980s?

June 2004

In the early 2000s, many private companies were working on building spaceships. SpaceShipOne (below) was the first privately-built ship to carry a person to space. Another company is working on the Goddard (right)—a ship designed to take off and land vertically, without needing wings.

N328KF

MAKING CONNECTIONS

1. **Analyzing** How has the United States benefited from the space program?

2. **Speculating** What kinds of private businesses might benefit from easy, inexpensive space programs?

New Social Activism

MAIN Idea Social problems affected many people during the 1980s, and new groups formed to try to solve them.

HISTORY AND YOU Does your school have organizations such as Students Against Drunk Driving? Read on to learn more about attempts to limit teen alcohol abuse.

The 1980s was a decade of wealth and prosperity. However, at the same time, many social problems continued to plague the nation, such as drugs, poverty, homelessness, and disease.

Social Problems

Ongoing problems with drug abuse in the 1980s made many neighborhoods dangerous. Drug users often committed crimes to get money for drugs. First Lady Nancy Reagan tried to discourage teen drug use with her "Just Say No" campaign. Drug use also spread from cities to small towns and rural areas.

Fighting Drugs in Schools As part of the effort to reduce drug use among teenagers, some schools began searching student bags and lockers to find concealed drugs. In 1984 one teen who had been arrested for selling drugs challenged the school's right to search her purse without a warrant. In 1985, in the case of *New Jersey* v. *T.L.O.*, the Supreme Court upheld the school's right to search without a warrant if it had reasonable cause to believe a crime was being committed. Although students did have a right to privacy, they did not have the same Fourth Amendment rights as adults. For similar reasons, in the 1995 case of *Vernonia School District* v. *Acton,* the Court held that random drug tests do not violate students' Fourth Amendment rights.

Efforts to Stop Drunk Driving Abuse of alcohol was also a serious concern. In 1980 **Mothers Against Drunk Driving (MADD)** was founded to try to stop underage drinking and drunk driving in general. In 1984 Congress cut highway funds to any state that did not raise the legal drinking age to 21. Within four years, all states complied.

PRIMARY SOURCE
The Farm Debt Crisis of the 1980s

Although the high interest rates of the 1980s helped reduce inflation, when they were combined with the low food prices of the era, they created a crisis for American farmers. Many farmers found themselves deeply in debt. Unable to make enough money to make their loan payments, they were soon forced out of business. By the end of the 1980s, the total number of farms in the United States had sharply declined.

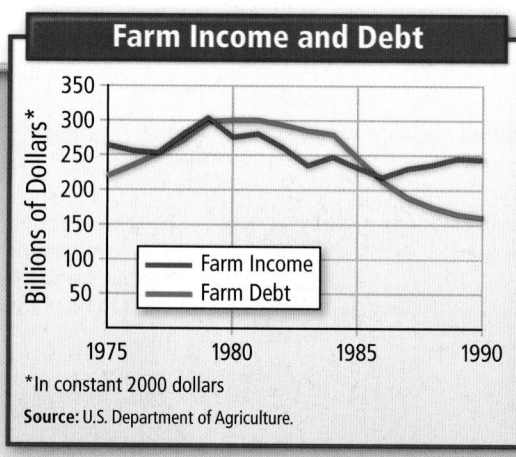

Farm Income and Debt

(Graph: Billions of Dollars* on vertical axis, ranging 50 to 350; years 1975, 1980, 1985, 1990 on horizontal axis. Two lines: Farm Income and Farm Debt.)

*In constant 2000 dollars

Source: U.S. Department of Agriculture.

◄ As farmers faced a debt crisis, some began holding demonstrations, such as this one in Washington D.C. in 1984.

Analyzing VISUALS

1. **Hypothesizing** What factors explain why farm debt increased between 1975 and 1980?

2. **Interpreting** What are the farmers at left complaining about?

The AIDS Epidemic Begins In 1981 researchers identified a disease that caused healthy young people to become sick and die. They named it "acquired immune deficiency syndrome," or **AIDS.** AIDS weakens the immune system, lowering resistance to illnesses such as pneumonia and several types of cancer. HIV, the virus that causes AIDS, is spread through bodily fluids.

In the United States, AIDS was first noticed among homosexual men, but it soon spread among heterosexual men and women. Many people were infected by sexual partners. A few got the disease from blood transfusions. Other victims included drug users who shared needles. Between 1981 and 1988, the Centers for Disease Control and Prevention identified more than 100,000 cases in the United States.

New Activist Groups

AIDS increased the visibility of the country's gay and lesbian community, but some homosexuals had been engaged in efforts to defend their civil rights since the 1960s. On June 27, 1969, New York City police raided a nightclub called the Stonewall Inn. The police had often raided the nightclub because of the sexual **orientation** of its patrons. Frustration among the gay and lesbian onlookers led to a riot. The **Stonewall Riot** marked the beginning of the gay activist movement. Soon after, organizations such as the Gay Liberation Front began efforts to increase tolerance of homosexuality.

Rock 'n' Rollers Become Activists Many musicians and entertainers in the 1980s began using their celebrity to raise awareness about social issues. To help starving people in Ethiopia, Irish rocker Bob Geldof organized musicians in England to present "Band Aid" concerts in 1984. In the next year, the event grew into "Live Aid." People in some 100 countries watched benefit concerts televised from London, Philadelphia, and Sydney, Australia. The organization's theme song, "We Are the World," was a best-seller. In the same year, country singer Willie Nelson organized "Farm Aid" to help American farmers who were going through hard times.

Senior Citizens Begin to Lobby Another group that became politically active in the 1980s was senior citizens. Decades of improvements in medicine had resulted in more Americans surviving to an older age. In addition, the birthrate had declined, so younger people represented a comparatively smaller proportion of the population. The fact that more Americans were receiving Social Security payments created budget pressures for the government.

Older Americans became very vocal in the political arena, opposing cuts in Social Security or Medicare. Because they tend to vote in large numbers, senior citizens are an influential interest group. Their major lobbying organization is the **American Association of Retired Persons (AARP),** founded in 1958.

✔ Reading Check **Summarizing** On what issues did some entertainers focus in the 1980s?

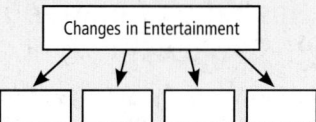

Section 3 REVIEW

Vocabulary

1. **Explain** the significance of: yuppie, discount retailing, Mothers Against Drunk Driving (MADD), AIDS, Stonewall Riot, American Association of Retired Persons (AARP).

Main Ideas

2. **Summarizing** How did retailing change in the 1980s?

3. **Listing** What are three social problems that gained focus in the 1980s?

Critical Thinking

4. **Big Ideas** What new innovations occurred in the consumer electronics industry in the 1980s?

5. **Organizing** Use a graphic organizer similar to the one below to list the changes in entertainment in the 1980s.

```
          Changes in Entertainment
         ┌──┬──┬──┬──┐
         ▼  ▼  ▼  ▼
        □  □  □  □
```

6. **Analyzing Visuals** Study the graph of the stock market rise on page 983. How is this graph indicative of what you have read about in this section?

Writing About History

7. **Persuasive Writing** Choose one of the social problems of the 1980s. Write a letter to members of your favorite band asking them to perform a concert to benefit your cause. Your letter should explain why the cause is important.

History ONLINE

Study Central™ To review this section, go to glencoe.com and click on Study Central.

Seattle

San Francisco

Los Angeles

San Diego   Phoenix

GEOGRAPHY & HISTORY

Urban America on the Move

After World War II, cities grew into vast metropolitan areas—a development referred to as
"urban sprawl." Inner cities, often inhabited by
lower-income people, lost tax revenue, resulting
in deteriorating infrastructure and shortages of
affordable housing. As the map shows, many
high-growth areas are in Southern Sunbelt states.

In response, some cities sought to improve
urban neighborhoods and encourage reinvest-
ment in the city core. These policies have had
only limited effect, as suburbs and new
"exurbs"—communities located in the country
beyond the suburbs, continue to grow.

How Has Urban Geography Affected Politics?

The rapid growth of the suburbs and exurbs
plays an important role in American politics.
Inner city communities tend to vote for
Democrats, while voters in outer suburbs and exurbs tend
to vote for Republicans. The reason for this pattern is
unclear. In part, it reflects the preference of many minorities who live in the inner city to vote for Democrats. In
addition, some political geographers believe that since
city-dwellers rely more on government services, they tend
to support liberal policies that favor government activism.
People in the suburbs and exurbs want more independence and more often distrust government—a conservative perspective. They believe large city governments have
done a poor job running schools and controlling crime.

▲ Urban sprawl, traffic congestion,
long commutes, and air pollution
are part of the price Atlanta paid
for rapid growth.

Existing development as of 1993
— Intense
— Moderate
Development since 1993
— Intense
— Moderate

Analyzing GEOGRAPHY

1. **Movement** Which regions experienced the most
growth after 1993?

2. **Human-Environment Interaction** How does the
urban geography of American cities shape voting
patterns and preferences?

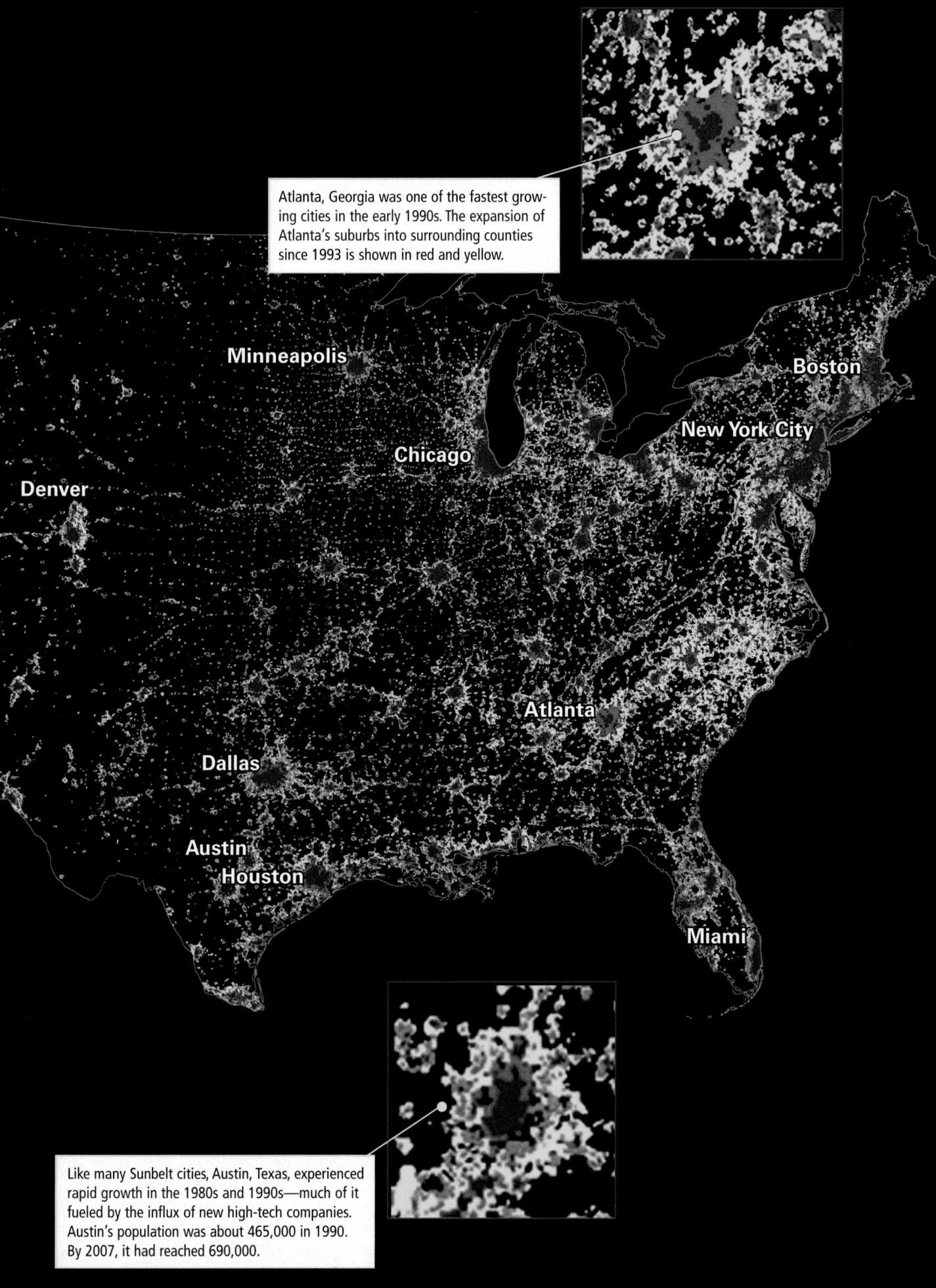

Atlanta, Georgia was one of the fastest growing cities in the early 1990s. The expansion of Atlanta's suburbs into surrounding counties since 1993 is shown in red and yellow.

Minneapolis

Boston

New York City

Chicago

Denver

Atlanta

Dallas

Austin

Houston

Miami

Like many Sunbelt cities, Austin, Texas, experienced rapid growth in the 1980s and 1990s—much of it fueled by the influx of new high-tech companies. Austin's population was about 465,000 in 1990. By 2007, it had reached 690,000.

Section 4

The End of the Cold War

In the late 1980s, the United States faced a series of international crises. The Cold War came to an end in Europe, but events in the Middle East soon led the United States into its first major war since Vietnam.

Place	Foreign Policy
Soviet Union	
China	
Panama	
Middle East	

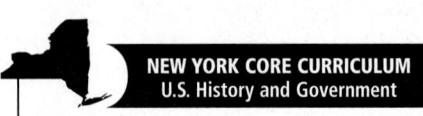

NEW YORK CORE CURRICULUM
U.S. History and Government

Unit 7:
VI.A.1.b Rise of a third party (H. Ross Perot)
VI.A.3 Foreign policy issues

The Soviet Union Collapses

MAIN Idea The Soviet Union's attempts at reforming its social and economic systems failed, leading to the collapse of the Communist eastern bloc.

HISTORY AND YOU What can you recall about the division of Europe after World War II? Read on to learn about the massive changes that took place in Eastern Europe at the end of the 1980s.

When Ronald Reagan left office, few Americans were thinking about foreign policy. Many generally wanted a continuation of Reagan's domestic policies—low taxes and less government action. When Republicans nominated George H. W. Bush for president in 1988, he reassured Americans he would continue Reagan's policies by making a promise: "Read my lips: No new taxes."

The Democrats hoped to regain the White House in 1988 by promising to help working-class Americans, minorities, and the poor. One candidate for the nomination, civil rights leader Jesse Jackson, tried to create a "rainbow coalition"—a broad group of minorities and the poor—by speaking about homelessness and unemployment. Jackson finished second in the primaries, the first African American to make a serious run for the nomination.

The Democrats nominated Massachusetts governor Michael Dukakis. The Bush campaign portrayed him as too liberal and "soft on crime." The Democrats questioned Bush's leadership abilities, but Bush had Reagan's endorsement and, with the economy still doing well, most Americans felt that Bush was the more able candidate. Bush easily defeated Dukakis in the general election, although Democrats kept control of Congress.

Voters had focused on domestic issues during the election campaign, but soon after taking office President Bush had to focus most of his time and energy on foreign policy as change swept through Eastern Europe and the Cold War came to an abrupt end.

Revolution in Eastern Europe

As president, Bush continued Reagan's policy of cooperation with Soviet leader Mikhail Gorbachev. By the late 1980s, the Soviet economy was suffering from years of inefficient central planning and huge expenditures on the arms race. To save the economy,

NATIONAL GEOGRAPHIC — Revolutions in Eastern Europe

◀ The Berlin Wall fell on November 10, 1989.

FINLAND

NORWAY

SWEDEN

North Sea

DENMARK

Tallinn

ESTONIA

Riga

LATVIA

LITHUANIA
Vilnius

RUSSIA

Moscow

Baltic Sea

5. Baltic States became independent, 1991

Minsk

BELARUS

4. Germany reunited, 1990

UNITED KINGDOM

NETH.

Elbe R.

Berlin

Oder R.

POLAND

Warsaw

1. Democratic elections, 1989

3. Berlin Wall torn down, Nov. 1989

EAST GERMANY

Kyiv (Kiev)

BELG.

LUX.

WEST GERMANY

Vistula R.

UKRAINE

Prague
CZECH REP.

SLOVAKIA
Bratislava

6. Czechoslovakia separated, 1993

Dnieper R.

FRANCE

LIECH.

SWITZ.

AUSTRIA

Budapest

MOLDOVA
Chişinău

HUNGARY

ROMANIA

Ljubljana
SLOVENIA

Zagreb

2. Non-Communist governments created, 1989

CROATIA

Belgrade

SAN MARINO

Adriatic Sea

ITALY

BOSNIA & HERZEGOVINA
Sarajevo

Bucharest

Danube R.

Black Sea

MONACO

Mediterranean Sea

YUGOSLAVIA

BULGARIA

Sofia

0   200   400 kilometers
0   200   400 miles
Lambert Azimuthal Equal-Area projection

Tiranë
ALBANIA

Skopje

MACEDONIA

GREECE

▲ Boris Yeltsin rallies the crowd against the military coup on August 19, 1991.

Analyzing GEOGRAPHY

1. **Regions** Which Eastern European countries abandoned communism first?

2. **Place** Why was the fall of communism in East Germany significant?

Gorbachev instituted **perestroika,** or "restructuring," and allowed some private enterprise and profit making.

The other principle of Gorbachev's plan was **glasnost,** or "openness." It allowed more freedom of religion and speech, enabling people to discuss politics openly. With Gorbachev's support, glasnost spread to Eastern Europe. In 1989 revolutions replaced Communist rulers with democratic governments in Bulgaria, Czechoslovakia, Hungary, Poland, and Romania. The tide of revolution then swept over East Germany, and at midnight on November 9, 1989, guards at the Berlin Wall opened the gates.

Within days, bulldozers leveled the hated symbol of Communist repression. Within a year, East and West Germany had reunited to form one nation—the Federal Republic of Germany.

The Soviet Union Collapses

As Eastern Europe abandoned communism, Gorbachev faced mounting criticism from opponents at home. In August 1991 a group of Communist officials and army officers tried to stage a coup—an overthrow of the government. They arrested Gorbachev and sent troops into Moscow.

In Moscow, Russian president **Boris Yeltsin** defied the coup leaders from his offices in the Russian Parliament. About 50,000 people surrounded the Russian Parliament to protect it from troops. President Bush telephoned Yeltsin to express the support of the United States. Soon afterward, the coup collapsed, and Gorbachev returned to Moscow.

The defeat of the coup brought change swiftly. All 15 Soviet republics declared their independence from the Soviet Union. Yeltsin outlawed the Communist Party in Russia. In late December 1991 Gorbachev announced the end of the Soviet Union. Most of the former Soviet republics then joined in a federation called the Commonwealth of Independent States (CIS). Although CIS member states remained independent, they agreed to form a common economic zone in 1993.

✓ **Reading Check** **Explaining** Why did Mikhail Gorbachev institute the policy of *perestroika*?

A "New World Order"

MAIN Idea Bush used his foreign policy expertise to deal with crises in China, Panama, and the Persian Gulf.

HISTORY AND YOU Do you remember learning about student protests in the 1960s? Read on to learn about a student protest in China.

After the Cold War, the world became increasingly unpredictable. President Bush noted that a "new world order" was emerging, and with it came several new crises in China, Panama, and the Middle East.

Tiananmen Square

Despite the collapse of communism in Eastern Europe and the Soviet Union, China's Communist leaders were determined to stay in power. China's government had relaxed

NATIONAL GEOGRAPHIC **The Persian Gulf War, 1991**

0   150   300 kilometers
0   150   300 miles
Lambert Azimuthal Equal-Area projection

3. Allied ground war against Iraqi troops, February 23–26, 1991

2. Operation Desert Storm begins, January 16, 1991

1. Buildup of Allied troops begins along Saudi Arabia/Iraq border, August 1990–February 1991

4. Cease-fire declared by President Bush, February 27, 1991

▲ *Even before the Gulf War, the United States was escorting oil tankers in the Persian Gulf to protect them from attack during the Iran-Iraq War.*

Analyzing VISUALS

1. **Explaining** Why do you think that U.S./UN troops staged their invasion of Iraq from Saudi Arabia?

2. **Specifying** What nations did Iraq attack with SCUD missiles during the war?

Iraq and occupied territory	Iraqi SCUD attacks	Allied troop buildup
Allied against Iraq	Allied air attacks	Allied troop movement
Neutral countries	Iraqi troop placements	Major oil fields

controls on the economy, but it continued to repress political speech and dissent. In May 1989, Chinese students and workers held demonstrations for democracy. The center of the protests was **Tiananmen Square** in Beijing, China's capital. At first, it appeared as if China were repeating the pattern of Eastern Europe and that communism might be ended peacefully. In early June, however, government tanks and soldiers crushed the protests in Tiananmen Square. Many people were killed and hundreds of pro-democracy activists were arrested. Many were later sentenced to death.

These events shocked the world. The United States and several European countries halted arms sales and reduced their diplomatic contacts with China. The World Bank suspended loans. Some U.S. congressional leaders urged even stronger sanctions, but President Bush resisted these harsher measures, believing that trade and diplomacy would eventually moderate China's behavior.

Panama

While President Bush struggled to deal with global events elsewhere, a crisis developed in Panama. In 1978 the United States had agreed to give Panama control over the Panama Canal by the year 2000. Because of the canal's importance, American officials wanted to make sure Panama's government was both stable and pro-American.

By 1989, Panama's dictator, General Manuel Noriega, had stopped cooperating with the United States. He also aided drug traffickers, cracked down on opponents, and harassed American military personnel defending the canal. In December 1989, Bush ordered American troops to invade Panama. The troops seized Noriega, who was sent to the United States to stand trial on drug charges. The troops then helped the Panamanians hold elections and organize a new government.

The Persian Gulf War

President Bush faced perhaps his most serious crisis in the Middle East. In August 1990 Iraq's dictator, **Saddam Hussein,** sent his army to invade oil-rich Kuwait. American officials feared that the invasion might be only the first step and that Iraq's ultimate goal was to capture Saudi Arabia and its vast oil reserves. American troops rushed to the Middle East and took up positions in Saudi Arabia in response.

President Bush persuaded other UN member countries to join a coalition to stop Iraq. Led by the United States, the United Nations imposed economic sanctions on Iraq and demanded that the Iraqis withdraw. The coalition included troops from the United States, Canada, Europe, and Middle Eastern nations. The UN set a deadline for the Iraqis' withdrawal, after which the coalition would use force to remove them. Congress also voted to authorize the use of force if Iraq did not withdraw.

On October 31, 1990, General Colin Powell, chairman of the Joint Chiefs of Staff, Secretary of Defense Dick Cheney, and other high-ranking officials met with President Bush. It was clear that Iraq would not obey the UN deadline. Powell presented the plan for attacking Iraq. Several advisers gasped at the numbers, which called for over 500,000 American troops. "Mr. President," Powell began, "I wish . . . that I could assure you that air power alone could do it but you can't take that chance. We've gotta take the **initiative** out of the enemy's hands if we're going to go to war." Cheney later recalled that Bush "never hesitated." He looked up from the plans and said simply, "Do it."

On January 16, 1991, the coalition forces launched Operation Desert Storm. Dozens of cruise missiles and thousands of laser-guided bombs fell on Iraq, destroying its air defenses, bridges, artillery, and other military targets. After about six weeks of bombardment, the coalition launched a massive ground attack. Waves of tanks and troop carriers smashed through Iraqi lines and encircled the Iraqi forces defending Kuwait.

The attack killed thousands of Iraqi soldiers, and hundreds of thousands more surrendered. Fewer than 300 coalition troops were killed. Just 100 hours after the ground war began, President Bush declared Kuwait to be liberated. Iraq accepted the coalition's cease-fire terms, and American troops returned home to cheering crowds.

Reading Check **Examining** Why did President Bush take action when Iraqi troops invaded Kuwait?

Domestic Challenges

MAIN Idea To reduce the deficit, President Bush raised taxes, an unpopular decision that helped Bill Clinton win the election.

HISTORY AND YOU How are your school and community designed to provide access for people who use wheelchairs? Read on to find out more about the Americans with Disabilities Act of 1990.

President Bush spent much of his time dealing with foreign policy, but he could not ignore domestic issues. He inherited a growing deficit and a slowing economy. With the Persian Gulf crisis, the economy plunged into a recession and unemployment rose.

The Economy Slows

The recession that began in 1990 was partly caused by the end of the Cold War. As the Soviet threat faded, the United States began reducing its armed forces and canceling orders for military equipment. Thousands of soldiers and defense industry workers were laid off.

Other companies also began **downsizing** —laying off workers and managers to become more efficient. The nation's high level of debt made the recession worse. Americans had borrowed heavily during the 1980s and now faced paying off large debts.

In addition, the huge deficit forced the government to borrow money to pay for its programs. This borrowing kept money from being

HISTORY AND GEOGRAPHY
The Election of 1992

The election of 1992 marked the first time since 1968 that no candidate won at least 50 percent of the popular vote and for much the same reason. A strong third party challenger, Ross Perot (below, center), took votes from both major candidates.

◀ The success of Perot's campaign surprised many Americans.

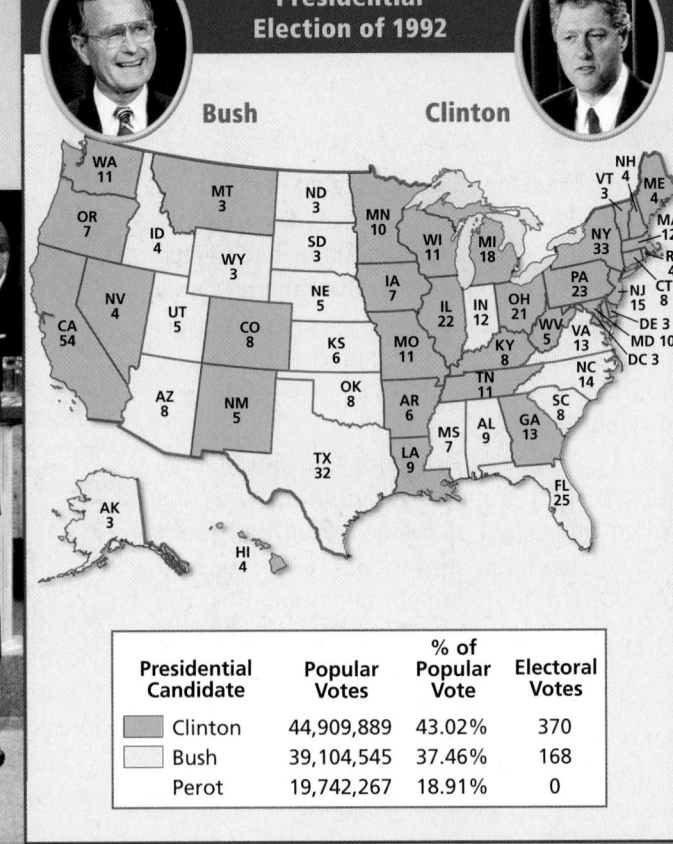

Presidential Election of 1992

Bush   Clinton

Presidential Candidate	Popular Votes	% of Popular Vote	Electoral Votes
Clinton	44,909,889	43.02%	370
Bush	39,104,545	37.46%	168
Perot	19,742,267	18.91%	0

Analyzing VISUALS

1. **Interpreting** What does the cartoon suggest about independent candidates?

2. **Speculating** What factors might explain Clinton's popularity in the Northeast?

available to businesses. The government also had to pay interest on its debt, money that might otherwise have been used to fund programs or boost the economy.

As the economy slowed, hundreds of savings-and-loan institutions collapsed. After President Reagan had allowed them to be deregulated, many had made risky or even dishonest investments. When these investments failed, depositors collected on federal programs to insure deposits. The cost to the public may have reached $500 billion.

Gridlock in Government

Shortly after taking office, Bush tried to improve the economy. He called for a cut in the **capital gains tax**—the tax paid by businesses and investors when they sell stocks or real estate for a profit. Bush believed that the tax cut would encourage businesses to expand. Calling the idea a tax break for the rich, Democrats in Congress defeated it.

Aware that the growing federal deficit was hurting the economy, Bush broke his "no new taxes" campaign pledge. After meeting with congressional leaders, he agreed to a tax increase in exchange for cuts in spending. This decision turned many voters against Bush.

The 1992 Election

Although the recession had weakened his popularity, Bush won the Republican nomination. Bush promised to address voters' economic concerns and he blamed congressional Democrats for the gridlock that seemingly paralyzed the nation's government.

The Democrats nominated Arkansas governor William Jefferson Clinton, despite stories that questioned his character and the fact that he did not serve in Vietnam. Calling himself a "New Democrat" to separate himself from more liberal Democrats, Clinton promised to cut middle-class taxes, reduce government spending, and reform the nation's health care and welfare programs. His campaign repeatedly blamed Bush for the recession.

Some Americans were not happy with either Bush or Clinton. This enabled an independent candidate, billionaire Texas businessman **H. Ross Perot,** to make a strong challenge. Perot stressed the need to end deficit spending. His no-nonsense style appealed to many Americans. A **grassroots movement**—groups of people organizing at the local level—put Perot on the ballot in all 50 states.

Bill Clinton won the election with 43 percent of the popular vote and 370 electoral votes. The Democrats also **retained** control of Congress. Bush won 37 percent of the popular vote, while Perot received 19 percent—the best showing for a third-party candidate since 1912—but no electoral votes.

As the first president born after World War II, the 46-year-old Clinton was the first person from the baby boom generation to enter the White House. It was his task to revive the economy and guide the United States in a rapidly changing world.

Reading Check **Summarizing** Why did President Bush lose popularity as the 1992 election approached?

Section 4 REVIEW

Vocabulary

1. **Explain** the significance of: perestroika, glasnost, Boris Yeltsin, Tiananmen Square, Saddam Hussein, downsizing, capital gains tax, H. Ross Perot, grassroots movement.

Main Ideas

2. **Explaining** How did perestroika and glasnost create conditions that led to the fall of the Soviet Union?

3. **Describing** What actions did the United States take in Panama in 1989?

4. **Determining Cause and Effect** How did the huge deficits from the Reagan years lead to economic problems under George Bush?

Critical Thinking

5. **Big Ideas** How did the economy affect the 1992 election?

6. **Organizing** Use a graphic organizer similar to the one below to list the causes of the recession of the early 1990s.

Budget Problems	Economic Problems	Foreign Developments

7. **Analyzing Visuals** Examine the map on page 992. Which nations have significant oil resources?

Writing About History

8. **Descriptive Writing** Suppose that you are traveling in West Germany in 1989 when the Berlin Wall is being torn down. Write a letter to a friend at home to describe the event and how you think it

History ONLINE

Study Central™ To review this section, go to glencoe.com and click on Study Central.

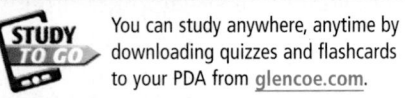

Causes of the New Conservatism

- The Cold War promotes strong foreign policy and an emphasis on minimal government interference in economics.
- Cold War fears of communism encourage many religious Americans to turn to conservative ideas.
- Many Americans are disturbed by the protests, demonstrations, and violence of the 1960s.
- The population growth in the Sunbelt increases support for conservative politicians.
- The rise of an evangelical movement willing to use politics to change society and defend its values helps mobilize conservative voters.
- Frustration with rising taxes and government regulation, especially in the South and West, turns many voters to conservative ideas.
- Both Western conservatives and Southern conservatives come to see the Republican Party as the more conservative party.

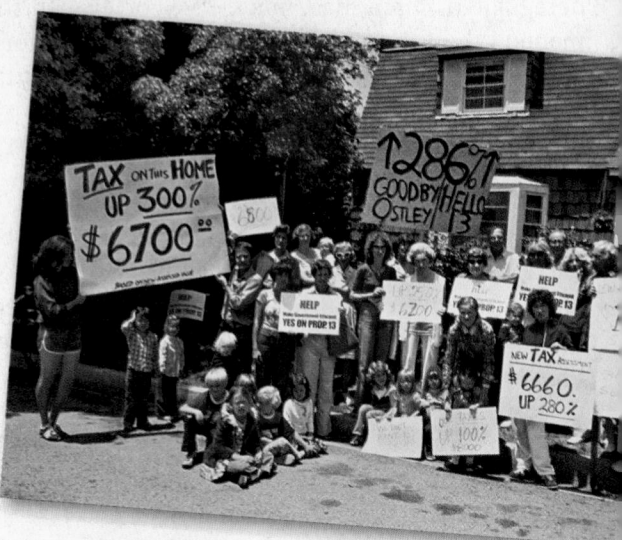

▲ Part of the new conservative movement drew support from Americans who were fed up with high taxes.

The Reagan Administration

- Ronald Reagan is elected president in 1980 and 1984.
- Reagan promotes supply-side economics and pushes large tax cuts through Congress.
- Many industries are deregulated, helping spur a boom in the oil, transportation, and communications industries.
- A political debate over cutting government programs rather than expanding them shapes the domestic politics of the era.
- Reagan's administration takes a strong anti-Communist stance in Latin America, the Caribbean, and the Middle East, providing aid to groups that resist communism.
- The nation begins a sustained military buildup to put pressure on the Soviet economy; in addition the United States begins work on anti-missile "Star Wars" technology.
- The failure to cut domestic programs, combined with increased military spending, drives the growing budget deficit to record levels.
- Energy prices fall, the economy grows rapidly, and stock market values soar.
- The farm debt crisis and deregulation of the banks leads to the collapse of many family farms, and many savings and loan institutions.
- Under great economic stress, the Soviet Union introduces perestroika and glasnost; communism falls across Eastern Europe in 1989, and then the Soviet Union collapses in 1991.

▲ The summit between President Reagan and Mikhail Gorbachev created an easing of tensions between the U.S. and Soviet Union.

NEW YORK REGENTS EXAM PRACTICE

TEST-TAKING

Read each answer choice and eliminate the ones that simply do not make sense for the given question.

Part I

Directions (1–10): For each statement or question, write on a separate sheet of paper the number of the word or expression that, of those given, best completes the statement or answers the question.

1 Which of the following groups, in general, believe that the government should regulate the economy to protect people from the power of large corporations?

(1) economists

(2) liberals

(3) conservatives

(4) televangelists

2 Which of the following new business models had a major impact on the economy starting in the 1980s?

(1) superstations

(2) wholesale retailing

(3) discount retailing

(4) direct mail

3 One main difference between liberals and conservatives is that, generally,

(1) conservatives believe in government regulation of the economy, while liberals do not.

(2) liberals believe in government regulation of the economy, while conservatives do not.

(3) conservatives believe that all power should be held by the national government, while liberals do not.

(4) liberals believe that all power should be held by the states, while conservatives do not.

4 Which of the following two groups had added their support to conservatives by the 1980s?

(1) African Americans and urbanites

(2) Northerners and Easterners

(3) Democrats and women

(4) Sunbelters and suburbanites

5 Critics of Reagan's economic policy referred to it as "trickle-down economics" because they

(1) believed the plan allowed wealth to "trickle down" to the middle and lower classes.

(2) ridiculed the idea that much wealth would "trickle down" to the middle and lower classes.

(3) believed that the plan would cause a great deal of wasteful government spending.

(4) agreed that the richest people would share their wealth with the neediest in society.

6 Which of the following technologies became available during the 1980s?

(1) the digital video recorder

(2) the video cassette recorder

(3) the personal digital assistant

(4) the digital watch

7 A major focus of U.S. social activism in the 1980s was

(1) gun control

(2) abortion

(3) drug abuse

(4) poverty

Need Extra Help?							
If You Missed Questions . . .	1	2	3	4	5	6	7
Go to Page . . .	968–970	983	968–970	971	976	985	986–987

[OVER]

8 The result of the failed Communist coup in Moscow in August 1991 was that

(1) Boris Yeltsin became president of the U.S.S.R.

(2) the Soviet republics declared independence.

(3) the Berlin Wall was taken down by bulldozers.

(4) the United States sent troops into Saudi Arabia.

9 In response to events in Tiananmen Square in China, the United States and other nations

(1) sent weapons and money to the rebels.

(2) halted arms sales and reduced their diplomatic contacts with China.

(3) made plans for a summit meeting with China.

(4) sent troops to free the imprisoned protesters.

Base your answer to question 10 on the graph below and your knowledge of Chapter 29.

Military Spending and the Deficit

In Hundreds of Billions of Dollars

— Federal Debt
— Total Federal Expenses
— National Defense

Sources: Departments of Commerce and Treasury; Office of Management and Budget.

10 How much money was spent on national defense in 1986?

(1) approximately 500 billion dollars

(2) more than 500 billion dollars

(3) approximately 250 billion dollars

(4) less than 250 million dollars

Part II Thematic Essay Question

Directions: Write a well-organized essay that includes an introduction, several paragraphs addressing the task below, and a conclusion.

Theme: The Reagan Presidency

In the late 1980s, the Cold War came to an end with the disintegration of the Warsaw Pact, the fall of the Berlin Wall, and the collapse of the Soviet Union.

Task:

- Describe the events in the 1980s on both sides of the Cold War that contributed to instability in the Soviet Union and Eastern Europe

- Evaluate the role of the Reagan administration's policies in bringing about the fall of the Soviet Union and the end of the Cold War

Guidelines:

In your essay be sure to:

- Develop all aspects of the task

- Support the theme with relevant facts, examples, and details

- Use a logical and clear plan of organization, including an introduction and a conclusion that are beyond a restatement of the theme

Part III Document-Based Question

This question is based on the accompanying documents. It is designed to test your ability to work with historical documents. Some of the documents have been edited for the purposes of the question. As you analyze the documents, take into account the source of each document and any point of view that may be presented in the document.

Historical Context:

During the 1980s President Reagan established a policy he referred to as "peace through strength" that some feel led to the fall of the Soviet Union and brought about the end to the Cold War.

Need Extra Help?			
If You Missed Questions . . .	8	9	10
Go to Page . . .	991–992	992–993	R16

Task:

Using information from the documents and your knowledge of United States history, answer the questions that follow each document in Part A. Your answers to the questions will help you write the Part B essay, in which you will be asked to

- Discuss the achievements and failures of Reagan's presidency
- Evaluate how Reagan's conservative politics and economic beliefs either strengthened or weakened the United States in foreign matters

Part A
Short-Answer Questions

Directions: Analyze the documents and answer the short-answer questions that follow each document on a separate sheet of paper.

Document 1

'I CAN'T BELIEVE MY EYES!'

Source: Edmund S. Valtman, Library of Congress, 1991

1 What is the cartoonist saying about Gorbachev's policies?

Document 2

The way I see it, there were two great triumphs, two things that I'm proudest of. One is the economic recovery, in which the people of America created—and filled—19 million new jobs. The other is the recovery of our morale. America is respected again. . . .

Common sense told us that when you put a big tax on something, the people will produce less of it. So, we cut the people's tax rates, and the people produced more than ever before. The economy bloomed. . . . Common sense told us that to preserve the peace, we'd have to become strong again after years of weakness and confusion. So, we rebuilt our defenses, and this New Year we toasted the new peacefulness around the globe. . . .

Source: Ronald Reagan, *Speaking My Mind*, Simon and Schuster, c. 1989

2 How did Reagan feel that his administration had preserved the peace?

Part B
Essay

Directions: Reread the task box at the top left and write a well-organized essay that includes an introduction, several paragraphs, and a conclusion. Use evidence from the documents in your essay. Support your response with relevant facts, examples, and details. Include additional outside information.

Guidelines:

In your essay, be sure to:

- Develop all aspects of the task
- Incorporate information from the documents
- Incorporate relevant outside information
- Support the theme with relevant facts, examples, and details
- Use a logical and clear plan of organization, including an introduction and a conclusion that are beyond a restatement of the theme

History ONLINE

For additional test practice, use Self-Check Quizzes—Chapter 29 at glencoe.com.

Need Extra Help?			
If You Missed Questions . . .	1	2	Essay
Go to Page . . .	R18	R19	R8

A Time of Change

1980–2000

President Bill Clinton looks over the new White House Web site on July 8, 2000

U.S. PRESIDENTS

U.S. EVENTS

WORLD EVENTS

1981
• IBM introduces their version of the PC or Personal Computer

1984
• Apple's Macintosh introduces the mouse and on-screen icons

1986
• Immigration Control and Reform Act passed

1991
• U.S. and other nations liberate Kuwait from Iraqi occupation

G. Bush
1989–1993

1980 1982 1984 1986 1988 1990 1992

1980
• Lech Walesa organizes trade union Solidarity in Poland

1987
• Soviet Union and United States sign INF Treaty

1989
• The Berlin Wall falls

1990
• The World Wide Web is developed in Switzerland.

How Has Technology Changed Society?

In the late twentieth century, the development of new technology, including personal computers, mobile phones, and the Internet, revolutionized the way people lived.

- *What other eras in American history experienced rapid technological change?*
- *Has the computer revolution changed society for the better? Why or why not?*

1993
- Mosaic, the first popular Web browser, is released

Clinton
1993–2001

1994
- U.S., Mexico, and Canada found NAFTA

1998
- House of Representatives impeaches President Clinton

1999
- Senate acquits Clinton

G. W. Bush
2001–2009

| 1994 | 1996 | 1998 | 2000 |

1993
- Israeli-Palestinian peace accord signed

1995
- Cease-fire signed in Bosnian war

1997
- Britain returns Hong Kong to China

FOLDABLES™

Identifying Technological Changes
Research how computers have changed the way Americans live. Organize the information you learn in a Layered-Look Book Foldable by the following categories: business, communications, and entertainment. Describe how computers are applied in each field and how they have changed the way people live.

The Computer Revolution
Business
Communications
Entertainment

History ONLINE Chapter Overview
Visit glencoe.com to preview Chapter 30.

The Technological Revolution

Guide to Reading

Big Ideas
Computers, Telecommunications, and the Internet The introduction of the first electronic digital computer in 1946 launched a technological revolution.

Content Vocabulary
- integrated circuit *(p. 1002)*
- microprocessor *(p. 1002)*
- telecommute *(p. 1003)*
- blogs *(p. 1005)*

Academic Vocabulary
- device *(p. 1002)*
- refinement *(p. 1003)*
- communications *(p. 1004)*

People and Events to Identify
- ENIAC *(p. 1002)*
- Silicon Valley *(p. 1002)*
- Steve Jobs *(p. 1002)*
- Bill Gates *(p. 1003)*

Reading Strategy
Categorizing As you read about the computer age, complete a chart similar to the one below to describe products that revolutionized the computer industry.

	How It Revolutionized Computer Industry
Microprocessors	
Apple II	
Macintosh	
Windows	

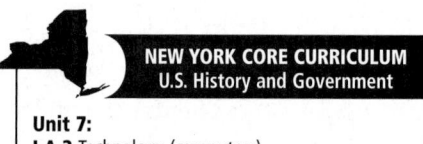

NEW YORK CORE CURRICULUM
U.S. History and Government

Unit 7:
I.A.3 Technology (computers)

The computers we use today bear little resemblance to the first electronic computers that were built in the 1940s. Since the 1980s, computer technology has advanced dramatically, with the creation of home computers and then the expansion of the Internet.

The Computer Changes Society

MAIN Idea A computer revolution changed the workplace and the way people communicate.

HISTORY AND YOU What computer devices do you use regularly? Read on to learn about the earliest electronic computers.

The development of electronic computers began at the end of World War II. The world's first electronic digital computer, called **ENIAC** (Electronic Numerical Integrator and Computer), went into operation in February 1946. ENIAC weighed over 30 tons and was the size of a small house. In early 1959, Robert Noyce designed the first **integrated circuit**—a complete electronic circuit on a single chip of silicon—which made circuits much smaller and very easy to manufacture. Noyce's company was located south of San Francisco. As new companies sprang up nearby to make products using integrated circuits, the region became known as **Silicon Valley.**

In 1968 Noyce and colleague Gordon Moore formed Intel, for "Integrated Electronics," a company that revolutionized the computer industry by combining on a single chip several integrated circuits containing both memory and computing functions. Called **microprocessors,** these new chips made computers much faster and smaller.

Computers for Everyone

Using microprocessor technology, Stephen Wozniak and his 20-year-old friend **Steve Jobs** set out to build a small computer suitable for personal use. In 1976 they founded Apple Computer and completed the Apple I. The following year they introduced the Apple II, the first practical and affordable home computer.

Apple's success sparked intense competition in the computer industry. In 1981 International Business Machines (IBM) introduced its own compact machine, which it called the "Personal Computer" (PC). Apple responded in 1984 with the revolutionary Macintosh, a new model featuring a simplified operating system using on-screen graphic symbols called icons, which users could manipulate with a hand-operated **device** called a mouse.

TECHNOLOGY & HISTORY

Computers Beginning in the late 1970s and continuing to the present, changes in computer and telecommunications technology have transformed how people live and work.

▲ Integrated Circuit

Without the integrated circuit, the computer and telecommunications revolutions would not have been possible. It allowed literally millions of tiny circuits to be mass produced and for manufacturers to greatly reduce the size of computer-based products.

Personal Computer ▶

The Apple Macintosh introduced in 1984 was the first mass-produced personal computer to use a mouse and on-screen icons to help users interact with the software. The new interface made computers far easier to use and encouraged Americans who were not technically trained to begin using computers. The first mouse (shown above) was invented by Douglas Englebart in 1964.

◀ Mobile Phone

Microprocessors and digital technology made small mobile phones (cell phones) possible. Combined with wireless access to the Internet, the cell phone allows people to stay in communication and to view videos, text messages, and photos no matter where they are.

Analyzing VISUALS

1. **Explaining** What aspects of life do computer-based devices make easier?
2. **Inferring** Why do you think it was important for integrated circuits to be so small?

As Jobs and Wozniak were creating Apple, 19-year-old Harvard dropout **Bill Gates** co-founded Microsoft to design PC software, the instructions used to program computers to perform desired tasks. In 1980 IBM hired Microsoft to develop an operating system for its new PC. Gates paid a Seattle programmer $50,000 for the rights to his software, and with some **refinements,** it became MS-DOS (Microsoft Disk Operating System). In 1985 Microsoft introduced the "Windows" operating system, which enabled PCs to use mouse-activated, on-screen graphic icons.

Compact computers soon transformed the workplace, linking employees within an office or among office branches. They became essential tools in almost all businesses. By the late 1990s, workers used home computers and electronic mail (E-mail) to **"telecommute,"** or do their jobs from home via computer.

New Telecommunications

A parallel revolution in telecommunications coincided with the development of personal computers. In the 1970s, the government started deregulating the telecommunications industry. Then, in 1996 Congress passed the Telecommunications Act, which allowed phone companies to compete with each other and to send television signals. It also allowed cable television companies to offer telephone service. This led to much greater competition, and many new technologies were developed.

One major telecommunications technology that became very popular was the cell phone. Cell phones had been invented in the 1940s, and the first large-scale cellular networks were built in the 1980s, but the phones were large and the service was very expensive. All that began to change in the 1990s.

History ONLINE
Student Web Activity Visit glencoe.com and complete the activity on the technological revolution.

Wireless digital technology made it possible to miniaturize cell phones, and they quickly became very popular. By the early 2000s, they were in widespread use around the world. Wireless digital technology also made it possible to manufacture small inexpensive satellite dishes that could receive video and radio beamed from orbit into people's homes.

Digital technology rapidly transformed many consumer products. Various companies developed music players, cameras, radios, televisions, and music and video recorders that used digital technology. Because they were digital and relied on computer chips, it became possible to connect them to each other and to computers. Modern cell phones, for example, often have digital cameras built in, and can send and receive E-mail and instant text messages. Computers can play the same videos that can be played on digital television. Further accelerating the interoperability and connections between the technologies was the rise of a global network of interconnected computers that came to be called the Internet.

Reading Check **Describing** How did digital technology change consumer products?

The Rise of the Internet

MAIN Idea A computer resource that linked government agencies developed into the Internet.

HISTORY AND YOU Have you ever used the Internet to do research for a class? Read on to learn about the origins of the Internet.

In 1969 the U.S. Defense Department's Advanced Research Project Agency created a system of networked computers known as ARPANET. The system linked computers at government agencies, defense contractors, and several universities, enabling them to communicate with one other.

In 1986 the National Science Foundation built NSFNet, a network connecting several super computer centers across the country. NSFNet was soon linked to ARPANET, and as the connections to other computer networks across the world grew, the system became known as the Internet. The Internet is not the World Wide Web or E-mail. Those are systems that use the Internet. The Internet is the physical network of computers connected together by phone lines, cable lines, and wireless **communications.**

PRIMARY SOURCE
The Rise of the Internet

As the Internet grew in size and people obtained access to faster computers and faster "broadband" connections, people began to use it for almost everything.

How People Use Computers

- E-mail or Instant Messaging
- Playing Games
- Listening to the Radio or Viewing TV or Movies
- Purchase Products or Services
- Take a Course Online
- Trade Stocks, Bonds, or Mutual Funds
- Bank Online
- Search for Products or Service Information
- Get News, Weather or Sports Information
- Search for Information on Health Services or Practices
- Search for Information about Government Services or Agencies
- Search for a Job

0 10 20 30 40 50 60 70 80 90 100
Percentage

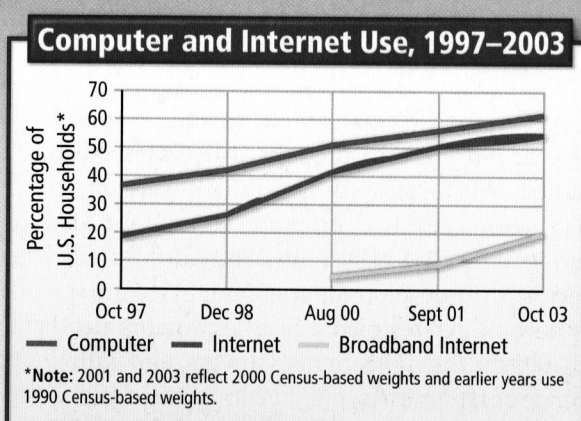

Computer and Internet Use, 1997–2003

Percentage of U.S. Households*

— Computer   — Internet   — Broadband Internet

*Note: 2001 and 2003 reflect 2000 Census-based weights and earlier years use 1990 Census-based weights.

Source: Economics and Statistics Administration.

Analyzing VISUALS

1. **Classifying** Which category of activities is the Internet used for the most?

2. **Hypothesizing** Is the growth in the use of the internet slowing or accelerating? Why might this be so?

As personal computers became cheaper and more widely available, more and more people began signing up with Internet Service Providers (ISPs) who could connect their computers to the Internet. By the late 1990s, the Internet had become wildly popular as businesses began experimenting with it to sell goods and services and to improve their productivity and communications. By 2007, more than 1 billion people were regularly using the Internet.

Birth of the World Wide Web

In 1990, researchers at CERN, a physics laboratory in Switzerland, developed a new way to present information on computers linked to the Internet. Known as the World Wide Web, this system used hypertext (what today are referred to as "links" on web pages) and could be accessed with software known as a web browser. The system allowed users to post information in the form of Web pages and click on links to jump from Web site to Web site.

Enthusiasm for the World Wide Web spawned a "dot-com" economy (from the common practice of using ".com" to designate the address of a business Web site). Seemingly rich with promise, a wide variety of dot-com companies made millions of dollars for stock investors without making any actual profits. Internet-related stocks helped fuel the prosperity of the 1990s, but dropped dramatically in 2000—a period that became known as the "dot-com bust" when many unprofitable online companies went out of business.

A few companies have, however, become major success stories. Amazon.com, founded by Jeff Bezos, has become a highly successful online bookseller. The companies Google and Yahoo both created search engines that help people locate information on the web. Many media companies have also found success on the web in the same way that they did in print and on television —by charging fees for advertising. A few have tried making money by offering music files for download, or by selling access to databases of information. Many traditional companies have begun using the Web to take orders from customers and to provide information about their products.

The Internet Changes Society

For many people, the World Wide Web has become more than just a source of information. It has become a way to build a sense of community. People with common interests visit Web sites about those interests and post comments and interact with each other.

Individuals and families share stories and photos about themselves on **blogs**—short for Web logs—Web sites that function as a kind of public diary or notebook. Web sites such as MySpace serve a similar function, while sites such as YouTube enable people to post video clips they want to share with others. Blogs have also led to a renaissance in essay writing and commentary as they enable people to publicly comment on news stories and other events. They have also helped mobilize people for political action. For many, accessing the Web has become a routine and important part of their daily life.

Reading Check Analyzing How have the Internet and World Wide Web changed society?

Section 1 REVIEW

Vocabulary

1. **Explain** the significance of: ENIAC, integrated circuit, Silicon Valley, microprocessor, Steve Jobs, Bill Gates, telecommute, blogs.

Main Ideas

2. **Describing** How have personal computers transformed the workplace?

3. **Contrasting** What is the difference between the World Wide Web and the Internet?

Critical Thinking

4. **Big Ideas** How have advances in telecommunications and the rise of the Internet affected the standard of living in the United States?

5. **Organizing** Complete a graphic organizer similar to the one below by listing developments that led to the technological revolution.

Technological Revolution

6. **Analyzing Visuals** Study the photograph of the Apple Computer on page 1003. How have computers changed since the 1980s?

Writing About History

7. **Descriptive Writing** Write two paragraphs describing the ways that you and your family use the Internet and how your way of life would be different without it.

History ONLINE

Study Central™ To review this section, go to glencoe.com and click on Study Central.

TIME NOTEBOOK

American Notes

KIM KOMENICH/GETTY IMAGES

In 1985, **RYAN WHITE** *became a symbol of the intolerance that is inflicted on some people suffering from HIV/AIDS.*

Ryan White was 13 years old when he learned that he had contracted HIV through blood products he was taking for hemophilia, a disease he had since birth. At the time, many people thought the AIDS virus could be passed by casual contact—by shaking hands, sneezing, or coughing. Even though AIDS can't be caught that way, people in Ryan's school in Kokomo, Indiana, were afraid to be near him. School officials banned him from classes, and Ryan had to fight in court to win the right to attend school.

In 1987, his family moved to another Indiana town, Cicero, where he was treated more kindly. Ryan died on April 8, 1990. At his funeral, a family friend, Rev. Ray Probasco, said: "It was Ryan who first humanized the disease called AIDS. He allowed us to see the boy who just wanted, more than anything else, to be like other children and to be able to go to school."

VERBATIM

"Just say no."

—NANCY REAGAN,
in 1983, launching her antidrug campaign

"Show me the money!"

—ACTOR CUBA GOODING, JR.'S CHARACTER,
in the 1996 movie Jerry Maguire

"Mr. Gorbachev, tear down this wall!"

—PRESIDENT RONALD REAGAN,
in 1987 addressing the head of the USSR while standing next to the Berlin Wall, which still divided East and West Berlin.

"Can we all get along?"

—RODNEY KING,
pleading in 1992 with the rioters in Los Angeles and other cities, after violence erupted following a jury's acquittal of the police officer who had beaten him.

"We are the world."

—FORTY-FIVE POP STARS,
including Lionel Richie, Ray Charles, and Bruce Springsteen, known as USA for Africa. The group recorded the song "We Are the World" in 1985 to raise money for Africans in need.

"I do not like broccoli. And I haven't liked it since I was a little kid and my mother made me eat it. And I'm President of the United States and I'm not going to eat any more broccoli."

—PRESIDENT GEORGE H. W. BUSH,
1990

FIRSTS IN TECH
Important Dates in the Technology Revolution

1981	1982	1983	1984	1985	1991	1995	1997
Columbia makes the first space shuttle flight	First use of emoticons in an e-mail: :-) and :-(	Music CDs go on sale in the United States — The first American cell phone system goes into operation	Apple Macintosh computer is released	Nintendo Entertainment System comes to America	World Wide Web is created by Tim Berners-Lee of Great Britain	Release of first DVDs (digital video disks)	Dolly the sheep is the first animal made by cloning adult cells

Steve Jobs presents the first Macintosh computer

AP PHOTO/PAUL SAKUMA

NASA

NAJLAH FEANNY/CORBIS

Time Capsule

In 1992, TIME magazine ran a short story, "Things to Show How We Live Now," as a way to highlight what was important to the public at the time. Here are 15 items from the list. How do they compare with what you think is important?

REMOTE CONTROL

GARTH BROOKS CD

8-MM CAMCORDER

CASH-MACHINE CARD

INFLATABLE GLOBE

DISPOSABLE CAMERA

DOLPHIN-SAFE TUNA

BAGGY JEANS

PALMTOP COMPUTER

SPF 15 SUNSCREEN

POCKET T-SHIRT

BOTTLED WATER FROM THE ALPS

IN-LINE SKATES

AIR BAG

BEEPER

JAMES KEYSER/GETTY IMAGES

Milestones

LOST, 1986. THE SPACE SHUTTLE *CHALLENGER* exploded 73 seconds after liftoff. Millions watched in horror as the 25th shuttle mission blew up, killing all seven crew members, including high school teacher Christa McAuliffe.

RECONCILED, 1992. U.S. PRESIDENT GEORGE H.W. BUSH AND RUSSIAN PRESIDENT BORIS YELTSIN formally declared an end to the Cold War.

RELEASED, 1981. FIFTY-TWO U.S. HOSTAGES IN IRAN were set free after 444 days in captivity. The crisis played a significant part in Jimmy Carter's failure to win a second presidential term.

AIRED, 1981. FORMER RADIO EXECUTIVES CREATED MTV (MUSIC TELEVISION). They knew that advertisers wanted to reach young people, who loved rock music. So they decided to run music videos on a cable channel.

ERUPTED, 1980. MOUNT ST. HELENS IN WASHINGTON STATE erupted after being dormant for 123 years. A stupendous explosion blew the entire top off the volcano.

NAMED, 1981. SANDRA DAY O'CONNOR became the first female justice on the U.S. Supreme Court after being appointed to the position by President Ronald Reagan.

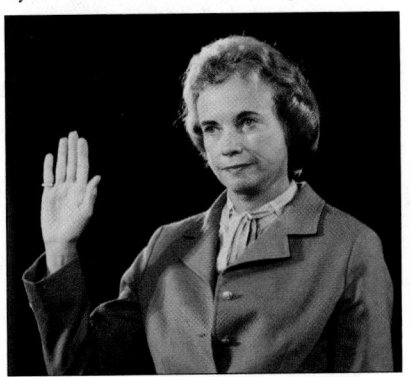

WALLY MCNAMEE/CORBIS

Justice Sandra Day O'Connor

HONORED, 1995. BALTIMORE ORIOLES SHORTSTOP CAL RIPKEN, JR. became a national hero just by going to work every day for 13 years. On September 6, 1995, Ripken showed up at his 2,131st game in a row, breaking the 1939 record set by Lou Gehrig.

NUMBERS

168 Number of people killed in the 1995 bombing of Oklahoma City's Federal Building by two Americans, Terry Nichols and Timothy McVeigh

12 Age of Valerie Ambrose, who won a NASA contest in 1997 by coming up with "Sojourner Truth" as the name for a robot explorer to Mars

11,000,000 Number of gallons of crude oil spilled into Prince William Sound by the tanker *Exxon Valdez* in 1989

NATALIE FOBES/CORBIS

An oil-soaked whale after the Exxon Valdez *spill*

20,000,000 Number of albums Michael Jackson's *Thriller* sold, making it the best-selling record of all time as of 1982

Forever Amount of time former player Pete Rose was banned from baseball after the discovery in 1989 that he was gambling on baseball games

CRITICAL THINKING

1. *Synthesizing* Do you think people's attitudes have changed towards people with HIV/AIDS since 1985? Explain your answer.

2. *Hypothesizing* Why might celebrities be better able than the "average" citizen to focus public attention on serious global issues and problems?

The Clinton Years

Guide to Reading

Big Ideas
Government and Society President Clinton pushed through laws to help families and strengthen gun control, but he also raised taxes and failed to reform health care.

Content Vocabulary
- perjury *(p. 1013)*
- ethnic cleansing *(p. 1015)*

Academic Vocabulary
- modify *(p.1009)*
- unprecedented *(p.1009)*
- participant *(p. 1015)*

People and Events to Identify
- AmeriCorps *(p. 1010)*
- Contract with America *(p. 1011)*
- Kenneth Starr *(p. 1013)*
- Dayton Accords *(p. 1015)*

Reading Strategy
Taking Notes As you read about the administration of President Clinton, use the major headings of the section to create an outline similar to the one below.

The Clinton Years
I. Clinton's Agenda
  A.
  B.
  C.
  D.
II.

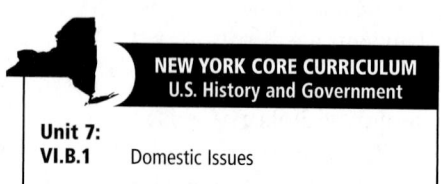

When William Jefferson Clinton was elected in 1992, he became the first Democrat to win the presidency in 12 years. After achieving only part of his agenda, he faced a new Republican Congress that had very different plans. His second term focused on foreign policy and scandal.

Clinton's Agenda

MAIN Idea President Clinton took office in 1993 with plans for improving health care, cutting the federal deficit, aiding families, and increasing gun control.

HISTORY AND YOU Do you know anyone who has worked for AmeriCorps? Read on to learn about the beginnings of this program.

Only 46 years old when he took office, Bill Clinton was the third-youngest person ever to serve as president and the first of the "baby boom" generation to reach the Oval Office. The new president put forth an ambitious domestic program focusing on five major areas: the economy, the family, education, crime, and health care.

Raising Taxes, Cutting Spending

As he had promised in his election campaign, Clinton focused first on the economy. The problem, in his view, was the federal deficit. Under Reagan and Bush, the deficit had nearly quadrupled, adding billions of dollars annually to the national debt. High deficits forced the government to borrow large sums of money, which helped to drive up interest rates. Clinton believed that the key to economic growth was to lower interest rates. Low interest rates would enable businesses to borrow more money to expand and create more jobs. Low rates would also make it easier for consumers to borrow money for mortgages, car loans, and other items, which in turn would promote economic growth.

One way to bring interest rates down was to reduce the federal deficit. In early 1993, Clinton sent Congress a deficit reduction plan. In trying to cut the deficit, however, Clinton faced a serious problem. About half of all government spending went to entitlement programs, such as Social Security, Medicare, and veterans' benefits. These programs are hard to cut because so many Americans depend on them. Faced with these constraints, Clinton decided to raise taxes, even though he had promised to cut them during his campaign. Clinton proposed raising tax rates for middle- and upper-income Americans and placed new taxes on gasoline, heating oil, and natural

The Debate Over Health Care

During his first term in office, President Clinton launched an ambitious program to reform the nation's health care system. The reforms faced much opposition and never materialized.

▲ President Clinton explains the proposed Health Security card in a speech to Congress in October 1993.

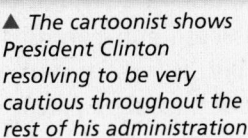

THE ACCIDENT

THE PAIN

THE EMBARRASSMENT

THE REHABILITATION

THE RECOVERY

THE RETURN TO THE SCENE OF THE ACCIDENT AND THE LESSON LEARNED.

I WILL BE SUPER CAUTIOUS FOR THE REST OF MY ADMINISTRATION.

HEALTH CARE REFORM

FOUND OUT YOU WEREN'T INSURED?

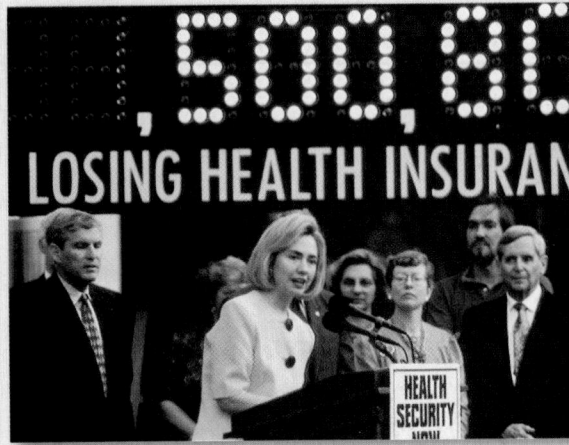

LOSING HEALTH INSURAN

HEALTH SECURITY NOW

▲ Hillary Clinton speaks about her health care plan in front of a counter showing one person losing health insurance every 1.17 seconds.

▲ The cartoonist shows President Clinton resolving to be very cautious throughout the rest of his administration.

Analyzing VISUALS DBQ

1. **Inferring** How does the cartoonist compare Clinton's failed attempt to change health care to an accident?

2. **Analyzing** Why does Clinton resolve to be cautious in the future?

gas. The tax increases were very unpopular, and Republicans in Congress refused to support them. Clinton pressured Democrats, and after many amendments, a **modified** version of Clinton's plan narrowly passed.

Stumbling on Health Care

During his campaign, Clinton had promised to reform the health care system. Some 40 million Americans, or roughly 15 percent of the nation, did not have health insurance. The president created a task force and appointed his wife, Hillary Rodham Clinton, to head it—an **unprecedented** role for a first lady. The task force developed a plan to guarantee health benefits for all Americans, but it put much of the burden of paying for the benefits on employers. Small-business owners feared they could not afford it. The insurance industry and doctors' organizations also opposed the plan and mounted a nationwide advertising campaign on television and radio to build public opposition to the plan.

Republicans argued that the plan was too complicated, costly, and relied too much on government control. Democrats were divided. Some supported alternative plans, but no plan had enough support to pass. Faced with public opposition, Clinton's plan died without a vote.

Families and Education

Clinton did manage to push several major pieces of legislation through Congress. During his campaign, he had stressed the need to help American families. His first success was the Family Medical Leave Act. This law gave workers up to 12 weeks per year of unpaid family leave for the birth or adoption of a child or for the illness of a family member.

Clinton also persuaded Congress to create the **AmeriCorps** program. This program put students to work improving low-income housing, teaching children to read, and cleaning up the environment. AmeriCorps incorporated the VISTA program that John F. Kennedy had created. AmeriCorps volunteers earn a salary and are awarded a scholarship to continue their education. In September 1994, the first group of AmeriCorps volunteers—some 20,000 in number—began serving in more than 1,000 communities.

Crime and Gun Control

Clinton had also promised to get tough on crime during his campaign, and he strongly endorsed new gun-control laws. Despite strong opposition from many Republicans and the National Rifle Association (NRA), the Democrats in Congress passed a gun-control law known as the Brady Bill. It was named after James Brady, President Reagan's press secretary who had been severely injured by a gunshot during the assassination attempt on the former president. His wife, Sarah Brady, became an advocate of gun control and lobbied Congress to pass the bill. The Brady Handgun Violence Prevention Act imposed a waiting period before people could buy handguns. It also required gun dealers to have police run a background check for a criminal record before selling someone a handgun.

The following year, Clinton introduced another crime bill. The bill provided extra funds for states to build new prisons, and put 100,000 more police officers on the streets. It banned 19 kinds of assault weapons and provided money for crime prevention programs, such as "midnight" basketball leagues that would get young people off the streets.

Reading Check **Explaining** Why did President Clinton's proposed health care plan fail?

Republicans Gain Control of Congress

MAIN Idea Republican victories in Congress led to conflicts between the executive and legislative branches of the federal government.

HISTORY AND YOU Have you ever refused to back down when you felt sure you were in the right? Read on to learn about a showdown between Congress and the president.

Despite his successes, Clinton was very unpopular by late 1994. He had raised taxes, instead of lowering them as he had promised, and he had failed to fix health care. Although the economy was improving, many companies were still downsizing. Several personal issues involving President Clinton further weakened

Debates IN HISTORY

Is a Balanced Budget Amendment a Good Idea?

One of the ideas that congressional Republicans put forth in the "Contract with America" was a balanced budget amendment to the Constitution. A balanced budget amendment would force Congress to pass a federal budget that balanced projected revenues and expenditures. Would such an amendment force Congress to be more responsible in how it spends the taxpayers' money, resulting in a more efficient, limited government? Or, would it dangerously limit Congress's ability to respond to economic and national security emergencies?

public confidence in him. In response, many Americans decided to vote Republican in 1994.

The Contract With America

As the 1994 midterm elections neared, congressional Republicans, led by Newt Gingrich of Georgia, created the **Contract with America.** This program proposed 10 major changes, including lower taxes, welfare reform, tougher anticrime laws, term limits for members of Congress, and a balanced budget amendment. Republicans won a stunning victory—for the first time in 40 years, they had a majority in both houses of Congress.

In their first 100 days in office, House Republicans passed almost the entire Contract with America, but they soon ran into trouble. The Senate defeated several proposals, while the president vetoed others.

The Budget Battle

In 1995 the Republicans clashed with the president over the new federal budget. Clinton vetoed several Republican budget proposals, claiming they cut into social programs too much. Gingrich believed that if Republicans stood firm, the president would back down and approve the budget. Otherwise, the entire federal government would shut down for lack of funds. Clinton, however, refused to budge, and allowed the federal government to close.

By standing firm against Republican budget proposals and allowing the government to shut down, Clinton regained much of the support he had lost in 1994. The Republicans in Congress realized they needed to work with the president to pass legislation. Soon afterward, they reached an agreement with Clinton to balance the budget.

YES

Strom Thurmond
U.S. Senator

PRIMARY SOURCE

"While Congress could achieve a balanced budget by statute, past efforts . . . have failed. It is simply too easy for Congress to change its mind. . . . The constitutional amendment is unyielding in its imposition of discipline on Congress to make the tough decisions necessary to balance the federal budget. Over the past half-century, Congress has demonstrated a total lack of fiscal discipline evidenced by an irrational and irresponsible pattern of spending. This reckless approach has seriously jeopardized the Federal government and threatens the very future of this Nation. As a result, I believe we must look to constitutional protection from a firmly entrenched fiscal policy which threatens the liberties and opportunities of our present and future citizens."

—Statement to the Judiciary Committee, February 16, 1994

NO

Bill Clinton
President

PRIMARY SOURCE

"The balanced budget amendment is, in the first place, bad economics. . . . [T]he Federal deficit depends not just on Congressional decisions, but also on the state of the economy. In particular, the deficit increases automatically whenever the economy weakens. If we try to break this automatic linkage by a Constitutional amendment, we will have to raise taxes and cut expenditures whenever the economy is weak. That not only risks turning minor downturns into serious recessions, but would make recovery from recession far more difficult. Let's be clear: This is not a matter of abstract economic theory. . . . A balanced budget amendment could threaten the livelihoods of millions of Americans. I cannot put them in such peril."

—Letter to Congressional leaders, November 5, 1993

DBQ Document-Based Questions

1. **Finding the Main Idea** Why does Senator Thurmond believe that a constitutional amendment, rather than simply a law, is necessary?

2. **Theorizing** How might Congress's "irresponsible pattern of spending" threaten the nation's future?

3. **Specifying** What specific reasons does President Clinton give to explain his opposition to the balanced budget amendment?

4. **Drawing Conclusions** Which argument do you find more convincing? Why?

In the months before the 1996 election, the president and the Republicans worked together to pass new legislation. In August Congress passed the Health Insurance Portability Act. This act improved health coverage for people who changed jobs and reduced discrimination against people who had pre-existing illnesses.

Later that month, Congress passed the Welfare Reform Act, which limited people to no more than two consecutive years on welfare and required them to work to receive welfare benefits. The law also increased child-care spending and gave tax breaks to companies that hired new employees who had been on welfare.

Clinton Wins Reelection

As the 1996 campaign began, Clinton took credit for the economy. The economic boom of the 1990s was the longest sustained period of growth in American history. Unemployment and inflation fell to their lowest levels in 40 years. The stock market soared, wages rose, crime rates fell, and the number of people on welfare declined. With the economy booming, Clinton's popularity climbed rapidly.

The Republican Party nominated Senator Bob Dole of Kansas, the Republican leader in the Senate, to run against Clinton. Dole chose as his running mate Jack Kemp, a former member of Congress from New York. Dole promised a 15 percent tax cut and attempted to portray Clinton as a tax-and-spend liberal.

H. Ross Perot also ran again as a candidate as he had in the 1992 election. This time he ran as the candidate of the Reform Party, which he had created. Once again Perot made the deficit the main campaign issue.

President Clinton won reelection, winning a little more than 49 percent of the popular vote and 379 electoral votes. Dole received almost 41 percent and 159 electoral votes, and Perot won about 8.4 percent of the popular vote and no electoral votes. Despite Clinton's victory, Republicans retained control of Congress. Two years later, after the 1998 elections, Republicans kept control of Congress, although the Democrats gained 5 seats in the House of Representatives.

✔ Reading Check **Identifying** What two reforms did Clinton and Congress agree to support?

Clinton's Second Term

MAIN Idea Clinton tried to focus the domestic agenda on the needs of children, but personal problems marred his second term.

HISTORY AND YOU Do you remember learning about the impeachment trial of Andrew Johnson? Read on to learn about the second president ever to be impeached.

During Clinton's second term, the economy continued its expansion. As people's incomes rose, so too did the amount of taxes they paid to all levels of government. At the same time, despite their differences, the president and Congress continued to shrink the deficit. In 1997, for the first time in 24 years, the president was able to submit a balanced budget to Congress. Beginning in 1998, the government began to run a surplus—that is, it collected more money than it spent.

Despite these achievements, Clinton's domestic agenda was less aggressive in his second term. Much of his time was spent on foreign policy and in struggling against a personal scandal.

Putting Children First

During his second term, Clinton's domestic agenda shifted toward helping the nation's children. He began by asking Congress to pass a $500 per child tax credit. He also signed the Adoption and Safe Families Act and asked Congress to ban cigarette advertising aimed at children. In August 1997, Clinton signed the Children's Health Insurance Program—a plan to provide health insurance for children whose parents could not afford it.

Clinton also continued his efforts to help American students. "I come from a family where nobody had ever gone to college before," Clinton said. "When I became president, I was determined to do what I could to give every student that chance." To help students, he asked for a tax credit, a large increase in student grants, and an expansion of the Head Start program for disadvantaged preschoolers.

Clinton Is Impeached

The robust economy and his high standing in the polls allowed Clinton to regain the initiative in dealing with Congress. By 1998, how-

Impeaching a President

The Constitution gives Congress the power to remove the president from office "upon impeachment for and conviction of, treason, bribery, or other high crimes and misdemeanors." The House of Representatives has the sole power over impeachment—the formal accusation of wrongdoing in office. If the majority of the House votes to impeach the president, the Senate conducts a trial. A two-thirds vote of those present is needed for conviction. If the president is being impeached, the chief justice of the United States presides.

▲ *House Judiciary Committee Chairman, Representative Henry Hyde, stands surrounded by boxes of evidence against President Clinton.*

▲ *Chief Justice Rehnquist is sworn in for the impeachment trial of President Clinton in the Senate.*

Analyzing VISUALS

1. **Hypothesizing** Why do you think the Founders required the House to impeach the president but the Senate to hold the trial?

2. **Theorizing** Why might impeachment only require a majority vote in the House, but conviction requires a two-thirds vote in the Senate?

ever, he had become entangled in a serious scandal that threatened to undermine his presidency.

The scandal began in Clinton's first term, when he was accused of arranging illegal loans for Whitewater Development—an Arkansas real estate company—while he was governor of that state. Attorney General Janet Reno decided that an independent counsel should investigate the president. A special three-judge panel appointed **Kenneth Starr,** a former federal judge, to this position.

In early 1998, a new scandal emerged involving a personal relationship between the president and a White House intern. Some evidence suggested that the president had committed **perjury,** or had lied under oath, about the relationship. The three-judge panel directed Starr to investigate this scandal as well. In September 1998, after examining the evidence, Starr sent his report to the Judiciary Committee of the House of Representatives. Starr argued

that Clinton had obstructed justice, abused his power as president, and committed perjury.

After the 1998 elections, the House began impeachment hearings. Clinton's supporters accused Starr of playing politics. Clinton's accusers argued that the president was accountable if his actions were illegal.

On December 19, 1998, the House of Representatives passed two articles of impeachment, one for perjury and one for obstruction of justice. The vote split almost evenly along party lines, and the case moved to the Senate for trial. On February 12, 1999, the senators cast their votes. The vote was 55 to 45 that Clinton was not guilty of perjury, and 50–50 on the charge of obstruction of justice. Although both votes were well short of the two-thirds needed to remove the president from office, Clinton's reputation had suffered.

Reading Check **Examining** What events led to the impeachment of President Clinton?

Clinton Foreign Policy

MAIN Idea During Clinton's second term, the United States worked to end violence in Haiti, southeastern Europe and the Middle East.

HISTORY AND YOU Do you remember when and why NATO was created? Read on to find out how the United States and NATO worked to resolve a crisis in southeastern Europe.

Although Clinton's domestic policies became bogged down in struggles with Congress, he was able to engage in a series of major foreign policy initiatives. On several occasions, President Clinton used force to try to resolve regional conflicts.

The Haitian Intervention

In 1991 military leaders in Haiti overthrew Jean-Bertrand Aristide, the country's first democratically elected president in many decades. Aristide sought refuge in the United States.

Seeking to restore democracy, the Clinton administration convinced the United Nations to impose a trade embargo on Haiti. The embargo created a severe economic crisis in that country. Thousands of Haitian refugees fled to the United States in small boats, and many died at sea. Determined to end the crisis, Clinton ordered an invasion of Haiti. With the troops on the way, former president Jimmy Carter convinced Haiti's rulers to step aside. The American troops then landed to serve as peacekeepers.

Bosnia and Kosovo

The United States also was concerned about mounting tensions in southeastern Europe. During the Cold War, Yugoslavia had been a single federated nation made up of many different ethnic groups under a strong Communist government. In 1991, after the collapse of communism, Yugoslavia split apart.

In Bosnia, one of the former Yugoslav republics, a vicious three-way civil war erupted

With the Cold War over, the Clinton administration focused on bringing stability to the Middle East and southeastern Europe, where religious and ethnic strife had contributed to ongoing violence. In addition, Clinton sent peacekeepers into Haiti to help rebuild the nation's democracy.

▲ Haitians gather outside the fence of the U.S. camp in Haiti to talk to American peacekeepers.

▲ Israeli Prime Minister Yitzhak Rabin and Palestinian leader Yasir Arafat shake hands after signing the 1993 Declaration of Principles.

▼ U.S. troops work with Bosnian Serbs in 1996 to set up boundaries between opposing forces.

Analyzing VISUALS

1. **Predicting** Do you think the United States should intervene in conflicts in the world? What problems can result from such a policy?

2. **Explaining** Why would the United States think intervening in Haiti and Bosnia was important to its own security?

between Orthodox Christian Serbs, Catholic Croatians, and Bosnian Muslims. Despite international pressure, the fighting continued until 1995. The Serbs began what they called **ethnic cleansing**—the brutal expulsion of an ethnic group from a geographic area so that only Serbs lived there. In some cases, Serbian troops slaughtered the Muslims instead of moving them.

The United States convinced its NATO allies that military action was necessary. NATO warplanes attacked the Serbs in Bosnia, forcing them to negotiate. The Clinton administration then arranged peace talks in Dayton, Ohio. The **participants** signed a peace plan known as the **Dayton Accords.** In 1996 some 60,000 NATO troops, including 20,000 Americans, entered Bosnia to enforce the plan.

In 1998 another war erupted, this time in the Serbian province of Kosovo. Kosovo has two major ethnic groups—Serbs and Albanians. Many of the Albanians wanted Kosovo to separate from Serbia. To keep Kosovo in Serbia, Serbian leader Slobodan Milosevic ordered a crackdown. The Albanians then organized their own army to fight back. Worried by Serbian violence against Albanian civilians, President Clinton convinced European leaders that NATO should use force to stop the fighting. In March 1999, NATO began bombing Serbia. In response, Serbia pulled its troops out of Kosovo.

Peacemaking in the Middle East

Although Iraq had been defeated in the Persian Gulf War, Iraqi President Saddam Hussein remained determined to hang onto power. In 1996 Iraqi forces attacked the Kurds, an ethnic group whose homeland lies in northern Iraq. To stop the attacks, the United States fired cruise missiles at Iraqi military targets.

Relations between Israel and the Palestinians were even more volatile. In 1993 Israeli Prime Minister Yitzhak Rabin and Palestine Liberation Organization leader Yasir Arafat reached an agreement. The PLO recognized Israel's right to exist, and Israel recognized the PLO as the representative of the Palestinians. President Clinton then invited Arafat and Rabin to the White House, where they signed the Declaration of Principles—a plan for creating a Palestinian government. Opposition to the peace plan emerged on both sides. Radical Palestinians exploded bombs in Israel and in 1995 a right-wing Israeli assassinated Prime Minister Rabin.

In 1998 Israeli and Palestinian leaders met with President Clinton at the Wye River Plantation in Maryland. They hoped to work out details of the withdrawal of Israeli troops from the West Bank and the Gaza Strip. The agreement they reached, however, did not address the ultimate dimensions of the Israeli withdrawal or the contested status of Jerusalem.

In July 2000, President Clinton invited Arafat and Israeli Prime Minister Ehud Barak to Camp David to discuss unresolved issues. Barak agreed to the creation of a Palestinian state in all of Gaza and about 95 percent of the West Bank, but Arafat rejected the deal. Beginning in October, violence again broke out between Palestinians and Israeli soldiers. The region was as far from peace as ever.

Reading Check **Identifying** In what three regions of the world did Clinton use force to support his foreign policy?

Section 2 REVIEW

Vocabulary

1. **Explain** the significance of: AmeriCorps, Contract with America, Kenneth Starr, perjury, ethnic cleansing, Dayton Accords.

Main Ideas

2. **Identifying** What were two reasons President Clinton's health care plan failed?

3. **Explaining** Why did the federal government shut down in 1995?

4. **Describing** How could Clinton be impeached but remain in office?

5. **Organizing** Complete a chart similar to the one below by explaining the foreign policy issues facing President Clinton in each of the areas listed.

Region	Issue
Latin America	
Southeastern Europe	
Middle East	

Critical Thinking

6. **Big Ideas** What did President Clinton do to help families during his presidency?

7. **Analyzing Visuals** Study the photograph on page 1013 of Clinton's impeachment trial. What elements in the photograph reflect the seriousness of the occasion?

Writing About History

8. **Persuasive Writing** Take on the role of a member of Congress. Write a letter in which you attempt to persuade other lawmakers to vote either for or against the impeachment of President Clinton. Provide reasons for your position.

History ONLINE

Study Central™ To review this section, go to glencoe.com and click on Study Central

A New Wave of Immigration

Guide to Reading

Big Ideas
Trade, War, and Migration A new immigration law allowed more people to immigrate to the United States.

Content Vocabulary
- migration chains *(p. 1016)*
- refugees *(p. 1017)*
- amnesty *(p. 1017)*

Academic Vocabulary
- illegal *(p. 1017)*
- allocate *(p. 1018)*
- resident *(p. 1018)*

People and Events to Identify
- Immigration Act of 1965 *(p. 1016)*
- Immigration Reform and Control Act of 1986 *(p. 1017)*
- Illegal Immigration Reform and Immigrant Responsibility Act of 1996 *(p. 1018)*

Reading Strategy
Determining Cause and Effect
Use a graphic organizer similar to the one below to list the effects of the Immigration Act of 1965.

```
        Effects of the
    Immigration Act of 1965
    ┌───────┬───────┬───────┐
    │       │       │       │
    └───────┴───────┴───────┘
```

NEW YORK CORE CURRICULUM
U.S. History and Government

...ew immigration patterns: Caribbean
...d Haitian immigration
...migrants; (Immigration
...ol Act of 1986)

In the late twentieth century, the number of immigrants in the United States hit an all time high. Large numbers of non-European immigrants changed the ethnic composition of the United States. Immigration—legal and illegal—emerged as a difficult political issue.

Changes in Immigration Law

MAIN Idea The Immigration Act of 1965 eliminated preferences for certain European immigrants; illegal immigration became a problem.

HISTORY AND YOU Do you remember the controversial elements of the National Origins Act of 1924? Read on to learn how the repeal of the national origins system led to major changes in American society which few people had anticipated.

After the introduction of the national origins quota system in the 1920s, the sources and character of immigration to the United States changed dramatically. For the next few decades, the total number of immigrants arriving annually remained markedly lower. The quota system which gave preference to immigrants from northern and western European countries, although occasionally modified by Congress, remained largely intact until 1965.

In the midst of the flurry of civil rights and antipoverty legislation of the mid-1960s, the **Immigration Act of 1965** received scant attention when it was enacted. The law abolished the national origins quota system. It also gave preference to skilled persons and persons with close relatives who are U.S. citizens—policies which remain in place today. The preference given to the children, spouses, and parents of U.S. citizens meant that **migration chains** were established. As newcomers acquired U.S. citizenship, they too could send for relatives in their home country. Also, for the first time, the legislation introduced limits on immigration from the Western Hemisphere. The act further provided that immigrants could apply for U.S. citizenship after five years of legal residency.

At the time of its passage, few people expected that the new law would radically change the pattern or volume of immigration to the United States. Supporters of the law presented it as an extension of America's growing commitment to equal rights for non-European peoples. As U.S. Representative Philip Burton of California stated, "Just as we sought to eliminate discrimination in our land through the Civil Rights Act, today we seek by phasing out the national origins quota system to eliminate discrimination in immigration to this nation composed of the descendants of immigrants." Supporters of the new law also assumed that the new equal quotas

CANADA

N.H.
Vt. Me.

Wash.

Mont. N. Dak.

Minn. Mass.

Ore. N.Y. R.I.

Ida. S. Dak. Wis. Mich. Conn.

Wyo. Iowa Pa. N.J.

ATLANTIC
OCEAN

Nev. Nebr. Ill. Ind. Ohio Del.
Md.

Calif. Utah Colo. Kans. Mo. Ky. W. Va.
Va.

Ariz. N. Mex. Okla. Ark. Tenn. N.C.

S.C.

Miss. Ala. Ga.

Tex.

La. Fla.

PACIFIC
OCEAN

MEXICO

Gulf of Mexico

**Number of unauthorized
immigrants**

	335,000 or more
	140,000–334,999
	85,000–139,999
	Fewer than 85,000

0   400 kilometers
0   400 miles
Albers Equal-Area projection

N
W   E
S

ARCTIC OCEAN

RUSSIA

70°N

ARCTIC CIRCLE

Alaska CANADA

60°N

180° Bering
Sea 160°W

140°W

50°N

0   800 kilometers
0   800 miles

PACIFIC OCEAN Albers Equal-Area projection

Hawaii

20°N PACIFIC
160°W OCEAN

0   200 kilometers
0   200 miles

Oblique Mercator projection 155°W

Analyzing GEOGRAPHY

1. **Place** According to the map, which states have the largest numbers of unauthorized aliens?

2. **Human-Environment Interaction** What are some geographic factors that could explain why some states attract more immigrants than others?

for non-European nations would generally go unfilled. In fact, immigration from non-European countries soared in subsequent decades.

In addition to those arriving through traditional immigration channels, some newcomers arrived in the United States as **refugees.** Beginning in 1948, refugees from countries ravaged by World War II were admitted, although they were counted as part of their nation's quota. The Cold War led to another class of refugees. According to the McCarran-Walter Act of 1952, anyone who was fleeing a Communist regime could be admitted as a refugee. Refugee policy was further broadened under the Refugee Act of 1980, which defined a refugee as someone leaving his or her country due to a "well founded fear of persecution on account of race, religion, nationality, membership in a particular group, or political opinion."

The growing problem of **illegal** immigration also prompted changes in immigration law. During the Reagan administration, Congress passed the **Immigration Reform and Control Act of 1986.** This law established penalties for employers who knowingly hire unauthorized immigrants and strengthened border controls to prevent illegal entry into the United States. It also established a process to grant **amnesty** (in other words, a pardon) and legal papers to any undocumented alien who could prove that he or she had entered the country before January 1, 1982, and had resided in the United States since then.

Despite these changes, illegal immigration persisted and the number of unauthorized immigrants continued to grow. By 1990, an estimated 3.5 million unauthorized immigrants resided in the United States. By the mid-1990s, Congress was debating new ways to combat illegal immigration.

The law that resulted from these debates was the **Illegal Immigration Reform and Immigrant Responsibility Act of 1996,** which made several changes to U.S. immigration law. First, it required families sponsoring an immigrant to have an income above the poverty level. Second, it **allocated** more resources to stop illegal immigration, by authorizing an additional 5,000 Border Patrol agents and calling for the construction of a 14-mile fence along the border near San Diego. Third, the law toughened penalties for smuggling people or providing fraudulent documents. Finally, the law made it easier for immigration authorities to deport undocumented aliens.

Another change in immigration law was spurred by the terrorist attacks of September 11, 2001. The USA Patriot Act of 2001 put immigration under the control of the newly created Department of Homeland Security. Furthermore, it tripled the number of Border Patrol agents, Customs Service inspectors, and Immigration and Naturalization Service inspectors along the Canadian border.

✓ **Reading Check** **Identifying** For what reasons may a foreigner be admitted to the United States as a refugee?

Recent Immigration

MAIN Idea In the late twentieth century, immigrants from Latin America and Asia outnumbered European immigrants.

HISTORY AND YOU Do you remember the reasons that some Americans objected to immigration in the late 1800s? Read on to learn how the debate resurfaced in the 1980s and continues today.

Although immigrants headed for all parts of the United States, certain states experienced a larger influx than others. In 1990, California, Texas, New York, Illinois, and Florida had the highest populations of foreign-born **residents.** High numbers of immigrants also increased the ethnic diversity of these states, as their Latino and Asian populations grew. Among the immigrants who arrived in the 1990s, just over 10 percent came from Europe. More than half of new immigrants came from Latin America, while approximately another 25 percent came from Asia. By 2001, the top five countries of origin for legal immigrants to the United States were Mexico, India, China, the Philippines, and Vietnam.

PRIMARY SOURCE
Securing the Border

After the attacks of September 11, 2001, many Americans became increasingly concerned about border security. Many agreed on the need for increased border patrols. Others proposed building a continuous wall from Texas to California to prevent illegal immigration. Critics of such proposals, however, claimed such actions would not stop people who were determined to enter the country illegally, but rather force them to take more dangerous risks.

▲ On May 27, 2006, a volunteer organization called the Minutemen Civil Defense Corps built a fence along the Mexican border on private property.

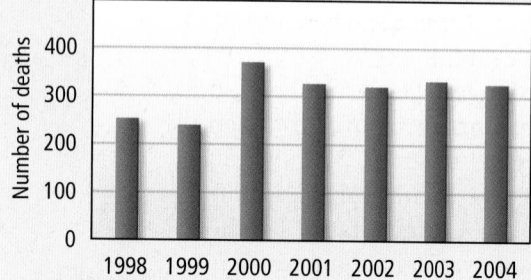

Deaths of Persons Attempting to Cross the Border Illegally

(Number of deaths)
400
300
200
100
0
1998 1999 2000 2001 2002 2003 2004

Source: United States Government Accountability Office.

Analyzing VISUALS

1. **Making Connections** Why do you think the organization pictured above decided to call themselves the "minutemen"?

2. **Theorizing** Do you think building a fence along the border would lead to fewer deaths? Why or why not?

Refugees added to the growing immigrant population. In the 25 years following the Cuban Revolution of 1959, more than 800,000 Cubans arrived in the United States. So many of these immigrants settled in the Miami, Florida, area that only the city of Havana, Cuba, is home to more Cubans. In addition, the Vietnam War created refugees. Some 600,000 immigrants from Vietnam, Laos, and Cambodia arrived in the decade after 1974.

In addition to the immigrants entering through legal channels, others arrived without official permission. The largest number of unauthorized immigrants came from Mexico, El Salvador, and Guatemala. The Reagan administration's amnesty program in 1986 had been designed to eliminate the problem of undocumented aliens, but over the next 20 years the number of unauthorized immigrants tripled. American public opinion divided over whether unauthorized immigrants should be able to obtain driver's licenses or send their children to public schools and receive other government services. Some believed that unauthorized immigrants should be deported. Others favored allowing them to apply for temporary work visas so the government could keep track of them, and permitting them to earn permanent residence if they learned English, paid back taxes, and had no criminal record.

In 2006, President George W. Bush made immigration reform a top priority, but members of Congress strongly disagreed over how to solve the problem. A bipartisan majority of the Senate favored legislation that blended tougher enforcement of immigration laws with some form of earned citizenship for the estimated 12 million undocumented aliens living and working in the country. The Senate bill included a provision that undocumented aliens who grew up in the United States and graduated from high school could apply for citizenship. Conservative Republicans who held the majority in the House objected that this would reward illegal behavior. The House rejected any form of amnesty and called for the United States to build a wall along its Mexican border— although the United States had already tripled the size of its border patrol without reducing illegal immigration. As Congress debated a bill that would subject unauthorized aliens to criminal prosecution, Latinos held rallies across the country, carrying signs that read: "We are not criminals."

Advocates of immigration reform promoted alternatives such as expanding quotas through a guest-worker program and establishing a means of legalization for those already in the country. Some undocumented aliens had lived in the United States for years, and had raised families here. Deporting them would mean separating husbands, wives, and children. Some undocumented aliens arrived as children and had lived in the United States most of their lives. Their own children, born in the United States, were native-born citizens even though their parents lacked legal status. Among those who became legal citizens, most wanted other family members to join them, so the reunification of families accounted for three-quarters of all legal immigration.

✓ **Reading Check** **Explaining** Why did some members of Congress oppose amnesty for undocumented aliens? Why did others support it?

Section 3 REVIEW

Vocabulary

1. **Explain** the significance of: Immigration Act of 1965, migration chains, refugees, Immigration Reform and Control Act of 1986, amnesty, Illegal Immigration Reform and Immigrant Responsibility Act of 1996.

Main Ideas

2. **Summarizing** What problems arose that caused changes in the immigration laws?

3. **Describing** What alternatives to immigration reform did advocates for reform suggest?

Critical Thinking

4. **Big Ideas** What two acts were instrumental in helping refugees?

5. **Organizing** Use a graphic organizer similar to the one below to list the immigration laws and what they intended.

Immigration Law	Intent
Immigration Act of 1965	
Immigration Reform and Control Act of 1986	
Illegal Immigration Reform and Immigrant Responsibility Act of 1996	

6. **Analyzing Visuals** Study the map on page 1017. Research the number of unauthorized immigrants in the United States and create a spreadsheet that lists the states where these immigrants settled and the estimated numbers in 2000 and 2005.

Writing About History

7. **Persuasive Writing** After reading about the problem of illegal immigration, write a letter to your representative in Congress explaining what you feel he or she should do about the problem.

History ONLINE

Study Central™ To review this section, go to <u>glencoe.com</u> and click on Study Central.

ANALYZING PRIMARY SOURCES

The New Immigrants

In the decades since the Immigration Act of 1965 was enacted, the number of immigrants in the United States has risen dramatically. By 2000, immigrants comprised more than 10 percent of the population. The largest groups of these new immigrants came from Latin America and Asia. Immigration has become a topic of political debate. Should the U.S. make it easier to immigrate legally? Should the U.S. decrease the number of persons allowed to immigrate? How should unauthorized immigrants be treated?

Study these primary sources and answer the questions that follow.

PRIMARY SOURCE 1

Oral Interview

"On our third attempt, my wife, children, and I escaped by boat from Vietnam and arrived in Hong Kong, where we remained for three months. Then my brother, who came to America in 1975, sponsored us, and we arrived in America in 1978. . . .

Although in America we live with everything free, to move, to do business, we still have the need to return to Vietnam one day. This is our dream. In Vietnam, before the Communists came, we had a sentimental life, more [mentally] comfortable and cozy, more joyful. . . .

Here in America, we have all the material comforts, very good. But the joy and sentiment are not like we had in Vietnam. There, when we went out from the home, we laughed, we jumped. And we had many relatives and friends to come to see us at home. Here in America, I only know what goes on in my home; my neighbor knows only what goes on in his home. . . . In America, when we go to work, we go in our cars. When we return, we leave our cars and enter our homes [and do not meet neighbors]. We do not need to know what goes on in the houses of our neighbors. That's why we do not have the kind of being at ease that we knew in Vietnam."

—Vietnamese immigrant

PRIMARY SOURCE 3

Oral Interview

"The buzzword is diversity. It's on TV, politics, and this school [university], but then people like me are seen as foreigners and worse, illegals. The logic is if you look Mexican you are an immigrant, don't speak English and are illegal. I get tired of saying that's not me, oh well, except for the Mexican part. I don't look at an Anglo with an Italian name and say, 'Hey, do you speak Italian and when did you come to the United States?'"

—Diana, second-generation Mexican American

PRIMARY SOURCE 2

Photograph, c. 2006

▼ *Tijuana (on the left) lies just south of San Diego; a fence marks the Mexico-U.S. border.*

PRIMARY SOURCE 4

Photograph, 2006

▼ *Jorge Urbina of Nicaragua and his brother Carlos take the oath of citizenship during a naturalization ceremony for 250 immigrants.*

PRIMARY SOURCE 5

Photograph, 2006

▼ *Woman protests illegal immigration.*

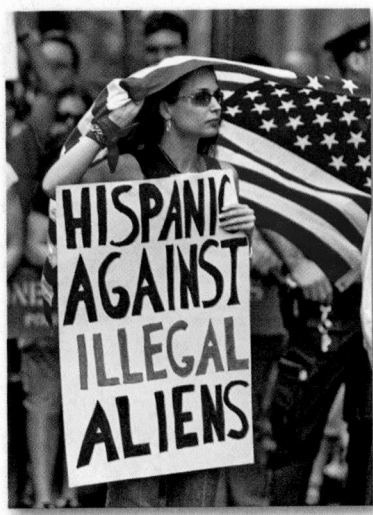

PRIMARY SOURCE 7

Photograph, 2006

▼ *Marchers oppose passage of a bill that would make it a felony to be in the country illegally.*

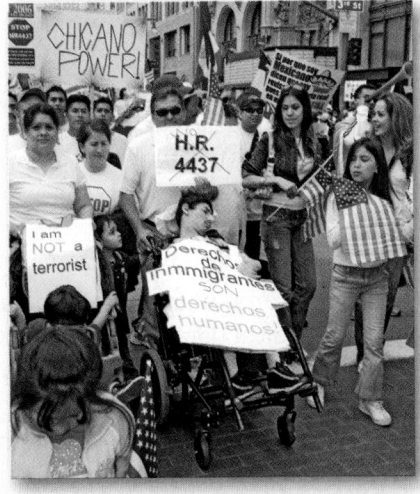

PRIMARY SOURCE 6

Oral Interview

"Usually we catch young men, who are looking for work to support their families back in Mexico. But more and more we are seeing entire families. They start coming around 7:30 P.M. . . . . A steady stream of people all night. We use our night-vision 'infrared' equipment to spot a lot of illegals who would otherwise go unnoticed. . . .

This time of year, in late winter, the aliens try to find work on farms in the Upper Rio Grande Valley. . . . Between New Year and June . . . many of the aliens we apprehend are usually agricultural workers or people heading for cities further north, like Denver or Chicago.

Perhaps our greatest concern is the trafficking of drugs tied to the smuggling of illegal aliens. Smuggling of all sorts has become big business in the border regions. . . . . We catch illegal immigrants who come from as many as eighty-five countries around the world. Even people from Eastern Europe, who are smuggled in for large fees through South America and Mexico City.

The great majority of them are decent people coming here to look for work. Their families' economic conditions are pretty bad in Mexico. You have to sympathize with them to a point. But if you open the border wide up, you're going to invite political and social upheaval."

—Michael Teague, U.S. Border Patrol

DBQ Document-Based Questions

1. **Contrasting** How does the speaker in Source 1 contrast his life in America with his life in Vietnam?

2. **Describing** Study the photograph in Source 2. Write a description of the Mexican side of the border and a description of the U.S. side of the border.

3. **Analyzing** Examine Sources 3 and 4. How do they reflect the ethnicities of the new immigrants?

4. **Speculating** Study the photograph in Source 5. What might be some reasons that the woman opposes illegal immigration?

5. **Making Connections** According to the speaker in Source 6, why do so many people risk crossing the border illegally? What other illegal traffic occurs at the border?

Section 4

An Interdependent World

Guide to Reading

Big Ideas
Economics and Society As the twentieth century drew to a close, world trade and environmentalism became increasingly more important during a period of globalization.

Content Vocabulary
- globalism *(p. 1022)*
- euro *(p. 1023)*
- global warming *(p. 1025)*

Academic Vocabulary
- cited *(p. 1024)*
- awareness *(p. 1025)*

People and Events to Identify
- North American Free Trade Agreement (NAFTA) *(p. 1023)*
- European Union (EU) *(p. 1023)*
- Asia Pacific Economic Cooperation (APEC) *(p. 1024)*
- World Trade Organization (WTO) *(p. 1024)*
- Kyoto Protocol *(p. 1025)*

Reading Strategy
Organizing Complete a graphic organizer like the one below to chart the major political and economic problems facing the world at the turn of the century.

Global Concerns

NEW YORK CORE CURRICULUM
U.S. History and Government

Unit 7:
VI.B.2.b United States in the global economy
VI.B.2.e United States—European relations: European Union (EU), NATO

As the world economy became more interconnected in the 1990s, Americans debated whether the elimination of trade barriers was more beneficial or detrimental for the nation. Concerns about environmental damage led to an international conference in Kyoto, Japan.

The New Global Economy

MAIN Idea Regional trade agreements, such as the North American Free Trade Agreement (NAFTA), reflected the growing interdependence of the global economy.

HISTORY AND YOU Do you remember how tariffs were a hotly debated issue in earlier periods of American history? Read on to learn about NAFTA and the fierce political debate it sparked.

In the 1990s Americans began to realize that their relationship with the rest of the world was changing. The economies of individual countries were becoming much more interdependent, and events in one part of the world could dramatically affect the economy of another country thousands of miles away. Computer technology and the Internet played a big role in forging this new global economy. So too did the conviction of many of the world's political and business leaders that free trade and the global exchange of goods contributed to prosperity and economic growth.

At the same time, the Internet and digital satellite technology helped link the world together culturally. For example, people in the United States could read Australian newspapers on the Web, while Chinese students could download American popular music, and an African doctor could consult a British medical database. This idea that the world is becoming increasingly interconnected is sometimes referred to as **globalism,** and the process is called globalization.

Selling American-made goods abroad had long been important to American prosperity. From World War II to the present, Republican and Democratic administrations have worked to lower barriers to international trade. They reasoned that trade helps the American economy: American businesses make money selling goods abroad, and American consumers benefit by having the option to buy goods that are less expensive than those made in the United States. Importing low-cost goods would also keep inflation and interest rates low.

Opponents warned that embracing the global economy would cause manufacturing jobs to move from the United States to nations where wages were low and there were fewer environmental regulations. They suggested that having cheap imports available to buy

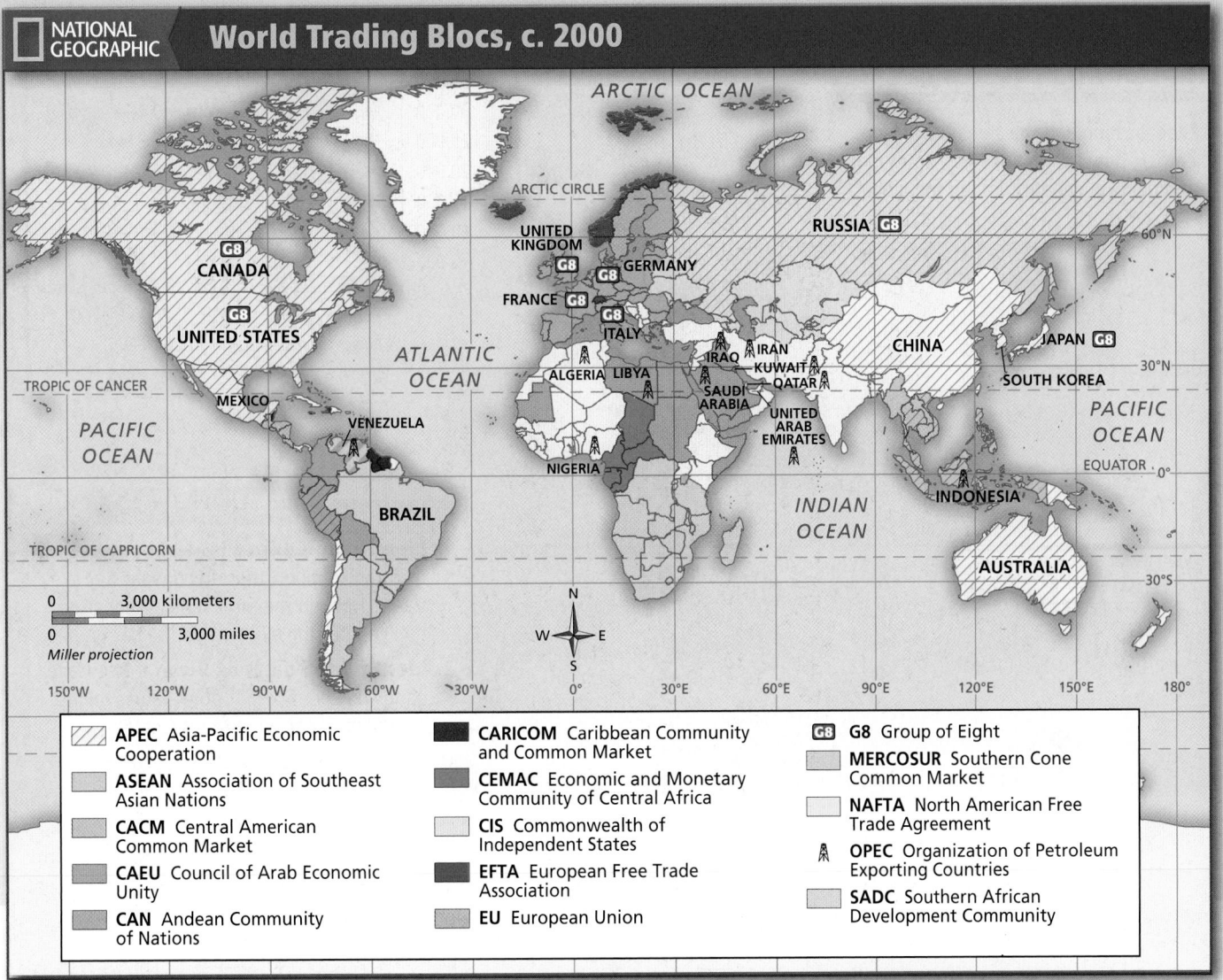

ARCTIC OCEAN

ARCTIC CIRCLE

RUSSIA G8

UNITED KINGDOM G8 GERMANY

CANADA G8

FRANCE G8 G8

UNITED STATES G8 ITALY

ATLANTIC OCEAN

IRAN

IRAQ KUWAIT

TROPIC OF CANCER

ALGERIA LIBYA QATAR

MEXICO

SAUDI ARABIA

CHINA

JAPAN G8

SOUTH KOREA

30°N

PACIFIC OCEAN

VENEZUELA

UNITED ARAB EMIRATES

PACIFIC OCEAN

EQUATOR 0°

NIGERIA

INDONESIA

BRAZIL

INDIAN OCEAN

TROPIC OF CAPRICORN

AUSTRALIA

30°S

0 3,000 kilometers
0 3,000 miles
Miller projection

150°W 120°W 90°W 60°W 30°W 0° 30°E 60°E 90°E 120°E 150°E 180°

APEC Asia-Pacific Economic Cooperation	**CARICOM** Caribbean Community and Common Market	G8 **G8** Group of Eight
ASEAN Association of Southeast Asian Nations	**CEMAC** Economic and Monetary Community of Central Africa	**MERCOSUR** Southern Cone Common Market
CACM Central American Common Market	**CIS** Commonwealth of Independent States	**NAFTA** North American Free Trade Agreement
CAEU Council of Arab Economic Unity	**EFTA** European Free Trade Association	**OPEC** Organization of Petroleum Exporting Countries
CAN Andean Community of Nations	**EU** European Union	**SADC** Southern African Development Community

would not help those Americans who no longer could find work because their industries had moved overseas. By the 1990s, the debate between supporters of free trade and those who wanted to limit trade had become an important part of American politics.

Regional Blocs

One way to increase international trade was to create regional trade pacts. In 1994 President Clinton convinced the Senate to ratify the **North American Free Trade Agreement** (NAFTA). This agreement joined Canada, the United States, and Mexico in a free-trade zone. With NAFTA in operation, exports of American goods to both Canada and Mexico rose dramatically. From 1993 to 2000, it is estimated that combined exports to those two countries rose from $142 to $290 billion, an increase of 104 percent.

Many Americans feared that NAFTA would cause industrial jobs to move to Mexico, where labor costs were lower. Some jobs were indeed lost, as foreign-owned factories, known as *maquiladoras*, opened in Mexico near the American border. At the same time, however, the unemployment rate in the United States began to fall and wages rose. Many American businesses upgraded their technology, and workers shifted to more skilled jobs or to the service industry.

Regional trade blocs also formed in Europe and Asia. In 1993, the **European Union** (EU) was created to promote economic and political cooperation among many European nations. The EU created a common bank and the **euro,** a common currency for member nations. The organization also removed trade barriers between its members and set policies on imports from nations outside the community.

Debating Free Trade

Globalization and the steady reduction of trade barriers between nations has led to many protests and political debates around the globe.

Rise of Global Trade and Global GDP

Source: *Australia's Foreign and Trade Policy White Paper.*

▲ Demonstrators in Seattle protest a meeting of the WTO on November 30, 1999.

Analyzing VISUALS

1. **Identifying Central Issues** How does the graph support those who want free trade? How do the protestors of globalization counter the evidence of the bar graph?

2. **Identifying Points of View** If free trade brings prosperity, what other values might opponents be seeking to protect?

Another trade bloc that came together in the early 1990s was the **Asia Pacific Economic Cooperation** (APEC). It includes most nations that have a coastline on the Pacific Ocean, including the United States, Canada, China, Japan, South Korea, Mexico, and Russia. APEC represented the fastest-growing region in the world and controlled 47 percent of global trade in 2001. APEC began as a forum to promote economic cooperation and lower trade barriers, but major political differences kept its members from acting together.

The World Trade Organization

In 1994 some 120 nations formed the **World Trade Organization** (WTO) to administer international trade agreements and help settle trade disputes. President Clinton convinced Congress to pass legislation enabling the United States to participate in the WTO. Supporters of the WTO **cited** benefits for American consumers, including cheaper imports, new markets, and copyright protection for the American entertainment industry. Opponents noted that the United States would be bound to accept the WTO's rulings in trade disputes even if they hurt the American economy. Despite their concerns, Congress passed the legislation.

Trade With China

China's huge population offered potential as a market for American goods, but many people had reservations about trading with China. These critics cited China's suppression of protests in Tiananmen Square in 1989, its record on human rights, and its threats to invade Taiwan. Despite these concerns, President Clinton argued that expanding trade with China would help bring it into the world community.

After negotiating a new trade agreement, Clinton urged Congress to grant China permanent normal trade relation status. Unions opposed the deal, fearing that inexpensive Chinese goods would flood U.S. markets; conservatives objected to China's military ambitions; and environmentalists worried about pollution from Chinese factories. Over such objections, the bill passed in late 2000.

✓ Reading Check **Analyzing** How did international trade change the world economy?

Global Environmentalism

MAIN Idea As scientists learned that certain chemicals could damage the Earth's ozone layer, they worked to ban their use; concern about global warming became a serious political issue.

HISTORY AND YOU Are there groups in your school or community that work to improve the environment? Read on to learn about efforts to reduce damage to the environment.

The rise of a global economy also increased **awareness** of environmental issues. Environmentalists began thinking of the environment as a global system. Increasingly, they began addressing issues that they believed were of global, not just local, concern.

Concern About Ozone

In the 1980s scientists discovered that chlorofluorocarbons (CFCs) had the ability to break down the ozone layer in the Earth's atmosphere. Ozone is a gas that protects life on Earth from the ultraviolet rays of the sun. At that time, CFCs were widely used in air conditioners and refrigerators. Environmental activists began to push for a ban on CFC production. In the late 1980s, public awareness of the issue increased dramatically when scientists documented a large ozone "hole" over Antarctica. In 1987 the United States and 22 other nations agreed to phase out the production of CFCs and other chemicals that might be weakening the ozone layer.

Global Warming

In the early 1990s, another global environmental issue developed when some scientists found evidence of **global warming**—an increase in average world temperatures over time. Such a rise in temperature could eventually lead to more droughts and other forms of extreme weather. A furious debate began over how to measure the Earth's temperature and what the results meant.

Many experts concluded that carbon dioxide emissions from factories and power plants caused global warming, but others disagreed. The issue became very controversial because the cost of controlling emissions would affect the global economy. Industries would have to pay the cost of further reducing emissions, and those costs would eventually be passed on to consumers. Developing nations trying to industrialize would be hurt the most, but economic growth in wealthier nations would be hurt, too.

Concern about global warming led to an international conference in Kyoto, Japan, in 1997. Thirty-eight nations and the EU signed the Kyoto Protocol promising to reduce emissions, but very few have actually complied with its requirements and reduced their emissions. President Clinton did not submit the Kyoto Protocol to the Senate for ratification because most senators were opposed to it. In 2001 President George W. Bush withdrew the United States from the **Kyoto Protocol,** citing flaws in the treaty.

Reading Check **Describing** Why did environmentalists think CFCs were dangerous?

Section 4 REVIEW

Vocabulary
1. **Explain** the significance of: globalism, North American Free Trade Agreement, European Union, euro, Asia Pacific Economic Cooperation, World Trade Organization, global warming, Kyoto Protocol.

Main Ideas
2. **Explaining** Why was China an important factor in world trade?

3. **Describing** What was the international response to concerns about global warming?

Critical Thinking
4. **Big Ideas** How did NAFTA affect exports of American goods?

5. **Organizing** Complete a graphic organizer by listing and describing the regional trade blocs that formed in the 1990s.

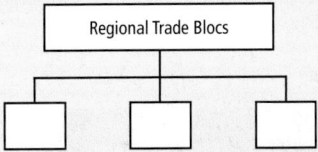

6. **Analyzing Visuals** Examine the image on page 1024. Why do some people or groups protest globalization?

Writing About History
7. **Expository Writing** Decide which issue of global concern is the most serious. In an essay, explain why you think it is the most serious problem, and provide some possible solutions.

Study Central™ To review this section, go to glencoe.com and click on Study Central.

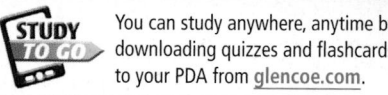
A Changing Society

The Technological Revolution

- The invention of the integrated circuit and microprocessors enables small personal computers built by Apple and IBM.

- The telecommunications revolution leads to the development of small portable cell phones, and digital video and audio players.

- The rise of the Internet and World Wide Web provide new ways for people to retrieve information, build communities, and do business.

A New Wave of Immigrants

- New immigration laws in 1965 and 1986 contribute to a rise in Hispanic immigration and an increase in immigrants from Asia, Africa, and the Middle East.

- The American population becomes increasingly culturally diverse.

The Rise of a Global Economy

- Free trade, in combination with the technological revolution, creates a new global marketplace.

- Increasing awareness of the global economy also sparks a new global environmentalist movement.

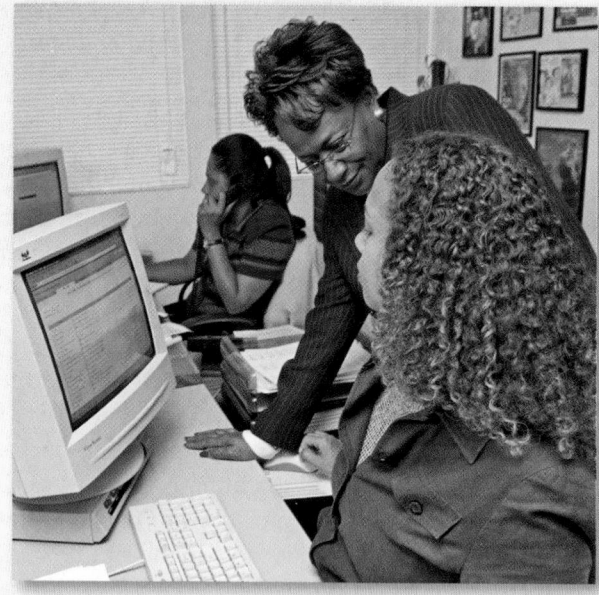

▲ Today, almost all businesses, such as this public relations firm, rely on computers to help employees perform their day-to-day duties.

The Clinton Years

First-Term Achievements and Failures

- Raised taxes to help cut the deficit
- Proposal for a national health care program fails
- Signed the Family Medical Leave Act into law
- Persuaded Congress to create AmeriCorps
- Signed the Brady Handgun Bill into law
- Worked with Republicans to push the Health Insurance Portability Act and the Welfare Reform Act through Congress

Second-Term Achievements and Failures

- Submits a balanced budget to Congress
- Convinces Congress to pass a new tax credit for children and a children's health insurance program
- Impeached on charges of perjury and obstruction of justice but is acquitted by the Senate

Foreign Policy Achievements

- Dispatched troops to Haiti to restore democracy
- Dispatched troops to Bosnia and bombed Serbia to end the civil war and ethnic cleansing that followed the breakup of Yugoslavia
- Mediated negotiations between Israel and the PLO

▲ President Bill Clinton delivers his State of the Union address to a joint session of Congress on January 24, 1995.

NEW YORK REGENTS EXAM PRACTICE

TEST-TAKING TIP

Consider each answer choice individually and cross out choices you have eliminated. You will save time and stop yourself from choosing an answer you have mentally eliminated.

Part I

Directions (1–11): For each statement or question, write on a separate sheet of paper the number of the word or expression that, of those given, best completes the statement or answers the question.

1 The government began to deregulate the telecommunications industry in the

(1) 1950s.
(2) 1960s.
(3) 1970s.
(4) 1980s.

2 In 1990, researchers at CERN developed a new way to present information known as

(1) the Internet.
(2) the computer.
(3) the Ethernet.
(4) the World Wide Web.

3 Democrats passed a law during President Clinton's administration that tightened gun control called

(1) the Gun Law.
(2) the Anti-Gun Bill.
(3) the Brady Bill.
(4) the NRA Law.

4 The Contract with America was proposed by

(1) Hillary Clinton.
(2) President Clinton.
(3) Al Gore.
(4) Newt Gingrich.

5 The Immigration Reform and Control Act of 1986 established

(1) admittance of any refugee fleeing a communist regime.
(2) legal papers to any undocumented immigrant who could prove he or she entered the country before 1982.
(3) the national origins quota system.
(4) allocation of more resources to stop illegal immigration.

6 The Illegal Immigration Reform and Immigrant Responsibility Act of 1996

(1) relaxed penalties for smuggling people or providing fraudulent documents.
(2) established more schools for immigrant children.
(3) allocated more resources to stop illegal immigration.
(4) called for a wall to be built at the U.S. border.

7 Since WWII, Republicans and Democrats have worked to lower barriers to international trade because

(1) it helps the American economy.
(2) it supports foreign policy.
(3) it moves manufacturing jobs overseas.
(4) it helps economically depressed countries.

8 Environmentalists were concerned about trade with China because

(1) anti-WTO protests would be held in Tiananmen Square.
(2) they believed the goods should be manufactured in the United States.
(3) the amount of pollution from Chinese factories.
(4) China had made threats to invade Taiwan.

Need Extra Help?								
If You Missed Questions . . .	1	2	3	4	5	6	7	8
Go to Page . . .	1003	1005	1010	1011	1017	1017–1018	1024	1024

[OVER]

Base your answer to question 9 on the graph below and your knowledge of Chapter 30.

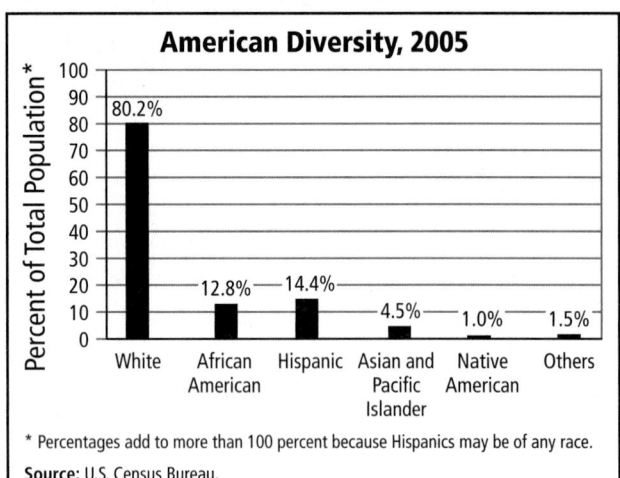

American Diversity, 2005

* Percentages add to more than 100 percent because Hispanics may be of any race.

Source: U.S. Census Bureau.

9   What group was the smallest percentage of the population in 2005?

(1) African American

(2) White

(3) Native American

(4) Multiracial

10 Which of the following is not an example of digital technology?

(1) cell phones that can receive emails

(2) MP3 players

(3) satellite radio

(4) newspapers

11 The North American Free Trade Agreement (NAFTA) joined Canada, Mexico and the United States in a free trade zone. Why was this beneficial?

(1) Exports to Canada and Mexico increased.

(2) Jobs were lost to Mexico.

(3) Unemployment in the United States rose.

(4) It provided free goods to Canada and Mexico.

Part II Thematic Essay Questions

Directions: Write a well-organized essay that includes an introduction, several paragraphs addressing the task below, and a conclusion.

Theme: The Technological Revolution

During the second half of the 21st century, the computer revolution began. By the 1990's scientists were making regular advances with technology that would lead to the technological revolution.

Task:

Identify three major technological advances during the 1990s and for each

- Discuss the history of the technological advance

- Describe the impact it had on the workplace, everyday life, or both

- Evaluate how your life would be different without it

Guidelines:

In your essay, be sure to:

- Develop all aspects of the task

- Support the theme with relevant facts, examples, and details

- Use a logical and clear plan of organization, including an introduction and a conclusion that are beyond a restatement of the theme

Part III Document-Based Question

This question is based on the accompanying documents. It is designed to test your ability to work with historical documents. Some of the documents have been edited for the purposes of the question. As you analyze the documents, take into account the source of each document and any point of view that may be presented in the document.

Historical Context:

President Clinton took office in 1992 with plans for improving health care, reducing the federal deficit, helping families, and strengthening gun control.

Need Extra Help?			
If You Missed Questions . . .	9	10	11
Go to Page . . .	R16	1002–1005	1023

Task:

Using information from the documents and your knowledge of United States history, answer the questions that follow each document in Part A. Your answers to the questions will help you write the Part B essay in which you will be asked to

- Evaluate President Clinton's effectiveness with his domestic and foreign policy initiatives
- Describe the early and late goals of the Clinton administration

Part A

Short-Answer Questions

Directions: Analyze the documents and answer the short-answer questions that follow each document on a separate sheet of paper.

Document 1

> The world is getting warmer, and by the end of the 21st century could warm by another 6 degrees Celsius (10.8 degrees Fahrenheit). . . . And climate scientists at the heart of the research are now convinced that human action is to blame for some or most of this warming. . . .
>
> Everywhere climatologists look—at tree-ring patterns, fossil succession in rock strata, ocean-floor corings…they see evidence of dramatic shifts from cold to hot to cold again…None of these ancient shifts can be blamed on humans. . . . There is still room for argument about the precise role of the sun or other natural cycles in the contribution to global warming. . . .

Source: *World Press Review,* February 2001

1 Based on this document, state the two opposing views of the cause of global warming.

Document 2

Source: Mike Luckovitch, *Atlanta Constitution*

2 What does the cartoon imply about Bill Clinton and the deficit?

Part B

Essay

Directions: Reread the task box at the top left and write a well-organized essay that includes an introduction, several paragraphs, and a conclusion. Use evidence from the documents in your essay.

Guidelines:

In your essay, be sure to:

- Develop all aspects of the task
- Incorporate information from the documents
- Incorporate relevant outside information
- Support the theme with relevant facts, examples, and details
- Use a logical and clear plan of organization, including an introduction and a conclusion that are beyond a restatement of the theme

History ONLINE

For additional test practice, use Self-Check Quizzes—Chapter 30 at glencoe.com.

Need Extra Help?			
If You Missed Questions . . .	1	2	Essay
Go to Page . . .	1025	1025	R18

Chapter 31

A New Century Begins

2001–Present

SECTION 1 America Enters A New Century

SECTION 2 The War on Terrorism Begins

SECTION 3 The Invasion of Iraq

SECTION 4 A Time of Challenges

On September 11, 2006, the Tribute in Light commemorated the fifth anniversary of the attack on the World Trade Center.

U.S. PRESIDENTS

U.S. EVENTS

WORLD EVENTS

November 2000
- A close vote in Florida causes a contested election

G. W. Bush 2001–

Sept. 11, 2001
- Terrorists attack World Trade Center and Pentagon

October 2001
- U.S. begins bombing Afghanistan
- Patriot Act enacted

January 2002
- President Bush signs No Child Left Behind Act

March 2003
- U.S. invades Iraq

2001

2002

2003

2004

2001
- Terrorists attack the Indian Parliament

2003
- Israel and PLO sign a cease fire

2004
- Tsunami in Indian Ocean devastates Indonesia and surrounding regions
- Terrorists bomb trains in Spain

How Does the Passage of Time Affect the Way Events Are Understood?

As the United States entered the twenty-first century, combating terrorism at home and abroad became a national priority. The attacks on the World Trade Center and the Pentagon resulted in wars in Afghanistan and Iraq. The wars as well as new security policies led to great controversy in American politics.

- *What previous events in American history have forced the nation to dramatically change its policies and actions?*
- *How should the United States respond to terrorism to prevent it from happening again?*

August 2005
- Hurricane Katrina devastates Louisiana and Mississippi; levies fail and New Orleans floods

January 2007
- Nancy Pelosi becomes first female Speaker of the House

November 2004
- George W. Bush defeats John Kerry in the election

2005   2006   2007

2005
- Terrorists bomb London subway system

2006
- Israel invades Lebanon to attack Hezbollah
- Over 1 billion people worldwide use the Internet

FOLDABLES™

Organizing Information Compile facts about the terrorist attacks at the World Trade Center and Pentagon on September 11, 2001. Then, make a Four-Door Book Foldable that explains what, where, when, and why these events occurred.

Why	What
When	Where

History ONLINE Chapter Overview
Visit glencoe.com to preview Chapter 31.

America Enters a New Century

Guide to Reading

Big Ideas
Government and Society A very close presidential election saw a shift in power in the White House, as George W. Bush became the forty-third President of the United States.

Content Vocabulary
- chad *(p. 1033)*
- strategic defense *(p. 1035)*

Academic Vocabulary
- priority *(p. 1035)*
- controversial *(p. 1035)*

People and Events to Identify
- Al Gore *(p. 1032)*
- George W. Bush *(p. 1032)*
- Ralph Nader *(p. 1033)*

Reading Strategy
Organizing Complete a graphic organizer similar to the one below by charting the key post-election events culminating in George W. Bush's victory.

In the election of 2000, Democrat Al Gore faced Republican George W. Bush. After a dispute over the outcome in Florida, Bush became president. Bush then focused on cutting taxes and introducing health care and education reforms.

The Election of 2000

MAIN Idea In one of the closest presidential races in history, involving vote recounts and the Supreme Court, George W. Bush became president.

HISTORY AND YOU Do you think the Electoral College should be modified or eliminated? Read on to learn how the 2000 election ultimately came down to a decision about Florida's disputed electoral votes.

As he prepared to leave office, President Clinton's legacy was uncertain. He had balanced the budget and presided over a period of rapid economic growth. His presidency was marred, however, by the impeachment trial, which had divided the nation and widened the divide between liberals and conservatives. In the election of 2000, that division led to one of the closest elections in American history.

The Candidates Campaign

The Democrats nominated Vice President **Al Gore** for president in 2000. Gore, a former senator from Tennessee, was regarded as a moderate and his Southern roots were expected to help him win votes in the South. For his running mate, Gore chose Senator Joseph Lieberman from Connecticut, the first Jewish American ever to run for vice president on a major party ticket.

The Republican contest for the presidential nomination came down to two men: Governor **George W. Bush** of Texas, son of former president George H.W. Bush, and Senator John McCain of Arizona, a former navy pilot and prisoner of war in North Vietnam. Most Republican leaders endorsed Bush, who was especially popular with conservatives. He easily won the nomination, despite some early McCain victories in the primaries. Bush chose Richard "Dick" Cheney as his vice presidential running mate. Cheney had served as President George H.W. Bush's Secretary of Defense.

The election campaign revolved around the question of what to do with surplus tax revenues. Both Bush and Gore agreed that Social Security needed reform, but they disagreed on the details. Both promised to cut taxes, although Bush proposed a much larger tax cut than Gore. Both men also promised to improve public education and to support plans to help senior citizens pay for prescription drugs.

Presidential Election of 2000

Gore — Bush

Presidential Candidate	Popular Votes	% of Popular Vote	Electoral Votes
Bush	50,456,002	47.88%	271
Gore	50,999,897	48.40%	266*
Nader	2,882,955	2.74%	0

*One Gore elector from Washington, D.C., abstained from casting an electoral vote.

▲ The recount of the vote in Florida meant vote counters had to examine ballots individually to determine the intention of the voter.

Analyzing VISUALS

1. **Making Generalizations** What characteristics do the states that voted for Bush share? What characteristics do the states that voted for Gore share?

2. **Assessing** Do you think the Florida ballot was easy to understand or confusing? Why?

Frustrated by what he viewed as the fundamental similarities between Bush and Gore, well-known consumer advocate **Ralph Nader** entered the race as the nominee of the Green Party. Nader was known for his strong environmentalist views and his criticism of the power of large corporations. Nader argued that both Bush and Gore depended on campaign funds from large companies and were unwilling to support policies that favored American workers and the environment.

A Close Vote

The 2000 election was one of the closest in American history. No candidate won a majority of the votes cast, but Gore received the most votes, winning 48.4 percent of the popular vote compared to 47.9 percent for Bush. (Nader won about 3 percent of the vote.) To win the presidency, however, candidates must win 270 electoral votes—not lead in the popular vote.

The election came down to the Florida vote—both men needed its 25 electoral votes to win. The results in Florida were so close that state law required a recount of the ballots using vote-counting machines. There were, however, thousands of ballots that had been thrown out because the counting machines could not read the voting cards. Gore then asked for a hand recount of ballots in several strongly Democratic counties. After the machine recount showed Bush still ahead, a battle began over the manual recounts.

Most Florida ballots required voters to punch a hole. The little piece of cardboard punched out of the ballot is called a **chad.** The problem for vote counters was how to count a ballot if the chad was still partially attached. On some, the chad was still in place, and the voter had left only a dimple on the surface. When looking at the ballots, vote counters had to determine what the voter intended—and different counties used different standards.

The Election of 2000

▲ The candidates are presented as two turkeys arguing over the results with closed captioning provided to translate what they are saying into what they really mean.

▲ The close presidential election of 2000 illustrated clearly how important it is for everyone to exercise the right to vote.

Analyzing VISUALS DBQ

1. **Evaluating** Based on the cartoon on the left, do you think the cartoonist supported Bush or Gore?

2. **Analyzing** Why are the three characters in the cartoon above angry at the man on the right?

Under state law, Florida officials had to certify the results by a certain date. When it became clear that not all of the recounts could be finished in time, Gore went to court to challenge the deadline. The Florida Supreme Court agreed to set a new deadline. At Bush's request, the United States Supreme Court then intervened to decide whether the Florida Supreme Court had acted constitutionally.

While lawyers for Bush and Gore prepared their arguments for the Supreme Court, the hand recounts continued. Despite having more time, not all of the counties where Gore wanted recounts were able to meet the new deadline. On November 26, Florida officials certified Bush the winner by 537 votes.

For more on *Bush* v. *Gore* read the case summary on page R58 in **Supreme Court Case Summaries.**

Bush v. Gore

Although Bush had been declared the winner in Florida, Gore's lawyers headed back to court arguing that thousands of ballots were still uncounted. The Florida Supreme Court ordered all Florida counties to begin a hand recount of ballots rejected by the counting machines. As counting began, the United States Supreme Court ordered the recount to stop until it had issued its ruling.

On December 12, in *Bush* v. *Gore,* the United States Supreme Court ruled 7–2 that the hand recounts in Florida violated the equal protection clause of the Constitution. The Court argued that because different vote counters used different standards, the recount did not treat all voters equally.

Both federal law and the Constitution require the electoral votes for president to be cast on a certain day. If Florida missed that deadline, its electoral votes would not count. The Court ruled 5–4 that there was not enough time left to conduct a manual recount that would pass constitutional standards. This ruling left Bush the certified winner in Florida. The next day, Gore conceded the election.

✔ **Reading Check** **Analyzing** Why did the U.S. Supreme Court stop the manual recounts in Florida?

Bush Becomes President

MAIN Idea George W. Bush supported the enactment of a tax cut, the No Child Left Behind program, and a strategic defense system.

HISTORY AND YOU Have new education policies affected the testing process at your school? Read on to learn more about No Child Left Behind.

On January 20, 2001, George W. Bush became the forty-third president of the United States. In his Inaugural Address, Bush promised to improve the public schools, to cut taxes, to reform Social Security and Medicare, and to build up the nation's defenses.

After taking office, the president's first **priority** was to cut taxes to try to boost the economy. During the election campaign, the stock market dropped sharply, unemployment began to rise, and many new Internet-based companies went out of business. Despite opposition from some Democrats, Congress passed a large $1.35 trillion tax cut to be phased in over 10 years. In the summer of 2001, Americans began receiving tax rebate checks that put about $40 billion back into the economy in an effort to prevent a recession.

Soon after Congress passed the tax cut plan, President Bush proposed two major reforms in education. He wanted public schools to give annual standardized tests, and he wanted to allow parents to use federal funds to pay for private schools if their public schools were doing a poor job. Although Congress refused to give federal funds to private schools, it did vote in favor of annual reading and math tests in public schools for grades 3–8. This law became known as the No Child Left Behind Act.

President Bush also focused on Medicare reform. By the summer of 2002, Congress had introduced a bill adding prescription drug benefits to Medicare. The bill was **controversial.** Some opponents feared it would cost too much, while others argued that it did not go far enough. The program finally became law in November 2003.

Congress also reacted to a rash of corporate scandals—the most famous taking place at a large energy trading company called Enron. Corporate leaders there cost investors and employees billions of dollars before the company went bankrupt. Congress passed a new law—the Public Company Accounting Reform and Investor Protection Act—also known as the Sarbanes-Oxley Act, after the members of Congress who introduced it. The law tightened accounting rules and toughened penalties for dishonest executives.

Shortly after taking office, President Bush also pushed for new military programs designed to meet the needs of the post–Cold War world. One program Bush strongly favored was **strategic defense**—the effort to develop missiles and other devices that could shoot down nuclear missiles. Bush argued that missile defense was needed because many hostile nations were developing long-range missiles.

As the debate about the nation's military programs continued in the summer of 2001, a horrific event changed everything. On September 11, 2001, terrorists crashed passenger jets into the World Trade Center and the Pentagon. A new war had begun.

Reading Check **Explaining** What was President George W. Bush's first priority when he took office?

Section 1 REVIEW

Vocabulary

1. **Explain** the significance of: Al Gore, George W. Bush, Ralph Nader, chad, strategic defense.

Main Ideas

2. **Paraphrasing** What did the U.S. Supreme Court decide in *Bush* v. *Gore?*

3. **Describing** What did the No Child Left Behind Act mandate?

Critical Thinking

4. **Big Ideas** What caused the vote-count controversy in Florida in the 2000 election?

5. **Organizing** Use a graphic organizer similar to the one below by listing President Bush's goals when he took office.

6. **Analyzing Visuals** Study the photos on page 1033. Explain how you would change the voting process following the controversy of the 2000 election.

Writing About History

7. **Persuasive Writing** Take on the role of a Supreme Court justice. Write a statement explaining how you voted in *Bush* v. *Gore* and why you took this position.

History ONLINE

Study Central™ To review this section, go to <u>glencoe.com</u> and click on Study Central.

Section 2

The War on Terrorism Begins

Guide to Reading

Big Ideas

Government and Society Acts of terrorism against the United States prompted George W. Bush to declare "War on Terror."

Content Vocabulary
- terrorism *(p. 1038)*
- state-sponsored terrorism *(p. 1039)*
- anthrax *(p. 1041)*

Academic Vocabulary
- resolve *(p. 1037)*
- interpretation *(p. 1038)*
- obtain *(p. 1040)*

People and Events to Identify
- Osama bin Laden *(p. 1037)*
- al-Qaeda *(p. 1037)*

Reading Strategy

Organizing Complete a graphic organizer similar to the one below to show causes of terrorism.

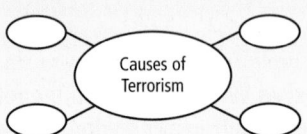

Causes of Terrorism

On September 11, 2001, terrorists attacked the United States killing over 3,000 people. The attacks united the nation as Americans worked to help the survivors. President George W. Bush and Congress launched a war on terrorism to prevent such attacks in the future.

September 11, 2001

MAIN Idea The terrorist attacks on the World Trade Center and the Pentagon shocked and alarmed Americans; almost immediately, combating terrorism became the nation's top priority.

HISTORY AND YOU Do you recall learning about the 1919 bombings that triggered government raids and roundups of foreigners? Read on to learn how the United States reacted to the more deadly attacks of 2001.

At 8:45 A.M. Eastern Daylight Time on September 11, 2001, a Boeing 767 passenger jet slammed into the North Tower of the World Trade Center in New York City. As people below gazed in horror, a second plane collided with the South Tower. Soon afterward, a third plane crashed into the Pentagon in Washington, D.C. At 9:50 A.M., the South Tower collapsed in a billowing cloud of dust and debris. The North Tower fell about 40 minutes later. The falling towers killed thousands of people, burying them beneath a vast mound of rubble.

The airplanes did not crash accidentally. Hijackers deliberately crashed them into the buildings. Hijackers also seized a fourth airplane, United Airlines Flight 93, probably hoping to crash it into the White House or the Capitol. Many passengers on Flight 93 had cell phones. After hearing about the World Trade Center, four passengers—Todd Beamer, Thomas Burnett, Jeremy Glick, and Mark Bingham—decided to do something. An operator listening over a cell phone heard Todd Beamer's voice: "Are you ready guys? Let's roll."

Soon afterward, Flight 93 crashed in a field in Pennsylvania. At that moment, Vice President Dick Cheney was in a bunker under the White House. After hearing Flight 93 had crashed, he turned to the others in the room, and said: "I think an act of heroism just took place on that plane."

A National Emergency

The attacks of 9/11, as the day came to be called, killed all 266 passengers and crewmembers on the four hijacked planes. Another 125 people died in the Pentagon. In New York City, nearly 3,000 people died. More Americans were killed in the attacks of September 11,

Turning Point

The Attacks of September 11, 2001

The terrorist attacks of September 11, 2001, altered the lives of millions of Americans and shifted the priorities of the federal government. At home the United States launched a new war against terrorists and their supporters. Globally, the United States took aggressive and preemptive steps to stop terrorism. At home, the balance between civil liberties and national security shifted, with passage of the USA Patriot Act, which gave broad new powers to the federal government.

MAKING CONNECTIONS How are the terrorist attacks and their aftermath still affecting American society and foreign policy?

Above, the South Tower of the World Trade Center bursts into flames after being struck by an airliner while the North Tower burns from an attack a few minutes earlier. At left, one side of the Pentagon was badly damaged. Part of the building later collapsed. At right, after the World Trade Center towers collapsed, the resulting debris coated the city with dust.

2001, than died at Pearl Harbor or on D-Day in World War II.

The attacks shocked Americans, but they responded rapidly to the crisis. Medical workers and firefighters from other cities raced to New York to help. Across the nation, Americans donated blood and collected food, blankets, and other supplies. Within weeks, Americans also donated over $1 billion. From around the world came sympathy. "We are all Americans!" wrote one French journalist.

Everywhere across the nation, Americans put up flags to show their unity and **resolve.** They held candlelight vigils and prayer services as they searched for ways to help. If the terrorists had hoped to divide Americans, they failed. As the Reverend Billy Graham noted at a memorial service, "A tragedy like this could have torn our country apart. But instead it has united us and we have become a family."

The American government also responded quickly to the crisis. All civilian airplanes were grounded. The armed forces were put on high alert. Across the nation, Americans in the National Guard left their civilian jobs and reported for duty. The Air National Guard began patrolling the skies over major cities, and Army National Guard troops were deployed to airports to strengthen security.

On September 14, President Bush declared a national emergency. Congress authorized the use of force to fight whoever had attacked the United States. Intelligence sources and the FBI quickly identified the attacks as the work of a man named **Osama bin Laden** and his organization, **al-Qaeda** (al KY•duh).

- 1. 1993 **Bomb at the World Trade Center kills 6**
- 2. 1995 **Bombs at a U.S.-Saudi facility in Riyadh kill 7**
- 3. 1996 **Bombing of Khobar Towers barracks in Dhahran, Saudi Arabia, kills 19 Americans**
- 4. 1998 **Bombings at U.S. embassies in Kenya and Tanzania kill more than 200**
- 5. 2000 **Attack on the USS *Cole* kills 17 American sailors**
- 6. 2001 **Hijacked airliners crash into the World Trade Center, the Pentagon, and a field in Pennsylvania killing nearly 3,000**
- 7. 2002 **Bombing in Bali, Indonesia, kills more than 200**
- 8. 2004 **Bombing of commuter trains in Madrid, Spain, kills 191**
- 9. 2004 **Attack on the U.S. Consulate in Jedda, Saudi Arabia, kills 5**
- 10. 2005 **Bombs on the London subway kill 52**
- 11. 2002–present **Ongoing attacks against coalition troops and civilians in Afghanistan**
- 12. 2003–present **Ongoing attacks against coalition troops and civilians in Iraq**

Middle East Terrorism and the United States

The attacks on the World Trade Center and the Pentagon were acts of terrorism. **Terrorism** is the use of violence by nongovernmental groups against civilians to achieve a political goal. Terrorist acts are intended to instill fear in people and to force governments into changing their policies.

Although there have been many acts of terrorism in American history, most terrorist attacks on Americans since World War II have been carried out by Middle Eastern groups. The reason Middle Eastern terrorists have targeted Americans can be traced back to events early in the twentieth century.

As oil became important to the American economy in the 1920s, the United States invested heavily in the Middle East oil industry. This industry brought great wealth to the ruling families in some Middle Eastern kingdoms, but most people remained poor. Some

became angry at the United States for supporting the wealthy kingdoms and families.

The rise of the oil industry also led to the spread of Western ideas in the region, and many Muslims feared that their traditional values were being weakened. New movements arose calling for a strict **interpretation** of the Quran—the Muslim holy book—and a return to traditional Muslim religious laws. These Muslim movements wanted to overthrow pro-Western governments in the Middle East and create a pure Islamic society. Muslims who support these movements are referred to as fundamentalist militants. Some militants began using terrorism to achieve their goals.

American support of Israel also angered many in the Middle East. In 1947 the UN divided British-controlled Palestine into two territories to provide a home for Jews. One part became Israel. The other part was to become a state for Palestinian Arabs, but fighting between Israel and the Arab states in 1948 left this territory under the control of Israel, Jordan, and Egypt. In the 1950s, Palestinians began staging guerrilla raids and terrorist attacks against Israel. Since the United States gave aid to Israel, it became the target of Muslim hostility. In the 1970s, several Middle East nations realized they could fight Israel and the United States by providing terrorists with money, weapons, and training. This is called **state-sponsored terrorism.** The governments of Libya, Syria, Iraq, and Iran have all sponsored terrorists.

The Rise of Al-Qaeda

In 1979 the Soviet Union invaded Afghanistan. In response, Muslims from across the world headed to Afghanistan to help fight the Soviets. Among them was a 22-year-old named Osama bin Laden. Bin Laden came from one of Saudi Arabia's wealthiest families. He used his wealth to support the Afghan resistance. In 1988 he founded an organization called al-Qaeda or "the Base." Al-Qaeda recruited Muslims and channeled money and arms to the Afghan resistance.

Bin Laden's experience in Afghanistan convinced him that superpowers could be beaten. He also believed that Western ideas had contaminated Muslim society and was outraged by Saudi Arabia's decision to allow American troops to be based on Saudi soil after Iraq invaded Kuwait.

At first, bin Laden ran al-Qaeda from camps in Sudan, but in 1996, he moved back to Afghanistan after the Taliban, a militant Muslim fundamentalist group, took power there. Bin Laden dedicated himself to driving Westerners out of the Middle East. In 1998 he called on Muslims to kill Americans. Soon afterward, his followers set off bombs at the American embassies in Kenya and Tanzania.

After these bombings, President Clinton ordered cruise missiles fired at terrorist camps in Afghanistan and Sudan, but bin Laden was not deterred. In 1999, al-Qaeda terrorists were arrested while trying to smuggle explosives into the United States in an attempt to bomb Seattle. In October 2000, al-Qaeda terrorists crashed a boat loaded with explosives into the *USS Cole,* an American warship, while it was docked in Yemen. Then, on September 11, 2001, al-Qaeda struck again, hijacking four American passenger planes and executing the most devastating terrorist attack in history.

✔ **Reading Check** **Explaining** Why was Osama bin Laden able to create a terrorist organization?

A New War Begins

MAIN Idea The war on terrorism involved halting terrorists' access to funding and launching a war in Afghanistan.

HISTORY AND YOU Does your school have plans for coping with an emergency? Read on to learn about the national response to the terrorist attacks.

In an address to Congress on September 20, 2001, President Bush demanded the Taliban regime in Afghanistan turn over bin Laden and his supporters and shut down all terrorist camps. The president then made it clear that although the war on terrorism would start by targeting al-Qaeda, it would not stop there. "It will not end," the president announced, "until every terrorist group of global reach has been found, stopped, and defeated." While Secretary of State Colin Powell began building an international coalition to support the United States, Secretary of Defense Donald Rumsfeld began deploying troops, aircraft, and warships to the Middle East.

The president also announced that the United States would no longer tolerate states that aided terrorists. "From this day forward," the president proclaimed, "any nation that continues to harbor or support terrorism will be regarded by the United States as a hostile regime." The war would not end quickly, but it was a war the nation had to fight:

PRIMARY SOURCE

"Great harm has been done to us. We have suffered great loss. And in our grief and anger we have found our mission and our moment. . . . Our Nation—this generation—will lift a dark threat of violence from our people and our future."

—President George W. Bush, *Address to Joint Session of Congress,* September 20, 2001

In a letter to the *New York Times,* Secretary of Defense Rumsfeld warned Americans that "this will be a war like none other our nation has faced." The enemy, he explained, "is a global network of terrorist organizations and their state sponsors, committed to denying free people the opportunity to live as they choose." Fighting terrorism would not be easy. Military force would be used, but terrorism had to be fought by other means as well.

For a longer excerpt from this speech read, "President Bush's Address to Joint Session of Congress, September 20, 2001" on page R57 of **Documents in American History.**

Responding to 9/11

After the attacks, Americans held vigils and prayer services to remember and honor those who had died. For months after the attacks, Americans closely followed the efforts of firefighters and rescue workers. Despite increased airport security, the attacks left some Americans wary of air travel.

At left, Alana Milawski, waves an American flag during a candlelight vigil in Las Vegas on September 12, 2001. Above, firefighters work in the rubble of the World Trade Center. The attacks led to an increase in airline security (right) resulting in long lines at airports while passengers waited to be screened.

Analyzing VISUALS

1. **Theorizing** Why do you think so many people participated in group vigils and memorials after the attacks?

2. **Evaluating** In what ways were Americans most immediately affected by the attacks of September 11, 2001?

Cutting Terrorist Funding One effective way to fight terrorist groups is to cut off their funding. On September 24, President Bush issued an executive order freezing the financial assets of several individuals and groups suspected of terrorism. As information about terrorist groups increased, more names and organizations were added to the list. President Bush asked other nations to help, and within weeks, some 80 nations had issued orders freezing the assets of the organizations and individuals on the American list.

Homeland Security and the Patriot Act

As part of the effort to protect the American people from further terrorist attacks, President Bush created a new federal agency—the Office of Homeland Security—to coordinate the dozens of federal agencies and departments working to prevent terrorism. He then appointed Pennsylvania governor Tom Ridge to serve as the agency's director.

The president also asked Congress to pass legislation to help law enforcement agencies track down terrorist suspects. Drafting the legislation took time. Congress had to balance Americans' Fourth Amendment protections against unreasonable search and seizure with the need to increase security. President Bush signed the antiterrorist bill—known as the USA Patriot Act—into law in October 2001. In cases involving terrorism, the law permitted secret searches to avoid tipping off suspects and allowed authorities to **obtain** a nationwide search warrant useable in any jurisdiction. The law also made it easier to wiretap suspects and allowed authorities to track Internet communications and seize voice mail.

In the months following the attack, the Office of Homeland Security struggled to coordinate all of the federal agencies fighting terrorism. In June 2002, President Bush asked Congress to combine all of the agencies responsible for the public's safety into a new

History ONLINE
Student Web Activity Visit glencoe.com and complete the activity on the war on terrorism.

department called the Department of Homeland Security. The plan called for the largest reorganization of the federal government since 1947, when Congress created the Department of Defense, the National Security Council, and the CIA.

The president's proposal led to an intense debate in Congress, and it did not pass until after the midterm elections in November 2002. The new Department of Homeland Security controls the Coast Guard, the Border Patrol, the Immigration and Naturalization Service, the Customs Service, the Federal Emergency Management Agency, and many other agencies. It also analyzes information collected by the FBI, the CIA, and other intelligence agencies.

Bioterrorism Strikes the United States As the nation struggled to cope with the attacks on the Pentagon and the World Trade Center, another terrorist attack began. On October 5, 2001, a newspaper editor in Florida died from an anthrax infection. **Anthrax** is a type of bacteria. Several nations, including the United States, Russia, and Iraq, have used anthrax to create biological weapons. Antibiotics can cure anthrax, but if left untreated, it can quickly become lethal.

Soon after its appearance in Florida, anthrax was found at the offices of news organizations in New York City. In Washington, D.C., a letter containing anthrax arrived at Senator Tom Daschle's office. It was now clear that terrorists were using the mail to spread anthrax. Traces of anthrax were found at several government buildings. Several postal workers who had handled letters containing anthrax contracted the disease, and two workers died. The FBI began investigating the attack, but no suspects were arrested.

The War in Afghanistan Begins

On October 7, 2001, the United States began bombing al-Qaeda's camps and the Taliban's military forces in Afghanistan. In an address to the nation, President Bush explained that Islam and the Afghan people were not the enemy, and that the United States would send food, medicine, and other supplies to Afghan refugees. The president also explained that the attack on the Taliban was only the beginning. The war on terrorism would continue until victory was achieved:

PRIMARY SOURCE

"Today we focus on Afghanistan, but the battle is broader. Every nation has a choice to make. In this conflict, there is no neutral ground. If any government sponsors the outlaws and killers of innocents, they have become outlaws and murderers, themselves. And they will take that lonely path at their own peril. . . . The battle is now joined on many fronts. We will not waver; we will not tire; we will not falter; and we will not fail. Peace and freedom will prevail. Thank you. May God continue to bless America."

—President George W. Bush, Address to the Nation, October 7, 2001

✓ Reading Check **Outlining** What steps did the president take in response to the terrorist attacks?

Section 2 REVIEW

Vocabulary

1. **Explain** the significance of: Osama bin Laden, al-Qaeda, terrorism, state-sponsored terrorism, anthrax.

Main Ideas

2. **Describing** What factors have contributed to the rise of Middle Eastern terrorist groups?

3. **Listing** What major actions marked the beginning of the United States' war on terrorism?

Critical Thinking

4. **Big Ideas** Why do Islamic fundamentalists in the Middle East disagree with U.S. foreign policy?

5. **Categorizing** Use a graphic organizer similar to the one below to list the responses of individual Americans and the federal government to the attacks on September 11, 2001.

Individuals — Response to 9/11 attacks — Government

6. **Analyzing Visuals** Study the map of terrorist attacks on page 1038. How would you describe the scope of al-Qaeda's operation?

Writing About History

7. **Persuasive Writing** The Patriot Act gave law enforcement new ways to fight terrorism. Write a letter to a newspaper explaining why you are either for or against giving up some freedoms in exchange for increased security.

History ONLINE

Study Central™ To review this section, go to glencoe.com and click on Study Central.

The Invasion of Iraq

Guide to Reading

Big Ideas

Trade, War, and Migration In an effort to fight terrorism, the United States launched attacks in both Afghanistan and Iraq.

Content Vocabulary
- weapons of mass destruction (WMD) *(p. 1044)*

Academic Vocabulary
- inspector *(p. 1045)*
- significantly *(p. 1046)*
- eliminate *(p. 1047)*

People and Events to Identify
- Northern Alliance *(p. 1042)*
- Khalid Shaikh Mohammed *(p. 1043)*
- "axis of evil" *(p. 1044)*
- Saddam Hussein *(p. 1045)*

Reading Strategy

As you read this section on the Invasion of Iraq, complete a graphic organizer similar to the one below to show the different groups in Iraq.

After the attacks of September 11, 2001, the United States invaded Afghanistan, the Central Asian nation that had sheltered many al-Qaeda members. In March 2003, the United States invaded Iraq and toppled the regime of Saddam Hussein.

The War on Terror Continues

MAIN Idea After forcing Taliban leaders in Afghanistan to flee, the United States and its allies sent more troops as peacekeepers and worked to create a stable and democratic government.

HISTORY AND YOU Can you think of a nation or region today where peacekeepers are stationed while a new government is established? Read on to learn about the role of peacekeepers in Afghanistan.

Less than a month after the September 11 attacks, the United States launched a war in Afghanistan with the goal of bringing down the Taliban regime that had sheltered Osama bin Laden and other members of al-Qaeda. Americans also hoped that bin Laden would be captured and brought back for trial in the United States.

While American warplanes bombed the Taliban's forces, the United States began sending military aid to the **Northern Alliance,** a coalition of Afghan groups that had been fighting the Taliban for several years. U.S. Special Forces also entered Afghanistan to advise the Northern Alliance and identify targets for American aircraft. The American bombing campaign quickly shattered the Taliban's defenses. The Northern Alliance then launched a massive attack. In December 2001, the Taliban government collapsed, and surviving Taliban fled to the mountains of Afghanistan.

Rebuilding Afghanistan

After the Taliban fled, the United States and its allies helped local Afghan leaders create a new government. Meanwhile, thousands of American and allied troops arrived to act as peacekeepers. In 2003 NATO took command of peacekeeping in Afghanistan.

Since 2002 Afghanistan has begun to slowly recover from decades of war. The economy has grown rapidly, although the people remain very poor. The United States and its allies have donated some $24 billion to help rebuild the country. In December 2004, Afghanistan held its first nationwide democratic election, and Hamid Karzai was elected president. One year later, the Afghan people elected a National Assembly. Despite these successes, Afghanistan continues to suffer from violence. Taliban insurgents have staged guerrilla

The War in Afghanistan

The United States invaded Afghanistan to overthrow the Taliban regime. Helping to establish a democratic government was the next step.

▲ American soldiers were sent to act as peacekeepers while the new Afghan government tried to establish order in the mountainous country.

▲ The new Afghan constitution granted equal rights to women, including the right to vote.

▶ Hamid Karzai was elected president in 2004.

Analyzing VISUALS

1. **Speculating** What part of their duties do you think these soldiers find most difficult?

2. **Predicting** How may voting rights for women affect the development of the new Afghan government?

attacks and suicide bombings. The Afghan government has little control over the mountainous regions of southern Afghanistan and fighting continues between NATO and Taliban forces in the south.

Bin Laden Goes Into Hiding

According to news reports, American intelligence agencies believe Osama bin Laden crossed into Pakistan to hide in the mountainous region of Warizistan where the local people were friendly to al-Qaeda and the Taliban. Between 2002 and 2006, bin Laden released a number of audiotapes and one videotape urging his followers to continue the fight.

Pakistan has not officially allowed American troops to enter its territory to find bin Laden, although news reports suggest U.S. Special Forces may be operating in the area. Pakistan has itself launched several military operations in Warizistan in search of al-Qaeda and Taliban forces. Although many al-Qaeda operatives have been arrested in Pakistan, Osama bin Laden remains at large.

Tracking Down Al-Qaeda

Since 2001, the United States and its allies have continued their worldwide hunt for al-Qaeda members. Hundreds of people have been captured or killed, including several top leaders of al-Qaeda. In November 2002, the CIA used an unmanned remote-controlled flying drone to fire a missile at a car in Yemen killing everyone in the vehicle. The car had been carrying top al-Qaeda leaders who had planned the attack on the USS *Cole* in 1998.

In 2003, Pakistan and the United States captured **Khalid Shaikh Mohammed**—one of the highest ranking members of al-Qaeda, and the man suspected of planning the September 11 attacks. Between 2002 and 2006, the American government believes that at least 10 major attacks by al-Qaeda, including at least three attacks on the United States and two on Great Britain, have been prevented.

✓ Reading Check **Describing** What strategy has the United States used to prevent the Taliban from regaining power?

Iraq and Weapons of Mass Destruction

MAIN Idea Concern that Iraq might be producing WMDs that could be given to terrorists led to an ultimatum.

HISTORY AND YOU Do you think the UN is an effective mediator of world affairs? Read on to learn about UN actions before the Iraq War.

The terrorist attacks of September 11, 2001 showed that groups such as al-Qaeda were determined to kill as many Americans as possible. President Bush and his advisers were deeply concerned that terrorist groups might acquire **weapons of mass destruction** (WMD). Weapons of mass destruction can kill large numbers of people all at once. Nuclear, chemical, and biological weapons are all examples of weapons of mass destruction.

During the Cold War, very few nations had weapons of mass destruction, and the United States relied upon a policy of deterrence to prevent their use. The United States announced that if any nation used weapons of mass destruction against the United States, the United States would counterattack with its own weapons of mass destruction. Deterrence worked during the Cold War, but the rise of state-sponsored terrorism created a new problem. If a nation secretly gave weapons of mass destruction to terrorists who then used them against the United States, the American military might not know where the weapons came from, or whom to attack in response.

The "Axis of Evil"

In his State of the Union speech in 2002, President Bush warned that an **"axis of evil"** made up of Iraq, Iran, and North Korea posed a grave threat to the world. Each of these nations had been known to sponsor terrorism, and was suspected of developing weapons of mass destruction. The president warned that "The United States of America will not permit the world's most dangerous regimes to threaten us with the world's most destructive weapons."

Of the three nations in the "axis of evil," the president and his advisers believed Iraq to be the most immediate danger. It had used chem-

THE Global War ON Terror, 2001–2007

Oct. 7, 2001
The United States launches attacks on Taliban positions in Afghanistan

March 20, 2003
American and coalition forces begin the invasion of Iraq

2001   2002   2003

Sept. 11, 2001
Terrorists highjack four planes and attack the World Trade Center and the Pentagon

Nov. 2002
UN Resolution warns Iraq to allow weapons inspectors to return

March 1, 2003
Khalid Shaikh Mohammed, suspected of planning the 9/11 attacks, is captured

Sept. 2003
Eleven countries form the Proliferation Security Initiative to intercept shipments of materials used to make weapons of mass destruction

ical weapons against the Kurds, an ethnic group in northern Iraq, and after the 1991 Gulf War, UN **inspectors** had also found evidence that Iraq had developed biological weapons and had been working on a nuclear bomb.

Between 1991 and 1998, Iraq appeared to be hiding its weapons of mass destruction from UN inspectors. In 1998 the Iraqi government ordered the inspectors to leave the country. In response, President Clinton ordered a massive bombing attack on Iraq to destroy its ability to make such weapons. Despite the attack, intelligence agencies continued to believe Iraq was hiding weapons of mass destruction.

An Ultimatum to Iraq

In 2002 President Bush decided the time had come to deal with Iraq. On September 12, he delivered a speech to the United Nations asking for a new resolution against Iraq. If Iraq's dictator, **Saddam Hussein,** wanted peace he would have to give up Iraq's weapons of mass destruction, readmit the UN weapons inspectors, stop supporting terrorism, and stop

oppressing his people. Although he was asking the UN to pass a resolution, the president made it clear that the United States would act with or without UN support.

While the UN Security Council debated a new resolution, President Bush asked Congress to authorize the use of force against Iraq, which it did. With the midterm elections only weeks away, Democrats wanted to focus on the nation's high unemployment rate and the slow economy. Instead, President Bush successfully kept the focus on national security issues. In 2002 Republicans picked up seats in the House of Representatives and regained control of the Senate.

Soon after the American elections, the UN approved a new resolution setting a deadline for Iraq to readmit weapons inspectors. It also required Iraq to declare its weapons of mass destruction, to stop supporting terrorism, and to stop oppressing its people. It threatened "serious consequences" if Iraq did not comply.

✔ Reading Check **Analyzing** Why did the United States think stopping the spread of weapons of mass destruction was linked to the war on terror?

Oct. 29, 2004
Osama bin Laden releases a video warning Americans that they will never have security if they continue their attacks

Oct. 2005
American deaths in the war in Iraq surpass 2,000

June 2006
Al-Zarqawi, the leader of al-Qaeda in Iraq, is killed in a U.S. attack

Jan. 2007
President Bush announces he will send 20,000 more troops to Iraq to restore order in Baghdad

2004 2005 2006 2007

Oct., 2004
Iraq Survey Group issues its final report concluding Iraq did not have weapons of mass destruction at the time the war began

Jan. 31, 2005
Iraqis go to the polls in their first free election

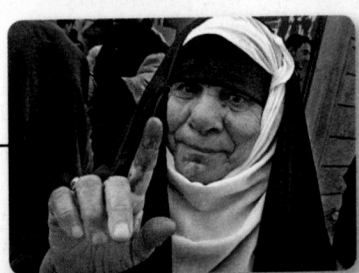

Analyzing TIME LINES

1. **Sequencing** Which happened first—the U.S. attack on Afghanistan or the invasion of Iraq?

2. **Specifying** When did Iraqis hold their first free election?

Confronting Iraq

MAIN Idea Coalition forces defeated the Iraqi military, but then factions in Iraq took up arms against coalition forces and each other.

HISTORY AND YOU In retrospect, do you believe the invasion of Iraq was justified? Read on to learn more about the different stages of the war.

In November 2002, Iraq agreed to readmit UN weapons inspectors. It then submitted a statement admitting it had weapons of mass destruction before the Gulf War, but denying it currently had weapons of mass destruction. Secretary of State Colin Powell declared that Iraq's declaration contained lies and was in "material breach" of the UN resolution.

As the United States and a coalition of some 30 nations prepared for war with Iraq, others at the UN Security Council argued that the inspectors should be given more time to find evidence of Iraq's WMD programs. By March 2003, the inspectors still had found nothing, and the United States began pressing the UN to authorize the use of force against Iraq.

France and Russia, two Security Council members with veto power, refused to back such a resolution. As war became imminent, world opinion divided between those who supported the United States and those who opposed an attack on Iraq. Around the world antiwar protestors staged rallies and marches. Several nations that had supported the United States in its war on terror, and had sent troops to Afghanistan, including France, Germany, and Canada, refused to join the coalition against Iraq. Saudi Arabia and Turkey—both American allies—refused to allow the United States to attack Iraq from their territories. The only nation bordering Iraq that granted permission to use its territory was Kuwait.

The Invasion Begins

On March 20, 2003, the U.S.-led coalition forces attacked Iraq. Over 150,000 American troops, some 45,000 British troops, as well as a few hundred special forces from Australia and Poland took part in the invasion.

Much of the Iraqi army dissolved as soldiers refused to risk their lives for Hussein. A few fierce battles took place, but the Iraqis were unable to slow the coalition advance **significantly.** On May 1, President Bush declared

PRIMARY SOURCE

The Invasion of Iraq

Overthrowing Saddam Hussein to ensure he could not give WMDs to terrorists was the primary objective of the invasion. Ousting his regime, however, proved easier than establishing a new government.

▲ *After decades of sham elections, Iraqi voters get to make real choices when they vote during Iraq's 2005 elections.*

▲ *U.S. and Iraqi soldiers face the difficult challenge of urban warfare in Iraq where the enemy can be very close, hiding behind walls or in buildings.*

Analyzing VISUALS

1. **Speculating** What do you suppose these soldiers hope to accomplish in fulfilling their duties?

2. **Predicting** Will regularly-scheduled elections lead to a more stable national government?

that the major combat was over. About 140 Americans and several thousand Iraqis had died. Saddam Hussein was captured in late 2003. After a prolonged trial, an Iraqi court found him guilty of ordering mass executions. He was executed in 2006.

Insurgents and Reconstruction

The quick victory did not end the fighting. Soon after the coalition took control of the country, small groups of Iraqis began staging bombings, sniper attacks, and sporadic battles against coalition forces. Some of the groups carrying out the attacks were former members of Saddam Hussein's military. Others were affiliated with al-Qaeda and other radical Muslim groups who believed the invasion offered a chance to build support in the Muslim world by organizing resistance to the Americans.

Some of the attacks were carried out by militias belonging to the different religious and ethnic groups in Iraq. The majority of Iraq's population is Shia Muslim, but there is a large Sunni Muslim minority as well. The Sunni are themselves divided between Sunni Arabs, who ruled the country under Saddam Hussein's leadership, and Sunni Kurds. The collapse of Hussein's dictatorship renewed old hostilities between these groups, forcing coalition troops to protect them from attacks from each other's militias.

Having gone to war in Iraq to overthrow a tyrant and **eliminate** the possibility of weapons of mass destruction being given to terrorists, the United States found itself trying to suppress an insurgency, prevent a civil war, and establish a new Iraqi government. The United States and its allies spent more than $30 billion to improve Iraq's electrical generating capacity, provide clean water, build schools, and improve health care, but insurgent attacks slowed these efforts. Despite the problems, Iraq's economy began to grow rapidly and a substantial improvement in living standards took place.

Between 2003 and 2006, insurgents killed over 3,000 American soldiers, many more than had died in the initial invasion. Many Americans had expected the war to be over quickly and as the fighting dragged on, support for the war began to decline. The failure to find any weapons of mass destruction also added to the growing controversy as to whether the war was a mistake.

American policy makers now faced a dilemma. If they pulled troops out too soon, Iraq might fall into civil war and provide a safe haven and breeding ground for terrorist groups. At the same time, the longer the United States stayed, the more its presence might stir resentment and support for terrorist groups. The best solution seemed to be to get a functioning and democratic Iraqi government up and running as fast as possible and then train its forces to take over the security of the country. As part of this plan, in January 2005, the Iraqi people went to the polls in huge numbers for the first free elections in their country's history. After much debate, voters then overwhelmingly approved a new constitution in October 2005.

Reading Check **Summarizing** Why did it prove so difficult to end the Iraq War quickly?

Section 3 REVIEW

Vocabulary

1. **Explain** the significance of: Northern Alliance, Khalid Shaikh Mohammed, weapons of mass destruction, "axis of evil," Saddam Hussein.

Main Ideas

2. **Explaining** Why did the United States send military aid to the Northern Alliance?

3. **Identifying** Why did Bush choose to focus military attention in Iraq?

4. **Summarizing** Why did fighting continue in Iraq after President Bush declared the major combat was over?

Critical Thinking

5. **Big Ideas** Why did the United States declare war on Afghanistan?

6. **Organizing** Use a graphic organizer to list the reasons why President Bush declared war on Iraq.

7. **Analyzing Visuals** Examine the photos on page 1046. How does the style of warfare in Iraq differ from the fighting in Afghanistan?

Writing About History

8. **Descriptive Writing** Suppose you are an Iraqi who has recently voted in your first election. Write a journal entry that explains how you feel following your vote.

History ONLINE
Study Central™ To review this section, go to glencoe.com and click on Study Central.

Section 4

A Time of Challenges

Guide to Reading

Big Ideas

Government and Society During President Bush's second term, the Republicans faced scandal and a national disaster that led to the Democrats gaining control of Congress in 2007.

Content Vocabulary

- "earmark" (p. 1054)

Academic Vocabulary

- monitor (p. 1051)
- procedure (p. 1052)

People and Events to Identify

- Abu Ghraib (p. 1048)
- Guantanamo Bay (p. 1050)
- National Security Agency (NSA) (p. 1051)
- John G. Roberts, Jr. (p. 1052)
- Samuel Alito, Jr. (p. 1052)
- Nancy Pelosi (p. 1055)

Reading Strategy

Taking Notes As you read about events from the 2004 election to the present day, use the major headings of the section to create an outline.

A Time of Challenges
I. The Election of 2004
II. Security vs. Liberty
   A.
   B.

After a close campaign, President Bush won a second term. His administration and the Supreme Court repeatedly clashed over the limits of executive authority in the war on terror. Scandals and frustration over Iraq helped Democrats win control of Congress in 2006.

The Election of 2004

MAIN Idea After a campaign that centered on the war in Iraq and the war on terror, Bush was reelected.

HISTORY AND YOU Have you ever participated in an election at your school? Read on to learn about the election of 2004 in which more voters turned out than had voted in other recent elections.

As the end of President Bush's first term neared, his popularity with Americans began to sink. In the months following the attacks of September 11, 2001, opinion polls showed that more than 80 percent of the public approved of the job he was doing. As the war dragged on in Iraq, and Osama bin Laden remained at large, his approval rating began to fall. The failure of inspectors to find any weapons of mass destruction in Iraq further weakened his support, as did the scandal at the Iraqi prison of **Abu Ghraib** where some Iraqi prisoners of war were abused by their American guards and interrogators. These events provided an opportunity for the Democrats to mount a serious challenge in the 2004 presidential election.

The war on terrorism and the war in Iraq dominated the election. President Bush and Vice President Cheney were renominated by the Republicans. The Democrats nominated Massachusetts Senator John Kerry for president and North Carolina Senator John Edwards for vice president.

Senator Kerry had fought in Vietnam and been decorated for valor, but he had returned from the war convinced of its futility. He joined Vietnam Veterans Against the War and testified before Congress against the war, a stand that angered many veterans and others who supported the war. Opponents used Kerry's actions in the 1970s against him in the 2004 campaign.

The candidates offered the nation a sharp choice. President Bush pledged to continue cutting taxes while building a strong national defense. He opposed abortion, supported limits on stem cell research, and called for a constitutional amendment to ban same-sex marriages. In contrast, Senator Kerry pledged to address domestic issues while pursuing the war on terror. He further promised to raise taxes on the wealthy to fund wider health care coverage, and to strengthen

The Election of 2004

▲ While the war on terror was the central issue of the campaign, Bush and Kerry differed on many issues, including stem cell research, Social Security, health care, and taxes. The two men held three debates during the 2004 campaign.

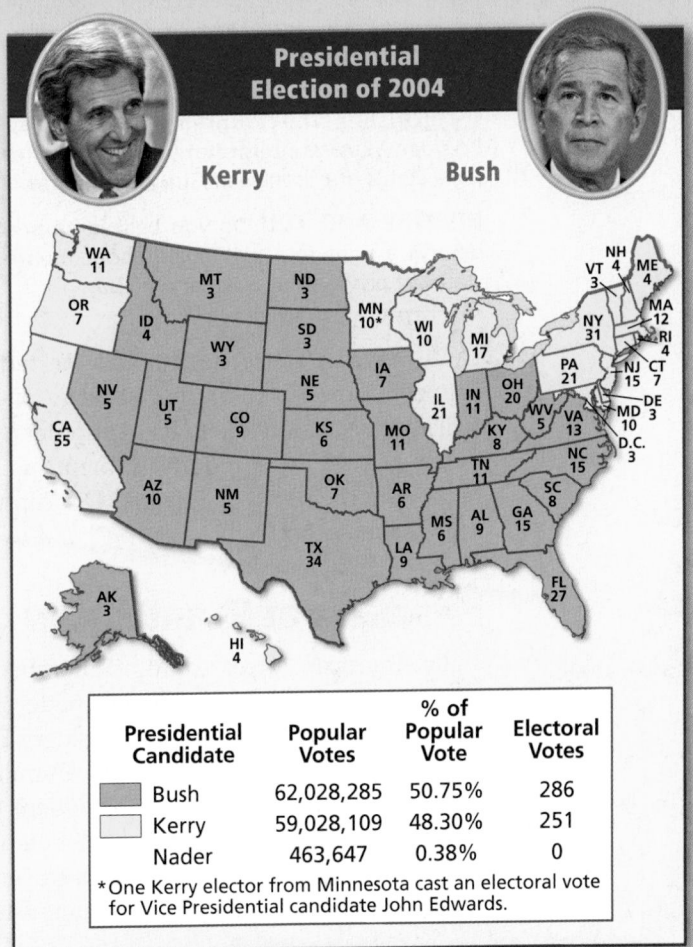

Presidential Election of 2004

Kerry

Bush

Presidential Candidate	Popular Votes	% of Popular Vote	Electoral Votes
Bush	62,028,285	50.75%	286
Kerry	59,028,109	48.30%	251
Nader	463,647	0.38%	0

*One Kerry elector from Minnesota cast an electoral vote for Vice Presidential candidate John Edwards.

Analyzing VISUALS

1. **Formulating Questions** If you had been the moderator of the debate, what questions would you have asked Bush and Kerry? Why?

2. **Theorizing** Why was Kerry more popular than Bush on the West Coast?

Social Security. He took the opposite stand from Bush on most social issues. Bush's campaign portrayed Kerry as an irresolute "flip-flopper" who could not be trusted with the nation's security. Kerry's campaign portrayed Bush as too stubborn and accused him of refusing to admit mistakes or change course when events required it.

Although the events of September 11, 2001, had united the nation emotionally, the country remained as divided politically as it had been in 2000. Bush's support was strongest in the South and on the Great Plains, as well as in rural areas and the outer suburbs of major cities. Kerry's base was in the Northeast and on the West Coast, as well as in cities and inner suburbs. Both candidates focused their efforts on a few key battleground states in the Midwest where voters were narrowly divided.

Both parties saw voter turnout as the key to victory. Election Day witnessed the highest voter turnout since 1968—nearly 61% of eligible voters went to the polls. Democrats won 8 million more votes than in 2000, but the Republicans gained 11.5 million. The election was decided in Ohio whose electoral votes both candidates needed to win. The vote was close enough that Bush was not declared the winner until the following day, having won the state by a little more than 100,000 votes. Nationwide, President Bush won a majority of the popular vote. His victory helped increase the Republican majorities in Congress as well. Despite the problems in Iraq, voters felt it safer to stay the course.

✔ **Reading Check** Analyzing Why did President Bush's popularity decline in the year before the 2004 election?

Security vs. Liberty

MAIN Idea The Supreme Court rejected President Bush's interpretation of the rights and legal status of prisoners at Guantanamo Bay.

HISTORY AND YOU Do you believe all prisoners deserve a right to a trial? Read about the unusual status of prisoners at Guantanamo Bay.

The war on terror heightened the tension between America's national security and its civil liberties. In order to prevent another major terrorist attack, was the government justified in limiting the rights of citizens? Did captured terrorists have any rights at all?

Prisoners at Guantanamo

As American forces captured members of al-Qaeda, a decision had to be made as to what to do with them. In 2004 President Bush decided to hold them at the American military base in **Guantanamo Bay,** Cuba, where they could be interrogated. Establishing detention facilities at Guantanamo proved controversial. Some people argued that the prisoners should have the same rights as Americans taken into custody in the United States, including the right to a lawyer, formal charges, and eventually a proper trial.

Rather than ask Congress for a law setting the rules for handling the detainees, the administration concluded that the president had the right as commander in chief to decide how detainees captured in combat should be treated. The administration insisted that the prisoners were illegal enemy combatants, not suspects charged with a crime, and as such, they did not have the right to appeal their detentions to an American court. The administration also declared that the rules regarding the treatment of prisoners, as specified in the Geneva Conventions, did not apply to terrorists since they were not part of any nation's armed forces.

Hamdan v. Rumsfeld

The Supreme Court disagreed with the administration. In 2004, in the case of *Rasul* v. *Bush,* the Court ruled that foreign prisoners who claimed they were being unlawfully

Abu Ghraib and Guantanamo Bay

The revelation that some American troops had mistreated prisoners at the Abu Ghraib prison in Iraq shocked many people. Photographs of prisoners being abused and humiliated diminished the international image of the United States. Similarly, the lack of judicial proceedings and the secrecy surrounding the detainees at Guantanamo Bay prompted international criticism.

▲ *Soldiers escort a detainee at Camp X-Ray at the military base at Guantanamo Bay, Cuba.*

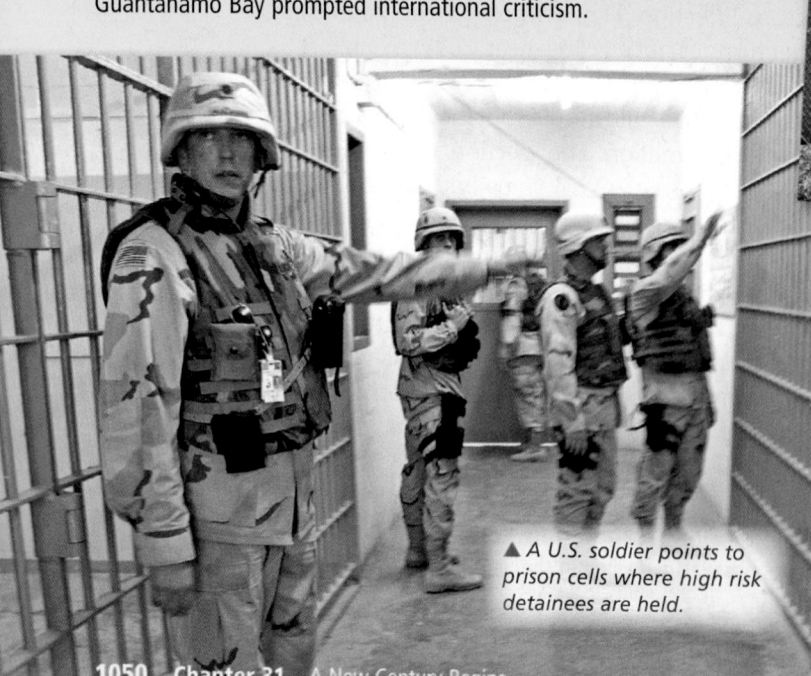

▲ *A U.S. soldier points to prison cells where high risk detainees are held.*

Analyzing **VISUALS**

1. **Interpreting** What might make a detainee "high risk"?
2. **Analyzing** In the photograph above, what elements show the level of security at the detention center?

imprisoned had the right to have their cases heard in court. The Bush administration responded by creating military tribunals to hear each detainee's case. In 2006 the Supreme Court struck this plan down in *Hamdan* v. *Rumsfeld,* arguing that the military tribunals at Guantanamo Bay violated both the Uniform Code of Military Justice and the Geneva Conventions regarding the treatment of prisoners of war.

President Bush then asked Congress to pass legislation establishing tribunals that met the Court's objections. In negotiations with Congress, the president agreed that prisoners would have the right to see the evidence against them, and any evidence obtained by torture would be inadmissible. The president also agreed to uphold the Geneva Conventions. Congress then responded with legislation that stated that non-citizens captured as enemy combatants would have no right to file writs of habeas corpus. This meant that as long as the tribunal had determined they were being lawfully held, they could be held indefinitely without trial.

Domestic Surveillance

As part of the war on terror, the **National Security Agency** (NSA) expanded its practice of **monitoring** overseas telephone calls. The NSA began wiretapping domestic calls made to overseas locations in those instances where they had good reason to believe that one party in the call was a member of al-Qaeda or affiliated with al-Qaeda.

When the *New York Times* broke the story of the wiretapping program in late 2005, it created a controversy. Civil rights groups feared the program would be abused and used to violate the privacy and Fourth Amendment rights of American citizens. Congress had created special courts to issue warrants in highly-classified security cases, but President Bush argued the courts were too slow and that he had the authority to expand wiretapping without warrants to help fight the war on terror. In August 2006, a federal judge declared the warrantless wiretapping to be unconstitutional. The federal government immediately appealed the case.

Reading Check **Explaining** Why did the Bush administration believe detainees at Guantanamo had no right to take their case to a U.S. court?

A Stormy Second Term

MAIN Idea Bush appointed two new Supreme Court justices; his second term was marred by a hurricane, the ongoing war, and scandals.

HISTORY AND YOU Do you remember Hurricane Katrina? Read on to learn how the handling of the crisis hurt the Bush administration.

Having won a second term with a majority of the popular vote, President Bush concluded the American people had given him a mandate to continue his policies. He began his second term by announcing plans to overhaul the Social Security system and to create a prescription drug program for senior citizens.

Debating Social Security

To build support for Social Security reform, President Bush pointed out that the baby boom generation would begin receiving Social Security in 2011. For decades, Congress had been warned that when baby boomers began retiring, the Social Security system would be in danger of collapse. The government would need to raise taxes dramatically, or greatly increase the deficit by borrowing money.

To fix Social Security, President Bush proposed that workers be allowed to put 4 percent of their income in private accounts rather than in Social Security. This money could then be invested in stocks and bonds. The president believed that private accounts would grow rapidly and help cover the expected shortfall in Social Security accounts. Bush's plan generated little enthusiasm in Congress. Democrats argued that the danger to Social Security was overstated and that privatizing any part of Social Security was dangerous. With the American public unenthusiastic, the plan was never brought to a vote in Congress.

Although his plan to reform Social Security failed, President Bush did convince Congress to enact a new prescription drug program for seniors. A major issue during the campaign had been the cost of prescription drugs for retirees living on a fixed income. Under the new program, provided by Medicare, people 65 and older can sign up for insurance that helps cover the cost of prescription drugs.

Conservatives worried that the plan would represent an enormous expansion of Medicare that the government could not afford. Democrats worried that the plan was too complex and did not go far enough in helping poor seniors. Despite the controversy, Congress enacted the plan.

New Supreme Court Judges

Although Republicans had gained four Senate seats in 2004, their majority of 55 still fell short of the 60 votes needed to end Democratic filibusters of President Bush's judicial nominees. Frustrated, Senate Majority Leader Bill Frist developed a plan to ban filibusters of presidential nominees. His plan called for Vice President Cheney, as the presiding officer of the Senate, to rule excessive debate on a nomination out of order. A simple majority of senators could then vote to uphold the vice president's ruling, rather than the 60 votes needed to stop a filibuster.

Worried that the plan would change Senate **procedures** too much, a bipartisan group of senators—the "Gang of 14"—forged a compromise. Under the plan, the seven Democratic members of the group agreed not to support a filibuster of the president's nominees solely because of their conservative ideology. They would support a filibuster only in extraordinary circumstances. In return the seven Republicans agreed not to support Frist if he tried to ban filibusters.

Early in Bush's second term, two vacancies occurred on the United States Supreme Court, enabling him to move the Court in a more conservative direction. First, Justice Sandra Day O'Connor announced her retirement. Although she had been appointed by President Reagan, Justice O'Connor had been a pivotal swing vote on the Court, sometimes siding with conservatives, sometimes with liberals. As her replacement, Bush nominated federal judge **John G. Roberts, Jr.,** who was well regarded in the Senate. Before the Senate could act, however, Chief Justice William Rehnquist died, and the president named Roberts to replace him. Roberts easily won Senate confirmation as chief justice.

Again attempting to fill Justice O'Connor's vacancy, President Bush nominated his White House counselor Harriet Miers. Although some Democrats regarded Miers favorably, conservative Republicans were unhappy with

Hurricane Katrina

Hurricane Katrina was one of the worst natural disasters in the history of the United States. The storm ravaged much of the Gulf Coast region. In New Orleans, the breach of the levies caused even more devastation.

▲ *An aerial photograph shows how the flooding in New Orleans ruined entire neighborhoods.*

her moderate views and lack of experience as a judge. As Republican opposition mounted, President Bush withdrew Miers' name and nominated federal judge **Samuel Alito, Jr.,** a well-known conservative justice. Democrats worried that Alito's strong views would shift the Court's balance, but the deal crafted by the Gang of 14 meant any filibuster would fail. The Senate voted 58 to 42 to confirm Alito.

Hurricane Katrina

On August 29, 2005, Hurricane Katrina smashed into the Gulf Coast of the United States, spreading devastation from Florida to Louisiana. The hurricane destroyed buildings, roads, and electrical lines, left thousands of people homeless, and cost at least 1,200 lives. Although the news media had given advance warning, many people had not evacuated the storm areas. Some stayed in their homes because they had ridden out previous storms, others because they wanted to protect their property, or because they were elderly and infirm. About 125,000 people in New Orleans had no cars and stayed behind.

▲ A man walks through the flooded Terme area of New Orleans. The breach of the levies left entire neighborhoods under several feet of water.

Analyzing VISUALS

1. **Explaining** Why did the flood cause so much damage to New Orleans?

2. **Speculating** Do you think this neighborhood can be restored to pre-flood conditions?

New Orleans Floods The fierce winds, rain, high tides, and storm surges leveled vast coastal areas of Mississippi and Alabama, but initially did only minor damage to New Orleans. Then, after the hurricane had passed, rising waters breached the levees that protected the low-lying city. As water flooded the city, those who had stayed behind were forced to flee onto their roofs, to await rescue.

As the water rose 15 feet in some neighborhoods, many people drowned. Thousands more took shelter in the convention center and at the Superdome, a covered football stadium. There they waited for days without much food, clean water, or information from authorities. City officials promised that buses would evacuate them, but days passed before the buses arrived. Some people began looting neighborhood stores.

The Government's Inadequate Response Television news broadcast scenes of the squalid condition of the survivors, asking why the government was failing to respond more quickly. The mayor of New Orleans was faulted for not issuing a mandatory evacuation until the storm was less than a day away, and for having failed to provide transportation for those who could not leave on their own. The governor of Louisiana engaged in a dispute with federal officials over who should take charge of the state's National Guard units. The Federal Emergency Management Agency (FEMA) seemed unprepared in its response. Only the Coast Guard seemed able to act, as its helicopters and boats began rescuing stranded citizens. Eventually troops and transportation arrived and moved the evacuees to other cities.

As New Orleans remained flooded, President Bush flew over the devastated areas a few days later. Photographs of the president viewing the scene from high above made him appear detached. The public also reacted critically when some members of Congress questioned whether it was worth the expense to rebuild New Orleans at a time when the United States was spending billions to reconstruct Baghdad. With polls showing a sharp drop in public confidence in his administration, President Bush fired the head of FEMA and then traveled to New Orleans to pledge federal funds for rebuilding the city.

People IN HISTORY

Condoleezza Rice
1954–

Born in Birmingham, Alabama, the same year as the landmark *Brown* v. *Board of Education* decision, Condoleezza Rice rose to become the first African American female secretary of state.

Before becoming involved in politics, Rice had a distinguished career in academia. She started her college studies at age 15 and went on to earn advanced degrees in economics and international studies. Dr. Rice then became a professor at Stanford University. Due to her expertise in Eastern and Central Europe, Rice served as an adviser on foreign affairs to President Ronald Reagan and President George H.W. Bush. She later returned to her post at Stanford.

When George W. Bush decided to run for president, he asked Rice to be his foreign policy adviser. During his first term, she served as head of the National Security Council and supported the attacks on Afghanistan and the invasion of Iraq. She became secretary of state during Bush's second term.

How did Rice's academic studies prepare her for her future role in politics?

Nancy Pelosi
1940–

Originally from Baltimore, Maryland, Nancy Pelosi's interest in politics began at an early age. Her father was a supporter of Democrat Franklin D. Roosevelt's New Deal and held political office.

Pelosi has spent most of her adult life in the San Francisco area. There, she attracted attention as an effective fund-raiser for the Democratic Party. She became the chair of the California State Democratic Party in 1981 and served for two years.

In 1987 she was elected to Congress in a special election to fill a vacancy caused by the death of her predecessor. The following year she was reelected for a full term and has held that office ever since.

In 2002 Pelosi was elected minority whip and tried to forge greater unity among different factions of her party. In that post, she emerged as one of President Bush's toughest critics. When the Democrats regained control of the House of Representatives after the 2006 elections, she became Speaker, the first woman elected to that post.

Why would Pelosi's position give her a platform from which to criticize the president?

Scandals in Congress

In 2005 Speaker of the House Dennis Hastert pledged that the 109th Congress would be "the Reform Congress." Very quickly, however, many voters grew disenchanted with the Republican majority in the Congress. Federal spending rose rapidly, in part because of the ongoing costs of the war in Iraq and partly because both Republicans and Democrats added **"earmarks"** to spending bills. These earmarks specified spending federal money for particular projects, such as building a bridge, or funding medical research, usually in their sponsors' own states and districts.

Congress also suffered a series of scandals. A prominent lobbyist, Jack Abramoff, pled guilty to bribing members of Congress. House Majority Leader Tom DeLay resigned after being indicted for violating campaign finance laws. California Representative Randy "Duke" Cunningham and Ohio Representative Ralph Ney also resigned after being convicted on corruption charges. Florida Representative Mark Foley gave up his seat after it was revealed that he had sent inappropriate E-mail to former House pages.

As the scandals broke, former Republican majority leader Richard Armey lamented that House Republicans, who had gained the majority in 1994 with big ideas, had descended to what he called "political point-scoring on meaningless wedge issues" such as same-sex marriage and flag burning, rather than getting control of earmarks, government spending, and budget deficits.

The 2006 Midterm Elections

The first two years of President Bush's second term had not gone well for his administration, or for Republicans in Congress. His effort to reform Social Security had failed. The public believed his administration had failed to respond adequately to Hurricane Katrina. Congress seemed awash in corruption scandals and unable to control spending. For many conservatives, Bush's support for a prescription drug plan and his decision to nominate Harriet Miers to the Supreme Court left them disenchanted with his leadership. Some were also angry about his plan to reform the nation's immigration system by creating a guest worker program and a path to citizenship for immigrants who had entered the country illegally. For most Americans, however, the single most important reason for their frustration with the government was the grim news coming daily from Iraq.

Problems in Iraq Ongoing suicide bombings, kidnappings, and attacks on American soldiers made Americans increasingly anxious about the situation in Iraq. A year earlier, many Americans had taken heart when large numbers of Iraqis had turned out to vote in democratic elections. The establishment of an Iraqi government gave some hope that the feuding sides might begin to work together. But while the Sunni Kurds and Iraqi Shia generally supported the new constitution, it had much less support among Sunni Arabs. Rather than bring peace, the number of sectarian attacks continued to rise after the elections. In February 2006, the bombing of the Shia Golden Mosque in Samarra set Sunni and Shia militias against each other. Iraq seemed poised on the edge of civil war.

The mounting violence led a majority of Americans to conclude they no longer approved of the president's handling of the war. Democrats in Congress demanded that the Bush administration set a timetable for withdrawing U.S. troops, a policy that President Bush described as "cut and run." When Republicans rejected a timetable and supported the president, they turned the congressional elections of 2006 into a referendum on the war.

The Democrats Gain Control of Congress Voters expressed their unhappiness with both the president and the Republican Congress in 2006. The Democrats won a majority in both the House and the Senate for the first time since 1992. House Democrats then elected California Representative **Nancy Pelosi** to be the first female Speaker of the House of Representatives.

When Democrats won control of Congress, President Bush acknowledged that his party had taken a "thumping" in the election. The day after the election, Secretary of Defense Donald Rumsfeld resigned. Rumsfeld had acknowledged that the administration's strategy in Iraq was not working and a change of course was needed. "In my view it is time for a major adjustment," Rumsfeld wrote. "Clearly what U.S. forces are currently doing in Iraq is not working well enough or fast enough."

President Bush chose Robert Gates to replace Rumsfeld and put a new commander—General David Petraeus—in charge of operations in Iraq. The president then announced a new plan to "surge" some 20,000 more troops to Iraq to restore order in Baghdad where most of the violence was concentrated. Led by Nancy Pelosi, and John Murtha—a Vietnam veteran and long-time opponent of the Iraq war—House Democrats passed a resolution opposing the strategy and began searching for ways to force the president to set a deadline for pulling troops out of Iraq. Whether or not the surge could work was unclear, but by the spring of 2007, what was clear was that Americans remained deeply divided over the war in Iraq and that its ultimate outcome remained uncertain.

✔ **Reading Check** **Analyzing** What events in the first two years of Bush's second term contributed to the Republicans losing control of Congress?

Section 4 REVIEW

Vocabulary

1. **Explain** the significance of: Abu Ghraib, Guantanamo Bay, National Security Agency, John G. Roberts, Jr., Samuel Alito, Jr., "earmarks," Nancy Pelosi.

Main Ideas

2. **Identifying** What issues did President Bush support in his reelection campaign? What did Kerry support?

3. **Explaining** What did the Supreme Court declare unlawful with the *Hamdan* v. *Rumsfeld* ruling?

4. **Describing** How did Bush propose to fix Social Security?

Critical Thinking

5. **Big Ideas** Why did Donald Rumsfeld resign as secretary of defense? Who did Bush choose to replace Rumsfeld?

6. **Organizing** Use a graphic organizer like the one below to list the reasons for Republican losses in the 2006 election.

> **Reasons for Republican Losses in 2006**
> I. The Election of 2004
> II. Security vs. Liberty
>   A.
>   B.

7. **Analyzing Visuals** Examine the photo on page 1049. Why do you think so many people voted in the 2004 election? Do you think voter turnout will remain high?

Writing About History

8. **Persuasive Writing** Write a journal entry describing current events that will be read by students 50 years in the future. Be clear and concise with your description of these events.

History ONLINE

Study Central™ To review this section, go to glencoe.com and click on Study Central.

STUDY TO GO — You can study anywhere, anytime by downloading quizzes and flashcards to your PDA from glencoe.com.

Causes of the Attacks of 9/11

- The rise of the oil industry in the Middle East makes many elites wealthy but leaves many people poor and resentful.
- The oil trade with Europe and the United States brings Western ideas and culture into the Middle East; many feel their traditional Muslim values are being undermined, and militant Muslim movements form.
- The founding of Israel in 1948 angers many Arabs, especially Palestinians. European and American support for Israel angers many in the Middle East.
- The Soviets invade Afghanistan in 1979; Muslims from across the Middle East, including Osama bin Laden, go to fight the Soviet troops.
- Osama bin Laden forms al-Qaeda to help drive the Soviets out of Afghanistan and all Westerners out of the Middle East.
- Iraq invades Kuwait leading to the deployment of American troops in Saudi Arabia, angering Muslim militants, including Osama bin Laden.
- The Soviet pullout from Afghanistan leads to a militant group, the Taliban, taking power and offering aid and shelter to bin Laden.
- Al-Qaeda, based in Afghanistan, stages a series of attacks on Americans, culminating in the attack on September 11, 2001.

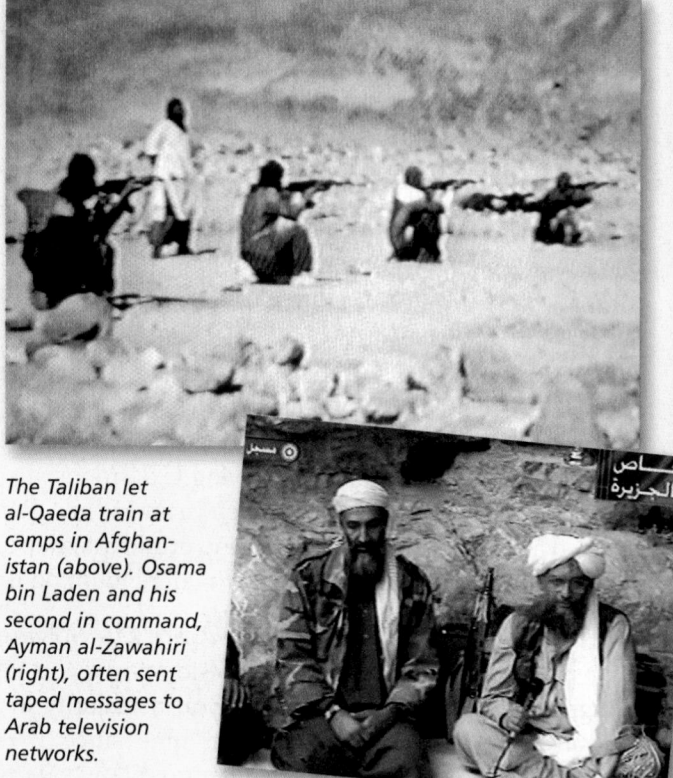

The Taliban let al-Qaeda train at camps in Afghanistan (above). Osama bin Laden and his second in command, Ayman al-Zawahiri (right), often sent taped messages to Arab television networks.

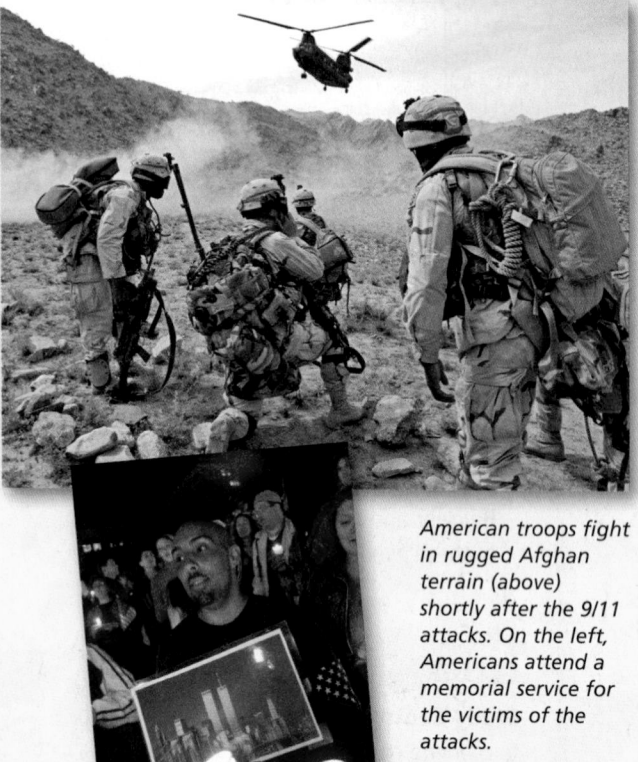

American troops fight in rugged Afghan terrain (above) shortly after the 9/11 attacks. On the left, Americans attend a memorial service for the victims of the attacks.

Effects of the Attacks of 9/11

- Initially, the 9/11 attack unifies Americans and leads to an outpouring of support to the people of New York.
- President Bush declares a global war on terror to put an end to terrorist groups that threaten Americans.
- The United States launches attacks on the Taliban and helps local forces overthrow their regime. NATO troops then enter Afghanistan to serve as peacekeepers.
- Congress passes the Patriot Act giving the FBI additional powers to help prevent another attack in the United States.
- Congress creates the Department of Homeland Security.
- The Bush administration decides that preventing terrorist groups from getting weapons of mass destruction is a high priority.
- The United States, backed by a coalition of allies, invades Iraq to destroy its weapons of mass destruction.
- The invasion of Iraq is controversial; many traditional allies do not support it, and it divides the American people.
- An insurgency begins in Iraq that keeps American troops fighting for several years.

NEW YORK REGENTS EXAM PRACTICE

Part I

Directions (1–11): For each statement or question, write on a separate sheet of paper the number of the word or expression that, of those given, best completes the statement or answers the question.

1 Which the following is under the control of the Department of Homeland Security?

  (1) Central Intelligence Agency (CIA)

  (2) Defense Intelligence Agency (DIA)

  (3) Federal Bureau of Investigation (FBI)

  (4) Federal Emergency Management Agency (FEMA)

2 After Bush took office, Congress passed which of the following educational reforms?

  (1) federal funding to parents to pay for private schools if their public school was performing poorly

  (2) annual standardized testing in reading and math for grades 3–8

  (3) prohibiting federally funded schools from discriminating against girls and young women

  (4) transporting children to schools outside their neighborhood to achieve a greater racial balance

3 After the bombing of American embassies in Kenya and Tanzania, President Clinton

  (1) ordered the invasion of Iraq.

  (2) created the office of Homeland Security.

  (3) ordered the bombing of terrorist camps in Afghanistan.

  (4) signed the Patriot act into law.

4 President Bush targeted Iraq, one of the three countries in the "axis of evil," before the other two countries because

  (1) Iraq was the most vulnerable.

  (2) Iraq was responsible for the September 11 attacks.

  (3) Iraq was believed to pose the most imminent danger to the United States.

  (4) Iraq attacked the United States first.

5 Which country was the only nation bordering Iraq to allow the United States to launch offensives from their territory?

  (1) Saudi Arabia

  (2) Turkey

  (3) Iran

  (4) Kuwait

6 During the 2004 presidential election, George W. Bush's support was strongest in

  (1) the northeast.

  (2) the South and the Great Plains.

  (3) the Midwest and Great Lakes.

  (4) all urban areas.

7 In 2005 the National Security Agency (NSA) expanded its practice of monitoring overseas calls to include domestic calls placed to overseas locations. This resulted in

  (1) overwhelming public support.

  (2) the arrest of many terrorists.

  (3) the NSA directors arrest.

  (4) a federal declaration of this practice's unconstitutionality.

Need Extra Help?							
If You Missed Questions . . .	1	2	3	4	5	6	7
Go to Page . . .	1041	1035	1039	1044	1046	1049	1051

[OVER]

Base your answers to questions 8 and 9 on the map below and on your knowledge of Chapter 31.

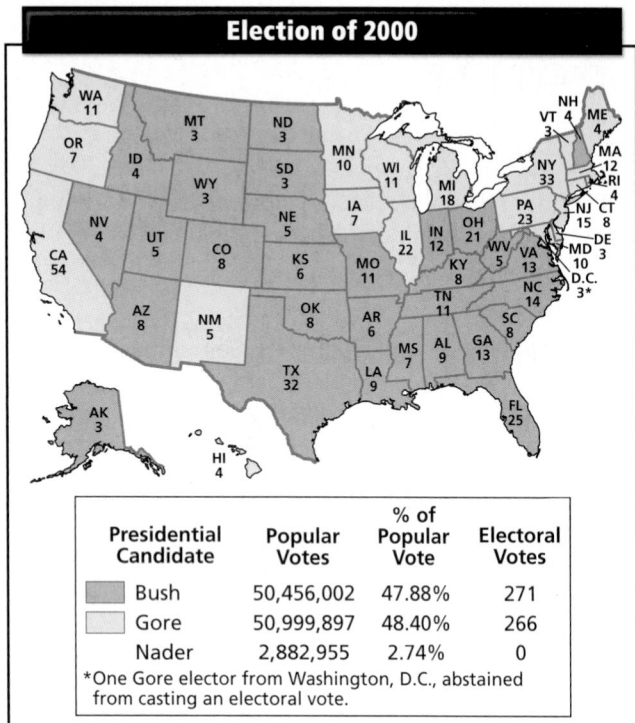

Election of 2000

Presidential Candidate	Popular Votes	% of Popular Vote	Electoral Votes
Bush	50,456,002	47.88%	271
Gore	50,999,897	48.40%	266
Nader	2,882,955	2.74%	0

*One Gore elector from Washington, D.C., abstained from casting an electoral vote.

8   In the election of 2000, George W. Bush won

(1) the popular vote

(2) fewer states than Al Gore

(3) a majority of electoral votes

(4) California and New York

9   Al Gore won fewer than half of the states, but the election was considered close because

(1) many of the states won by Bush has only a few electoral votes

(2) Gore won Texas and Florida, giving him 57 electoral votes

(3) Bush won the popular vote by such a small margin

(4) Gore won the South and Bush won the West, making it equal

Need Extra Help?		
If You Missed Questions . . .	8	9
Go to Page . . .	1033	1033

Part II Thematic Essay Question

Directions: Write a well-organized essay that includes an introduction, several paragraphs addressing the task below, and a conclusion.

Theme: The War in Iraq

The decision to invade Iraq as part of the war on terrorism was controversial. In 2006 the war became a central issue of debate, eventually deciding midterm elections.

Task:

Identify two reasons either in support or against the United State's continued presence in Iraq and for each

• Describe the long-term effects for the United States and the citizens of Iraq

• Evaluate how this opinion might be viewed by the rest of the world

Guidelines:

In your essay, be sure to:

• Develop all aspects of the task

• Support the theme with relevant facts, examples, and details

• Use a logical and clear plan of organization, including an introduction and a conclusion that are beyond a restatement of the theme.

Part III Document-Based Question

This question is based on the accompanying documents. It is designed to test your ability to work with historical documents. Some of the documents have been edited for the purposes of the question. As you analyze the documents, take into account the source of each document and any point of view that may be presented in the document.

Historical Context:

In October 2001, President Bush signed an anti-terrorist bill known as the Patriot Act. Although its intention was to protect the American people, controversy still surrounds some of the aspects of the bill.

Task:

Using information from the documents and your knowledge of United States history, answer the questions that follow each document in Part A. Your answers to the questions will help you write the Part B essay in which you will be asked to

- Discuss the Patriot Act and the reasons why Bush and Congress enacted the law
- Evaluate both the positive and negative aspects of this bill

Part A
Short-Answer Questions

Directions: Analyze the documents and answer the short-answer questions that follow each document on a separate sheet of paper.

Document 1

> If we were to take the position, reflected in provisions in the USA PATRIOT Act, that the government can invade our privacy and gather evidence that can be used against us based on no suspicion whatsoever that we've done anything wrong, but simply because the government wants to gather evidence as part of some generalized, 'anti-terrorism' or 'foreign intelligence' investigation, then we will have rendered that Fourth Amendment principle essentially meaningless.

Source: Congressman Bob Barr (R-GA),
"Problems with the USA PATRIOT Act"

1 Based on the Representative Barr's comments, what does he believe is violated with the Patriot Act?

Document 2

> Zero. That's the number of substantiated USA PATRIOT Act civil liberties violations. Extensive congressional oversight found no violations.
>   Intense public scrutiny has yet to find a single civil liberty abuse. Despite many challenges, no federal court has declared unconstitutional any of the Patriot Act provisions Congress is renewing.

Source: Congressman James Sensenbrenner (R-WI),
"No rights have been violated"

2 How does Representative Sensenbrenner differ from Representative Barr? Explain his position.

Part B
Essay

Directions: Reread the task box at the top left and write a well-organized essay that includes an introduction, several paragraphs, and a conclusion. Use evidence from the documents in your essay. Support your response with relevant facts, examples, and details. Include additional outside information.

Guidelines:

In your essay, be sure to:

- Develop all aspects of the task
- Incorporate information from the documents
- Incorporate relevant outside information
- Support the theme with relevant facts, examples, and details
- Use a logical and clear plan of organization, including an introduction and conclusion that are beyond a restatement of the theme

History ONLINE

For additional test practice, use Self-Check Quizzes—Chapter 31 at glencoe.com.

Need Extra Help?			
If You Missed Questions . . .	1	2	Essay
Go to Page . . .	R19	R19	1040–1041

Appendix

Contents

Skills Handbook

Skills Handbook
Table of Contents

Critical Thinking Skills

Social Studies Skills

Migrant mother and children in California, 1936

Identifying the Main Idea

Why Learn This Skill?

Finding the main idea in a reading passage will help you see the "big picture" by organizing information and determining the most important concepts to remember.

Learning the Skill

Follow these steps to learn how to make a valid generalization. Then answer the questions below.

> *In this nation I see tens of millions of its citizens . . . who at this very moment are denied the greater part of what the very lowest standards of today call the necessities of life. I see millions of families trying to live on incomes so meager that the pall of family disaster hangs over them day by day. . . . see one-third of a nation ill-housed, ill-clad, ill-nourished.*
>
> *It is not in despair that I paint you that picture. I paint it for you in hope—because the Nation, seeing and understanding the injustice in it, proposes to paint it out. We are determined to make every American citizen the subject of his country's interest and concern. . . . The test of our progress is not whether we add more to the abundance of those who have much; it is whether we provide enough for those who have too little.*

—Franklin D. Roosevelt, Second Inaugural Address, January 20, 1937

1. Determine the setting of the passage.

2. Skim the material to identify its general subject. Look at headings and subheadings.

3. Notice any details that support a larger idea or issue.

4. Identify the central issue. Ask: What part of the selection conveys the main idea?

As you read the material, ask yourself: What is the purpose of this passage—why was it written?

Practicing the Skill

1. On what occasion was this speech given?

2. When was this speech given?

3. What was the condition of the people mentioned in this passage?

4. What did Roosevelt think should be done about the situation discussed?

Applying the Skill

Bring to class an article about American history from the Internet or another source. Identify the main idea and explain why it is important.

Skills Handbook

Determining Cause and Effect

Why Learn This Skill?

Determining cause and effect involves considering *why* an event occurred. That helps you analyze how to encourage or prevent the same event in the future. A *cause* is an action or a situation that produces an event. What happens as a result of a cause is an *effect*.

The effect of pesticides on wildlife

Learning the Skill

To identify cause-and-effect relationships, follow these steps:

1. Identify two or more events or developments.

3. Identify the outcomes of events. Remember that some effects have more than one cause, and some causes lead to more than one effect. Also, an effect can become the cause of yet another effect.

> " . . . in 1957, there was a startling wildlife mortality in the wake of a mosquito-control campaign near Duxbury, Mass., followed by a pointless spraying of a DDT/fuel-oil mix over eastern Long Island for eradication of the gypsy moth. Next, an all-out war in the Southern states against the fire ant did such widespread harm to other creatures that its beneficiaries cried for mercy; and after that a great furor arose across the country over the spraying of cranberry plants with aminotriazole, which led to an Agriculture Department ban against all cranberry marketing just in time for Thanksgiving 1959. . . .
>
> Even before publication [of Rachel Carson's indictment of pesticides, Silent Spring,] Carson was violently assailed by threats of lawsuits and derision. . . . A huge counterattack was organized and led by . . . the whole chemical industry. "
>
> —*Time*, March 29, 1999

2. Decide whether one event caused the other. Look for "clue words" such as *because, led to, brought about, so that, after that, produced, as a result of, since, in the wake of, as a result.*

Look for logical relationships between events, such as "She overslept, so she missed her bus."

Practicing the Skill

Categorize the items below as *cause, effect, both,* or *neither.*

1. Rachel Carson published *Silent Spring*, criticizing chemical pesticides.

2. Duxbury's wildlife mortality rate rose significantly in 1957.

3. The gypsy moth is a common insect on Long Island.

4. The Agriculture Department banned cranberry marketing.

5. Southern states used pesticides to eradicate the fire ant.

6. The chemical industry threatened Carson with lawsuits.

Applying the Skill

In a newspaper, read an article describing a current event. Determine at least one cause and one effect of that event, and complete a flowchart like the one below.

| Cause | → | Event | → | Effect |

Making Generalizations

Why Learn This Skill?

Generalizations are conclusions that are usually accurate, based on the facts at hand. Generalizations are useful in studying history because they help you see trends. If you say, "Most Mexican immigrants to the United States in the early twentieth century worked in agriculture," that's a generalization. To support it, you could mention that federal funding of irrigation projects in the Southwest in 1902 gave rise to large farms requiring thousands of workers. Not all Mexican immigrants at that time became farmworkers, but many did.

Women workers install fixtures and assemblies to a tail fuselage section of a B-17 bomber at Douglas Aircraft Company's, Long Beach, California, plant.

Learning the Skill

To learn how to make a valid generalization, follow these steps:

1. Identify the subject matter.

2. Collect factual information and examples relevant to the topic.

The war years had a tremendous impact on women. . . . it was the first time I had a chance to get out of the kitchen and work in industry and make a few bucks. This was something I had never dreamed would happen. In Sapulpa [Oklahoma] all that women had to look forward to was keeping a house and raising families. The war years offered new possibilities. You came out to California, put on your pants and took your lunch pail to a man's job. In Oklahoma a woman's place was in the home, and men went to work and provided. This was the beginning of women's feeling that they could do something more.

—Sybil Lewis,
quoted in *The Homefront: America During World War II*

3. Identify similarities among these facts.

Use these similarities to form some general ideas about the subject.

Practicing the Skill

After reading the excerpt above, determine whether each generalization that follows is valid or invalid. Explain your answers.

1. During World War II, women did not want to work outside the home.

2. Women have careers only so that they can afford luxuries.

3. During the war, women had more choices in California than in Oklahoma.

Applying the Skill

Read three editorials in a newspaper and make a generalization about each.

Distinguishing Fact from Opinion

Why Learn This Skill?

To make reasonable judgments about what others say or write, it is important to distinguish facts from opinions. Facts can be proved by evidence such as records, documents, or historical sources. Opinions are based on people's differing values and beliefs.

Richard M. Nixon

Learning the Skill

To learn how to separate facts from opinions, follow these steps:

1. Identify the facts. Ask: Which statements can be proved? Where would I find information to verify this statement? If the information is a statistic, it may sound impressive, but you won't know if it's accurate unless you check the source.

> *In speaking of the consequences of a precipitate withdrawal [from Vietnam], I mentioned that our allies would lose confidence in America. Far more dangerous, we would lose confidence in ourselves. . . .*
>
> *In San Francisco a few weeks ago, I saw demonstrators carrying signs reading: "Lose in Vietnam, bring the boys home."*
>
> *Well, one of the strengths of our free society is that any American has a right to reach that conclusion and to advocate that point of view. But as President of the United States, I would be untrue to my oath of office if I allowed the policy of this Nation to be dictated by the minority who hold that point of view and who try to impose it on the Nation by mounting demonstrations in the street.*
>
> *. . . If a vocal minority, however fervent its cause, prevails over reason and the will of the majority, this Nation has no future as a free society.*
>
> —Richard M. Nixon speech, November 3, 1969

2. Identify opinions by looking for statements of feelings or beliefs. Opinions sometimes contain words like *should, would, could, best, greatest, all, every,* or *always.*

Practicing the Skill

The excerpt above is from a televised speech given by President Richard M. Nixon in 1969, when a Gallup poll showed that 58 percent of Americans believed the Vietnam War was a mistake. Reread the excerpt and answer the questions that follow.

1. Which statements in the passage are factual?

2. Which statements are opinions? Explain.

3. What was the speaker's purpose?

Applying the Skill

Watch a television interview. Then list three facts and three opinions that you hear.

Formulating Questions

Why Learn This Skill?

Asking questions helps you to understand and remember what you read. Learning increases when you ask yourself what is important about the topic and what you would like to know about the people, places, and events.

Jackie Robinson

Learning the Skill

Follow these steps to formulate questions:

1. Think of questions you would like to have answered.

> In 1947 life in America . . . was segregation. . . . But Jackie Robinson, God bless him, was bigger than all of that.
>
> . . . He had to be bigger than the Brooklyn teammates who got up a petition to keep him off the ball club, bigger than the pitchers who threw at him or the base runners who dug their spikes into his shin, bigger than the bench jockeys who hollered for him to . . . shine their shoes, bigger than the so-called fans who . . . wrote him death threats.
>
> . . . Somehow, though, Jackie had the strength to . . . sacrifice his pride for his people's. It was an incredible act of selflessness that brought the races closer together than ever before and shaped the dreams of an entire generation.
>
> —Henry "Hank" Aaron, holder of major-league career home-run record, *Time*, June 14, 1999

2. Ask *who, what, when, where, why,* and *how* about the main ideas, people, places, and events.

3. Reread the section to be sure all your questions have been answered.

Practicing the Skill

The excerpt above is about the first African American major-league baseball player. After reading it, use a chart like the one below and find the answers in the excerpt.

	Question	Answer
Who?		
What?		
Where?		
When?		
Why?		
How?		

Applying the Skill

Select any section of this textbook to read or reread. Make a question chart to help you ask and answer five or more questions about the section as you read.

Analyzing Information

Why Learn This Skill?

The ability to analyze information is important in deciding what you think about a subject. For example, you need to analyze the benefits of social services versus the benefits of small government to decide where you stand on the issue of Social Security.

Gloria Steinem (right) with Adelaide Abankwah, a Ghanian asylum-seeker, in 1999

Learning the Skill

To analyze information, use the following steps:

1. Identify the topic being discussed.

> *Having spent most of my adult life in social justice movements—from living in post-Gandhian India to working in the civil rights, farm worker and peace movements here, and most of all, in the feminist movement—I've seen constant proof that revolutions are like houses: They can't be built from the top down. Leaders can issue blueprints, which we then adapt to our needs or quietly sabotage. They can prevent us from following our own plan, divide the work force against itself and otherwise slow or stop progress. But what they can't do is create organic and lasting change from the top. Attempts to do so, even in the most authoritarian of systems, eventually end in reversion to old ways, as we see in the countries where Communism and artificial national boundaries were once imposed by Moscow.*

—Gloria Steinem, from *The Nation*, July 20–27, 1992

2. Examine how the information is organized. What are the main points?

3. Summarize the information in your own words, and then make a statement of your own based on your understanding of the topic and on what you already know.

Practicing the Skill

After reading the excerpt above, answer the following questions:

1. What topic is being discussed?

2. What are the writer's main points?

3. Summarize the information in this excerpt, and then provide your analysis, based on this information and what you already know about the subject.

Applying the Skill

Select an issue that is currently in the news, such as Social Security, oil prices, global warming, or taxation. Read an article or watch a news segment about the issue. Analyze the information and make a brief statement of your own about the topic. Explain your thinking.

Evaluating Information

Why Learn This Skill?

We live in an information age. Because the amount of information available can be overwhelming, it is sometimes difficult to tell which information is accurate and useful. To do this, you have to evaluate what you read and hear.

Soaring gas prices in the early 2000s frustrated consumers.

Learning the Skill

To figure out how reliable information is, ask yourself the following questions as you read:

" *The single biggest factor in . . . the increase in the inflation rate last year was from one cause: the skyrocketing prices of OPEC oil. We must take whatever actions are necessary to reduce our dependence on foreign oil—and at the same time reduce inflation.* "
—former president Jimmy Carter, January 23, 1980

" *Oil prices are so high, becuz big oil companys are tryng to goug us. Greedy oil executives, are driven up prices to get richer.* "
—on an individual's Internet "blog"

" *It's certainly clear that high oil prices aren't dulling demand for energy products. According to the Energy Dept.'s Energy Information Administration (EIA), U.S. demand for gasoline in June was 9.5 million barrels per day, a record.* "
—*BusinessWeek,* July 7, 2006

1. Is the author or speaker identified? Is he or she an authority on the subject?

2. Is there bias? Does the source unfairly present just one point of view, ignoring any arguments against it?

3. Is the information printed in a credible, reliable publication?

4. Is the information backed up by facts and other sources? Does it seem to be accurate?

5. Is it well written and well edited? Writing filled with errors in spelling, grammar, and punctuation is likely to be careless in other ways, too.

Also notice whether the information is up-to-date.

Practicing the Skill

After reading the statements above, rank them in order of most reliable to least reliable. Explain why you ranked them as you did.

Applying the Skill

Find an advertisement that contains text and bring it to class. In a brief oral presentation, tell the class whether the information in the advertisement is reliable or unreliable, and why.

Making Inferences

Why Learn This Skill?

To *infer* means to evaluate information and arrive at a conclusion. When you make inferences, you "read between the lines," or use clues to figure something out that is not stated directly in the text.

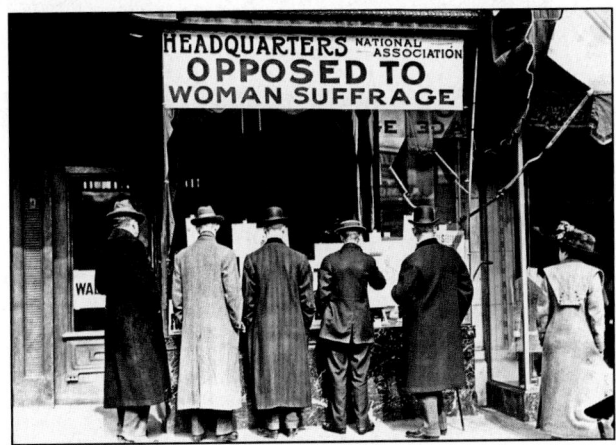

Men read posters at an office of the National Association Opposed to Woman Suffrage.

Learning the Skill

Follow these steps to make inferences:

1. Read carefully for facts and ideas, and list them.

> *Because the suffrage is not a question of right or of justice, but of policy and expediency. . . .*
>
> *. . . Because it means simply doubling the vote, and especially the undesirable and corrupt vote of our large cities.*
>
> *. . . Because the great advance of women in the last century—moral, intellectual and economic—has been made without the vote; which goes to prove that it is not needed for their further advancement along the same lines.*
>
> *. . . Because our present duties fill up the whole measure of our time and ability, and are such as none but us can perform. Our appreciation of their importance requires us to protest against all efforts to infringe upon our rights by imposing upon us those obligations which can not be . . . performed by us without the sacrifice of the highest interests of our families and our society.*
>
> —from Northern California Association Opposed to Woman Suffrage, 1912

2. Summarize the information.

3. Consider what you may already know about the topic.

4. Use your knowledge and insight to develop logical conclusions.

Practicing the Skill

After reading the statement above, answer the following questions:

1. What points do the authors make?

2. Which points does your experience contradict?

3. What inferences might you draw about the women who wrote the document?

Applying the Skill

Read an editorial printed in today's newspaper. What can you infer about the importance of the topic being addressed? Can you tell how the writer feels about the topic? Explain your answer.

Comparing and Contrasting

Why Learn This Skill?

When you make comparisons, you determine similarities among ideas, objects, or events. When you contrast, you are noting differences between ideas, objects, or events. Comparing and contrasting are important skills because they help you choose among several possible alternatives.

Learning the Skill

To compare or contrast items, follow these steps:

1. Select the items to compare or contrast.

2. To compare, determine a common area or areas in which comparisons can be drawn, such as topic, style, or point of view. Look for similarities within these areas.

3. To contrast, look for differences that set the items apart from each other.

Practicing the Skill

After studying the paintings above, answer these questions:

1. How are the paintings similar?

2. How are they different?

3. What do the answers to questions 1 and 2 tell you about the two artists' attitudes toward their subject?

Applying the Skill

Survey 10 of your classmates about an issue in the news, and summarize their responses. Then write a paragraph or two comparing and contrasting their opinions.

Detecting Bias

Why Learn This Skill?

Most people have a point of view, or bias. This bias influences the way they interpret and write about events and issues.

A politician running for reelection, for example, may claim the economy is strong because 20,000 new jobs were created last month. His or her opponent may say the economy is weak because 40,000 people also lost jobs last month. Recognizing bias helps you judge the accuracy of what you hear or read.

Southerners seize abolitionist literature from a local post office in South Carolina in the 1840s.

Learning the Skill

To recognize bias, follow these steps:

1. Consider the author's identity, location, and motivation. Does the writer or a group he or she represents benefit from an outcome supported in the article?

2. Identify statements of fact, if any.

"*The great conservative institution of slavery, so excellent in itself, and so necessary to civil liberty and the dignity of the white race, is one of the grand objects of our struggle. It should never be lost sight of, nor under any pressure should we ever take any step incompatible with the relation of master and slave. . . . Our theory is, that he is better off as a slave; and even if he were not, we could not safely have an emancipated class of them amongst us. Much less can we put arms in his hands. . . . Slavery afterwards would become impossible.*"

—Editorial from the Washington, Arkansas, *Telegraph,* January 13, 1865

3. Identify any expressions of opinion or emotion. Look for words with positive or negative overtones for clues about the author's feelings on a topic.

4. Determine the author's point of view.

5. Notice how the author's point of view is reflected in the work.

Practicing the Skill

Read the passage above and then answer the following questions:

1. What is the purpose of this passage?

2. What statements of fact and/or opinion are presented?

3. What evidence of bias do you find?

4. How does the author attempt to convince the audience?

Applying the Skill

Find an editorial in the newspaper that deals with a topic of interest to you. Apply the steps for recognizing bias to the editorial. Write a paragraph summarizing your findings.

Synthesizing Information

Why Learn This Skill?

Synthesizing information involves combining information from two or more sources. Each source may shed new light on other information.

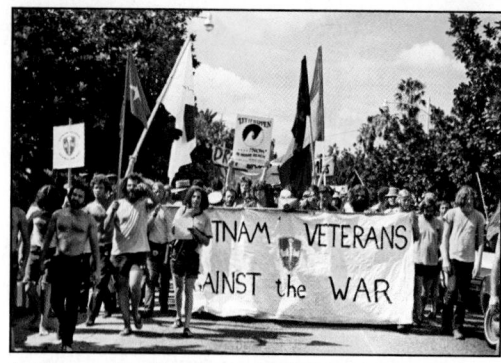

Antiwar rally, Miami Beach, Florida, 1972

Learning the Skill

Follow these steps to learn how to synthesize information:

1. Analyze each source separately to understand its meaning.

2. Determine what information and whose perspective each source adds to the subject.

Source A *We should declare war on North Vietnam. . . . It's silly talking about how many years we will have to spend in the jungles of Vietnam when we could pave the whole country and put parking stripes on it and still be home for Christmas.*

—future president Ronald Reagan, 1965

Source B *Vietnam presumably taught us that the United States could not serve as the world's policeman; it should also have taught us the dangers of trying to be the world's midwife to democracy when the birth is scheduled to take place under conditions of guerrilla war.*

—Jeane Kirkpatrick, future UN ambassador and foreign policy adviser to Ronald Reagan, 1979

Source C *People say we could have won the [Vietnam] war—we know we could not. People say the anti-war movement harassed and betrayed the soldiers . . . the people who supported the war, the folks who favored intervention, the people who sent us crusading against communism—they betrayed us, their own sons and daughters. Anti-war veterans are the witnesses against them . . . we saw the system was not working, we knew the war had to stop.*

—Ben Chitty, member Vietnam Veterans Against the War, April, 2000

3. Identify points of agreement and disagreement among the sources. Ask: Can Source B or C give me new ways of thinking about Source A?

4. Determine how the sources relate to each other.

Practicing the Skill

After reading the passages above, answer the questions that follow.

1. What is the main subject of each source?

2. Does Source B support or contradict Source A? Does Source C support or contradict source A? Explain.

3. Summarize what you learned from the three sources.

4. Which source do you consider the most reliable? Explain why.

Applying the Skill

Find two sources of information on any period of history that interests you. What are the main ideas in the sources? How does each source add to your understanding of the topic?

Drawing Conclusions

Why Learn This Skill?

A conclusion is a logical understanding that you reach based on details or facts that you read or hear. When you draw conclusions, you use stated information to formulate ideas that are unstated.

Victorian-era house for sale

Learning the Skill

Follow these steps to draw conclusions:

1. Read the text and labels carefully, looking for facts and ideas.

2. Summarize the information. List trends or important facts.

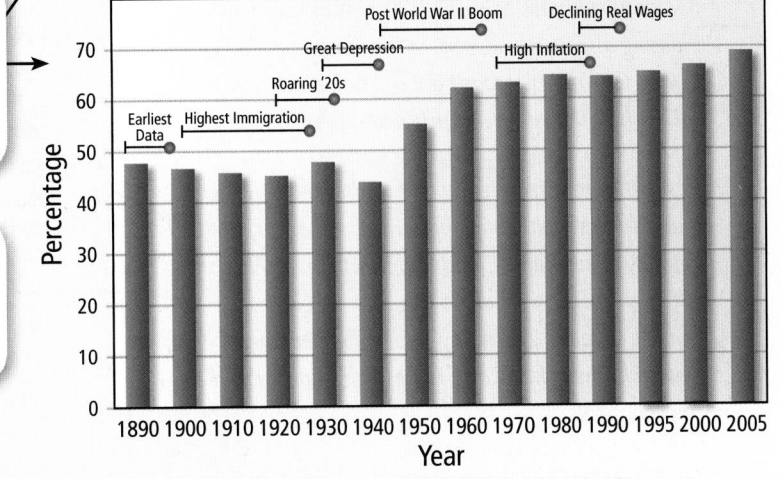

Homeownership in the U.S., 1890–2005

Post World War II Boom
Declining Real Wages
Great Depression
High Inflation
Roaring '20s
Earliest Data
Highest Immigration

Percentage

0 10 20 30 40 50 60 70

1890 1900 1910 1920 1930 1940 1950 1960 1970 1980 1990 1995 2000 2005

Year

Source: U.S. Bureau of the Census; U.S. Department of Commerce

3. Apply related information that you may already have.

4. Use your knowledge and insight to develop some logical conclusions.

Practicing the Skill

The bar graph above shows the percentage of Americans who owned their own homes during various time periods. Study the graph and answer the following questions:

1. When was the home ownership rate the lowest? Why do you think this was so?

2. During what 20-year period did home ownership rates increase the most? Why do you think this happened?

3. What conclusions can you draw about trends in home ownership?

Applying the Skill

Read one of the People in History profiles in this book. Using the information in the profile, what conclusions can you draw about the life of the person described?

Predicting Consequences

Lois Gibbs

Why Learn This Skill?

Predicting most future events is difficult, but the more information you have, the more accurate your predictions will be. Making good predictions will help you to make better decisions based on their likely outcomes. Using these skills can also help you to understand the outcomes of historical events.

Learning the Skill

To help you make predictions, follow these steps:

1. Gather information about the topic.

> *In the mid-1950s, the Niagara Falls board of education built an elementary school adjacent to a site where Hooker Chemical and Plastics Corporation had dumped more than 22,000 tons of toxic waste. Housing also was built next to the landfill, called Love Canal. Chemicals leached out of the landfill and, by 1976, had shown up in yards and basements.*
>
> *Residents were frequently sick and eventually were found to have extremely high rates of cancer, birth defects, miscarriages, and stillborns. In 1978 Lois Gibbs and other residents began a 3-year battle against Hooker and many levels of government, which claimed the health issues were not related to the chemicals.*
>
> *By 1980, President Jimmy Carter declared Love Canal a federal emergency and more than 1,000 families were relocated and paid for their homes. The tragedy led to "Superfund" legislation that collects taxes from gas and chemical companies, to be used to clean up similar sites.*

2. Use your experience and your knowledge of history and human behavior to predict what consequences could result.

3. Analyze each consequence by asking yourself: How likely is it that this will happen?

Practicing the Skill

1. Do you think the problem described in the passage is likely to reoccur elsewhere?

2. On what do you base your prediction?

3. What are the possible benefits and drawbacks of the "Superfund" legislation described in the passage?

Applying the Skill

Analyze three newspaper articles about an event affecting your community or the nation. Make an educated prediction about what will happen, and explain your reasoning. Then write a letter to the editor, summarizing your prediction. You may want to check back later to see if your prediction came true.

Reading a Special-Purpose Map

Why Learn This Skill?

Special-purpose maps show more than the location of places. They are useful because they show trends or movements of people or things in a concise, visual way.

Learning the Skill

To read a special-purpose map, follow these steps:

1. Read the title to see what topic is illustrated. If the time period being covered is part of the title, notice that.

2. Read the legend and any other text.

3. Notice the movement shown on the map, if any, including the direction of any arrows, where paths lead, or the concentration of several things in certain places.

4. Ask yourself: What have I learned from this map? What can I conclude from this information?

NATIONAL GEOGRAPHIC **Migration in the United States, 1940–1950**

Seattle
Portland
73,000
338,000
NORTH CENTRAL
319,000
NORTHEAST
385,000
1,188,000
WEST
Detroit 297,000
Chicago
New York City
San Francisco
Denver
614,000
1,113,000
449,000
427,000
Washington, D.C.
Los Angeles
San Diego
1,241,000
239,000
Memphis
SOUTH
Fort Worth Dallas
Baton Rouge
Mobile
Houston

Urban Population Increase, 1940–1947
- ☐ 400,000 and over
- ☐ 100,000–199,999
- ☐ 200,000–399,999
- ☐ 50,000–99,999
- ⬅ Population migration between regions

Practicing the Skill

Answer the following questions about the map above:

1. What period in history does the map cover?

2. Was the U.S. population fairly mobile or stationary during this time?

3. Name two cities that gained 400,000 or more residents.

4. From what part of the country did most immigrants to the West come?

Study the map on page 399. Then answer these questions:

Applying the Skill

Study the map on page 399. Then answer these questions:

1. Name three states through which Chief Joseph traveled in 1877.

2. What part of the country had the largest number of reservations at this time?

3. What does the map tell you about the compromises Native Americans made to the settlers?

Interpreting Graphs

Bar graphs are often used to compare quantities. By presenting similar categories of information visually, often on a grid, they make it easy to see the relationships among the categories.

Why Learn This Skill?

Being able to read bar graphs makes it easy to understand and analyze data quickly.

Learning the Skill

Follow these steps to learn how to understand and use bar graphs. Then answer the questions below.

1. Read the title to see what topic is being illustrated. Notice whether the period of time covered or other information is included within or just below the title.

2. Read the labels to see what categories are being compared, and what measure is being used; for example, dollars, thousands of people, bushels of grain, etc.

3. Notice the numbers that correlate to the ends of the bars.

4. Compare the lengths of the bars and draw a conclusion about the relationships being shown.

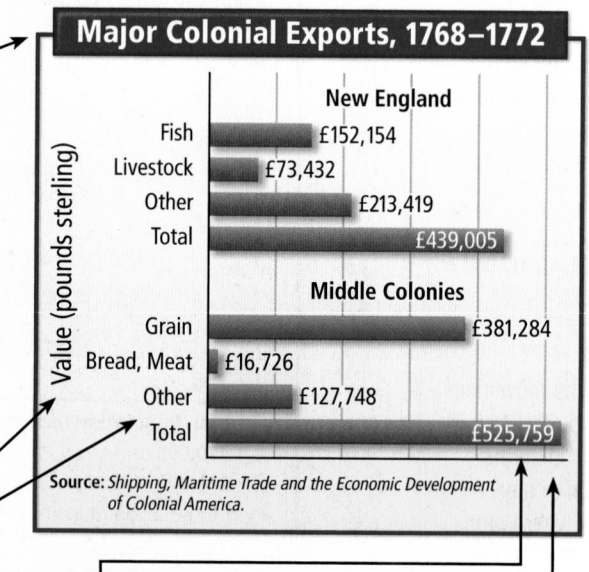

Major Colonial Exports, 1768–1772

New England
- Fish £152,154
- Livestock £73,432
- Other £213,419
- Total £439,005

Middle Colonies
- Grain £381,284
- Bread, Meat £16,726
- Other £127,748
- Total £525,759

Value (pounds sterling)

Source: *Shipping, Maritime Trade and the Economic Development of Colonial America.*

Practicing the Skill

1. What is the topic of this bar graph?

2. In what currency does the graph measure the products?

3. Which type of exports were the least valuable?

4. If you were going into the export business in 1770, which product would you want to export? Why?

Applying the Skill

Ask five students what their favorite food is. Then create a bar graph showing which foods are the most popular.

Sequencing Events

Why Learn This Skill?

Sequencing involves placing facts in the order in which they occurred. Sequencing helps you deal with large quantities of information in an understandable way. In studying history, sequencing can help you understand cause-and-effect relationships among events. This in turn helps analysts to predict outcomes of various events or policies.

John Wilkes Booth escaping Ford's Theatre after shooting President Lincoln

Learning the Skill

To sequence events, follow these steps:

1. Look for dates or clue words: *in 1920, later that year, first, then,* and so on.

2. Arrange facts in the order in which they occurred. Events are not always presented in sequential order. Ask: Would this logically have happened next?

Consider using an organizational tool such as a time line, which makes it easy to see the chronology as well as any cause-and-effect relationships between events.

> This evening [April 14] at about 9:30 P.M., at Ford's Theatre, the President, while sitting in the private box with Mrs. Lincoln . . . was shot by an assassin, who suddenly entered the box and approached behind the President.
>
> The assassin then leaped upon the stage brandishing a large dagger or knife, and made his escape in the rear of the theatre.
>
> . . . It is not probable that the President will live through the night.
>
> . . . Gen. Grant and wife were advertised to be at the theatre this evening, but he started to Burlington at six o'clock this evening.
>
> At a Cabinet meeting, at which Gen. Grant was present, the subject of the state of the country and the prospect of a speedy peace was discussed. The President was very cheerful and hopeful, and spoke very kindly of Gen. Lee and others of the confederacy.

–War Department statement of April 14, 1865, printed in *New York Times*, April 15

Practicing the Skill

Read the passage above and answer the questions that follow.

1. What dates or clue words in this passage help you determine the sequence of the events?

2. Complete a time line such as the one at right to show the sequence of events described in the selection.

Applying the Skill

Find a newspaper or magazine article about a recent event. Sequence the information presented in the article in a time line or chart.

First Event   Final Event

Interpreting Political Cartoons

Why Learn This Skill?

Political cartoons are drawings that express an opinion about public figures, political issues, or economic or social conditions. They appear in newspapers, magazines, books, and on the Internet. They are intended to convince readers of the artist's or the publication's opinion in an amusing way. Knowing how to interpret a political cartoon is useful because it helps you put issues and candidates in perspective.

Learning the Skill

To interpret a political cartoon, follow these steps:

1. Read the title, caption, conversation balloons, and other text to identify the subject of the cartoon.

2. Identify the characters, people, or symbols shown.

3. Ask yourself: What action is occurring? Who is taking the action?

4. Determine the cartoonist's purpose: is it to persuade, criticize, or just make people think? What idea is the cartoonist trying to get across?

5. Ask yourself whether the publication or the cartoonist has a bias that is being expressed in the cartoon.

Practicing the Skill

Study the cartoon. Then use the cartoon and your knowledge of history to answer the questions that follow.

1. What is the topic of the cartoon?

2. Who are the participants, and what are they doing?

3. What point do you think the cartoonist is trying to make? Is the cartoon relevant to any of today's political issues?

Applying the Skill

Bring a newspaper or magazine to class. With a partner, analyze the message and detect any bias in the cartoons you find.

Analyzing Primary Sources

Why Learn This Skill?

To determine what happened in the past, historians do some detective work. They comb through bits of written and illustrated evidence from the past to reconstruct events. These bits of evidence are called "primary sources." They include letters, diaries, photographs, newspaper articles, ads, and legal documents.

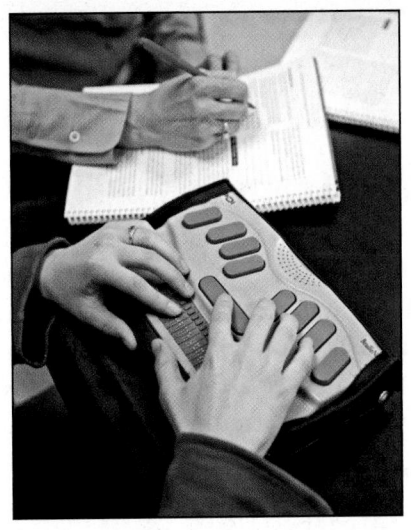

A blind student using a device to take notes in Braille

Learning the Skill

Primary sources yield several important types of information. They often provide details of events or personal perspectives. But remember: any source reflects only one perspective. Before drawing any conclusions, you should examine as many perspectives as possible. To analyze primary sources, follow these steps:

1. Identify the author, the publication, or the document.

2. Determine when and where the document was written or illustrated.

> *No person in the United States shall, on the ground of blindness or severely impaired vision, be denied admission in any course of study by a recipient of Federal financial assistance for any education program or activity; but nothing herein shall be construed to require any such institution to provide any special services to such person because of his blindness or visual impairment.*
>
> —United States Code, Title IX, Education Amendments of 1972

3. Read the document or study the illustration for its content. Try to answer the five "W" questions: Whom is it about? What is it about? When did it happen? Where did it happen? Why did it happen?

Practicing the Skill

The primary source above is a small part of a United States legal document. Read the source and then answer these questions:

1. When was the document written?

2. Who is affected by this document?

3. What is the purpose of this document?

4. Why do you think this document was written?

Applying the Skill

Find a primary source from your past, such as a photo, a report card, an old newspaper clipping, or your first baseball card. Bring the source to class and explain what it shows about that time in your life.

Analyzing Secondary Sources

Why Learn This Skill?

This textbook, like many other history books, is a secondary source. It was written by using primary sources to explain the topics covered. The value of a secondary source depends on how well the author has used those primary sources. Learning to analyze secondary sources will help you figure out whether they are presenting topics completely and accurately.

Painting of Mark Twain by John White

Learning the Skill

Read the passage to the right, which discusses the controversy over the United States's occupation of the Philippines after the Spanish-American War. To analyze secondary sources, ask yourself these questions:

1. Are there references to primary sources in the text? Who are the sources?

2. What insights or biases might these people have?

3. Does the author use the sources effectively to support his or her points?

4. Does the author consider different kinds of sources? Do they represent varying viewpoints?

> *... [The anti-imperialists] denounced the extension of American rule by force in the Philippines, not because of what it might do to the Filipinos, but because of what they were convinced it was bound to do to American democratic ideals. They saw in the American seizure and retention of the Islands 'the infamy of the doctrine that a people may be governed without their consent.'...*
>
> *... The expansionists' reply ... was the twin slogan: duty and destiny.... In the words of the archexpansionist Theodore Roosevelt: 'Peace cannot be had until the civilized nations have expanded in some shape over the barbarous nations.'*
>
> *... Mark Twain was one literary figure who was won over ... 'I left these shores at Vancouver,' he wrote, 'a red-hot imperialist. I wanted the American eagle to go screaming into the Pacific.... Why not spread its wings over the Philippines, I asked myself?...' But ... in 1900 he wrote to Joseph Twichell: 'Apparently we are not proposing to set the Filipinos free and give their islands to them.... If these things are so, the war out there has no interest for me.'*
>
> —Harold A. Larrabee, in *Historical Viewpoints*

Practicing the Skill

1. What primary sources does the author use?

2. Does the author cite where the quotations he used first appeared?

3. How reliable do you think these sources are?

4. Which source do you agree with?

Applying the Skill

In a newspaper or online, read an in-depth article about a topic that interests you. Then list the primary sources the article uses and analyze how reliable you think they are.

Foldables

FOLDABLES **Dinah Zike's Foldables** are three-dimensional, interactive graphic organizers used to help organize and retain information. Every chapter in your text uses a Foldable to help you identify and learn about the Big Ideas discussed in each section. The following pages provide complete folding instructions for the 14 different Foldables used throughout your Student Edition text.

Table of Contents

Basic Foldable Shapes

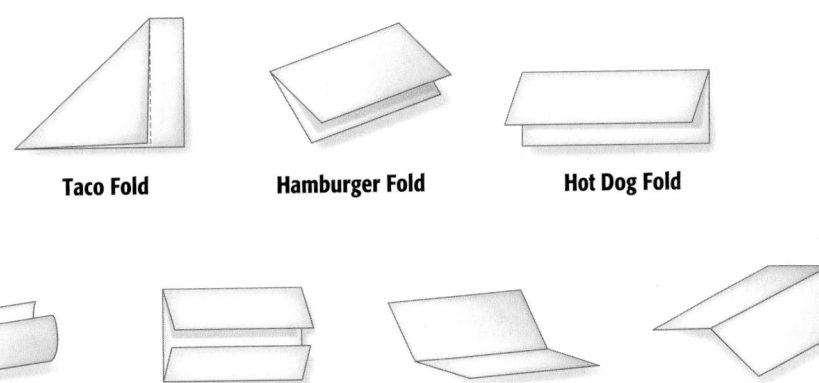

Taco Fold   Hamburger Fold   Hot Dog Fold

Burrito Fold   Shutter Fold   Valley Fold   Mountain Fold

Accordion Book

NOTE: *Steps 1 and 2 should be done only if paper is too large to begin with.*

1. Fold the selected paper into *hamburgers*.

2. Cut the paper in half along the fold lines.

3. Fold each section of paper into *hamburgers*, but fold one side one half inch shorter than the other side. This will form a tab that is one half inch long.

4. Fold this tab forward over the shorter side, and then fold it back away from the shorter piece of paper; in other words, fold it the opposite way.

5. To form an *accordion,* glue a straight edge of one section into the *valley* of another section.

NOTE: *Stand the sections on end to form an accordion to help students visualize how to glue them together. (See illustration.)*

Always place the extra tab at the back of the book so you can add more pages later.

Use this book for time lines, student projects that grow, sequencing events or data, and biographies.

Concept-Map Book

1. Fold a sheet of paper along the long or short axis, leaving a two-inch tab uncovered along the top.

2. Fold in half or in thirds.

3. Unfold and cut along the inside fold line(s) to create two or three flaps.

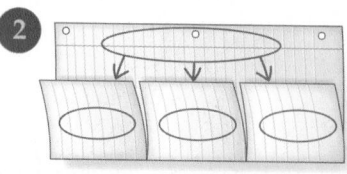

Folded Table or Chart

1. Fold the number of vertical columns needed to make the table or chart.
2. Fold the horizontal rows needed to make the table or chart.
3. Label the rows and columns.

Remember: Tables are organized along vertical and horizontal axes, while charts are organized along one axis, either horizontal or vertical.

Table

Chart

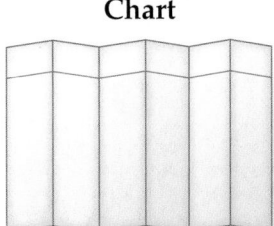

Four-Tab Book

1. Fold a sheet of paper (8½" × 11") in half like a *hot dog.*
2. Fold this long rectangle in half like a *hamburger.*
3. Fold both ends back to touch the *mountain top* or fold it like an *accordion.*
4. On the side with two *valleys* and one *mountain top,* make vertical cuts through one thickness of paper, forming four tabs.

Use this book for data occurring in fours.

Foldables

Four-Door Book

1. Make a *shutter fold* using 11" × 17" or 12" × 18" paper.
2. Fold the *shutter fold* in half like a *hamburger*. Crease well.
3. Open the project and cut along the two inside *valley* folds.
4. These cuts will form four doors on the inside of the project.

Use this fold for data occurring in fours. When folded in half like a *hamburger,* a finished *four-door book* can be glued inside a large (11" × 17") *shutter fold* as part of a larger project.

Half-Book

Fold a sheet of paper (8½" × 11") in half.
1. This book can be folded vertically like a *hot dog* or . . .
2. . . . it can be folded horizontally like a *hamburger.*

Use this book for descriptive, expository, persuasive, or narrative writing, as well as for graphs, diagrams, or charts.

Layered-Look Book

1. Stack two sheets of paper (8½" × 11") so that the back sheet is one inch higher than the front sheet.

2. Bring the bottom of both sheets upward and align the edges so that all of the layers or tabs are the same distance apart.

3. When all tabs are an equal distance apart, fold the papers and crease well.

4. Open the papers and glue them together along the *valley*, or inner center fold, or staple them along the *mountain*.

Foldables

Pocket Book

1. Fold a sheet of paper (8½" × 11") in half like a *hamburger*.

2. Open the folded paper and fold one of the long sides up two inches to form a pocket. Refold along the *hamburger* fold so that the newly formed pockets are on the inside.

3. Glue the outer edges of the two-inch fold with a small amount of glue.

4. **Optional:** Glue a cover around the *pocket book.*

   Variation: Make a multi-paged booklet by gluing several pockets side-by-side. Glue a cover around the multi-paged *pocket book.*

Use 3" × 5" index cards inside the pockets. Store student-made books, such as two-tab books and folded books in the pockets.

Foldables

Sentence Strips

1. Take two sheets of paper (8½" × 11") and fold into *hamburgers*. Cut along the fold lines making four half sheets. *(Use as many half sheets as necessary for additional pages to your book.)*
2. Fold each sheet in half like a *hot dog*.
3. Place the folds side-by-side and staple them together on the left side.
4. One inch from the stapled edge, cut the front page of each folded section up to the *mountain top*. These cuts form flaps that can be raised and lowered.

To make a half-cover, use a sheet of construction paper one inch longer than the book. Glue the back of the last sheet to the construction paper strip leaving one inch, on the left side, to fold over and cover the original staples. Staple this half-cover in place.

Shutter Fold

1. Begin as if you were going to make a *hamburger* but instead of creasing the paper, pinch it to show the midpoint.
2. Fold the outer edges of the paper to meet at the pinch, or mid-point, forming a *shutter fold*.

Use this book for data occurring in twos. Or, make this fold using 11" × 17" paper and smaller books—such as the half-book, journal, and two-tab book—that can be glued inside to create a large project full of student work.

Three-Tab Book

1. Fold a sheet of paper like a *hot dog*.
2. With the paper horizontal, and the fold of the *hot dog* up, fold the right side toward the center, trying to cover one half of the paper.
   NOTE: *If you fold the right edge over first, the final graphic organizer will open and close like a book.*
3. Fold the left side over the right side to make a book with three folds.
4. Open the folded book. Place your hands between the two thicknesses of paper and cut up the two *valleys* on one side only. This will form three tabs.

Use this book for data occurring in threes, and for two-part Venn diagrams.

Variation A:
   Draw overlapping circles on the three tabs to make a Venn diagram.

Variation B:
   Cut each of the three tabs in half to make a six-tab book.

Trifold Book

1. Fold a sheet of paper (8½" × 11") into thirds.
2. Use this book as is, or cut into shapes. If the trifold is cut, leave plenty of fold on both sides of the designed shape, so the book will open and close in three sections.

Use this book to make charts with three columns or rows, large Venn diagrams, or reports on data occurring in threes.

Two-Tab Book

1. Take a *folded book* and cut up the *valley* of the inside fold toward the *mountain top.* This cut forms two large tabs that can be used front and back for writing and illustrations.

2. The book can be expanded by making several of these folds and gluing them side-by-side.

Use this book with data occurring in twos. For example, use it for comparing and contrasting, determining cause and effect, finding similarities and differences, and more.

Vocabulary Book

1. Fold a sheet of notebook paper in half like a *hot dog.*

2. On one side, cut every third line. This results in ten tabs on wide-ruled notebook paper and twelve tabs on college-ruled.

3. Label the tabs.

Presents of the United States

In this resource you will find portraits of the individuals who served as presidents of the United States, along with their occupations, political party affiliations, and other interesting facts.

**The Republican Party during this period developed into today's Democratic Party. Today's Republican Party originated in 1854.

1 George Washington

Presidential term: 1789–1797
Lived: 1732–1799
Born in: Virginia
Elected from: Virginia
Occupations: Soldier, Planter
Party: None
Vice President: John Adams

2 John Adams

Presidential term: 1797–1801
Lived: 1735–1826
Born in: Massachusetts
Elected from: Massachusetts
Occupations: Teacher, Lawyer
Party: Federalist
Vice President: Thomas Jefferson

3 Thomas Jefferson

Presidential term: 1801–1809
Lived: 1743–1826
Born in: Virginia
Elected from: Virginia
Occupations: Planter, Lawyer
Party: Republican**
Vice Presidents: Aaron Burr, George Clinton

4 James Madison

Presidential term: 1809–1817
Lived: 1751–1836
Born in: Virginia
Elected from: Virginia
Occupation: Planter
Party: Republican**
Vice Presidents: George Clinton, Elbridge Gerry

5 James Monroe

Presidential term: 1817–1825
Lived: 1758–1831
Born in: Virginia
Elected from: Virginia
Occupation: Lawyer
Party: Republican**
Vice President: Daniel D. Tompkins

6 John Quincy Adams

Presidential term: 1825–1829
Lived: 1767–1848
Born in: Massachusetts
Elected from: Massachusetts
Occupation: Lawyer
Party: Republican**
Vice President: John C. Calhoun

7 Andrew Jackson

Presidential term: 1829–1837
Lived: 1767–1845
Born in: South Carolina
Elected from: Tennessee
Occupations: Lawyer, Soldier
Party: Democratic
Vice Presidents: John C. Calhoun, Martin Van Buren

8 Martin Van Buren

Presidential term: 1837–1841
Lived: 1782–1862
Born in: New York
Elected from: New York
Occupation: Lawyer
Party: Democratic
Vice President: Richard M. Johnson

9 William H. Harrison

Presidential term: 1841
Lived: 1773–1841
Born in: Virginia
Elected from: Ohio
Occupations: Soldier,
    Planter
Party: Whig
Vice President: John Tyler

10 John Tyler

Presidential term: 1841–1845
Lived: 1790–1862
Born in: Virginia
Elected as V.P. from: Virginia
Succeeded Harrison
Occupation: Lawyer
Party: Whig
Vice President: None

11 James K. Polk

Presidential term: 1845–1849
Lived: 1795–1849
Born in: North Carolina
Elected from: Tennessee
Occupation: Lawyer
Party: Democratic
Vice President: George M.
    Dallas

12 Zachary Taylor

Presidential term: 1849–1850
Lived: 1784–1850
Born in: Virginia
Elected from: Louisiana
Occupation: Soldier
Party: Whig
Vice President: Millard
    Fillmore

13 Millard Fillmore

Presidential term: 1850–1853
Lived: 1800–1874
Born in: New York
Elected as V.P. from: New York
Succeeded Taylor
Occupation: Lawyer
Party: Whig
Vice President: None

14 Franklin Pierce

Presidential term: 1853–1857
Lived: 1804–1869
Born in: New Hampshire
Elected from: New Hampshire
Occupation: Lawyer
Party: Democratic
Vice President: William R. King

15 James Buchanan

Presidential term: 1857–1861
Lived: 1791–1868
Born in: Pennsylvania
Elected from: Pennsylvania
Occupation: Lawyer
Party: Democratic
Vice President: John C.
    Breckinridge

16 Abraham Lincoln

Presidential term: 1861–1865
Lived: 1809–1865
Born in: Kentucky
Elected from: Illinois
Occupation: Lawyer
Party: Republican
Vice Presidents: Hannibal
    Hamlin, Andrew Johnson

17 Andrew Johnson

Presidential term: 1865–1869
Lived: 1808–1875
Born in: North Carolina
Elected as V.P. from: Tennessee
Succeeded Lincoln
Occupation: Tailor
Party: Republican
Vice President: None

18 Ulysses S. Grant

Presidential term: 1869–1877
Lived: 1822–1885
Born in: Ohio
Elected from: Illinois
Occupations: Farmer, Soldier
Party: Republican
Vice Presidents: Schuyler Colfax,
  Henry Wilson

19 Rutherford B. Hayes

Presidential term: 1877–1881
Lived: 1822–1893
Born in: Ohio
Elected from: Ohio
Occupation: Lawyer
Party: Republican
Vice President: William A.
  Wheeler

20 James A. Garfield

Presidential term: 1881
Lived: 1831–1881
Born in: Ohio
Elected from: Ohio
Occupations: Laborer, Professor
Party: Republican
Vice President: Chester A.
  Arthur

21 Chester A. Arthur

Presidential term: 1881–1885
Lived: 1830–1886
Born in: Vermont
Elected as V.P. from: New York
Succeeded Garfield
Occupations: Teacher, Lawyer
Party: Republican
Vice President: None

22 Grover Cleveland

Presidential term: 1885–1889
Lived: 1837–1908
Born in: New Jersey
Elected from: New York
Occupation: Lawyer
Party: Democratic
Vice President: Thomas A.
  Hendricks

23 Benjamin Harrison

Presidential term: 1889–1893
Lived: 1833–1901
Born in: Ohio
Elected from: Indiana
Occupation: Lawyer
Party: Republican
Vice President: Levi P. Morton

24 Grover Cleveland

Presidential term: 1893–1897
Lived: 1837–1908
Born in: New Jersey
Elected from: New York
Occupation: Lawyer
Party: Democratic
Vice President: Adlai E.
  Stevenson

25 William McKinley

Presidential term: 1897–1901
Lived: 1843–1901
Born in: Ohio
Elected from: Ohio
Occupations: Teacher, Lawyer
Party: Republican
Vice Presidents: Garret Hobart,
  Theodore Roosevelt

26 Theodore Roosevelt

Presidential term: 1901–1909
Lived: 1858–1919
Born in: New York
Elected as V.P. from: New York
Succeeded McKinley
Occupations: Historian, Rancher
Party: Republican
Vice President: Charles W.
  Fairbanks

27 William H. Taft

Presidential term: 1909–1913
Lived: 1857–1930
Born in: Ohio
Elected from: Ohio
Occupations: Lawyer
Party: Republican
Vice President: James S.
Sherman

28 Woodrow Wilson

Presidential term: 1913–1921
Lived: 1856–1924
Born in: Virginia
Elected from: New Jersey
Occupation: College Professor
Party: Democratic
Vice President: Thomas R.
Marshall

29 Warren G. Harding

Presidential term: 1921–1923
Lived: 1865–1923
Born in: Ohio
Elected from: Ohio
Occupations: Newspaper
Editor, Publisher
Party: Republican
Vice President: Calvin Coolidge

30 Calvin Coolidge

Presidential term: 1923–1929
Lived: 1872–1933
Born in: Vermont
Elected as V.P. from: Massa-
chusetts, Succeeded Harding
Occupation: Lawyer
Party: Republican
Vice President: Charles G. Dawes

31 Herbert C. Hoover

Presidential term: 1929–1933
Lived: 1874–1964
Born in: Iowa
Elected from: California
Occupation: Engineer
Party: Republican
Vice President: Charles Curtis

32 Franklin D. Roosevelt

Presidential term: 1933–1945
Lived: 1882–1945
Born in: New York
Elected from: New York
Occupation: Lawyer
Party: Democratic
Vice Presidents: John N. Garner,
Henry A. Wallace, Harry S.
Truman

33 Harry S. Truman

Presidential term: 1945–1953
Lived: 1884–1972
Born in: Missouri
Elected as V.P. from: Missouri
Succeeded Roosevelt
Occupations: Clerk, Farmer
Party: Democratic
Vice President: Alben W. Barkley

34 Dwight D. Eisenhower

Presidential term: 1953–1961
Lived: 1890–1969
Born in: Texas
Elected from: New York
Occupation: Soldier
Party: Republican
Vice President: Richard M.
Nixon

35 John F. Kennedy

Presidential term: 1961–1963
Lived: 1917–1963
Born in: Massachusetts
Elected from: Massachusetts
Occupations: Author, Reporter
Party: Democratic
Vice President: Lyndon B.
Johnson

U.S. Presidents

36 Lyndon B. Johnson

Presidential term: 1963–1969
Lived: 1908–1973
Born in: Texas
Elected as V.P. from: Texas
Succeeded Kennedy
Occupation: Teacher
Party: Democratic
Vice President: Hubert H.
  Humphrey

37 Richard M. Nixon

Presidential term: 1969–1974
Lived: 1913–1994
Born in: California
Elected from: New York
Occupation: Lawyer
Party: Republican
Vice Presidents: Spiro T. Agnew,
  Gerald R. Ford

38 Gerald R. Ford

Presidential term: 1974–1977
Lived: 1913–2006
Born in: Nebraska
Appointed as V.P. upon Agnew's
resignation; succeeded Nixon
Occupation: Lawyer
Party: Republican
Vice President: Nelson A.
  Rockefeller

39 James E. Carter, Jr.

Presidential term: 1977–1981
Lived: 1924–
Born in: Georgia
Elected from: Georgia
Occupations: Business, Farmer
Party: Democratic
Vice President: Walter F.
  Mondale

40 Ronald W. Reagan

Presidential term: 1981–1989
Lived: 1911–2004
Born in: Illinois
Elected from: California
Occupations: Actor, Lecturer
Party: Republican
Vice President: George H.W.
  Bush

41 George H.W. Bush

Presidential term: 1989–1993
Lived: 1924–
Born in: Massachusetts
Elected from: Texas
Occupation: Business
Party: Republican
Vice President: J. Danforth
  Quayle

42 William J. Clinton

Presidential term: 1993–2001
Lived: 1946–
Born in: Arkansas
Elected from: Arkansas
Occupation: Lawyer
Party: Democratic
Vice President: Albert Gore, Jr.

43 George W. Bush

Presidential term: 2001–
Lived: 1946–
Born in: Connecticut
Elected from: Texas
Occupation: Business
Party: Republican
Vice President: Richard B.
  Cheney

U.S. Presidents

United States Facts

The states are listed in the order they were admitted to the Union.

Washington, D.C.
Population: 572,059
Land area: 61 sq. mi.

Population figures are based on U.S. Bureau of the Census for 2000. House of Representatives figures are from the Clerk of the House of Representatives. States are not drawn to scale.

U.S. Territories

Puerto Rico
Population: 3,808,610
Land area: 3,425 sq. mi.

Guam
Population: 155,000 (est.)
Land area: 209 sq. mi.

U.S. Virgin Islands
Population: 121,000 (est.)
Land area: 134 sq. mi.

American Samoa
Population: 65,000 (est.)
Land area: 77 sq. mi.

1 Delaware
Year Admitted: 1787
Population: 783,600
Land area: 1,955 sq. mi.
Representatives: 1

2 Pennsylvania
Year Admitted: 1787
Population: 12,281,054
Land area: 44,820 sq. mi.
Representatives: 19

3 New Jersey
Year Admitted: 1787
Population: 8,414,350
Land area: 7,419 sq. mi.
Representatives: 13

4 Georgia
Year Admitted: 1788
Population: 8,186,453
Land area: 57,919 sq. mi.
Representatives: 13

5 Connecticut
Year Admitted: 1788
Population: 3,405,565
Land area: 4,845 sq. mi.
Representatives: 5
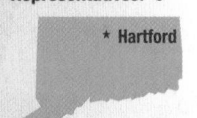

6 Massachusetts
Year Admitted: 1788
Population: 6,349,097
Land area: 7,838 sq. mi.
Representatives: 10
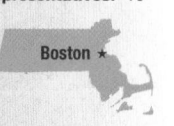

7 Maryland
Year Admitted: 1788
Population: 5,296,486
Land area: 9,775 sq. mi.
Representatives: 8

8 South Carolina
Year Admitted: 1788
Population: 4,012,012
Land area: 30,111 sq. mi.
Representatives: 6

9 New Hampshire
Year Admitted: 1788
Population: 1,235,786
Land area: 8,969 sq. mi.
Representatives: 2

10 Virginia
Year Admitted: 1788
Population: 7,078,515
Land area: 39,598 sq. mi.
Representatives: 11

11 New York
Year Admitted: 1788
Population: 18,976,457
Land area: 47,224 sq. mi.
Representatives: 29

12 North Carolina
Year Admitted: 1789
Population: 8,049,313
Land area: 48,718 sq. mi.
Representatives: 13

13 Rhode Island
Year Admitted: 1790
Population: 1,048,319
Land area: 1,045 sq. mi.
Representatives: 2
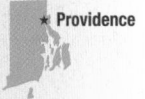

14 Vermont
Year Admitted: 1791
Population: 608,827
Land area: 9,249 sq. mi.
Representatives: 1

15 Kentucky
Year Admitted: 1792
Population: 4,041,769
Land area: 39,732 sq. mi.
Representatives: 6

16 Tennessee
Year Admitted: 1796
Population: 5,689,283
Land area: 41,220 sq. mi.
Representatives: 9
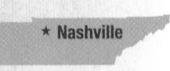

17 Ohio
Year Admitted: 1803
Population: 11,353,140
Land area: 40,953 sq. mi.
Representatives: 18

18 Louisiana
Year Admitted: 1812
Population: 4,468,976
Land area: 43,566 sq. mi.
Representatives: 7

19 Indiana
Year Admitted: 1816
Population: 6,080,485
Land area: 35,870 sq. mi.
Representatives: 9
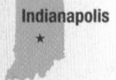

20 Mississippi
Year Admitted: 1817
Population: 2,844,658
Land area: 46,914 sq. mi.
Representatives: 4
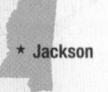

21 Illinois
Year Admitted: 1818
Population: 12,419,293
Land area: 55,593 sq. mi.
Representatives: 19

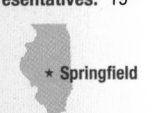
★ Springfield

22 Alabama
Year Admitted: 1819
Population: 4,447,100
Land area: 50,750 sq. mi.
Representatives: 7

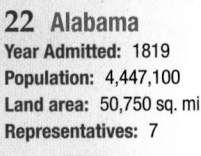
Montgomery ★

23 Maine
Year Admitted: 1820
Population: 1,274,923
Land area: 30,865 sq. mi.
Representatives: 2

★ Augusta

24 Missouri
Year Admitted: 1821
Population: 5,595,211
Land area: 68,898 sq. mi.
Representatives: 9

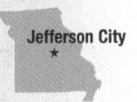
Jefferson City ★

25 Arkansas
Year Admitted: 1836
Population: 2,673,400
Land area: 52,075 sq. mi.
Representatives: 4

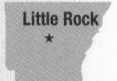
Little Rock ★

26 Michigan
Year Admitted: 1837
Population: 9,938,444
Land area: 56,809 sq. mi.
Representatives: 15

Lansing ★

27 Florida
Year Admitted: 1845
Population: 15,982,378
Land area: 53,997 sq. mi.
Representatives: 25

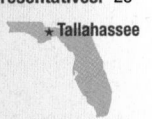
★ Tallahassee

28 Texas
Year Admitted: 1845
Population: 20,851,820
Land area: 261,914 sq. mi.
Representatives: 32

Austin ★

29 Iowa
Year Admitted: 1846
Population: 2,926,324
Land area: 55,875 sq. mi.
Representatives: 5

★ Des Moines

30 Wisconsin
Year Admitted: 1848
Population: 5,363,675
Land area: 54,314 sq. mi.
Representatives: 8

Madison ★

31 California
Year Admitted: 1850
Population: 33,871,648
Land area: 155,973 sq. mi.
Representatives: 53

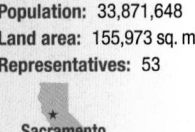
★ Sacramento

32 Minnesota
Year Admitted: 1858
Population: 4,919,479
Land area: 79,617 sq. mi.
Representatives: 8

Saint Paul ★

33 Oregon
Year Admitted: 1859
Population: 3,421,399
Land area: 96,003 sq. mi.
Representatives: 5

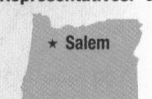
★ Salem

34 Kansas
Year Admitted: 1861
Population: 2,688,418
Land area: 81,823 sq. mi.
Representatives: 4

Topeka ★

35 West Virginia
Year Admitted: 1863
Population: 1,808,344
Land area: 24,087 sq. mi.
Representatives: 3

★ Charleston

36 Nevada
Year Admitted: 1864
Population: 1,998,257
Land area: 109,806 sq. mi.
Representatives: 3

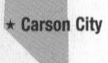
★ Carson City

37 Nebraska
Year Admitted: 1867
Population: 1,711,263
Land area: 76,878 sq. mi.
Representatives: 3

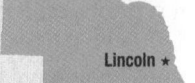
Lincoln ★

38 Colorado
Year Admitted: 1876
Population: 4,301,261
Land area: 103,730 sq. mi.
Representatives: 7

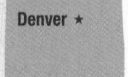
Denver ★

39 North Dakota
Year Admitted: 1889
Population: 642,200
Land area: 68,994 sq. mi.
Representatives: 1

Bismarck
★

40 South Dakota
Year Admitted: 1889
Population: 754,844
Land area: 75,898 sq. mi.
Representatives: 1

Pierre
★

41 Montana
Year Admitted: 1889
Population: 902,195
Land area: 145,556 sq. mi.
Representatives: 1

★ Helena

42 Washington
Year Admitted: 1889
Population: 5,894,121
Land area: 66,582 sq. mi.
Representatives: 9

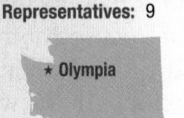
★ Olympia

43 Idaho
Year Admitted: 1890
Population: 1,293,953
Land area: 82,751 sq. mi.
Representatives: 2

★ Boise

44 Wyoming
Year Admitted: 1890
Population: 493,782
Land area: 97,105 sq. mi.
Representatives: 1

Cheyenne
★

45 Utah
Year Admitted: 1896
Population: 2,233,169
Land area: 82,168 sq. mi.
Representatives: 3

★
Salt Lake City

46 Oklahoma
Year Admitted: 1907
Population: 3,450,654
Land area: 68,679 sq. mi.
Representatives: 5

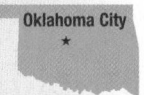
Oklahoma City
★

47 New Mexico
Year Admitted: 1912
Population: 1,819,046
Land area: 121,365 sq. mi.
Representatives: 3

★
Santa Fe

48 Arizona
Year Admitted: 1912
Population: 5,130,632
Land area: 113,642 sq. mi.
Representatives: 8

Phoenix
★

49 Alaska
Year Admitted: 1959
Population: 626,932
Land area: 570,374 sq. mi.
Representatives: 1

Juneau ★

50 Hawaii
Year Admitted: 1959
Population: 1,211,537
Land area: 6,432 sq. mi.
Representatives: 2

Honolulu ★

U.S. Facts

Documents of American History

TABLE OF CONTENTS

(right) Lincoln's drafts of the Gettysburg Address

Magna Carta

Signing the Mayflower Compact

Why They Matter

Documents are often public statements by a president or an official body, such as a legislature, on an important issue. They have become documents because they define a particular issue so well that Americans continue to refer to them. Many documents here address fundamental American beliefs, such as the rights of the individual and the proper limits of government. Other documents, such as the Monroe Doctrine or the Truman Doctrine, address the nation's position and responsibilities in the world.

Documents matter because they are guides to American government and values. Sometimes people study them to learn how Americans came to believe in certain principles. Other times people read documents simply because these writings express certain principles passionately.

Founding Documents of the American Republic

The first seven documents in this collection represent some of the founding documents of American democracy. Each contributed an essential building block for American political principles. Ultimately these principles were embodied in the Declaration of Independence, the Bill of Rights, and the Constitution.

DOCUMENT	WHY IT MATTERS
The Magna Carta In signing this charter in 1215, King John of England granted his subjects certain permanent liberties or rights, such as the right to a fair trial by a jury of their peers.	Over the centuries, English people believed that the Magna Carta gave them certain rights. They took this idea with them when they settled the American colonies. Some provisions of the Bill of Rights reflect ancient Magna Carta liberties.
The Mayflower Compact In 1620 the Pilgrims signed a compact while still aboard the *Mayflower*. This document laid out a plan for self-government the Pilgrims would use once they landed in America.	This document is the first plan for self-government put into effect in the English colonies. It reflected the idea that government should be based on a consensus of the entire community.
The Fundamental Orders of Connecticut Connecticut settlers agreed they would be governed according to a certain set of laws and through certain institutions. All citizens, not only those of a certain religion, could vote.	This document, the first written constitution drawn up in America, strengthened the colonists' beliefs about governing themselves.
The English Bill of Rights In 1689, after the Glorious Revolution, Parliament forced the king to accept this Bill of Rights guaranteeing basic civil rights.	This document clearly established that English subjects had certain rights and that the king could be removed from power for violating those rights.
Second Treatise of Government English philosopher John Locke wrote this document during the 1680s. One of his basic arguments was that government should be based on a contract between a ruler and those who are ruled. Rebellion is justified if a ruler violates the contract.	During the American Revolution, the colonists drew from Locke's theories of government and especially his ideas about the right to rebel.
The Virginia Statute for Religious Freedom This 1786 statute declared that the state of Virginia should not support Anglicanism or any other religious denomination.	The religious clauses of the Bill of Rights protecting the free exercise of religion and prohibiting an official religion were based on this statute.
The Federalist No. 10 In 1787 James Madison wrote this paper, one of a series arguing for stronger central government as reflected in the new Constitution.	The framework for American government today— a representative government with a strong federal government—was laid out in the Federalist Papers.

 *Use the **American History Primary Source Document Library CD-ROM** to find additional primary sources about American heritage.*

Documents

The Magna Carta

The Magna Carta, signed by King John of England in 1215, marked a decisive step forward in the development of English constitutional government. Later it served as a model for the colonists, who carried the Magna Carta's guarantees of political rights to America.

John, by the grace of God, king of England, lord of Ireland, duke of Normandy and Aquitaine, and count of Anjou: to the archbishops, bishops, abbots, earls, barons, justiciaries, foresters, sheriffs, reeves, ministers, and all bailiffs and others his faithful subjects, greeting. . . .

1. We have, in the first place, granted to God, and by this our present charter, confirmed for us and our heirs forever that the English church shall be free. . . .

9. Neither we nor our bailiffs shall seize any land or rent for any debt so long as the debtor's chattels are sufficient to discharge the same. . . .

12. No scutage [tax] or aid shall be imposed in our kingdom unless by the common counsel thereof. . . .

14. For obtaining the common counsel of the kingdom concerning the assessment of aids. . . or of scutage, we will cause to be summoned, severally by our letters, the archbishops, bishops, abbots, earls, and great barons; we will also cause to be summoned generally, by our sheriffs and bailiffs, all those who hold lands directly of us, to meet on a fixed day . . . and at a fixed place. . . .

20. A free man shall be amerced [punished] for a small fault only according to the measure thereof, and for a great crime according to its magnitude. . . . None of these amercements shall be imposed except by the oath of honest men of the neighborhood.

21. Earls and barons shall be amerced only by their peers, and only in proportion to the measure of the offense. . . .

38. In the future no bailiff shall upon his own unsupported accusation put any man to trial without producing credible witnesses to the truth of the accusation.

39. No free man shall be taken, imprisoned, disseised [seized], outlawed, banished, or in any way destroyed, nor will we proceed against or prosecute him, except by the lawful judgment of his peers and by the law of the land.

40. To no one will we sell, to none will we deny or delay, right or justice. . . .

42. In the future it shall be lawful . . . for anyone to leave and return to our kingdom safely and securely by land and water, saving his fealty to us. Excepted are those who have been imprisoned or outlawed according to the law of the land. . . .

61. Whereas we, for the honor of God and the amendment of our realm, and in order the better to allay the discord arisen between us and our barons, have granted all these things aforesaid. . . .

63. Wherefore we will, and firmly charge . . . that all men in our kingdom shall have and hold all the aforesaid liberties, rights, and concessions . . . fully, and wholly to them and their heirs . . . in all things and places forever. . . . It is moreover sworn, as well on our part as on the part of the barons, that all these matters aforesaid will be kept in good faith and without deceit. Witness the above named and many others. Given by our hand in the meadow which is called Runnymede. . . .

The Mayflower Compact

On November 21, 1620, 41 colonists drafted the Mayflower Compact while still aboard the Mayflower. It was the first self-government plan ever put into effect in the English colonies. The compact was drawn up under these circumstances, as described by Governor William Bradford:

"This day, before we came to harbor, observing some not well affected to unity and concord, but gave some appearance of faction, it was thought good there should be an association and agreement that we should combine together in one body, and to submit to such government and governors as we should by common consent agree to make and choose, and set our hands to this that follows word for word."

In the Name of God, Amen. We, whose names are underwritten, the Loyal Subjects of our dread Sovereign Lord King James, by the Grace of God, of Great Britain, France, and Ireland, King, Defender of the Faith, etc.

Having undertaken for the Glory of God, and Advancement of the Christian Faith, and the honor of our King and Country, a Voyage to plant the first Colony in the northern Parts of Virginia, Do by these Presents, solemnly and mutually, in the Presence of God and one another, covenant and combine ourselves together into a civil Body Politick, for our better Ordering and Preservation, and Furtherance of the Ends aforesaid; And by Virtue hereof do enact, constitute, and frame, such just and equal Laws, Ordinances, Acts, Constitutions, and Offices, from time to time, as shall be thought most meet and convenient for the general Good of the Colony; unto which we promise all due Submission and Obedience. In Witness whereof we have hereunder subscribed our names at Cape Cod the eleventh of November, in the Reign of our Sovereign Lord King James of England, France, and Ireland, the eighteenth and of Scotland, the fifty-fourth. Anno Domini, 1620.

Signing of the Mayflower Compact

The Fundamental Orders of Connecticut

In January 1639, settlers in Connecticut, led by Thomas Hooker, drew up the Fundamental Orders of Connecticut—America's first written constitution. It is essentially a body of laws and a compact among the settlers.

Forasmuch as it has pleased the Almighty God by the wise disposition of His Divine Providence so to order and dispose of things that we, the inhabitants and residents of Windsor, Hartford, and Wethersfield are now cohabiting and dwelling in and upon the river of Conectecotte and the lands thereunto adjoining; and well knowing where a people are gathered together the Word of God requires that, to maintain the peace and union of such a people, there should be an orderly and decent government established according to God, . . . do therefore associate and conjoin ourselves to be as one public state or commonwealth. . . . As also in our civil affairs to be guided and governed according to such laws, rules, orders, and decrees as shall be made, ordered, and decreed, as follows:

1. It is ordered . . . that there shall be yearly two general assemblies or courts; . . . The first shall be called the Court of Election, wherein shall be yearly chosen . . . so many magistrates and other public officers as shall be found requisite. Whereof one to be chosen governor . . . and no other magistrate to be chosen for more than one year; provided always there be six chosen besides the governor . . . by all that are admitted freemen and have taken the oath of fidelity, and do cohabit within this jurisdiction. . . .

4. It is ordered . . . that no person be chosen governor above once in two years, and that the governor be always a member of some approved congregation, and formerly of the magistracy within this jurisdiction; and all the magistrates freemen of this Commonwealth. . . .

5. It is ordered . . . that to the aforesaid Court of Election the several towns shall send their deputies.

. . . Also, the other General Court . . . shall be for making of laws, and any other public occasion which concerns the good of the Commonwealth. . . .

7. It is ordered . . . that . . . the constable or constables of each town shall forthwith give notice distinctly to the inhabitants of the same . . . that . . . they meet and assemble themselves together to elect and choose certain deputies to be at the General Court then following to [manage] the affairs of the Commonwealth; . . .

10. It is ordered . . . that every General Court . . . shall consist of the governor, or someone chosen to moderate the Court, and four other magistrates, at least, with the major part of the deputies of the several towns legally chosen. . . . In which said General Courts shall consist the supreme power of the Commonwealth, and they only shall have power to make laws or repeal them, to grant levies, to admit of freemen, dispose of lands undisposed of to several towns or person, and also shall have power to call either Court or magistrate or any other person whatsoever into question for any misdemeanor. . . .

Connecticut settlers on their way to Hartford

Documents

The English Bill of Rights

In 1689 William of Orange (pictured at right) and his wife Mary became joint rulers of England after accepting a list of conditions that later became known as the English Bill of Rights. This document assured the English people of certain basic civil rights and limited the power of the English monarchy.

An act declaring the rights and liberties of the subject and settling the succession of the crown. Whereas the lords spiritual and temporal and commons assembled at Westminster lawfully, fully and freely representing all the estates of the people of this realm did upon the thirteenth day of February in the year of our Seal of William and Mary Lord one thousand six hundred eighty-eight [-nine] present unto their majesties . . . William and Mary prince and princess of Orange . . . a certain declaration in writing made by the said lords and commons in the words following viz [namely]:

Whereas the late king James the second, by the assistance of divers evil counsellors, judges, and ministers employed by him did endeavor to subvert and extirpate the Protestant religion and the laws and liberties of this kingdom.

By assuming and exercising a power of dispensing with and suspending of laws and the execution of laws without consent of parliament. . . .

By levying money for and to the use of the crown by pretence of prerogative for other time and in other manner than the same was granted by parliament.

By raising and keeping a standing army within this kingdom in time of peace without consent of parliament and quartering soldiers contrary to law. . . .

By violating the freedom of election of members to serve in parliament. . . .

And excessive bail hath been required of persons committed in criminal cases to elude the benefit of the laws made for the liberty of the subjects.

And excessive fines have been imposed.

And illegal and cruel punishments inflicted. . . .

And thereupon the said lords spiritual and temporal and commons . . . do . . . declare that the pretended power of suspending of laws or the execution of laws by regal authority without consent of parliament is illegal. . . .

That levying money for or to the use of the crown . . . without grant of parliament for longer time or in other manner than the same is or shall be granted is illegal.

That it is the right of the subjects to petition the king and all commitments and prosecutions for such petitioning are illegal.

That the raising or keeping a standing army within the kingdom in time of peace unless it be with consent of parliament is against law. . . .

That election of members of parliament ought to be free. . . .

That excessive bail ought not to be required nor excessive fines imposed nor cruel and unusual punishments inflicted. . . .

The said lords . . . do resolve that William and Mary, prince and princess of Orange, be declared king and queen of England, France, and Ireland. . . .

Second Treatise of Government

English philosopher John Locke (above) wrote "Two Treatises of Government" in the early 1680s. Published in 1690, the "Second Treatise of Government" argues that government should be based on an agreement between the people and their ruler, and that if the ruler violates the agreement, a rebellion by the people may be justified.

Of the State of Nature

To understand Political Power right, and to derive it from its Original, we must consider what State all Men are naturally in, and that is, a State of perfect Freedom to order their Actions, and dispose of their Possessions, and Persons as they think fit, within the bounds of the Law of Nature, without asking leave, or depending upon the Will of any other Man. . . .

Of the Beginning of Political Societies

Men being, as has been said, by Nature, all free, equal and independent, no one can be put out of this Estate, and subjected to the Political Power of another, without his own Consent. The only way whereby any one divests himself of his Natural Liberty, and puts on the bonds of Civil Society is by agreeing with other Men to joyn and unite into a Community, for their comfortable, safe, and peaceable living one amongst another, in a secure Enjoyment of their properties, and a greater Security against any that are not of it. This any number of Men may do, because it injures not the Freedom of the rest; they are left as they were in the Liberty of the State of Nature. . . .

Whosoever therefore out of a state of Nature unite into a Community, must be understood to give up all the power, necessary to the ends for which they unite into Society, to the majority of the Community. . . .

Of the Dissolution of Government

Governments are dissolved from within . . . when the Legislative is altered. . . . First, that when such a single Person or Prince sets up his own Arbitrary Will in place of the Laws, which are the Will of the Society, declared by the Legislative, then the Legislative is changed. . . . Secondly, when the Prince hinders the legislative from . . . acting freely, pursuant to those ends, for which it was Constituted, the Legislative is altered. . . . Thirdly, When by the Arbitrary Power of the Prince, the Electors, or ways of Election are altered, without the Consent, and contrary to the common Interest of the People, there also the Legislative is altered. . . .

In these and the like Cases, when the Government is dissolved, the People are at liberty to provide for themselves, by erecting a new Legislative, differing from the other, by the change of Persons, or Form, or both as they shall find it most for their safety and good. For the Society can never, by the fault of another, lose the Native and Original Right it has to preserve itself. . . .

The Virginia Statute for Religious Freedom

This statute, excerpted below, was the basis for the religion clauses in the Bill of Rights. Thomas Jefferson drafted the statute, and James Madison guided it through the Virginia legislature in 1786. The issue it addresses arose when the new state considered whether citizens should continue to support the Anglican Church, as they had in colonial times, or whether they should support any or all other denominations.

Whereas Almighty God hath created the mind free; that all attempts to influence it by temporal punishments . . . tend only to beget habits of hypocrisy and meanness, and are a departure from the plan of the Holy author of our religion; . . . that the impious presumption of legislators and rulers, civil as well as ecclesiastical, who being themselves but fallible and uninspired men, have assumed dominion over the faith of others, setting up their own opinions and modes of thinking as the only true and infallible, and as such endeavouring to impose them on others, hath established and maintained false religions over the greatest part of the world, and through all time; . . . that to compel a man to furnish contributions of money for the propagation of opinions which he disbelieves, is sinful and tyrannical; . . . that our civil rights have no dependence on our religious opinions, any more than our opinions in physics or geometry; that therefore the proscribing any citizen as unworthy the public confidence by laying upon him an incapacity of being called to offices of trust . . . unless he profess or renounce this or that religious opinion, is depriving him injuriously of those privileges and advantages to which in common with his fellow-citizens he has a natural right; that it tends only to corrupt the principles of that religion it is meant to encourage, by bribing with a monopoly of worldly honours and emoluments, those who will externally profess and conform to it . . . :

Be it enacted by the General Assembly, That no man shall be compelled to frequent or support any religious worship, place, or ministry whatsoever, nor shall be enforced, restrained, molested, or burthened in his body or goods, nor shall otherwise suffer on account of his religious opinions or belief; but that all men shall be free to profess, and by argument to maintain, their opinion in matters of religion, and that the same shall in no wise diminish enlarge, or affect their civil capacities. . . .

Thomas Jefferson

The Federalist No. 10

James Madison (pictured at right) wrote several articles for a New York newspaper supporting ratification of the Constitution. In the excerpt below, he argues for the idea of a federal republic as a guard against factions, or overzealous parties, in governing the nation.

The latent causes of faction are thus sown in the nature of man; and we see them everywhere. . . . A zeal for different opinions concerning religion, concerning government, and many other points; . . . an attachment to different leaders ambitiously contending for preeminence and power . . . have, in turn, divided mankind into parties . . . disposed to vex and oppress each other than to cooperate for their common good. . . . But the most common and durable source of factions has been the various and unequal distribution of property. Those who hold and those who are without property have ever formed distinct interests in society. Those who are creditors, and those who are debtors, fall under a like discrimination. A landed interest, a manufacturing interest, a mercantile interest, a moneyed interest, with many lesser interests, grow up of necessity in civilized nations, and divide them into different classes, actuated by different sentiments and views. The regulation of these various and interfering interests forms the principal task of modern legislation and involves the spirit of party and faction in the necessary and ordinary operations of government. . . .

The inference to which we are brought is that the causes of faction cannot be removed and relief is only to be sought in the means of controlling its effects. . . .

By what means is this object attainable? Evidently by one of two only. Either the existence of the same passion or interest in a majority at the same time must be prevented, or the majority, having such coexistent passion or interest, must be rendered, by their number and local situation, unable to concert and carry into effect schemes of oppression. . . .

From this . . . it may be concluded that a pure democracy, by which I mean a society consisting of a small number of citizens, who assemble and administer the government in person, can admit of no cure for the mischiefs of faction. A common passion or interest will, in almost every case, be felt by a majority of the whole; a communication and concert results from the form of government itself; and there is nothing to check the inducements to sacrifice the weaker party or an obnoxious individual. Hence it is that such democracies have ever been spectacles of turbulence and contention. . . .

A republic, by which I mean a government in which the scheme of representation takes place, opens a different prospect and promises the cure for which we are seeking. . . .

The two great points of difference between a democracy and a republic are: first, the delegation of the government in the latter to a small number of citizens elected by the rest; secondly, the greater number of citizens and great sphere of country over which the latter may be extended.

The Federalist No. 51

The author of this Federalist paper is not known. It may have been either James Madison or Alexander Hamilton. The author argues that the Constitution's federal system and separation of powers will protect the rights of the people.

In order to lay a due foundation for that separate and distinct exercise of the different powers of government, which to a certain extent is admitted on all hands to be essential to the preservation of liberty, it is evident that . . . the great security against a gradual concentration of the several powers in the same department, consists in giving to those who administer each department the necessary constitutional means and personal motives to resist encroachments of the others. . . .

Ambition must be made to counteract ambition. . . . A dependence on the people is, no doubt, the primary control on the government; but experience has taught mankind the necessity of auxiliary precautions. . . . The constant aim is to divide and arrange the several offices in such a manner as that each may be a check on the other. . . . In the compound republic of America, the power surrendered by the people is first divided between two distinct governments, and then the portion allotted to each subdivided among distinct and separate departments. . . .

In a free government the security for civil rights must be the same as that for religious rights. It consists in the one case in the multiplicity of interests, and in the other in the multiplicity of sects. . . . In the extended republic of the United States, and among the great variety of interests, parties, and sects which it embraces, a coalition of a majority of the whole society could seldom take place on any other principles than those of justice and the general good. . . . It is no less certain than it is important . . . that the larger the society, provided it lie within a practical sphere, the more duly capable it will be of self-government.

The Federalist No. 59

In this Federalist paper, Alexander Hamilton explains why Congress, and not the states, should have the final say in how federal elections are conducted.

The natural order of the subject leads us to consider . . . that provision of the Constitution which authorizes the national legislature to regulate, in the last resort, the election of its own members. . . . Its propriety rests upon the evidence of this plain proposition, that every government ought to contain in itself the means of its own preservation. . . . Nothing can be more evident, than that an exclusive power of regulating elections for the national government, in the hands of the state legislatures, would leave the existence of the union entirely at their mercy. They could at any moment annihilate it, by neglecting to provide for the choice of persons to administer its affairs. . . .

It is certainly true that the state legislatures, by forbearing the appointment of senators, may destroy the national government. But it will not follow that, because they have a power to do this in one instance, they ought to have it in every other. . . . It is an evil; but it is an evil which could not have been avoided without excluding the states . . . from a place in the organization of the national government. If this had been done, it would doubtless have been interpreted into an entire dereliction of the federal principle; and would certainly have deprived the state governments of that absolute safeguard which they will enjoy under this provision. . . .

Washington's Farewell Address

Washington never orally delivered his Farewell Address. Instead, he arranged to have it printed in a Philadelphia newspaper on September 19, 1796. Designed in part to remove him from consideration for a third presidential term, the address also warned about dangers the new nation was facing, especially the dangers of political parties and sectionalism.

Washington preparing to leave office

Friends and Fellow Citizens:

The period for a new election of a citizen to administer the executive government of the United States being not far distant . . . I should now apprise you of the resolution I have formed to decline being considered. . . .

The unity of government which constitutes you one people is . . . a main pillar in the edifice of your real independence; the support of your tranquility at home, your peace abroad; of your safety; of your prosperity in every shape; of that very liberty which you so highly prize. But as it is easy to foresee that, from different causes and from different quarters, much pains will be taken, many artifices employed to weaken in your minds the conviction of this truth. . . .

The name of American, which belongs to you, in your national capacity, must always exalt the just pride of patriotism more than any appellation derived from local discriminations. . . .

In contemplating the causes which may disturb our Union, it occurs as matter of serious concern that any ground should have been furnished for characterizing parties by geographical discriminations: Northern and Southern; Atlantic and Western; whence designing men may endeavor to excite a belief that there is a real difference of local interests and views. . . .

Let me now take a more comprehensive view and warn you in the most solemn manner against the baneful effects of the spirit of party generally. . . . The alternate domination of one faction over another, sharpened by the spirit of revenge natural to party dissension . . . is itself a frightful despotism. . . .

Of all the dispositions and habits which lead to political prosperity, religion and morality are indispensable supports. . . . A volume could not trace all their connections with private and public felicity. Let it simply be asked where is the security for property, for reputation, for life, if the sense of religious obligation desert the oaths, which are the instruments of investigation in courts of justice? And let us with caution indulge the supposition, that morality can be maintained without religion. Whatever may be conceded to the influence of refined education on minds of peculiar structure—reason and experience both forbid us to expect that national morality can prevail in exclusion of religious principle.

The great rule of conduct for us, in regard to foreign nations, is in extending our commercial relations to have with them as little political connection as possible. . . .

In offering you, my countrymen, these counsels of an old and affectionate friend, I dare not hope that they will make the strong and lasting impression I could wish. . . . But if I may even flatter myself that they may be productive of some partial benefit. . . .

The Kentucky Resolution

The Alien and Sedition Acts of 1798 made it easier for the government to suppress criticism and to arrest political enemies. This Federalist legislation inspired fierce opposition among Republicans, who looked to the state governments to reverse the acts. Two states, Kentucky and Virginia, passed resolutions stating their right to, in effect, disregard federal legislation. The resolutions laid the groundwork for the states' rights often cited during the Civil War. Thomas Jefferson wrote the Kentucky Resolution, excerpted below, which was adopted in 1799.

RESOLVED, . . . that if those who administer the general government be permitted to transgress the limits fixed by that compact, by a total disregard to the special delegations of power therein contained, annihilation of the state governments, and the erection upon their ruins, of a general consolidated government, will be the inevitable consequence; that the principle and construction contended for by sundry of the state legislatures, that the general government is the exclusive judge of the extent of the powers delegated to it, stop nothing short of despotism; . . . that the several states who formed that instrument, being sovereign and independent, have the unquestionable right to judge of its infraction; and that a nullification, by those sovereignties, of all unauthorized acts done under colour of that instrument, is the rightful remedy; . . .

"The Star-Spangled Banner"

Francis Scott Key

During the British bombardment of Fort McHenry during the War of 1812, a young Baltimore lawyer named Francis Scott Key was inspired to write the words to "The Star-Spangled Banner." Although it became popular immediately, it was not until 1931 that Congress officially declared "The Star-Spangled Banner" as the national anthem of the United States.

O! say can you see, by the dawn's early light,

What so proudly we hail'd at the twilight's last gleaming,

Whose broad stripes and bright stars through the perilous fight,

O'er the ramparts we watch'd, were so gallantly streaming?

And the Rockets' red glare, the Bombs bursting in air,

Gave proof through the night that our Flag was still there;

O! say, does that star-spangled Banner yet wave,

O'er the Land of the free, and the home of the brave?

Fort McHenry flag

Documents

The Monroe Doctrine

When Spain's power in South America began to weaken, other European nations seemed ready to step in. The United States was developing trade and diplomatic relations with South America, and it wanted to curb European influence there. The following is a statement President Monroe made on the subject in his annual message to Congress on December 2, 1823.

The occasion has been judged proper for asserting, as a principle in which the rights and interests of the United States are involved, that the American continents, by the free and independent condition which they have assumed and maintain, are henceforth not to be considered as subjects for future colonization by any European powers. . . .

. . . We owe it, therefore, to candor and to the amicable relations existing between the United States and those [European] powers to declare that we should consider any attempt on their part to extend their system to any portion of this hemisphere as dangerous to our peace and safety. With the existing colonies or dependencies of any European power we have not interfered and shall not interfere. But with the Governments who have declared their independence and maintain it, and whose independence we have, on great consideration and on just principles, acknowledged, we could not view any interposition for the purpose of oppressing them, or controlling in any other manner their destiny, by any European power in any other light than as the manifestation of an unfriendly disposition toward the United States. . . .

Our policy in regard to Europe, which was adopted at an early stage of the wars which have so long agitated that quarter of the globe, nevertheless remains the same, which is, not to interfere in the internal concerns of any of its powers; to consider the government de facto as the legitimate government for us; to cultivate friendly relations with it, and to preserve those relations by a frank, firm, and manly policy, meeting in all instances the just claims of every power, submitting to injuries from none.

The Seneca Falls Declaration

One of the first documents to call for equal rights for women was the Declaration of Sentiments and Resolutions, issued in 1848 at the Seneca Falls Convention in Seneca Falls, New York. Led by Lucretia Mott and Elizabeth Cady Stanton, the delegates at the convention used the language of the Bill of Rights to call for women's rights.

We hold these truths to be self-evident: that all men and women are created equal; that they are endowed by their Creator with certain inalienable rights; that among these are life, liberty, and the pursuit of happiness; that to secure these rights governments are instituted, deriving their just powers from the consent of the governed. Whenever any form of government becomes destructive of these ends, it is the right of those who suffer from it to refuse allegiance to it, and to insist upon the institution of a new government. . . .

The history of mankind is a history of repeated injuries and usurpations on the part of man toward woman, having in direct object the establishment of an absolute tyranny over her.

Lucretia Mott

Now, in view of this entire disfranchisement . . . we insist that they have immediate admission to all the rights and privileges which belong to them as citizens of the United States. . . .

The Emancipation Proclamation

On January 1, 1863, President Abraham Lincoln issued the Emancipation Proclamation, which freed all enslaved persons in states under Confederate control. The Proclamation was a significant step toward the passage of the Thirteenth Amendment (1865), which ended slavery in the United States.

Whereas, on the 22nd day of September, in the year of our Lord 1862, a proclamation was issued by the President of the United States, containing, among other things, the following, to wit:

That on the 1st day of January, in the year of our Lord 1863, all persons held as slaves within any state or designated part of a state, the people whereof shall then be in rebellion against the United States, shall be then, thenceforward, and forever free; and the executive government of the United States, including the military and naval authority thereof, will recognize and maintain the freedom of such persons and will do no act or acts to repress such persons, or any of them, in any efforts they may make for their actual freedom.

That the executive will, on the 1st day January aforesaid, by proclamation, designate the states and parts of states, if any, in which the people thereof, respectively, shall then be in rebellion against the United States; and the fact that any state or the people thereof shall on that day be in good faith represented in the Congress of the United States by members chosen thereto at elections wherein a majority of the qualified voters of such states shall have participated shall, in the absence of strong countervailing testimony, be deemed conclusive evidence that such state and the people thereof are not then in rebellion against the United States.

Now, therefore, I, Abraham Lincoln, President of the United States, by virtue of the power in me vested as commander in chief of the Army and Navy of the United States, in time of actual armed rebellion against the authority and government of the United States, and as a fit and necessary war measure for suppressing said rebellion, do, on this 1st day of January, in the year of our Lord 1863, and in accordance with my purpose so to do, publicly proclaimed for the full period of 100 days from the day first above mentioned, order, and designate as the states and parts of states wherein the people thereof, respectively, are this day in rebellion against the United States. . . .

And, by virtue of the power and for the purpose aforesaid, I do order and declare that all persons held as slaves within said designated states and parts of states are, and henceforward shall be, free; and that the executive government of the United States, including the military and naval authorities thereof, will recognize and maintain the freedom of said persons. . . .

And upon this act, sincerely believed to be an act of justice, warranted by the Constitution upon military necessity, I invoke the considerate judgment of mankind and the gracious favor of Almighty God. . . .

Abraham Lincoln

The Gettysburg Address

President Abraham Lincoln delivered the Gettysburg Address on November 19, 1863, during the dedication of the Gettysburg National Cemetery. The dedication was in honor of the more than 7,000 Union and Confederate soldiers who died in the Battle of Gettysburg earlier that year. Lincoln's brief speech is often recognized as one of the finest speeches in the English language. It is also one of the most moving speeches in the nation's history.

There are five known manuscript copies of the address, two of which are in the Library of Congress. Scholars debate about which, if any, of the existing manuscripts comes closest to Lincoln's actual words that day.

Four score and seven years ago our fathers brought forth on this continent a new nation, conceived in liberty and dedicated to the proposition that all men are created equal.

Now we are engaged in a great civil war, testing whether that nation or any nation so conceived and so dedicated can long endure. We are met on a great battlefield of that war. We have come to dedicate a portion of that field as a final resting-place for those who here gave their lives that that nation might live. It is altogether fitting and proper that we should do this.

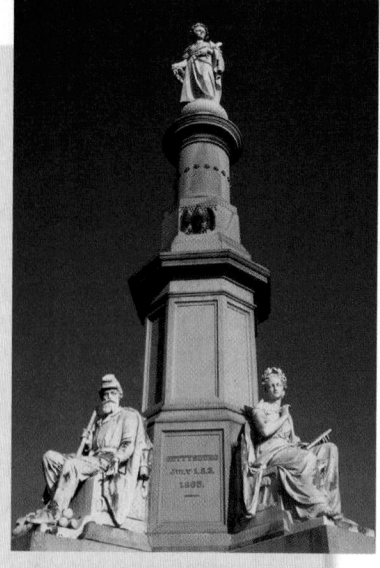

National monument at Gettysburg

But in a larger sense, we cannot dedicate, we cannot consecrate, we cannot hallow this ground. The brave men, living and dead, who struggled here have consecrated it far above our poor power to add or detract. The world will little note nor long remember what we say here, but it can never forget what they did here. It is for us the living, rather, to be dedicated here to the unfinished work which they who fought here have thus far so nobly advanced. It is rather for us to be here dedicated to the great task remaining before us—that from these honored dead we take increased devotion to that cause for which they gave the last full measure of devotion—that we here highly resolve that these dead shall not have died in vain, that this nation under God shall have a new birth of freedom, and that government of the people, by the people, for the people, shall not perish from the earth.

The Pledge of Allegiance

Students in a New York City school reciting the Pledge of Allegiance

In 1892 the nation celebrated the 400th anniversary of Columbus's landing in America. In connection with this celebration, Francis Bellamy, a magazine editor, wrote and published the Pledge of Allegiance. The words "under God" were added by Congress in 1954 at the urging of President Dwight D. Eisenhower.

I pledge allegiance to the Flag of the United States of America and to the Republic for which it stands, one Nation under God, indivisible, with liberty and justice for all.

Documents

President Harrison on Hawaiian Annexation

An early expression of American imperialism came in the annexation of Hawaii. With the support of the American government, a small number of American troops overthrew the Hawaiian monarchy in January 1893. The excerpt below is from President Benjamin Harrison's written message to Congress. He sent the message along with the treaty for annexation to Congress on February 15, 1893.

I do not deem it necessary to discuss at any length the conditions which have resulted in this decisive action. It has been the policy of the administration not only to respect but to encourage the continuance of an independent government in the Hawaiian Islands so long as it afforded suitable guarantees for the protection of life and property and maintained a stability and strength that gave adequate security against the domination of any other power. . . .

The overthrow of the monarchy was not in any way promoted by this government, but had its origin in what seems to have been a reactionary and revolutionary policy on the part of Queen Liliuokalani, which put in serious peril not only the large and preponderating interests of the United States . . . but all foreign interests. . . . It is quite evident that the monarchy had become effete and the queen's government is weak and inadequate as to be the prey of designing and unscrupulous persons. The restoration of Queen Liliuokalani . . . is undesirable . . . and unless actively supported by the United States would be accompanied by serious disaster and the disorganization of all business interests. The influence and interest of the United States in the islands must be increased and not diminished.

Only two courses are now open—one the establishment of a protectorate by the United States, and the other annexation, full and complete. I think the latter course, which has been adopted in the treaty, will be highly promotive of the best interest of the Hawaiian people and is the only one that will adequately secure the interests of the United States. These interests are not wholly selfish. It is essential that none of the other great powers shall secure these islands. Such a possession would not consist with our safety and with the peace of the world. This view of the situation is so apparent and conclusive that no protest has been heard from any government against proceedings looking to annexation.

The American's Creed

In the patriotic fervor of World War I, national leaders sponsored a contest in which writers submitted ideas for a national creed that would be a brief summary of American beliefs. Of the 3,000 entries, the judges selected that of William Tyler Page as the winner. In a 1918 ceremony in the House of Representatives, the Speaker of the House accepted the creed for the United States.

I believe in the United States of America as a Government of the people, by the people, for the people, whose just powers are derived from the consent of the governed; a democracy in a republic; a sovereign Nation of many sovereign States; a perfect union, one and inseparable; established upon those principles of freedom, equality, justice, and humanity for which American patriots sacrificed their lives and fortunes.

I therefore believe it is my duty to my Country to love it; to support its Constitution; to obey its laws; to respect its flag, and to defend it against all enemies.

The Fourteen Points

On January 8, 1918, President Woodrow Wilson went before Congress to offer a statement of war aims called the Fourteen Points. They reflected Wilson's belief that if the international community accepted certain basic principles of conduct and set up institutions to carry them out, there would be peace in the world.

We entered this war because violations of right had occurred. . . . What we demand in this war, therefore, is . . . that the world be made fit and safe to live in. . . .

The only possible programme, as we see it, is this:

I. Open covenants of peace, openly arrived at, after which there shall be no private international understandings of any kind but diplomacy shall proceed always frankly and in the public view.

II. Absolute freedom of navigation upon the seas, outside territorial waters, alike in peace and in war. . . .

III. The removal, so far as possible, of all economic barriers and the establishment of an equality of trade conditions among all the nations. . . .

IV. Adequate guarantees given and taken that national armaments will be reduced to the lowest point consistent with domestic safety.

V. A free, open-minded, and absolutely impartial adjustment of all colonial claims, based upon a strict observance of the principle that in determining all such questions of sovereignty the interests of the populations concerned must have equal weight with the equitable claims of the government whose title is to be determined.

VI. The evacuation of all Russian territory and . . . opportunity for the independent determination of her own political development and national polity. . . .

VII. Belgium . . . must be evacuated and restored. . . .

VIII. All French territory should be freed and the invaded portions restored, and the wrong done to France by Prussia in 1871 in the matter of Alsace-Lorraine should be righted. . . .

IX. A readjustment of the frontiers of Italy should be effected along clearly recognizable lines of nationality.

X. The peoples of Austria-Hungary . . . should be accorded the freest opportunity of autonomous development.

XI. Roumania, Serbia, and Montenegro should be evacuated; occupied territories restored . . . the relations of the several Balkan states to one another determined by friendly counsel along historically established lines of allegiance and nationality. . . .

XII. The Turkish portions of the present Ottoman Empire should be assured a secure sovereignty. . . .

XIII. An independent Polish state should be erected which should include the territories inhabited by indisputably Polish populations. . . .

XIV. A general association of nations must be formed under specific covenants for the purpose of affording mutual guarantees of political independence and territorial integrity. . . .

Discussion of the Fourteen Points at the Versailles peace conference

The Four Freedoms

President Franklin D. Roosevelt delivered this address on January 6, 1941, in his annual message to Congress. In it, Roosevelt called for a world founded on "four essential human freedoms": freedom of speech and expression, freedom of worship, freedom from want, and freedom from fear.

Just as our national policy in internal affairs has been based upon a decent respect for the rights and dignity of all our fellow men within our gates, so our national policy in foreign affairs has been based on a decent respect for the rights and dignity of all nations, large and small. And the justice of morality must and will win in the end.

Our national policy is this:

First, by an impressive expression of the public will and without regard to partisanship, we are committed to all-inclusive national defense.

Second, by an impressive expression of the public will and without regard to partisanship, we are committed to full support of all those resolute peoples, everywhere, who are resisting aggression and are thereby keeping war away from our Hemisphere. . . .

Third . . . we are committed to the proposition that principles of morality and considerations for our own security will never permit us to acquiesce in a peace dictated by aggressors. . . .

Let us say to the democracies, "We Americans are vitally concerned in your defense of freedom. We are putting forth our energies, our resources, and our organizing powers to give you the strength to regain and maintain a free world. We shall send you, in ever increasing numbers, ships, planes, tanks, guns. This is our purpose and our pledge." In fulfillment of this purpose we will not be intimidated by the threats of dictators that they will regard as a breach of international law and as an act of war our aid to the democracies which dare to resist their aggression. . . .

Caricature of President Roosevelt

In the future days, which we seek to make secure, we look forward to a world founded upon four essential human freedoms.

The first is freedom of speech and expression everywhere in the world.

The second is freedom of every person to worship God in his own way everywhere in the world.

The third is freedom from want, which, translated into world terms, means economic understandings which will secure to every nation a healthy peacetime life for its inhabitants everywhere in the world.

The fourth is freedom from fear—which, translated into world terms, means a worldwide reduction of armaments to such a point and in such a thorough fashion that no nation will be in a position to commit an act of physical aggression against any neighbor—anywhere in the world. . . .

The Truman Doctrine

President Harry S. Truman addressed a joint session of Congress on March 12, 1947, to request aid to fight Communist influence in Greece and Turkey. His message that communism had to be contained represents the central idea of American foreign policy during the Cold War.

The United States has received from the Greek Government an urgent appeal for financial and economic assistance. . . .

When forces of liberation entered Greece they found that the retreating Germans had destroyed virtually all the railways, roads, port facilities, communications, and merchant marine. More than a thousand villages had been burned. Eighty-five percent of the children were tubercular. Livestock, poultry, and draft animals had almost disappeared. Inflation had wiped out practically all savings. As a result of these tragic conditions, a militant minority, exploiting human want and misery, was able to create political chaos which, until now, has made economic recovery impossible.

Greece is today without funds to finance the importation of those goods which are essential to bare subsistence. Under these circumstances the people of Greece cannot make progress in solving their problems of reconstruction. Greece is in desperate need of financial and economic assistance to enable it to resume purchases of food, clothing, fuel and seeds. These are indispensable for the subsistence of its people and are obtainable only from abroad. Greece must have help to import the goods necessary to restore internal order and security, so essential for economic and political recovery. . . .

Meanwhile, the Greek Government is unable to cope with the situation. The Greek army is small and poorly equipped. It needs supplies and equipment if it is to restore the authority of the government throughout Greek territory. Greece must have assistance if it is to become a self-supporting and self-respecting democracy.

The United States must supply that assistance. We have already extended to Greece certain types of relief and economic aid but these are inadequate. There is no other country to which democratic Greece can turn. . . .

No government is perfect. One of the chief virtues of a democracy, however, is that its defects are always visible and under democratic processes can be pointed out and corrected.

The Government of Greece is not perfect. Nevertheless it represents eighty-five percent of the members of the Greek Parliament who were chosen in an election last year. . . .

Greece's neighbor, Turkey, also deserves our attention. The future of Turkey as an independent and economically sound state is clearly no less important to the freedom-loving peoples of the world than the future of Greece. The circumstances in which Turkey finds itself today are considerably different from those of Greece. Turkey has been spared the disasters that have beset Greece. And during the war, the United States and Great Britain furnished Turkey with material aid. Nevertheless, Turkey now needs our support.

. . . To ensure the peaceful development of nations, free from coercion, the United States has taken a leading part in establishing the United Nations. The United Nations is designed to make possible lasting freedom and independence for all its members. We shall not realize our objectives, however, unless we are willing to help free peoples to maintain their free institutions . . . against aggressive movements that seek to impose upon them totalitarian regimes. . . .

This is an investment in world freedom and world peace. . . . The seeds of totalitarian regimes are nurtured by misery and want. They spread and grow in the evil soil of poverty and strife. They reach their full growth when the hope of a people for a better life has died. We must keep that hope alive. . . . If we falter in our leadership, we may endanger the peace of the world—and we shall surely endanger the welfare of our own nation.

Brown v. Board of Education

On May 17, 1954, the Supreme Court ruled in **Brown** *v.* **Board of Education of Topeka, Kansas,** *that racial segregation in public schools was unconstitutional. This decision provided the legal basis for court challenges to segregation in every aspect of American life.*

These cases come to us from the States of Kansas, South Carolina, Virginia, and Delaware. They are premised on different facts and different local conditions, but a common legal question justifies their consideration together in this consolidated opinion.

In each of the cases, minors of the Negro race, through their legal representatives, seek the aid of the courts in obtaining admission to the public schools of their community on a nonsegregated basis. In each instance, they had been denied admission to schools attended by white children under laws requiring or permitting segregation according to race. This segregation was alleged to deprive the plaintiffs of the equal protection of the laws under the Fourteenth Amendment.

The plaintiffs contend that segregated public schools are not "equal" and cannot be made "equal," and that hence they are deprived of the equal protection of the laws. Because of the obvious importance of the question presented, the Court took jurisdiction. . . .

. . . Our decision . . . cannot turn on merely a comparison of these tangible factors in the Negro and white schools involved in each of the cases. We must look instead to the effect of segregation itself on public education.

In approaching this problem, we cannot turn the clock back to 1868 when the Amendment was adopted, or even to 1896 when *Plessy* v. *Ferguson* was written. We must consider public education in the light of its full development and its present place in American life throughout the nation. Only in this way can it be determined if segregation in public schools deprives these plaintiffs of the equal protection of the laws.

Today, education is perhaps the most important function of state and local governments. Compulsory school attendance laws and the great expenditures for education both demonstrate our recognition of the importance of education to our democratic society. . . . In these days, it is doubtful that any child may reasonably be expected to succeed in life if he is denied the opportunity of an education. Such an opportunity, where the state has undertaken to provide it, is a right which must be made available to all on equal terms.

We come then to the question presented: Does segregation of children in public schools solely on the basis of race, even though the physical facilities and other "tangible" factors may be equal, deprive the children of the minority group of equal educational opportunities? We believe that it does.

Linda Brown

. . . We conclude that, in the field of public education, the doctrine of "separate but equal" has no place. Separate educational facilities are inherently unequal. Therefore, we hold that the plaintiff and others similarly situated for whom the actions have been brought are, by reason of the segregation complained of, deprived of the equal protection of the laws guaranteed by the Fourteenth Amendment. . . .

"I Have a Dream"

On August 28, 1963, while Congress was debating broad civil rights legislation, Martin Luther King, Jr., led more than 200,000 people in a march on Washington, D.C. On the steps of the Lincoln Memorial, King gave a stirring speech in which he eloquently spoke of his dreams for African Americans and for the United States.

Martin Luther King, Jr., speaking at the march

Five score years ago, a great American, in whose symbolic shadow we stand, signed the Emancipation Proclamation. This momentous decree came as a great beacon light of hope to millions of Negro slaves who had been seared in the flames of withering injustice. It came as a joyous daybreak to end the long night of captivity.

But one hundred years later, we must face the tragic fact that the Negro is still not free. One hundred years later, the life of the Negro is still sadly crippled by the manacles of segregation and the chains of discrimination. . . .

There are those who are asking the devotees of civil rights, "When will you be satisfied?"

We can never be satisfied as long as the Negro is the victim of the unspeakable horrors of police brutality.

We can never be satisfied as long as our bodies, heavy with the fatigue of travel, cannot gain lodging in the motels of the highways and the hotels of the cities.

We cannot be satisfied as long as the Negro's basic mobility is from a smaller ghetto to a larger one. . . .

We cannot be satisfied as long as a Negro in Mississippi cannot vote and a Negro in New York believes he has nothing for which to vote.

No, no, we are not satisfied, and we will not be satisfied until "justice rolls down like waters and righteousness like a mighty stream." . . .

I say to you today, my friends, so even though we face the difficulties of today and tomorrow, I still have a dream. It is a dream deeply rooted in the American dream.

I have a dream that one day this nation will rise up and live out the true meaning of its creed: "We hold these truths to be self-evident; that all men are created equal."

I have a dream that one day on the red hills of Georgia the sons of former slaves and the sons of former slaveowners will be able to sit down together at the table of brotherhood.

I have a dream that one day even the state of Mississippi, a state sweltering with the heat of injustice and oppression, will be transformed into an oasis of freedom and justice.

I have a dream that my four little children will one day live in a nation where they will not be judged by the color of their skin but by the content of their character. . . .

And when this happens, when we allow freedom to ring, when we let it ring from every village and every hamlet, from every state and every city, we will be able to speed up that day when all of God's children, black men and white men, Jews and Gentiles, Protestants and Catholics, will be able to join hands and sing in the words of the old Negro spiritual, "Free at last! Free at last! Thank God Almighty, we are free at last!"

Gulf of Tonkin Resolution

On August 7, 1964, Congress passed the Gulf of Tonkin Resolution, which stood as the legal basis for the Vietnam War.

Resolved by the Senate and House of Representatives of the United States of America in Congress assembled,

That the Congress approves and supports the determination of the President, as Commander in Chief, to take all necessary measures to repel any armed attack against the forces of the United States and to prevent further aggression.

Section 2. The United States regards as vital to its national interest and to world peace the maintenance of international peace and security in southeast Asia. Consonant with the Constitution of the United States and the Charter of the United Nations and in accordance with its obligations under the Southeast Asia Collective Defense Treaty, the United States is, therefore, prepared, as the President determines, to take all necessary steps, including the use of armed force, to assist any member or protocol state of the Southeast Asia Collective Defense Treaty requesting assistance in defense of its freedom.

President Bush's Address to Joint Session of Congress, September 20, 2001

On September 11, 2001, terrorists crashed airplanes into the World Trade Center in New York City and the Pentagon in Washington, D.C. Thousands of people were killed. In his address, President George W. Bush announced a new kind of war against terrorism.

. . . On September the eleventh, enemies of freedom committed an act of war against our country. . . . Americans have known surprise attacks—but never before on thousands of civilians. All of this was brought upon us in a single day—and night fell on a different world, a world where freedom itself is under attack. . . .

The evidence we have gathered all points to a collection of loosely affiliated terrorist organizations known as al-Qaeda. . . . Our war on terror begins with al-Qaeda, but it does not end there. It will not end until every terrorist group of global reach has been found, stopped, and defeated.

Americans are asking: Why do they hate us? They hate what we see right here in this chamber—a democratically elected government.

Their leaders are self-appointed. They hate our freedoms. . . . By sacrificing human life to serve their radical visions—by abandoning every value except the will to power—they follow in the path of fascism, and Nazism, and totalitarianism. And they will follow that path all the way, to where it ends: in history's unmarked grave of discarded lies.

. . . We will direct every resource at our command—every means of diplomacy, every tool of intelligence, every instrument of law enforcement, every financial influence, and every necessary weapon of war—to the disruption and defeat of the global terror network. . . .

I know there are struggles ahead, and dangers to face. But this country will define our times, not be defined by them. . . . Great harm has been done to us. We have suffered great loss. And in our grief and anger we have found our mission and our moment. . . . Our Nation—this generation—will lift a dark threat of violence from our people and our future. We will rally the world to this cause, by our efforts and by our courage. We will not tire, we will not falter, and we will not fail.

The following case summaries explain the significance of major Supreme Court cases mentioned in the text.

Abington School District v. Schempp

(1963) struck down a Pennsylvania statute requiring public schools in the state to begin each school day with Bible readings and a recitation of the Lord's Prayer. The Court held that the Constitution's establishment clause leaves religious beliefs and religious practices to each individual's choice and expressly commands that government not intrude into this decision-making process.

Abrams v. United States

(1919) upheld a conviction under the Sedition Act and Espionage Act of 1917. The Court ruled that freedom of speech could be limited if there was a threat to the country.

Baker v. Carr

(1962) established that federal courts can hear suits seeking to force state authorities to redraw electoral districts. In this case, the plaintiff wanted the population of each district to be roughly equal to the population in all other districts. The plaintiff claimed that the votes of voters in the least populous districts counted as much as the votes of voters in the most populous districts.

Brown v. Board of Education

(1954) overruled *Plessy* v. *Ferguson* (1896) and abandoned the separate-but-equal doctrine in the context of public schools. In deciding this case, the Supreme Court rejected the idea that equivalent but separate schools for African Americans and white students would be constitutional. The Court stated that the Fourteenth Amendment's command that all persons be accorded the equal protection of the law (U.S. Const. amend. XIV, sec. 1) is not satisfied by ensuring that African American and white schools "have been equalized, or are being equalized, with respect to buildings, curricula, qualifications, and salaries, and other tangible factors."

The Court then held that racial segregation in public schools violates the equal protection clause because it is inherently unequal. In other words, the separation of schools by race marks the separate race as inferior. The ruling in this case has been extended beyond public education to virtually all public accommodations and activities.

Bush v. Gore

(2000) found that a manual recount of disputed presidential ballots in Florida lacked a uniform standard of judging a voter's intent, thus violating the equal protection clause of the Constitution. The Court also ruled that there was not enough time to conduct a new manual recount that would meet constitutional standards. The case arose when Republican candidate George W. Bush asked the Court to stop a hand recount. This decision ensured that Bush would receive Florida's electoral votes and win the election.

Chisholm v. Georgia

(1793) stripped the immunity of the states to lawsuits in federal court. The Supreme Court held that a citizen of one state could sue another state in federal court without that state consenting to the suit. The Court's decision created a furor and led to the adoption of the Eleventh Amendment, which protects states from federal court suits by citizens of other states.

Dred Scott v. Sandford

(1857) was decided before the Fourteenth Amendment. The Fourteenth Amendment provides that anyone born or naturalized in the United States is a citizen of the nation and of his or her state. In this case, the Supreme Court held that a slave was property, not a citizen, and thus had no rights under the Constitution. The decision was a prime factor leading to the Civil War.

Engel v. Vitale

(1962) held that the establishment clause (U.S. Const. amend. I, cl. 1) was violated by a public school district's practice of starting each school day with a prayer which began, "Almighty God, we acknowledge our dependence upon Thee." The Supreme Court ruled that religion is a personal matter and that government should not align itself with a particular religion in order to prevent religious persecution.

Escobedo v. Illinois (1964) held that Danny Escobedo's right to counsel, as provided by the Sixth Amendment, had been violated. Throughout police questioning, Escobedo asked repeatedly, but unsuccessfully, to see his attorney. The Supreme Court reversed Escobedo's murder conviction, holding that an attorney could have assisted Escobedo in invoking his Fifth Amendment right against self-incrimination. This case served as a forerunner to *Miranda* v. *Arizona*.

Gibbons v. Ogden (1824) made it clear that the authority of Congress to regulate interstate commerce (U.S. Const. art. I, sec. 8, cl. 3) includes the authority to regulate intrastate commercial activity that relates to interstate commerce. Before this case, it was thought that the Constitution would allow a state to close its borders to interstate commercial activity. This ruling says that a state can only regulate internal commercial activity, but Congress can regulate commercial activity that has both intrastate and interstate dimensions.

Gideon v. Wainwright (1963) ruled that poor defendants in criminal cases have the right to a state-paid attorney under the Sixth Amendment. The ruling in this case has been refined to apply only when the defendant, if convicted, can be sentenced to more than six months in jail.

Griswold v. Connecticut (1965) overturned the conviction of two Planned Parenthood employees charged with violating an 1879 state law banning the use of contraceptives. In deciding this case, the Court went beyond the actual words of the Constitution to protect a right—the right to privacy—which is not listed in the Constitution. The case also served as a forerunner to the *Roe* v. *Wade* decision that legalized abortion on the same basis.

Heart of Atlanta Motel, Inc. v. United States (1964) upheld the Civil Rights Act of 1964, which prohibits racial discrimination by those who provide goods, services, and facilities to the public. The Georgia motel in the case drew its business from other states but refused to rent rooms to African Americans. The Supreme Court explained that Congress had the authority to prohibit such discrimination under both the equal protection clause (U.S. Const. amend. XIV, sec. 1) and the commerce clause (art. I, sec. 8, cl. 3). With respect to the commerce clause, the Court explained that Congress had ample evidence to conclude that racial discrimination by hotels and motels impedes interstate commerce.

Korematsu v. United States (1944) allowed the federal government's authority to exclude Japanese Americans, many of whom were citizens, from designated military areas that included almost the entire West Coast. The government defended the orders as a necessary response to Japan's attack on Pearl Harbor. Yet, in upholding the orders, the Court established that government actions that discriminate on the basis of race would be subject to strict scrutiny.

Loving v. Virginia (1967) ruled that state laws that outlaw interracial marriages are unconstitutional under the Fourteenth Amendment. The Court explained that such laws violated the equal protection clause and deprived "citizens of liberty without due process of law." The Court went on to say, "Marriage is one of the basic civil rights of man, fundamental to our very existence and survival."

Mapp v. Ohio (1961) established that evidence seized in violation of the Fourth Amendment could not be used by the prosecution as evidence of a defendant's guilt at the federal, state, or local level.

Marbury v. Madison (1803) established one of the most important principles of American constitutional law. The Supreme Court held that the Court itself has the final say on what the Constitution means. It is also the Supreme Court that has the final say whether or not an act of government—legislative or executive at the federal, state, or local level—violates the Constitution.

Martin v. Hunter's Lessee (1816) affirmed that the Supreme Court has the authority to review state court decisions and is the nation's final court of appeal. The Supreme Court ruled that section 25 of the Judiciary Act of 1789 was constitutional. This section granted the Supreme Court appellate jurisdiction over state courts in certain situations, such as a state court denying the authority of federal law.

McCulloch v. Maryland (1819) established the basis for the expansive authority of Congress. The Supreme Court held that the necessary and proper clause (U.S. Const. art. I, sec. 8, cl. 18) allows Congress to do more than the Constitution specifically authorizes it to do. This case holds that Congress can enact almost any law that will help it achieve the ends established by Article I, Section 8 of the Constitution. For example, Congress has the power to regulate interstate commerce; the necessary and proper clause permits Congress to do so in ways not specified in the Constitution.

Miranda v. Arizona (1966) held that a person in police custody may not be held unless reminded of his or her rights. These rights include: 1) the right to remain silent, 2) the right to an attorney (at government expense if the person is unable to pay), and 3) that anything the person says after acknowledging that he or she understands these rights can be used as evidence of guilt at a trial.

The Supreme Court explained that a person alone in police custody may not understand, even if told, that he or she can remain silent and thus might be misled into answering questions. The presence of an attorney is essential.

Morgan v. Virginia (1946) challenged racial segregation in the South. Irene Morgan was convicted for refusing to give up her seat on an interstate bus bound from Virginia to Maryland. The Court ruled that the Virginia law posed an undue burden on interstate commerce and struck down the statute. However, segregation on southern buses continued on an informal basis.

National Labor Relations Board v. Jones and Laughlin Steel Corp. (1937) upheld President Franklin Roosevelt's New Deal legislation, the National Labor Relations Act, which allowed workers to organize unions in businesses operating or affecting interstate commerce. Employers were prohibited from discriminating against their employees because of union membership. Prior to this case, the Supreme Court had ruled much New Deal legislation unconstitutional. This ruling came less than a week after Roosevelt's proposed court-packing plan. The president intended on "packing" the Supreme Court with additional justices in order to obtain a pro-New Deal majority on the Court.

New York Times Co. v. Sullivan (1964) extended the protections afforded to the press by the free press clause (U.S. Const. amend. I). In this case, the Supreme Court held that a public official or public figure suing a publisher for libel (i.e., defamation) must prove that the publisher published a story that he or she knew was false or published the story in "reckless disregard of its truth or falsity," which means that the publisher did not take professionally adequate steps to determine the story's truth or falsity.

Norris v. Alabama (1935) overturned the conviction of Clarence Norris, an African American sentenced to death for a crime in Alabama. The Supreme Court held that the grand jury and trial jury had systematically eliminated African American jurors. Thus, the Court reversed the conviction because it violated the equal protection clause of the Fourteenth Amendment.

Northern Securities Company v. United States (1904) dealt with the application of congressional antitrust legislation. The party involved held three-fourths of the stock in two parallel railroad lines. By a narrow 5–4 decision, the Court upheld the application of the Sherman Antitrust Act. The Court ruled that the holding company clearly intended to eliminate competition between the two railroads, violating the constitutional right of Congress to regulate interstate commerce.

Plessy v. Ferguson (1896) upheld the separate-but-equal doctrine used by Southern states to perpetuate segregation after the Civil War officially ended law-mandated segregation. The decision upheld a Louisiana law requiring passenger trains to have "equal but separated accommodations for the white and colored races." The Court held that the Fourteenth Amendment's equal protection clause required only equal public facilities for the two races, not equal access. This case was overruled by *Brown* v. *Board of Education* (1954).

Regents of the University of California v. Bakke (1978) was the first Supreme Court decision to suggest that an affirmative action program could be justified on the basis of diversity. The Court explained that racial quotas were not permissible under the equal protection clause of the Fourteenth Amendment. However, the justices ruled that the diversity rationale was a legitimate interest that would allow a state medical school to consider an applicant's race in evaluating his or her application for admission. (Recent Supreme Court cases suggest that the diversity rationale is no longer enough to defend an affirmative action program.)

Reynolds v. Sims (1964) extended the one-person, one-vote doctrine announced in *Wesberry* v. *Sanders* to state legislative elections. The Court held that the inequality of representation in the Alabama legislature violated the equal protection clause of the Fourteenth Amendment.

Roe v. Wade (1973) held that women have the right under various provisions of the Constitution—most notably, the due process clause of the Fourteenth Amendment—to decide whether or not to terminate a pregnancy. The Court's ruling in this case was the most significant in a long line of decisions over a period of 50 years that recognized a constitutional right of privacy, even though the word *privacy* is not found in the Constitution.

Schechter Poultry Corporation v. United States (1935) overturned the conviction of the employers, who were charged with violating the wage and hour limitations of a law adopted under the authority of the National Industrial Recovery Act. The Court held that because the defendants did not sell poultry in interstate commerce, they were not subject to federal regulations on wages and hours.

Schenck v. United States (1919) upheld convictions under the Federal Espionage Act. The defendants were charged under the act with distributing leaflets aimed at inciting draft resistance during World War I; their defense was that antidraft speech was protected under the First Amendment.

The Supreme Court unanimously rejected the defense, explaining that whether or not speech is protected depends on the context in which it occurs. Because the defendants' antidraft rhetoric created a "clear and present danger" to the success of the war effort, it was not protected.

Stone v. Powell (1976) reversed a Court of Appeals decision that evidence was seized illegally and should therefore be excluded. The Court ruled that the defendant was provided a fair and legal opportunity to claim a Fourth Amendment violation before a trial jury. The trial jury found that the search was constitutional and the evidence should not be excluded. The Court stated, "Where the state has provided an opportunity for full and fair litigation of a Fourth Amendment claim, a state prisoner may not be granted federal habeas corpus relief."

Swann v. Charlotte-Mecklenburg Board of Education (1971) established a new plan to ensure that public schools were not segregated. Many school systems were slow to desegregate after *Brown* v. *Board of Education* and used various tactics to appear to be resolving the problem. This case ordered that busing students, reorganizing school boundaries, and racial ratios all be used as methods to obtain desegregated public school systems.

Sweatt v. Painter (1950) held that it was unconstitutional for African Americans to be denied admission to the University of Texas Law School based on race. An inferior law school established for African Americans did not give the state justification to deny admission to the main school. This act was a violation of the Fourteenth Amendment.

Wabash v. Illinois (1886) held that states have no authority to regulate railroad rates for interstate commerce. The Supreme Court held that the commerce clause (U.S. Const. art. I, sec. 8, cl. 3) allowed states to enforce "indirect" but not "direct" burdens on interstate commerce. State railroad rates were ruled "direct" burdens and therefore could not be enforced by states. The decision created a precedent by establishing rate regulation of interstate commerce as an exclusive federal power.

Wickard v. Filburn (1942) indicated how far the Supreme Court had come in complying with President Franklin Roosevelt's economic philosophies. The Court upheld specific parts of the Second Agricultural Adjustment Act. In its ruling, the Supreme Court held that marketing quotas could be applied to wheat that never left the farm. Using the commerce clause (U.S. Const. art. I, sec. 8, cl. 3) as the basis for its decision, the Court ruled that wheat that never left the farm still had an effect on interstate commerce. Farmers growing their own grain depressed the overall demand and market price of wheat. The decision further extended the power of the commerce clause.

Worcester v. Georgia (1832) overturned the conviction of Samuel A. Worcester, a missionary among the Cherokee. Worcester was imprisoned under a Georgia law forbidding whites to reside in Cherokee country without taking an oath of allegiance to the state and obtaining a permit. The Supreme Court voided the state law, ruling that the Cherokee were an independent nation based on a federal treaty and free from the jurisdiction of the state. Georgia ignored the decision, and President Jackson refused to enforce it, instead supporting the removal of the Cherokee to the Indian Territory.

American Literature Library

TABLE OF CONTENTS

What Is Literature?

Literature is art created with words. Some people use the term "literature" to include anything written—from newspaper articles and how-to books to pamphlets in a doctor's office. On the other hand, some insist that only creative writing can be literature. Still others suggest that some essays, or written opinions, and even speeches are of such high quality that they may be considered literature.

Just as there are many forms of the visual arts, there are many forms and styles of literature. Reading the literature of a certain period of history helps to bring the people and issues of the time to life.

A Good Story

Have you ever created a story to entertain a younger person? That's fiction: a story invented by the author. Writing that describes or explains real events or activities is referred to as "nonfiction."

The most popular type of fiction is the novel, a long story that usually has many people, or characters, and a complex plot, or action. Novels are written in prose, or everyday language, rather than poetry.

Some novels are inspired by actual events the author witnessed or people he or she has known. But a fiction writer is not attempting to report events or describe people accurately.

By telling a good story, the author tries to lead the reader to discover universal truths. Other types of fiction include short stories and novellas, or short novels.

Time and Timelessness

Some writers set their stories in the present; some write historical novels; others write science fiction tales set in the future. All writers hope their work expresses truths that will be valid long after their lifetimes.

Throughout history, writers have addressed major themes such as good and evil, freedom, religion, power, corruption, love, death, and the relationship of humans to the natural world. Works of literature from a specific period of history often reflect their time in several ways:

- the language used
- the form of the work
- the general attitudes of the characters and the issues they face
- the morality expressed by the outcome

Approaching Poetry

Poetry is writing that is intended first and foremost to evoke emotion, not just convey information or tell a story. The first job of poetry is to create feeling—not to stimulate thought. For this reason it often has a rhythm like music, and it is often easier to understand if read aloud.

Eighteenth- and nineteenth-century poets—and some modern ones—wrote in one of many traditional forms. Each form requires a certain rhyme frequency and pattern of accented syllables, or meter. It also requires a specific number of lines of certain lengths.

Modern poetry does not always follow these conventions; words do not always rhyme, and sometimes the rhythm is to be found in how the words are arranged on the page, not how they sound. Despite these modern touches, the poet's goal remains constant—to evoke specific emotions that illuminate some aspect of life.

The Eras of Literature in American History

Writers reflect world events and issues in their work. Some write directly about those events and issues. Others express values or beliefs that were changed by historical events.

The Early National Period During the early years of the United States, authors often wrote about the challenges of settling a new land. They also focused on religion, morality, and the new form of government. Native Americans already had a rich tradition of oral literature.

After the War of 1812, writers such as James Fennimore Cooper and Washington Irving created a uniquely American style of writing with tales of adventures in the New World. Ralph Waldo Emerson and Henry David Thoreau wrote of the spiritual power of nature.

The Civil War Era During the Civil War and in every decade since, the tragedies of that conflict and the nature of race relations in American society have inspired some of America's best writers, from Mark Twain and Harriet Beecher Stowe in the nineteenth century to William Faulkner and Richard Wright in the twentieth century, and contemporary writers such as August Wilson and Toni Morrison.

Naturalism and Realism As industrialization attracted immigrants from around the globe, writers created art out of the attainment—and the failure—of their dreams. In *The Rise of Silas Lapham*, William Dean Howells told the rags-to-riches story of a Northern industrialist. Early in the twentieth century, "realist" writers, such as Theodore Dreiser, aided the work of Progressive reformers by exposing the underside of industry and the lives of laborers. Other major writers of the era included Mark Twain, Henry James, Stephen Crane, and Edith Wharton.

Modernism in the 1920s and 1930s World War I and its aftermath challenged traditional values, family life, and individual identity. Perhaps the best-known writer of this era is Ernest Hemingway, who along with other "lost generation" writers such as John dos Passos, Gertrude Stein, and F. Scott Fitzgerald described their sense of disillusionment with modern life.

The era also witnessed the appearance of several major African American writers and poets, including Langston Hughes and Claude McKay, in what became known as the Harlem Renaissance.

The tragedy of the Great Depression and the struggles of average Americans to survive provided inspiration for many writers. John Steinbeck's novel *The Grapes of Wrath* about Dust Bowl refugees is perhaps best known.

The second world war spawned a flood of war novels as writers reexamined human beings' relationship to evil, religion, and the meaning of life in the wake of the Jewish Holocaust, and what such an event said about human nature and its capacity for evil.

The 1950s and 1960s In the 1950s, beat writers, such as Jack Kerouac and Tom Robbins, shunned the conformity and materialism of affluent postwar America in favor of spontaneity and experimentation. But history had more shocks in store for American society including the social upheaval of the 1960s, the Vietnam War, and the transformation of a society from one based on reading to a mass-media consumer culture.

Postmodern Writers of Today The events of the late twentieth century led to "postmodern" writing. Postmodern writers are skeptical about any single version of reality in the Information Age. Their writing is full of irony and doubt about modern culture.

Unit 1: Creating a Nation

When white settlers arrived in America, the Native Americans living there already had a highly developed civilization dating back thousands of years. They also had their own form of literature—not written, but handed down from generation to generation orally. A theme common to many Native American stories is their relationship to nature. Many are also parables—stories that use symbols or animals to teach lessons. "Bald Eagle Sends Mud-turtle to the End of the World," written down by Jeremiah Curtin, is an example of a parable.

The second selection here is a portion of a famous speech given by Chief Red Jacket (Native American name Sagoyoweha). Red Jacket was an influential leader of the Seneca nation and the Iroquois confederation of tribes from the 1770s until the 1820s. He fought on the side of the British during the American Revolution, but in the War of 1812, he influenced his people to support the United States.

An ardent advocate of the Native American mode of life, he opposed the introduction of white customs, laws, schools, and especially conversion of Seneca to Christianity. In 1820 or 1821 he successfully petitioned Governor Clinton for the removal of missionaries and white teachers from Buffalo Creek reservation near Buffalo, New York. This speech was given at an 1805 meeting to discuss establishment of missions among six Iroquois nations. In it, Red Jacket argues forcefully for the religious freedom that many white settlers had left Europe to enjoy.

forefathers: ancestors

"Bald Eagle Sends Mud-turtle to the End of the World"

Once upon a time, a bald-headed old man lived on the top of a mountain, and his wife and three children lived near a lake about half way to the summit of the same mountain.

Each day the old man went down to fish in the lake. On his way home he stopped and gave some of the fish to his wife, and thus they lived well and happily. After they had passed many years in this manner, the old man became curious to know how large the world is.

Being chief of his people he called a council, and said, "I want to know how large the world is. I wish some man would volunteer to find out."

One young man said, "I will go and find out."

"Very well," said the chief, "How long will you be gone?"

"I can't tell, for I don't know how far I shall have to travel."

"Go," said the chief, "and when you return you will tell us about your journey."

The young man started and after traveling two moons he came to a country where everything was white—the forests, the water, the grass. It hurt his feet to walk on the white ground, so he hurried back. When he reached home he notified the chief. The chief said, "I don't believe that he has been to the end of the world, but I will call a council and we will hear what he has to say."

When the people were assembled, the young man said: "I did not go very far, but I went as far as I was able." And he told all he knew of the White Country.

The chief said, "We must send another man." . . . Many men were sent, one after another, and each returned with a story a little different from that told by others, but still no one satisfied the chief. At last a man said, "I will start and I will go to the end of the world before I come back."

The chief looked at the man and saw that he was very homely, but very strong, and he said, "I think you will do as you promise. You may go." The chief called a council of the whole nation and each man agreed to make a journey by himself . . . The chief and his men went and were gone forty moons. When they came home a council was held and each told what he had seen. When the man came who had promised to go to the end of the world, he said, "I have been to the end of

Chief Red Jacket's Speech

Chief Red Jacket

the world, I have seen all kinds of people, all kinds of game, all kinds of forests and rivers. I have seen things which no one else has ever seen."

The chief was satisfied. He said, "I am chief of all the people, you will be next to me. You'll be second chief." This was the pay the man got for his journey. He took his position as second chief.

The old chief was Bald Eagle. The first man sent out was Deer. His feet were tender, he could not endure the ice and snow of the White Country. The homely man who went to the end of the world was Mud-turtle.

"BROTHER: Our seats were once large and yours were small. You have now become a great people, and we have scarcely a place left to spread our blankets. You have got our country, but you are not satisfied; you want to force your religion upon us. . . . You say that you are right and we are lost. How do we know this to be true? We understand that your religion is written in a book. If it was intended for us as well as you, why has not the Great Spirit given to us, and not only to us, but why did he not give to our **forefathers,** the knowledge of that book, with the means of understanding it rightly? We only know what you tell us about it. How shall we know when to believe, being so often deceived by the white people.

BROTHER: You say there is but one way to worship and serve the Great Spirit. If there is but one religion, why do you white people differ so much about it? Why not all agreed, as you can all read the book?

BROTHER: We do not understand these things. We are told that your religion was given to your forefathers, and has been handed down from father to son. We also have a religion, which was given to our forefathers, and has been handed down to us their children. We worship in that way. It teaches us to be thankful for all the favors we receive, to love each other, and to be united. We never quarrel about religion.

BROTHER: The Great Spirit has made us all, but He has made a great difference between his white and red children. He has given us different complexions and different customs. To you he has given the arts. To these He has not opened our eyes. . . . Since He has made so great a difference between us in other things, why may we not conclude that he has given us a different religion according to our understanding? The Great Spirit does right. He knows what is best for his children; we are satisfied. . . . We do not wish to destroy your religion, or take it from you. We only want to enjoy our own."

Unit 2: The Young Republic

Sixty years after declaring independence, American culture was still heavily influenced by Europe. In 1836 Ralph Waldo Emerson's groundbreaking essay, "Nature", established a new way for Americans to look at the world. For the first time in history, there was a roadmap showing how to escape from traditional cultures and build a new, American identity. A large part of that identity was the belief in individuality, expressed in another Emerson essay, "Self-Reliance," a portion of which follows.

Born in Boston in 1803, Emerson was descended from a long line of New England clergymen. He began his career as a Unitarian minister, but left the church because of doubts about orthodox doctrine. Still, he spent the rest of his life as a teacher of ethics, through his lectures and his writing.

Emerson wrote against the rising tide of American materialism and conformity in his time—themes that are as relevant today as they were a century ago. As he worded it, "Things are in the saddle/And ride mankind."

*Emerson is considered the father of a philosophical, religious, and literary movement called transcendentalism. Along with Walt Whitman, Henry David Thoreau, Margaret Fuller, and other writers of the day, Emerson believed that the divine spirit was present in every man and in all of nature. In nature, man could **intuitively** discover all universal laws at work. If God is good and just, then so is man. Evil exists only when man has an imperfect awareness of his essential goodness. This belief led some transcendentalists to social activism.*

intuitively: understanding immediately without the need of logic or rational thought

particulars: areas of life

asinine: marked by a failure to use intelligence or good judgment

loath: unwilling

hobgoblin: a mischievous goblin, or ugly sprite

gazetted: announced in a periodical

"Self-Reliance"
Ralph Waldo Emerson

What I must do is all that concerns me, not what the people think. This rule, equally arduous in actual and in intellectual life, may serve for the whole distinction between greatness and meanness. It is the harder, because you will always find those who think they know what is your duty better than you know it. It is easy in the world to live after the world's opinion; it is easy in solitude to live after our own; but the great man is he who in the midst of the crowd keeps with perfect sweetness the independence of solitude.

The objection to conforming to usages that have become dead to you is that it scatters your force. It loses your time and blurs the impression of your character. If you maintain a dead church, contribute to a dead Bible-society, vote with a great party either for the government or against it, spread your table like base housekeepers,—under all these screens I have difficulty to detect the precise man you are. And, of course, so much force is withdrawn from your proper life. But do your work, and I shall know you. Do your work, and you shall reinforce yourself. . . .

Well, most men have bound their eyes with one or another handkerchief, and attached themselves to some one of these communities of opinion. This conformity makes them not false in a few **particulars,** authors of a few lies, but false in all particulars. Their every truth is not quite true. . . . Meantime nature is not slow to equip us in the prison-uniform of the party to which we adhere. We come to wear one cut of face and figure, and acquire by degrees the gentlest **asinine** expression . . . the forced smile which we put on in company where we do not feel at ease in answer to conversation which does not interest us. The muscles, not spontaneously moved, but moved by a low usurping wilfulness, grow tight about the outline of the face with the most disagreeable sensation.

For nonconformity the world whips you with its displeasure. And therefore a man must know how to estimate a sour face. The by-standers look askance on him in the public street or in the friend's parlour. . . . but the sour faces of the multitude, like their sweet faces, have no deep cause, but are put on and off as the wind blows and a newspaper directs.

Ralph Waldo Emerson

and Galileo, and Newton, and every pure and wise spirit that ever took flesh. To be great is to be misunderstood.

. . . I hope in these days we have heard the last of conformity and consistency. Let the words be **gazetted** and ridiculous henceforward. . . . Man is timid and apologetic; he is no longer upright; he dares not say 'I think,' 'I am,' but quotes some saint or sage. He is ashamed before the blade of grass or the blowing rose. These roses under my window make no reference to former roses or to better ones; they are for what they are; they exist with God to-day. There is no time to them. There is simply the rose; it is perfect in every moment of its existence. . . . But man postpones or remembers; he does not live in the present, but with reverted eye laments the past, or, heedless of the riches that surround him, stands on tiptoe to foresee the future. He cannot be happy and strong until he too lives with nature in the present, above time.

. . . The other terror that scares us from self-trust is our consistency; a reverence for our past act or word, because the eyes of others have no other data for computing our orbit than our past acts, and we are **loath** to disappoint them. But why . . . drag about this corpse of your memory . . . ? Suppose you should contradict yourself; what then? It seems to be a rule of wisdom never to rely on your memory alone, scarcely even in acts of pure memory, but to bring the past for judgment into the thousand-eyed present, and live ever in a new day.

. . . A foolish consistency is the **hobgoblin** of little minds, adored by little statesmen and philosophers and divines. With consistency a great soul has simply nothing to do. He may as well concern himself with his shadow on the wall. Speak what you think now in hard words, and to-morrow speak what to-morrow thinks in hard words again, though it contradict every thing you said to-day.—'Ah, so you shall be sure to be misunderstood.'—Is it so bad, then, to be misunderstood? Pythagoras was misunderstood, and Socrates, and Jesus, and Luther, and Copernicus,

Unit 3: The Crisis of the Union

Harriet Beecher Stowe witnessed the harsh realities of slavery while living in Cincinnati, Ohio, just across the Ohio River from the slave state of Kentucky. Because of these experiences, she became an active abolitionist.

Before the Civil War, many Northerners believed slavery was a constitutionally guaranteed right, and that opposition to it endangered the Union. Even those who agreed with Stowe considered it dangerous to oppose slavery openly and assisted slaveholders in recovering fugitives.

Stowe believed they were able to do this because they did not understand what they were defending. While in church one day in 1851, after she had moved to Brunswick, Maine, she was overcome with a vision of a slave being beaten to death. Sobbing, she ran home and began writing Uncle Tom's Cabin.

The book depicts the life of a long-suffering enslaved person, and the slaveholders and fellow enslaved people in his life. Its 1852 publication attracted threat letters to Stowe, forced closings of bookstores that sold it, and initiated proslavery novels by Southern writers. When Abraham Lincoln met Stowe, he reportedly said, "So this is the little lady who made this big [Civil] war."

In the first year after publication, Uncle Tom's Cabin sold more than 300,000 copies in the United States. It became the best-selling novel of the nineteenth century, inspired songs and was presented as a play that is still performed today.

wormwood: A European plant whose leaves yield a bitter oil used to make a liqueur.

dray horse: a horse that hauls heavy loads

Uncle Tom's Cabin
Harriet Beecher Stowe

Harriet Beecher Stowe

In this excerpt the enslaved George is visiting his wife, Eliza. They were sold to different slaveholders, but have been allowed to visit each other when not working. George had been hired out to a factory, where he was treated well and had invented a work-saving machine. But when the slaveholder saw George's pride in his accomplishment, he moved George back to the plantation and gave him mindless physical work in order to restore his humility.

From Chapter 3

You are the handsomest woman I ever saw, and the best one I ever wish to see; but, oh, I wish I'd never seen you, nor you me!"

"O, George, how can you!"

"Yes, Eliza, it's all misery, misery, misery! My life is bitter as **wormwood;** the very life is burning out of me. I'm a poor, miserable, forlorn drudge; I shall only drag you down with me, that's all. What's the use of our trying to do anything, trying to know anything, trying to be anything? What's the use of living? I wish I was dead!"

"O, now, dear George, that is really wicked! I know how you feel about losing your place in the factory, and you have a hard master; but pray be patient, and perhaps something—"

"Patient!" said he, interrupting her; "haven't I been patient? Did I say a word when he came and took me away, for no earthly reason, from the place where everybody was kind to me? I'd paid him truly every cent of my earnings,— and they all say I worked well."

"Well, it *is* dreadful," said Eliza; "but, after all, he is your master, you know."

"My master! and who made him my master? That's what I think of—what right has he to me? I'm a man as much as he is. I'm a better man than he is. I know more about business than he does; I am a better manager than he is; I can read better than he can; I can write a better hand,—and I've learned it all myself, and no thanks to him,—I've learned it in spite of him;

and now what right has he to make a **dray-horse** of me?—to take me from things I can do, and do better than he can, and put me to work that any horse can do? He tries to do it; he says he'll bring me down and humble me, and he puts me to just the hardest, meanest and dirtiest work, on purpose!"

"O, George! George! you frighten me! Why, I never heard you talk so; I'm afraid you'll do something dreadful. I don't wonder at your feelings, at all; but oh, do be careful—do, do—for my sake—for Harry's! . . . O, George, we must have faith. Mistress says that when all things go wrong to us, we must believe that God is doing the very best."

"That's easy to say for people that are sitting on their sofas and riding in their carriages; but let 'em be where I am, I guess it would come some harder. I wish I could be good; but my heart burns, and can't be reconciled, anyhow. You couldn't in my place,—you can't now, if I tell you all I've got to say. You don't know the whole yet."

"What can be coming now?"

"Well, lately Mas'r has been saying that he was a fool to let me marry off the place; that . . . I shall take a wife and settle down on his place . . . or he would sell me down river."

"Why—but you were married to *me* by the minister, as much as if you'd been a white man!" said Eliza, simply.

"Don't you know a slave can't be married? There is no law in this country for that; I can't hold you for my wife, if he chooses to part us. That's why I wish I'd never seen you,—why I wish I'd never been born; it would have been better for us both,—it would have been better for this poor child if he had never been born. All this may happen to him yet!"

"O, but [my] master is so kind!"

"Yes, but who knows?—he may die—and then [our son] may be sold to nobody knows who. What pleasure is it that he is handsome, and smart, and bright? I tell you, Eliza, that a sword will pierce through your soul for every good and pleasant thing your child is or has; it will make him worth too much for you to keep."

The words smote heavily on Eliza's heart; the vision of the trader came before her eyes, and, as if some one had struck her a deadly blow, she turned pale and gasped for breath.

. . . "So, Eliza, my girl," said the husband, mournfully, "bear up, now; and good-by, for I'm going."

"Going, George! Going where?"

"To Canada," said he, straightening himself up; "and when I'm there, I'll buy you; that's all the hope that's left us. You have a kind master, that won't refuse to sell you. I'll buy you and the boy;—God helping me, I will!"

"O, dreadful! if you should be taken?"

"I won't be taken, Eliza; I'll *die* first! I'll be free, or I'll die!"

Eliza flees across the icy Ohio River

Unit 4: The Birth of Modern America

Carl Sandburg was the son of Swedish immigrants who settled in Galesburg, near Chicago. His father worked on the Chicago, Burlington and Quincy railroad at a time when advances in transportation, communications, and manufacturing technology were changing American commerce and life. By the end of the 1800s, the city had become an industrial hub for the lumber, grain, meatpacking, and mail-order businesses.

Sandburg's poem, "Chicago," captures the bustling activity of the city where many African Americans immigrated from the seg-regated South. It also exposes the evolving urban morality against which many Americans recoiled.

From the time he was a young boy, Sandburg had a variety of jobs—delivering mail, harvesting ice, laying bricks, thrashing wheat, and shining shoes. In 1897 he traveled as a hobo, seeing firsthand the sharp contrast between rich and poor. During his long career, he won two Pulitzer Prizes, one for poetry and another for a five-volume biography of Abraham Lincoln.

Following "Chicago" is a portion of an address by Samuel Clemens to the citizens of another city—his adopted home, San Francisco. It was written in 1866, as he pre-pared to revisit the town of his youth, Hannibal, Missouri. In this address, Clemens predicts the changes that he sees beginning to occur as San Francisco evolved from a "straggling town" to a modern **mecca** *for multicultural immigration.*

mecca: a center of activity sought as a goal by people with a common interest

heedlessly: without thinking

hither: here

"Chicago"
Carl Sandburg

Hog Butcher for the World,
    Tool Maker, Stacker of Wheat,
      Player with Railroads and the Nation's Freight Handler;
    Stormy, husky, brawling,
    City of the Big Shoulders:

They tell me you are wicked and I believe them, for I
    have seen your painted women under the gas lamps
    luring the farm boys.
And they tell me you are crooked and I answer: Yes, it
    is true I have seen the gunman kill and go free to
    kill again.
And they tell me you are brutal and my reply is: On the
    faces of women and children I have seen the marks
    of wanton hunger.
And having answered so I turn once more to those who
    sneer at this my city, and I give them back the sneer
    and say to them:
Come and show me another city with lifted head singing
    so proud to be alive and coarse and strong and cunning.
Flinging magnetic curses amid the toil of piling job on
    job, here is a tall bold slugger set vivid against the
    little soft cities;
Fierce as a dog with tongue lapping for action, cunning
    as a savage pitted against the wilderness,
        Bareheaded,
        Shoveling,
        Wrecking,
        Planning,
        Building, breaking, rebuilding,
Under the smoke, dust all over his mouth, laughing with
    white teeth,
Under the terrible burden of destiny laughing as a young
    man laughs,
Laughing even as an ignorant fighter laughs who has
    never lost a battle,
Bragging and laughing that under his wrist is the pulse.
    and under his ribs the heart of the people,
        Laughing!
Laughing the stormy, husky, brawling laughter of
    Youth, half-naked, sweating, proud to be Hog
    Butcher, Tool Maker, Stacker of Wheat, Player with
    Railroads and Freight Handler to the Nation.

Chicago grain elevator, 1900

"Farewell"
Samuel Clemens

"I am now about to bid farewell to San Francisco for a season, and to go back to that common home we all tenderly remember in our waking hours and fondly revisit in dreams of the night—a home which is familiar to my recollection, but will be an unknown land to my unaccustomed eyes. I shall share the fate of many another longing exile who wanders back to his early home to find gray hairs where he expected youth, graves where he looked for firesides, grief where he had pictured joy—everywhere change . . . where he had **heedlessly** dreamed that desolating Time had stood still! . . . And while I linger here upon the threshold of this, my new home . . . I accept the warning that mighty changes will have come over this home also when my returning feet shall walk these streets again.

I read the signs of the times, and I, that am no prophet, behold the things that are in store for you. Over slumbering California is stealing the dawn of a radiant future! The great China Mail Line is established, the Pacific Railroad is creeping across the continent, the commerce of the world is about to be revolutionized. California is Crown Princess of the new dispensation! She stands in the centre of the grand highway of the nations; she stands midway between the Old World and the New, and both shall pay her tribute. From the far East and from Europe, multitudes of stout hearts and willing hands are preparing to flock **hither;** to throng her hamlets and villages; to till her fruitful soil; to unveil the riches of her countless mines; to build up an empire on these distant shores that shall shame the bravest dreams of her visionaries. . . . Half the world stands ready to lay its contributions at her feet! Has any other State so brilliant a future? Has any other city a future like San Francisco?

"This straggling town shall be a vast metropolis; this sparsely populated land shall become a crowded hive of busy men; your waste places shall blossom like the rose, and your deserted hills and valleys shall yield bread and wine for unnumbered thousands; railroads shall be spread hither and thither and carry the invigorating blood of commerce to regions that are languishing now; mills and workshops, yea, and factories shall spring up everywhere, and mines that have neither name nor place to-day shall dazzle the world with their affluence. The time is drawing on apace when the clouds shall pass away from your firmament, and a splendid prosperity shall descend like a glory upon the whole land!

"I am bidding the old city and my old friends a kind, but not a sad farewell, for I know that when I see this home again, the changes that will have been wrought upon it . . . will be brighter, happier and prouder a hundred fold than it is this day."

San Francisco, 1890

Unit 5: Imperialism and Progressivism

*Theodore Dreiser and other writers, such as Frank Norris and Upton Sinclair, were Progressive Era "muckrakers." They exposed the scandals and corruption of urban American life at the turn of the twentieth century in a literary **genre** (ZHAHN•ruh) known as American Realism. In this style, writers present everyday life as it actually is, rather than in a **romanticized** style, as many earlier writers had done. Norris and Sinclair were also considered naturalist writers, since they believed that humans had to overcome their environment, their ego, and their "brute instincts."*

Dreiser was born "on the wrong side of the tracks," and learned early that middle-class Americans looked on his impoverished family as outsiders. Because of that, his writing shows a compassionate understanding of life's outcasts and failures, and sympathy for those who desperately crave wealth, love, and power. His famous novel, An American Tragedy, *follows the descent of an ordinary young man who commits a ruthless murder, and the social and political pressures that assail him.*

The life of Madeleine, an impoverished young woman, is the theme of this selection, from the short story "Sanctuary." In it we glimpse some of the urban conditions that inspired the work of many progressive reformers of the day.

genre: a category of artistic composition characterized by form, style, or content

romanticized: presented in a fanciful, imaginative way rather than based on fact

"Sanctuary"
Theodore Dreiser

Theodore Dreiser

Primarily, there were the conditions under which [Madeleine] was brought to fifteen years of age: the crowded, scummy tenements; the narrow green-painted halls with their dim gas jets, making the entrance look more like that of a morgue than a dwelling place; the dirty halls and rooms with their green or blue or brown walls painted to save the cost of paper; the bare wooden floors, long since saturated with every type of grease and filth from oleomargarine and suet leaked from cheap fats or meats, to beer and whiskey and tobacco juice. . . .

And then the streets outside—any of the streets by which she had ever been surrounded—block upon block of other red, bare, commonplace tenements crowded to the doors with human life, the space before them sped over by noisy, gassy trucks and vehicles of all kinds. . . .

In this atmosphere were always longshoremen, wagon drivers, sweepers of floors, washers of dishes, waiters, janitors, workers in laundries, factories—mostly in indifferent or decadent or despairing conditions. And all of these people existed, in so far as she ever knew, upon that mysterious, evanescent and fluctuating something known as the weekly wage.

Always about her there had been drunkenness, fighting, complaining, sickness or death; the police coming in, and arresting one and another; the gas man, the rent man, the furniture man, hammering at doors for their due. . . .

It is not surprising that Madeleine came to her twelfth and thirteenth years without any real understanding of the great world about her and without any definite knowledge or skill. Her drunken mother was now more or less dependent upon her, her father having died of pneumonia and her brother and sister having disappeared to do for themselves. . . .

The child actually went hungry at times. . . . a neighbor perceiving her wretched state and suggesting that some extra helpers were wanted in a department store at Christmastime, she applied there, but so wretched were her clothes by now that she was not even considered. . . . she was able to get a place as a servant in a family.

Those who know anything of the life of a domestic know how thoroughly unsatisfactory it is—the leanness, the lack of hope. . . . she had only the kitchen for her chief chamber or a cubbyhole under the roof. . . .

And then, as was natural, love in the guise of youth, a rather sophisticated gallant somewhat above the world in which she was moving, appeared and paid his all but worthless court to her. . . .

A single trip to Wonderland, a single visit to one of its halls where music sounded to the splash of the waves and where he did his best to teach her to dance, a single meal in one of its gaudy, noisy restaurants . . . were given to hope, a new and seemingly realizable dream of happiness implanted in her young mind. The world was happier than she had thought, or could be made so; not all people fought and screamed at each other. There were such things as tenderness, soft words, sweet words.

But the way of so sophisticated a youth with a maid was brief and direct.

. . . Often in this hour she thought of the swift, icy waters of the river, glistening under a winter moon, and then again of the peace and quiet of the House of the Good Shepherd, its shielding remoteness from life, the only true home or sanctuary she had ever known. And so, brooding and repressing occasional sobs, she made her way toward it . . . thinking of the pathetically debasing love-life that was now over— the dream of love that never, never could be again, for her.

* * *

The stark red walls of the institution stood as before, only dim and gray and cold. . . . She had come a long way, drooping, brooding, half-freezing and crying. More than once on the way the hopelessness of her life and her dreams had given her pause, causing her to turn again with renewed determination toward the river—only the vivid and reassuring picture she had retained of this same grim and homely place, its

restricted peace and quiet, the sympathy of Sister St. Agnes and Mother St. Bertha, had carried her on . . . the face of Mother St. Bertha, wrinkled and aweary, appeared at the square opening.

"What is it, my child?" she asked. . . .

"It is Madeleine. I was here four years ago. I was in the girls' ward. I worked in the sewing room."

She was so beaten by life . . . that even now and here she expected little more than an indifference which would send her away again. . . .

"Of course, my child," said the Mother, moving to the door and opening it. "You may come in. But what has happened, child?. . ."

"Mother," pleaded Madeleine wearily, "must I answer now? I am so unhappy! Can't I just have my old dress and my bed for tonight—that little bed under the lamp?"

"Why, yes, dear. . . . Now, my child," she said, "you may undress and bathe. . . . "

In a kind of dumbness of despair she … entered the warm, clean bath which had been provided. She stifled a sob as she did so, and others as she bathed. . . .

. . . Then she was led along other silent passages, once dreary enough but now healing in their sense of peace and rest, and so into the great room set with row upon row of simple white iron beds, covered with their snowy linen . . . beneath which so many like herself were sleeping.

. . . "Oh, Mother," she sobbed as the Sister bent over her, "don't ever make me go out in the world again, will you? You won't will you? I'm so tired! I'm so tired!"

"No, dear, no," soothed the Sister . . . "You need never go out in the world again unless you wish."

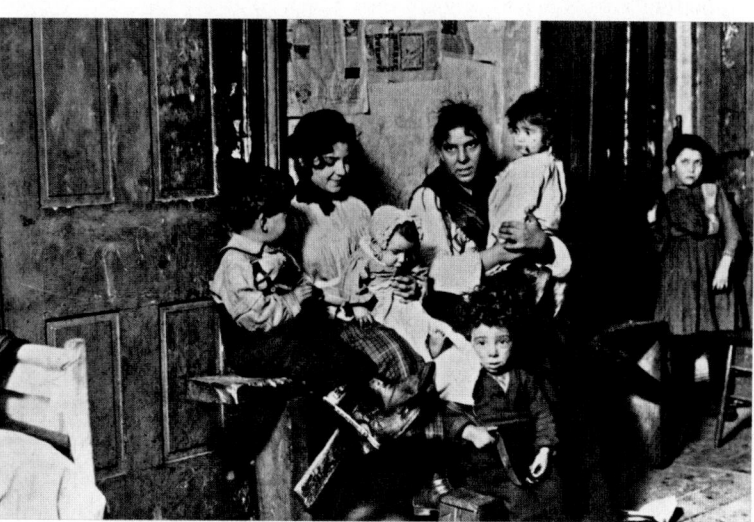

Family outside New York City tenement, 1890

Unit 6: Boom and Bust

Writers sometimes create works of fiction inspired by or based on actual events in the news. The story of Nicola Sacco and Bartolomeo Vanzetti, Italian immigrants convicted of murder in 1921, was the inspiration for this selection by John Dos Passos, written in 1936. Large demonstrations were held in support of Sacco and Vanzetti, who claimed they were convicted for being immigrants and anarchists—not for committing a crime. They were executed in 1927, inspiring this passage, as well as the novel, Boston, *by Upton Sinclair.*

Dos Passos used his wartime experience as an ambulance driver in France as the background for several antiwar novels. In his **trilogy,** *U.S.A, he used an experimental form—fragments of songs, news headlines, monologues, and fragments from the lives of unrelated characters—to depict American* **hypocrisy** *and materialism between the two world wars. Dos Passos often combines separate words into one to shade its meaning and for the flow of a line. His* **impressionistic** *writing influenced several generations of American and European novelists.*

The lines in italics in the following passage from U.S.A. *are from actual letters written by Sacco and Vanzetti.*

trilogy: a work of fiction or nonfiction written in three separately published parts, or books

hypocrisy: acting in a way that contradicts what you say you believe in

impressionistic: using vivid details to create a sensory impression rather than objective reality

wardheeler: a worker for a political boss in a ward or local area

U.S.A., "Sacco and Vanzetti Must Die"
John Dos Passos

S hall be the human race.

Much I thought of you when I was lying in the death house— the singing, the kind tender voices of the children from the playground where there was all the life and the joy of lib- erty—just one step from the wall that contains the buried agony of three buried

John Dos Passos

souls. It would remind me so often of you and of your sister and I wish I could see you every moment, but I feel better that you will not come to the death house so that you could not see the horrible picture of three living in agony waiting to be electrocuted.

The Camera Eye

they have clubbed us off the streets   they are stronger   they are rich   they hire and fire the politi- cians the newspapereditors the old judges the small men with reputations the collegepresidents the **wardheelers** (listen businessmen collegepresidents judges   America will not forget her betrayers) they hire the men with guns   the uniforms the policecars the patrolwagons

all right you have won   you will kill the brave men our friends tonight

there is nothing left to do   we are beaten   we the beaten crowd together in these old dingy schoolrooms on Salem Street shuffle up and down the gritty creaking stairs sit hunched with bowed heads on benches and hear the old words of the haters of oppression   made new in sweat and agony tonight

our work is over   the scribbled phrases   the nights typing releases the smell of the printshop the sharp reek of newsprinted leaflets   the rush for Western Union stringing words into wires the search for stinging words to make you feel who are your oppressors America

America our nation has been beaten by strangers who have turned our language inside out who have taken the clean words our fathers spoke and made them slimy and foul

their hired men sit on the judge's bench they sit back with their feet on the tables under the dome of the State House they are ignorant of our beliefs they have the dollars the guns the armed forces the powerplants

they have built the electricchair and hired the executioner to throw the switch

all right we are two nations

America our nation has been beaten by strangers who have bought the laws and fenced off the meadows and cut down the woods for pulp and turned our pleasant cities into slums and sweated the wealth out of our people and when they want to they hire the executioner to throw the switch

but do they know that the old words of the immigrants are being renewed in blood and agony tonight do they know that the old American speech of the haters of oppression is new tonight in the mouth of an old woman from Pittsburgh of a husky boilermaker from Frisco who hopped freights clear from the Coast to come here in the mouth of a Back Bay social-worker in the mouth of an Italian printer of a hobo from Arkansas   the language of the beaten nation is not forgotten in our ears tonight

the men in the deathhouse made the old words new before they died

If it had not been for these things, I might have lived out my life talking at streetcorners to scorning men. I might have died unknown, unmarked, a failure. This is our career and our triumph. Never in our full life can we hope to do such work for tolerance, for justice, for man's understanding of man as now we do by an accident.

now their work is over   the immigrants haters of oppression lie quiet in black suits in the little undertaking parlor in the North End   the city is quiet   the men of the conquering nation are not to be seen on the streets

they have won why are they scared to be seen on the streets? on the streets you see only the downcast faces of the beaten   the streets belong to the beaten nation   all the way to the cemetery where the bodies of the immigrants are to be burned   we line the curbs in the drizzling rain we crowd the wet sidewalks elbow to elbow silent pale looking with scared eyes at the coffins

we stand defeated America

Nicola Sacco and Bartolomeo Vanzetti being arrested

Unit 7: Global Struggles

Many Jews who survived concentration camps during World War II found it too painful to speak or write about their experiences until many years later. Elie Wiesel (vee•ZEHL) waited for 10 years to write the story of his experiences at Auschwitz, where his family was killed. The first passage is from his 1960 novel, Night. Wiesel was a teenager when the Nazis invaded his town of Sighet in Transylvania in 1944. He became a U.S. citizen in 1963, and won the Nobel Peace Prize in 1986.

World War II had shown the world an unprecedented scale of conflict. The science, technology, and industrialism—which were supposed to advance humanity—had been used instead for mass killing and devastation. It was not surprising that many postwar writers sought alternatives to traditional ways of thinking and writing.

*The Beat Generation—a term coined by Jack Kerouac—was the first modern **subculture,** or "alternative" culture. It was a group of writers during the late 1950s and early 1960s. Rejecting the intellectual, or mental, focus of traditional writing, the Beats sought spontaneity, emotion, and engagement in real, often gritty experience. Their writing has influenced artists, writers, rock musicians, and popular culture ever since.*

In 1947, Kerouac and a friend took a road trip around the country, which inspired his most famous novel, On the Road. Published in 1957, it expresses both the quest for experience and the pessimism of the Beats as they struggled to find meaning in the shadow of the atomic bomb.

subculture: a group that displays behavior different from that of society

Night
Elie Wiesel

Elie Wiesel

And then, one day all foreign Jews were expelled. . . .

Crammed into cattle cars by the Hungarian police, they cried silently. Standing on the station platform, we too were crying. The train disappeared over the horizon; all that was left was thick, dirty smoke.

Behind me, someone said, sighing, "What do you expect? That's war. . . ."

The deportees were quickly forgotten. A few days after they left, it was rumored that they were in Galicia, working, and even that they were content with their fate.

Days went by. Then weeks and months. Life was normal again. A calm, reassuring wind blew through our homes. The shopkeepers were doing good business, the students lived among their books, and the children played in the streets.

One day, as I was about to enter the synagogue, I saw Moishe the Beadle sitting on a bench near the entrance.

He told me what had happened to him and his companions. The train with the deportees had crossed the Hungarian border and, once in Polish territory, had been taken over by the Gestapo. The train had stopped. The Jews were ordered to get off and onto waiting trucks. The trucks headed toward a forest. There everybody was ordered to get out. They were forced to dig huge trenches. When they had finished their work, the men from the Gestapo began theirs. Without passion or haste, they shot their prisoners, who were forced to approach the trench one by one and offer their necks. Infants were tossed into the air and used as targets for the machine guns. This took place in the Galician forest, near Kolomay. How had he, Moishe the Beadle, been able to escape? By a miracle. He was wounded in the leg and left for dead.

On the Road
Jack Kerouac

Later in the afternoon we went out and played baseball with the kids in the sooty field by the Long Island railyard. We also played basketball so frantically the younger boys said, "Take it easy, you don't have to kill yourself." They bounced smoothly all around us and beat us with ease. Dean and I were sweating. At one point Dean fell flat on his face on the concrete court. We huffed and puffed to get the ball away from the boys; they turned and flipped it away. Others darted in and smoothly shot over our heads. We jumped at the basket like maniacs, and the younger boys just reached up and grabbed the ball from our sweating hands and dribbled away. We were like hotrock blackbelly tenorman *Mad* of American back-alley go-music trying to play basketball against Stan Getz and Cool Charlie. They thought we were crazy. Dean and I went back home playing catch from each sidewalk of the street. We tried extra-special catches, diving over bushes and barely missing posts. When a car came by I ran alongside and flipped the ball to Dean just barely behind the vanishing bumper. He darted and caught it and rolled in the grass, and flipped it back for me to catch on the other side of a parked bread truck. I just made it with my meat hand and threw it back so Dean had to whirl and back up and fall on his back across the hedges. Back in the house Dean took his wallet, harrumphed, and handed my aunt the fifteen dollars he owed her from the time we got a speeding ticket in Washington. She was completely surprised and pleased. We had a big supper. "Well, Dean," said my aunt, "I hope you'll be able to take care of your new baby that's coming and stay married this time."

"Yes, yass, yes."

"You can't go all over the country having babies like that. Those poor little things'll grow up helpless. You've got to offer them a chance to live." He looked at his feet and nodded. In the raw red dusk we said good-by, on a bridge over a superhighway.

"I hope you'll be in New York when I get back," I told him.

"All I hope, Dean, is someday we'll be able to live on the same street with our families and get to be a couple of oldtimers together."

"That's right, man—you know that I pray for it completely mindful of the troubles we both had and the troubles coming, as your aunt knows and reminds me. I didn't want the new baby, Inez insisted, and we had a fight. Did you know Marylou got married to a used-car dealer in Frisco and she's having a baby?"

"Yes. We're all getting in there now." Ripples in the upside-down lake of the void, is what I should have said. The bottom of the world is gold and the world is upside down. He took out a snapshot of Camille in Frisco with the new baby girl. The shadow of a man crossed the child on the sunny pavement, two long trouser legs in the sadness. "Who's that?"

"That's only Ed Dunkel. He came back to Galatea, they're gone to Denver now. They spent a day taking pictures."

Ed Dunkel, his compassion unnoticed like the compassion of saints. Dean took out other pictures. I realized these were all the snapshots which our children would look at someday with wonder, thinking their parents had lived smooth, well-ordered, stabilized-within-the-photo lives and got up in the morning to walk proudly on the sidewalks of life, never dreaming the raggedy madness and riot of our actual lives, our actual night, the hell of it, the senseless nightmare road. All of it inside endless and beginningless emptiness. Pitiful forms of ignorance. "Good-by, good-by." Dean walked off in the long red dusk. Locomotives smoked and reeled above him. His shadow followed him, it aped his walk and thoughts and very being. He turned and waved coyly, bashfully. He gave me the boomer's highball, he jumped up and down, he yelled something I didn't catch. He ran around in a circle. All the time he came closer to the concrete corner of the railroad overpass. He made one last signal. I waved back. Suddenly he bent to his life and walked quickly out of sight. I gaped into the bleakness of my own days. I had an awful long way to go too.

Unit 8: A Time of Upheaval

After two world wars many writers began to describe a sense of separateness from nature and a growing sense of personal alienation. The upheaval of societies and cultures brought about by the wars led to a feeling that morality was relative. In other words, what may be immoral in one situation could be considered moral in another situation. These themes, later called modernism by literary critics, showed up in many works of the time.

The early work of poet Adrienne Rich, who was born in 1929, seemed not to be part of this evolving modernist tradition, and wrote in careful, more traditional forms. By the 1960s, her work increasingly confronted themes such as women's role in society, racism, and the Vietnam War, and was written in free verse. In 1973, amid the feminist and civil rights movements, she wrote Diving Into the Wreck, Poems 1971–1972, which won the National Book Award the next year. The title poem uses the **metaphor** of a deep-sea diver to express the goal of looking deeply within to find the truth about ourselves.

Leroy V. Quintana is a New Mexico native of Mexican ancestry. His poetry draws on his experiences as a Chicano outsider in American society, subject to ethnic and socioeconomic discrimination. His poem here, "Natural History," reflects both his sensitivity to nature and the horrors of the Vietnam War, in which he served during 1967 and 1968.

metaphor: a figure of speech in which one word or image is used to mean something else

sundry: miscellaneous

crenellated: notched

"Diving into the Wreck"
Adrienne Rich

First having read the book of myths,
and loaded the camera,
and checked the edge of the knife-blade,
I put on
the body-armor of black rubber
the absurd flippers
the grave and awkward mask.
I am having to do this
not like Cousteau with his
assiduous team
aboard the sun-flooded schooner
but here alone.

There is a ladder.
The ladder is always there
hanging innocently
close to the side of the schooner.
We know what it is for,
we who have used it.
Otherwise
it is a piece of maritime floss
some **sundry** equipment.

I go down.
Rung after rung and still
the oxygen immerses me
the blue light
the clear atoms
of our human air.
I go down.
My flippers cripple me,
I crawl like an insect down the ladder
and there is no one
to tell me when the ocean
will begin.

First the air is blue and then
it is bluer and then green and then
black I am blacking out and yet
my mask is powerful
it pumps my blood with power
the sea is another story
the sea is not a question of power

I have to learn alone
to turn my body without force
in the deep element.

And now: it is easy to forget
what I came for
among so many who have always
lived here
swaying their **crenellated** fans
between the reefs
and besides
you breathe differently down here.

I came to explore the wreck.
The words are purposes.
The words are maps.
I came to see the damage that was done
and the treasures that prevail.
I stroke the beam of my lamp
slowly along the flank
of something more permanent
than fish or weed

the thing I came for:
the wreck and not the story of the wreck
the thing itself and not the myth

the drowned face always staring
toward the sun
the evidence of damage
worn by salt and away into this threadbare
    beauty
the ribs of the disaster
curving their assertion
among the tentative haunters.

This is the place.
And I am here, the mermaid whose dark hair
streams black, the merman in his armored
    body.
We circle silently
about the wreck
we dive into the hold.
I am she: I am he

whose drowned face sleeps with open eyes
whose breasts still bear the stress
whose silver, copper, vermeil cargo lies
obscurely inside barrels
half-wedged and left to rot
we are the half-destroyed instruments
that once held to a course
the water-eaten log
the fouled compass

We are, I am, you are
by cowardice or courage
the one who find our way
back to this scene
carrying a knife, a camera
a book of myths
in which
our names do not appear.

"Natural History"
Leroy Quintana

To cross a river meant leeches.
A company of NVAs crashing toward you
would be a troop of baboons.
A green snake named Mr. Two Step,
for the number you'd last after bitten.
It was said the NVAs carried flashlights.
One night frightening scores of them
turned out to be a swarm of fireflies.
The whir of birds' wings
turned out to be artillery rounds.
Threw stones at a cobra once,
the sun going down.
Fire at it
and the VC would know our position.
A VC moving slowly in the elephant grass
happened to be a water buffalo.
One night they overran the compound.
Loaded down with grenades, AK-47s
from North Vietnam, mines strapped to their
    chests:
these were only the mosquitos.
The VC only a little more than a whisper's
    reach away,
we called in the Cobras. They came in hissing,
cannons twice as fast as the old gunships.
It was also said the VC kept chickens leashed
    to strings.
So easily frightened they were perfect warning.
One night, shivering uncontrollably with fear,
knowing I would have to kill whatever was
    out there,
walking slowly, scratching.

Unit 9: A Changing Society

Dr. Maya Angelou is a poet, historian, author, actress, playwright, civil-rights activist, producer, and director. Born in St. Louis, Missouri, she has lived in many places. She was a newspaper editor in Egypt and Ghana, and has taught at the University of Ghana and, since 1981, at Wake Forest University in Winston-Salem, North Carolina.

*In the 1960s Dr. Martin Luther King, Jr., asked her to be the Northern coordinator for the Southern Christian Leadership Conference. Angelou gained fame in the United States when her **autobiographical** novel,* I Know Why the Caged Bird Sings, *received critical and popular success when it was published in 1969.*

*Like many modern writers, she focuses a harsh spotlight on characters' frailties, failures, and **dilemmas** in today's complex world. Unlike some, however, she also challenges our strengths and human potential. Former president Bill Clinton commissioned her to read her poem "On the Pulse of the Morning" at his 1993 inauguration. Although Angelou wrote her poem in the last decade of the twentieth century, it shows a focus on personal responsibility and peaceful coexistence that have been her lifelong quests and are her hopes for this millennium.*

autobiographical: written about the person's own life

dilemma: problems caused by a person's situation or world conditions

"On the Pulse of the Morning"

Maya Angelou

Maya Angelou

A Rock, a River, a Tree
Hosts to species long since departed,
Marked the mastodon.
The dinosaur, who left dried tokens
Of their sojourn here
On our planet floor,
Any broad alarm of their hastening doom
Is lost in the gloom of dust and ages.

But today, the Rock cries out to us, clearly, forcefully,
Come, you may stand upon my back
And face your distant destiny,
But seek no haven in my shadow.
I will give you no hiding place down here.

You, created only a little lower than
The angels, have crouched too long in
The bruising darkness,
Have lain too long
Face down in ignorance,
Your mouths spilling words
Armed for slaughter.
The Rock cries out to us today, you may stand on me,
But do not hide your face.

Across the wall of the world,
A River sings a beautiful song,
Come rest here by my side.

Each of you a bordered country,
Delicate and strangely made, proud,
Yet thrusting perpetually under siege.
Your armed struggles for profit
Have left collars of waste upon
My shore, currents of debris upon my breast.
Yet, today I call you to my riverside,
If you will study war no more. Come,
Clad in peace, and I will sing the songs
The Creator gave to me when I and the
Tree and the rock were one.
Before cynicism was a bloody sear across your
Brow and when you yet knew you still
Knew nothing.
The River sang and sings on.

There is a true yearning to respond to
The singing River and the wise Rock.
So say the Asian, the Hispanic, the Jew,
The African, the Native American, the Sioux,
The Catholic, the Muslim, the French, the
    Greek
The Irish, the Rabbi, the Priest, the Sheik,
The Gay, the Straight, the Preacher,
The Privileged, the Homeless, the Teacher.
They hear. They all hear
The speaking of the Tree.
Today, the first and last of every Tree
Speak to humankind. Come to me, here beside
    the River.
Plant yourself beside me, here beside the River.

Each of you, descendant of some
Passed-on traveller, has been paid for.
You, who gave me my first name, you
Pawnee, Apache, Seneca, you
Cherokee Nation, who rested with me, then
Forced on bloody feet, left me to the
    employment of
Other seekers—desperate for gain,
Starving for gold.
You the Turk, the Arab, the Swede, the
    German, the Italian, the Scot,
You the Ashanti, the Yoruba, the Kru, bought,
Sold, stolen, arriving on the nightmare,
Praying for a dream.
Here, root yourselves beside me.

I am that Tree planted by the River,
Which will not be moved.

I the Rock, I the River, I the Tree
I am yours—your Passages have been paid.
Lift up your faces, you have a piercing need
For this bright morning dawning for you.
History, despite its wrenching pain,
Cannot be unlived, but if faced
With courage, need not be lived again.

Lift up your eyes upon
This day breaking for you.
Give birth again
To the dream.

Women, children, men,
Take it into the palms of your hands.
Mold it into the shape of your most
Private need. Sculpt it into
The image of your most public self.
Lift up your hearts
Each new hour holds new chances
For new beginnings.
Do not be wedded forever
To fear, yoked eternally
To brutishness.

The horizon leans forward,
Offering you space to place new steps of change.
Here, on the pulse of this fine day,
You may have the courage
To look up and out and upon me, the
Rock, the River, the Tree, your country.
No less to Midas than the mendicant.
No less to you now than the mastodon then.

Here on the pulse of this new day
You may have the grace to look up, and out
And into your sister's eyes, into
Your brother's face, your country,
And say simply,
Very simply,
With hope,
Good morning.

Flag Etiquette

For Americans, the flag has always had a special meaning. It is a symbol of our nation's freedom and democracy.

Rules and Customs

Over the years, Americans have developed rules and customs concerning the use and display of the flag. One of the most important things every American should remember is to treat the flag with respect.

- The flag should be raised and lowered by hand and displayed only from sunrise to sunset. On special occasions, the flag may be displayed at night, but it should be illuminated.

- The flag may be displayed on all days, weather permitting, particularly on national and state holidays and on historic and special occasions.

- No flag may be flown above the American flag or to the right of it at the same height.

- The flag should never touch the ground or floor beneath it.

- The flag may be flown at half-staff by order of the president, usually to mourn the death of a public official.

- The flag may be flown upside down only to signal distress.

- When the flag becomes old and tattered, it should be destroyed by burning. According to an approved custom, the Union (stars on blue field) is first cut from the flag; then the two pieces, which no longer form a flag, are burned.

Continental Colors
1775-1777

First Stars and Stripes
1777-1795

Betsy Ross Flag
c. 1790

15-Star Flag
1795-1818

20-Star Flag
1818

Great Star Flag
1818

35-Star Flag
1863-1865

38-Star Flag
1877-1890

48-Star Flag
1912-1959

50-Star Flag
1960

Glossary/Glosario

- Content vocabulary terms in this glossary are words that relate to history content. They are **highlighted** yellow in your text.
- Words below that have an asterisk (*) are academic vocabulary terms. They help you understand your school subjects and are **boldfaced** in your text.

abandon • Americanization

English   ## Español

A

*abandon to withdraw protection, support, or help (p. 796)	*abandonar retirar la protección, el apoyo o la ayuda (p. 796)
abolition the immediate ending of slavery (p. 243)	abolición el final inmediato de la esclavitud (p. 243)
*academic associated with higher learning at a scholarly institution (p. 536)	*académico relacionado con los estudios superiores en una institución especializada (p. 536)
*access freedom or ability to obtain or make use of (p. 505)	*acceso libertad o capacidad de obtener o hacer uso de (p. 505)
*acquire to get as one's own; to come into possession or control of (p. 16)	*adquirir obtener como propio, tener la posesión o el control de algo (p. 16)
*adapt to change in order to meet the demands of a certain environment or circumstance (p. 390)	*adaptar cambiar para cumplir con las exigencias de cierto entorno o circunstancia (p. 390)
*adequate sufficient for a specific requirement; completed to its minimum requirements (pp. 567, 924)	*adecuado suficiente para un requisito específico, que se completa con los requisitos mínimos (pp. 567, 924)
*advocate to propose a certain position or viewpoint (p. 527)	*abogar proponer cierta posición o punto de vista (p. 527)
affirmative action an active effort to improve employment or educational opportunities for minorities (p. 953)	acción afirmativa un esfuerzo activo para mejorar las oportunidades educacionales y de empleo para las minorías (p. 953)
Agent Orange a chemical defoliant used to clear Vietnamese jungles during the Vietnam War (p. 889)	Agente naranja defoliante químico utilizado para limpiar las junglas vietnamitas durante la Guerra de Vietnam (p. 889)
agrarianism philosophy that agriculture and owning land is the backbone of the economy (p. 159)	agrarismo filosofía de que la agricultura y la propiedad de tierras son los elementos principales de la economía (p. 159)
agricultural revolution period when early Americans learned how to plant and raise crops (p. 4)	revolución agrícola período cuando los primeros americanos aprendieron plantar y cultivar la cosecha (p. 4)
alien a person living in a country who is not a citizen of that country (p. 166)	extranjero una persona que vive en un país del cual no es ciudadano (p. 166)
*allocate to set apart for something specific (p. 1018)	*asignar diferenciar para algo específico (p. 1018)
allotment a plot of land assigned to an individual or a family for cultivation (p. 403)	parcela un terreno asignado a un individuo o familia para su cultivación (p. 403)
*alternative existing or functioning outside the established cultural, social, or economic system (p. 961)	*alternativo que existe o funciona fuera del sistema cultural, social o económico establecido (p. 961)
*ambiguous to lack a definitive purpose (p. 208)	*ambiguo falta de un propósito definitivo (p. 208)
amendment a change to the Constitution (p. 109)	enmienda un cambio a la Constitución (p.109)
Americanization causing someone to acquire American traits and characteristics (p. 467)	americanización causar que una persona adquiera características y rasgos americanos (p. 467)

Glossary/Glosario

English	**Español**
amnesty the act of granting a pardon to a large group of people (pp. 356, 1017)	**amnistía** el acto de otorgar perdón a un número grande de personas (pp. 356, 1017)
amphtrac an amphibious tractor used to move troops from ships to shore (p. 742)	**amphtrac** un tractor anfibio utilizado para mover tropas desde barcos a la orilla del mar (p. 742)
anarchist a person who believes that there should be no government (p. 604)	**anarquista** una persona que cree que no debe haber ningún gobierno (p. 604)
annexation incorporating a territory within the domain of a country (p. 269)	**anexión** incorporar un territorio dentro del dominio de un país (p. 269)
*__annual__ occurring or happening every year (p. 202)	*__anual__ que ocurre o sucede cada año (p. 202)
annuity money paid by contract at regular intervals (p. 398)	**anualidad** dinero pagado por contrato en intervalos regulares (p. 398)
anthrax a bacteria used to create biological weapons (p. 1041)	**ántrax** bacteria utilizada para crear armas biológicas (p. 1041)
*__apparent__ appearing to be fact as far as can be understood (p. 651)	*__aparente__ que parece ser cierto dentro de lo que puede comprenderse (p. 651)
appeasement accepting demands in order to avoid conflict (p. 689)	**apaciguamiento** demandas aceptadas a fin de evitar conflictos (p. 689)
*__appropriate__ (adjective) especially suitable or compatible (p. 957)	*__apropiado__ (adjetivo) especialmente adecuado o compatible (p. 957)
*__approximately__ an estimation of a figure that is close to the actual figure (p. 403)	*__aproximadamente__ cálculo de un número cercano al número real (p. 403)
*__arbitrary__ existing or coming about seemingly at random or as an unfair or unreasonable act of will (pp. 829)	*__arbitrario__ que existe u ocurre aparentemente al azar o como un acto de voluntad injusto o irrazonable (p. 829)
arbitration settling a dispute by agreeing to accept the decision of an impartial outsider (pp. 432, 529)	**arbitraje** arreglar una disputa acordando aceptar la decisión de una persona imparcial (pp. 432, 529)
armistice a temporary agreement to end fighting (p. 569)	**armisticio** acuerdo temporal de paz para terminar con una lucha (p. 569)
*__assemble__ to bring together in a certain place for a particular purpose (p. 324)	*__reunirse__ congregarse en cierto lugar con un objetivo concreto (p. 324)
assembly line a production system with machines and workers arranged so that each person performs an assigned task again and again as the item passes before him or her (p. 596)	**línea de montaje** sistema de producción con máquinas y trabajadores arreglados para que cada persona haga su trabajo designado una y otra vez mientras el artículo pasa frente a ellos (p. 596)
assimilate to absorb a group into the culture of a larger population (p. 403)	**asimilar** incorporar a un grupo dentro de la cultura de una población más grande (p. 403)
*__assume__ to take for granted or as true (p. 696)	*__suponer__ dar algo por sentado o considerarlo verdadero (p. 696)
astrolabe a device used to determine direction, latitude, and local time (p. 16)	**astrolabio** instrumento usado para determinar la dirección, latitud y la hora de una localidad (p. 16)
attrition the act of wearing down by constant harassment or attack (p. 319)	**atrición** acto de desalentar por constantes ataques o acoso (p. 319)

*authorities those who have control over determining and enforcing what is right or wrong (p. 580)

autonomy the quality or state of being self-governing (p. 498)

*awareness the state of having or showing realization, perception, or knowledge (p. 1025)

*autoridades aquéllas que poseen control sobre la determinación y el cumplimiento de lo que es correcto o incorrecto (p. 580)

autonomía la cualidad o el estado de autogobernarse (p. 498)

*conciencia estado de poseer o mostrar comprensión, percepción o conocimiento (p. 1025)

baby boom a marked rise in birthrate, such as occurred in the United States following World War II (p. 801)

bailiff minor officer of the courts (p. 634)

bank holiday closing of banks during the Great Depression to avoid bank runs (p. 652)

bank run persistent and heavy demands from a bank's depositors, creditors, or customers (p. 631)

beats short for "beatniks"; a group of mostly white writers and artists who, in 1950s America, harshly criticized what they considered the sterility and conformity of American life, the meaninglessness of American politics, and the emptiness of popular culture (p. 807)

*benefit to be useful or profitable (p. 663)

benevolent society an association focusing on spreading the word of God and combating social problems (p. 237)

bilingualism the practice of teaching immigrant students in their own language (p. 925)

bill of rights a summary of fundamental rights and privileges guaranteed to a people against violation by the state (p. 113)

binding arbitration process whereby a neutral party hears arguments from two opposing sides and makes a decision that both must accept (p. 666)

black codes laws passed in the South just after the Civil War aimed at controlling freedmen and enabling plantation owners to exploit African American workers (p. 360)

black power the mobilization of the political and economic power of African Americans, especially to compel respect for their rights and to improve their condition (p. 872)

blacklist a list of persons who are disapproved of or who are to be punished or boycotted (p. 429)

blitzkrieg name given to sudden violent offensive attacks the Germans used during World War II; "lightning war" (p. 690)

blockade runner ship that runs through a blockade, usually to smuggle goods through a protected area (p. 322)

auge de nacimientos aumento marcado en la taza de natalidad, tal como ocurrió en Estados Unidos después de la Segunda Guerra Mundial (p. 801)

alguacil oficial en rango menor de las Cortes (p. 634)

feriado bancario cierre de bancos durante la Gran Depresión para evitar las corridas bancarias (p. 652)

corrida bancaria demandas constantes y numerosas por parte de los depo sitantes, acreedores o clientes de un banco (p. 631)

beats nombre corto para "beatniks", un grupo de escritores y artistas en su mayoría blancos quienes en la década de 1950 en Estados Unidos criticaban duramente lo que ellos consideraban la esterilidad y conformismo de la vida estadounidense, el sin sentido de la política estadounidense y el vacío de la cultura popular (p. 807)

*beneficiar ser útil o rentable (p. 663)

sociedad de beneficencia una asociación enfocada en llevar la palabra de Dios y combatir problemas sociales (p. 237)

bilingualismo la práctica de enseñar a estudiantes inmigrantes en su propio lenguaje (p. 925)

declaración de derechos resumen de los derechos y privilegios fundamentales que el estado garantiza al pueblo que no se violarán (p. 113)

arbitraje obligatorio proceso por el cual un partido neutral escucha argumentos de dos partidos opositores y toma una decisión que ambos deben aceptar (p. 666)

códigos negros leyes aprobadas en el Sur al terminar la Guerra Civil para controlar a los libertos y permitir a los dueños de plantaciones la explotación de los trabajadores afroamericanos (p. 360)

poder negro mobilización del poder económico y político de afroamericanos especialmente para imponer respeto por sus derechos y para mejorar su condiciones (p. 872)

lista negra lista de personas rechazadas o a las que se castigará o boicoteará (p. 429)

guerra relámpago nombre dado a los ataques repentinos ofensivos violentos que los alemanes usaron durante la Segunda Guerra Mundial (p. 690)

forzador de bloqueo un barco que navega a través de un bloqueo, usualmente para pasar contrabando a través de un área protegida (p. 322)

Glossary/Glosario

Glossary/Glosario

English	Español
blog online journal where an individual, group, or corporation presents a record of activities, thoughts, or beliefs (p. 1005)	**blog** publicación en línea donde un individuo, grupo o empresa presenta un registro de actividades, ideas o creencias (p. 1005)
blue-collar workers workers in the manual labor field, particularly those requiring protective clothing (p. 802)	**collar azul trabajadors** trabajadors de mano de obra, particularmente aquellos que requieren ropa protectora (p. 802)
blues style of music evolving from African American spirituals and noted for its melancholy sound (p. 618)	**blues** estilo de música que evolucionó de la música espiritual de los afroamericanos, distinguida por su sonido melancólico (p. 618)
bohemian a person (as an artist or a writer) leading an unconventional lifestyle (p. 610)	**bohemio** una persona (como artista o escritor) que lleva un estilo de vida poco convencional (p. 610)
bonanza farm a large, highly profitable wheat farm (p. 397)	**granja en bonanza** extensa granja de trigo que produce muchas ganancias (p. 397)
*****bond** a note issued by the government that promises to pay off a loan with interest (pp. 156, 470)	*****bono** una obligación emitida por el gobierno que promete pagar un préstamo con interés (pp. 156, 470)
bounty money given as a reward, as to encourage enlistment in the army (p. 321)	**recompensa** dinero dado para animar el alistamiento en el ejército (p. 321)
*****briefly** for a short time (p. 740)	*****brevemente** por poco tiempo (p. 740)
brinkmanship the willingness to go to the brink of war to force an opponent to back down (p. 783)	**política arriesgada** la buena voluntad para ir al borde de guerra para forzar a un oponente a que se retracte (p. 783)
broker state role of the government to work out conflicts among competing interest groups (p. 673)	**estado intermediario** el papel del gobierno para resolver conflictos entre grupos con intereses competitivos (p. 673)
budget deficit the amount by which expenses exceed income (p. 977)	**déficit del presupuesto** la cantidad por la cual los gastos exceden los ingresos (p. 977)
bull market a long period of rising stock prices (p. 629)	**bolsa al alza** largo período durante el cual los precios de acciones en la bolsa se incrementan (p. 629)
busing a policy of transporting children to schools outside their neighborhoods to achieve greater racial balance (p. 953)	**traslado** obligatorio la política de transportar estudiantes a escuelas fuera de sus vecindarios para alcanzar un balance racial (p. 953)

C

English	Español
cabinet a group of advisers to the president (p. 154)	**gabinete** grupo de consejeros al presidente (p. 154)
capital gains tax a federal tax paid by businesses and investors when they sell stocks or real estate (p. 995)	**impuestos a las ganancias del capital** impuesto federal pagado por inversionistas y negocios cuando ellos venden acciones y bienes raíces (p. 995)
caravel sailing ship capable of long-distance exploration (p. 16)	**carabela** buque capaz de explorar largas distancias (p. 16)
carpetbagger name given to many Northerners who moved to the South after the Civil War and supported the Republicans (p. 366)	**carpetbagger** nombre dado a muchos norteños que se mudaron al Sur después de la Guerra Civil y apoyaron a los republicanos (p. 366)
caucus system a system in which members of a political party meet to choose their party's candidate for president or decide policy (p. 224)	**sistema de junta** electoral sistema en el cual los miembros de un partido político se reúnen para escoger el candidato a la presidencia de su partido o para decidir políticas (p. 224)
cede to give up by treaty (p. 275)	**ceder** darse por vencido por un tratado (p. 275)

censure to express a formal disapproval of an action (p. 778)

chad a small piece of cardboard produced by punching a data card (p. 1033)

*challenger one who enters a competition (p. 941)

charter a constitution (p. 753)

checks and balances the system in which each branch of government has the ability to limit the power of the other branches to prevent any from becoming too powerful (p. 109)

circumnavigate to sail around (p. 19)

*circumstance a factor in a problem that determines its solution (p. 377)

*cite to point out as an example in an argument or debate (p. 1024)

*civil of or relating to citizens (p. 261)

closed shop an agreement in which a company agrees to hire only union members (pp. 434, 794)

cloture a motion that ends debate and calls for an immediate vote, possible in the U.S. Senate by a vote of 60 senators (p. 864)

*code a signal or symbol used to represent something that is to be kept secret (p. 724)

*collapse a sudden loss of force, value, or effect (p. 628)

*colleague a person who works in the same, or a similar, profession (p. 636)

collective a farm, especially in communist countries, formed from many small holdings collected into a single unit for joint operation under governmental supervision (p. 683)

*commentator one who explains, discusses, or reports in an expository manner, especially news on radio or television (p. 824)

*commissioner the officer in charge of a department or bureau of the public service (p. 368)

*commitment an agreement or pledge to do something in the future (p. 306)

committee of correspondence committee organized in each colony to communicate with and unify the colonies (p. 64)

commune a group living arrangement in which members share everything and work together (p. 913)

*communications the various medias and processes by which information is exchanged between individuals (p. 1004)

*community people with common characteristics living in the same area (p. 641)

censura expresar la desaprobación formal sobre una acción (p. 778)

agujereado pedazo pequeño de cartón producido taladrando una tarjeta de computadora (p. 1033)

*contendiente el que ingresa a una competencia (p. 941)

carta de privilegio una constitución (p. 753)

control y balances sistema en el cual cada ramo de gobierno tiene la habilidad para limitar el poder a los otros ramos para que ninguno vuelva a ser demasiado poderoso (p. 109)

circunnavegar navegar alrededor de (p. 19)

*circunstancia factor en un problema que determina su solución (p. 377)

*citar señalar como ejemplo en un argumento o debate (p. 1024)

*civil de los ciudadanos o relativo a ellos (p. 261)

taller cerrado acuerdo en el que una compañía contrata solamente a miembros del sindicato (pp. 434, 794)

clausura una moción que termina con el debate y requiere un voto inmediato, posible en el Senado de EEUU por un voto de 60 senadores (p. 864)

*código señal o símbolo utilizado para representar algo que se mantendrá en secreto (p. 724)

*colapso pérdida repentina de fuerza, valor o efecto (p. 628)

*colega persona que trabaja en la misma profesión o en una similar (p. 636)

granja colectiva una granja, especialmente en los países comunistas, formada por muchas tierras pequeñas reunidas en una sola unidad para operar conjuntamente bajo la supervisión del gobierno (p. 683)

*comentarista aquél que explica, discute o informa de manera expositiva, especialmente noticias por radio o televisión (p. 824)

*comisionado funcionario a cargo de un departamento o agencia de servicios públicos (p. 368)

*compromiso acuerdo o promesa de hacer algo en el futuro (p. 306)

comité de correspondencia comité organizado en cada colonia para comunicar entre las colonias y unificarlas (p. 64)

comuna un arreglo de vivienda en el cual los miembros de un grupo trabajan juntos y comparten todo (p. 913)

*comunicaciones los diferentes medios y procesos mediante los cuales se intercambia información entre individuos (p. 1004)

*comunidad personas con características comunes que viven en la misma área (p. 641)

Glossary/Glosario

English	Español
*compatible capable of existing in harmony (p. 919)	*compatible capaz de existir en armonía (p. 919)
*compensate to offset an error, defect or undesired effect (p. 242)	*compensar resarcir un error, defecto o efecto no deseado (p. 242)
*comprehensive covering a broad range of topics (p. 369)	*integral que cubre una amplia gama de temas (p. 369)
*concentrate to bring or direct one's powers, efforts, or attention toward a common objective (p. 690)	*concentrar orientar los poderes, esfuerzos o atención hacia un objetivo común (p. 690)
concentration camp a camp where persons are detained or confined (p. 698)	campo de concentración un campamento donde personas están detenidas o encerradas (p. 698)
*conference a meeting of two or more persons for discussing matters of common concern (p. 495)	*conferencia reunión entre dos o más personas para discutir asuntos de interés mutuo (p. 495)
conference committee a special joint committee organized to help the House and Senate work on a compromise bill acceptable to both houses (p. 124)	comité de conferencia una comisión paritaria especial organizada para ayudar a la Cámara y al Senado a forjar un compromiso de ley aceptable para ambas cámaras (p. 124)
*confine to enclose or restrain (p. 841)	*confinar encerrar o contener (p. 841)
*confirmation the process of supporting a statement by evidence (p. 978)	*confirmación proceso de sustentar una afirmación con evidencia (p. 978)
*conform to change in a way that fits a standard or authority (p. 802)	*adecuarse cambiar para ajustarse a un estándar o autoridad (p. 802)
*conformity agreement in form, manner, or character (p. 913)	*conformidad acuerdo en forma, modo o carácter (p. 913)
conquistador Spanish for *conqueror;* the men who led the expeditions to conquer the Americas (p. 20)	conquistador los hombres que condujeron las expediciones para conquistar las Américas (p. 20)
conscription requiring people to enter military service (p. 316)	reclutamiento requerir que personas ingresen en el servicio militar (p. 316)
consensus general agreement (p. 839)	consenso acuerdo general (p. 839)
conservative a person who believes government power, particularly in the economy, should be limited in order to maximize individual freedom (p. 968)	conservador una persona que cree que el poder del gobierno, particularmente en la economía, debe estar limitado para llevar al máximo la libertad individual (p. 968)
*constitute to be composed of, made up of, or formed from (p. 435)	*constituir estar compuesto de, hecho de o formado por (p. 435)
constitutional being in accordance with or regulated by a constitution (p. 170)	constitucional de acuerdo con una constitución o reglamentado por ella (p. 170)
*consumer a person who buys what is produced by an economy (p. 424)	*consumidor persona que compra lo que produce una economía (p. 424)
containment the policy or process of preventing the expansion of a hostile power (p. 766)	contención la política o proceso de prevenir la expansión de un poder hostil (p. 766)
contra Spanish for counterrevolutionary, an anti-Sandinista guerrilla force in Nicaragua (p. 979)	contra contrarevolucionario, la fuerza guerilla anti-Sandinista en Nicaragua (p. 979)
contraband goods whose importation, exportation, or possession is illegal (p. 554)	contrabando artículos de los que la importación, exportación o posesión es ilegal (p. 554)
*contract a binding legal document between two parties (p. 43)	*contrato documento legal vinculante entre dos partes (p. 43)

*contradiction a situation in which inherent factors, actions, or propositions are inconsistent or contrary to one another (p. 86)

*controversy a prolonged public dispute (p. 213)

*convention an assembly of persons who meet for a common purpose (p. 266)

*conventional nonnuclear (p. 830)

*convert to bring over from one belief, view, or party to another (p. 255)

*convince to bring to belief, consent, or a course of action (p. 776)

convoy a group that travels with something, such as a ship, to protect it (p. 567)

convoy system a system in which merchant ships travel with naval vessels for protection (p. 727)

cooperative a store where farmers buy products from each other; an enterprise owned and operated by those who use its services (p. 471)

cooperative individualism President Hoover's policy of encouraging manufacturers and distributors to form their own organizations and volunteer information to the federal government in an effort to stimulate the economy (p. 593)

*coordinate to harmonize or bring into common action, movement, or condition (p. 731)

corporation an organization that is authorized by law to carry on an activity but treated as though it were a single person (p. 422)

*correspondence communication by letters (p. 294)

"corrupt bargain" an illegitimate agreement between politicians (p. 215)

cost of living the cost of purchasing goods and services essential for survival (p. 576)

cost-plus a government contract to pay a manufacturer the cost to produce an item plus a guaranteed percentage (p. 716)

cotton gin a machine that removed seeds from cotton fiber (p. 202)

counterculture a culture with values and beliefs different than those of the mainstream (p. 912)

court-packing the act of changing the political balance of power in a nation's judiciary system whereby a national leader, such as the American president, appoints judges who will rule in favor of his or her policies (p. 670)

covert not openly shown or engaged in (p. 785)

*contradicción situación en la que acciones, propuestas o factores inherentes son incoherentes o contrarios entre ellos (p. 86)

*controversia discusión pública prolongada (p. 213)

*convención asamblea de personas reunidas con un fin común (p. 266)

*convencional no nuclear (p. 830)

*convertir cambiar una creencia, punto de vista o partido por otro (p. 255)

*convencer hacer creer, conseguir el consentimiento o lograr un curso de acción (p. 776)

convoy un grupo que viaja junto con algo, tal como un barco, para protegerlo (p. 567)

sistema de convoy un sistema en el cual barcos mercantes viajan con buques navales para protección (p. 727)

cooperativa tienda donde los granjeros compraban productos el uno del otro; empresa poseída y operada por los que usan sus servicios (p. 471)

individualismo cooperativo política del Presidente Hoover para alentar a los manufactureros y distribuidores a formar sus propias organizaciones y pasar información voluntariamente al gobierno federal en un esfuerzo para estimular la economía (p. 593)

*coordinar armonizar o realizar acciones o movimientos comunes o bien obtener condiciones comunes (p. 731)

sociedad anónima organización autorizada por ley a montar una actividad, tratada como si fuera una sola persona (p. 422)

*correspondencia comunicación a través de cartas (p. 294)

trato corrupto un acuerdo ilegítimo entre políticos (p. 215)

costo de vida el costo de comprar artículos y servicios esenciales para la supervivencia (p. 576)

costo más beneficio contrato del gobierno para pagar el costo de fabricación para producir un artículo más un porcentaje garantizado (p. 716)

despepitadora de algodón máquina que sacaba las semillas de las fibras de algodón (p. 202)

contracultura una cultura con valores y creencias diferentes de los de la cultura principal (p. 912)

recomposición de la corte acto de modificar el equilibrio político de poder en el sistema judicial de una nación mediante el cual un líder nacional, como el presidente estadounidense, nombra jueces que decidirán a favor de las políticas de éste (p. 670)

secreto no hecho o mostrado abiertamente (p. 785)

Glossary/Glosario

English	**Español**
creationism the belief that God created the world and everything in it, usually in the way described in Genesis (p. 608)	**creacionismo** la creencia que Dios creó al mundo y todo lo que hay en él, usualmente como se describe en Génesis (p. 608)
credibility gap lack of trust or believability (p. 892)	**barrera de credibilidad** falta de confianza (p. 892)
*__credit__ an amount or sum of money placed at a person's disposal by a bank on condition that it will be repaid with interest (p. 600)	*__crédito__ monto o suma de dinero que un banco pone a disposición de una persona con la condición de que se devolverá con intereses (p. 600)
*__creditor__ one to whom a debt is owed (p. 156)	*__acreedor__ aquél con quien se tiene una deuda (p. 156)
*__criteria__ standards on which a judgment or action may be based (p. 954)	*__criterios__ normas sobre las que puede basarse una opinión o acción (p. 954)
crop lien obligation placed on a farmer to repay a debt with crops (p. 377)	**derecho de cultivo** obligación impuesta a un agricultor para cubrir la deuda por medio de cosecha (p. 377)
*__crucial__ something considered important or essential (p. 326)	*__crucial__ algo que se considera importante o fundamental (p. 326)
*__currency__ paper money used as a medium of exchange (p. 471)	*__moneda__ dinero en papel que se utiliza como medio de cambio (p. 471)
customs duty a tax on imports and exports (p. 57)	**derecho de aduana** impuesto sobre importaciones y exportaciones (p. 57)

D

English	**Español**
de facto segregation segregation by custom and tradition (p. 851)	**segregación de facto** segregación por costumbre y tradición (p. 851)
debt peonage condition of sharecroppers who could not pay off their debts and, therefore, could not leave the property they worked (p. 377)	**esclavitud deudora** condición de aparceros que no podían pagar sus deudas y por lo tanto no podían abandonar la propiedad que trabajaban (p. 377)
*__decline__ a change to a lower state or level (p. 5)	*__disminución__ modificación a un nivel o estado inferior (p. 5)
deficit spending government practice of spending borrowed money rather than raising taxes, usually in an attempt to boost the economy (p. 662)	**gastos déficits** práctica del gobierno de gastar dinero prestado en vez de aumentar impuestos, usualmente una tentativa para levantar la economía (p. 662)
deflation a decline in the volume of available money or credit that results in lower prices, and, therefore, increases the buying power of money (pp. 428, 470)	**deflación** un decremento de la cantidad de dinero o crédito disponible el cual resulta en precios reducidos y por lo tanto aumenta el poder adquisitivo de la moneda (pp. 428, 470)
*__demonstration__ an outward expression or display (p. 245)	*__demostración__ expresión o exposición exterior (p. 245)
*__denial__ refusal to satisfy a request or desire (p. 331)	*__rechazo__ negativa a satisfacer una petición o deseo (p. 331)
*__deny__ to declare untrue (p. 608)	*__negar__ declarar que algo no es cierto (p. 608)
deport to expel individuals from the country (p. 580)	**deportar** expulsar del país a individuos (p. 580)
*__deregulation__ the act or process of removing restrictions or regulations (p. 949)	*__desregulación__ acción o proceso de eliminar restricciones o reglamentaciones (p. 949)
*__despite__ in spite of (p. 748)	*__a pesar de__ pese a que (p. 748)
détente a policy that attempts to relax or ease tensions between nations (p. 938)	**détente** una política que intenta relajar o borrar la tensión entre naciones (p. 938)

developing nation a nation whose economy is primarily agricultural (p. 785)

nación en desarrollo nación en donde la economía es principalmente agrícola (p. 785)

*__device__ a piece of equipment or a mechanism designed to serve a special purpose or perform a special function (p. 1002)

*__dispositivo__ pieza de un equipo o mecanismo diseñado para servir un propósito especial o para realizar una función específica (p. 1002)

direct primary a vote held by all members of a political party to decide their candidate for public office (p. 522)

elección primaria voto tomado por todos los miembros de un partido político para elegir a su candidato para un puesto público (p. 522)

discount retailing selling large quantities of goods at very low prices and trying to sell the goods quickly to turn over their entire inventory in a short period of time (p. 983)

ventas minoristas de descuento vender grandes cantidades de productos a precios muy bajos e intentar realizar ventas rápidas de productos para la rotación del inventario en un corto período de tiempo (p. 983)

*__discrimination__ to make a difference in treatment or favor on a basis other than individual merit (p. 478)

*__discriminación__ hacer diferencias en el trato o favorecer en base a toda cosa diferente del mérito individual (p. 478)

disenfranchise to deprive of the right to vote (p. 719)

privación civil privar el derecho al voto (p. 719)

*__disposable__ referring to the money remaining to an individual after deduction of taxes (p. 598)

*__disponible__ hace referencia al dinero que le queda a un individuo después de la deducción de impuestos (p. 598)

*__disproportionate__ lacking regularity or symmetry in size, degree, or intensity (p. 893)

*__desproporcionado__ que carece de regularidad o simetría en tamaño, grado o intensidad (p. 893)

*__distinct__ separate, apart, or different from others (p. 35)

*__distinto__ separado, apartado o diferente de otros (p. 35)

*__distribution__ the act or process of being given out or disbursed to clients, customers, or members of a group (p. 422)

*__distribución__ acción o proceso de repartir o desembolsar entre clientes, consumidores o miembros de un grupo (p. 422)

*__diverse__ being different from one another (p. 610)

*__diferente__ ser distinto de otros (p. 610)

dollar diplomacy a policy of joining the business interests of a country with its diplomatic interests abroad (p. 509)

diplomacia del dólar política de juntar los intereses comerciales de un país con sus intereses diplomáticos en el extranjero (p. 509)

*__dominance__ being in a state or position of command or control over all others (p. 54)

*__dominio__ encontrarse en un estado o posición de mando o control sobre todos los demás (p. 54)

domino theory the belief that if one nation in Asia fell to the Communists, neighboring countries would follow (p. 883)

teoría dominó la creencia que si una nación en Asia se derrumbara ante los comunistas, sus (p. 883)

dove a person in favor of the United States withdrawing from the Vietnam War (p. 895)

paloma persona a favor de que Estados Unidos se retirara de la guerra en Vietnam (p. 895)

downsizing reducing a company in size by laying off workers and managers to become more efficient (p. 994)

reducción de personal reducción del tamaño de una compañía despidiendo gerentes y trabajadores para llegar a ser una empresa más eficiente (p. 994)

*__draft__ to select a person at random for mandatory military service (p. 560)

*__conscripción__ selección de una persona al azar para el servicio militar obligatorio (p. 560)

dry farming a way of farming dry land in which seeds are planted deep in the ground where there is some moisture (p. 396)

cultivo seco manera de cultivar tierra seca plantando las semillas en la profundidad de la tierra donde hay algo de humedad (p. 396)

due process a judicial requirement that laws may not treat individuals unfairly, arbitrarily, or unreasonably, and that courts must follow proper procedures and rules when trying cases (p. 829)

proceso justo requerimiento judicial de que las leyes no deben tratar individuos injusta, arbitraria, o irracionalmente y que las cortes deben de seguir procesos y reglamentos justos al jurar casos (p. 829)

Glossary/Glosario

Glossary/Glosario

English	**Español**
duty a tax on imports (p. 101)	**impuesto** un impuesto sobre importaciones (p. 101)
dynamic conservatism policy of balancing economic conservatism with some activism (p. 798)	**conservatismo dinámico** política de alcanzar un balance entre el conservatismo económico y algún activismo (p. 798)

E

earmark specifications added by both Republicans and Democrats for the expenditure of federal money for particular projects (p. 1054)	**destino de fondos** especificaciones que tanto Republicanos como Demócratas añadieron para el gasto del dinero federal en proyectos particulares, por ejemplo, la construcción de un puente o la financiación de investigaciones médicas, generalmente, en sus propios estados y distritos (p. 1054)
economies of scale the reduction in the cost of a good brought about especially by increased production at a given facility (p. 422)	**economía a gran escala** reducción del costo de un producto a causa de la producción aumentada en una fábrica de producción (p. 422)
*__eliminate__ to remove or get rid of (p. 1047)	*__eliminar__ quitar o deshacerse de algo (p. 1047)
emancipation the act or process of freeing enslaved persons (pp. 89, 244)	**emancipación** el proceso de liberar a personas esclavizadas (pp. 89, 244)
embargo a government ban on trade with other countries (pp. 173, 946)	**embargo** prohibición gubernamental contra el comercio con otros países (pp. 173, 946)
*__emphasis__ a special importance given to an object or idea (p. 550)	*__énfasis__ importancia especial que se le da a un objeto o idea (p. 550)
empresario a person who arranged for the settlement of Texas in the 1800s (p. 264)	**empresario** persona que arreglaba el asentamiento de tierras en Texas durante los años 1800 (p. 264)
*__enable__ to make possible, practical, or easy (p. 178)	*__permitir__ hacer posible, práctico o fácil (p. 178)
encomienda system of rewarding conquistadors tracts of land, including the right to tax and exact labor from Native Americans (p. 22)	**encomienda** sistema de recompensar a los conquistadores con extensiones de tierra y el derecho de recaudar impuestos y exigir mano de obra a los indígenas americanos (p. 22)
*__encounter__ to come upon face-to-face as an enemy or adversary (p. 339)	*__encontrarse__ enfrentarse cara a cara como enemigos o adversarios (p. 339)
*__enforce__ to urge or carry out using force (pp. 67, 874)	*__hacer cumplir__ instar o llevar a cabo por medio de la fuerza (pp. 67, 874)
*__ensure__ to guarantee or make certain (p. 400)	*__asegurar__ garantizar o hacer certero (p. 400)
*__entity__ something having independent, separate, or self-contained existence (p. 813)	*__entidad__ algo que tiene una existencia independiente, separada y autónoma (p. 813)
entrepreneur one who organizes, manages, and assumes the risks of a business or enterprise (p. 415)	**empresario** persona que organiza, dirige y asume el riesgo de un negocio o empresa (p. 415)
enumerated powers powers listed in the Constitution as belonging to the federal government (p. 157)	**poderes enumerados** poderes nombrados en la Constitución que pertenecen solamente al gobierno federal (p. 157)
*__environmental__ having to do with the environment; the complex system of plants, animals, water, and soil (p. 532)	*__medioambiental__ relacionado con el medioambiente; el complejo sistema de plantas, animales, agua y suelo (p. 532)
envoy a person delegated to represent one country to another (p. 272)	**enviado especial** persona delegada para representar un país en otro (p. 272)

*equip to furnish with provisions; to make ready for action (p. 78)

*equipment the articles or physical resources prepared or furnished for a specific task (p. 762)

*erode to wear away at something until it fades (p. 554)

espionage spying, especially to gain government secrets (p. 558)

*ethnic relating to large groups of people classed according to common racial, national, tribal, religious, linguistic, or cultural origin or background (p. 444)

ethnic cleansing the expulsion, imprisonment, or killing of ethnic minorities by a dominant majority group (p. 1015)

euro the basic currency shared by the countries of the European Union since 1999 (p. 1023)

*eventually at an unspecified time or day; in the end (p. 8)

*evident clearly visible or understood (p. 223)

*evolution the scientific theory that humans and other forms of life have evolved over time (pp. 459, 608)

executive privilege principle stating that communications of the executive branch should remain confidential to protect national security (p. 944)

*expansion the act or process of increasing or enlarging the extent, number, volume, or scope (p. 491)

*explicit fully revealed or expressed and leaving no question as to meaning (p. 98)

*exposure the condition of being unprotected, especially from severe weather (p. 227)

extermination camp a camp where prisoners were sent to be executed (p. 698)

*extract to remove by force (p. 388)

*extraction the act or process of drawing or pulling something out (p. 196)

*equipar proporcionar suministros, alistar para la acción (p. 78)

*equipos artículos o recursos físicos preparados o proporcionados para una tarea específica (p. 762)

*erosionar desgastar algo hasta que desaparece (p. 554)

espionaje espiar, especialmente para obtener secretos gubernamentales (p. 558)

*étnico relativo a grandes grupos de personas clasificadas de acuerdo con características comunes de origen racial, de nacionalidad, tribal, religioso, lingüístico o cultural (p. 444)

purificación étnica expulsión, encarcelamiento o asesinato de minorías étnicas por un grupo mayoritario dominante (p. 1015)

eurodólar moneda básica compartida por los países de la Unión Europea desde 1999 (p. 1023)

*finalmente en un momento o día no especificado; al final (p. 8)

*evidente claro, sin la menor duda (p. 223)

*evolución teoría científica que los humanos y otras formas de vida se han evolucionado tras el tiempo (pp. 459, 608)

privilegio ejecutivo el principio de que las comunicaciones del ramo ejecutivo deben de permanecer confidenciales para proteger la seguridad nacional (p. 944)

*expansión acción o proceso de aumentar o ampliar la extensión, número, volumen o alcance (p. 491)

*explícito completamente revelado o expresado y sin dudas en cuanto a significado (p. 98)

*exposición la condición de estar desprotegido, especialmente del mal tiempo (p. 227)

campo de exterminación campo donde los prisioneros eran enviados para ser ejecutados (p. 698)

*extraer quitar algo por la fuerza (p. 388)

*extracción acción o proceso de sacar o separar algo (p. 196)

F

*facility something that is built, installed, or established to serve a particular purpose (p. 850)

fallout radioactive particles dispersed by a nuclear explosion (p. 781)

fascism a political system headed by a dictator that calls for extreme nationalism and racism and no tolerance of opposition (p. 682)

"favorite son" men who enjoyed the support of leaders from their own state and region (p. 214)

federalism political system in which power is divided between the national and state governments (p. 108)

*instalación algo que se construye, instala o establece para servir un propósito especial (p. 850)

caída radioactiva partículas radioactivas dispersadas por una explosión nuclear (p. 781)

fascismo un sistema político encabezado por un dictador que pide por nacionalismo y racismo extremo y poca tolerancia de la oposición (p. 682)

hijo favorito hombres que disfrutaban del apoyo do los líderes de su estado y región natales (p. 214)

federalismo sistema político en el cual el poder está dividido entre los estados y el gobierno federal (p. 108)

Glossary/Glosario

English	Español
feminism the belief that men and women should be equal politically, economically, and socially (p. 914)	**feminismo** la creencia que los hombres y las mujeres deben ser iguales política, económica y socialmente (p. 914)
filibuster an attempt to kill a bill by having a group of senators take turns speaking continuously so that a vote cannot take place (p. 864)	**filibustero** un atentado para acabar con un proyecto de ley hablando continuamente a turnos un grupo de senadores para que no pueda haber un voto (p. 864)
*__finalize__ to put in finished form (p. 193)	*__finalizar__ llevar algo a su conclusión (p. 193)
*__finance__ to provide money for a project (p. 664)	*__financiar__ proporcionar dinero para un proyecto (p. 664)
*__financier__ one who deals with finance and investment on a large scale (p. 104)	*__financiero__ el que maneja finanzas e inversiones a gran escala (p. 104)
fireside chats radio broadcasts made by FDR to the American people to explain his initiatives (p. 653)	**pláticas hogareñas** emisiones de radio transmitidas por FDR al pueblo americano para explicar sus iniciativas (p. 653)
flexible response the buildup of conventional troops and weapons to allow a nation to fight a limited war without using nuclear weapons (p. 830)	**respuesta flexible** formación de tropas y armas convencionales para permitir que un país entre en una guerra limitada sin usar armas nucleares (p. 830)
forage to search or raid for food (p. 337)	**forrajear** buscar alimento (p. 337)
foreclose to take possession of a property from a mortgagor because of defaults on payments (p. 643)	**ejecutar** una hipoteca tomar posesión de una propiedad por falta de pagos hipotecarios (p. 643)
*__formulate__ to prepare or devise according to a systematized statement or formula (p. 300)	*__formular__ preparar o crear de acuerdo con una fórmula o declaración sistematizada (p. 300)
fossil fuel a fuel formed in the earth from decayed plant or animal remains (p. 961)	**combustible fósil** un combustible formado en la tierra de los restos descompuestos de plantas o animales (p. 961)
*__framework__ a set of guidelines to be followed (p. 112)	*__marco__ conjunto de pautas por seguir (p. 112)
franchise the right or license to market a company's goods or services in an area, such as a store of a chain operation (p. 802)	**franquicia** derecho o licencia para comercializar los productos o servicios de una empresa en un área, como una tienda de operación en cadena (p. 802)
free enterprise system market economy in which privately owned businesses have the freedom to operate for a profit with limited government intervention (p. 197)	**sistema de libre empresa** economía de mercado en la que las empresas privadas tienen la libertad de operar para obtener una ganancia con poca intervención del gobierno (p. 197)
*__fundamental__ being of central importance (p. 658)	*__fundamental__ de central importancia (p. 658)

G

English	Español
*__gender__ term applied to the characteristics of a male or female (p. 915)	*__género__ término aplicado a las características de un ser masculino o femenino (p. 915)
general strike a strike involving all the workers in a particular geographic location (p. 577)	**huelga general** una huelga por todos los trabajadores de un lugar geográfico (p. 577)
*__generation__ a classification of people who share the same experience throughout their lives (p. 899)	*__generación__ clasificación de personas que comparten las mismas experiencias a lo largo de sus vidas (p. 899)
generation gap a cultural separation between parents and their children (p. 807)	**barrera generacional** una separación cultural entre padres e hijos (p. 807)
glasnost a Soviet policy permitting open discussion of political and social issues and freer dissemination of news and information (p. 991)	**glasnost** política soviética que permitía discusión abierta de temas políticos y sociales y diseminación más libre de noticias e información (p. 991)

globalism the idea that the world is becoming increasingly interconnected (p. 1022)

globalismo idea de que el mundo se encuentra cada vez más interconectado (p. 1022)

global warming an increase in average world temperatures over time (p. 1025)

calentamiento global aumento en la temperatura promedio mundial tras un período (p. 1025)

gold standard a monetary standard in which one ounce of gold equals a set number of dollars (p. 652)

patrón oro norma monetaria en la cual una onza de oro igualaba a un número fijo de dólares (p. 652)

gradualism theory that slavery should be ended gradually (p. 242)

gradualismo teoría de que la esclavitud debería terminarse gradualmente (p. 242)

graduated income tax tax based on the net income of an individual or business and which taxes different income levels at different rates (p. 473)

impuesto graduado de utilidades impuesto basado en los ingresos netos de un individuo o empresa en el cual la taza del impuesto se diferencia de acuerdo a diferentes niveles de salario (p. 473)

graft the acquisition of money in dishonest ways, as in bribing a politician (pp. 368, 455)

soborno adquisición de dinero de manera deshonesta tal como el sobornar a un político (pp. 368, 455)

grandfather clause a clause that allowed individuals who did not pass the literacy test to vote if their fathers or grandfathers had voted before Reconstruction began; an exception to a law based on preexisting circumstances (p. 478)

cláusula de abuelo cláusula que permitió votar a los que no aprobaron el examen de leer si sus padres o sus abuelos habían votado antes de que empezara la Reconstrucción; excepción a una ley basada en circunstancias preexistentes (p. 478)

***grant** to give or bestow upon, especially by a formal act (p. 26)

***conceder** otorgar o conferir, especialmente a través de un acto formal (p. 26)

grassroots movement a group of people organizing at the local or community level, away from political or cultural centers (p. 995)

movimiento local grupo de personas que se organiza a nivel local y popular lejos de centros políticos o culturales (p. 995)

greenback a piece of U.S. paper money first issued by the North during the Civil War (pp. 315, 470)

billete dorso verde billete de papel moneda de EEUU expedido por primera vez por el Norte durante la Guerra Civil (pp. 315, 470)

gross national product the total value of goods and services produced by a country during a year (p. 410)

producto nacional bruto valor total de bienes y servicios producidos por un país durante un año (p. 410)

***guarantee** a statement of assurance (p. 254)

***garantía** declaración de seguridad (p. 254)

guerrilla member of an armed band that carries out surprise attacks and sabotage rather than open warfare (pp. 511, 883)

guerrilla banda armada que usa ataques sorpresas o sabotaje en vez de la guerra organizada (pp. 511, 883)

guerrilla warfare a hit-and-run technique used in fighting a war; fighting by small bands of warriors using tactics such as sudden ambushes (p. 78)

guerra de guerrillas técnica de tirar y darse a la huida usada en combates de guerra; peleas por pequeñas bandas de guerreros usando tácticas tales como emboscadas repentinas (p. 78)

habeas corpus a legal order for an inquiry to determine whether a person has been lawfully imprisoned (p. 316)

hábeas corpus orden legal para una encuesta para determinar si una persona ha sido encarcelada legalmente (p. 316)

hacienda a huge ranch (p. 392)

hacienda un rancho extenso (p. 392)

hardtack a hard biscuit made of wheat flour (p. 331)

hardtack galleta dura hecha de harina de trigo (p. 331)

hawk someone who believed the United States should continue its military efforts in Vietnam (p. 895)

halcón persona que creía que Estados Unidos debía continuar sus esfuerzos militares en Vietnam (p. 895)

headright system in which settlers were granted land in exchange for settling in Virginia (p. 27)

derecho de terreno sistema en el cual los colonizadores recibían tierra a cambio de establecerse en Virginia (p. 27)

hedgerow row of shrubs or trees surrounding a field, often on a dirt wall (p. 746)

seto fila de arbustos o árboles cercando un campo a menudo sobre un muro de tierra (p. 746)

Glossary/Glosario

English	Español
hemispheric defense zone national policy during World War II that declared the Western Hemisphere to be neutral and that the United States would patrol this region against German submarines (p. 704)	**zona de defensa hemisférica** política nacional durante la Segunda Guerra Mundial que declaró que el Hemisferio Oeste fue neutral y que Estados Unidos patrullaría esta región en contra de submarinos alemanes (p. 704)
heretic a dissenter from established church beliefs (p. 29)	**hereje** disidente de creencias establecidas por la iglesia (p. 29)
hippies refers to young Americans, especially during the 1960s, who reject the conventions of established society (p. 912)	**hippies** se refiere a los jóvenes estadounidenses, especialmente durante la década de 1960, que rechazaban las convenciones de la sociedad establecida (p. 912)
hobo a homeless and usually penniless wanderer (p. 634)	**vagabundo** persona errante sin hogar y usualmente sin dinero (p. 634)
holding company a company whose primary business is owning a controlling share of stock in other companies (p. 426)	**compañía de valores** compañía de la cual el negocio principal es poseer el control de acciones en otras compañías (p. 426)
homestead method of acquiring a piece of U.S. public land by living on and cultivating it (p. 395)	**posesionar** método de adquirir una extensión de tierra pública de EEUU viviendo en ella y cultivándola (p. 395)
horizontal integration combining of many firms engaged in the same type of business into one corporation (p. 425)	**integración horizontal** asociación do firmas competitivas en una sociedad anónima (p. 425)
hydraulic mining method of mining by which water is sprayed at a very high pressure against a hill or mountain, washing away large quantities of dirt, gravel, and rock, and exposing the minerals beneath the surface (p. 389)	**minería hidráulica** método de minería mediante el que se pulveriza agua a alta presión contra una colina o montaña, lo que elimina grandes cantidades de suciedad, grava y rocas y expone los minerales que se encuentran debajo de la superficie (p. 389)

I

English	Español
*__ideology__ a system of thought that is held by an individual, group, or culture (p. 652)	*__ideología__ sistema de ideas que posee un individuo, grupo o cultura (p. 652)
*__ignorance__ the state of being uneducated, uninformed, or unaware (p. 215)	*__ignorancia__ el estado de ser inculto, ignorante o carecer de conocimiento (p. 215)
*__illegal__ not according to or authorized by law (p. 1017)	*__ilegal__ que no está de acuerdo con la ley o ésta no lo autoriza (p. 1017)
*__immigrant__ one who enters and becomes established in a country other than that of their original nationality (p. 442)	*__inmigrante__ aquél que ingresa y se establece en un país que no es su país de origen (p. 442)
*__impact__ to make a lasting impression upon an individual or group (p. 620)	*__impactar__ dejar una impresión duradera en un individuo o grupo (p. 620)
impeach to formally charge a public official with misconduct in office (p. 363)	**acusar** acusar formalmente a un oficial público de mala conducta en la oficina (p. 363)
imperialism the actions used by one nation to exercise political or economic control over a smaller or weaker nation (p. 490)	**imperialismo** acciones usadas por una nación para ejercer el control político o económico sobre naciones más pequeñas o débiles (p. 490)
*__implement__ to put into action; to assemble (p. 319)	*__implementar__ poner en acción (p. 319)
implied powers powers not specifically listed in the Constitution but claimed by the federal government (p. 157)	**poderes implícitos** poderes no nombrados específicamente en la Constitución pero reclamados por el gobierno federal (p. 157)
*__imply__ to express indirectly (p. 786)	*__insinuar__ expresar indirectamente (p. 786)
*__impose__ to establish authority by force (p. 307)	*__imponer__ establecer autoridad por la fuerza (p. 307)

*imposition something established or brought about as if by force (p. 238)

*imposición algo que se establece o se ocasiona por medio de la fuerza (p. 238)

impound to take possession of (p. 936)

confiscar tomar posesión de (p. 936)

impressment a kind of legalized kidnapping in which people are forced into military service (p. 173)

requisición un tipo de secuestro legalizado en el cual personas son forzadas a servir en el servicio militar (p. 173)

*incentive something that motivates a person into action (p. 450)

*incentivo algo que motiva a que una persona realice una acción (p. 450)

*incident occurrence of a happening or situation that is a separate unit of experience (p. 940)

*incidente acontecimiento de un suceso o situación que es una unidad separada de experiencia (p. 940)

*income a gain or recurrent benefit usually measured in money derived from capital or labor (p. 810)

*ingresos ganancia o beneficio recurrente que generalmente se mide en dinero proveniente de capital o trabajo (p. 810)

income tax a tax based on the net income of a person or business (p. 538)

impuesto de utilidades impuesto basado en el ingreso neto de una persona o empresa (p. 538)

indentured servant an individual who contracts to work for a colonist for a specified number of years in exchange for transportation to the colonies, food, clothing, and shelter (p. 34)

sirviente contratado individuo contratado para trabajar para un colono durante cierto número de años a cambio de transportación a las colonias, alimento, ropa y refugio (p. 34)

*indicate to point out, point to, or demonstrate the necessity of (p. 973)

*indicar señalar, describir o demostrar la necesidad de algo (p. 973)

individualism the thought that no matter what a person's background is, the person can still become successful (p. 458)

individualismo el pensamiento de que sin importar el origen de una persona, ésta puede ser exitosa (p. 458)

industrial union an organization of common laborers and craft workers in a particular industry (p. 429)

sindicato industrial organización de trabajadores comunes y obreros calificados en una industria (p. 429)

inflation the loss of value of money (pp. 58, 470, 946)

inflación pérdida del valor del dinero (pp. 58, 470, 946)

*initially of or relating to the beginning (p. 769)

*inicial relacionado con el comienzo (p. 769)

*initiative the right of citizens to place a measure or issue before the voters or the legislature for approval (pp. 523, 993)

*iniciativa derecho de los ciudadanos de poner una propuesta o tema ante los votantes o la legislatura para su aprobación (pp. 523, 993)

injunction a court order whereby one is required to do or to refrain from doing a specified act (p. 433)

medida cautelar orden judicial que exige o prohíbe la realización de una acción específica (p. 433)

*innovation a new idea or method (p. 396)

*innovación nueva idea o método (p. 396)

*insecurity the state of not being confident or sure (p. 766)

*inseguridad estado de desconfianza o indecisión (p. 766)

*inspector a person appointed to examine foreign facilities, usually in search of weapons (p. 1045)

*inspector persona designada para examinar instalaciones extranjeras, por lo general, en búsqueda de armas (p. 1045)

installment buying an item on credit with a monthly plan to pay off the value of the good (p. 633)

pago a plazos compra de un artículo a crédito con un plan de pago mensual para pagar el valor del artículo (p. 633)

*institute to initiate or establish something (p. 833)

*instituir iniciar o establecer algo (p. 833)

*institution an established organization or corporation (p. 236)

*institución organización o empresa establecida (p. 236)

insubordination disobedience (p. 535)

insubordinación desobediencia (p. 535)

insurrection an act of rebellion against the established government (p. 301)

insurrección un acto de rebelión en contra del gobierno establecido (p. 301)

*integrate to combine two previously separate things (p. 419)

*integrar combinar dos cosas previamente separadas (p. 419)

Glossary/Glosario

English

Español

integrated circuit a complete electronic circuit on a silicon chip that is small and easy to produce (p. 1002)

circuito integrado un circuito electrónico completo en un chip de silicona pequeño y fácil de producir (p. 1002)

*__intense__ existing in an extreme degree (p. 740)

*__intenso__ que existe en un grado extremo (p. 740)

*__intensify__ to become more frequent and powerful (p. 961)

*__intensificar__ volverse más frecuente y poderoso (p. 961)

interchangeable parts uniform pieces that can be made in large quantities to replace other identical pieces (p. 198)

partes intercambiables piezas uniformes que pueden ser hechas en grandes cantidades para reemplazar otras piezas idénticas (p. 198)

internationalism a national policy of actively trading with foreign countries to foster peace and prosperity (p. 687)

internacionalismo política nacional de intercambio comercial activo con países extranjeros para promover la paz y la prosperidad (p. 687)

interposition theory that a state should be able to intervene between the federal government and the people to stop an illegal action (p. 167)

interposición teoría que un estado debiera poder intervenir entre el gobierno federal y la gente para detener una acción ilegal (p. 167)

*__interpret__ to explain the meaning of complex material (p. 190)

*__interpretar__ explicar el significado de materiales complejos (p. 190)

*__interpretation__ the act or process of explaining or telling the meaning of (p. 1038)

*__interpretación__ acción o proceso de explicar o decir el significado de algo (p. 1038)

*__intervene__ to get involved in the affairs of another (p. 498)

*__intervenir__ involucrarse en los asuntos de otros (p. 498)

*__invest__ to put money into a company in order to gain a future financial reward (p. 629)

*__invertir__ colocar dinero en una empresa con el fin de obtener una recompensa financiera en el futuro (p. 629)

*__investigation__ a systematic examination or official inquiry (p. 591)

*__investigación__ examen sistemático o indagación oficial (p. 591)

*__investor__ one who puts money into a company in order to gain a future financial reward (p. 420)

*__inversor__ aquél que coloca dinero en una empresa con el fin de obtener una recompensa financiera en el futuro (p. 420)

Iron Curtain the political and military barrier that isolated Soviet-controlled countries of Eastern Europe after World War II (p. 765)

cortina de hierro barrera política y militar que aisló a los países de Europa Oriental controlados por los soviéticos después de la Segunda Guerra Mundial (p. 765)

isolationism a national policy of avoiding involvement in world affairs (p. 594)

aislacionismo política nacional de evitar el involucramiento en asuntos mundiales (pp. 594)

jazz American style of music that developed from ragtime and blues and that uses syncopated rhythms and melodies (p. 617)

jazz estilo de música americana que se desarrolló de ragtime y blues y que usa melodías y ritmos sincopados (p. 617)

Jim Crow laws statutes or laws created to enforce segregation (p. 478)

Leyes de Jim Crow leyes creadas para reforzar la segregación (p. 478)

jingoism extreme nationalism marked by aggressive foreign policy (p. 499)

patriotismo extremo nacionalismo marcado por la agresiva política extranjera (p. 499)

joint-stock company form of business organization in which many investors pool funds to raise large amounts of money for large projects (p. 25)

compañía por acciones forma de organización de negocios en la cual muchos inversionistas compran acciones para juntar grandes cantidades de dinero para grandes proyectos (p. 25)

judicial review power of the Supreme Court to determine whether laws of Congress are constitutional and to strike down those that are not (p. 170)

revisión judicial derecho de la Suprema Corte para determinar si las leyes del Congreso son constitucionales y para derribar aquellas que no lo son (p. 170)

Glossary/Glosario

*justify to prove or to show to be just, right, or reasonable (p. 732)

*justificar probar o demostrar que algo es justo, correcto y razonable (p. 732)

juvenile delinquency antisocial or criminal behavior of young people (p. 815)

delincuencia juvenil comportamiento antisocial o criminal de los jóvenes (p. 815)

kamikaze during World War II, a Japanese suicide pilot whose mission was to crash into his target (p. 743)

kamikase durante la Segunda Guerra Mundial un piloto suicida japonés de quien la misión fue chocar en su objetivo (p. 743)

kiva circular ceremonial room built by the Anasazi (p. 7)

kiva cuarto circular ceremonial construido por los Anasazi (p. 7)

*labor an action that produces a good or service (p. 17)

*mano de obra acción que produce un producto o servicio (p. 17)

labor union an organization of workers formed for the purpose of advancing its members' interests (p. 199)

sindicato organización de trabajadores formada con el propósito de promover los intereses de sus miembros (p. 199)

laissez-faire policy that government should interfere as little as possible in the nation's economy (p. 414)

laissez-faire política que el gobierno debe interferir tan poco como sea posible en la economía del país (p. 414)

land grant a grant of land by the federal government especially for roads, railroads, or agricultural colleges (p. 420)

concesión de tierras una concesión de terrenos por el gobierno federal especialmente para carreteras, vías de ferrocarril y colegios agrícolas (p. 420)

*legislation a proposed law to be voted on by a governing body (p. 523)

*legislación ley propuesta para que un órgano directivo la vote (p. 523)

*legislator one who makes laws as a member of a political, legislative body (p. 794)

*legislador aquél que elabora leyes como miembro de un órgano político legislativo (p. 794)

letters of marque licenses issued by Congress to private ship owners authorizing them to attack British merchant ships (p. 82)

patente de corso cédula autorizada por el Congreso para propietarios de naves privadas autorizándoles a atacar barcos mercantes británicos (p. 82)

*liberal a person who generally believes the government should take an active role in the economy and in social programs but should not dictate social behavior (pp. 936, 968)

*liberal persona que generalmente cree que el gobierno debe desempeñar un papel active en la economía y programas sociales pero que el gobierno no debe dictar el comportamiento social (pp. 936, 968)

*liberate to set free (p. 760)

*liberar dejar en libertad (p. 760)

*license permission or freedom to act (p. 173)

*licencia permiso o libertad de acción (p. 173)

*likewise in a like manner; similarly (p. 920)

*asimismo de la misma manera, igualmente (p. 920)

limited war a war fought with limited commitment of resources to achieve a limited objective, such as containing communism (p. 773)

guerra limitada guerra peleada con compromisos limitados de recursos para alcanzar un objetivo limitado, tal como la contención del comunismo (p. 773)

linkage policy of improving relations with the Soviet Union and China in hopes of persuading them to cut back their aid to North Vietnam (p. 898)

enlace política de mejorar relaciones con la Unión Soviética y China con la esperanza de persuadirlas a que redujeran su ayuda a Vietnam del Norte (p. 898)

lockout a company tool to fight union demands by refusing to allow employees to enter its facilities to work (p. 430)

cierre patronal práctica de una empresa para rechazar las demandas sindicales negándose a permitir a los empleados a entrar al área de trabajo (p. 430)

long drive driving cattle long distances to a railroad depot for fast transport and great profit (p. 391)

manejo largo conducción de ganado por largas distancias a estaciones de ferrocarril para la transportación rápida y grandes ganancias (p. 391)

Loyalist American colonist who supported Britain and opposed the War for Independence (p. 68)

lealista colono americano que apoyó a la Gran Bretaña y se opuso a la guerra para la independencia (p. 68)

Glossary/Glosario

Glossary/Glosario

English	Español
loyalty review program a policy established by President Truman that authorized the screening of all federal employees to determine their loyalty to the American government (p. 774)	**programa de verificación de la lealtad** política que estableció el presidente Truman y que autorizaba la investigación de todos los empleados federales para determinar la lealtad de éstos al gobierno estadounidense (p. 774)
lynching an execution performed without lawful approval (p. 480)	**linchamiento** ejecución hecha sin aprobación legal (p. 480)

M

English	Español
mandate authorization to act given to a representative (p. 348)	**mandato** autorización dado a un representante (p. 348)
*****manipulate** to operate or arrange manually to achieve a desired effect (p. 775)	*****manipular** operar o disponer manualmente para alcanzar un efecto deseado (p. 775)
manumission the voluntary freeing of enslaved persons (p. 90)	**manumisión** liberación voluntaria de personas esclavizadas (p. 90)
margin buying a stock by paying only a fraction of the stock price and borrowing the rest (p. 629)	**margen** comprar acciones pagando solamente una fracción del precio y pidiendo prestado el resto (p. 629)
margin call demand by a broker that investors pay back loans made for stocks purchased on margin (p. 629)	**llamada de reserva** demanda de un accionista a que los inversionistas paguen los préstamos hechos para la compra de acciones al margen (p. 629)
martial law the law administered by military forces that is invoked by a government in an emergency (p. 307)	**derecho marcial** derecho administrado por fuerzas militares que es invocado por un gobierno en una emergencia (p. 307)
mass media a medium of communication (as in television and radio) intended to reach a wide audience (p. 613)	**medios informativos** medios de comunicación (como televisión y radio) con la intención de llegar a la audiencia extensa (p. 613)
mass production the production of large quantities of goods using machinery and often an assembly line (p. 596)	**fabricación en serie** producción de grandes cantidades de productos usando máquinas y a menudo una línea de montaje (p. 596)
massive retaliation a policy of threatening a massive response, including the use of nuclear weapons, against a Communist state trying to seize a peaceful state by force (p. 783)	**represalia masiva** una política que amenaza una respuesta masiva, incluyendo el uso de armas nucleares, contra un estado comunista que trata de captar un país pacífico por la fuerza (p. 783)
*****media** a means of expression or communication, especially in reference to the agencies of mass communication—newspapers, radio, television, and the Internet (p. 892)	*****medios de comunicación** medios de expresión o comunicación, especialmente en referencia a las agencias de comunicación masiva periódicos, radio, televisión e Internet (p. 892)
*****mediate** an attempt to resolve conflict between hostile people or groups (p. 673)	*****mediar** intento de resolver un conflicto entre personas o grupos hostiles (p. 673)
mercantilism the theory that a state's power depends on its wealth (p. 40)	**mercantilismo** teoría que el poder de una estado depende de su riqueza (p. 40)
mestizo a person of mixed blood or ancestry (p. 262)	**mestizo** persona de ascendencia o sangre mixta (p. 262)
microprocessor a computer processor containing memory and computing functions on a single chip (p. 1002)	**microprocesador** procesador de computadora que contiene memoria y funciones de computación en un solo chip (p. 1002)
*****migrate** to move from one location to another (p. 558)	*****migrar** mudarse de un lugar a otro (p. 558)
*****migration** movement from one location to another (p. 24)	*****migración** desplazamiento de un lugar a otro (p. 24)
migration chain the process by which immigrants who have acquired U.S. citizenship can send for relatives in their home country to join them (p. 1016)	**cadena migratoria** proceso mediante el cual los inmigrantes que obtuvieron la ciudadanía estadounidense pueden llamar a sus familiares en sus países de origen para que se les unan (p. 1016)

militarism a policy of aggressive military preparedness (p. 549)

military-industrial complex an informal relationship that some people believe exists between the military and the defense industry to promote greater military spending and influence government policy (p. 787)

minutemen companies of civilian soldiers who boasted they were ready to fight on a minute's notice (p. 68)

missile gap belief that the Soviet Union had more nuclear weapons than the United States (p. 824)

Model T automobile built by the Ford Motor Company from 1908 until 1927 (p. 596)

*__modify__ to make changes or alter (p. 1009)

*__monitor__ to observe, oversee, or regulate (p. 1051)

monopoly total control of a type of industry by one person or one company (p. 425)

most-favored nation a policy between countries ensuring fair trading practices (p. 163)

muckraker a journalist who uncovers abuses and corruption in a society (p. 521)

mudslinging attempt to ruin an opponent's reputation with insults (p. 215)

multinational corporation large corporations with overseas investments (p. 802)

mutual assured destruction the strategy assuming that, as long as two countries can destroy each other with nuclear weapons, they will be afraid to use them (p. 981)

militarismo política de preparación militar agresiva (p. 549)

compejo militar industrial relación informal que algunas personas creen que existe entre lo militar y la industria de defensa para promover mayores gastos militares y para influenciar la política gubernamental (p. 787)

minutemen compañías de soldados civiles que se jactaban de que podrían estar listos para tomar armas en sólo un minuto (p. 68)

diferencia de proyectiles creencia que la Unión Soviética tenía más armas nucleares que Estados Unidos (p. 824)

Modelo T automóvil construido por la Ford Motor Company desde 1908 hasta 1927 (p. 596)

*__modificar__ realizar cambios o alterar (p. 1009)

*__controlar__ vigilar, supervisar o regular (p. 1051)

monopolio control total de una industria por una persona o una compañía (p. 425)

nación más favorecida política entre países asegurando prácticas de tratado de comercio justo (p. 163)

muckraker periodista que revela abusos y corrupción en una sociedad (p. 521)

mudslinging intentar arruinar la reputación de un adversario con insultos (p. 215)

corporación multinacional grandes corporaciones de inversión extranjera (p. 802)

destrucción mutua asegurada estrategia que supone que mientras dos países puedan destruirse mutuamente con armas nucleares, tendrán miedo de utilizarlas (p. 981)

Ⓝ

napalm a jellied gasoline used for bombs (pp. 749, 889)

national self-determination the free choice by the people of a nation of their own future political status (p. 570)

nationalism loyalty and devotion to a nation (pp. 181, 550)

nativism hostility toward immigrants (pp. 232, 446, 604)

*__network__ an interconnected system (p. 564)

*__neutral__ not aligned with any political or ideological group (p. 162)

nomad a person who continually moves from place to place, usually in search of food (p. 398)

nonimportation agreement a pledge by merchants not to buy imported goods from a particular source (p. 59)

napalm gasolina gelatinosa utilizada para bombas incendiarias (pp. 749, 889)

autodeterminación nacional es la libre elección que hacen los habitantes de un país sobre su propia situación política futura (p. 570)

nacionalismo lealtad y devoción a una nación (pp. 181, 550)

nativismo sentimientos de hostilidad hacia imigrantes (pp. 232, 446, 604)

*__red__ sistema interconectado (p. 564)

*__neutral__ no alineado con ningún grupo político ni ideológico (p. 162)

nómada persona que se mueve de un lugar a otro, generalmente en busca de alimentos o pastos (p. 398)

acuerdo de no importación compromiso por mercaderes de no comprar artículos importados de una fuente indicada (p. 59)

Glossary/Glosario

English	Español
*nuclear used in or produced by a nuclear reaction (p. 751)	*nuclear que se utiliza en una reacción nuclear o que ésta lo produce (p. 751)
nullification theory that states have the right to declare a federal law invalid (p. 167)	anulación teoría que los estados tienen el derecho de declarar inválida una ley federal (p. 167)

O

English	Español
*objective strategic position to be attained or a purpose to be achieved by a military operation (p. 83)	*objetivo posición estratégica por lograr o propósito por alcanzar mediante una operación militar (p. 83)
*obtain to gain possession of (p. 1040)	*obtener lograr posesión de algo (p. 1040)
*occupy to take control or possession of a location (p. 101)	*ocupar tomar control o posesión de un lugar (p. 101)
*ongoing being actually in process; continuing (p. 621)	*continuo que está en proceso, en curso (p. 621)
Open Door policy a policy that allowed each foreign nation in China to trade freely in the other nations' spheres of influence (p. 505)	política de Puertas Abiertas política que permitió a cada nación extranjera en China intercambiar libremente en las esferas de influencia de otras naciones (p. 505)
open range vast areas of grassland owned by the federal government (p. 390)	terreno abierto gran extensión de pastos propiedad del gobierno federal (p. 390)
open shop a workplace where workers are not required to join a union (p. 602)	taller abierto lugar de trabajo donde los trabajadores no son requeridos de ser miembros del sindicato (p. 602)
*orientation position relative to a standard (p. 987)	*orientación posición relativa a un estándar (p. 987)
*outcome something that follows as a result or consequence (p. 375)	*resultado algo que sigue como efecto o consecuencia (p. 375)
overlander someone who travels overland to the West (p. 256)	viajero persona que viaja al oeste por tierra (p. 256)
*overseas situated, originating in, or relating to lands beyond the sea (p. 177)	*extranjero situado en, originado en o relacionado con las tierras al otro lado del mar (p. 177)

P

English	Español
*participant one who takes part or shares in something (p. 1015)	*participante que forma parte de algo o que comparte algo (p. 1015)
party boss the person in control of a political machine (p. 455)	jefe de partido persona que lleva el control de la maquinaria política (p. 455)
penitentiary prison whose purpose is to reform prisoners (p. 238)	penitenciaría prisión cuyo propósito es de reformar prisioneros (p. 238)
*perception the capacity, degree, and accuracy of one's consciousness, awareness, or comprehension (p. 291)	*percepción capacidad, grado y precisión del conocimiento, conciencia o comprensión de una persona (p. 291)
perestroika a policy of economic and government restructuring instituted by Mikhail Gorbachev in the Soviet Union in the 1980s (p. 991)	perestroika política de reestructuración económica y gubernamental instituida por Mikhail Gorbachev en la Unión Soviética en los años 1980 (p. 991)
periphery the outer boundary of something (p. 725)	periferia frontera externa de algo (p. 725)
perjury lying when one has sworn under oath to tell the truth (pp. 776, 1013)	perjurio mentir cuando uno ha jurado decir la verdad (pp. 776, 1013)

*phenomenon an exceptional, unusual, or abnormal person, thing, or occurrence (p. 800)

philanthropy providing money to support humanitarian or social goals (p. 460)

*philosopher person who seeks wisdom or enlightenment (p. 234)

pietism movement in the 1700s that stressed an individual's piety and an emotional union with God (p. 47)

pillage to loot or plunder (p. 347)

pocket veto indirectly vetoing a bill by letting a session of Congress expire without signing the bill (p. 358)

polio abbreviated form of poliomyelitis, an acute infectious disease affecting the skeletal muscles, often resulting in permanent disability and deformity (p. 650)

political machine an organization linked to a political party that often controlled local government (p. 455)

poll tax a tax of a fixed amount per person that had to be paid before the person could vote (p. 478)

pool a group sharing in some activity; for example, among railroad owners who made secret agreements and set rates among themselves (p. 424)

popular sovereignty government subject to the will of the people (pp. 108, 120); before the Civil War, the idea that people living in a territory had the right to decide by voting if slavery would be allowed there (p. 285)

populism political movement founded in the 1890s representing mainly farmers, favoring free coinage of silver and government control of railroads and other large industries (p. 470)

poverty line a level of personal or family income below which one is classified as poor by the federal government (p. 810)

*practice to do something repeatedly so it becomes the standard (p. 415)

*precedent an earlier occurrence of something that may serve as a model for similar occurrences in the future (p. 363)

*predominant being most frequent or common (p. 232)

*prior happening before an event (p. 390)

prisoner of war a person captured in war (p. 333)

privateer privately owned ship licensed by the government to attack ships of other countries (p. 26)

*procedure a particular way of conducting or engaging in an activity (p. 1052)

---

*fenómeno persona, cosa o acontecimiento excepcional, inusual o anormal (p. 800)

filantropía proporcionar dinero para apoyar metas humanitarias o sociales (p. 460)

*filósofo persona que busca la sabiduría o la iluminación (p. 234)

piedad movimiento en los años 1700 que enfatizó la piedad individual y la unión emocional con Dios (p. 47)

saquear botín y robo (p. 347)

veto indirecto vetar indirectamente un proyecto de ley permitiendo que una sesión del Congreso expire sin firmar el proyecto (p. 358)

polio abreviatura de poliomielitis, una enfermedad infecciosa aguda que afecta los músculos esqueléticos y a menudo provoca discapacidad y deformidad permanente (p. 650)

maquinaria política organización aliada con un partido político que a menudo controlaba el gobierno local (p. 455)

impuesto de capitación impuesto de cantidad fija por cada persona, el cual tenía que ser pagado antes de que una persona pudiera votar (p. 478)

consorcio grupo compartiendo una actividad; por ejemplo, dueños de ferrocarril que tomaban acuerdos secretos y fijaban tipos entre ellos mismos (p. 424)

soberanía popular teoría política de que el gobierno está sujeto a la voluntad del pueblo (pp. 108, 120); antes de la Guerra Civil, la idea de que la gente que vivía en un territorio tenía el derecho de decidir votando si ahí sería permitida la esclavitud (p. 285)

populismo movimiento político fundado en los años 1890 representando principalmente a los granjeros que favoreció libre acuñación de plata y el control gubernamental de ferrocarriles y otras industrias grandes (p. 470)

línea de pobreza nivel de ingreso individual o familiar bajo del cual uno es clasificado por el gobierno federal como pobre (p. 810)

*práctica es la realización de algo repetidamente hasta que se convierte en hábito (p. 415)

*precedente acontecimiento anterior a algo que puede servir como modelo para acontecimientos similares en el futuro (p. 363)

*predominante más frecuente o común (p. 232)

*previo que sucede antes de un acontecimiento (p. 390)

prisionero de guerra persona capturada durante una guerra (p. 333)

buque corsario buque de propiedad privada autorizado por el gobierno para atacar a buques de otros países (p. 26)

*procedimiento método particular de llevar a cabo una actividad o participar en ella (p. 1052)

Glossary/Glosario

English	Español
*prohibit to make illegal by an authority (p. 694)	*prohibir cuando una autoridad dictamina que algo es ilegal (p. 694)
prohibition laws banning the manufacture, transportation, and sale of alcoholic beverages (p. 527)	prohibición leyes que prohibían la manufactura, transportación y venta de bebidas alcohólicas (p. 527)
*promote to advance in station, rank, or honor (p. 341)	*ascender progresar en puesto, rango u honor (p. 341)
propaganda the spreading of ideas about an institution or individual for the purpose of influencing opinion (p. 552)	propaganda diseminación de ideas sobre una institución o individuo con el propósito de influenciar la opinión (p. 552)
proprietary colony a colony owned by an individual (p. 27)	colonia propietaria colonia propiedad de un individuo (p. 27)
*prospective to be likely to, or have intentions to, perform an act (p. 394)	*potencial que hay probabilidades o se tienen intenciones de realizar una acción (p. 394)
protective tariff tax on imports designed to protect American manufacturers (p. 189)	arancel protectora impuesto en importaciones diseñado para proteger a los manufactureros americanos (p. 189)
protectorate a country that is technically independent but is actually under the control of another country (p. 490)	protectorado país que es técnicamente independiente pero que en realidad queda bajo el control de otro país (p. 490)
public works projects such as highways, parks, and libraries built with public funds for public use (p. 640)	obras públicas proyectos como carreteras, parques y bibliotecas construidos con fondos públicos para uso público (p. 640)
*publish to make a document available to the general public (p. 461)	*publicar hacer que un documento esté disponible para el público en general (p. 461)
pueblo Spanish for *village;* term used by early Spanish explorers to denote large housing structures built by the Anasazi (p. 7)	pueblo término usado por los primeros exploradores españoles para denotar grandes estructuras habitacionales construidas por los Anasazi (p. 7)
*purchase to gain by paying money or its equivalent (p. 702)	*comprar adquirir algo pagando dinero o su equivalente (p. 702)

R

English	Español
racism prejudice or discrimination against someone because of his or her race (p. 870)	racismo prejuicio o discriminación en contra de alguien por su raza (p. 870)
*radical one whose political views, practices, or policies are considered extreme (p. 162)	*radical aquél cuyas ideas, prácticas o normas políticas se consideran extremas (p. 162)
rationalism philosophy that emphasizes the role of logic and reason in gaining knowledge (p. 45)	racionalismo filosofía que enfatiza el papel de la lógica y la razón para obtener el conocimiento (p. 45)
*rationality the quality or state of being agreeable to reason (p. 912)	*racionalidad la cualidad o el estado de estar dispuesto a razonar (p. 912)
reapportionment the method states use to draw up political districts based on changes in population (p. 828)	nueva repartición método usado por los estados para formar distritos políticos basados en los cambios de población (p. 828)
recall the right that enables voters to remove unsatisfactory elected officials from office (p. 523)	elección de revocación derecho que permite a los votantes quitar del cargo a los oficiales elegidos que son inadecuados (p. 523)
recession an economic slowdown (p. 102)	recesión retraso económico (p. 102)
*recovery an economic upturn, as after a depression (p. 670)	*recuperación repunte económico, como sucede después de una depresión (p. 670)

referendum the practice of letting voters accept or reject measures proposed by the legislature (pp. 298, 523)

***refinement** the act or process of improving or perfecting (p. 1003)

refugee someone leaving his or her country due to a well-founded fear of persecution on account of race, religion, nationality, membership in a particular group, or political opinion (p. 1017)

***regime** a form of government (p. 688)

***register** to file personal information in order to become eligible for an official event (p. 859)

***regulate** to govern or direct according to rule (p. 530)

***reinforcement** to strengthen by additional assistance, material, or support (p. 268)

***reliable** dependable; giving the same results on successive trials (p. 40)

relief aid for the needy; welfare (p. 642)

***relocate** to move to a new place (p. 398)

***remove** to change the location or position (p. 835)

reparations payment by the losing country in a war to the winner for the damages caused by the war (p. 572)

repatriation being restored or returned to the country of origin, allegiance, or citizenship (p. 922)

republic form of government in which power resides in a body of citizens entitled to vote (p. 86)

***requirement** something essential to the existence or occurrence of something else (p. 362)

***resident** one who lives in a place for some length of time (p. 1018)

***resolution** a formal expression of opinion, will, or intent voted by an official body or assembly (p. 272)

***resolve** to come to an agreement (pp. 570, 1037)

***resource** material used in the production process, such as money, people, land, wood, or steel (p. 410)

***response** something said or done as a reaction (p. 787)

***restraint** the act of limiting, restricting, or keeping under control (p. 430)

***retain** to keep in possession (p. 995)

***revelation** an act of revealing to view or making known (p. 592)

revenue sharing federal tax money that is distributed among the states (p. 936)

referéndum práctica de permitir a los votantes aceptar o rechazar medidas propuestas por la legislatura (pp. 298, 523)

***refinamiento** acción o proceso de mejorar o perfeccionar (p. 1003)

refugiado persona que abandona su país debido a un miedo fundado de persecución a causa de su raza, religión, nacionalidad, pertenencia a un grupo en particular u opinión política (p. 1017)

***régimen** una forma de gobierno (p. 688)

***inscribirse** presentar información personal con el fin de ser elegible para un evento oficial (p. 859)

***regular** gobernar o dirigir según las normas (p. 530)

***refuerzo** fortalecer mediante asistencia, materiales o apoyo adicional (p. 268)

***confiable** fiable, que da los mismos resultados en pruebas sucesivas (p. 40)

asistencia pública ayuda para los necesitados; beneficencia (p. 642)

***trasladar** llevar a un nuevo lugar (p. 398)

***quitar** cambiar la ubicación o posición (p. 835)

indemnización pago hecho por el país perdedor de una guerra al país ganador por los daños causados por la guerra (p. 572)

repatriación acción de devolver o regresar a una persona a su país de origen, lealtad o ciudadanía (p. 922)

república forma de gobierno en el cual el poder reside en un cuerpo de ciudadanos con derecho al voto (p. 86)

***requisito** algo fundamental para la existencia o acontecimiento del algo más (p. 362)

***residente** que vive en un lugar durante algún tiempo (p. 1018)

***resolución** expresión formal de una opinión, deseo o intención votada por una asamblea u organismo oficial (p. 272)

***resolver** llegar a un acuerdo (pp. 570, 1037)

***recurso** material utilizado en el proceso de producción, como dinero, personas, tierra, madera o acero (p. 410)

***respuesta** algo que se dice o hace en reacción a algo (p. 787)

*** restricción** acción de limitar, impedir o mantener bajo control (p. 430)

***retener** conservar la posesión (p. 995)

***revelación** acción de divulgar para hacer ver o conocer (p. 592)

participación en los ingresos dinero de los impuestos federales que se distribuye entre los estados (p. 936)

Glossary/Glosario

English	Español
revenue tariff tax on imports for the purpose of raising money (p. 189)	**arancel de ingresos** impuesto en las importaciones con el propósito de recaudar dinero (p. 189)
*__revise__ to make changes to an original document (p. 702)	*__revisar__ realizar cambios a un documento original (p. 702)
revival large public meeting for preaching and prayer (p. 47)	**asamblea evangelista** reunión pública grande para predicar y rezar (p. 47)
*__revolutionary__ constituting or bringing about a major or fundamental change (p. 88)	*__revolucionario__ que constituye o provoca un cambio importante o esencial (p. 88)
right-to-work law a law making it illegal to require employees to join a union (p. 795)	**derecho a trabajar** ley que hace ilegal la demanda que los trabajadores se unan a un sindicato (p. 795)
rock 'n' roll popular music usually played on electronically amplified instruments and characterized by a persistent, heavily accented beat, much repetition of simple phrases, and often country, folk, and blues elements (p. 805)	**rock 'n' roll** música popular que generalmente se toca con instrumentos amplificados electrónicamente y se caracteriza por un ritmo persistente y pesadamente acentuado, muchas repeticiones de frases simples y a menudo elementos del Country, Folk y Blues (p. 805)
romanticism a literary, artistic, and philosophical movement in the 1700s emphasizing the imagination and the emotions, advocating feeling over reason, inner spirituality over external rules, the individual above society, and nature over environments created by humans (p. 234)	**romanticismo** movimiento literario, artístico, y filosófico del siglo XVIII que enfatizó la imaginación y las emociones, promoviendo el sentido en lugar de la razón, la espiritualidad interior en lugar de reglas externas, el individuo en lugar de la sociedad, y la naturaleza en lugar de medios ambientes credos por los humanos (p. 234)
*__route__ an established or selected course of travel or action (p. 15)	*__ruta__ curso de acción o viaje establecido o seleccionado (p. 15)

English	Español
safety net something that provides security against misfortune; specifically, government relief programs intended to protect against economic disaster (p. 673)	**red de seguridad** algo que proporciona seguridad en contra de desgracias, específicamente, programas de beneficencia gubernamentales para proteger en contra del desastre económico (p. 673)
satellite nations nations politically and economically dominated or controlled by another more powerful country (p. 765)	**países satélite** naciones política y económicamente dominadas o controladas por otro país más poderoso (p. 765)
scalawag name given to Southerners who supported Republican Reconstruction of the South (p. 366)	**scalawag** nombre dado a los sureños que apoyaron la Reconstrucción republicana del Sur (p. 366)
secede to leave or withdraw (p. 225)	**separarse** abandonar o retirar (p. 225)
secession withdrawal from the Union (p. 287)	**secesión** retiro de la Unión (p. 287)
secularize to transfer the use, possession, or control of something from church to civil authority (p. 261)	**secularizar** transferir el uso, la posesión o el control de algo de una iglesia a las autoridades civiles (p. 261)
*__secure__ free from risk of loss (p. 275)	*__seguro__ libre de riesgo de pérdida (p. 275)
sedition incitement to rebellion (p. 166)	**sedición** incitación a la rebelión (p. 166)
segregation the separation or isolation of a race, class, or group (p. 478)	**segregación** separación o aislamiento de una raza, clase o grupo (p. 478)
separate-but-equal doctrine established by the 1896 Supreme Court case *Plessy* v. *Ferguson* that permitted laws segregating African Americans as long as equal facilities were provided (p. 850)	**separados pero iguales** doctrina establecida por la Suprema Corte en el caso Plessy contra Ferguson en 1896 que las leyes que segregaron a los afroamericanos fueron permitidas si facilidades iguales fueron proporcionadas (p. 850)

separation of powers government principle in which power is divided among different branches (p. 108)

*series a number of events that come one after another (p. 640)

settlement house institution located in a poor neighborhood that provided numerous community services such as medical care, child care, libraries, and classes in English (p. 467)

sharecropper farmer who works land for an owner who provides equipment and seed and receives a share of the crop (p. 377)

siege a military blockade of a city or fortified place to force it to surrender (p. 337)

*significantly to affect something enough to be of some importance (p. 1046)

sin tax federal tax on alcohol and tobacco (p. 372)

sit-down strike method of boycotting work by sitting down at work and refusing to leave the establishment (p. 666)

sit-in a form of protest involving occupying seats or sitting down on the floor of an establishment (p. 852)

skyscraper a very tall building (p. 450)

slave code a set of laws that formally regulated slavery and defined the relationship between enslaved Africans and free people (p. 44)

smog fog made heavier and darker by smoke and chemical fumes (p. 959)

soap opera a serial drama on television or radio using melodramatic situations (p. 637)

Social Darwinism based on Charles Darwin's theories of evolution and natural selection, states that humans have developed through competition and natural selection with only the strongest surviving (pp. 459, 528)

sodbuster a name given to Great Plains farmers (p. 396)

*source the point at which something is provided (p. 606)

space race refers to the Cold War competition over dominance of space exploration capability (p. 832)

speakeasy a place where alcoholic beverages are sold illegally (p. 609)

special prosecutor a lawyer from outside the government appointed by an attorney general or Congress to investigate a government official for misconduct while in office (p. 944)

*specific restricted to a particular individual, situation, relation, or effect (p. 113)

separación de poderes principio de gobierno en el cual el poder está dividido entre diferentes ramos (p. 108)

*serie acontecimientos que suceden uno después de otro (p. 640)

casa de beneficencia institución establecida en una vecindad pobre que proveía numerosos servicios comunitarios tal como cuidado médico, cuidado de niños, bibliotecas, e instrucción en inglés (p. 467)

aparcero agricultor que labra la tierra para un dueño que proporciona equipo y semillas y recibe una porción de la cosecha (p. 377)

sitio bloqueo militar de una ciudad o un recinto fortificado para forzarlo a rendirse (p. 337)

*considerablemente afectar algo lo suficiente como para que sea de importancia (p. 1046)

impuesto pecadero impuesto federal sobre el alcohol y tabaco (p. 372)

huelga de brazos caídos método de boicotear el trabajo por medio de sentarse en el lugar de trabajo y de rehusar a abandonar el establecimiento (p. 666)

plantón forma de protesta ocupando las sillas o sentándose en el piso de un establecimiento (p. 852)

rascacielos edificio de gran altura (p. 450)

código de esclavos leyes aprobadas que regularon formalmente la esclavitud y definieron la relación entre los africanos esclavizados y la gente libre (p. 44)

smog niebla hecha más pesada y oscura por el humo y vapores químicos (p. 959)

novela drama en serie de radio o televisión utilizando situaciones melodramáticas (p. 637)

Darwinismo social se basa en las teorías de evolución y de selección natural de Charles Darwin y expresa que los humanos han evolucionado a través de la competencia y de la selección natural, donde sólo sobrevive el más fuerte (pp. 459, 528)

rompeterrón nombre dado a los granjeros de las Grandes Planicies (p. 396)

*fuente punto en el que se proporciona algo (p. 606)

carrera espacial se refiere a la competencia durante la Guerra Fría sobre el dominio de la exploración espacial (p. 832)

speakeasy lugar donde son vendidas clandestinamente bebidas alcohólicas (p. 609)

fiscal especial un abogado externo al gobierno nombrado por un procurador general o congreso para investigar a un funcionario del gobierno por mala conducta durante sus funciones (p. 944)

*específico limitado a un individuo, situación, relación o efecto particular (p. 113)

Glossary/Glosario

Glossary/Glosario

English	Español
speculation act of buying stocks at great risk with the anticipation that the price will rise (p. 629)	**especulación** acciones compradas con alto riesgo con la anticipación que los precios subirán (p. 629)
speculator person who risks money in hopes of a financial profit (p. 157)	**especulador** persona que arriesga dinero con la esperanza de obtener una ganancia financiera (p. 157)
sphere of influence section of a country where one foreign nation enjoys special rights and powers (p. 504)	**esfera de influencia** sección de un país donde una nación extranjera tiene derechos y poderes especiales (p. 504)
spoils system practice of handing out government jobs to supporters; replacing government employees with the winning candidate's supporters (p. 224)	**sistema de despojos** práctica de dar puestos gubernamentales a los partidarios; reemplazando a los empleados del gobierno con los partidarios del candidato victorioso (p. 224)
squatter someone who settles on public land under government regulation with the hopes of acquiring the title to the land (p. 254)	**colono usurpador** persona que se establece en tierras públicas bajo reglamento gubernamental con la esperanza de adquirir el título de propiedad (p. 254)
*__stability__ a state of peace; free from social unrest (p. 973)	*__estabilidad__ estado de paz, libre de inquietud social (p. 973)
stagflation persistent inflation combined with stagnant consumer demand and relatively high unemployment (p. 947)	**stagflación** inflación persistente combinado con la demanda estancada y una taza de desempleo alta (p. 947)
state-sponsored terrorism violent acts against civilians that are secretly supported by a government in order to attack other nations without going to war (p. 1039)	**terrorismo patrocinado por el estado** actos violentos en contra de civiles que son secretamente apoyados por un gobierno con el motivo de atacar a otras naciones sin entrar en la guerra (p. 1039)
steerage cramped quarters on a ship's lower decks for passengers paying the lowest fares (p. 443)	**tercera clase** cuarteles apretados de las cubiertas bajas de un barco para los pasajeros que pagan los pasajes más bajos (p. 443)
stock money or capital invested or available for investment or trading (p. 422)	**reserva** dinero o capital invertido o disponible para inversiones u operaciones comerciales (p. 422)
stock market a system for buying and selling stocks in corporations (p. 628)	**bolsa de valores** sistema para comprar y vender acciones de corporaciones (p. 628)
*__strategic__ necessary to or important in the initiation, conduct, or completion of a military plan (p. 885)	*__estratégico__ necesario o importante para iniciar, realizar o completar un plan militar (p. 885)
strategic defense a plan to develop missiles and other devices that can shoot down nuclear missiles before they hit the United States (p. 1035)	**defensa estratégica** plan para desarrollar proyectiles y otras armas que pueden derribar proyectiles nucleares antes de que estos golpeen en Estados Unidos (p. 1035)
strategic materials materials needed for fighting a war (p. 706)	**materiales estratégicos** materiales necesarios para una guerra (p. 706)
*__strategy__ a plan or method for achieving a goal (p. 472)	*__estrategia__ plan o método para alcanzar una meta (p. 472)
strike work stoppage by workers to force an employer to meet demands (p. 199)	**huelga** paro de trabajo por los trabajadores para forzar al empresario a satisfacer sus demandas (p. 199)
*__structure__ something that is composed or arranged into a unified whole, as a building or edifice (p. 346)	*__estructura__ algo compuesto o dispuesto como un todo unificado, como puede ser una construcción o edificio (p. 346)
*__submit__ to put forward for consideration or judgment (p. 73)	*__presentar__ presentar algo para consideración o fallo (p. 73)
*__subordinate__ one who is under the authority of a superior (p. 344)	*__subordinado__ aquél que está bajo la autoridad de un superior (p. 344)

*subsidy money granted by the government to achieve a specific goal that is beneficial to society (p. 842)

*subsidio dinero que otorga el gobierno para alcanzar una meta específica que beneficia a la sociedad (p. 842)

*substitute to put or use in the place of another (p. 59)

*sustituto colocar o utilizar en lugar de otro (p. 59)

subversion a systematic attempt to overthrow a government by using persons working secretly from within (p. 774)

subversión intento sistemático para derrocar un gobierno utilizando personas que trabajan secretamente desde adentro (p. 774)

*sufficient enough, adequate (p. 316)

*suficiente bastante, adecuado (p. 316)

suffrage the right to vote (pp. 223, 524)

sufragio derecho al voto (pp. 223, 524)

*sum a specified amount of money (p. 631)

*suma cantidad específica de dinero (p. 631)

summit a meeting of heads of government (p. 939)

cumbre junta de jefes de gobiernos (p. 939)

Sunbelt a new industrial region in southern California and the Deep South, developing during World War II (p. 730)

Región Solada nueva región industrial en el sur de California y el Bajo Sur que se desarrolló durante la Segunda Guerra Mundial (p. 730)

*supplement an addition to something, meant to make it complete (p. 331)

*complemento una adición a algo con la intención de completarlo (p. 331)

supply-side economics economic theory that lower taxes will boost the economy as businesses and individuals invest their money, thereby creating higher tax revenue (pp. 593, 976)

economía de oferta teoría económica de que los impuestos bajos levantarían la economía invirtiendo su dinero los negocios y los individuos, así creando un alto ingreso del impuesto (pp. 593, 976)

*survival the continuation of life or existence (p. 286)

*supervivencia continuación de la vida o existencia (p. 286)

*suspend to temporarily stop an operation (p. 634)

*suspender detener temporalmente una operación (p. 634)

*symbolize to represent, express, or identify by a symbol (p. 618)

*simbolizar representar, expresar o identificar por medio de un símbolo (p. 618)

*target something or someone fired on or marked for attack (p. 726)

*objetivo algo o alguien a quien se dispara o a quien se marca para atacar (p. 726)

task system a method of organizing enslaved labor wherein workers were given a specific set of jobs to accomplish every day, after which they were allowed to spend their time as they chose (p. 206)

sistema de tareas método de organización del trabajo esclavizado en el que se les asignaba a los trabajadores un conjunto de tareas para realizar cada día, y una vez finalizadas, eran libres de hacer lo que quisieran con su tiempo (p. 206)

teach-in an extended meeting or class held to discuss a social or political issue (p. 893)

plantón educacional junta o clase extendida para discutir un asunto político o social (p. 893)

*technique a method of achieving a desired task (p. 637)

*técnica método para lograr una tarea determinada (p. 637)

*technology the result of an improvement on an old or existing idea (p. 6)

*tecnología el resultado del avance de una idea antigua o ya existente (p. 6)

telecommute to work at home by means of an electronic linkup with a central office (p. 1003)

viajar electrónicamente trabajar en casa por medio de conexión electrónica con una oficina central (p. 1003)

televangelist an evangelist who conducts regularly televised religious programs (p. 973)

televangelista evangelista que transmite regularmente programas evangélicos por televisión (p. 973)

temperance moderation in or abstinence from alcohol (p. 238)

templanza moderación o abstinencia del uso del alcohol (p. 238)

tenant farmer farmer who works land owned by another and pays rent either in cash or crops (p. 377)

granjero arrendatario granjero que labra la tierra de un terrateniente y paga la renta ya sea con dinero efectivo o cosecha (p. 377)

English

tenement multifamily apartments, usually dark, crowded, and barely meeting minimum living standards (p. 453)

termination policy a government policy to bring Native Americans into mainstream society by withdrawing recognition of Native American groups as legal entities (p. 813)

terrorism the use of violence by non-governmental groups against civilians to achieve a political goal by instilling fear and frightening governments into changing policies (p. 1038)

*__theory__ a hypothesis meant for argument or investigation (p. 947)

time zone a geographical region in which the same standard time is kept (p. 419)

town meeting a gathering of free men in a New England town to elect leaders, which developed into the local town government (p. 38)

trade union an organization of workers with the same trade or skill (p. 429)

*__traditional__ relating to cultural continuity in social attitudes, customs, and institutions (p. 885)

transcendentalism a philosophy stressing the relationship between human beings and nature, spiritual things over material things, and the importance of the individual conscience (p. 234)

transcontinental railroad a railway system extending across the continent (p. 291)

*__transport__ to convey from one place to another (p. 693)

*__transportation__ method of travel from one place to another (p. 194)

triangular trade a three-way trade route for exchanging goods between the American colonies and two other trading partners (p. 38)

tribute a payment by one ruler or nation to another in acknowledgment of submission or as the price of protection (p. 6)

*__trigger__ to cause an action that causes a greater reaction (p. 455)

trust a combination of firms or corporations formed by a legal agreement, especially to reduce competition (p. 426)

Español

casa de vecindad apartamentos para varias familias, normalmente obscuros, apretados que apenas cumplen con los estándares mínimos de viviendas (p. 453)

política de terminación política gubernamental para traer a los Nativos Americanos dentro de la sociedad principal retirando el reconocimiento de los grupos Nativos Americanos como entidades legales (p. 813)

terrorismo el uso de violencia por grupos no del gobierno en contra de civiles para alcanzar una meta política impartiendo miedo y amenazando gobiernos para que cambien su política (p. 1038)

*__teoría__ hipótesis pensada para un argumento o investigación (p. 947)

huso horario región geográfica en la cual la misma norma horaria es mantenida (p. 419)

junta municipal asamblea de hombres libres de un pueblo de Nueva Inglaterra para elegir líderes la cual desarrolló en gobierno local (p. 38)

gremio organización de trabajadores con el mismo oficio o destreza (p. 429)

*__tradicional__ relativo a la continuidad cultural en las actitudes sociales, costumbres e instituciones (p. 885)

transcendentalismo filosofía que acentúa la relación entre los seres humanos y la naturaleza, cosas espirituales sobre las materiales y la importancia de la conciencia del individuo (p. 234)

ferrocarril transcontinental sistema de ferrocarril que se extiende a través del continente (p. 291)

*__transportar__ llevar de un lugar a otro (p. 693)

*__transporte__ método para viajar de un lugar a otro (p. 194)

comercio triangular una ruta comercial de tres ramas para intercambiar productos entre las colonias americanas y otros dos asociados comerciales (p. 38)

tributo pago de un gobernante o país a otro en reconocimiento de la sumisión o como precio por la protección brindada (p. 6)

*__desencadenar__ provocar una acción que desencadena una reacción mayor (p. 455)

cártel combinación de empresas o sociedades anónimas formada por acuerdo legal, especialmente para reducir la competición (p. 426) *ultimately in the end, finally, or eventually (p. 263)

*unconstitutional not in accordance with or authorized by the constitution of a state or society (p. 540)

unfair trade practices trading practices that derive a gain at the expense of the competition (p. 539)

*unify to bring a group together with a similar goal or thought pattern (p. 613)

union shop a business that requires employees to join a union (p. 795)

*unresolved not cleared up, understandable, or dealt with successfully (p. 903)

urban renewal government programs that attempt to eliminate poverty and revitalize urban areas (p. 811)

utopia community based on a vision of a perfect society sought by reformers (p. 234)

*última instancia al final, finalmente, o por último (p. 263)

inconstitucional que no está de acuerdo con la constitución de un estado o sociedad o no posee la autorización de ésta (p. 540)

prácticas comerciales injustas prácticas comerciales que ganan el beneficio perjudicando a la competencia (p. 539)

*unificar juntar a un grupo con un objetivo o patrones de pensamiento similares (p. 613)

taller sindicalizado comercio que requiere que los trabajadores se unan al sindicato (p. 795)

*no resuelto no esclarecido, no comprensible o tratado con éxito (p. 903)

renovación urbana programas gubernamentales que intentan eliminar la pobreza y revitalizar las áreas urbanas (p. 811)

utopía comunidad basada en una visión de la sociedad perfecta buscada por los reformistas (p. 234)

vaquero men who herded cattle on haciendas (p. 262)

*vehicle a means of carrying or transporting something (p. 717)

vertical integration the combining of companies that supply equipment and services needed for a particular industry (p. 425)

veto power of the chief executive to reject laws passed by the legislature (p. 109)

*via to have come by way of or through (p. 984)

victory garden gardens planted by American citizens during war to raise vegetables for home use, leaving more for the troops (pp. 556, 735)

victory suit a men's suit with no vest, no cuffs, a short jacket, and narrow lapels, worn during World War II in order to save fabric for the war effort (p. 732)

Vietnamization the process of making South Vietnam assume more of the war effort by slowly withdrawing American troops from Vietnam (p. 898)

vigilance committee group of ordinary citizens formed by local law enforcement officers whose goal is to find criminals and bring them to justice (p. 387)

*violation the disregard or breaking of the law (p. 688)

*virtually almost entirely; nearly (p. 699)

*visible what can be seen (p. 979)

vaquero hombres que conducían el ganado en las haciendas (p. 262)

*vehículo medio para llevar o transportar algo (p. 717)

integración vertical asociación de compañías que abastecen equipo y servicios necesarios a una industria particular (p. 425)

veto poder del jefe del ejecutivo de rechazar leyes aprobadas por la legislatura (p. 109)

*vía haber llegado mediante o a través de (p. 984)

huerto de victoria huertos plantados por ciudadanos americanos durante la guerra para cultivar vegetales para usar en casa así dejando más para las tropas (pp. 556, 735)

victory suit traje de hombre sin chaleco ni puños, con una chaqueta corta y solapas angostas que se vestía durante la Segunda Guerra Mundial para ahorrar tela para la guerra (p. 732)

vietnamización el proceso de hacer que el Vietnam del Sur asumiera más de los esfuerzos de la guerra sacando poco a poco a las tropas americanas de Vietnam (p. 898)

comité de vigilancia grupo de ciudadanos comunes formado por funcionarios locales encargados del cumplimiento de la ley, que deben encontrar criminales y ponerlos a disposición de la justicia (p. 387)

*violación ignorar o quebrantar la ley (p. 688)

*prácticamente casi por completo, por poco (p. 699)

*visible lo que puede verse (p. 979)

Glossary/Glosario

Glossary/Glosario

English	Español

war on poverty antipoverty program under President Lyndon Johnson (p. 839)

guerra contra la pobreza programa anti-pobreza bajo el Presidente Lyndon Johnson (p. 839)

weapons of mass destruction (WMD) weapons—including nuclear, chemical, and biological—that can kill large numbers of people all at once (p. 1044)

armas de destrucción masiva (ADM) armas, incluidas las nucleares, químicas y biológicas, que pueden matar una gran cantidad de personas a la vez (p. 1044)

*__welfare__ aid in the form of money or necessities for those in need, especially disadvantaged social groups (p. 936)

*__asistencia social__ ayuda en forma de dinero o necesidades para los necesitados; grupos sociales que se encuentran especialmente en desventaja (p. 936)

welfare capitalism system in which companies enable employees to buy stock, participate in profit sharing, and receive benefits such as medical care common in the 1920s (p. 602)

capitalismo de beneficencia sistema en el cual las compañías permiten a los trabajadores comprar acciones, compartir las ganancias, y recibir beneficios tal como atención médica, común en los años 1920 (p. 602)

white-collar jobs jobs in fields not requiring work clothes or protective clothing, such as sales (p. 802)

collar blanco trabajos trabajos que no requieren ropa de protección o de trabajo, asi como los vendedores (p. 802)

*__widespread__ having influence on or affecting a large group (p. 47); widely diffused or prevalent (p. 577)

*__generalizar__ influir sobre algo/alguien o afectar a un grupo numeroso (p. 577)

writ of assistance a search warrant enabling customs officers to enter any location to look for evidence of smuggling (p. 60)

escrito de asistencia documento legal que permitió a los oficiales aduanales entrar cualquier lugar en busca de evidencia de contrabando (p. 60)

yellow journalism type of sensational, biased, and often false reporting for the sake of attracting readers (p. 497)

periodismo amarillista tipo de reportaje sensacional, tendencioso, y a menudo falso con el propósito de atraer a los lectores (p. 497)

yeoman farmer owner of a small farm with four or fewer enslaved persons, and usually none (p. 205)

terrateniente menor dueño de una granja pequeña con cuatro o menos esclavos, normalmente ninguno (p. 205)

yuppie a young, college-educated adult who is employed in a well-paying profession and who lives and works in or near a large city (p. 982)

yuppie adulto joven educado en la universidad empleado en una profesión de buen salario y que vive y trabaja en o cerca de una ciudad grande (p. 982)

zoot suit men's clothing of extreme cut typically consisting of a thigh-length jacket with wide padded shoulders and peg pants with narrow cuffs (p. 732)

zoot suit vestimenta de hombre de corte extremo que consiste típicamente de una chaqueta a la altura de los muslos con hombreras anchas y pantalón pirata con bocamanga angosta (p. 732)

Glossary/Glosario

Italicized page numbers refer to illustrations. The following abbreviations are used in the index:
m = map; c = chart; p = photograph or picture; g = graph; crt = cartoon; ptg = painting; q = quote

Index

Index

Index

Index

Index

Index

Index

Index

Index

Index

Index

Index

Index

Index

Index

Index

Index

Index

Index

Index

Index

Index

XYZ Affair, 164–65

Index

Acknowledgments and Photo Credits

TEXT AND ART

637 Excerpt from *Dust to Eat: Drought and Depression in the 1930s* by Michael L. Cooper. Copyright © 2004 by Michael L. Cooper. Reprinted by permission of Clarion Books, an imprint of Houghton Mifflin Company. All rights reserved; **701** "Luther D. Fletcher" from *World War II: From the Battle Front to the Home Front, Arkansans Tell Their Stories*, copyright © 1995 by Kay B. Hall. Reprinted by permission of the University of Arkansas Press; **915** From The Feminine Mystique by Betty Friedan. Copyright © 1983, 1974, 1973, 1963 by Betty Friedan. Used by permission of W.W. Norton & Company, Inc.

Glencoe would like to acknowledge the artists and agencies that participated in illustrating this program: American Artists Reps Inc.; Deborah Wolfe Ltd/illustrationOnLine.com; GeoNova LLC.

PHOTO CREDITS

Abbreviation Key:
BC: Bettman/CORBIS
LOC: Library of Congress

Cover (tl)Steve Schapiro, (tc)CORBIS, (tr)National Portrait Gallery, Smithsonian Institution/Art Resource, NY, (cl)New York Historical Society/Library of Congress, (c)Thomas E. Franklin/Bergen Record/Getty Images, (cr)Carl Van Vechten/The Granger Collection, New York/Reprinted with permission of the Van Vechten Trust, (b)Collection of The Butler Institute of American Art, Youngstown, Ohio; **endsheet** (bl)photolibrary.com/Index Open, (bkgd)Getty Images; **vi** (t)SuperStock, (b)Boltin Picture Library/Bridgeman Art Library; **vii** (t)SuperStock, (c)Bridgeman Art Library, (b)akg-images; **viii** (t)Painting by Don Troiani, www.historicalartprints.com, (c)Art Archive/Metropolitan Museum of Art New York/Laurie Platt Winfrey, (b)Minnesota Historical Society/CORBIS; **ix** (t)Lowell Georgia/CORBIS, (c)William Henry Jackson/Cardoza Fine Art Gallery, (b)CORBIS; **x** (t)Nagasaki Museum of History and Culture, (c)The Granger Collection, New York, (b)CORBIS; **xi** (t)Howard A. Thain/Collection of the New York Historical Society/Bridgeman Art Library, (c)Roger-Viollet/Topham/The Image Works, (b)BC; **xii** (t)Mary Evans Picture Library, (c)BC, (b)SuperStock; **xiii** (t)Wally McNamee/CORBIS, (c)Bob Adelman/Magnum Photos, (b)Larry Burrows/Time Life Pictures/Getty Images; **xiv** (t)Eli Reed/Magnum Photos, (c)The White House/Handout/Getty Images, (b)Brooks Kraft/CORBIS; **xxviii** (t)Owaki/Kulla/CORBIS, (b)Pierce Rafferty/Petrified Collection/Getty Images; **xxix** (t)Dynamic Graphics Group/Creatas/Alamy Images, (b)Eric Foltz/iStockphoto; **A16** (t)ThinkStock/SuperStock, (cl)Janet Foster/Masterfile, (cr)Mark Tomalty/Masterfile, (bl)age fotostock/SuperStock, (br)Jurgen Freund/Nature Picture Library; **GH2** BananaStock/PictureQuest; **GH13** Copyright © 2008 by David W. Boles. All Rights Reserved; **GH16-1** Boltin Picture Library/Bridgeman Art Library; **2** (t)The Granger Collection, New York, (b)SuperStock; **2-3** BC; **3** (t)Stock Montage/Getty Images, (b)Michael Nicholson/CORBIS; **5** (l)Alison Wright/The Image Works, (r)Neil Setchfield/Getty Images; **6** (l)Art Archive/National Anthropological Museum Mexico/Dagli Orti, (r)Art Archive; **9** (tl)George Catlin/Getty Images, (tr bl)The Granger Collection, New York, (br)Photograph courtesy of the Schwarz Gallery, Philadelphia; **12** (t)CORBIS, (c)PunchStock, (bl)C Squared Studios/Getty Images, (br)Iconotec/Alamy Images; **13** (l to r, t to b)Getty Images, (2)LOC, LC-USZ62-242, (3)Ingram Publishing/Alamy Images, (4)Brand X Pictures/PunchStock, (5)Artville/Getty Images, (6)Alan and Sandy Carey/Getty Images, (7)Dynamic Graphics Group/IT Stock Free/Alamy Images, (8)PunchStock, (9)PhotoAlto/Getty Images, (10)CORBIS, (11)Getty Images, (12)Image Source Pink/Getty Images, (13)C Squared Studios/Getty Images, (14)LOC, LC-USZ62-242, (15)Creativ Studio Heinemann/Getty Images, (16)Alamy Images; **15** (l)National Maritime Museum, (c)CORBIS, (r)The British Museum/Topham-HIP/The Image Works; **17** Theodore de Bry/The Granger Collection, New York; **19** (l)The City of Plainfield, NJ, (r)The Granger Collection, New York; **21** (l)SuperStock, (r)Bibliotheque Nationale/Art Resource, NY; **22** Biblioteca Colombina, Sevilla; **25** (tl)Sheffield Galleries and Museums Trust, UK/Bridgeman Art Library, (tr)Adam Woolfitt/Robert Harding World Imagery/CORBIS, (b)National Maritime Museum, London; **26** (l)Stock Montage/Getty Images, (r)Association for the Preservation of Virginia Antiquities; **28** Private Collection; **30** (l)Kean Collection/Getty Image, (r)Schlesinger Library, Radcliffe Institute, Harvard University/Bridgeman Art Library; **35** Hulton Archive/Getty Images; **40** (l)Private Collection/Getty Image, (r)Getty Images; **44** The Granger Collection, New York; **45** (l)Ariadne Van Zandbergen/Getty Images, (r)Bridgeman Art Library; **46** BC; **48** (t)Erich Lessing/Art Resource, NY, (c)Association for the Preservation of Virginia Antiquities, (b)Private Collection; **51** BC; **52** (l)MPI/Getty Images, (r)Colonial Williamsburg; **52-53** SuperStock; **55** (t)LOC, LC-USZC4-5315, (b)LOC; **57** National Portrait Gallery, London; **58** The Granger Collection, New York; **59** Christopher J. Morris/CORBIS; **60** (tl)The Granger Collection, New York, (tr)John Carter Brown Library, (b)BC; **62** The Granger Collection, New York; **63** LOC, LC-DIG-ppmsca-01657; **65 66 67** BC; **69** The Granger Collection, New York; **71** (l)National Portrait Gallery/SuperStock, (r)The Granger Collection, New York; **72** (tl)William Walcutt, Pulling Down the Statue of George III, 1857/Lafayette College Art Collection, Easton, Pennsylvania, (tr)BC, (b)The Granger Collection, New York; **79** North Wind Picture Archives; **81** (t)BC, (b)Yale University Art Gallery/Trumbull Collection; **83** Fraunces Tavern Museum, New York City; **84 87 89** The Granger Collection, New York; **90** (l)Courtesy of the Massachusetts Historical Society, (r)The Granger Collection, New York; **92** (t)Hulton Archive/Getty Images, (c)SuperStock, (b)The Granger Collection, New York; **95** Picture History; **96** (t)Fraunces Tavern Museum, New York, (b)Picture Research Consultants; **97** National Postal Museum, Smithsonian Institution; **102** (l)The Granger Collection, New York, (r)Geoffrey Clements/CORBIS; **105** The Granger Collection, New York; **107** (l)American School/Bridgeman Art Library/Getty Images, (r)National Portrait Gallery, Smithsonian Institution/Art Resource, NY; **113** (l)LOC, LC-USZC4-4097, (r)Stock Montage/Getty Images; **114** The Granger Collection, New York; **116** (t)LOC, LC-USZ62-59464, (c b)The Granger Collection, New York; **119** American Antiquarian Society; **121** Comstock/PunchStock; **125 127** Brooks Kraft/CORBIS; **130** John Aikins/CORBIS; **150-151** Winterthur Museum; **152** National Museum of American History/Smithsonian Institution; **152-153** SuperStock; **153** Mary Evans Picture Library; **156** MPI/Getty Images; **157** (l)Art Archive/National Gallery of Art Washington/Laurie Platt Winfrey, (c)Huntington Library/SuperStock, (r)courtesy Winterthur Museum; **158** (l)Art Archive/National Gallery of Art Washington/Laurie Platt Winfrey, (r)Huntington Library/SuperStock; **163** LOC; **165** National Portrait Gallery, Smithsonian Institution/Art Resource, NY; **166** BC; **169** The Granger Collection, New York; **171** Stock Montage/Getty Images; **172** The Granger Collection, New York; **177** (t)The Granger Collection, New York, (cl)LOC, LC-USZC4-782, (cr)Bridgeman Art Library, (b)BC; **180** Anne S.K. Brown, Brown Military Collection/Brown University Library; **182** (t)North Wind Picture Archives, (b)SuperStock **185** LOC, LC-USZC4-2711; **186 186-187** The Granger Collection, New York; **189** The Landis Valley Museum; **191 192** The Granger Collection, New York; **195** Hermann J. Meyer/akg-images; **196** (l)BC, (r)Underwood & Underwood/CORBIS; **197** (l)Eric Long/National Museum of American History, Smithsonian Institution, (c)Photographer Unknown/SSPL/The Image Works, (r)The Granger Collection, New York; **198** (l)American Textile History Museum, Lowell, MA, (r)The Granger Collection, New York; **200** SuperStock; **203** (l)Art Archive/Yale University New Haven/Laurie Platt Winfrey, (r)National Museum of American History, Smithsonian Institution; **204** CORBIS; **205** (tl)The Granger Collection, New York, (tr)Carl G. Von Iwonski/Yanaguana Society gift/Daughters of the Republic of Texas Library (SC96.009A), (b)BC; **206** Collection of The New York Historical Society (48169); **208** The Granger Collection, New York; **210** The New York Public Library; **211** (t)BC, (b)Missouri Historical Society, St. Louis; **214** The Granger Collection, New York; **216** (t)The Granger Collection, New York, (b)Christie's Images/SuperStock; **219** LOC, LC-USZ62-41838; **220** David R. Barker/Ohio Historical Society; **220-221** Bridgeman Art Library, BC; **223** (tl)Collection of the New York Historical Society/Bridgeman Art Library, (tr)Art Archive/Chateau de Blerancourt/Dagli Orti, (c)BC, (b)The Granger Collection, New York; **224** The Granger Collection, New York; **225** (l)Monika

Graff/The Image Works, (r)Gary I. Rothstein/Reuters/CORBIS; 227 Super-
Stock; 228 (l)The Granger Collection, New York, (r)BC; 231 (t)The Granger
Collection, New York, (c)Mark Sexton/The Bostonian Society, (b)Museum of
the City of New York/CORBIS; 232 (l)Old Dartmouth Historical Society/
New Bedford Whaling Museum, (r)Picture History; 233 The Granger
Collection, New York; 234 BC; 237 CORBIS; 238 The Granger Collection,
New York; 239 (l)The Granger Collection, New York, (r)Museum of the City
of New York, Harry T. Peters Collection; 240 Art Archive/Culver Pictures/
Napoleon Sarony; 243 (t)BC, (c)Massachusetts Historical Society, Boston/
Bridgeman Art Library, (b)Schlesinger Library, Radcliffe Institute, Harvard
University/Bridgeman Art Library; 244 (l)Collection of J. Paul Getty
Museum, (r)The Granger Collection, New York; 245 BC; 246 CORBIS; 248
(t)Francis G. Mayer/CORBIS, (c b)The Granger Collection, New
York; 251 The New York Historical Society; 252 Texas Department of
Highways and Public Transportation; 252-253 akg-images; 255 Christie's
Images/CORBIS; 256 Bridgeman Art Library; 262 Courtesy of The
Bancroft Library/University of California, Berkeley, 1963.002:1350-
FR; 266 Texas State Library and Archives Commission; 267 (tl)Center for
American History/Barker Collection/University of Texas at Austin, (tr)Texas
State Preservation Board, (b)Texas Department of Transportation; 268 (t)Eri
c Beggs/Texas State Library & Archive Commission, (b)Randy Faris/
CORBIS; 271 (tl tc)The Granger Collection, New York, (tr)LOC, LC-USZ62-
10802, (b)LOC, LC-USZ62-1277; 273 (l)White House Historical Association,
(r)Library of Congress/Getty Images; 274 LOC, LC-USZC4-9950; 276 (t)The
Granger Collection, New York, (c)North Wind Picture Archives, (b)MPI/
Getty Images; 280-281 Painting by Don Troiani, www.historicalartprints.
com; 282 The Kansas State Historical Society, Topeka; 282-283 Art Archive/
Metropolitan Museum of Art New York/Laurie Platt Winfrey; 283 Chicago
Historical Society; 285 CORBIS; 286 (l)California State Library, Sacramento,
(r)LOC, LC-DIG-cwpbh-01232; 286-287 (br)The Granger Collection, New
York, (t)Bridgeman Art Library, (b)The Granger Collection, New York;
289 The Granger Collection, New York; 290 (l)Syracuse Newspapers/Dick
Blume/The Image Works, (r)BC; 292 CORBIS; 295 (t)LOC, LC-USZC4-
92049, (b)LOC, LC-USZ62-92031; 297 (l)LOC, LC-USZ62-79305, (r)The
Supreme Court of the United States Office of the Curator, #1991.402.2;
299 Picture History; 300 LOC, LC-USZ62-2890; 303 Steve Laschever/
Museum of American Political Life; 304 (l)BC, (c r)The Granger Collection,
New York; 305 (l)Bridgeman Art Library, (c)Henry Horner Lincoln
Collection, (r)Art Archive/Culver Pictures; 306 The Granger Collection,
New York; 308 (tl)Picture History, (tr)BC, (c)Library of Congress/Bridgeman
Art Library, (b)The Granger Collection, New York; 311 LOC, LC-USZC4-
7997; 312 Museum of the Confederacy; 312-313 Minnesota Historical
Society/CORBIS; 313 LOC, LC-DIG-cwpb-06233; 315 (l)Medford
Historical Society Collection/CORBIS, (r)BC; 317 (l)LOC, LCUSZ62-42025,
(r)LOC, LC-USZ62-132934; 318 (tl)Collection of David & Kevin Kyle/
Picture Research Consultants, (tc)Military & Historical Image Bank/Don
Troiani, (tr)Medford Historical Society Collection/CORBIS, (b)War
Department/National Archives/Time Life Pictures/Getty Images;
321 (l)LOC, LC-USZC4-708, (r)LOC, LC-USZC2-2124; 322 (t)LOC, LC-
USZC4-1910, (b)CORBIS; 323 G.H. Suydam Collection, Mss. 1394, Louisiana
and Lower Mississippi Valley Collections, LSU Libraries, Baton Rouge,
La.; 325 (t)CORBIS, (b)LOC, LC-USZ62-66616; 326 (tl)LOC, LC-USZC4-
1768, (tr b)BC; 329 (tl)CORBIS, (tr b)BC; 330 (l)BC, (r)CORBIS; 331 LOC,
LC-USZC4-507; 332 (tl)LOC, LC-USZC4-4582, (tr)LOC, LC-DIG-cwpb-
01195, (b)CORBIS; 334 LOC, LC-USZ62-100066; 335 LOC, LC-USZC4-
1425; 337 (l)LOC, LC-USZC4-1754, (r)US Naval Academy Museum/Beverly
R. Robinson Collection/US Naval Historical Center; 338 BC; 339 CORBIS;
340 (l)Hulton-Deutsch Collection/CORBIS, (r)LOC, LC-DIG-cwpb-04402;
345 CORBIS; 346 (t)LOC, LC-DIG-cwpb-02226, (b)BC; 348 (l)BC, (r)The
Granger Collection, New York; 350 (tl)The Granger Collection, New York,
(tr)Bridgeman Art Library, (cl)CORBIS, (cr)Kunstler Enterprises, Ltd.,
(bl)LOC, LC-USZC4-1519, (br)Picture History; 353 LOC, LC-USZ62-
132749; 354-355 Art Archive/National Archives, Washington DC, (t)LOC,
(b)Art Archive/Musee d'Orsay Paris/Dagli Orti; 357 (t)CORBIS, (cl)Art
Archive/National Archives, Washington DC, (cr)LOC, LC-USZ62-128709,
(b)LOC, LC-DIG-ppmsca-05704; 359 (l)CORBIS, (r)Cook Collection/
Valentine Museum; 361 (tl)Flip Schulke/CORBIS, (tc)Flip Schulke/Black
Star, (tr)AP Images, (b)BC; 367 (tl)The Granger Collection, New York,
(tr b)The Granger Collection, New York; 368 (l)Mother Bethel African
Methodist Episcopal Church/Scurlock Records, Archives Center, National
Museum of American History, Smithsonian Institution, (r)The Granger
Collection, New York; 369 Patrick Zachmann/Magnum Photos;

370 (l br)The Granger Collection, New York, (tr)Dallas Historical Society/
Bridgeman Art Library; 373 (t)LOC, LC-USZC4-8345, (b)LOC; 374 (l)Super
Stock, (r)Art Archive/Culver Pictures; 374-375 LOC, LC-USZC4-2623; 376
CORBIS; 378 (t)Picture History, (b)CORBIS; 381 LOC, LC-USZC4-
5606; 382-383 William Henry Jackson/Cardoza Fine Art Gallery; 384 The
Granger Collection, New York; 384-385 Lowell Georgia/CORBIS; 388 LOC,
LC-USZ62-9889; 389 (t)Calvin Larsen/Photo Researchers, (b)Scott T. Smith/
CORBIS; 391 BC; 392 (l)Art Archive/Bill Manns, (r)Getty Images;
395 Minnesota Historical Society/CORBIS; 396 (l)State Historical Society
of Wisconsin, (r)akg-images; 401 (l)Getty Images, (r)CORBIS; 402
(l)CORBIS, (r)The Granger Collection, New York; 404 (t b)The Granger
Collection, New York, (c)CORBIS; 408 National Railway Museum/Science
& Society Museum; 408-409 LOC, LC-USZ62-77541; 412 (t)Mary Evans
Picture Library, (bl)The Granger Collection, New York, (bcl)Time Life
Pictures/Getty Images, (bcr)BC, (br)Schenectady Museum; Hall of Electrical
History Foundation/CORBIS; 413 (tl)BC, (tr)Mary Evans Picture Library,
(b)George Eastman House 414 (l)LOC, LC-USZ62-99122, (r)LOC, LC-
USZ62-99407; 417 (tl)Union Pacific Museum, (tr)Private Collection, Peter
Newark American Pictures/Bridgeman Art Library, (bl)Getty Images,
(bc)Union Pacific Museum, (br)BC; 420 Getty Images; 423 BC; 426 (l)
SuperStock, (r)CORBIS; 429 (t bl)CORBIS, (br)Hulton Archive/Getty
Images; 434 CORBIS 436 (t)Union Pacific Museum, (c)CORBIS, (b)Hulton
Archive/Getty Images; 439 Stock Montage/Hulton Archive/Getty
Images; 440-441 CORBIS; 441 (l)Shore Line Trolley Museum Library,
Sprague Collection, (r)London Stereoscopic Company/Getty
Images; 444 (l)Michael Maslan Historic Photographs/CORBIS, (c)The
Granger Collection, New York, (r)Art Archive/Culver Pictures; 446 The
Granger Collection, New York; 448 (t)Picture Research Consultants,
(b)Brown Brothers; 449 OSU Cartoon Research Library 451 (l)CORBIS,
(c)LOC, LC-USZ62-54088, (r)Museum of the City of New York/
CORBIS; 452 Hulton-Deutsch Collection/CORBIS; 453 (l)CORBIS, (c)The
Granger Collection, New York, (r)BC; 454 The Granger Collection, New
York; 459 (l)LOC, LC-USZ62-15566, (r)Frank & Marie Wood/The Picture
Bank; 460 Geofferey Clements/CORBIS; 461 Museum of Art, Rhode Island
School of Design; Jesse Metcalf and Walter H. Kimball Funds; 463 (l)The
Granger Collection, New York, (r)Getty Images; 465 (l)CORBIS, (r)Duke
University; 466 (l)The Granger Collection, New York, (r)AP Images; 471 The
Everett Collection; 472 The Granger Collection, New York; 474 (l)Getty
Images, (c r)CORBIS; 477 The Granger Collection, New York; 479 Snark/
Art Resource, NY; 480 Brown Brothers; 482 (t)Brown Brothers, (c)Picture
Research Consultants, (b)Lewis W. Hine/George Eastman House/Getty
Images; 485 Picture Research Consultants; 486-487 Franklin D Roosevelt
Library; 488-489 CORBIS; 491 (t)CORBIS, (b)The Mariners' Museum/
CORBIS; 493 (l)Nagasaki Museum of History and Culture, (r)James G.
Evans/Chicago History Museum (1932.21); 494 (l)Hawaii State Archives,
(r)The Granger Collection, New York; 497 (tl)LOC, LC-USZ62-99767, (tr)The
Granger Collection, New York, (b)Kurz & Allison/The Granger Collection,
New York; 498 BC; 499 (l)Hulton Archive/Getty Images, (r)LOC;
501 (l)LOC, LC-USZ62-62631, (r)Getty Images; 502 (l)LOC, LC-USZC4-
5392, (r)LOC, LC-USZ62-91465; 505 The Granger Collection, New
York; 506 BC; 507 Koichi Kamoshida/Getty Images; 510 The Granger
Collection, New York; 513 Morton Beebe/CORBIS; 514 (t)BC, (c b)Time
Life Pictures/Getty Images; 517 CORBIS; 518 (t)Museum of the City of
New York Print Archives, (b)Key Color/Index Stock Imagery; 518-519 Jessie
Beals/Schlesinger Library, Radcliffe Institute, Harvard University/
Bridgeman Art Library; 521 (t)BC, (b)Hulton-Deutsch Collection/
CORBIS; 522-523 LOC, LC-USZ62-56437; 524 (t)LOC, LC-USZ62-46713,
(bl)LOC, LC-USZ62-106109, (br)LOC, LC-ISZ62-28195; 525 BC; 526 (l)
Keystone/Getty Images, (r)UNITE HERE Archives, Kheel Center, Cornell
University; 529 LOC, LC-USZC4-434; 531 The Granger Collection, New
York; 533 (l)BC, (r)The Granger Collection, New York; 534 CORBIS; 537
(t)CORBIS, (b)The Granger Collection, New York; 540 (t)Underwood &
Underwood/CORBIS, (b)BC, (c)LOC, LC-USZ62-83858,
(b)CORBIS; 545 LOC, LC-USZC4-6425; 546 (t)The Mariners' Museum/
CORBIS, (b)BC; 546-547 BC; 547 BC; 550 (l)CORBIS, (c r)BC; 551 BC;
553 (l)LOC, LC-DIG-ggbain-05650, (r)CORBIS; 554 (t b)BC, (c)CORBIS;
557 (l)BC, (c)Swim Ink 2, LLC/CORBIS, (r)K.J. Historical/CORBIS; 559
BC; 560 (l)LOC, LC-USZ62-116442, (r)LOC, LC-USZC4-2426; 562 (t)LOC,
LC-USZC4-1539, (b)LOC, LC-USZC4-9928; 563 UNC University Library;
566 (l)Australian War Memorial Negative Number, E00921, (r)Hulton-
Deutsch Collection/CORBIS; 567 569 BC; 572 (l)By Permission of the
Marcus Family, (r)Library of Congress/© 1919, The Washington Post.

Reprinted with permission; 577 Underwood & Underwood/CORBIS; 578 Brown Brothers; 579 Neville Elder/CORBIS; 580 (l cr)White House Historical Association, (cl)Underwood & Underwood/CORBIS, (r)CORBIS; 582 (t)BC,(cb)CORBIS; 585 Chicago Tribune; 586-587 Howard A. Thain/Collection of the New York Historical Society/Bridgeman Art Library; 588 CORBIS; 588-589 Roger-Viollet/Topham/The Image Works; 589 National Air and Space Museum/Smithsonian Institution; 591 592 The Granger Collection, New York; 597 (tl)Hirz/Getty Images, (tr)FPG/Hulton Archive/Getty Images, (cr)Topham/The Image Works, (bl)FPG/Getty Images, (br)The Granger Collection, New York; 598 (l to r)Hulton Archive/Getty Images, (2)The Image Works, (3)SSPL/The Image Works, (4)Ohio Historical Society; 599 (tl)Mary Evans Picture Library, (tr)LOC, LC-USZ62-119950, (c)Huntington Library/SuperStock,(b)Minnesota Historical Society; 600 The Granger Collection, New York; 601 (l)Frank & Marie-Therese Wood, (r)The Granger Collection, New York; 602 Hulton Archive/Getty Images; 605 (l)BC, (r)LOC, LC-USZ62-52584; 606 Underwood & Underwood/CORBIS; 607 (l)Mary Evans Picture Library, (r)Columbus Dispatch/Ohio Historical Society; 608 (l)Library Of Congress/Getty Images, (r)CORBIS; 611 Francis G. Mayer/CORBIS; 612 (tl)Culver Pictures/SuperStock, (tc)National Archives, (tr)Art Archive/Culver Pictures, (b)The Kobal Collection; 617 (tl)Carl Van Vechten/The Granger Collection, New York/Reprinted with permission of the Van Vechten Trust, (tr b)The Granger Collection, New York; 618 (l)Art Archive/Culver Pictures, (r b)Frank Driggs Collection/Getty Images; 619 (l)Frank Driggs Collection/Getty Images, (c)Sasha/Getty Images, (r)Underwood & Underwood/CORBIS; 622 (t)Mary Evans Picture Library, (c)Frank Driggs Collection/Getty Images, (b)General Photographic Agency/Getty Images 625 Library of Congress/© 1925, The Washington Post. Reprinted with permission; 626-627 BC; 627 BC; 629 (l)The Granger Collection, New York, (r)LOC, LC-USZ62-24155; 630 Hulton-Deutsch Collection/CORBIS; 631 (l)BC, (r)American Stock/Getty Images; 635 (l)Chicago History Museum,(r)Hulton Archive/Getty Images; 636 (l)BC, (r)Margaret Bourke-White/Time Life Pictures/Getty Images; 639 Russell Lee/CORBIS; 641 (l)The Granger Collection, New York, (r)Getty Images; 642 (tl)BC, (tr)AP Images, (b)Picture History; 644 (t)Mary Evans Picture Library, (c)BC, (b)Scherl/SVBilderdienst/The Image Works; 647 John T. McCutcheon/The Granger Collection, New York; 648 (t)CORBIS, (b)akg-images; 648-649 BC; 649 BC; 651 Underwood & Underwood/CORBIS; 653 BC; 654 (tl)Picture History, (tr)LOC, LC-USF34-032948-D, (b)MPI/Getty Images; 655 (tl)B, (tr)Underwood & Underwood/CORBIS, (b)BC; 657 (l)Tom Brakefield/Getty Images, (r)CORBIS; 658 The Granger Collection, New York; 660 Illustration by Peter Arno/Copyright © 1933 Condé Nast Publications; 661 (l)LOC, LC-DIG-ppmsca-12896, (r)Illustration by Garretto/Copyright © 1934 Condé Nast Publications; 663 (l c)BC, (r)The Granger Collection, New York; 665 (l)The Granger Collection, New York, (r)CORBIS; 666 669 BC; 671 The Granger Collection, New York; 672 (tl)BC, (tr)courtesy FDIC, (b)courtesy FHA; 674 (t)Underwood & Underwood/CORBIS, (c)U.S. Forest Servic, (b)BC; 677 678-679 The Granger Collection, New York; 680 Keystone/Getty Images; 680-681 Mary Evans Picture Library; 681 (t)United States Holocaust Memorial Museum, (b)LOC, LC-USZ62-89348; 685 (t)Art Archive/Reina Sofia Museum, Madrid, (b)BC; 686 BC; 689 CORBIS; 691 (l c)BC, (r)The Granger Collection, New York; 692 (tl)Art Archive, (tr b)BC; 695 Mary Evans Picture Library, (bkgd)Roger Foley; 696 (l)Yivo Institute for Jewish Research, (r)Yad Vashem Photo Archives, courtesy of USHMM; 696-697 Roger Foley; 697 (l)AFP/Getty Images, (r) National Archives: Suitland, courtesy of USHMM; 698 700 USHMM; 701 (l)USHMM, (r)By Permission of Alexandre Oler, the son of the Artist. Nice, France; 703 (l)The Granger Collection, New York, (r)LOC, LC-USZ62-52601; 704 SuperStock; 706 (t)CORBIS, (b)MPI/Getty Images; 708 The Granger Collection, New York; 711 Chicago History Museum; 712 712-713 BC; 713 CORBIS; 715 BC; 716 Getty Images; 718 BC; 719 (l)US Army Photo, (r)BC; 720 (l)Peter Stackpole/Time Life Pictures/Getty Images, (r)CORBIS; 723 CORBIS; 725 Art Archive/National Archives Washington, DC; 726 (t)CORBIS, (b)Art Archive; 729 (l)LOC, LC-DIG-fsac-1a34953, (c)Getty Images, (r)CORBIS; 730-731 John Vachon/Anthony Potter Collection/Getty Images; 733 Getty Images; 734 (l)United Artists/The Kobal Collection, (c)Walt Disney Pictures/The Kobal Collection; 734 (r)CORBIS; 738 (t)BC, (bl)CORBIS, (br)Getty Images; 739 (t)Art Archive, (b)ullstein bild/The Granger Collection, New York; 740-741 742 CORBIS; 748 Digital Stock/CORBIS; 749 (tl b)CORBIS, (tr)Naval Historical Foundation; 751 (l)Art Archive/Culver Pictures, (r)Getty Images; 752 CORBIS; 754 (l)LOC, LC-DIG-fsac-1a35223, (r)Digital Stock/

CORBIS; 757 Dr. Seuss Collection/Mandeville Special Collections Library/University of California, San Diego; 758 (t)BC, (b)Picture Research Consultants; 758-759 BC; 759 Smithsonian Institution; 761 The Granger Collection, New York; 763 (l)BC, (r)Hulton-Deutsch Collection/CORBIS; 767 Getty Images; 769 Time Life Pictures/Getty Images; 771 BC; 772 The Granger Collection, New York; 775 CORBIS; 777 (l)Weber and Beyer/CORBIS, (r)The Granger Collection, New York; 779 BC; 780 (t)LOC, LC-USZC4-4431, (c b)BC; 783 (l c)CORBIS, (r)U.S. Air Force Photo; 784 (tl)NSSDC/NASA, (tr)The Granger Collection, New York, (bl)BC, (br)Donald Uhbrock/Time Life Pictures/Getty Images; 786 (tl)NASA Dryden Flight Research Center, (tr)Time Life Pictures/Getty Images, (b)CORBIS; 788 (t)Picture Research Consultants, (b)BC; 791 Ross Lewis Milwaukee Public Library; 792 (t)FPG, (b)CORBIS; 792-793 SuperStock; 793 Natural Museum of American History/Smithsonian Institution; 795 (l)Getty Images, (r)CORBIS; 797 CORBIS; 798 (tl)Masterfile, (tr)Time Life Pictures/Getty Images, (bl)J R Eyerman/Time Life Pictures/Getty Images, (br)Marvin Koner/CORBIS; 801 (l)Time Life Pictures/Getty Images, (r)CORBIS; 803 BC; 804 (l)BC, (c)National Museum of American History/Smithsonian Institution, (r)The Kobal Collection; 806 (tl)Brown Brothers, (tr br)Michael Ochs Archives/CORBIS, (c)Photofest, (bl)BC; 811 (tl tr)Time Life Pictures/Getty Images, (b)AP Images; 812 BC; 813 Thomas Hoepker/Magnum Photos; 814 National Archives; 816 (t)SuperStock, (b)Time Life Pictures/Getty Images; 819 B. Wiseman/from Hey, Can't You Forget Business? by Charles Preston, ©1953, E.P. Dutton & Co., Inc.; 820-821 Wally McNamee/CORBIS; 822 (tl)Art Resource, (tc)Getty Images, (tr b)AP Images; 822-823 Time Life Pictures/Getty Images; 825 827 BC; 831 George Silk/Time Life Pictures/Getty Images; 832 (l)Getty Images, (c)CORBIS SYGMA, (r)CORBIS; 833 (l)CORBIS SYGMA, (cl)BC, (cr r)CORBIS; 834 (tl)Rene Burri/Magnum Photos, (tr)AP Images, (b)Carl Mydans/Time Life Pictures/Getty Images; 839 (l)John Dominis/Time Life Pictures/Getty Images, (r)CORBIS; 840 Americorps VISTA Archives; 841 Corporation photo by Peter Shifter, Office of Public Affairs/AmeriCorps; 844 (t)Ameri-Corps Archive, (c)Carl Mydans/Time Life Pictures/Getty Images, (b)Flip Schulke/Black Star; 847 A 1965 Herblock Cartoon, copyright by The Herb Block Foundation; 848 (l)Carl Iwaski/Time Life Pictures/Getty Images, (r)Art Resource, NY; 848-849 Bob Adelman/Magnum Photos; 849 Collection of Janice L. and David J. Frent; 851 Time Life Pictures/Getty Images; 853 Carl Iwasaki/Time Life Pictures/Getty Images; 855 (t br)Don Craven/Time Life Pictures/Getty Images, (bl) Flip Schulke/CORBIS; 856 CORBIS; 859 (l) CORBIS, (r)AP Images; 860 (t br)BC, (bl)Don Craven/Time Life Pictures/Getty Images; 861 (tl)Charles Moore 1963/Black Star, (tr)Steve Schapiro, (b)BC; 863 Bill Hudson/AP Images; 865 Francis Miller/Time Life Pictures/Getty Images; 866 Flip Schulke/CORBIS; 868 Eve Arnold/Magnum Photos; 869 The Everett Collection; 871 (l)Atlanta Constitution, 1964, Clifford H. "Baldy" Baldowski Editorial Cartoons. Courtesy of the Richard B. Russell Library for Political Research and Studies, The University of Georgia Libraries, (r)A 1967 Herblock Cartoon, copyright by The Herb Block Foundation; 873 (l)Robert Parent/Time Life Pictures/Getty Images, (c)AP Images, (r)Flip Schulke/CORBIS; 876 (t)Carl Iwaski/Time Life Pictures/Getty Images, (c)Francis Miller/Time Life Pictures/Getty Images, (b)Flip Schulke/CORBIS; 879 Jon Kennedy/Arkansas Democrat-Gazette; 880 (t)Art Resource, NY, (b)Naval Historical Foundation; 880-881 Larry Burrows/Time Life Pictures/Getty Images; 884 (tl)BC, (tr)AFP/Getty Images, (b)AP Images; 887 (l)POPPERFOTO/Alamy Images, (r)CORBIS; 888 (t)MPI/Getty Images, (b)Larry Burrows/Time Life Pictures/Getty Images; 891 (l)BC, (r)AP Images; 893 (l)Library of Congress/Tom Francis Darcy, Newsday/Reprinted with permission from LA Times Reprints, (r)Atlanta Constitution, Oct. 18, 1965, Clifford H. "Baldy" Baldowski Editorial Cartoons. Courtesy of the Richard B. Russell Library for Political Research and Studies, The University of Georgia Libraries; 894 (l) Bernard Gotfryd/Getty Images, (c)Hulton Archive/Getty Images, (r)Paul Fusco/Magnum Photos; 896 (tl)Bob Gomel/Time Life Pictures/Getty Images, (tc)CORBIS, (tr c)BC, (b)Bernard Gotfryd/Getty Images; 899 (l)John Filo, (c)David Kennerly/BC,(r)Dirck Halstead/Time Life Pictures/Getty Images; 901 (l)BC, (c)The Granger Collection, New York, (r)Time Life Pictures/Getty Images; 902 (l)Alex Wong/Getty Images, (r)Sal Veder/AP Images; 904 (t)AP Images, (c)Art Archive/Dept Defence Washington, (b)Wally McNamee/CORBIS; 907 Photo by DeAlba/Washington Daily News/Lyndon Baines Johnson Library; 908 (l)Art Resource, NY, (r)Charles Gatewood/The Image Works; 908-909 Take Stock; 909 AP Images; 911 BC; 912 (l)Vince Streano/CORBIS, (r)Andrew DeLory/Hulton Archive/Getty Images; 915 (l)BC, (r)Charles Gatewood/The Image Works; 917 AP Images;

918 BC; 921 CORBIS; 922 LOC, LC-USF33-012870-M5; 923 (l)CORBIS, (r)Jim Sugar/CORBIS; 924 Arthur Schatz/Time Life Pictures/Getty Images; 926 (t c)BC, (b)Steve Northup/Time Life Pictures/Getty Images; 929 Jack Knox Estate/OSU Cartoon Research Library; 930-931 Michael Goldman/Master-file; 932 (l)Hulton Archive/Getty Images, (r)BC; 932-933 AP Images, Tom Ebenhoh/Black Star; 935 (l)A 1968 Herblock Cartoon, copyright by The Herb Block Foundation, (r)Atlanta Constitution, 1968 Oct. 17, Clifford H. "Baldy" Baldowski Editorial Cartoons. Courtesy of the Richard B. Russell Library for Political Research and Studies, The University of Georgia Libraries; 937 (l)BC, (r)Time Life Pictures/Getty Images; 938 (t)Dirck Halstead/Liasion/Getty Images, (b)AFP/Getty Images; 941 (tl)Adam Woolfitt/CORBIS, (tcl)Dennis Brack/Black Star, (tc tcr b)BC, (tr)Robert Maass/CORBIS; 943 Mark Godfrey/The Image Works; 944 (l)A 1973 Herblock Cartoon, copyright by The Herb Block Foundation, (r)Atlanta Constitution, 1973, Clifford H. "Baldy" Baldowski Editorial Cartoons. Courtesy of the Richard B. Russell Library for Political Research and Studies, The University of Georgia Libraries; 947 (l)Jason Laure/Woodfin Camp/Time Life Pictures/Getty Images, (c r)BC; 949 (l)Brown Brothers, (r)Karl Schumacher/Time Life Pictures/Getty Images; 950 (tl)David Rubinger/CORBIS, (tr)M. Lipschitz/AP Images, (bl)MPI/Getty Images, (br)Sergio Gaudenti/Kipa/CORBIS; 953 (l)AP Images, (r)Scherl/SV-Bilderndienst/The Image Works; 954 (l)PA/Topham/The Image Works, (r)Charles Gatewood/The Image Works; 956 (l)Wally McNamee/CORBIS, (c)Ed Kashi/CORBIS, (r)Brand X/SuperStock; 959 (l c)BC, (r)Charles E. Rotkin/CORBIS; 960 (l)A 1975 Herblock Cartoon, copyright by The Herb Block Foundation, (r)Hulton Archive/Getty Images; 962 (t)Charles Gatewood/The Image Works, (c)BC, (b)Julian Wasser/Time Life Pictures/Getty Images; 965 Ranan R. Lurie, Cartoonews International Syndicate, New York City; 966 (t)AP Images, (b)Peter Turnley/CORBIS; 966-967 Eli Reed/Magnum Photos; 967 Lana Harris/AP Images; 969 (l)Gary McCoy/Cagle Cartoons, (r)Chris Slane/Cagle Cartoons; 972 (t)Index Stock Imagery, (bl)Cynthia Johnson/Time Life Pictures/Getty Images, (bc)Annie Griffiths Belt/CORBIS, (br)Joe Raedle/Newsmakers/Getty Images; 975 (t)Atlanta Constitution, 1976 Apr. 6, Clifford H. "Baldy" Baldowski Editorial Cartoons. Courtesy of the Richard B. Russell Library for Political Research and Studies, The University of Georgia Libraries, (b)Atlanta Constitution, 1981 Oct. 18, Clifford H. "Baldy" Baldowski Editorial Cartoons. Courtesy of the Richard B. Russell Library for Political Research and Studies, The University of Georgia Libraries; 977 (l)Wally McNamee/CORBIS, (r)Roger Ressmeyer/CORBIS; 978 (tl)Wally McNamee/CORBIS, (tr)Bob Daughtery/AP Images, (b)BC; 980 (tl)Robert Nickelsberg/Time Life Pictures/Getty Images, (tr)Dirck Halstead/Time Life Pictures/Getty Images, (b) CORBIS; 983 (l)Eli Reichman/Time Life Pictures/Getty Images, (r)Bob Krist/CORBIS; 984 NASA/AP Images; 985 (inset)Blue Origin, (bkgd)HANDOUT/epa/CORBIS; 986 BC; 988 AP Images; 991 (l)Stephen Ferry/Liasion/Getty Images, (r)Diane-Lu Hovasse/AFP/Getty Images; 992 Thomas Hartwell/Time Life Pictures/Getty Images; 994 (tl)Owen Franken/CORBIS, (tr)Markowitz Jeffrey/CORBIS SYGMA, (c)Wally McNamee/CORBIS, (b)Mike Lane/Cagle Cartoons; 996 (t)Tony Korody/Time Life Pictures/Getty Images, (c)BC, (b)Alain Nogues/CORBIS SYGMA; 999 LOC, LC-DIG-ppmsc-07960; 1000 (tl)Roger Ressmeyer/CORBIS, (tr)Spec. Robert Elliott/CORBIS, (b)David Brauchli/Reuters/CORBIS; 1000-1001 The White House/Handout/Getty Images; 1003 (tl)Ed Young/CORBIS, (tr)Douglas Engelbart/Bootstrap Alliance, (bl)TWPhoto/CORBIS, (br)Roger Ressmeyer/CORBIS; 1009 (l)TOLES © 1997 The Washington Post. Reprinted with permission of UNIVERSAL PRESS SYNDICATE. All rights reserved, (tr)Wally McNamee/CORBIS, (br)Markowitz Jeffrey/CORBIS SYGMA; 1011 (l)Terry Ashe/Time Life Pictures/Getty Images, (r)SuperStock; 1013 (l)Wally McNamee/CORBIS, (r)Joe Marquette/AP Images; 1014 (tl)Peter Turnley/CORBIS, (tr)Les Stone/CORBIS SYGMA, (b)Leif Skoogfors/CORBIS; 1018 David Kadlubowski/CORBIS; 1020 (l)Fred Greaves/Reuters/CORBIS, (r)Carlos Barria/Reuters/CORBIS; 1021 (t)Stanley Rogouski, (b)Michael Newman/PhotoEdit; 1024 Hamilton Karie/CORBIS SYGMA; 1026 (t)Michael Newman/PhotoEdit, (b)Ron Edmonds/AP Images; 1029 TOLES © 1998 The Washington Post. Reprinted with permission of UNIVERSAL PRESS SYNDICATE. All rights reserved.; 1030 (l)Alan Diaz/AP Images, (c)Evan Vucci/AP Images, (r)Dimas Ardian/Getty Images; 1030-1031 Michael Macor/San Francisco Chronicle/CORBIS; 1033 (tl tc)Ron Sachs/CNP/CORBIS, (tr)Colin Braley/Reuters/CORBIS, (b)Najlah Feanny/CORBIS; 1034 Daryl Cagle/Cagle Cartoons; 1037 (t) Reuters/Sean Adair/CORBIS, (bl)Ron Sachs/CNP/CORBIS, (br)Stan Honda/AFP/Getty Images; 1038 AP Images; 1040 (t)Matthew McDermott/CORBIS, (bl)Reuters/CORBIS, (br)Steve Liss/CORBIS; 1043 (t)Alexandra Boulat/VII/AP Images, (bl)Scott Peterson/Getty Images, (br)David Guttenfelder/AP Images; 1044 (t)Ali Haider/AP Images, (b)Reuters/Jeff Christensen/CORBIS; 1045 (tl)Al Jazeera via APTN/AP Images, (tr)Lynsey Addario/CORBIS, (b)Wathiq Khuzaie/Getty Images; 1046 (l)Lauren Frayer/AP Images, (r)Khalid al-Mousily/Reuters/CORBIS; 1049 (l)Shaun Heasley/Reuters/CORBIS, (c)Charles W. Luzier/Reuters/CORBIS, (r)Brooks Kraft/CORBIS; 1050 (l)Khampha Bouaphanh/Knight Ridder/Tribune/Pool/Reuters/CORBIS, (r)Brooks Kraft/CORBIS; 1052 Smiley N. Pool/Dallas Morning News/CORBIS; 1053 Rick Wilking/Reuters/CORBIS; 1054 (l)Wathiq Khuzaie/Getty Images, (r)Nancy Kaserman/ZUMA/CORBIS; 1056 (t)AFP/Getty Images, (cl)Kamal Kishore/AP Images, (cr)Al Jazeera/AP Images, (b)Evan Agostini/ImageDirect/Getty Images; 1059 Olie Johannson/Political Cartoons; R2 LOC, LC-USF34-T01-009095-C; R3 Art Shay/Time Life Pictures/Getty Images; R4 LOC, LC-DIG-fsac-1a35337; R5 Wally McNamee/CORBIS; R6 Photo File/MLB Photos/Getty Images; R7 Stan Honda/AFP/Getty Images; R8 Getty Images; R9 CORBIS; R10 (l)Comstock/CORBIS, (r)Art Archive/Reina Sofia Museum, Madrid; R11 CORBIS; R12 R13 BC; R14 Harry Scull Jr./Getty Images; R17 The Granger Collection, New York; R18 Clifford K. Berryman/National Archives; R19 Scott Lituchy/Star Ledger/CORBIS; R20 Smithsonian Institution/CORBIS; R29 through R33 White House Historical Association; R33 (br)Official White House Photo by Eric Draper; R36 (t)Illinois State Historical Library, (b)Private Collection; R39 Private Collection; R40 The Wadsworth Atheneum; R41 R42 Bridgeman Art Library; R43 R44 National Portrait Gallery, Smithsonian Institution/Art Resource, NY; R46 Chicago Historical Society; R47 (t)Maryland Historical Society, Baltimore, Maryland, (b)National Museum of American History/Armed Forces History Collections/Smithsonian Institution; R48 Picture Research Consultants; R49 LOC; R50 (t)Andre Jenny/Focus Group/PictureQuest, (b)BC; R52 National Portrait Gallery, Smithsonian Institution, Washington, D.C./Art Resource. N.Y.; R53 Courtesy Franklin D. Roosevelt Library; R55 Carl Iwaski/Time Life Pictures/Getty Images; R56 Francis Miller/Time Life Pictures/Getty Images; R58 R60 Getty Images; R61 Picture Research Consultants; R65 Stock Montage/Getty Images; R67 (t)Stock Montage/Getty Images, (b)Frans Lanting/CORBIS; R68 BC; R69 Collection of the New York Historical Society/Bridgeman Art Library; R71 (t)Erling Larson/Getty Images, (b)Henry Guttmann/Getty Images; R72 Keystone/Getty Images; R73 General Photographic Agency/Getty Images; R74 Ray Fisher/Time Life Pictures/Getty Images; R75 Hulton Archive/Getty Images; R76 Stephen Jaffe/AFP/Getty Images; R80 Mitchell Gerber/CORBIS; **Time Line Presidential Paintings** White House Historical Association.